COLLIER'S
ENCYCLOPEDIA

TWENTY VOLUMES
With Bibliography and Index

EVERETT O. FONTAINE
Director of Publications

WILLIAM T. COUCH
Editor-in-Chief

Library Consultant and Advisory Editor
LOUIS SHORES

Consultant for Canada
ROBERT H. BLACKBURN

1957

Volume 2

P. F. COLLIER & SON CORPORATION
NEW YORK

LIBRARY OF CONGRESS CATALOG CARD NUMBER 57-5090

CFN

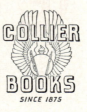

COLLIER
BOOKS
SINCE 1875

DISTRIBUTED IN CANADA BY

P. F. COLLIER & SON LTD.

MANUFACTURED IN THE UNITED STATES OF AMERICA

CONTRIBUTORS TO VOLUME TWO

A.Cu. **Alden Cutshall,** B.Ed., M.A., Ph.D.
Associate Professor of Geography, University of Illinois.

A.C.S. **Alexander C. Soper,** A.B., M.F.A., Ph.D.
Professor of the History of Art, Bryn Mawr College.

A.C.T. **Alfred C. Tan,** B.A. (National Wuhan U., China), M.S., M.A.
Editor, Chinese News Service, New York, N. Y.

A.E.A. **A. E. Alexander,** B.S., Ph.D.
Director, Gem Trade Laboratory, Inc.; Consulting Ceramic Engineer, Electric Auto-Lite Co., Champion Spark Plug Co.

A.E.R. **Antony E. Raubitschek,** Ph. D. (U. of Vienna).
Associate Professor of Classics, Princeton University.

A.Gr. **Albert Greenberg**
Everglades Aquatic Nurseries, Tampa, Fla.

A.G.B. **Arthur G. Bills,** B.A., Ph.D.
Professor of Psychology, Head of the Department of Psychology, University of Cincinnati.

A.G.Br. **Ashbel G. Brice,** B.A., M.A.
Editor and Associate Director, Duke University Press.

A.G.G. **Allan Garfield Gruchy,** B.A., M.A., Ph.D.
Professor of Economics, University of Maryland.

A.H. **Archibald Henderson,** A.B., A.M., Ph.D., Litt.D., D.C.L., LL.D.
Former Professor of Mathematics, Former Head of the Department of Mathematics, University of North Carolina.

A.H.G. **Allan H. Gilbert,** Ph.D.
Professor of English Literature, Duke University.

A.H.Sw. **Alfred H. Sweet,** A.B., A.M., Ph.D.
Linn Professor of History, Washington and Jefferson College.

A.J.J. **A. J. Jaffe,** Ph.D.
Statistician, U. S. Bureau of the Census.

A.K.L. **Alan K. Laing,** B.A., B.S. in Arch.
Professor of Architecture, University of Illinois; Editor, *Journal of the Society of Architectural Historians.*

A.L. **Anna Lavaska,** B.A.
Instructor in Russian, University of Washington.

A.L.H-Q. **Alfred Lawrence Hall-Quest,** B.A., M.A., Ph.D.
Former Professor of General Education, New York University; Former Research Specialist in Adult Education, Carnegie Corporation.

A.Me. **Alfred Metraux,** D.Litt. (U. of Paris).
Research Assistant in Anthropology, Yale University.

A.M.Cl. **Arthur Melville Clark,** M.A., D.Phil. (Oxford U.), D. Litt. (Edinburgh U.), F.R.S.E.
Reader in English, Edinburgh University.

A.P.J. **Alfred Procter James,** A.B., B.A. (Oxford U.), M.A. (Oxford U.), A.M., Ph.D.
Professor of History, University of Pittsburgh.

A.S.M. **Alfred S. Myers**
Free Lance Writer.

A.Sv. **Arthur Svihla,** A.B., M.S., Ph.D.
Professor of Zoology, University of Washington.

A.T.MacA. **Archibald T. MacAllister, Jr.,** A.B., Ph.D.
Associate Professor of Italian, Director of Language Instruction, Princeton University.

A.V. **Amry Vandenbosch,** Ph.B., Ph.D.
Professor of Political Science, University of Kentucky; Advisory Editor, *Far Eastern Quarterly.*

A.W.Bu. **Ardath Walter Burks,** B.A., M.A., Ph.D.
Assistant Professor of Political Science, Rutgers University.

A.W.Gr. **Albert Woodruff Gray,** B.A., LL.B.
Free Lance Writer.

A.W.Van B. **A. W. Van Buren,** A.B., Ph.D.
Emeritus Professor of Archaeology, American Academy in Rome.

B.B. **Brand Blanshard,** B.A., M.A., B.Sc. (Oxford U.), Ph.D.
Professor of Philosophy, Yale University.

B.C.G. **Barbara Crawford Glasrud,** B.A., M.A.
Former Senior Resident, Bryn Mawr College.

B.L. **Bartholomeus Landheer,** Cand. Juris. (U. of Leyden), Ph.D. (U. of Vienna).
Visiting Professor of Sociology, University of Alabama; Former Head, Research Department, Netherlands Information Bureau, New York, N. Y.

B.La. **Bruno Lasker**
Expert and Author on Asiatic Affairs; Free Lance Writer.

B.M.M. **Rev. Bruce Manning Metzger,** A.B., Th.B., Th.M., A.M., Ph.D.
Associate Professor of New Testament, Princeton Theological Seminary; Member, Board of Managers, American Bible Society; Editorial Secretary, *Theology Today.*

B.Pr. **Benfield Pressey,** A.B., A.M.
Professor of English, Dartmouth College.

B.S.H. **B. Smith Hopkins,** A.B., A.M., Ph.D., D.Sc., LL.D.
Emeritus Professor of Chemistry, University of Illinois.

B.W.Z. **Benjamin W. Zweifach,** B.S., M.S., Ph.D.
Associate Professor of Physiology in Medicine, Cornell Medical College.

C.B.B. **Chandler B. Beall,** B.A., Ph.D.
Professor of Romance Languages, University of Oregon.

C.C.H. Colbert C. Held, A.B., A.M.

Graduate Student, Graduate School of Geography, Clark University.

C.D. Charles Duffy, Ph.B., M.A., Ph.D.

Pierce Professor of English, Chairman of the Department of English, University of Akron.

C.DeB. Cornelius De Boe, A.B., A.M., Th.B., Ph.D.

Professor of Philosophy and Christian Ethics, School of Theology, Temple University.

C.E.J. Chester E. Jorgenson, B.A., M.A.

Associate Professor of English, Wayne University.

C.E.K. Charles E. Kellogg, Ph.D.

Chief, Division of Soil Survey, Head Soil Scientist, U. S. Department of Agriculture.

C.H.Cu. C. H. Curran, B.S.Agric., M.A., D.Sc.

Curator, Department of Insects and Spiders, The American Museum of Natural History.

C.H.Go. Cyrus H. Gordon, A.B., M.A., Ph.D.

Professor of Assyriology and Egyptology, Dropsie College.

C.H.Wo. Carol H. Woodward, B.A.

Editor, *The Journal*, New York Botanical Garden.

C.M.D. Christopher M. Dawson, B.A., Ph.D.

Associate Professor of Greek, Yale University.

C.O.O. C. O. Oakley, B.S., M.S., Ph.D.

Professor of Mathematics, Haverford College.

C.R.S. Charles Robbins Schroeder, B.S., D.V.M.

Assistant Director, Animal Industry Section, Lederle Laboratories Division, American Cyanamid Company; Former Veterinarian, New York Zoological Park.

C.S.Sp. C. Sumner Spalding, A.B., M.A., B.S.

Music Cataloger, Library of Congress.

C.T.F. Rev. Charles T. Fritsch, A.B., Th.B., Ph.D.

Assistant Professor of Old Testament, Princeton Theological Seminary.

C.T.H. Charles T. Haven

Former Technical Assistant, Johnson Automatics.

C.T.M. Charles T. Murphy, A.B., M.A., Ph.D.

Associate Professor of Classics, Head of the Department of Classics, Oberlin College.

C.W.D. Caleb W. Davis, A.B., A.M.

Free Lance Writer.

C.W.Do. Carroll W. Dodge, A.B., A.M., Ph.D., D.H.C.

Professor of Botany, Washington University; Mycologist, Missouri Botanical Garden.

D.D.M. Donald D. Millikin

Former Major, United States Army; Former Free Lance and Technical Writer.

DeL.F. DeLancey Ferguson, B.A., M.A., Ph.D.

Professor of English, Chairman of the Department of English, Brooklyn College.

D.F.P. Donald F. Putnam, B.S.A., Ph.D. (U. of Toronto).

Associate Professor of Geography, University of Toronto.

D.G. Rabbi David Graubart, B.S., M.A., D.D., Ph.D.

Rabbi and President, The Bet Din (Ecclesiastical Court) of the Chicago Council of the United Synagogue of America; Lecturer in History, College of Jewish Studies.

D.G.G.K. Donald G. G. Kerr, B.A., Ph.D. (U. of London).

Professor of History, Mount Allison University.

D.J.G. Donald J. Grout, A.B., A.M., Ph.D.

Professor of Music, Chairman of the Department of Music, Cornell University.

D.N.W. Donald N. Wilber, A.B., M.F.A. in Arch.

Associate Professor of Classical Studies, The Asia Institute.

D.R. Dana Rush

Free Lance Writer; Former Staff Writer, *Current Biography*.

D.T. Day Tuttle

Associate Professor of Drama, Department of Theatre. Smith College.

E.A.M. Ernest A. Moody, B.A., M.A., Ph.D.

Associate Professor of Philosophy, Graduate School, Columbia University.

E.A.R. Edward A. Ryan, S.J., A.B., S.T.L.

Professor of Church History, Woodstock College.

E.B.A. Elsie B. Allen

Free Lance Writer.

E.B.D. Edward B. Dunford, LL.B., LL.D.

Special Lecturer, Yale School of Alcohol Studies; General Counsel, Temperance League of America.

E.B.H. Edward B. Ham, B.A., M.A., Ph.D. (Oxford U.).

Professor of French, Department of Romance Languages, University of Michigan.

E.C.R. Edward C. Raney, B.S., M.S., Ph.D.

Associate Professor of Zoology and Fishery Biology, Cornell University.

E.C.S. Erwin C. Stumm, A.B., A.M., Ph.D.

Assistant Professor of Geology, Associate Curator of the Museum of Paleontology, University of Michigan; Former Member, U. S. Geological Survey.

E.E.B. Elizabeth E. Bacon, B.A., Ph.D.

Lecturer in Anthropology, University of California; Former Research Analyst, Iran and Afghanistan, U. S. Department of State.

E.G.DaC. Ernesto G. Da Cal, B.S., Litt.Ph.L. (U. of Madrid).

Assistant Professor of Romance Languages, New York University.

E.G.H. Rev. Elmer G. Homrighausen, A.B., Th.B., M.A., Th.M., Th.D.

Thomas Synnott Professor of Christian Education, Princeton Theological Seminary.

E.H. Einar Haugen, B.A., M.A., Ph.D.

Professor of Scandinavian Languages, University of Wisconsin.

E.J.C. Edward J. Cottrell, Jr.

Assistant to the Chief of Press, Army Public Information Division.

E.J.J. Edward J. Jurji, B.A., M.A., Ph.D., Th.B.

Associate Professor of Islamics and Comparative Religion, Princeton Theological Seminary; Lecturer in Oriental Languages, Princeton University.

E.L.F. E. Lee Fairley, B.M., M.M.

Music Specialist, U. S. Department of State; Associate Editor, *Notes,* Music Library Association; Program Annotator, National Symphony Orchestra.

E.L.Sh. Estelle L. Sharp

Garden Consultant, Berwyn, Pa.

E.P. Ernest Posner, Ph.D. (U. of Berlin).

Director, School of Social Sciences and Public Affairs, The American University.

E.Po. Eric Ponder, M.B., Ch.B., M.D., D.Sc. (Edinburgh U.).

Attending Physician in Medicine, Nassau Hospital.

E.P.C. Eugene Parker Chase, A.B., B.A. (Oxford U.), M.A. (Oxford U.), Ph.D.

Professor of Political Science, Lafayette College.

E.R.A. E. R. Adair, B.A., B.A. (Cambridge U.), M.A. (Cambridge U.).

Professor of History, McGill University; Former President, Canadian Historical Association.

E.R.C. Emily Read Cheston

Garden Consultant; Lecturer on Horticultural Subjects.

E.S. Eric Schroeder

Keeper of Islamic Art, Fogg Museum, Harvard University.

E.S.B. Edgar Sheffield Brightman, A.B., A.M., S.T.B., Ph.D., Litt.D. LL.D.

Borden Parker Bowne Professor of Philosophy, Boston University; Permanent Chairman, Board of the Graduate School, Brown University.

F.A.C.,Jr. Fenner A. Chace, Jr., A.B., A.M., Ph.D.

Curator of Marine Invertebrates, U. S. National Museum.

F.Br. Rev. Frederick Bronkema, A.B., B.D., Th.M., Th.D., Ph.D.

Professor of Theology and Philosophy, Bob Jones University.

F.C.C. Frank C. Campbell

Member, Circulation Department, *Notes,* Quarterly Journal of the Music Library Association.

F.C.H. Fred C. Hamil, B.A., M.A., Ph.D.

Assistant Professor of History, Wayne University.

F.E.F. Frederic Everett Faverty, A.B., M.A., Ph.D.

Professor of English, Chairman of the Department of English, Northwestern University; Editor, Northwestern University Press.

F.E.L. F. E. Lord, A.B., A.M., Ph.D.

Director of Special Education, Michigan State Normal College; Lecturer in Education, University of Michigan.

F.J.R. Frank J. Roos, Jr., Ph.B., Ph.D.

Professor of Art, University of Illinois.

F.P.Ma. Frank Pelletreau Mathews, A.B., M.D.

Assistant Physician, Assistant Clinical Professor of Public Health, Yale University.

F.R.F. F. Raymond Fosberg, A.B., M.Sc., Ph.D.

Professorial Lecturer in Botany, George Washington University; Research Associate, Department of Biology, Catholic University of America.

F.V. Fernand Vial, Bac.-es-Lettres (U. of Aix-en-Provence), M.A., Ph.D.

Associate Professor of French, Chairman of the Department of Romance Languages, Fordham University.

F.W.B. Francis William Buckler, B.A., M.A. (Cambridge U.), S.T.D.

Professor of Church History, Oberlin College.

G.A.B. George A. Barrois, S.T.D., Th.D.

Associate Professor of Biblical Literature and Theology, Princeton Theological Seminary.

G.B. Giuliano Bonfante, Ph.D. (U of Rome).

Professor of Romance Languages, Princeton University.

G.Bu. Glen Burch, A.B., M.A.

Executive Director, Film Council of America; Former Associate Editor, *Film Forum Review;* Former Editor, *Adult Education Journal,* American Association for Adult Education.

G.C.F. George Clyde Fisher, A.B., LL.D., Ph.D.

Former Curator of the Hayden Planetarium, The American Museum of Natural History.

G.C.V. George C. Vedova, B.A., M.A., Ph.D.

Professor of Mathematics, Chairman of the Department of Mathematics, Newark College of Engineering.

G.E.B. George Edgar Burford, B.S., M.D.

Attending Anesthetist, St. Luke's Hospital; Anesthetist, Babies Hospital; Anesthetist, Woman's Hospital, New York, N. Y.

G.E.D. George E. Duckworth, A.B., M.A., Ph.D.

Giger Professor of Classics, Princeton University.

G.F.E. Major George Fielding Eliot, B.A.

Military Affairs Expert; Author; Columnist, New York *Post Home News.*

G.F.H. George Frederick Howe, A.B., A.M., Ph.D.

Chief, Mediterranean Unit, Historical Division, U. S. Department of the Army.

G.G. George Gamow, Ph.D. (U. of Leningrad).

Professor of Theoretical Physics, The George Washington University.

G.H.DeC. George H. De Chow

Major, United States Army; Member, U. S. Department of the Army General Staff.

G.H.K. George Harmon Knoles, A.B., M.A., Ph.D.

Associate Professor of History, Stanford University.

G.L.D.V. G. L. Della Vida, Ph.D. (U. of Rome).

Professor of Arabic, Graduate School of Arts and Sciences, University of Pennsylvania.

G.M.C.   **G. Miles Conrad**, B.A., M.A.

Editor, Graphic Science Associates, Inc.; Former Assistant Curator, Comparative and Human Anatomy, The American Museum of Natural History.

G.McL.H.   **George McLean Harper, Jr.**, B.A., M.A., Ph.D.

Garfield Professor of Ancient Languages, Chairman of the Department of Classics, Williams College.

G.M-S.   **Geoffrey Mott-Smith**

Perpetual Member, National Laws Commission of the American Contract Bridge League.

G.M.Sm.   **Gertrude M. Smith**

Garden Consultant, Montclair, N. J.

G.R.S.   **Gordon R. Silber**, A.B., Ph.D.

Professor of French and Italian, Chairman of the Department of Modern Languages, Union College.

G.R.W.   **Gordon R. Willey**, B.A., M.A., Ph.D.

Anthropologist, Bureau of American Ethnology, Smithsonian Institution; Member, Institute of Andean Research.

G.Str.   **Georg Strandvold**

Associate Editor, *The Decorah-Posten*.

G.T.   **Griffith Taylor**, B.S., B.M.E., Sc.D. (U. of Sydney), A.B. (Cambridge U.)

Professor of Geography, Head of the Department of Geography, University of Toronto.

H.A.S.   **Hayden A. Sears**, B.S.

Colonel, United States Army; Director of Instruction, The Armored School, Washington, D. C.

H.Bl.   **Rabbi Herbert Bloom**, B.A., M.H.L., Ph.D.

Rabbi, Temple Emanuel, Kingston, N. Y.; Jewish Chaplain, Wallkill Prison, New York.

H.B.W.   **H. Bunker Wright**, A.B., M.A., Ph.D.

Associate Professor of English, Miami University; Lecturer in English, University of Cincinnati.

H.C.K.   **Hilmar C. Krueger**, Ph.D.

Associate Professor of History, University of Cincinnati.

H.C.S.   **H. C. Sauvain**, B.S., M.B.A., D.C.S.

Professor of Finance, Chairman of the Department of Finance, Indiana University.

H.E.Be.   **Henry E. Bent**, A.B., M.S., Ph.D.

Professor of Chemistry, Dean of the Graduate Faculty, University of Missouri; Former Secretary, Association of American Universities.

H.F.H.   **Harry F. Harlow**, B.A., Ph.D.

Professor of Psychology, University of Wisconsin.

H.F.R.   **Harris Franklin Reeve**

Assistant to the Director, Flight Safety Foundation.

H.G.De.   **Herbert G. Deignan**, B.A.

Associate Curator, Birds, U. S. National Museum.

H.G.M.   **Harlan Goldsbury Metcalf**, A.B., M.A., Ph.D.

Professor of Physical Education, Head of the Department of Recreation and Outdoor Education, State Teachers College, Cortland, New York.

H.H.Wa.   **Hyatt Howe Waggoner**, A.B., A.M., Ph.D.

Associate Professor of American Literature, The University of Kansas City.

H.L.B.   **Henri L. Brugmans**, Lic. ès L., D. de l'U. de Paris, Elève Titulaire.

Associate Professor of French, Acting Chairman of the Department of Languages, Hofstra College.

H.L.C.   **Howard Lester Cooke, Jr.**, A.B.

Resident Critic in Painting, Princeton University.

H.L.Sh.   **Harry L. Shapiro**, A.B., A.M., Ph.D.

Chairman, Department of Anthropology and Curator of Physical Anthropology, The American Museum of Natural History; Professor of Anthropology, Columbia University.

H.M.M.   **Henry Miller Madden**, A.B., Ph.D.

International Refugee Organization, Linz, Austria.

H.M.V.   **Harold M. Vinacke**, A.B., Ph.D.

Professor of International Law and Politics, University of Cincinnati.

H.N.A.   **Hubert N. Alyea**, A.B., A.M., Ph.D.

Associate Professor of Chemistry, Princeton University.

H.N.Ho.   **Harry N. Howard**, A.B., M.A., Ph.D.

Adviser, Division of Greek, Turkish, and Iranian Affairs, U. S. Department of State.

H.R.H.   **Henry Russell Hitchcock**, A.B., M.A.

Professor of Art, Smith College; Lecturer in Architecture, Massachusetts Institute of Technology.

H.S.   **Henry Semat**, B.S., A.M., Ph.D.

Associate Professor of Physics, College of the City of New York.

H.Sc.   **Harold Schlosberg**, A.B., M.A., Ph.D.

Professor of Psychology, Brown University.

H.Si.   **Harry Silver**

Member, New York State Bar.

H.S.R.   **Hugh S. Rice**, B.S., A.M., Ph.D.

Research Associate, Hayden Planetarium, The American Museum of Natural History.

H.T.Jr.   **Harry Tschopik, Jr.**, A.B., M.A.

Assistant Curator of Ethnology, The American Museum of Natural History.

H.T.D.   **Hans T. David**, Ph.D. (U. of Berlin).

Professor of Musicology and Theory, School of Music; Chairman of the Department of Music, College of Arts and Sciences, Southern Methodist University.

H.T.K. **Rev. Hugh Thomson Kerr, Jr.,** S.T.B., M.A., Ph.D.

Associate Professor of Systematic Theology, Princeton Theological Seminary.

H.W.F. **Harry W. Freeman,** B.S.

Metallurgical Engineer, U. S. Department of the Navy.

I.H. **Irving Herman,** B.S.

Ordnance Engineer, Office of the Chief of Ordnance, U. S. Department of the Army.

J.A.Bo.,Jr. **John A. Borneman, Jr.**

Associate Professor of Homeopathic Pharmacy, Hahnemann Medical College.

J.A.Br. **James Arnold Brussel,** B.S., M.D., (Assoc.) A.C.P.

Assistant Director, Willard State Hospital, Willard, N. Y.

J.A.L. **James A. Lane,** B.S., M.S.

Chief, Reactor Evaluation Staff, Atomic Energy Commission; Director, Reactor Engineering Division, Oak Ridge National Laboratory.

J.A.L.M. **Juan A. L. Marichal,** B.A., M.A.

Instructor in Romance Languages, The Johns Hopkins University.

J.A.P. **James Arthur Prescott,** C.B.E., D.Sc. (U. of Adelaide).

Professor of Agricultural Chemistry; Director, Waite Agricultural Research Institute, University of Adelaide.

J.C.Wi. **J. Christy Wilson,** A.B., M.A., Th.M., D.D.

Director of Field Work and Associate Professor in Ecumenics, Princeton Theological Seminary.

J.C.Wis. **John C. Wister,** A.B., D.Sc.

Director, Arthur Hoyt Scott Horticultural Foundation, Swarthmore College; Director, John T. Tyler Arboretum, Lima, Pa.

J.D. **John Diebold,** M.B.A., A.B., B.S.

President, John Diebold & Associates, Inc.; editorial associate, *Automatic Control.*

J.D.H. **Rev. John D. Herr,** B.Arch., B.D., Th.M., Th.D.

Minister, Philadelphia Conference of the Methodist Church; Professor of Systematic Theology, School of Theology, Temple University.

J.E.F. **Johnson E. Fairchild,** B.A., M.A.

Professor of Social Philosophy, Head of the Division of Social Philosophy, Cooper Union; Former Instructor in Geography, Hunter College.

J.E.Hi. **John Eric Hill,** A.B., Ph.D.

Former Assistant Curator of Mammals, American Museum of Natural History.

J.E.Mo. **James Ernest Moffat,** A.B., A.M., Ph.D.

Professor of Economics, Special Administrative Assistant to the President, Indiana University.

J.E.V. **James E. Vance, Jr.,** A.B.

Graduate Student, Graduate School of Geography, Clark University.

J.F. **Rev. Jack Finegan,** B.A., M.A., B.D., M.Th., L.Th. (U. of Berlin).

Professor and Head of the Department of Old Testament and New Testament Literature and Interpretation, Director of the Palestine Institute of Archaeology, Dean of the Summer Session, Pacific School of Religion.

J.F.R. **John Fraser Ramsey,** M.A., Ph.D.

Professor of European History, University of Alabama.

J.G. **Joseph Geschelin,** B.S. in M.E.

Detroit Editor, Chilton Publications (*Automotive Industries, Motor Age,* and *Commercial Car Journal*).

J.Ga. **John Gassner,** B.A., M.A.

Chairman, Play Department, Dramatic Workshop of the New School for Social Research; Lecturer in Dramatic Arts, Columbia University.

J.Go. **John Goheen,** B.A., Ph.D.

Associate Professor of Philosophy, Chairman of the Department of Philosophy, Queens College.

J.G.D.C. **J. Grahame D. Clark,** B.A., M.A., Ph.D. (Cambridge U.).

University Lecturer in Archaeology, Cambridge University; Editor, *Proceedings of the Prehistoric Society.*

J.G.J. **John G. Jenkins**

Professor of Psychology, Chairman of the Department of Psychology, University of Maryland.

J.G.VanD. **James Grote Van Derpool,** B.S., M.A.

Professor of Library Service, Head of the Avery Architectural Library, Columbia University.

J.G.W. **Joseph Garnett Wood,** Ph.D. (U. of Cambridge), D.Sc. (U. of Adelaide).

Professor of Botany, University of Adelaide.

J.H.M. **John H. Madison,** B.S.

Colonel, Coast Artillery Corps, United States Army; Director of Instruction, Antiaircraft and Guided Missile Branch, The Artillery School, Fort Bliss, Tex.

J.H.P. **J. Hugh Pruett,** A.B., L.H.D.

Director, Astronomical Observatory, University of Oregon.

J.I.C. **John Irwin Cooper,** B.A., M.A., Ph.D.

Associate Professor of History, McGill University.

J.J. **Jotham Johnson,** A.B., Ph.D.

Associate Professor of Classics, Chairman of the Department of Classics, New York University.

J.J.T. **James J. Talman,** B.A., M.A., Ph.D.

Chief Librarian, Associate Professor of History, University of Western Ontario.

J.J.VanN. **John James Van Nostrand,** A.B., M.A., Ph.D., LL.D.

Professor of Ancient History, University of California.

J.L. **Jerome Lederer,** B.S. in M.E., M.E.

Director, Flight Safety Foundation, Inc.; Technical Adviser, United States Aviation Underwriters; Fellow, Institute of the Aeronautical Sciences.

J.M.P. **John Musser Pearce,** Ph.B., M.D.

Professor of Pathology, Professor of Pathology in Surgery, Cornell University Medical School; Attending Pathologist, New York Hospital.

J.R.To. **Joseph Richard Toven,** A.B., A.M., Ph.D.

Assistant Supervisor of University Admissions, Assistant Professor of Spanish, New York University.

J.S.By. **Janet S. Byrne,** B.A., M.A.

Assistant, Department of Prints, Metropolitan Museum of Art.

J.Se. **Janet Searles,** M.A.

Free Lance Writer in the field of Chemistry.

J.S.R. **Joseph S. Roucek,** B.A., M.A., Ph.D.

Professor of Political Science and Sociology, Chairman of the Department of Political Science and Sociology, University of Bridgeport.

J.T.I.   **J. Theron Illick,** Ph.D.

Associate Professor of Zoology, Syracuse University.

J.W.   **John Wild,** Ph.B., M.A., Ph.D.

Professor of Philosophy, Harvard University.

J.W.A.   **James W. Atz,** A.B.

Assistant Curator, New York Aquarium, New York Zoological Society.

J.W.Bo.   **Rev. John Wick Bowman,** A.B., A.M., B.D., Ph.D.

Robert Dollar Professor of New Testament Interpretation, San Francisco Theological Seminary.

J.W.D.   **John William Dowling,** B.A,. M.A., B.A. (Oxford U.), M.A. (Oxford U.).

Assistant Professor of Philosophy, Rutgers University.

J.W.F.   **John W. Flight,** B.A., B.D., M.A., Ph.D.

Professor of Biblical Literature, Haverford College.

K.B.   **Klaus Berger,** Ph.D.

Assistant Professor of Art, University of Kansas City.

K.B.T.   **Kendall B. Taft,** BA., MA., Ph.D.

Professor of American Literature, Chairman of the Department of English and Speech, Roosevelt College.

K.J.C.   **Kenneth John Conant,** M.Arch., Ph.D.

Professor of Architecture, School of Design, Division and Department of Fine Arts, Harvard University.

K.K.L.   **Kenneth K. Landes,** B.S., A.M., Ph.D.

Professor of Geology, Chairman of the Department of Geology, University of Michigan.

K.McK.   **Kenneth McKenzie,** A.B., A.M., Ph.D., Doctor (U. of Padua).

Emeritus Professor of Italian, Princeton University.

K.R.S.   **Kendon R. Smith,** A.B., A.M., Ph.D.

Associate Professor of Psychology, Pennsylvania State College.

K.V.G.   **K. V. Grinius**

Instructor in Russian, Department of Romance Languages, Syracuse University.

L.A.V.   **Louis A. Vaczek**

Member, Foreign Service of Hungary; Instructor in Hungarian Language and Literature, Graduate School, Columbia University.

L.B.   **Lucienne Blanjean,** A.B., A.M.

Special Student, Graduate School of Geography, Clark University.

L.E.N.   **Leslie E. Neville**

Director, Standard Aeronautical Index, Institute of the Aeronautical Sciences.

L.G.   **Lucius Garvin,** A.B., A.M., Ph.D.

Professor of Philosophy, Oberlin College.

L.M.B.   **Lester M. Beattie,** A.B., A.M., Ph.D.

Professor of English, Carnegie Institute of Technology.

L.N.R.   **Louis N. Ridenour,** B.S., Ph.D.

Professor of Physics, Dean of the Graduate College, University of Illinois.

L.P.C.   **L. P. Chambers,** M.A., B.D., Ph.D.

Associate Professor of Philosophy, Washington University; Former Professor of Philosophy and Psychology, Robert College, Constantinople.

L.R.   **Lincoln Rothschild,** A.B., A.M.

Assistant Professor of Art, Chairman of the Department of Art, Adelphi College; Lecturer on the History of Art, Art Students League of New York.

L.S.   **Leslie Spier,** B.S., Ph.D.

Professor of Anthropology, University of New Mexico.

L.T.R.   **Laurence T. Rogers,** A.B., M.A., Ph.D.

Professor of Health Education, George Peabody College.

L.T.S.   **Lucy T. Shoe,** A.B., M.A., Ph.D., F.A.A.R.

Associate Professor of Art, Archaeology, and Greek, Mount Holyoke College.

L.W.B.   **Lorne W. Barclay,** B.A., M.A., L.H.D., B.D.

National Director of Publications, Boy Scouts of America; Editor, *Scouting Magazine.*

L.W.L.   **Lane W. Lancaster,** B.A., M.A., Ph.D.

Professor of Political Science, Chairman of the Department of Political Science, University of Nebraska.

M.A.G.   **Rabbi Morris A. Gutstein,** B.S., Ph.D., D.H.L.

Rabbi, Congregation Shaare Tikvoh, Chicago, Ill.; Lecturer in American-Jewish History, College of Jewish Studies.

M.A.S.   **Mirza Ahmad Sohrab**

Founder and Director of the New History Society and the Caravan of East and West, Inc.

M.Bi.   **Margaret Bieber,** Ph.D. (U. of Bonn).

Former Associate Professor of Fine Arts and Archaeology, Columbia University.

M.Br.   **Manuel Brussaly,** B.A., M.A., Ph.D.

Assistant Professor of Romance Languages, New York University.

M.B.E.   **M. B. Emeneau,** B.A., B.A. (Oxford U.), M.A. (Oxford U.), Ph.D.

Professor of Sanskrit and General Linguistics, University of California; Editor, *Journal of the American Oriental Society.*

M.B.H.   **Mohamed B. Hifny,** B.A., M.A.

Graduate Student, Graduate School of Geography, Clark University.

M.E.McD.   **Mary E. McDonnell,** B.A.

Drama, Art, and Society Editor of *The Villager.*

M.G.N.   **M. Graham Netting,** B.S., M.A.

Curator of Herpetology, Assistant Director, Carnegie Museum; Assistant Professor of Geography, University of Pittsburgh.

M.H.Sm.   **Maurice H. Smith,** M.L.S.

Librarian, Institute of the Aeronautical Sciences.

M.Je. Merrill Jensen, B.A., M.A., Ph.D.
Professor of History, University of Wisconsin.

M.K. Michael Kraus, B.S.S., Ph.D.
Professor of History, College of the City of New York.

M.L.F. Martin L. Faust, A.B., A.M., Ph.D.
Professor of Political Science, Chairman of the Department of Political Science, University of Missouri.

M.L.S. Milton L. Shane
Member of staff, Modern Language Department, George Peabody College for Teachers.

M.Mo. Margaret Morrell, B.A.
Associate Editor, *American Astrology* Magazine.

M.Sr. Montgomery Schuyler, B.S. in C.E.
Free Lance Writer.

M.S.M. M. S. Marshall, B.Sc., M.A., Ph.D.
Professor of Bacteriology, School of Medicine, College of Dentistry, College of Pharmacy, University of California.

M.Wi. Mulford Winsor
Director, Arizona State Library and Archives.

N.C.S. Nathan Comfort Starr, A.B., B.A. (Oxford U.), M.A. (Oxford U.), A.M., Ph.D.
Professor of English, Chairman of the Division of English and Theatre Arts, Rollins College.

N.D.H. Neal D. Houghton, B.S. in Ed., A.M., Ph.D.
Professor of Political Science, University of Arizona.

N.F.R. Norman F. Ramsey, B.A., B.A. (Cambridge U.), M.A. (Cambridge U.), Ph.D.
Associate Professor of Physics, Harvard University; Associate Head of the Physics Department, Brookhaven National Laboratory, Upton, L. I., N. Y.

N.J.B. N. J. Berrill, B.Sc., Ph.D., D.Sc. (U. of London).
Strathcona Professor of Zoology, McGill University.

N.J.T. Neil J. Twombly, S.J., A.B., S.T.L.
Professor of Latin, Jesuit Novitiate, Wernersville, Pa.

N.L.H. Norman L. Hill, A.B., M.A., Ph.D.
Professor of Political Science, University of Nebraska; Member, Executive Council, American Society of International Law.

O.S.Fj. Olaf S. Fjelde, B.S., M.A.
Professor of Architecture, University of Illinois.

O.W.H-Q. Olga Wilbourne Hall-Quest, B.S., M.A.
Teacher of Remedial Reading and Director of the Testing Program, The Masters School, Dobbs Ferry, N. Y.

P.C.P. Paul C. Potter, B.S.M.E.
Member, Engineering Staff, General Motors Corporation.

P.E.J. Preston E. James, M.A., Ph.D.
Professor of Geography, Syracuse University.

P.F. Paul Forchheimer, M.A.
Teacher, Beth Jacob High School, Brooklyn, N. Y.; Member, American Anthropological Association.

P.G.G. Paul G. Gelrud, B.S., M.A., Ph.D.
Associate Professor of Music, University of Manitoba; Chairman, Theory Committee, Western Board of Music.

P.H. Paul Honigsheim, Ph.D. (U. of Heidelberg).
Professor of Sociology, Anthropology, and Foreign Studies, Michigan State College.

P.J.B. Rev. Philip J. Boyle, S.J., A.B., S.T.L.
Assistant Pastor, Mambajao, Misamis Oriental, Philippine Republic.

P.S.D. Paul S. Dull, B.A., Ph.D.
Assistant Professor of Political Science and History, University of Oregon.

R.A.B. Robert A. Brotemarkle, A.B., A.M., Ph.D.
Professor of Psychology, Chairman of the Department of Psychology, Director of the Psychological Laboratory and Clinic, University of Pennsylvania; Diplomate in Clinical Psychology, American Board of Examiners in Professional Psychology.

R.A.N. Robert A. Nisbet, Ph.D.
Associate Professor of Sociology, University of California.

R.A.P. Richard Alexander Parker, A.B., Ph.D.
Associate Professor of Romance Languages, New York University.

R.A.W. Richard Alan Waterman, A.B., M.A., Ph.D.
Assistant Professor of Anthropology, Northwestern University.

R.B. Ruth Blair
Executive Secretary, Atlanta Historical Society.

R.Da. Royden Dangerfield, B.S., Ph.D.
Professor, National War College; Former Professor of Political Science, University of Oklahoma.

R.F. Rosalie Feltenstein, B.A., M.A.
Free Lance Writer.

R.G.B. Robert G. Bowman, A.B., Ph.D.
Associate Professor of Geography, State University of Iowa.

R.G.M. Richard G. Monges, B.Sc.
Assistant Professor of French and Italian, New York University.

R.G.W. Robert Gale Woolbert, A.B., A.M., Ph.D.
Professor of History, University of Denver; Book Review Editor, *Foreign Affairs*.

R.H.B. Robert H. Baker, Ph.D.
Professor of Astronomy, University of Illinois; Former Research Associate, Harvard Observatory.

R.H.L. Ralph H. Lutz, A.B., LL.B., Ph.D.
Professor of History, Dean of Graduate Study, Stanford University.

R.J.K. Robert Joseph Kerner, A.B., A.M., Ph.D., LL.D., Litt.D.
Sather Professor of History, Director of the Institute of Slavic Studies, University of California.

R.J.N. Robert J. Niess, A.B., A.M., Ph.D.
Assistant Professor of French, Harvard University.

R.J.O'C. Robert J. O'Connell, S.J., A.B., S.T.L.
Graduate Student, Fordham University.

R.L.P. Robert Leet Patterson, A.B., A.M., B.D., Ph.D.
Professor of Philosophy, Duke University.

R.L.S. **Robert L. Scranton**, A.B., A.M., Ph.D.
Associate Professor of Classical Archaeology, Emory University.

R.M. **R. Matthes**, B.S.S.
Head of the Commercial Division, W. R. Grace & Co.

R.Ma. **Robert Mainhardt**, B.S., M.S.
Staff member, University of California Radiation Laboratory.

R.M.K. **Richard M. Keith**
Member of the Faculty, School of Music, Howard University.

R.M.L. **Robert M. Loebelson**
Military Editor, American Aviation Publications.

R.M.Y. **R. M. Younger**
Director, Australian News and Information Bureau, New York.

R.Ne. **Rexford Newcomb**, B.S., M.Arch., M.A.
Professor of the History of Architecture, Dean of the College of Fine and Applied Arts, Director of the Bureau of Community Planning, University of Illinois.

R.S.B. **Richard S. Bowman**, B.S.
Assistant Professor of English, Director of Dramatics, Public Events Officer, Cooper Union.

R.S.M. **Robert Stuart Mathews**, A.B., M.A.
Free Lance Writer in the field of Biology.

R.S.Y. **Rodney Stuart Young**, A.B., M.A., Ph.D.
Professor of Archaeology, Head of the Department of Archaeology, University of Pennsylvania.

R.T. **Ruthven Todd**
Author; Free Lance Writer.

R.Ta. **René Taupin**, Ph.D.
Associate Professor of Romance Languages, Hunter College.

R.T.H. **Robert T. Hatt**, Sc.B., Ph.D.
Director, Cranbrook Institute of Science; Former Assistant Curator of Mammals, American Museum of Natural History.

R.V.S. **Ronald V. Sires**, A.B., Ph.D.
William Kirkman Professor of History, Whitman College.

R.W.,Jr. **Raymond Walters, Jr.**, A.B., M.A., Ph.D.
Member of the Editorial Staff, *Saturday Review of Literature*.

R.W.H. **Ralph Warner Hammett**, B.S., M.Arch.
Professor of Architecture, University of Michigan.

R.W.K. **Ruth Wedgwood Kennedy**, B.A., Diploma (Oxford U.).
Lecturer in Art, Smith College.

S.A. **Sherman Abrahamson**, B.A., M.A.
Member of the Staff, Environmental Research Division, Quartermaster Corps, Washington, D. C.

S.A.W. **Selman A. Waksman**, M.Sc., Ph.D., Sc.D., LL.D., M.D. (hon.).
Professor of Microbiology, Rutgers University; Discoverer of Streptomycin.

S.C. **Sidney Cowell**
Free Lance Writer in the field of Music.

S.D. **Sami Dayan**, B.A., M.A.
Instructor in Philosophy, Syracuse University.

S.D.At. **Samuel D. Atkins**, A.M., Ph.D.
Associate Professor of Classics and Sanskrit, Princeton University.

S.E.B. **Samuel E. Braden**, A.B., M.A., Ph.D.
Associate Professor of Economics, Indiana University.

S.G. **Stephen Gilman**, B.A., Ph.D.
Associate Professor of Romance Languages, Ohio State University.

S.G.I. **Samuel Guy Inman**, A.B., A.M., LL.D.
Advisor to U. S. Department of State, U. S. Office of Education, League of Nations, Pan American Conference, Bogotá Conference.

S.Gl. **Samuel Glasstone**, B.Sc., M.Sc., Ph.D., D.Sc. (all U. of London).
Professor of Chemistry, Boston College; Consultant, U. S. Atomic Energy Commission.

S.H. **Sidney Hook**, B.S., M.A., Ph.D.
Professor of Philosophy, Chairman of the Department of Philosophy, New York University; Lecturer, New School for Social Research.

S.H.M. **Samuel Holt Monk**, Ph.D.
Professor of English, Chairman of the Department of English, University of Minnesota.

S.K.W. **Samuel K. Workman**, B.A., Ph.D.
Associate Professor of English, Illinois Institute of Technology.

S.P.J. **S. Paul Johnston**, B.S. in M.E.
Director, Institute of Aeronautical Sciences.

S.VanV. **Samuel Van Valkenburg**, Ph.D. (U. of Zurich).
Professor of Geography, Director of the Graduate School of Geography, Clark University.

T.A.B. **Thomas A. Brophy**, S.J., A.B., S.T.L.
Professor of Dogmatic and Ascetic Theology, Dean, Woodstock College.

T.A.S. **Thomas A. Sebeok**, B.A., M.A., Ph.D.
Assistant Professor of Linguistics, Indiana University.

T.B.J. **Tom B. Jones**, A.B., M.A., Ph.D.
Associate Professor of History, University of Minnesota.

T.E.DeS. **Thomas E. De Shazo**
Colonel, United States Army; Assistant Commandant, The Artillery School, Fort Sill, Okla.

T.F.Ha. **Talbot Faulkner Hamlin**, B.A., B.Arch.
Professor of Architecture, Columbia University.

T.G.T. **Theodore G. Tappert**, A.M., B.D., D.D., Litt.D.
Professor of Church History, Philadelphia Lutheran Theological Seminary.

T.M.P. **Thomas Marc Parrott**, A.B., A.M., Ph.D. (U. of Leipzig).
Emeritus Professor of English, Princeton University.

T.R.H. **Thomas Robson Hay**, B.S., E.E.
Writer in the field of American History.

U.P.H. **U. P. Hedrick**, B.S., D.S.C., LL.D.
Director Emeritus, New York State Agricultural Experiment Station.

V.A.T. **Victor A. Tiedjens**, B.S., M.S., Ph.D.
Director, Virginia Truck Experimental Station; Former Associate Professor of Vegetable Gardening, Rutgers University.

V.B.H. **Virgil B. Heltzel**, A.B., M.A., Ph.D.
Professor of English, Northwestern University; Editor, *Northwestern University Studies*.

V.H.C. Victor H. Cahalane, B.Sc., M.F.

Chief, Biology Branch, National Park Service; Former Director, Cranbrook Institute of Science.

V.L.L. Victor L. Loosanoff, B.S., Ph.D.

Director, U. S. Fish and Wildlife Service Biological Laboratory, Milford, Conn.; President, National Shellfisheries Association.

V.M. Vincent Marcellino, B.S., J.D.

Assistant Counsel, New York City Rent Commission.

V.M.D. Vincent M. Downey, M.D.

Major, USAF; Chief, Department of Internal Medicine, School of Aviation Medicine, Randolph Field, Texas.

W.B.H. William B. Hesseltine, B.A., M.A., Ph.D., Litt.D.

Professor of History, University of Wisconsin.

W.B.T. William Bertram Turrill, D.Sc. (U. of London).

Keeper, Herbarium and Library, Royal Botanic Gardens, Kew, Surrey, England.

W.C. Woodstock College

A group of Philosophy and Theology Students directed by Professors of Woodstock College, Woodstock, Md.

W.C.Ro. Rev. William Childs Robinson, A.B., A.M., B.D., Th.M., Th.D.

Professor of Historical Theology, Columbia Theological Seminary.

W.D.B. W. D. Brush, B.S., M.A., Ph.D.

Former Member, U. S. Forestry Service.

W.D.Co. Walter D. Cocking, M.A., Ph.D.

Chairman, Board of Editors, American School Publishing Corporation; Member, Committee of the American Council on Education on Educational Plants.

W.D.T. William Darby Templeman, A.B., A.M., Ph.D.

Professor of English Language and Literature, University of Southern California.

W.E. William Ebenstein, LL.D. (U. of Vienna), Ph.D.

Associate Professor of Politics, Princeton University.

W.E.A. William Eugene Anderson, B.A.

Free Lance Writer.

W.E.M. William E. Milligan, B.A.Sc.

Associate Professor of Metallurgy, Yale University.

W.Fr. Wolf Franck, A.M.

Free Lance Writer; Reference Assistant, Music Division, New York Public Library.

W.F.B. William F. Boericke, A.B.

Mining Consultant, Hayden Stone & Company; Former Chief Valuation Engineer, Bureau of Mines, Government of the Philippines.

W.H.B. William H. Berry, M.D., F.A.C.S.

Associate Attending Surgeon, St. Luke's Hospital; Attending Surgeon, Sea View Hospital, New York, N. Y.

W.I. Wilton Ivie, B.S., M.S.

Editor, Technocracy, Inc., New York, N. Y.; Former Curator of Spiders, University of Utah.

W.J.Ha. William J. Hamilton, Jr., B.S., M.S., Ph.D.

Professor of Zoology, Cornell University.

W.Li. William Lichtenwanger, B.M., M.M.

Assistant Reference Librarian, Music Division, Library of Congress; Associate Editor, *Notes;* Chairman, Southeastern Chapter, American Musicological Society.

W.M.W. W. Menzies Whitelaw, B.A., B.D., A.M., Ph.D.

Professor of History, Chairman of the Department of History, American International College; Former Associate Professor of History, University of Saskatchewan.

W.M.Wa. William M. Walton, Ph.D.

Instructor in Philosophy, Yale University.

W.N.P. W. Norman Pittenger, S.T.B., S.T.M., S.T.D.

Instructor in Christian Apologetics, General Theological Seminary; Former Lecturer in Religion, Columbia University.

W.N.W. William N. Woodbury, Ph.B.

Assistant Chief Engineer, Virginia Bridge Company.

W.O.S. William O. Shanahan, A.M., Ph.D.

Associate Professor of History, University of Notre Dame.

W.R. William Ringler, A.B., Ph.D.

Assistant Professor of English Literature, Princeton University.

W.R.W. William R. Weems, B.S. in A.E., S.M.

Associate Professor of Aeronautical Engineering, Massachusetts Institute of Technology.

W.S.P. William S. Parsons

Rear Admiral, United States Navy.

W.S.V. Wayne S. Vucinich, A.B., M.A., Ph.D.

Assistant Professor of History, Stanford University.

W.T.G.,Jr. William Travis Gibb, Jr., M.D.

Assistant Clinical Professor of Medicine, School of Medicine, The George Washington University.

W.Y.T. W. Y. Tindall, A.B., A.M., Ph.D.

Associate Professor of English, Graduate School, Columbia University.

The following members of the staff contributed articles to this volume.

A.J.	Aline Jordan		**M.V.K.**	Marie V. Kowalk
A.P.	Arthur Perrow		**S.D.M.**	Shirley D. Margolius
A.W.	Alice Waldo		**S.T.S.**	Sally Topping Sun
F.G.P.	Franklyn George Palmer		**T.R.**	Theodore Ryder

THE PRONUNCIATION SYSTEM

The system employed to indicate pronunciations in this encyclopedia is based on the alphabet of the International Phonetic Association. Inasmuch as the sounds that occur in the various languages of the world far exceed in number the letters of the English alphabet, any system designed to represent all these sounds must have recourse to a set of symbols that may or may not be closely related to the familiar alphabetical characters. The International Phonetic Alphabet has two notable advantages: it is widely known beyond the boundaries of any one nation, and it is readily applicable to all the languages of the world.

Certain modifications of the International Phonetic Alphabet have been considered desirable for the purposes of this encyclopedia. Thus, instead of the symbols ʃ, ʒ, θ, and ð, with which many readers are unacquainted, the more familiar combinations *sh, zh, th,* and *th* have been employed. This modification violates the excellent principle that a single sound should be represented by a single character, but it makes the transcriptions easier for the ordinary reader to comprehend; wherever the letters that form these combinations are to be pronounced consecutively and separately, a raised period is set between them. A modification of opposite nature is introduced in the use of the single letter *j* to represent a combination of sounds which might also be transcribed *dʒ* or *dzh;* this modification, like the previous one, has been made for the purpose of simplifying the system for English readers. The consonantal sound *y,* for the same reason, is represented by the letter *y* rather than the letter *j.* In the table of vowel equivalents, the symbols *ö* and *ü* have been adopted from German for the rendering of certain vowels that occur in German and other languages but not in English, the assumption being that readers of foreign languages will generally find these symbols more illuminating than they would find alternative phonetic equivalents. In the use of the symbol *r,* no attempt has been made to distinguish between variations in the pronunciation of the sound that it represents; it is assumed that each reader will give to the symbol *r* precisely the pronunciation that he gives to the letter *r* in a written word. Furthermore, the single symbol χ has been used to represent not only the palatal voiceless fricative found, for example, in the German word *ich,* but also the velar voiceless fricative found in the German word *ach;* since, as a rule, the vowel that precedes the fricative automatically makes the sound that follows it either palatal or velar, it is unnecessary to indicate the distinction by phonetic symbols.

TABLE OF EQUIVALENTS

CONSONANTS

Phonetic Symbol	Sound Represented
b	*bob*
d	*did*
f	*forfeit*
g	*gag*
h	*hothouse*
j	*judge*
k	*cake*
l	*loyal*
m	*mime*
n	*none*
p	*prop*
r	*roar*
s	*sauce*
sh	*hashish*
t	*trot*
th	*thirty-three*
th	*other than this*
v	*vivid*
w	*woodwork*
y	*yesteryear*
z	*prizes*
zh	*pleasure, azure*
ŋ	*singing*
χ	(Ger.) *ich, ach*

THE PRONUNCIATION SYSTEM

Vowels

Phonetic Symbol	Sound Represented
ɑ	father, car
ɑ̃	(Fr.) élan, en
ɒ	what, not
a	ask, answer; (Fr.) attacher
æ	hat, back
æ̃	(Fr.) vin, main
e	fate, elite
ɛ	yet, spell
ə	maker, ago
ɜ	first, burn
i	eve, benzine
ɪ	if, sting
o	note, old
õ	(Fr.) bon, rompre
ö	(Ger.) schön, böse
ɔ	orb, all
œ	(Fr.) leur; (Ger.) können
œ̃	(Fr.) brun, lundi
u	rule, prune
ü	(Fr.) cru; (Ger.) grün
ʊ	bull, bush
ʌ	but, son

Diphthongs

ai	cry, spine
au	prow, loud
ɔi	toy, point

The tilde (˜), wherever used, indicates that the vowel above which it appears is nasalized.

In the application of this system in the encyclopedia, indications of pronunciation are restricted to article heads, particularly to those that may be supposed to present difficulties in pronunciation. In these cases the phonetic symbols are printed in square brackets following the head, and stresses are indicated by accents placed immediately after stressed vowels, a heavy or a light accent indicating respectively a primary or a secondary stress. When more than one pronunciation of a given word is in wide use, the variations appear in the phonetic transcription.

The phonetic symbols are intended to serve as a flexible guide to pronunciation, not as a standard of correct usage. Usage varies so greatly in the English language between different groups of society, between different localities, and between different nations speaking the same language, that the selection of a norm is, for the purposes of an encyclopedia, practically out of the question. Users of the encyclopedia may find distinctions in pronunciation which they do not themselves observe in their ordinary speech, but in such cases the system of transcription is sufficiently flexible to admit variations. For example, many speakers, especially in the United States, pronounce the vowel in *what* virtually as they pronounce the *a* in father; the encyclopedia's symbol for the vowel in *what* is ɒ, but when these speakers encounter that symbol in a phonetic transcription, they will presumably give it approximately the value of the symbol ɑ wherever it occurs.

COLLIER'S ENCYCLOPEDIA

ANEGADA PASSAGE, a body of water in the extreme northern part of the Leeward Islands of the West Indies, between the Virgin Islands on the west and the islands of Anguilla and St. Martin on the east. The passage is used as a route to the Panama Canal by ships coming from Europe. The name is derived from Anegada, one of the British Virgin Islands.   J.E.F.

ANEMIA [əni′miə], a term which describes a condition in which either the number of red cells in the blood or the amount of contained hemoglobin is reduced. Normally there are approximately 5,000,000 red cells per cubic millimeter of blood in men, and 4,500,000 in women, these figures being subject to a variation of about 700,000 in both directions. Each 100 cc. of blood contains about 16 gm. of hemoglobin in males and 14 gm. in females; these values may be 2 gm. above or below the average and still be normal. Children have normal values of about 80 per cent of those of the adult. The normal 14 to 16 gm. of hemoglobin, according to sex, is often spoken of as "100 per cent"; if the hemoglobin content of the blood falls much below this, or the number of red cells much below the normal number, anemia results.

Types of Anemia. There are anemias which are diseases in their own right and anemias which are only symptoms of other diseases. The first kind includes pernicious anemia, iron deficiency anemia, and several others. The second and more common kind is sometimes called "secondary," and is often caused by blood loss, either visible or concealed; sometimes it is caused by toxic processes and may be one of the first indications of cancer. Anemia, indeed, like headache and change in bowel habits, is one of the conditions which is apt to be treated as trivial although it may be a sign of serious underlying disease.

Nutritional Anemia. Red blood cells are made in the bone marrow and are largely composed of the iron-containing protein, hemoglobin. Their manufacture is accordingly dependent on the supply of substances from which protein is built and on the supply of iron. If the available amount of either of these is reduced over a sufficiently long period, a nutritional anemia gradually develops. This type of anemia is met with under conditions of extreme poverty, in inadequately rationed communities, and occasionally as a result of dietary peculiarities such as an almost exclusive carbohydrate diet. It used to be common in young women in domestic service; now it is most often met with in undernourished children, in women during pregnancy, and in cases in which the absorption of iron is interfered with because of gastric and intestinal disturbances. It can nearly always be cured by giving iron compounds, adding protein to the diet, and correcting gastro-intestinal abnormalities when they exist.

Chronic Anemia. Some chronic anemias are difficult to distinguish from nutritional anemia and are caused by interference with red cell and hemoglobin production by toxins from chronic infections, kidney disease, cancer, or the habitual use of certain drugs. Their treatment depends on the removal of the toxic cause.

Pernicious Anemia. In pernicious anemia, sufficient red cells and hemoglobin are made in the marrow, but the normal development of the cells does not take place, and they are not delivered into the blood stream because there is lacking a specific anti-anemia factor, derived from a reaction between the food and an unknown substance present in normal gastric juice. Once formed, the anti-anemia factor is absorbed from the intestine, stored in the liver, and used by the marrow for the development of red cells. Lack of the anti-anemia factor may come from a deficient diet, from faulty absorption in the intestine (in the disease called sprue), or from inability of the liver to store it. In its most common form, however, the fault lies in the absence of the unknown substance, normally found in gastric juice. This deficiency may run in families, and it is often associated with blue eyes and premature grayness of the hair. It can be successfully treated with liver or its extracts, which contain the anti-anemia factor and supply the deficiency. This type of anemia was termed "pernicious" before the curative effect of liver and its extracts was known.

Hemolytic Anemia. Other types of anemia are caused by red-cell destruction. The most common is the anemia following blood loss, which may be visible or concealed, as when it takes place from ulceration in the gastro-intestinal tract. A form of anemia which results from the destruction of red cells in the blood stream itself is less common; this is called a hemolytic anemia. A form of hemolytic anemia occurs in the newborn baby whose father's blood possesses the Rh factor (Rh positive) and whose mother's blood lacks it (Rh negative); under these circumstances the mother may become sensitized to the Rh factor, and may produce anti-Rh substances which destroy the red cells of the baby. The destructive agents are usually bacterial toxins or organic poisons, but sometimes the red cells themselves are abnormally easily destroyed because of an inherited weakness of structure. Sometimes an overactivity of the spleen results in an abnormally high rate of red-cell destruction. The treatment of these anemias depends on removing the cause, if it is possible to do so, just as in post-hemorrhagic anemias the treatment consists in removing the cause of the bleeding.   E. Po.

ANEMOMETER, *See* METEOROLOGY (*Weather and Weather Observations*).

ANEMONE [ənε′məni], a large genus of perennial herbs of the crowfoot family, many commonly called wind-flowers. Possibly one hundred species are widely scattered throughout the temperate zones, many native to southern Europe. About twenty-five occur in North America. Some are low, delicate, spring flowers of the eastern woods, others, like the American pasqueflower, native to the northern central states, are larger, hairy-stemmed, with creamy or lavender flowers 2½ in. broad. Florists force various European varieties for winter bloom, such as *A. coronaria,* with stiff stems and red, blue, white, or purple flowers 2 in. across, and *A. fulgens,* scarlet with black stamens. *A. sylvestris* has white nodding fragrant flowers. *A. pulsatilla,* the pasqueflower of Europe, resembles the American *A. patens.* All these are low-growing, not exceeding 2 ft. The hardy *A. japonica* is 3 or 4 ft. with branching graceful stems and many white, rose, or lavender open flowers sometimes 3 in. across in autumn.   J. C. Wis.

ANESTHESIA [ænəsthiˈsiə; ænəsthiˈzhiə], a bodily state in which sensations are greatly reduced or absent and in which pain is therefore absent. The search for relief from pain during surgery started before the Christian Era. Only a limited success was achieved. The drugs used included marijuana, alcohol, and opium. Modern anesthesia began in the decade of 1840 to 1850. It is regarded by many as the most important American scientific contribution up to, and possibly since, that time. Credit for the discovery was divided between William T. G. Morton of Massachusetts, Horace Wells of Connecticut, and Crawford Long of Georgia.

The word anesthesia means insensibility. As generally employed the word refers to the establishment of pain relief by one of a variety of methods during surgery. Anesthetist refers to a technician who administers anesthesia. Anesthesiology denotes that specialty of medical practice, one of the fifteen recognized by the American Medical Association, which deals chiefly with pain relief during surgery, and includes resuscitation and therapy by gaseous or local anesthetic drugs (blocking agents). Ordinarily one of two methods is chosen to establish pain relief for surgery, general anesthesia or nerve block anesthesia.

GENERAL ANESTHESIA

General anesthesia implies loss of consciousness. It is produced by drugs administered by inhalation, by vein, by rectum, and occasionally by subcutaneous injection and by mouth. Electrical anesthesia as well as hypnotism were studied with provocative but largely ineffectual results. Only the first three of these methods were used in 1949 with regularity.

Inhalation Anesthesia. Inhalation anesthesia was used most frequently. A large number of gases and vapors were found capable of establishing a reversible loss of consciousness (anesthesia), and new ones were appearing in 1949. Many produced intolerable or toxic effects. Only seven inhalation agents achieved regular employment. The most important were ethyl ether, nitrous oxide, and cyclopropane.

Muscular Relaxation. First it should be stated that a major technical problem, after questions of pain relief and safety are satisfied, centers around establishing relaxation in anesthetized muscles, particularly the abdominal muscles. Muscular relaxation by no means automatically accompanies anesthesia, and yet it is considered as a requisite in most instances for performing accurate surgery. Skill of the administrator enters at this point. However, certain agents, no matter how skillfully handled, lack the necessary potency to produce relaxation.

Ether. Ether (the original ethyl ether of Long and Morton) delivers excellent relaxation. Further, it possesses a wide margin of safety between the anesthetic and lethal concentration. Unfortunately, at times it proves irritating to the lungs and is disagreeable when inhaled. Ether occasionally affects other organs adversely and is particularly unsuited for the individual who is debilitated or acutely ill.

Nitrous oxide. Nitrous oxide can be inhaled without discomfort. It generally produces no morbid effect on pulmonary (lung), hepatic (liver), or renal (kidney) function. Unfortunately, however, the gas delivers no relaxation and only a limited anesthesia. The administration is frequently accompanied by a dangerous deficiency of oxygen.

Cyclopropane. Cyclopropane is the most recently introduced (1933) inhalation agent unquestionably destined to survive critical usage. It is respirable without producing discomfort or irritation. Anesthesia develops rapidly. Relaxation, while adequate for most surgery, is less effectively established than that following the use of ether. At times cyclopropane affects certain organs adversely. And as is true of all commonly used inhalation agents, except chloroform and nitrous oxide, cyclopropane has to be administered with due precautions against explosion.

Chloroform. This agent has been used to produce anesthesia and its use was popular in England. However, it is much more dangerous to use than ether, causing a fall of blood pressure and a depression of the respiratory center.

Intravenous Anesthesia. Many drugs when injected intravenously produced general anesthesia. The intravenous technique, from considerations related to safety, soon became limited to drugs derived from barbituric acid. Pentothal was the most commonly used agent. Wide employment of this drug during World War II was associated with the advantages of availability under field hospital conditions, small bulk, nonexplosibility, and ease of administration. Disadvantages were related to the limited relaxation and occasional untoward respiratory responses produced, and to the ease of establishing accidental overdosage.

Curare. The use of curare intravenously should be mentioned. This exotic alkaloid, possessing no anesthetic properties, was introduced to anesthesiology in 1943 and rapidly achieved wide recognition. The drug was known for many years as an arrow poison used by certain South American Indians. It was first studied scientifically in 1850 by the great physiologist Claude Bernard, who showed that the poison killed by paralyzing the muscles of the victim. Transposed to anesthesiology, the muscular paralysis and relaxation proved subject to accurate control and was relatively devoid of aftereffects. The resulting muscular relaxation produced excellent working conditions for the surgeon. This made possible the use of lighter, hence safer and less toxic levels of anesthesia.

Rectal Instillations. Anesthesia by rectal instillation was formerly popular. Ether in oil was selected for prolonged operations but it has been displaced by more modern methods. However, since 1926 a preparation trade-marked "Avertin" has been frequently used. This drug establishes a deep preliminary sedation. Then one of the standard agents is used to follow up the sedation and complete the anesthesia. Rectal instillations are often used when the patient is nervous, the agent being administered in an enema.

NERVE-BLOCK ANESTHESIA

Nerve-block anesthesia includes three types of procedure which establish anesthesia of a circumscribed part of the body without producing loss of consciousness. This is accomplished by injecting nerve-blocking chemicals into contact with the nerves to the part. These three procedures are known as local anesthesia, block or regional anesthesia, and spinal anesthesia. They are differentiated by the site on the nerve at which the block takes effect.

Local Anesthesia. Local anesthesia means the establishment of a peripherally placed block at the nerve endings. This procedure is usually selected for simple operations, but on proper indication can be employed for abdominal surgery and other major procedures. When it is used thus, pain relief is not always complete.

Block Anesthesia. Block, or regional, anesthesia means the interruption of conduction along the course of a nerve. Continuous caudal anesthesia, frequently used in obstetrics since 1943, furnishes an example of this method. In this instance the nerves carrying sensation from the pelvis are blocked at a location near the spinal cord. Other examples are brachial plexus block in the neck, and mandibular block in the mouth. These procedures are frequently used for operations on the arm and in dentistry. Block anesthesia usually produces a minimal functional disturbance. Yet the technical difficulties encountered, and the discomfort at times produced, make the method less than ideal. Sensitivity to the blocking agent used (typical ones are procaine and metycaine) is occasionally encountered.

Thermal Block. Block anesthesia effected by sharply lowering the temperature of a limb through the use of ice has been used on occasion in recent years. With the aid of a sedative, adequate anesthesia resulted. The method was credited with slowing the progress of infection as well as preserving the viability of impaired tissues.

Spinal Anesthesia. Spinal anesthesia implies that the nerve is blocked at the point where the component parts leave the substance of the spinal cord and are still surrounded by spinal fluid. The blocking agent is injected into the spinal fluid. Many nerves are thus blocked by a single injection. Spinal anesthesia produces excellent muscular relaxation. Little toxicity is associated with the small quantity of the agent required, even on the impaired organs of debilitated individuals requiring extensive surgery. Nevertheless, the disadvantages of the method are formidable. As a result of diffusion within the spinal fluid the anesthetic drug occasionally produces a widespread effect. The end result is circulatory collapse and respiratory failure. Direct injury to a nerve by the needle or agent is known to occur.

RESUSCITATION AND THERAPY

Other phases of anesthesiology, besides the relief of pain during surgery already considered, include resuscitation and therapy by gases, vapors, and blocking agents. These practices are naturally interrelated because the methods and agents employed are for the most part identical.

Resuscitation. Resuscitation, of course, has to be carried out by the person available when and where the need arises. However, urgent situations that require special attention are frequently encountered at the average hospital. Under ideal conditions resuscitation differs greatly from the simple procedure of manual artificial respiration called upon, for instance, by an emergency such as drowning. Reliance is placed on technical procedures such as intubation of the trachea (windpipe). Aspiration of secretions assures a clear airway. The lungs are ventilated by use of oxygen, oxygen-enriched air, and occasionally other gases, under controlled pressure. A special apparatus is used for this purpose. The circulation is supported, and specific treatment, if any, is instituted.

Inhalation Therapy. Therapy by the use of gases and vapors constitutes a growing phase of anesthesiology. For example, in one hospital oxygen therapy was used almost twice as frequently during 1946 as five years earlier. Helium, carbon dioxide, and aerosols (vaporized suspensions of materials such as penicillin suitable for inhalation) find employment on an enlarged scale.

Block Therapy. The injection of local anesthetic drugs, and alcohol when a permanent destruction of a nerve is desired, is used to treat painful conditions that otherwise require no surgery. The pain of heart disease has been approached by this method. Occasionally, a nerve block is done for a curative as well as a palliative effect. For example, the temporary blocking of nerves supplying a leg impaired by thrombophlebitis (a painful infection of a vein) produces improvement. The good effect is due not only to the relief of pain but also to the improvement in the circulation resulting from the effect of the block. G. E. B.

ANEURIN, or **ANEIRIN** [ɑ'nɛʊrin, ɑ'nairin], Welsh poet, who flourished about the year 600, was author of the oldest and longest Cymric epic poem, *Gododin*. Of his family and his life there is much conjecture and a number of interpretations. He attended St. Cadoc's College in Llancarvan, was an accepted bard, and was present at the Battle of Cattraeth. The great epic relates the story of this battle, in which the Saxons defeated the Britons, who were, according to the poet, too drunk on their "blue mead" to fight. Of the poem only 900 lines are extant, and their obscurity has produced many interpretations and editions. John Williams translated the work in 1852 under the title of *Y Gododin, poem of the battle of Cattraeth;* Thomas Stephens translated *Gododin* with a life of the author in 1888; and T. Gwenogvrvn Jones translated it in 1908.

ANEURYSM. *See* HEART (*Diseases of the Heart and Circulatory System*).

ANFU CLIQUE [ɑ'nfu'], members of a faction of northern Chinese militarists, who, after the death of Yuan Shihk'ai, organized the Anfu Club, ostensibly to work for the election of Hsu Shih-chang to the presidency of China in 1918. The clique remained dominant in Chinese politics until 1920. It used its power to enrich its members, largely through Japanese loans negotiated through the Japanese financier Nishihara. The clique was considered pro-Japanese and was held responsible for concessions made by the Chinese government to Japan. H. M. V.

ANGEL, in monotheistic religions, a supernatural being intermediate between God and man. In the Hebrew-Christian tradition, the word "angel" signifies not the nature of the creature, which is pure spirit, but its function or office, for both the Hebrew *malakh* and the Greek ἄγγελος mean simply "a messenger" and are used of both earthly and heavenly messengers. In addition to the word *malakh,* the Old Testament contains several other expressions which refer to beings that come under the category of angels, namely, "sons of God" (Job i:6), "sons of the mighty" (Ps. lxxxix:6), "watchers" (Dan. iv:17), "mighty ones" (Joel iii:11), and "the holy ones" (Zech. xiv:5 R.V.). Three expressions, "the host of heaven" (Deut. xvii: 3), "the host of the Lord" (Josh. v:14), and "the host of the high ones on high" (Isa. xxiv:21 R.V.), suggest the regimentation of enormous numbers of angelic beings in a heavenly army (see also Job xxv:3). The names of two are given in the Book of Daniel: Gabriel (viii:16) and Michael (x:13 and xii:1); and the apocryphal books contain the names of other angels and archangels (i.e., chief angels). In the Book of

Tobit, Raphael is one of the seven holy angels who present the prayers of the saints and who go constantly in and out before the presence of God (Tob. xii:15). In II Esdras are mentioned Jeremiel (iv:36), Phaltiel or Psaltiel (v:16), and Uriel (x:28). Many other names occur in the pseudepigraphical literature, especially in I Enoch, and in magical papyri or amulets. The angelology of the Old Testament, being influenced by Zoroastrianism, developed with unbridled extravagance in the later Jewish writings of the Talmuds, the Midrashim, and the Cabala.

In the New Testament, besides the general term ἄγγελοι, or "messengers," reference is made to "spirits" (Heb. i:14), "principalities" and "powers" (Rom. viii:38; Eph. vi:12), and "thrones" and "dominions" (Col. i:16). Michael is here called an archangel (Jude ix). Jesus rather frequently refers to angels, indicates that they are of neither sex (Matt. xxii:30), and once speaks of guardian angels (Matt. xviii:10), though he does not declare that each child has his own angel. Wicked angels are those who, probably through overweening pride, sinned and fell (II Pet. ii:4 and Jude vi). No explicit statement is made in the Bible that angels have wings. Jewish and Christian angelology was taken over into Mohammedanism and was there mingled with many animistic beliefs. Many present-day ideas among English-speaking peoples regarding the appearance of angels have been derived from John Milton. *See also* ARCHANGEL; CHERUBIM; GABRIEL; MICHAEL; RAPHAEL; SERAPHIM; URIEL.

B. M. M.

ANGELFISH, a name applied to a group of fresh-water species, *Pterophyllum,* which live in South America, and a group of marine fishes, *Holacanthus,* which has the East Indies as its center of distribution. The former is a beautiful small fish of the family Cichlidae, highly prized by aquariists. It is a compressed and somewhat circular fish, with long, filamentous extensions on the tail and lower fins which reach

NEW YORK ZOOLOGICAL SOCIETY PHOTO

ANGELFISH (PTEROPHYLLUM EIMEKII)

far beyond the body. Three dark vertical streaks on the body and fins serve to break the continuity and to hide the fish from view when among aquatic plants. The eggs are deposited on aquatic vegetation. When hatched, the young remain attached to a leaf by means of a viscous thread extending from its head. The parents often take them into the mouth and then blow them onto another leaf.

The salt-water angelfishes are large and highly colored species, often being scarlet or blue, with long extensions from the dorsal and anal fins. Although most of them are found in the East Indies, others also are found in the warmer portions of all oceans.

E. C. R.

ANGELICA, a large genus of tall, perennial herbs of the parsley family. There are forty or more species, chiefly native to the northern hemisphere, possibly twenty to the United States. *Angelica archangelica,* 6 ft. high with finely divided leaves, is used both medicinally and, when the stalks are candied, as a confection. Stems, grown like celery, are used for food in northern Europe. Angelica is cultivated as a vegetable in Iceland. Some varieties are grown in gardens

PLANT INDUSTRY STATION. BELTSVILLE. MARYLAND

Dried specimen of Angelica archangelica showing seed, stem, and finely divided leaves

for subtropical effects. *A. atropurpurea,* purple stemmed, 6 ft. high, grows from Newfoundland to Iowa. *A. hendersoni,* shorter and thicker, is native to the Pacific states. J. C. Wis.

ANGELICA TREE, Hercules' club or devil's walking stick, are common names of *Aralia spinosa,* a large, very spiny, aromatic shrub of the ginseng family, native from New York to Florida. Thickset spiny stems, with leaves 2 to 3 ft. broad, divided into many leaflets, and clusters 3 to 4 ft. long of small white flowers which bloom in August, give a tropical effect. The Chinese angelica tree, *A. chinensis,* similar but more picturesque, is widely planted for ornament. It quite often escapes and grows wild. J. C. Wis.

ANGELICO, FRA GIOVANNI [ɑnjɛ'liko], Italian painter, was born near Florence in 1387. At the age of twenty he entered the Dominican convent at Fiesole with his brother, a calligrapher. The tranquility of his monastic life from 1409 to 1418 was interrupted by ecclesiastical politics but he may well have learned to illuminate manuscripts during that time. His first known paintings, in 1423, are the exquisite reliquaries for the church of Santa Maria Novella, Florence, which hang in the Museum of San Marco, Florence, and in the Gardner Museum, Boston. In 1433, he executed the well-known altarpiece with its frame of music-making angels, now at San Marco, for the Florentine Linen Weavers' Guild. In 1436, Cosimo de' Medici gave the architect Michelozzo the commission to restore the Convent of San Marco as a new residence for the Fiesolan friars; Angelico undertook, with several assistants, the frescoed decorations of the courtyard, the chapter room, the upper corridors, and the individual cells. The renovation was completed by 1443. Pope Nicholas V, who had known Angelico in Florence when the artist was cataloguing the library of the Convent of San Marco, gave him, in 1447, a commission to fresco the *Life of St.*

Lawrence and St. Stephen in the Pope's chapel in the Vatican. In the summer of the same year Angelico began the ceiling of the Chapel of San Brixio, Orvieto, but left it unfinished. On the completion of his work in Rome, in 1449, he returned to Fiesole as prior of the monastery where he had passed his novitiate. He died in Rome in 1455.

A spontaneous piety and gladness of spirit pervade all Angelico's paintings. His workmanship in tempera, in gold, and in fresco has the rare perfection of work done joyfully for the greater glory of God. He was sufficiently responsive to the humanistic spirit of his time gradually to temper the serene medievalism of his early style with a gentle naturalism which could visualize both a radiant landscape, such as that in *Deposition,* at San Marco, and the touching gratitude of the mendicants in the Vatican frescoes. R. W. K.

ANGELL, JAMES BURRILL [e′njəl] (1829-1916), American college president and diplomat, was born on his father's farm at Scituate, R. I., Jan. 27, 1829. Graduating from Brown University in 1849, he was professor of modern languages and literature there from 1853 to 1860. He then served as editor of the *Providence Journal* until 1866, when he became successively president of the universities of Vermont (1866-1871), and Michigan (1871-1909), where he was an advocate of coeducation. Angell served on the Anglo-American Fisheries Commission (1887-1891). As minister to China in 1880 and 1881, he negotiated a new immigration treaty; he was also minister to Turkey (1897-1898). He died at Ann Arbor, Mich., Apr. 1, 1916. M. Sr.

ANGELL, JAMES ROWLAND (1869-1949), American educator and psychologist, was born in Burlington, Vt., on May 8, 1869. He was graduated from the University of Michigan in 1890, where he was prominent in athletics and excelled in the then new subject of psychology. He later studied at Harvard and at Halle, Berlin, Vienna, and Paris. Angell taught philosophy at the University of Minnesota in 1893 and psychology at the University of Chicago from 1894 to 1919, also serving as dean of the university faculties from 1911 to 1919 and as acting president for the year 1918-1919. His fame as a psychologist rests upon his championship of biological functionalism as incorporated in his *Psychology* (1904) and in numerous later articles, which show the influence of William James and John Dewey. Under his direction, the department of psychology at Chicago became notably productive of work in experimental, animal, and theoretical psychology and also made significant contributions in the field of mental tests.

After serving as president of the Carnegie Corporation from 1920 to 1921, Angell became president of Yale University, a position he held until 1937. He was known as the creator of the "New Yale" and was the first nonalumnus to be president of that institution. Under his able administration, thirty-five new buildings were erected and the endowment was quadrupled. He also built up the Yale Law School and established the Yale Institute of Human Relations. After his retirement from Yale, Angell served as educational consultant and public service counselor of the National Broadcasting Company and as general director of its Inter-American University of the Air. He was also national president of the English-Speaking Union from 1939, director of the Hall of Fame for Great Americans from 1944, and an officer in other scientific and humanistic institutions. His *American Education* was published in 1937. Angell died at Hamden, Conn., near New Haven, on Mar. 4, 1949. M. Sr.

ANGELL, NORMAN (1874-   ), English journalist, author, and lecturer, was born Ralph Norman Angell Lane at Holbeach, Lincolnshire, Dec. 26, 1874. He was educated first privately and later at the Lycée de St. Omer in France. After spending one year at the University of Geneva he traveled to the United States, where for six years he was a cowboy rancher and prospector in the West. His last year in America before returning to Europe in 1898 was spent in newspaper work and research on the causes of the Spanish-American War. In Europe he pursued a career in journalism, serving as correspondent for American papers, and from 1899 to 1903 he served as editor of Galignani's *Messenger.* From 1903 to 1905 he was on the staff of the Paris *Éclair.* In 1905 he was appointed general manager in Paris for the *Daily Mail.*

Angell's whole career was largely devoted to the promotion of international peace. Following the publication of his famous book, *The Great Illusion* (1910), which was translated into twenty languages, a movement known as "Norman Angellism," seeking the realization of the ideas expressed in this book, developed in Great Britain, France, and Germany, and a foundation was established for the promotion of those ideas. During World War I, Norman Angell was one of the founders of the Union of Democratic Control, which demanded a workable peace and open diplomacy. In 1919 Angell attended the Second Socialist International at Bern. From 1928 to 1931 he was editor of *Foreign Affairs.* In 1929 he was elected to Parliament from North Bradford as a Labor Party candidate. He was knighted in 1931. In 1933 he was awarded the Nobel Prize for peace jointly with Arthur Henderson. Since 1928 he has been a member of the Council of the Royal Institute of International Affairs. He also served on the Executive Committee of the League of Nations. Sir Norman Angell is the author of no less than thirty books. His earliest work was *Patriotism under Three Flags: a Plea for Rational Politics* (1903). His other works include: *Peace Theories and the Balkan War* (1912), *The Foundations of International Polity* (1914), *The Dangers of Half Preparedness* (1916), *The Economic Chaos and the Peace Treaty* (1919) *The Public Mind* (1926), *The Money Game* (1928), *The Story of Money* (1930), *The Unseen Assassins* (1932), *From Chaos to Control* (1933), *America's Dilemma* (1940), *What Kind of Peace* (1941), *Let the People Know* (1943), and *The Steep Places* (1947). S. D.

ANGELO, MICHAEL. *See* MICHELANGELO BUONARROTI.

ANGERONA [anjəro′nə], an ancient Roman goddess whose significance had various aspects. Sometimes known as the goddess of silence, she was represented with her finger laid upon her closed lips. She was also known as the goddess who relieved men from pain, especially angina or quinsy; or as the protective goddess of the city of Rome and guardian of the secret of its holy name. She was also known as the spirit of the new year or of the returning sun. She bears resemblances to Acca Laurentia, originally an Etruscan earth goddess and the nurse of Romulus and Remus, and to Ops, the goddess of fertility and abundance. Her festival, the Angeronalia, or Divalia, was held on December 21 in the temple of Volupia, the goddess of pleasure. R. F.

ANGERS, DAVID D'. *See* DAVID, PIERRE JEAN.

ANGERS [ã′zhe′], a city in western France, the capital of the department of Maine-et-Loire, situated on the Maine River, about 45 mi. northeast of Nantes. It is the ancient capital of Anjou, and its people continue to be known as Angevins. In Gallo-Roman times it was known as Juliomagus, and in the ninth century it became the chief residence of the counts of Anjou. In the twelfth century it came into the possession of the English king, but in 1204, after unsuccessfully laying seige to Angers, which had remained loyal to Philip Augustus, the contender for the French rights, King John of England was forced to give up Angers. The city again suffered from the English invasion of France in the fifteenth century, and in the sixteenth century it was the scene of fighting during the religious wars. During the Vendéan royalist insurrection in 1793 the Angevins took up arms against the royalists, who were repulsed near by. After the Battle of Waterloo the city was occupied by the Prussians. During World War II the section surrounding the railroad station suffered considerable damage, but the numerous historic monuments and museums escaped injury. The city was captured in 1944 by United States General George Patton, who made it the limit of his southern flank in his march eastward towards Germany.

Angers is considered one of the most beautiful cities in France, and it has monuments of great historical and architectural interest. Most outstanding is the Cathedral of St. Maurice, begun in the second half of the twelfth century and completed in the thirteenth century. Though its façade is disproportionately narrow, the cathedral as a whole is an imposing Gothic structure, set in a commanding position. The interior has an unusually broad nave, undivided by aisles, and lighted through splendid medieval glass. The earliest stained glass dates from 1170, and there are also beautiful windows of the thirteenth and fifteenth centuries. The nave has domed vaulting built in the transitional style of the twelfth century. The fame of the cathedral lies in its unrivaled collection of Gothic tapestries, especially the fourteenth-century series of the Apocalypse.

The St. Jean Hospital, founded about 1155 by Henry II of England, contains an archaeological museum. The Logis Barrault, a mansion built in the fifteenth century, houses the public library, the Musée David with works by the noted native sculptor David d'Angers, a natural history museum, and a picture gallery. The Castle of Angers, built chiefly in the thirteenth century and partly demolished in the sixteenth and subsequent centuries, continues as an excellent example of an imposing feudal stronghold. The Hôtel Pincé, or Hôtel d'Anjou, is considered the finest private mansion of the sixteenth century standing in Angers and has an interesting collection of antiquities. Of additional interest are the St. Aubin Tower, the main tower of an old Benedictine abbey, the Préfecture, occupying the old abbey buildings, and the churches of La Trinité and St. Serge. The city's educational institutions include the Université Catholique de l'Ouest.

The city has been called the Black City because of the extensive slate quarries near by, which furnish employment to many of the city's residents. The varied industrial output includes textiles, rope, sailcloth, farm machinery, liquors, cables, and shoes. Angers also serves as the trade center for the district's wines, cereal grains, vegetables, horses, cattle, and wool. Pop. 1954, 102,142.   S. Van V.

ANGEVINS, THE. *See* PLANTAGENETS.

ANGHIERA, PIETRO MARTIRE D' [aŋgye'əra] (c. 1457-1526), Italian geographer and historian, commonly known as Peter Martyr, was born at Arona in northern Italy probably Feb. 2, 1457. In 1477 he became secretary to the governor of Rome, and ten years later removed to Spain. He was present at the taking of Granada from the Moors in 1492, and in 1501 he went on a diplomatic mission to the sultan of Egypt. Ordained a priest in 1494, he served as tutor to the children of Ferdinand and Isabella. From 1505 until his death in 1526 he held the post of dean of the chapter of the Cathedral of Granada. In 1520, Anghiera was appointed royal chronicler, and later served on the Council for the Indies. He knew many of the great explorers of his time, including Columbus. His principal works are *Opus epistolarum,* letters dealing with contemporary events, and *De rebus oceanicis et novo orbe decades,* on early American discovery. He died in October 1526, in Granada.
                                                                    F.C.H.

ANGILBERT [æ'ŋgɪlbɜrt] (d. 814), Frankish poet and abbot of Saint-Riquier, was born probably between 740 and 750, of noble parentage. He was raised at the court of Charlemagne, where he was a pupil of Alcuin, and achieved fame as a contemporary "Homer." He retired to the abbey of Saint-Riquier in 790, becoming abbot in 794. He acted as ambassador for Charlemagne on three known occasions, and was witness to the signing of his will in 814. Angilbert is also said to have been the father of Nithard, the historian, through a union with Berthe, daughter of Charlemagne. He died in Saint-Riquier on Feb. 18, 814. His poetry consists of several epitaphs and inscriptions, a poem addressed to Pepin (796), and the poem *Charlemagne et le pape Léon,* usually attributed to Angilbert.   C.W.D.

ANGINA PECTORIS. *See* HEART (*Diseases of the Heart and Circulatory System*).

ANGIOSPERMS. *See* FLOWERING PLANTS; PLANT SYSTEMATICS.

ANGKOR [æ'ŋkɔr; ʌ'ŋkɔr], site of the ancient capital of the Khmer kings, rulers of the earliest known inhabitants of Cambodia, in the southwestern part of Indochina, in the northern part of central Cambodia. It is just north of the lake Tonle Sap. The site is famous for two areas of ancient ruins known as Angkor Thom, a fabulous ruined city located at 13° 25′ N. lat. and 103° 48′ E. long., and Angkor Vat, a great temple about a mile away. Both the town and the temple, remnants of the Khmer civilization, were probably built between A.D. 800 and 900 by King Yazecarman.

Angkor Thom, the city, is thought to have been populated by as many as 1,000,000 people. It covered about 5¼ sq. mi. and was surrounded by a large and ornamental stone wall. Most of the history of the city was carved on the stone wall and on the sides of buildings. The city was built around a large, centrally located temple which had 50 towers. There are also ruins of many ornate palaces and temples.

Angkor Vat, the temple, is considered one of the most beautiful buildings in southern Asia. Although the temple is large, it has extremely graceful, delicate lines, and it is much ornamented with carvings. The building, surrounded by a moat and approached by a causeway 1,800 ft. long leading to its main gate, is built of blocks of laterite faced with sandstone and can be described as a broad-based, stepped pyramid culminating in a building having five acorn-shaped towers. The central tower is 213 ft. high. The shrine of Vishnu within the temple is reached by 38 steps, each 2 ft. high. There are many courtyards, and the rooms within the building are ornamented with carvings.

The ruins, almost covered by tropical forest, were lost, or unknown, until 1858-1860, when it was rediscovered by A. H. Mouhot, a French naturalist.   J.E.F.

ANGLE. A plane angle is the geometric figure formed by a line rotating in a plane from one position to another, for example from OA to OB_1 in the figure. The angle AOB_1 may be of any magnitude, depending on the amount of ro-

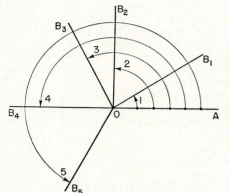

tation, and positive or negative, according as the rotation is counterclockwise or clockwise. The lines OA and OB_1 are called the sides and the point O the vertex of the angle. On other surfaces angles are thought of as formed by intersecting geodetic lines of the surface. For example, spherical angles are formed at the intersections of great circles of the sphere. Other extensions of the notion of angle are dihedral angle, formed by two intersecting planes; trihedral angle, formed by three planes that meet in a point; and, in general, polyhedral angle, formed by any number of planes greater than two that meet in a point. These are also known as solid angles.

Units of measure for plane angles are the degree, the angle subtended at the center of a circle by one-360th of the circumference; the radian, subtended by an arc equal to the radius; and the mil, subtended by one-6,400th of the circumference. Each of these offers certain computational advantages in its special field, degrees in navigation, radians in mechanics, and mils in gunnery. G. C. V.

ANGLER, *Lophias piscatorius,* also called fishing frog or goosefish, a fish found on both sides of the Atlantic. It is characterized by a large flattened head and an enormous, upturned, well-toothed mouth. An outstanding feature is the slender spine or fishing rod tipped with a leaf-like flap of skin located on the front of the head. This flap is said to act as a lure for its prey. Adults reach a length of 4 ft. and a weight of 70 lb. The eggs are shed in large ribbon-shaped, mucous sheets, from 20 to 30 ft. long and 2 to 3 ft. wide, which float at the surface. Over a million eggs may be laid by a single female. The young float at the surface. E. C. R.

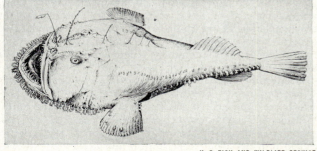

ANGLER

ANGLES or **ANGLI,** a Teutonic people so closely akin to the Saxons that after their settlement in Britain the two terms became interchangeable. Writing in A.D. 98, the Roman historian Tacitus mentions the Angles, among other German tribes, as inhabiting the north-western seaboard of Germany, but he gives no indication as to their exact geographical location. Bede, in A.D. 731, states that they came to Britain from a country called Angulus, lying between the territories occupied by the Jutes and the Saxons. The Anglo-Saxon chronicler Aethelweard identified the place with eastern Schleswig, a part of which still bears the name Angeln. Further confirmation of this appears in English traditions concerning certain ancestors of the royal families of Mercia and Wessex, who also appear in Danish tradition in connection with Schleswig. Most modern scholars accept the Schleswig origin of the Angles.

During the 5th century the Angles, in company with the Jutes and Saxons, invaded Britain in great numbers, after which time their name does not appear among the German tribes of the continent. By far the greater part of present-day England, which gained its name from them, was occupied by the Angles. Along the Trent, and in the Midlands, to the west and north, the Middle English settled in the country later known as Mercia. North of the Humber, and extending into the southern part of Scotland, the land was occupied by other Angles, known as Northumbrians, who developed into two kingdoms, Deira and Bernicia. For several centuries the kingdoms of the East Anglians, the Mercians, and the Northumbrians, played a prominent part in English history. F. C. H.

ANGLESEY [æ′ŋgəlsi], a wild island county located in the Irish Sea off the northwest coast of Wales and separated from Carnarvonshire on the mainland to the southeast by Menai Strait which is 14 mi. long and varies in breadth from 200 yd. to about 1 mi. Some authorities derive the name from *ongull,* Norse for fiord. Anglesey, second smallest of the Welsh counties, with an area of 276 sq. mi., extends about 28 mi. east to west and about 20 mi. north to south. It is the only county of North Wales whose terrain is not mountainous, as it comprises the much reduced foundation of an ancient highland consisting of somewhat older rocks than those across the Strait. The island is partly barren and waste, notably lacking in trees, and subject to fogs. On the north and west coasts especially, the cliffs are high and rugged, while the south shore is low and subject to flooding. The highest elevation is Holyhead Mountain, over 700 ft., on Holyhead Island.

When the Romans reached Wales in 55 B.C., Anglesey, or Mona as it was then called, was inhabited by a remnant of the Iberic stock, precursors of the Celts. In A.D. 78, Julius Agricola all but exterminated the Druid priests who had made the island their headquarters; even their sacred groves have disappeared. Megalithic remains—fortified camps, dolmens, and tumuli—are plentiful, particularly near the Menai shore, as are the inscribed stones and stone crosses of later eras. The county is primarily agricultural. Cattle are exported, along with butter, cheese, and hides. There is an active export of mineral products, including copper, gray marble, granite, lead, potter's clay, magnesia, sulphur, and coal. The county owes its importance to the fact that for many years it has proved the most convenient point of departure for Dublin. Pop. 1952, 50,960. A. H. Sw.

ANGLESITE [æ′ŋgləsait], the name applied to naturally occurring lead sulphate, $PbSO_4$. This mineral was first observed on an island, Anglesey, off the coast of Wales, in 1783. It occurs most commonly in white or gray masses coating or replacing galena (lead sulphide). Because of its lead content, anglesite is heavy (specific gravity: 6.3) and has a brilliant luster when pure. It is easily fused, producing a lead button in a reducing flame. Anglesite is found throughout the world as a product of the oxidation of galena. Ordinarily it is a very minor ore of lead, but in arid regions where the zone of oxidation is thick, as in Australia, a considerable quantity may be produced.   K. K. L.

ANGLICANISM, a term used to describe the Christian bodies which are in communion with the English see of Canterbury, use a similar Prayer Book, and maintain a similar theological orientation and the same form of government or polity. The Anglican Communion has branches in all parts of the world, its American representative being the Protestant Episcopal Church in the United States of America.

The Church of England, *ecclesia anglicana,* became a distinct part of the Catholic Church in 1536, when Parliament passed an act by which loyalty to the Roman see was made illegal in the realm. This act brought to a completion a series of steps taken largely under Henry VIII and Thomas Cranmer, Archbishop of Canterbury, designed to sever all allegiance to the Pope at Rome. Dissatisfaction with the papacy had been rife in England long before this, as the statutes *Provisors* and *Praemunire* indicate; these protested against and made unlawful the payment of fees to the papacy by appointees to episcopal sees and largely reduced the Roman control of the English Church. The immediate occasion for the action under Henry was his desire to remarry, but this was not the significant reason for the separation, which historians, among them G. Constant, the Roman Catholic author of *The Reformation under Henry* (1941), recognize as inevitable in view of the discontent in Britain for a century past.

After passing through the vicissitudes of the Protestant reform in the reign of Edward VI, the restoration of Romanism under Mary Tudor, and the return of Anglican principles with the accession of Elizabeth, England reached a settlement in 1559 under Elizabeth, by which the distinctively Anglican position was established. The theological justification of this settlement is found in Richard Hooker's famous *Laws of Ecclesiastical Polity,* and its classical expression was given by the so-called Caroline divines, Laud, Andrewes, Jewel, Bramhall, and others, whose writings have conveniently been edited in a selection entitled *Anglicanism* (1937). The Anglican Church was introduced into America with the Jamestown settlers in Virginia, but bishops were not secured for the American colonies until after the Revolution.

The Anglican Communion, now numbering some forty million adherents including the membership in the established Church of England, is often described as "the bridge Church." It maintains traditional Catholic worship, centering in the Eucharist, or Holy Communion, the sacramental and liturgical stress characteristic of the undivided Church, the traditional Apostles' and Nicene creeds, and a ministry of bishops, priests, and deacons with emphasis upon the apostolic succession. At the same time it is also a reformed church, with strong influence upon it from the Protestant tradition springing from the Reformation on the Continent.

The principal mark of identity in the Anglican Communion is the Book of Common Prayer; despite modifications introduced by the several sister churches, in America, Canada, South Africa, Scotland, and New Zealand, for example, the service book is rooted in the tradition established by the first English Prayer Book of 1549. The fact of a common ministry is another mark of identity, all bishops, and hence all of the lower clergy, being in communion with the see of Canterbury, although that see has no primacy other than one of honor. A conference held every ten years at Lambeth Palace, to which all bishops are invited, acts as a kind of supreme court, but its decisions are advisory only. Each national Church or regional division is self-governing. The doctrinal position of Anglicanism, on the whole, is "high," although a strong element in the communion has been the evangelical or "low church" wing, which tends to minimize ceremonial and to emphasize the importance of "personal" religion and commitment to Christian truth.

In the United States, there are approximately 2,500,000 communicants and adherents to the Episcopal (or Anglican) Church. All are in communion with the Archbishop of Canterbury.   W. N. P.

ANGLING. *See* Fishing.

ANGLO-EGYPTIAN SUDAN [suda′n; sudɑ′n], the territory which was known as the Egyptian Sudan until 1898, when native uprisings were put down by Anglo-Egyptian military expeditions, and which has since been under the joint sovereignty of Great Britain and Egypt. It is a part of a larger region in Africa known as the Sudan, which stretches south of the Sahara and Egypt from Cape Verde on the Atlantic to Massaua on the Red Sea and which is divided into a number of states, all under the control of foreign powers. The political boundaries of the Anglo-Egyptian Sudan are Egypt to the north; the Red Sea, Eritrea, and Ethiopia to the east; Kenya, Uganda, and the Belgian Congo to the south, and French Equatorial Africa and Libya to the west. In the present article the term Sudan is used to indicate the Anglo-Egyptian condominium only, an area of about 969,600 sq. mi.

Geographical Features. The Sudan is traversed from south to north by the Nile, and all the great tributaries of that river are either partly or entirely within its borders. The country enclosed by the Nile, the Atbara, and the Blue Nile is very fertile. The northern portion of the Sudan is practically all desert, while the southern portion is fertile, abundantly watered, and in some places densely forested. The coast line along the Red Sea is over 400 mi. long and contains few good harbors. The climate is extremely hot; there is considerable summer rainfall in the central and southern regions.

Ethnology and Population. The population is sparse and unevenly distributed. It was estimated at 8,500,000 before the period of the Mahdi despotism in the late nineteenth century; however, in 1905, the estimate was 1,853,000. Since then, with more stabilized conditions, there has been a rapid increase, and the official estimate in 1950 was 8,350,000. The north of the Sudan is mainly occupied by Hamitic and Semitic tribes, classed as Arabs; the southern area is primarily inhabited by pagan Negroid tribes, speaking Sudanic languages; the remainder, found chiefly in the middle zone, are Nubian and other mixed races. About 20 per cent of the population in the south is Christian. The standard of living is at best on a simple level and is frequently primitive. Islam is the predominant religion in the non-Negroid areas.

Economic Resources and Activities. *Agriculture and Other Industries.* The main crops are millet and cotton, which are produced in the irrigated districts of the north. Considerable quantities of peanuts and sesame are also grown. Gum and rubber are the chief forest products; the Sudan provides about 80 per cent of the world's gum arabic. Elephant hunts yield marketable ivory, and camels, sheep, and cattle are used both domestically and for export. Irrigation is done for the most part by river-side water wheels turned by oxen. The Gezira scheme, which was put into effect in 1925, provided an irrigated district of 1,000,000 acres on the banks of the Blue Nile, watered by means of a dam across the river at Sennar and a system of canals. By 1939, it had accounted for 25 per cent of the total revenue of the country. Agricultural production has also been aided by the Resettlement and Compensation Scheme and the Gash Board and Pump Irrigation schemes.

Minerals. The Sudan is fundamentally a poor country, and, except for the salt found mainly near Port Sudan and negligible quantities of gold, there are no important deposits of minerals, which limits industrial development. Small deposits of iron ore, lignite, and copper exist.

Communications. North of Khartoum, the capital, at the junction of the White and Blue Nile, the chief means of communication is by railway; south of that city by steamer. There are two trunk railways, one connecting Sennar, above Khartoum, with Wadi Halfa, on the Egyptian border, the other connecting El Obeid, southwest of Khartoum, with Port Sudan on the Red Sea, opened in 1906. There is a total of 2,056 mi. of railway, owned by the state as are the steamers operating on 2,325 mi. of the Nile and its tributaries. There is an extensive telegraph system. Khartoum is also an important railway junction.

Finance. The Egyptian pound ($£E$), worth approximately $2.87 in 1952, is the monetary unit. The 1951-1952 budget provided £E24.8 million revenue and £E17.8 million expenditure. The foreign debt as of Dec. 31, 1949, was £E12.3 million, of which £E5.3 million was owed to Egypt.

Trade. Sudan does not participate in the Imperial Preference arrangement. Egyptian goods have free entry. Trade in 1950 amounted to £E26.8 million in imports and £E33.2 million in exports. The United Kingdom and India are the principal importers and buyers of Sudanese exports. The most important imports are sugar, coffee, tea, cotton goods, and fuel. Chief exports are cotton (69 per cent), gum (8 per cent), cottonseed (6 per cent), and livestock (5 per cent).

Government. The role of the Sudanese government is that of trustee for the Sudanese people. The governor-general, appointed on the recommendation of the British, has full legislative power. Since 1921 the policy has been to admit the native to a share in government. In 1944 a Provincial Council was set up in each of the six northern provinces. In the same year an Advisory Council for the Northern Sudan was created, with a view "to associating Sudanese public opinion with central government policy"; its members are natives of the country; it meets twice a year. Similar councils were established in 1948 in three southern provinces. In that year an Executive Council and a Legislative Assembly were also set up. The Assembly has 65 elected members, a number of ex-officio members, and is allowed no more than 10 nominated members. The Moslem north has about three times the representation of the pagan south. The Executive Council comprises from 12 to 19 members and is responsible to the governor-general for the executive and administrative affairs of the government. The ordinance of June 19, 1948, stipulated that all members of the Legislative Assembly and under-secretaries serving under ministers are to be Sudanese. The Executive Council, 6 Sudanese and 6 Europeans, initiates legislation, which, when rejected by the Assembly, it may submit to the governor-general.

Divisions and Chief Towns. The Sudan is divided into mudiria, or provinces; these are in turn divided into mamuria, which vary considerably in size. The capital, Khartoum, is built in the fork formed by the junction of the White and Blue Niles. Other important towns are Omdurman, the old Mahdi capital; El Obeid, an important market center; and Port Sudan.

Education. Elementary education is given in village schools. Arabic is the language of instruction. There are primary schools in the chief towns where English, Arabic, and mathematics are taught. Gordon College at Khartoum provides vocational teaching, as well as training in law, medicine, engineering, education, and agriculture. Protestant and Roman Catholic mission schools provide education in the vernacular among the pagan Negro tribes.

History. There is no recorded history of the southern regions of the Sudan until the Egyptian conquest in the nineteenth century. The northern regions were the sites of various independent states, which gradually became Arabized after the eighth century. The conquest of Nubia, or northern Sudan, was undertaken by Mohammed Ali in 1820. It was accomplished in two years, and Egyptian domination was extended over a larger area in succeeding generations. Turko-Egyptian occupation lasted until 1885, when the Mahdi, Mohammed Ahmed, captured Khartoum. After this victory the Mahdist movement swept the entire Sudan, and with the subsequent withdrawal of British and Egyptian forces the Mahdi's rule was unchallenged. There followed a period of harsh and despotic rule, marked by constant strife and warfare within the country. This lasted until 1898, when an Anglo-Egyptian force defeated the Mahdist army. An agreement was signed in 1899 establishing the joint sovereignty of Great Britain and Egypt. This agreement was confirmed by the Anglo-Egyptian Treaty of 1936, although it was subjected to frequent criticism by Egyptian nationalists.

After World War II there was much controversy over the status of the Sudan. The country's political parties agitated for dominion status within Egypt (the Internal Struggle Front, or Unionists), for independence from both Egypt and the United Kingdom (the Independence Front), for union with Egypt (Ashigga), and for independence and self-government (the Umma, or Nation, Party). The elections of November 1948 were accompanied by violence. When the Legislative Assembly met for the first time in December 1948 it elected Miralai Abdullah Bey Khalil, Secretary of the Umma Party, its chairman, in effect the premier. The British, as another aid to Sudanese self-government, withdrew its officers from the Sudanese army. On Dec. 15, 1950, a motion for immediate independence was defeated by a single vote in the Assembly. The Egyptian government, from 1946, pressed for the outright incorporation of the Sudan, even taking the matter to the United Nations Security Council, which failed to act. In 1951 the party urging self-government had the greatest political strength.   W. S. V.

ANGLO-SAXONS, the modern name for the descendants of Germanic peoples who settled in Britain in the fifth and sixth centuries A.D., after the withdrawal of the Roman armies. They came from the coasts of Holland, Germany, and Denmark. According to tradition, Hengist and Horsa led the first band, which settled in Britain in 449. By the end of the sixth century the Saxons had established a series of kingdoms which occupied the south of England as far north as the River Stour, with the exception of Kent, which was settled by the Jutes. The east coast, from the Stour to the Firth of Forth, was occupied by the Angles, most numerous of all, who also conquered the Midlands. The various kingdoms were brought under the control of the West Saxon kings in the tenth century.   F. C. H.

AIRCRAFT OPERATING CO. OF AFRICA. LTD. , FROM EWING GALLOWAY

LUANDA, CAPITAL OF ANGOLA

ANGOLA [æŋgoˈlə], a Portuguese colony on the west coast of Africa, situated between the Congo and Kunene rivers. It is bounded on the north and northeast by the Belgian Congo, on the east by Northern Rhodesia, and on the south by Southwest Africa. It has approximately 1,000 mi. of coast line and an area of 481,226 sq. mi. The enclave of Cabinda, established by the Portuguese-Congolese agreement of Feb. 14, 1885, lies just north of the Congo River and is separated from the rest of Angola by a thin corridor of Belgian Congo territory.

Physical Features. On the west, Angola has a coastal plain which varies in width from 30 to 100 mi. Parallel to this are several inland plateau areas, trending north and south, the highest of which is the Benguela Highland, with altitudes exceeding 7,500 ft. In general, the highland regions average between 4,000 and 6,000 ft. above sea level, where the hot climate is sufficiently tempered to be suitable for Europeans. The plateau descends in the east to lowlands. In the northeast these lowlands form part of the Congo watershed; in the southeast they drain into the Zambezi River and the lakes of northern Bechuanaland. The principal rivers are the Cuanza and the Kunene, emptying into the Atlantic; the Kasai and the Kwango, tributaries of the Congo; and the Cubango-Okovanggo, flowing into Lake Ngami. Although some of these streams are navigable by light-draft vessels, only the lower Cuanza carries traffic of any volume. The generally flat coast line affords few natural harbors. In the south are the Bay of Tigers and Pôrto Alexandre. Lobito, in the central coastal area, has a good harbor, recently developed to serve as the oceanic terminus of the Benguela Railway; Luanda, in the north, has a harbor protected by an offshore island.

Climate. The climate varies considerably between regions. Along the coast, little rain is brought by the west winds because of the cold Benguela Current. Luanda has an average annual rainfall of 12 in.; Lobito, 9 in.; and Mossamedes, in the far south, 1 in. The highland zone is well watered, with from 40 to 60 in. of rain annually. The wet season usually runs from October to May. In the south and southeast, precipitation is light and irregular. Temperatures also are influenced by altitude and by the Benguela Current, but in general are high because of the country's proximity to the Equator. Only the highlands are suited to European settlement.

Flora and Fauna. The natural vegetation of Angola is most dense in the north. Along the coast the palms thin out below Luanda, and south of Benguela the littoral zone becomes increasingly arid. Tropical forests containing valuable timber cover large areas of the highlands north of the Cuanza River, while on the Benguela plateau there are many deciduous trees. To the south and east, open savannas prevail.

The fauna includes a wide assortment of African animals, such as elephants, rhinoceroses, giraffes, lions, and baboons, and many kinds of antelopes and birds. Some of the game animals, however, are far less numerous in Angola than in former years.

Population. In 1950 Angola had a population of 4,111,-796, including Europeans, mulattoes, and natives. The mixed groups are confined largely to the coastal zone. The natives are almost entirely Bantu Negroes, divided into various tribes and subtribes; in the southeast a few Bushmen are encountered. The principal population centers are the capital, São Paulo de Luanda (also Luanda), with 141,647 inhabitants in 1950; Lobito, the colony's chief port, 23,897; Nova Lisboa, the proposed capital, 28,296; Benguela, 14,690; and Mossamedes, 4,926.

Government. Angola is administered by a governor-general who resides at Luanda. He is assisted by a council, to which some of the members are elected by local economic organizations; all members are Portuguese nationals. The governor-general is responsible to the minister of colonies in Lisbon. The colony is divided into five provinces: Luanda, Malanje, Benguela, Bié, and Huila. These are subdivided into fourteen administrative districts, which are again subdivided into civil circumscriptions. For judicial purposes, the colony consists of nine districts, with a court of appeal at Luanda.

The Angolan monetary unit is the angolare, equivalent to the Portuguese escudo, valued at four cents. As of Dec. 31, 1946, the colony had a public debt of 1,014,636,000 angolares, of which 846,299,000 angolares were owed to the Portuguese government. The budget usually shows an excess of expenditures over revenues because of capital investments made to develop the country's resources.

In 1945 the military force of Angola consisted of 112 officers and 2,440 men, most of whom were natives.

Economic Life. Agriculture, stock raising, and fishing are the major economic pursuits in Angola. The soil generally is fertile and, because of the diversity of climate, can produce crops typical of both the tropical and temperate zones. The natives grow beans, manioc, and corn, the latter being exported in some volume. European-operated plantations cultivate coffee, oil palms, sugar cane, cotton, and sisal. Rubber formerly was Angola's leading export, but its production declined to almost nothing after World War I. The central highlands afford the best conditions for stock raising, not only because of the climate but also because the tsetse fly is detrimental to the industry elsewhere. European breeds of sheep, cattle, goats, horses, and hogs have been introduced and are raised in quantity.

Several of the southern ports are headquarters for extensive fisheries carried on by Portuguese, who sell their catch in the

BY EWING GALLOWAY, NEW YORK

Angolan natives relax over a game of "chess." The board consists of a slab with twenty-eight square troughs. Beans or seeds are used as men, with two in each rear trough when the game begins.

Belgian Congo and on São Thomé and Principe islands. The colony has various mineral resources, including copper, gold, iron, and coal, but most are undeveloped. In 1940, 28,865 tons of coal were exported. Diamonds are mined in small quantities in the Luanda area.

Foreign Trade. Over half the colony's foreign commerce is carried in vessels of the Portuguese National Navigation Company, subsidized by the government. In addition, trade between Angola and Portugal is encouraged by extensive reciprocal tariff reductions. In 1946 imports were valued at 799,580,000 angolares, and exports at 962,251,000 angolares. The principal imports were textiles, foodstuffs, coal, and hardware; the exports were chiefly coffee, corn, diamonds, sugar, and palm oil.

Transportation. Angola's major ports are Lobito, Luanda, Benguela, and Mossamedes. The chief railroad is the Benguela Railway, completed in 1931, running from Lobito, via Benguela and Nova Lisboa, to the Belgian Congo, a distance of 1,162 mi. Other lines extend from Luanda to Malange, 389 mi.; from Pôrto Amboim to Gabela, 70 mi.;

and from Mossamedes to Sá da Bandeira, 155 mi. All of these lines run from the coast inland for varying distances, and none of them is connected with any of the others. However, the primary highway system, comprising nearly 25,000 mi. of roads, provides a network covering most of the colony, particularly the Benguela Highland. These roads were built largely by natives working off their hut and head taxes, and serve as feeders for the railroads. Angola is connected with other parts of Africa as well as with Western Europe and the United States by steamship lines.

Labor Conditions. Regulation of native labor long has been a major problem in Angola. Few natives have voluntarily sought employment beyond their own tribal communities, and the government has felt obliged to use compulsion on behalf of private recruiters, as well as in order to provide labor for road building and other public works. By various acts and codes, notably the Colonial Charter of 1930, the government has circumscribed the duty of officials to assist private recruitment while upholding its own right to exact labor in partial payment for taxes. In recent years the mines and industrial establishments of Rhodesia and the Union of South Africa have attracted Angolan laborers. In the less accessible interior, slavery and the slave trade continued into the twentieth century.

Religion and Education. Angola constitutes a Roman Catholic diocese, with Luanda as its see. Catholic missionary activity has been carried on since the end of the fifteenth century. More recently various Protestant sects have entered the field, including several American denominations. The colony's very small educational facilities for natives are provided almost entirely by these missions. Most of the natives are pagans and illiterate. For the European population there are a number of primary, secondary, and professional schools in the larger towns. The colonial authorities have not encouraged the use of native languages.

History. The Portuguese were the first Europeans to visit Angola. Diogo Cam discovered the mouth of the Congo River in 1482 and later explored the coast to the south. Penetration by the Portuguese originally was confined to the north, where they acquired influence over the powerful Mwani Congo, said to rule a vast domain from Bonza Congo, renamed São Salvador when it became the center of Catholic missionary activities. This African kingdom later lost its prosperity and importance when invaded by a barbarous people from the interior, and Portuguese interest was shifted southward.

Luanda was founded in 1575, and the ecclesiastical center was moved there from São Salvador in 1627. Benguela was settled in 1617 and henceforth the middle seacoast of the colony became the center of a lucrative slave trade with the Americas, notably Brazil. The subjugation of the Bantu states on the plateau and in the interior was a long and costly process. Although Mossamedes was founded in 1785, the Huila Highlands behind it were not occupied for nearly a century thereafter. The scramble of European powers for possessions in Africa in the early 1880's obliged Portugal to establish her territorial claims by the effective occupation of many remote districts. Boundary treaties were made with France and Germany in 1886, Great Britain in 1891, and Belgium in 1927; the treaty with Great Britain was modified in 1905 by an arbitral award of King Victor Emmanuel III of Italy.

Between 1640 and 1648 the Dutch established several footholds on the Angolan coast, but eventually were dislodged by forces from Brazil. On the eve of World War I, Germany and Great Britain were on the point of signing a treaty in which the former was recognized as having paramount economic interests in Angola. After World War I the Fascist government of Italy showed marked interest in the undeveloped resources of Angola. Portugal managed to preserve its sovereignty, but subsequent Portuguese efforts to develop the colony were greatly handicapped by a lack of capital and of local initiative. Consequently, many of the large-scale business activities in Angola are foreign-owned. Under the Salazar regime, the Portuguese government has renewed its efforts to promote the colony's economic development and to tie it more closely to the homeland.   R. G. W.

ANGORA. *See* ANKARA.
ANGORA CAT. *See* CAT, DOMESTIC.
ANGORA GOAT. *See* GOATS, DOMESTIC.

ANGOULÊME [ã'gu'lɛ'm], a city in west central France, the capital of the department of Charente, situated on a height between the Charente and Anguienne rivers, about 80 mi. northeast of Bordeaux. The city existed during Roman times and was known as Iculisma. During the Hundred Years' War it was contested by the English and the French, the English finally being expelled in 1353. In 1515 it became part of a duchy created by Francis I, who had been the count of Angoulême. In 1568 both the Huguenots and Catholics persecuted the populace, and the community suffered greatly during the ensuing religious wars. In 1534 John Calvin visited the city and began his studies which formed the basis of his famous *Institutes of the Christian Religion.* During World War II the section surrounding the railroad station in southwestern Angoulême was greatly damaged. The city is noted for the Cathedral of St. Pierre, one of the most interesting Romanesque-Byzantine churches in southern France. It was begun in the eleventh century and largely rebuilt in the twelfth. Damaged during the wars of religion, it was repaired in the seventeenth century and restored by Abadie between 1866 and 1875. The rich sculpture of the west front is especially noteworthy, and the carving throughout the cathedral is of marked elegance. The high square tower of the north transept is considered the most beautiful external feature. Covered by three great domes, the nave is among the largest in southwestern France. Famous inhabitants of Angoulême include Marguerite d'Angoulême, sister of Francis I, queen of Navarre, and the author of *Heptameron,* and Jean Louis Guez de Balzac, author. Cognac distilleries and paper mills comprise the city's chief industrial establishments. Pop. 1954, 43,170.
                                                    S. Van V.

ANGOUMOIS [ã'gu'mwa'], former French province in southwestern France, bounded by the provinces of Poitou on the north, Limousin on the east, Guyenne on the east and south, and Saintonge and Aunis on the west. The ancient capital was Angoulême. The surface is undulating, and hilly in the northeast. At the time of the Roman occupation of Gaul, it was the territory of the Gallic tribes, the Santones and Pictons. It was conquered by the Visigoths in A.D. 417, and by the Franks under Clovis in 507. It was part of the kingdom of Aquitaine under Charlemagne's empire. It was made a county by Charles the Bald about 850, and was united to the French crown by King Philip the Fair of France in 1307. It was claimed by King John of England in the name of his wife, Isabella of Angoulême, but was acknowledged as English territory only from the treaty of Brétigny in 1360. In 1371 it became a fief of the dukes of Berry, a branch of the French royal family. It was annexed

to France when Francis I, who was then Count of Angoulême, ascended the French throne in 1515. From the reign of Louis XIV one of the sons of the royal family held the honorary title of Duke of Angoulême. In 1790 the department of Charente was formed from the province of Angoumois. *See also* CHARENTE.   M. V. K.

ÅNGSTROM, ANDERS JONAS [ɔ'ŋström] (1814-1874), Swedish physicist, after whom the unit used in measuring the wave length of light is named (1 angstrom = 10^{-8} cm.), was born Aug. 13, 1814, at Lögdö, Sweden. He was educated at the University of Uppsala, where he became *privatdozent* in physics in 1839. In 1843 he was made observer at Uppsala Observatory, and in 1858 he took the chair in physics at Uppsala, which he held until his death. Ångström was one of the founders of spectroscopy. In a paper delivered to the Stockholm academy in 1853, he deduced that an incandescent gas emits light of the same wave length as it will absorb. After 1861 he studied particularly the spectrum of the sun. He announced the presence of the element hydrogen in the sun's atmosphere in 1862, and in 1868 published his famous map of the solar spectrum, which remained authoritative for many years despite its wave length errors of about one part in 7,000. These arose because Ångström referred his measurements of wave length to a meter bar that was slightly too short. In 1867 he was the first to investigate the spectrum of the aurora borealis. He died June 21, 1874.   L. N. R.

ANGUS (FORFAR) [fɔ'rfər; fɔ'rfɑr], a maritime county, or shire, in eastern Scotland, with an area of 873 sq. mi. It is bounded by the counties of Aberdeen and Kincardine on the north, Perth on the west, the Firth of Tay on the south, the North Sea on the east. The Braes of Angus in the north are crossed by beautiful glens; in the southwest, near the Firth of Tay and almost parallel to it, are the Sidlaw Hills; in between is the fertile valley of Strathmore. There are sandy coasts from Dundee to Arbroath, fertile soils from the Sidlaw Hills to the coast on the east and south, and wasteland in the northwest which is in deer forests or sheep walks. Dundee, the chief city, is the third largest in Scotland in population, and second only to Glasgow in manufacturing. Its principal industries are jute and linen manufactures. Near Forfar is the Forfar Loch, on whose shores the last battles between the Picts and Scots were fought. Kirriemuir is a linen-weaving town celebrated as "Thrums" in the novels of Sir James Barrie, who was born there. Shakespeare laid the scene of *Macbeth* in Glamis Castle, Macbeth being Thane of Glamis. Glamis Castle is the property of the Earl of Strathmore, and Queen Elizabeth, youngest daughter of the Earl and consort of King George VI, spent many summers there when she was a girl. The population of Angus in 1952 was 275,843.   S. Van V.

ANHALT [ɑ'nhɑlt], a duchy set up in central Europe by Frederick Barbarossa in 1180 and given to Bernard of Anhalt, originally comprised territory east of the Weser River and extended westward into Saxony between Leipzig on the south and Berlin to the north. The duchy, particularly in its western half, had been largely settled by Dutch and Flemish bishops and their flocks as a part of the archbishopric of Magdeburg. The original duchy was divided by death and inheritance, but in time was reunited in one degree or another until in 1863, due to the death of heirs of rival reigning houses, all the territory came under one ruler, who took the title of Duke of Anhalt.

One *Landtag* (diet) was set up for the government of all the duchy. In 1871, when the German Empire was constituted, the duchy of Anhalt became one of the twenty-five constituent states. After the close of World War I, on July 18, 1919, the duchy received a constitution and designation as the Free State of Anhalt in the German Republic, with an elected diet and a five-member state council, whose chairman bore the title of president. When Hitler came to power and the Nazis gained control of Germany, Anhalt, by virtue of the Unification Act of Apr. 7, 1933, became a state in the Third Reich and the area was reduced to the status of an administrative unit. Following the defeat of Hitler and as a result of the decision of the Potsdam Conference in July 1945, Anhalt was combined with surrounding areas, with a substantially increased population, under the name Anhalt-Saxony. The enlarged territory, as an administrative unit, was entirely within the Russian zone of occupied Germany.

The duchy of Anhalt proper has an area of 2,500 sq. mi. with a population of about 450,000, most of whom are Protestants. Its principal cities are Dessau, the capital, on the Elbe River, which flows through the duchy in a general southeast to northwest direction, Zerbst, Bernberg, Köthen, and Ballenstedt. Agricultural products, particularly beet sugar and wheat, lignite or brown coal, potash salt mines, chemical works, and electric generating plants are the most important business operations. R. H. L.

ANHINGA [ænhɪˈŋgə], any of three or four species of fish-eating birds of the genus *Anhinga,* allied to the cormorants, but having a longer, more slender neck and a sharp-pointed bill. Adults are mostly black, varied with silvery gray or brown on the neck and upper parts. They inhabit fresh-water streams, lakes, and swamps. Anhingas are expert swimmers and divers and pursue their prey beneath the surface with extraordinary speed and agility. They occur in the warmer regions of the New World, Africa, Asia, and Australia. The American species, *A. anhinga,* ranges from the southern United States to northern Argentina. It is often known as the water turkey, an allusion to the broad fan-shaped tail adorned at the tip with a conspicuous light band, or the snakebird, because of its habit of swimming with the body submerged, the long, slender head and neck appearing like a snake rising out of the water. H. G. De.

ANHWEI [ɑˈnhweˈ], a province in the eastern part of central China, 54,810 sq. mi. in area. It is surrounded by five provinces: Kiangsu, on the north and east; Chekiang and Kiangsi, on the south; and Hopeh and Honan, on the west. Most of Anhwei is flat, almost level country, with the exception of the 8,200 ft. Kaunlung Shan range in the southwest and the 5,900 ft. Hwang Shan in the southeast. The level lands are along the Hwei River and its tributaries, and Hungtze Lake on the northeastern boundary. The Hwei River serves as a dividing line between northern and southern China. The northern part of the province, which lies in the region of the former route of the Hwang River, is composed of alluvial land. This agricultural region has suffered varying fortunes from floods and the shifting courses of the river. Cotton and wheat are grown in the north; and rice and mulberries for silkworms, in the south. Hwaining on the Yangtze is one of the more important towns in the province. The estimated population of Anhwei in 1949 was 20,500,000. J. E. F.

ANHYDRITE [anhaiˈdrait], a mineral so named because it is composed of anhydrous calcium sulphate, $CaSO_4$. The hydrous form of this compound is the mineral gypsum.

Unlike gypsum, however, anhydrite is not exploited commercially to any great extent, although it was reported as far back as 1933 that this mineral could be used as a fertilizer and in the manufacture of ammonium sulphate and commercial plaster. Anhydrite is usually light colored and massive, looking like limestone, but not effervescing in acid. It has a hardness of 3, whereas gypsum's is only 2. Anhydrite usually occurs in sedimentary beds, precipitated from evaporating brines. Calcium sulphate is less soluble than salt, therefore anhydrite is precipitated first and occurs beneath salt and is more widespread than the latter mineral. Anhydrite is rarely found in hydrothermal veins, which were formed at relatively high temperatures. Sedimentary anhydrite is found in all of the geological basins which were occupied by evaporating seas in the past. Examples are the Prussian salt basin in Germany, basins in northern New York and Michigan, and the Permian basin. The latter occupies parts of western Kansas, Oklahoma, and Texas, and eastern New Mexico. K. K. L.

ANICETUS, ST. [æˈnɪsiˈtəs] (d. 166), pope, is said to have been a Syrian from Emesa. During his pontificate, 155-166, Justin worked at Rome, and Valentine and Marcion carried on their Gnostic propaganda there. Bishop Polycarp came to Rome to treat with Anicetus regarding the date for the celebration of Easter. Although no agreement was arrived at, there was at that time no break between Rome and the churches of Asia Minor. Although he was canonized, it is very doubtful that Anicetus died a martyr. His feast is April 17. E. A. R.

ANICOR. *See* INDOCHINA.
ANILINE. *See* ORGANIC CHEMISTRY.
ANIMAL ELECTRICITY. *See* BIOELECTRICITY.

ANIMAL MAGNETISM, a theory of ancient origin which holds that magnets have therapeutic action and that animal life is similarly endowed, was revived in modern times by Franz (or Friedrich) Mesmer (1734-1815), an Austrian physician. In developing his hypothesis, Mesmer first resorted to mechanical means in the treatment of his patients. His experiments, which were performed in a large tub into which projected large rods for the patients to grasp, were discarded when he came to believe in his own occult powers. Following his announcement that magnetism flowed through his own body, Mesmer laid claim to the efficacy of various curative techniques; these included the magnetizing of a glass of water from which a patient could drink and be healed, and the magnetization of a tree so that its influence, conveyed by cords extending from its branches, could be felt by a sensitive patient stationed beneath it.

Mesmer's method was to induce a crisis and then allay it. Commissions, selected to examine his claims, reported that the effects were the result of imagination, or of what is now known to be suggestion. Mesmer is recognized as the founder of mesmerism, which developed into the scientifically established phenomenon of hypnotism, but his methods and claims regarding animal magnetism were denounced by a group of physicians and scientists appointed by the French government and remain without trustworthy support. A. J.

ANIMAL PAINTING. The representation of animals in art is common to all periods of the world's history, but it assumed special prominence in those countries where particular importance was attached to animals for reasons traceable to religion, warfare, or sport.

The earliest known representations of animals are the expressive colored drawings of paleolithic animals on the walls of caves in southern France and in Spain, such as those discovered at Altamira in 1879. In ancient Egypt, animals were frequently represented either as cult images (often in hybrid form) or, as in the murals in the tombs of Beni-

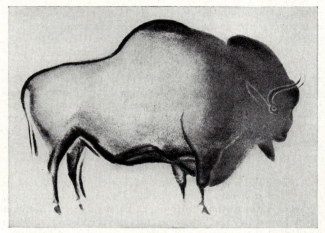

STANDING BISON
PAINTING FROM THE CAVES OF FONT-DE-GAUME, FRANCE

Hassan, for their own sake. In Assyria, where hunting and horsemanship had an important bearing on the art of war, animals were the most common subjects of portrayal.

In the paintings of Classical antiquity animals were frequently represented, but they were of minor importance in these compositions, and, with the exception of the horse, their likenesses were executed with indifferent success. Similarly in medieval art, animals were frequently subjects in illumi-

A YOUNG HARE
PAINTING BY ALBRECHT DÜRER (1471-1528)

nated manuscripts, and they were represented often for their own sake as well as to illustrate religious themes. But most medieval versions of animals are decoratively abstract; they are not based on a close study of the beasts represented.

With the revival of interest in nature during the Italian Renaissance, the study of animals became a specialty with certain artists, notably Pisanello (c.1385-1455), the first real animal painter in Western art, and Leonardo da Vinci (1452-1519), whose studies of horses remain among the best ever made. Albrecht Dürer (1471-1528) is the next great animal painter in the European tradition; he portrayed all forms of animal life from insects to horses with extraordinary accuracy.

During the seventeenth century in Holland, animal painting enjoyed great popularity; cows, hens, cocks, hares, and other animal subjects were painted both dead and alive, with

DEER IN FOREST
PAINTING BY ROSA BONHEUR

painstaking fidelity, by Albert Cuyp, Adriaen Van de Velde, Melchior d' Hondecoeter, Jan Weenix, and many other genre painters. Again during the Romantic period of French painting, in the nineteenth century, there were specialists in animal painting, such as Théodore Géricault (1791-1824), who owned race horses and painted them with great skill and understanding. During this period, also, hunting and racing scenes attained great popularity in both England and America, and a number of animal painters of merit specialized in this type of picture.

In England, Sir Edwin Landseer (1802-1873), as a painter of deer and sporting dogs, and A. J. Munnings (1878-   ), as a painter of horses and hunting scenes, are important in the history of animal paintings; in the United States, Frederic Remington (1861-1909) specialized in Western ranch scenes, while in Germany Frans Marc (1880-1916) has shown that animals can be represented truthfully in other ways than by attempting photographic accuracy. France also in this period produced several outstanding animal painters, among whom Rosa Bonheur (1822-1899) and Constant Troyon (1813-1865) are the best known.

Animal painting has played an important part in Chinese

art. Beginning with the work of Chao Mêng-Fu (1254-1322) of the Sung Dynasty, the horse has been among the most favored subjects of Chinese painters; and each dynasty has produced a number of artists whose fame rests on consummate skill in this field. H. L. C.

ANIMAL PSYCHOLOGY, also known as comparative psychology, the scientific study of the behavior of animals other than man. This branch of psychology concerns itself with two types of investigations: field studies, in which animals are observed in the wild state under natural living conditions; and laboratory studies, in which the behavior of animals is investigated under rigidly controlled scientific conditions. Although the behavior of subhuman animals may be studied because of sheer curiosity and interest in their behavior as such, the more common purpose of the scientific student of animal behavior is to gain information that will bear on broad psychological laws directly or indirectly applicable to our understanding of all animals, especially man.

Early History. The first extensive records concerning the behavior of animals were compiled by Aristotle (384-322 B.C.) in six separate volumes, of which *Historia animalium* is the most extensive. Characteristics of the behavior of no less than 500 different species are described. The range of topics is wide, covering such aspects as the development of the embryo, breeding, mating and nesting habits, temperamental and intellectual characteristics, and social organization. No work of comparable importance in the field of animal psychology appeared in the next 2,000 years.

The Roman naturalists, Pliny and Plutarch, living in the first and second centuries, A.D., supplemented material taken from Aristotle with limited anecdotal and observational evidence of their own. Plutarch, particularly, was interested in stressing the high intellectual achievement of the subhuman animal, but many of the remarkable performances which he claims to have observed have never been recorded by any person since.

Additional observational material on animal behavior was reported in written form, both in England and on the European continent, by such late Renaissance writers as Joannes Rosarius and Michel DeMontaigne. The gradual development in both the biological and medical sciences, from this time on, provided a background from which the scientific study of animal behavior was to arise.

Darwin & Evolution. The effect of Charles Darwin's theory of evolution, which was first presented in complete form in his *Origin of the Species* (1859), was to give a tremendous impetus to research in animal psychology. Darwin attempted to show the evolution of emotional expression in his book *Expression of the Emotions in Man and Animals* (1872). George J. Romanes' book, *Mental Evolution in Animals* (1883), presented a similar thesis for the evolution of intellectual abilities. Even though no comparable book concerning the possible evolution of patterns of social behavior in animals appeared, interest in this theme was aroused by Darwin's theory of evolution and has continued steadily since then.

Early Controlled Laboratory Studies. Investigation of animal behavior, in which the activities of subhuman animals were observed under carefully and precisely controlled conditions, using specially designed apparatus, appeared first in the last quarter of the nineteenth century. Researches of this type were originally carried out on lower animal forms. John Lubbock (1883) tested the sensory capacities of ants, wasps, and bees under rigid scientific conditions. Jacques

Loeb, in 1890, described "forced" tropistic responses of single-celled animals to light stimulation. Loeb's theory of tropistic behavior was of particular importance to animal psychology because of his emphasis on the machine-like behavior of animals and because of his demonstration that animal behavior could be described in quantitative and mathematical terms.

The year 1898 was of particular importance to animal psychology, for it marked the beginning of laboratory researches on higher animal forms, including the mammals. In this year, Edward Lee Thorndike began the publication of his studies on the learning of problem boxes by chickens, cats, dogs, and monkeys, and L. Kline published a careful account of the development of behavior in the infant rat. At about the same time, W. S. Small was beginning his studies on the maze learning of rats.

The growth of animal psychology during the twentieth century was steady and rapid. Robert Means Yerkes began his series of truly remarkable studies on animal forms, extending from the fishworm to the chimpanzee. No less remarkable was his construction of a series of machines which ranged from equipment for studying visual discrimination in mammals to the multiple-choice apparatus for measuring their learning and thinking processes.

Psychologists were quick to realize that these accurate, precise, and controlled measures of learning and other intellectual processes could be utilized in studies of brain functions. The investigations of Victor Franz, in the second decade of the twentieth century, on the effect of brain damage on learning and intelligence in rats, cats, and monkeys were later extended and amplified by his co-worker, Karl S. Lashley.

During the same period, the Russian physiologist, Ivan P. Pavlov, carried out a series of highly analytical studies on learning in the dog, studies which he systematized and formalized in his theory of conditioned reflexes.

Quantitative investigation of motivation was initiated by a provocative study by Curt Paul Richter in 1927, which revealed the cyclical nature of the drive mechanisms and their probable relation to the body's internal environment: the chemical composition of the blood and tissue fluid. Quantitative comparisons of the strengths of the various drives were made shortly afterward by F. A. Moss, and by C. J. Warden and associates, using the obstruction method. Strength of drive was measured in terms of the animal's willingness to accept the punishment of an electric shock in order to attain a reward that could satisfy the drive.

Brief descriptions of the pioneering efforts of animal psychologists in the fields of the sensory processes, learning, intelligence, drives and motives, and brain functions must be taken as merely representative of a large body of behavioral researches on animals. Equally successful initial studies on such important topics as instinctive functions, heredity, emotional behavior, neuroses, and social organization were carried out by other psychologists in the field. In historical summary, it may be stated that a truly remarkable development took place in the first three decades of the twentieth century. At the beginning of this century, animal psychology did not exist as a recognized and independent field of scientific investigation. Thirty years later, animal behavior research laboratories had been established in almost every major university in the United States and in many universities in Europe; basic problems had already been solved; and the apparatus, techniques, and methods for programs of research on most fundamental problems in psychology had been outlined.

Field Studies of Animal Behavior. Field studies of animal behavior have not been carried out extensively by trained psychologists. This is in part due to the fact that field studies are expensive and time-consuming and demand unusual patience and fortitude on the part of the experimenter if they are to be successful.

Fortunately, adequate field studies have been made on a number of representative species of subhuman primates, and these studies provide valuable information concerning the nature of the social organization of man's near relatives. The primates are the animal order which includes the monkeys, the anthropoid apes, and man. The monkey species which have been studied are the Central American howler monkey; the rhesus monkey, the sacred monkey of India; and the Hamadryas baboon, a very large, dog-faced monkey living in Africa.

Hamadryas baboons, in the wild state, form large bands which may total a hundred or more, the largest subhuman social groups found anywhere in the world. These large bands are probably family groups consisting of a strong, vigorous male, his "harem," and children. The size of the harem is apparently related to the strength and vigor of the male. "Bachelor" baboons may follow at a discreet distance, representing a constant threat to the family head.

Such well-integrated family groups do not characterize the rhesus monkey bands, which appear to be organized in heterosexual groups of 10 to 70 members. Several males are found in each social group, and the males are outnumbered two or three to one by the females—a typical characteristic of subhuman primate groups. No particular male has exclusive possession of any one female.

The howler monkeys form closely knit groups averaging about 20 members. These monkeys have been described as communistic. Unlike the Old World monkeys, which frequently engage in fights leading to mutilation and death, the howler monkeys have never been seen to quarrel. Our interpretation of this domestic bliss may be marred, however, by the fact that the howler monkeys are entirely promiscuous and show no semblance of domestic organization.

The social life in the wild of two anthropoid apes, the gibbon of Siam and the chimpanzee of equatorial Africa, has been studied. The gibbon is strictly monogamous. Father, mother, and two infants form the typical family. The family life appears to be placid, normally, though the gibbon is known to give vent to fits of explosive rage.

The exact nature of the family life of the elusive chimpanzee is not known with certainty. It is thought that chimpanzees live in small groups of a dozen or less, and that each group consists of a polygamous male, his wives, and their children.

The best of the field studies have been made by C. R. Carpenter, who has demonstrated that even such elusive animals as monkeys and apes can be kept under almost continuous observation for days at a time. Carpenter's detailed field studies enabled him to plot the howler monkey's day. These sensible creatures get up at daybreak, retire at sunset, and take two long siestas during the day. Both howler monkeys and gibbons live in defined geographical territories. They have favorite trees, favorite areas for nesting and feeding, and established "highways" to and from these areas. Though no subhuman animal has language of a human type, Carpenter was able to describe about 15 different vocalizations possessed by the howler monkeys. These vocalizations had a useful role in the maintenance of social relationships between parents and children, and between various adults of the larger social group.

Later Laboratory Studies of Animal Behavior. Laboratory studies of animal behavior are carried out in large part because the study of subhuman animals offers certain intrinsic advantages over that of human beings as experimental subjects. The typical laboratory studies subsequently described in this article were selected to illustrate these inherent advantages.

Pavlov. One advantage of subhuman animals as laboratory subjects for psychological study lies in the greater simplicity of their behavior. The behavior of the human being is so complex that much of what he does almost defies analysis. But basic scientific behavioral laws obtained from experiments on animals may reveal fundamental principles that aid in analyzing the more complicated behavior of man. This fact is well illustrated in the field of learning by the classical studies carried out by Pavlov. Pavlov was interested in the laws governing the formation of learned associations. Using dogs as subjects, he studied the salivary response which is elicited innately by the stimulus of food in the mouth. Pavlov observed that many other stimuli such as light and sound, which did not originally call forth the salivary response, would do so after temporal pairing of these new stimuli, which he called conditioned stimuli, with the presence in the mouth of food, which he called the unconditioned stimulus. Using this basic technique, Pavlov was able to make detailed studies of the fundamental mechanisms which underlie all learning, and was able to demonstrate common principles determining such widespread phenomena as generalization of the learned stimuli, the effect of internal and external distractions, time relationships in stimulus association, neurotic behavior, and sleep.

Pavlov's original conditioning studies have been greatly extended by American workers, using other animals and other basic responses. Clark L. Hull and his co-workers have taken Pavlov's basic learning principles and have demonstrated that they are adequate to describe learning in animals ranging from rat to man. The basic Pavlovian laws operate even in human verbal learning, as demonstrated in the classical paired associates method, where learned associations between paired words in a series are studied. Workers in the United States have also investigated intensively a greater number of conditions associated with learning than did Pavlov, giving special emphasis to the physiological conditions which underlie the motivation to learn.

Inheritance. A second advantage shown by subhuman animals over man, as subjects for certain types of psychological investigations, lies in their shorter life cycle. This is particularly true for studies of psychological inheritance. In man, a single generation encompasses a period of about 30 years. Experimental studies of the inheritance of psychological traits need to cover from five to ten generations at a minimum to be truly effective. In the case of man, this requirement would mean a period of 150 to 300 years, a period well beyond the life span of any experimenter. A generation of rats is produced in a hundred days, and ten generations can be studied within a three-year period.

Using rats as subjects, R. C. Tryon studied the inheritance of intelligence, defined as the ability to learn a complicated maze. This investigator tested a large number of rats on the maze, and then, for 18 successive generations, bred maze-bright (rapid learning) rats with other maze-bright rats, and maze-dull (slow learning) rats with other maze-dull rats. Differences between the groups became progressively greater for seven generations, and, by the seventh generation, there was practically no overlapping between the maze-bright and maze-dull groups. In other words, by this time, with few exceptions, the poorest of the maze-bright rats were superior to the best of the maze-dull rats. From the seventh generation on, no further separation of the two groups could be obtained. Such a study is extremely thought-provoking, since it showed that a particular kind of intelligence was in large part inherited. But two other facts appear to be of equal importance. There were limits to the improvement which could be obtained merely by selective breeding. Furthermore, the maze-bright rats did not show any unusual intelligence for other kinds of problems, such as those involved in discrimination learning or problem boxes.

Controlled Experimentation. Greater control can ordinarily be exerted over both the external and internal environmental conditions of the subhuman animal than over those of the human being. Man has long pondered over the effect of the early environmental influences on animal behavior. Complete isolation represents a drastic difference from a normal early environment. It is impractical to rear a human child in total isolation, but infant animals of other species have been raised under these conditions.

Baby rats and baby chimpanzees have been raised not only in complete isolation, but also in a totally dark environment. This environment had little demonstrable effect on the visual response of the rats when they were tested after maturity. The chimpanzees, however, experienced much greater difficulty. When first permitted to respond to visual stimuli, they showed only the most rudimentary reflex visual capacities. Great difficulty was experienced in teaching these animals to learn very simple visual associations, though after the first problem was mastered, later problems were learned with somewhat greater ease. Either the early dark environment exerted a much more profoundly depressing effect upon the chimpanzee than on the rat or else early learning is actually slower in the higher mammal than the lower mammal.

Certain behavior patterns in animals are not present at birth but appear later in the life cycle. Patterns associated with sex behavior are classical examples of such delayed responses. The degree to which these responses are innate or learned can be determined only by isolating animal subjects from other members of their species and studying them during a period that approximates the time that the pattern is known to appear in animals raised under normal conditions. C. M. Louttit and C. P. Stone carried out such studies of the sexual responses of the guinea pig and rat, respectively. In these latter rodents it appeared that experience had little effect, if the animal was otherwise healthy and normal. Overt sex behavior occurred in both the male and the female the first time that association was offered with a member of the opposite sex. Speed of appearance of the response pattern, and the form of the response pattern, did not differ in the rodents reared in isolation from those allowed previous heterosexual association with others of their particular species.

Animals as Operative Subjects. A fourth advantage possessed by subhuman animals as laboratory subjects for psychological study lies in the fact that it is permissable to carry out operative procedures on subhuman animals that could not be carried out on man.

Much of our knowledge of the functioning of the nervous system in learning and thinking has been obtained through joint operative and behavioral studies. The lobes in the frontal part of the brain have long been thought to be intimately concerned with the functioning of the more complex thinking processes. This hypothesis was tested by C. F. Jacobsen, using procedures of the general type described

above. Monkeys and chimpanzees were trained on both simple learning problems and complex thinking problems, and the effect of destruction of the frontal lobes was then experimentally tested. Complex thinking processes involving such functions as use of recent memories and the use of tools were much more gravely affected by destruction of the frontal lobes than simple learning processes. Destruction of other parts of the brain produced no greater loss on the performance of complex intellectual problems than it did on the performance of simpler learning problems.　H. F. H.

ANIMAL SCULPTURE. Besides the human figure, animals provide the only natural form that is both complex and concise organically and sufficiently implies life and movement to serve as a fit subject for sculpture in the round.

JAGUAR
SCULPTURE BY ANNA HYATT HUNTINGTON

In Egypt, each god was symbolized by an animal, and these animals often became the subject of sculptural representation, the god frequently being represented with an animal's head on a human body. The body of the Great Sphinx at Giza is that of a lion while its head is that of a man, possibly intended to represent King Menkure (reigned c. 2800 B.C.). Sphinxes with animal heads are also found.

Similar combinations occur in Mesopotamia, where winged man-headed bulls and winged representations of gods and kings are common. In both these regions, where human forms are represented in relief sculpture by rather rigid conventions, accessory animals are often done with much greater realism of form and action.

In the anthropocentric cultures of Greece and Rome, animals were less important, though sculptures of sacrificial animals are recorded, notably a cow by the leading fifth-century sculptor, Phidias. Animals shown as human accessories in relief sculpture are very skillfully done, as in the frieze of the Panathenaic Procession on the Parthenon in Athens. Horses, which were regarded as symbols of politico-military power, were frequently portrayed. The variety of subject matter fostered by private patronage in the Hellenistic Period includes some animal sculpture like the playful *Boy and Goose* of Boëthus (second century B.C.).

In medieval sculpture, animals are used symbolically. Three of the four evangelistic symbols are the bull, lion, and eagle, and these recur constantly, with typical decorative formalization, throughout Romanesque sculpture. In Lombard Romanesque and in related schools of southern France, columns are often rested on the backs of lion-like beasts, representing sin being crushed by the Church.

Animals are often used in Far Eastern sculpture, both natural and fantastic; the horse and camel were accorded particular attention after their introduction by the Mongols under Genghis Khan.

During the nineteenth century, widespread interest in sculptured animals of all sorts came into prominence as part of the search for strange and dramatic subject matter. Among the many artists who reflect this interest, particular mention may be made of Antoine Louis Barye (1795-1875), French sculptor, who specialized in the sculpture of wild animals. *See also* EQUESTRIAN SCULPTURE. L. R.

ANIMAL SYSTEMATICS, the classification of animals based upon the principle introduced by Carolus Linnaeus in the eighteenth century, found in the tenth edition of his *Systema naturae,* published in 1758. He introduced various categories called phyla, classes, orders, genera, and species. The total number of kinds of animals listed by Linnaeus was slightly over four thousand. Shortly after the outbreak of World War II, a group of British zoologists was successful in publishing a list of all known animals with their scientific names in a set of four volumes. The total number of animals listed numbered about one million.

The classification of animals enables the zoologist to give to each individual a scientific name which is recognized by scientists throughout the world. In 1895 the International Congress of Zoologists, meeting in Holland, set up a permanent Commission on Nomenclature to prepare an International Code of Nomenclature. This code serves as a guide to help prevent confusion and duplication in the choice of suitable descriptive names for newly discovered animals. Animals are placed in their various categories according to certain fundamental structural similarities. Structures having a common origin are said to be homologous. A study of such structures is known as homology. It is essential that a distinction be made between homology, similarity of origin, and analogy, similarity of function. For example, the arms of man, forelegs of a cat, and wings of a bird are essentially similar in the structure of their bones, blood vessels, nerves, and muscles and so are homologous, although in function they are widely different. On the other hand, the wings of a bird and the wings of a butterfly are similar in function, i.e., analogous, but are very greatly different in structure and hence are not homologous. The various phyla, classes, orders, genera, and species recognized today are not identical to those used by Linnaeus. This might be expected. A better knowledge of the developmental stages of animals, i.e., their embryology, is the chief reason for this difference. Homology is dependent upon embryology.

Classification of Man. As an example of classification, a man is called an animal by biologists because he requires complex organic food and so is placed in the animal kingdom. He also possesses three striking fundamental characteristics, a dorsal tubular nerve cord, and, during his embryonic development, a notochord, a stiff rodlike structure, and gill slits. Man, together with all other animals with such characteristics, is placed in a category called the phylum Chordata. Upon examining these chordate animals during their embryonic as well as their adult life, it is discovered that they differ among themselves in certain respects. Those possessing a brain case and a segmented spinal column, as does man, are called vertebrates and are placed in the subphylum Vertebrata. Some vertebrates have at least two characteristics in common, hair and a muscular diaphragm. All such animals therefore are placed in a single category, the class Mammalia. Since man comes under this category, he is placed in this class. Dogs and cats also are mammals for the same reasons. But it can be seen that some mammals possess four generalized limbs or appendages, each having five digits with cupped nails. These are called Primates. Man therefore is placed in the order Primates, as are the apes, monkeys, and lemurs. Again, among the Primates there are differences sufficiently important to enable them to be divided into two categories called families, the Simidae and the Hominidae. The family Hominidae is characterized by many features, including a brain of large size and with great functional ability; a flat or vertical face; teeth which tend to be even in size; short arms; opposable thumb well developed; two arches in the foot; and the big toe not opposable. Man, possessing these characteristics, is placed in the family Hominidae.

There remain the two categories, genus and species. A species can be defined as a group of animals having many similar characteristics but differing from all other individuals in various ways. Since all members of a species are genetically related they can breed with one another to produce offspring which resemble their parents. Examples of well-known species are man, robin, and the grass frog. A genus can be defined as a group of species that have certain characteristics in common, or as a single species which is quite distinct from its relatives. Since there are no significant structural differences among the races of man, they are all placed in one genus, *Homo,* meaning man, and in one species, *sapiens,* meaning wise. All men therefore are given the scientific name, *Homo sapiens.* This method of using two words, generic and specific, to name an animal is credited to Linnaeus and is termed binomial nomenclature.

PHYLA AND CLASSES OF ANIMALS

The principal animal phyla are well agreed upon today by zoologists, but for some of the less well-known, often highly specialized or degenerate animals, there is less general agreement concerning their classification. These debatable groups will be pointed out. The twenty-one phyla listed are those generally recognized.

Protozoa (Gr. *protos,* πρῶτος, first; *zoon,* ζῷον, animal). Von Siebold in 1845 used the term Protozoa to include only the one-celled animals as distinguished from the many-celled animals, the Metazoa. Protozoa literally means the first animals, most of which are single-celled. Only a few are colonial or live in groups more or less closely associated. Protozoa are aquatic organisms, usually microscopic, and possess no organs in the ordinary sense. Some are highly organized and possess specialized structures called organelles. The colonial Protozoa are often classed as plants and possess yellow, green, or brown chromatophores.

Each protozoan animal resembles structurally an individual cell of a metazoan, or many-celled, animal but differs in that it performs all the essential functions characteristic of the higher or many-celled animals. The colonial Protozoa differ from the many-celled animals in that the cells of the colony are essentially alike and behave more or less as individual units. Colonial forms are said to result from an incomplete division of the cells during reproduction. Because the Protozoa are individual cells composed of a mass of nucleated protoplasm, they are said to be on the protoplasmic level of organization. Protozoa differ from each other in one significant characteristic, their locomotor structures. These structures permit the formation of five classes.

Sarcodina (Gr. *sarcodes*, σαρκώδης, fleshy). The Sarcodina are characterized by having temporary protoplasmic projections for locomotion and food-getting called pseudopodia.

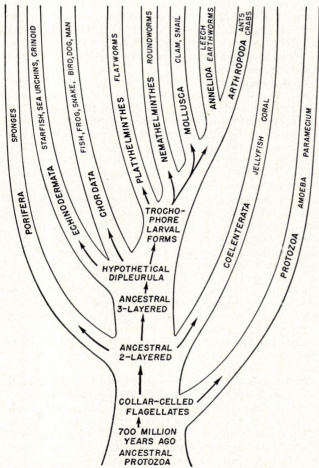

Phylogenetic tree of animals, showing approximate relationship among the great animal groups

They are mostly marine and may or may not have a secreted shell or skeleton. They are the amoebas.

Mastigophora (Gr. *mastix*, μάστιξ, whip; *phoros*, φόρος, bearing). The Mastigophora are often called flagellates because they all possess at some time during their life cycle long, whiplike permanent protoplasmic projections called flagella. This is the class which includes colonial Protozoa, and the trypanosomes.

Sporozoa (Gr. *spora*, σπορά, seed; *zoon*, ζῷον, animal). The Sporozoa possess no structures for locomotion, pseudopodia, cilia, and flagella being absent in the adult individual. The Sporozoa are almost all parasitic animals, of which the malarial parasite is an example.

Ciliata (L. *cilium*, eyelash). The Ciliata are characterized by possessing cilia, short permanent protoplasmic projections, used for locomotion and securing food. They also usually possess a definite mouth and gullet. *Paramecium* is perhaps the best-known member of this group.

Suctoria (L. *sugo*, to suck). The Suctoria possess no cilia in the adult stage but have long sucking tubes called tentacles. They are usually sessile, that is, fixed and nonmotile animals. There is no popular name associated with this group.

Porifera (L. *porus*, pore; *ferre*, to bear). The phylum Porifera contains the sponges and includes the lowest of the many-celled animals. They are sessile, aquatic, usually colonial animals, possessing very few specialized structures. The body wall, which consists of two cellular layers, an outer dermal and an inner gastric flagellated epithelium, is perforated by numerous pores through which water enters the single large cavity. A single large opening of this cavity is the exit for the water. Skeletal fibers or spicules are characteristic body-wall structures. No nerve cells are present. The basal portion of some of the epithelial cells are contractile and function as muscle cells. The phylum is characterized by three structural features: the reversal of the germ layers, the dermal epithelium being entodermal in origin and the gastric epithelium being ectodermal in origin; a simple or complicated system of canals and cavities lined with flagellated cells; and the presence of calcareous, siliceous, or spongin spicules. The cells in the body of the sponge are intimately associated, yet not to the extent that tissues are recognized. The Porifera therefore are said to be on the cellular level of organization. Three classes of Porifera are recognized. The distinguishing characteristics lie in the nature of the skeletal fibers, or spongin.

Calcarea (L. *calx*, lime). The Calcarea are marine sponges of small size possessing calcareous spicules with one ray, three rays, or four rays.

Hexactinellida (Gr. *hex*, ἕξ, six; *aktis*, ἀκτίς, ray). The Hexactinellida are the glass sponges; they possess siliceous spicules which are usually six-rayed.

Demospongiae (Gr. *demos*, δῆμος, a crowd; *spongos*, σπόγγος, sponge). The Demospongiae are mostly marine, only a few being fresh-water forms. Most of these are very large animals. This class may possess a skeleton of siliceous spicules which are not six-rayed, or of elastic spongin fibers, or a combination of both of these types of spicules, or both may be lacking. The commercial sponge and the fresh-water sponge belong to this class.

Coelenterata (Gr. *koilos*, κοῖλος, hollow; *enteron*, ἔντερον, intestine). The Coelenterata are the lowest of the Metazoa with recognized tissues and therefore are said to be on the tissue level of organization. They are characterized by possession of a single cavity, an enteron or digestive cavity, the body wall of which consists of an outer dermal epithelium of ectodermal origin and an inner gastric epithelium of entodermal origin. Between these two cellular tissues is a noncellular structure of variable thickness called mesoglea. In the dermal epithelium are special stinging structures called nematocysts. These are unique structures. Coelenterates are either single or colonial, and are all radially symmetrical. These are the first animals to possess nerve cells. These nerve cells are structurally connected to form a nerve net. Muscle cells are modified epithelial cells as in the Porifera. Three classes of Coelenterata are recognized.

Hydrozoa (Gr. *hydro*, ὑδρο-, water; *zoon*, ζῷον, animal). Hydrozoa include coelenterates, called the hydroids, single or colonial, and medusae, or small jellyfish, with a contractile structure called a velum.

Scyphozoa (Gr. *skyphos*, σκύφος, cup; *zoon*, ζῷον, animal). The Scyphozoa include the true jellyfish or medusae, with velum lacking. There are usually eight notches on the margin of the jellyfish. The hydroid stage is lacking or modified.

Anthozoa (Gr. *anthos*, ἄνθος, flower; *zoon*, ζῷον, animal). Anthozoa are coelenterates in which only the hydroid stage is present. They may be solitary, as the sea anemone, or colonial, as are the corals. The digestive or gastrovascular cavity is divided by septa.

Ctenophora (Gr. *kteis*, κτείς, comb; *phoros*, φόρος, bearing). Ctenophora are commonly called comb jellies because of their eight ciliated bands used for locomotion, or sea walnuts due to their shape. Because of certain structural features such as apparent radial symmetry, a single gastrovascular cavity, and gelatinous mesoglea, they used to be grouped with the Coelenterata, but the following structures permit the relatively few species involved to be placed in a separate phylum. These structural differences are: ciliated ectoderm and entoderm; eight rows of ciliated bands; aboral sense organs; absence of nematocysts; and a recognized biradial symmetry. It is thought the Ctenophora probably arose from coelenteratelike ancestors. There are only about eighty to one hundred species.

Platyhelminthes (Gr. *platys*, πλατύς, flat; *helmins*, ἕλμινς, worm). The Platyhelminthes are the lowest of the many wormlike groups of animals. This group is much advanced over those already mentioned. It is bilaterally symmetrical, with an anterior-posterior axis and dorsal-ventral surfaces. It possesses a nervous system consisting of anterior ganglia and nerve cords extending along the long axis of the body. It has a definite third embryonic germ layer, the mesoderm, which makes it triploblastic and produces for the first time true muscles as well as other organs. It has internal sex organs with permanent ducts and copulatory organ. And it has an excretory system consisting of branched tubules beginning with flame cells and emptying to the outside through a permanent excretory pore. A flame cell is a special shaped cell with cilia whose movements cause waste fluids to move along the tubules. Animals higher in the evolutionary scale also possess some of these characteristics, but the Platyhelminthes differ in that no true coelom is present and the alimentary canal, when present, is branched and possesses only one opening. This and all the later phyla possess organs and are said therefore to be on the organ level of organization. There are four classes often recognized.

Turbellaria (L. *turbella*, confusion). Turbellaria are mostly free-living or nonparasitic; only a few are ecto- and endoparasitic. This class is characterized by possessing ciliated epidermis. The best-known members are the planarians.

Trematoda (Gr. *trematodes*, τρηματώδης, having holes). The Trematoda are all parasitic and are commonly called flukes. They are characterized by possessing a variable number of suckers on the ventral surface, while cilia are absent.

Cestoidea (Gr. *cestus*, κεστός, girdle; *eidos*, εἶδος, form) are all endoparasitic and are commonly called tapeworms. They are characterized by the absence of any alimentary canal; the body is usually made up of divisions called proglottids, with cilia absent.

Nemertinea (Gr. *Nemertes*, Νημερτής, a nymph). The Nemertinea are mostly free-living marine animals and are commonly called ribbon worms. Because there is present an alimentary canal with mouth and anus, a blood vascular system, and a reproductive system in which the sexes are separate, some zoologists place the nemerteans in a special phylum. But they resemble the flatworms in that there is no segmentation and no coelom. Also the nervous system, excretory tubules with flame cells, and a trochophore larval stage (a minute, transparent, free-swimming, pear-shaped organism with two rows of cilia at the large end whose beat suggests a rotating wheel) all resemble those in the flat-worm group. They are therefore grouped under the Platyhelminthes.

Nemathelminthes (Gr. *nema*, νῆμα, thread; *helmins*, ἕλμινς, worm). Nemathelminthes are the unsegmented roundworms. This characterization distinguishes them from the flatworms, on the one hand, and the annelids or true worms, on the other. They also possess a very resistant cuticle and an alimentary canal with a mouth and anus. The sexes are usually separate. Their numbers are tremendous and among the Metazoa are said to be second only to the insects in this respect. Some of the familiar members are the vinegar eels, guinea worm, and trichina. All roundworms are placed under one class, the Nematoda (Gr. *nema*, νῆμα, thread; *eidos*, εἶδος, form), whose characterizations are also those mentioned above.

Acanthocephala (Gr. *acantha*, ἄκανθα, spine; *kephale*, κεφαλή, head). Acanthocephala resemble most closely the Nemathelminthes. A careful comparison of these two groups therefore would help in determining their right taxonomic position. The Acanthocephala are all parasites, the adult stage living in the intestine of any vertebrate from fish to mammal while the larval stage lives in arthropods, usually insects. They are commonly known as spiny-headed worms, or burhead worms. There are at least five important ways in which the three hundred odd species of this group differ from the roundworms. They are: a proboscis with recurved spines, hence the name spiny-head; the absence of any alimentary tract at any time; the presence of circular muscles which, with the longitudinal muscles, permit extension and contraction; ciliated nephridia, or excretory tubules; persistent paired testes but temporary ovaries, the sexes being separate as in the roundworms. These structures are so different from anything found in the Nemathelminthes, their nearest relatives, that most zoologists would place them in a phylum by themselves. When this is done, the few hundred species are all placed in one class, the Echinorhynchidea (Gr. *echinos*, ἐχῖνος, spiny; *rhynchion*, ῥυγχίον, snout).

Gordiacea (L. *Gordius*, in reference to "Gordian knot"). Also called Nematomorpha, the Gordiacea are the horsehair worms or snakes. They resemble more closely the roundworms than do the Acanthocephala and therefore by some zoologists are grouped as a class under the Nemathelminthes. This is done because of the body form, the presence of cuticle, longitudinal muscles, though incomplete, a complete digestive tract in larval stages, and the absence of any circulatory, respiratory or excretory systems. They will be considered a separate phylum here because the coelom is lined with epithelium of mesoderm origin and filled with parenchyms; a single nerve cord is present; and the reproductive organs are separate from their ducts. When considered a separate phylum, two classes are recognized.

Gordididea (L. *Gordius*; Gr. *eidos*, εἶδος, form). The Gordididea are fresh-water and terrestrial worms, with their posterior ends bilobed or trilobed.

Nectonematoidea (Gr. *nectes*, νήκτης, a swimmer; *nema*, νῆμα, thread; *eidos*, εἶδος, form). The Nectonematoidea are marine worms, with their posterior ends unforked.

Rotatoria or **Rotifera** (L. *rota*, wheel). The Rotatoria consist of over a thousand known species. They are common in fresh-water pools, while a few are marine. They are for the most part microscopic and free-living. A few live in tubes and a few are parasitic. Because of the direction of the beating cilia on the anterior end of their body they are commonly known as wheel animalcules. This arrangement of cilia on the anterior end of the animal, the absence of cilia on the rest of the body, and the moving pharynx are distinguishing characteristics. Posteriorly, the body commonly possesses a forked tail or toes in which is a cement gland by which it can attach itself to objects. A pair of short sensory tufts, the lateral antennae, are usually present near the posterior part of the body. The alimentary canal can be complete and differentiated or incomplete. The excretory organs consist of two long coiled, branched nephridia with flame cells. These tubes open into a bladder which contracts periodically, eliminating its contents. There is a dorsal nerve ganglion but no cord. The sexes are separate but the male is usually very small or may be absent. The female possesses a well developed ovary. Reproduction therefore may be both parthenogenetic (by virgin reproduction) and sexual. There is no larval stage. The animals in this group show a remarkable variation in their structural features which is said to suggest a long geologic history. No fossils are known by which to verify this statement. Three classes can be recognized.

Seisonidea (Gr. *seison,* σείσων, an earthen vessel; *eidos,* εἶδος, form). The Seisonidea are characterized by possessing no lateral antennae or toes, by having two ovaries, and by having the male fully developed. There are only two species known.

Bdelloidea (Gr. *bdella,* βδέλλα, leech; *eidos,* εἶδος, form). The Bdelloidea consist of forms with no lateral antennae, with toes absent, or with as many as four. Females have two ovaries and males are unknown.

Monogononta (Gr. *monos,* μόνος, single; *gonos,* γόνος, reproduction). The Monogononta consist of animals with two lateral antennae and of toes, none to two. The females have one ovary and the males are usually present but degenerate.

Gastrotricha (Gr. *gaster,* γαστήρ, belly; *thrix,* θρίξ, hair). Gastrotricha is a small group of something over one hundred species. They are microscopic animals found in quiet, fresh and marine water, usually on bottom plant debris. In movement they resemble some Protozoa. The body is indistinctly divided into a head, neck, and trunk. The dorsal convex surface possesses numerous fine spines. The posterior end is forked and possesses cement glands whose substance enables the animal to attach itself temporarily. Gastrotricha also possess certain features common to the flatworms: a ventral body with a flat and ciliated surface, the cilia being used for locomotion; excretory organs consisting of two coiled unbranched nephridial tubes which begin with a flame cell; and an anterior nerve ganglion connected with two ventral nerves extending the length of the body. Like roundworms, the Gastrotricha possess a straight digestive tract having a mouth and an anus. Only females are known among the fresh-water forms and the marine forms are hermaphroditic. No larval stage is known. There is no popular name associated with this group.

Echinodera (Gr. *echinos,* ἐχῖνος, spiny; *deire,* δειρή, neck). This group, also known as Kinorhyncha, consists of about thirty species of small marine worms measuring up to one millimeter, and is usually considered a separate phylum. They were formerly grouped under a phylum, the Trochelminthes, now not generally recognized. The body is segmented externally only into thirteen to fourteen segments. The anterior end possesses a short retractile proboscis. The digestive canal is straight and possesses a mouth and anus. There are two excretory tubes, each with a flame cell, opening dorsally. The nervous system comes from ectoderm and consists of a dorsal ganglion with a ventral cord having a ganglion in each body segment. The sexes are separate. These characteristics are sufficient grounds for placing these

few species under a separate small phylum. There is no popular name associated with this group.

Bryozoa (Gr. *bryon,* βρύον, moss; *zoon,* ζῷον, animal). The Bryozoa, Brachiopoda and Phoronidea have a number of structures in common so that they are sometimes grouped under one phylum, the Molluscoidea, and yet they differ sufficiently to be placed in separate phyla. Most bryozoans are marine and colonial, while a few live in fresh water. They are commonly known as moss animals because some are mat-like in appearance. Superficially they resemble the hydroids, or Coelenterata, but they are much more advanced. Many fossil forms date back over four million years. Bryozoa are bilaterally symmetrical, nonsegmented, possess three embryonic germ layers and usually a well developed coelom. At the anterior of each animal is a rounded prominence, the lophophore, with its fringe of ciliated hollow tentacles which circulate water for respiration and propel minute particles of food to the mouth. The larval stages resemble a trochophore. Two classes are recognized.

Endoprocta (Gr. *endon,* ἔνδον, within; *proktos,* πρωκτός, anus). Endoprocta are characterized by having the mouth and anus both opening within the lophophore, by the absence of a coelom, and by nonretractile tentacles.

Ectoprocta (Gr. *ectos,* ἐκτός, outside; *proktos,* πρωκτός, anus). Ectoprocta are characterized by the mouth and anus opening outside the lophophore and by the presence of a well-developed coelom, a retractile lophophore, and colonies which are bushy, incrusting, or gelatinous.

Brachiopoda (Gr. *brachion,* βραχίων, arm; *pous,* πούς, foot). The living brachiopods are marine, solitary, sessile, bivalved animals. They differ from the mollusks or shellfish in various ways, one of which is that the valves are dorsal-ventral instead of lateral. Geologically they are very old; fossil forms date back five hundred million years. One of the seventy living genera, *Lingula,* is very similar to its ancestors dating back four million years. It is therefore considered the oldest living genus of animals. The Brachiopoda are commonly called lamp shells because the concave valve resembles the old Roman oil lamp. The one outstanding structural characteristic is the lophophore which consists of two coiled arms on which are ciliated tentacles whose functions are the same as those of the Bryozoa. A large coelom is present, as are contractile blood vessels. The larval stage resembles a modified trochophore. Two classes are recognized.

Inarticulata (L. *in,* not; *articulus,* small joint). The Inarticulata are characterized by having the two valves nearly alike, by the absence of a hinge and beak, and by the presence of an anus.

Articulata (L. *articulus,* small joint). The Articulata are characterized by having valves very unlike, with a hinge, and usually with a beak for the peduncle, the structure whereby the animal attaches itself permanently to the substrate. An anus is absent.

Phoronidea (Gr. *Phoronis,* Φορωνίς, surname of Io; *eidos,* εἶδος, form). There is only one genus of this phylum and about a dozen species. These are sessile, marine, wormlike organisms and may attain a length of six inches. Each animal lives in a leathery or membranous tube secreted by itself. The anterior end is crowned with a horseshoe-shaped lophophore with its double row of ciliated tentacles which can be retracted within the tube. The digestive canal is U-shaped, and the coelom is composed of six large compartments. Two ciliated nephridia are present as well as contractile blood vessels containing cells red with hemoglobin. A nerve ring is located at the base of the tentacles. Both male and female sex organs are in each animal. There is a free-swimming larva, the actinotrocha, which resembles a trochophore. There is no popular name associated with this group.

Chaetognatha (Gr. *chaite,* χαίτη, bristle; *gnathos,* γνάθος, jaw). This is a small group of marine animals consisting of a half-dozen known genera and about thirty known species; they are very widely distributed. In size they measure from 20 mm. to 70 mm. in length. They live near the surface of the ocean, move about rapidly, and are known as arrowworms. They are transparent and are also called glass worms. This phylum is characterized by structures not unique to the group but rather common to a number of various animal phyla. They are bilaterally symmetrical, non-segmented animals and lack cilia on the body surface. The body possesses a head, trunk, and tail with lateral and caudal fins. The mouth is surrounded by two lobes with curved bristles or hooks used to capture food. The coelom is large and divided into three parts; striated muscles are present but circulatory; respiratory and excretory systems are absent. The nervous system consists of a pair of cerebral ganglia and one large ventral ganglion located in the mid-region of the trunk. The anus is located anterior to the tail, a characteristic found only in the chordates. Male and female sex organs are found in each animal. In development, a typical gastrula stage is formed while the coelom is produced by lateral outpushings from the gut cavity, a chordate characteristic. This is truly a mosaic animal group.

Annelida (L. *annellus,* little ring). Of all the wormlike animals that have been mentioned, the annelids are the best developed in many ways. They represent the true worms which are characterized by being segmented, usually externally and internally. They have paired hairlike bristles, or setae; a large, well-developed body cavity, or coelom; a closed blood system with red blood; excretory organs consisting of coiled paired tubules, the nephridia, located in almost every segment; and a ventrally located, solid nerve cord with ganglia segmentally arranged. Five classes are recognized.

Archiannelida (Gr. *archaios,* ἀρχαῖος, primitive; L. *annellus,* little ring). The Archiannelida are small in size and are either degenerate or primitive marine worms. Segmentation is chiefly internal, and parapodia, leaf-like lateral body projections, and setae are usually absent. There is usually a trochophore larval stage. There is no popular name associated with this group.

Polychaeta (Gr. *polys,* πολύς, many; *chaite,* χαίτη, bristle). The Polychaeta are mostly marine and are the best developed in many ways of all the annelids. Many are tube dwellers. Segmentation is external and internal, with parapodia and setae. There is a distinct head with sense organs. A trochophore larval stage is present. Some of the members of this class are the Palolo worms, clam worms, and the sea mouse.

Oligochaeta (Gr. *oligos,* ὀλίγος, few; *chaite,* χαίτη, bristle). The Oligochaeta are found chiefly in fresh water and moist soil. External and internal segmentation is pronounced, and setae are few on each segment, but there are no parapodia. No head is present. Development is direct; thus there is no larval stage. The earthworm belongs to this class.

Hirudinea (L. *hirudo,* leech). The Hirudinea are the leeches which are found in salt or fresh water or on land. The body is usually somewhat flat with a posterior sucker and sometimes a small sucker surrounding the mouth at the anterior end. No tentacles or parapodia are present and most often no setae. Development is direct, there being no larval stage.

Gephyrea (Gr. *gephyra,* γέφυρα, bridge). Gephyrea are a small group of marine worms with sausage-shaped bodies. Segmentation is not pronounced. They all have a nonsegmented ventral nerve cord. Some zoologists place this group in a separate phylum but there are good reasons for including the group as a class under the Annelida. Some members of the class are segmented in their larval stages and have a segmented nerve cord; others possess a few pair of setae and nephridia. There is also a trochophore larval stage. Fishermen call members of this group, which are used for bait, doodles.

Onychophora (Gr. *onyx,* ὄνυξ, claw; *phoros,* φόρος, bearing). This phylum contains about seventy known species restricted in their geographical distribution to Mexico, Central America, the West Indies, and South America. It has sometimes been considered a class under the Annelida and at other times under the Arthropoda. For reasons to be mentioned, it is now generally classified as a phylum and considered a possible link between the true worms, the Annelida, and the jointed, legged animals, the Arthropoda.

Peripatus, the most common representative of the Onychophora, resembles the annelids structurally in its simple gut, its segmentally arranged nephridia, its eye structure, and its ciliated reproductive tubules. Peripatus also possesses striking arthropod structural characteristics, such as jaws derived from modified appendages, a dorsal heart with ostia surrounded by a cavity called a hemocoele, and a coelom which is restricted to the regions occupied by the nephridia and reproductive ducts. It also possesses tracheae, as do the insects.

The Onychophora might well be placed under the phylum Arthropoda were it not for the fact that it has striking structural characteristics of its own. These are: a single pair of jaws, an unsegmented body, the arrangement of the tracheal openings, the nature of the skin texture, and non-jointed appendages. From these facts it might be concluded that the Arthropoda have arisen from a wormlike stock through the medium of the group Onychophora.

Arthropoda (Gr. *arthron,* ἄρθρον, joint; *pous,* πούς, foot). The Arthropoda is the largest phylum numerically of the entire animal kingdom. Any invertebrate with jointed appendages belongs to this phylum. Some other distinguishing characteristics of the Arthropoda are the chitinous exoskeleton secreted by the epidermis, striated muscles, and the absence of cilia. Five classes are recognized under this phylum.

Crustacea (L. *crusta,* a hard shell). Crustacea are characterized by having the function of respiration performed by means of gills; they usually have one pair of appendages on each body segment variously modified, two pairs of antennae, and two sex openings on the posterior part of the thorax. Their habitat is either marine or fresh-water or terrestrial. This class includes the crabs, crayfish, and lobsters.

Insecta (L. *insectum,* cut into). The Insecta are characterized by having three pairs of legs on the thorax, and mouth parts consisting of one pair of mandibles, one pair of maxillae and a labium. This is the largest class of the phylum and includes the flies, butterflies, moths, beetles, and grasshoppers.

Arachnoidea (Gr. *arachne,* ἀράχνη, spider; *eidos,* εἶδος, form). The Arachnoidea are distinguished from the other classes of the Arthropoda by the presence of four pairs of legs on the cephalothorax, a fused head and thorax, and one sex opening on the second abdominal segment, and by the absence of antennae and mandibles. This class includes spiders, scorpions, and horseshoe crabs.

Chilopoda (Gr. *cheilos,* χεῖλος, lip; *pous,* πούς, foot). The Chilopoda is a relatively small class which includes the

BONGO

LION

ZEBRA

GIRAFFE

MANDRILL

ELEPHANT

HIPPOPOTAMUS

GORILLA

CAMEL

PAINTED FOR COLLIER'S ENCYCLOPEDIA BY BOB KUHN

ATLANTIC WALRUS

COYOTE

WHITE-TAILED DEER

BEAVER

BISON OR BUFFALO

RACCOON

GRIZZLY BEAR

WOLVERINE

BIGHORN

PRONGHORN

MOOSE

PUMA

PAINTED FOR COLLIER'S ENCYCLOPEDIA BY BOB KUHN

PECCARY

AGOUTI

GIANT ARMADILLO

KINKAJOU

JAGUAR

HOWLER MONKEY

CHINCHILLA

TAPIR

SLOTH

MANED WOLF

GIANT ANTEATER

LLAMA

PAINTED FOR COLLIER'S ENCYCLOPEDIA BY R. F. KUHN

MAMMALS OF ASIA AND AUSTRALIA

TIGER

LEOPARD

ORANGUTAN

PANDA

KANGAROO

DUCKBILLED PLATYPUS

BLACK BUCK

CUSCUS

RHINOCEROS

WATER BUFFALO

PAINTED FOR COLLIER'S ENCYCLOPEDIA BY BOB KUHN

centipedes. They are characterized by possessing a head and a long segmented body, a pair of legs on each segment, and mouth parts consisting of a pair of mandibles and two pairs of maxillae.

Diplopoda (Gr. *diplous*, διπλοῦς, double; *pous*, πούς, foot). The Diplopoda consists of the millipedes. These are characterized by having usually two pairs of legs on each body segment, mouth parts consisting of one pair of mandibles and maxillae, and one sex opening on the third segment near the head.

Mollusca (L. *mollis,* soft). The Mollusca, or shellfish, are soft-bodied animals possessing a ventrally located muscular foot of some sort, a dorsal visceral mass and in most cases a head. The mouth of many possesses a radula, a rasping ribbon-like structure. The coelom is reduced as a hemocoele. There is no segmentation. A trochophore larval stage is present in most of the classes. This phylum is composed of five classes dependent upon such characteristics as the nature of the foot, the organs of respiration, the mantle, and the shell, a secretion product of the mantle.

Amphineura (Gr. *amphi*, ἀμφί, both; *neuron*, νεῦρον, nerve). The Amphineura, or chitons, are marine animals and have an elongated, elliptical body, convex on the dorsal and flat on the ventral surfaces. On the dorsal side are usually eight overlapping calcareous plates. The mouth possesses a radula. Many pairs of gill filaments are present and tentacles are absent. As the class name indicates, the nerve cord is double, one on each side of the body. The larval stage is usually a trochophore. This group is considered the most primitive class of the mollusks.

Scaphopoda (Gr. *skaphe*, σκάφη, boat; *pous*, πούς, foot). Scaphopoda, the tooth or tusk shells, are marine forms. The shell is a slightly curved tubular structure open at both ends. This may attain a length of two and one-half inches. Gills are absent; the mantle assumes the function of respiration. A radula also is absent. The larval stage resembles a trochophore.

Gastropoda (Gr. *gaster*, γαστήρ, belly; *pous*, πούς, foot). Gastropoda include the slugs, snails, whelks, and limpets. The body, including the visceral mass and shell, is often spirally coiled, either sinistrally or dextrally. The shell or external skeleton may be absent. There are present a distinct head with tentacles, one pair of eyes, and gills or a lung for respiration. The mouth possesses a radula, and a larval stage is absent.

Pelecypoda (Gr. *pelekys*, πέλεκυς, hatchet; *pous*, πούς, foot). Pelecypoda includes the oysters, clams, and scallops. They are characterized by having two valves as their external skeleton. Head, jaws and radula are absent. The muscular foot is usually hatchet-shaped; the gills are usually platelike. The larval stage resembles a trochophore.

Cephalopoda (Gr. *kephale*, κεφαλή, head; *pous*, πούς, foot). Cephalopoda includes squids, sepia, nautili, and octopuses. The shell may be external, internal, or absent. The head is large with conspicuous, highly developed eyes. The foot is modified into eight or ten arms, or tentacles, located on the head. The mouth possesses horny jaws and a radula. Development is direct, there being no larval stage.

Considering the phyla up to this point, it is interesting to observe evidence of evolutionary relationship. It will be noticed that a trochophore larval stage is common to many of the invertebrate animals. For example a trochophore is to be found among the marine flatworms, the nemerteans, brachiopods, bryozoans, mollusks, and some of the annelids. The larval stage of the phylum Phoronidea is called an actinotrocha and resembles a trochophore. The other very

large invertebrate phylum, the Arthropoda, or jointed, legged animals, was shown to be related to the Annelida, the true worms, by the fact that the phylum Onychophora has characteristics common to both. These facts would indicate that most of the invertebrate animal phyla have arisen from a common worm stock.

Echinodermata (Gr. *echinos*, ἐχῖνος, spiny; *derma*, δέρμα, skin). The phylum Echinodermata, the last of the invertebrates, has a possible evolutionary connection with the next higher and last group of animals, the chordates. The phylum Chordata is the one to which man, the vertebrate, belongs. Evidence for this relationship is found in the presence of the following chordatelike characteristics: the mesoderm forms as lateral outpushings from the primitive gut; the skeleton, which is an endoskeleton and not an exoskeleton, is of mesodermal origin; the adult anus is derived from the embryonic blastopore; the mouth is a new structure formed by an ectodermal inpushing, the stomodeum. The larvae of some echinoderms also resemble similar stages of some of the chordates.

The presence of these many resemblances has resulted in the formulation of the Echinoderm Theory for the origin of chordate animals. These chordate characteristics seen in the echinoderm group nevertheless should not be considered complete evidence that the chordates have arisen from the echinoderms. The theory is very suggestive but leaves too many problems still unsolved. Some important features of the echinoderm group include a change from a basic bilateral symmetry to radial symmetry with a consequent sedentary mode of life; a much reduced blood and nervous system; a unique water-vascular or ambulacral system including contractile tube feet; and the absence of any segmentation. Five classes are recognized.

Crinoidea (Gr. *krinon*, κρίνον, lily; *eidos*, εἶδος, form). Crinoidea, the sea lilies, or feather stars, usually possess a stalk for permanent or temporary attachment while the five arms are generally branched.

Asteroidea (Gr. *aster*, ἀστήρ, star; *eidos*, εἶδος, form). The Asteroidea are the starfish or sea stars. Their arms, numbering from five to fifty, are usually not sharply marked off from the central disc. The madreporite, the exit of the water-vascular system, is aboral in position; the ambulacral grooves are open, and pedicellariae, microscopic pincerlike structures on the body surface, are present. The starfish are sluggish in their movements.

Ophiuroidea (Gr. *ophis*, ὄφις, snake; *eidos*, εἶδος, form). Ophiuroidea are the serpent or brittle stars. The central disc is rounded and the five slender, very flexible arms are sharply marked off from the disc. The madreporite is oral; the anus is absent; and there are no pedicellariae. They are active in their movements.

Echinoidea (Gr. *echinos*, ἐχῖνος, spiny; *eidos*, εἶδος, form). Echinoidea include the sea urchins, cake urchins, and sand dollars. This group is also pentamerous but without free arms, the body being somewhat hemispherical or disc-like in shape. The endoskeleton consists of calcareous plates firmly sutured in a regular pattern.

Holothuroidea (Gr. *holothourion*, ὁλοθούριον, sea cucumber; *eidos*, εἶδος, form). Holothuroidea are the sea cucumbers and are so called because of their superficial resemblance in shape to the cucumber. Tentacles which are pentamerous surround the mouth. The body wall is a thin or thick muscular structure containing very fine scattered calcareous particles. No spines nor pedicellariae are present.

Chordata (Gr. *chorde*, χορδή, string). All animals of the phylum Chordata exhibit at least four distinguishing structural characteristics. These are: (1) the presence at some time in their life cycle of a dorsal, stiff, rodlike structure called the notochord; (2) a dorsal hollow nerve cord; (3) gill slits in the walls of the pharynx; (4) a ventrally located heart. The vertebrate animals belong to this phylum, of which there are seven recognized classes.

Cyclostomata (Gr. *cyklos*, κύκλος, circle; *stoma*, στόμα, mouth). Cyclostomata are jawless vertebrates including the lampreys and hagfishes. They possess a circular suctorial mouth with rasping, horny, teethlike structures. The body is elongated, eel-shaped, and has no appendages. The notochord persists throughout life. There is a single median olfactory pit and from six to fourteen pairs of gills, each in a separate pouch. The skin possesses no scales.

Chondrichthyes (Gr. *chondros*, χόνδρος, cartilage; *ichthys*, ἰχθύς, fish). Chondrichthyes include the sharks and rays. They are characterized by having a nonterminal mouth with jaws, an endoskeleton of cartilage, five to seven pairs of gills in separate slits with no gill covers, a spiral valve structure in the intestine, and a notochord which persists throughout life. They possess a tough skin with placoid scales.

Osteichthyes (Gr. *osteon*, ὀστέον, bone; *ichthys*, ἰχθύς, fish). Osteichthyes include all the bony fish. The mouth is usually terminal and four pairs of gills are present in a common cavity covered with an operculum. Appendages usually include median and paired lateral fins with no pelvic girdle present. An air bladder is usually present. Scales of the skin are either of a cycloid, ctenoid, or ganoid type.

Amphibia (Gr. *amphi*, ἀμφί, dual; *bios*, βίος, life). Amphibia include the frogs, toads, salamanders, and caecilians, the limbless forms. The endoskeleton is largely ossified. In most cases there are two pairs of limbs for walking or swimming. The Amphibia are thus the lowest of the Tetrapoda. Two nostrils join directly with the mouth cavity. Gills are present sometime during the life cycle. Ten pairs of cranial nerves are present. The heart is three-chambered, including two auricles and one ventricle. The skin is soft and has no external scales.

Reptilia (L. *reptilis*, creeping). Reptilia include the lizards, snakes, turtles, crocodiles, and alligators. The skeleton is fully ossified. Two nostrils open into the nasal cavity and respiration is by means of lungs. Twelve pairs of cranial nerves are present. The heart consists of two auricles and partly divided ventricles; the crocodile has a heart with four chambers. The skin is dry, usually with scales or scutes. Fertilization is internal, usually by a copulatory organ. In development, the embryonic membranes include an amnion, chorion, yolk sac, and allantois. These structures are adaptations to a terrestrial mode of life.

Aves (L. *aves*, bird.) Aves include all the birds. They are warm-blooded. The body is covered with feathers and the skeleton is completely ossified. Two pairs of limbs are present, the anterior pair usually modified as wings, the posterior pair modified for perching, walking, or swimming. The mouth possesses a beak, or bill, and no teeth. Only the right aortic arch persists as the systemic artery, and the heart is four-chambered. Respiration is by means of lungs and these are connected to air sacs in the body cavity. No urinary bladder is present. Fertilization is internal, but no copulatory organ is present. Embryonic membranes are the same as in the reptiles and for the same reason.

Mammalia (L. *mamma*, breast). Mammalia, warm-blooded, suckling animals, are characterized by the presence of mammary glands, hair and a diaphragm. The heart is four-chambered; only the left aortic arch persists. The red blood cells are non-nucleated. Teeth are usually present, set in alveoli in the jaws and modified according to their food habits. Fertilization is internal and is achieved by means of a copulatory organ. Embryonic membranes consist of amnion, chorion, and allantois. The yolk sac is vestigial since the source of food is the mother.   J. T. I.

ANIMATISM. *See* PRIMITIVE RELIGION.
ANIMISM. *See* PRIMITIVE RELIGION.
ANION. *See* ELECTROLYTES.

ANISE [æ'nɪs], *Pimpinella anisum,* a small annual of the parsley family, native to Mediterranean countries, cultivated widely as a condiment plant, especially in southern Europe, Tunisia, India, and South America. The aromatic seeds are

PUBLICITY ASSOCIATES. INC.

Anise, an annual which regularly attains a height of two feet

used for flavoring and yield a fragrant oil useful in cooking and medicine. The tiny, yellowish flowers are on slender branching stems. Young plants resemble the young growth of celery.   J. C. Wis.

ANISE TREE, *Illicium,* a handsome, evergreen shrub of the magnolia family, with anise-scented foliage, grown as ornamentals in warm climates. *I. floridum* of the southern United States has nodding purple flowers.   J. C. Wis.

ANJERO-SUJENSK. *See* ANZHERO-SUDZHENSK.

ANJOU, a former province in western France, bounded by the provinces of Maine on the north, Touraine on the east, Poitou on the south, and Bretagne on the west. Its capital city was Angers. The topography is that of a plateau bisected by the Loire Valley. Spurs of the Armorican Massif protrude over the western border of Anjou. There are plains in the western part of the province, and in the south are the lower basins of the Mayenne and Sarthe rivers. Many megolithic remains indicate early habitation of this area by prehistoric man. The Andes, or Andecavi, who later occupied this region, were conquered by Fabius, a lieutenant of Caesar, thereafter coming under Roman domination. Under the reign of Valentinian III (419-455) the territory detached itself from the Empire of the West and entered into the American Confederation, changing the imperial name of its principal city, Juliomagus, to Andegavia, which in medieval times became Angers, and the region became known as Angou, or Anjou.

Toward 720 appeared the first count of Anjou, Rainfroy, who had borne arms against Charles Martel, but who was nevertheless able to maintain the title of count. In the ninth century the Vikings invaded and pillaged Anjou, and in later years the people of the province were engaged in frequent combat with the Bretons and Normans. Geoffrey V, eleventh count of Anjou, who was surnamed Plantagenet because he habitually wore a sprig of the broom plant in his cap, married Mathilda, daughter of Henry I, King of England, in 1128, thereby transmitting the countship of Anjou to their son, who ascended the throne of England as Henry II. The kings of England kept Anjou in their possession until 1203, when Philip Augustus seized it from King John. In 1246, Louis IX gave Anjou as an appanage to his younger brother, Charles, who established an Angevin dynasty on the throne of Naples and the Two Sicilies in 1266. Marguerite, the daughter of Charles, brought Maine and Anjou as a dowry to Charles of Valois, whose son, on becoming king of France under the name of Philip VI, united the two provinces to the crown in 1328. In 1297 a peerage was attached to the countship of Anjou by Philip IV, and it was made into a duchy by John the Good in 1360. It was appanaged to his son Louis, who became king of Naples. When René, second son of Louis II and lord of Anjou and Provence, died in 1480, Louis XI annexed Anjou to the French crown. During the French Revolution the province fought against the Republicans in the Vendée Wars. In 1790 the department of the Maine-et-Loire was formed from the province of Anjou.   S. Van V.

ANKARA or **ANGORA** [a'ŋkara, æŋgɔ'rə], the capital city of Turkey, situated at an altitude of 3,100 ft., near the west central part of the country on the Anatolian Plateau. Ankara is connected with all parts of Turkey, and with the East and Europe, by road, rail, and air routes. It is about 300 mi. southeast of Istanbul. The Ankara River, a tributary of the Sakarya River, flows through the old part of the city, which occupies the steep slopes of several craggy sections of an old volcanic plug. Protected by mountains to the north, Ankara's winter temperatures rarely fall to freezing, and there is little wind or snow. The summer days are dry and hot; the nights, however, are cool. The average annual rainfall is about 20 in. The surrounding countryside is almost barren, but there are a few willow and poplar trees along the streams. Grass and flowers bloom during the short spring season. With the improved transportation and communications, the plains to the south and west are becoming more settled and productive in cereal raising and grazing, which are the chief agricultural activities. Vegetables and fruits, especially pears, apricots, and apples, are also grown. Mohair from the Angora goat, other wools, and hides are exported.

Primarily a seat of government and a residential city, Ankara's industries include agricultural machine shops, flour mills, wine and beer distilleries, and plants for the production of cement, tractors, and airplane engines. There are also some home industries.

The region of Ankara has been inhabited since Paleolithic and Neolithic times. It was part of the Hittite empire

STATUE OF KEMAL ATATURK IN ANKARA SQUARE, ANKARA. AT THE LEFT IS THE STREET LEADING TO THE OLD QUARTER OF THE CITY.

as early as the seventeenth century B.C. After the Hittites came the Phrygians, who renamed the city Ancyra. Then came the Lydians for a short period, followed by the Persians. Alexander the Great lived here for a time after capturing Gordium, farther west. Later the city, then called Galatia, was the principal settlement of the Gallic tribe of the Tectosages and the mixture of conquered peoples in the surrounding territory.

Following two centuries of alternate peace and conflict with the Romans and two short periods under the King of Pergamum and then Mithradates, King of Pontus, the city came under Roman rule in 25 B.C. Ankara was taken by Chosroes II, Shah of Persia, and attacked several times by the Arabs, and, early in the ninth century, by Harun Al-Rashid. After the defeat of the Byzantine army at Malazgirt in 1071 by the Seljuk army, the Seljuks took the city. The Crusaders held it for eighteen years. In the fourteenth century, Ankara fell to the Ottoman Sultan Murad I. It was held in 1402 by Tamerlane after defeating Sultan Bayazid I, but passed again to the Turks in 1403. Ibrahim Pasha seized it in 1832 on his campaign against the Sultan, and held it for a short time.

A fifteenth century A.D. closed market on the slope of the citadel hill contains pre-Hittite and Hittite basreliefs, sculpture, pottery, metal articles and jewelry. There are many remains from Roman and Byzantine times. The foremost is the Temple of Rome and Augustus, in the center of the city, said to have been built in the first century A.D. by Galatian princes in honor of Augustus. On its walls is the famous inscription, the Monumentum Ancyranum, recording the activities of this great emperor. The temple was altered and used as a church in Byzantine times. In the fourth century, the Emperor Julian was given an ovation when he visited the city. The Julian Column is said to commemorate this visit. There are extensive foundations of baths of the early third century. The old part of the city is crowned by the picturesque walled citadel; in the walls of the citadel remnants of early sculpture and architecture are found.

In 1920, Ankara became the headquarters of the Young Turk movement, which had started the previous year and was led by Mustafa Kemal Pasha. The Turkish Grand National Assembly was established and included partisans from the old parliament at Istanbul (Constantinople), which had been dissolved. On Oct. 13, 1923, the city superseded Istanbul as the capital of Turkey. At that time, it was essentially a village of the Middle Ages. A complete process of modernization has taken place, and Ankara has come to rank with other capitals. The University of Ankara, founded in 1935, is in the new city, as are the Atatürk Memorial Mausoleum, the opera house, the ethnographical museum, the national library, two new mosques, hospitals, parks, a stadium, and a hippodrome. The Mausoleum, situated above a spacious court paved with marble, has a 1,000-ft., tree-lined approach and crowns the garden-terraced ridge of Rasateppe. The new city and the suburbs spread out onto the plains and hills to the southwest. The ministries and most of the embassies and legations are along the upper section of two-and-a-half-mile-long Atatürk Boulevard, which begins in the central square in the business section and ends at the heights of Çankaya, where the President's residence is located. Pop. 1950, 286,781.

ANLACE. *See* ARMS AND ARMOR.

ANNABERG [ɑ'nɑbɛrχ], a manufacturing town in the German state of Saxony, 55 mi. southwest of Dresden on the northern slopes of the Erz Gebirge or Ore Mountains. It was founded as a silver-mining town in 1496; however, silver mining ceased near the end of the nineteenth century. In a mining region, uranium, bismuth, cobalt, and tin are found nearby. Annaberg became the lace center of Germany after the introduction of lace making in 1561; it is also a center for silk, ribbon, braid, and hosiery. Other manufactures include glass and cardboard. After World War II, Annaberg was placed in the Soviet zone of occupation and is now a city of East Germany. Pop. (est. 1938), 19,800.

ANNA COMNENA [æ'nə kɒmni'nə] (1083-1148), Byzantine historian, daughter of Alexius I Comnenus, was born in Constantinople, Dec. 1, 1083. While the emperor was dying, she and her mother Irene tried to induce him to disinherit his son and give the crown to Anna's husband, Nicephorus Briennius. After her brother succeeded to the throne, Anna conspired against him, but was stripped of her fortune when the plot was discovered. After the death of her husband, she retired to a convent in 1137 and began writing the history entitled the *Alexiad*. A rambling chronicle of her father's reign, 1081-1118, it completes the history written by her husband. Although she was carefully educated in the learning of the Greeks, her work lacks scientific detachment, and is filled with exaggeration and gossip extolling the family of which she was a member. F. C. H.

ANNA KARENINA [ɑ'nɑ kɑrɛ'nyɪnɑ], a Russian novel, one of the major works of Leo Tolstoy, first appeared as a serial in the *Russian Messenger* (1875-1877) and was first published in book form in 1878. It contains an excellent portrayal of the life of the nineteenth-century nobility of Russia. Anna, the heroine, a beautiful and romantic woman married to a celebrated but unemotional public official much older than herself, falls desperately in love with Alexei Vronsky, a handsome young officer. Having abandoned husband and child for Vronsky, Anna, distraught by remorse and jealousy, commits suicide.

In his portrayal of Anna's lapse from moral rectitude, Tolstoy achieved a degree of objectivity not ordinarily displayed in his other major novels. Perhaps of even greater significance than the plot and artistic merit of the work is the portrayal of Tolstoy himself in the character of Levin, which reveals Tolstoy in the process of transition from *War and Peace* to *Confession,* and is, therefore, an indispensable aid in the complete study of Tolstoy's life and literary career. *Anna Karenina* has been adapted many times to the stage and screen, and has been a popular vehicle for some of the more important actors and actresses of Europe and America.

A. L.

ANNAM [ənɑ'm], one of the former three federated states of Vietnam (Annam, Cochin China, and Tonkin), which is one of the three associated states of Indochina (Cambodia, Laos, and Vietnam). The territory of Annam forms a long strip of isolated coastal plain on the South China Sea, with a background of tall mountains which separate it from Laos. It has an area of 57,838 sq. mi. Cam Ranh Bay, on the southeast coast, has an excellent natural harbor. Rice is the chief crop. Annam's mineral deposits include iron ore, ferromanganese, chrome, tin, zinc, lead, antimony, phosphates, and bauxite. It produces some coal. The climate in the southern part is tropical; in the northern part the dry season, from November to May, is relatively cold. Typhoons are frequent and violent.

Ethnology and Population. The population of Annam was 6,751,462 in 1951. Except for some tribes of Mois in the mountains, the population is nearly all Annamese, a mixture of Mongolians with the indigenous Moi tribes. Chinese numbered about 16,000 and Europeans about 5,000. Hue, the capital, and Tourane, its port, are important cities. Buddhism is the predominant religion.

History and Government. Between 200 B.C. and A.D. 1000, Annam was under the domination of China. During this period many Chinese came into the country and intermarried with the Annamese. Having already ceded Cochin China to France, Tu-duc, Emperor of Annam, in 1874 signed a treaty by which he placed his country under French protection, but a decade later Annam joined China in a war against France. By treaties in 1884 and 1885 at the conclusion of this war, Annam and Tonkin became protectorates of France. The emperor retained nominal power, but the actual administration was exercised by a Resident Superior, directly responsible to the Governor-General of the Indochinese Union. He was assisted by Residents in each of the provinces, and a council with advisory powers. Traditional native administrations continued to exist side by side with the French administration. Annam, as all of Indochina, was occupied by the Japanese during World War II. At the conclusion of the war, Annamese nationalists overthrew Bao Dai, the Emperor of Annam, and declared the independence of the Republic of Vietnam in September 1945. After several months of hostilities the French government recognized the republic in an agreement of Mar. 6, 1946, but only as a part of the Indochinese Federation and the French Union. Subsequent negotiations to implement the agreement broke down, largely over the status of Cochin China, which Vietnam hoped to incorporate in its territory, and the amount of autonomy to be enjoyed by Vietnam. The Communist-trained president of Vietnam, Ho Chi Minh, launched a civil war in December 1946, his party being known as the Viet Minh. French forces succeeded in holding the chief cities, and native pro-French groups in June 1948 launched Vietnam, originally including only Annam and Tonkin but joined by Cochin China in April 1949. In June 1949, Bao Dai returned as Emperor of Vietnam, backed by the French, and Vietnam was granted the status of an autonomous state within the French Union. At the Geneva Conference in 1954, the northern half of Vietnam was awarded to Ho Chi Minh's government for administration. It was agreed that a plebiscite covering all of Vietnam would be held in 1956 to determine whether the Communist government of the north or the non-Communist government of the south shall rule. *See also* Indochina; Vietnam. A. V.

ANNAMESE [ænəmi'z; ænəmi's], a language spoken in Indochina by sixteen million people, who inhabit the Tonkinese delta in the north, the plain of Cochin China in the south, and the long coast line between. It is a typical monosyllabic, noninflecting, tonal language. Among its characteristic features are the following: a grammar marked by rigid rules of word order; four clearly distinguished parts of speech, namely, nouns, verbs, conjunctions, and a class of words used at the end of a sentence to mark a special function of the sentence, such as to ask a question or express a doubt; an extensive use of classifying words when nouns are counted; and a complex use of kinship terms instead of pronouns. Annam has been under strong Chinese political influence for almost two thousand years, and the language is full of Chinese loan words. Of the non-Chinese part of the lexicon, some words are clearly allied to the Mon-Khmer vocabulary, some to the Thai, and some, as far as is known, to neither. There is a suspicion that the basic part of Annamese is very distantly related to the Thai group.

The Annamese language was written from the fourteenth century onward in modified Chinese characters. In the seventeenth century missionaries invented a Roman transcription which is now the official written medium of the language. It is very exact and well adapted for the promotion of universal literacy in the Annamese-speaking part of Indochina.

M. B. E.

ANNA PERENNA [æ'nə pərɛ'nə], an early Roman goddess, traditionally the sister of Dido. Anna went to Italy after Dido's death and she was welcomed by Aeneas, but his wife Lavinia was jealous of her. Dido warned her of her danger in a dream and she drowned herself. She was then worshipped as a river nymph. She was also known as the goddess of the complete circle of the year, as her name indicates. Her festival, a holiday of revelry and licentiousness, was celebrated on March 15, when sacrifices were made to her in order that the year might be completed with good fortune. She had a sacred grove on the Via Flaminia. There are references to her worshippers in Ovid and in Silius Italicus. R. F.

ANNAPOLIS [ənæ'polɪs], capital city of Maryland and the county seat of Anne Arundel Co. on the Severn River near Chesapeake Bay, 32 mi. northeast of Washington, D.C. Annapolis is most widely known as the site of the United States Naval Academy. It was founded by Puritans in 1649 and first called Providence. It subsequently became Anne Arundel Town, and in 1694 was renamed Annapolis in honor of the Princess Royal (later Queen Anne). In 1708 it was incorporated as a city. Located in Annapolis are the Church of St. Anne (1695) and St. John's College (1784). General Washington resigned his commission to the Congress of the Confederation at the old State House on Dec. 23, 1783; and in this historic building, shortly afterward, the Congress ratified the Treaty of Paris, which ended hostilities with Great Britain. It was here, also, in 1786 that the Annapolis Convention was opened. The Hall of Records preserves historical documents, and Historic Annapolis, an active historical society, is working to restore many eighteenth-century houses which were built when Annapolis was considered the "Athens of America." The city carries on a busy mercantile trade and supports a shipyard near by. Pop. 1950, 10,047 (exclusive of the U.S. Naval Academy). *See also* United States Naval Academy.

ANNAPOLIS CONVENTION, a meeting of delegates from Virginia, New York, Pennsylvania, New Jersey, and Delaware, held at Annapolis, Md., Sept. 11-14, 1786, to discuss the question of commercial regulations for all the states. There had been talk of a general convention ever since 1780, but this was the first actual meeting of the five states. The call was issued early in 1786 by the Virginia legislature. However, a good deal of suspicion existed regarding the motives of the leaders of the convention: men such as Alexander Hamilton and James Madison. Northern merchants, who wanted national regulation of commerce, claimed that the leaders were aristocrats who were more interested in political schemes than in commerce. Some legislatures thought Congress was the proper body to propose measures for strengthening the Confederation, and in fact Congress was busy during 1786 preparing sweeping amendments to the Articles of Confederation.

When the twelve delegates from the five states met, they took the position that the representation was inadequate for the purpose and drafted a report calling for another convention to meet in Philadelphia in the spring of 1787. They argued in their report that any steps that might be taken with regard to commerce would affect all parts of the government and make necessary a general change in the Articles of Confederation. They suggested that the delegates to the proposed convention be given wider powers. This report, sent to Congress and to the governors of all the states, was at first ignored. Then, as a result of Shays's Rebellion, it was acted upon by Congress, which issued a call for a convention to meet in Philadelphia in the spring of 1787. M. Je.

ANNAPOLIS ROYAL, the county town of Annapolis Co., Nova Scotia, Canada, situated at the head of Annapolis Basin, about 75 mi. west of Halifax. It is the oldest permanent white settlement in North America north of Florida. The Basin was visited by Pierre de Monts and Samuel de Champlain in 1604. A fort, which in later years was restored, was built on the north side of the harbor in 1605. Known as Port Royal, the community was the stronghold of the French in Acadia for a century. The British captured it in 1654 and held it for four years. The French then reoccupied the town. In 1690 the British again took the town and this time held it for seven years before the French once more reoccupied it. The British regained it in 1710 and changed the name from Port Royal to Annapolis Royal in honor of Queen Anne. Until Halifax was founded in 1749, it served as the British headquarters in Nova Scotia. The town is of historical interest as a place of reputed "firsts," for it is known as the site of the launching of the first vessel built in North America, of the first water-power grist mill, of the first conversions of Indians to Christianity, of the first drama written and staged in the non-Spanish Western Hemisphere, and of the first social club, called Champlain's Order of the Good Time. In 1917 the site of the old fort was set apart as Fort Anne National Park. The Dominion Atlantic Railway serves the town. Pop. 1951, 784. D. F. P.

ANNAPOLIS VALLEY, a long, deep, narrow valley in Annapolis Co., Nova Scotia. The valley, which is about 8 to 10 mi. wide, is immediately east of and practically parallel with the Bay of Fundy. The port of Digby is at the southwestern end of the valley, which extends northeastward for about 45 mi. Annapolis (Annapolis Royal), the county seat, and Bridgetown and Middleton are the other towns in the valley. The valley is formed on a soft sandstone which lies between a small traprock ridge to the northwest and a granite upland to the southeast. The trap ridge separates the valley from the Bay of Fundy. The Annapolis River, which has its headwaters in several small lakes in the central (granite) upland, flows north into the valley, where it makes an abrupt turn to the southwest and enters the Bay of Fundy between Digby and Port Wade. The lower part of the river has been drowned or embayed, and this estuary is up to 5 mi. wide and about 23 mi. long. The mouth of the estuary is narrowed by 500-ft. cliffs to a width of about one-half mile. The river has a strong tidal current and the Bay of Fundy is ice-blocked during part of the year. As a result, Digby and Port Wade have not developed into large ports, but there is considerable fishing and local shipping. The valley is noted for its beauty and historical background, both of which attract tourists. Apple growing is the major economic activity. The valley is protected from strong winds and averages up to 5° F. warmer than the more exposed eastern regions. Annapolis Valley has a cool spring and a warm fall.

Annapolis, the first French settlement in Canada, was founded by Sieur de Monts in 1605 as Port Royal. It was captured and held by the British twice before it was permanently acquired in 1710 and renamed Annapolis Royal. Digby was founded in 1785 by United Empire Loyalists.

D. F. P.

ANN ARBOR, county seat of Washtenaw Co. in southern Michigan, a college community and trade center for a large agricultural area. Ann Arbor was platted in 1824 and incorporated as a city in 1851. It is the seat of the University of Michigan, founded in 1837, and the center of its cultural activity. Annual events are the May Festival (six concerts), the Spring Drama Festival, and the Choral Union Series. Water power supplied by the Huron River serves the city's varied industries. Manufactures include automobile accessories, broaches and broaching machines, machine parts, cameras, plastics, bearings, and precision instruments. Pop. 1950, 48,251.

ANNATES, ANNATS [æ′nets, æ′næts] (Med. Lat. *annatae* from Lat. *annus,* a year), in ecclesiastical law, the first fruits of a benefice. When administration of the Western church was centralized in the thirteenth century, the collation of benefices (not only bishoprics and abbacies but even canonries and parishes) was increasingly reserved to Rome and made the occasion of the payment of a tax into the Apostolic Camera (papal treasury). The term "annates" originally designated only the payments made on the granting, outside of consistory, of minor benefices; but in the 15th century it came to include all monies paid on the occasion of the collation of any benefice by the pope. Frequently levied by 14th century popes in financial straits, much criticized in the Council of Constance (1414-1418), annates in the original sense disappeared with the gradual transformation of the system of benefices. They have come to be levied only on certain bishoprics according to the provisions of current Concordats or of the Bulls establishing new dioceses. *See also* BENEFICE.

N. J. T.

ANNATTO [ɑnɑ′to], also called orleano, arnotta, or annotta, is a yellowish-red dye obtained from the pulpy seedcoverings in the fruit of *Bixa orellana,* a medium-sized tree with large, entire, heart-shaped leaves and showy, pinkish or rose-colored flowers borne in terminal clusters. The tree is native to northern South America but cultivated in tropical Asia and Africa. Annatto is used for dyeing silk and cotton and for coloring cheese and butter.

J. A. Bo.

ANNE (1665-1714), Queen of Great Britain and Ireland and younger daughter of James II, was born at St. James's Palace, London, Feb. 6, 1665. Her mother, Anne Hyde, died in 1671, and Anne spent a rather sickly and not too happy childhood. On July 28, 1683, she was married to Prince George of Denmark. One of the ladies of her bedchamber, Sarah Jennings, wife of Colonel Churchill, who later was to become duke of Marlborough, became her intimate friend. A staunch Protestant, Anne took the side of William of Orange in 1688, and at his death in 1702 she became queen of England. During her reign Marlborough successfully fought the War of the Spanish Succession, and at home in 1707 the union with Scotland became effective. Inclining to the Tories and the High Church, Queen Anne did not get on well with her Whig ministers, and she strongly disapproved of the trial of Henry Sacheverell in 1708. The influence of Mrs. Abigail Masham, who at this time succeeded the Duchess of Marlborough in the Queen's affections, did much to bring about the fall of the Whigs and to place in power Robert Harley, Earl of Oxford. Anne was a fat, dull woman, little interested in literature or the arts, and both weak and obstinate, often replacing political intelligence by personal prejudice; yet at times she was generous and had the good of her country at heart. She died at Kensington Palace, Aug. 1, 1714.

E. R. A.

ANNEALING OF METALS. *See* METALLURGY, PHYSICAL.

ANNECY [a′nsi′], a city in southeastern France, chief city of the department of Haute-Savoie and the seat of a bishopric, located at the foot of the Semnoz Mountains, on Lake Annecy, about 70 mi. northeast of Lyon and 21 mi. south of Geneva, Switzerland. An ancient city dating from Gallo-Roman times, it reached its peak of development under the reign of the dukes of Savoy in the sixteenth century. It is a city of arcades, and one of the famous landmarks is the Palais de L'Ile, a palace constructed between two arms of the Thiou River. Annexed to France in 1860, Annecy has become a popular summer resort. The tourist trade is the city's chief source of income. There are also manufactures of jewelry, ball bearings, and watchbands. In 1728 Jean-Jacques Rousseau, at the age of sixteen, came to live at Annecy with Mme. de Warrens, and portions of his *Confessions* relate to his life at the resort. Pop. 1954 (city), 33,114; commune, 45,000.

S. Van. V.

ANNELID WORMS [æ′nəlɪd], elongated, bilaterally symmetrical animals with a mouth just beneath the front tip and an anus at the hindmost end, and with a body divided regularly into a large number of segments or rings which are visible externally. The segmentation extends inward as membranes or septa which are pierced by the long straight intestine, the dorsal and ventral blood vessels, and the nerve cord along the ventral side. A pair of excretory organs (nephridia) occur in each segment, and reproductive organs are repeated in many of them. The brain lies in front of and above the mouth, and is joined to the ventral nerve cord by short nerves passing on either side of the esophagus. There is a swelling of the nerve cord in each segment where a pair of lateral groups of nerves emerge to operate the locomotory appendages. These may be in the form of minute bristles above, or the bristles may be borne on projections called parapodia (lateral feet) and may be accompanied by paddlelike extensions. The bristles are used mainly in burrowing; the paddle or leaf processes, in swimming. There are three main groups, the most primitive, colorful, and fantastic being the exclusively marine polychaetes. The other two groups are the leeches (Hirudinea), and the relatively drab but exceedingly important oligo-

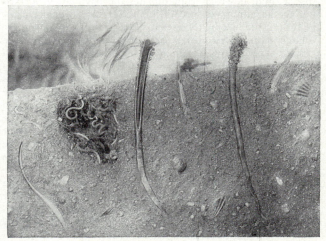

Diopatra cuprea, plumed worm in sectional tube, and Cistenides gouldi, *or trumpet worm, in a sandy, muddy bottom near Woods Hole, Massachusetts*

chaetes, typified by the earthworms, which are of critical value in the creation of soil.

Polychaetes. The marine polychaetes, relatively simple in their internal structure, are externally handsome, even beautiful. The fanworms and featherworms live in vertical, parchment-like, sand-covered tubes of their own making, never leaving except to extend their multicolored plume of palmlike tentacles from the upper open end. A group expanded looks like a patch of flowers. They are so sensitive to light that a passing shadow sends them flashing down within their tubes. Somewhat similar worms precipitate lime from the sea water to form protective tubes and can plug the open end with a corklike structure of their own body. Another, *Chaetopterus*, lives in a parchment-like tube completely buried in the sand except for two open ends. They fan a current of water through this tube for

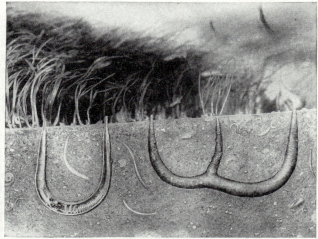

Section of sea bottom of a shallow, muddy cave showing annelids, Chaetopterus pergamentaceus, *in parchment tube and burrows*

feeding and respiration. Many of the less conspicuous polychaetes reproduce asexually as well as by egg production. Some merely break apart, and each part grows a new head or tail region. Others develop a new head part way down the body which forms a new individual when the hind part breaks away. Others may form a chain of such individuals that will eventually separate. Some of the minute fresh-water oligochaetes also reproduce in this manner.

Oligochaetes. The oligochaetes probably have a marine ancestry, but are essentially fresh-water and semiterrestrial animals. Somewhat degenerate externally, they have lost even the simple eyes of the polychaete, and the parapodia are reduced to barely visible bristles. Internally they are far more complex, having a digestive tract divided into pharynx, crop, gizzard, and intestine, capable of handling the soil that they swallow. Since the tiny delicate larvae of marine forms cannot survive in fresh water or in the soil, a complex reproductive apparatus is present. This involves the presence of both male and female sexual glands in the same individual. The mechanism provides for the exchange of sperm and for the laying of relatively yolky eggs. These eggs are capable of developing directly into miniature adults, within protective cocoons.

Hirudinea. Leeches are rather closely related to the oligochaetes. They have the same external degeneration, and similar internal reproductive elaboration, but they have acquired anterior and posterior suckers in connection with their bloodsucking and semiparasitic habits. *See also* BLOODWORM; EARTHWORM; FIREWORM; LEECH; PALOLO WORM; SEA MOUSE.   N. J. B.

ANNE OF AUSTRIA (1601-1666), Queen of France, was born in Madrid, Sept. 22, 1601, the daughter of Philip III of Spain. At the age of fourteen she was married to Louis

ANNE OF AUSTRIA

XIII of France. In 1633, when the king's chief minister, Richelieu, was ill, there was a conspiracy to replace him, and it was suspected that some of the plotters also intended to murder the king and place his brother, Gaston, on the throne. Anne was implicated in the conspiracy, but her guilt was never proven. She was later accused of carrying on a treasonable correspondence with her brother, Philip IV of Spain. She signed a confession that she had secretly corresponded with Philip, but denied sending him treasonable information. Cardinal Mazarin succeeded Richelieu as chief minister when the latter died, and when Anne assumed the regency for her five-year-old son Louis XIV upon the death of Louis XIII in May 1643, she retained Mazarin as her chief minister. The queen and her minister dealt successfully with the last stages of the Thirty Years' War, settled by the Peace of Westphalia in 1648, and with the civil conflict, the Fronde, defeating the proponents of a constitutional government for France in 1653. In 1659 the Peace of the Pyrenees was concluded with Spain, settling the Pyrenees as the boundary of the two countries and the ownership of the Flanders and Netherlands territories. On the death of Mazarin in 1661, Louis XIV, then past twenty-one years of age, ended the regency and assumed power in his own right. Anne, as Queen Mother, withdrew from the forefront of public affairs. She died in Paris, Jan. 20, 1666.   W. Fr.

ANNE OF CLEVES. *See* Henry VIII.
ANNE OF RUSSIA. *See* Russia, History of.
ANNEXATION MANIFESTO OF 1849. *See* Canadian-American Relations.

ANNISTON, the county seat of Calhoun Co., located in the lower Appalachian Mountains of northeastern Alabama, 57 mi. east of Birmingham. The city lies in a cotton-growing area in which cattle raising and dairying have made great gains. Iron ore, limestone, and timber are natural resources of the area. Anniston was founded by Samuel Noble and Alfred Tyler in 1872 and incorporated in 1879. The city government is administered by a commission. Diversified manufactures include foundry and machine-shop products, iron pipe, chemicals, soap, cotton goods, yarn, wearing apparel, electronic tubes, and paper wallboard covering. Fort McClellan stands approximately 5 mi. north of the city limits. Pop. 1950, 31,066.

ANNOBÓN [ɑ'nobo'n], an island possession of Spain in the Gulf of Guinea, some 200 mi. off the coast of Gabon, French Equatorial Africa. It was discovered by a Portuguese navigator on New Year's Day of 1473, hence its original name, Anno Bon. Annobón is a partly submerged volcanic mass, rising in places to an elevation of 3,000 ft. above sea level. Its area of 7 sq. mi. is covered with luxuriant vegetation, including several species of commercially valuable trees. Located less than two degrees south of the Equator, the island has a hot, moist climate. Annobón was uninhabited when discovered but was later settled by Negroes from the mainland, whose descendants now inhabit the island. Some of them work seasonally on nearby Fernando Po. Annobón was ceded by Portugal to Spain in 1778, but only in 1885, when Germany was about to seize the island, did the Spanish government occupy it effectively. It is administered from Bata, in Río Muni, as part of a subdivision of Spanish Guinea. Pop. 1950, 1,802.   R. G. W.

ANNONA [æno'nə], a levy on the produce of the soil established by Diocletian (Roman emperor A.D. 285-305). The tax was paid annually in kind, and its assessment was based on the findings of a land census taken every fifteen years. Grain lands, vineyards, orchards, and other types of agricultural land were subject to taxation in this manner.   T. B. J.

ANNUITY [ənyu'ɪti], in the ordinary meaning of the legal term, the right to the payment of a specific sum of money at stated intervals, usually annually or at shorter periods. In modern practice, annuities are generally created by will as a form of legacy, or purchased from an insurance company as an investment. The person entitled to receive the annuity is known as an "annuitant."

When a testator bequeaths the income from a fund to a legatee, his gift embraces only net profits, or return after the deduction of all proper expenses and charges, and, therefore, is indeterminate in amount. The gift of an annuity from a fund, however, contemplates the payment of a fixed sum to the annuitant, permitting resort to the principal of the fund if the income therefrom should prove insufficient.

Theory and Principle. Annuity contracts have become a major type of investment in recent years. Although such contracts are issued almost exclusively by insurance companies, in theory the annuity policy is the very antithesis of the life insurance policy. From the viewpoint of the individual who takes out a life insurance policy, such an undertaking shifts the risk of his premature death to the insurance company, for the benefit of his dependents or other beneficiaries. Thus the individual, by carrying life insurance, creates an estate in the future by his payments of stated insurance premiums, which are themselves in the nature of annuity payments to the insurance company. From the viewpoint of the individual annuitant, on the other hand, the annuity contract generally represents the investment of a present estate by transferring it to the company in return for the undertaking of the latter to pay a fixed sum during the life of the annuitant, or some other period such as the life of the annuitant and, afterward, during the life of a named survivor. The annuitant assumes the risk of premature death, since the lump-sum consideration paid to the company is not recoverable. As noted by the United States Supreme Court in *Helvering* v. *Le Gierse* (312 U. S. 531), "from the company's viewpoint, insurance looks to longevity, annuity to transiency."

Although diametrically opposed in theory, life insurance and annuity contracts closely supplement each other as means of personal protection. Life insurance policies often contain annuity features, providing for the payment of an annuity to the insured upon his reaching a given age, or containing survivorship annuity clauses. As a general rule, annuity payments are not apportionable. Thus, even though the annuitant survives until, say, a day or two before the due date of an annual payment, the estate of the annuitant cannot recover for the proportional part of the period prior to the annuitant's death. In the case of a survivorship annuity, however, the survivor who lives to the next date when payment is due may recover the entire current annuity payment.   H. Si.

ANNUNCIATION, FEAST OF THE, a church festival commemorating the announcement of the incarnation of Jesus Christ, is regarded in the Eastern Churches as a feast of Christ and celebrated on various dates; it is considered a feast of the Virgin Mary in the West, where since early times it had been celebrated on March 25, sometimes called Lady Day. It was long one of the days commonly taken as the start of a new year, particularly in England before the Norman Conquest and from 1155 to 1752, when Great Britain accepted the Gregorian calendar.   W. C.

ANNUNCIATION OF THE VIRGIN MARY. In the Scriptures, the Gospel of St. Luke (i:26-38) recounts that God, through the Angel Gabriel, announced to Mary, a virgin betrothed to Joseph, that she would conceive of the Holy Ghost a child to be called Jesus and the Son of God. First troubled, then objecting that she knew not man, Mary, reassured by the angel, acquiesced.

In popular devotion, the Annunciation suggested the Ave Maria, was epitomized in the Angelus, and figures in the

Rosary. In art the Annunciation was represented, perhaps from the second, certainly from the fourth century, in frescoes, mosaics, ivories, medallions, wood-carvings, and manuscript illuminations; it was sculptured monumentally on the portals of Gothic cathedrals; and it inspired varied treat-

ANNUNCIATION OF THE VIRGIN
PAINTING BY ROGER VAN DER WEYDEN (c.1400-1464)

ments by Fra Angelico, Van Eyck, Grünewald, Rubens, Poussin, and many other painters. *See also* ANNUNCIATION, FEAST OF THE; AVE; JESUS CHRIST; JOSEPH; MARY, THE VIRGIN. N. J. T.

ANNUNZIO, GABRIELE D'. *See* D'ANNUNZIO, GABRIELE.

ANNUS MIRABILIS: THE YEAR OF WONDERS, 1666 [æ'nəs mɪre'bɪlɪs], a poem by John Dryden in celebration of the English naval victories over the Dutch in 1665 and 1666 and of the courage of London during the Great Fire of 1666. Indirectly replying to malcontents who interpreted the fire as a sign of divine disapproval of the monarchy, Dryden here expressed his loyalty to the throne and his confidence in the destiny of England as a great commercial power. S. H. M.

ANOA [ano'ə] (*Anoa*), a little buffalo that lives in the Celebes. The mountain anoa, *A. fergusoni,* which lives on

the peaks, is the smallest of all cattle—only 25 to 30 in. tall. The common anoa, *A. depressicornis,* stands about 39 in. high and is dark brown to blackish. Its very sharp, nearly straight horns are longer than those of the mountain anoa, and may measure up to 15⅜ in. in length. Its disposition is also much more fierce. Shy, but vicious, it is dangerous if attacked. An inhabitant of dense forests, its range is decreasing due to the extension of agriculture. A close relative, the timarau (*A. mindorensis*), lives in the Philippines. *See also* BUFFALO. V. H. C.

ANOKA [əno'kə], a city in southeastern Minnesota, the county seat of Anoka Co., situated on the Mississippi and the Rum rivers, 18 mi. northwest of Minneapolis. The community, incorporated in 1878, is a trade center for the surrounding farm population, which specializes largely in dairying and truck farming. Transportation facilities are provided by the Northern Pacific and the Great Northern railways. Anoka is a popular summer resort. The manufacture of ammunition is the city's major industry. Other industries produce farm implements of all kinds, wood products, fibre furniture, sashes and doors and dairy products. Pop. 1950, 7,396.

ANOMIA. *See* APHASIA.
ANORTHOSITE. *See* GABBRO; FELDSPAR.
ANOXIA. *See* AIRPLANE PRESSURIZATION; AVIATION MEDICINE.

ANQUETIL DU PERRON, ABRAHAM HYACINTHE [ãkti'l dü pe'rɔ̃'], French Orientalist, was born in Paris Dec. 7, 1731. Having acquired in his studies a good knowledge of Oriental languages, including Arabic, Hebrew, and Persian, Anquetil happened to see an Indian Avestan manuscript that he could not decipher. Thereupon he decided to visit India and, enlisting in a French expeditionary force, he reached Pondichéry Aug. 10, 1755. From there he went in 1758 to Surat, where he stayed until Mar. 15, 1761. During these years he succeeded in learning from Parsi priests their traditional lore concerning their sacred book, the Avesta, and even received from them about one hundred manuscripts in Avestan, Pahlavi, and Sanskrit. Anquetil returned to France in 1762, and in 1771 he published in Paris the first translation of the Avesta in three volumes, preceded by the description of his adventurous journey (*Zend-Avesta, ouvrage de Zoroastre, contenant les idées théologiques, physiques et morales de ce législateur*). The surprise was great, and several scholars, among them the highly regarded William Jones, denounced Anquetil as a forger. But although the interpretation of Anquetil is frequently wrong, and his knowledge of Pahlavi and Avestan quite imperfect, he has the great merit of having revealed to the West the sacred book of the Parsis, a text of immeasurable value for history, linguistics, and religious studies. Other important works of Anquetil are: *Législation orientale* (Amsterdam, 1778); *Recherches historiques et géographiques sur l'Inde* (1786); *L'Inde en rapport avec l'Europe* (1790); *Oupnekhat, sive arcanum tegendum* (2 vols., 1802-1803) ("The Secret that must not be revealed"). Anquetil was courageous, daring, honest, and full of enthusiasm for science, although at times he was excessively melancholic and hypersensitive, living in extreme poverty and deliberately shunning society. He died in Paris on Jan. 17, 1805, and posterity has, on the whole, refuted the charges of his contemporary detractors. G. B.

ANSCHLUSS. *See* AUSTRIA (*History*).

ANSELM, ST. [aˈnsɛlm] (c.1033-1109), archbishop of Canterbury, was born at Aosta in Piedmont of noble Lombard parents. Leaving home because of his father's harshness, he finally settled at the renowned Abbey of Bec in Normandy, where in 1060 he became a monk and in 1063 succeeded his master Lanfranc as prior. Chosen abbot of Bec in 1078, he visited his abbey's possessions in England, where he won many friends. Upon the death of Lanfranc as archbishop of Canterbury, the king, William Rufus, resisted the general desire for Anselm, kept the see vacant four years, until 1093; and even then he consented to the consecration of Anselm only because he supposed himself to be on his deathbed. Then William Rufus recovered to repent his decision, for Anselm demanded that he be invested with the insignia of his office by the Pope and not by the King. Though the quarrel was smoothed over, Anselm went to Rome in 1097, where he remained until William's successor, Henry I, recalled him in 1100. The dispute over lay investiture was revived, however, and was not settled until 1107, when it was agreed that the bishops should do homage to the king for their lands but must be invested with the symbols of their spiritual functions by the Church. Anselm died at Canterbury, Apr. 21, 1109, and was canonized in 1494.

In the realm of thought, Anselm's achievement was threefold. In the field of Christian dogma he elaborated a revolutionary interpretation of the doctrine of the Atonement, according to which the sacrifice of Christ was a ransom offered not to the Devil—as had previously been believed—but to God. The new theory quickly won general acceptance. In considering the problem of the relation between reason and faith, Anselm, inspired by the teaching of St. Augustine, maintained that faith is the necessary presupposition of rational speculation. His celebrated phrases, "Faith seeking knowledge," *fides quaerens intellectum,* and "I believe in order that I may know," *credo ut intelligam,* became watchwords of the Augustinian school, and the majority of his successors before the advent of St. Albertus Magnus and St. Thomas Aquinas deferred to his opinion. His supreme achievement, however, was the formulation of the ontological argument, which professes to show that the very conception of God involves his existence, an argument which has been repeatedly restated, championed, and attacked by eminent philosophers since his time. Anselm's important writings include the *Monologion,* the *Proslogion, De veritate,* and *Cur Deus homo*—the last containing his famous exposition of the theory of Redemption.   R. L. P. and W. C.

ANSELM (ANSELMUS) OF LAON (d. 1117), French theologian of the eleventh century, probably born in Laon. He studied at the Benedictine abbey of Bec in Normandy and may also have studied under St. Anselm of Canterbury, with whom he is often confused. In 1076 he taught theology in Paris and was commended by Pope Gregory VII for reviving interest in the Scriptures in that city. Toward the close of the century he returned to Laon to become head of the cathedral school. His pupils included William of Champeaux and Peter Abelard, and the school became famous, attracting students from all parts of the country. His teachings were based strictly on a dogmatic interpretation of the Scriptures, and he was known as "the doctor of doctors." Anselm refused several offers of bishoprics and honorary titles. His most notable work was an interlinear glossary of the Scriptures, which for years remained the most valuable contribution of its type. He died in Laon on July 15, 1117. His previously unpublished *Sententiae* were edited by G. Lefèvre in 1894.   C. W. D.

ANSHAN [ɑˈnshæn], a city in the Chinese province of Liaoning, in southern Manchuria. The city is located in the south central part of the province a short distance south of Mukden, at 39° 45′ N. lat. and 119° E. long. Anshan is on the fertile Manchurian Plain about 140 ft. above sea level and has a continental type of climate. The winters are long, cold, dry, and windy, while the summers are short and warm. The average annual temperature is 44° F., and January, the coldest month, averages 9° F., while July, the warmest month, averages 75° F. An average of 26 inches of precipitation falls a year, but the rainfall is variable. July is the wettest month, with about 6 inches of rain. The fertile Manchurian Plain supports a variety of crops, such as soybeans, wheat, millet, grain sorghum, corn, cotton, and sugar beets; horses, cattle, sheep, donkeys, and mules are grazed. In spite of the agricultural wealth of the surrounding area, Anshan is not a noted farm center. Its fame is derived from its 300- to 500-ft. thick deposits of red hematite in the immediate environs. With the huge coal deposits of near-by Fushun, the proximity of the large city of Mukden, and the excellent railroad connections, it was natural for Anshan to be developed into one of the largest iron and steel centers in the world. The steel mills were developed by the South Manchurian Railroad Corporation interests in 1918. After the Japanese seized Manchuria and set up the state of Manchukuo in 1932, the steel mills were enlarged and became the Showa Steel Company. The pig iron output in 1933 was about 430,000 tons, and in 1941 Showa had a capacity of 1,750,000 tons of pig iron and about 1,000,000 tons of steel. Steel production has varied considerably. The Japanese utilized this plant during World War II, and it was one of their major sources of steel. During the war Allied war prisoners, including some captured during the Philippine campaign, were kept in a prison camp at Anshan. Late in the war some damage was done to the plant by Allied bombing. After the defeat of Japan, Anshan, as well as Manchuria, was returned to China. In 1948 the city was captured by the Chinese Communist armies. The city's population has varied considerably. Pop. 1940, 213,865.   J. E. F.

ANSON, GEORGE ANSON, BARON (1697-1762), English admiral, was born at Shugborough, parish of Colwich, in Staffordshire, on Apr. 23, 1697. In 1712 he entered the navy as a volunteer; by 1724 he had reached the rank of captain, and in 1740 he was made commodore and put in command of a small fleet which had been organized to operate against the Spaniards in the Pacific. Two of the ships failed to round Cape Horn, and one was wrecked. With the remaining three, Anson did great damage to Spanish commerce off the Pacific coast of America. Because his crews were much reduced by death and sickness, he destroyed two more ships, and in his flagship, the *Centurion,* sailed back to England. On the journey around the Cape of Good Hope he captured a Spanish galleon with a cargo of great value. Reaching England in 1744, he was made a rear admiral and a lord of the admiralty. In 1747 he defeated a French fleet off Cape Finisterre and was made a baron. Except for a few months in 1756-1757, he was a member of the admiralty board until his death, becoming first lord in 1751 and admiral in 1761. Anson had great administrative ability; he improved naval equipment and dockyards, reformed naval discipline, and created the modern corps of marines. The success of the British navy in the Seven Years' War was largely the result of Anson's fight against corruption and inefficiency. He died at Moor Park, Hertfordshire, June 6, 1762.   E. R. A.

ANSONIA, a city of New Haven Co., in southwestern Connecticut, on the Naugatuck River, 68 mi. northeast of New York City. It was founded in 1840 and named for Anson Green Phelps. At one time it belonged to the township of Derby. It received its charter as a borough in 1864, as a town in 1889, and as a city in 1893. The New York, New Haven and Hartford Railroad supplies transportation. Ansonia is an important industrial center noted for its copper and brass fabrication. Other manufactures are electrical appliances, machinery, metal specialties, wire, and screw-machine products. Pop. 1950, 18,706.

ANSWER. *See* LEGAL PROCEDURE.

ANT, a member of the Hymenoptera, which includes bees and wasps. The ant is characterized by a slender waist at the base of the abdomen, swollen to form one or two "beads" or conspicuous enlargements. Most ants are wingless, but the sexual forms are fully winged, and most of them mate in the air. After mating, and locating a place suitable for a new home, the queen either bites or rubs off her wings and establishes a nest, caring for her offspring until they are mature. She then resigns herself to egg laying, producing only workers until the approach of the mating season. Sexual forms are then produced, those of all near-by nests emerging within a day or two of each other. In the red wood ant, *Formica rufa,* and others, the queen is unable to form a colony without the aid of workers, and returns to the old nest, where several queens may be present at one time. Others, such as the narrow-headed ant, *F. exsecta,* may move to a near-by location with a group of workers.

The number of types of a single species of ant occurring in one nest is variable, depending upon the species. In some kinds there are only three forms—queen, male, and worker, the workers being undeveloped females. In the most complicated nests there may be as many as 29 different forms. There may be several types of queens, including forms that never develop wings, and there may be more than one type of male. The greatest diversity occurs among the workers. These vary in size and form: the ordinary workers are the kind generally seen; in the soldiers, which fight and crush seeds to be used as food by their sisters, the mandibles are greatly developed, and the heads large. There may be several types of soldiers, and there is a more or less pronounced gradation in the size of head and mandibles between the small workers and the large soldiers.

Ant nests occur almost anywhere, and many contain from a few dozen to a half-million inhabitants. Most nests contain hundreds of individuals, but those of Pharaoh's ant, *Monomorium pharaonis,* a nomadic ant which keeps moving in order to remain always in close proximity to its food supply, are often composed of fewer than a hundred individuals, and as many as ten queens may be present in a colony of this size. This ant has been widely distributed by commerce, and is a serious household pest in the United States.

The ponerine ants, Ponerinae, are carnivorous, feeding upon other insects. Their nests are generally small, often containing only about 20 individuals. They are often observed singly. They are able to sting, while other ants bite. The jumping ants of Australia belong to this group. They can jump several inches. Some of them are fully an inch long.

The driver, or army, ants belong to the Dorilinae. They march in armies and have no permanent nests, the young being carried with them on their travels. They attack all animal life in their path, and many peoples welcome them because they destroy the vermin in their dwellings.

The Myrmicinae include the harvester ants, which gather and store seeds for food, and the parasol or fungus ants, which cut leaves and carry them to their nests to make a foundation upon which they grow their fungus food. They build sunken roadways several inches wide and often a half a mile long between their nests and their leaf supply.

The Formicinae include mound-building ants, so common in the American countryside, and the strange green ants of the Old World that build nests in trees, using their larvae to sew the leaves together. The honey ants also belong in this group; certain members of the nest are used as honey chests, being fed nectar which is stored in their greatly distended abdomens to serve as food for members of the colony during the cold season.

The Argentine ant, a pest in the southern states, belongs to the Dolichoderinae, in which the prothorax is very narrow. It is of tropical origin and infests houses, gardens, and fields, doing enormous damage.   C. H. Cu.

ANTAEUS [anti'əs], in Greek mythology, a mighty giant of Libya, son of Poseidon and Gaea (Earth). Heracles, wrestling with him, perceived that his strength was renewed from contact with his mother Earth and only by lifting him in the air was he finally able to crush him to death. G. E. D.

ANTAKYA or **ANTIOCH** [ɑ'ntɑki'yɑ, a'ntiɒk], a city in the extreme southern extension of central Turkey, located on the Orontes River about 18 mi. northeast of the river mouth at 36° 5′ N. lat. and 36° 12′ E. long. It lies about 500 mi. southeast of Ankara, on a fertile plain practically surrounded by the approximately mile-high peaks of the Amanus Range.

Northeast of Antakya is the swamp-fringed lake of the same name. The city has a typical Mediterranean climate consisting of short, cool, wet winters and long, hot, dry summers. The temperature averages about 80° F. during the summer months and about 45° F., with frost, in winter. The precipitation is between 20 and 30 in. a year, almost all of which occurs in November, December, January, and February. Agriculture, in spite of the climatic handicap, is an important industry of the environs, and wheat, sesame, durra, chick peas, cotton, some melons and vegetables, olives, and small fruit are grown. Licorice root, both wild and cultivated, is one of the specialties of the district. Sheep, goats, donkeys, and camels are raised. Manufacturing consists chiefly of tanning, leather work, including the making of shoes, soap manufacture, food processing, and handicraft work.

Antakya, the ancient Antiochus, was a great and famous city which lost its world importance because of the shift of trade following the modern development to the Atlantic and Pacific regions, the silting of the harbor, the increase in size of ships, the decrease in importance of the hinterland, and the lack of modern communication facilities. The city was founded by Antigonus about 307 B.C., but Seleucus Nicator destroyed the town in 301 B.C., and, utilizing the ruins, built a new city several miles to the south of the old site. This second city is believed to have been copied after Alexandria. The first great flourishing of the town occurred under Antiochus I, from 280 to 261 B.C. It became a great Eastern capital of the Roman Empire. Most of the great Romans visited the city, and it became a great artistic, administrative, and commercial center. After Jerusalem, which had been retaken by the Jews in 66 B.C., was recaptured and destroyed by the Romans in 70 B.C., Antakya, then Antioch, became the great city of Christendom. Peter and Paul worked in the city, the term Christian first being applied to Paul's converts there about 20 years after the crucifixion of Jesus of Nazareth, and 40 mi. from the city St. Simeon Stylites performed his feat of living on top of a pillar. Earthquakes and wars helped to destroy the city, and the Arabs took it in 638. But after a long siege, Crusaders captured it in 1098, and the city became the capital of a Latin principality. The Turks recaptured it in 1517. The city was taken by the Egyptians in 1840, was regained later by the Turks, and was occupied by the English field marshal, Edmund H. H. Allenby, in 1918. In 1920 it became part of the French mandate, but during World War II was ceded to Turkey. Pop. 1950, 30,385.

J. E. F.

ANTANANARIV. *See* TANANARIVE.
ANTARCTICA. *See* POLAR REGIONS.

ANTARES [əntɛˈəriz], also designated α Scorpii, the bright, reddish star in the constellation Scorpius, which, from the latitude of the United States, is low in the south in the late twilight of early July. The name means "similar to Ares" (Mars), since the star and Ares rival each other in redness. Its color indicates a relatively low temperature of around 3,000° C. With a diameter of approximately 350,000,000 mi., Antares is rated as a supergiant star. It is one of the four largest stars in the sky measured by Michelson's interferometer. If Antares were placed at the center of the solar system, the outer limits of the star would extend almost to the orbit of Mars. Its density is very low, probably less than one-millionth that of the sun, but its luminosity is considerably over 1,000 times that of the sun. Its distance is about 250 light-years. A red nebula, believed to be lighted by the star, has been discovered extending 1° north of Antares. *See also* SCORPIUS.

J. H. P.

ANT BEAR, the great anteater, *Myrmecophaga jubata,* largest of the true anteaters, distributed throughout Central and South America. The ant bear derives its name from its supposed habit of crushing its enemies to death, like the bear, with its powerful forelegs. Measuring about 4 ft. long, exclusive of the long, bushy tail, this completely edentulous mammal has a dark gray coat of coarse, long hair, showing a black band from the chest to the middle of the back. Its slender and viscous tongue may be protruded as far as 18 in. to catch white ants, upon which it feeds. Entirely terrestrial, the ant bear is a powerful runner, but generally burrows into the earth to escape pursuit. The female bears one at birth, the young animal being carried on her back during its slow growth.

G. M. C.

ANTEATER, any of several species of edentate mammals of the family Myrmecophagidae of South and Central America. These animals have, typically, a tubular mouth without teeth, a worm-like, long tongue, and powerful burrowing claws on the hind foot and on the third digit of the forefoot, used in excavating white ant hills in its marshy habitat. Nocturnal in habit, unsocial and stupid, this family of mammals spends much time in sleep, and like other insect-eating animals, is able to bear famine for long periods. Members of the family include the great anteater, *Myrmecophaga jubata,* or ant bear; and the tamandua, or *Tamandua tetradactyla,* a smaller, arboreal form having a scaly, slightly prehensile tail.

ANTELOPE [aˈntəlop]. Any of almost 100 species of artiodactyl mammals of the family Bovidae. Eight of the 11

subfamilies of the Bovidae consist of antelopes, while one, the Caprinae, contains not only the sheep and goats but also the saiga, the chamois, and *Panthalops,* the latter often being referred to as antelopes. It is impossible to devise a definition of the term antelope which is adequate for the members of all of the subfamilies. In general, however, the antelope

KEYSTONE VIEW CO.

PRONGHORN ANTELOPE

subfamilies may be described as bridging the structural gap between sheep and goats on one hand and cattle on the other. Antelopes vary in size from the eland (*Taurotragus oryx*) which stands five or six feet at the shoulder, to the pygmy antelope (*Antilope pygmaeus*) which is less than one foot in height. Although antelopes resemble deer in many respects, they differ markedly in the nature of their horns, which are hollow at the base and set upon a solid bony core like those of cattle. These horns are permanent and are not renewed annually as are those of deer. Regardless of size, almost all of the living species of antelope are peaceable, timid animals distinguished for their agility and fleetness.

KEYSTONE VIEW CO

GROUP OF SOUTH AMERICAN ANTEATERS

According to the researches of G. E. Pilgrim (1941), antelopes (Gazellinae) evidently arose in Central Asia whence they were dispersed into India, Asia Minor, and Africa, with a few species entering Europe and western China. Antelopes, in the restricted sense, are missing from the New World where their place is taken by their close relatives, the pronghorn antelope (*Antilocapra*) and the Rocky Mountain goat (*Oreamnos*). Just as antelopes bridge the anatomical gap between sheep and goats, and cattle, so, too, does the range of their various habitats. Some, like the goats, are found only in the most inaccessible mountain regions; some inhabit the plains; while others, like cattle, dwell in jungles and deep forests. Although many classifications of the Bovidae had been proposed, none had been completely satisfactory for they had necessarily been based upon recent species alone. Ever-increasing knowledge of the fossil Bovidae, however, has enabled what appears to be a more natural classification of the family to be established. Pilgrim, in his exhaustive monograph *The Fossil Bovidae of India* (1939), summarizes his researches in the following classification:

Section	Subfamily	Representative forms
Antilocaproidea	Antilocaprinae	Pronghorn antelope (*Antilocapra*)
Aegodontia	Caprinae	goat (*Capra*)
		sheep (*Ovis*)
		saiga (*Saiga*)*
		(*Panthalops*)*
		chamois (*Rupicapra*)*
	Ovibovinae	musk-ox (*Ovibos*)
	Neotraginae*	klipspringer (*Oreotragus*)*
		royal antelope (*Neotragus*)*
		dik-dik (*Madoqua*)*
	Gazellinae*	gazelle (*Gazella*)*
		black buck (*Antilope*)*
	Alcelaphinae*	hartebeeste (*Alcephalus*)*
		gnu (*Connochaetes*)*
	Hippotraginae*	sable (*Hippotragus*)*
		addax (*Addax*)*
		beisa (*Oryx*)*
	Reduncinae*	waterbuck (*Kobus, Onotragus*)*
		reedbuck (*Cervicapra*)*
	Cephalophinae*	duiker (*Cephalophus*)*
Tragelaphoidea	Tragelaphinae*	bushbuck (*Tragelaphus*)*
		kudu (*Strepsiceros*)*
		eland (*Taurotragus*)*
	Boselaphinae*	nilgai (*Boselaphus*)*
		four-horned antelope (*Tetracerus*)*
	Bovinae	cattle (*Bos,* etc.)

* Groups generally included among the antelopes. V. H. C.

ANTENNAS. *See* INSECTS; RADIO; TELEVISION.

ANTENOR [anti'nɔr], Greek sculptor of the late sixth century B.C. who worked at Athens. He executed the original bronze statues of Harmodius and Aristogiton, slayers of the tyrant Hipparchus, in 510 B.C. When Xerxes sacked Athens in 480 B.C., he carried these statues off to Persia. They were restored to Athens by Alexander the Great. Copies now extant are of the statues by Critias and Nesiotes, which replaced those of Antenor. It is improbable that his composition was as vigorous. Antenor's name occurs on the base for a draped female figure found on the Acropolis, and his style can be surmised from characteristics common to other figures found there. He was one of the most celebrated sculptors of the early Attic school. *See also* TYRANNICIDES.
R. F.

ANTENOR [anti'nɔr], a legendary Trojan known as one of the wisest elders in Troy. When Menelaus and Ulysses came to Troy as ambassadors, he welcomed them. Because he was the head of the Trojan peace-party and advised that Helen be sent back to Menelaus, the Greeks spared his life when they captured the city. A later legend makes him a traitor to the city. According to various accounts, after the war he rebuilt Troy, founded Patavium on the western coast of the Adriatic, or settled at Cyrene. In the legend of Brutus, mythical founder of England, the descendants of Antenor are encountered in Italy.
R. F.

ANTHEIL, GEORGE [a'ntail] (1900-   ), American composer, was born July 8, 1900, in Trenton, N. J. After studying with Ernest Bloch and others, Antheil resided in Europe for several years and there gained a reputation for experimental compositions in an ultra-modern vein, notably his *Ballet mécanique* (1925). Antheil returned to the United States in 1933 and established himself in Hollywood, Calif., in 1936. In the latter place, although he has not been exclusively connected with motion pictures, he has written scores for *The Plainsman* (1936) and *The Spectre of the Rose* (1946). Notable among his other works are four symphonies; two operas, *Transatlantic* (1929) and *Helen Retires* (1932); ballets; piano and violin concertos; chamber music; many magazine articles; and an autobiography. E. L. F.

ANTHEM, a choral composition for two or more voices set to an English text of a sacred nature. It is usually extra-liturgical, having in English churches approximately the same function as the motet has in the Roman Catholic Church. The modern anthem originated in the early Anglican church and spread from this source; today it is in use in most English-speaking Protestant churches. A verse anthem is one containing occasional passages for solo voices, while a full anthem is choral throughout. The term is often used loosely to indicate any song of praise, as in "the national anthem." R. M. K.

ANTHOCYANIN. *See* GLYCOSIDES.

ANTHONY, ST. (c. 250-c. 356), the founder of Christian monasticism, was born in the Faiyum (upper Egypt). At twenty he began imitating the Egyptian hermit ascetics, engaging, tradition says, in strange conflicts with the demons. At thirty-five he withdrew to complete solitude at Pispir for twenty years. After instructing and organizing numerous disciples, he retired to the desert near Thebes for the last forty-five years of his life. A biography of St. Anthony by St. Athanasius is authentic. The position accorded him after the fourth century was due to his commanding personality and high character, "without cowardice, without gloom, without formality, without self-complacency" (Cardinal Newman), at once enthusiastic and moderate. His feast is celebrated Jan. 17. N. J. T.

ANTHONY OF PADUA, ST. (1195-1231), Franciscan wonder-worker, was born at Lisbon, joined in 1210 the

Canons Regular of St. Augustine, and in 1220, desirous of martyrdom, entered the Franciscan Order so that he might preach to the Saracens. Appointed in 1224 to teach theology, he attained fame in Italy rather as a preacher, combating fearlessly and discreetly not only heresy but the obstinate vices of luxury, avarice, and tyranny. Of him are recounted many miracles, some legendary, many certainly historical. He died at Vercelli, June 13, 1231, his relics being transferred to Padua in 1263. He is invoked for aid in finding lost objects; his feast is celebrated June 13.   N. J. T.

ANTHONY, SUSAN BROWNELL (1820-1906), feminist and woman's rights advocate, was born in Adams, Mass., Feb. 15, 1820, of Quaker stock. After a cursory education in the local schools she became a neighborhood teacher, later moving with her family to Rochester, N. Y. She began teaching in Canajoharie (N. Y.) Academy in 1846, met Lucretia and Abigail Mott and Elizabeth Cody Stanton, and in 1848 joined with them to hold the first Women's Rights convention in Seneca Falls, N. Y. In 1850 Miss Anthony gave up teaching to devote all her time to the cause of women's rights. In addition, she joined the Temperance and antislavery movements. As an ardent abolitionist she was mobbed in Buffalo, N. Y. but continued her efforts throughout the Civil War. She urged enactment of the Fourteenth Amendment to the Constitution and at the presidential convention of the Democratic party in 1868 proposed a resolution endorsing woman suffrage. She helped to organize the National Woman's Suffrage Association in 1869 and was executive secretary, vice-president, and, from 1892-1900, president. She lectured constantly in support of the movement. In the presidential election of 1872 Miss Anthony and fourteen other women voted, claiming the right to do so under the Fourteenth Amendment. The votes were thrown out, Miss Anthony was arrested, and the case was heard without a jury, in the United States Circuit Court for the northern district of New York. Miss Anthony was found guilty, and a fine of $100 and costs was imposed, which she refused to pay. In the meantime, in 1868, she had started a newspaper, *The Revolution,* but it failed as a commercial venture. She continued her lecturing, traveling constantly throughout the United States, and in 1883 went to Europe. In 1888 she organized the International Council of Women, spoke at the Chicago World's Fair in 1893, toured California with Anna Shaw, and worked steadily with Ida Husted Harper and others in the cause of woman's suffrage. In 1899 she again went to Europe, but in 1901 resigned the presidency of the National Woman's Suffrage Association and returned to her home in Rochester, N. Y. She engaged in a campaign to raise funds for the education of girls at the University of Rochester, wrote the fourth volume of the *History of Woman Suffrage,* and went to Berlin in 1904 in the interest of woman's suffrage. She died in Rochester, N. Y., on Mar. 13, 1906.

ANTHOXANTHIN. *See* GLYCOSIDES.

ANTHOZOA. *See* ANIMAL SYSTEMATICS; COELENTERATA.

ANTHRACENE. *See* ORGANIC CHEMISTRY.

ANTHRACITE. *See* COAL; COAL MINING; FUELS.

ANTHRAX [an'thræks], also called splenic fever or charbon, a highly fatal, rapidly acting, infectious disease of men and animals. In animals, the death rate ranges from 50 to 100 per cent. Anthrax is spread by infected animal by-products and feedstuffs, by scavenger birds (especially buzzards), by migrating wild animals, by streams draining anthrax-infected soil, and also by contact with sick animals. Animals usually become infected by contaminated drinking water or forage or through the bites of blood-sucking insects. Water, forage, and soil are contaminated by discharges from diseased animals or from dead animals that are left exposed. Anthrax in carnivorous animals is usually the result of feeding on anthrax-infected carcasses.

Cause. Anthrax is caused by a bacterium, *Bacillus anthracis,* which produces spores that are particularly resistant. They may remain alive in the soil for many years. Once soil is contaminated, therefore, it can, for all practical purposes, be regarded as a permanent source of anthrax infection.

Occurrence. Anthrax is one of the oldest and most destructive diseases recorded in history. It exists on all continents, in tropical as well as polar regions. It is particularly prevalent in man and animals in the Mediterranean area. The antiquity of the disease in Asia Minor and North Africa is demonstrated by the existence of naturally immune species of sheep. So-called "anthrax districts" of large dimensions exist in many parts of the world. The disease is most prevalent when flies and other insects are numerous. All warm-blooded animals are susceptible to anthrax. In the United States, anthrax occurs principally in cattle; however, infections in horses, mules, sheep, goats, and swine are not uncommon. Dogs, cats, and mink occasionally are infected.

Symptoms. Symptoms vary according to the kind of animal and the acuteness of the disease. Anthrax in cattle may be confused with blackleg, malignant edema, hemorrhagic septicemia, poison, and other causes of sudden death. In cattle, sheep, and goats, the onset may be so sudden and death may occur so quickly that few clinical symptoms are observed; or animals may be found dead without showing previous signs of disease. In these very acute cases, there is sudden staggering, collapse, bloody discharges, convulsions, and death, usually after 1 or 2 days. In subacute cases, symptoms include restlessness, followed by depression, lack of appetite, high fever, rapid breathing, and unsteady gait. Bloody discharges from the body openings are common. Soft swellings, that pit on pressure, may appear on the neck, chest, flanks, or back. Animals may die after 3 to 5 days or completely recover. Anthrax should be suspected in any sudden livestock deaths occurring on premises where a history of anthrax exists. In horses and mules, the first symptom may be hot, painful swellings about the neck or abdomen which rapidly increase in size. High temperature, chills, colic, loss of appetite, depression, and blood-stained discharges are observed. Swine are quite resistant to anthrax. In an infected herd, some die without showing previous signs of disease, but the larger percentage of visibly sick animals usually recover unless death from suffocation results from the rapidly progressive swellings that usually develop about the throat of a stricken animal.

Control. Anthrax can be prevented by preseasonal immunization of all animals in areas where anthrax is known to exist, as well as in adjacent areas. Animals dead of anthrax and the contaminated material about them should be burned completely or buried deeply in quicklime. Caution should be observed by the person disposing of carcasses or handling infected animals, since anthrax is transmissible to man, causing malignant carbuncles. In the treatment of the disease, antianthrax serum has questionable value. Antibiotics and chemotherapy, including penicillin and sulphonamides, have been used successfully.   C. R. S.

ANTHROPOGEOGRAPHY. *See* ANTHROPOLOGY.

ANTHROPOLOGY, the study of man's physical characteristics and his behavior from both a comparative and an historical viewpoint. All varieties of men and all manners of life, regardless of location, period of time, or race, must of necessity be included in such a general view. Anthropology is concerned with the whole history of man from the earliest times, both as an animal and as following fixed and traditional modes of behavior, but its interest centers in form, function, and processes of development rather than in the history as an end in itself.

The subject matter is so vast that anthropology shares its inquiries with other fields of study, such as psychology, history, and biology. Where the historian is interested in tracing the history of events in terms of personalities, politics, and economic situations, the anthropologist searches for parallels of situation and sequences of change with a view to formulating regularities of human conduct. Economists and sociologists also share this general approach, but they are concerned with values, with deciding which of several kinds of life is preferable as a course for future action. Where the biologist is interested in placing man in relation to other animals—both with respect to evolution and the determination of man's anatomical and physiological distinctiveness—the anthropologist seeks to learn the specific history of each racial and subracial variety, the reasons for anatomical differences and resemblances, and their bearing on human behavior. The psychologist is concerned with man's mental and neural equipment in order to discover the way it operates, how it may be trained by learning, and the mechanisms of thinking. The anthropologist's task is that of defining what is learned according to established norms of behavior in each community.

Early Theories. Anthropology had its beginnings when early explorers found men of quite diverse sorts in previously unknown parts of the world. Their interest was one of comparison with Europeans at home. Beetle-browed savages, dark of skin, unclad, uncouth in manner, and lacking equipment were held to be a lower species of animal with a mentality incapable of developing arts of life like those of contemporary Europeans. In those pre-Darwinian days the explanation usually invoked was derived from theology: that differences in physique and lowliness of life were the consequences of moral depravity or original sin.

Scientific investigation began in the mid-nineteenth century as the indirect result of a spirit of religious enlightenment, coupled with a growing knowledge of geological history and the development of the doctrine of organic evolution. Fossil remains of men and varieties of living men were then seen in evolutionary perspective as forms derived, along various branching lines of descent, from lower animals of geologically ancient times. At once this broad view was applied to account for the sequence of stone tools of early times, the remains of ancient and Classical civilizations, and the contemporary culture of Mid-Victorian Europe. Accordingly it was held that cultures (the characteristic modes of life in each period and in each region) formed an evolutionary series and that all races had followed the same line of development in all parts of the world. Primitive peoples of varying degrees of complexity of life, peasant communities, and beliefs thought to be survivals from earlier times were all assigned places in this series as representative of its various stages. It was generally assumed that the organic development of man and the development of his mentality went hand in hand with cultural evolution, that, in fact, the culture of a people could be adduced as evidence of their stage of mental evolution. It is significant that the early anthropological writers—J. J. Bachhofen, Sir Edward Burnett Tylor, Lewis Henry Morgan, and Sir Walter Baldwin Spencer—did not make their position wholly clear on this point, the most vital element in their formulation.

Modern Concepts. Criticism of the view that all peoples had followed a single path of cultural development began toward the end of the nineteenth century and grew apace in the early decades of the twentieth. While it was recognized that the beginnings of culture had been rudimentary and that there had been accumulation, notably in the material arts, it became increasingly clear that the presence of elements in a people's culture was caused overwhelmingly by transmission from other groups rather than solely by a people's own inventiveness. It was thus recognized that a people's culture was in large part not the product of its own originality and hence could not be taken to indicate its stage of mental evolution. Furthermore, it was fully demonstrated that essentially similar traits in various cultures had had a diversity of origins and developed along different ways. This conclusion made it impossible to speak of a single line of universal culture growth and to assign each people to a particular developmental stage in it. On the biological side it was recognized that all races were variants of a single species, *Homo sapiens,* from at least neolithic times onward. Mental testing and an analysis of cultural behavior indicated that there were no vital differences between races, though they might differ in minor ways.

Aims. Thus the aims of anthropology shifted, largely through the influence of Franz Boas in America, from merely assigning places to racial types and cultural forms in a universal sequence, to a detailed investigation of how the forms developed. The task became one of minute observation and recording. As a consequence, the bulk of the vast anthropological literature is descriptive of the manifold phrasings of life in all parts of the world, of details and relations in the past as revealed by archaeology, and an endless series of measurements and comparisons of bodily types. The second largest ingredient is historical reconstruction of the sequence of particular forms in each locality, a history based on documentary evidence, archaeology, and inference controlled by logical safeguards. Some progress has been made in abstracting general relations and processes from particulars, but the vastness of the field and the relatively small number of anthropologists have hampered accomplishment.

Subfields. Investigations have followed special interests, so that the field is now divided into recognized parts. Physical anthropology deals with the relations of the early races of man to their living descendants, the physical characteristics of local races, the inheritance of certain physical traits, and the influences—both internal and environmental—during growth in producing the adult racial types. Archaeology traces the manner of life in earlier days from such objects (tools, houses, etc.) as have survived the ravages of time. While the remains are for the most part those that relate to material existence, much has been done to envisage their use in social situations and religious thought. It is obvious that archaeology is closely linked to ethnology, the study of the customs and behavior of living races. In this subfield, comparisons of cultures have led to the formulation of specific histories and general processes. Analysis has been many-faceted, from a consideration of the form of culture traits to investigations of the interrelations of form and function in society. A recent shift has given attention to the individual in cultural situations, the permissible varieties of personal expression provided by a culture, and the formation of personality as fixed by culturally determined behavior. The last has given assistance to psychiatrists and psychoanalysts, who are concerned largely with personality problems. General linguistics has become a separate branch in view of the exceedingly numerous language types differing fundamentally from the European and Asiatic languages traditionally studied by the philologists. General linguists are interested not only in the structure of particular languages, but view the whole of language as an essential part of culture.

Applied Anthropology. The application of some aspects of anthropological knowledge to problems of human organization is known as applied anthropology. Its roots lie in the activities of anthropologist advisors dealing with native affairs in British and Dutch colonies and in sociological interests in community and personal organization. The Society for Applied Anthropology has for its announced object "the promotion of scientific investigation of the principles controlling the relations of human beings to one another, and the encouragement of the wide application of these principles to practical problems." Its area of special interest lies in "the fields of business and political administration, psychiatry, and social work," and it offers consultant services for federal and private agencies. Some authorities find it difficult to see the dividing line between applied anthropology and sociology.

Anthropogeography. Anthropogeography is the aspect of geographic study concerned with human life in relation to the totality of geographic factors—climate, physiography, soil conditions, and plant and animal life. Whereas anthropology emphasizes the selective principle of culture and personal volition in relation to nature, anthropogeography concentrates on the various facets of the geographic environment in shaping man's activities. Stress is placed on economic life, inventions, and material existence and, to a lesser extent, on political situations as affected by geographic elements.

Basic Conclusions. Some fundamental conclusions of modern anthropology are: (1) all living races are varieties of a single species, substantially alike in contrast to their collective distinctiveness from other animals; (2) inborn mental capacities are approximately equivalent in the various races; (3) cultures are historic products taking form as the result of many determining factors; and (4) culture determines modes of behavior in both action and thought to an overwhelming extent and in subtle and intimate ways. *See also* ARCHAEOLOGY; ETHNOLOGY; PRIMITIVE CULTURE; PRIMITIVE SOCIETY; PRIMITIVE RELIGION.   L. S.

ANTHROPOMETRY [aˈnthropɒˈmətri], the standardized technique of measuring the human body clothed in its tissues. The procedures employed for measuring the cleaned skeleton are known as osteometry and those for the bony skull as craniometry. Anthropometry is based on the recognition of anatomical landmarks on the body and head which serve as termini or guides for various dimensions. These landmarks are either specific points or well-defined regions and developments; upon their precise definition depends the comparability of measurements taken by different observers. International agreements, the last drawn up at Geneva in 1912, have maintained a considerable degree of consistency among the various anthropometrists working in different parts of the world. The basic equipment is calipers and tape, although various specialized instruments are in use for specific purposes. In addition to measurements, observations on qualitative and nonmeasurable traits are also included in anthropometry, but standards and scales of various kinds are generally employed to aid the eye wherever possible. Anthropometric techniques are necessary in any study of the human body that involves size proportion and various morphological developments. Consequently they are generally an essential part of the equipment of those who investigate race, growth, constitution, genetics, nutritional status, and cognate subjects.   H. L. Sh.

ANTHROPOMORPHISM [aˈnthropomɔˈrfɪzəm], the ascription of human form or attributes to what is not human, especially to God.

In primitive thought, the objects of nature were supposed to be animated with a conscious life force, akin to what man found in himself. This view is called animism. The beginnings of religion are discernible in man's first approach, with an attitude of persuasion or petition, to the animistic life force. Objects of worship were soon endowed with human form, and most religions, especially in their popular early forms, were anthropomorphic. The gods of Homer were conceived on the pattern of exalted men, sharing men's feelings and even their moral defects; the early Biblical God spoke to Adam while "walking in the garden in the cool of the day." Xenophanes launched an attack on anthropomorphism in the sixth century B.C., contemporary with a like attack by Deutero-Isaiah (Isa. xliv:9-20), based on the prohibition of idolatry in the Decalogue. Plato's devastating critique of Homer's anthropomorphism in Books II and III of the *Republic* is grounded on moral and rational objections.

Both philosophy and religion have moved away from anthropomorphism. This is true of the Greek and Judaeo-Christian traditions, and notably of Hinduism. The tendency is toward a view of deity as superhuman, spiritual, ideally perfect, and without bodily form.

Critics, however, urge that any philosophy or religion that finds reason and goodness in God retains vestiges of a refined anthropomorphism. This charge is directed against both idealism and theism. The usual reply is that all knowledge—scientific, philosophical, or religious—must be based on human experience and reason; hence, anthropomorphism is unavoidable. The question should be: what kind of anthropomorphism, critical or uncritical? And the answer to this, it is said, depends on the relations between human experience and reality: what human experiences, if any, afford models of the real; what anthropomorphism is false, what true?   E. S. B.

ANTHURIUM [anthuˈriəm], a genus of highly ornamental tropical American aroids called tailflower by florists.

COURTESY OF AMERICAN MUSEUM OF NATURAL HISTORY, NEW YORK

ANTHURIUM, OR ARTIST'S PALLET

Many of them are characterized by a brilliant red spathe subtending the spikelike spadix which bears the individual flowers. Others are noteworthy for the perfection of pattern in their large, often velvety leaves. In greenhouse cultivation they require a hot, humid atmosphere and a rich but porous soil. Given these conditions, the species with red spathes will flower almost continuously.   J. C. Wis.

ANTIAIRCRAFT DEFENSE, the ground defense against aircraft which is a component of the air-defense combat team. It supplements fighter aircraft in the defense of field forces and vital installations located in the communications zones and in the zone of the interior. Its development in relative combat effectiveness has paralleled that of air power. During World War II, antiaircraft artillery units were attached or assigned to divisions, corps, and armies in all theatres and were deployed on an extensive scale. In general, deployment at all levels is based upon established priorities which are determined as a result of critical analysis of hostile capabilities, matériel available, and relative importance of the objective to the defender. Antiaircraft artillery was habitually landed with the assault waves in amphibious operations during World War II in order to provide early defense of the beaches, landing craft, shipping, and beach maintenance areas. Combat reports have shown that antiaircraft artillery, properly disposed at adequate scale and effectively controlled, can inflict losses on conventional combat aviation which are beyond the enemy's operational tolerance over an extended period of time. Antiaircraft guns and automatic weapons were widely used by both sides in World War II against ground targets, supplementing the work of the regular field artillery. This use became more frequent, on the Allied side, as, toward the end of the war, German air power declined in strength and ground targets became more important. In the Korean war, where hostile air power has rarely appeared over areas occupied by United Nations forces, the use of antiaircraft weapons in ground missions has become habitual.

Matériel and Technique. Modern antiaircraft weapons in the U. S. Army include guns of 75-mm., 90-mm., and

120-mm. caliber, 40-mm. automatic weapons, the .50-caliber machine gun, and guided missiles. The 75-mm. "Sky-Sweeper" gun is a fully automatic piece, with a built-in radar direction device so that each gun can be operated singly if required. Details as to characteristics of this weapon had not been made public as late as August 1952, although the gun was then in production and in course of issue to troops. The 90-mm. gun and mount, weighing approximately 16 tons in traveling position, and towed on a two-bogie trailer by tractor, has a sustained road speed of 20 m.p.h. Ten minutes are required for emplacement and an additional ten minutes for orientation and preparation for firing. Under combat conditions, the gun is fortified by digging in or by constructing a revetment. This latter operation requires approximately six hours. The gun has a rate of fire of from 20 to 24 rounds per minute, has a muzzle velocity of 2,700 f.p.s., and fires a projectile weighing 25 lb. to a maximum range of 33,000 ft., vertical, and 57,000 ft., horizontal. Limits of elevation are from —10° to 80°, with a traverse of 360°. It is equipped with an automatic fuse-setter which functions as the projectile is loaded. The gun battery, which is the firing unit, consists of four guns.

The 120-mm. antiaircraft artillery gun has been developed to increase the hitting power and effective ceiling of the gun defense. This weapon with mount weighs approximately 30 tons, is towed on a two-bogie trailer, and requires approximately one hour to emplace and orient. It has a muzzle velocity of 3,100 f.p.s. and fires a 50-lb. projectile at the rate of 12 rounds per minute to an altitude of 46,000 ft. While designed primarily for employment in static positions, it is classified as mobile. Position-finding equipment is similar to that employed with the 90-mm. gun, with necessary modifications made in the director to accommodate the higher muzzle velocities developed. The firing battery consists of four guns which are employed as a single unit.

Prediction and Fuse-Cutting. When firing is conducted at night or under conditions precluding visual observation, the target is located by radar and its position determined in terms of slant range, azimuth (bearing), and angular height. This information is transmitted in the form of potentiometer data to an electronic director, or computer, which solves instantaneously, for the firing, data consisting of firing azimuth, quadrant elevation, and fuse range. The remote-control system transmits the firing data instantaneously and continuously to the four guns, which are automatically pointed in azimuth and quadrant elevation for firing at the future position of the target corresponding to the position determined initially by the radar.

Mechanical-type time fuses are automatically set on the fuse data received from the director as the projectile is loaded. A "dead time" of the order of four-tenths second exists in the system as a result of the elapsed interval from the time of fuse cutting to firing the round. This systematic error is corrected in the director. A tracking head is provided as an auxiliary means for transmitting azimuth and angular height to the radar and director under conditions permitting visual tracking. The director is capable of computing firing data based on target speeds of zero to 600 m.p.h. Gun-laying radars in current use will track automatically in range, azimuth, and angular height. The effectiveness of the entire system is dependent upon precise orientation and synchronization of all components; application of ballistic corrections for parallax, muzzle velocity, air density, wind direction, and velocity; and adjustment corrections in terms of azimuth, elevation, slant range or altitude, and fuse. The director solves the prediction problem on the

ACME NEWS PICTURE
A manually-operated 90-millimeter antiaircraft gun

assumption of constant speed and the rectilinear course of
the target at a constant altitude or a constantly changing
altitude during the time of flight of the projectile; consequently, the initial bursts are usually the most effective,
prediction having been accomplished prior to evasive action
by the hostile aircraft. The employment of variable time or
proximity fuses has materially increased the effectiveness of
antiaircraft artillery gunfire. These fuses each contain a
miniature radar which actuates the firing mechanism when
the projectile passes sufficiently close to the target to permit
functional reception of the reflected radar impulses. Thus,
under ideal operating conditions, the systematic probable
error is decreased by eliminating the time fuse probable
error. An additional advantage to the defense accrues when
employing proximity fuses, since only those rounds which
are close enough for destructive effect will detonate in the
vicinity of the target. Evasive action by an enemy plane is
therefore less probable.

Automatic Weapons. Automatic weapons are provided
in antiaircraft artillery ground defense for the attack of low-
flying aircraft. They are characterized by high rates of fire,
ease and speed of tracking in elevation and azimuth, and
high mobility. The 40-mm. gun and mount weighs approximately three tons and is towed by a standard 2½-ton
truck. Emplacement for firing with the director requires
from 15 to 30 min.; if on-carriage sights are employed, it
can be prepared for firing in from 3 to 5 min. Firing is
conducted manually at the rate of 60 rounds per minute or
automatically at 120 rounds per minute. The projectile,
weighing 1.96 lb., contains a tracer element which facilitates adjustment and is provided with a supersensitive point
detonating fuse. A self-destructive element is also incorporated in the projectile to insure an air burst. A mechanical
type of director is employed, with the towed 40-mm. gun
utilizing azimuth and elevation rates established by tracking
the target and slant ranges determined by a range finder
mounted on the director. These data are utilized to compute
firing azimuth and quadrant elevation, which are transmitted and applied to the individual gun through an electrical and oil gear system. On-carriage sights which compute lead angles in the slant plane containing the longitudinal axis of the target give hit expectancies which are
commensurate with those obtained with the director. On-
carriage sights permit a more immediate engagement of
the target and, in general, are preferred by seasoned battery
commanders, particularly when engaging high-speed aircraft on short warning. Modern, standardized, automatic
weapon equipment of United States forces includes a twin
40-mm. gun mounted on a light chassis. On-carriage sights
were used with this equipment.

The .50-caliber machine gun, employed singly or in multiple mounts of four, is used to supplement the automatic
weapon defense. The multiple caliber .50 machine gun,
mounted in a standard half-track vehicle and capable of
firing at the rate of 1,200 rounds per gun per minute, is one
of the most effective antiaircraft weapons. The reflector
type of on-carriage sights and tracer stream observation are
used for fire control. The automatic weapons battery contains eight 40-mm. towed guns or eight dual 40-mm. units,
depending upon type, and eight quadruple .50-caliber machine gun units. Firing is normally conducted by individual
unit.

Searchlights. By 1949, the standard 60-in. searchlight was
in an obsolescent stage as antiaircraft artillery equipment.
Its employment was generally limited to spread beam illumination. Radar, in the military service, was first employed as

a target-locating device for searchlights. Since gun director
input data could be obtained from these searchlight radars
in reasonably accurate form, they served as interim equipment for firing at unseen targets until the more precise gun-
laying radars were developed.

Warning Systems. Under the system employed by the
United States, long-range warning of the approach of hostile
aircraft is furnished antiaircraft artillery by the general Aircraft Warning Service (A.W.S.) operated by Air Force signal personnel. This information is broadcast and otherwise disseminated from the Air Defense Controls Center
(A.D.C.C.), or Tactical Air Control Center (T.A.C.C.),
and is monitored by all Antiaircraft Operations Rooms
(A.A.O.R.) integrated into the system and within broadcast
range. Short-range warning is obtained from the Antiaircraft
Artillery Intelligence Service (A.A.A.I.S.), which includes
visual observation posts, search radars, and all antiaircraft
agencies organized and equipped to obtain and transmit
warning intelligence by wire or radio to higher, lower, and
adjacent operations rooms to include A.D.C.C. and T.A.C.C.
The effectiveness of the defense depends directly on the
accuracy and timeliness of early warning. With the advent
of supersonic aircraft and missiles, it constitutes a vital element in the defense organization.

Tactical and Operational Control. The tactical disposition of antiaircraft artillery units employed with the field
forces is controlled through the AA brigade, group (regiment) battalion, and battery chain of command based on
directives issued by army, corps, and division artillery commanders. Those units deployed in the communication zone
are controlled through similar command channels in con-
formity with the directives of the air defense commander.
Operational control is provided by the establishment of Inner
Artillery Zones (I.A.Z.) and Gun Defended Areas (G.D.A.),
for each of which definite "rules for engagement" are prescribed. A controller located in the combined air corps-anti-
aircraft artillery control center at air force level has delegated
authority to impose restrictions on antiaircraft fire. In the
absence of this restriction, aircraft violating the I.A.Z or
G.D.A. are immediately engaged.

For the defense of the continental United States, antiaircraft weapons are organized under the Anti-Aircraft
Command, which is divided into three subordinate commands—Eastern, Central, and Western. The Anti-Aircraft
Command is under the operational direction of the Air Defense Command of the Air Force, which controls the interceptor squadrons and the warning system.

Guided Missiles. The penetration of the sonic barrier
by jet-propelled aircraft and the production of long-range
jet bombers capable of carrying atomic weapons have posed
new problems for antiaircraft defense. A defensive weapon
capable of tracking, overtaking, and destroying a target flying
at supersonic speeds must obviously be capable of superior
speed and must also be equipped with a fire control system
which will reduce to the lowest possible time-denominator
the processes of decision involved in moving the missile
from the ground to the target. The antiaircraft guided missile is the result of this new defensive requirement, and the
U. S. Army in 1952 placed the first commercial production
order for weapons of this type, after eight years spent in
research and experiment.

The new weapon (named Nike) is described as a medium-
range, supersonic antiaircraft rocket with a guidance system
capable of directing it to any target within its reach. First
acceleration on take-off is provided by a "booster" which
drops away by aero-dynamic pressure as soon as its limited

supply of fuel is exhausted, leaving the rocket to continue under the power of its own motor.

Guidance systems for antiaircraft missiles are of two general types: (1) beam-riding systems, in which a radar beam is directed on the target and the missile is made to follow the beam until it intercepts the target; and (2) homing systems in which the missile is fitted with a "seeker head," which is attracted to sources of heat or sound, or which emits radio pulses that are reflected from the target and guide the missile.

Troops units of the Anti-Aircraft Command for the operation of guided missiles are organized in batteries, battalions, and groups on the general system of other antiaircraft artillery units. The 1st Guided Missile Group, which is located at Fort Bliss, Texas, established the pattern for organization and training of guided missile units, and this parent organization has supplied the nucleus of trained personnel to its offspring guided missile units located throughout the country. J. H. M. and G. F. E.

ANTIBES [ã'ti'b], a famous fortified seaport in the department of Alpes-Maritimes, in southeastern France, on the Mediterranean Sea, 11 mi. southwest of Nice. It was founded by the Greeks about 340 B.C. and was called Antipolis. The city later became a Roman colony, was destroyed by the Saracens in the ninth century, and finally came into the possession of the counts of Provence. The Marquis de Vauban fortified Antibes with the Fort Carré or Square Fort, which withstood the sieges of 1746 and 1815. Of historic interest are Gallic Roman remains in the city hall, remains of a Roman theatre, an aqueduct, and a sixteenth century citadel. Fruits, olives, grapes, and tobacco are grown, although Antibes is considerably more important as a winter resort. Pop. 1954, 27,064. S. Van V.

ANTIBIOTICS [a'ntɪbaɪɒ'tɪks], chemical substances produced by microorganisms which have the capacity to inhibit the growth of and even to destroy bacteria and other microorganisms, in dilute solutions. The antimicrobial action of an antibiotic is selective in nature, some organisms being affected and others not at all or only to a limited degree; each antibiotic is thus characterized by a specific antimicrobial spectrum or range of activity against different bacteria and other microorganisms. The selective action of an antibiotic is also manifested against animal cells, different antibiotics varying greatly in their toxicity to animals and in the effect upon blood and other body fluids. Antibiotics also vary greatly in their physical and chemical properties and in their mode of action upon bacteria and other microorganisms. Because of these characteristics, some antibiotics have remarkable chemotherapeutic potentialities and can be used for the control of various microbial infections in man and in animals.

FORMATION

Certain bacteria, fungi, actinomycetes, and algae have the capacity of exerting antagonistic effects upon the growth of other microorganisms; they produce chemical substances, or antibiotics, which are responsible for this action. The property of producing antibiotics is not characteristic, however, of a given genus or even of a given species, but rather of specific strains of certain organisms. Thus, the ability to produce penicillin, streptomycin, or other antibiotics is characteristic of certain strains of *Penicillium notatum* and *P. chrysogenum,* of *Streptomyces griseus,* and of certain other microbes. There are also differences between various antibiotic-producing strains, these differences being either

quantitative or qualitative in nature, different strains yielding different forms of a given antibiotic—as in the case of the various forms of penicillin which are produced by different strains of the species *P. notatum, P. chrysogenum, Aspergillus flavus, A. parasiticus,* and others. Maximum yields of a given antibiotic may be produced by one strain under surface or stationary conditions of culture, and by another in submerged or shaken cultures. Some organisms are capable of producing more than one antibiotic: *Pseudomonas aeruginosa* yielding pyocyanase, pyocyanin, pyolipic acid, and pyocompounds; *Bacillus brevis,* gramicidin and tyrocidine, the mixture being known as tyrothricin; *P. notatum,* penicillin and penatin; *A. flavus,* penicillin and aspergillic acid; *A. fumigatus,* fumigatin, spinulosin, fumigacin (helvolic acid), and gliotoxin; *Streptomyces griseus,* streptomycin, mannosido-streptomycin, actidione, and streptocin; *S. rimosus,* oxytetracycline and rimocidin. The same antibiotic also may be produced by different organisms, as in the case of gliotoxin which is produced by species of *Gliocladium, Trichoderma, A. fumigatus,* and others. Different organisms or strains may produce various chemical modifications of the same antibiotic, as in the case for the various penicillins or the different forms of streptomycin. A large number of antibiotics now have been isolated and described. Among the bacteria, both nonsporeforming and sporeforming organisms have the capacity to produce antibiotics. Among the actinomycetes, the capacity of producing antibiotics is largely limited to the genus *Streptomyces.*

INOCULATING INITIAL CULTURE PLATES

Production by Nonsporeforming Bacteria. Pyocyanase was the first antibiotic isolated by Rudolf Emmerich and Löw in 1899 from a group of bacteria known first as *Bacillus pyocyaneus* and more recently as *Pseudomonas aeruginosa.* Other nonsporeforming bacteria also produce antibiotics which vary greatly in their chemical nature and antibacterial properties. This can be illustrated by the colicines, which are produced by different strains of *Escherichia coli.*

Production by Sporeforming Bacteria. Various sporeforming bacteria produce a variety of antibiotics. Strains of *B. subtilis* yield subtilin, subtilysin, bacitracin, eumycin, and others; *B. brevis,* tyrothricin; *B. polymyxa* (*B. aerosporus*), polymyxin (aerosporin); *B. mycoides, B. mesentericus,* and *B. simplex* give rise to a variety of ill-defined substances designated as bacillin, simplexin, and colistatin, and by other names. Many of them are active against fungi.

Production by Fungi. Fungi are among the most important antibiotic-producing organisms. In addition to penicillin, they yield mycophenolic acid (the first antibiotic isolated from fungi), penicillic acid, gliotoxin, clavacin, aspergillic acid, citrinin, chetomin, polyporin, viridin, penicidin, and many others.

Production by Actinomycetes. Since the discovery of penicillin, the most important antibiotics that have found application as chemotherapeutic agents have come from the actinomycetes. Nearly 125 compounds have now been isolated or described. Some of these have found extensive application in the treatment of human and animal infectious diseases. These antibiotics include streptomycin, chloramphenicol, the tetracyclines, erythromycin, and neomycin. Some of these antibiotics are active largely upon bacteria; others, like actidione, fradicin, and nystatin, are active against fungi; still others are active against rickettsiae and some of the larger viruses.

Production by Other Forms. Certain algae also have been found capable of producing antibiotic agents. Only one, chlorellin, had been described by 1949. Lichenin and usnic acid, products of lichens, also may be mentioned. Higher green plants and animals also form antibacterial substances, which have properties similar to those of true antibiotics. The plant products have been described as phytoncides; they include allicin, tomatin, and various others. Among the animal products which possess antibacterial properties lysozyme occupies an important place. To what extent protozoa, maggots, and other animal forms that have the capacity of digesting living bacteria and fungi produce substances which possess antibioticlike properties, still remains

COURTESY OF CHARLES PFIZER CHEMICAL CO.

INCUBATION OF CULTURES

to be determined. Certain microorganisms also are capable of producing substances which inhibit the growth of or destroy viruses, including phages, and tumor cells. Recently, certain specific compounds, notably actinomycin, azoserin, sarcomycin and certain others, have been found to produce a specific effect against certain neoplasms, including lymphogranulomas and sarcomas.

CHEMICAL NATURE

Various systems of classification of antibiotics have been proposed. These are based upon the origin of antibiotics, their solubility, toxicity to animals, or chemical nature. The last system appears to be the most logical. Antibiotics have been classified as lipoids, pigments, polypeptides, sulphur-bearing compounds, quinones, and ketones, on an organic basis. On the basis of their chemical structure, antibiotics have been grouped as follows:

I. Compounds containing carbon, hydrogen, and oxygen.
   1. C_6 group—$C_6H_6O_4$—Kojic acid
   2. C_7 group—$C_7H_6O_4$—Clavacin
   3. C_8 group—$C_8H_{10}O_4$—Penicillic acid
   4. C_{11} group—$C_{11}H_{10}O_5$—Gladiolic acid
   5. C_{15} group—$C_{15}H_{14}O_6$—Javanicin
   6. C_{32} group—$C_{32}H_{44}O_8$—Fumigacin (Helvolic acid), etc.

II. Compounds containing carbon, hydrogen, oxygen, and nitrogen.
   1. C_{12} group—$C_{12}H_{20}O_2N_2$—Aspergillic acid
   2. C_{13} group—$C_{13}H_{10}O_2N_2$—Pyocyanin
   3. C_{21} group—$C_{21}H_{39}O_{12}N_7$—Streptomycin
   4. C_{41} group—$C_{41}H_{56}O_{11}N_8$—Actinomycin

III. Compounds containing carbon, hydrogen, oxygen, nitrogen, and sulphur.
   1. $C_9{}^+$ group—$C_9H_{11}O_4SN_2 \cdot R$—Penicillin
   2. C_{13} group—$C_{13}H_{14}O_4N_2S_2$—Gliotoxin

IV. Compounds containing chlorine.
   1. $C_{19}H_{15}O_5Cl_3$—Ustin
   2. $C_{17}H_{17}O_6Cl$—Griseofulvin
   3. $C_{11}H_{12}O_5N_2Cl_2$—Chloramphenicol

A large number of other antibiotics are produced by microorganisms; many of them had not been isolated or purified by 1954. A few had been synthesized, including pyocyanin, clavacin, and, most important of all, penicillin and chloramphenicol. However, all the penicillin used to 1954 in chemotherapy was produced biologically, although most of the chloramphenicol used in chemotherapy is synthesized. Some of the chemical modifications of antibiotics have also found extensive application. This is true of dihydrostreptomycin, derived from streptomycin, and of tetracycline, derived from chlorotetracycline.

MODE OF ACTION

Antibiotics are said to be largely bacteriostatic agents, inhibiters of growth, although some are markedly bactericidal or even bacteriolytic. Many antibiotics, such as actinomycin and clavacin, are highly toxic to animal tissues; a few, notably the penicillins, are either nontoxic or, like streptomycin, possess only limited toxicity. Some, like tyrothricin, are hemolytic, dissolvers of red blood cells; others, like chetomin, are inactivated by the body cells. Some are not soluble in water; hence, their application may be limited to the treatment of surface or local infections. Since antibiotics are characterized by their selective action upon bacteria, none can be used as a general disinfectant against all bacteria. Penicillin is active largely upon cocci and various gram-positive bacteria and spirochetes, but it has only little activity against the gram-negative rod-shaped bacteria and the acid-fast bacteria. Streptomycin is active against bacteria found both among the gram-negative and the gram-positive organisms, including the bacteria causing tuberculosis. Neither penicillin nor streptomycin is very active against fungi and viruses, although the first has some activity against the larger viruses, such as psittacosis and vaccinia, and the second is active against rickettsiae and granuloma inguinale. Other antibiotics, however, notably chloramphenicol, the tetracyclines, and erythromycin, are highly active upon rickettsiae and the larger viruses. Some antibiotics are highly active upon fungi but not upon bacteria and actinomycetes. Some are active upon neoplasms.

Point of Action. Various theories have been postulated concerning the mechanism of growth-inhibition or the mode of action of antibiotics upon bacteria. This varies with the antibiotics. In most cases, the effect consists in interference with cell multiplication or cell division. The antibiotic may also interfere with the nutrition of the bacterial cell by substituting for one of the nutrients, or by interfering with the utilization of special cell constituents or essential growth factors. The antibiotic may affect cell respiration or certain other enzyme mechanisms; it may influence surface tension of bacteria, or it may combine with certain groupings essential for bacterial multiplication, such as the sulphydryl groups.

Resistance to Antibiotics. Many of the bacteria have the capacity of adapting themselves to the effect of certain antibiotics upon continued contact with them; this leads to the development of resistant strains of such bacteria. Cultures of *Staphylococcus aureus* which originally have been sensitive to penicillin may become resistant. *Mycobacterium tuberculosis* strains originally sensitive to streptomycin may develop resistance to this antibiotic. A culture of an organism that has become resistant to one antibiotic still may remain sensitive to others.

CHEMOTHERAPEUTIC USE

Antibiotics have revolutionized medical practice. Among the various antibiotics that have found extensive application as chemotherapeutic agents, penicillin, streptomycin, chloramphenicol, the tetracyclines, erythromycin, and carbomycin are most important. This is also true to a lesser extent of tyrothrycin, bacitracin, and neomycin. Certain other antibiotics appear to offer definite promise.

Penicillin. Penicillin has found extensive application in the treatment of infections caused by staphylococci, namely, osteomyelitis, suppurative arthritis, bronchitis, empyema, endocarditis, furuncles, laryngotracheitis, mastitis, meningitis, otitis media, peritonitis, suppurative pneumonia, burns, septicemia, sinusitis, tonsillitis, wounds, and many others. Penicillin is also effective in the treatment of a variety of infections caused by hemolytic streptococci, pneumococci, anaerobic streptococci, gonococci, meningococci, anaerobic clostridia (gas gangrene), diphtheria, and the anthrax organisms, spirochetes, and syphilis, and a variety of other bacteria. Most actinomycetes are also sensitive to penicillin. However, it is not effective in mixed infections caused by gram-negative bacteria or in malaria, tuberculosis, virus infections, fungus diseases, and many others. The toxic manifestations to penicillin are limited largely to conditions of allergy.

Streptomycin. Streptomycin has been applied in the treatment of a variety of infections. Meningitis, endocarditis, laryngotracheitis, and urinary tract and pulmonary infections caused by Pfeiffer's bacillus, *Hemophilus influenzae,* respond favorably to treatment. Meningitis, bacteremia, and urinary tract infections due to susceptible strains of *Escherichia coli, Proteus vulgaris, Klebsiella pneumoniae* (Friedlander's bacillus), *Aerobacter aerogenes,* and *Pseudomonas aeruginosa* have been benefited by the use of streptomycin. Meningitis due to susceptible strains of *Salmonella* and tularemia respond well to its use; and it has been found helpful in the treatment of the following ailments, although its clinical position has not yet been clearly defined: peritonitis, liver abscesses, bile duct infections, and empyema due to susceptible organisms; tuberculosis; chronic lung infections due predominantly to gram-negative bacteria; endocarditis

caused by penicillin-resistant, streptomycin-sensitive pathogens; and pneumonia due to *Klebsiella pneumoniae.* Among the limitations of streptomycin are a certain degree of toxicity, which may result in dizziness, deafness, or other reactions, and a rapid development of resistance to it by the infecting organism. The former have been largely overcome by reducing the amount and frequency of the dosage, and the latter, by combining streptomycin with PAS and INH, in the treatment of tuberculosis.

Capping and inspecting ampules under sterile conditions

Chloramphenicol, Tetracyclines, Erythromycin, and Carbomycin. These antibiotics, especially the tetracyclines, have certain similar biological properties, as shown by the cross-resistance of various bacteria and by their respective antimicrobial spectra. They are usually given by mouth. They have found extensive application in the treatment of numerous infections caused by bacteria, rickettsiae, and some of the larger viruses. These include typhoid fever, various forms of typhus fever, spotted fever, gonorrheal infections, syphilis, brucellosis, urinary tract infections, lymphogranuloma venereum, infectious hepatitis, herpes zoster, trachoma, and various others.

Other Antibiotics. Among the other antibiotics that have found important applications in chemotherapy, mention should be made of tyrothricin, polymyxin (aerosporin), bacitracin, and neomycin. Due to their somewhat greater toxicity, they are used primarily for surface applications and by oral administration, and only to a lesser extent by the parenteral route. They are active against a great variety of infectious diseases.

Other Utilization. Antibiotics are also finding extensive application in veterinary practice, in the treatment of plant seed and in certain plant diseases (pear blight, bean and pepper blights), in the feeding of animals, notably chickens, turkeys, and swine, in the preservation of bull semen, and in the purification of virus preparations.

The chemotherapeutic use of antibiotics has opened new vistas in combating diseases caused by microorganisms.

S. A. W.

ANTICHRIST, one who denies or opposes the name and rights of Christ. In the New Testament John alone uses the term (I John ii:18, 22; iv:3; II John vii), but the idea appears in the Gospels in references to false Christs (Matt. xxiv:5, 23, 24; Mark xiii:21, 22), in Paul's mention of "that man of sin" (II Thess: ii:3), and in the Apocalypse in allusions to "the beast" (Rev. xi:7; xiii; xvii:8 ff.). Some scholars have found antecedents of Antichrist in the Babylonian dragon-myth and in the Jewish mythology regarding Beliar (Belial). During the history of the Church, various individuals and institutions were deemed apostate by certain Christians and were called the Antichrist. The earliest embodiment of the spirit of Antichrist was held to be the Emperor Nero, for the cryptic cipher 666 in Revelation xiii:18 is the equivalent, by gematria, of "Nero Caesar" when written in Hebrew characters. Since then, by dint of ingenious calculation, the apocalyptic number has been made to yield the name of almost every heretic or persecutor of the Church. Luther, Calvin, Zwingli, and many of their followers have regarded the Pope as the Antichrist.   B. M. M.

ANTICIPATION, in music, the playing of a note slightly ahead of time, a common practice in ragtime and jazz and in the Viennese waltz, where it occurs at the second beat of the accompaniment. Anticipation, as the term is employed in harmonic analysis, refers to a chordal tone played somewhat ahead of time so that it clashes with the preceding chord, as at the word "and" toward the end of *Annie Laurie*.
W. Li.

ANTICLERICALISM. *See* CHURCH AND STATE.

ANTICOSTI ISLAND, a large island occupying the eastern portion of the Gulf of St. Lawrence and forming part of the province of Quebec, Canada. It is approximately 150 mi. long and less than 40 mi. wide, about equal in size to the island of Corsica. Anticosti Island is well forested and its topography is undulating and low, very little of it rising above 500 feet. It is formed of rock structures which were laid down during the Ordovician and Silurian periods, similar to those found in the adjacent peninsula of Gaspé. There are no long rivers on Anticosti Island, and as a result the forests have been difficult to work for pulp or lumber. The climate is rather cool and not very favorable for crops. The population of only a few hundred is mostly engaged in fur trade or fishing. Henry Menier, a French industrialist, bought the island in 1895 and built a short railway and a wharf, but was unable to exploit his possession profitably.   G. T.

ANTIETAM, BATTLE OF [anti'təm], an engagement of the Civil War resulting in the repulse, Sept. 17, 1862, of Gen. Robert E. Lee's first effort to invade the North. After defeating Gen. John Pope at the second Battle of Manassas (Bull Run), Lee prepared to invade the North, partly in the hope that Maryland would be won for the Confederacy. On September 5 he crossed the Potomac with 51,844 men. He then divided his army, sending Gen. T. J. (Stonewall) Jackson to capture Harpers Ferry. In this emergency, Lincoln placed Gen. G. B. McClellan in command of the Union army. With 75,316 troops, McClellan advanced so slowly that Lee had time to reunite his forces and take a strong position on Antietam Creek, near Sharpsburg, Md. McClellan attacked on the morning of September 17, and the Confederates beat off successive attacks throughout the day. By evening Lee had lost 13,533 men and McClellan 12,469. Although neither side could claim a victory, Lee had lost ground and more than one-fourth of his army. The following day, when McClellan failed to renew the battle, Lee began an orderly withdrawal across the Potomac.   M. K.

ANTI-FEDERALISTS, at first, opponents in the American states to the ratification of the Federal Constitution, following its adoption by the Constitutional Convention meeting at Philadelphia in 1787, and, subsequently, advocates of states' rights. The Anti-Federalists comprised a numerous and influential segment of the population in each state; they succeeded in New York in delaying the state's ratification, until after ten other states had voted for the new document, and prevented the ratification of the Constitution by the North Carolina and Rhode Island conventions until 1789 and 1790 respectively. The voting of the Declaration of Independence by the Second Continental Congress in 1776 had been delayed partially because several representatives favored erecting a strong central government to supplant the authority of England prior to a declaration of separation. These aims were thwarted a second time in the writing and ratification by the states of the Articles of Confederation, which generally represented the political aspirations of the agrarian and small-propertied elements supporting the war against England. The Anti-Federalists favored a continuance of the Articles of Confederation and the strong state governments permitted under that constitution. They feared that in the contests between the states and the new central government envisaged under the Constitution, the states would lose their sovereign powers. Moreover, they distrusted the new Constitution, since it provided no bill of rights. Following the inauguration of the new Federal Government in 1789, the Anti-Federalists became the opposition party, accepted the leadership of Thomas Jefferson in national politics, and provided the principal support of the Democratic-Republican Party, subsequently the Democratic Party.   G. H. K.

ANTIGEN. *See* BACTERIOLOGY.

ANTIGO [a'ntɪgo], the county seat of Langlade Co. situated on Spring Brook in northern Wisconsin, 32 mi. northeast of Wausau. It is on the watershed between the St. Lawrence and Mississippi rivers amid beautiful country with an abundance of lakes and trout streams. The Menominee Indian Reservation lies 10 mi. to the east. Antigo was founded about 1882 and chartered as a city in 1885. It has the mayor-alderman form of government. Among its manufactures are gears, shoes and lasts, and veneers. It is also a shipping center, served by the Chicago and North Western Railroad, for large quantities of dairy products, grain, and potatoes produced in the vicinity. Antigo is the seat of the Langlade County Teachers College. Pop. 1950, 9,902.

ANTIGONE [antɪ'gəni], a tragedy by Sophocles presented about 441 B.C. Antigone, daughter of the dead Oedipus, following the dictates of custom and religion, but disobeying the edict of Creon, regent of Thebes, attempts to inter her traitor brother Polynices, slain in an unsuccessful attempt to capture Thebes. For this attempt she is sentenced to solitary confinement for life, and Haemon, Creon's son and Antigone's fiancé, cannot persuade his father to reverse the sentence. The prophet Tiresias warns Creon of dire things to happen if Polynices is not buried and Antigone released, however, and Creon is finally persuaded to permit a proper burial. But it is too late to avert tragedy, for Antigone has already committed suicide. In despair, Haemon slays himself, and Eurydice, Creon's wife, follows her son in death upon hearing of his suicide. *Antigone* is a play of conflict and contest. Antigone, unfeminine, arrogant, proud, recklessly self-sacrificing, but, near the end, showing human weakness that wins sympathy and pity, is the representative of the higher and infallible divine law. Creon, developing as the play advances from a well-intentioned ruler into an intemperate tyrant, is the representative of fallible human law. The result of the conflict between these two forces is the utter defeat and humiliation of Creon. *See also* OEDIPUS; SEVEN AGAINST THEBES, THE. S. D. At.

ANTIGONIDS [antɪ'gonɪdz], a Macedonian dynasty founded by Antigonus Monophthalmos (Antigonus the One-Eyed) (382-301 B.C.), a general whom Alexander the Great had made satrap of Phrygia. After the death of Alexander in 323, Antigonus wanted to control all, or at least a portion, of Alexander's empire, and when the Regency disintegrated after 316 B.C., Antigonus disputed the spoils with Cassander, Lysimachus, and Seleucus. On two occasions Antigonus and his son, Demetrius Poliorcetes (c. 338-283 B.C.), were on the point of uniting the major part of Alexander's empire under their control. In 312 B.C., Antigonus held Asia Minor and was about to invade Macedonia while Demetrius invaded Egypt, but Demetrius was defeated by Ptolemy and Seleucus at Gaza, and Antigonus had to abandon his Macedonian campaign. Later, after Antigonus and Demetrius had established themselves in Greece and won Macedonia (303-302 B.C.), they were defeated by a coalition of Ptolemy, Seleucus, and Lysimachus at Ipsus in Asia Minor, where Antigonus was killed in 301 B.C. Between 301 and 285 B.C., Demetrius tried to carry out his father's plan for world empire. By virtue of his control of the sea and his foothold in Greece, he was able to effect the conquest of Macedonia and become king in 294 B.C. Later, however, he was driven out by Lysimachus and Pyrrhus and forced to take refuge in Asia Minor. Here he was captured by Seleucus in 285 B.C. He died in prison two years later. Antigonus Gonatas (c. 320-239 B.C.), the son of Demetrius, was apparently with his father when he took Macedonia in 294. Antigonus, then about twenty-six years old, reigned for Demetrius in Greece. As king of Macedonia until his death in 239 B.C., Antigonus controlled the Aegean and eastern Greece as far south as Corinth. A convert to Stoicism and a patron of the arts, he was one of the most enlightened rulers of the Hellenistic period. The Antigonids who succeeded Antigonus Gonatas were Demetrius II (ruled 239-229 B.C.), Antigonus Doson (ruled 229-221 B.C.), and Philip V (ruled 221-179 B.C.). These rulers gradually lost influence as a result of the rise of the Aetolian and Achaean leagues in Greece and the advance of Rome into the eastern Mediterranean. Philip V fought two wars against the Romans; his kingdom never recovered from the crushing defeat at Cynoscephalae in 197 B.C. Perseus, the son of Philip and the last of the Antigonids, reigned from 179 to 168 B.C. He made a futile last stand against the Romans (171-168 B.C.), but was decisively defeated in the Battle of Pydna in 168 B.C. After this, the Romans divided Macedonia into four republics under Roman control. T. B. J.

ANTIGONISH [antɪgonɪ'sh], the county town of Antigonish Co., Nova Scotia, Canada, on the Canadian National Railways, about 33 mi. east of New Glasgow. Founded in 1784 by disbanded members of the Royal Regiment of Nova Scotia Volunteers, it received an influx of Highland Scottish immigrants in 1795 and the following years. Their descendants make up most of the population in eastern Nova Scotia. Antigonish was incorporated as a town in 1888. St. Francis Xavier University, founded in 1853, and St. Ninian's Cathedral, built in 1878, make Antigonish the cultural and religious center of eastern Nova Scotia. Workers from the university initiated credit unions and study groups among fishermen and miners of this section. Pop. 1951, 3,196. D. F. P.

ANTIGONISH MOVEMENT, an important adult education venture, closely aligned with the co-operative movement that originated at St. Francis Xavier University in Antigonish, Nova Scotia. Aptly termed "adult education for action," the movement drew its initial inspiration from the work of Father J. J. Tompkins, who in the 1920's organized small study clubs and fought illiteracy in some of the poverty-stricken fishing villages along the coast. Informal courses in co-operation, handicrafts, and credit-union management, all with a view to acquainting the people with the principles of mutual self-help, were given, and libraries were developed. The local co-operatives and credit unions that were developed as a result of these teachings succeeded in raising the economic level of the people, and other poverty-ridden sections of the province asked for similar assistance. As a result, St. Francis Xavier University in 1928 organized an extension department which not only carried the pattern of education for action into scores of villages in the Maritime Provinces but also helped communities in other parts of Canada and in the United States to develop similar programs. G. Bu.

ANTIGUA [anti'gwa], officially known as Antigua Guatemala, the capital of the department of Sacatepéquez, in south central Guatemala, Central America, situated in a valley at the base of the volcano of Agua, about 27 mi. southwest of Guatemala City, at 14° 34′ N. lat. and 90° 45′ W. long. Two other volcanoes, the Fuego and the Acatenango, are visible from the city, which lies in the center of a coffee-growing region at an altitude of 5,000 ft. Capital of the republic until 1773, when it had a population of over 80,000, the city was wrecked by an earthquake, and the administration was removed to the city of Guatemala. The interesting public buildings include the Palace of the Captains General, the city hall, the cathedral, built in 1534, and the University of San Carlos Borromeo, founded in 1678. The town is reached in less than an hour by highway from Guatemala City. Pop. 1950, 10,691.

ANTIGUA, an island of the West Indies located between Guadeloupe and Barbuda. Largest of the British Leeward Islands Colony, it is roughly circular in shape and has an area of 108 sq. mi., with a 200-ft. limestone plateau in the northern part and volcanic mountains 1,330 ft. high in the southwest. The climate is dry, limiting the raising of sugar cane to the area containing moisture-retaining clays in the central part of the island. Cotton provides the second most important crop. St. John's (est. pop. 11,000) is the capital, chief port, and largest town. Antigua was sighted by Columbus in 1493 and settled by the British in 1632. In 1940 the United States Government leased an area near Parham Harbor for a naval base. Two other islands, Barbuda and Redonda, are included in the Antigua Presidency. The population of Antigua in 1949 was 40,777, principally Negroes. J. E. F.

ANTIHISTAMINIC DRUGS. *See* PHARMACOLOGY.

ANTI-LEBANON MOUNTAINS, a range between the Lebanon Republic and Syria, paralleling the Lebanon Mountains. This folded, sedimentary range has four main ridges and forms the eastern edge of the rift valley of El Bekaa. The range has an average elevation of about 6,000 ft. In the extreme south, Mount Hermon rises 10,000 ft. above sea level. The range is cut by the Barada River, which provides water for the city of Damascus, located at the eastern edge of the mountains. J. E. F.

ANTILLES [æntɪl'ɪʒ], a name for the West Indies, commonly divided into the Greater Antilles, comprising Cuba, Jamaica, Hispaniola (Haiti and Dominican Republic), and Puerto Rico; and the Lesser Antilles, comprising the Leeward and Windward groups, and the smaller islands that form an arc between Puerto Rico and South America.

ANTI-MASONIC PARTY, an American political party originating in New York state in the 1820's, whose principal tenets consisted of opposition to Freemasonry and to the appointment of Masons to public office. The movement had its beginnings in the kidnapping on Sept. 12, 1826, of William Morgan, of Batavia, N. Y., following his declaration of intent to publish a book revealing the secrets of the Society of Freemasons. The conspirators took Morgan to Fort Niagara, N. Y., where all trace of him was lost. A body, reputed to be Morgan's, but later proved to be the corpse of Timothy Monro, washed ashore some forty miles from Fort Niagara and served for a time as proof of foul play to Morgan.

In the meantime, anti-Masonic sentiment spread rapidly throughout the upper half of western New York, and entered local politics as a divisive issue. For a time anti-Masonry excited little or no interest outside of New York, although in that state the National Republican Party named a state ticket containing the names of no Masons. An Anti-Masonic Convention met at Utica, N. Y., in 1828, and nominated a ticket pledged to oppose Masonry. The slate received a scant poll; but the party increased rapidly, becoming by 1830 the second largest political group in New York state. An Anti-Masonic Party convened at Baltimore, Md., in September 1831 (the first national nominating convention in American history), and nominated William Wirt for the presidency. The convention, in a long address to the people, borrowed the passage from the First Inaugural of Thomas Jefferson, in which he declared sixteen essential principles of democracy. The address charged that Freemasonry subverted these principles. The party received a small vote in the canvass of 1832, winning the electoral vote of Vermont only.

During the ensuing decade, anti-Masons drifted into the Whig organization, forming a powerful faction within that party of factions and the Anti-Masonic Party declined about as rapidly as it had arisen. G. H. K.

ANTI-MONOPOLY PARTY, an American political party organized at Chicago, Ill., May 14, 1884, to participate in the presidential contest of that year, a forerunner of the Populist Party. Farmers, especially Grange members, had organized Anti-Monopoly parties, sometimes called Reform or Independent parties, during the 1870's. These generally demanded reforms of a political and economic nature, and in some instances succeeded in securing enactment of legislation regulating the railroads, as the Granger laws. The 1884 convention nominated Benjamin F. Butler of Massachusetts for President on a platform demanding laws for the regulation of interstate commerce, the popular election of United States senators, free trade, a graduated income tax, a labor bureau, industrial arbitration, payment of the national debt as it matures, and "fostering care" for agriculture. When Butler accepted the presidential nomination of the Greenback-Labor Party, the Anti-Monopoly Party lost its identity. G. H. K.

ANTIMONY [a'ntɪmoni], symbol Sb (Lat. *stibium*), a chemical element which is a member of Group V-A, the nitrogen family, of the periodic table. There are three allotropic modifications of the element, the stable form being a silvery-white metallic-looking solid.

Properties. Antimony is an amphoteric element. It resembles nonmetals in being brittle, in being a poor conductor of heat and electricity, and in yielding stable anions like $SbO_4^{\equiv}$. It also shows metallic properties in its brilliant luster and in its ability to form alloys and to give up three valence electrons, forming Sb^{+++}.

When heated in air, antimony melts, forming brilliant globules looking like mercury. On solidifying, it expands slightly. The heated metal combines slowly with oxygen, giving a white smoke of the oxides Sb_2O_3 and Sb_2O_4. It combines directly with the halogens and sulphur. With various metals, it forms antimonides such as that of copper, CuSb, in which its valence is —2, and iron, Fe_2Sb_3, in which its valence is —3. It does not dissolve in hydrochloric acid; nitric acid converts the metal into oxides.

PROPERTIES OF ANTIMONY

Atomic number	51
Atomic Weight	121.76
Stable isotopes	121, 123
Density (g./ml.), 20°C.	6.62
Melting Point, °C.	630.5
Boiling Point, (1 atm.)°C.	1,440
Specific Heat (cal./g.)	0.050
Heat conductivity, 0-30°C.	0.042
Linear coefficient of thermal expansion	10.8
Young's modulus of elasticity (lb./in.²)	11.3
Hardness (Mohs' scale)	3-3.3
Electrical Resistivity (microhm-cm.) 20°C.	41.7

Applications and Compounds. *Alloys.* Antimony is used principally in making alloys, usually with tin and lead. It adds to the metal's hardness and provides the property of expansion on solidification. Such alloys are useful in making sharp castings for type metal. One per cent of antimony added to lead gives the metal covering for telephone cables; 12 to 15 per cent antimony gives hard lead or antimonial lead, used in battery plates and in acid lines; and 13 to 30 per cent antimony, alloyed with tin and lead, gives type and linotype metal which expands slightly on solidifying, thus ensuring a sharp imprint. Other alloys usually containing antimony include bearing metal, pewter, britannia metal, and stereotype metal.

Oxides. The trioxide, Sb_2O_3, is formed by burning the metal in air; the pentoxide, Sb_2O_5, by repeated heating of the metal in nitric acid; and the tetroxide, Sb_2O_4, presumably antimonous antimonate, $Sb(SbO_4)$, by heating either of the other oxides in air. The oxides form weak acids similar to those of arsenic. The salts of antimony acids are easily hydrolyzed. The trioxide is also weakly basic, forming salts with acids like the nitrate, $Sb(NO_3)_3$, and the sulfate, $Sb_2(SO_4)_3$.

Other Compounds. Potassium antimonyl tartrate (tartar emetic), $KSbO \cdot C_4H_4O_6$, is used in medicine and in dyeing cloth. Antimony trichloride, $SbCl_3$, known as butter of antimony because of its consistency, forms a deliquescent crystalline mass which fumes in the air and is readily hydrolyzed, giving the insoluble oxychloride SbOCl. This reaction is easily reversed by hydrochloric acid. Stibine, SbH_3, is a colorless gas produced when a soluble antimony salt is introduced into a hydrogen generator. It is an analogue of ammonia (NH_3), phosphine (PH_3), and arsine (AsH_3), but it is less stable than these compounds. Antimony trisulphide, Sb_2S_3, is used in veterinary medicine and in the manufacture of pyrotechnics, matches, and paints. B. S. H.

ANTINOMIANISM [aˈntɪnoˈmɪənɪzəm], a word meaning "against law." It is applied to a heresy which begins with an undervaluing of the moral law of God and which often leads to immoral teaching and practice. Antinomian tendencies are found in the Gnostics, in the mystical sects of the Middle Ages, in Agricola, in the Libertines, in the Familists, in the Ranters, in Mrs. Anne Hutchinson, and in various schools of Perfectionism. Antinomianism exaggerates the difference between the Old and New Testaments and denies the obligatory nature of the Ten Commandments for Christians. It sees in the law only a covenant of works and so rejects it in every form as work-righteousness, or legalism. It perverts the teaching of the Apostle Paul by magnifying certain of his statements to the neglect of others. The Apostle says, in Galatians, that the law is a schoolmaster to lead us to Christ that we may be justified by faith. Thus the believer is not "under law" as a means of earning righteousness, and the law no longer holds terrors and torments for him, for in the New Testament dispensation of grace, the righteousness of Christ is freely given to him by faith. So far the Antinomian follows Paul, but he slights Paul's further contention that the law is the will of man's loving Heavenly Father, the criterion by which the child of God continually examines himself that he may seek the power of the Holy Spirit for sanctification and that accordingly the law is good and the commandment to follow it is holy and just. To Paul, the believer comes to love God first as the Saviour, the grace-giver, but he loves the same God when he finds that He is also the lawgiver; and loving the lawgiver, he loves the law which God the Saviour has given. Properly understood, the will of the Creator is always law for the creature, and He has given the moral law to restrain transgression, to reveal sin and lead to the Saviour, and to guide the life of faith.

W. C. Ro.

ANTINOÜS [antɪˈnoəs], the most insolent of the suitors of Penelope in Homer's *Odyssey;* the first of the suitors to be slain by Odysseus.

G. E. D.

ANTIOCH. *See* ANTAKYA.

ANTIOCH [aˈntɪɒk], a city in north central California, in Contra Costa Co., on the San Joaquin Deep Waterways, about 39 mi. northeast of Oakland. Silica sand and gravel are found in the vicinity. The city was settled in 1849, and its name was adopted in 1851 at a picnic attended by the community's entire populace of forty. In 1871 Antioch experienced a severe fire, but by 1872 the city was rebuilt and was incorporated in that year. Transportation is furnished by the Atchison, Topeka & Santa Fe and by the Southern Pacific railroads. In addition to making paper containers, the chief manufacture, the city's industries comprise packing and canning of the tomatoes, peaches, and asparagus grown in the region. Pop. 1950, 11,051.

ANTIOCH, SIEGE OF, an important action of the First Crusade. It began Oct. 21, 1097. The Christians were too few to surround the city and shut off the supplies constantly brought in to the Moslem garrison. The siege continued in desultory fashion throughout the winter, under trying conditions for the besiegers. In the spring of 1098, an Italian fleet arrived with supplies and siege engines, enabling the Crusaders to invest the city closely. It might have held out for many months if Prince Bohemond I had not been able to bribe a Turkish officer to open one of the gates. On June 4, 1098, the Crusaders entered the city, just five days before they were themselves besieged by a large force brought up by Kerboga, the emir of Mosul. The Christians were soon starving, but inspired by the discovery of a sacred relic, the Holy Lance, they combined under the leadership of Bohemond on June 28 to gain a decisive victory over the Mohammedans.

F. C. H.

ANTIOCH COLLEGE, a privately controlled, coeducational, nonsectarian liberal arts college in Yellow Springs, Ohio, 18 mi. east of Dayton. It was chartered in 1852; first instruction was offered the same year under Horace Mann, the institution's first president. All courses in this accredited

ANTIOCH HALL, ANTIOCH COLLEGE

institution are on the co-operative work-study plan, which provides for alternate periods of work and study as an integral part of education, supplementary to the academic program. This co-operative plan places students in approximately 500 positions in 30 states. Each job is usually held by two students who alternate. Arrangements are in effect with several medical, professional, and art schools, such as the Yale School of Drama, the Harvard Medical School, and the Western Reserve School of Nursing, whereby certain courses in these institutions may be counted toward obtaining a degree from Antioch.

Degrees offered are A.B. and B.S. in liberal arts and may be earned in five years. Each academic year under the Antioch plan consists of two alternate academic periods of eight weeks each and two alternate academic periods of twelve weeks each; the summer vacation lasts ten weeks.

Another unique feature at Antioch is the Community Government, to which all students and faculty members belong and contribute. Community Government, through Community Council (the student-faculty legislative body) and the community manager, a student, controls an expenditure of $50,000 a year. It owns and operates a bookstore, sets up and administers campus standards of conduct, furnishes an extensive program of social activities, maintains a fire squad, formulates and enforces fire and traffic rules, maintains insurance on students' belongings, allocates funds to extracurricular activities, and operates a transportation bureau and various other activities.

Dormitory facilities were provided for more than half of the student body in 1949, when an additional dormitory and apartments were constructed.

Scholarship and student-loan funds are available. The co-operative plan, administered by the personnel department, supersedes the usual forms of self-help, since students earn wages under the co-operative plan. *For statistics see* COLLEGES AND UNIVERSITIES.

J. R. To.

ANTIOCHUS [antɑi'okəs], the name of several kings of the Seleucid Dynasty, the founder of which was Seleucus Nicator, a general under Alexander the Great. The most noteworthy of these kings were:

Antiochus I (Soter). Antiochus I, who reigned 281-262 B.C., came into power after the assassination of his father, Seleucus Nicator. He repelled an invasion by the Gauls from the north, and fought the Egyptians under Ptolemy in the south. The chief concern of his reign was the problem of keeping the Seleucid Empire together, and defending it against encroaching neighbors.

Antiochus II (Theos). Antiochus II, who reigned 262-247 B.C., continued the struggle with the Egyptians, but finally made peace by marrying Berenice, daughter of Ptolemy Philadelphus of Egypt.

Antiochus III (The Great). Antiochus III, who reigned 223-187 B.C., was a nephew of Antiochus II. He defended the empire against Molon and Achaeus, who had attempted to usurp control, and in defeating them restored the eastern boundaries and Asia Minor to the empire. He was, however, defeated by the Egyptians at Raphia in 217. From 212 to 205 he fought the Parthians and the Bactrians and was finally forced to make an inconclusive peace. In 198 he again went to war with the Egyptians, this time conquering Palestine and Coele-Syria. He had by then regained possession of all the original territory of the Seleucid Empire. In 192, against the advice of Hannibal, who had sought refuge in his kingdom, he crossed over to Greece at the invitation of the Aetolian League. This brought him into contact with the Romans, who requested him to withdraw and at his refusal defeated him at Thermopylae in 191 and vanquished his fleet. In the following year he was again defeated by the Roman general L. Scipio, at Magnesia in Asia Minor, and in 188 Antiochus sued for peace. Under the terms of the treaty he lost his entire fighting forces and all the territory west of Mount Taurus which he had regained for his empire. He was murdered in 187 while plundering the temple in Elymais for funds with which to pay indemnities to the Romans. The reign of Antiochus III marked the high point as well as the beginning of the decline of Seleucid influence in the affairs of the ancient world.

Antiochus IV (Epiphanes). Antiochus IV, who reigned 175-164 B.C., had been given as a hostage to the Romans in 188. Through the intervention of Eumenes, he succeeded his brother Seleucus III to the throne in 175. From 171 to 168 he fought a successful war against the Egyptians, who had sought to regain Palestine and Coele-Syria. He subsequently laid siege to Alexandria and would have taken over complete control of Egypt, but the Romans, fearing any such expansion of another empire, forced him to relinquish his ambitions. Antiochus Epiphanes acquired a reputation for cruelty by his efforts to Hellenize the Jews. The persecutions which they suffered brought about the Maccabaean revolt, instigated by Mattathias and his sons, and marked the rebirth of active Judaism. Antiochus died during an abortive campaign into Persia in 164 B.C.   C. W. D.

ANTIOPE [antɑi'opi], in Greek mythology, the name of two women. The more famous was the daughter either of the river god Asopus or of Nycteus, king of Thebes, and the mother by Zeus of the twins Amphion and Zethus. Persecuted by Lycus, king of Thebes, and his jealous wife Dirce, she escaped to her sons, who as herdsmen had been commanded by Dirce to tie Antiope to the horns of a bull. Learning that Antiope was their mother, however, they killed Lycus and had Dirce dragged to death by the bull. Another Antiope was a princess of the Amazons and later the wife of Theseus. *See also* AMAZONS; THESEUS.
    G. E. D.

ANTIOQUIA [ɑ'ntio'kyɑ], the second largest department of Colombia. With an area of 25,419 sq. mi., it lies in the heart of the mountain district, west of the Magdalena River, and is traversed by rivers and the central mountain range. It is most important as a manufacturing center, but it is also an important center for mining and agriculture. Nearly one fourth of the coffee exported from Colombia comes from Antioquia and brings a high price. The forests contain hardwood and rubber. The department has five good-sized cities besides the capital, Medellín, which, with an estimated population in 1949 of 185,000, is second only to Bogotá in the republic. Between thirty and forty other towns have populations of 10,000 or more. In more than 300 manufacturing plants, large and small, Antioquia produces cotton and woolen textiles, iron ware, shoes, soap, candy, sugar, and other products. Private wealth is considerable and the banking institutions are important. Hotels are excellent; theatres and plazas, attractive. The University of Medellín is a leading educational center. Antioquia has also numerous private schools and special institutions for vocational education. Est. pop. 1949, 1,400,000.   S. G. I.

ANTIPATER [antɪ'pətər] (d. 319 B.C.), Macedonian general, was born soon after 400 B.C., the son of Iollas, a general under Philip of Macedon. Antipater served under both Philip and Alexander the Great, and he was as much a political as a military figure. In 346 he was sent as ambassador to Athens by Philip, and in 338 he was again sent to Greece to negotiate the Treaty of Chaeronea. When Alexander departed for Asia (the campaign of 334-323) he appointed Antipater acting regent of Macedonia. During this regency Antipater successfully suppressed a Thracian uprising and, at Megalopolis in 330, quelled a Spartan insurrection led by King Agis. Owing to dissension between him and Olympias, mother of Alexander, Antipater was summoned to Asia in 324, the intention being that Craterus should replace him as regent, but the death of Alexander in 323 interrupted this scheme, and he returned to Macedonia as joint governor with Craterus. That same year he participated in a campaign against the Greeks, known as the Lamian War, and defeated them at Crannon in 322, obtaining the submission of Athens. Demosthenes, the orator and leader of the rebellious Athenians, subsequently committed suicide. The following year Antipater formed an alliance with Ptolemy, governor of Egypt, and departed for Asia to suppress Perdiccas, who was seeking to usurp control of the empire. Perdiccas, however, was murdered, and Antipater ruled as supreme regent for two years. Antipater died in 319, after appointing Polyperchon as his successor, passing over his own son Cassander.   C. W. D.

ANTIPHONY [antɪ'fəni] is (1) the singing or playing of music by separate and alternating groups of performers, or (2) music so sung or played. The term was originally used in connection with Catholic Church chants called antiphons, which were sung by alternating choirs.   F. C. C.

ANTIPODES [antɪ'podiz], a scientific as well as a popular term that refers to two places or any two things diametrically opposite. Geographically, the term is applied to any two points on the earth's surface that are located exactly opposite each other. These opposite points could be joined by an imaginary straight line that passes through the center of the earth. An antipodal position assumes that there are 180° of longitude between the two points and that one point is as many degrees of latitude south of the equator as the other point is north of the equator, or vice versa as the case may be. For example, south of New Zealand is a group of small islands (49° 38′ S. lat. and 178° 30′ E. long.) that are named Antipodes because they are on the opposite side of the globe from the southeast coast of England. Actually, the antipodal position of 49° 38′ S. lat. and 178° 30′ E. long. is 49° 38′ N. lat. and 1° 30′ W. long. which is closer to Cherbourg, France, than to England. The British commonly refer to New Zealand as the Antipodes, because the New Zealand Islands are close to being on the opposite side of the globe from the British Islands. Some other examples of antipodal locations are as follows: Kergulen Island in the Antarctic Ocean at 49° 30′ S. lat. and 70° E. long. is exactly opposite 49° 30′ N. lat. and 110° W. long., which is a point just southeast of Medicine Hat, Alberta. St. Paul Island in the Indian Ocean at 38° 42′ S. lat. and 77° 34′ E. long. is an antipode of 38° 42′ N. lat. and 102° 26′ W. long., which is the location of a point near Cheyenne Wells, east central Colorado.

J. E. F.

ANTIPODES ISLANDS, an isolated group of small, rocky islands in the South Pacific Ocean southeast of South Island, New Zealand (49° 38′ S. lat. and 178° 30′ E. long.). The total area is about 24 sq. mi., but the islands are strung out over a distance of four to five miles in a north-south line. The group was discovered in 1800 by Captain Waterhouse of the British naval vessel *Reliance* while homeward bound from Port Jackson, Australia. Later the islands became an important base for sealers. The name Antipodes was given to the group because it is located on the globe diametrically opposite to England. The islands, which are uninhabited, are nesting places for petrels and penguins. The group is included in the geographical boundaries of New Zealand.   R. G. B.

ANTI-RENT PARTY, a political party organized in 1842 in the state of New York as a means of abolishing by state action the leasehold system inherited from the patroon era. Much farm land in the older counties of Albany, Columbia, Delaware, Schoharie, and others, included in great estates, had been subdivided and leased in perpetuity or for very long periods of time in return for ground rent paid in kind, labor, and money; the landlords exacted certain feudal dues in the case of transfers of leaseholds (or other contingencies) amounting in some instances to a quarter or a third of the realized sale of the leasehold.

The anti-rent agitation, which swept the affected areas from 1839 to 1846, broke into violence when the heirs of Stephen Van Rensselaer attempted to collect about $400,000 in delinquent rents and dues. Disguised as Indians, bands of farmers terrorized the district and tarred and feathered or abused sheriffs and deputies attempting to force collections, serve writs of ejection, or make arrests. The agitation increased in intensity and eventuated in some bloodshed, while the state sought to preserve law and order by authorizing the use of militia. Following its organization in 1842, the Anti-Rent Party gained control of several counties and in 1846 elected its candidate, John Young, nominally a Whig, to the governorship. By the end of 1846, the state amended its constitution to prohibit new feudal tenures, and the courts declared "one-quarter sales" illegal. A general conversion of old leases into ownership in fee simple resulted.   G. H. K.

ANTI-SALOON LEAGUE OF AMERICA, an interdenominational temperance movement, officially organized Dec. 17, 1895, which had begun in Ohio and in the District of Columbia in 1893 to outlaw the saloon through local option. As no-license areas increased, state-wide prohibition became the objective. Later, when the United States Supreme Court reversed earlier decisions and held that the states were without power to regulate interstate liquor traffic, the league supported both the Wilson Act (1890) and the Webb-Kenyon Act (1913) to make liquors introduced into states subject to state police power.

The growth of prohibition sentiment and the delay in securing a satisfactory ruling from the Supreme Court upholding the right of the states to protect themselves from liquor shipped in interstate commerce caused the Anti-Saloon League at its convention in Columbus, Ohio, in 1913, to advocate a prohibition amendment to the United States Constitution. A resolution for such a constitutional amendment, offered by Sen. Morris Sheppard of Texas in the Senate and by Representative E. Y. Webb of North Carolina in the House, was ratified by the legislatures of 46 of the 48 states and became part of the federal Constitution as the Eighteenth Amendment, Jan. 16, 1919, to be effective one year later.

The League, directed by Wayne B. Wheeler, was aggressive in its support of legislation to enforce the Eighteenth Amendment. Forty-seven of the states at some period enacted state enforcement laws, and special or local acts were enacted in most of the areas of the remaining state. Notable among the measures enacted by Congress, which the League supported, was the Volstead Act (1919).

With the repeal of the Eighteenth Amendment by ratification of the Twenty-first Amendment on Dec. 5, 1933, the League began a campaign for local-option legislation and urged Congress to enact measures to protect the states against the importation of liquor for delivery or use therein, as prohibited by the second section of the new amendment.

At the national convention in Pittsburgh, Pa., on Jan. 20, 1948, the name of the organization was changed to The Temperance League of America, with headquarters in Washington, D. C.   E. B. D.

ANTISANA [ɑ′ntisɑ′nɑ], a volcanic peak 18,714 ft. high, 30 mi. southeast of Quito in the Ecuadorian Andes. Although apparently inactive, it is thought by some to be the source of occasional quakes felt in Quito. Its base covers a large area, and its snow-capped summit is marked by two cones.   P. E. J.

ANTISEPTIC [a′ntisɛ′ptɪk], any substance which prevents the growth of microorganisms. A compound which actually kills microorganisms is a disinfectant, or germicide. Since many substances may fulfill the requirements of both, depending on the concentration, time, temperature, and other factors of application, the terms are often used interchangeably. In general, antiseptics are used in or upon a living animal or plant, where their usefulness depends upon their ability to suppress viral, bacterial, fungous, or protozoal growth without harming the host harboring these parasites. Disinfectants are of most use in sanitation and public health; antiseptics, in medicine. Destruction of higher parasites (worms, mites, and insects) is defined as disinfectation. A deodorant or insecticide may or may not be antiseptic, and vice versa. The complete destruction of all forms of microorganisms, with their spores, is called sterilization.

It is primarily with bacterial and protozoal diseases, rather than those of viral origin, that antiseptics are concerned. Viruses and rickettsiae exist in the host's body within living cells. Any substance destroying viruses in the body would tend also to destroy the invaded cell and many others. An exception may be made of the antiviral action of some of the newer antibiotics.

Death of Bacteria. Much research has gone into this problem, since it concerns not only treatment and prevention of disease, but also agriculture, food preservation, fermentation, and the like. Methods of inhibiting or killing bacteria may be divided into physical and chemical. Examples of the former are light, drying, and heat. Antiseptics are all chemical inhibitors. When bacteria are treated either by a killing degree of heat or by a chemical disinfectant, death of the whole culture is not immediate, since vulnerability to the killing agent varies from one bacterial cell to another. When death rate is plotted against time, it is evident that many bacteria are killed immediately, with a sharp drop thereafter, gradually flattening out in a characteristic parabolic curve. Spore-bearing bacteria are harder to kill. Some bacterial species, as the tubercle bacillus, have waxy, protective constituents, or capsules, which render them relatively resistant to drying and to antiseptic agents.

Chemical antiseptics attack the bacterial cell in a variety of ways. Examples are the surface-tension depression of soap and water on bacterial cell membranes, alteration of bacterial hydrogen-ion concentration (pH) by acids and alkalies, coagulation of bacterial proteins by minerals and many other protoplasmic poisons, selective toxic dyeing action, and oxidation.

Standardization of Antiseptics. Since so much variability exists in the rapidity and thoroughness of action of different antiseptics, and since bacteria vary so in their susceptibility, it seems desirable to standardize each antiseptic by comparison to a selected "yardstick" of antiseptic action. Such a yardstick is the phenol coefficient. Phenol, or carbolic acid, is, historically, the prototype of all antiseptics. Dr. Joseph Lister, the great British surgeon, discovered this use for phenol in 1867, when he found that soaking his hands, instruments, and his patients' skin with phenol, prior to operation, tremendously reduced the rate of postoperative infection. The phenol coefficient of any antiseptic is determined by dividing the reciprocal of its minimum killing concentration by the reciprocal of the minimum killing concentration of phenol against the same organism under the same conditions. The following familiar antiseptics are listed in order of their diminishing phenol coefficients: merphenyl nitrate, metaphen, merthiolate, bichloride of mercury, hexylresorcinol, tincture of iodine, Lysol, Mercurochrome, Dakin's solution, Formalin, Pepsodent antiseptic, Listerine antiseptic, and hydrogen peroxide. Antiseptics which are also aromatic compounds related to phenol include the cresols, resorcinol, guaiacol, and thymol.

Antiseptic Dyes. Since microorganisms vary greatly in their staining qualities and in their affinity for certain dyes, many compounds of this class have been found to be antiseptics. For instance, the gram-positive bacteria have a strong attachment for gentian violet, an aniline dye, which also inhibits their growth. Other examples of this class are acriflavine (active particularly against gram-negative bacteria), methylene blue, and the azo dyes, the latter being particularly useful as urinary antiseptics. The antimalarial yellow-dye drug atabrin should be included in this category.

Oxidizing Agents. Various compounds liberate nascent oxygen, which is very destructive to bacteria. Examples are potassium permanganate, hydrogen peroxide, and sodium perborate, all efficient skin and mouth antiseptics, particularly against anaerobic bacteria. The halogens, chlorine and iodine, in solution, also are oxidizing agents. The element iodine in standard 7 per cent alcoholic solution (tincture) is the most widely used of all skin antiseptics; it has recently been shown to be as effective and less irritating in ½ per cent solution. The related compound iodoform has a limited surgical use. Chlorine compounds used as antiseptics (largely in infected wounds) include Dakin's solution (a hypochlorite), dichloramine-T, and Azochloramid.

Metallic Compounds. This category is of interest because it includes certain highly selective or specific compounds. Many are used in vulnerable sites of the body, like the eye or the blood stream, because of their wide difference of toxic action on host tissue and invading organism. Mercury, bismuth, and arsenic in various organic and inorganic compounds have an honorable history in the treatment of syphilis. Ehrlich's famous antisyphilitic arsenicals Salvarsan and Neosalvarsan ("606" and "914") have modern analogues in Mapharsen (antisyphilitic); Carbarsone and Acetarsone (active against amoebic dysentery); and Tryparsamide (used against African sleeping sickness). Pentavalent antimony, as in the drug Neostibosan, similarly inhibits the protozoan cause of leishmaniasis. One per cent solution of silver nitrate has a highly specific action against the gonococcus, hence its wide use in the eyes of new-born babies to prevent gonorrheal blindness. Organic silver in the form of Argyrol, Neosilvol, and Protargol have wide use in rhinolaryngology and urology. A cheap and powerful coagulant germicide is mercuric chloride (bichloride of mercury), with a limited use as an antiseptic when in high dilution (1/10 per cent or less). Less dangerous and corrosive mercurial antiseptics are the organic synthetics merthiolate, metaphen, and the red dye Mercurochrome.

Miscellaneous Antiseptics. Two alkaloids (plant extractives), quinine and emetine, should be mentioned for their remarkable action against the protozoa of malaria and amoebic dysentery, respectively. Certain alcohols (ethyl, isopropyl), glycol, and glycerol are moderately antiseptic. Seventy per cent is the optimum antiseptic concentration of the widely used ethyl alcohol. Formaldehyde has a special action as a urinary antiseptic when combined with ammonia as methenamine (Urotropin). Various weak acids (boric, benzoic, and undecylinic) have specialized uses, especially as skin fungicides. Para-amino-benzoic acid, Paba, shows promise in controlling rickettsial diseases. Investigation of antiseptic properties of sulphonic acid derivatives led to the discovery of the powerful antiseptics, the sulphonamides. These, with penicillin, streptomycin, and other mold derivatives are given special treatment elsewhere. *See also* ANTIBIOTICS; BACTERIOLOGY; MALARIA; RICKETTSIA; VIRUS.

F. P. Ma.

ANTI-SLAVERY. See ABOLITIONISTS.

ANTITRUST LAWS, FEDERAL. See BUSINESS ORGANIZATION AND MANAGEMENT.

ANTIUM. See ANZIO.

ANTLIA [a'ntliə], the Air Pump, a newly-discovered constellation located immediately south of Hydra and centered at about declination −32°. It is composed of faint stars only. Antlia is visible in the southern sky from any point in the United States.

J. H. P.

ANT LION, is the name given to the various members of the family Myrmelionidae, of the order Neuroptera. The adults have four wings with many long veins and numerous crossveins, and the antennae are conspicuously clubbed; and if the Ascalophidae are included, the antennae are long.

The insects resemble damsel flies; in some, the hind wings are greatly modified to form long "tails." In the American species, the wings are similar, and the adults fly with a motion that suggests a lazy helicopter. The most interesting phase in the life of an ant lion is the larval, or doodle-bug, stage. The majority of the larvae of ant lions build funnels in the soil in sheltered places, such as under bridges, boards, or on the broad leaves of plants. Their victims fall into these; they may be ants or any other crawling creature. The soil is kept loose so that when the victim attempts to crawl up the sides, it finds itself in great difficulty. Should it succeed in nearing the top, the doodle-bug, using its long, strong proboscis, throws soil above the struggling victim, thus causing it to fall back. If the victim comes within reach of the mandibles, it is grasped and held until its body is sucked dry. The larva is provided with forwardly directed hooks and spines in order to hold itself in its burrow. Other related forms live in sand, debris, or on foliage, and ambush their prey. C. H. Cu.

ANTOFAGASTA [ɑ'ntofɑgɑ'stɑ], an important seaport in northern Chile, the capital of the province of the same name, about 650 mi. north of Valparaiso. It is northern Chile's most important commercial center. The many minerals mined in the area—the most important being nitrate, its by-product iodine, and copper from Chuquicamata, about 160 mi. inland—are shipped from Antofagasta. In addition, more than 50 per cent of Bolivia's exports and 30 per cent of its imports pass through the port. Vessels anchor off shore, and landing is by boat. There are rail connections to La Paz, Bolivia, and in 1947 a railroad to northern Argentina was being completed. The Pan American World Airways also provides air transport facilities connecting Antofagasta with Arica, Chile, and with Salta, Argentina. Pop. 1949, 52,000. S. G. I.

ANTOINE, ANDRÉ [ã'twa'n] (1858-1943), French actor and stage director, was born in Limoges, Jan. 31, 1858. Having gone to work at the age of twelve, he acquired only a haphazard education, largely through frequenting libraries and museums and attending Taine's lectures on the history of art. In 1875 he became a paid claqueur at the Comédie-Française in Paris; presently he was employed there as a supernumerary, took evening classes in diction and recitation, and staged student productions, but he was denied admission to the acting course at the Conservatoire. After five years of military service, he returned to Paris, joined the amateur Cercle Gaulois while working for a gas company, and in 1887 organized the Théâtre Libre for the purpose of producing new plays.

With the Théâtre Libre, Antoine achieved distinction as a character actor, director, and manager, discovering new playwrights such as Eugène Brieux, Georges de Porto-Riche, and François de Curel, and introducing the masterpieces of European realistic drama to the French public. Although disinclined to commit himself exclusively to the naturalistic dramatists of the school of Zola, he was nevertheless the first to produce their works. Influenced by the Meiningen Company, which was famous for its realistic settings and mob scenes, he became an advocate of its techniques and carried stage realism further than anyone before him. He banished conventional painted backdrops and built solid, authentic scenery; employed lighting from above instead of footlights; stressed the playing of all roles in character, with natural speech and gestures; allowed the actor to turn his back to the audience when occasion arose; and abolished the actor's practice of stepping out of the stage background, posing for the audience, and making tableaux.

After losing control of the Théâtre Libre, Antoine established the Théâtre Antoine in 1897 and in 1906 moved to the state-subsidized Odéon. He resigned from the Odéon shortly before the outbreak of World War I, but continued to exert an influence on the French theatre as a dramatic critic. He died at Pouligneu, Brittany, Oct. 21, 1943. *See also* THÉÂTRE LIBRE. J. Ga.

ANTONELLI, GIACOMO [ɑntonɛ'lli] (1806-1876), Italian cardinal, was born at Sonnino, April 2, 1806. He began his ecclesiastical studies at Rome, later changing to law. He distinguished himself in the Vatican diplomatic service and became a minister of state. Ordained deacon in 1840, he was created cardinal by Pius IX and made premier of that Pope's first constitutional ministry in May 1848. He arranged the flight of Pius to Gaeta; there he became papal secretary of state and, returning to Rome with the Pope in 1848, retained his power up to the time of his death, Nov. 6, 1876. Until 1870 he was practically the temporal ruler of the Papal States. W. C.

ANTONELLO DA MESSINA [ɑ'ntonɛ'llo dɑ messi'nɑ] (c. 1430-1479), Sicilian painter of the early Renaissance in Italy, was born at Messina about 1430, the son of a sculptor, Giovanni di Michele degli Antoni.

The style of Antonello shows that the artist was versatile and that he was impressed by the products of foreign schools of art with which he came in contact. Early influences upon his art appear to have been Flemish, although it is not known whether he traveled to Flanders or whether he studied northern works of art which reached Italy. The small size of his portraits, the precise detail of such works as his *Annunciation,* at Syracuse in Sicily, and his oil-glaze technique seem to be Flemish traits. In 1475 he worked in Venice and Milan, returning to Messina where he died at the age of forty-nine in 1479.

Antonello's style and technique had a strong influence upon Renaissance painters in Italy and the north. Among his most famous works are the *Crucifixion,* in Antwerp, the portrait called *Il Condottiere,* in the Louvre, Paris, the *Pietà* in the Correr Museum, Venice, and fragments of his most ambitious project, the San Cassiano Altarpiece in Vienna. B. C. G.

ANTONINUS, ST. [a'ntonai'nəs] (1389-1459), Archbishop of Florence, was born at Florence, Italy, Mar. 1, 1389, as Antonio Pierozzi. He became a Dominican in 1405 and held various administrative posts from 1414 to 1446. In 1436 he established at Florence the famous convent of St. Mark, assisted as theologian at the Council of Florence in 1439, and was forced by Pope Eugene IV to accept the archbishopric of Florence, which he ruled with zeal and kindness from 1446 until his death, May 2, 1459. His principal work, on moral theology, and the later part of his world history are valuable historical sources. He was canonized by Pope Adrian VI, May 31, 1523. His feast is May 10. N. J. T.

ANTONINUS PIUS (TITUS AURELIUS FULVUS BOIONIUS ARRIUS ANTONINUS) (A.D. 86-161), who became Roman emperor in A.D. 138, was born in A.D. 86, the son of the Roman consul Aurelius Fulvus. Antoninus was a sound and careful administrator who, after years of public service, was chosen by the Emperor Hadrian to be his successor. His long and peaceful reign was marked by accord with the senate, humanitarian reforms, and the strengthening of

Rome's frontier defenses. When he died after a brief illness in A.D. 161, Antoninus was succeeded by his adopted sons, Marcus Aurelius and Lucius Aurelius Verus.　　　T. B. J.

ANTONY, MARK or **MARCUS ANTONIUS** (c. 83-30 B.C.), Roman general and statesman, was born about 83 B.C. Marcus Antonius, the third generation to bear this name, achieved his first success through Julius Caesar. Raised in quick succession from quaestor, to augur, and tribune, he espoused Caesar's cause so violently that when civil war broke out he was excluded from the senate. After a brief disagreement, Antony again sided with Caesar and was consul with him in 44 B.C. at the time of Caesar's death. He aroused the people against Caesar's murderers and forced them to flee from Rome. At first Antony refused to ally himself with Caesar's heir, Octavian, who had the support of Caesar's veterans. As a result Octavian sided with the senate and took the field against Antony, whom he defeated at Mutina in 43 B.C. Later, however, because the senate did not reward him suitably for his services, Octavian joined with Antony and Lepidus in the Second Triumvirate. The triumvirs overawed the senate and carried out a program of confiscation and execution; one of their first victims was Cicero. Next, Antony and Octavian moved against Brutus and Cassius in Thessaly, where the two principal assassins of Caesar were wiped out in the second battle of Philippi in 42 B.C. While the Second Triumvirate was in existence from 43 to 33 B.C., Antony was responsible for the Roman provinces in the East, and it was there that he met Cleopatra. After Antony's first wife, Fulvia, died, he married Octavia, the sister of Octavian, as a pledge of friendship with Octavian. Antony was now formally assigned the government of the East, which he signalized by brilliant although unprofitable campaigns against the Parthians in Mesopotamia. About 38 B.C., he divorced Octavia and married Cleopatra. After this, Octavian and Antony became bitter enemies, but there was no open conflict until six years later. In 37 B.C., the triumvirate was renewed for five years, but Antony's notorious infidelity to Octavia and his grant of kingdoms and provinces to Cleopatra alienated his supporters in Rome and led the senate to declare war against Cleopatra. With a large fleet and army, Antony and Cleopatra occupied Actium on the west coast of Greece with the object of invading Italy. Octavian and Agrippa, however, blockaded the Egyptian forces in Actium and precipitated the famous sea battle of 31 B.C., from which Antony and Cleopatra both fled to Egypt. In 30 B.C., when Octavian pursued them to Alexandria, Antony committed suicide upon receipt of a false rumor that Cleopatra was dead.　　　T. B. J.

ANTONY AND CLEOPATRA (1607-1608), a tragedy by Shakespeare. Based on Plutarch's *Lives,* it is a grand panorama of the struggle for power between Rome and the Orient, combined with a dramatic treatment of one of the great love stories of history. It represents in some ways a reversion from Shakespeare's tragedies of the inner life, which culminated in *Macbeth,* to the historical tragedy, set, like *Julius Caesar,* in the world of action. It is in this sense a chronicle play, but a chronicle play with a difference. Shakespeare here suppresses battle scenes and single combats to dwell upon the relation of the two great lovers, not only to each other, but also to the world for which the contest is being waged. The decisive battle of Actium is fought off stage and the subsequent reunion of the lovers is presented in full detail; after Antony's death, the entire last act is devoted to Cleopatra's hopeless struggle with Octavius and her final suicide. Antony is raised by the intensity of his passion to

heroic stature, and Cleopatra has been called "Shakespeare's most sovereign creation." Most of the other characters are swiftly sketched, but Enobarbus, created from a mere hint in the source, is a realistic and cynical commentator on the action, and the Clown of the last act is a Warwickshire peasant who has somehow strayed with his fatal asp into the palace of Cleopatra.

Coleridge asserts that *Antony and Cleopatra* is "by far the most wonderful" of Shakespeare's historical plays; "there is not one in which he has followed history so minutely, and yet there are few in which he impresses the notion of angelic strength so much." This "angelic strength" springs largely from the magical music of Shakespeare's dramatic verse. It is by the spoken word that he conducts the action, portrays the characters, and lifts the whole into the sphere of poetic tragedy.　　　T. M. P.

ANTRIM [a'ntrɪm], in Northern Ireland, the northernmost county of Ireland, bounded on the north and east by the North Channel. On the south lie counties Armagh and Down, the boundary passing through Lough Neagh and along the Lagan River; and on the west are counties Tyrone and Londonderry, the dividing line passing through Lough Neagh and, for 27 mi., along the Bann River. The eastern two thirds of the county is a tableland of basaltic trap, broken by numerous valleys, rising in the northeast to the flat domes of Slievenance (1,782 ft.) and Trostan (1,817 ft.) and farther north in the fine isolated dome of Knocklayd (1,695 ft.). Hills form a broken rim to the basalt plateau, extending on the east from Ballycastle south to Larne, thence along Belfast Lough to Lisburn, and on the west in Londonderry from Magilligan near the entrance to Lough Foyle south to the Sperrin Mountains. Between the two edges is a broad fertile basin whose sunken upper portion is occupied by Lough Neagh, largest freshwater lake in the British Isles, with an area of 153 sq. mi. and a depth of 40 to 50 ft. At the northwest corner is the outlet of the Lough, the Lower Bann, the termination of Ulster's most extensive river system, flowing northward through a rich, well-wooded valley. The final miles and mouth of the Bann are in County Londonderry. Soon after leaving Lough Neagh the Bann expands into Lough Beg, in which are several islands. A low north-and-south ridge divides the trough between the Sperrins and the Antrim plateau into two valleys. The western valley is that of the Bann, and the eastern is occupied by the Main River, flowing south for 25 miles into Lough Neagh. Along the Antrim coast the exposed edges of basalt have been carved into deep glens, "the Glens of Antrim"—Glenshesk, Glendun, Glencorp, Glenaan, Glenballyemon, Glenariff, Glencloy, and Glenarm. The grandest is Glenariff, 4 mi. long and 1,000 ft. deep. A picturesque road skirts the coast from Carrickfergus to Ballycastle. The coastal cliffs approach 400 ft. in height and occasionally, notably at Giant's Causeway in the north, present marvelous columnar structures. Here are 40,000 columns, mostly hexagonal. The chief headlands, north to south, are Bengore Head, Fair Head, Garron Point, and Ballygalley Head. Off the north coast are Rathlin Island and the Skerries; off the east coast, the Maiden Rocks. The Lagan River, 22 mi. long, flows into Belfast Lough, 12 mi. long and 3 mi. broad. At the northeast corner of this lough is Island Magee, a north-south peninsula behind which is Lough Larne. Other major lakes are Lough Guile near Ballymoney, Portmore Lake east of Lough Neagh, and Lough Mourne north of Carrickfergus. Bogs are large and numerous. The Lagan Canal connects Lough Neagh with Belfast Lough. The extreme dimensions of Antrim are 54½

FLAX, SHEAVED AND STACKED IN THE FIELDS TO DRY, COUNTY ANTRIM, NORTHERN IRELAND

mi. north-south and 30 mi. east-west. Its area is 1,176 sq. mi., including over 81 sq. mi. of fresh water.

The January temperature ranges from 40° to 41°F., July temperature from 57° to 60°F., and annual average temperature from 42° to 50°F. January rainfall ranges from 3 to 6 in., July rainfall from 3 to 4 in., and the mean annual rainfall from 30 to 60 in.

The county name is derived from the town of Antrim, which probably means "one tribe" or "one habitation." The northern part was the ancient territory of Dalriada, commonly called the Route. The south was part of Dalaraidhe, later called North Clandeboy, which with South Clandeboy in County Down was the territory of the O'Neills. The district along the coast from Larne to Ballycastle—"the Glens of Antrim"—belonged to the O'Donnells.

There is coal at Ballycastle and salt-mining near Carrickfergus. Iron ore from the hills between Larne and Cushendall is shipped from Larne and other ports to seaports in Cumberland and Wales and on the Firth of Clyde. The staple industries, which occupy most of the population, are spinning linen and cotton yarn, and linen and cotton weaving. Belfast is the second largest Irish city, the foremost industrial city of Ireland, and the capital and premier city of Northern Ireland. Its rapid growth is of quite recent occurrence, and it is rather devoid of historical monuments, associations, or interest. Belfast has regular passenger steamer service to Fleetwood, Liverpool, Heysham, Ardrossan, Greenock, and Ayr. The Great Northern, Midland, and Belfast and County Down railways link Belfast with other towns in Antrim and in counties Londonderry and Down. It is the principal seat of the linen industry of the United Kingdom. Shipbuilding is its second largest industry. In 1947 the Belfast and Govan yards broke a record of 33 years' standing by launching 16 vessels totaling 183,509 tons. Among the city's other products are whisky, tobacco, and rope. Its proximity to the great mining areas of Scotland and the north of England permits the inexpensive importation of iron and coal. The population of the county

borough of Belfast increased from 438,086 in 1937 to a total of 450,800 by the census of 1953.

Carrickfergus (pop. 8,650 in 1952), north of Belfast, with its Norman castle and limestone quarries, was prominent years before the capital. Lisburn (pop. 14,778 in 1951) on the Lagan is a linen center, as is Ballymena (pop. 14,165 in 1951). Antrim (pop. 1,628 in 1937) is about one mile east of Lough Neagh. Larne (pop. 11,976 in 1952), on the coast north of Belfast, has a marine zoological station. Portrush (pop. 4,166 in 1951), near the Giant's Causeway, is a watering place with a coastguard and lifeboat station. There are important salmon fisheries along the coast.

Antrim attained its maximum population of 360,875 in 1841, the inhabitants of Belfast Town accounting for 75,308 of this figure. The county population in 1953, exclusive of the county borough of Belfast, was 232,700. Antrim returns two members to the British House of Commons in London.

J. I. C.

ANTUNG [ɑ'ndʊ'ŋ], one of the nine Manchurian provinces, was established in China in 1945 after the end of Japanese occupation. It was carved out of the old Liaoning Province and is situated on the Chinese-Korean border. Tunghua is its capital. The people in Antung speak a dialect belonging to the northern Mandarin system and very similar to the standard national language, Kuoyu. Antung has an area of 26,300 sq. mi. and in 1947 had a population of 3,213,894.

History. The history of Antung is closely associated with that of the old Liaoning Province. During the period of the Contending States, 403-221 B.C., the whole region of Liaoning belonged to the kingdom of Yen. This region later was placed under the viceroyalty of Liaotung, Liaohsi, and Antung during the Ch'in (255-206 B.C.), Han (206 B.C.-A.D. 220), and T'ang (A.D. 618-907) dynasties, respectively. It became a province, known as Fengtien, in the Ch'ing Dynasty (A.D. 1644-1912). In 1929 the name of the province was changed to Liaoning. Three years later Liaoning became a part of the puppet state, Manchukuo, after the Japanese invasion of Manchuria in September 1931.

Topography and Climate. The province of Antung is a highland formed by the Changpai Mountains, which stretch across the region toward the northeast, with its highest peak, Paitou Shan (8,900 ft.), located north of Changpai County. The Yalu River, 500 mi. long, constitutes a natural boundary on the east between Antung and Korea. The Yalu starts in the hills of the Changpai Mountains, in the eastern part of Kirin Province, and empties into the Yellow Sea at Antung City. The Sungari River, on the northern side of the Changpai Mountains, flows northward to Kirin Province. The average temperature of the province is 42° F. Annual rainfall ranges from 27 in. in the northern part of the province to 39 in. in the south.

Economic Resources and Activities. *Timber and Agricultural Products.* Timber is the principal product of the province. The Yalu River Valley has a forest of about 2,000,000 acres, most of which has been little exploited. Soybeans are produced around Hailung and Tungfeng in the north. Rice, corn, and tobacco are produced around the port city of Antung; and kaoliang around the Tunghua area. Ginseng, a medical herb found in the mountains, has an annual production of 440,000 lb. Fish of various kinds are abundant along the 300-mi. coast of the province between the cities of Antung and Chuangho.

Coal and Minerals. The province abounds in coal deposits, which constitute about 20 per cent of the total reserve in the nine provinces of Manchuria. Coal deposits at Yentung alone are estimated at 30,000,000 tons. Iron ores at Talitzekou are estimated at 70,000,000 tons, containing 63 per cent of iron, while those at Chitaokou are estimated at 10,000,000 tons, containing 53 per cent of iron. Tin found at Fengcheng, in the south of the province, was developed by the Japanese during the puppet regime, with a monthly output of 12,000 tons. Gold ores are found and refined in the Huinan area and areas north of Chinyan. Other mineral resources include lead and tungsten from Kwantien, copper from Huinan, and alum from Fengcheng.

Transportation. The railway network consists of four major lines totaling about 400 mi. The Antung-Shenyang (Mukden) line, 162 mi. from Antung City to Shenyang, in Liaoning Province, is connected with railways of northern Korea. The Meihokow-Chian line, 152 mi., is roughly parallel to the Antung-Shenyang Railway. The Hailung-Yungchi line, 115 mi., crosses from Hailung, in the northern part of the province, to Yungchi, in Kirin Province. The Shenyang-Hailung line, 131 mi., links the Meihokow-Chian line at Meihokow. A small section of the Szepingkai-Shahokow line, in Liaopei Province, extends into the province between Tungfeng and Shahokow. Highways in this province connect Antung City with Kwantien and Fengcheng; Hailung with Tunghua and Fusung; Huanjen and Tunghua with Shenyang, in Liaoning Province; Fengcheng with Chuangho, in Liaoning Province; and Tungfeng with Sifeng, in Liaopei Province. The Yalu River is navigable for about 400 mi. in its lower sections. The upper section is navigable by log raft only when the river is flooded in the autumn. These rafts glide downstream to Antung City, carrying soybeans, kaoliang, and millet to market and bringing back cotton, silk, kerosene, matches, piece goods, and other daily necessities. The rapids in the upper sections have been harnessed in several places to generate electric power. The Suifeng hydroelectric power plant, built over the Yalu, is capable of generating 700,000 kw.

Cities. Tunghua, the provincial capital, is the second largest city in the province with a population of approximately 50,000 in 1947.

The city of Antung is the largest city and the province's only seaport. In 1947 it had approximately 220,000 residents. It is the gateway from Korea to China and is located on the western bank of the Yalu River, about 20 mi. north of the river's mouth and the Bay of Korea, at 39°59′ N. lat. and 124°30′ E. long. Directly opposite the city on the eastern bank of the river are the Korean cities of Gishu and Shingishu. Antung became a treaty port and open to foreign trade in 1903. The port is closed by ice from the end of November through March, and not until the Antung-Shenyang railroad line was completed was the port very active. When Japan took over the control of Korea, the Japanese became interested in the port, and they enlarged and developed it. This was carried on more extensively when the Japanese established the puppet state of Manchukuo in 1932. As a result of improvements, ships can anchor in the deeper water, less liable to freeze, south of the city at Tatung Harbor, but the water is still too shallow to allow large steamers to anchor. For centuries rafts of timber from the hinterland have been floated down the river to Antung for transshipment to other ports in China and overseas. Lumber has figured prominently in the city's industrial life. There are numerous saw mills, and matches and paper pulp are important local products. The city is noted for its large mills producing silks and silk yarns, and at Antung, too, the region's soybeans are processed in the local bean mills.   A. C. T.

ANTWERP (Fr. Anvers, Flem. Antwerpen) [a′ntwзrp, ãvɛr, ɑ′ntvɛrpən], a province and the capital city of that province located in northern Belgium.

The modern city of Antwerp is the country's leading port and commercial center and ranks second in population after Brussels. It is situated at 51°13′ N. lat. and 4°25′ E. long., on the Schelde River, about 26 mi. north of Brussels, and about 50 mi. from the sea. Before World War II it was considered to have had one of the finest harbors in the world, and it ranked among the foremost ports in Europe.

In A.D. 726 Antwerp was a small trading town. It was destroyed by the Normans in 826, but it became very important in the twelfth century. At the end of the fifteenth century, with the silting and closing of the Zwijn and the decline of Bruges, the foreign trade houses were transferred to Antwerp, which rose in importance and enjoyed a fabulous prosperity. Under Charles V (1500-1558) it was the greatest seaport of Europe, even surpassing Venice. In 1576 religious uprisings broke out in the port, as in every other part of Belgium, and the Spanish destroyed the city. Six thousand citizens were killed in "the Spanish fury." Trade almost disappeared after its capture by Parma in 1585. The Treaty of Münster in 1648 closed the Schelde to navigation to favor Amsterdam. This was relaxed under French rule from 1795 to 1814. In 1803 Napoleon found a ruined city and, realizing its strategical importance, assigned 2,000,000 francs for the construction of new docks. In 1830 the Belgian insurgents captured the city, but the citadel was still held by a Dutch garrison which bombed the city and damaged it severely. In December 1832 the Dutch surrendered. Trade revived after 1863 when the trade restrictions of 1648 were removed and the growth of Antwerp steadily continued until the outbreak of World War I. It was then the third port in importance in the world. In October 1914 after ten days of heavy bombardments the city surrendered. On May 18, 1940, during World War II, Antwerp was again occupied by the German

THE HARBOR AT ANTWERP, BELGIUM'S LEADING PORT

army. During the war the port was virtually idle for four years. The city and port facilities were severely damaged by thousands of flying bombs, but the public buildings escaped with little serious damage.

The city is fortified by strong ramparts and numerous citadels and forts. The most noteworthy edifice is the Cathedral of Notre Dame, one of the largest and finest specimens of Gothic architecture in the Low Countries. Its façade was only slightly scarred by World War II activity. It was begun in 1352 and continued during the fifteenth and sixteenth centuries. It contains three famous paintings by Peter Paul Rubens, *The Descent from the Cross, The Elevation of the Cross,* and *The Assumption.* The Church of St. James contains the tomb of Rubens. Other important buildings are the city hall, in the Renaissance style, the Bourse, the Archers' Guild Hall, and the Steen, part of the old tenth-century castle. The Maison Plantin, a typical ancient Flemish house, was the home of the famous fifteenth-century printer Christophe Plantin; it has been maintained as a museum. In the Fine Arts Museum there is an excellent collection of Flemish and Dutch paintings, many representing the school of painters famous in Antwerp in the seventeenth century. Noted among the painters of this era were Peter Rubens, Anthony Van Dyck, Jacob Jordaens, the two Teniers, and the Brueghels. The city's zoological garden has one of the largest collections of rare animals and birds in Europe.

Antwerp is not only a leading port but also an important industrial center where export products are manufactured. The principal industries include diamond cut-ting, sugar refining, distilling, shipbuilding, ship repairing, and the manufacture of chocolate, biscuits, margarine, soap, candles, tobacco, oil, and chemical products. Pop. 1952, (city) 261,405; (province) 1,330,103.   L. B.

ANTWERP, SIEGE OF, a German assault on Antwerp, Belgium, during World War I. The city was the last important place in Belgium still under the control of King Albert, and the Belgians were determined to hold it. The assault began on Sept. 28, 1914, when German howitzers bombarded the surrounding area. Day by day more of the defending forts fell. The Belgians pleaded for help, and on October 4 and 5 the British sent more than 6,000 men, most of them poorly trained. The reinforcements were of little help, and by October 7 the situation had become hopeless. The Belgian government left by boat for France, and, as bombardment of the city began, most of the residents left in confusion. The Germans began their occupation of the city on October 9.   M. K.

ANUAK. *See* AFRICAN PEOPLES.

ANUBIS [ənyu′bɪs], the mortuary god of Ancient Egypt, was conceived as a jackal who devoured the dead. The jackal was at first a deity, later becoming a divinity and showing but a faint trace of his animal origin. As god of the Necropolis at Siut (Lycopolis), Anubis was subject to the city-god Upawat (Bath-Opener), a wolf-deity and sun-deity. With Thoth, he shared the function of conducting the dead through Amenti (Hidden Place—the West), the region of the dead where the soul was taken to the hall of Osiris and considered by forty-two judges who sent it to Aaru or condemned it to torment.

The Book of the Dead, written by Pharaohs of the Fifth and Sixth Dynasties, was incorporated later in the Papyrus of Ani, a collection that sheds light on the religious belief of the middle Eighteenth Dynasty, and deals with the hereafter. Chapter 125 portrays Ani, followed by his wife, Tutu, bowing humbly in the great hall of judgment. In the corner is the balance operated by the jackal-headed Anubis. On the left scale-pan is Ani's heart, while in the other is a feather symbolizing truth and righteousness.

Anubis, whom the Greeks identified with Hermes, is commonly described as a son of Osiris. In the company of Osiris, he attained great recognition. A very ancient deity of the dead, Anubis is represented prowling among the graves in the desert surrounding Siut.   E. J. J.

ANVERS. *See* ANTWERP.

ANXIETY, one of the few medical terms that covers a symptom, an affliction, and an emotional response. It is applicable, likewise, to both normal and pathogenic affective manifestations. The difference between the latter two depends on the provocative cause, the time element, and the individual himself. Anxiety over the safety of a loved one who is serving in a combat unit during war is understandable. Continuance of that reaction following cessation of hostilities is questionably normal. Anxiety from without, i.e., precipitated by a real stress, disappointment, or challenge, is to be expected if the precipitating factor is proportionate to the apprehension. Anxiety from within, i.e., arising purely within the individual's psyche (mind) is definitely an indication of neurosis. It is currently accepted that the mentally ill person reacts to his unconscious conflict with fear, which, to the neurotic, is not a socially tolerated emotional response; as an affective presentation of instinctual drives, it is overtly converted into anxiety. This apprehensive, worrying, troubled expression is surcharged with tension and consists chiefly of emotion.

Psychoanalysts claim that instincts have ideational forms of presentation, and that, in the process of repression, the ideational expression of an instinct disappears from the conscious sphere, if it is there, or remains in the unconscious if that is where it is hidden. Three courses are accordingly possible for instinctual, ideational presentation: (1) complete suppression, (2) appearance in the guise of a particular type of affect, or (3) transformation into anxiety. Many psychiatrists object to the ambiguous intermixture of anxiety and fear in clinical literature. However, there is little doubt that the former is an outward expression of inner, unconscious fear. Sigmund Freud (1856-1939) postulated three situations which were almost certain to precipitate a later manifestation of anxiety: loss of a loved object, the castration complex of children following a parental scolding or punishment for normal sexual curiosity or activity, and the superego (conscience) or social fixation.

As an emotional expression, anxiety is commonly encountered in its maximal strength, i.e., intense, marked, extreme. Its logical and its psychical origins are well covered by Eugen Bleuler, who said, "Anxiety undoubtedly has different sources. In many cases it is plainly connected with respiratory difficulties as seen in diseases of the heart, in the respiratory organs, and in the blood. Furthermore, anxiety is undoubtedly connected in some way with sexuality, a fact which we knew for a long time, but which Freud made clearer."

Anxiety may be attached to definite thoughts or ideas; it may exist without any ideational association, in which case it is referred to as free-floating anxiety. It is often accompanied by physical signs, such as short, rapid breath, accelerated pulse, sweating, and alternating flushing and pallor, all of which indicate a close organic-physiologic association with the adrenal glands, the sympathetic nervous system, and possibly the subthalamic nuclei in the brain. Investigators, particularly Jules Hymen Masserman, have been investigating these interrelations by fear-producing stimuli in laboratory animals.

Clinically, the commonest type of neurosis encountered is the anxiety state, in which the patient presents an overwhelming reaction of anxiety manifested physically as diarrhea, urinary frequency, palpitation of the heart, tremor, or some other such symptom. Anxiety neurosis is a condition in which anxiety syndromes are characterized by definite, circumscribed attacks affecting some bodily system such as the cardiovascular, respiratory, or mental. In the latter, there is always a fear of impending disaster, such as incipient insanity, or incurable cancer. Anxiety neurosis is best known as that subdivision of neurosis including all the well-recognized phobias or fears, such as claustrophobia, agoraphobia, and syphilophobia.

Treatment of anxiety conditions includes formal psychoanalysis, narcosynthesis, and individual psychotherapy which is based on lengthy, periodic interviews encompassing a common-sense approach. Hypnosis during World War II was used as an emergency measure; but as a means toward permanent cure it usually fails and accordingly meets with disapproval. Therapeutic adjuvants include encouragement, reeducation, occupational therapy, physiotherapy, and, if the patient has a depressive component to his reaction, electric shock treatment. *See also* AMNESIA; HYPNOSIS.   J. A. Br.

ANYWAK. *See* AFRICAN PEOPLE (ANUAK).

ANZHERO-SUDZHENSK [ʌnzhɛˈərə suĵeˈnsk], a coal-mining and industrial town in the Kemerovo *oblast'* (region) of the Russian Soviet Federated Socialist Republic. It lies about 150 mi. northeast of Novosibirsk, at the point where the Trans-Siberian Railroad crosses the northern section of the Kuznetsk coal basin. Because of the need of Anzhero-Sudzhensk's coal for the railroad, the town developed industrially at the beginning of the twentieth century, much earlier than the southern sections of the Kuznetsk basin and long before any industrialization of Siberia. Today, the manufacture of mining equipment, glass, and chemicals is also important. Pop. (est. 1950), 85,000.   G. A. T.

ANZIO [ɑˈntsio], a small fishing port and resort town on the Tyrrhenian Sea, 30 mi. south of Rome, in the province of Rome, in central Italy. It is situated at the end of a promontory, on low ground at the southern extremity of the Agro Romano. The city of Nettuno adjoins Anzio. In addition to being a fishing center, Anzio is important largely as a bathing resort and the site of many villas, principally of well-to-do people from Rome. The city is almost wholly modern and is connected by rail with Rome.

In ancient times the town of Anzio was known as Antium. Apparently occupied as early as the Iron Age, Antium was taken by Rome after long resistance in 341 B.C. Nero, who was a native of the town, built a large villa there, as did many Roman aristocrats. He also had a circular port constructed, later destroyed by the Saracens. During the Middle Ages the port was abandoned for the more easily defensible one at Nettuno. In 1378 a Genoese fleet was defeated off Anzio by the Venetians under Vittor Pisani. The port of Anzio was rebuilt at the end of the seventeenth century and later, but it served only the local fishermen.

The two cities were very badly damaged during World War II. When the Allied drive up the Peninsula stalled before Cassino during the winter of 1943-1944, General Harold Alexander created a diversion behind the German lines by effecting a landing at Anzio and Nettuno. This operation, begun early on Jan. 22, 1944, achieved momentary success, but soon the Allied forces were pinned in their small beachhead zone, from which they were freed only late in May by the general advance on Rome. Pop. 6,950.

R. G. W.

AOMORI [ɑ'omori], a port on the northern coast of Honshu Island, Japan, at the head of Aomori Bay, and the capital of the prefecture of Aomori. The city has cold winters and warm summers, the temperature averaging between 25° and 30° F. during the cold months of the year and about 68° F. in summer. The winter months are cloudy and unpleasant, and there is considerable snowfall. Between 40 and 60 in. of rain fall every year. The city is a transshipment point for Honshu-Hokkaido trade, and there are train ferries that connect four times daily with Hakkodate on the northern island of Hokkaido. Aomori was declared an open port in 1906. It was destroyed by fire in 1910 and was subsequently rebuilt as a modern city with broad streets, modern shops, and shipyards. Aomori is the market center for the Tsugaru Plain; lumber, rice, textiles, tobacco, oil, and apples are exported. Aomori Prefecture alone produces about 60 per cent of Japan's apple crop. The municipal park and the Uto-jinsha Shinto shrine are well known. Pop. 1954, 114,529.

J. E. F.

AORTA. *See* ARTERY; HEART.

AOSTA, EMANUELE FILIBERTO, DUKE OF [aɔ'sta] (1869-1931), Italian military leader, Prince of Savoy and cousin of King Victor Emmanuel III, was born in Genoa, on Jan. 13, 1869. Until the birth of the Prince of Piedmont in 1904, he was heir to the Italian throne. During World War I, he commanded the Third Army which was stationed on the extreme right flank of the Italian line which faced the Austrians in northern Italy. The Duke of Aosta maintained his positions until a break through the Second Army's lines by the Austrians at Caporetto, Oct. 24, 1917, compelled him to retreat hastily to new positions, lest he be cut off and trapped against the Adriatic Sea. General Luigi Cadorna, commander in chief of the Italian forces, was held responsible for this defeat, and was relieved of his command. For a time it was thought that the Duke of Aosta would replace him, but General Armando Diaz was chosen for this post instead. In October 1918, the Duke of Aosta, still at the head of the Third Army, participated in the victory at Vittorio-Veneto. He was for some years president of the Opera Nazionale Dopolavoro, and in June 1926 was made a marshal of Italy. He died in Turin, July 4, 1931.

E. B. A.

AOSTA, a province and also a capital city in northwest Piedmont in northern Italy. Becoming a duchy in 1302, the country remained, thereafter, under the rule of the Savoy dynasty.

City. Aosta is situated in the Val d'Aosta near the confluence of the Buthier and the Dora Baltea rivers at an altitude of 1,800 ft. above sea level, and is about 50 mi. northwest of Turin (Torino). Since early times, Aosta has been important as the meeting point of the transalpine routes over the Great and the Little Saint Bernard passes to France and Switzerland. Aosta lies in a pleasant valley surrounded on three sides by some of the highest peaks in the Alps, including Mont Blanc, the Matterhorn, and the Gran Paradiso.

Aosta is chiefly an administrative center and market place for its region. It is the starting point for a variety of excursions to scenic and sports areas in the surrounding mountains. The tourist trade is a lucrative source of income, and during

Cobblestone city street in Aosta, Italy

World War I the abundance of electricity encouraged the growth of iron works using the ore of Cogne. There is a railway line from Turin which has been extended to Pré Saint Didier, with the possibility that some day it will be joined by a tunnel under Mont Blanc with the French railway system. Following the Roman plan, the city is laid out with straight streets crossing at right angles. There are numerous remains of the Roman city, including the Pretorian Gate, the Arch of Augustus, a theatre and amphitheatre, and the old walls (especially on the west and south). Among the interesting medieval buildings are the cathedral (begun before the twelfth century) and the Collegiata of Sant'Orso, with its cloister and priory.

When the Romans conquered the Val d'Aosta from the Ligurian-Celtic tribes—the Salassi—about 25 B.C., they set up Augusta Pretoria as a rectangular walled camp garrisoned by three thousand Pretorians. After the Romans came the Goths, Byzantines, Lombards, Franks, and Burgundians —with Saracen forays doing much damage. By the eleventh century the authority of the local bishop was replaced by the House of Savoy. Except for brief intermissions of French occupation (1691, 1704-1706, 1798-1799, 1800-1814), the country remained under the rule of the Savoy dynasty after 1302. The secondary branch of the family is headed by the dukes of Aosta. Pop. 1947, 23,322.

Province. The province of Aosta, created in 1927 and comprising 107 communes, had in 1936 an area of 1,837 sq. mi. It is thus sparsely populated, due primarily to its Alpine topography. It lies almost entirely within the basin of the Dora Baltea and its numerous tributaries and the Val di Locana (Orco River). There is a zone of level plain where these streams emerge from the mountains. Otherwise, the terrain is very irregular, culminating in some of Europe's highest peaks and most extensive glaciers. Despite these unfavorable natural conditions, agriculture and pasturing constitute the basis of economic life, producing grain, fruit, forage crops, and wine. Small holdings are predominant in the area. Industry has expanded in recent decades, primarily because of abundant water power. Textile plants (cotton and rayon) are found at Châtillon, Pont, Cuorgnè, and Ivrea.

The language commonly spoken by the natives in the mountainous part of the province is a French (Provençal) dialect. In the upper valley of Gressoney, just below Monte Rosa, a German dialect is found. Pop. 1947, 225,981.

R. G. W.

AOUDAD [a'udad], *Ammotragus lervia,* a mountain sheep. It has several other names: auri, Barbary sheep, and maned sheep. It inhabits mountainous regions of northern

YLLA PHOTO

AOUDAD, OR BARBARY SHEEP

Africa. This animal is 3 ft. high at the shoulder and is clothed in sandy to deep-reddish hair which in the ram becomes a mane, 6 to 13 in. long, on the neck, chest, and upper forelegs. Its horns are heavy at the base, sweep sharply back and out, and taper to sharp points. They measure about 21 in. along the curve. Because of overgrazing and hunting, aoudads have become rare in Egypt and Libya. The survivors are confined to the roughest and most isolated cliffs of the Atlas Mountains.

V. H. C.

APACHE. *See* INDIAN TRIBES, NORTH AMERICAN.

APACHE PLUME, *Fallugia paradoxa,* a native western shrub of the rose family, so named because of the similarity of the feathery heads of its fruit to war bonnets of the Apache Indians. It is used in gardens but is valued chiefly

on the range because of the persistent or evergreen character of the foliage for foraging cattle and also because of its usefulness as an erosion control. It grows wild 2 to 4 ft. high, or as high as 7 ft. under cultivation. The leaves are palmate with 3 to 7 lobes, and the flowers are white. The Tewa Indians used the brush in bundles as brooms, and the straight stems to make arrow shafts. The apache plume is found in Utah, Colorado, Arizona, and western Texas.   J. C. Wis.

APALACHEE. *See* INDIAN TRIBES, NORTH AMERICAN.

APALACHEE BAY [æpəlæ'tshi], an indentation of the Gulf of Mexico into northwestern Florida. It extends from Deadman's Bay on the east to St. George Island on the west, a distance of 85 mi., and extends about 40 mi. in a north-south direction. Franklin, Wakulla, Jefferson, and Taylor counties of Florida extend around the northern boundary of Apalachee Bay. The Ochlockonee and Aucilla rivers drain into the bay. The capital of Florida, Tallahassee, is about 25 mi. north of Apalachee Bay.   J. E. F.

APALACHICOLA RIVER [æ'pəlæ'tshɪko'lə], a river flowing from southwestern Georgia across northwestern Florida, a distance of about 90 mi. It empties into Apalachicola Bay, part of the Gulf of Mexico. The river is formed by the junction of the Chattahoochee, which forms the southern Alabama-Georgia boundary, and the Flint rivers in Seminole Co., Ga. The Apalachicola may be navigated by small boats, and the mouth of the river and Apalachicola Bay form a region famed for shellfish-gathering and sport fishing. The town of Chattahoochee, Fla., is at the northern end of the river and that of Apalachicola is near the southern end, on the bay of the same name.   J. E. F.

APAR. *See* EDENTATA.

APARRI [apa'rri], a Philippine municipality composed of an administrative center and ten barrios or districts, in the province of Cagayan, on the island of Luzon. It is situated on the Cagayan River near its mouth, about 50 mi. north of Tuguegarao, the provincial capital, and 285 mi. northeast of Manila. The town, the only port of entry and only free port of northern Luzon, is the northernmost of the larger Philippine municipalities, and it is the best entrance into the fertile Cagayan valley, which is the leading tobacco-producing district of the archipelago. Other significant crops are rice and corn. Lumbering, fishing, and grazing (cattle) are also important economic interests. Aparri has an irregular street pattern, but there is the customary public square, or plaza. A firm sandy beach fronts the city and a low sea wall, ½ mi. long, has been built between the beach and the town. The mouth of the river is sometimes blocked by sand bars and other silt deposits so that entrance is possible only by pilotage. There is a good highway southward to Tuguegarao and on to Manila, but there is no railroad in the Cagayan valley. Drinking water is obtained from artesian wells. During World War II the first Japanese landing in the Philippines, on Dec. 10, 1941, was at Aparri. On June 23, 1945, airborne Allied forces landed near the town to help defeat the Japanese remaining in the Cagayan valley and terminate the Luzon campaign. Pop. 1948 (town) 10,125.

A. Cu.

APARTMENT HOUSE. *See* HOUSING.

APATITE [æ'pətait], a phosphate mineral named by the German mineralogist, Abraham G. Werner, in 1790. The name is derived from a Greek word meaning to deceive, in allusion to the ease with which apatite can be mistaken for aquamarine, amethyst, and other minerals. Apatite is composed of calcium phosphate, plus calcium fluoride or calcium chloride or both. It is often in well-formed crystals which are prismatic in shape and hexagonal in section. Apatite is number 5 in the mineral scale of hardness. It appears in a wide range of colors, especially in shades of green, blue, and brown. Apatite is commonly present in all types of igneous rocks, but usually in microscopic crystals. At Kiruna, Sweden, this mineral is intermixed with magnetite in an iron ore deposit that has been ascribed to magmatic segregation. Larger crystals of apatite occur with calcite, phlogopite, and other minerals in pegmatites in Ontario and Quebec, Canada. It was at one time mined extensively for fertilizer phosphate in this area. More recently, large deposits on the Kola Peninsula, U.S.S.R., have been exploited for phosphate. Smaller production has been reported from Chile, Sweden, and Virginia, in the United States.   K. K. L.

APE, a term used until the sixteenth century as the equivalent of monkey. Today, the word is largely restricted to primates having no tails, or, in the terminology of science, to the anthropoid apes: the gorilla, the chimpanzee, the orangutan, and the gibbon.   R. T. H.

APE MAN OF JAVA. *See* EVOLUTION OF MAN.

APELDOORN [ɑ'pəldorn], a city in the northeastern part of the province of Gelderland, in the Netherlands, about 16 mi. north of Arnhem. It is the largest municipality of the country, with an area of over 85,000 acres, comprising the villages of Apeldoorn, Beekbergen, Loenen, as well as other small communities. It is on the northern border of the Veluwe in a region of beech and pine forests and heather. Near it is Het Loo, summer palace of the Dutch royal family, situated among extensive parks and forests. Apeldoorn, which is connected by canals with Zwolle and Dieren, has a number of small industries. They manufacture copperware, paper, ink, soap, paint, and metalware, but the city is mostly known as a residential and tourist city with beautiful parks and pleasant suburbs. Near-by Kootwijk has a powerful radio transmitter. Apeldoorn was mentioned as early as 793. In World War II it was liberated in 1945, after a short fight, by Canadian troops. Pop. 1952, 68,700.   B. L.

APELLES [əpɛ'liz], Greek painter of the fourth century B.C., was born about 370 at Colophon in Asia Minor. He studied at Ephesus and under Pamphilus in the school at Sicyon, where the training, which aimed at accuracy and technical perfection, included arithmetic, geometry, optics, and color effect. Apelles practiced his art continually, letting no day pass without drawing at least one line. He worked at Ephesus, Cos, and Rhodes, at the courts of Philip and Alexander of Macedon, and at the court of the first Ptolemy in Alexandria. His time of highest achievement was between 332 and 329, when he served as court painter to Alexander the Great, but he continued to work for the Diadocni, the successors of Alexander and lived at least until 300 B.C. He acquired the reputation of being the greatest painter of antiquity and of having a style that combined some charm and grace with grandeur and dignity. Of his character many stories have been told, among them the report that he exhibited his pictures in order to hear criticism. By another account, he once corrected his representation of a sandal because a cobbler criticized it, but when the same man found

fault with the leg he rebuked him with the comment "Shoemaker, stick to your last."

The most celebrated of Apelles' portraits of Alexander was one in the temple of Artemis at Ephesus, depicting Alexander as Zeus with a thunderbolt in his hand, the hand seeming to protrude from the surface of the picture. Other portraits showed Alexander on his spirited horse, Bucephalus; another on a triumphal car with the demon of war; another with Victory and the Dioscuri, Castor and Pollux. Other pictures also used allegories and personifications. *The Calumny,* described by Lucian, inspired a painting by Botticelli and a drawing by Raphael. In another painting a thunderstorm was depicted by means of a combination of three personifications, Bronte, thunder, Astrape, lightning, and Keraunobolia, thunderbolts.

Other famous portraits by Apelles were those of Archelaus with his wife and daughter; of Antigonus on horseback, painted in profile, so that his one blind eye was hidden; of himself; and of Pankaspe, a beautiful woman whom Alexander had given over to the artist when he perceived that Apelles had fallen in love with her. The same Pankaspe, or Phryne, was Apelles' model for the celebrated *Aphrodite* in the sanctuary of Asclepius at Cos, a painting showing the goddess rising from the sea (anadyomene), wringing the sea foam out of her hair. This picture was taken by Augustus to Rome and placed in the temple of Caesar; when it decayed in the time of Nero it was replaced by a copy made by Dorotheus. Another famous picture by Apelles, also later taken to Rome, was a representation of Heracles with averted face. In Apelles' picture showing a procession and the sacrifice of a bull in Cos, the realistic rendering of men and animal by the artist was stressed by the poet Herondas.

Apelles used only four main colors, Melian white, Attic ocher, red from Sinope, and black from burned ivory, but these were modified by his invention of a thin, transparent glaze, which lent austerity to the colors and softened their brilliance. The stories about the protruding hand of Alexander and the averted face of Heracles show that he experimented with difficult foreshortenings and perspective problems. The best idea of his style is to be gained, probably, from mosaic found in the house of the Faun in Pompeii and removed to Naples. It represents the decisive battle between Alexander and Darius and is probably a copy of a painting in four colors by Philoxenos of Eretria which was commissioned by King Cassander after 318 and before 297 B.C. It shows foreshortenings suggesting the *Alexander* and the *Heracles,* particularly in the horses, which are seen from the front and from the back. The four colors show many mixtures and intermediate tones like reddish and yellowish gray, brown and brownish violet; there is no blue, and the general effect is sober and restrained.   M. Bi.

APENNINES [æ'pənainz], a mountain range extending along the entire Italian Peninsula. At their northwestern end the Apennines merge into the Maritime Alps between Liguria and Piedmont. From this junction they run generally eastward, with the Po Valley to the north, until they reach the Adriatic Sea below Rimini. Here they turn in a somewhat more southerly direction and form the backbone of the Italian Peninsula as far as the Strait of Messina. Their aggregate length is about 800 mi., while the width varies according to the distinction between the main range and its subsidiary spurs and plateaus.

The Apennines may be divided into three main parts—northern, central, and southern—each divisible into smaller sections. The northern group consists of the Ligurian and

Assisi, Italy, famous old hill town in the central Apennines

Tuscan Apennines (the latter are also known as the Tusco-Emilian Apennines.) The Ligurian segment runs east to the Pass of La Cisa near to La Spezia and attains a maximum elevation of nearly 10,000 ft. It is pierced by several passes carrying historic highways or railway lines. The Tuscan Apennines continue southeastward to the Montefeltro region near the headwaters of the Tiber, with its high point (7,100 ft.) in Monte Cimone. A subsidiary range, known as the Apuanian Alps and noted for its marble quarries at Carrara, lies between the principal chain and the Tyrrhenian Sea in northwest Tuscany.

The central Apennines, the widest and highest section, extend south to the valley of the Sangro River. In the north they culminate in Monte Vettore (8,100 ft.) in the Sibillini Mountains. To the south the Apennines divide into three roughly parallel ranges. The eastern spur comprises the Gran Sasso d'Italia, of which Corno Grande (9,500 ft.) is the highest peak in the Apennines, and the La Maiella group, exceeding 9,000 ft. These heights are snow-covered much of the year, and a winter-sports area has been developed around the Gran Sasso. The middle range includes the Monte Reatini and the peaks of Terminillo and Velino. The westernmost comprises the summits Sabini and Simbruini, north of Rome, where the highest elevations approximate 7,000 ft. The central section, highest and widest of the Apennine Plateau, presents difficult highway and railroad engineering.

South of the Sangro the identity of the ranges is less pronounced. The Matese massif, rising to 6,700 ft., lies north of Naples. From Abruzzi and Molise southward the Apen-

nines desert the east coast, although they fringe its central portion. The main range trends south through Lucania and into Calabria, where it rises to over 6,000 ft. in the Sila and in the culminating massif of Aspromonte on the toe of Italy overlooking the Strait of Messina.

In the north and west the Apennines form a divide between the Tyrrhenian and Adriatic watersheds. In the central section, where there is a diversity of ranges, the divide is more complex, and further south it is complicated by the intrusion of the Ionian watershed. Only in central Italy do the Apennines give rise to rivers of importance, such as the Arno, Tiber, Pescara, Sangro, and Volturno. Here are the principal sources of water power. These are being exploited with increasing thoroughness. Elsewhere the streams are too short and their flow is too subject to seasonal fluctuation to provide a secure basis for hydroelectric industry. However, it is in these drier areas that the water in Apennine streams is utilized for irrigation purposes, both in the north and the south.

The Apennines are singularly devoid of valuable mineral deposits. Once they were heavily wooded, but the long process of deforestation has now destroyed most of the original stands of both deciduous and evergreen timber. Recent attempts to restore some of the forest cover have not materially halted the devastation wrought by erosion on mountain fields and pastures. The pasturing of sheep and goats, and to a lesser extent of cattle, is still carried on widely in the Apennines, and in some places prevails the ancient custom of transhumance—the migration of flocks and shepherds from mountain to plain in the fall, and reversely in the spring.

R. G. W.

APEX OF THE SUN'S WAY. *See* SOLAR MOTION.

APHASIA [əfe′zhiə], a term including all motor or sensory disturbances of language caused by a brain lesion, usually thrombosis or hemorrhage, but not including disturbances caused by the faulty innervation of musculature necessary for speech, or by involvement of the sense organs themselves, or by mental defect. Speech implies the physiologic activity of three associated centers in the brain: (1) Broca's area, situated in the third frontal convolution on the left side in righthanded persons, the center for motor images of words; (2) Wernicke's area, in the first temporal convolution and supramarginal gyrus of the parietal lobe, on the left side, the center for phonetic verbal images; and (3) posteriorly, in the occipitoparietal lobe (near the visual area), the center for visual verbal images. Aphasia results from a lesion of Broca's area; word deafness, or "sensory aphasia," from a lesion of Wernicke's area; and word blindness, from a lesion of the occipital lobe or of the angular gyrus in the parietal lobe. While a lesion in nerve pathways or in peripheral organs may cause speech loss or impairment, the "mental" speech power remains uninvolved. A lesion affecting Broca's and Wernicke's areas may produce altered speech and the inability to perform phonetic expression.

Clinicians do not agree on theories of aphasia. One school regards aphasia as a disorder of symbolic formulation and expression, the pattern it assumes being dependent on the specific modes of behavior which are disturbed or impaired. Another category includes all changes in motor behavior and speech as apractic (apraxia, the inability to perform purposeful acts) and receptive disturbances as forms of agnosia (the inability to recognize sounds or objects). Aphasia is also regarded as a disorder of basic mental functioning, aphasic symptoms being considered as expressions of a single functional disorder involving loss of the ability to comprehend the essential nature of a process, to differentiate "figure" and "ground."

Expressive aphasia is associated with frontal lobe centers adjacent to motor areas (mouth and tongue for speech, hands and eyes for writing; receptive aphasia is linked to the posterior portion of the brain where sensory areas (the parietal, occipital, and temporal lobes) are located. Both may be involved in expressive-receptive aphasia. Amnesic aphasia, actually true amnesia, implies a mnemonic defect and, accordingly, has no definite localization in the brain. Aphasia and agraphia (the loss of motor speech and of motor writing) imply involvements of their respective centers, but the patient's ability to recognize symbols or words or objects heard and seen remains intact. Word deafness does not signify impairment of the hearing apparatus. The patient hears everything that is normally audible, but his brain center cannot interpret what is heard. If the auditory center is damaged, the patient will talk meaninglessly, a "gibberish," since he cannot interpret sound. He may be able to read aloud, thanks to his visual center; he may be able to describe objects but not name them (anomia); and he may even be able to repeat words. The using of wrong words is termed paraphrasia. Thus, a patient may desire a pen and call it a key. Alexia, or word blindness, signifies an intact visual system but the inability to interpret what is seen. An alectic patient is like the average American who sees all that is written on a Chinese laundry ticket, but can make no sense of the symbols. Apraxia is the inability to perform purposeful movements, even though the neuromuscular system is undamaged.

Thus motor or expressive aphasia includes aphasia (replacing the older term "aphemia," or loss of power of speech), agraphia, and amimia (the inability to gesticulate). Sensory or perceptive aphasia includes word deafness and alexia. Other clinical descriptive terms for various aphasic phenomena are: alalia, the inability to produce sounds; anarthria, the inability to produce articulate speech; asyllabia, the inability to form syllables from individual sounds; aphrasia, the inability to mold separate words into phrases; and syntactic aphasia, the inability to arrange words into sentences.

Because the common etiological lesion of aphasia is a thrombosis of, or hemorrhage from, a cerebral vessel, the scope of the damage is usually larger than a particular center, and other signs and symptoms are present in addition to the speech disorder. These include evidences of paralysis or paresis, unconsciousness, alteration of reflexes, bladder and bowel incontinence, and changes in the personality.

Hysterical patients may develop a pseudo-aphasia, but this is seldom noted because speech involvement in the neurotic is, like all other neurotic syndromes, complete; that is, speech is lost, not impaired. The organic aphasic patient never loses his speech completely. He is always capable of at least some sound. *See also* AMNESIA. J. A. Br.

APHELION [əfi′liən], the point in a comet's or a planet's orbit farthest from the sun. The earth is in aphelion at about July 2 each year. The aphelia of certain long-period comets lie far beyond the orbit of the outermost planet, Pluto.

APHEMIA. *See* APHASIA.

APHID [ə′fɪd] or **PLANT LOUSE,** is the name applied to any member of the family Aphididae, of the order Hemiptera. They suck the juices of plants, feeding mostly on the leaves and tender shoots, but a few kinds feed on tender bark, others on roots. They may do considerable damage. Many aphids have alternate hosts, feeding upon one kind of plant at one season, upon another the rest of the year. In temperate regions, such common species as the peach aphid, *Myzus persicae,* the green apple aphid, *Aphis pomi,* and many others pass the winter as eggs on woody plants. The eggs hatch in the spring, giving rise to stem mothers, which reproduce parthenogenetically. Their offspring may be winged or wingless, the winged forms migrating to herbaceous plants on which several parthenogenetic generations

Close-up of a colony of green aphids feeding on the undersides of bean leaves.

occur. Toward fall, the aphids migrate back to the primary host and give rise to a generation that develops sexual forms. These mate, and the eggs are laid on the bark. This procedure may be greatly modified in warmer regions: in South Africa the peach aphid is always wingless and migrates from host to host by crawling over the ground. The mealy plum aphid, *Hyolopterus arundinis,* has alternate hosts in cool regions, but in warm regions may live the year around on a single host.

The majority of aphids, such as those occurring on maple, oak, and so on, do not have alternate hosts, but sexual forms are produced in the fall; in many tropical species sexual forms are unknown.

The woolly aphids and gall aphids are sometimes placed in the family Eriosomatidae. The wooly apple aphid, *Eriosoma lanigerum,* is primarily a bark feeder, but also lives on the roots of elm. In warm regions they may not develop sexual forms, but in the North, eggs are produced in the fall. In Europe, it is known as American blight. Several genera produce galls on poplar; the winged forms migrate to herbaceous plants. C. H. Cu.

APHIS LION is the name given any member of the Neuropterous family Chrysopidae. The adults are of a delicate green color, and the veins form a beautiful irregular network that has earned for them the name lacewings. Most of them are quite innocuous, but some have a glandular secretion that is obnoxious and most resistant, even strong soap failing to remove the odor. There are about 500 different kinds, their wing expanse varying from ¼ inch to almost 3 inches. The eggs are appended at the end of long, slender stalks, often in attractive rotary patterns, apparently for the purpose of preventing the newly hatched young from eating each other or the unhatched eggs. When the young hatch, they crawl down the "stem" and go in search of plant lice. Even when first hatched they have long, strong mandibles with which to catch aphids and suck their juices. Other insects also serve as food. When full grown, the aphis lion builds a round white cocoon, attached to leaf, bark or refuse, in which to transform to the adult stage, the adult emerging from a circular opening at the top of the cocoon.   C. H. Cu.

APHRASIA. *See* APHASIA.

APHRODITE [æ'frodɑi'ti], in Greek mythology and religion, the goddess of love and beauty, identified by the Romans with Venus. In Homer's *Iliad* she was the daughter of Zeus and Dione; according to later poets, she sprang from the foam of the sea, a birth which explains her name (Gr. *aphros,* foam) and one of her titles, Anadyomene. Many of her attributes indicate an Asiatic origin;

COURTESY OF THE METROPOLITAN MUSEUM OF ART

APHRODITE GENETRIX   APHRODITE URANIA

she is identified with the Assyrian Ishtar and the Phoenician Astarte. The legend that she landed at Paphos in Cyprus or at Cythera, an island near Laconia, accounts both for the fact that her oldest seats of worship were in Cyprus and Cythera, and that she had the titles Cypris ("the Cyprian"), Cytherea, Paphia, Amathusia, and Idalia, the last three titles deriving from places in Cyprus. Sacred to Aphrodite were the sparrow, dove, and swan. She was the wife of Hephaestus, but was faithless to him and took Ares as a lover; Homer relates in the *Odyssey* how the intrigue was discovered and the pair caught in a net by Hephaestus, who called together the other gods to ridicule the lovers. Aphrodite also loved the mortals Anchises and Adonis. Her girdle, the cestus, made those who wore it irresistible; Hera, for instance, borrowed it to divert Zeus's attention from the Trojan conflict. Aphrodite was worshipped in Greece as goddess of the sky under the name Aphrodite Urania, and as goddess of all the people under the name Aphrodite Pandemos; this two-fold worship later gave rise to a distinction between Aphrodite Urania as a goddess of pure love and Aphrodite Pandemos as a goddess of sensual lust. Aphrodite had a famous sanctuary on Mount Eryx in Sicily, and this was honored by the Romans, who looked upon Aphrodite, the mother of

Aeneas, as their ancestress. In works of art Aphrodite was often represented with her son Eros, or Cupid; many beautiful statues of the goddess were made in antiquity, and the most famous of existing statues is the Aphrodite of Melos (the Venus de Milo), now in the Louvre. *See also* ADONIS; AENEAS; ANCHISES; EROS; PARIS; TROJAN WAR.   G. E.D.

APHTHOUS FEVER. *See* FOOT AND MOUTH DISEASE.

APIA [ɑpi'ɑ; ɑ'piɑ], the principal town and seaport of Western Samoa, a mandate in the southern Pacific Ocean administered by New Zealand. The town is located on the northern shore of Upolu Island, on a bay, at 13° 50′ S. lat. and 171° 50′ W. long. It has a tropical marine climate, and it presents a picturesque setting among the coconut and other palm trees on the bay, with native villages at either end of the community. Between 1860 and 1889 Western Samoa was ruled jointly by representatives of Great Britain, the United States, and Germany. In 1889, just as Western Samoa passed to Germany as a colony, a hurricane swept Apia harbor on March 15, destroying the United States cruisers *Vandalia* and *Trenton* and the German battleships *Adler* and *Eber*. Many lives were lost, and the skeleton of the *Adler* remains in the harbor as a reminder of the disaster. On Aug. 30, 1914, a New Zealand expeditionary force occupied Apia and all of Western Samoa, which never returned to German control. After World War I Western Samoa was officially mandated to New Zealand. During World War II Apia was an active naval base for Allied forces. It has steamer service to New Zealand, and there is also interisland service. Ships anchor in the harbor, and passengers and cargo must be transferred to the mainland by small boats. Apia is the center of political and commercial activity in Western Samoa. The New Zealand government maintains high-powered radio stations at the town. There are many points of interest surrounding the town. At near-by Mulinu'u are a native museum and several monuments of interest which Robert Louis Stevenson mentioned in his *A Footnote to History*. Vailima, about 4 mi. distant, was Stevenson's home, and 500 ft. above it, on Mount Vaea, is Stevenson's tomb. In Apia's environs there are many beautiful pools and waterfalls. Also in the area surrounding Apia there are several large coconut plantations.
                                              J. E. F.

APICULTURE. *See* BEE.

APIS [e'pis] (Eg. *api*), a sacred bull worshipped by the ancient Egyptians, as early as the Fourth Dynasty (c. 2600 B.C.), as an embodiment of the god Ptah of Memphis. Apis was idolized as an image of the soul of Osiris, and the center of his worship was Memphis. He was believed to have been engendered by the moonbeam and to be reborn each time he died. Apis appeared to the people with a beetle on his tongue and the figure of an eagle on his back. He was embalmed and accorded an elaborate funeral and buried in the rock-hewn Serapeum in the Necropolis of Memphis. When his soul passed to the world beyond, it was known as Osiris.

Apis, called Serapis, was adopted by the Greeks and was eventually worshiped throughout the Roman Empire; the Golden Calf of the Hebrews may have been derived from him. As Serapis, the bull was encircled by a serpent, emblem of immortality. In Rome the Temple of Serapis and Isis was erected on the Campus Martius, not far from the Pantheon, about A.D. 39. It was a vast structure, built on the site occupied now by the church of Sant' Ignazio, a section of the Collegio Romano.   E. J. J.

APO [ɑ'po], an extinct volcano, the highest mountain in the Philippine Archipelago, with an elevation of approximately 10,000 ft. It is located in the south central part of Mindanao Island west of Davao Gulf (7° N. lat.; 125° 17′ E. long.). R. G. B.

APOCALYPTIC LITERATURE [əpɒkəlɪ'ptɪk], as a fully developed type of Jewish literature, first appeared during the Hellenistic period. The word "apocalyptic" is derived from a Greek verb which means "to uncover" and refers to the intent of this literature, namely, to reveal the divine purpose for the present and future. Arising in times of personal or national distress, apocalyptic books sought to encourage faith and hope in God as the only vindicator of the oppressed and judge of the wicked. Thus apocalypticism attempted to present a philosophy of history which would "justify the ways of God to man." Its scope was broader than that of prophecy proper, which was ordinarily limited in time and space; apocalyptic visions were as wide as the universe and as unlimited as time. Though the ethical element is not lacking, chief stress is laid not on what people must do, but on what they may expect.

Characteristic motifs in apocalyptic literature are the transcendental concept of God, his operation through intermediary spirits (angels and demons), a pessimistic outlook upon the fortunes of this world, and an optimism regarding the ultimate triumph of God's purposes over all evil and the establishment of his kingdom. A peculiarity of this type of literature is that it conveys its message by means of mysterious symbols. Thus, persons and nations are represented by sheep, bulls, birds, and wild beasts; and events in history are represented by the operations of nature, such as falling stars, earthquakes, and violent storms. At times the imagery, from the standpoint of Western logic, becomes grotesque, as, for example, the beast with seven heads and ten horns (Rev. xiii:1). Within the Bible notable apocalypses are included in Daniel vii-xii, Zechariah xii-xiv, Mark xiii (with parallels in Matthew and Luke), and the Book of Revelation.

Important apocalyptic writings outside the Bible, all attributed to famous personages in order to command a wider hearing, are the following. The Book of Enoch (I Enoch) was written originally in Hebrew or Aramaic by at least five Palestinian authors during the two centuries before Christ; it has been preserved in Ethiopic and partly in Greek and Latin. The Book of the Secrets of Enoch was written by an Alexandrian Jew during the first half of the first Christian century; it has been preserved only in Slavonic manuscripts. Both these books devote much attention to angelology, demonology, and cosmology. The Apocalypse of Peter, written in Greek by a Christian about the middle of the second century, is noteworthy for introducing into Christian literature pagan ideas (Orphic and Pythagorean) of heaven and hell, vividly describing the rewards of the faithful and the torments of the damned. The Sibylline Oracles, a chaotic medley of pagan, Jewish, and Christian material, now extant in twelve books of Homeric hexameter verse, were written between 180 B.C. and A.D. 350.
B. M. M.

APOCRYPHA [əpɒ'krɪfə] (Gr. ἀπόκρυφος, hidden), a name variously applied to one or more categories of books lying outside the Hebrew scriptural canon. In its broadest use it is applied to all quasi-scriptural books which are excluded from Holy Writ. By Protestants it is usually applied specifically to the fourteen books that were included in the Septuagint, the Bible of the early Christian church, but were excluded from the Hebrew canon. This use of the term is avoided by Roman Catholics, who apply it rather to pseudepigraphical works that have never formed part of the Bible. The books generally called the "Apocrypha" by Protestants are termed "deuterocanonical" by Catholics; the books generally called the "Apocrypha" by Catholics are variously designated by Protestants, one term in general use being "Apocryphal Literature." The ancient rabbinical designation of uncanonical books was "outside books"; the name "Apocrypha" was given to them by St. Jerome, whose Latin version of the Bible is known as the Vulgate. Some of these books were written in Hebrew, others in Aramaic or Greek, and some of them contain Christian elements.

The books termed Apocryphal by Protestants and deuterocanonical by Catholics have formed a part of English Bibles since 1382. They were included in the King James Version of 1611, but they are usually omitted in the English Revised Version and the American Revised Version. The Puritans disapproved of them because they did not form part of the original Hebrew text. The Septuagint, however, which was the Greek version of the Jewish Bible, did contain these books, and from the Septuagint they found their way into the Latin Vulgate of St. Jerome. Originally they were distributed among the various Old Testament books to which they formed supplements, but in 1534 Luther, in his German Bible, originated the custom of grouping them as a separate unit between the Old and the New Testaments. The Catholic English Old Testament, however, still retains them scattered as in the Vulgate. They bear the following titles: First and Second Esdras; the Additions to Daniel, comprising the Hymn of the Three Holy Children, Susanna, and Bel and the Dragon; The Rest of the Book of Esther, Baruch with The Epistle of Jeremiah; The Prayer of Manasseh; First and Second Maccabees; Tobit; Judith; Ecclesiasticus; and The Wisdom of Solomon.

The books to which the name "Apocrypha" is given by Catholics form a vast body of writings of uncertain date and unknown authorship. Some of them exist only in fragments, and some have entirely disappeared and are known only through references in other works. In general usage these writings are classified under the two headings Old Testament Apocryphal Literature and New Testament Apocryphal Literature, according to the absence or presence of Christian elements within them.

There are naturally no complete lists of these writings, but some are more important than others. Among those usually classified in Old Testament Apocryphal Literature are the *Psalms of Solomon*, the Jewish portions of the *Sibylline Books, Enoch*, the *Assumption of Moses*, the *Syriac Apocalypse of Baruch*, the *Greek Apocalypse of Baruch*, the *Book of Jubilees, the Testaments of the Twelve Patriarchs*, the *Martyrdom of Isaiah*, the *Testament of Job*, several writings on the subject of Adam and Eve, the *History of Johannes Hyrcanus*, and various other legendary and apocalyptic works. Among those usually classified as New Testament Apocryphal Literature are a number of gospels, including the *Gospel of Nicodemus*, the *Gospel of Thomas*, the *Protevangel of James*, the *Gospel According to the Egyptians*, and the *Gospel According to the Hebrews*; certain *Acts*, including those of John, Thomas, and Paul, and the *Didache*, a book on the teachings of the Twelve Apostles; various epistles ascribed to Clement, Ignatius, Polycarp, Paul, and others; and a large body of apocalyptic writings, which include the Christian portions of the *Sybylline Books, The Shepherd of Hermas*, the *Apocalypse of Peter*, the *Apocalypse of Paul*, and the *Testament of Abraham. See also* PSEUDEPIGRAPHA.

APOGEE [æ′poji], the point in the moon's orbit farthest from the earth. Because of the eccentricity of the orbit, the distance from the earth to the apogee may be some 31,000 miles greater than the distance to the perigee. *See also* Perigee.   H. S. R.

APOLLINAIRE, GUILLAUME [a′pɔ′li′nɛ′r] (1880–1918), French poet, novelist, and dramatist, was born Aug. 26, 1880, in Rome. His real name, Kostrowitski, came from his mother, who was of Polish origin; his father's identity is unknown. He was educated at the Lycée Saint-Charles in Monaco. In 1898 he went to Paris, where he published his first poems in the *Revue Blanche* and *La Plume.* His first volume of verse, *Alcools,* appeared in 1913. His poetry, which initially showed the influence of Symbolism, is impregnated with nostalgia for Paris as it had been in bygone years. During World War I Apollinaire wrote most of the poems published in *Calligrammes.* He had accepted the war joyfully as a magnificent manifestation of modern beauty. He revived the old technique of the *graffiti,* and, composing drawings with written words, he tried to make poetry an art of space as well as of time.

Apollinaire was the spokesman of Cubism, and his book, *Les Peintres cubistes* (1913), presented the new painters to the public. Cubism was, in his view, an art on a universal scale, contrasting with the art on a human scale that had prevailed up to his time. His prose works include *Le Poète assassiné* (1916) (English translation, *The Poet Assassinated,* 1923), *La Femme assise* (1920), and a book of short stories, *L' Hérésiarque et Cie* (1910). In 1917 his *Mamelles de Tirésias,* "a surrealist drama," was staged. He died in Paris, Nov. 9, 1918, during an influenza epidemic.   R. Ta.

APOLLO [əpɒ′lo], one of the most important and many-sided of the ancient Greek divinities. Apollo was the son of Zeus and Leto and the twin brother of Artemis; he was born on Delos, whither Leto had fled, persecuted by the jealousy of Hera. According to tradition, Delos, which had earlier been a floating island, now became stationary, being chained to the bottom of the sea, and was henceforth an important center of Apollo's worship and the seat of one of his oracles. Among Apollo's many aspects, several are significant. He was the god of vengeance, who, with bow and arrows, sent pestilence and death. He was the god of agriculture and vegetation and protector of flocks and herds; as such his epithet Lyceian is explained by some as "wolf-slaying" (Gr. *lykos,* "wolf") by others as "Lycian-born," or "god of light." He was the god of prophesy; after slaying the Python he was worshipped as Pythian Apollo at Delphi, where his famous oracle existed and the Pythian games were held in his honor, and in this aspect he conferred the gift of prophecy upon Cassandra, Helenus, and other mortals. As the god of healing, who could avert disease and misfortune, Apollo was the father of Asclepios (Aesculapius) and was later identified with Paeon, the physician of the gods in Homer. In another manifestation, Apollo was the god of music and song, the leader of the Muses; and in still another, he was the god of colonization and founder of cities and laws, thus acting as the protector of civil order. Finally, he was the god of the sun; in the earliest period the sun god Helios was distinguished from Phoebus Apollo, but Apollo was later considered the god of light and identified with foreign sun gods. The epithet Phoebus, "shining," may refer to the brightness of the sun, or to Apollo's physical beauty, or to his moral purity.

Apollo's influence upon Greek thought was very great

and his worship stimulated the more humane and artistic side of Greek life. His attributes were the bow, the lyre, and the tripod; the laurel and the palm also were sacred to him. There were numerous representations of the god in Greek art, from the archaic statues of the sixth century B.C. to those of the later period in which he appears as the ideal of youthful manliness and beauty. His worship was taken over by the Romans, who dedicated a temple to him in 430 B.C. and instituted games in his honor (the *ludi Apollinares*) in 212 B.C. He became one of the chief Roman gods in the age of Augustus, who erected a temple to him on the Palatine. Numerous adventures and love affairs were related of Apollo; he was the father of Asclepios by Coronis, of Orpheus by the muse Calliope, and of Aristaeus by the nymph Cyrene. *See also* Cassandra; Clytië; Daphne; Hyacinthus; Linus; Marpessa; Marsyas; Midas; Niobe; Oracle; Phaëthon; Tityus.   G. E. D.

APOLLO BELVEDERE [bɛlvədi′r; be′lvede′re], a famous marble statue in the part of the Vatican museum called Belvedere. The statue was found about 1550 and was much admired by Bernini and other artists of the day. Montorsoli,

APOLLO BELVEDERE

a pupil of Michelangelo, restored the hands but did so wrongly, for the right hand was not empty but held a laurel branch, and the left hand held a bow, as testified by the quiver on the back of the figure. The statue was thus intended to depict the two aspects of Apollo, the god who punishes wrong-doers and purifies repentant sinners. Both Dürer and Rubens used poses based on the statue in their work, and Winckelmann praised it as a classical masterpiece.

The original statue was probably created by Leochares in the fourth century B.C. The copy is related to the Ganymede of that master, and an Apollo of Leochares is known to have stood before the temple of Apollo Patroos at Athens. The Vatican statue is considered rather too elegant and dry to do justice to the original, but there is a better copy of the head in Basel, Switzerland.   M. Bi.

APOLLODORUS OF DAMASCUS [əpɒ′lodɔ′rəs], Roman architect who flourished in the first quarter of the second century of the Christian Era, was a Syrian Greek by birth. He was invited to Rome by Trajan, and the great buildings that he erected there made him one of the most famous architects of the ancient world. In a treatise, now lost, he described his method of constructing a bridge over the Danube in Dacia for the Emperor Trajan in A.D. 104-105. His greatest achievement was the Forum of Trajan, built in 112-113. This was a monumental composition, combining an arched entrance, a court surrounded by colonnades, the many-columned Basilica Ulpia, and two library buildings flanking the colossal Trajan column, which was covered with a spiral band of relief recording Trajan's campaigns. Apollodorus added, besides, a large market area of arcaded and vaulted shops opening from corridors on three stories. He combined the principles of his native Hellenistic Greek and his adopted Roman architectural styles with rare originality and ingenuity. In the public baths that he built in Rome he developed the vault in forms that influenced most later Western architecture. He clashed, however, with Trajan's successor, Hadrian, who, himself an architectural designer, resented Apollodorus' biting criticism of his plans for the Temple of Venus and Roma and ordered his exile and death.   L. T. S.

APOLLONIUS OF PERGA [æpəlo'niəs] (c.262 B.C.-c.200 B.C.), Greek geometer, from Perga in Pamphylia, was the first important writer on the subject of conic sections. He wrote eight books on the subject and was perhaps the first to use the terms parabola, hyperbola, and ellipse. The locus of a point, the ratio of whose distances from two fixed points is a given constant, is a circle and is known as the circle of Apollonius. He was a student in the Alexandrian school of mathematics, in which Euclid had taught.   C. O. O.

APOLLONIUS OF RHODES (c. 305-235 B.C.), Greek epic poet, was born in Alexandria or possibly in Naucratis in Egypt near the end of the fourth century B.C. He was a pupil of Callimachus and while still young decided to write an epic poem on the adventures of the Argonauts. His first draft met with the disapproval not only of his teacher, but also, apparently, of the Alexandrian literary world. Apollonius retired discomfited to Rhodes, where his teaching of rhetoric and his epic verse gained him honorary citizenship. On the death of Zenodotus about 260, he was invited by Ptolemy Philadelphus to become head of the Alexandria Library. Here he engaged in critical, scholarly work and published his *Argonautica* in a revised form. He died shortly after Callimachus and is said to have been buried next to him in the Museum.

The theory, once widely held, that a bitter personal feud existed between Apollonius and Callimachus, requires modification in view of later evidence drawn from papyri and closer study of ancient documents. Apollonius was only one, though an important one, among several writers who opposed the theories of Callimachus. They did not subscribe to Callimachus' belief that certain genres in which perfection had already been reached (notably the Homeric epic) should be avoided, and they ignored his advice to strike out along new lines and concentrate on smaller, more precise forms. Apollonius in his *Argonautica* unwittingly supplied a justification of Callimachus' theories. Unable to maintain the grand sweep of the heroic epic, he shows himself at his best in short, episodic passages like the Rape of Hylas, Polydeuces' encounter with Amycus, or the sketch of Aphrodite as a charming housewife with a spoilt child, Eros. The great third book owes more to its picture of young Medea in love than to any heroic qualities. With his interest in erudition

and curious lore, and his capacity for short dramatic sketches, Apollonius is, in fact, a typical Alexandrian who misjudged his powers. *See also* ARGONAUTICA.   C. M. D.

APOLLONIUS OF TYANA [tai'ənə], Greek philosopher of the first century, was born at Tyana, in Cappadocia, probably in the same year as Jesus of Nazareth. Apollonius was educated at Tarsus and at the temple of Aesculapius in Aegae, where he became a Neo-Pythagorean. He traveled extensively in Asia Minor, India, Spain, Africa, Rome, and Greece, in the tradition of the Pythagorean mystic and disputant, and became famous for his wisdom. He was imprisoned by Emperor Domitian for treason, but escaped, reputedly by miraculous means. He is supposed to have founded a school at Ephesus, and to have died either there or at Rhodes or Crete, having led a pious and ascetic life for close to a hundred years. The only record of his life is by Flavius Philostratus of Lemnos, written about A.D. 216 at the request of the Empress Julia Domna and purporting to be based on some letters of Apollonius and the journal of his traveling companion, Damis. The story is presumed to be a religious romance with a partial element of historical truth. It has been denounced as a heretical attempt to rival the Christ story, in view of the coincidence of birth dates and the supposed similar marvels attending the birth of Apollonius, together with his ability to perform miracles. However, as with Virgil's *Messianic Eclogue,* the story of Apollonius probably ties in with the popular mythology of divinely attended births and the contemporary prevalence of itinerant preachers and seers.   C. W. D.

APOLLYON [əpɒ'lyən], the destroyer (Rev. ix: 11) in John Bunyan's *Pilgrim's Progress,* who tries to prevent Christian's flight from his dominions but retreats after a combat in the Valley of Humiliation.   H. B. W.

APOLOGETICS [əpɒ'lojε'tıks], the department of Christian theology concerned with the rational defense of the Christian interpretation of life. The term "apologetics" is derived from the Greek word ἀπολογία, "apologia," meaning a verbal or rational defense. The New Testament writers use the same word and its derivatives in describing Christians as the defenders of the faith. An apologist is one who formally undertakes the task of apologetics. The writings of the apologist are known as apologies.

A brief survey of the history of Christian apologies will enable one to see the great value of apologetics in Christian theology. In the apologetic period (100-254) the outstanding apologetic writings were Irenaeus' *Adversus haereses* ("Against Heresies") and Origen's *Contra Celsum* ("Against Celsus"). Augustine (354-430) during the polemic period (254-730) contributed his great work *De civitate Dei* ("The City of God"), for the purpose of stating and defending the Christian philosophy of history. In the course of the years Thomas Aquinas (1225-1274), the great Catholic theologian, added his *Summa contra Gentiles* ("Against the Unbelievers") in defending the faith, against Mohammedanism in particular. The Protestant revolt against Roman Catholicism was ably defended by Philip Melanchthon in *Apology of the Augsburg Confession* (1531), and by John Calvin in *The Institutes of the Christian Religion* (1536); Robert Bellarmine (1524-1621) was among the most distinguished of the Roman Catholic apologists. Perhaps the best defense against the Rationalists' attacks during the seventeenth and eighteenth centuries was offered by Bishop Joseph Butler in *The Analogy of Religion* (1736), but William Paley's

View of the Evidences of Christianity (1794) was widely read. In the nineteenth century the skirmishes occasioned by the theory of evolution, philosophy of naturalism, higher criticism, and comparative religion resulted most notably in J. H. Newman's well-known *Apologia pro vita sua* (1864), in which he justified his entrance into the Roman Church, but they produced no outstanding positive apologies for the Christian religion. In 1919 Karl Barth rallied the apologists to an aggressive proclamation of the unique message of Christ in the New Testament. The prevailing tendency among contemporary apologists is to declare the Christian philosophy of life the key to the true meaning of existence.

The perennial task of apologetics is to defend the eternal truth as expressed in Christian theology against false and inadequate philosophies of life. Its first duty is to demonstrate on the grounds of reason that Christianity is the true philosophy of life. Its second duty is to show that the Christian interpretation is the basis for all the special sciences, such as physics, psychology, sociology, aesthetics, ethics, and religion. Its third duty is to defend with reason the Bible as the primary source for our knowledge of the truth as God has revealed it in Christ; this duty implies that apologetics must deal with the problems involved in theological teachings of miracles, revelation, prophecy, and the inspiration of the Scriptures.

Apologetics is a vital factor in the effective proclamation of Christianity. It upholds and defends the truth in Christ as indispensable in the pursuit of goodness. The apologist has a passion for the winning of unbelievers to faith in Christ as the way, the truth, and the life. He is concerned with strengthening the faith of the doubting Christian. He understands that the truly Christian example is the best defense of the faith. In carrying on this great frontier work of Christianity, the apologist must have a mind to grasp philosophy, the heart of a pastor, and an exemplary life that reflects the power of God in Christ to make men perfect.

C. De B.

APOLOGIA PRO VITA SUA. *See* Newman, John Henry.

APOLOGUE. *See* Fable.

APOMORPHINE. *See* Alkaloids; Poisons.

APONOGETON CRISPUS [æ'ponoji'tən], a strikingly beautiful, translucent aquarium plant with long knifelike leaves, the edges of which are rippled. It blooms on a long stem in the shape of a shepherd's crook, which comes out above the water. Native to Ceylon, it will grow in gravel or sand.

A. Gr.

APOSTASY [əpɒ'stəsi] (Gr. ἀποστασία: ἀπό, from, στῆναι, stand), in general the complete abandonment of one's faith, professions, principles or party; in particular it is the total desertion of one's religion. In the early Christian Church apostasy was regarded as one of the sins whose forgiveness was left to God alone; absolution of apostates by the Church was first admitted in the second half of the third century. With the Christianization of the Roman Empire, apostasy was punished by loss of civil rights. Flavius Claudius Julianus (c. 331-363), known as Julian the Apostate, was brought up to profess the Christian faith but secretly abandoned it when he was twenty. As emperor (from late 361), he openly favored a pagan restoration, the failure of which is epitomized in the unauthentic words attributed to him, *Vicisti Galilaee!* ("Thou hast conquered, Galilaean!"). In the Middle Ages apostates were classed with heretics and similarly punished. In the (1918) Code of Canon Law of the Roman Catholic Church, the same penalties, principally excommunication, are prescribed for apostasy "from the faith" (defined as the total desertion of the Christian faith), heresy (defined as the pertinacious denial or calling in doubt of an article of faith), and schism (defined as the refusal of obedience to the Pope or of communication with members of the Church subject to him). Apostasy "from religion" (defined as the crime of a religious bound by perpetual vows who illegitimately leaves a religious house with the intention of not returning, or who, although leaving the house legitimately, remains away with the intention of withdrawing himself from religious obedience) is punished by excommunication and other penalties. The term *apostasia ab ordine* (i.e. from Holy Orders) is sometimes used to designate the abandonment by a cleric of the clerical dress and state, an action variously punished according to circumstances.

N. J. T.

A POSTERIORI. *See* A Priori.

APOSTLE [əpɒ'səl], a member of the select group, originally commissioned by Jesus Christ, which took the leading part in evangelism and in the administration of the primitive Christian Church. The twelve disciples of Jesus formed the nucleus of the band (Luke vi:13; Mark vi:7, 30; Matt. x:1-5), their functions being those of preaching and healing (Mark vi:7-13; Matt. x:5-8). With the organizing of the Church the task of administration was added to these primitive duties (Acts vi:1-6; xv:2, 4, 6, 22). At the same time a few additional names, Paul and Barnabas among them, were added to the original twelve with a view to the enlarged mission throughout the Roman Empire. In the New Testament only Paul (Gal. i:1; I Cor. xv:9) and Luke (Acts xiv:4, 14) bear witness to this more general use of the term; Paul indicates his claims to its use in his own case (I Cor. ix:1-7). The later *Didache* (about A.D. 100) testifies to the use of "apostle" for a missionary in the Gentile world.

The apostles from the first were the center of the Church's life—of its "preaching," "teaching," "breaking of bread" (the common meal), and "fellowship" (Acts i:8; ii:42). Through them the teachings of Jesus were transmitted to his Church (Mark iv:10-12; I Cor. xi:23-26; xv:3-11; II Peter iii:2). In the lists of Church officials they were always given the first rank (I Cor. xii:28; Eph. iv:11). With the "prophets" they formed the foundation of the Church (Ephesians ii:20; Rev. xxi:14). With the close of the first century their office was discontinued and men assuming the title were branded as liars (Rev. ii:2).

J. W. Bo.

APOSTLES' CREED, THE, a formula which contains the fundamental beliefs of the Christian Church, expressed in brief statements or "articles" traditionally considered as twelve in number. The subject of innumerable commentaries (among the older being those of Rufinus, Nicetas, and Cyril of Jerusalem) and of much modern critical research (e.g., by Caspari, Hahn, Kattenbusch, Harnack, Burn, Voisin, and Vacant), the Apostles' Creed, whatever its precise origin and antiquity, is considered by the Roman Catholic Church as an official document. Nearly all theologians of the Eastern Orthodox Churches deny its ecumenical authority. Protestant scholars, who accept it merely as representative of the teaching of Apostolic times, have been especially diligent in investigating its origin.

N. J. T.

APOSTLE SPOON, one of a set of thirteen spoons bearing representations of Christ and the twelve Apostles. These are distinguished by their traditional emblems, a key or fish for St. Peter, a chalice for St. John, a butcher's knife for St. Bartholomew, a saw for St. Simon, and so forth. They are heard of first in the sixteenth century, were more in vogue in England than elsewhere, and were given by sponsors as baptismal gifts. Allusions to them occur in the English drama, e.g., "Come, come, my lord, you'd spare your spoons" (*Henry VIII,* Act 5, scene 3).   N. J. T.

APOSTOLIC CONSTITUTIONS, THE, a collection of ecclesiastical regulations held to have been composed by the apostles of Jesus Christ and promulgated by St. Clement, the fourth pope of Rome. In reality it was assembled and edited about A.D. 400 by an unknown author in Syria or Constantinople. This editor was apparently an Arian. The Quinisext Council (692) rejected most of the *Apostolic Constitutions* as having been interpolated by heretics, but this condemnation left undecided the question of the authenticity of the original collection. Consequently the work did not lose the high esteem in which it had come to be held, and in excerpts it found its way into the legal codes of the Eastern Church.

The *Apostolic Constitutions* is a lengthy work composed of eight books and may be divided into three parts. The first part, comprising the first six books, reproduces, with occasionally capricious alterations, the *Didascalia,* a work composed very probably in northern Syria in the early third century. This part treats of bishops, deacons, deaconesses, and widows, of various points of doctrine and discipline, and of schisms and heresies. The second part includes only book seven. It reproduces in an adapted and expanded form the *Didache* or *Teaching of the Twelve Apostles,* which dates from the early second century, and was composed probably in Syria. Besides its garbled version of the *Didache,* this seventh book contains liturgical matter from unknown sources and a list of the earliest bishops which is probably derived from earlier works which are now lost.

The third and most interesting part of the *Apostolic Constitutions* is the eighth book, which is based almost entirely on the *Apostolic Tradition* of St. Hippolytus of Rome, who died in 235. This part treats of charisms and gives formulae for various ordinations and consecrations. In the formula of the consecration of a bishop the entire liturgy of the Mass is included, and this is the most ancient complete Mass extant. There are also instructions on confessors, virgins, widows, and exorcists. Finally there is a collection of canons on various subjects, among them the so-called *Canons of the Apostles,* which are probably the work of the compiler of the *Apostolic Constitutions.*   E. A. R.

APOSTOLIC DELEGATE, a legate sent by the Holy See not to a government but to the Roman Catholic hierarchy of a country, to keep the Roman pontiff informed concerning the condition of the Church and to serve as his representative in certain ecclesiastical affairs. Apostolic delegates in the United States have been Francesco Satolli (1893-1896), Sebastianni Martinelli (1896-1902), Diomede Falconio (1902-1911), Giovanni Bonzano (1911-1922), Pietro Fumasoni-Biondi (1922-1933), all created cardinals at the end of their terms, and Amleto Giovanni Cicognani (1933-   ), who was born in Italy in 1883, ordained priest in 1905, attached to the Curia Romana in 1922, and consecrated titular Archbishop of Laodicea in 1933.   N. J. T.

APOSTOLIC FATHERS, the general name customarily given to those Christian writers of the last two decades of the first century and the first half of the second, known or considered to have had personal contact with the apostles or to have come within their unmodified influence. The list of writers included under this title varies according to the norms of scholars. The most important are the three first-century bishops, St. Clement of Rome, St. Ignatius of Antioch, and St. Polycarp of Smyrna. Their writings are chiefly hortatory, in the form of letters intended for individuals or for local churches. Their great value is in their antiquity, bearing witness to the faith of the early Christians in the chief mysteries of the Divine Unity and Trinity, and in forming the link of tradition that binds the apologies of the second century with the New Testament.   W. C.

APOSTOLIC SUCCESSION, the principle underlying the theory that the ministry of the Christian Church is a divinely appointed and historically continuous steward of the doctrine, discipline, and worship of Christianity from apostolic times (i.e., the first century of the Church's life). This conception is maintained by the Eastern Orthodox, Roman Catholic, and Anglican Communions, all of which lay stress on the succession of ministers secured through the historic episcopate. A similar theory, held by some Calvinists, maintains that the succession is given through the presbyter, whose office is equated with that of the bishop. The Ordinal of the Anglican Communion, found in the Book of Common Prayer, implies that the apostolic succession through the episcopate is the means of securing a continuous life for the Church. Associated with this whole idea is emphasis on "tactual succession," or the unbroken line of episcopal ordinations from apostolic days. A modern variant of the theory is that the episcopate is the external sign or sacrament of the internal dynamic succession of the Church's life as "Body of Christ"; this view is held by many twentieth-century Anglo-Catholic divines.   W. N. P.

APOTHEOSIS [æ′pothi′osɪs; apɒ′thio′sɪs], the deification of a mortal. Many rulers in the Greco-Roman world and in the Orient have been honored as divine, some of the most notable in the Greek world being Philip II of Macedon, Alexander the Great, and certain successors of Alexander. Julius Caesar was deified in 42 B.C. at the instigation of Augustus Caesar, and thereafter the Roman Senate formally elevated to the rank of the gods not only deceased emperors but several living emperors and favorites of the imperial household as well.   B. M. M.

APPALACHIAN MOUNTAIN SYSTEM [æpələ′tshɪən; æpəle′tshɪən], a rugged highland area of eastern North America, extending from the Gaspé Peninsula and St. Lawrence River Valley in Quebec, Canada, southwestward for approximately 1,500 mi. to Alabama. The Appalachian system includes a large number of mountains, plateaus, and valleys. The Appalachians are bordered on the north by the St. Lawrence lowland, on the east and south by the coastal plain, and on the west by the interior lowlands. The width of the Appalachians varies from place to place, but in general the system is about 80 to 100 mi. wide in the northern part and about 300 to 350 mi. wide in the south. The elevations vary from about 300 to 400 ft. above sea level at the eastern edge, or fall line, to 6,711 ft. at Mount Mitchell in the Black Mountains of North Carolina.

The system contains many types of rock formations of different geologic ages. Its four major physiographic provinces, from east to west, are the Piedmont; the Blue Ridge, or Older Appalachian Mountains; the Valley and Ridge, or Younger

Appalachian Mountains; and the Appalachian Plateau Province, of which the Ozark plateaus and the Ouachita Province of Missouri and Arkansas are considered outliers. Within each of these large subdivisions are many subregions, and the whole problem of Appalachian nomenclature is confused by the use of local names and terminology. In other cases it is difficult to draw exact boundary lines between physical features and between provinces. Some of the dissected Appalachian Plateau areas are higher and more rugged than some of the flat-topped mountain areas, and part of the Great Valley is about 2,000 ft. above sea level, which is about the maximum elevation of some of the Highland area. The whole Appalachian system is further divided into a northern (New England) and a southern district. Perhaps the most outstanding characteristics of the Appalachian system are that the major features have a generally northeast-southwest trending axis and that the major provinces are more or less parallel to each other. In many respects the southern Appalachians are more typical than the northern.

The Appalachians were formed by a series of uplifts, foldings, and erosion, all of which took place over long periods of time during different geologic ages and which affected rocks of different hardness. The Older Appalachians were uplifted during Proterozoic and Paleozoic times and were higher than the present mountains. These mountains were eroded for a long time, and sediments were washed down and deposited in the sea, which then extended on either side. Near the end of the Paleozoic Era the consolidated sediments on the west were folded up into the Younger Appalachians. The whole area was then subjected to several cycles of erosion, one particularly widespread cycle resulting in the even-summit levels and flat-topped areas of the Cretaceous peneplain. Continental glaciation further affected the northern section of the Appalachian system; and many of the swamps and lakes and the drainage pattern, as well as the rocky boulder-strewn fields of New England, are the result of continental glaciation.

The Appalachian system has had a tremendous effect on the economic history of the United States. The long, densely forested mountains hampered westward expansion, thus giving the thirteen seaboard colonies time to consolidate. The roles played by the Cumberland and other gaps and by valleys such as the Mohawk-Hudson-Champlain and the Shenandoah in the development, history, and economy of the United States are almost incalculable. East-west overland transportation is still restricted and hampers the development of parts of the Appalachian system.

Piedmont Province. The Piedmont, or foothill province, is the most easterly of the Appalachian system and lies between the coastal plain on the east and the Blue Ridge, or Older Appalachian, Province on the west. It extends from the Hudson River Valley in New York State south to Alabama. From north to south the Piedmont increases in width as well as in importance. The northern portion is about 50 mi. wide, whereas the southern section in North Carolina is about 125 mi. wide. Southwestward from South Carolina the Piedmont narrows and ends in central Alabama.

As the name suggests, the Piedmont is a foothill region, that is, a transition zone between the coastal plain and the mountains. In general, the Piedmont is an undulating plain that slopes eastward from its western border (approximately 1,200 ft. above sea level) to the eastern border (300 to 400 ft. above sea level). Most of the Piedmont, particularly in the south, is underlain by hard crystalline rock with a complicated structure. Gneiss, schist, quartzite, and some granite, gabbro, and limestone, all more or less crystalline, are the most common types of rock. This area was uplifted, eroded, and peneplained, and the general levelness and even summits of the Piedmont are caused by erosion rather than structure. At the eastern border of the Piedmont is a fall line where the rivers and streams fall from the harder and higher crystalline rock onto the softer coastal-plain sediments. In some places on the Piedmont the more resistant rock remains standing above the general level, forming a series of low, rounded, even-summit hills. Part of the Piedmont, particularly in New Jersey, Pennsylvania, and Virginia, and in scattered areas of the Carolinas, is underlain by the Newark series of Triassic red sandstone. In the northern section of the Appalachians, the Connecticut River Valley of Connecticut and Massachusetts and the Annapolis Valley of Nova Scotia are underlain by this sandstone. This area has gentle slopes and is more of a lowland than the rest of the Piedmont. However, in the Triassic sandstone areas there are numerous trap ridges, which break up the lowland character of the sandstone belts. The major part of the sandstone area in New Jersey, Pennsylvania, and Virginia is enclosed by four prominent crystalline ridges called prongs. To the northwest is the Reading Prong, to the northeast the Manhattan Prong, to the southeast the Trenton Prong, and to the southwest is the Carlisle Prong.

The soil of the Piedmont varies from place to place. Most of it is reddish and not particularly fertile except in the favored limestone belts and some of the Triassic sandstone valleys. In the Piedmont, agriculture is fairly diversified, but there are several major-crop regions. In the south, tobacco is the main crop; in northern Virginia, Maryland, and Pennsylvania, apple growing and livestock raising are the principal agricultural activities; whereas at the northern end, farming, including wheat, corn, and livestock is important.

The most important cities of the Piedmont are Lancaster and York, Pa.; Lynchburg and Charlottesville, Va.; and Winston-Salem, N. C. Along the eastern or coastal-plain side of the fall line are manufacturing and commercial cities that have been developed because of the water power available at the fall line, the proximity to tidewater, and the good shipping facilities. Some of the more important of these cities are, from north to south: Newark, New Brunswick, and Trenton, N.J.; Philadelphia, and Chester, Pa.; Wilmington, Del.; Baltimore, Md.; Washington, D.C.; Richmond, Va.; and Columbia, S.C.

The Blue Ridge Province or the Older Appalachian Mountains. The Older Appalachian Mountains, or Blue Ridge Province, lies between the Piedmont on the east and the Valley and Ridge Province on the west. This province contains the highest and most majestic as well as the oldest section of the Appalachian system. The area is composed of crystalline, igneous, and metamorphic rocks and ancient granite, as well as gneiss and schist. The mountain structure is extremely complicated and irregular. There is a large number of mountain ranges within the province, of which some of the more important are the Blue Ridge, which forms the steep escarpment and ridge along the eastern border of the province, the Pisgah Ridge, and the Bald, Stone, Iron, Unaka, Great Smoky, and Black mountains. In the Black Mountains, which are transverse to the general trend of the Appalachians, is Mount Mitchell, 6,711 ft. above sea level, the highest peak in the Appalachian system. Within the jumble of worn-down, somewhat rounded, but nonetheless majestic mountain ranges are small basins, plains, and coves, in which most of the inhabitants of this sparsely settled area live. The Asheville Basin is well known as a resort center.

Because of its higher elevation the Blue Ridge Province

Looking toward Hanging Rock State Park, South Carolina, from Caesar's Head, near the southern end of the Appalachians

has cooler and wetter climatic conditions than the surrounding regions. The area is densely forested; trees that are typical of the northern states, such as spruce, birch, hemlock, and white pine, grow on the mountaintops, and yellow pine and other southern trees grow along the flanks of the mountains. In places, there are stands of beech, oak, and hickory. In the Great Smoky Mountains some tremendous first-growth trees are still standing, and the whole region has a dense underbrush of wild scenic interest. It is a region of retreat for human beings. In the coves and valley settlements some remnants of Elizabethan language, songs, and customs still prevail.

The Valley and Ridge Province, or the Younger Appalachians. The Valley and Ridge, or Younger Appalachian Province, is located between the Older Appalachian or Blue Ridge on the east and the Appalachian Plateau on the west. This region has a more or less continuous northeast-southwest trending valley, which might be called the single feature that gives continuity to the whole Appalachian system. Associated with this valley is a series of long, narrow, parallel, folded sedimentary mountains, separated by deep and steep valleys. These sedimentary ridges are the result of folding, erosion to a peneplain surface, and then uplift with renewed erosion. Streams were formed on the peneplain surface, and when uplift occurred the streams were able to maintain their original course across the ridges. In many cases the headwater streams of the rivers that flow in the valleys, parallel with the ridges, intercepted or cut off the streams flowing across the mountains and so diverted the water. This left wind gaps through the mountains. Cumberland Gap is one of these. Long, narrow, tightly folded anticlines and synclines, many of them zigzag or cigar-shaped ridges, are found in the area. The western border of the

Valley and Ridge Province is formed by the Adirondack and Catskill mountains and by the abrupt wall of the Allegheny Front and the Cumberland Escarpment. The northern end of this province is the St. Lawrence River Valley, which connects with the Champlain Trough and the Hudson River Valley in New York and the Kittatinny Valley in New Jersey, the Lebanon and Cumberland valleys in Pennsylvania and Maryland, the Shenandoah Valley in Virginia, the Tennessee Valley in Tennessee, and the Coosa Valley in Georgia and Alabama, all of which combine to form the Great Appalachian Valley.

Much of the Great Valley is underlain by limestone, and much of it is extremely fertile and productive. The primary products of the area are corn, wheat, hay, and livestock; cotton in the south; and apples and other fruits, mainly in the north. There are fine highways and railroads. The Great Valley served as a highway for Indians and then later for the pioneers who went south through the valley and west through the Cumberland Gap. During the Civil War the Great Valley was a marchway and battleground for the Confederate and Union armies; some towns in the northern edge of the valley changed hands over seventy times during the course of the war.

The Valley and Ridge Province is a famous industrial district because of the north-south transportation facilities and the near-by or present sources of iron, coal, limestone, shale, and, on either side of the valley, lumber. Among the important industrial centers are Harrisburg and Bethlehem, Pa.; Hagerstown, Md.; Roanoke, Va.; Chattanooga, Tenn.; and Birmingham, Ala. Although the valley and the mineral-bearing ridges are prosperous regions, in sharp contrast are the large sections of long, narrow, steep parallel ridges, which hamper human use and occupancy.

The Tennessee River, in cutting crookedly through the Appalachian Range, forks to form Williams Island.

The Appalachian Plateau Province. The Appalachian Plateau Province is the most westerly of the Appalachian provinces. Its eastern boundary is a remarkable and fairly continuous escarpment called the Allegheny Front. This steep ridge extends from New York to Tennessee and forms a definite boundary to the Appalachian Plateau Province. The Appalachian Plateau here slopes rather gently westward and merges with the Ohio Valley and the Central Lowland area. The plateau is underlain by more or less horizontal sandstone and conglomerate beds, and erosion and stream gullying have cut the surface into a rugged region that seems to be more mountainous than parts of the Appalachian Mountains. In West Virginia and Kentucky the Appalachian Plateau is about 4,000 ft. above sea level and has deep valleys that make the area seem like a jumble of mountains. In New York, the Catskill Mountains are on the edge of the plateau, as are the Pocono Mountains of Pennsylvania and New Jersey.

The northern part of the Appalachian Plateau is called the Allegheny Plateau and the southern part the Cumberland Plateau. The Allegheny Plateau extends from the Helderberg Escarpment, which is on the southern edge of New York State, south to the Cumberland River; and the Cumberland Plateau extends from the Cumberland River south to the Tennessee River. The main difference between the two plateaus is that the northern, or Allegheny Plateau, has been much more deeply dissected and is therefore rugged and more mountainlike.

The whole Appalachian Plateau area has deposits of coal, iron, and some oil and natural gas, but the terrain makes transportation difficult. Pittsburgh is the major plateau city. The Pennsylvania Railroad crosses the Allegheny Front near Altoona, Pa., and the famous horseshoe curve is one example of the engineering problems presented by the Allegheny Front.

The New England physiographic province forms the northern end of the Appalachian system. It extends from the Gaspé Peninsula and St. Lawrence River lowland, on the north, southward to New York City. The western border is the Hudson-Champlain Valley, and the eastern boundary is the Atlantic Ocean. In southern New England, bordering Long Island Sound, there is a narrow coastal plain, but this is not typical of the New England Province. The major divisions within the New England Province are the New England uplands, which correspond to the Piedmont region to the south. The New England upland is a low hilly belt which gradually increases in elevation to the west, where it is about 2,000 ft. above sea level. The bedrock is largely composed of hard, ancient, crystalline gneiss, granite, quartzite, and schist.

The whole upland region is divided into two sections, east and west, by a fault valley—the Annapolis River Valley in Nova Scotia and the Connecticut River Valley in New England. Both areas are Triassic sandstone districts with trap ridges, and they correspond to the Triassic sandstone areas of New Jersey, Pennsylvania, and Virginia. The eastern part of the New England upland is fairly low but has occasional monadnocks such as Mount Monadnock of southern New Hampshire and Mount Wachusett in Massachusetts. In the eastern uplands are two prominent structural basins, the Boston and the Narragansett. West of the New England hilly belt are two roughly parallel north-south trending mountain regions separated by the Connecticut River Valley. The most easterly are the White Mountains which are the

The White Mountains and the Franconia Mountains, New Hampshire, part of the Appalachian System

BROWN BROTHERS

highest and most imposing mountains of the northern Appalachians. The White Mountains are formed by the erosion of anticlinorium and extend from southern New Hampshire northward, bending eastward into Maine, Quebec, and New Brunswick and forming the Maine-New Brunswick highland. Of the many ranges within the White Mountains, the Presidential Range is the highest and best known. This range contains Mount Washington, the highest peak in the northeastern area, 6,293 ft. above sea level; Mount Adams, 5,798 ft.; Jefferson, 5,725; Monroe, 5,390; and Madison, 5,380. This range and the White Mountains district comprise a famous tourist and resort area.

West of the White Mountains and the Connecticut River Valley are the Green Mountains. This folded range of mountains extends from northwest Connecticut northward through west Massachusetts and Vermont, and then curves to the northeast into Canada, forming the Notre Dame and Shickshock Mountains. Their greatest development is in Vermont, where the summit elevations vary between 2,000 and 4,000 ft. above sea level. The Green Mountains, like the White Mountains, are forest-covered and form a well-known winter and summer resort area. The Green Mountains correspond to the Older Appalachians in the Southern Appalachians. The Newer Appalachian, or the Appalachian Valley and Ridge section, is represented in New England by the Taconic Range and the Little Hoosic Valley and in New York State by the Rensselaer Plateau and the Hudson Valley.

The surface features of the whole New England district have been altered by glaciation, and the whole region is overlaid with glacial till. The mountains have been rounded off, and deltas, moraines, eskers, drumlins, and kames have been formed. New England is noted for the large number of lakes and ponds formed by the glacier and for the large number of stones and boulders left by the ice when it melted. The drainage pattern has also been altered by glaciation.

The New England section has a cool to cold but humid and moist climate. It is rather heavily forested, principally with birch, beech, maple, hemlock, white pine, and some oak. These forests are valuable for flood control, scenic beauty, wild-life protection, paper pulp manufacturing, and lumbering. Other forest products are the maple sugar and syrup of Vermont, and the Christmas trees grown throughout the mountain regions. Agriculture has been hampered by physical conditions but New England is a good dairy region and has areas of specialized agriculture such as the Aroostook Valley, a potato district, and the Connecticut River Valley, a tobacco and onion district. Apple growing is also important, and the Annapolis Valley of Nova Scotia is also a famous fruit-growing region. Because of the many small and large streams, New England has abundant water power. Many of the early towns developed around small waterfalls, which were utilized to turn water wheels. Because of this power source, the bracing climate, and the difficulty of agriculture, manufacturing developed, and the New England district has a large number of important manufacturing cities. Shipbuilding and fishing are also important activities along the drowned coast of New England, and marble and granite quarrying are important economic activities in Vermont and New Hampshire.   J.E.F.

APPALACHIAN TRAIL, an extensive foot-trail for the recreation of hikers and campers that runs generally through the wilderness along the crest of the Appalachian Mountains near the Atlantic Coast of the United States. It is about 2,020 mi. long, originating at Mt. Katahdin in central Maine, traversing fourteen states, and terminating at Mt. Oglethorpe in northern Georgia.

The idea of a continuous foot-path through the wilderness can be traced to Benton MacKaye, forester, author, and philosopher, of Shirley Center, Mass., who published an article proposing such a trail in October 1921. As it exists today, the Trail was completed in 1937 with subsequent minor deviations of route. As a route for foot travel only, it is the longest marked path in the world. With the exception of National and State forests and parks traversed, the Trail is mainly on privately owned land by consent of the owners. To be continuous, the Trail sometimes follows existing roads in crossing valleys from one ridge to another, but such roads constitute a negligible fraction of the Trail mileage. For the marking of the Trail route itself, white paint blazes on trees and rocks are used along with a few board signs, giving directions, distances, and termini.

A long-range program for the development of Trail shelters at intervals of a moderate day's journey, was begun in 1937 and is still in progress. General maintenance and improvements to the Trail are undertaken by local outdoor clubs and other interested organizations.   A. P.

APPARITION, the visual perception of animate or inanimate objects that usually do not have external existence. Although it is true that most apparitions can be classified as illusions and hallucinations, cautious psychologists admit that there are extrasensory phenomena that cannot be scientifically explained. Experiences defined as clairvoyance and second sight, for example, present difficulties which cannot be wholly removed by calling them illusory or hallucinatory. A notable example is the experience of Emanuel Swedenborg (1688-1772), ennobled in 1719 by the Swedish Crown for his achievements in science and technology. About 1743 he experienced visions which initiated his devotion to psychical and spiritualistic research, the results of which became the foundation for the widely numerous sect of Swedenborgians. Swedenborg, with what he believed to be supporting evidence, had had numerous visions, many of which cannot be scientifically disproved.

Viewed as hallucinations, apparitions are the effects of a variety of causes. Victims of brain and nerve disorders, of high fever, and of alcoholism frequently experience hallucinations, delirium tremens being a well-known condition. Drug addicts frequently report fantastic visions. Vivid dreams at times are so realistic, particularly during the period before full wakefulness, that they have an objectivity which the individual sometimes asserts is actually real. Other types of apparitions or hallucinations may occur in relation to a near or distant dying person with whom one has had intensely emotional contacts. While such apparitions are usually explained in terms of telepathy or clairvoyance, in most instances they are manifestations of long-existing unconscious anxiety, expectancy, or sense of loss, fear, or hope suddenly projected into apparitional form, either by coincidence or because stimulated by some free association which initiates a memory chain dominated by a revival of emotions similar to those current during the original experience. Such projections of memory are likely to be intensely vivid in highly sensitive and emotionally unstable individuals.

From early times, belief in ghosts has affected human behavior. Many long-continuing efforts have been made by the Society for Psychical Research to obtain evidence for the survival after death and rational explanations for avowed experiences with ghosts. Sir Oliver Lodge (1851-1940) in England, James Hyslop (1854-1920), founder of the American Society of Psychical Research, and William James (1842-1910) have been among many other notable investigators of the possibility of communication between the human and spectral worlds. No scientifically valid evidence of such a possibility has ever been found.

Belief in the objectivity of apparitions probably is based on the age-old belief in angels, demons, and spirits as recorded in the sacred books of various religions. Although the Egyptians believed strongly in immortality they do not appear to have believed in direct communication with the departed. To what degree the ancient Hebrews were influenced by Zoroastrian angelology and demonology is problematical, but the Bible contains numerous references to angels and demons. Christian theology, in its teachings of the Holy Ghost or Holy Spirit, emphasizes the reality of the spiritual world. Among the Mohammedans, Hebrews, and Christians, conceptions of spirits merge in a further elaboration of theological doctrine.

In most parts of the world, from early times to the present, man has been conditioned from childhood to accept the reality of a world beyond the mundane. So predisposed, many individuals do not question experiences which to them can have no other explanation than that they are contacts with the supernatural. Such experiences, however, can be explained largely as products of emotional disorders or of vivid imagination in which fear plays a major role. Open-minded students of mental and emotional phenomena admit, however, the possibility of other explanations which wait upon further research into the psychically unknown. A. L. H-Q.

APPEAL. *See* Legal Procedure.
APPEARANCE. *See* Legal Procedure.
APPENDECTOMY. *See* Appendicitis.

APPENDICITIS [əpɛ'ndɪsai'tɪs], an inflammation and infection of the vermiform process, or appendix. The disease was first recognized in 1759, but not until 1886 was the clinical entity brought before the medical profession. An interesting fact is that the disease is much more common among civilized people than primitive ones.

Cause. The appendix is a blind pouch and such pouches are prone to become infected. The *Streptococcus* is supposed to be a cause of infection in some cases and the *Bacillus coli* in others. Appendicitis is due to a mixed infection of both these bacteria. Many foreign bodies are found in acute appendicitis and may be a contributing cause. These foreign bodies consist of such things as dry feces, pins, intestinal worms, and even birdshot which have been found in persons who have eaten wild game.

Symptoms. The appendix is attached to the first portion of the colon, which is called the caecum. One end is free and it may lie in any one of nine positions. Consequently, the symptoms vary greatly in types and severity. Sometimes a patient may experience very few symptoms, yet the appendix may become inflamed and even rupture. The typical symptoms are pain around the umbilicus with nausea and vomiting. The pain shifts and localizes to the right lower quadrant of the abdomen. Pain is elicited if pressure is applied over the appendix, and the muscles become involuntarily spastic. The white blood count rises to fifteen thousand or more and temperature is only slightly elevated.

Treatment. If the diagnosis is positive, the infected organ should be removed. This can be done through any number of lower abdominal incisions. The most common

APPIAN WAY
(Left) *Circus of Maxentius and tomb of Cecilia Metella* (Right) *Tomb of St. Urbanus and the Temple of Jupiter*

one is a muscle-splitting incision in which muscle fibers are separated and not cut. The appendix is removed by ligating the vessels, cutting across the appendix base, and inverting the stump with a chromic catgut suture placed in a circular fashion about it. Drains are seldom used even if the appendix is ruptured. Sulphanilamide is placed around the area if the organ has ruptured. The mortality is very low in cases operated on before rupture occurs. An acute appendix may subside, recur, or rupture and form a localized abscess becoming walled off by a pad of fat known as the omentum, or the infection may spread throughout the abdomen and cause a generalized peritonitis.

Chronic Appendicitis. This is a questionable entity and covers a multitude of symptoms referable to the right lower quadrant of the abdomen. An operation is justified only when all other causes of the pain are eliminated. An X ray of the appendix is of no value in diagnosing either acute or chronic appendicitis. W. H. B.

APPENDIX. *See* APPENDICITIS.

APPENZELL [ɑ'pəntsɛl], a northeastern canton of Switzerland, has been entirely surrounded by the canton of St. Gallen since 1803. It consists of two half cantons: Interior Appenzell (Inner Rhoden, Inner Rhodes) to the south, with an area of 67 sq. mi. and a population of 13,300 in 1953; and Exterior Appenzell (Ausser Rhoden, Outer Rhodes) to the north, with an area of 90 sq. mi. and a population of 48,500 in 1953. Appenzell joined the Swiss Confederation in 1513 but withdrew from it in 1597 in order to separate Catholic Interior Appenzell from Protestant Exterior Appenzell. German-Swiss is spoken in both parts. Most of the area is a rather large, rolling plateau dominated by Mount Säntis (8,216 ft.) on the southern border. Dairying is the chief occupation, though Appenzell embroideries have long been famous. The town of Appenzell (pop. about 5,000) is the capital of the interior unit; Herisau (pop. 13,601); near the northwestern border, has succeeded the more easterly village of Trogen as the capital of Exterior Appenzell. On the last Sunday in April, the *Landesgemeinden* (local legislative assemblies of the two half cantons) conduct their business in ancient and picturesque open-air meetings. S. Van V.

APPERCEPTION, the process by which the individual assimilates new ideas or impressions into his thinking. It requires the unifying action of his previously organized ideas, called the "apperceptive mass." It differs from attention, which is the bringing of impressions into clear focus. It is related to perception, because it influences what is perceived and how it is interpreted. A botanist, hearing the

word "root," thinks of something quite different from what the mathematician does. First used by Leibnitz, later popularized by J. F. Herbart in the sense defined above, it gained wide usage in educational theory to describe the selective function of cultural habits on mental growth. The word rarely appears in textbooks written after 1920, being replaced by "set" and "perception." A. G. B.

APPIA, ADOLPHE [ɑ'ppyɑ] (1862-1928), Swiss scenic artist, writer, and theoretician of the theatre and opera, was born in Geneva, on Sept. 1, 1862. Appia was largely responsible, along with Gordon Craig, for the revolution in the theory and practice of stagecraft that has simplified and illuminated the European and American stage since 1900. In his books, *Die Musik und die Inscenierung* (1899), *La Mise-en-scène du drame wagnérien* (1895), and his final testament, *L'Oeuvre d'art vivant* (1921), Appia applied to the setting, as Thomas H. Dickinson has observed, a space law as absolute as the time law of music. Dickinson adds that he went further and showed how the space law of the setting and the lighting could be co-ordinated with the time law of the music through the medium of the living and moving actor. The actor, in this scheme, was conceived as moving always in light.

Some of Appia's finest designs were done for productions of *Orfeo ed Euridice* at Hellerau in Saxony (1912-1914); *Tristan und Isolde* at La Scala, Milan (1923); and *Das Rheingold* and *Die Walküre* at Basel, Switzerland (1924-1925). Puritan, mystic, and Dionysiac, Appia strove all his life for a theatre and a drama that could be justly called, in his own words, "the cathedral of the future." D. T.

APPIAN WAY, one of the best known ancient Roman roads in Italy. Its construction was the work of Appius Claudius the Censor in 312 B.C. The road ran from Rome southward to Capua; it was later extended across the peninsula by way of Beneventum, Tarentum, and Brundisium. Like other Roman roads, the Appian Way was remarkable for its straightness and its permanence. A cement of gravel and lime laid upon a solid base and then covered with large paving blocks produced a remarkably durable road which withstood centuries of military and civilian travel. The convex surface drained readily, and like most Roman roads constructed in this manner it was always passable. T. B. J.

APPLE, *Malus,* a tree of the rose family, bearing probably the most important fruit in the world. Wild apples of the whole Northern Temperate Zone are the parents of modern varieties. Most cultivated apples derive from either *Malus pumila,* the common apple, or in some cases from *M. baccata,* the Siberian crab, both of which have been cultivated since antiquity. Charred remains of apples have been found in the prehistoric Swiss lake dwellings. Apple wood is very heavy, hard, and moderately strong. A cubic foot of the air-dry wood weighs about forty-six pounds. It is used principally in the making of handsaw handles and turned articles.

CRAB APPLES

Some species of crab are native to North America; these include *Malus ioensis,* the Prairie crab, from which the Soulard crab apple, particularly hardy in cold regions, was developed in 1868. The wild sweet crab of the eastern states has more recently given rise to varieties including Matthew's

COURTESY OF UNITED STATES FOREST SERVICE

Crab apple tree in blossom, with detail of leaf, blossom, and fruit

crab, the Charlotte, and the Nieuwland. The crab apple tree has come into favor for ornamental planting because of its pleasing form and masses of bloom followed by decorative fruits, the latter being in some cases useful in jelly making and in all cases attractive to wild life. Many varieties and species have been introduced, especially from China and Japan, but also from Korea, Assam, Siberia, the Himalayas, and Italy. The crab apple trees are somewhat more wiry in structure than the common apple and have more open clusters of flowers, varying from white to deep rose, and from single to semidouble and double with glossier, shorter-stalked leaves. Both the apple and crab apple are characteristically round-headed, medium-sized trees.

COMMON APPLES

Growing Regions. The eating apple is commercially important in most temperate climates, including Australasia, with the greatest production in North America. Most Canadian provinces and all of the United States, except the Gulf states and the hottest portions of the western states, are adapted to apple raising and comprise the principal apple-growing regions of the world. The oldest such area extends in a broad belt from Nova Scotia through Massachusetts to Michigan. Quality of fruit and its ripening characteristics, together with the health, productivity, and longevity of orchards, make this section a highly favored one for this purpose. The piedmont and highlands of Virginia and West Virginia are the center of a similar region. The West Coast from British Columbia through Washington, Oregon, and California has more recently come to be a great apple region, while other younger areas, including the Ozarks and intermountain districts between Montana and New Mexico, are proving to be good areas for commercial production.

Varieties. The apple has produced a great range of varieties, and modern methods of storing and shipping are being adapted to make use of the characteristics of each variety. Studies of the natural ripening processes of the picked fruit have made possible the controlling of ripening rates. The use of automobile trucks making short trips for small loads is a factor in encouraging greater variety in planting than was customary when very large crops of a small number of varieties of winter apples constituted the only shipping apples. The present broader distribution of harvesting from early summer through late fall has resulted in the planting of a greater assortment of varieties and has facilitated the labor problems involved: small forces of workers may be given continuous employment, while formerly, large numbers of pickers were needed for only short periods each fall. The wide range of variety characteristics is remarkable: the Bonum thrives in the South; the Baldwin, in the North; the Yellow Newton, in limestone soils; and the Gravenstein, in light soils. Some are usable for cooking only (Fallawater); others are dessert apples, like the Jonathans; others, like the Fall Pippin, are general-purpose apples. In the north the season of ripening has extended from July (Early Strawberry apple) to April, when Winesaps in natural storage are ready for eating. In texture, apples vary from extreme juiciness (Fameuse) to mealiness (Rome). In size, the Pomme Gris may weigh two ounces, while a record specimen of the coarser Gloria Mundi weighed more than two pounds and sold for fourteen pounds sterling when it was exhibited in London. A number of newer varieties have gained favor while at the same time the position of older favorites such as Baldwin, Primate, Northern Spy, McIntosh, and Wealthy has remained stable. Most varieties grown in the United States have been developed locally, the sites of the original trees of some varieties having been marked with tablets or monuments.

Uses. The apple maintains enormous popularity as a fruit to be eaten raw and in pies. It is used in many other ways for the table, a fact which gives rise to large commercial utilization in the making of apple butter and jelly as well as in canning; considerable quantities are dried, largely for export, along with raw apples, to countries of Europe and South America. Other great markets are for vinegar and for beverages, including cider, juice, wine, and brandy. Apple trees are widely used in planting home grounds, with dwarf varieties and espaliered specimens (trained against walls or on trellises) becoming popular, as they have long been in Europe. Apple varieties are dwarfed by grafting or budding them on Doucin or Paradise apple stocks.

Cultivation. For commercial or home orchard planting, there are several considerations. Apples thrive on any well-drained soil suitable for wheat, corn, or potatoes. Rolling or elevated lands are preferable to low sites, as they are less subject to frost during the blooming period. Preference for fall versus spring planting varies in different sections. Varieties differ in the age at which they will bear, from Oldenburg in 2 or 3 years, to Esopus in 9 or 10. Apple trees do not reproduce true to type from seeds, so that it is necessary to have nursery-grown stock, propagated by grafting and budding. These may be developed to salable size in known varieties in one season's growth. Trees should be set 40 feet apart. The space between may be used for peach trees to be grown for a period of ten years, after which time the peach trees will have served their usefulness and may be cut out, having provided some income toward the cost of tillage. Surface crops, such as strawberries, melons, tomatoes, and cabbage, may be grown among apple trees for two or three years. Quick-maturing varieties of apple trees may be set between the more permanent trees if the grower is careful to cut these new trees out when their space is needed by the permanent trees. To facilitate harvesting, commercial plantings are not planted with other fruit trees. Apples suffer from insects and fungous diseases, for the control of which sprays are used.

U. P. H. and W. D. B.

Production. Apple production of leading states in the United States on a ten-year average from 1943 through 1952 was as follows (in thousands of bu.): Washington, 28,232; New York, 14,009; Virginia, 8,897; California, 8,324; Michigan, 6,698; Pennsylvania, 6,074; West Virginia, 3,558; Illinois, 3,088; Ohio, 3,060; total, leading states, 81,940; total for United States, 105,802. The general tendency has been for production to decline: in the five years preceding 1950, for example, average country-wide production was over 120,000 thousand bu. Extreme years were 1939, in which almost 130,000 thousand bu. were produced, and 1945, with a yield of only 66,796 thousand bu. The price to farmers per 48-lb. bu. averaged $2.25 in the 1943-1952 period.

APPLE BORER, one of the long-horned beetles, *Saperda candida,* belonging to the family Cerambycidae, characterized by its rich brownish color and two broad white stripes extending from the head to the tip of the wing covers. The beetle occurs east of the Rocky Mountains, and attacks a variety of trees, including apple, quince, pear, mountain ash, hawthorn, and chokecherry. Before the introduction of the apple, it probably lived chiefly on hawthorn, which is still a favorite food plant. Occasionally, it becomes a serious pest in orchards. The female makes an incision in the bark of the tree with her mandibles, lays an egg and covers it with a gummy fluid. The young larva bores into the tree and spends the first season tunneling in the sapwood. The second summer it bores deeper into the solid wood, and the third it bores outward and constructs an enlarged chamber just beneath the bark, where it passes the winter, the adult emerging the following spring.   C. H. Cu.

APPLESEED, JOHNNY. See CHAPMAN, JOHN.

APPLES OF SODOM, a phrase used figuratively to describe anything disappointing. Various ancient writers told of beautiful fruits which, when plucked, proved to be full of ashes. Apples growing by the Dead Sea, sometimes called Dead Sea fruit, are so described by the French traveler Jean Thévenot and also by Josephus, Strabo, and Tacitus. They may have referred to gallnuts produced by the sting of the insect *Cynipes insane.* The small tomatolike yellow fruits of the spiny shrub *Solanum sodomeum* are often called apples of Sodom.   J. C. Wis.

APPLETON, SIR EDWARD VICTOR (1892-   ), English physicist, was born in Bradford, Yorkshire, Sept. 6, 1892. His discoveries in physics made possible the development of radio-locating devices that were first used in World War II. He entered St. John's College, Cambridge, but left to serve in the British Army in World War I. Having developed an interest in radio while serving as a signal officer, he began to study it when he returned to Cambridge after the war. He was appointed assistant demonstrator in experimental physics at the Cavendish Laboratory in 1920 and sublector at Trinity College in 1922. In 1924 he was appointed professor of physics at London University and was named professor of natural philosophy at Cambridge in 1936. After demonstrating the existence of the Kennelly-Heaviside layer and measuring its height, Appleton discovered a layer that existed 90 mi. above the Heaviside layer and that was capable of reflecting radio short waves around the world. This reflector of waves, which he demonstrated to be but one of many which formed the ionosphere, came to be known as the Appleton layer. Appleton was made a Fellow of the Royal Society in 1926 and knighted in 1941. His awards include the Morris Liebman Prize by the American Institute of Radio Engineers in 1929, the Faraday Medal from the Institute of Electrical Engineers in 1946, and a Nobel Prize in 1947 for his work on the physics of the atmosphere. Appleton was appointed permanent secretary of the Department of Scientific and Industrial Research at the beginning of World War II. This virtually placed him in control of all phases of scientific research in Great Britain. After the war he was appointed to committees studying atomic energy and the use of scientific manpower. He became a member of the government's television committee and served as chairman of the National Committee for Radio Telegraphy.   S. D.

APPLETON, the county seat of Outagamie Co. in eastern Wisconsin, is situated on the Fox River, 109 mi. north of Milwaukee. It was founded as a village in 1846, incorporated in 1853, and chartered as a city in 1857 in consolidation with two other villages. It has the aldermanic form of government. Appleton is the seat of Lawrence College and the Institute of Paper Chemistry, the only research center of its kind for the paper industry in the United States. In 1954 the Institute acquired the Dard Hunter Paper Museum from Massachusetts Institute of Technology. Abundant water power produced by a 33-ft. fall of the Fox River accounts for Appleton's thriving paper and pulp mills and its many related industries which turn out paper products, paper mill machinery, felts, and wire cloth. Other manufactures include wood, metal, and concrete products, knitted goods, and dairy products. Pop. 1950, 34,010.

APPLIED MECHANICS. See ANALYTICAL MECHANICS; POWER TRANSMISSION.

APPLIED PSYCHOLOGY, the term used to describe those phases of psychology which deal with practical problems. In pure psychology the researcher is never asked whether his investigations have to do with useful ends. He may, and does, work on any problem that increases his knowledge of human behavior. While his researches may ultimately find very useful application, this does not concern him while his investigations are under way. The applied psychologist, on the other hand, finds his problems in the everyday practical affairs of men; he seeks constantly to aid in solving practical problems. The contrast between pure and applied psychology may be made clearer by illustration. The pure psychologist has worked on such problems as how we learn new skills, why square tables look square when the image on the eye is not square, and how people judge the lapse of time. Investigations on such topics provide the psychologist with a systematic analysis of human behavior. At the time they are undertaken, however, it is not of such importance that they would seem to have practical usefulness. The applied psychologist, on the other hand, has worked on such problems as how to select taxi drivers, how long to make a line of type, and how to make airplane instruments more readable. Some of his work is done in the laboratory, but much of it must be done in the field. Wherever he works, he is interested in useful outcomes. Thus the applied psychologist may do research in a factory on the causes of labor turnover. He may serve in a school as counselor on choice of vocation. He may be called in to advise army or navy officials on the problem of adapting gunsights to the limitations of human eyesight. The applied psychologist may use facts and methods developed by the pure psychologist. He may, for example, utilize the known laws of learning in writing a manual for salesmen. Likewise, he may take what the pure psychologist has discovered about color-vision and use it to prevent confusion between the colors of jerseys on the basketball court. On the other hand, he may, and often does, develop his own methods and discover his own facts. Thus the applied psychologists who have sought to develop methods of measuring the size of the radio audience have developed new devices, new methods, and new principles. In this way it often happens that applied psychology, while receiving help from pure psychology, contributes in its own right to the over-all growth of psychology as a study of human behavior.   J. G. J.

CLINICAL PSYCHOLOGY

Clinical psychology is a basic background of applied psychology employed in educational, vocational, mental, emotional, and social guidance and adjustment of normal individuals, the subnormal or so-called mentally deficient, and the abnormal or psychoneurotic and psychotic. In dealing with the abnormal, the clinical psychologist is usually a member of the modern diagnostic and therapeutic team, most frequently composed of a psychiatrist, a clinical psychologist, and a social case worker.

Purpose. In contrast to systematic experimental psychology, which has as its main purpose the discovery of the general principles or laws of behavior based upon the average or common pattern of behavior revealed by many persons, clinical psychology has as its main purpose the discovery of the specific capacities and reactions of an individual. It is sometimes referred to as the study of individual differences, and its techniques of investigation arose out of the nature of these differences; this study had its scientific origins in the work of Francis Galton and J. McKeen Cattell.

Clinical psychology studies and applies itself to the interorganized patterns of behavior in the human individual. Gathering its materials and techniques primarily from psychology, it also deals with the materials of education, the medical sciences, the social sciences, and all factors which influence individual personality; it is based upon the results of scientific research in the study of human behavior. Its methodology involves the analysis of the competencies, efficiencies, and proficiencies of the individual through clinical diagnoses, tests, and diagnostic teaching. It proceeds through the postanalytical diagnosis of the reactions of the individual to the prognosis of the future performance of the individual. Its purpose is to enable the individual to accomplish his highest level of attainment through the corrective, directive, preventive, and creative production of patterns of preferred behavior in the developing integration of his personality.

History. Clinical psychology is one of the late nineteenth-century developments of the age-old study of human behavior. Fundamentally scientific in its methods, it was dependent upon the origins of modern scientific experimental and systematic psychology.

During the 1870's a new scientific and experimental concept of psychology was emerging from philosophical psychology. Wilhelm Wundt exploited this concept by the establishment of the first psychological laboratory for experimentation and research at the University of Leipzig in 1879. In the United States by 1876, William James had set up what is commonly referred to as "James' room for demonstrational experiments" at Harvard University. G. Stanley Hall established the second psychological laboratory at John Hopkins University in 1883. Cattell, Wundt's first laboratory assistant, started work in psychophysics at the University of Pennsylvania in 1886, and by 1887 had established the third psychological laboratory. The laboratory at Johns Hopkins closed shortly, leaving the one at Pennsylvania the oldest in continuous activity in America. On Jan. 1, 1889, Cattell was appointed professor of psychology at Pennsylvania, occupying the first chair in the new profession.

Application. The concept of applied psychology, which Wundt termed typically American, also was coming into prominence. Among those attracted thereby was Lightner Witmer, who, during his graduate studies with Wundt, sought to do his doctoral work on an applied problem. Wundt required Witmer to do his dissertation on an experimental problem in aesthetics, dealing with the concept of the golden section, known to the Egyptians. Witmer returned to Pennsylvania determined to develop the application of scientific methods to individual human behavior. During the academic year 1894-1895 Witmer held a seminar on child psychology, discussing the typical problems of early human behavior. In March 1896 he was challenged by a public school teacher to solve the individual difficulties of a chronic bad speller. This, his first clinic case, gave impetus to the development of the postanalytic diagnosis based on clinical observation during remedial training. In the fall of 1896, Witmer presented to the American Psychological Association a new method of research and instruction, which he called "the clinical method in psychology and the diagnostic method of teaching." He pointed out that clinical psychology is based upon the results of the examination of many human beings, one at a time, and that the analytic method of discriminating mental abilities and defects leads to an ordered classification of the observed behavior by means of postanalytic generalizations. He asserted that "the psychological clinic is an institution for social and public service, for original research, and for the instruction of students in psychological orthogenics, which includes vocational, educational, correctional, hygienic, industrial, and social guidance."

Qualitative Emphasis. Clinical psychology, then, awaited the development of specific testing devices for the investigation and measurement of specific mental abilities, aptitudes, attitudes, and patterns of mental, emotional, motor, and social behavior. It has been confused frequently with its techniques or tools, more commonly known as psychometric devices, and is thought by some to be limited to so-called scores obtained through psychometric examination.

Clinical psychology's basic point of view, however, is qualitative. This qualitative emphasis upon the teleological or purposive concept of human behavior is best stated by Witmer: "A psychological diagnosis is an interpretation of the observed behavior of human beings. . . . Human psychology is an examination of man's spiritual nature. The unit of observation is a performance, but the unit of consideration is personality, defined by the perfectability of behavior, which is measured or estimated in units of progress which men make toward the perfection which they prefer." This is not to imply that clinical psychology has in any wise avoided the quantitative point of view; it has, however, been most insistent upon the proper understanding of the usefulness and limitations of this approach. Quantitative measures are clearly and precisely defined. They tell us the amount of behavior performed and what status this production gives to the individual when he is compared to his standard group or level and both within the limits of determinable probabilities. This gives an excellent answer to what the individual did and where this performance places him in his group distribution. They give no information whatsoever on how he did what he did. Knowledge of the how of behavior is the result of a postanalytic diagnosis based upon clinical observation. It alone permits a functional qualitative interpretation, based upon the experience of the clinician.

New Methods. The methodology of clinical psychology has been enriched by the experience of the years. Fundamentally it is determined by the same postanalytic diagnostic or remedial teaching or training. Its emphasis has been predominantly "corrective." For years this corrective approach was pursued largely through "directive" methods. More recently, greater emphasis has been placed upon the indirect method, which Witmer characteristically called the "creative." Few have understood that by this method Witmer meant the purposeful self-direction of the individual who, with an understanding of his acting self, moves on from one "stage of perfection" or attainment to the higher levels of achievement of which he is capable.

Professional preparation for clinical psychology is given in over 35 graduate schools today, and includes academic, practicum, research, and internship training over a period of four years leading to the doctoral degree. R. A. B.

Psychotechnology. The name "psychotechnology" is applied by certain social scientists to the fact-finding aspects of applied psychology, to distinguish these fact-finding phases from the work of the practitioner who deals primarily with the treatment of specific, individual cases.

The psychotechnologist is a fact-finder, while the psychological practitioner aims at helping solve individual cases as they are laid before him. Thus, the research technologist may spend ten years in measuring the effects of radio programs on the behavior of children. The practitioner, by contrast, will be asked to advise Mrs. Jones what to do about her eight-year-old son who bites his fingernails while listening to exciting programs. The technologist in the field of psychology limits himself to controlled research methods which allow him to state the probable error of his results. The practitioner in psychology, on the other hand, may or may not use any of the facts or methods developed by the research specialist. In general, he will use any source of information that seems likely to help solve the problem laid before him by his client.

The term "psychotechnology" has never gained any great currency in the United States. Such terms as "human engineering" and "biomechanics" have been coined in an attempt to find a more suitable name for this research field. Because there seems to be real significance in differentiating between the technological researcher and the practitioner in the field, some suitable name will doubtless be finally adopted.

J. G. J.

APPOGGIATURA [əpɒˈjətuˈrə], in modern musical parlance a term for melodic "nonharmonic" tones (tones foreign to the chord with which they are played) at an interval of a second above or below the succeeding tone with which they are phrased. During earlier periods the appoggiatura was notated and executed in a variety of different ways. In music written since the early nineteenth century two distinct types are found: the long appoggiatura, written out in exact notation and discernible only through harmonic analysis; and the short appoggiatura, indicated by a small grace note with a stroke across its stem, played sometimes before, sometimes on the beat. *See also* GRACE NOTE.

W. Li.

APPOMATTOX COURT HOUSE [æˈpəmæˈtəks], scene of the capitulation, April 9, 1865, of the Confederate Army of Northern Virginia to the Union forces under Gen. Ulysses S. Grant. On April 2, Gen. Robert E. Lee directed the evacuation of Petersburg, and on the following day the Confederate Government left Richmond. Federal forces under Gen. Godfrey Weitzel occupied Richmond, while Grant's army followed the retreating Confederates. As Lee moved towards Lynchburg, Grant moved more rapidly and cut him off. On April 8, at Appomattox Station, Union cavalry seized Confederate supply trains; the failure of expected supplies to arrive at Amelia Court House left the Confederate troops without food. On the following day, Gen. P. H. Sheridan's cavalry blocked the road for Lee's escape. Lee, accepting the arguments of his staff that surrender was inevitable, arranged to meet Grant at the McLean house in the village of Appomattox Court House. Casualties, captures, and desertions had reduced Lee's army to 26,765 men. These he surrendered to Grant, under terms which granted parole to all the men until exchanged. Grant also permitted Confederate officers to retain their privately owned side arms, and officers and men to keep horses and mules which were their personal possessions. The same terms were accepted by other Confederate commands which surrendered quickly after hearing of Lee's capitulation. In all, 174,223 men were paroled under these terms. On April 10, 1940, to commemorate the ending of the war between the states, Appomattox Court House was established as a national historical monument, with an area of 968 acres. Restoration of the village to its 1865 appearance was undertaken by the National Park Service. W. B. H.

APPONYI, COUNT ALBERT [ɑˈponyi] (1846-1933), Hungarian statesman, was born at Vienna, May 29, 1846, the son of the political leader, Count György Apponyi (1808-1899). In 1872 he entered Parliament, where he served as a member of the Conservative National Party. This began a political career which was furthered by his remarkable oratorical ability. In 1899 he joined the Liberal Party, and two years later was elected president of the Chamber of Deputies. In 1904 he left the Liberal Party, reorganized the National Party, and joined the coalition which brought about the fall of the Tisza cabinet in 1905. He introduced free elementary education when he was Minister of Education from 1906 to 1910 and during World War I. After World War I he represented Hungary at the Trianon Peace Conference in 1920 and later headed the Hungarian delegation to the League of Nations, where his linguistic gifts and oratory made a profound impression. His *Memoirs* (English translation) was published in 1935. Among his other works were *Aesthetics and Politics, The Artist and The Statesman* (1895); *A Brief Sketch of the Hungarian Constitution, and of the Relations Between Austria and Hungary* (1919); *The American Peace*

GENERALS GRANT AND LEE DISCUSS THE TERMS OF LEE'S SURRENDER AT APPOMATTOX COURT HOUSE

and Hungary (1919); *Hungarian Foreign Policy* (1921); and *Justice for Hungary* (1928). He died at Geneva, Feb. 7, 1933.
                                                                H. M. M.

APPURTENANCE, in law, is a thing belonging to another thing, as principal, and which passes as incident to the principal thing. The term "appurtenances" is commonly used in deeds conveying title to land and buildings. It is an expression of limited connotation and generally has reference to easements and servitudes necessary to the enjoyment of the land conveyed. The word "appurtenances" in a deed has been held not to include such items as electric refrigerators or gas ranges, or the personal property of the seller. It is apparent, therefore, that in case of possible doubt or controversy, the parties to an agreement of purchase and sale should not rely solely upon the expression "appurtenances" to define their intendment as to incidentals but should employ specific terms to enumerate the items included in and excluded from the transaction.   H. Si.

APRA, a leftist political party organized in Peru after the overthrow of the dictator Augusto Leguía in 1930. The organizers were Victor Raul Haya de la Torre and other university students. They gave it the full name of *Alianza Popular Revolucionaria Americana* ("American Popular Revolutionary Alliance") and included among its principles the internationalization of the Panama Canal; the limitation of foreign capital in, and the unification of, Latin-American republics; the distribution of land to the Indians; and social justice to the underprivileged. Practical measures suggested by the party chief, Haya de la Torre, included redistricting of the political divisions of Peru to correspond more nearly to the economy of each section, strengthening

of the programs of public health and the labor movement, participation of women in political life, and separation of church and state (but encouragement, rather than discouragement, of the spiritual work of the churches). When Haya and a group of fellow students at San Marcos University, in Lima, were expelled by President Leguía, who ruled Peru dictatorially from 1919 to 1930, Haya went to Mexico, which at that time was in the midst of a reform movement. After studying the Mexican Revolution Haya traveled in Russia, as well as in other European countries, meanwhile keeping in touch with the underground movement in Peru.

When Leguía was overthrown in 1930, Haya returned and was a candidate for the presidency, but was ruled out by an allegedly unfair count. Official opposition to APRA grew, and many of its members including Haya were imprisoned, while others fled to Chile and elsewhere. They urged left-wing elements to join them in continent-wide political and economic reforms. APRA parties were soon organized in Chile, Cuba, and other Latin-American nations. In 1945, having accepted from President Manuel Prado an assurance of freedom of action in the presidential elections of that year, APRA joined with a number of leftist groups (but not with the Communists, whom the party had always opposed) to elect their candidate, Dr. José Bustamante of Arequipa. APRA then changed its name to the People's Party to overcome old prejudices. Haya, who had retained the loyalty of his group to a remarkable degree, decided that it would be better for him and his fellow Apristas not to accept cabinet posts but to work for reforms through the party members in Congress and in other posts, and he brought about the adoption of this program.   S. G. I.

APRAXIA. *See* Aphasia.

APRICOT, a fruit and ornamental tree or shrub of the rose family, genus *Prunus*. The fruiting apricot, *P. armeniaca*, though for a long time cultivated in Armenia, is a native of west Asia. It was introduced to Europe during the reign of Alexander the Great. The fruit is intermediate between the peach and plum, having the tender, though not fuzzy, skin of the peach, but a smooth stone, thickened at the edge, and firm, sweet flesh of deep, pinkish yellow. It is prized as a dessert fruit for use raw, canned, or dried, with a considerable part of the commercial crop being dried. Both canned and dried apricots are exported to Europe, largely from California. Washington and Oregon also have commercial orchards. The tree is as hardy as the peach, and may accordingly be grown in a majority of the states, but it is planted in limited numbers in regions other than the West Coast for the reason that the fruit is often destroyed by spring frosts. This can be avoided to some extent by planting the trees on the north or west side of a building in order to retard early blossoming. It should be possible to grow them rather well in the southern states. A well-drained soil suitable to apple growing is the same type as that preferred by the apricot. *Prunus mume,* a flowering apricot from Japan and China, was introduced in 1884. It is similar in form to *P. armeniaca,* both being round-headed and attaining a height up to 30 ft. *P. armeniaca* has red-brown bark, and *P. mume* gray-green bark. The fruit of the latter, which is yellow-green, is not edible. The flowers are fragrant, and in different varieties come in both pink and white and single and double blossoms. U. P. H.

APRIL. *See* Calendar.
APRIL FOOLS' DAY. *See* Holidays and Holy Days.

A PRIORI [e' prɪɔ'raɪ; ɑ' prɪɔ'ri] (Latin *a,* "from," and *priori,* "that which comes before"), a term used in philosophy to denote the kind of knowledge derived from intellect or reason as contrasted with that which comes from sense experience, called *a posteriori*. Kant noted two earmarks of a priori knowledge, universality and necessity. Take the proposition: $7 + 5 = 12$. It is universal, in the sense that it has no exceptions. It is necessary, in the sense that it must be true; we can see that $7 + 5$ could not conceivably equal anything else but 12. Neither of these characteristics is present in knowledge that comes from sense experience; our knowledge that snow is white, for example, is not an insight that snow could not be other than white, hence we can never be sure than an exception will not occur. Empiricist logicians like John Stuart Mill have tried to explain a priori knowledge by saying that logical necessity is nothing but firm habit; we have found two attributes going together so regularly that we have formed a fixed association between them. Most logicians consider this unconvincing. The school of logical positivists grants the existence of a priori knowledge but holds that it is only a way of making explicit what we already mean (12 is only another way of saying $7 + 5$) and that it gives no knowledge of the outer world. On the other hand, rationalists find in a priori insight the most revealing as well as the most certain form of knowledge. B. B.

APSE. *See* Architectural Terms.

APSIDES, LINE OF [æ'psɪdiz], in a planet's orbit, the line connecting the aphelion and perihelion points with the sun. It is the major axis extended indefinitely. In a satellite's orbit the line of apsides is the major axis extended similarly and passing through the satellite's primary—the planet. H. S. R.

APTERYX [æ'ptərɪks], any one of a small group of flightless birds of the family Apterygidae, allied to the ostriches, emus, and extinct moas. The several species are restricted to New Zealand. They are about the size of a domestic fowl and have a long, straight or slightly curved bill, short, stout legs, and no visible wings or tail; the hairlike plumage is gray or brown. Among their many anatomi-

FREDERIC LEWIS

APTERYX

cal peculiarities is the position of the nostril, almost at the tip of the bill. All the species live in dense, dark forests in burrows; they come out at night to feed on earthworms, which are procured by using the sensitive bill as a probe. They lay two white eggs of extraordinary size; while the bird itself weighs about four pounds, each egg may weigh 14 or 15 ounces and may be five inches long and three inches broad. Owing to destruction of its habitat and persecution by such alien predators as dogs and cats, all the species are becoming very rare, except on certain small offshore islands to which they have been introduced in recent years in an effort to preserve the species. In New Zealand they are known as "kiwis" or "kiwikiwis," a Maori name imitative of their call. H. G. De.

APUANIA [ɑ'pua'niɑ], a province and the administrative commune in that province, in north central Italy, in the northwestern corner of Tuscany. The province contains 446 sq. mi. and comprises only fifteen communes. It consists of two parts which are geographically quite distinct. The larger subdivision, known as Lunigiana, is made up of fourteen communes and occupies the basin of the Magro River behind La Spezia. On the north the Lunigiana is bounded by the main range of the Apennines, which in this section attain 6,000 ft. elevations. Most of the population lives in small villages or in scattered dwellings. The chief town is Pontremoli. The principal agricultural products of the region are cereals, grapes for wine, olives, and chestnuts, and livestock is raised on a large scale. Industries are small, and manufactures are only for the local market.

The small zone consisting of only the commune of Apuania is situated between the crest of the north Apuanian Alps and the Tyrrhenian Sea, and it has a coast line of approximately 12 mi. along the sea. In 1938 the commune was formed by the amalgamation of the three older communes of Carrara, Massa, and Montignoso. This is the section in which are found the famous Carrara marble quarries. Pop. (Gov't est. 1942), 205,917. R. G. W.

APULEIUS (APPULEIUS), LUCIUS [æ'pyuli'yəs], Roman philosopher, rhetorician, and novelist, was born c. A.D. 125 at Madauros in Numidia. Educated at Carthage and Athens, Apuleius practiced law in Rome. Returning to Africa, he married Aemilia Pudentilla, whose family accused him of winning her by magic arts. His defense survives in a book called *De magia* ("On Magic") or *Apologia*. Apuleius' philosophy was Neoplatonic, influenced by the oriental mysticism of the cult of the Egyptian Isis. His extant works are *Apologia, Metamorphoses* (or *The Golden Ass*), *De deo Socratis, De dogmate Platonis, Florida* (excerpts from his speeches), and possibly *De mundo*. The *Metamorphoses,* his masterpiece, exerted a strong influence on later fiction. *See also* GOLDEN ASS, THE.   G. McL. H.

APULIA [əpyu'liə] (Ital. Puglia, or Le Puglie), a modern region and an ancient district of Italy, lying along the lower Adriatic coast from the Monte Gargano Promontory southeastward to the tip of the Salentine Peninsula. Modern Apulia, with an area of 7,440 sq. mi., includes the smaller regions of Capitanata, Terra di Bari, and Terra d'Otranto; or the provinces of Foggia, Bari, Brindisi, Lecce, and Taranto. Apulia is bounded on the north and northeast by the Adriatic Sea; on the east by the Strait of Otranto; on the south by the Ionian Sea; on the southwest by the Gulf of Taranto and the Lucania and Campania regions; and on the west by the Abruzzi and Molise region.

Topographically Apulia consists of the mountainous peninsula of Monte Gargano; the prairie-like Tavoliere of Foggia; the terraced limestone Murgian Hills; the coastal plain between the latter and the sea, extending from Barletta to Brindisi; and the low and fairly level Salentine Peninsula, known as the heel of Italy. The high point in Monte Gargano has an elevation of 3,480 ft., and that in the Murgian Hills around 2,200 ft. The highest elevations in Apulia are in the Neapolitan Apennines, which form the western border of Foggia province. The region has a coast line of some 800 mi. with but few naturally good harbors, Brindisi and Taranto being the best. Shifting sand bars along parts of the coast offer hazards to navigation. The climate varies somewhat with altitude and latitude but in general may be said to include hot summers and moderate winters. The annual rainfall averages between 20 and 30 in., most of which comes in the early winter and runs off rapidly or disappears into the ground, as in the limestone areas in the center and south. There are thus few permanent streams south of the Afanto River, which divides Capitanata from the Terra di Bari. The Tavoliere of Foggia is crossed by a number of small rivers that descend from the Apennines. Because of these climatic conditions, the Mediterranean brush, or *macchia,* is the typical form of natural vegetation. Forests occur only in eastern Monte Gargano and in certain areas of the Murgian Hills.

The People. The population of Apulia in 1949 was estimated to be 3,000,000, representing an increase of two and one-half times in the preceding century. The population is very unevenly distributed, there being wide areas with a very low density in the hills and on the Tavoliere of Foggia. Bari province, with nearly 500 persons per sq. mi., is the most densely populated; and Foggia province, with less than 200, the most sparsely inhabited. The density of the region as a whole, however, is only slightly inferior to that of all Italy. The tendency to live in urban communities, common throughout southern Italy, is so accentuated in Apulia that only 8 per cent of the people live in scattered dwellings. The proportion of towns with over 10,000 inhabitants is high and indicates the extent of urban concentration even in ex-

clusively agricultural areas. The principal towns are Bari, Brindisi, Taranto, and Barletta.

Economic Life. Agriculture is not only the foremost economic activity of Apulia but provides a basis for most of its industrial production. Since climate is a governing factor, only those crops that can resist long dry spells or have short and early growing seasons are raised. The former include the olive, the grape, the almond, and the fig; while the latter consist largely of wheat and oats. The olive is found over about one fifth of Apulia, which produces about one third of Italy's total output of olive oil. Apulia is second among the Italian wine-producing regions and first in the production of almonds and figs. It is a principal source of cherries. Extensive wheat-growing, especially on the Tavoliere of Foggia, is a development of the decades preceding the middle of the twentieth century. Apulia is first among Italian regions in the production of oats, and second in barley.

The total area under cultivation was increased under the Fascist regime through reclamation, the stamping out of malaria, and other projects designed to restore land to human use. More important in improving living conditions is the remarkable Apulian Aqueduct, which brings the pure water of the upper Sele River, in the provinces of Avellino and Salerno, through the Apennines in a series of tunnels, to most of the cities and towns of the region. The water in the Aqueduct also develops some electricity.

Livestock raising, particularly of sheep, was of prime importance up to the nineteenth century, when the pastures of Capitanata were plowed and sown to wheat. A million sheep are found in Apulia, with smaller numbers of goats, cattle, and other animals. Fishing is carried on by Apulians on the opposite shore of the Adriatic as well as in home waters.

Manufactures are largely confined to such food products as olive oil, wines, milled cereals, and canned fruits and vegetables. Foundries, metallurgical works, and ship-servicing industries are found in the major ports. The latter, in order of their tonnage of freight before World War II, were: Bari, Taranto, Barletta, Brindisi, and Monopoli. Bari alone handled about one third of the total water-borne commerce of Apulia. There is a railroad network of some 900 mi. in length. The highway system has been much improved.
                                                                   R. G. W.

HISTORY

The early tribes of Apulia were the Daunii in the north and the Peucetii in the south. These were Italic tribes having close political connections with the Samnites. The origin of the Apulian tribes appears to have been Illyrian, and their dialects are generally classified as Messapic, although a long inscription in Oscan has been found at Bantia. The Apulian people were exposed to Greek influences in the Classical Period after the foundation of Tarentum (c. 708 B.C.). Their religion was modified, and they began to make pottery which they decorated in the prevailing Greek fashion. Apulia became Roman territory after the Second Punic War, during which it was the scene of Roman-Carthaginian conflicts, notably the battle of Cannae (216 B.C.), Hannibal's famous victory on the banks of the Ofanto River. The Romans long regarded the area as lacking in culture, despite the fact that the poets Livius Andronicus (fl. third century B.C.) and Quintus Ennius (239-c. 169 B.C.) had their origin there.

After forming part of the Roman domain for some seven centuries, Apulia was fought over in the fifth century A.D. by Goths, Lombards, Saracens, and Byzantines. In the eleventh century, under the rule of Norman adventurers, Apulia became a duchy. The Normans were succeeded by the Hohenstaufen rulers. Most famous of these was Frederick II (1194-

1250), who erected a number of fortresses and castles, including Castel del Monte and Lucera, and spent much of his amazing career there.

Further wars were engendered by the claims and counterclaims of the houses of Anjou, Aragon, and Hapsburg; but Apulia managed, nevertheless, to enjoy occasional periods of respite and prosperity. The Venetian Republic obtained trading privileges in Apulian ports, an arrangement that proved to be mutually advantageous. Beginning in 1734, the Bourbons established their rule over the region; and during the early decades of the Bourbon period Apulia contributed many illustrious men to the political and cultural life of the Kingdom of the Two Sicilies, of which Apulia was then a part. During the early nineteenth century, Apulia also contributed leaders to the various liberal and revolutionary movements that ended in the Unification of Italy in 1860. In 1861 Apulia was added to the Kingdom of Italy. Since that date, the region has made progress in returning the land to cultivation, in raising the standard of living and education, and in uniting the life of Apulia with that of the rest of Italy.   T. B. J. and R. G. W.

APUS [e′pəs], the Bird of Paradise, a modern constellation which is also called Avis Indica. It is entirely south of declination —70° and extends almost to the south celestial pole. It is centered at about right ascension 16 hr. Apus cannot be seen from latitudes north of Mexico City.   J. H. P.

AQABA [ɑ′kabɑ], the only seaport of Transjordan, in the extreme southwestern part of the country at the point where Transjordan, Palestine, Egypt, and the Hejaz meet at 29° N. lat. and 34° 40′ E. long. The port lies at the head of the Gulf of Aqaba, which is a northeastern continuation of the Red Sea, and is probably part of the Rift Valley, a down-faulted area that extends northward as the Dead Sea, the Jordan Valley, and the Sea of Galilee. Aqaba has a desert climate and receives a few inches of rain a year. The summer temperatures are extreme: from 95° to 100° F. during the day. The humidity from the Red Sea and the Gulf of Aqaba adds to the discomfort. There is a great range between day and night temperatures, and in the winter the nights are cool. Aqaba has a small fresh-water supply from underground drainage and some run-off water in the wadis that drain into the gulf. The vegetation of the surrounding area includes palm trees and melons. Fishing is of some importance as a subsistence industry. Aqaba is a local trading port for small vessels that ply the Red Sea coast. It is a transshipment point for goods, but primarily it is a meeting place for pilgrims between the northern part of the Near East and Mecca.

Aqaba has a strategic location because it is the only port and because four frontiers meet near by. It has had a long history and was quite important in ancient times. In the Bible (I Kings ix:26), Solomon is reported to have built a navy at Ezion-geber, an old city site near Aqaba. The Romans made Aqaba (Aelana) an important city in the province of Arabia and built a road northward to Petra. After numerous ups and downs the port fell to Turkey, but Egypt wanted and claimed it in the nineteenth century because pilgrims from Egypt had always used Aqaba as a port en route to Mecca. The Egyptians eventually gave the port back to Turkey, but during World War I Thomas E. Lawrence (Lawrence of Arabia) led a brilliant land attack on the Aqaba fort and captured it for the Allies. After considerable disagreement over the boundary lines Aqaba was placed within Transjordan. It has been a useful port for political exiles from the surrounding countries. In 1948 and 1949 the port and its surroundings figured in the war against the new state of Israel, the border of which, as established by the United Nations, closely approached Aqaba.   J. E. F.

AQABA, GULF OF [ɑ′kabɑ], a gulf at the northeastern end of the Red Sea, between the Sinai Peninsula and Hejaz. It is about 110 mi. long and 15 to 20 mi. wide. The northern end of the gulf is the common boundary of Egypt, Palestine, Transjordan, and Hejaz. It is believed that the Gulf of Aqaba is a rift valley. The land on either side of the gulf is rugged, arid, and sparsely populated. The entrance to the gulf, which is by way of the Strait of Tiran, is blocked almost completely by the islands of Sonafir and Tiran. The important port city of Aqaba, in Transjordan, lies at the head of the Gulf of Aqaba.   J. E. F.

AQUAMARINE [ækwəməri′n], a blue or sea-green mineral, a variety of beryl, beryllium aluminum silicate, $Be_2Al_2(SiO_3)_6$. It has a hardness of $7\frac{1}{2}$-8 and a density of 2.70. Crystallizing in the hexagonal system, aquamarine has indices of refraction of 1.57-1.58. This popular gem stone is found in very large crystals, often weighing several pounds. Fine aquamarine, when cut, is usually clear and flawless, thereby differing from its dark-green relative, emerald, which is rarely flawless. Genuine aquamarine is sometimes heat-treated to improve color; this treatment, however, may result in an off-colored sea-green tone, which gives an unnatural look to the gem.

Synthetic Aquamarine. A very fine synthetic aquamarine is manufactured today. This mineral is spinel, the magnesium aluminate. Synthetic spinel is single-refracting, having an index of refraction of 1.730. By means of this factor and the use of special color filters, the real can be readily told from the spurious. The finest gem aquamarine is obtained from Brazil and the Island of Madagascar. *See also* BERYLLIUM.   A. E. A.

AQUA REGIA [æ′kwə ri′dzhiə], "royal water," is a mixture of one volume of nitric acid and two to four volumes of hydrochloric acid, depending upon the intended application. Commercial mixtures are generally made using 35° Baumé nitric acid and 22° Baumé hydrochloric acid in a 1:4 ratio by volume. Essentially, nitric acid as a strong oxidizing agent liberates the chlorine from hydrochloric acid according to the reaction

$$\underset{\substack{\text{Hydrochloric}\\\text{acid}}}{3HCl} + \underset{\substack{\text{Nitric}\\\text{acid}}}{HNO_3} = \underset{\substack{\text{Nitrosyl}\\\text{chloride}}}{NOCl} + \underset{\text{Water}}{2H_2O} + \underset{\text{Chlorine}}{Cl_2}.$$

Since the chlorine is thus present in the nascent state, aqua regia is a much more active reagent than chlorine water proper.

Aqua regia owes its name to the fact that it is capable of dissolving gold and platinum. It is used primarily for this purpose, as in the extraction of platinum from its ores. In determining the approximate gold content of an article made from alloys containing copper or silver, the mark made by the article on a touchstone, a black siliceous rock, is compared with marks made by alloys of similar composition. To facilitate this comparison, the marks may be moistened with aqua regia of a composition such that it does not attack alloys above a given gold content, 75 per cent for example. Below this titer, or strength, it is possible to distinguish differences in alloy composition to 1 per cent. Such a method, although rather crude, may give satisfactory control of gold alloys of known composition.   J. Se.

AQUARIUM, an object or place in which aquatic animals, principally fishes, are kept captive for public or private exhibition.

Historical Development. Although the word aquarium itself was not used in the established sense until 1852, fishes have been kept in captivity since at least 2500 B.C., when the Sumerians maintained them in ponds for food. Romans of the first century of the Christian Era had pet marine fishes, while the Chinese domesticated the goldfish in their Sung Dynasty (960-1278). All these fishes were kept in ponds or pools, however, and it was not until the latter quarter of the eighteenth century that goldfish bowls became popular in England, goldfish most likely having been introduced there from China at the close of the previous century.

Domestic Aquaria. With the adoption of the idea of growing aquatic plants in tanks along with fishes, the popularity of the hobby grew in England and Scotland during the

COURTESY OF THE NEW YORK ZOOLOGICAL SOCIETY

GOLDFISH IN AN AQUARIUM

1850's. Nathaniel Bagshaw Ward, English botanist and originator of the Wardian case for transplanting delicate plants; Robert Warington, English chemist; and Philip Henry Gosse, English clergyman and naturalist, among others, contributed to this popularity. From England the fancy spread to the Continent. By 1865 there was at least one dealer in aquarium fishes in New York City, but not until after 1900 did the hobby become at all widespread in the United States. At the beginning of the twentieth century the only exotic fishes available to the fancier were a few neotropical catfishes, the climbing perch, the paradise fish, a gourami, a snakehead, a cichlid, and the goldfish. Thereafter, however, an ever-increasing number of small, tropical fresh-water species, now called singly tropicals, was introduced into Germany, which was the acknowledged leader in this field until World War II. Since the war the United States has been the center of both the hobby and the large importing, exporting, fish-breeding, and tank-and-appliance-manufacturing businesses connected with it. In 1948 approximately 150 different species of tropicals and 40 kinds of aquatic plants were commercially available for home aquaria in the United States.

Public Aquariums. The first public aquarium consisted simply of a series of standing marine and fresh-water aquaria, arranged in a conservatory-like building in Regent's Park, London. The Fish House, as it was first known, was opened in 1853 and contributed much toward popularizing the keeping of small home aquaria. Within the next 15 years several more public aquariums were started on the British Isles and the Continent; however, none of these, nor the

one in Regent's Park, survived. The experience gained from them nevertheless established the basic practices of aquarium management, such as circulation, aeration, filtering, and storage of water. In 1871 the aquarium at Blackpool, England, was opened, and in 1872 similar institutions at Brighton, England, and Frankfort, Germany, were completed. The Naples aquarium was opened in 1874. By 1929 there were at least 45 public aquariums in operation throughout the world. Since then no accounting has been made.

The first public aquarium in the United States was a small, commercial establishment in New York City, sponsored by P. T. Barnum, which was opened in 1856. It did not last long, nor did a similar commercial aquarium that followed it in 1876. In 1896 New York City opened a municipal aquarium in the remodeled building that had been, in turn, Fort Clinton, Castle Garden, and an immigration station at Battery Park. The New York Aquarium, for many years the world's largest, occupied these quarters until 1941, when it was temporarily established in the Lion House of the New York Zoological Park, pending the erection of a new building. The largest aquarium in the world in 1948 was the John G. Shedd Aquarium at Chicago, which had been opened in 1929. It had 132 larger exhibition tanks and 65 smaller ones, with a total capacity of more than 450,000 gal. and with reservoirs capable of holding an additional 2,000,000 gal. A radical departure from the conventional architecture of public acquariums is Marineland, opened near St. Augustine, Fla., in 1938. Previously all aquariums had consisted of halls, flanked by walls into which series of openings for the exhibition tanks were inserted and behind which the tankmen and engineers performed their duties. Marineland, called by its designers an "oceanarium," consists of two very large outdoor tanks. The larger is about 100 x 50 x 18 ft., arranged with ramps and portholes so that visitors can see such large-sized aquatic exhibits as porpoises and sharks both from above and below the surface of the water.

Maintenance. There is a popular misconception that plants in a standing, fresh-water aquarium function in the oxygenation of the water and that they balance the fish in this respect. This is not true, because any deficiency of that gas in the tank's water is quickly made up by oxygen from the atmosphere. The presence of plants, while beneficial in many ways, actually lessens the number of fish that can be maintained in any given aquarium, because plants consume oxygen and give off carbon dioxide just as animals do, at night or on dark days.

Because of the difficulties inherent in the proper maintenance of sea water, small marine aquaria have never become popular. Sea water "deteriorates" from the effects of storage and the waste products of animals living in it, and most marine organisms are very sensitive to chemical changes in their environment—much more so than the fresh-water species generally kept in home aquaria. Marine fishes and invertebrates, therefore, will not live in captivity unless means are employed to keep their water relatively unaltered. This means circulating, filtering and aerating the water, all in a completely nonmetallic water system. The water system is the heart of a public aquarium. Unless a dependable and continuous supply of clear and chemically suitable water is available for their exhibits, aquariums are dependent on closed circulations, in which water is stored, treated if necessary, and then used over and over again, being recirculated through tanks, aerators, filter, and reservoir. The accumulation of metabolic wastes, the presence of toxic metals and other poisons, the spread of infectious diseases and parasites among the exhibits, and the maintenance of relatively unstable sea water are some of the problems arising from the use of such closed circulations.

There are four different, and sometimes opposing, aspects to almost every item used in a public aquarium: (1) it must satisfy the visitors and provide them with entertainment and, if possible, education; (2) it must meet the physical requirements of the exhibits, so that they can thrive in captivity; (3) it must be practical to work with and to maintain, so that tankmen and engineers can operate efficiently; and (4) it must be feasible to construct and not too expensive.

J. W. A.

AQUARIUS [əkwɛ'əriəs], the Water Bearer, a large zodiacal constellation, mostly south of the celestial equator and extending from right ascension 20.5 hr. almost to 24 hr. Its symbol ♒ forms the eleventh sign of the zodiac, which the sun enters on Jan. 20. It contains no conspicuous star, the brightest being of third magnitude. The most noticeable asterism, the Water Jar, is a small Y composed of four stars

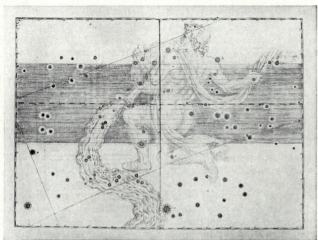

AQUARIUS, THE WATER BEARER

(fourth and fifth magnitudes) astride the celestial equator. In middle north latitudes, Aquarius is in the south in late October around 8 P.M. local civil time (l.c.t.). Among the numerous stars of this group, there are several telescopic doubles of contrasting colors. It also includes M 2, the globular cluster of thousands of stars, 45,000 light-years from the earth.

In mythology, Aquarius was pictured as an old man pouring water from his jar into the mouth of the Southern Fish.

J. H. P.

AQUEDUCTS. *See* BRIDGES; WATER SUPPLY.
AQUEOUS HUMOR. *See* EYE.
AQUILA. *See* ARNO, ARN or AQUILA.

AQUILA (ADLER), JOHANN KASPAR [æ'kwɪlə] (1488-1560), German religious reformer, was born in Augsburg, Aug. 7, 1488. He was educated in Italy, Switzerland, and the universities of Leipzig and Wittenberg. In August 1514 he entered the ministry and became a pastor at Bern. From 1514 to 1516 he served as military chaplain with Franz von Sinckengen during the campaigns of Worms and Metz, after which he was appointed pastor at Jengen, near the town where he was born. When he announced his conversion to the Lutheran cause, he was imprisoned by order of the bishop of Augsburg. After he was freed he proceeded to Wittenberg, where he became professor of Hebrew. He also

became acquainted with Luther, whom he helped in the task of preparing a translation of the Old Testament. In 1527 he was appointed pastor at Saalfeld and soon afterward became Protestant bishop in that town. He attended the Diet of Augsburg in 1530. In 1548 Aquila was an outspoken opponent of the Interim, an action which aroused Charles V against him; he was then forced to seek refuge at Rudolstadt. In 1550 he was appointed dean of the Collegiate Institute at Schmalkalden and in 1552 found it possible to return to his bishopric. He died at Saalfeld, Nov. 12, 1560.   E. B. A.

AQUILA or **AQUILA DEGLI ABRUZZI** [ɑ'kwilɑ de'lyi ɑbru'tsi], officially L'Aquila, a province and also a capital city in the mountains of central Italy, in the department of Abruzzi e Molise.

The City. Aquila lies on a shoulder of one of the foothills of the Gran Sasso at an elevation of 2,150 ft. and is 58 mi. northeast of Rome. It overlooks the valley of the upper Aterno River, a tributary of the Pescara, which empties into the Adriatic Sea.

Because of its situation in the midst of high mountains, Aquila has long and cold winters. The annual precipitation is around 28 in.; the late fall is the wettest season, but no month is without rainfall. Formerly a center for handicraft industries, such as lace-making, Aquila has become essentially an administrative center for a large province and a market place for the adjacent farming and pasture lands. Its only railway service is provided by a branch line from Terni to Sulmona; Aquila thus has come to depend largely on busses for intercity traffic. The population has grown very little in the last century. Indeed, during the late Middle Ages, Aquila is said to have had from fifty to sixty thousand inhabitants and to have been the second city in the Neapolitan domain. Beginning in the sixteenth century it declined, and, though temporary periods of revival ensued, Aquila never regained its former size and glory. Disastrous earthquakes in 1315, 1349, 1452, 1501, 1646, and 1703 and the ravages of pestilence contributed to the city's decline. There are several churches of historic and artistic value, including the Cathedral, San Bernardino, and the Basilica of Santa Maria di Collemaggio, described as the outstanding example of Abruzzi architecture, begun in 1287 in Roman-Gothic style. The highest point in the city is crowned with a massive castle built by the Spanish in the early sixteenth century.

Aquila was founded in the thirteenth century and soon acquired, through numerous rebellions and by participating in the wars of the era, a considerable degree of self-government, though nominally it was under the succession of Hohenstaufen, Angevin, Aragonese, and Spanish sovereigns who ruled over southern Italy. Aquila became so powerful that it waged war on its own account, made treaties on its own authority, and from 1382 to 1556 coined its own money. During this period it was a textile center and became famous for its international trade in wool, silk, and saffron. In 1482 a pupil of Gutenberg set up in Aquila one of the first printing presses in Italy. In 1529, the army of Charles V of the Holy Roman Empire sacked Aquila, its liberties were revoked, and never again did it prosper as before. Pop. (est. 1947), 59,349.

The Province. The province of Aquila, comprising 104 communes, contains 1,943 sq. mi. The terrain consists of parallel mountain ranges and the valleys between them. Among the latter the most important are the upper and middle reaches of the Aterno and the Conca di Fucino. The latter once contained Lago Fucino, largest lake in central Italy, which was drained in the nineteenth century to provide 40,789 acres of fertile land. The province also includes the upper valleys of the Sangro, Liri, and Salto. The mountains include the Gran Sasso d'Italia (9,600 ft.), La Maiella (9,100 ft.), and Monte Velino (8,200 ft.). Cereals, potatoes, and, in the Fucino basin, sugar beets are cultivated on the arable land. Grapes, olives, and fruit are also grown. On the slopes sheep raising is extensively carried on. Only 8 per cent of the population lives outside urban settlements. Noteworthy towns in the province, with their populations, are Sulmona, a railroad center (21,289) and Avezzano (18,463). Pop. (off. est. 1947), 371,000.   R. G. W.

AQUILA [æ'kwɪlə], the Eagle, a fairly large constellation, seen partly in the Milky Way, astride the celestial equator and centered at right ascension 19.5 hr. From northern latitudes, Aquila is due south in early October about 7 P.M. local civil time (l.c.t.). Among its numerous stars are several telescopic doubles of contrasting colors and the bright star Altair. M 11, a beautiful open cluster of tiny stars, more correctly included in Scutum, is sometimes listed in Aquila. In 1918, a temporary star, or nova, of magnitude —1.2 appeared in Aquila.

In mythology, Aquila was the eagle which Zeus sent to carry the beautiful boy Ganymede from earth to be his cupbearer in the abode of the gods. Aquila was finally placed among the stars. *See also* ALTAIR.   J. H. P.

AQUILA OF PONTUS (second century A.D.), a pagan scholar born in Pontus, Asia Minor, was first converted to Christianity and then became a proselyte to Judaism. The church father, Epiphanius, claims that Aquila was related to Hadrian, who commissioned him to rebuild Jerusalem as the city "Aelia Capitolina" in 128. It was then that he came under the influence of Rabbis Akiba, Eliezer ben Hyrcanus and Joshua ben Hananiah, who are said to have been his teachers.

Aquila's most notable contribution was his literal Greek translation of the Bible, in which he rendered the Hebrew word for word into Greek, disregarding linguistic idioms. The translation appeared in the year 170 and was accepted by the Jews as the official Greek version in contrast with the Septuagint, which was unpopular at the time because of its use by the Greek-speaking Christians. Aquila's complete translation is no longer extant, but a great many fragments of it have been preserved, and parts of his original translation of Kings and Psalms have been discovered in the *Genizah,* a collection of ancient manuscripts found in the synagogue at Fostat, near Cairo, Egypt.   M. A. G.

AQUILEIA [ɑ'kwile'ya], a small town in Udine province, northeastern Italy, one of the great cities of the Roman Empire and, after the fall of the latter, the seat of a patriarchate. It lies on the small Natissa River only a few miles north of the Lagoon of Grado in flat, almost marshy, country, 22 mi. northwest of Trieste. The town is connected by rail with Udine, the provincial capital.

Occupied originally by Veneto-Illyrians and Celts, the site was made a Roman military colony in 183 B.C. and became a stronghold against barbarian invasions from the north and east. By the time of Augustus (63 B.C.-A.D. 14) it had grown greatly, having become not only a military but also a naval base and the capital of the Tenth Imperial Region, Venetia et Histria. After Diocletian (A.D. 245-313) it possessed a mint and was frequently selected by the emperors as a place of sojourn. Through its port passed a large part of the trade with the Danubian countries. As the Empire began to decline, Aquileia was several times contested among aspirants

to the imperial title and menaced by barbarian incursions. In 452 the city was devastated by Attila, but only after the Lombard invasion was it abandoned by its patriarch in 568 for the nearby island-city of Grado. With the return of more peaceful conditions by the eleventh century, the patriarchs returned to Aquileia and rebuilt part of the ruined city. The port was reopened and several religious edifices were erected, notably the cathedral.

The patriarchs, combining temporal with ecclesiastical duties, came to spend less and less time in Aquileia, which meanwhile had acquired certain municipal liberties. The severe earthquake of 1348 damaged the city, and after the Austrian occupation in 1509 Aquileia declined to the status of a forgotten village. In 1751 the papacy decreed the suppression of the patriarchate, thus reducing the town to virtual extinction. The process of uncovering the artistic and historic treasures of Aquileia through archaeological explorations began in the nineteenth century and was carried on with increased momentum in the twentieth.

Among the more important monuments is the Basilica, in Romanesque style, which was built between 1021 and 1031 on the site of a previous church. It was later altered to include Gothic and Renaissance features. Inside are pavement mosaics (probably of fourth century), various frescoes, and a crypt. Also notable are the remains of Santa Maria della Libera, the Archaeological Museum, and the site of the ancient port. Pop. 1,350.   R. G. W.

AQUINAS, ST. THOMAS [ə'kwai'nəs] (1225-1274), Italian theologian and Scholastic philosopher, was born at Roccasecca, the family castle near Aquino, early in 1225. He attended the abbey school of the Benedictines at Monte Cassino and completed his studies in liberal arts at the University of Naples. After entering the Dominican order, he was sent to Paris and Cologne for his novitiate and theological training, and it was at this time that he came under the tutorship of St. Albert the Great. In 1252 he returned to the Dominican convent of St. James in Paris, and four years later he was appointed to one of the chairs of theology reserved for the Dominicans by the University of Paris. During the years 1254-1256 he commented on the *Four Books of the Sentences* of Peter Lombard and composed his short treatise, *On Being and Essence.* To this period in Paris belongs also his unfinished commentary on the celebrated treatise of Boethius, *On the Trinity.* This little work is the *locus classicus* for his teaching regarding the classification, interrelation, and methodology of the sciences of his time. He set down also the literary resumé of the first of his several disputations conducted as a professor of theology — the "disputed questions" *On Truth.* From the earliest days of his teaching it became apparent to his contemporaries that he was laying the foundations of a veritable revolution in theology and philosophy. The insights he had achieved even at that early age were to remain, with but slight modifications and refinements, the very core of his mature thought.

Thomas returned to Italy in the summer of 1259 and remained there at Anagni, Orvieto, Rome, and Viterbo for nine years; during much of this time he was present at the papal court as lecturer. His meeting at Orvieto with his fellow Dominican, William of Moerbeke, led to William's translation of the writings of Aristotle from Greek originals and to Thomas' series of commentaries, in which there is a careful effort to arrive at the real thought of the Philosopher. During this period he wrote his so-called "philosophical" *summa,* the *Summa Against the Gentiles,* a work that was intended primarily as a teaching and study manual for

Dominican missionaries. He began also his most mature and most celebrated work, the so-called "theological" *summa,* the *Summa of Theology,* which he had not completed when he ceased to write on Dec. 6, 1273. In the beginning of this monumental synthesis of Christian thought, Thomas outlines his intention "to set forth briefly and clearly the things which pertain to sacred doctrine . . . for the instruction of beginners" and his endeavor to treat "of God; of the rational creature's movement towards God; of Christ who as man is our way to God." To this period also belongs the literary resumé of the "disputed questions," *On the Power of God.*

In the fall of 1268 Thomas was recalled to Paris to enter into a strenuous struggle against a new form of Aristotelianism, Latin Averroism, which had arisen within the Faculty

the soul alone so called, since it is a part of the human species" (*Sum. Theol.* I:75.4). Thus man as a knower is a composite subject, and if one is to speak strictly he should not say that the senses know or that the intellect knows, but that man knows through these powers. The human soul is united to the body primarily that the human being may be essentially complete. Man, in his role as knower, however, needs the body also, in order to acquire knowledge through the medium of his sense organs. The human subject communicates with the external world first by means of his sense organs, which attain the reality that exists outside of him. In so far as it animates the body, the human soul is on the same level as external material forms and can enter into society with them. The composite is acted upon by those

Thomas Aquinas defending the Dominican Order against the attacks of the University of Paris before Pope Alexander IV and an assembly of prelates and scholars at Anagni in 1256

of Arts as a powerful current of thought. In 1270 he wrote his firmly worded treatise, *On the Unity of the Intellect Against the Averroists.* In 1272 he was recalled to Italy to establish a new house of studies for the Dominicans at Naples. There he wrote his unfinished "compendious treatise on Christian teaching," the *Compendium of Theology.* On his way to the Council of Lyons, to which he had been called as consultant by Pope Gregory X, he died in the Cistercian (Benedictine) monastery of Fossanuova on Mar. 7, 1274.

Philosophy. For Thomas, God's effects are singular things, subsistent beings, technically known as *supposita* or "subjects." The act of existing belongs properly to that which has existence, to that which is subsisting in its own existence.

Only subjects exist, then, with the accidental modifications (accidents) which inhere in them and the operations which emanate from them. That which exercises an act of existing in any essence is a subject of that essence. Essence is that which a thing is; subject or *suppositum* is that which exercises existence and action; "action belongs to the *suppositum* and the individual. Hence action . . . presupposes the subject which operates" (*Sum. Theol.* III:7.13). The designation, "that which exists" (and acts), is reserved for the subject alone.

In composite beings the subject is the whole being, as in the case of man the subject is the whole man; for the notion of part is incompatible with the notion of subject. "Hence a hand, or a foot, is not called a subject . . . nor, likewise, is

material objects. Through the senses man receives the materials upon which the intellect acts in order to abstract therefrom its concepts. Concepts are drawn actively from the sense data by the mind, and these concepts are the means whereby the knower can know what things are. Because concepts are means, "though the human intellect does not know singulars as such, it does have a proper knowledge of things, since it knows them through their essences" (*On Truth* II.4). Philosophy attempts to perceive those features of the essences of things that are above the purely sensible plane. The intellect by its own strength disengages from sense experience those essences.

The operation we have been considering is what Aristotle called the "simple gaze of indivisibles" or "simple apprehension." For Thomas, knowledge is completed only in the judgment which restores essences to existence or to the world of subjects. The proper function of the judgment is to affirm existence. The first operation, simple apprehension, is for the sake of the second operation, wherein knowledge is perfected. Truth belongs properly to the judgment and is based on the act of existing rather than on the essence: in other words, "truth follows the existence of the thing" (*On Truth* I:1).

For Thomas, being is the proper object of the intellect, but the intellect encompasses that object diversely in the acts of simple apprehension and judgment. In the first act the intellect expresses being in that which is its intelligible constitution, essence, whereas in the second act it expresses being

FRONTISPIECE FROM THE *ORATIO HABITA* BY THOMAS AQUINAS

in that which is its act, existence. The act of existing of each being is more intimate to it than its intelligibility. Existence is the ultimate act of being itself, and because of this it is also the ultimate act of being intelligible; "the first thing conceived by the intellect is being, because everything is knowable only inasmuch as it is actually" (*Sum. Theol.* I:5.2). In order to conceive the real in its integrity, we must therefore conceive being as signifying the coincidence of essence and existence. Within the range of our experience, there is no real being which is not an actually existing essence and an existent which is conceivable through its essence. Thus in every being there is a proportion between that which is and the act by which it exists. This diversity of relations to the act of existing gives an intrinsically proportional value to the very concept of being which is implicitly manifold: in predications all univocal names are reduced to one first nonunivocal, analogical name, which is "being" (*Sum. Theol.* I:13.5). From the consideration that the act of existing is limited by an essence which is distinct from it, we must infer the reality of a cause that is its own act of existing: "it must be that all things which are diversified by the diverse participation of being, so as to be more or less perfect, are caused by one First Being, Who possesses being most perfectly . . . from the fact that a thing is being by participation, it follows that it is caused. Hence such a being cannot be without being caused. . . . But since to be caused does not enter into the concept of being taken absolutely, that is why there exists a being that is uncaused" (*Sum. Theol.* I:44.1). A created essence is really distinct from its act of existing,

as potency is really distinct from the act that actuates it; for if it were its own existence it would be Existence itself and not a created being.

According to Thomas the only possible explanation for the presence of such finite beings is that they have been freely given existence by Him who is. This idea of creation quite distinctly separates Greek and Christian thought, since for the principal Classic Greek philosopher the universe was uncreated and eternal. At the summit of actuality is the Pure Act of existing: existence distinct from every other existence through its own purity. After the First Being there are beings whose acts of existing are diversified in so far as they are the existences of this or that being. The first effect of the Creator is the act of existing; all other effects presuppose it and are founded on it. The Creator wills to communicate His existence to other beings by way of likeness. As a generous and all-wise Creator He gives to the creatures that He causes to exist all that their essences require and all that they need to attain their end. The act of existing expands into activity in every being, just as the Good activates and attracts to Himself the universal order of beings. The good is essentially diffusive of itself, both as an end which attracts other beings to itself and as an efficient cause. This aptitude or propensity to communicate itself is contained in the very notion of goodness. It is because God is absolute goodness that He "communicated His goodness to created things in such a way that one thing can communicate to another what it has received" (*Cont. Gent.* III: 69).

In the thirteenth century the so-called Augustinian thinkers tended to depreciate the universal natural order in order to glorify the Creator. They seemed to fear that should they grant efficacy to created causes they would make creatures too independent of the Creator and thereby detract from His all-powerfulness. For Thomas, on the contrary, to detract from the creature's perfection is to detract from the perfection of the divine power. Such a position is incompatible, moreover, with the divine wisdom; it would not be a wise thing to create powerless causes. "This detracts from the universal order which is woven together by the order and connection of causes, while the First Cause, from the abundance of its own goodness confers upon other things not only that they may be, but also that they may be causes" (*On Truth* XI: 1).

In their historical setting these statements are freighted with connotations of bitter struggles. For Thomas, however, they are deeply rooted in the metaphysic of being. Goodness is coterminous with being, and there is in being a tendency to expand and pass beyond itself, to communicate to another the perfection that it has.

As a young theologian, Thomas had already noted how unreasonable it would be to admit that God has created man lacking the ability to know natural truths without special assistance (illumination) from God. Against Avicenna and the Augustinian "Illuminationists" Thomas stated that man acquires a knowledge of the unknown through his own intellectual light and the first concepts intuitively known, which are compared to that light as tools to a builder. The whole certitude of knowledge arises from the certitude of principles. Conclusions are known to be valid when they are resolved into their principles.

In this way "philosophy is founded upon truths made manifest by the light of natural reason. God's supernatural gifts (the gifts of grace) are added to nature in such a way, however, that they do not destroy nature but rather bring it to perfection. Hence the light of faith does not destroy the natural light of knowledge, which is inborn in us. It is, therefore, impossible that the things which belong to philosophy should be contrary to the things that belong to faith. Otherwise, either one or the other would be false; and since God is the author of both faith and nature, God would be the author of falsehood to us; which is impossible" (*On the Trinity* II: 3.).

Faith is not opposed to knowledge, it is a kind of knowledge. It is founded wholly on the testimony of God and derives infallible certitude from this fact. The act of faith is the act of assenting to the revealed truth because it has been spoken by God. The assent of him who has faith is unshakeable, but it requires the determinative action of the will (moved by grace). When that which the reason apprehends—for example, the first principles of knowledge—is such that it naturally assents thereto, it is not in the knower's power to assent or dissent. Such knowledge (knowledge by science) and faith cannot, therefore, be in the same subject and about the same object. It is thus manifest that Thomas does lift faith above reason; he never fails to stress the transcendant nature and incomparable dignity of the word of God. But in order to do so he does not lower reason. Though he does put the supernatural infinitely higher than the natural, he does not lower the natural. For Thomas there is but one proper method of inquiry and that is to handle philosophical problems as a philosopher and theological problems as a theologian. This method would seem to invite contradiction, yet his faith and his philosophy grow into an organic unity because they both spring from the same divine source.

Summary. Thomas broke sharply from the so-called Augustinian tradition, which was essentially a form of Neoplatonism, albeit a Platonism in which many Aristotelian notions had found a place. His work represents the renewal of Christian thought in the light of a metaphysic and theology whose conceptual systematization was expressed in terms of the principles of Aristotle. He transfigured Aristotle, however, emending him wherever he felt necessary. Perhaps the most fundamental change made by him was his extension of Aristotle's doctrine of potency and act to the relation between an essence and the act of existing which actualizes it. He maintains that, historically speaking, it was not Aristotle but Christian revelation that established the act of existing as the "act of every act and the perfection of every perfection" (*On the Power of God* VII: 2), the deepest layer of reality and the supreme attribute of the divinity: *I am Who am* (*Exod.* III: 13-14). Thomas saw that it is the act of existing which establishes and determines the nature of the intelligible structure of reality. His philosophical indebtedness to Aristotle should not be minimized. One has only to read his theological works to realize the esteem in which he held the philosopher. Yet it is in the Aristotelian commentaries that we read "the study of philosophy is not for the purpose of knowing what men have thought but to get at the truth of the matter" (*De coelo* I: 22).

Thomas himself was anxious to listen to all the arguments arising from a philosophical disagreement, "as nobody can judge a case unless he hears the reasons on both sides, so he who has to listen to philosophy will be in a better position to pass judgment if he listens to all the arguments on both sides" (*In metaph.* III). In order to preserve the wisdom of Augustine, Thomas disputed with its professed protagonists and urged them to abandon the whole Platonic approach, while in order to save the philosophy of Aristotle, he commented on it and recast it. He considered Averroes no faultless interpreter of Aristotle. While the Averroists were convinced that not a word could be altered in the works of

Aristotle or Averroes, Thomas tried to convince them that their ill-guided conviction was destructive of philosophy.

Aquinas had great commentators like Cajetan (1470-1534) and John of St. Thomas (1589-1644), but it was not until the twentieth century and the appearance of the work of such scholars as Etienne Gilson and Jacques Maritain that the spirit of his philosophy was recaptured in all its originality and vitality.   W. M. Wa.

AQUINAS COLLEGE, a privately controlled coeducational, accredited college of arts and sciences affiliated with the Catholic Church, at Grand Rapids, Mich. First instruction was given by this institution in 1886 as Novitiate Normal. A charter was granted in 1923, when the school merged with a college at Marywood and adopted the name of Sacred Heart College. After several additional changes in name the present name was adopted in 1940, when it began operating as a four-year institution.

Degrees offered are A.B., B.S., B.Mus., and B.S. in education. Terminal and preprofessional training are offered in education, secretarial science, medicine, biology, engineering, law, and business administration. Three centers of study are located, respectively, in three parts of the city. Late afternoon, evening, and Saturday courses are available to accommodate those who are unable to attend regular classes.

Scholarship aid is available, some of it open only to graduates of Catholic high schools in Grand Rapids. Residence halls are available for about 20 per cent of the women students. No residential facilities are available for men. *For statistics see* COLLEGES AND UNIVERSITIES.   J. R. To.

ARA. *See* ARAS.

ARA [e'rə], the Altar, the constellation immediately south of Scorpius and extending southward nearly to declination —70°. At least part of it was so named in ancient times. The constellation is visible south of the Tropic of Cancer.
                                                                                J. H. P.

ARABESQUE. *See* ARCHITECTURAL TERMS.

ARABI, AHMAD [ərɑ'bi] (1839-1911), Egyptian army officer and revolutionary leader, was born in Lower Egypt of poor parents in 1839. Commissioned in the Egyptian army in 1862, he served in the Abyssinian War of 1875 and joined a secret officers' movement headed by Ali Rubi, which aimed to rid the army of Turkish officers. In 1878 he was encouraged by Khedive Ismail to raise anti-Christian disturbances and was remunerated with a wife from the khedive's harem and the command of a regiment. During the reign of Khedive Tawfik he led discontented elements against the Khedive and Anglo-French control. As a result of a military demonstration led by Arabi in September 1881, Khedive Tawfik was forced to increase army pay, replace Riaz Pasha with Sherif Pasha as premier, and convoke an assembly of notables. In 1882 Arabi became undersecretary of war, then minister of war in Mahmud Sami's cabinet, and was created a pasha. As minister of war, he armed the forts of Alexandria and usurped powers that made him virtually a dictator. British and French naval squadrons anchored at Alexandria in June 1882, and rioting directed against foreigners, particularly Europeans, broke out in the city. The British bombed the Alexandria forts on July 11, British troops were landed, and Arabi's army was defeated at Tel-el-Kebir on September 11. Arabi was captured in Cairo and tried on December 3. He pleaded guilty, his sentence was reduced from death to banishment, and he spent almost twenty years on the island of Ceylon. In May 1901 he was pardoned by Khedive Abbas II. He died in Cairo, Sept. 21, 1911.   W. S. V.

ARABIA. *See* Arabian Peninsula; Saudi Arabia.

ARABIAN DESERT, a term applied to the interior of the Arabian peninsula and adjacent areas. It is subdivided into several deserts, among them the Syrian in the north, the Nefud in the central part, and the Rub' al Khali, or Great Sandy Desert in the south. The section of northeastern Egypt between the Nile and the Red Sea is also called the Arabian Desert.

Syrian Desert. Occupying the whole of northern Arabia above 30° N. lat., the Syrian Desert is classed as a geographi-

An oil well derrick rises above the sands of the Arabian Desert just north of Abqaiq.

cal unit with Arabia, although politically it belongs to Palestine, Syria, and Iraq. It extends from the border of Palestine to the edge of the Euphrates Valley. With a general elevation of 1,860 ft., the Syrian Desert has a small but regular rainfall. Its black-colored flint sand is dotted with pasture along the Wadi Hauran, which in rainy seasons forms a succession of pools from the Jebel Hauran to the Euphrates River. The broad depression of the Wadi Sirhan crosses from northeast to southwest, 500 ft. below the average level of the desert. The town of Jauf, with a 1939 population of 10,100, has rich palm groves.

Nefud Desert. The northern edge of the red sands of the Nefud Desert, following 30° N. lat., stretches east and west for a distance of 400 mi.; from north to south the region is about 200 mi. With a general elevation of 3,000 ft., the Nefud is a continuous area of sand blown into high, longitudinal sandbanks and dunes, with valleys 10 to 12 mi. wide. The northern part of the Nefud Desert is granitic and compact and has a small but regular rainfall. Although almost waterless, the Nefud is richer in pasture than any other part of the Arabian Desert. The sandhills are dotted with bushes and succulent plants, like the adar.

Rub' al Khali. The Rub' al Khali sometimes is called the Great Arabian Desert. Consisting of yielding, towering slopes of soft sand, the Rub' al Khali is passable only to camels. Only the northern fringe is visited by Bedouin tribes after the rains, when the sands produce herbs; on the northern fringe of the desert, gazelles, wolves, and hyenas are found.

Arabian Desert in Egypt. The Arabian Desert extends from the Nile River to the Red Sea, and from 26° to 29°

N. lat. In the southern part of the desert the Wadi Kenneh runs from north to south and the Wadi Fatira from west to east.   J. E. F.

ARABIAN NIGHTS, THE, a famous collection of Arabian stories, also known under the title *One Thousand and One Nights,* which is a more exact translation of the original title, *Alf layla wa-layla.* According to a pattern which is standard in Indian works of this kind, but is also found in the ancient Near East, the different stories in the collection are included in a simple and arbitrary framework, which gives the book a semblance of unity; in the case of the *Arabian Nights,* all the stories are recounted to King Shahriyār by his wife, Scheherazade, during one thousand and one nights. Chronological consistency is, however, entirely disregarded, and while Shahriyār is said to have lived in the fabulous age of pre-Islamic Persia, many of the stories belong to the Islamic Age and are located in Baghdad, Basra, and Cairo, all of which were founded long after the rise of Islam.

The problem of the origin, growth, and final redaction of the *Arabian Nights* has not yet been finally solved. Obviously the book has undergone many changes and did not take its present shape until a comparatively recent time, perhaps not earlier than the eighteenth century. The manuscripts used by Galland at the end of the seventeenth century were different from those on which nineteenth-century editions were based. On the other hand, the existence of a book of tales entitled *One Thousand Nights* in which the major role was played by a woman called Shīrazād is well attested as early as the tenth century, and some ancient manuscripts bearing the same title, but much shorter than more recent versions and differing considerably from them in their arrangement and contents, have been recently discovered. Besides the introductory story, which establishes the framework, some others are undoubtedly of Indian origin. We must assume, therefore, that an old book consisting chiefly of fairy tales, one in which the number "one thousand" should not have been taken at face value, met such a success in the Arabian world that a series of storytellers endeavored, in different ages and places, to inflate it by the insertion of new material drawn from the most varied sources, and even substituted new stories for some old ones, which were discarded.

As it now exists, the *Arabian Nights* is made up of a chaotic mass of heterogeneous matter, assembled from all quarters of Oriental tradition. As such it affords the discerning reader the most complete picture available of the diverse agents that were instrumental in the growth of Moslem civilization. Within the work several groups of stories characterized by certain common features can be singled out: (1) fairy tales, and tales of a purely fantastic character, ultimately of Indian or Persian origin; (2) stories centering on Baghdad and often linked to the Caliph Harun al-Rashid and his minister Ja'far, although with no true historical contents; many of them are love stories in a romantic and mawkish vein, the ultimate origin of which has recently been shown to be the Greek love novel of the Hellenistic-Byzantine age; (3) "bourgeois" stories, often humorous and ludicrous, sometimes even lewd, generally located in Cairo at the time of the Mameluke Sultans (thirteenth to sixteenth century). Besides these main themes, an extraordinary number of narratives formerly composed and published as independent works has been incorporated in the *Arabian Nights,* such as the adventures of Sinbad the Sailor; the story of the wise Ḥayqār, which is derived from an old Aramaic book of which there is evidence from as early as the fifth century B.C.; the novel of the knight al-Nu'man, an epic-romantic tale connected with the wars against the Crusaders; and many more.

The *Arabian Nights,* therefore, lacks unity, and its literary merit varies widely from one tale to another. Some are unpolished and popular, some present extremely well-arranged plots, a keen insight into human psychology, and a remarkable skill in narration; unfortunately the names of their authors, some of whom undoubtedly were gifted artists, have fallen into oblivion. Arabian literary criticism, however, always considered fiction an inferior type of literary production, to be despised and neglected by a well-educated public; the *Arabian Nights* was reserved, therefore, to the vulgar taste of the populace until it was rediscovered, as it were, by European scholars and through its unparalleled popularity in the West became the most significant gift of the Arabs to world literature.

The West became aware of the existence of the *Arabian Nights* through a French translation published by Antoine Galland in Paris from 1704 to 1717. Upon Galland's work most translations in other Western languages depend. In 1825-1843 the Arabic text was printed in Breslau, Germany, by M. Habicht, who also gave a German translation in 1840. In 1839-1841 the great English Arabist, E. W. Lane, published a masterful translation, unfortunately incomplete, to which he gave the title *Arabian Nights Entertainments;* it is based on a printed edition which had appeared in Cairo in 1835. Other English translations were given by John Payne (1882-1884, from the Calcutta edition of 1839-1841) and R. F. Burton (1885-1889). Burton's translation, which attained a wide popularity, is largely dependent upon Payne's and often reproduces it literally. A French translation by J. C. Mardrus (1899), which claims to be literal and to preserve the flavor of the original, is actually a free adaptation of doubtful taste. The German translation by E. Littmann (1921-1928), with a learned introduction, is of a very high scholarly standard.

Two of the most popular stories in Galland's translation, those of Aladdin and Ali Baba, are missing in all manuscripts and prints. For a long time Galland was suspected of forgery, until the original texts were discovered. The problem of the relationship of the different manuscripts of the *Arabian Nights* is a very involved one; the greatest progress toward its solution has been made through the outstanding studies of the American scholar, D. B. Macdonald. *See also* ALADDIN; ALI BABA; SCHEHERAZADE; SINDBAD THE SAILOR.

G. L. D. V.

ARABIAN PENINSULA, the southwestern extremity of Asia. Located between 12° and 32° N. lat. and 35° and 60° E. long., the peninsula is about 1,400 mi. long, has a maximum width of 1,300 mi., and contains approximately 1,000,000 sq. mi., an area equivalent to a little less than one third of that of the United States. The peninsula is bounded on the north by Iraq and Jordan and on all other sides by water. On the west is the narrow Red Sea, and in the southwest the 23-mi.-wide strait of Bab el Mandeb separates Arabia from Africa. On the south are the Gulf of Aden and the Arabian Sea. The Gulf of Oman, Strait of Hormuz, and the Persian Gulf are on the east.

Physical Features. The peninsula is a tilted block, or plateau, covered by sediments with occasional outcrops of lava and granite. The plateau slopes from the west to the east, with the western rim beginning at distances varying from 10 to 20 mi. inland from the Red Sea coastal plain. This plateau has a general elevation of from 4,000 to 5,000 ft. but a mountain range parallels the Red Sea, and in the south, from Mecca almost to Aden, the elevation is about 8,000 ft.

A few peaks in the extreme south reach 9,000 ft. In Oman, on the southeastern extremity of the peninsula, there is a small range of mountains, including Jebel Sham, a peak rising to 9,900 ft.

The interior of the Arabian Peninsula is not well known, and relatively little exploration has been done because of the great heat, dryness, and the distrust of the inhabitants. It is known, however, that the plateau is not an absolutely flat surface; there is considerable local relief, and there are several ranges of low mountains, such as Jebel Shammar and Jebel Tuwaiq.

There are no permanent rivers, but there are many wadies or dry stream beds, that carry off the water when it rains. Some of these wadies are important because they drain into oases.

Climate. The Arabian Peninsula is one of the great desert areas of the world. The entire peninsula is hot and dry al-

EWING GALLOWAY

Cratertown Mosque on the outskirts of Aden, a seaport on the Arabian Peninsula.

most all of the time. During the winter months the nights are fairly cool and there is a large diurnal difference in temperature. If it were not for the cool nights, desert travel would be extremely difficult.

Most of the peninsula receives less than 8 in. of rainfall a year, but there are large areas which receive less than 3 in. The areas of slightly higher rainfall are on the mountain tops, particularly the mountains of Yemen and Aden, where about 15 in., and sometimes as much as 20 in., of rain fall every year. This area is called Arabia Felix, or "Lucky Arabia." The rain comes in the winter over most of the peninsula, but Arabia Felix also receives rain in late summer from the monsoons.

The town of Aden, on the southwest coast, has an average annual temperature of 83° F. Daytime temperatures of over 100° F. are the rule rather than the exception. The average annual rainfall at Aden is 1.9 in. yearly.

Although the whole peninsula is dry, there are different degrees of dryness that are important. Distinction is made between the true desert, the dry steppe, and the oasis regions. The true desert is divided into many different areas named for their physical characteristics, such as the Nefud, or the deep sand and gravel desert in the north central part. The Dahanah is a gravel plain, and part of the 400- to 500-mi.-wide Rub' al Khali (the abode of emptiness) desert in the south is a Dahanah type. The dry steppe areas occupy most of the outer edges of the peninsula and consist of plains that support clumps of grass and a few hardy plants. They are utilized by the nomadic tribes. In the Nejd, or central plateau region, there is a group of oases that receive water draining from surrounding mountain areas.

Economic Life. Agriculture is limited to the raising of sheep, goats, camels, asses, and horses and the growing of wheat, millet, barley, and some dates. Arabia Felix is noted for coffee (inland from Mocha) and some tobacco, but agri-

OIL REFINERY AT RAS TANURA IN SAUDI ARABIA

culture is largely a subsistence matter, and there is a constant search for grass and water to nourish the flocks.

Oil is the largest export item and the major economic resource of the peninsula. The chief oil deposits are the Bahrein Island field, off the central Persian Gulf coast, and the nearby Damnar field. There are also some local fisheries and pearl-fishing grounds. Another great source of income is the tourist trade. About 500,000 Moslems annually make pilgrimages to the Holy City of Mecca to worship the famous Black Stone in the Kaaba.

Political Divisions. The major political division of the Arabian Peninsula is the Kingdom of Saudi Arabia, with about 600,000 sq. mi. The British protectorate of Aden is the second largest political area, with about 112,000 sq. mi.; and the Sultanate of Masqat and Oman, is third with 82,000 sq. mi. Other divisions are the Kingdom of Yemen, 75,000 sq. mi.; the Sheikdom of Kuwait, 1,930 sq. mi.; the Sultanate of Bahrein Island, 213 sq. mi.; Aden Colony (Br.), 80 sq. mi.; and the Qatar and Trucial coast sheikdoms, whose areas are unknown. The estimated population of all of the peninsula is between 7,000,000 and 8,000,000.

ARABIAN PHILOSOPHY. *See* Philosophy (*Medieval Philosophy*).

ARABIAN SEA, a northwestern extension of the Indian Ocean, lying between India on the east and Arabia on the west. The Gulf of Oman connects the Arabian Sea with the Persian Gulf; on the west the Gulf of Aden connects

with the Red Sea. The distance from the Arabian to the Indian coast at the broadest part of the sea is 1,500 mi. The southern boundary is indefinite, as the Arabian Sea merges with the Indian Ocean between 10° and 15° N. lat. Soundings of 13,000 to 16,500 ft. have been made. There are several smaller gulfs on the coast of India such as the gulfs of Cutch, which is north of the Kathiawar Peninsula, and Cambay, which is south of it. The Indus, flowing from northwest India, and the Narbada and Tapti, both flowing from central west India, are the most important rivers to empty into the Arabian Sea. Cyclonic storms coming from the Indian Ocean blow during the months of May, June, and July. The chief products shipped are silk, wool, spice, sugar, grain, cotton, carpets, silverware, petroleum, and opium. J. E. F.

ARABIC LANGUAGE. Arabic is spoken over an area which extends from the fringes of the Iranian highland westward to the African coast of the Atlantic Ocean, and from the southern slopes of the mountain range in Asia Minor and the eastern and southern coast of the Mediterranean, southward to the Indian Ocean and the northern part of Africa. It is the official language of all independent Arab states, Iraq, Syria, Lebanon, Transjordan, Saudi Arabia, Yemen, and Egypt; it is also official, either alone or together with French, English, or Italian, in many other countries with semi-independent status or under foreign sovereignty, namely, Palestine, Tunisia, Algeria, Morocco, Libya, the Anglo-Egyptian Sudan, Zanzibar, and the minor states on the Arabian Peninsula.

On the borders of the Arabic linguistic area, other languages dovetail with it: Turkish in northern Syria and northwestern Iraq, Kurdish and Persian in Iraq, Hebrew in Palestine, several Nubian and Nilotic languages in the Anglo-

A dhow, an Arab trading ship, sails the Persian Gulf.

Egyptian Sudan, and, especially, Berber in North Africa. Represented in Libya by scanty enclaves, Berber expands fanwise westward through Tunisia, Algeria, and Morocco and prevails in the south of the last-named country, although most people who have Berber as their native tongue are actually bilingual. In Arabia, the vernaculars of a few ethnic groups on the southern coast are offshoots of the ancient South Arabic language. On the other hand, Arabic is spoken by some isolated communities within the borders of other linguistic areas. This is true of southwestern Iran and some less notable Iranian areas, the southern Anglo-Egyptian Sudan, Zanzibar, French Senegal, and a few centers in Uganda, Tanganyika, and the Belgian Congo.

Although reliable statistics are lacking for certain countries, it is estimated that about sixty million persons speak Arabic as their mother tongue. A much larger number understand or even speak and write Arabic, either as a language of trade —as in some parts of Ethiopia and Somaliland, in East Africa and Madagascar, and, to a lesser extent, in West Africa—or as the religious language of Islam in all Moslem countries. In this latter case the knowledge of Arabic is restricted to the learned. The relatively recent Westernization in the culture of the Moslem countries and the rise of nationalism have impeded the spread of Arabic beyond its earlier linguistic area.

Until the seventh century of the Christian Era, Arabic was the language of northern and central Arabia; its spread over the area which it now covers was not the consequence of a gradual mass migration but the result of the sudden invasion and conquest which followed the rise of Islam, when the previous languages of Iraq, Syria, Palestine, Egypt, and North Africa gradually yielded to the language of the ruling minority. Thus, the majority of the present speakers of Arabic are by no means Arabs in their ethnical background, except, of course, the inhabitants of Arabia and a number of Arab nomadic tribes which settled in the Near East and North Africa and avoided intermarriage with sedentary groups. On the other hand, the Persians and the Turks in the East and the Berbers in Africa, although politically subdued by the Arabs and converted to the Arab religion, successfully resisted the linguistic impact of their conquerors; the same holds true for other more remote peoples in eastern and central Africa, as well as in central and eastern Asia, who were converted to Islam later. Nevertheless, all Moslems, whatever language they may speak, have added thousands of words borrowed from Arabic to their vocabulary. In some countries, such as Spain and Sicily, which the Arabs had conquered and from which they were later driven, Arabic lost ground, but it was spoken as late as the eighteenth century on the small island of Pantelleria, south of Sicily, and it is still spoken in Malta, which was lost to the Arabs in the twelfth century.

Arabic, or more specifically North Arabic, belongs to the Semitic family. Its closest affinities are with South Arabic and Ethiopic. With these it may be considered as forming a South Semitic group, differentiated from the North Semitic group of Akkadian, Canaanite, and Aramaic, but this division is far from clear-cut and should not be overemphasized. Because of its isolation, both geographical and historical, Arabic, together with South Arabic, is more archaic than the other Semitic languages, especially in its phonetics. Among the proto-Semitic features preserved by Arabic are: most spirant, fricative, and "emphatic" consonants; the short final vowels, and, as a result, a fully developed system of nominal declension; and a complete passive conjugation. On the other hand, Arabic has lost the last of the three proto-Semitic sibilants (s, $\check{s}$, $\acute{s}$) which Canaanite and South Arabic have preserved. Nasalization, or the so-called nunation, of final vowels in certain nominal inflections, an internal, or "broken," plural of nouns, a wide development of verbal forms, a specific form of comparative adjective, and other morphological features may be peculiar innovations within the South Semitic group.

Dialects. The classical, or literary, Arabic, which was basically the language spoken in central Arabia in the sixth and seventh centuries of the Christian Era, as is evidenced by the Koran and a number of texts in verse and prose, was molded into a rigid grammatical system as early as the end of the eighth century. It is still used in writing and is practically unchanged throughout the Arab world, but it is seldom spoken except on formal occasions and on the radio. Dialectical differentiation arose at a very early date, however, and we are informed about certain peculiarities in the speech of different tribes even before the rise of Islam. In all likelihood, the living language of the Arabs never precisely matched classical Arabic, which, in a way, should be considered as having been affected by the development of a literary style to the same degree as were the Greek literary dialects. Therefore, the history of the dialects, which today are the only colloquial languages, is a long one, although evidence is lacking for a precise demonstration except in Spain and a few other areas. An impact of the linguistic substrata, as with Aramaic in Iraq and Syria, Coptic in Egypt, Berber in North Africa, is also undeniable, but it has not yet been ascertained in every detail.

At present, the Arabic dialects fall into three groups: dialects of Arabia proper, which are more archaic than the others and may be compared to the dialects of the nomadic Bedouins outside of Arabia, who speak a more archaic language than their sedentary neighbors; Eastern dialects, in Iraq, Syria, and Egypt; and Western dialects, from Libya westwards. To the last group belongs the dialect spoken in Malta, which made extensive borrowings from the Italian, and especially the Sicilian, vocabulary and is the only Arabic dialect which developed into a literary language and adopted the Latin script. Many changes in phonetics, morphology, and syntax are common to all dialects. The most remarkable are the loss of all short final vowels and the consequent loss of the nominal declension and the modal conjugation; the loss of the passive; the shrinking of the verbal system; and a great simplification in the subordinate clauses. Others are peculiar to each group or to the single dialects. The differences between dialects are often very great, and while a Syrian easily understands an Egyptian, an uncultivated Iraquian would find it difficult to carry on a conversation with a Moroccan.

The Written Language. The first evidence of North Arabic, though it occurs in a form noticeably different from the standard language, is offered by the Lihyanite, Thamudene, and Safaitic inscriptions from Hejaz and Transjordan, which range from about the second century B.C. to about the fifth century of the Christian Era. Their script is an offshoot of the South Arabic alphabet. The earliest written document in Arabic proper is a funerary inscription in the Nabatean script, found near Nemarah in Transjordan and dated A.D. 328. After that, with the exception of two later inscriptions, both Christian, from the sixth century, it is necessary to go down to the Koran in order to find written evidence of Arabic. The Arabic script developed from the Nabatean, stressing its cursive aspect, and attained a high level of calligraphic elegance in its various types (*kufic, naskhi,* etc.). Not only the Arabs but all Moslem peoples, whichever their language, adopted this script; and it is only recently that Turkey and some Central Asiatic republics of the Soviet Union, whose languages belong to the Turkish group, have switched to the Latin alphabet. Arabic script is written from right to left.

In its origin Arabic was the language of the uneducated yet bright and gifted Bedouins, who accomplished outstanding achievements in poetry. Through the foundation of the Arabian Empire and the spreading of Islam, it became a highly sophisticated instrument, capable of expressing the most complex thoughts in science and philosophy, and produced an extensive literature. Although it has failed to keep pace with the trend of Western civilization during the last four centuries, it has received a vigorous stimulus during recent decades and has proved itself able to respond to new technical and cultural needs. The social and political changes in the Arab world and the increase in literacy among its inhabitants are adding momentum to the development of this new phase in the history of the Arabic language.

South Arabic. Under the conventional head "South Arabic" scholars designate a group of slightly differentiated dialects, evidence of which is given by inscriptions found in South Arabia from at least the beginning of the first millennium B.C. South Arabic, with its main branches, the Minaean, Sabaean, Qatabanian, and Hadramawtian, was the language of the South Arabian civilization as it flourished down to the sixth century of the Christian Era, when it was superseded by the North Arabic of Islam. North Arabic is now spoken all over Arabia, but in certain remote regions of the southern coast and on the island of Socotra certain vernaculars (Mehri, Shkhawri, and Soqotri) are still in use, and these undoubtedly go back to the old South Arabic language.

South Arabic is only imperfectly known, both because comparatively few examples have survived and especially because its script does not indicate vowels. It shares most of the features of North Arabic but in some of its branches presents certain peculiarities: inflectional nasalization through -m instead of -n (the so-called *mimation*), s instead of h as pronominal suffix, and s instead of a as prefix of the causative form of the verb. In its vocabulary, South Arabic presents many similarities to Ethiopic.   G. L. D. V.

ARABIC LITERATURE.

ARABIC LITERATURE. The role of the Arabs in world civilization depends on and is linked to the rise and spread of Islam and the foundation of the empire of the Caliphs. Before the time of Mohammed (570-632), however, the Arabs already possessed an important literature which was largely poetical. This pre-Islamic literature was never surpassed by the great achievements of the later ages and has remained in the judgment of the Arabs themselves the paragon of aesthetic perfection. With the rise of Islam, new modes of literary expression developed, and the old ones underwent essential changes through the influence of a deeply modified social environment and of various foreign cultures. Though literary activity has been considerable, the greatest contribution which the Islamized Arabs made to the progress of the human mind lies in the fields of religion and science. A learned literature of a tremendous magnitude, to be compared in volume only to the Chinese, the Indian, and medieval Latin, bears witness to the undaunted zeal of the Arabs for science and scholarship; no field, from rhetoric to mathematics and from philosophy to sports and games, remained untouched by them, and the indebtedness of Western civilization to Arabic science is well known. The following discussion will not, however, consider this aspect of Arabic literature, but will confine itself to poetry and artistic prose.

THE PRE-ISLAMIC AGE

The information which we possess about the history of the Arabian peninsula previous to the rise of Islam is poor and full of gaps. Nothing is known about the existence of a literature in the kingdoms of Southern Arabia (Minaean, Sabaean, and Himyarite), the earliest cultural centers in that country. If they had any, which is most likely, it was irretrievably lost during their decline, from the third to the sixth centuries of the Christian Era. In the age of social and po-

litical depression which ensued, the nomadic element, which had always existed in Arabia, gained the ascendancy. The Bedouins, roaming in the desert or pushing toward the borders of the Byzantine and Persian empires in Syria and Mesopotamia, where some of their tribes became sedentary and grew into petty kingdoms, came to be the essential factor in Arabian life. Although the level of their material culture was very low, their intelligence was keen, and their aesthetic and emotional reactions were prompt and alert. They developed a language of extraordinary richness and precision which, in a later age, proved fit for the subtlest philosophical and scientific shades of thought. For the time being they used their speaking ability to express themselves in a style both simple and abundant. We still possess, carefully preserved by later philologists, some samples of their public speech, wise sayings, and historical narration. The last, generally dealing with the fights among tribes and the deeds of tribal heroes, in its dignified and yet realistic expression is often reminiscent of the best Hebrew prose in the historical books of the Old Testament.

Poetry, however, shows the pre-Islamic genius at its highest. Long epic poems remained unknown to the Arabs; even their longest poems, called "kasidas," do not exceed one hundred distichs. Although the subjects treated by the poets are various, their stylistic presentation follows certain patterns which are scarcely, if ever, ignored. Hence, there is in Arabic poetry a certain monotony, which, however, is counterbalanced by an unsurpassed variety in verbal profusion. The main topics are self-praise, praise of the tribe, scorn and satire, love (generally the lament for the departure of the beloved), grief over dead heroes (a mode much cultivated by women), and, above all, the fresh and immediate description of desert nature, with its dangers and terrors, its rough and yet picturesque landscape, its thorny bushes, and its wild animals.

The oldest samples of Arabic poetry go back to the beginning of the sixth century of the Christian Era, only one hundred years before the rise of Islam. Practice of poetry must, of course, have been much older, and the loss of many an ancient poem may be due to the lack of written records; it would seem, however, that the "classical" style took its final shape only at that time. This style is characterized by a system of metrics with rigorously defined rules, based, like Greek and Latin metrics, on the length of the syllable; a no less rigorous rhyme scheme, requiring a single rhyme through the whole length of each poem and a conventionalized style and vocabulary. These features bear witness to the high degree of ripeness and refinement attained by the poets of the desert in spite of their uncouthness and illiteracy; the poets who dwelt in cities, curiously enough, attained no such proficiency.

Philologists of later generations, when the golden age of Arabic poetry was long past, eagerly gathered ancient poems, and edited them in the form of dewans (divans)—collections of poems by a single poet or a group of poets belonging to the same tribe—or as anthologies of specimens selected because of their high artistic standard. Among the latter we may mention the *Aṣmaʿiyyāt,* the *Mufaḍḍaliyyāt* (of which we possess an excellent English translation), the *Mudhahhabāt* ("The Golden Ones"), and, the shortest and most famous of all, the *Muʿallaqāt,* seven poems of considerable length which were considered the highlights of pre-Islamic poetry. Of their authors the best known are ʿAntara, the fierce warrior, an-Nābigha adh-Dhubyānī, the eulogist of the Christianized kings of Syria and Mesopotamia, and Imraʾalqays, the dispossessed scion of a royal family, who died as an exile.

THE KORAN

For Moslems, as for Mohammed himself, the Koran is the living word of God, and as such it not only contains the eternal Truth but also represents the most perfect achievement of literary style. That the Koran was inimitable became a dogma, and two men who were bold enough to challenge its uniqueness, Ibn al-Muqaffa' and Abu'l-'Alā' al-Ma'arrī, were branded as blasphemous and heretical. To the Western critic, however, the literary value of the Koran is uneven; in its most ancient chapters (suras), where religious emotion is at its peak, and the dominant motifs are the praise of God's all-pervading majesty and the frightful expectation of the Day of Judgment, Mohammed appears as an artist, even in the choice of his formal means of expression, a kind of rhythmic and rhymed prose (saj'), which he borrowed, substantially improving its original awkwardness, from the form of the forecasts of the Arab soothsayers. Although this feature is preserved until the more recent parts of the Koran, in them it loses much of its vigor and freshness and gradually deteriorates into a purely ornamental technique. A spirit of dignified grandeur permeates the whole of the book, the traditional arrangement of which runs almost contrary to the chronological sequence, and sometimes attains a powerful effect; however, especially in the most recently recorded sections, mostly devoted to legal and ritual matters, eloquence falls into rhetoric. Nevertheless, the immense influence of the Koran upon the development of the later Arabic style makes of this earliest Arabic work a cornerstone, not only of the religion of the Arabs, but also of their literature. The period during which the Koran was composed (or, as Moslems would say, "revealed") covers more than twenty years, from about A.D. 610 to the year of the Prophet's death, 632.

THE CLASSICAL PERIOD OF ARABIC LITERATURE

Poetry. Through the sweeping conquest of Byzantine- and Persian-held territory from the deserts of Central Asia to the African shores of the Atlantic Ocean, the Arabs, in a century or so, entirely changed their social environment and cultural outlook. Nevertheless, the impact of the new way of life on literature was not as sudden and thorough as one might have expected. Since, for a long time, literature consisted chiefly of poetry, and since the artists who were responsible for it were nomadic Arabs who remained faithful to their traditional customs even when they had settled in Syria, Iraq, or Persia, the greatest part of the poetic remains dating from A.D. 632 to 750, or from the early Islamic age to the fall of the Ommiad dynasty, reproduces, with only minor changes, the stylistic patterns of the pre-Islamic period. Not even the new religion modified these patterns substantially, and although poetry was also used as a political tool in the civil strife which soon disrupted the unity of the Islamic community, its formal aspect was scarcely altered. The three greatest poets of the age of the Ommiad caliphs, Jarīr, al-Farazdaq, and al-Akhtal, who was Christian, might have belonged, but for some slight innovations, to a much older time.

However, we may already perceive the beginning of a new manner in some poets who gave up the description of desert life, such as Omar ibn Abī Rabī'a (died 718), an inspired painter of romantic and sometimes frivolous love, and especially the caliph Walid II (died 743), whose poems describe in a light vein the pleasures of love and wine, substituting short and popular meters for the classical ones.

This trend gained momentum during the earlier period of the Abbasside dynasty, when the Arab civilization finally lost the specific Bedouin character of its origin. While some poets kept faithful to the time-honored schemes of pre-Islamic tradition even when they dealt with contemporary subjects, others were able to find new forms for the expression of new feelings, and a few succeeded in giving an artistic shape to issues which had been entirely beyond the horizon of ancient poetry, such as ethics, religion, and philosophy. As examples of the first kind we may mention Abū Tammām (died 845), al-Buhturī (died 897), and, much later, al-Mutanabbī (died 965), the greatest of them all, in whose poems the style and spirit of the past found artistic expression. Abū Nuwās (died c. 810), whose chief subjects are the pleasures of sensual love, drinking, and hunting, is the typical representative of the new style, a true poet in spite of the lewdness of some of his verses. In Bashshār Ibn Burd (died 784), of doubtful Islamic orthodoxy, with strong leanings toward the Iranian concept of an eternal fight between the principles of Good and Evil, and in Abu'l-'Atāhiya (died 825), who gave a pointed expression to deeply ascetic feelings, philosophy and religion take their rightful place in poetry. Much later, Abu'l-'Alā' al-Ma'arrī (died 1057), the blind poet, emphatically asserted in a highly sophisticated style the inadequacies of all religions and, in his respect towards every manifestation of life that led him to vegetarianism, revealed the influence of Neoplatonic and Indian ideas.

The new developments, however, failed to call for an essential change in the poetical horizon of the Arabs. The stylistic tradition, which put its highest ideal in the servile imitation of ancient models, was never entirely overcome by the individual efforts of isolated personalities. In the hundreds and hundreds of dewans produced during the later centuries in the wide area, extending from Spain to Persia and Turkey, where Arabic was used as a literary language, no realization of a new artistic trend can be found. Only in two fields, which the conventionalized pattern of style had neglected, does a genuine spirit reveal itself—in the mystic (sūfī) poems and the popular love songs. The most perfect representative of sufistic poetry, Omar Ibn al-Fāriḍ (died 1235), although he did not attain the heights of the Persian mystic poets, succeeded in approaching the ineffable intoxication of the soul delving into God's Oneness. New metrical forms, the most typical of which is the gazel, a four-verse stanza with a refrain, were introduced or developed to express the pains and pleasures of love in a light and unsophisticated vein and in a language close to the language actually spoken by the people. This poetry, which has survived to the present day as a mere unwritten production of dialect literature, is almost entirely lost in its earlier samples. The dewan of the Spanish poet Ibn Guzman (died 1160) is the only extensive collection that has escaped destruction; besides love it contains satire and realistic pictures of everyday life. Gazel poetry, coupled with the theory of Platonic love which also flourished in Spain and found its expression in poetry, is not unlikely to have stimulated the development of Provençal poetry.

Literary Prose. The native eloquence of the Arabs and their fondness for expressing themselves in a highly elaborate speech were the chief reasons for the development of a prose style in which the main consideration is manner rather than substance. During the first century after the rise of the Arabic empire, political issues were still publicly debated, and political eloquence flourished. It disappeared entirely with the growth of authoritarian government and, instead, religious, ethical, and literary eloquence developed in the form of sermons (khuṭbas) and admonishments (mawā'iz), either actually delivered or fictitious, and lectures on the most varied topics. The highly centralized public administration raised the position and influence of the clerks and secretaries who were responsible for the writing of official letters, and they became the main bearers of an encyclopedic culture. In the highly cultivated and refined environment of Baghdad, the capital of the Abbasside caliphate and the greatest international metropolis of that age, the literary essay developed and was brought to its most complete fruition by al-Jāḥiẓ (died 868), one of the most brilliant authors in Arabic literature. Besides dealing, in his major works, with such topics as rhetoric and natural history—never, however, systematically, but rather striving for variety—he wrote a great number of small tracts, indulging in anecdotes, learned quotations, and niceties. In his real, although not always deep, interest in Greek science and philosophy and Persian wisdom and legend, and in his careful study of ancient Arabic lore and poetry, al-Jāḥiẓ responds to the Arabic ideal of *adab,* a term which could be approximately rendered by "the gentleman's culture" and which ultimately is a blend of the Arab, Greek, and Persian intellectual legacy, the three elements that shaped Islam into a world civilization. A great portion, and perhaps the most entertaining, of Arabic literature (for example, *The Book of the Misers* by the same al-Jāḥiẓ) consists of *adab* works, wide collections of anecdotes and aphorisms arranged under different headings and either embracing the whole range of the subject or dealing with a special aspect of it. *The Sources of Stories* by Ibn Qutayba (died 884) and *The Precious Necklace* by the Spaniard Ibn 'Abd Rabbihi (died 940) are among the finest examples of this variety of literature. Ibn Qutayba is also responsible, among other numerous works, for *The "Adab" of the Secretary,* a kind of handbook dealing with all the subjects that a public official was supposed to know; and this literary type had a wide success until a much later age. Indeed, at that early period we find already developed a characteristic feature of most Arabian authors—the variety of their achievements and their striving for an all-embracing knowledge. This is only one of the aspects which Islam has in common with the European medieval frame of mind.

In its striving for a purely formal perfection, Arabic literature emphasized the use of rhymed prose, which, as we have seen, had been the stylistic form of the Koran and was widely employed from the tenth century on. Besides being used in innumerable sermons, lectures, and epistles, this peculiar style reached its peak in the so-called *Maqāmāt,* or "Sessions," one of the most original and successful productions of the Arabic literary genius, although its lack of significant content makes it little palatable to most Western readers. First introduced, as it seems, by al-Hamadhānī (died 1008), the *Maqāmāt* literature attained its ultimate shape through the unparalleled linguistic and stylistic mastery of al-Ḥarīrī (died 1122). The works of al-Ḥarīrī consist of fifty chapters, in each of which a curious type of swindler appears in different cities and under various disguises and through his shrewd tricks and baffling grandiloquence succeeds in cheating his audience and filling his pockets. The story, however, is only a pretext for an amazing display of stylistic effects attained by an unbelievable accumulation of rare words and expressions, proverbs and sayings, alliterations and puns. The success of al-Ḥarīrī's *Maqāmāt* was tremendous; imitations of them not only were produced in Arabic until very recent times but also in other languages, among them Hebrew. On the other hand, their hero, the eloquent thief, seems to have offered a model for the Spanish picaresque novel.

Together with the practice of poetry and literary prose, the Arabs, besides building up an elaborate grammatical system and collecting in huge dictionaries the wide treasures of their language, developed a keen interest in the theory of the use of human speech for artistic purposes. Literary criticism began, in a quite primitive and unsystematic manner, as an attempt at a comparative appraisal of the merits of different poets; it was stimulated by the fight over the legitimacy of the new school of poetry, which was going its own way and disregarding the time-honored tradition of the pre-Islamic poets. Later on, the influence of Greek theory helped to build up a complete system of rhetoric which, although it lacks a deep insight into the nature of art, nevertheless takes full cognizance of the basic problems of aesthetics and tries to solve them along the line of a consistent philosophy. In his introduction to an extensive collection of biographies of poets, Ibn Qutayba stresses the contrast between the ancient and the new style; Ibn al-Mu'tazz (died 908) set up a definite theory of artistic expression independently of the Greek precedents; and Qudāma Ibn Ja'far (died c. 931), whose approach to poetry was influenced by the Greeks, was responsible for the earliest theoretical work on artistic prose.

POPULAR LITERATURE

Neither epic nor fiction nor drama ever developed in the Arabic world as the achievements of individuals. They throve, nevertheless, as anonymous expressions of an artistic trend, to the extent that some of their products rank with the most important Arab additions to world literature.

Fiction was, indeed, used more than once (the *Maqāmāt* themselves arose from the framework of a novel) as a medium for the attainment of other aims, as, for instance, the allegory of two mystic novels by Ibn Sīnā (Avicenna) or the expression of a philosophy in the famous *Hayy Ibn Yaqẓān* of Ibn Tufayl (died 1185), which contains the story of an infant who, abandoned on a desert island, by the simple use of inborn reason attains the knowledge of the supreme truth. A journey in the nether world, the *Epistle of Forgiveness* by Abu'l 'Alā' al-Ma'arrī in which has been seen a possible source of the *Divine Comedy,* appears to be a novel, but actually the narrative serves only as a pretext for a discussion of literary topics. Such works cannot be considered in the category of Arabic fiction, nor should the animal tale, *Kalīla and Dimna,* one of the earliest and most famous items of the literary prose, be so regarded, not only because it actually is a translation from the Middle Persian (and ultimately from the Indian Panchatantra), but also because its purpose is chiefly didactic.

However, the *Thousand and One Nights* is fiction and, because of its composite character, presents a stupendous variety of subjects and styles which enable us to appraise the uncommon skill of the Arabs in description and psychological analysis, as well as their ability to develop and bring to an end the most entangled situations. Although some of these stories are of foreign origin, they have been reshaped in an Arabic mold, and there is among them a whole group of stories centering in Cairo that are Arabic in origin. The authors of some of the stories in the *Thousand and One Nights* were accomplished artists, and their names deserved to escape oblivion.

A quite different type of fiction should be called "epic," in spite of its being written in prose. It arose from an historical situation not very different from those which stimulated the birth of the epic in many other countries; an issue in which national or religious security was at stake awakened the recollection of the heroic deeds of the past, and these were recounted with legendary embellishments and with implicit reference to the present. The struggles of the Arabs against the Byzantine empire in the ninth century of the

Christian Era, and against the Crusaders in the twelfth, were responsible for the anonymous composition of sundry historical romances dealing with the early conquests of the Arabs and with the half-mythical feuds and expeditions of the pre-Islamic age. Some have entered the collection of the *Thousand and One Nights*. The warlike migration of the nomadic tribes Sulaym and Hilāl from Egypt to North Africa in the eleventh century has been idealized in an entire cycle of epic tales. The exploits of the Egyptian sultan Baybars I (reigned 1260 to 1277) against the Tatars and the Crusaders took the shape of a romance which bears his name. The literary history of these works is extremely involved and has not yet been entirely elucidated. From an early kernel, through the successive addition of episodes sometimes entirely strange to the subject, works of tremendous size and disconnected contents have arisen, in which the original unity is totally lost. Such are the romances of 'Antara, originally the story of the pre-Islamic poet and warrior, Sayyid Baṭṭāl, a legendary besieger of Constantinople, of Sayf Ibn Dhī Yezen, a legendary king of Yemen, and others. Although quite popular in style and not important for their artistic attainments, these works cannot be neglected in a general survey of Arabic literature. Their failure to arouse the interest of some gifted artist who would have raised them to the dignity of true poetry was obviously due to the suffocating yoke of the acknowledged literary rules.

Mention of the scanty remnants of Arabic drama may be brief. Although this variety of literature has perished almost entirely, a few of the preserved plays seem to date from the fourteenth or fifteenth centuries. They were performed as shadow plays rather than on the stage, and are probably of foreign origin; they took on, however, a distinctively Arabic appearance and thrived especially in Egypt. Although they never developed into a theatre of real artistic significance, they are interesting as examples of realistic description.

LITERARY ASPECTS OF NONLITERARY WORKS

History and geography, as well as works of and on religion, lie outside the limits of literature, considered from a purely artistic point of view; nevertheless, some artistic elements can be found in them. A clear-cut difference between an historical anecdote, as found in the *adab* books, and a continuous historical report is hard to draw. Arabic works on history are mostly clusters of reports on the events of the past rather than critical investigations. In the oldest of these —among them may be mentioned the works of Ibn Isḥāq (died 768) for the biography of Mohammed; al-Balādhurī (died 892) for the history of the early conquests and of the Arabian tribes; aṭ-Ṭabarī (died 923) for universal history to the end of the tenth century of the Christian Era—the author himself never appears, his only task being to collect and present the best possible sources. As a result, the reports are fragmentary, unsophisticated, and very often endowed with a powerful gift of graphic immediateness. Later historians, to the degree that they are not mere compilers of previous works and deal with happenings of their own time, often exhibit the same appealing quality. Only in later times, and chiefly under the impact of a court life encouraging flattery of the reigning sovereign and his dynasty and ministers, does history degenerate into void rhetoric. The only Arabic historian who attempted to explain history as the natural result of social environment, Ibn Khaldūn (died 1406), was a great philosopher but a very poor writer.

Most works on geography, a field intensively cultivated by the Arabs, are sheer descriptions and lack any artistic value. However, we find among them a few personal narratives of travelers who, without being professional writers, were able to report on their experiences in a spontaneous and attractive way. The Spaniard Ibn Jubayr, in the twelfth century, left an extremely personal account of his pilgrimage to Mecca and of the various countries through which he had traveled. In the fourteenth century, a North African, Ibn Baṭṭūṭa, "the Marco Polo of the Arabs," recounted his travels and adventures through the whole Moslem world, Constantinople, Russia, India, and China in an unpretentious yet colorful style which is full of charm.

The reports of the experiences of some outstanding mystics, such as al-Ghazzālī (died 1111) and Ibn al-'Arabī (died 1240), although written with the purpose of teaching or edifying, are often so vivid in their actualization of the unseen, so keen in their inquiry into the depths of the human soul, and so powerful in their rendering of religious emotion, that they must be reckoned as important literary achievements in spite of the nonliterary character and aim of the works where they are found.

As a whole, Arabic literature lacks artistic personalities of world significance. It is somewhat fragmentary, and more enjoyable in its details than in its whole compositions. Too much in it is the mere result of a subtle but ultimately void play with words and images, for even the best of the Arab writers were unable to escape the tyranny of a too sophisticated stylization. Nevertheless, when they succeeded in being natural and spontaneous, these writers proved capable of shaping artistic values of lasting significance. In the description of nature, in the analysis of feelings and emotions, and in the fresh narration of human events and experiences, they have often attained the highest reaches of aesthetic expression.

CONTEMPORARY LITERATURE

A decided decline in creative power is noticeable in Arabic literature as early as the twelfth century of the Christian Era. From the fourteenth to the end of the nineteenth century, although poetry and literary prose never ceased to be cultivated, there is hardly a name that deserves mention as that of a true poet or significant creative writer. During the last generation there occurred a renascence of Arabic creativity, and this has continued to grow in importance. Under the impact of Western culture and paralleling the rebirth of the political world of the Arabs, a new literature has arisen. Its first achievements followed closely, and perhaps too slavishly, the model offered by European, chiefly French, literature. Gradually, however, some among the most gifted Arab authors have succeeded in blending happily their own tradition and the new spirit aroused by the West. A new style has been born, and new literary modes, unknown to classical Arabic literature, have been introduced. Novels, short stories, plays (both for the stage and the screen), and essays are published at a continuously accelerated tempo. A characteristic aspect of this young literature is that it is produced on the same scale by both Moslem and Christian Arabs and that many important additions to it have come from Arabs residing in North and South America. Among the outstanding forerunners of this movement was Jurjis Zaydān (died 1914), a Syrian-born resident of Egypt. Among poets the first place belongs to the Egyptian Ahmed Shawqī (died 1932), followed by the Syrian Khalīl Jabrān (Kahlil Gibran) (1883-1931), whose *The Prophet* is familiar to many English-speaking readers. Among leading prose writers are the brothers Taymūr—Muhammad (died 1921), chiefly a playwright, and Mahmūd (born 1889), a novelist —and Ṭāhā Husayn (1889-   ), a learned and brilliant essayist.   G. L. D. V.

ARABIC MUSIC, the name broadly applied to the music of most Islamic peoples. Two areas of Arabic music exist, the smaller that of southern Spain, the larger a vast domain embracing North Africa, Arabia, Syria, Palestine, Turkey, Iraq, and Iran. The Andalusian music of Spain differs from that of the larger area chiefly in having a closer kinship with European music, but pure Arabic music is basically nonharmonic and employs a great many more tones within the octave than are found in the European scale.

Little is known of the antecedents of Arabic music before the dawn of the Christian Era, but it is apparent that by this time a considerable musical development had already taken place. There is evidence to indicate that as civilization advanced, the main stream of influence was, for the most part, from Iran to Arabia, and Iranian music in turn has much in common with Hindu music. At the opening of the Christian period, in any case, Mecca, Ukaz, and Medina were the musical centers of the Arabic world, and to these towns came poets and minstrels from all parts of the peninsula; musicians trained in this area found great favor in foreign courts, and singing girls were invariably found in the household of any Arab of social pretensions.

With the rise of Islam, music came under a technical religious ban, but this was never successfully enforced. Mohammed himself participated in introducing the cantillation of the Koran, employing the legal fiction that this kind of sacred song was merely a modulation of the voice which could be mastered without musical training. He also instituted the musical *adhān,* or call to prayer. The *nauh,* or elegy, was also valuable to Islam, as was the war song, and in addition to these officially sanctioned types, almost all the "forbidden" kinds of secular music apparently survived as well.

Since the seventh century, the diffusion of Arabic music has been linked with the spread of Islam. The first theoretical writing, largely based on classical Greek theory, began with the eighth century and culminated in the works of al-Fārābī (A.D. 870-950). Later writers of note were Safi a Dīn, of the thirteenth century, and Abd-el-Kadir, who wrote in the fifteenth. Theoretical writings were somewhat handicapped by the lack of a system of musical notation, but they nevertheless reached a point of refinement matched only by Greek writers in the same field.

Early Arabic musical instruments were the lute, or *mizhar;* the psaltery, or *mi'zafa;* the flute, or *qussāba;* the reed pipe, or *mizmār;* and the tambourine, or *duff.* During the early Islamic period the *tanbur,* a long-necked, two-stringed lute related to the Persian *tambur* and the Hindu *tambura,* was introduced. The lowest one-eighth of its lower string was divided by frets into five equal parts; the higher string was tuned to the second fret of the lower. The *tanbur* was also sometimes fretted so that one whole tone was divided into three equal distances. The harp, or *jank,* became popular, especially in Iraq, and the trumpet, or *būq,* also appeared. Among the instruments of percussion, in addition to the *duff,* were small metal castanets, *sunnuj sazhira,* with which dancers accompanied themselves, the stamping staff, or *qadib,* and a whole family of drums known generically as *tabl.*

Tunings of the modern Arabic stringed instruments vary with localities and with individual musicians. The most important modern Arabic stringed instruments are the four- or five-stringed lute, or *'ud;* the "spike fiddle," or *rabāb,* a one-stringed fiddle with a parchment-covered resonating head; and the dulcimer, or *santir.* Of these the *'ud* is the only one with frets. Since the beginning of the nineteenth century there has been a tendency to place these frets approximately a quarter tone apart, although according to the earlier theory of al-Fārābī, the octave should have but seventeen intervals.

In traditional music, Arabic musicians employ a system of melody patterns, or *maqāmāt,* which are linked with localities, with times of day, and with seasons of the year. These are comparable to the *rags* of Hindu music, although they are not so clearly formulated. Rhythmic patterns similar to the *tals* of Hindu music are also used and are expressed mainly on the drums and tambourines. Since the last quarter of the nineteenth century Arabic music has been considerably influenced by ideas from Europe, and this influence is most noticeable in the music of the marching bands, in which European instrumentation is employed, particularly in urban areas.

Traditionally, Arabic musicians are held in low esteem. The one brief exception occurred early in the Islamic era, from about 750 until well into the ninth century, when the courts were crowded with professional musicians, who were treated with great generosity and favor. In addition to famous virtuosi, both instrumental and vocal, there were two classes of lesser musicians at this time, the ordinary instrumentalists and the singing girls. These were either slaves or freemen and were attached to the virtuosi as accompanists. The singing girls were taught by the virtuosi, most frequently at their schools of music. Discussions on the theory of music by both the musical virtuosi and the philosophers were not uncommon, and during this Golden Age a phonetic musical notation began to be established. At the music school founded by Ziryab the curriculum of the pupils was divided into three parts. First, the rhythm, meter, and words of a song were taught to the accompaniment of a musical instrument. Then the melody in its simple state was mastered. Finally, the variations, quavers, and glosses so characteristic of Arabic music were introduced. The musical academies flourished briefly, then died out.

Musicological theory continued to be taught at the universities in connection with mathematics and the sciences, but musicianship itself went into a decline until the advent of the phonograph in the twentieth century. Since about 1910, a few musicians have succeeded in becoming famous throughout the Arabic world, largely as the result of this rise of the recording industry, and at the beginning of World War II, this industry was beginning to center around the person of Abd-el-Wahab, in Cairo, Egypt. Most of this recorded Arabic music is well tinctured with European themes, but the folk music of rural areas in Syria, Arabia, Iraq, and Egypt has presumably remained unchanged.   R. A. W.

ARABINOSE. *See* SUGAR CHEMISTRY.
ARABI PASHA. *See* ARABI, AHMAD.

ARABIS [æ'rəbɪs], a genus of about 100 species of low-growing plants in the mustard family, several of which, chiefly of European origin, are in cultivation in flower gardens. Most common is *A. albida,* wall rock-cress, also occasionally the more slender *A. alpina,* mountain rock-cress, both of which flower in early spring in the north. They are especially suited to rock gardens, where, after their flowers have passed, they mask their surroundings with soft green foliage. The numerous fragrant white flowers, ½ in. across, with four petals each, are borne in terminal clusters. A long-lasting double form occurs and there are pink flowers in this and related species. Plants are easily propagated by division, seed, or cuttings. The species mentioned are hardy, thriving even in poor soil.   J. C. Wis.

ARAB LEAGUE, a regional bloc of eight Arab states: Egypt, Jordan, Syria, Lebanon, Iraq, Saudi Arabia, Yemen, and Libya, organized in 1945 and representing a population of about 34,200,000 in an area of 2,172,000 sq. mi.

Origins. The Arab awakening of the 19th century and the Arab revolt against Turkey in World War I, together with the establishment of independence of the member states in the years following World War I, formed part of the movement to recreate and reintegrate the Arab community, with its common past, common religion, common language,

which threatens peace between member states or any member state and a country outside the League. The Council also considers proposals of the committees.

Activities. Since its organization in 1945 the League has become the spokesman for Arab and Moslem interests. It has supported independence movements in Syria, Lebanon, Algeria, Tunis, Morocco, and Libya, and, since September 1951, it has supported Egypt's efforts to oust the British forces from the Suez Canal zone. It has also steadily opposed the Israeli movement in Palestine, going to war,

Arabs throng a Moorish desert market on a road outside Marrakech, western Morocco.

and in part, its common racial stock, which culminated in the formation of the Arab League in 1945. In the preceding year, representatives of Egypt, Iraq, Syria, Lebanon, Jordan, Saudi Arabia, and Yemen, which later became the charter members of the League, met at Alexandria and issued a protocol for the establishment of the league. On Mar. 22, 1945, a covenant, establishing the League and based on the protocol, was signed by the seven charter members. (Libya joined the League in March 1953.)

Purposes. The purposes of the League are "to strengthen the ties between the participant states, to co-ordinate their political programs in such a way as to effect real collaboration between them, to preserve their independence and sovereignty, and to consider in general the affairs and interests of the Arab countries." Another purpose of the League is the collaboration of the member states in economic and financial matters, in communications, and in cultural affairs, and in matters relating to nationality, public health, and social and other questions. The original covenant also provided for co-operation between the Arab League and the United Nations, then being formed.

Organization. The Arab League consists of a Council on which each state has one vote; a number of special committees; and a permanent secretariat, headed by a secretary general, at Cairo. The Council normally meets twice a year and, among other things, acts as mediator in any dispute

unsuccessfully, in 1948-1949, to prevent the partition of Palestine. Defeated militarily, it has continued its economic blockade of Israel, often to the detriment of its own members. The League has aided Jordan against Israeli attacks, voting special funds for Jordan's defense. Under the League's auspices, an Arab collective security pact went into effect in August 1952, and in 1953 the members authorized the formation of an Arab army of 150,000.

Although the problems of Arab refugees, of Jerusalem, and of Israel consume much of their time, the League members have, since 1949, greatly increased their efforts toward effecting social and economic reforms in the Arab states. In May 1953 an Arab economic conference discussed common Arab problems in currency, finance, agriculture, industry, and trade. H. C. K.

ARABS, a term used to describe several groups of people. The term is applied loosely to numerous inhabitants of North Africa and of the Near and Middle East, i.e., to all those who have a racial, linguistic, or religious kinship to the inhabitants of the Arabian Peninsula. More frequently and more accurately, the term is applied to the people of the Arabian Peninsula alone. The Arabs of the interior desert and those of the mountains of Yemen and Hadhramaut are considered the purest types; the rest show Turkish, Negroid, Hamitic, and Jewish features and characteristics.

ORIGINS AND EARLY HISTORY

Origins. The question of the original home and origin of the Arabs has brought forth two answers, seemingly contradictory, but also reconcilable. East Africa has been suggested as the earliest home of a Semitic-Hamitic community by one group, and southwest Arabia as the original Semitic and Arabic home by another. It is possible that the Semitic group migrated from East Africa to South Arabia at an early date, and that after that date various Semitic groups, including the Arabs, migrated from Arabia during the ancient and medieval periods. However, Arabists prefer south-

Conical huts made of wheat straw serve as dwellings for these Berbers in Morocco.

west Arabia as the earliest home of the Arabs and suggest that the Arabs and other Semitic groups migrated from that original home, during the ancient and medieval eras, into East Africa and the Fertile Crescent. This is the generally accepted explanation. Arab traditions attempt to establish genealogies beginning with Shem and Ishmael. Other Semitic or semi-Semitic groups are the well-known Babylonians, Assyrians, Chaldaeans, Amorites, Phoenicians, Hebrews, and Aramaeans.

Early History. The earliest historical references to the Arabs are found in non-Arabic sources. Inscriptions of the Babylonian rulers Naram-Sin (c. 2450 B.C.) and Gudea (c. 2350 B.C.) contain the first records of Arabia and the Arabs. Both refer to Magan (in modern Transjordan) as a source for stone and wood for their temples. Egyptians throughout the second millenium sought copper and turquoise from Mt. Sinai and frankincense, myrrh, and aromatic woods from South Arabia. During the same period portraits of Arabian Bedouins appear in Egyptian reliefs.

Arabic inscriptions date back to about 700 B.C., and they number about 3,000. They indicate the commercial nature of the earliest Arabian kingdoms of southwest Arabia. Although the chronology is vague, the Minaean Kingdom existed from c. 1200 to 650 B.C., and it was eventually included in the more important Sabaean Kingdom (c. 950-115 B.C.). The records of the neighboring states similarly show the peaceful or at least unsuccessful military nature of these Arabian states. Both Assyrian and Chaldaean tribute lists

record Arab contributions of gold, frankincense, myrrh, precious stones and woods, camels, and donkeys. To the ancient Persians, the Arabs apparently never fell victims. Old Testament references to the Arabs generally are descriptive of their commercial and pastoral life, and are not indicative of belligerent relations. The third of the early Arabian kingdoms, the Himyarite Kingdom, maintained itself to c. A.D. 525, but during its existence both Greeks and Romans successfully plundered the Arab caravans on land and broke the Arab commercial monopoly on the Red Sea. This weakening of Arab prosperity, and the Byzantine and Persian attacks, caused tribal unrest and disunity in the Himyarite Kingdom. The Arabs, for a century before Mohammed, were in an anarchical state. Mohammed (570-632) brought unity and leadership to the Arabs along the Red Sea, and after his death the Arabs expanded beyond the peninsula, eventually extending their authority westward to Spain and the Atlantic and eastward to India and the Indus.

SOCIAL LIFE

Physique and Character. The Arabs are usually well proportioned, strong, muscular, and slender; they are brown to almost black in color. The Arab face has distinctive lines; it is oval and somewhat long, with an aquiline nose. The eyes, a striking feature, are dark and deep-set, under bushy and heavy eyebrows. Men usually have their heads shaven but let their beards and mustaches grow.

Intellectually, the Arabs are of high ability, but that ability has not been tested or developed by an adequate educational system. Similarly, the Arabian poetic sense is not appreciated sufficiently by Westerners because of linguistic difficulties. Socially, the Arab presents some curious contradictions according to Western standards. As a host, the Arab is courteous and hospitable, but as an enemy he may be cruel and vengeful, and the well-treated guest of one day may find himself plundered the next day by his recent host. And although the Arab has deep regard for his children, his camel and horse may enjoy preference in a period of crisis.

Food and Drink. The Arab is simple, almost ascetic, in

his food habits. Well-cooked rice and raisins are served with various meat dishes like mutton, lamb, locusts, chicken, and wild fowl. Vegetable soups and stews are also favorite dishes. All types of fruits and nuts are eaten. Milk is provided by the camel, sheep, and goat. Wine and alcohol are very seldom drunk. However, coffee is the national drink and the symbol of welcome. Two or three cups of coffee are usually drunk at dinner, and on formal occasions coffee is followed by a cup of sweetened or minted green or black tea. Coffeehouses and coffeerooms are common throughout Arab lands. The food is served in dishes on great mats or oilcloth, placed on the floor, and eaten with spoons or the right hand. The diners sit cross-legged, so that the feet are hidden from view. Again on formal occasions, a servant offers warm water, towel, and soap to the dining guests, and a censer with burning incense is passed around.

Clothing. Arab clothing varies with economic status and geographical location. For men, the green or white turban, or a simple handkerchief kept on by a band, forms the headdress. An outer gown, yellow, brown, or black, reaching from shoulders to ankles and held around the waist by a wide sash, is worn over a shorter shirt or loose drawers. Sandals usually cover the feet. Arab women appear in similar dress, without the turban, but with some form of veil and generally with considerable gold and silver jewelry.

Dwellings. The village Arabs usually live in sun-dried brick houses, whitewashed or ochre-tinted, at times of two or three stories and usually with a flat roof. The poorest Arabs are satisfied with wattle huts, roofed with palm leaves. The Bedouin Arabs of the desert live in tents, "the houses of hair" of the camel and goat.

Tribal Customs. The Bedouins call themselves "people of the tent," but the Bedouin tent is more than a mere dwelling place; it is also a social and political unit. It is the home of a single family, and several families form a clan and several related clans form the tribe. From family to tribe, blood-relationship is the bond of union, as is vaguely indicated by the "ibn" ("son of") and "banu" ("children of"), so common in Arabian nomenclature. At the head of the tribe stands the sheik, the senior member in wisdom and general personal qualifications, if not always in age. His position rests upon the good will and respect of his followers, and all important decisions are subject to the tribal council, composed of the heads of the tribal families or "tents." It is the tribe which holds the communal rights to water and pasturages. Each member of the tribe is bound to protect these rights of the tribe and uphold the tribal honor. Any injury committed against a member of the tribe by someone outside the tribe must be avenged, and therefore blood feuds are almost interminable; at times, peace is established through the payment of a blood fine, a *diya*.

The intertribal conflicts over pasture and water rights and almost incessant blood-feuds, both connected with family pride, have always been the chief obstacles to Arab unity and have been a serious challenge to the modernization program of King Ibn Saud and his son and successor, King Saud. The same factors may account for the curious military history of the Arabs. They make excellent individual fighters but poor leaders; they are very skillful and courageous in sporadic raids and attacks, but show less ability in military strategy and organized fighting.

Status of Women and Family Customs. The status of women among the Arabs is gradually improving. All women still wear some form of veil. Polygamy is allowed by Koranic tradition, as long as the husband can provide for all of his wives equally well and as long as he cherishes

all equally. The Arab has deep regard for his children, and a special day is set aside for an amusement excursion and holiday for the father and his children. Most holidays are religious holidays; a very gay three-day festival follows the

ROBERT Y. RICHIE FOR ARABIAN AMERICAN OIL COMPANY

Arab herdsmen and their black sheep on a street in Hofuf, capital of Hasa Province, Saudi Arabia

period of abstinence in the month of Ramadan. Among recreations are football, basketball, horse racing, and hunting.

ECONOMIC LIFE

Economically, the Arabs must be divided into two distinct groups, those who live in the coastal areas of the Arabian Peninsula, in which farming can be done, and those who are limited to the vast interior desert, in which little agriculture can be carried out, except in the oases.

Coastal Arabs. The Arabs who live along the seacoast, that is, in Hejaz, Asir, Yemen, Hadhramaut, and Oman, are generally confined to a rather narrow coastal strip between the sea and the hills that border the desert plateau. These hills keep the rain within the coastal areas and so permit farming, which is also promoted by the rich alluvial soil brought in by the desert wadies (streams). The farming Arabs are usually settled in small villages in the foothills at the edge of the vast plateau. In these farming areas of the plains and in the desert oases several crops are found. Dates are grown almost everywhere, and as many as twenty varieties have been discovered; grain sorghums, too, are raised, some in the desert having a scrubby growth of only three feet, others, however, reaching seventeen feet. Wheat and rice are interchangeably staple products and foods; wheat was originally a main food item, but it was gradually replaced by rice; then, during World War II, wheat again surpassed rice in production and popularity. The farmers of Yemen and Asir raise excellent coffees, and the farmers everywhere have plots for potatoes, tomatoes, eggplant, okra, radishes, onions, beans, and squash. Fruit orchards yield bananas, apricots, peaches, figs, pomegranates, oranges, limes, pears, and apples. Both vegetables and fruits are raised for domestic and local use. Generally, however, the farmer can export only dates and coffee. Most of the agricultural fields must be watered from irrigation ditches and wells. Some dams in use today to store the water were constructed in the eighth century. In most areas, the water table is only eight to twelve feet below the surface, so the Arabs can easily dig wells.

BARBARY COAST ARABS ON A SUNNY STREET IN ALGIERS

Bedouin Arabs of the Interior. In the vast interior plateau, the Bedouin Arabs live much as their ancestors lived since their trek into the desert. The almost limitless sands, the intense heat, the poor soil, and the lack of water all have helped to isolate the Bedouins from the rest of the world and to make them the purest of all of the Arabs and Semites. Hence, they are subject to tenacious, age-old traditions and customs. In fact, the desert Bedouins look with considerable contempt upon the coastal Arabs and other civilized, but to them less fortunate, people.

The Bedouins are nomads, leading their families and herds from one oasis to another and often fighting other Bedouins for pasturage and water. Among these cultivable spots of the desert they maintain a regular schedule. For travel, for food, or for profit, the Bedouins prize the camel most of all. It, too, furnishes them the hair for clothes and for tents. They also raise sheep, goats, donkeys, and horses, but the horses are used only for riding and racing, and never for heavy work. Sheep and goats furnish food and materials for clothing, carpets, and rugs; goat's hair, too, is used for tents. The Bedouins seldom raise cattle. Of necessity, the Bedouins must raise some foodstuffs, but generally they look upon farming, mining, and manufacturing as undignified. *See also* ASIATIC TRIBES; ISLAM; SAUDI ARABIA.

H. C. K.

ARACAJÚ [ɑrɑ'kɑzhu'], a port city in central Brazil, capital of the state of Sergipe, situated about 920 mi. northeast of Rio de Janeiro, and about 6 mi. from the coast, at the mouth of the Continguiba River. It is the chief port and leading commercial city of the state. The city's tropical beauty and colonial character make it interesting. The Sergipe Historical and Geographical Institute possesses a museum and a fine library. Extensive limestone quarries are found near by. The main products of the district are sugar and cotton, which are exported. The city, founded in 1855, has tanneries, cotton mills, and coconut and sugar factories. Pop. 1950, 68,686.

S. G. I.

ARACHNE [əræ'kni], in Greek mythology, a maiden of Lydia who excelled in weaving and challenged Athena to compete with her. Arachne filled her web with the love affairs of the gods, and Athena in anger destroyed the web. Arachne hanged herself and was transformed by the goddess into a spider.

G. E. D.

ARACHNIDA [əræ'knɪdə], a class of air-breathing terrestrial arthropods, related to the crustaceans and insects, but distinct from both. Representatives of this class are among the oldest land animals on the earth, dating back to the Silurian period. Many species of spiders fossilized in Baltic amber closely resemble living forms. The Arachnida usually have the head and thorax fused together into one part, the cephalothorax. The abdomen may be soft and undivided, as in the spiders and mites, or covered with chitinous shields and segmented, as in the scorpions. The cephalothorax bears six pairs of appendages: four pairs of legs; a pair of pedipalpi, which are used as feelers or grasping organs in most arachnids; and a pair of chelicerae, which are used as jaws, since the Arachnida have no true jaws. There are no antennae. The eyes are always simple. In some orders, the abdomen is extended into a long tail, as in the scorpions and whip scorpions. The reproductive organs open at the front end of the abdomen, in which respect the Arachnida resemble the crustacea and differ from the insects. The young are usually hatched from eggs, but are born alive in the scorpions.

The extant Arachnida are grouped in nine orders: Araneae (spiders), Acarina (mites and ticks), Scorpionida (scorpions), Phalangida or Opiliones (daddy longlegs), Chelonethida (false scorpions), Solpugida (sun spiders), Pedipalpida (whip scorpions), Ricinulei (ricinuleids), and Microthelyphonida (microwhip scorpions). Other fossil orders are known. The order most numerous in species is the spiders, followed in descending order by the mites, daddy longlegs, false scorpions, and scorpions. The others are only occasionally encountered.

All of the Arachnida, with the exception of a few mites, are carnivorous, usually living on insects and other small

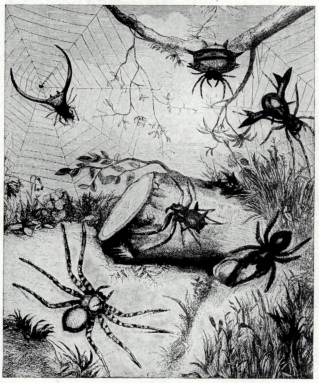

ARACHNIDA

(Upper left) Spiny Crab Spider, Gasteracantha arcuata. *(Lower left) Huntsman Spider,* Selenops celer. *(Center) Crab Spider,* Epicadus heterogaster. *(Top center) Spiny Crab Spider,* Gasteracantha cancriformis. *(Upper right) Microthena. (Lower right) One of the Trapdoor Spiders,* Cteniza nidulans.

animals, most of which are captured alive. Only fluids from the victims are sucked into the stomach, no solid parts being swallowed. Most of the Arachnida have poison glands, though few are harmful to man. The black widow spider and its close relatives are the most poisonous of the spiders; the bite is very painful in its effects, and an occasional death is reported. Some of the larger tropical tarantulas are considered dangerous, but those of the southern and western United States have a bite that is seldom more consequential than the sting of a wasp. The scorpions, of which only a few are highly poisonous, are capable of inflicting a painful sting by means of a sharp spine on the end of the tail. The vinegarroon, a large whip scorpion of the southwestern United States, is nonpoisonous, contrary to popular belief. Some ticks carry disease organisms.

The Arachnida are common wherever insects occur. They extend north of 80° N. lat.; they live as far up as any life on high mountains; and spiders have been collected from air-

planes many thousands of feet up in the air, where they float in the wind attached to pieces of gossamer. The warmer areas of the earth abound in species and individuals.

The study of arachnids is technically known as arachnology, but for practical reasons it is usually considered as a branch of entomology. The large collections in the United States are located at the universities of Harvard, Cornell, Yale, and Utah and at the American Museum of Natural History and the United States National Museum. The largest foreign collections are located in London, Paris, and Berlin. For scientific study, arachnids are best preserved in 85-95 per cent grain alcohol, into which the specimens are dropped alive. No further care or preparation is necessary for most of them, except to see that the alcohol which kills the arachnids amounts to several times the volume of the specimens. *See also* GOSSAMER; MITES; SPIDER; TICKS. W. I.

ARAD [ɑ′rɑd], the capital of the Romanian district of the same name, situated on the Mureşul River, in western Romania, at 46° 11′ N. lat. and 21° 19′ E. long., at the edge of the Hungarian lowland, about 140 mi. southeast of Budapest and about 115 mi. southwest of Cluj. The possession of Arad has been contested several times. In 1551 it was conquered by the Turks, in 1685 by the Austrians, and in 1849 by the Hungarians. In 1920 it came into the possession of Romania. Since then, Arad has developed into a center of commercial and industrial activity. Its favorable location at the junction of the Hungarian lowland and the Transylvanian highlands provides the city with better facilities and raw materials for manufacturing than other cities of the Hungarian lowland to the west. As a cultural center, it is the seat of a Greek Orthodox bishopric, and it has a theological seminary, several normal schools, and libraries. Included among its many industries are the manufacture of railroad cars, machines, automobiles, furniture, leather goods, and flour mills. Its population includes many Magyars. Pop. (est. 1949), 82,800. S. A.

ARAFURA SEA [ɑ′rɑfu′rɑ], an extension of the Indian Ocean north of Australia and south of New Guinea. On the east, the Arafura Sea meets the Torres Strait; on the west, it merges with the Timor Sea. There are several islands in this area: the Aroe Islands, Timor Laoet, Frederik Hendrik, Melville, and Bathurst. The sea is very shallow and is notoriously dangerous for shipping, but it is regularly crossed from Sydney and Brisbane to Singapore and Colombo. The region in which the Arafura Sea is located is well known for its pearl and pearl-shell fisheries. J. E. F.

ARAGO, DOMINIQUE FRANÇOIS JEAN [a′ra′go′] (1786-1853), French physicist, was born Feb. 26, 1786, at Estagel, Perpignan, eastern Pyrenees. After being educated at the municipal school of Perpignan and at the École Polytechnique, he became secretary of the Paris Observatory. Through the influence of Pierre Simon de Laplace, he was commissioned, with J. B. Biot, to complete the geodetic measurements then being supported by the French government. Arago's work in the Balearic Islands on this assignment coincided with the French invasion of Spain, and in the resulting turbulence Arago was captured and imprisoned for some months. In 1809 Arago became professor of analytical geometry at the École Polytechnique and was made an astronomer at the Royal Observatory. In 1830 he became director of the observatory and perpetual secretary of the Academy of Sciences. In the same year he entered the Chamber of Deputies from the district of Seine-Inférieure.

UNIVERSITY OF ZARAGOZA, AT ZARAGOZA, CAPITAL CITY OF ARAGON

After the revolution of 1848, he joined the Provisional Government as minister of war and marine.

Arago's scientific work was mainly in the fields of magnetism and optics. He discovered the phenomenon of eddy currents induced in a conducting medium by the motion of a near-by magnet. He also proved the connection of the aurora borealis with variations in the strength of the earth's magnetic field. With Augustin Jean Fresnel and Friedrich Heinrich Alexander von Humboldt, Arago espoused the wave theory of light in the early years of the nineteenth century. He made many experiments on the polarization of light, and discovered the ability possessed by quartz to rotate the plane of polarization of light. He died in Paris, Oct. 2, 1853.   L. N. R.

ARAGON, LOUIS [a'ra'gɔ̃'] (1897-   ), French poet, novelist, and journalist, was born in Paris on Oct. 3, 1897. During his early career as a Dadaist and Surrealist poet he produced such volumes as *Feu de joie* (1920) ("Fireworks"), *Anicet* (1921), *Le Paysan de Paris* (1926) ("The Parisian Peasant"), and *Traité du style* (1928) ("Treatise on Style"), which were revolutionary in content and method. In 1930 he became a Communist and renounced pure literature in favor of partisan journalism. His incendiary poem, *Front rouge* (1931) (*The Red Front*, 1933), brought him a suspended prison sentence and caused his final break with his former Surrealist allies.

During World War II Aragon was France's leading Resistance poet, and at that time he published *Le Crève-Coeur* (1941) ("Heartbreak"), *Les Yeux d'Elsa* (1942) ("Elsa's Eyes"), and *Le Musée Grévin* (1943) ("The Grévin Museum"), which reflect his return to the classic themes of love and patriotism. As a novelist he is best known for *Les Beaux Quartiers* (1936) (*Residential Quarter,* 1938) and for *Aurélien* (1944), a love story containing a detailed picture of contemporary society, published in translation with the original title in 1946.   R. J. N.

ARAGON [æ'rəgɒn; ɑ'rɑgo'n], a former kingdom in northeastern Spain, and, until 1833, one of the old Spanish administrative units. The territory is divided into the modern provinces of Zaragoza, with an area of 6,611 sq. mi.; Huesca, 5,849 sq. mi.; and Teruel, 5,721 sq. mi. It is bounded on the north by France, on the east by Catalonia and Valencia, on the south by New Castile, and on the west by New Castile and Navarra. Geologically, Aragon is a continuation of Navarra. It is bordered by the Pyrenees, but most of it lies in the dry basin of the Ebro River. The region has rich deposits of gypsum, slate, marble, and clay, and salt areas so vast that they preclude extensive cultivation of the land. The only considerable oases in this desolate area lie along the banks of the Ebro River and in the alluvial plain above and below the city of Zaragoza (Saragossa). The peasants cultivate olives and grapes and make wine.

The northern parts of Aragon ascend toward the central crest of the Pyrenees, with the magnificent peaks of Maladetta rising to 11,169 ft., and Mount Perdido to 10,998 ft. The streams rising in the mountains become important rivers as they flow through the adjoining provinces and have been harnessed for hydroelectric power. The rain is very scanty, because the cold northwestern wind, *cierzo,* and the hot southeastern wind, *bochorno,* lose all moisture as they traverse the mountains; thus the plain has a continental climate, with hot summers and cold winters. Conservation of the water supply and production of electrical energy from the Pyrenean rivers have helped to better the standard of living in some districts. In general, nine tenths of the population live along the banks of the Ebro and its tributaries.

The Aragonese have preserved their national culture to a considerable degree. Their national dance, the *jota,* is performed at village festivals, and the national costume, consisting of knee breeches supported by a sash, white stockings, and red head-cloth covered by a broad brimmed hat, is seen in all country districts. The estimated populations of the Aragon provinces in 1947 were: Zaragoza, 637,099; Huesca, 224,580; and Teruel, 219,518.

History. In common with the rest of Spain, Aragon has a long history of conflict and invasion. The chief city, Zaragoza (Saragossa), capital of the ancient kingdom of Aragon and of the province that bears its name, has a famed history. It was founded by the Roman Emperor Augustus, and in A.D. 476 was captured by the Goths. In the early eighth century it fell into the hands of invading Moors and was given as a prize to the Berbers. In 777 the Arabian viceroy of Barcelona enlisted the help of Charlemagne in trying to wrest the province from the caliph of Córdoba, but without success. In the ninth century Aragon's Gothic counts threw off Carolingian control and joined Navarra. Aragon became completely independent in 1035 under Ramiro I and during the next hundred years gradually extended its territory at the expense of the Moors, with the help of recruits from the French principalities to the north. In 1076 Navarra was annexed, and in 1137 Aragon and Catalonia were united through the marriage of their sovereigns. James I (1213-1276) conquered the Balearic Islands, beginning the creation of an Aragonese Mediterranean empire. By 1340 Sardinia, Sicily, and Naples had been added. In 1469 Ferdinand II of Aragon married Isabella of Castile, and ten years later the two kingdoms were united.   J. S. R.

ARAGONITE [əræ'gənait; æ'rəgənait], a mineral named for the province of Aragon, in Spain. The composition of aragonite is calcium carbonate, $CaCO_3$, the same as the much commoner mineral calcite. It differs from calcite in its orthorhombic crystallization; calcite is rhombohedral and possesses a distinctive cleavage. Crystals of aragonite may be so intergrown as to form a pseudohexagonal aggregate. This mineral is relatively unstable and tends in time to alter to calcite. Aragonite occurs in nature as an organic secretion in the interior of shells (mother of pearl), in hot spring deposits, and as a saline precipitate, associated with anhydrite or gypsum.   K. K. L.

ARAKI, SADAO [a'ra'ki'] (1877-   ), Japanese soldier, was born near Tokyo, May 26, 1877, the son of a poor agrarian family. From his student days he was brilliant, ascetic, and resembled the traditional samurai. As president of the Military Staff College, Araki became the idol of the young officers' clique. He was minister of war, 1931-1933, and education minister, 1938-1939. Araki was a personifica-

tion of militarism and is credited with popularizing Japan's mission as an extension of *Kodo* (the Imperial Way). He was among those who directed the invasion of Manchuria and China and among the first to demand Japan's withdrawal from the League of Nations. In 1945 he was indicted as a war criminal, and on Nov. 12, 1948, was given a life sentence for his participation in the exploitation of Manchuria.   A. W. Bu.

ARAKS [ara's], variously called the Araxes (especially in ancient times), Aras, Ara, and, by the Armenians, Yerash, a stream in the Transcaucasus Mountains which forms part of the boundary between the U.S.S.R. and Turkey and between the U.S.S.R. and Iran. Rising on the northwest slopes of the Bingoel Dagh south of Erzurum in eastern Turkey, the Araks flows through the wild, dry, Armenian mountains and plateau in an easterly direction. In its lower course it flows into the flat Kura Valley, a hot, semiarid plain. It formerly joined the lower Kura River, but in 1896-1897 it opened an additional course directly to the Caspian Sea southwest of the Kura mouth, and it now empties through both channels. Approximately 590 mi. long, its channel through the mountains is relatively narrow, but it broadens on the Kura plain. Draining about 34,200 sq. mi., it receives as left-bank tributaries the Zanga (draining Lake Gokcha, or Sevan), Arpa, and Bergushet, and as right-bank tributaries the Ak and Kara Su. The Araks is the principal stream of Armenia, although its mountain course and shallow depth prevent navigation. In the spring it is heavily swollen by meltage from mountain snows and runs swiftly. The Armenian capital of Yerevan (or Erivan) is situated on the Zanga tributary.   C. C. H.

ARALAC. *See* SYNTHETIC FIBERS.

ARALIA [əre'liə], a genus of perennial herbs, shrubs, or small trees of the ginseng family, scattered throughout the world, some in the United States, many in the Pacific islands. They are often spiny with much divided foliage and big clusters of creamy flowers. Some have medicinal value and many are cultivated as ornamentals. Hercules club, *A. spinosa,* the spikenard, *A. racemosa,* and wild sarsaparilla, *A. nudicaulis,* are native to the United States. *See also* ANGELICA TREE.   J. C. Wis.

ARAL SEA [ara'l; æ'rəl], a lake of 24,500 sq. mi. in the south-central part of the Kazkh Soviet Socialist Republic of the Soviet Union. It is situated between the Kirghiz Steppe and Soviet Turkestan at 45° N. lat and 60° E. long. It is the second largest salt-water lake in the world, ranking after the Caspian Sea, which lies 210 mi. to the west. It measures 165 mi. from north to south and 150 mi. from east to west; its deepest part, 220 ft., is in the west near the 300-ft. escarpment of the Ust Urt plateau. On the south and east the Aral Sea is bordered by sand wastes and the deltas of the only entering rivers, the Syr Darya (Jaxartes River), in the northeast, and the Amu Darya (Oxus River), in the south. Along the eastern shore are many islands and marshes, owing to the lake's shallowness. The surface is 160 ft. above sea level and 245 ft. above the Caspian Sea, into which it flowed in glacial times. It now has no outlet. The climate of the Aral depression is cold in winter and freezes the northern part of the lake, but is very hot in summer. The annual rainfall is only 4 to 8 in.; hence the basin is very arid. Although navigation of the Aral Sea is difficult, owing to severe local storms with strong northeast winds, some fishing is carried on. As a result of its low salinity, the lake contains many fresh-water fish. Kazalinsk, near the mouth of the Syr Darya, is the nearest population center, with Chimbai and Kungrad in the Amu delta.   J. E. V.

ARAMAIC [ærəme′ɪk], a term broadly designating a number of closely related Northwest Semitic dialects. Aramaic did not spread by force of arms, for the native states of Syria never attained wide dominion; nor was it the medium of any great ancient literature. The first steps of its extraordinarily widespread dissemination occurred during the second millennium B.C., through the medium of trade. By the early part of the first millennium B.C. Aramaic had become the international and diplomatic language of the Near and Middle East, gradually ousting Assyro-Babylonian, Phoenician, Hebrew, and the other Semitic languages of the Fertile Crescent. It attained its maximum diplomatic prestige in the Achaemenian Empire of Persia, wherein it was used as the interprovincial language from India to Egypt between the sixth and fourth centuries B.C. It became a language of post-Biblical Judaism, on a par with Hebrew. Parts of the Old Testament and much of rabbinical literature are in Aramaic, and when Christianity arose, it was in an Aramaic milieu. Jesus preached in Aramaic. The churches of Asia, such as the Nestorian, Chaldean, and Maronite, produced literature and liturgies in Syriac, as most Christian Aramaic is called. Paganism, though on the decline, also survived in an Aramaic environment; thus the Mandaeans of Babylonia have preserved until the present time their holy books in their own particular Aramaic script and dialect.

The Islamic Conquest in the seventh century of the Christian Era doomed Aramaic. Since then Arabic has more and more displaced the Syro-Aramaic dialects, which are now spoken by only a few thousand persons, mostly Christians, in Kurdistan and Syria.

Although the Syro-Aramaic literature is enormous and of great historical importance, it does not include any original world classics. It was, however, the translation into Aramaic of Greek philosophy, especially that of Aristotle, and its subsequent rendering into Arabic, that made possible the brilliant intellectual age of medieval Islam.

Aramaic was written, for the most part, in the consonantal alphabet used in Hebrew. However, one Aramaic text on clay, from Babylonia, dating from about the second century B.C., is written in syllabic cuneiform script, which provides vowels as well as consonants.

In most Aramaic dialects a number of sound shifts have taken place. Unaccented short vowels in open syllables are dropped. Semitic unvoiced *th* (as in English "thing") has become *t*; voiced *th* (as in "this") has become *d*; and two of the Semitic emphatic consonants have undergone drastic change.

The noun has two genders, masculine and feminine; three states, absolute (standing alone), construct (before a genitive), and emphatic (with suffixed article); and, as a rule, two numbers, singular and plural. The dual survives vestigially. The suffix of the feminine absolute plural, *-ān,* is peculiar to Aramaic.

The definite article in Aramaic is suffixed *-ā.* The suffix making nouns masculine plural emphatic (i.e., with the article) is *-ayyā* in some dialects and *-ē* in others; thus it is *-ayyā* in Official Aramaic, the diplomatic language of the Achaemenian Empire, which includes the Aramaic of the Old Testament, whereas it is *-ē* in Mesopotamian dialects

such as the Syriac of the Christians and the Talmudic speech of the Jews.

The word for "son" is *bar* in Aramaic, while nearly all of the other Semitic languages have *-n* instead of *-r* as the last consonant; similarly the numeral "two" is *trēn,* whereas nearly all of the other Semitic languages again have *-n-* for the *-r-.* However, South Arabic dialects coincide with Aramaic respecting the *r* of these two words.

Most verbs are limited in their inflection to six conjugations, for example, the normal triconsonantal root *qtl* "to kill." The conjugations for this verb are: (1) the simple active *qtal,* (2) the simple reflexive *itqtel,* (3) the intensive active *qattel,* (4) the intensive reflexive *itqattal,* (5) the causative *aqtel,* and (6) the causative reflexive *ittaqtal.* Though the causative prefix is most often *a-, ha-* occurs dialectally, and many special verbs regularly take *sha-.* The reflexive of *shaqtel* causatives is *ishtaqtal.*

The normal prefix, third person masculine, with verbal forms of the imperfect tense, is *y-* as in the other Semitic languages; but in Syriac it is *n-.* However, such phenomena are not rigid criteria of dialect. In Jewish Babylonian Aramaic not only *y-* and *n-,* but also *l-* are found. An interesting example of interdialectal mixture is the incantation literature written on bowls in Babylonia during the first six centuries of the Christian Era. As the personal names, divine and demonic invocations, scripts, and general contents show, Jewish, Aramaic, Christian Syriac, and pagan Mandaean existed side by side; and in each of the three dialects are found forms derived from the other two.

Aramaic is one of the important languages in world history, and its influence has been great, as striking evidence of which is the use of hundreds of Aramaic words as ideograms in Pehlevi or Middle Persian.   C. H. Go.

ARANDA, PEDRO PABLO ABARCA DE BOLEO, COUNT OF [ara′nda] (1718-1799), Spanish statesman, was born Dec. 18, 1718 (according to some versions, Aug. 1, 1719), near Huesca, of a noble family. He was educated at Bologna and Parma, and the early part of his life was spent in military service, in which he made a distinguished record, and in travel. He commenced his political career as ambassador to Portugal in 1755 and in 1760 was appointed ambassador to Poland. He was captain general of Valencia when summoned by King Charles III to assist in the suppression of an uprising in Madrid in 1766. After restoring order he was appointed president of the council of Castile and in this capacity instituted many reforms. Following the lead of Pombal in Portugal and Choiseul in France, he expelled the Jesuits from Spain in 1767. He also curbed the Inquisition, and improved agricultural, economic, and social conditions. Aranda had considerable influence with the king, and though a remarkably capable administrator he was a man of inflexible purpose, using harsh and ruthless methods. It was his genuine desire to restore the political and economic strength of Spain, but his edicts aroused discontent both among the poor, who suffered under his severity, and the rich, who had been deprived of their spoils. In addition, his arrogance as a member of the nobility made him many political enemies. When he was blamed for Spain's humiliation in the Falkland Islands incident of 1773, he found it politically expedient to resign and was appointed ambassador to France. He remained in Paris until 1787, during which time he helped negotiate the Paris Treaty of 1783 and played an important role in the negotiations regarding the American Revolution. In 1792 he became president of the council again for a short time and then held other political posts, but in 1794 he was exiled to Jaen because of his open sympathy with the French Revolution. He died at Epila, Aragon, in 1799. C. W. D.

ARANEAE. *See* ARACHNIDA.

ARANHA, OSWALDO [əræ′nyə] (1894-   ), Brazilian politician and diplomat, was born in Alegrete, state of Rio Grande do Sul, Feb. 15, 1894. He was educated in the Military School of Rio de Janeiro, 1908 to 1911, and the Law School of Paris, 1912-1914, then did graduate work in the University of Brazil, 1914-1916. After practicing law in Rio Grande do Sul, he was elected to the state legislature in 1927 and two years later became a member of the cabinet of the governor, Getulio Vargas. Aranha joined Vargas in the revolution of 1930 and was Minister of Justice, 1930, and Minister of Finance, 1931-1934. He served as ambassador to the United States, 1934-1938, when he was recalled to serve as Minister of Foreign Affairs. In that position, which he occupied from 1938 to 1944, he exercised strong influence in controlling German and Japanese colonists in Brazil and finally brought his country into the war on the side of the United Nations. As the Minister of Foreign Affairs in Brazil's war cabinet, defender of the Monroe Doctrine at Inter-American conferences, and advocate of democracy and friendship with the United States, Aranha has become one of the outstanding diplomats in America. His strong stand for democracy led to a break with Vargas in 1945, but he continued to have a great influence in his country and the rest of Latin America. He was appointed to représent Brazil on the Security Council of the United Nations in 1946, and was president of the U.N. Assembly, 1947-1948. S. G. I.

ARANJUEZ [ɑrɑ′nhweʹth], a city in the province of Madrid, in central Spain, noted for its royal palace and park. It lies in a fertile plain, 30 mi. south of Madrid, on the left bank of the Tagus River, just above the confluence of the Jarama. Temperatures rise to 115° F. in the summer and malaria has long been a menace. Under the monarchy Aranjuez was a spring residence of the royal family. The surrounding district, irrigated by waters from the Tagus, produces fruits and vegetables for the near-by capital, and strawberries and asparagus are exported abroad. The city was laid out on a gridiron pattern, unusual in Spain, with straight and spacious streets. Aranjuez is on the Madrid-Alicante railway, with branches running to Cuenca and Toledo.

The principal monument is the royal palace, which was begun in the late fourteenth century by the Grand Master of the Order of Santiago. Isabella the Catholic made it a favored place of sojourn, and under Philip II it was enlarged, beautified, and made a royal residence. The palace was badly damaged by fires in 1660, 1665, and 1748, but it was rebuilt and refurnished in a more modern style; new wings were added by Charles III. The extensive gardens occupy both banks of the Tagus and the island, Isla, just below the rapids. Later additions were built under Charles IV, who, with his minister Manuel de Godoy, was compelled to relinquish his power while at the palace in 1808. Thereafter, the palace and grounds fell into relative neglect. Aside from the palace, there is the Casa del Labrador, richly decorated with objects of art. Aranjuez was the scene of a treaty signed on May 1, 1745, by Spain, the Two Sicilies, France, and Genoa concerning the military contribution and territorial claims of the latter during the War of the Austrian Succession. Pop. 1940, 21,771. R. G. W.

ARANY, JÁNOS [ɒ′rɒny], Hungarian epic poet, was born in Nagyszalonta (now Romania), Mar. 1, 1817, and died in Budapest, Oct. 28, 1882. When he was four years old, his father, a very poor peasant, started teaching him the alphabet. With great sacrifice on the part of his parents, he was sent to the college at Debrecen, where he won scholastic honors. In 1836, before graduation, he joined a group of traveling actors but soon returned home disillusioned. He married and became a teacher and later a notary of his town.

Arany's first composition, a long satirical poem, *The Lost Constitution* (1846), won a prize, and the next year his noble epic, *Toldi,* won him national fame. In 1847 he finished *Toldi's Eve.* From 1851 to 1860 he was professor at Nagykörös, where, although never happy, he wrote his finest ballads. After moving to Budapest, in 1860, he wrote *Buda Halala* (1864) ("The Death of Buda"), based upon the Hun myths and Attila. In 1865 he became secretary of the Hungarian Academy of Sciences. Grief over the death of his daughter in 1865 and bad health stopped his writing for ten years, but in 1879 he finished *Toldi's Love,* the middle part of his trilogy, and in the last part of his career he wrote some of his finest epics.

Meditative by nature, Arany created a popular, simple, story-telling art, joining to the folksong the artistic finish of polished verse. His work is characterized by perfection of form, depth of thought and feeling, and love of country. Some of his poems have been translated into German and *The Death of Buda* into English; Arany's own translations from Goethe, Tasso, Shakespeare, and Aristophanes are outstanding. L. A. V.

ARAPAHO. *See* INDIAN TRIBES, NORTH AMERICAN.

ARAPAIMA [ærəpaiʹmə], *Arapaima gigas,* a giant fish of South American rivers. It exceeds 400 pounds in weight. The maximum length is about 15 feet. The arapaima is probably the largest strictly freshwater fish in the world. It has enormous scales. The dorsal and anal fins are located far back on the body, characteristics of its family, the Osteoglossidae. The arapaima is common in the rivers of the Amazon region, where it is highly esteemed as food. The mass of small uniform teeth on the floor of the mouth are dried and used by the natives as a rasp for grating vegetables. E. C. R.

ARAQ. *See* ARAK.

ARARAT [æ′rəræt], an occasionally active volcano situated in the Armenian Knot of central eastern Turkey. Lying in the plain of Aras, the eastern slope of Ararat forms the point of contact between the Armenian Soviet Republic, Turkey, and Iran. The craterless volcano of Mt. Ararat consists of two peaks: Little Ararat, 13,100 ft., on the southeast, and Great Ararat, 16,916 ft., on the northwest. The peaks are seven miles apart. On the northeast slope of Mt. Ararat lies a deep, crater-like chasm. Light vegetation is found up to 11,000 ft., pasture tract from there to about 13,000 ft., where Alpine flora begins. The upper 4,500 ft. of the Great Ararat is covered with perpetual snow. Little Ararat is free from snow in September and October. Mt. Ararat is the traditional resting place of Noah's Ark. In November 1948 the discovery of the remains of a petrified ship on the 11,000-ft. level of Mount Ararat was reported from Istanbul, Turkey. Believing that this ship might be the original Noah's Ark, American and British archaeologists gained the consent of

Mount Ararat is seen across the Turkish-Soviet border from Yerevan, capital of the Armenian Soviet Socialist Republic.

the Turkish government to explore the site, but when *Pravda*, in Moscow, accused the proposed expedition of planning espionage, the Turkish consent was withdrawn in May 1949.

J. E. F.

ARAS, TEVFIK RÜŞTÜ [ɑrɑ's] (1883-   ), Turkish diplomat and statesman, was born Tevfik Rüştü Bey at Cannakkale in 1883. He was educated at Üskûb (Skoplje) in Serbia and in Istanbul and received medical degrees from the universities of Beyrouth and Paris. His first public employment was as an inspector of the Turkish board of health; later he became inspector-general of public health of Salonica. During the first Balkan War, while serving as a surgeon in the Turkish army, he was captured by the Serbs. Before World War I he was inspector-general of public health of the Ottoman Empire and during that war served in the Turkish army. A follower of Kemal Atatürk, he participated in the Turkish war for independence, 1919-1923. He was elected deputy from Smyrna (Ismir) to the first national assembly of Turkey; the Congress of the Committee of Union and Progress selected him its secretary-general. In 1923 he was elected to the *Kamutay* (Parliament) of New Turkey, again as deputy from Smyrna, and became secretary of the foreign affairs committee considering the Treaty of Lausanne. He was president of the commission directing the Greco-Turkish migrations, and served as Turkish minister of foreign affairs from 1925 to 1938. He promoted the Balkan Entente, was twice president of the League of Nations assembly, and led the Turkish delegation that signed the Straits Convention, July 1936, insuring Turkish sovereignty over the Dardanelles.

He resigned as foreign minister after the election of Ismet Inönü as president, and was appointed Turkish ambassador to Great Britain, serving from 1939 to 1942. In 1950 he was named a member of the United Nations Palestine Conciliation Commission.

T. R.

ARAS. *See* ARAKS.

ARAUCANA, LA. *See* ERCILLA, ALONSO DE.

ARAUCANIAN [æ'rɔke'niən], a fierce, warlike independent Indian race which inhabited the central valley of Chile. Its members are famous as the only Indians whom the Spanish were unable to conquer. Again and again, for more than 300 years, these warriors defeated the Spanish invaders. Their greatest leader was named Caupolicán, who won his place by his unusual strength and courage.

These Indians, with nothing but sticks and stones, charged organized Spanish troops with their guns and cannon, and often won the battle. It was not until late in the nineteenth century, after more than three hundred years of resistance, that the Araucanians were finally conquered and became a part of the Republic of Chile.

The union of Spanish and Araucanian blood, as well as the long struggle between these peoples, partly explains the strength and energy of the Chilean character. The Indians still have their own settlements in the province of Temuco, where about thirty thousand live today.

A. Me.

ARAUCARIA [æ'rɔkɛ'əriə], a genus of handsome evergreen trees of great height and symmetrical habit, native to South America, Australia, and the Pacific islands. They are valuable for timber and for their resins. Several species are planted for ornament in very mild regions, including southern Florida and California, and young specimens are popular greenhouse plants. The stiff leaves are scalelike and pointed, or flat, generally overlapping. The huge, woody cones, with large seeds are used for food. Valuable species include the Chile pine or monkey puzzle tree, *A. araucana*, and the Norfolk Island pine, *A. excelsa*, a magnificent tree growing sometimes to 220 ft. *See also* CONIFERS.

J. C. Wis.

ARAWAK. *See* INDIAN TRIBES, SOUTH AMERICAN.

ARAXES. *See* ARAKS.

ARBALEST. *See* ARCHERY.

ARBELA, BATTLE OF [ɑrbi'lə] (331 B.C.), fought at Gaugamela, near Arbela in Assyria, where the army of Alexander the Great encountered the much larger army of the Persian king, Darius III, on Oct. 1, 331 B.C. (The precise date is fixed by an eclipse which occurred a few days before the battle.) The victory of Alexander was a decisive one because it opened the way for his invasion of Babylonia and, subsequently, Persia. At Arbela the Persians made their last real stand against Alexander; after that, the resistance he encountered was never so determined nor so well organized. It was at Arbela that Alexander's army had to face the formidable scythed chariots of the Persians, which operated on much the same principle as the modern lawnmower. When Alexander, however, noticed that these chariots were drawn by stallions, he cleverly threw the enemy line into confusion by causing a mare to be loosed on the battleground.

T. B. J.

ARBITRAGE, the practice of simultaneous purchase in one market and sale in another to take advantage of differences in prices. It is widely conducted in the organized stock and commodity markets, in the precious metals, and in foreign exchange. For example, an arbitrager might purchase British pounds with dollars in New York and at the same time sell pounds for dollars in London. The effect is to reduce or eliminate the very price difference that offered the original inducement. Arbitrage thus strengthens the tendency toward equalization, except for transportation costs, of the price of a given article in all markets. S. E. B.

ARBITRANTS, THE, a comedy by Menander, presented at Athens about 300 B.C. Pamphila, wife of a young Athenian, Charisius, has given birth to a child, about five months after the marriage. Her husband has been absent at the time and she has abandoned the baby in the country, but Charisius has learned the facts from his slave Onesimus. Charisius, instead of divorcing his wife, plunges into a life of riotous indulgence. Pamphila's gruff old father, Smicrines, who knows nothing of the baby, is outraged and tries to get his daughter to leave her husband. In the meantime, the baby has come into the possession of a peasant, and among the trinkets or "birth-tokens" which were left with the infant is a ring which Onesimus recognizes as belonging to his master Charisius. As the facts are gradually revealed to the characters, it turns out that the father of the child is actually Charisius himself, who had unwittingly violated Pamphila at a night festival the year before. Hence, husband and wife are happily reunited. C. T. M.

ARBITRATION, the submission of a matter in dispute between sovereign nations or between private individuals to persons selected by the disputants for decision instead of resorting to warfare or litigation in the courts.

INTERNATIONAL ARBITRATION

As a rule arbitral tribunals for the settlement of disputes between nations include one or two judges from each disputing nation and one neutral judge or umpire. The precise arrangements governing the selection of judges, the procedure to be followed, the submission of evidence, the hearings, the place of meeting, and the date when the award should be delivered, are all made in the agreement to arbitrate, known as the *compromis*. Arbitration is best fitted for the treatment of disputes of a legal nature in which the disputants are in disagreement as to their rights or duties under international law or treaties. Generally, therefore, an arbitral tribunal bases its award on international law. It is possible, however, for the parties to set up in the *compromis* special rules to be followed by a tribunal in arriving at a decision. An agreement to arbitrate implies a willingness to accept an award as binding.

Arbitration is an old procedure. It was used among the city-states of ancient Greece and among those of medieval Europe. Then it was abandoned for several centuries, to be revived by the United States and Great Britain in the Jay Treaty in 1794, where provision was made for the arbitration of several controversies. It was resorted to increasingly in the nineteenth century, particularly by the United States and Great Britain. Among arbitrations of special interest to the United States were the following: the Alabama Claims Case, 1872 (United States and Great Britain); the Bering Sea Case, 1893 (United States and Great Britain); the Pious Fund Case, 1902 (United States and Mexico); and the Alaska Boundary Case, 1903 (United States and Great Britain). In 1899 a Permanent Court of Arbitration was set up at The Hague, providing a panel of names from which judges might be chosen by disputants. N. L. H.

CIVIL AND COMMERCIAL ARBITRATION

Civil and commercial arbitration is the submission of a disputed matter to a selected person or persons for determination, in lieu of litigation between the parties to the dispute. The object of the substitution of arbitration for the ordinary judicial process, generally, is to avoid the delay and vexations incident to trial by court and jury, to preserve amicable relations between the disputants, and to have the decision, called an award, rendered by a person or persons who are familiar with the activity to which the controversy relates.

A contract to arbitrate a controversy thereafter arising, or the submission to arbitration of an existing controversy, may designate a person or persons as the joint selection of the parties, to serve as the arbitrating tribunal; or, as an alternative, each party may choose his own arbitrator, and empower him to join with the arbitrator chosen by the adverse party in selecting a third arbitrator.

At common law, in the United States, arbitration agreements were easily disregarded, such agreements being deemed revocable by either party before the actual award was made. Indeed, legal climate favorable to the flourishing of the practice of arbitration did not exist in the United States until the enactment of the New York State Arbitration Law of 1920. This law not only supplied statutory implementation for agreements for submission of existing disputes to arbitration but furnished sanction for arbitration clauses in contracts relating to future disputes. Such sanction, although essential to the development of arbitration as an important adjunct to trade and commerce, had hitherto been lacking in arbitration statutes. Under the New York law, submissions to arbitration and contracts to settle by arbitration a controversy thereafter arising between the parties (except as to title to real estate) are irrevocable save upon such grounds as exist at law or in equity for the revocation of any contract; such contracts and submissions must be in writing; actions brought in disregard of arbitration agreements may be stayed; the courts may appoint an arbitrator or umpire where a party to an arbitration agreement has failed to do so; arbitrators may require the attendance of witnesses before them; and judgment may be entered by court order upon the arbitration award. The award made in due course may be attacked in court only upon the ground that it was procured by fraud or corruption or that the arbitrators refused to hear pertinent and material evidence or were otherwise guilty of prejudicial misbehavior.

The judgment of the arbitrators relating to the law and the facts of the controversy is not reviewable by the courts. The arbitrators are thus cloaked with powers of final determination, more absolute than those possessed by trial judge, jury, or governmental administrative board.

When a controversy is submitted for adjudication to a regularly constituted court of law, appellate procedure may be applied to obtain a review of the correctness of the trial judge's rulings or the evidentiary sufficiency to support the determination. Generally, also, the decisions of governmental agencies or officers, are subject to judicial review of varying scope. However, error of judgment on the part of arbitrators with respect to law or facts is a risk assumed by parties submitting or agreeing to submit controversies to arbitration. This risk constitutes an offset to the advantages generally incidental to arbitration as a means of resolving civil and commercial controversies.

Arbitration statutes patterned upon the New York law have been enacted by Congress (Title 9, United States Code, section 1-14) and by the states of New Jersey, Massachusetts,

California, Pennsylvania, Louisiana, Arizona, Connecticut, New Hampshire, Rhode Island, Michigan, Washington, Wisconsin, and Oregon.

In the jurisdiction in which arbitration has been accorded by statute a firm legal foundation, it has become an important and salutary institution. Chiefly responsible for this realization of the potentialities of arbitration as an advantageous substitute for litigation has been the American Arbitration Association, founded in 1926, which succeeded in winning the co-operation and support of representative trade and business organizations for arbitration under the association's auspices, as a preferential mode of adjusting contractual disputes. Arbitration, as thus sponsored by leading economic and civic organizations and organized and administered by the American Arbitration Association, offers to business disputants the services of specialized arbitrators and adjudication under established rules of procedure.

England. In England, commercial arbitration has been traditional among members of various exchanges and trade associations long antedating the enactment of the English Arbitration Act of 1889, which is comparable to the American statutes designed to promote the practice of arbitration. Moreover, the English courts for many years prior to the adoption of the English Arbitration Act no longer treated arbitration agreements with the juridical disparagement which characterized the attitude of American courts in the absence of express statutory mandate to sustain arbitration agreements. Organized arbitration in England is centered in the London Court of Arbitration.

Canada. Arbitration statutes in the Canadian provinces (except in Quebec) are modeled after the English Arbitration Act. Arbitration of controversies arising in the course of trade and commerce between Canadian and American business concerns is promoted by the existence and functioning of a private international agency, the Canadian-American Commercial Arbitration Commission, established jointly by the American Arbitration Association and the Canadian Chamber of Commerce. *See also* ARBITRATION, PERMANENT COURT OF; INTERNATIONAL COURT OF JUSTICE; LEAGUE OF NATIONS; UNITED NATIONS.   H. Si.

ARBITRATION, PERMANENT COURT OF, a list of qualified jurists, established in 1899, from which disputing governments, by agreement, might select special arbitration tribunals. Haphazard but increasing use of international arbitration during the nineteenth century brought general recognition of a need for an organized system for settling disputes. At the Hague Conference in 1899 a so-called "permanent court" was arranged by treaty for this purpose. It was improved in 1907 but never became a real court. The thirty governments which became parties to the treaties of 1899 and 1907 were permitted each to designate the names of not more than four jurists. From this list, any two disputing governments could select one or more arbitrators. The treaties also prescribed rules of procedure. About a dozen cases had been arbitrated under this system by 1920 when the establishment of the Permanent Court of International Justice tended to reduce the importance of the previously established "court," which, nevertheless, continues to supply judges to the U. N. International Court of Justice.   N. D. H.

ARBOR DAY. *See* HOLIDAYS AND HOLY DAYS.

ARBORVITAE [ɑrˈbɔrvaiˈti], tree of life, the name used for the genus *Thuja,* evergreen trees. Of some half dozen species, two are native to North America, the others

to eastern Asia. Countless horticultural varieties of *Thuja,* of slow growth and compact habit, have been developed. The narrow, pyramidal outline of the forest arborvitae has disappeared in many garden forms which may be low and bushy, sometimes even globular, with drooping branches and variegated foliage. The leaves, aromatic when crushed,

ARBORVITAE

are tiny, and scalelike in flattened feathery branchlets. The cones are erect and very small.

The American arborvitae, *T. occidentalis,* sometimes called northern white cedar, is found from Nova Scotia to Saskatchewan and southward to Virginia, usually in swamps and along streams. It grows to 60 ft. The coarse-grained wood, which is slow to decay under moist conditions, is used for fence posts, railway ties, and shingles.

The giant arborvitae, *T. plicata,* sometimes called the canoe cedar, is native from northern California to Alaska and east to Montana. It reaches 200 ft., having a huge buttressed trunk sometimes 15 ft. through at the base. The bark is cinnamon-red; the branchlets droop slightly at the tips. The wood is heavily lumbered. Wood and bark were important in Indian economy. The most familiar Asiatic species is the Chinese arborvitae, *T. orientalis.* It differs from the American species in carrying its flat branchlets in vertical instead of horizontal planes. The arborvitae was brought to Europe in the eighteenth century. *See also* CONIFERS.

J. C. Wis.

ARBROATH [ɑrbroˈth], a royal burgh and seaport on the east coast of Scotland, situated in Angus, at the mouth of the Brothock River, on the North Sea, 17 mi. northeast of Dundee. It was made a royal burgh in 1186, and was chartered in 1599. The town, sometimes called Aberbrothock, contains the ruins of Arbroath Abbey, founded in 1178 by William the Lion, who was buried in it. Arbroath is the Fairport of Sir Walter Scott's *Antiquary,* in which the Abbey hospice also figures. Near by is a fine example of Pictish sculptured stones. Local industries include fishing, shipbuilding, and the making of canvas, sailcloth, and coarse linens. Pop. 1952, 19,540.   A. S. M.

ARBUTHNOT, JOHN [ɑrbʌˈθnət; ɑˈrbəθnɒt], (1667-1735), Scottish physician and minor prose writer, was born near Bervie, Kincardineshire, in 1667. He completed his education at Oxford and Aberdeen in 1696 and thereafter pursued his career as physician and wit in London, where he won both popularity and respect. In the Royal Society

JOHN ARBUTHNOT

FROM AN OLD ENGRAV-
ING BY CHARLES JERVAS

he associated with Isaac Newton and Hans Sloane; as physician to Queen Anne, he was intimate with Jonathan Swift and Robert Harley. Many of his writings are lost, but some of his generally slender scientific works survive, including a witty rebuttal of Woodward's account of the Deluge and dissertations on mathematical learning, probability, coins and weights, ailments, and air. In satire, his ironical *Art of Political Lying* (1712) and *The History of John Bull* (1712), a merry allegory of war between the Allies and France, reveal him as a shrewd pamphleteer. In collaboration with Pope, Gay, and Swift, Arbuthnot also contributed substantially to various "Scriblerus" satires. Though learned, he was free from pedantry, and his desultory production displayed independence, modernity, a thrifty style, and tolerant humor. He died Feb. 27, 1735, in London.   L. M. B.

ARBUTUS [ɑrbyuˈtəs], a group of trees and shrubs of the heath family, native to mild regions of the northern hemisphere. Smooth red bark, peeling in large flakes, shining evergreen foliage, clusters of red to white flowers, and red berries make them popular as ornamentals. *See also* MADROÑA.   J. C. Wis.

ARBUTUS, TRAILING, *Epigaea repens,* a member of the heath family, known as mayflower or ground laurel, is a low, creeping woody plant of woods, hillsides, and sand barrens of eastern North America. Small clusters of waxy, pinkish white, intensely fragrant flowers appear in very early spring among the bronzed leaves of the previous season. New bright green leaves appear in early summer. Ruthless picking threatens the plant with extermination.   J. C. Wis.

ARCADIA or **ARKADHÍA** [ɑrkeˈdiə; ɑrkɑthiˈa], a department in the center of the Peloponnesus in southern Greece. It is an elevated plateau about 50 mi. long and from 35 to 41 mi. wide, surrounded by mountains. Those in the western part of the region are high and bleak, forested, and thinly populated. The mountains of the eastern part are lower; grain, and grapes for wine, are raised in the fertile plains between the mountains. The area, often called the "Switzerland of the Peloponnesus," is for the most part inaccessible except by mule path. A railroad crosses the southern part from the plain of Argos, touching at the city of Tripolis and the town of Megalopolis, and then continues on to Messenia. In the north a railroad of the cog type climbs 2,200 ft. in 12 mi. to the plateau of Arcadia. It is a land of small, primitive stone villages scattered among the valleys, and cropland is often created by building terraces. Tripolis was built on the territory of the ancient cities of Mantinea, Pallantion, and Tegea. Megalopolis was anciently an important city state, but it is now a small village. The ancient Arcadians, isolated from the rest of Greece by their walls of mountains, were known for their simple habits, piety, hospitality, kindness, and love of music. The Roman poets exaggerated these qualities to present Arcadian shepherds as the ideal of innocence and virtue, and later European poets continued this practice. Pop. 1951, 154,361.   S. Van V.

ARCADIA, a city in southern California, in Los Angeles Co., about 20 mi. northeast of Los Angeles and 8 mi. east of Pasadena. It was founded and incorporated in 1903 and

TRAILING ARBUTUS OR MAYFLOWER, EPIGAEA REPENS

is administered by a mayor and council. Although primarily a residential city, it manufactures, principally, sashes and doors, beverages, and airplane tools. Large orange and walnut groves are located in the vicinity, and the city has a Pony Express museum. Pop. 1950, 23,066.

ARCADIA [ɑrkeˈdiə; ɑrkɑˈdia], a pastoral romance by the Neapolitan humanist Jacopo Sannazaro. It is essentially a late fifteenth century work, though it was first officially printed in 1504. It consists of twelve poems set in a framework of florid prose, rich in epithet and Classical allusion. The prose passages describe the life, pastimes, and rites of conventionalized shepherds, represented as in a vaguely situated Arcadia, visited by the author under his academic name of Sincero. Generally romantic and melancholy in tone, the prose passages contain no real plot but serve principally to furnish background and motivation for the singing of the poems by one or more of the characters. These poems, or eclogues, vary widely in subject, style, and meter and represent, through skillful imitation, the ancient masters of the bucolic tradition as well as certain Italian poets of the fourteenth and fifteenth centuries. Once enormously popular, today the *Arcadia* is remembered as a chief source of that stream of pastoral literature which includes Honoré d'Urfé's *Astrée,* Miguel de Cervantes' *Galatea,* Jorge de Montemayor's *Diana,* and Edmund Spenser's *Shepheardes Calender.*

A. T. MacA.

ARCADIA, a pastoral prose romance by Sir Philip Sidney (1554-1586), first published posthumously in 1590. Reminiscent of ancient Greek, medieval, Italian, and Spanish romances, among them those of Sannazaro and Montemayor, the work, though carefully contrived, is yet leisurely and complicated in plot. It abounds in descriptive passages, is interspersed with songs, and contains much of the author's serious thought on a number of significant topics. Its style is picturesque but extravagant, often noble in expression, yet at times marred by strained conceits. It was one of the Elizabethan works most widely read by succeeding generations, furnished plots for a number of plays, notably *The Arcadia* (1640) by James Shirley, and was the source of the subplot concerning the earl of Gloucester in *King Lear.*

V. B. H.

ARC DE TRIOMPHE, the most famous of the triumphal arches, located at the end of the Avenue des Champs Élysées in the center of the Place de l'Étoile in Paris, France. Twelve radiating avenues intersect at the place, hence the name "The Star." Standing in the middle of the square, the arch commemorates the victories of Napoleon I, by whose decree it was built. Construction was started in 1806 by J. F. Chalgrin, who worked from his own architectural sketches, and was carried on after his death by L. Goust, J. N. Huyot, and G. A. Blouet, with construction completed in 1836. The arch is 160 ft. high, 150 ft. wide, and 72 ft. deep; inspired by Roman architecture, its grandeur is enhanced by a multiplicity of columns and sculptures depicting important French battles. Since the interment of a French unknown soldier beneath the main arch in 1920 and the lighting of a perpetual flame, the Arc de Triomphe has served as a setting for military memorial ceremonies for both World Wars.

P. N.

ARCE, MANUEL JOSÉ [aʹrse] (c.1786-1847), first president of the Central American Confederation, was born in San Salvador in either 1786 or 1787 and was educated in Guatemala. He was imprisoned in 1811 for participating in a conspiracy to secure the independence of El Salvador, and when a second attempt in 1814 again failed, he was imprisoned for five years. At the refusal of El Salvador in 1821 to follow the lead of Guatemala and submit to annexation by Mexico, Arce was named head of the army, and in two successful battles defeated the Guatemalan generals Nicolás Avos Padilla and Manuel de Arzú but was himself later defeated by the Mexican general Vicente Filísola and was forced into exile in the United States. In 1824 he returned to Guatemala, restored order in Nicaragua after a civil uprising, and was elected first president of the United Central American Provinces in 1825. As president his popularity waned, he was accused of betraying the liberals, and he was deposed by Gen. Francisco Morazán, taking refuge in Mexico in 1829. Aided by the nobility he made two abortive attempts, in 1831 and 1833, to return to power. In 1840 he returned to El Salvador as a candidate for the presidency. Failing to win the election, he tried to overthrow President Juan J. Guzmán but was defeated by Gen. Francisco Malespín at Comtepique in 1843 and again banished. He later returned to El Savador where he died on Sept. 14, 1847.

C. W. D.

ARCHAEOLOGY, the study of the material culture of extinct races of man.

Chronology. The conventional chronological divisions are the Paleolithic ("Old Stone"), Mesolithic ("Middle Stone"), Neolithic ("New Stone," featured generally by the introduction of pottery and therefore sometimes called the "Ceramic Age"), the Bronze Age, and the Iron Age. Some scholars recognize an Eolithic ("Dawn Stone") Age, prior to the Paleolithic, and a Chalcolithic ("Copper-Stone," otherwise known as "Aëneolithic" or "Subneolithic," with first appearance of metal) Age between the Neolithic and the Bronze Age. A major demarcation is provided by the introduction of writing, cultures having no decipherable written records being termed "prehistoric," the others "historic" cultures. In western Asia and Egypt, writing appears about the beginning of the Bronze Age; in Greece, Italy, and the West, not until the end of the Bronze Age or even well into the Iron Age.

Divisions. Archaeology covers many thousands of years and all the land surfaces of the earth except the polar zones; consequently, no archaeologist pretends to competence in the whole field. Students tend to specialize in one of the four main geographical-chronological divisions into which archaeology naturally falls: (1) Prehistoric Archaeology of the Old World, comprising Europe, Asia, and Africa to the beginning of written history; (2) Oriental Archaeology, covering Asia, especially western Asia (Iran, Iraq, Anatolia, Syria, Palestine, and Arabia, to which is often linked Egypt), from the beginning of written records to the Roman or Byzantine period; (3) Classical, or Mediterranean Archaeology, consisting of Greece, Italy, and the other areas falling within the limits of the Roman Empire (that is, the lands bordering the Mediterranean), from the beginning of written history to the time of Constantine (A.D. 337); and (4) American Archaeology, comprising the pre-Columbian cultures of North, Central, and South America.

Temporal and spatial subdivisions are created at will, such as Egyptian, Aegean (the prehistory of the coasts and islands of the Aegean Sea), Danubian, Hittite, Italic, Celtic, Hellenistic, Byzantine (the Near East and Adriatic from Constantine to the capture of Constantinople and Trebizond), Slavic, Scandinavian, Maya, and Inca; but archaeologists who specialize in such subdivisions usually do so as a side line to a principal occupation in one of the general fields.

Purposes of Archaeology. Archaeology as a science has no independent existence. It exists solely to provide the raw materials of history in the broadest sense. Historical disciplines which have acquired new evidence from archaeological investigations include cultural, political, economic, and social history; chronology; mythology; cultural anthropology; history of religion, art, and architecture; epigraphy; numismatics; literature; linguistics; physical anthropology; zoology; botany; and geology. Many archaeological finds, of course, yield information in more than one of these categories. Thus, an Attic vase found in an Etruscan tomb may furnish data on the technology of ceramics, the art of painting, trade connections between Athens and northern Italy, a basis for dating the tomb, and, in the painted scene itself, an otherwise unreported mythological concept. A Syracusan coin found in Corinth, besides being an exquisite specimen of a so-called minor art, may provide evidence for trade connections, monetary weights and standards, and the official and religious symbolism of the issuing city. An inscription may contain a text important to political and social history and chronology, as well as otherwise unrecorded linguistic data. In the absence of formal historical narrative, the history of a city may be reconstructed in astonishing detail from the evidence produced from its own soil, and for this kind of reconstruction the archaeologist draws upon every type of artifact. Coins and inscriptions are especially useful for dating, but coinage is a comparatively late invention (seventh century B.C.) and not invariably reliable; in their absence building forms and construction techniques, pottery, lamps, and many classes of minor finds may be drawn upon. Handles of the jars in which Rhodian wine was exported, certified authentic by official stamps, have provided excellent dating criteria where even coins were indecisive.

The prehistorian works in the absence of historical records. Here he may occasionally have some clue from linguistic patterns or even direct assistance from legends, as in "Homer" 's account of the siege of Troy, now recognized as based, at least in part, on actual events. More often the prehistorian is without any other evidence than the results of the excavations, which by definition contain no decipherable written texts. In such investigations, the smallest artifact may be valuable, the precise level of a single pottery fragment of decisive importance in determining the sequence and relative dating of strata and even of entire cultures. Some prehistorians have in consequence acquired such perfected field techniques that workers in this field generally feel themselves a cut above archaeologists working in the historic periods.

History. *First Phase.* In most parts of the world, the collapse of the Roman Empire in the fifth century of the Christian Era was followed by total loss of interest in the past; the ancient monuments, and the languages and literatures of the people who made them, were ignored or completely forgotten. Even in medieval Europe, interest in material remains was so undeveloped that public opinion permitted the large-scale destruction of older monuments in order to obtain their materials. Marble sculptures were sent to the kilns to be burned to lime; marble and limestone structural and decorative elements were stripped from public and private buildings, either for lime or for re-use as found; the noncalcareous stones were ripped out and re-used whole, or broken into smaller fragments for use in rubble masonry; bronze statues and ornaments were melted down; lead waterpipes and even lead pins and clamps were pried out and melted; and ancient bricks were laboriously separated from their mortar. Where severe population shrinkage has occurred, as in Central America, human agencies have not been a serious factor in the destruction of ancient ruins. The monuments of western Asia, whose principal building material was mud brick, unbaked, almost valueless for re-use, suffered relatively less damage from human agents, and relatively more from weathering.

The Renaissance in Italy saw a partial reversal of the trend; the poet Petrarch (1304-1374) collected Roman coins, and Cyriacus of Ancona (1391-c. 1450) made drawings of buildings and copied inscriptions in southern Italy and Greece. The revival of sympathy for Latin literature and the resulting search for earlier manuscripts were stimulated by the capture by the Turks of the Byzantine capital of Constantinople in 1453 and the exodus of those Greeks who found means to escape with their possessions. Libraries of Latin and Greek manuscripts were formed in Italy and western Europe, and the concurrent development of printing saw editions of Latin classics among the earliest printed books; the intellectual revolution which followed the appearance of the first printed books was enriched by the texts of Vergil, Horace, Cicero, Plautus, Lucretius, Livy, and Tacitus, while Renaissance architecture rested heavily upon the Roman

tradition and the treatise of the archconservative Augustan architect Vitruvius.

In such an antiquarian atmosphere the illustrative value of material relics of the Classical period came to be recognized. The methodical destruction of ancient buildings was not stopped at once—it is not entirely prevented today—but several popes and influential individuals acquired first

COURTESY OF THE METROPOLITAN MUSEUM OF ART

Silver Ladle and Jug (Greek, IV-III Century B.C.)

small, then larger, collections of sculpture from the Baths of Caracalla, Hadrian's villa at Tivoli, and other ruined Roman buildings. Word got around among country folk that such pieces had more value whole than burned or broken, and a long series of informal, unrecorded excavations by farmers and self-appointed purveyors to the wealthy began. Most Roman cities in Italy were explored during this period or later. For the moment, however, this wave of cultural activity did not spread far beyond the borders of Italy; elsewhere, ancient ruins continued to be subject only to sporadic pillaging by farmers and rural masons in quest of building materials. In the following centuries, private collectors in France and England assembled objects from Italy and even Greece; Charles F. M. Olier, Marquis of Angevilliers and Nointel, visited Athens in 1674, and an artist in his company made drawings of the Parthenon sculptures; and Jacques Spon, French physician, and George Wheler or Wheeler, an Englishman, visited Greece and the Aegean islands in 1675-1676; but no real change in the dilettante attitude toward ancient art took place until the middle of the eighteenth century.

Second phase. In the eighteenth century several events laid the foundations for new approaches to the study and appreciation of the past: the discovery of large numbers of painted vases, presently identified as of Greek and finally as of Attic (Athenian) workmanship, in the tombs of Etruria in north central Italy; the discovery of Herculaneum (1738) and Pompeii (1748), as buried by the ashes from Vesuvius in A.D. 79; and the visit of the English painter and architect, James Stuart, with Nicholas Revett, to Athens (1751-1754) and their eventual publication, in four volumes (1761-1816), of the monumental *Antiquities of Athens,* followed by the expedition to Asia Minor sponsored by the Society of Dilettanti and the publication of the *Antiquities of Ionia.* These discoveries did not immediately lead to the establishment of a new art or science of archaeology (J. J. Winckelmann, who published his *History of Ancient Art* in 1763, has been hailed as the founder of archaeology, but he is more accurately to be described as the first scientific historian of art); for the moment, the Pompeii and Herculaneum finds led to a wave of clandestine excavation aimed at the embellishment of the palaces and villas of near-by Naples, while the ruins of the Athenian Acropolis presently touched off the Greek Revival movement in architecture. The larger lessons—that at Pompeii and Herculaneum as nowhere else could be studied the everyday life of ordinary citizens, their living rooms, gardens, kitchens, workshops, taverns, plumbing, markets, wayside shrines, and carnal pleasures, and that in Greece could be observed masterpieces of architecture and sculpture finer, by maturing standards, than those of Rome—did not have an immediate broad impact; but, though latent, these criteria were thenceforth spread upon the record, and further developments were to serve to bring them into true perspective.

In 1799 soldiers of Napoleon discovered, near the Rosetta mouth of the Nile, a stone with three inscriptions, now called the Rosetta Stone. In 1803 Lord Elgin removed the Parthenon marbles from Athens to London. As in the case of Pompeii and Herculaneum, these excited only local curiosity at the time; the Elgin marbles, after prolonged discussion, were purchased for the British Museum, where their artistic merits began gradually to be recognized, while the import of the Rosetta texts, in Greek and two scripts of Egyptian, was not known until 1822 when the French scholar Jean François Champollion reported his discovery of the phonetics and thus of the structure and vocabulary of the Egyptian language. These all served to contribute to the gathering momentum of antiquarian studies.

Formal excavations, with informed and generally conscientious antiquarians rather than antiquities dealers in charge, and with public rather than private collections as the beneficiaries, now began. Since these enjoyed official approval or even governmental sponsorship, the excavators could work without haste and with the object of removing entire deposits, instead of single pieces out of context. Techniques and doctrines improved slowly; whole or nearly whole vases were admitted to preservation, and coins and lamps, and even fragmentary inscriptions were collected as observed; but the dirt moved was not sifted, allowing many small finds to go unobserved, little effort was made to differentiate occupation levels, and field records were incomplete, scanty, or not kept at all. In the period from 1811 to 1870 such sites as the following were explored in this manner: the temple of Aphaia, on the Greek island of Aegina in 1811; Corneto, Chiusi, Cervetri, Orvieto, and Vulci in Etruria from 1827 to 1828; Nineveh and Babylon, in Mesopotamia, by Austen Henry Layard, British archaeologist, author, and diplomat, from 1845 to 1847 and in 1849 and 1850; the Acropolis of Athens from 1832 to 1836; and the Tomb of Mausolus ("Mausoleum") at Halicarnassus in 1846 and 1857. Another landmark in this period was Henry Rawlinson's deciphering of the Persian text of the great trilingual inscription of Darius I at Behistun, in Persia; since this was in cuneiform, it provided clues which enabled Rawlinson to decipher Neo-Babylonian cuneiform, and Edwin Norris to decipher Median, the third language of the Behistun monument.

Third phase. Up to 1870 archaeologists had been motivated primarily by the desire to discover new artistic treasures; sculptures, wall paintings, painted vases, mosaics, figurines, sarcophagi, and architectural masterpieces. Renown in the field was the achievement of the individual, not of teamwork, and the way to fame was to be identified as the dis-

coverer of a masterpiece. The use of the more pedestrian archaeological finds, particularly those of Pompeii, to illustrate Classical civilization was a subordinate consideration, but the deliberate application of archaeological method to the solution of purely historical problems had hardly been tried. The reorientation of archaeological objectives which began in 1870 was the work of one man, and an amateur at that—Schliemann.

Heinrich Schliemann (1822-1890) was a German who, having made a substantial fortune in commerce, happened to be in California on July 4, 1850, the day that state was admitted to the Union, thereby acquiring United States citizenship. He was a vigorous, charming, tenacious, and ruthless man, of incisive and penetrating intellect. Among a score of languages, he had learned Latin and Greek, and had read the Homeric poems in Greek. Rejecting the then traditional view that the *Iliad* and *Odyssey* were works of fiction, he argued that the poems described real people and events, and that the site of Troy could be located and identified from internal descriptions in the *Iliad*.

In 1870 he began the excavation of the mound of Hissarlik, commanding the Dardanelles, in northwestern Asia Minor, which he excavated at various times until his death. He dug a large trench through the entire heart of the mound, revealing the stratification of numerous successive occupation levels, founded the science of Greek prehistory, and satisfied himself that Hissarlik was Troy. He is said to have been the first field archaeologist to keep careful notes of the progress of the work and the location of finds, now a routine procedure. Mindful of Schliemann's lack of technical preparation, many scholars refused, even after his discovery of the famous Circle Graves at Mycenae in Greece, to acknowledge the value of his materials or the justness of his views; but the subsequent excavations at Hissarlik by Schliemann's architect, Wilhelm Dörpfeld, from 1893 to 1894, and Carl Blegen, from 1932 to 1938, have left no room for doubt.

Schliemann had shown what light the excavation of an entire site might be expected to throw on the immense and complex problems of ancient culture; the modern phase of archaeology begins with him. Austrian expeditions under Alexander Christian Leopold Conze excavated the sanctuary of the Great Gods at the Greek island of Samothrace in 1873 and 1875; a German expedition supervised by Ernst Curtius excavated the sanctuary of Zeus at Olympia in southern Greece from 1875 to 1880; the Berlin Museum excavated in Asia Minor the Hellenistic capital of Pergamum from 1878 to 1886 and intermittently after 1900, the small Hellenistic town of Priene from 1895 to 1899, and the Classical and Hellenistic metropolis of Miletus after 1899; and the Archaeological Institute of America excavated Assus in Asia Minor from 1881 to 1883. During this period the first archaeological schools (French, German, American, British, and Austrian) were founded in Athens and Rome. These in turn undertook excavations, the American School in Athens excavating the sanctuary of Hera at Argos in 1892 and 1893, the important Classical city of Corinth sporadically since 1896, and a number of lesser sites; the French School in Athens, at Delos from 1877 to 1894 and from time to time after 1902 and at Delphi after 1893; and the British School in Athens, at Megalopolis in 1890 and 1891 and at Sparta after 1906. Hiller von Gaertringen, a German, excavated at his own expense the Greek island city of Thera on Santorin from 1896 to 1901, and Sir Arthur Evans, an English archaeologist, began in 1900 his memorable excavations at the Palace of Minos at Cnossus in Crete, which with the evidence from other excavations resulted in the reconstruction of the rich Bronze-Age (prehistoric) culture now known as Minoan. The Greek Archaeological Society excavated Epidaurus beginning in 1881, Eleusis beginning in 1882, and the deposits on the Acropolis of Athens from 1885 to 1891. Since none of these sites has been entirely cleared and since work either is continuing or may be expected to be resumed, terminal dates are given only for those excavations considered to be permanently abandoned.

The techniques of excavation, recording, and interpreting developed in international rivalry on Greek sites were subsequently applied to the great mounds of Mesopotamia (Nippur, Babylon, Asshur, Nineveh, Kish, Ur, and Erech), and then to sites in Elam, Palestine, Anatolia, Egypt, and the Mediterranean cultures generally. The modern phase reached its peak during the period of abundance in the 1920's, when Harvard, Yale, the University of Pennsylvania Museum, the Oriental Institute of the University of Chicago, the Museum of Fine Arts, Boston, the Metropolitan Museum, New York, the University of Michigan, and many other public and private institutions in this country and Europe competed in the field for the sites of the potentially greatest dramatic interest to specialist and layman.

Selection and Identification of Sites. In the past, sites have usually been selected for excavation because of their prominence in the pages of history; since Ur, Babylon, Kish, Asshur, Nineveh, Palmyra, Megiddo, Thebes, Cnossus, Ephesus, Pergamum, Constantinople, Troy, Athens, Corinth, Mycenae, and Rome were at various periods important political or commercial centers, it could be assumed that they were *ipso facto* cultural centers, once, and possibly still, containing admirable artistic products; this assumption has been regularly proved correct by excavation, and similarly in the case of important religious foundations such as Delos, Delphi, Epidaurus, and Olympia. Other cities which even at their peak were of secondary commercial or political, and therefore historical, importance, such as Dura-Europus, Priene, Olynthus, Pompeii, and Herculaneum, owe their archaeological appeal to accidents of preservation, frequently coupled with extraordinary circumstances of destruction (Olynthus was taken by storm by Philip of Macedon, 348 B.C.; Pompeii and Herculaneum, deeply covered by volcanic ash, A.D. 79; and Dura-Europus, taken by storm by Shapur, A.D. 256).

In the case of prehistoric sites such considerations hold only for those sites standing at the threshold of written history (for example, Cnossus, Troy, and Mycenae), whose traditions carried over into the historic period; the contemporary name of no Paleolithic, Mesolithic, or Neolithic station is known. Here the considerations governing the decision to excavate are the apparent depth of the deposit (a deep deposit usually presents a sequence of cultures, of total importance for relative dating), location with reference to known or probable trade routes, and surface finds or the yield of trial trenches.

The question most often asked of the archaeologist by laymen, "How do you know where to dig?" is really two questions: "How do you know where an ancient city lies buried?" and "Having determined the location of an ancient city, how do you decide what part of it to dig?" For the first, the answer is simple: an ancient city is virtually impossible to conceal. Historical records describe the location of many ancient cities, with reference to familiar topographical features, so precisely that no confusion is possible. In many parts of the Old World, local traditions have continued ancient site names in use down to modern times. In the stone-building and brick-building cultures of the Mediterranean, substantial remains of columns, walls, or fortifications, often

structures known from their descriptions by ancient authors, are frequently visible above ground. In the mud-brick cultures of western Asia, the mounds formed by successive occupation levels stand conspicuous in the level plains of the desert. Even sites occupied for brief periods display large quantities of stone artifacts or potsherds on the surface. Since 1918 air photography has been effectively applied to archaeological exploration. Thus O. G. S. Crawford, a British pioneer in this field, has discovered, in the British Isles, hundreds of Roman and pre-Roman village and camp sites, roads, cemeteries, and other man-made topographical features; R. P. Poidebard has traced Roman roads and forts in Syria; a University of Pennsylvania Museum expedition located many pre-Columbian sites in the roadless jungles of Central America; and Erich Schmidt of the Oriental Institute of the University of Chicago photographed dozens of known ruins and discovered many previously unknown sites in Iran.

In answer to the second question, the selection of the precise spot within a site to start work may introduce the element of chance. At Mediterranean sites, surface indications often reveal the pretentious temples, public buildings, and decorations characteristic of civic centers ("agora," "acropolis," or "forum"). Lacking such indications, the archaeologist may proceed by marking out on the surface strips four to six or more feet wide and fifty, a hundred, or more feet long, often two such strips in the shape of a +. These, the "trial trenches" of excavation reports, are then dug to bedrock or sterile soil. If any important building lies underneath, one or both trenches should reveal it. Trial trenching may be continued, prior to the thorough excavation of any one building, until the major characteristics of the site, walls and gates, streets, block plan, business and residential areas, principal structures, and over-all dimensions, are well understood. In very deep deposits, vertical shafts through the successive strata may be substituted for trial trenches. Once the principal features of the site are understood, excavation may proceed building by building, block by block, or by arbitrary plots (in what is called a "grid") surveyed and marked on the surface for the excavator's convenience.

Preservation of Antiquities. In most parts of the world, rain or ground water makes the soil moist through part of the year. Alternate wetting and drying is very destructive to most vegetable and animal products; under such conditions cloth, paper, leather, and objects of wood or fiber decompose rapidly, whereas oyster and other shells, teeth, and horn are usually, and bones are often, admirably preserved. Of mineral products, the metals generally are well preserved; gold remains untarnished, and silver, copper, tin, zinc, and lead usually corrode only slightly, though in some soils copper and bronze may corrode badly. Iron corrodes so heavily that objects of iron are often unrecognizable, except under conditions where vegetable and animal products are preserved. Of worked stones, those exposed on the surface suffer from abrasion as well as weathering, but most stones below ground are well preserved, though some, the gypsums for example, tend to swell and crack when moist for long periods. A major factor in structural damage, particularly in tropical and subtropical jungles, but encountered to some degree in nearly all archaeological areas, is the growth of trees and shrubs, which take root and spread in cracks and in joints between stones or bricks, and may cause the collapse of superstructure or foundations.

Manufactured objects whose components are of mineral origin tend to resist decomposition in all soil conditions. This group includes some of the classes of artifact most important to the historian, for many such objects in the process of manufacture underwent decoration, and both the decorations and the processes of manufacture revealed by inspection of the fabric yield valuable clues for dating and for the study of intercultural relations. Among such objects are, above all, pottery and other ceramic products, and glass, while under favorable conditions structural stucco and wall plaster may preserve important architectural and decorative details, particularly if original coloring has survived, as in the mural

A Classical Etruscan silver amphora is inscribed and decorated with gold (Suthma, IV-III Century B.C.).

paintings found in Egypt, Iraq, Turkestan, the Crimea, Macedonia, Etruria, Pompeii and Herculaneum, Rome, Ostia, and other sites of Roman date, Central America, and the American southwest. Sculptures of molded plaster have been found in Greco-Roman contexts in the eastern Mediterranean and western Asia, while Afghanistan and Turkestan have Greco-Buddhist sculptures in the same medium.

In those regions of scanty or no rainfall, where throughout the historical period the subsoil has remained dry, as in the desert regions of Africa, Central Asia, and the southwestern states, materials usually considered perishable may be found astonishingly well preserved. Thus in Arizona and New Mexico ancient basketry, cloth, wood, and human mummies have been found; the Turkestan deserts have yielded similar finds and also large numbers of parchment manuscripts, regarded as sensational because they include texts in two dialects of Tocharian, a previously unknown language of Indo-European affiliations, and other "new" languages. One of the extraordinary developments of the last half-century has been the discovery of immense numbers of papyrus documents, mainly in Greek, in the trash heaps of the Greco-Roman towns of Egypt. Such finds, containing both literary texts and social and economic material, have drawn to such areas archaeological attention wholly out of proportion to their natural place in the history of culture.

Elsewhere special circumstances have made possible the excellent preservation of perishables. Substantial finds of papyri, for instance, have been made at Auja el Hafir (ancient Nessana) in the Negeb, a district subject to heavy winter rains, where a collapsing roof fell in such a way as to furnish shelter for the deposit beneath; and at Dura-Europus, on the middle Euphrates, where the surface soil appears to resist penetration by water. An entire library on papyrus was discovered during the early excavations at Herculaneum; here the special condition was that the fall of ash

during the Vesuvian eruption (A.D. 79) coincided with a heavy rain, so that the streets and houses of Herculaneum were filled and covered with a river of warm mud which presently hardened into impervious rock. In addition to the papyri, the houses of Herculaneum have yielded substantial elements of wood, oxidized and fragile, but sufficiently recognizable to make possible the reconstruction of stairs, balconies, screens, doors, furniture, and garden trellises, while in several gardens identifiable remains of plants have been found. At Pompeii itself, the deep (sixteen to twenty feet) fall of dry ash buried most buildings completely, and the consequent preservation of the architecture and furnishings of the city has astonished modern visitors; but in all sections of the city surface rains have penetrated freely and such perishables as wood and textiles are actually rare; a series of inscribed wax tablets is a notable exception.

Occasional tantalizing finds have been made of sealed jars containing documents or other historically valuable relics, as at Avroman in Persia, which yielded three or more parchments inscribed in Greek, and more recently (1947) in a cave near the Dead Sea, which produced a series of eleven Hebrew manuscripts, remarkable for their extraordinary preservation as well as for their historical uniqueness, competent scholars having assigned them to the second century B.C., a thousand years earlier than any other Hebrew manuscripts. A tomb in northern Italy produced a unique find, a glass vessel in the shape of a bird, hermetically sealed and containing a small quantity of wine of the Roman period.

Another special condition leading to extraordinary preservation is provided by perpetual frost, as in the Altai Mountains of western Asia, where ancient tombs built above the frost line have been found to contain the frozen bodies of human beings, horses, dogs, clothes and trappings, food, and other objects normally considered perishable. Ice fields in northern Siberia, at the edge of the Arctic Circle, have yielded carcasses of mammoths whose flesh has been eagerly eaten by dogs.

Where objects are kept continually wet, remarkable preservation may occur; thus the bogs of Scandinavia, particularly Denmark, have yielded an increasing number of coffins containing human bodies in such good condition that the contents of the stomachs could be identified, and with clothing and woolen articles in excellent preservation. English and Irish bogs have produced occasional finds of this sort, and stream beds in England and elsewhere have given up such finds as the wooden pilings of bridge and wharf structures and the wooden hulls of ancient boats.

Caves occasionally provide conditions of extreme dryness with consequent excellent preservation of their contents, as in the case of a cave found in 1946 in France, containing human and animal footprints and coproliths dating apparently from the Upper Paleolithic Period. Since most of the geological formations of the circum-Mediterranean lands are limestone, the caves were generally formed by water and are more or less constantly penetrated by water, so that conditions of total dryness are rare. Tombs, both above ground and underground, are artificial caves, and when skillfully built may resist penetration by water; the famous tomb of Tutankhamen, in the Valley of the Kings, is only one of hundreds of tombs discovered in Egypt, notable because its original rich contents were preserved entire. The mural paintings preserved in the tombs of Tarquinia and other Etruscan sites are among the most admired examples of this art. Tombs of the Classical period in the Crimea have yielded coffins of wood, and comparable finds are occasionally made from Asia to the Andes.

Field Techniques of Recovery and Protection. In digging any ancient site, the excavator keeps constantly in mind the possibility of coming upon fragile articles such as sculpture, pottery, glass, jewelry, ivory, and bone; perishable articles such as textiles, wood, and plaster; and very small articles such as coins, gems, and beads. When he observes that an occupation stratum likely to contain such objects has been reached, correct procedure is to withdraw all but the most skillful and careful workman from the spot; the excavator may prefer to do the actual digging himself. Work then proceeds slowly, with the small hand-mattock or trowel, or even with hunting knife or whiskbroom as tools. Table utensils such as spoons and dinner knives are often diverted to such uses. Where an object is found in partial disintegration, as ivory or bone articles often are, very careful search for small particles is made, the removed earth is passed through a fine screen, and, as successive fragments are revealed, numerous photographs to facilitate eventual restoration are made. Many excavators make it a practice to pass all excavation dirt through a screen made of hardware cloth.

Such field conditions as heavy rains, the untrustworthiness of workmen, or the presence of scavenger dogs or hyenas

(Left) Scene from a boar hunt (Late Minoan III, 1350-1100 B.C.) (Right) Cupbearer, part of a procession from the palace of Cnossos, Crete (Late Minoan II, 1500-1350 B.C.)

(who, for instance, will gobble greedily at ancient bones), may make it undesirable to leave an important deposit overnight for further clearing on succeeding days. Or, such discoveries as human skulls, bones and jewelry crushed into a mass as in the Royal Tombs at Ur, may require that the actual work of removal and preservation be carried out under laboratory rather than field conditions. In such cases, the object may be removed in one mass with its enclosing dirt. In order to obtain a rigid package which will sustain transportation, the usual procedure is to dig around the deposit and undercut it so that it stands on a pedestal or column of unexcavated earth; the shape suggests that of a mushroom. A topless, bottomless wooden box of appropriate size is then placed around it. This container is filled with plaster of Paris. Undercutting of the pedestal is completed and the whole mass is then turned over in one piece. The remaining unplastered surface is plastered, top and bottom boards are screwed in place, and the package is ready for transportation. This method of packing, which was used by Charles L. Woolley, the English archaeologist, in recovering the treasures of the Royal Tombs at Ur, and by Charles Watelin in removing primitive wooden objects, such as carts, from the lower levels of Kish, has since been widely adopted. Various waxes may be used in the same way with equal suc-

cess, provided that the package will not be exposed to extremes of heat during transportation. Where paleontological specimens are found encased in rock formations, the comparable procedure, of quarrying out the rock in blocks of size convenient for transportation, is followed; the actual freeing of the specimens may then be carried out with requisite care in the laboratory.

Mural paintings on mud or plaster require special techniques; at sites where as expressions of art they are more important than any other class of find, they are of special concern. At centers readily accessible under present conditions of travel, modern procedure is to preserve them in place by consolidating the walls on which they are painted, and by building a roof to shelter them from rain and sunlight; at Pompeii and Herculaneum, for instance, the shelter reproduces the form of the original roof, so that the visitor may see the paintings in a semblance of their original setting. In the case of such finds at places now considered hazardous, difficult, or inconvenient of access, such as Dura-Europus on the Euphrates and Chinese Turkestan, the doctrine is in dispute; some advocates, arguing that constantly improving air transportation will shortly make such places easy of access and that easing political tensions will make the frontiers more readily passable, urge that murals be preserved *in situ* as at Pompeii. Up to the present, however, those responsible for the decision have considered it preferable to move paintings to areas where public security is considered to meet Western standards.

The removal of paintings from plaster or mud walls requires unusually delicate procedure and great manual skill. The normal process is to face the painted surface with waterproofed cloth or paper. A second wall of cement or plaster is then built up against the painted wall. This double wall, with the painted surface carefully sandwiched in the middle, is then sawn out in convenient sections, having due regard for the integrity of individual figures in the painting, and meticulously crated for transportation. Where the painted wall is so thick that complete sections through both walls would be inconveniently bulky or heavy, or where it is desirable not to destroy the whole thickness of the original wall, a further vertical cut may be made by the saw in a plane parallel to the painted surface, producing sections of convenient thickness.

Even where a perishable object has completely vanished, it may be found to have left an impression in the fill. In such event, the archaeologist may be able to recover its form by treating its impression as a mold, pouring liquid plaster of Paris into the hole. This of course requires great care lest the walls of the impression collapse before plaster can be poured. This has been a familiar device at Pompeii, where in recent years doors and battens, door frames, furniture, and, in one exceptional example, the forms of the wooden household gods in a family shrine have been recovered by this procedure. In such circumstances the original metal members, such as nails, pins, studs, hinges, handles, and locks, are often held in place by the packed fill, and are found gripped in their original positions in the plaster replica when the latter is freed; this has yielded priceless evidence on Roman carpentry and cabinetmaking, and hardware. At Ur, Woolley used the same technique to recover the shapes and decorations of musical instruments and other fragile objects of perishable materials, in one instance so successfully that he obtained recognizable casts of the impressions left by the strings of a harp.

In the moist soil of England, objects such as wooden posts and stakes and human bones have decomposed so completely that to the untrained eye no trace of the original remains. But if the soil is undisturbed, its composition at such points is different from that immediately adjacent, and it has been a triumph of English prehistorians that they have learned to detect these dim shadows in the ground so effectively that they have recovered from them the plans and dimensions of wooden buildings and, of skeletal remains, at least their size, position, and orientation. Scandinavian archaeologists recovered the form and accurate dimensions of a buried Viking galley from the relative positions in the earth of the nails which held the planking to the frame, though every trace of timber had disappeared.

Personnel. There are no rigid conventions regarding the personnel of a field expedition. A typical excavation required the services of a field director and a recorder for the finds, and technical assistance in surveying, planning, photography, and restoration. Under ideal conditions, there is a field assistant in charge of each sector where actual digging is going on, and in some excavations the finds are so numerous as to require one or more assistant recorders. On the other hand, staff members frequently fill two or more functions, as when the photographer directs the work of one trench or the field director acts as his own surveyor-architect. Budgetary considerations have always played an important part in such matters, and particularly when salary, transportation, and living expenses are at high levels; many apprentices have joined expeditions for expenses only, without salary. A well-staffed expedition would perhaps be comprised of five salaried staff members: field director, assistant field director or field assistant, recorder, assistant recorder and photographer, and surveyor-architect. Women are accepted in any of these capacities and have taken part in the great majority of modern expeditions.

Labor is usually recruited on the spot; with instruction, local farmers usually become good diggers, and the best are entrusted with the areas where fragile objects are most likely to be found. Foremen are often engaged to work away from home, as therefore more apt to serve the interests of the excavators. Excavation is a slow, expensive process; from ten to twenty workmen may be required to remove the earth loosened by one pickman. The extremes are provided by Egypt and Iraq, where gangs of five hundred are not unknown, and the American southwest, where the technical staff may do all the excavating without the assistance of paid labor. A gang of forty to sixty is an economical median.

Recording. Several systems of recording the finds of an excavation or surface exploration are in use. The ultimate aim of any system of recording has been described as one which would enable a later worker to reverse the process of excavation, replacing the dirt and all finds in the exact locations and positions they had held when originally discovered. This goal is impossibly romantic, but such excavating as the University of Michigan's at Karanis in the Fayum, in Egypt, and the American School excavations in the Athenian Agora, and such excavators as Wace, Blegen, and Hetty Goldman are known for the exquisite precision of their field records.

The basis of field recording is the field journal, a day-by-day narrative of the progress of the excavations, with measurements and provisional sketches of all constructions found in place and all noteworthy finds, often supplemented by small field photographs for maximum identification. Here the ideal calls for notes so complete that if the excavation were unexpectedly halted overnight and not resumed, a scholar who had never seen the site could prepare a complete and accurate publication of all buildings and finds discovered up to the moment of suspension. The field journal is often prepared in several copies, to provide control copies for local officials and to guard against the risk of loss.

Alongside the field journal is the field inventory, which is a list of the finds in their order of accession. Inventory numbers assigned may be in simple numerical order, but some excavators make of them a complex code, where, for example, M49-E9-246 may represent the name of the site (M), the season or campaign (1949), the square (E9) on the surveyor's grid where the find was made, and the sequence number of the object so listed. In modern excavations the field inventory may be kept in file-card form, often in quadruplicate, one set to be filed by categories (for example, sculpture, pottery, glass, lamps, coins, figurines, inscriptions, or architectural fragments) for the convenience of the person who will publish or study the category of his special interest, the second set to be filed by buildings or other proveniences, so that the person publishing an account of a building may have a handy list of the separate finds made at that building, and the third and fourth sets to be deposited with the local authorities and the sponsoring institution as an inventory control and record of the eventual disposition of the finds.

The development of the Leica-type camera has greatly increased the effectiveness of field recording. The film's compactness in handling, developing, and storing has endeared it to explorers wrestling with problems of limited space and transportation difficulties. From the small negatives contact prints may be made in quantity, for affixing to the field journal, to the field inventory cards, and to the inventory of photographic negatives essential to all large operations; from the same negatives may also be made enlargements as desired for the information of correspondents, preliminary publication, and press releases, pending ultimate photography under studio conditions.

Disposition of Finds. The antiquities codes of most countries do not specifically forbid the export of national antiquities, but several countries—notably Italy, Greece, and Turkey—taking advantage of the prestige attached to digging in their soil, have adopted a policy of releasing no antiquities for export. Elsewhere, as in Egypt, Cyprus, Palestine, Syria, Iraq, and Iran, the antiquities codes authorized, and official policy until recently permitted, foreign excavators to export one half of the portable finds. Where such division is permitted, the manner of effecting it is simple; the field director or other representative of the foreign institution divides the finds of a campaign or series of campaigns into two lots, and the representative of the local government takes his choice of the lots. This method also protects the government's interest when, as sometimes has happened, a campaign has produced a single masterpiece and other finds of mediocre interest.

In an access of nationalism, several countries which formerly permitted equal divisions have now rescinded this provision. Where the new policy is in effect, such institutions as museums, which for continued financial support of field excavations depend upon a regular flow of new discoveries for study, publication, and exhibition, have been forced to abandon field operations. Since, in such countries as Egypt, Syria, Iraq, and Turkey, native archaeologists have now been trained to European standards of competence, government-sponsored field work will continue and reports will be made available, though the appearance of excavation reports in such languages as Turkish and Arabic suggests that the Western student will have to become even more polyglot than in the past. There is an indirect result, however, with unhappy implications: museums deprived of the opportunity to replenish and enhance their collections by scientific exca-

(Left) Woman carrying a casket (Late Minoan III, 1350-1100 B.C.) (Right) Side of a painted sarcophagus (Cretan, 1350 B.C.)

vations are apt to re-enter the antiquities market, thereby giving renewed stimulus to clandestine, unrecorded excavations, and to other activities of professional dealers in antiquities, including the forgery of works of art.

Sponsorship. Among the European countries, archaeological work is generally conducted directly by government agencies or under the direct supervision of a government agency. Archaeological expeditions from the United States are sponsored almost entirely by learned institutions such as universities, museums, antiquarian societies such as the Archaeological Institute of America, various state societies, and schools of archaeology or ancient studies. Where museums sponsor excavations, it is with the hope of obtaining art objects for display and publication, in addition to historical material. Funds are supplied mainly from private sources, endowment, specific individual gifts, or educational foundations such as the Carnegie, Rockefeller, and Bollingen Foundations, and the Viking Fund; however, the United States government, through the Smithsonian Institution, has financed important excavations, and several state governments, acting through state universities or museums, have supported excavations at Indian or other sites within their own borders. In 1949, the tendency to use Federal and state funds appeared to be on the increase. A few expeditions have been financed and conducted by private individuals.

Archaeological Institutions. The Archaeological Institute of America was founded in 1879. It publishes a technical quarterly, the *American Journal of Archaeology;* a popular quarterly, *Archaeology;* an annual *Bulletin;* and an informal *Newsletter.* The Institute has sponsored seven schools of ancient studies: the American School of Classical Studies at Athens; the Classical School of the American Academy in Rome; the American Schools of Oriental Research in Jerusalem and Baghdad; the School of American Research, Santa Fe; the American School of Prehistoric Research, with field offices in London, Paris, and Algiers; and the Center of Near Eastern Studies, to be located in Cairo. The American Anthropological Association and the Society

for American Archaeology are particularly identified with field work and research in the archaeology of the Americas. Most states and most countries have both public archaeological agencies and private archaeological or antiquarian societies.

J. J.

PREHISTORIC OLD WORLD ARCHAEOLOGY

Prehistoric archaeology, the science of reconstructing human history before the appearance of inscriptions or written documents by study of material traces, such as pottery, implements, and weapons of flint, stone, or metal, burials, and remains of fields and houses, is of quite recent origin. The people of Classical times speculated in a poetical way on the remote ages of man; those of the Middle Ages gave no thought to them at all. Interest in material remains of the past was first stimulated at the time of the Renaissance when men began to seek out the art and monuments of Classical antiquity. During the centuries which followed, interest began to spread to the antiquities of the barbarous peoples from whom the nations of northwestern Europe had sprung, but it was not until the closing decades of the eighteenth century that research into the prehistoric origins of human society began to be carried on in a scientific manner.

For a hundred years or so, excavators devoted themselves almost entirely to the exploration of burial mounds, an activity which had really grown out of treasure seeking and ultimately from tomb robbing. Even so, methods of excavation gradually improved and the actual finds accumulated to the point at which they began to demand classification. In 1836 the Danish archaeologist, Christian Jurgensen Thomsen, first demonstrated in a guide to the collections at Copenhagen, by the so-called Three-Period System, the successive existence of periods during which stone, bronze, and iron were the leading materials in use for toolmaking.

An immense stimulus was given to prehistoric research by the publication of Charles Darwin's *Origin of Species* (1859) and by Thomas Huxley's ardent advocacy of it. Previous to this, many discoveries of flint implements associated with remains of extinct animals had been made, as in the Somme

Valley of France, and at Kent's Hole, Torquay, England, but these had generally been ignored or ascribed to the Flood. Once the biological evolution of man over long periods of time was accepted by men of science, however, such discoveries were no longer anomalous, but were eagerly sought. From this time forward intensive research was directed to discovering the earliest steps by which man and his hominid forebears ascended from brutishness toward a civilized existence.

Already by 1865 sufficient progress had been made for it to be possible for Sir John Lubbock (later Lord Avebury) to distinguish two main stages in the Stone Age, namely, an immensely long Paleolithic, or Old Stone, Age during which man subsisted by hunting and gathering, and a much shorter Neolithic, or New Stone, Age in which he cultivated the soil and domesticated animals. During the following generation or two the main divisions of the Bronze and Iron Ages were worked out, and the existence of a Mesolithic Period intermediate between the Paleolithic and Neolithic was recognized. The significance of western Asia and of the Nile Valley as sources of higher civilization had been accepted during the nineteenth century, but especially fruitful excavations were carried out during the period 1918-1939 in Syria, Assyria, and Sumer following the eviction of the Turks as a result of World War I. During the same period the search for the earliest races of human culture was extended over the whole of Asia as far east as China, Burma, Siam, and Java, as well as over the greater part of Africa.

THE STONE AGES

The Paleolithic, or Old Stone, Age. The earliest definite traces of tool-making hominids date from early in the Pleistocene Period of geological time, perhaps half a million years ago, and are referred by prehistorians to the Paleolithic, or Old Stone, Age, although some authorities postulate a still earlier stage, which they call the Eolithic, or Dawn Stone, Age. They base their hypothesis on the chipped flints called eoliths.

The Lower Paleolithic. At first development was so slow as to be almost imperceptible, and it reveals itself mainly in refinements in the technique of flaking flint and stone. In fact, flint and stone implements are almost the sole memorial of thousands of generations of prehistoric men. This is only fitting, since such tools were the most effective means whereby early man was able to supplement his limbs in the age-long struggle with his external environment.

Three principal types of flint work and stone work date from Lower Paleolithic times. The first type consisted of pebble industries. Rough chopperlike tools were produced by striking a few flakes off natural pebbles in such a way as to produce working edges. Primitive pebble industries have been found in China (Choukoutien), Burma (Anyathian), Siam (Fingnoian), Java (Pajtitanian), Northwest India (Soan), and East Africa (Oldowayan and Kafuan). The second type comprised the core industries. Here a more regular working edge was formed by reducing a nodule, removing flakes from both faces. The finished implements or cores are often referred to as hand axes (French *coup de poing,* German *Faustkeil*), but in view of the uncertainty as to whether they were in fact held in the hand directly or mounted on a handle, some authors speak of them as bifaces. The core industries were centered in Africa, where they have been studied in Kenya and elsewhere, but they were also found in south Asia from Palestine to southern India and during interglacial periods they spread into the ice-free parts of Europe, as in the Abbevillian and Acheulian

cultures. The flake industries made up the third type. In these the finished implement was made from a flake struck from a previously prepared nodule and the core itself was discarded as waste. Such industries centered in Europe east of the Rhine and in Asia north of the mountain axis, but they also spread into western Europe, as in the Clactonian, Levalloisian, and Mousterian cultures, and into parts of Africa. Many hybrid core and flake industries are known.

Most examples of Lower Paleolithic industries are found loose in geological deposits without associated finds; the possibility of learning more about these remote times rests on the discovery of products of flint industries associated with organic materials including remains of early hominids and of their game animals. Already some such discoveries have been made, as when Lower Paleolithic core tools were found in old lake beds in Spain and in east Africa together with the bones of extinct animals killed by the ancient hunters.

The closest insight into the life of Lower Paleolithic man is given by the discoveries at Choukoutien near Peiping (Peking), where deposits over 160 ft. thick that filled collapsed caves have been carefully examined. The cave dwellers, who belonged to a group of primitive anthropians, made rough pebble tools, knew the use of fire (ash strata were encountered throughout the deposit), and utilized animal bones, although they apparently did not shape or work them. With such primitive equipment Peking man, who was right-handed and apparently capable of uttering crude cries, succeeded in dominating other animals. Deer (*Euryceros pachyosteus* and *Pseudaxis grayi*) were the commonest food animals, but remains of bison, a kind of musk ox, gazelles, horses, wild boars, leopards, tigers, hyenas, bears, rhinoceroses, and elephants were also found. The fact that remains of Peking man were found in dismembered condition mixed with animal bones and that the skulls had been opened for the extraction of the brain suggests that cannibalism was practiced.

Very little is known about the life of the earliest exponents of the flake-tool tradition, but at the close of Lower Paleolithic times in Europe the Mousterians, whose flint work belonged predominantly to this tradition, although evidences of core-tool methods have been found, sought shelter in caves and under rock shelters, while at about the same time the Levalloiso-Mousterians of Palestine inhabited the caves of

COURTESY OF THE AMERICAN MUSEUM OF NATURAL HISTORY, NEW YORK

Paleolithic painting of a horse and hind incised in the rock walls of the cave of Altamira, Spain

ANCIENT ART

COURTESY OF THE METROPOLITAN MUSEUM OF ART

(Upper left) Glazed and decorated hippopotamus is representative of Egyptian ceramics of the XII Dynasty, about 1950 B.C. It is 4½" high.
(Center left) Assyrian art of the time of Nebuchadnezzar II, 605-562 B.C., is exemplified in a frieze from Royal Procession Street, Babylon.
(Upper right) A charming example of Egyptian wood carving, this statuette of an offering bearer is from the XI Dynasty, about 2000 B.C.
(Lower left) The combat of Herakles and Triton is depicted on a Greek water jar (hydria) from the last quarter of the 6th century B.C.
(Lower right) A Greek kylix (banquet drinking cup), familiar example of Athenian art, dated about 470 B.C., shows women folding clothes.

Mount Carmel as at Et Tabūn. In physical character the Mousterians were Neanderthaloid creatures with strongly developed brow ridges, poorly formed chins, and slouching gaits. The Tabūn people, although sharing certain Neanderthaloid features, were more closely related to the modern type of man (*Homo sapiens*). On the whole the culture of these groups was at much the same general level as that of Peking man; the only marked exception is that they accorded burial to their dead, but the absence of personal adornments or of any trace of graphic art shows that they lacked the aesthetic sense which is one of modern man's most cherished and characteristic traits.

The Upper Paleolithic. In some parts of the Old World the Lower Paleolithic traditions persisted down to the end of the Pleistocene period, as in Egypt, where a Levalloisian culture continued to evolve without interruption. Elsewhere, notably in southwestern and central Europe and in parts of western Asia, new and infinitely more fertile cultures made their appearance in Upper Paleolithic times. Then for the first time there was manifested what we can recognize as the spirit of modern man, a spirit embodied in races of indubitably *Homo sapiens* character. The Upper Paleolithic peoples of these favored regions revealed a fertility of invention and a tempo of progress quite unlike anything that went before. Numerous cultures can be distinguished of varying distribution, the most complete sequence being that established in the caves of France and northern Spain: namely, the Aurignacian, consisting of Chatelperronian, the Middle Aurignacian (Aurignacian proper), and the Gravettian; the Solutrian; and the Early, Middle, and Late Magdalenian. In southern Europe and north Africa we find distinct cultures called, respectively, the Capsian and the Grimaldian, in Britain the Creswellian, and in northern Germany the Hamburgian.

Especially in limestone regions caves and rock shelters were much used, but it is likely that light shelters in the open were made during seasonal migrations in pursuit of game. In regions where caves were lacking, as in large parts of southern Russia, quite elaborate houses were constructed, often with the floor scooped out of the earth, as at Gagarino. Although the flint industries of the several cultures vary widely, they are all based fundamentally on the production of blades and burins, or gravers. Bone and antlers were employed for making implements, weapons, and ornaments of a wide variety of forms. Specific hunting weapons, including spears and spear throwers, harpoons, and bows and arrows, as well as primitive fishing gear, appear for the first time.

The hunters had a keenly developed aesthetic sense. They decorated themselves with necklaces, bracelets, and girdles of perforated shells (sometimes brought from distant seas), animals' teeth, fish vertebrae, and carved bone, and some of them wore feather headdresses and knee bands; they engraved many of their most prized objects, whether spear throwers or arrow straighteners, of bone or antlers; they carved bas-reliefs

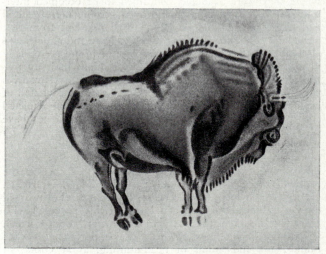

Stationary polychrome bison, one of many paintings from the cave of Altamira, Spain

and figurines; and they engraved and painted the walls and ceilings of their caves in a manner which has attracted the admiration of modern observers. No doubt an important impulse behind this cave art was the anxiety to control by magical means the wild animals on whom the lives of the hunters depended, to secure their fertility, and to ensure their capture in the chase. Indeed, there is evidence in the art itself of organized ritual with masked dancers and individuals akin to sorcerers or priests. Finally, the elaborate ceremonial burials, in which the dead were arrayed in their finery, provided with implements and weapons, and liberally scattered with red ochre, emblematic of blood, indicate some belief in life after death.

The Mesolithic, or Middle Stone, Age. The transition from Pleistocene to Holocene times was marked by profound changes in the external environment of early man. Ice sheets contracted on a dramatic scale, the earth's crust recovered where it had previously been depressed under the weight of ice, and the release of vast masses of water from melted ice brought about a general rise in ocean levels, all of which implied substantial changes in the shape of land and sea. Again, the shift of climatic zones brought about biological changes of world-wide range, temperate forests replacing arctic tundra and even invading land formerly covered by ice and, further south, subtropical desert encroaching on the former parkland and setting up stresses which may have led to the beginning of farming and so have made possible the whole future of civilization.

Before passing on to consider the origins of the Neolithic way of life, something must be said of the Mesolithic hunter-fishers, who survived the break-up of the Pleistocene and ushered in the world as we know it. Although their mode of life was essentially similar to that of their Upper Palaeolithic forebears, certain groups in northwestern Europe developed the resources of the seacoast to an extent previously unknown, taking such fish as cod and haddock. In this con-

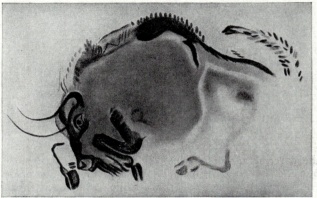

A recumbent bison recorded by primitive man on the walls of the cave of Altamira, Spain

nection one may note the introduction of boats, both dugout and skin, nets, and fishhooks (as distinct from gorges). Other innovations included compound tools, with flints set into slots, and raised sledges in the polar region. It is possible that some inventions, such as pottery in northern Europe, may have spread among Mesolithic groups from regions nearer the original centers of Neolithic culture. Caves and rock shelters, where they were available, continued to be occupied intermittently, but settlement in the open became more general and traces of huts and of coastal shell middens from that period are common. The engraving of bone and antlers, and also of amber, continued among certain groups, especially in northern Europe, where the Maglemosians built up patterns by means of small pits, apparently made by bow-drills as among the Eskimos; most of the engravings consisted of geometrical patterns, but occasionally animals were depicted and many schematic representations of human beings have been found, including some made in the pit technique on amber pendants, which were presumably of magical significance. A few amber figurines of animals are also known. Indications of a belief in a nonmaterial world include the painted pebbles from the tunnel of Mas d'Azil, in Ariège, France, which have been compared with the churingas of the Australian aborigines; and burials richly provided with grave-goods, such as the Natufian remains at Mount Carmel, in Palestine. Sometimes crowns of deer antlers, as at Téviec, France, and indications of head-hunting, as at Ofnet, in Bavaria, have been found in Mesolithic graves.

The Neolithic, or New Stone, Age. One of the greatest changes in human history was the invention of farming, the transformation of a parasitical mode of life based on hunting, fishing, and gathering, into a productive one in which man availed himself of the controlled increment of crops and herds. The Neolithic revolution, as it is sometimes called, involved a new attitude on the part of man toward his external environment and provided a basis on which successive urban civilizations could be reared. Disregarding the problem of the origins of farming in the Far East and in the New World, it is generally agreed that the change must first have been made somewhere in the region between the Nile Valley, the Oxus (modern, Amu Darya), and the Indus.

Attempts have been made in the past to deduce the earliest centers through study of the distribution of the wild species from which domesticated animals and plants are thought to have been bred. A more direct and certain method is that of archaeological excavation. This has so far revealed three main regions where primitive farmers were established before 4000 B.C., if not in some cases before 5000 B.C. The first of these regions was the Nile Valley, where the sites of Merimde-Benisalame, Fayūm, and El Badari (seat of the Badarian culture) have been excavated. The Fertile Crescent, the narrow strip of fertile land from Palestine around the northern rim of the Arabian desert to Mesopotamia, is demonstrated by the finds at Tell Hassuna near Mosul, Iraq, and those at Mersin, Turkey, to be the second. The third zone consists of the plateau of Iran and its borderlands. Its culture is evidenced by the two tells at Sialk, Iran, and the two mounds at Anau near Merv, Turkmen Republic, U.S.S.R.

Although differing in many details, the primitive farming cultures revealed by archaeology in these areas share a number of common features. (1) Technically they were founded on the working of flint and stone and of substances capable of being shaped by these. Metal, where it was used at all, was merely hammered into shape and employed to make small objects, mainly pins and beads. (2) Subsistence was based mainly on the harvesting of wheat and barley and on products derived from cattle, swine, and sheep. Among tools employed in connection with cereal growing were reaping sickles, consisting of wooden or bone handles slotted to hold flint teeth, and saddle querns for grinding the corn, comprising a rubber and a lower slab. (3) Economic life was organized in local units and in fact centered to a great extent on households. Food was produced for local consumption, and raw materials were mostly those locally available, as a rule only substances small in bulk and of magical or ceremonial character being traded from a distance. The practice of farming and especially the growing of cereals, however, made it possible to even out the food supply more adequately and silos of clay or basketry, generally sunk in the ground, were a common feature. (4) The only important division of labor was that between the sexes, and the small size of communities precluded much specialization of function. Handicrafts, which included making pottery by hand and weaving, were carried on domestically. (5) Settlements were not yet permanently fixed, and houses were made of comparatively flimsy materials, such as reeds or skins.

It was, indeed, the character of the earliest farming settlements which has made remains of them difficult to locate. In western Asia the only traces so far found have been those at the bases of the settlement mounds or tells, remains which date as a rule from the period at the very beginning of permanent settlement. These, because of their depth, have seldom been adequately explored.

Although the earliest beginnings of farming cannot yet be accurately dated, there is little doubt that a Neolithic stage of culture already existed by 5000 B.C. in Syria, Assyria, and neighboring regions and probably also on and around the Iranian plateau and in the Nile Valley. In Europe evidences of Neolithic culture are not met with until over two thousand years later and then only in Greece, at about 2000 B.C. In fact urban civilizations based on Bronze Age technology, with established dynasties and the beginnings of recorded history, appeared before the first grain was sown in Europe, and Mesolithic savages still roamed much of the continent while sophisticated townsfolk chaffered in the bazaars or worshipped in the temples of Ur or Tell Asmar.

In parts of Europe, notably in the southeast, farming peoples were able to colonize virtually uninhabited territory, but over most of the western and northwestern regions they encountered an aboriginal population sufficiently powerful in many cases to give their own distinctive impressions to the Neolithic cultures which developed. Another obstacle was

COURTESY OF THE METROPOLITAN MUSEUM OF ART

Found at Vaphio (Minoan I-III, 1600-1100 B.C.): prehistoric gold cups with repoussé decorations depicting bulls, frequent theme of Aegean culture

the covering of forest which established itself during the phase of optimum climate known as the Atlantic phase. Although varying according to altitude and soil, the forests fell into the same three zones recognizable today; namely, Mediterranean evergreen, deciduous trees, and, in the polar zone, coniferous birch. During prehistoric times the north-

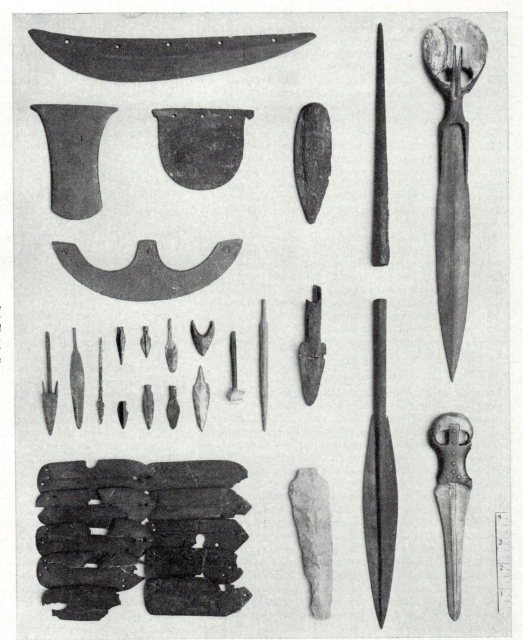

Egyptian artifacts: bronze blades from battle axes; arrow heads of bronze, flint, and wood; bronze scales from armor; flint and bronze spear heads; and bronze daggers with inlaid bone handles

ern limit of cultures based on farming was set by the margins of the deciduous forest running through southern Norway, south central Sweden, and southwestern Finland; to the north there persisted an Arctic Stone Age based on trapping and fishing, many elements of which may be traced from Scandinavia across northern Eurasia to North America. Further south, farming spread at the expense of the forest which was cleared by fire and axe. In the Mediterranean zone, where the forests had little power of resistance, deforestation rapidly ensued, but in the deciduous zone there was initiated a regular regime of clearance by burning and temporary cultivation, followed by the clearance of a new patch and the regrowth of forest trees in the abandoned area. This shifting cultivation, in which the potash from the burning played an important part and in which the chief crops were wheat, barley, and millet, was accompanied by the breeding of cattle and swine, both of which found their chief food in the forest. Except in areas where open grazing was available, sheep played only a subsidiary role and breeding of horses was quite absent among most Neolithic groups. Hunting, fishing, fowling, and plant-gathering continued to augment the food supply, and especially in coastal areas they were often of great importance.

European settlement mounds like the tells of eastern Asia are confined to Greece and the countries of southeastern Europe. Over most of the continent settlements were abandoned at fairly frequent intervals and communities rarely exceeded three hundred persons. The commonest type of house was built on a rectangular plan with timber posts, including a row down the middle to carry a gable roof, the walls being made from split timbers, wattle and daub, or turf. Where the material was available, houses were sometimes built by the use of dry-stone construction, as at Skara Brae. In Switzerland, villages were often built on piles on the margins of lakes, and the excavation of these lake villages has told us much about the food and implements and equipment made from wood, bone, and bark, because many perishable materials are preserved owing to the moist conditions. Where, as in the Rhineland, different cultures came into contact, village sites were often defended by palisades and earthworks.

Handicrafts included the working of flint and stone, the making of pottery by hand, weaving, wood-working, leatherwork, and the preparation of bark, bast, and similar substances. Flint was mined from the parent chalk, and stone was quarried, while Neolithic trade was extended to raw materials, notably flint and stone, and occasionally even to artifacts like pottery.

Over most of Europe the dead were inhumed singly, but the practice of building family tombs from great stones (megaliths) was propagated from the Mediterranean, where rock-cut versions are also commonly found, and spread around the Atlantic coasts as far as the west Baltic area. Engravings on the megalithic tombs and associated structures include representations of women, as well as schematic designs. Figurines and symbols indicative of fertility cults were especially common in the Neolithic peasant cultures throughout southeastern Europe.

THE BRONZE AGE

Long before Neolithic culture had begun to spread over Europe, the earliest urban communities had arisen in parts of western Asia and in the Nile Valley. Based ultimately on farming, which was soon improved by the introduction of the traction plough and irrigation, the civilizations whose successive traces are found in the tells or settlement mounds of the Fertile Crescent give evidence of many improvements in technology. The most notable of these was the introduction of metallurgy to supplement and ultimately to displace the working of flint and stone. The practice of casting copper and later of working bronze involved a certain specialization of labor, other signs of which are visible in the large-scale production of high-grade pottery turned on the wheel and baked in large, well-regulated kilns, and in the high degree of skill shown in the carving of stone. Permanency of settlement is implied, not only in the height of the settlement mounds, but also in the character of the buildings themselves; flimsy tents and shelters were replaced by houses of clay and ultimately of bricks, and temples of reeds or mats were ultimately transformed into great structures of stone masonry. In Egypt the growing wealth of the Predynastic people was most clearly reflected in the increasing size and elaboration of tombs, a process which was only carried to its conclusion in the Great Pyramids. Progressively wider territories were drawn upon to supply the raw materials needed for a rapidly evolving technology, and it is notable that southern Mesopotamia, which saw some of the most striking progress, is deficient in nearly all of the materials needed to equip complex urban civilizations. Hand in hand with trade went the use of personal seals and ultimately of the writing needed to maintain accounts and records, as well as means to improve communications, including sailing vessels and wheeled vehicles. Equally notable was the elaboration of warfare and the emergence of ever larger political entities, starting with cities and growing to empires. At the same time great religions with priests and elaborate temples developed from the crude nature

cults of the Stone Age, kingships emerged and around 3000 B.C. historical dynasties were established.

Metallurgy spread to Crete and the Greek mainland from Egypt and western Asia shortly after 3000 B.C. In Crete there developed the remarkable Minoan civilization with its royal palaces and largely undeciphered scripts, but leadership in the eastern Mediterranean passed to the Greek mainland around 1600 B.C., where the brilliant Mycenaean civilization flourished for some four centuries. Knowledge of the working of copper and bronze was spread among the barbarous peoples of western, central, and ultimately of northern

Double - handled Mycenaean gold cup, thought to be from Thebes (1450-1100 B.C.)

COURTESY OF METROPOLITAN MUSEUM OF ART, NEW YORK

Europe by 1000 B.C., largely through the operation of trade from the Mediterranean. Thus, Anatolian demand first caused the copper and tin of Hungary and Bohemia to be won and the native metallurgy which arose in due course was modelled on Asiatic prototypes. Again, the first metal objects to reach the Baltic were made in central European workshops and were traded for Jutland amber, much of which ultimately found its way to the Mycenaean area. Alluvial gold was another substance sought by civilized peoples, and trade in that commodity made Ireland important during the early Bronze Age of western Europe. The range of trade connections at this time is well illustrated by the discovery in burial mounds in Wessex, southern England, of objects made from Irish gold, Danish amber, and Egyptian faïence and, conversely, by the occurrence in graves at Mycenae of bronze halberds of Irish pattern and of amber discs with gold beading resembling those from the Wessex.

THE IRON AGE

The elaboration of iron working and the general adoption of wrought-iron tools occurred in parts of western Asia that had already been civilized for a long time. The first European region in which iron working was practiced was Greece, which was already on the road to Classical civilization. During the Mycenaean Period iron was still a precious substance, doubtless imported from Asia, and it was during the period of transition (1200-900 B.C.) that iron swords came to be buried more and more frequently with the dead; the use of iron became general in Greece with the beginning of the early Geometric Period around 900 B.C. It was by Greek and Etruscan colonists that iron working was brought to south and central Italy, probably by 700 B.C. Thence it spread among the still prehistoric Villanovan and Este peoples of northern Italy, crossed the Alps, and became general through Europe during the later stage of the Hallstatt culture.

The diffusion of iron working and the consequent transformation of the old Bronze Age technology was brought about partly by the spread of the Hallstatt culture westward down the Rhine, across France, and into Iberia, and eastward to the Oder and Vistula, and partly by the spread of the Scythian nomads across southern Russia and into central Europe. All the while, also, the culture of the prehistoric iron-users was being quickened by influences from Greek and Greco-Etruscan civilization, notably from the Greek colony at Marseille and from across the Alps.

The working of these diverse influences, Greek, Etruscan, and Scythian, on the Hallstatt tradition brought about the start, about 400 B.C. in southwestern Germany and neighboring areas, of a distinctively Celtic style of art in which Classical motives were transmuted by the native genius to produce a new, unique synthesis. The La Tène culture spread rapidly eastward over the Danubian territories into southeastern Europe and ultimately into Asia Minor, and westward over France, Belgium, and Britain. Many of its lowlier artifacts, such as pottery and wooden bowls, bore the imprint of the new style which was most lavishly displayed on the ornaments and weapons of the leading families.

Farming remained the basis of economic life among the communities of the prehistoric Iron Age, but this was now carried on more intensively. The worsening of climate which affected extensive areas of northwestern Europe during the Sub-Atlantic period caused, it is true, a temporary contraction of the farming zone in parts of Scandinavia, but even where conditions were adverse, the means were greater. Thus iron scythes were available to cut the hay fodder needed in order to feed livestock in stalls for a longer period. The general use of iron tools made possible many improvements in agriculture, facilitating forest clearance and ultimately, at the end of the prehistoric period, resulting in plows capable of cutting and turning the sod. At the same time many devices from the Classical world helped to ease daily work: rotary querns made it possible to grind corn more quickly; the lathe assisted the wood worker; and the potter's wheel lightened the potter's labor. With improving food supply and growing population went increasing subdivision of labor and greater volume of trade, the latter reflected in the coinage minted during the last two centuries B.C. Society was organized on a tribal basis, and the many hill forts and fortified refuges testify to intertribal warfare. Such conditions favored the rise of a class of warrior chieftains, who accumulated much of the surplus wealth, and it was for these that the finest objects of La Tène art were made. The progressive extension of the Roman Empire brought under control the whole Celtic world with the notable exception of Ireland and parts of Scotland, and Roman influence, furthered in part by trade, affected profoundly the Teutonic barbarians beyond the frontiers of the empire. J. G. D. C.

NEW WORLD ARCHAEOLOGY

Areas. Following lines of archaeological interest rather than strict geographic limits, New World archaeology is regarded as divided into three regions: (1) the North American region, comprising all of America north of Mexico; (2) the Middle American region, including Mexico, Guatemala, British Honduras, and portions of Honduras and Salvador; and (3) the South American region, embracing all of South America as well as the West Indies and the portions of Central America not included in the Middle American region.

NORTH AMERICA

America north of Mexico lies wholly within the Temperate and Arctic zones. It is a vast region of striking physiographic and climatic contrasts. On the west is the great Cordilleran mountain complex with its intervening semiarid plateaus and desert basins. Eastward from the mountains are the Plains, the Mississippi system, and the woodlands of the East. The Appalachians form a low mountain border near the Atlantic.

Northward, into Canada, the woodlands finally give way to the cold, barren polar zone.

Archaeological Research. There has been some casual North American archaeology since the days of the first European colonization of the eastern seaboard, but organized research did not begin until about 1870. Modern archaeology in North America dates from the period 1912-1918, when interest began to focus on problems of culture chronology and distributions. In the succeeding thirty years archaeological excavations and analyses have progressed most in the southwestern United States, the Eskimo or far northern area, and parts of the eastern United States. For many sections, such as the enormous interior of Canada, little is known of the archaeology. In all regions prehistoric Americanist studies have been characterized by attempts to connect with, and interpret by means of, the ethnographic investigations among historic or modern American Indians.

The Paleo-Indian. *Origin.* Present archaeological and geological evidence indicates that the New World was first populated about 15,000 years ago by people of a Mongoloid stock emigrating from northeast Asia across the Bering Strait. At this time, during the last stage (Wisconsin) of the Pleistocene, the Bering Sea lowlands and the Arctic Coast were not glaciated, and there was an open corridor extending down the eastern slopes of the Rocky Mountains. The earliest American inhabitants, prototypes of the later American Indians, probably crossed from Siberia and found their way south along the Mackenzie River into the Great Plains. A second passage was also open between the Rockies and the Coast Range. Correlations between Old and New World cultures have not been specifically established, but the tools and weapons from the Paleo-Indian sites have a generalized resemblance to those of the transition stage between the end of the Paleolithic and the beginnings of a full Neolithic. These comparisons are, however, with Europe and not with northeastern Asia. A closer synchronization of Old and New World culture development is expected when more is known of north Asiatic archaeology.

Artifacts. The most reliable evidences of the Paleo-Indian are those pertaining to the Folsom Complex or assemblage of chipped stone artifact types. These have been found at three principal stations, all in the Great Plains: Folsom and Clovis, N. M., and Lindenmeier, Colo. At each site distinctive fluted and carefully chipped projectile points and two types of knives have been found associated with fauna now extinct in the region and under geological conditions signifying the wet period at the close of the Pleistocene. The artifacts and the campsites are those left by a people with a hunting economy. Presumably these early hunters moved eastward into the Mississippi Valley, since Folsom-like points have been found in many parts of the eastern United States; however, these finds have not been in geological contexts comparable to those of the West. Another early projectile type is the Yuman, named from a county in eastern Colorado. The Yuma points are not fluted, are somewhat different in shape from the Folsom, and are characterized by fine transverse flaking. They are definitely later than the Folsom type, and while some may belong to the early Recent geologic stage, others date even later. The Sandia Cave projectile type, from near Albuquerque, N. M., is apparently even older than the Folsom type. These points are characterized by a single notch on one side of the base. So far, however, no other sites of a "Sandia Complex" have been found. A number of other finds, chiefly in the West, are of equal antiquity to Folsom or occupy an intermediate position between these late Pleistocene hunters and the much later sedentary agriculturists. Some of these are the Ventana Cave discoveries of southern Arizona, the Abilene and Clear Fork Complexes of Texas, the Gypsum Cave finds near Las Vegas, Nev., the Cochise cultures of southeastern Arizona, and the Pinto Basin and Lake Mojave remains from the southern California desert. The Cochise and Pinto Basin-Lake Mojave artifacts reflect a gathering rather than a hunting economy. Unfortunately, there is no clear-cut evidence of human remains in association with Folsom artifacts. Human skulls or skull fragments of possible Pleistocene date have been recovered in Arizona, Texas, and Minnesota; and these, while within the range of the physical type of the modern American Indian, have a number of primitive morphological characteristics.

Eastern North America. *Archaic Period.* The temporal relationship of the preceramic or Archaic periods of eastern North America to the Paleo-Indian Folsom Complex of the West is unknown. Since, however, there is no appreciable time hiatus between the Eastern preceramic and ceramic horizons, it is believed that the old hunting cultures

CHARLES PERRY WEIMER

SERPENT MOUND, ADAMS COUNTY, OHIO

of the East are considerably later than those of the West. Some of the better-known cultural foci of the Eastern Archaic are Lamoka Lake, N. Y.; Indian Knoll, Ky.; the prepottery levels of the Ozark Bluff-Dwellers; and Tick Island, Fla. The Archaic is characterized by its hunting equipment: large chipped stone points, atlatl weights (bannerstones and boatstones), plummets, and net-sinkers. There is evidence that toward the end of the Archaic Period crude fiber-and-sand-tempered pottery made its appearance in eastern North America.

Burial Mound Stages. The next stage of Eastern prehistory is the Burial Mound I. Agriculture probably made its appearance at this time, presumably an innovation from Middle America. The idea of a prepared log-covered tomb within an earth mound, or an earth mound raised over the dead, suddenly appeared in seven places in the East. It is not known if the burial-mound concept was introduced from Middle America or Asia, or whether it developed independently in the East. Many of the old hunting devices continued over from the Archaic. Tchefuncte (Louisiana) and Adena (Ohio Valley) are typical Burial Mound I groups. The Burial Mound II Stage represents the florescence of burial-mound building and of the type of social, political, and economic organization upon which Burial Mound society was based. Pottery became more elaborate and plentiful; work in stone, copper, and bone reached an artistic peak; and the treatment of the dead dominated ceremonial life. The Ohio Valley Hopewell culture is the most brilliant example

of the Burial Mound II Stage, but similar culture groups were in existence in many parts of the East.

Temple Mound Stages. Temple Mound I Stage marks the introduction of the great truncated pyramidal mounds which were surmounted by temples and chiefs' houses. Improved agricultural techniques made for population expansion, and larger political units came into existence. The spread of the temple-mound idea and all that it represented, together with Mississippian culture, was probably carried out by an actual population migration from the central Mississippi Valley into nearly all parts of the East. Such great temple-centers as Etowah (Georgia), Aztalan (Wisconsin), and Cahokia (Illinois) were begun during this stage. Temple Mound II saw the crystallization of this system, a tendency for the temple centers to become urban centers, and the eventual decline of native Eastern culture under the impact of the Europeans, beginning about 1540. The following culture sequence and dates of the East follow conventional estimates: Temple Mound II, (A.D. 1500-1700); Temple Mound I, (1300-1500); Burial Mound II, (900-1300); Burial Mound I, (500-900); Archaic, (?-A.D. 500).

Southwestern United States. Unlike eastern North America, a horticultural economy was a precarious subsistence adjustment in the semiarid southwestern United States. The severity of the environment was an important limiting and directing factor in aboriginal cultural development in Arizona and New Mexico, and in adjacent Mexico, Utah, Nevada, and Colorado. This accounts to a large extent for the cultural self-containment of the Southwest and for its essential homogeneity. There are three main streams of cultural development which correspond to subregions and to subecological zones. In the desert of southern Arizona are the remains of the Hohokam tradition; in the plateau country of the North, centering around the intersection of the Arizona-Utah-New Mexico-Colorado boundary, is the Anasazi tradition; and in mountainous country of the Mogollon Rim, running from southwest New Mexico northwestward into Arizona, is the center of the third or Mogollon tradition. All three of these cultural stocks are characterized by sedentary communities, agriculture, and pottery. There is no close connection with the earlier Paleo-Indian groups, although there are some indications that the earliest Hohokam and Mogollon periods developed out of a late Cochise culture base.

Hohokam Culture. Hohokam pit-houses were made of wood, grass, and earth, and the villages were composed of several scattered houses. The dominant influence in Hohokam ceramics was the decoration of buff ware with red paint. The dead were cremated. In the second, or Colonial, Hohokam period extensive irrigation canals were dug and ceremonial ball courts, similar to those of Middle America, were constructed. Snaketown, in southern Arizona, is the best known of the Hohokam sites. In the Classic Hohokam Period there was an abrupt change in many aspects of the culture as the result of an invasion of people from the Anasazi region to the north. Compound "apartment house" units tended to replace the simple villages of scattered houses. The big compound dwellings were made of puddled adobe. Hohokam culture seems to have disintegrated after 1400, possibly as the result of pressure from the seminomadic Apache Indians. Quite possibly some of the descendants of the Hohokam are the modern Pima and Papago Indians who live in the region today.

Anasazi Culture. In the Anasazi area the culture history of man can be traced from early Basketmaker Period beginnings down to the present-day Pueblo Indians (Hopi and Zuñi).

COURTESY OF SANTA FE RAILWAY

This ruined pueblo on the floor of Frijoles canyon in Bandelier National Monument, New Mexico, is comprised of the remains of 200 to 300 rooms of crude masonry around a circular plaza some 150 ft. in diameter. Three kivas, circular subterranean ceremonial chambers, are sunk into the northeast side of the plaza.

The earliest houses in the north were also of the pit or semi-subterranean type, and a gradual evolution can be traced from small villages of these up to the great compound villages. Pueblo Bonito (New Mexico) and Mesa Verde (Colorado) are two outstanding examples of the latter. The dominant strain in Anasazi pottery is the motif of black decoration on a white ground, as opposed to the red-on-buff of the Hohokam. Interment was the rule in disposal of the dead. The construction of underground ceremonial chambers or kivas was a common custom. After about A.D. 1400 there was a contraction of Anasazi populations into a few centers where their descendants, the modern Pueblo Indians, live today.

Mogollon Culture. The Mogollon is the least known of the three major Southwestern prehistoric traditions, but its archaeological significance appears to be very great. It is most likely that the main movements of influence from Mexico into the Southwest came up the Mexican Sierra Madre Mountains into the Mogollon region. Culturally it is not so distinctive as either the Hohokam or the Anasazi, and appears to have been a blend of the two. On the other hand, this less specialized quality of Mogollon may indicate that it is the parent stock from which the other two diverged and specialized in their particular environments. Between A.D. 900 and 1000 influence from the Anasazi became very strong in the Mogollon, and the subsequent Mimbres culture type was the outgrowth of this fusion. Sometime after 1200 the Mimbres people deserted the area and moved south into Chihuahua. The long slow growth, the climactic flowering, and the gradual shrinkage or decay characterize all three of the Southwestern culture stocks. The growth and flowering most likely coincided with the experimentation and final achievement of an economic balance connected with agriculture under extremely difficult environmental conditions. The decay and contraction may have been the result not only of

the marauding Apaches and Navahos, but also of prolonged drought periods. Table I presents the conventional sequence dates for the three Southwestern culture growths:

TABLE I.

	Anasazi	Hohokam	Mogollon
1800 A.D.	Pueblo V	Pima	
1600			
1400	Pueblo IV		Chihuahua
1200	Pueblo III	Classic	
1000	Pueblo II	Sedentary	Mimbres / Three Circle
800	Pueblo I		San Francisco
600	Modified Basketmaker	Colonial	Georgetown
400			Pine Lawn
	Basketmaker	Pioneer	

Great Plains. This area is the open grassland extending from the Rocky Mountains to the forested borders of the Mississippi Valley, and from Texas north to Canada. Archaeological research has shown that the later cultures, those following the early Paleo-Indian Folsom hunters in this region, are linked to both the eastern United States and to the Southwest. These linkages, however, are of a general sort, and prehistoric life on the Plains developed as a fairly self-contained and integrated unit. At Signal Butte, in western Nebraska, there is evidence of a hunting people who occupied a time position somewhere intermediate between the Folsom horizon and the horticultural tribes. Between A.D. 500 and 1000, domesticated food plants were introduced into the area, and direct Eastern influences are found near Kansas City in the form of Hopewell-type burial mounds and artifacts. From 1300 to 1600 a rich horticultural subsistence was established by the Upper Republican and Nebraska prehistoric cultures. After 1600 the introduction of the horse changed the sedentary-horticultural way of life in the Plains, and the Indians became mobile hunters. The Pawnee, Sioux, and other historic or modern Indian groups of the area are their descendants.

Far West. The prehistoric peoples of the Far West, like their historic descendants, were hunters, fishers, and gatherers

Tuzigoot ruin, near Clarkdale, Arizona, contains many implements, jewelry, and pottery of the original dwellers. The original building was begun in A.D. 1000 and abandoned in A.D. 1400. Since then eighty-six ground floor rooms have been excavated and two council chambers have been reconstructed.

who did not practice agriculture. The region is diversified both naturally and culturally. A culture sequence from central California stretches from somewhere in the vicinity of 1000 B.C. up to historic times. The sequence shows a gradual increase in artifacts connected with hunting, fishing, and gathering as well as ornamental objects. Stone and shell were the principal materials. Pottery, never important, appears very late in the sequence as an imported idea from the East. The crafts in which the most was accomplished were basketry and steatite carving. In the Plateau area, between the Cas-

cade and Rocky Mountains, the prehistoric remains suggest a similar economic orientation, as do those of California. Almost nothing is known of culture chronology. Presumably the Plain and Northwest Coast influences observed in the modern tribes of this area are the result of rather recent diffusions. There seems to have been some tradition of ornamental carving in the area, and in some sections stone and bone tools are decorated with life forms. The archaeology of the Northwest Coast region, from northern California to southern Alaska, is little known, but the available evidence suggests that the prehistoric people along these shores lived in much the same way as their historic descendants. They were a hunting and fishing people, lacking agriculture and pottery. They were wood craftsmen, and wood was used for utensils, canoes, and houses. Modern Northwest Coast houses, canoes, totem poles, and incidental manufactures are a continuation of this tradition.

Far North. The Eskimo and Eskimo culture is spread from northeastern Siberia to Greenland. The severe polar environment has been a crucial factor in the set and direction of aboriginal subsistence and culture in the Far North. Although regional and chronological variations exist, they are essentially minor in terms of the total context. Archaeologists have attempted to rationalize a "basic Eskimo" culture by eliminating traits which appear late in the sequences. Their conclusions are that Eskimo culture developed in Siberia and was brought to the New World by the latest of the Mongoloid immigrants of prehistoric times. The original Eskimo culture is believed to have been based upon hunting, fishing, and collecting, with more of an orientation toward the land than the later Eskimo periods indicate. Stone and bone tools were used, and bone harpoon points were common. Houses were simple tent-shelters or semisubterranean constructions. Subsequently the Eskimo spread down the Pacific Coast into southwestern Alaska and eastward, eventually reaching Greenland, where they came in contact with medieval Norse settlements between A.D. 1200 and 1400. Asiatic influences probably continued intermittently for some time after the first Eskimo were established in America. This may have been by way of the Bering Strait or across the Aleutians. In the early periods, especially in the Northwest, there was an elaboration of ivory carving strongly suggesting Asiatic stimulation. Later there was somewhat of an artistic decline, but technological proficiency increased, as indicated by tools and equipment. By historic times the Eskimo had achieved one of the most remarkable cultural adjustments to a difficult climate that has ever been recorded. Table II gives conventional sequence estimates for the Eskimo:

TABLE II.

	Northwestern	Southwestern	Eastern
1800 A. D.			
	Modern	Modern	Modern
1600			
		Late Aleut	
		Late Kachemak	
1400	Post-Punuk		
			Inugsuk
			Thule
1200			
1000			

Table II (Continued)

	Northwestern	Southwestern	Eastern
800	Punuk-Birnirk	Middle Aleut	
		Middle Kachemak	
600			Dorset
400			
200	Old Bering Sea Ipiutak	Early Aleut Early Kachemak	
0	Okvik		
	Hypothetical Original Eskimo Culture		

MIDDLE AMERICA

Area and Environment. The archaeological culture area of Middle America includes Mexico south of the 27th parallel, Guatemala, British Honduras, and portions of Honduras and Salvador. Both the northern and southern boundaries are defined, somewhat vaguely, in terms of prehistoric distributions. On the north the cultural influences of Central Mexico thin out and disappear somewhere short of influences spreading southward from the Southwestern United States; on the south the Maya influence merges with the cultures of Southern Central America in Honduras and Salvador. Middle America, as defined, is either mountainous and temperate or low and tropical. Along the Gulf of Mexico and the Caribbean Sea there is a low-lying jungle belt which extends inland into the Yucatán Peninsula as far as central Guatemala. On the Pacific side the mountains are much nearer the ocean. Inland are high plateaus and valleys.

Archaeological Research. Investigations have centered in the Valley of Mexico, in the Maya area of the Yucatán Peninsula and Guatemala, in Oaxaca, and in southern Vera Cruz. There has also been some work in northwestern and northeastern Mexico, but many rich archaeological zones have not been systematically studied. Among these are west-central Mexico, central Vera Cruz, and the region south of Mexico City. Research has not yet demonstrated the time and manner in which the prehistoric cultures of Middle America influenced, and were influenced by, those of North or South America. That there were connections is not doubted, and the determination of these relationships remains one of the most fascinating problems for American archaeologists.

The Paleo-Indian. The most convincing evidence of early man in Middle America was reported in 1946 by De Terra. Two horizons of lithic tools and weapons have been found in late Pluvial and post-Pluvial strata in the Valley of Mexico. The earlier of these, the San Juan industry, was associated with extinct fauna. Possibly it correlates in time with the Folsom Complex of North America. The later horizon, the Chalco, may be approximately contemporaneous with the Cochise culture of southern Arizona. The Chalco, like the Cochise, suggests a small-game hunting and gathering culture as opposed to the big-game hunters of the Pluvial.

Central Mexico. *Middle Cultures.* The earliest agricultural periods of the Valley of Mexico have been designated both as the Archaic and as the Middle Cultures. The latter term is more appropriate in view of the fact that earlier evidences of man's occupation are being brought to light. In the earliest sites of the Middle Cultures there is evidence of settled community life in large permanent villages, and maize agriculture is seen to have been well established. Ceramic craftsmanship is competent, with monochrome and incised pottery predominating; hand-made figurines are extremely common. Toward the end of the Middle Cultures specialized religious centers appear. The great terraced mound of Cuicuilco was built at this time.

Teotihuacán Culture. The Middle Cultures were succeeded by the Classical Toltec or Teotihuacán culture. The origins of this civilization lay partly in the preceding Middle Periods and are partly attributable to migrations of new people into the Valley of Mexico from the outside, probably from Puebla to the south or Michoacán to the west. The Teotihuacán Period was one of artistic virtuosity and architectural magnificence. The famous stucco-covered or cloisonné pottery was made at this time. The mold was introduced for the manufacture of pottery figurines. Toward the end of the Teotihuacán Period new religious, and probably political, ideas made themselves felt, and the general unrest of the times culminated in the desertion of the great site. Azcapotzalco and Tula succeeded Teotihuacán as the leading centers of the area.

Chichimec Culture. This was the beginning of the Chichimec Period, an interval of even greater social and political unrest in the Valley of Mexico. It was during this time that many of the Central Mexican tribes moved southward. These emigrants were the "New Toltecs" as distinct from the Classical or "Old Toltecs" who built the pyramids at Teotihuacán.

Aztec Culture. Out of the confusion of the Chichimec Period the Aztecs, or Tenochas, emerged as the dominant power in the Valley of Mexico. In many respects they were less civilized than their predecessors, the people of Teotihuacán. Art and architecture, although abundant, lost something in aesthetic quality. The cultural interest of Aztec times had shifted to war and empire-building. When the Spaniards arrived in 1519, the Aztecs dominated a large part of Mexico from their capital at Tenochtitlán.

Other Central Mexican Regions. During this long cultural development in the Valley of Mexico other regions of Central Mexico were probably experiencing parallel changes. In Puebla the huge pyramid of Cholula was an important religious site during the "New Toltec" Era, and it is quite likely that earlier deposits will eventually be found there. Northwest of Mexico City, in the Tarascán area, recent investigations have shown prehistoric sequences paralleling in age and partially in content those of the Valley of Mexico. Less spectacular in architecture, the Tarascán region was an important center for lacquer and copper work in the later periods. Eastward from the Valley of Mexico, in central Vera Cruz, is an area occupied by Totonac peoples at the time of the Conquest. It is not known how long they had been there, but cultural connections between central Vera Cruz and the Valley of Mexico can be demonstrated back to the early Teotihuacán Periods. The region is known for its curious carved stone "yokes."

Northwest Mexico. To the northwest of the Valley of Mexico, in Colima, Jalisco, Nayarit, southern Guanajuato, Zacatecas, Durango, and Sinaloa, the archaeology, although regionally distinct, stems from the Valley of Mexico, Michoacán, and Puebla. Most of the materials so far recovered date from the latter half of the Central Mexican sequences, after the decline of Teotihuacán. Many of the sites, even as remote as Sinaloa, can be attributed to emigrants from Central

Montezuma Castle, a true cliff dwelling in an excellent state of preservation, fifty-five miles from Prescott, Arizona, was set aside as a national monument, December 8, 1906. A ranger is pointing out the ruins at the base of the cliff.

Mexico during the Chichimec Period of unrest. This does not mean that earlier periods are not likely to be found in these areas; on the contrary, connections northward into the prehistoric cultures of the southwestern United States will probably be found on an earlier time level.

The Huasteca. The Huasteca is the area in lowland Vera Cruz and adjacent Tamaulipas at the mouth of the Panuco River. The modern city of Tampico is in the vicinity. At the time of the Conquest a Mayan-speaking group of Indians lived in this territory. Culturally, they were not like Maya, lacking the architectural and intellectual accomplishments of the Yucatecán-Guatemalan people. A long sequence in the Huasteca shows some very interesting cross-relationships. In the two earliest periods, which are thought to be approximately coeval with the Valley of Mexico Middle Cultures, the ceramics are monochrome and bear close relationship with the earliest pottery of the lowland Maya. The third Huasteca Period has affinities with the early periods at Teotihuacán; the fifth period correlates in ceramics with the "New Toltec" expansion into the Maya area and with the Chichimec Period in the Valley of Mexico. Strangely enough, the sixth and final Huasteca Period bears no close kinship to Aztec culture. The ceramics are quite distinct from anything known in Mexico. This is the style commonly called Huasteca pottery. It has been found as far north along the Gulf Coast as the Texas border. The Huasteca appears to have been an area which maintained some degree of cultural independence but which, from time to time, was strongly influenced by affairs in the principal centers of Middle America. The area has special interest as it is here that connections between the southeastern United States and Middle America were eventually to be uncovered.

Oaxaca. The mountains and valleys of the Pacific slope south of Mexico City, in the state of Oaxaca, were the home of two important cultural traditions, the Zapotec and the Mixtec. Monte Alban, one of the most picturesque sites in Middle America, was the ancient Zapotecan capital, abandoned before the arrival of the Spanish. The earliest Monte Alban period has the less specialized art, the monochrome ceramics, and the absence of imposing structures that characterize the Central Mexican Middle Cultures and the earliest Maya area periods. Subsequently, a distinctive Zapotecan style was evolved in pottery, architecture, and sculpture; its closest ties were with the early classic period of the Maya but it was, nevertheless, a local development. This, and the centuries which followed, were the great period of Monte Alban and the Zapotecs. The abandonment of Monte Alban by the Zapotecs was probably the result of their conquest by the Mixtecs from near-by Mitla. There is evidence of a very brief Mixtec period at Monte Alban. One of the most interesting features of Zapotec culture is the presence of glyphs and numerals in the earliest Monte Alban period. Whether this was due to Maya influence or whether the Zapotecs participated in an early widespread system of glyph writing is unknown. In any event, Zapotec writing apparently never developed beyond a simple stage. Mitla, noted for its geometric stone wall frescoes and cruciform tombs, was not founded until Monte Alban was well advanced into the third period. The city was conquered by the Aztecs in the fifteenth century. Oaxacan civilizations are noted for their fine metalwork of the late periods. Some students have seen South American and Central American influences in this as well as in certain pottery designs from the region. Because of its geographical position it may have been a point of contact for traders coming from the south by sea.

Southern Vera Cruz. This area, and certain distinctive

stone sculptures found therein, have been referred to as Olmec. This is an old tribal designation mentioned in Aztec histories. Its applicability to the archaeological remains of the southern Vera Cruz area has been questioned, and, recently, the term La Venta has been standardized as the name for the archaeological culture of the region. Some of the most striking art of Mexico, particularly in stone sculpture, is of

COURTESY OF PAN AMERICAN WORLD AIRWAYS SYSTEM

El Castillo, famed Mayan pyramid-temple at Chichen Itza, Yucatan, dedicated to the Feathered Serpent, patron deity of Chichen Itza.

this Olmec or La Venta style. The "cat-face," "baby-face," "negroid," and "mongoloid" motives are characteristic. These do not imply a direct connection with the Mongoloid or Negroid races of the Old World; they are used merely as descriptive labels. Another notable feature of La Venta culture is the presence of occasional bar-and-dot numeral dates, comparable to those of the Maya system. One of these dates is inscribed on the famous Tuxtla statuette; another was discovered by Dr. M. W. Stirling at the site of Tres Zapotes. The latter is of the seventh cycle of the Maya "long-count" and is the earliest inscribed date yet to be found in Middle America. The associated ceramics at Tres Zapotes indicate that the seven cycle date is contemporaneous with pottery similar to that of the earliest periods of the Maya area, before the Maya began to carve dates upon stone. Later ceramic periods at Tres Zapotes and other La Venta type sites correlate chronologically with Classic Maya, Teotihuacán, and the third period of Monte Alban. It is believed that most of the fine stone sculpture mentioned above dates from middle Tres Zapotes periods and is contemporary with Classic Maya.

The Maya. The Maya area is probably the most famous archaeological region of the New World. Its prehistory can be most conveniently divided into three zones: the highlands of Guatemala; the lowland Petén of Guatemala; and the lowlands of the Yucatán Peninsula. The ceramic styles of the highlands and the lowlands are quite similar, but the well-known architecture, the stone sculpture, the stelae, and the "long-count" dating system are found only in the lowlands. In all parts of the Maya area there are evidences of early ceramic periods comparable to those of the Valley of Mexico Middle Cultures, early Huasteca, early Tres Zapotes, and early Monte Alban. In the highlands this horizon is known as the Miraflores, in the lowlands, as Mamon and Chicanel. The Maya Classic or "Great" Period follows these simpler cultures and at approximately A.D. 1000 the old Maya tradition was broken by invasions from Central Mexico. An outstanding Maya site of the highlands is Kaminaljuyu, near Guatemala City; typical Classic sites of lowland Guatemala are Palenque, Uaxactún, and Tikal; and in Yucatán such sites as Chichen Itza and Uxmal were founded as typically Maya centers but were captured and rebuilt by the Mexicans. A phenomenon of Maya history was the shift of populations

COURTESY OF THE AMERICAN MUSEUM OF NATURAL HISTORY

The Aztec Calendar Stone, based on the calendar of the early Maya, embodies the history of the world and is thought to record certain mythological events important to the Aztec religion.

out of the Petén and adjacent areas of Honduras into Yucatán. This seems to have taken place at about the time of the Mexican Conquest. Soil exhaustion has been offered as one explanation for this desertion of the southern cities; possibly the invading Mexicans had something to do with it; in any event, lowland Maya civilization centered in Yucatán after

A.D. 1000. Although it was previously believed that this northward migration was into virgin territory, more recent evidence has shown that the Maya were in Yucatán as early as the Chicanel Period.

Art and Architecture. Maya architecture is expressed in the theocratic temple centers. These sites, administrative and religious capitals rather than actual cities, were usually grouped on a prepared platform. Steep pyramids were built on the platform in various plaza-type arrangements, and the actual temples were constructed on the tops of the pyramids. Great solid architectural masses, like the platforms or pyramids, were constructed of earth and rubble and faced with limestone masonry. Temples and palaces were also constructed with rubble fill between walls in some instances. Walls were carefully faced with limestone blocks set in place with slaked-lime cement. Characteristic Maya architectural features include the corbelled rather than the true arch, the flying facade, and the roof-comb. The last two are massive ornamental features added to the tops of temples or palaces to give added height and dignity. Sculpture, both carved and plastic, was characteristically in relief. Life forms, distinctly conventionalized, and geometric elements were both used in decoration. Ceramics of the Classic Maya are artistically painted in three or four colors. Priests, warriors, and dignitaries are often represented in various ceremonial attitudes.

Writing and Time-Counting. The outstanding intellectual achievement of the New World was the Mayan system of writing and time-counting. The recording of time was made possible by a system of hieroglyphs or rudimentary writing combined with a considerable knowledge of astronomy. In addition to these two factors the Maya had made use of the *tzolkin* or *tonalamatl,* a permutation system with two numbering series, 20 and 13. This cycle or *tzolkin* was widespread in Middle America, undoubtedly very old, and not necessarily a Maya invention. It will be recalled that the La Venta or Olmec civilization had developed a similar time-counting system as early, or possibly even earlier, than the Maya. In any event, the Maya carried the cyclic permutation, along with all aspects of the calendar and of writing, to much greater heights than did any other aboriginal American people. With these basic elements the Maya had evolved a sys-

TABLE III.

	Valley of Mexico	Oaxaca	Southern Vera Cruz	Lowland Maya	Highland Maya
A.D. 1500	Aztec	Monte Alban V	Cerro de las Mesas (Upper)	Mexican Absorption	Mexican Absorption
		Monte Alban IV			
	Chichimec			Mexican Occupation	Mexican Occupation
A.D. 1000	Teotihuacán { V IV III II I	Monte Alban III		Tepeu	Pamplona Amatle
		Monte Alban II	Cerro de las Mesas (Lower)	Tzakol	Esperanza
A.D. 500	*Middle Cultures* Cuicuilco Ticemán Copilco Zacatenco	Monte Alban I	Middle Tres Zapotes (La Venta style) Lower Tres Zapotes	Chicanel Mamom	Miraflores

TEMPLE OF THE SUN, A PRE-INCA RUIN AT MACCHU PICCHU, PERU

tem of reckoning time over periods of several hundreds of years as early as A.D. 300. Glyph dates were carved on stone and painted on pottery. Table III correlates Maya relative chronology with other areas of Middle America.

SOUTH AMERICA

The Andes form the western backbone of South America. In Chile and Peru they constitute a high wall separating a narrow coastal strip on the Pacific from the Amazonian drainage or the lowland plains of the east. There are occasional intermontane valleys and high plateaus or *punas* within the Andean block, and these regions have been important places of human habitation in past as well as present times. In the north the Andes divide and finger out into the Colombian jungles. The other two highland areas of South America are in the Guianas and in southeastern Brazil. Neither area compares with the Andes, both being only relatively high, dry plateaus rising above the tropical lowlands. Much of eastern South America is tropical lowland, centering on the Amazonian and Orinocan river systems. In the southeast there are low temperate plains around the Paraná River system. Parts of the flat lands of the Gran Chaco of Paraguay, Bolivia, and Argentina are semiarid and desolate; parts are more like the tropical lowlands. In the south the pampas and the Patagonia region of Argentina are chiefly flat grasslands with a temperate climate.

Archaeological Research. Archaeological investigation in South America has centered in Peru and highland Bolivia. Considerable work has been done in Argentina, and the West Indies have recently been intensively studied. There

has been a smattering of excavation and analysis in Chile, Ecuador, Colombia, Central America, and Venezuela. The vast interior of the Amazonian drainage region is virtually untouched.

The Paleo-Indian. A number of evidences of early man have been recorded from South America. Near Managua, Nicaragua, bison tracks and human footprints have been found in volcanic deposits. Since the bison has long been extinct in Central America, this association of tracks argues for considerable antiquity of man in this part of the New World. Another find is the Punin skull of Ecuador. This also came from volcanic ash in possible association with extinct fauna. Physically, the skull is an archaic Indian form and could be quite ancient, although this evidence is not conclusive in establishing a relative date. The volcanic deposit cannot be dated with the accuracy comparable to the dating of glacial activity in North America; hence the find remains suggestive of antiquity but nothing more. Association of a human skeleton with extinct Pleistocene fauna was demonstrated in South America with the announcement of the Confins man from Minas Geraes, Brazil. The finds were made in a cave under the cover of several feet of sedimentary deposits and stalagmitic overburden. No chronological estimates can be given, but this is an extremely important find. Interesting finds, including the association of extinct fauna with human artifacts, have been made in southern Patagonian caves. The projectile points, in this case, although unlike those in later horizons in southern South America, are not the North American Folsom, Sandia, or Yuma types. The dating of the Patagonian remains has been placed at 3,000 to about 5,000 years ago. This estimate was based upon geological observations including land uplift, lake subsidence, and volcanic activity. As indicated, the physical nature of the early inhabitants of South America, as revealed by Punin, Confins, and Lagoa Santa (Brazil) finds, was that of a dolichocephalic early American Indian type. The whole question of the Paleo-Indian in South America will revolve around the matter of geological correlations between South America and North America. Unquestionably, man has been in South America for several thousand years; whether or not the South American remains found in association with fauna generally considered characteristic of the Pleistocene will be adjudged coeval with North American Folsom finds remains to be seen.

Central Andes. The archaeology of the Central Andes is exceedingly rich and has been demonstrated to have great chronological depth. In prehistoric times the Peruvian coast and highlands and the adjacent highlands of Bolivia were the most densely occupied regions of the New World. Conservative estimates place the population of the Inca Empire, just before the Spanish Conquest, at six to seven million persons. Sequentially, the area can be divided into six major temporal and cultural horizons.

First Stage. The earliest inhabitants, who lived along the coast as well as back in the highlands, were hunters, gatherers, and fishers. This type of life probably went on for several hundred years before the advent of maize horticulture. The first domestication of maize is an unknown reference point in New World prehistory, but some authorities have hypothesized that the eastern slopes of the Andes or the lowlands of Bolivia may have been the original location. In any event, its appearance in Peru is estimated at somewhere between 1000 B.C. and the beginning of the Christian era. With the advent of agriculture, Central Andean culture underwent a rapid transformation. Population increased and stable village life became possible.

Second Stage. This leads to the second major stage of prehistory for the area, generally known as the Chavín horizon. Chavín culture is remarkably uniform over a considerable area. The type site is Chavín de Huantar in the Central Andes. The Chavín site is known for its stone structures and sculpture, but the art style represented there, dominated by the feline motif, is very similar to that of the stucco sculptures of the Nepeña Valley of the coast and the Cupisnique ceramic art of the Chicama, another coastal valley. Linkages have already been demonstrated between Chavín ceramics and those of the earliest pottery period of Ancon. In brief, the Chavín horizon, the first pan-Peruvian period following the prehorticultural, appears to be the one in which the basic sedentary-horticultural arts and crafts were spread throughout the Central Andes. In addition, a distinctive art style based on the "cat-god" motif unifies the horizon.

Third Stage. The third major horizon is the one in which a number of the Peru-Bolivian regions attained their peak in arts, crafts, and in some cases, architecture. Nazca, with its excellent textiles and polychrome ceramics, is the south coastal culture of this horizon; Classic Tiahuanaco is a south highland parallel; Mochica (Early Chimu), with its brilliant emphasis on ceramic sculpture, is the north coast equivalent. Recuay in the central highlands, Early Lima on the central coast, and the slightly earlier Paracas Cavernas culture of the south coast probably fall into this developmental bracket. It appears to have been a period of local classicism, small kingdoms, and society dominated by both religious and secular forces.

Fourth Stage. The fourth horizon probably represents the first pan-Peruvian empire. Its point of origin is unknown, but the art style from which it takes its name is closely related to the south highland Tiahuanaco type. The influence seems to have spread from either the central or south highlands down to the south coast and northward to the centers of the Mochica culture in the Moche and Chicama valleys. Big religious centers and temples of the old local cultures were taken over and rebuilt or reused as a result of this new cultural force. Pachacamac, an old Early Lima center on the central coast, and Moche, a Mochica temple on the north coast, are two such examples. Both sites became Tiahuanaco burying grounds. It seems quite likely that the Tiahuanaco obliteration of the styles which had preceded it represents an actual conquest and invasion in many parts of the Central Andes.

Fifth Stage. The fifth horizon is marked by the resurgence of localism. The art styles of this period are often blends of the old local cultures with the Tiahuanacoid. Chimu of the north coast is one of the best known. The Chancay style of the central coast and the Ica style of the south coast are examples of such styles and cultures that arose after the subsidence of the Tiahuanacoid influence.

Sixth Stage. The sixth horizon, and the only one that can be timed with accuracy, is the Incaic. The Incas began to expand their empire from around Cuzco, their capital in the Central Andes, about A.D. 1438. By 1527 they had brought under their control all the coastal and highland territory from Quito, Ecuador, to the Rio Maule in Chile. Evidences of Inca influence are seen in the ceramics and architecture of the areas which they overran. Table IV presents conventional dating estimates and correlations in Central Andean archaeology:

TABLE IV.

	North Coast	Central Highlands	Central Coast	South Coast
1530 A.D.				
	Inca		Inca	Inca
	Chimu	Inca	Chancay	Ica
1000	Tiahuanacoid	Tiahuanacoid	Tiahuanacoid	Tiahuanacoid
	Mochica	Recuay	Early Lima	Nazca B
500				
	Gallinazo Salinar	White-on-red	Interlocking White-on-red	Nazca A Paracas Cavernas
0	Chavín	Chavín	Chavín	

Southern Andes. The archaeological culture area of the Southern Andes lies to the south of the Peru-Bolivia region; it embraces the highlands of northwest Argentina and the northern two thirds of Chile. The physiography is similar to the Central Andes; the climate is both colder and drier.

Atacameño Culture. Two principal culture types dominate the Southern Andes. In the north the Chilean provinces of Tacna, Arica, Tarapacá, Antofagasta, and Atacama, and parts of the northwest Argentine provinces of Los Andes, Salta, and Jujuy, comprise the region of the Atacameño. Today the descendants of the old Atacameño Indian stock have become Europeanized, but the name is used to apply to the archaeological remains of the district. This Atacameño culture was oriented around agriculture and herding. Agriculture was precarious in the area, and it centered in the few favorable little coastal valley oases where irrigation was possible. The Chilean valleys are much smaller than those of coastal Peru. Herding was confined to the llama and alpaca. Villages were rather small and consisted of a few stone houses within an enclosure wall. Woodwork was their most distinctive craft, with carved wooden tablets and nose tubes for taking snuff as characteristic artifacts. Pottery was polychrome and apparently derived from Central Andean inspirations, dating from late Tiahuanaco times.

Diaguita Culture. The other principal culture, the Diaguita, also named for tribes long assimilated, lies to the south. It is found mainly in Argentina, in the provinces of Salta, Tucumán, Catamarca, La Rioja, and San Juan, but it also extends through the Chilean provinces of Atacama and Coquimbo. Diaguita culture was essentially agricultural. Diaguita populations were larger, the country more favorable, and the material wealth greater than was the case for the Atacameño. Work in copper, bronze, gold, and silver was fairly common and competent. Ceramics, particularly those of the earlier Diaguita periods, show affinities to the Central Andes.

Other Cultures. Other cultures or tribes of the Southern Andes include the peoples of the Quebrada de Humuhuaca in northwest Argentina and the Araucanians of central Chile. Both were agriculturalists and both show relationships to the Atacameño and Diaguita. In the vicinity of Arica, on the north Chilean coast, and farther south around Taltal, evidences of earlier cultures have recently been found. Some of these are preceramic and prehorticultural and relate, in a general way, to the prehorticultural horizon of the Peruvian coast types.

Northern Andes. The northern Andes area is one of great cultural diversification and complexity. The prehistoric cultures were rich but seem to have been intensely regionalized; no widespread stylistic phenomena, such as those which characterize the Central Andes, have been noted. The highlands of Colombia and Ecuador compose the area, which differs from the Central or South Andean block in being divided into several intermontane valleys, many of which are tropical in part. Except for the Ecuadorian coast, it seems to have been an area of relatively small settlements and, with the exception of the Chibcha in Colombia, of little large-scale political unification. Relative chronologies are only in the formative stages of research, but general trends in ceramics and other crafts show simple beginnings with plain or incised wares, the introduction of negative painting, combined negative and positive painting, and a return to simple plastic treatment (incision and appliqué). The craft peak was in the middle periods of three-color negative-positive painting. Cast gold, for which Colombia is famous, was particularly elaborate at this time. The Quimbaya style is the most noted. The earlier periods are known for carved stone monuments such as those at San Agustín in southern Colombia and for the painted underground tombs of the nearby Tierradentro region. Although unplaced chronologically, the rich Manabí culture of the Ecuadorian coast may have certain affiliations with San Agustín. Throughout, the lack of specific stylistic resemblances to the Central Andes is striking and curious.

Southern Central America. The cultures of southern Central America have a general resemblance to those of the Northern Andes. Ceramics, though not identical in style, bear affinity; metallurgy, especially goldwork, shows a definite linkage. In Panama, Costa Rica, and Nicaragua most of the archaeological materials which have been recovered to date probably belong to the period just before the Spanish Conquest. The Coclé culture of Panama is one of the most famous. At one cemetery of this culture several tombs disclosed dead chieftains buried with amazing splendor. Wives and retainers had apparently been killed and thrown into the tomb; gold ornaments abounded; polished and gold-mounted stones, including emeralds, were typical. The inferences are those of rich, if small, kingdoms. Another distinctive culture zone, noted for its excellent polychrome pottery, lies in Nicaragua and Costa Rica. This is the Nicoya. It is probably related distantly to the Coclé ceramic style, although it may be chronologically earlier. In Honduras, on the Ulua River, the streams of influence from the south and north merge. Ceramic styles which may relate to Nicoya are found contemporaneous with Classic Maya pottery. Underneath the finer painted wares are incised styles which vaguely suggest the early incised pottery of Middle America and South America.

Venezuela-Guianas. The archaeology of Venezuela and British Guiana is less rich in material remains than that of either the Central or Northern Andes. Like the latter, it has no imposing above-ground structures or great pyramids. In western Venezuela there are relationships between the prehistoric ceramics of that area and ceramic styles of Colombia; to the east, around Lake Valencia and on the Orinoco River, the pottery styles are quite different, and it is clear that here is another important focus of cultural development in South America. It seems most likely that Arawakan-speaking Indians occupied the middle and lower Orinoco and the Venezuelan coast for many centuries before the Conquest. They were tropical forest agriculturists skilled in the ceramic arts. Most of the Venezuelan and Guianan pottery styles probably were Arawakan. These styles are typically incised or modeled rather than painted although some red and white painting occurs in the earlier periods. There is a general trend from broad-lined, bold incision to less well executed, fine-line incised designs. The late period culture around Lake Valencia is, perhaps, the most spectacular. It is represented by mounds, artificially constructed for burial, urn burials, and distinctive female figurines. There is no way to estimate reasonably the age of the Venezuelan cultures. Absence of European artifacts or trade materials would indicate that they date earlier than A.D. 1500.

West Indies. The West Indies were populated from northeastern South America, particularly the Venezuelan area, in prehistoric times. The earliest cultures are preceramic and nonhorticultural. In western Cuba the Indians lived in this fashion until the time of the Conquest, but elsewhere in both the Greater and Lesser Antilles the pottery-making horticulturists had driven out or subdued the earlier peoples. The linguistic affiliations of the early people are not known, but the later predominant linguistic stock throughout most of the Antilles was the Taino, an Arawakan affiliate. The linguistic connections with mainland South America are further substantiated by the archaeology, since the dominant art styles in pottery and stone carving are related to the pottery of the Orinoco. In spite of these mainland influences, West Indian prehistoric culture appears to have developed independently to a large extent. The strongest ties to Venezuela are in the late ceramic periods; the early ceramic periods, particularly those of Haiti, Jamaica, and the Bahamas, may represent local development. Shortly before the Conquest, marauding Caribs began to push out into the West Indies, and they were establishing themselves in the Lesser Antilles by 1492. Their archaeology has not yet been distinguished. In general, the prehistoric peoples of the West Indies were much like their South American tropical forest kinsmen in that they lived in small villages and subsisted chiefly on manioc rather than maize. There are no mounds or large architectural features from the aboriginal past in the West Indies. The peak of West Indian civilization was achieved in Puerto Rico, probably in the two centuries immediately before the arrival of Columbus.

Amazon Basin. Large prehistoric populations lived in villages along the Amazon and its tributaries in prehistoric times. There are few evidences of these settlements in the way of above-ground architectural features, but rich refuse deposits and large cemeteries attest to ancient habitation. On the lower Amazon and the adjacent Atlantic Coast there are several cultural foci, each of which is known largely through styles of pottery. On the large island of Marajó, at the delta of the Amazon, several mounds have yielded very ornate modeled and painted pottery vessels and figurines. These represent the Marajó style. Its influences are seen in distant parts of the Amazonian drainage. The modern pottery of the tropical forest Indians who today inhabit the jungles of eastern Peru is very similar in design. Relationships have been pointed out with the prehistoric painted wares of Venezuela and the West Indies. In eastern Bolivia there are similar styles on the prehistoric level. On Marajó its chronological position is unknown except that it is definitely pre-Spanish. As for the mounds, it is not known if these are simply refuse piles or whether they are artificial tumuli for the express purpose of burying the dead. A second important stylistic focus is at the confluence of the Amazon and Tapajoz. This is known as the Santarem. As opposed to the Marajó style, it emphasizes modeling and incising rather than painting. Its closest known affiliations are with the broad-lined incised styles of the Orinoco and the West Indies. Near Trinidad, in eastern Bolivia, on the Upper Madeira drainage, an unusual pottery style was discovered a number of years ago in the lower levels of a refuse mound. This is known as the Lower Velarde style. Although other types of the area resemble Marajó, the Velarde style is distinctly different. It is a polychrome ware, and the vessels are often supported by tetrapods. Its relationships to Andean ceramics have been postulated by some, but these surmises have not been conclusive. There is reason to believe that it is reasonably old, antedating A.D. 1000. It is generally conceded that the cultural stimuli for the Amazonian area proceeded southward along the coast from Venezuelan centers, entered the mouth of the Amazon, and subsequently spread throughout the drainage. There has yet been no adequate demonstration of prehistoric contact between the tropical forest and the Andean cultures.

The Paraná. It is supposed that the earlier inhabitants of the Paraná River were a hunting and fishing people without agriculture. They buried their dead in small natural hillocks along the river bank, and their most distinctive manufacture was modeled and linear-punctated pottery of a relatively crude sort. Sometime before the European Conquest the river was invaded by the Guaraní peoples, probably coming down the coast from Brazil. These people were farmers and made painted pottery. As a cultural focus the Paraná is important because the ceramic traditions of the earlier inhabitants of the river banks were diffused throughout southern South America.

Southern South America. The Argentine pampas and Patagonia comprise southern South America. In aboriginal times these people lived a seminomadic existence, and the archaeological sites, except those near the mouth of the Plata River, are little more than campsites or flint-working stations. The area abounds in chipped and groundstone work reflective of a hunting and gathering economy. Projectile points, knives, scrapers, various skin-dressing tools, stone mortars, and bola stones are typical. Pottery is found from the Plata south of the Straits of Magellan. In general it be-

comes less common and more simply made and decorated as one proceeds southward. In the pampas the pottery types are much like those of the earlier period on the Paraná; farther to the south this similarity is less apparent. There is no relative dating of these cultures. It is known merely that they continued, with some modifications, such as the advent of the horse, for about 200 years or more after the invasion of the Europeans. Presumably, they date several centuries before the Conquest. *See also* CLASSICAL ARCHAEOLOGY.

G. R. W.

ARCHAEOPTERYX. *See* AVES; BIRDS.
ARCHAEORNITHES. *See* BIRDS.
ARCHANGEL. *See* ARKHANGELSK.

ARCHANGEL [ɑ'rke'njəl]. The word "archangel" (the chief angel) appears in the Greek translation of Daniel and twice in the New Testament: Jude 9, where Michael is so named, and I Thessalonians iv:16. The number of archangels varies from four—Michael, Raphael, Gabriel, Phanuel (Book of Enoch xl:9)—to seven—Uriel, Raphael, Raguel, Michael, Saraquael or Sariel, Gabriel, and Remiel or Hieremihel (Book of Enoch xx). Only Michael and Gabriel appear in the Old and New Testaments. The number four is probably earlier than seven, since only four archangels have genuinely early Israelite names and the number seven may have been taken from late Persian sources. In Revelation viii:2, xv:1, and xxi:9, the seven angels who stand before God are no doubt the seven archangels. The well-organized angelic host of later Judaism was led by these chief angels, who were admitted into the immediate presence of God and formed His secret council. *See also* GABRIEL; MICHAEL; RAPHAEL; URIEL.

C. T. F.

ARCHBALD, a borough in Lackawanna Co., in northeastern Pennsylvania, on the Lackawanna River, about 10 mi. northeast of Scranton. The borough, incorporated in 1877, had the mayor-council form of government in 1950. A glacial pot hole about 20 ft. in diameter and 40 ft. in depth is a feature of the borough. The Delaware & Hudson and the New York, Ontario & Western railroads provide freight and transportation facilities for the community. Coal mining, which began in the locality about 1846, is the chief occupation. Pop. 1950, 6,304.

ARCHBISHOP (Gr. *archi*, chief; *episcopos*, bishop, hence the adj. *archiepiscopal*), originally the senior bishop or the bishop of the original see of a province, having little more than priority among equals. The title dates from the fourth century A.D. Gradually the archbishop acquired jurisdiction over the rest of the bishops in the province by virtue of Roman imperial usage or by the process of the elevation of his assistants to full diocesan status. In the Protestant Episcopal Church of America the title has been definitely avoided, and that of presiding bishop is conferred on an official elected for a fixed period instead of for life.

F. W. B.

ARCHDEACON, in Christian churches, the chief or ruler of the deacons of a diocese, originally only in deacon's orders, but later a senior priest. The duties and prerogatives of the archdeacon have varied greatly at different times and in different churches. In the Church of England the office retains something of its early importance, its duties comprising the general discipline, arrangements, and finances of the diocese, but in the Episcopal Church in the United States it is of rare occurrence, and in the Roman Catholic Church it is no more than a titular office. In the

Middle Ages, especially in the opening years of the thirteenth century, the archdeacon was an official of considerable power, having in some instances the authority to hold court and impose penance. A medieval proverb to the effect that an archdeacon is beyond the hope of salvation may reflect a popular impression of the manner in which the prerogatives were exercised. F. W. B.

ARCHDIOCESE [ɑrtshdɑi'osiz], the jurisdiction and administration of an archbishop, usually called a province. An archdiocese consists of a collection of dioceses. The additional authority implied in the title was marked in the Middle Ages, as it still is in the Church of Rome, by the gift of the pallium, a vestment which the Pope wears at Mass and then places on the shoulders of the archbishop. The jurisdiction of an archdiocese carried with it the limited jurisdiction of the papal legate (*legatus natus*), and these powers have been retained in the Church of England by the Archbishop of Canterbury. F. W. B.

ARCHEOZOIC ERA. *See* GEOLOGY.

ARCHER, WILLIAM (1856-1924), British dramatist and critic, was born in Perth, Scotland, Sept. 23, 1856. He was educated at Edinburgh University and from 1884 to 1905 was dramatic critic for the *London World*. Archer was an early proponent of Ibsen's plays, and his edition of Ibsen in English became standard when it was completed in 1912. As a practicing dramatist, he scored a notable success in 1920 with his melodrama *The Green Goddess*, and as a critic he is remembered for his *The Old Drama and the New* (1923). Archer died Dec. 27, 1924. B. Pr.

ARCHER FISH, *Toxotes jaculator*, a handsome fish of the family Toxidae, found in coastal areas and mouths of rivers in the Burma-Malay area. It is widely known from its habit of shooting down insects and other small organisms from overhanging vegetation by means of a well directed drop of water shot from the mouth. The force necessary to propel the water is supplied by a quick closing of the

COURTESY OF NEW YORK ZOOLOGICAL SOCIETY

ARCHER FISH

gill covers. A deep groove along the middle of the roof of the mouth is converted into a tube when the tongue is applied to the roof of the mouth. The paper-thin tip of the tongue acts as a valve and regulates the flow of water from the end of the tube. Thus, with the tip of the jaws protruding from the surface, a drop of water is ejected very accurately to a distance of four feet to bring down its prey. Large archer fish can project a drop as far as 10 to 12 feet, although not accurately. Sometimes insects are pursued and shot down in flight. E. C. R.

ARCHERY. The term "archery" comes from the Latin *arcus,* a bow, and in modern usage covers the equipment and procedure of shooting with all types of bows and arrows for war, hunting, or sport. The military use of the sling for throwing stones by hand can be grouped with archery, since tactical use of slingers and bowmen was very closely allied in ancient and medieval warfare.

History. In a broad sense it may be said that the first cave man who caught up a rough stone and hurled it at his antagonist of the moment, man or beast, invented the whole series of projectile weapons and their ammunition. The bow in its several types and the hand and staff sling were by far the commonest of missile weapons before the use of gunpowder. While the bow as a means of propelling a light dart or arrow was probably an original invention and not an adaptation from some other piece of equipment, it is simple enough to have been made at the very earliest stages in man's development. The origin of the bow probably predates the Stone Age. The earliest bows had arrows with tips of charred wood instead of chipped stone arrowheads. Widespread use of the bow also indicates that it was made independently in many parts of the world. In fact, the only primitive races that were not acquainted with it were the aborigines of Australia and New Zealand.

For centuries the Egyptians were famous for their mounted archers, and the Babylonians, Persians, and Scythians were also adept with the bow. The Greeks and Romans largely employed mercenary archers from various Eastern nations, e.g., the Scythian archers who guarded some of the later Roman emperors. In the Middle Ages the English were regarded as the greatest archers, but contemporary Egyptians and Turks were also highly proficient, as the Crusaders discovered.

In the Western Hemisphere, the American Indians were able hunters with bows and arrows. However, their effectiveness was not due to their skill as archers, or to the excellence of their weapons, which were often crude, but to their unusual ability to stalk within close range of an enemy or game. They contributed greatly to the development of field archery.

TYPES OF BOWS

Basically, there are two types of bow, with several variations of each type. These are the simple hand bow in several lengths and designs and the crossbow, also made in a number of styles. The plain hand bow is by far the oldest and has always had the widest use. References to it appear in the earliest known writings and drawings all over the world. It is found in Biblical writings and in the preserved documents of all the ancient races. The Greeks and Romans used it during most of their history as a standard item of their military equipment.

Plain Bow. *Early Construction.* In its simplest form the bow was a single piece of springy wood, seasoned and shaped so that a string attached to its two ends caused it to bend in a regular curve, with the center of the bowstave farthest from the string. The dart or arrow consisted of a straight shaft with two or more directing feathers at the rear end and a notch at the tip into which to fit the string. A metal point was usually fitted to the front end of the shaft. Sometimes this was barbed so as to retain the arrow in the wound; sometimes it was blunt-ended for shooting birds. Small rounded or fluted section points, well waxed, were used in the Middle Ages for the penetration of armor. The power of a bow is usually given in "pounds pull." This is the number of pounds of force necessary to draw an arrow of normal length back so that only the metal tip projects beyond the front of

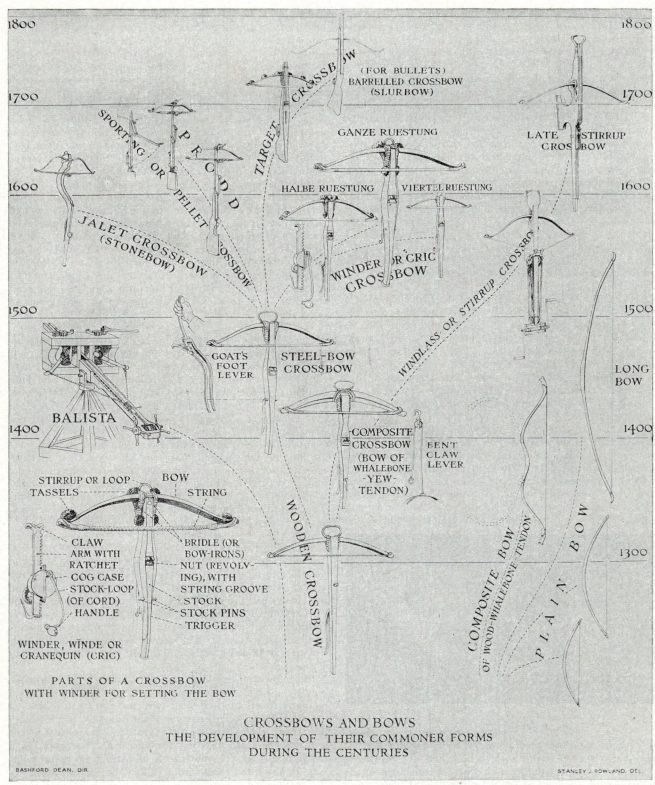

CROSSBOWS AND BOWS
THE DEVELOPMENT OF THEIR COMMONER FORMS
DURING THE CENTURIES

BASHFORD DEAN, DIR.

STANLEY J. ROWLAND, DEL.

COURTESY OF THE METROPOLITAN MUSEUM OF ART. NEW YORK

the bowstave. Modern target or hunting bows usually pull between 40 and 80 lb., occasionally up to 100 lb. Military bows of the Middle Ages, were, on the average, more powerful.

Composite bows, built up by glueing together several pieces of wood or other springy material, such as horn, and reinforcing them with bands of sinew were also fairly common, as were bows of recurved or double-curved shape, designed to give extra strength and length of pull in relation to their over-all dimensions. Most early bows averaged from 4 to 5 ft.

in length. The Japanese used a longer built-up bow, designed so that the center of the pull was well below the actual center of the bow. This construction enabled their relatively short warriors to use a long bow. Peoples who used the bow on horseback favored the short, powerful, composite bows, since compactness was a valuable characteristic that facilitated use by mounted bowmen.

Tactical Use. In most ancient armies and in Europe prior to the Norman Conquest, archers were considered relatively unimportant auxiliaries, especially in open-field battles. In such cases their harassing fire was delivered from the flanks of the armies, and the main fighting was done by the heavily armed infantry or cavalry. Missile fire from ambush was considered good tactical practice, and in siege operations archers were considered of especial value. It was their job, by shooting from the walls, to hinder as much as possible any operation of the besiegers within range; or, if supporting the attack, to keep the defenders from the walls while they were being stormed by the assault parties, and to protect the works and engines from the counterfire of the enemy.

General European Types. Most of the European bows of the period before the Norman Conquest were of short to medium length, from 3 to 5 ft. for the most part. They were of simple, single-material design, strung with an even curve from tip to tip. The bow was a common hunting weapon and was used for killing all kinds of birds and animals. It was used more for military purposes in the northern and Scandinavian countries than in England and, consequently, was better developed in the North.

Norse and Norman Bows. It is probable that the Norse bows of the tenth and eleventh centuries were among the best in Europe. Consequently, the archers who invaded England with William the Conqueror carried, as a result of their Norse origins, weapons far superior to the bows used by the forces of King Harold II. Norman archers are shown in the Bayeux Tapestry using bows about 4½ ft. in length. These archers are credited with an important part in the invasion, since their arrows fell behind the shields of the defenders, killing Harold, among others.

English Longbow. In England, the period from shortly after the Norman Conquest to the latter part of the reign of Queen Elizabeth was that of the greatest development of the bow and its most extensive use as a military weapon. The true English longbow had probably been developed to almost its maximum efficiency by the late twelfth or early thirteenth century. Since it usually requires some time for the tactical value of a new weapon to be appreciated, the greatest use of the longbow for military purposes was during the Hundred Years' War, 1337-1453, and the Wars of the Roses, 1455-1485. The English archer and his skill were certainly the deciding factors in such battles as Crécy, Poitiers, and Agincourt.

Although the feats of Robin Hood and his Merry Men are probably mostly legendary, the English bowman of this period was the backbone of the most powerful infantry armies then existing, and the first type of foot soldier that was able to withstand and repulse the charge of the armored knights who had previously swept all before them. The usual archer carried a single-piece, evenly curved bow, normally of yew wood, about 6 ft. long with a pull between 80 and 150 lbs.—the true longbow. He also had a sheaf of "cloth-yard" arrows about 30 in. in length, although the cloth yard as a unit of measure varied considerably at different periods. He usually wore a jack or brigandine of mail and a steel cap and carried a sword and sometimes a leaden-headed mallet for the double purpose of dispatching a wounded enemy

and driving pointed stakes into the ground to form a palisade for defense.

At Crécy in 1346 there were about ten thousand archers on the field in the English army, but it is probable that only slightly more than half of them were actually engaged, since a considerable number were in the king's reserve and did no fighting. Contemporary accounts describe "arrow flights that darkened the sky," and such a figure of speech is not without some foundation in fact. When it is considered that an estimated six thousand effective bowmen at Crécy had a capacity of about seven shafts per minute per man, with a useful range against the armor of the period of about 250 yds., the "rain of arrows" becomes a potent reality. The advance of the heavily armed cavalry, over rising ground rendered soft by a recent rainstorm, met, by simple arithmetic, a fire of 42,000 shafts per minute, piercing armor, bringing down horse and rider to be trampled by other horses maddened by their wounds, and throwing the whole French advance into a deadly chaos. Consequently, Crécy was a slaughter of the French cavalry and a memorable victory for English infantry.

After Crécy, for two hundred years or more, the English archer made the longbow and the power of infantry felt and respected wherever he went. Only with the rise of firearms was the bow superseded, and then by a weapon that was at first far inferior to it in power, range, accuracy, and speed of fire—in everything, in fact, except the terror which it inspired by the roar and flash and the magic powers attributed to it.

Range of Plain Bows. While the range of early missile weapons was usually exaggerated in contemporary manuscripts, it is certain that the longbow was commonly used in practice for "shooting at the clout," a white cloth stretched on a hoop, at 220 yds.; and for "shooting at the butts," a mark placed on an earthen backstop, at ranges of over 50 yds. Effectiveness of sheaf and flight arrows in warfare ranged from 250 to 300 yds., and recorded shots of 400 yds. and over have been made in both ancient and modern times. A Turkish official shot 480 yds. with a double-curved composite bow of horn in 1795, and modern bowmen have duplicated this range.

Crossbow. *Types and Operation.* The crossbow, in appearance, is like a small catapult, with a bow mounted crosswise on a stock to be put to the shoulder like a gun. The bow is usually short and very powerful in relation to its length. In the early types, the bow was nearly always composite and frequently recurved; later, the bow was usually of steel. The crossbow was also commonly called an arbalest and sometimes, especially in the case of the lighter hunting types which shot stones, a prod, or prodd.

In the simplest form of the crossbow, the string was drawn back by hand and held in position by a nut or roller pivoted in the stock. This nut had two notches: one for the string, and one for a simple trigger that came out below the stock in the form of a long lever which was squeezed up against the stock to release the roller and fire the piece. The arrow was short and heavy-headed. It was provided with "feathers" of leather or thin bone rather than actual bird feathers. It was usually called a bolt or "quarrel," from the French *carré*, meaning square, in reference to the head, which was a square or diamond section. When the feathers were set curving, so that it would spin in flight, it was called a vireton. It was placed in a groove in the stock with its butt resting against the string.

As the bows became more powerful, mechanical means were necessary to draw back the string. At first, a stirrup was provided at the front of the stock; the stirrup was held down with one foot while a hook in the belt was put over the string and the bow bent by straightening the back. Another arrangement known as a "goat's foot lever" was also used. This utilized a jointed lever operating over studs in the stock of the bow: the claw of one part of the lever engaged the string, and the other, riding on the studs, provided power to bend the bow when the outer end of the lever was drawn back.

In even stronger bows, two types of windlass were used. One was the cranequin, which slipped over the stock from the rear and engaged the string with the hooked end of a toothed arm that was drawn back by turning a long-handled ratchet gear. The other used a regular pulley windlass, with two handles and a block-and-tackle system of cords and pulleys: the windlass frame was fitted to the butt of the crossbow stock and wound up with both hands, while the front of the stock rested on the ground and was held in place with a stirrup. This type was called the *arbalest a tour* and was the most powerful crossbow in use. Light hunting crossbows or prods were used even for killing small birds, and one type, with a double string supporting a small pouch in its center, shot stones or lead balls.

Use in Europe. While it existed in ancient times, the crossbow was not commonly used in Europe, either for the chase or warfare, until late in the eleventh century. It is not shown in the Bayeux Tapestry, although some contemporary accounts of the Norman Conquest refer to its use. King Richard I is supposed to have introduced it to the English army, and was himself killed with a bolt from one in a foreign war. A papal bull dated 1139 forbade its use between Christian adversaries as being too deadly a weapon for knightly combat but permitted its use against the Saracens.

The arbalest as a military weapon was more popular in central Europe and Italy than it was in England, where the longbow was always foremost in public esteem. The most powerful of the crossbows had a pull of nearly 1,200 lbs., although, because of the limited length of the bow, the travel of the string was only about 8 or 9 in. The extreme range of the big windlass crossbows was between 450 and 500 yds. The usual military field-crossbow would average from 300 to 350 yds. The principal advantage of the crossbow for military purposes was that it could be used by relatively weak and unskilled men and still give good results; this was because it was bent mechanically and was aimed from the shoulder like a gun, so that its bolts could be delivered fairly accurately without the skilled longbowman's lifetime of practice. In fact, the crossbow sometimes was fitted with elaborate adjustable sights with adjustments for both windage and elevation, and with a very delicate set of hair triggers.

The crossbow, however, was much slower in operation than a longbow. This was especially true of the more powerful models, since the winding of the windlass limited them to about one shot per minute against six or seven for a longbow in skilled hands. The crossbow also was more vulnerable to the rain, since its string could not be readily removed and protected. A rainstorm that wet the strings of the weapons used by the Genoese crossbowmen in the French army at Crécy was one of the many factors contributing to the English victory, although it is probable that the storm helped more by softening the ground and slowing up the French knights. While the range of the Genoese fire was reduced, the English archers were superior to the Genoese even at their best.

Crossbows remained in military use in Europe for about the same length of time as longbows and were fairly common army equipment until the last quarter of the sixteenth century. They were used for sport and hunting long after they ceased to be military weapons.

Chinese Repeating Crossbow. A relatively modern type of crossbow was the repeating, or magazine, crossbow used by the Chinese as a military weapon as late as the last quarter of the nineteenth century. This was a regular crossbow of medium power, with an attached cocking lever and a box holding a dozen arrows mounted above the string and arrow groove. Each time the string was drawn back, an arrow dropped into the groove ready to be fired. It was an ingenious device, but was ineffective against the repeating rifles of the Japanese in the first Sino-Japanese War.

Modern Target Uses. In some parts of Europe, especially Belgium and Switzerland, crossbows are still used for target shooting. The modern bows have stocks like guns, very fine trigger pulls, and adjustable sights. Shooting at the "popinjay," a small figure of a bird mounted on a high pole, is a common type of modern crossbow shooting. Some of the Continental shooting clubs claim to be a thousand years old.

C. T. H.

ARCHERY AS A SPORT

Archery is becoming increasingly important as a physical education activity because by varying the strength of the bow it can be adapted to the strength of the individual; it can be enjoyed all seasons of the year; it can be purchased with satisfaction by individuals, families, or larger groups; and its tackle can be made in home or school workshops.

Equipment. *The Target.* The regulation target for archery is a circular disk of unthreshed rye or other straw at least 4 ft. in diameter and 6 or more in. thick. It has an oilcloth or canvas face, with concentric rings of different colors. The "gold" is a bull's-eye of this color 9.6 in. in diameter at the center of the target. Arrows hitting the gold score nine points. Surrounding the gold are four concentric circles, each 4.8 in. wide. The colors of the circles from the gold outward are red, blue, black, and white. The arrangement of circles, their colors, and their widths are shown in Fig. 1. Arrows landing in the red score seven points; in the blue, five; in the black, three; and in the white, one. Arrows which pass entirely through the face of the target, or bounce off, score five points, regardless of where they hit the target.

Tackle. Bows and arrows and other equipment classed together as archery tackle are shown in Figs. 2, 3, and 4.

Bow and Arrow Woods. The best woods for making bows

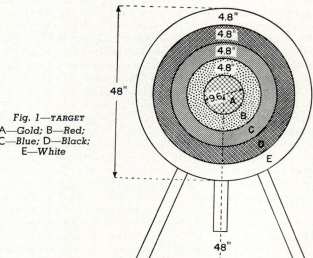

Fig. 1—TARGET
A—Gold; B—Red;
C—Blue; D—Black;
E—White

are Osage orange, yew, lemonwood, and Tennessee red cedar. Lemonwood (dagame) is imported from Cuba in large quantities and from it most of the commercial bows are made. Other good bow-woods native to the United States are sassafras, black locust, and hickory.

The best arrows are made from Port Orford cedar, Norway pine, Douglas fir, Sitka spruce, and Alaska cedar. White birch was once used almost entirely for hunting and roving arrows but, because of its weight and tendency to warp, was generally supplanted by the other lighter woods.

Shooting. *Point-of-Aim System.* In using the point-of-aim system, shown in Fig. 5, the archer aims in the general direction of the target but specifically at a small object or

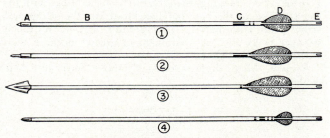

Fig. 2—COMMON ARROW TYPES AND PARTS

(1) Target arrow; (2) Roving arrow; (3) Hunting arrow; (4) Flight arrow. A—Pile or point; B—Shaft; C—Crest; D—Fletching; E—Nock

aiming point, such as the handle of an icepick, which is stuck into the ground between the archer and the target, or in the target itself, depending upon the physical characteristics of the archer and upon the range at which he is shooting. This object is known as the point-of-aim and acts as his front sight; the pile or point of the arrow when fully drawn and anchored is the rear sight.

To shoot, a right-handed archer stands erect with the left side of his body toward the target. The bow is held in the left hand, with the arm practically straight in a side horizontal position pointing toward the target. The head is turned 90° to the left, so that it also faces the target; the feet, hips, and shoulders face 90° to the right of the target. The arrow is nocked at the proper point on the string and the latter is gripped by three finger tips of the right hand, with the index finger above the arrow and the long and ring fingers below. Before aiming and releasing the arrow, it is drawn to the anchor, which for most target archers is a position in which the string snugly touches and bisects the middle of the nose and the chin, while the top of the index finger is under and against the lower surface of the jawbone. The right elbow should be kept in line with the arrow. Having

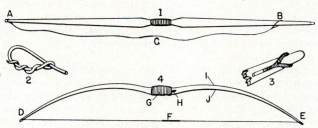

Fig. 3—PRINCIPAL PARTS OF THE BOW

(1) Unstrung bow: A—Timber hitch, a method of securing string to lower tip or nock of bow, B—Loop, C—String; (2) Close-up of timber hitch; (3) Method of looping or nocking loop of string to upper nock or tip of bow; (4) Bow ready for use: D—Lower tip; E—Upper tip; F—Serving; G—Handle; H—Arrow plate; I—Back; J—Belly

anchored the arrow, the archer raises or lowers his bow and body above the waist until the point-of-aim is seen just above the pile, or point of the arrow. The arrow is then released by simultaneous extension of all three fingers at the anchor. If the point-of-aim has been properly placed and the archer's release is correct, the arrow will hit the gold or bull's-eye. If

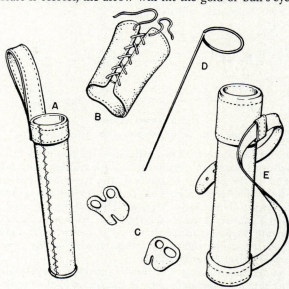

Fig. 4—SUPPLEMENTARY EQUIPMENT

A—Quiver for target arrows with belt attachment; B—Armguard or bracer; C—Finger tabs; D—Wire ground quiver; E—Hunting quiver with shoulder strap

the arrow goes too high, the point-of-aim should be moved toward the archer; if it goes too low, the point-of-aim should be moved toward the target. For lateral corrections, the point-of-aim should be moved to the right or left, away from the direction of error. Immediately after the release, an archer should hold his position, with the bow arm up and the right hand near the chin, for a brief "follow-through."

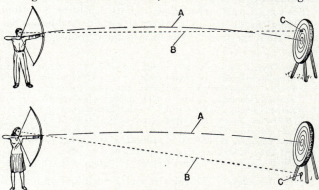

Fig. 5—POINT OF AIM SYSTEM

A—Flight of arrow; B—Line of sight; C—Point of aim

Sight System. In using the sight system (Fig. 6), a bow-sight is pasted, taped, or otherwise fastened to the surface of the bow above the handle. Horizontal elevation marks for distances from 10 to 100 yd. are often marked across the bow to act as guides for placing the sight. These marks must be established for each bow and set of arrows by practice at known distances from the target.

The same anchor position and other fundamentals used in point-of-aim shooting are employed in the sight method. Final adjustments of the sight at a given distance are made according to hits made by the first arrows. If an arrow goes too high, the bar on the sight is moved higher to lower the bow; if the arrow goes too low, the sight is lowered to raise the bow. If the arrow goes too far to the left, the bar is pushed to the left, or, conversely, to the right, if the error is in that direction. When the arrows consistently hit the gold, the sight is properly adjusted.

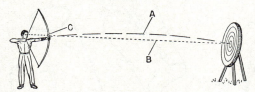

Fig. 6—SIGHT SYSTEM
A—Flight of arrow; B—Line of sight; C—Bow-sight.

Instinctive System. The instinctive system, used by the American Indian and others for hunting, differs from other systems in the position of the bow, the type of anchor, and sighting. The bow, instead of being held vertical, is tilted to the right about thirty degrees. The full-drawn arrow is anchored higher, closer to the right eye, so that the nock of the arrow is usually just above the right corner of the mouth, with the tip of the right index finger resting snugly against the lower ridge of the cheekbone.

The sighting is done with both eyes open, concentrating on the smallest observable spot in the center of the target or game, with no thought of sights. However, the same fundamentals of full draw, consistent anchor, releasing, and follow-through are essential for good shooting. The instinctive system is best for all phases of field archery, with the possible exception of archery golf.

Target Archery. In target archery, one of two major divisions of archery in the United States, participants generally use either the point-of-aim or the sight system of shooting. The annual national tournament of target archery's governing body, the National Archery Association, includes the following events:

Rounds. Target archers shoot rounds, consisting of various combinations of arrows released at certain established distances from the target. The most popular rounds are listed below:

York (men): 72 arrows at 100 yds.; 48 at 80 yds.; 24 at 60 yds.
Metropolitan (men): 30 arrows each at 100, 80, 60, 50, and 40 yds.
American (men, women): 30 arrows each at 60, 50, and 40 yds.
Columbia (women): 24 arrows each at 50, 40, and 30 yds.
National (women): 48 arrows at 60 yds.; 24 arrows at 50 yds.
Metropolitan (women): 30 arrows each at 60, 50, 40, and 30 yds.
Junior American (boys): 30 arrows each at 50, 40, and 30 yds.
Junior Columbia (girls): 24 arrows each at 40, 30, and 20 yds.
Men's Team Round (four men): 96 arrows at 60 yds.
Women's Team Round (four women): 96 arrows at 50 yds.

Clout Shooting. The clout is a target marked and scored like the regular archery target, but it is twelve times as large, having a diameter of 48 ft. instead of 48 in. It is laid out horizontally on the ground, with a white flag in its exact center. Men shoot 36 arrows from a distance of 180 yds. Requirements for women are less exacting; they shoot 36 arrows from a distance of 120 yds.

Wand Shooting. The standard wand is a white pole of soft wood, 2 in. in diameter. This is stuck vertically in the ground, so that 6 ft. of its length projects above the surface. Men shoot 36 arrows at the wand from 100 yds. Women and juniors shoot 36 arrows from 60 yds. This event was derived from the legend of Robin Hood's feat of splitting the willow wand at 100 paces.

Flight Shooting. In this event, contestants strive to shoot the greatest distance. Specially designed bows and arrows are used. So that the event will not be limited to those able to pull heavy bows, it is conducted in various classifications based on the drawing weight of bows. This weight is the number of pounds of pressure required to draw a bow to the full length of the arrow, which is generally 28 in. The classifications for men are: (1) bows up to and including 50 lbs.; (2) bows up to and including 65 lbs.; (3) bows up to and including 80 lbs.; (4) bows of all weights; and free style. Women's bow-weight classifications for flight shooting are: (1) bows up to and including 35 lbs.; (2) bows up to and including 50 lbs.; (3) bows of all weights; and free style.

In free-style shooting, the archer lies on his back, with his feet strapped to the bow handle. He draws the string and arrow with both hands. This permits the use of much stronger bows and the attainment of greater distance than with the regular style.

Records. Men's flight-shooting distance records and their holders are:

Class 1: 640 yds., Jack Stewart.
Class 2: 557 yds., 8.5 in., C. L. Haugen.
Class 3: 601 yds., 1 ft., 7 in., I. L. Baker
Class 4: 625 yds., 1 ft., 8.5 in., Jack Stewart.
Free Style: 719 yds., 2 ft., Paul Perry.

Women's flight-shooting distance records and their holders are:

Class 1: 433 yds., 2 ft., 1 in., Blanche Stewart.
Class 2: 505 yds., Evelyn Haines.
Class 3: 474 yds., 1 ft., 3 in., Verne Trittin.
Free Style: 575 yds., 2 ft., Eunice Modlin.

Field Archery. Archers most interested in field archery develop the so-called "instinctive" system of shooting, used always at unmeasured distances. The following events are included in field archery:

Hunting. It is legal to hunt deer and small game in season with the bow and arrow in any place where hunting with the gun is allowed. Conservation authorities in many states encourage bow-and-arrow hunting of deer on state-owned areas both as a conservation measure and, in some instances, as a means of reducing overcrowded herds. Also, in an increasing number of states, seasons for bow-and-arrow hunting of deer precede the gun hunting seasons.

Roving. This phase of the sport involves roaming the fields alone or with a few other archers and shooting informally at such objects as leaves, small sticks, stumps, or pieces of paper. These are picked at random, without knowledge of their distance.

Field Archery Courses. In field archery the bow is used in shooting arrows at animate or inanimate objects, at unknown, unannounced, and not predetermined distances. Most field archers are primarily interested in hunting and spend much of the time outside of hunting seasons roving or shooting on field archery courses (rovers) in preparation for hunting.

Such courses are built in units of fourteen targets, two fourteen-target units constituting a round. Distances between posts (shooting positions) and targets vary between 20 ft. and 80 yds. Targets of four different sizes are used, their faces ranging from 6 in. to 24 in. in diameter, the largest being for the targets at the greatest distance. The face of the target consists of a white bull's-eye surrounded by a black ring. The width of the black ring is always one half the diameter of the bull's-eye. A black aiming spot with a diameter one third that of the bull's-eye is painted on the middle of the bull's-eye. Four arrows are shot at each target from the same or different posts. An arrow in the bull's-eye scores five points and one in the black ring scores three points.

Archery Golf. Archery golf was first played on a regular golf course, archers competing with golfers. The archers shot their arrows into the cups on the green, and the golfers putted into the cups. Later, to protect the cups, a white sponge-rubber ball four inches in diameter was placed just off the green, and archers hit this in order to "hole out." As in golf, the low score won. Other adaptations of this game have used targets with double faces and bull's-eyes four inches in diameter.

Pope-Young Hunting Round. In the Pope-Young hunting round, 36 broadheads or hunting arrows are shot at six targets at six different distances, with a 45-second time limit for each six arrows.

Archery Organizations of the United States. The first archery club in America, known as the United Bowmen, was formed in 1828 in Philadelphia. In 1879 the National Archery Association was formed and held its first national archery tournament in Chicago, at which Will Thompson won the championship. The National Field Archery Association was organized Aug. 4, 1939, by George Brommers, of Bellevue, Wash.; John L. Yount, of Redlands, Calif.; and Earl Grubbs, of Los Angeles, Calif. It grew rapidly, and in August 1946, when the first National Field Archery Tournament was held, it had a membership of 4,500. The first president was A. J. Michelson, of Flint, Mich. The first men's national champion field archer was Dr. Erwin C. Pletcher, of Bakersfield, Calif., and the first women's national champion was Babe Bitzenburger, of Los Angeles. H. G. M.

ARCHIANNELIDA. *See* ANIMAL SYSTEMATICS.

ARCHIL [ɑrʹkɪl], also orchil, orseille, a purple dye obtained from the lichen *Roccella tinctoria* and other lichens. These are often called orchella weed or dyer's moss, and are found chiefly along the coasts of Mozambique, Madagascar, Angola, and the Mediterranean coast of Africa. The dye is obtained by the maceration for several days of the lichens with diluted ammonia and the probable addition of potassium or sodium hydroxide. After the proper fermentation has occurred, sulphuric acid and sodium chloride are added. The resultant dye is dried and powdered, but may be obtained as a liquid or paste. It is used as a dyestuff, especially for modifying the tinctorial value of other dyes, such as indigo. A satisfactory dye for marble, archil was formerly used for staining wool. It is the basis for litmus, a chemical indicator. J. A. Bo., Jr.

ARCHILOCHUS [ɑrkɪʹlokəs] (fl. c. 650 B.C.), Greek lyric poet, was born at Paros in the early seventh century B.C. of an aristocratic father and a slave mother. He was approximately contemporaneous with Callinus, with whom he shares the credit of having developed the elegiac couplet as a poetic form. A soldier of fortune, he had an adventurous life, finally dying in battle in Paros.

Archilochus' poetic activities covered many fields, but he was famous as the earliest of the iambic writers and noted for his furious invective and keen satire, though invective and satire are not unusually prominent in the verses preserved. His lampoons are said to have driven to suicide the family of a certain Lycambes, whose daughter, Neobule, had refused to honor her promise to marry Archilochus, probably because of his lowly birth. Archilochus' trochaic poems consist chiefly of narrative. The content of his elegies, on the

other hand, varies from expressions of consolation to a professional soldier's careless disregard of military regulations or his cheerful suggestion that an abandoned shield is nothing if the soldier himself escapes. In all these forms we may regard Archilochus as a pioneer who introduced system into verse forms already popularly practiced. A further innovation was his use of the epodic form, a couplet consisting of two dissimilar lines, the second generally shorter than the first. A papyrus fragment of this sort invokes some vivid curses on an enemy.

Not only are Archilochus' meters close to popular song; the use of animal fable, the frequent appearance of conversational passages, and the scanty use of epic material point to the same source of inspiration. The poems give us our first real self-portrait of a poet who put into his verses what he himself felt—his hates and loves, his pleasures and griefs—with superlative vigor of expression. C. M. D.

ARCHIMANDRITE [ɑ'rkɪmɑ'ndrɑit] (Gr. ἄρχω, I rule, μάνδρα, enclosure, monastery), in the Byzantine rite, is (1) the superior of one or more monasteries (the Western abbot or abbot general), or (2) an administrative official of a patriarchate or diocese (the Western Roman prelate or diocesan official), or (3) a distinguished priest honored with the title. N. J. T.

ARCHIMEDES [ɑ'rkɪmi'diz] (c. 287-212 B.C.), Greek mathematician and inventor, was born at Syracuse in Sicily about 287 B.C. He was a friend and perhaps a kinsman of Hiero and Gelon, kings of Syracuse. He studied at Alexandria, and thus came in contact with the work of Eratosthenes and his slightly older contemporary, Aristarchus of Samos. Archimedes became known particularly for his mechanical and hydrostatic contrivances. He wrote a series

ARCHIMEDES

of mathematical works on the sphere and cylinder, on conic sections, on the measurement of circles, and on the center of gravity of planes, all of which he worked out in geometrical methods of proof.

Archimedes is famous for his solution of the problem of King Hiero II's crown, in which silver was mixed with gold. While in his bath he noticed that his outstretched legs lost weight in the water. Experiments with other objects showed him that the weight lost was equal to the weight of the water displaced. A body which lost all its weight had exactly the same weight, or the same specific gravity, as the water it displaced. He applied the same idea to Hiero's crown and measured the volumes of water displaced respectively by the crown itself, by the same weight of pure gold, and by the same weight of pure silver. In this way, he found the specific gravity of the crown and was thus able to tell how much gold and silver it contained. It is said that he was so pleased with his discovery that he leaped from the bath and paraded the street exclaiming "Eureka!" (I have found it!)

Archimedes was credited with the invention of a spiral pipe or screw for raising water. He is said to have raised a ship with a lever, and to have offered to raise the earth if a fulcrum were given him. He also experimented with some sort of burning mirror which terrified the Romans at the siege of Syracuse, where he was reputedly killed as he contemplated mathematical formulas in the sand. The influence of Archimedes on geometry is evident in his ten extant treatises and by references to six other works. The extension of some of his theorems, following Euclid, became the equivalent of introductory integral calculus. Cicero, when quaestor of Sicily in 75 B.C., found the tomb of Archimedes, marked by a sphere inscribed in a cylinder.　　C. O. O.

ARCHIPENKO, ALEXANDER [ʌrxɪpyeˈnkɔ] (1887-　　), Russian-American sculptor, was born May 30, 1887, in Kiev, Russia. He rebelled against formal academic procedure in his early study of art at the University of Kiev, in Moscow, and at the École des Beaux-Arts in Paris, and worked independently in France until 1919 when he took an exhibition of his work on a tour of Europe. He founded an art school in Berlin in 1921 but moved it to New York in 1923, later joining the faculty of the New Bauhaus established in Chicago by L. Maholy-Nagy. He held his one-hundreth one-man show in 1953. Archipenko's style involves severe simplifications of form in the modern manner, apparently influenced by the work of Constantin Brancusi. He has also done some painting and invented a form of kinetic painting or sculpture called "archipentura," which is moved by a concealed electric motor. He is director of Arko Studios, which create architectural decorations.

　　　　　　　　　　　　　　　　　　　　L. R.

ARCHITECTURAL ORDERS. An order consists of a column and its entablature. The column has three parts: the base, the column, and the capital. The entablature's three parts are the architrave, the frieze, and the cornice. The orders are derived from wooden forms that were gradually transformed into stone, as is shown by rows of stone plinths in many excavations that indicate the presence of wooden columns which they once supported. The architrave was originally a wooden lintel, and the triglyphs of the Doric order were the ends of ceiling beams. The origin of the volutes of the Ionic order is controversial. The functional school of thought asserts that they were derived from doubled circular beam ends, which were later transformed to cushion capitals or stilt blocks, on which were carved spirals inspired by the annular rings of the former beam ends. The decorative school asserts that they were derived from natural forms.

Classic Proportions. There are five Classic orders—the Doric, Ionic, Corinthian, Tuscan, and Composite. In *De architectura,* written near the end of the first century B.C., Vitruvius gave rules for the proportions of the then known orders, the Doric, Ionic, and Corinthian. After his manuscripts were printed, about the year 1486, Renaissance architects followed his example by making strict rules or canons for the proportions of the five orders, including pedestals and balusters for each. The best-known of the Renaissance books are *Cinque ordini d'architettura,* printed in 1563, by Gia-

como Barocchio, called da Vignola; and *I Quattro libri dell' architettura,* published in 1570, by Andrea Palladio. The system of proportion used is the module, a measurement equal to one-half the diameter of the shaft taken at its lower part. Modules were further divided into parts called minutes, ranging from a twelfth to a sixtieth of a module.

The canons were derived from the measurements of existing Classical examples, but since each author used his individual proportions, there was considerable variation in both the proportions and the taste used in detailing them. For example, Palladio prescribes 19 modules for the height of the Corinthian column, whereas Vignola prescribes 20. Known examples of the Roman Corinthian order vary from 17½ to 20⅕ modules for the same dimension.

The canons attempt to give a model order with ideal proportions. Thus they are a useful average from which deviations can be made as dictate requires. Somehow the architects of succeeding ages fostered the mistaken notion that the canons are inalterable and must be copied with the greatest fidelity. But even those who made the rules did not always follow them, because such determining factors as material, usage, and character of design often required a reproportioning of the parts to achieve the desired effect.

Since the rebirth of Classicism during the Renaissance, the Classic orders have been used continuously, with great facility and imagination shown in their application. Attempts have been made to design a sixth order, but none has persisted. It is interesting to note American attempts to create capitals using native flora and fauna instead of the Mediterranean acanthus. Benjamin H. Latrobe (1762-1820) designed tobacco and corn capitals, both of which are found in the National Capitol at Washington. It is said that he also designed a cotton capital. In the vestibule of the Nebraska state capitol, begun in 1922, are capitals designed by the sculptor Lee Lawrie, containing wheat, corn, and bulls.

Greek Orders. *Doric.* The Greek Doric order is characterized not only by its rectilinear forms but also by the beauty of its interrelated proportions. The short column is 5½ diameters high on the Parthenon. It has no base, but the entasis begins at the bottom and runs the length of the shaft. The architrave and frieze do not quite line up vertically with each other or with the upper diameter of the shaft. Triglyphs line up with the center of the columns, except at the end, where they are placed at the corner. There is a minimum of carved moldings, but the entasis of the shaft, the sensitive echinus of the capital, the anta moldings, and the bird's-beak molding of the cymatium are just enough to give the order refinement.

Ionic. The Greek Ionic order is slender and graceful. The column is about nine diameters high. Attic and Ionian bases were used. The capital has larger volutes than the Roman Ionic, and the band connecting them dips down at the center. The frieze was often filled with processions of figures, as on the Erechtheum and the Temple of Nike Apteros, both on the Acropolis at Athens. The cornice was relatively thin, with a simple *cyma reversa* for a bed mold and a *cyma recta* for the cymatium. Later, as on the Mausoleum at Halicarnassos, the dentils typical of the Roman Ionic appeared in the bed molds.

Corinthian. The Greek Corinthian order was of late development. Though elaborate, it was used mostly on smaller works, like the monument to Lysicrates at Athens. The Romans developed this order into one of great size and splendor.

Roman Orders. The accompanying illustrations show Vignola's proportions of the Roman orders, using the diameter and module. It is to be noted that the height of the

THE CLASSIC COLUMNS
(1) Tuscan; (2) Doric; (3) Ionic; (4) Corinthian; and (5) Composite

(AFTER VIGNOLA)

entablature equals one-fourth the height of the column. The entasis is confined to the upper two-thirds of the column, with the lowest third straight. The diameter of the shaft just below the capital is five-sixths diameter. The lower face of the architrave and the frieze always line up with the upper diameter of the column.

Doric. The Roman Doric shaft has either twenty or twenty-four semicircular flutes, separated by narrow flat bands (the arris), or flutes in the form of shallow segmental channels, meeting each other in sharp edges. In general, Roman columns were not fluted if made of fine colorful marble which was enhanced by polishing. The triglyphs on the frieze are separated by square, often decorated metopes. The triglyphs are centered above the columns and are equally spaced between columns. There are two types of cornice, the denticulated containing a row of dentils in the bed molds, and the mutular containing the bracketlike mutules.

Ionic. The Roman Ionic order (and the Corinthian and Composite as well) uses twenty-four semicircular flutes for the shaft. The capitals contain the spiral volutes, which are connected front to back by a double vase-shaped cushion. The Scamozzi Ionic capital, omitting the cushion, has four volutes projecting diagonally at each corner and dying into the sides of the abacus.

Corinthian. The Corinthian, the Roman's favorite, and the Composite are the tallest orders. The Corinthian was usually used on a large scale. It has the most involved cornice, containing not only dentils but also the S-shaped brackets known as modillions. During the Renaissance, many beautiful variations of its capital, known as Corinthianesque, were devised.

Tuscan. Tuscan, the shortest and plainest of the orders, is in reality only a simplified form of the Roman Doric. The columns are usually unfluted. A notable example is found in the colonnade around the forecourt of St. Peter's Basilica in Rome, built between 1655 and 1667.

Composite. The Composite order developed in later Roman times. Its capital contains the two superimposed rows of acanthus leaves of the Corinthian with the Ionic capital placed above them. *See also* ARCHITECTURAL TERMS; COLUMN; MOLDING. O. S. Fj.

ARCHITECTURAL RENDERING. *See* RENDERING, ARCHITECTURAL.

ARCHITECTURAL STYLES. This article defines and describes many styles of architecture employed through the ages and includes the historical development and application of each. The principal styles are discussed under separate alphabetical listings, as indicated at the end of this article.

BAROQUE

The Baroque, an elaborate and grandiose style of architecture and decoration, was inaugurated in Italy during the latter half of the sixteenth century. Its plastic but unarchitectural curves, both in plan and elevation, are particularly contrary to a classic taste. The interiors are marked by exaggerated and badly scaled ornament, featuring broken curved pediments, contorted sculpture, and much gilding.

The Jesuits adopted Baroque for their churches and were instrumental in spreading it throughout most of continental Europe, where it succeeded the Neoclassic style of the earlier Renaissance. The work of Galeazzo Alessi (1512-1572) at Genoa and Milan and that of Giacomo Barocchio da Vignola (1507-1573) at Rome typifies the transition between the two styles. The playful stuccoed brick palaces erected by Alessi at Genoa, in which advantage has been taken of sloping sites

and pleasant vistas, are more fascinating than any ecclesiastical architecture produced during the period.

Baroque in full flower may be seen at Rome in the work of Carlo Maderna (1556-1639), Giovanni Lorenzo Bernini (1598-1660), and Francesco Borromini (1599-1667); at Venice in that of Baldassare Longhena (1604-1682). Baroque was the dominant style in France during the reign of Louis XIV, which lasted from 1660 to 1715. Under Louis XV (1710-1774), Baroque developed into Rococo, characterized by lighter and even more fantastic forms. The German states and the Low Countries took up these styles at the corresponding periods. The extravagant Churrigueresque was the Spanish equivalent of the Baroque, which found no counterpart in England except in certain reflections introduced by Dutch or Flemish builders. The vogue was carried to the New World by the militant missionary orders, and it found great popularity in the mission churches of Brazil and the Spanish colonies. In simplified form, more recently known as Mission style, it reached what is now Florida, Texas, New Mexico, Arizona, and California.

Conspicuous monuments of the Baroque movement in Italy include the churches of Santa Maria della Vittoria by Maderna and Santa Agnese by Borromini, in Rome, and Santa Maria della Salute by Longhena in Venice. This last example, with its competing domes, represents discrepancies in scale. The huge inverted spiral brackets which flank the larger of these domes are particularly questionable as architectural motifs. Occasionally, however, a masterful composition like Bernini's colonnades leading to Saint Peter's, Rome, compensates for many gaudy and less brilliant conceptions.

Germany and the Low Countries suffered particularly at the hands of the Baroque, whole towns presenting repetitious, unbroken, unarchitectural façades. Structures like the Pellerhaus in Nuremberg (1605) are typical.

The acme of European sculpturesque architecture was the Churrigueresque. José Churriguera (1650-1723) appears to have delighted in fanciful plastic form for its own sake with little consideration of its fitness for a work of architecture. Spreading to Latin America, these fanciful Hispanic forms, modified to meet New World conditions and executed by Indian workmen, brought forth a series of ecclesiastical monuments which, for their abandonment of functional principles, their rich and voluptuous sculptural decoration, and their vibrant color, transcend anything the Baroque was able to produce in Europe. This peak was reached during the eighteenth century in Mexico, where abundant examples are extant.

In each nation to which it spread, the Baroque, after a period of vigor, was gradually superseded by a grammatical, if cold and unconvincing, return to Classic forms. R. Ne.

COLONIAL

American Colonial architecture is divided into several national types, flourishing in different regions and at various periods.

English. The English Colonial, from 1607 to about 1790, differs somewhat between the northern and southern colonies in materials, elevation, and floor plans. About 1725, the New England style changed from a simple elevation and a Jacobean source, with overhanging second stories and a compact floor plan, to the use of the Palladian Roman detail popularized earlier in England by Inigo Jones and Sir Christopher Wren. This later English Colonial is commonly called Georgian. The seventeenth-century New England house was well adapted to its severe climate; it had a central chimney with several fireplaces, an interior porch, and small windows with diamond-shaped leaded panes and shutters.

Wood was the common building material because it was readily available. Multiple gables were common, as in Salem, Mass., as was also the lean-to at the rear. The New England farmhouse remained quite simple, even into the nineteenth century, often combining the various outbuildings into an L-shaped assembly. In contrast, the early Colonial house of the southern colonies was made of brick, because of the availability of clay in such places as the tidewater area of Virginia. The earlier Jacobean style was not so common in the South, although Bacon's Castle in Isle of Wight County, Va., is an excellent brick example of this type. The typical southern plantation house of about 1725 had elaborate cornices and moldings in the Georgian style. From the beginning, the southern Colonial house had an open floor plan, due to the need of air circulation in the summer. There were normally numerous outbuildings, including a kitchen, work buildings, and slave quarters.

Dutch. The Dutch Colonial style prevailed from 1614 to about 1673 in New Amsterdam (New York), the Hudson River valley, and Long Island. The urban type was distinguished by step gables and a low stoop set close to the street. The farmhouses were normally low, with a broken pitch to the roof, which at times even curved over the porch. This steeply pitched roof is the most characteristic feature of modern imitations of Dutch Colonial.

German. German Colonial, which flourished from 1683 until the Revolution and even later, was confined almost exclusively to Pennsylvania, notably along the Delaware River and the Lehigh Valley, as well as at Germantown. The various German religious groups that began to arrive in the latter part of the seventeenth century commonly built communal structures, such as the old Moravian Seminary at Bethlehem, Pennsylvania. This type of structure normally lacked elaborate detail and was functional in plan. Brick and stone were used in Germantown and Philadelphia. The William Penn House in Fairmount Park, Philadelphia, is a good example of the late seventeenth-century house of the central colonies. Half timbering was sometimes used in the central colonies as well as in New England. This form of construction consisted of a frame of timbers pegged together, the intervening space being filled with clay. Most half-timber houses have since been covered with clapboards.

French. French Colonial architecture, common in New Orleans and the Mississippi Valley from 1608 to 1803, was primarily of the stockade type. Domestic structures sometimes took the form of a low hip-roofed building, often having walls constructed of posts set in the ground, as at Ste. Geneviève, Mo., on the Mississippi below St. Louis. The urban courtyard type is well exemplified by numerous structures still standing in the old French Quarter, New Orleans.

Spanish. Spanish Colonial architecture ranges widely in time, from 1565 to 1850, and in location, primarily in Florida, the Southwest, and California. The Spanish developed the mission system with the characteristic Mission architecture, well exemplified in California, Arizona, and Texas. One of the best examples is the mission at Santa Barbara in California. It is built around a patio on three sides—the church on one, and a covered arcaded walk in front of the cells on the other two sides. Architectural embellishment was generally saved for the church door and the windows. *See also* Georgian, *infra*. F. J. R.

CURVILINEAR

Curvilinear designates a style of English Gothic architecture current in the first half of the fourteenth century. Its rich and varied character is indicated by its frequent classification as a subdivision of the broader Decorated style. It is also called Late Decorated. It succeeded the Geometric style in England, and was followed by the Perpendicular, although features of one style often lingered and terminal dates are only approximate. As with other phases of the English Gothic, identifying characteristics are found chiefly in the window treatment and vaulting.

In Curvilinear window tracery, flowing curves and ogee arches replace the simpler circles, trefoils, and spherical triangles of the Geometric style. Centerpieces, when present, are shaped like hearts or leafed stems. Examples of curvilinear tracery may be seen in the west window of York Cathedral and the Bishop's Eye of Lincoln Cathedral.

In Curvilinear vaulting, liernes, or connecting ribs, became popular and continued so even after the introduction of fan vaulting. Examples may be seen in the south transept of Gloucester Cathedral and in St. George's Chapel, Windsor. In some instances the structural ribs of the lierne vault were retained, but frequently the ribs lost all structural significance and became merely surface decorations. *See also* Flamboyant, *infra*. A. K. L.

DIRECTOIRE

Directoire style refers to a minor vogue in architecture, furniture, and decoration popular about the time of the French Directorate (1795-1799), from which it derives its name. Occurring between the downfall of the monarchy and the establishment of the Napoleonic empire, the style was transitional, discarding the elaborately decorative forms of the Louis XVI style in favor of a Classic simplicity. The superfluous ornament, so characteristic of the arts of the late monarchy, was abandoned, and both architecture and furniture presented purer forms executed in less expensive materials. Charles Percier and Pierre F. L. Fontaine, later the architects of Napoleon, were proponents of the style, as was the painter Jacques Louis David (1748-1825), whose portrait of Madame Récamier is generally considered emblematic of this era.

Interiors with unbroken expanses of waxed or painted wood were used with moldings and other simple ornamental parts based upon Graeco-Roman forms. The rich tapestries, brocades, and damasks of Louis XVI were replaced by chintzes, cotton prints, and wallpaper. R. Ne.

EARLY ENGLISH

Early English is a descriptive term for English Gothic architecture of approximately the first half of the thirteenth century. The most distinguishing characteristics of the style are found in its window treatment and vaulting.

Early English windows are of the lancet type, tall and narrow with pointed heads instead of the semicircular heads used in the earlier Norman Romanesque style. They appear as early as 1170. Because of them, Early English Gothic is frequently called Lancet. Used singly at first, they were soon grouped in two, three, or even five, as in the famous Five Sisters in York Cathedral. By grouping several lancets under a common dripstone and by piercing the blank wall space between their pointed heads, plate tracery resulted, in which the shape of the opening determines the pattern. Further reduction of the wall areas separating the windows resulted in bar tracery about the middle of the thirteenth century and marks the beginning of the Geometric style.

Early English vaulting is of simple design, employing pointed transverse, diagonal, and wall ribs over rectangular bays. The continuous horizontal ridge rib became almost universal in England during this period, defining the ridge line of the vault and emphasizing the great length of the English Gothic church. A few examples of tiercerons or auxiliary intermediate ribs also appear in the Early English period.

Moldings of the Early English style are bold and deeply undercut. Ornament is simple and, where foliage is employed, vigorously conventionalized.   A. K. L.

EARLY REPUBLICAN (FEDERAL)

"Early Republican" is a term used to designate the architecture of the young American republic between the Declaration of Independence and 1820. The term "Federal" is sometimes applied to the same period, as is also "Post-Colonial." In general the style may be described as an attempt to adapt later Georgian forms to the fuller social demands of the newborn nation. The protagonists of the movement were Charles Bulfinch of Boston and Samuel McIntire of Salem. In Bulfinch's work one senses a combination of the French Renaissance and the light decorative motifs developed by the brothers Adam in England. McIntire also developed a personalized style showing even more of the Adam influence. Others who worked in this vein were Isaac Damon, Philip Hooker, John McComb, Peter Banner, Ithiel Town, and James Hoban. Outstanding examples of the style are the Pierce-Nichols house at Salem, Mass., completed in 1801; "Homewood" in Baltimore (1800); the Massachusetts State House, Boston (1808); the New York City Hall (1814); University Hall at Harvard University (1813); Park Street Church, Boston (1809); and Center Street Church, New Haven (1814).   F. J. R.

ELIZABETHAN

Elizabethan is a style of early English Renaissance architecture more or less contemporaneous with the reign of Elizabeth (1558-1603). Transitional in nature, it followed the Tudor forms of the reigns of Henry VII and Henry VIII and foretokened the oncoming Anglo-Classic of Inigo Jones and Sir Christopher Wren. The style can be compared with the architecture of the Francis I period in France (1515-1547) in that each is still somewhat medieval in mass and plan though Classic in detail. Many Gothic features, such as tower, the oriel, large mullioned windows, pierced or traceried parapets, and huge chimney stacks, were retained.

Elizabethan mansions were of E- or H-shaped plan containing a great hall, a so-called long gallery on the second floor, broad staircases, and often a chapel, surrounded by garden terraces and formal gardens containing box, yew, and other ornamental trees. Exterior walls were treated by the application of Classic orders used somewhat freely as at Kirby Hall in Northamptonshire and the Bodleian Library, Oxford. Interior walls were covered with wooden panels and ceilings were elaborately modeled in plaster. The walls were perforated with large mullioned windows glazed with small diamond-shaped leaded panes, and doors somewhat classically treated, as at Hatfield House or Kirby Hall. Roofs were high pitched or low, sometimes both upon the same design. Dormers were frequently used, and there were many chimneys, sometimes masked by classic columns.

Among the famous Elizabethan mansions are Charlecote in Warwickshire (1558); Knole (1570); and Penshurst Place (1570-1585) in Kent; Longleat (1567) and Longford Castle (1580) in Wiltshire; Burghley House in Northamptonshire (1575-1589); and Montacute House in Somerset (1580-1601). Among the collegiate structures are those built by Ralph Simons at Cambridge (Sidney Sussex College Courtyard, the courtyard of Saint John's College, and Nevill

Court in Trinity College) and those of Thomas Holt at Oxford (Merton, Wadham, Oriel, and Jesus colleges). A good many Elizabethan town houses, several of them of half-timber construction, still remain in London, Chester, York, and the older provincial towns.   R. Ne.

EMPIRE

Empire style refers to a style of architecture, furniture and decoration developed under the encouragement of Napoleon I during the first French Empire (1804 to 1815). Essentially of Classical origin, it attempted to recapture for France something of the grandeur that characterized the arts of the imperial period at Rome. Basically, the forms were Roman, some even Pompeian, but with these were incorporated decorative motives from Egypt, in remembrance of the Emperor's Egyptian campaign. The architecture was likewise based upon antique models, as can be seen by an examination of the works of the principal court architects of the era, Charles Percier (1764-1838) and Pierre F. L. Fontaine (1762-1853), who worked in a somewhat refined manner indicating the influence of the brothers Adam of England. Perhaps the most important example of their architecture is the north wing of the Tuileries. The building, with its thin pilasters supporting great pediments, exhibits certain discrepancies of scale that mark its designers as decorators rather than architects. However, the vogue set by Percier and Fontaine prevailed in France down to about 1840, when it was followed by the related Neo-Greek phase of French Classicism championed by Henri Labrouste.

The furniture of the period, which was squarish and massive, made great use of applied bronze ornaments reflecting Pompeian origins. Ivory inlays were also popular. When

ELIZABETHAN STYLE
Gainford Hall, Durham, England

curves were involved, these were large and robust. Heavy embroidered textiles with Classic ornament and Napoleon's monogram were much employed. The throne of the Emperor was a decorative masterpiece in this style.   R. Ne.

FLAMBOYANT

The Flamboyant style (from Old French *flambe,* flame) is the latest phase of medieval Gothic architecture, extending from about 1373 (chapel of the Cardinal de la Grange, Amiens Cathedral) into the early sixteenth century. The late thirteenth-century Gothic style was somewhat dry and hard as a result of the lavish decorative use of linear tracery and gable designs. English designers as early as 1322 (at Ely) and for some time afterward introduced reverse curves to soften this effect. Their work is called Curvilinear, or Late Gothic. The same idea was developed with greater verve by the French and the Flemings. Flame-like forms (*soufflet* and *mouchette*) in tracery and other decoration suggested the name Flamboyant for the style. Tracery forms were used decoratively on walls, parapets, buttresses, pinnacles, gables, and vaults, often with great bravura, and with effects which are rightly described as lacework in stone. There were no real novelties in plan or structure, but the schemes were often piquant and very ingenious. The skill of the designers and their masons was very great. Sometimes they succumbed to the temptation of stunting, and in the sixteenth century the effects were sometimes overwrought and weedy. In Portugal, for instance, lopped trees, seaweed, and chains sometimes replaced the elaborate Flamboyant moldings. Occasionally, the piers are cylindrical without capitals, in contrast to the usual intricate and subtle profiles. Superb wood carvings, including altarpieces, stalls, and screens of extraordinary intricacy and beauty, tombs, and sumptuous stained glass, were produced in Flamboyant times. In contrast to older work in the style of Chartres, the glass has relatively large individual pieces and the designs are rather pictorial, but the color effects are usually gorgeous. The figure sculpture tends to be heavy, with masses of drapery in involved compositions, particularly in Flanders and Germany.

Flamboyant churches abound. Examples: parts of the cathedrals of Amiens, Rouen, Evreux, Limoges; parish churches at Lépine, Rouen (St. Maclou), Abbeville (St. Vulfran), Caudebec-en-Caux; the famous Chartreuse at Champmol near Dijon. There are important examples of Flamboyant civic architecture at Rouen, the Palais de Justice; at Compiègne, the town hall; at Bourges, the house of Jacques Coeur; and at Paris, the Hôtel de Cluny. *See also* CURVILINEAR, *supra.*   K. J. C.

GEOMETRIC

Geometric style is a term used to describe the Gothic architecture of England in the latter half of the thirteenth century, although the characteristic Geometric window tracery appears before 1250 and continues after 1300. The term was one of those selected by nineteenth-century architectural historians in their attempt to identify and classify periods of English Gothic construction. It and the Curvilinear which followed are frequently treated as subdivisions of the Decorated period and are called Early Decorated and Late Decorated by some. Although variably defined as to date and not completely descriptive, the terms continue as part of the phraseology of English Gothic architecture.

Geometric window tracery is composed of stone mullions or bars so arranged as to form recognizable geometric figures such as circles, trefoils, quatrefoils, and the like. When this tracery lacks a circular centerpiece, the foliations form the dominant lines of the tracery pattern. Examples may be seen in the Angel choir of Lincoln Cathedral (erected between 1255 and 1280) and the Lady chapel of Exeter (1308). Vaulting of the Geometric period is marked by the use of additional intermediate ribs (tiercerons), which rise from the piers to meet in pairs along the longitudinal ridge rib and, less frequently, along a transverse ridge rib. The Exeter Cathedral nave (1280) is a noteworthy example.   A. K. L.

GEORGIAN

"Georgian," named for the first three Georges of Great Britain, is a term commonly applied to architecture in the American colonies from about 1720 to the Revolution. The style is derived from the form of decoration introduced into England in the seventeenth century by Inigo Jones and Sir Christopher Wren, which in turn is based mainly on the use of Roman decorative motifs as published by Andrea Palladio in Venice in 1570. The early Colonial style was simple in comparison with the Georgian and evidenced a greater variety between the northern and southern colonies than did the later style. Georgian forms are distinguished by formality and an elaboration of Classic detail, both inside and outside of houses, churches, and public buildings. Such elaboration was possible because the colonies had prospered in their first century, and wealth was concentrated in the New England coastal towns and the tidewater plantations of the South.

Before the Revolution there were no trained architects, and yet the handling of proportion, detail, and plan was almost uniformly good in all the colonies. The reason lay in the belief that a knowledge of architecture and its practice was a necessary part of every gentleman's training. The gentlemen-designers were aided by numerous builders' handbooks, which simplified and codified the use of the Roman and Renaissance orders. As long as they followed the symmetrical proportions of elevation and Classic detail as outlined in these books, they could not go wrong stylistically. Such handbooks account for the comparative unity in the use of this style between the northern and southern colonies in the fifty years before the Revolution. The same motifs were used on the churches and public buildings as were used in domestic structures. The exteriors almost invariably had heavy cornices with as elaborate a pedimented doorway as could be afforded. Pilasters were common inside and out, and the mantels, overmantels, and staircases received much attention.

Southern Georgian is well exemplified in the restored town of Williamsburg, Va. Mount Pleasant, in Fairmount Park in Philadelphia, is one of the best examples of the style in the central colonies. Portsmouth, N. H., and Cambridge, Mass., also have numerous good examples of this style. Carpenter's Hall, Independence Hall, and Christ Church in Philadelphia are all excellent examples of the use of the classic orders in the Georgian mode. *See also* Colonial, *supra.*   F. J. R.

GOTHIC REVIVAL

Gothic Revival refers to the widespread and highly conscious imitation of Gothic styles that reached its height during the second quarter of the nineteenth century, when it was one of several equally significant Romantic reactions against a predominantly Greek discipline of design. Although Neo-Gothic buildings were constructed in all western European countries during the nineteenth century, in both Americas, and by Europeans in Africa and Asia, the Gothic

Revival, formally so called, is peculiarly an Anglo-Saxon matter. In England in the 1850's and 1860's, so many new buildings were being designed intentionally in medieval style, and so original and vital was the Gothic work of a few architects that for a time the Gothic Revival could seem comparable with the revival of ancient Roman architectural forms in the Italian Renaissance.

Early Exponents. Probably the first neo-medieval structures were the artificial ruins built by Sanderson Miller and others in the new naturalistic English gardens of the second quarter of the eighteenth century, in places where real ruins were not available. The first Gothic Revivalists were amateurs. In the middle of the century, Horace Walpole gave prestige to a playful fake medievalism by altering and adding to his house, Strawberry Hill, in an eclectic and decorative way. In the design of the chief Gothic monument of the late eighteenth century, Fonthill Abbey, the extravagant client, William Beckford, was undoubtedly as important as the architect, James Wyatt (1746-1813). By the 1820's, both in England and in America, many new churches had pointed arches and pinnacles, although they remained in plan and structure nearly identical with the Protestant churches and meetinghouses of the eighteenth century.

Pugin's Influence. Chiefly for nationalistic historical reasons, the competition for the new British Houses of Parliament in the mid-1830's required Gothic or Elizabethan design. The winner, Sir Charles Barry (1795-1860), otherwise a leader in the reintroduction of Italian Renaissance forms, employed A. N. W. Pugin (1812-1852) to detail the Perpendicular Tudor ornamentation that veiled his eminently academic plan. Paradoxically, Pugin soon was propagandizing for the humble emulation not of the late Gothic, but of the English Decorated style of the early fourteenth century, as the only path to architectural salvation. A convert to Catholicism, Pugin had intense—and barely separable—feelings concerning religion and architecture. The English Roman Catholics then had little money for building, and the phenomenal number of churches Pugin began around 1840 proceeded slowly, yet the new standards Pugin proclaimed soon made earlier Gothic Revival work look childish. He stressed the need for good materials and for expert craftsmanship, the essential importance of truth in the expression of structure, function, and materials, as well as other obligations which were ethical as much as aesthetic. A great Frenchman, Viollet-le-Duc (1814-1879), more archaeologist than architect, paralleled the rationalism, if not the moralism, of Pugin's thought later in the century.

The interests of the Cambridge Camden Society and of other similar Anglican groups inspired by Pugin were related to, but not identical with, the program of doctrinal reform, or re-emphasis, of the Oxford movement in the Church of England. These interests lay in the detailed study of the ritual, the symbols, and the entire physical investiture of the medieval church. The influence of these groups was enormous and had the effect of establishing the Puginian version of the Gothic Revival in the Anglican community. Strangely enough, the Nonconformists in England and the dominant non-Anglican sects in America, although they could hardly accept the doctrinal implications of the Camdenian position, tended also to follow the new path.

The best of the buildings Pugin was able to complete—St. Giles, Cheadle, the Roman Catholic cathedrals of Birmingham and Nottingham, and his own model church of St. Augustine, Ramsgate—have intrinsic as well as derivative architectural virtues. But the Camdenians were academics, hunting heresy in architecture, and the formula they imposed was on the whole a dreary one. Almost equally dreary was the secular Gothic employed throughout the mid-century for most country houses and schools where the taste of parsons and their co-workers controlled. The ablest and most original minds among the new generation of architects in the mid-century, however, concentrated on such work.

Secular Applications. It was unfortunate that other equally serious problems of the age, such as the use of new materials, the provision for new functions, and the solution of inherited problems such as slums, were left to less able architects, who paid only lip service to the ideals of the leaders of the revival. William Butterfield (1814-1900) and G. E. Street (1824-1881) were recognized as the most individual and sincere of the Gothic Revival architects. Though they and others ransacked the medieval monuments of the Continent for ideas, their work was markedly original in massing, in space composition, and in treatment of polychromatic materials. The most successful architect of the period, Sir George Gilbert Scott (1811-1878), was not in their class as a designer, but he and Alfred Waterhouse (1830-1905), because of their very pliability and lack of aesthetic finesse, were able to carry the second stage of the revival out of the church field into municipal buildings, railroad stations, and other types, often with ludicrous results.

Although some of the finest Gothic Revival churches were not built until the 1860's, by younger architects such as James Brooks (1825-1901), John L. Pearson (1817-1897), and G. F. Bodley (1827-1907), it was other men who made the final contribution of the Gothic Revival to the general development of architecture in England. Philip Webb (1831-1915), W. Eden Nesfield (1835-1888), and Norman Shaw (1831-1912) really applied the basic principles of the revival, considered as a living movement and not a mere program of imitation, as well as its subtle and eclectic aestheticism to domestic problems. Webb's Red House of 1859 for William Morris, the last great critical writer of the revival, and a series of houses by Shaw in the late 1860's and the 1870's displayed new standards of convenience in planning and new refinements of scale and handicraftsmanship in materials. But in the 1870's the basis of their inspiration shifted to later and later models and is characteristically called Queen Anne. Henceforth, the Gothic Revival was largely confined to churches and ceased to be, even in the Anglo-Saxon world, a general stylistic movement.

Significance. Thus the Gothic Revival was a short-lived renaissance, producing a relatively small number of memorable monuments, chiefly churches. Even so, it has influenced later thinking about modern architecture, though its ideals have been transmuted to include respect for new materials as well as old, or sometimes have even been inverted in the insistence that no architecture can be other than a sham if it is based on past models.

In America the Gothic Revival was partially a reflection of its stages in England: Richard Upjohn corresponds to Pugin and the Camdenians, though lacking Pugin's eminence; whereas Henry Hobson Richardson is the counterpart of Webb and Shaw, though far greater than they. But America produced only minor figures to compare with Butterfield and Street in England.

In other countries, with the great exception of Viollet-le-Duc, perhaps only the name of the Dutchman Petrus Cuypers (1827-1921) has individual significance. His work parallels the line that led from the High Victorian Gothic of the 1860's to the later Queen Anne style.   H. R. H.

Carpenter's Gothic. Carpenter's Gothic refers to the wooden Gothic architecture fashioned by carpenters during the Gothic Revival era of American architecture. Whereas in Victorian England the Gothic Revival was largely of masonry, in America masonry was not deemed necessary. New England and the Midwest erected many examples in wood with battened walls and lacelike bargeboards. In fact, the prominent American architect Richard Upjohn, designer of the present Trinity Church in downtown New York, furnished designs for wooden Gothic churches and other struc-

CARPENTER'S GOTHIC STYLE

tures. Upon such buildings traceried (jigsawed) porticos, balconies, and finials were widely employed. Towers, turrets, oriel windows, porte-cocheres, and conservatories completed these fanciful creations, which were popular between the 1830's and the Civil War.   R. Ne.

GREEK REVIVAL

Greek Revival style spread widely over the Western world. It began after the first systematic and accurate publication in the second half of the eighteenth century of descriptions of ancient Greek buildings and was stimulated and made popular later by the general interest in the Greek War of Independence (1821-1833). The early publications, such as Stuart and Revett's *Antiquities of Athens* (1762-1830), J. D. Leroy's *Les Ruines des plus beaux monuments de la Grèce* (1770), and that of the Society of Dilettanti, *Antiquities of Ionia* (1797-1821), revealed to architects and the interested public alike a new architectural world. It was distinguished by extraordinary sensitiveness, restraint, purity of detail, and simple power of composition. At last the scholars saw the real origin of Classic form, and that Roman work, which had energized the Renaissance and was still powerful in the Roman Revival, was only a degenerate copy of the Greek. Thus, advanced taste everywhere turned to Greek forms for inspiration.

Application in England and Germany. The new Greek inspiration had its earliest architectural expression in England and Germany. The Potsdam Gate in Berlin (1777) had a modified Greek Doric order as its essential feature. The studies made by David Gilly for a monument to Fred-

erick the Great made superb creative use of the new inspiration, as did the work of Friedrich Schinkel.

In England the new style crept in gradually, at first only in the hesitant occasional use of Greek orders in buildings otherwise conservative. By the end of the eighteenth century it was in the ascendant and deeply affecting the work of John Soane, who used Greek precedent in the most unconventional and creative way, as in the Bank of England. A large number of others, including Philip Hardwick, the Wyatts, and Wilkins, were similarly influenced.

Much of the best Greek Revival work in England and Scotland was in small towns and the newly growing spas and resorts. In these it lasted well into the nineteenth century, with some of its most original works in Glasgow as late as the 1850's. In its more monumental and official aspects, it is best represented by the great colonnaded front of the British Museum (1825-1827) by Robert Smirke and the High School in Edinburgh by Thomas Hamilton.

Application in France. In France, the Greek Revival had little direct effect, for the persistent Roman tradition of the École des Beaux Arts, admiration for the Napoleonic monuments, and an emerging sense of logic in design were too powerful; however, deep study of Greek work was made. Certain architects attempted to found a new school of creative form, which they called *Neo-Grèc,* by applying to their contemporary problems, materials, and building techniques the same logic, delicacy, and imagination that they conceived to be the basis of Greek achievement. Characteristic *Neo-Grèc* buildings are the west front of the Palais de Justice, by Viollet-le-Duc, the greater part of the École des Beaux Arts, by Jacques Félix Duban, and the Bibliothèque Ste Géneviève, by Henri Labrouste.

Application in Russia and the United States. The Greek Revival was most influential in Russia and the United States, with extensive building under way and no controlling existing tradition. In both countries Greek inspiration was used with the greatest freedom as an incentive to creative design. The enormous series of monumental structures which make Leningrad one of the greatest of architectural cities evidenced much use of Greek inspiration.

In Moscow, the Crimea, and the Ukraine, almost all the buildings erected by the nobles or the court after 1800 were similarly based. Both foreign architects (Delamothe and de Thomon) and Russians (Vorinikhin, Stassov, Zaharov, and others) had a part in this program. From their work a Classic Revival style of definitely national character was born.

In the United States, Benjamin Latrobe first used Greek forms in the Bank of Pennsylvania, Philadelphia (1799-1800), and in most of his subsequent work in the United States Capitol, and elsewhere, the Greek influence is dominant. His pupils, Robert Mills and William Strickland, working in many parts of the country, made a Greek-inspired architecture the national style for public buildings. The period 1820-1850 saw a freely adapted, Greek-inspired style generally used in houses, business buildings, and churches, although Gothic and Italianate forms disputed its supremacy after 1830.

The influence of the books of John Haviland, the later books of Asher Benjamin, and especially the books of Minard Lafever did much to account for this countrywide character. Details developed from them can be found in New England, the Central States, the South, and all through the Middle West and the Mississippi Valley. In public work, the buildings are frequently vaulted throughout in masonry. Important architects of the period include Ithiel Town, A. J. Davis, Martin Thompson, James Dakin, James Gallier, D. Morrison, and Isaiah Rogers.   T. F. Ha.

JACOBEAN

Jacobean, the second style of Renaissance architecture in England, corresponds with the reign of James I (1603 to 1625). A development of the Elizabethan style, Jacobean was the result of a gradual capitulation to Classic forms as the Italian Neoclassicism of Palladio became better known in

JACOBEAN STYLE
Jacobean Manor House, Bramshill (Surrey), England

England. However, since Jacobean builders did not understand Classic design, the style is characterized by much questionable ornament and by mishandling of the orders of architecture. As in the Elizabethan style, interior decoration and furniture followed architectural design closely and developed appropriate forms.

The architect, John Thorpe, stands out as the great exponent of this vogue, of which his famous Holland House in Kensington, London (1607), is a notable model. Charlton House in Wiltshire (1607); Bramshill, Hampshire (1607-1612); Audley End in Sussex (1603-1616); Ashton Hall, Warwickshire (1618-1635); Bolsover Castle in Derbyshire (1613); and Blicking Hall in Norfolk (1620) likewise are outstanding examples.   R. Ne.

LOMBARD

Lombard architecture, as a style, refers to the Romanesque style employed in Lombardy in northern Italy. It had to do mostly with churches, and is characterized by attenuated pilasters, blind arcading, and archlike corbeling along the eaves and rakes of the roofs; also for cupolalike towers toward the back, at the crossing, which were the exterior expression of domes on squinches to admit light near the chancel. Square campanile towers topped by spire-like roofs were sometimes a feature, though they had no definite location and were generally detached from the main body of the church. These also were decorated with pilaster strips, arcaded corbels, and a few simple arched openings at the top.

Portals were often protected by small gabled porches with columns resting on the backs of grotesque lions.

Decoration and sculpture were based on both Byzantine and Teutonic sources, although, compared with some districts in France, sculpture was only sparingly used. Brick, stone, and marble were used in construction, and groin-ribbed vaulting was experimented with in order to make these buildings as permanent and fireproof as possible.

Lombard was one of the most creative of the Romanesque styles and influenced contemporary work in southern Italy, Germany, central and southwestern France, and Normandy. Lanfranc of Pavia, who had charge of construction work of many of the monasteries of Normandy in the eleventh century, is given credit for Lombardian influence there. It was no doubt Lombard vaulting that contributed to the solution of Gothic construction in northern France and England toward the end of the twelfth century. *See also* ROMANESQUE ARCHITECTURE.   R. W. H.

MUDEJAR

Precisely defined, a Mudejar [muthe′har] is a Moslem who lives, unconverted, as a vassal in a Christian state. By extension, the term has come to describe the Christian edifices of Spain which were executed in the Moslem or Moorish style of that country.

Spain, overrun by the Moslems in the early eighth century, was the birthplace of a brilliant Moorish culture, architecture, and art. The reconquest of the Iberian Peninsula by the Christian kings was completed by the middle of the thirteenth century with the exception of the kingdom of Granada, in the extreme south, which held out until 1492. Before this reconquest the artistic styles of the two religions had tended to remain separate and distinctive, although as early as the twelfth century a few churches had been built in the Moorish style. Immediately after the reconquest the existing mosques were turned into churches, but soon scores of new churches were erected. These churches were built and decorated by Moorish craftsmen, who continued the deep-rooted tradition and forms of their own art.

In spite of the severance of this Mudejar style from its Moorish background and its tendency towards decadence, the style displayed a remarkable persistence and a high level of virtuosity. The greater cathedrals were henceforth built by masters brought from the northern centers of Gothic art; however, this art never became firmly established in Spain. Although Mudejar style admitted some Gothic forms and details, there was no fusion of the two.

The Mudejar style was displayed in churches, church towers, city walls, and palaces and other secular buildings. The style had two levels of expression: one in the less important structures erected by Moslem craftsmen resident in the various towns, the other in the splendid palaces built by master workmen brought in for the purpose from Granada or even from North Africa. A notable example of the palace style is the Alcázar at Seville.

The materials of construction were brick and cut stone; those of decoration were carved wood, carved and painted plaster, and polychrome tiles. The Moorish horseshoe arch continued in favor, and the complicated geometrical ornament so characteristic of all Moslem art spread its fantastic forms over the surfaces of walls, vaults, and ceilings.

The Mudejar style reached its liveliest expression in the region of Aragon. Characteristic Mudejar monuments of the thirteenth century survive at Teruel and Arevalo; of the fourteenth century in the palaces at Seville and Toledo; of the fifteenth century in the palaces at Segovia; and of the sixteenth century, in a diluted form, in the cathedrals at Segovia and Salamanca. The style declined in the sixteenth century (the Mudejares were expelled from Spain in 1502); and although traces of it persisted into the Renaissance, it tended to merge with its logical and spiritual successor, Churrigueresque. D. N. W.

NORMAN

Norman architecture, as a style, has reference to the Romanesque style of Normandy and England. It is evident mostly in churches and is characterized by heavy construction and geometrical ornament, particularly edgings around arches of chevrons and dogtooth zigzags. Sculptures and leaf ornament are seldom seen except as importations, such as a sculptured portal in the Le Mans Cathedral. Exteriors are generally characterized by twin flanking towers on the west façade and by high lantern towers at the crossing.

Many of the structural characteristics are similar to, and were derived from, Lombardy. The Normans used groin-ribbed vaulting and the alternate system of plan. But whereas the Lombards were never successful in developing their vaulting so as to buttress properly and at the same time allow clerestory lighting, the Normans brought this to a satisfactory conclusion in the middle of the twelfth century. They had found the key to Gothic construction.

In England, the style was characterized by heavier piers and bulkier façades than in France. English plans were generally longer and often used double transepts and a Galilee porch, as at Cluny in Burgundy. French churches put greater emphasis on height, but neither the French nor English modifications were accented until after the development of the Gothic.

It was in the late twelfth century that France and England began to go separate ways. At this time, English work gave up much of its Norman character, while French Norman continued to differentiate itself from the work of the rest of France by high, square, lantern towers that were generally topped by simple pitched roofs. *See also* ROMANESQUE ARCHITECTURE. R. W. H.

PERPENDICULAR

The Perpendicular (also called Rectilinear by nineteenth-century historians) was a style of Gothic architecture current in England between 1350 and 1500. Like other stylistic phases of the English Gothic, it may be most quickly identified by its vaulting and window tracery. However, most architectural details of this period reflect the vertical and rectangular character suggested by the names Perpendicular and Rectilinear.

Perpendicular window tracery emphasizes the vertical line by extending the vertical bars, or mullions, to the window head. The window head itself was frequently four-centered, and since the vertical mullions gave additional strength, windows were increased in size. Horizontal bars divided the windows into rectangular panels. The glassworkers, benefiting from the rectangular frames thus formed, and perhaps even initiating such development, filled the resulting glass rectangles with representations of saints and angels. One of the largest Perpendicular windows is the east window of Gloucester Cathedral, 72 ft. high and 38 ft. wide.

Perpendicular vaulting continued the lierne vault of the Curvilinear period, but also employed the fan vault. This latter type first appeared in the cloister of Gloucester, built between 1351 and 1377. In it each rib is alike in curve, length, and spacing. Fan vaults were sometimes constructed with ashlar filling between the ribs and sometimes with thin

stone panels which had the ribs carved upon them. In some examples, such as the Chapel of Henry VII at Westminster Abbey, the transverse rib was enlarged and served as the major vault support.

Wooden roofs in the Perpendicular period were frequently of the hammer-beam type, in which short beams projecting

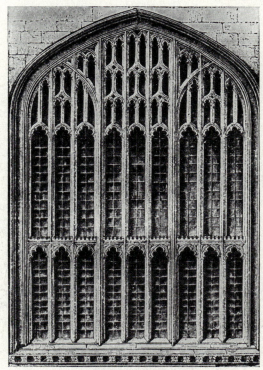

PERPENDICULAR STYLE
King's College Chapel, Cambridge, England

from opposite walls serve as supports for the principal roof truss, making a tie beam unnecessary. This type is brilliantly exemplified by Westminster Hall, erected in 1399, in which a span of 68 ft. was achieved without any intermediate support.

Perpendicular parapets and buttresses are dominated by vertical lines and rectangular shapes. Ornament likewise tends toward conventionalized angular form in contrast with the undulating naturalism of the preceding Curvilinear period. A. K. L.

RÉGENCE

Régence [re'zhã's] was a style of architecture and decoration popular in France during the regency of Philip, Duke of Orleans, from 1715 to 1723. It was a transitional period between the stately Classicism of the period of Louis XIV and the bizarre Rococo of the reign of Louis XV. The period was characterized by an increasing use of curves and a growing disregard for Classic dignity, the Classical orders being decreasingly used. Interiors were painted white and embellished with gilded moldings, cartouches, and similar ornaments. R. Ne.

ROCOCO

Rococo is a somewhat florid vogue of decoration originating in France during the early eighteenth century. The term is derived from the French word *rocailles,* "rock or shell designs," which was applied to such artificial designs as the grottoes and cascades in the gardens of Versailles. The grammar of ornament of this playful and graceful style was based upon the curves of natural forms like shells. Balance and regularity of rhythm were avoided in favor of a sportive playfulness and sparkling caprice. Historically, it was an extreme form of the Baroque movement and appeared originally as a protest against the heavy pomp of the Louis

ROCOCO STYLE

XIV style. For a half century the vogue remained gay and spontaneous, or occasionally odd; then a reaction set in and the designs became calmer and less sportive. They retained their charm and gracefulness, however, until the Neoclassic reaction set in.   R. Ne.

ROMAN REVIVAL

The Roman Revival, an important international architectural movement from about 1770 to 1830, was based on the new knowledge of ancient Roman architecture which came from an increasingly scientific archaeology and from the dramatic excavations of Pompeii and Herculaneum. Its popularity was the result of a growing dissatisfaction with the dying Baroque and Rococo tradition. Moreover, it expressed the dynamic upsurge of feeling that accompanied a revolutionary era. Many were finding in the ancient Roman Republic an inspiration for solving the current confusions; what more natural than to choose Roman forms as a new inspiration in architecture? By 1840, however, the Roman Revival had run its course, being superseded by the Greek Revival or by medieval romanticism in the form of the Gothic Revival.

France. In France the movement reached its height in the great Paris monuments of the Empire—the arches of the

Étoile (by J. F. T. Chalgrin) and of the Carrousel (by Charles Percier and P. F. L. Fontaine), the colonnade of the Chambre des Députés (by Poyet), the Bourse (by Alexandre Brogniart), and the Madeleine (by Vignon and Huvé)—and Roman and Pompeian inspiration exerted a compelling influence on the austerely rich interiors and graceful furniture of Percier and Fontaine. This Empire style in turn gave rise to much similar work of the early nineteenth century throughout Europe and even in the Americas. At the same time, a turning toward simple geometric forms, appearing earlier in the revolutionary designs of Claude Nicolas Ledoux, was deeply affecting all architectural composition and especially the design of the smaller houses; this movement produced a vast number of quiet, dignified, modest yet elegant buildings in cities and suburbs until almost the middle of the century.

England. The traditional conservatism of England kept Palladianism alive there longer than on the Continent, and the early popularity of Greek detail prevented any such wholesale Roman adaptations as those of Napoleonic France. Yet the Roman enthusiasm showed in a general reduction in Baroque detail, a growing love of plain surface, a more sophisticated decorative use of Classic architectural forms, and the introduction of Roman and Pompeian details, as well as in a love of monumental plans. Both architecturally and decoratively, the movement reached a climax in the work of the brothers Adam, in such great monuments as St. George's Hall at Liverpool (by Harvey L. Elmes), the University at Edinburgh (by Robert Adams), and, in a totally different vein, in the quiet houses and the interiors and furniture usually termed Regency (after the regency of the Prince of Wales, later George IV, from 1810 to 1820, during George III's final madness). Ideals of Roman grandeur also deeply influenced some of the work of the most creative architect of the period, Sir John Soane, as in the grand interiors of the Bank of England.

Germany. The early interest of German architects in Greek detail limited the scope of the German Roman Revival, but triumphal arches and gates were built and many German buildings show the effect of a study of Roman plans. Friedrich Schinkel, who summarized in his work all the tendencies of his time, was deeply influenced by Roman work, as his designs for Schloss Orianda and the Nicolai Kirche in Potsdam show, though his expression, like Soane's, was always personal and creative. Other designers, such as Persius and later Gottfried Semper, show the same influence, and in Hamburg and North Germany there was much building of a quiet, restrained type not unlike that of the English Regency and under similar influences.

Russia. The movement permeated all northern Europe. The Scottish architect Cameron took it to Russia, and many great buildings there by Russian, French, and Italian architects show its influence, though the fully developed St. Petersburg Classic revival is as much influenced by Greek as by Roman precedent.

United States. In the United States the Roman Revival was limited by the persistence of the Colonial tradition, but it is dominant in some of the architecture of Thomas Jefferson, as in the University of Virginia and the Virginia Capitol, and in plan and concept it deeply affected the designs for the United States Capitol and for early statehouses. The popularity of the low, wide dome in the United States is due to Roman influence. Elsewhere the movement appears merely as a distant reflection of Adam detail, as in some of the work of Charles Bulfinch and Samuel McIntire.

T. F. Ha.

TUDOR

Tudor, the late or final period of Gothic architecture in England, was current between 1485 and 1558, or during the reign of the Tudor monarchs Henry VII, Henry VIII, Edward VI, and Mary I. The architecture of the reign of Elizabeth, who was also a Tudor, is generally called Elizabethan.

The Tudor period witnessed a decrease in the amount of church building, the secularization of the monasteries, and the widespread erection of manor houses. Increasing prosperity led almost inevitably to the general secularization of life and the demand for greater comfort and convenience in domestic arrangements.

Tudor window tracery and vaulting generally continues the Perpendicular style. Openings frequently employ the Tudor or four-centered arch and are often enclosed by rectangular frames. Increased horizontality is especially noticeable in domestic architecture, where several windows are grouped under one horizontal dripstone. Square-headed mullioned windows were also employed. Fireplaces with four-centered arches and heraldic carvings became common. These necessitated chimneys, which display wide variety. Pinnacled gables and carved finials add to the picturesque silhouette of the typical Tudor manor house. Brick, stone, and half-timber are the common materials of the larger dwellings. Equally pleasing are the plaster and half-timber walls of the less pretentious cottages.

Here and there Italian Renaissance details were incorporated among the prevailing late Gothic forms. Italian craftsmen were employed on a number of projects, but they were not liked and most of them had departed by the middle of the sixteenth century. The magnificent wood screen in King's College Chapel, Cambridge, is evidence of their ability.

A. K. L.

VICTORIAN

In Great Britain and her Dominions the name "Victorian" is generally given to the characteristic architecture of the mid-nineteenth century, though the reign of Queen Victoria spanned the years 1837 to 1901. Since Americans continued in this period to follow English stylistic developments almost as closely as in Colonial times, the term "Victorian" is not improperly used also for much mid-nineteenth-century American architecture.

The vitality of the Victorian age, so evident in other fields, is admirably expressed in its architecture, and certain of the finest individual monuments deserve the sort of respect usually reserved for work of earlier periods. Yet individualism rampant seemed incapable of concerted architectural effort. In the Victorian architectural story lie the origins of most of the twentieth-century functional and structural problems and even perhaps some hints of the aesthetic dilemmas of the later period.

A purely Victorian style can hardly be isolated, since most Victorian architects worked in some relation to the recognized styles of the past. Serious attempts at basic originality were always peripheral. The lack of adequate archaeological documentation—particularly evident in America—and a characteristic taste for rich and striking effects, however, generally produced results which can hardly be mistaken for the work of earlier centuries.

Exhibition Buildings. Men of engineering, not architects, produced occasional monuments in metal and glass which were peculiar to the age and of very considerable intrinsic distinction. The Crystal Palace, designed by a gardener-engineer, Sir Joseph Paxton, for the first great international exposition in London in 1851, fired the imagination of the age and was imitated in various countries within the next few years. One of these imitations, New York's Crystal Palace, dated from 1853.

Churches. The Victorian age was by no means purely an industrial and scientific age; it was also very religious. Churches were built in greater numbers than ever before to take care of an expanding population. By the mid-century, medieval styles were generally used for churches even by the evangelical sects that had earlier rejected Gothic models as tending to Roman Catholic practice.

Many factors tended to produce edifices of great complexity of interest: asymmetrical exterior compositions, massed about towers with spires of striking silhouette; various experiments first in compound and later in unified interior space; elaborate enrichment with polychromatic materials and painted decorations or with boldly plastic details and naturalistic carvings. In the hands of a few masters, such as William Butterfield and G. E. Street in England, the results sometimes represent the most original artistic achievement of the age. But in imitative and provincial hands Victorian churches are notorious for their confusion.

Commercial Buildings. Midway between the exhibition buildings of the Victorian Age, on the one hand, and the churches on the other (with which educational buildings and, in England, country mansions can be grouped), lies the world of Victorian commercial architecture. In America, cast iron was very freely used for exteriors as well as for interiors, but the stylistic forms were generally derived from the Renaissance vocabulary and the iron was actually sanded and painted to imitate stone. In England brick or stone shells were erected around the interior skeletons of cast and wrought iron, because English architects realized that iron alone would not stand up against the extreme heat of urban conflagrations (as those of the early 1870's in America proved) and also because prestige demanded monumental expression in masonry. Although the general frame of design was usually Renaissance, the best commercial architects utilized freely the polychromy and plastic enrichment of the more aesthetic church architects. The need for additional light in offices, above all, led to much originality in arcaded compositions; while in such buildings as exchanges, which required large covered courts, iron and glass were used with more subtlety and refinement than in such engineering work as railroad station sheds. Two masterpieces that may be mentioned are the courts of Bunning's Coal Exchange in London of 1846 and of Brodrick's Corn Exchange of 1861 in Leeds, both Italianate in exterior design. A less happy venture in iron and glass was the Gothic court of the University Museum at Oxford by Deane and Woodward, 1855.

Houses. Domestic design before the late 1860's was the least successful field of Victorian architecture in England. The "model" dwellings, built to replace the incredible slums of the eighteenth and early nineteenth centuries, never caught up with the building of new slums. They often seem today little better than slums themselves, despite their philanthropic intention. The middle classes were housed chiefly in double houses which were either pathetically tawdry in their illiterate embellishments or grim in their barren shapelessness. Urban row houses, whatever their economic level, represented a positive decline in almost every way (except for advances in plumbing and heating) from those of the preceding Georgian age. In the characteristic detached houses of America, however, the vogue of the "Tudor cottage" or "Italian villa" encouraged a freer sort of planning. The important "Queen Anne" development in domestic architecture, though it began in the heart of the Victorian age, pointed toward the post-Victorian future.

Public Buildings. Public architecture in both England and America was pretentious and expansive, usually lacking the structural innovations and the curious dignity of the best commercial work and the subtle if perverse aestheticism of the churches. In this field the model of Napoleon III's new Louvre was frequently imitated. Indeed, in the 1860's, elements of French Second Empire style, notably the high mansard roof and pavilion composition, were used in all sorts of structures. *See also* Gothic Revival, *supra*.   H. R. H.

For related studies see also: AEGEAN ARCHITECTURE; ARCHITECTURE, HISTORY OF; BYZANTINE ARCHITECTURE; CHINESE AND JAPANESE ARCHITECTURE; EARLY CHRISTIAN ARCHITECTURE; EGYPTIAN ARCHITECTURE; ETRUSCAN ARCHAEOLOGY; GOTHIC ARCHITECTURE; GREEK ARCHITECTURE; INDIAN ARCHITECTURE; MAYAN ARCHITECTURE; MEXICAN ARCHITECTURE; MOHAMMEDAN ARCHITECTURE; NEAR EASTERN ARCHITECTURE; PERSIAN ARCHITECTURE; RENAISSANCE ARCHITECTURE; ROMAN ARCHITECTURE; ROMANESQUE ARCHITECTURE; SYRIAN ARCHITECTURE.

ARCHITECTURAL TERMS.

ARCHITECTURAL TERMS. This article defines and describes architectural forms, components, and devices. A historical record and typical applications are generally included. Supplementary information is noted by means of cross references at the end of the complete article, and after some terms.

Apse, the semicircular or polygonal termination of a basilican church, used in various forms from Early Christian times to the present. It constitutes a focal point in the physical arrangement of the church and in the liturgy, framing the high altar, which is customarily placed on its diameter or chord. Although the semicircular apse was employed in England, it is rare after the twelfth century, and its identity as a separate element is lost in the typical English rectangular termination called chancel or presbytery. In France and on the Continent, generally, the apse remained as a separate visible element.

Early examples still exist in Rome, Ravenna, and other Mediterranean centers. These consist of a semicircular wall (sometimes polygonal or square on the exterior) covered by a half dome. The wall was frequently faced with colored marble and the half dome incrusted with glass mosaic. In the early medieval period, painting took the place of mosaic, and the apse was pierced with arches opening into the processional or ambulatory aisle that came to encircle it. With the development of Gothic vaulting, the apse became taller, its enframing arch became pointed, and the half dome was replaced by stone ribs and panels, also frequently painted. The Renaissance returned to the early basilican church type but with many variations and an infinite variety of embellishment. In America, regions colonized under French or Spanish influence often employed the apse in their church designs. Those stemming from England regularly employed the rectangular chancel. Most of the former types of apse are represented in contemporary church design. Some achieve refreshing newness of form, as in the chapel at Kelham, Newark, England. Others emulate the finest medieval examples. *See also* Choir, *infra*.   A. K. L.

Arabesque, a kind of ornamentation consisting of a complex overlapping and interlacing pattern of geometrical devices, flowers, foliage, or fruit and sometimes including human and other faunal forms, these last-named types being more specifically called grotesques. Though applied to an element much used in Oriental, particularly Saracenic art, the term "arabesque" has no definite historic connotation and is applied to any complicated ornamental pattern. Persian and Moorish ceramics and architecture afford many examples of the general nonfaunal patterns of ornament that gave rise to the term. Such designs, distinctly Islamic in origin, became highly popular in Europe between the fifteenth and seventeenth centuries. Western designers employed painted, inlaid-wood, and bas-relief arabesques composed of Greek and Roman grotesque designs. Such ornamental patterns were used even as decoration for the Classical derived Renaissance orders of architecture, particularly for the ornamentation of panels, pilasters, and sometimes of columns.   R. Ne.

Arcade, a term applied to a series of consecutive arches, usually of the same size, combined to form a single architectural motif. It is used structurally when it supports the wall above and decoratively when it is applied to a wall without acting as a support. When used for heavier construction, as on aqueducts and bridges, the arches in Roman architecture were supported by heavy piers. The result was heavy and crude. Therefore, to give the arcades more grace, the so-called Roman arcade was developed. This motif consists of arches whose piers contain engaged columns supporting an entablature which runs over the arches, the order being used as a superimposed decoration and having no structural meaning. An example of this motif is found on the Colosseum in Rome, built A.D. 70 to 82.

In later Roman times, the piers were omitted and the arcades were supported directly by columns with the impost in the form of a full or abbreviated entablature. An early example of this arrangement is found in the Palace of Diocletian at Split (Spalato), Yugoslavia, built A.D. 300. This new motif was much more open and graceful than the Roman arcade and consequently was much used in Early Christian and Byzantine architecture to separate the nave from the side aisles of churches. It continued in use through all the medieval period and the Renaissance. It was used also in cloisters, as at Monreale, Sicily (1174); on façades, as in the cathedral at Pisa (1063-1092), adorned with superimposed rows of small freestanding arcades, and for courtyards and porches, as in the Cancelleria in Rome (1495-1505) and the municipal palace at Genoa (1564). The interesting interlaced arcades of the medieval period are exemplified by those applied on the interior walls of Peterborough Cathedral, England (1117 to 1190), and in Christ Church, Oxford (1158-1180).   O. S. Fj.

Arch, in architecture, a structural device used to span an opening in a wall. The arch is composed of several wedge-shaped stones, called voussoirs, which press sidewise, one against the other, resulting in an outward pressure or thrust which must be abutted by sufficient material at the sides of the arch lest it collapse.

The arch principle was known to the ancient Egyptians and Assyrians, who used it mainly for sewers. It was not until the times of the Etruscans and Romans, however, that the arch was fully developed and used as a dominant architectural feature. During the Italian Renaissance, metal tie rods with a turnbuckle were often used, especially at the corners of an arcaded porch, to make up for the lack of abutment. The term "arch" is also applied to openings in walls imitating arch shapes but not using the dynamic principle.

Parts. Besides the voussoirs in general, the parts of the arch are as follows:

1. The impost, the first stone immediately below the voussoirs. It is often accentuated by moldings or decorative carving.

2. The springer, the lowest voussoir, resting on the impost. It contains the stilt, a short straight vertical surface between the impost and the point where the curvature of the arch begins, known as the spring line.

3. The keystone, the central voussoir at the top of the arch. When it is inserted, the arch stones are locked in place and the arch is completed. Its importance is often accentuated by decorative carving or by modeling in it the much-used **S**-shaped scroll.

4. The intrados, the inner line of the voussoirs. The voussoirs or arch stones usually intercept equal arcs on the intrados, although sometimes they are made in an alternate pattern.

5. The extrados, the outer line of the voussoirs, which appears only when the arch is molded

6. The soffit, the underside of the arch

T. RICKMAN

ARCH

(Left) *Ely Cathedral, England;* (Right) *Selby Abbey Church, England*

Forms. With use, the arch has been made to assume a wide variety of shapes, as follows:

1. The triangular arch, consisting of two wedge-shaped stones, found on one side of the Lion's Gate at Mycenae (about 1400 B.C.) sometimes called the Saxon arch, because of its prevalence in Saxon architecture

2. The semicircular, or Roman, arch

3. The pointed, or Gothic, arch, consisting of two intersecting circle segments

4. The segmental arch, whose intrados is a circle segment with a small rise from the impost to the center of the arch

5. The flat arch, composed of wedge-shaped stones but whose lower edge is a straight horizontal line

6. The horseshoe-shaped arch, prevalent in Moorish architecture

7. The elliptical arch, employing three or five centers, as found in Elizabethan and early French Renaissance architecture

8. The parabolic arch, found in late European and American architecture

9. The ogee arch, which uses a double reverse curve for its inner outline   O. S. Fj.

Attic, in Classic architecture, a term used to designate (a) a low story or parapet above the main order on the façade of a building, or, (b) more generally, that part of a building just below the roof. The term, probably derived from Attica in Greece, is among architects sometimes known as an Athenian story. Attics vary considerably in size and architectural treatment, but in height are generally one fourth that of the order below. They are divided, as are parapets, pedestals, and balustrades, into molded plinths, dies, and upper rails. Such stories were popular in Roman architecture and were used with excellent monumental effect upon Roman public buildings. Particularly effective was their use upon triumphal arches, where, ornamented with bas-relief sculpture or freestanding statues, they also bore the dedicatory inscriptions. During the Italian Renaissance, attic

stories were revived and given a new and important emphasis. In smaller compositions a balustrade often fulfills the same decorative purpose as the attic.   R. Ne.

Baldachino (Baldaquin), from Italian *baldacchino,* denotes in architecture a shelter of canopy form over a tomb or an altar. It takes its name from the fact that such canopies were hung with rich fabrics of oriental silk from Baldacco (Bagdad). Such a canopy, also known as a ciborium, is usually constructed of four columns of wood, bronze, or marble connected at the top by an entablature from which lambrequins of rich fabrics may or may not be suspended. Excellent early examples are found in the Early Christian basilicas of Italy, where this form of marking a holy spot was most popular.

The baldachino continued popular during the Romanesque era, but its use died out during the Gothic period. Its popularity returned with the Renaissance, when many rich examples were erected, especially in Italy. Perhaps the best known baldachino of this style is that in bronze designed by G. L. Bernini as a canopy for the altar of St. Peter's basilica in Rome. This, like many other examples, has spiral bronze columns. Frequently, the columns were of richly colored marbles selected for their unique veining. The baldachino over the altar of the basilican church of Santa Maria Maggiore in Rome has angelic figures above the columns together with the papal insignia, the cross surmounting a crown.   R. Ne.

Baluster, denoting a short column with base, shaft, and capital. A series of balusters used to support a top member

BALUSTER

Gondi Palace, Florence, Italy

or rail forms a balustrade. The term should not be used for railings using other than balusters to support the top member. Balustrades are used as railings on parapets, porches, terraces, retaining walls, and staircases. The thinness of the balustrade makes it necessary to introduce occasional piers as stiffening members. The baluster was developed as a diminutive column during medieval times. During the Renaissance period each order was assigned a baluster. The shafts were vase-shaped; for the Corinthian order a double-vase form placed end to end was used.   O. S. Fj.

Base, in architecture, the lower member of a pier, wall, or column. Functionally, it spreads the superimposed weight over a larger area and thereby lessens the pressure per unit area on the surface below.

The base of a pier or wall may consist of the lowest stone course, or it may be elaborated in height and contain decorative moldings, or panels. The term is also applicable to the lower finish of an interior wall, as in "baseboard."

In Classic orders, it is the lower member of a column and appears on all orders except the Greek Doric. It consists of a square flat block, the plinth, on which rest moldings circular in plan. Classic bases are confined to a few types, like the Attic and Doric. The Attic base has, above the plinth, two torus moldings separated by a scotia. The Doric base has, above the plinth, a large torus with a bead molding above it. The Tuscan order uses a simplified Doric base, and the Corinthian and Composite orders use variations of the Attic base.

In medieval architecture, column bases were extremely varied. Some were extremely low and simple; others were high and decorated with series of moldings. Polygonal shapes were common in Gothic architecture.   O. S. Fj.

BATTLEMENT
Carcassone, France

Battlement, a parapet with embrasures (open spaces) surmounting the walls of fortified buildings; later used as a decorative feature. Battlements early appeared in military architecture and constituted well-defined motifs of Assyrian, Babylonian, and Persian buildings. When war was waged with spears, bows and arrows, and battering rams, the battlement was effective, inasmuch as its merlons (solid parts) protected the warriors while they hurled missiles through the crenels or embrasures. Battlements were not important in Greek fortifications, but they reappeared in Roman architecture and continued popular down through the Middle Ages. The castellated architecture of Italy, France, and England shows many and highly developed battlemented forms which persisted long after the technique of warfare had changed. Indeed, with the Gothic Revival toward the middle of the nineteenth century, battlemented towers and turrets reached the United States, where they were much used for armories, prisons, and college buildings.   R. Ne.

Bay, (a) a unit or principal compartment of a building usually indicated on the plan as the area delineated by walls or by other supports, such as piers or columns; (b) a principal division of the façade, set off by vertical members, like pilasters or columns; (c) a compartment of a medieval vault; or (d) a windowed bay or recess in a room. When windowed bays project from an outer wall and are carried upon corbels or brackets, they are designated as "oriels." Bay windows date from the Gothic period. They had been used in great profusion in the manors and town houses of early Renaissance England but were less popular from the time of Sir Christopher Wren on. As plant conservatories and as simple additions to rooms, bay windows found considerable favor in America during the middle and late nineteenth century.   R. Ne.

Bed Mold, in Classic architecture, the molding or group of moldings at the top of a frieze or a wall to support the corona; the lower member of the cornice. It varies as between the several orders of architecture but usually takes the form of a cymatium. More generally, the term refers to any molding below a deep projection. *See* Cornice, *infra.*   R. Ne.

Buttress, a masonry prop or counterbalance, formed by thickening the walls at intervals to resist the thrust of an arch, vault, or roof. It is an essential element of Gothic architecture although appearing earlier and used later. By its employment, maximum strength is achieved with a minimum quantity of masonry. Among the earliest examples are the buttresses of the Basilica of Constantine, Rome (A.D. 312). Other examples exist in Syria, Milan, and Ravenna. The medieval buttress, however, was a reinvention rather than a derivative from Rome. Early medieval churches, such as San Ambrogio, Milan, employed flat pilaster strips at regular intervals as buttresses. Until these acquired more depth than breadth, however, they were of slight value. Sometimes elongated columns were used as apse buttresses, as at St. Pierre, Aulnay.

With the advent of Gothic, interior vault thrusts were greater and were concentrated against the outer walls at definite points. The economical absorption of these thrusts by masonry props perpendicular to the walls marks a salient difference between Gothic and Romanesque architecture. Romanesque masons had depended on walls seven to nine

T. RICKMAN

BUTTRESS
Merton College Chapel, England

feet thick for resistance to vaulting and had fearfully limited the size of their windows. Gothic masons reduced the function of walls between buttresses to mere screens against the weather, permitting them to become glass instead of stone. The significant beginnings of the flying buttress (*See* Flying Buttress, *infra*), are found in Caen, Normandy, and at Durham, England. This type of buttress was widely employed in France (and throughout Europe), where the high vaults necessitated a veritable forest of masonry props often arranged in flights and stages. The lower vaults of the English allowed their masons to build lower and simpler buttresses or even to continue the Romanesque reliance on thick clerestory walls, as at Salisbury, where they measure seven feet.

Buttresses form an important element of Gothic tower design, although they were generally omitted in Italy. These tower buttresses were placed at the corners either perpendicular to the walls or on the diagonal. They usually terminated in pinnacles and were built with several stages, each projecting farther as it came nearer the ground and each stage protected by moldings to prevent weather erosion. *See also* MASONRY STRUCTURES.   A. K. L.

Candelabrum, denoting a large candleholder or decorative shaft to support a group of candles or oil lamps. During Roman times candelabra figured as decorative architectural ornaments and were executed in a variety of materials, notably carved marble and cast bronze. A common type consisted of a low pedestal borne upon lion's-claw feet out of which arose a shaft decorated with acanthus leaves or other bas-relief ornament, which in turn carried the candle socket or a circular shelf for the lamps. The decorative possibilities of the candelabrum fascinated the artists of Renaissance Italy, who revived its use. The term applies also to branched candlesticks.   R. Ne.

Capital, in architecture, the top of the three divisions of the column. It acts as a stilt block to spread the bearing for the lintel. Favored by the dignity of a high position, it has

T. RICKMAN

CAPITAL

(Left) *York Cathedral;* (Right) *Cloisters, Norwich, England*

become a beautiful accentuating feature. Aesthetically, it arrests the speed of the eye as it travels up the column and forms a pleasant transition to the horizontals of the lintel above. The Classic orders derive their names from the forms of their capitals—Doric, Ionic, Corinthian, Tuscan, and Composite. *See also* ARCHITECTURAL ORDERS; COLUMN. O. S. Fj.

Chandelier, denoting, originally, a candleholder; later, any lampstand for candles, oil, gas, or electricity, but especially a branched frame of metal, wood, glass, or other material suspended from a ceiling to support lamps. Hanging lamps go back to the Middle Ages, when they appear to have been fashioned mainly of wood. However, as metal became more plentiful, iron, bronze, brass, and silver chandeliers made their appearance. As an architectural embellishment, chandeliers were fashioned in designs to accord with the style of the structure in which they were used. In Europe

during the seventeenth and eighteenth centuries, and in France particularly, the chandelier reached an elaborate decorative development with lavish glass or rock-crystal pendants, ropes, and drops, which by reflection multiplied the effect of the lights.   R. Ne.

Chimney (from Latin *caminus,* Old French *cheminée*), the device by means of which the smoke and fumes of fires employed to heat buildings are conducted outside the structure. When fire was first taken inside the cave man's dwelling, no effort was made to remove the smoke. In time, however, as men constructed habitations, a hole in the roof served this purpose. The Romans heated the rooms and bathing pools in their great public bathhouses by means of furnaces under the floors with flues in the walls. In northern Europe, however, the primitive hole in the roof appears to have been employed as late as the twelfth century, at which time castles were still heated by open fires upon iron and stone dogs in the middle of the great hall. It was not until the fire was removed to a recess in the wall (the fireplace) that correct venting was obtained. Usually this was accomplished by means of flues built in the wall to carry the smoke above the roof of the structure.

During the thirteenth and fourteenth centuries, flues began to receive architectural treatment. With the multiplication of fireplaces and the necessity of venting each by a flue, groups of flues appeared upon the roof. Then architects recognized the advisability of housing these flues in a single stack or chimney and according it an architectural treatment in accord with the rest of the structure. Thus in French and English Late Medieval and Renaissance architecture the chimney became a monumental and in some cases an elaborate feature, as in the chateaux de Blois and Chambord in France or Kirby Hall, Hampton Court Palace, and Burleigh House in England.

In the pioneering days of western movement in America, the chimneys of many log cabins were constructed of sticks and mud or of logs chinked with clay and mortar. Until the general adoption of other heating devices, fireplaces, and consequently chimneys, remained prominent in architectural composition. Even in a large part of new construction, this importance survives in decorative fireplaces and chimneys.   R. Ne.

Chimney Piece, a recess into, or a hood projecting from, a wall to shelter a fire grate, collect the smoke and fumes arising from the fire, and conduct them to a flue which will exhaust them to the outside air; any decorative embellishment of the fireplace, such as a mantel. The chimney piece was a late development in northern European architecture. It received its fullest artistic attention in France and England, where it became the principal focal feature of important interiors. If there was a hood, frequently it ran up to the ceiling and was elaborately ornamented. If there was no hood, rich wood carving or sculptural relief embellished the overmantel. During the Renaissance the orders of architecture figured highly in fireplace ornamentation. In warm countries, like Italy and Spain, chimney pieces were treated with restraint and delicacy, but in the chateaux and palaces of the French Renaissance they were lavishly decorative. The early English chimney pieces were simple in treatment, but from about 1600 onward they became highly elaborate until the return of restraint under the brothers Adam, late in the eighteenth century.   R. Ne.

Choir, sometimes known as chancel, that portion of a church set apart for the clergy and choir and once separated from the place of the worshippers by a screen (*cancellus*) or rail. The term choir is derived from the

Greek χορός (Latin *chorus*) and refers to the singing element, first in the Greek drama and later applied to the singing worshippers in Christian rituals. As the Christian service developed, the various functions of worship were reflected in specific architectural arrangements, and the choir became a well-defined part. Thus in the church of San Clemente in Rome, which dates from the eleventh century but preserves the plan of fifth-century churches, the choir is set off by a low marble screen.

As Romanesque and Gothic architecture developed, more and more attention was bestowed upon the choir, particularly in France and England, where richly carved choir stalls, elaborate paneling, and beautifully wrought rood screens were featured. The choirs of York, Durham, Ely, Lincoln, Wells, and Canterbury cathedrals and Westminster Abbey are particularly beautiful. In some English churches, such as the Norwich Cathedral, the choir extends beyond the transepts and into the nave, and in Spanish Gothic cathedrals the choir generally extends beyond the crossing and transepts. Barcelona, Toledo, and Burgos are representative examples. The space in the choir at the rear of the high altar, sometimes provided with a small altar and used as a chapel, is called the retrochoir, less frequently the angels' choir, as at Lincoln Cathedral. *See also* Apse, *supra*.   R. Ne.

Choir Screen, a screen used to separate the choir of a church from the aisles and nave. On the north and south of the medieval cathedral the screen was usually faced by the choir stalls. On the west it marked the termination of the choir and provided a background wall, or reredos, for the altar used by the lay congregation. When this western screen was surmounted by a rood cross it was called the rood screen. This, however, was sometimes a separate screen placed one or two bays west of the choir screen. The liturgical needs of the Renaissance and contemporary churches have often preserved the medieval architectural arrangement.

Built of stone or wood, choir screens paralleled general architectural development. Thus, round-arched tracery and openings characterize the screens of the Romanesque period, whereas Gothic screens employ the pointed arches, cusps, and crockets of the Gothic style current at the time of building. Some of the finest Renaissance choir screens are found in the churches of Spain. Called *rejas,* they are usually of gilded wrought iron and unbelievably rich.   A. K. L.

Clerestory (Clearstory), the upper windows and/or window wall of a hall or church. The roofing of aisles, galleries, or subsidiary chambers ordinarily reaches about to the sills of the clerestory windows, and the vault or ceiling of the main hall is close above these windows on the interior. The most famous examples are the great hypostyle hall of the Temple of Karnak, Egypt, of the Nineteenth Dynasty, with huge stone-lattice screens; the central hall of the Palace of Darius at Persepolis (480 B.C.), destroyed; the Basilica Nova of Maxentius and Constantine in Rome (fourth century A.D.), now a ruin. Old St. Peter's in Rome, also dating from the time of Constantine, but demolished in the fifteenth century, set the style for big clerestory windows in churches. Stained glass, first used importantly about 1140, made necessary the larger windows which the new Gothic style of architecture was able to provide.

Other examples of the clerestory in churches include Santa Sabina, Rome (425), a typical large Early Christian basilica, whose windows were originally filled with gypsum screens; Hagia Sophia, Constantinople (begun 532), with forty windows at the base of the dome and others in the great lateral tympana; Autun Cathedral (1119 to 1146), a Burgundian Romanesque structure, with small windows under a masonry vault, resulting in a dark interior, and probably leaded glass in screens of wood; Chartres Cathedral (1194 to 1260), which is Gothic and has plate tracery and leaded glass, and whose clerestory is world-famous for its filling of thirteenth-century stained glass. St. John the Divine, in New York, is a good modern example in the Gothic style.
                                              K. J. C.

Colonnade, a series of columns of the same height, spaced at regular intervals and carrying an architrave. The columns usually form a straight line or a circular shape. When used all the way around a building, court, or garden, they form a peristyle. When used as an entrance porch projecting from the wall of the building, they form a portico. The columns may be relatively short or tall, but when stone is used the limitations of the material limit the length of the lintel and therefore the intercolumniation to a distance of from ten to twelve feet. The resulting narrower proportions of the space between tall columns accentuates their height and dignity. The simple and impressive Classic colonnades were composed of single columns. During the Renaissance, columns doubled side by side were introduced, creating a new, less formal effect. Examples of these are found on the east façade of the Louvre and on the main entrance of St. Paul's Cathedral in London.

In Greek work, to overcome the impression of crowding, the columns were spaced wider apart at the center of the colonnade and the space between them gradually diminished toward the ends of the colonnade. To increase the feeling of stability, the columns were not plumb but leaned inward slightly toward the center, the corner column leaning inward the most. *See also* ARCHITECTURAL ORDERS; COLUMN.
                                              O. S. Fj.

Corbel, a projection from the face of a wall, supporting a weight. Corbels may be individual supports, like brackets, or continuous bands of moldings. Frequently, in battlemented architecture, a series of projecting corbel blocks support arches that carry the superimposed crenelated parapet. In Romanesque architecture, arcaded cornices, belt courses (horizontal bands), and eaves galleries or passages are carried upon plain or ornamental corbel blocks. Corbels as supports for statuary and even as places from which to spring vaults or arches were much used in medieval architecture. The kindred corbel table is a projecting wall supported by a row of corbels and forming a parapet. Corbels in the form of consoles (scroll-shaped brackets) or modillions were used during the Italian Renaissance.   R. Ne.

Cornice, a term having several meanings: (1) a project-

T. RICKMAN

CORNICE

ing horizontal feature at the top of a wall which extends the roof so that water will drip away from the building; (2) a finish at the top of an interior wall, forming a decorative transition from the wall to the ceiling; (3) the uppermost of the three divisions of the Classic entablature. The cornice on Classic orders consists of the bed molds supporting the projecting corona, which, in turn, has a molding above it called the cymatium.

In hot climates, the cornice is given a great overhang to protect the walls from the sun. In the contemporary solar house a large overhang is so arranged as to protect the walls and openings from the sun in summer but to admit the solar light and heat in winter.

The several materials used in cornice construction add great variety to its forms. Classic cornices were usually of stone with decorative tile forming the gutter. In the brick cornices of North Italian Romanesque architecture, interesting variations using patterns suitable to brick were used. Medieval stone cornices were often supported by corbels decorated with grotesques. In carpentry, the open cornice is one where the roof rafters are left exposed. The boxed cornice is one where the rafters are covered on the outer edge and underside with boards and moldings to give greater similarity to the Classical cornice. On a skyscraper, where they cannot serve their function, cornices are omitted as unnecessary. *See also* Entablature, *infra*. O. S. Fj.

Crocket, a projecting leaf ornament commonly used in the structure or ornamentation of column capitals and on the raking edges of the gables, spires, pinnacles, and dripstones

T. RICKMAN

CROCKET
Winchester Cathedral, England

of Gothic architecture. Early examples appear in the nave capitals of Noyon Cathedral (c. 1174) and in the stalk foliage of the east transept piers at Lincoln Cathedral (1192). In both France and England, the simple incurved leaf changed to more naturalistic foliage about 1250, assuming an undulating ogee profile. Conventionalized stiff square leaf forms were usual in England after 1350.

At first used on spires to emphasize the edges, crockets came to serve the useful purpose of steppingstones during and after the fourteenth century. By them, the steeple jack could reach all parts of a spire without costly scaffolding. A. K. L.

Crypt (Latin *crypta*, from Greek κρυπτὸς, hidden), a burial vault partly or wholly underground, particularly under the floor of a church. *Crypta,* at first used to designate any vaulted compartment, attained a specialized meaning in early Christian times, when the vaulted burial places in the catacombs were thus named. After Christianity was legalized early in the fourth century, many of the churches were erected over the burial places of saints or martyrs. Thus, as churches multiplied, it became a common prac-

tice to inter the bodies of holy men or women within church buildings. In time, a subterranean chamber for such burials was considered an essential part of the church. Hence, most of the great churches in medieval and modern Europe have crypts; and in America St. John the Divine in New York, St. Albans in Washington, and some others follow this precedent. R. Ne.

DONJON
Chateau Niont, France

Donjon, the keep of a medieval castle as distinguished from a dungeon or prison. In the castles of western Europe, the donjon was regarded as the fortress, the embattled walls being considered as auxiliary defenses. In the Near East, however, and particularly in crusaders' castles, each enclosing wall was considered as a fortress and the keep was looked on as a last-ditch refuge. In some eastern castles the donjon is just a larger tower, so located in the defense system as to flank the main walls. This idea of flanking towers was incorporated into western European castles during the twelfth century. In some cases, however, the keep was at the heart of the castle surrounded by from one to three distinct enceintes. Although many donjon towers were rectangular or polygonal in plan, round towers in time became the most popular. Splendid examples were built in both England and France, the famous donjon of the now-destroyed Château of Coucy in France being outstanding. This feature of the medieval castle has figured in picture and story and remains perhaps the most dramatic aspect of castle architecture. R. Ne.

Egg and Dart, a highly stylized motif consisting of alternating oviform and dartlike or tonguelike members, carved or painted on the surface of a molding. It was originated by the Greeks, borrowed by the Romans, and revived during the Renaissance. By some, it has been held to have a phallic origin and significance, but, like the bead and reel, the leaf and tongue, and other alternating ornaments of Classic architecture, it appears to have derived from purely decorative considerations. In general, the ornamentation of Greek moldings was designed to correspond with and enhance the profile or contour of the molding. Thus, the egg and dart was applied to that convex profile known as the ovolo. The flatter leaf and tongue, on the other hand, was applied to the half-convex, half-concave *cyma reversa*. The egg and dart was

EGG AND DART
Erectheum, Athens, Greece

used not only in straight moldings, but also in the echinus of the Ionic order, where, as on the moldings, it received polychromatic treatment. R. Ne.

Elevation, in architecture, a drawing or design that depicts a structure, or part thereof, as it is projected upon a vertical plane parallel to a principal face of the structure; the drawing of any façade of a structure. Buildings of rectilinear plan are considered to have four elevations, generally labeled front, rear, and ends. However, doors, windows, and other parts of structures may be selected for more detailed delineation on elevation drawings, which, accompanied by plan and section drawings, completely explain a structure or any part of it. These conventional projections are the documents, generally reproduced in blueprint, that are furnished by the architect to the general contractor and other craftsmen as guides to the correct erection of a structure which the architect may have also delineated by a perspective, a drawing which sets forth the same edifice as it might appear in natural three-dimensional space. It should be pointed out that, as a geometrical projection, the elevation does not represent a façade as it will actually appear to any observer but as a diagram that sets off correct widths and heights of the part represented. Elevation drawings, embellished with trees and colored to simulate the finished structure are sometimes made to do duty for a true perspective. R. Ne.

Encaustic Painting, a once common decoration practice in ancient times by which colors suspended in wax were applied and fixed by the application of heat. This technique appears to have been employed in Egypt, Greece, and Rome for mural decoration, portrait painting, and the polychromatic treatment of sculpture and architecture. It is believed that much of the mural decoration at Herculaneum and Pompeii was executed in this medium, three varieties of which the elder Pliny describes in his *Historia naturalis*. There is good evidence that the polychromatic adornment of Greek white-marble statues and buildings was accomplished by this means. The technique here was probably that of applying tinted hot wax by means of a brush to the part to be colored, after which the excess wax was removed and the surface polished by rubbing it with sheep's wool. Although encaustic painting was highly prized as an exterior treatment on buildings and ships, where it resisted the sun's heat and the weathering

effect of salt water, its principal application was upon the porous plaster walls of Greek and Roman houses, where backgrounds of red or black were particularly popular. The Egyptians applied encaustic color to mummy cases. Various attempts have been made by enthusiasts to revive this art, which is almost lost, although colored wax crayons are still used in certain schoolroom exercises and various electrically heated devices are available for burning the color in. Some encaustic decoration of textiles is carried on, but here the wax is used only as a vehicle to dye the textile, after which it is removed by a hot iron and blotting paper. R. Ne.

Entablature, horizontal members supported by the columns of an order. It has three parts: the lower is the architrave, forming the lintel; above this is a flat surface called the frieze; the top member, consisting of projecting moldings, is the cornice. A wall, with or without columns, may be capped with a complete entablature. If this motif is too ponderous, greater lightness may be achieved by omitting the frieze, or, more rarely, the architrave. The caryatid porch of the Erechtheum at Athens has an entablature with the frieze omitted.

In the rules for proportioning the orders, Vignola (Giacomo Barocchio) made the entablature one fourth the height of the column. On the Ionic, Corinthian, and Composite orders, Andrea Palladio and Vincenzo Scamozzi tended to make the entablatures successively less high, in proportion to the column height, than on the Doric and the Tuscan. C. Normand's system of proportioning the height of the entablature to the actual height of the column seems very reasonable, since a cornice at a greater distance from the eye tends to foreshorten more than a lower one. *See also* Cornice, *supra;* Frieze, *infra.* O. S. Fj.

ENTABLATURE

Section of the entablature and capital of the Temple of Castor, Rome, Italy

COURTESY OF METROPOLITAN MUSEUM OF ART

Fan Vault, a type of English Gothic vault of the late fourteenth, fifteenth, and early sixteenth centuries. Examples also occur in Baltic countries. It is primarily decorative rather than structural and consists of inverted conoids shaped like half trumpets or funnels which rise from the capitals of regularly spaced columns. The fan shape also results from the half revolution of a four-centered arch about one vertical side, but this was not its origin. In a fan vault each radiating rib has exactly the same length, curve, and spacing. Seen from below, the circumferential ribs appear as a series of concentric half or whole circles. These vaulting conoids are arranged in various combinations, some quadrant, some half, and some whole. At the interstices of the conoids, a pendant, a heraldic device, or a flat-ribbed panel was usually employed.

Structurally, the ribs served little purpose. Where grouped closely together, several were often carved on one stone. Where the ribs were farther apart, the space between them was sometimes filled in by panels. Sometimes a half panel extended from either side of a rib and formed an integral part of it.

The origin of the fan vault may be traced to the cloth palls suspended over fourteenth-century tombs. First translated into wood and then into stone, these canopies had diminutive representations of the intricate vaults of the time carved on their undersides. The trumpet shape accomplished the desired effect with less effort. The earliest example of a full-scale fan vault occurs in the cloister of Gloucester Cathedral, built between 1351 and 1377. From this it developed rapidly. In Henry VII's chapel (1500 to 1512) at Westminster Abbey, the fan vault reached its ultimate expression. Here transverse ribs pierce the lacelike vault, and the vaulting conoids (complete circles) spring from pendants that seem to hang in mid-air. Actually, the vault is all panel but creates the illusion of insubstantiality.   A. K. L.

Finial, a decorative terminal element of a pinnacle, spire, gable, canopy, or bench end. Finials are most common in Gothic architecture, where they were designed with infinite variation of the crocket or leaf motif. Animal forms and foliated crosses and, during Renaissance times, the candelabrum were also used.   A. K. L.

Flèche, a slender spire; more specifically, the arrowlike wooden spire rising above the crossing roof of nave and transepts in a French Gothic church. Wooden spires existed in Europe as early as the eighth century, as at the monastery at Centula (St. Riquier), France, and were common by the thirteenth century. In France the great height of the vaulting

PINNACLE AND FLÈCHE

(Pinnacle, left) Peterborough, England; (Flèche, right) Notre Dame, Paris, France

made the construction of a stone tower over the crossing perilous, though a number of churches were so designed and some actually built, as at Beauvais. Wood, covered with lead, achieved a similar effect without the difficulty and danger involved with a stone tower.

The flèche of Amiens Cathedral, dating from the sixteenth century, is the only large early one remaining in France. It rises about 150 ft. above the roof ridge and is of heart oak covered with lead, which was once painted and gilded. It weighs 551 tons. The intricate carpentry involved in the construction of such a spire is amazing and indicates careful consideration of wind stresses as well as weight. The flèche of Notre Dame, Paris, rebuilt in the nineteenth century by Viollet-le-Duc, follows the design of the original spire. *See also* Pinnacle, *infra.*   A. K. L.

Flying Buttress, a masonry prop using a half arch to support a diagonal bar whose upper end opposes any tendency of a wall to overturn and whose lower end is anchored in a rectangular mass of masonry. It is usually used to resist the outward thrust of an arch or vault in Gothic architecture. In the flying buttress, Gothic architects created the paradox

FLYING BUTTRESS
Reims Cathedral, France

of a vital structural element exposed to the destructive forces of weather. It is one of the most organic, most vulnerable, and most beautiful elements of Gothic architecture.

Direct predecessors of the developed flying buttress are found above the side aisles but under the aisle roofs of Durham and Norwich cathedrals in England and in the church of St. Trinité, Caen, France. By 1140, the buttress appeared above the aisle roof of the abbey church of St. Denis, France. This higher elevation made it possible for the buttress to oppose the vault thrust at a more effective level. The exact point at which the thrust was delivered was not capable of computation, however, and to be sure of opposing it Gothic builders placed a stiffening column or pilaster against the clerestory wall and rested the buttress against this. Sometimes superimposed ranges of buttress were employed for added support.

The lower end of the flying buttress rapidly developed from a simple masonry mass (e.g., St. Leu-d'Esserent), to a projecting gable, to a multipinnacled form such as Reims Cathedral. The addition of a pinnacle added weight and stability. It is most efficient when placed toward the inner side. In buttresses of two flights, intermediate piers bearing pinnacles were employed. The diagonal stone bars of the buttresses were covered with coping stones to deflect water or channeled to conduct water. Often they were decorated with crockets. *See also* Crocket, *supra.*   A. K. L.

Frieze, an architectural element functioning as: (1) a long horizontal band containing decoration; (2) the middle member of the entablature of the Classic orders. In the Doric order, the frieze is flat, and contains triglyphs and metopes. Triglyphs, vestiges of wooden beam ends, are spaced on center with, and at regular intervals between, the columns. They project slightly from the surface of the frieze and contain two shallow V-shaped channels and two half channels at the edges, all separated by flat surfaces of uniform width. The sum total of three channels gives the name triglyph. The intervening metopes are square or very nearly so. They may be decorated with figure sculpture, as on the Parthenon, or with rosettes, animal skulls, or shields. The other orders have friezes which are usually long, flat surfaces, either left plain or decorated with acanthus scrolls, garlands, figure sculpture, rosettes, or inscriptions. Occasionally, the frieze is not flat but shaped in the form of a convex curve, and is known as a pulvinated frieze. *See also* Entablature, *supra.*   O. S. Fj.

Galilee, a medieval church porch or vestibule church. The widely used Cluniac monastic processional liturgies included a station in a porch before the main door of the church, after which the leader went ahead into the church "as Christ before his disciples into Galilee" after the Resurrection. From this circumstance the porches came to be called galilees and in some cases developed into elaborate antechurches. The term is often loosely used; thus the so-called galilee of Durham Cathedral (c. 1175) is really a congregational chapel, but it occupies the position that was proper to the ritual galilees.

The Galilee station accounts in part for the sculptural development of the medieval church portal. On the interior portals, carved and painted subjects related to the Resurrection naturally appeared when Romanesque sculpture was developed in the late eleventh century. By the early twelfth century, very imposing compositions were achieved (like that at Cluny, which is 62 ft. high), and before the middle of that century they were appearing on the exterior façades of the galilees (at the abbey church of Vézelay, for example), whence they came into the scheme of the Gothic church (as at Chartres and St. Denis, and others later).   K. J. C.

GARGOYLE
Cathedral of Notre Dame, Reims, France

Gargoyle, an architectural element whose primary purpose is the discharge of water. Although used by the Greeks and Romans, the gargoyle was reinvented by Gothic architects and played a role of paramount importance. Its simplest form is a pierced stone block projecting as far beyond the wall as possible to throw the water far away from vulnerable surfaces. Carved to resemble grotesque monsters, satiric demons, and various other forms, they testify to the vivid imaginations of the medieval sculptors.   A. K. L.

Gate, in architecture, an opening for passage into an enclosure such as a yard or a walled city; the structure erected over or about such an opening. Ingress and egress, especially from temples or other sacred enclosures, bridges, and cities, have from early times been considered in the nature of a rite and the gate has carried a corresponding symbolism. The pailous of China, the torii of Japan, the triumphal arches of the Romans, and the city gates of medieval and Renaissance cities are architectural expressions of this symbolism.

An early example of such commemorative structures was the famous Ishtar Gate of the city of Babylon, a great arch flanked by battlemented walls which were sheathed with colorful ceramic façades setting forth mythical animals. Another important early city portal was the Gate of the Lions at Mycenae in Greece, formed of upright stones spanned by a heavy lintel some 16 ft. long; the triangular space above

the gate is ornamented by a bas-relief of lions heraldically flanking a primitive column.

The Propylaea or monumental entrances to the sacred area of the Acropolis at Athens may also very properly be considered as gates. However, it was left to the Romans to bring the commemorative entrance to its fullest decorative development. Probably the best known of these triumphal gateways are the arches of Titus (A.D. 81), Septimus Severus (204) and Constantine (312) in Rome. Erected by the Roman emperors and great militarists in honor of their victories, these gates were either single-arched or triple-arched. The surface was given over to bas-relief sculpture relating to the campaigns with ample space for dedicatory inscriptions. Most of the important centers of the Roman world were graced with such arches, which formed the entrances to forums, bridges, and roads, and which are not to be confused with Roman city gates like those at Trier (Treves), Autun, or Split (Spalato), which combined various defensive and commemorative functions.

Since fortifications were an important means of defense until after the invention of gunpowder, most medieval cities had elaborate gates. Many of these have been preserved, either as actual portals or as historic relics long since outgrown by modern traffic. Jerusalem, Rome, Paris, and various Continental and English cities retain such entrances. Memorial gates borrowing the symbolism of ancient portals have been erected in modern times. Examples: the Arc de Triomphe de l'Étoile in Paris (1806), the Brandenburg Gate in Berlin (1784), and the Washington Arch in New York City (1895). *See also* Torii, *infra.*   R. Ne.

Groin, in architecture, the arris, or sharp edge, formed by the meeting of two vaults or vaulted surfaces. Perhaps the simplest type of groin is that formed by intersecting semicircular vaults placed at right angles to each other. This type is ordinarily called a groined vault, but vaults with groins can be formed by other geometrical penetrations. A vault oblong in plan can be covered by a groined vault, provided the groins are so profiled as to meet at a common point at the apex of the vault. If a tunnel vault is intersected by a similar vault of smaller span, the penetrations into the larger vault result in arrises or groins, but the vault is not called a groined vault.

The Romans were the world's greatest exponents of simple groined vaults, those in the Basilica of Constantine and the great bathhouses of Rome being outstanding. During the medieval period few simple groined vaults were used; at that time structural ribs replaced the groins, which are the weakest points of a vault. *See also* Vault.   R. Ne.

Grotesque, a fanciful exaggeration of human or animal form used as a decorative device.

Grotesques are almost as old as recorded history; for example, a two-headed eagle was found in the ruins of Lagash in Babylonia. Among the Greeks, the man-horse or centaur, the satyr, and the faun are well known. The winged sphinx of Egypt descended through the Persians to Baghdad and the Moslems and through Byzantium to western Europe, where it appears in early medieval sculpture. The winged bull of Assyria reached western Europe through the same channels.

One example, among hundreds, of the fantastic and contorted carving of the Romanesque period is the central column of the entrance to the church at Souillac, France. Column capitals from the Baltic to the Adriatic illustrate the same imaginative spirit, and the chimerical forms of Gothic architecture, such as those on the parapet of Reims Cathedral, represent its extension into a later age. Likewise in the decorative panels and capitals of the Renaissance, one finds bird-headed animals and other animal-like forms growing out of leafy foliage or intertwined with it.

A splendid quality of grotesque ornament also appears in the Pacific basin, as in the early relief carvings and bronzes of China and in the carved wood forms of northwest North America and the South Pacific islands. Some of these represent, as in ancient Greece, the forces of living nature; others reflect the decorative fancy of the artist.   A. K. L.

Half-Timber Work, a northern European system of construction having its frame and principal supports of timber, but with its interstices, or spaces in between, filled in with

HALF-TIMBER WORK

masonry (stone or brick) or lathwork and plaster. Some French examples go back to the twelfth century, and by the thirteenth century the system had attained a complete development, both technically and artistically.

Technique. The frame, usually of oak, was tenoned and pinned together. Sometimes a wall was framed on the ground, then raised into place and pinned to the other sections. This system of house framing was popular in England when the colonists came to America, where it persisted with modifications until it was superseded by balloon framing, developed in the Middle West about 1833. In England and America the infilling, or wall material, was often of wattle and daub, a sort of basket wickerwork plastered with mud, or of clay and straw rolled together. This rough work was plastered with clay, whitewashed inside, and covered with a thin coating of lime plaster on the outside. Sometimes the infilling consisted of sun-dried or burned brick which was stuccoed outside and plastered within.

The colonists soon found, however, that the wattle and daub and other such materials as had been used to fill the frames of houses in old England would not answer the purpose in the rigorous climate of New England. Therefore, they devised a covering material of wood. These clapboards, rived from short logs, were found so efficacious in shedding water and keeping out the wind that they were generally adopted for covering wooden structures. When sawmills came into use and it was possible to cut this material in long lengths, siding or weatherboarding evolved.

Examples. During the fifteenth and sixteenth centuries, northern Europe, particularly England, gave increasing decorative attention to half-timber façades. Many fine examples of half-timber houses are still extant in France and Germany, where they function as town dwellings, and in England, where often they appear as country places as well. Although many excellent English types coming down from medieval

days still remain, the more elaborate types date from the Renaissance period. Simply framed, undecorated half-timber façades are seen in the cloisters of Queen's College, Cambridge, on the Old Five Gables at Stratford-on-Avon, where the library and Shakespeare's house are almost as simple, and on Saint William's College at York. Harvard House at Stratford, God's Providence house (1652), and Bishop Lloyd's Palace, all in Chester, and St. Peter's Hospital at Bristol are highly ornate examples, the last-named edifice exhibiting many gables, carved wood sculpture, ornate bargeboards, and decorative half-timber and plaster patterns. In the late work such patterns are rather a surface ornament than a functional or structural expression. Imitation half-timber is sometimes seen in America, where the timbers are simply boards planted on a plastered wall.   R. Ne.

Hall, a large room or building used for public purposes, the manor house of a landed proprietor, a college or university building, an assembly hall, a vestibule, a corridor or passage. In feudal England the principal interior apartment in the residence of a lord, king, or chieftain was known as the hall or great hall. In times of stress, a lord could use this forerunner of the living room as a place to bed his retainers on a shakedown of straw. The hall also served as banquet room and general gathering place for the lord and his vassals. The lord occupied a dais at one end of the room. Before the days of chimneys, the fire was kindled upon the stone floor in the center of the hall, the heat and smoke being vented through a louver upon the roof. Upon occasion, a minstrel's gallery was constructed above one end of the room, in which traveling entertainers sang their lays. Such halls with music galleries carried over into the early English Renaissance period, as at Hatfield House, Hertfordshire, dating from 1611. Westminster Hall, near the Houses of Parliament in London, is a remnant of a medieval palace destroyed by fire in 1834. This structure, with hammer beams projecting like brackets from the sides to support the roof, gives an excellent idea of the great hall of a medieval royal residence. Begun in 1099 by King William Rufus, the hall survived many vicissitudes until it was almost wholly rebuilt by Richard II in 1394, of whose period it may be considered typical. The great hall at Hampton Court Palace is another good example.

The hall remained an important feature of English domestic architecture until about the end of the Gothic era, when the addition of smaller apartments, more easily heated, led to its decline. In smaller extent it lingered as a reception place, then degenerated into a vestibule and finally a passage to a growing complexity of smaller rooms.

English baronial castles and manor houses are often called halls. Examples: Haddon Hall, Hardwick Hall, Kirby Hall. Likewise in the United States, notably in the South, country houses and landed estates are so designated. Throughout the United States such terms as "town hall," "city hall," and "grange hall" are in current use. American college buildings are ordinarily called halls, as Nassau Hall at Princeton, and Holworthy Hall at Harvard.

In early Colonial times in America, the large living room was called a hall, and the vestibule in front of the stairway was known as a porch. However, when a passage was pushed through the house from front to rear, the old hall became a parlor and the elongated vestibule came to be termed a hall. In the South the hall was widened and given a new importance more in keeping with its medieval function. Popularly, however, "hall" still remains a term for "corridor."   R. Ne.

Impost, the capping stone of the wall or pier on which the arch rests. Its top surface is preferably placed a short distance below the spring line of the arch to give it a stilt. The impost may be formed by a flat projecting band, with or without moldings, or, as in the orders of architecture, a complete or an abbreviated entablature. The canons for the various orders of architecture have a special form of impost moldings for each. *See also* Arch, *supra;* Entablature, *supra;* ARCHITECTURAL ORDERS.   O. S. Fj.

Inglenook (Chimney Corner), a recess or corner by a fire, particularly one adjacent to a grate or fireplace. Usually it is a recessed place for the fire, with a step or two leading from the main floor of the room down to the level of the hearth, or with a high-backed bench on either side of the fire. Many early fireplaces were so large that the benches could actually stand within the fireplace proper, the walls of which would catch and reflect the heat. In more recent architectural practice, the inglenook is apt to be still larger, a room or alcove within a room, but with the grate in a comparatively small separate recess in the middle of the end wall.

Inglenooks are more popular and functional in England and on the Continent than in the United States, since grate fires are in more general use there. However, the feature has been imported along with certain styles of English domestic architecture. It was given a particular importance in the late nineteenth-century revival of earlier domestic forms that took place during the arts and crafts movement, under the leadership of William Morris in England. The motif, adapted to American use, was popular in the so-called craftsmen houses about 1900.   R. Ne.

JUBE

St. Peter's Church, Louvain, Belgium

Jube, a chancel screen or rood screen, or particularly the gallery above such a screen. The chancel screen separates that portion of the church set apart for the clergy and choir from that part devoted to congregational worship. The chancel gallery or rood loft, as it is sometimes called, was used for the reading of the Gospel. Since the deacon uttered the words *jube Domine benedicere* before his reading, the name "jube" was applied to this exercise and to the place where it was conducted.   R. Ne.

Keystone, the central voussoir of an arch. After the lower stones of the arch have been set, the inserted keystone locks the arch into place. Structurally its importance is no greater than that of any other voussoir, but its central position is advantageous for decoration. It may project from the other voussoirs, be decorated with scroll forms, or sculptured in relief or in the round. In Saxon (triangular) arches the keystone is absent, since the arch is formed by a pair of symmetrical stones. Often the pointed Gothic arches are formed similarly when bosses are not used.   O. S. Fj.

Lunette, in architecture, a structural or decorative mural area of a shape resembling a crescent or half moon. The term may be used to describe a door transom, a window head, a recess containing a painting, or a molded decorative wall panel. The shape may be a semicircle, a flatter chord of a circle, or a semiellipse. The lunette form, first used in Roman arcuated architecture, was popular also in Renaissance architecture and its later derivatives.   R. Ne.

Minaret, a monumental tower found in Mohammedan countries. It was historically evolved from local prototypes such as church, hermit, and lighthouse towers in western Islam, ziggurats in Iraq, and pillars and perhaps cult towers in other parts of the East. Minarets were often built in or near mosques, both for ornamental purposes and for the call to prayer. They were erected also in deserts as watchtowers and guideposts to caravans, but their richness and scale (the Kutb at Delhi is 270 feet high) really preclude a utilitarian explanation. Eastern minarets in general are windowless, round shafts with balcony heads; those of Syria and countries farther west are usually habitable towers with rooms and windows.   E. S.

Misericord (Miserere), a small rest or projection on the underside of a seat in a monastic or cathedral choir, giving a partial support during the long parts of the office when the seats were raised and the clergy were expected to remain standing. In early Christian times only ceremonial seats were provided, and this was true in the early monastic choirs. In northern lands, walls were built around the choirs as a protection from draughts in the icy winter interiors. In Gothic times canopied individual stalls were provided; lifting the seat would bring the misericord into position. Medieval fancy decked them with carvings, not invariably edifying but almost always interesting because of their inventiveness and informality. Examples may be found in Toledo Cathedral, Amiens Cathedral, and Westminster Abbey.

Misericord also denotes a small dining room set aside for the use of monks who were given special dietary dispensations to build themselves up.   K. J. C.

Modillion, a decorative horizontal bracket under the corona of the Corinthian cornice. It is in the shape of an S scroll with the heavier end at the back. Its underside usually has an acanthus leaf following the profile of the scroll. At the Maison Carrée, Nîmes, dating from 16 B.C., the scroll is

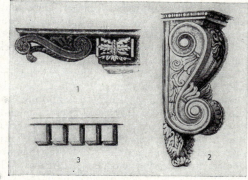

(1) MODILLION (2) CANTALIVER (CANTILEVER); AND (3) DENTIL

T. RICKMAN

reversed, with the heavier part at the outside. Modillions are spaced so as to form a square between them on the underside of the soffit of the cornice. The modillion should not be confused with the mutule of the Doric order. *See also* Entablature, *supra;* ARCHITECTURAL ORDERS.   O. S. Fj.

Mortuary, a room set aside for the reception of a body awaiting burial. Mortuary chapels appear to have been parts of medieval monasteries and churches, and in medieval Latin this room was designated as *domus morturia*, house of the dead. Currently the term is used to designate a burial chapel operated by a mortician, otherwise called a funeral home or a funeral parlor; also a morgue. R. Ne.

Mullions, in architecture, the vertical molded members by which windows are divided into lights; in Gothic architecture, the stone frames into which the leaded glass was set; in modern windows, the division between the sash. Loosely used, the term denotes the enframing divisions of a window, and may apply even to the radiating bars in a rose window or the stone tracery of Gothic architecture. Indeed, the term has been applied to vertical members in a paneled wainscot or stair rail.

In Gothic architecture, window tracery varies with the period, and therefore the corresponding mullions present varying profiles or sections. Likewise, when the larger Renaissance windows were divided into smaller lights, appropriately molded mullions were devised. These mullions became exceedingly important as design elements and by their patterning controlled the scale of the design. With the modern production of glass in large sheets, the importance of mullions has decreased, but in certain historic styles mullions are indispensable. R. Ne.

Narthex, an entrance vestibule preceding the nave of a Christian church, especially those churches of the Early Christian and early medieval periods. The narthex was almost universal in Early Christian churches, serving as a transition between the atrium, or entrance courtyard, and the church proper. It was less sacred than the church and was used by catechumens before their admission to the full rites of the church. In Rome the narthex was separated from the atrium by an open colonnade or arcade. In Byzantine churches it was more enclosed and brilliantly decorated with mosaic.

Elaborate development of the narthex occurred in the Cluniac churches of Burgundy. In these it was often two stories high and several bays long, and constituted practically an antechurch. Since it usually was the last element built, it often exemplified more advanced design and construction than the church itself. In later periods the importance of

the narthex decreased, and its place was taken by the galilee porch in England or by an entrance vestibule incorporated within the body of the church. This latter arrangement is common in contemporary church architecture. A. K. L.

MULLION

Cathedral of Pisa, Italy

Nave, the arm of a church between the entrance and the choir, usually long in proportion to width and flanked by aisles. When accompanied by aisles, it is partially separated from them by a colonnade or arcade and lighted by windows placed in the wall above it. Although without seating arrangements until late medieval times, the nave has generally been provided with seats or pews since then. It is primarily the place for the congregation. In contemporary architecture, emphasis is placed upon accommodation, sight lines, acoustics, and ease of circulation, as well as aesthetic values.

A. K. L.

Oriel, a bay window usually semicircular or semipolygonal in plan, projecting from an upper story and supported upon corbels or brackets. Such windows were particularly popular in late medieval and early Renaissance times. The semicircular example at Bramshill House, Hampshire, dating from 1603, is typical of the latter period. Sometimes

NARTHEX

Church of the Madeleine, Vézelay, France

ORIEL
*Church of St. Sebastian,
Nürnberg, Germany*

such windows project over the entrances of city gates, castles, and collegiate structures, and frequently they extend through several stories. Although American prototypes are modeled principally after those in England, oriels were also used during contemporary periods in French and German architecture. Such ground-supported bay windows as those at Hinchingbrooke Hall, England, are not correctly called oriels.

R. Ne.

Overdoor and **Overmantel,** terms employed in decoration, wherever paneling, painting, or other mural embellishment is important. Overdoor treatment may consist simply of the ornamentation of a transom, the development of an elaborated molded panel, or the use of a pictorial or other decorative painting. In any case, the treatment is made to accord with the general period *décor* and color scheme.

The overmantel, being an embellishment of a focal social and decorative element, the fireplace, is vastly more important. Although the term may be extended to include the decorative hoods above Italian and Spanish Renaissance mantels, it usually denotes only the treatment accorded the chimney pieces in the more northern climates of France and England. From the time of Francis I of France, who reigned from 1515 to 1547, and in England from the time of Elizabeth and James I (1558 to 1625), overmantels have received elaborate treatment. During the Anglo-Classic (Restoration) and Georgian (eighteenth-century) periods, pedimented enframements to receive oil portraits or other paintings were popular. This vogue, exported to the colonies, resulted in pleasant developments in American Georgian architecture.

R. Ne.

Pediment, in Classic architecture, the triangular gable end of buildings or a similar shape used over a door or window. The pediment is framed with a cornice that splits at the lower angles of the pediment, with the cymatium (top molding) continuing up the slanting cornice but omitted on the lower (horizontal) cornice. The Greeks used pediments only on the ends of buildings, but the Romans used them also over doors, windows, and niches, often alternating triangular and segmental shapes, both of which are found in the interior of the Pantheon at Rome.

Tympanum. The flat triangular surface bounded by the cornices is called the tympanum. Though sometimes left plain, it is usually decorated with sculpture. Its triangular shape poses real decorating problems, but on the Parthenon the succession of recumbent, kneeling, seated, and standing figures was formed into a masterful composition that has served as a model.

Acroteria. At the summit of the pediment and above its lower ends the Greeks placed acroteria, low flat blocks supporting decorative sculpture. Apparently the Greeks never placed their gods in these positions, but it was common practice for the Romans to do so.

Broken Pediments. Pediments have been used profusely in the Renaissance and Neoclassic styles. During the Baroque period the fantastic broken pediment was developed, with the raking (slanting) cornice broken back and the void between the ends filled with a cartouche (a stone in the form of a flat piece of paper with the ends curling), urn, niche, or bust. The cornice segments themselves were often in the form of a reverse curve; occasionally they were even reversed so that they faced outward instead of inward. *See also* Cornice, *supra.*

O. S. Fj.

Pendentive, a structural device used in architecture to support a dome over a square plan. Known since the second century (at Kusr-en-Nûreijîs, in Palestine), the pendentive was perfected by Byzantine builders and first used on a grand

scale in the church of Hagia Sophia, Constantinople (erected 532 to 537). A set of four pendentives based on the corners of the square is required to support the dome. In geometrical terms, these pendentives are formed by the remaining sections of a hemisphere when it is cut by the sides and top of a half-cube whose base is inscribed within that of the hemisphere. The four remaining sections of the hemisphere will then meet to form hemispherical arches, and their tops will join to form the circle upon which the dome is set. This design permits continuous support of the dome and carries its downward and outward thrust through the pendentives to the four corner piers or walls of the square plan. Once perfected, this method gave flexibility to domical planning on a grand scale. It permitted such complex domical structures as Hagia Sophia, Constantinople, St. Mark's, Venice, and subsequent domical structures like the new St. Peter's, Rome, to be built with freedom of planning and structural security of method.

Throughout succeeding styles, the pendentive proved the ideal method of support for domes covering a square plan unit. It allows the dome to be (a) continuous with the pendentive, by not using the theoretical horizontal cutting plane, (b) supported directly on the pendentives, or (c) raised above the pendentives on a drum, as was frequent in late Byzantine and subsequent work. *See also* Squinch, *infra;* BYZANTINE ARCHITECTURE; DOME.

J. G. Van D.

Pier, a substantial building support built of masonry or concrete. The pier was necessitated by exhaustion of the supply of antique columns in the Early Christian period

PIER

T. RICKMAN

Early English piers: (Left to right) *Lincoln Cathedral; Netley Abbey; North Transept, Westminster Abbey; and Beverley Minster*

and by the new structural requirements of Byzantine and Romanesque buildings. It was larger than the Classical column and depended more on its mass than on precise calculation and craftsmanship. Under such crushing loads as the dome and half domes of Hagia Sophia, Constantinople, begun A.D. 532, some form of massive support was necessary. The four brick piers carrying Hagia Sophia's domes answered this requirement, and for the next 1,400 years similar piers were used to support domes. The weighty vaults of the Romanesque church likewise created a need for support which columns could not meet. In such a church as San Ambrogio,

Milan, erected between 1088 and 1125, eight arches converge at regularly spaced points along the nave. The cruciform piers used at these points of convergence reflect the forces transmitted by the arches, and are called compound or clustered piers. In Gothic times the clustered pier was altered in two ways. First, as the number of arches was increased and the shape of each arch section was elaborated, the pier moldings were likewise increased and elaborated. Secondly, the pier was simplified and the arch moldings were allowed to disappear in it. The Gothic pier was slenderized to as little as one-nineteenth the area of the Romanesque pier. Gothic pier capitals underwent constant modification, and in the late Gothic period they were often entirely omitted.

In the early skyscrapers of the 1880's, piers of solid masonry were used to carry the tremendous weight of the multiple floors and soaring walls. Rapid technical advance led to the use of cast-iron or steel columns in the core of these piers and a consequent reduction in their size. Steel reinforcement likewise became an essential element of concrete piers for bridges, industrial buildings, and other structures, with some amazing reductions in pier sections as exemplified by the bridges of Robert Maillart in Switzerland. A. K. L.

Pilaster, a flat mass projecting from a wall and corresponding in detail of base, entasis, and capital to the order with which it is used. When fluted, Roman examples show five, seven, or nine flutes, and the projection from the wall is usually the width of one flute. The pilaster is a Roman development and is particularly a feature of Roman and Renaissance architecture. Renaissance pilasters were frequently ornamented with an arabesque of bas-relief. The pilaster should not be confused with its Greek counterpart, the anta, which is the enlargement of the end of a wall and has its own capital and base moldings, which differ from those of the columns with which it is used. O. S. Fj.

Pinnacle, a turretlike termination used at the junction of walls and atop buttresses. Its value in weighting the corners of towers and the like was recognized in Norman times, and, as a stabilizing adjunct to buttresses, somewhat later. Curiously, however, pinnacles were frequently placed toward the outer edges of flying buttresses instead of toward the inner edges, where their weight would be more effective in counterbalancing the thrust of the buttress arches.

Once introduced, they developed from square, circular, and polygonal forms to traceried pinnacles and open tabernacles enriched with sculpture and multitudinous crockets. In general, pinnacles embody the stylistic characteristics of their period and region. *See also* Flèche, *supra.* A. K. L.

Plan, in architecture, a drawing or design made to scale to show the scheme or arrangement of a projected or existing structure; a section taken at the level of the openings of a building upon a plane parallel to the floor which sets forth the arrangement of rooms or other parts. A plan is a specific projection of a structure and must be used in conjunction with elevation and section drawings to obtain a complete delineation of any three-dimensional object such as a building. The general term "plan," sometimes used to indicate all these drawings, is technically inaccurate.

Each floor, as well as the roof, of a structure requires a special plan to delineate its arrangement and to set off its over-all and detailed dimensions, carefully scaled upon some generally accepted scheme of measurement. As a usual thing, general plans as documents for the builder are laid out upon a scale of ¼ in. to the foot; plot plans and surrounding land arrangements are at a scale of $\frac{1}{16}$ in. to the foot. In Great Britain and the United States, architects' drawings observe the English method of measurement. In countries using the metric system, architects' drawings are scaled accordingly.

In connection with detailed drawings of such items as doorways, windows, and interior details and furnishings, plans drawn at a larger scale (1 in. to the foot or even full size) are furnished with elevations for a complete delineation of the parts.

Down through the history of building delineation, certain conventions have been adopted to represent a structure or its parts. Indeed, before the wide use of photographic blueprints as a means of reproducing structural documents, certain colors were used in the drawings to represent the various materials. Thus brick walls were red on plans, frame walls were yellow, stone walls were green, and so on. Now, in place of colors, certain conventional hatchings are used to indicate materials. Doors, windows, steps, and mechanical equipment have likewise been conventionalized upon plan delineations, thus making blueprint reading a special skill. *See also* Elevation, *supra;* Section, *infra.* R. Ne.

Post and Lintel, a system of construction using wood, stone, or metal, in which the wall or superstructure is carried on horizontal beams (lintels) whose ends are supported by vertical posts or columns. This ancient system preceded the arch and vault, is found in Egyptian architecture, and is the principal system in Classical and Neoclassical column architecture. The post and lintel system limited the size of rooms and consequently was superseded by the vault in Roman times. O. S. Fj.

Quatrefoil, an ornamental device common in Gothic architecture, consisting of four symmetrically arranged leaves or lobes divided by cusps. It is most often bounded by a circle, occasionally by a square; it also appears as an unbounded, pierced opening in panels of wood, stone, or metal. A. K. L.

Rib, a projecting band or arch used in the construction of a vault. Ribs are usually of masonry, though sometimes fashioned of wood or other material. The brick arches or ribs used in the construction of Roman concrete vaults and Byzantine brick vaults were so deeply embedded as to be practically invisible. In Romanesque construction, arches of brick and stone were employed to make a ribbed skeleton, usually arranged in plan like an **X** inscribed within a square. Such a skeleton eliminated the necessity of a temporary wood supporting vault, for it permitted the vault cells to be filled in one at a time. The ribs also emphasized the lines of the vault, minimizing minor irregularities in the webs and adding much to the total aesthetic effect.

Romanesque ribs of the eleventh and twelfth centuries are bold and simple. Transverse ribs were at first made broader than the diagonal ribs. Moldings soon developed as part of the rib, and triangular as well as quadrangular sections were employed. Carved ornament, such as the billet, zigzag, and rosette, was added occasionally, and polychromy became common.

Gothic ribs are more complex and generally more slender. In English Gothic architecture, the number of ribs was increased, with tierceron, lierne, ridge, and fan ribs supplementing the transverse, diagonal, and wall ribs of the Romanesque and early Gothic periods. The intersection of these ribs at the vault crown was often marked by a keystone or boss. Islamic architecture likewise affords splendid examples of rib development, both structural and decorative, and undoubtedly contributed to the medieval architecture of Western Europe. A. K. L.

Rinceau, a running spiral motif occurring in Mediterranean ornament from the time of the Egyptians and Cretans to the end of the Roman Empire. It reappeared with the revival of Classic motifs during the Renaissance. Applied to friezes and other flat bands in Classic architecture, perhaps the most popular version was a Roman scroll clad in the foliage of the acanthus plant with deep-cut rosettes at the eye of the spiral. Though generally applied to horizontal members, occasionally it was used to decorate unfluted pilasters and door jambs. It supplied the same decorative function that the simpler Greek honeysuckle ornament had fulfilled. Generally encountered as carved bas-relief, it appeared also in floor mosaics, intarsia (wood inlaid in wood), and even painted ornament. In modern ornamentation it recurs in various forms.   R. Ne.

RUSTICATION
Riccardi Palace, Florence, Italy

Rustication, in architecture, refers to masonry stones whose edges or joints are cut back square or beveled, but whose faces are left rough or have recessed joints. Such rustic rough-surfaced stones have been used extensively for retaining walls and the lower stories of buildings. The decorative types of rustication have been used on all parts of the exterior of buildings.

During the Renaissance, many types of recessed joints, such as square, splayed, and rounded, plus stone faces formed in flat pyramidal shapes, were developed. Rustication was applied to the architectural orders, where it was added to the proportion of the column, with the bottom of the joints indicating the original column shape. Quoins, the cornerstones of buildings, were often rusticated, while the remaining wall surface was left smooth.

During the Baroque period, vermiculation, or wormlike sinkages on the face of the stone, and dripping stalactite surface decoration were used, the latter being a favorite motif for grottos and fountains.

Examples of Italian work containing rustication are the Aqua Claudia, in Rome, and the Pitti Palace in Florence, the latter having various types of rusticated walls and columns. The Louvre in Paris contains vermiculation, and the Medici Fountain in the Luxembourg Gardens, in Paris, contains both vermiculation and stalactite ornament. O. S. Fj.

Sconce, a wall bracket designed to hold one or more candles, or other lamps. The history of the sconce is not clear, but means of holding a light upon a wall date back to antiquity. Made of wood or metal, the sconce was important in early American Colonial homes, where it was frequently fashioned of tin or pewter. Sometimes it took the form of a single candle socket attached to a molded panel. At other times tall, scalloped reflectors stood behind the candle holders. These reflectors were perforated with a hole by means of which the sconce was hung upon the wall. Thus the flame was protected from drafts and the light was thrown into the room. After kerosene lights came into vogue, silvered glass reflectors were used behind the contemporary wall-bracket lamps.   R. Ne.

Section, in architecture, a drawing or a design depicting a structure as if cut by a plane perpendicular to the walls and floors, showing the internal arrangement. Sectional drawings, used in conjunction with plans and elevations, are necessary to delineate a structure completely and set forth the intention of the architect. Sections of a structure are taken at various advantageous points to explain the detailed inner arrangements of a building. The principal sections are those taken through an edifice upon its principal axes. On these documents, ceiling heights, floor thicknesses, and other internal measurements are set forth. In more elaborate structures, sections of such important parts as stairways, fireplaces, balconies, or other unusual arrangements are supplied. Also, in connection with elevation drawings of doors, windows, vestibules, or other detailed parts, sectional drawings are necessary to explain the part. These are usually drawn at larger scale than general sections, which usually correspond in scale with the plans and elevations. Conventional hatchings to indicate the various materials in section have been adopted. *See also* Elevation, *supra;* Plan, *supra.*   R. Ne.

Sedilia (plural of Latin *sedile,* seat), seats, generally in a group of three, for the use of the officiating priests between the parts of a service. They were generally of masonry and were recessed into the wall on the south side of the chancel of English churches of the Romanesque and Gothic periods. *See also* Stall, *infra.*   R. Ne.

T. RICKMAN

SEDILIA

Spandrel, a term used to designate several wall areas, as follows: (a) the triangular space between the curve of an arch and a rectangle enclosing it, (b) the triangular spaces between the arches of an arcade, or (c) the panels below or above windows in modern steel-framed or concrete-framed structures. Down through history, the spandrel has been an area open to decorative embellishment with bas-relief, mosaics, and even inscriptions. In modern rectangular framed buildings, such spaces are often filled with brick panels, sculptured marble inserts, or bronze or aluminum plates. Perhaps the world's most celebrated decorative spandrels are the terra-cotta medallions with which the Della Robbias embellished the Foundling Hospital at Florence, Italy. The Certosa at Pavia likewise has interesting spandrels, with the figures approaching full-round sculpture.

R. Ne.

Squinch, a structural device used in various forms to support a dome or lantern over a square or polygonal plan. Its earliest type is represented by successively corbeling out the upper courses (level ranges) of masonry in the corners of the apartment to be covered, so that they tend to form a circular stone course, approximating the soffit (underside) of the dome. The downward and outward thrust of the dome is thus transferred through the squinches to the supporting walls or piers. A second solution is effected by constructing small diagonal arches in the upper corners which thus convert that portion of the walls to a polygonal form approaching more nearly a circle. A third solution, closely related to the second, is accomplished by using small semi-domes, termed "pseudopendentives" (or vaulted variations of these), to effect the transition from the round plan of the dome to the square or polygonal form of its primary supports. The squinch is only a partial solution to the problem of supporting a dome on a square plan, which was not perfectly solved until the development of the pendentive. The squinch occurs in Roman architecture (e.g., Villa Adriana, Tivoli), Persian architecture (e.g., the palace at Sarvistan), Byzantine architecture (e.g., St. Luke of Stiris, Phocis), Romanesque architecture (e.g., Le Puy-en-Velay, France), Mohammedan architecture (e.g., Sultan Hassan Mosque, Cairo), and to a minor extent in Gothic architecture as a support for octagonal superstructures. *See also* Pendentive, *supra;* ARCHITECTURAL STYLES (Byzantine); DOME.   J. G. Van D.

Stalactite Work, an intricate plastic enrichment of niches, squinches, domes, and soffits in general, peculiar to Mohammedan architecture, and a striking instance of the style's ornamentalization of structural detail. The earliest examples, at Rakka, Syria, and excavations near Nishapur, Persia, indicate that it was primarily a fantasy in plasterwork

SPANDREL

T. RICKMAN

or brickwork, possibly developed from the Hellenistic conch, and not an elaboration of the Iranian eleventh-century squinch with oversailing quarter domes. Forms vary greatly; but alternation and superimposition of prismatic niches, giving an effect like that of honeycomb cells cut on the bias, is general. Stalactites are worked in carved and painted plaster, in stone, in tile mosaic, and in wood.   E. S.

Stall, a compartment set off within a structure for some specialized purpose, like an enclosure for a horse or other animal in a stable; a booth for the sale of foodstuffs or other merchandise in a market; a place for the sale of books; and particularly the enclosed seats for the use of the clergy within the choir or chancel of a church or a cathedral. Stalls are not to be confused with sedilia. Choir stalls, generally of wood and often elaborately carved, were provided with projecting elbows and misericords (misereres). The sides of the choir stalls were often ornamented with wood bas-reliefs of Biblical scenes of Gothic geometrical ornament and surmounted by foliated finials. Frequently the ledge of the misericord was also beautifully carved. Some choir stalls were supplied with canopies. The stalls in Henry VII's chapel and the abbey choir at Westminster are particularly elaborate. The bishop's seat,

COURTESY OF METROPOLITAN MUSEUM OF ART

STALACTITE WORK
The Alhambra, Granada, Spain

usually called the throne, was generally more elaborate than those of the clergy. *See also supra:* Choir; Misericord; Finial; Sedilia.   R. Ne.

Tierceron, a type of vaulting rib. A bay of English nave vaulting commonly has a plan resembling the British union jack. The top and bottom lines are the transverse ribs which divide the bays from one another; the ends are the wall ribs, above the windows; the + form represents the ridge ribs at the crown of the vault, and the × represents the diagonal ribs. Additional diagonals are sometimes run from the corners up to the ridge ribs, and these are called tiercerons. In addition, there are often small crisscross ribs called liernes or binding ribs. The liernes often made a net-like pattern in Germany, and affected gorgeous starlike shapes in Spain. Such a structure was easy to cover with the thin stone Gothic vaulting webs. The French, who invented Gothic vaulting, preferred larger panels or severies (usually only four to a bay), which they built by clever masonwork, thus avoiding the intricate ridge, tierceron, and lierne ribs. *See also* ARCHITECTURAL STYLES.   K. J. C.

Torii, the typical form of symbolic gateway erected in shrines of the Shinto sect in Japan. Its origin is not known, but like some types of Shinto sanctuary buildings, its use down to modern times has reproduced a design obviously inherited from a primitive age. The basic elements of the torii are two pillars and two beams surmounting them, the topmost being longer. A number of standard variations modify the austerity of the original design. The traditionally favored material is the fine cypress, hinoki, which may either be left its natural color or painted in red and black. Exceptional torii have been made of stone or metal, and in modern Japan reinforced concrete is often used. Size varies widely; the shrine precincts may contain from one to several hundred examples.   A. C. S.

Tracery, the structural and decorative subdivision of the window openings characteristic of Gothic architecture though employed in other periods and regions. Similar or identical interlacements were also applied to walls and screens.

Grouping of Lancets. In western Europe the development of tracery dates from early Gothic times, when two or three lancets (tall slender windows undivided by mullions) were grouped together. This arrangement solved the practical need for more light at a time when large glass areas

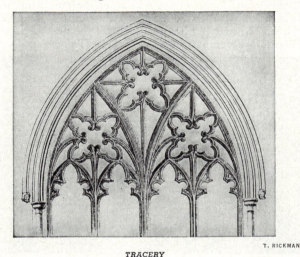

TRACERY

Chartham, England

T. RICKMAN

were impractical because of high wind pressures and inadequate technique. Such an arrangement of grouped lancets may be seen in the aisle window of Warmington, England, where each window has its own dripstone, though the group is also protected by one common dripstone.

Plate Tracery. A pierced opening in the wall above the lancets carried the development a step further. Multiplication of these piercings and elaboration of their shapes into trefoils or quatrefoils resulted in what is called plate tracery. In this, the openings, rather than the separating panels between the openings, create the visual impression. The circular western window at Chartres (c. 1194), filled with rich glass, is a magnificent example of such tracery. Its great size (36 ft. in diameter) was made possible by the unusually fine quality of stone employed.

Bar Tracery. In regions lacking stone of the quality used at Chartres, the masons developed curved bars of stone with which to subdivide large window areas. No doubt the desire for more slender divisions between the openings likewise contributed to this change. Whatever the reasons, by the year 1225 bar tracery was fully developed, with slender colonnettes instead of stone panels separating the openings. A comparison of the western rose window of Notre Dame, Paris, with that of Chartres clarifies the difference between plate and bar tracery.

Late Gothic Types. From these relatively simple patterns of the early thirteenth century, window tracery became increasingly complex. In England it was Geometric, Curvilinear, and Perpendicular; in France, Rayonnant and Flamboyant. Curvilinear tracery of England is marked by free flowing curves in contrast to the circles and circle segments of the Geometric period. The Perpendicular usually has uninterrupted mullions rising to the head of the arch which emphasize the rectilinear nature of its pattern. In Rayonnant tracery of France, the bars acquire a willowlike slenderness, and the pattern assumes a radiating character as at St. Urbain, Troyes. The Flamboyant (literally, "flaming") prob-

ably stemmed from the English Curvilinear and because of its flamelike pattern acquired its descriptive name. An excellent example may be seen in the western window of Sainte Chapelle, Paris.

Improvement in the design of the separating bars or mullions made possible a reduction in their width. Whereas earlier mullions had width and depth approximately equal, depth was increased in later mullions, thereby offering maximum resistance to the wind. Inasmuch as the glass of the window obscured the view of one-half the depth of each mullion, the increase in mullion depth was also aesthetically advantageous, creating stronger shadows and a more pronounced three-dimensional effect. A distinctly charming variation of Gothic tracery is that achieved by doubling the window openings, the outer one glazed, the inner unglazed. Care was taken to vary the tracery of the two openings but with consideration of total effect. A good example is found in the eastern transept of Durham Cathedral.

Use on Furniture. Tracery as a decorative device for walls, screens or other pieces of ecclesiastical or domestic furniture is common throughout Europe. It parallels the development of window tracery, though often executed in wood rather than stone. The wood choir stalls and stone reredos of Beverley Minster, England, illustrate the unusual richness of such tracery decoration.

Development in the Near East. In the East and in the Mediterranean world, pierced slabs of stone were used in window openings before the Christian Era. In Byzantine and Islamic architecture such pierced openings were enriched by the insertion of colored glass. Sometimes stucco panels were used instead of stone. In Islam and Asia, as in western Europe, tracery developed into patterns of unbelievable intricacy. Probably nowhere can work of greater delicacy or richness be found than that of the ten sandstone windows of the Sidi Sayyad mosque (built about 1500) at Ahmadabad, India. Almost equally brilliant is the pierced marble screen around the cenotaph of the Taj Mahal.

Modern Types. In the nineteenth and twentieth centuries, repetition of the tracery patterns developed by former periods has been most common. With increasing frequency, however, new designs have appeared. A suggestion of the aesthetic effects obtainable may be seen in some of the textile-block houses of Frank Lloyd Wright and in the work of other contemporary architects. An example of metal tracery, in which advertising is used as a part of the design, is offered by De Volharding, The Hague, by architect Jan Buys.

A. K. L.

Triforium (literally, "pierced stage"), one of the elements of the interior elevation of a Romanesque or Gothic church nave, corresponding in level to the aisle roofing. Romanesque and Early Gothic churches often have a triforium arcade with openings on the roof space above the aisles. In Gothic work from about 1160 there is often a triforium gallery, really a vaulted second-story aisle with the roof space above it. Such a triforium gallery may in turn have above it a triforium arcade or passage which, with the aisles and the great windows or clerestory, makes what is called a four-story interior elevation (example, Laon Cathedral). From about 1180 the successful application of flying buttresses made the triforium gallery unnecessary; it was replaced by an arcade and triforium passage in the thickness of the wall closing off the aisle roof space from the nave as in the cathedral at Chartres. With a high triforium story and a flat or pitched aisle roof, it was possible to introduce windows in the outside wall of such a passage, thus producing the glazed triforium, as at Beauvais.

K. J. C.

Triglyph and Metope, alternate ornaments and spaces in the frieze of the Doric order. A triglyph is a rectangular tablet, slightly projecting and having two vertical channels of V section called glyphs. There are also two corresponding chamfers or half channels on the vertical sides which are considered to be a third glyph. Triglyphs are repeated

METROPOLITAN MUSEUM OF ART

TRIGLYPH AND METOPE
Parthenon, Athens, Greece

alternately with the metopes. A metope is the space between two triglyphs. Such spaces are often carved for adornment. *See also* ARCHITECTURAL ORDERS.

Volute, in architecture, a spiral or scroll. It is a frequently occurring ornament in architecture and architectural decoration and forms the principal motif of the Ionic order. The introduction of the volute into art and its wide geographical distribution have been the subject of many investigations. Two theories concerning its appearance in art are held: (1) that it is a derivation from natural forms and (2) that it is the result of technical processes. The latter view is held by ethnologists, who cite the use of the motif as decoration on Indian pottery and baskets constructed upon a spiral pattern. This theory has been extended to account for its incorporation into the Ionic order by projecting the early stone bolster-cap form back to a possible wooden origin. *See also* ARCHITECTURAL ORDERS.   R. Ne.

Wainscot, a facing of any material on the lower portion of an interior wall; also, in British usage, fine oak or other wood panels applied to interior walls. When plain, plastered, or painted walls are divided by a chair rail, that part of the wall below the rail, is called a wainscot. It has been the custom to surface this portion with a material other than that used above the rail. In Georgian (eighteenth-century British) architecture, wainscots were of wooden panels, but as these increased in cost, matched or beaded boarding was substituted. Later, Lincrusta (canvas treated with linseed oil and stamped with decorative patterns), tile, linoleum, and various fabrics were employed in contrast to the plaster or wallpaper above the chair rail.   R. Ne.

See also ABBEY; BAPTISTERY; BASILICA; CAMPANILE; CARAVANSARY; CASTILE (CHATEAU); CATACOMBS; CHAPEL; CLOISTER; COLUMN; DOME; DOOR AND DOORWAY; MOLDING; PAGODA; STUPA; VAULT; VILLA; WINDOW.

ARCHITECTURE, HISTORY OF. The quest for shelter led man first to seek the protection of trees, overhanging rocks, and caves. Cave dwellings in many parts of the world bear testimony of such use. Slowly, however, man learned how to construct his own shelters, and thus was born the art of architecture. The first primitive habitations were devised as shelters from rain and wind and as barriers against wild beasts and human adversaries. They provided space in which early man could sleep and in which he could spend his time when circumstances forced him indoors. In its rudest form, such a habitation was little better than the brush lair of the beast, incorporating few of the functions connoted by the modern term "house" and none of the aspects included in the concept "home."

In the beginning only the physical comfort of man was considered. But in time the mind, as well as the body, required satisfaction. Beauty became a consideration in the design of human shelter, and architecture became a fine art as well as a useful art. Aesthetic considerations became important very early in human history. In fact, long before the hunters and fishers forsook the cave dwellings of southwestern Europe, they were decorating these caverns with colorful mural paintings.

Thus architecture became an index to both the life and the thought of an age or a race. Down through human history, man's aims, ambitions, and ideals have been built into the structures which he has reared to symbolize his relationship to his fellows and to his gods. Man has always been religious. Whereas his earliest monuments, the house and the tomb, had to do with the shelter of his living or dead body, almost as early he erected some sort of a sanctuary within whose sacred precincts he attempted, by certain rites, to propitiate those unseen forces which he believed inhabited his environment and guided his destinies. These three early architectural types—domestic, sepulchral, and religious—long satisfied man's needs. However, as human society slowly diversified its activities, new social functions called into being new types of structure.

Architecture is not only a function of human utility; it is also a function of its environmental background. Environment is a complex matter, but no study of the history of architecture as a whole, or of any style or period, can neglect it. Simple investigation indicates that a given environment can be divided into two primary parts: the natural setting (the land) and human influence (the people). To be sure, human life is itself a function of the natural environment; but for the purposes of this discussion these influences may be considered coequal. The natural setting exerts its influence through geography and topography, through geology, which determines the building materials and natural resources in general, and through climate. Human influence on architecture is reflected in the history, religion, and social, political, and economic systems of a people.

All these environmental and cultural factors have a direct bearing upon social expressions and should be considered in the evaluation of a given architectural style or period.

NATURAL INFLUENCES

Geography. Geography determines the location of art centers and conditions the exchange of ideas. Proximity of the sea has much to do with expression in the arts. Commerce and intercourse disseminate learning. Thus places fronting the sea are favored gateways through which the arts and learning of other lands pass. Usually such cities present an advanced architecture. Seafaring peoples, other things being equal, usually have been more highly civilized than those who did not travel so widely. For example, the arts throve early in Crete and Greece. In contrast, the character and individuality of Egyptian architecture were precisely what they were because of Egypt's geographical isolation.

Ancient Egypt was a country hemmed in by natural barriers. On the west was the great Lybian Desert, the shifting sands of which constantly encroached upon the fertile green

Pyramid of Uxmal, Yucatan, Mexico, with Holy Temple on Top

ribbon of the Nile valley. On the north the delta alluvium offered an almost impassible swampy barrier to intercourse; on the east were the Red Sea and the Arabian Desert, and on the south the ever-menacing Ethiopians. By virtue of this isolation, the Egyptians were a highly distinctive people socially, religiously, culturally; and their greatest expression —architecture—was characteristic.

Greece constitutes a splendid example of the effect of geography upon a race, and consequently upon the architecture of that race. Situated at the heart of the ancient world, Greece was within easy reach of most of the ancient Mediterranean cities. The land of Hellas was so broken up into mountains and valleys that communication by land was difficult; hence communication by sea early became popular, the more so because no spot in Greece lay many miles from the coast. Although the terrain was not conducive to political unity, the bond of blood relationship always remained strong among the Hellenes. Other bonds were religion and social custom. A long history in the islands and peninsula and before that in Asia Minor and the Balkan area had made of the Greeks a strong, individual, energetic, artistic, enterprising, and self-assertive race. Their architecture is dignified, serene, and sturdy. It is severe and simple in line, because the Greek was a practical and rational person as well as a lover of beauty. The Greek temple, a model of structural and aesthetic perfection, is perhaps the world's best example of architectural appropriateness. Greek architecture expresses the effect of the solemn, bare mountain fastnesses of northern Greece, a land wrested inch by inch from a preceding race of kindred origin.

Geology. The geology of a country determines its mineral resources, which include its building stones. To an extent, also, it predetermines its flora, often an important source of construction materials. Egypt's eternal monuments are a product of the country's geology. The absence of wood for use in building made it necessary to utilize more durable materials such as limestone, sandstone, and granite (syenite). These materials not only imparted much to the architectural character but also, in conjunction with a beneficent

climate, account for the survival of many ancient Egyptian structures.

The Tigris-Euphrates basin likewise furnishes a splendid example of the effect of geology upon architectural form. This whole area, with the exception of the hills of Armenia, possessed no stone. Being largely an alluvial deposit in what had been, until recent geologic times, the upper waters of the Persian Gulf, the country was too young geologically to support a developed forest growth. However, mud made possible an architecture of sun-dried brick, which was gradually transformed into an architecture of burned brick. The discovery of deposits of a natural asphalt was helpful, and the eventual importation of gypsum blocks and the bringing of cedar logs from Lebanon made possible a more complete architectural expression. Nevertheless, the possibilities and the limitations of ceramic production set the pattern of valley architecture.

The fine white marbles of Greece contributed to the perfection of Greek architecture, for they are among the noblest of building materials and favor extreme purity of line and refinement of detail. Since they are less refractory than granite and more durable than gypsum, besides being agreeable to the eye and comparatively easy to work, they gave the Greeks a great advantage over the Egyptians and the Assyrians. Obviously, architecture in Greece was immensely favored by geology.

Climate. Perhaps no environmental factor has a wider influence upon people, and therefore upon human shelter, than has climate. In hot dry countries, precautions against the heat and glare of the sun—courts and other shade-producing devices, such as porches, canopies, and awnings—are necessary. Since there is little rain and no snow, flat roofs are practical. As one goes northward, steeper roofs, smaller openings, the absence of courts, the addition of chimneys, and greater compactness of plan become apparent.

Down through the ages, climate has so potently influenced architectural form that certain of these forms are associated only with definite climatic environments. In lands like Egypt, the brilliant sunshine and the nullification of shadows by reflected light have modified architectural form and made necessary polychromatic differentiation of architectural surfaces. Color has played an important role in architecture, partly because of its aid to vision in the differentiation of forms and partly because of its considerable emotional effect upon the beholder.

COLOR IN ARCHITECTURE

Color in architecture is introduced either through the intrinsic color of the structural materials or as applied pigment. All the great styles of architecture down to the Renaissance made wide use of color both externally and internally.

Egyptian. In Egypt, architectural polychromy is apparent in every direction, because everything in Egyptian art was colored in some way. The peculiar Egyptian climate has been held responsible for the emphasis upon color and the comparative simplicity of form. With scarcely any rainfall and a glaring white sun, reflected light from the white sands practically destroys all shadows and nullifies the effect of projections. Thus architecture had, of necessity, to make its appeal largely through color. Architectural forms, consequently, were large in conception, bold in execution and simple in form, but brilliant in color. Every wall, cornice, column, or ceiling was rich with a profusion of varicolored designs. Finish of gypsum plaster was placed on the surfaces of the buildings, and it was upon this plaster coat that the architectural decorator worked. The paint was of a water variety and the palette consisted of pigments of red, yellow, blue, green, brown, black, and white. Gold leaf was also employed.

Mesopotamian. Whereas the predominant colors of the Egyptians were red and yellow, the chief color of the Mesopotamian peoples was blue. This preference is perhaps best illustrated by the beautiful tiles recovered at the site of Sargon's palace at Khorsabad, near modern Mosul, Turkey. The Tigris-Euphrates basin furnished nothing in the way of building materials except earth. As a consequence the ceramic arts developed early, and the Babylonians, the Assyrians, and their successors, the Persians, witnessed the evolution of the potter's art from simple mud bricks to the glorious tiles for which Persia has long been famous.

Of course the Assyrian palette was limited by the colors that could be produced in ceramic materials, and as a consequence blues, yellows, and whites are by far the most frequent. Grounds were usually blue, with figures in yellow and flesh tints rendered in burnt sienna. White and black were used as separators. As in Egypt, the color was flat, not graded or shaded, and there was no attempt to represent a succession of planes. Whereas the Egyptian artist colored his subjects to simulate nature, the Mesopotamian did not. Of the animal figures upon the famous walls of Babylon, some were yellow with white manes and others were yellow with green manes.

Greek. Modern knowledge of Greek polychromy dates mainly from the middle of the nineteenth century. Its use is explained by the brilliant light of the country, which destroys the effect of sculptural relief and makes some polychromatic differentiation necessary, especially on the narrower portions of white-marble entablatures. In the archaic period, about the sixth century B.C., color was used lavishly. With the perfecting of form, color was applied with increasing restraint, being treated with much delicacy and refinement during the Age of Pericles, about a hundred years later. The Greeks were always careful not to allow a delight in beautiful things to seduce them into senseless or unreasonable profusion. Architectonic rather than pictorial considerations dictated color emphasis; it was subordinated to architectural effect.

The colors used were red, blue, yellow, and green. Red and blue were the most predominant and were used in almost equal proportions. Color was not used in large areas but was broken into bits and alternated with brilliant high lights of the fine white Pentelic marble or relieved by the glint of bronze, silver, or gold. Used thus, the colors, seen from a distance, were blended into a delightful monochrome. An ancient traveler has described the aspect that the Acropolis presented to one approaching from Piraeus as resembling a great iridescent pearl glistening under the bright sunshine of Hellas.

Color decoration was carefully worked out in connection with the Doric order, although tradition did not bind the Greek architect as did the hard-and-fast rules of the Egyptians. The triglyphs seem to have been preferably of blue, the mutules of blue relieved by guttae of gold. The metopes, whether decorated or not by sculpture, were red. Various fasciae and cymae were decorated with painted running honeysuckle ornaments in red and green.

It is improbable that color was much used below the capital of the order, that is, on the weight-bearing members. It appears to have been confined almost exclusively to the entablature and pediment, those parts of the structure which, by virtue of their small dimensions and comparatively great distance from the eye, needed definition in so vibrant a sunlight. In this way the sensitive Greek, characteristically correcting imperfections of vision with delicate refinements in form, found a means to overcome the effect of diminution produced by distance and to give to his structure the aspiration that results from a use of interesting form or color above the eye.

Roman. Roman polychromy stemmed from that of the Greeks but never equaled it in fineness. The Romans were so destructive of their earlier work that scarcely any remnant of applied external color survives from the days before the introduction of colored marble. This latter means of coloration won over the Roman architect completely. Even after two thousand years, Rome is full of precious materials imported from the ends of the Roman world to grace her imperial structures. To be sure, few of them any longer embellish the original buildings; medieval Christians used old pagan structures as quarries for the materials in their churches. Many a Christian church contains interior colonnades that originally graced some pagan temple or basilica, and many a floor mosaic presents colorful marble disks sawed from the drums of old Roman columns.

Byzantine. Under the influence of the Christian Church, polychromatic decoration in the interiors of churches reached a high level of achievement, particularly on the part of the Byzantine mosaicists (sixth to thirteenth centuries). But with the development of colorful interiors came also a decline in external coloration. This decline, which had already set in during the Western Empire, operated at Byzantium to produce in Santa Sophia, one of the most colorful interiors that the world has seen, together with a somewhat colorless exterior.

Medieval Italian. Although Early Christian and Byzantine buildings were generally dull externally, the medieval Italian buildings that stemmed from the same tradition were quite otherwise. One of the world's most colorful exteriors is that of St. Mark's Church in Venice. Venice produced not only colorful architecture but also a long list of painters famed as colorists. The Venetian love of color results from a beautiful geographical setting and a long commercial contact with the Orient. The exterior of Saint Mark's is as splendidly decorated as the interior, being overlaid with shafts of porphyry and verd antique with capitals of alabaster and encrusted with mosaics and gilding. In this structure the Roman method of applying skin-deep beauty achieves a complete climax.

Besides using this encrusted decoration, the Venetians also applied paint to the façades of their palaces. In fact, the Ca' d'Oro Palace gets its name from the fact that it was illumined with color and gilt. The document showing the specifications for this coloring, still extant, is extremely valuable for the light that it sheds upon medieval technical processes, and leaves little question as to just what parts of the façade were of red, ultramarine, white, or gold.

What has been remarked of Venice in particular was true of Italy in general during the Romanesque and Gothic periods. The buildings of both periods present examples of polychromatic variation accomplished both by the use of colored materials and by means of applied paint. Well-known examples of the first class of variation are such churches as San Miniato and the cathedral at Florence and various churches at Lucca, Pisa, Pistoia, and even as far east as Bologna. These buildings exhibit exterior walls paneled in dark green and white, or green, white, and red marble, relieved here and there by panels of colored mosaics. The little church at Sparone, the Cathedral of Piacenza, and the Church of San Zeno at Verona retain distinct traces of applied pigment.

Medieval French. Somewhat surprisingly, color was also generally loved and used in the somewhat duller climates of northern France and England. It appeared on exteriors in France as far back as Gallo-Roman times and continued throughout the medieval period and during the Renaissance down to the time of Louis XIV. Viollet-le-Duc, who restored Notre Dame in Paris, between 1845 and 1856, found numerous traces of color on that structure. The three doors of the façade, with their tympana, were painted and gilded, and

EGYPTIAN CITADEL; MOSQUE IN BACKGROUND
BADGER - GUILLUMETTE

the sculpture around the doors, the gallery of the kings, the arcades under the towers, and the great rose window were once radiant with color. The large gables of the transept also show unmistakable evidences of painting. According to Paul Sédille, the same was true of most of the French churches of the thirteenth, fourteenth, and fifteenth centuries.

PHILIP GENDREAU. N. Y.
THATCHED-ROOF COTTAGE, DEVONSHIRE, ENGLAND

Modern Avoidance of Color. With the revival of the Classics during the Italian Renaissance, color was largely lost sight of. Indeed Palladio, the guiding spirit of the later Renaissance and the man responsible for many of the ideas that eventually filtered into England and, through England, into her American colonies, proclaimed in defense of his white buildings that white was more acceptable to the gods. This doctrine, coupled with the further sobering influence of Puritanism, not only in the mother country but also in America, may account for the extreme timidity in the use of color on the exteriors of buildings.

CULTURAL INFLUENCES

History. The history of a nation has a great influence upon its art. If a nation is warlike, its art will be martial, perhaps even brutal. If a nation's story is a record of peace, the essays of the artists are likely to be passive in nature. Rome's victories were the themes of the sculptors of the imperial city, and commemorative architecture in the form of triumphal arches, commemorative columns, and memorials to victorious generals graced the nation's forums. Assyria's palaces were as martial as its people were warlike.

Religion. No single influence has more completely dominated the character of art than has religion. The great temples of antiquity and the matchless cathedrals of the Middle Ages are the direct architectural concomitants of the religious fervor of these respective ages. Indeed, during the Middle Ages the artists and craftsmen were trained by the Church, and, until the middle of the twelfth century, science, letters, the arts, and enlightenment generally were the monopoly of religious bodies. Monks and the pupils of monks were the architects of many of the great cathedrals of medieval Europe.

Social, Political, and Economic Conditions. The social and economic patterns of a nation likewise vastly influence the architecture of that nation. Egypt's great works of architecture would have been impossible under a social organization that did not reduce the great bulk of the population to the status of slaves. A vast labor pool was available

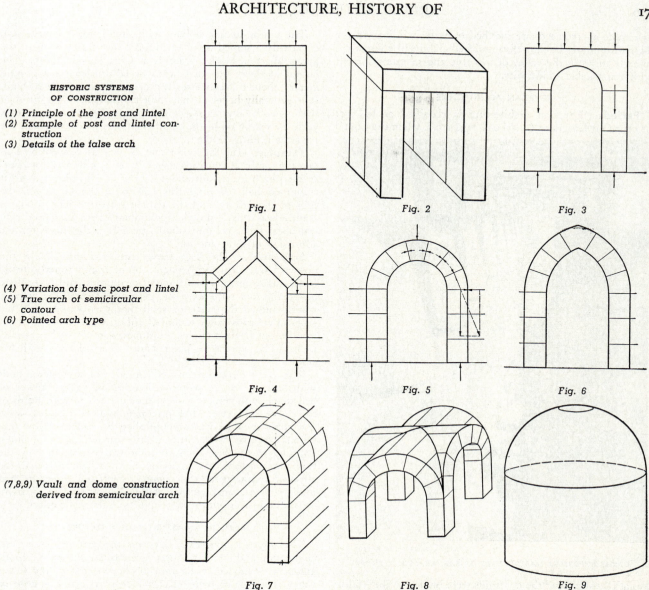

HISTORIC SYSTEMS
OF CONSTRUCTION

(1) *Principle of the post and lintel*
(2) *Example of post and lintel construction*
(3) *Details of the false arch*

Fig. 1   Fig. 2   Fig. 3

(4) *Variation of basic post and lintel*
(5) *True arch of semicircular
contour*
(6) *Pointed arch type*

Fig. 4   Fig. 5   Fig. 6

(7,8,9) *Vault and dome construction
derived from semicircular arch*

Fig. 7   Fig. 8   Fig. 9

for work upon public edifices. This fact, coupled with the existence of a strongly centralized and despotic government, made possible the erection of monuments out of all proportion to the nation's economic potential. In the Tigris-Euphrates basin, the Assyrians, a sturdy, cruel, warlike people, indulging in many wars with their neighbors, conquering many races, and carrying away prisoners to labor upon the public works of the realm, were able to erect structures which would have been impossible under any other social scheme.

FUNDAMENTAL PRINCIPLES

Until modern times the constructive systems which made possible the world's architecture were of two general types: (1) the static (post and lintel, columnar, or trabeated) and (2) the dynamic (arch and pier, arched, or arcuated).

The principle of the post and lintel is illustrated in Fig. 1. It will be noted that the weights and counterweights, in obedience to gravity, act vertically with no tendency toward lateral or sidewise action. This is the simplest system of raising a structure and is the type that always results when man spans the distance between two supports by a single member (*see* Fig. 2). It is not necessarily the only form that a static system may take, as is shown in the false arch in Fig. 3.

When the simple lintel is replaced with two members that lean against each other, as in Fig. 4, lateral thrusts are set up as indicated by the arrows. These lateral thrusts must always be abutted or combated by equal and opposite thrusts or counterthrusts. Until the introduction of structural materials strong in tension, this was the all-compelling concern of the builder.

Fig. 5 shows the true arch of semicircular contour and Fig. 6 a pointed arch, both popular dynamic shapes down through the ages. Figs. 7, 8, and 9 show the architectural forms (vaults and domes) that derive from the semicircular arch. These fundamental structural principles characterize architecture from the beginning down to modern times.

HISTORIC SYSTEMS OF CONSTRUCTION

At what place and at what time man took his first steps toward the fabrication of architecture will probably never be known with certainty. However, in the eastern Mediterranean there were three early centers of culture with distinguished architectural expressions: Egypt, the Tigris-Euphrates basin, and the Greek archipelago. Although dates as remote as 4500 B.C. are ascribed to early buildings in the Tigris-Euphrates basin, a distinguished architecture also arose in early times in the valley of the Nile and maintained itself with remarkable uniformity.

EGYPTIAN ARCHITECTURE

Periods. Egyptian architecture is classified as follows: (1) the Old Kingdom (c. 3200-c. 2134 B.C.), when the capital

SCREEN TRAVELER. FROM GENDREAU

GREAT HYPOSTYLE HALL, TEMPLE OF KARNAK, LUXOR, EGYPT

was at Memphis and the pyramids were built; (2) the Middle Kingdom (c. 2134-1788 B.C.), with the capital at Thebes, in which period the rock-cut tombs at Beni Hassan and the temples at Baubastis and Karnak were begun; (3) the Hyksos Invasion (1788-1580 B.C.) during which no important buildings were erected; (4) the brilliant New Kingdom (1580-1150 B.C.), with the capital at Thebes, during which the great temples at Karnak, Medinet, Abū Simbel, Luxor, and Abydos and the tomb-temples at Deir el Bahari were built; (5) the Decadence, Restoration, and Persian periods (1150-332 B.C.), with little building; and (6) the Ptolemaic Period (332-30 B.C.), with the capital at Alexandria, when the temples at Edfu, at Denderah, and on the island of Philae revived Egypt's glory. After 30 B.C. Egypt was no longer a national power.

Tombs. Egypt is well endowed with limestone, sandstone, and granite, which were used to advantage in important structures. The huts of the peasants, however, were largely made of unburned brick and consequently have not survived. Egyptian life centered around religion; therefore those structures having religious significance, such as temples and tombs, were of paramount importance. Indeed, it is these tombs and temples, built to last throughout eternity, that afford information concerning Egyptian architecture.

The tombs, at first oblong with sloping sides (mastabas), eventually assumed a full pyramidal form, as is seen in the great limestone-block pyramids at Giza outside Cairo. The largest of these, that of Cheops or Khufu, covers a ground area of about thirteen acres and originally stood 482 ft. high. It is generally believed that these monuments were finished with smooth outer casings. The pyramids are of solid stone, with the exception of the tomb chambers for royalty and the passages leading to them.

Temples. The Egyptian temple was as conventional as was the tomb. It consisted generally of a columned forecourt fronted by huge pylons and a gate as an entrance to a great columned hall. Beyond this hall were the sanctuary, the cells of the priests, and the temple treasury. The principal feature was this hypostyle (columned) hall, in whose central aisles taller columns made possible a clerestory for the admission of light and air.

Structure. The Egyptians employed principally the post-and-lintel structural system. Stone beams rested directly upon square piers or heavy circular columns, and upon these beams the roof slabs were set. A coping around the exterior walls retained the earth or sand that was placed upon the roof. Pyramids and temples, alike, were built without mortar, but in the temples the stones were dressed to precise joints. The piers were plain, paneled, or adorned with the effigy of a god.

The massive columns carried capitals (1) of clustered buds with lotus, palm, or papyrus decorations, (2) of flower or bell shape with similar embellishments, or (3) with heads of the goddess Hathor. The ornamentation of surfaces, walls and columns alike was accomplished by means of low bas-relief, executed with little regard for architectural lines. Painting of the bas-reliefs in color was necessitated by the brilliant sunshine and reflected light, which defeated the effect of architectural projections. Egyptian architecture was massive, mysterious, eternal, static. No other style of architecture compares with it in simple, bold dramatic effect.

BABYLONIAN-ASSYRIAN ARCHITECTURE

The Tigris-Euphrates valley was the seat of a very old civilization and the home successively of a number of important peoples. Since civilization developed first in the lower valley (Chaldea or Babylonia), which was devoid of stone or of much tree growth, the architecture here was originally of unburned earth and later of burned (ceramic) materials. After commerce developed upon the twin rivers, and especially during the zenith of Babylon, building stone was imported from the north. Architecture in the valley divides itself into the following periods: (1) the Early City-State Era (5000-2250 B.C.), during which time the temples of the sun god at Sippar, the sea god at Eridu, the moon god at Ur, and the palace of Gudea at Lagash were all erected; (2) the Old Babylonian (Chaldean) Kingdom (2250-1750 B.C.) with temples at Babylon and Borsippa; (3) the Kassite Interruption (1750-1100 B.C.); (4) the Assyrian Empire (1650-606 B.C.) with the capital at Nineveh, during which time the temple of Anu-Adad at Asshur and the great palaces at Calah, Khorsabad, and Nineveh were erected, and (5) the Neo-Babylonian Empire (606-538 B.C.) with the capital at Babylon, where were built the great temple of Marduk, the processional street, the palace of Nebuchadnezzar, and the famous Hanging Gardens.

The earthen-built Assyrian-Babylonian architecture was massive, military, noncolumnar. Temples were in the form of stepped pyramids with a small shrine for the deity at the top and a palace for the priests near by. Palace plans were

TEMPLE OF CERES OR OF VESTA
Greek Architecture in Pesto, Italy

labyrinthine, the long rooms surrounding large open courts. The chief architectural effect was achieved by sheer walls, embattled and palisaded, set atop huge platforms reached by ramps up which the king and his lords might drive their chariots. Ornamentation was accomplished principally by wainscots and mural decorations of glazed, colored tiles or of low bas-relief of the king and his lords at war, on the hunt, or at the banquet table.

PERSIAN ARCHITECTURE (558–33 B.C.)

Persian culture was based upon that of the Tigris-Euphrates, and thus there are noticeable resemblances in architectural expression. However, Persia, being situated in a terrain that provided both excellent stone and wood, in time developed a well-defined columnar system with saddle-back capitals ornamented with heads of bulls, horses, and griffins. The Persians employed their materials as follows: stone for door and window frames, platforms, steps, and ramps; marble for columns, sculpture, and bas-reliefs; brick (burned, colored, and glazed) for wall facings (cores were of unburned bricks), and wood for beams, girders, and roof coverings.

Decorative ceramics, based directly upon the achievements of Mesopotamian peoples, were carried to a high state of perfection, as the Archers' Frieze in the Louvre demonstrates. Great emphasis was placed upon palaces and reception rooms like the great hypostyle or audience halls built at Persepolis by Darius and Xerxes. The palaces of Darius, Xerxes, and Artaxerxes at Susa and Persepolis, the summer and winter capitals, were likewise lavish in extent and ornamentation. Their architecture was commanding, formal, and monumental. Other types were rock-cut and structural tombs, monumental gateways, and fire altars called into being by the fire worship of the Zoroastrian religion.

AEGEAN (CRETAN) ARCHITECTURE

Aegean architecture centered on the island of Crete, at whose capital, Knossos, successive sea kings built palaces. Cretan power was based upon naval supremacy, and Crete seems to have been the home of the world's first great sea power. The commerce based upon this power made possible the exchange of goods and ideas, and, therefore, exotic traits exhibit themselves in Cretan architecture. Court life was splendid, and the elaborate palaces give an index to the island's social scheme.

In Cretan palaces, which were of two or three stories, broad staircases and large courtyards were important. The sanitary arrangements were ingenious, the royal baths and latrines being served by sewer pipes of salt-glazed tile. Cleaning and inspection were made possible by manholes. Palace plans were complicated, resembling a group of small houses about a court rather than a well-thought-out unified scheme. The Greek legend of the labyrinth and its tortuous passages was based upon this trait in Cretan architecture.

The decorative system, which featured mural painting, appropriately included references to the sea, with squids and flying fish taking their places alongside charioteers, cup-bearers, hunters, and animals. One columnar support, larger at the top than at the bottom, is sometimes regarded as the prototype of the Greek Doric order.

GREEK ARCHITECTURE

Numerous references have already been made to Greek (Hellenic) architecture, which is believed to have had its beginning in the Homeric age (about 1000 B.C.) but which came to full flower during the rule of Pericles, between 460 and 430 B.C., with the erection of such masterpieces as the Parthenon, the Erechtheum, and the Propylaea on the Acropolis at Athens. Greek architecture is generally divided into the following periods: (1) Homeric Age, 1100-750 B.C.; (2) Archaic Period, 750-470 B.C.; (3) Hellenic Period, 470-338 B.C.; (4) Hellenistic Period, 338-146 B.C.; and (5) Roman Period, after 146 B.C.

Orders. The trabeated system of construction was brought to perfection in the three Greek orders of architecture: the Doric, the Ionic, and the Corinthian. Generally thought to have been derived from wooden prototypes, the Doric and the Ionic show various stages of development before perfection was achieved at Athens. The Greeks, sensitive to optical illusion, made adjustments in their forms to counteract the awkward effects that straight lines often produce. Thus a composition was considered subjectively rather than objectively.

Ornament. The Greeks handled architectural ornament with greater restraint than any race since their time. They developed a grammar of ornament based upon native faunal and floral motifs and applied it so expertly that it enhanced rather than detracted from the structural logic. Such ornament was introduced in sculptural embellishment and in polychromy. The use of color on the orders became highly conventional but was handled with great delicacy and restraint.

Types of Structure. The Greek social system, which was more elaborate than any down to its time, called into being a great variety of structures, among which the temples were the most important. Temples were built upon two plans, rectangular and circular. The general arrangement of the former called for a *pronaos* or portico, the *naos* or worshiping chamber, and a place for the temple treasure surrounded by a peristyle with from four to twelve columns across the front. The Parthenon, with eight columns at the front and seventeen along the flanks, is generally considered the best solution. Civic usage called for a *boulouterion* or council chamber; a *prytaneum* to house the public fire; *stoae,* the long colonnaded shelters around the *agora* or market place; and gymnasiums, stadiums, theatres, and gateways. In addition there were residences, shops, and tombs and other sepulchral monuments. Among the great monuments should be mentioned the Parthenon, the Erechtheum, the Theseum, the temple of Zeus at Olympia, the Propylaea, the Tholos at Epidaurus, the temple of Niké Apteros, the Tower of the Winds, the theatres of Dionysus at Athens and at Epidaurus, the Mausoleum at Halicarnassus, and the stadium at Athens.

ROMAN ARCHITECTURE

Greek architecture was not confined to the Greek archipelago but spread to Sicily and the mainland of Italy (Magna Graecia), where it profoundly influenced architectural expression in Rome. During its early history, this expanding city-state touched the lands of the Etruscans on the north and Magna Graecia on the south. Roman architecture may be divided into the following periods: (1) Etruscan Influence, 616-212 B.C.; (2) Greek Influence, 212-27 B.C.; (3) Augustan Age, 27 B.C.-A.D. 14; and (4) Imperial Period, A.D. 14 to the fifth century.

Structure. The Romans used a mixed system of construction. To the trabeated method of the Greeks they added the arcuated system of the Etruscans, in time bringing the latter to a brilliant climax and using the former in a reminiscent mood as mere architectural decoration. In the process, however, they added to the Doric, Ionic, and Corinthian orders, a simpler order known as the Tuscan, and a more complicated one (the Composite) made by combining elements of the Ionic and Corinthian.

Mastering the arch, the Romans developed (1) the barrel or tunnel vault, (2) the cross or groined vault, and (3) the dome (*see* Figs. 7, 8, and 9). The development of excellent stonework, good brick, and concrete made possible the erection of great structures at a speed hitherto unknown in the history of building. As imperial power developed and Rome became master of the world, a growing complexity of society called for a variety of structures that in number and size transcended anything the Greeks may have envisioned.

Types of Structure. Temples, though numerous, were not so important as in past architectures. Like those of the Greeks, they took both rectangular and circular shapes, the finest examples of the latter being the Pantheon, which has the largest masonry dome ever constructed (span, 142 ft.). The public structures included theatres, amphitheatres, circuses, stadiums, thermae (public baths), basilicas for legal and commercial business, forums, and rostrums. Other civic monuments were city walls, gates, aqueducts, fountains, triumphal arches, and commemorative columns. Then there were palaces, villas, insulae (apartment houses), and simpler town dwellings and shops.

Prominent Buildings. In its heyday, Rome was the paramount power in the world, and Roman architecture was distributed over Syria, North Africa, France, Spain, and Great Britain. Among the foremost Roman architectural achievements are the Colosseum, the Circus Maximus, the thermae of Caracalla and Diocletian, the basilicas of Julius Caesar (Basilica Julia), Trajan, and Constantine, the Forum Romanum, the Forum of Trajan, the Pantheon, and the Mausoleum of Hadrian, all in Rome; the Maison Carrée, the aqueduct Pont du Gard, and the amphitheatre at Nîmes, France; and the great Temple of the Sun at Palmyra and the Temple of Jupiter at Baalbek, in Syria.

Characteristics. Roman architecture was grand in conception, magnificent in scale, and lavish in execution. Versatility and engineering prowess were outstanding characteristics, although ornament was at times overdone and decadent. Rome's great contribution was the arch and its derivatives. Here was the starting place of the groined vault, which was to be brought to perfection by the medieval architects.

EARLY CHRISTIAN ARCHITECTURE

Out of Roman pagan forms grew two early Christian styles of architecture, (1) the so-called Early Christian style, which found expressions in Syria, in Italy, and among the Coptic churchmen of Egypt, and (2) the Byzantine style, with its center at Constantinople, the ancient Byzantium.

Italian (A.D. 300-1000). Christianity came as a vitalizing influence to the decadent forms of late Roman art. Through its influence that dying style was converted into an expression that was again living and dynamic. To be sure, new forms were not immediately developed, but old Roman forms were appropriated and given new meaning. Principal among these was the Roman basilica (courthouse), which was taken over as a worshiping place. The basilica was admirably adapted to Christian usage: the long aisles made possible the many processionals; all architectural lines converged upon and accentuated the altar; the priest faced the congregation while speaking; the apse, a semicircular projection at the rear, afforded seats for the clergy, the priest taking the seat of the Roman quaestor and the presbyters,

BASILICA OF CONSTANTINE, ROME, ITALY

twelve in number, occupying the seats of the Roman assessors (jury). In its full development the Christian basilican church was characterized by the following features: (1) an atrium or forecourt with a basin for ablutions, (2) a narthex or vestibule for penitents, (3) a nave with side aisles, lighted by a clerestory, (4) a *bema* (the forerunner of the transept), and (5) an apse with altar and other ecclesiastical appointments.

The early Christians continued the late Roman habit of encrusting the interiors with beautiful materials. Walls, floors, and other surfaces were well adapted to mosaic art and painted ornament. A conventional grammar of ornament, based upon Christian symbolism, was worked out. The original St. Peter's Basilica (A.D. 300) and the churches of St. John Lateran, Santa Maria Maggiore, San Clemente, and St. Paul-Outside-the-Walls, all in Rome, are typical of this era.

Byzantine (A.D. 330-1453). In A.D. 330 Constantine moved the capital of the Roman Empire to the Hellespont and renamed the ancient city of Byzantium "Constantinople." The new Byzantine style of architecture that soon developed became, after the division of the empire, the official style of the Eastern Empire and of the Greek Catholic Church, so that it spread into Greece, Syria, the Balkans, and Russia.

At Constantinople a dome-crowned central plan, in contradistinction to the basilican plan of the Roman Catholic Church, became the popular arrangement and in time gave rise to such monuments as the magnificent church of Hagia Sophia, one of the great triumphs of Christendom.

The Byzantine plan, normally square, had great piers at the corners. From these sprang pendentives (triangular vaulting) to carry a low dome lighted by a row of windows in its base. This square central space was usually amplified by great apses on the four sides crowned by semidomes which in turn helped to buttress the central dome. However, the dome of Hagia Sophia, 107 ft. in diameter, is less in span than the later great domes of Florence Cathedral, St. Peter's in Rome, and St. Paul's in London.

Byzantine architects considered every interior surface available for encrusted decoration. Floors were covered with mosaics of marble, walls were wainscoted with colored marbles, and vaults, pendentives, and domes were lined with colorful glass mosaics, often with gold grounds. Even columns, when used, were of beautifully veined and colored marbles.

Whereas the Byzantine style confined its great monuments to the areas above indicated, certain reflections found their way back into Italy at places which enjoyed commerce with the East. Thus such monuments as the churches of St. Mark's at Venice and San Vitale at Ravenna exhibit unmistakable Byzantine traits. In the Balkans and Russia, the style, influenced by indigenous conditions, brought forth edifices like those at Moscow—the Cathedral of Novgorod and the churches of Saint Savior, the Virgin, the Assumption, and St. Basil.

SARACENIC ARCHITECTURE (A.D. 641 TO DATE)

While the Early Christian and Byzantine architectures were arising in response to Christian zeal north of the

FLEMISH ARCHITECTURE, YPRES, BELGIUM

Mediterranean, a new style to house the followers of Mohammed was slowly developing in Arabia, Syria, Egypt, Persia, Turkey, India, North Africa, and Spain.

Decoration. The Saracens were not great builders by nature; therefore they appropriated existing constructive systems wherever they went. However, they were among the world's great decorators. Nearly every inch of surface inside their buildings was encrusted either with colorful marble veneers, glazed tiles, stamped plaster bas-reliefs, rich inlays of rare woods or even embellishments in semiprecious stones. Since the depiction of human or animal forms was held idolatrous, decorations ran to intricate geometrical patterns and floral forms.

Types of Structure. In addition to homes (complicated because of the practice of polygamy) and shops, the principal structures were mosques (temples), tombs, madrasahs (schools), hospitals, and caravansaries (khans) or hospices built upon caravan routes to protect merchants from desert robbers.

The mosque, following specifications from the Koran, exhibited the following features: (1) a forecourt with a fountain for ablutions, (2) a prayer hall where the faithful prayed while facing Mecca, (3) minarets or towers from which, in the absence of bells, the muezzin (Mohammedan crier) called the people to prayer, and (4) living quarters for the criers and their families. Sometimes a school or the tomb of a saint was attached.

Prominent Buildings. The Saracenic style was generally fanciful, colorful, and typically oriental. It showed various traits in the different countries; but courtyards, arcades, and other shade-producing features, together with domes, frequently lofty and of pointed outline, were universal. Among the notable Saracenic buildings are Dome of the Rock, Jerusalem; Mosque El Walid, Damascus; the mosques of Ibn-Tulun, Sultan Hassan, and El Muayyad, all in Cairo; the Mosque of Córdoba and the Alhambra at Granada, Spain; the mosques at Tabriz, Isfahan, and Ardebil in Persia; the mosques of Suleiman I, Ahmed I, and Yeni Djami at Constantinople; various great mosques in Mohammedan India; and the matchless Taj Mahal at Agra.

ROMANESQUE ARCHITECTURE (A.D. 1000-1200)

While the Byzantine style was developing in the Eastern Empire, great changes were taking place in the West. By A.D. 476, the Roman Empire in the West had succumbed to the inroads of the northern barbarians, and, by the eighth century, the Mohammedans were battling the Christians around the Mediterranean.

The Roman Church, as Europe's only unified institution, was the civilizing and educative agency of medieval times. Science and art were in the hands of monks, who were often the architects of churches and cathedrals. Indeed, down to the thirteenth century, architecture was regarded as a sacred science.

Types. Christian architecture had made such changes that the style dating from around A.D. 1000 must be called by a different name. The term "Romanesque" is now generally used to denote this style, which, growing out of the Early Christian, gradually was transformed into the Gothic. However, down through the years antiquaries have used many terms to designate variants of the Romanesque. In north Italy the term "Lombard" is used; in Norman France and England, "Norman"; in western Germany, "Rhenish"; in pre-Conquest England, "Saxon"; in Charlemagne's empire, "Carolingian." The term "Round-arched Gothic" has also been used to describe this transitional style, which spread over western Europe, embracing France, Italy, Sicily, England, Spain, and Germany, with some influence in Portugal and Scandinavia.

Characteristics. Some general traits of the Romanesque may be noted here. Whereas Early Christian churches had been largely wooden-roofed, Romanesque builders aspired to make the house of God as imperishable as possible. To this end the Roman groined vault was revived. At first only the side aisles were vaulted, but in time the naves were likewise covered in square bays, two bays of the side aisles synchronizing with one bay of the nave. Masonry semi-domes continued to be the covering for the apse. The church of San Ambrogio in Milan may be taken as the first milestone in this long development of medieval vaulting, which came to a complete solution during the Gothic period. Lombard building methods, imported into France, gave rise to a series of contributions to this problem in such churches as Abbaye aux Hommes and Abbaye aux Dames at Caen, Notre Dame at Morienval, and Abbey St. Denis and St. Germain des Prés at Paris.

Italian. Among the great monuments of the Italian Romanesque are San Zenone at Verona, the cathedrals of Piacenza, Pisa, and Monreale, the Leaning Tower and the

ST. MARK'S, VENICE, ITALY

METROPOLITAN MUSEUM OF ART

baptistery at Pisa, San Stephano at Bologna, San Michele at Lucca, San Pietro and Santa Maria at Tuscania (Toscanella), and the Palatinate Chapel at Palermo. The Romanesque style in central Italy was influenced by Roman models, and that in southern Italy and Sicily by Byzantine and Saracenic forms.

French. In France regional differences and the lack of national unity operated to divide the Romanesque into several local schools, all more or less concerned with the central problem of vaulting churches in stone. Some schools used tunnel vaults, some domes upon pendentives, and some groined vaults with or without ribs. Buildings presenting groping but brilliant solutions of the vaulting problem are St. Trophime at Arles, St. Front at Perigueux, Le Puy Ca-

thedral, St. Sernin at Toulouse, the abbeys at Caen, and the Abbey St. Denis near Paris, already mentioned.

English. When the Normans under William conquered England in 1066, the French Romanesque was introduced into Great Britain, where the cruder Saxon Romanesque was already flourishing. Soon the cathedral churches at Canterbury, Gloucester, Durham, Norwich, Hereford, Peterborough, and Ely were erected in the imported manner, competing in size and splendor with the great Romanesque churches of France. English vaults in general followed French models, both the quadripartite and sexpartite ribbed types being used. The Norman style in England, as in France, formed the basis upon which a subsequent national Gothic style was predicated. In both countries the Romanesque was heavy and round-arched, crude in ornament, picturesque, groping, and transitional.

German. The German Romanesque style, though of foreign origin, was reflective of German medieval traits. Neither brilliant nor daring in conception, it was honest in construction and of excellent craftsmanship. Such buildings as the cathedrals at Mainz, Speyer, and Worms, the Church of the Apostles at Köln, and various Romanesque castles are the best architectural expression of the German people before modern times.

GOTHIC ARCHITECTURE (1150-1500)

French. French Gothic architecture, which may be considered the logical development of the Romanesque, is generally divided into three periods, based not upon the character of the vaulting but upon the patterns of the window tracery, which form a convenient though superficial index to the style. These periods are (1) thirteenth century—Primary or Gothique; (2) fourteenth century—Secondary or Rayonnant; and (3) fifteenth century—Tertiary or Flamboyant. The thirteenth century was the ascendant period, the fourteenth century the crest (best), and the fifteenth century

ST. PETER'S HOSPITAL, ENGLAND

PETERBOROUGH CATHEDRAL; NORMAN ARCHITECTURE IN ENGLAND

the decline or ultradecorative period. France was the original home of the Gothic and the last country to give it up. Île de France, a former province comprising Paris and its environs, produced the style's noblest monuments.

Organic structure was the keynote of the style. There is every indication that the builders thought of their building as enclosed space rather than as plastic monuments in stone. Structural logic dictated form; and although architectural ornament became increasingly important, it was never allowed to transcend architectonic values. Vaults, constructed with pointed rather than round arches, were either quadripartite or sexpartite and were carefully sustained by flying buttresses, the space between the piers in many cases being filled with stained glass. A careful balance between thrust and counterthrust made possible the poet's paradox of "roofs of stone above walls of glass." Ornamentation of the great churches and cathedrals was carried out by (1) the decorative handling of structural features like piers, parapets and flying buttresses, (2) the use of sculpture, both in the round and as bas-relief, and (3) the use of color, first, in painted and gilded ornament and, second, in great stained-glass windows.

This magnificent style, which may be described as structurally logical, daring and brilliant in construction, and reflective of religious fervor and civic pride, brought forth such masterpieces as the cathedrals of Chartres, Paris (Notre Dame), Bourges, Rouen, Rheims, and Amiens, and such churches as Sainte Chapelle in Paris and St. Ouen in Rouen. These are the flower of man's efforts at building.

English. English Gothic architecture embraces almost the same span of time and, like the French, is generally dated by its window tracery. However, whereas French vaulting remained simple and structural, English vaulting went in

for elaborate ornamentation. Moreover, since many English churches were covered with wooden roofs, these also came in for highly decorative treatment. This "flowering out at the top" led the eye heavenward; in the French cathedrals this aspiring effect was achieved by the sheer height of the vaults (120 to 130 ft.) and the vertical fluting of the piers. Although in many respects the Gothic in England cannot compare with that of France, it exhibits a variety of massing and detail that is delightfully natural and pleasing. The structures seem also to step down in scale to human dimensions and are thus more intimate and understandable than the towering structural treatment of France.

At the time of the break between Henry VIII and the Pope in the 1530's, many monasteries were transformed into cathedrals, yet retaining many monastic features, such as cloisters, chapter houses, and refectories, not found in French cathedrals. Also many churches underwent additions or alterations in subsequent periods, resulting in a mixture of styles and causing confusion in attempts at classification by period. Among the great Gothic cathedrals are those at Wells, Lincoln, York, Worcester, and Salisbury, and sizable portions of Canterbury, Gloucester, Exeter, Lichfield, and Norwich. Westminster and other abbeys, parish churches, chapels, and the educational buildings at Oxford and Cambridge also illustrate the prowess of English medieval builders.

German. German Gothic, though developing some striking characteristics and perhaps even a national feeling, may be regarded as an importation from France rather than an outgrowth of the preceding Romanesque. The excellent craftsmanship that contributes a human interest to the structures should not be mistaken for architectural achievement. The more important of the monuments include the cathedrals at Köln, Regensburg, Strassburg, Ulm, and Augsburg, St. Stephen in Vienna, and Liebfrauenkirche in Nürnberg. Similar observations may be made of the Gothic of the Low Countries, which has many structures celebrated in legend and story.

Italian and Spanish. Neither the Italians nor the Spaniards ever understood the Gothic style, which was a frank importation from the north. It was considered barbaric by the Italians, although they produced such large-scale Gothic monuments as the cathedrals of Florence and Milan. In Spain the great examples of the era are the cathedrals at Burgos, Toledo, and Seville. Both Italy and Spain paid only lip service to Gothic structural logic but characteristically produced lovely ornamental details, good examples of which are the marble and mosaic decorations on Giotto's tower in Florence.

RENAISSANCE ARCHITECTURE (1420-1700)

A competition for the completion of Arnolfo's Cathedral of Santa Maria del Fiore in Florence led to the design of the first considerable monument of the Renaissance. This was Brunelleschi's dome of Florence, under construction from 1420 to 1464. This masterful work revived an old Roman form, the dome, but employed pointed arches, rather than the semicircular forms of the Roman Pantheon. The Gothic architects had learned that pointed arches and vaults have less lateral thrust than the lower semicircular arches and vaults, and Brunelleschi profited by this knowledge. Not only did he construct a pointed dome; he also contrived a system of internal reinforcement to offset the lateral thrust at the base of the dome. Thus he obviated external buttressing. With buttresses not necessary, he could raise the dome upon a huge octagonal drum 137 ft. in diameter, making of it a dominant motif and setting the pattern for the subsequent domes of St. Peter's Basilica in Rome, St. Paul's Cathedral in London, and the United States Capitol in Washington.

Italy. Starting at Florence, where a restless cultural quest had turned men's attention to the glories of Greek and Roman literature and art, the vogue spread first throughout Italy, then to France and Spain and eventually to England and Germany. The Florentine Renaissance reached its peak about the year 1500, when leadership passed to the Roman school, followed by a colorful twilight terminating in the Venetian school of the sixteenth century.

The Renaissance in Italy was characterized by a revival of classic Roman architecture and the adaptation of its forms to the solution of new problems called for by a developing society. The new philosophical system, in which man and his worldly interests were made central and dominant, was bound to have a profound influence upon architecture. Although highly reminiscent, the Renaissance laid the basis for modern architecture.

France. Spreading to France, where it was championed by royalty, the Renaissance adapted itself to French demands and brought forth a respectable group of monuments, among which were the famous châteaux of the Loire Valley. In time, French architects took a leading place in the propagation of the Renaissance vogue.

England. England, farther away and, after the break with Rome, less interested in Italian matters, was tardy in taking up Renaissance forms. Indeed, before English architects awakened to the charms of revitalized Classic forms, Venice had already assumed leadership in Italy. The architecture of the late Renaissance master, Palladio, was imported into England by the court architect, Inigo Jones. Once it was adopted, the English were faithful to the neo-Classical style, which with modifications has remained popular down almost to the present. Under the name "Georgian" the style was imported into the American colonies, where it may be considered to have been the main form from about the year 1720 until after the achievement of American independence.

Spain. In Spain likewise, the Renaissance took firm hold and brought forth a score of interesting monuments. It came into vogue during the exultant sixteenth century following the final expulsion of the Moors and the discovery of America and was at its heyday during the period of the colonization of Latin America. Strong indigenous variants of this already cosmopolitan Hispanic style grew up in South and Central America, Mexico, and in the territories which are now the states of Florida, Texas, New Mexico, Arizona, and California.

Baroque and Classical Revival. During the blatant terminal Baroque period of the waning Renaissance many sculpturesque but vulgar buildings were erected throughout the areas above enumerated. With greater emphasis upon decorative embellishments than upon architectonic logic, the public soon tired of its excrescences and welcomed a second return to Classic purity. This ushered in the Classical Revival (the emphasis this time being placed largely upon Greek precedent), which spread throughout those areas which had once been Renaissance territory. As would be expected, this brought forth responses in Italy, France, England, Spain, Germany, and the young American republic. Such examples as the Church of the Madeleine in Paris, the British Museum in London, the Brandenburg Gate in Berlin, the Campo Santo at Milan, and the old Custom House in Philadelphia are representative. In the United States the Greek Revival was the national style down until the time of the Civil War.

OLD STATE HOUSE, HARTFORD, CONN.

MODERN ARCHITECTURE (1750 TO DATE)

Beginning about 1750, a series of important inventions, among them the steam engine, revolutionized manufacturing and transportation. These changes in industrial methods were bound to introduce social and economic maladjustments, some of which still plague the world. This changeful social picture, coupled with the introduction of a whole new group of structural materials, has introduced problems for the architect, the magnitude of which he has not faced since the days of the early Renaissance. This movement in architecture, admittedly groping and uncertain, is termed modern or contemporary architecture.

In most countries, from about 1860 until World War II, architecture took an eclectic trend, resulting in the stylistically mixed "battle of the styles." Meanwhile, industry was developing new building materials (iron, steel, glass, concrete, bronze, ceramics, and plastics) to express the new social patterns induced by a mechanized economy. Architects soon discovered that the new materials required a handling entirely different from that accorded the time-honored brick and stone; and, too, that each new material had definite physical and aesthetic possibilities and limitations. From this development and the further realization that social usage should determine the form of buildings, emerged a whole new philosophy and practice of architecture which has, for want of a better term, been called "functionalism."

The first experiments with iron and glass as worthy architectural materials date back over a century, when in 1811, the architects Brunet and Bélanger replaced the wooden dome of the Halles au Blé in Paris with one of iron construction. The use of structural glass was first promoted by Sir Joseph Paxton in botanical gardens, then in the great Crystal Palace of London in 1851. Although concrete as a structural material had been known since Roman times, the French and English were the first to explore its great possibilities as a worthy architectural material. It was not until the 1890's, however, that Portland cement became cheap and plentiful.

Between 1860 and 1870, cast-iron and wrought-iron structural shapes made great inroads into architecture. However, steel was not to influence building markedly until a process was perfected that rendered it cheap enough to be used as a major framing material. After about 1887, the steel frame and the skyscraper were evolved. The same story, with

GRUNDTVIG MEMORIAL CHURCH, COPENHAGEN, DENMARK

modifications, is being written of aluminum and possibly also of other materials. The great need of human shelter spurs builders, and industry in general, to find new and cheaper construction materials.

The aesthetic solution of a new material is not immediately apparent, and the modern architect is not expected to arrive at conclusive solutions without some experimentation. In each civilized nation of the world this problem is being attacked, and new expressions are emerging from the various environmental and social settings.

In Paris, starting with the National and Ste. Genevieve libraries, one may trace in the Bon Marché (store) and the Eiffel Tower significant contributions to the expression of metal in architecture. The churches of the brothers Perret at Le Raincy and Montmagny are interesting essays in reinforced concrete. And, in even a more modern palette, the cousins Pierre Jeanneret and Le Corbusier (C. E. Jeanneret) and a host of others have given us fresh interpretations.

In England the work of Philip Webb, Norman Shaw, C. F. A. Voysey, C. R. Mackintosh, and A. H. Mackmurdo pointed in the direction of the later achievements of Easton and Robertson in the Royal Horticultural Hall, and Ellis and Clark in the Daily Express Building.

In Germany the works of Alfred Messel, Peter Behrens, Joseph Olbrich, and Otto Wagner laid the foundations of a

modern movement which produced many competent designers and culminated finally in the famous Bauhaus which, though disbanded by Hitler, continued to have considerable international influence; exponents such as Richard J. Neutra, Walter Gropius, and Mies van der Rohe taught or practiced in the United States.

Scandinavia and the Netherlands have each made significant contributions, the former furnishing excellent exemplars in the City Hall at Stockholm by Ostberg and the Concert Hall at Göteborg by Bjerke, the latter in the Utrecht Post Office by Crouwel and the New Exchange at Amsterdam by Berlage. In Italy, under Mussolini, architects were afforded an opportunity to produce outstanding examples of modern architecture in buildings for the University of Rome, stadiums, and other Fascist state structures.

Although most architectural movements in the United States have stemmed from European beginnings, this cannot be said of the nation's modern movement. Indeed, much that has occurred in Germany and the Low Countries appears to have been inspired by the works of Louis Sullivan and Frank Lloyd Wright, forward-looking Chicago designers. Sullivan is generally considered the father of American modernism, and Chicago, the first center of the movement. In such early structures as the Chicago Auditorium, the Wainwright Building in St. Louis, and the Guaranty Trust of Buffalo, Sullivan practiced his basic philosophy that "form should follow function," meanwhile preaching his doctrine to a group of young designers who had settled in Chicago, among them Wright. Others who have made definite contributions to American modernism are Irving K. Pond, Dwight Perkins, George G. Elmslie, George Maher, Walter Burley Griffin, William L. Steele, Bernard Maybeck, Bruce Goff, Louis Mulgardt, Bertram G. Goodhue, Barry Byrne,

MODERN ARCHITECTURE: THE CHICAGO TRIBUNE BUILDING

WURTS BROTHERS

PENTHOUSE TERRACE OF THE MUSEUM OF MODERN ART, NEW YORK CITY

Raymond M. Hood, Howe & Lescaze, R. M. Schindler, Paul Schweikher, and George Fred Keck.

Nor must one omit the names of men like William Le Baron Jenney, Daniel H. Burnham, and William Holabird, who achieved the structural knowledge that made possible the steel frame and America's modern contribution, the sky-scraper. Of the many buildings that constitute milestones in this development, the Tacoma Building (1888), Chicago, was the first structure with a complete steel frame, and the 1,245-ft. Empire State Building in New York became the world's tallest building.

Contemporary architecture is in the hands of a competent generation of architects in several countries. Western Europe, South America, Mexico, Sweden, and the United States are all making significant contributions to modern design. Indeed, as a result of the efforts of these practitioners, what has been called an international style has arisen.

ORIENTAL STYLES

Apart from the architectures that characterize Western culture or in one way or another touch the Christian tradi-tion, three other great architectural styles arose in India, China, and Japan.

Indian. The temple architecture of India has generally been classified by cults as follows: Buddhist, Jain, and Hindu. Of the first class, only rock-cut examples remain; therefore, little is known of their structural counterpart. The typical Buddhist temple consisted of a nave with side aisles terminat-ing in an apse in which stood the object of veneration. Such temples were popular from 250 B.C. to A.D. 600.

Jain architecture flourished from 1000 to 1300. The Jain temple consisted usually of a small idol-cell, containing a cross-legged figure of the saint, faced by a dome-crowned entrance porch.

The earliest of the Hindu temples date from the sixth century after Christ. The heyday of the style falls between 1000 and 1300, though good examples were built as late as 1750. The northern Hindu type, perhaps the most pic-turesque, consists of a rectangular idol cell crowned by a high curved pyramidal tower decorated by horizontally stratified ornament. An entrance porch usually marks the façade.

Besides the temples and their adjacent monasteries, there were sacred enclosures (rails), memorial mounds (stupas), and commemorative columns. Lesser monuments included palaces, tombs, and landing places (ghats along the sacred rivers with their shrines, shelters, and kiosks).

Chinese. Through the influence of Buddhism, which spread to China, Chinese architecture derives some traits from India; but whereas Indian architecture was largely of stone, Chinese architecture shows every evidence of a wooden origin. The simple structural system was that of great tile-clad wooden roofs held aloft upon wooden columns, be-tween which walls of wood, marble, or brick were then inserted. Built upon high platforms, Chinese temples and palaces were generally of one story with open-timber roofs covered with glazed tiles of blue, green, yellow, or black. The columns were lacquered in red, while the roof timbers were elaborately decorated with color and gilt. Palace and temple groups were symmetrical and formal in arrange-

ROCKEFELLER CENTER, NEW YORK CITY
The 70-story RCA building towers above the other buildings in the development.

ment. The temple group at Peiping, of which the circular Temple of the Happy Year is a central feature, is an outstanding sacred shrine. The Summer Palace in the western hills outside Peiping is an interesting domestic group. Characteristically Chinese are the pagodas (towers), three to thirteen stories in height, and the pailous (gates), both commemorative types. These may be of brick or stone and are sometimes sheathed with colorful tiles. Tea houses, bridges, city walls, and tombs comprise other Chinese architectural types.

Japanese. Since Japan is culturally the child of China, its architecture is derived from Chinese prototypes. The same system of construction prevails, also the same use of lacquered columns, illumined brackets, and tile-covered roofs. The architecture tends to be on a smaller scale, however. Moreover, there are no brilliant glazed tiles as in China, the dominant color being gun metal. The pagoda is as popular as in China but is generally of from five to seven stories. The pailou of China becomes the torii gate in Japan, formed of two circular posts surmounted by a curved beam. One of the great charms of Japanese architecture is its harmony with carefully planned landscape settings. *See also* Architectural Styles; Architectural Terms.   R. Ne.

ARCHITRAVE. *See* Architectural Orders; Architectural Terms.

ARCHIVES [ɑ'rkaivz], records considered worthy of permanent preservation. The term, a collective noun derived from the Greek word *archeion* (government building), originally applied to the records of government agencies (public archives) but later was extended to include the records of institutions (institutional archives), corporations and business firms (business archives), and families and individuals (family and personal archives). The term is also used to designate the agency charged with the custody, preservation, and administration of archival material after it has become noncurrent, and the building in which archives are housed. A person engaged in the administration of archival material is called an archivist.

Archives have a twofold character and use. They are, in the first place, evidence of the activities and legal rights of organizations or individuals and, when current, may become important for the maintenance of legal rights and of policies. Public archives are, at the same time, indispensable for the protection of property and of other legal rights of the citizen. Secondly, archives constitute an unsurpassed source of information concerning the political, social, economic, and technological developments of the past: information that is prerequisite to the understanding of the evolution and problems of modern society. The holdings of many archival establishments originated centuries ago, but it would be entirely misleading to think of archives as rare documents that are of interest to antiquarians only. The records of the War Production Board of World War II are archives, just as are the parchments of the chancery of the English kings of the thirteenth century.

Easily the most important category of archives is the public archives, which, in the United States, include the permanently valuable records of the federal, state, local, and municipal governments. Certain public records are published in printed or processed form, bearing the imprint of government agencies, and are often termed "government documents" by the librarian. Such government publications, when distributed to the public, however, are not archives. Retained as a record set by the originating agency, or in the files of other agencies, they may be considered a part of their archives. In any case, only a fraction of a government's archives becomes accessible in printed or processed form as government publications. A distinction should be made also between archives and historical manuscripts. Papers of families and individuals that lack the organic character of true archives, and isolated items of this kind, assembled as the result of collecting activities rather than accumulated in the course of the conduct of public or private business, are called historical manuscripts.

Archival Development in Europe. Just as writing was invented to meet the needs of the early administrator and accountant, rather than those of the scholar, the keeping of archives developed as an administrative technique in the urban cultures of the Euphrates and Tigris valleys. Clay tablets bearing cuneiform characters, constituting the texts of official proclamations and laws, of judicial decisions, and contracts between private persons, constitute the earliest archives that have been preserved. In Greece and republican Rome, the various magistrates continued the practice of keeping archives, which reached a high level of perfection in the bureaucratized administration of the Roman and Byzantine empires. The Catholic Church inherited its methods of keeping archives from the imperial authorities, while, during the period of feudalism, the keeping of archives fell into decay in the rest of Europe. First revived in the Hohenstaufen-Anjou Kingdom in southern Italy and in the city states of the north, archive keeping became a necessary part of administrative technique in evolving the national states of Western and Central Europe, each office setting up its own archives. However, as statesmen realized the administrative advantages of concentrating archives in one place, Spain, Austria, and a few other countries consolidated the archives of different offices in the custody of special archival agencies. Examples of such agencies include the General Archives of Simancas in Spain, established in 1543, and the Archives of the Dynasty, State, and Court in Vienna, established in 1749.

The concept of the archival agency as a service agency emerged in more perfect form during the French Revolution, when France created its National Archives (*Archives nationales*) as the depository for records of the central government, past and present, and later provided archival agencies for the safekeeping of the records of provincial and local governments in each province or department (*archives départementales*). It was the French Revolution, too, which gave all citizens the right to inspect government archives, thus expressing the truth that such archives are the property of the people whose legal rights and past history they preserve. As archives acquired the dignity of national monuments, and as historians became increasingly eager to have access to them, the more progressive states of Europe made provision for a state-wide system of archival service. While such a system had to be adapted to the particular governmental structure of a given country, it normally included:

(1) a national archival agency to care for the archives of the central government; (2) provincial archival agencies for the records of the intermediate levels of government; and (3) municipal and other local archives, frequently supervised by officers of the national archival administration.

Before World War II, most European countries were noteworthy for the excellence of their archival administration and for the richness of their archival contents. The splendid archives of the British government, so important for the Colonial period of the United States, were readily available to American and other scholars in the Public Record Office in London. France, the Netherlands, and Belgium had, in addition to their national archival establishments, complete networks of provincial depositories that also exercised supervision over municipal and local archives in their respective areas. Italy was in the process of building up an equally comprehensive system, while the archival system of Spain was still lacking in completeness and organization. Sweden, Norway, Denmark, and Finland had national archival centers in their capitals, supplemented by a number of provincial establishments. Germany, maintaining its *Reichsarchiv* in Potsdam and archival administrations in the different states, applied the concept of public archives service within the framework of a federal government, as did Switzerland, which maintained federal archives in Berne and state archives in its various cantons. Remarkable progress toward the realization of a national archives system had also been made in Poland, Czechoslovakia, and Hungary. In Russia, previously little affected by developments in Western and Central Europe, the Bolshevik Revolution, because of the disestablishment of the tsarist administrative machinery and the inheriting of its records, resulted in the setting up of archival administrations and archival depositories on the Soviet Union and on all lower levels of government, corresponding exactly to the complicated hierarchy of governmental units.

Among institutional archives, the Secret Archives of the Vatican became of outstanding importance when Pope Leo XIII opened its doors to scholars in 1881. Toward the end of the nineteenth century, increasing attention was given to business archives, and depositories for their preservation were established by firms, chambers of commerce, and other interested groups in Germany, the Netherlands, Switzerland, and Belgium. Archives of private families are especially rich and numerous in Germany, England, and Austria. In spite of precautions taken by both the Axis countries and the Allies, World War II was bound to inflict heavy and irreparable losses on European archives, particularly on those of Germany and Poland.

Archives in the United States. Until the beginning of the twentieth century, the United States, a youthful member of the community of nations, unencumbered as such by the records of an extended past, was little concerned with the preservation of its archives. Though the executive branch of the Federal Government had long clamored for a storage building to house its overflowing records, the movement for a national archives succeeded only after the elite of American scholarship, organized in such groups as the American Historical Association and the Carnegie Institution of Washington, had joined the executive agencies of the government in urging Congress to make provision for the nation's archives. The names of J. Franklin Jameson and Waldo G. Leland, to mention only two of the prominent leaders of the movement, will forever be associated with the magnificent National Archives building on Constitution Avenue in Washington, D. C. Appropriations for this building were included in the

Second Deficiency Act, approved July 3, 1926, and the cornerstone was laid by President Herbert Hoover on Feb. 20, 1933.

The National Archives is headed by the Archivist of the United States and is staffed by about 350 employees. Operating under the National Archives Act, approved June 19, 1934, it is charged with taking over, preserving, and making accessible the permanently valuable noncurrent records of the Federal Government, including maps, motion pictures, photographs, and sound recordings. By July 1, 1948, more than 800,000 cu. ft. of records had been transferred to the custody of the National Archives, this quantity, however, constituting only a small part of the total records of the government, then estimated at about 15,000,000 cu. ft. In fact, the greatest problem facing the National Archives has been to cope with the enormous physical bulk of federal records and to salvage, for permanent preservation, those of enduring value. To achieve this end, the National Archives has assisted government agencies in developing disposal schedules that make it possible to destroy worthless records after given periods of time, and it has urged such agencies to adopt measures that facilitate the segregation of the permanently valuable records for transfer to the National Archives. Records thus transferred are carefully fumigated, cleaned, and stored in windowless stack areas, where they are kept under conditions of ideal temperature and humidity. In accordance with acknowledged principles of archival administration, the National Archives has arranged its holdings in about 250 "record groups," each group containing the records of one of the major bureaus, or independent agencies, of the Federal Government. Within these groups, records are kept in their original order: that is, they are not broken up and classified to fit into a subject arrangement, such as one would find in a library. Records pertaining to the Civil War, for instance, are stored in many different record groups where they may be traced with the help of the *Guide to the Records in the National Archives.* Check lists and inventories give more detailed information about the contents of each record group. The enormous wealth of information in the records in the National Archives is intensively used by agencies of the government, by scholars, and by other interested persons. While government agencies may borrow records, private persons must inspect them in the search rooms, or they may obtain photostat or microfilm copies of them. The National Archives, to a limited extent, gives information from the records in response to mail or telephone requests. During the first fifteen years of its existence, the National Archives has accomplished the great achievement of concentrating in its custody practically all the valuable noncurrent records of the Federal Government. Its methods and techniques, particularly the lamination process used for repairing and protecting papers, have attracted the attention of archivists of all countries.

Although all the states have made some provision for the preservation of their archives, not many of them maintain well-organized archival agencies. In 1949, outstanding state archival agencies included: the Archives Department of the Illinois State Library in Springfield, Ill.; the Maryland Hall of Records in Annapolis, Md.; the Archives Division of the Virginia State Library in Richmond, Va.; and the Hall of Records in Dover, Del.

Since the beginning of the century, local archives have been well cared for in a few states, especially in Connecticut and New York. In others, the earlier local records have been deposited in the state archival agencies; or the state archival agencies have received photostat or microfilm copies of the more important records.

Other Parts of the World. During the nineteenth and twentieth centuries, many other countries awoke to the importance of their archives and established special agencies for the preservation and administration of such records. Among these countries were those of Latin America; China, maintaining splendid archives in the Palace Museum in Peiping; and most of the Dominions, and some of the Crown Colonies, of the British Commonwealth of Nations. In 1946, the United Nations established its archives at Lake Success on Long Island; and, two years later, effective steps were taken at a meeting in Paris toward creating a world-wide organization of archivists.   E. P.

ARCHON [ɑ'rkɒn], an important elected official found in many Greek states of the Classical period. In Athens, for example, there were nine archons who were at first elected annually but who in the fifth century were chosen by lot. The principal archon at Athens was the *archon eponymus,* who was the chief civil and administrative official. The *polemarch,* or war archon, served as commander in chief of the army; later, he was president of the board of generals (*strategoi*). The *archon basileus,* or king archon, was in effect a high priest and, in homicide trials, the presiding judge. The functions of the remaining six archons were largely judicial. *See also* ATHENIAN CONSTITUTION.
                                                                T. B. J.

ARCHPRIEST, formerly the ranking priest of a large rural district. In its eventual development the office was confounded with that of rural dean (vicar forane), whose duty is in general to facilitate relations between clergy and bishop. The title is used inaccurately for the assistant priest at certain solemn masses.   N. J. T.

ARC LAMPS. *See* ELECTRIC LIGHTING.
ARCO. *See* MUSICAL TERMS.

ARCOT [ɑrkɒt'], a city in southeastern India, in the state of Madras, located at 12° 55' N. lat. and 79° 24' E. long., on the Palar River, about 35 mi. southwest of Madras. It is the administrative center of the North Arcot District. Arcot has a warm climate all year, and it receives between 30 and 50 in. of rainfall a year. The agricultural district surrounding the community is productive, and rice is the major crop. Arcot formerly was an industrial and commercial center of some importance, but its economic development has declined, and it has become a local market and administrative center. The old community is primarily noted for the activities occurring in and around it during the British conquest of India. It was the capital of the Carnatic Kingdom. In the middle of the eighteenth century there was a war between rival contenders for the throne, one being actively backed by the British and the other by the French. In 1751 the British forces were besieged in Trichonopoly, about 150 mi. south of Arcot; to raise this siege Robert Clive and about 500 men attacked and captured Arcot. This victory caused a large number of the attacking force at Trichonopoly to abandon the siege and march on Arcot, which they besieged in turn. Thus the British force at Trichonopoly was saved. In 1758 the French captured Arcot, but in 1760 the British recaptured it. In 1780 the frequently contested city was taken by Haidar Ali, the Mohammedan prince of India and ruler of Mysore. In 1801 the British finally gained full control of the whole Carnatic region, including Arcot. Pop. 1951, 21,124.   J. E. F.

ARCTIC EXPLORATION. *See* POLAR REGIONS.

ARCTIC OCEAN, an almost completely landlocked body of water (5,400,000 sq. mi.) surrounded by the continents of North America, Europe, and Asia. The lands encircling it are, in clockwise direction, the Soviet Union; Norway; the Republic of Iceland; Greenland, a colonial possession of Denmark; Canada; and Alaska. Lying entirely within the Arctic Circle, the Arctic Ocean contains a continental shelf of which the islands of Navaya Zemlya, Franz Josef Land, and Greenland are a part. Aside from these and other smaller island groups, the ocean remains a vast waste of pack ice, formed during the winter, spring, and fall months. Glacial ice, the source of icebergs, originates largely on Greenland. Icebergs, however, comprise only about one third of the ice content of the Arctic Ocean, and are found mainly in the Greenland Sea.

Contained within the boundaries of the Arctic Ocean are the Kara and Barents seas, off the coast of Siberia in the Soviet Union; the Greenland and Beaufort seas, off Greenland and Canada; and the East Siberian and Laptev seas, off the coast of the Soviet Union. Baffin Bay, Davis Strait, and Hudson Bay likewise are contained within the Arctic Ocean, falling within its southernmost boundary (59° 47′ N. lat.). Chief tributaries of the Arctic are the Nelson and Mackenzie rivers from Canada, and the Lena, Yenisey, and Ob from Siberia.

Although the polar basin itself has not been entirely charted because of the abundance of polar ice on its surface, soundings off the broad continental shelf indicate depths in several places over 100 fathoms, while in the Greenland Sea soundings of 2,000 fathoms have been made.

Little marine life is supported in those sections of the ocean covered with ice the year around because the comparatively little light seeping through is not enough to encourage plant growth. In the more open areas, however, seals, polar bears, whales, and numerous species of fish abound.　S. T. S.

ARCTIC REGION. *See* POLAR REGIONS.
ARCTIC WARFARE. *See* WARFARE.

ARCTURUS [ɑrktuˈrəs], also designated α Boötis, the brightest star (magnitude 0.24) in the constellation Boötes. It is visible from all but the most southern latitudes. In middle north latitudes it rises considerably north of east early in March at 8 P.M. local civil time (l.c.t.). It is orange in color and is at the lower tip of a large kite-shaped figure.

Arcturus received much publicity in 1933, when its rays were used to turn on the lights at the opening of Chicago's Century of Progress Exposition. Since this star was considered approximately 40 light-years distant (later measurements have reduced this to 33 light-years) the light received in 1933 was said to have left Arcturus during the Columbian Exposition, held at Chicago in 1893. *See also* BOÖTES.
　J. H. P.

ARC WELDING. *See* WELDING.

ARDEBIL [ɑrdəbiˈl], a city in northwestern Iran, in the province of Azerbaijan, 76 mi. northeast of Tabriz and 44 mi. west of the Caspian Sea. It is chiefly noted as the city from which came the famous Safavid Dynasty of the Persian kings. Shah Abbas the Great, a contemporary of Queen Elizabeth of England, was a tireless builder who enlarged and embellished the tomb, at Ardebil, of Sheikh Safi, the progenitor of the line. Also at Ardebil is the tomb of Shah Ismail I, first of the dynasty to rule all of Iran. There was a long colonnade, decorated in tile faïence and leading to a mosque, to a museum, and to towers above the tombs. All sections but the approach have been repaired, and they are being maintained by the Persian government. The cover of the tomb of Sheikh Safi, one of the finest examples of handweaving in the world, has been moved to the government museum in Tehran. The famous Ardebil carpet, displayed in the Victoria and Albert Museum in London, came from the mosque facing the tomb of Sheikh Safi and is considered one of the finest examples of the rug weaver's art. The Jameh, or Mosque of the Congregation, largely in ruins, dates from the fourteenth century, and parts of it are probably from the earlier Seljuk Period (eleventh, twelfth, and thirteenth centuries). The region of Ardebil was a center of population from prehistoric times, as is evidenced by burials on numerous elevations. The graves are surrounded by huge natural stones, and in them are found bronze weapons and other articles which show a very high degree of workmanship. Prehistoric pottery is often found by local diggers, but no scientific excavations had been made in the region by 1949.

Finds of hoards of coins and other remains show that Ardebil was also a prominent place in Parthian as well as in early Islamic times.

Formerly an important Asiatic trade center, Ardebil's commercial position has been declining steadily. It has become a center for local trade, and there is some trade passing through the city on its way to the Soviet Union. Pop. 1944, 63,406.　J. C. Wi.

ARDÈCHE [aˈrdɛˈsh], a department in south central France, with an area of 2,140 sq. mi., bounded on the north by the departments of Loire and Isère, on the east by the department of Drôme, on the south by the department of Gard, and on the west by the departments of Lozère and Haute-Loire. The Cévennes Mountains are in the western part of the department. The Vivarais mountain region also is largely in the department of Ardèche, where offshoots become the Boutières in the northeast, the Coiron in the east, and the Tanargue in the south. The mountains are mostly of volcanic origin; some still produce noxious vapors, and warm springs issue from them. The principal rivers are the Rhône, in the east, which is navigable, the Ardèche, the Erieux, and the Doux. The principal agricultural products are mulberry leaves for silkworm culture, and wine grapes. The wines of the Côtes du Rhône and of St. Péray are the best in the department. Grains, vegetables, and fruits are also grown. There are extensive chestnut plantations, and figs and olives are grown in the south. There are silk factories at Privas, Aubenas, and Annonay. Iron is mined in the region around Privas, the prefecture, and lime and cement are quarried. A strong fortress in the sixteenth century, Privas was razed by Louis XIII in 1629 because a Calvinistic revolt started there. Vals-les-Bains, in the valley of the Volane, is famous for its cold mineral springs. The region was part of the province of Languedoc before the department was created in 1790. Pop. 1954, 249,077.　S. Van V.

ARDENNES, a department situated in north central France, with an area of 2,020 sq. mi., bounded by Belgium on the north, and by the departments of Meuse on the east, Marne on the south, and Aisne on the west. The highest elevations are the forests of Ardennes in the northeast and Argonne in the southeast. The climate is cold and humid. The principal rivers are the Meuse, the Aisne, the Bart, and the Aire. The department is mostly forest plains and pasture land. In the fertile valleys of the central and southern sections grain is grown. There are important quarries of slate, marble, potter's clay and sand, and iron mines. The metallurgic industry is one of the most important in the department, with steel, copper, bronze, zinc, and aluminum foundries. The Meuse Valley is a center for manufacturing small metallic articles such as nails and kitchen utensils. The cloth trade founded in the sixteenth century is still flourishing. Sedan is the textile center. Mézières, the prefecture, is a medieval fortified town separated from the seventeenth-century commercial town of Charleville by the Meuse. Mézières withstood a siege by a Prussian army of 20,000 for 42 days in 1815. It was invested three times in the Franco-Prussian War in 1870 and surrendered after bombardment in 1871. Ardennes was the only French department completely occupied by the Germans during World War I. Both Mézières and Charleville were occupied by the Germans in August 1914. Sedan was the scene of a French military disaster in September 1870, ending the Franco-Prussian War. It was also the scene of the French victory of November 1918, and the first breach of the Maginot Line in World War II occurred here. Rethel, of Roman origin, was partly burned by the Germans in August 1914 and occupied by the Germans until November 1918. In 1790 the department was created from part of the old province of Champagne and small parts of the provinces of Picardy and French Flanders. Pop. 1954, 280,490.   S. Van V.

ARDENNES [aˈrdɛˈn], a region of worn-down mountains of the Hercynian system, now high plateaus, in southeastern Belgium, Luxembourg, and northern France. The mountains range from 1,500 to 2,000 ft. in elevation. The ancient Gauls gave the name of Ardennes to a large wooded area which began at the banks of the Seine and the Oise and extended up to the Rhine in the east. Caesar called it Arduenna Silva, and it then extended from the Rhine and the region of the Treviri up to the Escaut River and the territory of the Remi. Today, the region covers most of the area south of Namur and Liége, Belgium, extends over the Belgian province of Luxembourg, and crosses the border into France and Luxembourg. It forms a broad, low arch, rising abruptly northward above the Famenne depression, and, gently inclining to the southwest, gradually disappearing under the softer secondary formation of the Lower Luxembourg cuesta land. It consists of shales, sandstones, and quartzophyllites of the Cambrian and Devonian periods, with no calcareous rocks, which explains the infertility of the soil. At many points the crest of the arch has been lowered by stream erosion, and isolated domes appear. The decomposition of the Cambrian shales and phyllites produced a waterproof clay soil. Where the drainage is poor, sphagnum bogs grow; the accumulated peat was long exploited as a fuel. The Hautes-Fagnes, on the Baraque-Michel flat top, is the largest and the most characteristic of these boggy areas. It is also covered with heather and blueberry bushes; its solitude and wide horizons attract many nature students. The other flat summits are covered partly with bogs, heather lands, and forests. The forest of St. Hubert is one of the most beautiful in Europe. The slopes of the arch are cut by deep valleys and ravines densely wooded. The alluvial plains of the main rivers are used as pasture land or are cultivated. The Semois River region is well known for its fine tobacco. Spa and Malmédy on the slopes of the Hautes-Fagnes, Bouillon on the Semois, La Roche and Houffalize on the Ourthe, and Stavelot and Quarreux on the Ambleve are tourist centers. Slate is quarried, especially at Herbeumont, Martelange, and St. Vith. Wood is exploited intensively; dairy products, tobacco, and fresh-water fish are also commercially important. The region is inhabited largely by Walloons, a sturdy, dark-complexioned, French-speaking people. Because of the great number of wild animals, particularly deer and wild boar, hunting in the forests is popular.

The Ardennes was the scene of the exploits of the four sons of Aymon, or Haimon, of Dordogne, a vassal of Charlemagne, who had presented them with a magnificent horse, on whose back the four brothers were able to ride at one time. Their adventures were described by William Caxton in *The Foure Sonnes of Aymon* (c. 1489). The region was also the scene of many military engagements. It was the buttress against the eastern invasion in 1792, and it contributed to the defeat of the French at Sedan in 1870, when the army of Napoleon III was surrounded on the southern slopes. In 1914, the Germans under Gen. Max von Hausen marched through the Ardennes into France, while in November 1918 the plateau became the strategic point where the Allies cut the German lateral communications. In World War II the

WORLD WIDE PHOTOS

CASTLE OF BOURSCHEID IN THE ARDENNES, LUXEMBOURG

Allies were caught in the forest of the Ardennes on Dec. 16, 1944, at the start of the Battle of the Bulge. The German attack required a rearrangement of Allied supplies and a rapid redeployment of forces. The battle raged for a month in the frozen forests of the Ardennes, but the Germans failed to reach the English Channel, their objective.   L. B.

ARDERNE, JOHN (c.1307-c.1390), surgeon, was born in England, about 1307, and resided at Nottingham from 1349 until 1370, when he moved to London. Tradition claims that he was educated at Montpelier, France, and was a military surgeon with the English forces during the early years of the Hundred Years' War; also that he was present at the Battle of Crécy, in 1346. His work on the treatment of the fistula was first published in 1376. The following year, he published *De cura oculorum*. At this date, his work on clysters may have already been published. He ranked as a Master of Surgery, a class below that of medieval doctors of physic, but above the grade of barbers and apothecaries, and he is reported to have introduced certain new methods of operating.   A. W. Gr.

ARDMORE, a city and the county seat of Carter Co. It is 98 mi. south of Oklahoma City and is the oil metropolis for southern Oklahoma. The surrounding farms raise livestock, wheat, corn, and cotton. Founded in 1887, Ardmore was incorporated in 1898. Carter Seminary, a federal school for Indian girls, is in Ardmore. The Atchison, Topeka & Santa Fe and the St. Louis-San Francisco railroads supply transportation. The industries include oil refining, flour milling, and the manufacture of cotton-seed oil. Pop. 1950, 17,890.

AREAL LINGUISTICS [ɛ'əriəl lɪŋgwɪ'stɪks], a linguistic theory which has introduced a new method, based on geographical distribution, for the investigation of the chronological relationship between two equivalent linguistic forms, sounds, or words. The theory was developed by Giovanni Campus, Matteo Bartoli, and other Italian scholars on the basis of Jules Gilliéron's *Atlas linguistique de la France.* The nature and scope of the theory appear from an examination of its premises and conclusions.

First Areal Norm. In Romance languages, for example, there are many cases in which the distribution of the forms is more or less as follows:

Iberia	Gaul	Italy	Dacia
mus	sorex	sorex	sorex
comedo	manducare	manducare	manducare
metiri	mensurare	mensurare	mensurare
foetere	putere	putere	putere
final *-s*	no *-s*	no *-s*	no *-s*

The listing of the forms in the first column indicates that the modern representatives of these forms are found mostly, or exclusively, in Iberia (for example, Old Sp. *mur,* Sp. *comer, medir, heder, cantas*); the listing of the forms in the three remaining columns indicates that the modern representatives of these forms are found mostly, or exclusively, in Gaul, Italy, and Dacia, or, roughly, in modern France, Italy, and Romania. As a result, Iberia is said to constitute an isolated area. In these cases, and in the vast majority of instances in which Iberia diverges from the other Romance areas, it preserves, or preserved, the older of the two linguistic forms, evidence as to the relative age of the forms being drawn from the works of Latin authors, from inscriptions, from the testimony of grammarians, and from linguistic deductions of other kinds. On the basis of these and innumerable other cases, the first areal norm may be formulated as follows: when two linguistic phases—of forms, words, sounds, expressions, or idioms—are preserved each in a different area, one of the areas being isolated, the isolated area preserves the older phase. An area can be more or less isolated for social, political, religious, or commercial reasons, but the usual reasons are of a geographic character. Islands and mountainous areas are much more isolated than continental regions and plains; the country is more isolated than the city; villages are more isolated than towns, towns more isolated than big cities.

Second Areal Norm. The second areal norm may be illustrated by the following examples:

Iberia	Gaul	Italy	Dacia
fervere	bullire	bullire	fervere
formosus	bellus	bellus	formosus
magis fortis	plus fortis	plus fortis	magis fortis
tunc	ad illam horam	ad illam horam	tunc
angustus	strictus	strictus	angustus

The listing in the first and fourth columns indicates that in Iberia (mainly Spain and Portugal) and Dacia (i.e., Romania) the legitimate descendants or close relatives of these words predominate, or even dominate without competition; in Gaul and Italy, on the other hand, the types in the second and third columns are found much more frequently, or

even exclusively. Thus Spanish has *hervir, hermoso, más fuerte, entonces,* and *angosto;* but French has *bouillir, beau, plus fort, alors,* and *étroit,* and Italian has *bollire, bello, più forte, allora,* and *stretto.* As in the case of the first areal norm, it can be shown that the types predominant in the lateral areas of Iberia and Dacia are older than the types predominant in the central areas of Gaul and Italy. The second areal norm indicates, accordingly, that as between a lateral area and a central area, the lateral area preserves the older linguistic phase. The logical reason for this fact is readily understood. If the hypothesis that the central type is older than the lateral type were accepted, it would be necessary to assume that two distant regions such as Iberia and Dacia, entirely separated from each other, created the same innovation independently; this assumption is not impossible, but it is obviously most unlikely. The other hypothesis, that the central type is the innovation, is on the contrary both likely and natural; it leads to the plausible assumption that a central innovation, originating either in Italy or in Gaul, expanded over the whole central territory and in that area eliminated more or less completely the older type, which resisted in the more remote lateral areas.

General Considerations. Areal linguistics has formulated other areal norms in addition to the examples cited. Developed by Italian linguistic scholars, it has proved an invaluable tool for the investigation of past phases in the history of language. In the case of languages such as the Romance group, where the parent language is known to some extent through historical documents, it confirms, corrects, or completes the existing stock of knowledge; in other cases, such as proto-Indo-European, where a dead language must be reconstructed by exclusively linguistic means, it provides an excellent instrument of research. *See also* LINGUISTIC GEOGRAPHY.

G. B.

ARECUNA. *See* INDIAN TRIBES, SOUTH AMERICAN.

ARENDAL [ɑ'rɛndɑ'l], a port in southern Norway, capital of Aust-Agder Fylke (county), located 125 air miles southwest of Oslo, on the Skagerrak in the lee of the island of Tromoy at the mouth of the Nid River in a region of rolling wooded hills. First mentioned around 1500 as a place for export of timber, the town was incorporated in 1723 and was the most active shipping town in Scandinavia in the days of the sailing vessel. Today it is both a shipping and industrial center, exporting wood products, fish, and stone. The houses are mainly of wood, the town hall being one of the largest wooden structures in Norway. Pop. 1952, 11,712.

AREOPAGITICA. *See* MILTON, JOHN.

AREQUIPA [ɑ'reki'pɑ], a department and its capital city in southwestern Peru.

The City. The city of Arequipa is located on the Chili River at 16° 20′ S. lat. and 71° 25′ W. long., 746 mi. southeast of Lima. The city is beautifully situated 7,550 ft. above sea level, in a fertile oasis amid arid uplands, surrounded by great volcanic mountains. It is at the foot of snow-capped El Misti, also known as El Volcan de Arequipa, which is surrounded by the Chachani and Pichu-Pichu mountains. Arequipa, the third city in Peru in commercial importance and the second in population, has gained a wide reputation for its beauty not only because of its surroundings but also because of its buildings, most of which are constructed of the white or pink volcanic rock (*sillar*) of the vicinity and are

EL MISTI, "THE GENTLEMAN," RISES ABOVE AREQUIPA, GATEWAY TO THE LAND OF THE INCAS

primarily in Spanish Baroque architecture fused with the Indian style. The whiteness of the buildings has resulted in the city's sobriquet, "The White City." Arequipa enjoys a mild, dry climate with an average temperature of 74° F. during the day and 58° F. in the evening. The rainy season occurs between December and the end of March. The city was important in

A mosaic-tiled plaza fronts Arequipa's twin-towered Cathedral

the Inca Empire when it served as a stopping place for travelers en route from Cuzco to the Pacific Ocean. It was refounded in 1540 by Francisco Pizarro. He named it Villa Hermosa de la Asunción, but its original Indian name prevailed. The city has been subjected to numerous earthquakes in its history, the one in 1868 virtually destroying it. As a result, most of the buildings are one-storied. Because of the clear atmosphere, Harvard University established an observatory on El Misti in 1891, however this was moved in 1927 to South Africa. The religious and cultural life of southern Peru is centered in Arequipa, which is the seat of a bishop and the site of an official university. It also has a branch of the National Conservatory of Music and a normal school. The twin-towered cathedral, founded in 1612 and largely rebuilt in the nineteenth century, is considered a masterpiece of simple dignity and beauty, while the small Jesuit Church of La

Compañia is very decorated and elaborate in comparison. Many tourists are attracted to Arequipa because of the numerous Indian villages, interesting ruins, and hot springs in the city's environs.

Mollendo and Matarania, both approximately 110 mi. southwest, are Arequipa's ports through which much of its manufactures are sent. Matarania was opened in 1947, having been under construction for approximately ten years. This port, which in 1949 contained only dock facilities, was built to supplement the docking facilities at Mollendo because of the rough seas encountered in the latter's harbor and the frequent washing away of its jetty, which forced the ships to anchor off shore and use barges to bring in their passengers and cargo. Goods are shipped to and from Arequipa to Mollendo by rail, but until the completion of the railroad which was in the process of construction in 1949 at Matarania, goods from the new port were conveyed by motor. Arequipa ranks after the Lima-Callao district as a center for manufacturing. The local industries produce canned milk and other foods, textiles, leather, soap, flour, beer, and candles. The city is the market place for the sheep raisers and farmers in the district, and at all times the visitor will find the natives with their produce traversing the city's streets in their varicolored costumes, on foot or atop llamas. The city is connected by rail with Lima, Puno, Mollendo, and La Paz, Bolivia, and it has air service provided by the Faucett and the Pan American World air lines. In 1943 its airport, which had been privately owned, was taken over by the Peruvian government. Pop. (est. 1947), 91,590.

The Department. The department of Arequipa, with an area of 21,947 sq. mi., is bordered on the northwest by the department of Ica; on the north by Ayacucho, Apurimac, and Cuzco; on the east by Puno and Moquegua; and on the south and west by the Pacific Ocean. In some places the coast is rocky, with steep precipices, whereas in other sections it consists of arid plains. The interior is composed of high valleys dominated to the north by the Andes and their counterforts. The department is watered by the Lomas, Ocoña, Majes, and Vitor rivers. Mining and agriculture are the chief industries. Among the mineral products are gold, silver, copper, lead, iron, borax, gypsum, and opal, while the chief agricultural products are wheat, maize, potatoes, alfalfa, barley, sugar cane, and fruits. Cattle, sheep, and goats are grazed.

Manufacturing is carried on principally in the city of Arequipa. Coast ports are Mollendo, Chala, Atico, Acoño, Camaná, Quiloa, and Islay. The southeastern part of the department is traversed by the Southern Railway of Peru. The department is divided into the provinces of Arequipa, Cailloma, Islay, Camaná, La Unión, Condesuyos, and Castilla; it is subdivided into 77 districts. Pop. 1947, 302,161.

S. G. I.

ARES [ε'əriz], in Greek mythology, the son of Zeus and Hera and one of the Olympian deities. He personified wild conflict, took his delight in war and bloodshed, and was the god of war or warlike frenzy. He was hated by the other divinities for his savage character, especially by Athena, who encouraged Diomedes in the Trojan war to attack and wound the god. In battle he was often attended by his sister Eris, goddess of discord, and by Enyo, goddess of war, who is variously described as his sister, daughter, or wife. In Homer, Ares was the lover of Aphrodite, and Hephaestus, Aphrodite's husband, caught the guilty pair in a net. According to another version, Ares was the husband of Aphrodite, and their children included Eros, god of love, and Harmonia, who became the wife of Cadmus. At Athens, Ares had a temple at the foot of the Areopagus, where, according to legend, he had been tried by the gods for murder and acquitted.

The myths concerning Ares are surprisingly few; originally a Thracian deity, he never developed social or moral importance, as did such a god as Apollo. Ares was sometimes worsted in conflict, by Diomedes, for instance, whom he encountered in battle, and by Heracles, with whom he fought to avenge the death of Cycnus. The Romans identified Ares with Mars, their own god of war. *See also* APHRODITE; CADMUS; DIOMEDES; HEPHAESTUS; MARS OR MAVORS; TROJAN WAR.

G. E. D.

ARETHUSA [ærəthyu'zə; ærəthyu'sə], in Greek mythology, a nymph of Elis who was pursued by the river god Alpheus. Aided by Artemis, she fled to Sicily, where she took the form of a spring in Ortygia, an island near Syracuse. Alpheus, flowing under the sea, was there united with her.

G. E. D.

ARETHUSA, *A. bulbosa*, a small bulbous orchid growing in bogs of eastern North America. The stem grows to 10 in. and bears one narrow leaf and one, or rarely two, large violet-scented, fringed, rose-pink flowers. The arethusa is also called dragon's-mouth and Indian pink.

J. C. Wis.

ARETINO, PIETRO [ɑ'reti'no] (1492-1556), Italian man of letters, was born at Arezzo of a humble family in 1492. He studied painting as a youth at Perugia and went in 1517 to Rome, where he soon discovered how to use his pen to promote his own career and interests. Pope Leo X and Cardinal Giulio de' Medici took him under their protection, and upon Leo's death (1521) Aretino conducted a vigorous campaign in favor of the cardinal's election by writing *pasquinate* ("pasquinades"), satirical poems posted around the statue of "Pasquino" or circulated on printed flyers. The election of Adrian VI caused him to leave Rome for north Italy, but the election of Giulio as Pope Clement VII two years later allowed him to return to Rome with new prestige. Enmities which he incurred and indiscretions which he committed forced him soon to leave the papal court (1525), and he joined his friend Giovanni delle Bande Nere in the north. On the latter's death in the following year Aretino took up residence in Venice, where he remained,

except for brief trips, until his own death, October 21, 1556.

In Venice, Aretino won wealth, fame, and the friendship of kings and emperors, diplomats, writers, and artists (among them Titian, who was his devoted friend) through his vigorous, sensual personality and the power of pen and printing press. Historians have called him the first journalist because

PIETRO ARETINO

of the influence he acquired through his writings, but it should be remembered that this influence rested upon blackmail and that he sold his services to the highest bidder. He had two principal weapons: the "prognostications," the vogue of which had been established by almanac-like predictions by astrologers, which were circulated at the beginning of each year among the courts of Italy in manuscript or printed on a single sheet; and letters which were circulated in pamphlet form or in collected volumes. Armed with these weapons, Aretino solicited the favor and the gifts of the powerful in return for his support. Those who did not yield to this pressure, or whose gifts were surpassed by a more generous rival, soon found themselves the target of ridicule and vituperation or learned that Aretino had published dire predictions about the future of their party or cause.

The amorality of Aretino's career as a publicist is matched by many aspects of his personal life and by the indecency of some of his writings. On the other hand, some of his dialogues, his five comedies (*La Cortegiana*, 1521; *Il Marescalco*, 1527; *La Talanta* and *L'Ipocrito*, 1542; *Il Filosofo*, 1546), and his verse tragedy *Orazia* (1546) have greater merit and significance. The *Orazia*, based on an episode of Roman history, has, in fact, been considered the best Italian tragedy of its century. The comedies contain some lively scenes, effective satire, and realistic elements, but they are structurally weak.

G. R. S.

AREZZO [ɑre'tso], a province and also a capital city in an agricultural area in eastern Tuscany, north central Italy.

The City. Arezzo, 55 mi. southeast of Florence, is located near the point where the Chiana Canal empties into the upper Arno and has an elevation of 900 ft. above sea level. The climate shows a fairly wide seasonal range and the annual rainfall averages around 36 in.

Arezzo is chiefly an agricultural center for the surrounding area. There are railway repair shops, furniture factories, woolen mills, and other industries of local importance. Communications are provided by the main Florence-Rome railway and several branch lines. The city is on a gentle slope, straddling the Castro torrent. The older town, constructed by the Medici, is within the former circuit of the walls. At its highest point are the remains of the Medici fortress, from which several streets fan out to the west, south, and east. In general, the town is Renaissance and modern in appearance. The newer quarters are near the railway station to the south. Among the notable monuments of Arezzo are the Church of San Francesco (fourteenth century), with

SANTA MARIA DELLA PIEVE, IN AREZZO, ITALY

Piero della Francesca's frescoes of the *Story of the Cross;* Santa Maria della Pieve (twelfth and thirteenth centuries), with campanile and a remarkable façade and apse; the Cathedral, started in the late thirteenth century in the Gothic style; the Palazzo Pretorio, containing a museum and picture gallery; the Palazzo della Fraternità dei Laici (built between 1375 and 1460); and the loggia of Santa Marie delle Grazie, south of the city.

In Etruscan and Roman times, Arezzo was known as Arretium and was an important and prosperous city; few remains survive of these eras. On emerging from the Dark Ages in the eleventh century, Arezzo created a commune and by the thirteenth century had acquired a wide domain, under the active political guidance of her bishops. But Florence was determined to annex the domains of the Aretines, and, after numerous political vicissitudes in the fourteenth century, finally succeeded in buying it by the beginning of the fifteenth century. Subsequent revolts failed to shake Florentine control. Arezzo was the home of several illustrious men, including the satirist Pietro Aretino (1492-1556) and the painter and biographer Giorgio Vasari (1511-1574). Pop. 1947, 65,778 (city and environs).

The Province. The province of Arezzo, comprising 39 communes, has an area of 1,236 sq. mi. It contains the upper valley of the Arno, most of the Val di Chiana, and the uppermost basin of the Tiber. In the southeast it reaches the shore of Lake Trasimeno. The province is thus partly mountainous and partly hilly, with only small areas that could be called plains. Agriculture is the leading occupation, with cereals, wine, and olives as the chief products. Cattle, sheep, and silkworms are raised, and in the mountains are chestnut forests. Mining and manufacturing are of limited importance. Except for Arezzo, there are no other towns in the province with as many as 10,000 inhabitants, though several are historically or artistically interesting, such as Cortona, Sansepolcro, Bibbiena, and Camaldoli. Pop. (est. 1949), 325,000.   R. G. W.

ARGALI [ɑ'rgəli], *Ovis ammon,* a mountain sheep of central Asia. One of the dozen or more subspecies is the Marco Polo sheep, named in honor of the famous traveler. The great flaring horns of the argali curl more than a full circle and in rare instances measure as much as 75 in. along the curve. These are the finest hunting trophies of all wild sheep. Argali are more lightly built than the Rocky Mountain bighorns, but most races are taller. They stand 42 to 53 in. high at the shoulder. The buffy to dark-brown summer coat is replaced by a pale, even white covering in winter. Because of excessive hunting, most subspecies of argali are threatened with extinction.   V. H. C.

ARGELANDER, FRIEDRICH WILHELM AUGUST [ɑ'rgəlɑ'ndər] (1799-1875), German astronomer, was born at Memel, Mar. 22, 1799. In 1820 he was made assistant to Friedrich Wilhelm Bessel at the University of Königsberg, where he worked on stellar surveys. He had a deep urge to undertake scientific investigations, and became director of the observatory at Helsingfors, Finland, in 1832. His researches on the proper motions of stars confirmed Sir William Herschel's idea that the solar system is moving toward Hercules. In 1837 he became professor of astronomy and director of the observatory at the University of Bonn, where he remained until his death, Feb. 17, 1875. Argelander's greatest work was the *Bonner Durchmusterung,* a catalogue of all northern stars to the 9th magnitude (over 324,000), together with a large atlas showing these stars.   H. S. R.

ARGENTEUIL [ɑ'rzhɑ̃'tœ'y], a city in northern France, in the department of Seine-et-Oise, 5 mi. northwest of Paris, on the Seine River. It is an old town built around a nunnery founded in the seventh century. One of the more famous abbesses was Theodada, daughter of Charlemagne, and another famous inmate was Héloïse, who went into retreat in this nunnery after the death of Abelard. What is believed to be a tunic of Jesus Christ is on display in the church. In the city there are a few metallurgical industries, and in the environs are asparagus farms and vineyards. During World War II the city suffered some war damage. Pop. 1954, 63,376.   S. Van V.

ARGENTINA or **LA ARGENTINA** [ɑ'rhenti'nɑ, ɑ'rjənti'nə] (c. 1888-1936). Spanish dancer, was born Antonia Mercé about 1888 in Buenos Aires, Argentina, where her parents, professional dancers from Spain, were appearing. The family returned to Madrid when Antonia was two years old; she began studying dancing under her father's tutelage at the age of four and appeared as a soloist at Córdoba at five. She combined ordinary schooling with lessons at the Conservatory of Madrid, because her mother wished her to be a singer. She preferred dancing, however, and at eleven she was *première danseuse* at the Royal Theatre, Madrid. At seventeen she left the opera to devote herself to Spanish dancing instead of opera ballet, and she made such a success that she was the only dancer to be voted into the Ateneo (Atheneum) at Madrid. She then toured Europe until the outbreak of World War I in 1914. During the war years she toured the Western Hemisphere, being especially successful in the Latin American countries. After the war she returned to Paris and gave many recitals, first in small halls and finally at the Opéra. Between 1928 and 1936 she made six tours of the United States. She was generally credited with reviving Spanish dancing as a recognized art form. One of her most popular dances was performed

LA ARGENTINA

NICKOLAS MURAY

to the music of the Fire Dance from Falla's *El Amor Brujo* ("Love, the Magician"). She died suddenly July 18, 1936, at Villa Miraflores, near Bayonne, France.   F. G. P.

ARGENTINA [arjənti'nə; a'rhenti'na], a republic occupying most of the tapering southern half of South America east of the Andes Mountains. It is bounded on the north and northeast by Bolivia, Paraguay, and Brazil; on the east by Uruguay and the Atlantic Ocean; on the west by Chile; and on the south by the converging lines of the Atlantic Ocean and Chile. Argentina is about one third the size of the United States, the second in size of the Latin American republics, and the eighth largest country in the world. Politically, the republic is divided into 1 federal district, 14 provinces, and 10 territories (listed with areas and populations in the following table), comprising a total area of 1,074,209 sq. mi.

Political Divisions	Area sq. mi. (1947)	Population (1947)
Federal District	74	3,000,371
Provinces		
Buenos Aires	118,752	4,408,373
Catamarca	38,540	145,216
Córdoba	65,195	1,455,222
Corrientes	34,500	570,907
Entre Ríos	29,427	776,380
Jujuy	20,548	166,783
La Ríoja	35,691	109,386
Mendoza	58,239	590,548
Salta	59,759	290,063
San Juan	33,257	260,714
San Luis	29,632	167,620
Santa Fe	51,354	1,700,026
Santiago del Estero	52,222	574,383
Tucumán	8,697	604,526
Territories		
Chaco	38,468	408,897
Chubut	65,354	53,986
Comodoro Rivadavia*	37,741	51,444
Formosa	28,778	112,056
La Pampa	55,382	166,929
Misiones	11,506	244,123
Neuquén	36,324	84,738
Río Negro	78,383	132,726
Santa Cruz	77,843	24,491
Tierra del Fuego	7,996	4,921
Total	1,074,209	16,104,929

*Formed from part of the territory of Chubut in 1946.

PHYSICAL GEOGRAPHY

Argentina stretches some 2,300 mi. from the hot scrub forests of the Chaco on the margin of the tropics in the north, to cold, windswept Tierra del Fuego in the south. Within this vast territory Argentine geographers recognize four major physical regions: the Andes Mountains, which, except in the far south, cover most of the western third of the country; the North, including the Argentine portion of the Gran Chaco and the land between the Paraná and Uruguay rivers; the Pampas, the great central plains; and Patagonia.

The Andes. In the northwest, the Andes Mountains include the southern part of the altiplano, a high region of dry intermontane basins; and the *puna,* a high undissected east-sloping plateau, both of which extend northward into Bolivia. Several broad valleys or *quebradas,* breaching the eastern front of the *puna,* provide access to the high country beyond. North of Tucumán is a zone of parallel front ranges, separated by north-south depressions and lying between the *puna* and the Chaco. The piedmont from Tucumán southward to Mendoza is a dry region composed of north-south ranges and broad basins with salt flats or lakes called salinas along their bottoms. Rainfall in this northwest highland and piedmont area is low and decreases southward from 29.4 in. annually at Jujuy to 3.3 in. at San Juan. With the exception of an "island" of heavier rainfall at Tucumán, settlement and agriculture are completely dependent on irrigation water from Andean rivers. Annual temperatures average between 62° and 68° F. The range between the

COURTESY OF MOORE MCCORMACK LINES

Argentina's lovely Lake Nahuel Huapí

El Tronador Glacier, "The Thunderer," near Bariloche in the Argentine lake region, derives its name from the roaring avalanches that hurtle down its sides.

average of the hottest month, January, and of the coldest month, July, is the greatest in South America: close to 30° F. at several stations.

The North. The region between the Andean piedmont and the Río Paraguay-Paraná is part of the Gran Chaco, which extends northward from about 30° S. lat. into eastern Bolivia, Paraguay, and western Brazil. The Chaco is a great lowland plain with few prominent surface features, composed mostly of alluvium from the erosion of the Andes. Across the Argentine Chaco flow the Pilcomayo, the Bermejo, Salado del Norte, and Dulce, sluggish rivers with braided courses which flood the land on either side during the summer rainy season. Some of the highest temperatures in South America have been recorded in the Chaco. The January average at Santiago del Estero is 83.1° F. Seasonal variation is nearly 30° F. Rainfall is heaviest in the east but decreases toward the west. At Santiago del Estero the annual rainfall of about 20 in., concentrated in the hot season, is evaporated rapidly, and agriculture is possible only in the floodplain of the Río Dulce. The vegetation of the Chaco is scrub forest interspersed with patches of savanna. Among the scrub trees is the quebracho, valuable as a source of tannin. The red quebracho of the Santiago area, containing less tannin than the true quebracho of the eastern Chaco, is useful for its hardwood.

The land between the Paraná and Uruguay rivers in the northeast, called by some writers "Argentine Mesopotamia," is composed of gently rolling grassy plains and swampy forest-filled valleys. Summers are hot and rainy, and winters are mild. The shifting, shallow-channeled Paraná floods annually, and settlements in Mesopotamia have been largely limited to patches of high ground close to the main channel of the river. In the far northeast the territory of Misiones projects like an arm onto the Paraná plateau, separating Paraguay and Brazil. Rivers dropping over the hardened lava edges of the plateau have produced spectacular waterfalls.

The Pampas. The Pampas are the great expanse of level plains lying south of the Chaco and east of the Andean piedmont. They cover Buenos Aires Province, parts of the provinces of Santa Fe, Córdoba, and San Luis, and La Pampa Territory. A distinction is commonly made between the Humid Pampa of the wetter east and the Dry Pampa of the west. These plains are composed of a deep accumulation, reaching 985 ft. at Buenos Aires, of loose erosional material resting on top of a buried hilly surface of granite and other crystalline rock. The Córdoba Hills, the Sierra del Tandil, and the Sierra de la Ventana are the only conspicuous protrusions of this buried surface. Otherwise, important relief features are absent. Along the Paraná-La Plata, from Rosario to the mouth of the Plata, a steep bluff, the *barranca*, rises abruptly about 100 ft. above river level. For some 130 mi. westward there is an imperceptible rise to 500 ft. elevation. The slope is more apparent as the Córdoba Hills are approached. At the base of the hills the plain is about 1,300 ft. above sea level. To the southwest there is a gradual decrease of elevation from the crest of the *barranca* to the zone of swamps along the southern Río Salado. The Córdoba Hills mark an approximate boundary between the Humid and the Dry pampas, for to the east, ground water is abundant, while to the west and south it is far below the surface. In the northeastern part of the Humid Pampa annual rainfall is a little below 40 in.; at Buenos Aires it is 37.9 in. and is evenly distributed throughout the

PENGUINS DOT THE PATAGONIAN SHORE. MILLIONS OF THE BIRDS LIVE HERE AND IN MAGELLAN STRAIT.

year. Toward the southwest and west the amount of rainfall decreases; at Bahía Blanca it is 21.5 in.; and at Córdoba it is 28.2 in., with more and more of a concentration in the summer months, from December to February. In general, winters are mild and summers are hot, with a growing season varying from 300 days along the Paraná-La Plata shore to about 140 days south of Bahía Blanca. When first seen by the Spaniards, the eastern Pampa was covered with tall prairie grass gradually merging in the west with the *monte,* an area of impoverished scrub trees and short grass. The Humid Pampa has become an area of plowed cropland and thick-sodded European pasture grasses.

Patagonia. South of the Río Colorado lie the cool, dry, windswept plateaus of Patagonia. A number of deep canyons, crossing the plateaus from west to east, provide shelter from the constant winds and a supply of ground water for the few ranches of Patagonia. A more intensive grazing area is found in the Pre-Andean Depression, a discontinuous series of lowland basins between the plateaus and the eastern front of the Andes, where rainfall is higher than on the desert plateaus. The territory of Neuquén, in the northwest corner of Patagonia, is a part of the lake region of Argen-

tina, which attracts tourists from all parts of the world. Lake Nahuel Huapí is visited by motor car or launch, which takes the traveler through some of the most gorgeous scenery of the snow-capped Andes into the Chilean lakes of Todos Santos and Llanquihue, all of which belong to the same natural system. The Argentine government has made this a national park and built fine hotels, chalets, and small inns for tourists, who find many attractions, such as skiing, fishing, mountain climbing, golf, and horseback riding.

P. E. J.

Flora. Argentina is characterized by much more floristic and vegetational diversity than might be expected from the relatively uniform topography. Climatic diversity, resulting from the great range in latitude from the tropics in the extreme north to subantarctic Tierra del Fuego in the south, as well as from a position in the rain shadow of the Andes, seems responsible for much of this variation. Some is also correlated with diversity of substratum.

As would be anticipated, the peripheral regions of the country are, floristically, extensions of the adjacent provinces of surrounding countries. In the northeast, the Misiones forests are a continuation of the south Brazilian deciduous

AVERAGE TEMPERATURE AND RAINFALL FOR SELECTED ARGENTINE STATIONS

Station		Jan.	Feb.	March	April	May	June	July	Aug.	Sept.	Oct.	Nov.	Dec.	Year
Santiago del Estero	T.	83.1	80.6	76.6	70.3	62.8	55.9	56.7	60.6	67.5	72.3	77.5	80.6	70.4
Alt. 623.4	Rf.	3.3	3.0	3.0	1.3	0.6	0.3	0.2	0.2	0.5	1.4	2.5	4.1	20.4
Córdoba	T.	73.9	72.3	68.5	62.1	55.8	49.6	50.5	53.4	58.6	63.3	68.4	72.1	62.4
Alt. 1,387.8	Rf.	3.7	5.0	3.2	2.1	1.1	0.2	0.6	0.6	0.9	2.2	4.0	4.6	28.2
Mendoza	T	74.5	71.6	67.5	59.4	52.0	45.5	46.4	50.0	56.1	61.9	68.0	71.6	60.4
Alt. 2,477	Rf.	0.9	1.3	1.1	0.5	0.4	0.4	0.2	0.3	0.5	0.7	0.7	0.7	7.7
Buenos Aires	T.	73.6	72.5	68.7	61.3	55.0	49.6	48.9	51.1	55.0	59.9	65.8	70.9	61.0
Alt. 82.0	Rf.	3.1	2.8	3.9	4.8	2.8	2.0	2.1	2.2	2.9	3.3	4.0	4.0	37.9
Bahía Blanca	T.	74.5	71.6	67.5	60.1	53.1	47.1	46.4	48.9	53.6	59.2	66.4	71.8	60.0
Alt. 82.0	Rf.	2.2	2.4	2.2	3.5	1.1	0.6	0.9	0.7	0.7	3.4	1.9	2.0	21.6
Santa Cruz	T.	58.6	57.6	54.7	47.7	40.8	35.2	35.2	38.3	43.5	48.7	52.9	56.3	47.5
Alt. 39.4	Rf.	0.6	0.3	0.4	0.6	0.4	0.5	0.4	0.6	0.3	0.3	0.4	0.7	5.5

Alt. = Altitude in feet.   T. = Temperature in degrees Fahrenheit.   Rf. = Rainfall in inches.

and Araucaria forests. The savannas, or parklands, of the Paraná Basin are continuous with similar formations in southern Brazil, Paraguay, Bolivia, and northern Uruguay. The strip of tropical and subtropical forest between the savannas of the Chaco and the Andes in the Tucumán region is a part of the great Bolivian jungle. The *puna,* or Andean desert of the higher mountains from Bolivia to Aconcagua, is equivalent to the *puna* of Peru, Bolivia, and Chile. It is related also to the vast Patagonian Steppe, which occupies most of southern Argentina. Along the relatively low crests of the southern Andes is a strip of the Magellanic or subantarctic *Nothofagus* forest, in the northern portion of which are stands of the monkeypuzzle (*Araucaria araucana*) and enormous and ancient trees of the Sequoia-like *Fitzroya cupressoides.* The famous prairie-like pampas of the Buenos Aires region are continued across the Río de La Plata in Uruguay. The only really distinctive floristic regions of the country are the western desert scrub and the Patagonian Steppe. The former has interesting affinities with the southwestern desert scrub of North America, including common dominance by the creosote bush (*Larrea divaricata*).

Argentina's vegetation types generally reflect climatic regions. The country is characterized by grasslands, scrub, savanna, and desert vegetations of dry climates. Only small areas are mesophytic. It is the vast fertile grassland that is the basis of much of the country's agricultural wealth.

Tropical forests of a mesophytic character occur in the northeast and northwest, in the provinces of Misiones and Tucumán, with large trees and dense canopies of lianas. These are scarcely wet enough to be called rain forests, but are truly tropical jungles. A small portion of the Misiones area is dominated by the picturesque Paraná pine (*Araucaria angustifolia*), an important timber tree. Otherwise the forests are very mixed and do not contain large stands of single species.

Between and to the south of these two forests lies an extensive area of diversified savanna, divided by various students into an eastern Parque Mesopotámica and a western Parque Chaqueña, the latter in the famous Gran Chaco region contiguous to that of Paraguay. Palm savanna covers extensive areas in the Chaco and certain parts of the eastern section; the several quebrachos (*Schinopsis* and *Aspidosperma*) also dominate many localities. Grasslands alternate with gallery forests along rivers, and local edaphic variations are reflected in more or less xerophytic types of vegetation. Many arborescent legumes, especially species of *Prosopis,* are found in both sections. A southward extension of this region, lying west and southwest of the pampas and practically reaching the Atlantic at the south, has been termed the Bosque Pampeano, but differs only in detail from the Chaco.

The pampas are tall-grass prairies on deep fertile loess soil, dominated by grasses of numerous genera, with a liberal admixture of broad-leafed herbs. Arborescent vegetation is practically absent. Owing to the agricultural value of this land, the original vegetation is nearly a thing of the past. It is here that Argentina's huge wheat crops are grown.

The northern half of the Argentine Andes is high, and is dominated above the timber line by the harsh xerophytic bunch grass of the *puna,* locally alternating with cushion plants and dwarf shrubs. In the southern half of the country this sterile vegetation descends to low altitudes and becomes even more sparse, with dwarf shrubs and broad-leafed herbs more common; there it is termed the Patagonian Steppe.

Between the Andes and the savannas to the east, in the rain shadow of the mountains, is the Monte Occidental, or western desert scrub. *Larrea divaricata* and other xeromorphic shrubs and cacti are the dominant growth forms, and the spacing is wide. Generally the area is a true scrub desert.

Along the crest of the southern Andes the temperate Chilean rain forest, known as the Magellanic or Fuegian beech forest, enters Argentina. The evergreen beeches (*Nothofagus*) and various gymnosperms constitute a luxuriant forest, which, however, does not descend far on the eastern slopes. This small area forms an important part of Argentina's timber resources.   F. R. F.

THE PEOPLE

Origins of Inhabitants. The inhabitants of Argentina, as of all other Spanish American republics, developed from a combination of aborigines, Spanish colonists, and African slaves. Unlike the highly civilized Indians on the west coast of South America and in Mexico, the earlier inhabitants of Argentina and other parts of the east coast were wandering tribes, who developed few permanent centers of life and no literature. Early Spanish settlers entered the country from three directions: from the sea at Buenos Aires, from the west over the Andes Mountains from Chile, and from Peru through the region that later became Bolivia.

The governing and intellectual classes maintained their Spanish traditions and family life and developed a highly cultured civilization and great landed estates and mines which made them rich. They maintained their families in patriarchal dignity. Unions with Indian women produced the mestizo, who comprises a large segment of the population. From this mixture of Spanish and Indian blood came the famous gauchos, who for two centuries were to Argentina what the cowboys were to the western frontier of the United States. The same warfare between the Indian and the white man took place in the southern republic as in the northern. Likewise, the warfare was ended in the same way, by the organized drive of a trained army of whites against bands of individualistic Indian braves. This happened in Argentina around the middle of the nineteenth century.

The complete transformation of Argentina from a mestizo country into a white one took place in the nineteenth century. This was accomplished under the leadership of Domingo Faustino Sarmiento, Juan Bautista Alberdi, and Bartolomé Mitre, who believed, as Sarmiento pointed out in his books *Facundo* and *Conflicto y armonías de las razas en América,* that the gaucho, the mestizo with predominant Indian blood, must be ruled by the Euro-Argentine, the latter reinforced by the introduction of large additional streams of migrants from Europe. José Ingenieros, Argentine sociologist, in his *Sociología argentina* states that in 1852 the Argentine federation had 800,000 people, made up of 553,000 mestizos, 100,000 Indians, 15,000 Negroes, 110,000 mulattoes, and 22,000 whites. By 1914 it had 7,885,237 people, with the racial ratios so far changed that 4,000,000 were whites, 3,000,000 mestizos, 300,000 mulattoes, and 40,000 Indians. The 1932 estimate of Argentina's population was 11,846,655, with only 1,000,000 non-whites. In 1949, it was estimated that the total population of Argentina was over 16,000,000 and that of this total about 89 per cent were of European origin, 9 per cent of mixed Indian and European origin, and 2 per cent of Indian origin.

It was during the two administrations of President Julio Argentino Roca that immigration was most active. During his first year of office in 1880, 27,000 foreigners came to Argentina; by 1889 a high point was reached when 219,000 were received. General Roca, before he became president,

ARGENTINA
Index to Physical Features and Points of Interest

TOPOGRAPHIC FEATURES

Islands, Peninsulas, Capes, Mountains, Plateaus, Valleys, etc.

HYDROGRAPHIC FEATURES

Lakes, Rivers, Creeks, Bays, Straits, Seas, etc.

SPECIAL POINTS OF INTEREST

Parks, Monuments, Ruins, Dams, Sites, Buildings, etc.

ARGENTINA

For Northern Argentina, see map of Bolivia and Paraguay.

BRAZIL

URUGUAY

Montevideo

La Plata

Avellaneda

Buenos Aires

ENTRE RIOS

Paraná

Rosario

Santa Fe

Rafaela

CORDOBA

Córdoba

Río Cuarto

Villa María

Mercedes

SAN JUAN

San Juan

Mendoza

MENDOZA

San Rafael

SAN LUIS

San Luis

LA PAMPA

Santa Rosa

LA RIOJA

BUENOS AIRES

Mar del Plata

Tandil

Bahía Blanca

Tres Arroyos

Necochea

Olavarría

Azul

NEUQUÉN

Neuquén

RIO NEGRO

Viedma

Carmen de Patagones

General Roca

Golfo San Matías

PENÍNSULA VALDÉS

Golfo Nuevo

Pto. Madryn

Trelew

Rawson

CHUBUT

Esquel

CHILE

COQUIMBO

Ovalle

Valparaíso

Viña del Mar

Santiago

O'HIGGINS

COLCHAGUA

CURICÓ

TALCA

LINARES

MAULE

ÑUBLE

Chillán

CONCEPCIÓN

Talcahuano

Concepción

Lota

BIO-BIO

Los Angeles

ARAUCO

MALLECO

Temuco

CAUTÍN

VALDIVIA

Valdivia

OSORNO

Osorno

LLANQUIHUE

Puerto Montt

CHILOE

ISLA CHILOE

Castro

Ancud

PACIFIC OCEAN

Pacific Ocean

Longitude West of Greenwich

BRAZIL

PARAGUAY

Asunción

FORMOSA

Posadas

Corrientes

Resistencia

CHACO

BOLIVIA

Sucre

PERU

JUJUY

Jujuy

SALTA

Salta

TUCUMÁN

Tucumán

Santiago del Estero

CATAMARCA

Catamarca

Tropic of Capricorn

ANTOFAGASTA

Antofagasta

ATACAMA

Copiapó

Iquique

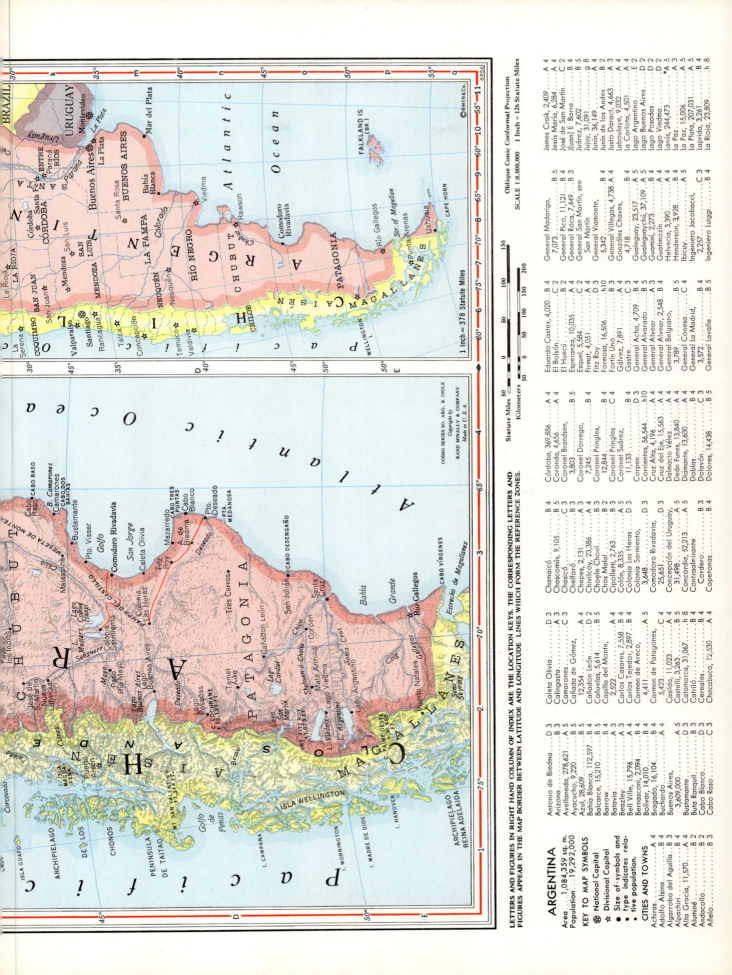

ARGENTINA

Area....1,084,359 sq. m.
Population...19,292,000

KEY TO MAP SYMBOLS

⊛ National Capital
☆ Divisional Capital
● Size of symbols and type indicates relative population.

CITIES AND TOWNS

LETTERS AND FIGURES IN RIGHT HAND COLUMN OF INDEX ARE THE LOCATION KEYS. THE CORRESPONDING LETTERS AND FIGURES APPEAR IN THE MAP BORDER BETWEEN LATITUDE AND LONGITUDE LINES WHICH FORM THE REFERENCE ZONES.

Oblique Conic Conformal Projection
SCALE 1:8,000,000   1 Inch = 126 Statute Miles

1 Inch = 378 Statute Miles

COSMO SERIES SO. ARG. & CHILE
Copyright by
RAND M?NALLY & COMPANY
Made in U.S.A.

©RM&CO.

Achiras....A 4
Adolfo Alsina...B 4
Algarrobo del Aguila...B 3
Alpachiri...B 4
Alta Gracia, 11,570...B 4
Aluminé...B 2
Andacollo...B 2
Añelo...B 3

Antonio de Biedma...D 3
Arizona...A 3
Avellaneda, 278,621...A 5
Ayacucho, 9,220...B 5
Azul, 28,609...B 4
Bahía Blanca, 112,597...B 4
Balcarce, 15,210...B 5
Barrow...B 4
Batavia...A 3
Beazley...A 3
Bell Ville, 15,796...A 4
Bernasconi, 2,094...B 4
Bolívar, 14,010...B 4
Brogado, 16,104...B 4
Buchardo...A 4
Buenos Aires, 3,609,000...A 5
Bustamante...D 3
Buta Ranquil...B 3
Cabo Blanco...D 3
Cabo Raso...D 3

Caleta Olivia...D 3
Calingasta...A 3
Camarones...C 3
Cañada de Gómez, 12,354...A 4
Cañadon León...D 2
Cañuelas, 15,614...B 5
Capilla del Monte...B 4
Carlos Casares, 7,558...B 4
Carlos Tejedor, 2,897...B 4
Carmen de Areco, 4,411...B 4
Carmen de Patagones, 5,423...C 4
Casilda, 11,023...A 4
Castelli, 3,263...B 5
Catamarca, 31,067...A 3
Catiló...B 4
Cereales...B 4
Chacabuco, 12,530...A 4

Chamaicó...B 4
Chascomús, 9,105...B 5
Chasicó...C 3
Chelforó...A 3
Chepes, 2,131...A 4
Chivilcoy, 23,386...A 4
Choele Choel...B 3
Chos Malal...B 2
Cipolletti, 2,763...A 5
Colón, 8,335...A 4
Colonia Las Heras...D 3
Colonia Sarmiento, 3,648...D 3
Comodoro Rivadavia, 25,651...D 3
Concepción del Uruguay, 31,498...A 5
Concordia, 52,213...A 5
Contraalmirante Cordero...B 3
Copetonas...B 4

Córdoba, 369,886...A 4
Coronda, 4,656...A 4
Coronel Brandsen, 3,803...B 4
Coronel Dorrego, 7,245...C 4
Coronel Pringles, 12,844...B 4
Coronel Suárez, 11,133...B 4
Corpen...B 4
Corrientes, 56,544...h10
Cruz Alta, 4,196...A 4
Cruz del Eje, 15,563...A 4
Dalmacio Vélez...A 4
Deán Funes, 13,840...A 4
Diamante, 13,600...A 5
Doblas...B 4
Dolavón...C 3
Dolores, 14,438...B 5

Eduardo Castex, 4,020...B 4
El Bolsón...B 2
El Huecú...A 2
Esperanza, 10,035...A 4
Esquel, 5,584...C 2
Firmat, 4,051...A 4
Fitz Roy...D 3
Formosa, 16,506...h10
Fortín Uno...B 4
Gádvez, 7,891...A 4
Gastre...B 3
General Acha, 4,709...B 4
General Alvarado...B 5
General Alvear, 2,548...B 4
General Belgrano, 3,789...B 4
General Conesa...C 4
General La Madrid...B 4
General Lavalle...B 5

General Madariaga, 7,073...B 4
General Pico, 11,121...B 4
General Roca, 7,449...B 3
General San Martín, see San Martín
General Viamonte, 5,342...A 4
General Villegas, 4,738...A 4
Gonzáles Chaves, 4,718...B 4
Gualeguay, 23,517...A 5
Gualeguaychú, 37,109...A 5
Guamini, 2,273...B 4
Guatimozín...A 4
Helvecia, 3,390...A 4
Henderson, 3,928...B 4
Ibicuy...B 5
Ingeniero Jacobacci, 2,257...C 3
Ingeniero Luiggi...B 4

James Craik, 2,409...A 4
Jesús María, 6,284...A 4
José de San Martín...C 2
Juan E Barra...B 5
Juárez, 7,602...B 5
Jujuy, 31,091...g 8
Junín, 36,149...A 4
Junín de los Andes...B 3
Justo Daract, 4,663...A 4
Laboulaye, 9,032...A 4
La Carlota, 4,501...A 4
Lago Argentino...E 2
Lago Buenos Aires...D 2
Lago Posadas...D 2
Lago Viedma...*A 5
Lanús, 244,473...A 5
La Paz, 15,006...A 5
La Plata, 207,031...A 5
Laprida, 3,261...B 4
La Rioja, 23,809...h 8

ARGENTINA Continued

Las Coloradas ... B 2
Las Flores, 9,287 ... B 5
Las Lajas ... A 3
Las Pipinas ... B 2
Las Plumas ... C 3
Las Rosas, 6,153 ... A 4
Las Varillas, 5,950 ... A 4
La Union ... B 3
Lavalle ... B 4
Leleque ... C 2
Limay Mahuida ... B 4
Lincoln, 12,695 ... A 4
Loberia, 7,916 ... B 5
Lobos, 8,372 ... B 4
Lomas de Zamora, 125,943 ... A 5
Los Cerrillos ... A 3
Luján, 115,113 ... A 4
Lujån, 3,542 ... B 4
Macachín ... A 4
Mackenna ... B 5
Magdalena, 4,114 ... C 3
Maipú, 5,469 ... B 5
Malanzán ... A 3
Malargüe ... B 3
Malaspina ... C 3
Maquinchao ... C 3
Marcos Juárez, 9,556 ... A 4
Mar del Plata, 114,729 ... B 5
María Grande, 3,400 ... A 4
Mata Armilla ... D 2
Maza ... B 4
Mazarredo ... D 3
Médanos, 2,229 ... B 4
Mendoza, 97,496 ... A 3
Mercedes (Buenos Aires prov.), 16,932 ... A 5
Mercedes (San Luis prov.), 25,912 ... A 3
Meridiano ... A 3
Milagro ... A 3
Monte Caseros, 11,409 ... A 5
Monte Coman ... A 3
Morón, see Seis de Septiembre
Morteros, 5,593 ... A 4
Nahuel Huapi ... C 2
Nahuel Niyeu ... C 3
Nahuelquir ... B 2
Navarro, 2,547 ... A 4
Navia ... B 4
Necochea, 17,808 ... B 5
Neuquén, 7,498 ... B 3
Nogoyá, 12,051 ... A 4
Norquinco ... C 2
Nueva Lubecka ... C 2
Nueve de Julio, 13,678 ... B 4
Olascoaga, 2,358 ... B 4
Olavarría, 24,204 ... B 4
Ordoquí ... A 4
Paraná, 84,153 ... A 4
Paso del Limay ... C 2
Paso de los Indios ... C 2
Pedro Luro ... B 4
Pehuajó, 13,537 ... B 4
Pergamino, 32,382 ... A 4

Picún-Leufú ... B 3
Pigüé, 5,869 ... B 5
Pinas ... A 3
Porteña ... A 4
Posadas, 37,588 ... h10
Puán, 3,191 ... B 4
Puerto Arroyo Verde ... C 3
Puerto Belgrano ... B 4
Puerto Deseado ... D 3
Puerto Madryn, 3,441 ... C 3
Puerto Pirámides ... C 3
Puerto Visser ... D 3
Punta Alta, 19,852 ... B 4
Punta de Vacas ... A 3
Quemú Quemú, 3,564 ... B 4
Quequén, 4,760 ... B 5
Quilmes, 115,113 ... *A 5
Quines, 3,038 ... A 3
Rafaela, 23,665 ... A 4
Rauch, 5,274 ... B 5
Rawson ... C 3
Realicó ... A 4
Recalde ... B 4
Remecó ... B 4
Resistencia, 52,385 ... h10
Retamito ... C 3
Río Colorado, 3,304 ... B 4
Río Cuarto, 48,706 ... A 4
Río Gallegos, 5,880 ... E 3
Río Primero ... A 4
Río Tercero, 10,683 ... A 4
Rivadavia, 5,643 ... D 3
Rivadavia, 4,925 ... B 4
Rivera, 2,569 ... B 4
Rojas, 6,608 ... A 4
Rosario, 467,937 ... A 4
Rosario Tala, 10,584 ... A 4
Rufino, 10,987 ... A 4
Saavedra, 2,130 ... B 4
Saladillo, 7,586 ... B 5
Salliqueló, 3,938 ... B 4
Salsacate ... A 3
Salta, 67,403 ... G 8
Sampacho, 3,554 ... A 3
San Agustín ... A 4
San Antonio Oeste, 3,847 ... C 3
San Carlos ... C 3
San Carlos, 6,562 ... C 2
San Cristóbal, 9,071 ... A 4
San Enrique ... B 4
San Fernando, 44,666 ... *A 5
San Francisco, 24,354 ... A 4
San Isidro, 90,086 ... *A 5
San Jaime ... A 4
San Javier, 2,961 ... A 5
San José de Feliciano, 7,643 ... A 4
San Juan, 82,410 ... A 3
San Julián, 3,050 ... D 3
San Justo ... A 4
San Justo, 88,853 ... *A 5
San Lorenzo, 11,109 ... A 4
San Luis, 25,147 ... A 3
San Martín, 8,748 ... A 3

San Martín (General San Martín), 269,514 ... *A 5
San Martín de los Andes, 2,366 ... C 2
San Nicolás [de los Arroyos], 25,926 ... A 4
San Pedro, 12,798 ... A 4
San Rafael, 28,847 ... B 3
San Salvador, 3,532 ... E 3
Santa Cruz ... E 3
Santa Fe, 168,791 ... A 4
Santa Isabel ... B 3
Santa Rosa (Mendoza prov.) ... A 3
Santa Rosa (San Luis prov.), 3,564 ... A 3
Santa Rosa, 2,999 ... A 4
Santa Rosa [de Toay], 14,623 ... B 4
Santiago del Estero, 60,039 ... C 3
Sastre, 2,308 ... A 4
Sauce, 3,017 ... A 5
Seis de Septiembre (Morón), 110,344 ... *A 5
Serrezuela ... A 3
Sierra Colorada ... C 3
Sunchales, 5,048 ... A 4
Tamel Aike ... D 2
Tandil, 32,309 ... B 5
Tapalqué, 3,018 ... B 4
Tecka ... C 2
Telén ... B 3
Telsen ... C 3
Toay, 2,457 ... B 4
Tornquist, 2,782 ... B 4
Trelew, 10,987 ... C 3
Trenque Lauquén, 10,887 ... B 4
Tres Algarrobos ... A 4
Tres Arroyos, 29,996 ... B 5
Tres Cerros ... D 3
Tres Lomas, 3,425 ... B 4
Tucumán, 194,166 ... h 8
Tunuyán ... A 3
Tupungato ... A 3
Udaquiola ... B 5
Ushuaia, 1,950 ... p 8
Valcheta ... C 3
Vedia, 3,676 ... A 4
Veinticinco de Mayo ... A 4
Veinticinco de Mayo, 9,063 ... B 3
Venado Tuerto, 15,947 ... A 4
Viamonte ... A 4
Vicente López, 149,958 ... *A 5
Victoria, 17,771 ... A 4
Victorica ... B 3
Victorino de la Plaza ... B 4
Viedma, 4,683 ... C 4
Villa Constitución, 9,183 ... A 4
Villa Crespo, 4,289 ... A 4
Villa del Rosario, 4,461 ... A 3

Villa Dolores, 13,835 ... A 3
Villa Federal, 9,158 ... A 5
Villaguay, 17,607 ... A 4
Villa Huidobro ... B 4
Villa Iris, 2,422 ... B 4
Villalonga ... B 4
Villa María, 30,362 ... A 4
Villa Valeria ... B 3
Vivoratá ... B 5
Winifreda ... B 4
Zapala, 3,387 ... B 2
Zárate, 35,197 ... A 5

PROVINCES

BUENOS AIRES ... B 4
 Area ... 116,322 sq. m.
 Pop. ... 5,069,000

CAPITAL FEDERAL [Federal District] ... A 5
 Area ... 77 sq. m.
 Pop. ... 3,611,000

CATAMARCA ... h 8
 Area ... 45,829 sq. m.
 Pop. ... 172,000

CHACO ... C 3
 Area ... 38,041 sq. m.
 Pop. ... 607,000

CHUBUT ... C 3
 Area ... 87,237 sq. m.
 Pop. ... 123,000

CÓRDOBA ... A 4
 Area ... 64,894 sq. m.
 Pop. ... 1,808,000

CORRIENTES ... A 5
 Area ... 33,544 sq. m.
 Pop. ... 624,000

ENTRE RÍOS ... A 5
 Area ... 28,487 sq. m.
 Pop. ... 926,000

FORMOSA ... g10
 Area ... 28,778 sq. m.
 Pop. ... 177,000

JUJUY ... g 8
 Area ... 22,962 sq. m.
 Pop. ... 229,000

LA PAMPA ... B 3
 Area ... 55,103 sq. m.
 Pop. ... 188,000

LA RIOJA ... A 3
 Area ... 35,691 sq. m.
 Pop. ... 123,000

MENDOZA ... A 3
 Area ... 58,239 sq. m.
 Pop. ... 752,000

MISIONES ... h11
 Area ... 11,514 sq. m.
 Pop. ... 331,000

NEUQUÉN ... B 3
 Area ... 36,429 sq. m.
 Pop. ... 112,000

PATAGONIA ... D 3
 Area ... 102,010 sq. m.
 Pop. ... 63,000

RÍO NEGRO ... C 3
 Area ... 78,220 sq. m.
 Pop. ... 180,000

SALTA ... g 9
 Area ... 59,757 sq. m.
 Pop. ... 377,000

SAN JUAN ... A 3
 Area ... 34,910 sq. m.
 Pop. ... 334,000

SAN LUIS ... A 3
 Area ... 28,520 sq. m.
 Pop. ... 183,000

SANTA FE ... A 4
 Area ... 51,127 sq. m.
 Pop. ... 1,977,000

SANTIAGO DEL ESTERO ... h 9
 Area ... 56,243 sq. m.
 Pop. ... 576,000

TUCUMÁN ... h 8
 Area ... 10,425 sq. m.
 Pop. ... 750,000

CHILE

Area ..... 286,322 sq. m.
Population 15,932,995

CITIES AND TOWNS

Achao, 707 ... C 2
Alicahue ... A 2
Ancud, 6,410 ... C 2
Angol, 14,292 ... B 2
Antofagasta, 62,272 ... g 7
Arauco, 2,707 ... B 2
Barraza ... B 2
Bulnes, 5,147 ... B 2
Calbuco, 2,049 ... C 2
Cañete, 3,137 ... B 2
Cartagena, 2,384 ... A 2
Castro, 6,283 ... C 2
Cauquenes, 14,849 ... B 2
Chanco, 1,931 ... B 2
Cherquenco, 1,677 ... B 2
Chillán, 52,576 ... B 2
Colbún ... B 2
Colliguilli, 4,057 ... A 2
Coltauco ... A 2

Combarbalá, 2,112 ... A 2
Concepción, 119,887 ... B 2
Constitución, 8,285 ... B 2
Copiapó, 19,535 ... h 7
Coronel, 17,372 ... B 2
Corral, 5,525 ... C 2
Corte Alto ... B 2
Cunco, 2,728 ... B 2
Cuncumen ... A 2
Curacautín, 9,201 ... B 2
Curanilahue, 3,995 ... B 2
Curepto, 1,739 ... B 2
Curicó, 26,773 ... A 2
Dalcahue ... C 2
El Volcán ... A 2
Galvarino, 1,209 ... B 2
Huentelauquén ... A 2
Illapel, 8,266 ... A 2
Iquique, 39,576 ... g 7
La Calera, 13,047 ... A 2
Lagos, 2,106 ... B 2
La Ligua, 3,178 ... A 2
Las Cabras, 1,032 ... A 2
La Serena, 37,618 ... A 2
La Unión, 9,830 ... C 2
Lautaro, 9,255 ... B 2
Lebu, 3,827 ... B 2
Lepihué ... B 2
Licantén ... A 2
Linares, 19,624 ... B 2
Liucura, 1,094 ... B 2
Llico ... A 2
Loncoche, 5,061 ... B 2
Los Andes, 19,162 ... A 2
Los Ángeles, 25,071 ... B 2
Los Sauces, 2,158 ... B 2
Los Vilos, 1,305 ... A 2
Lota, 40,475 ... B 2
Mariposas ... B 2
Melipilla, 11,525 ... A 2
Molina, 6,123 ... B 2
Monte Patria ... B 2
Mulchén, 7,324 ... B 2
Nacimiento, 2,815 ... B 2
Navidad ... A 2
Nueva Imperial, 6,450 ... B 2
Osorno, 40,120 ... C 2
Ovalle, 17,573 ... A 2
Papudo ... A 2
Parral, 10,717 ... B 2
Pemuco, 1,703 ... B 2
Petorca, 1,098 ... A 2
Petrulnué ... B 2
Pitrilquín ... B 2
Pitrufquén, 4,982 ... B 2
Polcura ... B 2
Puerto Aisén, 3,767 ... D 2
Puerto Montt, 28,944 ... C 2
Puerto Natales, 8,140 ... E 2
Puerto Varas, 5,797 ... C 2
Punta Arenas, 34,440 ... B 2
Puyehue ... B 2
Quillota, 22,640 ... A 2
Quilpué, 16,332 ... B 2
Quintero, 5,563 ... B 2
Rancagua, 39,972 ... A 2

Ranco ... A 2
Recinto ... B 2
Rengo, 9,115 ... A 2
Riñihue ... B 2
Río Bueno, 6,259 ... C 2
Rupanco ... C 2
Saavedra ... B 2
Salamanca, 2,819 ... A 2
San Antonio, 18,394 ... A 2
San Bernardo, 37,221 ... A 2
San Carlos, 11,094 ... B 2
San Felipe, 15,476 ... A 2
San Fernando, 17,598 ... A 2
San Javier, 7,006 ... B 2
San Rosendo, 3,315 ... B 2
Santa Bárbara, 2,292 ... B 2
Santa Cruz, 2,132 ... A 2
Santiago, 664,575 ... A 2
 (*1,348,283)
Sewell, 9,009 ... A 2
Talagante, 7,966 ... A 2
Talca, 55,059 ... B 2
Talcahuano, 54,782 ... B 2
Temuco, 51,497 ... B 2
Toltén, 1,014 ... C 2
Tomé, 18,228 ... B 2
Traiguén, 8,806 ... B 2
Valdivia, 45,128 ... C 2
Valparaíso, 218,829 ... B 2
 (*310,000)
Vichuquén ... A 2
Victoria, 10,671 ... B 2
Villarrica, 7,036 ... B 2
Viña del Mar, 85,281 ... B 2
Yungay, 3,671 ... A 2

PROVINCES

ACONCAGUA ... B 2
 Area ... 3,940 sq. m.
 Pop. ... 128,378

AISÉN ... D 2
 Area ... 34,357 sq. m.
 Pop. ... 26,262

ANTOFAGASTA ... g 8
 Area ... 47,515 sq. m.
 Pop. ... 184,824

ARAUCO ... B 2
 Area ... 2,222 sq. m.
 Pop. ... 72,289

ATACAMA ... h 7
 Area ... 30,843 sq. m.
 Pop. ... 80,113

BIO-BÍO ... B 2
 Area ... 4,343 sq. m.
 Pop. ... 138,292

CAUTÍN ... B 2
 Area ... 6,707 sq. m.
 Pop. ... 365,072

CHILOÉ ... C 2
 Area ... 9,052 sq. m.
 Pop. ... 100,687

COLCHAGUA ... A 2
 Area ... 3,423 sq. m.
 Pop. ... 139,531

CONCEPCIÓN ... B 2
 Area ... 2,201 sq. m.
 Pop. ... 411,566

COQUIMBO ... A 2
 Area ... 15,401 sq. m.
 Pop. ... 262,169

CURICÓ ... A 2
 Area ... 2,215 sq. m.
 Pop. ... 89,432

LINARES ... B 2
 Area ... 3,791 sq. m.
 Pop. ... 146,257

LLANQUIHUE ... C 2
 Area ... 7,107 sq. m.
 Pop. ... 139,986

MAGALLANES ... E 2
 Area ... 52,285 sq. m.
 Pop. ... 55,119

MALLECO ... B 2
 Area ... 5,512 sq. m.
 Pop. ... 159,419

MAULE ... A 2
 Area ... 2,172 sq. m.
 Pop. ... 72,181

ÑUBLE ... B 2
 Area ... 5,487 sq. m.
 Pop. ... 251,342

O'HIGGINS ... A 2
 Area ... 2,746 sq. m.
 Pop. ... 224,593

OSORNO ... C 2
 Area ... 3,867 sq. m.
 Pop. ... 123,059

SANTIAGO ... A 2
 Area ... 6,559 sq. m.
 Pop. ... 1,754,954

TALCA ... B 2
 Area ... 3,722 sq. m.
 Pop. ... 173,693

TARAPACÁ ... g 8
 Area ... 21,346 sq. m.
 Pop. ... 102,789

VALDIVIA ... C 2
 Area ... 7,723 sq. m.
 Pop. ... 232,647

VALPARAÍSO ... C 2
 Area ... 1,860 sq. m.
 Pop. ... 498,254

* Not shown on map. Index key denotes approximate location.　　* Population including suburbs.　　† Includes 87 persons in Antarctica.

had led a campaign to eliminate the Indians, which resulted in their being reduced to a small number living in the north. The seizure of Indian property marked the beginning of a period of great Argentine prosperity. The government came into possession of many square miles of farm and pasture lands, much of which it divided among the soldiers who had engaged in the campaign and the politicians who had advertised it. The value of the land quickly multiplied. Capital poured into the country and new developments in steam navigation brought Europe nearer. Exports of grain increased, and Argentina gained the reputation of being one of the richest countries in the world. In spite of financial crises and political upheavals, the reports of continuous prosperity brought European immigrants in steady streams until the outbreak of World War I. Since then, immigration from central Europe has not been sufficient to affect the evolution of the country, although the entrance of European refugees has had some influence. Dr. Alejandro Bunge in his *Seventy Years of Argentine Immigration* points out that of the 5,740,000 immigrants entering the country during that period, Italians and Spaniards constituted 79.6 per cent. The Italians alone constituted as much as 45 per cent, but they were also the group more inclined to return to the homeland. In fact, the passing of Italians and Spaniards back and forth across the Atlantic led to the use of the term *golondrina* or "swallow" immigrant.

In 1940 approximately one-fifth of the population was European born, and in 1947 a Five Year Plan sought to encourage 250,000 additional agricultural immigrants, principally from the Latin countries of Europe. Argentina was forming a robust blend of the many different nationalities, led by the three Latin groups—Italians, Spaniards, and French—followed by English, Germans, Swiss, Austrians, Poles, Scandinavians, and Slavs, in the order named. As José Ingenieros put it: "A new Argentine race is being formed by a combination of social and psychological variations which the Argentines impose on Europeans who come to live in our land. There is an Argentine tradition. It is not indigenous, neither is it colonial: it was born with our nationality; it was enriched by our thinkers; it plays on new generations."

Language. The language of the country is Spanish, although Italian, French, English, German, and Portuguese are auxiliary tongues.

Religion. Relations between church and state in Argentina are different from those of any other American republic and are somewhat difficult for a foreigner to understand. The Constitution states that "The Federal government supports the Roman Catholic Apostolic Church." Argentine authorities insist, however, that this statement does not mean that Roman Catholicism is the official religion, but rather that it continues the colonial tradition, in which the nation exercised almost complete control of ecclesiastical matters, with power to limit the church's dominance over the state. For the same reason the Constitution provides that the president, who must be a Roman Catholic, names the bishops of the cathedrals from lists submitted by the Senate, approves or rejects papal decrees, and submits to the Pope the names from which he must choose certain chief members of the hierarchy. There are one cardinal, seven archbishops, and fifteen suffragan bishops. Full religious freedom is guaranteed and practiced. The Socialist Party is anticlerical, and a large number of intellectuals and labor union members profess no religion. Argentine Protestants number around 200,000 and have churches in all the principal towns. Schools and colleges begun by American mission boards are gradually being taken

The Kavanaugh Building, Argentina's tallest, on San Martín Plaza, Buenos Aires

over by Argentine communities. Spiritualism and Oriental cults have considerable influence in the cities. In 1946 President Perón departed from the long-established lay character of public instruction and decreed the teaching of the Roman Catholic religion in all schools.

Distribution of Inhabitants. Approximately two thirds of Argentina's population (17,111,000 in 1950) live in the Humid Pampa. Over half of this population is in 25 cities and towns of over 20,000 inhabitants, chief among which is Buenos Aires, the largest city of the Southern Hemisphere. The density of rural population is surprisingly low, exceeding 100 per sq. mi. only in a few spots near Buenos Aires. Densities up to 60 per sq. mi. are found in a zone extending 200 mi. west of the capital, but most of the Humid Pampa has a rural density of only 10 to 25 people per square mile. The only other areas of considerable population density are the oases along the eastern piedmont of the Andes, principally Tucumán, Catamarca, La Rioja, San Juan, Mendoza, and San Rafael. Perhaps 10 per cent of Argentina's population is concentrated in these oases. Another 5 or 6 per cent of the population is found in Entre Ríos Province, the southernmost part of Mesopotamia. The Chaco is scantily inhabited. Most of the permanent settlements are found along the southern and eastern margins, focusing on Santiago del Estero and Resistencia. There are small pioneer

A cattle roundup takes place on the estancia El Pelado fifty miles outside Buenos Aires

CHARLES PERRY WEIMER

colonies along the railroads extending northwestward into the forest from Resistencia and Formosa. Patagonia, which occupies over 28 per cent of Argentine territory, has only about 2 per cent of the population, mostly located in the irrigated oases of the Colorado, Negro, and Chubut rivers.

Buenos Aires, with a population in 1947 of 3,000,000, is the third largest city of the Americas and has succeeded Paris as the largest Latin city in the world. Other leading cities of Argentina are: Rosario, with a population of 464,688; Córdoba, 351,644; Avellaneda, 279,572; La Plata, 217,738; Santa Fe, 168,011; Tucumán, 152,508; Mendoza, 105,328; and Mar del Plata, 104,513.

Social Divisions of Inhabitants. In few countries is the population so clearly divided as it is in Argentina between the residents of Buenos Aires, who are known as *porteños,* or "people of the port," and those living in the rural sections and smaller towns. Until the development of the railroads in the latter part of the nineteenth century there was actual war between the two. With the development of industry in many of the smaller cities, this division began slowly passing away. Other social divisions remain, however.

The *estancieros* are the owners of the great estates, who raise the wheat, meat, linseed, sheep, corn, and other products for which Argentina is known the world over. Up to the ascendancy of Colonel Juan D. Perón to the presidency in 1946, they dominated Argentina.

The gauchos are the cowboys who herd and care for the cattle on the great ranches of the *estancieros.* The gauchos once led a migratory, picturesque life and were the authors and source of inspiration of the songs, dramas and games that have passed into the folklore of the nation; but the gaucho has been reduced in the ignominious status of a peon on the great estates. To take his place with the gaucho has come the sharecropper, often a foreign immigrant who moves from one great farm to another seeking better conditions. A new epoch in the social life of Argentina began when the government fostered regularly organized foreign colonies in the mid-nineteenth century. The Swiss formed the first of the colonies in the rich north; then in rapid succession came the Germans, the French, the Russians, and later the Welsh, who went to Patagonia. From these colonists, who have become more Argentine than the Argentines themselves, arose a growing middle class comprising the carpenters, merchants, small farmers, and schoolteachers.

The city dwellers live in a different world, with the exception of the rich *estancieros* who have palatial homes in Buenos Aires as well as on their ranches and often on the French Riviera. To the urban population has been added a considerable number of rural laborers who heard of the higher wages offered by the rapidly growing factories and came crowding into the city tenements. The industrialists,

not only in Buenos Aires but also in cities like Rosario, Córdoba, and Mendoza, had by 1947 come to occupy a dominant place in open conflict with the *estancieros,* who wished to continue the dominance of agriculture and the exchange of raw products for luxury goods from foreign lands. Where the latter were aristocrats—pro-Catholic, anti-United States, anti-Socialist, and anti-Protestant—the former held international or national opinions, depending on which favored business.

The middle class has become larger in Argentina than in any other Latin American republic and is estimated at thirty-five per cent of the total population. This class includes the clerks in stores and government offices, small merchants, doctors, lawyers, tailors, and editors.

Labor in rural sections is largely unorganized, with little class consciousness. Industrial labor was organized at the beginning of the twentieth century under the influence of the young Socialist Party led by such reformers as Juan B. Justo and Alfredo Palacios, the first Socialist elected to congress in any American republic. Organization increased rapidly under the leadership of the first president of the Radical Party, Hipólito Irigoyen. The Argentine General Federation of Labor (C.G.T.) reported 465,000 members in 1935. The Federation joined the Confederation of Latin American Workers (C.T.A.L.) when this movement was ini-

AN ARGENTINE GAUCHO

COURTESY OF
MOORE MC CORMACK LINES

tiated in Mexico under the leadership of Lombardo Toledano in 1938. It was a strong supporter of the Allies, until disbanded by the Fascist regimes of Ramón Castillo and Pedro P. Ramírez. When Perón came into power, he reorganized the C.G.T. and made it the official backer of his regime. The situation was described thus: "Labor is the government, and the government is labor." Leaders of the unions soon became restive under government control and moved toward an independent existence, when President Perón limited the freedom of action and settled strikes by force.

In no other country except France do the intellectuals exercise such large influence. As university professors, writers, lawyers, doctors, engineers, scientists, poets, and editors, they have largely dominated the thinking of the nation. Their leadership was challenged by Perón, who, on the charge that the intellectuals were the enemies of the New Order, dismissed 1,100 professors from the six national universities during the first year of his administration. He also took harsh measures against another seat of their power, the conservative newspapers *La Prensa* and *La Nación*.

ECONOMIC RESOURCES AND ACTIVITIES

Producing Regions. The Humid Pampa, together with Entre Ríos Province, produces the larger part of Argentina's principal export commodities. In the period immediately preceding World War II over 50,000,000 acres were sown to grain crops, principally in this area. Wheat acreage was approximately 17,500,000, and corn over 15,000,000. The remaining acreage was in flaxseed, oats, rye, barley, and sunflower seed. In 1945-1946 the total grain acreage was only two thirds of the prewar average, or about 31,000,000 acres. The Humid Pampa may be divided into four major districts. The first one is the pastoral district, located in the southeast between Mar del Plata and Tandil. Here 80 per cent or more of the land is devoted to livestock ranching without agriculture. High-grade mutton and wool sheep are raised, and it is the chief breeding area for beef cattle. There is no part of the Humid Pampa, however, in which less than 40 per cent of the land is used for pasture. The principal commercial wheat district extends in a broad crescent along the western side of the Humid Pampa from Santa Fe to Bahía Blanca. Wheat production is combined with livestock ranching and the cultivation of alfalfa as a feed crop. Corn predominates in a central zone some 145 mi. east and west and 155 mi. north and south, centering on the river port of Rosario. This district produces an amount of corn second only to that of the North American corn belt. The district around Buenos Aires is one of truck and dairy farming and also fruit production. Dairying is concentrated on the rich pastures southeast of Buenos Aires, and orchards along the floodplain of the Paraná and on the islands near the junction of the Paraná and the Uruguay. Entre Ríos Province produces wheat and corn and has become the leading flaxseed-producing area and one of the major sources of wool export. Corrientes Province in the northern part of Mesopotamia is purely pastoral. The far northern territory of Misiones is chiefly important for its production of *yerba maté,* a popular herb beverage of southeastern South America. In addition to its production of quebracho extract and quebracho logs, the Chaco is producing an increasing quantity of cotton. The principal areas are the pioneer settlements along the two railroads of the northern Chaco and around Santiago del Estero. The principal commercial products of the oasis settlements of the Andean piedmont are sugar cane and wines. The Tucumán district produces 70 per cent of Argentina's sugar. South of Tucumán are the vineyard oases

of La Rioja, Catamarca, San Juan, Mendoza, and San Rafael. Unlike Tucumán, where sugar cane occupies more than 60 per cent of the cropland, only 30 per cent of the irrigated land of the vineyard oases is planted for vines. A larger acreage, about 40 per cent, is devoted to alfalfa for the fattening of range cattle, the traditional activity of the piedmont. Most of Patagonia is devoted to sheep raising on ranches measured in thousands of square miles. Tiny ports along the coast are used for shipment of the wool. The principal crop of the river oases is alfalfa, used for fattening the small concentrations of cattle of the Río Negro and Río Chubut. In the Río Negro oases a part of the irrigated land is also devoted to vineyards and pear orchards.

Economic Background. The people of Argentina are more mindful of economic factors than are the people of any other South American republic. This awareness began in colonial days, when its people were far removed from the aristocratic cultural centers, such as Lima and Mexico City, which derived their riches from gold and silver mines and their art, science, and education directly from Spain and Rome. The citizens of Buenos Aires developed a large, if illegal, trade with England, France, and Holland. Argentina's fight for independence from Spain was inspired more by commercial than by political motives. Thus, very early, foreign trade became the dominant influence in Argentine life, as it has continued to be.

The cattle industry became important when the first Spanish settlers, following an attack by the Indians, were forced to let their few horses and cattle run wild on the prairies. In a few decades these wild animals had grown into hundreds of thousands. At first they were hunted by the gauchos largely for their hides. When barbed wire was manufactured, large cattle ranches were established, owned by the *estancieros* and served by the gauchos. The British, who

CHARLES PERRY WEIMER

Some of the world's finest beef is processed at this modern meat-packing plant in La Plata

made the first loan to Argentina in 1824, began building railroads into the cattle country in the 1860's. Land values skyrocketed. The British erected packing houses in Buenos Aires and in 1877 shipped the first chilled meat to London.

About the same time it was discovered that the pampas, like the great prairies of Kansas, were suited for growing wheat, and Argentina was on its way to becoming one

A HERD OF WOOLLY SHEEP, A COMMON SIGHT IN THE ARGENTINE

of the richest countries in the world, its economy clearly established. Wheat and meat, far more valuable than the gold and silver in which other Latin American countries had put their trust, were sold at great profit to England, France, Germany, and other industrial countries, which paid for them by sending farm machinery, clothes, chemicals, and luxury goods to the Argentines. This was the classic colonial economy of the nation, which was defended by the powerful agricultural barons until the Revolution of June 4, 1943. This economic system was aided especially by the British, who controlled the shipping, developed the ports, and ran the banks that furnished the necessary credits to the great *estancieros* and the government. Later, rival capital came from Germany, the United States, and other countries. Other investors, especially those from the United States, gradually replaced the British, who finally sold their railway holdings to the Argentine government in February 1947.

In spite of the objections of the agriculturists, Argentina began to industrialize during World War I. Ships were unavailable to carry grain and meat to Europe, and the countries at war needed all their manufactured goods. There was nothing for Argentina to do but burn corn in locomotives, let wheat rot, and start manufacturing necessities at home. This marked the time also when United States capital began to displace European money, which was no longer available.

Livestock Industry. Cattle raising and the shipping of meat early became the dominant industry and the recognized business of gentlemen in Argentina. The annual stock show of Buenos Aires is still the most important social event in that city. Farming for a long time was considered the business of foreigners and poor people. Before the *frigorificos,* as the Argentines call packing houses, were developed, the sale of hides was the most profitable part of the business. With the development of the freezing process, an enormous business began with Europe. This placed a premium on improved stock, and the native animals were rapidly improved by the addition of the best meat-producing stock, such as Shorthorns and Herefords imported from Great Britain. Cattle raising in Argentina received a further stimulus through the spread of alfalfa cultivation. In 1945 the livestock in the country included 34,010,300 cattle, 56,181,800 sheep, 7,473,300 horses, and 8,009,700 swine.

The first meat regularly exported from Argentina was jerked beef. The first refrigerator ship docked at Buenos Aires in 1876 and initiated the export of frozen meat,

chiefly mutton. By 1889, a million carcasses of frozen mutton were being exported yearly. During this period, live cattle were being shipped to Europe to be slaughtered there. Later, the freezing plants prepared and shipped frozen beef as well as mutton; but not until 1901 did the export of chilled beef in quantities begin. The building of huge modern meat-packing plants by American and English companies has greatly changed the meat trade in Argentina. Frozen beef is still shipped in large quantities, but chilled beef has taken the lead. The exports of beef in 1928 totaled 515,846 metric tons; and of mutton, 18,000 metric tons. In the years preceding the outbreak of World War II in 1939, slaughtering of livestock in Argentine *frigorificos* was approximately as follows: cattle, 4,000,000 to 4,400,000; sheep, 5,200,000 to 5,800,000; hogs, 1,000,000 to 1,400,000. Total slaughtering, including *frigorificos,* was estimated at 7,069,000 cattle and 7,838,500 sheep in 1938. In 1946, exports included 226,811 metric tons of chilled and frozen beef, 72,511 tons of tinned corned beef, 125,020 tons of mutton, and 21,900 tons of pork. Argentina is also one of the world's chief sources of cattle hides and calfskins, producing about 6,000,000 of the former and 1,000,000 of the latter annually. In 1946, 119,908 tons of hides were exported. These and other animal by-products—horsehair, hog bristles, and so forth—helped to raise the value of livestock exports to nearly 44 per cent of the total.

The Argentine livestock industry has been almost entirely dependent upon the British market, which ordinarily absorbed about 90 per cent of all Argentine meat exports. The industry was thus seriously threatened when Great Britain in 1931 and 1932 abandoned its historic free trade policy for a system of combined imperial preference and tariff protection for British livestock raising and agriculture. Quotas were placed upon imports of meat from Argentina for the first time in 1933. In 1936 the British government levied duties on Argentine meats to grant further protection to empire and home producers. To meet this threat to the industry, the Argentine government established the National Meat Board and other government agencies to improve the grade of Argentine meat products while keeping production costs as low as possible. At the same time, the government exerted every effort to retain its predominant position in the British market and to find additional export markets in Germany, the United States, and other industrial countries. The refusal of the United States to permit the entry of

Argentine fresh meat into the American market proved a source of irritation and controversy throughout the decades from 1920 to 1940.

Dairy Industry. By 1948 dairying in the eastern districts of Buenos Aires had advanced notably. After meeting local requirements, the dairying districts export butter in such quantities as to make it one of the major sources of that

CHARLES PERRY WEIMER

In Mendoza the milkman brings the cow right to the door. Although pasteurized milk is available throughout most of Argentina, often fresh milk is preferred.

product in international trade and follow up this advantage by supplying the outside world with considerable amounts of cheese.

Farming. Farming developed as a dominant industry when, in the middle of the nineteenth century, wheat and corn began to be grown on the pampas. Here are located the great farms which often include tens of thousands of acres and are cultivated by modern machinery with mass production techniques. Other sections have developed as producers of special crops. Tucumán in the north is noted for sugar production. Cotton has likewise grown to be an important crop in the northern tropical areas, as have oranges, which formerly came entirely from Paraguay.

Mendoza is the center of the important grape and wine industry. Farther south in the Río Negro valley fruit growing has developed. Patagonia, long famous for its sheep, has discovered that with irrigation, it can produce wheat, corn, and other staple crops. President Perón made an important place in his Five Year Plan of 1946 for great irrigation projects and called a number of American engineers to aid in the development of dams which are expected to transform sparsely developed sections into flourishing communities. The president pointed out that in spite of the large production of crops such as wheat, corn, alfalfa, and linseed, there remain immense farming possibilities—that of the total area of Argentina, only a third was being used, and of this amount only 25 per cent was in any sense adequately cultivated. The new plan calls for diversified crops, intensified cultivation, and greater attention to forestation.

Minerals. The lack of important coal resources in Argentina is a serious handicap. The only important petroleum fields are near the coast in Patagonia, 900 mi. south of Buenos Aires, and in the northern province of Salta. Production at the Comodoro Rivadavia field dates only from the early years of the twentieth century, when men drilling for water for their flocks in the coastal desert struck a heavy oil of excellent quality. With the assumption of control by the government, the aspect of the barren coast changed. In a waste

of sand, oil derricks soon arose, and Comodoro Rivadavia has grown to a community of more than 50,000 people. Though the annual production of 3,473,120 cubic meters in 1947 does not fill Argentine requirements, the field is an important source of fuels for the country. Tungsten deposits yielding 8 to 10 per cent of the world's supply are worked in the north central part of the country. Unimportant quantities of gold, silver, copper, lead, and zinc have been mined in the mountains of the West, but the difficulties of transportation and the long distance from the principal markets do not make these operations profitable. Small quantities of salt, borax, and antimony are mined, and in 1947, uranium ore was discovered in La Heras in the province of Mendoza.

Industrialization. The struggle between the *estancieros,* who made their fortunes under the old colonial economy, and the industrialists, who received their start during World War I when neither exports nor imports were available, continued unabated during the great depression of the 1930's and World War II. The industrialists gradually won the battle. In 1940 they received official endorsement when the government authorized the Bank of the Nation to issue credits to industrial concerns. President Perón emphasized this victory in 1946 by placing industrialization as point number one in his Five Year Plan. By encouraging manufacturing, it is not to be supposed that any overwhelming industrial program like that developed in the United States and Germany will ever dominate Argentine economy. There is no basis for a heavy iron and steel industry, for both high-grade iron and coal are lacking. Also, the small populations in Argentina and nearby countries do not offer sufficient markets to encourage the mass production necessary to meet foreign competition.

The most important industries developed have been those connected with the processing of agricultural and pastoral products, the outstanding examples being the packing houses, wineries, sugar refineries, and flour mills. Textile mills have grown rapidly since 1930, producing cotton, silk, rayon, and woolen goods. In 1941 there were 57,940 industrial establishments, employing 852,154 manual workers, but only 53 factories employed over 1,000 people.

A secondary iron and steel and nonferrous metals industry, using scrap and imported pig, sheet, and bars, has made rapid headway. Among its products are hardware, boilers, structural steel, railway equipment, and office furniture. Other important manufactures include cement, glass products, cosmetics, paints, inks, matches, and industrial alcohol. Nearly one-third of all industrial establishments are in the city of Buenos Aires. Buenos Aires, Córdoba, and Santa Fe are the chief industrial provinces but Tucumán, Mendoza, and Entre Ríos also have considerable industrial interests.

The Central Bank's comparative estimate of agricultural and industrial production shown in the table below, indicates how far Argentina has progressed from a purely agricultural country.

AGRICULTURAL AND INDUSTRIAL PRODUCTION OF ARGENTINA
(Millions of Dollars)

	VALUE OF TOTAL OUTPUT		NET VALUES CREATED BY PROCESSING	
	Agriculture	*Industry*	*Agriculture*	*Industry*
1935	725	825	537	325
1939	750	1,207	600	437
1943	837	1,950	650	675

The proportion of industrial products in total exports, which was 2.95 per cent in 1939, rose to 13.0 per cent in

1942, and was as high as 19.4 per cent in 1943. This expansion is even more impressive when it is considered that total exports increased from $393,300,000 in 1939 to $548,066,000 in 1943, and to $1,333,025,000 in 1947.

The value of industrial production in 1914 was $455,750,-000, and in 1944 it was $2,025,000,000. Of the $487,500,000 value of Argentine agricultural livestock production in 1914, $177,500,000 or 35 per cent was utilized in local industry; of the $837,500,000 production in 1943, $680,750,000 or 81 per cent was utilized.

Foreign Trade. Foreign trade is the life blood of Argentina's economy. While the foreign trade of the United

CHARLES PERRY WEIMER

Many tons of grain are shipped annually from this dock near Rosario on the Paraná River.

States amounts to only about 10 per cent of the nation's commerce, Argentina's trade with other nations averages one third of all Argentine buying and selling. Since most of its business was done with Europe, many economists predicted that failure to sell its surpluses during World War II would bankrupt the nation. In the years during and immediately following World War II the truth of this prophecy was not evident, as new markets found in the United States and other American republics, plus a better balancing of agriculture and manufacturing, made the nation more prosperous than ever.

The high degree of prosperity reached by Argentina despite shipping shortage and other difficulties during the war was manifested by foreign trade returns for 1944. These showed that during that year the value of Argentine exports reached the record figure of $590,106,000. This compares with $548,066,000 in 1943 and with $350,113,000 in 1938, the last complete peacetime year. The figure for 1944 slightly exceeds that of $577,749,000 registered in 1937, when good crops in Argentina, coinciding with poor crops elsewhere, brought about the best year in Argentine history. The balance of trade in 1944 also reached an unprecedented figure in Argentina's favor. It totaled $338,303,000 as compared with $312,554,000 in 1943 and only $188,328,000 in 1937, the highest prewar level. The large excess of Argentina's exports over imports in the preceding two years enabled the country to repatriate in 1944 over £27,500,000 worth of loans from Great Britain. The Argentine treasury repatriated $53,000,000 in gold from New York between November 1943 and the middle of August 1944, when its gold holdings in New York still amounted to $429,000,000. Argentine credits in London were estimated at £70,000,000 at the beginning of 1947. Great Britain continued to be Argentina's best customer, buying 37 per cent of the latter's

total exports in 1944. The United States followed with 22.2 per cent, and Brazil with 9.3 per cent. Brazil at the same time became Argentina's chief supplier, furnishing 34.2 per cent of the latter's total imports. The United States was second with 15.1 per cent and Great Britain third with 8 per cent. Argentine trade in 1944 with Great Britain gave the former a favorable balance of $215,452,000 and with the United States of $96,113,000. By 1947, Argentina's foreign trade had reached a new high, totaling over $2,670,000,000. In 1948 Argentina made a sustained effort to extend trade relationships with other countries. The total number of European and American nations with which Argentina had trade treaties reached twenty-three in that year. Although Argentina refused to sign the Havana Trade Agreement sponsored by the United States, Argentina's trade relations with both the United States and Great Britain were strengthened during the year. In spite of all efforts, however, it became apparent to the Perón administration early in 1949 that the huge amounts of credit that Argentina had acquired during World War II, when exports had far exceeded imports, had been exhausted by government spending after the war. In an attempt to bolster the country's economic structure, Perón discharged his chief economic adviser, Miguel Miranda; reorganized the National Economic Council; and halted all foreign trade until an estimate of the situation could be made. It was discovered that Argentina had spent more than $1,000,000,000 of its accumulated foreign exchange, which had amounted to $1,722,000,000 at the end of 1945. Realizing that the nation was losing its position in world trade and facing depletion of its resources, the Economic Council decided to abandon much of President Perón's Five Year Plan.

Foreign Investments. The Perón government stated in 1946 that Argentina sold to foreign countries goods which on the average amounted annually to about $100,000,000. But the amount taken out of the country annually by foreign investors was $125,000,000, $25,000,000 more than the country received for all it sold abroad. This was the reason, the government declared, that it was absolutely necessary to nationalize industry.

During the long history of foreign capital in Argentina, beginning with the first British loan in 1824, international financial relations have been much better than in most South American republics. Argentina has established the enviable reputation of never having defaulted on a government loan. Until World War II, Great Britain was the chief source of both bank loans and investments. The United States then supplanted Great Britain as the principal source of new foreign capital, but British banks and investors continued to control by far the largest part of the total foreign capital invested. Prior to the outbreak of World War II in 1939, the total foreign capital invested in Argentina was estimated at £800,000,000, of which £500,000,000 was British and £85,000,000 French. Of this sum, £264,598,600 was invested in railway securities and £64,031,246 in Argentine government bonds. The average interest return on all British capital was estimated at 2.4 per cent. Beginning with 1914 the National City Bank of New York and other United States banking institutions furnished the bulk of the capital entering Argentina until the world economic and financial depression began in 1929. During the post-World War I years, the Argentine federal government borrowed approximately $470,000,000 in the United States in long and short term issues, and the Argentine provinces and municipalities borrowed an additional $145,000,000. The federal debt was serviced regularly throughout the 1929-1935 depression, but some of the provinces and municipalities defaulted temporarily on dollar loans which had been underwritten in the United States.

Direct investments by citizens and corporations of the United States in Argentina were estimated at $381,900,000 in 1943, divided as follows: public utilities and transportation, $181,800,000; manufacturing, $101,000,000; petroleum, $38,600,000; trade, mining, and smelting, etc., $160,500,000. Dollar loans to Argentine governmental units—federal, provincial, and municipal—amounting to some $84,100,000 were outstanding in 1943, making a total of about $466,000,000 of United States investments in Argentina, exclusive of unestimated but substantial holdings of local peso securities in the hands of American investors.

Plans for the new Perón government to control more completely the economic life of the country were soon in evidence. Increased profits in staples sold to other countries were early demanded by the government, especially in meat, linseed oil, and fats, which were greatly in demand. Foreign businessmen claimed that former Nazi financial experts were behind this scheme. One of the first implications of the Perón nationalization plans appeared in the new economic pact signed with Great Britain. The British economic mission sent to negotiate the pact had great difficulty because of the stiff demands of Argentina. Great Britain agreed to buy all but 17 per cent of Argentina's exportable surplus meat at an advance of 7½ cents over the price then in effect. Argentina was allowed to use a part of its £120,000,000, deposited in London for payment for Argentine wartime sales, to pay off its national debt, and to receive interest payment on the amount that remained in London. It was tentatively agreed in regard to the British-owned railroads in Argentina, which had been in poor condition for many years, that a new company, part British and part Argentine, was to be formed to finance and manage them. This proposed settlement proved unsatisfactory, however, and protracted bargaining for the sale of the railroads to the Argentine government followed. It was generally agreed that the rolling stock and other properties were completely run down and that any real modernization would involve more financial outlay than British stockholders, who had been losing money on their investment for some time, would be willing to advance. The Argentine government offered $500,000,000 which was half of what the British asked for the railroads. On Feb. 12, 1947, it was announced that Argentina had acquired control of the 16,000 mi. of railroad and their related properties for about $100,000,000 more than originally offered.

Britain thus continued as the principal purchaser of Argentine meat and retained a considerable amount of Argentine trade but lost many of the exclusive advantages it had formerly enjoyed as the largest investor in Argentina. As a part of the nationalization plans, the Perón administration bought outright for the sum of $95,000,000 the telephone system of Buenos Aires, owned by the International Telephone and Telegraph Company, with the latter retaining the sole right of sale of materials to the government. The nationalization plans included not only industries in the communication and transportation fields that are of key military importance, but also power and cement plants, and other industries.

Banking and Government Finance. The monetary unit of Argentina is the paper peso, written m$n, which bore a rate of exchange of approximately twenty cents in United States money before the depression of 1951. Currency consists of bronze one- and two-centavo pieces, and nickel five-, ten-, twenty-, and fifty-centavo pieces. Paper notes are issued in denominations from fifty to one thousand pesos.

During the early years of Argentine independence, the Bank of the Province of Buenos Aires, a bank of issue, played an important part in the development of the Argentine livestock industry. In the great financial and political crisis of 1890 it was forced to suspend operation, but it was subsequently reorganized as one of the leading banks of the republic. The National Bank was organized in 1873, with the federal government contributing half the capital. It financed the development of many industries. In 1891 it became the Bank of the Argentine Nation (Banco de la Nación) to transact the business of the federal government. Until 1935 it served as fiscal and financial agent of the government, while at the same time operating as a commercial bank in competition with other nonofficial institutions. Although deprived of its official function in 1935, the Bank of the Argentine Nation remained the largest domestic banking institution, with a capital in 1939 of 165,409,300 paper pesos and a reserve of 36,472,900 paper pesos. Its commercial banking business was nearly as large as that of all the other banks combined. As of Jan. 1, 1937, there were 45 banks having a capital of 1,000,000 paper pesos or more, including 23 domestic, 9 provincial, and 12 foreign banks.

The Caja de Conversión (Gold Conversion Office) was established in 1896 as an independent governmental agency charged with exclusive control of the printing and issuing of paper money, the receipt of gold, safeguarding of the gold reserves, and similar functions.

The financial crisis of the early 1930's brought far-reaching banking and currency reforms. The Central Bank of the Argentine Republic was established, the organic laws of the National Mortgage Bank and Bank of the Argentine Nation were revised, an Institute for the Liquidation of Bank Investments was established, and for the first time in Argentine history the commercial banks were made subject to regulation under a general banking law.

In December 1934 the federal government was given the right to collect internal consumption taxes on a wide range of specified products which had previously been levied by the provinces. The federal government also undertook to assume the debt of each province that agreed to divert to the national government from its share in federal internal taxes a sum sufficient to cover the service of its debt. These reforms modernized and strengthened the financial structure of the country.

The whole financial system of Argentina was reorganized by President Juan Perón in 1946. The new program was based on the three ideas which Perón had announced as his platform before he was elected president, (1) restriction of foreign capital and nationalization of industry, (2) government control of finances, and (3) greater sharing of wealth with the common man. A series of decree laws completely modified the banking laws and brought the government much larger control over both domestic and foreign financial institutions. The first of these decrees on March 25, 1946, nationalized the Central Bank, which formerly was owned, half by the government and half by private banks, including a number of United States banks. The private banks were reimbursed, and the Central Bank was given control of all bank deposits of the country. Under the decree, all deposits were guaranteed by the government and were held in private institutions serving merely as agents of the Central Bank. By a second decree law, issued May 24, 1946, the Central Bank was directed to work on the problem of maintaining a high level of employment of the human and material resources of the country and to take over various institutions, such as the Bank of the Argentine Nation, responsible for farm production and commerce, and the National Mortgage Bank, which is authorized to grant loans for building. The Argentine Reinsurance Institute was created as a monopoly on all reinsurance business, with extensive limitations placed on all foreign insurance companies. A number of privately operated institutions, such as the Argentina Trade Promotion Corporation, were liquidated, and a Securities Commission was formed to authorize quotations on new issues of securities.

Another far-reaching move was made in July 1946, when the government announced that it would pay off the national debt and be prepared to make loans to neighboring countries. This was made possible through the use of funds which Argentina had accumulated in New York and London from payments for the war materials sold to the United Nations. The amount of this credit in New York, blocked by the United States Government for some two years but released following the election of President Perón, was $644,000,000. Nearly an equal sum was also in London. It was estimated that by December 1946 Argentina had paid $130,000,000 to New York bankers, which practically closed out its dollar indebtedness. Argentine branch banks in neighboring countries began at the same time to announce that credits were available for governments and institutions. Thus Argentina passed for a time, at least, from a debtor to a creditor nation. By 1948, however, Argentina's dollar surpluses created by exports during the war had vanished, and the country's economy tottered on the precipice of inflation and a dollar shortage. The Central Bank suspended the transfer of dollars to pay for imports, and in early 1949, when the shortage became critical, further measures were taken to prevent spending and to protect dwindling currency reserves. It was ruled that all imports must be paid for only through funds granted by the Central Bank, and all loopholes permitting the importation of nonessential goods were closed. Argentina found itself in almost desperate need of dollars; and, as Perón had stated that he would never accept a foreign loan and as Argentina was not a member of the World Bank, the acquisition of such funds became a severe problem.

Central Banking System. The Central Banking System of Argentina as it appeared in 1948 was composed of six institutions as follows: (1) the Banco Central, entirely government-owned and functioning as a bank of issue and as the depository of all the deposits of the commercial banks of the nation; (2) and (3) the Banco de la Nación and Banco de Credito Industrial Argentino, owned by the government, which guarantees their liabilities (the first, with enormous resources, aids in developing commerce, agriculture, and cattle raising; the second, one of the world's most important banks, aids in the development of industry); (4) the Banco Hipotecario Nacional, government-owned and financing real estate and land development; (5) the Instituto Argentina para la Promoción del Intercambio (I.A.P.I.), owned by the government for the promotion of exportation of grains, meats, quebracho, hides, and vegetable-oil products, with the right to purchase abroad for government dependencies; and (6) the Instituto Mixto de Inversiones Inmobiliarias (I.M.I.M.), with a capital subscribed half by official banks and half by commercial banks, which regulates the issuance of securities and stabilizes stock exchange quotations.

Taxation. Argentina, like most Latin American republics, collects the largest part of its revenue from indirect levies, the largest being import tariffs. Other important taxes are those on incomes (graduated from 2 per cent on incomes from m$n 1,250 to m$n 2,500, to 22 per cent for incomes of m$n 250,000), sales, excessive profits, returns from the national lottery, and all insurance operations, and the ordinary taxes of various kinds.

Government Revenue and Expenditures. The 1948 budget, sent to Congress at the end of June 1947, called for the over-all expenditure of m$n 6,200,800,000 to be financed as follows: m$n 3,091,600,000 from general income; m$n 1,146,500,000 from bond sales; and m$n 1,962,800,000 corresponding to the various autonomous units, which should support themselves from their own income. Expenses to be covered by general income during 1948 were up m$n 425,000,000, 16 per cent over 1947. This increase was attributed principally to increased salaries of personnel (up 61.6 per cent), to new services, and to higher costs of purchases in world markets. Estimated revenue for the same period was placed at m$n 3,092,000,000.

Depression. The whole picture of Argentine trade began to change about 1950. The United States, which had already superseded Great Britain, in capital investments, took first place in trade, with Great Britain second and Brazil third. The American Continent thus became Argentina's principal market, in spite of the dour prewar prophecies of the economists who had insisted that this could never happen. Droughts and bad management changed the nation's favorable balance of trade, amounting to 216 million pesos in 1950, to an unfavorable balance (more imports than exports) of 2.6 billion pesos in 1951, with the country's favorable exchange balance falling rapidly. This situation contributed to further inflation. The cost-of-living index increased 38 per cent, indicating a considerable drop in real wages. The Argentine public, the greatest meat-eaters in the world (247 lb. per capita in 1950 as against 145 lb. in the United States), were shocked when meatless days were announced in 1952, as were the British when their meat shipments were cut 50 per cent. At the same time, no wheat and little wool (formerly the nation's greatest moneymakers) could be exported. It would be wrong, however, to accept this as permanent, for droughts do not last forever, and it cannot be expected that Argentina will continue to accept fundamental mismanagement of its riches.

Transportation. The principal port of Argentina is Buenos Aires, which receives most incoming shipments. Rosario on the Paraná handles a large part of the agricultural exports. Other ports for ocean vessels are La Plata, Bahía Blanca, and Santa Fe. A large fleet of steamers is in operation on the Plata connecting Buenos Aires with Montevideo. Smaller river steamers ascend the Paraguay-Paraná to Asunción, Paraguay, and to Corumbá in Brazil, and the Alto Paraná to Porto Mendes, Brazil.

Many efforts were made to build a merchant marine, but until 1941 it was only embryonic. At that time the Argentine State Merchant Marine was created through the purchase of sixteen former Italian ships that were interned in Argentine waters. Since then used ships have been purchased from other countries; in 1948 there were approximately one hundred ships.

Argentina has a well-developed railroad system, though rolling stock and equipment suffered serious deterioration during the years following the depression and during World War II. In 1946 the Argentine government bought control of the British-owned lines, in 1947 it took over the French-owned lines, and in March 1948 the government became owner of the country's entire railroad system, totaling 26,568 mi. The principal railroads radiate from Buenos Aires,

VESSELS CROWD ALONG THE NUEVO PUERTO DOCKS IN BUENOS AIRES.

serving almost all the important towns of the Humid Pampa, the Andean piedmont, and the southern and eastern Chaco. Trans-Andean railroads run from Mendoza to Los Andes, Chile, via a tunnel through the Uspallata Pass, and from Salta to Antofagasta, Chile. Other international lines connect Buenos Aires with La Paz, Bolivia, and Asunción, Paraguay.

Of a total of some 250,000 mi. of highways, about 13,000 may be classified as paved, principally focusing on Buenos Aires. Argentina has within its borders 3,252 mi. of the Pan American Highway. The principal section is that between Buenos Aires and Santiago de Chile. Other sections within Argentina lead to La Paz, Asunción, and Rio de Janeiro. An average of 38,000 workmen are employed in the building and upkeep of the road system.

In the Five Year Plan, $27,000,000 were set aside for highways; $200,000,000 for railway equipment; and $25,000,000 for river transportation.

International airlines connect Buenos Aires with the United States, Montevideo, Asunción, La Paz, and Santiago and also serve the interior cities of Córdoba, Mendoza, Tucumán, and Salta. Argentine lines provide domestic services and connections with Asunción, Montevideo, and Rio de Janeiro. The Department of Civil Aeronautics reported that in 1942 the activities of the various air services established in Argentina made 4,488 trips; flew a total of 9,626 hours and carried 55,000 passengers, 197,420 pounds of mail, and 526,295 pounds of packages or freight. The Five Year Plan of President Perón included the opening of government-directed airlines to New York, London, Moscow, Paris, Madrid, and Cairo.

GOVERNMENT AND POLITICS

Constitution. Argentina is governed under a federal system somewhat similar to that of the United States, which served as its model. In Argentina, however, the local entities, called provinces, do not participate, as such, in the amendment of the Constitution. Moreover, under the constitutional provisions which permit the federal government to intervene in the provinces in order to insure the republican form of government, the governors of the fourteen provinces have become the political agents of the president.

The Constitution, written in 1853 and amended in 1860, 1866, and 1898, contains numerous guarantees to individuals and property, including freedom of worship, but the Roman Catholic Church is the established church, and the president and vice-president must belong to it. The president, whose powers are somewhat more extensive than those of the president of the United States, is chosen indirectly by an electoral college for a term of six years and is debarred from immediate re-election. He must have an independent income of 2,000 pesos per year and be at least thirty years of age.

As president he is the supreme head of the nation and has the general administration of the country in his charge. He is, in addition, the immediate and local head of the capital of the nation. He appoints the magistrates of the Supreme Court and exercises the right of national patronage in the appointment of the bishops for cathedral churches on Senate recommendation. With the concurrence of the Supreme Court he grants or refuses passage of decrees of the Supreme Pontiff of Rome. He cannot leave the country without permission of Congress. In 1949, the Constitution was revised to permit the president to succeed himself, to authorize certain limitations on foreign investors, to give women the right to vote, and to enlarge the rights of labor.

National Congress. The National Congress consists of the Senate and the Chamber of Deputies. The Senate is made up on the basis of equal representation of the provinces, two senators being chosen by the legislature of each province. The Federal District of Buenos Aires also has two senators selected by a special electoral college. The senatorial term is nine years and indefinite re-election is permitted, one third of the Senate being renewed every three years. A property qualification is required for senators, but not for members of the lower house, who are elected by direct popular vote for a term of four years.

Ministries. The Constitution of Argentina provides for a Cabinet of eight ministers. Because of the limitation in number and the rapid increase in governmental functions, one minister in the Argentine Cabinet may have supervision over two different departments.

In addition to the ministries, four executive offices, ranking as ministries, were created in 1943, 1944, and 1945; they are the secretariats of the Presidency, Labor and Social Welfare, Industry and Commerce, and Aeronautics, respectively. The Secretariat of the Presidency assists in co-ordinating the activities of the various ministries, is liaison officer between them and the president, and is responsible for the general publicity issued by the government. The Ministry of Labor and Social Welfare was created to further the interests of labor, keep national production running smoothly, generally plan and co-ordinate the social policy of the nation and take charge of immigration and of industrial and social hygiene. The Ministry of Industry and Commerce includes the National Power Administration, and the National Institute of Technology.

Justice. The judicial power is vested in a Supreme Court of Justice and other lower tribunals which Congress may establish. The latter include federal courts of appeal and courts of first instance. Each province has its own judicial system. The members of the federal Supreme Court of Justice are chosen by the president with the consent of the Senate. The Constitution also provides that the Supreme Court of Justice shall "take cognizance of and decide on all cases involving points governed by the Constitution and laws of the nation." It is within the province of the Supreme Court to take cognizance of or decide on cases of treason, cases involving interpretation of the Constitution, cases concerning foreign ambassadors, treaties with foreign nations, and cases not entirely within the jurisdiction of the various provinces of the nation.

Local Government. The Constitution provides that the provinces are to retain the power not delegated to the federal government and "that which they may have expressly reserved by special covenants at the time of their incorporation." Each province is given the power to enact its own constitution and to provide for its own institutions of government. But such rights are often limited by intervention of the Executives.

Political Parties. Prior to the coming to power of General Perón, the three main political parties in Argentina were the Radical Civic Union, the National Democrats, and the Antipersonalists.

At the time of his election as president on Feb. 24, 1946, General Juan Perón was supported by a Labor Party and a faction of the Radical Party. His opponent, Dr. José P. Tamborini, headed a coalition of Radical, Socialist, Progressive, Democratic, and Communist parties. After President Perón's inauguration, a movement was started to incorporate all of the supporters of the administration into a single party, the Union Party. This name was later changed to the Perón Party. In 1948, 102 out of the 152 deputies supported Perón, and in the Senate 28 out of 30 supported him.

Armed Forces. Service in the Argentine army is compulsory for all male citizens from the age of twenty to forty-five. For the first ten years men are enrolled in the First Line Army, then pass into the National Guard, closing their service with five years in the Territorial Guard. All of the military organization has been greatly strengthened since the army took over the national government in 1943. Under Perón, military strength has been continued.

The peacetime strength of the regular army is 100,000.

There is also a trained reserve of about 300,000. There are 100,000 officers and men on one-year active service, followed by nine years in the active reserve; 215,000 in the National Guard; and 75,000 in the Territorial Force, which is called up in war. The republic is divided into six military districts, garrisoned by six divisions, three cavalry brigades, and two mountain detachments (all half-strength peacetime nuclei). The army represents 0.6 per cent of the population and provides one soldier for every ten square miles of territory.

The Argentine air force aspires to hemispheric leadership south of the Rio Grande. In the spring of 1946 a British aviation mission arrived in Buenos Aires, and since then Argentina has been a large customer of British aircraft manufacturers. Long-range Vikings, four-engine Lincolns, and various jet models, including eighteen twin-jet Gloster Meteor fighter bombers were in use in 1948. Domestic aircraft manufacture centers around Córdoba. The air force is under the Aviation Ministry departments but has its own autonomous command organization. Major air bases are located at El Palomar, Córdoba, Mendoza, and Paraná, and there is a paratrooper school at Córdoba. Naval aviation is separate under the Ministry of Marine, with air bases at Belgrano, Punta Indio, Fuerta Barragán, Mar del Plata, and Madryn. Chief training establishments are at El Palomar and Córdoba.

The Argentine navy consisted of about 11,500 men in 1948. It possessed two 27,720-ton battleships, three cruisers, eleven destroyers, three submarines and a number of smaller vessels. A new naval construction program, adopted in 1946, called for one aircraft carrier, one cruiser, four destroyers, three submarines, ten patrol craft, and one supply vessel. Former German military missions have been replaced by United States experts. The Perón regime has made strenuous efforts to modernize the military establishment. In 1946 the military expenses were reported to be 44.2 per cent of the national budget. The 1948 budget listed m$n 334,000,000 for the three military branches. Although Argentina was denied all Lend Lease aid during World War II because of its sympathy with the Nazi regime, beginning in 1947 the United States extended aid to the country.

International Relations. Argentina is a member of the United Nations and of the Pan American Union. The Argentine delegation at the Ninth International Conference of American States at Bogotá in 1948 took a leading role, under the guidance of Dr. Juan A. Bramuglia, Minister of Foreign Relations. In the United Nations, in 1949, the Argentine delegation, under the general leadership of Dr. José Arce, backed by a large permanent delegation, called for a general conference to eliminate the veto and opposed the partition of Palestine and the isolation of Franco Spain from the U.N. Dr. Arce served a term as president of the Security Council, and his delegation showed a desire to contribute to the solution of the struggle between the U.S.S.R. and the Western Powers.

Argentina, under President Perón, has signed an unusually large number of international treaties, most of which were of an economic nature. The first group of treaties was with neighbors in Latin America, providing for Argentine credits and interchange of products. Later treaties embraced relations with European and Asiatic countries.

United States. Argentina and the United States have always had difficulty in co-operating. Economic rivals with the same things to sell, both believing themselves entitled to lead in inter-American affairs and with little inclination to surrender any supposed right, they are usually on opposite sides in Pan American gatherings. In neither World War did Argentina join with the United States. The Perón regime was the object of open criticism by U. S. Ambassador Spruille Braden. His successor, George Messersmith, who went from Mexico to Buenos Aires in 1946, formed a close friendship with President Perón in his effort to clear up differences between the two countries. A favorable reaction brought the attendance of Argentina at the Rio de Janeiro Conference in 1947 and the Pan American Conference in Bogotá in 1948, with the signing of the important Continental Defense Pact. Assistant Secretary of State Edward G. Miller, Jr., had long conferences with President Perón in 1950; and a frank discussion of differences brought a commission to Washington to work on a detailed economic exchange. To aid Argentina to pay the large sums due to American merchants, the Export-Import Bank extended a credit of $125 million, a move that was criticised as aid to a dictatorship and defended as facing the practical question of keeping unity in the hemisphere, which wounded Argentine pride. When American officials strongly criticised the closing of the Argentine daily, *La Prensa,* the old differences again developed. After three American businessmen—James Bruce, Stanley Griffin, and Elsworth Bunker—had tried their hands at improving relations from 1947 to 1951, a career diplomat—Alfred Neufer—was dispatched in 1952 with instructions to do little more than watch the situation. Recently President Perón has added labor attachés to his embassies to preach the doctrine of "the middle way," which means condemnation of both Soviet and American warlike movements.

CULTURAL DEVELOPMENTS

Publishing. Argentina has 2,737 periodicals, classified as follows: 313 daily newspapers, 1,638 periodicals in newspaper form, and 786 magazines. In relation to its population Argentina ranks high in the consumption of printing paper. The republic has become the world's center for the publication of Spanish literature. However, the severe censorship and the closing of most of the free press, including the famous *La Prensa,* reduced the nation's reputation as a publishing and cultural center.

Education. Argentina, with over 17,000,000 inhabitants, has approximately 20,550 primary schools where attendance is compulsory and tuition free. Approximately 2,800,500 pupils are enrolled under 114,300 teachers. There are also approximately 40,000 university students and about 245,000 in secondary, normal, industrial, and art schools. The institutions of higher learning are the national universities of Buenos Aires, La Plata, Córdoba, Litoral, Tucumán, and Mendoza. The annual cost of education in Argentina reaches the sum of $300,000,000.

Libraries and Museums. Argentina has 1,700 public libraries and 86 museums, among them one of the richest paleontological museums in the world.

HISTORY

The early history of Argentina, which lies on the east coast of South America, gave no such promise of development as did Peru and other west coast countries, with their background of highly developed aboriginal civilizations and rich mines of silver and gold. The Indian tribes that inhabited the Argentine plains lived in small independent bands and were largely occupied with hunting the guanaco, an animal related to the llama. When the Spaniards arrived some Indian groups were in a period of decadence, while others had conquered people of higher culture. Argentina lacked rich tropical verdure and precious minerals, and the magnificent prairies which later were to make Argentina

the richest of all South American countries were not appreciated in the early days.

Discovery and Colonial Period. The early Spanish discoverers were largely interested in the Caribbean area and Central America. The discovery of Brazil was accidentally made by Portuguese on their way down the African coast, and Spanish ventures in the South Atlantic were primarily to find routes to the Pacific Ocean and the Malayan Archipelago. It was not until 1516 that Juan Díaz de Solís, a Spanish navigator, first landed on the shores of the Río de la Plata. He visited a small island in that river, which he named Martín García and which later came to serve as an important strategic center for the Argentine navy. He was killed by Indians when he landed, and his companions lost no time in returning to Spain. Ferdinand Magellan, a Portuguese employed by Spain, entered this enormous estuary four years later, in 1520, but, when he was convinced that it did not lead to the Pacific Ocean, he turned south to complete the circumnavigation of the globe.

Sebastian Cabot, in 1526, was the first to ascend the Río de la Plata and go north into the Paraná and Paraguay rivers. He was greatly pleased by the reception given him by the Indians, and, because they presented him with silver trinkets, he believed that the land was filled with silver and called the estuary Río de la Plata, or Silver River. Another Spanish explorer, Diego García, ascended the river a little later and the two expeditions met and quarreled. Both returned to Spain without accomplishing anything of a permanent nature. The few settlers left at the small fort of Espiritu Santo were soon killed by the Indians. The next expedition from Spain was a large and well-planned one under the leadership of a rich nobleman of great ability, Pedro de Mendoza. He reached the site of the present Buenos Aires in February 1536. At first the Indians were friendly, but they soon quarreled with their visitors and attacked them with great ferocity. After a trial trip up the Paraná, Mendoza became discouraged and started back to Spain; he died on the way. Expeditions under Juan de Ayolas and Domingo Martínez de Irala were sent north by Mendoza in search of gold. Ayolas probably reached Peru, but on his return was killed by Indians. In 1536 Irala founded Asunción, present capital of Paraguay, the first permanent Spanish settlement in eastern South America. It was not until 1580 that Juan de Garay, with an expedition of sixty men from Asunción, refounded Buenos Aires.

The refounding of Buenos Aires proved to be the most important event in the history of Argentina, and one of the most important in the development of Spanish America. In the seventeenth century the colony settled down to the monotonous life imposed by the monopolistic policy of Spain and by the jealousy of the Lima merchants. In 1617 Buenos Aires was separated from Asunción and made a province. The Buenos Aires *cabildo,* a kind of self-perpetuating town council under which local elections were held, often took advantage of its great distance from the viceroy in Lima and acted with daring independence. This led to the decision of Charles III of Spain to form the new independent viceroyalty of La Plata in 1776. Buenos Aires was made the capital of this powerful Atlantic region of the Spanish empire, with the areas which became Argentina, Uruguay, Paraguay, and Bolivia composing its territory. Already Buenos Aires had developed clandestine trade with England and other European countries, which included the importation of liberal books describing political developments in France and the North American colonies. Liberals fleeing from persecution in Spain, British seeking new commercial opportunities, and world travelers from other nations found it easy to enter Buenos Aires, which became the most cosmopolitan center of Spanish America. Even in colonial days dissension began to develop between the *porteños* and the aristocratic ecclesiastical-minded landowners who came from Peru to found the interior northern cities of Córdoba, Tucumán, Salta, and Chuquisaca.

The period of the viceroyalty was one of rapid progress. Its prosperity attracted the attention of the British, who towards the end of the viceregal period in Buenos Aires were

Grenadier Guards parade in Buenos Aires. They are palace guards and wear the uniform of Argentina's first regiment commanded by Gen. San Martín, hero of the Liberation.

at war with Napoleon and with Spain, his ally. In 1806 an English expedition captured the city of Buenos Aires. The viceroy who fled before the British was declared deposed by a *cabildo abierto,* an open town meeting, in Buenos Aires. The inhabitants of the city chose Santiago de Liniers, later to become viceroy, as their leader in a popular movement to oust the British. The invaders were soon expelled, and a second attempt at invasion in 1807 failed. These victories of the citizens of Buenos Aires gave them a marked degree of self-confidence.

The Revolution. When Napoleon invaded Spain and deposed Ferdinand VII in favor of Joseph Bonaparte, an Argentine national assembly was called, Viceroy Cisneros was deposed, and the country decided to appoint a junta to rule in the name of Ferdinand until he was restored to his throne. The date of that decision, May 25, 1810, is celebrated as Argentine Independence Day and the *Revolución de Mayo* is one of the country's most important events. During the next seventeen years, constant fighting between the revolutionists and loyalists continued. The growing conviction that Argentina must become completely free from Spain and organize a republic came to a head at a congress which met at Tucumán on July 9, 1816, and framed a declaration of independence for the United Provinces of Río de la Plata.

The man who did most to bring about this declaration was General José de San Martín, often called "the Saint of the Sword" because of his patriotic, unselfish character. Born in northern Argentina, he entered the Spanish army when he was thirteen and campaigned in several European countries. Returning to his native soil to fight for its independence, he decided that local campaigns were useless unless the Spanish troops could be driven from their stronghold in Lima. Keeping his plans secret, he devoted two years to training an army in Mendoza at the foot of the Andes. When all was ready he led his force secretly across the high Andes and conquered the Spanish troops in Chile. Next he moved

his victorious army to Peru, captured the royalist center of Lima and on July 28, 1821, declared Peru independent. There still remained, however, a strong Spanish force in South America, and San Martín went to the Ecuadorian city of Guayaquil to propose a united move with General Simón Bolívar, who was moving south after having liberated Venezuela, Colombia, and Ecuador. Bolívar proved unwilling to join forces with San Martín, who, seeing the danger of an incipient rivalry, returned to Lima and resigned his command. After thus making way for Bolívar, San Martín returned home. In Buenos Aires he found such rivalries that he bade his friends good-by, and with his daughter went to France, where he lived until his death on Aug. 17, 1850. A few years later his native land repatriated his remains and buried them in the Buenos Aires Cathedral.

Dissension in Argentina continued. The territories later known as Uruguay, Paraguay, and Bolivia refused to accept the leadership of Buenos Aires and set up independent governments. Two parties strove for control of the remaining territory, which later became the Argentine Republic: the Unitarians who desired a united central government with Buenos Aires as the capital, and the Federalists who desired a loose federation of the provinces, with Buenos Aires sharing port and tariff privileges with the rest of the country.

The first great civilian president was Bernardino Rivadavia, who was elected in 1826. Brilliant and progressive, he introduced a series of educational, ecclesiastical, social, and judicial reforms. But as an advocate of the new centralized constitution he was unable to carry with him the *caudillos,* political bosses of the provinces, and was forced to resign in 1827. The next strong man was Juan Manuel de Rosas, who ruled with an iron hand from 1829 to 1852. In spite of his cruelty, his wholesale exiling of liberals, and his dominance over the other *caudillos,* he failed to bring unity to the country. Rosas was finally defeated by a coalition led by one of his former henchmen, General Justo José Urquiza, and was exiled to England in 1852.

The Republic. Argentina's first representative constitution was written in 1853 by a group of distinguished patriots, led by returned liberal exiles such as Juan Bautista Alberdi, Bartolomé Mitre, and Domingo Faustino Sarmiento. Ten years later, under General Mitre, the country accepted the Constitution and began the life of a united republic, with Buenos Aires as the capital. Mitre was the first Argentine president to serve out his full term (1862-

THE PLAZA CONGRESO, BUENOS AIRES

1868). Under him began the progress which has marked the development of the republic. It has been said that Mitre served Argentina as George Washington did the United States. If so, his successor, Sarmiento (1868-1874), rendered service similar to that of Thomas Jefferson.

In 1880 Buenos Aires was made the federal capital and Julio Roca, who had won renown in a war against the Indians in Patagonia, became president. At the end of his term he favored the candidacy of his brother-in-law, Miguel Juárez Celman. Celman's presidency was marked by graft and corruption, and the Union Cívica, a radical party, was formed to oppose the conservative party in power. The Union Cívica in 1890 fomented a revolution which led to the resignation of Celman. In the next year payments on the foreign debt were suspended and bankruptcy was imminent. Luis Sáenz Peña, a compromise candidate, was elected in 1892, but resigned in 1895 because of opposition to his methods. The continued growth of industry and agriculture eased the situation and assisted in the material recovery of the country.

The progress initiated in this period included building of railroads, colonization by European immigrants, importing of registered livestock, shipping of refrigerated meat abroad, rise of land values, and development of foreign commerce. The reverse side of the picture showed a long series of "aristocratic presidents" who invariably selected their successors, intervened in the provinces, encouraged excess spending and graft, and favored the rich landholders. As the distinguished rector of the University of La Plata, Dr. J. V. Gonzalez, described it: "To be a great citizen, a great patriot, a great tribune, signified in the language of that period to be a bully and a hero capable of marching with fixed bayonets, eliminating all obstacles, and taking possession of polls, ballot boxes, and registers."

President Roque Sáenz Peña, harkening to the demand for electoral reform, risked his political life in 1912 by putting through Congress the law of the secret ballot, one of the greatest political reforms in the republic's history. This law made it possible for the majority party, the Radicals, to elect and install as president the party leader, Hipólito Irigoyen. His administration (1916-1922) was noted for the great attention given to social questions and education, although his lack of administrative experience and his individualistic traits weakened his record. After a six-year intervening period (1922-1928) during which his fellow-Radical, Dr. Marcelo T. de Alvear, was chief executive, Irigoyen was elected for his second term in 1928. He was then eighty years old and was so incapable of facing the problems brought on by a world depression that the army drove him out of office and substituted General José F. Uriburu. This returned the nation to the old days of controlled elections and favors for the rich landholders.

The 1932 elections controlled by General Uriburu brought General Agustín P. Justo to power. In 1938, by a similar process, Dr. Roberto M. Ortiz was elected president and Ramón Castillo, vice-president. President Ortiz started on a program to return the country to democratic processes. But in 1942 he was compelled because of illness to surrender the government to a reactionary vice-president, Castillo, who played completely into the hands of the Nazis, the clericals, and the extreme nationalists. On June 4, 1943, a military group overthrew the government and installed General Arturo Rawson as president, but the next day Rawson resigned in favor of General Pedro P. Ramírez. All efforts to swing Argentina into World War II on the side of the United Nations failed until early in 1945.

These changes in the presidency were a product both of local political conditions and personal rivalries and of the international situation created by the beginning of World War II in September 1939. Strong Nazi German penetration into Argentina caused much criticism to be directed against

Argentina for alleged pro-Nazi sympathies. The government proclaimed its neutrality, but continued to be accused of

CHARLES PERRY WEIMER

Christ of the Andes, at Uspallata Pass on the Argentina-Chile border, commemorates the settling of the boundary dispute between the two countries.

harboring Nazi fifth columnists. The rejection, on Jan. 4, 1940, of a reciprocal trade agreement with the United States and the apparent attitude of government, army, and business gave same validity to the charges of Nazism. Ramírez abolished all political parties and broke relations with the Axis, Jan. 26, 1944, after disclosing German spy activities in Argentina. A clique of Argentine officers, apparently fearing war with Germany, replaced Ramírez with General Edelmiro J. Farrell on Feb. 24, 1944. His regime was embarrassed by diplomatic nonrecognition and by the rise to power of Colonel Juan Perón. Perón came to power as a strong champion of labor who was not above the use of fascist methods. To win recognition and dispel the taint of fascism, his government declared war on Germany, Mar. 27, 1945; it was invited back into the Pan American Union, signed the Act of Chapultepec, Apr. 4, 1945, and was admitted to membership in the United Nations. In elections held Feb. 24, 1946, Perón was elected president and his inauguration took place on June 4, 1946. He initiated a Five Year Plan that pointed toward industrialization; major programs included increased immigration, irrigation projects, and greater participation of labor in the riches of the country.

Argentina began to return to nearly normal life, after the abnormal conditions which had prevailed since the death of President Roberto Ortiz in 1942. While President Perón continued his strong-arm methods, he seemed to move closer to constitutional government and to the encouragement of private enterprise. The Argentines as much as ever were ruling their country. However, the aristocratic landowners, who had been in control during the last eighty years, were being as soundly abused as labor had been in the past.

Perón led Congress in the impeachment of the Supreme Court on the charge that it favored former illegal governments and laws. He discharged some 1,100 university professors because, he alleged, they were standing against a modern approach to education and were using the universities for political purposes. He pushed through a law requiring that the Roman Catholic religion be taught in all schools, public and private, although the Constitution guarantees religious freedom. Several opposition newspapers were closed, and others were forced to support the government.

A major crisis of the Perón regime occurred in 1951, seven years after he, as a young colonel, had marched with the army into Buenos Aires. In less than two years he had been elected president of the Republic, and with the enormous credits piled up during the war years he began a large spending program: buying railroads and other public utilities from foreigners, building up merchant marine and military power, constructing public works, and taking over the management of foreign trade from private enterprise. For a while, everything attempted by Perón and the beautiful Señora Eva Perón, known as "Evita," seemed to succeed. In 1951 these extravagances reached the limit for even such a rich country as Argentina. The crisis was introduced by a two-year drought, which severely cut such vital exports as wheat and cattle. A sharp depression unbalanced all economic life and sent the peso, which for a quarter of a century had remained at around four to the dollar, down to twenty-eight to the dollar. With presidential elections nearing, Perón forced on the country his own candidacy, with his wife as vice-president. An army revolt compelled Señora Perón to withdraw, but Perón was re-elected, with complete backing in the new Senate and overwhelming support in the House of Deputies.

However, his new tenure of office was short-lived, despite the continued support of the army and the trade-union movement. The death of his wife in 1952 and worsening economic conditions served to decrease popular support for Perón, as did his anti-clerical campaign, begun early in 1955. In June of that year the navy revolted, and the army, in suppressing the revolt, took control of the regime, although Perón remained at the head of the government until September 19, when he was forced to flee the country after a four-day uprising. Gen. Eduardo Lonardi became provisional president until November 13, when Army Chief of Staff Gen. Pedro Aramburu took command of the government.

S. G. I.

ARGENTITE [ɑˈrʤəntait], a primary silver mineral, of the composition silver sulphide, Ag₂S. It has a metallic luster but differs from most other metallic minerals in that it is sectile and malleable. On charcoal, argentite can be fused, yielding sulphur dioxide and a silver button. This mineral was first described by Agricola in 1529, who named it after the Latin word for silver, *argentum*. Argentite occurs in low and intermediate temperature hydrothermal veins. It has been a leading source of silver in such famous mining districts as Freiberg, Saxony; Guanajuato, Mexico; and Comstock and Tonopah, in the state of Nevada.   K. K. L.

ARGININE. *See* PROTEINS.
ARGO. *See* JASON.
ARGON. *See* GASES, INERT.

ARGONAUT, a cephalopod mollusk having the scientific name of *Argonauta argo* and belonging to the same order as the octopus. It lives in tropical and subtropical seas where it floats at the surface, submerging if disturbed.

V. L. L.

ARGONAUTICA [ɑrgənɔˈtɪkə], a Greek epic poem of the third century B.C. by Apollonius of Rhodes. It narrates the story of Jason, who sailed on the *Argo* from Iolcus

COURTESY OF THE MUSEUM OF NATURAL HISTORY
Argonaut or Paper Nautilus, a cephalopod related to the octopus

in Thessaly to Colchis on the Black Sea to secure the Golden Fleece with the magic help of Medea. The remarkable account in Book III of the growth of Medea's love for Jason inspired the Dido-Aeneas episode in Vergil's *Aeneid*. An incomplete *Argonautica* by the Latin epic poet Valerius Flaccus, is also extant. *See also* APOLLONIUS OF RHODES; JASON.

C. M. D.

ARGONAUTS. *See* GOLDEN FLEECE, THE; JASON.

ARGO NAVIS [ɑˈrgo neˈvɪs], an unusually large constellation discovered in ancient times and situated between right ascension 6 hr. and 11 hr.; some parts of it are too far south to be seen from middle north latitudes. In modern times astronomers have divided Argo into various smaller groups. In 1947, four such groups—Pyxis, the Compass; Puppis, the Stern; Vela, the Sails; and Carina, the Keel—were recognized by the Nautical Almanac Office and the American Astronomical Society. Telescopically, rich portions of the Milky Way are included in these boundaries. Canopus, the second star in apparent brightness, is in Carina. Argo Navis (ship *Argo*) is named after the ship that carried the fifty heroes to Colchis in search of the Golden Fleece. *See also* CANOPUS; CARINA; PUPPIS; PYXIS; VELA.   J. H. P.

ARGONNE [aˈrgɔˈn], a plateau comprising portions of the departments of Ardennes, Meuse, and Marne in northeastern France and providing a natural barrier between the former provinces of Lorraine and Champagne. A rocky, heavily forested area, the Argonne is 10 mi. wide and stretches 44 mi. in a southeast-northwest direction; its eastern boundary is marked by steep cliffs, and its western slope is traced by the Aisne. The Aire and its tributaries divide the plateau longitudinally. As a field of military operations, the Argonne has long figured in French history. Bitter fighting raged in its 25-mi. wooded section during the campaign of Dumouriez in 1792 and in the Franco-Prussian War of 1870. The Battle of the Argonne in September 1918 gave the Allies ample evidence of the strength of the American

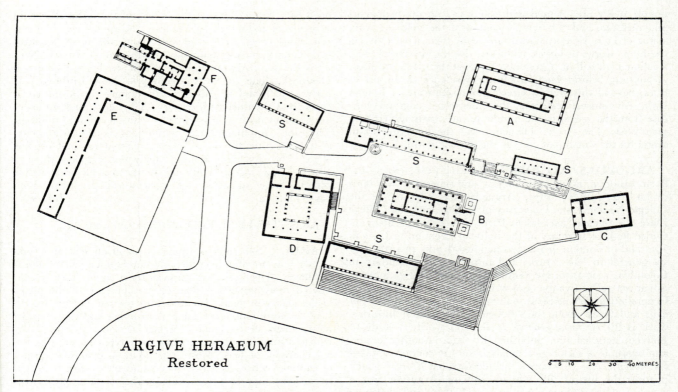

ARGIVE HERAEUM
Restored

ARGIVE HERAEUM, SANCTUARY OF HERA, AT ARGOS

(A) Archaic temple; (B) Classical temple; (C) Ceremonial hall; (D) House of Priestesses; (E) Gymnasium; (F) Roman Bath; (S) Stoas

Expeditionary Force when the American First Army and the French Fourth launched simultaneously an attack on the German positions in the woods of the Argonne. The French approach from the west, timed with the American push from the east, resulted on Oct. 10 in the disruption of German lines of communication. The Argonne-Meuse operation was brought to a victorious finish with the Allies in control. German losses: 847 cannon, 3,000 machine guns, 26,000 prisoners. The American army suffered 117,000 killed and wounded but the success of the campaign led the way to further Allied gains which were a deciding factor in the German suit for an armistice.   M. V. K.

ARGOS [ɑ'rgɒs], the name of several places in Greece, the most important being the city in the eastern part of the Peloponnesus at the head of the Gulf of Argolis, and on the western edge of the Argive Plain, with a population in 1951 of 13,163. The city lies about four miles from the coast, below two hills, Larisa and Aspis, which constitute its natural defense. Argos is one of the chief settlements in the Argolid, the district of the watershed centering on the plain. The border areas of the Argolid are hilly with some moderately arable land; the plain itself is alluvial and fertile, famous in modern times for melons and in legend for horses. The coast is unfit for modern port activities, except at Nauplia.

The history of the Argolid begins early, with a Neolithic culture dating from before 3000 B.C. During the Middle and Late Helladic Periods (c. 2000-1000 B.C.), it was the most powerful region in Greece. Tiryns and Mycenae (which gave its name to the culture of the later years of this epoch) left remains more impressive and rich than did Argos, but Mycenaean tombs and a fortified palace have been found on and around the Larisa, and the great legendary cycles of Agamemnon, Hercules, and others recognize the important

position of Argos in those times. The invading Dorians brought in new blood, and in the eighth and seventh centuries Argos, enjoying power and prosperity under landed aristocracy based on agriculture, dominated the Argolid. Tradition holds that the historically momentous introduction of coined money into Greece in this period was accomplished by a certain King Pheidon, possibly the one who ruled Argos.

The great power of the city was broken by Sparta in the sixth century, and thenceforth it played only an auxiliary role in Greek history. In the fifth and fourth centuries it was neutral or favored Athens in the wasting struggle with Sparta; in Hellenistic times it was important to the warring parties for its strategic position on a main route into the heart of the Peloponnesus. Under the Romans it was quietly and moderately prosperous. During the Middle Ages its political position improved, and the fortifications on Larisa were powerfully rebuilt. In the late years of Turkish rule, a colony of Albanians was settled in the land, and in the War of Independence in the 1820's Argos was a center of revolutionary activity.

Between 1902 and 1930 investigations of the Classical remains at Argos were carried on for the French Archaeological School by the Dutch archaeologist C. W. Vollgraf. Vollgraf examined a sanctuary of Apollo and Athena on the Aspis, remains of civic buildings in the town, and a theatre and the Mycenaean remains on the Larisa. The American School of Classical Studies excavated more important ruins at the Argive Heraeum, the great sanctuary of Hera, about five miles to the northeast. Sir Charles Waldstein largely cleared the sanctuary itself in 1892-1895, and in 1925-1928 Carl W. Blegen studied prehistoric tombs on the near-by Prosymna Hill. The sanctuary spread over three terraces: on the highest was an early archaic Doric temple, destroyed by fire in 423 B.C.; on the second was its successor, a Doric temple richly ornamented with sculptures on the pediments and metopes, and this temple contained the gold-and-ivory statue of Hera by Polycleitus, ranked by the ancients among the finest works of Greek sculpture. Facing the temple was a colonnaded hall of uncommon form; at the side were stoas. A building behind was possibly the residence of the priestesses; beyond this were a Greek gymnasium and a Roman bath. An unusual feature of the ensemble is a grand staircase from the lowest to the middle terrace, surmounted by a great stoa. The Argive Heraeum was the most important center for the worship of Hera in the ancient world. R. L. S.

ARGUEDAS, ALCIDES [ɑrge'dɑs] (1879-1946), Bolivian historian, novelist, sociologist, and statesman, was born in La Paz, July 15, 1879. Arguedas was educated at the Colegio Nacional, the University of La Paz, and the Collège Libre des Sciences Sociales in Paris. His political career included posts as secretary of the Bolivian Legation in Paris in 1910 and in London in 1914; as national deputy in 1916; consul general in Paris, 1925; and minister plenipotentiary to Colombia, 1929-1930. He ventured into the field of journalism at the age of twenty. As a writer he was a follower of the Generation of '98 in Spain—always struggling to point out evils and bring about their reform. His greatest historical work is his *Historia general de Bolivia*, a critical study of Bolivian national life, published in 1922. Another important work is a sociological analysis of his country entitled *Pueblo enfermo*. His novels include *Raza de Bronce,* which pictures the life of the Aymara Indian. Arguedas was a member of the Bolivian Academy of Letters, and chairman of the Liberal Party. He died in Chulumani, May 6, 1946. S. G. I.

ARGUS [ɑ'rgəs], in Greek mythology, a name variously applied. The most familiar Argus was the hundred-eyed guardian appointed by Hera to watch Io after the latter's transformation into a heifer; charmed to sleep by Hermes, he was slain and his eyes became ornaments on the tail of the peacock, the bird of Hera. Another Argus was the son of Phrixus and builder of the *Argo*, the ship of the Argonauts. Odysseus' dog, who recognized his master upon his return to Ithaca after an absence of twenty years and then died of joy, was also called Argus. *See also* Io; Jason. G. E. D.

ARGYLL [ɑrgai'l], a maritime county, or shire, in the central part of western Scotland. The second largest Scottish county, Argyll is bounded by the counties of Inverness on the north; Perth, Dumbarton, and the Firth of Clyde on the east; the North Channel on the south; and the Atlantic Ocean on the west. It includes nearly all the Inner Hebrides, and the mainland extends from the Firth of Clyde to Inverness-shire. Numerous inlets of the sea extend inland to form a ragged series of peninsulas. Argyll reaches to within 20 mi. of the Irish Sea. The surface is nearly all mountainous, and Ben More and Jura are the highest island peaks, while Ben Cruachan is the highest inland peak. Herring fishing and sheep grazing are the chief occupations. Slate is extensively quarried and exported. There are large distilleries in Islay and Campbelltown. The county sends one member to Parliament. Pop. 1952, 61,487. S. Van V.

ARHUACO. *See* Indian Tribes, South American.

ÅRHUS [ɔ'rhus], the principal port of Jutland and the second largest city of Denmark, located in eastern Jutland on the Kattegat, 100 mi. west of Copenhagen, on an open bay, Århus Bugt, at the mouth of the Århus River, in a region of rolling glacial deposits and moraines. The surrounding scenes are considered among the most beautiful in Denmark, having many lakes and extensive forests. Near by is the 500-ft. Himmelbjerg, one of the highest points in Denmark. The city was a bishopric (now Lutheran) as early as 948, and its cathedral, the longest in Scandinavia, dates from the thirteenth century. The Old Town, an open-air museum near Århus, contains many medieval buildings. The king's summer palace, Marelisborg, is close to the city, as is Kal Castle, the scene of the imprisonment of Gustavus Vasa. The city manufactures chiefly metal goods; there is also a large vegetable-oil and margarine factory. Århus exports large quantities of agricultural products. Pop. 1953, 118,232. J. E. V.

ARI, THE LEARNED. *See* Thorgilsson, Ari.

ARIA, a solo song composed to a given text and sufficiently long to allow considerable development of the musical ideas. The perfected musical form in an aria is considered more important than close adherence to the meter of the poetry or detailed reflection of the sense of the words. It is the amplitude of its musical structure and the frequent requirement of the more spectacular sorts of vocal skill which distinguish the aria from such types of song as the air, chanson, or lied. Most arias occur in operas, oratorios, or cantatas, where as a rule they stand in contrast to recitative. They may be accompanied either by a single instrument or, more commonly, by an orchestra.

In form, an aria may follow any desired musical scheme. A favorite is the *da capo* aria, consisting of a first section followed by a shorter and less elaborate part somewhat contrasting in mood, after which the first section is repeated from the beginning (*da capo*), sometimes with added embellishments. This was the standard form for arias in the eighteenth century, the golden age of solo singing, though within this prevailing pattern many modifications and subtypes were distinguished. In the seventeenth century the word aria was used to designate simple stanzaic songs as well as others of many different musical styles and forms. It was also used occasionally for instrumental pieces in dance rhythms, especially in ballets and suites of the early eighteenth century. In the course of the nineteenth century the aria gradually lost its earlier distinct outlines until in the later music dramas of Wagner it was completely absorbed into a kind of irregularly rhythmed, variegated vocal line intimately attached to the text and forming with the orchestra an integral part of the whole musical texture. Recently composers have shown a tendency to return to the more formal, distinct aria of classical times, though in freer structural patterns and in a modern musical idiom. D. J. G.

ARIADNE [æriæ'dni], in Greek mythology, the daughter of Minos, king of Crete, and Pasiphae. Ariadne fell in love with Theseus when he came to Crete to slay the Minotaur and gave him a thread to guide him through the labyrinth. After slaying the Minotaur, Theseus carried her off but abandoned her on Naxos where she later married Dionysus. Another version relates that she was slain at Naxos by Artemis. *See also* Minotaur. G. E. D.

ARIANISM [ε'əriənɪzəm], a heresy rejected by the Council of Nicaea, 325 A.D., named after Arius, presbyter of Alexandria. Of the person of Christ, Arius said that there was a time when He was not, thus denying his preexistence and

ARIADNE

making him a creature of consubstantial rather than of the same nature with, the unbegotten Creator. It is therefore called subordinationism, in that it represents Christ not as the mediator of creation, coequal and coeternal with God, but rather as a medium of creation, God's intermediary agent, the first created of all creatures yet not fully God. Christ is thus represented as a demigod, even though it is granted, in this view, that his personality is unique not merely in function but also in its supramundane nature, and even though it is recognized that he is spotless and sinless and is to be the final judge of the world. This heresy opens the door to polytheism and destroys the Christian Trinitarian monotheism. The view that it embraces constitutes a denial of God's true immanence in Christ, for it signifies that Christ works for God, but his work is not God's work of salvation, that he rules as God's tributary king, but is not God's personal ruling presence.

According to Arianism, since there was a time when Christ was not, God became Father only at the creation of the Son; the Logos, the Son of God, therefore, was created. Arius called the Logos the Wisdom of the Father, but he is not the immanent wisdom; he is only a created being who shares in God's immanent wisdom. Arius therefore believed in two wisdoms, and in all this he made the Logos a creature rather than the Creator. Since the nature of the creature is changeable, so is the Logos, but God perceived by foreknowledge that he would merit goodness and made him spotless. The similarity between the view of Arius and that of Dynamistic Monarchianism lies in the fact that what the latter taught of Jesus as a man, the former taught of him as an intermediary being. Arianism is therefore a form of heretical Monarchianism; it is a denial of Trinitarian Christianity in favor of a one-person God.

The greatest Church opponent of Arianism was Athanasius, who set himself against its subordinationism and maintained the consubstantial deity of Christ with the Father, rejecting the idea that Christ is like the Father (homoiousion) only in will, energy, name, and wisdom. For Athanasius the salvation of man was endangered by this heresy. Only in the deity of Christ could he find a firm basis for our salvation. *See also* ARIUS; NICAEA, COUNCILS OF.   F. Br.

ARICA [ar'ka], the most northerly port in Chile, in Tarapaca Province, located about 375 mi. north of Antofagasta and about 39 mi. south of Tacna. The ownership of

the city was the subject of much dispute between Peru and Chile, until 1928, when the port was awarded to Chile. The "Morro de Arica," on the south side of the harbor is a historical landmark of a battle which occurred during the war against Peru and Bolivia in 1880. Built at the foot of the 400-foot *morro* (headland), with the Andes often clearly in view, Arica has become a popular resort. There is no rain in summer or winter, and water must be brought down from the mountains. The port owes its importance to its site as Bolivia's nearest outlet to the Pacific; from it are shipped Bolivian borax, tin, wolfram, antimony, sulphur, copper, hides, and agricultural produce. The Azapa Valley, which it serves, is fertile and is known particularly for its oranges and bananas. In the city itself, tropical fruits are grown. Rail and air facilities connect the city with Tacna, Peru, and Bolivia. Pop. (est. 1949), 15,000.   S.G.I.

ARIDED. *See* DENEB.

ARIÈGE [a'riɛ'zh], a department in southern France, bounded by the departments of Haute-Garonne on the north and west, Aude on the northeast, Pyrénées-Orientales on the southeast, and Andorra and Spain on the south, with an area of 1,890 sq. mi. The department is mountainous, the chief summits being the Pic d'Estax, 10,302 ft., and the Montcalm, 10,102 ft. Branches of the Pyrénées Mountains extending east-west separate the department into two valleys, watered by the Ariège and Salat rivers. The climate is mild and temperate in the north, but has extremely cold winters and oppressively hot summers in the mountains. The northern part has fertile soil, on which grain, forage plants, fruits and vegetables, and grapes are grown. In the forests and pastures of the southern mountains, cattle, horses, sheep, and goats are raised. There are rich iron mines and iron works. Marble, gypsum, slate, and talc are quarried, and coal is mined. In the Touyre Valley wool spinning is an industry. The factories of the Hers Valley are important centers for making horn products. The principal exports of the department are horn combs, woolen cloth, talc, and marble. Foix, at the confluence of the Ariège and Arget rivers, was the capital of the Counts of Foix in the Middle Ages, and their ruined castle, partly twelfth century and partly fourteenth century, dominates the town. The mineral springs of Ax-les-Thermes were known to the Romans; Audinac and Aulus also have mineral springs. St. Girons, at the confluence of the Salat and Baup rivers, is an industrial town. Pamiers, on the Ariège, is noted for its iron foundries. Prehistoric relics have been found in a cave near Mas -d'Azil, which is ¼ mi. long and 160 to 260 ft. high. Ariège is formed from the province of Foix, and part of Languedoc. Pop. 1954, 140,010.   S. Van. V.

ARIES [ɛ'əriiz], the Ram, a zodiacal constellation located somewhat north of the celestial equator and centered at right ascension 2.5 hr. Its symbol ♈ forms the first sign of the zodiac, which the sun enters about March 21. In the second century B.C., the sun, at the beginning of spring, was viewed as among the stars of "the First of Aries," or its western part. Precession has since moved this equinoctial point about 30° westward into Pisces; but astrologers and some others still speak of this new position as the Sign of Aries. This constellation contains no stars brighter than the second magnitude, but a little triangle composed of the brightest stars in the constellation attracts instant attention.

In Greek mythology, Aries was the Ram with the Golden Fleece which carried the royal children, Phrixis and Helle, away from the fury of their stepmother. After the sacrifice of the Ram, the Argonautic expedition was organized to recover its Golden Fleece.   J. H. P.

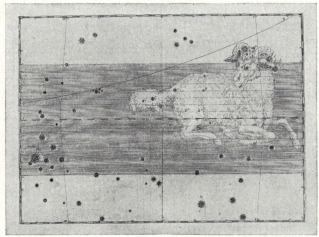

AMERICAN MUSEUM OF NATURAL HISTORY
ARIES, THE RAM

ARIKARA. *See* Indian Tribes, North American.
ARIOSO. *See* Musical Terms.

ARIOSTO, LODOVICO [a'rɪɔ'sto] (1474-1533), Italian Renaissance poet, was born in Reggio, Sept. 8, 1474, and spent most of his life in Ferrara. In 1500 the death of his father left him to care for nine younger brothers and sisters, and he presently entered the service of the Este family. Here, for more than a year, he was in charge of the garrison of Canossa, a part of the Este domain, but in 1503, he assumed, in the service of Cardinal Ippolito d'Este and of Duke Alfonso, a more responsible position, which entailed various journeys to Rome for negotiations with Popes Julius II and Leo X. He also embarked upon his literary career at about this time and in 1508 produced at the court of Ferrara his comedy entitled *La Cassaria.* This he followed in 1509 with his *I Suppositi,* which was performed also in Rome before Leo X in 1519, and with his other comedies, *Il Negromante* (1520), *La Lena* (1529), and the unfinished *Gli Studenti.* Ariosto's love for Alessandra Benucci, whom he married late in life, dates from about 1513, but his son Virginio, born in 1509 and legitimized about 1530, was the child of Orsolina Sassomarino. In 1519 the Duke of Ferrara laid claim to property that Ariosto expected to inherit from his uncle Rinaldo, and this action prolonged the poet's financial difficulties to the end of his life. From 1522 to 1525 Ariosto was Commissario in the Garfagnana, an Este possession at the headwaters of the Serchio. He died at Ferrara, June 6, 1533.

Much of Ariosto's early verse is in Latin, but his greatest work, the *Orlando furioso,* is in Italian, and his composition of this masterpiece occupied much of his literary energy during his later years. From the various editions of the work itself, from autograph manuscripts of the material he added for an edition of 1532, and from various letters, it is possible to give some indication of just how the work was composed. When Ariosto started work on the material in 1504, he seems to have intended no more than a continuation of Boiardo's *Orlando innamorato,* and there is no indication that the *Furioso* was independently conceived, or even given a name, until its first printing. Between 1504 and 1516 he composed nearly forty cantos, in addition to much else that he reserved for publication later, but in the midst of the final

canto he seems to have come to a point beyond which he could not satisfy himself. Consequently, when he acceded to the demands of influential friends to publish the work, he devised a conclusion that was only temporary and permitted publication of the first edition in 1516.

During the five years before a second edition appeared, Ariosto made numerous minor revisions in his work, changing some of the locutions from Ferrarese into Tuscan and making a number of strictly poetical changes. These revisions were not drastic, however, or even consistent, for many non-Tuscan forms were retained and new ones added, and indeed most of the cantos of the second edition correspond, stanza by stanza, to those of the first. After 1521, the revisions became more extensive. Six cantos were added in the third edition of 1532, partly composed of material rejected for the 1516 edition, and five further cantos were published after Ariosto's death. The poem as a whole, then, is unfinished, yet it does not seem incomplete, and its incidents are woven together with extraordinary skill. The old charge of confusion which has been advanced against the work is the result of hasty reading and of a demand for an Aristotelian unity that Ariosto never intended.

Ariosto did not attempt to print his lesser works, and such comedies as were published during his lifetime were unauthorized. The *Satires,* which are sometimes surprisingly frank in their comments on great men, were perhaps intended only for circulation in manuscript. The *Orlando furioso*

LODOVICO ARIOSTO

was clearly Ariosto's chief concern, and to it most of his career was devoted. He did not hesitate to borrow from his own minor works to improve his masterpiece, and from his lyric poetry, especially, much was taken over into the *Furioso.* In one instance he converted an entire poem from terza rima to octaves for this purpose, and his unpublished verse in general served as a store of material upon which he drew for use in the poem that formed the center of his life. *See also* Orlando Furioso.   A. H. G.

ARIOVISTUS (fl. 71-58 B.C.), German chieftain, king of the Suebi, who crossed the Rhine into Gaul about 71 B.C. to aid the Sequanians against the Aeduans, the leading tribe of the Gauls. Ariovistus then brought in more Germans and defeated an attempt of the Gauls to drive him back into Germany. Julius Caesar, appealed to by the Gallic tribes, defeated the Suebi under Ariovistus in 58 B.C. near Vesontio (modern Besançon) and thus brought security to the Gauls along the middle and upper Rhine.   G. E. D.

ARISTARCHUS OF SAMOS [æ'rɪstɑ'rkəs], Greek philosopher, mathematician, and astronomer, flourished in Alexandria, roughly from 280 to 264 B.C. He is said to have been the first to hold the theory that the earth moves around the sun, and because of this belief he was accused of impiety by Cleanthes (c. 300–c. 220 B.C.), a Stoic philosopher. His only surviving work, a discourse called *On the Magnitudes and Distances of the Sun and the Moon,* with a commentary by Pappus, sets forth a geometrically correct method of estimating the relative distances of the sun and the moon. The results, however, are incorrect because of the primitive instruments with which Aristarchus worked. Aristarchus' heliocentric theory is not mentioned in this treatise, but there is a reference to it in the *Arenarius* of Archimedes (c. 287–212 B.C.), which suggests that his work anticipated that of Copernicus.   R. F.

ARISTEAS [æ'rɪsti'əs], mythical ancient Greek poet and teacher of Homer. The island of Proconnesus was credited with being Aristeas' birthplace, though this, together with his life and works, are matters of legend. He was a poet, possibly a contemporary of Cyrus, and widely traveled. According to Herodotus and others, he could perform such wonders as causing his soul to leave his body at will. Aristeas appeared at different periods in the history of ancient Greece: as a predecessor of Homer (ninth century B.C.); as his teacher; and later as the author of the poem *Arimaspeia,* fragments of which were preserved in the works of Longinus and Tzetzes, though Aristeas' authorship was denied even by the ancient Greeks themselves. More than three centuries after the appearance of that work he was reported to have founded a city in southern Italy. Aristeas was regarded as the favorite of Apollo.   E. B. A.

ARISTIDES [æ'rɪstai'diz] (c.530–468 B.C.), Athenian statesman and general, was born about 530 B.C. He was one of the Athenian commanders who defeated the Persians at the Battle of Marathon in 490 B.C. As a political opponent of Themistocles, Aristides favored the building of a strong army at Athens instead of the big navy which Themistocles successfully advocated. When the policy of Themistocles finally received popular approval, Aristides was ostracized, in 483 B.C. He was recalled from exile in 480 B.C. during the Persian invasion crisis, when he participated in the Battle of Salamis and commanded a squadron in the continuing naval warfare against the Persians. As the Greek allies turned from Spartan to Athenian leadership in 477 B.C., Aristides shared with Themistocles the honor of forming the Delian League. It was a sincere compliment to the integrity of Aristides that the allies accorded him the task of fixing the annual assessment of member-state ships and funds which members were to pay for the maintenance of the league. Aristides' equitable settlement of these matters gained for him the title, the Just, by which he is still remembered. He died in poverty in 468 B.C., and was buried at Phalerum.   T. B. J.

ARISTOCRACY, etymologically, a word meaning rule by the best. To the Greeks, who invented the term, it meant rule by a noble class, presumably superior to the majority of their fellow citizens. According to Plato, aristocracy was the rule of men distinguished by their virtue and the contribution they could make to the welfare of the state. In Aristotle's classification aristocracy was a good form of government, the rule by the able and unselfish minority, in contrast to rule by a selfish minority, which he considered a perverted form of government and called oligarchy. In modern usage, aristocracy has come to mean rule by persons possessing special privileges before the law and able to pass on their authority to their children. It also refers to the class of persons so privileged.   E. P. C.

ARISTOLOCHIA [ærɪstələ'kiə], a large genus of the birthwort family, widely distributed in warm regions. Some are native to the United States, many to South America. Most are woody climbers. The flowers have strangely bent calyx tubes that imprison pollinating insects. The pelican-flower, *A. grandiflora,* has a variety, *sturtevanti,* with flowers often 20 in. across. The Dutchman's pipe, *A. durior,* with big heart-shaped leaves and small, inconspicuous, but curious flowers, is much planted for its heavy foliage. J. C. Wis.

ARISTOPHANES [æ'rɪstɒ'fəniz], a Greek comic poet of the fifth century B.C., the greatest and only representative of Old Attic Comedy whose works are still extant. He was born probably not long after 450 B.C., since he tells us that he was very young when he produced his first play (427 B.C.). There is some question as to whether he was of pure Attic parentage; certain ancient evidence connects him with Aegina, and he was once accused of being of foreign extraction. But all his life he felt and wrote as a true Athenian citizen. Brought up in the stimulating atmosphere of the Periclean Age, he reflects in his comedies the wide versatility and keen intellectual curiosity of the typical fifth-century Athenian. As a youth he saw the outbreak of the fatal Peloponnesian War (431–404 B.C.), which was to end in the destruction of the Athenian Empire and the fall of the Periclean democracy. His first play was produced in the name of Callistratus, an experienced playwright or actor-manager; several of his later plays were also produced through others, but the reasons are unknown. He won his first victory in dramatic competition at the Lenaean festival of 425 B.C. with *The Acharnians* and thereafter was one of the most successful comic poets at Athens. His literary

ARISTOPHANES

career continued uninterrupted until his death shortly after 385 B.C. There is almost no evidence concerning his private life. We know that he was married and had two or three sons, one of whom, Araros, followed his father's career as a comic writer.

Works. Eleven plays remain in existence out of forty-four known in antiquity. The poet-dramatist's literary activity may be divided into the following periods:

Early Period. From 427 to 421 B.C. Aristophanes devoted

himself largely to political satire. The extant plays of this period, with dates of production, are *The Acharnians*, 425; *The Knights*, 424; *The Clouds*, 423; *The Wasps*, 422; and *Peace*, 421. All of these plays except *The Clouds* were directly concerned with the political situation; in particular, they bitterly attacked the demagogues of the radical faction, the Athenian jury-system and passion for litigation, and above all the war with Sparta. The period ends with the Peace of Nicias, which the comedy *Peace* was written to celebrate.

Middle Period. From 420 to 404 B.C. Aristophanes wrote mainly plays of fantasy and literary criticism. Examples are *The Birds*, 414; *Lysistrata*, 411; *Thesmophoriazusae*, 410; and *The Frogs*, 405. *Lysistrata*, with its eloquent and amusing plea for peace, is an exception to the prevailing tone of these plays. In general, Aristophanes occupied himself with fantasies like the Utopia in mid-air of *The Birds* or with parody and criticism of Euripides.

Late Period. This period, which lasted from 404 to 385 B.C., contains broad social comedy, with less direct and personal satire. The *Ecclesiazusae* (Women in Parliament), written in 393, satirizes some of the communistic social orders proposed by certain contemporary philosophers, while the *Plutus* (388) exhibits the results of restoring the sight of the blind god of wealth. With this play Greek comedy enters the period known as Middle Comedy.

Nature and Structure. The plays of Aristophanes were written in terms of the contemporary political life of Athens. The scene is usually set in Athens, the time is the present, and references to contemporary figures and events abound. The themes are usually drawn from the current life of the city. On this solid basis of reality Aristophanes then builds plots that are improbable and fantastic: characters fly to heaven on a beetle or descend to the Underworld. The indecency and the lusty, Rabelaisian humor which form so large an element in the plays are perhaps survivals of primitive fertility ritual; but doubtless Aristophanes and his audience took conscious pleasure in an indecent joke for its own sake.

The earlier plays exhibit certain features of form and structure characteristic of Old Attic Comedy. The prologue, which is regularly in iambic trimeters, sets forth the idea or principle which the comedy is to study; the leading character, who often embodies this principle, conceives some daring, fantastic plan which he tries to carry out. In this attempt he comes into violent conflict either with the chorus or some other character who represents the opposing principle. There follows a series of closely connected scenes in longer meters, interspersed with lyric songs of the chorus. This series consists of (1) the *parodos*, the entrance of the chorus in rapid, violent evolutions, often leading to a physical attack on the characters; (2) the *agon*, a static scene of formal debate, which usually leads to the victory of one of the opposing principles; and (3) the *parabasis*, a nondramatic address to the audience made by the chorus and its leader. The subject matter is often praise of the poet and satiric political comments. The second half of the play usually consists of loosely connected scenes of a farcical nature, designed to exhibit the results of the victorious principle in action. A favorite motif is the introduction of a series of intruders who try to secure the benefits of the new order for themselves. The final scene, or *exodos*, usually contains revelry, with song and dance.

These elements appear in almost all the comedies, but by no means in a rigid order or without variation. The *agon* may be postponed until the second half, or the issue left undecided; in either case the dramatic suspense is increased, and the farcical scenes of the second half continue the development of the plot. In the later plays the *parabasis* becomes dramatic, i.e., spoken in character throughout, and is integrated into the action. In general, however, Aristophanes is careful neither of probability nor dramatic illusion; characters enter or leave and events succeed each other at the whim of the playwright, and the characters address the audience directly, bringing them into the dramatic situation. The unity of the plays depends not so much on the unity of a single action as on the unifying effect of a single controlling idea, to which all the events and episodes are related.

Thought. Aristophanes, like all great comic writers, tends to represent the feelings of the average man of good sense against the pretensions of various charlatans, imposters, and eccentrics who set themselves apart from or above the common man. Hence his comedies present an instinctively conservative point of view. In politics he attacked all the leading statesmen of the democratic faction, and in general the plays recommend a return to the political situation of Greece before the development of the full, radical democracy under Pericles. Aristophanes particularly criticized the use of state funds to pay the citizens for their services to the state, such as serving on juries or on embassies; and he deplored the dependence of the citizen-body during the war years on these state jobs. He also urged a more generous treatment of Athens' allies and a united front of the Greeks against the common enemy, Persia. In education and literature he satirized the tendencies of the sophists, the rationalism and realism of later tragedy as represented by Euripides, and the high-flown, unconventional style and music of the new school of dithyrambic poetry. Aristophanes took an earnest and serious view of literature and art, stressing mainly their moral and didactic functions. From this point of view, his last extended attack on Euripides in *The Frogs* was based on his feeling that Euripides had lessened the dignity and moral value of tragedy. *See also* BIRDS, THE; CLOUDS, THE; FROGS, THE; LYSISTRATA.

C. T. M.

ARISTOPHANES OF BYZANTIUM (c.260-c.180 B.C.), Greek critic and grammarian, lived for most of his life at Alexandria. There, in about 200 B.C., he became librarian of the Museum, the great library established by Ptolemy I. In this post he produced critical editions of Homer and Hesiod, of the chief lyric, comic, and tragic poets, and of Plato. Of these, only his arguments, or plot summaries, to the plays of Aristophanes and the tragic poets survive. Aristophanes also wrote on miscellaneous subjects suggested by his study of comedy, such as proverbs, masks, and Athenian courtesans. As a grammarian, he compiled collections of unusual words and introduced many used in textual criticism. As a scholar, he is notable for his work in establishing the Alexandrian "canon" of outstanding authors.   G. McL. H.

ARISTOTLE [ǽrīstŏ'təl] (c.384-322 B.C.), Greek teacher and philosopher, was born at Stagira in 384 or 383 B.C. and died at Chalcis in 322 B.C. He studied almost twenty years at Plato's Academy and probably taught there for some years. After leaving the Academy, he was the tutor of Alexander the Great, before the young Macedonian prince embarked on his campaign of world conquest. As founder of the Lyceum at Athens, which continued many centuries after his death, Aristotle made an important contribution to education in the ancient world. He planned and organized far-reaching projects of empirical research, supported by Alexander and carried out by himself and his students, which led to many basic discoveries in the fields of the natural sciences. But his greatest achievements lay in the field of philosophy. Developing Platonic thought along new lines, he formulated certain basic concepts and principles of realistic philosophy which have played a peculiarly important role in the history of Western culture.

The Life of Aristotle. Aristotle's father was a doctor of Stagira, the personal physician of King Amyntas II in near-by Macedonia. After the early death of his parents, Aristotle was brought up by a relative, Proxenus, in Atarnea.

ARISTOTLE

At the age of eighteen, he went to Athens and joined Plato's Academy, where he remained for almost twenty years until Plato's death in 347 B.C. During this time, he gained an exact knowledge of Platonic philosophy, its Socratic and pre-Socratic roots, and many related disciplines. There is good evidence for the belief that he taught rhetoric at the school, and possibly other subjects as well. During this period, he wrote several dialogues defending Platonic philosophy in a popular style adapted to a wide public. It is probable that the logical works, the *Physics,* and portions of the treatise on the soul (*De anima*) were also written at this time.

There is no foundation for the widespread legend that there was a deep tension and possibly even an open break between Aristotle and Plato during the latter's lifetime. Even after Plato's death, Aristotle considered himself to be a Platonist. In a moving passage of the *Nicomachean Ethics,* written much later in the full maturity of his thought, he expresses a deep sense of friendship and obligation to Plato and his students.

About 348-347 B.C., however, Speusippus was chosen as Plato's successor. Many members of the Academy, including Aristotle, disapproved of this decision, and with his friend, Xenocrates, he left the Academy to join a small Platonic circle that had been gathered together by Hermias, the ruler of Assus, a small city in Asia Minor. Here, and a little later at Mytilene, on the island of Lesbos, he engaged in teaching and research. Criticizing the doctrines of Speusippus, he began to work out an interpretation of Plato which, he thought, would be truer to the mature philosophy of his teacher as well as to the facts of nature. He now became more closely associated with Hermias and through him brought his philosophy to bear upon concrete politics, in accordance with the basic, practical interest of Platonism.

Hermias was a political ally of King Philip of Macedonia, the father of Alexander. It was probably through this connection that Aristotle was invited in the year 343-342 to become the tutor of the young prince, then thirteen years of age. He accepted this offer and moved to the Macedonian capital, where, in accordance with the life and teachings of Plato, Aristotle made the most of all opportunities to bring philosophy to bear upon the concrete exercise of political power. Very little is known of the intimate relationship between these two men. From the evidence we have, it is probable that Aristotle recognized the tragic separation of the small Greek city-states and the desperate need for political union, but he probably disapproved of Alexander's vast schemes of world conquest. So when Alexander ascended the throne in 336 B.C., Aristotle returned to his home in Stagira and after a year was drawn back to Athens.

Though he still felt himself to be a Platonist, his thought had now developed in a new direction, definitely opposed to that of Plato's successors and to certain aspects of Platonism. These criticisms were expressed in the dialogue *On Philosophy* and in the earliest portions of the works we now know as the *Metaphysics,* the *Ethics,* and the *Politics.* Feeling his own thought to be moving in a direction opposed to current Academic teaching, he founded a new school, the Lyceum, in the northeast part of Athens. Like the Academy, this school was devoted not only to teaching but also to independent investigation and research. Here Aristotle gathered around him a group of able students and assistants and guided them in a most intensive and far-reaching program of co-operative philosophical and scientific activity. This lasted for twelve years and was the climax of the master's career.

The results of these co-operative investigations were extraordinarily fruitful. Aided by specimens and information gathered by assistants who accompanied Alexander on his distant expeditions, Aristotle and his school made many important observations and discoveries, which left a lasting mark on the history of many sciences and laid new foundations for others. But the leader of the school devoted even more attention to the underlying disciplines of philosophy. Most of the philosophical writings by Aristotle that we now possess were composed during this period.

At the sudden death of Alexander in 323 B.C., a surge of anti-Macedonian sentiment swept through Athens and the other Greek cities. Aristotle's friendship with Philip and Alexander, as well as his expressed political convictions, which were not in sympathy with the intense patriotism of the local city-state, endangered his status. Threatened with prosecution, he left the city in order to keep the Athenians, as he put it, from sinning a second time against philosophy. He went to Chalcis on the island of Euboea, where he possessed some inherited property, and died there after a brief illness in 322 B.C.

The Aristotelian Writings. The writings of Aristotle fall into two sharply differentiated groups. First, there are the popular or exoteric works, most of them probably in dialogue form, and intended for a large reading public. These were composed for the most part during the period when Aristotle was a student at the Academy. They survive at present only in the form of fragments quoted by later authors, and even their titles convey the intimate tang of Platonism. They include the *Eudemus* or *On the Soul,* a dialogue *On Justice,* the *Statesman,* the *Sophist,* the *Menexenus,* and the *Symposium.* In addition, there is the *Protrepticus,* an exhortation to philosophy, well known in ancient times, which was modeled after a certain portion of

ARISTOTLE AND HIS PUPIL,
ALEXANDER THE GREAT

Plato's *Euthydemus* and in turn became the model for Cicero's *Hortensius,* which, as St. Augustine says in his *Confessions,* aroused him from his dogmatic slumber, and changed the whole course of his career by turning him to philosophy. We also possess a few fragments of another popular work, *On Philosophy,* which was written later, during the second stage of Aristotle's development at Assus. These works are all written in a simple style with great care for literary expression. They were widely read in ancient times and established Aristotle's reputation as a Platonic author of great fervor and eloquence, a reputation very difficult to understand, since the writings we possess belong to a very different category and were not meant to be widely read. They were meant to be heard by Aristotle's students and assistants, first the smaller group at Assus, and then the larger group at the Lyceum in Athens. Modern historical scholarship, particularly the work of Werner Jaeger, has now made it clear that these writings, as they now survive, are not philosophical and scientific "works," in the sense which this word conveys to us today. Their precise mode of origin cannot of course be established beyond all doubt, but the following is the most probable theory of their nature.

Aristotle certainly gave regular lectures on a wide variety of topics to students and associates. These lectures were often repeated from year to year. Apparently Aristotle was in the habit of composing written versions, which he read to a specially trained audience, often with extemporaneous explanations and comments. These written lectures were circulated in the school and used for individual study. What we now possess as a supposed single work on a single topic is rather a collection of many different written lectures on this topic, often covering a considerable span of time. These versions were pieced together into single works by later editors. In some cases, it is probable that portions of a single text may be notes taken down by listeners, or original Aristotelian lectures, revised and edited by students. There is no reason to doubt, however, that the greater part of this literature was originally written by Aristotle himself to be heard or read by a well-trained group of those co-operating with him in

the great research program of the Lyceum. This explains the difficulty which the modern reader faces when he plunges into the translations of these works. For they are full of unexplained, technical terms and abbreviations well known to a trained student, but unfamiliar to a modern reader, and they often represent several different versions of one topic, written during an interval in which Aristotle's thought was developing; this leads to many apparent inconsistencies. Then, too, these versions were often pieced together in an arbitrary and artificial manner by later editors, having little understanding of their original nature and purpose. And, finally, the original texts were probably badly damaged during the period of the Roman civil wars and may owe their survival only to a queer accident of fate. As a result, the process of reconstructing the original texts, undertaken by the later Roman editors, was a task of great difficulty, subject to many errors and confusions. Nevertheless, it has been possible, by patient philosophical study, to recover the basic Aristotelian doctrines and the general drift of his thought.

From the standpoint of subject matter, the writings fall into four major groups. First, there are the logical treatises now commonly referred to as the *Organon.* These include the *Categories,* the *De interpretatione,* the *Prior* and *Posterior Analytics,* and the *Topics.*

Second, there are the writings on natural philosophy and science. The most important of these are the treatise *On Coming Into Being and Passing Away,* the *De caelo,* the *Physics, De historia animalium, De partibus animalium, De generatione animalium,* and the *De anima* on human nature. Aristotle himself wrote no treatise on plants, but such a work was undertaken by his student, Theophrastus.

Third, there is the collection now known as the *Metaphysics.* Aristotle did not use this title, but referred to the field as that of "first philosophy." The *Metaphysics* is a set of lectures written by him during the late development of his thought at Assus and during his final period at Athens.

Fourth, there are the works on ethics and politics, to which the *Poetics* and the *Rhetoric* are subordinated. The most important of these are the *Eudemian Ethics,* composed during the second period; the *Nicomachean Ethics,* during the last Athenian period; the *Politics,* consisting of different lectures written over a long period of time; the *Rhetoric;* and the fragmentary *Poetics.* Except for his account of the Athenian Constitution, Aristotle's great work on *City Constitutions* and several historical treatises have been lost.

The Philosophy of Aristotle. Aristotle does not mention logic as a definite part of philosophy. He conceives of it as a methodological instrument involved in all science and philosophy rather than as a philosophical doctrine. Hence the later concept of "tool" (*organon*), though not used by Aristotle himself, is probably true to his own thought. Its consideration clearly belongs at the beginning. Aristotle divides philosophy itself into the theoretical part, concerned with the attainment of truth apart from all desire, and the practical part, concerned with reason and desire, working together for an understanding and attainment of the human good. Theoretical philosophy is divided into three parts: the study of changing being (physics and natural science, including the science of man); the study of abstract, mathematical being (the various branches of mathematics); and first philosophy, the study of being qua being (which we call metaphysics).

No special treatises by Aristotle on number and figure have survived, and the following discussion will be limited to the four branches: logic, the method of rational thought; physics, the theoretical study of changing being; first philosophy; and finally, practical philosophy. We shall consider these disciplines in this order, trying to indicate in each case the chief concepts and doctrines that can be culled from the texts as distinctively Aristotelian.

Aristotelian Logic. The logic of Aristotle is divided into three parts: (1) that concerning the basic modes of being that are apprehended by single concepts and definitions (cf. the *Categories*); (2) that concerning the union and separation of these modes of being that are expressed by the judgment (the *De Interpretatione*); and (3) that concerning the way in which the mind can pass by reasoning from truth that is known to truth that is unknown (the *Prior* and *Posterior Analytics*). For Aristotle, thought is not the construction or creation of some new entity by the mind, but rather the assimilation or apprehension of something external to the act of thought. The concept is an identification of the mind with some mode of being, and the judgment is an expression of the union of such modes in actual existence. Finally, the principles of demonstration, the law of contradiction, and that of excluded middle govern science in the deduction of true conclusions, because these principles actually govern all being.

The basic modes of being and the kinds of concepts corresponding to them are listed in the *Categories* and the *Topics* as ten in number: (1) substance, such as man or horse; (2) quantity, as three feet long; (3) quality, as grammatical; (4) relation, as greater than; (5) place, as in the Lyceum; (6) time, as yesterday; (7) situation, as sitting; (8) having, as being armed; (9) action, as cutting and burning; and (10) passion, as being cut or being burned. In the *Posterior Analytics,* however, and elsewhere, "situation" and "having" are omitted, and an eightfold list is given.

Extramental things really exist in these ways, as substances, qualities, quantities, relations, and so forth. The basic concepts, here enumerated, grasp each of these modes of being precisely as it is, but in a state of abstraction or isolation from the rest, with which it is always combined *in rerum natura.* Hence no single concept by itself is true or false. It is simply some mode of external existence grasped in abstraction.

Only the proposition, or judgment, not the isolated concept, is true or false. It uses the logical structure of subject and predicate to combine or to separate two categorical concepts. If the modes of being are actually combined or separated in this way, then the proposition is true. If not, it is false. Since the laws of contradiction and excluded middle hold of all existence, two such modes of being must be either united or not united, and any given predicate must be either truly assertible or truly deniable of any given subject.

All science is universal, but it has to be attained by induction from sense experience of the individual substance and its individual properties. Sometimes we may apprehend two kinds of being combined together in a given sense experience, but can discover no necessity in this connection. The proposition expressing such an accidental connection in a universal form is only probably true. The dialectical methods by which such probable opinions may be expanded, attacked, and defended are studied in the *Topics.* Science in the strict sense is something quite different. It is dealt with in the *Posterior Analytics.*

As soon as certain subjects and certain predicates are gained by induction from experience and clearly grasped, the mind is able to see that they are necessarily connected. This is true, for example, of the law of contradiction, which asserts that a given reality cannot at the same time, and in the same respect, both be and not be. As soon as we clearly grasp being and nonbeing, we see that they necessarily exclude one another. The premises of science in the strict sense are self-evident in this way and require no proof. The first step in the establishment of any true science is the discovery of such necessary connections, which are not purely accidental, and which are expressed in necessary propositions. Then further knowledge can be deduced from these evident principles by syllogistic reasoning.

This process is described and analyzed in the *Prior Analytics.* Deduction or demonstration is the means by which the mind passes from what is already known to what is unknown. This can happen only through the discovery of some middle term. Thus, suppose we wish to demonstrate that x is z, which is not self-evident. The only way this can be done is to discover two premises, x is y, and y is z, which are already known to be self-evident, or to be deducible from self-evident premises. If we know two such premises, involving the crucial, middle term y, then we can demonstrate the desired conclusion, not otherwise. Thus if we know that Socrates is human, and that being human is to be mortal, we can demonstrate that Socrates is mortal, through the middle term, human. The mind cannot rest until it understands that things are necessary in the sense that they cannot be otherwise. Hence the aim of all science is to attain such necessary knowledge.

The first step is a careful, inductive examination of the confused objects of sense that surround us, and the clear apprehension and definition of the kinds of being in which we are interested. The next step is the discovery of necessary connections between these entities. The final step is the deduction of further truths. If we find only accidental connections, these of course may be stated and deductively elaborated. But they will yield only probable conclusions, for such conclusions will be no stronger than the premises. Science depends upon the discovery of evident premises, which require no proof.

Natural Philosophy. The whole world of nature is characterized by a never-ending flux or change, and Aristotle's philosophy of nature is based upon an analysis of process. Every change is discontinuous. It begins with the absence of something that is acquired in the process. Thus, the building of a house begins with something unformed and ends with an ordered structure or form. Hence, an initial privation and a final form are necessarily involved in all change.

But change is also continuous, for we never observe something coming out of nothing. In order to explain this factor of continuity, Aristotle argues, as against Plato, that it is necessary to recognize the existence of a third factor that underlies the passage from privation to form. He calls this substratum, matter. In the case of the building of the house, this is the wood and other raw material. In the case of the making of a statue, it is the bronze that was present at the beginning in a privative state and that is still present underlying the finished form.

Aristotle distinguishes four kinds of change. The most fundamental is that in which a new substance, capable of existing in itself, comes into being. This can occur only through the destruction of some preceding substance or substances. Only the pure potency of matter underlies such change. But any material substance, once it is in existence, has a capacity for further changes in its attributes or accidents. These accidental changes fall into three types: (1) of quality, (2) of quantity, and (3) of place. The last is involved in all the other kinds of change. Every transformation is also measured by time, the number of change. Such a temporal measure requires a mind that can remember the past, anticipate the future, divide such intervals into parts, and compare them with one another.

Every natural entity that has emerged from the processes of change has two intrinsic causes on which its natural existence necessarily depends. These are the underlying matter (like the bronze of the statue) from which it evolved, and the specific form or structure that makes it the kind of being it is (like the shape of the finished statue). In addition to these intrinsic causes, matter and form, there must also be some extrinsic, efficient cause (like the movements of the sculptor), which impose the form on the matter. Finally, there must be an ultimate end (like the idea of the statue in the mind of the sculptor), which directs the efficient cause, or causes, to act in a certain, determinate way.

Change is the actualization of that which is potential; hence, nothing that moves can move itself. Every mobile being requires some extrinsic efficient cause to account for its origin and to sustain it in being. This is true of the physical universe as a whole, which Aristotle held to be everlastingly in motion. In order to explain this motion, it is necessary to recognize the existence of a first, unmoved mover, not subject to change. When the necessary effects of two or more independent causes coincide in the same matter, unpredictable chance events occur, but for the most part the events of nature follow a regular order, which makes natural science possible. This order and harmony, which holds for the most part throughout the world of nature, also leads to the conclusion that there is a stable and intelligent first cause.

In astronomy, Aristotle was of course deeply influenced by the prevailing scientific views of the time. He held that the earth is at the center of the physical cosmos. It is surrounded by revolving spheres, in terms of which the planetary motions are explained. The outermost sphere is that of the fixed stars. This is moved directly by an aspiration to the first unmoved cause, which, lacking all material potency and imperfection, is wholly immaterial and immobile in nature. Even the heavenly bodies are moving and, therefore, material, but they are made up of purer matter than that of the sublunar regions.

Different levels of material substance are found in these regions. First, there are the basic elements and their combinations, which make up the realm of nonliving substances. These are moved only by external causes. Then there are the living organisms, of which plants are first, possessing organically differentiated parts, which can act upon one another. Thus, plants are not merely increased and generated by external causes, but grow of themselves and reproduce themselves.

Animals exercise these vegetative functions, but they are also endowed with sense organs by which they are able to take account of things in the environment, seeking what is able to foster their activity and fleeing what is injurious. The higher material organisms are built up on the lower ones and probably emerge from them by a gradual process of change, though Aristotle is not altogether unambiguous on this point.

The highest earthly entity is man, and the whole treatise, *De anima,* is devoted to a study of his nature. Aristotle is quite clear that man is a material being and definitely a part of nature. Like all other natural entities, therefore, he is composed of an underlying matter from which he has emerged, the human body, and a certain form or structure animating it, the human soul. As in the case of any other natural entity, this form and this matter are not two things merely put in juxtaposition but two essential parts, each existing by virtue of the other, in one composite individual. Thus, the gold of the ring and its circular structure are not two things, but one gold ring. In the same way, the human soul and the human body are two essential, intrinsic causes of one single entity, or natural substance, the individual man.

Though it is one, the human soul, the form of man, is built up of three united parts. First, there is the vegetative part, which enables the human being to nourish himself, to grow, and to reproduce the species. Then there is the animal part, which enables him to sense, to desire sensory objects, and to move about from place to place like the other animals. Finally, built on these as the apex of human nature, there is the rational part, which enables man to perform those most extraordinary and distinctive functions which differentiate him from all the other animals. Each of these parts necessarily develops the essential accidents or faculties which it requires to activate itself. Thus, the vegetative soul is responsible for the different organs and faculties of nutrition, growth, and reproduction; the animal soul is responsible for the organs and faculties of sense and locomotion; and the rational soul is responsible for the nonphysical faculties of intellect and rational choice or will.

Knowing must not be confused with making. Cognition does not involve the construction of anything new, but rather the assimilation by the noetic faculty of something already in physical existence, precisely as it is. Forms exist physically in the individual matter, which restricts them to a certain place and time. Thus, the human form exists in this way in the matter of each individual human body. But through his cognitive faculties, a human being can assimilate the forms of such things without their matter. Thus, while remaining physically distinct from other material things, a man can noetically unite himself with them in a nonmaterial way, becoming a microcosm, reflecting the natures of all things within his fragile being on the mirrors of his mind.

Sense is restricted to a certain, limited range of forms and apprehends them only as they are confused together in a concrete, physical influence. But reason is not so restricted. It can apprehend any form whatsoever and can free its essence from everything else with which it is associated in sense experience. This act of rational insight, or abstraction, however, cannot be performed without the prior activity of sense and imagination.

When some particular sense experience is conjured up by the imagination, the active intellect can shine upon it like a light and illumine some nature, which is present in it, all alone by itself, freeing it from everything irrelevant to its essential nature. Reason can also illumine every other real element in the thing, impressing its pure, abstract species on the receptive intellect that is present in every man. Then, by making judgments, which combine these natures as they are actually combined, the intellect can build up a composite conception of the whole entity, precisely as it is. This rational faculty not only can gain a theoretical understanding of all things in this way; it can also work with human appetite in enabling men to perfect by action their original natures. In fact, without this rational guidance of appetite, human nature cannot perfect itself at all. The study of this process of perfection belongs to practical philosophy.

First Philosophy. First philosophy is the study of the first causes of things. The most basic reality, of which all else is a limited determination, is being itself. All the categories are restricted kinds of being; hence, Aristotle defines first philosophy as the study of being qua being. Physical science regards things so far as they are sensible and changing, but being does not have to be restricted in this way. Mathematical science regards things so far as they are quantitative, but being is not necessarily quantitative, and first philosophy is not restricted to any such limited object. It regards things so far as they are. Hence, all things whatsoever come within its purview, whether they be changing or nonchanging, and whether they be quantitative or nonquantitative. It is from this point of view alone that we can attain the clearest possible understanding of the most basic structure of the world.

Plato's followers, and Plato himself, in certain statements of his philosophy, had held that the ultimate causes of all things were to be found in certain ideas or abstract essences which existed apart from the changing things of the natural world. Aristotle subjects this view to a careful criticism and finally rejects it, asking why any such world should exist. It would be only a futile doubling of the world of individual substances, and the view that science knows such separate universals leads to skepticism, for then science will not know the individual entities of this world, which we need to know. For these and other reasons, Aristotle rejects the Platonic view that in addition to individual men and individual houses there is a universal man in himself, and a universal house in itself, which exist apart from their instances. But his criticism does not end in a mere negation. Like Plato, Aristotle still defends the existence of formal structures. But instead of inhabiting a separate world of their own, they exist materially in the individual things they determine. The form or essence of a thing dwells in the thing as its inherent nature, which brings it out of potency into definite act.

That which exists, the foundation of real existence, is, therefore, not an abstract essence but an individual substance, such as this tree or this man, and the core of Aristotle's treatise on metaphysics, Books VII, VIII, and IX, deals with this central topic. The individual, or primary substance, is a whole made up of matter and form, each of which makes its own contribution to the total, single entity. The matter acts as a substratum, giving the thing a place in the flux of nature. The form determines and actualizes the matter, making it an entity of a certain kind. When abstractly understood by the intellect, this form is the definition, or essence, of the substance, and it may be predicated of the primary substance. All the other categories, such as place,

time, action, quantity, quality, and relation inhere in primary substance as its accidents. They cannot exist in themselves but only in the substance which sustains them.

The word "being" has many senses. There is the being that things have as objects before the mind. Then there is the being that things have as existing *in rerum natura,* but this being also has its subdivisions, the most important of which is potential contrasted with actual being. Before a thing actually exists, it exists as a potentiality in its various causes. This power, or capacity to exist, is not nothing, but it is a being that is incomplete or unfinished. Even when a material substance emerges into the world from its causes, it is still in an unfinished, or imperfect state of potency. But the formal nature that determines it makes it tend to full completion and actualization. Every nature is tending, seeking to perfect itself—every nature, that is, except the highest nature of the unmoved mover, God; Book XII of the *Metaphysics* is concerned with this first cause of all finite existence.

This first mover of the cosmos must be fully in act, and must lack all potency, otherwise it would have to be actualized by something prior to itself. Since change is the actualizing of potency, this being must be changeless, eternal, and lacking in matter, which is a kind of potency. Such an immaterial being must then be an intellect, not dependent upon alien entities to constitute the objects of its reflection, but contemplating its own perfect being. Striving for no end beyond itself, it maintains an eternal activity within itself and is thus able to function as the ultimate end toward which all imperfect beings strive and tend. This fully active and perfect being is the climax and the center of the Aristotelian metaphysics. It is only insofar as the imperfect beings of the cosmos share to some degree, each according to its limitations, in this perfection that they have real existence.

Practical Philosophy. Theoretical philosophy and science are the pursuit of truth for its own sake alone. Practical philosophy is the pursuit of truth for the sake of guiding human action. Such action has three divisions: (1) the transitive action, which passes outside the agent into some external entity, which it molds or perfects; (2) the immanent action of the human individual by which he strives to perfect himself; and (3) the immanent action by which human individuals co-operate to perfect themselves in a human community. Aristotle wrote treatises dealing with each of these kinds of action.

Rhetoric is the art of acting on others in discourse and argument in such a way as to produce belief and conviction. Aristotle's *Rhetoric* deals with this art, which is really subordinate to *Politics.*

He follows Plato in judging what we call "fine art" to be imitative in character. But the aim of the art is not to produce a photographic replica of some individual reality; it is rather to reveal what is universal and essential in it, with everything accidental subordinated, as far as possible. But the artist is not a scientist. His aim is not merely to reveal the truth, but to provide the beholder with a peculiar pleasure derived from the apprehension of truth in a fitting material example, with a means of purifying his emotions, particularly those of pity and fear, and with a powerful instrument to serve the ends of moral education. These topics are treated in Aristotle's *Poetics,* important parts of which have been lost.

All the other creative arts are subordinated to action, for their products are manufactured not for their own sake, but only to be used in the actual living of life, the proper direction of which is the object of individual ethics. This topic is first dealt with by Aristotle in the *Eudemian Ethics,* but more maturely and thoroughly in the *Nicomachean Ethics*.

Like any other material substance, the individual man is endowed with a complex nature, which tends to complete or perfect itself from the very start. Unlike these other substances, however, his nature does not include a set of fixed tendencies which lead him automatically to his goal. Instead of such drives, his nature has been endowed with the faculty of reason, which can truly apprehend the ultimate goal and guide him to it. The individual human being, however, must operate his own rational faculty by himself and train his various appetites to be guided by this faculty. This he can do, for nature has provided man with the means of discovering his own goal for himself and of freely guiding himself to this goal.

The common name for this goal, which is known with more or less clarity by all men, is happiness. Happiness is the complete activation of all parts of human nature, guided by reason, for the whole span of a human life. Such a life will require certain material things as the instruments of action, and, even more, it will require that all our raw tendencies to respond and act be moderated by the guiding influence of reason, which must enter into every phase of our conduct. Finally, it will include pleasure, which crowns all activity, whether it be good or bad, but which crowns particularly the rational or virtuous activity that is in accordance with human nature.

The most important factor in the achievement of human happiness is the learning of the basic moral virtues, and most of the *Nicomachean Ethics* is concerned with this topic. A moral virtue is a rational habit or firm tendency to desire and act in accordance with sound deliberation. Unless we establish such rational habits in every phase of our lives, it will be only by luck that we shall ever perform a sound act. The first step in the establishment of such a habit must come from the outside. Thus, the parents may begin by punishing the child when he performs a selfish act and by rewarding him when he performs a generous act. But the child will not have learned true generosity until he learns to understand why the act should be performed, until he chooses to perform it for its own sake, and until he finally gains pleasure from its performance. Only then will reason have penetrated into this area of conduct to such a degree that the rational action at last springs up spontaneously from within the living character without requiring external support. Moral training is not complete until every natural mode of response and action has thus been rationalized.

Our modes of passive response belong to three different groups. First, we are excited by our own inner states. Thus, we all have a natural tendency to pursue whatever gives us pleasure. This response needs to be moderated and toned down by rational reflection and deliberation until we possess the virtue of temperance. We also have a natural tendency to resist what thwarts and obstructs our activity, and this tendency needs to be stirred up and intensified until we possess the habit of courage. In the second place, external things excite in us a tendency to possess them and to keep them; this tendency needs to be relaxed by the rational virtue of generosity. The external praise and blame of others also excites us; this tendency needs to be further aroused and intensified until we gain not only the respect of others, but, what is more difficult, our own self-respect. Finally, we are all excited by the feelings of others and their actions upon us, and these social tendencies need to be rationalized and purified into the virtues of friendliness.

When these passive modes of response, or passions, are under rational control, we can then step out into the public world and act upon others in such a way as to give to each, including ourselves, precisely what reason demands. This is the virtue of justice, which orders all our public actions with others to the common good, without making any unreasonable exceptions or giving ourselves any undue advantages. The activities of two individuals, thus treating each other justly, may be further crowned, if they are thrown much together, by the gift of friendship, the greatest natural good that can be possessed by any man; for when we share the thoughts and activities of a friend, our own thought is enriched and our own activity intensified. We love him as we love ourselves, not for the sake of any particular good that he can do us or pleasure that he can give us, but for himself, for his own sake and the genuine virtue within him.

With our passions rationally moderated by the virtues of temperance, courage, generosity, self-respect, and friendliness, with our public acts governed by the virtue of justice, and with a moderate amount of external instruments of action and reasonable good fortune in the possession of friends, a happy life may be lived. But the most important part of happiness is pure insight and contemplation; this alone can grasp the true end of human life and the natural order of action it necessitates; for without a clear insight into the nature of the true end, the more clever and efficient we are in reaching the wrong goal, the worse off we really are. Hence the intellectual virtues of contemplation and prayer underlie all the rest. They require less physical support; they may be pursued most continuously and autonomously by the individual man; they are crowned by the purest pleasures and possess the greatest intrinsic worth; they are the expression of what is most distinctive in our nature and of what is at the same time most divine.

Man is by nature a political animal, requiring the co-operation of his fellows in order to approximate his own highest possible perfection. This happy life can be achieved only with others in an interlocking, interdependent mode of combined activity—the common good. This common good, as a whole, takes precedence over the individual good, which is a part of it; politics must dominate individual ethics. The proper aim of politics is to attain the happiness or virtuous activity of all citizens. The subordination of everything to military conquest or to the acquisition of material goods rests upon a misunderstanding of the nature of man. Economics, the art of acquiring and producing material goods, has a legitimate subordinate place in the common life but should never be pursued as an end in itself, or beyond the point demanded for the satisfaction of justifiable needs. Usury, for instance, is a perversion, producing nothing.

Aside from the ideal state, considered in the eighth and ninth books of the *Politics,* Aristotle recognizes six basic types of political organization: monarchy, aristocracy, and polity, and their three perversions, tyranny, oligarchy, and democracy. Monarchy, the rule of one man who is preeminent in virtue, and aristocracy, the rule of many who excel in virtue, are sound forms of government when they really exist, but this is rarely the case. On the other hand, aristocracy mixed with oligarchy (rule of the rich), and oligarchy mixed with democracy, have often occurred, and the constitutions of such mixed or compromise states are relatively sound.

When a king, who should rule for the common good, uses authority and power for what he conceives as his own benefit, tyranny, the worst of all social corruptions, arises. Pure oligarchy is another egotistical, one-sided form of government, in which the rulers exercise their power for the further accumulation of wealth. Because they excel in wealth, the oligarchs assume that they also excel in other more important respects, and thus are led to error and ruin. Freedom is equally shared by all the citizens in a democracy. Because they are equal in this respect, the democrats assume that they are also equal in other respects; this is false and leads to irrationalism and confusion. But of the three one-sided and distorted forms of government, tyranny, oligarchy, and democracy, the last is the least perverted and dangerous.

In such distorted forms, it is impossible to be both a good man and a good citizen. In the sound forms, monarchy, aristocracy, and polity, it is possible to be a good and useful citizen without being a good man, because of a ruling minority, which plays the major political role. But in the ideal state, the whole citizen body exercises rule over itself. This requires that all participate not only in the peculiar virtues of citizenship, but in the general human virtues. It requires the establishment of a most elaborate system of education for the whole citizen body, capable of training them in the intellectual and moral virtues.

The ultimate aim of politics must be to approximate this ideal social order, in which every citizen participates in a rule of law and reason. But in the distorted forms that are actually given in human history, the politician must strive to avoid the perverted extremes by judiciously mixing oligarchy with democracy and thus to achieve a more or less stable mean in which peace and order make further education and social advance possible.

Rhetoric is an instrument of the political art, and Aristotle's treatise on this subject should be read together with the *Politics*. Rhetoric is the art of persuasion, which takes two distinct forms. In the first, the discourse is addressed to a purely theoretical listener and must take an argumentative form. In the second, the discourse is addressed to a listener from whom a decision is sought. Such practical discourse has two subvarieties: first, there is legal discourse concerning some past occurrence which is to be judged; second, there is political discourse about some future act. Each type of situation has its own proper rules and methods.

Aristotle's thought was guided by a profound sense of the reality existing independently of all human opinion and desire, together with a deep trust in the capacity of human reason, when properly exercised, to know this reality as it is. These two convictions combined to produce in him an extraordinary readiness to follow the empirical facts wherever they led him and a remarkable capacity for discerning and describing their essential structure. The great edifice of theoretical and practical doctrine that he erected has survived many periods of bitter attack by alien ways of thought, as well as many periods of ignorance and neglect; today it is still studied and cultivated and lives a vigorous life in the minds of men.   J. W.

ARISTOTLE'S CLASSIFICATION. *See* GOVERNMENT.

ARITHMETIC, the branch of mathematics dealing both with the art of computing with figures and with the theory of number. The word itself is derived from the epithet ἀριθμητική (*arithmetike*) of the phrase ἡἀριθμητική τέχνη (*he arithmetike techne*), "the arithematic art." Originally the word referred to the theory or science of numbers as distinguished from practical computing which was called λογιστική (*logistike*) from the word λόγος (*logos*), "ratio" or "reason."

Arithmetic may be regarded as a set of operations, such as addition, subtraction, multiplication, division, extraction of roots, etc., performed on numbers in order to solve problems of daily life. It may also be regarded as a theoretical science built up by logical inference from assumptions about certain defined entities. For the person who wishes to make only practical use of arithmetic, memorization of rules may be sufficient; for the person who would acquire knowledge of the science, memorization will be of help, but it alone will not be sufficient.

The reader will find the following explanations helpful:

1. *Principle of position.* According to this principle, the meaning of a numeral or symbol of a digit depends on its position. In the number 237, for example, the meaning of 2 is two hundred; in 327, it is twenty.

2. *Symbols.* Some of the mathematical symbols will be familiar to the reader, such as $-$ for minus, $+$ for plus, $\div$ for divided by, $=$ for equals, and $\times$ and $\cdot$ for multiplied by. Others may be less familiar. These include: $\neq$, for does not equal; $>$, is greater than; $<$, is less than; $\leq$, is less than or equals; $\lesseqgtr$, is less than, equals, or is greater than; $\equiv$, is identical to.

3. *Numbers.* A natural number is a whole number without regard to sign, that is, whether it is positive or negative. An integer is a whole number with a sign, plus or minus. The system of integers includes the negative whole numbers, zero, and the positive whole numbers.

MODERN ARITHMETIC

The arithmetic taught in schools today is characterized more by utility and practicality than theory and logical development. The topics usually dealt with are:

1. Number Names and Counting,
2. Numerals and the 10-scale of Notation,
3. The Fundamental Operations,
4. Fractions,
5. Factoring,
6. Greatest Common Divisor and Least Common Multiple,
7. Ratios and Proportions,
8. Progressions,
9. Decimal Fractions,
10. Percentage,
11. Recurring Decimals,
12. Extraction of Roots,
13. Continued Fractions,
14. Other Scales of Notation.

These subjects are not all equally developed in our schools; the higher aspects of some of them are relegated to more advanced studies, particularly the Theory of Numbers, Number Systems, and Series.

1. Number Names and Counting. To count one must have names for the various numbers. We use the names one, two, three, four, and so on, for the first few numbers. Since there are so many numbers that we are not able to name them all, the device of grouping is used. After ten is reached in counting, we start over again with ten-and-one or eleven, ten-and-two or twelve, ten-and-three or thirteen, ten-and-four, etc., until ten-and-ten or two tens—called twenty—is reached. Then we begin over again, repeating one, two, three, . . . after the name twenty, until thirty is reached and in the same way, forty, fifty, sixty, . . . until ten tens, which is called one hundred, is reached. The result is to establish a set of denominations—units, tens, hundreds, thousands, etc.—in which ten of any denomination make one of the next higher order.

2. Numerals and the 10-scale of Notation. The symbols we use for the units are the Hindu-Arabic numerals: 1, 2, 3, 4, 5, 6, 7, 8, 9, and 0. According to the nomenclature described above, the symbol for ten is 10; for twenty, 20. In general, any big number is expressed by a symbol of many digits. The first digit at the left shows how many of the highest denomination are in the number; the second digit shows how many of the next lower denomination there are, and so on, ending with a digit at the right showing how many units are in the number. Thus, the symbol for three hundred and forty-seven thousand, five hundred and eighty-two is 347,582; the meaning of the symbol 3,576 is three thousand, five hundred and seventy-six. When a denomination is absent from a number, 0 is placed in its position. The symbol 3,506, therefore, means three thousand, five hundred, no tens, and six. We do not read it this way; instead of saying "no tens," we just do not mention the tens, but the meaning is the same. Since ten of any denomination make one of the next higher order, the symbol 3,576 corresponds to the statement:

$$3,576 = 3(10)^3 + 5(10)^2 + 7(10) + 6.$$

3. The Fundamental Operations. This term includes the operations of addition and its inverse, subtraction, and the operations of multiplication and its inverse, division.

Addition. In this operation, numbers which are added are called addends; their total is the sum. In order to engage in the operation of addition, it is necessary either to have memorized the addition tables or to know how to conduct the time-consuming process of finding sums by counting. In the following discussion, the assumption is made that the addition tables have been memorized. The sum of two natural numbers is another natural number which contains as many units as the other two together. To find the sum of two natural numbers, such as 437 and 925, the numbers to be added are written the one under the other, so that the units, tens, hundreds, etc., of the one are under the corresponding unit of the other.

$$\begin{array}{r} 437 \\ 925 \\ \hline 1,362 \end{array}$$

The units are added first. The addition of 7 and 5 gives 12, which is interpreted as 2 units and 1 ten, and the computer writes 2 in the units column and carries 1 ten to add to the tens column. Addition of this column gives 5 to which is added the 1 carried over from the units column, so that the computer writes 6 in the tens column. Since the figures in the column of the hundreds add up to 13 hundreds or 1 thousand and 3 hundreds, 3 is written in the position of the hundreds and 1 in the position of the thousands. Thus, the computer finds the sum to be one thousand, three hundred and sixty-two. This example above makes use of all the important ideas that are involved in the addition of whole numbers.

Subtraction. This operation is inverse to that of addition. It is loosely considered as taking something away from something else. The number which is taken away from another is called the subtrahend; the one from which it is taken, the minuend; their difference is the remainder. If m and n are two natural numbers, m being greater than n, the difference $m - n$ is defined as the natural number s which, added to n, produces m. In symbols this becomes $m - n = s$, if $n + s = m$. Hence, to find the difference, $795 - 633$, the number is found which, added to 633, will produce 795. The subtrahend is written under the minuend so that the units, tens, hundreds, etc. of one fall under the units, tens, hundreds, etc. of the other. First, the units of the subtrahend are taken away from the units of the minuend. Thus, 3 units taken away from 5 units leaves 2 units. The computer writes 2 below the subtrahend in the column of units. In the tens

column, 3 from 9 leaves 6; in the hundreds column, 6 from 7 leaves 1, and the computer arrives at the remainder, 162.

$$\begin{array}{r} 795 \\ -633 \\ \hline 162 \end{array}$$

When the number in the minuend is smaller than the number in the corresponding column in the subtrahend, it is necessary to borrow from the next higher column. In subtracting 758 from 1,383, for example, the units number in the subtrahend is larger than in the minuend. Instead of subtracting 8 units from 3 units, 1 ten is borrowed; 8 units are now subtracted from 13 units, and the computer writes 5 in the units column of the remainder. As the result of borrowing, there are 7 tens in the minuend rather than 8. Since this number is larger than the tens in the subtrahend, their subtraction is straightforward, and the computer writes 2 in the tens column of the remainder. The situation in the hundreds column is the same as was found in the units. It is necessary to borrow from the thousands column; 7 hundreds are then subtracted from 13 hundreds; 6 is written in the hundreds column of the answer, and nothing is left in the thousands column. The remainder is 625. As a check the

$$\begin{array}{r} 1,383 \\ 758 \\ \hline 625 \end{array}$$

answer is added to 758. Their sum is 1,383, proving that the subtraction was correctly performed. Variations on this method occur in any standard textbook.

The fact that the difference $m - n$ exists in the system of natural numbers only if m is greater than n led to the creation of a larger number system—the system of integers or whole numbers which includes the positive and negative whole numbers and zero. In this system the difference $m - n$ exists whether $m > n$ or $m \leq n$.

Multiplication. This operation is one of repeated addition and is, therefore, the product of the integer m by the integer n. This is denoted by $m \times n$, mn, $m \cdot n$, or $m(n)$. These symbols are defined by, for example, $m \times n = m + m + m + \ldots$ to n terms. Since by definition nm is the same as mn, we also have $m \times n = n + n + n \ldots$ to m terms. This fact enables us to attach a meaning to the product of $m \times (-n)$. Although the definition would require us to add m to itself $(-n)$ times—which makes no sense—$m \times (-n)$ can be rewritten $(-n) \times m$ which means the sum of $(-n)$ to m terms. This meaning is acceptable; it means the negative integer $-mn$.

Multiplication of the number 645 by the number 237 is shown below. The number 645 is the multiplicand; 237, the multiplier; the answer is their product. To begin, the

$$\begin{array}{r} 645 \\ 237 \\ \hline 4515 \\ 1935 \\ 1290 \\ \hline 152865 \end{array}$$

number 5 units is multiplied by the number 7 units to give 35 units—knowledge of the multiplication table is clearly essential. The computer writes 5 in the units column and carries 3 tens to add to the tens. Next, 4 tens are multiplied by 7 units. To the 28 tens so obtained is added the 3 carried over, giving 31 tens, and the computer writes the 1 and carries 3 hundreds. Then 6 hundreds are multiplied by 7 units, giving 42 hundreds, to which is added the 3 hundreds carried over. The result is 45 hundreds, which the computer writes as 5 hundreds and 4 thousands by putting these numerals in the proper columns. The resulting number, 4515, is the first partial product. Two more partial products are obtained by multiplying the multiplicand by the remaining numbers 3 and 2 (in that order) of the multiplier. Only this time, because the 3 is 3 tens, the next partial product is written one position to the left of the previous one; because the 2 is 2 hundreds, the third partial product is placed two positions to the left of the first. Then the three partial products are added, yielding the final product, 152,865. Every multiplication can thus be treated.

Division. Division is the inverse of multiplication. To indicate the division of the integer m by the integer n, the symbol $m \div n$ or m/n is used. The result of division is called the quotient; m is the dividend, and n the divisor. The quotient of m/n is defined to be the integer c which, if it exists, satisfies the condition $n \times c = m$. It is clear that the quotient of an integer divided by an integer is not always an integer; these are the cases where c does not exist, at least, not as an integer.

Division of m by n is given by an example in which the dividend is the integer 81,765 and the divisor, the integer 237. The dividend is written down and, on either side of the number, a box is drawn. In one box, preferably the left one, the divisor is written; in the right one, the quotient. The computer now finds how many times the divisor goes into the three-digit number 817. Since by estimation it will go three times, 237 is multiplied by 3 and the product subtracted from 817. The difference is 106, a number less than the divisor, meaning that 237 will not go in the trial dividend 817 more than 3 times. The symbol 3 is written in the box to the right as the first figure of the quotient. The next digit of the dividend is brought down to form the new trial dividend, 1066, and the computer finds how many times the divisor 237 will go into it. Four is tried. The divisor is multiplied by 4; the product subtracted from 1066; the difference is found to be 118, showing that 4 is the next figure of the quotient. Then the next digit of the dividend is brought down, and the procedure outlined above is repeated; the number 345 is thus obtained as the quotient. To check the result the divisor is multiplied by the quotient. This shows whether the product is equal to the dividend, as the definition of division requires.

$$
\begin{array}{r|r|r}
237 & 81765 & 345 \\
& 711 \\ \hline
& 1066 \\
& 948 \\ \hline
& 1185 \\
& 1185 \\ \hline
& 0
\end{array}
$$

In this example the division gave an integer. As a rule m/n is not an integer; the operation of division on members of this number system does not always produce a member of the system. For this reason, another number system, that of the "rational numbers," was created. The quotient of any two members of this system is a member of the system. The sole exception is where the divisor is the number zero. The operation is then regarded as meaningless. Division by zero is not defined in any number system, for, taking division as the inverse of multiplication, the symbol m/o would mean a number c such that $o \times c = m$. This means $o = m$ for any finite number c. There would be no number c which made nc equal to m, if n were zero; hence, there would be no meaning to the mark m/o—in other words, the sign m/n is meaningless if $n = o$.

Rational numbers are those that have the form m/n where m and n are integers. The full arithmetic of the rational numbers is developed in the secondary schools on an intui-

tive basis. It is explained, for example, that if a thing is divided into n equal parts, and m of these parts are taken, then m/n represents the part of the whole that is taken. This kind of development leaves much to be desired. For instance, the very definition of m/n leads one to believe that $m \leq n$, since, obviously, no more parts than there are can be taken. For an adequate development of the Rational Number System, or of any of the other number systems, the postulational method or the logical method of the Peano-Frege-Russel school must be resorted to. Since the latter is the one most widely used, a few examples of its use in the creation of the rational number system will be given.

It will be seen that in the development of the system, the fundamental operations are taken care of. Terms such as a, b, c, etc. are used rather than 1, 2, 3, etc. because the latter are specific and the object here is to state assumptions and definitions that apply in all cases involving numbers in which the stated conditions are met. The reader might experiment with numbers in place of letters to see how elementary the development is, for, in what follows, knowledge of the system of integers is presupposed.

1. *Definition.* If m and n are integers and $n \neq o$, the rational number m/n means the relation of x to y, where x and y are any two integers satisfying the condition $ym = xn$.

2. *Definition.* $m/n = p/q$, if $mq = np$.

3. *Theorem.* If $m/n = p/q$ and $p/q = r/s$, $m/n = r/s$.
Proof. By (2) above, $mq = np$ and $ps = qr$. Hence, $mqs = nqr$, whence $ms = nr$ and, thus, $m/n = r/s$.

4. *Definition.* By the "sum" of m/n and p/q is meant the rational number $(mq + np) / nq$, if it exists.

5. *Theorem.* The sum of m/n and p/q, as defined, exists and is unique.
Proof. From the properties of integers, the integer $mq + np$ exists and is unique, nq exists and is unique, and, since $n \neq o$ and $q \neq o$, then $nq \neq o$. Hence, by (1) above, $(mp + nq) / nq$ is a unique rational number.

Theorem. There is a unique rational number $U \equiv u_1/u_2$ such that, for any rational number $X \equiv x_1 x_2$, $X + U = X$.
Proof. The rational number o/u_2 satisfies the condition because $o/u_2 + x_1/x_2 = \frac{(ox_2 = u_2 x_1)}{u_2 x_2} = \frac{(o + u_2 x_1)}{u_2 x_2} = \frac{u_2 x_1}{u_2 x_2} = x_1/x_2$. Conversely, if any rational number $V = v_1/v_2$ satisfies the condition, it must be the number o/u_2. For, if $X + V = X$, or $\frac{(v_1 x_2 + v_2 x_1)}{v_2 x_2} = x_1/x_2$, then $v_1 x_2 x_2 + v_2 x_1 x_2 = v_2 x_2 x_1$, whence $v_1 x_2 x_2 = o$. From this and the fact that $x_2 \neq o$, it is seen that $v_1 = o$, whence v_1/v_2 is o/v_2 which is equal to o/u_2. Thus, the number U is unique.

The system of rational numbers can be further developed by this strict and formal method. Division is defined in this system also as the inverse of multiplication.

4. Fractions. As the name implies, fractions are pieces or parts of units. The symbol m/n represents the ratio to the whole of m of the n equal parts into which the whole has broken or subdivided. It is a rational number. In a "proper fraction," m the numerator is less than n the denominator, as $2/3$. An "improper fraction" is one in which the numerator is greater than the denominator, as $5/4$.

The fundamental operations may be carried out with fractions. Addition of fractions which have the same denominator is easily performed; their numerators are simply added together, as

$$1/16 + 5/16 + 7/16 = \frac{1 + 5 + 7}{16} = 13/16.$$

If the fractions have different denominators, however, the

operation becomes more complex. It is necessary to change the terms so that they all have the same denominator. This is done by finding the lowest common denominator, the smallest number which is a multiple of each of the given denominators. For example, in the addition of 2/3, 1/6, and 3/5, the lowest common denominator is 30.

$$2/3 = 20/30$$
$$1/6 = 5/30$$
$$3/5 = 18/30$$

$20/30 + 5/30 + 18/30 = 43/30$, an improper fraction.

Subtraction of fractions is carried out in the same way as addition. If the denominators of the fractions are alike, the numerators are simply subtracted: $10/13 - 2/13 = 8/13$. If unlike denominators are involved, the lowest common denominator must be found.

$$7/8 - 3/4 = \frac{7-6}{8} = 1/8$$

It is not necessary to find the lowest common denominator in the multiplication of fractions. Instead the numerators are multiplied, as are the denominators separately. The product is simplified if possible. This is called reducing the fraction. It consists of dividing both terms by the largest integer that will divide them both exactly.

$$5/6 \times 4/9 = 20/54 = 10/27.$$

Division of fractions is the inverse of their multiplication. If m/n is divided by p/q, the quotient is defined as r/s which fulfills the requirement that $(p/q) \times (r/s) = m/n$ or $pr/qs = m/n$. It can be found from this and from the properties of integers that $r/s = mq/np$. This shows that to divide m/n by p/q, one inverts p/q and multiplies.

$$3/4 \div 7/8 = 3/4 \times 8/7 = 24/28 = 6/7$$

"Mixed numbers" and "complex fractions" are also met with. A mixed number is the sum (or difference) of a whole number and a fraction, such as $4 + 2/3$ or $10 - 1/8$. Since an integer may be looked upon as a fraction having the denominator 1, m may be treated in any operation in the same manner as the rational number $m/1$. Thus, a mixed number is nothing but the sum (or difference) of two rational numbers, for example, $4 + 2/3 = 4/1 + 2/3 = \frac{3 \times 4 + 1 \times 2}{1 \times 3} = \frac{12 + 2}{3} = 14/3$, an improper fraction.

A complex fraction is the quotient of a mixed number or sum of fractions by another mixed number or sum of fractions, as $\frac{4 - 2/3}{3 + 1/4}$. It can be converted into a simple fraction:

$$\frac{4 - 2/3}{3 + 1/4} = \frac{4/1 - 2/3}{3/1 + 1/4} = \frac{\frac{3 \times 4 - 1 \times 2}{1 \times 3}}{\frac{4 \times 3 \times 1 \times 1}{4 \times 1}} = \frac{\frac{12 - 2}{3}}{\frac{12 + 1}{4}} = \frac{10/3}{13/4}$$

$$= 10/3 \times 4/13 = 40/39.$$

5. Factoring. At the beginning of a discussion of factoring it is convenient to state a few simple definitions. A number is said to be a "prime number" if it is not exactly divisible by any number other than itself and the number 1. There is an infinite number of prime numbers, the first few being 1, 2, 3, 5, and 7. Two or more numbers are said to be "factors" of another, if their product is that number. Thus, 3 and 4 are factors of 12; so are 2 and 6, but only 2, 2, and 3 are called *the* "prime factors" of 12. The definite article "the" is used because it is shown (in higher arithmetic) that the decomposition of a number into its prime factors is unique. The principal uses to which factoring is put are in the reduction of fractions to their lowest terms, in finding the greatest common divisor of two or more numbers, and in finding their least common multiple. The first of these uses is given in reducing the fraction 36/48 to its lowest terms

thus: $36/48 = \frac{2 \times 2 \times 3 \times 3}{2 \times 2 \times 3 \times 2 \times 2} = \frac{2}{2} \times \frac{2}{2} \times \frac{3}{3} \times \frac{3}{2 \times 2}$
$= 1 \times 1 \times 1 \times 3/4 = 3/4$.

6. Greatest Common Divisor and Least Common Multiple. These two phrases are usually abbreviated to g.c.d. and l.c.m., respectively. The g.c.d. of two or more numbers is the greatest number that will divide them all exactly. It may be found by decomposing each of the numbers into its prime factors and taking the product of all the different factors common to all the decompositions, each prime being taken the least number of times that it occurs in any decomposition. Thus, making use of the decompositions given above for the numbers 36 and 48, the prime 2 is taken twice and the prime 3 once; their product, $2 \times 2 \times 3$ or 12, is the g.c.d. of the numbers.

There is another way to find the g.c.d. of two numbers. It is Euclid's method. The two numbers, a and b, are taken so that $a > b$; a is divided by b yielding a quotient and the remainder r_1. Then, b is divided by r_1, with remainder r_2. The last divisor obtained is divided by the last remainder until a division is reached which leaves no remainder. The last divisor used is the g.c.d. To find the g.c.d. of the numbers 120 and 36, for example, 120 is divided by 36. The quotient 3 and the remainder 12 are obtained; 36 is next divided by 12 to give 3 and no remainder. The last divisor, 12, is the g.c.d.

The l.c.m. of two or more numbers is the least number that is exactly divisible by them all. It is the product of all the different primes that occur in their decompositions, each prime being taken the greatest number of times that it occurs in any decomposition. Thus, decompositions of the numbers 36, 48, and 60 gives

$$36 = 2 \times 2 \times 3 \times 3$$
$$48 = 2 \times 2 \times 2 \times 2 \times 3$$
$$60 = 2 \times 2 \times 3 \times 5,$$

and, hence, the l.c.m. is $2 \times 2 \times 2 \times 2 \times 3 \times 3 \times 5 = 720$.

7. Ratios and Proportions. The ratio m/n of two numbers, m and n, has been discussed as a rational number. The statement of equality of two ratios, such as $m/n = p/q$, is called a proportion. Proportions are also written $m:n = p:q$ or $m:n::p:q$. The theory of proportions is of ancient origin; it appears, fully developed, in the works of Euclid. Many and varied uses of proportions are found in the works of early mathematicians and scientists.

There is a tendency, nowadays, to write a proportion, such as $y/x = a/b$, in the form $y/x = k$, where k represents a/b, to connect it with the theory of variation. From the form $y/x = k$, it follows that $y = kx$, which is read as the statement "y is proportional to x," k being looked upon as a constant of proportionality. This is valid, of course, but it is modern and foreign to Greek thought. Archimedes has shown that if two weights, W and w, balance each other at distances D and d, respectively, from a fulcrum, then $W/w = d/D$. The problem is to find the weight, W, which at a distance of two ft. from the fulcrum, will balance a five-lb. weight four ft. on the other side of the fulcrum. Solving the proportion for the weight W gives $W = kw$, where k is the ratio of the distances, 4/2 or 2, and w is the given weight. Thus, $W = 2 \times 5$, and the answer is 10 lbs.

8. Progressions. The most useful of the progressions studied in secondary schools are the arithmetic and the geometric ones. The former is $a + (a + d) + (a + 2d) + (a + 3d) + \ldots + (a + \overline{n-1}\, d)$; the latter is $a + ar^2 + ar^3 + \ldots + ar^{n-1}$. In each, a is the first term and n is the number of terms. In the arithmetic progression, d is the common difference; in the geometric one, r is the common ratio.

Formulas are developed for the sum of n terms. For the first, the sum is $\frac{2a + (n\text{-}1)\, d_n}{2}$, for the second $\frac{a\,(1\text{-}r^n)}{1\text{-}r}$.

Applications are in banking, annuities, and other subjects, as shown in the following examples. A man starts on a job with a salary of \$5,000 a year. Annually he receives an increase of \$200. The problem of finding the total of his earnings after 10 years is recognized as one in which the sum of an arithmetic progression is wanted. The first term of the progression is 5,000, the common difference is 200, and the number of terms is 10. The formula for the sum, the total of the man's earnings, thus becomes:

$$\frac{2 \times 5{,}000 + (10\text{-}1) \times 200}{2}\,10 = \frac{10{,}000 + 1{,}800}{2} = 59{,}000.$$

A problem involving the use of a geometric progression is that of finding the money amassed at the end of 10 years by a man who deposits \$200 in a bank the first of every January for 10 years. The rate of interest is four per cent compounded annually. The solution is obtained by substituting in the geometric progression 200 for the first term, 1.04 for the common ratio, and 10 for the number of terms. Accordingly, the man has to his credit $\frac{200\,[(1.04)^{10} - 1]}{(1.04 - 1)} = \$2{,}401.$

9. Decimal Fractions. In the 10-scale, a unit in any position is equal to ten of the units in the next position to the right. If, therefore, a digit is written in the position immediately to the right of the units position, it denotes tenths of a unit. One written in the position next to the right of this one represents tenths of a tenth or hundredths, and so on. In a sequence of digits, a dot or decimal point is put immediately after the digit that represents units. The digits to the left of the dot then represent whole numbers and those to the right, decimal fractions, such as tenths, hundredths, thousandths, etc. Hence, the number 23.57 represents twenty-three and fifty-seven hundredths. Some prefer to read this as two-three-point-five-seven. Numbers containing digits on both sides of the decimal point can be added, subtracted, multiplied, and divided like whole numbers.

10. Percentages. The use of percentages is involved in problems which call for finding the value or magnitude of a ratio m/n as so many out of a hundred. A vendor of peaches, for example, eats one peach for every three that he sells. Out of every four peaches, he eats one and sells three; therefore, out of every hundred he eats twenty-five. The percentage of his stock that he eats is found by setting up the proportion $1:4 = x:100$. This gives $4x = 100$, since the product of the means equals the product of the extremes, and $x = 25$.

In general terms, the ratio m/n is converted into a rate per hundred (a percentage) by setting up the proportion $m:n = x:100$ and solving for x. An alternative method is just to divide m by n decimally. Thus, in the specific example given above, 1 is divided by 4 to give 0.25, the meaning of which is 25 per hundred. The inverse problem is also studied. In a class of 80 students, for example, 15 per cent failed. To find the number of students who failed, 80 is multiplied by 0.15; the answer is 12. Percentages are useful in problems on profit and loss, interest, and discount.

11. Recurring Decimals. In converting an ordinary fraction to a decimal fraction it sometimes happens that the same figure will recur endlessly. This occurs in $1/3 = 0.3333\ldots$. It may also happen that a set of figures will recur endlessly, as in $3/11 = 0/272727\ldots$, or that a set of figures will recur endlessly after a few other figures that do not recur, as in $5/6 = 0/8333\ldots$. Such decimal fractions are called recurring decimals. The chief problem that arises

in connection with these decimals is that of finding the ordinary fraction, if any, to which the recurring decimal is equal. It was the practice until recently to assume that every such decimal can be expressed as an ordinary fraction—the Pythagoreans made a similar assumption concerning certain numbers now called irrational. To find, for example, the rational number m/n which the recurring fraction $0.323232\ldots$ is assumed equal to, the following procedure is followed. First, one writes $m/n = 0.323232\ldots$; multiplying both sides by 100 gives

$$\begin{aligned}(100)\,(m/n) &= 32.323232\ldots\\ &= 32 + 0.323232\ldots\\ &= 32 + m/n\end{aligned}$$

and, therefore, $(99)\,(m/n) = 32$
whence, $m/n = 32/99$, the answer.

In the case of the recurring decimal $0.8333\ldots$
$$\begin{aligned}m/n &= 0.83333\ldots\\ 100\,(m/n) &= 83.3333\ldots\end{aligned}$$
and $10\,(m/n) = 8.3333\ldots$
whence, by subtraction, $(90)\,(m/n) = 75$
and, thus, $m/n = 75/90 = 5/6$, the answer.

The lack of rigor involved in this method has caused the adoption of another procedure based on the sum of an infinite geometric progression. It has already been shown that the sum of n terms of $a + ar + ar^2 + ar^3 + \ldots$ is $\frac{a\,(1\text{-}r^n)}{1\text{-}r}$ Now, if r is less than 1, the power r^n gets smaller and smaller as n increases. This means that the sum $\frac{a\,(1\text{-}r^n)}{1\text{-}r}$ gets closer and closer to the value $\frac{a}{1\text{-}r}$ provided $r < 1$. The recurring decimal $0.83333\ldots$ is again considered and, thus,

$$\begin{aligned}0.8333\ldots &= 0.8 + 0.3333\ldots\\ &= 8/10 + 3/100 + 3/1{,}000 + 3/10{,}000 + \ldots\\ &= 8/10 + 3/100 + (3/100)\,(1/10)\\ &\quad + (3/100)\,(1/10)^2 + \ldots.\end{aligned}$$

The recurring decimal has thus been expressed as the sum of an ordinary fraction and an infinite geometric progression whose common ratio is less than 1. It can now be written·

$$0.83333\ldots = 4/5 + \frac{3/100}{9/10} = 4/5 + 1/30 = 5/6.$$

The result is the same as before, only this time the procedure cannot be questioned.

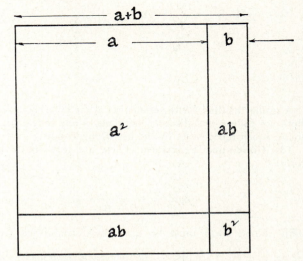

12. Extraction of Roots. Roots are extracted by processes based on the relations $(a + b)^2 = a^2 + 2ab + b^2$ for the square root and $(a + b)^3 = a^3 + 3a^2b + 3ab^2 + b^3$

for the cube root. If the square root of a number, N, is wanted, N is thought of as being equal to A^2; thus, what is wanted is A, which is found first as a, a rough approximation of A, the difference between the two being b. Then an approximate value, b_1, of b is found, so that $a_1 = a + b_1$ is a better approximation of A. Another correction b_2, is next made so that $a_2 = a_1 + b_2$ is still a better approximation, and so on. The procedure is continued until either A has been found exactly—which will happen if N is a perfect square—or a sufficiently close approximation has been obtained. This method, expressed as a set of rules, and illustrated by an example, is as follows:

1. The given number, for example 235225, is separated into periods of two figures each, 23/52/25. There will be as many figures in the square root as there are periods in the number—three figures in this case.

2. The biggest perfect square contained in the first period is found—16 above; the square root of this square is the first figure of the root—four in this example.

3. This square is subtracted from the first period, the difference is 7; the next period, 52, is brought down to form the first trial dividend, or 752.

4. The first figure found is doubled and a zero annexed to it to form the first trial divisor, 80.

5. The trial dividend is divided by the trial divisor; the quotient is the next figure of the root, or 9, disregarding the remainder.

6. A zero is annexed to this quotient; the quotient is added to the number thus formed; the sum is multiplied by the quotient, and the product subtracted from the trial dividend; but, if this product is greater than the trial dividend, the quotient is reduced by 1 and the resulting quotient is treated as originally directed in this step. In this case $80 + 9 = 89$; $89 \times 9 = 801$; but $801 > 752$; therefore, 9 is reduced by 1; $9 - 1 = 8$; $80 + 8 = 88$; $88 \times 8 = 704$; $704 < 752$; therefore, 8 is the second figure of the root.

7. The next period is brought down to form the new trial dividend, 4825.

8. Steps (4), (5), (6), and (7) are repeated.

9. The procedure is continued until the square root or a sufficiently close approximation has been found. In the case considered, the process ends with the exact square root, 485.

The various operations described above are shown below:

23/52/25	485		80		80		960
16			+9		+8		+5
752			89		88		965
704			×9		×8		×5
4825			801		704		4825
4825							
0							

A similar method for the extraction of the cube root exists. Both are falling into disuse, since roots of any index can be found much more easily by the use of logarithms.

13. Continued Fractions. These are fractions of the form:

$$\cfrac{1}{a + \cfrac{1}{b + \cfrac{1}{c + \dots}}} \qquad \text{or} \qquad \frac{1}{a} + \frac{1}{b} + \frac{1}{c} + \frac{1}{d} + \dots$$

This second form must be carefully distinguished from $\frac{1}{a} + \frac{1}{b} + \frac{1}{c} + \frac{1}{d} + \dots$. In the secondary schools, these fractions are studied when continued only to a finite number of steps; it is then pointed out that they do not differ essen-

tially from complex fractions. In higher arithmetic, however, they are studied even when continued indefinitely.

The number $1/a$ is called the first convergent; $\cfrac{1}{a + 1/b}$ or $\cfrac{b}{ab + 1}$ is the second, and so on. The convergents are alternately greater (the odd ones) and less (the even ones) than the value to which the fraction converges. The theory of these fractions has few practical applications.

14. Other Scales of Notation. It will be recalled that in the grouping used in the 10-scale notation, 10 of any denomination made one of the next higher order. If twelve of any denomination had been chosen instead to make one of the next higher order, twelve numerals, such as 1, 2, 3, 4, 5, 6, 7, 8, 9, t, e, 0—t representing ten and e eleven—would have been necessary. In this case the meaning of $3t06$ would be $3(12)^3 + t(12)^2 + 0(12) + 6$ or three great gross, ten gross and six. The number 23.57 would mean two dozen and three, five twelfths and seven grossths. The last word in the previous sentence is rather awkward, but, if the 12-scale ever came into general use, the word would become quite common place. Fractions, in the 12-scale, would probably be called "duo-decimals."

In these ways of grouping, called scales of notation, the number of times a denomination is taken to make one of the next higher order is called the base of the scale. In the 10-notation, the base was 10; in the example given above, the base was 12. The first is called the denary scale; the second, the duodenary. There is, however, no uniformity as yet in the names of the scales of notation. The denary scale is also called the decimal scale; the duodenary the duodecimal scale. It seems wise to abandon both nomenclatures and adopt the practice, used by some, of calling a scale an n-scale if n is its base. In the past, scales with bases of 10, 12, 20, and 60 have been used. The binary or 2-scale is gaining use in scientific work. The base used most extensively is 10, although there is some interest in replacing this by 12. Among the advantages claimed by the advocates of the 12-scale are greater divisibility of numbers and more direct, or natural, applications. Astronomers, in the past, have found the 60-scale more convenient; one suspects that navigators would find the 12-scale more convenient.

All processes that may be performed on the 10-scale have corresponding processes on any other scale. To find the product 257×23 in the 12-scale, for example, the numbers are written as in ordinary multiplication, a line is drawn, and the partial products 749 and $4e2$ are found.

$$
\begin{array}{r}
257 \\
23 \\
\hline
749 \\
4e2 \\
\hline
5669
\end{array}
$$

Multiplication of 3 by 7 gives 19 or one dozen and nine; the computer writes 9 and carries 1. (Of course, $3 \times 7 = 21$ in the decimal system, but this is reduced to the notation of the 12-scale.) Continuing the multiplication gives: $3 \times 5 = 13$, $13 + 1 = 14$, 4 is written down, and 1 is carried; $3 \times 2 = 6$, $6 + 1 = 7$, 7 is written. Next, multiplying by 2 in the tens column of the multiplier gives: $2 \times 7 = 12$, one dozen and two, 2 is written, and 1 is carried; $2 \times 5 = t$, $t + 1 = e$, e is written; $2 \times 2 = 4$, 4 is written. The partial products, 749 and $4e2$, are then added as in ordinary addition, but observing that $e + 7 = 16$. To check the product, use could be made of a device analogous to that of casting out nines, except that in this scale one could cast out elevens.

Casting out nines depends upon the fact that the remainder obtained by dividing a number by 9 is the same as that found by dividing the sum of its digits by 9. It is used chiefly as a check in multiplication; 274×38, for example, yields the product 10,412. To check this result, the digits in 274 are added, casting away each 9 as it occurs: $2 + 7 = 9$, which is cast away; 4 is left. A diagram is made, and the remainder 4 is written in the right section. The multiplier 38 is treated in the same way: $3 + 8 = 11$ or 9 and 2. The 9 is cast out and 2, the remainder, is written in the diagram across from the 4. The product itself is then subjected to the same procedure: $1 + 0 + 4 + 1 + 2 = 8$. The sum is 8, which is written at the bottom of the diagram. This number is compared to the product of the remainders from casting out 9 in the multiplier and multiplicand (the number at the top of the diagram). The two are identical; the original multiplication checks.

$$\begin{matrix} & 8 & \\ 2 & \times & 4 \\ & 8 & \end{matrix}$$

It will be clear now that use of the 12-scale or any other scale with ease and rapidity calls for the memorization of new addition and multiplication tables. In constructing tables for the 12-scale, the digits 1, 2, 3, 4, 5, 6, 7, 8, 9, *t, e,* 10 are placed in the top row and in the first column as shown. The symbols *t* and *e* are used to indicate that between 0 and the first number with two digits there are 11 numbers having only one digit. In order to maintain the positional relation, zero is part of the symbols representing one dozen (10), two dozen (20), three dozen (30), etc. The sum of any two numbers—one from the first column, the other from the first row—is written at their intersection in the addition table. In the multiplication table, the product of these two numbers appears at their intersection. For example, addition of 6 and 7 is written as 11 or one dozen and one (this is 13 in the 10-scale). Multiplication of 6 and 7 is the addition of 6 to itself 7 times; 36 is written at the intersection of these two numbers in the multiplication table. The number

Addition Table for the 12-scale

	1	2	3	4	5	6	7	8	9	t	e	10
1	2	3	4	5	6	7	8	9	t	e	10	11
2	3	4	5	6	7	8	9	t	e	10	11	12
3	4	5	6	7	8	9	t	e	10	11	12	13
4	5	6	7	8	9	t	e	10	11	12	13	14
5	6	7	8	9	t	e	10	11	12	13	14	15
6	7	8	9	t	e	10	11	12	13	14	15	16
7	8	9	t	e	10	11	12	13	14	15	16	17
8	9	t	e	10	11	12	13	14	15	16	17	18
9	t	e	10	11	12	13	14	15	16	17	18	19
t	e	10	11	12	13	14	15	16	17	18	19	1t
e	10	11	12	13	14	15	16	17	18	19	1t	1e
10	11	12	13	14	15	16	17	18	19	1t	1e	20
11	12	13	14	15	16	17	18	19	1t	1e	20	21
12	13	14	15	16	17	18	19	1t	1e	20	21	22

Multiplication Table for the 12-scale

1	2	3	4	5	6	7	8	9	t	e	10
2	4	6	8	t	10	12	14	16	18	1t	20
3	6	9	10	13	16	19	20	23	26	29	30
4	8	10	14	18	20	24	28	30	34	38	40
5	t	13	18	21	26	2e	34	39	42	47	50
6	10	16	20	26	30	36	40	46	50	56	60
7	12	19	24	2e	36	41	48	53	5t	65	70
8	14	20	28	34	40	48	54	60	68	74	80
9	16	23	30	39	46	53	60	69	76	83	90
t	18	26	34	42	50	5t	68	76	84	92	t0
e	1t	29	38	47	56	65	74	83	92	t1	e0
10	20	30	40	50	60	70	80	90	t0	e0	100

36, it is remembered, means 3 dozen and 6 or 42 in the 10-scale.

Though it is true, theoretically, that any whole number may be used as the base of a scale of notation, there are practical considerations which more or less force the selection to one of a few. Questions of divisibility, appropriateness to predetermined uses, etc., must be satisfied. It is desirable, also, that *n* be small, though not too small.

A number written in any scale may be converted to an equivalent number in any other scale. The number 1,397 of the 12-scale is converted to the 10-scale as follows:
$$1,397 = 1(12)^3 + 3(12)^2 + 9(12) + 7,$$
which equals $1,728 + 432 + 108 + 7$ or 2,275 in the customary decimal scale. To convert a number, say 2,275, to the 12-scale, it is repeatedly divided by 12, noting the remainders. These remainders, read backwards after the last quotient, give the desired number. Thus,

```
12 | 2275
12 |  189  —remainder 7
12 |   15  —remainder 9
12 |    1  —remainder 3
12      0  —remainder 1
```

The required number is 1,397.

HISTORY

Ancient Egypt. The earliest written records of arithmetic operations are found in the papyri of Egypt, notably that of Ahmes (c.3,000 B.C.) They disclose a knowledge of the addition of fractions, of arithmetic and geometric progressions, and of simple algebraic equations. These, however, appear only as solutions of stated, simple problems; there are no examples of logical development, axioms, deductions, generalizations, or adequate symbolism. Papyri written 2,000 years after Ahmes show no improvement.

Babylonia. The deciphering of Babylonian tablets reveals an arithmetic comparable to that of the Egyptians. It also reveals numeration by 60's and a knowledge of the principle of position. Introduction of this principle into the then young art of arithmetic was an important contribution. To show that a certain position was vacant, the zero was devised. It seems probable that the Babylonians used the zero in their calculations. Certain it is the Hindus did, and the Arabs, who borrowed the zero and numerals from the Hindus and passed them on to the Western World.

Ancient Greece. Greek arithmetic may be said to have begun with Pythagoras (c. 580-500 B.C.) and his school. The properties of numbers were studied by dot representations at first, as shown by the following representations of the odd numbers 1, 3, 5, and 7:

The first fits into the second to form the square :: or four; the first and second together fit into the third to form the square :⦙: or nine; the first, second, and third together fit into the fourth to form the square ⦙⦙⦙⦙ or 16, and so on.

Thus, it was deduced that the sum of the first *n* odd numbers is n^2 or, in symbols,
$$1 + 3 + 5 + 7 + \ldots + (2n - 1) = n^2.$$
Here the symbol $(2n - 1)$ has been used to indicate the *n*th odd number. If *n* is 2, the symbol gives the second odd number; if *n* is 3, the symbol gives the third, etc.

In the Pythagorean theory of ratios and proportions, numbers are represented by line segments and the products of two numbers by rectangles. These representations made it possible to perform graphically such operations as additions, subtractions, multiplications, and extractions of roots. In the graphical arithmetic of the Pythagoreans, there was an underlying assumption, namely, that a line consists of juxtaposed, indivisible dots or points, and that its length is proportional to the number of points it contains. This assumption led to the belief that the ratio of a line segment to another line segment was necessarily equal to the ratio of a whole number to another whole number. Then, it was discovered that there are numbers that cannot be represented in this manner. These numbers are called irrational numbers and their discovery is definitely attributed to the Pythagoreans. As to the method of discovery, however, opinions differ. The following method, which is most generally accepted, is the one given by Aristotle.

Pythagoras had proved that, for any right-angled triangle the square of the hypotenuse equals the sum of the squares of the two sides. This result may be pictured thus:

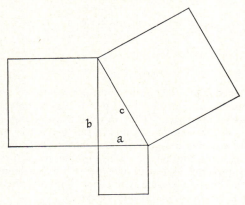

where a and b are the two sides and c is the hypotenuse. The relationship between the sides a and b and the hypotenuse c of any right-angled triangle is $a^2 + b^2 = c^2$. If a is 3 and b is 4, then c is the square root of 25; if a is 2 and b is 3, then c is the square root of 13. In the first, the sum $a^2 + b^2$ is a perfect square; in the second, it is not.

It follows that in the case of the unit square, which is a square of side 1, the diagonal is $\sqrt{2}$. If, as the Pythagoreans had assumed, a line segment bears to any other line segment a ratio which is equal to the ratio of a whole number m to another whole number n, then $\sqrt{2/1} = m/n$, that is, there must exist whole numbers m and n such that $m/n = \sqrt{2}$.

If the fraction m/n is in its lowest terms, then m and n are not both even. Squaring both sides of this equality gives $m^2/n^2 = 2$, which may be written $m^2 = 2n^2$. The right-hand member of this term is clearly even for any number multiplied by 2 is even; whence, the left-hand side m^2 is even also. From this it follows that m itself is even—if it were odd, its square would be odd. Since m is even, it may be written as $2s$, where s is another integer. Therefore,

$$m^2 = 2n^2 \text{ leads to}$$
$$4s^2 = 2n^2$$
whence,
$$2s^2 = n^2.$$

This means that n^2 and n also, is even. Thus, both m and n are even. This contradicts the original hypothesis that m and n are not both even. Therefore, $\sqrt{2}$ is not equal to a fraction m/n since the supposition that it is leads to a contradiction. It will be noticed that in this argument use has been made of the principle of contradiction in logic, namely, that a statement leading to a contradiction is false.

This was the way, according to Aristotle, that the Pythagoreans discovered there are line segments, and therefore numbers that express their lengths, which do not bear to one another a ratio of a whole number to a whole number. There are numbers which are not of the form m/n, the assumption being throughout that to every length on a straight line there corresponds a number which expresses its magnitude. Some of these numbers are of the form m/n; they are called rational numbers since they can be expressed as ratios of a whole number to a whole number. Some can not; these are called irrational.

The discovery of irrational numbers made the Pythagorean theory inapplicable to ratios a/b, where a and b are incommensurable magnitudes. A higher number system is developed in Book V of the *Elements* of Euclid. Known now to be due to Eudoxus (born c. 408 B.C.), the theory deals with a set C of magnitudes, a, b, c, ... about which the following assumptions are made explicitly or tacitly:

1. if $a = b$ and $b = c$, then $a = c$;
2. if $a > b$ and $b > c$, then $a > c$;
3. of the relations $a > b$, $a = b$, and $a < b$, one and only one holds;
4. if a and b are elements of C, then $(a + b)$ is also an element of C;
5. if $a < b$, there exists a number n such that $na > b$.
6. if a and b satisfy condition (5), then the ratios a/b and b/a exist.

After the ratios a/b are established by these assumptions, "equality" and "inequality" of ratios are defined thus:

Definition 1. If for every pair m and n of whole numbers, $ma \gtreqless nb$ according as $mc \gtreqless nd$, then $a/b = c/d$.

Definition 2. If for some pair of whole numbers m and n, $ma > nb$, but $mc \lesseqgtr nd$, then $a/b > c/d$.

The number system created by this theory of ratios is a more comprehensive one than that of the rational numbers, for in the ratio a/b, a and b are magnitudes given not necessarily by whole numbers or rational numbers, but by any numbers that satisfy assumptions (1) to (5) above. Assumption (5) of the list given above is one of the fundamental principles of infinitesimal analysis; its former name, "Archimedean Axiom" is now yielding to the more correct name, "Eudoxian Axiom."

The theory of proportions, as improved by Eudoxus (for the former one was applicable only to whole numbers and rational ones), became the most powerful tool of analysis in ancient mathematics. The skill that was developed in solving problems and proving theorems by means of proportions is phenomenal. This tool was used by Euclid, Aristarchus, Apollonius, Archimedes, and Ptolemy and reappears as late as 1638 in Galileo's *Two New Sciences*.

Practical arithmetic or the rules of computing solutions to practical problems was never developed in any outstanding manner by the Greeks. Their attitude towards mathematics was of a loftier, more philosophic nature; practical arithmetic was deemed vulgar and childish. Perhaps this is the reason why their system of numeration and notation was so cumbersome. The Greek numerals were the letters of their alphabet, plus three additional symbols: the σταῦ, ς, for the number 6; κόππα, ϙ, for 90; the σαμπτ, ⅃, for 900.

The Greek numerals and their corresponding values in our notation are:

α	β	γ	δ	ϵ	ς	ζ	η	θ
1	2	3	4	5	6	7	8	9
ι	κ	λ	μ	ν	ξ	o	π	ϙ
10	20	30	40	50	60	70	80	90

ρ	σ	τ	υ	ϕ	χ	ψ	ω	λ
100	200	300	400	500	600	700	800	900

${}_{\iota}\alpha$	${}_{\iota}\beta$	${}_{\iota}\gamma$	${}_{\iota}\delta$	
1,000	2,000	3,000	4,000	etc.

$\overline{\mathrm{M}}$	${}_{\beta}\overline{\mathrm{M}}$	${}_{\gamma}\overline{\mathrm{M}}$	
10,000	20,000	30,000	etc.

The clumsiness of mathematical operations in this system is shown by a multiplication carried out in the manner presented by Eutocius, a commentator of the 6th century of the Christian era. Derivation of the first partial product is readily seen by following the operation in our symbols; how the second was obtained may be confusing unless it is remembered that this is an interpretation in our symbols of the Greek ones. Thus 5 tens multiplied by 3 hundreds gives 15 thousand. In our symbols, this is simply 15,000; in the Greek symbols, it had to be written as ${}_{\alpha}\mathrm{M}$ or 10,000 and ${}_{\iota}\epsilon$ or 5,000. It will be noticed that the principle of position and zero are not used.

$\tau\nu\beta$		352
$\tau\nu\beta$		352
$\theta\mathrm{M}\alpha\mathrm{M}\epsilon$	χ	$90000 + 15000 + 600$
${}_{\alpha}\mathrm{M}_{\iota}\epsilon$	${}_{\iota}\beta\phi\rho$	$10000 + 5000 + 2000 + 500 + 100$
$\chi\rho\delta$		$600 + 100 + 4$
${}_{\iota}\mathrm{M}_{\beta}\mathrm{M}_{\iota}\gamma\psi\delta$		123904

The Romans also used the letters of their alphabet as numerals. In this system a new principle of notation appears. When a letter is written before one of higher value, its value is subtracted from the higher one. Thus, IV means 5 — 1 or 4; XL means 50 — 10 or 40; XC means 90; CD means 400; CM, 900, and so on. The Romans contributed nothing, however, to arithmetic.

Medieval Era. The Hindu-Arabic numerals, with the use of zero and the principle of position firmly established, became three important elements in the computational techniques of present-day arithmetic; they appear together for the first time in the works of Al-Khwarazmi (c. A.D. 825), a native of Khwaram (Khiva). Adelard of Bath (c. A.D. 1125) translated Al-Khwarazmi's arithmetic into Latin, as did John of Seville (c. A.D. 1150.) Leonardo of Pisa published the *Liber Abaci* in 1202. It contained a much expanded arithmetic, but one still based upon the arithmetic of the Arabs. Maximus Planude introduced this arithmetic in Constantinople. From John of Seville's translation *Liber Algorismi,* all later books on arithmetic were called books of algorism. Through a further confusion with the Greek word (*arithmos* = number), the barbarism "algorithm" came into being. The meaning of this word in mathematics is restricted now to an arithmetic process or set of processes by which a desired result is computed, for example, Euclid's algorism for the extraction of the square root, etc. Simultaneously with the establishment of the principle of position and the use of zero in computations came the adoption (and adaption to local needs) of the abacus (Greek *Abax* meaning "a counting board") for performing fundamental operations easily and quickly. The use of the abacus was widespread in the Middle East and China, and it remained in use in Europe until the end of the 16th century, when it was finally superseded by written computations.

Advance in the underlying theory of arithmetic was rapid after the 16th century. New symbols, extended number systems, new theories, and new algorisms brought arithmetic to its present state. *See also* ABACUS; DIVISOR, LOWEST COMMON; DUODECIMAL SYSTEM; LOWEST COMMON MULTIPLE; NUMBERS, THEORY OF; SERIES,   G. C. V.

ARIUS [ərɑɪˈəs; ɛˈərɪəs] (A.D. 256-336), early Christian leader, was born in Libya (or Alexandria) in 256. His name is associated with Arianism, a belief which held heretical ideas about the nature of Christ. Arius who was tall, lean, learned, morally exemplary, a fine orator, and inclined to be disputatious, was educated in the theological school of Antioch under the distinguished scholar Lucian. This school was noted for its emphasis upon (1) the historical and inductive method of religious investigation and (2) the unity and transcendence of the Godhead. Combined with these two characteristics was a tendency to regard Jesus Christ as a created being and subordinate to the Father, a tendency that had its effect upon Arius.

Arius became a presbyter in Alexandria, in charge of a church named Baucalis. In 318 he disagreed with his bishop, Alexander, on the nature of Christ, and as a result he was condemned with his friends at a synod at Alexandria in 320 or 321 and banished. Leaving Alexandria, he was received by two powerful churchmen, Eusebius of Caesarea and Eusebius of Nicomedia, who sympathized with his view. Both Bishop Alexander and Arius, who was aided by Eusebius of Nicomedia, defended their positions vigorously, until the churches in the East were greatly disturbed. The controversy became so universal that the Emperor Constantine, now military master of the East and the West, called the first General Council of the Church at Nicaea to decide the issue in May 325. Three parties emerged at the Council: the Arian, led by Eusebius of Nicomedia; the Alexandrian; and the moderate, led by Eusebius of Caesarea. The Council banished Arius to Illyria, condemned Arianism, and affirmed that the Christ was "begotten, not made," "of one essence [homoousian] with the Father." The unity of the Church seemed achieved.

However, controversy continued. Arius returned from banishment through the favor of the Empress Constantia and presented a new creed to the Emperor, which seemed like a retraction of his heretical views. The Emperor commanded that Arius be restored to his position in Alexandria, which Athanasius, who was then bishop of Alexandria, refused to do. Charged with insubordination, Athanasius was banished to Gaul in 335. The opposition to Arianism seemed broken, and the bishops decided to restore Arius to the fellowship of the Church through a formal ceremony. The aged Arius died in Constantinople in 336, before the ceremony took place, perhaps because the emotional stress was too great. His friends thought he had been poisoned, but his enemies regarded his death as the act of a vengeful Providence.

The principal work of Arius is *Thalia* ("The Banquet"), in which he defends his doctrine in prose and poetry. The document is lost and the knowledge of his writings comes through his critics. Arianism continued in the Church for many years, particularly in the Christianity of the Germanic tribes; Ulfilas, "the apostle to the Goths," was the Arian missionary to these peoples. *See also* ARIANISM; NICAEA, COUNCILS OF.   E. G. H.

ARIZONA, a southwestern border state of the United States, popularly known as the Grand Canyon State. Its name comes from the Papago Indian word meaning "little spring." Lying between 109° and 115° W. long. and 31° and 37° N. lat., Arizona is irregular in shape and is bounded on the west by California and Nevada, the Colorado River being the separating line for most of the boundary; on the north by Utah; on the east by New Mexico; and on the south by the state of Sonora, Mexico. Its northeast corner is the only place in the United States where four states join

(Arizona, New Mexico, Colorado, and Utah). In size almost equal to the total area of the New England states plus the state of New York, Arizona ranks fifth in the nation, covering 113,909 sq. mi., of which approximately 400 sq. mi. are water surface. The state is 375 mi. long and 340 mi. wide.

THE GREAT SEAL OF THE STATE OF ARIZONA

Arizona entered the Union on Feb. 14, 1912, the 48th state to achieve statehood. The state motto is *Ditat Deus* (God enriches); the state flower is the waxlike bloom of the saguaro cactus; the state tree is the palo verde; and the state bird is the cactus wren. Arizona has 14 counties, Coconino County (18,573 sq. mi.) being the nation's second largest county; (San Bernardino County in California is the largest).

GEOGRAPHIC FEATURES

Topography. Arizona is a complex of plateaus, mountains, deserts, and plains with elevations varying from 90 ft. above sea level near Yuma to 12,611 ft. at the summit of Humphreys Peak in the San Francisco Mountains north of Flagstaff. The mean altitude is 4,100 ft. The state has three principal topographic regions which are parts of the Colorado Plateaus, the Sonoran Desert, and the Mexican Highlands.

The Colorado Plateaus lie in the northern and northeastern part of the state and occupy approximately two fifths of its total area. With elevations ranging from 5,000 ft. on the plains to over 10,000 ft. on the high peaks, the plateaus are characterized by deep chasms cut by torrential streams, table-like mesas, basins enclosed by infacing cliffs, terraces rising above the plain, brilliantly colored deserts, and lofty mountain peaks. The most unusual feature of the plateau region is the Grand Canyon in the northwestern part of the state. North of the canyon is a series of plateau terraces descending from east to west like huge steps, each step being about 1,000 ft. high. They are successively the Kaibab Plateau, 9,000 ft. high and 35 mi. wide, bordered on the east by the Marble Canyon of the Colorado and on the west by an almost vertical cliff; the Kanab, ending at the west with the Toro-weap escarpment; the Umkaret, which has about 160 volcanic cones and Mt. Trumbull rising nearly 2,000 ft. above it; and Shivwits, separated from the Umkaret by the Hurricane Ledge and terminating at the west with the Grand Wash Cliffs.

South of the Grand Canyon is the San Francisco Plateau, an area of 2,000 to 3,000 sq. mi. covered by lava flows and dotted with several hundred volcanic cones. Its general level is 5,000 to 7,000 ft. above sea level. Directly north of Flagstaff the San Francisco Mountains rise 5,000 ft. above this level.

In the northeastern part of the state is the Navajo section,

which takes its name from the Indian reservation. It is noted for the Echo Cliffs, which lie immediately east of the Grand Canyon; for the Black Mesa, a tableland in northern Navajo and Apache counties, 60 mi. in diameter and having outfacing cliffs 2,000 ft. high; and for the Painted Desert east of the Little Colorado River.

The second distinct topographic area comprises the southwestern portion of Arizona, known locally as the Gila Desert. A part of the Sonoran Desert, the region consists of widely separated, short mountain ranges and desert plains which slope uniformly to the south and west. More than half of the Gila Desert is below 2,000 ft. in elevation; a considerable area is below 1,000 ft. The lower course of the Gila River flows across it before joining the Colorado at Yuma.

Arizona's third topographic region is a mountainous area which occupies the southeastern part of the state and extends diagonally, in a northwesterly direction, from the Mexican border to the Colorado River, north of the Gila Desert. A volcanic escarpment known as the Mogollon Rim parallels these mountain ranges as far as central Arizona and separates the region from the northern plateau area. The highlands are a combination of basins, called bolsons, and ranges similar to those of the Gila Desert but distinguished therefrom by higher altitudes, less desert region, larger mountains, and a greater number of rivers. Intermediate between these highlands and the extreme desert to the west is found the most productive agricultural section of the state. The Gila River and its tributaries supply water to irrigate the extensive valley areas.

Mountains. Among Arizona's numerous mountain ranges, the highest points are Humphreys Peak (12,611 ft.) and Agassiz Peak (12,340 ft.), in the San Francisco range; Baldy Peak (11,590 ft.) and Greens Peak (10,115 ft.) in the White Mountains, in eastern Arizona; and Mt. Graham 10,713 ft.), in the Pinaleno Mountains, in southeastern Arizona.

Rivers and Lakes. Arizona's principal river is the Colorado, which enters the state near the center of the north boundary, flows south and west through the Grand Canyon, then south until it empties into the Gulf of California. Other important rivers are the Little Colorado, the Virgin, and the Williams, all three tributaries of the Colorado; the Gila, which flows through the southern part of the state from east to west and enters the Colorado at Yuma; the San Pedro, Salt, Agua Fria, and Hassayampa, all tributaries of the Gila; and the Verde, an affluent of the Salt, from which Phoenix derives its water supply. The streams of the desert area, fed by heavy rains in May and June, dry up almost entirely during the rest of the year. The Santa Cruz, flowing north past Tucson, terminates in the desert before reaching the Gila.

Arizona has few natural lakes, the principal ones being Mormon Lake and Lake Mary, both in Coconino County, but it has a number of artificial lakes, formed by dams constructed in the rivers for purposes of flood control, irrigation, and power development. The largest artificial lakes are Lake Mead, on the state line between Nevada and Arizona, formed by the Hoover Dam on the Colorado River at the western end of the Grand Canyon; Roosevelt Reservoir, formed by Roosevelt Dam in central Arizona on the Salt River; San Carlos Reservoir, in southeastern Arizona on the Gila River; and Lake Pleasant, in western Arizona formed by Lake Pleasant Dam on the Agua Fria River.

VIEW OF THE GRAND CANYON FROM ITS HIGHEST SPOT, POINT IMPERIAL ON THE NORTH RIM

Geologic Phenomena. Arizona has many unusual topographic features, of which the Grand Canyon is the most spectacular. Cut by the Colorado River, which winds through it for more than 200 mi., the canyon is more than a mile deep and in some places 15 mi. wide. The most scenic part of the canyon lies within the Grand Canyon National Park.

A WINTER CARROT FIELD NEAR YUMA

The Painted Desert is another unique topographic area. An arid plateau with little vegetation, the desert is about 15 mi. wide and extends for more than 100 mi. north of Winslow along the east side of the Little Colorado River and Marble Canyon. Known as Asa-ma-unda ("the country of departed spirits") by the Hopi Indians, the region is marked by low mesas with naked marls and soft rocks of red, chocolate, vermilion, pink, buff, and gray colors.

The Petrified Forest, a national monument, is located near Adamana in northeastern Arizona. Here are the remains of huge fallen trees that stood in prehistoric times and have been metamorphosed to brilliantly colored stone.

Sunset Crater, near Flagstaff, is an inactive volcanic crater scarred by lava flows; it is the site of a lava cave which contains ice at all seasons. Other areas of geologic interest include Oak Creek Canyon, called the Little Grand Canyon, and Meteor Crater, both in Coconino County; Monument Valley, in Navajo County; and the pinnacles and balanced rocks found in the Chiracahua National Monument, in Cochise County.

Climate. The local climates of Arizona, created by the vastness of its territory, its dissimilarity of surface, and differences of elevation above sea level, are many and varied, but all are characterized by dryness and clearness. The mean annual temperature of the state is 61.5° F. In the north at an altitude of 5,000 ft. and upward the mean annual temperature is 45.7° F.; in the south central plains, at about 1,000 ft., the mean annual is 69.7° F. Summer temperatures average 69° F. in the northern counties of the state, and 88° F. in the southwest. The average maximum for these areas and for the season is 85° F. in the north and 104° F. in the southwest. The lower Gila Valley, in Yuma County, which has suffered temperatures of 130° F., has the hottest weather and the least rainfall. The northern winter average stands at 34° F., with a minimum at 19° F. In the southwest, the average winter temperature is 54° F., with an average minimum set at 36°

F. Rainfall is heaviest in the high plateau area which registers an annual average of 31 in. The low plains section records an average annual rainfall of 8 in., dropping to a minimum of 2.5 in. Little snow is seen except in the northern plateau region. The heaviest fall, measured on the north rim of the Grand Canyon, is recorded as 119 in. The growing season varies from 266 days in the Salt River valley to 311 days in the Yuma valley.

Soils. The soils of almost all of Arizona's 73,000,000 acres are fertile. The high plateaus and mountains of the northern, eastern, and central parts are heavily forested or covered intermittently with brush and grasslands upon which many herds of cattle, sheep, and goats subsist. The semiarid areas of the south and west, which have 90 per cent of the arable lands, are dependent upon irrigation for their fertility. The soils of the plains and valleys, brought from the surrounding mountains by water and wind, vary from heavy clay to coarse sand, with sand loam and silt loam predominating. Containing large quantities of potassium and adequate phosphate, their fertility is readily manifested by irrigation. Because of scant vegetation and little accumulation of organic matter from plant debris, humus and nitrogen are usually deficient, a condition quickly corrected by means of green manure crops.

Forests. In the area between the desert and the evergreen forests of the mountains in the southwest and in the north central portion of the state are found scattered growths of juniper, piñon, and several species of evergreen oak. At

Navajo woman and child in Monument Valley, Arizona

altitudes of 5,000 to 7,000 ft., except for the San Francisco peak region, there stretches an evergreen coniferous forest, its heaviest growth extending southeast from south of the San Francisco peaks to the New Mexico border. At higher altitudes, from 7,000 to 9,000 ft., ponderosa pine predominates. Above this, some deciduous species, mainly oak and aspen, mingle with Douglas fir and Engelmann spruce. In the

DESERT CACTI FRINGE SAN CARLOS LAKE IN SOUTHERN ARIZONA

canyons far below are thickets of ash, cherry, cottonwood, sycamore, walnut and willow.

Arizona's seven national forests, the Apache, Cococino, Coronado, Kaibab, Prescott, Sitgreaves, and Tonto, covering a total of 11,427,008 acres, have attained major importance as recreational areas, with over one million visitors annually using them for camping, hunting, and fishing. In addition, over 200,000 cattle, horses, sheep, and goats graze on the forest ranges.

Flora. Arizona's plant life ranges from the subtropical organ pipe cactus of the southwestern desert to the snowbank primrose blossoming in the snow of the San Francisco mountains at 12,000 ft. Most spectacular of Arizona flora are the numerous cacti. The largest of the group is the giant saguaro, which grows 50 ft. high and is found in veritable forest stands. The pure white, waxy blossom of this mammoth column is the state flower. Other varieties of cacti are the cholla, called the "jumping cactus" because its sharp spines are so easily detached; the bisnaga, or barrel cactus, from which candy is made, and which derives its common name from its shape and from the fact that palatable water may be secured from the crushed pulp of its head; several varieties of opuntia, or prickly pear; and the ocotilla, which has long green wands decorated with brilliant red flowers.

Closely akin to the cacti are the yuccas, conspicuous among which are the Joshua tree and the Spanish bayonet. Sagebrush, typical of northern deserts, is found north of the Grand Canyon, and shad scale occurs in heavy alkaline areas. Creosote bush, or greasewood, is a common shrub of the southwestern portion. Black brush occurs in the southeast, and drought-resistant mesquite, palo verde, and ironwood trees are found in the arid areas. The mesquite has been called the most useful desert tree. Its wide spreading branches form shelter for man and livestock; its long pods of beans serve as food for man and stock; the bark has medicinal properties; and the wood is valuable for fence posts and fuel. Of great economic value also are the native grasses, upon which depends the state's range industry. Blue grama is usually found only at high altitudes, but galleta grass is more widely distributed. In the lower areas the mesquite grasses prevail—black and crowfoot grama, curly mesquite, and tabosa grass. Large areas for the preservation of desert flora have been set aside in the Organ Pipe Cactus National Monument south of Ajo and the Saguaro National Monument near Tucson.

Fauna. The animal life of Arizona is plentiful, though not in great variety. In the pine forests, the Rocky Mountain mule deer are found; in the mesquite, cactus, and grassland of the southern and western areas, the Mexican mule deer and the burro deer; in the chaparral-covered foothills of rough mountain ranges, the Arizona whitetail deer. Herds of antelope share range pastures with domestic cattle. In the western desert mountains, below the yellow pine, desert bighorn sheep and, farther south, short-tailed Gaillard bighorn are found. The javelina, peccary, or wild pig is the smallest of Arizona's big game. Elk and buffalo are also numbered with the big game, but they are not native. The elk, well distributed over the Mogollon Plateau, were imported in 1913; the buffalo are found in

FPG

AN OPEN PIT COPPER MINE IS WORKED AT MORENCI, ARIZONA

House Rock Valley and are state owned. The black or brown bear is classed as a game animal, and its range corresponds to the forested areas. Predatory animals include the mountain lion, lynx, bobcat, jaguar, and ocelot, and of the dog species, the coyote and the lobo, or timber wolf. Rodent species, many almost extinct, include the beaver, muskrat, porcupine, tree squirrels, prairie dog, chipmunk, ground squirrel, pack rat, pocket gopher, and kangaroo rat. Jack rabbits and cottontail rabbits are the small game animals.

Arizona has about 400 species of birds, including winter and summer visitors and about 150 permanent residents. Among the game birds are the Merriam wild turkey, the Gambrel quail, and several species of doves. Birds of prey include numerous varieties of eagles, vultures, hawks, owls, and an interesting member of the cuckoo family, locally named the road runner, which is an omnivorous feeder on small reptiles and insects. Reptilian fauna includes the poisonous Gila monster, a slow-moving, awkward lizard, as well as many other lizards, several species of rattlesnakes, and the king and gopher snakes.

ECONOMIC RESOURCES AND ACTIVITIES

Mining. With an annual return from mining of $200,000,000 (five-year average, 1948-1953), Arizona is a leading state in the production of essential metals, copper, lead, zinc, silver, and gold. The state is responsible for about 40 per cent of the total copper production of the United States.

The earliest mining operations of any extent were developed during the nineteenth century by the Mexicans who worked the silver deposits in the mountainous region of the southeast. About 1860, placer deposits of gold were discovered and exploited along the lower courses of the Colorado and Gila rivers; later, around 1880, a rich gold lode was discovered and worked at Tombstone. Copper mining was instituted at Bisbee in 1880, and until other copper mines were opened at Jerome, Globe, and Morenci, Bisbee produced the major part of Arizona's copper output. Several of the richest copper lodes have been exhausted, but operations have been diverted to lower-grade ores, and Arizona's copper resources are by no means depleted. Relatively low-

MONUMENTAL BUTTES IN TSELANI, ARIZONA, ABOUT 35 MILES NORTH OF GANADO

EWING GALLOWAY

ARIZONA
Index to Physical Features and Points of Interest

TOPOGRAPHIC FEATURES
Islands, Peninsulas, Capes, Mountains, Plateaus, Valleys, etc.

Apache, peak, 7,684'	D 3
Baboquivari, mountains	D 3
Baker, butte, 8,182'	B 3
Baldy, peak, 11,590'	C 4
Bangs, mountain, 7,500'	A 2
Barnes, peak, 5,028'	D 3
Bill Williams, mountain, 9,264'	B 2
Black, mesa	A 3
Black, mountain, 5,583'	C 3
Black, mountains	B 1
Black, peak, 1,656'	B 1
Bradshaw, mountains	B 2
Carrizo, mountains	A 4
Castledome, mountains	C 1
Chinle, valley	A 4
Chiricahua, peak, 9,795'	D 4
Chuska, mountains	A 4
Cochise Head, mountain, 8,100'	C 4
Coconino, plateau	B 2
Colorado, plateaus	A 2
Crossman, peak, 4,340'	B 1
Dellenbaugh, mountain, 6,750'	A 2
Diablo, canyon	B 3
Floyd, mountain, 7,500'	B 2
Four Peaks, mountain, 7,691'	D 2
Galiuro, mountains	C 3
Gila, mountains	C 4
Gila Bend, mountains	C 2
Gothic, mesas	A 4
Graham, mountain, 10,720'	C 4
Grand, canyon	A 2
Grand Wash, cliffs	A 2
Greens, peak, 10,115'	B 4
Harcuvar, mountains	C 2
Highest Point in Arizona, 12,655'	B 3
(Humphreys Peak)	
Hopi, buttes	B 3
Hualpai, mountains	B 2
Hualpai, peak, 8,266'	B 2
Humphreys, peak, 12,655'	B 3
(Highest Point in Arizona)	
Iron, mountain, 6,075'	C 3
Kaibab, plateau	A 2
King's Crown, mountain, 6,075'	D 2
Lemmon, mountain, 9,185'	C 3
Logan, mountain, 7,700'	A 2
McDowell, mountain, 4,022'	D 2
Maple, peak, 8,302'	C 4
Marble, canyon	A 3
Maricopa, mountains	D 1
Mazatzal, mountains	B 3
Mazatzal, peak, 7,888'	B 3
Miller, peak, 9,445'	D 3
Mineral, mountain, 3,350'	D 2
Mogollon, plateau	B 3
Music, mountain, 6,761'	B 2
Natanes, plateau	C 3
Navajo, mountain, 10,416'	A 3
Oak Creek, canyon	B 3
Painted, desert	A 3
Pastora, peak, 9,420'	A 4
Peacock, mountains, 6,268'	B 2
Peloncillo, mountains	C 4
Pinal, mountains	C 3
Pinal, peak, 7,850'	D 3
Roof, butte, 9,576'	A 4
Rose, peak, 8,787'	C 4
Santa Catalina, mountains	C 3
Santa Maria, mountains	B 2
Sauceda, mountains	C 2
Sheep, mountain, 3,150'	C 1
Sierra Ancha, mountains	C 3
Spud Rock, mountain, 8,590'	C 3
Sulphur Spring, valley	C 4
Table, mountain, 6,145'	C 3
Table Top, mountain, 4,373'	C 2
Tipton, mountain, 7,364'	B 1
Tritle, mountain, 7,793'	B 2
Turret, peak, 6,000'	B 3
Virgin, mountains	A 2
Weaver, mountains	B 2
Woolsey, peak, 3,199'	C 2
Wrightson, peak, 9,432'	D 3

HYDROGRAPHIC FEATURES
Lakes, Rivers, Creeks, Bays, Straits, Seas, etc.

Agua Fria, river	C 2
Big Sandy, river	B 2
Black, river	C 3
Carrizo, creek	B 4
Chevalon, creek	B 3
Chinle, creek	A 4
Clear, creek	B 3
Colorado, river	A 3
Corn, creek	B 3
Fish, creek	D 2
Gila, river	C 2
Hassayampa, creek	C 2
Havasu, creek	B 2
Havasu, lake	B 1
Kanab, creek	A 2
Leroux, wash	B 3
Little Colorado, river	B 3
Moenkopi, wash	A 3
Oraibi, wash	A 3
Pari, river	A 3
Pinto, creek	D 3
Pleasant, lake	C 2
Pueblo Colorado, wash	B 4
Puerco, river	B 4
Queen, creek	D 2
Roosevelt, lake	C 3
Salt, river	C 3
San Carlos, reservoir	C 3
San Francisco, river	C 4
San Pedro, river	C 3
San Simon, creek	C 4
Santa Cruz, river	C 3
Santa Maria, river	B 2
Verde, river	B 3
Waterman, wash	D 1
White, river	C 3
Williams, river	B 2
Zuni, river	B 4

SPECIAL POINTS OF INTEREST
Parks, Monuments, Ruins, Dams, Sites, Buildings, etc.

Camp McDowell, Indian reservation	C 3
Canyon De Chelly, national monument	A 4
Casa Grande, national monument	C 2
Chiricahua, national monument	C 4
Cliff Dwellings	A 3
Colorado River, Indian reservation	C 1
Dinosaur Tracks	B 3
Early Notorious Mining Camp, near Tombstone	D 3
Extinct Volcanoes and Lava Beds	B 4
Fort Apache, Indian reservation	B 3
Fort Mohave, Indian reservation	B 1
Ghost Town of the Colorado, near Quartzsite	C 1
Gila Bend, Indian reservation	C 2
Gila River, Indian reservation	C 3
Gillespie, dam	C 2
Grand Canyon, national monument	A 2
Grand Canyon, national park	A 2
Hoover, dam	A 1
Hopi, Indian reservation	A 3
Hualpai, Indian reservation	B 2
Imperial Diversion, dam	C 1
Kaibab, Indian reservation	A 2
Laguna, dam	C 1
Lowell Observatory, Flagstaff	B 3
Maricopa, Indian reservation	C 2
Meteor, crater	B 3
Montezuma Castle, national monument	B 3
Morelos, dam	C 1
Navajo, Indian reservation	A 3
Navajo, national monument	A 3
Old Butterfield Stage Station, near Dome	C 1
Organ Pipe Cactus, national monument	C 2
Papago, Indian reservation	C 2
Parker, dam	B 1
Permanent Mirage, Willcox Dry Lake, near Willcox	C 4
Petrified Forest	A 4
Petrified Forest, national monument	B 4
Pictograph Rocks	C 2
Pictured Rocks	C 3
Pipe Spring, national monument	A 2
Saguaro, national monument	C 3
Salt River, Indian reservation	D 2
San Carlos, Indian reservation	C 3
San Xavier, Indian reservation	C 3
San Xavier Del Bac Mission, near Tucson	C 3
Sunset Crater, national monument	B 3
Tonto, national monument	C 3
Tonto Natural Bridge	B 3
Tumacacori, national monument	D 3
Tuzigoot, national monument	B 3
University of Arizona, Tucson	C 3
Walnut Canyon, national monument	B 3
White Mesa Natural Bridge	A 3
Wupatki, national monument	B 3

CITIES AND TOWNS

Aguila, 147..........C 2
Ajo, 5,817..........C 3
Alpine, 250..........C 4
Alzona Park, 2,000..D 2
Amado, 150..........D 3
Anita, 22..........B 2
Apache, 45..........B 4
Apache Junction, 20..D 2
Arivaca, 150..........C 3
Arizola, 100..........C 3
Arlington, 25..........C 2
Artesia, 40..........B 2
Ash Fork, 675..........B 2
Ashurst, 175..........C 4
Avondale, 2,505..........D 1
Aztec, 50..........C 3
Bagdad, 800..........B 2
Bakersville, 350..........B 4
Bannon, 100..........C 3
Bapchule, 150..C 3, D 2
Barr, 15..........D 2
Bellemont, 35..........B 3
Benson, 1,440..........D 3
Bisbee, 3,801..........D 4
Blue, 125..........E 4
Bon, 10..........E 2
Bonita, 100..........C 4
Bosque, 22..........E 1
Bouse, 100..........C 2
Bowie, 600..........C 4
Buckeye, 1,932..C 2, D 1
Bylas, 636..........C 4
Cactus, 125..........C 3
Calva, 75..........C 4
Cameron, 25..........B 3
Camp Verde, 450..........B 3
Cane Beds, 45..........A 2
Casa Grande, 4,181..C 3
Cascabel, 50..........C 4
Cashion, 100..........D 1
Castle Hot Springs, 50..C 2
Cavecreek, 175..........C 3
Centerville, 250..........B 2
Central, 290..........C 4
Chandler, 4,887*..C 3, D 2
Chandler Heights, 300..D 2
Chinle, 140..........A 4
Chino Valley, 350..........B 3
Chloride, 719..........B 1
Choulic, 104..........D 3
Christmas, 129..........C 3
Cibecue, 35..........B 3
Clarkdale, 1,609..........B 3
Claypool, 1,177..C 3, D 3
Clay Springs, 154..........B 3
Cleator, 46..........B 2
Clemenceau, 300..........B 3
Clifton, 3,466..........C 4
Cochise, 65..........D 4
Concho, 458..........B 4
Congress, 100..........B 2
Constellation, 23..........B 2
Coolidge, 4,306..C 3, D 2
Coolidge Dam, 25..........C 3
Cornfields, 42..........B 4
Cortaro, 25..........C 3
Cottonwood-Clemenceau,
  1,626..........B 2
Crown King, 50..........B 2
Crozier, 35..........B 1
Cyclopic, 10..........B 1
Dateland, 50..........C 2
Desert Wells, 10..........D 2
Dock, 35..........D 2
Dome, 50..........C 1
Dos Cabezas, 262..........C 4
Douglas, 9,442..........C 4
Dragoon, 60..........C 3
Drake, 10..........B 2
Duncan, 941..........C 4
Eagar, 637..........B 4
Eden, 215..........C 4
Elfrida, 38..........C 4
Elgin, 44..........D 3
El Mirage, 1,111*..........D 1
Eloy, 3,580..........C 3
Emery Park, 250..........C 3
Escuela, 150..........C 3
Espero, 30..........C 4
Estrella, 20..........E 1
Fairbank, 30..........D 3
Feldman, 40..........C 3
Flagstaff, 7,663..........B 3
Florence, 1,776..C 3, D 2
Florence Junction, 15..D 2
Fort Apache, 150..........C 4
Fort Defiance, 645..........B 4
Fort Grant, 150..........C 4
Fort Huachuca, 1,500..D 3

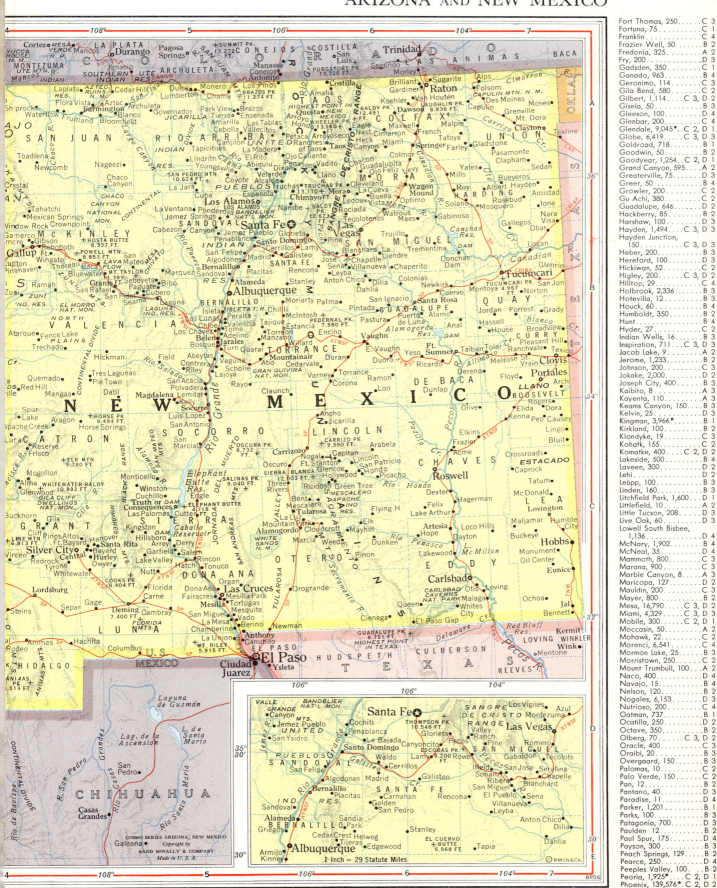

Statute Miles
Kilometers

Lambert Conformal Conic Projection
SCALE 1:3,674,000   1 Inch = 58 Statute Miles

1 Inch = 29 Statute Miles

8R56

ARIZONA *Continued*

Picacho, 100....C 3
Pima, 824....C 4
Pine, 70....B 3
Pinedale, 192....B 3
Pinetop, 300....B 4
Pirtleville, 898....D 4
Plenty, 35....B 4
Polacca, 600....B 3
Pomerene, 300....C 3
Portal, 100....D 4
Poston, 25....D 2
Prescott, 6,764....B 2
Quartzsite 150....C 1
Queen, 95....D 2
Queen Creek, 20....D 2
Quijotoa, 10....C 2
Ray, 594....C 3, D 3
Redington, 50....C 3
Red Rock 50....C 3
Rillito, 50....C 3
Rimmy Jims, 50....B 3
Rimrock, 25....B 3
Rittenhouse, 50....D 2
Rock Point, 5....A 4
Rock Springs, 200....B 2
Roll, 300....C 2
Roosevelt....C 3, D 3
Rowood, 842....C 2
Ruby, 30....D 3
Sacaton, 584....C 3, D 2
Safford, 4,378*....C 4
Sahuarita, 200....D 3
St. David, 700....D 3
St. Johns, 1,469....B 4
St. Michaels, 50....B 4
Salome, 75....C 2
San Carlos, 100....C 3
San Luis, 38....C 1
San Miguel, 256....D 3
San Simon, 700....C 4
Santan, 206....C 3, D 2
San Xavier, 26....D 3
Sasabe, 75....D 3
Sawmill, 50....B 4
Scottsdale, 2,032..C 3, D 2
Second Mesa, 300....B 3
Sedona, 280....B 3
Seligman, 764....B 2
Sells, 789....D 3
Sentinel, 78....C 2
Serape....D 2
Sheldon, 75....C 4
Short Creek, 90....A 2
Show Low, 450....B 3
Shumway, 80....B 3
Shungopavy, 450....B 3
Signal, 25....B 2
Silverbell, 6....C 3
Skull Valley, 200....B 2
Snowflake, 929....B 3
Solomon, 753....C 4
Sombrero Butte, 5....C 3
Somerton, 1,825....C 1
Sonora, 1,821....C 3, D 3
South Tucson, 2,364....C 3
Springerville, 689....B 4
Sunglow, 15....D 4
Sunnyslope, 4,420....D 2
Sunset, 50....C 3
Supai, 230....A 2
Superior, 4,291....C 3, D 3
Tacna, 7....C 1
Taylor, 400....B 3
Tempe, 7,684....C 3, D 2
Thatcher, 1,284....C 4
Theba, 150....C 2
Thompson, 20....D 2
Tiger, 998....C 3
Tolleson, 3,042....D 1
Tombstone, 910....D 3
Tonalea, 9....A 3
Tonto Basin, 50....C 3
Topawa, 304....D 3
Topock, 55....B 1
Toreva, 100....B 3
Tortilla Flat, 56....D 2
Tubac, 500....D 3
Tuba City, 150....A 3
Tucson, 60,268*....C 3
Tusayan, 20....B 2
Tuweep, 44....A 2
Twin Buttes, 74....D 3
Vahki, 50....D 2
Valentine, 80....B 2
Valle, 10....B 2
Vamori, 127....D 3
Vernon....B 4
Vicksburg, 15....C 2
Waddell, 600....C 2, D 1
Walker, 60....B 2
Warren, 2,610....D 4
Wellton, 150....C 1
Wenden, 80....C 2
Whipple, 400....B 2
Whiteriver, 200....C 4
Wickenburg, 1,736....C 2
Wide Ruin, 25....B 4
Wikieup, 100....B 2
Willaha, 10....B 2
Willcox, 1,266....C 4
Williams, 2,152....B 2
Window Rock, 400....B 4
Winkelman, 548....C 3, E 3
Winona, 6....B 3
Winslow, 6,518....B 3
Wittmann, 60....C 2
Wolf Hole, 10....A 2
Woodruff, 225....B 3
Woolaroc, 60....C 4
Wooley, 10....D 3
Yarnell, 75....B 2
Young, 200....B 3
Yucca, 60....B 1
Yuma, 9,145....C 1
Zeniff, 20....B 3

COUNTIES

Apache, 27,767....B 4
Cochise, 31,488....D 4
Coconino, 32,910....B 2
Gila, 24,158....C 3
Graham, 12,985....C 3
Greenlee, 12,805....C 4
Maricopa, 331,770....C 2
Mohave, 8,510....B 1
Navajo, 29,446....B 3
Pima, 141,216....C 2
Pinal, 43,191....C 3
Santa Cruz, 9,344....D 3
Yavapai, 24,991....B 2
Yuma, 28,006....C 1

NEW MEXICO

Area.....121,666 sq. m.
Population......681,187

CITIES AND TOWNS

Abeytas, 120....B 5
Abiquiu....A 5
Abo, 300....B 5
Acme, 125....C 6
Adelino, 400....B 5
Alameda, 1,792....B 5, D 5
Alamo, 49....B 6
Alamogordo, 6,783....C 6
Albert, 36....B 7
Albuquerque, 96,815 B 5, D 5
Alcalde, 325....A 5
Algodones, 290....B 5, D 6
Alma, 95....C 4
Alps, 89....A 7
Amalia, 350....A 6
Amistad, 35....B 7
Anal, 43....B 6
Ancho, 100....C 6
Animas, 150....D 4
Anthony, 1,800....D 5
Anton Chico, 435 B 6, D 7
Apache Creek, 15....C 4
Arabela, 80....C 6
Aragon, 200....C 4
Arch, 200....B 7
Archuleta, 35....A 5
Armijo, 4,516....D 5
Arrey, 298....C 5
Arroyo Hondo, 541....A 6
Arroyoseco, 727....A 6
Artesia, 8,244....C 6
Atarque, 10....B 4
Aztec, 885....A 5
Azul, 5....D 7
Baca, 75....B 4
Bayard, 2,119....C 4
Belen, 4,495....B 5
Bennett, 225....C 7
Bent, 200....C 6
Berino, 300....C 5
Bernalillo, 1,922....B 5, D 6
Bibo, 215....B 5
Blanchard, 100....B 6, D 7
Blanco, 80....A 5
Bloomfield, 619....A 4
Bluewater, 250....B 5
Bluit, 50....C 7
Bosque, 150....B 5
Brazos, 200....A 5
Brilliant, 400....A 6
Broadview, 64....B 7
Buckeye, 289....C 7
Buckhorn, 100....C 4
Buena Vista, 140....B 6
Bueyeros, 50....B 7
Cabezon, 69....B 5
Cambray, 75....C 5
Canjilon....A 5
Canyon, 175....B 5, D 5
Canyoncito, 60....D 6
Capitan, 575....C 6
Caprock, 100....C 7
Capulin, 300....A 7
Carlsbad, 17,975....C 6
Carnahan, 100....D 6
Carne....C 5
Carrizozo, 1,389....C 6
Causey, 69....C 7
Cebolla, 100....A 5
Cedar Crest, 100....D 6
Cedar Hill, 200....A 5
Cedarvale, 5....B 6
Central, 1,511....C 4
Cerrillos, 660....B 5, D 6
Chaco Canyon, 100....A 5
Chacon, 400....A 6
Chama, 919....A 5
Chamberino, 210....C 5
Chapelle, 300....B 6, D 7
Chaperito, 100....B 6
Chilili, 100....B 5
Chimayo, 1,800....B 6
Chloe, 150....B 5
Cienega, 43....C 6
Cimarron, 855....A 6
Clapham, 12....A 7
Claunch, 50....B 5
Clayton, 3,515....A 7
Cleveland....A 6
Cliff, 161....C 4
Cloudcroft, 251....C 6
Clovis, 17,318....B 7
Cochiti, 50....D 6
Colmor, 150....A 6
Colonias....B 6
Columbus, 251....D 5
Conchas Dam, 550....B 6
Contreras, 70....B 5
Corona, 530....B 6
Costilla, 971....A 6
Coyote, 300....A 5
Crossroads, 2....C 7
Crownpoint, 90....B 4
Crystal, 7....A 4
Cuba, 733....B 5
Cubero, 500....B 5
Cuchillo, 200....C 5
Cuervo, 150....B 6
Cutter, 20....C 5
Dahlia, 25....B 6, D 7
Datil, 61....B 5
Dawson, 1,206....A 6
Dayton, 105....C 6
Deming, 5,672....C 5
Dereno, 4....B 7
Derry, 200....C 5
Des Moines, 282....A 7
Dexter, 784....C 6
Dilia, 250....B 6, D 7
Dixon, 800....A 6
Dona Ana, 500....C 5
Dora, 100....C 7
Dulce, 150....A 5
Dunken, 10....C 6
Dunlap, 5....B 6
Duoro, 15....B 6
Duran, 300....B 6
Dwyer, 120....C 5
Eagle Nest, 300....A 6
East Vaughn, 423....B 6
Edgewood, 40....D 6
Elida, 430....C 7
Elk, 17....C 6
Elkins, 20....C 6
El Paso Gap, 5....C 6
El Pueblo, 100....D 7
El Rito, 707....A 5
Encino, 408....B 6
Engle, 50....C 5
Ensenada, 375....A 5
Espanola, 1,446....B 5
Estancia, 916....B 5
Eunice, 2,352....C 7
Fairacres, 200....C 5
Farley, 175....A 6
Farmington, 12,449*....A 4
Felix....C 6
Fence Lake, 75....B 4
Field, 59....B 5
Flora Vista, 250....A 4
Florida, 15....C 5
Floyd, 50....B 7
Flying H, 35....C 6
Folsom, 206....A 7
Forrest, 110....B 7
Fort Bayard, 750....C 4
Fort Stanton, 490....C 6
Fort Sumner, 1,982....B 6
Fort Wingate, 100....B 4
Frazier, 37....C 6
French, 103....A 6
Frisco, 105....C 4
Fruitland, 300....A 4
Gabaldon, 150....D 7
Gage, 12....C 4
Galisteo....B 5, D 6
Gallegos....B 7
Gallup, 9,133....B 4
Gamerco, 600....B 4
Gardiner, 300....A 6
Garfield, 200....C 5
Gibson, 250....B 4
Gila, 200....C 4
Gladstone, 9....A 7
Glencoe, 200....C 6
Glenrio, 80....B 7
Glenwood, 100....C 4
Glorieta, 500....B 6, D 8
Golden, 75....D 6
Governador, 35....A 5
Grady, 130....B 7
Grants, 2,251....B 5
Green Tree 363....C 6
Grenville, 102....A 7
Griegos, 100....D 5
Guadalupita, 520....A 6
Hachita, 200....D 4
Hagerman, 1,024....C 6
Hanover, 800....C 4
Hassell, 50....B 7
Hatch, 1,064....C 5
Hayden, 100....B 7
Heck Canyon, 250....A 6
Helweg, 175....D 6
Hickman, 4....B 5
Hillsboro, 350....C 5
Hobbs, 13,875....C 7
Hollywood, 100....C 6
Hondo, 200....C 6
Hope, 186....C 6
Horse Springs, 60....C 4
Hot Springs, see Truth or Consequences
House, 144....B 7
Humble City, 61....C 7
Hurley, 2,079....C 4
lifeld, 31....D 6
Ione, 8....B 7
Isleta, 804....B 5
Jal, 2047....C 7
Jarales, 1,199....B 5
Jemez Pueblo, 650 B 5, D 5
Jemez Springs, 740....B 5
Jicarilla, 100....C 6
Jordan, 200....B 7
Kelly, 100....B 5
Kenna, 105....C 7
Kingston, 58....C 5
Kinney, 75....E 5
Koehler, 25....A 6
La Bajada, 15....D 6
La Cueva....B 6
Laguna, 500....B 5
La Jara, 300....A 5
Lajoya....B 5
Lake Arthur, 380....C 6
Lake Valley, 55....C 5
Lakewood, 75....C 6
La Liendre, 100....B 6
La Luz, 150....C 6
La Madera, 150....A 5
La Mesa, 601....C 5
Lamy, 235....B 6, D 6
Laplata, 300....A 4
Las Cruces, 12,325....C 5
Las Palomas, 73....C 5
Las Tablas, 150....A 5
Las Vegas (city), 7,494....B 6, D 7
Las Vegas (town), 6,269....B 6, D 7
La Union, 300....D 5
La Ventana, 122....B 5
Ledoux, 300....B 6
Lemitar, 600....B 5
Levy, 40....A 6
Leyba, 125....B 6, D 6
Lincoln, 200....C 6
Lindrith, 30....A 5
Lingo, 98....C 7
Llano, 300....A 6
Loco Hills, 100....C 6
Logan, 400....B 7
Lon, 25....B 6
Lordsburg, 3,525....C 4
Los Alamos, 9,934....B 5
Los Chavez, 100....B 5
Los Lunas, 889....B 5
Los Pinos, 125....A 5
Los Vigiles, 60....D 7
Loving, 1,487....C 6
Lovington, 3,134....C 7
Luis Lopez, 50....C 5
Lumberton, 350....A 5
Luna....C 4
McDonald, 40....C 7
McIntosh....B 5
Madrid, 800....B 5, D 6
Maes, 100....B 6
Magdalena, 1,297....B 5
Malaga, 701....C 6
Maljamar, 100....C 7
Malpie, 8....A 6
Mangas, 45....B 4
Manzano, 500....B 5
Marcia, 50....C 6
Marquez, 100....B 5
Maxwell, 404....A 6
Mayhill, 450....C 6
Melrose, 936....B 7
Mentmore, 300....B 4
Mescalero, 200....C 6
Mesilla, 1,264....C 5
Mesilla Park, 500....C 5
Mesquite, 197....C 5
Mexican Springs, 42....B 4
Miami, 150....A 6
Mills, 136....A 6
Mogollon, 800....C 4
Monero, 500....A 5
Montezuma, 30....C 7
Monticello, 175....C 5
Montoya, 100....B 6
Monument, 76....C 7
Mora, 1,400....B 6
Moriarty, 75....B 5
Moses....A 7
Mosquero, 583....B 7
Mountainair, 1,418....B 5
Mountain Park, 200....C 6
Mount Dora, 250....A 7
Nageezi, 25....A 5
Nambe, 879....B 6
Nara Visa, 250....B 7
Newcomb, 37....A 4
Newkirk, 250....B 6
Newman, 100....C 7
Nogal, 100....C 6
Norton, 8....B 7
Nutt, 41....C 5
Obar, 50....B 7
Ochoa, 20....C 7
Oil Center, 100....C 7
Ojo Caliente....A 5
Ojo Feliz, 150....A 6
Old Albuquerque, 1,119....D 5
Olive, 10....C 6
Optimo, 200....B 6
Organ, 100....C 5
Orogrande, 75....C 5
Oscuro, 45....C 5
Otis, 50....C 6
Paguate, 520....B 5
Palma, 50....B 6
Park View, 795....A 5
Pasamonte, 7....A 7
Pastura, 200....B 6
Pecos, 1,241....D 6
Penablanca, 508....B 5, D 6
Penasco, 627....A 6
Pep, 47....C 7
Peralta, 573....B 6
Petaca, 150....A 6
Picacho, 300....C 6
Pie Town, 40....B 4
Pine, 260....B 6, D 6
Pinehaven, 75....B 4
Pinon....C 6
Pinos Altos, 150....C 4
Pintada, 100....B 6
Placitas, 200....B 5, D 6
Pleasant Hill, 75....B 7
Polvadera, 300....B 5
Ponderosa, 100....B 5
Portales, 8,112....B 7
Puerto de Luna, 150....B 6
Quarai, 200....B 5
Queen, 75....C 6
Quemado, 375....B 4
Questa, 1,341....A 6
Ramah, 298....B 4
Ramon, 4....B 6
Ranches of Taos, 1,386....A 6
Ranchvale, 75....B 7
Raton, 8,241....A 6
Rayo, 15....B 5
Red Hill, 3....B 4
Redrock, 125....C 4
Rehoboth, 150....B 4
Rencona, 119....B 6, D 6
Reserve....C 4
Ribera....D 7
Ricardo, 75....B 6
Riley, 60....B 5
Rincon, 476....C 5
Rociada....B 6
Rodeo, 150....D 4
Rogers, 87....C 7
Romero, 50....D 7
Rosebud, 10....B 7
Roswell, 25,738....C 6
Rowe, 30....D 6
Roy, 1,074....B 6
Ruidoso, 806....C 6
Sabinoso, 85....B 6
St. Vrain, 120....B 7
Salem, 250....C 5
San Acacia, 123....B 5
San Antonio, 400....C 5
Sandia Park, 80....D 6
Sandoval....B 5, D 5
San Felipe, 670....B 5, D 6
San Fidel, 200....B 5
San Ignacio, 75....B 6
San Jon, 362....B 7
San Jose, 500....B 6, D 7
San Marcial....C 5
San Mateo, 500....B 5
San Miguel, 200....C 5
San Miguel, 200....D 7
San Patricio, 100....C 6
San Pedro, 21....D 6
San Rafael, 300....B 5
Santa Fe, 27,998 B 6, D 6
Santa Rita, 2,135....C 4
Santa Rosa, 2,199....B 6
Santo Domingo Pueblo, 1,169....B 5, D 6
San Ysidro, 26....D 5
Scholle, 100....B 5
Seama, 100....B 5
Seboyeta....B 5
Sedan, 55....A 7
Sena, 130....B 6, D 7
Separ, 44....C 4
Serafina, 82....D 7
Shiprock, 125....A 4
Silver City, 7,022....C 4
Socorro, 4,334....B 5
Soham, 7....D 6
Solano, 68....B 6
Springer, 1,558....A 6
Spur Lake, 45....C 4
Stanley, 75....B 5, D 6
Steins, 60....C 4
Sugarite, 300....A 6
Tafoya, 200....A 6
Taiban, 100....B 6
Tajique, 350....B 5
Taos, 1,815....A 6
Tapia, 20....E 7
Tapicitoes, 100....A 5
Tatum, 688....C 7
Tecolote, 100....D 7
Tecolotenos, 200....B 6
Texico, 691....B 7
Thoreau, 250....B 4
Three Rivers, 37....C 5
Tierra Amarilla, 787....A 5
Tijeras, 150....D 6
Toadlena, 49....A 4
Tohatchi, 100....B 4
Tome, 250....B 5
Tonuco, 150....C 5
Torrance, 30....B 6
Torreon....B 5
Tortugas, 400....C 5
Trechado, 100....B 4
Trementina, 500....B 6
Tres Lagunas, 11....B 4
Truchas, 694....A 6
Trujillo....B 6
Truth or Consequences, 4,563....C 5
Tucumcari, 8,419....B 7
Tularosa, 1,642....C 5
Turn, 400....B 5
Tyrone, 200....C 4
Vadito, 350....A 6
Vado, 225....C 5
Valencia, 350....B 5
Vallecitos, 275....A 5
Valley Ranch, 20....D 6
Van Houten, 542....A 6
Varney, 200....B 6
Vaughn, 1,356....B 6
Veguita, 600....B 5
Velarde, 600....A 5
Villanueva, 560....B 6, D 7
Virden, 146....C 4
Wagon Mound, 1,120....B 6
Waldo, 50....D 6
Waterflow, 200....A 4
Watrous, 500....B 6
Weed, 80....C 6
Whites City, 100....C 6
Whitewater, 75....C 4
Willard, 296....B 5
Winston, 100....C 5
Yates, 25....A 7
Yeso, 150....B 6
Youngsville, 250....A 5
Zuni Pueblo, 2,563....B 4

COUNTIES

Bernalillo, 145,673....B 5
Cafron, 3,533....C 4
Chaves, 40,605....C 6
Colfax, 16,761....A 6
Curry, 23,351....B 7
De Baca, 3,464....B 6
Dona Ana, 39,557....C 5
Eddy, 40,640....C 6
Grant, 21,649....C 4
Guadalupe, 6,772....B 6
Harding, 3,013....B 7
Hidalgo, 5,095....D 4
Lea, 30,717....C 7
Lincoln, 7,409....C 6
Los Alamos, 10,476....B 5
Luna, 8,753....C 5
McKinley, 27,451....B 4
Mora, 8,720....A 6
Otero, 14,909....C 6
Quay, 13,971....B 7
Rio Arriba, 24,997....A 5
Roosevelt, 16,409....B 7
Sandoval, 12,438....B 5
San Juan, 18,292....A 4
San Miguel, 26,512....B 6
Santa Fe, 38,153....B 5
Sierra, 7,186....C 5
Socorro, 9,670....C 5
Taos, 17,146....A 6
Torrance, 8,012....B 5
Union, 7,372....A 7
Valencia ,22,481....B 4

* Population according to special census taken since 1950.

grade ores are profitably mined by open-pit methods at Morenci, Ajo, Bisbee, and Miami; underground mines are also operated in these places, as well as at Superior, Ray, and Bagdad.

Prior to World War II, over nine hundred mines were primarily employed in producing gold, but these have been converted to producing more essential minerals, and both gold and silver are now derived only as by-products. Lead and zinc ores are mined at Bisbee, Humboldt, Dragoon, and Elfrida. Manganese, tungsten, and molybdenum deposits are plentiful but relatively undeveloped, as are the deposits of asbestos and barite. Complementary to the mining industry, various types of building stone and aggregates, including granite, tufa, bentonite, feldspar, gypsum, mica, and perdite, are quarried.

Agriculture. Although for many years mining was Arizona's leading industry, agriculture now yields higher gross returns than any other industry. Despite a dry climate, Arizona has vast areas of productive farm land; irrigation has reclaimed more than 1,000,000 acres of arid land, of which approximately half is irrigated from reservoirs built behind river dams in large-scale federal and state projects such as the Salt River Valley, the San Carlos, and the Yuma projects. In addition to these reservoirs, wells are used to irrigate large areas in Maricopa, Graham, Pinal, Pima, Cochise, Santa Cruz, and Yuma counties.

Farming in Arizona is conducted on a large scale, with highly mechanized commercial farms employing Indians and migratory workers from Mexico, Oklahoma, and Texas. Cotton, alfalfa, and vegetables are the principal crops, with grains and fruits of secondary importance. Lettuce and muskmelons are the largest vegetable crops; grain sorghums, barley, wheat, and oats comprise the major cereal crops; and the fruit crops are grapefruits, oranges, lemons, and grapes. From all crops an annual gross return of more than $250,000,000 (five-year average, 1948-1953) is realized.

About one third of Arizona's annual income from agriculture, or about $85,000,000, is derived from animal husbandry. Natural grasses and extensive ranges provide suitable grazing land for stock raising. Beef cattle and sheep raising are the principal animal industries, with ranch holdings of about 900,000 head of cattle and 450,000 head of sheep. The annual wool clip is about 3,000,000 pounds, and mohair production from goats is around 420,000 pounds. Horses, mules, and hogs are also raised. Although dairy and poultry farms supply local markets, Arizona now imports butter, eggs, and poultry.

Manufacturing. Arizona's manufacturing interests are closely related to the state's mineral, agricultural, and forest resources. Sawmills at Flagstaff and Williams produce lumber and timber products, and Phoenix is a meat-packing center. Processed foods, bread and bakery products, cottonseed oil, and artificial ice are important manufactures. Stimulated by the war needs, manufacturing increased during World War II, and new plants were built for the manufacture of aluminum extrusions, aircraft and aircraft parts, and precision instruments. With the conversion of wartime

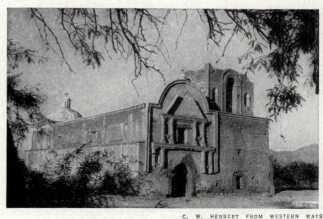

C. W. HERBERT FROM WESTERN WAYS

Ruins of the Tumacacori Mission, Arizona

plants to peacetime production and the establishment of new industries, postwar manufacturing employs more people than mining, and the gross value of manufactured products increased steadily from $117,000,000 in 1947 to $292,000,000 in 1952.

Colorado River Projects. Arizona's outstanding economic development is the utilization of the vast irrigation and hydroelectric power possibilities of the Colorado River. Five dams, Hoover, Davis, Parker, Headgate Rock, and Imperial, have been constructed in the Colorado River by the United States Bureau of Reclamation for the purpose of flood control, irrigation, and water and power supply. Since the inception of the plan, Arizona and California have been in disagreement over the distribution of water and power rights. At present both states are benefiting from the facilities, but the final settlement will determine to what extent Arizona will be able to expand both as a manufacturing and an agricultural state. Hoover Dam at Boulder Canyon is the highest dam in the world, and Lake Mead behind it is the largest artificial lake. The Boulder power plant has an ultimate capacity of 1,332,300 kw. Imperial is a diversion dam from which a 125-mile irrigation canal, when completed, will carry water to vast areas of Arizona's desert land in the Gila project. Both Davis and Parker dams are used for river regulation and power generation. Headgate Rock is a diversion dam for the Colorado River Indian Reservation.

Reclamation transforms a desert area. Through the Canal, the Colorado River water flows all the way from Arizona to California's Imperial Valley and is deflected at bridges to citrus groves and fields.

PHOENIX, ARIZONA, AND THE STATE CAPITOL BUILDING (INSET)

Commerce. Arizona's commerce consists mainly of inter-state shipments of mining, lumber, and agricultural products. Cotton, wool, and mohair are marketed for textile manufacturing, and winter citrus and vegetable crops find markets in eastern cities. Large shipments of copper as well as other metals and lumber are sent to out-of-state manufacturing centers. The climate of the south in winter and of the north in summer, together with unique scenic attractions and all-year highways, attracts many tourists. Indians and novelty manufacturers make souvenirs, blankets, rugs, baskets, and pottery for sale to tourists. The expansion of Arizona's commercial activities is evidenced by increased excise tax collections, outbound interstate shipments, clearing house transactions, trade licenses, construction permits, and motor travel. Retail sales, excluding interstate transactions and direct farm products sales, increased from $162,000,000 in 1939 to $517,000,000 in 1946, and to $1,031,926,668 in 1952.

Communications and Transportation. Arizona's transition from an isolated frontier wilderness to a modern commonwealth is typified by its advance in transportation and communication. When the territory was organized in 1863, the ox, the mule, and the horse supplied the motive power for all modes of conveyance. There were no roads north of the Gila, and south of it there was only a trail to the California gold fields. Today transcontinental railways, bus-lines, airways, and truck routes span the state; feeder lines afford unlimited connections, and paved highways supply ready means of private transportation. Mail, telegraph, telephone, radio, and television round out a complete communications system. The Atchison, Topeka, and Santa Fe railway crosses the northern part of the state, and the Southern Pacific, the southern part; both enter Phoenix, the capital. American Buslines, Greyhound Lines, and Santa Fe Trailways furnish regular bus transportation. American Airlines and Trans-World Airlines afford means of air travel to all pats of the world. State-wide feeder airlines are operated at Bonanza and Frontier airlines, serving the major cities of the state. The state highway system includes more than 4,000 mi. of paved highways, which, with 2,500 mi. of other surfaced roads and 2,000 mi. of national forest, park, monument, and reservation roads, afford convenient access to all points.

GOVERNMENT AND POLITICS

Structure. The legislative branch of the government consists of a Senate of 28 members, chosen by counties, and a House of Representatives, membership in which is based upon the number of votes cast but is limited at 80. The constitution, ratified in 1911, also reserves to the people the power to propose, to enact, or to reject laws and amendments to the constitution, under the initiative and referendum. Regular sessions of the legislature convene annually

234

the second Monday in January, but special sessions may be called by the governor. The executive department consists of the governor, secretary of state, state auditor, attorney-general, and superintendent of public instruction, each elected for a term of two years. The judicial department is composed of a supreme court, superior courts in the various counties, and justices of the peace in precincts. The supreme court, originally composed of three justices, was, by an act of the 1947 legislature, effective in 1949, increased to five.

Until 1942 Arizona was represented in Congress by its two senators and a single member of the House of Representatives. Under the Reapportionment Act, the census of 1940 gave Arizona an additional seat in the House of Representatives.

Legislation. Arizona's legislature has shown a consistent trend in improving local conditions by passing laws relating to the protection of miners; hours and conditions of labor in hazardous occupations; hours and conditions of labor of women and minors; compensation for occupational injuries and diseases of workmen; assistance for the aged, the needy blind, and dependent children; prohibition of gambling and of houses of prostitution; regulation of liquor traffic; measures for the protection of agriculture, horticulture, and animal husbandry, and for the support of advancement of education.

The course of legislation by the people, under the powers of the initiative and referendum, has been distinguished rather for its negative than its affirmative achievements. Of 135 proposals voted on, by far the greater number were rejected. Amendments to the constitution which received approval include reinstatement of the provision for recalling judicial officers, removed upon the insistence of President Taft; equal suffrage; execution of death sentences by use of lethal gas; and workmen's compensation. Among proposals rejected were: creation of a one-house legislature by abolishment of the senate; abolition of direct primaries; four-year terms for state and county officers; creation of public offices; bond issues; and tax limitations.

EDUCATIONAL AND SOCIAL CONDITIONS

Education. Arizona's educational system, built upon a broad and strong constitutional foundation, consists of kindergarten schools, common schools, high schools, junior colleges, state colleges, and the University of Arizona at Tucson. It also embraces a school for the deaf and the blind, at Tucson. The state colleges, located at Tempe and Flagstaff respectively, emphasize the training of teachers. They confer bachelor and master of arts degrees in education, and bachelor degrees in arts and in science. Elementary and secondary schools are maintained on the basis of equality of opportunity, the state bearing a part of the cost. A continuing annual appropriation provides $95.00 per pupil in common schools and in high schools. The common schools also enjoy the benefit of a grant of four sections of land in each township. Income from rentals and from investment of the proceeds of sales of school lands assists in maintenance of the schools.

Enrollment in elementary schools is above 175,000. Methods of bilingual education receive particular attention because of the considerable number of children of Spanish-speaking families. Children of Indians residing off the reservations are taught in the common schools, though most Indian pupils are educated in reservation schools or in government schools at Phoenix and Tucson. In secondary schools, with an enrollment of more than 50,000, citizenship,

physical education, and vocational training are emphasized. Salaries of teachers average $3,900. Enrollment in junior colleges is more than 2,500; at state colleges, 6,000; and at the University of Arizona, 6,000. The school for the deaf and blind has approximately 200 pupils.

Social Measures. Provisions for safeguarding the public health, caring for the physically and mentally incapacitated, rehabilitating handicapped persons, assisting the needy, training juvenile offenders, and protecting workers feature Arizona's social service program. Institutions maintained for such purposes are: the State Hospital for the Insane, at Phoenix; the Home for the Aged and Infirm Arizona Pioneers, and the Home for Disabled Miners, at Prescott; the State Welfare Sanitorium, for tuberculars, at Tempe, and the State Industrial School, for juvenile offenders, at Fort Grant. Administered by the state Board of Social Security and Welfare, assistance is provided for the needy aged, blind, dependent and crippled children, and relief of various types extended to other persons in distress. The state Department of Health has charge of an expanding program, in which the federal government participates, for curbing and preventing infectious and communicable diseases. Training of mentally or physically disabled persons in occupations which will make them self-supporting is carried on by the Superintendent of Public Instruction, with federal co-operation. The Employment Security Commission administers the fund for the compensation of unemployed workers. In addition to this well-rounded official program of social welfare, volunteer organizations devoted to social betterment, such as parent-teacher associations and children's clubs, are active and influential.

PLACES OF INTEREST

Grand Canyon, Arizona's most famous attraction, is located in Grand Canyon National Park and contains 105 mi. of the Colorado River. The Canyon itself has an average depth of about one mile and is 217 mi. long and from four to 18 mi. wide. Almost as famous are the Painted Desert, in north central Arizona, which is nearly 200 mi. long and from 15 to 30 mi. wide; and the Petrified Forest, a national monument containing petrified wood, formed from prehistoric conifer trees. Other national monuments in the state include the Canyon de Chelly, Casa Grande, Montezuma Castle, Navajo, Tonto, Tuzigoot, Walnut Canyon, and Wupatki monuments, all containing examples of prehistoric cliff dwellings or pueblos. Chiricahua National Monument is a wilderness of unusual rock shapes; Organ Pipe Cactus and Saguaro national monuments are interesting for their cacti displays; Pipe Spring National Monument contains a historic Mormon fort; and Tumacacori National Monument has an old Spanish mission building.

POPULATION

In 1950 the United States census credited Arizona with a population of 749,587. Of these, 415,108, or 55.4 per cent were urban. The principal cities are Phoenix, with a population of 106,818 in 1950; Tucson, 45,454; Mesa, 16,790; Amphitheatre, 12,664; Douglas, 9,442; Wakefield, 8,906; Glendale, 8,179; Tempe, 7,684; and Prescott, 6,764.

Racial and Ethnic Groups. The total foreign-born white population in the state, according to the 1950 census, was 45,594, with the principal countries of origin as follows:

Mexico	24,917	Germany	1,825
Canada	2,904	U.S.S.R.	1,756
England and Wales	2,218	Italy	1,600
		Poland	969

"OLD FAITHFUL," A PETRIFIED TREE AT THE PETRIFIED FOREST NATIONAL MONUMENT IN HOLBROOK, ARIZONA

The total population of the state included 654,511 white persons, 65,761 Indians, 25,974 Negroes, 1,951 Chinese, and 780 Japanese.

Occupational Groups. The main industry groups of the total of 238,695 employed persons in the state in 1950 were as follows:

Retail trade	43,317	Manufacturing	20,986
Agriculture	35,196	Construction	20,444
Professional and related		Personal services	19,615
services	24,023	Public administration	12,727
Transportation,		Mining	10,490
communication, and		Wholesale trade	9,059
other public utilities	21,132		

HISTORY

Explorations. In the latter part of 1535 or early in the following year Álvar Núñez Cabeza de Vaca, member of the ill-fated Florida expedition of the Spanish explorer Pánfilo de Narváez, found his way, with three companions, across Texas and possibly the southeast corner of what is now Arizona, to the Spanish colony at Cullacán, Mexico. He was the first European to enter Arizona, and his report led to further expeditions to explore the region. In 1539 Estebanico, one of the Cabeza de Vaca party, guided Fray Marcos de Niza back over the trail to confirm Cabeza's report, and in 1540 Francisco Vásquez de Coronado, at the head of a company of young Spanish adventurers seeking the fabled "Seven Cities of Cíbola," viewed the Grand Canyon and visited the Hopi Indians in their northern villages. Spanish explorers in search of precious metals and Jesuit and Franciscan friars on missionary errands traveled the state at intervals during the next two centuries. Juan de Oñate in 1604-1605 traversed the state to the mouth of the Colorado. Jesuit missions were founded at San Xavier del Bac in 1700 and at Guevavi in 1732, the first by Padre Eusebio Kino. A presidio established in 1752 at Tubac was removed in 1776 to a village of Indians on the site of Tucson, the first permanent white settlement. An almost constant state of war between the Spaniards and the Indians and between the Apaches and other Indians existed during the years of Spanish occupation. All the missionary settlements except Tubac and Tucson were finally abandoned. American traders and explorers began to penetrate Arizona during the first quarter of the nineteenth century, and were followed by a small number of settlers.

Political Development. At the end of the war with Mexico, in 1848, as part of the terms of settlement, the por-

tion of Arizona north of the Gila River became United States territory. The discovery of gold in California and the resulting importance of the California seaports emphasized the value of travel routes in the strip south of the Gila still held by Mexico. In 1854, by the Gadsden Purchase, this area was added to the domain of the United States. The crude mining operations carried on within the new acquisition immediately attracted eastern capital. Settlements were established on the Santa Cruz River, and mines were opened. Congress had included the strip north of the Gila in the Territory of New Mexico, formally organized in 1850, and had later attached also the Gadsden Purchase area. Agitation soon arose for the creation of the Territory of Arizona, on the ground that the settlements south of the Gila were too far distant to receive consideration from the New Mexico legislature, sitting at Santa Fe. This demand, opposed on the ground of the insignificance and unimportance of the area, was urged unceasingly until Feb. 24, 1863, when President Abraham Lincoln approved the act creating Arizona Territory.

The first and most pressing objective of the settlers of the new territory, attracted in great numbers by reports of gold discoveries, was to curb the activities of the hostile Indians. This struggle, which continued for more than twenty years, did not prevent the residents of Arizona from fighting for a higher political status.

Statehood. As early as 1877 a demand for statehood was voiced, although it was not until 1889 that the first bill for that purpose was introduced in Congress. Because of eastern opposition to the free coinage of silver, coupled with objections based upon partisan considerations, the battle for statehood was prolonged. A bill was passed in 1906 to provide for the admission of Arizona and New Mexico as a single state, subject to the approval of the two territories separately. This measure was overwhelmingly rejected by Arizona. In 1910 an enabling act was passed authorizing Arizona and New Mexico to hold conventions and draft constitutions, but for Arizona the statehood struggle was not yet ended. The enabling act provided that the constitutions should be subject to approval by Congress and the President. A resolution of Congress approving the Arizona constitution was vetoed by President W. H. Taft on the ground, specifically, that it contained a provision for the recall of judicial officers, which he declared to be "destructive of free government." By way of compromise, Congress passed and the President signed a resolution providing for approval of the constitution upon the

"THE WHITE HOUSE," A CLIFF DWELLING IN ARIZONA'S CANYON DE CHELLY

adoption by the people of Arizona of an amendment eliminating the recall of the judiciary. This requirement was met, and on Feb. 14, 1912, the President issued a proclamation by which Arizona became the forty-eighth state. At the next succeeding election the offensive provision was reinstated but in only one instance has the power to recall judicial officers been exercised. This occurred when a presiding judge became mentally incapable of performing the duties of his office, and the recall was employed to create a vacancy.

Politically Arizona is classed as a Democratic state. Fifteen Democratic governors have been elected, but only three Republican executives, in 1918, 1920, and 1928. In both houses of Congress the state has been, with a single exception, continuously represented by Democrats. The exception was in 1920, when Ralph H. Cameron, territorial delegate at the time the Enabling Act was passed in 1910, defeated the veteran Marcus Aurelius Smith for the Senate. He served but one term.

Military Activities. In February 1862, during the Civil War, a small detachment of Baylor's Texas Rangers, bent upon the capture of California for the Confederacy, occupied the pueblo of Tucson and proceeded west. California volunteers dispatched eastward precipitated a small engagement known as the battle of Picacho, and the invaders were dispersed.

The bloody Apache war, brought to an end only with the capture and deportation in 1886 of the treacherous and cruel chieftain, Geronimo, and his band, marked a dark era in Arizona's history. The services of the United States Army and some of the nation's most illustrious military figures, including Gen. George Crook, Gen. Nelson A. Miles, and Gen. James H. Carleton, were required to defeat Geronimo. Many of Arizona's pioneer settlers as well as companies of Pima and Maricopa Indians, who were at war with the Apaches, supplemented the army in the bitter conflict. Geronimo was taken to Florida and later permitted to remove to Oklahoma.

Arizona's military fame rests in considerable measure upon its record in the war with Spain in 1898. The regiment of volunteer cavalry which gained renown as "Roosevelt's Rough Riders," was composed largely of Arizona volunteers. The regimental flag, made by Phoenix women, when unfurled on the heights of Daiquiri became the first United States flag flown on Cuban soil. It is exhibited today in the state capitol at Phoenix.

World War I produced the renowned Arizona flying ace, Frank Luke, Jr., whose name and fame were perpetuated by a monument and by one of the largest air training fields of World War II, named in his honor.

Arizona's National Guard regiment, the 158th Infantry, gained fame in World War II as the "Bushmasters," described by Gen. Douglas MacArthur as "the greatest fighting combat team that ever deployed for battle." The Arizona organization was inducted into service Sept. 16, 1940. After

237

a year's intensive training and a year spent in defense of the Panama Canal Zone, the Bushmasters, reinforced by officers and men from various states, achieved brilliant successes in the Pacific, at Arawe, Wakdi-Sarmi, Noemfoor, Lingayen Gulf, Batangas, and Legaspi. Bushmasters' Day is annually celebrated in Arizona.

Reactivated in October 1946, the Arizona National Guard consists of a fighter squadron and the 158th Combat Team, the latter embracing the 158th Infantry, an engineer corps, a field artillery battalion, an ordnance company, and a band. State headquarters are at Phoenix.

Archaeologic and Historic Sites. Archaeological exploration in Arizona has revealed remarkably well-preserved remains of the culture of a prehistoric people. A cliff-dwelling people, they built communal dwellings in the faces of vertical cliffs, high above the canyon floors, and cultivated the fertile valleys at the bottom with skilfully contrived irrigation systems. Many of these almost inaccessible sites have been discovered in remote canyons and have been converted into national monuments to preserve the ruins and permit people to view them. Montezuma Castle, on the Verde River south of Flagstaff, is a cliff dwelling that was built in a natural crevice of the cliff 80 ft. above the canyon floor and housed probably 300 people. Other cliff-dweller sites that have been discovered include the Keet Seel ruin, part of the Navajo National Monument in Navajo County; Canyon de Chelly in Apache County, Tonto ruins in Gila County, and Walnut Canyon in Coconino County.

A ruin that may antedate the cliff dwellings was discovered near Florence and is known as Casa Grande. This ruin consists of a large adobe structure with many rooms, courts, and plazas, surrounded by a wall. Other similar ruins farther north are Tuzigoot, on the Verde River near Clarksdale, and Wupatki, on the Little Colorado northeast of Flagstaff.

The principal historic sites are Tumacacori National Monument, which is a restored Franciscan mission of the seventeenth century; Coronado Trail, route of the Coronado expedition of 1540; and Apache Trail to Roosevelt Dam and Lake.

Cultural Development. Arizona's civilization has evolved from the life of a frontier mining and cattle territory to that of a modern state with large cities and a highly mechanized agricultural and industrial economy. However, much of the distinctive character of the Southwest has been retained. Rodeos are held annually in the large cities and many of the smaller cattle towns, and many people wear the traditional cowboy hats and boots. Indian cultures have been carefully preserved on the Hopi, Navajo, and Apache reservations, and Mexican and Spanish influences are evident in architecture and street and place names. Many of the public buildings are of Spanish architecture, and residential areas show the influence of both Spanish and ranch-type architecture.

Scientific research in Arizona has been enhanced by the state's extraordinary resources for field studies. Geologic surveys have been made of the Grand Canyon, the Painted Desert, and other unusual physical features; archaeological studies have been made of the cliff dwellings and prehistoric ruins; and the various Indian tribes have been the subject of many anthropological studies.

Because Arizona has an unusually dry and clear atmosphere, it is a suitable location for astronomical study. The Lowell Observatory, which was founded at Flagstaff in 1894, by Dr. Percival Lowell, is famous for observations of Mars and the discovery in 1930 of the planet Pluto. Steward Observatory at Tucson is the seat of the discovery of the Douglass tree-ring method of determining climatic cycles. The Southwestern Arboretum, near Superior, was founded by William Boyce Thompson for experiments in desert plant life from all parts of the world.

Interest in the arts has been stimulated by Arizona's recent popularity as an artists' and writers' colony. Many artists, attracted by climate and scenery and seclusion, have established residence and are exhibiting their work locally. Agencies for the dissemination and refinement of culture—churches, schools, libraries, museums, and educational, historical, musical, and artistic associations—are found in every community. M. Wi.

ARIZONA, UNIVERSITY OF, a land-grant state university, accredited, coeducational, and publicly controlled, at Tucson, Ariz. The 94-acre campus is in the city of Tucson and there are five agricultural research centers at other points in the state. The university's charter was granted in 1885,

KEN SHARP

ENGINEERING COLLEGE, UNIVERSITY OF ARIZONA

and instruction began in 1891. Degrees granted include B.A. and B.S. in liberal arts; B.S. in business administration, public administration, civil, electrical and mechanical engineering, agriculture, home economics, mining engineering, mining, geology, and metallurgical engineering; A.B. or B.S. in education; B.F.A., B.Mus., and LL.B. The new school of pharmacy granted its first degrees in 1949. The M.A. and Ph.D. degrees are offered in the graduate college.

Among the notable buildings on the campus are the Arizona State Museum, established in 1893 as a territorial museum and made part of the university in 1912, when Arizona became a state. This building contains collections pertaining to the anthropology of the state and to the flora, geology, and history of the Southwest.

Residential facilities were available for approximately one third of the students in 1949. Some scholarship and loan help is extended to students who qualify, but 80 per cent of this aid is restricted to Arizona residents. *For statistics see* COLLEGES AND UNIVERSITIES. J. R. To.

ARK, a chest or closed receptacle, a word used to translate two different Hebrew words in the Bible: *tēbah* and *arōn*.

Ark (*tēbah*), in the Book of Genesis, designates the vessel that Noah built to save himself and his family from the flood. Noah's ark, made of "gopher" wood, was three hundred cubits long, fifty cubits wide, and thirty cubits high

(Gen. vi:14-22). The casket of bulrushes in which the infant Moses was placed "in the flags by the river's brink," because of Pharaoh's decree that all newborn Hebrew male children be drowned, is also called an ark (*tēbah*) (Exod. ii:3).

The ark of the covenant (*arōn*) was the chest made by the Israelites, during their wandering in the desert, to contain the tablets of the Ten Commandments, the covenant between God and Israel, made on Mount Sinai (Deut. x:2). It was made of acacia wood, overlaid with gold inside and outside, and it had a cover of pure gold upon which were sculptured two cherubim facing each other and spreading their wings over the entire cover; it was two and a half cubits long, a cubit and a half wide, and a cubit and a half high (Exod. xxv:10-22). The ark was the most sacred religious symbol of the Israelites, and was placed in the Holy of Holies in the tabernacle in the desert, in the sanctuary in Shiloh, and finally in the *debir,* or the innermost chamber, of the Holy of Holies in King Solomon's temple in Jerusalem. The ark was carried by priests or Levites (Num. iii:32), with staves drawn through rings attached to the corners on both sides (Exod. xxv:14). At times the ark was carried in battle (Josh. vi:4; I Sam. iv:3; II Sam. xi:11). The ark was captured by the Philistines (I Sam. iv:11) and, according to tradition, miraculously returned to the Israelites. It was then placed in the house of Abinadab in Kirjath-jearim, until it was removed to Jerusalem.

In post-biblical times, the holy ark (*arōn ha-ḳodesh*) is a closet in which the scrolls of the Law, or Torah, are kept. It is placed in, or along, that wall of the synagogue to which the worshippers turn in prayer—in most synagogues, the eastern wall. The *ner tamid,* or the perpetual light, is suspended in front of it. The ark, symbolic of the Holy of Holies of the temple in Jerusalem, is the most sacred part of the synagogue and when it is opened, the congregation rises. The curtain, or *paroket,* that covers it is reminiscent of the curtain which separated the Holy of Holies from the Holies in the temple.

Synagogues in various parts of the world have boasted some very ornate arks. An historic ark, from Fostat in Egypt, dating from the tenth century is found in the Museum of the Jewish Theological Seminary of America. *See also* NOAH. D. G. and M. A. G.

ARKADELPHIA [ɑrkədɛl'fiə], a city and the county seat of Clark Co., in southwestern Arkansas, situated on the Ouachita River, 66 mi. south of Little Rock. Founded in 1836, the city was incorporated in 1856 and had the mayor-council form of government in 1951. Arkadelphia lies in an agricultural area where livestock, cotton, hay, peanuts, and corn are raised; pine and hardwood are found in the region. Industries include dairying and the production of lumber, cottonseed oil, flour, and clothing. The city is the seat of Ouachita College, and Henderson State Teachers College. Transportation is provided by the Missouri Pacific Railroad. Pop. 1940, 5,078; 1950, 6,819.

ARKANSAS. *See* INDIAN TRIBES, NORTH AMERICAN.

ARKANSAS [ɑ'rkɛnsɔ], a south central state of the United States, named for the Quapaw or Arkansas tribe of Sioux Indians. Once known as the Bear State, it was officially named The Wonder State in 1923. Its location is between 33° and 36° 30′ N. lat. and 89° 40′ and 94° 42′ W. long. In the shape of a rough square, it is bounded on the north by Missouri, on the east across the Mississippi River by Tennessee and Mississippi, on the south by Louisiana, and on the west by Texas and Oklahoma. It comprises an area of 53,102 sq. mi., of which 52,725 are land and 377 inland water surface. In size among the states it ranks twenty-sixth.

GEOGRAPHIC FEATURES

Topography. The topography of Arkansas is varied and has two distinct features—the mountainous northwest and the low-lying plains of the east and the south. The northwestern section is a highland region through which flows the

Arkansas River. The Ozark Plateau lies north of the river, and the Ouachita Mountains are on the south. The Ozark region has two divisions. Springfield Plateau, 1,000 to 1,500 ft. high, extends from beyond the Missouri boundary south into northern Arkansas. Gently rolling hills and canyon-like valleys diversify its surface. The Boston Mountains, covering a belt about 35 mi. wide and 200 mi. long from east to west, overlook the Springfield Plateau from a steep north-facing escarpment. The mountain tops consist of a tableland 2,200 ft. high, cut into numerous ridges by narrow ravines 500 to 1,400 ft. deep. Their southern face has a moderate slope toward the valley of the Arkansas River.

The Ouachita Mountains, lying south of the Arkansas, cover a belt 50 to 60 mi. wide which extends into Oklahoma. They consist of a series of narrow parallel ridges having sharp, uneven crests, separated by wide basins. Their height increases from 750 ft. near Little Rock to 2,850 ft. at the western border.

Between the Ozark and Ouachita regions is the Arkansas Valley. It is a fairly level plain 30 to 40 mi. wide and 300 to 600 ft. above sea level.

The Gulf Coast Plain extends across the southern and eastern parts of the state, a rolling plain ranging in elevation from 100 to 700 ft. and sloping toward the southeast. Its most prominent feature is Crowleys Ridge, 12 mi. wide and 400 ft. high, in the northeastern corner. The St. Francis Basin in the northeast corner of the state and the strip of land contiguous to the Mississippi River, extending the entire length of the eastern border, are parts of the Mississippi Alluvial Plain and subject to floods. The state is drained by the Mississippi River and its tributaries, the St. Francis, White, Arkansas, Ouachita, and Red rivers, of which the Arkansas is the largest and most important. There are no natural lakes of importance in the state but five large reservoirs—Nimrod Reservoir, Lake Norfork, Lake Catherine, Lake Hamilton, and Blue Mountain Reservoir—have been formed by river dam construction.

Arkansas has a mean elevation above sea level of 650 ft.

CYPRESS SWAMP ON THE MISSISSIPPI RIVER NEAR HELENA, ARKANSAS

FROM EWING GALLOWAY, NEW YORK

Blue Mountain on the boundary between Polk and Scott counties, and Magazine Mountain in Logan County, both 2,850 ft., have the highest altitudes. The lowest point, 55 ft., is in Ashley County, where the Ouachita River enters Louisiana.

Climate. Arkansas has a relatively mild climate with long summer seasons and short, mild winters. The average annual temperature of the state is 61.4° F. Little Rock, the capital, in the center of the state, has a normal mean temperature of 41.4° F. in January and 80.9° F. in July, with —12° F. the lowest temperature on record and 118° F. the highest. In the mountains temperatures are lower in both winter and summer. Unlike the lowlands, the mountains have cool summer nights, and snowfall, which averages 5.6 in. for the state, amounts to 10.4 in. in the mountains. The average rainfall for the state is 48.25 in. Most of the precipitation comes during the winter and spring months and at times results in floods. In spite of the heavy precipitation,

PUBLICITY DIVISION, ARKANSAS RESOURCES AND DEVELOPMENT COMMISSION

A stand of pine timber in the Piedmont area of southwest Arkansas. Forestry experts claim that pine timber grows faster in this area than anywhere in North America.

63 per cent of the days are sunny during the average year, as recorded at Little Rock. The growing season, between frosts, ranges from 176 days in the mountains to 241 days in the lowlands, with an average for the state of 211 days or about 7 months.

Soil. Although all but 15 sq. mi. of Arkansas is of sedimentary or alluvial origin, the state's soil varies greatly. Limestone, sandstone, shale, clay, sand, and chalk soils are found. In the lowlands east and south of Little Rock, black soil produces rich crops of cotton, corn, and rice. Northwest of Little Rock the soil is sandy, but in some areas of this region there are highly fertile loams. The mountains are in some places fertile with soils based on shale, but in the mountainous region of the Ozark Plateau soils derived from masses of conglomerates have no fertility. In the southwest, in the Red River Valley, the soil is a heavy, sticky clay and is relatively poor.

Erosion is a serious threat to the soil of Arkansas, for an area of 12,216,000 acres, or 36 per cent of the total, has lost one-fourth of its top soil and requires curative treatment. Another 3,286,000 acres require preventive treatment.

Forests. Arkansas was once heavily timbered, with an estimated 50,000 of its 53,102 sq. mi. covered by forests. Vast areas of the original timber stand have been removed by extensive lumbering operations, until approximately only one third of the state is now in forests and woodlands. Two national forests, Ozark and Ouachita, preserve 3,586,665 acres of forest land, and the state forests, parks, and recreational areas protect an additional 19,800 acres. Because of its diverse topographic regions, Arkansas has a variety of trees, of which the more important timber trees are yellow, shortleaf, and loblolly pine; oak, of which there are 47 varieties; cottonwood; cypress; red gum, and ash.

Flora and Fauna. Arkansas has 2,600 types of native plants, in addition to many naturalized ones. Twenty-six varieties of orchids grow in the state, and water lilies and passion flowers are abundant. The American bell flower, the crimson catchfly, the cardinal flower, blue lobelia, phlox, verbena, wild hydrangea, hibiscus, aster, and yellow jasmine grow in the east. The state flower is the apple blossom.

Arkansas lies in two faunal zones. The major portion of the state is in the Gulf State zone, while the area in the northwestern corner of the state is in the lower Appalachian zone. The more spectacular fish of this region are the paddlefish, the alligator gar, and the Mississippi catfish. Freshwater angling is good, for black bass, rock bass, warmouths, crappies, and several species of sunfish are abundant. Alligators at one time were common in the swampy regions

ARKANSAS

Index to Physical Features and Points of Interest

TOPOGRAPHIC FEATURES

Islands, Peninsulas, Capes, Mountains, Plateaus, Valleys, etc.

Bear, mountain, 1,350'.................C 5
Big Rock, mountain, 519'.............D 6
Blue, mountain, 2,800'................C 1
   (One of Highest Points in Arkansas)
Boston, mountains.....................B 2
Caddo, mountains.....................C 2
Cossatot, mountains..................C 2
Cowan Knob, mountain, 2,281'.........B 2
Cross, mountains......................C 1
Glazypeau, mountain..................C 5
Granite, mountain, 536'...............D 6
Gulf Coastal, plain....................C 4
Hemmed In, hollow...................A 2
Highest Points in Arkansas, 2,800'
   (Magazine Mountain).............B 2

(Blue Mountain)......................C 1
Irons, mountain ,1,600'...............B 3
Kymes, mountain, 1,800'.............B 1
Magazine, mountain, 2,800'..........B 2
   (One of Highest Points in Arkansas)
Moss, mountain, 1,150'...............C 3
Muddy Creek, mountain..............C 2
Mulberry, mountain, 2,127'..........B 3
Ozark, escarpment...................B 4
Ozark, plateau........................A 2
Petit Jean, mountain..................B 3
Petit Jean, mountain..................C 2
Pilot Knob, mountain, 2,345'.........B 2
Pilot Knob, mountain, 1,977'.........C 1
Poteau, mountain, 2,600'............C 1
Purdham, hill.........................D 6

Raspberry, peak, 2,360'..............C 1
Rich, mountain........................C 1
Sharp Top, mountain, 1,685'.........C 2
Sherman, mountain, 2,250'..........A 2
Shinall, mountain, 1,100'.............D 5
Skylight, mountain, 1,900'...........B 1
Stevenson, mountain, 1,800'........B 1
Swain, mountain, 1,800'.............A 2
Trap, mountain, 1,120'...............D 5
West, mountain, 1,420'...............C 5
White Oak, mountain.................C 2
White Oak, mountain, 2,050'.........B 2
Woods, mountain, 1,927'.............B 2

HYDROGRAPHIC FEATURES

Lakes, Rivers, Creeks, Bays, Straits, Seas, etc.

Arkansas, river.......................C 4
Bakers, bayou........................D 6
Bartholomew, bayou.................C 4
Big, bayou............................D 4
Big, creek.............................C 5
Big Cornie, creek.....................D 3
Black, river...........................B 4
Bodcau, creek........................D 2
Boeuf, river...........................D 4
Buffalo, river.........................B 3
Bull Shoals, reservoir................A 3
Cache, river..........................B 4
Caddo, river..........................C 2
Cadron, creek........................B 3
Catherine, lake.......................C 3
Chicot, lake...........................D 4
Cossatot, river........................C 1
Crooked, creek.......................A 3
Current, river.........................A 5
Cypress, bayou.......................B 4
Des Arc, bayou.......................B 4
De View, bayou.......................B 4
Dorcheat, creek......................D 2
Dutch, creek..........................C 2

Fort Smith, lake......................B 1
Fourche, creek........................D 5
Fourche La Fave, river...............C 2
Hamilton, lake........................C 2
Hill, lake..............................D 6
Hurricane, creek......................C 3
Illinois, bayou........................B 2
Illinois, river.........................A 1
Kings, river...........................A 2
Lagrue, bayou........................C 4
L'Anguille, river......................B 5
Lee, creek............................B 1
Little, river...........................B 5
Little, river...........................D 1
Little Mazarn, creek..................D 5
Little Missouri, river.................D 2
Little Red, river......................B 4
   Middle, fork.....................B 3
Long, creek...........................A 2
Mason, bayou........................D 4
Mazarn, creek........................C 5
Meto, bayou..........................C 4
Mississippi, river.....................D 4
Moro, creek...........................D 3
Mulberry, river.......................B 2

Nimrod, reservoir.....................C 2
Norfork, lake.........................A 3
Old River, lake........................D 6
Osage, creek..........................A 2
Ouachita, river........................D 3
Petit Jean, creek......................B 2
Plum, bayou...........................D 6
Poteau, river..........................C 1
Prairie, bayou........................D 6
Red, river.............................D 2
Rolling, fork...........................C 1
St. Francis, river......................C 5
Saline, river...........................C 1
Saline, river...........................D 3
   South, fork........................C 6
Smackover, creek.....................D 2
Spring, river...........................A 4
   South, fork........................A 4
Strawberry, river.....................A 4
Sulphur, river.........................D 1
Two Prairie, bayou...................D 6
War Eagle, creek......................A 2
Wattensaw, bayou....................C 4
White, river.......................A 2, C 4

SPECIAL POINTS OF INTEREST

Parks, Monuments, Ruins, Dams, Sites, Buildings, etc.

Arkansas Agricultural and Mechanical
   College, Monticello...............D 4
Arkansas State College, State College....B 5
Big Hurricane, cavern................A 3
Blue Mountain, dam and reservoir.......B 2

Carpenter, dam.......................D 6
Diamond, cave........................B 2
Diamond Mine, Murfreesboro..........C 2
Hot Springs, national park............C 2
Medicinal, springs....................B 3
Melbourne, cave......................A 4

Mystic, cavern........................A 2
Norfork, dam..........................A 3
Remmel, dam..........................D 6
Treasure, cave........................C 1
University of Arkansas, Fayetteville.......A 1

ARKANSAS

Area..... 53,102 sq. m.
Population..... 1,909,511

KEY TO MAP SYMBOLS

- ✪ State Capital
- ○ County Seat
- ⬡ Cities over 100,000
- ● Size of symbols and type indicates relative population.

CITIES AND TOWNS

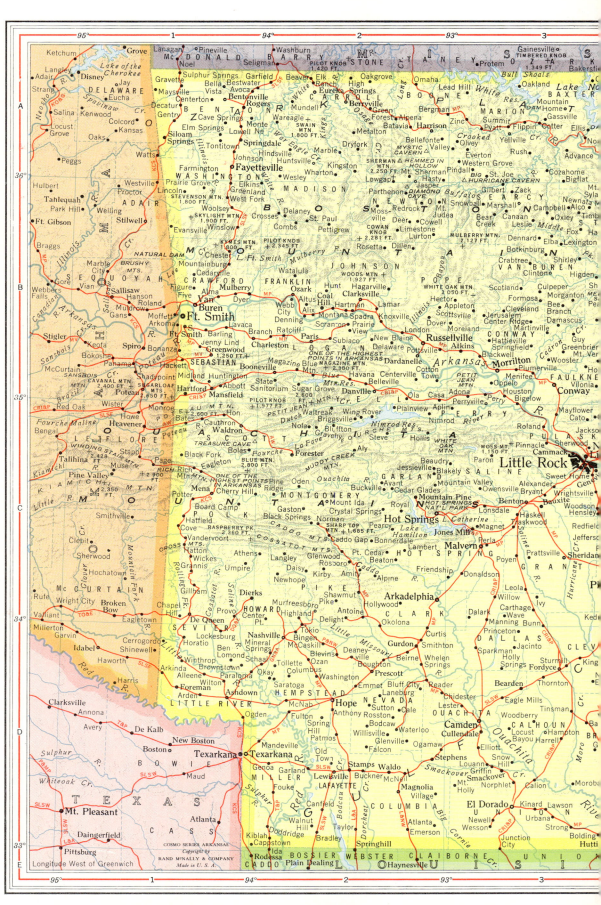

ARKANSAS

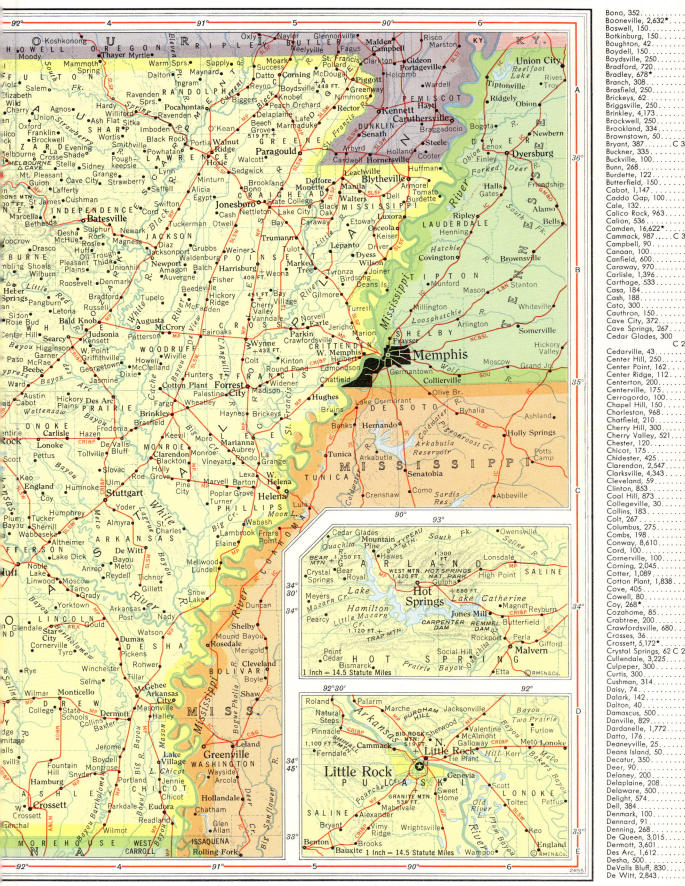

ARKANSAS *Continued*

Diaz, 200 ... B 4
Dierks, 1,253 ... C 1
Dillen, 45 ... B 2
Dixie, 150 ... B 4
Doddridge, 500 ... D 2
Donaldson, 500 ... C 3
Dover, 510 ... B 2
Drasco, 150 ... B 4
Driver, 400 ... B 5
Dryden, 43 ... *B 5
Dumas, 2,512 ... D 4
Dyer, 398 ... B 1
Dyess, 2,300 ... B 5
Eagle Mills, 225 ... D 3
Eagleton, 50 ... C 1
Earle, 2,375 ... B 5
Edgemont, 89 ... B 3
Edmondson, 283 ... B 5
Egypt, 250 ... B 5
Elaine, 744 ... C 5
El Dorado, 24,477★ ... D 3
Elizabeth, 214 ... A 3
Elkins, 350 ... B 1
Elk Ranch, 50 ... A 2
Elliott, 100 ... D 3
Ellis, 250 ... A 3
Elm Springs, 217 ... A 1
El Paso, 300 ... B 3
Emerson, 523 ... D 2
Emmet, 482 ... D 2
England, 2,136 ... C 4, E 6
Enola, 250 ... B 3
Etowah, 300 ... B 5
Eudora, 3,072 ... D 4
Eureka Springs, 1,958 ... A 2
Evansville, 163 ... B 1
Evening Shade, 360 ... A 4
Everton, 198 ... A 3
Fairoaks, 160 ... B 4
Fargo, 200 ... C 4
Farmington, 149★ ... A 1
Fayetteville, 17,071 ... A 1
Felsenthal, 203 ... D 3
Ferndale, 50 ... D 5
Figure Five, 150 ... B 1
Fisher, 289 ... B 5
Flippin, 646 ... A 3
Fordyce, 3,754 ... D 3
Foreman, 1,007 ... D 1
Forester, 818 ... C 2
Formosa, 190 ... B 3
Forrest City, 7,607 ... B 5
Fort Smith, 56,312★ ... B 1
Fouke, 336 ... D 2
Fountain Hill, 320 ... D 4
Fourche, 51 ... *C 3
Fox, 50 ... B 3
Franklin, 100 ... A 4
Fredonia, 406 ... C 4
Friendship, 179 ... C 3
Fulton, 385 ... D 2
Furlow, 50 ... D 6
Galloway, 110 ... C 6
Gamaliel, 250 ... A 3
Garfield, 83 ... A 2
Garland, 351 ... D 2
Garner 250 ... B 4
Gassville, 273 ... A 3
Gateway, 97 ... *A 1
Genevia, 2,200 ... C 3, D 6
Genoa, 150 ... D 2
Gentry, 729 ... A 1
Gentry City, see Gentry
Georgetown, 250 ... B 4
Gifford, 50 ... D 6
Gilbert, 51 ... B 3
Gillett, 774 ... C 4
Gillham, 207 ... C 1
Gilmore, 500 ... B 5
Glendale, 100 ... D 4
Glenville, 185 ... D 2
Glenwood, 843 ... C 2
Gould, 1,076 ... D 4
Grady, 517 ... C 4
Grange, 250 ... B 4
Grannis, 193 ... C 1
Gravelly, 300 ... C 2
Gravelridge, 200 ... D 3
Gravette, 894 ... A 1
Greenbrier, 375 ... B 3
Green Forest, 738 ... A 2
Greenland, 164 ... B 1
Greenway, 288 ... A 5
Greenwood, 1,634 ... B 1
Griffin, 40 ... D 3
Griffithville, 207 ... B 4
Grubbs, 313 ... B 4
Guion, 219 ... B 4
Gurdon, 2,390 ... D 2
Guy, 300 ... B 3
Hackett, 440 ... B 1
Hagarville, 200 ... B 2
Halley, 149 ... D 4
Hamburg, 2,655 ... D 4
Hampton, 838 ... D 3
Hanover, 280 ... B 3
Hardy, 599 ... A 4
Harrell, 342 ... D 3
Harrisburg, 1,498 ... B 5
Harrison, 5,617★ ... A 2
Hartford, 865 ... B 1
Hartman, 418 ... B 2
Haskell, 209 ... C 3
Hasty, 56 ... A 2
Hatfield, 364 ... C 1
Hattieville, 120 ... B 3
Hatton, 160 ... C 1
Havana, 348 ... B 2
Hawes, 63 ... C 5
Haynes, 250 ... C 5
Hazen, 1,270 ... C 4
Heber Springs, 2,109 ... B 3
Hector, 300 ... B 3
Helena, 11,236 ... C 5
Hensley, 750 ... C 3
Hermitage, 398 ... D 3
Hickory Plains, 200 ... C 4
Hickory Ridge, 345 ... B 5
Higden, 115 ... B 3
Higginson, 131 ... B 4
Highland, 110 ... C 2
Hindsville, 165 ... A 2
Holland, 185 ... B 3
Hollis, 200 ... C 2
Holly Grove, 761 ... C 4
Holly Springs, 85 ... D 3
Hollywood, 120 ... C 2
Hon, 150 ... C 1
Hope, 8,605★ ... D 2
Horatio, 776 ... D 1
Hot Springs, 29,307 ... C 2, C 6
Houston, 291 ... B 3
Howell, 200 ... B 4
Hoxie, 1,855 ... A 5
Huff, 150 ... B 4
Huffman, 200 ... B 6
Hughes, 1,686 ... C 5
Hulbert, 300 ... B 5
Humnoke, 263 ... C 4
Humphrey, 629 ... C 4
Hunt, 50 ... B 2
Hunter, 286 ... B 4
Huntington, 744 ... B 1
Huntsville, 1,010 ... A 2
Huttig, 1,038 ... D 3
Imboden, 447 ... A 4
Ingalls, 300 ... D 3
Ingram, 50 ... A 3
Ivy, 150 ... C 3
Jacinto, 150 ... D 3
Jacksonport, 215 ... B 4
Jacksonville, 3,007★ C 3, D 6
Jamestown, 84 ... *B 4
Jasmine, 45 ... B 4
Jasper, 407 ... B 2
Jefferson, 175 ... C 3
Jennie, 200 ... D 4
Jenny Lind, 750 ... B 1
Jericho, 150 ... B 5
Jerome, 82 ... D 4
Jerusalem, 250 ... B 3
Jessieville, 150 ... C 2
Johnson, 350 ... A 1
Johnsville, 105 ... D 3
Joiner, 596 ... B 5
Jonesboro, 16,310 ... A 5
Jones Mills, 1,069 ... D 6
Jordan, 53 ... A 3
Judsonia, 1,122 ... B 4
Junction City, 1,013 ... D 3
Kedron, 75 ... C 3
Keevil, 150 ... C 4
Keiser, 522 ... B 5
Kensett, 829 ... B 4
Keo, 200 ... C 4, E 6
Kerr, 75 ... D 6
Kiblah, 195 ... D 2
Kimberley, 46 ... *C 2
Kinard, 150 ... D 3
Kingsland, 337 ... D 3
Kingston, 208 ... A 2
Kinton, 250 ... B 5
Kirby, 300 ... C 2
Knobel, 417 ... A 5
Knoxville, 250 ... B 2
La Crosse, 150 ... A 4
Lafe, 100 ... A 5
Lafferty, 200 ... B 4
La Grange, 500 ... C 5
Lake City, 783 ... B 5
Lake Dick, 320 ... C 4
Lake Village, 2,484 ... D 4
Lamar, 555 ... B 2
Lambrook, 150 ... C 5
Laneburg, 100 ... D 2
Lavaca, 373 ... B 1
Lawson, 96 ... D 3
Leachville, 1,454★ ... B 5
Lead Hill, 110 ... A 3
Leola, 313 ... C 3
Lepanto, 1,683 ... B 5
Leslie, 610 ... B 3
Lester, 250 ... D 3
Letona, 164 ... B 4
Lewisville, 1,273★ ... D 2
Lexa, 500 ... C 5
Lexington, 100 ... B 3
Limestone, 250 ... B 2
Lincoln, 771 ... B 1
Linwood, 100 ... C 4
Little Rock, 107,331★ C 3, D 6
Lockesburg, 714 ... D 1
Locust Bayou, 50 ... D 3
London, 353 ... B 2
Lonoke, 2,068★ ... C 4, D 6
Lonsdale, 91 ... C 3, C 6
Louann, 291 ... D 3
Lowell, 341 ... A 1
Lowgap, 200 ... A 2
Lundell, 300 ... C 5
Lurton, 117 ... B 2
Luxora, 1,302 ... B 6
Lynn, 500 ... A 4
Mabelvale, 580 ... D 5
McAlmont, 150 ... D 6
McCaskill, 122 ... D 2
McClelland, 500 ... B 4
McCrory, 1,115 ... B 4
McDougal, 150 ... A 5
McFadden, 100 ... B 4
McGehee, 4,348★ ... D 4
McHue, 200 ... B 4
McNab, 206 ... D 2
McNeil, 597 ... D 2
McRae, 414 ... B 4
Madison, 718 ... B 5
Magazine, 503 ... B 2
Magness, 229 ... B 4
Magnet, 150 ... C 3, D 6
Magnolia, 9,255★ ... D 2
Malvern, 9,243★ ... C 3, D 6
Mammoth Spring, 870 ... A 4
Mandeville, 300 ... D 2
Manila, 1,729 ... B 5
Manning, 375 ... C 3
Mansfield, 869 ... B 1
Marble, 150 ... A 2
Marcella, 89 ... B 4
Marche, 200 ... D 5
Marianna, 4,530 ... C 5
Marion, 883 ... B 5
Marked Tree, 2,878 ... B 5
Marmaduke, 643 ... A 5
Marshall, 1,189 ... B 3
Martinville, 250 ... B 3
Marvell, 1,121 ... C 5
Masonville, 75 ... D 4
Mayflower, 293 ... C 3
Maynard, 216 ... A 5
Maysville, 250 ... A 1
Melbourne, 568 ... A 4
Mellwood, 250 ... C 5
Mena, 4,445 ... C 1
Menifee, 175 ... B 3
Metalton, 50 ... A 2
Midland, 356 ... B 1
Mineral Springs, 751 ... D 2
Minturn, 138 ... B 4
Moark, 125 ... A 5
Monette, 1,114 ... B 5
Monroe, 150 ... C 4
Montana, 300 ... B 2
Monte Ne, 100 ... A 1
Monticello, 4,501 ... D 4
Montrose, 344 ... D 4
Moreland, 200 ... B 3
Morganton, 95 ... B 3
Moro, 189 ... C 5
Morobay, 75 ... D 3
Morrilton, 5,483 ... B 3
Moscow, 200 ... C 4
Mossville, 25 ... B 2
Mountainburg, 405 ... B 1
Mountain Home, 2,217 ... A 3
Mountain Pine, 1,155 ... C 2, C 5
Mountain Valley, 130 ... C 2
Mountain View, 1,043 ... B 3
Mount Holly, 400 ... D 3
Mount Ida, 566 ... C 2
Mount Judea, 150 ... B 2
Mount Olive, 100 ... B 3
Mount Pleasant, 250 ... B 4
Mount Sherman, 200 ... A 2
Mount Vernon, 250 ... B 3
Mulberry, 952 ... B 1
Mundell, 135 ... A 2
Murfreesboro, 1,079 ... C 2
Nady, 200 ... D 4
Nashville, 3,548 ... D 2
Natural Steps, 85 ... D 5
Nettleton, 1,382 ... B 5
Newark, 913 ... B 4
New Blaine, 200 ... B 2
New Edinburg, 175 ... D 3
Newell, 375 ... D 3
Newhope, 250 ... C 2
Newnata, 500 ... B 3
Newport, 6,254 ... B 4
Nimmons, 199 ... A 5
Nimrod, 100 ... C 2
Noble Lake, 100 ... C 4
Nola, 150 ... C 2
Norfolk, 431 ... A 3
Norman, 401 ... C 2
Norphlet, 653 ... D 3
North Little Rock, 49,588★ ... C 3, D 6
Norvell, 372 ... B 5
Oakgrove, 100 ... A 2
Oakland, 80 ... A 3
Oden, 133 ... C 2
Ogamaw, 300 ... D 2
Ogden, 296 ... D 1
Oil Trough, 850 ... B 4
Okay, 150 ... D 2
O'Kean, 165 ... A 5
Okolona, 458 ... C 2
Ola, 880 ... B 2
Old Town, 200 ... D 2
Olmstead, 50 ... C 3
Olvey, 85 ... A 3
Omaha, 91 ... A 2
Oppelo, 30 ... B 3
Osceola, 5,006 ... B 6
Otwell, 50 ... B 5
Owensville, 100 ... C 3, C 6
Oxford, 79 ... A 3
Oxley, 132 ... B 3
Ozan, 124 ... D 2
Ozark, 1,757 ... B 2
Palestine, 420 ... C 5
Pangburn, 669 ... B 4
Paragould, 9,668 ... A 5
Paraloma, 186 ... D 1
Paris, 3,731 ... B 2
Parkdale, 385 ... D 4
Parkin, 1,414 ... B 5
Paron, 62 ... C 3
Parthenon, 300 ... B 2
Patmos, 300 ... D 2
Patterson, 357 ... B 4
Peach Orchard, 327 ... A 5
Pearcy, 250 ... D 5
Pea Ridge, 268 ... A 1
Pearson, 85 ... B 3
Perla, 270 ... C 3, D 6
Perry, 284 ... B 3
Perryville, 674 ... B 3
Pettigrew, 150 ... B 2
Pettus, 210 ... C 4, D 6
Pickens, 105 ... D 4
Piggott, 2,558 ... A 5
Pike, 123 ... C 2
Pindall, 200 ... A 3
Pine Bluff, 37,162 ... C 3
Pine City, 105 ... C 4
Pine Ridge, 45 ... C 2
Pinnacle, 75 ... C 3, D 5
Plainview, 637 ... C 2
Pleasant Plains, 153 ... B 4
Plum Bayou, 100 ... C 3
Plumerville, 550 ... B 3
Pocahontas, 3,840 ... A 5
Point Cedar, 150 ... C 2, D 5
Pollard, 165 ... A 5
Poplar Grove, 169 ... C 5
Portia, 349 ... A 4
Portland, 517 ... D 4
Potter, 250 ... C 1
Pottsville, 224 ... B 3
Poughkeepsie, 300 ... A 4
Powhatan, 120 ... A 4
Poyen, 253★ ... C 3
Prairie Grove, 939 ... B 1
Prairie View, 225 ... B 2
Prattsville, 130 ... C 3
Prescott, 3,960 ... D 2
Princeton, 112 ... D 3
Provo, 175 ... C 1
Pyatt, 257 ... A 3
Quitman, 345 ... B 3
Ratcliff, 213 ... B 2
Ravenden, 245 ... A 4
Ravenden Springs, 197 ... A 4
Reader, 79 ... D 2
Readland, 125 ... D 4
Rector, 1,855 ... A 5
Redfield, 291 ... C 3
Redrock, 100 ... B 3
Reyburn, 50 ... D 6
Reydell, 100 ... C 4
Reyno, 292 ... A 5
Rich Mountain, 51 ... C 1
Rison, 953 ... D 3
Rockport, 159★ ... D 6
Roe, 300 ... C 4
Rogers, 5,222★ ... A 1
Rohwer, ... D 4
Roland, 500 ... C 3, D 5
Rondo, 194 ... C 5
Roosevelt, 110 ... B 4
Rosboro, 84 ... C 2
Rose Bud, 150 ... B 3
Rosetta, 130 ... B 2
Rosie, 150 ... B 4
Rosston, 100 ... D 2
Round Pond, 1,800 ... B 5
Rover, 200 ... C 2
Rudy, 97 ... *B 1
Rush, 100 ... A 3
Russell, 241 ... B 4
Russellville, 8,166 ... B 2
Rye, 250 ... D 4
Saffell, 150 ... B 4
St. Charles, 313 ... C 4
St. Francis, 292 ... A 5
St. James, 40 ... B 4
St. Joe, 187 ... A 3
St. Paul, 136 ... B 2
Salem, 687 ... A 4
Saratoga, 110 ... D 2
Schaal, 300 ... D 2
Scotland, 288 ... B 3
Scott, 375 ... C 3, D 6
Scottsville, 250 ... B 3
Scranton, 283 ... B 2
Searcy, 6,445★ ... B 4
Sedgwick, 196 ... B 5
Selma, 300 ... D 4
Shawmut, 50 ... C 2
Sheridan, 1,893 ... C 3
Sherrill, 263 ... C 4
Sherwood 717 ... D 5
Shiloh, 41 ... B 3
Shirley, 259 ... B 3
Sidney, 120 ... A 4
Sidon, 150 ... B 4
Siloam Springs, 3,837★ ... A 1
Sitka, 50 ... A 4
Slovac, 50 ... C 4
Smackover, 2,495 ... D 3
Smithton, 175 ... D 2
Smithville, 250 ... A 4
Snowball, 130 ... B 3
Snow Hill, 100 ... D 3
Snow Lake, 96 ... C 4
Snyder, 75 ... D 4
Social Hill, 150 ... D 6
South Fort Smith, 1,885 ... B 1
Spadra, 300 ... B 2
Sparkman, 964 ... D 3
Springdale, 5,835 ... A 1
Springfield, 250 ... B 3
Spring Hill, 200 ... D 2
Stamps, 2,552 ... D 2
Star City, 1,296 ... D 4
State College, 800 ... B 5
State Sanatorium, 300 ... B 2
State Schools, 500 ... D 4
Stella, 108 ... A 4
Stephens, 1,283 ... D 2
Steve, 218 ... C 2
Strawberry, 250 ... B 4
Strong, 839 ... D 3
Sturmill, 150 ... D 3
Stuttgart, 8,062★ ... C 4
Subiaco, 191 ... B 2
Success, 311 ... A 5
Sugar Grove, 214 ... B 2
Sulphur Rock, 179 ... B 4
Sulphur Springs, 543 ... A 1
Summit, 268 ... A 3
Supply, 30 ... A 5
Sutton, 150 ... D 2
Sweet Home, 694 ... C 3, D 6
Swifton, 539 ... B 4
Sylamore, 100 ... B 3
Tamo, 52 ... C 4
Taylor, 547 ... D 2
Texarkana, 19,733★ ... D 1
Thida, 200 ... B 4
Thornton, 668★ ... D 3
Tichnor, 50 ... C 4
Tie Plant, 250 ... D 6
Tillar, 239 ... D 4
Timbo, 100 ... B 3
Tinsman, 118 ... D 3
Tokio, 250 ... C 2
Tollette, 200 ... D 2
Tollville, 100 ... C 4
Toltec, 75 ... D 6
Tomato, 300 ... B 6
Tontitown, 203 ... A 1
Traskwood, 199 ... C 3
Trumann, 4,133★ ... B 5
Tucker, 165 ... C 4
Tuckerman, 1,338★ ... B 4
Tulot, 400 ... B 5
Tumbling Shoals, 100 ... B 3
Tupelo, 188 ... B 4
Turner, 45 ... C 4
Turrell, 670 ... B 5
Tyro, 60 ... D 4
Tyronza, 656 ... B 5
Ulm, 131 ... C 4
Umpire, 83 ... C 1
Union, 500 ... A 4
Unionhill, 150 ... B 4
Urbana, 800 ... D 3
Valentine, 180 ... C 3, D 6
Valley Springs, 200 ... A 3
Van Buren, 6,413 ... B 1
Vandervoort, 600 ... C 1
Vanndale, 800 ... B 5
Village, 150 ... D 2
Vilonia, 215 ... B 3
Vineyard, 100 ... C 5
Viola, 206 ... A 4
Wabash, 115 ... C 5
Wabbaseka, 375 ... C 4
Walcott, 85 ... A 5
Waldenburg, 125 ... B 4
Waldo, 1,491 ... D 2
Waldron, 1,292 ... C 1
Walnut Hill, 175 ... D 2
Walnut Ridge, 3,106 ... A 5
Waltreak, 100 ... C 2
Ward, 364 ... B 4
Wareagle, 95 ... A 2
Warm Springs, 40 ... A 4
Warren, 6,905★ ... D 3
Washington, 344 ... D 2
Watalula, 125 ... B 2
Waterloo, 300 ... D 2
Watson, 309 ... D 4
Wave, 75 ... C 3
Webb City, 135 ... B 2
Weiner, 644 ... B 5
Weona, 800 ... B 5
Wesley, 65 ... A 2
Wesson, 245 ... D 3
West Crossett, 289 ... D 4
Western Grove, 184 ... A 3
West Fork, 351 ... B 1
West Helena, 6,107 ... C 5
West Memphis, 15,776★ ... B 5
West Point, 115 ... B 4
Wharton, 100 ... A 2
Wheatley, 406 ... C 4
Whelen Springs, 192 ... D 2
Wickes, 401 ... C 1
Widener, 187 ... B 5
Wilburn, 300 ... B 4
Wild Cherry, 100 ... A 3
Williford, 213 ... A 4
Willisville, 150 ... D 2
Willow, 125 ... C 3
Wilmar, 746 ... D 4
Wilmot, 721 ... D 4
Wilson, 1,301 ... B 5
Wilton, 328 ... D 1
Winchester, 198 ... D 4
Wing, 105 ... C 2
Winslow, 248 ... B 1
Winthrop, 284 ... D 1
Wiville, 100 ... B 4
Woodberry, 250 ... D 3
Woodrow, 165 ... B 3
Woodson, 350 ... C 3
Woolsey, 100 ... B 1
Wooster, 140 ... B 3
Wortis, 200 ... A 4
Wrightsville, 500 ... C 3, D 6
Wynne, 4,142 ... B 5
Yellville, 697 ... A 3
Yoder, 100 ... C 4
Yorktown, 380 ... C 4
Zack, 150 ... B 3
Zinc, 99 ... A 3

COUNTIES

Arkansas, 23,665 ... C 4
Ashley, 25,660 ... D 4
Baxter, 11,683 ... A 3
Benton, 38,076 ... A 1
Boone, 16,260 ... A 2
Bradley, 15,987 ... D 3
Calhoun, 7,132 ... D 3
Carroll, 13,244 ... A 2
Chicot, 22,306 ... D 4
Clark, 22,998 ... C 2
Clay, 26,674 ... A 5
Cleburne, 11,487 ... B 3
Cleveland, 8,956 ... D 3
Columbia, 28,770 ... D 2
Conway, 18,137 ... B 3
Craighead, 50,613 ... B 5
Crawford, 22,727 ... B 1
Crittenden, 47,184 ... B 5
Cross, 24,757 ... B 5
Dallas, 12,416 ... D 3
Desha, 25,155 ... D 4
Drew, 17,959 ... D 4
Faulkner, 25,289 ... B 3
Franklin, 12,358 ... B 2
Fulton, 9,187 ... A 4
Garland, 47,102 ... C 2
Grant, 9,024 ... C 3
Greene, 29,149 ... A 5
Hempstead, 25,080 ... D 2
Hot Spring, 22,181 ... C 2
Howard, 13,342 ... C 2
Independence, 23,488 ... B 4
Izard, 9,953 ... A 4
Jackson, 25,912 ... B 4
Jefferson, 76,075 ... C 3
Johnson, 16,138 ... B 2
Lafayette, 13,203 ... D 2
Lawrence, 21,303 ... A 4
Lee, 24,322 ... C 5
Lincoln, 17,079 ... D 4
Little River, 11,690 ... D 1
Logan, 20,260 ... B 2
Lonoke, 27,278 ... C 4
Madison, 11,734 ... B 2
Marion, 8,609 ... A 3
Miller, 32,614 ... D 2
Mississippi, 82,375 ... B 5
Monroe, 19,540 ... C 4
Montgomery, 6,680 ... C 2
Nevada, 14,781 ... D 2
Newton, 8,685 ... B 2
Ouachita, 33,051 ... D 3
Perry, 5,978 ... C 3
Phillips, 46,254 ... C 5
Pike, 10,032 ... C 2
Poinsett, 39,311 ... B 5
Polk, 14,182 ... C 1
Pope, 23,291 ... B 2
Prairie, 13,768 ... C 4
Pulaski, 196,685 ... C 3
Randolph, 15,982 ... A 4
St. Francis, 36,841 ... B 5
Saline, 23,816 ... C 3
Scott, 10,057 ... C 1
Searcy, 10,424 ... B 3
Sebastian, 64,202 ... B 1
Sevier, 12,293 ... D 1
Sharp, 8,999 ... A 4
Stone, 7,662 ... B 3
Union, 49,686 ... D 3
Van Buren, 9,687 ... B 3
Washington, 49,979 ... A 1
White, 38,040 ... B 4
Woodruff, 18,957 ... B 4
Yell, 14,057 ... B 2

* Not shown on map. Index key denotes approximate location.

★ Population according to special census taken since 1950.

ARKANSAS RESOURCES & DEVELOPMENT COMMISSION

HARVEST TIME IN ARKANSAS

along the rivers but now are almost extinct. The soft-shelled turtle is a characteristic reptile of the swamps. One of the most attractive birds of the region is the bobwhite. The wild turkey is still to be seen in the heavily wooded regions, and many species of ducks pass through the state on migration.

Two of the most interesting small mammals of the state are the opossum and the raccoon, which are found throughout the state. Otter are found in some areas. Bobcats are

TRIANGLE PHOTO SERVICE

Hauling logs in Wabash, Arkansas

reasonably abundant in the less settled regions. One of the handsomest animals of the region is the spotted skunk. The only large game animal still numerous is the white-tailed deer.

ECONOMIC RESOURCES AND ACTIVITIES

Minerals and Mining. Petroleum, coal, natural gas, and bauxite, a valuable ore of aluminum, are Arkansas' chief mineral products. With mineral production for 1951 estimated at $118,693,000, Arkansas ranked high among the states in bauxite and petroleum production. The state produces over 1,000,000 long tons of bauxite annually—approximately 90 per cent of the entire production for the United States. In 1952 coal production was 873,000 short tons, and production of crude petroleum was 1,236,480,000 bbl. Natural gas production in 1951 was 44,656,000,000 cu. ft., and natural gasoline in 1952 was 110,880,000 gal. Manganese and mercury deposits are also worked.

Various other minerals of less commercial importance are mined. Among these are limestone, sandstone, granite, and quartzite for building material, novaculite for whetstones, marble, and phosphate rock. Mineral waters are extensively bottled, and diamonds in limited quantities have been found in Pike County near Murfreesboro. The mine located there, now inactive, is one of the few places in the United States where diamonds have been obtained.

Agriculture. Arkansas is primarily an agricultural state, with 57 per cent of its population living on farms, and a total farm income in 1952 of over $592,000,000. Fifty-four per cent of the state's total area, or 18,871,244 acres, is in farmland, which was appraised in 1948 at $1,500,000,000, an average of $6,500 per farm.

The principal farm crop is cotton, which is raised in the Arkansas River Valley south of Little Rock and in the eastern portion of the state along the Mississippi River. Approximately 2,000,000 acres are planted in cotton annually, and in 1952 the yield was about 1,550,000 500-lb. bales.

Corn, oats, potatoes, sweet potatoes, hay, and forage crops are raised mainly in the northern part of the state, and in 1953 the corn production amounted to 11,849,000 bu. Arkansas is one of the leading producers of strawberries. Other agricultural crops are vegetables (mainly tomatoes and watermelons), soybeans, peanuts, peaches, apples, pears, and grapes. A unique agricultural industry is the cultivation of roses for perfumes.

Rice is another important crop, with production in 1953 totaling 11,786,000,000 lds. For the raising of rice, irrigation systems have been built in the eastern part of the state. Three-fourths of the Arkansas rice crop is produced north of the Arkansas River and east of Little Rock in Lonoke, Poinsett, and Prairie counties, which have 76 per cent of the irrigated acreage.

In 1949 Arkansas had 419,101 acres under irrigation with an investment in irrigation works of $14,171,467. More important than irrigation systems are the artificial drainage works. These works involved a total of about 4,701,000 acres in 1950.

Animal Industry. In 1954 the state had 1,566,000 head of cattle, of which 485,000 were milch cows; 374,000 hogs and pigs; 95,000 horses; 87,000 mules; and 44,000 sheep and lambs. On Arkansas farms there were also more than 7,310,000 chickens and 39,000 turkeys. The value of livestock and livestock products sold in 1949 was $48,396,000. The income derived from dairy products was $17,011,000; from all poultry products, $30,221,000.

Manufacturing. Although Arkansas is primarily an agricultural state, manufacturing and industrial interests

TRIANGLE PHOTO SERVICE

Operating a cotton picker in an Arkansas cotton field

are an important part of the economy. In 1948 there were 2,100 manufacturing establishments in the state, about half of which were classified as plants or factories of small size and output. In 1952 a total of 77,996 workers were employed in industry, and the income derived from all industries was $386,472,000. The principal industries are furniture manufacturing, woodworking, petroleum refining, cottonseed oil and meal processing, fruit and vegetable canning, meat packing, textile manufacturing, railway equipment production and repair, and mineral water bottling. Of the 89 industries mentioned in the 1940 United States Census, in value of output the first five ranked: furniture, $41,433,196; cottonseed oils and meals, $17,340,000; petroleum refining, $14,327,000; food preparation products, $8,998,000; and nonalcoholic beverages, $5,441,196.

Fisheries. The Mississippi River and its tributaries are fished commercially, the annual catch being around 15,-

000,000 lbs. The most important commercial species are buffalo fish, catfish, carp, crappie, sheepshead, and paddlefish. A federal fish hatchery at Mammoth Springs and a state hatchery at Lonoke propagate fish and stock creeks and rivers with black bass, sunfish, crappie, and rainbow trout.

Commerce. In 1948 Arkansas had a wholesale trade involving 2,147 establishments, 14,705 employees, $35,808,000 in payrolls, and sales of $851,613,000. While concentrated in Little Rock and Fort Smith, some of this wholesale trade was widely scattered over the state. In retail trade for the same year the state had 22,243 stores, 22,517 active proprietors of unincorporated businesses, 54,451 employees, $85,176,000 in payrolls, and sales of $1,083,262.

Finance and Banking. In 1952 the state revenue was $145,574,000, of which $99,589,000 came from taxes, $38,640,000 from intergovernmental sources, and $7,345,000 from miscellaneous sources. Total expenditures for the same year amounted to $138,019,000, of which $46,039,000 was spent for education, $34,900,000 for highways, $24,674,000 for public welfare, and $6,384,000 for health and hospitals. The net debt of Arkansas at the end of 1952 was $131,063,-000. The state collected a total of $102,492,000 in taxes in 1953.

Arkansas had 230 banks in 1952, with total assets of about $992,500,000 and deposits of $926,300,000. Of these, 53 were national banks, having assets of about $525,112,000 and deposits of $490,677,000; 177 were state banks with resources of over $364,722,000 and deposits of more than $340,470,000. In addition, there were 8 state building and loan associations and 34 federal savings and loan associations, which had resources well above $46,000,000.

Transportation. Arkansas is well provided with transportation facilities. By 1951 there were 64,621 mi. of roads, of which 28,266 mi. were surfaced. On highways the 1951 expenditure was $40,765,000.

The railway mileage of the state in 1952 was 4,270 miles, a decrease since 1910 of 991 mi. The principal railroads are the Missouri Pacific, the St. Louis-San Francisco, the Rock Island, and the Kansas City Southern. Busses are extensively used for urban and interurban passenger traffic. Arkansas has an extensive river system of navigable waterways on the Mississippi, Arkansas, and Red rivers, but water transportation is seldom used except on the Mississippi. By 1953 the state had 80 airports, of which about one half were suitable for commercial aircraft, 21 municipally owned, and 11 totally lighted.

Communications. Arkansas had 203,000 telephones

Hereford cattle herds are seen throughout the whole of Arkansas. The livestock industry reaps one of the state's major farm incomes.

LITTLE ROCK, ARKANSAS, AND THE STATE CAPITOL BUILDING (INSET)

in 1951, 50 broadcasting stations in 1953. Arkansas is well supplied with oil and gas pipe lines, water system lines, electric light and power lines, and sewage pipe lines.

GOVERNMENT AND POLITICS

Structure of Government. Under the constitution of 1874, as amended, the legislature consists of two houses, a Senate of 35 members and a House of Representatives of 100 members. The term of senators is four years and of representatives two years. The General Assembly meets in biennial sessions subject to extension by a two-thirds vote of each house. On extraordinary occasions the governor may convene a special session. State officers include a governor, lieutenant governor, secretary of state, treasurer, auditor, and attorney-general, elected for two years. Numerous additional state officers are selected by nomination and confirmation. The judicial power is vested in a supreme court, circuit courts, county and probate courts, and justice-of-the-peace courts.

Congressional Representation. Arkansas, with 2 United States senators and 7 representatives (6 after the 1952 elections), has an electoral-college vote of 9 (8). Since 1876 the state national voting has been uniformly Democratic.

Political Movements and Legislation. During the dominance of the Democratic Party in Arkansas, political movements have been concerned mainly with state problems. Many movements such as railway regulation, initiative and referendum, women's suffrage, and higher school taxes have been reflected by amendments to the constitution of 1874. Questions of suffrage and civil service have agitated the political scene. Efforts to encourage manufacturing in the state have been featured in politics since 1925.

Corporation laws, educational legislation, initiative and referendum, poll tax and suffrage laws, and a vigorous corrupt-practices law are outstanding legislation of the last 75 years. A constitutional amendment and legislation have provided for temporary exemption from taxes to encourage the establishment of new industries.

National Guard. The constitution of 1874 provided for a state militia of all able-bodied male persons between the ages of 18 and 45, and permitted the formation of volunteer companies. Later the militia became the Arkansas National Guard, headed by an adjutant general. Unlike the majority of states, Arkansas has not a state guard distinct from the old militia organized as the Arkansas National Guard.

SOCIAL AND CULTURAL ACTIVITIES

Education. In Arkansas the earliest educational facilities were missionary Indian schools. Every sixteenth section of public land became available for education in 1819, and legislation to establish a system of common schools was passed in 1843. Private academies were more in vogue before 1860, with 90 chartered between 1836 and 1860. The constitutions of 1868 and 1874 laid the basis of later public education. Public schools in 1890 numbered more than 2,500 with about 240,000 pupils. Arkansas Industrial University was opened in 1872 and renamed the University of Arkansas in 1899. Educational legislation of 1903 defined and provided for the improvement of public school standards.

In 1950, there were 407,084 pupils enrolled in Arkansas' public schools. Another 8,073 pupils were enrolled in the state's private schools. The number of public schools was 2,566, and the number of teachers, 12,845. Of these schools, 1,983 were elementary, and 583 were secondary. There were, in addition, 79 private and parochial schools. In the public schools, the average number of pupils per teacher was 27.6; teachers' salaries averaged $1,801. State expenditures for public schools were $54,354,000.

Of the 23 colleges, universities, and professional schools as of 1950, 12 were publicly-controlled and 11 were private institutions. The leading public institutions of higher

243

Hot Springs National Park, Arkansas, one of the nation's most famous health resorts

learning are the University of Arkansas at Fayetteville; Arkansas Agricultural, Mechanical and Normal College for Negroes, Pine Bluff; Arkansas State College, Jonesboro; Arkansas Polytechnic College, Russellville; Arkansas Agricultural and Mechanical College, Monticello; Southern State College, Magnolia; Arkansas State Teachers College, Conway; Henderson State Teachers College, Arkadelphia. Leading private institutions are Ouachita College, Arkadelphia; Harding College, Searcy; Hendrix College, Conway; Subiaco Academy, Subiaco; College of the Ozarks, Clarksville; St. John's Seminary, Little Rock; John Brown University, Siloam Springs; Arkansas College, Batesville; Philander Smith College for Negroes, Little Rock.

Social Measures. Arkansas is well provided with institutions and other measures of public welfare. It has a state board of health, schools for the blind and deaf at Little Rock, a tuberculosis sanatorium at Booneville, and a hospital for nervous diseases at Little Rock. In progressive penology it is far advanced. Arkansas abandoned the leasing of convicts in 1910, and later removed its prisoners from penitentiary buildings and established them on farms where they engaged in agriculture and noncompetitive industry. Similar provision was made for juvenile offenders, white and Negro, male and female, and a reformatory for women was organized at Jacksonville. Child labor laws and wages and work-hour laws for women were put on the statute book in 1915, and genuine efforts for the improvement of Negro welfare have been made. Arkansas also implemented the Social Security Act of 1935 with ten programs of social security. In 1948 the state's agency for unemployment compensation received from the Federal Government $498,000 to cover adminstration expenses and paid out, from a fund derived from a state tax, benefits totaling $3,377,733.

Historic Sites. Probably the most famous place in Arkansas is Hot Springs, where, adjoining the resort city, an area containing 47 mineral springs was set aside as a special reservation in 1832 and established as a national park in 1921. Use of the spa's thermal waters is controlled by the national government. Among other springs in the state, that at

Mammoth Spring in north Arkansas is one of the largest in the world, flowing 200,000,000 gallons a day. The sunken lands of northeast Arkansas caused by the New Madrid earthquake of 1811-1812 are geologically famous. Arkansas Post, the oldest settlement in the state, on the Arkansas River below Pine Bluff; Helena, a river port and battlefield; and Elkhorn, a great battlefield of 1861, are well known historically.

POPULATION

Over-all Statistics. The population of Arkansas, according to the 1950 census, was 1,909,511. Of this population, 1,278,920 were rural and 630,591 urban. Between 1920 and 1950, the urban percentage increased from 16.6 per cent to 33 per cent, a common trend in the United States. The state in 1950 had 64 urban places with a population of more than 2,500 each.

Counties. Of the 75 counties of Arkansas only one has a population of over 100,000: Pulaski with 196,685. Mississippi and Jefferson counties, the next most populated, had 82,375 and 76,075, respectively, in 1950.

Major Cities. In 1950, of the 64 urban places of more than 2,500 population only one, Little Rock (102,213), had a population exceeding 50,000; only four others, Fort Smith (47,942), North Little Rock (44,097), Pine Bluff (37,162), and Hot Springs (29,307), more than 25,000; and only seven others, El Dorado (23,076), Fayetteville (17,071), Jonesboro (16,310), Blytheville (16,234), Texarkana (15,875), Camden (11,372), and Helena (11,236), more than 10,000.

Ethnic and Racial Groupings. The population of Arkansas in 1940 contained 1,458,392 native whites, 7,692 foreign-born whites, 482,578 Negroes, 278 Indians, 432 Chinese, and three Japanese. Of the foreign-born whites, 2,015 were from northwestern Europe, 3,022 (mainly German) from central Europe, 462 (mainly Russian) from eastern Europe, 1,037 (mainly Italian and Greek) from southern Europe, and the remaining 1,156 largely from Canada, Mexico, and Palestine-Syria.

Religious Groups. Arkansas in 1936 had 4,278 Christian churches or congregations with 4,179 edifices and 565,995 members. The value of the 4,179 edifices was $20,-282,516, with an indebtedness of $2,111,785 upon 645 churches. These data include 2,256 Negro or part Negro congregations, 1,939 Negro church edifices, 1,471 rural and 93 urban, of which the value of 1,715 was $4,273,157, and an indebtedness of $382,293 on 268. Of the 482,578 Negroes of Arkansas, 217,123 were church members, most of them Baptists or Methodists. There were in 1936 in Arkansas 12 Jewish congregations, with a total of 4,224 members and nine edifices, eight of which reported an indebtedness of $239,000. Little Rock had two Jewish congregations with a total of 2,500 members and Fort Smith one congregation of 350 members. Arkansas in 1936 had 52 different denominations.

Occupational Groups. Occupational statistics for Arkansas show a trend away from agricultural occupation. The data for 1940 showed the following occupational groups: professional and semiprofessional, 24,657; farmers and farm managers, 191,607; proprietors, managers, and officials except farms, 73,100; clerical, sales, and kindred workers, 46,700; craftsmen, foremen, and kindred workers, 32,524; operatives and kindred workers, 42,722; service workers, 53,356; farm laborers and foremen, 54,605; laborers except farm and mine, 43,321; occupation not reported, 3,937; a total of 569,728 employed or 29 per cent of the population.

PLACES OF INTEREST

Hot Springs. The nation's first national park. More than a million gallons of mineral-laden water with an average temperature of 143° F. flow daily from 47 springs at the base of Hot Springs Mountain.

Old State House. A magnificent example of pre-Civil War southern architecture in Little Rock. The building is now maintained by the state and houses the Arkansas Museum of History and the State Archives.

Lakes Norfolk and Bull Shoals. These are large reservoirs created by great power and flood control dams in north central Arkansas on the White River, near the Missouri border. Both are well stocked with fish.

Bauxite Mines. Located a few miles southwest of Little Rock, these are the only known important deposits of this vital ore in the United States.

The "Arkansas Ozarks." Situated in northwest Arkansas, these are rugged, forested hills, canyons, and valleys, which are highly regarded for hunting and fishing. They are especially colorful in spring and fall.

Territorial Capitol. This is the fully restored meeting place of the last Arkansas Territorial Legislature at Little Rock. Originally built in 1820, the restored area includes 13 buildings.

Petit Jean State Park. The park is located on a beautiful mountain in west central Arkansas near Morrilton. It is cleft by a canyon with a 75-ft. waterfall.

HISTORY

Explorations. The Spanish explorer Hernando de Soto was the first European to explore Arkansas. Having traveled up the Mississippi, de Soto spent several months during the winter of 1541-1542 exploring the eastern part of Arkansas. The region was not visited again until 1673 when Marquette and Joliet, the French explorers, came down the Mississippi and explored the country around the mouth of the Arkansas River. In 1682 La Salle came to the same area on his way down the Mississippi, and in 1686 de Tonti, La Salle's lieutenant, left a party of his men to establish Arkansas Post and

An open hot spring registers a temperature of 115° F.

trade with the Indians along the Arkansas River. John Law attempted to establish a colony under the auspices of the French at Arkansas Post in 1718, but the venture failed. La Harpe came to the region and traveled up the Arkansas River, visiting the site of Little Rock in 1722 and leaving a permanent garrison at Arkansas Post. A settlement was made at the mouth of White River in 1766 and at Helena in 1797. The region of present Arkansas had a population of 368 in 1799.

Development. Originally French, but having been ceded to Spain in 1762, the region was retroceded to France in the treaty of San Ildefonso signed in 1800. In 1803, it was purchased by the United States as part of the Louisiana Purchase and the next year occupied by United States troops. Further explorations were made, mainly along rivers, and new settlements were established. The region was set apart as the District of Arkansas in 1806, and it had a population of 1,062 in 1810. On the admission of Louisiana as a state in 1812, the Arkansas region became Arkansas County of the Territory of Missouri, and in 1819 it became the Territory of Arkansas. Meanwhile settlement continued, and the population reached 14,273 in 1820. By 1830 the population had doubled. In 1836 a convention drew up a constitution, and Arkansas was admitted to the Union, June 16, 1836, as the twenty-fourth state. Population tripled between 1830 and 1840, and farms, villages, and local governmental units spread over the state. Commerce, industry, education, and the professions were begun. By 1850 the population had reached 209,897, and by 1860 it had increased to 435,450. During the Civil War Arkansas seceded on May 6, 1861, and joined the Southern Confederacy, but not without hesitation and serious opposition from unionists of the state. Confederate and Union forces contested control of the state, and pitched land battles, river expeditions, naval attacks, and numerous guerrilla skirmishes took place. By 1863 the Union forces recovered a large part of the state. A loyal antislavery government was established in 1864, but the state was not readmitted until June 23, 1868. Under "carpet bag" rule anarchy prevailed for some time, finally developing into armed conflict between the supporters of the Republican and Democratic candidates for governor. In 1874 a new constitution was adopted. Since the close of the Civil War the state's history has been largely without dramatic incidents. Exceptions to this have been the "Agrarian Revolt" of the 1880's and 1890's, and the Populist movement which, for a time, threatened the political hegemony of the conservative plantation owners and businessmen. Arkansas's recent history has been a story of rapid urbanization of its population and industrialization of its economy.

Military Activity. Indian warfare between whites and Indians in the region of Arkansas never became extensive. The original Indians made treaties and retired westward. The eastern Indians, removed to the west under President Jackson, stopped for a while in the region but eventually settled in the Indian Territory. Their passage through the state was not accompanied by serious disorder or bloodshed.

An Arkansas regiment served in the Mexican War, while a battalion at home protected the borders of the state. In the Civil War, Arkansas raised 25 regiments and 15 battalions of infantry, 10 regiments and 17 battalions of cavalry, and three battalions of artillery for the Confederacy. In addition, the state furnished four regiments of infantry, four of cavalry, and a battalion of artillery of white men, and four regiments of Negroes for the Union. Arkansas furnished two regiments for the Spanish American War. World War I drew into United States military services 71,862 Arkansans, including the Arkansas National Guard, most of them former civilians who were trained at hurriedly built cantonments located in or near Arkansas, one of which, Camp Pike, near Little Rock, included 100,000 trainees. Participating to the fullest extent of its resources in World War II, Arkansas had contributed about 200,000, 194,000 men and 3,000 women to the armed forces of the United States.   A. P. J.

ARKANSAS, UNIVERSITY OF, an accredited, coeducational, state-controlled institution located in Fayetteville, Ark., a community of 17,000. The school of medicine is at

At the University of Arkansas, in Fayetteville, "Old Main" (left) is the oldest building on campus, the Student Union (right) one of the newest.

Little Rock, 200 mi. away from the main campus. The university was chartered in 1872 as the Arkansas Industrial University, and the name was changed to the University of Arkansas in 1899.

Liberal arts courses lead to degrees of B.A., B.S., B.Mus., and B.S. in social welfare; the college of business administration grants B.S. and B.A. degrees; the college of engineering courses lead to a degree of B.S. in chemical engineering, civil engineering, electrical engineering, and mechanical engineering. The college of agriculture, including home economics, confers B.S.A. and B.S.E. degrees; the college of education confers a B.S.Ed.; the school of law confers B.S. in law and LL.B. The medical school grants an M.D. degree. Graduate degrees include M.A. and M.S.

There is but one undergraduate scholarship available. A number of graduate assistantships are offered and there is a substantial loan fund. Residential facilities are provided, and new buildings for both men and women were under construction in 1949 to meet the increasing demand. *For statistics see* COLLEGES AND UNIVERSITIES.   J. R. To.

ARKANSAS AGRICULTURAL AND MECHANICAL COLLEGE, a state-controlled, coeducational, accredited, technical college on a campus of 796 acres in Monticello, Ark., a town of 4,500, approximately 75 mi. south of Pine Bluff. The charter was granted in 1909, and instruction started the following year. Degrees of B.A. in liberal arts and B.S. in business administration, education, physical education, and sciences are offered. A two-year course in applied forestry leading to a Certificate of Forest Technician is available. There is some scholarship and loan assistance for which only residents of the state of Arkansas are eligible. Dormitory facilities are available for all students. *For statistics see* COLLEGES AND UNIVERSITIES.   J. R. To.

ARKANSAS CITY [ɑrkɑ'nzəs], a city in southern Kansas, in Cowley Co., situated on the Arkansas River, 56 mi. southeast of Wichita. The city was founded as Creswell in 1870 and incorporated as Arkansas City in 1872. A division point on the Atchison, Topeka and Santa Fe, the city is also served by the Midland Valley, the Missouri Pacific, and the Frisco Lines railroads. Oil and gas deposits are in the vicinity, while wheat, corn, and livestock are raised in the area. The city's industrial products include refined oil, oil-field equipment, flour, candy, and packed meat. It is the seat of Arkansas City Junior College. The government school for Chillocco Indians, a few miles away in Oklahoma, and Gueda Medicinal Springs are points of interest. Pop. 1950, 12,903.

ARKANSAS RIVER [ɑ'rkənsɔ; ɑrkɑ'nzəs], 1,450 mi. long, one of the major western tributaries of the Mississippi River. If every bend in the river is counted, the total length is about 2,000 mi. The Arkansas River has its headwaters near Tennessee Pass on the eastern side of the Continental Divide in west central Colorado. The headwater streams, fed by rain, snow melt, and glacial lakes, have their origin about 10,000 ft. above sea level in the Sangre de Cristo, Sawatch, and Culebra mountains. The river flows generally southeastward, and in the mountains it has an average fall of 40 ft. per mile. Near Canyon City, Fremont County, Colo., the river has cut one of the deepest canyons in the United States, the Royal Gorge. In eastern Colorado the gradient of the river decreases as it flows out of the mountains, and changes from a youthful, rushing mountain stream to a more mature river flowing between broad banks across Kansas, northeastern Oklahoma, and central Arkansas. It flows into the Mississippi River in southeastern Arkansas, 37 mi. north of Arkansas City. The major tributaries are the Huerfano, Purgatoire, Big Sandy, Salt Fork, Verdigris, Neosho, Canadian, and Cimarron rivers. The Arkansas has a high-water period during the spring and early summer, and floods have been quite common. During the rest of the year the river dwindles away and almost disappears. At Little Rock, Ark., the water level may vary 26 ft. between high and low water. The river is no longer important for navigation but supplies water for irrigation to a large plains area. The principal cities located on the banks of the Arkansas are Pine Bluff, Little Rock, and Fort Smith, Ark.; Tulsa, Okla.; Wichita, Kan.; and Pueblo, Colo.   J. E. F.

ARKANSAS STATE COLLEGE, a state-controlled, accredited, coeducational, multiple-purpose institution occupying grounds of more than 1,000 acres at Jonesboro, Ark., a city of 20,000 in the northeastern part of the state. Degrees awarded are the B.A., B.S., B.F.A., B.Mus., B.S.A., B.S.Ed., B.M.E., and the M.S.Ed. The Master of Science in Education was first offered in 1955. Courses on the junior college level are given at a branch campus located at Beebe. Scholarship funds are limited. Modern housing for single and married students is available. *For statistics see* COLLEGES AND UNIVERSITIES.

ARKHANGELSK [arχa'ngɛlsk], sometimes Archangel, the name of both an oblast (region) and a city on the northern coast of the Russian Soviet Federated Socialist Republic, in the northwestern Soviet Union.

The City. Arkhangelsk is an important seaport and lumber city on the Dvina River, 25 mi. from its mouth on Dvina Bay, which is part of the White Sea. It is approximately 630 mi. northeast of Moscow, at 64° 35' N. lat. and 40° 50' E. long. Lying on low moraine hills, the city extends for several miles along the right bank of the Dvina, with numerous saw-mills and factories on both sides. At the southern end of the city is the imposing eighteenth-century monastery of the Archangel Michael, from which the town received its name. The five-domed Troitzky Cathedral was built from 1709 to 1793; other churches are scattered through the older part of the city. There are also a large library, a forestry institute, a northern regional museum with noteworthy natural history and ethnographical collections, and a polytechnic college.

About one third of the Soviet lumber export trade is carried on from Arkhangelsk, since lumber is shipped there from an area including not only the Arkhangelsk oblast but adjacent regions as well. Although the port is ice-free only from May to October, ice-breakers can open the harbor in winter, except in unusually severe weather. The long summer days, 18 to 21 hours in length, permit extended loading periods for the lumber ships. Industry too is predominantly concerned with timber: about 150 sawmill units, as well as plywood factories, pulp and paper mills, and other woodworking plants, cover the waterfront and land around the city with thousands of stacks of lumber every spring. Other industries include chemical plants, tanneries, rope mills, and fisheries. Furs, leather, flax, and butter are also exported, but up to 80 per cent of Arkhangelsk's exports are timber and wood products. The port also serves as the base for the northern sea route and is the starting-point for many polar expeditions.

Norman settlements were established in the area in the tenth century, but the importance of Arkhangelsk dates from the founding of an English trading post there in 1553. The growth of the city dates from 1584, and it became a provincial capital in 1708. Until the eighteenth century, Arkhangelsk was Russia's only seaport and developed rapidly as the center of trade with England and Holland. With Russian

seizure of the Baltic coast and opening of the great harbor of Leningrad (then St. Petersburg), Arkhangelsk declined because of the suppression of its trade, but it revived in the late nineteenth century, when, in 1897, the first railroad to open up the Arctic in Russia was built from Moscow through Vologda to Arkhangelsk. In 1918-1919, Arkhangelsk was a center of anti-Bolshevik intervention by British and other Allied troops. During World War II the port was greatly expanded. Thousands of tons of matériel were received through the harbor from the United States and other allied countries. Pop. (est. 1950), 325,000.   C. C. H.

The Region. The oblast of Arkhangelsk is situated in the northern section of the Russian Soviet Federated Socialist Republic. Its area of 229,400 sq. mi. includes the Nenets National Okrug (district), the islands of Franz Josef Land, Novaya Zemlya, Vaygach, and Kolguyev in the Barents Sea, and the Solovetskiye islands in the White Sea. The region is traversed by great northward-flowing rivers, the Onega, Dvina, Mezen, and lower Pechora. The section north of the Arctic Circle lies in the tundra zone and is desolate and unproductive; the remaining part, the taiga or forest zone, is 65 per cent forested land, and has areas of fertile alluvial soil along the rivers where flax and cereals are raised. Reindeer breeding and fishing are the chief occupations in the tundra zone, but the primary economic significance of the entire oblast consists in its lumber production. Winter temperatures are lowest in the European section of the region (January average —4° F.). Other population centers beside the port are Molotovsk and Kotlas. Pop. (est. 1954), 1,200,000.   W. S. V.

ARKWRIGHT, SIR RICHARD (1732-1792), British inventor, was born Dec. 23, 1732, in Preston, Lancashire, the youngest of thirteen children in a family of humble circumstances. He received a meager formal education at local schools and from his uncle. At an early age he was apprenticed to a barber. In 1750 he moved to Bolton, set up shop as a barber, and, securing a secret formula

SIR RICHARD ARKWRIGHT

for dyeing hair, soon had a thriving business. He gradually developed an interest in spinning machinery, and, in 1767, with the help of John Kay, a clockmaker from Warrington, Arkwright constructed his first "spinning-frame," a machine for spinning with rollers, which was the first to produce cotton thread of sufficient tenuity and strength to be used as warp. In 1769 he erected a spinning mill in Nottingham and took out his first patent. Two years later he built another mill at Crompton, in Derbyshire, where

COURTESY OF FRENCH EMBASSY, INFORMATION DIVISION

View of St. Honorat des Aliscamps, a monastery at Arles, France

he could make use of water power in place of the horses, which had heretofore been the sole means of power. By 1775 he had made several improvements in his machine to permit carding, drawing, and roving in one continuous operation, and he applied for another patent. Arkwright erected more mills in other parts of the country but, in spite of the success of the machines, his patents were infringed upon to such an extent that he was threatened with financial ruin. In addition, he was meeting with opposition from other manufacturers and from workers who resented the new labor-saving devices. One of his mills at Chorley was sacked. In 1781 he took his case to the courts, charging nine manufacturers with infringement of patent. The case dragged on for several years, and in 1785 was finally settled against him. He lost his letters of patent on the grounds that his specifications had been deficient, that his was not a new invention, and that he had borrowed his ideas from James Hargreaves, of "spinning-jenny" fame, and from Thomas Highs. In spite of these setbacks, his business continued to increase and to accumulate for him a modest fortune. This was largely due to Arkwright's persistence and prodigious energy, together with his remarkable skill as a manager. Arkwright's mills were the origin of the factory system, as we know it today. In 1790 he installed a Boulton and Watt's steam engine in the Nottingham mill. He was knighted in 1786. He died Aug. 3, 1792, at unfinished Willersley Castle, the home he had been building in Crompton.   C. W. D.

ARLES [a′rl], a city in southern France, the capital of an arrondissement in the department of Bouches-du-Rhône, 45 mi. northwest of Marseille, on the Rhône River. The city, founded between the fifth and second centuries B.C., developed rapidly under Rome. Under Honorius it was the seat of the prefecture of Gaul and much later the capital of Euric the Visigoth. In the eighth century Arles was plundered by the Saracens, and in the tenth century it became part of the Kingdom of Burgundy, later known as the Kingdom of Arles. In the twelfth century it flourished as a free city like the Italian civic republics. Its commerce and navigation prospered. In 1251 the city came under French domination. Arles has been the seat of numerous synods, the most famous occurring in 314, when the first general council of the Western Church was called by the Emperor Constantine to settle the dispute between the Catholics and Donatists. During the Middle Ages Arles was enriched architecturally, the Cathedral of St. Trophime being one of the best examples. It is considered the most beautiful Romanesque church in Provence. Most of the structure dates from the twelfth century, and of particular beauty are the cloister, the west porch, and the main portal. Archaeologically, Arles is one of the richest and most interesting cities in France, and as a consequence it has become a popular tourist spot. The historical sites include the well-preserved Roman amphitheatre; a fortress built by the Arabs, of which several towers remain; the Musée Lapidaire, with one of the finest collections in France of Gallo-Roman antiquities; an ancient cemetery known as the Aliscamp, consisting of an avenue (the only one remaining of ancient Arles) bordered by tombs; and the Muséon Arlaten, with its collection of Provençal arts and crafts. During the excavations at Arles, many works of art have been discovered, the most famous being the Venus of Arles, which was taken to the Louvre in Paris and is one of the most perfect and best known of the Venus statues. During World War II the northern section of the city was badly damaged. The port is of little importance, and the community depends on the tourist trade for most of its income. It is a market center for the region's wheat, grapes, and vegetable oils. Pop. 1954, 23,776.   S. Van V.

ARLINGTON, a town in Middlesex Co., in eastern Massachusetts, adjoining Cambridge and Somerville, approximately 5 mi. northwest of Boston. Truck farming is carried on in the area, and the manufactures in the town itself include interior woodwork, boxes, and textile machinery. Near-by Arlington Heights is a health resort. The neighborhood has many memorials of the Revolutionary War period in which it played a prominent part. Arlington was the home of Cyrus Dallin, sculptor, and John T. Trowbridge, writer. The town, which was originally a part of Cambridge, became West Cambridge in 1807 and in 1867 was named Arlington. The Boston and Maine Railroad supplies transportation. Pop. 1940, 40,013; 1950, 44,353.

ARLINGTON HEIGHTS, a village in northeastern Illinois, situated in Cook Co., in a truck gardening and dairying area, 22 mi. northwest of Chicago. Founded in 1836, it was incorporated as a village in 1887. Transportation is furnished by the Chicago and North Western Railroad. Local industries produce radio parts, school seats, blackboards, concrete blocks, milk cans, and canned food products. Pop. 1950, 8,768.

ARLINGTON HOUSE. *See* LEE MANSION.

ARLINGTON NATIONAL CEMETERY, the national burial ground of America's honored dead, situated at Arlington, Va., on the banks of the Potomac River, facing Washington, D.C. In this national shrine, occupying an area of 1,100 acres, are the graves of American heroes, distinguished statesmen, and military and naval leaders, from the time of the American Revolution through World War II.

THE INVINCIBLE ARMADA

FROM A PAINTING BY O. W. BRIERLY

HISTORICAL PICTURES SERVICE

Military memorials include the Tomb of the Unknown Soldier representing all the dead of World War I, the last resting place of more than two thousand unknown dead from the Civil War, and the graves of over one hundred and fifty men blown up with the battleship *Maine* in Havana Harbor. Among the graves of distinguished Americans are those of General Philip H. Sheridan, hero of the Civil War; Robert Todd Lincoln, son of the martyred president; Admiral Robert E. Peary, discoverer of the North Pole; and former President William Howard Taft.

The United States Government did not acquire title to Arlington until 1883, although its use as a cemetery began in 1864. The land was formerly a part of the estate of George Washington Parke Custis, the adopted son of George Washington, and was acquired by the government upon the pay-

CHARLES PHELPS CUSHING

TOMB OF THE UNKNOWN SOLDIER, ARLINGTON NATIONAL CEMETERY

ment of $150,000 to G. W. Custis Lee, who then relinquished his claims. The sarcophagi and monuments of Arlington include the Temple of Fame, the Confederate Monument, the Maine Memorial, and the Arlington Memorial Amphitheater, erected through the efforts of the Grand Army of

the Republic. Arlington House, the former mansion of General Robert E. Lee, modeled from the temple of Theseus in Athens and used as a Union hospital during the Civil War, stands on a hill two hundred feet above the Potomac. It commands a sweeping and inspiring view and is itself a magnificent landmark easily discernible from the city of Washington. The Fields of the Dead, with row upon row of plain headstones, contain the graves of thousands of soldiers and sailors slain in American wars.   J. E. F.

ARLON [a′rlɜ′] (Flem. Aarlen), the chief town in the province of Luxembourg, in extreme southeastern Belgium, about 4 mi. west of the Duchy of Luxembourg and 12 mi. north of the French border, above the source of the Semois River. It is situated on a hill, which is dominated by the Church of St. Donat, and is a market center for the agricultural produce of the region. The town, probably of Celtic origin, became the Roman station of Orolaunum on the road connecting Reims and Trèves. In 1671 Sebastien de Vauban fortified Arlon, damaging the old Roman walls. The provincial museum in Arlon contains relics of the Roman occupation. Pop. 1952, 11,726.   L. B.

ARMADA, THE SPANISH OR INVINCIBLE, the name given to the fleet sent by Philip II in 1588 to convoy an army assembled in Flanders for the invasion of England. The expedition may truly be called a tragedy of errors. One of the first errors was Philip's refusal to accept the aid of French and Scottish Catholics. Another was the substitution of the divided plan, military and naval, for the unified plan suggested by the great Spanish admiral, the Marquis of Santa Cruz. In 1587 came the daring raid by Sir Francis Drake on the unprotected port of Cádiz, and the destruction of shipping in that harbor. Again, all details of preparation had to be submitted for approval by King Philip in Madrid. This delayed progress and encouraged inefficiency. It also broke the spirit and ultimately took the life of Santa Cruz, who had nominal charge of assembling and equipping the fleet.

The Armada finally began sailing from Lisbon on May 18, 1588, under the command of the inexperienced Duke of Medina Sidonia. Unfavorable weather forced another delay.

At long last, the Armada sailed from La Coruña on July 12. The guiding hand of Philip was still upon the fleet, since his explicit orders gave directions from which the duke could not deviate. The fleet of 130 vessels of all sizes, aggregating about 59,000 tons, carried about 22,000 soldiers and 8,100 sailors. It was sighted off Lizard Head, southwest England, on July 20. Passing Plymouth, the Armada was harried by the English forces under the Lord High Admiral Howard of Effingham, and Hawkins, Drake, Frobisher, Seymour, and Wynter. The English ships were smaller; but superior seamanship, heavier guns, and a position to windward gave them the advantage in a running battle. On July 26 the Armada reached Calais. There the hoped-for union with the 25,000 troops under the Duke of Parma was prevented by a strong Anglo-Dutch squadron. English fire ships forced the Spaniards out of Calais harbor on July 28. Thence they sailed, with the wind from the north, followed to the Firth of Forth by the English. Discouragement drove the Armada around the north of Scotland rather than east to Bremen, as some of the captains recommended. Gales and disease reduced the expedition to half its original strength on the long journey home.

The defeat of the Armada saved England from invasion, and ruined Philip's hope of financial return on his ten-million-ducat investment. His heretical Dutch subjects were encouraged in their long struggle for liberty. The underlying motive of Philip, however, was neither economic nor political. It appears, here as elsewhere, to have been religious. Certainly the victory was hailed as a triumph of Protestant over Catholic. There was no immediate challenge to the sea power of Spain, nor did her colonial empire suffer. But the failure of Philip did mark the end of an aggressive foreign policy.   J. J. Van N.

ARMADILLO [ɑrmədɪ′lo], any of several edentate mammals of the family Dasypodidae, ranging in large numbers from Mexico and Texas south to Patagonia. Provided

W. P. TAYLOR FROM U. S. FISH AND WILDLIFE SERVICE

ARMADILLO

with short, muscular legs and powerful digging claws, the armadillo will generally escape capture by burrowing. It has characteristic armor plate on the dorsal surface and employs this covering by rolling up when attacked. The armadillo has a few upper and lower teeth without true roots. Nocturnal in habit, its eyes are weak, but its senses of smell and hearing are acute. It feeds upon insects, worms, fruits, roots, and sometimes carrion. Species range in size from 5 in. to 3 ft. All armadillos are edible. *See also* EDENTATA.

      G .M.C.

ARMAGH [ɑrmɑ′], the southernmost county of Northern Ireland and a city within that county.

The County. County Armagh is the smallest in Northern Ireland, with an area of 512 sq. mi. It is bounded on the south by County Louth, on the southwest by County Monaghan, on the northwest by County Tyrone, and on the north by Lough Neagh. Tidewater just reaches the county at the head of Carlingford Lough on the southeast. From the flat, boggy land near Lough Neagh in the north, the low, fertile, gently undulating surface rises to the granitic hilly districts of the south and southeast. Slieve Gullion (1,893 ft.), highest summit in the county, is a fine detached mountain affording a splendid view. Camlough (1,385 ft.), in the Newry Mountains, is separated from it by a deep valley. The Fews Mountains are a long, low range culminating in Armaghbreague (1,200 ft.) near Newtown Hamilton. Anglesey (1,349 ft.), in the southeast, is on the County Louth border. The northwestern boundary with Tyrone is formed by the Blackwater River, entering Lough Neagh somewhat west of the mouth of the Upper Bann, 12 miles of which flows across Armagh. The other rivers are the Callan, a tributary of the Blackwater, and the Cusher, a tributary of the Bann. North and west of Crossmaglen are Loughs Patrick, Kiltybane, Lisleitrim, and Cullyhanna. Camlough lies between Camlough Mountain and Slieve Gullion. Clay Lake is near Keady. Bordering Lough Neagh are Loughs Gullion, Derrylileagh, Derryadd, and Annagariff. The Newry Canal skirts the county on the east.

The average January temperature is 40° F., average July temperature 60° F., and the annual average temperature ranges from 46° to 50° F. January rainfall ranges from 2 to 4 in., July rainfall from 3 to 4 in., and mean annual rainfall from 30 to 40 in. The county is served by the Great Northern Railway Board.

The county name comes from that of the town Armagh, which is derived from the Irish *Ard-Macha* (Macha's Height). Macha was a semi-mythical heroine who founded the palace of Emania about 300 B.C. Armagh was part of the ancient kingdom of Oriel. The eastern part, Oirthera, meaning "eastern people," was the territory of the O'Hanlons. The name is perpetuated in the baronies of Orior. The old territory of Hy Niallain is now represented by the baronies of O'Neilland. On the shore of Lough Neagh, around the mouth of the Bann, was the ancient district of Hy Breasail or Clanbrassil. Among notable antiquities of Armagh are an early Irish and medieval ruined church at Killevy near Newry, an early Irish stone cross at Tynan, and earthworks at Navan Fort (Emania) and at Armagh (ancient Irish).

Important cities in the county are Lurgan and Portadown on the Bann, both devoted chiefly to the manufacture of linen. Red marble and standstone are quarried throughout the county. The county attained its maximum population, 232,393, in 1841. By 1937 the total decrease amounted to 53.2 per cent of this figure. It returns one member to the House of Commons in London and four members to the House of Commons in Belfast. Pop. 1953, 113,900.

The City. Armagh, the city, lies about 89 mi. northwest of Dublin. It is built on two hills, the one surmounted by a Roman Catholic cathedral, and the other by an Episcopal cathedral; the two structures face each other across the roofs of the town. According to tradition, St. Patrick founded his church in Armagh in 432, and the city became a synod as early as 448, since when it has been the ecclesiastical center of the country. It flourished, and early became the country's most important center. Successive Danish and English attacks then reduced the importance of the town, which was sacked five times between 839 and 1092 by the Danes alone; Armagh then suffered in the religious wars waged between the English and the Irish. An ancient cathedral built about 444 suffered particularly, and finally, in 1566, was laid in ruins by Shane O'Neill. After the middle of the eighteenth century something of the city's former prosperity returned. Linen weaving is the principal industry, and red marble and limestone are quarried in the vicinity. Institutions in the city include an infirmary, hospitals, a lunatic asylum, schools, and a famous astronomical college. Pop. 1951, 9,279. J. I. C.

ARMAGNACS [aʹrmaʹnyaʹk], a French political and military faction that emerged after the assassination in 1407 of the Duke of Orleans by John the Fearless of Burgundy as the result of rivalry for control in the council of regency. The head of the party was Bernard VII, Count of Armagnac, whose daughter married the new Duke Charles of Orleans, and who was a powerful figure at the French court. The Burgundians were strong in the north and northeast, and many great nobles of the south of France joined the Armagnac faction to combat the preponderant influence of the Burgundian duke.

In August 1413, the Armagnacs gained control of the government and led a feudal reaction which ruined any hope of reform. This made a renewal of the war with England inevitable. Two years later Henry V of England landed in Normandy, and in October he defeated the flower of the French chivalry at Agincourt. The Burgundians returned to power in 1418 and massacred the Armagnacs in Paris, including their leader, Bernard VII. The following year the Duke of Burgundy was assassinated at the bridge of Montereau while negotiating with the Dauphin (later Charles VII) and the Armagnacs for an alliance against the advancing English. The Burgundians then allied themselves with the English, and the Armagnacs, with the Dauphin at their head, became the national party. Conciliation between the two factions did not come until the Peace of Arras in 1435. In 1444-1445 a large army of Armagnac adventurers was lent to the Emperor Frederick III by Charles VII to use against the Swiss in what came to be called the Armagnac War. They were completely defeated near Basel, in the battle of St. Jakob on the Birs River.   F. C. H.

ARMAVIR [aʹrmavɪʹr], a town in the Krasnodar *Kray* (Territory) of the Russian Soviet Federated Socialist Republic, on the left bank of the Kuban River, 170 mi. southeast of Rostov-on-Don. Founded in 1848 on the fertile Kuban steppe, it rapidly developed as a trade center and, later, as an industrial center, closely tied with the farming of the surrounding region. The manufacture of agricultural implements and the processing of food are the major industries. Tobacco, woodworking, and textiles are also important. In addition, Armavir is a noted railroad junction, connecting the Black Sea port of Tuapse with the main North Caucasian line. Pop. (est. 1950), 80,000.   G. A. T.

ARMENIA [ɑrmiʹniə], a region which includes (1) Soviet Armenia, called the Armenian Soviet Socialist Republic and (2) a wider ethnographic area comprising Soviet Armenia and Turkish Armenia. The latter consists of six Turkish districts (vilayets): Van, Erzurum, Sivas, Diyarbakir, Bitlis, and Kharput. Ancient Armenia (Armenia Minor) included also the areas which were later embraced within the vilayets of Adana and Trabzon.

ARMENIAN S.S.R.

The Armenian Soviet Socialist Republic (S.S.R.) occupies an area of 11,500 sq. mi. in the center of Soviet Trans-

SOVFOTO

Rocky terrain in the Zangezun area of the Armenian S.S.R.

caucasia, bordering the Georgian S.S.R. in the north, the Azerbaidzhan S.S.R. on the east, Turkey in the southwest and Iran in the southeast. The Nakhichevan' A.S.S.R. which belongs to the Azerbaidzhan S.S.R. also forms part of the southern border. The country is mountainous, occupying the northeastern section of the Armenian Highlands, or Plateau, which extend far west and south outside the Soviet Union. The Araks River and its affluent the Arpa-Chay form the international border of the Armenian S.S.R. in the southwest and south. Within the borders of the Republic the Plateau reaches from 5,000 to 7,000 ft. in elevation and is traversed by ranges and volcanic peaks. The highest of these is Alagez (or Aragats), an extinct volcano with an altitude of about 13,500 ft. Earthquakes are not uncommon, and in 1926 a severe disturbance damaged the industrial center of Leninakan.

Due to the generally high elevation, which includes numerous mountain barriers, the Armenian Republic has a continental climate with dry hot summers (average July temperature from 62° to 75° F.) and cold winters (average January temperature from 10° to 15° F.). The average yearly rainfall is 12 to 25 in. Climate differences are very great, depending on local surface conditions and on the elevation. Soils in the river valleys are of an alluvial and partly volcanic origin and afford good yields under irrigation. The elevated sections are steppe-like with predominant black-earth and chestnut soils. Still higher lie the Alpine meadows. These are used for pastures by Armenian herds and by the livestock of neighboring regions.

Among the mineral deposits, copper, mined near Alxaverdy and in the Zangezun area (Kafan mines) is of major importance, the Armenian S.S.R. ranks third in the total output of copper in the Soviet Union. Molybdenum, zinc, and non-metallic minerals such as limestone, pumice, volcanic tuffs, and marble are also exploited.

In the absence of mineral fuel, the importance of rivers as sources of hydroelectric power is of particular interest. The chief river of Armenia, the Araks, forms the frontier with Turkey and Iran and is little utilized. One of its tributaries, however, the Razdan (formerly called the Zanga), is the only outlet of Lake Sevan. The Razdan lies at an altitude of 6,250 ft. and joins the Araks after a course of about 65 mi. and a drop of 3,300 ft. Along its course four hydroelectric stations are already in operation. A subterranean tunnel, in which turbines will develop water power, is under construction.

SOVFOTO

Generator shop of the Yerevan Electro-Machine Building Plant

This series of hydroelectric plants provide cheap power for industry. Among the users are an aluminum plant and chemical factories (notably a synthetic rubber plant). Agriculture, too, is a consumer, and irrigated fields, mainly in the Yerevan areas, are steadily increasing. A hydroelectric plant constructed on the Dzora River supplies power to the copper refineries at Alaverdi. Other branches of industry include textiles, cement, glass, ceramics, machine manufacturing, lumbering, canning, sugar, and wine.

The best farm lands of the Armenian Republic are in the irrigated lands in river valleys, where cotton, tobacco, and orchard trees are cultivated. On the unirrigated slopes of the mountains and on most of the steppes, vineyards, orchards, cereals (mainly wheat and barley), sugar beets, and potatoes are grown. The Leninakan steppe, in the west, and the Lori steppe, in the north, are the main farming areas on the Armenian Plateau. Elsewhere, in the higher sections of Armenia, livestock (chiefly sheep and goats) is raised for the production of cheese, wool, meat, and skins. Sericulture is widespread in the Yerevan area. Fishing is important at Lake Sevan where trout are abundant.

There is only one railroad line in the Armenian Republic. Entering the north from Tbilisi, the capital of the Georgian S.S.R., it turns to Leninakan, near the west frontier of Armenia, and follows the Araks River along the southern border of the Armenian Republic and the Azarbaidzhan S.S.R. From this line, short terminal lines lead to Yerivan, Artik, and Kafan. In the rest of the country, highways are the only means of transportation. The greater part of the population is Armenian (about 83 per cent), followed by Azerbaidzhanians (about 10 per cent), and Russians and Ukrainians (about 4 per cent). Several thousand Armenians were repatriated from the Near East and the United States during the period from 1947 to 1949. Many Armenians live in the two other Soviet Republics of Transcaucasia, as well as in the Northern Caucasus of the R.S.F.S.R. Yerevan is the capital.

HISTORY

Origins. The Armenians have a mixed racial origin, stemming from a people calling themselves Khaldians,

perhaps related to the Hittites, and two Indo-European peoples, the Phrygians and Cimmerians, who entered the region in the eighth century B.C. and gave the original inhabitants their Aryan language.

Religion. The Armenians are Christians, St. Gregory the Illuminator having converted their King Tiridates (c. 238-314) before 303. The Bible was translated into Armenian by St. Mesrob in the fifth century. The Armenian church dignitaries constituted a separate Gregorian Christian Church after they refused to agree to the decrees of the Council of Chalcedon in 451. The Armenian Gregorian Church had at its head the catholicos (primates) at Ejmiadzin, near Yerevan, and to them the Armenian patriarchs at Jerusalem and Constantinople were subordinated.

Political History. In the course of Armenian history, Assyrians, Medes, Persians, Romans, Parthians, Greeks, Arabs, Turks, and Russians have conquered, ruled, and divided among themselves the lands inhabited by the Armenians. In spite of this, the Armenians managed to retain a considerable autonomy and developed a tenacious nationalism in the centuries of foreign domination. The brief periods of national independence date from about the ninth century B.C. to the sixth century B.C., when Armenia became a nominal satrap of the Persian Empire. The region was conquered in large part by Alexander the Great in 331 B.C., and then divided between the Greek, Roman, and Persian empires until Tigranes the Great (94-56 B.C.) again secured its independence over a wide area under the Arshakuni line. Armenia then acted as a buffer between Rome and Persia. The acceptance of Christianity by King Tiridates led to conflict with Zoroastrian Persia and the weakening of Armenia, which was divided between the Romans and Persians in the fourth century. The Armenian catholicos at times held together the nation, especially in the eighth century. Finally the princes of the Bagratuni line under Ashot I united the country in the ninth century and maintained a precarious rule against Arabs and Seljuk Turks. The latter established their rule toward the end of the eleventh century but were succeeded by the Mongols in 1240. Many Armenians migrated elsewhere, and the Kingdom of Lesser Armenia lasted until 1375. Timur overran Armenia at the beginning of the fifteenth century, to be followed by Turkomen, and later the Ottoman Turks, who had established their domination by the middle of the sixteenth century. In the seventeenth century the Persians reacquired a part of Armenia. The Armenians were organized under the Turks as a millet (non-Moslem community), and received a form of religious and national autonomy, which was extended by the Turkish authorities in 1862.

The Russian advance into the Caucasus engulfed Georgia in 1801, and the Armenian nation was faced with a new problem. It soon became a policy of the Russians to absorb all of Armenia, and the British policy was to prevent it. The Russo-Persian War of 1828 brought Russian rule to Persian Armenia, the plain of Yerevan and Ejmiadzin, where the Russians assisted the Armenian Church and introduced a modern state apparatus as a contrast to the Turkish. The Armenians prospered under Russian rule. After the Russo-Turkish War in 1877-1878, Russia proposed the annexation of the rest of Armenia, but the proposal was successfully opposed by the British under Disraeli at the Congress of Berlin in 1878 since Armenia controlled the road from Constantinople to India. Russia, however, acquired Ardahan, Kars, and Batum (Batumi). The British had previously concluded secretly the Cyprus Convention, in which, in return for the occupation of the island of Cyprus, they

SOVFOTO

LENIN SQUARE IN YEREVAN, CAPITAL OF SOVIET ARMENIA

promised to defend Turkey's territorial integrity with special reference to its Asiatic frontiers and to protect the Christians among others. The British insisted that this protection be extended to the Armenians by provisions in the Treaty of Berlin in 1878. However, little resulted from these provisions.

In 1885 the foundations of the Hunchak revolutionary society, to be followed by the Daschnak in 1890 at Tiflis, began the renaissance of Armenian nationalism, which led to the massacres in 1894-1896 under the suspicious Turkish sultan Abdul-Hamid II, who feared an Armenian revolt, and again under the Young Turks in 1909 and 1915.

Soviet Russia ceded Batum and Kars to the Turks by the Treaty of Brest-Litovsk on Mar. 3, 1918, while the Bolsheviks began sovietizing the regions of the Caucasus in 1918-1920. President Wilson declined an American mandate for a large Armenia proposed at the Peace Conference of Paris by Armenian representatives. Taking advantage of the Russian Revolution, the Armenians proclaimed their independence. Exhausted Turkey was obliged to accept this as an accomplished fact. Armenian independence was recognized by the Treaty of Sèvres (Aug. 10, 1920). Frontiers were to be fixed on recommendation of President Wilson. But the Turkish revolutionary movement under Mustapha Kemal refused to recognize these treaty provisions. Squeezed between the Soviet Union and the Turks, the republic of Armenia was obliterated by them. Armenian Marxian groups facilitated the Soviet objectives. In December 1920 the Soviet Armenian government was established at Yerevan, and Armenia, Georgia and Azerbaidzhan were set up in what was known as the Transcaucasian Soviet Socialist Republic. The Treaty of Mar. 16, 1921, between the Soviet Union and Turkey established the present frontiers between the two countries, and assigned Kars and Ardahan to Turkey. Batum retroceded to Russia. The Soviet-Turkish Treaty of 1921 completely sealed the fate of the Armenians in Turkey, and the friendly relations between the Soviet

Union and Turkey, confirmed by a twenty-year treaty in 1925, offered little hope of Armenian independence. In 1936 the Transcaucasian Republic was divided into three constituent republics—Armenia, Georgia, Azerbaidzhan. Since that time Armenia has been assigned the status of a Soviet Socialist Republic, whose paper rights are extensive. Actually the "republic" is completely integrated into the Soviet system which does not allow for the slightest particularist tendency or departure from Communism as interpreted by the Kremlin. During World War II, some Armenians went over to the Germans, but it is difficult to ascertain with any degree of precision the number of such persons. In March 1945, Soviet Russia denounced its treaty of friendship with Turkey and soon thereafter demanded not only the military control of the Turkish Straits, but, in the name of its Armenian people, it demanded the cession of Kars and Ardahan.   R. J. K. and W. S. V.

ARMENIAN, an Indo-European language known from the fifth century of the Christian Era in an uninterrupted tradition. Armenian-speaking peoples had lived in Armenia for several centuries before that date, however, for they are already mentioned in the great Bisutūn cuneiform inscriptions of Darius the Great in the sixth century B.C. According to Herodotus, the Armenians were "Phrygian colonists," and Eudoxus adds that their language strongly resembled Phrygian. This is apparently confirmed by the few Phrygian texts we possess, for they indicate that Armenian has many characteristics in common with Phrygian, among others the following: 1) *$\bar{e}$ becomes *i*; 2) *$\bar{o}$ becomes *u*; 3) *n and *m become *an* and *am*; 4) *k becomes *s* (the satem character); and 5) initial and intervocalic *s* becomes *h* (and then frequently disappears). In both languages there also occurs 6) a sound shift very similar to the Germanic one, although without any apparent historical connection, by which, for example, t becomes th, d becomes t, dh becomes d, p becomes ph. Armenian also weakens the occlusion of some sounds. Further characteristics which Armenian shares with Phrygian are 7) the vocalic prosthesis, 8) the participle in -menos, 9) the verbal augment (e-), 10) the element -sm- in the pronouns, and 11) the r-forms in the verbal system. These and other facts seem to make of Armenian a sort of Phrygian dialect. Some of these characteristics (5, 7, and 8, and, in part, 2, 3, and 9) are also common to Greek and partly to Iranian and Slavic, a relationship that clearly defines the linguistic position of Armenian and shows that it corresponds to the geographic location of the language.

Among the specific innovations of Armenian are the loss of the gender distinction and the shift of the accent to the Indo-European penult (*ébberet *ebéret), which, after the general Armenian loss of all final syllables, became the last syllable of the word (ebér). Today Armenian is an oxytonic language, like French.

Armenia has been for several centuries subjected to Iranian domination or Iranian influence. Iranian, and especially Pehlevi, words have entered into Armenian in such an enormous number that until Hübschmann's fundamental work, in *Zeitschrift für vergleichende Sprachforschung,* XXIII, Armenian was considered as an Iranian dialect. There are also in Armenian several Greek and Syriac words of a religious nature, but the Greek words penetrated in part through Pehlevi. The oldest Armenian text is the translation of the Bible, dating from the fifth century. There are a few fragments of pagan epics, perhaps one century older than this translation.

Armenian is divided now into two main dialects, Western, which is spoken in Anatolia, Constantinople, and Europe, and Eastern, which occurs in Armenia proper. The main characteristic of Western Armenian is that all voiced stops become voiceless, *grabar* thus becoming *krapar.* Armenian has a special alphabet, mainly derived from Greek, but with several new signs of obscure origin for sounds that Greek did not possess. It has thirty-six letters, including two later additions, and was invented in A.D. 406 by Bishop Mesrob (or Maštoc) with the help of a Greek scribe called Rufinos.

Before the great Turkish massacres of 1894-1896, 1909, and 1915-1920, the Armenians numbered probably around 4,000,-000 persons; they may now number something over 2,000,000: 1,400,000 in Transcaucasia, about 200,000 in Syria, about 100,-000 in Turkey, 100,000 in America, 70,000 in Irak, 50,000 in Persia, and perhaps 200,000 in other countries, notably Romania, with 11,000, and Greece, with 34,000. The city of Constantinople has about 50,000 Armenians. *See also* PHRYGIAN. G. B.

ARMENIAN LITERATURE.

ARMENIAN LITERATURE. Of pre-Christian Armenian literature the few traces extant consist only of some inscriptions, and mythical tales preserved by writers of the fifth century of the Christian Era. The bulk of the ancient inscriptions so far recovered in Armenia are the work of the Urartians, who occupied the country before the coming of the Armenians; thus the history of Armenian literature before the fourth century of the Christian Era remains almost wholly unknown. Continuing studies by Armenian scholars should, however, soon add much to our knowledge of this period.

Recorded Armenian literature, which begins with the fourth century of the Christian Era, may be described as consisting of four periods of intense activity, with intermediate periods during which foreign invaders ravaged the country and decimated the population. These intermediate periods were not devoid of literary activity; but, on the whole, only works of secondary merit were produced. This literary production included histories describing the wars of the Arabs, Byzantines, and Persians, and the more terrifying invasions of Mongols and Turks from Central Asia; theological controversy; and an abundance of religious poetry describing the sufferings of the people and calling on God for help.

The four main periods of literary activity are: (1) the fifth century of the Christian Era, the so-called Golden Age of Armenian literature, which was preceded by the conversion of Armenia to the Christian faith in 276, the literary activity of this period being given special impetus by the invention in 406 of the Armenian alphabet by Bishop Mesrob, which makes possible the use of Armenian instead of Greek, Persian, and Syriac as the medium of literary expression; (2) the twelfth century, known as the Silver Age, which followed the founding of the Armenian kingdom of Cilicia by emigrants from devastated Armenia, resulting in contact with the Crusaders and, through them, with western Europe; (3) the eighteenth and nineteenth centuries, with the extension of the use of printing at Ejmiadzin, Constantinople, and elsewhere; and (4) the second quarter of the twentieth century, with intense literary activity, especially in Soviet Armenia. A few names more or less arbitrarily selected out of hundreds will suffice to give an idea of the type of literary activity of each period.

To the fourth century belong such works as the sermons of Krikor Lousavoritch (Gregory the Illuminator), who converted the nation to Christianity; Agatankeghos' history of the introduction of Christianity to Armenia; Zenop Klag's life of Sourp Krikor (St. Gregory); and Pavsdos Puzant's history of contemporary Armenia. The introduction of the Armenian alphabet at the opening of the fifth century led to the translation of the Bible and many other works, including those of Eusebius and Josephus, into Armenian. Among the original works of this period may be mentioned Yeznig's refutation of the Greek philosophers: Yeghishé Vartabed's romanticized life of Vartan Mamigonian, who died about 450, successfully resisting an attempt of the Persians to force fire worship on the Armenians; and Moses Khorenatsi's monumental history of Armenia from the days of Adam to his own day, containing old myths and semihistorical tales, and for centuries accepted as authentic.

To the early eleventh century belongs Krikor Naregatsi's *Dirge* (*Voghperkoutiun*) describing in vivid poetic imagery the sufferings of his people and calling on God for salvation. Equally vigorous in style are the writings of Krikor's grandson, Krikor Makistros, including religious correspondence, a grammar, and translations from Plato. During the twelfth century the spoken ("wordly") tongue (*ashkharhapar*) developed into a literary medium, and the literary tongue (*krapar*) became confined mainly to religious works. The most popular of the writers of this period is Nerses Shnorhali (the Graceful), who left many religious prose works but is best known for his poetry on religious and secular themes. Also important are Mekhitar Heratsi's treatise on fever, Mekhitar Kosh's text on jurisprudence, and Nerses Lampronatsi's life of Shnorhali. At this time there reappeared poems on valor, love, and beauty which had, since the fifth century, been almost entirely replaced by poems in praise of saints and martyrs and hymns to God.

Printing in Armenian was begun at Ejmiadzin in 1512, at Constantinople in 1570, and elsewhere in that and the next century. But the most extensive printing of Armenian books was carried on in the Mekhitarist monastery of St. Lazare, near Venice, founded in 1717, and later in the companion monastery in Vienna. From these presses came many original works on a variety of themes, including the first Armenian dictionary, a new translation of the Bible, and also translations of such foreign classics as Homer, Vergil, Tacitus, Milton, Racine, and Voltaire; their chief work, however, was a compilation of the Armenian classics.

During the eighteenth and nineteenth centuries, Armenian literary activity was almost at a standstill throughout the Ottoman Empire except at Constantinople, which, as capital, enjoyed special privileges in which the Armenians shared. Catholic and Protestant missionaries fed the Armenians' native love of learning, and American missionaries translated the Bible into the spoken tongue. But in Russian Armenia, which was made up of less than one fifth of the historic Armenian homeland and which had been annexed by Russia late in the nineteenth century, and among the Armenians of the Dispersion there was considerable literary activity. Every variety of literary work was accomplished during this period, but whatever their medium the writers were mainly preoccupied by one theme, the liberation of Turkish Armenia from the Ottoman yoke. Typical of this interest are the works of "Raffi" (Hagop M. Hagopian), whose essays and novels, though banned, were much esteemed in Turkish Armenia. Since 1925 Soviet Armenia, relieved of the obsession which had hitherto characterized the history of the Armenian people, has evidenced extraordinary activity in every form of literature, including the new art of the cinema. Research, not only in natural science but also in archaeology and anthropology, is throwing new light on the history of the people. Illustrative of this are the five volumes, on which several scholars have collaborated, of the *History of the Armenian People from the Beginning to the Present Day;* and also Hrachia Ajarian's *Etymological Dictionary of the Ancient Armenian Language.* The hitherto suppressed genius of the people seems to be flowering in a renaissance of Armenian literature.   L. P. C.

ARMENIAN QUESTION. The Armenian Question had its more recent origins in the treaties of San Stefano and Berlin, which followed the Russo-Turkish War of 1877-1878. The Russians occupied the six Armenian vilayets, and Armenian nationalism was stimulated. In 1880, a revolutionary organization known as the Defenders of the Fatherland was organized in Erzurum. A few years later, in 1885, the Armenakan society was organized, and in 1887 the Hunchagian Party appeared. The Armenian Revolutionary Federation (Dashnaktzoutun) was formed in 1890.

The Armenians expected outside assistance in their design to break away from Ottoman misrule and were led to commit a number of disloyal acts. In August and September 1894, a series of massacres occurred in the vicinity of Sassun as a result of an uprising which was put down with ferocity by Kurdish irregular cavalry (Hamidieh regiments). The massacres soon spread, and in October and November 1895 there were outbreaks at Trabzon, Erzurum, Bitlis, Kurun, Maras, and elsewhere. The essential cause of the massacres lay in the failure of the European powers to secure the reforms envisaged by the Treaty of Berlin for the Asiatic provinces of the Ottoman Empire. The massacres caused an outcry in Europe, and ultimately Sultan Abdul-Hamid II appointed an investigating commission, joined by British, French, and Russian delegates, which produced a minor reform program. In August 1896 after an attack on the Ottoman Bank in Istanbul, a massacre of Armenians occurred in the Ottoman capital, in which 4,000 to 6,000 Armenians were killed. By the end of 1896 it was estimated that as many as 200,000 had been massacred in the eastern provinces.

With the advent to power of the Young Turks in 1908, there was hope for improvement of the lot of the Armenians, but in April, 1909, there were massacres at Adana and other places of "little" Armenia, provoked by demonstrations which aroused the Moslem inhabitants. Intermittent attacks took place in the following years, climaxed by the more general massacres in June and July 1915 during World War I. Difficulties continued in the region of Armenia until after the end of the war. The Treaty of Sèvres, Aug. 10, 1920, which proved abortive, provided for an independent Armenia, and President Wilson was asked to set the boundary lines of the new state. On Nov. 29, 1920, an Armenian republic was established, and a treaty was signed with Turkey on Dec. 3, 1920, by which Kars and Ardahan went to Turkey, while Armenia was limited to the province of Yerevan. In 1922 it formed part of the Transcaucasian Soviet Socialist Republic but in 1936 became a separate Soviet Socialist Republic.   H. N. Ho.

ARMIDA [armi'da], a pagan enchantress in Tasso's *Jerusalem Delivered* who hinders the Crusaders by luring away the best knights. She falls in love with one of her victims, Rinaldo, and wafts him to a fairy isle of delight. Her love and grief finally make her an engaging figure. C. B. B.

ARMILLARY SPHERE [a'rmiɛ'ri], an ancient astronomical instrument, actually a skeleton celestial globe. An armillary sphere had a polar axis, horizon and meridian rings, the celestial equator, ecliptic, and a zodiac, also a few hour circles and parallels of declination. Some armillary spheres could be turned on their polar axis. Occasionally they are still constructed for decorative purposes.   H. S. R.

ARMINIUS (c. 17 B.C.-A.D. 19), a prince of a German tribe, the Cherusci, and, because of his victories over the Romans, a German national hero, often called Hermann in modern times. He served in the Roman army (A.D. 1-6), where he attained the rank of *eques,* or knight, and gained Roman citizenship; returning to Germany about A.D. 7, he organized native forces against the Romans and in A.D. 9 annihilated three legions of about 20,000 men under the Roman general Publius Quinctilius Varus at the battle of Teutoburg Forest. Although the exact site of the battle is not known, a colossal statue of Arminius was erected in 1875 to commemorate the victory. The defeat of Varus was a great blow to Roman plans for the occupation of Germany. The attempts of Germanicus Caesar to regain the lost territory were unsuccessful and the northeastern boundary of the Roman empire became the Rhine instead of the Elbe. Arminius was assassinated by one of his relatives as he was attempting to become the leader of the Cherusci. G. E. D.

ARMINIUS, JACOBUS [armi'niəs] (1560-1609), Dutch theologian, was born at Oudewater, South Holland, on Oct. 10, 1560, and died at Leiden on Oct. 19, 1609. Arminius, whose name is the Latinized form of Hermanns or Hermansen, studied at the University of Leiden and, while visiting in Switzerland, at Geneva and Basel, where he was soon recognized as a leading interpreter of Calvinism.

Before he was thirty years of age, Arminius was recalled to the Netherlands, and there, for fifteen years, he occupied the pulpit of the Reformed Church in Amsterdam. In 1603 he was appointed a professor of theology in the University of Leiden, the chief training center for ministers of the Dutch Reformed Church. Until this time his views were never questioned; on the contrary, he was everywhere respected and admired as a man and as a scholar.

Arminius became involved in theological controversy when a minister of Haarlem by the name of Koornheert raised certain objections to the current interpretation of Calvin's doctrine of predestination. Arminius was requested to prepare a convincing reply against this outburst, but the more he studied the question the more his own views changed. The issues at stake had to do with refinements of Calvin's

JACOBUS ARMINIUS

theology on which there were differences of opinion, such as predestination, God's foreknowledge, the nature and extent of man's sin, and the doctrine of the atonement. Through a study of Paul's Epistle to the Romans, Arminius became convinced that the doctrine and promise of Dutch Calvinism was much more rigid and scholastic than either Calvin's writings or the Scriptures would warrant. In this controversy many able thinkers were ranged on opposite sides: Franciscus Gomarus, a colleague of Arminius at Leiden, was the chief advocate of the orthodox position; Simon Episcopius, Arminius' successor at Leiden, and Hugo Grotius, the celebrated authority on international law, were spokesmen for a more liberal and modified Calvinism.

The Arminian group, shortly after the death of their leader, presented their case to the ecclesiastical authorities in the form of a "Remonstrance," which set forth five points that were taken as essential to a right understanding of Calvinism. These had to do with: (1) conditional predestination, (2) universal atonement, (3) saving faith, (4) resistable grace, and (5) the uncertainty of perseverance.

The orthodox party called a general synod at Dort in 1619 to discuss this Remonstrance, and while delegates came from Reformed Churches in Great Britain as well as from the Continent, the assembly was dominated by the conservative element which immediately condemned the errors of Arminius, depriving the Arminian pastors and teachers of their ecclesiastical standing. In connection with this synod, a statement in reply to Arminianism was drawn up; this was known as the "Canons of Dort," and it set forth the strict Calvinistic position on all the points raised in the Remonstrance.

Arminianism was thus formally defeated, but it was given legal status in the Netherlands after the death of Prince Maurice of Nassau in 1625, and it continued to exist as a separate Church, mainly in Rotterdam and Amsterdam.

The later history of Arminianism is not easily followed because it became related in different ways to the Socinian or unitarian movement on the Continent, and the evangelical revival associated with John Wesley and Methodism in Great Britain and America, though in each instance the original attack upon Calvinism had ceased to be the motivating principle. Arminianism thus came to be loosely related with a liberal as opposed to a conservative attitude in theology. The strength of Arminianism lay in its refusal to be bound by a rigid scholastic system of doctrine; its weakness was due to the fact that it had no definite body of doctrine which it could call its own.   H. T. K.

ARMISTICE DAY. *See* Holidays and Holy Days.
ARMOR. *See* Armored Troops; Armor, Naval; Arms and Armor.

ARMOR, NAVAL, the protective or defensive covering of the vital parts of a ship. From the earliest days of armed fighting ships, attention has been given to the protection of hulls against gunfire. As fire power increased, naval armor underwent progressive changes, the material ranging from wrought iron to high quality, heat-treated alloy steel.

Armor Requirements. The armor on modern ships is the result of careful balancing of the protection that is required against the permissible weight that can be allotted to the armor. The vital parts of the ship that require protection are the waterline, steering gear, prime movers, ammunition, guns, and fire-control equipment. Exposed personnel must be protected against shell fragments, splinters, and small caliber projectiles. The type of armor that is selected depends upon the anticipated missile that will be used against the ship. Ships can be expected to be attacked by torpedoes, rockets, projectiles, bombs, and radio guided missiles.

Armor Design. In general, there are two classes of steel armor. One class has an extremely high surface hardness on the face, with a tough ductile back that prevents the plate from shattering under impact. The other is substantially homogeneous throughout and is designed for toughness and strength. The purpose of the armor hardened on the face is to break up projectiles and render them incapable of penetration. The homogeneous armor has great resistance to explosive charges and to projectiles that strike at glancing angles.

Improved bombing techniques in World War II, which employed both dive bombing and heavier bombs with armor-piercing heads, made it necessary to give the decks of large fighting ships additional armor protection. Notwithstanding the fact that decks of vessels were armored against glancing attacks of projectiles, it was considered essential to provide additional armor on other decks above the main armored deck. In this manner, additional strength would be provided, together with protection against small bombs and fragments. Since there is always a possibility that a bomb may enter a funnel, protection is afforded by the use of armor plate gratings or bars in the smoke escape or air intake passages.

Armor, generally, is not designed to carry any of the stress load of the ship. At times, however, special armor is made to carry stress loading for bulkheads or decks. The tendency has been to design ships with the armor on the inside of the hull instead of outside. This method of design reduces the drag of the ship in the water and facilitates the extending of armor below the waterline. By means of suitable joints, the heavy armor on the ship is made into a continuous box, open only on the bottom. The guns are encased in armored turrets, which are connected to the main armored deck by means of barbettes.

Manufacture and Testing. Heavy armor usually is forged to shape, but, in the United States, armor under six

NAVAL ENGAGEMENT BETWEEN THE MERRIMAC AND MONITOR

inches thick in flat plates may be rolled. The composition of the steel used for armor is high in nickel and chromium and contains other elements that permit the steel to be hardened deeply. A hard face on armor is obtained by the use of carburizing and differential hardening. The homogeneous armor is heat-treated so as to obtain about the same hardness throughout the plate. Samples of all armor manufactured are given a gunfire or ballistic test at a proving ground.   H. W. F.

ARMORED TROOPS, a military formation of combined arms in which tanks are supported by all other ground arms and services in such proportion and combination as will most readily enable it to conduct mobile warfare. The primary purpose of such formations is the execution of offensive operations against an enemy, usually for the purpose of accomplishing a break-through or of effecting a penetration of the hostile lines to destroy vital rear installations and communications or to secure important terrain objectives, the possession of which is desirable or essential to the further profitable prosecution of a war or campaign. The largest armored formations generally employed in World War II were the armored divisions. In modern practice, special armored formations have been organized at the battalion level for furnishing direct tank support within infantry divisions. At corps and division levels, respectively, light armored regimental and battalion organizations are provided for reconnaissance missions. Such smaller formations may be assigned individual tactical missions but in general do not operate independently or at any great distance from the parent division.

In World War II, armor played an important part in all theatres, on many diversified types of terrain, under a wide range of climatic conditions, and in varying types of operations. Without it, either in its primary offensive role or in its secondary supporting role, conclusive successes were seldom achieved. A careful analysis of the major Continental campaigns shows clearly that strategic ground successes were never achieved without the powerful contribution of armor in the spearhead role.

The tank is the basic armored vehicle in the modern plan of mobile warfare. The major supporting ground arms, combined with the tank to enable it to prosecute mobile combat, are armored infantry, artillery, and engineers, with their soldiers transported in armor-protected personnel carriers or self-propelled gun mounts. The supporting services consist of ordnance maintenance troops, ammunition supply personnel, and the necessary unarmored transport and personnel to assure a continued availability of necessary fuel and lubricants during any period of active operations. Medical units, when used in armored formations, furnish necessary aid facilities and evacuation of sick or wounded personnel.

Development of Armor Principle. The idea of the use of armor plate for personnel protection is not new. It was prevalent in the days of savagery, when some personal protection was achieved by the use of a shield of skins; in Biblical times, when certain warlike tribes used chariots of iron; and in the Middle Ages, when complete suits of body armor made their appearance. Although in the first century B.C. the Ulstermen invaded Connaught with "three strong, stout, battleproof towers on wheels," their motive power being thirty Danish stallions apiece, it was not until the fifteenth century that a movable hull, offering a sort of armored protection to its crew against missiles, was generally conceived.

In 1456, the Scots appeared with a war cart which not only encased its crew but also shielded the horses; in 1482, Leonardo da Vinci conceived of a covered chariot powered by men turning by hand an offset shaft similar to the crankshaft of today. Succeeding developments included an attempt in the nineteenth century to use steam, but the necessity for stopping every few minutes to replenish the water and get up more pressure rendered this source of power undependable, and hence impractical. A tank was also designed for use in

Modern armored troops in action in Europe during World War II

the Crimean War in 1854 but was abandoned as being too barbarous. Before World War I, major world powers turned down various types of armored caterpillar vehicles demonstrated to them. It was not until September 1916 that the tank made possible by the partial perfection of the internal combustion engine first went into action on a battlefield. Initial credit for the use of the tank belongs to the British, who put this type of combat vehicle into action on the Somme front in France. Their efforts were immediately followed in 1917 by the introduction of similar units in both the French and American armies.

World War II Armor. Armor employed in World War II forced the development and employment of fluid techniques that were directly opposed to the static concepts that had prevailed in World War I prior to introduction of the tank. The armored fighting vehicle (tank) is designed to provide mobile firepower on the battlefield while at the same time furnishing sufficient armored protection to its operating personnel to permit them to engage the enemy at close range. Mobility is a quality second in importance only to the firepower potential of the tank. It implies economy in fuel consumption, ability to carry a large amount of fuel and operate continuously over a period of many hours, and the possession of sufficient power to insure vehicular agility on the battlefield. This mobility makes it a difficult target and enables it to take full advantage of such protective cover and concealment as the terrain may afford. The firepower potential of the tank is based on the penetrating characteristics of its main weapon, its capacity to stow sufficient ammunition for both its main armament weapon and those of its secondary armament, and the ability of its crew to sustain a high rate of accurately delivered fire. This firepower characteristic is of primary importance. The third characteristic of the tank, i.e., armored protection for the crew, must be balanced between those of firepower and mobility. Because of weight, it cannot be great enough to provide absolute protection for the crew, but it must be sufficient to give them reasonable protection against the smaller caliber hostile weapons and insure them sufficient peace of mind so that they may devote their attention to the elimination from the battlefield of automatic weapons and direct fire weapons of larger caliber and thus assure more rapid progress to either supported or accompanying infantry.

Tanks of World War II were divided into three general classes—light, medium, and heavy—and ranged in weight from 10 to 12 tons to 65 to 70 tons. They carried armor plate up to 6 in. or more in thickness and mounted tank guns from 37-mm. to 120-mm. in caliber. In the modern tank, adaptability to roads and cross-country ability combine to produce maneuverability, while mechanisms steer the vehicle and point its guns. Its performance includes the ability to span ditches, clamber vertical walls or banks, knock down trees and hastily constructed unmined obstacles, and ford water courses with firm bottoms. Its actions are limited by swampy or boulder-strewn terrain, suitably constructed tank obstacles and mines, the capacity or width of bridges across unfordable water courses, and the ability of its operators to keep the tank mechanically sound and adequately supplied with fuel and lubricants.

Effect of Combined Arms. Armored combined arms formations must be mobile in the extreme if they are to be employed on strategic offensive operations. If, on the other hand, they are to be employed on limited tactical missions, they need possess only the mobility of the troops they support. Armored formations have been both land-borne and water-borne in the past. Broadening their powers of mobility through technological advancement to make them airborne is a future projected development. World War II precipitated the development of various ship-to-shore methods of transporting armored vehicles and of special amphibian combat vehicles. These speculative amphibious ideas culminated in the successful water-borne invasions of Africa, Sicily, Italy, and France and the island-hopping operations of the Pacific. There is no reason to suppose that their counterparts, using air as the operating medium, cannot be developed in even more effective terms. World War II began on a mobile scale that shook the world. It ended on a mobile scale that brought defeat to its most foresighted proponents. Armor fully justified its development and existence, success falling to the side with armored preponderance on the ground and superiority in the air, as demonstrated by the early Axis successes and the final Allied victory. The surprise which can be achieved through the employment of large armored formations on offensive missions in the hostile rear creates a shock effect on the morale of the enemy in both his military and civilian ranks. The use of these armored combined arms teams launched against successive vital objectives of strategic value, the shocks increasing in tempo and in violence amply supported by and co-ordinated with air and slower moving ground formations, breaks the national will to resist and materially hastens the conclusion of international hostilities.

While the introduction of armored formations to the battlefield did not change the basic principles of warfare, it did restore the power of mobility to the battlefield. Armored organization in the U. S. Army after World War II tended to increase the allotment of armor to infantry divisions. The standard infantry division had a battalion of medium tanks and a reconnaissance company with light tanks under the direct control of division headquarters, and each of the three infantry regiments also included a company of medium tanks. The armored division included four medium tank battalions and four infantry battalions, plus a reconnaissance unit. Armored cavalry regiments were assigned to corps and army headquarters for reconnaissance and raiding missions. In the Korean War, large armored formations were not employed, as the terrain was unsuitable for their use; the role of armor was largely confined to direct support of infantry operations—anti-tank defense, fire support, patrolling, counterattack. The tactics of the tank-infantry patrol became highly developed. *See also* TANKS.   H. A. S.

ARMORICA or **AREMORICA** [ɑrmɔ'rɪkə], the early name for the northwest coast of France between the Loire and the Seine rivers. This was the scene of Caesar's campaign against the Veneti in 56 B.C. In the fifth century A.D., the term Armorica was applied only to Brittany, whereas previously it had included part of Normandy as well. T. B. J.

ARMOUR, JONATHAN OGDEN (1863-1927), American meat packer and industrialist, was born in Milwaukee, Wis., Nov. 11, 1863. He entered Yale University in 1881 but did not graduate, going instead to Chicago to work in his father's meat-packing firm. He was made a partner in 1884; after the death of his father in 1901, Jonathan Armour became the head of Armour & Company. Under him, Armour & Company developed into one of the biggest concerns in the United States. In 1923 he resigned as president of Armour & Company and became chairman of its board of directors. He was a director in many other companies and a trustee of the Armour Institute of Technology, founded by his father in 1893. He died in London, Aug. 16, 1927. S.D.

ARMS, JOHN TAYLOR (1887-1953), American etcher, illustrator, and architect, was born Apr. 19, 1887, in Washington, D.C. He studied architecture under Désiré Despradelle at the Massachusetts Institute of Technology, receiving his B.S. degree in 1911 and his M.S. in 1912. While working as an architect, he began to draw and etch in his spare time, and after World War I he made art his vocation. On his travels in France, Spain, and Italy, Arms studied medieval churches, and it is for his accurately rendered etchings of Gothic churches that he is best known. His book, *Handbook of Print Making and Print Makers,* was published in 1934. He died in New York City on Oct. 13, 1953. J. S. By.

ARMS AND ARMOR, terms used here to refer to those means of offense and defense in warfare which were in use prior to the development of firearms. More recent usages will be discussed elsewhere, as indicated at the end of this article. The bow is treated separately under ARCHERY.

ARMOR

Primitive Armor. Primitive armor in the less civilized parts of the world has been made up of many curious substances, largely dependent on the materials at hand. Almost complete suits of basketwork armor were used through the South Sea Islands, and mail coats of overlapping plates of tur-

tle or tortoise shell were defensive devices in the Philippines. American Indians used breastplates of shells, finely strung sections of porcupine quills, wampum, and bead work; this had some defensive value. Heavy leather garments were common in many parts of the world and formed a good defense against the relatively blunt weapons frequently used.

Partial Armor. Partial armor of metal plates was fairly widely used in the early civilizations and particularly in ancient Greece and Rome. This included the beautifully shaped helmets and leg pieces or greaves used by the ancient Greeks in combination with molded breast and back plates, worn over leather jackets. In Greece, there apparently was some feeling that the wearing of armor was cowardly, and, in some countries, restrictions were placed on sizes and shapes of either shields or breastplates simply because it was not heroic to protect certain portions of the body. The Romans, however, were practical and used a very well-made cuirass of leather and metal plates which protected the main part of the body, leaving the arms and legs free for quick movement. They also carried a good-sized square shield and wore well-shaped helmets of metal or metal-reinforced leather, which, in conjunction with their short, two-edged swords and deadly javelins, made them the most effective fighting units of their period.

With the fall of the Roman Empire and the beginning of the Dark Ages, armor making in the civilized part of the world declined, along with the other arts and sciences, and armor consisted mostly of quilted garments of leather or cloth strengthened and supported at vulnerable points by metal plates or rings, when such metal was available. By the time of the Norman Conquest, the Central European knights who crossed the channel were equipped, according to the Bayeux Tapestry, with defensive garments, fairly well reinforced with metal rings or plates. Very little chain mail, possibly none, existed at this time; but, shortly after the Norman Conquest and for the next two hundred years, chain mail became common and formed the largest part of the defensive equipment of Continental and English wearers of armor.

Chain Mail. Chain mail consisted of garments made of interlocked rings of chain, in which each ring was interlocked with a number of other rings and riveted to retain it in position. These garments took the form of a loose shirt, with arms to the wrists and skirts to about the length of the knee, and a pair of leggings, supported at the waist, which completely covered the feet as well as the lower and upper legs. The shirt was called a hauberk, and the leggings were called chausses. These names also applied to the similar garments of reinforced cloth or leather which had preceded them. The Norman shield and the shields following the Conquest for some years were long and pointed for use on horseback to cover as much of the left side of the rider as possible.

Various authors give different periods for the age of complete chain, but this type of armor undoubtedly appeared shortly after the Norman Conquest and was generally in use one hundred years later. It was the commonest and most complete type of defense for another hundred years or so, certainly until between 1250 and 1300. It was expensive, as each link of the chain had to be beaten out by hand, bent, and riveted into position. The art of wire drawing was not learned until shortly after 1300, when it was reputedly invented by Rudolph of Nürnberg.

Chain mail, completely covering the body and including a cap, or coiffe-de-maille, usually worn over a small steel cap, was a fairly good defense against an actual cut, but it had numerous disadvantages. It put most of the drag of its

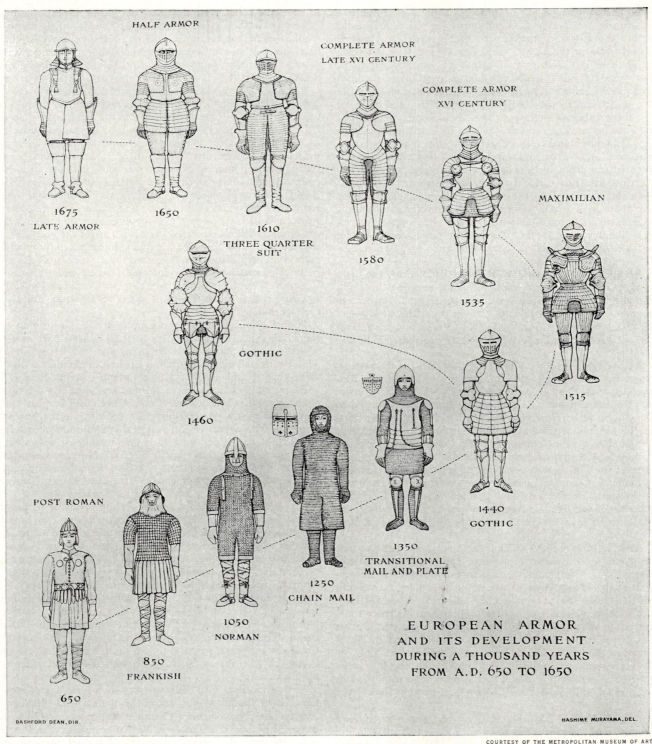

HALF ARMOR

COMPLETE ARMOR
LATE XVI CENTURY

COMPLETE ARMOR
XVI CENTURY

MAXIMILIAN

1675
LATE ARMOR

1650

1610
THREE QUARTER
SUIT

1580

1535

1515

GOTHIC

1460

1440
GOTHIC

1350
TRANSITIONAL
MAIL AND PLATE

POST ROMAN

1250
CHAIN MAIL

1050
NORMAN

EUROPEAN ARMOR
AND ITS DEVELOPMENT
DURING A THOUSAND YEARS
FROM A.D. 650 TO 1650

850
FRANKISH

650

BASHFORD DEAN, DIR.

HASHIME MURAYAMA, DEL.

weight on the shoulders and waist of the wearer; it reduced the crushing and shocking effect of a blow to only a limited extent; and because of its confining nature, it was about the worst type of equipment to wear in the East, although it was the common armor during most of the crusades. Worn over heavy leather-padded garments, it was extremely hot and stifling, and the chafing of chain mail chausses on the inside of the legs and thighs of the mounted men caused infected sores.

Because of the poor quality of resistance of chain mail to shock and smashing blows, reinforcements to it began to appear from the middle to the late thirteenth century. Although it is impossible to provide current proof, it is probable that flat or slightly shaped plates, called plastrons-de-fer, were worn as chest protectors beneath what appears, from illustrations on contemporary brasses, to have been a simple chain shirt. The shape of the coiffe-de-maille on the head obviously indicates that helmets of various shapes, commonly called pot-de-

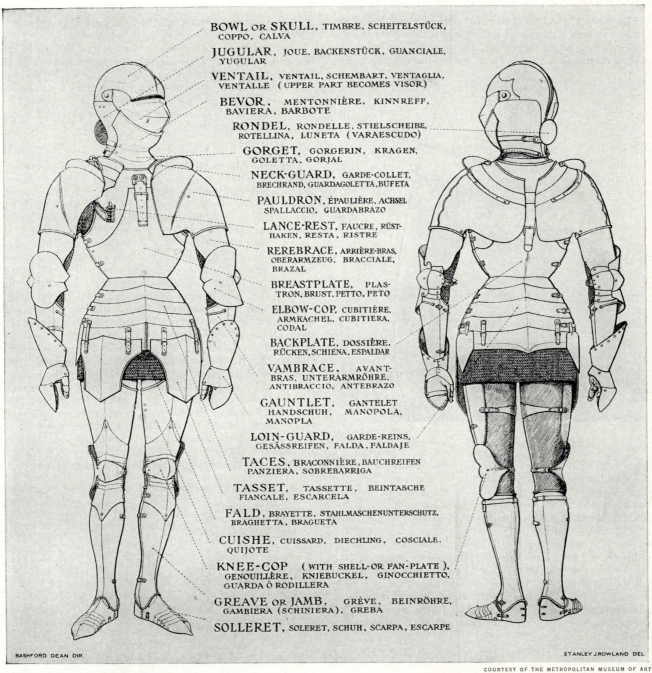

BOWL OR SKULL, TIMBRE, SCHEITELSTÜCK, COPPO, CALVA

JUGULAR, JOUE, BACKENSTÜCK, GUANCIALE, YUGULAR

VENTAIL, VENTAIL, SCHEMBART, VENTAGLIA, VENTALLE (UPPER PART BECOMES VISOR)

BEVOR, MENTONNIÈRE, KINNREFF, BAVIERA, BARBOTE

RONDEL, RONDELLE, STIELSCHEIBE, ROTELLINA, LUNETA (VARAESCUDO)

GORGET, GORGERIN, KRAGEN, GOLETTA, GORJAL

NECK-GUARD, GARDE-COLLET, BRECHRAND, GUARDAGOLETTA, BUFETA

PAULDRON, ÉPAULIÈRE, ACHSEL, SPALLACCIO, GUARDABRAZO

LANCE-REST, FAUCRE, RÜST-HAKEN, RESTA, RISTRE

REREBRACE, ARRIÈRE-BRAS, OBERARMZEUG, BRACCIALE, BRAZAL

BREASTPLATE, PLAS-TRON, BRUST, PETTO, PETO

ELBOW-COP, CUBITIÈRE, ARMKACHEL, CUBITIERA, CODAL

BACKPLATE, DOSSIÈRE, RÜCKEN, SCHIENA, ESPALDAR

VAMBRACE, AVANT-BRAS, UNTERARMRÖHRE, ANTIBRACCIO, ANTEBRAZO

GAUNTLET, GANTELET, HANDSCHUH, MANOPOLA, MANOPLA

LOIN-GUARD, GARDE-REINS, GESÄSSREIFEN, FALDA, FALDAJE

TACES, BRACONNIÈRE, BAUCHREIFEN PANZIERA, SOBREBARRIGA

TASSET, TASSETTE, BEINTASCHE FIANCALE, ESCARCELA

FALD, BRAYETTE, STAHLMASCHENUNTERSCHUTZ, BRAGHETTA, BRAGUETA

CUISHE, CUISSARD, DIECHLING, COSCIALE, QUIJOTE

KNEE-COP (WITH SHELL- OR FAN-PLATE), GENOUILLÈRE, KNIEBUCKEL, GINOCCHIETTO, GUARDA Ó RODILLERA

GREAVE OR JAMB, GRÈVE, BEINRÖHRE, GAMBIERA (SCHINIERA), GREBA

SOLLERET, SOLERET, SCHUH, SCARPA, ESCARPE

BASHFORD DEAN DIR.

STANLEY J. ROWLAND DEL.

COURTESY OF THE METROPOLITAN MUSEUM OF ART

COMPLETE SUIT OF ARMOR OF THE SECOND HALF OF THE FIFTEENTH CENTURY

fer, were usually worn beneath them. Because armor was used almost exclusively on horseback, the knee was a very vulnerable point, and, to a lesser degree, the elbow. Therefore reinforcements of plate or leather surrounding these joints began to appear on the outside of chain mail during the late thirteenth century.

Jousting Armor. For tilting or jousting purposes, a large helmet called a heaume was also worn, covering completely the inner pot-de-fer and the coiffe-de-maile. The heaume had only narrow eye slits for vision and was extremely ponderous and heavy, so that, while it was occasionally used in battle, it was confined very largely to the jousting field. It was relatively shapeless, but it was a helpful defense against a blow

on the head from a five-pound, iron-spiked ball on the end of a three-foot shaft. During the next one hundred and fifty years, these original pieces were augmented by plates which spread completely over the chain defenses, particularly their outer surfaces. These plates received their names from the part of the body they covered and were usually adaptations of French terminology, since this was the "classical" language in Europe at the time.

Gothic and Maximilian Armor. This transition period culminated between approximately 1275 and 1440, by which time Gothic plate armor of simple and beautiful lines typifying the arches and points of general Gothic design was the accepted equipment of the mounted knight. The surface of this armor was relatively smooth but characterized by angles to carry thrusts away from the body of the wearer. It also specialized in peculiar pieces of equipment, such as the pig-faced basinet, which emphasized this characteristic. The visor of this basinet extended to a sharp point, giving the general appear-

COURTESY OF THE METROPOLITAN MUSEUM OF ART

GERMAN JOUSTING ARMOR (CIRCA 1500)

ance of the snout of a pig. Gothic appeared in its best form by the second quarter of the fifteenth century and remained the basic design until about 1500. The effigy of Sir Richard Beauchamp, Earl of Warwick, dated c. 1454, is one of the finest representations of this form of armor. It gave way after a brief transition period between 1500 and 1525 to the typical Maximilian armor of the last three-quarters of the sixteenth century. This was characterized by extensive fluting for strength and lightness, and extremely complete coverage of the body by very finely articulated plates. The wearing of chain mail beneath the armor, except in the form of gussets sewn on a leather undergarment at the various joints, was no longer necessary because of the completeness of the plate coverage.

Decadence of Armor. Elaborate parade armor for both mounted and foot fighting appeared at this period, and the decadence of armor began partly because of attempts to simulate the elaborately puffed and slashed clothing and bulbous footwear of the period. The Elizabethan "peasecod" doublet was simulated in steel, and other exaggerations were common. The use of firearms in military combat was also beginning to disrupt the system of tactics which depended upon armored knights and, for this reason principally, heavy armor began to disappear, although from the early to middle seventeenth century, three-quarter armor and half armor were still commonly worn by officers and nobles and some classes of troops. As long as pikemen were in use, simple armor in the form of helmets, back, breast, and high pieces supplemented their leather garments as defensive equipment. The last surviving remnants of armor were the back and breast plates, or cuirasses, of the cuirassiers, or heavy cav-

alry, used in European armies even during the nineteenth century, although much of this equipment became mere parade ornament after its useful life had ceased.

The feudal system was founded on armor and castles, the one protecting the person and the other the domain of the noble, and its breakdown was caused as much by the arms and artillery that rendered these two forms of defense obsolete as by the centralization of political power that brought nations and national unity out of a loosely woven system of small separate baronies.

EDGED WEAPONS

Swords. The sword, which for thousands of years was a mark of authority as well as a practical fighting weapon, undoubtedly evolved as a metal enlargement of the "dagger stones" or long sharp stones found in prehistoric dwellings. Swords may be divided essentially into two types: the straight and the curved blade. Most of the earlier types found in ancient Egypt and Greece took the straight form, although in many cases the blade was double-edged and leaf-shaped, curving on each of its surfaces equally to a forward section heavier than that near the hilt, and then coming to a fairly fine sharp point. The Roman legionaries used a sword with a straight, short, double-edged blade, and, as indicated by early manuscripts on fencing, the legionaries were taught to use both cut and thrust in conjunction with defense by the shield on the left arm. Most of these earlier swords had rudimentary hand guards in the form of slight swellings at either end of the grips. Longer iron swords in the hands of the Central European barbarians were used principally for hacking, more or less as an ax is used. The curved blade undoubtedly was a development of an ax-type blade, with the ax head cut off by paralleling the outer curve of the blade along the inside of the ax head, leaving the point and a narrow blade.

The advantage of a curved blade is a more cutting effect

COURTESY OF THE METROPOLITAN MUSEUM OF ART

Complete suit of armor for horse and man, dated 1548, made for the Duke of Saxony

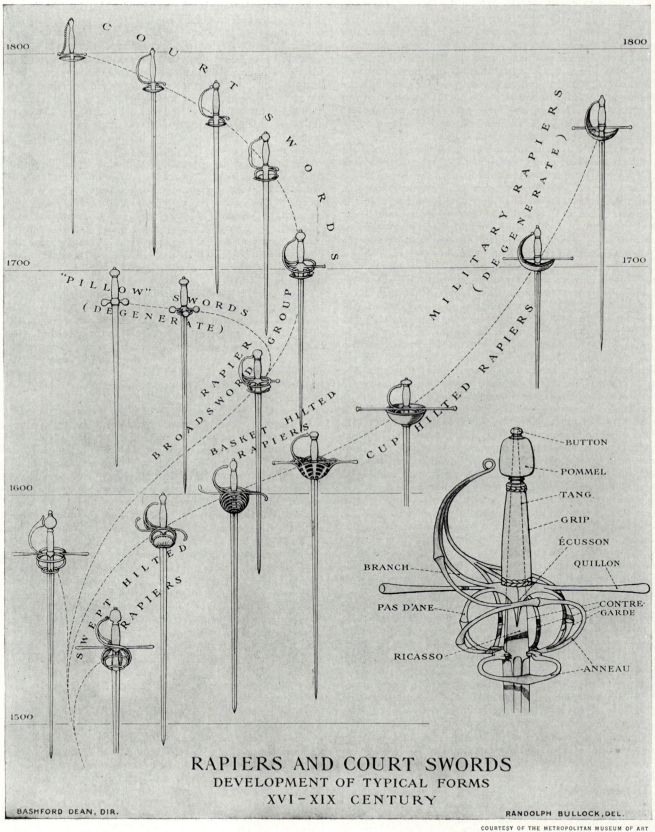

1800

1700

1600

1500

COURT SWORDS

"PILLOW" SWORDS (DEGENERATE)

RAPIER-BROADSWORD GROUP

BASKET HILTED RAPIERS

SWEPT HILTED RAPIERS

CUP HILTED RAPIERS

MILITARY RAPIERS (DEGENERATE)

BUTTON
POMMEL
TANG
GRIP
ÉCUSSON
QUILLON
BRANCH
CONTRE-GARDE
PAS D'ANE
RICASSO
ANNEAU

RAPIERS AND COURT SWORDS
DEVELOPMENT OF TYPICAL FORMS
XVI - XIX CENTURY

BASHFORD DEAN, DIR.

RANDOLPH BULLOCK, DEL.

with a straight, hacking blow without the necessity for draw-ing the blade at the same time the blow is made. It was more common in the East than in Europe and was probably brought back from the crusades by the first crusaders in about 1100; it became the falchion, one of the few curved weapons used during the knightly period in Europe. The simple cross-hilted sword, with its quillons standing out for some distance on each side, was the universal weapon of the crusaders. It was straight-bladed and double-edged, of varying weights and sizes, and was designed in both one- and two-hand types, approximately three to five feet in length.

As armor began to disappear from common civilian attire, more attention was paid to fencing, and further hand guards were necessary to protect the sword hand of the user, since his sword had become a shield as well as an attacking weapon. The first guards were small rings, called pas-d'âne, added to the guard below its level so that one or two fingers could be put through them, and side rings for the protection of the rest of the hand. These developed further in two ways. One devel-opment was toward the complete cup hilt or swept hilt rapier, which had a series of rings and counter guards ending with the knuckle bow but opening toward the pommel, so that the sword could be used as an elongation of the arm for a straight thrust. The other grouping of guards became the basket hilt, which surrounded the hand on three sides, allow-ing the grip to be held only in the manner of an axe. This type of hilt was designed for swords used primarily for cut-ting rather than thrusting. The Scotch claymore and the Venetian schiavone are two examples of this latter type. The cup hilt form, usually accompanied by a long, narrow, dia-mond-sectioned blade, was developed between 1550 and 1600, forming the rapier, or gentleman's sidearm, of the period. The small sword, or court sword, which followed the lighter transi-tion rapiers and flamberges used during the first half or three-quarters of the seventeenth century, had a small, simplified hilt and a light blade of hollow, triangular section for stiff-ness and lightness of the point. This was the common dress sword of a gentleman from the last quarter of the seven-teenth century through the eighteenth century until swords were no longer worn. It is the basis of the modern épée and the fencing foil or dueling sword of Europe; as a lightened version of the single-edged blade, usually straighter than in its earlier form, it has become the dueling saber. The heavy horseman's saber of recent times is a military version of the single-edged and usually slightly curved blade, since it is primarily a cutting rather than a thrusting weapon.

Fencing both followed and influenced the style of swords and became faster and more scientific as the swords became lighter and more manageable. Up to the middle of the seventeenth century, it was fairly common to use a left-handed auxiliary, such as a dagger, cloak, or small shield, to offset the slowness and clumsiness of the sword. After that date, the light, fast sword and straight-line play made these earlier appendages unnecessary, and fencing more and more approached its modern techniques. Although, from a point of view of pure combat, it is probable that modern fencing might be classed as somewhat decadent, it is a far more scientific sport in its modern form than it was in earlier times, when life and limb depended on the swordsman's ability.

Daggers. The short-bladed, edged, and pointed weapon is commonly called a dagger. More specific classification by blade types identifies the dagger as a double-edged weapon, the knife as a single-edged weapon, and the stylette, or stiletto, as a weapon for thrusting, having three or more edges or a round, pointed blade.

In early and primitive forms, the double-edged blade was often leaf-shaped, like the sword, in straight-bladed designs. Oriental daggers were frequently curved like oriental swords, although often double-edged completely to the hilt. Far Eastern, heavy, short weapons, such as the bolo, parang, or barong of Malaysia and the Philippines, were widened to a heavy section at the front and had a single cutting edge. They were used almost entirely for a chopping form of combat with no thrusting, as was the kukri knife of the Gurkhas, in India, which was curved to a very wide forward section of the blade, was sharpened on its inner edge, and had a relatively blunt point.

European "knightly daggers," following the wide-bladed Anglo-Saxon seax or scramasax, took a number of peculiar forms, including a very sharp, pointed stiletto type of weapon called the misericord, or "dagger of mercy," which was used for dealing the blow of mercy to a fallen knight and was shaped to penetrate chain and plate armor. Another was the anlace, or cinquedea, a dagger with a very wide, tapering double-edged blade, which took its second name from the fact that the upper part of the blade was supposed to be five fingers in width.

Small light daggers with typical double-edged blades were commonly called poniards from their size and general char-acteristics rather than special shape. A generic word for the short, single-edged fighting weapons of the British Isles is the skene (Welsh) or skean (Scottish). These were single-edged blades of varying length, and, in the case of the Scottish skeandhu, or black knife, a very short weapon usually worn at the top of the stocking. A typical Scottish general purpose arm was the dirk, a single-edged blade with-out a guard, which usually was worn in an ornamented sheath that also carried a fork as an eating utensil.

In the development of swordplay during the sixteenth and seventeenth centuries, the dagger was commonly used as a left-hand auxiliary, and special forms for this purpose had large guards and strong hilts. From its use, this type was commonly known as a *main gauche,* or left-hand dagger and in the more elaborate Spanish forms had a side guard of pierced or solid metal coming completely over the knuckles and up to the pommel, as well as long quillons. These weapons were used for both attack and defense, with the rapier in the right hand and the swordsman operating more or less in the fashion of a boxer who guards essentially with one hand and launches his main attacks with the other but can strike a blow from either side. With the advent of the faster sword-play and smaller swords, daggers were discarded and had disappeared from general civilian dress in most of Europe by the beginning of the eighteenth century. However, they have always been popular with frontier or primitive people all over the world and, as hunting and "scalping" knives, were used in America throughout the eighteenth century and in the first part of the nineteenth century. Perhaps one of the most famous American examples was the bowie knife, designed by Col. Bowie, of Texas, who lost his life in the Battle of the Alamo. This was typical of the weapon-tool knives of the period utilizing a relatively straight blade with a single edge running to a slight curve at the point, a short false edge at the back, a small cross guard, and a well-shaped grip. Hunting knives of similar design are still in use. The dagger, as a weapon, has never appealed as much to the Anglo-Saxon races as it has to the Latin and Eastern peoples, and it is still probably more widely used in Spain, Italy, and the Orient than in Northern Europe and America. As a personal defense weapon, it was superseded by revolvers and automatic pistols.

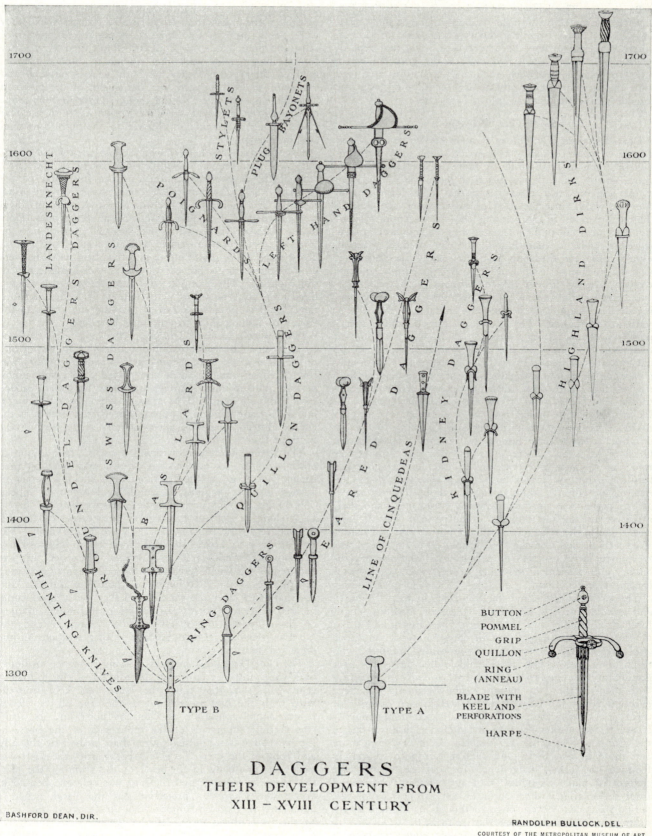

1700

1600

STYLETS

PLUG BAYONETS

LEFT HAND DAGGERS

POIGNARDS

LANDESKNECHT DAGGERS

SWISS DAGGERS

1500

RONDEL DAGGERS

BASILARDS

QUILLON DAGGERS

EARED DAGGERS

KIDNEY DAGGERS

LINE OF CINQUEDEAS

HIGHLAND DIRKS

1700

1600

1500

1400

HUNTING KNIVES

RING DAGGERS

1400

BUTTON
POMMEL
GRIP
QUILLON

RING
(ANNEAU)

BLADE WITH
KEEL AND
PERFORATIONS

HARPE

1300

TYPE B   TYPE A

1300

DAGGERS
THEIR DEVELOPMENT FROM
XIII – XVIII CENTURY

BASHFORD DEAN, DIR.

RANDOLPH BULLOCK, DEL.

Bayonets. The bayonet in its basic form is believed to have been invented by Marshal Vauban, of France about 1641. It takes its name from the town of Bayonne, in France, where it is said to have been first used. The first type of bayonet was inserted in the muzzle of the gun and had a plug-type handle. Between 1680 and 1700, the later type with the ring or socket attachment for slipping over the muzzle of the barrel came into general use.

SHAFTED WEAPONS

Classification. The type of weapon known generically as a lance or spear, consisting of a shaft varying in length from two or three to twenty-five or more feet, and a head or point, usually of different material from the shaft, is so simple and universal in adaptation that it has been used all over the world since the most primitive times. In general, shafted weapons in use among the ancient and modern civilized races fall into three categories. These are: (1) the lance or pike, a long-shafted, simple, pointed weapon, usually used for thrusting but occasionally for throwing; (2) the javelin or assegai, a short-shafted, simple, pointed weapon, usually thrown with or without mechanical assistance; and (3) the various complex-bladed, cutting or thrusting shafted weapons of the medieval infantry.

Infantry Lance. The spearman, armed with a metal-pointed weapon having a wooden shaft, was the common infantryman of most of the well-organized armies of the ancient civilizations. His spear or lance point was usually a lozenge or diamond section, sharply triangular or leaf-shaped, fitted with some form of socket to attach it firmly to the shaft, and made of bronze or relatively soft iron. Its over-all length varied from 5 or 6 ft. in types which could be used for both throwing and thrusting to the 15- or 20-ft. lances of the famous phalanx of Alexander the Great of Macedon. These latter extended past four or five ranks of footmen and presented to the hapless enemy a bristling front of points backed by the weight of the massed formation. The average length of infantry lances at this period was probably between 6 and 9 ft., and their extensive use as the standard infantry arm was at least partly due to the relatively small amount of rare and expensive metal needed to make their heads. Also, the sword was surrounded with an aura of nobility and was reserved for officers and noblemen in many armies, even after metal became more common.

The ancient Greeks and the Roman light-armed infantry and auxiliary troops used light lances of medium length for both thrusting and throwing. The "barbarian" tribes of central Europe, Great Britain, and the Norse countries also used a good proportion of spear-armed infantry, who threw their spears with considerable range and force as a preliminary to hand-to-hand combat, as well as thrusting with them in the close fighting. The Germanic "Framea" encountered by the Romans was a well-known example of this type. During the period of chivalry, extending roughly from A.D. 800 to 1600, the pike or footman's lance was one of the commonest arms of the infantry. As it was used more and more by the Swiss and central European mercenary footmen to form "hedgehogs" for defense against the charges of mailed knights, its length gradually increased from the relatively short spear of the earlier part of this period to 25 ft. or even longer, although its average length during the Middle Ages was from 10 to 15 ft.

With the decline in use of armor and edged weapons in battle and the gradually increasing appearance of firearms of all sizes and types, pikes were retained after most other shafted weapons had disappeared; pikemen were used to protect the musketeers from cavalry charges while they were going through the slow and complicated process of reloading their ponderous muskets. Pikes used by infantry for repelling cavalry were long enough to catch the horsemen on their points when the butts were grounded, and the shafts slanted outward over the shields of the pikemen crouching on one knee behind them. Three or four ranks of pikemen so disposed, with the longer shafts in the rear ranks, made a formidable obstacle to the most powerful cavalry charge.

Protecting the musketeers was the last tactical use of the pike. It was rendered completely obsolete in the latter part of the seventeenth century by the invention of the bayonet. The bayonet made every musketeer his own pikeman at a moment's notice and replaced, with an edged weapon, the last of the infantryman's shafted weapons. Only in one place was the thrusting pike still used, and then in the form of a short version called a "half-pike." This was on board ship, where most cutting and thrusting weapons were used in short forms because of the crowded conditions of ship fighting. The half-pike was a common naval weapon during the days of sailing ships with their tactics of short-range artillery broadsides and of carrying the attack to the enemy by lashing ships together and boarding.

Horseman's Lance. The use of the long spear or lance by horsemen also is of extreme antiquity. In the armies of the Greeks and Romans and their opponents, cavalry was considered an auxiliary arm and played a relatively unimportant part in most battles, but most horsemen carried some form of lance. This practice was adopted throughout the ancient Central European and British armies as the rise of chivalry began to affect military tactics during the ninth and tenth centuries.

The mailed horseman, wearing a sword, in addition to other weapons, as evidence of wealth and nobility, then began to emerge as the backbone and striking power of armies, and the panoply of knighthood began to appear. The knight of this period carried a lance between 9 and 12 ft. long as part of his regular equipment, but it still differed very little from the spear of the infantryman. The Bayeux Tapestry (1066) shows the mounted knights of Duke William of Normandy carrying lances. However, they are depicted as still wielding them in the early manner, grasping the middle of the shaft with the thumb to the rear and the shaft back over the shoulder so that the weapon could be used either for thrusting or throwing. Armored infantry, or dismounted knights, on both the English and the Norman sides are shown holding similar weapons in the same manner.

The later "knightly" method of using the lance on horseback came into use in about the middle of the thirteenth century. From that time, the lance was held near its butt, with the butt under and to the rear of the elbow. It was aimed across the neck of the horse and its thrust was entirely the result of the movement of the horse as the weapon was supported rather than pushed by the arm and body of the user. To give a better grip, the shaft was thickened gradually to the level of the front of the grip, the grip was recessed, and the butt was enlarged behind it. Sometimes a circular protection for the hand, called a vamplate, was added immediately in front of the grip. In the later tilting form, called a *bourdonesse,* the heavy shaft was made hollow to reduce weight and make it easier to "splinter a lance" when the jousts were held for glory and honor only.

Infantry Pole Arms. Long-shafted arms, or "pole arms," with heads of more complicated design than simple pointed blades, also date far back as military weapons. The "trident" or three-pointed spear, derived from a fishing spear, was used in Roman times, and trident-and-net men were powerful contenders in the Roman gladiatorial games. Simple agricultural tools, such as forks, long-handled billhooks, or axes, also lent themselves to military use. Especially in the days of well-armored knights, it was desirable for the infantryman to have on the blade of his shafted weapon a hook for dismounting passing cavalry and a heavy edge for long-distance chopping. Consequently, many variations and combinations of hooks, points, and bill or ax edges were devised.

One of the best known of the pole arms was the halberd. It was made in various lengths, but its head was fairly well standardized. It had a wide ax-type blade with a concave cutting edge, a hook at the rear with sharpened edges, and a spear or pike point at the top. In about an 8-ft. length it was one of the favorite weapons of the Swiss infantry during the fourteenth, fifteenth, and sixteenth centuries. It was also one of the ceremonial or parade weapon forms that survived beyond its period of practical use as part of the regimental insignia of noncommissioned infantry officers long after the general adoption of firearms. The glaive and guisarme were early bladed forms with extending spikes, commonly used from the twelfth to the fourteenth centuries. The spontoon had a broad, pike-shaped blade with equal, upcurving projections on both sides. This weapon was also used up to the eighteenth century as a badge of office of infantry noncommissioned officers. The vouge was an early, long ax-blade type of weapon in which the top of the blade came to an extended point. The spetum or ranseur was generally similar to the spontoon, as was also the partisan. The battle-ax was a favorite weapon of knights in full armor, fighting on foot either in battle or in tourneys. It had a short pike point, a sharp spike at the rear, and usually a cluster of four short, thick spike points at the front, although it was sometimes supplied with a small, heavy ax blade like a halberd. It nearly always differed from the halberd, however, in that the shaft was seldom more than 5 ft. long.

These combination shafted weapons, with their formidable array of hooks, points, and edges, were popular infantry arms, and deadly ones, during the period of the development of armor into complete plate. However, they lost much of their superiority to the simple pike when opposed to the complete plate of the late sixteenth century and the shock tactics of the period. Consequently, they disappeared from regular use while the pike survived into the seventeenth century as a support for musketeers.

Javelins or Throwing Spears. The second group of spears, including types intended primarily for throwing, also dates from remote antiquity. They are usually called javelins or darts. They were, for the most part, less than 6 ft. in length and sometimes not more than half that. The carrying of two or more javelins per man was the usual military procedure; the weapons were thrown at the advancing enemy at ranges of from 20 to 50 or 60 yd.

The famous Roman pilum, variously translated as "javelin" or "pike," was between 5 and 6 ft. in length, with a long iron head, a short wooden shaft, and an iron spiked butt. Two were carried by each heavy-armed Roman infantryman or legionary, in addition to the short sword or gladius. They were usually thrown at ranges up to 50 yd. and were heavy enough to penetrate the average "barbarian's"

shield. They could also be used as thrusting or stabbing weapons in close fighting.

A javelin or dart very similar in size and weight to the pilum, although usually without the spiked butt and sometimes supplied with "feathers" of wood or leather, was used as a missile for the catapult type of throwing engine of the period. While these were largely siege engines, carroballistae, or "cart catapults," were used by the Roman armies as infantry-accompanying, mechanical missile throwers or "field guns." They consisted of light catapults resembling big crossbows mounted on small carts, and the missiles were discharged between the two horses that drew them. With trained teams and operators, they were deadly weapons, since the heavy, 5-ft. javelins they shot had a range of several hundred yards and would penetrate any shield or armor in use.

A lighter throwing spear or dart was also used by the ancient Greeks and Romans. This was called the *ankule* by the Greeks and was the *amentum* in Roman terminology. It was provided with a loop or thong, attached near the rear end of the shaft, into which the first two fingers of the throwing hand were hooked to give more impetus to an overhand throw. It had greater range than the pilum, but less penetrating power because of its lighter weight.

A common feature of the lighter types of throwing spears, especially among the ancient Mediterranean and later central European armies, was the use of an easily bent head or one attached so that it would break off from the shaft if it struck the ground. This feature prevented javelins of this type from being picked up and thrown back by foes. The angon, of the Central European tribes of the first five or six centuries of the Christian Era, was a heavier weapon, and the direct descendant of the Roman pilum introduced at the time of the Roman conquest of the area.

Another form of javelin used contemporaneously with the angon had a very short, spike-butted shaft and a long, heavy, double-edged blade. Instead of being hurled point first, it was thrown with an over-arm motion, so that it turned over and over in the air and struck with a slashing rather than a stabbing blow. Similar use was made of the francesque (francisca), the short fighting ax of the Franks. Up to the time of the Norman conquest and later, even figures in the knightly armor of the period are depicted as carrying several short javelins. Weapons of this type, up to six in number, are commonly shown in use in conjunction with regular knightly equipment of all types; so apparently missile spears as well as lances were used by all branches of the military at this time.

Although the throwing spear was abandoned for battle purposes not long after the Norman conquest, it was used in hunting and had a curious revival as a weapon of war after the Battle of Poitiers in 1346, when the French knights, dismounted and fighting on foot, cut off their lance shafts for easier handling. These short spears were called lancegays at this time, from the Arabic zagaye, a javelin, more commonly found in English as assegai, an African tribesman's throwing spear. They apparently were commonly used by knights, but were considered such dangerous and unfair weapons that a king's edict was issued against them in 1383.

Superiority of the English, or more properly Welsh, longbow and clothyard arrow over all other shafted missile weapons, the development of armor and battle tactics, and finally, the introduction and improvement of firearms contributed to the decline and eventual disappearance of the throwing spear as a military weapon in Europe and Great

Britain well before the end of the period of chivalry. It was, however, used as a weapon of the chase in some parts of Europe, and especially in the Norse countries, well into the seventeenth century.

THE SLING AS A MISSILE WEAPON

The sling was the other common missile weapon of the period before gunpowder. The slingers and archers of early armies were usually grouped together among the light armed auxiliaries and were used for the same tactical purposes.

Traditional Hand Sling. Essentially, the sling (*fundis*) of the Romans consisted of two pieces of cord or thong about 3 ft. long, connected by a pouch of leather. A loop in one cord was slipped over one finger, and the loose end of the other cord was held in the same hand. A stone or some other missile was placed in the pouch, the sling was whirled around the head one or more times to gain momentum, and then the loose end was released, propelling the stone on its flight. The sling could be composed entirely of one piece of material, broadened at the center instead of composite.

This general type was the traditional sling of David, the shepherd, with which he killed the giant Goliath of Gath. It changed little from its original form during the entire period of its use. It was a part of the equipment of the Greek, Roman, and other ancient armies, as well as those of medieval times. Missiles of lead were used by the Romans. Some have been found bearing the name of an intended victim: during the period of the Roman civil wars, molds were cut so that *Feri Pompei* ("Strike Pompey") could be read on the surface.

Staff Sling. A later version of the sling, called the "fustibal," or staff sling, was used extensively in the Middle Ages. This was simply a regular sling with one cord fixed to the end of a stout staff about 5 ft. long. It was used by slipping the loop of the free end of the cord over the end of the staff and giving the staff a simple overhand swing. The free end slipped off and discharged the missile in the pouch at the top of the swing. The staff sling would handle heavier missiles than the hand sling, but both regular and staff slings were used for throwing grenades and other missiles until the early part of the sixteenth century. The range of the sling was about equal to that of the bow; its accuracy in the hands of skilled troops was high, although the usual exaggeration of its powers is to be found in the old manuscripts. *See also* ARCHERY; ARTILLERY; ENGINES OF WAR; FIREARMS; SPORTING ARMS.   C. T. H.

ARMS AND THE MAN, one of the "pleasant" plays in G. B. Shaw's *Plays: Pleasant and Unpleasant* (1898) and the most universally popular of his dramas, presents in lucid form a comedic satire on war as romance. The time is the period of the war between Serbia and Bulgaria in 1885, and the scene is laid in the home of the Petkoffs, an ancient Bulgarian family.

Raina Petkoff, who is a young girl of highly romantic temperament, is the fiancée of Sergius Saranoff, an officer in the Bulgarian army. In the dead of night Captain Bluntschli, a Swiss soldier of fortune of the Serbian army, breaks into Raina's bedroom, hotly pursued, and pleads for assistance. The conflict of the play arises between the common-sense realism of the professional soldier Bluntschli and the romantic gallantry of the posturing Sergius. Raina, a sentimental girl who has been spoiled by adulation, is fascinated by the downright Swiss and eventually discards the luckless Sergius in favor of the wealthy Bluntschli, the inventory of whose property includes six huge establishments with accompanying furniture, including ten thousand knives and forks.   A. H.

ARMSTRONG, DANIEL LOUIS (1900-   ), American Negro jazz trumpeter, was born July 4, 1900, in New Orleans and as a youth absorbed the intoxicating jazz for which the city is noted. After a period of playing on the riverboats, he went to Chicago in 1922, first playing with "King" Oliver. Since that time he has been one of the outstanding figures in hot jazz. His performances represent the epitome of technical mastery and imaginative improvisation. He is the author of *Satchmo* (1954), an autobiography. *See also* JAZZ.   C. S. Sp.

ARMSTRONG, EDWIN HOWARD (1890-1954), electrical engineer and inventor of frequency modulation (FM), was born in New York City, Dec. 18, 1890. He graduated in electrical engineering from Columbia University in 1913. Armstrong started his career as an assistant in the electrical engineering department of Columbia University (1913-1914), joined the staff of the University's Marcellus Hartley Research Laboratory, and from 1914 to 1935 conducted the experiments which have helped to revolutionize radio. During World War I he served as a captain and a major in the Signal Corps, and since 1934 he has been professor of electrical engineering at Columbia University. Armstrong is credited with the invention of the regenerative circuit for high frequency oscillations (1912) and the superheterodyne (1918). His invention of the superregenerative circuit in 1920 achieved immediate use in police and military radio. In 1925 he began his work on the correction of static in radio, which resulted in the achievement of frequency modulation. In 1937 Armstrong set up his own FM station in Alpine, N.J., and in March 1953 he announced the development of a "multiplex" technique whereby several different programs could be transmitted simultaneously on a single FM channel. In recognition of his work, the Radio Club of America established an annual award, the Armstrong Medal. He died by suicide in New York City on Feb. 1, 1954.
    M. E. McD.

ARMSTRONG, SAMUEL CHAPMAN (1839-1893), American educator, was born of American missionary parents in Hawaii, Jan. 30, 1839. After graduating from Williams College in 1862, he entered the Union army in the Civil War, where he commanded a company of Negro troops and rose to the rank of colonel at the age of twenty-five. In 1868 he founded the Hampton Normal Agricultural and Industrial Institute (now Hampton Institute), at Hampton, Va., for educating Negroes, and later Indians, under a system combining study with gainful work. He headed the institute until his death, in Hampton, May 11, 1893.   M. Sr.

ARMY, that portion of the organized armed force of any state which is equipped and designed to fight on land, as distinguished from the navy and the air force. Originally, the word "army" meant the entire military organization of a nation, but more recently it has been applied only to land forces. This definition still holds good, although the pressure of modern techniques and weapons has tended to reduce the sharpness of distinction between the three major services.

Origin. The identification of the army as a separate entity within the body politic begins very early in recorded history. In ancient Egypt and ancient China there were already organized armies under the control of the respective rulers. In India, a warrior caste, second only to the priesthood in rank, developed. The warlike kings of Assyria had well-arranged armies of cavalry, chariots, and foot soldiers. Cyprus and Persia carried military organization to the highest degree which it was to reach in any Asiatic state until the Mongol Empire arose under Genghis Khan. It was Greece, however, that produced the first of the three great revolutionary developments of warfare: (1) discipline; (2) gunpowder; and (3) the airplane.

Greek Armies. The Greek spearman, disciplined and drilled, standing in steady formation or maneuvering under the orders of experienced officers, proved an obstacle against which the hordes of Persia beat in vain. Originally the Greek "hoplite," the heavy-armed spearman of the phalanx, was a citizen-soldier, not a professional warrior. Every young man was required to undergo a year or more (usually two years) of military training in most of the free Greek cities. In Sparta, which was little more than a barrack-state, all male citizens were primarily soldiers, and training went on incessantly. When an emergency arose, a Greek city could instantly put into the field a force of thoroughly trained men, who were, moreover, citizens fighting for their own homes and liberties. Slaves could not ordinarily be soldiers, though in great stress exceptions were made to this rule. However, men whose circumstances did not permit them to acquire the heavy arms and armor of the hoplite could fight as light-armed soldiers, operating on the flanks or in advance of the phalanx and using such missile weapons as bows, slings, and javelins to a considerable extent. The tremendous defeats which the Persian armies suffered at Marathon, Plataea, and elsewhere as a result of Greek discipline made a profound impression throughout the ancient world.

This caused Asiatic kings, in their quarrels with each other, to seek the services of Greek mercenaries. Thus a professional warrior class arose in many Greek cities, with captains of renown selling their services to Eastern despots for fixed sums and established periods of time, on the basis of being able to raise stipulated numbers of troops. Xenophon, who was a professional officer of this type, has left a very clear picture of the Greek mercenary soldier of his day in his *Anabasis*. As in the case of Rome centuries later, the wealthier cities of

SPARTAN AND EGYPTIAN MILITARY COSTUME COMPARED

Greece came to find it convenient to hire mercenaries to do their fighting for them, while the citizens took their ease at home. It is hardly surprising, therefore, that the liberties of the Greek citizen did not last very long under this system.

Macedonian Phalanx. The rise of the warrior kings of Macedonia was based on a different military plan. The discipline was there, but it was a discipline based on devotion to the throne. To a more perfect organization, both tactical

and logistical, than any Greek state had yet developed, was added the territorial recruitment of men by districts, each district being obligated to furnish a given number of young men for the army each year. The Macedonian phalanx, as developed by Philip of Macedon from the tactics of the great Theban general, Epaminondas, was by far the most formidable army the world had yet seen.

It had as its base the solid body of spearmen, traditional to Greek tactics, but formed sixteen files deep and divided

MACEDONIAN SOLDIERS IN PHALANX

carefully into companies, battalions, and regiments capable of maneuvering either separately or together. The flanks, always the most sensitive part of the phalanx, were protected by bodies of foot soldiers called peltasts, armed with swords and shields. The light-armed troops were still farther to the flanks. But the real advance made by Philip, and brought to perfection by his son Alexander, was the use of cavalry in connection with the phalanx. Hitherto the ponderous, slow-moving mass of armored infantry had lacked the power to follow up its successes and bring about the final destruction of the enemy after he had broken himself against its ironclad ranks. The scarcity of horses in Greece had not encouraged the development of the cavalry arm. In Macedonia, however, horses were plentiful, and the heavy cavalry of Philip and Alexander gave decisive quality to their battles by providing the means to pursue and destroy a shattered foe. Alexander also gave great attention to supply organization, and it was under him that organized bodies of engineer troops, as well as an organized medical service, first made their appearance on the battlefield.

Roman Army. The Roman army, like the armies of the Greek states, was originally a citizen militia. Its early organization was similar to that of the phalanx, but it soon began to adopt a more open order, more maneuverable on broken ground (always difficult with the phalanx), and able to change front quickly to a flank. The basic tactical unit was the maniple of 120 men, in which only the reserve was armed with long spears, most of the infantrymen having swords and shields, like the Greek peltasts, and javelins which they hurled into the enemy ranks as they attacked. The short sword and the prowess of the individual swordsman were basic in Roman tactics, as contrasted to the eighteen foot spear and the steadiness of the mass in Macedonian tactics.

The major unit of the Roman army was the legion, composed of ten cohorts (battalions), each of which had three maniples. With its tactical flexibility, its ability to make the best use of the ground, and its high quality of individual training, discipline, and spirit, the legion proved superior to the phalanx on almost every occasion when the two met. How-

FROM AN ENGRAVING BY HENRI-PAUL MOTTE

HISTORICAL PICTURES SERVICE

HANNIBAL CROSSING THE RHONE RIVER EN ROUTE TO INVADE ITALY

ever, the political system which had produced the phalanx had degenerated by that time, and the great successes of the legions were gained in general either against old-style Asiatic armies or the fierce but undisciplined tribes of northern Europe. The principal exception was the series of wars with Carthage known as the Punic Wars.

ROMAN INFANTRY SOLDIERS

HISTORICAL PICTURES SERVICE

Carthaginian Army. The army of Carthage was composed almost entirely of mercenaries. The merchant-citizens of Carthage were not inclined to the tedium of military duties, and their wealth might have been wrested from them long before it was, except for the fact that Carthage managed to produce a few military leaders of the very first order, or, as in the case of the Spartan general, Xanthippus, was able to hire them. By the genius of these generals, and by the use of her vast wealth to hire soldiers from other lands, Carthage managed not only to prolong her existence for centuries but to expand her empire until it included, at its greatest extent, Sicily, Sardinia, and Spain, as well as most of north Africa. It should be noted that Carthaginian aversion to military service did not extend to the navy and that the fleet was a vitally important factor in Carthage's expansion. Of her three great struggles with Rome, the second was the decisive contest.

During the Second Punic War, the great Carthaginian general, Hannibal, invaded Italy with an army of Gallic, Spanish, and African mercenaries and nearly succeeded in destroying the Roman Republic. He failed, despite his overwhelming victories of the Trebia, Lake Trasimene, and Cannae, largely because his home government would not support him adequately. Tactically, Hannibal's victories were due to his masterly combination of steady infantry formed in battalion squares with intervals between them, heavy cavalry for the decisive stroke when the enemy had spent himself against the squares, and light cavalry for the pursuit. The Roman cavalry of the time was neither very numerous nor very good. Basically, however, these victories were the product of a personal leadership of so transcendent an order that it infused a whole army of mercenaries from many lands with the spirit of the great general. When Hannibal was finally beaten at Zama, there was no one to take his place, and the Carthaginian state crumbled.

Later Roman Armies. While the survival of Rome under the stress of invasion and defeat was a tribute to the Roman soldier and the Roman spirit, it was hardly a tribute to the Roman system of command. This was largely responsible for Cannae and illustrates the difficulties of a free people trying to reconcile democratic liberties with the necessities of military control. The Greek city-states had made a practice of appointing ten generals to command in daily rotation. With the Romans, the two civilian officers (consuls) who exercised the executive power for a year were also the military commanders. In a small war, one consul took the field with one or two legions while the other stayed at home to govern; in a great war, both consuls took the field, and commanded the army on alternate days. The legion, under the Republic, had no designated commander, but was led by six tribunes, who commanded in pairs, changing daily. The reason for this complicated and perilous system was a republican fear of putting too much power in the hands of one man, but the qualities of the Roman citizen-soldier saved Rome, even under this system.

The civil wars, the rise of personal leadership, and finally the Empire changed the character of the Roman army. When Augustus had disposed of all rivals and ruled alone, he had no wish to keep the legions close at hand. He sent them to the frontiers, where they were permanently stationed; and, inevitably, their ranks became more and more filled with mercenaries. In Italy, a home guard, the Praetorians, was the only force. These troops made and deposed emperors at their pleasure; or, on occasion, generals marched in with their legions from the frontiers and took over power in Rome. The system of command was changed. The general, or imperator, now commanded an army; a legion was commanded by a legatus, with a quaestor as his chief of staff. But the legions were no longer Roman. When the Western Empire went down at last under barbarian assault, the Eastern Empire lingered on for a thousand years, maintained largely by the development of a system of military organization and administration on the territorial model. The horse-archer, combining mobility and fire power, was the mainstay of the Byzantine armies.

In general, however, throughout the whole period of ancient history, hand-to-hand combat and shock decided battles. The Greek spear and the Roman short sword dominated the battlefield in succession. Missile weapons were for the most part weak and of short range, used for harassment rather than decisive effect. It is perhaps significant that the most effective missile weapon used by organized armies from the days of Cyrus down to those of Trajan was the Roman pilum, or javelin, which was hurled at a distance of only a few yards. The Byzantine horse-archer, heir of the Parthians, was the forerunner of an era yet to come, in which men would find ways of killing each other at greater and greater distances and in greater numbers with an expenditure of less time and effort.

Feudal Armies. The break-up of the Western Empire, the rise of the "barbarian" kingdoms, and the excellent but ephemeral military system of Charlemagne gave place in turn to the coming of feudalism. Feudalism was a military as well as an economic system, but it was, paradoxically, a system which developed soldiers rather than armies. Personal address-at-arms was the essential qualification for knighthood, but the fragmentation of loyalties and the rampant individualism of chivalry precluded true military organization, of which the basis is discipline. Every knight or petty baron was required to bring a given levy of fighting men at the call of

his suzerain, but he was required to keep them in the field no more than three months in a year, and this made sustained long-term operations impossible. Europe was plagued with thousands of little armies, the personal retainers of knights, counts, and earls. These, which were for the most part little more than castle guards, were the professional rank-and-file of the times. For the rest, the "levies" were an ill-armed, ill-

HISTORICAL PICTURES SERVICE

ROMAN SOLDIERS STORMING A TEUTONIC POSITION
FROM THE VICTORY PILLAR OF MARCUS AURELIUS AT ROME

disciplined rabble, to be ridden down without mercy by the armored knights, as they were on scores of battlefields. As for command and control, every knight felt himself as good as any other and had something to say about how things were to be done. Only a leader with great personal prestige—such a warrior king as Edward III of England, or Louis IX of France—could take the field with a feudal army and carry through a plan to its objective.

The weapons of the knight were the lance, a one-encounter weapon which shattered at the first shock; thereafter he used the sword, mace, or battle-ax in close personal combat, depending on his armor for defense. He was impervious to such feeble weapons as might be possessed by peasant levies, unless he fell from his horse, when the weight of his armor would render him helpless. This vast superiority in weapons was a means of enforcing feudalism; a few knights and nobles with small bodies of personal retainers could rule over thousands of peasants and villagers.

In the great towns matters were somewhat different. As trade grew, bringing wealth with it, the cities formed burgher militia forces. Forbidden the trappings of chivalry and lacking horses, militiamen were trained as solid infantry corps, armed with pike or halberd. These proved quite capable of dealing with the charges of armored cavalry, as feudal knights discovered in encounters with the Flemings, the Swiss, or the Scots. The city militia had no golden spurs, but they had discipline.

Meanwhile, in England, the development of the longbow brought to the battlefield for the first time a missile weapon of real effectiveness at comparatively long ranges. The result was far-reaching. At Crécy, at Poitiers, at Agincourt, the armored chivalry of the continent went down in bloody ruin before the hail of English arrows, and in England the rise of political freedom was not unconnected with the fact that the common man possessed a cheap, readily obtainable weapon.

The longbow's reign was cut short, however, by the appearance of gunpowder, the second of the great military developments. The longbow had already undermined the foundations of English feudalism; gunpowder wiped out the system in all of Europe. It gave the king, who alone had the money to build foundries and acquire great numbers of cannon, the means of battering down the castle walls of recalcitrant nobles. As hand-carried firearms came more and more into use, the armored knights became simply targets for mus-

HISTORICAL PICTURES SERVICE

Battle of Crécy, August 26, 1346, in which England, under Edward III, defeated France, under Philip of Valois, as depicted in the Chronicles by Froissart

kets in the hands of common soldiers. Armies again came into being—national armies, composed of the three arms: infantry, cavalry, and artillery. All of these were dependent in varying degrees on a combination of fire power and mobility, a combination which still rules the battlefield.

Revival of Professional Armies. The armies which emerged from the twilight of feudalism were small according to modern standards. Examples were the *condottieri,* or mercenary bands of Italy; the Landsknechts of Germany, from whom are derived many of the modern military customs; and the Swiss, who like the Greeks had commercialized their prowess as citizen-soldiers. Such groups predominated during the period of transition from feudalism to nationalism, but their military importance diminished as the great states of Europe began to take form, as cannon gave the kings power to deal with rebellious nobles, and as muskets increased the value of the enlisted foot soldier. The growth of armies and the growth of nations went hand in hand, and the new professional soldier was a trained man enlisted in the service of his king for a fixed period of time rather than a vassal performing a hereditary duty toward his liege lord for a few weeks in the year. Thus sustained campaigns became possible, and with them, continuity of military policy. The study of the art of war revived and took on new meaning. Purely military careers, as distinguished from the combined military-civil careers of the Romans and of feudal times, could now be sought after, with reasonable promise of advancement and without the hazard of mercenary employment—indeed with the full inspiration of patriotic duty. This was the age of Turenne and Condé, of Gustavus Adolphus and Tilly, and later of Marlborough, Eugene, and Saxe. The professional soldier and professional officer came once more into a prominence which they had not known, except, perhaps, in the

Eastern Empire and among the Mongols, since the barbarian tide swept over Italy a thousand years before the first cannon was used on a western battlefield.

The first and for many years the best of the new armies was that of Spain. It gave primary recognition to the creation of good infantry; its tactical organization sought the combination of fire power (musketeers) and shock or defensive steadiness (pikemen), with cavalry as the arm of the decisive moment. It remained for Gustavus Adolphus of Sweden to add to this a highly organized and highly mobile artillery, with light guns attached to the infantry units, as well as heavier guns in the traditional "artillery train." Gradually the character of armies began to change from that of small bodies of regular troops, permanently maintained and augmented in time of war by levies obtained by local impressment or hastily offered bounties, to larger regular establishments with traditions and a character of their own. The Spanish "tercios" or regiments had their counterpart in France, England, Prussia, and Holland. But an army, however large, was still a collection of regiments or smaller units, and there were no brigades, divisions, or army corps in the modern sense until the time of Napoleon. On the battlefield, the army usually fought in three parts: the right wing, the left wing, and the center. The provision of a reserve was the exception rather than the rule, although wing commanders sometimes maintained a second line or even a third. It was unusual for the wing commanders to be assigned until the day of battle was actually at hand. But these were days of small armies, largely because the bad roads and horse-drawn transport could not supply large ones, and the whole of a given battlefield could be kept under the eye of the commander. Staff officers scarcely existed, except for supply and administration. The staff of the commanding general were mere messengers, and when an army was given a "second-in-command," it was rather to keep a check on the commander than to provide him with a capable executive officer.

Promotion in time of war might be swift enough and based to some extent on merit displayed in the field, but promotion in peacetime was a matter of court favor, or of outright purchase of commissions. It was inevitable that a kind of dry-rot should begin sapping the foundations of the military structure—a formalism which in the field was curiously like the formal maneuverings of the Italian condottieri three centuries before, when a battle might be decided by the loss of two or three men after weeks of skirmishing and countermarching. Even the military genius of Frederick the Great did not bring this era of formalism to an end; it only adopted the military practices of the age to a more ardent spirit and to the concepts of a more flexible and inventive mind.

Revolutionary Armies. It remained for the wars of the American and French revolutions, people's wars fought in the name of liberty, to break down the barriers that time and custom had erected and to bring about the next great change in the character of armies: the change from the period of the professional soldier to that of the nation in arms, which meant the return in full force to the citizen-soldier concept of the Greeks, the Romans, and even the cavemen, with military service again part of the duty of every citizen.

The knell of the old military formalism was sounded at the battle of Valmy, where the raw levies of France, although having fled in disgraceful panic from the sight of a few Prussian hussars, contrived to stand firm in a major battle. The Prussian troops could not bring themselves to drive home their charge against an enemy who was obviously outmaneuvered and doomed but did not seem to know it, and actually the

BATTLE OF ILLKIRK, FRANCO-PRUSSIAN WAR (1870-1871)

battle was little more than a cannonade. The French won because the officers of the old army's artillery, always considered a second-class arm, had for the most part stayed with the Revolutionary government while those of the infantry and cavalry had fled. Thus at Valmy the French at least had reliable artillery, and since the dry-rot of formalism kept the Prussian infantry from closing, the best artillery won. Valmy was a curtain-raiser for the machine age of warfare which was yet to come.

Armies of the Napoleonic Era. The Revolutionary armies of France were defending a government which did not yet know how to govern, but within a few years they became the instrument of a despot who was, unfortunately for Europe, a great military genius. In the use which he made of his artillery and in his introduction of the higher units of organization (brigade, division, and corps), Napoleon gave form to the armies of the nineteenth century. After his time, artillery ceased to be an arm officered by "grimy mechanics," and armies ceased to be merely unwieldy aggregations of regiments and squadrons. But perhaps the most far-reaching military development of the Napoleonic era was one which Napoleon did not initiate, but which was adopted in Prussia as a measure of defense against him.

This was the *Krümper* system, by which conscripts were called up on a territorial basis and in classes according to age. After completing their training, they returned to their homes and became part of an enrolled army reserve, subject to recall whenever an emergency occurred. The Prussian government adopted this plan in order to evade Napoleon's restriction on the size of the Prussian army. But the *Krümper* system became, eventually, the model plan for the "nation in arms," by which the states of Europe were able to mobilize their entire manpower when, fifty years later, the development of railways reached a stage which permitted armies of large size to be moved quickly and efficiently to the scenes of action and kept supplied with food and arms.

Growth of Conscript System. At the end of the Napoleonic wars there was a return to the old regular armies of the eighteenth century, but this was a temporary reaction. Most countries, during this interim period, kept up citizen militia forces of one sort or another, partially trained, partially equipped, and usually separate from the regular forces. But in Germany, and especially in Prussia, after the collapse of the revolutionary movements of 1848, the revival of the *Krümper* system began to build up large trained reserves which were directly associated with the regular army. With these reserves, Bismarck easily won his three wars against Denmark, Austria, and France, and brought about the union of the German states to form the most powerful military empire Europe had yet seen.

Faced by this menace, the other large states of continental Europe had little choice except to follow suit. In consequence, within a few years after the Franco-Prussian War of 1870-1871, the principle of the nation in arms had been incorporated into the military systems of France, Italy, Austria-Hungary, and Russia, and to some extent into the military systems of the lesser continental states. Every able-bodied European was now a trained soldier, at least in theory. In his young manhood he spent two or three years in military service, and thereafter, until he became middle-aged, he was a reservist, subject to call in an emergency and belonging to a regiment or other unit; his uniform, weapons, and equipment were carefully stored away in the barracks of his district.

In some of the smaller countries, i.e., the Scandinavian states and the Netherlands, the initial period of service was much less. Switzerland retained her national militia, with no regular troops but with every citizen trained under a system of short-term, intermittent calls. Belgium alone of the continental countries adhered to the old plan of a small regular army and a separate citizen militia until the approach of war in 1913, when the change was made too late. The Balkan countries for the most part had the "nation in arms" system, although in these countries and in Russia smaller numbers of available able-bodied men were trained and organized.

Europe had become an armed camp under a shadowy but terrible portent called "mobilization." Mobilization is the process of calling up the reservists. An example of its working may be taken from the French Army of 1914. At that time the peacetime strength of a French infantry battalion was about 550 officers and men. Each battalion had assigned to it about 2,000 reservists of the "first reserve," that is, men ranging up to 29 years of age, in the first to sixth year of reserve service. The war strength of the battalion was slightly over 1,000. On mobilization, the reservists reported to the barracks and were issued their arms and uniforms. Of the 2,000 available, 450 were added to the peacetime battalion to bring it up to full war strength, each of the four companies expanding from about 125 to about 250 men. This left 1,550 reservists. Of these, 1,000 formed a reserve battalion, ready for immediate service; reserve officers and noncommissioned officers were always available, there being a carefully organized system for training these leaders in time of peace. The remaining reservists formed the "depot," as a reservoir of replacements for both the first-line and reserve battalions, and to undertake the training of additional recruits.

The immediate practical effect of mobilization was, therefore, to quadruple the peacetime strength of the French infantry. Comparable though not identical results were obtained with the other arms by this process. Thus any major military power of the continent, by the simple process of setting this machinery of mobilization in motion, could within forty-eight hours expand an army of, say, 500,000 men, to an army of 2,000,000 men, fully ready for active service. Germany, as was proven in 1914, could do better than this; German expansion was about five-fold. It followed that if any great power ordered mobilization, its neighbors were in self-defense compelled to follow suit, or risk being attacked by overwhelmingly superior numbers. This situation was reflected in the outbreak of war in August 1914. Once fear and uncertainty had been translated into starting mobilization, the effect was infectious.

Armies in World War I. These great national armies fought World War I, depending for victory on masses of infantry and masses of guns to support them, backed up by the entire industrial effort of the nations concerned in order to supply the rifles, guns, and ever increasing amounts of ammunition. The railway and, to an increasing extent, the motor truck, made the movement of these supplies possible.

The war began under leaders who drew their ideas of tactics from Napoleon and the period up to 1870, but a change had taken place in armaments which was to stultify their early hopes and plans. The Napoleonic wars had been fought with muzzle-loading weapons of comparatively short range and slow rates of fire. Subsequent wars in Europe and America had brought the breech-loader to the battlefield, but it was during the period of profound peace from 1871 to 1914 that the magazine rifle, the quick-firing field gun, and above all the machine gun had been developed. These weapons had been tried out in Manchuria, Cuba, the Philippines, and South Africa, but their effect on the massive deployments of a European war had not been accurately appraised. It was discovered that infantry could no longer advance in the open against field fortifications defended by machine guns and that no amount of artillery support enabled the attack to do more than make a minor penetration into a system of trenches arranged in suitable depth and with adequate underground shelter for the defenders. Increasing the mass of the attacking infantry merely increased the casualties. The answer was to

be found, not in more men, but in better machines to overcome the mechanical power of the machine gun.

This resulted (1) in the return of armor to the battlefield after an absence of some three centuries; and (2) in the development of the airplane as a combat weapon, able to overpass ground obstacles and bring fire directly to bear on crucial targets. The internal-combustion engine provided the necessary lightweight element of driving power for both purposes. War passed into the third dimension and became more than ever dependent on a close association between the tactician, the engineer, and the inventor. Armies lost the simplicity of the old division into the three arms of infantry, cavalry, and artillery. They became aggregations of specialist units, highly organized and each trained for a special task, and associated together in higher formations based on minimum basic requirements of fire power and mobility, with large pools of additional specialist units to be attached as the needs of each new mission might require.

Prior to World War I, however, the American and British armies had not undergone the same metamorphosis as those of the continent of Europe. Both the United States and Great Britain had clung to the old system of a small regular army and a separate force of volunteer, half-trained citizen militia of very uncertain quality. Neither was able to put into the field anything except its regular troops when an emergency came. A long period of time was required to expand and fully train the citizen forces upon which both countries really depended, and although the small regular armies of these countries were perhaps the most efficient forces of their size anywhere in the world, and far superior in quality to the conscript armies of the Continent, they were much too small to accomplish any major mission of war against a "nation in arms." Consequently, Great Britain, going to war in August 1914, was unable to make a major military effort in France until July 1916; and the United States, going to war in April 1917, fought its first major battle in France in September 1918.

Effects of World War II. A similar situation prevailed in World War II. Great Britain came to the brink of war in the summer of 1939 in no better military condition than in 1914; and the United States, precipitated into war by the Japanese bombing of Pearl Harbor in December 1941, did not achieve a full-scale military effort in Europe until the summer of 1944. World War II destroyed the military systems of Germany and of Japan, which alone of the Asiatic states had adopted the "nation in arms" system. It likewise wrecked, through defeat and occupation, the military system of France and of several other European states. American and British armies demobilized as soon as the war ended.

In 1948, the only major "nation in arms" was the Soviet Union. Two of Russia's satellite states, Poland and Yugoslavia, had armies of the same type, under closely linked Russian supervision. Other satellite armies were limited by treaty or were less closely controlled from Moscow.

But by 1950 the armies of Western Europe were reviving under the tensions of the cold war and the impetus of substantial American aid. The tendency was toward the creation of temporary covering forces kept at something like full strength while the "nation in arms" system was rebuilt behind this shield. The United States, Great Britain, and Canada, associated with the western European powers (France, Italy, Belgium, Holland, Luxembourg, Denmark, Norway, Iceland, and Portugal) in the North Atlantic Treaty Organization, contributed substantial forces. In 1951, Turkey and Greece were admitted to membership in N.A.T.O. and the treaty limitations on Italian armament were set aside. A more far-reaching step was taken in February 1952, when the North Atlantic Council meeting at Lisbon, Portugal, voted unanimously for the creation of a "European army" to include French, Belgian, Dutch, Luxembourg, and Italian units with which troops of the West German Federal Republic were to be associated under a common command and wearing a common uniform. Outside of N.A.T.O., Spain and Sweden retain the "nation in arms" system in full operation, and the Swiss still have their formidable citizens militia.

The British have retained conscription since the end of World War II. While the withdrawal of British troops from India, Pakistan, Palestine, and Burma has reduced the extent of British overseas commitments, others have arisen in Egypt, Malaya, Hong Kong, and Korea, together with a sharp increase in the number of British troops in Germany as part of the N.A.T.O. covering force. At the close of 1951 almost all of the British regular army was serving outside the United Kingdom.

The United States has been forced to resume Selective Service on a two-year basis, and the Korean crisis compelled the mobilization of considerable elements of the National Guard and Organized Reserve. In February 1952, a plan for a system of universal military training to provide a steady flow of basically trained recruits was again being considered by Congress.

The treaty of peace with Japan (1951) opens the way for a limited revival of Japanese defense forces.

Characteristics of Modern Armies. In general, the modern army, even more than the army of World War I, is a collection of specialists and small, highly trained units armed with weapons of a power almost unimaginable even twenty years ago. Fire power and mobility still rule the battlefield, but the modern army possesses fire power and mobility to a very high degree indeed. The semiautomatic rifle and the light machine gun are replacing the bolt-action repeater. Even the smallest infantry "teams" have both automatic and high-angle weapons. The recoilless rifle has given infantry a hand-carried weapon superior in striking power to cannon of World War I that were drawn by a tractor or six horses. The range and rate of fire of artillery has been enormously increased, and all artillery is now either self-propelled or motor-drawn. The horse has vanished from the battlefield, and there is an increasing tendency for all ground troops to be either motorized or air-borne; the development of air-borne tactics threatens to do away with the importance of terrain obstacles, once the very framework of tactical patterns.

The organization of the modern army is concerned with the grouping and co-ordination of these fast-moving and powerful weapons to produce the maximum effect, allowing for flexibility to meet ever varying conditions and a quick-moving enemy. Even the World War II distinctions between infantry divisions and armored divisions are fading, as more tanks are given to infantry divisions and more infantry to armored divisions.   G. F. E.

ORGANIZATION OF UNITED STATES ARMY

Basic Units. The modern organization of the ground army is based on the battle-tested standard measuring stick, the "division," which is the smallest tactical and administrative unit containing combined arms.

Infantry organization begins with the nine-man rifle squad. Three rifle squads, with a weapons squad, form a rifle platoon. Three such platoons form a rifle company, plus a weapons platoon. This platoon includes a mortar section and the 57-mm. recoilless gun section. Three rifle companies and a

heavy weapons company with heavy machine guns and 81-mm. mortars, form a rifle battalion. Three rifle battalions compose a rifle regiment, which also includes a company of heavy mortars and a tank company.

Three of these regiments together, adding the division artillery and service units, establishes the ground organizational fighting unit, the infantry division. The basic unit of artillery is the battery of six guns. Three or four batteries form a battalion, and the artillery of a normal infantry division includes four battalions. If it is an airborne division, certain attachments, such as radar units and parachute maintenance units, are added and heavy equipment is deleted. If it is an armored division, three combat commands, each with a tank battalion, one or two armored infantry battalions, and supporting artillery and other units, are substituted for the regiments to form a balanced fighting unit, a division.

The infantry division contains about 18,500 troops at war strength, and includes, organically, in addition to the basic combat units mentioned, antiaircraft, tanks, engineer and medical units, and its own signal, military police, ordnance, quartermaster, and reconnaissance units of company size.

Modernization since World War II has resulted in the addition of armor to the infantry division, and in the case of the armored division infantry units have been increased. In the airborne division, the basic infantry division concept has been maintained, with the exception that certain heavy equipment has been deleted, as well as the personnel for that equipment. The new air-borne division is completely air-transportable.

Above the ground-division level is the corps. The corps is a tactical headquarters, and concerns itself with administration only when absolutely necessary, or when pertaining to its own corps troops. A typical corps is a flexible unit and may consist of any number of divisions, the usual number being from two to four, depending entirely upon its mission. The modern corps headquarters is of moderate size, comprising approximately 70 officers and a detachment of approximately 100 enlisted men. To maintain itself in the field, it has a headquarters company. The corps does not have organic service troops. The signal, military police, and ordnance units are attached and detached as necessary. A corps artillery headquarters, which is designed to command and utilize heavy field guns as attached, usually from army artillery, is organic to the corps.

The army headquarters is much better known to the layman than the corps headquarters. The function of these headquarters is that of higher command, and the issuing of combat missions and objectives to the several corps under their command. The army is an administrative headquarters and as such, controls and influences to a large extent the logistical impetus in battle. A typical army will ordinarily consist of two or more corps, and a considerable number of administrative and service troops.

The army group will normally command two or more armies in combat operations. While units from the army level down to the squad are organized under standard tables of organization, such is not the case with the army groups and higher. The army group is a flexible unit, and its size is entirely dependent upon its mission and the number of troops which it controls. Like a corps, it is a tactical unit. The army group considers over-all strategy on the battlefield and determines strategic orders and over-all objectives.

Department of the Army. The Department of the Army, under the National Security Act of 1947, is charged with the administration of the ground forces of the United States. It retains most of the features of the former War Department, except that the Army Air Forces was transferred

A MASS PARACHUTE LANDING IN SOUTHERN FRANCE BY AMERICAN PARATROOPS DURING WORLD WAR II

to a Department of the Air Force. Both departments, together with the Department of the Navy, are to be supervised and co-ordinated by the Secretary of Defense.

The Secretary of the Army, under the direction of the Secretary of Defense, represents the President, who is Commander in Chief of the Armed Forces. The Chief of Staff is the immediate advisor to the Secretary of the Army on all army matters and is charged by law with the planning, development, and execution of the military program. The Chief of Staff commands all components of the Army of the United States and is responsible to the Secretary of the Army for the co-ordination and direction of the Department of the Army general and special staffs. He is a member of the Joint Chiefs of Staff and of the War Council.

The Chief of Staff directs the activities of the Army General Staff, assisted by a Vice Chief of Staff, a Deputy Chief of Staff for Administration, a Deputy Chief of Staff for Plans, and the Comptroller of the Army. These, with the Secretary of the Army and the Under and Assistant Secretaries, form the Army Policy Council.

Below the Deputy Chiefs of Staff are four Assistant Chiefs of Staff, as follows: G-1, Personnel; G-2, Intelligence; G-3, Operations; and G-4, Logistics. Functioning under broad directives laid down by the President, the Secretary of Defense, the Secretary of the Army, and the Chief of Staff, these officers supervise at the Army Department level the over-all policies of the Army within their respective spheres of responsibility.

Operating below the General Staff level are a number of special, technical and administrative staff agencies. The Chief of Information and the Chief of Legislative Liaison work directly under the Chief of Staff. The special staff includes the Chief of the National Guard Bureau, the Executive for Reserve and R.O.T.C. Affairs, the Inspector General, the Chief of Military History, the Judge Advocate General, and the Chief of Finance.

The Technical and Administrative Services, which operated under the Army Service Forces during World War II, are operated in a staff relationship similar to that of the special staff divisions. Their chiefs, however, are commanders as well as staff officers. Their command responsibility lies principally in their training and procurement functions. They are charged with the training of their particular type of personnel and operate their own schools, over which they retain command. In addition, these chiefs carry out procurement functions, and in some cases, operate procurement facilities, such as arsenals. They include the Adjutant General (administration, records, personnel matters), the Quartermaster General (supply), the Chief of Transportation, the Chief of Ordnance, the Chief of Engineers, the Chief Signal Officer, the Surgeon General, and the Chief of the Chemical Corps.

The activities of the Department of the Army are integrated with the activities of the agencies, which were established during World War II for over-all command, such as the Joint Chiefs of Staff. It is the responsibility of the Chief of Staff to carry out the decisions of the Joint Chiefs of Staff as far as they affect the army; the General Staff, in turn, is charged with implementing decisions of the Chief of Staff.

Peacetime Territorial Organization. The continental United States is known in military terms as the Zone of the Interior. It is divided into six army areas, with headquarters as follows: First Army, Governors Island, New York; Second Army, Fort Meade, Maryland; Third Army, Atlanta, Georgia; Fourth Army, San Antonio, Texas; Fifth Army, Chicago, Illinois; Sixth Army, San Francisco, California.

These army headquarters, trimmed to as efficient a peacetime organization as possible, consistent with the work load, command all ground units within their military boundaries and take charge of the civilian components program throughout the United States. In addition, they are adequately prepared to conduct field training and large-scale maneuvers during summer and winter training periods.

Situated within these army areas and their coterminous air-defense areas, under the Department of the Air Force, are the separate installations directly under the command of the chiefs of each respective Technical and Administrative Service. This organization is the foundation of the peacetime military establishment.

Distribution of the Army. At the end of World War II, the United States Army was reduced from a wartime "high" of about 8,200,000 officers and men (including the Army Air Forces) to 670,000 as of June 30, 1949. But the Korean War brought rapid expansion; a strength approaching 2,000,000 was reached in 1952.

This figure included a total of 20 divisions and 18 regimental combat teams, with supporting corps and army troops, antiaircraft artillery, and overhead and service units. On Dec. 31, 1951, the Seventh Army in Germany included the equivalent of 6 divisions, and the Eighth Army in Korea and Japan had 8 divisions plus a division of Marines. Other combat elements of the Army were stationed in Alaska, Iceland, the Hawaiian Islands, Okinawa, Berlin, Austria, Trieste, the Panama Canal Zone, and Puerto Rico. In the United States were 6 divisions and several regimental combat teams. The Anti-Aircraft Command in the United States was greatly expanded in 1951 and 1952, chiefly by federalization of National Guard anti-aircraft artillery units. *See also* ANTI-AIRCRAFT DEFENSE.

ORGANIZATION OF OTHER ARMIES

Canada. The Canadian Army consists of:

1. The Active Force, corresponding to the Regular Army in the United States. In 1952 its strength was 49,000 officers and men. It includes such famous units as the Royal Canadian Regiments, Princess Patricia's Canadian Light Infantry, and the Royal Twenty-second Regiment. Former cavalry units, such as the Royal Canadian Dragoons, and Lord Strathcona's Horse, are now armored regiments.

2. The Reserve Force, corresponding to the National Guard in the United States. Armory drills, special courses of instruction, and annual training in summer camps are provided. Reserve Force strength in 1952 was 47,000.

3. The Supplementary Reserve, corresponding to the Class "A" Organized Reserve units in the United States. The Supplementary Reserve provides the additional elements required to complete army organization on mobilization.

Officer candidates for active and reserve forces are trained in the Canadian Officers Training Corps, in which 4,110 men were enrolled during 1951-1952.

For home defense there is also the Reserve Militia, which receives little or no training in time of peace, except for such members as belong to officially recognized rifle associations.

The organization of units, drill, and technical training

are virtually identical with those of the British Army. The Chief of Staff of the Canadian Army is responsible to the Minister of National Defense for the military command and administration of the army. There are five regional commands, each under a general officer, with headquarters respectively at Halifax, Montreal, Oakville, Winnipeg, and Edmonton and additional "area headquarters" located at Quebec, Fredericton, London, Regina, and Vancouver.

During World War II the Canadian Army furnished three infantry divisions and two armored divisions, which fought with distinction in Italy and western Europe. A total of 709,007 officers and men served in the Canadian Army during the war, in addition to 21,618 members of the Canadian Women's Army Corps. Peak wartime strength was 481,500. Casualties in killed and wounded totaled 74,374.

As the result of the Korean crisis and Canada's responsibilities under N.A.T.O., the Active Force was greatly expanded in 1950-1951. A reinforced brigade group was sent to Korea, where it forms part of the British Commonwealth Division of the United Nations Command, and another reinforced brigade group went to Germany as Canada's contribution to the N.A.T.O. defense forces.

Great Britain. The basic unit of the British Army is the division, quite similar in organization to the American division and of similar types (infantry, armored, airborne). The administration of the Army is under the Secretary of State for War, a subordinate of the Minister of Defence. The Chief of the Imperial General Staff is the chief military officer. The United Kingdom is divided into territorial commands for administrative purposes. The principal overseas commands are the Middle East Command, the Far East Command, and the British Army of the Rhine (in Germany). At the close of 1951, 4 divisions (3 of them armored) were in Germany, with brigade groups in Berlin, Austria, and Trieste; about 3 divisions were in the Middle East; 1 division was in Malaya, plus a division largely composed of Gurkha troops; and 2 brigades were in Korea. Home defense was almost wholly left to the Territorial Army, which on mobilization could furnish, in 1952, 12 divisions— 9 infantry, 2 armored, and 1 airborne. In 1952, however, a new infantry division of regular troops was being formed in the United Kingdom. The anti-aircraft defense of the United Kingdom is also a responsibility of the Territorial Army, though the Anti-Aircraft Command is under Royal Air Force operational control.

Colonial defense forces (locally recruited) include the King's African Rifles in East Africa, the Royal West African Frontier Force, the Sudan Defense Force, and the Malay Regiment.

Union of Soviet Socialist Republics. The Soviet army organization is similar in principle to that of the United States as far as tactical units are concerned. The Minister of the Armed Forces is the administrative chief of all Soviet armed forces; there is a Chief of Staff and the usual staff officers and departments, as well as territorial commands. At the end of 1951 there were believed to be 175 active divisions, of which about 30 were armored. Most of these divisions were maintained at reduced strength.

G. F. E.

ARMY, UNITED STATES. *See* ARMY.

ARMY PERSONNEL. *See* MILITARY PERSONNEL.

ARND or **ARNDT, JOHANN** [ɑ'rnt] (1555-1621), German Lutheran theologian, was born in Edderitz, near Ballenstedt, Anhalt. He attended the University of Helmstedt in 1576, and subsequently the universities of Witten-

A pontoon bridge spans the Rhine River, at Arnhem, the Netherlands

berg, Strasbourg, and Basel. In 1582 he returned to Ballenstedt to become a teacher and the following year was appointed pastor at Badeborn, Anhalt. He was dismissed in 1590 for refusing to comply with certain doctrinal changes ordered by the Duke Johann Georg of Anhalt and moved to Quedlinburg. In 1599 he became pastor of St. Martin's Church in Brunswick and in 1608 pastor at Eisleben. In 1611 he was appointed General Superintendent of the Lüneburg church system at Celle. He produced the first volume of *Vom wahren Christenthum* in 1605 (*True Christianity,* 1646), and completed the work in 1609. It aroused some controversy, for Arnd asserted that the orthodox doctrines were insufficient and that the true Christian ideal consisted of a mystical union of the soul with God. He was thus a precursor of Pietism. Among his other works, *Paradiesgaertlein aller christlichen Tugenden* (1612) (*The Garden of Paradise,* 1716) is most worthy of note. He died at Celle on May 11, 1621.   C. W. D.

ARNHEM [ɑ'rnhɛm], the capital city of the province of Gelderland, in the south central Netherlands, located on the right bank of the Lek River, a branch of the Rhine, at the foot of the diluvial hills of the Veluwe, a pleasant region of forests and moors which possesses great scenic beauty. It is situated at 51° 59′ N. lat. and 5° 55′ E. long., about 15 mi. southeast of Utrecht. The municipality of Arnhem, comprising also the village of Schaarsbergen, has an area of over 16,000 acres. It is a large communications center, with railroads to Utrecht, Nijmegen, Zevenaar (where lines cross to Germany), and Dieren (connecting Arnhem at this point with Apeldoorn and Zutphen). Near Westervoort, about 3 mi. southeast of the city, a railroad and motor vehicle bridge crosses the Geldersche Ijssel, and in 1948 there was a pontoon bridge across the Rhine River where the construction of a permanent bridge was planned.

Historically, Arnhem is not mentioned prior to the thirteenth century. It received city rights in 1233 and later be-

came a member of the Hanseatic League. Its further history was rather quiet until it was for a large part destroyed in World War II. In September 1944 Allied, chiefly British, parachute troops tried in vain to conquer the city and gain control of its strategic river crossings. Arnhem's ancient buildings—Devils House, Great Church, Eusebius Church, Walpurgus Church—were all heavily damaged. In 1948 they, like the rest of the damaged city, were in the process of restoration.

Arnhem is an administrative and military center and a large industrial city. Its industries produce steam engines, iron and copper, precision instruments, carriages, rayon, tin, leather, beer, and salt. There is also a shipbuilding yard. The city is the seat of the well-known Netherlands Heath Company, which is concerned with the reclamation of wasteland. In the summer Arnhem and its surroundings draw many tourists. The Netherlands Open Air Museum in the vicinity is a popular tourist spot, and the parks and forests near by are considered the finest in the Netherlands. Pop. 1952, 108,619.   B. L.

ARNICA, a large group of perennials of the family Compositae, mostly native to northwestern America. A few species are grown in gardens. The tough, brown rootstock of mountain arnica, *A. montana,* of northern and central Europe, yields tincture of arnica, a popular remedy for sprains and bruises. The flowers are dark, golden yellow on two-foot stems.   J. C. Wis.

ARNO, ARN or **AQUILA** [æ'kwɪlə] (c. 746-821), first archbishop of Salzburg and a leading churchman of the reign of Charlemagne, was born in Bavaria late in the first half of the eighth century. Ordained in 776, he was named bishop of Salzburg in 785. Although a Bavarian, he was a friend and perhaps a disciple of Alcuin, several of whose letters are addressed to him. In 787 Arno went to Rome as an agent of Tassilo III, Duke of Bavaria, and when, after

Tassilo's revolt and defeat, Charlemagne annexed Bavaria to his empire, the bishops of the country asked for Arno as primate. The emperor consented, and in 798 Pope Leo III gave Arno the pallium, with jurisdiction over Freising, Ratisbon, Passau, Neuburg, and Laibach. Arno held provincial synods at Riesbach in 799, 804, 807, and 810; he was also in charge of the missions in Kärnten and Pannonia, the latter province being then overrun by the Avars. In 799, Leo III fled the violence of his enemies at Rome and was received in Germany by Charlemagne, who had Arno and Archbishop Hildebald of Cologne accompany the pope to Rome, there to investigate the charges made against him. Arno's opinion seems to have been unfavorable to Leo, but the matter was finally referred to Charlemagne, who accepted the pope's disavowal of guilt. Arno also introduced the Carolingian Renaissance into Bavaria, where he assembled a library of 150 manuscripts and sent a number of students to Tours. He died Jan. 24, 821. E. A. R.

ARNO [ɑ'rno], the most important river in Tuscany and the second largest in peninsular Italy. It rises on the southern slopes of Monte Falterona in northeastern Tuscany, passes near Arezzo and through Florence and Pisa, and empties into the Tyrrhenian Sea about 8 mi. below Pisa. Its length is 163 mi. and the area of its basin 3,150 sq. mi. Upstream from Florence the valley of the Arno is narrow, but below it widens into a level and fertile plain. The volume of water fluctuates very greatly; in summer the stream appears nearly to dry up. It is navigable for light craft to Pontedera. The larger tributaries of the Arno, proceeding upstream, are the Era, Elsa, Bisenzio, Sieve, and Chiana, whose valley is drained by the Chiana Canal and contains in its upper reaches the small lakes of Montepulciano and Chiusi. R. G. W.

ARNOBIUS [ɑrno'biəs] (A.D. 300), Christian rhetorician and apologist, was born at Sicca in Numidia, Africa. He flourished during the reign of Diocletian. Arnobius was the author of the *Adversus Nationes,* also known as the *Adversus Gentes,* which he wrote, it was said, to convince his bishop of the sincerity of his conversion to Christianity. In this work, composed of seven books, he argued that the Christians were not to be blamed for the ills of the time, as the pagans argued they were, but that the ills were caused by pagan opposition to Christianity. The Christian doctrines of Arnobius are hardly to be called orthodox; for example, he held that heathen gods did exist, but that they were subordinate to the Christian God. The soul, which he did not believe to be the work of God but of subordinate beings, he did not consider immortal; he thought it capable of immortality only by virtue of special grace. The *Adversus Nationes* is, however, of very great historical value, for in it Arnobius described in great detail the religious practices, gods, and beliefs of the pagan Greco-Roman religions. The absence of scriptural references is to be noted in his work. His writings were listed as apocryphal. E. B. A.

ARNOLD, BENEDICT (1741-1801), American soldier and traitor, was born in Norwich, Conn., Jan. 14, 1741, the descendant of a distinguished New England family. Apprenticed to a druggist at the age of fourteen, he twice ran away to join the British colonial forces in the French and Indian War, but on one occasion deserted. At twenty-one he became a druggist and bookseller at New Haven, Conn., eventually venturing into profitable smuggling and speculation in the West Indies trade. With the outbreak of the Revolu-

tion, Arnold led a militia company to Cambridge, Mass. Commissioned a colonel, he shared with Colonel Ethan Allen leadership of the expedition that captured Fort Ticonderoga in the spring of 1775. That summer he led a force of his own and captured the fort at St. Johns. With Wash-

BENEDICT ARNOLD

ington's permission he undertook an attack on Canada via the Maine woods the following autumn. The march, made against great odds, failed because Arnold's force and another headed by General Richard Montgomery were so weakened that they were unable to capture Quebec. Nevertheless, the desperate effort gave the Americans another year to prepare for the British invasion of 1777. Retreating to Crown Point, Arnold got together a fleet of small vessels with which he met the British on Lake Champlain in 1776. Although he was defeated, his resistance helped to block the British plan to cut New England off from the middle colonies. The following year he successfully repulsed an attempted invasion of Connecticut by a British force under General Tryon. A few months later he was in the thick of battle at Saratoga, where he was wounded leading troops in the victory over General Burgoyne. After he was placed in command of Philadelphia in 1778, his career was less heroic. He adopted an extravagant manner of living and ran heavily into debt. He was nettled because he had been repeatedly passed over in the matter of promotion, and he entertained grievances against Congress and the civil authorities of Pennsylvania and Massachusetts. These factors led him to begin, in the spring of 1779 or earlier, a treasonable correspondence with the British, especially with Sir Henry Clinton. Arnold and his second wife, the former Peggy Shippen of Philadelphia, provided the enemy with data about American military plans and strength, for which they received payment. Arnold's plan to deliver West Point, which he then commanded, to the enemy in 1780 was detected, and he fled to the British in New York. A year later he led a British force in marauding his native Connecticut and then was transferred to Virginia. After Cornwallis' surrender, Arnold and his wife moved to England, where they were highly unpopular. He spent his last days in disgrace and want, frustrated in numerous projects for new military and commercial careers. He died in London, June 14, 1801. R. W., Jr.

ARNOLD, BION JOSEPH (1861-1942), American engineer, a pioneer in electric railroading, was born at Casnovia, near Grand Rapids, Mich., Aug. 14, 1861. He attended the University of Nebraska, 1879-1880, and graduated in 1884 from Hillsdale College in Michigan. He did graduate work there and at Cornell University. Arnold was chief designer for the Iowa Iron Works at Dubuque, Iowa, and a mechanical engineer with the Chicago and Great Western Railway, after which he became a consulting engineer at the Chicago office of the General Electric Company. He was assigned in 1893 to design and build the intramural elevated electric railway at the Chicago Exposition and in the same year organized the Arnold Engineering Company. In 1901 he was appointed by New York City to submit a plan for the electrification of railroad approaches to the city and in 1908 became a member of the New York City subway commission. He had been appointed consulting engineer to the city of Chicago in 1902 and was assigned to rebuild the city's street railways. He became chairman of the board of supervisors of Chicago's railway system in 1907. Arnold also served as consulting engineer to numerous railroads and cities in the United States. He was a member of Navy and Army advisory boards before and during World War I and served in the aviation section of the Signal Corps, attaining the rank of colonel. Arnold invented many devices for improvement of electrical railroad operation. He was president of the American Institute of Electrical Engineers, 1903-1904, and president of the Western Society of Engineers, 1906-1907. He died in Chicago, Jan. 29, 1942.   S. D.

ARNOLD, EDWIN (1832-1904), English author and journalist, was born on June 10, 1832, at Gravesend. In 1853 his first publication, *Poems Narrative and Lyrical,* appeared. Arnold received his bachelor's and master's degrees from Oxford University in 1854 and 1856 respectively and became principal in 1856 of a British college near Bombay. There he studied Indian, Turkish, and Persian languages and published *Education in India: a Letter* (1860) and a translation from Sanskrit, *The Book of Good Counsels* (1861). He returned to England in 1861 and for twenty-eight years did editorial work for the *Daily Telegraph.*

Arnold's extensive travels are reflected in many of his writings. His works include *India Revisited* (1886); numerous books of poetry, history, and travel inspired by the Near East, India, and Japan; and a novel of India, based on fact, *The Queen's Justice* (1899). His best-known work is *The Light of Asia* (1879), a colorful epic poem, in blank verse, of the life and teachings of Gautama. Arnold died in London, Mar. 24, 1904.   W. D. T.

ARNOLD, HENRY HARLEY (1886-1950), American general, was born at Gladwyne, Pa., on June 25, 1886. He was graduated from the United States Military Academy at West Point in 1907 and as a second lieutenant of infantry served in the Philippine Islands until October 1909. Soon after his return to the United States, Arnold was detailed to the aviation section of the Signal Corps. In June 1912, Lieut. Arnold established an altitude record—6,540 ft.—and won the Mackay Trophy in 1912 for a nonstop flight from College Park, Md., to Washington Barracks, D. C., to Fort Myer, Va., and return, a distance of 30 mi. In 1916 he was promoted to the rank of captain. He was the first to fly air mail and to observe artillery fire from a wireless-equipped plane. During World War I, he was assistant director, Office of Military Aeronautics, in command of 30 training schools, 15,000 officers, and 125,000 enlisted men. Arnold was graduated from the Army Industrial College in 1925 and from the Command and General Staff School in 1929. A lieutenant colonel in 1931, he commanded March Field, at Riverside, Calif. Arnold won a second Mackay Trophy in 1935 for his leadership of an Army Alaska flight in 1934. He

became assistant chief, Army Air Corps, in 1936; chief, as a major general, in 1938; deputy chief of staff for Air in 1941; and, as a lieutenant general, was appointed commander of all Army Air Forces in March 1942. In March 1943 he was made full general, with all flying services of the Army under his direction until his retirement in 1946.

During World War II, General Arnold was responsible for the organization, equipping, training, and general direction of the entire United States Army Air Corps and in this capacity was instrumental in building the largest and most powerful air force in the world. His air-force service covered the entire period of development of aviation from the first flight by the Wright Brothers at Kitty Hawk, N. C., to flights of thousands of powerful, fully armed war planes and commercial planes capable of transporting 200 or more passengers over long distances. For his leadership of a 77-hr. flight, from Brisbane to San Francisco in September 1942, General Arnold received the Distinguished Service Medal. He was also awarded the Distinguished Flying Cross and had the longest record of continuous flying in the army. He was author of the "Bill Bruce" series of aviation stories, of *Airmen and Aircraft* (1926), and in collaboration with General Ira Eaker, of *This Flying Game* (1936), *Winged Warfare* (1941), and *Army Flyer* (1942). General Arnold, a member of the National Defense Council, held the rank of permanent General of the Army and the rank of permanent General of the Air Force. He died near Sonoma, Calif., Jan. 15, 1950.   T. R.

ARNOLD, MATTHEW (1822-1888), English poet, critic, and essayist, was born Dec. 24, 1822, at Laleham. He was the eldest son of Dr. Thomas Arnold, who achieved fame as an historian and, from 1828 onward, as headmaster of Rugby. Matthew studied under an uncle at Laleham; was sent to Winchester School in 1836; attended Rugby from 1837 to 1841, where he wrote the prize poem *Alaric at Rome* (1840); and attended Balliol College, Oxford, from 1841 to 1844, where he wrote the Newdigate prize poem *Cromwell* (1843). He was elected a Fellow of Oriel College in 1845, taught at Rugby, and then served, from 1847 to 1851, as private secretary of the Marquis of Lansdowne, minister in charge of the administration of public instruction. Through Lord Lansdowne, Arnold was appointed inspector of schools, and he fulfilled the often arduous duties of the inspectorship from 1851 to 1886, undertaking, during the same period, two five-year terms (1857-1867) as Professor of Poetry at Oxford University. He died suddenly, of heart failure, in Liverpool, on Apr. 15, 1888.

The preceding brief account of Arnold's career clearly indicates his long concern with formal education. He was sent, moreover, on three official missions (in 1859, 1865, and 1885) to inspect formal methods of education on the Continent, and he published notable and influential reports on his findings. But in addition to these and other efforts in behalf of the schools, Arnold untiringly contributed to the education of his age in other directions. Little is known about his personal life, for he desired that no biography of him be written. In 1851 he married Frances Lucy Wightman, daughter of Judge Sir William Wightman, and the union was a happy one. Descriptions of Arnold's personal appearance indicate that he was broad-shouldered, almost burly, with a bronzed face that suggested his love of the outdoors, and a deep-toned, rich, well-modulated voice; his facial features, which were fine and strikingly aristocratic, presented an expression of kindly sympathy united with moral determination.

Arnold published *The Strayed Reveller and Other Poems by A.* in 1849, and three years later he brought out a second volume, similarly signed, entitled *Empedocles on Etna and Other Poems.* The second collection included two long poems, *Empedocles on Etna* and *Tristram and Iseult,* which contain eloquent lyrical and descriptive sections; it also included numerous sonnets and longer lyrics of great beauty, among them *A Summer Night, Self-Dependence,* and *The Buried Life. Poems by Matthew Arnold, A New Edition* (1853), Arnold's first signed work, has for its preface an essay which is justly famous in the history of literary criticism; in it Arnold urges that poetry should have nobility of subject, clarity of construction, and a dominant wholeness of impression. This volume included *Sohrab and Rustum* and *The Scholar-Gipsy. Poems . . . Second Series* (1855) included *Balder Dead.* In 1858 Arnold published the poetical tragedy *Merope,* written with the deliberate intention of shaping an English tragedy upon classical Greek lines; the effort was not especially successful, for the play lacks unity and intensity. *New Poems* (1867) included four notable elegies: *Rugby Chapel, A Southern Night, Thyrsis,* and *Stanzas from the Grande Chartreuse.* Arnold wrote little poetry after 1867, but collected editions of his poems appeared in 1869, 1877, 1881, and 1885. *Poetical Works of Matthew Arnold* was published posthumously in 1890. Although the poems do not bulk large in Arnold's total literary output, they possess for the most part vivid imagery, exactness and often superb simplicity of diction, sincerity, and restrained purposefulness.

Among the publications that resulted from Arnold's lectures at Oxford are *On Translating Homer* (1861), *On Translating Homer: Last Words* (1862), and *On the Study of Celtic Literature* (1867). In 1865 he published *Essays in Criticism,* in which he carried on an open campaign against narrowness and materialism, calling the combination "philistinism." From 1867 to the end of his career, he wrote almost exclusively on social problems, his articles making their first appearance in magazines. His services in this field were recognized by Gladstone, who in 1883, as Prime Minister, granted him an annual pension of £250. *Culture and Anarchy* (1869) presented Arnold's most famous articles, which promulgated his doctrine of "culture" as a striving after perfection in the employment of all four of the chief human passions or powers. Similar in general subject is his *Friendship's Garland* (1871), mostly a collection of letters published from 1866 to 1870 in the *Pall-Mall Gazette.* He wrote numerous articles on live religious topics, and collected them in *St. Paul and Protestantism* (1870), *Literature and Dogma: an Essay Towards a Better Apprehension of the Bible* (1873), *God and the Bible: a Review of Objections to "Literature and Dogma"* (1875), and *Last Essays on Church and Religion* (1876). Other volumes, which collected Arnold's further remarks on literature and social-ethical problems, included *Mixed Essays* (1879), *Irish Essays and Others* (1882), *Discourses in America* (1885), *Essays in Criticism, Second Series* (1888), *Civilization in the United States* (1888), and *Essays in Criticism, Third Series* (1910). *Discourses in America* contained lectures Arnold gave in America during a profitable tour in 1883 and 1884.

Arnold's poetry and, especially, his prose have contributed to establish his fame as a maker of felicitous and memorable phrases. His prose, whether directed to literature, politics, social problems, education, or religion, is generally vigorous and tactful, talkative and impressive, urbane and pleasing, yet always insistent that every one develop an unrestricted concern for the best both in literature and in living. Among the qualities which have contributed to his high reputation as an author may be mentioned the extraordinary clarity of his style and the skill with which he applied principles which

MATTHEW ARNOLD

BROWN BROTHERS

were drawn from a wide culture to the problems of contemporary life. *See also* BALDER DEAD; SOHRAB AND RUSTUM; THYRSIS.   W. D. T.

ARNOLD, THOMAS (1795-1842), English clergyman, educator, headmaster of Rugby School, England, and father of the poet Matthew Arnold, was born in Cowes, Isle of Wight, June 13, 1795. When sixteen, he entered Corpus Christi College at Oxford on a scholarship. Four years later he was selected a fellow of Oriel College, Oxford, where he spent four years. Arnold's early views were directed to the Church, and in 1818 he took deacon's orders. A year later he left Oxford University and settled in Laleham, where he later married. While in Laleham he prepared students for universities and devoted much of his time to studying the Classics and writing. In 1828 Arnold became headmaster of Rugby and gained for that school a wide reputation as a builder of body, mind, and spirit. He continued his literary activities and took a vital interest in public and ecclesiastical affairs. Among his best works are *Roman History* (uncompleted), *Sermons,* and his edition of Thucydides. In 1841 he left his position at Rugby and became professor of history at Oxford, where he remained until his death, June 12, 1842. He was buried under the communion table in the chancel of Rugby Chapel.   A. S. M.

ARNOLD, a manufacturing community of approximately 442 acres located in the metropolitan area of Pittsburgh, lies on the Allegheny River in Westmoreland Co., southwestern Pennsylvania. It was incorporated as a borough in 1896 and as a city in 1936 and is governed by a mayor and council. Arnold is served by the Pennsylvania Railroad. Glass and aluminum production are among its principal industries. Pop. 1950, 10,263.

ARNPRIOR, a town in Renfrew Co., Ontario, Canada, located at the confluence of the Madawaska and Ottawa rivers, 40 mi. west of the city of Ottawa, on the Trans Canada Highway. Founded as a mill site by Scottish colonists in 1831, it became a village in 1862, and was incorporated as a town in 1892. The Canadian Pacific and Canadian National railways serve the town. Its manufactures include felts, blankets and other woolens, office furniture, and building materials. Pop. 1951, 4,381.   D. F. P.

ARNSTEIN, KARL [ɑ'rnstain] (1887-   ), Czech airship designer, was born in Prague on Mar. 24, 1887, and obtained the degree of doctor of engineering at the University of Prague. His early work in stress analysis in Strasbourg won the attention of the Zeppelin company in Friedrichshafen, Germany, with which he worked from 1915 to 1924, leaving as chief engineer to join the Goodyear Tire and Rubber Company in the United States. He was a director and vice president in charge of engineering of the Goodyear-Zeppelin Corporation from 1924 to 1939 and since 1939 has been a director, vice president, and chief engineer of the Goodyear Aircraft Corporation. He has designed about seventy airships, and his designs for two large rigid airships won competitions held by the United States Navy. He directed the construction of the *Akron* and the *Macon,* begun in 1926 for the United States Navy, and supervised the design and construction of the large airship dock at Akron. His techniques of stress analysis, which were first applied to bridges and to the cathedral at Strasbourg and later to rigid airships, have been applied to airplane materials and structures. He has contributed numerous articles to the technical press.

M. H. Sm.

ARNULF [ɑ'rnulf] (c.850-899), German king and Holy Roman emperor, the illegitimate son of Carloman, King of Bavaria and Italy. At the death of his father in 880 he inherited Carinthia, and in 887 forced the abdication of Charles the Fat and was himself elected King of Germany (Ostfranken). He defeated the Normans at Löwen-on-the-Dyle in 891, and from 892 to 893 waged an indecisive campaign against Zwentibold (Zvatorpluk), Prince of Moravia, and Rudolph of Burgundy, who sought to assert their independence. In 894, at the request of Pope Formosus, he marched into Italy and fought Guido of Spoleto, who menaced the Pope and disputed Arnulf's claim to power in Italy. He was forced to retire, owing to severe military losses, but the following year returned, defeated Guido, and in 896 was crowned emperor by Formosus. He died in Regensburg, Dec. 8 (or Nov. 29), 899, and was succeeded by Louis the Child, his legitimate son and the last of the Carolingians in Germany.

C. W. D.

AROE or **ARU** [ɑ'ru], an island group in the Moluccas between New Guinea and Australia, 134° 40′ E. long., 6° S. lat.; area, 3,244 sq. mi. The islands are mostly of coral formation and are covered with virgin forest. Sago palms, coconut trees, and casuarinas flourish. There are many wild pigs. Agricultural products are rice, tobacco, and sugar cane. The natives also catch and sell the feathers of the abundant birds of paradise and engage in pearl and shark fishing. Tanabesar, the largest island, is 122 mi. from north to south and 58 mi. at its maximum width, but three wide, shallow channels practically split it into six parts. There are also about a hundred islets in the group. On one of these, west of Tanabesar, is Dobo, the seat of government and a trading town. The Royal Packet Navigation Company connects the islands with New Guinea. The population is estimated at 20,000, including about 600 Chinese, who are in charge of most of the trade. The majority of the natives, of Papuan race, are pagans. Before World War II the Aroes were part of the residency of Amboina in the Netherlands Indies. From 1942 to 1945 they were under Japanese occupation, the Dutch returning at the end of World War II. By the Cheribon Agreement of Mar. 25, 1947, the Aroes became the easternmost part of the autonomous state of East Indonesia, geographically the largest unit of the Republic of Indonesia.

AROIDS. *See* Arum.

AROMATIC COMPOUNDS. *See* Organic Chemistry; Petroleum.

ARONSON, NAOUM [a'rənsən] (1872-1943), Russian sculptor, was born at Kreslavka, Russia, in 1872. He studied at the Vilna Art School. Aronson refused the Russian Minister of Public Instruction's offer to send him to art school in St. Petersburg and studied in Berlin and briefly at L'École des Arts Décoratifs, Paris. He resided in Paris for fifty years. He executed the only bust for which Grigori Rasputin posed. His bronze bust of Ludwig van Beethoven was placed before the composer's birthplace in Bonn. Both this work and his portrait-bust of Count Leo Tolstoy (c. 1910) illustrate Aronson's intuitive and reasoning comprehension of temperament. His bust of Louis Pasteur won a French government-sponsored nation-wide contest upon the occasion of Pasteur's centenary (1923). This bust, a good likeness and an indubitable work of art, is in the Institut Pasteur in Paris. For his bas-relief, *France and Her Colonies,* displayed at the Paris World Exposition of 1937, Aronson received the Officers' Cross of the Legion of Honor. France also appointed him chevalier, Société des Amis de la Musique Juive. Other notable works were bronze busts of Foch and Lenin; a nude female figure, *Mystic Silence* (Salon of 1912, Beaux Arts); bust of a peasant woman, *Old Silesienne* (Leningrad); *Adolescence,* a group; marble bust, *The Martyr* (Leningrad); *Angel's Head;* bronze bust of Turgenev; *A Symbolic Figure of Russia,* a bronze male figure; bust, *The Slav Thinker;* marble, *Maiden from Vendée* (Paris); marble statue, *The Drowned Lovers;* bronze bust, *The Ancient;* and several marble portrait-busts of youths. He designed a fountain in the Place de la Concorde, Paris. Aronson left Paris in 1940 and reached the United States in 1941. Critics called him the successor of Rodin. He died in New York City Sept. 30, 1943.

T. R.

AROOSTOOK WAR [əru'stuk], a boundary dispute that almost led to war between Maine and New Brunswick in February 1839. The boundary agreed upon in the Treaty of Paris, 1783, had been based on faulty geographic knowledge and could not be drawn. Lumbermen advancing from either side into the Aroostook Valley, in the disputed area, came into conflict. All attempts at settlement, even arbitration in 1831 by the king of the Netherlands, failed. Incidents in 1837 and 1838 caused the two legislatures to make large defense appropriations and to send armed forces to the border. Irregular bands, active on both sides, even captured some prisoners. Before any real disaster occurred, however, General Winfield Scott of the United States Army succeeded in settling difficulties by negotiation. His peace proposals were accepted by the lieutenant-governor of New Brunswick, Sir John Harvey. The boundary was finally determined satisfactorily in the Webster-Ashburton Treaty of 1842.

D. G. G. K.

ARPEGGIO [ɑrpɛ'jo], in music, the playing of any chord in harp fashion—that is, with each tone succeeding the other in rising sequence. In notation, the arpeggio may be indicated by a wavy line placed before the chord, or it may be written out in grace notes. Written in ordinary notes and played in strict time, the arpeggio is a favorite form of piano or harp accompaniment to a melody.

W. Li.

ARPHAXAD [ɑrfæ'ksæd], in the Old Testament, the third son of Shem and grandson of Noah. Arphaxad was the grandfather of Eber, lineal ancestor of Abraham and traditionally the ancestor of the Hebrew people, thus linking the Hebrew people to Shem. Some critics maintain that Arphaxad also designates a name of a people or a region near Armenia and ancient Assyria, the native lands of the Chaldeans, in whose country Abraham was born.

Arphaxad is also the name of the king of the Medes, in the first chapter of the Book of Judith, against whom King Nebuchadnezzar waged war. Arphaxad was defeated and killed by Nebuchadnezzar. A number of attempts have been made to identify him with various known kings of the Medes—Deioces, Astyges, or Ahasuerus, the last king of the independent Medes. M. A. G.

ARRAH [ɑ′rrɑ], a city in northeastern India and the headquarters of the Shahabad District, located on the Ganges Plain, between the Ganges and Son rivers in the western part of Bihar State, 33 mi. west of Patna. The city is in a famous rice-growing region; barley, corn, sugar cane, and linseed are also grown. During the Sepoy Mutiny, in 1857, Arrah was the scene of a bitter struggle between British contingents and the local chieftain Baba Kuer Singh, leading a strong force of natives. Pop. 1951, 64,205.

ARRAN [æ′rən], an island in Buteshire, Scotland, on the Firth of Clyde, 19 mi. long and from 8 to 10½ mi. wide, with an area of 166 sq. mi. The surface in the northwest is mountainous; the highest elevation, Goatfell, is 2,866 ft. above sea level. The mountainous terrain is well known for rare botanical specimens, and the island is of unusual geological interest. It also has prehistoric stone circles and relics of Viking invasions. Robert the Bruce landed on Arran in 1302 and from there went to Turnberry to begin the fight for Scottish freedom. Today dairying, potato growing, and fishing are the chief occupations, and tourism is important. Pop. (est. 1952), 4,450.

ARRAS [a′rɑ′s; æ′rəs], the capital of the department of Pas-de-Calais in northern France, located 112 mi. north of Paris on the Scarpe River. Before the Roman rule, Arras was the principal town of the Atrebates tribe. Its history is linked with that of Artois, of which it was the chief town. Its Burgundian inhabitants were banished by Louis XI of France, when the town was ceded to him in 1182. In 1493 the city was given to Maximilian of Austria and remained under the rule of the Hapsburgs until 1640, when it was taken by the French. During the Middle Ages the city was famous for its rug works and tapestries, especially for a type of tapestry hanging which brought the word "arras" into use. The city was the birthplace of the famous revolutionist Maximilien de Robespierre. During World War I, the city was the scene of fierce combat, and was virtually destroyed in a campaign in the spring of 1917, although it remained in Allied hands. In World War II, the Germans captured the city in 1940, and the British army liberated it in August 1944. The city's industries include flour mills, oil refineries, and metalworking plants. Pop. 1954, 36,242. S. Van V.

ARRAS, BATTLE OF, a battle marking the beginning of the Allied spring offensive on Apr. 4, 1917, in World War I. It was decided that the British, under General Sir Douglas Haig, were to attack in the Arras region of France. To the south, the French also were to engage in the offensive. After four days of heavy bombardment, the British infantry on April 9 made great gains. But the weather was on the side of the Germans. Rainfall made the ground muddy, slowing down the Allied advance, while the Ger-

COURTESY OF FRENCH EMBASSY, INFORMATION DIVISION
LA PETITE PLACE, ARRAS, FRANCE

mans were able to bring up reserves and strengthen their lines. To the south, the French attack did not go well. The British continued their attacks mainly to divert troops from the French sector. The engagement came to an end May 4. Many prisoners were taken, but the British losses were severe, over 130,000 casualties in all. The Allies gained the major objectives around Arras, but the battle was not a success, owing to the weather, the failure of the French to the south, and the strength of the German reserves. M. K.

ARREST, in criminal law, is the taking of a person into custody that he may be held to answer for a crime. Primarily a law enforcement function of peace officers, arrests may be made by private persons as well under given conditions. Thus, at common law, both peace officers and private persons are authorized to make an arrest for a felony or breach of the peace committed in their presence; however, a peace officer possesses the additional right of making an arrest upon reasonable belief that a felony has been committed, and that the person arrested committed it, whereas the private person may justify an arrest upon reasonable belief only if a felony actually has been committed. When a peace officer executes a warrant of arrest, duly issued by a magistrate, the warrant itself is the officer's justification. Recent statutes have enlarged officers' rights to arrest without a warrant to include misdemeanors, and in some instances enlarged and in others further limited the arrest making powers of private persons. *See also* CRIMINAL LAW. H. Si.

ARRHENIUS, SVANTE AUGUST [arre′nɪʌs] (1859-1927), winner of the Nobel prize in chemistry for 1903 for his theory of electrolytic dissociation, was born at Wijk, near Uppsala, Sweden, Feb. 19, 1859, and died in Stockholm on Oct. 2, 1927. Showing great mathematical ability as a child, he attended the local schools at Uppsala, graduating from the university there in 1881. Afterward he went to Stockholm to study under Erik Edlund, who attempted to discourage Arrhenius from the pursuit of chemistry. In 1884 his thesis was accepted with little enthusiasm, although it was this same dissertation which subsequently won for him the Nobel prize. Shortly thereafter, a copy of his thesis reached Wilhelm Ostwald in Riga. Ostwald's reputation as a first-class physical chemist was already established, and in him the young Arrhenius found a staunch champion. Had it not been for the espousal of the Arrhenius theory by Ostwald, it might well have been completely rejected. Following a visit to Uppsala by Ostwald, Arrhenius worked in the latter's laboratory at Riga for a year. By 1887 the electrolytic theory had been sufficiently completed for a careful exposition, which appeared in the first volume of the *Zeitschrift für physikalische Chemie*. At this time, the young Dutch chemist J. H. van't Hoff joined Ostwald and Arrhenius. It is said that this publication ranks in importance with Madame Curie's announcement of her discovery of radium; yet hers was accorded instant approval and praise by the scientific world, whereas that of Arrhenius met with violent opposition and ridicule. Arrhenius presently moved to Amsterdam to work with van't Hoff, and later to Leipzig with Ostwald to continue his studies on this revolutionary hypothesis. To this famous laboratory flocked many scientists who were later to champion the theory of ions, which was to have a profound influence upon the chemical thinking of theoretical chemists during the first decade of the twentieth century. The adherents were dubbed "the wild army of ionians." Arrhenius met violent opposition by Mendeleev and his "hydrate" school, as well as by Kahlenberg and his students at Wisconsin. By 1925, Arrhenius' theory had been so extensively altered by the more exact treatment of Debye and Hückel that it was essentially outmoded, but it had served as a valuable groundwork.

From 1887 to 1902, Arrhenius was rector of the University of Stockholm. From 1891 to 1895, he was a lecturer there, and from 1895 to 1902, he served as professor. In 1904, he lectured on immunochemistry at the University of California. In 1905, he accepted the directorate of the Nobel Institute for Physical Chemistry at Experimentalfältet, near Stockholm, a position which he held until his death in 1927.

In spite of the many objections by his opponents, many honors were accorded Arrhenius. Besides the Nobel prize already mentioned, he was awarded the Davy medal in 1910, the Willard Gibbs medal in 1911, and the Faraday medal in 1914. He was a delegate to the Louisiana Purchase Exposition, St. Louis, in 1904, and was made a foreign member of the Royal Society (London) in 1910.

Arrhenius had a wide circle of friends who were always hospitably received in his laboratory. He was eagerly sought in scientific discussion groups, not only for his erudition but also for his humor and good-fellowship. His researches in the field of immunochemistry, notably in the chemistry of the toxins, were important. He originated the theory of the pressure of light. He was interested in astronomical problems, especially in the ever-popular question of life on Mars and other worlds, and included astrology within his range of active interests. *See also* ELECTROLYTES.   H. N. A.

ARRIAN (FLAVIUS ARRIANUS) [æ'riən] (c. A.D. 95-c. 180) was born in Nicomedia, Bithynia, Greece, before

A.D. 100. He belonged to a distinguished family and his father had received Roman citizenship. Arrian studied in Nicopolis in Epirus (near the modern city of Preveza) with the philosopher Epictetus, whose teachings he recorded and later published. He then went to Rome and entered upon a brilliant career under the emperor Hadrian. He was consul in A.D. 130 and later governor of Cappadocia but finally retired to Athens, where he received honorary citizenship, was chosen archon for the year 147-148, and died after 171-172. In Athens he wrote books and became known as the imitator of Xenophon. Following Xenophon, he wrote a hunting book, *Cynegeticus,* and an *Anabasis of Alexander;* his other works include the *Periplus of the Euxine,* studies on the Black Sea, and *Indica,* a study on India.   A. E. R.

ARROWHEAD, a genus, *Sagittaria,* of aquatic perennials of the water plantain family. Most of the approximately thirty species are found in temperate and tropical

Arrowhead, Sagittaria latifolia, in blossom

America, chiefly the northern part. Some are grown as ornamentals in shallow water for their attractive leaves, shaped like arrowheads, and showy three-petaled white flowers. The Chinese grow the Old World arrowhead, *S. sagittifolia,* for its edible starchy tubers. It is widespread in Europe and Asia, and grows 3 to 4 ft. tall. In California, the Chinese grow the similar broad-leafed plantain, *S. latifolia,* common in North America, known as the tule potato. It was formerly used as food by the Iroquois Indians. The South American giant arrowhead, *S. montevidensis,* is grown as an ornamental and is naturalized in California and the southeastern states.   J. C. Wis.

ARROWHEAD, the piercing point or head of an arrow. Among the Indian tribes of the New World, arrowheads were made of stone, antler, bone, fire-hardened wood, and occasionally metal. They were affixed to the shaft end by various techniques, usually involving binding with cord or sinew. There is a great range of size, from tiny flint points of ½ in. to the huge palmwood points, 2 or 3 ft. long, of some of the Indians of the tropical forests of South America. Popularly the term is applied to all projectile points, spear and dart as well as arrow tips. Projectile points of some sort were possessed by all American Indians from earliest to historic times.   G. R. W.

ARROWROOT, *Maranta arundinacea,* a perennial of the maranta family, native to South America, naturalized in southern Florida. Cultivated in the tropics for its starchy rootstock, it is an important source of commercial arrowroot and tapioca. The plant grows to 6 ft., with long, pointed leaves and small, scattered white flowers. Starchy products obtained from various other plants are included under the general name arrowroot.   J. C. Wis.

ARROWWOOD, the common name of various North American trees or shrubs, the straight stems of which were used for arrow shafts by the Indians. One example is *Vi-*

Flowers and fruits of Arrowwood, Viburnum dentatum

burnum dentatum (honeysuckle family) widely found in moist ground from New Brunswick to South Carolina. From its roots grow numerous slender straight stems. J. C. Wis.

ARROYO DEL RIO, CARLOS ALBERTO [arro'yo thel ri'o] (1893-   ), statesman, educator, and president of Ecuador, was born at Guayaquil on Nov. 27, 1893. He was graduated from the University of Guayaquil and received the degree of doctor of jurisprudence in 1914. He was appointed secretary of the board of education of the province of Guayas in 1913 and in 1917 he became secretary of the council of the canton of Guayaquil. A year later Arroyo became a member of the Provincial Board of Education and was a member of the Board of Public Welfare in 1920. In 1921 and 1922 he was head of the canton of Guayaquil.

Arroyo's career as an educator began when he was offered a chair of sociology at the University of Guayaquil in 1918, later being appointed professor and dean of civil law and rector of the university. In 1922 and 1923 he was elected to the national legislature from the province of Guayas and then became president of the Chamber of Deputies. In 1924 he was elected to the Senate. When, on Nov. 17, 1939, President Mosquera Narvaez died, Arroyo was president of the Senate and in that capacity became acting president. He was nominated as the presidential candidate of the Liberal Party in 1939, a nomination he had refused at previous elections. He was elected president of Ecuador on Jan. 12, 1940. Throughout his career Arroyo championed democracy and Pan-Americanism. In January 1942 his country broke diplomatic relations with the Axis powers. He was forced to resign on May 29, 1944, by revolutionary forces supporting former president José Velasco Ibarra, who assumed power in Ecuador on May 31, 1944. Arroyo resumed his teaching in 1944.   S. D.

"ARSENAL OF DEMOCRACY," a term used by President Franklin D. Roosevelt to describe the World War II role of the United States prior to Pearl Harbor. In a radio speech on Dec. 29, 1940, the President declared that the victory of Great Britain over Nazi Germany was essential to the defense of the United States; therefore the United States must become "the arsenal of democracy," from which to supply Great Britain and her allies with war materials and equipment. This was to be done even at the risk of retarding the United States' own armament program. The domestic economy was drastically reorganized by a number of governmental agencies working in co-operation with the Lend-Lease Administration, which came into existence on March 11, 1941.   R. W., Jr.

ARSENIC [a'rsənɪk], symbol As, a steel-grey, brittle, crystalline chemical element which is a member of Group V-A of the periodic table. This group begins with the typical nonmetal nitrogen and ends with bismuth, which is almost wholly metallic in nature. The third member of the group, arsenic, is somewhat amphoteric, but its nonmetallic properties are much more pronounced than its metallic characteristics. It resembles the metals in appearance and forms some valuable alloys, but it forms the negative ions $AsO_3^{\equiv}$ and $AsO_4^{\equiv}$ characteristic of a nonmetal.

Properties. *Physical.* Arsenic is obtained as a by-product of the smelting of ores, particularly those of copper, lead, and iron. It is almost wholly lacking in ductility, malleability, tensile strength, and ability to conduct heat and electric current. When heated, it begins to show a definite vapor tension at 100° and sublimes readily at 615° C. Its vapor has a faint yellowish color and an odor resembling garlic. The density of the vapor at 644° C. indicates that the molecule is As_4. At higher temperatures the molecules dissociate, and at 1,700° C. the formula is As_2. There are three solid allotropes, but only the gray, brittle mass is stable at room temperature.

PROPERTIES OF ARSENIC

Atomic number	33
Atomic weight	74.91
Stable isotopes	75
Density (g./ml.) 15° C.	5.7
Melting Point (36 atm.) °C.	814
Specific Heat (cal./g.)	0.082
Linear coefficient of thermal expansion (10-90° C.)	3.86
Hardness (Mohs' scale)	3.5
Electrical Resistivity (microhm-cm.) 0° C.	35

Chemical. Arsenic tarnishes slowly in moist air and, when heated, begins to burn at about 180°, giving off a dense white smoke of the oxide As_2O_3. Arsenic can be made to combine directly with chlorine, bromine, iodine, and sulphur; it combines with some of the metals, forming arsenides. Arsenic dissolves in hydrochloric acid only in the presence of air, a behavior explained by the assumption that the formation of As_2O_3 as an intermediate compound is essential. Concentrated nitric acid attacks arsenic vigorously, giving arsenic acid, H_3AsO_4.

Alloys. A small amount of arsenic, usually less than one per cent, appears in such alloys as arsenic bronze and speculum metal. In the manufacture of shot, if 0.5 per cent of arsenic is added to molten lead, the fluidity of the metal is increased, giving more nearly spherical drops as it falls in the shot tower. When solidified, the lead is hardened by the arsenic, so that the shot has greater penetration in use. Arsenic added to brass increases its fluidity; the tensile strength, rigidity, hardness, and resistance to corrosion of various alloys are increased by a small addition of arsenic.

Compounds. Arsenic forms compounds in which its valence ranges from -3 to $+5$, with the exception of -1. Its water soluble compounds are toxic. The treatment for arsenic poisoning is to produce vomiting, then to give milk or white of egg. In small doses, arsenic compounds are valuable in medicine for the treatment of disease of the skin and respiratory organs. They are also used in pigments, in printing and dyeing calico, in tanning leather, for preserving hides and museum specimens, in glass manufacturing, and for protecting crops against insect enemies.

Arsine. Arsine, AsH_3, is a colorless gas produced when a soluble arsenic compound is put into a flask in which hydrogen is being generated. Although the formula of arsine suggests a close relationship to ammonia (NH_3), there is little resemblance, since arsine is only slightly soluble in cold water, has no basic properties, and is easily decomposed by heat. Arsine is intensely poisonous. Some of its derivatives are: diphenylchlorarsine, $(C_6H_5)_2AsCl$, known as "sneeze gas"; arsphenamine, or salvarsan, and neoarsphenamine, or neosalvarsan, effective in the treatment of syphilis, relapsing fever, Hodgkin's disease, and Vincent's angina.

Halide. Arsenic trichloride, $AsCl_3$, a volatile colorless liquid, is formed by the direct union of the elements. When water is added it is completely hydrolyzed, and the resulting arsenious acid readily yields the anhydride, As_2O_3.

Sulphides. Arsenic forms three sulphides, As_2S_2, As_2S_3, and As_2S_5. The disulphide is found in nature as the mineral realgar. The corresponding synthetic compound is used in pyrotechnics, especially Bengal fire. The trisulphide, As_2S_3, is the mineral orpiment; the synthetic compound is used in pyrotechnics and in dehairing skins in the production of leather. The pentasulphide, As_2S_5, not found in nature, is precipitated as a yellow powder when hydrogen sulphide is added to a solution of arsenic acid in concentrated hydrochloric acid. Its main use is as a pigment.

Oxides. Arsenious oxide, As_2O_3, is formed by burning arsenic or roasting arsenical ores. It is the most important compound of arsenic and is the substance commonly called white arsenic or by the simple name "arsenic." At ordinary temperatures it is a crystalline mass that sublimes at 125 to 150° C. This behavior is used to purify the material. Arsenious oxide is the anhydride of the weak arsenious acid, H_3AsO_3; salts of this acid, the arsenites, are valuable insecticides. Paris green contains copper arsenite, $Cu_3(AsO_3)_2$.

Arsenic oxide, As_2O_5, may be prepared by heating the trioxide in nitric acid. It is a white hygroscopic powder that dissolves in water, forming arsenic acid, H_3AsO_4. The arsenates are valuable insecticides, especially useful in destroying pests such as the gypsy moth and the boll weevil. *See also* PHOSPHORUS.   B. S. H.

ARSENIUS AUTORIANUS [ɑrsiʹniəs ɔtoʹrieʹnəs] (c. 1204-1264 or 1273), patriarch of Constantinople, was born in that city about 1204. He was educated at a monastery in Nicaea, and later lived in retirement at a monastery near Lake Apollonias in Bithynia. In 1254 he was summoned by the Emperor Theodore II Lascaris, who appointed him patriarch. When the Emperor died four years later, Arsenius became one of the two guardians of his son John. The other guardian was murdered by Michael Paleologus, who finally usurped the throne. Arsenius escaped, but was induced to return and resume his duties as patriarch. When Michael ordered that John Lascaris, the rightful heir to the throne, be blinded, Arsenius, conscience-stricken, excom-

municated the usurper. Michael, after vainly attempting to obtain the patriarch's pardon, had him deposed and exiled to the island of Proconnesus. There he died, Sept. 30, 1273. (According to Fabricius he died in 1264.) In 1268 a new patriarch was appointed at Constantinople. When he absolved the emperor, a schism was created in the Greek Church, known as the "Arsinian" schism. It lasted until 1315.   E. B. A.

ARSENOPYRITE [ɑrsənopaiʹrait], or Arsenical Pyrites, is the most widespread arsenic-bearing mineral. Its composition is iron arsenide-sulphide, $FeAsS$. Arsenopyrite is characterized by a silver-white color and an arsenical (garlic) odor when struck with a hammer. Crystals, when present, are pseudo-orthorhombic, with a pyramidal aspect. Arsenopyrite may be mined for its arsenic content, but it is more often exploited because of associated gold, silver, copper, or tin, in which case the arsenic may be obtained as a smelter by-product. Arsenopyrite is a typical high-temperature vein mineral. It is less commonly found in contact metamorphic deposits and pegmatites. Important localities for arsenopyrite include the Black Hills of South Dakota and Jardine, Montana. It is found in many other mining districts in the western states, in Bolivia, in Saxony, and in Cromwell, England.   K. K. L.

ARSINE. *See* ARSENIC.

ARSON, "the malicious and voluntary burning of the house of another by night or by day," is Lord Coke's common-law definition. Because this crime has such destructive force and so widely endangers human life, it was always regarded as a most serious offense and always, at common law, as a felony. Under the English statute of the reign of Henry VI, the willful burning of houses, under special circumstances, was branded as high treason. In early times the punishment was death, and in the reign of Edward I the sentence was executed by burning the guilty person to death. The statutes adopted in almost all jurisdictions define arson to include the burning of one's own home. In those states where statutes do not define arson, the common law is followed. The burning must be willful and malicious, otherwise it is only a trespass.   V. M.

ART, PHILOSOPHY OF, the branch of philosophy which deals with the theory of art creation, art experience, and art criticism. The term "aesthetics," which is sometimes used interchangeably with "philosophy of art," ordinarily covers not only philosophical but also psychological and technical inquiries in the field of art.

Nearly all of the great philosophers, from Plato and Aristotle on, have devoted attention to the function and value of art and the analysis of the art experience. Two problems in particular have occupied those who have sought philosophical understanding of art: (1) the determination of the nature of the impulse to art creation and enjoyment, with a view to distinguishing artistic activity from other spheres of human interest, and (2) the determination of artistic standards of value and bases of criticism, especially the determination of the significance and proper application of such terms as "beauty," "ugliness," "sublimity," and "gracefulness."

The two problems are not independent of each other. Indeed, there are those who define art creation as the production of the beautiful. Other writers, however, insist that the fundamental concern of the artist is to make his creations vivid or effective or expressive, and that his concern with beauty is incidental. Perhaps art creation is most commonly interpreted as the expression or communication of the feelings or insights or values that the artist finds within his own experience.

The nature of such expressive activity, however, is variously interpreted by opposing schools of theorists. Thus emotionalist writers, following the lead of Tolstoy, interpret art as the language of the emotions. Croce and the members of the idealist school of aestheticians think of art as the expression of intuitions, of images and impressions which are unique and individual, the process of expression occurring entirely within the mind—so that the physical work of art is merely a kind of memorandum or reproduction of the mental activity. Other theorists, appealed to particularly by the abstractionist artists, maintain that the artist gives concrete expression to certain pure forms or relations, the significance of which lies in their internal organization alone and not in their content or their representative meaning.

In striking contrast to this last position is the theory of the contextualists, like John Dewey, who see art as so closely integrated with the life environment from which it arises, and within which it is enjoyed, that it can be understood only in terms of the social meanings inherent in it. Related to this view are those theories which interpret artistic experience as the fulfillment of wishes, unconsciously harbored by the artist, and objectified, according to Freud's hypothesis, in a disguised or sublimated form in the work of art. Mention should also be made of the play theory of art, which regards art creation as a sophisticated and serious manifestation of the play instinct, the conscious illusion of the artist replacing the unconscious make-believe of the child.

Theories of art criticism fall into two main groups which may be designated as objective and subjective respectively. Objective theories of criticism tend to regard beauty, or whatever quality is held to be valuable in the contemplation of art, as belonging to the art object in entire independence of the experience of the contemplator. Thus the excellence or artistic merit of a drama or a painting or a symphony would be an inherent quality of it and would simply be discovered by the discriminating awareness of the critic. Good taste would consist in the ability to perceive and enjoy the intrinsic excellence of such works of art. Objective definitions of beauty range from those that refer to it in mystical or religious terms to those that seek to reduce it to a mathematical formula.

Subjective theories of criticism define beauty in terms of the kind of response produced by the art object in the spectator. Such response may be evaluated in terms of its pleasantness, its vividness, its coherence, or its completeness. Theories of this type tend to deny that there are any standards of beauty or of good taste that transcend the special conditions of any given place or period. Appreciation of works of art is held to be relative to the cultural inheritance and the psychological peculiarities of the individual. In this view, the function of criticism is not to delineate absolute and unchanging excellencies in art products, but rather to call the attention of those who possess appreciative capacities to the features in works of art that may be expected to satisfy those capacities. *See also* AESTHETICS.   L. G.

ARTEMIS [ɑ′rtəmɪs], one of the most important of the Greek goddesses, called Diana by the Romans. She was the daughter of Zeus and Leto, born with Apollo, her twin brother, on Delos, and hence called Delia or, from Mount Cynthus in Delos, Cynthia. Artemis was in many respects the feminine counterpart of Apollo and had the names Phoebe and Pythia, which compare with Phoebus Apollo

and Pythius Apollo. Armed like Apollo with bow and arrows, she, too, punished offenses, assisting her brother, for example, in slaying the children of Niobe; she was also a goddess of healing and purification, and, as goddess of seafarers, she brought fair weather to travelers. Artemis has been considered a goddess of nature and vegetation, and

ARTEMIS

in this aspect she sent the Calydonian boar to ravage the fields when Oeneus failed to give her a harvest offering; more recent views make her originally a non-Hellenic goddess of wild animals, probably connected with the Minoan Lady of Wild Things. A further indication of the goddess' antecedents is the fact that Britomartis, one of Artemis' attendants, was a Cretan goddess. Various other non-Greek divinities were identified with Artemis, the most famous being Artemis (Diana) of the Ephesians, a goddess whose maternal character was very unlike that of the Hellenic Artemis.

To the Greeks, Artemis was goddess of hunting, goddess of chastity, and protectress of youth and maidens. She was connected also with childbirth and hence called Eileithyia. Just as Apollo was identified with Helios, god of the sun, so Artemis in later legend was identified with Selene, the moon goddess, in which capacity she loved the beautiful shepherd Endymion. In works of art Artemis is usually represented as a huntress with bow and arrows, accompanied by a dog or a deer. *See also* APOLLO; ARETHUSA; CALYDONIAN HUNT; ENDYMION; IPHIGENIA; NIOBE; ORION; SELENE; TROJAN WAR.   G. E. D.

ARTEMISIA [ɑrtəmɪ′zhə], a genus of aromatic plants in the family Compositae, mostly perennial herbs commonly known as wormwood. The group includes the shrubby sagebrushes, *A. tridentata* and other species, of the western United States; absinthe, *A. absinthium;* southernwood or old man, *A. abrotanum,* long grown in herb gardens; tarragon, *A. dracunculus,* used for flavoring salads; mugwort, several species, among them *A. vulgaris,* which is a persistent weed; and several species known as cudweed. The wormwood of the Bible belongs to the same genus. A number of artemisias, among them *A. albula,* silver king, and *A. stelleriana,* called beach wormwood, old woman, or dusty miller, are used in gardens for the effect of their finely cut silvery leaves. Most of the species are shrubby in stature and gray-leaved. The flowers are inconspicuous, consisting of small tight heads of yellow disk florets.   C. H. Wo.

ARTEMOVSK [ɑrtyiˈmɔfsk], formerly Bakhmut, a mining and industrial town in the Ukrainian Soviet Socialist Republic, in the southwestern portion of the Soviet Union. It lies approximately 125 mi. to the southeast of Kharkov in a depression on the left bank of the Bakhmut, a small tributary to the Donets River. It was settled in the latter half of the seventeenth century when salt springs were discovered there and was surrounded by a wooden wall in 1703. Damaged in World War II fighting, it was occupied by Nazi forces for several months. It is a rail junction, and its industries produce coal, salt, alabaster, mercury, iron and steel, textiles, glass, pottery, flour, cement, and fireproof brick. Pop. (est. 1950), 60,000.   C. C. H.

ARTERIOSCLEROSIS. *See* HEART (*Diseases of the Heart and Circulatory System*).

ARTERY, a vessel serving to convey blood from the heart to different organs and tissues of the body. The largest artery is the aorta, which extends from the heart alongside the vertebral column. Branches of the aorta represent the major arteries: the pulmonary, to the lungs; the carotid, to the head and neck; the coeliac, to the stomach and liver; the mesenteric, to the intestines; and the renal, to the kidneys. The arteries are not only pipe lines or conduits through which blood, under pressure, is pumped to all parts of the body, but are elastic structures whose walls can actively contract and aid in the distribution of blood. These functions are reflected in the structure of the arterial wall. The inner surface consists of flattened, elongated cells joined together by a cementing material to form a smooth lining for the vessel lumen. Immediately adjacent is a layer of delicate interlacing fibrils intermingled with spindle-shaped muscle cells. A meshwork of relatively coarse, collagenous fibers surrounds the vessel, and imparts to the wall its unusual elastic strength. The muscle layer, which is thickest in the larger arteries, becomes progressively thinner with the successive branching of the vessels until, in the arterioles, their ultimate subdivisions, only a single layer of muscle cells is closely applied to the endothelium. *See also* CIRCULATORY SYSTEM; HEART.   B. W. Z.

ARTESIA [ɑrtiˈzhə], a city of Eddy Co., in southeastern New Mexico, situated 42 mi. south of Roswell, about 3,350 ft. above sea level. Oil wells are near by, and Artesia is in a mountain resort district. Settled in 1903, the city was incorporated in 1905. It is served by the Atchison, Topeka & Santa Fe Railway. Artesia is a wool-trading center in a diversified farming area. Agricultural activities include raising cotton, alfalfa, sheep, and goats. The local industries comprise oil refining, its storage and pipe-line shipping, and the bottling of beverages. Pop. 1950, 8,244.

ARTESIAN WELLS. *See* WATER SUPPLY.

ARTEVELDE, JACOB VAN [ɑˈrtəveldə] (c.1290-1345), Flemish statesman, was born in Ghent about 1290. He first appeared as a political leader in 1337, when revolution broke out in Ghent as the result of the English King Edward III's embargo on the export of wool from England. The Flemish cities were dependent on English wool for their textile industries, and thousands of weavers were thrown out of work. Edward III had shrewdly counted on revolution to overthrow the count of Flanders, who was under French control. Artevelde, a prominent cloth merchant, induced Ghent, Bruges, Ypres, and a number of other towns to form a league for neutrality. The league's first step was to sign a commercial peace with England. Artevelde virtually became dictator of Flanders by defeating the efforts of the count, backed by the pope and the king of France, to overthrow him. By 1340 the federation organized by Artevelde had grown to include many towns and provinces in the Netherlands. Discarding the policy of neutrality, Artevelde induced the towns to form a close political alliance with the English, even recognizing Edward III as the lawful sovereign of Flanders. As a result of this alliance and Artevelde's able administration, trade flourished and the Flemish towns became rich and powerful. Artevelde's proposal to substitute the English Black Prince, son of Edward III, for the count of Flanders led to an insurrection in Ghent. It was during this insurrection that Artevelde, while at the height of his power, was murdered, July 24, 1345.   F. C. H.

ARTFUL DODGER, THE, nickname of Jack Dawkins, a young pickpocket in Dickens' *Oliver Twist;* a pupil of Fagin, he befriends Oliver.   DeL. F.

ARTHRITIS [ɑrthraiˈtɪs], a term loosely applied to inflammatory, metabolic, or degenerative diseases involving one or more joints. The most important forms may be classified in respect to the rapidity of their course, as (1) acute, (a) infectious arthritis; (2) less acute, (a) syphilitic arthritis and (b) tuberculous arthritis; (3) recurrently acute, (a) gout and (b) rheumatic fever; (4) chronic (arthritis deformans), (a) osteoarthritis and (b) rheumatoid arthritis. Discussed below are infectious, osteo, and rheumatoid arthritis.

Acute Infectious Arthritis. The acute infectious type is usually traceable to the invasion of the joint capsule by one of the common disease-producing bacteria. Since the joint lubricating fluid (synovial fluid) is an excellent culture medium for many bacteria, they soon proliferate in it and produce a hot, red, swollen, and painful joint. The swelling comes both from inflammation of tissues surrounding the joint and from increased secretion of the joint fluid. This fluid, when removed by a hypodermic needle, is found to be cloudy from the presence of white blood cells and bacteria. The infecting organism may reach the joint via the blood stream from an inflammatory area elsewhere in the body, as pneumonia, gonorrhea, or a boil; or it may be introduced by a penetrating wound. The joint, if not treated, may become permanently stiff (ankylosed). Treatment includes aspiration, irrigation, possibly surgical drainage, and the use of the appropriate antibiotic, either singly or in combination. Choice of the latter is governed by sensitivity tests. In approximate order of frequency, the following agents may cause infectious arthritis: gonococcus, streptococcus, pneumococcus, staphylococcus, meningococcus, dysentery, typhoid, influenza, and undulant fever bacillus (Brucella).

Osteoarthritis. Osteoarthritis, also called degenerative, hypertrophic osteoarthrosis, is a very slowly developing disease of mature years, usually occurring in persons over fifty. Typically it seems to be the result of wear and tear on the protective cartilage covering the articulating surfaces of bones. Overweight, faulty posture, and a lifetime of hard manual work predispose to it. Commonly affected are the lower spine, the hip joints, and the knees, because of the particular weight-bearing strain on these joints. As the cartilage gradually wears away toward the bone, spurs and lips grow from the irritated bone, the presence of which may be compared to rust inside an iron hinge. Characteristic and diagnostically useful in osteoarthritis are the Heberden's nodes, which are small, bony knobs appearing about the terminal finger joints. There is seldom swelling or increase of fluid in the joint, and rarely fusion. Pain is variable, X rays often revealing osteoarthritic changes in a symptom-free joint. Though no permanent cure is at hand, severe

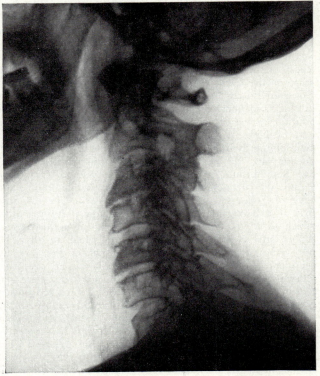

COURTESY OF MICHAEL D'AMICO, M.D.

Extensive hypertrophic arthritis of the cervical spine, showing marked narrowing of the third cervical intervertebral space indicating herniation or rupture of the intervertebral disc.

crippling is rare. Some improvement usually follows rest, weight reduction, protection of joints by suitable braces, physiotherapy, and hydrotherapy.

Rheumatoid Arthritis. Rheumatoid arthritis, which includes atrophic, ankylosing, and chronic infectious, is by far the most important of all types because it is so prevalent, crippling, and deforming, yet so little is known of its cause and cure. This disease usually begins at about thirty-five years of age, and is three times commoner in females than in males. It is seen especially among the poor. Some hereditary predisposition is manifest, the characteristic arthritic-prone person being thin, narrow-chested, and of poor muscular development. The microscopic picture of this type of arthritis includes a fibrinoid degeneration of collagen (connective tissue matrix substance). This is also seen in rheumatic fever, scleroderma, periarteritis nodosa, and other rarer diseases now called the "collagen diseases."

The disease commonly begins after a physical or emotional shock, fatigue, exposure, or infection. The latter, in some distant body focus (teeth, tonsils, sinuses, gall bladder, or prostate) was thought until recently to be the usual cause of rheumatoid arthritis, but substantial proof is lacking. However, the arthritic process itself seems infectious, as evidenced by the associated symptoms of fever, elevated white-blood-cell count, accelerated blood-sedimentation rate, and, often, rise of blood antibodies against the hemolytic

streptococcus. In these respects it closely resembles rheumatic fever; the two are often difficult to differentiate. No organism has ever been consistently demonstrated in rheumatoid arthritis; joints are usually sterile.

After a period of vague ill-health and anemia, first one joint, then another, insidiously becomes stiff and painful. Fingers, hands, and knees are common sites, often symmetrically involved. In the fingers the joints gradually develop a characteristic cigar or sausage-shaped swelling. This is due to thickening of joint-lining synovial membrane and joint capsule. Joint cartilage gradually thins out, and the continued painful, protective spasm of surrounding muscles gradually pulls the joint into flexion, which becomes "frozen" in this position as the joint fuses (ankyloses). X-ray studies in advanced cases show narrowing of joint spaces, and loss of substance (atrophy) of neighboring bone.

Many varieties of rheumatoid arthritis have been described, among them a childhood form (Still's disease), a form associated with an enlarged spleen (Felty's syndrome), and a form associated with urethritis and conjunctivitis (Reiter's disease). A special form starting in the lower spine of young men (Marie-Strümpell's ankylosing spondylitis) is not rare. The end result of this disease, when untreated, is complete rigidity of the spine and a flattening of its curves (poker spine). A feature of Marie-Strümpell's disease is its susceptibility to cure by deep X-ray treatment, if the treatment is used at an early stage.

A new era in the treatment of all the collagen diseases, including rheumatoid arthritis, dawned in 1949. Cortisone, given either by injection or by mouth, and the cortex-stimulating drug, ACTH (adreno-cortico-tropic-hormone, or corticotropin), given by injection, were found to keep the inflammatory symptoms in abeyance for the duration of the treatment, and if skillfully tapered off after a month or so, often effected at least a partial permanent cure. Disadvantages of these hormones are their high cost, and a long list of possible dangerous side reactions. The one drug that seems most nearly to approach a permanent cure is one of the salts of gold as introduced entirely on empirical grounds by Forestier in 1932. Good practice at present is to produce quick symptomatic relief with the hormones, and overlap this effect with a series of about 20 injections of a gold salt until the total dose of metallic gold is calculated to be one gram. Even under the best circumstances, rheumatoid arthritis is prone to relapse, and courses of these drugs may have to be repeated. The basic hygienic principles of good treatment closely resemble those used in managing pulmonary tuberculosis. Rest of the whole body, preferably in a warm, dry climate, is purposeful; rest of the acutely inflamed joint by splints, plus gentle physiotherapy to prevent ankylosis, is mandatory. The arthritic patient tends to be undernourished and anemic. The former condition calls for a high-caloric, high-vitamin diet (particularly the vitamin-B complex and vitamin D). The anemia often requires iron and transfusions. Finally, as in all forms of arthritis, the pain-killing properties of aspirin and other salicylates are always gratifying, and usually safe for the patient.   F. P. Ma.

ARTHRODIUM. *See* JOINT.

ARTHROPODS [ɑ'rthropɒds], a major group or phylum of animals, usually characterized by a segmented body, an external skeleton, and jointed limbs. Included in the phylum are the crustaceans (crabs, lobsters, shrimps, sow bugs, barnacles), arachnids (spiders, mites), myriapods (thousand legs), insects, and a few smaller and less well-known classes of invertebrate animals. It is by far the largest phylum of the animal kingdom, probably comprising more than 800,000 described species or about 80 per cent of all known animals. Arthropods are found in all parts of the

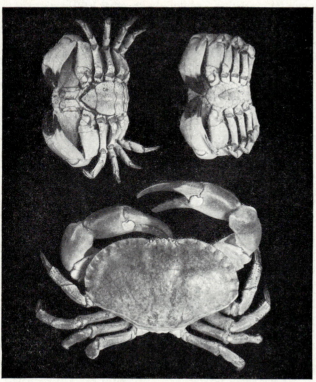

COURTESY OF THE AMERICAN MUSEUM OF NATURAL HISTORY

European pocket crab, Cancer pagurus, *an arthropod belonging to the class Crustacea*

world, from well above the timber line on mountain ranges to the deepest parts of the oceans. Wherever found, they are important economic factors, whether injurious or beneficial. On land, the vast number of both individuals and species of insects is well known. Man's constant struggle against the destructive species, and his indebtedness to the beneficial forms that pollinate plants and the parasitic ones which help control the destructive forms, is obvious. Less often recognized is the role of the predominant aquatic forms, the crustaceans, in the economy of the sea and bodies of fresh water. Not only do the crabs, lobsters, and shrimps furnish food for human consumption, but the smaller forms are the basic food on which most aquatic animals from the smallest fish to the largest whales are directly or indirectly dependent. *See also* ANIMAL SYSTEMATICS.   F. A. C., Jr.

ARTHUR, KING. *See* ARTHURIAN LEGENDS; ROUND TABLE, THE.

ARTHUR, CHESTER ALAN (1830-1886), twenty-first President of the United States, assumed that office upon the death of James A. Garfield on Sept. 19, 1881. He was born Oct. 5, 1830, one of a large family. His father, William Arthur, was a schoolteacher and Baptist clergyman who came to the United States from northern Ireland by way of Canada. His mother was Malvina Stone Arthur, daughter of a farmer who lived near the border of Vermont in the Province of Quebec. Arthur's birthplace, at one time

a subject of dispute among his biographers, was in a parsonage in Fairfield, Vt.

Early Career. After graduating in 1848 from Union College, Schenectady, N.Y., Arthur taught school in Vermont and then studied law until, in 1854, he was admitted to the bar of New York. Five years later he married Ellen Lewis Herndon of Fredericksburg, Va., and New York City, the daughter of a distinguished officer in the navy. His boyhood associations had been those of an antislavery Whig, and he was an early member of the Republican Party in New York. Arthur was an ardent Unionist, although his wife was from the South and one of his sisters was married to an official of the Confederate government. During the first two years of the Civil War he served on the military staff of Governor Edwin D. Morgan of New York, first as engineer in chief and later as quartermaster general. In the former position he was responsible for constructing defenses for the port of New York, and in the latter for equipping and maintaining thousands of troops from New York State. During the early Reconstruction period Arthur was a conservative Republican. As an adherent of Ulysses S. Grant, he became the party chief in New York City while holding the office of Collector of the Port of New York. His role was that of a lieutenant in Roscoe Conkling's party machine, which in 1880 supported General Grant for a third term. Arthur first received national attention when, in 1877, he was removed from his office as collector of the port by President Rutherford B. Hayes for violating an executive order requiring all federal officials to refrain from participation in party management. The removal was resisted unsuccessfully in the Senate after being at issue for almost a year.

The Republican national convention of 1880, after nominating Garfield for president, selected Arthur as the candidate for vice-president. The nomination was followed by a successful election; on Mar. 4, 1881, Arthur was sworn in and assumed the only office to which he was ever elected.

COURTESY OF FRICK ART REFERENCE LIBRARY

CHESTER ALAN ARTHUR

FROM A PAINTING BY DANIEL HUNTINGTON

He presided over a special session of the Senate, and was among Garfield's opponents in a patronage controversy at the time the President was shot by an assassin.

Presidency. Arthur's succession to the presidency, with a term of more than three and one-half years before him, was greeted with many expressions of anxiety or dismay. Nevertheless, he surpassed the expectations of those who had known him only as a machine politician. His course of action was marked by good sense rather than weakness or vindictiveness. All but one of Garfield's cabinet were replaced by men of Arthur's own selection without lowering the average merit of the group. Influential Republicans charged with conspiracy to defraud the postal service were diligently prosecuted in the "Star Route Trials." Arthur vetoed an extravagant appropriation for public works, as well as two bills restricting immigration, and devoted surplus federal revenues to reducing the public debt. To administer the new Civil Service Act of 1883, he appointed an able commission and gave it firm support. These actions did not win popularity for his party or for him, and the Congressional elections of 1882 resulted in a Democratic landslide.

The first ships of the modern United States Navy were constructed during Arthur's administration, while steps were also taken toward the manufacture within the country of naval armament for such vessels, which had previously been imported. To revise the tariff laws, Arthur appointed at Congressional instigation a tariff commission which reported a series of recommendations in December 1882. The law, signed Mar. 3, 1883, made little change in the average level of tariff rates, but brought them up to date. Reciprocal trade treaties which lowered tariff duties were negotiated with Mexico and Spain, and negotiations with Great Britain were far advanced when Arthur's administration ended. The freer trade was to apply to goods originating in the United States and in the Caribbean area, with a preference to goods carried in ships of the same nationality. The treaties failed to receive Congressional support. A similar treaty with the Hawaiian Islands was, however, extended on terms which gave the United States control of Pearl Harbor.

Arthur signed a treaty which involved the conveyance by Nicaragua to the United States of sole control over an isthmian canal to be constructed across Nicaragua; in return, the United States was to furnish money and protection to Nicaragua. Since this treaty conflicted with the Clayton-Bulwer Treaty between the United States and Great Britain, its ratification would have raised serious difficulties. Grover Cleveland, Arthur's successor, withdrew it from the Senate before it had been ratified. Arthur's popularity improved each year of his presidency, but he was denied a renomination in 1884 and retired on Mar. 4, 1885, with the advent of the first Democratic president to be chosen since the election of 1856. An effort by friends to procure his election to the Senate by the New York legislature was unsuccessful. Mrs. Arthur had died in 1880, before his nomination to the vice-presidency. Arthur retired to New York City in poor health, and died there Nov. 18, 1886. One son and one daughter survived him. He was buried near Albany, N.Y.

G. F. H.

ARTHURIAN LEGENDS. The origin of the legends of King Arthur is all but lost in the mists of early British history. Though no contemporary reference survives, it is probable that there was a Celtic chieftain named Arthur who succeeded in temporarily stemming the tide of Anglo-Saxon invasion in the early part of the sixth century. He is mentioned in Nennius' ninth-century chronicle, *Historia Britonum,* as a successful leader, not a king, in twelve battles against the invaders. As the years passed, the Britons began to embroider the exploits of Arthur, probably assisted by shadowy suggestions of a Celtic culture-divinity, and possibly even the recollection of a Roman Artorius. Arthurian material of the sort found in the early medieval *Ancient Books of Wales* and *The Mabinogion* was widespread enough among the Celts of Britain, and probably Armorica, to provoke William of Malmesbury's slighting allusion in his *Gesta Regum Anglorum* (1125) to the Britons' nonsensical tales about Arthur. These tales largely ignored the historical Arthur. He had now become a king, ruling in a land of fantastic adventure and associated with certain well-known Arthurian figures: Kay, Gawain, and Bedivere.

To this body of inchoate legend Geoffrey of Monmouth gave permanent direction in his epoch-making *Historia Regum Britanniae* (c.1137). In what purports to be a chronicle, Geoffrey describes Arthur, the son of Uther Pendragon,

FROM A MURAL PAINTED BY EDWIN A. ABBEY COURTESY OF THE BOSTON PUBLIC LIBRARY

THE KNIGHTS DEPARTING IN QUEST OF THE HOLY GRAIL

as a great king, the conqueror of Europe from Italy to the Baltic. Here also is the story of Queen Guinevere's adultery with Mordred, of Arthur's last great battle against Mordred, who had attempted to usurp his power, and his departure for Avalon to be healed of his mortal wound. Merlin, the sage and enchanter, a descendant of the youthful seer Ambrosius in Nennius' chronicle, plays an important part in Arthur's life. The bold inventions of Geoffrey immediately focused attention on the Arthurian story.

The pseudohistorical approach was continued in Wace's *Roman de Brut* (1155), in which the Round Table was introduced in its primitive form, and in Layamon's *Brut* (c.1200). Meantime the legends were elaborated by French writers of romances. The Celtic hero, Tristram, was the central figure in twelfth-century poems by Béroul and Thomas of Brittany. Geoffrey's contemporary, Chrétien de Troyes, developed Arthurian themes elaborately and originally in six poems, adding two elements of great importance: the great hero Lancelot, destined to supplant the Celtic Gawain as the leading knight of Arthur's court; and a somewhat primitive form of the Holy Grail, now beginning to emerge in a blending of archaic pagan and medieval religious belief. Robert de Boron added explicit Christian symbolism to the Round Table and the Grail in his trilogy, *Joseph of Arimathea, Merlin,* and *Perceval.* And in the "Vulgate Cycle" of the thirteenth-century French prose-romances, Lancelot took his traditional place in the story. He replaced Mordred as Guinevere's lover and by his union with King Pelles' daughter fathered Galahad, whose Christian asceticism made him a worthy successor to Perceval as the Grail hero.

Thus the familiar narrative situations of the Arthurian legend were well established by the end of the thirteenth century, and over the whole was cast the coloring of chivalric conventions and the code of courtly love. Solidly established in this way, the story of the "Flower of Kings" was widely used by medieval romancers, not only in England but throughout a large part of Europe as well. Malory's *Le Morte d'Arthur* (1485), which drew the legends into one body of English prose, has kept Arthur vitally alive in literature and the other arts down to our own day.   N. C. S.

ARTICHOKE, also globe artichoke, *Cynara Scolymus,* a thistle-like plant belonging to the family Compositae. Much valued as a choice vegetable, the edible parts of the plant are the immature flower and surrounding leaves. A native of the Mediterranean countries, its origins nevertheless have

ARTICHOKE

been traced to parts of Asia. Artichokes are propagated from sprouts or suckers, growing best in rich, well-drained soils in foggy climates at temperatures between 60° and 85° F. In the United States production is confined mostly to small areas in California. The artichoke is not easily grown, since it is exacting in its soil and climatic requirements.

ARTICHOKE, JERUSALEM, *Helianthus tuberosus,* the edible part of a species of sunflower known to the Hurons and other Indians of eastern North America. Unlike the globe artichoke, the edible portion of the Jerusalem artichoke is the underground tuber. Long since popular in both the United States and France as a basic food, its importance as a salad and cooking vegetable has increased in recent years. As the tubers have been found to contain inulin, which, upon hydrolysis, is broken down into levulose, Jerusalem artichokes are satisfactory in diabetic diets. Their high carbohydrate content gives them also considerable market value for the making of sugar, starch, and alcohol. They grow well in the sandy loam soils of the Mississippi Valley, particularly in the corn-belt states. They are propagated from small tubers. The tubers which have not been dug will live over the winter and sprout in the spring. There are a number of good varieties available. They are easily grown and will produce well even in the poorer soils.   V. A. T.

ARTICLE, a part of speech which has the function of limiting the application of a noun to a particular object or idea. If the particular object or idea is specifically identified, the definite article is used, as in *the roof of the house* or *the wine we drank yesterday;* if it is not specifically identified, the indefinite article is used, as in *a proof, a house,* or *a wine of good quality.* In both cases, one particular object is signified, despite the fact that when the indefinite article is used, the particular object is one of a vast category of objects. If no article is used, the category itself is signified, as in *Virtue is its own reward* or *Life is a dream,* which may be compared with *to make a virtue of necessity* and *the life of a soldier.*

The article seems to be a relatively recent achievement of culture, and in many languages it does not exist. Certainly Proto-Indo-European had no article, and Proto-Germanic, Proto-Greek, and even historical Latin, Sanskrit, and Old Iranian had none; it is also lacking in modern Baltic and in the Slavic languages, except Bulgarian. The article is still an exceptional form in language, and the fourth-century Gothic translation of the Bible by Ulfilas shows it just developing, as a comparison with the Greek original makes clear; the situation is the same in Old Icelandic. The indefinite article always appears later than the definite, Modern Icelandic having the latter, for example, but not the former.

The definite article regularly develops from a deictic pronoun, as can still be seen in English, where *the* has the same stem as *that* or *there.* The same development is observable in German *der da* and *der dort,* in Greek ὅ-δε, and in the Romance languages, most of which use an article derived from *ille.* Some of the Romance languages derive the article from *ipse,* but this word certainly passed through a deictic stage, as in the Spanish *ese,* the Southern Italian *issu,* and elsewhere. The indefinite article always develops from a semantic weakening of the numeral *one;* this weakening is sometimes even phonetic, as in the English *a house,* from Old English *ān hūs,* and the same phenomenon can be observed in some German and Modern Greek dialects and in Coptic.

There is hardly any doubt that the article spread throughout Europe from one center, Greece. It probably reached the Germanic languages through Latin, where it was accepted to a certain extent in the spoken language at least as early as the first or second century of our era. From Greece it also penetrated directly into Bulgarian, although Old Bulgarian does not have it.

The article is sometimes preposed to the noun or adjective, as in Greek, English, German, and the Western Romance languages, but it is sometimes postposed, as in Romanian, Bulgarian, and the Scandinavian languages. Its function is the same, however, in either case.

Among the Western European languages, French has gone farthest in the adoption of the article, requiring it, in fact, with practically any noun. While the Englishman can omit the article in *I drink water, I see dogs,* and so can the Italian, the German, and the Spaniard, the Frenchman has to say *je bois de l'eau, je vois des chiens.* With few obvious exceptions, such as *un pont en pierre,* forms without the article survive only in proverbs like *loups et agneaux ne vivront pas ensemble,* and usually in proper names, although this is not true of forms like *Le Havre, La Ferté,* or *La Spezia.*

The psychological reason for the creation of the article in culturally advanced societies has been clearly stated by A. Sommerfelt in his book *La Langue et la société.* Pointing out that Latin *petra* means at once "the stone," and "a stone," Sommerfelt maintains that the article was created only when the need was felt to distinguish the general meaning from the concrete case. For the mind of primitive man, then, incapable of generalization and abstraction, there is no difference between the stone he sees in front of him or talks about and stone in general. He never drinks water, in fact; he drinks only the specific water that he has before him.

Outside of the Indo-European domain, it is significant that among the Finnic languages only Hungarian, which is surrounded by Indo-European tongues and strongly Indo-Europeanized in its whole structure, has the article. Proto-Semitic had no article, and none was ever used in the two opposite fringe languages of the Semitic area, Assyrian in the North and Ethiopic in the South. The central languages, Aramaic, Hebrew, and Arabic, have developed articles, but each has a different one, Hebrew having *ha,* Arabic having *al,* and Aramaic having a postpositive *-ā,* this diversity offering one more proof that the article did not exist in the mother tongue. The older Hebrew language as reflected in its poetry makes very sparing use of the article, and Ugaritic has no article at all. In Egyptian the definite article appears first in the vulgar language of the Middle Kingdom, and the indefinite, as usual, at a later date. G. B.

ARTICLES, THIRTY-NINE. *See* THIRTY-NINE ARTICLES OF THE ANGLICAN CHURCH.

ARTICLES OF CONFEDERATION. The thirteen Articles of Confederation were the first constitution of the United States, serving as a framework of government from Mar. 1, 1781, when they were ratified, until Mar. 4, 1789, when government began under the Constitution written by the Convention of 1787.

Essentially the Articles were drawn up to govern a "confederacy" in which "each state retains its sovereignty, freedom, and independence." The states entered into "a firm league of friendship," but in the process too much power was retained by the individual state and not enough was delegated to the central government. The result was a confederation in which the individual members, for all practical purposes, agreed as long as it was to their interest to agree, but in times of disagreement a state's freedom of action, without interference by the central government, was hardly impaired or restricted.

Controversial Issues. *States' Rights.* The idea of union was an old one among the Colonies, and many plans had been proposed during the eighteenth century. As the controversy with Great Britain moved toward an open break, the necessity of some form of union became apparent to the Americans generally; but they could not agree on the kind of union they wanted. One group wanted a government that left all power in the hands of the states; the other wanted a government which could force the states and their citizens to do its bidding. This issue was debated in 1776 and 1777 as the Articles were written. The first draft provided for a strong central government; the final draft, sent to the states for ratification in November 1777, provided for a weak central government of strictly delegated powers. The believers in the power of the states had won out.

Representation, Taxes, and Western Lands. Members of Congress disagreed over three other main issues. One they called "representation"; that is, how many votes the various states should have in Congress. The states with large populations wanted representation according to population, and the smaller states wanted representation by states. The latter won on this issue. The second issue was the basis upon which the states should levy taxes for common expenses. Some delegates, particularly the northern ones, wanted taxes levied according to population, whereas the southern states wanted taxes levied according to land values, on the ground that their population was large but poor. Land values, they held, were the best index to wealth. The northern delegates argued that population was the best index. Eventually, taxation according to the value of improved lands was adopted as the means of apportioning expenses. The greatest single issue was that of control of western lands. Five of the states had definite western boundaries, and hence no western lands. The rest had charters giving them claims, however vague, "to the South Seas." The states without such claims wanted all western lands given to Congress. The states with such claims, led by Virginia, insisted that Congress could not interfere with the lands of the states. It was this dispute over control of the West that delayed the ratification of the Confederation until 1781. Maryland alone refused to ratify until Congress got control of the West. Virginia refused to give up control. Complicating the issue was the fact that land speculators from landless states like Maryland had staked out claims in the region demanded for Congress. Their influence was such that their particular claims in the West were always exempted from the land that was supposed to be surrendered. Virginia, however, finally ceded her claims to the region northwest of the Ohio, and Maryland then ratified the Articles of Confederation on Mar. 1, 1781. M. Je.

ARTICLES OF FAITH, in Judaism. Under the influence of other religious and philosophical systems, Jewish thinkers began to formulate the principles or articles of faith in Judaism. Saadia Gaon, in the tenth century, examined the following nine concepts: *Creatio ex nihilo,* the Unity of God, prophecy, freedom of the will, merit and guilt, the soul and its destiny, the resurrection, the redemption of Israel, and immortality.

Maimonides (1135-1204) formulated thirteen articles of faith which have been generally accepted. The first five deal with the conception of God: (1) His existence, (2) His unity, (3) His incorporeality, (4) His perpetuity, and (5) His sole title to be worshipped. The next four deal with revelation: (6) the reality of prophecy, (7) the absolute supremacy of Moses as prophet, (8) the divine origin of the Torah, and (9) the immortality of the Torah. The last four treat of retribution: (10) omniscient providence, (11) reward and punishment, (12) the advent of the Messiah, and (13) the resurrection of the dead.   M. A. G.

ARTICULATION. *See* Joint; Musical Terms; Phonetics.

ARTIFICIAL LIMBS. *See* Prosthetic Devices.

ARTIFICIAL RESPIRATION. *See* First Aid.

ARTIGAS, JOSÉ [arti'gas] (1764-1850), Uruguayan army officer and nationalist leader, was born in Montevideo, June 19, 1764. Although a captain in the Spanish army in Uruguay, Artigas organized and led an army of Gauchos in an attempt to overthrow the Spanish regime. This attack coincided with the revolutionary movement of 1811 in Buenos Aires, and was sponsored by factions both in Argentina and Brazil. Having defeated the royalist forces, Artigas compelled them to take up a defensive position within the city of Montevideo, but a truce, established by the armistice of Oct. 20, 1811, called a temporary halt to hostilities and Artigas withdrew across the Plata. However, a year later the young officer was given fuller authority in a renewed attack and the siege of Uruguay's capital city was resumed. Long in disagreement with his allies, Artigas broke completely with them in January 1814 over the question of national organization. In 1816 Brazil invaded Uruguay and, with his army decimated by four years of war, the Uruguayan patriot was defeated in the Battle of Paso del Calatan, Jan. 4, 1817. He fought on for three years, but was routed finally at Tacuarembo, Jan. 22, 1820, and forced to surrender. Throwing himself on the mercy of the Paraguayan dictator, José Francia, by whom he was given asylum, Artigas devoted the rest of his life to farming and philanthropy, and when in 1841 the president of Uruguay invited him to return he refused, saying he wished to die in Paraguay. Artigas was, however, the inspiration which ultimately led to the formation of the Republic of Uruguay. He died at his country home, Ibiray, near Asunción, Paraguay, Sept. 3, 1850.   A. J.

ARTILLERY. The term artillery comes from the old French *artiller*, "to fortify," and in its broad sense means munitions of war, especially missile-throwing equipment of all kinds. In its more specific usage, it is applied to guns or firearms of larger than hand-size, firing projectiles by means of gunpowder. Such weapons are usually called cannon, from the Latin *canna*, meaning a hollow reed, which is descriptive of the barrel; and in several languages derivatives of this word are still used for the barrel of any firearm, even of small size, i.e., French *canon*, Spanish *cañón*, and Italian *canna*. The term also applies to a modern military organization that bombards distant targets with heavy weapons, provides effective support for infantry, or provides antiaircraft or seacoast defense.

HISTORY

Origin and Introduction of Cannon. Like gunpowder, cannon developed from the use of the series of combustibles usually called Greek fire and the accessories used with it. As the composition of Greek fire improved, it was placed in the breech end of hollow tubes, and when ignited, it blew its less volatile elements out on the opposition in flaming chunks. Greek fire thus developed into crude gunpowder, and the tubes used with it became missile projectors or true cannon. As with Greek fire, gunpowder and cannon, because of the prevalence of necessary raw materials, originated in the East and then spread to Europe—in the latter case, through contacts established by the Crusades and the conquests of the Moors in Spain.

Gunpowder of a reasonably practical formula seems to have been known about to some extent in Europe during the thirteenth century, and cannon as definite projectile-propelling engines are mentioned in rare instances in mid-thirteenth-century European manuscripts. Cannon undoubtedly existed in Seville, Spain, in 1247, and one dating from 1258 was preserved until recently in the Castle of Coucy, France. Except for a few such isolated instances, cannon were unknown to the average European noble or soldier in the thirteenth century, and, except in a restricted way, they exerted no general influence on the military strategy or tactics of that period.

The fourteenth century may be accepted as the true beginning of the era of gunpowder and cannon in military affairs, since more general notice of them appears in the early part of the century and their influence was felt more and more as the century progressed. Among the earliest references to cannon in this century is the record of their use by Ferdinand of Castile at the siege of Gibraltar in 1308. An illuminated manuscript dated 1326 and preserved at Christchurch, England, shows a "firepot" in the shape of a vase lying on its side with an arrow or bolt issuing from its neck. This piece is supposed to be of Flemish origin, as were many of the fourteenth-century cannon. Also, Edward III of England is recorded as using "Crakys of Warre" against the Scotch in 1327. Another contemporary account places cannon in the hands of the Germans at the Siege of Ciridale in Italy in 1331. While there is some disagreement in this case, the Black Prince is generally credited with using three small cannon as field pieces at the Battle of Crécy in 1346. These cannon were blamed by the French for a defeat more logically attributed to other causes, chief among them good English archery and poor French generalship.

COURTESY OF THE METROPOLITAN MUSEUM OF ART

A fifteenth century English cannon of tube and ring construction. Bore: 1.084 in. Weight: 45 lbs.

Fourteenth-Century Artillery. *Bombards.* The four-teenth-century guns and their successors for the next hundred years or more were at first made up of circular bundles of longitudinal iron bars surrounded by rings or hoops which were driven over the bars while red-hot and shrunk into place as they cooled. Rolled tubes of iron were also strengthened by hoops in the same way. The early guns were called "bombards," from the Italian *bombo et ardore*, meaning thunder and lightning, and *vogheleer* or *veugliere* by the Dutch and Flemings.

The bombards of hooped construction were usually short and sometimes of large, sloping bore, with a powder chamber smaller than the bore. In appearance, if not in use, the bombard was the prototype of the true mortars which apparently were invented in Germany in about 1435, and certainly were classified by Charles VIII in 1490. The usual missile of the fourteenth century was an arrow or bolt, or a round stone ball, although iron shot is mentioned as being used in 1391. Another early name for cannon was the *cerbotain,* apparently applied to pieces of a type longer and straighter than the bombard and mounted on some type of movable carriage for siege work. A curious variety of the bombard was the *bombardo cubito,* or elbow-joint bombard, with its movable powder chamber at right angles to the bore holding the ball. Cast guns of copper and tin were made at Augsburg in 1378. Breechloaders of wrought iron, with separate breech chambers which were loaded with powder and ball out of the gun and wedged into place by crossbars inserted in the breech frame, were also in use, both as small swivel-mounted guns and fixed pieces of considerable size. Long guns of medium size were usually attached to wooden frames by a number of straps, almost as a musket barrel is fixed to a stock, and these frames in turn were sometimes mounted movably on further supports or wheeled carriages instead of having the gun barrels mounted directly on trunnions. Big breechloaders were mere tubes with their separate chambers dropped into place at the rear and wedged against the heavy blocks or bitts that made up the breech end of their wooden frames. Most of the early examples of these bigger pieces had no wheels and could be moved only by levers and man power.

Ribaudequins. Another early type was the ribaudequin, developed late in the fourteenth century. This consisted of a movable cart mounted with a combination of small guns and pike points. It was used for the next hundred and fifty years as a protection for infantry against cavalry and to provide fire power at the outset of a battle. One such piece carried 144 barrels, arranged to be fired in banks of 12. Ribaudequins were useful until the superior musket fire of the sixteenth century made these small-caliber mobile pieces obsolete. Generally, the fourteenth century was one of de-

A fifteenth century French mortar wrought from a single piece of iron. Bore: 6.815 in.

velopment of cannon types, experimental tactical use, and the general military acceptance of the idea of using guns and gunpowder; the guns themselves did not have much capacity for killing men, destroying fortifications, or forcing important military decisions.

Fifteenth-Century Artillery. *Trend in Guns.* The fifteenth century was one of consolidation and expansion of previous ideas. While relatively few new types appeared, use of the many developments of the fourteenth century spread from isolated instances to relatively common practice. The ribaudequins and war carts mounting small cannon were used extensively, and hooped iron guns of considerable size were made in both breech- and muzzle-loading designs. As already stated, mortars, as distinct from cannon both in design and use, also appeared, probably in the early part of the century and certainly by the end of it. In the process of development, huge bombards, bigger in bore than anything made since, and of both built-up and cast construction, began to appear. Among these, the famous "bombard of Ghent," named the "Dulle Griete," had a 25-in. bore; a huge Russian piece, although only 9 ft. long, had a bore of 36 in.; and the Mons Meg, built at Edinburgh Castle in 1460, shot a stone ball weighing 350 lb. While these guns were of enormous size, they were of relatively light construction, rarely weighing more than eight tons. This was because of the poor quality and low strength of the early powder and the relative lightness of stone as a ball component.

First Great Artillerists. One of the most powerful concentrations of early artillery during this period was at the siege of Constantinople in 1453. The Turkish Sultan, Mohammed II, concentrated a total of 68 cannon on this age-old citadel of European power in the East. The biggest of these was the great bombard, "Basilica," 30 in. in bore and requiring 60 oxen and 200 men for moving. Cast for the Sultan by the Hungarian cannon founder, Urban, it took two hours

A fifteenth century French mortar of wrought iron stave and hoop construction. Bore: 7.75 in.

to load it with a 1,600 lb. stone ball. It had no carriage or support of any type and was aimed at its objective by being installed on a mount of dirt, sloping upward and facing the enemy. It had a range of about a mile.

Eleven of the Sultan's other guns were of great size, shooting balls of from 500 to 1,000 lb., and most of the others were at least two-hundred-pounders. These guns were set up in fourteen batteries trained on the triple land-walls protecting the four-mile-wide neck of the peninsula on which Constantinople was built. Under their ponderous and deliberate fire, the city built by Constantine in the 330's and conquered only once, by "Latin" Crusaders in 1204, fell within two months. The era of the castle or stronghold capable of withstanding almost indefinitely any previous siege engine was brought to an end, and with it the whole feudal system. Some of the guns that accomplished this first demonstration of power were still in the hands of the Turks in 1807 and were firing 700-pound stone balls at the English fleet.

Following Mohammed II, the next great artillerist was Charles VIII of France. Progress had been slow during the last half of the fifteenth century, but Charles provided then a significant step in the gathering of equipment for his invasion of Italy in 1495. He took with him a siege train that not only embodied the best features of the guns of that century, but added a new element, mobility. Mohammed's cannon were cast close to their point of use and dragged painfully into position at great expense of time and man power; Charles' went from France and down the length of Italy at a fair rate of speed in a siege train capable of reducing promptly any castle or walled city that opposed him. His guns were still moved ponderously by ox teams whose drivers were not soldiers but carters, but at least they were of a design, as were their carriages, that could be hauled with a fair degree of facility.

Charles, among other reforms, adopted improved gun carriages, set up schools for gunners, made cast bronze cannon of improved shape and strength, and consistently used cast-iron balls for his missiles. He also classified his guns by size and type, listing weights of guns and projectiles and designating mortars as weapons separate from cannon. Since then the mortar has been constantly in use with various modifications of its tactical employment, but not of its type of high-angle fire. Essentially, it is short-barreled and of big bore in relation to the weight or velocity of its ball. It was developed for high-angle fire with a large, low-speed projectile, and was first used with the typical stone balls of its period.

Sixteenth-Century Artillery. *Improvements in Design.* The sixteenth century brought many improvements in cannon design and use. Cast guns with trunnions for mounting them flexibly on portable carriages were increasingly used as the century progressed. In 1525, Peter Bawde cast the first cannon so made in England. Cannon were more accurately classified in all armies and became a part of royal standard army equipment instead of being, as had often been the case previously, the personal property of masters of artillery who owned them and rented them out, like the mercenary soldiers of the period. Gunners' assistants and drivers were still stray peasants picked up by the wayside, since guns were still suspect and it was considered a waste of valuable soldiers to expose them to such uncertain weapons.

Increasing numbers of decisive battles were definitely influenced by the use of field guns. Among these, in the early part of the century, were the battles of Ravenna in 1512, Marignano in 1515, and Pavia in 1521. A visitor to the Tower of London in 1515 reported 400 cannon there, most of them mounted on wheels. Especially in Germany, wheel-mounted breechloaders of medium size were in use, with a breechlock consisting of a heavy pin passing through the breech of the barrel and the breechblock from side to side. This breech-locking design was invented by a man named Cotter and its identifying element has since been put to many industrial uses under the name of the "cotter pin."

Invention of Gunner's Quadrant. Niccolò Tartaglia in Italy, between 1537 and 1546, invented the gunner's quadrant for aid in aiming and demonstrated that guns shot farthest when trained at an angle of 45°. He also first described the continually curving trajectory of a ball, pointing out that at no time did it travel on an absolutely level course.

Classification of French Guns. In 1551, the French artillery was listed as composed of six standard sizes, ranging from the cannon, about 10 ft. long, weighing 5,300 lb., and shooting a ball of 33 lb., down to the falconet, about 6 ft. long, weighing 410 lb., and shooting a 1-lb. ball. Case shot, or canister, was used at this time; this consisted of a metal container of bore diameter filled with small balls which could be loaded and fired as a unit but flew apart as soon as it left the muzzle.

First Explosive Shells. Explosive shells were invented in the Netherlands before the middle of the century. At this period they were used entirely from mortars in high-angle fire. They were made up of a hollow iron case filled with gunpowder and exploded by a fuse entering the charge through a hole in the case. In the first examples, the fuse was loaded outward toward the muzzle of the mortar and lit before the propelling charge was fired. This system had obvious drawbacks, especially in case of a misfire of the main charge, and in about 1580 the single-ignition shell was introduced. This shell had its fuse ending in a cone of highly inflammable material that was loaded on top of the powder in the propelling charge and ignited by its explosion.

Early Naval Artillery. Naval gunnery also made its first great strides in the sixteenth century. Late fifteenth- and early sixteenth-century ships had been armed with heavy, clumsy-framed, breech-loading bombards with no wheels. These guns were usually mounted on the upper deck and had little or no way of adjusting them for range. Between the middle and the latter part of the century the typical naval gun, with its two- or four-wheeled carriage and cast muzzle-loading barrel attached to the carriage by trunnions so as to be adjustable for elevation by driving in and out the quoin supporting its breech, began to appear. The small breech-loading swivel guns, called minions and murderers, were still used for mounting on the poop and quarter railings and other strategic points for repelling boarders, but heavy cannon of advanced design shooting balls from 1 to 66 lb. in weight were mounted in broadside formation; these fired through gunports from the lower decks and also from bow and stern chase positions. Number, size, and weight of the guns varied with the size of the ships, but the bigger warships carried between 30 and 50 guns of respectable size and power.

The defeat of the Spanish Armada in 1588 was largely due to the fire power of the English ships and the line-of-battle, relatively long-range artillery tactics that they used. By this type of attack they were able to sink many of the Spanish galleons outright and drive the others from their objectives northward into the storm that caused their final destruction. Ships more and more were becoming gun platforms, to be maneuvered at long range until an advantage was obtained, instead of being used as seagoing battlefields, to be brought together at the earliest opportunity so that an essentially land-type battle could be fought on their decks.

Seventeenth-Century Artillery. *Sizes and Types of Guns.* The following list of artillery sizes and types describes guns in use in about 1600. These types had been developing for the previous forty or fifty years and were to change but little in the next fifty. Their effective range probably varied from 400 or 500 yd. to three times that in

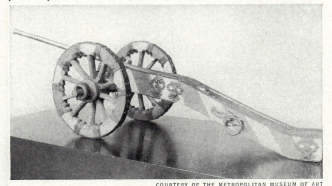

COURTESY OF THE METROPOLITAN MUSEUM OF ART

A model of a seventeenth century Turko-Austrian cannon. The carriage has been reinforced with ornamental bands of wrought iron, and the barrel inlaid with silver.

the largest sizes, but because of problems of sighting and variations in powder strength, they were normally used well inside their effective limits.

ARTILLERY USED IN 1600

Names	Bore of Cannon (in.)	Weight of Metal (lb.)	Weight of Shot* (lb.)	Weight of Powder (lb.)
Cannon Royal	8½	8,000	66	30
Cannon	8	6,000	60	27
Cannon Serpentine	7	5,500	53½	25
Bastard Cannon	7	4,500	41	20
Demi Cannon	6¾	4,000	33½	18
Cannon Petro	6	4,000	24½	14
Culverin	5½	4,500	17½	12
Basilisk	5	4,000	15	10
Demi Culverin	4	3,400	9½	3
Bastard Culverin	4	3,000	5	5¾
Sacar	3½	1,400	5½	5½
Minion	3½	1,000	4	4
Falcon	2½	660	2	3½
Falconet	2	500	1½	3
Serpentine	1½	400	¾	1½
Rabinet	1	300	½	¾

* Lead-shot weights listed above appear in some cases to be out of proportion with bore sizes. These are probably safe weights of powder and metal in the form of bar or cannister rather than the actual weights of ball loads.

Further Improvements. Seventeenth-century developments included the invention by the French in about 1620 of the limber for holding ready-prepared powder charges and balls, operating as a unit with a particular gun, and a greater understanding of the principles of trajectory, ball travel, and air resistance, from the writings of such men as Galileo, Edmund Halley, and Sir Isaac Newton.

The greatest genius in the use of artillery in the seventeenth century was Gustavus Adolphus of Sweden. Between 1620 and 1630, he developed the tactical use of light- and medium-weight field artillery in conjunction with infantry in open-field battles to a degree that was not improved upon for over one hundred years. He made a definite division of types and limited his field artillery to 4-, 9-, and 12-pounders,

using the lighter pieces as battalion, and the heavier as regimental, guns. He also used his guns in a far greater ratio to infantry than his opponents. Using grapeshot or canister at infantry ranges, he improved drill and loading techniques until he was able to fire his artillery about a third faster than the muskets of the period could be discharged. He redesigned both guns and carriages to make them lighter and more manageable than the earlier types.

Introduction of Howitzer. No other major changes were made until 1693, when a new type of wheel-mounted field piece was developed and classified by the Dutch. This was the howitzer, a short-barreled gun of light weight in relation to its bore. In length, it was between the mortar and the standard field gun, and it could be used for either horizontal or high-angle fire. It employed a relatively light powder charge and had only about half the velocity of a regular gun, but it was an effective and versatile piece for mobile short-range use. The classification has remained since, modified to breech-loading form.

Developments in Naval Gunnery. Seventeenth-century naval artillery changed little in type from that of the end of the sixteenth century, but as ships of war became larger, more and heavier guns were carried. Hundred-gun three-deckers with 42-pounders in battery on the lower gun deck began to appear. Special shot used against rigging, such as bar shot or chain shot, were standard loads, and bundles of short iron bars wrapped up in rope yarn to the diameter of the bore of a gun was also destructive to enemy rigging or personnel. In addition to cannister and grape (clusters of larger balls held together in the bore by a single bolt between caps of wood), bags of loose scrap iron called sangrenel were common missiles.

Eighteenth-Century Artillery. *Advances in Methods.* There were few general changes in artillery in the early eighteenth century, but in 1742 Benjamin Robins published in England his *New Principles of Gunnery,* which was the greatest single advance in the theory of ballistics up to that time. Frederick the Great of Prussia, in the middle of the century, also made new and constructive changes in the use of field artillery. In 1759 he introduced horse artillery, with gunners and drivers both mounted, so that pieces could maneuver with the cavalry; he also used the field howitzer more extensively than any of his predecessors, massing 45 of them in one battery at Burkersdorf in 1762.

In the next few years general reforms were made in the artillery of all nations following the lead of Frederick the Great. In France, General Jean Baptiste Vaquette de Gribeauval reorganized the French artillery on a new and improved system in 1776. He specified that field pieces should be 4-, 8-, and 12-pounders, and 6-in. howitzers; siege guns were built in sizes up to 12-in. mortars. All carriages were built as much as possible on the interchangeable system, and improved methods of using horses were introduced. The British army introduced horse artillery in 1793, and in 1794 departed from the long-established custom of using civilian drivers; a regular army driver corps was established in that year, and drivers and gunners both rode on the horses or limbers, so that the whole organization was far more mobile and amenable to discipline.

Changes in Ships-of-War. Ships-of-war improved during the eighteenth century and cast-iron guns of good quality, ranging from 4- or 5-pounders up to 32-pounders were the general rule. Range adjustment was by quoins under the breech, and the guns were secured to the side of the ship by heavy breech ropes through or around the cascabels, which limited their recoil, and by side tackles to run them into the ports after they had been sponged with water and reloaded. Extreme range was probably between 1,500 and 2,500 yd., but most naval battles were fought at distances ranging from less than 1,000 yd. to pistol range. Cast-iron round shot was the standard type of long-range missile, but it was frequently heated red-hot before firing

BROWN BROTHERS

An American Revolutionary War cannon at Valley Forge Park, the site of Washington's winter encampment, 1777-1778

so that it would set fire to sails, powder magazines, or enemy ships.

A special type of naval gun, paralleling the howitzer in general function, was the carronade. This was a short, light gun, of large bore in relation to its weight, invented by Gascoigne and named after the Carron iron works in Scotland, where carronades were first cast in about 1770. They were adopted by the English navy in 1779. Their range was about half that of a long gun of corresponding bore, but they were popular as spar-deck armament because of their light weight and consequent ease of handling. Their usual attachment to the carriage was by means of a loop at the bottom of the barrel, forward of the point of balance; this was pinned to a relatively flat four-wheeled carriage by a through-bolt.

Nineteenth-Century Artillery. *New Explosive Shells.* The nineteenth century brought greater changes in all types of armament than any other period. Until then, artillery had been improved in tactical use and convenience, but changed relatively little in basic principles in three hundred years. At its close, most of the modern features of guns, large and small, had been incorporated in at least rudimentary form. One of the first innovations was the adoption in 1803 by the British artillery of spherical, explosive case shot. This had been invented some fifteen years earlier by Lieutenant Henry Shrapnel, and has since been called "shrapnel" after his name. In its original form, it consisted of a round shell case with a thin compartment separating a charge of powder from a number of lead balls which filled a major part of the case; the fuse was inserted in the powder chamber and designed to explode the shell at a predetermined distance while in the air above the heads of opposing troops.

Explosive shells of all types came into more extensive use as the century progressed, and horizontally-firing guns began to be designed to handle shells as their regular missiles, with solid shot for use only on special targets. The United States coast defense "Columbiads," of 10- and 15-in. bore, designed in about 1812 by Colonel Bomford of the

Ordnance Department, were intended especially for the use of shells and were adaptable to either high-angle or direct fire. In 1822 the Frenchman, Henri Joseph Paixhans, also designed large-bore guns with explosive shells which were used on ships-of-war as well as for coast defense.

Napoleon's Artillery Methods. In the realm of field guns, Napoleon Bonaparte, in the early decades of the century, used the greatest concentration of muzzle-loading mobile guns at infantry ranges ever assembled on a battlefield. The musket fire of Napoleon's armies was relatively poor, but he offset this and won battles by using great numbers of 6- and 12-pounder field pieces almost wheel to wheel, firing continuous blasts of grape and canister. Since cannon at that period fired about twice as many rounds per minute as infantry muskets, and 6- and 12-pounders shot a formidable quantity of musket balls in the form of canister which outranged effective musket fire by several hundred yards, his system proved effective.

Increase in Gun Sizes. In the second quarter of the century, naval and siege guns began to increase considerably in size and strength in order to handle safely shells of 10-, 15-, and even 20-in. diameters. Between 1840 and 1860 built-up guns of several full- or part-length tubes of iron and steel were experimented with, among them the British Armstrong guns and the American Blakely. These were forerunners of types used during the next twenty or thirty years. Improved forms of cast guns were also developed, including the Dahlgren bottle-shaped and Rodman guns, both smoothbores of interior diameters between 10 and 20 in. Extreme ranges were still for the most part under 3,000 yds., and reasonable accuracy could not be expected at much more than half that.

Development of Rifling. Between 1855 and 1860 rifled cannon were developed and introduced into most armies for field and siege work; they also had naval uses. This was one of the major steps forward, since it nearly doubled the accurate range of most sizes of cannon and also made possible the use of the elongated or "cylindro-conoidal" projectile in both solid-shot and shell types. Most of the rifled cannon of the 1850's and 1860's were muzzle-loading, using conical shells with either studs or other projections cast on their surfaces to fit the rifling grooves, or having at their bases copper or brass driving flanges which were expanded into the rifling by the discharge of the powder. Shells of all types were increasingly used, including conical shrapnel, Armstrong segmental shells with central bursting charges, and various designs of powder-filled explosive shells.

Improvement of Fuses. This trend, covering increased ranges, called for improved fuses, and a number of types were developed. In principle, they still resembled the original single-ignition fuses of 250 years before, but in detail they were greatly improved. The general type was a tubular case of wood or metal about 1 in. in diameter and 3 or 4 in. long. This tube was inserted in the base of the shell and contained one or more trains of tightly-rammed, slow-burning powder which would burn at a fairly accurately known rate per inch. The inner end of the train communicated with the bursting charge, and the outer end was ignited by the explosion of the propelling charge of the gun; the time of burning was controlled by cutting or boring through the case of the fuse to bring the fire from the burning train into contact with the bursting charge at the proper time. In use, the fuse was cut or bored for the time desired and driven into the fuse-holder in the base of the shell just before the shell was loaded into the gun. Some fuses were designed so that, if they did not burst the shells in the air, they would

A Union Army mortar in front of Petersburg, Va., during the American Civil War

explode them immediately on contact with any hard surface; others were simple percussion nose-fuses, designed to burst the shells on contact only.

Shaping of Shells. A few of the rifled guns of this period were breechloaders, and some used shells cast in the shape of the specially designed rifled bore; i.e., the Whitworth breech-loaders, which had hexagonal bores and used shells cast to fit them, and the Lancaster muzzle-loaders, with bores in the form of spiraled ovals instead of being rifled. Guns were fired either by percussion locks and primers flashing into a vent communicating with the powder charge, or by the older method of igniting priming powder in a depression at the top of the vent hole.

Among the best known of the American rifled guns of the Civil War period were the Parrot muzzle-loading rifles of from 3- to 10-in. bore. They shot elongated shells, weighing from 10 to 250 lb., and having expanding brass driving skirts. Velocities were about 1,000 ft. per sec. The range of a 6.4-in., 100-pounder Parrot rifle is given in contemporary material as 3,100 yd., effectively outranging the smoothbores of the same period by better than two to one.

Use of Mortars. Mortars continued to be used, especially large-bore models for siege work and for occasional naval mounting on mortar-ships which were designed to bombard shore defenses but were of very little use in a general naval engagement. An unusual example of this type of weapon was the Mallet sectional mortar cast in 1858; this was 8 ft. long, had a 36-in. bore, and weighed 50 tons. It shot a 2,400-lb. spherical shell with a bursting charge of 480 lb. of gun-powder and a propelling charge of 70 lb.

American Civil War Guns. The artillery of the Civil War consisted of horse-drawn field guns with bores up to 4 or 5 in., field howitzers up to 8 in., regular siege mortars up to 15 in., and big naval and siege guns up to 15 and 20 in. Most of these were smoothbore, but there was a fair percentage of rifled long guns. Siege and fortification guns were mounted on wooden or iron carriages capable of accurate adjustment for range or traverse. The simple quoin had been replaced by the elevating screw, a long screw pivoted in the carriage and passing through the threaded cascabel, thus allowing very fine adjustment for elevation. Casemate guns fired through ports in fortifications, like those on the lower decks of naval vessels; guns mounted *en barbette* fired over the walls with a greater range of lateral fire. The extensive use of shells on shipboard doomed the wooden warship, and, in the field, bursting standard shells near the ground and conical shrapnel in the air increased the range of artillery casualties to personnel to nearly two miles from the batteries.

Horse-drawn field guns of battery D, Fifth U.S. Artillery, go into action against the Confederate line near Fredericksburg, Va., during the American Civil War.

A "Big Bertha," the famous 42-centimeter Krupp cannon used by the German artillery during World War I, was named for Frau Bertha von Bohlen, head of the Krupp family.

Pickett's famous charge at Gettysburg was under the shell-fire of General Winfield Scott Hancock's 173 cannon for nearly all of its 1½-mi. advance from the Confederate lines, so that Pickett's valiant 15,000 were badly cut up long before musket range was reached.

An example of the effect of shell-firing naval guns of large size was provided by the engagement between the *Alabama* and the *Kearsarge* during the Civil War. Action was opened at 900 yd., but the *Alabama* was sunk principally as a result of the bursting of one 11-in. spherical shell from a smooth-bore gun which struck almost precisely at her water line from a range of 800 yd.

Franco-Prussian War Artillery. The Franco-Prussian War was lost by the French for many reasons, one of which was the superiority of the Prussian ordnance. This consisted mainly of Krupp breech-loading field guns, fitted with steel shields to protect the gunners who had no occasion to get out in front of them. These guns made short work of the French muzzle-loaders and of the "secret weapons" of the French, the mitrailleuses, which were crude machine guns resembling cannon and used by the French at cannon ranges, and even against cannon, although their missiles were only showers of small-caliber rifle bullets.

Developments after 1870. The period from 1870 to 1900 was one of increasingly powerful and larger guns for naval and fortification use. Guns were built of composite metals and methods of manufacture included jackets of varying lengths shrunk into place, or strengthening layers of wire wound and welded over relatively thin cores. Weights increased to upward of 100 tons. These guns were mounted in shore batteries but also were used on shipboard, where they changed not only the methods of mounting but the designs of ships. Between 1870 and 1900 the ironclad warship, in addition to becoming far larger and better armored, abandoned the "broadside" type of gun mount and placed its relatively few but enormously heavy guns in revolving turrets or barbette armor-clad mounts. Muzzle- and breech-loading guns were both in use after 1870, but the latter replaced the former as the period progressed. Most of the heavy breechloaders used an interrupted-screw type of breechblock, and this has remained the strongest breech closure system. The development of smokeless powder between 1885 and 1895 added greatly to the power and range of guns and also made necessary further increases in the strength of guns. One example of the use of the heavy rifled guns on the early ironclads was the bombardment of the forts at Alexandria, Egypt, by the British fleet in 1882. Fire was opened at ranges of from 1,500 to 4,000 yd., and the forts were reduced with relatively little damage to the ships; the land batteries were numerically superior to the ships' guns firing against them, but they were composed mostly of old-fashioned smoothbore muzzle-loaders.

In the realm of smaller guns, corresponding improvement was taking place. The mechanically-ignited, nose-positioned time fuse, accurately adjustable for varying ranges, was invented in France in 1877, and at about this time small field pieces up to 3- or 4-in. bore began to use fixed ammunition in conjunction with their breech-loading systems. The next step was the development between 1890 and 1895 of the rapid-fire gun, first for naval and then for land use. The usual rapid-fire gun had a recuperator or recoil brake of spring, or spring and hydraulic action, fitted between the gun barrel and its mount. Recoil of the gun did not move the mount, and in many examples the movement of the gun barrel in relation to the mount cammed open the breechblock and ejected the empty shell case; the barrel was returned to battery by spring action. In some models, throwing in a loaded shell caused the breechblock to close, making the gun ready for firing. The French 75-mm. field gun model of 1897 was a good example of this type of gun. Later it was used extensively during World War I in the tremendous artillery bombardments that were characteristic of that conflict. While sustained fire at rates of not over 6 or 8 shots per minute was the normal procedure with guns of this type, the American artillerymen using these guns in France sometimes reached a speed of 30 shots per minute for brief periods of firing.

Fuses also improved constantly during this period. In

A United States Army 155-mm. howitzer is prepared to fire against a German-held town during World War II.

some cases their firing mechanisms were partly made by watch companies, and they could be set to fire surely and accurately at any one-fifth of a second during the travel of the shell.

Artillery in World Wars I and II. *Development of Shells.* The further development of smokeless powder and high explosives such as TNT, amatol, picric acid, and similar compounds, and the use of poison gas, culminated in World War I in fairly well standardized types of shells. Shrapnel, with a range of 5,000 or 6,000 yds., burst in the air with a shotgun effect over troop concentrations; it lost much of its usefulness where such concentrations did not exist. High explosives, with nose-positioned time or delayed-action percussion fuses, were fired against fortifications or matériel and either burst long enough after hitting to allow penetration or, if used for antiaircraft fire, burst in the air at a preset height. Armor-piercing shells were essentially heavy and strong in the nose, with a relatively small bursting charge fired by a delayed-action base fuse. Gas shells were used to lay down a concentration of gas beyond the range of direct projectors and had only enough of a bursting charge to release the gas they contained. Incendiary or tracer compounds could be added to most of the above types for ob-

servation and burning effect and were used principally for aircraft and antiaircraft fire.

Comparison of Basic Weapons. In general, guns used in World Wars I and II were similar, but improved carriages, sights, operating equipment, and target-locating devices increased their efficiency tremendously in the second conflict. For example, the French 75 in World War I had a range of about 7,500 yd., and its mount was designed for very little elevation and to be drawn by horses at about 6 m.p.h. The same basic gun in World War II had a range of over 13,000 yd., and a split-trail mount capable of 40° of elevation; with its rubber-tired wheels, it could be hauled by motor truck at speeds up to 50 m.p.h.

Howitzers of 75-mm. and 105-mm. bore and relatively light weight became excellent medium-range, all-purpose weapons which, in the case of the "pack howitzers," could be disassembled for movement by airplane. Muzzle velocities of most of the field howitzers were between 1,200 and 1,500 ft. per sec. in comparison with 2,000 ft. or so for the regular field guns. During World War II improved antitank weapons added about a third to this speed in standard-sized weapons and produced velocities up to 5,000 ft. per sec. in some specially built small-bore guns. In mounting guns up to 90 mm. on tanks, the muzzle brake, a new recoil-control feature, was added, especially in German and Russian weapons. The muzzle brake was made in several designs on arms of all sizes, but in principle it was an attachment to the muzzle of a gun barrel that pocketed some of the gas from the discharge, so that its forward thrust on the brake would reduce the recoil of the gun. Fieldpieces of World War II ranged in size to the 155-mm. gun, based on the French M1918, throwing a 95-lb. shell 26,000 yd.

Automatic Cannon and Machine Guns. Two new developments in ordnance prior to and during World War II were the application of automatic action to relatively large cannon, principally for aircraft and antiaircraft work, and the invention of the recoilless gun. Machine guns in World War I reached a size of about .50 cal. in low-velocity loads; experimental guns of this caliber in regular rifle velocity were being developed. Also low-velocity pom-poms or Maxim automatic guns in 1- and 1½-in. cal. were used to some extent in anti-

United States self-propelled caterpillar mounted with an 8-in. howitzer (Mark IX, model 1921)

The United States Army's 1918 model of a 3-in. antiaircraft gun, with its auto-trailer carriage

BROWN BROTHERS

aircraft fire, although they were large and extremely clumsy in relation to their power. Antiaircraft fire by single-shot, quick-firing, 3-in. guns on high-angle mounts was practiced by artillerymen of all combatant nations, but even against the slow-speed, low-flying planes of the period it was notoriously ineffective.

Between the two wars various .50-cal. machine guns employing velocities comparable to regular rifle ammunition (2,500-3,000 ft. per sec.) were perfected. These required relatively little alteration of the design of existing machine guns of rifle caliber, but a group of larger automatic cannon from 20-mm. to 40-mm. cal. embodied definitely new designs. Several types of 20-mm. (.787-in.) automatic cannon were developed, including the Oerlikon and Hispano Suiza, both used for ground and airplane mounting. These fired at a cyclic rate of about 600 shots per minute, with a muzzle velocity of about 2500 ft. per sec. and used explosive, tracer, and incendiary shells, as well as armor-piercing solid shot. An American 37-mm. aircraft cannon was also developed but was never very popular, since its velocity was in the old 1,200-ft. class. One of the best of the ground-mount antiaircraft automatic guns was the 40-mm. Bofors Swedish gun. This shot 2-lb. explosive shells at a cyclic rate of about 120 rounds per minute; Bofors were commonly mounted on ships for antiaircraft fire in banks of four, firing simultaneously and being controlled for direction and discharge as a single unit.

Antiaircraft Batteries. Control and speed of fire of the larger antiaircraft guns, ranging from 3 in. to 5 in. in bore, were also greatly improved. Batteries of four guns of the latest quick-firing types were set up with electrical controls and radar aiming devices. A gun in this class was not fully automatic, but its quick-firing features were developed to the point where it was only necessary for the loader to throw a shell into the tray; the gun was then loaded and fired and the shell ejected by spring and recoil action. Batteries were pointed and control-fired by radar-directed electrical equipment. Another great improvement was the proximity fuse, a closely guarded secret developed after entry of the United States into World War II. This was a fuse that, instead of being set for distance before firing, had as part of its mechanism a miniature radio set that sent out a continuous impulse as the shell traveled towards its mark; the echo of this impulse, returning to the shell as it arrived within effective

bursting range of the mark, operated the firing mechanism and exploded the shell.

Naval Antiaircraft Guns. Since improved aircraft were the greatest menace to warships in the extensive naval war in the Pacific during World War II, upper decks of battleships and aircraft carriers bristled with antiaircraft artillery of all types, capable of spewing up a veritable inverted rain of tracers, explosives, and incendiaries in calibers from .50 to 5 in. Although the guns and shells used in World War II were basically similar to those of World War I, the development of automatic fire, radar sighting, and proximity fuses produced antiaircraft fire which so far eclipsed that of World War I as to make a comparison difficult.

Recoilless Rifle. The recoilless gun, or, as it was officially described, the "57-mm. and 75-mm. Rifle, Recoilless," was developed during World War II by the United States Ordnance Department, and was used in both calibers by United States forces during the latter part of the war. The 57-mm. model weighed 45 lb. and could be fired from the shoulder or a light bipod; it threw a 3-lb. shell 4,300 yd. and had a muzzle velocity of 1,200 ft. per sec. The 75-mm. model weighed 105 lb. and was shot from a light machine-gun tripod; it threw a 14-lb. shell 7,200 yd. and had a muzzle velocity of 1,000 ft. per sec. The principle involved use of a pierced shell case, so that some of the gases from the propellent charge spurted to the rear through specially shaped vents in the breech at the time of firing and thus counteracted the normal recoil. The gunners could not stand behind it and its rearward flash, and the cloud of dust stirred up by the discharge disclosed its position to enemy observers. It was, however, a completely new source of low-angle fire, mobile enough for use in advanced positions against tanks or field fortifications.

Improved Mortar Types. Mortars were prominently revived during the last stages of both World Wars I and II. In the trenches in World War I the need of a short-range, high-angle weapon was immediately apparent. At the beginning of the war most nations had rather unwieldy big-bore weapons of the type weighing about 1,000 lb. and shooting shells weighing between 150 and 200 lb. up to ranges of 1,000 yd. or more. While these mortars shot shells comparable to those from guns weighing ten times as much and were reasonably adaptable to trench use, they were still too bulky for the most effective results. Late in the war the

United States Army 120-mm. anti-aircraft guns (M1) are demonstrated at the Army Proving Grounds at Aberdeen, Md.

U.S. ARMY PHOTO

English Stokes mortar, prototype of all later trench mortars, made its appearance.

This type of mortar resembles a piece of stovepipe on a bipod mount. Its effectiveness lies in its shell, which is a winged projectile similar in appearance to an airplane bomb, but carrying at its base its own propellant and bursting charges. The tube or barrel is a definite reversion to the older types of mortars, since it is muzzle-loading and smooth-bore, but it is not chambered like the older weapons and has a fixed firing pin at the breech. The bipod is accurately adjustable for range and is equipped with a sight and spirit level; the base plate supports the breech on any kind of terrain and keeps the tube from moving around with each shot. Two sizes still used by the United States Army are the 61-mm. mortar, weighing 39 lb. but breaking down into three light loads, and the 81-mm. mortar, weighing 134 lb. but also breaking down into three loads. Extreme ranges are between 1,200 and 3,000 yd., with shells weighing from 3 to 14 lb. Mortars are set up for high-angle fire, and the shells are dropped down the muzzle; the primer of the propellant charge strikes the fixed firing pin and is exploded. Adjustment for distance is made by regulating the amount of propellant used with the shells, as well as by changing the angle of the barrel. A large mortar, with a 4.2-in. rifled barrel, uses a shell with an expanding soft-metal driving band

WIDE WORLD PHOTO

Shown in firing position with its mount and sighting equipment is a modern American 155-mm. mortar, used for the penetration of semipermanent fortifications at long ranges.

to grip the rifling instead of fins to control the flight. The rate of fire is as fast as the shells can be dropped down the muzzle, since no other firing procedure is required.

Naval and Coastal Guns. In the other extreme, the biggest guns in modern artillery are the naval and seacoast guns in the turrets or disappearing mounts of battleships or fortifications. These have changed little in principle since 1900 but have greatly increased their effective range. The 12- and 16-in. types of naval and coast-defense guns have ranges between 40,000 and 55,000 yd., with shells weighing between 1,000 and 2,500 lb. The efficiency of these modern guns was demonstrated at Oran, during World War II, when, from a

BROWN BROTHERS

A German 150-mm. trench mortar used in World War I

range so distant that attacking Allied forces were below the horizon, an enemy battleship was put out of action by one radar-directed salvo.   C. T. H.

UNITED STATES ARMY ARTILLERY

The sections immediately following pertain to various phases of artillery as exemplified in the practices and organization of the United States Army.

CLASSIFICATION OF WEAPONS

Artillery weapons are classified in the three general categories of light, medium, and heavy.

Light Artillery. Light artillery pieces include the 75-mm. pack howitzer, organic to airborne and mountain

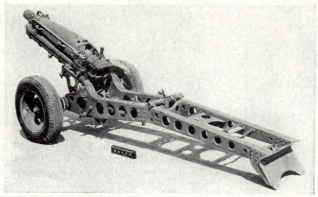

U.S. ARMY PHOTO

A UNITED STATES ARMY 75-MM. PACK HOWITZER

divisions, and the 105-mm. howitzer, which is the standard direct support weapon in the infantry and armored divisions. Three battalions with the latter weapon are organically assigned to each division. Rockets up to 4.5 in. in diameter are classified as light artillery but are rather a special-purpose weapon and are not organic to divisions; they are organic to army artillery. Targets usually attacked by light artillery are enemy personnel, installations under light overhead cover, and any enemy formation or installation which may threaten or impede advancing infantry or tanks.

Medium Artillery. In the medium class, the principal weapon is the 155-mm. howitzer. The companion piece for this howitzer in World War II was the 4.5-in. gun, since

obsolete. One 155-mm. howitzer battalion is organically assigned to each infantry and armored division for a general support role to reinforce the fires of the three 105-mm. howitzer battalions. This medium battalion is also employed by corps and army. Targets usually attacked by these weapons include enemy artillery, command posts, communication centers, and supply installations. The 155-mm. howitzer is considered a good weapon for destruction missions.

Heavy Artillery. Heavy artillery includes the 155-mm. gun, the 8-in. howitzer, the 240-mm. howitzer, and the 8-in. gun. Heavy artillery is employed by corps and army. These weapons are employed in counterbattery fire against enemy artillery, for destruction of heavy emplacements, in long-range interdiction and harassing missions, and for attacking sensitive areas, such as supply points, rail or trucking centers, and ammunition and fuel dumps deep in enemy territory. Some of the important detailed characteristics of artillery weapons are set forth in the table below.

ARTILLERY AMMUNITION

Artillery ammunition comprises all ammunition used in firearms of caliber greater than .60 in., with the exception of rockets. Such ammunition normally consists of a projectile, a propelling charge (propellant) to drive the projectile out of the weapon, and a primer to start the burning of the propelling charge. A fuse or other device may be used on the projectile to initiate action at the time desired.

Classification. Artillery ammunition is classified as service, practice, blank, and drill ammunition. Service ammunition is used in combat. Practice ammunition is used for training purposes, such as target practice and simulated combat. It usually consists of a projectile which has the same ballistics as the one being simulated but which is inert or harmlessly loaded. Blank ammunition contains no projectile and is used for salutes and simulated fire. Drill ammunition simulates the weight and contour of service ammunition but is completely inert, having no propelling charge. It is used for training in the handling of ammunition and the loading of weapons.

There are three types of rounds in use. The fixed round, or cartridge, consists of a cartridge case containing the propelling charge and a primer, firmly crimped to the projectile, which is usually already fused. This is handled as a unit in packing, shipping, loading into the weapon, and firing. Most United States ammunition of caliber smaller

CHARACTERISTICS OF FIELD ARTILLERY WEAPONS

		75-mm. Howitzer	105-mm. Howitzer	4.5-in. Rocket Launcher	155-mm. Howitzer	155-mm. Gun	8-in. Howitzer	240-mm. Howitzer	8-in. Gun
Weight of Piece (Tons)	Towed	.72	2.49	.64	6.35	15.05	14	49.41	51.86
	Self-Propelled	..	19.5	..	21.5	41.5	41.5	64.5	67.0
Time to Emplace in Firing Position (Minutes)	Towed	3	3	2	5	30 to 360	30 to 360	60 to 360	60 to 360
	Self-Propelled	..	½	..	1	1	1	3	3
Weight of Projectiles (Pounds)		14.7	33	42	96.1	95.1	200	360	240
Rate of Fire (Shells per Gun per Minute)	Maximum	6	4	16	3	1	1	1	1
	Normal	3	2	16	1	½	½	½	½
Effective Diameter of Burst (Yards)		30	50	50	60	60	80	100	80
Range (Yards)		9,610	12,205	5,200	16,355	25,715	18,510	25,255	35,490

A UNITED STATES ARMY 240-MM. HOWITZER

U.S. ARMY PHOTO

than 105-mm. is of this type. The semifixed round contains all the components of the fixed round in one assembly, but the cartridge case is not crimped to the projectile. It is thus possible to remove the projectile easily in the field in order to adjust the propelling charge for zone firing. Ammunition for the 60-mm. and 81-mm. mortars constitutes a special class of semifixed round. This is because the propelling charge increments are accessible for adjustment for zone fire. In this type of round there is no cartridge case. The primer is in the rear of the boom which carries the fins, and the powder increments are attached to the fins or to the fin shaft. Semifixed rounds are used in certain United States 75-mm. and 105-mm. ammunition, as well as in the mortar shell mentioned. In separate-loading ammunition, as the name implies, the projectile is loaded into the weapon first, and the propelling charge follows. This charge may be contained in a separate cartridge case, also containing the primer and a closing plug. In some types, the charge is contained in a cloth bag, and the primer is inserted into the firing mechanism of the gun. Separate-loading ammunition is used in all United States ammunition larger than 105 mm.

BROWN BROTHERS

Workers charging shells in a Belgian munitions plant during World War I

Propelling Elements. *Charges.* Propelling charges are composed of a quantity of propellant, with an igniter, in a suitable container. Modern propellants may be nitrocellulose, double-base (mixture of nitrocellulose and nitroglycerine), or FNH (Flashless, Non-Hygroscopic) powder. The latter is either nitrocellulose or double-base powder, with certain additives which decrease the hygroscopicity of the powder and cause it to produce cooler products of combustion. United States ammunition uses powder in the shape of cylindrical grains; these usually are perforated with one or more holes parallel to the axis of the cylinder. The size of the grains, and the perforation, which leaves "webs" of powder between the holes, have an effect on the manner and rate of burning of the powder. The composition of a powder may determine whether it is relatively smokeless or relatively flashless; it is difficult to obtain both conditions at once. Choice of powder composition, grain size, web size, and perforation are matters to be decided in the case of each projectile in each weapon. It is necessary to control the rate of pressure developed in the weapon.

Primer. The primer provides the flame which initiates the propelling charge. Percussion primers, most extensively used in United States Army ammunition, are activated by the impact of a firing pin on the sensitive parts of the primer. Electric primers, used largely in United States seacoast and naval ammunition, are activated by an electric bridge in the primer. Most artillery primers also contain an igniter charge, usually black powder, which throws a hot flame into the propelling charge.

Cartridge Case. The cartridge case serves several purposes. First, it contains the powder, and protects it from loss or contamination. Second, it acts as an obturator in many weapons. It expands in the chamber of the weapon, helping to seal the chamber against the loss of propelling gases through the breech. Third, it holds the various components of the fixed round together, so as to make handling, loading, and firing quick and convenient operations. Cartridge cases are usually made of brass but may also be made of steel.

Cartridge cases for ammunition for United States recoilless weapons are perforated to permit powder gases to flow out of the case to the vent ports of the weapon. In other respects, such ammunition is similar to conventional types.

Fuses. Fuses provide the essential initiating action in most projectiles. They are classified as to location on the projectile as point or base fuses, and with respect to functioning, as time, impact, or proximity fuses. The commonest type is the point detonating fuse, which functions directly on impact. According to the quickness of functioning after impact, these fuses are classed as delay, instantaneous, or superquick. A fuse which functions on very light targets is called supersensitive.

Time fuses function at a preset time after firing, without necessarily impacting the target. The fuse timing mechanism may be mechanical, such as clockwork, or it may be timed by the burning of an internal element. Time fuses may be set, by hand or by a special device called a fuse setter, to function at any time over a certain range.

Fuses generally consist of a series or train of explosive elements, initiated by a primer or detonator activated by a striker or firing pin. Each element is successively larger and less sensitive, until a booster charge, last in the train, detonates the shell filler or ignites the expeller charge, as the case may be. The booster may be part of the fuse proper, or it may be a separate but connected unit.

Safety Devices. Safety devices are incorporated into all United States fuses. A "bore safe" fuse is one which cannot function until the shell is fired and out of the bore of the gun. A "detonator safe" fuse is one in which the main charge cannot be activated until the shell is fired, even if the detonator in the fuse should be set off accidentally. A fuse with "delayed arming" cannot function until the shell is a certain distance from the weapon. This prevents injury to the gun crew if the shell were to strike an obstruction, such as a tree, near the gun.

Shell Stabilization. To achieve accuracy in flight, projectiles must be stabilized by one of two means. Rotated projectiles are fired from a rifled weapon and spin rapidly in gyroscopic fashion. Fin-stabilized projectiles do not rotate but are kept from tumbling by the action of the fins.

The typical rotated projectile has a cylindrical body and a pointed nose, which may be conical but more usually is of a special curved shape called an ogive. The nose may be a windshield, or the fuse itself may constitute the nose. The tail of the projectile may be "square," or it may have a slight conical taper called a boattail. Toward the rear is a rotating band (sometimes more than one) which imparts rotation to the shell by meshing with the rifling of the weapon and which prevents powder gases from blowing by the projectile. The band may be brass, copper, iron, mild steel, or other material. The conventional band is engraved by the rifling of the weapon. In some types, called "preengraved," the engraving (cuts for the rifling) is done in manufacture. At the front of the cylindrical portion is the bourrelet (ridge), which bears against the lands (bore) of the gun. A rear bourrelet is also used in some designs. Tracer elements are used at the rear of some projectiles to enable gunners to observe their flight.

The typical fin-stabilized mortar shell is streamlined in both the front and rear. A shaft, known as the boom, projects from the rear of the shell, carrying the fins, primer, and powder increments.

Types of Projectiles. Following is a brief discussion of a number of types of service projectiles in general use by the United States.

High-Explosive (HE) Shell. The high-explosive shell consists of a steel casing filled with a high explosive such as TNT. A fuse initiates the explosion, which is usually transmitted to the high explosive filler by means of a booster. The HE shell produces a blast effect and at the same time hurls fragments at high velocity. The size and velocity of the fragments may be controlled to some extent by the design of the shell, wall thickness, the steel used, and the type and the quantity of explosives. This type of shell is the most versatile and widely used projectile. To use the HE shell against personnel or aircraft, time, impact, or proximity fuses may be employed. The HE shell of small caliber is fused for direct impact against aircraft. Against buildings, lightly armored targets, and fortifications, the HE shell is fitted with a delay fuse to explode after the shell has penetrated the target. Against concrete, a special fuse permits deep penetration before detonation. The HE shell is made in nearly all calibers of United States Army ammunition.

Chemical and White Phosphorus (WP) Shell. Similar to the HE shell, the chemical and white phosphorus shell consists of a thin steel shell filled with white phosphorus or a chemical agent. A steel burster casing along the shell axis contains a small high-explosive burster charge which fragments the shell and spreads the contents. The charge is detonated by a point detonating fuse through a burster initiator. Modern WP shells are made to match the ballistics of the corresponding HE shell, and are used for "spotting" or ranging and for creating smoke screens. Since white phosphorus makes an easily visible white smoke cloud and pillar, the point of burst may be determined fairly accurately. These shells are very effective in placing a quick but shortlived smoke screen in front of a point target. They are made in most calibers from 57-mm. to 155-mm.

Smoke Shell. Two types of shell are used specifically for making smoke screens. The base-ejection type has two or more canisters which are ejected by the action of a time fuse and burn as they fall on the ground. Most shells of this type are loaded with HC mixture, which gives a dense gray screen. The base-emission type contains the smoke mixture directly in the shell and has no fuse. The mixture is ignited through a delay pellet by the powder gases in the gun. These types are made for various weapons in calibers from 75-mm. to 155-mm.

High-Explosive Antitank (HEAT) Shell. The high-explosive antitank shell is a special type of HE shell in which the explosive is shaped as a "hollow charge." By virtue of the shape of the charge, part of the force of the explosive is concentrated in a jet which is capable of blasting a hole through armor. These shells are made largely in the medium calibers from 57-mm. to 105-mm.

Armor-piercing (AP) and Armor-piercing Capped (APC) Shot. Both armor-piercing and armor-piercing capped shells are made of very hard and strong heat-treated steel. The head is usually harder than the rest of the shot, and the body is so treated as to be very tough. An armor-piercing cap is placed in front of the nose in some designs to aid in overcoming face-hardened armor plate. A windshield is usually placed at the very front of the projectile to give it good ballistics. These shots are solid and contain no explosive; however, after penetration of armor, they usually retain enough velocity to cause considerable damage inside of a tank. Armor-piercing and armor-piercing capped shot are made only for highvelocity guns.

High-Explosive Armor-piercing Shot (HEAP). High-explosive armor-piercing shot is similar to AP shot but has a small cavity in the rear, containing high explosive. A base

KRUPP WORKS, THE FAMOUS GERMAN MUNITIONS FACTORY, AS IT APPEARED DURING WORLD WAR I

detonating fuse initiates the explosive charge after penetration of the target has occurred. The heavy structure and excellent physical properties of the shot give it penetrating qualities nearly as good as the solid shot, while the high explosive charge enables it to cause more damage after penetration. This type of shot is made in various calibers from 57-mm. up to 16-in. Most effective seacoast ammunition is of this type, which is particularly effective against armored vessels.

Hypervelocity Armor-piercing Shot (HVAP). One of the major achievements of World War II, hypervelocity armor-piercing shot, can penetrate much heavier armor than any other type of armor-piercing projectile of the same caliber. The heart of this ammunition is a tungsten carbide core, very dense, hard, and strong. Because of the light materials used in the remainder of the shot, called the carrier, the shot as a whole weighs less than an HE shell of the same caliber and achieves a higher velocity in the same gun. The core achieves its penetrating power partly because of its higher velocity, but in greater measure because of its physical characteristics. In 1947 this type was standard only for 76-mm. and 90-mm. tank guns.

Incendiary Shell. As the name implies, the incendiary shell is filled with a mixture capable of igniting inflammable targets. It may be combined with an HE filler to make a high-explosive incendiary (HE-I) shell, in which the high explosive blasts open the target, such as a gas tank, and the incendiary ignites it or its contents. In 1947 this type was used only in ammunition for 20-mm. guns.

Canister. The canister consists of an arrangement of slugs, usually steel balls, in a sheet-metal can. It has no explosive filling and no fuse. When fired, the case breaks up as it leaves the weapon, and the slugs scatter in a conical pattern like shot from a shotgun. It is used to fire pointblank at an attacking enemy in defense of a gun position, and to clear lanes of fire through underbrush. Use of this type is declining.

Illuminating Shell. The illuminating shell is used to light up a target or observation area. A time fuse initiates an expelling charge at the desired height, which ejects the assembly in the shell. The assembly consists of a parachute, a high-intensity illuminating candle, and supporting shrouds. The assembly falls slowly as it burns. These shells are made in a number of calibers for infantry and field-artillery weapons from 60-mm. to 155-mm.

Atomic Shell. In 1952 it was officially announced that an artillery piece capable of firing an atomic shell had been developed by the U. S. Army. There was, however, no indication as to when weapons of this type might be expected to go into service.

Manufacture. United States ammunition is designed and manufactured with the aim of making an intrinsically dangerous product as safe as possible. Every component is designed to have the requisite strength to prevent premature functioning of the ammunition. Safety devices are built into fuses, boosters, and other components, even though they complicate manufacture. Great care is given to the drawing of tolerances and details of construction. Rigid inspection standards are enforced on metal parts and explosive components and fillers. Propelling charges are carefully tested, weighed, and loaded according to the weight zones of the projectile. Packing and packaging of ammunition is such as to provide safe arrival in the field. It is also considered that accuracy and proper functioning of the ammunition are nearly as important as safety, and extensive measures are taken to insure them. I. H.

ORGANIZATION

Modern Organization. Artillery organization in the American army is divided into two classifications: division artillery and nondivisional artillery.

Division Artillery. Division artillery is that artillery which is organically a part of the division. In the airborne or mountain division, it consists of three 75-mm. pack-howitzer direct support battalions and one 105-mm. howitzer general support battalion. In the infantry or armored division, it consists of three 105-mm. howitzer direct support battalions and one 155-mm. howitzer general support battalion. The direct support battalions are so called because each is paired with one of the three infantry regiments or tank battalions to form a combat team. The primary mission of the direct support artillery battalion is to render continuous and close support to its team member. The general support battalion is so called because its primary mission is to assist, with its heavier projectiles, any one, or all three, of the direct support battalions in the execution of their primary missions. Division artillery in the infantry or armored division organically includes an antiaircraft battalion armed with 40-mm. and .50-caliber automatic antiaircraft weapons. This battalion has the primary mission of protecting the division against hostile air action.

Army and Corps Artillery. Division artillery strength is the minimum for independent action in combat. For sustained and heavy combat, the divisions must be materially augmented in artillery strength. The total combat strength, therefore, is not measured only in the number of divisions but must include the reinforcing and supporting troops in corps and armies. Because it is not feasible or economical to provide organically in each division all the additional artillery strength required under all circumstances, a pool of reinforcing and supporting artillery is assigned to each army, army group, or theatre of operation. Army artillery organizations include all calibers used by field artillery, antiaircraft, and coast artillery. Artillery from this pool is allotted to the corps for combat operations on a rather uniform scale. The only artillery units organic to the corps are the corps artillery headquarters and an observation battalion, which perform the functions of providing the facilities for command, fire direction, counterbattery, survey, and tactical employment of the artillery units allotted by the army to the corps. This system of pooling artillery in the army and suballotting it to corps in quantities and calibers required for the corps mission affords great flexibility. On occasion, the corps may further suballot some of its allotted battalions by attaching them directly to its divisions when conditions demand that direct support battalions be reinforced.

Tactical Subdivisions. The basic tactical artillery organization is the battalion. This is standard for division and army artillery. The standard battalion consists of a headquarters battery; three firing batteries, usually designated as A, B, and C; and a service battery. Army artillery is permanently organized into regiments and brigades. The group organization of World War II was found to be too loose and haphazard, and, as a result, it had been decided in 1947 to resume the regimental formation. The regiment normally consists of four battalions; the brigade, of four regiments. Since the army does not usually retain control of its field artillery units but allots them to corps for combat, and since corps already possess adequate artillery command facilities, it has been found that there is small need for field artillery brigade headquarters. However, some may be organized for special purposes, such as task forces. In organization for combat and in order to gain the desired grouping of calibers and flexibility of fire for a particular mission, battalions are freely exchanged between regiments, and regiments between corps, on a temporary basis. Standard organization, training, and technique permit this to be done with the greatest facility.

The army antiaircraft artillery is organized into battalions, regiments, and brigades. Brigade organization in this branch is essential because of the relatively independent action of antiaircraft artillery. The army does retain combat control of major parts of its antiaircraft artillery due to the many key installations in the army zone which must be protected.

Artillery Scale for a Typical Army with Strength of Three Corps, Each with One Armored and Two Infantry Divisions

Type Unit	Number	Total
Antiaircraft Artillery Brigade	1 per Corps plus 2 per Army	5
105-mm. Howitzer Battalion (Self-Propelled)	1 per Division plus 1 per separate Armored Regiment	12
155-mm. Howitzer Battalion (Towed or Self-Propelled)	2 per Infantry Division (1 per Airborne Division) plus 3 per Corps	21
155-mm. Gun Battalion (Towed or Self-Propelled)	1 per Division plus 1 per Corps	12
8-inch Howitzer Battalion (Towed or Self-Propelled)	1 per Infantry Division plus 2 per Corps	12
240-mm. Howitzer Battalion (Towed or Self-Propelled)	2 per Corps plus 1 per Army	7
8-inch Gun Battalion (Towed or Self-Propelled)	1 per Army	1
4.5-inch Rocket Battalion	2 per Corps	6
Observation Battalion	1 organic per Corps	3

History. The history of the organization of the American artillery may be divided into four phases. The first artillery units organized in the Continental Army during the Revolutionary War were batteries, averaging six guns each. One of these batteries, organized by Alexander Hamilton, has seen continuous service and is the oldest American military organization. It is known currently as Battery D, Fifth Field Artillery. The original type of battery organization lasted until the Civil War, when the artillery battalion, numbering three or four batteries at that time, came into being. The tactical concept of employment of artillery was that field batteries were maneuvered on the battlefield to positions that afforded good fields of fire, while the infantry formed along the flanks of the artillery in order to protect or support it in the defense. In the offense, the artillery first fired a preparation, after which the infantry advanced. The artillery displaced forward by rapid stages, taking new firing positions along the flanks of, or in gaps between, advancing infantry units until the objective was gained.

BROWN BROTHERS

American Civil War artillery ready for action

Men of the United States 197th Field Artillery Battalion, 30th Infantry Division, gather around a 105-mm. howitzer as the 100,000th shell is fired against the enemy somewhere in Belgium during World War II.

Artillery technique was by direct laying, i.e., the gunner sighted directly at his target in the same manner as the rifleman. The range and accuracy of weapons did not permit close supporting overhead fire.

The period from about 1880 to 1900 produced revolutionary improvements in weapons, propellants, and projectiles in all the armies of the world. Improved technique kept pace. At the time of the Spanish-American War, the American artillery had perfected the indirect laying technique and developed overhead fire procedure. In indirect laying, the gunner sets a predetermined angular value on the scale of his panoramic sight and traverses the cannon until his sight is on a fixed aiming point. The calculated value of the angular setting causes the cannon to be pointed at the desired target. One vast improvement of indirect laying opened the new field of unobserved fire, i.e., by using data determined from maps, fire could be placed on unseen targets.

From colonial times until 1900, the artillery was a single branch of the service, with batteries designated as field type, to accompany the army in the field, or seacoast type, permanently emplaced to protect harbors and other critical points of the seacoast. By 1907 new developments and techniques had produced sufficient variance within the types of artillery to cause the artillery arm to be broken into two separate arms, the Field Artillery and the Coast Artillery. Batteries, currently numbering four guns each, were formed into battalions, and battalions into regiments. By World War I, the United States had regiments formed into brigades, one of which was organically a part of each division. The heavy caliber guns were formed into brigades of corps and army artillery. The development of the airplane brought the need for a defensive artillery weapon, and, in 1921, the antiaircraft artillery was created as a branch of the Coast Artillery.

In 1935, as a result of the great improvements in fire power of automatic weapons, the War Department conducted experiments in tactical organization with a view to reducing the cumbersome 28,000 man "square" division to a lighter striking force with equal fire power. The "triangular" division was adopted, with the two infantry brigades of two regiments each reduced to three unbrigaded infantry regiments, and the artillery brigade of three regiments reorganized as four separate artillery battalions. In 1942 the army artillery brigades were reorganized into separate battalions, and the regiments were replaced by a new unit, the group. Battalions were not permanently assigned to groups but were attached in numbers of from two to six for periods of combat; this was thought to afford the greatest flexibility and conservation of artillery strength.

By 1940 the development of the armored division had brought a corresponding development in armored self-propelled artillery, used for the direct support of tanks. Armored divisions were assigned three battalions of self-propelled artillery. One important innovation in armored artillery organization which affected postwar artillery organization was the six-gun battery, as opposed to the traditional four-gun battery in other types of field artillery. Based on the success of this arrangement in World War II, the six-gun battery had become standard for field artillery. Experience in World War II also indicated that there was no real need for the separate branches of artillery, and, consequently, they were integrated again into a single arm.

TECHNIQUE AND TACTICS

Types of Missions. The primary mission of the division artillery is to assist its team members in combat by instantly attacking those enemy formations that can harm them or interfere with their missions. The mission of the corps artillery, which is drawn from an army pool and organized into corps, is to reinforce by adding density and depth to the division artillery fire; to attack and destroy the enemy artillery; to disrupt enemy organization and plans by attacking with fire power his attacking forces and his reserves, and to deny him routes and critical areas; to isolate the enemy locally on the battlefield within the limits of range of the pieces; and, by shock action of massed artillery fire, to destroy him or his will to fight.

Observation and Fire Control. In executing these missions, certain procedures and techniques are followed. An artillery observer from the direct support battalion accompanies each front-line infantry and tank company. Also at each supported battalion and regimental command post there is an artillery liaison officer. Through a very complete radio and wire net, these officers call down and control the desired quantity of artillery fire on close-in targets as they are located, and thus the fire from the direct support battalions is continuously placed where it will best aid the supported troops. Two light aircraft with observer pilots are also assigned to each artillery battalion. In World War II these air spotters were eminently successful in locating and bringing artillery fire on targets hidden from ground observers. The fire of its batteries is controlled in each battalion through a fire-direction center. Calls for fire come from any of the observers, usually by radio direct to the fire-direction center, which instantly transmits data to the firing batteries to cause fire to be placed on the target. Based on the information included in the call for fire, the fire of all three batteries may be placed on a single target, or each battery may fire on a separate target. Nor is this by any means the limit of the amount of fire that may respond to the call of a single observer. Through communication systems established between battalions, between division artilleries, and between corps artilleries, the fire of all artillery units within range can be brought down on a single target located by any one of scores of observers distributed along the front or in the air. Another application of massed artillery fire is the familiar T.O.T., or time on target. When it is desired to hit a target or area with a devastating volume of surprise fire, the procedure is as follows. The location and description of the target to be hit, the type and amounts of ammunition to be fired, and the exact second it is desired to have the fire hit the target are predetermined and dispatched to the battalions which are to take part in the shoot. Each battalion fire-direction center computes data for its batteries. When the range to the target is determined, the time of flight for each projectile is known. By subtracting the time of flight from the announced T.O.T., each battery fires at the split second which will assure that all projectiles land on the target simultaneously. This technique, perfected by American artillery in World War II, produces extremely effective results on an enemy. While the fire of all of the

division and corps artillery may be massed on single targets, the division artillery will normally be occupied in attacking close-in targets whereas the corps artillery will penetrate more deeply into enemy territory in a relentless search for additional targets.

The reliability of artillery lies in the fact that once it joins the battle its fire is available around the clock. No condition of weather gives it pause. It is limited only by its maximum range and the ammunition tonnage which can be delivered to the firing positions.   T. E. De S.

ARTILLERY IN OTHER COUNTRIES

Great Britain. In the British Army all artillery formations belong to the Royal Regiment of Artillery, which is a purely ornamental title. British artillery is organized in "troops" of from four to six guns, batteries of two or three troops, and field regiments of three or four batteries. The field regiment comprises the artillery component of a division. Thus the British troop corresponds to the United States battery; the battery, to the battalion. The standard weapon of the British divisional artillery is the 23-pounder howitzer, a weapon not unlike the American 105-mm. howitzer. The British also use heavier weapons in both the gun and howitzer classes, mountain or pack artillery, and seacoast batteries. Antiaircraft artillery was highly developed in Great Britain during World War II for obvious reasons and was under the operational control of the Fighter Command of the Royal Air Force, so that a single headquarters became responsible at all levels of command for the air defense of the whole island and of separate localities.

France. The artillery of the French Army was being reorganized in 1947 in accordance with the lessons of World War I. Its organization in batteries, battalions, and regiments is similar to that of the United States Army.

Soviet Russia. A striking characteristic of the army of the Union of Soviet Socialist Republics (U. S. S. R.) is the use of great masses of guns under a single command—the so-called artillery division, which, in World War II, sometimes comprised as many as 1,000 guns. *See also* ANTIAIRCRAFT DEFENSE; COAST DEFENSE; MACHINE GUN; NAVAL GUNNERY.   G. F. E.

ARTILLERY PLANT, *Pilea microphylla,* annual or biennial of the nettle family, native to Florida and tropical America. It is grown in the South and in greenhouses for its graceful sprays of tiny, glossy leaves. In sunlight, the mature staminate flowers burst open like little explosions, discharging the pollen.   J. C. Wis.

ARTIODACTYLS [ɑ'rtiodæ'ktɪlz], even-toed, hoofed mammals. The group includes the deer, antelope, cattle, sheep, goats, and swine. All of these animals stand on the tips of their third and fourth toes, which are equal in size and bear the weight equally. Each toe is encased in a separate hoof. The first toe of each foot has disappeared. The second and fifth toes are rudimentary or small, and are located high on the sides or rear of the foot. There they rarely furnish any support except perhaps in soft ground; they are used in this way by such animals as pigs and caribou. These two toes are usually called dew-claws. Like other hoofed mammals, artiodactyls feed almost exclusively on vegetation, and the majority prefer grass and other herbs. Most of them have no upper canine teeth and no upper incisors. The latter are replaced by a tough pad, against which the lower incisors are able to cut, twist, and tear off the food. Most artiodactyls have long legs and are swift runners. They generally put up little defense, relying on their speed to keep away from enemies, and on their keen eyes, ears, and noses to warn them of danger. The vast majority of the species, or at least the males, are armed with either horns or antlers. The greatest diversity of species, as well as number of individuals, is found in Africa. Several species of deer, and of course domesticated cattle, sheep, goats, and swine, have been imported into Australia, the only continent where artiodactyls have never occurred naturally. *See also* UNGULATES; RUMINANTS.   V. H. C.

ARTOIS [aʹrtwaʹ], formerly a province in northwestern France, bounded by the provinces of Flanders on the northeast and Picardy on the south and southwest and by the English Channel on the northwest. Like Flanders, it was divided into Walloon and Flemish sections by the Lys River. The terrain is mostly flat but is traversed from southeast to northwest by low hills forming the watershed between the basin of the North Sea and the English Channel. The name Artois was derived from the Atrebates, who inhabited it at the time of Caesar. The capital was Arras. When Baldwin I, count of Flanders, married Judith, daughter of the Carolingian king, Charles the Bald, he received Artois as Judith's dowry. It belonged to the counts of Flanders until 1180, when Philip Augustus of France married Isabel, daughter of Count Thierry d'Alsace, and received Artois as her dowry. In 1322 Artois passed to the House of Burgundy as a result of the marriage of Oto (Otto) IV to the daughter of Philip V of France. It passed with part of the Burgundian domains to the royal house of Austria in 1477. Louis XI claimed Artois with other parts of Burgundy in the same year, on the death of the duke of Burgundy, but it was retained by the Austrian royal house. The French conquered Artois, and the conquest was recognized in the Treaty of the Pyrenees in 1659. After the French Revolution, Artois was formed into most of the department of Pas-de-Calais. *See also* BURGUNDY; PAS-DE-CALAIS.   S. Van. V.

ARTSYBASHEV, MIHAIL PETROVITCH [ʌʹrtsɪbaʹshəf], Russian novelist, was born in the Ukraine, Oct. 18, 1878, and died as a political emigré in Warsaw, Mar. 3, 1927. His ancestry, like that of many Russians, shows a complex origin, with a strong strain of Tatar blood. His mother was Polish.

Artsybashev at first followed a career as a painter, even attaining some repute as a caricaturist, but subsequently devoted himself to the writing of short stories, followed by novels and plays. His first short story, *Pasha Tumanov,* was published in 1901.

Like many other expressions of the realistic school, his writings show Russian life frankly and even brutally. Very often his literary expression, although deep and vividly colored, degenerates into a quite naked exhibit of a society of dissolution, a morbidly exaggerated picture of crime and sexual folly. Some of his novels deal with incurable tuberculars, as, for instance, in *Bunt* ("Mutiny"), *Smert Lande* ("Death of Lande"), or *Sanin.* At the age of twenty-five he published his first substantial novel, *Sanin,* which at once gained him a national reputation. This work showed him already in revolt against social restraints, away from oppression and conventional regimentation.

Among Artsybashev's novels and plays done before 1912 are *Rabotchi Shevyrev* ("Worker Shevyrev"), *Poslednei Tcherty* ("At the Extreme Limit"), *Revnost* ("Jealousy") and *Voyna* ("War"). Some of his writings deal with episodes taken from the bloody repression of revolutionary movements by the Tsarist government. Such are *Krovavoye Pyatno* ("Bloody Spot"), *Na Byelom Snyegu* ("On the White Snow"), *Odin Den* ("One Day"), *Tchelovyecheskaya Volna* ("Human Wave"), and other short stories.

For having left Soviet Russia, and for having attempted to discredit revolutionary ardor by acknowledging revolutionary frustration in some of his writings, Artsybashev was considered a negative personality by the Soviet government. He was repeatedly sued before courts, and his novels, in many instances, were confiscated as immoral. He was the father of Boris Artzybasheff, Russo-American illustrator and writer.   K. V. G.

ARUBA [ɑruʹbɑ], an island of about 69 sq. mi., a part of the Netherlands West Indies territory of Curaçao, situated in the Caribbean Sea at 12° 30′ N. lat. and 70° W. long.,

COURTESY OF STANDARD OIL COMPANY OF NEW JERSEY

A Divi-Divi tree, Caesalpinia coriaria, commonly known as the "one-way tree," dominates an Aruban landscape. The constant winds of the Caribbean blowing from the east account for the direction of tree growth.

165 mi. northeast of Maracaibo, Venezuela, and 50 mi. west by north of the island of Curaçao. Aruba was formed by a capping of limestone on top of ancient crystalline rocks. Much of the softer limestone has been eroded away, leaving a series of low limestone hills and ridges. The highest elevation on the island is a little over 600 ft. above sea level. The northeastern and northern coasts are cliffed, and the southern coast is fringed by coral. The island is within the path of the Northeast Trade Winds, but because of its low elevation these winds deposit little moisture. The average annual rainfall is approximately 20 in., and November is the wet month, with about 5 in. of rain. The average temperature is 81° F., varying between 78° F. in January and 83° F. in September. Because of the low rainfall, high temperature, high evaporation rate, and rapid run-off of water, the island is semiarid and the natural vegetation is limited to grass, cacti, agaves, mangrove swamps, and some palms. Agriculture is limited to small truck gardens, papayas, mangoes, coconuts, aloes, a few citrus fruits, guavas, and watermelons. Some sorghum is also grown. Goats, sheep, cattle, donkeys, and pigs are the most common farm animals. Phosphate of lime and a little gold have been found on the island, but these deposits have decreased in amount and value to the point of being economically unimportant.

The Spanish occupied Aruba early in the fifteenth century but were driven out by the Dutch about 1634. Since that time the Dutch have held the island continuously except for a period of British rule during the Napoleonic Wars. In the Colonial period Curaçao, including Aruba, enjoyed a profitable slave trade, but slavery was abolished during the first part of the nineteenth century and Aruba went into a decline. The economic and world importance of the island was revived in 1925, when American, British, and Dutch oil interests built oil refineries there, convenient to the Maracaibo Basin oil field. Crude oil is imported in shallow-draft tankers from the Maracaibo district and from Colombia, East Venezuela, and Trinidad. The oil is refined, and gasoline, Diesel oil, and fuel oil are exported to Europe and the United States. Machinery and food are imported. The oil companies have built small towns, schools, roads, docks and other facilities for their employees. The island has a cosmopolitan population of Americans, western Europeans, Negroes, Chinese, and Hindus. Dutch, Papiamento (a local dialect), and English are spoken. The population of Aruba in 1870 was 3,792; in 1915, 9,204; in 1938, 28,155; and in 1948, about 39,000. The capital and principal city is Orangestad, which has cable, radio, plane, and ship connections with South America and the rest of the world.

J. E. F.

ARUM [ɛ'ərəm], also called aroids, a large family of plants with possibly 100 genera and about 1500 species. They are chiefly tropical, although the eastern wild flowers,

Jack-in-the-pulpit, Arisaema triphyllum, a typical arum from central Africa

jack-in-the-pulpit, *Arisaema triphyllum,* and skunk cabbage, *Symplocarpus foetidus,* belong to this family, and there is one species on the Pacific coast, the western skunk cabbage, *Lysichitum camtschatcense.* Many species are grotesque in appearance. Some, like the calla lily, *Zantedeschia aethiopica,* are ornamental, and a few yield important food products. What is usually considered the flower is, in reality, a white or colored bract protecting the club-like spadix, on which are crowded the tiny true florets. The tuberous roots often contain starch, and become edible after

WATER-ARUM, OR NORTH AMERICAN WILD CALLA, CALLA PALUSTRIS

cooking removes the bitter taste of the raw root. Dasheen or taro, *Colocasia esculenta,* has been grown as a vegetable in the South since 1913. Vautia or malanga, species of *Xanthosoma* native to tropical America, are cultivated like taro. In Hawaii taro tubers and poi, a fermented paste made from the tubers, are staple foods, and the leaves and young shoots are used as greens. In England, the cuckoo-pint or lords-and-ladies, *Arum maculatum,* is sometimes cultivated. It has handsome but poisonous red fruits, and the root yields an edible starch called British arrowroot or Portland sago.

J. C. Wis.

ARUNDEL [æ'rəndɛl], a small market town and municipal borough, forming with Shoreham the parliamentary division of Sussex, England, on the Arun River, 58 mi. southwest of London and four miles from the coast. At the time of the Domesday Book it was recorded as being a prosperous town and port. William the Conqueror granted the town to Roger de Montgomery in the eleventh century, and Montgomery built the castle for which the town is famous. The town was severely damaged by fire in 1338, but it was soon rebuilt. The castle was frequently assaulted in the ensuing centuries, particularly during the seventeenth century, but was restored by Charles, the Duke of Norfolk, in the late eighteenth and early nineteenth centuries. He made it one of the most beautiful castles in England. Of additional note is the Church of St. Nicholas, which is built in the Perpendicular style. Pop. 1952, 2,580.

A. W.

ARVIDA, a city in Chicoutimi Co., Quebec, Canada, situated on the Saguenay River, about 65 mi. from its confluence with the St. Lawrence River and 102 mi. north of Quebec, on the Canadian National Railways. Because of the excellent water-power resources of the Saguenay River, this site was chosen for the erection of one of the largest aluminum refineries in the world, to which the ore is brought by ship from British Guiana. Arvida was established and incorporated in 1926. Pop. 1951, 11,078.

D. F. P.

ASA [e'sə], a king of Judah, ruling from 918 to 877 B.C. He opposed every form of idolatry and removed the idols that his father had introduced into the land. He was attacked by Baasha, king of Israel, but his ally, Ben-hadad, king of Syria, came to his assistance and forced Baasha to leave Judah in peace. Asa died after reigning forty-one years, and was succeeded by his son, Jehoshaphat.

M. A. G.

ASAFETIDA [æsəfɛ'tɪdə], also called devil's dung or food-of-the-gods, a gum resin obtained by incising the living rhizomes and roots of *Ferula assafoetida* and of other species of *Ferula* found in Persia, Turkestan, and Afghanistan. The soft mass or irregular lumps have a characteristic odor and bitter taste. In medicine, it is used in hysteria, hypochondriasis, and intestinal flatulence.

J. A. Bo.

ASAHIGAWA [a'sa'hɪgawa], the most important city in interior Hokkaido, the most northern of the Japanese islands. It lies on the upper course of the Fukagawa River, in the west central part of the island. Asahigawa has a mean annual temperature of 41.5° F., while January, the coldest month, averages 14.2° F. An average of 42 in. of rain falls every year, and snow falls heavily in winter. Because the Asahigawa district has a warmer and somewhat less cloudy summer season than the rest of Hokkaido, it produces a variety of agricultural crops, including oats, rice, potatoes, beans, peas, buckwheat, rye, and a little wheat. Rice is the major crop. Since the city is a railroad center, and the main junction point of interior Hokkaido, it has railroad yards and shops. It is also an administrative center, and was a military headquarters and a horse procurement center for the Japanese army towards the end of World War II. For these reasons the city developed rapidly. It is noted for cleanliness and for its right-angled street pattern. Asahigawa has a small gas company, an alcohol plant, paper pulp mills, an aluminum-casting plant, a power station, a radio station, and, just north of the city, an airport. Principal products are lumber, *sake* (rice wine), woodenware, cotton textiles, machinery, and tools.

There has been an Ainu village near the site of Asahigawa for a long time; a remnant of this village exists about 2.5 mi. outside the city. The modern development of the city of Asahigawa started late in the nineteenth century, after the introduction of railroads. The near-by 40-acre Tokiwa Park is a winter resort and a popular ski center. Pop. 1954, 126,073. J. E. F.

ASANSOL [ɑ'sʌnso'l], a city in eastern India, located in west Bengal, near the Bihar-Bengal boundary line, 132 railroad miles northwest of Calcutta. The city is near the Damodar River, at the eastern edge of the Chota Nagpur Plateau. It has a cool, dry winter season, the average January temperature being 60° F. The rest of the year is either hot and dry, or hot and wet. Between 50 and 100 in. of rain fall during the summer season. Asansol is a large railway center and the hub of a highly industrialized area, the principal industries being iron and steel refractories, the manufacture of ceramics, electric cables, railway locomotives, glass, aluminum, cycles, cotton textiles, and articles from by-products of coal. There are numerous coal mines around the city and one of the few pig-iron and steel producing centers of India is at nearby Burnpur-Kulti. During World War II there was a large Indian and U.S. military establishment at Asansol. Pop. 1951, 76,277.
J. E. F. and M. R.

ASAPH [e'səf], in the Old Testament, a Levite and musician, whom King David appointed as chief of certain Levites who were "to minister before the ark of the Lord, and to record, and to thank and praise the Lord..." (I Chron. xvi:4-7). The name of Asaph appears in the superscription of twelve of the Psalms (l and lxxiii-lxxxiii). The Sons of Asaph, a group of Levites tracing their ancestry and function to Asaph, figure as singers in the first temple in the days of Solomon (II Chron. v:12) and King Josiah (II Chron. xxxv:15) and in the second temple in the days of Ezra and Nehemiah (Ezra ii:41; Nehemiah vii:44).

Asaph is also the name of a recorder in the court of King Hezekiah (II Kings xviii:18; Isa. xxxvi:22) and of the keeper of King Artaxerxes' forests to whom Artaxerxes addressed a letter directing him to supply Nehemiah with timber for the rebuilding of Jerusalem (Neh. ii:8). In addition there is a group of Korahite Levites, called the Sons of Asaph, of whom some acted as doorkeepers, mentioned in the Book of Chronicles (II Chron. xxvi:1). M. A. G.

ASBESTOS, a town in Richmond Co., Quebec, Canada, 75 mi. east of Montreal, in the hilly region usually known as the Eastern Townships. The Canadian National Railways furnishes transportation. Its chief industry, after which the town is named, is the quarrying and processing of asbestos rock fiber. Pop. 1951, 8,190. D. F. P.

ASBESTOS. *See* AMPHIBOLE GROUP; SERPENTINE.

ASBJØRNSEN, PETER CHRISTEN [ɑ'sbyörnsən] (1812-1885), Norwegian folk-tale collector, was born in Oslo, Norway, Jan. 15, 1812. Though he spent most of his life as a forester, zoologist, and popular scientific writer, he is remembered chiefly for his collaboration with Jørgen Moe in the collection and publication of folk tales. Their joint col-

PETER CHRISTEN ASBJØRNSEN

lection *Norske Folkeeventyr* (1841) ("Norwegian Folk Tales") was followed by Asbjørnsen's unaided compilations, *Norske Huldreeventyr og Folkesagn* (1845-1847) ("Norwegian Fairytales and Folklore"), and *Norske Folkeeventyr* (1871). These collections were a treasure house for Norwegian authors, particularly for Ibsen in his *Peer Gynt,* and changed the course of Norwegian literary style. Asbjørnsen died in Oslo, Jan. 5, 1885. *See also* MOE, JØRGEN. E. H.

ASBURY, FRANCIS [æ'zbɛri] (1745-1816), Anglo-American Methodist preacher and bishop, was born in Handsworth, Staffordshire, England, on Aug. 20, 1745. At thirteen he became apprenticed to a harness maker. In time he adopted the Methodist faith and, feeling a call to preach, became a local preacher at the age of eighteen.

In 1771 Asbury came as a missionary to America, where his qualities of leadership soon distinguished him. During the Revolutionary War he had to go into hiding in Delaware, since he was suspected of Tory sympathies, but the suspicion proved to be unfounded. The Baltimore Conference of 1784 consecrated him a general superintendent, but

JOHNS MANVILLE PHOTO

ASBESTOS MILL, ASBESTOS, QUEBEC, CANADA

SCENE ON ASCENSION ISLAND

soon he referred to himself as bishop, a title first used by the Conference of 1787.

Asbury believed in itinerant preaching and set a good example of it himself, for he traveled thousands of miles on horseback, visiting communities from New Hampshire to Georgia; to him, along with Thomas Coke, belongs much of the credit for the rapid spread of Methodism in the United States. He left a journal that sheds valuable light on American social life in his period. Asbury died on Mar. 31, 1816, at Spottsylvania, Va.   J. D. H.

ASBURY COLLEGE, an accredited, privately controlled, coeducational college of arts and sciences located on an 18-acre campus in Wilmore, Ky., a town of 2,300. Asbury College was chartered in 1890, and first instruction was given in the same year. The A.B. degree is offered. No scholarship aid is available, but students are required to earn up to one half of their expenses in farm work and other duties for the college. In addition, there is a fund for student loans. Residential facilities are ample. Students must spend one year of their course in residence. *For statistics see* COLLEGES AND UNIVERSITIES.   J. R. To.

ASBURY PARK, a resort city in Monmouth Co., on the Atlantic coast in east central New Jersey, 50 mi. south of New York City. Founded in 1869 and named after Bishop Francis Asbury, it was chartered as a city in 1879. The summer tourist trade is the city's prime industry. To accommodate the influx of visitors there are a great number of boarding houses and hotels. The two convention halls on the boardwalk are open all year for conventions, sporting events, and dances. Rail transportation is provided by the Central Railroad of New Jersey and the Pennsylvania Railroad. Manufactures include confectionery, beverages, leather sportswear, and window shades. Pop. 1950, 17,094.

ASCENSION [əsɛ'nshən], a small, volcanic, oval island resting on the submarine Challenger Ridge. It is 38 sq. mi. in area. Situated in the South Atlantic at 7°53′ S. lat. and 14° 18′ W. long, it lies halfway between Africa and South America. It was discovered by Juan de Nova, a Portuguese mariner, on Ascension Day in 1501. The English took possession of the still uninhabited island in 1815, and in that year stationed a garrison to block Napoleon's escape from St.

Helena which is 800 mi. to the southeast. With the death of Napoleon in 1821, the garrison was removed. The island was administered by the British Admiralty until November 1922, when the administration was transferred to the Colonial Office and annexed to the colony of St. Helena. The island lies in the path of the southeast trade winds and has a mild climate with temperatures averaging about 73° F. in summer and 60° F. in winter. Green Mountain, the principal peak, 2,820 ft., is surrounded by a tableland, 1,200 ft., which is covered with extinct volcanoes. It is only in this peak's fertile soil that bushes, trees, and green vegetables have been cultivated. Ascension is bare and hilly, receives little rainfall, and consists mostly of volcanic cinders, craters, and lava fields. The Quartermaster of the United States Army Air Forces in 1944 selected the desolate island as the first place to test the practicality of hydroponic gardening. Five vegetables—cucumbers, lettuce, radishes, tomatoes and green peppers—were successfully raised in black cinder beds which were irrigated with distilled sea water mixed with chemicals. Ascension's strategic importance on the main route to the East declined when the Suez Canal was opened in 1869. In World War II it became a major airbase on the airline between South America and Africa, and played an important role in winning the Battle of Africa. British civilians who maintain the cable station comprise the major population. Georgetown in the northwestern part of the island is the only settlement. The island is famous as a breeding ground for sea turtles and the sooty tern, or the wideawake. Prior to World War II such government as existed was exercised by a resident magistrate who was regularly the manager of the cable station. During the war a special representative was sent from St. Helena to administer the government.   W. M. W. and S. Van V.

ASCENSION DAY, the Thursday, forty days after Easter, on which is commemorated Christ's ascension, placed by tradition at Mount Olivet near Bethany. The earliest documentary evidence for the observance of the feast is of the fifth century, which presents it as already long observed. Pictorial representations of the event narrated in the Acts are found in fifth-century diptychs (hinged tablets) and frescoes. The Eastern Churches know the feast as the Analepsis (taking up); the Roman liturgy ranks the day among the highest feasts, and marks its celebration with a vigil and an octave. Connected with the liturgical solemnity were certain customs, including the blessing of beans and grapes during the Canon of the Mass, the extinction of the paschal candle, triumphal processions, and, in some churches, the elevation of a figure of Christ through an opening in the church roof, symbolizing the Ascension. W. C.

ASCETICISM [əsɛ'tısızəm], the principles or the way of life of the ascetics. The word is derived from the Greek ἄσκησις, which meant originally the training of athletes but was applied by the Stoics to moral discipline. It connotes always a variable amount of austerity. Asceticism is found among the primitives and in several religions or cultures like Islam, Buddhism, and others. It often derives from dualistic conceptions which assume that there is an unavoidable tension between spirit and matter, the latter being regarded usually as evil. Self-inflicted chastisements, fasting, abstaining from certain foods, refraining from luxury or from pleasurable activities, and observing silence are common practices.

Christian ascetics, while sharing in these mortifications, are inspired by specific desires for ethical and religious perfection. Their purpose is to bring human sinfulness under control and to discipline the body and to make it an organ fit for a Christlike life; as a rule they consider austerity and penance merely as means toward these ends. Extraordinary mortifications have been and still are regarded by some as having special merit, or as constituting a propitiation for the guilt of sin; but such views are radical deviations from Christian asceticism as such. G. A. B.

ASCHAFFENBURG [ɑʃɑ'fənburχ], an industrial and commercial town in northwest Bavaria, west central Germany, 25 mi. southeast of Frankfurt. It lies on the navigable Main River at the west foot of the Spessart forested highlands. It was a Roman settlement and, from about 982, a residence of Frankish kings and Mainz ecclesiastics; it was annexed to Bavaria in 1814. Most of the town's quaint old buildings were largely destroyed by bombs and artillery during World War II. The massive seventeenth-century palace, an important example of the German Renaissance architecture, was totally ruined. Its library contained rare books and manuscripts, and the picture gallery had excellent paintings. There was considerable traffic in the river port, while extensive industries produced paper, metals, clothing, beer, cellulose, and spirits. After World War II, Aschaffenburg was placed in the United States occupation zone. Pop. 1953, 51,300. C. C. H.

ASCHAM, ROGER [æ'skəm] (1515-1568), English scholar, was born in Kirby Wiske, Yorkshire, in 1515. He was tutored in the house of Sir Humphrey Wingfield and about 1530 entered St. John's College, Cambridge, where he studied under Sir John Cheke and was appointed to a fellowship upon his graduation. In 1545 he published *Toxophilus*, a dialogue on bodily exercise and recreations, with special reference to archery, and the next year he succeeded Sir John Cheke as public orator of the university. In 1548 he became tutor to Princess (later Queen) Elizabeth and served, 1550-1553, as secretary to Sir Richard Morrison, ambassador to Charles V. Upon his return home from extensive travel on the Continent, he was, despite his professed Protestantism, made Latin secretary to Queen Mary. In 1553 he wrote a *Report . . . . of the Affaires of Germany,* published in 1570, and in 1555 resumed his Greek studies with Princess Elizabeth. In 1563 he began *The Scholemaster,* completed just before his death on Dec. 23, 1568, and pub-

lished by his widow in 1570—an influential work concerned with the private education of young gentlemen and with a method of teaching Latin by "double translation." Ascham's attacks on rhyme, medieval romances, and Italian books and travel, and his discussion of "quick and hard wits" and of literary imitation are noteworthy features of the work. His style marks a distinct advance in English prose in its purity of diction and its well-constructed, trenchant sentences. His Latin and Greek works were published posthumously. V. B. H.

ASCIDIANS or **SEA SQUIRTS** [əsɪ'diənz], a class of tunicates which is exclusively marine, obscurely related to vertebrates. Ascidians attach their bases to surfaces of rocks, wharves, and ship bottoms. They are found throughout the world, from the intertidal zone to the edge of the

COURTESY OF THE AMERICAN MUSEUM OF NATURAL HISTORY
Cluster of ascidians attached to a log of wood

continental shelf, and a few forms are found even in the oceanic abyss. Solitary and compound forms are equally common, the latter usually forming encrusting mats consisting of numerous small individuals embedded in a common matrix and derived from a single egg. Every individual, whether large and solitary or a minute constituent zooid of a compound colony, has two apertures. One of these serves as the mouth, leading into the branchial chamber with its perforated walls through which the sea water is filtered. The strained water is ejected through the second, or exhalant, aperture, and the trapped food particles are wrapped into a cord of mucus and passed on to the intestine. The blood is peculiar in containing large concentrations of salts of the element vanadium. All are hermaphroditic, having functional ovaries and testes in the same individual. The eggs develop, not directly into anything resembling the adult, but into tiny tadpolelike larvae possessing the forerunner of the vertebrate backbone and other features suggestive of their relationship to the vertebrates. The larvae live for a few days at the most and then settle on the sea floor to metamorphose into the attached condition of sea squirts.

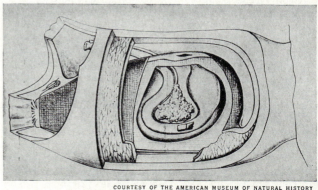

COURTESY OF THE AMERICAN MUSEUM OF NATURAL HISTORY
Cross-section showing interior of an ascidian

Many are able also to reproduce by a process of budding, forming either social groups of common parentage or true colonial organisms. Colors are usually drab, but some species found in tropical waters are among the most vivid and beautifully colored of all marine animals.   N. J. B.

ASCOLI, GRAZIADIO ISAIA [aʹskoli] (1829-1907), Italian linguist, was born in Gorizia, then in the Austro-Hungarian Empire, on July 16, 1829. He pursued his linguistic studies with diligence and in addition became an active Italian patriot, constantly advocating the reunion of his native Gorizia with the Italian state. He taught from 1861 onward in the University of Milan. After receiving innumerable honors in Italy and abroad, he died in Milan on Jan. 21, 1907. Ernesto Parodi called him in an obituary "the greatest linguist in Italy and perhaps in the world."

A man of extraordinary learning and activity, Ascoli cultivated many linguistic fields, including the Indo-European, Semitic, Dravidian, Turkish, and Chinese. He specialized, however, in Celtic and Romance languages and he left upon these fields, and upon the broader one of Indo-European, such traces of his genius that by the time of his death they were entirely transformed. His work on the Irish glosses of Milan would be sufficient to assure the glory of any linguist. He solved, in the main, the problem of the Indo-European velar sounds, the most important and debated question of all Indo-European linguistics; his studies on the Romance languages, especially Franco-Provençal, Rhaeto-Romance, and the Italian dialects, were the basis for all later investigation in those fields. His classification of Italian dialects is the first great study of languages in geographical terms, anticipating the great movements of linguistic geography and neolinguistics. Ascoli was a staunch opponent of the neogrammarians and in his opposition to their views, as in other departments of his thinking, especially his famous substrate theory, he anticipated the work of later generations of linguists. *See also* AREAL LINGUISTICS; LINGUISTIC GEOGRAPHY; NEOGRAMMARIANS; NEOLINGUISTICS.   G. B.

ASCOLI PICENO [aʹskoli pitsheʹno], a province and also a capital city in an agricultural area in the southern Marches of central Italy.

The City. Ascoli Piceno, 53 mi. south of Ancona, is situated in an excellent defensive position on a wedge-shaped tongue of land at the confluence of the Tronto and Castellano rivers, at an altitude of 500 ft. above sea level. The city is on the eastern side of the Monti Sibillini, part of the high Apennines, and lies 16 mi. west of the Adriatic Sea. There is a considerable variation of temperature between summer and winter, and the average annual rainfall is 36 in.

Ascoli Piceno is not only an important commercial center for a wide agricultural area, but has some industrial specialities of its own. The waters of the Tronto produce electricity at the Venamartello-Acquastanta plant; there are electric furnaces, chemical plants, and food processing establishments. The city is world famous for its scientific production of silkworm eggs. Before World War II Ascoli was the source of two thirds of Italy's total output of this valuable item, for which the climatic conditions in the Tronto valley are especially propitious. Ascoli Piceno lies along the Via Salaria, shortest route from Rome to the Adriatic, and contains several interesting Roman monuments, such as the Porta Binata and the Ponte Romana over the Tronto. From the Middle Ages date the Palazzo del Popolo and the churches of San Francesco and San Vincenzo e Anastasio. The cathedral was started in the fifteenth century

and the baptistery in the sixteenth. After World War I the new Vittorio Veneto quarter was created across the Tronto, and during this period much building activity was carried on by the Fascist government. Among the city's schools are a classical lyceum, the Stabili, and a professional school, the Sgarilia. A short branch line formerly connected Ascoli with the main Adriatic coastal railway at Porto d'Ascoli, but this has been abandoned.

Ascoli Piceno was, as its name indicates, a center of the Piceni. In 286 B.C. it fell under Roman sway and, after taking a leading part in the Social War between Rome and her Italian allies between 90 and 88 B.C., it was rigorously punished. The disintegration of the Roman Empire ushered in the Goths, then the Lombards, who included Ascoli Piceno in their Duchy of Spoleto. Later the local bishops set up their own temporal rule, but by 1185 Ascoli Piceno became a free commune. As elsewhere in central Italy, the political life of the city was kept in turmoil by contending families and parties, including the division between Guelphs and Ghibellines. When Ascoli acquired a port on the Adriatic, the neighboring city of Fermo was stirred into a bitter enmity that led to two and a half centuries of wars between the rival towns. In the fourteenth and fifteenth centuries a series of *signori* ruled Ascoli, but in 1502 papal dominion was established and, with the exception of the Napoleonic Era, lasted until 1860, when the Marches joined the newly established kingdom of Italy. Pop. 1947, 45,834 (city and environs).

The Province. The province of Ascoli Piceno contains 72 communes with an area of 807 sq. mi. and a population (off. est.) in 1947 of 326,000. A southern province in the Marches, it runs from the lower Tronto to the lower Chienti River, and from the Adriatic to the Apennines, where it reaches at Monte Vettore an altitude of 8,050 ft. The terrain is partly mountainous and partly hilly, with a narrow coastal zone. The river valleys tend to be rather narrow. Agriculture is the chief livelihood, the four principal products being wheat, corn, grapes, and potatoes. There is little except local industrial or commercial activity. San Benedetto del Tronto is the leading Adriatic fishing port and, like Grottammare and Porto San Giorgio, is a much-visited bathing resort. San Benedetto had in 1936 a population of 12,337. The only other important city in the province is Fermo (pop. 9,295).   R. G. W.

ASCOMYCETES. *See* FUNGI.
ASCORBIC ACID. *See* VITAMINS.

ASEN [aseʹn], or Assen, the most important medieval Bulgarian dynasty (1185-1258), which was established by the twin brothers Ivan Asen (d. 1196) and Peter Asen (d. 1197). By 1187 the brothers had won control of northern Bulgaria. Kalojan, their younger brother, ruled 1197-1207. He finished the conquest of Bulgaria in 1201 and established friendly relations with Pope Innocent III. The greatest ruler of the dynasty was Ivan Asen II, who, during his reign from 1218 to 1241, conquered Macedonia, Epirus, and most of Albania and Serbia. The last of the Asenid house was Caliman II, who ruled in 1257-1258.   R. F.

ASEXUAL GENERATION. *See* REPRODUCTION, ANIMAL; REPRODUCTION, PLANT.

ASH, the common name of a large genus, *Fraxinus,* of timber and ornamental trees belonging to the olive family. There are about 65 species, largely restricted to temperate regions of the Northern Hemisphere, and about 20 species are native to the United States. While a few are shrubby, they are mostly small to medium-sized trees, and some grow to timber size, attaining heights of 60 to 120 feet and trunk diameters of 2½ to 6 feet. They are characterized by a thick, furrowed bark, yellow-green-colored branchlets with deciduous, opposite, odd-pinnately compound leaves, small flowers in clusters, and a narrow winged fruit called samara.

Most species of ash bear inconspicuous greenish flowers, but the Himalaya ash, *F. floribunda,* of Central Asia, the foothill ash, *F. dipetala,* of the California mountains, and the southwestern flowering ash, *F. cuspidata,* of the Mexican border, bear showy white flowers. Those of the last-named species are extremely fragrant.

Of the seven timber-producing species in the United States, four furnish more than 90 per cent of the ash lumber cut. White ash, *F. americana,* and green ash, *F. pennsylvanica* var. *lanceolata,* which grow over nearly all of the eastern United States, provide the "white ash" of commerce, which is heavy, hard, strong, stiff, and tough and is especially adapted for shovel and spade handles and long handles for forks, hoes and rakes. It is also valued highly for baseball bats, snowshoes, tennis racket frames, paddles, and oars. Black ash, *F. nigra,* of the northeastern United States, furnishes wood that is somewhat lighter and less strong and tough than "white ash" and is suitable for interior finish of houses and offices and furniture and cabinet work in general. Oregon ash, *F. oregona,* of the Pacific coast is of only local importance.

The total stand of ash saw timber in the United States has been estimated at 8,016,200,000 board feet. In 1946, the total cut of ash lumber in the United States was approximately 132,700,000 board feet, and about half as much more was used in the form of logs by handle manufacturers.

AMERICAN ASH

COURTESY OF THE
NEW YORK BOTANICAL GARDENS

The white ash is frequently planted for shade and ornament in the eastern United States, as are also the European ash, *F. excelsior,* an important timber tree sometimes 120 feet high with numerous foliage varieties, and the flowering ash, *F. ornus,* of southern Europe. The waxy exudations from the trunk and leaves of the last-named species furnish the manna used in medicine. The Chinese ash, *F. chinensis,* yields the Chinese white wax.

The name ash is applied to various nonrelated trees: the mountain ash, *Sorbus* species, of the rose family; the poison ash, *Toxicodendron vernix,* of the cashew family; the cape ash, *Ekebergia capensis,* of the mahogany family; the bitter ash, *Simaruba excelsa,* of the quassia family; and the mountain ash or giant eucalyptus, *Eucalyptus regnans,* of the myrtle family.   W. D. B.

ASHANTI [əsha'nti], a division of the Gold Coast in British West Africa, formerly an independent kingdom. It is bounded on the west by the French Ivory Coast, on the east by the British-mandated territory of Togoland, on the north by the Northern Territories of the Gold Coast, and on the south by the Gold Coast Colony. Its area is 24,379 sq. mi.

The Black Volta, a major river approximately 800 mi. long, rising in the French Ivory Coast, forms the northern boundary of Ashanti before its confluence with the White Volta. Below a 50-mi. stretch through the Northern Territories, the Volta proper becomes the northeastern and eastern border of Ashanti. The Pra River, a major tributary, forms part of the southern boundary of Ashanti, and its tributaries, the Ofin and Anum, are probably the most important rivers of the Gold Coast, considered agriculturally. In the rainy season the Ofin is used for floating timber to the railroad to Dunkwa. The river valleys are fertile. The northern edge of the forest area follows the Volta and Afram rivers, thence proceeds northwest to the Ivory Coast boundary. The terrain consists of steep, timbered ridges. North of the forest is open grassland, with rivers bordered by dense trees. The forest is seasonally well watered; many small rivers, dry at other times, flow during the rains, from May to October. The grassland streams flow only for a few hours directly following rain, when they flood. There are few notable mountains or highlands; roughly one-half of the entire Gold Coast is less than 500 ft. above sea level, and most of the rest below 1,000 ft. In southwest Ashanti, along the Gold Coast Colony border, are hills. The Mampong Scarp is in the north, on the line separating forest and park. Another range cuts across western Ashanti. Lake Bosumtwi occupies a deep, nearly circular depression 21 mi. southeast of Kumasi. Five miles in diameter, it has a maximum depth of 233 ft., and the sides rise abruptly 600 to 700 ft. above the surface. The lake is probably the result of subsidence, as evidence of volcanic origin is lacking. Most of the Ashanti hills range about 1,500 ft., with a few peaks of 2,500 ft.

The forest belt is warm and moist. Moist southwesterly winds (monsoons) penetrate farthest north from June to September, the rainiest season; dry northeasterlies, the harmattans, bearing dust from the Sahara, penetrate farthest south, even beyond the coast, in January and February. A brief dry period intervenes in August. Normally, the relative humidity is high, but the harmattan brings about a loss of moisture—as much as 63 per cent in 24 hours—and more than doubles the daily range of temperature. Both of these changes are severe to Europeans. At Kumasi, the capital, mean rainfall in 1946 was 58 in.; mean max. temp., 86.2°; mean relative humidity, 84 per cent. But Kumasi has registered temperatures as low as 45° in the shade.

West African Airways connects Kumasi with Tamale, capital of the Northern Territories, and with Takoradi and Accra on the coast of the colony. A 3 ft., 6 in.-gauge railroad runs 366 mi. from Takoradi to Kumasi to Accra. There are 2,714 mi. of all-weather roads, of which 2,078 mi. are gravel. There are in addition dry-weather roads, ferries, and bridges. The confluence of the Black and White Volta is 280 mi. from the sea. The Volta is navigable for light-draft launches as far as Akuse, and at some seasons for canoes as far as Yeji.

In the west there are rich forests of mahogany, and the cleared fertile areas are devoted to fruit trees and oil palms. Rubber and gum copal are gathered. Eastern Ashanti, a comparatively dry, open, undulating savanna, is good pasture land. The products are chiefly maize, yams, bananas, piassava, peanuts, and cocoa, all grown in the south. Sheanuts are grown for local consumption. Exports include cocoa, gold, diamonds, manganese ore, timber, rubber, and hides (other than cattle).

Ashanti's population at the 1948 census was 818,944, of whom 817,782 were Africans. Kumasi ranked second among Gold Coast cities with 78,483, of whom 77,689 were Africans. Other large towns are Kete-Krachi, Mampong, Bekwai, Juaso, Sunyani, and Wenchi. The confederated tribes are the Mampong, Juabin, Bekwai, Adansi, Kokofu, Nsuta, Offinsu, Kumarvu, Ejisu, and Agona, each with its own head chief.

The administration is vested in the governor of the Gold Coast, the chief commissioner of Ashanti, the assistant chief commissioner, and four district commissioners for the districts of Bekwai, Kumasi, Mampong, and Wenchi-Sunyani. Ashanti is a confederacy within the Gold Coast federation. The constitution of the Gold Coast federation, as established in 1951, substantially increased the elected representation of Ashanti in the federal legislative council and made Ashantians eligible for election to departmental headships and thus for membership in the responsible executive council, which assists the appointed governor of the Gold Coast with the administration of the federation. Supreme court jurisdiction was extended to Ashanti in 1935. Local government is in the hands of native authorities, chiefs, councils of elders, and subchiefs, who hold their rank through heredity and election by their people, and whose powers have legal force through government recognition. There is no government interposition in their selection—only in the appointment of statutory native authorities. Subject to the supervision of administrative officers, the native authorities make by-laws, and maintain order and the general welfare of their people.

There were in 1946 four government-supported, coeducational primary schools, with wholly African staffs, and many mission-assisted schools. Primary schools emphasize craftwork, but all schools teach agriculture. A daily newspaper is published in Kumasi.

The Ashanti are a distinctive people, the largest unified group in the Gold Coast. From small beginnings they extended their authority by arms and diplomacy, creating a splendid military organization that was rarely defeated. Europeans on the coast first mentioned them about 1700. Their first contact with the British occurred in 1806 when the Ashantis reached the coast during a war with the Fantis. Kumasi had a British resident, later withdrawn, in 1817. Between 1826 and 1873 the Ashanti often invaded the Gold Coast in the prosecution of tribal wars. In 1874 Sir Garnet Wolseley in a brief campaign captured and burned Kumasi and concluded the Treaty of Fomena. In 1896, following a threatened invasion of the Gold Coast, Sir Francis Scott marched to Kumasi, encountering no resistance. A resident was established there, and Prempeh, the king, who had refused terms, was exiled to the Seychelles. In 1900, the disappearance of the symbol of Ashanti unity, the Golden Stool, preservation of which was regarded as a duty, coupled with the intervention of the governor, necessitated renewed military operations against the Ashanti nation. Ashanti was

formally annexed in 1901, and in 1902 the boundaries of the three divisions of the colony were fixed and the laws of the Gold Coast extended to Ashanti. Frequent petitions for the return of Prempeh were submitted. In 1924 these were granted, and in 1926 he became head chief (Omanhene) of Kumasi, being succeeded upon his death in 1931 by his nephew, Osei A. Prempeh II. Upon restoration of the Ashanti Confederacy in 1935, Prempeh II became Asantehene.

S. Van V.

ASHBURTON, ALEXANDER BARING, 1ST BARON [æ'shbɜrtən] (1774-1848), English financier, politician, and statesman, was born in London on Oct. 27, 1774. He sat in the House of Commons from 1806 to 1835 and supported free trade, though in later years he changed his opinion. He was strongly against parliamentary reform. He was president of the Board of Trade from 1834 to 1835 under Sir Robert Peel and in 1835 was made 1st Baron Ashburton of the second creation. In 1842 he was sent to the

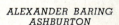

ALEXANDER BARING
ASHBURTON

United States, where he negotiated the Webster-Ashburton treaty, which settled the disputed boundary between Maine and Canada. He died at Longleat, May 13, 1848.   E. R. A.

ASHEBORO [æ'shbɜro], a town and the county seat of Randolph Co., in central North Carolina, about 26 mi. south of Greensboro. The Norfolk Southern Railway supplies transportation. Tobacco and corn are among the region's leading products, and furniture and hosiery are manufactured. Once the home of Andrew Jackson, Asheboro was incorporated in 1796. Pop. 1950, 7,701.

ASHER, in the Old Testament, the eighth son of Jacob, borne to him by Zilpah, the handmaid of Leah. He had four sons and one daughter (Gen. xlvi:17) and was the head of a large tribe, numbering 41,500 fighting men at the time of the Exodus from Egypt (Num. i:41). This number increased to 53,400 before the invasion of Palestine (Num. xxvi: 47). The tribe seems to have enjoyed a prosperity derived from the rich land it possessed near the Phoenician cities, which offered good markets and profitable commerce.   M. A. G.

ASHEVILLE, a city in western North Carolina, the county seat of Buncombe Co., is located at the junction of the Swannanoa and French Broad rivers in the midst of the splendor of the Blue Ridge Mountains. It is popular as a resort and health center. Asheville was founded in 1794 and incorporated in 1797. Among the points of interest in

ASHEVILLE, NORTH CAROLINA

EWING GALLOWAY

the vicinity are the Biltmore estate, the Great Smoky Mountains National Park, Mount Mitchell, the highest peak east of the Rockies, the rhododendron gardens at Craggy Mountain, Pisgah National Forest, a Cherokee Indian reservation, and Chimney Rock Mountain. In or near the city are the graves of O. Henry, short-story writer; Thomas Wolfe, novelist; and Bill Nye, humorist. During World War II the city served as the world headquarters for the Army Airways Communications System and the Army Air Forces Weather Service.

The Asheville-Biltmore College and St. Genevieve-of-the-Pines Junior College are located in Asheville. Near the city is the Oteen Veterans Hospital.

The Delta and the Capital air lines and the Southern Railway System furnish transportation. Asheville is the trade center for the surrounding agricultural, mining, and lumber district. The city's factories produce furniture, paper, textile bleaches, cotton products, hose, rayon, homespun, blankets, processed mica, and leather. Pop. 1950, 53,000.

ASHI [əshī'] (352-427), Babylonian amora, and editor of the Babylonian Talmud. He became head of the Sura rabbinical academy, a position he held for over fifty years. His prestige as a scholar and a man of wealth and eminent social position restored the importance of the academy and made of Sura a political and religious center. He is said to have spent close to sixty years in compiling all the material on the *Mishnah* and adding the *Gemara,* or commentary. His work was completed by Rabina, two generations later, and their redaction of the Babylonian Talmud, or *Babli,* is considered definitive.   C. W. D.

ASHIKAGA, TAKAUJI [ashıkaga] (1305-1358), Japanese military leader, was the founder of the Ashikaga shogunate. Betraying first the Hojo family, by deserting to Emperor Daigo II in the latter's successful attempt to overthrow the Hojo regency in 1333, Takauji soon betrayed Daigo, driving him from Kyoto in 1336 after the Battle of Minato-gawa and setting up Emperor Komyo in his place. Takauji became shogun (military dictator ruling in the name of the emperor) in 1338. The remainder of his life was spent in fighting a civil war to maintain his shogunate. He died in 1358, but the war fought in the names of the rival lines of emperors continued until 1392. Because of his betrayal of Daigo II, Takauji became a despised figure in Japanese history.   P. S. D.

ASHIKAGA, a city in central Honshu, the main island of Japan, located in the Tochigi Prefecture, near the northwestern end of the Kwanto Plain. It is on a tributary of the Tone River about 50 miles northwest of Tokyo. Formerly, the city was a cultural center with a classical school founded in the ninth century and restored in 1429. Some of the school's ancient Chinese books can be found in the local library. The city has long been a commercial center for silk and cotton mills and today is the country's largest producer of export silk textiles. Mufflers, scarves, and handkerchiefs of spun silk crepe, Fuji silk, organdy, and taffeta are notable exports. The library and Ashikaga Gokko, the temple to Confucius, are places of interest. Pop. 1954, 89,766.

ASHKENAZIM [æshkənæ'zım], the name applied to German and East European Jews and to all Jews who follow the religious rites and customs established by them.

The term Ashkenazim is often used in contradistinction to Sephardim, or those who use the Spanish and Portuguese ritual. Ashkenazim also differ from Sephardim in their pronunciation of Hebrew. The expulsion of the Jews from France in 1306 forced a great number of them into Germany, which became the new center of Jewish life, and gradually they went to Bohemia, Hungary, and other parts of Europe. Today by far the greatest number of Jews are Ashkenazim. *See also* SEPHARDIM.   H. Bl.

ASHKHABAD [a'shχaba'd], an *oblast* (region) of the Turkmen Soviet Socialist Republic, located in the southern part of the Soviet Union along the Iranian border, and the capital city of the Turkmen S.S.R. The area of the *oblast* is about 45,000 sq. mi., the largest part of it falling within the Kara Kum desert, where economic activity is restricted to the output of sulphur, the operation of a sulphur-processing plant, and sheep raising (mainly the karakul breed). The smaller section in the south lies along the northern slopes of the Kopet-Dag mountains, dotted with small oases. Intensive agriculture has been developed here, especially the cultivation of wheat, grapes and other

Pictorial Arts Museum, at Ashkhabad, capital of the Turkmen Soviet Socialist Republic, U.S.S.R.

The city of Ashkhabad is the capital of the Turkmen S.S.R. and the economic center of the *oblast* and the Republic. Founded in 1881, it now has cotton-ginning and milling, as well as silk-spinning plants, a large glass factory, meat-packing plant, wineries, metal and leather works, and flour mills. It is the site of the Turkmen University, the Academy of Sciences, and many research and higher educational institutions. Pop. est. 1950, 133,600.

ASHLAND, a city in northeastern Kentucky, in Boyd Co., on the Ohio River, about 120 mi. east of Frankfort. It is served by the Chesapeake & Ohio Railroad and river craft. A picturesque park containing several ancient Indian mounds is the center around which the entire city is built. Among the deposits of the region are iron ore, asphalt, and coal, and there are many natural gas wells, even within the city limits. Ashland's industrial output includes sheet steel, steel culverts and other steel products, petroleum products, coke and other by-products, sole leather, shoes, brick, and tile. Pop. 1950, 31,131.

ASHLAND, a city and the county seat of Ashland County, in north central Ohio, 13 mi. northeast of Mansfield, in a fertile farming area. The town, platted in 1815, was first called Uniontown; in 1822 it was renamed Ashland and was incorporated in 1844. It has the council-manager type of government. Ashland College, a coeducational institute, was chartered in 1878. Ashland is served by the Erie Railroad. Local manufactures include rubber goods, stock and poultry feeds and remedies, agricultural equipment, paper boxes, and auto parts. Another industry is commercial printing. Pop. 1950, 14,287.

ASHLAND, a borough in Schuylkill Co., in east central Pennsylvania, about 88 mi. northwest of Philadelphia. The borough, incorporated in 1857, has rail facilities furnished by the Reading line. A statue based on Whistler's painting of his mother is located in Ashland. The area is a rich coal region, and coal mining is a leading occupation of the borough. Local factories produce mine pumps and perforated metal. Pop. 1950, 6,192.

ASHLAND, a city in northern Wisconsin, the county seat of Ashland Co., situated on Chequamegon Bay, an arm of Lake Superior, approximately 65 mi. east of Duluth, Minn. Potatoes and grain constitute the principal crops of the region. Ashland was settled in 1854 and incorporated in 1887. It is the seat of Northland College. Lake steamers and the Chicago and North Western, the Chicago, St. Paul, Minneapolis and Omaha, the Minneapolis, St. Paul & Sault Ste. Marie, Northern Pacific Railroad, and the Duluth South Shore & Atlantic railroads supply transportation. Local industries include granite finishing, shipping of coal and iron ore, and the manufacture of paper. Pop. 1950, 10,640.

ASHLAND COLLEGE, an accredited, coeducational college of arts and sciences controlled by the Brethren Church, located in Ashland, Ohio, an industrial and residential city of 14,287, 65 mi. southwest of Cleveland. The institution was chartered and opened for instruction as Ashland University in 1878. In 1888 it was reincorporated as Ashland College. Degrees offered are A.B., B.S. in Ed., B.S. in Business Administration, and B.Mus. Under the "Ashland Plan" some class work requires business, industrial, and professional participation. Scholarship and loan funds are avail-

fruit, cotton, and silkworms. Livestock and horse breeding is also important. The area is known on the export market for its carpet weaving. The Trans-Caspian Railroad crosses the *oblast* in its southern section; automobiles, airplanes, and camel caravans are also in general use. The population of the *oblast* (est., 1954, 360,000) consists mostly of Turkmen tribes, some of which are still semi-nomadic. Others are Uzbeks, Russians, and Kazakhs.

able, and substantial opportunity for self-help is provided. There are no residential facilities for men students. There are additional private dwellings to supplement present residence halls for women. *For statistics see* COLLEGES AND UNIVERSITIES.   J. R. To.

ASHLEY. *See* SHAFTESBURY.

ASHLEY, a borough in Luzerne Co., in central Pennsylvania, 3 mi. south of Wilkes-Barre, situated in a coal region. Founded in 1810, the community adopted its present name in 1871. It is served by the Central Railroad of New Jersey, which has repair shops in the borough. Coal mining is Ashley's chief occupation. Pop. 1950, 5,243.

ASHLUSLAY. *See* INDIAN TRIBES, SOUTH AMERICAN.
ASHMEDIA. *See* ASMODEUS.

ASHTABULA [æʃtəbyuˈlə], a city and lake port in northeastern Ohio, on Lake Erie at the mouth of the Ashtabula River, about 55 mi. northeast of Cleveland. The first permanent white settlement was made on the site about 1801. Incorporated as a village in 1831, Ashtabula received its city charter in 1891. Ashtabula has the mayor-council form of local government. The harbor is the transfer point for iron ore being shipped from the upper lake regions to the Pittsburgh district mills and for coal from the western Pennsylvania and Ohio fields being sent to lake markets. Rail transportation is provided by the New York Central, the New York, Chicago and St. Louis, and the Pennsylvania lines. Shipyards, railroad shops, iron and steel works, and tanneries comprise the city's major industries. Ashtabula is the Indian word meaning "fish river," and fishing is an important industry in the city. The county is one of the state's leading dairy and grape-growing areas, and in the city's immediate vicinity there are large vegetable greenhouses. Pop. 1950, 23,696.

ASHTAROTH [æˈʃtərɒθ], the plural of the Hebrew 'Ashtōreth, the Phoenician-Canaanite goddess Astarte, deity of fertility, reproduction, and war. By the use of the plural, as was so, also, with the god Baal, the name served as a general designation for the female deities of the Canaanites. Certain passages in the Old Testament (I Sam. xii:10 and I Sam. xxxi:10) suggest the possibility that "Ashtaroth" was used as a plural of majesty, so that the goddess was glorified through her own name by her adherents. The word "Ashtaroth" was also used as a place-name to designate the shrine of the goddess; the site, 21 mi. east of Lake Galilee, has been identified with the modern Tell Ashtarah.
                                        E. J. J.

ASHTAVAKRA [ɑʃtəvɑˈkrɑ], hero of a story in the *Mahābhārata,* longest of the Hindu epic poems, was the son of a man named Kahoda, who was so absorbed in his studies that he neglected his wife. Ashtavakra, even before he was born, rebuked his father for this. To punish him, Kahoda condemned him to be born crooked. Ashtavakra (*ashtan* meaning "eight" and *vakra* meaning "crooked") consequently was born crooked in eight places. Later, at the court of King Janaka, Kahoda and a Buddhist sage met in a verbal duel. It was held on the condition that the man who lost the argument would be drowned, and Kahoda paid the penalty. When Ashtavakra reached the age of 12, he determined to avenge his father. He defeated the Buddhist sage and demanded that he be drowned. The Buddhist then confessed that he was the son of Varuṇa, the water god, and

that he had been sent by his father in the guise of a Buddhist sage to obtain, in the manner described, Brahmans to officiate at Varuna's sacrifices. Kahoda was restored to life, and he asked his son to bathe in the Samanga River. As soon as Ashtavakra did so, his crookedness disappeared and he became straight.

The Vishnu *Purāṇa* tells how, prior to this, Ashtavakra was standing one day in a river, doing penance, when water nymphs saw him and worshiped him. Ashtavakra was pleased, and he promised to grant them the first thing they asked. They asked for the best of men to be their husbands, and when Ashtavakra presented himself they laughed because he was crooked. Although he could not recall his promise, Ashtavakra condemned them to fall into the hands of thieves.
                                        E. B. A.

ASHTON-UNDER-LYNE, a municipal and parliamentary borough of Lancashire, England, on the Tame River, located 6½ mi. east of Manchester. Its name is derived from the Old English *æsc* (ash, or spear) *tūn* (an enclosed place) and from the Latin *subter lineam* (under the line), in recognition of the fact that it is below the original boundary of Northumbria and Mercia. As a baronial manor, it was granted by William I to Roger de Poictou, but it soon passed into the barony of Manchester. Although it was incorporated as a borough in 1847, it had been considered a borough for many years before. A church is mentioned as being in the community in 1261. Portions of the Church of St. Michael's, largely restored after 1840, date from about 1413, when the construction of the edifice was begun. Since the introduction of the cotton industry in 1769, Ashton-under-Lyne has been an important manufacturing center. In addition to cotton weaving, the local industries include silk weaving and dyeing and the manufacture of hats, iron products, and machinery. Pop. 1952, 45,720.   A. W.

ASHUR. *See* ASSUR.

ASHURBANIPAL [ɑˈʃʊrbɑˈnipɑl], king of Assyria from 669 to 626 B.C. During his long reign the Assyrian Empire attained its farthest limits, although the period saw also the beginnings of imperial disintegration. Early in his reign Ashurbanipal held Assyria, Babylonia, Syria, Palestine, and Egypt; to this realm he added the territory of Elam. Perhaps the first warning of the impending fall of Assyria was the successful revolt of Egypt shortly before 660 B.C. This was followed eight years later by a Babylonian insurrection led by the Assyrian governor, Ashurbanipal's own brother. The expense of quelling this revolt and of carrying out the Elamite campaign which followed was probably the immediate cause for the recession of Assyrian power. Although Ashurbanipal was as fierce and warlike as any of the Assyrian kings who preceded him, he was also well-educated and a patron of culture. His forty-three year reign, marked by excessive wealth and splendor, also saw the rise of art and literature. In his inscriptions he boasted that he had "a large ear for learning," that he learned to read and write, to interpret the language of the stars, and to penetrate the mysteries of multiplication and division. One of his own tablets reads: "The beautiful writings in Sumerian that are obscure, in Akkadian that are difficult to bear in mind, it was my joy to repeat." Many students of antiquity regard Ashurbanipal's own inscriptions as among the finest examples of early writing still in existence. He was the founder of two large libraries at Nineveh which contained important historical records and religious texts, as well as the royal correspondence. The Nineveh libraries also included a

ASHURBANIPAL AND HIS QUEEN IN THE GARDEN

heretofore unrivaled collection of poetry, history, science, religion, lexicography and works on grammar.   T. B. J.

ASHURNASIRPAL II [ɑ'ʃʊrnɑ'zɪrpɑl], king of Assyria, reigned from about 885 to 860 B.C. As a great warrior king, he advanced and strengthened the frontiers of Assyria. He also carried the Assyrian standards to the shores of the Mediterranean and brought back fifteen thousand Aramaean captives. The palace which Ashurnasirpal built at Calah (Kalakh) was a magnificent structure with bronze-plated

ASHURNASIRPAL II

gates and was furnished with costly objects of gold, silver, and ivory. Many inscriptions and sculptured reliefs which now adorn numerous museums in the United States and Europe came from Calah and its palace.   T. B. J.

ASH WEDNESDAY, the first day of the Lenten fast, the Day of Ashes, so called because on this day the faithful, according to ancient custom, receive on the forehead the sign of the cross marked with blessed ashes. This sacramental of the Roman Catholic Church recalls to the faithful their final end and symbolizes the need of contrition and penance during Lent. The blessed palms which remain from the previous Palm Sunday are burned, and the ashes obtained are blessed for the ceremony before the principal Mass on the Day of Ashes. In the ancient Church the ceremony was marked by a penitential procession after the distribution of ashes. For several centuries only public penitents received the blessed ashes. This custom of the Church is not without precedent in the Old Testament, which frequently describes the penitent sinner as wearing a penitential garb of sackcloth and sprinkling himself with ashes as a sign of humility and sorrow for sin. *See also* FAST DAYS; HOLIDAYS AND HOLY DAYS; LENT.   R. J. O'C.

ASH WEDNESDAY, a poem by Thomas Stearns Eliot, first published in 1930. It signalizes the acceptance of the Christian account of man's destiny, an achievement toward which Eliot had been working for many years. The images of the poem refer to two contrasting moods of the poet: his recollection of his struggles before the return of faith, and his tentative exploration of the value of faith. Thus, in Part III of the poem, the figure of the stair allows Eliot to summarize his painful return towards faith; and in Parts II and IV the "Lady" seems to be that Wisdom (the *Sophia* of Christian revelation) whose company may well be beneficial to the poet. Partly in rhymed, partly in unrhymed verse, *Ash Wednesday* is one of Eliot's most melodic and evocative works.   H. H. Wa.

ASIA, the largest continent in the world, with a total area of 16,235,000 sq. mi. A part of the vast land mass which includes Europe and Africa, it has the largest population of the continents and has some of the most densely as well as the most sparsely inhabited areas of the world. It also has the highest mountains, the deepest depressions, the greatest peninsulas, and some of the coldest and hottest and the driest and wettest places on the surface of the earth. Historically, Asia has had a tremendous influence on the history of mankind. The origin of the name is uncertain, but it is probable that it was derived

THE VILLAGE OF CRATER, ADEN

from ancient Assyrian or Hebrew sources. The early Greeks divided the known world into only two parts, Europe and Asia, the latter including Libya (Africa), but their geographers left no key to the origin of the name Asia.

Asia extends northward to Cape Chelyuskin, 77° 35′ N. lat., and the low, swampy northern coast, mosquito infested in summer and solidly frozen in winter, is bordered by the Kara, the Laptev (Nordenskiöld), and the East Siberian seas, all part of the Arctic Ocean. Off the northern coast are many islands, the largest of which are the Severnaya Zemlya Islands, the Novosibirskiye (New Siberian) Islands, and Wrangel Island. In the extreme northeast, the 56-mi.-wide Bering Strait separates Cape Dezhneva (East Cape), Siberia, from Cape Prince of Wales, Alaska. It is probable that Asia and North America were at one time joined at this point.

The eastern coast of Asia extends about 6,000 mi. southward from East Cape to Singapore Island on the southern tip of the continent. From north to south, the major bodies of water that border Asia are the Bering Strait, Gulf of Anadyr (Anadir), Bering Sea, Sea of Okhotsk, Tatar Strait, Sea of Japan, Korea Strait, Yellow Sea and Gulf of Pohai, East China Sea, Formosa Strait, Gulf of Tonkin, South China Sea, and Gulf of Siam, all part of the Pacific Ocean. East Cape, the most eastern Asiatic point of land, is in the Western Hemisphere, at 170° W. long., almost on the Arctic Circle, but the coast line trends southwestward, and Singapore Island at the southern tip is at 103° 45′ E. long. The major peninsulas on this coast are the Kamchatka, Korean, Liaoting, Shantung, Liuchow, and Malay

peninsulas, and Cape Cambodia. Many islands fringe the entire eastern coast, forming an almost continuous chain. From north to south, these include the Kuril Islands, Sakhalin Island, the main Japanese islands, the Ryukyu Islands, the large island of Formosa, Hainan Island, and the Philippines.

Southern Asia is bordered by the Strait of Malacca, Gulf of Martaban, Bay of Bengal, Gulf of Mannar, Gulf of Cambay, Arabian Sea, Gulf of Oman, Persian Gulf, and Gulf of Aden. India, Arabia, and the peninsula formed by Burma, Indochina, Siam, and Malaya are the three large southern projections of Asia, and Ceylon is a large island just east of the southern tip of India. The extreme southwestern tip of Asia, at the boundary of Aden and Yemen, is separated from Africa by the 20-mi.-wide Strait of Bab el Mandeb.

Western Asia is bordered by the Red Sea, Suez Canal, Mediterranean Sea, Aegean Sea, the Dardanelles, Sea of Marmara, the Bosporus, and the Black Sea. The Dardanelles separate the most western point of Asia from Europe. Between the Black Sea and the Ural Mountains, which form the traditional boundary between Asia and Europe, the boundary line is not definite. Some geographers believe that the boundary line of Asia extends from the Black Sea to the Caspian Sea, north along that body of water to the Ural River, and then to the Ural Mountains. Other geographers accept a diagonal line extending northeastward from the Bosphorus to the Ural River bend, and then north along the Ural Mountains to the Kara Sea. However, division between Europe and Asia is not very

323

Sugar-loaf mountains dominate the rice paddies of Kwangsi Province, China.

well defined, and there is a strong geographical argument for considering Europe as a peninsula of Asia. J.E.F.

HISTORICAL GEOLOGY

Present Physiographic Regions. The great subcontinent of Asia is divided into five major physiographic regions. (1) The Angara Shield, in north central Siberia, consists of a large well-dissected region on Archeozoic and Proterozoic igneous and metamorphic rocks. (2) The northern plains, an eastward continuation of the Baltic plains of northern Europe, are cut by the Ural Mountains and extend eastward to the Angara Shield and southward to Turkestan. They are mainly composed of flat, sedimentary rocks. (3) The central ranges and plateaus, a series of mountain chains and intervening highlands, border the south end of the northern plains and the Angara Shield. They are composed largely of folded or elevated Paleozoic and Mesozoic rocks and extend from Afghanistan through Tibet and the Gobi Desert to Manchuria on the northeast, and through China and the Malay Peninsula on the southeast. (4) The southern range comprise the mountains of Turkey and Iran (Persia), the Himalayas, and the islands of the East Indies, then swing north to form the Philippines, the Japanese islands, and the eastern margin of Siberia. They are composed mainly of folded sedimentary rocks of which the majority are of Mesozoic and Cenozoic age. (5) The southern plateaus, comprising Arabia and all of India south of the Himalayas, are large granitic blocks covered in places by lava flows and alluvial deposits.

Archeozoic and Proterozoic Eras. Much of the Archeozoic and Proterozoic history of Asia is obscure, and even where the rocks are exposed at the surface they are unmapped over large areas. It is known, however, that thick sediments were deposited in north central Siberia and that at the end of the Proterozoic these were folded and metamorphosed to form a series of mountain ranges and uplands which subsequent erosion has reduced in elevation to form the Angara Shield.

Paleozoic Era. In the early Paleozoic, epeiric seas were widespread over Asia. Cambrian, Ordovician, and Silurian seas covered most of Siberia, even overlapping the Angara Shield. Much of southern Asia was also below water, but Arabia and southern India were land masses and remained so throughout most of subsequent geologic history. Two large troughs were present and thicker sediments accumulated in them. One of these was the Ural geosyncline, extending from north to south in the position of the present Ural Mountains. The other extended east-west across southern Siberia.

At the end of the Silurian there was a general uplift and withdrawal of the seas. The formations that had been deposited in the regions surrounding the Angara Shield were folded and elevated to form a series of arcuate mountain ranges, causing the shield to become an elevated land mass throughout the rest of geologic time. In the early Devonian the seas were confined to the two troughs, but later spread over western and southern Siberia, northern India, and China.

In the late Paleozoic the eastern part of the Tethys Trough became an extensive seaway. It extended from the Caucasus eastward across Persia, Afghanistan, northern India, southern China, and Indochina, emptying into the south Pacific. The southern end of the Ural Trough connected with the Tethys Trough at this time. Many terrestrial rocks were deposited in southern Siberia during this interval. Toward the end of the Paleozoic the Ural Mountains were formed by the folding of the sediments that had accumulated in the Ural Trough. Several other mountain ranges were elevated in Siberia south and east of the Angara Shield.

Mesozoic Era. During most of the Mesozoic the Tethys Trough was almost continuously under water, but after the Triassic the easternmost end of the trough shifted southward and emptied into the Indian Ocean in the vicinity of eastern India and Burma. Over most of the era an epeiric sea covered northeastern Siberia east of the Angara Shield. Thick continental sands and clays were deposited in central Asia, especially in southern Siberia, Mongolia, and northwestern China. At the end of the Mesozoic, Asia was elevated without extensive mountain building.

Cenozoic Era. In the early part of the Tertiary a great sea extended from the Arctic across western Asia along the east flank of the Ural Mountains, connecting at its southern end with the Tethys Trough. The latter was also submerged and thick marine sediments were deposited in it. In the middle of the period the strata that had been accumulating in the Tethys Trough during many geologic periods were squeezed and folded to form the impressive Himalaya Mountains. This tremendous deformation caused complete withdrawal of the seas.

No extensive ice sheet developed in northern Asia during the Quaternary period, but smaller ice fields were present and the mountain ranges were heavily glaciated. During the interglacial periods the Arctic Ocean spread southward over parts of northern Siberia and deposited strata of sand and clay. Thick continental deposits, produced by erosion of the Himalaya and other mountain ranges, are widespread in central and southern Asia. At the end of the Quaternary period the ice fields melted away and the continent of Asia assumed its present form. *See also* GEOLOGY. E.C.S.

TOPOGRAPHY

General Relief. All of the various features of relief are found in Asia, but in general the continent consists of a series of plateaus flanked by high mountains. The dominant area of relief is a triangular-shaped mass composed of high

THE GREAT WALL OF CHINA VIEWED FROM THE EAST OVER THE TOP OF THE NANKING PASS

LINDSLEY F. HALL

THE AGHA JARI ROAD TO SAR-I-BAND TAKES A WINDING ROUTE AMONG THE LOW, BARREN HILLS OF AFGHANISTAN

RAYMOND WILSON

FISHING ON CHINA'S HSIANG RIVER

mountains, plateaus, and uplands that extends southward from the Dzhugdzhur (Stanovoi) Mountains in the northeast to the northern part of Indochina, and westward to the Pamir Knot. This triangle is bounded on the north by the plains of Siberia and on the west by the Kirghiz Steppe; on the east is a series of offshore islands formed by the tops of folded mountains and volcanoes that are part of a "belt of fire" around the Pacific Ocean. On the south are two great peninsulas: one composed of Indochina, Siam, the Federation of Malaya, and Burma; the other of India. On the southwest is the great peninsula of Arabia and the Near East.

Mountains. One of the interesting features of the relief of Asia is that there are two orographic or mountain centers from which extend most of the major mountains. One of the mountain knots, the Armenian Knot, is in eastern Turkey and Armenia, centering around Mount Ararat. The other mountain knot, the Pamir Knot, is located on the boundary of northwestern India, Afghanistan, the Tadzhik S.S.R., and of Sinkiang, China. The mountains connected with the Armenian Knot are the Caucasus Mountains, the Pontus and Taurus mountains that enclose the plateau of Anatolia, and, indirectly, the Lebanon and Anti-Lebanon mountains that border the Arabian plateau. Eastward from the Armenian Knot extend the Elburz and Zagros chains that enclose the plateau of Iran and are almost connected with the Pamir Knot by the Sulaiman Range and the Hindu Kush located in Baluchistan and Afghanistan. From the Pamir Knot, some of the highest and greatest mountains of the world extend eastward; the Tien Shan constitute the northernmost boundary of the Tarim Basin, and the Karakoram and Altyn Tagh ranges mark the southern boundary. The Kunlun Mountains flank the northern edge of the Tibetan plateau and extend into China as the Tsin Ling Mountains, while the Himalaya Range forms the southern boundary of Tibet and extends into southwest China, northern Burma, and eastern India. In the north central area, the Plateau of Mongolia is bordered on the west and north by the Altai Mountains, Sayan Mountains, and Yablonovy Mountains, while the

eastern border is formed by the relatively low Greater Khingan Mountains. North of the Amur River are the Dzhugdzhur and Verkhoyansk mountains of northern Siberia. Except for the northernmost mountains, most of the ranges are high, steep, and spectacular, rising abruptly from oceans, plateaus, or plains. The Elburz rise from the Caspian Sea coast, 85.5 ft. below sea level, to the 18,375-ft. summit of Mount Demavend. The Pontus, Taurus, and Lebanon mountains rise to elevations of 9,000 and 10,000 ft. above the Mediterranean seacoast. Even the low Judean Plateau of Palestine, varying in elevation between 3,000 and 3,500 ft., has a steep scarp that drops over 4,000 ft. to the Dead Sea, 1,293 ft. below sea level. The Himalayas rise to 29,028 ft. (Mount Everest) above the low plain of the Ganges River of northern India.

Most of these mountains are relatively young, folded and faulted sedimentary series of Tertiary origin. In some places volcanism has greatly affected the orography, and in many cases the sediments have been metamorphosed. Geologists who believe in the continental drift theory hold that many of the high mountains of Asia have been formed by the folding of sediments against the edge of stable, ancient crystalline blocks, such as those of Arabia and peninsular India. It is well established that there is a belt of folded mountains and volcanoes that encircles the Pacific Ocean, and this accounts for the offshore islands.

Plateaus. The plateaus of Asia vary in elevation from 2,000 ft. to 15,000 ft., but most of them are mountain-bordered, and most contain a series of basins; some of the plateaus are formed by tilted blocks, such as that of Arabia, which tilts eastward, as does also the Deccan plateau of India, the upturned edges of which form the Eastern and Western Ghats. The major plateaus are those of Arabia, Anatolia, Iran, Deccan, Tibet, Yünnan (southwestern China), and Mongolia.

Plains and Rivers. The major plains of Asia are in the north and west. In the north, swampy tundra and muskeg and taiga flats slope gently northward to the Arctic Ocean, and are crossed by great rivers, such as the Ob, Yenisey, Khatanga, Olenek, Lena, Yana, Indigirka, and Kolyma. In the west, the Kirghiz Steppe and the Turkestan area, combined under the Kazakh or Kazakhstan S.S.R., form a shallow basin area containing salt lakes, into which flow such rivers as the Amu Darya (Oxus), and Syr Darya. Other plains areas are narrow coastal plains that border much of the continent, and the broad flood plains of rivers. The broad river plains of Asia are the most important areas of the continent as far as human habitation, agriculture, and history are concerned. Rivers which have supported great agricultural and urban densities since the early history of mankind include the Jordan of Palestine; the Orontes of Lebanon and Syria; the Euphrates and the Tigris of Iraq; the Indus, including the Punjab, and the Ganges and Brahmaputra, of India; the Irrawaddy and Salween of Burma; the Menam of Siam; the Mekong and Red rivers of Indochina; and the Si, Yangtze, and Hwang Ho (Yellow) rivers of China. Some of these rivers have cut great gorges thousands of feet deep, such as those of the Indus, Salween, Mekong, and Yangtze rivers.

Lakes. There are many large lakes in Asia in addition to the Caspian Sea, the largest inland sea in the world. Among the important lakes are the Dead Sea and other salt lakes such as Tuz and Van in Turkey, Urmia in Iran, and Hamun-i-Helmand on the border between Iran and Afghanistan. Other great lakes are Balkhash and Issyk-Kul in the Turkestan area; Lop Nor, the lake in Sinkiang that has twice shifted its location; the beautiful Koko Nor of China; and Lake Baykal (Baikal) in Siberia. Many of these lakes, located in arid or semiarid basins, are salty, and their size and volume fluctuate considerably. Other large and fluctuating lakes are the Tonle Sap of Indochina, and the Poyang, Tunting, Tai, and Hungtse lakes of China.

CLIMATE

Asia, because of its size and mountains, has many different types of climate, but most of the continent is cold and arid during the winter and hot and arid in the summer. There are small areas of true tropics on the southwest coast of India and in the lower Ganges and Assam valleys, in Burma, the Malay Peninsula, and much of Indochina, but there is a vast expanse of arid to semiarid land that extends from the Red Sea coast of Arabia to the Kamchatka Peninsula, and from the Arctic Ocean to the Himalayas, west of China. This entire region receives less than 20 in. of rainfall a year, and a great part of this area is formed by such deserts as the Arabian, the Seistan of Iran and Afghanistan, the Thar of India, the Taklamakan in the Tarim Basin, and the Gobi in Mongolia, all of which receive less than 5 in. a year. With the exception of the Black Sea coast of Turkey, the summits of the Lebanon and Judean plateaus, and Arabia Felix, the only areas of Asia that receive much rainfall are in the south and southeast. The only areas that have about 80 in. of rain a year are the Malabar coast of southwestern India and the lower Ganges Valley; Assam, where Cherrapunji, on the Assam plateau, has the second highest rainfall in the world, averaging over 424 in. annually; the Arakan and Tenasserim coast of Burma; the Malay Peninsula and Indochina; and some parts of the coast of southeastern China.

The cold pole of the world is in northeastern Asia, in the middle course of the Lena River, in the Verkhoyansk region, where the average annual temperature is 3.4° F. The summer temperatures in this area average 56.1° in June, 60.3° in July, and 51.6° in August, but during the winter the average temperatures range as follows: December, —34.1°; January, —51.3°; February, —48.1°; and March, —23.8°.

Most of interior Asia has bitterly cold subzero but dry winters, and even central and northern Iran and eastern and central Turkey have cold winters. Most of the previously mentioned mountains and high plateaus also have cold winters because of their elevation. In the summer the situation is reversed and most of interior Asia has temperatures between 70° and 80° F., and some of the true deserts, such as the Arabian, Seistan, and Thar deserts, have temperatures up to 125° F. The area around the Persian Gulf is notorious for its heat and high humidity, and Aden has an almost constant temperature of 90° F.; the true tropical areas have a fairly constant temperature average of about 80° F. annually and are uncomfortable because of their high humidity.

There are many reasons for the various climates of Asia, but the simplest and most inclusive is that the interior of Asia, because of its great size, is farther from the temperature-modifying influence of large ocean bodies. The result is that during the winter, when the earth mass of Asia cools rapidly, the temperature drops and the air above the earth contracts and becomes slightly heavier, forming a high-pressure area, so that the wind blows out toward the lower pressure area over the warmer oceans. This causes a shift of cold, dry air to move out across the continent. In the summer the opposite situation develops. The land mass heats quickly and the air expands and rises, causing a lower pressure, so that the moist air from the ocean moves in over the land; but, because of the size of Asia and the mountain barriers, much of the rain falls on the fringes and eastward-facing mountain slopes, leaving the interior hot and dry. This alternating wind system is a monsoon type: the outblowing, or winter monsoon, is cold and dry; the inblowing, or summer monsoon, is warm and moist. In some areas the outblowing monsoon brings heavy rainfall when it has passed over a body of water and blows across an island or coast line, such as northwestern Japan or the Gulf of Tonkin area. There is a monsoon wind system south of the Himalayas that centers about India and Burma and accounts for the cool, dry winters and hot, wet summers, as well as the distribution of rainfall on the Western Ghats, the Assam Plateau, and the Arakan and Tenasserim coasts. Ceylon and part of the Carnatic coast region receive outblowing monsoon, or winter, rainfall.

Southern Asia, particularly the Malay Peninsula, is so far south that it lies within the tropics and receives heavy convectional showers with the passage of the direct rays of the sun to the north and south. Western Asia, the Near East from Turkey and the Levant coast to Iran, comes under the Mediterranean climatic type, having long, hot, clear, dry summers and short, cool, cloudy, and rainy winters. This climatic type affects strongly the northern Mediterranean coast and westward-facing mountains. Parts of Iran and the Kirghiz Steppe-Turkestan area receive a light spring rainfall, possibly from the evaporation of snow, which provides a source of moisture. Cyclonic storms occasionally travel across the Mediterranean Sea into the interior of southwestern Asia; they also move across the plains of northern Asia and along the Yangtze Valley. The southeastern coast of Asia is affected by typhoons in late summer.

Such an explanation of the rainfall and climate is oversimplified and generalized, since there are innumerable complicated local climatic types with many different causes. The exploration of the climate of Asia is just beginning. In southwest China, for example, 100-mi.-an-hour upper winds are a common occurrence in the mountain areas, and

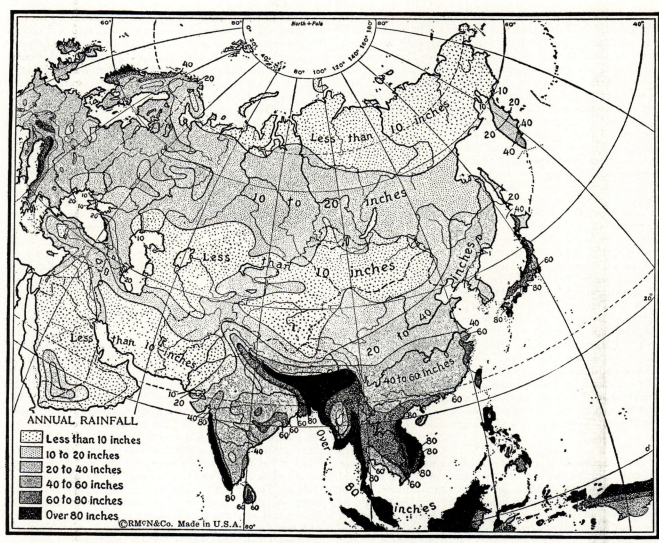

ANNUAL RAINFALL
Less than 10 inches
10 to 20 inches
20 to 40 inches
40 to 60 inches
60 to 80 inches
Over 80 inches
©RM°N&Co. Made in U.S.A.

in east and central China the cloudy, misty, hot weather is caused by the stagnation of the tropical Pacific air mass. When this air mass comes in contact with a cold air mass, the warm air overrides the cold, causing rainfall. In the Szechwan Basin of western China the clouds are low and the region is almost always under haze, fog, and drizzle. Mount Omei, in southwestern Szechwan, receives 300 in. of rainfall a year. The Basin of Mandalay receives only from 20 to 40 in. of rain a year and has become an important area because of this low rainfall. There are many other separate climatic regions, and the relief has a great effect on the local climate and therefore on the inhabitants. For example, in India, on the slopes of the Himalayas, there is a line of resort towns that parallels the great river valley towns, and the wealthier inhabitants migrate to these resorts to escape the summer heat. A similar arrangement of towns is found along the coast of Lebanon.   J. E. F.

SOILS

Across northern Asia there is a broad strip of tundra, generally treeless and having an ever-frozen subsoil. Only tiny areas in favored places are cultivated. Large parts are mountainous and swampy.

Southward lies an enormous area of podsols. This landscape, called the taiga, is a relatively thin forest containing a

mossy ground cover and many swamps. Many of the soils are weakly developed, and they are erratically underlain with permanently frozen subsoil. The rise of modern agri-

ALEXANDERSON (CNS). PAUL GUILLUMETTE, INC.

Harvesting wheat in Szechwan Province, China

TERRACED RICE PADDIES BORDER A SECTION OF CHINA'S "BURMA ROAD" NEAR TIEN LAKE.

CNS PHOTOS. PAUL GUILLUMETTE

cultural technology is pushing farming into the better parts of this huge area.

Further south are discontinuous zones of degraded chernozem, used for mixed farming, and of chernozem used for cereals and mixed farming. The black, slightly leached chernozem soils are highly fertile. Yields are limited by the uncertain climate. The growth of industry and transportation in this area will improve management and yields.

Between the chernozem and the desert lies a broad band of chestnut soils. These soils are dark brown, fertile, and only slightly leached. In moist years, yields are good, but drought years are frequent. In favored places, the soils may be irrigated for excellent yields of a wide variety of crops. The effects of drought can be ameliorated with better machine tillage, windbreaks, strip cropping, terraces, and local structures to impound the water.

In western and central Asia there are great areas of desert soils. Most of these soils are useless for agriculture, yet throughout these areas there are good deep soils along the streams that can be irrigated where water is available. The use of modern engineering could expand the irrigated land considerably.

Throughout the subhumid and semiarid parts, there are scattered spots of salty soils, especially in low lands where seepage or flood waters evaporate and leave the salts leached out of higher land.

In China there are important, densely populated areas of gray-brown podsolic and related soils somewhat like those of western Europe and eastern United States. The area is traversed by great streams and has broad strips of fertile, alluvial soil. In the western part, many of the streams have cut deeply into a mantle of wind-blown silt. Here erosion control is seriously needed. Although the soils support an enormous population, and have done so for centuries, yields could be greatly increased by better fertilization and by the application of other scientific methods in place of the present comparatively primitive farming practices.

In southern Asia there are a great many kinds of tropical soils. The poorest of these is the ground-water laterite, found on undulating landscapes having alternating wet and dry seasons. The few inches or feet beneath the surface are thoroughly leached. Beneath, there is a mass of highly weathered, doughy soil material that is saturated in the wet season. When exposed through erosion, or in other ways, the material hardens to a slaglike rock. Then there are areas of red, pervious soils developed from basic rocks, such as basalt and dolorite, that are highly productive when fertilized and otherwise well managed. In India especially, there are relatively fertile, nearly black, heavy soils (the "black cotton" soils) used extensively for cotton and small grains. Of great importance are the large and small bodies of alluvial soils along the streams. Many of the hilly soils are quite fertile, as the leached surface material is eroded away as it forms. Their use requires terraces or mixed plantings to prevent excessive runoff. Then there are a host of intermediate soils. A large part of the rice which is grown there is "paddy" rice, grown

BOTANICAL ZONES
OF ASIA

↟ = Coniferous forest
♀ = Broad-leafed forest
⟙ = Dry forest
▦ = Tundra and high-mountain vegetation
⸖ = Steppe and desert grass
✲ = Scrub woodland, thorn scrub
✿ = Tropical rain forest, monsoon forest
▦ = Desert

©R M⁰N & Co.
90° Made in U.S.A.

on the alluvial or other soils that may be ponded naturally or through irrigation.

The lands of southern and southeastern Asia are very densely populated. Farming methods are crude, and generally farmers have too little land for full employment. Progress requires increased industrialization, to employ the "extra" people now on farms and to produce the machinery, fertilizers, and other materials that are essential to an efficient agriculture. C. E. K.

FLORA

Asia is not only the largest of the continents but the only one to stretch from the polar regions almost to the equator. It has the highest mountains on the earth's surface and the greatest variety and range of climates. Hence its flora is rich and diverse, and its vegetation includes that of the arctic tundra, of the evergreen and deciduous temperate forests, of the steppes, of desert areas, of high mountain plant zones, and the different kinds of tropical and subtropical forests. In all this vast area it is estimated that there are well over 100,000 distinct species of seed-bearing plants. There is some evidence that central Asia is the original home of the flora of the temperate parts of the Northern Hemisphere. It is certain that some regions have been subjected to great climatic modifications in the course of geological time; these changes were partly correlated with such physiographic

changes as the uplift of the Himalaya Mountains. It is impossible to treat the flora of Asia as a unit, but the close correlation between climate and vegetation enables some broad subdivisions to be made. In many areas, however, the influence of man, mainly destructive, on the natural vegetation has been great, and in others different climates are juxtaposed, giving a patchwork of floras and communities of vegetation when these are viewed as mapped on a surface. In a concise account, therefore, it seems best to compromise by using both botanical and geographical subdivisions of the continent.

Arctic Tundra. The whole northern fringe of continental Asia and all the islands off the mainland are treeless. The vegetation is often dominated by mosses and lichens or by arctic grasses and sedges. In places there are richer "meadows" with monkshoods, saxifrages, asters, gentians, sea pinks, louseworts, and other plants producing gay flowers in the short summer season. Boggy depressions, pools, and lakes are frequent, but the ground is frozen solid most of the year, and only the surface thaws in summer. In sheltered and otherwise particularly favorable habitats, dwarf willows and birches may form a low scrub, and members of the heath and whortleberry families are widespread.

Siberian Taiga. South of the tundra, and separated from it by a very irregular and sometimes ill-marked boundary, but extending west to east across the continent, is a broad, sometimes broken belt of coniferous forests. The trees of this belt consist mainly of relatively few species of spruce, *Picea;* fir, *Abies;* pine, *Pinus;* and larch, *Larix.* The exact composition of the forests and the nature of the undergrowth depends largely on the drainage and the altitude. In some places birches and poplars are mixed with the conifers. In West Siberia there are large marshy areas and dense undergrowth. Where the ground is drier, shrubby layers are absent in the forests, which are taller and more open. In East Siberia the country is more undulating, and marshes are rarer, but the long and cold winter and strong drying winds lead to poor tree growth.

Towards the south, in some localities, the taiga passes into mixed woods where the conifers are partly replaced by broad-leaved deciduous trees, such as oaks, elm, walnut, maples, poplars, ash, birch, and lime. These mixed woods and patches of woodland dominated by deciduous trees partly represent, in diminished form, the broad belt of summer green forests characteristic of Europe. Passing into wooded steppes, they form a transition between the closed forests of the north and the treeless steppes of the south.

Steppes. Extensive areas of so-called "grasslands" devoid of trees cover large parts of Central Asia from Manchuria to the European part of the U.S.S.R. Generally the winter is cold; the summer, hot and dry. A typical genus in the flora is comprised of the feather grasses, *Stipa.* Common species of feather grass have long feathery awns and grow in tufts 3 to 6 ft. tall; frequently the earth is bare between clumps. These grasses have little economic value, but many other plants are associated with them. Members of the pea family (species of *Astragalus* and *Oxytropis*), meadow rues (*Thalictrum* spp.), umbellifers, labiates, anemones, chenopods, lilies, and numerous other plants are intermingled with the steppe grasses, and, for a short period in early summer, their flowers provide a gay carpet of many colors. Where the water table is somewhat higher during much of the year, a shrub steppe may develop, including low bushes of roses, honeysuckle, dwarf almond, and species of *Daphne* and *Spiraea.* Frequently, during periods of diminished water supply, the steppes become semidesert. Then the plant communities become more open, and wormwoods, *Artemisia* spp., dominate the monotonous landscape.

Deserts. With relatively insignificant breaks, there is a belt of desert and semidesert country from Arabia across Iran, through southern Siberia east to the Gobi Desert in Mongolia. The Arabian Desert, apart from the Sahara, is the most extreme desert on the earth. It contains many square miles almost devoid of plant life. Most of the central Asian deserts, on the other hand, have a sparse and sometimes seasonal vegetation. After rare rains a flora of ephemerals may pass through their life histories in a few weeks. Other plants occur as widely scattered individuals, of dwarf form, having reduced leaves and deeply penetrating roots. There are desert grasses bearing wiry foliage, members of the chenopod and knotgrass families. In sand-dune country the "saxaul," *Haloxylon ammodendron,* grows as a tree or shrub, singly or in small groups. Tamarisks also form bushes or brushwood. Where saline water accumulates, salt-desert vegetation may be lush, and chenopods, including species of *Salicornia, Suaeda,* and *Atriplex,* may form a greensward. Oases occur on or near desert margins, or along reduced water courses marked by poplars, tamarisks, and other trees and shrubs.

The high interior plateau of Tibet has a very severe continental climate, internal drainage, and salt or brackish lakes. The entire known flora comprises only about 50 seed-bearing plants, none of them woody. They are widely scattered and form open communities only. The outer plateau has extensive grazing grounds. The flora of the eastern river gorges is rich, with varied, often beautiful, and sometimes lush vegetation.

Mountain Regions. Of exceptional interest are the mountain floras of Asia. In the Altai, above the forest region, they include about 460 species. Many of these species are also found in the Arctic. Tall grass meadows containing a great variety of species are succeeded by so-called alpine meadows of low-growing plants, passing into tundra, the vegetation of which is finally composed mainly of mosses and lichens. The Tien Shan has a dry climate, and steppelike and tundralike communities are characteristic. Large parts of the Pamir are covered with semidesert communities, but in valleys and sheltered spots there are groves of willows and birches, and meadows containing many flowering plants occur where water is available. At the highest altitudes the vegetation may be matlike.

The great ridge of the Himalayas shows, on its southern face, long belts of vegetation reaching from the tropical communities below, through subtropical and moist-temperate to dry-temperate forests, and finally to high mountain scrub and herbaceous communities, up to the permanent ice and snow. There are floristic differences between the western and eastern Himalayas, a dividing line occuring in Nepal which is botanically the least known part. Rhododendrons are especially characteristic of the eastern Himalayas, where the flora passes into that of mountainous western China. The high mountain flora has numerous species of primula, gentian, saxifrage, asters, anemones, monkshoods, blue poppies, and many other often beautiful flowering herbs.

Mediterranean Asia. Mediterranean plant communities fringe Asia Minor, Syria, and Palestine. These include variants of the macchia, or maquis, of evergreen, hard-leaved shrubs. Inland there are steppes, semideserts, and even deserts in Syria, and, farther east, in Iraq and Iran. An interesting, isolated, luxuriant forest is found on the northern slopes of the Elburz Mountains in northern Iran, containing many relict types. The flora of most of Afghanistan is almost unknown.

Eastern Asiatic Temperate Zone. The greater part of eastern China is intensively cultivated; only fragments of the original vegetation are left. In the hills and mountains of western China, however, there exists the richest temperate flora in the world, composed of about 20,000 species of seed-bearing plants. There are forests of conifers, including *Abies, Pinus, Picea, Tsuga, Larix,* and *Cephalotaxus;* mixed montane forests of oaks and pines; and deciduous forests, including species of most of the woody genera known in the Northern Hemisphere. The forests are often rich in bamboos. Shrubs and herbs are just as abundantly represented. There are numerous rhododendrons, barberries, lilies, primulas, roses, vines, honeysuckles, gentians, ragworts, louseworts, poppies, irises, anemones, and many other flowering plants. An interesting fact is that there is a marked affinity between the flora of China and that of eastern North America. Special mention must be made of two very ancient plants: the maidenhair tree, *Ginkgo biloba,* which has survived only in China and Japan, and, even in these countries, probably only under cultivation; and the conifer known as *Metasequoia glyptostroboides,* which has been called "a living fossil," since it is apparently closely related to plants known only as fossils. In the extreme south the flora is subtropical to tropical. The absence of barriers to the migration of floras from north, south, and west explains in part the great floristic wealth of western China.

Over 6,000 species of seed-bearing plants are known from Japan, and the flora has many endemics and a high proportion of woody plants. The northern and central regions have a temperate vegetation including coniferous and mixed broad-leaved forests; the vegetation of the southern region is sub-tropical, and includes figs, evergreen laurels, and oaks. There

LINDSLEY F. HALL

ANCIENT CAMPHOR TREE, ST. JOHN'S UNIVERSITY, SHANGHAI

is a rich high-mountain flora. In the Formosan lowlands the vegetation is tropical.

The Indian Subcontinent. India and Burma, south of the Himalayas, have tropical floras. In northwest India and Burma there are more or less desert areas, and, in the broad sense, also some infiltration of Mediterranean types. The Gangetic plain is highly cultivated, but the Ganges Delta has the peculiar vegetation of the Sundribuns, largely swamp

LINDSLEY F. HALL

TAMARIND TREE, ZOOLOGICAL GARDENS, CALCUTTA

forests containing mangroves associated with many other tropical trees, especially "Sundri," *Heritiera minor.* On the west side of Peninsular India there are evergreen, equatorial forests; elsewhere there are monsoon and dry forests. Assam has the richest flora of any Indian province, and its flora, like that of northern Burma, includes many Chinese types. Lower Burma is much cultivated. Ceylon has a flora essentially like that of southern India, but it includes a number of plants limited to the island. The total flora of India and Burma exceeds 20,000 species of seed-bearing plants.

Indochina. A tropical vegetation of dense forests, principally mangroves, tropical rain forest, monsoon forest, and pine forest, is characteristic of Indochina. Dipterocarps and legumes are very important constituents of the primary rain forests; the former, of monsoon forests. Much of the forest has been destroyed or modified by man. Savanna vegetation, produced by cultivation and fires, has replaced monsoon forest over considerable areas.

Malaysia. This region, including the Malay Peninsula and the Malay Archipelago, has a flora estimated at 45,000 species of seed-bearing plants. In densely populated areas, like parts of Java, the natural vegetation has been destroyed; except on the highest mountains, this vegetation is, or was, forest. Beach and mangrove forests occur in the coastal districts. In the

LINDSLEY F. HALL

Flame Tree in Post Office Square, Penang, Federation of Malaya

lowlands there is a luxuriant, tropical, evergreen rain forest and, where there is a marked dry season, a deciduous monsoon forest. The former is particularly well developed in Sumatra, where the tallest story of trees may be 190 ft. high, towering over two lower stories of woody plants below. Orchids, ferns, and other plants occur as epiphytes. There is a mixture of a very large number of tree species in which none is dominant. Various types of secondary vegetation range from rejuvenating forest to scrub, fern brakes, and coarse grassland. Much of the monsoon forest has been transformed by fires into savanna. In the mountains there is a well-marked altitudinal zonation in the flora, the composition and history of which is very different from that of the low-land vegetation, where plants belonging to genera characteristic of temperate latitudes appear, such as buttercups, *Ranunculus,* and violets, *Viola.*   W. B. T.

FAUNA

Regions. The continent of Asia encompasses part of one zoogeographic region and all of another. All of the continent east of the Urals and south to the Himalaya Mountains lies within the Palaearctic region, as does the whole of Europe. South of the Himalayas, from the northwest boundary of India eastward to Indochina and southward through the Malay Peninsula and including most of the Malay Archipelago (Malaysia) to the island of Bali, especially Java, Sumatra, Borneo, and the Philippines, lies the Oriental region.

ORIENTAL REGION

By definition, therefore, the fauna of northern Asia shares with Europe many of the same forms and, in addition, they both contain many elements which are found in the Nearctic

(North America). The Oriental region, although very characteristic, receives some elements of the Palaearctic fauna; and even though it is separated from the Ethiopian region, many elements of the latter have infiltrated. The sharpness of Wallace's line (from Alfred R. Wallace), dividing the Australasian region from the Oriental, is remarkable. The marked affinities between the fauna of the island of Madagascar, which lies in the Ethiopian region, and the Indian fauna have led many zoogeographers to postulate a land bridge, Lemuria, connecting the two in ages past.

Mammals. The most characteristic mammals of the Oriental region are the anthropoids. The gibbons (*Hylobates, Symphalangus*), the only anthropoids that characteristically walk erect, are widespread throughout Malaysia from Assam southward through the archipelago to Borneo, Sumatra, and the Sulu Islands. The giant orangutans (*Pongo*), the largest of the anthropoid apes, are restricted to Borneo and Sumatra. Other Primates distributed throughout the region are the specter lemur, or tarsier (*Tarsius*), of Borneo, Java, Sumatra, Celebes, and the Philippines; the slow loris (*Loris*) of Ceylon and southern India; the loris (*Nycticebus*) of Malaysia and the Philippines; several apes (*Pithecus, Pygathrix*), shared with the Palaearctic; and *Simias* and *Nasalis,* the latter from Borneo and the former from the island of South Pagi, west of Sumatra.

Although not restricted to the Oriental region, the Bengal tiger (*Panthera tigris*) is one of the most characteristic mammals of the subcontinent. Its range extends throughout northeastern India, Burma, Siam, and the Malay Peninsula; it also extends northward (as the Siberian tiger) to Siberia, Manchuria, and Korea, in the Palaearctic. The typically African lion (*P. leo*) has extended its range to include Palaearctic Asia and northwestern India. The leopard (*P. pardus*) and the cheetah (*Cynaelurus jubatus*) are both found in the Oriental region and are shared with the Palaearctic and Ethiopian regions.

Probably the most widely known of Oriental animals is the Indian elephant (*Elephas indicus*), the species most generally included in circuses and zoological parks.

The Oriental region possesses at least two rhinoceroses—*Rhinoceros unicornis,* the Indian species, and *R. sumatrensis,* the Sumatran form. This family of perissodactyls is shared with the Ethiopian region. Another perissodactyl of great interest, especially so because its nearest relative is a resident of South America, is the Malayan tapir (*Tapirus indicus*).

There are many characteristic Oriental artiodactyls. The zebu, or Brahmany bull (*Bos indicus*), is a native of India and the adjacent countries. East of the Brahmaputra River is found the gayal (*Bubalus frontalis*); and in Burma, the Malay Peninsula, and some of the larger islands of the archipelago is found the banteng, or Javan ox (*B. sondaicus*). The Indian buffalo (*B. bubalus*) is a familiar part of the Oriental scene. Two notable antelopes are found in India—the nilgai (*Boselaphus tragocamelus*) and the very small four-horned antelope (*Tetraceros quadricornis*). Among the deers should be mentioned the axis deer (*Cervus axis*), the sambar (*C. unicolor*), and the tiny muntjac, or barking deer (*Cervulus muntjac*). Among the smallest of the ungulates are the chevrotains, several of which are found in the Oriental region, notably the Indian species (*Tragulus meminna*) and the Malayan species (*T. javanicus*). Of the pigs, *Sus cristatus* is typical, and the babirusa (*Babirusa alfurus*) is unique.

The pangolins (*Manis*) range throughout the Oriental region. Among the characteristically Oriental rodents are the flying squirrels (*Pteromys*) and the porcupine (*Atherura*). In addition to members of the cat family, there are

several other typically Oriental Carnivora: the Indian civet (*Viverra civetta*), which extends to southern China and the islands of Malaysia; the renowned snake killer of India, the mongoose (*Herpestes mungo*); the hyena (*Hyaena striata*), which enters India; the Indian jackal (*Canis aureus*); the

L. GREEN FROM GENDREAU

A Ceylon native using an elephant to pull a heavy roller

wild dog, or dhole (*C. deccanensis*); and the badgers (*Mydaus, Arctonyx*).

Birds. Among the characteristic birds of the Oriental region, babbling thrushes (Timeliidae) and pheasants are, with a few exceptions, confined to this region; the cuckoos are a widespread group and have at least eighteen genera in the region; and the bee eater (*Nyctiornis*) is confined. Though the parrots are abundant, only the genus *Psittinus* is unique. The remarkable owl *Photodilus* is found here, as is the highly characteristic surgeon bird (*Hydrophasianus*), which is related to the jaçana (*Parra*) of the New World. The ralline (cranelike) birds are not abundant.

The pheasants deserve a further mention, since it is from their numbers that the domestic chickens have been derived. There are four species of jungle fowl (*Gallus*): the red (*G. gallus*), the Ceylon (*G. lafayetti*), the gray (*G. sonnerati*), and the Javan (*G. varius*). It is from the red jungle fowl, which ranges throughout northern India, through Malaysia to the island of Sumatra, that the domestic breeds have arisen.

Reptiles. The reptiles of the Oriental region are represented by the estuarine crocodile (*Crocodilus porosus*) of the tidal estuaries of the Bay of Bengal and by the long-snouted gavial (*Gavialis gangeticus*) of India; cryptodiran (hidden-necked) and trionychoid (soft-shelled) turtles are found throughout the Orient. The geckos are especially widespread throughout India and Malaysia and are typified by the fringed gecko (*Ptychozoon*). Among the agamids should be noted the flying dragon (*Draco volans*). Monitor lizards (Varanidae) spread throughout the Australasian and Oriental regions. Various species of chameleons are also present.

Wild swine receive their daily feeding at the Khas Odi, a royal shooting box in Udaipur, north-western India.

The cobra (*Naja tripudians*) is typical of the Oriental Colubridae. The Malayan reticulated python (*Python reticulatus*) and the Indian python (*P. molurus*) are characteristic Oriental Boidae.

Amphibians. Among the typical Amphibia of the region are included the flying frogs of southeastern Asia (*Rhacophorus*) and the wormlike caecilians.

Fish. The fish fauna of India and Malaysia includes numerous carp (Cyprinidae), of which the mahseer (*Barbus*) is the giant; featherbacks (Notopteridae); numerous members of the cichlid family; ambassids, such as the glassfish (*Ambassis lala*); and the anabantids of the order Labyrinthici, so frequently met with in the aquaria of North American fanciers, such as the Siamese fighting fish (*Betta splendens*), the paradise fish (*Macropodus*), and the gouramis (*Colisa, Trichogaster, Helostoma*).

PALAEARCTIC REGION

The open lands of central Asia and the heights and plateaus of the Himalayas are within the Palaearctic region, and, as has been noted, share their fauna with Europe. Asiatic Palaearctica has, in turn, been subdivided into the Siberian and Manchurian subregions.

Mammals. The Siberian subregion includes as characteristic animals the yak (*Bos grunniens*), the antelopes *Procapra* and *Panthalops*, the musk deer (*Moschus*), the reindeer (*Rangifer*), the sable (*Mustela*), the wolverine (*Gulo*), and the mole (*Nectogale*). The second subregion, the Manchurian, contains several unique genera. The deer *Hydropotes* and *Elaphodus* are endemic. The raccoon dog (*Nyctereutes*), an unusual canid, and two interesting procyonids, the panda (*Ailurus*) and the giant panda (*Ailuropoda*), are also typically Manchurian forms. The otter (*Lutronectes*) is peculiar to the subregion.

The artiodactyls are very well represented in the Asiatic Palaearctic by numerous wild sheep, goats, and antelopes. The argali (*Ovis ammon*), the urial (*O. vignei*), and Blandford's sheep (*O. blandfordi*) are representative of the sheep. The tur (*Capra cylindricornis*), the markhor (*C. falconieri*), the pasang (*C. aegagrus*), the tahr (*Hemitragus*), and the takin (*Budorcas*) are all Asiatic goats of the Palaearctic. Among the antelope genera represented are *Addax, Procapra, Saiga, Panthalops,* and the chamois (*Rupicapra*).

Among the typically Palaearctic insectivore genera which populate Asia are *Talpa, Scapto chirus, Scaptonyx,* and *Anurosorex*.

Both species of the Old World camels are represented in Asia: the one-humped, or Arabian (*Camelus dromedarius*), and the Bactrian, or two-humped (*C. bactrianus*).

Especially noteworthy, because of its association with man, is the presence of the wild horse in Mongolia (*Equus caballus*) which is unquestionably of the same species as the domestic horse. The Asiatic wild ass (*Equus hemionus*) is found in central Asia, Iran, and Syria.

Asia is unique in having one species of fresh-water seal (*Phoca sibirica*) which inhabit the huge inland Lake Baykal. Another unique species (*P. caspica*), the Caspian seal, enjoys water that is only slightly salt.

The Primates are represented in Palaearctic Asia by only a few genera in the east, the rhesus (*Macaca*) and the douc langur (*Pygathrix*), shared with the Oriental region, and by the snub-nosed langur (*Rhinopithecus*).

Birds. The avifauna is, like the mammalian, Eurasiatic. The starlings (*Podoces*) are, in general, confined to the Siberian subregion, whereas the pheasants, although shared with the Oriental, are highly characteristic of southern China. The birds of Palaearctic Asia are similar to those of Europe.

Reptiles. The typical reptiles of Asia are largely restricted to the Oriental region.

Amphibians. Among the Amphibia, the Asiatic salamanders (Hynobiidae), range from the Urals to Kamchatka and Japan and from northern Siberia south to Turkestan and Hupeh. The giant salamanders of the family Cryptobranchidae are represented in China and Japan by *Megalobatrachus*. The most primitive of the Salamandridae, *Tylototriton,* is found both in Yünnan and the island of Okinawa.

Numerous other salamandrids are typical of the Asiatic fauna.

The discoglossid frogs are represented by *Bombina* in China and *Barbourula* in the Philippines. Among the pelobatid toads typical of Asia are *Megalophrys, Scutiger, Aelurophryne,* and *Ophrophryne.* Bufonids are represented by *Nectophryne* and *Pseudobufo.* The true frogs (Ranidae) are represented, except for *Rana* itself, by the members of one subfamily (Cornuferinae). Typical genera are *Micrixalus, Staurois,* and *Cornufer.*

Fish. The most widespread family of Asiatic fishes is the Cyprinidae (carps). Among the many other notable fishes should be mentioned the Chinese paddlefish (*Psephurus*), very closely related to the North American *Polyodon,* and the giant huso sturgeon (*Acipenser huso*), which is said to be the largest of all fresh-water fishes (a weight of 2,250 lb. has been recorded). The fishes of Asia are similar to those of Europe and North America.

POPULATION

Asia, excluding that part of the Union of Soviet Socialist Republics lying east of the Urals, contains an estimated population of over 1,200,000,000, perhaps one half of the world total. The largest country is China, with a population of about 462,800,000. India, consisting of the Dominion of India, with some 337,000,000 persons, and Pakistan, with about 70,000,000, contains more than 400,000,000. Japan, with 78,627,000, has the next largest population.

Distribution and Density. The Near East, defined as those countries on the Asiatic continent west of Pakistan, is

An Afghan trader, one of many who band together in caravans to transport goods through the Khyber Pass

estimated to have a population of approximately 68,000,000 persons, and the Far East, which is taken as including the islands off the coast of southeast Asia, but which excludes Australia, New Zealand, and the small Pacific islands to the east, contains more than 1,140,000,000. Most of the countries in the Near East are comparatively small; some have only around 100,000 persons. The largest are Turkey and Iran, each of which is estimated to contain about 17,000,000 (only the former has reliable data).

The Near Eastern countries are not densely settled; for example, the population per square mile is approximately 27 in Iran, 28 in Afghanistan, 41 in Iraq, and 59 in Turkey. The countries of the Far East, on the other hand, are considerably larger and more densely settled. Thus, Java may have a density approaching 1,000 persons per square mile; Japan, 531; and India, 256. Asia as a whole (excluding the U.S.S.R.) has a density of about 118 persons per square mile. The United States, in comparison, has a density of about 49 persons per square mile.

The Asiatic population tends to be concentrated along the coasts; the mountainous interior of the continent is largely empty. The following areas comprise the interior of the continent: Afghanistan, Bhutan, Nepal, the Mongolian Peoples Republic, the western Chinese provinces, and Tibet. In this territory are approximately 40,000,000 persons, or between 3 and 4 per cent of the total Asiatic population, excluding the U.S.S.R. In terms of land surface, however, perhaps between one quarter and one third of the continent is included here. The semiarid regions of the Near East are also relatively lightly settled, particularly in comparison with the humid southeast.

Growth. It is estimated that in 1650 the total world population was about 500,000,000; the population of Asia numbered over 300,000,000, or about 60 per cent of the total. Under the influence of the Industrial Revolution and the settlement of the Western Hemisphere, the other continents of the world grew at a faster rate than did Asia. Accordingly, it is thought that over the last 300 years the population of Asia, excluding the U.S.S.R., increased about three and one-half times, whereas the population in the rest of the world increased some five times.

Birth and Death Rates. Asia, having to a large extent a subsistence and nonindustrialized economy, provides but a very low standard of living for most of its peoples. Accordingly, as among all largely illiterate and impoverished people, both the birth and death rates are very high. For all of Asia the birth rate may be about 40 or more per 1,000 population annually. Japan, where the statistics are fairly accurate, reported a rate of under 30 before World War II, a rate of about 30 during the war years and a rate of 35 in 1947. This country is the only industrialized nation of Asia and may have the lowest birth rate of any major Asiatic nation. Because, however, of the lack of any reliable statistics for any country except Japan, it is difficult to determine whether the over-all Asiatic birth rate has been decreasing. While it is clear that there has been a decrease in Japan, there is no positive evidence that the rate has decreased substantially in any other major areas.

The Asiatic death rate is also very high and, like the birth rate, may be two or more times greater than the corresponding rates in western Europe and North America. The death rate in Asia, excluding China, may be approximately 30 deaths per 1,000 population. In Japan, which may have the lowest rate of any major country in Asia, the death rate was reported at about 17 per 1,000 population before World War II, and decreased to 15 in 1947; life expectancy at birth was

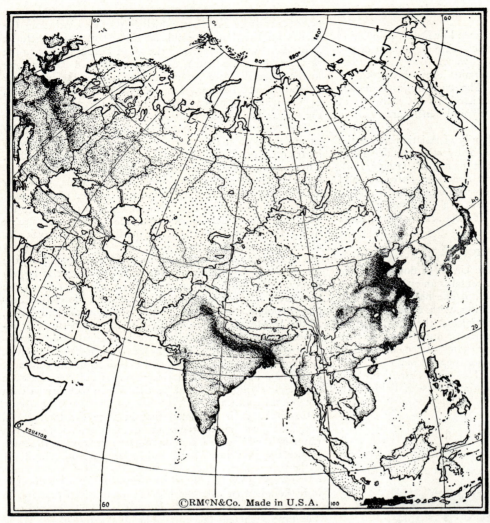

*RELATIVE
POPULATION DENSITY IN ASIA*

©RM^cN&Co. Made in U.S.A.

calculated as about 45 years (1926-1930). In India, by contrast, the death rate is so much higher that life expectancy at birth was estimated at only about 26 years (1921-1930); this figure compares with an expectancy of almost 60 years in the United States at that time. In China there is reason to believe that the death rate may be about as high as the birth rate; accordingly, it is thought that the Chinese population may remain substantially unchanged in size.

Both the birth and the death rates, but particularly the latter, fluctuate considerably from year to year; accordingly, the rate of population change from year to year also fluctuates quite erratically. During years of good harvest and few epidemics or wars, the death rate may fall considerably and the population increase in size through an excess of births over deaths. In years of bad harvest, epidemics, or wars, the death rate may increase to the point where previous population gains are almost if not quite wiped out. In China over the years, it would seem that the deaths tend to equal the births; in the remainder of Asia there appears to be a net excess of births over deaths, although in any given year in any specific area the reverse may be true. It is difficult to foresee to what extent the population of Asia may increase in the future. To the degree that the economy remains substantially unchanged, it is not likely that there will be much population increase. However, given peaceful conditions, increased development of available natural resources, and

the introduction of modern agriculture and manufacturing, it is possible for the population-supporting capacity of Asia to increase.

The population data for this vast continent are so grossly inadequate that any but very approximate estimates of its demographic characteristics are impossible. China, contain-

TRIANGLE PHOTO

Country Scene in Korea

(Top, left) Priests and priestesses leave the Inari-Jinja shrine at Fushimi, near Kyoto. Dedicated to the rice goddess, Inari shrines stand in every Japanese village. This one, built in 717, is considered the oldest in Japan.

(Top, right) Geishas chat in a Kyoto garden.

(Above) A view of the center of Tokyo showing the famous Nihonbashi (Bridge of Japan), which spans the Sumida River.
(Right) Brightly clad native women, their heads shaded from the hot glaring sunlight, harvest tea near Shizuoka, Honshu.

(Above) The circular, blue-roofed Temple of Heaven is located in Peiping, China's former capital and historically most famous city. Quietly decorative, the temple is Confucian.

(Right) A colorfully robed Buddhist priest solemnly performs the Long Life Ritual in the Lama Temple. The huge smiling Buddha image may be seen above the richly ornamented altar.

(Below) Sampans and junks are crowded into busy Shanghai harbor, resting from fishing and cargo-hauling duties. Shanghai's skyline and waterfront are seen across the water.

PHILIP GENDREAU. N. Y.

PREPARING KARAKUL SKINS FOR TANNING, IN BAGHDAD, IRAQ

ing perhaps 40 per cent of the total (and about one-fifth of the total world population), has never had a census, and estimates of its population vary from 350,000,000 to more than 500,000,000. It is assumed here that the population is approximately 450,000,000 and has remained at this size over the last several decades. During the 1930's a number of reasonably accurate censuses were taken in several countries, particularly in India, Ceylon, Japan, the Philippines, Turkey, and several smaller countries. During the 1940's India and several other nations took censuses at one time or another. In comparison with the data available for Europe, the Western Hemisphere, and Oceania, however, the information for Asia must be considered highly unsatisfactory. With respect to vital statistics, i.e., birth and death rates, the data are even less satisfactory than the total head counts. Japan and Palestine may be the only countries having reasonably complete counts of all births and deaths. Because of the major inadequacies in the basic data, statistics and conclusions must be considered only as estimates. *See also* ASIATIC TRIBES.   A. J. J.

EXPLORATIONS

Little is known of the earliest explorations in Asia. Typical are those recorded in the Scriptures as having been undertaken by Moses: he went with a small party to find water in the desert land of Rephidim (Exodus xvii); and he organized a reconnaissance survey to "spy out the land of Canaan" (Numbers xiii). Only an acute need for food, water, or soil persuaded men to penetrate the unknown. The weak sought places of refuge; the strong sought places of larger resource.

Much later, though still in times for which there are no contemporary records, expeditions began to trace the origins of articles that appeared on the market too sparsely or intermittently: the sources of precious stones and metals, of rare woods, foods, and spices, of elephant tusks, of manufactures, and of slaves. Often several purposes were combined. A party sent out to find a suitable mountain pass for a military campaign would also be on the lookout for possible allies and enemies and send back reports on the size and character of remote populations. Pilgrims in search of magic returned with rumors of fabulous cities. News brought by one set of travelers gave impetus to later expeditions by others.

Peoples were separated by fear and suspicion. Each tried to isolate the core of its settlement or the seat of its government from attack. As a result, such contacts as were made usually took place at the marginal meeting of cultures: the returning soldier, pilgrim, or merchant brought back a wealth of hearsay about distant places, but only a small kernel of firsthand observation. His tales spoke of marvelous cities of

Tomb of Darius the Great (558-486 B.C.), at Nagsch-e-Rustem near Persepolis, Iran

gold and mountains of jade, of dragons and unicorns, of giants and of gods walking on earth. Sometimes the truth gained less acceptance than the fable.

A more systematic pursuit of geographical knowledge in Asia began with large-scale irrigation—the need of following streams to their source—and with navigation beyond the familiar coast lines. Expeditions were sent out not only for immediate purposes, but also to obtain mapping data. And at a remarkably early age men wandered far in search of knowledge for its own sake: thus the emissaries of powerful rulers in Mesopotamia, Persia, India, and China braved untold hazards to seek out temples and oracles, to obtain a talisman, and later to sit at the feet of men famed for insight and to bring back holy books. In the fourth millennium B.C. Sumer (southern Iraq) and Egypt knew of each other. China was in touch with central and western Asia at least through the greater part of the Chou Dynasty (1027-256 B.C.) Toward the end of that era caravan routes served for the exchange of China's most precious product, silk, for gems and metal goods. Europe was as marginal to the known world of Asia as America was to that of Europe before the seventeenth century of the Christian Era.

Eastern Contacts of Greece and Rome. Although the civilization of the Mediterranean Basin had to some extent been unified by trade and conquest even in prehistoric times, what lay beyond the coastal margin was almost unknown, even after some products from the western coast of Africa and from Asia Major had already entered into the commerce of the region. Until about the eighth century B.C., Greek explorers rarely ventured far from a seaport or a navigable river. Like the Phoenicians, from whom they had acquired most of their knowledge of lands and peoples, they

had little incentive for extended overland travel. Yet, the Phoenicians, when they founded the colony of Carthage in the ninth century B.C., were already carrying on a trade reaching from Spain to India. The nature of that trade is described in the Book of Ezekiel.

Herodotus (c. 490-430 B.C.), the Greek historian, also was an outstanding geographer. His travels took him to the coasts of the Black Sea, to Ecbatana and Susa in the heart of the Persian Empire, to Babylon, and to Egypt by way of Tyre. His topographical descriptions are circumstantial, and he was curious about strange manners and customs. In the following centuries the plantation of Greek colonies along the shores and on many islands of the Mediterranean was an aid to a more far-flung reconnoitering of lands under alien control. Herodotus had got as far as the mouth of the Indus River and had followed the road built by Darius the Great from the Euphrates to the Mediterranean, a distance of some 1,500 mi. A generation later, another Ionian, Hecataeus of Miletus, traveled over part of the same route and, like his predecessor, combined geographical and ethnological with historical studies. Of his *Travels Around the World* only fragments have been preserved.

It was not until Alexander the Great (356-323 B.C.) waged his successful campaign against Persia and established his rule from Egypt to India that the West obtained an approximately true idea of the geography of the Near and Middle East. He organized many expeditions to mountains and valleys so little known that he did not dare take his main army through them without more precise knowledge. Not only Alexander's campaigns but also the journeys of ambassadors from many parts of the world to his camp began to build up a more substantial body of information. More than that, they helped to diffuse over a large part of western Asia a humanistic Hellenic civilization and so prepared the way for a more disinterested and exact exploration. However, of the regions north and east of India, and indeed of the greater part of the subcontinent itself, Europe remained ignorant for many more centuries. Megasthenes, a historian sent in 302 B.C. by one of Alexander's successors, Seleucus I (Nicator), on a mission to Patna, India, stayed there for several years and wrote a book on the flora, fauna, and customs of the land, of which only fragments remain.

Ancient China and the West. Chinese knowledge of India and central Asia at that time probably was no more extensive and no more accurate. For example, a book written in the third century B.C. describing the campaigns and travels of the Chou emperor Mu Wang (c. 965-928 B.C.) is almost entirely legendary. The reigns before the first Han Dynasty (206 B.C. to A.D. 25) were too preoccupied with questions of security to become very curious about the *terra incognita* beyond the adjacent regions from which the attacks of barbarians came.

Within the Chinese Empire the building of highways and the organization of postal stages facilitated travel even in early Han times. The minute pictorial description of everything seen by imperial officers on their journeys to outlying provinces became through the centuries an unusual feature of Chinese art. It was not, however, until the Emperor Wu-ti of the Later Han Dynasty, who came to the throne in A.D. 140, subjected Korea, Annam, and Sinkiang, that contacts with the more distant seats of civilization were cultivated. One of his ministers, Chang Ch'ien, sent to secure a treaty of mutual aid with the Iranian tribes in the southern part of the Gobi Desert against the Huns, was captured by these enemies and returned after ten years of captivity, the first of a long line of Chinese emissaries to bring news of Turkestan and Tibet. Later he was sent even farther afield and returned with geographical information that served to extend the ancient silk road from Bactria beyond the Pamirs to Ferghana—that is, to the very borders of the Persian Empire.

From this period dates the first reliable evidence of an exchange of products between China and the Near East. References to Persia became more frequent in Chinese literature. Pan Ch'ao, a Later Han general (c. A.D. 31-102), subjected not only the Huns but also the desert peoples to the west of them and secured direct access to the Caucasus and the Caspian Sea. One of his officers, commissioned to proceed to Rome, got only as far as the head of the Persian Gulf; but through its now regular contact with Mesopotamia, China gained increasing knowledge also of Europe.

The chief impetus to Chinese exploration did not come from glimpses of Mediterranean culture, but from those of Indian culture. Under Ming Ti, second emperor of the Eastern Han Dynasty (A.D. 28-75), began a succession of expeditions to India for the study of Buddhism. After an interruption of two centuries, during which both Rome and China were disturbed by internal disorders, Chinese explorations in central and western Asia were resumed under the Wei emperors. Fa Hsien, a Buddhist priest of the beginning of the fifth century, may have been the first educated Chinese to visit India by the more southerly land route through Burma, to study and translate Sanskrit texts, later also to publish an account of his travels. About the same time, Buddhist missionaries began to come to China.

Not until the conquest of the Turkis by the founder of the T'ang Dynasty, in the seventh century, did Chinese exploration again reach the Caspian Sea. The greatest explorer of this period was Hsüan Tsang (c. 600-664). He crossed both the Tien Shan and the Hindu Kush mountains, reached the Ganges, visited some of the most famous monasteries and, after studying Sanskrit, returned by way of the Pamirs and Kashgar with 657 sacred texts and 150 relics. He was probably the first Chinese to describe with a fair degree of accuracy the civilization of northern India.

The next great Chinese explorer was, first of all, a theologian. The Buddhist monk I-ching in 671 sailed on a Persian ship to Sumatra, then a part of the Hindu empire of Shrivijaya, famed for its art and learning. After a visit to the Nicobar Islands, where he observed people of a much more primitive culture, he reached northern India and collected a large Sanskrit library, which he took back to China some years later. Diplomatic missions between China, India, Indonesia, and Japan at this time were frequent. Although most of the maritime trade was in the hands of Arabs, whose colonies and ports of call were scattered from the African coast to Canton, Chinese shipping in the seventh and eighth centuries occasionally extended as far as the mouth of the Euphrates. There was, indeed, in T'ang times (618-907) an intense interest in geographical knowledge, stimulated in part by visits of ministers and missionaries from every part of the known world.

The Crusades. Like the Chinese, so the Mediterranean peoples had, since the days of Alexander, gained geographical knowledge mainly through war and to a much smaller extent through trade. Rome's eastern neighbors were peoples with old civilizations whose maritime and overland connections were fully developed, so that for many centuries they continued to act as intermediaries between Europe and Asia. Just as Buddhism had given the impetus to extensive travel in the Far East, so in the early Middle Ages the rise of the Caliphate and its missionary ardor pro-

vided the incentive for renewed travel in the Near and Middle East. In the eighth century its power extended beyond Afghanistan as far as Kahgar. Overland travel brought Arab explorers to China itself, and Arab sailors were familiar with its southern coast. In the tenth century, strong Arab settlements in Ceylon and Indonesia brought Islamic

PHOTO BROWN BROTHERS

A granary in the Caspian Sea region of Iran. Circular disks on top of poles are to prevent rats from destroying the grain.

culture even closer to the Far East, while Europe's knowledge of Asia remained clouded by legend. Before the Crusades the world map of Ptolemy, produced about A.D. 150, had undergone little change.

The Crusades contributed mainly, of course, to a more accurate knowledge of Asia Minor. Cut off for a millennium from direct contact with central and eastern Asia, Europe was unprepared for the evidences of great contemporary civilizations in India, southeast Asia, and China, when at last the opportunity arose to cut out the intermediaries. That opportunity was the Mongol invasion of all western Asia and a large part of Europe in the thirteenth century.

In 1245 Pope Innocent IV sent a Franciscan, John Plano de Carpini, to Mongolia, or Tartary, as it was then called. This emissary traveled by way of Bohemia, Poland, and Russia around the northern end of the Caspian Sea and of the Aral Sea along the western extension of the Tien Shan mountains—over a more northern route than that customarily followed by the caravans—and reached the Grand Khan's camp at Karakorum five months after leaving Kiev. He returned after a stay of less than four months over almost the same route, and his contributions to geographical knowledge were remarkably accurate (His account of lands and peoples seen, *Liber Tartarorum,* was not published as a whole, however, until 1839.)

A few years later King Louis IX of France, then engaged in the Sixth Crusade against the Saracens, i.e., Turks, sent another envoy to the Mongol emperor: William de Rubruk, also a Franciscan. This traveler went by sea to Constantinople and the Crimea, but from Russia he followed almost the same route as his predecessor. On his return trip he rediscovered what Herodotus had already known, that the Caspian was an inland sea and not an extension of the Persian Gulf, as the medieval map-makers had insisted it was. Rubruk's description of central Asia also failed to reach a wide public. His *Itinerarium* was first published, in part, in 1598-1599.

Marco Polo. More famous than either of these travel books was to be the lively account of his experiences by a young Venetian merchant, Marco Polo (c. 1254-c. 1324). His grandfather, discontented with the prices he had to pay in Baghdad for Russian furs destined for the London trade, had opened a branch office in Soldaia, the main port of the Crimea. His father and uncle, finding the Tartars who had invaded Russia favorably disposed to trade with the West, decided to cut out some more of the middlemen by making a buying trip in the interior. When war broke out behind them between Tartars and Saracens, they considered it safer to go all the way to the Far East and return by sea. Following the established route to Turkestan, they attached themselves to a caravan that was returning to the capital of China, where they were received as distinguished foreigners by the progressive ruler Kublai Khan. They returned as his official envoys to the pope with a request that he send out a hundred missionaries. But there was to be an election in Rome, and the delivery of their message was delayed. When they set out again, as ambassadors of the new pope to the Grand Khan, they took with them 17-year-old Marco. This time they selected a more southern route through central Asia, still well north of the Himalayas, and spent almost four years on the journey. All three remained in China, accompanied the ruler on several expeditions, and went on political missions for him. Marco evidently became a favorite of the Khan. During his years of service he made many long journeys, some of them extending overland into Tibet and Burma, and by sea to India and Ceylon. When he was about 30 years old, Marco governed the city of Yangchow for three years and gained insight into Chinese life such as no European had ever had. He was 45 when at last it became possible to return to Europe, with a commission to escort an imperial princess on her marriage trip to Persia. This journey, along the China and Annam coasts through the Strait of Malacca to the Nicobar Islands, then to Ceylon and along the west coast of India to the Persian Gulf, and so to the Black Sea and home to Venice, took the Polos four years. In 1296, while a prisoner of Genoa, Marco dictated the story of his adventures. Circulated in manuscript and later in printed form, it profoundly influenced geographers and explorers, including Columbus.

Other East-West Contacts. Exchanges between Europe and the Mongol Empire continued. John of Monte Corvino (c. 1247-c. 1328) went as a missionary and not as an explorer, but his letters described what he saw on the way in Persia, southern India, and Ceylon. Later he organized a Christian community at the Mongol summer capital and became its archbishop. In the remaining 40 years of Mongol rule, before the collapse of the dynasty, other European missionaries appeared in China. The friar Jordanus traveled through Persia and India and also visited Cambodia. The friar Odoric, after extensive land journeys in the Middle East, sailed by the already familiar route to Canton, traversed China from south to north, spent three years in Peiping, and returned by the silk route through Tibet; he became famous for his description of Lhasa, the Lamaist capital. Merignolli, sent to the Grand Khan by Pope Benedict XII, made both voyages by sea and added to geographical confusion with erroneous identifications of river systems, lakes, and ocean bays. Niccolò de' Conti, of Venice, was the last great merchant adventurer to add substantially to the knowledge of India, which he penetrated from the Gulf of Cambay in the west and, after rounding the tip, from the mouth of the Ganges in the east. From India he went to Burma overland, and on his homeward voyage he visited Java, the Arabian coast, and Egypt.

In the Middle East the rise of the western Mongolian Empire under the great warrior Timur, better known in English literature as Tamerlane (c. 1336-1405), had created a new incentive to direct relations between Europe and central Asia. The Spanish diplomat Gonzáles de Clavijo sailed with a letter from Henry III of Castile to Constantinople and Trebizond, then traveled overland to Tabriz and through the Kara Kum Desert to Samarkand, the new ruler's capital. He wrote of the marvelous postal connections, with a hundred horses in readiness at some of the stations, and described the wealth of Turkestan in glowing terms. A German prisoner of war, Hans Schiltberger, in the early years of the fifteenth century took part in some of Tamerlane's campaigns and later in a *Reisebuch* described expeditions that had taken him as far as Siberia and, perhaps, India.

Era of Maritime Discovery. *Portuguese and Spanish Exploration.* With the disruption of Mongol rule over western Asia and the failure of the Crusades, the idea of a direct

GEMMA COHN-WIENER

A broach, a typical Bombay coastal ship for light haulage

sea route to India and the Far East occupied many minds in Europe. This time Portuguese explorers took the lead. Following reports of shipmasters who, after a century of surveys of the African coasts, had rounded the Cape of Good Hope ten years earlier, Vasco da Gama (c. 1469-1524) set out from Lisbon in 1497 with four ships, sailed to the easternmost point of Africa, there took on an Arab pilot, and was the first European to cross the Indian Ocean to Calicut. This port had become the chief entrepôt for the export to Europe of gems, woods, essences, spices, and fabrics, collected in different parts of India and also in Burma, Siam, Ceylon, Sumatra, and Malaya. The return voyage with a rich cargo seems to have been uneventful. On a second voyage, made with fifteen ships in 1502, da Gama planted a number of small colonies; and in 1524 he assumed administrative control over them, the first European empire in southern and eastern Asia.

Each further advance of the Portuguese, and there were

A JAVANESE TEA ESTATE

SCREEN TRAVELER, FROM GENDREAU

many, produced new knowledge which, despite their strenuous effort to maintain a monopoly, they could not long keep from the rest of Europe. But the interior of India, Malaya, Borneo, Siam, Cochin China, and the Large Sunda Islands, which they claimed for their trade, remained untraveled and unknown. Even the small settlement established first at Canton, then at Macao, to facilitate penetration of China produced little new information about that vast country, though a few Dominican and Franciscan missionaries braved Chinese opposition and settled in the interior. Not until after the union of Portugal with Spain, in 1580, was China really explored.

An Italian and a Portuguese entered the service of Spain to find a way to the Far East by sailing west. Columbus' magnificent failure preceded the success of Magellan. Leaving San Lucar in 1519 with five ships, Magellan at first mistook the mouth of the La Plata for the rumored southern passage to the other side of the world, then correctly identified the strait which bears his name, and passed through it to the Pacific. He discovered the Philippine Islands and took possession of them in the name of the king, but was killed by a treacherous ruler of Cebu. Only one of his ships completed the return voyage to Spain, the first vessel to circumnavigate the globe.

Ludovico di Varthema, of Bologna, a soldier of fortune in Portuguese service, already had distinguished himself by being the first European to describe what went on in the holy city of Mecca when he undertook a commission to proceed to India through Persia and to explore the Deccan. He also traveled extensively in Indonesia. Like him, Duarte Barbosa, a Portuguese, prepared himself by language study; he secured valuable information in India and in the coun-

tries east and north of Malacca which was published some years later. Mendes Pinto, of the next generation, got as far as Japan and also visited China, Siam, and Burma, after extensive explorations in the Middle East, to collect material for a travel book published in 1614. Gasparo Balbi, a Venetian, went overland to India and spent three years in Burma, or Pegu, as it was called at that time. His travel book, published in 1590, gave the first authentic news of that country.

English Exploration. About this time English explorers got into the picture. Anthony Jenkinson went to Moscow in 1557, then north of the Caspian Sea through western Turkestan, returning over much the same route. On a second journey in 1562 he collected much new information about outlying parts of Persia. Two other Englishmen, John Newberry and Ralph Fitch, took northern India for their field of investigation; Fitch also visited Pegu and Malacca. Francis Drake, whose principal claim to fame lies elsewhere, visited the Moluccas, Celebes, and Java in 1579. Thomas Coryat, an Oxford scholar, was one of the first of that long line of Englishmen of leisure who, traveling mainly for pleasure and self-education, picked up and published an immense store of interesting knowledge.

Dutch, French, and German Exploration. Jan Huyghen van Linschoten (1563-1611), one of the first Hollanders to travel extensively in Asia, though better known for his Atlantic exploits, excelled in accurate description of what he saw in the Portuguese Empire. Several Frenchmen, too, among them Tavernier, Thevenot, and Chardin, went to India and, taking diverse overland routes, supplemented the already substantial knowledge of the Middle East. In the early part of the seventeenth century there was indeed a steady stream of travel between Europe and southern Asia; and although this was not to any large extent motivated by scientific curiosity, it did feed the craving for news from Asia in that romantic age.

In the second half of the century occidentals of great ability often filled administrative posts in India and beyond; with better opportunities to check rumors and to follow special trends of interest, they produced a larger body of authentic data. For example, Engelbert Kaempfer, a German physician and naturalist, lived long enough in Siam and Japan to write a history of these countries and to describe with fair accuracy their contemporary life. With the establishment of the English and Dutch East India companies, even visits to places somewhat remote from the commercial routes became more frequent and more rewarding, both in adventure and in reliable information. At about this time a new motive entered into Asian exploration in addition to those which survived from ancient times, the motive of sport.

Missionary Exploration. In Siam, China, and Japan propagation of the Christian faith had the largest by-product of new knowledge. Jesuit missionaries attached to the court of the Mogul emperor, Akbar the Great, developed the strategy of expediting conversion by becoming intimates, in other Eastern countries too, of courtiers and learned men. In this way they became well informed on matters which by now all cultured Europe was eager to hear more about. Despite prohibitions, Jesuit, Dominican, and Franciscan missionaries traveled everywhere and penetrated far into Tibet, Mongolia, and Manchuria. One of the last of the missionary adventures which have provided Europe with reliable facts about little-known places and peoples was that of the Lazarist Fathers, Huc and Gabet. After a long residence in Mongolia these men decided in 1844 to find out more about Lamaism by visiting Tibet. The story of their journey north of the Great Wall and over the Koko Nor through Sinkiang to Lhasa, and of their sojourn in that forbidden city, has become a classic of travel literature.

Northern Routes. Cut off by the Portuguese from eastern Asia, Dutch and English merchant adventurers early conceived the idea of reaching that distant region by a northern sea route. Already somewhat familiar with the northern Atlantic and with the White Sea, they were not appalled by the particular inhospitality of these near-arctic regions. To get to China by sailing along the unknown northern shores of Asia or America seemed entirely feasible with the geographical knowledge possessed at the end of the sixteenth century. But that knowledge was fragmentary, and in spite of many attempts both the northwest and the northeast passages to Cathay remained dreams. Eventually it was Russian enterprise that succeeded in the quest. During the first part of the seventeenth century most of the great rivers of Siberia were followed as far as they were navigable, and the north coast of Asia was roughly charted. In 1648 Deshnev sailed around the continent's most eastern cape and at Anadirsk established an outpost for further inland exploration. Subsequent semimilitary expeditions reached the Amur River and, in spite of Manchu opposition, established trading posts in that area. An inland route to the Amur Basin was found in 1643 by the Cossack Poyarkoff who followed the Yenisei River as far as possible, crossed Lake Baykal, and proceeded east along the Selenga and Shilka valleys.

At the end of the century the major geographical features of eastern Siberia were known. Kamchatka had been annexed, and the search for a defensible warm-water port on the Pacific had begun. Throughout the eighteenth century Siberia and central Asia were objects of continued research in which Swedish, German, and Danish, as well as Russian explorers, took part. Vitus Bering, a Danish navigator (1680-1741) was employed by Peter the Great to chart the strait between Asia and America which was later to be named for him. He missed America by a mile in 1728 because of foggy weather, but on a second voyage in 1741 he followed the coast of Alaska for some distance.

Nineteenth- and Twentieth-Century Exploration. Though the fur trade had given the original impetus to expeditions across Siberia, timber and mineral resources later proved of far greater economic importance. Moreover a growing desire to share in the wealth of southern Asia led Russian explorers under imperial auspices to pay ever greater attention to the topography, the peoples, and the climatic conditions of central Asia, and to study possible means of access to India. Further exploration of eastern Siberia, Mongolia, and Manchuria was undertaken mainly with a view to colonial settlement, so as to establish a firm and economically self-supporting basis for Pacific trade. Moreover, since the days of the Empress Catherine I (1684-1727), Russia shared with the rest of Europe an intense awareness of the value of correct knowledge of Asia on general grounds of cultural liberalism.

Of the nineteenth-century explorers in Russian Asia, the two most celebrated are Nicolai Muraviev, who in 1854 set a group of scientists to work on a thorough survey of the Amur River region, and Prince Peter Kropotkin (1842-1921), who spent many years in the study of Manchuria and Turkestan. Because of its high mountains and barren wastes, central Asia remained almost a closed book during the greater part of the nineteenth century. Peter P. Semënov, a Russian geographer (1827-1914), was the first to map the whole range of the Tien Shan. An Englishman, Robert Shaw, penetrated Chinese Turkestan; other English explorers surveyed Tibet and the northern borders of India.

Outer Mongolia and the Altai Mountains gradually gave up their secrets. Sir Francis E. Younghusband (1863-1942) stands out in the group of Altai explorers by the wealth and readability of his published reports. Sir Aruel Stein (1862-1943) was pre-eminent for archaeological discoveries which established the trade routes and cultural contacts between the Far East and the Mediterranean in ancient times. An American diplomat in China, William W. Rockhill (1854-1914), made two expeditions to Mongolia and Tibet under the auspices of the Smithsonian Institution. The German geologist and geographer Ferdinand von Richthofen (1833-1905) made detailed reports of northern and western China during 1860-1862. Sir Henry Rawlinson, Sir Percy Sykes, and many more followed the trails of earlier explorers in Persia and Turkestan. An American, Roy Chapman Andrews, after earlier expeditions in Alaska, Borneo, and Korea, gained renown chiefly by his geological studies in China, Mongolia, Tibet, and central Asia between 1916 and 1930, and by his discovery in the Gobi Desert of some of the oldest known forms of human and animal life. The Swedish geographer, Sven Hedin, at first mainly interested in Mesopotamia and Persia, later became famous for his travels between 1893 and 1933 in Turkestan, Mongolia, and Tibet.

Inland Arabia largely remained untraveled by occidentals until the twentieth century. Of the explorers who crossed and recrossed its central plateau, the Nejd desert, the best known is Gertrude Bell (1868-1926), archaeologist and diplomat. Her knowledge of the Bedouins was unmatched. Like her, Thomas Edward Lawrence, better known as

"Lawrence of Arabia" (1888-1935), started out as an archaeologist before he became ethnologist, diplomat, and military strategist. More recently other important discoveries have been made in Arabia, partly through the use of air travel as a means of reconnaissance; but the most important recovery of the seat of an ancient civilization was made by Bertram Thomas on camelback. It was he who demonstrated the location of the Biblical city of Ophir.

Up to the time of World War II scientific expeditions continued to fill in empty spaces in the map of Asia, to make tentative contours more certain, to identify places of antiquity, to show what changes in climate and fertility had taken place through the ages, hence also to explain many historical events and movements. Military strategy, politics, and economic advantage still motivate many studies, although not without by-products in other branches of learning. The book of Asian discoveries is not yet closed. As throughout history, exploration of the continent still beckons to men of daring and disciplined curiosity.

HISTORY

Background of Social Evolution. Asia has the oldest and largest population of all the continents and a recorded history that goes back some five thousand years. Its vast territory has been the scene of never-ending interaction between man and his environment, and present-day Asia contains examples of almost every stage in the growth of civilization. The slow evolution of Asian societies, at times intensified by the impact of external forces, such as the expansion of Western empires, has in the main reflected changes in the relation between human needs and natural resources. Much of the continent permits only meager livelihoods. As long as the dwellers in its deserts and tundras, its high mountains and tropical marshes, remained separate from each other and did not increase too rapidly, they could enjoy a certain degree of security; but this state was conditioned by close adherence to the established ways, and there was little progress. Only when populations outgrew resources and large numbers were forced out of their habitat, when there was contact between groups with different backgrounds of experience, could cultural cross-fertilization take place. Sometimes aggressive newcomers would force their institutions on conquered peoples. Sometimes the civilization of those subjected would be superior and prevail, so that in time the traits brought by the sturdier tribes disappeared. More often an amalgam of contributions from both sources occurred. Where this process recurred again and again, as in the valleys of the Tigris and Euphrates, the Yellow River, or the Ganges, civilizations with characteristics of their own emerged; new tastes and beliefs, arts, and forms of organization evolved that cannot be ascribed to earlier sources.

Asian history, therefore, is largely one of internal adjustments. Where conditions have remained relatively unchanged over many centuries, as in the northern and eastern parts of Siberia, there has been little history. But where noticeable changes occurred, migrations originated and spread both conquest and cultural transition far afield. Causes of such movements included changes in climate; the denuding of pastures and woodlands; the drying up of irrigation systems, as in central China and Mesopotamia; decimation of populations by war and abduction, as in Farther India and in Asia Minor; and reversal of the relative power of neighboring peoples through technical progress, as in Persia. Sometimes the effects of new contacts were immediate and beneficial, as when trade between pastoral hill peoples and lowland agriculturists enriched both with new ideas as well as material enjoyments; sometimes old, established culture patterns were wiped out.

These currents, observed in historic times, were continuations of migrations and adaptations to new environments in prehistoric times, when, largely because of the receding ice cap in central Asia, lakes and rivers dried up and the wild vegetation and fauna upon which primitive man depended for his food thinned out. The major lines of the great population movements through tens of thousands of years are gradually being reconstructed by modern science from human bones and culture remains, such as chipped stones and fragments of early pottery, long hidden under layers of mineral matter; also sometimes from allusions to earlier homes found in ancient myths. In the main, the migratory trends were to the east and south and west of the high plateaus that lie north of the Tsinling, Himalaya, and Hindu Kush mountains. These early homes of diverse racial groups are themselves separated from each other by the Kunlun, Tien Shan, and Altai mountains in the east, the Pamirs in the center, and the Elburz and Caucasus in the west.

The great civilizations of historic times arose where, with the growth of population, the fertility of wide river valleys and a warm but not too humid climate made possible intensive land uses, a differentiation of occupations, and specialized arts. These were in China, northern India, and Mesopotamia. Although the peninsulas of Asia Minor, Arabia, lower India, Indochina, and Korea and the archipelagos of Indonesia and Japan also have given rise to civilizations, these are younger and are largely derived from the three ancient seats of civilization.

As a result, the eastern and southern lowlands of Asia, comprising less than one tenth of the total area of the continent, have a population almost three times as high as the average population of the world's total land area. India, with an average population density of 256 persons per square mile, and China contain the majority of Asia's population. Central Asia still supports only about one person per square mile, Siberia less than five. As a further result, the more favored lands, always in danger of fresh invasions from the hinterland, in turn repeatedly gave rise to large outward movements, which, in prehistoric times and since, populated the islands of the Pacific, and in modern times have sent streams of migrants to such distant underpopulated regions as parts of the Americas, Africa, and Australia.

Human ingenuity and not instinctive reactions have guided the distribution of the human species. Each migratory movement followed the beacon of ascertained opportunity. From Inner Asia down the rivers east and south, or westward over the few passes wide enough to permit the grazing of herds, men drifted millennium after millennium. These migrations and their consequences make up most of the history of Asia. Annals tell of wars which, time and again, brought areas larger than Europe or the United States of America under the rule of tribes which, though of obscure origin, were endowed with bravery, lust for adventure, and some method of aggressive warfare—such as the use of mounted troops, against which peace-loving peoples had no adequate defense. Much less is known about the more gradual drifts of nomad peoples down the rivers and over the plains. Such slow advance in historic times frequently followed the routes of trade. Colonialism is not an altogether modern development. From the most ancient times, the caravan and the caravel have connected one civilization with another, even though the volume of trade has never been great compared with that made possible by modern means of transportation.

LINDSLEY F. HALL

A BLINDFOLDED WATER BUFFALO WORKS AN IRRIGATION WHEEL NEAR SHANGHAI.

First Historic Period. At the dawn of recorded history, some three thousand years B.C., most Asians lived by the collection of such food as nature afforded, sometimes in abundance but more often sparingly. The arts of hunting and fishing already were well advanced. The dog, the pig, and various bovine species had been domesticated over a wide area. But even the wealthier tribes, with fairly large herds, rarely engaged in agriculture other than an occasional slashing of the brush over a few acres of level land and the planting of seeds with pointed sticks. Only a few river valleys, especially those of the Indus, the Yellow River, and the Tigris and Euphrates, had settlements large and permanent enough to give rise to organized states. Peaceful, continuous occupation of fertile land required the recognition and enforcement of law, sometimes the fortification of towns. The nomadic peoples also had codes to regulate the rights to property. But a long evolution of social institutions separates the complex statutes of the Babylonian city-states from the rough-and-ready law of the nomad tribes. These states had developed far beyond the arbitrary jurisdiction of individual chiefs when Hammurabi, the sixth Amorite king of Babylonia, codified them in the second millennium B.C. At that time, the lower Euphrates Valley already had experienced several conquests; and, under a line of Akkadian kings descended from Sargon I, the original conqueror, peace had prevailed long enough to permit the development of an elaborate system of waterworks.

For China, in spite of many finds of extremely old remains, historical records are much less ancient. Its civilization began in central North China, in the basin of the Hwang Ho or

Yellow River, on the relatively elevated plains of the present Shansi, Shensi, and Honan provinces, where the river, fed by numerous streams which deposited a fine sediment, often changed its bed and left expanses of fertile soil that could be worked with primitive tools. Embankments and ditches were the first manifestations of permanent settlement, and probably also of the first experiments in the transition from dry to wet cultivation of cereals. Millet was the principal grain food, hemp the first plant cultivated for textile uses. Hunting and fishing still occupied much of the men's time, while the women cultivated the fields and also raised pigs. A clan system early resulted from the need for social order and for a long period was ruled by women, who were custodians of the essential agricultural processes and properties.

Over most of Asia roamed nomad tribes. They were always in potential conflict and were thus concerned with the arts of war no less than those of peace. Throughout Asian history this state of military preparedness gave the tribesmen of the highlands and deserts the advantage which, despite lesser numbers, looser discipline, and ruder equipment, they often had over the more settled valley dwellers. Thus, rapidly ascending the ladder of recorded history, it is found that in the middle of the eighteenth century B.C. Kassite highlanders from Elam, north of the Persian Gulf, descended into the Sumerian realms of Babylonia, which, by gradually merging with the Akkadian and Semitic inhabitants, they were to dominate for almost six centuries. At about the same time, also, the Hittites, swarming through the defiles of the Caucasus, invaded Asia Minor and reduced to slavery the more

A LUMBER ENTERPRISE ON THE LIU RIVER, CHINA

primitive native Anatolians. The Hittites were perhaps the first people in western Asia to forge iron weapons. And from the mountain-bordered plateau of Iran an Aryan-speaking people penetrated the Indus Valley, gradually spread over the Ganges Valley, and pushed southward the smaller, dark-skinned Dravidian-speaking folk who, in prehistoric times, had wrested the land from much more primitive Australoid groups.

Formation of Empires. Not all of the areas ascribed in early days to the domination of great warrior tribes were actually ruled by them. It was not until about 1500 B.C., for example, that the first authentic dynasty arose in China, that of the Shan or Ying. Having mastered not only the forging of bronze weapons and armor but also the art of writing and other instruments of civilization, this ruling group was so superior to the simple peasant folk that a feudal system naturally resulted. The dynasty was not, however, of long duration. Four centuries later another militant group, the Chou, driven from their native heath in the northwest by drought, invaded the fertile Honan plain and, though much less advanced in civilization, dethroned the Shan. In the course of six centuries, until the middle of the fifth century B.C., the Chou gave unified rule to a much larger area than the Shan had held. They strengthened the responsibilities of the various feudal classes and succeeded for a long time in warding off further attempts at invasion from the border lands.

The Hittites, in Asia Minor, suffered the impact of foreign imperialism in the middle of the thirteenth century B.C., when Egypt—under Ramses II, most famous of the Phar-

aohs—extended its dominion over all of Phoenicia and Palestine. However, the Hittites were able to resist and kept most of Syria. The Egyptian Empire was over-expanded and soon lost all its dependencies in Asia.

The Phoenician city republics, first appearing in about 1600 B.C., exemplify another type of empire building, one based on sea power. They founded and for centuries held numerous small colonies along the shores accessible to them, the most famous of which was Carthage. The Phoenician trade eventually extended along both sides of the Mediterranean Sea as far as Spain, and even beyond the Pillars of Hercules (Strait of Gibraltar) to the British Isles.

The millennium before the birth of Christ brought dynastic history to its height in Palestine under the Jewish kings David and Solomon, the latter powerful enough to lay tribute on Arabia. It also witnessed the mythical founding by a descendant of the sun goddess of a dynasty in Japan that is one of the few that still remain in existence. In the same period the Assyrian Empire expanded, and under Sargon II destroyed the northern kingdom of Israel and laid tribute on Judaea. The latter theocratic state was to suffer even more from the land hunger of its northern neighbors; for, when the Medes and Babylonians had subdued the Assyrian Empire, Nebuchadnezzar, the second Chaldean king of Babylonia, took all of Palestine and led Jewish families to captivity in Babylonia. His rule, like that of the famed Lydian king, Croesus, was not to be of long duration. The point to be noted, however, is that throughout western Asia a rapid improvement in methods of warfare, including not only the use of cavalry but also of heavy artillery, made con-

SHWE DAGON PAGODA, RANGOON

quests speedier than they had been in earlier times, so that much wider areas came under the sway of ambitious monarchs. The dynasties they founded were correspondingly precarious. Feudal political systems might, when based on the prowess of a knightly upper class, rule relatively small realms for long periods; they rarely succeeded in holding down peripheral peoples.

In 539 B.C., Persia, newly emerged from its historical obscurity, destroyed the city of Babylon and, under Cyrus the Great, vastly expanded its realm. Under Cyrus' successor, Darius I, the westward advance of the empire overran Thrace and threatened Hellenic civilization until it was stopped in 490 B.C. by the battle of Marathon. With the naval defeat of Xerxes I at Salamis, in 480 B.C., Persia was forever repulsed from Europe. A little more than a century later, it became the dependency of a European power when Alexander the Great conquered all of Persia and entered India by the route familiar to previous invaders.

Birth of World Religions. Zoroaster, founder of the religion associated with the worship of fire, flourished in Persia in about 600 B.C. At about the same time, Lao-tse founded the Taoist school of religion in China; and only a generation later Gautama, from whom stemmed Buddhism, was born in India. Confucius, who identified divine worship with the service of humanity, was born about 551 B.C. This was the period, too, following the Jewish captivity, when in Judaea the ancient beliefs of Israel received a new and warmer, less ritualistic, interpretation.

It should not be generalized from these coincidences that some mystic thread goes through the affairs of men, which, in distant places and under unlike conditions, makes for militancy in one period and for contemplation and the advance of morality in another. The poets, thinkers, and prophets did not flourish solely in times of peace; and some of the great military strategists have also been known as wise rulers and initiators of social reforms. Alexander the Great, when he reopened one of the land routes to the Far East, was fired by admiration for those evidences of oriental culture which had come to eastern Europe from earlier times. Fifty years after

his death, there arose in India a great emperor, Asoka, who, having conquered Bengal and Orissa, made the religion of the gentle Buddha the official creed of his state. Confucius was a politician as well as a philosopher; his belief in the need for harmony in personal relations as the essential condition of the state's security came to him with sorrow over the bitter internecine strife and battle between rival feudal states that characterized his time. His disciple Mencius, although several generations removed, carried the thought further. He was the first to formulate the rules of education and logical procedures through which the desired state of internal and external harmony might be achieved.

The feudal division of China was followed by two dynasties which greatly advanced civilization. Under the Ch'in (221-206 B.C.) the empire was reunited, the excesses of feudalism were abolished, and the Great Wall was built, by the junction of existing sectional walls, to aid the empire against invasion from the north and also to prevent the colonization of the northern grasslands by land-hungry Chinese peasants. The latter movement, however, was to recur from time to time, giving rise to border troubles. Under the Han (206 B.C. to A.D. 220), imperial rule once again expanded to the north, and to the Korean peninsula, while exploring expeditions sent to the west reached the Caspian Sea. But it was the building of the Grand Canal, linking the inner provinces of the empire, which became the key to internal security. It was during this dynasty that a full trade developed between China and the Roman Empire, both by land and by sea.

In the long perspective of history, the inner development of the two empires at the extremes of Asia is more noteworthy than are their conquests. What made the reign of Augustus (27 B.C. to A.D. 14) illustrious was not the expansion of the Roman Empire to the deserts of Arabia and to the banks of the Euphrates but the efficiency of the civil service, the reform of the tax system, a novel tolerance of diverse religious beliefs (without which Christianity could not have obtained its original foothold), and a high regard for the cultural contributions of the Orient. While the Chinese philosophers, themselves public officials, made their influence felt on current affairs, it was not until many centuries had passed that the teachings of the Buddha were to affect the cultural evolution of Asia.

Era of Disintegration. In A.D. 70 Jerusalem was destroyed. Consolidation of the eastern provinces of the Roman Empire continued during the first two centuries of the Christian Era under the so-called "good emperors," especially Trajan and Marcus Aurelius. But the empire's inner cohesion was lost. Its division into a western and an eastern, largely Asian, realm, first evident when Constantine the Great (c. 280-337) ruled from an eastern capital, was completed with the death of Emperor Theodosius in 395. In the Far East, likewise, a powerful empire split. The Chin dynasty (265-415) for a time reunited China but could not resist repeated attacks from neighboring peoples to the west and the north. Among the successful invaders were a Central Asian people, the Turks, or Turkis, who a century later were to establish an empire of their own in Turkestan.

The Sui dynasty (589-618) still followed in the tradition of building and perfecting great public works but lost a war waged to enforce the payment of tribute by Korea. Eventually it was ousted by invaders of Tatar origin later known as the T'ang, who for three hundred years (618-907) gave China one of its most brilliant dynasties. The T'ang subjected the eastern Turks and included in their realm most of Manchuria, northern Korea, Inner and Outer Mongolia, Turkestan, part of Tibet, Tashkent, Samarkand, Bukhara, Fergana, and Annam; above all, they achieved new heights in administration, education, and literature. It was in this period that Buddhism spread over a vast area, including Japan, and brought with it arts and, in some countries, institutions and ideas far in advance of those which the native peoples had developed from their own resources.

Again overexpansion of imperial power brought its eventual defeat. The T'ang dynasty was followed by five short-lived military dictatorships which lasted until 960, when, once more with emphasis on honest, centralized civil administration and Confucian social ideals, the Sung dynasty (960-1279) revived something of the old splendor. In the end, however, it was unsuccessful in its resistance to the continuing invasions of pastoral and warrior tribes from Mongolia and the Amur region.

In the first millennium of the present era, a new prophet arose in western Asia whose followers were destined to carry both destruction and cultural advance to distant lands. Mohammed (570-632) founded a religion; his followers founded an empire. Omar I, the second caliph of Arabia (c. 581-644), defeated the Persians, conquered Syria and Palestine, and invaded Egypt. The Ommiad dynasty of Arabia (661-750) transferred the capital from Medina to Damascus and for a time united the Moslem world. Following conquest after conquest along the north coast of Africa, the Arabs, joined by Moorish allies, invaded Spain. Caliph Harun al-Rashid (c. 764-809), a contemporary of Charlemagne, has become famous through *The Arabian Nights*. This was the Golden Age of Islam. But already the inevitable disruption of over-expanded empire had set in, and in the next few centuries it was to take the form of frequent insurrections and the establishment of separate caliphates. During the Abbasside caliphate, which ruled from Baghdad between 750 and 1258, scientific knowledge spread over a territory extending from Spain to India. It was only after the capture of Baghdad by Mongol infidels from central Asia in the last-named year and the overthrow of the Abbasside caliphate that Islam lost its civilizing influence.

In Asia no less than in Europe, the early Middle Ages

Seventeenth-century turreted wall, Mukden, Manchuria

were truly the Dark Ages. East and west, nomad horsemen rode roughshod over the tender shoots of a nascent universal culture. Seljuk Turks, a western branch of the same racial group that had given so much trouble to T'ang China, left the steppes beyond the Caspian Sea, conquered most of Asia Minor, and in 1072 captured Jerusalem. It was this uncouth military regime which, whatever other causes there may have been, provoked the revulsion to Islam in western Europe and produced the Crusades (1095-1291). The reconquest of Jerusalem and the establishment of a Christian kingdom there only briefly interrupted a Turkish regime that was to last for six centuries. But for a time the Turks themselves were menaced by the inroads of another mounted host from central Asia, the Mongols, who captured Baghdad in 1258 and there overthrew the Abbasside caliphate.

These Mongol horsemen were the westernmost advance of an army that was to engulf a large part of Asia and Europe. Under Genghis Khan (1162-1227), they and their allies invaded China, Manchuria, Korea, and southeast and south-central Asia and occupied northern India and eastern Russia. Under Kublai Khan, grandson of Genghis Khan and first emperor of the Mongol (Yüan) dynasty, what remained of the Chin empire was subjected. A good deal is known about the state of eastern Asia during Kublai Khan's reign from the excellent notes made by Marco Polo, the Venetian merchant, on his travels. Of course, not all the evidences of an advanced civilization which surprised this young European can be ascribed to the Mongol rulers. Like others who had come from the north to usurp the Dragon Throne, they took over much of the Chinese law, administrative organization and methods, and cultural refinement that had developed in earlier times. But the Mongols, like their predecessors, could not resist the temptation to expand their rule. Rumors of the wealth and splendor of Japan, which in 1192 had come under the actual rule of a shogunate established at Kamakura by Yoritomo, although the imperial dynasty continued to reign, induced the Mongol emperor to attempt the island empire's conquest. His army and navy were decisively defeated, and the attempt was never repeated.

Again a cycle fulfilled itself. Toward the end of the fourteenth century the Mongols were driven back from their western outposts; some of their advance groups were converted to Islam, and trade through Persia and Arabia was broken. At home in China, inflation and neglect of farm

Sacred cows gather in the street before the Singh Durwaza (Lion Gate) of Jagannath Temple in Puri, State of Orissa, India.

347

prosperity had led to rebellion. The central system of civil administration and military preparedness no longer functioned. A new dynasty arose, the Ming (1368-1644), which effected civil and military reforms, restored the Grand Canal as an artery of internal trade and tax collection in kind, established military outposts in Manchuria and Mongolia, and ushered in a new era of achievement in literature and art.

At the end of the fourteenth century, India, also, was invaded. The old capital at Delhi was destroyed by Tamerlane, a Mongol-Turkish prince of Samarkand (c. 1336-1405) who already had brought under his sway a large part of the former Mongol Empire: Turkestan and Persia, and everything to the west up to the very gates of Moscow (1381). Later this prince was also to invade Syria and Anatolia, finally being defeated by the Turks at Angora (1402).

Impact of the West. The Moorish conquest of Spain was one of the stimulating factors in that revival of ancient learning in Europe which was later signalized by the term Renaissance. Other influences from Asia seeped in with trade. From ancient times, two caravan routes had carried to Europe the more precious and less bulky products of oriental craftsmanship, such as silk textures and carved gems. There had also always been a sea-borne trade, but this had taken on much greater dimensions when Arabia dominated the Persian Gulf and the Indian Ocean. With the rise of Venice as Phoenicia's successor in Mediterranean shipping, and with the growth of merchant adventuring in northern Europe, a keener desire for Asian products had been created, along with a greatly improved network of transportation facilities to get them. The era of discoveries was based on the new science and on better seamanship. There was little definite knowledge in Europe as yet as to the exact places where the silks and spices, rare woods, and other commodities in demand had their origin, but there was a great deal of curiosity, heightened by fantastic tales by mariners. The search was destined greatly to increase the contacts between Europe and Asia, to recast the relative power position of nations, and to cause the disintegration of Asian societies that had matured in isolation from the currents of world happenings.

Again it is necessary to condense the events of centuries. In 1493 Pope Alexander VI, as arbitrator between Portugal and Spain in the clash between their expansionist ambitions, divided the New World between them in such a way as to permit Spanish colonization of almost every part of the Americas but to make sea access to India and China practically a Portuguese monopoly. Thus it was Portuguese enterprise which opened up southern Asia to European maritime trade. A few of the noteworthy dates are Vasco da Gama's arrival at Calicut, India, after rounding the south cape of Africa, in 1498; the occupation of Malacca by Alfonso de Albuquerque in 1511 and his establishment of a trading post at Ormuz, Persia, in 1515; establishment of the first trading post at Canton in 1517; discovery of the Philippine Islands by Ferdinand Magellan in 1521; foundation of the colony of Macao on the south coast of China in 1537; and the first landing in Japan in 1542. Each new Portuguese foothold in Asia became at once a starting point for missionary and for mercantile advances.

Later in the sixteenth century an English adventurer, Sir Francis Drake, was to round the south cape of America and, after following most of the west coast, to cross the Pacific and reach the Indies from the east (1579). It was a century of competition literally to the death between the seafaring nations of Europe for the trade of south and eastern Asia. Yet there was almost no penetration inland once a port had been established. Indeed, even three centuries later, at the

outbreak of World War II, not all the territories in Asia claimed by European powers as dependencies were fully administered by them. The charters granted to the English East India Company in 1600 and the Dutch East India Company in 1602 made profit the sole motive of such colonization as took place. But clashes of interest were inevitable, and costly campaigns of subjugation eventually followed milder policies.

For the first time, in the sixteenth century, the northern half of Asia enters significantly into world history. Diverse Mongol and Turkish tribes had long since found the passes through the Ural Mountains and had used the wide steppes between the Caspian Sea and the Urals to spread over the Russian plains. But it was not until 1480 that a Muscovite grand duke, later known as Ivan the Great, threw off the domination of the Tatars and founded an empire that was to reverse the process of migration and subjection. In 1579 the Cossack leader Yermak seized the Tatar fort of Sibir. Seven years later occurred the first settlement of Russian peasants in Siberia. Fifty years later, in 1637, the Russians fortified a trading post as far east as Yakutsk, and in 1648 Simon Dejneff led one of many Russian expeditions to the extreme northeast of the continent. Three years later, Khabaroff descended the Amur River and secured trade concessions from China. The Treaty of Nerchinsk followed in 1689 and for a long time regulated both the overland trade and the boundaries between Russian Siberia and China. In 1741 Vitus Bering, a Dane in Russian service, rediscovered the strait between Asia and North America later named for him.

These events must not be interpreted to mean that all of the territory between the Urals and the Pacific came under effective Russian rule. That rule for a long time was not intact, even on the European side. In 1683 the Ottoman Turks brought their invasion of Europe to the very gates of Vienna, and it was not until 1829, by the Treaty of Adrianople, that Turkey, after two wars, surrendered to Russia most of its Caucasian territory. Only in 1844 did the last of the Kirghiz tribes submit to Russian rule, and the Siberian territory north of the Amur, from the mouth of the Argun to the mouth of the Amur, was not definitely ceded by China until the Treaty of Aigun, in 1858. It was not until 1867 that Turkestan, the source of so much aggression through the centuries, was fully incorporated into the Russian Empire.

The Russian impact on Asia differed from that of other European powers; it was continental and it was exerted over vast expanses of territory that could never be expected to be densely populated or to produce an abundance of cultivated crops. Settlement took place for political and trading purposes. The world over, Siberia has become known as the region of penal colonies made up in large part of political offenders and their families; only in very recent times has the desire to exploit more fully the forest and mineral resources of Siberia led to large-scale transfers of population from European Russia, so planned as to make each area as self-sufficient as possible. Such transfers have involved the promotion of agriculture and of consumer industries calculated to insure the prosperity and stability of peasant communities.

Era of National Consolidation. From the seventeenth century on, Asia's history belongs to an era that has not yet closed. It is the era, first, of increasing European interference, which was to find its climax early in the twentieth century, but also the era of political, economic, and social transformation under the influence of that interference. Two forces are at work: the impact and the reaction. Both make for a crys-

A public outdoor laundry in
Bombay, India

LINDSLEY F. HALL

tallization of Asian society around new nuclei of national formation.

British India, the Netherlands Indies, French Indochina, and the Spanish Philippines, once scattered collections of ports of call, trade stations, small protectorates, and smaller possessions, became solidified. China, too, in spite of its growing weakness under the later rulers of the Manchu or Ch'ing dynasty (1644-1911), more and more assumed the outward behavior, if not all the substance, of a nation.

Opening of the Suez Canal, in 1869, further changed Asian-European relations by undercutting the role of Arab and other Near Eastern peoples as intermediaries between East and West, but in particular by reducing the cost of mass transportation and thereby encouraging large-scale agricultural, mining, and industrial enterprise in Asia with European capital. Industrialization of the West had produced a greatly increased demand for raw materials of many kinds. When the characteristic methods of modern industry were

transplanted to Asia, they helped to disrupt traditional social patterns. New wants were stimulated and disturbed the traditional social patterns: for example, by inducing individuals to work for wages far from their homes. Some of the foreign influences undoubtedly were beneficial: in many places regulated relations between employers and employees took the place of feudal subservience, and more attention was paid to health and welfare. At first superficial in its effects, the adoption of occidental ideas and methods often had unforeseen effects. New problems arose when, with better sanitation, death rates dropped while birth rates remained unchanged, so that in many regions the population has become far too large to live by tending fields or herds in the traditional ways. Missionary teaching motivated rebellious movements, such as had occurred often before, with a religious sense of social justice and so helped undermine long-established political systems. When large-scale modern enterprise came to rely on migratory Asian labor, it loosened the ties that bound the peasant to his soil. Emigration and the growth of prosperous oriental communities in many parts of the world produced centers from which advanced ideas and the seeds of revolution were returned to the homelands in Asia. The effect of Western education was similar, even when administered with the sole purpose of training oriental, that is, cheaper, personnel for foreign enterprises; always there were unintended by-products of learning.

Nationalism grew apace. The two East India companies had been disbanded; the governments which succeeded them could gain in efficiency only by substituting more and more the interest of the dependent territory for that of the metropolitan power as the principal motive in the formation of policies. Borderlands were incorporated into colonies where that was possible. Where circumstances made it advisable, controls were concealed through the maintenance of the indigenous government, which, however, accepted "protection," along with "advisers" in key positions. Where a buffer area between rival empires became involved in the struggle for power, the rivals divided it into spheres of "interest" or "influence," as in Manchuria and parts of the Middle and Near East. The ultimate progression was from the "sphere

ALEXANDERSON FROM GUILLUMETTE

Coolies at work in a bituminous coal mine in Yunnan Province,
China

The high-walled Tomb of Sheik Omar in a desert cemetery, Baghdad, Iraq

of interest" or the protectorate to annexation as a colony, as the circumstances of international politics permitted.

Throughout the seventeenth, eighteenth, and nineteenth centuries, political events in Asia also reflected shifts of power in other parts of the world. Portugal, reduced to a lower rank in Europe, lost all but fragments of its Asiatic possessions. Portions of India, Malaya, and the Indies were handed back and forth between Great Britain, France, and Holland with the shifting fortunes of the Napoleonic wars. Spain lost a war in the Western Hemisphere, and the United States took over the Philippines. Russia lost its privileged position in Manchuria when, in 1905, it lost a war, not to China but to Japan. Korea was annexed by Japan in 1910, having first been detached from China in 1894 and accepted by the other Powers, first as a sphere of Japanese influence and then as a protectorate, after the Russo-Japanese War. Having supported Japan to that point because of fear of Russian aggrandizement in the Far East, the Western Powers raised no objection when Japan extended the protectorate into a colony.

The main currents of Asian history in recent times can best be seen, then, by following these two lines of development: first, the growing weakness of characteristically Asian political and social institutions under the pressures from without; second, the growing, and over much of the continent only incipient, absorption of Western concepts of the good life, and with it a growing revolt against foreign rule and economic exploitation.

Thus, the formal abolition of clan military feudalism in Japan in 1871, following the Restoration of Meiji in 1868; the adoption of compulsory elementary education in 1872; and the laying of the foundations for an industrial economy are more important landmarks in Japan's history than were either the victories over China in 1895 and over Russia in 1905 or the short-lived occupation of Manchuria from 1932 to 1945, and of most of Southeast Asia from 1942 to 1945.

Similarly, the achievement of Indian and Burmese independence in 1947 is more memorable than the crowning of Queen Victoria as Empress of India in 1877. The French annexation of Annam in 1885 was only one step in empire building, while establishment of the Viet-Nam Republic in 1946, however incomplete, may well prove to be the birth of a new nation. After World War I, European powers established mandates over large parts of the Turkish Empire; greater significance must be attached, however, to the achievements of the Turkish revolution under Kemal Pasha in 1919, which carried forward the Young Turk movement of 1908. Both helped to light the spark of national independence throughout the Near and Middle East. The idea of the right of self-determination of peoples, as applied in the Philippines, caught hold in Indonesia and has had to be applied by the Dutch in the reformation of their colonial empire. China, after the First Opium War, was forced in 1842 to cede Hong Kong to the British and to concede extraterritorial rights to the Western trading nations; but the final abolition of these rights in 1943, the overthrow of the Manchu dynasty in 1911, the "Northern Expedition" in 1925-1927 (resulting in the establishment of the National Government), and the recognition of China as a leading member of the United Nations, in 1945, are the memorable dates.

Nor should one overstate the importance of such events as the establishment, between World War I and World War II, of the states of Iraq and Manchukuo. Frequently, trends are more significant than specific events. Throughout Asia, in addition to the trend toward independence and self-government, there is a movement to modernize communications facilities. Completion of the Trans-Siberian Railway in 1905 and of the Trans-Iranian Railway in 1938 were only steps in the opening up of Inner Asia. The building of railways and motor roads, the introduction of the telegraph, the telephone, and radio telegraphy, and of the kerosene lamp and the electric light in such countries as India and China, have begun

350

to produce a chain of social as well as economic consequences of fundamental importance in the lives of the peoples of Asia. No longer are they restricted to production for a local market nor to the satisfaction of their needs from local production where this change has been made. Of even greater importance, they can begin to draw on the world for ideas and methods of production and distribution instead of remaining dependent on the ideas and practices crystallized in purely local custom. New methods of production and distribution offer an opportunity for social changes in the direction of higher living standards for the masses.

Geographical and climatic differences remain to affect the rate of speed at which diverse Asian peoples find their way into the modern world society. But as new avenues of contact and exchange are opened up, even those as yet little removed from a primitive tribal mode of life are drawn out of their isolation. Illustrative of this historic process is the demand, everywhere, for modern education. More than any other part of the world, Asia at this stage exemplifies a history that is visibly in the making.   B. La.

ASIAGO, BATTLE OF [ɑziɑ′go], the name given to an engagement fought in the spring of 1916, during World War I, along the plateau of Asiago in the Alps between Austria and Italy. The object of the Austrian attack was to cut off the communications of the Italian army under General Luigi Cadorna. The Italian troops were not sufficiently prepared for an attack, although they took hasty measures to strengthen their position. On May 14, a heavy bombardment was started by the Austrians under General Franz Conrad, and his troops began to move forward. The attack was at first successful, but the Austrians hesitated in their offensive, thereby giving the Italians time to bring up reserves. Conrad's troops continued to advance, but at a slower pace, and their losses were great. Early in June, at the request of the Italians, the Russians attacked Luck, in Austrian Poland, and the Austrians had to retreat both there and in Italy. Casualties on both sides were heavy, and neither won a definite victory.   M. K.

ASIA MINOR, a designation generally applied to the peninsula forming the western extremity of Asia. It is also sometimes called Anatolia, although, strictly speaking, Anatolia comprises the central section of the peninsula. Asia Minor, including Anatolia, lies wholly within modern Turkey, and is bounded on the north by the Black Sea, on the west by the Sea of Marmara, the Bosporus, and the Dardanelles, and on the south by the Mediterranean. On the east it is bounded by a line running eastward from below the Gulf of Iskenderun to the Euphrates River, up that stream to the Tchoruk (Chorokh), and thence to the Black Sea. Thus about 20 per cent of the land area of Turkey lies east and southeast of Asia Minor proper.

The surface is an elevated plateau, dotted with salt lakes, sloping generally toward the seas on the north and west with mountain ranges increasing in number and height toward the east, the most prominent of which is the Taurus range. The rivers run generally north into the Black Sea and westward into the Aegean Sea. The total area of Asia Minor is about 200,000 sq. mi.

History. The earliest known history of Asia Minor dates from about 3000 B.C. The country was dominated by the Hittites between the years 2000 to 1200 B.C. When attacked from the west by the Indo-European Thracians, and from the east by Phrygians and Armenians, the weakened empire was easy prey for the invading Lydians and later for the Persians coming both from the west and the east. In this period Troy, in extreme western Asia Minor, flourished, the sixth city, that of Homer's Iliad, being destroyed about 1180 B.C.

Persian and Greek Rule. By 500 B.C. the Persians, led by Darius I, had overrun Asia Minor and moved on westward into Greece and Egypt. Xerxes I continued his father's war against the Greeks and in the process stormed Thermopylae, conquered Athens, and was defeated at Salamis and then at Plataea. During this period occurred the famous March of the Ten Thousand, chronicled by Xenophon, from whom, together with Herodotus, most of our information concerning Asia Minor of this period is derived. The Persian control of Asia Minor was interrupted by the conquests of Alexander the Great in the fourth century B.C., but, with the death of the conqueror and the lack of a direct heir, the Persians gradually restored their rule in eastern Asia Minor while Egypt, under the Ptolemies, controlled much of the western coastal areas. During the period of paramount Greek influence (c. 1000-500 B.C.), the western half of Asia Minor was divided into spheres of influence, dominated by important centers of commerce and by the infiltration of tribes coming from the west across the Dardanelles. Among these were certain Celtic tribes under Brennus which, in the third century B.C., established themselves in the area called Galatia and located their capital city at Ancyra, the modern Angora, now Ankara.

Roman and Christian Rule. The defeat of the Seleucid ruler, Antiochus III, at Magnesia in 190 B.C. by the brothers Scipio, firmly established Roman rule in Asia Minor, where it continued with varying degrees of authority for nearly one thousand years. It was not until 133 B.C. that the first Roman province, Asia, was formed to include western Asia Minor. The rise of Pontus in northeastern Asia Minor under Mithradates I for a time threatened Roman rule, but Mithradates was defeated and driven from his country by Pompey, and most of the kingdom became a part of the Roman

The Bosporus, dividing Istanbul, Turkey, from Asia Minor, in the foreground

ROBERT CAPA · MAGNUM

Empire. Asia Minor prospered under Roman rule, and, by the fourth century of the Christian Era, Diocletian had united the provinces into groups called dioceses. The coming of Christianity caused further changes, the seven Christian Churches of Asia being built up in this period of Roman rule. By the close of the sixth century, Asia Minor had become wealthy and prosperous, but centuries of peace had softened the powers of resistance of both rulers and people. The Persian monarch, Chosroes II, invaded Asia Minor, 616-626, and for a time threatened Constantinople, the capital of the Eastern Roman or Byzantine Empire set up in A.D. 395. Heraclius, the East Roman emperor, managed to restore Byzantine power by leading his army into Kurdistan in southeastern Asia Minor and thence into Persia.

Arab and Turkish Rule. But an enemy more dangerous than Persia or Egypt began to move eastward. In A.D. 668, the Arabs laid siege to Constantinople, and, urged on by the power of Islam, were soon threatening to put an end to Roman Byzantine rule in Asia Minor. From the east came the Seljuk Turks, who had been driven from central Asia through Persia onto the plains of Mesopotamia. In the latter part of the eleventh century they had established themselves in Cappadocia in eastern Asia Minor and at Nicaea. During the twelfth century, the Turks ruled in various districts throughout Asia Minor, and the struggle for power and over-all dominance was among the various Turkoman tribes, rather than with a common enemy, the Roman Byzantine emperor in Constantinople. In this struggle for power the Osmanli Turks eventually gained supremacy and gradually extended control over all of Asia Minor. Their power was interrupted by Mongolian incursions in the early part of the fifteenth century. But on the death of Timur, the leader of the invaders, the Osmanli power, after a prolonged struggle, was re-established. By the end of the century Constantinople had fallen, and the last vestige of Roman power had been swept away. The later history of Asia Minor is that of Turkey and the Ottoman Empire.

The marchings and countermarchings, the pillage and burning, of warring tribes and armies over a long period of years, followed by an influx of nomadic Turkish tribes, had done much to destroy the cultivated acres, the livestock, and many towns and historic monuments. Whole provinces of land passed out of cultivation, the natives fled to the mountains or to the towns, and in time many of them became nomads. The Mongols, who came in the fifteenth century, completed the destruction of anything left by the Turks and leveled towns in their path that had been rebuilt. Entire Christian communities were wiped out, and the remaining traces of the once-flourishing Hellenic civilization (c. 1000-500 B.C.) almost completely disappeared. The use of the Turkish language was rigidly enforced, and wholesale conversions to Islam took place under Osmanli sultans. Asia Minor was left bare and desolate, and centuries of Osmanli rule did nothing to restore it to its former productiveness. *See also* ASIA; NEAR EAST.   J. E. F.

ASIATIC TRIBES. Asia, the most populous continent of the world, presents also the most complex pattern of racial mixtures. Of the three primary racial stocks—Mongoloid, Caucasoid, and Negroid—the first is most numerous. The popular conception of these stocks, as representing respectively the yellow, white, and black races, is an oversimplification; for countless centuries, in almost every part of the world, they have been continuously dividing and subdividing into progressively smaller groups with mixed physical characteristics. In intermixing, these subgroups have in-

evitably acquired different ways of living and different beliefs—in other words, different cultural patterns.

Among the most important cultural characteristics is language, and it is through language similarities that the anthropologist has been able to trace the origins of many diverse peoples or tribes. This article, therefore, classifies the Asiatic peoples in terms of their linguistic affiliations, besides dealing with their other ethnic characteristics.

The following are the principal linguistic families of the Asiatic mainland:

1. The Indo-Iranian, which, roughly speaking, occupies that part of Asia bounded on the west by Turkey, on the

Buddhist priest, from Ayutthaya, Siam

north by Turkestan and Tibet, on the east by Burma, and on the south by the Arabian Sea and the Persian Gulf. It does not, however, include southern India.

2. The Ural-Altaic, which embraces almost all of the Asiatic territory of Turkey and the Soviet Union, as well as parts of Chinese Turkestan, Mongolia, and Manchuria.

3. The Dravidian, which covers most of southern and southeastern India.

4. The Semitic, which prevails in southwestern Asia, south of Asia Minor and west of Iran.

5. The Sinitic, which covers most of China, Tibet, Burma, and Siam.

In addition to these principal language families, which include all but a relatively small number of the Asiatic peoples, certain other interesting groups are described, such as the Ainu and the Paleo-Siberians of northeastern Asia and the Mon-Khmer of southeastern Asia. The Japanese, the Indonesians, and other island peoples off the Asiatic mainland are dealt with in separate articles.

INDO-IRANIAN

Afghans. The Afghans, or Pathans, are a people of Indo-Iranian speech who are the ruling group in Afghanistan and who extend over into the Northwest Frontier Province of India. A distinction between Afghan and Pathan has been made on the basis of dialects, Afghans being defined as those who speak the western Pushtu dialect, Pathans the eastern Pukhto. By another definition, this time politico-geographical, the term "Afghan" is applied to those living in Afghanistan, "Pathan" to the related peoples on the Indian side of the border. The linguistic and political divisions do not entirely coincide. Afghans and Pathans are essentially the same people.

The origin of the Afghans is obscure. They appear to result from a mixture of Iranians, Turks, and, particularly among the eastern tribes, of "Indians," who in turn were probably of mixed origin. The Afghans first appear in history as a people at the beginning of the eleventh century, when they were listed as being enrolled in the army of Mahmud of Ghazni, who reigned from 998 to 1030. At that time their territory extended from Ghazni eastward through the Suleiman Mountains toward the Indus. In the fifteenth century there was a movement from Ghazni into the Kabul Valley and thence eastward to the Peshawar valley and into the adjacent mountains. A more southerly move-

AFGHAN TRADER

TRIANGLE PHOTO SERVICE

ment from the Suleiman Mountains carried Afghans into the Punjab, where the Lodi, a Ghilzai tribe, in 1450 established a dynasty at Delhi. The Afghans did not achieve political importance in Afghanistan until the beginning of the eighteenth century, when the Ghilzai under Mir Wais established an independent state at Kandahar.

The Afghans are divided into a number of major groups, which in turn are subdivided into tribes, subtribes, and sections. They are an extremely independent and democratic people. Tribal khans and subtribal *maliks*, or chiefs, enjoy only limited authority, and not only tribes, but often sections of tribes were until recent years split by feuds into hostile factions. Since Abdur Rahman Khan, who ruled from 1880 to 1901, first began to unify Afghanistan, there has been a gradual relinquishment of feuds and a growth of national solidarity. Although Afghanistan now has a European-style constitution and parliament, the king still meets in council with the tribal khans and receives their advice.

The Afghans are traditionally a pastoral people. While retaining their tribal organization, some have settled down and become agriculturists; others plant crops near their permanent villages, but migrate with their herds during a part of the year. The nomads live in black tents of the Arab type. Most Afghans are Sunnite Moslems, though a minority follow Shiite tradition. In the cities, women have adopted the Persian veil, which covers the figure to the feet. In the country they cover their faces with a shawl when strangers approach. Although very modest in demeanor, they exert considerable influence within the family group.

The largest and most important group of Afghans is the Durani, formerly called Abdali, to which the royal family belongs. Their territory is centered in Kandahar province, along the lower courses of the Helmand and Argandab

rivers. The Duranis dwelling in the fertile river valleys are settling down and becoming agriculturists. Those living in the more arid regions, extending southeast from Kandahar to the borders of Baluchistan, remain nomads. Another important group is the Ghilzai, who live east of the Durani in the region of Ghazni. They extend southeast from Ghazni to the borders of Waziristan. Many scholars believe the Ghilzai to be descended from the Khalaj, a Turkic tribe which had already moved south of the Syr Darya, or Jaxartes River, in the seventh century. Although this derivation is doubtful, the Ghilzai probably do represent a mixture of Iranian Tajiks with some of the Ghuzz, Khalaj, or other Turks who entered the country between the eleventh and fourteenth centuries to fight in the armies of Ghazni and Ghor. The Ghilzai are largely nomadic. In the winter they move with their herds into the Indus River Valley.

In the mountains between Kabul and Peshawar, and north of the Khyber Pass, live the Mohmands and Yusufzai. The Mohmands, whose hills are arid and infertile, supplement the produce of crude agriculture by acting as carriers of goods along the trade routes. They are somewhat more aristocratic than most Afghans, having well-established lines of hereditary khans. The Yusufzai, who extend into Swat and across the Indus to the east, are agriculturists, every man having an hereditary share in the land. Among the Yusufzai of Swat the women go unveiled and appear to have more authority than the men.

Along the Khyber Pass are the Afridi. They differ from the usual Afghan type and probably represent the descendants of an aboriginal mountain people which was absorbed by the Afghans in their northern advance. The Afridi are for the most part pastoral. In addition to large herds of cattle, sheep, and goats, they also breed donkeys and mules. They cultivate some crops in their summer villages, moving down into the plains for winter pastures. Their sections are engaged in continual feuds; and as late as 1939, Afridi raids necessitated the temporary closing of the Khyber Pass.

South of the Khyber Pass are a number of groups: the Orakzai, Shinwari, Bangash, Zaimukht, Chamkanni, Turi, Wazirs, and Mahsuds. The Chamkanni and Shinwari are said to be of Persian origin, while the Orakzai, Turi, and Wazirs are believed to represent a mixture of Turks with an ancient Indian population. The Bangash have a tradition of Arab descent, although they are Afghan in physical type. The Bangash are principally agriculturists; the remainder, nomadic or seminomadic pastoralists. Unlike most Afghans, the Turi are in religion strongly Shiite; some Orakzai, Bangash, and Chamkanni are also Shiite. The Wazirs are remarkable for their tribal solidarity and absence of internal feuds.

Baloch. The Baloch are an Iranian people living mainly in Baluchistan, between Iran and the Indus River. They speak a language related to Persian, though it has some features characteristic of Eastern Iranian, and in physical type they resemble the Iranian Tajiks. Shortly after the Arab conquest in the seventh century, the Baloch moved into the modern Kerman province of Iran from an earlier home near the Caspian Sea. In the tenth century they moved eastward into Seistan and Makran, and in the thirteenth, under pressure of Genghis Khan's armies, some continued again farther east. In their present territory the Baloch are separated into two geographical groups, with a block of Brahui tribes between the two. The western Baloch dwell in the provinces of Makran and Seistan and extend north halfway up the eastern side of Iran. The eastern section extends from the longitude of Quetta eastward toward the Indus and northward to about 31° N. lat. Many Baloch are also to be found across the Indus in the southern Punjab and northern Sindh in India, but these have lost their language and tribal organization.

The Baloch are pastoral nomads, moving along a regular annual circuit in their arid territories to find pastures for their sheep, goats, cattle, and camels. Many of the western Baloch remain true nomads, dwelling the year around in tents of woven black goat wool and practicing no agriculture. The eastern Baloch have tended to settle down and take

KASHMIRIAN WOMAN

TRIANGLE PHOTO SERVICE

up agriculture. They almost never live in cities, however, although the tribal chiefs maintain fixed residences which may be in trading centers. In winter the eastern Baloch live in the plains in clusters of flat-roofed mud or stone houses, around which they plant some crops. In summer they move to the mountains, where they occupy little enclosures of loose stones over which a temporary roof of matting is spread. In addition to weaving the cloth for their tents, the women do fine embroidery and weave pile rugs which are reminiscent of Turkoman rugs in design. The Baloch are divided into tribes, called *tuman,* under a hereditary chief, or *tumandar.* These tribes are divided into subtribes and the latter into sections of related families. The chief's authority is based on the respect which he can command. Subtribes or sections who disapprove of him may attach themselves to another tribe. Blood feuds, which usually originate in the abduction of a woman or in a murder, are an important feature of tribal life. Before the pacification of Baluchistan by the British in the late nineteenth and early twentieth century, a Baloch man gained prestige by leading raids for cattle and other booty. Like the other inhabitants of Baluchistan, the Baloch are nominally Sunnite Moslems, but follow many Shiite Moslem practices.

Bhils. The Bhils are a people who speak various dialects of Gujarati and live in the hill ranges of Khandesh (central India), southern Rajputana, and Gujarat. In physical type they are below medium height, dark-skinned, and broadnosed. The Bhils are considered to be the aboriginal inhabitants of southern Rajputana and parts of Gujarat, and until the twentieth century several dynasties of Rajput princes received their marks of sovereignty on succession from a Bhil. The chiefs and landholders of the Bhil country belong to a caste composed of descendants of Rajput-Bhil intermarriage, and into the nineteenth century Rajputs would accept food from pure Bhils. With the spread of orthodox Hinduism in Rajputana, however, Bhils became an impure caste because

they ate beef. They serve as village watchmen in the occupational caste system. When the plundering Mahrattas occupied central India in the eighteenth century, they treated the Bhils with such cruelty that many became brigands and highway robbers, swooping down to raid the plains from strongholds in the hills. Their chiefs, who were their leaders in wars and raids, exercised absolute power. Since the middle of the nineteenth century the Bhils have gradually settled down and given up brigandage. While a few own villages or are settled as tenant farmers, the majority have become farm servants. In the seventeenth century the Moghul Emperor Aurangzeb forcibly converted some of the Bhils to Islam; however, both Hindu and Moslem Bhils have similar customs. The Moslems employ Brahman priests for their ceremonies, and the Hindus give cult attention to Moslem saints.

Gujars. The Gujars are a numerous and important Indo-Iranian-speaking pastoral people in western India. They are found chiefly in the Punjab and Rajputana, but also extend as far east as Oudh and the Central Provinces. They are believed to be descended from the Gurjaras, a people associated with the Ephthalite Huns who entered India in the fifth and sixth centuries. Between the ninth and eleventh centuries there were a number of Gujara kingdoms in western India. Babur, who founded the Moghul dynasty of India at the beginning of the sixteenth century, wrote of the hordes of Gujars and Jats who poured down from the hills to steal cattle, and in the seventeenth century Babur's descendant, the Emperor Jahangir, wrote that the Gujars lived on milk and curds and seldom tilled the land. Even today the western Gujars are primarily cattle breeders, with a reputation for appropriating their neighbors' animals, although those to the east have become competent agriculturists. The Gujars have no distinctive physical type, owing to intermixture with other peoples in India. Like the Rajputs, the Gujars practiced female infanticide and hypergamy. In the caste system the Gujars rank slightly below the Jats and above the Ahirs, although they will eat and

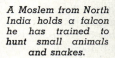
A Moslem from North India holds a falcon he has trained to hunt small animals and snakes.

COHN - WIENER

drink with members of both these related castes. About four fifths of the Gujars are Hindu, the remainder Moslem. Both employ Brahman priests to propitiate their family guardian spirits.

Hazara Mongols. In the central mountains of Afghanistan live the Hazara Mongols, believed to be descendants of Mongol military garrisons originally stationed in the surrounding plains by the sons and later descendants of Genghis Khan. They were pushed back into the mountains by Afghans and Uzbeks. The Hazaras speak an archaic Persian in which some Turkic and Mongol words have been retained. Unlike most of the peoples of Afghanistan, who are Sunnis, the Hazaras are Shia Moslems of the "twelver" sect. Their villages of flat-roofed mud or stone houses, built around a central courtyard and backed by a protective wall, are at the edge of the narrow valley floors where barley, wheat, and legumes are raised. On the barren mountainsides above the village, sheep and goats are pastured. A few oxen for plowing and an occasional riding horse are kept. The Hazaras are divided into a number of regional tribal groups, the most important of which are the Dai Zangi, Dai Kundi, Besud, and Jaghuri. These tribes in turn are divided into subtribes and sections. Altogether, the Hazaras are estimated to number about 500,000. Chiefs inherit their position in some tribes, in others are elected. In either case they may be deposed if unpopular. The Hazaras have never been united under a single leader, and often there are chiefs only for the subtribes, not for the tribe as a whole. Marriages take place by preference between cousins or neighbors in near-by villages. Because of the high bride-price, women are often twenty-five years old, and men thirty-five, before they marry. Women, though retiring in manner, enjoy a status not inferior to their husbands. They may inherit and administer property.

Kafirs. In the mountainous country astride the border of northeastern Afghanistan and the Northwest Frontier Province of India live a tribal people known as the Kafirs. They speak a language known as Dardic, of Aryan origin. The Kafirs are said to be mainly descended from tribes of eastern Afghanistan. They are divided into three groups: the Siah Posh; the Waiguli, about whom little is known; and the Presungali, who represent the ancient population of the area. The Kafirs live in wooden houses two or more stories high and often decorated by elaborate carving. The women cultivate the small fields, where they raise millet, maize, wheat, and some barley, while the men herd cattle, goats, and sheep when not engaged in feuds and raids. The Kafir tribes are kin groups with a strong and responsible feeling of solidarity. In addition, there is a well-developed class system based primarily on economic status. The Kafirs have slaves, partly descendants of aboriginal inhabitants and partly war prisoners, who live in a segregated section of the village. Among the Siah Posh themselves, rich men may become *jast,* or elders, by going through a two-year period of elaborate and costly rituals and banquets. An elder may, by still further ostentation and expenditure of wealth, attain the rank of *mir.* The status of other individuals is determined by the wealth and number of male adults in their kin group. A man too poor to afford more than one wife receives scant consideration. Tribal affairs are managed theoretically by the elders in council, in practice by two or three of the most respected elders. Important matters are debated by all the men of the tribe. The Kafirs formerly worshiped a number of gods, including a supreme creator god and, most popular, a war god; shrines dedicated to one or more of the gods were to be found in every village. The dead were deposited in wooden boxes, amid much wailing, dancing, and feasting, and a year later a wooden statue of the deceased was erected with similiar ritual at the edge of the village.

Kurds. The Kurds, of whom there are about 4,000,000, inhabit the wide arc of the Taurus and Zagros ranges from northern Syria, through eastern Turkey and northern Iraq, into western Iran. They are believed descended from a people known variously as Guti, Qurti, and Karduchoi, who

were living in these mountains in 2,000 B.C. The original Guti have, however, become greatly mixed with Armenians, Semites, Iranians, and Turks. The Kurds speak a western Iranian language which is divided into three mutually incomprehensible dialects. Very few Kurds are true nomads. Some are permanently settled in villages of flat-roofed mud or stone houses; others spend the winters in villages, where they raise some crops, but live in black tents when they accompany the flocks to summer pastures. Among the settled Kurds and some of the seminomads, the old tribal organiza-

Tightly turbaned Kurdish man of Baghdad

tion has broken down and the hereditary khans have become government officials or wealthy landowners of the territory which once belonged to the tribe. The Kurds have never been united into a single tribal confederation, although a Kurd, Salah al-Din, known to the Crusaders as Saladin, built a sultanate in the twelfth century which extended from the Tigris to the Nile. In the time of the Ottoman Empire and Safavid dynasty a number of Kurdish states were established, the last two of which, Sulaimaniya in what is now Iraq, and Ardalan in Iran, disappeared in the nineteenth century. Most Kurds are of the Shafi'i school of Sunnite Moslems except in Iran, where several tribes belong to the radical Shiite sect of Ahl-i Hakk or Ali Ilahi. Contrary to normal Islamic practice, Kurdish women take an active part in family and tribal affairs. Among the Kalhur in Iran they have even on occasion ruled their tribe.

Lur. In the mountains of southwestern Iran the Lur have given their name to the province of Luristan. Believed by some scholars to be descended from the Lullubi, who inhabited these mountains in the second millenium B.C., the Lur themselves claim a Persian origin. They now speak an Iranian language related to Persian, and it is probable that the ancient Lullubi became mixed with Persians in the first millennium B.C., just as in the Islamic period the Lur are known to have absorbed many subtribes of Kurd, Turkish, and Arab origin. Linguistically and culturally they are closely related to their neighbors in the southern Zagros Mountains, the Bakhtiyari, Mamassani, and Kuhgalu tribal confederations. Three sections of the Mamassani are permanently settled, living in villages of wattle huts where they are engaged in cultivating rice. Even these retain a tribal organization under khans and kadkhodas, or tribal chiefs, and the majority of the other Lur-speaking groups remain nomads, living in black tents of the Arab type and migrating with their sheep and horses from summer quarters in the mountains to winter quarters in the lower valleys. Many plant crops in the spring before leaving the winter quarters. The Bakhtiyari, though divided since the nineteenth century into Chahar Lang and Haft Lang groups, have considerable solidarity under an hereditary *ilkhan*. The tribes of Lur proper and the Kuhgalu are divided into a number of tribal sections which shift their allegiance from one leader to another in an ever changing pattern of factions. All Lur are officially Shiite Moslems. Many belong to the radical Ahl-i Hakk or Ali Ilahi sect. The women go unveiled.

Nepalese. Nepal, the independent state which lies along the southern slope of the Himalaya Mountains between India and Tibet, has a mixed population which reflects its geographical position. The majority of the people are Mongoloid in physical type, but, particularly in western Nepal, an Indian Caucasoid element is seen. The official language of the country, Nepali, belongs to the Indo-Iranian family, but many of the peoples speak Tibeto-Burmese languages. Hinduism and Tibetan Buddhism are represented, as well as animism among the more primitive tribes. The class stratification of the Hindu caste system has been taken over by the Buddhists, but even the Hindus observe few of the food tabus commonly associated with caste. In Nepal the usual house is a two-room dwelling of stone or mud, with a veranda. In the mountains the roof is often of thatch. Among some groups agriculture is supplemented by stockbreeding. The pastoralists are not nomadic, however, but send the cattle and sheep to the upper pastures in summer with shepherds. The women have great freedom, not only to work in the fields with the men, but to talk and joke with them. This freedom does not imply sexual license, however. Dancing and singing play an important part in Nepalese social life, and the men have a reputation as ardent gamblers.

The term Gurkha, which is sometimes used to designate Nepalese in general but which applies more precisely to the Nepalese regiments in the Indian army, is derived historically from the princely dynasty which was established in the eighteenth century. It is not the name of a people. In accordance with Hindu caste custom, each of the several peoples has acquired a definite status position in a ladderlike social system. The top rung is held by the Brahmans, who, as in India, form the priestly class. They are said to be descendants of Indian Brahmans who fled to Nepal in the twelfth century to escape the Moslem invasion of India. They speak Nepali and are Caucasoid Indian in physical type. Next in the social scale come the Thakurs, a small group claiming princely descent, who have Mongoloid features. Third in rank, but of great importance in government administration, are the Chetris (from the Hindu *kshatriya*, "warriors"). They are said to be descended from early Brahman immigrants who intermarried with native hill women. They speak Nepali and are of mixed physical type, with the Caucasoid slightly predominating. They monopolize the government service and higher officer ranks of the army. Following the Chetris are two tribal groups, the Magars and Gurungs, who are found chiefly in central Nepal. Both are Mongoloid and both speak Tibeto-Burmese languages. The Magars, who are the more Hinduized of the two, are agriculturists. The Gurung, who are Buddhists, combine agriculture with stockbreeding. Whereas the Hinduized peoples cremate their dead, the Gurung practice burial in village cemeteries. During the harvest season Gurung boys and girls meet freely at the village dancing hall. Ranking below these tribes are the Newars, the most numerous group in Nepal, and by tradition the oldest residents of the country. Their features show Mon-

goloid traits with some Indian admixture; their language is Tibeto-Burmese. The Newars are the craftsmen and traders of the country. Whereas the hill tribes depend chiefly on maize, barley, and millet, the Newars raise rice in carefully irrigated terraces. About two thirds are nominally Buddhists; the remainder, Hindus. The whole community, including the priests, participates in the festivals of both religions. The Limbus, who dwell in eastern Nepal, are said to speak a Munda language, but this is open to question. They are neither Hindu nor Buddhist, but have tribal priests who officiate at sacrifices, weddings, and funerals, and are called on to cure sickness caused by evil spirits. At the bottom of the social ladder are the Rais and several other hill tribes, about which little is known.

Ossetians and Tate. Two tribes of the Caucasus, a region in which most people speak Caucasian, belong to the Iranian language family. These are the Ossetians and the Tate. The Ossetians, who live in the central Caucasus, are believed to be descended from the ancient Alans. They are breeders of sheep and cattle and live in two-storied stone houses, the cattle being kept on the first floor, the family living on the second. Of note in their religion is an annual ritual to the devil, and the Persian custom of jumping over a fire at New Year's time. The Tate, who are found in the Transcaucasian Republic of Azerbaidzhan, are believed to be either Persian immigrants or Iranicized Turks. By their own tradition they are descended from Persians exiled after a revolt against the Sassanid dynasty which lasted from A.D. 226 to 641. They speak an aberrant form of Persian.

TAJIK FOLK SINGER

SOVFOTO

Tajiks. Before the expansion of Turkic-speaking peoples in the first millenium of the Christian Era, both eastern and western Turkestan were populated by people speaking eastern Iranian languages. They were gradually absorbed or pushed aside by the Turks. Of those who were displaced, some 3,000,000 descendants, known as Tajiks, are found in the mountain areas around Fergana, Samarkand, and Bukhara, and in Afghanistan. They are agriculturists, skillful in irrigation, and are also active in trade. They are for the most part Sunnite Moslems, but vary from Moslem practice in some ways: there is almost no polygamy, and the bride-price is divided between the girl's father, to whom it is usually paid, and her mother's brother. The women are seldom veiled, and the men do not wear turbans. One group of Tajiks, living in the high valleys of the Pamirs, are known as Galchas. The languages spoken in the various valleys, although belonging to the eastern branch of Iranian languages, differ greatly from the plains Tajik dialects. Because of these linguistic peculiarities the Galchas are believed to be descended from the ancient Sogdians. Galchas are Shiite Moslems. Some belong to the Persian "twelver" sect, others to the Ismaili "sevener" sect.

Tajik actress costumed for a musical play

SOVFOTO

Veddas. In the interior of the island of Ceylon, off southern India, live the primitive Veddas, a people who resemble in physical type the aborigines of Australia. They speak an Indo-Iranian language. The people are very short, often below five feet in height. The Veddas formerly were primitive nomads, living in rock shelters or temporary brush shelters. Today they are more or less sedentary, living in huts and practicing agriculture. The men hunt with the bow and arrow, and the women make a very crude pottery. The Veddas are divided into clans or kinship groups which trace descent through the mother. When death occurs, the corpse is abandoned and the spot is not revisited by the family for a number of years. The spirits of the dead are believed to return in dreams.

URAL-ALTAIC

Finno-Ugrian. *Cheremiss (Mari).* The Cheremiss are a Finno-Ugrian-speaking people who live in the Middle Volga region of Russia in communities scattered among the Mordvin. They call themselves Mari. They are able agriculturists and breeders of horses and cattle. The mountain Cheremiss, west of Kazan, also keep bees, hunt, and fish. Their religion, before the Russian Revolution, was a mixture of shamanism, Islam, and Christianity. In 1941 there were 500,000 Mari, over half of them in the Mari Autonomous Soviet Socialist Republic.

Mordvin (Mordovian). The Mordvin are a Finnic-speaking agricultural people who live in the central Volga region of Russia. In 1941 they numbered a million and a half, most of them in the Mordovian Autonomous Soviet Socialist Republic.

Permians. The Permians are a Finnic-speaking people who live just west of the Urals. One branch, the Votyak, occupy the Soviet Komi-Permiak National District along the Kama; the other branch, the Zyrians (Komi), live to the north in the Komi Autonomous Soviet Socialist Republic. Except for some of the northern Zyrians, who are nomadic reindeer-breeders, the Permians are agriculturists, artisans, and traders.

Vogul (Mansis). The Vogul are related to the Ugrian Ostyak, who live on the eastern slope of the northern Ural Mountains in western Siberia. The Ostyak Vogul National District, under which these two groups are governed, is the largest national district in the Soviet Union. The Vogul are called Mansis by the Soviet government.

Mongol. The Mongols are a people of Mongoloid physical type and Mongol language who dwell in northeastern central Asia. Their origin is obscure. They did not adopt writing until the thirteenth century, and since their language bears many similarities to Tungus and Turkic, transliterations in Chinese records before that date leave the linguistic affiliations of early "northern barbarians" in doubt. By descriptions of physical type the ancestral Mongols may be readily distinguished from the Caucasoid Turks, but not from the Mongoloid Tungus. It is believed that at least some of the Huns may have been Mongol. The Khitans, who had a dynasty in north China from 916 to 1125, may have been either Mongol or Tungus. It was not until the rise of a Mongol empire under Genghis Khan at the end of the twelfth century, and the adoption of writing, that the Mongols achieved an undisputed identity in history.

Chinese records disclose that the people who founded the Mongol Empire in the twelfth century occupied the present Mongolia, which in the eighth century had been ruled by Turks. Some of these Mongols had settled down and adopted Chinese customs. Others were pastoral nomads, while still a third group consisted of woodland-dwelling peoples. It is probable that the Mongols were originally northern woodland dwellers who gradually adopted pastoral nomadism and moved into the plains as these were vacated by the westward movements of Turkic peoples. Under their great leader, Genghis Khan, the nomadic Mongols conquered an empire which at its height included all of China and extended westward to the Mediterranean and eastern Europe. The armies of Genghis Khan and his successors in the West included

A NATIVE OF INNER MONGOLIA

TRIANGLE PHOTO SERVICE

many Turks as well as Mongols. Indeed this last great westward nomadic movement in Asia swept all but the sedentary town-dwelling Turks out of eastern central Asia and brought into the steppes of western central Asia peoples who, though Turkic-speaking, were Mongoloid in physical type. After the breakup of the Mongol Empire, the Mongols became localized in Mongolia and its borderlands. They are divided into five main dialect groups: the Chahar or Charkhar, in Inner Mongolia and Manchuria; the Khalkha, who dwell in Outer Mongolia; the Buryat, who occupy territory east and west of Lake Baykal in southern Siberia; the Kalmuck, or Western Mongols, who are centered in the Sinkiang province of China; and the Mongol tribes of northwest Tibet, such as the Tsaidam Mongols.

The Mongols are for the most part pastoral nomads: in felt-covered tents they follow their herds of horses, cattle, camels, sheep, and goats along a regular annual circuit of pastures. Their staple diet consists of milk products, and meal and tea which they obtain by barter. This is supplemented by wild game, sheep, or horse flesh. They are organized into tribal groups which they believe to be descended from a common ancestor. Under the Manchus (1644-1911), the tribes of the Chahar and Khalkha were organized into "Banners" which fought as military units. The Mongols are ruled by princes claiming descent from Genghis Khan. After the rise of the Manchu dynasty in 1644, the position of these princes among the eastern Mongols was confirmed by the Chinese government, and in turn the princes confirmed by appointment the succession of the hereditary tribal and section chiefs. Among the Buryat under Russian rule, up to the time of the Russian Revolution in 1917, the position of hereditary tribal chiefs was strengthened by their appointment as Russian officials. Tribal affairs are regulated by councils of civil and religious officials called and presided over by the princes. A man may marry anyone except his own mother, sister, or daughter. Formerly, a man might marry as many wives as he wished, but since the beginning of the nineteenth century only the Buryats have practiced polygamy to any extent. Marriages were usually late because of the high bride-price.

The conversion of the Mongols to Tibetan Buddhism in the sixteenth century exerted a profound influence on their social and economic life. It is estimated that one third of the male population of the Mongols are Buddhist priests or monks. The withdrawal of this large proportion of the people from productive economic employment, plus the diversion of funds and supplies for the support of the temples and monasteries, has impoverished the Mongols. The Buddhist rule, which forbids marriage to the clerics, is accompanied in practice by extramarital license which has robbed Mongol women of their thirteenth-century reputation for chastity and fidelity. As a religious system, Buddhism has made little contribution. The priests, ignorant and often illiterate, practice curing and soothsaying much after the fashion of pre-Buddhist Mongol shamans.

Buryat. The Buryat Mongols live in the Lake Baykal region of southern Siberia. Those living south and east of Lake Baykal are nomadic cattle breeders and belong to the Yellow Hat sect of Lamaist Buddhism. Those to the west remain shamanistic, but under Russian influence have become settled agriculturists. The Buryats form the Buryat-Mongolian Autonomous Soviet Socialist Republic and the Agin Buryat Mongol and Ust-Ordin Buryat Mongol National Districts.

Chahar. The Chahar, also known as Charkhar, were once the ruling tribe of southern Mongolia. They became impoverished by the encroachment of Chinese colonists on their former pastures. In the nineteenth century some were transported to Sinkiang province in China, where a reservation was established for them by the Chinese government.

Hsien Pei. The Hsien Pei, a people of uncertain origin, appeared in what is now western Manchuria in the first century B.C. During the following century they pushed into Outer Mongolia, displacing the Hsiung Nu. In the second century a Hsien Pei tribal confederation conquered southern Siberia and eastern Manchuria, and invaded Korea on the east and Dzungaria on the west, thereby weakening the once powerful Hsiung Nu empire. In the fourth century one group of Hsien Pei established a state in what is now Hopei Province. The Hsien Pei have been variously described as Korean, Tungus, Mongol, and Turkic, with modern opinion favoring Mongol or Turkic.

Kalmuck. Kalmuck is the name commonly given to the western branch of the Mongols, who live chiefly in the Dzungaria region of Sinkiang. They call themselves Oirat. The Kalmuck are also frequently called the Eleut, or Dzungar, after the Eleut tribe and its Dzungar subtribe which con-

Kalmuck woman from Southern Russia

SOVFOTO

quered an empire in the seventeenth and eighteenth centuries, when they invaded Tibet, Yarkand, Samarkand, Bukhara, and the western steppes. The Torgut, another Kalmuck tribe, in 1632 crossed the Volga River and settled northwest of the Caspian Sea. A part of their descendants remain there, and between 1935 and World War II, were organized into the Kalmuck Autonomous Soviet Socialist Republic. In 1770 a part of the Volga Torgut fled eastward again and settled on the slopes of the Altai Mountains and the Tien Shan, in Dzungaria and in Russian territory. While some Kalmucks are included in the Oirat Autonomous Region of the Soviet Union, the native population of that region consists chiefly of the so-called "Kara Kalmuck," who are not Mongol, but Turkic-speaking people of mixed origin.

Khalkha. The Khalkha, who inhabit Outer Mongolia, were organized in 1927 into the Mongolian People's Republic, nominally an independent state having close relations with the Soviet Union.

Naimans. The Naimans are a Mongol tribe which moved from the Orkhon River in Mongolia to the region of the upper Irtysh in southern Siberia, where they already were established in the thirteenth century. Scholars believe that the Naimans were the first to adapt to the Mongol language the Aramaic script used by the Turkic Ulghurs. The Naimans survive in their upper Irtysh home as a tribe of the Kazakh.

Samoyed. The Samoyed, also known as Nentsi, are skilled, nomadic, reindeer breeders who occupy the frozen tundra from the Khatanga River of north central Siberia to the Kola Peninsula in northernmost Europe. One branch, the Ostyak Samoyed, wander in the northern forests east of the Ural Mountains. Although the Samoyed language resembles that of the Finns, the exact relationship has not yet been determined. In the forest belt spreading east and west from the Upper Yenisey River are several tribes believed to be Samoyeds who have undergone Turkish influence. These are the Beltir, Koibal, and Karagas.

Tungus. The Tungus are divided into two main branches, the northern, or Tungus proper, and southern, represented by the Manchus. The northern Tungus are scattered over eastern Siberia, from Manchuria to the Arctic Ocean and from the Sea of Okhotsk on the Pacific to the eastern tributaries of the Yenisey River. They have tended to adopt the culture of their neighbors: some are sedentary coastal fishermen, others nomadic reindeer-breeders. Those

Tungus man of Siberia, hunter and reindeer breeder

SOVFOTO

living near the Buryat Mongols and Yakut are horse- and cattle-breeding nomads. In the Transbaykal region are sedentary agriculturists whose ancestors in the eighteenth century made up Cossack regiments in the Russian army. The best-known Tungus tribes are the Lamut, east of the Kolyma River in eastern Siberia, and the Goldi, on the Lower Sungari River in Manchuria. Whatever their economy, the Tungus resemble the Manchus and Mongols and differ from the Paleo-Siberians in being organized into exogamous clans or extended kinship groups.

Manchu. The Manchus are a southern Tungusic people who gave their name to Manchuria. Like the Chinese, who have long been their neighbors, they are sedentary agriculturists; the pig is their chief food and sacrificial animal, and the chicken is similarly used. Also like the Chinese, but unlike the northern Tungus and Mongols, they do not use milk. The Manchus are divided into clans of related families, under an elected chief, and make annual sacrifices to their clan ancestors and spirits. A Manchu homestead is owned by the extended family, not by an individual, and the family chief who administers the property may be either a man or a woman. A Manchu dynasty, under the name of Ch'ing, ruled China from 1644 to 1911.

Turkic. The word "Turk," which comes from the Chinese *Tu-küe,* first appears in history as the name of a nomadic people which in the sixth century ruled an empire extending from Mongolia to the Black Sea. The name probably applied originally only to a single tribe, or to the ruling family of that tribe. It came to be used for Turkic-speaking peoples in general by the Moslem Arabs, who encountered the Turks in the seventh and eighth centuries. The Orkhon inscriptions of the eighth century, the earliest dated records written in Turkish, place the eastern Turks proper, or Türk-Oghuz, as masters of Mongolia, with the Uighur to the east of them, the Karluk to the west, and the Kirghiz

dwelling in the Minusinsk region of the Upper Yenisey River in Siberia. The areas now known as Chinese and Russian Turkestan were then inhabited by Iranian-speaking peoples, although some Turks began to move down and settle in the southern oases in the ninth century. In the middle of the eighth century the Türk-Oghuz power in Mongolia was overthrown by the Uighur. In 840 the Uighur, in turn, were forced out of Mongolia by the Kirghiz, although Uighur groups established two other kingdoms: one in the present Kansu province of China, which lasted until the eleventh century; the other near Beshbalik (the modern Tihwa, or Urumtsi, in Dzungaria), which survived until the fourteenth century. The Kirghiz, the last Turkic people to rule Mongolia, were conquered by the Khitans in the first quarter of the tenth century.

While the eastern Türk, Uighur, and Kirghiz struggled for control of Mongolia, other Turkic tribes were already moving into the West. The western Türk had extended their power to the Black Sea in the sixth century. When the Moslem Arabs invaded western Turkestan in the seventh and eighth centuries, they found two Turkic groups, the Khalaj and the Karluks, south of the Jaxartes River, now known as the Syr Darya, while the steppes to the north were dominated by Turkic nomads. In the ninth century the Pechenegs crossed the southern Urals into the Volga region. Between the eighth and eleventh centuries a number of groups generally called Oghuz or Ghuzz moved into western Asia. The great migrations of the eleventh century carried the Ghuzz into Iran and across to the Mediterranean, their descendants becoming the Turkoman and the Azerbaijani and Osmanli Turks, and across southern Russia to the Balkans. The last great purely Turkic migration in the West was that of the Kipchak, who in the eleventh century moved southward from the Irtysh River region of western Siberia into what is now Kazakhstan. From the time of Genghis Khan's western conquests in the first quarter of the thirteenth century the westward-moving nomads were of Mongol admixture, although they became Turkic in speech. In modern times few Turks are found in eastern central Asia, other than the sedentary Turki, whose ancestors began to settle in the oasis towns there as early as the ninth century.

The Turks are of Caucasoid physical type, not Mongoloid, as has sometimes been assumed. The "typical" Turk is described as very broad-headed, brunet, and with a luxuriant beard. The Kirghiz, however, were described as late as the eleventh century as being fair-complexioned, blond, and blue-eyed. The modern Turkomans are very long-headed, like an Iranian type. It is probable that peoples of more than one type became identified with the Turks through adoption of their language and inclusion in their tribal confederations. Little is known of Turkic culture before the eighth century. In the eighth century the Turks were pastoral nomads, a way of life they had probably borrowed from Iranian-speaking neighbors. Some scholars claim that the Turks knew how to work iron from early times; others deny this. The Turks were organized into tribes and tribal confederations, the more important of which had a leader called the *khaghan,* or khan. The dynasties were short-lived, however, and the confederations unstable. The culture of modern Turkic groups is described under the names of the various tribes.

Azerbaijani Turks. In Iranian and Russian Azerbaijan there are some 6,000,000 Turks who speak a Turkic dialect very closely related to that of the Turkomans and the Osmanli Turks. Like the latter, they are believed to be descended from Ghuzz Turks who moved westward into the area in the eleventh century. Most of those in Iran are permanently settled. Others are seminomads. In winter they live in villages of one- or two-storied mud houses, on the flat roofs of which fodder is stored, and they plant crops in the fields around the village. In summer they live in felt-covered tents while tending their herds of cattle, sheep, and camels in pastures. The Azerbaijani are Shiite Moslems of the orthodox "twelver" sect.

Bashkir. The Bashkir are a Turkic-speaking people found in the southern Ural Mountains of the Soviet Union. They may originally have been Finno-Ugrian in speech. Between

Siamese man

TRIANGLE PHOTO SERVICE

the tenth century, when they were first mentioned by Arab geographers, and the thirteenth, when they were conquered by the Mongols, the Bashkir were a strong and independent people, often at war with their neighbors, the Bulgars and Pechenegs. In 1556 they voluntarily became vassals of Russia. Many of the Bashkir have long been settled, with an economy based on agriculture, cattle breeding, and beekeeping, but others remained pastoral nomads into the twentieth century. In 1941 there were 885,000 Bashkir in the Bashkir Autonomous Soviet Socialist Republic.

Gagauz. The Gagauz are a Turkic-speaking people found in scattered groups in Bessarabia, Romania, Bulgaria, and Turkey. They are believed to be descended from the Kara Kalpak, a branch of the Ghuzz Turks, who in the eleventh century settled in the Balkans and southern Russia, where they were converted to the Orthodox Christian religion. Although the modern Gagauz live in isolated and inhospitable groups and speak Turkic exclusively in the home, they are not generally distinguishable in dress or customs from their non-Turkic neighbors.

Kara Kalpak. The name "Kara Kalpak" is applied to a Turkic people who lived south of the Russians in the twelfth century and who may be the ancestors of the present Kara Kalpak. The latter, first recorded in the seventeenth century as living on the Syr Darya (Jaxartes River) in Russian Turkestan, now make up the population of the Kara Kalpak Autonomous Soviet Socialist Republic south of the Aral Sea. Some are cattle-breeding pastoral nomads who live in dome-shaped felt tents; others are sedentary agriculturists, and those on the shores of the Aral Sea are fishermen. Groups of 20,000 each are also found in Samarkand and Fergana. Among those Kara Kalpak who retain their old tribal subdivisions, some have clan names found also among the Kazakh and Uzbek.

Karluk (Qarluq). The Karluk was one of the first Turkic tribes of central Asia to move south of the Oxus. In the seventh century A.D. Arab invaders found Karluk living in Badakhshan, in the northeastern part of the present Afghanistan. The Orkhon inscriptions of the eighth century mention them as living in western Mongolia, and at the end of that century they established power in Semirechia, the eastern part of modern Kazakstan. In the thirteenth century there was a Karluk kingdom north of the Ili River and another in Ferghana. When Timur (d. 1404) invaded India, he stationed garrisons of Karluk soldiers in what is now the Hazara district of the North West Frontier Province, where their descendants are still found. A few Karluks also live in the Qattaghan and Badakhshan provinces of Afghanistan.

Kashkai. The Kashkai of Iran are the last strong Turkic nomadic tribal confederation to survive in Asia. They are descended from parts of two different Turkic groups: the Khalaj, who were reported to be living in southern Afghanistan in the tenth century, and from Turks who came into Iran from eastern Turkestan in the thirteenth century with the Mongol *ilkhan*, Hulagu Khan. The several tribes which form the Kashkai confederation lived in western Iran for a time before being removed to Fars Province by Shah Ismail Safavi early in the sixteenth century. They were not united under a single *ilkhan* until the third quarter of the eighteenth century, and since that time have been a political power in Iran. Their summer and winter quarters occupy about a third of Fars Province, with the Khamseh confederation on the east, and the Bakhtiyari and Kuhgalu tribe of Lur on the west. Some Kashkai sections have absorbed Kurd, Lur, and Bakhtiyari subtribes. Their language is similar to that of the Azerbaijani Turks. Except for some Khalaj, who have become sedentary agriculturists, most of the Kashkai live in tents of woven, black goats' hair, and move with the seasons to find pasture for their sheep, goats, horses, and camels. The women weave fine rugs. Kashkai are Shiite Moslems, like the Persians, but are not at all fanatic. The women go unveiled, and the religious men who minister to the Kashkai are village-dwelling Persians and Lurs. Unlike most Moslems, the Kashkai are almost entirely monogamous. Blood feuds, common among most nomadic tribes, are unknown among the Kashkai, and there is an unusual sense of communal solidarity among the 90,000 people who constitute the Kashkai federation.

Kazakh. The Kazakhs, formerly also known as Kirghiz and Kirghiz Kaisak, are the Turko-Mongol people who inhabit the vast domain of western central Asia now called Kazakhstan. The term "Kazakh" first appeared in the Turkic language in the fifteenth century, when it meant "robber" or "adventurer." Shortly thereafter it was applied to the tribal group which now bears the name. In the fifteenth century, Abu'l Khair (d. 1468) formed a tribal confederation of the conglomeration of Turkic and Mongol tribes then roaming the steppes of western central Asia. Some were recent arrivals from eastern central Asia; others had moved eastward when expelled from southern Russia by Muscovite armies. From this Uzbek confederation the Kazakhs split off about 1465-1466. In the seventeenth century they held power over their present domain as well as over Tashkent and Fergana. By the end of that century the Kazakhs had separated into the Great, Middle, and Small *ordas*. This division, which is primarily geographical rather than political, remains to the present. The Kazakhs are Mongoloid in physical type, but speak a western Turkic dialect related to that of the Kirghiz, Bashkir, and Siberian and Volga Tatars. Many of them remained true nomads until after the Russian Revolution, dwelling the year round in felt-covered, dome-shaped tents, and following a regular seasonal route of migration to obtain fresh pastures for their horses, sheep, goats, cattle, and, in the south, camels. Except for some, living near Russian or Iranian agriculturists, they planted no crops, subsisting on a diet of milk products and mutton. Such grain or rice as was eaten was obtained by trade. Since the seventeenth century there has been no sultan over all the Kazakhs. Tribal chiefs were elected, normally from the family of the preceding khan. A chief's authority depended on his personal and family prestige. Families descended from Genghis Khan claimed special privileges and married among themselves, whereas in other families a man could not marry anyone descended from the same ancestor within seven generations. The Kazakhs were shamanistic in religion until the Russian Revolution, although nominally they were converted to Islam in the eighteenth century.

Khalaj. The Khalaj are a Turkic tribe which had already moved south of the Oxus River, now known as the Amu Darya, by the seventh century. In the tenth century the Khalaj were reported by Istakhri, the Arab geographer, to have been living in southern Afghanistan "since ancient times." One branch of their descendants is represented in the Kashkai of Iran, and in the belief of some scholars the Afghan tribe of Ghilzai is also descended from the Khalaj.

Kipchak. The Kipchak were a Turkic people who, from their eleventh-century home on the Irtysh River, spread out over what is now Kazakhstan, possibly thereby starting the movement of the Ghuzz Turks to the south and west. They were known to Russians as Polovtsi, to Western Europeans as Comans. The name "Kipchak" was later applied to the Mongol Empire of the Golden Horde, but Kipchak political power came to an end with the Mongol period. Kipchak subtribes are found among the Kazakh and Uzbek, while small independent Kipchak groups are reported to live in Fergana and in northwestern Afghanistan.

Kirghiz. The Kirghiz, also called Kara Kirghiz, are a central Asian people who first appeared in history as the Kien Kuen in Chinese sources of the second century. In the eighth century they were mentioned in both the Turkic Orkhon Inscriptions and in Chinese records as living in the Minusinsk region of the Upper Yenisey River. The Turkic Yenisey inscriptions have been attributed to the Kirghiz. In 840 they invaded Mongolia and conquered the Turkic Uighur empire which they found there. In the early eighteenth century, under the empire of the Jungars, the Kirghiz were moved south from the Yenisey to their present range in the southern Tien Shan range, the Alai and Fergana mountains, and the Pamirs. Chinese records of the seventh to tenth centuries show that the Kirghiz already spoke Turkic at that period. Up to the eleventh century both Chinese and Arab accounts describe them as having blond or red hair, light complexions, and blue eyes. Today they are distinctly Mongoloid in physical type. Early Moslem reports indicate that they were not a settled people; some were hunters, some stock-breeding nomads. In recent centuries the Kirghiz have been pastoral nomads, migrating seasonally among the mountains and living in felt-covered tents. Their herds include sheep, camels, horses, and, in the higher altitudes, yaks. Only some of the Kirghiz practice agriculture. They are nominally Sunnite Moslems, but continue to be served by shamans rather than by Moslem priests. Those Kirghiz in the Soviet Union, of whom there are about 900,000, are organized in the Kirghiz Soviet Socialist Republic, where they constitute two thirds of the population.

Kumyk, Balkarians, and Karachai. The Kumyk, Balkarians, and Karachai are Turkic-speaking peoples who live in the Caucasus, where most of the tribes speak Caucasian. The Kumyk, who form the chief element of the population of the Soviet republic of Daghestan, in the eastern Caucasus, speak some thirty-seven dialects of a primitive Turkic. They are thought to be descendants of the medieval Khazars. Traditionally stock breeders and fishermen, they are now taking up agriculture. The Balkarians and Karachai, in the northern Caucasus, speak related languages.

Native woman of Nikko, Japan, carrying gravel

TRIANGLE PHOTO SERVICE

Nogai. The Nogai are a small Turko-Mongol nomadic group living on the lower Volga in southern Russia. They first appeared as a tribal confederation west of the Volga in the sixteenth century, after the breakup of the Golden Horde. In the seventeenth century most of the Nogai were driven by the Kalmucks eastward across the Volga, where culturally they gradually became a part of the Kazakhs. Under the Soviet regime, they were united with this tribe politically. A few Nogai are found in the Cherkess Autonomous Region of the north Caucasus.

Taranchi. The Taranchi, a people of mixed Turkic and east Iranian origin, are found in eastern Kazakhstan. Taranchi is the Turkic word for agriculturist. It was applied first to a group of colonists who were moved by the Chinese government from Kashgaria to the Ili River Valley in the eighteenth century. In 1882 most of them moved from Chinese to Russian territory, where they were considered good agriculturists and artisans. They have no autonomous political unit in the Soviet Union, one group being included in Kazakhstan, another in Turkmenistan.

Tatar. Tatar, frequently miscalled Tartar, is a name originally applied to the Mongols. It appeared in the Turkic Orkhon inscriptions of the eighth century, where it referred apparently to Mongol tribes living southwest of Lake Baykal. In accounts of the Mongol conquests of the thirteenth century, the Mongols were universally called Tatars by Chinese, Moslem, Russian and Western European writers. Peoples of Mongol origin and language appear to have called themselves Tatars until after the time of Genghis Khan, when the name was replaced by that of Mongol in central Asia and Mongolia. The Turkic-speaking people of the Golden Horde in southern Russia, whose chiefs were descended from Genghis Khan's son Juchi, continued to be called Tatar, and later Russians and Western Europeans applied the term to all Turkic peoples except the Osmanli

Turks. By extension of this usage in the sixteenth and subsequent centuries, the term "Tatar" again came to be applied to the Mongols, and also to the Manchus. As a proper name, it is used only by certain Turkic-speaking groups in Russian territory:

1. The Astrakhan, Kazan, and Krim (Crimean) Tatars. Turkic in speech and Caucasoid in physical type, these groups in southern Russia are descended from Turks who established kingdoms in their present homes after the disintegration of the Golden Horde in the fifteenth century. After

Korean man

SOVFOTO

the Russian Revolution of 1917 the Kazan and Krim Tatars were organized respectively into the Tatar and Crimean Autonomous Soviet Socialist Republics.

2. The Siberian Tatars. After the breakup of the Golden Horde, a nomadic Tatar kingdom arose in western Siberia, near the present town of Tobolsk. These Tatars were probably Turko-Mongols, like their southern neighbors, the Kazakhs. It was the depredations of these Siberian Tatars which inspired the first Russian conquest of Siberia at the end of the sixteenth century.

3. Altaian Tatars. In the northern Altai Mountains of southern Siberia live a small number of tribes speaking archaic Turkic dialects, some of whom are Turkic in origin, while others show an admixture of Turks with Yeniseians and Samoyeds. The Teleut, Telengut, and Kara Kalmuck, the last of which are called Oirat under the Soviet regime, are nomadic cattle breeders; other groups are woodland hunters or reindeer breeders. The Altaian Tatars include the Abakan Tatars, the Kumandins, Lebeds, and Shors.

Turki. The Turki are the Turkic-speaking sedentary inhabitants of modern Sinkiang, in Chinese central Asia, who make up 70 per cent of the population of that province. They are also sometimes called Uighur, and may be at least in part descendants of the medieval Uighur Turks. They live in towns of flat-roofed mud houses and cultivate the irrigated oases of Kashgar and other cities of southern Sinkiang. They are Sunnite Moslems, but the women are unsecluded. Since the days of Marco Polo, they have been noted for their love of music, story-telling, and other entertainment.

Turkoman. The Turkoman is one of a Turkic-speaking group of tribes who occupy a strip of territory extending from the southeast shores of the Caspian Sea to Afghan

Turkestan. Like the Azerbaijani and Osmanli Turks, the Turkomans are believed to be descended from that wave of Ghuzz Turks who moved into western Asia in the eleventh century. Unlike most Turkic peoples, the Turkomans are noticeably long-headed in physical type, thus indicating a considerable admixture with Iranians. They are divided into six independent tribes: the Yomud, on the eastern shores of the Caspian; the Goklan, along the Atrek River on the Iranian-Soviet border; the Salor, just east of the Goklan, around Serakhs; the Saryk, who extend along the Murghab River into Afghanistan; the Tekke, living around Merv; and the Ersari, whose territory is north and east of Merv near Bukhara. Many of the Yomuds along the Caspian are settled fishermen, while the Goklan are sedentary agriculturists. For a long time many of the other tribes have been seminomadic; they live in felt-covered tents and cultivate the grain, fruits, and vegetables which form an important part of their diet. In addition to horses, for which the Turkomans are renowned, they raise sheep, goats, and camels. Before the coming of the Russians the Turkomans did not have hereditary khans. Community affairs were regulated by a council of old men, and the raids which made the Turkomans the terror of their sedentary neighbors were led by self-chosen temporary leaders. The slaves captured in these raids were usually sold in the markets of Turkestan rather than kept within the tribe. Marriage frequently took place within the subtribe, in order to keep the high brideprice within the group. The women, who went unveiled even before the Russian Revolution, enjoyed great freedom of action. Turkomans were nominally Sunnite Moslems of the Hanefite school, but did not observe such Moslem rules as they found inconvenient. Scattered among the Turkoman tribes were sheiks, sayids, and khojas, who claimed Arab descent and married only among themselves. Turkoman priests were drawn from this group, which enjoyed considerable prestige.

Uighur. The Uighur, a Turkic tribe, was first mentioned in the Orkhon inscriptions (eighth century of the Christian Era) as living in eastern Mongolia. At that time they conquered Mongolia, with a capital on the Orkhon River, where the Mongols later built their capitol of Karakorum. Pushed out of Mongolia by the Kirghiz in the ninth century, they formed two kingdoms: one at Beshbalik endured until the fourteenth century; the second, in Chinese territory, was conquered by the Tangut (Tibetans) in the eleventh century. The descendants of this latter kingdom still form a small group in northern Tibet, where they speak an old Turkic dialect. The Uighur were converted to Manichaeism by Sogdian missionaries, from whom they adopted the Aramaean alphabet. This they transmitted to the Mongols and Manchus. The modern Turki of Sinkiang are also sometimes called Uighur.

Uriankhai. In the Yenisey Basin between Outer Mongolia and Siberia, live an aboriginal Yeniseian people known variously as Uriankhai, Soyot, and Tuva. They have lost their own language; a few of them speak Mongol, the remainder an archaic Turkic. In physical type some show pronounced Mongol admixture; others are Caucasoid in type. Of five Uriankhai tribal groups, three are chiefly woodland hunters, living on wild game and on vegetable foods which the women collect. Part of two other groups are nomadic reindeer breeders. The reindeer are remarkably tame, returning to camp each evening, and never mating with wild reindeer. The reindeer are kept for transportation, both riding and pack, and for milk, but are seldom killed for meat. A few of the Uriankhai under Mongol influence raise sheep, goats, horses, and cattle. Except for the sheep breeders, who live in Mongol-type felt-covered yurts, the Uriankhai live in birchbark-covered conical tents. Some near Mongolia have become Buddhists; the remainder are shamanists. In 1921 the country of the Uriankhai was recognized by the Soviet government as an independent Tannu Tuva People's Republic. In 1945 it was announced that Tannu Tuva had joined the Soviet Union as an Autonomous Region.

Uzbek. The Uzbek are a Turkic-speaking people in central Asia who occupy a strip of land extending southeast from the Aral Sea into Afghan Turkestan. The Uzbek nation was founded in the second half of the fifteenth century by nomads who, after the breakup of the Golden Horde, moved eastward from southern Russia into the plains of the Oxus River, or Amu Darya. In the sixteenth century Uzbeks founded the khanates of Khiva and Bukhara, which lasted until the Russian Revolution. The Uzbek khanate of Kokand, which included Tashkent and Fergana, was founded toward the end of the eighteenth century and taken over by the Russians in the 1870's. In Afghan Turkestan a number

Thin, long braids, tightly plaited, effect a simple hairstyle for a woman of the Uzbek Soviet Socialist Republic.

of small Uzbek khanates remained independent until the last quarter of the nineteenth century. In 1941 there were about 5,000,000 Uzbeks in the Soviet Union, most of them in the Uzbek Soviet Socialist Republic. The Uzbek population of Afghan Turkestan is estimated at 200,000. The Uzbeks, originally Turko-Mongol, have intermarried with the original Iranian population of Turkestan, and have acquired many Iranian customs. Comparatively few Uzbeks remain nomadic or seminomadic, though at the end of the nineteenth century many of the village-dwelling agriculturists still retained much of the old, nomadic tribal organization. The cities of Bukhara and Khiva, which until the middle of the nineteenth century were important trading centers and noted for certain crafts, were thoroughly Iranicized in culture. Uzbeks are Sunnite Moslems of the Hanefite school, and before the Russian Revolution the khans enforced rigid adherence to the Koranic law in Bukhara and Khiva.

Yakut. The Yakut occupy the vast expanse of northeastern Siberia from the Lena to the Kolyma rivers, and from the Arctic Ocean to a thousand miles southward. The estimated population in 1941 was 340,000. The Yakut are believed to be descended from Turks who were pushed north in the thirteenth century by Mongols, with whom they intermarried. A horse cult suggests that they were formerly horse-breeding pastoral nomads. They are now chiefly semisedentary cattle-

breeders, with permanent winter and summer dwellings. They live in birchbark-covered conical tents in summer, and in semisubterranean earth huts in winter. Some Yakut in the far north breed reindeer for use in transportation, but they do not use reindeer milk. In religion the Yakut are shamanistic.

Yürük. The Yürük are nomadic Turkish tribes found in Turkey and occasionally in the Balkans. They are believed to have mixed little with non-Turkic peoples since they moved into their present home from central Asia, although a few tribes in Anatolia speak Kurdish. Although nominally Moslems, the Yürük retain many pagan rites and beliefs. They raise sheep and goats, sometimes cattle, and some tribes are breeders of horses and camels. Many groups supplement stock breeding with hunting or a little agriculture. They live in tents of woven goats' wool.

DRAVIDIAN

Badagas. The Badagas are an agricultural tribe living in the Nilgiri Hills of southwestern India. They speak a language resembling Kanarese, a Dravidian dialect, and are said to be descended from Kanarese colonists from Mysore. In physical type, however, they more nearly resemble the neighboring Todas and Kotas than Kanarese. In terraced fields which are carefully cultivated and manured, the Badagas plant in rotation bearded wheat, barley, and onions. The women do much of the field work, while the men work elsewhere as plantation coolies or artisans. Although the Badagas provide the dairying Todas with grain, they have their own cattle and buffaloes, and, like the Todas, maintain dairies under celibate priests. Every Badaga family has a barter relationship with a Kota family, from which it receives its agricultural implements, pottery, and other manufactured articles in exchange for an annual present of grain and potatoes. The Badagas provide grain and a buffalo for Kota funerals, and Kota musicians play at Badaga marriages and funerals. The Badagas also pay an annual tax to their primitive neighbors, the Kurumba, whom they call in to serve as witch doctors. The Badaga village consists of a kinship group living in a row of huts under a single continuous thatched or tiled roof. The headman, the richest man in the village, is assisted by a council of elders in the administration of village affairs. Funerals are the occasion for a celebration, with music and dancing. A calf is led around the bier three times, to draw off the sins of the deceased; it then is considered a sacred animal which is allowed to roam freely, and may neither be sold nor killed. At long intervals an elaborate memorial ceremony for dead ancestors is held by all the Badagas of the Nilgiri Hills.

Brahui. In central Baluchistan, forming a compact population block between the eastern and western Baloch, are the Brahui tribes. They are of the same general physical type as the Baloch, though somewhat stockier in build, and their culture is similar to that of the Baloch. The Brahui are remarkable because their language belongs to the Dravidian family, which is spoken chiefly in peninsular India.

The Brahui are by their own tradition of mixed origin. Three tribes are said to be of Afghan origin; two others claim to be Mamassani and Kurds, respectively, from Iran; four are related to the Jats of India; and finally, two tribes are said to be descended from the original inhabitants of the country. The evidence suggests that the indigenous tribes gave their language to the western nomads with whom they became merged. The name "Brahui" goes back only to the eighteenth century, when the several tribes were organized into a confederation under a single khan. The Brahui formed two confederations, both under the leadership of the Khan of Kalat. They consider themselves of lower social status than the Baloch; the Khan's family normally speaks Balochi, and there is a tendency for the tribesmen to adopt that language.

Chenchus. The Chenchus, among the most primitive folk remaining in India, live in southeastern Hyderabad, in the hills called the Eastern Ghats. They are of mixed physical type and speak Telugu, a Dravidian language. In 1941 they numbered 3,865. Although many have taken up primitive agriculture or stock breeding, a few continue to live by hunting and collecting wild plants. Their weapons are the bow and arrow and the knife, and their only clothing a scanty loin cloth. Toddy, a fermented drink made from the flower buds of the mahua tree, is consumed in quantity at all feasts.

Gonds. The Gonds are one of the largest Dravidian-speaking tribes of India. They number some 3,000,000, of which a large part dwell in the Central Provinces. Between the fourteenth and seventeenth centuries most of what became the Central Provinces was ruled by Gond dynasties, but a movement of Hindu farmers into the best lands, beginning in the sixteenth century, gradually pushed the Gonds back into the hill lands which they now occupy. Members of the Gond tribe have developed into occupational castes of ironworkers, fortunetellers, minstrels, and carpenters, but a majority of the tribe are farm laborers. The Maria Gonds of Bastar, who may not be true Gonds, practice a crude, semi-nomadic jungle agriculture. The Gonds have shrines in their houses to the spirits of dead ancestors, to the cobra god, and to the sun, as well as to numerous guardian spirits. The tribal gods are worshiped at "the threshing-floor of the gods," an open space near each village. Up to the middle of the nineteenth century the Gonds practiced human sacrifice. Although the Gonds eat all kinds of meat, including snakes and ants, and are given to excessive drinking, they have not become village menials or scavengers, and so are not considered as impure in the Hindu caste scale as are many aboriginal tribes.

Irulas. The Irulas are a primitive Dravidian-speaking people who live in the Nilgiri Hills of southern India. They are short and flat-nosed, and have very dark skin. Many have taken service as plantation laborers, but in their native state the Irulas live by hunting and collecting, sometimes supplementing the game and wild yams by a crude agriculture. They obtain their digging sticks, as well as jewelry, from neighboring Kota tribesmen. Kurumbas, members of a Nilgiri tribe skilled in sorcery, are employed to officiate at Irula funerals.

Khonds. The Khonds are a Dravidian-speaking tribe who inhabit mountainous country in Bihar, Orissa, and northern Madras in eastern India. Although the Khonds in the neighboring plains have been Hinduized, those in the mountains avoid Hindu contacts. They live in scattered villages surrounded by fields, burning over new patches of jungle for cultivation every two years. The Khonds are known for the human sacrifice which they practiced until the middle of the nineteenth century. Some sacrificial victims were obtained as children by purchase, others voluntarily consecrated by father or guardian, while still others were the children of victims. They were kept, often for years, until they reached adulthood, and treated with great affection and deference. At least once a year one village or group of villages made a sacrifice, so that the head of every Khond family might annually obtain a shred of sacrificial flesh for his fields. After several days of ceremonial drinking and dancing, the victim, often stupefied by opium, was strangled or squeezed

to death, or sometimes cut up alive. Portions of the flesh were then quickly carried to all the villages, where a part was buried ritually by the village priest and the remainder apportioned among the householders to be buried in the field of each. This was supposed to assure growth to the crops and prosperity to the village. After human sacrifice was abolished, a buffalo or lamb was substituted in some places.

Kotas. The Kotas are a tribe inhabiting seven villages on the Nilgiri Plateau of southern India, who speak a Dravidian dialect similar to that of the Todas. The Kotas are as able cultivators as their neighbors, the agricultural Badagas, but they are especially known as an artisan tribe. The men are skilled blacksmiths, jewelers, carpenters, tanners, and rope-makers, while the women make baskets and crude pottery on a potter's wheel. Each Toda, Badaga, Irula, and Kurumba settlement in the Nilgiris has its Muttu Kota, a Kota family or families who provide manufactured wares in return for carcasses of cattle and buffalo, clarified butter, grain, and other produce. The Kotas, who have no meat tabus, eat the flesh of the carcasses and sell the horns and roughly tanned hides. The Todas keep buffaloes, but may not milk cows nor drink milk in their own village. The cows are milked by priests.

Kurumbas. The Kurumbas are a primitive tribe found in the Nilgiri Hills, Coorg, and Mysore in southern India. They depend on hunting and the collecting of wild plants for subsistence. They act as musicians for ceremonies among neighboring tribes, officiate as priests at Irula funerals, and are greatly feared by the Todas and Badagas for their supposed powers as sorcerers.

Oraons. The Oraons are a primitive Dravidian-speaking tribe found on the Chota Nagpur Plateau of east central India. They are a cultivating tribe, and claim to have introduced the plow to Chota Nagpur. Many of them have lost their land to Hindus, becoming tenant farmers or landless agricultural laborers. Because they will eat almost all foods except beef, they are considered impure by the Hindus. Where they live as laborers in Hindu villages, they are segregated and often are not allowed to draw water from the village well. When they live apart from the Hindus, their culture is similar to that of their neighbors, the Kolarian-speaking Mundas.

Todas. The Todas, like the Badagas, Irulas, and Kotas, live in the Nilgiri Hills in the western part of southern India. They differ both in appearance and in customs from most of the aboriginal tribes of India. Above medium height, they have a straight, narrow nose, and luxuriant wavy hair and beards. The Toda economy and religion is centered around the breeding and keeping of buffaloes; they scorn all agricultural work. The typical Toda village consists of three dwellings, a dairy temple, and a cattle pen where the buffalo calves are kept at night. The houses are shaped like a barrel sawed in half lengthwise. The curved walls are of bamboo covered with thatching, the straight front and back walls of solid blocks of wood. Only men may milk the buffaloes, and women are allowed to approach the dairy only at appointed times to receive buttermilk. In addition to the regular village herds, there are sacred herds of buffalo used for an elaborate ritual. At intervals the buffalo herds are conducted away from the village, partly to find new pastures, partly to visit certain sacred spots. Sometimes all the inhabitants of the village accompany their herds, sometimes only the dairymen and one or two male assistants. The sacred herds follow special paths over which no woman may walk. The Todas eat no meat. The grain which forms the basis of their diet is received as tribute from the Badagas. Wild vegetables are collected to supplement the grain and milk products. The Todas practice polyandry. When a girl marries a man, she also becomes the wife of his brothers. Formerly this was associated with female infanticide. As women have become more plentiful with the suppression of infanticide, polyandry has sometimes been combined with polygyny, with the result that a group of brothers may have two or more wives in common.

SEMITIC

Arabs. The name "Arab" is a Semitic word meaning "desert" or "dweller in the desert." In Biblical times the word had two usages: in the first it applied specifically to the nomadic dwellers of Arabia; in the second it was used to refer more generally to all inhabitants of the Arabian Peninsula. Under the Ommiad caliphate (661-749) of Islam the term "Arab" came also to refer to anyone who professed Islam and who spoke Arabic. These three meanings continue in use to the present day.

Arabia is, as far as is known, the home of the Semitic-speaking peoples of whom the Arabs are a branch. In the middle of the third millennium B.C., Semitic peoples began to move northward out of Arabia. First to go were the Akkadians, followed by the Babylonians and Assyrians. The first Arabians to develop a civilization known to modern scholars were the South Arabians. The kingdoms of Ma'in, Kataban, Saba, and Hadramaut, in turn or at times simultaneously, flourished as caravan centers from about the twelfth century B.C. to the early centuries of the Christian Era. When a route through the Red Sea replaced the overland trade route, their prosperity collapsed, although Hadramaut later developed trade relations by sea with Indonesia. In the fourth century B.C. the Arabic Nabataeans established a kingdom in north Arabia, with its capital and caravan center at Petra, south of the Dead Sea, and five hundred years later the Arab city-state of Palmyra flourished as far north as central Syria. The sedentary people of the

Agricultural worker of Khuzistan, Iran

southern kingdoms spoke and wrote in a South Arabic language. The Nabataeans and Palmyrenes kept their records in Aramaic, the language of a Semitic people who had preceded them northward into Syria. It was not until the sixth century of the Christian Era that North Arabic acquired its own system of writing, and only in the seventh century, when Mohammed founded the religion of Islam, did the north

Arabians achieve their great place in history. With the propagation of Islam, northern Arabs migrated eastward as far as India and Turkestan. In the west they moved through North Africa into Spain. Today, except for individual holy men and a few small colonies, no Arabs remain east of the province of Khuzistan in southwestern Iran. North Africa, on the other hand, has become an Arabic-speaking area. The north Arabs of Asia extend from southern Arabia to northern Syria, and from the Mediterranean to southern Iran.

It is estimated that only one fifth of the Arab popu-

Bedouin chief, a nomadic desert Arab

COURTESY OF THE
AMERICAN MUSEUM OF
NATURAL HISTORY

lation is nomadic. Nevertheless, since the culture of the sedentary Arabs is in general similar to that of the non-Arabs of the area, it is more appropriate to describe here the "dwellers of the desert," the nomads. The characteristic which distinguishes the Arab from other pastoral nomads is his preoccupation with the camel. The best known of the Bedouins, as the camel-breeding nomads are called, are the great Shammar and Anaze groups, some sections of which gradually moved northward between the end of the seventeenth and middle of the nineteenth centuries from their home in Nejd, in central Arabia, into Mesopotamia and Syria. They live the year round in pavilionlike tents of woven black goats' hair. While they take great pride in the purebred horses which they use both for raids and for war, their great wealth is in their vast herds of camels. Some of them, like the Rwala, one of the most powerful of the Anaze tribes, keep no sheep at all. Others leave their flocks with shepherds when they move into the true desert during the winter rainy season. They practice no agriculture, obtaining grain from sedentary villages near which they camp during midsummer. Camel milk, curds, and cheese form an important part of the diet, but camels are killed for meat only on special occasions. Next to camel and horse breeding, the chief occupation of the Bedouins is raiding and warfare. The horses which are trained with such care have no economic usefulness, but are kept for the greater mobility they give in raids. A chief's prestige, and that of his tribe, depends to a considerable extent on the ability to steal the camels of hostile tribes and protect their own herds from similar thefts. Weak tribes pay tribute to their stronger neighbors for protection. Often, through loss of camels and tribal pastures, tribes or sections of tribes are forced to turn to agriculture and become seminomads.

All the Anaze believe themselves to be descended from a

common ancestor. They are divided into northern and southern branches, and these in turn are subdivided into tribes,
of which the Rwala is the best known. The *âl* or *beni,* as
the tribe is variously called, is the largest kinship group having a sense of group responsibility for its individual members.
Outside the great tribal confederations, the *âl* is often an
independent unit, and not a subdivision of a larger social
grouping. A smaller and more closely integrated kin group
is the *ahl,* which includes a man's ancestors for three generations back, their descendants, and his own descendants for
three generations. The *âl* or *beni* is ruled by a sheik or chief
who usually inherits the position. Chieftainship does not
necessarily pass from father to son, but normally remains
within a definite family. If the chief is incompetent, however, the tribe may attach itself to a stronger leader in another family. Bedouins respect purity of descent to such an
extent that in effect they observe caste distinctions in marriage. The Shammar and Anaze consider themselves to be
of pure descent, and would not permit one of their members
to marry into a less pure tribe. Other tribes are ranked
according to the purity of descent, down to such outcast tribes
as the Huteim, living northeast of Medina, with whom no
Bedouin tribe would intermarry although they are a numerous tribe following the same camel-breeding pastoral life as
the true Bedouins. Negro slaves, who enjoy a great deal of
freedom, form a separate caste group in marriage, as do the
blacksmiths who work for the Bedouins. Bedouin women
go unveiled, and young people have ample opportunity to
become acquainted and choose their own mates. A man has
first right to marry his father's brother's daughter, however,
and his permission is required before she may marry anyone
else. Although the religion of Islam arose among the Arabs
and was first propagated outside Arabia by the tribesmen,
the Bedouins are very halfhearted Moslems except for the
Wahabis under Ibn Saud. The ritual daily ablutions and
prayers required by Islam are ignored. While they make
vows to Allah to gain a favor, they also believe in a malevolent
sun goddess and her benevolent spouse, the moon god. Sorcerers may receive power either from Allah's spokesmen or
from ancestral spirits.

The above describes in general the Bedouin Arab. Not
all Arab nomads are Bedouin, however. On the Tigris and
Euphrates plains most of the tribes are shepherds, with
no camels and few horses. They devote themselves to the
raising of sheep or, in a few cases, of cattle and buffaloes.
Because sheep are slow, and require more water than camels,
the shepherds do not venture out into the true desert but
follow a fairly restricted annual circuit in the pasture lands
between the rivers and the desert. Many spend the summer
in permanent mud or wattle houses along the river, where
they plant some crops. There is considerable variation from
group to group in the relative importance of herding and
agriculture. Some live in their black tents the year round;
if they plant crops, these are left to the care of hired laborers
during the winter while the group is migrating with the
flocks. At the other extreme, some groups devote most of
their time to agriculture and send the flocks out with shepherds. The shepherds are a peaceful folk and are usually
left unmolested by their warlike Bedouin neighbors, to whom
they pay tribute. In Syria some tribes have vast flocks of
sheep and goats and few camels, but sufficient horses to
protect their flocks. From Palestine southward into Arabia
there is a gradual increase in the numbers and cultural importance of the camel. Many tribes breed both sheep and
camels. A majority of these tribes, however, appear to be
seminomads rather than true nomads; that is, they main-

tain more or less permanent quarters during a part of the
year and plant some crops. There is a general tendency for
these seminomads to give increasing attention to their crops
at the expense of the herds until they finally become sedentary *fellahin,* or peasants, or drift along the caravan routes
into the cities.

One group of nomads in Arabia, the Sulubba, or Sleb,
differ so greatly in culture from both the shepherds and the
Bedouins that their Arabic origin has sometimes been
questioned by various authorities. The Bedouins look on
them as Arabs, however. The Sulubba are to be found in
the area extending southward from Damascus and Mosul
to Jauf on the west and the Persian Gulf on the east. Such
few horses or camels as they may own appear to be of recent
acquisition. Traditionally they live by hunting the gazelle
and other game, and by breeding a particular type of white
ass. Their small tents, and often their clothing, are made
of skins. They migrate north and south following the movements of the gazelle which they hunt. Although they usually
set up their tents in hidden ravines, out of sight of the
Bedouins, they sometimes visit Arab camps to beg. The men
occasionally work as tinkers for the Bedouins and are often
employed as guides because of their intimate knowledge of
the steppe land which they roam.

Assyrian Christians. The Assyrian Christians are a Nestorian community found principally in northern Iran and
in Turkey. Until approximately the middle of the nineteenth
century their history was roughly parallel to that of the
Chaldean Christians. Before World War I the Assyrians had
established a cultural center at Urmia (now Rezaiyeh) in
northwestern Iran. During the war they fought both the
Turks and their Kurdish neighbors, with the result that
Urmia was destroyed and the Assyrian community scattered.
Few remain in Iraqi Kurdistan, where their active hostility
to Islam culminated in a massacre of them in 1933.

Chaldean Christians. The modern Chaldean inhabitants
of northern Iraq and Iran are unrelated to the ancient Chaldeans who flourished in southern Mesopotamia. They are
descended from the Assyrians, a Semitic people who reigned
in northern Mesopotamia between the fourteenth and seventh
centuries B.C. They are called Chaldeans because they are
members of the Chaldean Uniate Church, an offshoot of the
Nestorian Church, which acknowledges the pope, but otherwise follows its own ritual and is governed by its own
religious hierarchy. In the centuries after the Assyrians were
defeated by Babylon in 607 B.C., many gradually drifted from
their homeland in the northern Mesopotamian plains into
the highlands of Kurdistan. They were converted to Christianity sometime during the early centuries of the Christian
Era. In A.D. 409 they were permitted by a decree of the Sas-
sanian Persian emperor, Yezdigird, to establish semiautono-
mous Christian governments in Kurdistan. When, in 480,
many eastern Christians seceded from the Imperial Church of
Byzantium and founded an independent Nestorian Church,
the Assyrians were among them. In 1552 there were two
claimants for the patriarchate of the Nestorian Assyrians.
When the claimant favored by the highlanders succeeded to
office, the plainsmen appealed to the pope, who appointed
the second claimant "Patriarch of the East." Thus two rival
congregations arose among the Assyrians, the Church of the
Mountains (Mar Shimun) and the Church of the Plains
(Mar Elia). Around the beginning of the eighteenth century
the Church of the Plains was brought more closely under
the authority of Rome, which gave it the name of the Chaldean Uniate Church. In 1845 the Ottoman government
recognized the desire of the Chaldean plainsmen to establish

a *millet,* or administrative unit, distinct from that of the highland Nestorian Assyrians. This completed the separation of the two Assyrian communities.

During World War I both the Chaldeans and Assyrians, as the Nestorians continue to be called, were persecuted as Christians by the Turks. In addition, the highland Assyrians became involved in a struggle with their Kurdish neighbors. As a consequence, both Chaldean and Assyrian communities were scattered. In 1947 there were estimated to be about 83,000 Chaldeans in Iraq, 50,000 of them in the Mosul district, the remainder in Baghdad, Basra, and Kirkuk. About 8,000 were to be found in Turkey and 4,000 in Iran. The language of the early Nestorian Christians was Aramaic, a Semitic language. The Chaldeans and Assyrians speak and write in Syriac, a modern descendant of Aramaic.

Hadramauts. Hadramaut, on the southern edge of the Arabian Peninsula, has a mixed population. Most numerous are the so-called Bedouins or Qahtani, who consider themselves purer Arabs than either the Yemeni or the northern Arabs. Some are sedentary, living in the skyscraper castles which are characteristic of Hadramaut and Yemen, and which are large enough to house a whole subtribe. Some are nomadic camel-breeders; a greater number are seminomadic. But neither nomads nor seminomads use the black tent of the northern Arabs. While on migration they sleep under the stars, surrounded by a ring of camels. When not traveling, the prosperous live in houses, the poor in caves. The Bedouin men wear only a narrow brown loincloth, but supplement this scanty costume by dyeing their bodies blue with indigo. The women wear trousers and shirt, and adorn their faces with yellow turmeric, touches of henna, and red, green, and black paint. The Hadramaut population also includes the so-called Arabs proper, the tribes of which claim an origin in Yemen or north Arabia. These Arabs live in the towns, under tribal sultans. The rich derive their income from fields cultivated by slaves, or from remittances sent by merchant relatives in Singapore or Batavia. Often when these merchants return home they bring with them Malayan wives and children. Poorer members of the Arab group are artisans and servants. Their ancestors are said to have come individually from north Arabia. A small, highly influential group of north Arabians are the Sayyids, who claim descent from Mohammed through his grandson Hussein. They are looked on as sacred, and their touch is believed to cure. Only they can safely act as mediators in the constant intertribal wars which occupy the tribal sultans. The slaves who cultivate the fields for the Arab landowners are the descendants of Negroes brought from Africa. They are not only employed as field laborers, fishermen, and boatmen, but also constitute the personal armies and real strength of the tribal sultans.

Yemeni. The people of Yemen, an isolated kingdom in the southwestern corner of the Arabian Peninsula, differ in many ways from the Arabs of north Arabia. They are city and town dwellers, not nomads, and devote themselves to agriculture and trade. Around the towns are vineyards and orchards of peaches, apricots, pomegranates, and other fruits. On the plateau, fields are carefully cultivated to yield crops of wheat, barley, lentils, and peas. Along the terraced escarpment which leads from the plateau down to the coast, the coffee is raised which forms Yemen's chief export, as well as *qat,* a narcotic to which the city-dwellers are often addicted. Along the coastal plain much of the land is too sandy for cultivation. Camels are the chief pack animals used for the transportation of goods, but they are not as numerous as among the northern Arabs, and they are never ridden.

Horses are owned only by the wealthy. The principal animals are the hump-necked cattle, which provide the farmers with beef, milk, and hides, as well as being used for ploughing; goats; and fat-tailed sheep. Donkeys are used for riding. Only upper-class townsmen wear the flowing kaftans of the north Arabians. In the cities the women completely veil their heads in lengths of brightly printed cloth; elsewhere they go unveiled. On the plateau farmers wear knee-length kilts and wide-sleeved shirts of blue cotton, while their wives wear shirts and baggy pantaloons of the same material. On the warm coastal plain a loincloth suffices for all but aristocratic men.

The Yemeni are divided into a number of class or caste groups, each of which forbids its members to marry outside the group. At the top of the social ladder are the Imam, who is at once high priest and king, and the royal family, who claim descent from Mohammed through his grandson Hussein. Also included in this top class are the sayyids, who also claim descent from Mohammed, though not through the same line as the Imam. Below this Mohammedan stratum, drawn from north Arabia, are the tribes. Although the Yemeni are sedentary, the tribal structure is similar to that of the pastoral nomads to the north. The tribe is a group of related families who trace descent in the male line, under the leadership of an hereditary sheik. The tribe is divided into smaller kinship groups, each of which occupies a separate castle or fortified village and has its own hereditary sheik. In the large towns is found a third and lower social class, called the Beni Khoms ("Sons of the Five"). Traditionally the Beni Khoms belong to the five trades of bloodletter, barber, bath attendant, butcher, and tanner. Actually they include a number of other occupations. Each occupational group has its own sheik. As a symbol of their degraded social position, the Beni Khoms are forbidden to wear silk or to ride a horse. The fourth and lowest class consists of the primitive Hojeri, who are found only along the southern escarpment and on the coast. They are usually Negroid in physical type, and of unknown origin. They own no land and have no political rights, but are not slaves. There is also to be found in Yemen a considerable Jewish colony. Most of the Jews live in San'a and the other cities, where they are engaged as merchants and craftsmen, although there are a few Jewish agricultural communities. The Jews are subject to the disabilities first imposed on nonbelievers by the Ommiad Caliph Omar II, who ruled from 717 to 720, but they have the privilege of being governed by their own chief rabbi and are not liable to military service, as are the Moslem Yemeni.

Although Yemen is a strongly Moslem state, the people have a number of cult practices which are non-Islamic. Sacrifices of black cattle are made to the spirits of springs, rocks, and trees, and in an annual fertility festival black heifers are led through the village streets, their horns festooned with flower garlands. Illness, which is believed to be caused by evil jinn, is cured by special jinn doctors or shamans. One particularly malevolent jinni causes madness, and can be dispossessed of his victim only by an especially trained shaman, assisted by a curing society made up of former patients.

SINITIC

Chinese. *Hakkas.* The Hakkas are found in the southeastern Chinese provinces of Kwangtung, Kwangsi, Kiangsi, and Fukien. Although their customs are essentially Chinese, they live in communities apart from other Chinese and maintain a separate social identity. Their language is a distinctive and somewhat archaic one, more closely related to northern Chinese dialects than to those of their present neighbors. The name Hakka, which means "strangers" or "guests," implies that they are immigrants into the regions which they now occupy. According to the traditions and

Chungking tailor

CNS PHOTOS
PAUL GUILLUMETTE

family records of the Hakkas, their ancestors were living in western Shantung at the end of the Chou dynasty. During the struggles which brought the Ch'in dynasty to power in the third century B.C., the Hakkas fled south of the Yellow River into Honan, and later moved more gradually into Kiangsi, Chekiang, and Fukien, where they settled. A second southward movement took place at the end of the T'ang dynasty (A.D. 618-907), and a third during the Sung dynasty (A.D. 960-1279). The Hakkas appear to have drifted into Kwantung as wandering farm laborers during the Sung and succeeding Mongol periods. The Hakkas are farmers who usually occupy hilly and less fertile districts and eke out their rice crops with sweet potatoes. Their women never adopted the Chinese custom of foot-binding and consequently have been able to work in the fields. Polygamy is uncommon among them, and girls are seldom sold as slaves and concubines, as is often the case among impoverished Chinese. The Hakkas have added to their meager income as farmers by further migration. While the women remained to take care of the farm and family, the men have migrated as laborers to foreign countries. The Hakkas form one of the chief elements of the overseas Chinese population in southeast Asia and Indonesia, and Hakkas are to be found as far afield as Ceylon, South Africa, the West Indies, California, and South America.

Miao. The Miao people are found in Yünnan, Szechwan, Kweichow, and Kwangsi provinces of China, in the interior of Hainan Island, and in northern Tonkin and Laos in French Indochina. The relationship of the Miao language to other languages in the area has not yet been determined. The Miao do not possess a true script, but use crude symbols for written communication. The Miao live in the mountains, usually between 3,000 and 6,000 ft., and clear and burn over fresh fields as the old ones become exhausted. At intervals the whole village moves to another mountain slope and builds new houses of tamped earth or plank. Their staple crops are maize and buckwheat. They raise pigs for market, horses, buffaloes, oxen, chickens, ducks, and geese. Riding horses are treasured, and never sold. Once a year, after the harvest, parties of men go down to market in the plains.

Marriages are arranged by families without consulting the young people, and take place before the planting season. The young couple lives sometimes with the groom's family, sometimes with the bride's. Burial of the dead is preceded by the sacrifice of several buffalo or oxen, and by a three-day feast. The Miao have village chiefs, who direct the planting, and sometimes a tribal chief. The Miao believe in a creator god, and also in nature spirits which must be placated. Shamans are called on chiefly to direct funeral ceremonies and to insure success in time of war.

San Tak. In the Fukien and Chekiang provinces of southeastern China are found remnants of a pre-Chinese population known variously as San Tak, Sia Ming, Sia Bo, Yü, and sometimes, incorrectly, as Hakka. They live in isolated hill communities apart from the Chinese and, although Mongoloid, differ considerably from the Chinese in appearance. They have a tradition of having sprung from the marriage of a princess with a dog, a tradition which they share with the Nias of Sumatra, the Kalangs of Java, and certain tribes of Formosa, Hainan, and the Ryukyu Islands. They are said to worship an image of their dog-headed ancestor on the first day of the New Year. The San Tak raise sweet potatoes and a little tea and hill rice, clearing new fields every two or three years. Many of the men have adopted Chinese dress, but the women wear an elaborate headdress which distinguishes them from the Chinese.

Tai. The Tai people number approximately 20,000,000 and are spread over a large area of southeast Asia. There are an estimated 9,850,000 in Siam, slightly over 1,000,000 in Burma, and the remainder are found in French Indochina, on the island of Hainan, and in the southern Chinese provinces of Yünnan, Kweichow, Kwangsi, and Kwangtung.

Paint streaks on the face of this Formosan girl indicate her married status.

TRIANGLE PHOTO SERVICE

Those in Burma are called Shan, and the Siamese and Lao call themselves Thai, rather than Tai. The Tai in southeast Asia began to move out of their home in China around the eighth century, and groups are still drifting southward. The Tai are Mongoloid in physical type, with straight black hair, slightly slant eyes, high cheek bones, and usually flat noses. In addition to the Thai and Shan, they are divided into a number of groups, such as the White, Black, and Red Tai, the Tai Nua, Lu, Youn, Tho, and Khamti, who are distinguished from each other by the colors of their costumes. The Tai are agriculturists. Those living in the river valleys have irrigated rice fields, while those in the mountains burn over new fields every two or three years for digging-stick cultivation. Water buffalo are used for plowing, and oxen, poultry, and pigs for sacrifices and food. The women weave cotton and silk cloth, and many of the tribes have their own metal workers. Tattooing is widespread. The Tai are Buddhists, but some continue

A Haiphong docker, Indochina

their ancestor cult and belief in multiple souls and spirits which must be propitiated.

Khamti. The Khamti are a Tai-speaking people found in northern Burma and, since the nineteenth century, in northeastern Assam. They live in great multifamily houses raised from the ground on piles. While some work in the fields, most engage in hunting or trade. Buddhist priests of the Burmese Hinayana persuasion have more influence than chiefs, and all boys are educated in the village temple schools.

Lao. The valleys in the middle Mekong River in French Indochina and the upper Menam River in Siam are inhabited by a Tai people, the Lao. The Yun, or western Lao, live in Siam. The Lao kingdom was founded in 1353, and in the early years of the eighteenth century was divided into two kingdoms, Luang-Prabang and Vien-Tiane. The Lao are a fairly sophisticated people. Many engage in trade while their land is cultivated by hired laborers or, formerly, slaves. Rice is the staple food of the Lao, who season it with fresh or salt fish paste. Fowl, eggs, and buffalo meat are eaten only at festivals, when rice beer or distilled rice liquor is also served. The Lao are skilled hunters of elephants, which they kill for ivory or meat, or capture to train. Craftsmen make glazed pottery and tiles, and cast copper. Villages own long dugout racing canoes, gilded and lacquered, which are brought out for festivals. Their rectangular pile houses of bamboo, often multifamily, are surrounded by large gardens. Lao society is divided into two classes: nobles, who are descendants of former kings, and commoners. The two groups do not intermarry. Slaves formerly were obtained by capture or purchase. The Lao are Hinayana Buddhists but retain some Hindu deities who have become identified with animistic cult spirits. The temples serve as village schools and as hostels for travelers.

Tangut. Tangut is the name of two tribes in different parts of Asia. One was a Tibeto-Burmese-speaking people who established the kingdom called Hsi Hsia which, from A.D. 982 to its overthrow by Genghis Khan in 1227, ruled over the Ordos Region, the present Kansu province, and part of modern Shensi in western China. The name Tangut is thought to be of Turkic origin. The present-day Tangut

are a pastoral, nomadic people, Tibetan in speech and customs, who dwell in northeastern Tibet. The Tangut live in pavilionlike tents of woven goat- or yak-hair, unlike their Mongol neighbors who dwell in dome-shaped felt-covered tents. They practice no agriculture, but obtain by barter the meal which is a staple of their diet.

Tibeto-Burmese. *Abor.* The Abor are a warlike people who inhabit the Abor Hills, on the borderland between Assam and Tibet. They speak a language belonging to the North Assam branch of Tibeto-Burmese.

Bodo. The Bodo are a Tibeto-Burmese-speaking people found in western Assam. They are divided into the Mech and Kachari, along the Bhutan border; the Garo, who live in the Garo hills east of the Khasi tribes; the Chutiyas, who live in two small tracts northwest of the Naga Hills; and the Tipperas, who are found north of Chittagong in eastern Burma. The Koch are a Garo group who have become partially Hinduized. The Kacharis raise rice in irrigated fields and keep pigs in numbers. Fishing supplies an important element in their diet, and they do considerable hunting. The village organization of the Bodo is democratic, and there are no formal chiefs. Among the Garo a man may acquire a special social status of *nokma* by giving a series of ritual feasts. Such a *nokma* often presides when the villagers assemble to debate issues of concern to the community. There is no special priesthood; village elders officiate at religious ceremonies. Among the Garo, heads were formerly taken in war, and the skulls kept in the house of the *nokma*.

Bot. The Bot or Bhotiya, as they are called in India, are the Tibetan peoples who live along the Indian-Tibetan borderlands from western Nepal through Ladak, in northern Kashmir. The Bot on the lower slopes of the Himalayas

Tibetan Lama with prayer wheel

live in sedentary villages of two- and three-storied stone houses of the Tibetan type, and the mountainsides are carefully terraced to enable the people to cultivate barley and such other crops as will grow in the harsh climate. At a higher altitude, between 9,000 and 12,000 ft., agriculture becomes subordinate to stock-breeding and trade. The Bots dwelling here are seminomads, alternating between winter homes in the lower valleys and summer residences high on the bleak mountainsides. Groups of related villages usually migrate in bands, and while on the march they live in tents. The women remain in their summer or winter villages and occupy themselves with weaving various woolen materials, for which they have a high reputation. While some of the men go out with the flocks of sheep and goats, others make trading expeditions into Tibet in the summer and down into India in the winter. In Ladak the Bot, like the Tibetans, practice polyandry; one woman marries two or three brothers. In other parts of the area polygamy is common, men having several wives. The Bots of Ladak, and most of the semi-nomads elsewhere, are Lamaist Buddhists. Many of those farther south have become Hinduized and employ Brahman priests for their ceremonies.

Kachins. "Kachin" is the name applied by the Burmese and Europeans to a people who called themselves Chingpaw. The Kachins are one of the largest and best-known tribes of Burma, and are the chief inhabitants of the region north of Myitkyina, though they are also found in other areas. They have a state of their own within the Burmese Union. In World War II the Kachins, alone among the Burmese, succeeded in repulsing the Japanese north of Myitkyina, later fighting under American leadership. They speak a Tibeto-Burmese language related to Naga, Kuki-Chin, and Lolo.

Kuki-Chin. The Kuki and Chin are Tibeto-Burmese-speaking people of Mongoloid physical type found in the

TRIANGLE PHOTO SERVICE

Heavily armed head man of a Burma hill tribe, with his wife and three daughters

Chittagong Hill tracts of eastern Bengal, the Chin Hills of western Burma, and the Lushei Hills, Manipur, and Cachar, in Assam. Those in Assam entered their present territory in recent times. The Old Kuki, the first arrivals in Assam, were pushed into the borderland in the eighteenth century by the Lushei Kuki, who in turn moved westward under pressure from the Chin. The Chin occupy permanent villages. The Lushei and Kuki, who practice a seminomadic jungle agriculture, move their fortified hilltop villages every four or five years. Hunting and fishing provide an important

part of their diet, for the mithan, or domesticated bison, are killed only for special feasts. Each village is an independent unit. Among the Lushei and Chin the hereditary village chief theoretically has absolute power over his people, although in practice dissatisfied subjects may move to another village if the chief becomes too autocratic. Among the Old Kuki the elected chief is primarily a priest, while administrative matters are dealt with by a council of village elders. The Lushei chiefs have *boi,* or dependents, who work for the chief in return for support and protection. The more democratic Old Kuki have neither. All the Kuki-Chin tribes believe in a benevolent creator god, but propitiatory sacrifices are made chiefly to the numerous malevolent spirits who threaten the welfare of the tribe.

Lahu. The Lahu are a Tibeto-Burmese-speaking people of Upper Burma, related to the Mosos and Lolos.

Lepchas. The Lepchas are a Mongoloid people believed to be the original inhabitants of Sikkim, a state on the southern slopes of the Himalayas between Nepal and Bhutan. Although the country has been largely taken over by migrants from Nepal and Tibet, about 25,000 Lepchas remained in 1931, equally distributed between Sikkim and the neighboring Indian district of Darjeeling. The Lepchas speak a Tibeto-Burmese language and live in isolated farmsteads or clusters of not more than four houses. Their two-roomed houses, built of bamboo, are raised from the ground by stone piles. They now have vegetable gardens and irrigated rice terraces, but these are recent innovations. Wet rice was not introduced until about 1920. The older type of digging-stick forest cultivation is still practiced. The Lepchas raise cattle, used for milking and plowing, and pigs and goats, which provide food and sacrifices. The watchdogs are regarded with affection. According to their own tradition, the Lepchas were nomadic hunters until the seventeenth century. While hunting has become a sport rather than an important source of food, an elaborate ritual is still observed by all who hunt. Each village has a headman who is elected by the villagers from the family of the preceding headman. He advises the people, looks after the poor, entertains visitors, and in general acts as the village father. The position of administrator of village affairs is held by a representative of each family in turn. The Lepchas are Tibetan Buddhists, but in addition to lamas there are shamans who are called in at every occasion to deal with the supernatural spirits which inhabit the Lepcha world.

Lolos. The Lolos are a Tibeto-Burmese-speaking people scattered through the mountains of Szechwan, Kweichow, Yünnan, and probably eastern Sikang provinces in China, and in upper Tonkin and Laos in French Indochina. There are about 2,000,000 Lolos. Their stronghold is the Ta Liang Shan plateau in southwestern Szechwan, which the Chinese administration has been unable to penetrate. Lolo is the name of one tribe, but has been applied by Europeans to all members of the group. Closely related in language and culture are the Moso, Lisu, and Sifan. Those Lolos living in the plains have been strongly influenced by their Chinese neighbors. Those in the mountains live in thatched plank houses and practice a shifting agriculture, in which maize, buckwheat, sweet potatoes, and beans are the chief crops. In addition to goats, which are very numerous, the Lolos raise cattle, donkeys, horses, pigs, and sheep. Except for one group which makes cheese, milk is not used. Distilled spirits are made from various cereals and drunk at meals. Clothes are woven from hemp, and some groups make felt. Among some tribes there is a caste distinction between Black Lolos, nobles of "pure" descent; White Lolos, commoners; and slaves, who are not of Lolo origin. These groups do not intermarry. Elsewhere "Black" is applied to Lolos uninfluenced by Chinese culture and "White" to those who have adopted Chinese customs. Among others, the distinction between Black and White is a matter of costume, after the fashion of the Red and White Tai. Except in war, when an elected chief is given full authority, village leadership is usually informal. Around the Ta Liang Shan Plateau, however, there seem to be hereditary feudal chiefs. The Lolos believe in a benevolent creator god and have a weakly developed ancestor cult, but their religion is chiefly animistic.

Mishmi. The Mishmi are a group of seminomadic tribes living on the Tibet-Assam border. They are Mongoloid in physical type and speak a language of the Tibeto-Burmese stock. Women and slaves cultivate the soil, and the men hunt.

Mosos. The Mosos are a Tibeto-Burmese-speaking people found in Yünnan province in China and in northern French Indochina and Burma. Their language is closely related to that of the Lolos, and they appear to represent a branch of the Sifan.

Nagas. The Nagas live in the hills of eastern Assam and in the Upper Chindwin region of Burma. They show some Mongoloid traits in physical type, speak dialects of a language which belongs to the Assam-Burmese branch of Tibeto-Burmese, and in culture are akin to the peoples of southeast Asia.

The Nagas are divided into a number of distinct tribes, of which the best known are the Angami Nagas, the Semas, Rengmas, Lhotas, and Aos. While the Naked Rengmas and some of the Angamis raise wet rice in carefully cultivated terraces, most of the Nagas practice a crude digging-stick horticulture in jungle clearings. They keep mithan, a domesticated bison, for trade and food for feasts, and cattle to provide meat. Pigs roam everywhere; dogs are eaten, although in general they are well treated. The Lhota Nagas are particularly skillful hunters. Since the Nagas are a warlike people, the villages are usually built on hilltops and surrounded by stockades with outlying ditches, pitfalls, and sharpened bamboo skewers to retard the advance of an enemy. The Angamis live in sturdy wooden houses built on the ground, with a high front gable which is often carved, while the Ao and Lhota Nagas have lighter bamboo houses raised from the ground on piles. The Naga tribes are divided into clans or extended kinship groups, several of which may be represented in a single village. A man is expected to marry a girl from another clan, and usually from another village. The Ao Nagas have a girls' dormitory in each village, where the girls receive young men at night. Other tribes do not have the dormitory, and among the Sema Nagas a girl who has an affair before marriage brings a much lower bride-price than her chaste sister. Among the Angami Nagas the chiefs have little authority, since most decisions are made by the clan council of elders. Among the Sema, on the other hand, the hereditary chief has great authority. The commoners owe him service and may not leave the village without his consent, although in return the chief looks after their welfare, finds wives for them, and supplies food in times of scarcity. The Nagas practice headhunting. A young man may not marry until he has taken a head, and the heads of all enemies killed in battle are displayed, among some groups, suspended from special trees outside the village, among others, in dwellings, on the porch of the chief's house, or in the bachelor's house. Although the heads are looked on chiefly as a proof of valor, the killing of victims is also considered to bring prosperity to the community.

OTHER LINGUISTIC FAMILIES

Caucasian. The Caucasus Mountains, because of their height and inaccessibility, have acted as a haven for several ancient peoples and cultures. A majority of the population speaks languages of the Caucasian language family, which is quite generally believed to have extended through the highland region from Anatolia into the Iranian plateau. Among the inhabitants are also peoples speaking archaic dialects of Iranian and Turkic. In religion some of the people are Moslems, others Greek Orthodox Christians, while a few are Roman Catholics. Whatever their ostensible religion, most groups retain the gods and cult practices of their pagan ancestors. In economy, most of the Caucasian peoples are stockbreeders who practice agriculture, though some are primarily agriculturists and a few are pastoral nomads. The trait shared by almost all these peoples has been a fierce desire to maintain their independence from outside control. Brigandage and blood feuds were common into the twentieth century.

Among the south Caucasian peoples are the Georgians, Mingrelians, Lazes, and Svanetians. The Georgians, or Grusians, are the most numerous, with a population of 2,362,000 in 1941. Though the three formal religions of the area are represented among the Georgians, they still seek rain by a pagan ceremony in which girls are harnessed to a plow. The Svanetians, whom the Greek geographer Strabo described in the first century B.C. as the brave and ferocious Swans, still carry on feuds which make useful the high watchtowers under which their small stone houses are clustered. Their most important deity is a pagan hunting god. The Lazes, who live on the southeastern shore of the Black Sea, have been Christians since the sixth century of the Christian Era and have been under Turkish rule since the beginning of the nineteenth century. They are good sailors, and also practice agriculture.

The north Caucasian language group includes the Chechen, Ingush, and Khevsur. The Chechen and Ingush believe that the dead continue to live in the tombs which are kept near the family home. The Khevsur, because of the medieval chain armor and swords which they used into the nineteenth century, are reputed to be descended from a band of European crusaders who were stranded in the Caucasus in the Middle Ages. There is no real basis for this belief. The Khevsur live in one-room houses, which they share with their oxen, goats and sheep. There are separate houses, apart from the dwellings, where women go for childbirth. At religious ceremonies sheep are sacrificed, and beer or arrack, a distilled liquor, is drunk.

The northwest branch of the Caucasians is represented by the Cherkess (Circassians) and Abkhazians. The Cherkess, who call themselves Adighe, migrated to Turkey in large numbers after the Russian conquest of the Caucasus, and there is also a Circassian colony in Transjordan. There remain 125,000 Cherkess proper in the Adygei and Cherkess Autonomous Regions in the Caucasus, although the Kabardin branch of the Cherkess are estimated to number 172,000 in the Kabardino-Balkarian Autonomous Soviet Socialist Republic and the Cherkess Autonomous Region. The Cherkess formerly practiced only stockraising, being famous for their horses, and a little agriculture. For the worship of their pagan gods they had no temples, but made sacrifices in sacred groves. They had a rigid class system, with princes, nobles, commoners, and serfs. Many of the Kabardin princely families are descended from Georgian, Armenian, and Mongol immigrants into the region. A fourth branch of the Caucasians comprise the Lesghins and Avars of Daghestan, in the eastern Caucasus. The Avars raise excellent grapes. In the spring, they have their first plowing ceremony, before the fields may be cultivated, and in the fall a ritual picking of grapes which precedes the harvest.

Solid brass coils weighing more than twelve pounds encircle the neck of a woman of the Palaung tribe, Burma. Worn since childhood, the ornament has pressed in her collar bones and lengthened her cervical vertebrae.

TRIANGLE PHOTO SERVICE

Kolarian. A number of tribes of India speak a language of the Kolarian stock, which is unrelated to either Indo-Iranian or Dravidian, the two great language stocks of India. A suggested relationship with the Mon-Khmer languages of Burma and Cambodia remains to be proven. The Kolarian-speaking peoples in general are referred to as "Kol," and include the Munda, Ho, Santal, Savara, and Korku tribes. "Kol" is also applied specifically to a Kolarian-speaking tribe dwelling along the Vindhya Kaimur Plateau in central India.

Ho. The Ho are a Kolarian-speaking tribe found in the Singhbum district of southern Bihar in India. Their culture is similar to that of the Mundas.

Korku. The Korku are a Kolarian-speaking tribe found in the Central Provinces and Berar, Bhopal, and Chota Nagpur, in India. They are separated from the Mundas and other Kol tribes by an expanse of Dravidian tribes, and differ somewhat in culture from their eastern relatives. They live by hunting and a crude jungle agriculture, or hire out as farm laborers. Their hereditary village priests are employed by neighboring Hindu villages to propitiate local deities.

Mundas. The Mundas are a numerous aboriginal people inhabiting the Chota Nagpur Plateau of east central India. They are short and sturdy in build, long-headed, and have a dark brown skin, thick lips, broad nose, and scanty beard. They formerly practiced a seminomadic form of agriculture in jungle clearings, but are now sedentary agriculturists who cultivate their fields with cattle-drawn plows. The Munda villages consist of a few homesteads built on high points above the rice fields. Around each homestead is a garden in which vegetables are grown. Each village has a house where unmarried youths sleep, and some have a girls' dormitory. An open space serves for meetings, both formal and informal, of the villagers. Adjoining the village is the cemetery, and a short distance away the sacred grove which serves as the village temple. The Mundas are divided into totemistic kinship groups, or *kili,* of people descended from a common ancestor. Each *kili* has a special tabu regarding the animal or plant after which the *kili* is named or with which it is associated. Into the nineteenth century, and in some regions until later, groups of from ten to twenty-five

neighboring villages were organized into *parhas,* or communes. Each *parha* was governed by a group of officials which included an hereditary chief, a tax collector, and a village priest. The dead are cremated, after which the bones are collected and kept for an annual ceremony in which the bones of all villagers who died during the year are buried. The Mundas believe in a supreme and benevolent deity, Sing Bonga, whose name is invoked before every important religious ceremony, but who receives sacrifices only in times of calamity. Each village has its guardian spirits which, in return for proper sacrifices made in the sacred groves, will insure health and prosperity. The family ancestors act as household guardians to whom the head of the family gives ritual attention. The spirits of people who died a violent death are malevolent, and must be appeased, and there are many nature spirits who may be either good or evil, but who must also be propitiated.

Santals. The Santals are a large Kolarian-speaking tribe found in western Bengal, northern Orissa, and the Santal Parganas of eastern Bihar in India. In language, physical type, and customs, they resemble closely the Mundas of Chota Nagpur, to whom they are related.

Savara. The Savara are a hill tribe found in the Eastern Ghats, in the northern part of the Madras Presidency in India. Their speech is Kolarian, which has been strongly influenced by the Dravidian Telugu language. The Savara, unlike many Kolarian-speaking tribes, are industrious agriculturists who raise wet rice on hillside terraces and cultivate their fields with cattle-drawn plows. They do not usually own the land, but pay rent to absentee landlords. The Savara are divided into several subcastes which are chiefly occupational in nature. In addition to agricultural work, one subcaste does the weaving for the tribe, another the iron work, a third makes the grain baskets, and a fourth the pottery, which is used both for cooking and for household fetishes. One group has no occupational specialization, but holds itself superior to the others because its members do not eat beef. Each village community has two hereditary chiefs. One, called "the great man," is the chief proper; the second acts as high priest. The presence of both is essential at all weddings, funerals, and harvest festivals, and they preside over the council of village elders, which deals with such matters as property and marital disputes. The dead are cremated, after which the bones are buried and a miniature spirit hut is erected over them. Every second year the village holds a great feast to the dead. After twelve days, in which the people fast during the day and dance and feast at night, there is a great slaughter of buffaloes, and all the houses in which death has occurred are burned. They believe that after this ceremony the souls of the dead can cause no more trouble.

Mon-Khmer. The peoples of Mon-Khmer speech include the Jakun, Sakai, and Semangs of the Malay Peninsula; the Khasis of Assam; most of the Moi tribes of French Indochina; the Chams of French Indochina and Siam; the Nicobar Islanders; and the Palaung and Wa, two tribes found in the Salween River basin of Burma and Siam. Mon proper is spoken by the Talaing on the Gulf of Pegu in Burma, and Khmer by the Cambodians.

Chams. The Chams are remnants of a people that once owned a great kingdom during the first millennium of the Christian Era in what is now Annam and French Indochina. After centuries-long warfare with the Annamese and Cambodians, Champa ceased to exist as a political power in the fifteenth century. It is survived by some 20,000 Chams in Annam and by some 90,000 who have at various times migrated to Cochin China, Cambodia, and Siam. The Chams are taller than their neighbors, the Annamese and Cambodians, and have fine, often wavy, hair. The language of the Chams is of a mixed character, containing Mon-Khmer as well as Indonesian elements. Some scholars have stressed its Mon-Khmer affinities, while others prefer to place it with the Indonesian branch of the Malayo-Polynesian family. The Chams live in large multifamily pile houses, usually beside a river or lake, and cultivate paddy rice. Plows are drawn by water buffalo, and goats and chickens are raised for use as sacrificial animals. The villages are governed by an elected council of notables. The Chams differ from both Annamese and Cambodians in that they trace descent and inherit property through the mother rather than the father. Some of the Chams in Annam are nominally Hindus, the remainder, Moslems; all retain much of their pagan religion. A part of their fields is cultivated ritually in a "rice mother" cult like that found among Indonesian tribes. They believe that a person has several souls, and give considerable attention to propitiating nature and ancestral spirits. Shamanistic priestesses obtain their power for curing and foretelling the future from a moon goddess.

Jakun. Jakun is the general name given to the primitive proto-Malaysian tribes of the Malay Peninsula, of which the best-known groups are the Besisi, Mantra, Benua, and Blandas. The Land Jakun, or Orang Bukit, vary somewhat in culture from group to group, but in general they are seminomads who hunt, fish, and collect wild fruits and vegetables in addition to practicing a crude agriculture. Their tiny one-room houses, usually raised from the ground on piles, are abandoned when a community shifts to clear new plots in the jungle. For travel on the rivers, they use dugout canoes. In hunting the Jakun use the blowgun, with poisoned arrows, and the spear. Formerly the Jakun made bark cloth; the men wore a loincloth, the women a cloth wrapped around the waist and reaching to the knee. Now they wear garments of cotton trade cloth, often made after the Malay fashion. Groups of jungle villages are united under a chief called *Batin,* who arbitrates disputes referred to him by the village chiefs, acts as judge, and officiates at weddings. The Sea Jakun, called Orang Laut, live among the coastal islands off the Malay Peninsula.

Khasis. The Khasis are a group of tribes in the Khasi and Jaintia Hills of west central Assam. They are the only group in Assam who speak a Mon-Khmer language. The Khasis raise wet rice in the valley bottoms, but sow the seeds broadcast in the mud rather than transplanting seedlings, as is done in Burma. They also grow oranges and lemons, and it was from the Khasi Hills that oranges were carried by Arab traders to Syria, whence they became known to the western world. Unlike most of the tribes of Assam, the Khasis trace descent through the mother, and the mother is head of the family. When a girl marries, the husband takes up residence with her family or, among some tribes, continues to live at his mother's home and visits his wife only at night. Groups of Khasi villages are organized into small states under an hereditary *siem,* or ruler, who acts on the advice of a council. The Khasis have no tradition of headhunting, but formerly practiced human sacrifice.

Moi (Kha). In the mountains of French Indochina are a number of tribes called Moi by the Annamese, Kha by the Lao. They differ somewhat in physical type, language, and culture, differences which seem to indicate varying absorption or influence of a number of Lao, Cham, Australoid, and Negrito elements. The languages of some of the tribes (Radè, Djaraï, and a few others) are predominantly Indonesian, while those of the majority of the tribes belong to the Mon-Khmer family. Except for one primitive hunting group the Moi practice a crude digging-stick agriculture, but cultivated plant foods are supplemented in their diet by game and some fish. In hunting, the characteristic weapon is the crossbow with poisoned arrows. Such oxen, buffalo, pigs and fowl as are kept are used chiefly for sacrifices. Many tribes weave cotton cloth, although a few still make bark cloth. Some smelt iron ore; others make tools from imported iron. Crude pottery is not uncommon. The men wear loincloths, the women, wrap-around skirts tucked in at the hips. Most groups live in multifamily pile houses. The Radès and Djaraïs, who resemble Chams closely, have matrilineal succession and inheritance, and when a man marries he lives with his bride's family. Most of the tribes, however, are patrilineal and patrilocal. Villages are governed by a village chief, usually hereditary, advised by the village elders. The members of a tribe unite only for common action in war. The dead are buried in wooden coffins, and a roof or little house is built over the grave for the soul. The Moi believe that not only people but animals also have several souls, some of which survive after death. On all occasions animals are sacrificed and rice wine libations made to placate potentially harmful spirits. Some tribes sacrifice human slaves.

Mon (Talaing). The Mon were among the first peoples of southeastern Asia to adopt the culture of India, particularly Hinayana Buddhism. It was they who converted the Burmese, and later the Thai, to that religion. Mon is the name they themselves use, while they are known to the Burmese as Talaing. The Mon formerly occupied the Irrawaddy River delta, the region on the lower Sittang and Salween rivers, the region now called the Amherst District in the northern part of Tenasserim, and, until the tenth century, the Menam Plain in Siam. In the seventh or eighth century they also conquered the upper Menam Valley and maintained themselves there until the end of the thirteenth century. A large number of the Mon were exterminated in a long struggle with the invading Shans and Burmese. To-day, except for scattered groups in Siam, they survive as a people only in the Tenasserim area, where in 1931 they numbered 305,394.

Nanai child of the Soviet Far East

SOVFOTO

Nicobarese. The Nicobarese live on the Nicobar Islands, which lie between Sumatra and the Andaman Islands in the Bay of Bengal. Two thirds of the population is found on Cay Nicobar, the northernmost island of the group. The people are below average height, have straight to wavy hair, and are slightly Mongoloid in appearance. The Nicobarese cultivate gardens and keep pigs and fowl. Their diet includes coconut, a kind of breadfruit, yams, sweet potatoes, fish, and wild fruits. Pork and fowl are eaten only at feasts. Their thatched houses stand on piles from five to eight feet from the ground, and the villages are kept remarkably clean. The Nicobarese make excellent canoes. The best are made on the island of Chowra, where the people have a monopoly on the making of big racing canoes, as well as of pottery. Annually, the people of the other islands make an expedition to Chowra to obtain the year's supply of pottery, as well as such racing canoes as are required. The Nicobarese have no larger social unit than the village. The man who commands respect because of superior intelligence and ability acts as informal headman, and justice is administered by an assembly of elders.

Palaung. The Palaung are Mon-Khmer-speaking people found in the Shan States of Burma. The Palaung, Wa, Lawa, Lamet, and other tribes of the region speaking related dialects totaled 176,024 in 1931. Because of language similarities they are sometimes grouped with the Wa, but culturally they are very different. The Palaung are Buddhist and far less primitive.

Sakai (Senoi). The Sakai are a primitive hill people who live in the Malay Peninsula south of the Semangs. They are short and brown-skinned, with wavy hair, and speak a Mon-Khmer language. Some are nomadic, living by hunting and collecting and finding shelter in tree huts or caves. Others have adopted a seminomadic jungle agriculture and live in huts raised from the ground on piles. The chief weapon of the Sakai is the blowgun with poisoned arrows. The men wear a loincloth, the women a brief wrapper of bark cloth. The tribe has great fear of death; when someone dies the encampment is burned down and the group moves to a new spot. The Sakai are adopting the culture of their proto-Malaysian neighbors, the Jakun, and frequently intermarry with members of the latter group.

Semangs. The Semangs are primitive Negritoes who live in the mountains of the Malay Peninsula. They are divided into bands, each with its customary territory, within which family groups wander. They encamp in palm-leaf shelters, and live by hunting small game and collecting such vegetable food as wild yams and durian fruit. Most of their utensils are made from bamboo and other jungle plants. Their characteristic weapon is the blowgun, with poisoned darts, although this has been replaced in recent years by the bow. The men wear bark loincloths, the women girdles of twined leaves.

Wa. Most of the Wa are found in northeastern Burma. Some have become Buddhist, but a large block, particularly the so-called Wilde Wa, are pagans and headhunters, and have a very archaic culture which in many respects resembles that of the Nagas of Assam and northwestern Burma.

Paleo-Siberian. In far northeastern Siberia are a number of tribes with similar cultures which are frequently grouped under the name of Paleo-Siberian. They include the Chukchi, Koryak, and Kamchadal, who speak closely related languages; the Gilyak, whose language is said to be related to those spoken by American Indians of the northwest coast; and the Yukaghir and Chuvantzy. Those of the Chukchi, Koryak, Yukaghir, and Chuvantzy who live on the coast have permanent settlements and engage in the hunting of sea mammals and in fishing for a livelihood. They formerly lived in half-underground earth huts. Those sections of the tribes dwelling inland are reindeer breeders who

in summer range along the barren tundra of the far north and in winter seek shelter in the edge of the woodland belt to the south. They do not milk their reindeer as do the Tungus, Altaians, and southern Samoyeds. The reindeer of the Paleo-Siberians are only half-domesticated, and while the Chukchi and Koryak use them for drawing sledges, in general the reindeer are chiefly of importance for the meat and hides they supply.

Until the establishment of the Russians in eastern Siberia the Kamchadal, Gilyak, and some of the Yukaghir were primitive nomads, who hunted in the woodland forests dur-

SOVFOTO

A Chukchi, inhabiting the Chukotski Peninsula in northeastern Siberia, hunts sea mammals on the shore of Zima Bay.

ing the winter and moved down the rivers in spring to catch the fish which formed an important part of their diet. The reindeer breeders also depend to a lesser extent on hunting, fishing, and the collecting of wild roots to supplement their diet. All the Paleo-Siberians breed dogs, which they use for drawing sledges, and also as sacrificial animals. The inland people live in skin-covered tents which are either conical or of a clumsy dome shape. Paleo-Siberians live in small hamlets or nomadic camps of related families. There is no larger social unit, although intermarriage takes place between neighboring villages and camps. The Paleo-Siberians believe that all nature is animated. There are "masters" of the rivers and forests, and a multitude of other nature spirits, some good, some malevolent, to whom sacrifices are made. The Koryak and Kamchadal believe certain mountains or cliffs to have been the ancestors of their tribes. Among the Chukchi and Koryak a member of each family acts as shaman in family ceremonials, in addition to the more general professional shamans who are able to cure sickness, foretell the future, and work magic through the power of spirits who are believed to enter the body of the shaman and speak and act through him. Both men and women may be shamans.

Unrelated Tribes. *Ainu.* The Ainu are believed to have occupied at one time most of the Japanese Archipelago, from which they were gradually pushed northward or absorbed by the ancestors of the Japanese. The few remaining Ainu inhabit northern Hokkaido, Sakhalin, and the southern Kurile Islands. Because they have abundant beards and body hair, unlike the surrounding Mongoloid peoples, they are called "hairy" Ainu. Formerly, they lived in half-buried earth huts, as did the Paleo-Siberians of the Asiatic mainland. The coastal people are fishermen; those inland, hunters. Both raise some millet, but also collect wild fruits and vegetables. The dog, which they train to help in fishing, is their only domestic animal. Material for clothes is woven from elm bark fiber on a belt loom. In marriage either the girl or the man may propose, and the young couple live with the family of whichever made the proposal. The mother's brother, not the father, is the real head of the family. The Goddess of Fire and the "Divine Husband" are guardian deities of the home, and in every ceremony libations of millet beer are made to ancestor and guardian spirits. The Ainu are famous for their bear cult, in which they bring up a bear cub with the care and affection

One of the Ainus, original inhabitants of Japan

given a child, then kill it ritually and eat its flesh in a feast in which the bear itself is supposed to participate.

Andaman Islanders. The Andaman Islands, in the Bay of Bengal, are inhabited by a primitive Negrito people. They are very short, with black skins and frizzly hair, and have been shown to be related to the Semang of the Malay Peninsula. The Andamanese are grouped into a number of small seminomadic bands which own the territory within which their camps are located. They practice no cultivation, but depend on the fruits of hunting and collecting. Affairs of the village are regulated by its older members. A man or woman may acquire influence in the village because of personal quali-

Ainus give their morning salutation

ties which win the respect of the villagers, but his or her position is purely informal. Young people are allowed sexual freedom, but once a marriage is blessed with children, it is usually permanent. The Andamanese supernatural world is peopled with spirits of the jungle and sea who are believed to be ghosts of the dead who cause sickness and death. Nature deities include the moon and his wife, the sun; the southwest monsoon; and, most important in the latitude of the Andamans, the northeast monsoon, called Biliku or Puluga, who is regarded as a female deity in the northern islands, a male in the southern. In 1931 only 460 Andamanese survived.

Hunzas. In the high Pamir Mountains, beside the arduous caravan route which leads from Kashmir to Chinese Turkestan, live the Hunzas and Nagirs. They speak a language, Burushaski, which has no known relatives. They are Caucasoid in physical type, and probably represent an ancient population element which has been preserved only in this rugged mountain haven. The Hunzas are agriculturists. They painstakingly terrace the mountain slopes to obtain tiny fields for their crops, and build long aqueducts in order to water them. Barley, millet, wheat, and buckwheat supply the ingredients of their mixed-grain bread, and dried apricots form an important element in the diet. Cows furnish a small amount of milk, and a cheese is made from goat's milk. The Hunzas live in villages of flat-roofed houses, with three or four houses set within a walled courtyard. In the summer the young men go into the mountains to herd the sheep, goats, and cattle. The people are divided into clans, several of which may be represented in one village. All the marriages in the country take place on one Wedding Day, which is held in mid-December each year. The Hunzas are governed by an hereditary Mir. They have long been Shia Moslems, and toward the end of the nineteenth century they were converted to the Ismaili Shia sect. Nevertheless they retain many non-Islamic customs. In the spring there is a great sowing festival, during which the Mir ritually sows the first barley and plows the first furrows. The end of the harvest is marked by a thanksgiving prayer and feast, and at the winter solstice is another great ceremony. Dancing is an important part of every ceremonial occasion.

Although the Nagirs are closely related to the Hunzas both in language and culture, the two groups are traditionally unfriendly toward each other. The fact that the Hunzas are now Ismailis while the Nagirs remain orthodox Shias has intensified their aloofness. Intercourse is limited to occasional trading expeditions and to intermarriage between the royal families of the two peoples.

Min Chia. The Min Chia are a non-Chinese people who inhabit the Tali Plain of Yünnan province in China. Linguistic relationships have not yet been established. Their economy is based on wet-rice cultivation. They raise cattle, and are one of the few peoples in China who use milk. There is considerable specialization in occupation. Those living around the lake near Tali are fishermen. In one locality a crude pottery is made, in another iron pots, and in a third wooden furniture. These manufactured products are brought to Tali for sale at the fairs which are held at frequent intervals. Although the Min Chia are under Chinese administration, they avoid Chinese courts of justice, settling all matters among themselves. Village schools are held in the temples. The Min Chia pantheon includes a Buddhist goddess, a Taoist god, and several local deities. Cult attention is also given by the family to its ancestors, and by each village to its founder.

Yeniseians. The Yeniseians are an almost extinct people

found along the eastern tributaries of the Yenisey River in Siberia. They speak a language of unknown affiliations, and show non-Mongoloid physical traits. The Uriankhai, who now speak a Turkic language, are of Yeniseian origin, as are some of the Altaian Tatars. The one surviving group to retain its own language and culture into the twentieth

Ude of the Soviet Far East wearing ancient national costume

SOVFOTO

century is the Ket, also known as Kott or Yenisey Ostyak. They are woodland hunters who live in tents of birch bark.

See also ALANI; CHAMARS; CHUVASH; DOMS; EPHTHALITE HUNS; EVENKI; GOLDEN HORDE; GHUZZ TURKS; HSIUNG-NU; INDONESIAN PEOPLES; JATS; KHITAN; PARSIS; PECHENEGS; RAJPUTS; SAKA; SARMATIANS; SART; SCYTHIANS; YUE-CHI.

E. E. B.

ASIR [asi'r], a province of the kingdom of Saudi Arabia, extending for 230 mi. along the southeastern shore of the Red Sea, between the province of Hejaz and the independent imamate of Yemen. Geographically it consists of two parts, a coastal plain about 40 mi. in width which continues the Tihama Plain of Hejaz, and a mountainous area which rises abruptly to about 9,000 ft. and then descends gradually to about 3,600 ft. to join with the Nejd Plateau. It comprises about 40,000 sq. mi. and has a population of about one million. The lowland plain is hot and barren, but the inland hills and wadis enjoy a temperate climate and abundant rainfall, 10 to 12 in. annually, the highest in Arabia.

Most of the inhabitants live as farmers in the mountain area. Najran, in the southeastern corner of the province, is one of the richest agricultural areas of the kingdom, and the largest wheat crops are harvested there. In this area the slopes of the mountains are carefully terraced to prevent erosion. Unfortunately, the area is almost inaccessible from the sea; the roads, actually paths, are impassable even for donkeys. Asir has the traditional Arab crops, but, in addition to wheat, it is outstanding for sorghums, which reach 17 ft. in height. Like Yemen, it is famous for its coffee. Most of the cattle of the kingdom is raised in Asir; angora goats are found only in this province. Industry is limited to basket weaving and pottery making.

Only two cities are of significance. Jizan is the best port of the province; on its southern edge rock salt is still mined in primitive fashion, and timber is brought from the interior for the construction of dhows. Abha, the capital, a city of 15,000, is located in the very fertile Wadi Abha, about 7,000 ft. above sea level. Many buildings at Abha have horizontal layers of schist jutting out about 18 inches from their walls at 18-inch intervals to prevent the erosion of the mud and stone walls during the heavy rains.

Both King Ibn Saud of Arabia and Imam Yahya of Yemen sought control over the area, but in 1926 Asir sheiks asked for and received the protection of the former. In 1932 the province was formally included in the kingdom of Saudi Arabia. Two years later Ibn Saud again had to fight Yemenite efforts to control the area, while British naval forces kept the Italians from intervening on behalf of Yemen. H. C. K.

ASK [a'sk], in Nordic mythology, first man created by the Gods, and father of the human race. In the *Voluspa,* one of the Eddic poems, it is recounted how the gods Odin, Hœnir, and Lodur (Loki) had discovered the forms of Ask and Embla (ash and elm) lying inanimate. (According to some accounts they had been fashioned out of ash and elm trees by dwarfs and had been abandoned until the gods found them and gave them life.) Odin gave Ask and Embla life and soul, Hœnir gave them reason, and Lodur gave them heat and color. "Spirit gave Odin, Thought gave Hœnir, Blood gave Lodur and color fair." Thus did Ask and Embla become the first man and woman created by the gods. According to other versions, it was Odin and his brothers, the gods Vili and Ve, who had found the two trees by the seaside, and from them had created Ask and Embla. Some scholars believe that Hœnir and Lodur were but different names for the gods Vili and Ve, brothers of Odin. All accounts agree, however, that Ask was created from an ash tree and Embla from an elm. E. B. A.

ASKIN, JOHN (1734-1815), British trader with the Indians and merchant of the Old Northwest, was born in northern Ireland in 1734 of Scotch descent, served in the British army in America during the Seven Years' War, and before 1761 became a merchant in Albany, N. Y. He frequently visited Detroit and Mackinac as one of the first British traders in the Northwest after the fall of New France. He also established himself in the transport business, and furnished Montreal traders in the region with supplies. In 1780 Askin removed permanently to Detroit, and became an important factor in the Indian trade. Because of his British sympathies, after Detroit was transferred by the British to the United States in 1796 he became dissatisfied, and in 1802 moved across the river into Canada. The *John Askin Papers,* published in 1928 and 1931, are valuable for the information they contain concerning the fur trade in the area. Askin died at Walkerville, Ontario, Canada, in 1815.

J. J. T.

ASMA'I, AL- [ælæs'mæi] (740-828), Arabian scholar and writer, whose full name in Arabic was al-Asma'i 'Abd-al-Malik ibn-Quraib, was born in Basra in 740 of a poor family. He studied diligently under various teachers in his youth and eventually became sought after as a tutor. Al-Asma'i was remarkable for his memory and for his mastery of the languages of the desert peoples. He took care to collect ancient poetic works so that they might be preserved for posterity. His fame became so great that Harun al-Rashid, greatest of the caliphs of Baghdad, engaged him as tutor to his son, and al-Asma'i became the intellectual leader of the court at a time when Baghdad was the center of Arabic culture. Most of the scholar's works deal with subjects rather arbitrarily and are never exhaustive. He is noted for a history of the kings of Arabia and Persia before Islam. Among his few surviving works are *Book of Distinction, Book of the Wild Animals, Book of the Sheep,* and *Book of the Horse.* In his later years he retired

ASMARA, CAPITAL OF ERITREA

to Basra, having accumulated considerable wealth, and died there in 828. A. S. M.

ASMARA [ɑsmɑ'rɑ], the capital city of Eritrea, in northeastern Africa, about 75 mi. southwest of Massaua. It is situated at 7,765 ft. above sea level and has a mild climate with the temperature fluctuating between a maximum mean of 73.6° F. and a minimum mean of 55° F. The annual rainfall averages about 20 in. with the rainy season in the summer months. Asmara presents the appearance of an Italian rather than an African city because of its impressive public buildings and handsome villas. The native population has been relegated to its own quarters. A narrow-gauge railroad runs east to Massaua on the Red Sea and northwest through Cheren to Agordat. Good roads lead to Massaua, Cheren, and, in Ethiopia, Addis Ababa and Gondar. In 1935 an overhead cableway was installed from Asmara to Massaua to carry material for war against Ethiopia. Under this same impulse Asmara was endowed with industrial facilities and machine shops which, after the British conquest of Eritrea in the spring of 1941, proved useful in World War II to the Allies in the Middle East theatre and along the trans-African air route to India. A considerable number of American technicians made Asmara their headquarters as did the British Military Administration.

Before the Italian occupation in 1889, Asmara was only a small village. After the Italian failure to conquer Ethiopia, which culminated in the battle of Aduwa (Mar. 1, 1896), Asmara became the seat of the civil administration of the colony. Between 1936 and 1941 it was the capital of the *governo* of Eritrea, which included the Tigré and Danakil provinces of Ethiopia. In 1951 the United Nations approved the federation of Eritrea with Ethiopia, a plan accepted by Eritrea and Ethiopia in 1952.

Approximately 50,000 of the city's population prior to World War II were Italians, the rest being for the most part natives speaking Tigrinya and professing Coptic Christianity. There were also small communities of Sudanese, Arabs, Indians, and Greeks. Pop. (est. 1940), 85,000. R. G. W.

ASMODEUS [æ'zmodi'əs], or Ashmedai, a figure in the demonological lore developed in post-Biblical Jewish tradition. He is probably related to the Persian Aeshma deva, the demon of rage and lust, and the name itself seems to come from the Persian word meaning covetous. He also appears as the king of demons, sometimes being identified with Satan himself, sometimes, by the Greeks, with Apollyon. He is a prominent figure in the Talmud, especially in the legends concerned with Solomon, and was often known as the spirit of marital unhappiness or jealousy. In the apocryphal book of Tobit is the story of his passion for Sara, the daughter of Raguel. She was married seven times, and on each occasion Asmodeus killed her husband on their wedding night. Tobias finally drove the demon away by burning the heart and liver of a fish. R. F.

ASNIÈRES [ɑ'nyɛ'r], a suburb in north central France, northwest of Paris on the left bank of the Seine River, in the department of Seine. It is a center of numerous villas and the headquarters of Parisian boating and rowing enthusiasts. The Château of Asnières contains many excellent examples of the paintings of François Boucher. Boats and perfumes are the principal manufactures. Pop. 1954, 77,838.

ASO [ɑso], a volcanic mountain 5,492 ft. high, in the central part of Kyushu, the southernmost island of Japan. Mount Aso is a dormant volcano noted for its large crater which has an area of about 100 sq. mi. The volcano has been dormant for so long that many thousand Japanese have moved into the crater area.   J. E. F.

ASP, a name confusingly applied to two very different poisonous snakes, a large cobra and a small viper. Cleopatra's asp, the asp of classical writers, was the snake now miscalled

COURTESY OF THE AMERICAN MUSEUM OF NATURAL HISTORY

English viper, Vipera berus, one of the European asps

the "Egyptian" cobra, *Naja haje,* which actually occurs from Morocco and Arabia to South Africa. Its neurotoxic venom kills relatively painlessly, so the asp was customarily used for humane executions in ancient Alexandria. Today "asp" generally designates one of the European vipers, especially the long-snouted *Vipera ammodytes aspis.*   M. G. N.

ASPARAGUS, a genus of the family *Lilaceae,* native of Central Europe and the steppes of Russia. A herbaceous perennial, its species, numbering 150, include about twenty developed for ornamental purposes. Of the garden varieties, the most common is Asparagus *officinalis,* known for centuries before being domesticated. The woody, thick-rooted crowns bear buds which produce tender spears. These are cut when 6 to 8 in. high. Feathery branches, tall and ornamental, result as the stems mature. Short leaf-like branches develop and function as leaves when the stalk reaches a height of 18 to 20 in. Plants may be either pistillate or staminate. Wind carries pollen from the male to the female plant, on which red berries, containing one to eight seeds, are formed.

Generous feeding, care, and good, friable soil are essentials to the growth of the choicest stalks. Limestone and decaying vegetable matter provide the richest soil, which must be well drained and deeply dug. Eastern or southern exposure should combine with ample space between plants. Sandy limestone soil in northern states produces the best yields.

In areas where the plants are not dormant part of the year, small spears are produced, and plantations short-lived. Only large one-year roots should be planted; these are grown from seed. In commercial fields, plants are set 6 to 8 in. deep, 2 ft. apart in rows 4 to 5 ft. apart; in gardens, depth may be 4 in. and distance between plants as little as one foot each way. No stalks should be cut until the third year. In the north, beds may continue productive for thirty to fifty years.
                    V. A. T.

ASPARAGUS BEETLE. The common asparagus beetle is *Crioceris asparagi,* which is blue-black with reddish thorax and connected yellow spots on the elytra. The adults hibernate in sheltered places, emerging about the time the asparagus shoots appear. They begin feeding and egg-laying at once. The larvae attack the tender shoots and later feed on the leaves and stems. The adult of the spotted asparagus beetle, *Crioceris 12-punctata,* has similar habits, but it delays egg-laying until the berries form, the larvae living in the berries and moving from one to the other as the food supply becomes exhausted. The eggs of *C. asparagi* are laid in conspicuous rows along the leaves and stems; those of *C. 12-punctata* are laid on their sides along the branches, and, being green in color, are not readily seen.   C. H. Cu.

ASPARAGUS FERN, *Asparagus plumosus,* a climbing plant of the lily family, a native of South Africa, widely grown by florists for its decorative greenery. The stem branches into fine, feathery sprays of delicate, soft, ferny green; the leaves reduce to small scales, as in the closely related garden asparagus. There are several horticultural varieties.   J. C. Wis.

ASPASIA [æspe′sha; æspe′zha] (c.470-410 B.C.), the mistress of Pericles, was a native of Miletus, Ionia, who came to Athens to establish a school of rhetoric. She appears to have been a brilliant and educated woman whose intellectual charms moved even Socrates and whose physical charms Pericles found irresistible. Pericles, already the father of two sons, divorced his Athenian wife and lived openly with Aspasia. The product of this union, the younger Pericles, was not eligible for Athenian citizenship until his father

THOME · DR. LASCOFF

ASPARAGUS OFFICINALIS

FROM A PAINTING BY JEAN LÉON GÉRÔME   COURTESY OF THE NEW YORK PUBLIC LIBRARY

ALCIBIADES IN THE HOUSE OF ASPASIA

secured the repeal of his own law of 451 B.C. requiring Athenian parentage on both sides. Like other close associates of Pericles, Aspasia was often attacked by his political opponents. She was accused of maintaining a group of slave girls for hire as courtesans. It is said that she was tried for impiety, but that Pericles undertook her defense and secured an acquittal. Aspasia died in Athens.   T. B. J.

ASPEN, the name distinguishing several widely distributed species of poplars having tremulous leaves. The de-

sign of the leafstalks, slender, flattened, and very flexible, allows the thin, papery foliage to respond to the slightest air current. The American aspen, *Populus tremuloides,* called also quaking asp, has the widest range of any American tree, from Labrador to the Yukon and south to Kentucky, and along mountain ranges to Mexico. This aspen and the related black willow, *Salix nigra,* are the only native trees spanning the continent from Maine to California. Commonly a small tree, the aspen may grow to 100 ft. It is important in natural reforestation. Appearing as the first growth on burnt-over land, it develops quickly, protecting the young stages of more permanent trees. The soft, white wood is cut chiefly for wood pulp. The flowers appear in drooping catkins before the leaves, with male and female flowers on separate trees. The European aspen, *P. tremula,* is a forest tree throughout northern Europe, and in Asia reaches the Arctic Circle. The trembling of the aspen leaves has been the subject of many literary references. J. C. Wis.

ASPERGES [æspɜ'rdzhiz] (Lat., thou shalt sprinkle), a ceremony used in the Roman Catholic Church before High Mass. It is named after the first word of the antiphon (Psalms 1:9) intoned by the celebrant before he sprinkles the altar, clergy, and people with holy water. The instrument used for the sprinkling is sometimes called an asperges.
    N. J. T.

ASPERGILLOSIS. *See* MYCOSES.
ASPHALT. *See* ENGINEERING MATERIALS.

ASPHODEL [a'sfodɛ'l], a small genus, *Asphodelus,* of annual and perennial herbs of the lily family, natives of the Mediterranean region and India. They have clumps of narrow basal leaves and stalks with clusters of white flowers.

COURTESY OF U.S. FOREST SERVICE

ASPEN, POPULUS TREMULOIDES

The white asphodel, *A. albus,* with flower-stalks 3 to 4 ft. tall, is among the best known of those grown for ornament. The asphodel of the ancients is the yellow asphodel, *Asphodeline lutea,* which, in Greek mythology, was the flower of the dead. The name was also applied to the wild English daffodil, and the word daffodil is derived from it. Some believe the asphodel of the Greek poets to be the poet's narcissus, *Narcissus poeticus.* J. C. Wis.

ASPIDISTRA [æ'spɪdɪ'strə], a genus of lily, having about six species, native to eastern Asia. Vigorous roots send up stiff, shining strong-veined leaves, and interesting, brownish flowers, about 1 in. across, are borne close to the ground. The common aspidistra, *A. elatior,* with leaves 3 to 4 in. wide and 1 to 2½ ft. long, thrives in Florida, especially near water. In the North, it is much grown as a house or decorative plant. As it will endure very unfavorable conditions, it is often called cast-iron plant. A variegated form with white striped leaves is interesting, as no two leaves are ever exactly alike. J. C. Wis.

ASPIDIUM [æspɪ'diəm], a botanical name formerly given to a group of several hundred species of true ferns, mostly tropical. They are now divided among three genera, *Cyrtomium, Dryopteris,* and *Polystichum.* The male fern, *Aspidium,* or *Dryopteris filixmas,* yields a drug, aspidium, long used as a remedy for tapeworm. The marginal shield fern, *Dryopteris marginalis,* also is a source of the drug.

Many beautiful woodland ferns of North America are included in *Dryopteris* and *Polystichum. Cyrtomium* includes the popular house holly fern, *C. falcatum.* G. M. Sm.

ASPLENIUM. *See* SPLEENWORT.

ASPROMONTE [ɑ'spromo'nte], a mountainous mass forming the southern end of Calabria, and attaining an elevation of 6,400 ft. in Montalto. It is popularly described as the toe of Italy. Aspromonte is marked by a series of four terraces, *piani,* indicating successive stages of its emergence from the sea in this area, long noted for its severe seismic disturbances. Aspromonte stands in a zone of generally light precipitation — about 20 in. at Reggio Calabria. Because of its altitude, however, it receives an annual rainfall aggregating 50 in. on the peaks. There is thus during the rainy winter months a heavy runoff, and this has worn deep but short watercourses, *fiumaras.* During the summer these are nearly or completely dry. Snow covers the summit of Aspromonte from November to June. The higher slopes were once covered by a vast forest of pines, beeches, and other hardy trees, but deforestation has now denuded wide areas, and only the beeches remain. The lower slopes are dotted with towns and villages, but these go no higher than the 3,000-ft. level. In a few towns on the southern side of the massif, Greek is still spoken. Aspromonte was the scene, in August 1862, of the brief combat between the troops of the Italian government and the band collected by Garibaldi to march on Rome. R. G. W.

ASQUITH, HERBERT HENRY, 1ST EARL OF OXFORD AND ASQUITH [a'skwɪth] (1852-1928), English statesman, was born at Morley, in Yorkshire, Sept. 12, 1852. Educated at the City of London School and at Balliol College, Oxford, he was admitted to the bar in 1876 and become a queen's counsel in 1890, having made his reputation as junior counsel to the Parnell Commission in 1889. He entered Parliament in 1886 as a Liberal and was home secretary under W. E. Gladstone from 1892 to 1895. When Joseph Chamberlain raised the question of tariff reform, Asquith campaigned for free trade and as a result was made chancellor of the exchequer under Sir Henry Campbell-Bannerman from 1905 to 1908. In his final budget he introduced old age pensions. In 1908 he became prime minister, and in August 1911, as the result of the rejection of the budget, his Parliament bill abolished the veto power of the House of Lords. His Irish Home Rule bill was not so successful; he allowed himself to be intimidated by Ulster's threat of resistance by force; his difficulties were postponed by the outbreak of World War I in July 1914, and the bill was not enforced. In 1915 the Asquith cabinet was vigor-

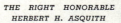

THE RIGHT HONORABLE HERBERT H. ASQUITH

ously attacked for the shortage of munitions and the naval failure at Gallipoli. A coalition cabinet proved no more successful, and the resignation of David Lloyd George and other members brought about its fall in December 1916. In the 1924 election Asquith was defeated, and in 1925 he entered the House of Lords as Earl of Oxford and Asquith. In 1926 he split finally with Lloyd George and the majority of the Liberal Party. He died at his country home in Oxfordshire, Feb. 15, 1928. E. R. A.

ASS, *Asinus,* or donkey, a small relative of the horse and the zebra. Its very long ears vary in length from 7 to 12 in. The animals are 3½ to 4½ ft. high at the shoulder. Their thick, rather long hair is buffy or gray, and they have short, upstanding, black manes. The back stripe and tail tuft are black. The progeny of a stallion ass and a mare horse is the mule.

Asses were domesticated by the Egyptians and other people of the eastern Mediterranean region as early as 4,000 B.C. The characteristics of ill-treated, poorly bred, domesticated asses and mules have caused their names to become synonyms of stupidity and obstinacy. Carefully bred and cared for, asses and mules are intelligent draft and saddle animals.

When left in the wild state, asses are swift runners and are extremely alert and wary. Sociable animals, they live in family groups or small bands, or occasionally in herds of one hundred or more individuals. They inhabit arid regions, usually sandy plains or stony, rolling hills, and feed on herbs, grass, and the leaves and twigs of shrubs. Wild asses are still common in many parts of eastern Africa, western Asia, and Mongolia. Small numbers remain in western India, but asses have been exterminated in the wild state from northern Africa, southern parts of the Soviet Union, and much of Asia Minor. V. H. C.

ASSAB [asɑ'b], a small port on the Red Sea coast, in southern Eritrea, near the Strait of Bab el Mandeb, about 270 mi. southeast of Asmara. Assab is located in an arid and unproductive region but its bay is protected by a number of offshore islands. It was the first point on the African continent acquired by Italy, having been purchased by Giuseppe Sapeto in 1869 for the Rubattino Steamship Company, one of the predecessors of the Italian Line. Assab was intended as a coaling station for Italian shipping on the routes to the Orient, which had been opened up by the completion of the Suez Canal. It was regarded as an Italian counterpart to the British position at Aden, 150 mi. to the east. The territory held by the company was expanded in 1879-1880, and in 1882 it was taken over by the Italian government, but Assab never became the commercial center that had been planned. A treaty of friendship between Italy and Ethiopia in 1928 envisaged the cession of free port facilities to the latter in Assab and the construction of a modern highway to Dessie and the Abyssinian plateau. But it was only after the conquest of Ethiopia in 1936 that steps were taken to improve the harbor of Assab, to build a modern city on spacious and ambitious lines, and to construct the road to the interior. The Fascist government planned to make Assab the principal outlet for central Ethiopia, but World War II put an end to this project. After the defeat of Italy in 1943 the Ethiopian government laid claim to Assab. Before the war there were about 1,000 Italians included in the city's population, which was composed mostly of Danakil. Pop. (est. 1949), 10,000.   R. G. W.

ASSAI. *See* Musical Terms.

ASSAM, a constituent state in northeastern India, bordered on the southeast by Manipur and Burma, on the southwest by Pakistan, on the northeast by West Bengal, and on the north by Bhutan and Tibet. It covers an area of 53,261 sq. mi. Consisting largely of the Brahmaputra River valley, the state comprises the entire western course of the river and is surrounded by mountain ranges on all sides. On the north rises the eastern section of the great Himalayan range, and on the south lies the Assam Range, consisting of a series of hills, named from their peoples, running southwest from the Himalayas between India and Burma and broadening out into the Naga Hills in the central section, and then curving southward to form the Cachar and Lushai hills. A spur running west from the Naga Hills includes the Jaintia, Khasi, and Garo hills, the western extension of the latter causing the southward bend of the Brahmaputra. This spur is about 200 mi. long, with a general elevation of 3,300 ft., though Japuo Peak in the Naga Hills rises to 9,990 ft., and on the south the hills rise sheer from the Sylhet plain (Surma valley). The Brahmaputra, called the Tsangpo in Tibet and then the Dihang, enters Assam through gorges at the northeast corner of the state. Its valley, an alluvial plain about 450 mi. in length and 50 mi. in average breadth, is subject to flooding during the rainy season. The region is also subject to severe earthquakes, that of Aug. 15, 1950, having caused at least 1,500 dead and over $50,000,000 damages, as well as floods and dammed rivers.

The state's climate is generally moderate, but the rainfall is fairly heavy, and the town of Cherrapunji on the south face of the Khasi Hills, receives the second highest recorded rainfall in the world, averaging nearly 500 in. of rain a year. Characteristic trees are those of temperate climates—pine, oak, chestnut, and magnolia—and rhododendrons and orchids grow in the woods. The first native Indian tea plants were found in Assam in 1821, and famous tea plantations, the chief source of wealth to the state, are on the slopes leading to the Brahmaputra valley. Rice, jute, cotton, and potatoes are also cultivated. Industrial development has been slow, though deposits of coal, limestone, oil, and iron are found, and the forests produce high grades of timber.

The chief towns are Shillong, the state capital, and Gauhati. The small town of Sadiya in the extreme northeast, is the starting point for roads through Sikang to West China, and Ledo, also in the northeast, is the starting point of the famous Ledo Road, built during World War II and going through Burma to China. The inhabitants of Assam are an extremely heterogeneous group. They comprise many different tribes, speaking no less than 101 distinct languages, the two chief being Assamese and Bengali, and belonging to a variety of religious groups, of which Hindus and Mohammedans are predominant.

Assam was formed into a strong independent kingdom by the invading Ahoms in the thirteenth century. During the seventeenth century it successfully resisted the attacks of the powerful Mohammedan rulers of Bengal. Early in the nineteenth century Assam became a Burmese dependency and in 1826, following the First Anglo-Burmese War, was ceded to Great Britain by the Treaty of Yandabo. It remained a British protectorate under the lieutenant-governor of Bengal until 1874, when it was erected into a separate chief commissionership. On the partition of Bengal in 1905, a Province of Eastern Bengal and Assam was created under a lieutenant-governor, but in 1912 Assam was reconstituted as a separate province, and in 1921 a governorship was created. In 1937 it was constituted an autonomous province. During World War II Assam served as a shipment point for Allied supplies to China and near Kohima the westward advance of the Japanese was halted in 1944. Under the terms of the India Independence Act of 1947 almost the whole of the predominantly Mohammedan Sylhet district was assigned to Pakistan. The Indian constitution of 1950 provided that the state of Assam include in its jurisdiction the Khasi States and the Assam tribal areas. Pop. 1951, 9,043,707.   C. W. D.

ASSAMESE [æsəmi'z; æsəmi's], an Indian dialect of the Indo-Iranian family, closely related to Oriyā and Bengālī. Assamese is spoken in the valley of the Brahmaputra, from the borders of Cooch Behar in the west to Dibrughar in the east, by about 1,717,500 persons. It has a literature dating from the fifteenth century, which consists of works on medicine, dramas, religious poetry, translations of the *Mahābhārata* and *Rāmāyana,* and even historical works. Historical writing in Indian literature other than Assamese is found only in the Rajputana chronicles in the Rājasthānī dialect.

One of the main characteristic features of spoken Assamese is that, being entirely surrounded by Tibeto-Burman dialects, which do not separate dental consonants from cacuminals, it has likewise lost this distinction; thus the Assamese pronounce *du-tä* ("two") instead of *du-ṭä.* The language has also lost, like modern French, the affricates *č* and *čh,* which have become *s,* and the affricates *ǰ* and *ǰh,* which have become *ž.* In Assamese, the sign *ph* is pronounced *f,* and *s, s,* and *ś* are all pronounced χ (like German *ch* or Arabic *kh*).   G. B.

ASSASSIN BUG, is the name given to any member of the Reduviidae, a family of true bugs of the suborder Hemiptera. Almost all are predaceous, feeding upon other insects, and a few have developed the bloodsucking habit. When they capture their prey, they paralyze it by injecting a highly toxic poison, then suck the blood and soft tissues. The largest species in the United States is the wheel bug, *Arilus cristatus,* which has a semicircular crest on the back of its thorax, and is capable of inflicting an extremely painful bite. The species of *Triatoma* and *Rhodnius* suck the blood of human beings, and several of them are carriers of Chagas disease, which is often deadly. The blood suckers are commonly known as kissing bugs because they usually bite humans near the mouth. The bite itself does not transmit the disease, but it causes itching, and scratching the injured area rubs the bug's excrement into the wound. If the bug is diseased, infection follows. The marked bedbug hunter is common in homes in North America, where it normally feeds on bedbugs and other household pests, but it has the same biting habits as do the disease-carrying forms.

C. H. Cu.

ASSASSINS [əsæ'sinz], from Arabic *"hashshāhīn,"* or addicts of the drug *hashīsh* (hemp), a secret order of religious fanatics, originating in the Ismā'ili branch of the Shiite sect. Founded in Iran by the Persian, al-Hasan ibn-al-Sabbāh, a Fatimid missionary (died 1124), the movement was one of propaganda with little regard for spiritual objectives. In its graded system of authority, the *Shaykl-al-Jabal,* known to the Crusaders in popular translation as the "Old Man of the Mountains," was chief of operations, aided by two groups of subordinates, the Grand Priors, and, below them, the contingents of desperadoes ready to do or die in blind obedience to the command of their chief.

From Alumūt, their mountain stronghold in the northwest of Qzavin in Iran, taken by Hasan in 1091, the Assassins in the next two hundred years spread their militant anarchical influence through many parts of the Moslem world by establishing a chain of hill forts in northern Iran and Syria and by pursuing a policy of secret assassination against their enemies. Among the first victims was Hasan's old schoolfellow, Nizam al-Mulk, patron of learning and vizier of the sultan, Malik Shah, who had sent two unsuccessful expeditions against the order.

Toward the close of the eleventh century the Assassins gained a foothold in northern Syria, where the hill fortress of Masyād (or Masyāf) served them as an impregnable citadel. Their chief in Syria, Rashīd-ad-Dīn Sinān (died 1192), who in turn had become the "Old Man of the Mountains," terrorized the invading Crusaders in a campaign of systematic murder.

In 1256 the Persian strongholds of the order were destroyed by the Mongols under Hulagu. Sixteen years later in 1272 those in Syria were demolished by the Mameluke ruler, Baybars I, and the Assassins of Syria were scattered abroad. Some remnants of the sect exist today in northern Syria, Iran, Zanzibar, Uman, and India. In India they are known as "Khojas" and "Mawlas," acknowledging the Agha Khan of Bombay, who claims descent from the seventh Shiite Iman, Ismail, as their titular head.

E. J. J.

ASSAULT AND BATTERY. An assault is an unlawful threat or attempt to do violence to the person of another; battery is the actual hostile and willful touching of the other's person. Mere words, no matter how provocative, do not constitute an assault. At common law, the person who was the object of assault and battery may bring an action against the wrongdoer and recover monetary damages. In some jurisdictions, exemplary damages, in addition to the compensation for the actual injury, are provided for by statute, particularly where the wrongful act was malicious, or was accompanied by insult or gross violence. Such damages are usually large, and are intended to deter the wrongdoer from repeating the offense. Many statutes define assault separately from "assault and battery," and make them two distinct offenses, punishable as felonies or misdemeanors varying with the intent of the wrongdoer and the manner in which the offense is committed. The intent to injure another must always be proved in a criminal prosecution. The use of force in self-defense, however, does not make one guilty of assault and battery, unless the person defending himself employs excessive force, far more than is reasonably necessary to repel the initial attack upon him.   V. M.

ASSAYING, a method of quantitative analysis for the determination of precious and rare metals in ores, concentrates, furnace products, both intermediate and finished metals, alloys, precipitates, and industrial sweepings. It is based essentially on a series of separations, extractions, and collections obtained by the addition to the material under test of suitable dry fluxes and reagents and subsequent fusion of the resulting charge in suitable refractory containers and furnaces. Previous to the development of modern wet analytical chemical methods, fire-assaying procedures were used for quantitative determination of many of the more common heavy base metals, particularly copper, lead, tin, and mercury.

History. Assaying is an ancient practice; surprisingly complete descriptions of the principal operations appear in the early treatises pertaining to the art of metal extraction and refining. Reliable English translations of two of these are available: the *Pirotechnia* of Vannoccio Biringuccio translated from the first Italian edition of 1540 by Cyril Stanley Smith and Martha Teach Gnudi, and *De Re Metallica* of Agricola (Georg Bauer) translated from the first Latin edition of 1556 by Herbert Clark Hoover and Lou Henry Hoover. Both authors emphasized the importance of careful sampling, preparation of reagents, and assaying in order to control and develop economic and efficient extractions of the metals and to determine the purity of the final metallic products. It is noteworthy that in these early days, the similarity between assaying procedures and those operations common to commercial lead smelting and refining was recognized and emphasized.

The great appreciation of the monetary and ornamental value of gold and silver in early times resulted in the development of methods of extraction, of casting, and of working these metals together with the application of assaying procedures. Later, when the more modern procedures of wet chemical analysis superseded the fire-assay procedures for the heavy base metals, it was still the custom to apply the term "assaying" to these newer methods. Consequently, the term has been applied in a general way to all procedures which had for their object the determination of metals in ores and metallic products.

In modern practice, fire assaying is chiefly concerned with the determination of silver and gold, and less frequently, because of their rarity, with the five rare metals—ruthenium, rhodium, palladium, iridium, and platinum. All seven of these metals are relatively high in price, and all are quoted in units of ounces troy. On the other hand, the raw ores from which gold is extracted are normally estimated and reported in tons avoirdupois. The existence of two units of different dimension in the latter system has occasioned further complication. In countries where the metric system prevails, it is customary to report precious and rare metal contents in terms of grams or kilograms per metric ton (1,000 kg.).

Ore-Sample and Extracted-Metal Ratio. In order to facilitate the work of the assayer, it was recognized that some readily workable relationship must be established between the quantity of ore taken for assay and the weight of the metal extracted during the assay operation. In the case of gold, these final weights are small and normally less than one milligram, since at $35 per ounce troy an ore containing one ounce of gold is considered a rich ore, although in terms of per cent the amount would be expressed as 0.00343. This relationship has been developed on the basis of the following definitions:

1 oz. troy	= 31.103481 grams
	= 1.09712 oz. avoirdupois
	= 480 grains troy
1 lb. troy	= 373.2420 grams
	= 13.1657 oz. avoirdupois
	= 12 ounces troy
	= 5,760 grains troy
1 lb. avoirdupois	= 16 oz. avoirdupois
	= 7,000 grains troy
1 ton avoirdupois (short)	= 2,000 lb.
	= 14,000,000 grains troy
1 oz. troy	= 480 grains
Then	$\frac{14,000,000}{480} = 29,166.66$

If the last figure above is called an assay ton and if the units of weight employed are milligrams, then 1 assay ton = 29.166 grams and the following relationship holds:

$$\frac{1 \text{ oz. troy}}{1 \text{ short ton avoirdupois}} = \frac{1 \text{ mg.}}{1 \text{ assay ton}}$$

In a similar manner, a comparable unit for use with the long ton avoirdupois of 2,240 lb. can be established. Weighing samples in assay tons or fractions of that unit and final gold and silver products in milligrams gives the required ounces troy per ton avoirdupois with minimum calculation. However, it should be obvious that assaying ores for gold is essentially a trace-element method of determination.

Because of the relatively large initial weights of material taken for assay and the extremely small weights of the final metallic product, or bead, two distinctly different types of balances are required. The first, the pulp balance, is capable of weighing large loads, 1 assay ton or more, where very limited sensitivity is required. The other is limited in load capacity to a maximum of 0.50 gram but has great sensitivity, sufficient to permit the weighing of the bead to 0.01 mg. Balances of the latter type have been for many years the finest product of the balance manufacturer's skill.

Sampling. All assay procedures are primarily based upon the prior acquisition of a representative sample of the material to be analyzed. This should be adequate in quantity for analytical purposes and of such a degree of particle fineness as to permit the reproducible selection of an assay portion. Experience has shown that for most gold ores the maximum size of particle in the final sample (pulp) should be smaller than the opening in a 100-mesh sieve, or of the order of 0.0058 in. (0.147 mm.). All assay results are based upon thorough drying of the samples. Similarly, the sampling of metallic materials must conform to the principles of good sampling techniques.

Furnaces and Fuels. Two general types of furnace have been developed. In the pot furnace, the crucible with its charge rests directly on the fuel bed or on a special base and is exposed to direct contact with the products of combustion. One form uses coke exclusively, while gas and oil are used in various modifications. Pot furnaces are restricted to the collection fusion and are unsuitable for cupellations. The muffle furnace is provided with a container, or muffle, which contains the charged crucibles free from contact with the products of combustion. Muffle furnaces require long-flame fuels such as bituminous coal, gas, or oil. Such a furnace, with proper fluxing of the charge, attains an adequate temperature for the collection fusion, about 1,200° C., and also provides sufficient control of temperature and air draft to permit of the operation of cupellation. Temperatures during this latter operation vary between 825 and 950° C., depending upon the stage of lead elimination.

Collection of Precious Metal in a Lead Button. *By Fusion in a Crucible.* In fusion assay a charge is prepared by mixing together 1 assay ton of the ore; a source of lead, usually lead monoxide (PbO); suitable fluxes; and, if the ore is nonreducing, a reducer. If the ore is too powerful as a reducer and will liberate more lead than is desirable (more than 25 grams), an oxidizer is introduced into the charge. The latter is thoroughly mixed, transferred to a refractory crucible of adequate capacity, and inserted into either a muffle or a pot furnace.

Fluxes may be either acid or basic, depending upon the character of the ore. Acid flux is usually powdered silica (SiO_2), but borax glass ($Na_2B_4O_7$) may be substituted for a portion of this former. Basic fluxes are made up of the low-melting-point lead monoxide, sodium carbonate (Na_2CO_3), and sodium bicarbonate ($NaHCO_3$) or the more costly similar potassium salts. Fire assaying does not normally make use of the relatively cheap but higher-melting-point iron oxide and lime as basic fluxes. However, these compounds may be present in the ore, and the corresponding silicates would then be found in the slag. Reducing ores derive the property of reducing metallic lead from lead monoxide from their content of natural sulphide. When sulphides are absent, a reducer must be added; the choice may be made from charcoal, flour, sugar, starch, argols, or sulphur.

By Scorification. In the scorification assay the charge consists of metallic granulated lead and the ore. Most of the lead is mixed with the ore and the balance is placed on top of the mixed portion contained in a small, shallow, saucer-like refractory vessel. The fusion is carried on in a muffle furnace. It is essentially a melting and strongly oxidizing operation. The excess metallic lead oxidizes, and the resulting lead monoxide reacts to dissolve the oxides formed from the oxidation of the base-metal sulphides present in the ore. Oxidation of the lead is continued until the excess lead is reduced to button dimensions.

The objects of both of the operations are to secure complete decomposition of the ore, liberation of the gold and silver, collection of the precious metals in a metallic lead button, and the formation of a thinly fluid slag. Preliminary separation of the two products is accomplished in the molten state by taking advantage of the difference in their specific gravities. Final separation is made after solidification by tapping the two-layered casting at the interface. Ideally, all the precious metals should be in the button and the slag should contain all the gangue (valueless portions of the ore) and fluxes.

Cupellation. In cupellation the collecting lead of the button is removed by an oxidizing fusion in a muffle furnace, with the resulting lead monoxide being absorbed in the porous cupel container. The latter, when made in the laboratory, is a compressed molded product of water-moistened bone ash, neat cement, or bone ash and cement. Patent or magnesia cupels, marketed under various names, also are available. The cupel must be sufficiently porous to absorb the molten litharge (fused lead monoxide) formed by the oxidation of the collector lead and yet remain impervious to the molten silver-gold alloy bead. Control of temperature

LUCIUS PITKIN, INC.

TYPICAL ASSAYING WORKSHOP

is most critical during this operation, since high temperatures decrease the imperviousness by increasing the extent to which the cupel is wet by the precious metals; whereas low temperatures result in complete termination of the oxidation reaction. The latter development is called "freezing" and is accompanied by solidification of the oxide film before absorption can take place. Termination of the cupellation is evidenced by a series of physical phenomena, the last of which is a dulling of the bead. The cupel is then removed from the furnace.

The small precious-metal bead is removed from the cupel by small bead pliers, flattened by squeezing, and then further flattened by hammering on a small anvil. The small plate so obtained is clean and ready for weighing on the bead balance. The resulting weight in milligrams is a composite of all the silver and gold in the ore.

Further refinement in the result can be obtained by "parting," the separation of the silver from the gold. The parting agent is normally nitric acid of various degrees of dilution varying from 1 part of acid to 9 parts distilled water up to 3 parts of acid to 2 parts of distilled water. All the reagents must be free from gold-dissolving substances, particularly chlorine-liberating materials, and the ratio of silver to gold must be approximately 3 to 1. Once the acid ceases to react at a temperature slightly below boiling, the parting is considered to have been completed. The silver

nitrate solution is removed by decantation, and the sponge-like gold bead is cleaned by frequent decantation washes, drained dry of water, dried by heating, and finally annealed by heating to red heat over a Bunsen burner or in a muffle. The annealing converts the reddish-gold sponge to a bright, compact, crystalline normal-colored gold bead. This bead is transferred to the pan of the bead balance and weighed to the nearest hundredth of a milligram. Silver is obtained by difference, subtracting the weight of the gold from the combined weight of silver and gold. The final report is obtained by converting the weights to milligrams per assay ton of ore, which is by definition equivalent to ounces troy per ton avoirdupois.

Gold and Silver Alloys. The foregoing selection of a typical ore assay has illustrated the more complicated all-assay procedure. Alloys of gold and silver may be assayed with fewer operations in some cases but nevertheless adhere to the sequence of collection of the gold and silver in a lead button and subsequent cupellation. The five rare metals are normally collected in a final gold or silver bead and subsequently separated by a series of wet operations involving the use of a number of reagents of selective action.

Fine bullion assays are normally comparison assays. That for silver is the so-called mint or Gay-Lussac method of solution in nitric acid and titration with standard sodium chloride solutions standardized against fine silver standards.

Gold bullion assays are normally restricted to cupellations after a preliminary cupellation has been run to determine the approximate fineness. Based upon these data, a synthetic or "proof" assay is run conjointly with another cupellation of the unknown bullion. The loss or gain of the proof is applied to the bullion assay in order to compensate for any errors introduced during the cupellation.

Commercial gold alloys are based upon a scale of carats, where 24-carat gold is equivalent to fine gold. Thus a 16-carat gold alloy is $^{16}/_{24}$ or 66⅔ per cent gold. A very ancient method of checking the hallmark, or official designation, of the alloy is by use of scratch needles and the touchstone, also known as basanite. The needles are tipped with standard gold alloys. Comparison scratches are made on the touchstone, and these streaks are then treated with a standard-strength acid. Like behavior of the scratches classifies the unknown with the standard alloy.

Despite the ancient origin and development of the fundamental principles of assaying, it is interesting to note that this method of analysis still continues to function as the commonly accepted method of controlling the extraction of gold and silver and the other rare metals. This longevity is the resultant of a number of factors, chiefly the importance of gold and silver in ancient times, the intensive early investigations resulting from demand, the low concentration of the metals required to make commercial ores, and the speed with which a large number of samples can be assayed. Technological advances have resulted in reagents of higher purity, improved equipment for containing the charges during fusion, improved furnaces with more effective combustion control, and high-quality bead balances. Essentially, assaying has always been a highly sensitive, readily reproduced, and extremely accurate method of trace analysis for gold and silver. W. E. M.

ASSESSMENT, the listing and appraisal or valuation of the taxable items subject to a given tax. The term is also used to indicate the actual levying of a tax, but this is hardly the accepted technical meaning. Although common to all forms of taxation, assessment procedure encounters the most serious difficulties in the taxation of property according to value. The universal dependence of local governments in the United States upon this form of taxation adds particular significance to the problem of property assessment. The fundamental difficulties are the increasing complexity of the nature of property and the discretionary elements involved in the determination of values. Specific sources of dissatisfaction have been poorly qualified assessors, the practical impossibility of assessing personal intangible property (stocks, bonds, mortgages), and the wide variations in taxable values in relation to actual values. Improvements in assessment procedure have been effected in some jurisdictions by the introduction of mechanical rules and formulas, by more state supervision and control of local assessment practices, and by substituting a system of classified property taxes for the general property tax. Original assessments are made by local assessors, usually elected. Such assessments are subject to review by local boards of equalization, by the courts, and by state tax commissions. Public utilities are generally assessed initially by state rather than local authorities. M. L. F.

ASSIDEANS or **HASIDAEANS** [æ′sɪdi′ənz, hæ′si-di′ənz], a Jewish sect or group of "pious ones" that became prominent during the age of the Maccabean revolt (second century B.C.). They are mentioned three times in the Books of the Maccabees (I Macc. ii:41; I Macc. vii:13; and II Macc. xiv:6). Opposed to all foreign impact upon what they believed to be pristine Judaism, the Assideans pitted themselves against those Jewish groups which tended to yield to Hellenistic influences and, under the leadership of Judas Maccabaeus, they also aligned themselves in the foreground of the battle to win independence from the Greco-Syrian hosts.

The Assideans were noted for their extreme piety, but, when those who would not resist on the Sabbath were slain in a surprise attack by the enemy, the Assideans joined those that defended themselves on the Sabbath, in accordance with the principle, followed throughout Jewish history, that the preservation of life supersedes the observance of the Law. They emphasized the virtue of meditation, coming to the synagogue an hour before the stated time to prepare themselves properly for prayer. Although active in the liberation of the Jews, the Assideans never assumed the proportions of a political party and as an organized group they ceased to exist soon after the Maccabean period, although many of their ideas pervaded Jewish thinking in later times. Their stress upon joy in the Law and their great piety have left their imprints on Jewish life. H. Bl.

ASSIGNATS [a′si′nya′; æ′sɪgnætz], interest-bearing bonds, based on land, used as currency during a phase of the French Revolution. When the financial crisis, which was the reason for summoning the States-General (Estates-General) of 1789, continued unsolved, the National Assembly was forced to take drastic steps. At the suggestion of Talleyrand and with aid from Mirabeau, the Assembly voted on Nov. 2, 1789, to seize the church lands, and, at Mirabeau's suggestion, to use them as the basis for bonds, bearing 5 per cent interest, which might be exchanged for land. The bonds so returned to the treasury were to be burned. The plan, as originally proposed, was simple and practical, if no further paper money had been issued and if the original issue had been redeemed promptly and retired as first contemplated. However, many investors hesitated to accept the bonds, and so in 1790 the Assembly undertook to clear the mortgages from the land and to give the assignats the force of legal tender. It was believed that not only would the state debt be eliminated by the sale of land, but also that a large class of new landowners would be created who would be bound by self-interest to the Revolution. In this latter aim, the Assembly was successful, but as a financial transaction the measure failed. The large amounts of land-bonds on the market reduced their value, and the assignats were over-issued, there being eventually 1,800,000,000 livres of them in circulation. The result was inflation which produced a severe economic crisis. By the middle of 1792, the assignats were being quoted at a loss of 60 per cent in value. In 1796 the government was forced to repudiate the whole issue. J. F. R.

ASSIGNMENT, in law, in its most general sense, a transfer to another of a claim, right, or interest. An assignment for benefit of creditors is a transfer by a debtor of his property to an assignee in trust for the purpose of having the proceeds applied toward payment of the assignor's debts. Colloquially, the bare term "assignment" is often used to indicate an assignment for benefit of creditors, and particularly, when it is said of a merchant that he has "made an assignment," it is generally intended to convey the information that he has made a general disposition of his property and suspended his business in consequence.

Even under modern statutes and decisions, which generally have liberalized the right of assignment of claims and rights, certain matters remain in the category of nonassignability. Thus, contracts involving personal relations, such as those between master and servant, are generally nonassignable. Business contracts involving the element of special reliance upon a party's skill are nonassignable to the extent that the performance of another may not be substituted for that of the person whose special skill was bargained for in the original agreement. Moreover, a provision prohibiting assignment in a contract, otherwise assignable, is generally enforceable. The right to sue another to recover damages for personal injuries remains generally nonassignable although the proceeds of judgment recovered in an action for personal injuries may be assignable. Other claims for damages also generally remain nonassignable, if they are of the type of chose in action which does not survive the death of the person who has suffered the damage.

In the case of wages and salaries, the modern statutes, as an exception to the trend toward liberalization of the right of assignment, have restricted such assignments and subjected them to detailed regulation, out of regard to considerations of social security.   H. Si.

ASSIMILATION, SOCIAL, the processes by which individuals become psychologically and culturally identified with a social order. In its fullest sense social assimilation is identical with socialization. In its commonest sociological usage the term is applied to the interaction between an immigrant group and a native population leading toward the incorporation of the former in the social organization of the latter. Unlike legal citizenship, social assimilation is a slow process, involving subtle changes in attitudes, customs, and institutions. The natural reluctance of the incoming group to abandon its language, beliefs, and institutions frequently is matched by suspicion on the part of the native population, and successful assimilation generally requires two or more generations, with modifications occurring in the culture of both immigrant and native groups. Assimilation is slowest where there are differences of race or color, or where there is a strong religious resistance.   R. A. N.

ASSINIBOIA [æsɪ'nɪbɔi'ə], a town in the grazing region of Saskatchewan, Canada, situated on the Canadian Pacific Railway, 79 mi. south of Moose Jaw. It is the retail shopping center for the surrounding territory. The local industrial establishments include six grain elevators, a flour mill, a planing mill, and a creamery. Two hospitals are located in the town. Pop. 1951, 1,938.   D. F. P.

ASSISI, ST. FRANCIS OF. *See* FRANCIS OF ASSISI, ST.

ASSISI [ɑssi'zi], an historic town and religious center in Umbria, central Italy. The city, 15 mi. southeast of Perugia, spreads along a spur of Monte Subasio at an elevation of 1,300 ft. above sea level, overlooking the valley of the Topino River, a tributary of the upper Tiber.

The population of the city has been almost stationary since the seventeenth century. Assisi itself has changed little in appearance since the Middle Ages, when it first acquired fame as the home of St. Francis. It has no commercial or industrial importance, and much of its income is from tourists and pilgrims. The railway station in the valley, 2½ mi. distant, provides local service on a branch line to Foligno and Terontola. Except for a few main thoroughfares, the streets in the city are narrow, winding, and usually steep. At the northwest end of town is the Church and Convent of St. Frances, erected in 1228-1253. This famous edifice is comprised of two churches, one on top of the other. Some of the chapels in the lower church are richly decorated with frescoes by Simone Martini, P. Lorenzetti, and other noted artists. It contains the tomb of St. Francis, discovered in 1818 under the altar of the crypt. The upper church has a high, single Gothic nave, adorned by the frescoes of Giovanni Cimabue and Giotto di Bondone, especially the latter's celebrated twenty-eight episodes from the life of St. Francis. Other noted churches in Assisi are Santa Chiara (Gothic of the thirteenth century); the Cathedral of San Rufino (ninth century); and the basilica of Santa Maria degli Angeli, beautified with work by A. della Robbia, on the spot where St. Francis died and where his order originated. Crowning the

Church of St. Francis in the famous hill town of Assisi, central Italy

hill above the town is the fourteenth-century *rocca,* or castle, from which there is a remarkable view.

Known as Asisium, the town was of some consequence in Roman times, evidenced by remains of a theatre and amphitheater. In 545 it was destroyed by the Goth Totila. After the arrival of the Lombards a few years later, Assisi fell under the rule of the Duchy of Spoleto and remained there until the twelfth century. However, in the preceding century, there had already begun an interminable series of wars whereby the near-by city of Perugia sought to take Assisi against other states and the will of the city's inhabitants. During his brief pontificate, from 1198 to 1216, Innocent III temporarily reimposed papal rule. Soon there began another series of wars, revolts, conquests, pillaging, and mass murders that continued until Pope Paul III, 1535-1549, established the uncontested dominion of the Holy See. Though the city lost its municipal liberties, it gained a modicum of tranquility.

St. Francis (1182-1226), probably the most appealing of all the Italian medieval saints, lived and labored in and around his native Assisi, bringing it imperishable glory. Artistically the golden era of Assisi was the fourteenth century, and it was noted for its glass and gold work as well as for the beauty of the decorations of its churches. In the convent attached to the churches of St. Francis, a magnificent library of books, manuscripts, and music was collected; later this collection became part of the communal library. Pop. (city), 4,686; (commune), 22,514.   R. G. W.

ASSISTANCE, WRIT OF. *See* WRIT OF ASSISTANCE.

ASSOCIATION, THE, an agreement adopted by the First Continental Congress in 1774, which provided that there should be no importation of British goods or importation or purchase of any slave after Dec. 1, 1774, and that there should be no exportation of American goods to Great Britain, Ireland, or the West Indies after Sept. 10, 1775, except rice to Europe. The signers also agreed to stop all orders for European goods, to encourage sheep raising, to give up extravagance and dissipations such as horse racing and cockfighting, and also to give up the wearing of excess mourning at funerals in order to save cloth. The association called on local committees to see to the observance of the agreement, once it had been signed by local citizens, and to publish in the papers as enemies of American liberties the names of those who violated it. The association was of great importance in the revolutionary movement since it furnished a common activity for people throughout the colonies. It gave a sanction of sorts to revolutionary organizations outside the regular legislatures and courts of the colonies. The organizations that sprang up everywhere to enforce it in time became revolutionary governments. The non-importation, non-exportation agreements were so effectively enforced that imports were almost completely stopped by 1775. English merchants were panic-stricken, but the British government refused to yield as it had at the time of the Stamp Act in 1765. It decided that the issue of political control over the colonies had to be settled once and for all.   M. Je.

ASSOCIATION OF AMERICAN UNIVERSITIES, an organization which originated in an informal conference held by representatives of fourteen universities Feb. 28, 1900, "for the purpose of considering matters of common interest relating to graduate study."

Membership. The original enrollment consisted of the following members: University of California, Catholic University of America, University of Chicago, Clark University, Columbia University, Cornell University, Harvard University, Johns Hopkins University, Stanford University, University of Michigan, University of Pennsylvania, Princeton University, University of Wisconsin, and Yale University. Gradually additional institutions were invited to become members on the basis of quality of their graduate work, the number of departments giving advanced degrees, and the distinction of the faculty. There are no hard and set criteria for membership. Invitations are sent on the basis of the opinion of faculty members of institutions already in the association. The 1949 membership was as follows: Brown University, California Institute of Technology, Catholic University of America, Clark University, Columbia University, Cornell University, Duke University, Harvard University, Indiana University, Johns Hopkins University, McGill University, Massachusetts Institute of Technology, Northwestern University, Ohio State University, Princeton University, Stanford University, State University of Iowa, University of California, University of Chicago, University of Illinois, University of Kansas, University of Michigan, University of Minnesota, University of Missouri, University of Nebraska, University of North Carolina, University of Pennsylvania, University of Rochester, University of Texas, University of Toronto, University of Virginia, University of Wisconsin, Washington University, and Yale University.

Functions. The Association holds an annual meeting, always at the invitation of some member institution and attended usually by the president and the dean of the Graduate School of each institution. These meetings have been concerned with methods of improving the quality of graduate work, the establishment of appropriate standards for advanced degrees, and the problem of training graduate students for positions as college teachers. Many other matters dealing with foreign students, patent policy, and fellowships have been discussed and reported in the association's annual *Proceedings.*

Accreditation. In 1913 the association undertook the task of accrediting institutions giving the bachelor's degree. This has led to the annual publication of a list of approved institutions whose qualified graduates are admitted to graduate schools of the association. This work dates back to a letter written in July 1904, by the faculty of the University of Berlin, in which the statement was made that all bachelors' degrees from American colleges would be accepted, but that graduate work would be accepted only from institutions which were members of the Association of American Universities. In practice, the rule was interpreted to mean that bachelors' degrees would be accepted by the University of Berlin, and later by similar action in other universities on the continent, only when received at institutions which were members of the association. This created undue hardship for nonmember institutions; as a result, in 1913 the association undertook to "recommend to the Prussian Kultusministerium and the corresponding ministries of the other German states that, for the present, there be recognized as the equivalent of the German Maturitätszeugnis, not only the bachelors' degrees conferred by the members of the association, but also the degrees of those other American colleges and universities which were on the accepted list of the Carnegie Foundation or which were certified by the Foundation as of equivalent standing but excluded from its accepted list for other than educational reasons. . . ." From 1913 until 1923 the association added an appreciable number of institutions to the list of the Carnegie Foundation. In 1923 the association decided to inspect each new institution before putting it on the list, and for this purpose received a grant from the Carnegie Corporation. From 1923 to 1946 the cost of the inspections was borne to a large extent by the institutions seeking approval, but after 1946 the association increased its dues in order to cover an appreciable part of the cost. The original purpose of the classification work has long since ceased, but it has been continued on account of its significance in establishing standards for undergraduate work and in encouraging appropriate student training. H. E. Be.

ASSOCIATION OF IDEAS, a term used to denote the mental process by which ideas are related in such a way that the later recall of one tends to evoke the others. It was the central explanatory doctrine of the British school of associationists. They made it the main integrating principle of mental life in contrast to the concept of faculties, like the faculty of memory, or to any such dynamic process as the Herbartian "apperception." Association psychology, founded by Thomas Hobbes and John Locke in the latter part of the seventeenth century, proved to be an effective weapon in the hands of the British empiricists in their struggle against the older rationalistic psychology. The movement was furthered by David Hume (1711-1776); by David Hartley (1705-1757), who gave the associative process a physiological basis in his nerve-vibration doctrine; by the Scottish school; by James Mill (1773-1836); and by Alexander Bain (1818-1903), under whose brilliant advocacy it reached its culmination. The use of the principle of association as an explanatory concept to account for the integration of the complex elements of consciousness is found in such American schools as Structuralism and Functionalism. It even appears in a somewhat disguised form in Behaviorism, if the concept of "ideas" be replaced by that of stimuli and responses.

Association doctrine rests on the "laws of association," a set of empirically derived laws which state the conditions under which ideas are first related and later recalled together. The first statement of such laws was made by Aristotle, who formulated the principles of similarity, of contrast, and of contiguity in time and space. These have been called the "primary" laws in contrast to the "secondary laws" which were added later. Thomas Brown (1778-1802), the Scottish associationist, added three secondary laws, to account for the conditions under which the primary laws operate, namely: frequency, recency, and intensity. Others are primacy and vividness. Sir William Hamilton (1730-1803) added the concept of reintegration, the principle by which an idea tends to reinstate all the elements which were originally presented with it in experience. H. L. Hollingworth (1880) revived this concept as a more comprehensive principle than conditioning to account for many abnormal phenomena, involving unconscious reference.

The main objection raised by the enemies of association psychology against the laws of association as a set of explanatory principles is that they are descriptive rather than causal, and state logical rather than psychological relations. The Gestaltists, Max Wertheimer, Kurt Koffka, and Wolfgang Kohler, all objected to the atomistic conception of mental life which assumes that ideas are bound together. They emphasized the wholeness of mental life which is only separated into elements by an artificial process of analysis. Physiological and neurological theories of "associative bonds" and "synaptic resistance changes" tended to support an associationistic psychology. Dynamic theories, such as K. S. Lashley's, or the "holistic" concepts of K. Goldstein, are in opposition.
A. G. B.

ASSOCIATION OF UNIVERSITY PROFESSORS, AMERICAN, founded Jan. 1, 1915, for the purpose of ensuring academic freedom. Membership in the A.A.U.P., as the organization is usually designated, is open to all college and university teachers and to graduate assistants and students of eligible institutions. The list of eligible institutions is based primarily on the approved list of established accrediting agencies. Election to membership of an eligible individual is based on a nomination made by one member. The declaration of the association, as endorsed in 1926, states that a university or college may not impose any restraint upon a teacher's freedom to investigate or to expound within his own subject specialty. Likewise, a college or university should recognize that a teacher, in speaking or writing off the campus, is entitled to the same freedom that all other citizens have. In 1940 these principles of academic freedom were reaffirmed. Up to 1949, 13 institutions had been blacklisted for violations of academic freedom. Of these, three were state universities; three, private; one, municipal; and the remainder, private or state colleges. A blacklisted institution may lose its accredited status, thereby losing also its prestige among teachers and patrons. In practice, however, the blacklisting affects chiefly the institution's administrative policy as effected by the board of trustees, or the president, or both, or by a particular department. While no college or university is wholly indifferent toward the association's rating, it is true that several institutions have remained on the blacklist for years without any apparent effect on their ability to attract students.

The headquarters of the association are located at 1101 Connecticut Ave., Washington, D. C.   O. W. H-Q.

ASSOCIATIONS AND CLUBS. *See* SOCIETIES, ASSOCIATIONS, AND ORGANIZATIONS.
ASSOCIATIVE FIBERS. *See* BRAIN.
ASSUAN. *See* ASWÂN.

ASSUMPTION, FEAST OF THE, also called in ancient liturgy the Falling Asleep, or Repose. The feast, according to Roman Catholic teaching, commemorates the bodily taking up of the Virgin Mary into Heaven, following the reunion of her soul with her body after her death. The doctrine of the Assumption was defined as an Article of Faith by Pope Pius XII in an Apostolic Constitution dated Nov. 1, 1950. This Papal Bull was issued in response to numerous petitions from all parts of the Catholic world for the definition of a dogma that had universal belief from the early ages of the Church. From the sixth to the eleventh centuries, Fathers of the Church in the East and West preached homilies commemorating the Assumption with a directness which leaves no doubt as to their faith. Since the sixth century the Catholic Church has celebrated the feast in its liturgies on August 15. Other testimony to the feast is found in Latin martyrologies and Greek monologies. The subject has been painted by great artists and has inspired poets. *See also* HOLIDAYS AND HOLY DAYS; MARY, THE VIRGIN.   R. J. O'C.

ASSUR (ASHUR) [a'shur], capital of ancient Assyria, now an important archaeological site and ruin near the small town of Sharquat in the central part of northern Iraq. The ruins of Assur are situated in a low hilly area on the western bank of the upper Tigris River about 160 mi. north by west of Baghdad. Assur had become a strong city by 1300 B.C.   J. E. F.

ASSYRIA. *See* BABYLONIA AND ASSYRIA.
ASSYRIAN ART. *See* BABYLONIAN AND ASSYRIAN ART.
ASSYRIAN CHRISTIANS. *See* ASIATIC TRIBES.

ASTARTE [æstɑ'rti], the Phoenician goddess of fertility and erotic love. The Greek name, "Astartē," was derived from Semitic, "Ishtar," "Ashtoreth." Astarte was regarded in Classical antiquity as a moon goddess, perhaps in confusion with some other Semitic deity. In accordance with the literary traditions of the Greco-Romans, Astarte was identified with Seléne and Artemis, and more often with Aphrodite. Among the Canaanites, Astarte, like her peer Anath, performed a major function as goddess of fertility. The prestige of Astarte and Anath as powers over fertility surpassed that of any other deities among ancient peoples.

Egyptian iconography, however, portrayed Astarte in her role as a female, warlike goddess, massacring mankind, young and old. She is represented on plaques (dated 1700-1100 B.C.) as naked, in striking contrast to the modestly garbed Egyptian goddesses. An Egyptian text of the New Empire refers to Astarte and Anath as "the great goddesses who conceive, but do not bear."   E. J. J.

ASTER, a genus of the family Compositae with about 250 species. Some are native to Europe, Asia, and South America and about 200 to North America, chiefly in the north-

NEW ENGLAND ASTERS

COURTESY OF THE NEW YORK
BOTANICAL GARDENS

eastern portion and the Rocky Mountain region. About 45 are native to New York and perhaps 20 to California. They are coarse-growing, often strikingly handsome, autumn-blooming perennial herbs, with numerous flower heads, commonly in showy clusters. Each flowering head is composed of a central disk of minute yellow florets, surrounded by many fine rays of white, purple, red, or blue. Asters grow in great profusion along roads or in waste fields, often mixed with goldenrod. Many are cultivated as garden ornamentals. Among the Old World species are *A. tataricus,* tall, pale blue, and *A. alpinus,* a low-growing rock plant. Some of the best-known American ones are the New England aster, *A. novae-angliae,* with large purple clusters; the smooth blue aster, *A. laevis;* and the New York aster, *A. novi-Belgi,* a rich violet-blue. The common aster of the Pacific states, *A. chilensis,* is white, varying to blue or lavender.   J. C. Wis.

ASTER, CHINA, *Callistephus chinensis,* a member of the family Compositae, is a handsome annual, widely grown commercially and by amateurs for its late summer bloom. In 1731, it was introduced into Europe from China by the Jesuit missionary, Pierre d'Incarville, as a single white, blue, or violet flower. Seeds of red and double varieties followed soon afterward. The plants were very popular and widely grown. As the main supply of seed and many improved varieties came from Germany, certain varieties were called German asters for many years. The first China asters were tall, stiff-flowered, with quilled petals, which have in later years been replaced by loose, flat-rayed, fluffy varieties show-

ing their close relationship to chrysanthemums. It is now possible to grow dwarf and tall, early or late, single and double varieties in all tints from pure white to deep purple and red. There is no yellow. Most of the seed now comes either from California or New York. China asters are easily cultivated, but have of late years been widely attacked by a virus disease known as "the yellows." It is important to plant disease-resistant varieties.   E. L. Sh.

ASTHMA. *See* RESPIRATORY DISEASES.

ASTI [ɑ'sti], a province and also a capital city in the hilly Monferrato region in Piedmont, northwestern Italy.
The City. Asti is situated on the left bank of the Tanaro River at an elevation of 400 ft., and 28 mi. southeast of Turin (Torino). The city is on the main railway line from Turin to Alessandria. Before the province of Asti was created in 1935, the city of Asti was part of the province of Alessandria.

Asti is famous for its grapes and wines, for which it is a big market; livestock and raw silk are also sold. Local industries produce sundry items, such as bicycles, matches, stoves, and textiles. The principal monuments include the Baptistry of San Pietro (twelfth to thirteenth centuries), the Cathedral (Gothic of the fourteenth century), and the Palazzo Alfieri, built in honor of the Italian tragic dramatist, Conte Vittorio Alfieri, who was born in Asti in 1749. A number of houses date back to the thirteenth century.

Originally a Roman *municipium,* Asti suffered greatly during the successive Germanic invasions of northern Italy. Later, during the conflict between the Holy Roman Empire and the communes, Asti wavered but eventually confirmed her municipal liberties and expanded her trade. Beginning in the thirteenth century, family quarrels led to outside intervention by Milan and the rulers of Monferrato and Savoy. Even after the latter won out in the sixteenth century, Asti continued to be fought over during the successive wars. Pop. 1947, 52,733 (city and environs).
Province. The province of Asti, created in 1935 and comprising 105 communes, has an area of 586 sq. mi. It consists largely of the hilly country of Monferrato and Le Langhe, drained by the Po River and its tributary, the Tanaro. The only city with a population above 8,000 is Asti, the capital city. Most of the land is quite fertile, with wheat, corn, grapes, and fruit as the outstanding products. The region is noted for its wines, especially a sparkling wine, Asti spumante. A big hay crop encourages livestock raising, and many families supplement their incomes with silkworm culture. Industries are largely local in importance. Pop. (off. est. 1947), 233,000.   R. G. W.

ASTIGMATISM. *See* EYE.

ASTILBE [əstɪ'lbi], a genus of ornamental plants of the saxifrage family, closely resembling the goatsbeard, *Aruncus sylvester,* also several of the spiraeas and filipendulas. All these groups are placed in the rose family. Except for one species, native in southeastern United States, *A. biternata,* most of the astilbes originate in Asia. Garden hybrids, however, have been developed chiefly in Europe, and are known principally as *A. arendsii, A. rosea,* and *A. lemoinei.*

The minute flowers of deep rose, pink, or ivory-white are carried in rather dense yet delicate spires of bloom above the sharply toothed, dark-green leaflets. Petals are generally five, sepals four or five, stamens eight, ten, or occasionally five. The plants are sometimes sold in florist shops under the name of spiraea. Propagated by division or seed, they are thoroughly hardy herbaceous perennials, easily cultivated outdoors in rich soil where abundant water is provided.

J. C. Wis.

ASTON, FRANCIS WILLIAM (1877-1945), British physicist, was born at Harborne, Birmingham, Sept. 1, 1877. After being educated at Malvern College and Birmingham and Cambridge universities, he was elected to a fellowship at Trinity College, Cambridge, and in 1909 became assistant lecturer in physics at Birmingham University. Following up the work of J. J. Thomson, who first showed that the atoms of a given chemical element could differ in weight, Aston spent his life in devising more and more powerful ways for investigating the isotopic constitution of the elements; that is, identifying the atomic species making up each of the chemical elements found in nature. He constructed the first mass spectrograph and with its aid discovered hundreds of isotopes. In 1922 he won the Nobel Prize in chemistry and in 1938 was awarded the Royal Medal of the Royal Society. He died Nov. 21, 1945, in Cambridge, England.

ASTOR, JOHN JACOB (1763-1848), American merchant, was born July 17, 1763, in Waldorf, Germany, the youngest of four sons. His father was a butcher of spend-

JOHN JACOB ASTOR

thrift habits, and John Jacob's early years, working in his father's store, were years of hardship and privation. In 1780 he made his way to London and found employment with his brother, George Astor, who had left home several years earlier and opened a workshop for the manufacture of musical instruments. After two years John Jacob had saved enough money to buy passage to America, and in 1783 he sailed for Baltimore. During the voyage a shipboard acquaintance told him of the money to be made in furs in the United States, and upon arrival Astor consequently sought employment in that business, finding it at Robert Browne's fur store in New York City. He applied himself diligently and soon was entrusted with the purchase of furs from the Indians and the seasonal trips to Montreal to obtain furs from the trappers. By 1786 Astor had learned enough about the business to open his own shop on Water Street. This rapidly became a thriving enterprise, especially after he had established connections in London, which, besides providing a valuable outlet for his furs, also enabled him to buy merchandise for resale in the United States at a profit. In addition, he contracted to represent his brother's concern, Astor and Broadwood, in America, and he sold "furs and pianos"; thus he became the first regular dealer in musical instru-

ments in New York. Astor soon had enough money to purchase a ship, which enabled him to enter the profitable China market, receiving valuable return cargoes of tea and silks.

In 1811 Astor organized an expedition to establish "Astoria," a coastal depot at the mouth of the Columbia River, as part of a contemplated line of trading posts from the Great Lakes to the Pacific, and thence to China. The story of this settlement, the difficulty with the Indians, the loss of the first ship of the expedition, and the capture of the settlement by the British in the War of 1812, has been told by Washington Irving in *Astoria* (1836). This was, however, Astor's only real loss during that war, for his ships continued to slip through the blockade unmolested, and he invested in government loans at a considerable profit to himself. Large as his earnings were in the fur business, the bulk of Astor's fortune came from his investments, chiefly in real estate. He bought and resold property on Manhattan Island, on the fringes of the rapidly expanding city, such as Richmond Hill (Aaron Burr's estate) and Eden Farm, on which is now located Times Square. The celebrated Morris estate trial is an illustration of his business acumen. The Roger Morris estate in Putnam County had been confiscated by the state during the Revolutionary War, but Astor discovered that Morris had held only a lifetime interest in the estate, and for $100,000 Astor bought the rights of the heirs. The legality of this transaction was upheld by the courts in 1827, and, despite the fact that Daniel Webster and Martin Van Buren had acted as counsel for the state, it was obliged to pay Astor approximately $500,000 for his rights. Astor drove a hard bargain, he carefully scrutinized his investments, he ruthlessly foreclosed on mortgages, and he lived frugally and unostentatiously. It is not surprising, therefore, that he became the richest man of his day, and at the time of his death in New York, on Mar. 29, 1848, he had amassed a fortune of some $20,000,000. In his will he left $50,000 to his native village of Waldorf, $70,000 for sundry philanthropic purposes, $400,000 to the city for the founding of the Astor Library, and the remainder to his son, William B. Astor (his eldest son being mentally deficient), who later doubled the family fortune.

C. W. D.

ASTOR, NANCY WITCHER LANGHORNE, VISCOUNTESS (1879-   ), British politician, was born at "Mirador," Greenwood, Va., on May 19, 1879. In 1897 she married Robert Gould Shaw of Boston but divorced him in 1903. In 1906 she married Waldorf Astor, the son of William Waldorf Astor, an American who had become a British subject. On his father's death in 1919, he became 2nd Viscount Astor, and was forced to retire from the House of Commons. Lady Astor was elected in his place as Conservative member for Plymouth, and so became the first woman to sit in the British Parliament. At first she concentrated her attention on seeking reforms in connection with the welfare of women and children; in this she had some success, but her preaching of a temperance which amounted to prohibition gained her nothing but polite derision. She served her constituency vigorously, and was consistently re-elected until 1945, since which time, she has been interested in public affairs but has held no public office.

E. R. A.

ASTORGA [astɔ'rga], a city and see of a bishop in León Province, in northwestern Spain, about 60 mi. southwest of León. It is situated about 2,850 ft. above sea level, near the Gerga Torrent (an affluent of the Esla and Duero rivers), on the eastern slopes of the Montañas de León. As-

ASTORIA, OREGON, AS AN EARLY FUR-TRADING STATION

torga lies at the junction of the Madrid-Salamanca-La Coruña railway with the line running to León, both of which follow ancient highways long used for military and trading purposes. There are several small industrial plants, and the city serves as a market for the surrounding region. The principal monument is the cathedral, built in the fifteenth and sixteenth centuries. Its Renaissance façade is of interest. Parts of the city walls still survive.

Astorga became an episcopal see as early as the third century. The Goths, and later the Moors, destroyed the city, but the site was resettled in the ninth century. It stoutly resisted a siege by the French from March 21 to April 22, 1810. Pop. 1940, 14,523. R. G. W.

ASTORIA, a port city and the county seat of Clatsop Co., Oregon, situated at the mouth of the Columbia River, about 80 mi. northwest of Portland. It is served by the Spokane, Portland & Seattle Railway and is on the route of the West Coast Airlines. Lumber, flour, and fertilizer milling are leading industries. Dairying and salmon canning are also important activities. Astoria was founded in 1811 by the John Jacob Astor expeditionary parties and is said to be the oldest city in the Northwest. Pop. 1950, 12,331.

ASTRAEA [æstri'ə], in Greek mythology, daughter of Zeus and Themis and goddess of justice, who fled from earth when men grew wicked. She became the constellation Virgo. *See also* AGES OF MAN. G. E. D.

ASTRAGALUS [æstræ'gələs], a genus of about 1,500 herbs and shrubs of the pea family, growing in dry soils throughout the world, except in Australia. A few are sparingly cultivated for their heads of somewhat pea-like white, yellow, or purple flowers. The common forms are low herbs, with small leaflets, called "milkvetch." Several western Asiatic species yield gum tragacanth, while the so-called Swedish coffee is made from the seeds of a European species. Several species from the Great Plains of the United States are called "locoweed" from the peculiar disease that their consumption produces in cattle, and several other western kinds are poisonous. J. C. Wis.

ASTRAKHAN [æ'strəkæ'n, ɑ'straχɑ'ny], the name of an *okrug,* or district, and the administrative center of that district in the Stalingrad Region of the Russian Soviet Federated Socialist Republic, in the southwestern Soviet Union.

The City. The city is a fishing port situated on an island formed by branches of the Volga River in its great delta in the northwest Caspian Sea. It is about 135 mi. southeast of Stalingrad. Behind Astrakhan lies a low area of salt marshes in the Caspian depression, and the city is 70 ft. below sea level. Since the town is only slightly higher than the average level of the Volga, earthen dikes 14 ft. high are required to prevent flooding in spring. Although the location is unhealthy and bad epidemics have occurred, it was inevitable that a large city should develop at the Volga's mouth in order to handle the great volume of trade, to transship goods from seagoing ships to river boats, and to carry on the great fishing industry.

Established in the thirteenth century on a bank of the Volga River 7 mi. north of the present site, it became the capital of a Tatar khanate. Tamerlane destroyed Astrakhan in 1395, and the city was rebuilt on the island on which it now stands to afford necessary protection against marauding nomads. Taken from the Tatars by Ivan the Terrible in 1557, it successfully withstood a Tatar attempt in 1660 to retake the city, but it fell ten years later to the robber Cossack, Stenka Razin. As an advance base for Peter the Great's campaigns against Persia, Astrakhan expanded considerably, gaining in industry and trade. Pestilence and destructive fires often caused temporary declines in prosperity, but growth was continuous. During the civil conflict between 1917 and 1920, the city was a strong defensive point against the anti-Bolshevik leader Denikin. Fighting in World War II occurred west and northwest of Astrakan.

On the highest elevation is the sixteenth-century kremlin; within its walls is the Uspensky Cathedral, completed in 1710. Among several large squares, the former Alexander Square is noteworthy. In the city hall is the Peter Museum, containing natural-history and other collections. The Ichthyological Museum south of the kremlin contains excellent exhibits of Caspian fish. Mosques and Roman Catholic, Greek Orthodox, and Lutheran churches are among

KIROV SQUARE IN ASTRAKHAN

SOVFOTO

the city's religious institutions. A university was founded here in 1919.

Astrakhan derives its importance from its location at the mouth of Russia's greatest waterway. Goods moving between European Russia and central Asia on Caspian Sea boats are transferred at Astrakhan to and from smaller Volga boats. There is large-scale trade in timber, petroleum, fish, caviar, cotton, carpets, grain, salt, rice, dried fruits, and manufactured goods, making the city the second greatest Caspian port. While the harbor is a busy one, excessive silting of the channel detracts from the value of the port and prevents entry of large vessels. As a fishing center, Astrakhan ranks first in the Soviet Union; the Volga delta is the sturgeon and caviar center of the world. In addition to the fishing, Astrakhan does considerable processing and canning of fish products. Melons and wine are produced in the area, and there are shipbuilding yards in the city. The population is greatly mixed, including Armenians, Persians, Tatars, Russians, and Kalmuks. Pop. (est. 1950), 325,000.

The District. The Astrakhan Okrug is bounded on the northeast by the okrugs of West Kazakhstan and Guryev, on the southeast by the Caspian Sea, on the south by Gronzy Okrug, on the southwest by Stavropol Krai, on the west by Rostov Okrug, and on the northwest and north by Stalingrad Okrug. The district is divided into two arid steppe areas by the Volga River, which flows generally southeastward in a series of channels, the principal being the Akhtouba, and forms a delta of 2,500 sq. mi. covered by a network of narrow outlets. Alluviums are causing the delta to increase at the rate of 308 ft. a year into the Caspian Sea. The temperature averages 19.2 degrees F. in January and 77.3 in July. In ravines adjoining the Volga are belts of land suitable for agriculture, which in some years produce good crops, although not in sufficient quantity to satisfy the needs of the district. Rainfall is unreliable and famines often occur. The main industry is fishing, carried on in the Caspian Sea and in the Akhtouba, which is one of the richest fishing regions in the world. The vogla, a variety of shad, together with pike, carp, sturgeon, herring, and other fish are caught. Salt from deposits at Lake Baskunchak is used in fish-curing. The Volga forms the chief means of transport in the district. Pop. (est. 1954), 700,000.   C. C. H. and W. S. V.

ASTRINGENTS. *See* PHARMACOLOGY.

ASTROLOGY, in the widest sense, the discipline which formulates general concepts of the universe, based on the assumption of a correspondence between the movements of the sun, moon, and planets in the heavens and the movements of life on earth. In the long history of its development and application, astrology has been variously defined as a science, a pseudo science, an astral theology, and an art, and it is still so defined by the conflicting branches of its advocates as well as its opponents. Actually, each one of these definitions describes the subject accurately at a different phase of its history and practice, so that a precise definition of astrology cannot properly be separated from a review of its history.

Primitive Development. Astrology appears to have its beginning in the primitive man's realization of the wonder of the waxing, waning, and eclipses of the moon, and a recognition of the correspondence of the seasons of the year with the sun's arrival at the equinoctial and solstitial points. These are the most easily observed celestial data, and are of overwhelming importance as soon as a people begins to cultivate the soil. In Sumeria and Babylonia, where records extend back to 2500 B.C., in China to at least 2300 B.C., and in the Mayan civilization, the chronology of which is questionable, astrology consisted at first solely of observing and tabulating these solilunar data, and from them predicting the time and circumstances of their recurrence. This effort, which was truly scientific in the modern sense of the word, was followed shortly by attempts to correlate the solilunar data with weather conditions. It was but a short step further to add the correlation of the solilunar phenomena with mundane occurrences, such as famine, natural disasters, war and peace, and victory and defeat. One step more carried the correspondence to the developments in the life and fortunes of the ruling personage. That belief in such correspondence has survived into modern times is evidenced in sketches of the life of Adolf Hitler.

In a stage of civilization in which the sun and moon were regarded as supernatural it was inevitable that their movements should have been enhanced with the trappings of a celestial religion. The scientific data then became merely a means of determining in advance the wishes of the gods, thus establishing astrology's transition to an astral religion. Not that purely astronomical investigation stopped; on the contrary, it accelerated and acquired an almost unbelievable degree of accuracy, considering the lack of instruments and higher mathematics. But as a greater body of data was accumulated, the speculative thought of the priest-astrologers, under whose direction it was gathered, ranged into wider and wider theological conceptions and naive conclusions. All primitive astrologies consist of virtually the same material: rules for weather and mundane predictions, lucky and unlucky days, and set formulas for traditional activities and rituals. Mayan astrology apparently never progressed beyond this point, Chinese astrology remains in substantially the same stage, and there is little evidence to support the contention that Babylonian astrology achieved a much broader interpretation before being supplemented by Greek thought. Certainly, however, the Babylonians' contribution to astronomical data is unquestioned. By the second century B.C., they were able to construct, in advance, ephemerides (tables of planetary positions in the signs, heliacal risings and settings, and times and places of conjunctions and oppositions of the planets). Perhaps the major contribution of the Babylonians to later thought rests upon their conclusion, drawn from the invariable cycles of the celestial bodies, that the world is eternal.

Greek and Hellenistic Contributions. In the interchange of culture between Greece and the Near East that followed upon the conquests of Alexander the Great early in the fourth century B.C., Babylonian (Chaldean) astrology arrived and offered to Greek thinkers, who were primarily preoccupied with the nature of the universe, a conception which was not only based on demonstrable data but which also presented a broad enough frame of reference to embody many of the theories already crystallized. Empedocles' four elements—fire, air, earth, and water—were immediately correlated with the four astrological elements of the same names. The cosmogony of Plato and the metaphysic of Aristotle raised astrology almost to the status of a divine science. These theories of the origin of being were largely responsible for the high regard in which astrology was held, not only in ancient and medieval times, but also after the revival of Greek culture in the Renaissance. Perhaps even more important to the later life of astrology was the Stoics' concept of the unity of the microcosm (man) and the macrocosm (the universe), which offered a reasonable basis for the correspondence between celestial cycles and cycles in human activities. The Greeks, by thus transferring astrology from the realm of national or meteorological conditions to the affairs of the individual, gave a new vitality to the subject and established that branch of the astrology, genethliacal (nativity) or judicial (planetary-influence) astrology, through which it is most generally known to this day. The last great Greek astronomer, Claudius Ptolemy, who flourished in Alexandria during the second century of the Christian Era, also contributed greatly to the survival of astrology. His most famous books, the *Almagest* and *Tetrabiblos,* were standard textbooks of astrology and astronomy for twelve hundred years after his time; in fact, his *Tetrabiblos* is still in use as an astrological textbook.

Judicial Astrology. Judicial astrology, already well developed at the time of Ptolemy, deals with the relationship between the positions of the sun, moon, and planets and the life of an individual. It had its philosophical basis in the concept that man is a miniature replica of the universe, and that therefore each individual reflects in himself and his circumstances the pattern of the heavens at the time of his birth; and conversely that the pattern of the heavens at that time describes the individual.

Horoscope. A horoscope is an illustration of the heavenly pattern of the sun, moon, and planets at a given moment of time from a given longitude and latitude on the earth. The individual was, and still is, considered to be placed in the center of the "wheel," since in Ptolemy's astronomy the earth was a sphere around which the celestial bodies revolved. The wheel of the horoscope shows twelve spokes or dividing lines, although the sphere is actually divided into two separate sets of twelvefold divisions, which conventionally are projected on a flat surface as if they existed in one plane.

Zodiac. The primary division of the celestial sphere is the zodiac, a hypothetical band extending 8° on each side of the ecliptic (the apparent path of the sun around the earth), which is divided into 12 equal divisions, or signs, of 30°. The Babylonians devised the zodiac about 500 B.C., and assigned to each sign the name of the constellation which occupied the greater part of the 30° area at that time. The starting point of the zodiac, at 0°, is Aries, followed by Taurus, Gemini, Cancer, Leo, Virgo, Libra, Scorpio, Sagittarius, Capricorn, Aquarius, and Pisces, at 30° intervals. Because of precession of the equinoxes, 0° Aries no longer coincides with the constellation Aries; but astrology maintains that the starting point of the zodiac, which was originally based on solar movement, should continue to coincide with the vernal equinox (the passage of the sun on its northward journey over the point where the ecliptic cuts the equator). The zodiac itself is subdivided into four triplicities or elements, arrived at by inscribing within the circle four equilateral triangles whose apexes coincide with the equinoctial and solstitial points, and placing the signs outlined by the points of each triangle in one classification. Starting with the vernal equinox, the fire signs Aries, Sagittarius, and Leo are defined by the first triangle; Cancer, Scorpio, and Pisces, the water signs, by the triangle whose apex is the summer solstice; Libra, Aquarius, and Gemini, the air signs, by the autumn equinoctial point; and Capricorn, Taurus, and Virgo, the earth signs, by that of the winter solstice.

Houses. The spokes on the wheel are the dividing lines between the houses of the horoscope. House division is a method of dividing the visible and invisible hemispheres either in terms of time or space. Either method trisects the celestial arc that appears at a given moment at a given latitude between the eastern horizon (ascendant) and the upper meridian (midheaven). Thus, the twelvefold division of the houses is based on the earth's daily rotation on its axis, whereas the twelvefold division of the zodiac is based on the sun's apparent yearly motion. Therefore, the movement through the zodiac, which is a universal experience, is basic and relates principally to character—the Aries type, the fire type, and so on. In contrast, the movement of the houses, which is completed in 24 hours, relates to the circumstances of the individual—the first house, personality; the second, financial prospects; the fourth, home, and so on. Each planet is considered to describe a type of activity. For example, Mercury describes mental ability, speech, and writing; Venus, affection. The moon governs the emotions. Each planet also rules two signs (the sun and moon rule one each). In addition, the planet which rules the sign on a house rules that house and its circumstances. Interpretation of planetary positions is further refined by consideration of the planets' angular relationships to each other (called aspects), the major aspects being 0°, 60°, 90°, 120°, and 180°. There are also a number of subdivisions of both the zodiac and the houses which were used by ancient astrologers and are still in use by the Hindus, and refinements of many types.

A Typical Horoscope. The accompanying illustration shows the horoscope of the United States of America, erected for 2:21 A.M., Local Civil Time, July 4, 1776, at Philadelphia,

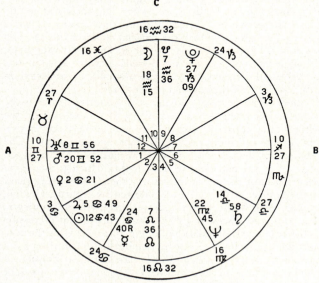

HOROSCOPE OF THE UNITED STATES

Pa., 75° 8′ W. long., 39° 57′ N. lat. *A* indicates the eastern horizon or ascendant, *B* the western horizon or descendant, and *C* the upper meridian or midheaven. The figures around the center of the horoscope indicate the houses; thus the first house lies just under the horizon, the second below the first, and so on. The figures to the right of the planets' symbols give the positions of the planets in geocentric longitude, while the figures and symbols in the outermost circle give the degrees of the zodiac cut by the planes of the great circles of the houses.

Application to Inorganic Matter and in Medicine. The Greeks applied astrology to all levels of the material world, assigning rulership over different minerals, plants, colors, precious stones, and other phenomena to planets and signs. In accordance with their microcosm-macrocosm concept, each sign of the zodiac rules a part of the body, and the planets rule various physical functions; this is the origin of the "celestial man" who decorates popular almanacs and drugstore windows. Medical astrology was so widely accepted that even in medieval times it was not considered possible for a physician to practice without the knowledge and use of astrology.

Divinatory Astrology. After the fall of the Roman Empire, astrology languished, nurtured perhaps as a secret knowledge by Jewish scholars of the Alexandrian school, by whom it is presumed to have been introduced into the Mohammedan world. In the eighth century, Harun-al-Rashid ordered a translation into Arabic of Ptolemy's *Almagest.* Construction of observatories followed rapidly at Baghdad, where the greatest of Arabic astrologers, Albumazar, studied in the ninth century, and at Cordova and Toledo after the Moorish invasion of Spain. The Arabs, however, with their fatalistic

orientation, relegated the judicial astrology of the Greeks to a minor place, developing in its stead divinatory or horary astrology. Divinatory astrology encompasses elections (selection of the proper time for action) and questions on any subject—recovery of lost property, when to invest money, and so on. A chart is erected for the exact hour and minute the question is asked, and the answer is determined from the distribution of the planets on it. Elections consist of selecting a time when the planetary positions indicate success for the particular venture. Although divinatory astrology is based on a concept similar to that of the judicial astrology of the Greeks—that the heavens at the moment illustrate the conditions below—it is limited by an almost numberless set of intricate rules which allow for little deviation, either in interpretation or action.

Decadence. Astrology came into medieval Europe via the universities of Spain, to which scholars began to flock in the eleventh and twelfth centuries, and where they translated the *Almagest* and *Tetrabiblos* of Ptolemy and *Introductorium in Astronomiam* of Albumazar. The astrology that developed in Europe from the twelfth through the sixteenth centuries, despite its almost universal acceptance by scholars and its position as a vital part of medieval literature, had little resemblance to the reasoned conclusions of Ptolemy. Divinatory astrology was emphasized, judicial astrology was vitiated by an admixture of Semitic mysticism, and toward the close of this period astrology became allied more and more closely with magic. The discovery of the heliocentric system by Copernicus in the sixteenth century, and the growth of scientific inquiry and knowledge in the seventeenth and eighteenth centuries, discredited astrology first with astronomers, then with scientists in other fields. Moreover, the obvious charlatanry of many of its practitioners helped to throw it into disrepute. The invention of printing in the 1400's permitted the publication of ephemerides and trigonometrical tables, so that the astrologer no longer had to know astronomy and higher mathematics to practice his art; thus the door was opened to anyone who could read, add, and subtract. A close reading of the early modern opponents of astrology reveals that opposition was directed more against astrologers than against the subject itself. It is significant that no astrological literature has survived between Ptolemy's *Tetrabiblos* of the second century, and the writings of William Lilly and his pupil, John Gadsbury, in the mid-1600's.

MODERN SCHOOLS

Moralistic. Scattered interest in astrology continued, especially in England, during the Renaissance and the eighteenth century, but the real beginning of modern astrology dates from 1820 and 1822, when two translations in English of *Tetrabiblos* appeared. Then, toward the end of the nineteenth century, the rise of theosophy, which adopted astrology, supplied the next impetus with the publication of the works of Alan Leo in England; and Rosicrucianism, with its flavor of medieval mysticism and ancient Masonry, accomplished the same end in America. These two movements, through the wide distribution of their literature, may be said to have been the initiators of the semireligious, or at least moralistic, astrology which is widely followed today. The two main lines of modern astrology, however, as developed since World War I, originated in America: astrological physics and astrological meteorology, which are in essence throwbacks to the natural astrology of the Babylonians, and psychological astrology, which is akin to much of Greek thought, though clothed in terms of modern psychology.

Physical Astrology. The term "physical astrology" is

applied to any astrology based on a theory of a cause-and-effect relationship between the physical body of a planet and conditions of life on earth. Astrological physics utilizes some of the recent concepts of interspatial physics and electrodynamics, namely, that man, the earth, the sun, the fixed stars, and the planets are charged bodies with magnetic fields of varying intensity; and that the relative movements of the sun and planets in space cause changes in the phase angles of the "magnetic-field couplings," thus changing the "power factor" at the various angular relationships.

Astrological Meteorology. Astrological meteorology, a theory based on the tidal and gravitational pull of the sun and moon and the planets, is the only branch of present-day astrology that can rightly be termed a science, in that it consists of empirical conclusions derived from a correlation of weather and astronomical data collected daily and recorded over decades. It confines itself to weather forecasting, whereas astrological physics has been applied mainly to earthquakes, fires, floods, and so on. Astrological meteorology has met with a degree of success in application, and has aroused more interest among meteorologists and scientists in other fields than any other branch of astrology. In method and purpose, it approaches closely the early astrology of the Babylonians.

Astrological Biology. Astrological biology, loosely placed under the heading of physical astronomy, is a theory that allocates certain mineral salts to the sun, moon, planets, and, in some cases, to the earth. The determination of the salts needed to maintain a healthful balance is arrived at according to the placement and relationship of the planets in a horoscope erected for the time and place of birth. Lunar planting, or planting when the moon is in certain signs and phases (the moon in a water or earth sign in first and second phase is considered most favorable for growth), should also be classified as a physical astrology.

Psychological Astrology. Psychological astrology is essentially the judicial astrology of Ptolemy's time; the same general interpretations, applied to modern life, are retained. The major difference is that the emphasis is now placed wholly on the individual; he continues to maintain his unity of rhythm with the rhythm of celestial cycles, but the universal or archetypal characteristics of the planetary interpretations are considered as potentials rather than foreordained factors, both in relation to his innate character and to his circumstances. The final sovereignty of the free will of the individual to develop and use the potentials of his horoscope is thus supposedly accomplished (though opponents of astrology protest that connecting man to the rhythm of the universe is in itself an *a priori* denial of his free will). Plotinus and his contemporaries (third century A.D.) moved in this direction by holding that the "stars" are signs, not causes; but despite this lip service to the free will of man, it remained for the most part an abstract doctrine, divorced almost completely from the actual practice of horoscopy.

Modern philosophical thought has also led to the development of a *Gestalt* approach to the horoscope, by which it is considered an integrated pattern rather than so many separate parts. In addition, astrological factors or groups of factors have been correlated with psychological complexes and concepts—with the inferiority and superiority complexes, the masculine urge, and the abnormal parental bonds, of Alfred Adler; with the four psychological types, and the anima and animus of Carl Jung; and with theories of other psychologies. Moreover, the modern interest in cycles, now under investigation by scientists, has also led to a new method of "prediction" by astrology that is not unlike the predictional methods of the scientists; the cyclic return of planets to a given

position is related to the general circumstances that prevailed at previous returns, with due regard paid to the interlinking of the different planetary cycles.

As an example of the difference in interpretation between medieval astrology and that of the modern psychological school, the medieval astrologer would say that the early life of a person born with Saturn ascending in the eastern horizon would be filled with hardships, ill health, perhaps poverty, whereas the modern advocate of psychological astrology would interpret the same position as suggesting unsureness and an overanxiety to please, so that the person might take on unnecessary responsibilities to prove his competence or to make himself feel needed. By relating the position of Saturn to other factors in the horoscope, the sense of inferiority might be traced to a broken home, an unhealthy bond with one of the parents, the superiority of brothers or sisters, and so on. Where medieval judicial astrology emphasized the destiny of the individual, at best trying to find means of avoiding the worst, modern psychological astrology emphasizes self-knowledge as a therapy, and the possibility of development of the potentials of the horoscope at the highest level.   M. Mo.

ASTRONOMICAL INSTRUMENTS. In astronomy the basic field work is accomplished by observation of celestial objects. The work is done largely by means of telescopes and accessories, and by spectographs and other instruments. All of these, for professional work, are housed in an observatory.

TELESCOPES

The telescope is the principal instrument. There are two chief kinds: the refractor and the reflector.

Refractors. Refracting telescopes vary in size from the small spyglass to the 40-in. model at the Yerkes Observatory, at Lake Geneva, Wis. Essentially a refractor consists of only a few parts.

Objective. The large lens, or objective, is the most important and expensive feature. Ordinarily it consists of two lenses used together, a positive and a negative element placed nearly (and sometimes altogether) in contact. The elements are composed of different kinds of glass and are of different physical properties so that the image will be as nearly perfect as possible. In the apochromat, a special highly corrected objective, there are three lenses, and the corrections are the finest obtainable; but apochromats are not made in the very large sizes. The focal length of the objective is comparatively long; in the normal astronomical objective it is 15 times the diameter of the glass.

Ocular. The only other essential optical element in the refractor is the ocular, or eyepiece, a very small and short-focus lens which is used to magnify the primary image formed by the objective. It is slipped into a sliding sleeve in the eye end of the telescope. Oculars are compound, being composed of two separate lenses (Huygens and Ramsden types), or three lenses, one separated from the other two which are cemented together (Kellner type); or in the most highly corrected type, of four lenses (orthoscopic). Various oculars may be used with the same objective, according to the need of the observer and the conditions of the atmosphere at the time. Magnification achieved is expressed by $m = F/f$, where F is the focal length of the objective and f is the focus of the ocular. The shorter the focus of the eyepiece, therefore, the higher the magnification given with the same objective. High magnifications for a certain instrument are difficult to use, since the irregular refractive phenomena of the atmosphere are thereby intensified, and ordinarily a

SCHMIDT TELESCOPE, CLEVELAND, OHIO

given telescope is not used at magnifications or "powers" of more than 50 per inch of diameter of objective. The lowest power that shows the necessary details gives the best results. The image is inverted, but the inversion is of no consequence for sky objects, and an erecting system of lenses like that in small terrestrial telescopes and field glasses is purposely not used.

Reflectors. The reflecting telescope has for its principal optical element a concave mirror as large in diameter as convenient, arranged at the bottom of the telescope tube. The sides of the latter may be closed as in small telescopes, or composed of an open framework as in the larger sizes. In all types of reflectors the end toward the sky is open. There are different models of reflectors, each named after its inventor. In the Newtonian type, the rays of light from the parabolic mirror converge and fall onto a prism or a small,

optically flat mirror within the telescope tube and near the open end. From this surface they are reflected at right angles to the side of the tube where the ocular is mounted; thus the observer looks into the instrument at right angles to the tube. In the Cassegrainian form, the light rays converge onto a small hyperbolic mirror instead of a flat one, and then they are reflected back to the main mirror. This has a hole in the center, thus allowing the image to be inspected with the eyepiece from a point behind the mirror. Instead of the hole arrangement, the Nasmyth modification has a small mirror reflecting the image out at the side of the tube, near the large mirror, as in the Mount Wilson 100-in. instrument.

The Newtonian and Cassegrainian are the commonest forms of reflectors. Occasionally others are made. In the Gregorian model, the small secondary is of concave elliptical section, the rays going through a central hole in the mirror as in the Cassegrain type. The secondary mirror, however, is placed farther from the large mirror and the tube is longer. In the Herschellian telescope the mirror is tilted off axis and the image is viewed from the rim at the open end of the tube as one looks down toward the mirror. The coudé form, which literally means "bent like an elbow," is used in some of the largest telescopes, including the 200-in. instrument at Mount Palomar, Calif. The largest instruments are often arranged so that the telescope may be used interchangeably in two or more systems. The coudé arrangement has a plain mirror at the intersection of the polar and declination axes, so that the light-rays are reflected down the polar axis and received in a fixed location, that is, a room where various accessory instruments may be used with it, and which may be a more comfortable observing situation.

Mounting. The mounting is an essential feature of any telescope. In the altazimuth mounting, often used with small portable telescopes, the telescope is usually mounted on a tripod and the observer can move the tube in different directions. While this mounting is comparatively light in weight, its facilities and use are somewhat limited; photography is impossible. The equatorial mounting is far heavier and less convenient and is used typically for fixed and observatory telescopes. There are two axes: a polar axis arranged parallel to the earth's axis, around which axis the telescope can turn in hour angle, following the stars; and a declination axis (at right angles to the polar axis) around which the telescope moves in declination. When an equatorial telescope is properly arranged and oriented, the observer may follow a celestial object in its diurnal movement merely by turning the slow-motion screw in hour angle; or if, as in observatory installations, the telescope is fitted with a driving clock, the clockwork mechanism then holds the image continually in view. Small telescopes up to about 5 in. diameter are mounted on tripods or stands, whereas an observatory instrument commonly is fixed on a pier, which affords a heavier and more stable support for the long, heavy, telescope tube.

Finders. Telescopes 3 in. in diameter and larger are commonly supplied with a finder, a small telescope mounted on the tube of the main telescope, of low magnification and wide field of view; it is adjusted so that the object in the middle of the field of the finder is also in the middle of the field of the main telescope. Thus a finder helps locate a faint object by centering it quickly so that it may be examined in the main tube.

OTHER INSTRUMENTS AND ACCESSORIES

Clocks. Clocks are an essential feature of an astronomical observatory. Only two kinds of time are kept by them: mean solar and sidereal. The mean-time clocks are simply high precision clocks running on normal standard time. They are used for general purposes, including the timing of observations. Sidereal clocks measure time by the apparent motion of the "fixed" stars. All time used for civil purposes over the earth is obtained by star observations made with the aid of sidereal time. Aside from the fundamental determination of time itself, the sidereal clock is used for finding latitude and longitude and for miscellaneous purposes. If the local sidereal time is known, together with the right ascension and declination of an invisible object, the telescope may be pointed at the object. An observatory clock is by far the most accurate clock made. It is large and usually beats seconds; its dial has 24 hours, and it has an accurate second hand. Often it has an electric connection to be used with the chronograph or with other instruments.

Chronograph. A chronograph is an excellent means of recording astronomical observations accurately and permanently. A revolving drum covered with a sheet of paper causes a pen to trace a continuous line on the sheet. The main observatory clock is connected with this device, and an electric contact marks off each second. Radio time signals may be connected when desired, to compare the clock reading with official time. Any series of observations involving time, as for example star transits, may be run onto the chronograph, and such signals are recorded as breaks in the otherwise continuous record of minutes and seconds on the sheet. Ordinary readings are 0.01 sec., but readings to 0.001 sec. may be obtained with accuracy.

COURTESY OF AMERICAN MUSEUM OF NATURAL HISTORY

COELOSTAT

Coelostat. The coelostat is an auxiliary instrument composed of two plain mirrors of fine workmanship and special mounting, so arranged that the main telescope (or other instrument) may remain in a fixed position. One mirror is equatorially mounted, in a situation open to the sky. Following the heavenly objects in their diurnal movement, it reflects the light rays into a second mirror, which in turn throws the rays into the telescope.

Transit Instrument. The transit instrument is made to observe the passage of stars (and occasionally other objects) across the meridian, as in time determinations. It is a telescope mounted with its axis in an east-and-west line, and capable of swinging accurately in the meridian plane. Various adjustments (pivots, levels, adjusting screws) are so arranged as to make it an instrument of precision. The objective is usually about 3 or 4 in. in diameter, and the eyepiece end has an ocular fitted with a system of cross hairs or spider lines. When a star crosses the reticle (system of lines), the observer makes contact with an electric circuit and this makes a signal on the chronometer, thus affording a permanent time record. An improved type of eyepiece for this work is the transit micrometer, described below.

Meridian Circle. A larger and more rigorously made instrument is the meridian circle. This device is a transit of the greatest precision, having a specially made graduated circle that turns with it, by which the declination of the object can be read.

Zenith Telescope. The zenith telescope is of about the same size as the transit instrument, but for accurate determination of the latitude it makes use of the difference between equal zenith distances of stars. Stars are observed to the north and to the south of the zenith, the telescope

COURTESY OF AMERICAN MUSEUM OF NATURAL HISTORY
MERIDIAN CIRCLE

being reversed between observations. Very sensitive levels and a micrometer eyepiece are essential parts.

Altazimuth. An altazimuth is a telescope like the transit instrument but with both vertical and horizontal circles. Altitude and azimuth of an object can be measured; and with the time recorded, the right ascension and declination may be computed. The latitude, longitude, and meridian can also be determined with the altazimuth.

Photo Zenith Tube. The photo zenith tube is allied functionally to the transit instrument. It is used at a few stations to photograph stars near the zenith, in order to obtain time determinations of the utmost accuracy. By using photography, errors due to the personal equation (the observer's human shortcomings) and other causes are largely eliminated.

Filar Position Micrometer; Measuring Engine. The filar position micrometer is a relatively small but important attachment used at the eye end of the telescope. It is a measuring instrument of great accuracy consisting essentially of one or more fine fixed wires, together with movable wires,

an ocular, and a small source of illumination for the wires. Various screws orient the apparatus and align the star. The distance between an observed body and a near-by star whose position may be accurately known can be measured. Or the direction of one of the objects from another (position angle)

COURTESY OF THE AMERICAN MUSEUM OF NATURAL HISTORY
PHOTO ZENITH TUBE

may be measured, as in double-star observing. Planetary diameters, satellite measures, comet and asteroid positions, and the relative position of a faint object near a bright one may also be ascertained. Such applications as these have particular reference to a large-scale view or small field on the sky. When a small scale and larger area are involved, the photographic plate is commonly used, and measurement is made on the finished plate with a measuring engine (machine).

Transit Micrometer. The transit micrometer, as used on the transit instrument and meridian circle, has a movable wire guided by hand to follow continuously a star crossing the meridian. Electric signals record on the chronograph the times when the star thus crosses each of several fixed wires. With this instrument, personal error is greatly reduced.

ASTROPHOTOGRAPHY

Several combinations of camera and telescope are used in astrophotography. If an ordinary visual refractor is used, the best results are secured by the use of yellow filters and color-sensitive plates, because the objectives are corrected mainly for yellow rays.

Photographic Telescope; Astrograph. A photographic telescope is a refractor having the objective corrected for the blue-violet rays, to which the "ordinary" photo plate is highly sensitive, and in this case no filter is necessary. In several large telescopes, as at Meudon and Potsdam, such a photographic refractor is mounted together with a visual refractor on the same axis, thus effectually making a twin telescope. More complicated objectives composed of four lenses, arranged in the fashion of a portrait lens in outward appearance, are designed purely for photographic use on the sky. Their focal lengths are usually shorter than those of refractors, yet they are long-focus lenses compared with normal photo objectives. These lenses are known as astrographic lenses or doublets, and the complete instrument is an astrograph. Typical uses for astrographic outfits are in asteroid photography and in the photography of stellar regions for star charts.

Schmidt Camera. Reflecting telescopes, especially the large ones in observatories, are used photographically with the plate fixed commonly (but not always) at the Newtonian focus, and sometimes at the prime focus. The Cassegrain and coudé foci are not as often used for direct photography. The plates are shifted by movement of the plateholder when "guiding" is being done, by watching a star image through an eyepiece at the margin of the field. The Schmidt camera (or telescope) has a spherical mirror instead of a paraboloid, and a correcting plate of specially figured glass placed near the sky end of the telescope, to overcome aberrations. Such an instrument is made in small and large sizes. Its field of view is relatively very large, say 25°, and the "speed" or relative aperture is very large, $f/1$ and even faster. However, the tube length is longer than that of the average reflector, and the plates or films must be fitted into a curved surface. Several modifications of the Schmidt camera occur, with variations in the correcting plate, mirror system, and other specifications.

Astrocamera. When an ordinary or even a special camera of normal focal length is attached to the outside of an equatorial telescope, it becomes an astrocamera. The angle of view is wider than in other types mentioned. (The field of sharp focus of a reflecting telescope is relatively very small.) When an astrocamera is in use, the telescope itself is used to guide the whole instrument and hold a star on the crosshairs of the eyepiece. Thus a field of view covering a large number of square degrees is obtained and at times a whole constellation may be photographed. A good example of the use of an astrocamera is the photographing of a comet with tail extending over several degrees of the sky.

Spectrograph. The spectrograph is an exceedingly important instrument in professional astronomy. Indeed, some observatories specialize on research in stellar spectroscopy almost exclusively. Photographs made with this tool reveal, in the arrangement of the spectral lines, the elements composing the various stars. Such photos may be made in a few minutes or several hours, according to the star's brightness. The pattern of spectral lines formed by a gaseous element in the laboratory is always the same: a certain element repeatedly gives lines spaced at definite wave-length intervals in the band of electromagnetic radiation. When exactly the same pattern is found in the spectra of the sun or a star, the inference is that this element exists there also. In a spectroscope (the visual counterpart of the spectrograph), either a prism or train of prisms, or else a grating of thousands of fine lines close together, is used to separate the star's light into its spectral colors. In a spectroscope the light enters the instrument at the eye end of a telescope, through a slit only a few thousandths of a millimeter wide, passes through a collimator lens where the rays become parallel, then through one or more prisms, and finally through another lens in the view telescope, where the spectra are focused and magnified by the eyepiece. If the eyepiece is replaced by a photo plate, the instrument becomes a spectrograph. As used on the large reflectors, this may be a large and complicated apparatus and very costly. It has special lenses and prisms that are transparent to ultraviolet radiation. The spectral colors are not of special importance; it is the positions of thousands of lines crossing the spectral band that assume significance. On each side of a stellar spectrum, a comparison spectrum made from a laboratory arc light always is recorded at the time of making the stellar spectrogram, for positive identification of the lines from the star. The arc spectra are frequently made under special conditions of pressure and other factors, thus giving the astronomer a clue to the physical condition of the stars.

The instrument just described is a slit spectrograph. An objective prism may be installed instead, whereby commonly a narrow-angled prism is put before the main telescope objective. By this means, the spectra of many stars in the field can be photographed simultaneously and kept for reference, for purposes of classification though not for measurement. The spectra are long bands which would be narrow ordinarily, but they are purposely widened by mechanical adjustment of the telescope.

Spectroheliograph. The spectroheliograph, a very ingenious contrivance, is used in researches on the sun, at observatories specializing in this kind of work. In effect it is a spectrograph which admits only one spectral line at a time as coming from the image of the sun's disk. The first slit is at the focal plane of the objective of a large telescope. The light from the one spectral line passes through an optical system of lens, grating, another objective, and then another slit, behind which the photo plate is placed. Thus only a very narrow part of the spectrum is used at one time, and the solar surface at this point is photographed in the light of but one chemical element, as for example calcium. In practice, the optical system as a whole is moved steadily, so that the first slit passes successively over all parts of the sun's image, and a spectrogram is made that represents the entire solar surface in this one element.

Coronagraph. The coronagraph is a specially designed telescope made for the observation of the sun's corona at any

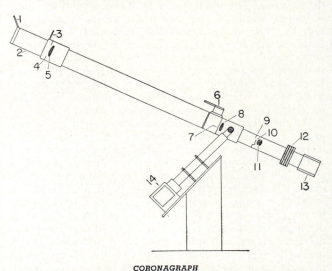

CORONAGRAPH

(1) Cover; (2) Dew cap; (3) Guider lens; (4) Diaphragm A; (5) Objective lens; (6) Photoelectric guiding mechanism; (7) Occulting disk; (8) Field lens; (9) Diaphragm B; (10) Screen; (11) Photocamera lens; (12) Balancing weights; and (13) Spectrograph

time, without waiting for a total solar eclipse. It was invented by Bernard Lyot of the Paris Observatory, who used it in the exceptionally clear atmosphere of the branch observatory at the Pic du Midi. A few coronagraphs have also been constructed and installed in Switzerland and the United States. The intensity of light from the corona is scarcely greater than the light from the sky near the sun, so that various ingenious features are included in the coronagraph, to destroy traces of stray light accompanying an optical system. In Lyot's instrument, particular attention is paid to having lenses that are free of even minor defects. In front of the main objective is a diaphragm. The image of the sun, formed by this lens, is thrown onto an occulting disk, which cuts out most of the sun, leaving only the chromosphere, prominences, and corona. Back of the occulting disk is a field lens which forms an image farther down the tube, and this image is picked up by the camera objective which finally projects it onto a photo plate. The instrument may be used photographically or visually, or spectrographic equipment may be used to record the coronal lines.

Comparators. The blink microscope (or comparator) is an apparatus for the examination of stellar photo plates made on the same region of the sky. The two plates are shown to the eye in rapid succession by movement of a lever. Thus changes in the configuration of the objects, as for example movement by a suspected planet, are immediately detected by apparent relative motion; or new objects become apparent by their alternate appearance and disappearance. Essentially the blink microscope consists of an elaborate arrangement of microscope, prisms, lenses, standards to hold the plates, and illumination for the latter. Other instruments are the stereo-comparator, to measure rectangular co-ordinates; the spectro-comparator, for measurement of displacement of spectrum lines; and the ordinary co-ordinate measuring machine. All these instruments of precision may be very complicated and costly.

Photometers. Photometers are light-measuring instruments with which to measure stellar magnitudes or difference of magnitude between two stars. Several forms are in use. A wedge photometer is one of the simple kinds, in which a wedge of dark glass is inserted at the focal plane of the telescope. The observer adjusts the wedge until the intensity of the star is equal to that of an artificial star arranged near by. The wedge is previously calibrated, and readings on the wedge are made. An alternative procedure, superior when feasible, is to compare the star of unknown magnitude with one whose magnitude has been determined previously. In the polarizing photometer, the apparent brightness of a star and that of an artificial one are equalized by sending their light through a polarizing-prism system.

The photometers just described are used in visual photometry. In photographic photometry, the brighter the star image on a plate, the brighter the stellar magnitude. One method of obtaining magnitudes is to compare the image of the star of unknown magnitude with images of near-by stars of known magnitude used as standards. Graduated scales of star images are also used. In this work, special frames ("star-counting machines"), illuminate and magnify the negatives; measurement of density requires the use of the densitometer in its different forms. A microdensitometer tracing is a record, made photographically, of the density changes in a spectrum as the spectrum plate moves under a narrow slit. The photoelectric photometer is more elaborate; it measures objectively, and records photographically, the depth of blackening of the photo plate made on stars. The photoelectric cell installed in instruments gives the highest accuracy and is used in stellar photometry of precision. Very sensitive photocells in conjunction with large telescopes are able to measure magnitudes that are reliable to about $\frac{1}{100}$ magnitude.

Thermocouple. The thermocouple is an extremely sensitive instrument to record all radiations, including the infrared, visible, and ultraviolet regions. It utilizes a junction of very minute pieces of unlike metal (such as platinum and

bismuth), the free ends of which are connected to a galvanometer. The instrument is placed in the focus of a large reflector, the heat from the star or planet falling on an exceedingly small surface and setting up a minute electric current. The latter is read off and is proportional to the intensity of the radiation in the original source. By this means, actual heat from the planets and stars is recorded. The instrument has to be vacuum-enclosed in order to prevent escape of radiation to the surroundings. *See also* OPTICAL INSTRUMENTS; PHOTOMETRY; SPECTROSCOPY.   H. S. R.

ASTRONOMY, the science of the stars, is concerned with the nature and content of the stellar universe. It deals with the planets (including the earth); with their satellites, such as the moon, and with comets and meteor swarms that also revolve around the sun. It views the stars as distant suns and records how they are often assembled in pairs and clusters and into the vast structure called the galactic system. It looks beyond the Milky Way to survey millions of other stellar systems millions of light-years away. As a physical science, it is interested in the physical properties and chemical compositions of the celestial bodies. It supplements, by its more extensive inquiries, the information acquired in the narrow confines of physical and chemical laboratories.

DAWN OF ASTRONOMY

Astronomy is the oldest of the sciences. Its early cultivation was stimulated by the beauty and mystery of the starry scene, which was intimately associated with the ancient religions and mythologies. It was natural that primitive peoples, who spent much time out of doors, should become acquainted with the celestial bodies and their more obvious ways. Another incentive to watch the skies was the idea of some, but not all, early peoples that the destinies of nations were revealed by the heavenly bodies. When it became evident that there was no correlation between the two, astrology degenerated into a pseudo science. The astrologers then began to cast personal horoscopes, no longer watching the heavens but depending on rule books for guidance.

Importance of Stars. The stars were useful to early peoples, as they are to modern civilization. As they rose and set they told the time of night, and foretold the seasons, although today astronomers observe the stars with instruments of remarkable precision. Once, the same stars guided voyagers over the seas and deserts, and, while early methods of celestial navigation lacked the accuracy attained by the modern navigator with his sextant and tables, they served the same purpose and used the same stars. The practical value of astronomy was an important reason for its early cultivation.

Early Observations. Through the mists that beclouded the doings of people before the times of the early Greek philosophers, can be found glimpses of some progress in astronomy. It is not always easy to decide what discoveries originated with the early Greek philosophers and what they learned from the people of Mesopotamia. Certainly, it was obvious in very early times that the stars rise and set and move westward daily across the sky. It was also well known that particular groups of stars march slowly westward from night to night at the same hour, so that different groups are in view in the different seasons. Moreover, the cause of this was understood to be the sun's annual eastward motion around the heavens. The position of the ecliptic, the circular apparent path of the sun, was fairly well determined by measuring the lengths of shadows at noon through the year. The fact that the circle is tilted, so that the sun goes north and south as well, was known to cause the changing seasons. The importance of the zodiac was recognized, and it was understood that this band of the heavens, 16° wide, through which the ecliptic runs centrally, contains not only the sun but the moon and usually all the bright planets. These planets—Mercury, Venus, Mars, Jupiter, and Saturn—were also familiar as they moved around through the zodiac, although there was some confusion about the first two because they appear at times in the west after sunset and at other times in the east before sunrise.

Origin of Nomenclature. Some of the groupings of stars known as constellations are mentioned in the Book of Job and in the poems of Homer, dated three thousand years ago —constellations such as the Great Bear and Orion. Most of the conspicuous star figures were undoubtedly recognized and named by people of Mesopotamia in much earlier times. Those dippers, crosses, and other geometrical patterns outlined by the stars were named after animals of the Tigris-Euphrates valley, and after representatives of certain vocations, e.g., the Hunter and the Charioteer. The Greeks later took over the plan, changing some of the names to fit characters of their mythology.

Listing of Constellations. The first orderly description of the original constellations that survives is found in the *Phenomena,* written by the minor Greek poet Aratus about 270 B.C. The complete list of the forty-eight is contained in Ptolemy's *Almagest,* dated about A.D. 150. In both books the stars are designated in terms of their rank among mythological figures, and, on such authority, the ancient symbols of animals and heroes dominated the star charts and globes up to fairly recent times. They have now practically disappeared from modern charts and only their names remain. Meanwhile, the areas unoccupied by the original constellations, including the region around the south pole of the heavens which the primitive observers could not see, have been filled with additional constellations. Most of the newer ones are areas devoid of conspicuous configurations of stars. Eighty-eight constellations are recognized today, and of these seventy are visible, at least in part, in the latitude of New York. Boundary lines appear on modern star maps, separating the constellations in the manner of boundaries between the different countries of the earth. To the astronomers the constellations are areas of the heavens, but to many people they remain conspicuous geometrical figures outlined by stars, just as they were in primitive times.

Ideas of the Universe. Ideas of the construction of the universe were introduced in very early times. In these, the earth was the central and most important feature, and the sky required support to keep it from falling down. The first ideas were fantastic, and were succeeded by more realistic ones, in which attempts were made to represent things as they seemed to be. Persons who lived in narrow valleys, or along the shores of the Mediterranean Sea, could readily imagine a flat, oblong earth supporting by pillars at its four corners the oblong canopy of the heavens. Other peoples imagined a flat, circular earth, with the sky resting around its rim like an inverted blue bowl. Such static constructions did not interpret very well the daily westward movements of the celestial bodies.

THE SPHERE OF THE STARS

Greek Philosophers' Concepts. As early as the sixth century B.C., the Greek nature philosophers proposed a plan of the universe which developed into the following form. The earth is a stationary globe and the sky around it is a great spherical shell, on whose inner surface the stars are set like jewels. They are the "fixed stars," or stars fixed on the sphere in their familiar patterns. The sphere of the stars is supported by a long axis thrust through the earth, and around which it turns daily from east to west, causing the celestial bodies to rise and set. It is possible that the globular earth was favored at first as suitable to match the sphere of the stars. In the same period, however, proofs of the earth's rotundity were being cited by scholars, such as Aristotle. They observed that the superstructure of the incoming

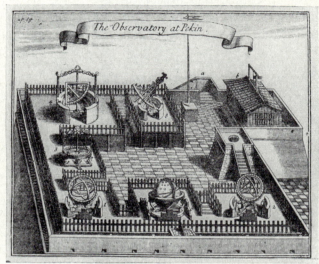

Ancient observatory at Pekin (Peiping), China
REPRODUCED FROM A WOODCUT FROM LE COMTE'S *VOYAGE TO CHINA* (1698)

ship is seen before the hull appears over the horizon; that the earth's shadow on the moon during a lunar eclipse is a shadow such as a globe would cast; and that, as one travels south, stars come into view which were not seen at home. This evidence showed, at least, that the earth's surface is curved and not flat.

Earth's Circumference. Measures of the earth's circumference were also undertaken by Greek scholars. The best known of these was made in the third century B.C., by Eratosthenes, at Alexandria. He observed that the sun, at noon during the time of the summer solstice, stood a fiftieth of the circumference of the heavens from its zenith, while at Syene (Aswan), 500 mi. to the south, it was said to be directly overhead. With this as a basis, his measurement of the circumference of the earth came out as 25,000 mi. Thus, the globular form of the earth was recognized long before the time of Columbus, whose belief that he had reached India was based on another measurement of the earth's size, which was much too small.

Rotating-Sphere Theory. The rotating sphere of the stars was an improvement on any idea that had preceded, because it assigned to a single cause the daily motions of all the celestial bodies. For more than two thousand years thereafter, up to and even beyond the time of Copernicus, the stellar area stood almost unquestioned as the boundary of the universe. Even today, when we know that it has no tangible existence, the rotating celestial sphere remains as a very useful convention in astronomy and navigation. It is the device used to represent the positions of the celestial bodies on globes and in projection on plane maps. Their places are denoted with reference to circles on the celestial sphere, just as places of towns and ships are denoted in relation with the terrestrial sphere.

Equator System of Circles. The circles imagined on the celestial sphere for denoting the places of the stars are similar in position to those of the earth; they are based on the celestial equator. The earth's axis extended to the celestial

AMERICAN MUSEUM OF NATURAL HISTORY

JOHANNES HEVELIUS WITH QUADRANT
This seventeenth century observing instrument was used to measure declination.

sphere fixes its two poles. The north celestial pole is directly above the north point of the horizon and nearly halfway up to the zenith for observers in the latitude of New York. It is closely marked by Polaris, the north star, at the end of the Little Dipper's handle. The south celestial pole is equally as far below the south horizon. Halfway between these poles is the celestial equator, the great circle of the sky directly over the earth's equator. Hour circles run from pole to pole all around, like the terrestrial meridians. The position of a star is denoted with reference to these circles by giving its right ascension and declination. These resemble longitude and latitude on the earth; they are measured along and at right angles to the celestial equator. Instead of the meridian of Greenwich, from which longitude is reckoned, the hour circle through the vernal equinox is employed for right ascension, the position of the sun's center when it crosses the celestial equator at the beginning of spring. The circle of the ecliptic is inclined 23.5° to the celestial equator, and so crosses it at the two opposite equinoctial points.

Thus, on its axis, which inclines upward toward the north for people living in middle northern latitudes, the celestial sphere seems to rotate from east to west daily, just as people of former times supposed it actually did rotate; the stars rise and set. Toward the north, their daily circles are more and more above the horizon, until they are entirely visible. Within a circular region centered in the north celestial pole, they wheel around without setting. Conversely, toward the south the daily circles are more and more out of sight. Within a circular region centered in the south celestial pole, the constellations, such as the Southern Cross, go around without coming up into view. Observers watching the celestial bodies moving around them can readily forget that it is they who are moving and that the daily rotation of the heavens is simply the scenery passing by.

Other Systems. Although the system described above is the one most commonly used for denoting the places of the stars, it is not the only one. A system based on the horizon is often used in problems of astronomy, navigation, and surveying. Nor was the equatorial system of circles the first to be employed. Ancient astronomers, who were particularly interested in the sun, moon, and planets, reckoned their places with reference to the ecliptic, and named their co-ordinates celestial longitude and latitude. Consequently, when the equator system came into use in the Middle Ages, the astronomers had to invent different names for the new co-ordinates, which they called right ascension and declination.

PROBLEM OF PLANETARY MOTIONS

Basis of Inquiry. Although the rotating celestial sphere represented quite well the daily motions of the "fixed stars," it did not, by itself, account for the movements of the "wanderers", a term denoting the sun, the moon, and the five bright planets. It was observed that these bodies, in addition to their daily rising and setting, kept moving generally eastward against the turning background of the constellations. The sun and moon move always in that direction among the stars at somewhat variable speeds, but the planets occasionally halt and countermarch toward the west for a time before resuming their eastward progress. Such behavior required explanation. The planetary bodies were supposed to revolve around the central, stationary earth between it and the rotating sphere of the stars. In order of increasing distance from the earth, they were identified as: the moon, Mercury, Venus, the sun, Mars, Jupiter, and Saturn. This arrangement was chosen because it is the order of decreasing swiftness of their movements. Saturn, the most remote of the bright planets, was considered to be almost as far away as the stars. Early Greek philosophers proposed the problem: by what combinations of uniform circular motions centered in the earth could the observed movements of the planetary bodies be represented? It was a problem destined to be the major subject of inquiry in astronomy during the following two thousand years. The purpose was to formulate geometrical machinery for interpreting these movements and also for predicting planetary phenomena for the future. Uniform circular motion was prescribed, partly because it seemed a dignified procedure for heavenly bodies but mostly because the circle is the simplest figure for calculations.

Unsuccessful Solution by Eudoxus. One solution of the problem was proposed by Eudoxus in the fourth century B.C. The motion of each planet was controlled by a set of spherical shells. The first shell of each set was attached to the long axis of the celestial sphere and thus rotated daily from east to west, causing the planet to rise and set. The

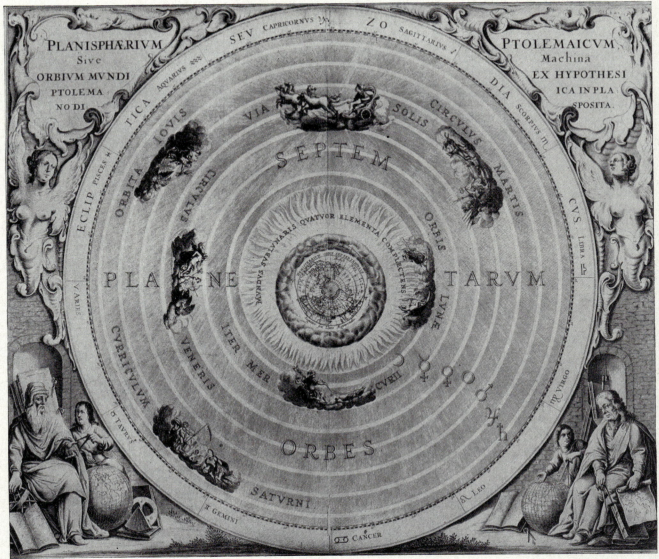

THE PTOLEMAIC SYSTEM

second shell shared the motion of the first and also rotated slowly eastward on an inclined axis, causing the planet to move along the ecliptic. The third shell, on which the planet was set, was another factor in its motion. Although the plan was adopted and improved by the great Aristotle, it proved unsuccessful because it kept each planet always at the same distance from the earth.

Ptolemaic System. The second and more enduring solution of the planetary problem was instituted by the mathematician Apollonius, in the third century B.C. It was favored by Hipparchus, who worked in the following century on the island of Rhodes. That most famous of all ancient observers applied the plan particularly to the motions of the sun and moon. It was extended by Ptolemy (Claudius Ptolemaeus) at Alexandria in the second century A.D. to represent the motions of the planets. On this account, and also because it is explained in detail in his celebrated book, the *Almagest,* the whole construction came to be known as the Ptolemaic system. It is a scheme of eccentrics and epicycles. To simplify the account, only the second and principal feature is noted here. The motion of Jupiter

among the stars provides an example. This planet completes its eastward circuit of the heavens once in twelve years. It turns at intervals of a year and a month and goes back toward the west for a time before resuming the eastward advance. In the Ptolemaic plan, a fictitious planet moves in a circle, the deferent, around the central earth once in twelve years. Meanwhile, Jupiter itself goes around the fictitious planet in a smaller circle, the epicycle, once in the shorter period. The result is the looped motion of Jupiter among the stars noted by observers. The other planets have similar deferents and epicycles.

There were some restrictions on the plan to keep the predicted motions of the planets in agreement with their actual motions. It was necessary, for instance, that the fictitious planets Mercury and Venus remain on the line joining the sun and earth, so that the planets would oscillate to the east and west of the sun's place as evening and morning stars—as they are observed to do. It was also necessary that the line joining each of the outer planets to its fictitious planet remain parallel to the line joining the sun and the earth. In addition, the Ptolemaic system did not picture

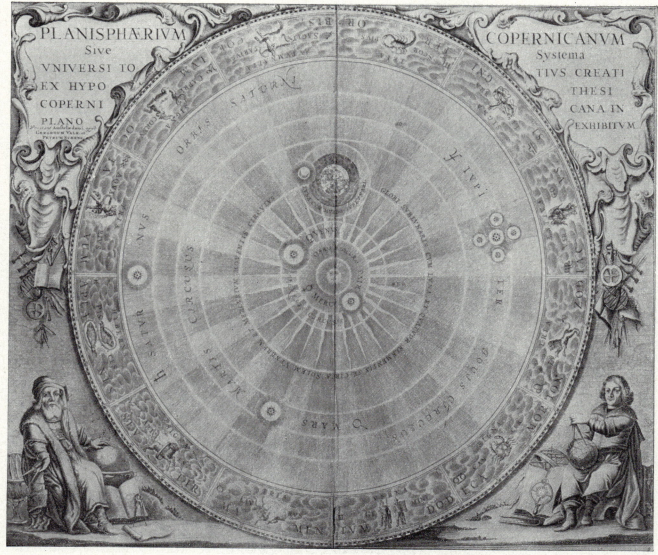

THE COPERNICAN SYSTEM

very clearly the daily westward motions of the planets. It prescribed somewhat vaguely a *primum mobile,* a shell outside the sphere of the stars which rotated westward daily and imparted its motion not only to that sphere but also to the planets within it.

Work on Geocentric Theory. For many centuries thereafter, the efforts of astronomers were devoted to improving the specifications of the geocentric system, so as to bring the predicted positions of the planets into better agreement with the observed ones. After the decline of classical culture and before the revival of learning in Europe, the work was carried on chiefly in the Arabian dominions. New epicycles were added to the construction, until each planet was provided with from forty to sixty, and the system had become too cumbersome. It had been evident to the scholars all along that the yearly motion of the sun around through the zodiac could be produced equally as well by the revolution of the earth around the sun. The rising and setting of the celestial bodies could be caused by the earth's daily rotation on its axis. An occasional scholar, as Aristarchus of Samos, in the third century B.C., had even proposed that

the earth is in motion, but such ideas were not in accord with the common sense of the times and received little attention. Growing dissatisfaction with the geocentric theory, however, had brought more inclination to re-examine the postulates behind it.

THE HELIOCENTRIC SYSTEM

Copernican Theory. In his book published in 1543, Nicholas Copernicus the Polish scholar (1473-1543) presented his theory that the planets revolve around the sun and that the earth is one of the planets. He retained the original idea of uniform circular motion, so that some epicycles were still required to represent the nonuniform movements of the planets among the stars. However, the largest epicycles of the geocentric system, which accounted for the looped motions of the planets, were no longer needed, because the loops were explained by the earth's revolution. The new plan was simpler. It also seemed simpler to suppose that the earth rotates daily rather than the larger celestial sphere. But no convincing proof could be offered that the earth had any motion at all. In the Copernican system, the sun

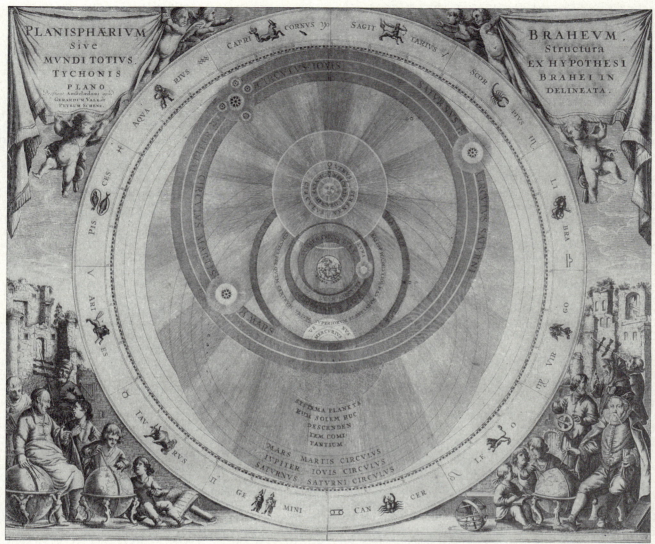

THE TYCHONIC SYSTEM

instead of the earth was the central feature. The membership of the planetary system, in order of distance from the sun, was now: Mercury; Venus; the earth, accompanied by its satellite, the moon; Mars; Jupiter; and Saturn. Beyond Saturn was the sphere of the stars, fixed as the stars seemed to be upon it. The daily westward movement of the celestial sphere became simply the passing of the scenery as the earth rotates eastward.

Tycho's Study of Parallax. If the earth goes around the sun, the stars should show evidence of parallax—a difference in direction as viewed from different places in the orbit. The stars would seem to oscillate slightly during the year. So reasoned the celebrated Danish astronomer Tycho Brahe. At his fine observatory on the little island of Hven, toward the end of the sixteenth century, Tycho and his assistants were unable to detect the parallaxes of the stars. Thus, the celestial bodies themselves seemed to dispute the correctness of the heliocentric theory. The difficulty was the failure to comprehend the vast distances of the stars, which made their parallaxes very small. Actually, they are much too small to have been observed with Tycho's instruments, equipped with plane sights. The telescope had not yet

been invented. Failing to observe evidence of the earth's motion, Tycho proposed a compromise system in which the earth was stationary. The moon and sun revolved around the earth, and the sun's orbit was the common deferent of the orbits of all the other planets. The Tychonic and Copernican systems were equally effective in representing planetary configurations, and it was impossible to decide between them until telescopic evidence became available.

Tycho's Contributions. Tycho's constructive contribution to the knowledge of planetary motions was his repeated observations of the positions of the planets in the sky, and their right ascensions and declinations, which he continued for a period exceeding twenty years. As it turned out, it was fortunate that he paid particular attention to Mars, because it has a more eccentric orbit than most bright planets.

Kepler's Laws. After Tycho's death in 1601 his records were entrusted to the German astronomer John Kepler (1571-1630), who continued the work. Kepler undertook, at first, to represent the observed positions of the planets by combinations of deferents, epicycles, and eccentrics, but was unable to bring the calculated and observed positions into satisfactory agreement. At length, he tried elliptical orbits having the sun at one focus and was successful to an encouraging degree. In 1618, he had formulated three empirical laws concerning the motions of the planets. Kepler's laws are as follows:

(1) The orbit of each planet is an ellipse with the sun at one of its foci.

(2) Each planet revolves so that the line joining it to the sun sweeps over equal areas in equal times.

(3) The squares of the periods of revolution of any two planets are in the same proportion as the cubes of their mean distances from the sun.

Kepler's first law declares that the planets revolve around the sun instead of the earth, but does not necessarily include the earth as one of the planets. In this respect it might follow the Tychonic system. It states that the orbits are ellipses instead of the traditional circles. The second law shows that a planet revolves faster in the part of its orbit that is nearer the sun. Thus, the nonuniform motions of the planets no longer required epicycles for their interpretation. The third law is a useful relation between the periods of the planets and their mean distances from the sun. As given here, it is useful for calculating distances in the planetary system, when one distance is established as the yardstick. This yardstick, the earth's mean distance from the sun, is known as the astronomical unit and has a length of 93,003,-000 miles.

Effect of Laws. The problem of the planetary motions had been concerned, up to this time, with kinematics, the geometry of bodies in motion. The plan of the orbits was prescribed without explanation of why the planets moved in such orbits. After the formulation of Kepler's laws, however, the problem soon became one of dynamics, and the inquiry turned from the courses alone to the forces which controlled the motions in these courses.

THE LAW OF GRAVITATION

Galileo's Conclusion. The Italian scientist Galileo Galilei (1564-1642) is known for his pioneer studies concerning bodies in motion. He questioned the traditional idea that rest is the natural state and motion the enforced one. He concluded that a body left to itself continues moving uniformly in a straight line; and that it is only when its motion is altered, either in speed or direction, or both, that the body is acted on by a force. Inquiry into where the force originates is the next and logical step.

Newton's Laws of Motion. Galileo's conclusion had an important part in the three laws of motion formulated in 1687 by the English scientist Sir Isaac Newton (1642-1727). The laws are:

(1) Every body persists in its state of rest, or of uniform motion in a straight line, unless it is compelled to change that state by a force impressed on it. (Inertia.)

(2) The change of motion is directly proportional to the force impressed, and it takes place in the direction of the straight line in which the force acts.

(3) To every action there is always an equal and contrary reaction.

Newton's second law is the definition: force equals mass times acceleration, where acceleration is the rate of change of velocity, that is to say, directed speed. The first law says that where no force is impressed there is no acceleration. The third law states that the mutual forces exerted by two bodies are equal and opposite; or the law of the conservation of momentum.

Newton's Law of Gravitation. In terms of these laws of mechanics, Newton undertook to explain Kepler's empirical laws of the planetary motions. Since the path of a planet is always curving, the planet is always acted on by a force. From Kepler's law of equal areas it is easy to show that the force is directed toward the sun; the planet continually falls toward the sun and, accordingly, revolves around it instead of going away on a straight course. Further studies revealed the character of the force. The sun attracts a planet with a force that is proportional directly to the product of the masses of the two and inversely to the square of the distance between their centers. By the third law of motion, the planet attracts the sun with an equal force. Newton proved, in addition, that the earth's attraction for things around it, from the moon to an apple, operates according to the inverse-square rule. He concluded that he had discovered a universal law of gravitation and formulated it as follows:

Every particle of matter in the universe attracts every other particle with a force that varies directly as the product of their masses and inversely as the square of the distance between them. This premise is the basic law by which the motions of the celestial bodies can be explained and their future progress predicted. The implications of the law of gravitation, particularly as they apply to the planetary system, were studied by Newton and those who followed him. Especially noteworthy are the contributions of the distinguished continental mathematicians Leonhard Euler, Jean Le Rond d'Alembert, Joseph Louis Lagrange, and Marquis Pierre Simon de Laplace, during the eighteenth century. The problem of planetary motions is highly complex, because any particular planet is attracted not only by the sun but also by all the other members of the system. In practice, it is simplified by the preponderant mass of the sun and the wide separation of the planets. The orbit of a planet relative to the sun, or of a satellite around its planet, can be calculated in the first approximation as though they were alone in the universe. This is the problem of two bodies, which can be completely solved.

The law of gravitation requires that the orbit of a body in the sun's vicinity be a conic. In the case of a permanent member of the solar system, it must be an ellipse having the sun at one focus. The law further requires that the line joining the planet to the sun sweep over equal areas in equal times. This is Kepler's second law, which is equivalent to the law of the conservation of angular momentum. When the positions of a planet among the stars have been observed on three occasions the orbit can be calculated by formulae based on the law of gravitation. The elements of the elliptic orbit of a planet are the six specifications which define it uniquely. They are: (1) the inclination of the orbit to the ecliptic, (2) the longitude of the ascending node reckoned from the vernal equinox, (3) the longitude of the perihelion point measured from the node, (4) the length of the semi-major axis, (5) the eccentricity of the orbit, and (6) the time of perihelion passing. The first two elements denote the position of the orbit plane, while the third element fixes the orientation of the orbit in the plane. The fourth gives the size of the orbit and the fifth its shape. The sixth permits the position of the planet in its orbit to be calculated for any particular time, and accordingly, its place in the heavens, as observed from the earth at that time. By such procedure, when allowance is made for perturbations caused by the other members of the planetary system, the positions of the sun, moon, and planets in the sky are computed in advance in the various almanacs for use of astronomers and navigators.

Problem of Three Bodies. The problem of three bodies is more complex than that in which only two are considered, because the motion of a particular planet around the sun is perturbed by the attraction of a third body. A common perturbation is the westward regression of the nodes of the planet's inclined orbit, the nodes being the two points where the planet crosses the ecliptic plane. Another perturbation is the advance of the perihelion point; the major axis of the elliptic orbit slowly rotates in the direction of the planet's revolution. A famous case of this sort is the advance of Mercury's perihelion, which is caused mostly by the disturbance of Venus. It has long been known that the perihelion of Mercury's orbit advances faster than is predicted by the law of gravitation. Attempts to account for the discrepancy included the suggestion that it might be an additional perturbation caused by a planet as yet unseen within Mercury's orbit. But the search for such a planet during total solar eclipse was unsuccessful. Finally, in 1915, Albert Einstein explained that the faster advance of the perihelion is required by his theory of relativity. This is one of the few instances where the predictions of celestial events by Newtonian mechanics and the relativity theory are sufficiently different to be subject to the test of observation.

THE SOLAR SYSTEM

The solar system comprises the sun and the numerous smaller bodies that revolve around it. These include: the nine principal planets and their attendants, or satellites, of which about thirty are known; the thousands of minor planets, or asteroids; the comets; and the meteor swarms. The principal planets in order of increasing distance from the sun are: Mercury, Venus, the earth, Mars, Jupiter, Saturn, Uranus, Neptune, and Pluto. The first two are called inferior planets because they revolve inside the earth's orbit; those outside the earth's orbit are superior planets. Five principal planets are brilliant, starlike objects in the heavens. Termed "wandering stars" by the ancients, they have been well known ever since observant people have watched the skies. Saturn is the most remote of the bright planets, and, until toward the close of the eighteenth century, there was no reason to suppose that there were other planets still more remote.

Discovery of Uranus. The discovery of Uranus in 1781 by the English astronomer William Herschel was accidental and unexpected. He was exploring a region of Gemini through his telescope when he came upon an object which seemed too large to be a star, and which proved to be moving among the stars. Surprise at the discovery increased when it later became evident that Uranus was departing from the path prescribed for it by calculations in which the perturbations by known planets had been carefully included. The knowledge of its actual path was expedited by the finding of records showing as many as twenty observations of its positions among the stars during the hundred years preceding its discovery. Each time Uranus had been set down simply as a star.

Discovery of Neptune. Neptune was discovered by Urbain Jean Joseph Leverrier, a French astronomer, in 1846. Examining the discrepancies between observed and calculated positions of Uranus, he concluded that they were perturbations caused by an unknown planet. He calculated that planet's place in the sky, and invited astronomers at the Berlin Observatory, where a star chart of the particular region was available, to look for the planet near the specified position. There, through the telescope, they found a starlike object in the constellation Aquarius which was not recorded in the chart. The discovery of Neptune, made at Leverrier's desk and verified by the observers, is a famous example of the detection of celestial bodies before they are seen, and of confidence in the law of gravitation.

Discovery of Pluto. Pluto, the most remote known planet, was discovered at the Lowell Observatory in 1930. Slight residual discrepancies in the motion of Uranus had suggested the search for another planet beyond Neptune. The planet was first detected in the photographs by Clyde William Tombaugh as a tiny star of the fifteenth magnitude. The discovery could scarcely be called accidental because the search for the planet had been in progress for many years. Yet, the mass of Pluto seemed too small to have caused the irregularities of Uranus, which promoted the search.

Regularities of Planets. The motions of the more massive planets and satellites exhibit interesting and probably significant regularities. The orbits are not far from circular and are nearly in the same plane, so that these planets never depart far from the ecliptic. Among the principal planets, Pluto, which in its small size and mass is a somewhat disappointing addition to this category, departs most from these regularities. All planets revolve from west to east around the sun. Laplace argued that such an orderly arrangement of the solar system in space must have resulted from a simple plan of development, and, in 1796, he proposed his celebrated nebular hypothesis of the evolution of the system.

Laplace's Nebular Hypothesis. The nebular hypothesis began with a globe of tenuous gas, extending out beyond the present distance of the most remote planet and in slow rotation. As the globe contracted under the urge of gravity, it accordingly rotated faster and bulged more at its equator. The centrifugal effect of the rotation became so great, eventually, that the extended ring of gas around the equator was abandoned. Other gaseous rings were left behind successively by the shrinking globe. These assembled to form planets, and some, while they were still balls of gas, abandoned additional rings, which became their satellites. The central mass became the sun, and by this successive but simple process the solar system developed with its observed regularities.

Weakness of Hypothesis. This hypothesis does not account for the motions of many small and faint members of the solar system, discovered since the time of Laplace. It does not, for example, explain the tangled confusion of orbits of the asteroids. Ceres, the first of these minor planets to become known, was discovered in 1801, and many hundreds have since been added to the list. Many asteroids revolve in a fairly orderly way between the orbits of Mars and Jupiter; others have highly eccentric and inclined orbits, including one which ventures out as far as Saturn, and a number crossing the earth's orbit. Comets and meteor swarms are even more extreme, with elongated orbits often extending from the vicinity of the sun out beyond the most remote planet. Details of the nebular hypothesis are not consistent with recognized physical principles, in particular the law of the conservation of angular momentum, and the kinetic theory of gases. As an example, the present total angular momentum of the solar system is only a small percentage of what it had to be, when the material which formed the planet Neptune was abandoned. Moreover, the present total resides mostly in the giant planets, whereas it should, by the Laplace hypothesis, be mostly in the sun. The second inconsistency raises the question of whether it is possible for a ring of tenuous gas to assemble and form the beginning of a planet. Finally, in view of these and other difficulties, the nebular hypothesis was discarded.

Other Hypotheses. More recent hypotheses of the evolution of the planetary system have sought to be in accord with the foregoing troublesome principles, but have not always succeeded. The encounter theory, first formulated about 1900 by Thomas C. Chamberlin and Forest R. Moulton as the planetesimal hypothesis, began with a passing star. This star came so near the sun that, by excessive

AMERICAN MUSEUM OF NATURAL HISTORY
ARMILLARY SPHERE OF EUROPEAN DESIGN

tidal action, it tore loose enough of the sun's material to form the planetary system. But if the disturber came near enough to cause such damage to the sun, it could not, by its revolution, impart the necessary amount of angular momentum to the system. An alternate idea that the star brushed against a former companion of the sun may deliberately avoid the first physical difficulty, but remains involved with the second one.

A hypothesis currently under scrutiny supposes that the gaseous material which formed the planets was emitted from the sun by a sort of safety-valve action when it became too hot. Much of the hydrogen and helium could escape into outer space, taking with them any unwanted amount of angular momentum. However, the problem of the evolution of the solar system is not yet solved.

DISCOVERIES WITH TELESCOPES

Galileo's First Instruments. Galileo, in 1609, was the first to employ the telescope for the examination of the celestial bodies. He recognized its important bearing on astronomy when he heard of the discovery by a Dutch spectacle maker of an optical system that brought a distant object in the landscape nearer the observer. Two of the telescopes he assembled and used are preserved in a museum in Florence. They are little spyglasses having lenses less than 2 in. in diameter. With these, Galileo was able to observe celestial sights never before seen. His discoveries of features of the planetary system and of the stars mark the beginning of the great advances in astronomy which the telescope has made possible.

Through the telescope, the bright planets are magnified into disks on which appear some surface or atmospheric features. Planets and satellites invisible to the naked eye are brought into view, while the magnification allows measurements to be made more precisely. When a telescope is used as a camera, with a plateholder replacing the eyepiece, recordings of the celestial events are made for repeated study. By exposing the film for a long time, otherwise invisible objects are disclosed on the film plate. The spectroscope, thermocouple, photocell, and other devices attached to the telescope can supplement the information obtained in the direct view. The refracting telescope, in which all the optical parts are lenses, was gradually improved after Galileo's time, particularly by the introduction of the achromatic objective in 1758. The making of large refractors began with the work of the German optician Joseph von Fraunhofer, near the beginning of the nineteenth century. The largest instrument of this type is the 40-in. refracting telescope of Yerkes Observatory. Meanwhile, the reflecting telescope has attained much greater size; in this type the objective is a concave mirror. The largest telescope in the world is the 200-in. reflecting telescope on Palomar Mountain, California, installed in 1947-1948.

Galileo's Discoveries. One of Galileo's discoveries with the new telescope was that the planet Venus, like the moon, shows the whole cycle of phases, from new to full, and back to new again. This would be expected of an inferior planet in the heliocentric system, and also in Tycho's plan, but not in the Ptolemaic system, as Galileo pointed out. Mercury also shows phases through a somewhat larger telescope. Despite its lack of atmosphere, the markings on Mercury's surface are indistinct, even with modern telescopes. They seem to keep the same places on the sunward hemisphere, suggesting that the planet rotates on its axis and revolves around the sun in the same period of eighty-eight days. The surface of Venus cannot be seen through the thick atmosphere of the planet, which contains markings clearly brought out in photographs through violet filters.

The mountains of the moon were first seen by Galileo. They are invisible without the telescope, although the irregularities of the sunrise line they cause are plainly visible to the naked eye. Most of those mountains form the circular walls of the lunar craters, as Galileo noticed, and there has been difference of opinion as to their origin. Some scientists have viewed the craters as scars caused by the fall of great meteors; others consider them as products of vulcanism, features which might well be expected on the surface of a small and rapidly cooled airless body, where there has been no weathering to erase them.

The four bright satellites of Jupiter were discovered by Galileo. Seven other very faint ones have been detected, so that the giant planet now has the greatest number of known attendants; the three outer satellites revolve from east to west around the planet. The dark streaks across the disk of Jupiter parallel to its equator were not noticed until 1630. Turning to Saturn, Galileo saw what seemed to be two appendages on either side of the planet's disk. In 1655, Christian Huygens (1629-1695) in Holland concluded that Saturn is encircled by a flat ring in the plane of its equator; in 1675 at Paris, Jean Cassini (1625-1712) noticed a fine dark line dividing the ring into two concentric ones; and, in 1850, Wm. C. Bond (1789-1859) of Harvard Observatory detected the faint crepe-like ring inside the other two.

Observations of Mars. The surface features of Mars are too difficult to have been seen with Galileo's telescopes. They began to be observed soon after the middle of the seventeenth century. White caps spread around the poles in the winter, and large blue-green blotches also show seasonal changes. The markings soon established the rotation period of 24 hr. 37 min. Narrower dark markings, the "canals" of Mars, were first seen in 1877 by the Italian astronomer Giovanni Schiaparelli (1835-1910), and became the subject of much controversy as to their natural or artificial status. In that year, also, the two small satellites of Mars (Deimos and Phobos) were discovered by Asaph Hall (1829-1907) at the Naval Observatory in Washington.

ORIGINS OF SIDEREAL ASTRONOMY

Early Inquiries. Sir William Herschel (1738-1822), of England, was a prominent pioneer in the study of the stellar system toward the close of the eighteenth century. Before his time, the attention of astronomers had been given chiefly to the planetary system, and interest during the century had taken two major directions: the mathematical investigations of the planetary motions, following the formulation of the law of gravitation; and study of the features of the planets, as displayed through the telescope. The stars had been useful as landmarks for fixing the paths of the planets in the sky, and, of course, as aids in timekeeping, surveying, and navigation. It was generally supposed that very little could be learned about the stars themselves. Nevertheless, some progress had been made in that field before Herschel's time.

Copernicus' proposal of the earth's rotation on its axis had disposed of the rotating sphere of the stars. Probably no distinguished scientist after him believed in the reality of the celestial sphere of the ancients. Since the stars were no longer imagined to circle the earth daily, they could be considered to be farther away, and at varying distances. Also, the promotion of the sun to the dominant role in the planetary system prepared the way for the idea that the stars might well be remote suns, perhaps also attended by systems of planets.

Edmund Halley (1656-1742), for whom a famous comet was named, was the first to show, in 1718, that the stars are not fixed. He pointed out that Sirius, Arcturus, and some other bright stars had moved as far as the apparent breadth of the full moon from the places assigned them in Ptolemy's ancient catalog.

Herschel's Inquiries. By 1783, the proper motions of thirteen stars were available, and with these data Herschel demonstrated that the sun is in motion relative to the stars around it. The stars seem to be opening out from a point in the constellation Hercules, which is roughly marked by the bright star Vega. This point is the solar apex, toward which the sun is moving along with its planetary system. Beginning in 1650, with Mizar in the handle of the Great Dipper, a few stars which appeared single to the naked eye had been casually recorded as being separated into pairs through the telescope. Herschel discovered many hundreds of additional doubles, which he first thought were unrelated, except as they happened to have nearly the same direction from the earth. By 1803, however, he had observed that the members of one of the pairs, the bright star Castor, were mutually revolving around a common center. Thus began the study of visual binary stars—physically related pairs revolving in accord with the law of gravitation. Many binaries, too close to be separated with the telescope, have been discovered in more recent times and studied by means of the spectroscope. Some of these, such as the well-known winking star, Algol, have been found to eclipse mutually as they go around.

Construction of Universe. The chief subject of Herschel's

sidereal inquiries was the construction of the universe. Do the stars continue on out into space indefinitely? Or is the stellar system bounded, and, if so, what is its form and size? These were specific points of inquiry. In 1750, Thomas Wright (1711-1786), of Durham, England, had proposed the "grindstone theory" of the universe, based on the appearance of the Milky Way. He pictured the stellar system as having the form of a rather thin circular disk, with the sun near its center. The philosopher Immanuel Kant (1724-1804) set forth about the same idea in 1755, and emphasized the

ORIENTAL ARMILLARY SPHERE
This device was used in ancient times to measure declination and right ascension.

thought that the nebulae were other milky ways exterior to the earth's stellar system. But these were speculations, and Herschel undertook to solve the problem observationally. His procedure was to count the numbers of stars visible in the field of his 19-in. reflecting telescope when it was directed successively to various parts of the heavens. He made 3,400 such gauges in all.

Herschel supposed that the distances to the boundary of the stellar system in the different directions were proportional to the cube roots of the counted numbers. The model of the system which resulted was like a grindstone, abruptly indented at many points of its circumference, where the counts were made in the dark rifts of the Milky Way. At these points, where few stars could be seen, the boundary was not far away, according to the assumption. The method was too simple, as its author soon came to realize, and the result added little to the speculations which had preceded. Herschel inaugurated the investigation of the structure of the galactic system, and his approach by means of star counts is employed today in improved form.

Detection of Parallaxes. The importance of the parallax method for determining the distances of stars was understood by the early investigators. The change in direction of a star as the earth goes around the sun is inversely proportional to its distance from the earth. The difficulty is the vast distance of the stars, which makes the parallax of even the nearest star extremely small. Tycho undertook to observe the parallax effect to prove the heliocentric theory but was unsuccessful. After the earth's revolution had been established in another way, the astronomers kept trying to detect the parallaxes with instruments of increasing accuracy. In 1838, Friedrich Bessel, at Königsberg, Germany, was the first to do so; he measured the parallax of the star 61 Cygni. In the present century, thousands of stellar parallaxes have been determined by photographic methods developed by Frank Schlesinger in 1903.

SPECTROSCOPIC ASTRONOMY

Spectrum Studies. The use of a spectroscope was inaugurated in 1814 by Joseph von Fraunhofer (1787-1826), the German optician, who was the first to observe the dark lines of the solar spectrum. He mapped several hundred lines along the spectrum, from red to violet, and labeled prominent ones with letters of the alphabet. In 1823, he examined the spectra of some bright stars and saw that they are also interrupted by dark lines. He noticed that the pattern of lines is different for stars of different colors. The

AMERICAN MUSEUM OF NATURAL HISTORY
ORIENTAL QUADRANT AND CELESTIAL GLOBE

significance of the dark lines remained unknown until 1859, when the German physicist Gustav Robert Kirchhoff (1824-1887), professor of physics at Heidelberg and Berlin universities, explained that they are frequencies abstracted chiefly by the atmospheres of the sun and stars. Some additional lines are produced as the light comes down through the earth's atmosphere. Each gaseous chemical element in the same conditions absorbs the same unique array of dark lines that it emits as bright lines.

Solar Spectrum. Examinations of the solar spectrum have thus far identified two thirds of the ninety-six known chemical elements in the sun's atmosphere. Hydrogen is by far the most abundant element, not only in the atmosphere but presumably in the body of the sun as well; helium is second. When the sun is in total eclipse, the spectrum of the glowing atmosphere is a pattern of bright lines, resembling, with some exceptions, the usual dark-line pattern. Helium lines are present only in the bright-line spectrum. This element was first recognized during the total eclipse of 1868, and was not identified on the earth until 1895. The spectroheliograph, invented in 1892, is employed for photographing the sun's chromosphere and prominences outside eclipse. The more recently designed coronagraph can also provide photographs of the inner corona outside eclipse.

Planetary Atmospheres. Studies of the atmospheres of planets are made by comparing the spectra of the sunlight they reflect with the spectrum of the sun itself. Any additional dark lines in the planetary spectra are abstracted in those atmospheres. By this means, it is known that the atmosphere of Venus is heavily charged with carbon dioxide. The spectrum of Jupiter's atmosphere shows conspicuous bands of methane and ammonia. The spectra of the atmospheres of Saturn, Uranus, and Neptune also contain methane bands. The disappointing feature of these recent inquiries (at least to people who like to speculate on life in other worlds) is that no other planetary atmosphere, except that

of the earth, gives much evidence of containing either free oxygen or water vapor.

Photographic Studies of Stellar Spectra. An extensive program of photographic studies of stellar spectra, begun at Harvard Observatory in 1885, has continued to the present time. The spectra of more than 250,000 stars have been examined, largely under the direction of Annie Jump Cannon (1863-1941). One product of the program was the discovery that the spectra of most stars fall into a single unbroken sequence from the blue to the red stars, and that the progression in the patterns of lines is caused chiefly by diminishing temperature of the stars along the sequence. At the beginning of the present century, it was supposed that the sequence might represent the track of stellar development. Stars condensed out of nebulae, and were very hot at first; then, as they gradually cooled and contracted, they changed in stages from blue to yellow, to red, and, finally, became dark. This early idea of stellar evolution was contradicted by the discovery that some red stars are the largest and most tenuous of all.

Spectrum Luminosity. H. N. Russell, at Princeton Observatory in 1913, made a spectrum-luminosity diagram, in which the spectral classes of stars are arrayed with respect to the absolute magnitudes—the magnitudes these stars would have if they were all placed at the distance of thirty-two light-years. Most of the points are in a rather narrow band, extending diagonally across the diagram. They are the stars of the main sequence, of which the sun is a member. Above the band, especially at the red end of the sequence, are the more luminous and larger giant stars, and still higher are the great supergiants. Later, white stars were found and given their places in the diagram far below the corresponding stars of the main sequence. These are the feebly luminous, small, and very dense dwarf stars.

Stellar Hypothesis. The course of stellar development is at present highly conjectural. A working hypothesis pictures the stars as condensing out of the cosmic dust. They emerge as large and very tenuous red supergiants; then, by compression and by certain atomic transformations in their relatively cool interiors, they gradually attain the stability of the main sequence, where they spend most of their lives. At this stage, their central temperatures have become so high that hydrogen in their interiors can be transformed to helium, releasing energy at a rate sufficient to keep them shining steadily for a very long time. When their hydrogen is nearly exhausted, they collapse to become very dense dwarf stars, a process in which they are unstable enough to explode from time to time into the ephemeral splendor of novae. This, it has been pointed out, is conjectural.

Manifestations of Doppler Effect. Spectroscopic astronomy is often concerned with velocities in the line of sight. The Doppler principle, first announced in 1842 in the case of sound by Christian Johann Doppler (1803-1853), was later shown to have the following effect in the spectra of the celestial bodies: when the source of light is approaching the observer, the lines of its spectrum are displaced to the violet from their normal places; when the source is receding, the lines are displaced to the red. The amount of the displacement is proportional to the speed of approach or recession. By this means, the radial velocities of the stars are determined. Very close binary stars are detected by the oscillations of their spectrum lines. Pulsations of stars such as the Cepheid variable stars are observed as the gases in front of the stars alternately approach and recede from the earth. These are a few examples of the manifestations of the Doppler effect.

SYSTEM OF THE MILKY WAY

Co-operative Star Counts. The modern exploration of the galactic system, or system of the Milky Way, began in 1906, when the Dutch astronomer Jacobus Kapteyn (1851-1922) invited the co-operation of his colleagues in the plan of selected areas. He chose 206 areas scattered uniformly over the heavens. It was like Herschel's plan of star gauges, but the counts were to be made with respect to the magnitudes of the stars, and with the guidance of other data. The work had not progressed far when one of the sources of confusion in the original inquiry was explained. Edward E. Barnard (1857-1923), at Yerkes Observatory, a pioneer in the photographic study of the Milky Way, concluded in about 1910 that the dark rifts were the obscuring effects of cosmic dust clouds. In 1922, Edwin P. Hubble, at Mount Wilson Observatory, explained that the bright nebulae are areas of this material illuminated by neighboring stars. Where the stars are sufficiently hot, or hotter than spectral Class B1, they stimulate the gases in the material to fluorescence, as in the great nebula in Orion. Where the stars are cooler, the nebular light is mostly the reflected starlight, as with the nebulosities surrounding stars of the Pleiades. These observations made it evident that the regions containing dark and bright nebulae should be avoided or investigated with caution.

Meanwhile, in 1917, Harlow Shapley, then at Mount Wilson, had facilitated the explorations by formulating the period-luminosity relation of the Cepheid variable stars. Whenever the period of the light fluctuation of one of these pulsating stars is observed, the star's absolute magnitude can be determined by the relation. If it is one of the short-period Cepheids, which are abundant in some globular star clusters, the absolute photographic magnitude is zero, regardless of the period; and, whenever the absolute magnitude becomes known, the distance is easily calculated. Shapley employed the new method for finding the distances of the globular clusters. Given also their directions, he could then picture the arrangement of the globular cluster system. The center of that array proved to be far from the sun in the direction of Sagittarius. Assuming that the cluster system is concentric and coextensive with the whole assemblage of stars, he announced the following features of the system of the Milky Way: (1) the galactic system is isolated in space; (2) the sun is far from the center of the system, as indicated by the globular clusters, and also by the greatest brightness of the Milky Way in the direction of its center in Sagittarius; (3) the system is much extended in the directions of the Milky Way.

Results of Star Counts. The results of star counts in the selected areas, published in 1928 by Frederick Seares, at Mount Wilson, confirmed the much-flattened form of the system and the eccentric position of the sun within it; they also showed that the sun is near the principal plane of the system. They suggested that the sun is situated in a lesser assemblage of stars of considerable size and population, which has been called the "local system." All the modern investigators, thus far, had recognized the presence of the obvious dust clouds, but they had supposed that interstellar space was otherwise transparent.

In 1930, Robert Julius Trumpler (1886-   ), at Lick Observatory, showed from his studies of the open star clusters that dust is widespread throughout the galactic system, particularly near the central line of the Milky Way. Since 1930, the star counts have not been confined to the selected areas. Bart Jan Bok (1906-   ), at Harvard Observatory, and his associates in the newer plan have undertaken to count the stars to the fifteenth magnitude in all parts of the Milky Way. The distances and effectiveness of the obscuring dust clouds in the various directions are being determined by observing the amounts in which the stars behind them are reddened by the dust. By analysis of the counts, the star-density gradients are derived, showing how the number of stars per unit volume of space varies with increasing distance from the sun. The numbers decrease in most directions, which means that the region of the sun is relatively rich in stars. However, toward Cygnus, and

ASTROLABE
This instrument was used to measure angles, either vertical or horizontal.

in the opposite direction toward Carina, both of which are at right angles to the direction of the galactic center, the numbers remain fairly constant for considerable distances. This could mean that the sun is situated in an arm of a spiral system.

The Galactic System. Although the picture of the galactic system is not complete, very satisfactory progress has been made in the few decades since the beginning of its modern exploration. The system contains one hundred billion stars. It is widely extended around its equator, where the diameter is 100,000 light-years. The sun is situated near the equatorial plane of the system and some 30,000 light-years from its center. From the earth's place in the system, the center lies in the direction of the constellation Sagittarius—in that part of the Milky Way which people in the Northern Hemisphere see in the southern sky on summer evenings. The galactic system probably has the form of a two-armed spiral, like the many spiral systems seen outside it. In its general form, it could be said to resemble the great spiral in Andromeda. A remarkable and somewhat disturbing feature is that it seems to be larger than any of the exterior spirals. Also, its texture is smoother than the variety in the Milky Way might at first suggest. Many of the spectacular "star clouds" of the Milky Way are partial openings in the obscuring dust clouds, but some of the brighter areas, such as the Scutum cloud, are actually clouds of stars.

The galactic system is rotating on its axis, as its flattened form suggests. In the whirl of the system, the sun is speeding in the direction of Cepheus at the rate of 175 mi. a second, but, even with this fast motion, it requires more than two hundred million years to circle once around the galactic center. In the space where the sun and planets are traveling, the period of the rotation increases with increasing distance from the center. Thus, the stars somewhat closer in are moving past the earth, and those that are further than the earth from the center are falling behind. A second category of objects, including the globular clusters, form a less flattened system than the main body to which the sun belongs. These objects are going around so much more slowly than the earth that they seem to be speeding swiftly in the opposite direction.

THE EXTERIOR SYSTEMS

Identification of Nebulae. Immanuel Kant's speculation that the nebulae might well be other milky ways far outside the known galactic system was found to be partly correct. Photographs of more recent times proved that these hazy patches among the stars are very numerous, and are separated into two classes, which have come to be known as galactic nebulae and extragalactic nebulae. The former are concentrated toward the Milky Way, like most objects in the galactic system; the latter seem to avoid the Milky Way. Many of the extragalactic nebulae appear as spirals in the photographs and were accordingly called spiral nebulae. Their status remained uncertain for a long time because their distances were unknown. They might, for instance, be near by and be small enough to be ancestors of planetary systems, as some people conjectured; or, again, they might be the "island universes" of Kant's imagination.

Studies of Spirals. Hubble, at Mount Wilson Observatory in 1924, succeeded in resolving into stars in his photographs parts of the great spiral in Andromeda and much of a neighboring spiral. He observed that some of the stars are the useful Cepheid variables, and, with the aid of the period-luminosity relation, determined their distances. The two spirals mentioned, which are the nearest of all to the earth, were found to be 750,000 light-years away. They are, accordingly, outside the galactic system, and are themselves vast systems of stars. Thus, the extragalactic nebulae of the earlier observers are extragalactic in space, as well as in their distribution over the face of the sky.

Three fourths of the exterior systems near enough to show their structures are spirals. The normal type has two arms emerging from opposite sides of the nucleus and coiling around it in the same sense and the same plane. Nearly circular in the flatwise view, they look like spindles when they are presented edgewise to the eye of an observer. In about 20 per cent of the spirals, the arms start abruptly from the extremities of a short bar, which looks as though it were thrust through the nucleus. Both types can be arranged in sequences, from spirals having conspicuous nuclei and thin, tightly coiled arms, to those with small nuclei and large, loosely coiled arms. The spirals are rotating, as shown by their flattened forms and also by their spectra. Hubble latterly proposed the working hypothesis that all are rotating in such a manner that their arms are trailing.

Another 20 per cent of the exterior systems resemble spirals without arms. These "elliptical systems" vary in form from approximate spheres to those resembling spindles and looking as though they might be about to develop arms. Like the spiral nuclei, they are great assemblages of stars. In photographs with the 100-in. telescope on Mount Wilson, Walter Baade (1893-   ) resolved into stars some of the nearer elliptical systems and also central parts of the Andromeda spiral. He finds that these stars, like those of the globular clusters of the galactic system, belong to a type of population which differs considerably from that of the stars around us. They have no supergiants among them, and the giants include the short-period or cluster-type Cepheids.

Irregular Systems. The remaining systems are of the irregular type represented by the two satellites of the galactic system. These are the two Magellanic clouds, near the south pole of the heavens, where they are plainly visible to the naked eye. They show no evidence of rotational symmetry, and no resemblance to the spiral and elliptical systems which might suggest evolutionary connection.

Distribution of Systems. Counts of exterior systems in the photographs in selected areas by Hubble, at Mount Wilson, and in larger regions of the heavens by the Harvard observers, show that very few systems are to be seen near the Milky Way. The appearance of any systems at all in this region suggests that the obscuring dust is patchy. The numbers increase toward the galactic poles. If the dust could be swept away, it seems probable that the systems would appear rather uniformly distributed over the face of the sky, aside from their occasional obvious clustering. The nearest and, accordingly, the most conspicuous of the clusters, at the distance of seven million light-years, is contained in the constellation Virgo. The distribution of the exterior systems through space is also fairly uniform, as far as can be observed with present means. Photographs with the 100-in. Mount Wilson telescope can reach to the distance of five hundred million light-years. To that distance, there is no evidence of thinning out of the systems, which might herald the approach to the boundary of their assemblage. Within the present visible universe, there are one hundred million systems, according to Hubble, and their average separation is two million light-years. Further evidence is awaited from the 200-in. telescope on Palomar Mountain, which should extend the radius of observation to one billion light-years.

In addition to the large clusters of systems, such as the Virgo cluster, there are small groups. The galactic system belongs to a group of a dozen or more systems contained in a volume of space not more than a million light-years across. This fortunate arrangement for the investigator makes the systems of the local group closer to the earth than the average separation of the systems generally. The group includes the great Andromeda spiral and the neighboring spiral in Triangulum, as well as several elliptical and irregular systems.

Hubble's Deduction. The most surprising result of the studies of the exterior systems is concerned with the displacements of their spectral lines toward the red by amounts which increase with increasing distances of the systems from the earth. Viewing the displacements as Doppler effects, and after making allowance for the effects of the galactic rotation, Hubble showed in 1929 that the velocity of recession of the systems increases by 100 mi. a second for each million light-years added to the distance. If these actually are Doppler effects, the conclusion would be that the universe is expanding; or, in other words, that the systems are drawing apart. Also, if the universe has been expanding at the above rate since it began, students can look backward and calculate that the beginning occurred two billion years ago. But this conclusion might be premature.

R. H. B.

ASTROPHYSICS. *See* STARS.

ASTURIAS [astu′rias], the name of a former kingdom of Spain, and of the old northern province which is conterminous with the modern Spanish province of Oviedo. The Prince of Asturias was the title formerly conferred upon the heir apparent to the Spanish throne. The province, with an area of 4,206 sq. mi., borders the Bay of Biscay and is bounded on the west by Galicia, on the south by León, and on the east by the Basque provinces. Its physical features and geological formations resemble those of Galicia. The Cantabrian Mountains, an extension of the Pyrenees, form its southern border, while on the north a line of formidable cliffs overlooks the Bay of Biscay. All the available land is cultivated, but the soil is poor despite a rainfall which is above the average for the rest of Spain. Consequently, the province is devoted mostly to pasture land for horses, cows, and mules, the latter being one of its most notable products. Farming yields chiefly maize, while the warm climate supports olives, figs, and citrus, as well as the more northern types of fruits, especially apples, from which cider is made for export to other provinces. The fishing industry is an important source of livelihood. There are rich deposits of anthracite in several sections of the province, but these have not been mined because of lack of transportation facilities. Resources also include deposits of iron, sulphur, and cinnabar. The coastal plains yield large quantities of peat and amber. Since the province can barely support its population, the Asturians are scattered over Spain, especially as domestic servants.

Oviedo, the capital, a bishopric and the seat of a university, is a beautiful town with gardens and avenues, favored with a temperate and rainy climate. Founded in 757 by Fruela I as a fortress defending the Pass of Pajares, it became the capital of Christian Spain in 810, when the Asturian kings were expelled from León. With the reoccupation of León in 1002, Oviedo's importance declined. It is still economically important, however, as the center of the Asturian coal and iron fields. The chief Asturian seaport, Gijón, is a well-known summer resort. It has an excellent harbor, the safest between Vigo and Pasajes. It afforded a refuge, in 1588, to the defeated remnants of the Spanish Armada. Mieres, across the Pajares, is an important iron-smelting center. The population of the province on July 1, 1946, was 862,345.

History. The history of the province is connected with the expulsion of the Moors from Spain. The attacking Moors, while pursuing the Christians who were retreating into the mountains, were caught in a trap in the glen of Covadonga, where they lost the best elements of their army. This first victory of the Christians over the invaders inspired the defenders with new hope. In 718, Pelayo was chosen chief and began the fight which eventually led, after 800 years, to the expulsion of the Moors from Spain. Hence, the Asturians claim to be the cradle of Spain's nationalism. In 1388, John I honored this claim and, at the request of John of Gaunt, conferred the title of Prince of Asturias upon his oldest son, thereby establishing a tradition of the monarchy.

J. S. R.

ASUNCIÓN [ɑsuˈnsyoˈn], the capital and chief city and port of Paraguay, situated in the southern part of the country, on the Paraguay River near its confluence with the Pilcomayo River, about 935 rail mi. northwest of Buenos Aires, Argentina. Settlement in the vicinity began in 1536, and the city was founded in 1537 with the building of a fort on the site. This occurred before Paraguay was a nation and eighty years prior to the founding of Buenos Aires. The city is built largely on the Bay of Asunción, which extends eastward from the river. The majority of dwellings are one-storied and in the traditional Spanish style with patios and fountains. Most of the buildings date from the nineteenth century, and those of note are the Archbishop's Palace with its collection of historical and ecclesiastical antiquities, the Godoy Museum, the Church of the Incarnation, which is built on one of the city's highest hills and dominates the port, and the government

buildings. The Oratorio de la Asunción, in the Italian Renaissance style, is a soldier's memorial, and the Panteon Nacional, which opened in 1937, contains the remains of many of the nation's heroes, including the Unknown Soldier. The city has many beautiful parks, including the Botanical Garden and the Carlos Antonio López Park. Asunción is the seat of a university, a normal school, and International College. In the 1940's, as a gesture of friendship, the United States government inaugurated an extensive health and cultural program for the nation, with headquarters in the capital.

Colonnaded government house at Asunción, capital of Paraguay

Merchandise is shipped to Asunción by steamer from Buenos Aires where it is transferred to lighter-draft vessels for shipment to inland river ports. Because of the scarcity of railroads and highways, these river steamers frequently are the only means of transportation for the interior. In addition, Asunción has rail connections with Buenos Aires and air service to that city and to Rio de Janeiro. Local factories produce canned goods, quebracho extract, cotton textiles, shoes, soap, hats, cigars, and furniture. There are numerous plants that pack yerba maté for export. Pop. of Asunción district 1945, 130,067.

S. G. I.

ASVINS [æˈsvɪnz], twin gods of Vedic Hindu mythology. They are believed to be of Zoroastrian origin and bear strong resemblances to the Dioscuri, Castor and Pollux, of Greek and Roman mythology. They are described as young and beautiful gods of the dawn and are called the youngest of the gods and the children of the sun and the ocean. They were benefactors of mankind and functioned as physicians and dentists. There are many hymns in their honor in ancient Vedic literature, but they are of little importance in modern Hindu religion.

R. F.

ASWÂN [ɑswɑˈn], sometimes Assuan, a city and province of the same name in Upper Egypt. The city is the capital of the province, which is the southernmost in Egypt and is located near the borders of Nubia, on the right bank of the Nile River, at the First Cataract. The city is situated about 40 mi. north of the Tropic of Cancer and 590 railroad mi. south of Cairo. The province contains approximately 363 sq. mi., and farming is carried on by irrigation which has been made possible by the huge Aswân Dam, completed in 1902 above the city at the First Cataract. The dam is the most important irrigation structure in Egypt, and in 1948 the Aswân reservoir had a capacity of 5,500,000,000 cubic meters of water. In that year a plan was under way to exploit the hydroelectric power of the reservoir. The dam was heightened and lengthened in 1912 and again in 1934, bringing its total length to 6,970 ft. and its height to 174 ft. As a result of the raising of the dam, the famous island of Philae, with the beautiful temple of Isis, is under water most of the year.

The city is a center for trade with the Sudan. South of it is El Shellâl, the southern terminus of the Egyptian railways, from which start the steamers to the Sudan. Aswân is a noted winter health resort and also a famous tourist spot in Egypt. Ancient remains abound in the vicinity, and the city's colorful bazaars are further tourist attractions. Among the chief sites of interest are the catacombs, on the left bank of the river, and the island of Elephantine in front of the city,

with its numerous ancient remains. In the city's environs are red granite quarries, which in ancient times provided the stones for the obelisks and huge statues of the Pharaohs. The granite is called syenite after the ancient city of Syene.

A community existed on Aswân's site as early as the sixth century B.C. By Roman times the community, known as Syene, was an outpost against attacks by desert tribes. It became a center for Coptic Christians, and there are numerous ruins of Coptic convents in the district. After the Turkish conquest of Egypt in the sixteenth century, the Turks established a garrison at the city's site, and from that time until the end of the nineteenth century Aswân was an important military post. The city figured prominently during the Mahdia Rebellion in the 1880's and 1890's. As a result, it was occupied by British and Egyptian troops. Pop. 1947 (province), 290,842; (city), 26,343.   S. D. M.

ASYNCHRONOUS MACHINES. *See* ALTERNATING-CURRENT MACHINES.

AS YOU LIKE IT (1600), a comedy by Shakespeare. It is a dramatization, with additions and alterations, of Thomas Lodge's *Rosalynde* (1590), a pastoral romance of the type that Sir Philip Sidney's *Arcadia,* published 1590, made popular in Shakespeare's England. Shakespeare himself, however, was not at all inclined to accept the artificial conventions of the pastoral; in this gay comedy he ridicules them in the characters of Silvius and Phebe, and he transforms Lodge's sentimental heroine into the merry, witty, and warm-hearted Rosalind of the play. Two characters, original with Shakespeare, have only a slight connection with the plot and are essentially "humours." One of these is Touchstone, the jester, a part written for Shakespeare's new fellow-actor, Armin; the other is the melancholy Jacques, a representative of the malcontent spirit appearing in Elizabethan literature about this time. The peculiar charm of *As You Like It* is the atmosphere of the good greenwood, ringing with song, in which Shake-

speare has set the action. Yet the best scenes between Rosalind and Orlando are in prose; Shakespeare had come to realize that prose rather than verse is the proper speech for lovers who are neither passionate nor sentimental.

T. M. P.

ASYÛT [ɑsyu't], sometimes Assiut, a city in Upper Egypt, capital of the agricultural province of the same name. Situated on the western bank of the Nile River, about 248 mi. by rail south of Cairo, it is the largest city in the Nile Valley south of the capital. It is famous for its ornamental wood,

Aswân Power Dam, on the Nile, Upper Egypt

EWING GALLOWAY

ivory work, and furniture, and the city's ivory bazaar is a unique feature. Asyût Barrage, a magnificent construction north of the city, supplies the Ibrahmia Canal with irrigation water. There are handsome churches and mosques in the city, which is one of the chief centers of the Coptic Christians, and a division of the University of Al-Azhar is in Asyût. The city has both rail and air connections with Cairo, and it is the northern terminus of the caravan route from Darfur across the desert. The province of Asyût covers approximately 812 sq. mi. Pop. 1947 (province), 1,374,454; (city), 90,103.

ATACAMA. *See* INDIAN TRIBES, SOUTH AMERICAN.

ATAHUALPA

ATAHUALPA [ætəwɑ'lpə] (c. 1500-1533), the last of the Inca rulers, was born in the city of Quito about 1500. He was the illegitimate son of the Inca emperor, Huayna Capac, and of the daughter of the Indian chief of Quito. After the death of his father, Atahualpa and his half-brother, Huascar, became engaged in a civil war to decide who should be emperor. Huascar was finally defeated in 1532. It was at this time that the Spanish conqueror, Francisco Pizarro landed in Peru and sent word to Atahualpa to meet him. Atahualpa promised to visit Pizarro in the plaza at Cajamarca. When the emperor, with a small escort, marched into the plaza, he found himself surrounded by the Spaniards fully armed with guns. Vicente de Valverde, a priest, accompanied Pizarro and demanded that Atahualpa swear allegiance to the God of the Christians. When Atahualpa refused he was seized and imprisoned. A mock trial was held, and the emperor was promised his freedom if he would fill the room where he was imprisoned with gold. Runners to all parts of the empire brought back more than enough gold to pay his ransom. However, other excuses were made and finally Atahualpa was put to death, Aug. 29, 1533. After Atahualpa's death the Inca Empire disintegrated.   S. G. I.

ATALA [a'ta'la'], the title, and the name of the heroine, of a short Romantic novel by François René de Chateaubriand, first published in 1801. Intended originally to be an episode of *Le Génie du Christianisme* (1802), it was issued separately in advance, because, the author alleged in the preface, some pages of proof had been lost.

The story is related by an old Indian, Chactas, to a young Frenchman, René, whose life history in turn forms the parallel novel *René*. Chactas, captured by a hostile tribe and condemned to the stake, is rescued by Atala, a young Christian girl. The latter loves Chactas but has taken a vow to her mother to devote herself to God. Unable either to keep the vow or to break it, she poisons herself after confessing her sin to Father Aubry, the missionary, who following her burial is burned alive by the Indians.

The novel is notable for its harmonious and picturesque style and for its pioneer depiction of passion against the exotic natural background of primitive America. *See also* RENÉ.   R. A. P.

ATALANTA [ætəla'ntə], the name of two heroines in Greek mythology.

The Boeotian Atalanta, daughter of Schoeneus and famed for her swiftness of foot, agreed to marry the suitor who conquered her in a foot race, but death was the penalty for those who failed. Hippomenes received from Aphrodite three of the golden apples of the Hesperides and won the race by dropping them one by one before Atalanta, who could not resist stopping to pick them up. The lovers forgot to thank Aphrodite, however, and were transformed into lions by the goddess Cybele.

The Arcadian Atalanta, daughter of Iasius and Clymene, was abandoned at birth and reared by huntsmen. She became skilled in the use of bow and arrow, took part in the Calydonian hunt, and was long devoted to Artemis, but she later yielded to love and accepted Melanion as a husband. These two Atalantas were often confused, and the story of the foot race and the golden apples was told of Melanion as well as of Hippomenes. *See also* CALYDONIAN HUNT.
                                        G. E. D.

ATAMASCO LILY [ætəmæ'sko], *Zephyranthes atamasco,* amarylis, known also as the zephyr flower, or fairy lily. It grows in moist soil from Pennsylvania to Florida, and is a handsome, bulbous plant, readily cultivated in pots or gardens. Narrow shiny leaves appear in early spring with the single white or purplish lily-like flowers borne on hollow stems about a foot high.   J. C. Wis.

ATARGATIS [ətɑ'rgətɪs], a Syrian goddess of fecundity, especially prominent in Hierapolis; she was known to the Greeks as Dea Syria or Deasura. Her cult has been described in a treatise by Lucian. In certain aspects she was the counterpart of the Phoenician Astarte and the Greek Aphrodite. Her worship was carried by Syrian merchants to Greece and Italy, and during the third century she became prominent in Rome through the influence of the Syrian empresses. Atargatis generally appeared as a fish goddess and was later identified with the great nature goddesses, Rhea and Cybele. Her rites were performed by men dressed as women, and there are many legends about her, chiefly of an astrological character. In her various aspects, she represents either water or earth as the source of life; she was sometimes also known as the protecting deity of various communities.   R. F.

ATBARA [ɑ'tbɑrɑ], a town in eastern Anglo-Egyptian Sudan, the capital of Atbara District in Berber Province, located on the right bank of the Atbara River, about 250 mi. southwest of Port Sudan. The district occupies only 4 sq. mi., with the town its nucleus. The town's economic activity centers chiefly around the Sudan Government Railways, for which it is the headquarters and an important junction point. There are large railroad workshops in the community, and the curriculum of Atbara's technical school is based upon the requirements of the railroad. The town is also a cotton center and the site of a hospital. There is air service to other communities in the Sudan. At Atbara are the graves of many of the British soldiers who died of wounds as a result of the Battle of Atbara, Apr. 8, 1898, during the Sudan campaign. Pop. (est. 1948), 44,300.   A. D.

ATBARA, the northernmost of the several tributaries of the Nile. It rises in northwestern Ethiopia and, after joining the Tacazze River, its greatest affluent, flows northwestward and reaches the Nile at Atbara, south of Berber. It has a torrential flow during part of the year, but is reduced to a series of pools from December to June. Its swift current prevents navigation, even in the flood season. It carries a great amount of silt.   S. Van V.

COURTESY OF OFFICE OF PORT AND PUBLIC RELATIONS, CHARLESTON, NORTH CAROLINA
ATAMASCO LILY, ZEPHYRANTHES ATAMASCO

ATCHAFALAYA [ətshæ'fəlai'ɑ], an important river of south-central Louisiana, having an extremely complicated pattern and flowing southward from the Red River into

U.S. Highway 71 crosses the Atchafalaya Swamp near Krotz Springs, Louisiana.

Atchafalaya Bay off the Gulf of Mexico. The Atchafalaya begins as an overflow of the Red River near Naples in Avoyelles County and also receives water from tributary streams south of the Red River. Its course generally parallels the Mississippi and is within the valley of the master drainage river. During the early history of the Mississippi its lower course was west of its present river site. Gradually the Mississippi moved eastward to its present position, and the Atchafalaya now flows in the general area of the old course of the Mississippi. The Atchafalaya flows across a low, wet, swamp area, part of its course being a maze of meanders, bayous, oxbows, and waterways. During flood season the waters of the Mississippi and Red rivers back into the Atchafalaya, which thus acts as a distributary and helps relieve the flood stage at New Orleans.

Although there are no big cities situated on the banks of the Atchafalaya River, there are a large number of small

towns such as Jacoby, Melville, Krotz Springs, Morgan City, Berwick, and Patterson.   J. E. F.

ATCHISON, a city in northeastern Kansas, the county seat of Atchison Co., on the Missouri River, situated 22 mi. southwest of St. Joseph, Mo. The city was founded by antiabolitionists in 1854 and incorporated in 1858. It was the birthplace of Amelia Earhart Putnam, the aviatrix. The Atchison, Topeka and Santa Fe Railroad was organized in Atchison, and along with the Chicago, Burlington & Quincy, the Chicago, Rock Island & Pacific, and the Missouri Pacific railroads it provides shipping facilities for the city's industries and the grain, truck crops, and fruit raised in the vicinity. River craft also furnish transportation. The factory output includes locomotives, plumbing supplies, leather goods, industrial alcohol, canvas goods, dairy products, flour, and dried eggs. Pop. 1950, 12,792.

ATE [e'ti], in Greek mythology, the blind folly that led gods and men into rash and disastrous acts. Ate was personified as a goddess, the daughter of Zeus and of Eris, goddess of discord.   G. E. D.

A TEMPO. *See* MUSICAL TERMS.

ATHABASKA [æthəbæ'skə], a lake and river in west central Canada. The name is derived from the reeds which grow in great profusion in the muddy deltas of the river and the rich soil shallows of the lake. In the Cree Indian language Athabaska means "where there are reeds."

The lake is situated partly in Alberta and partly in Saskatchewan. It lies to the extreme north of these provinces in 59° N. lat., between 106° and 110° W. long., and its surface is 697 ft. above sea level. The elongated lake is 195 mi. long from east to west, and its width varies from 5 to 35 mi. Its surface area measures approximately 3,100 sq. mi. At the western end the lake is shallow, but it is deep elsewhere and is navigable at all points. The Athabaska River enters the lake near its southwestern extremity, and at the northern shore of this extremity the lake flows into the Slave River. The surrounding region is generally rocky and poor farming country, but it is good fishing and hunting country. Wild game abound in the district, and Fort Chippewyan, situated on the north side of the lake, is one of the oldest northern fur-trading posts in western Canada.

The Athabaska River is situated wholly in Alberta. It rises on the eastern slopes of the Rocky Mountains near the Yellowhead Pass, in the extreme western part of the province, and flows in a northeasterly direction for approximately 740 mi. until it empties into the lake. The Clearwater, McLeod, Lesser Slave, and Pembina rivers are the Athabaska's most important tributaries.   G. T.

ATHALIE [a'ta'li'], a French five-act tragedy in verse by Jean Baptiste Racine (1639-1699). It was the author's last work, written at the request of Madame de Maintenon for the pupils of the school of Saint-Cyr, where it was produced for the first time in 1691. The story of *Athalie* is derived from the Bible. Athalie has usurped the throne of Judah after massacring all her grandchildren except Joas. The play tells of the struggle of the high priest, Joad, against Athalie, in order to place Joas on the throne. Finally, Athalie is killed by the mob, and Joas is crowned in the temple of Jerusalem. Voltaire, although criticizing the play for its implications, called it the "masterpiece of the human mind." In contrast to all of Racine's works, except *Esther,* all reference to earthly love is absent from *Athalie.* Its lyric passages, expressing deep religious feeling, are justly famous. H. L. B.

ATHANARIC [əthæ'nərɪk] (d. 381), ruler of the Visigoths, who called himself "Judge of the Tervingians," was the son of Rothesteus. A pagan, Athanaric would not tolerate the spread of Christianity among the Goths, and his rule was marked by the ruthless persecution of all who professed the new faith. In 367 he was at war with the Roman emperor Valens, as a result of his aid to the usurper Procopius, and at the cessation of hostilities three years later the Danube River was declared their common boundary. Athanaric also fought against Fridigern, a rival ruler of the Visigoths. In 375 the invading Huns forced him to retreat into the Transylvania mountains, but when he was simultaneously attacked by the Ostrogoths in 380 he sought refuge with the emperor Theodosius I in Constantinople. He died Jan. 25, 381, two weeks after his ceremonial reception in Constantinople.   C. W. D.

ATHANASIAN CREED, THE [æthəne'zhən], once attributed to St. Athanasius and sometimes called the *Quicumque,* from its first word (Latin, "Whosoever"), is a formulary of faith characterized by precise expressions concerning the Trinity and the Incarnation. It is considered to have been composed by a Latin writer, probably in Gaul, after the emergence of Nestorianism (430) and before the death of St. Caesarius of Arles (543), since it lays special emphasis on the Incarnation and is mentioned in a letter of Caesarius. Used liturgically after the tenth century, it appears in the Roman Breviary at Prime for Trinity Sunday and the minor Sundays after Epiphany and Pentecost, and in the Church of England it is recited on certain feasts.
                                                            W. C.

ATHANASIUS, ST. [æthəne'zhiəs] (c. 296-373), Bishop of Alexandria, Confessor and Doctor of the Church, was born in 296 in Alexandria. Athanasius, known in his lifetime as the "Father of Orthodoxy," was the greatest champion of the Church's doctrine of the Incarnation. Early brought into contact with the ecclesiastical authorities of Alexandria, by his wisdom he impressed the bishop, Alexander, who made him his secretary and a member of his household. In his very first books, *Contra gentes* and

ST. ATHANASIUS

FROM THEUET'S
*Portraits et vies des
hommes illustres,* 1584

Oratio de Incarnatione, between 318 and 323, was evidenced the key concern of his life, devotion to the Incarnation.

Athanasius accompanied Alexander to the Council convoked at Nicea in 325 against Arius and Arianism. This council used the term "homoousios" against Arianism to express the character of orthodox belief in the person of Christ, by defining Him to be identical in substance or coessential with the Father, hence truly God. The abilities of the youthful Athanasius displayed in the Nicean debates, his courage, and his sincerity distinguished him, and he was chosen Bishop of Alexandria.

Some time afterwards Eusebius, the Arian Bishop of Nicomedia, began to intrigue against Athanasius, alleging

ATHABASKA VALLEY, ALBERTA, CANADA

COURTESY OF THE CANADIAN NATIONAL RAILWAYS

various ecclesiastical and political charges, which were, however, clearly refuted. Nevertheless, Athanasius was exiled in February 336 to Trèves where he remained for over two and a half years.

Exiled on three other occasions through the intrigues of the Eusebians, Athanasius nevertheless managed to be present in his see for various periods, the longest being from 346 to 356. Only in the last years of his life did he hold comparatively tranquil possession of his see. He died at Alexandria in 373. Beloved and greatly esteemed by his people, he continued to affirm the divinity of Christ, to which his whole life had been dedicated, and which was the subject of his chief dogmatical work, the *Discourses against the Arians* (generally dated 356-359). P. J. B.

ATHEISM, a doctrine which denies the existence of any supernatural power or powers. The early history of atheism is buried in obscurity because of the loose and vague connotations of the term. The ancient Greeks sometimes used it to designate belief in strange or foreign gods, as well as disbelief in the existence of any gods. The Epicureans were occasionally taxed with atheism because they believed that although gods exist, they neither govern human affairs nor are concerned with them. Atheism, as a denial of the existence of any gods, took on the character of a broad intellectual movement in the nineteenth century in consequence of left-wing Hegelian higher criticism of the Bible, notably in the work of David Friedrich Strauss, Bruno Bauer, and Ludwig Feuerbach. Through their influence on Marx, atheism became associated with the international socialist movement, and through the teachings of Marx and Lenin it became an integral part of the state philosophy of the Soviet Union. The growth of atheism was intensified, especially in Anglo-American countries, by the spread of the doctrine of evolution and the organization of Free-Thought and Rationalist societies.

Strictly speaking, one may be sure that the existence of anything cannot be logically disproved, but those who have denied the existence of gods maintain that no valid rational arguments or empirical evidence have been found which indicate the existence of God or gods. Atheists distinguish themselves from agnostics, who profess doubt about divine existence or about the capacity of the human mind to consider the question, in their assertion that the negative evidence is sufficient to warrant disbelief. They maintain that the same methodological considerations which lead people to disbelief in the existence of elves, fairies, and leprechauns justify disbelief in the existence of God or gods.

In the history of religious thought many thinkers have been denounced as atheists: Spinoza, whose conception of God differed from the one generally held in his time, is a famous example. The word atheism has been in such bad odor and illogically associated with all sorts of unethical and antisocial conduct in so many quarters, that few people have had the courage to declare themselves atheists openly. Many twentieth century writers who employ the term God manifest less belief in religious dogmas than thinkers like Paine and Shelley who were widely regarded as atheists in their time. On the other hand, some atheists criticize the social role which churches have played in the past, under the impression that such criticism constitutes a logical reply to arguments for theism. Formally, considerations pointing to the allegedly good or evil practical effects of religious belief are irrelevant to the truth of religious doctrine, including the assertion of divine existence.

On the whole, and with important exceptions, individuals and movements that have called themselves atheistic, or who have been regarded as such, have been closely allied with the general movements for intellectual advancement and social progress of their time. The philosophic basis of atheism is materialism or naturalism. Some materialists and naturalists, however, have repudiated the designation of atheism as implying a too radical separation of man from nature, and have continued to use the term God in their own special naturalistic sense. *See also* THEISM. S. H.

ATHELSTAN [æ'thəlstæn] (895-940), English king and grandson of King Alfred, succeeded his father, Edward, as king of the West Saxons and Mercians in 925. He annexed Northumbria, made the princes of Wales do homage, invaded Scotland, and defeated King Constantine. In 937 a revolt of his subject princes was crushed at Brunanburh, probably in Northumbria. Athelstan was really the first king of all the English and was so powerful that five European princes sought his sisters in marriage. A considerable body of law was left by Athelstan. He died at Gloucester, Oct. 27, 940. E. R. A.

ATHENA or ATHENE [əthi'nə, əthi'ni], one of the most important goddesses of Greek mythology, identified by the Romans with Minerva, the Italian goddess of arts

HEAD OF THE
ATHENA LEMNIA

AFTER PHIDIAS

COURTESY OF THE
METROPOLITAN MUSEUM
OF ART

and crafts. Athena was often called Pallas Athena, or simply Pallas. In origin, she was a pre-Hellenic goddess, probably the protectress of the citadel of some Mycenaean prince. Her birth is variously recounted: she sprang in full armor from the head of Zeus which Hephaestus had split open with an axe (the common version); she issued from a cloud burst asunder by Zeus; she was the daughter of the river god Triton, whence the epithet, "Triton-born." Athena was the patroness of numerous Greek cities, chief among which was Athens, where the festival of the Panathenaea was celebrated in her honor. According to legend, in the time of Cecrops, Poseidon and Athena each desired possession of the city, which was to be assigned to the divinity offering the most useful gift; Poseidon gave the horse, but Athena planted the olive tree, whereupon the city was awarded to her and named Athens.

As protectress of cities, Athena was necessarily a goddess of warfare, but of defensive and prudent warfare as opposed to brute force and rashness, which was represented by Ares. In the Trojan conflict, Athena fought on the side of the Greeks and against Ares and Aphrodite. She was also goddess of agriculture and navigation, of peaceful pursuits in general, and, in particular, of the female arts and industries of spinning and weaving; in addition she was patroness of the arts and the inventor of the flute, which she was said to have thrown away because it distorted her features. As goddess of wisdom, Athena was looked upon as a moral and righteous divinity, and her influence upon Greek thought was most beneficial. Among her attributes were the helmet, the aegis, the spear, the olive branch, and

ATHENA PARTHENOS

the owl, and she was represented in statues as helmeted, with the aegis on her breast and a spear in her hand. *See also* ARACHNE; TROJAN WAR. G. E. D.

ATHENAGORAS [æðənæ'gərəs], Christian apologist of the second century. About his life the only reliable information is that contained in the title to his *Apology* or *Embassy for the Christians,* by "Athenagoras the Athenian, Philosopher and Christian," which is inscribed "to the Emperors Marcus Aurelius Antoninus and Lucius Aurelius Commodus . . . ." From internal evidence it is possible to estimate the date of composition as approximately A.D. 177. Philip of Side, in his *Pamphylia* (c. 425), claims that Athenagoras was the first director of the catechetical school at Alexandria, but this is extremely doubtful. The *Apology* is a plea for justice for the Christians and a denial of the accusation that they were atheists and cannibals and practiced incest. Athenagoras also wrote a *Treatise on the Resurrection,* probably after the *Apology,* in which he upholds the Resurrection on the basis of God's power and man's nature. In point of style Athenagoras ranks high among the apologists. His arguments are philosophically sound and presented in a lucid, elegant, and forcible manner. C. W. D.

ATHENIAN CONSTITUTION, in the fifth century B.C., was the most democratic of ancient Greece. Before 500 B.C., the Athenian government had already gone through a long period of evolution, which had begun with monarchy, passed through aristocratic and timocratic stages, and progressed to the verge of democracy. Perhaps as late as 750 B.C., the Athenians retained the primitive Indo-European monarchical form, in which there was a king who func-

tioned as war leader, high priest, and judge; a council of the elders, who advised the king; and an assembly of the people, the ecclesia, which included all citizens able to bear arms. About 750 B.C., however, due to the concentration of land in the hands of a few people, political power passed into the control of a minority of landed aristocrats, who transformed the council, called the Areopagus, into a major governing body, which usurped the powers of the king and the popular assembly. Thereafter, the council annually chose magistrates who performed the duties formerly reserved for the king, and the kingship was abolished. The new aristocratic magistrates were called archons. They were: a civil executive, the *archon eponymous;* a war leader, the *archon polemarchos;* and a high priest, the *archon basileus.* Later, six more archons, the *thesmothetae,* were added; these were judges and the keepers of the laws. During this period the popular assembly almost ceased to function.

Timocracy. In the seventh century B.C., with the introduction of coinage and the growth of commerce, the aristocratic form of government became essentially a timocracy, with political power concentrated in the hands of the wealthy aristocracy. The citizens were classified according to their income, the lowest class being the *thetes,* the peasants and workers with an income of less than 200 measures of grain. These had no political rights. Great dissatisfaction developed among many Athenians because of this virtual disfranchisement, and to avert a revolution the famous statesman Solon was elected archon with extraordinary powers for the purpose of revising the constitution. Political offices and membership in a new Council, the Council of the Four Hundred, were still open only to the three wealthier classes (*pentakosiomedimni, hippeis,* and *zeugitae*); to this extent Solon's constitution was still timocratic, but he laid the foundations of democratic government by permitting the lowest class of citizens, the *thetes,* to participate in the popular assembly and also to serve as jurors in the law court, called the Heliaea, which heard appeals from sentences of the magistrates involving penalties of death, exile, or heavy fines. This last was perhaps the most important innovation of all, for the citizens as a whole could now try magistrates after retirement for misconduct in office. The Council of the Four Hundred was elected annually; one hundred councilors were chosen from each of the four Athenian tribes. The council advised the archons and prepared measures to be submitted to the assembly for enactment into law. The old council, the Areopagus, was now relegated to the position of a minor law court; it was composed of ex-archons.

About 508 B.C., the Athenian constitution was made more democratic by the reforms of Cleisthenes, who abolished the Council of the Four Hundred in favor of a new council, the boule, or Council of the Five Hundred. In this, councilors were chosen annually by lot, fifty from each of the ten new tribes created by Cleisthenes on a geographical basis to take the place of the four older tribes. Cleisthenes also added new magistrates, the Board of the Ten Generals (one from each tribe), who directed military affairs.

New Structure. In the fifth century, during the Age of Pericles, the Athenian constitution culminated in a democracy, the organization of which may be described as follows: *Executive.* The most important officials were the ten generals, annually elected. The generals were not only military leaders but also recognized heads of political parties. Pericles, for example, was almost continuously in office as the principal general, the *strategos autokrator,* elected by the people as a whole. The archonship had declined in importance. In the fifth century the nine archons were judges

VIEW OF ATHENS TOWARD THE ACROPOLIS, SHOWING THE PARTHENON (LEFT) AND HALL OF THE VIRGINS (RIGHT)

and predominantly municipal officials chosen by lot each year. Other executive functions were exercised by boards or committees, also chosen by lot: the treasurers of the various temples, contractors, financial boards, police, and prison commissioners, and those who regulated the market place in Athens and the Piraeus.

Legislative. The Council of the Five Hundred (boule) drafted measures to be presented to the people for legislative action, but the boule could also enact ordinances which were effective for a period of one year. The boule, in addition, had the general supervision of military and financial affairs and was supposed to see that the laws of the state were properly enforced. The ecclesia, or popular assembly, was a legislative, elective, judicial, and deliberative body. It made the laws, elected the generals, received foreign ambassadors, and might even sit as a court (the Heliaea).

Judicial. Although there were special courts in Athens (the ephetae, Areopagus, and others), the main judicial business was carried on by the *dikasteria,* the jury courts, composed of panels of citizen jurors who sat almost daily under the presidency of the archons. Before these jury courts came all civil suits and most criminal suits involving citizens, Athenian allies or subjects, or foreigners who became involved in cases in which citizens of Athens were concerned.

The Athenian government was a democracy in the sense that all the citizens of Athens (not allies, subjects, or resident aliens) were able to participate in governmental affairs. Pay for councilors and jurymen made it possible for the poorer citizens to serve, and the rotation of most offices by the use of the lot meant that almost every citizen had an opportunity to fill several posts during his lifetime. Furthermore, the widespread use of the committee system increased the number of positions in which citizens might serve. *See also* CLEISTHENES; DICASTERY; SOLON.   T. B. J.

ATHENS [æ'thənz], the capital of modern, and the most important city of ancient, Greece, lies at 38° N. lat. and 23° 45′ E. long. in the Attic plain, closed in on three sides by mountains, Hymettus to the east, Pentelikon to the northeast, and Parnis to the north. To the southwest and west the plain opens on the Saronic Gulf, three miles from the city at the nearest point. The partially sheltered bay of Phaleron, with its broad sandy beach, offers a convenient landing place for small craft, while the excellent, deep harbor at Piraeus offers safe shelter for larger vessels. The plain is bisected from north to south by a low ridge, the ancient Anchesmus, which ends at the south in the conspicuous peak of Lycabettus and the flat-topped rock of the Acropolis. West of the latter rise the lower hill, the Areopagus, and the long ridge which comprises three low peaks, the Hill of the Muses to the east, the

Hill of the Nymphs to the west, and the Pnyx between. Small springs seep out at the foot of the Acropolis to south and west, and a larger one at the north foot of the Areopagus. The ancient city was traversed by a brook, the Eridanus, which rose at the foot of Lycabettus and flowed out of the town toward the northwest. The plain is watered by the Cephissus and Ilissus streams, the former rising in Pentelicon and passing to the west of the city, the latter in Hymettus and passing just to the east. The plain itself is fertile and comparatively well watered; conditions were therefore favorable for primitive settlement centering on the Acropolis as a strong place of refuge with an adequate supply of water, easy to defend against enemies by land, and at a safe distance from surprise by raiders coming from the sea.

THE ARCHAEOLOGY OF ANCIENT ATHENS

The Primitive Period. Wells and other remains from the Neolithic period prove that the Acropolis and its slopes were inhabited as early as the fourth millennium before Christ. Although the ancient Athenians boasted that they were autochthonous, that is, sprung from the soil of their land, the native inhabitants were amalgamated with invaders and conquerors from the north during the Early and Middle Bronze Ages. Both these periods, known also as Early and Middle Helladic, are represented in Athens by wells and graves which are clustered on the north and west slopes of the Acropolis and the Areopagus. In the Late Bronze Age (Late Helladic Period) the ruling family had its palace on the Acropolis. Tombs containing objects of ivory and gold have been found on the north slope of the Areopagus and assigned to this royal family, but the finds are poor compared with those of contemporary Mycenae and Tiryns. In the thirteenth century B.C. heavy fortification walls were built around the Acropolis. The invasions from the north, which have been equated with the traditional "Dorian invasion," destroyed the flourishing cities of central Greece and the Peloponnesus and brought Mycenaean culture to an end, but they seem to have by-passed Attica and Athens, which remained unconquered. The Athenian claim of autochthony may have been based on this immunity.

The period between the twelfth and the seventh centuries B.C. was a dark age for Athens as well as elsewhere in Greece. Graves along the Eridanus near the Dipylon Gate show that the technique and decoration of pottery declined; in these graves iron objects appear. Somewhat later tombs in the same cemetery indicate a change of culture: cremation was practiced, objects made of iron are more abundant, and a new style of pottery appears. This improved pottery became the decorative style known as Geometric, which reached its highest development in Athens. The grave offerings of the later part of the eighth century B.C. include scarabs and objects of gold and ivory, and the pottery reveals patterns and designs of Eastern art; all this suggests a reopening of trade relations with the Orient, and this is confirmed by the first appearance of alphabetical inscriptions.

The great innovations of the seventh century, the introduction of coinage and the spread of alphabetical writing, apparently came to Athens at second hand through her more active neighbors, Aegina, Corinth, and Chalcis. The Attic pottery of the seventh century (Protoattic or Early Attic) reflects the influence of all these places, sometimes badly jumbled together, but before the end of the century the characteristic Attic Black-Figured ware had emerged. The figures, usually mythological, were painted black and glazed against a reddish clay background; red was used for the hair and beards of men, and white for the flesh of women.

This style became the standard for sixth-century Athenian pottery, which soon captured the markets of southern Italy and Etruria and dominated them for two centuries.

The Sixth Century B.C. The first of the three great building periods of Athens occurred when public works on an extensive scale were carried out under the rule of Pisistratus and his sons. The sixth-century buildings on the Acropolis were destroyed by the Persians in 480 B.C., but the foundations have been discovered of the temple of Athena Polias, which stood close to the later Erechtheum. The building was approximately one hundred feet long and has been identified with the "Hecatompedon" or "hundred-foot temple," to which there are references in both literature and inscriptions, but the identification is not certain. Erected in the first half of the sixth century, the temple of Athena was beautified by Pisistratus and his son Hipparchus.

At the north foot of the Areopagus a famous fountain house was built, called Enneacrunus (the "nine-spouted"). During the recent American excavations of the Agora, or market-place, foundations of this building were uncovered just outside the southern limits of the Agora proper. In the Agora itself a large public building, rectangular in plan, has been found, dating also from the period of Pisistratus. This was probably a law court, perhaps the famous Heliaea, where the Athenian jurors listened to the pleas of the litigants. Numerous bronze ballots, some for acquittal, others for condemnation, have been found in this area.

The most ambitious project of the regime seems to have been the temple of Olympian Zeus on the banks of the Ilissus southeast of the Acropolis. Work was probably started after the death of Pisistratus himself, and the temple was left unfinished; the Athenians apparently regarded it as a task imposed by tyrants and so abandoned the project after their fall. The temple seems to have been planned as an Ionic structure and measured about 135 by 350 ft.—an enormous structure, comparable in scale to the sixth-century Ionic temples of Artemis at Ephesus and of Hera at Samos.

About 525 B.C. Athens introduced a new style of pottery, the Red-Figured ware; the decorated figures were left in the reddish clay color, with details drawn in with thin lines, while the background was painted black. Another style, with white background, was developed, but the red-figured pottery remained predominant for almost two centuries.

The Fifth Century B.C. With the fall of the tyrants and the restoration of democracy, a new *bouleterion* was erected in the Agora for the Council (*boule*), and a new meeting place on the Pnyx was established for the popular assembly of citizens (*ecclesia*). The popularity of the institution of ostracism, by which any citizen deemed dangerous to the state could be sent into exile for ten years by the vote of his fellow citizens, is attested by the discovery of numerous ostraca, bearing the names of prominent Athenians such as Aristides and Themistocles scratched on potsherds. The voting was done in the Agora, but large dumps of the votes have been found in the area to the south of the market-place proper, and outside the Dipylon Gate to the north.

Traces of the siege of Athens by the Persians in 480 B.C. have been recognized in bronze arrowheads, their points turned by striking against the walls and the rock of the Acropolis. After the withdrawal of the Persians from Greece, Themistocles urged the fortification of Athens with strong walls. This wall is best preserved in the northwest, in the neighborhood of the Dipylon Gate and the cemetery, where a number of Archaic sculptures and gravestones have been found built into it, thus confirming the statement of the historian Thucydides that every sort of material was used as it came to hand. The course of the Themistoclean wall may be conjectured by the presence of graves which must have lain outside, since the Athenians had religious regulations forbidding burials within the city. The cemeteries were clustered outside the various gates. At the Ceramicus, near the Dipylon Gate, numerous steles of the fifth and fourth centuries B.C., carved with relief representations of

Other buildings which added to the beauty of the Acropolis in the fifth century include the small Ionic temple of Athena Nike, planned by the architect Callicrates; the great Propylaea, or entrance gate, on the west side of the hill, designed by Mnesicles; and, constructed some years after the death of Pericles, the Erechtheum, which united a number of ancient sanctuaries in a single structure and which is

Ruins of the Propylaea, the marble gateway to the temples on the Acropolis.

EWING GALLOWAY

the departed, have been uncovered. The Dipylon Gate, as we know it, dates from late in the fourth century. Other important gates in the wall were the Sacred Gate (adjoining the Dipylon), where began the Sacred Way to Eleusis, the Piraeus Gate to the south and west, and the Acharnian Gate to the north.

The walls of the Piraeus were also built under Themistocles and were repaired by Conon in the fourth century. Before the middle of the fifth century the Long Walls were built to link the fortifications of Athens with those of the Piraeus. The Long Walls were three in number: the north wall, the Phaleric Wall, and the middle wall. The first of these was the earliest, extending directly from Athens to the Piraeus. The Phaleric Wall went to the coast on the east side of Phaleron Bay. On the advice of Pericles the Athenians abandoned this wall and built the south or middle wall, thus reducing the area to be defended. The Long Walls proper, consisting of the north and middle walls, were parallel throughout most of their course, about 550 ft. apart. Their length was about 4½ mi., protected at frequent intervals by towers. Few remains of the Long Walls are extant.

The second great architectural period of ancient Athens was in 450-430 B.C. under the direction of Pericles. The Acropolis was rebuilt with far greater splendor than it had known before the destruction by the Persians. The most famous of the new structures was the great Doric-style temple to Athena, the Parthenon, designed by the architect Ictinus. This, the most beautiful of Greek temples, became a church, then a mosque, and was well preserved until 1687, when a gunpowder explosion destroyed the central portion of the temple and left it in its present ruined condition.

famed for the perfection of its workmanship; especially beautiful are its Ionic capitals and the caryatids of the "porch of the maidens."

Just west of the Agora stands the Doric temple of the god Hephaestus, built entirely of Pentelic marble. This, the best preserved of all Greek temples, was mistakenly identified as the Theseum, since the metopes at the east end represented the exploits of Theseus. The real Theseum, where the bones of the hero were deposited, lay somewhere to the north of the Acropolis but has never been found. Among the foundations uncovered in the Agora by the American excavations in recent years is that of a late fifth-century building of several rooms (probably fourteen) which has been tentatively identified as the *thesmotheteion,* the offices and dining quarters of the six *thesmothetae,* or officials in charge of the law courts.

The contrast between the public buildings and the private dwellings in fifth-century Athens was very great, and the ancient writers themselves comment on the difference between the mean appearance of the streets and houses and the magnificence of the public monuments. The streets were narrow and winding, having been rebuilt after the Persian invasion without plan, and the houses were mostly of sun-dried brick, turning blank walls to the outside and getting their light from central courtyards. The streets as revealed by the American excavations are sometimes only two meters wide—little more than six feet. But some of the important streets of the city were more impressive. The street from the Dipylon Gate to the Agora was bordered by monuments, and the Panathenaic Way, leading from the Altar of the Twelve Gods in the Agora to the Acropolis, was a broad street lined on both sides by statues and dedications, the scene each year of the Panathenaic procession when a new peplos, or robe, for the statue of Athena was carried in state to the Acropolis. Along the Street of the Tripods, which went around the east end of the Acropolis to the theatre of Dionysus on the south side, the winners of the dramatic contests set up tripods to record their victories. One of these monuments, that of Lysicrates, dating from the second half

of the political and religious life of the city. The great prestige of her past led friendly rulers of the wealthy eastern kingdoms to adorn the city with many splendid monuments. In the third century B.C. Ptolemy Philadelphus, King of Egypt, built a gymnasium and a library near the Agora. The kings of Pergamum were distinguished as benefactors. Attalus I dedicated a number of bronze statues on the Acrop-

The Erechtheum, an ancient temple on the Acropolis

EWING GALLOWAY

of the fourth century, is still well preserved in its original position to the east of the Acropolis. It is a small circular structure decorated with engaged Corinthian columns, on the top of which the tripod itself stood.

The Fourth Century B.C. With the defeat of Athens at the end of the Peloponnesian War, the Long Walls and those of the city and the Piraeus were destroyed. The victory of Conon over the Spartans at Cnidus in 394 B.C. revived Athenian ambitions; the city walls and the Long Walls were restored, the Phaleric Wall being definitely abandoned at this time. The walls of the Piraeus as we know them today date mostly from the restoration by Conon.

The third quarter of the fourth century saw considerable building activity under the leadership of Lycurgus, a contemporary of Demosthenes. The first stone theatre of Dionysus was constructed beneath the south cliff of the Acropolis, replacing the earlier wooden building, and the Panathenaic Stadium outside the city on the south side of the Elissus was completed. From this period also dates the final arrangement of the Pnyx. In the fifth century the *bema,* or speaker's platform, had faced south toward a slope in the hill forming a curved auditorium, where the citizens sat on the ground or on cushions. Early in the fourth century the auditorium was changed to face the south and the speakers on the *bema* stood with their backs to the sea. In the time of Lycurgus the auditorium was enlarged and made more accessible by the construction of passages on the south side and of a stair and ramp on the north side. Two long stoas, or colonnades, fronting on wide terraces, were planned on the summit of the hill to afford shelter from rain and to provide strolling places for the citizens before and after the meetings of the assembly; these were partially built but never completed because a new stretch of city wall was carried over the area which they were to have occupied.

The Hellenistic Period. With the loss of political liberty, the architecture of Athens ceased to be an expression

olis, and his brother Eumenes constructed a long stoa to the west of the theatre of Dionysus, where the audiences could stroll in a sheltered place. In the second century, Attalus II built a magnificent stoa along the east side of the Agora. This structure, 382 ft. long, was of two floors with a row of 21 shops and a broad porch in front on each floor; the supporting columns were of the Doric order on the first floor and Ionic on the second. In front of the building was a broad, unroofed terrace, where spectators could watch the processions on their way to the Acropolis. The most ambitious undertaking of the Hellenistic kings was the attempt of Antiochus Epiphanes of Syria to complete the great temple of Olympian Zeus begun nearly four centuries earlier by the sons of Pisistratus. The new temple was left unfinished by the death of the benefactor. Some of the columns were taken to Rome by Sulla after the siege of 86 B.C. and there used in the rebuilding of the temple of Jupiter on the Capitoline Hill.

The Roman Period. Athens, adorned both with the monuments of her own past and with the gifts of the Hellenistic kings, was at the peak of her splendor by the end of the second century B.C. For siding with King Mithridates in a war against Rome, she was besieged and captured by Sulla in 86 B.C. The dockyards and arsenals of the Piraeus were destroyed, and Athens became a city of the Roman empire without independent power. So great was her prestige and the influence of her schools, however, that she continued to receive the gifts of wealthy patrons. In the first century B.C. Andronicus of Cyrrhus built his Horologium, now known as the Tower of the Winds, an octagonal structure decorated with reliefs personifying the winds which blow from eight different directions. The building stands at the north foot of the Acropolis; most of the space between it and the Stoa of Attalus was occupied by the Roman Agora, or Market of Caesar and Augustus, under whose auspices it was built.

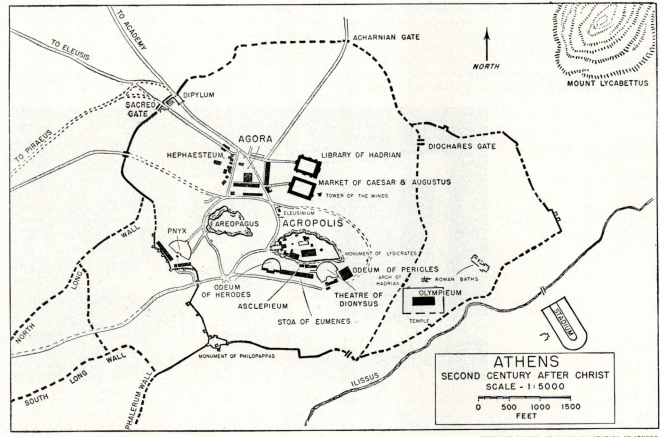

The third and last important building period of ancient Athens came in the reign of the Roman emperor Hadrian (A.D. 117-138). An entire new quarter was added to the city to the east, and the wall was extended to enclose it. Southeast of the Acropolis an arched gate was built, bearing on its inner face the inscription "This is the Athens of Theseus, the old city," and on its outer face "This is the city of Hadrian, not of Theseus." Hadrian completed and dedicated the temple of Olympian Zeus in A.D. 130 or 131. As finally finished it was one of the largest temples in the Greek world, a structure measuring about 355 by 135 ft. Fifteen of the original 108 columns of Pentelic marble, about 56 ft. in height, are still standing. Hadrian also built a library in the old city north of the Roman Agora. Herodes Atticus, a contemporary and friend of Hadrian, reconstructed the Panathenaic Stadium with seats of Pentelic marble and also built an Odeum, or music hall, at the western end of the Stoa of Eumenes below the Acropolis. In the Odeum, which seats about 5,000 persons, dramatic and musical performances are still presented. These monuments of the second century of the Christian Era were the last important additions to the ancient city.

Foreign interest in the antiquities of Athens began in the seventeenth century, when British and French architects, artists, and topographers traveled to Greece to record monuments, several of which were later destroyed. The Turks, who controlled Athens from 1458 to 1833, were not interested in Greek antiquities and allowed Lord Elgin early in the nineteenth century to take from the Acropolis the famous collection of sculptures now in the British Museum. With the liberation of Athens from the Turks there began the period of conservation, excavation, and restoration of the ancient city. The Greek Archaeological Society was founded in 1837, and the foreign archaeological schools have undertaken excavations and restorations in various parts of the city. The excavations of the American School in the Greek Agora were still in progress in 1955, this being their twentieth season of work in the area. Because of the many finds (over 60,000 catalogued objects) a permanent museum is needed, and for this purpose the Stoa of Attalus II is being reconstructed. The building, when completed, will provide an adequate museum for the objects discovered in the excavations, give modern visitors an excellent idea of the design of an ancient stoa, and afford a splendid view of the newly excavated Agora of ancient Athens. *See also* ACROPOLIS; AGORA; GREEK ARCHITECTURE; GREEK ART; PARTHENON.

THE HISTORY OF ANCIENT ATHENS

The Primitive Period. The early history of Athens is obscure. Archaeological evidence proves that the site was inhabited as far back as the fourth millennium B.C. and that it was a center of Mycenaean culture in the latter part of the second millennium, but less prosperous than Mycenae and Tiryns. The invasions from the north which destroyed the other Mycenaean cities seem to have spared Attica and Athens. According to Athenian tradition, Attica was originally composed of several independent sovereignties which later merged into a single community, and the hero Theseus was credited with the unification of the country. Athens was ruled by kings until, as elsewhere in Greece, the monarchy was supplanted by an aristocracy. The archonship, or chief magistracy, became an annual office in 683 B.C. The archons were three in number and were later increased to nine by the addition of six *thesmothetae,* or judges.

The social structure at this time was almost feudal, with a few landowning families (*Eupatridae,* or nobles) holding most of the land of Attica and controlling the magistracies, and the rest of the population (*Georgi,* or peasants, and *Demiurgi,* or public workers) reduced to a condition approximating serfdom. The development of foreign trade in the seventh century B.C. brought an increased emphasis on wealth, and new classifications were established, determined by the annual yield of landed property: *pentakosiomedimni,* those with an income of 500 medimni of corn; *hippeis,* or knights, with an income between 300 and 500 medimni; and *zeugitae,* or teamsters, with an income of at least 200 measures. The poorer peasants and workers were known as *thetes;* although citizens, they had no political rights. The introduction of coinage increased the conflict between the rich and the poor. About 632 B.C. Cylon seized the Acropolis and attempted to make himself tyrant but was overthrown. The continued distress of the people led in 621 B.C. to the appointment of Draco as a legislator with power to draw up criminal laws. Although his laws were noted for their severity, their codification benefited the lower classes and deprived the nobles of their exclusive control of legal knowledge.

The Sixth Century B.C. The condition of the small farmers and the free laborers grew worse. Forced to borrow money on their land or on their persons, many citizens were reduced to slavery, and a revolution and the establishment of a tyranny seemed imminent. In 594 B.C., however, Solon, a member of the wealthiest class in the state, was elected archon with power to remedy the social and economic evils. His reforms were enlightened and far-reaching: he cancelled all mortgages and debts in which the debtor's person had been pledged, and he forbade the future borrowing of money on such pledge; he established a Council of 400 to prepare the business to be submitted to the Assembly; and, whereas the political offices and membership to the Council were open only to members of the first three classes, Solon permitted the *thetes* to participate in the Assembly and to serve as jurors in the law courts. Athens was not yet a democracy, but Solon laid the foundations of democratic government by his constitutional reforms; and his economic legislation, by improving the conditions of the poorer classes and encouraging commerce, introduced a period of material prosperity. Because of his statesmanship Solon was considered one of the Seven Wise Men of Greece, and since he expressed his political and ethical views in verse, he was honored as the first Athenian poet.

Party strife again broke out after Solon's archonship, and in 561 B.C. Solon's friend, Pisistratus, who had conquered Salamis and annexed it to Attica, seized control of the state and established a tyranny. He and his sons Hippias and Hipparchus ruled, with interruptions, until 510 B.C. This was a period of great prosperity for Athens. Pisistratus preserved many features of Solon's constitution, maintained peaceful relations with other states, and established settlements along the Hellespont, thus taking the first steps on the road to an Athenian empire. He and his sons encouraged both agriculture and industry and initiated a building program which included temples to Athena on the Acropolis and a great temple to Olympian Zeus southeast of the Acropolis; the latter structure was not completed until the time of the Roman emperor Hadrian six centuries later.

Upon the death of Pisistratus, his oldest son Hippias succeeded to the rule and was assisted by another son Hipparchus. They encouraged literature by bringing to Athens the leading poets of the day, among them Simonides and Anacreon. A conspiracy against the Pisistratids, headed by Harmodius and Aristogiton, resulted in the assassination of Hipparchus in 514 B.C. The conspirators were put to death, but Hippias, embittered by the loss of his brother, now became a harsh and despotic ruler. The Athenians, aided by Sparta, overthrew the tyrant in 510 B.C., bringing to an end the rule of the Pisistratids.

After a short period of confusion during which an attempted Spartan intervention was crushed, Cleisthenes, as leader of the people, introduced a series of reforms (508-507 B.C.) which made Athens a democracy in the fullest sense: he abolished sectionalism by creating ten artificial tribes, each tribe being composed of citizens from the city, the coast, and the inland hills, and he established as the supreme administrative authority a new Council of 500, representing every part of Attica, since each tribe contributed fifty members. The Ecclesia, or Popular Assembly, had the power of declaring war and making treaties; it passed laws only on matters already proposed and discussed by the Council, but it could order the Council to bring a certain matter before it at its next meeting. According to tradition, Cleisthenes was responsible for the institution of ostracism, by which a citizen could be condemned to leave Athens for ten years; the earliest recorded instances of ostracism date from about twenty years later, after the battle of Marathon.

Sparta, hostile to the new democracy, invaded Attica in 506 B.C. and was repulsed. Conflicts with both Thebes and Chalcis resulted in Athenian victories and the acquisition of part of the Chalcidian plain. The rising power of Athens led it to support the Ionian cities of Asia Minor in their revolt against the Persians in 499 B.C. After burning Sardis, the Greeks were defeated by the Persians and the Athenians returned home. Eretria also had sent ships to Asia Minor, and the intervention of the two Greek cities led to action by the Persians to obtain revenge.

The Fifth Century B.C. With the outbreak of the Greco-Persian Wars the history of Athens begins to merge with the general history of Greece. But it is important to remember that the campaign of Darius against Greece was undertaken primarily to punish Athens and Eretria for taking part in the Ionian revolt and that the victory over the Persians at Marathon in 490 B.C. was won chiefly by the Athenians. Marathon has been called a triumph for Greece and for Europe; it was first and foremost a triumph for Athenian democracy, and the enormous prestige and self-confidence which Athens gained at this time were strong factors in her rise to power later in the century.

Under the leadership of Themistocles Athens built up a strong naval force. The second Persian War broke out in 480 B.C. when Xerxes invaded Greece from the north and defeated the Spartans at Thermopylae. Themistocles persuaded the Athenians to evacuate Athens, after which the city was captured and plundered by the Persians, but the destruction of the Persian fleet at Salamis proved the wisdom of Themistocles' naval policy and added still more to Athenian prestige. By the naval victory at Mycale in 479 B.C., in which the Athenians took an active part, the Greek cities of Asia Minor were freed from Persian control.

When in 447 B.C. the Greek cities of the Aegean islands and the coasts of Thrace and Asia Minor formed a league for mutual defense against Persia, they naturally placed themselves under the leadership of Athens, now the greatest naval power of Greece. The smaller states, instead of furnishing ships, paid a sum of money each year into a common treasury, located on the sacred island of Delos. The league was known as the Delian League, or the Confederacy of

THE ACADEMY OF SCIENCE IN ATHENS

Delos. More and more it came under the control of Athens; as member states attempted to withdraw or to oppose Athenian supremacy, they were conquered and deprived of their autonomy. Since most cities contributed money rather than ships, the Athenians used the money to increase their own naval forces and looked upon the contributions as tribute paid by subject states. In 454-453 B.C. the treasury of the League was transferred from Delos to Athens and the confederacy, as such ceased to exist. Athens was now in effect the head of an empire composed of more than 200 tribute-paying cities in the Aegean Sea and the Hellespont.

Meanwhile, at Athens the destruction caused by the Persian invasion was repaired. Both Athens and the Piraeus were fortified with strong walls, and the Long Walls were built to connect Athens with the sea, which she controlled, and to make her secure from attack by land. Public indiscretions committed by Themistocles resulted in his ostracism, and Cimon, who had risen to prominence through military victories over the Persians in Asia Minor, became the most important statesman in Athens. He favored maintaining good relations with Sparta, believing that Athens should retain control of the seas but that Sparta, as head of the Peloponnesian League, should continue to be supreme on the mainland of Greece. His oligarchical sympathies, however, aroused the opposition of the younger statesmen of the democratic party, the leaders of which were Ephialtes and Pericles. Accused of being pro-Spartan, Cimon was ostracized and banished (461 B.C.), and the murder of Ephialtes shortly after left Pericles as the leader of the Athenian democracy for the next thirty years, a glorious period for Athens known as the Age of Pericles, or the Golden Age.

In spite of its imperial policy abroad, Athens under Pericles became an absolute democracy at home. The state was governed by laws passed by the popular assembly. The laws were drawn up by committees appointed by the Assembly and then were brought before the Council of 500, which submitted them to the Assembly for ratification. The court, or Heliaea, was open to all citizens, with the 6,000 jurors, 600 from each of the ten tribes, divided into panels of 501; the odd number was to prevent a tie, since the decision was by majority vote, and the large number of jurors made bribery impossible. On one occasion the entire group of 6,000 jurors participated in the trial. Although income and capital taxes were unknown, the richer citizens were required to equip and man ships, to perform specified religious duties, and to provide choruses for the festivals in honor of Dionysus.

Although Athens prospered under Pericles, especially from the tribute of the subject cities of what had formerly been the Delian League, she suffered occasional reverses. An Egyptian expedition (459-454 B.C.), sent to assist Egypt in its revolt against Persia, ended in the loss of a large fleet. The war with Persia had been continued in the East and ended in 448 B.C. with the peace of Callias; Athens agreed to cease her attacks on Persian possessions, and Persia in turn promised not to molest by land or sea the Greek cities of Asia Minor. The Spartans, who, as leaders of the Peloponnesian League, controlled numerous cities in the Peloponnesus and central Greece, continued, however, to be hostile to Athens because of its democratic government and its widespread empire. The democratic factions of other Greek cities sought the support of Athens, and the aristocratic party in each city looked to Sparta for assistance. The territory on the mainland of Greece held by Athens for a short time included Boeotia, but the country was lost by the battle of

426

Coronea in 447 B.C. The Thirty Years' Peace of 445 B.C. between Athens and Sparta provided that Athens should give up most of her continental allies and territory, but Sparta acknowledged the existence of the Athenian maritime empire. Neither state was to interfere with the other, but neutral states could join whichever alliance they chose.

Under Athens, the entire Aegean area prospered, since the subject cities enjoyed peace and the protection of the Athenian navy. Commerce with Egypt, Sicily, and Italy brought to the Greek cities the choice products of other lands. But in spite of their prosperity, the cities resented the loss of their independence and they objected to both the necessity of paying tribute and the presence of Athenian garrisons. Attempts at revolt, such as that of Samos in 440-439 B.C., were promptly and harshly crushed, and Athens extended its power by establishing new colonies on the coast of the Black Sea and in southern Italy.

Increasing hostility between Athens and Sparta, and, more specifically, Athenian interference between the Dorian city of Corinth and her colony Corcyra, resulted in the outbreak of the Peloponnesian War in 431 B.C. The Spartans and their allies invaded Attica by land and devastated the crops each year, at which time the country people fled within the fortifications of Athens for protection; Athens retaliated by ravaging the Peloponnesian coast with her fleet each year and cutting off Spartan commerce. The famous Funeral Oration of Pericles, as given by the historian Thucydides, expresses the grief of the statesman for the citizens who perished in the first year of the war. The great plague occurred at Athens in 430 B.C., at a time when the city was overpopulated, and a third of the citizens perished. Pericles himself died the following year. The war dragged on inconclusively until 421 B.C., when the Peace of Nicias brought a temporary cessation of hostilities. Fighting was renewed three years later. Athens received a crushing blow: In 415 B.C., at the instigation of Alcibiades, who later fled to Sparta in disgrace, she had fitted out a great naval expedition against Syracuse in Sicily and had reinforced this with a second fleet. After keeping Syracuse under siege for two years, the Athenian fleet was finally defeated in 413 B.C.; besieged and defeated in the harbor of Syracuse, the Athenians attempted to retreat by land but were either killed or sold into slavery. The famous fragment of an Athenian comic dramatist, "He is either dead or a schoolteacher," refers to this event, with the survivors being compelled as slaves to teach Greek literature to the youth of Sicily.

After the disaster at Syracuse Athens lost many of its possessions, with numerous Greek cities now joining the side of Sparta. The Athenians fought on, winning a great naval victory at Arginusae, south of Lesbos, in 406 B.C., but a new Spartan fleet under Lysander defeated the Athenians at Aegospotami the following year and then blockaded the Piraeus, compelling the city to surrender. Thus ended the Athenian Empire and the supremacy of Athens in the Greek world. The Thebans and the Corinthians wished to destroy the city and enslave her citizens, but Sparta favored more generous treatment. By the terms of the peace of 404 B.C. Athens lost its fleet, was compelled to destroy the Long Walls and the fortifications of the Piraeus, and acknowledged the leadership of Sparta on land and sea. An oligarchical form of government, the Rule of the Thirty, was established at Athens under Spartan instigation, but it degenerated into such a bloody despotism that it was soon overthrown (403 B.C.) by Thrasybulus and a band of Athenian patriots who then restored the democracy.

In the fifth century, and especially during the Age of Pericles, Athens became the literary and artistic center of Greece. Drama flourished, and the impressive trilogies of the tragic writer Aeschylus, dealing with the nature of divinity and the relation of man to the gods, were followed by the tragedies of Sophocles and Euripides, more concerned with ethical and emotional themes. No other writers of tragedy equalled these three dramatists until William Shakespeare produced his tragedies in Elizabethan England 2,000 years later. The comedies of Aristophanes in the latter part of the century were political, literary, and philosophical satires; composed with striking wit, they have not been surpassed either in ancient or in modern times. In historical writing, the Athenian Thucydides wrote an account of the Peloponnesian War to 411 B.C., which, in its analyses of both individuals and states, has seldom been rivalled in acuteness and intellectual depth. Athens was outstanding not only in literature but in sculpture and architecture. Under Pericles, the construction of the Parthenon and the Propylaea on the Acropolis gave both architects and sculptors a free hand. This was the age of the sculptor Phidias and the architects Ictinus and Callicrates, and their achievements mark the highest point of Athenian, and Greek, art.

The Fourth Century B.C. The continuing conflicts between other Greek cities presently enabled Athens to regain part of her losses; she restored the Long Walls and again built up a navy. By siding with Thebes against Sparta prior to the Theban victory at Leuctra in 371 B.C. and by supporting Sparta against Thebes from 369 B.C. on, she helped to maintain a balance of power on the Greek mainland. The supremacy of Thebes came to an end with the battle of Mantinea in 362 B.C. Being strong at sea and still controlling Thrace and the Hellespont, Athens by the middle of the century was again a strong power in Greece and took the lead in resisting the encroachments of Philip of Macedon. The famous *Philippics* of the orator Demosthenes were delivered at this time. The victory of Philip at Chaeronea in 338 B.C., which placed Macedonian garrisons in Thebes, Corinth, and other cities, left Athens untouched but deprived her of her possessions in the northern Aegean. After the death of Alexander the Great in 323 B.C., many Greek cities revolted from Macedon. Athens, taking a prominent part in the revolt, was defeated the following year and forced to receive a Macedonian garrison. This marks the end of Athens as an important military power.

Athens' quick recovery from the disastrous defeat by Sparta in 404 B.C. made the fourth century a period of great material prosperity and the city remained the cultural center of Greece. The outstanding Athenian sculptor of the age was Praxiteles, famed for his ability to express emotion. Drama continued to flourish, especially comedy, with a shift of emphasis from political and literary satire to more social and mythological themes. Oratory was represented by Lysias, Isaeus, and Isocrates and reached its heights with Aeschines, who favored Philip of Macedon, and Demosthenes, the greatest of Greek orators and the bitter opponent of Macedon. The anti-Macedonian policy of Demosthenes received eloquent support from the orators Hyperides and Lycurgus. In spite of the trial and death of Socrates in 399 B.C. philosophy and science prospered. Fourth-century Athens is distinguished for two of the greatest philosophers of all time: Plato, the founder of the Academy and the author of numerous *Dialogues* on ethical and political themes, the best-known being the *Republic* and the shorter Socratic dialogues which give an insight into the life and method of his teacher; and Aristotle, Plato's pupil and the founder of the Lyceum. Aristotle, seeking to systematize all human knowledge, composed works on logic, rhetoric, ethics, politics, poetics, physics, metaphysics, and many other branches of science. The contributions of Plato and Aristotle rank among the greatest which ancient Athens has made to the modern world.

The Hellenistic and Roman Periods. Athens was able to reinstate its democratic form of government but it had

VIEW OF MOUNT LYCABETTUS FROM THE ACROPOLIS

little influence, being overshadowed by the Hellenistic kingdoms of Macedon, Syria, and Egypt, and by the Aetolian and Achaean Leagues in Greece, which opposed Macedonian domination. With the growth of Alexandria in Egypt and the establishment there of a great library, Athens lost her supremacy in literature, scholarship, and science, but comic drama continued at the hands of Menander and other New Comedy poets, and the successors of Plato and Aristotle continued to teach philosophy at the Academy and the Lyceum. Theophrastus, Aristotle's successor, not only wrote on botany, physics, and metaphysics but composed a series of *Characters* which became famous and were imitated by numerous French and English writers in the seventeenth and eighteenth centuries. Added vitality was given to philosophical studies at Athens by the founding of two more schools about 300 B.C.—that of Stoicism by Zeno and of Epicureanism by Epicurus. These two schools prospered and claimed many adherents among both Greeks and Romans during the next five centuries. Stoicism particularly, with its doctrine of an all-powerful, all-loving World Soul which could be identified with Zeus, the leading divinity of the Greek Pantheon, and with its emphasis upon virtue, justice, and the world-wide brotherhood of man, claimed the allegiance of the more thoughtful and responsible citizens of the ancient world before the acceptance of Christianity.

Athens was respected and revered for her past achievements in literature, art, architecture, and philosophy. Wealthy Hellenistic kings, especially of Egypt and Pergamum, adorned the city with new monuments. During the rise of Rome and its conflicts with Macedon and the Greek states, Athens remained a free city and kept itself free from international disputes. When war broke out between Rome and Mithridates the Great, King of Pontus, Athens sided with Mithridates. The city was besieged by the Roman general, Cornelius Sulla, and captured in 86 B.C. The city was looted and left poverty-stricken. However, it was still respected for

its philosophical schools, and many Romans, including the orator Cicero, his son, and the poet Horace, went to Athens to study philosophy. In the early Roman Empire, visits to Athens continued to be fashionable, and in the second century of the Christian Era the emperor Hadrian adorned the city with many new structures and completed the great temple of Olympian Zeus, begun by Pisistratus in the sixth century B.C. *See also* CLEISTHENES; GREECE; GREEK ART; GREEK LITERATURE; PERICLES; SOLON; THEMISTOCLES.

From the Decline of Rome to the War of Liberation. Athens was captured and sacked by the barbarian Heruli, a Gothic tribe, in A.D. 267 and the entire northwestern quarter of the city was devastated. The Athenians learned to their sorrow that the Roman Empire was no longer strong enough to defend them and they themselves were no longer numerous enough to man the long circuit of the ancient walls. They accordingly built a new and much contracted city wall, the so-called Valerian Wall, behind which they could take shelter. Materials of every sort, taken from the buildings destroyed by the barbarians, were incorporated into the new wall.

In the fifth century Athens had something of a revival, owing perhaps to the continuing influence of her schools. But Christianity, accepted by the Roman emperor Constantine in the early fourth century, had already shown itself a strong rival to both ancient learning and pagan beliefs. At about the same time that the Parthenon and the Hephaesteum were converted to the churches of Hagia Sophia and St. George, the emperor Justinian in A.D. 529 closed the Athenian schools of philosophy. Athens became now merely the seat of a provincial bishopric.

After the capture of Constantinople by the Crusaders in 1204, Athens became part of the Frankish duchy of Otho de la Roche and his successors; the Franks were followed in 1311 by the Catalans, and in 1387 the Florentine Nerio Acciajuoli became duke. This series of rulers turned the Acropolis into a mediaeval fortress, built a palace on the Propylaea, and put a high watchtower on the bastion of the Nike temple. The city fell to the Turks in 1456, but the Acropolis held out with stubborn resistance until 1458. The devastation of the city was increased during the nearly four centuries of Turkish rule. The Turks made a practice of storing gunpowder in the buildings of the Acropolis. As a result, the Propylaea were largely destroyed in 1656 in an explosion caused by lightning; and the Parthenon, which had been converted into a mosque, was blown up in 1687 during the siege of the Acropolis by the Venetian doge, Francesco Morosini.

In the fight for Greek independence the Greeks captured the Acropolis and took control of the city in 1822, but the Turks regained it in 1826. In the bombardment which preceded the Turkish capture, the Erechtheum was damaged considerably and the choragic monument of Thrasyllus was destroyed; fortunately this monument was already known from drawings made in the eighteenth century by English architects. When Prince Otto of Bavaria was crowned king of Greece in February 1833, the Turkish garrison still remained on the Acropolis, refusing to leave until the Greek government settled Turkish property claims. As the government could not raise the money, the garrison continued to occupy the stronghold. In April when 300 Bavarian troops entered Athens, the Turks gave up the Acropolis without collecting their claims, and the city then came completely under Greek control. In 1834 Otto made Athens the capital of the kingdom, and from this date the history of the city becomes part of the history of modern Greece.   G. E. D.

MODERN ATHENS

Modern Athens is the capital and chief city of Greece and of the *nomos* (department) of Attica. An electric railway to Piraeus, its seaport, 5 mi. distant, makes the two cities almost one. When the city of Athens passed from Turkish control and was designated as the capital of the newly established kingdom of Greece in 1834, it was a mere village of huts clustered about the Acropolis, with a population of about 15,000. It was selected as the capital principally for historical reasons. The plan of the new city was largely the work of the German engineer Schaubert. It is a modern city with wide, well-paved streets. The most important shops and office-buildings are found on or near the streets that link Constitution Square, on which the Parliament Building faces, and Concord Square, originally the center of the shopping district. The Royal Palace is near Constitution Square, as are several museums. The National Museum houses some of the richest treasure of Greek art, and Mycenaean and Egyptian antiquities. Other noteworthy buildings are the Palace of Justice, the University of Athens, the Polytechnic Institute, and the National Academy. Athens is surrounded by suburbs—particularly Glyfada, Old Phaleron, Psychico, and Kifissia—many of them admired for their gardens and flowering shrubs.

The decades from 1910 to 1930 were particularly remarkable in the growth of Athens. In 1912, after the defeat of Turkey, and by the Treaty of Lausanne in 1923, Greece doubled her territories and population, and Athens assumed a front-rank position among Balkan capitals. It not only became a political center of great importance but also the banking, commercial, and industrial center of a wide area. Piraeus, its port, shared with Athens a rise to importance in the Mediterranean and became one of the world's busiest ports and the chief point of export and import for the Greek islands and Greek mainland. Its principal industries are shipbuilding, flour milling, brewing, distilling, wine making, soap manufacture, and carpet weaving. There are also rapidly expanding textile mills, chemical plants, food-products and cigarette factories, and metal-working establishments. The chief exports of Athens and Piraeus include olive oil, tobacco, wine, raw hides, carpets, fruits, and some minerals. Among the imports are wheat, finished metals and manufactured goods, fish and animal products, coal, lumber and wood products, motor vehicles, machinery, and paper.

In World War II, the Germans entered Athens on Apr. 27, 1941, and occupied the port of Piraeus and Athens until October 1944, when British and native guerrilla forces drove them out. Industrial plants suffered considerable damage by German and Allied bombing, as well as by systematic looting. The Germans in their withdrawal destroyed nearly all the wharves and cranes, many warehouses, and ships. In December 1944 and January 1945 Athens was the scene of sharp street-fighting (the "Battle of Athens"), traces of which may still be seen on the walls of many houses. The public buildings and historic monuments were not damaged during the disorders of the 1940's. Pop. 1951, 565,084.

ATHENS, a city in northeastern Georgia, the county seat of Clarke Co., in the Piedmont region of the state, located about 70 mi. northeast of Atlanta. Farming is the principal occupation in the surrounding region, and cotton, corn, potatoes, and small grains are the chief products. The city was founded in 1801, at the time of the land purchase for the site of the University of Georgia, and was incorporated in 1806. It is governed by a mayor and ten councilmen. Points of interest in Athens and its vicinity include Memorial Hall, erected in memory of students of the University of Georgia who lost their lives in World War I; the University Chapel, built in 1832; the home of Dr. Crawford Long, one of the first users of ether as an anesthetic; and the home of Martha Atlanta Compton, for whom Atlanta was twice named, once as Marthasville, then as Atlanta. Athens' industrial life primarily revolves around the cotton grown in the district. Textile production is the largest industry, and cotton yarn, sheeting, flannel, upholstery and curtain material, and tire fabrics constitute the chief items of output. Local plants also produce hosiery, bedspreads, wearing apparel, cottonseed products, flour, and millwork. Pop. 1950, 28,180.

ATHENS, a city in southeastern Ohio, the county seat of Athens Co., on the Hocking River, 76 mi. southeast of Columbus. Bituminous coal is mined in the surrounding region, and there are fruit, livestock, and dairy farms in the vicinity. In 1801 the campus of Ohio University, the oldest college in the Northwest Territory, was laid out on its present site, which was then a virgin forest. The university received its charter in 1804 and opened its doors to students in June 1808. Local industries manufacture flooring, office equipment, meat products, printed matter, and binding machines. Pop. 1950, 11,660.

ATHENS, a city and the county seat of McMinn Co., in southeastern Tennessee, about 60 mi. southwest of Knoxville. It was laid out in 1823, incorporated in 1868, and has the mayor-council form of government. It is the seat of Tennessee Wesleyan Junior College. The Southern and the Louisville and Nashville railroads provide transportation. Cotton, pine, and harwood timber are the principal resources of the region. Among the products manufactured are furniture, cotton and woolen textiles, paper boxes, hosiery, insecticides, stoves, and farm implements. Pop. 1950, 8,168.

ATHERTON, GERTRUDE FRANKLIN (HORN) [æ'thərtən] (1857-1948), American novelist, was born in San Francisco, Calif., Oct. 30, 1857. Educated at private schools, including Sayre Institute, Lexington, Ky., in 1876

GERTRUDE ATHERTON

INTERNATIONAL NEWS PHOTO

she married George Henry Bowen Atherton of Dedham, Mass. Shortly after her marriage she published articles and a novelette in the San Francisco *Argonaut,* and articles and stories in the *News Letter.* Her husband died in the late 1880's. Mrs. Atherton removed to New York and launched upon her literary career. She lived for seven or eight years in

England and six years in Munich. She was interested in politics, world affairs, and civic affairs. Her most popular books were *The Conqueror* (1902); *The Immortal Marriage* (1927); *Dido, Queen of Hearts* (1929); *Rezánov* (1906); *The Splendid Idle Forties,* short stories of Old California; *Adventures of a Novelist* (1932), an autobiography; *California: An Intimate History* (1914); *The Avalanche* (1919); and *Black Oxen* (1923). Her own favorite of her writings was *Tower of Ivory* (1910). By 1941 she had written some forty books. Mrs. Atherton died in San Francisco, June 14, 1948.   T. R.

ATHERTON TABLELAND, an extensive plateau in northeastern Queensland, Australia, rising from 2,000 to 4,000 ft. above sea level. The eastern brim of the plateau lies about 10 mi. southwest of the port of Cairns, at approximately 17° S. lat. and 145° E. long. The level to gently rolling land contains large tracts of fertile volcanic soil, considerable mineral wealth, and a good year-round water supply. Despite its location in the tropics, the climate is cool and invigorating. Maize and a wide variety of temperate zone fruits and vegetables grown on the plateau supplement the tropical crops produced on adjacent lowlands; European breeds of beef and dairy cattle thrive in the temperate climate. The proximity of lakes and mountain scenery to the populous coastal lowlands have made the tableland a popular tourist spot. Lumbering and mining are locally important.   R. G. B.

ATHETOSIS [æthəto'sɪs], also known as "mobile spasm," is a neuromuscular symptom complex arising from involvement of the basal ganglia and central ovale of the brain. The condition is usually a congenital one, caused either by maldevelopment or by birth injury, and may be generalized in its symptoms, or confined to one side of the body. Athetosis may result from a brain tumor involving the basal ganglia and central ovale, or from infection, such as encephalitis or syphilis affecting those regions. Whereas choreic movements are jerky and affect the peripheral parts of the arms and legs, and trunk movements are briefer and swifter, athetotic manifestations are wormlike, writhing and undulating in nature, and commonly begin at an earlier age. A typical case of athetosis reveals facial muscles distorted by grimaces, the tongue writhing and spasmodically protruding. The patient has marked difficulty in phonation and swallowing. Peripheral segments show the most movement. Typically, the arm is adducted and rotated inwardly, the elbow partially flexed, while fingers and wrist are extremely flexed with the exception of the thumb, which is adducted and extended. If the movement is unilateral, the patient will persistently try to hold the writhing limb with his unimpaired hand in a vain attempt to control the excessive, vermiform motion. When involved, the leg is similarly affected (both legs may be affected), the foot showing the defect known as equinovarus, a combination of equinus and varus. The former reveals the patient walking on the toes or the anterior part of the foot; the latter walking on the outer border of the foot, the sole turned inward. At rest, the patient is completely free of all athetotic movement. There is no specific treatment. Sedation may be indicated. Re-education under physiotherapy guidance, over a long period of time, seems to hold some promise.   J. A. Br.

ATHÍNAI. *See* Athens.

ATHLETE'S FOOT, epidermophytosis, tinea pedis **or** tinea interdigitalis, caused by fungi of the genus *Epidermo-* *phyton* or sometimes by certain yeasts, is a chronic infection of the outer, horny layer of moist skin, especially in the folds, and is commonest on the feet. A small blister (vesicle) appears at the site of inoculation (usually between the toes) and breaks, exposing a small, raw area surrounded by the drying horny layer which peels away, exposing more tissue. The fungus tends to grow radially, producing successive crops of blisters at the margin and healing in the center, often accompanied by itching (pruritus) or burning sensations. The circular appearance of the lesions is clearer in the crotch (jockstrap itch, tinea cruris), in the armpits or under the breasts. On the soles of the feet, owing to the thicker horny layer, the blisters are deeper and break less easily. The organisms may also invade the toenails, causing discoloration and scaling. When yeasts are the infecting agents, the lesions are moister and are oftener found between the fingers, especially on people who work with their hands in water for considerable periods, such as laundresses, dishwashers, and washers in the fruit-packing industry. These cases also resemble dermatitis of chemical origin and may be distinguished by the case history or by isolating the organism in culture. The disease is spread by the scales of epidermis or of nails, where the organisms may survive up to a year. Since the organisms grow rapidly in wool, silk, and leather, articles of clothing incompletely sterilized serve as reservoirs of infection or reinfection. Scratching the itching lesions often results in autoinoculation to other sites or in secondary infection with other organisms. This disease is very common among soldiers, students, and athletes (whence the name), as it is often contracted in shower and locker rooms or about swimming pools. The crotch infections are usually contracted from unsterilized towels or interchange of athletic clothing. Since the fungi grow only in the horny layer of the epidermis where penetration of antiseptics is very difficult, a keratolytic agent such as salicylic acid is combined with the antiseptic to soften and remove the outer portion of the horny layer, thus enabling the antiseptic to reach and kill the fungus. Serious cases should be prescribed for by a physician.   C. W. Do.

ATHLETIC SPORTS. *See* Sports.

ATHLONE [æthlo'n], or Ath Luain, a city on both sides of the Shannon River, in County Westmeath, Eire, about 78 mi. west of Dublin. The city is connected internally by various bridges. Athlone is an agricultural center, and it thrives on its water-routed trade with Limerick and Dublin and on the sporting fisheries of the region. A canal and lock have obviated rapids in the river, making it navigable 71 mi. above the town. There are cotton factories and a number of sawmills in Athlone; the city's famous woolen mills were burned in 1940. The castle and a stone bridge in the city date from 1210. During the reign of Elizabeth, Athlone was made the seat of the presidency of Connaught, and when the Irish rebelled against English Protestant rule in 1641, the town was unsuccessfully besieged. Athlone was incorporated by James I, and sent two representatives to the Irish Parliament; until 1885 it sent a representative to the Imperial Parliament. In 1688 the town was twice besieged by adherents of James II. The fortifications were materially strengthened in 1797 by the English, who feared another uprising. Portions of town walls built in 1567 survive; also the ruins of a Franciscan foundation and of the ancient Abbey of St. Peter. Pop. 1952, 9,015.

ATH LUAIN. *See* Athlone.

ATHOL [a'thɒl], a town in northern Massachusetts in Worcester Co., 82 mi. northwest of Boston, situated on Miller's River. Settled as Pequoiag in 1735, the town was incorporated in 1762 as Athol, being named after Atholl, Scotland. It is located on the historic Mohawk Trail. Transportation is furnished by the Boston and Maine Railroad. The chief manufactures of this industrial community are tools, toys, coated fabrics, furniture, and shoes. Pop. 1950, 9,708.

ATHOS [æ'thɒs; e'thɒs], a mountain, the "Holy Mountain" of the Orthodox Church, situated on the southern end of the eastern peninsula of the Chalcidice trident near Thessaloniki, Greece. This sacred mountain, which stands 6,347 ft. above the Aegean Sea, is the site of a religious colony founded in the latter part of the ninth century by Peter the Athonite. The oldest of the twenty monasteries on the peninsula, Lavra, was founded in 963, and the newest, Stavroniketa, was founded in 1542. The colony was under the sovereignty of the Byzantine emperors until the fifteenth century, when it was ruled by the Turks. It enjoyed local autonomy under both regimes. In 1912 it was occupied by the Greeks. In 1926 the Greek government recognized the community as a theocratic republic, consisting of a council of 4 members and of an assembly of 20 members. The community has its own police force of about 24 men. No women or female animals are allowed within the 30 sq. mi. that comprise the religious community. Athos was also sacred to Zeus and is sometimes designated "the Thracian watchtower of Athoan Zeus."

S. Van V.

ATJEH. *See* ACHIN.

ATKINSON, GEORGE FRANCIS (1854-1918), American botanist, was born in Raisinville, Mich., Jan. 26, 1854. He was graduated from Cornell University in 1885

and returned there seven years later as an assistant professor of botany. In 1896 he became head of the department, a post he held until his death. When the American Botanical Society was founded in 1907, Atkinson was elected its first president. Among his writings are *Botany for High Schools, College Textbook of Botany, The Biology of Ferns,* and *Studies of American Fungi.* Atkinson died Nov. 15, 1918, in Tacoma, Wash.

J. C. Wis.

ATLANTA, a city in northwestern Georgia, the state capital and the county seat of Fulton Co. Situated on a spur of the Blue Ridge Mountains, Atlanta is known as the Gate City of the South. Because of its altitude of 1,050 ft. and its location south of 34° N. lat., the city has a mild and equable climate. The first settlement of Atlanta was in 1837 around the terminus of a state owned railroad and was called Terminus. In 1843 its name was changed to Marthasville and in 1845 to Atlanta. With the outbreak of the Civil War, Atlanta became one of the strategic cities of the Confederacy, as it was a principal munitions and supply center. The city was captured by General Sherman in September 1864 and was burned on November 15. Early in December the Confederates reoccupied Atlanta and began rebuilding the city. Sufficient progress was made by 1881 to hold a World's Fair and Great International Cotton Exposition. The Piedmont Exposition of 1887 and the International Exposition of 1895 were also held in the city. Among the city's many educational institutions are Georgia Institute of Technology, Emory University, Clark College, Morehouse College, and the Atlanta division of the University of Georgia. The Atlanta Art Institute, High Art Museum, the Atlanta Symphony Orchestra, and many libraries contribute to the cultural life of the city. Atlanta is headquarters for the Sixth Federal Reserve District and the southeastern headquarters for many large insurance

SHANNON RIVER BRIDGE AT ATHLONE, IRELAND

UNDERWOOD - STRATTON

THE SIEGE OF ATLANTA
FROM THE CYCLORAMA MURAL AT ATLANTA, GEORGIA

LANE BROTHERS

companies. The city is a major merchandise market for the southeastern states. Its industries are diversified, the chief products being textiles, apparel, chemicals, paper and paper products, beverages, food products, candy and confectionery, iron and steel, and printing and publishing. Eight railroads and twelve airlines provide transportation. The city is governed by a mayor and council. The population was considerably increased in 1952 when the area of Atlanta was increased by annexation from 37 to 128 sq. mi. Pop. 1950, 331,314. A. J.

ATLANTA, SIEGE OF, July 20-Sept. 2, 1864, was a campaign in the American Civil War against the principal railroad and supply center in Georgia. The city had been fortified by Col. L. P. Grant, a civil engineer who had been born and reared in Maine, had come South in the early 1840's to help build the Georgia railroad, and had settled in Atlanta.

On July 17 Gen. William T. Sherman's Union army of approximately 100,000 men advancing southward from Dalton, Ga., crossed the Chattahoochee River and took positions north of Atlanta. The impetuous but crippled Confederate Gen. John B. Hood, who had just replaced Gen. Joseph E. Johnston as commander of the 50,000 troops which had resisted Sherman's advance, attacked the Federals at Peach Tree Creek July 20 but was beaten off with a loss of some 5,000 men. Two days later Gen. Hood threw his battle-tired men, who had marched 15 mi. the night before, against McPherson's army to the east of the city in an engagement known as the Battle of Atlanta, later immortalized in a remarkable panoramic painting now exhibited in the L. P. Grant Park. This bloody but indecisive movement was

called by Gen. Blair of the Federal forces "a very bold and a very brilliant one . . . very near being successful." On the 28th the Confederates attacked the Union men in the battle of Ezra Church, a short distance to the west of the city, but they were again repulsed. The Southern losses in this engagement were estimated at more than 2,700, while the Northern losses amounted to only 600. From July 20 until late in August Gen. Sherman besieged the city, shelling it intermittently from the north and west and seeking always to reach the two railroads on the south. After winning the Battle of Jonesboro 20 mi. south of Atlanta on September 1, he succeeded and the following morning Atlanta was formally surrendered. R. B.

ATLANTA UNIVERSITY, in Atlanta, Ga., an accredited, coeducational, privately controlled graduate school for Negroes. Instruction began in 1865, two years before the institution received its charter. Work in the old Atlanta University was first undertaken in the Jenkins Street School and in a railroad car which had been purchased at Chattanooga by the American Missionary Association. In 1929 Atlanta University and Morehouse and Spelman Colleges were affiliated under a university plan, and Morris Brown, Clark, and Gammon Colleges have since been incorporated into the Center. The system provides a complete education through professional and graduate work with a master's degree, one year of residence being required for the graduate degree.

Courses are offered in the school of education, including a laboratory school for nursery, kindergarten, and elementary studies; in the school of social work; in the school of business administration; in the school of library science; and

EWING GALLOWAY. NEW YORK

PEACHTREE STREET, ATLANTA, GEORGIA

in the graduate school of arts and sciences. An adult education program is offered under the sociology department. Five of the affiliated colleges occupy adjoining campuses, which together are considered one of the interesting sights

ADMINISTRATION BUILDING, ATLANTA UNIVERSITY

of the city. The A.B. and M.A. degrees are offered, and occasionally a Ph.D. is granted. *For statistics see* COLLEGES AND UNIVERSITIES.   R. B.

ATLANTIC, a city and the county seat of Cass Co., in southwestern Iowa, situated about 85 mi. west of Des Moines. The city was chartered in 1869. Transportation is supplied by the Chicago, Rock Island & Pacific Railroad. Atlantic is the trade center for an excellent farming region and has poultry-feeding yards, packing houses, and a canning factory for corn and green beans. Pop. 1950, 6,480.

ATLANTIC CHARTER, a declaration made in a joint statement issued on Aug. 14, 1941, by President Franklin D. Roosevelt and Prime Minister Winston S. Churchill following a meeting held aboard the *U.S.S. Augusta,* somewhere in the North Atlantic, Aug. 9-12. The Charter sets forth the principles upon which the United States and the United Kingdom proposed to shape their national policies during the period of World War II and the postwar period. The text of the statement follows.

The President of the United States of America and the Prime Minister, Mr. Churchill, representing His Majesty's Government in the United Kingdom, being met together, deem it right to make known certain common principles in the national policies of their respective countries on which they base their hopes for a better future for the world.

First, their countries seek no aggrandizement, territorial or other;

Second, they desire to see no territorial changes that do not accord with the freely expressed wishes of the peoples concerned;

Third, they respect the right of all people to choose the form of government under which they will live; and they wish to see sovereign rights and self-government restored to those who have been forcibly deprived of them;

Fourth, they will endeavor, with due respect for their existing obligations, to further the enjoyment by all States, great or small, victor or vanquished, of access, on equal terms, to the trade and to the raw materials of the world which are needed for their economic prosperity;

Fifth, they desire to bring about the fullest collaboration between all nations in the economic field with the object of securing, for all, improved labor standards, economic advancement and social security;

Sixth, after the final destruction of the Nazi tyranny, they hope to see established a peace which will afford to all nations the means of dwelling in safety within their own boundaries, and which will afford assurance that all the men in all the lands may live out their lives in freedom from fear and want;

Seventh, such a peace should enable all men to traverse the high seas and oceans without hindrance;

Eighth, they believe that all of the nations of the world, for realistic as well as spiritual reasons, must come to the abandonment of the use of force. Since no future peace can be maintained if land, sea or air armaments continue to be employed by nations which threaten or may threaten aggression outside of their frontiers, they believe, pending the system of general security, that the disarmament of such nations is essential. They will likewise aid and encourage all other practicable measures which will lighten for peace-loving peoples the crushing burden of armaments.   R. Da.

ATLANTIC CITY, a seashore resort city of Atlantic Co., on the southern coast of New Jersey, about 52 mi. southeast of Trenton, situated on a narrow sand island separated from the mainland by the New Jersey Inland Waterway and tidal flats. Atlantic City was settled about 1790. First used for summer residences about 1845, it grew rapidly and was incorporated as a city in 1854. Notable for its wide sandy beach, a boardwalk 8 mi. long, recreation piers, and many hotels, it is one of the most popular Atlantic seaboard resorts and convention cities. It has been estimated that more than ten million vacationists, who furnish the chief source of the city's income, visit this all-year-round resort annually. One of its most popular yearly features is the "Miss America" beauty contest. It was in Atlantic City that saltwater taffy was first made, and its manufacture is one of the city's leading industries. The Pennsylvania Railroad provides rail transportation for the city. Pop. 1950, 61,657. (*See illustration on following page.*)

ATLANTIC OCEAN, the body of water separating the continents of Europe and Africa from North America and South America. The name "Atlantic" may have been derived from Atlantis, the mythical lost continent supposed to have been covered by the Atlantic Ocean, or from the Atlas Mountains.

The Atlantic Ocean, which is surpassed in area only by the Pacific Ocean, has an area that is variously estimated as between 41,000,000 and 41,400,000 sq. mi. The Atlantic is unique among oceans in that it has an unusually large number of indentations in the form of seas, large bays, and gulfs, particularly in the northern part. Also, it receives water from a larger drainage area than any other ocean. The Atlantic is further characterized by its rather small number of islands.

NORTH ATLANTIC

Boundaries and Shore Line. The Atlantic Ocean is divided into the North Atlantic and the South Atlantic. For lack of a definite zone of demarcation between the two, the equator is sometimes used as an arbitrary and imaginary dividing line, though oceanographically the South Atlantic Ocean extends to about 5 to 8° N. lat. The northern boundary is also indefinite, but the Arctic Circle is usually used for this purpose.

The North Atlantic Ocean has a very irregular shore line. Its northern section is rather narrow and is connected with the Arctic Ocean by three narrow straits. On the northwest, the Atlantic connects with Baffin Bay and the Arctic Ocean by Davis Strait, 220 mi. wide at the Arctic Circle. In the north central section, Denmark Strait, between Greenland and Iceland is only 260 mi. wide. In the northeast, there is the 760-mi.-wide passage between Iceland and Norway, sometimes called the Norwegian Sea. There are two large eastern indentations of the Atlantic Ocean. The northeastern extension of the Atlantic begins with the North Sea, between Great Britain, Denmark, and Germany, and extends eastward

THE FAMOUS BOARDWALK AT ATLANTIC CITY, NEW JERSEY

by way of the Skagerrak and Kattegat straits to the Baltic Sea and the Gulf of Bothnia and the Gulf of Finland. The portion of the Atlantic Ocean which separates Ireland from Great Britain is called the Irish Sea, with North Channel and St. George's Channel the connecting straits. The English Channel separates Great Britain from France and Belgium and connects the North Sea and the Atlantic Ocean. The Atlantic bordering western France and northern Spain is the Bay of Biscay. The large southeastern extension of the North Atlantic, the Mediterranean-Black Sea basin, extends eastward 2,500 mi. From the Strait of Gibraltar eastward, the Mediterranean is subdivided into local bays and seas such as the Gulf of Lions, the Ligurian Sea (including the Gulf of Genoa), Tyrrhenian Sea, the Strait of Messina, and the Adriatic, Ionian, and Aegean seas. The Dardanelles, Sea of Marmara, and Bosporus connect the Mediterranean with the Black Sea. In the southwestern part of the North Atlantic basin are the Caribbean Sea, Gulf of Mexico, and Straits of Florida; in the central part are numerous small bays and sounds such as Pamlico Sound, Barnegat, Chesapeake, and Delaware bays, and Long Island Sound; and on the northwest are the Bay of Fundy and Gulf of St. Lawrence, Strait of Belle Isle, Hudson Strait, and Hudson Bay.

Islands. The larger islands entirely in the North Atlantic basin are Iceland; the British Isles, which are a part of the continent of Europe; the Azores; Madeira and the Canary

GREENLAND ICEBERGS IN DISKO BAY

and Cape Verde Islands; and the West Indies, with the large islands of Cuba, Haiti (Hispaniola), Jamaica, and Puerto Rico. From Florida northward on the western edge of the Atlantic, most of the islands, such as the Bahamas, Long Island, Nantucket, Martha's Vineyard, Cape Breton Island, Prince Edward Island, and Newfoundland, are closely related to North America; the Bermuda group, about 600 mi. east of North Carolina, forms a notable exception.

Floor. Along the edges of the ocean basin is the continental shelf, broad in some areas (over 200 mi. wide in certain sections) and much narrower in others. Across the continental shelf are deep Grand Canyon-like gorges which usually occur opposite the mouth of a large river. These canyons may have been formed by rivers when the continent was at a higher level, becoming submarine canyons when the edges of the continent were submerged and became the continental shelf. Other explanations of these canyons involve subsurface currents and earthquakes.

The floor of the North Atlantic, like most ocean basins, has a varied topography of submarine ridges, plateaus, depths, and gorges. Most of the ocean floor is covered to a depth of from 200 ft. to several miles with fine mud and ooze ranging from dark blue to bluish green in color. There are some rocky, gravel and sand, and red-clay bottom areas, but they are relatively small compared with the total area.

Along the northern edge of the Atlantic basin, a submarine ridge extends from Iceland to Scotland; and in the western North Atlantic are the elevated plateaus which form the Grand Banks fishing grounds. In the north central part of the Atlantic, between the Grand Banks and Iceland, lies the large so-called telegraph plateau. South of this plateau is the narrow Mid-Atlantic Ridge, which extends in a rough **S** shape from Iceland southward under the North Atlantic and South Atlantic. Some of the peaks rise from 10,000 to 12,000 ft.

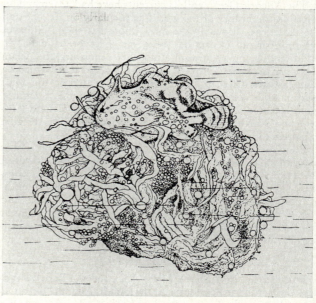

A nest of Sargassum fish, Histrio histrio

above the ocean floor. Most of this ridge is at least a mile below sea level, but the islands of the Azores, São Paulo, Ascension, and Tristan da Cunha are peaks of the Mid-Atlantic Ridge.

In the western part of the North Atlantic and extending around the Caribbean Sea is a disconnected submarine ridge which extends from northern South America to Central America, and the high parts of this ridge form the West Indian islands. Associated with this arc-shaped ridge and roughly parallel with it are Bartlett Deep, 21,036 ft., between Cuba and Jamaica and Haiti, and the Brownson Deep, north of Puerto Rico; the latter is 30,246 ft. below sea level in its Milwaukee Depth, the deepest place that had been found in the Atlantic Ocean through 1950. Sounding and recording devices developed during World War II are speeding the work of studying the floor of the ocean.

Currents. The ocean currents in the North Atlantic move in a clockwise manner. The major parts of this great system are the warm northward-flowing Gulf Stream, the West Wind Drift, the Canary Current, and the North Equatorial Current. The Gulf Stream flows from the Straits of Florida and the island of Cuba northward along the coast of the United States and at about 40° N. lat. bends to the northeast as the West Wind Drift. The West Wind Drift divides into two sections; the northeastward flowing section is known as the North Atlantic Drift, and the southward-flowing part forms the Canary Current. The North Atlantic Drift keeps the coast of Norway and all of northwestern Europe warmer than would normally be expected in latitudes corresponding to those ranging from Nova Scotia to southern Greenland. The Canary Current moves southward and southwestward off the coast of Africa. This current moves to the southwest and joins the North Equatorial current, which moves westward to the West Indies and joins the Gulf Stream. Just north of the Equatorial Current is a calm

→ Warm currents
∿→ Cold or cool currents

CURRENTS OF THE ATLANTIC OCEAN

and weed-filled area known as the Sargasso Sea. Along the Atlantic coast of northern North America is the cold Labrador Current, which moves south from Labrador and Baffin Bay and hugs the shore of North America, bringing cold water to the New England beaches.

The Atlantic Ocean and its currents have had a tremendous effect on the history of the world, particularly on Europe and the Americas. Probably the most important single influence of the Atlantic Ocean has been its effect on climate. In addition to being a source of atmospheric moisture, the Atlantic, with its warm and cold currents, has great influence on temperatures. For example, the warm water of the Gulf Stream and West Wind Drift keeps northwestern Europe from becoming a barren subarctic region. The Canary Current and North Equatorial Current helped to carry the first explorers to North America.

Prior to the development of large ships, the Atlantic was a formidable barrier. Since the sixteenth century, however, the North Atlantic has become the greatest ocean of commerce, and great nations have developed around it. In addition to its influence on climate, discovery, transportation, and communication, the Atlantic Ocean has provided throughout the years a tremendous number of fish and shellfish to help feed the great population along its shores.

SOUTH ATLANTIC

Boundaries and Shore Line. Like the northern boundary, the southern boundary of the South Atlantic Ocean is not well defined. Some authorities consider that the Atlantic extends south to the Antarctic ice sheet; others use the imaginary line between Cape Horn, South America, and the Cape of Good Hope, Africa, as the southern boundary. The South Atlantic Ocean has a much more regular coast line than the North Atlantic, and there are almost no major indentations that carry the marine influence deep into either Africa or South America. The Gulf of Guinea is the only major gulf or bay along the African coast, and along South America there are few large bays. The southern tip of South America, Tierra del Fuego, has an irregular and island-fringed coast. In South America are some smaller gulfs such as San Jorge and San Matias and several large river-mouth bays such as those of the Plata, Amazon, and Orinoco.

Islands. There are no major islands in the South Atlantic Ocean, but there are a few isolated islands such as Fernando Noronha, Ascension, São Paulo, St. Helena, the Tristan da Cunha group, and in the extreme south, Bouvet, the Sandwich group, South Georgia, the South Orkneys, and the Falklands.

Floor. In addition to the Mid-Atlantic Ridge there are two major submarine ridges in the South Atlantic: the Walvis (Walfisch) Ridge extends from the southwestern tip of the coast of Angola to Tristan da Cunha, where it joins the Mid-Atlantic Ridge; and the Rio de Janeiro Ridge, which is not a continuous mountain range, extends from Tristan da Cunha toward Rio de Janeiro.

Currents. The major current in the South Atlantic moves counterclockwise. The South Equatorial Current moves from east to west and divides east of the horn of Brazil. The northern branch drifts along the northern coast of South America into the Caribbean; and the southern branch, the warm Brazil Current, moves southward along the coast of Brazil, where it joins the Southern Hemisphere West Wind Drift, or Antarctic Current, which flows eastward and northeastward. Part of this cold current divides and moves north along the coast of Africa as the cold Benguela Current, which eventually joins the Southern Equatorial Current.

The warm Guinea Current flows southward along the coast of northwestern Africa and thence into the Gulf of Guinea.

J. E. F.

ATLANTIC PACT. See NORTH ATLANTIC TREATY ORGANIZATION.

ATLANTIC UNION COLLEGE, a privately controlled, coeducational college of arts and sciences related to the Seventh-Day Adventist Church and located on a 350-acre campus in South Lancaster, Mass., a community of 3,500. It was established in 1882 as South Lancaster Academy and chartered in 1918 as Lancaster Junior College. The present name was adopted in 1922. Degrees offered are the A.B. in liberal arts and the B.S. in nursing, elementary education, home economics, and dietetics. Many students work to earn some part of their expenses in school industries (farm, press, bindery) and offices, and boarding students live in college dormitories or approved homes. *For statistics see* COLLEGES AND UNIVERSITIES.

ATLANTIS [ætla′ntɪs], a legendary island in the Atlantic Ocean west of the Pillars of Hercules, mentioned by Plato in his *Timaeus* and *Critias*. The tradition related that the armies of Atlantis invaded the Mediterranean area nine thousand years before the birth of Solon and were defeated by the Athenians and their allies. Later, because of the wickedness of its inhabitants, the island disappeared beneath the sea. Similar legends are told of other lands sinking beneath the waters—Lyonnesse, off the Cornish coast, for example, and the lost Breton city of Ys. The Greek tradition of the Isles of the Blest in the western seas may be related to the legend of Atlantis.   G. E. D.

ATLAS [æ′tləs], in Greek mythology, the son of the Titan Iapetus and Clymene and the brother of Prometheus and Epimetheus. He was the father of the nymphs the

ATLAS

COURTESY OF THE
METROPOLITAN MUSEUM OF ART

Pleiades, the Hyades, and the Hesperides; according to Homer, he was also the father of Calypso. As a penalty for aiding the Titans against Zeus, Atlas was condemned to hold up the heavens with his head and hands. According to another version, he was turned into a mountain by Perseus, who punished him for inhospitality by showing him the Gorgon's head. *See also* HERACLES; TITANS.

G. E. D.

ATLAS, a series of mountain chains in northwestern North Africa, extending from the extreme southwestern section of Morocco (Cape Nun), to Cape Bon on the north-

VIEW OF THE ATLAS MOUNTAINS NEAR BUIRA, ALGERIA

EWING GALLOWAY, NEW YORK

eastern tip of Tunisia. The Atlas system in Morocco forms a barrier between the northwestern plains fronting on the sea and the northwestern Sahara Desert. Its main ridge, extending from the vicinity of Agadir on the Atlantic Ocean east-northeast to the Algerian border, is called the High or Great Atlas (Fr. *Grand Atlas*), and attains a predominant altitude exceeding 10,000 feet. The highest peak, Djebel Toubka (13,665 ft.), is in the western part. Separated from the High Atlas by the Sous Valley to the south is the parallel ridge called the Anti-Atlas; and extending northeast from the High Atlas is the ridge known as the Middle Atlas (*Moyen Atlas*). The lower chains in Algeria and Tunisia are the Maritime or Tell Atlas (*Atlas tellien*) along the Mediterranean coast, with its numerous subsidiary ranges, attaining an altitude of 7,572 ft. at Lella Khedidja in the Kabylie massif; and the Saharan Atlas (*Atlas saharien*), forming an extension of the High Atlas from eastern Morocco to the vicinity of Tunis. The highest peak of northern Algeria is Djebel Chélia (7,641 ft.) in the Aurès massif of the Saharan Atlas. The two mountains chains in Algeria are separated by the Hauts Plateaux, a great highland, and almost merge in the Cape Bon region of Tunisia.

Despite the high altitude of the High Atlas range, there are only a few peaks that remain entirely snow covered throughout the whole year. Dense pine, cedar, oak, and cork forests predominate on the northern slopes of the lower peaks, while the southern flanks, facing the Sahara, are generally barren. The climate, one of extremes, produces on the north, where the rainfall is adequate, vegetation that is largely European in type. The other side, however, fanned constantly by hot Sahara winds, is largely African desertic, while the peaks and crests of the range are essentially alpine in character.

Deep erosion in several places has created numerous winding passes. In the central portion, however, for a distance of about 100 miles, there are no breaks of sufficient size to permit caravan passage. Between the Sous and the Tensift basins in the southwestern sector, however, two such gaps occur. This area, although not considered so imposing as the Alps, nevertheless is generally higher. The southern slopes are predominantly granite; however the range also contains formations of porphyry, limestone, marble, and basalt. The difficult terrain of the Atlas in Morocco and Algiers long delayed the subjection of their Berber inhabitants and the scientific exploration and exploitation of the region.

R. G. W.

ATLATL (NAHUATL) [aʹtlatəl, naʹwatəl], an implement used for hurling a lance or spear. Its essentials are a hook at one end for engaging the butt of the spear and a handgrip for holding at the other. The mechanical principal is that of an extension to the throwing arm, giving the missile much greater propulsive force. The atlatl was used in many parts of the New World. In the eastern United States it was the characteristic weapon of the Archaic and Burial Mound stages, prior to A.D. 1200, after which it was superseded by the bow and arrow. In Mexico and Peru it was one of the most important fighting weapons from early to late times.

G. R. W.

ATMOSPHERE, the term applied to the gaseous envelope which surrounds the earth. The term is used in contradistinction to the lithosphere, the solid portion of the earth, and the hydrosphere, the liquid portion. The exact thickness of the atmosphere is unknown, but there is evidence that it extends some several hundred miles beyond the earth's surface, and it is believed that it may extend 1,000 mi. or more. The composition of the atmosphere at any considerable distance beyond the earth's surface differs in condition and composition from that found at the surface. The lower section, called the troposphere, extends to a height of about 8 mi., but varies in different places. It extends 11 mi. above the equator and only 4 mi. above the poles; at latitude 45° it is about 6 mi. above the earth's surface. The troposphere is characterized by differences in temperature, winds, clouds, and dust. At the surface of the earth the atmosphere is a mechanical mixture of gases which is divided into 78 parts nitrogen, 21 parts oxygen, and one part water vapor, inert gases, and carbon dioxide. The composition of air changes with altitude; the heavier molecules are more abundant near the earth's surface and become relatively rarer at greater heights.

Variation in Air Composition by Altitude

	6.5 mi.	12 mi.	60 mi.
Nitrogen	78.02%	81.24%	2.95%
Oxygen	20.99	18.10	0.11
Carbon dioxide	0.03	0.01	....
Water	0.01	0.02	0.05
Hydrogen	0.01	0.04	95.58
Argon	0.94	0.59	....
Helium	....	....	1.31

In addition to sustaining animal and plant life the atmosphere has a great effect on the weathering of the earth's surface and causes all types of physical and chemical reactions. The density of the atmosphere is not uniform. The pressure is greatest at sea level and when measured by a mercurial barometer is about 29.92 in., but usually fluctuates between 29 and 30 in. and rarely goes much above or below those figures. Every increase of 900 ft. in elevation produces a decrease in pressure of about 1/30.

The earth is heated by short-wave radiant energy from the sun, called insolation, and the earth then radiates long-wave terrestrial energy which is absorbed by the atmosphere. Only 15 per cent of insolation is absorbed directly by the atmosphere. The temperature of the atmosphere at the earth's surface varies between about 90° F. below zero and about 135° F. above zero. In the troposphere, the temperature decreases steadily with increasing elevation. The circulation of the atmosphere is caused by unequal heating of the earth's surface, which is caused by the differences in the intensity of solar radiation received in different latitudes and by the differences of the duration of daylight. These two factors are controlled by the inclination of the earth's axis and the yearly revolution of the earth about the sun. Heated air expands and rises, while cooling causes contraction and the air becomes heavier. The resulting differences cause low- and high-pressure areas, and air moves laterally from a high-pressure area to a low-pressure one. These movements of air are called winds. The greater the difference in air pressure, the greater is the wind velocity. There is a variety of local winds, but the major wind belts are the polar easterlies, the prevailing westerlies, and the northeast and southeast trades; in southeastern Asia there is a well-developed monsoon wind belt.

The upper limit of the troposphere is called the tropopause; convection currents do not rise above this point and there is little change in temperature within the tropopause. The area above the tropopause is the stratosphere, which extends upward for about 50 mi. The temperature at the lower level of the stratosphere varies. The lowest recorded temperature is 112° F. below zero, and winds, clouds, dust, and a regular temperature lapse rate are absent. The stratosphere ends at the stratopause and above the stratopause is the ionosphere. *See also* METEOROLOGY.   J. E. F.

OPTICAL PHENOMENA

Optical phenomena of the atmosphere include a variety of effects arising from a variety of causes. Lightning, the commonest of these sights, which occurs in connection with thunderstorms; the striking aurora borealis and aurora australis; and refraction are discussed in separate articles. Other such phenomena of particular interest include rainbows, halos, parhelia and arcs, coronas, glories and Brocken specters, mirages, St. Elmo's fire, noctilucent clouds, green flashes, and crepuscular rays.

Rainbows. Rainbows are usually thought of as the most beautiful examples of atmospheric effects. An ordinary rainbow is a huge arc of colors in the heavens observed typically when the sun shines on a part of the sky that is filled with drops of water—for example, at places where it is raining. The bow of colors appears like a spectrum, but the colors are rarely if ever purely spectral, for they tend to overlap and become mixed, so that all the standard "colors of the rainbow" (red, orange, yellow, green, blue, indigo, violet) are not always present. In fact, ordinarily the physical features of a rainbow differ from one bow to another, giving a wide variety in appearance. They all have one invariable feature: the center of the arc is always on a straight line, extended, from the sun to the observer.

The primary rainbow is the main arc, having the most brilliant colors, the red on the outside and violet inside. The inner radius subtends an angle of approximately 40° and the outer radius 42°. At times this is the only bow visible, but frequently a secondary rainbow appears outside the main arc, the respective radii here being about 51° and 54°. This rainbow is not nearly so vivid in color as the first, and the red and violet edges are changed about, with the red inside in the secondary bow. The supernumerary bow is a series of narrow arcs parallel to and inside of the primary rainbow or else outside of the secondary bow. The color of these faint arcs is rather indefinite, and usually red and green predominate.

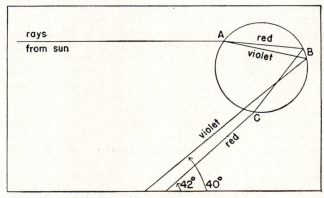

FORMATION OF PRIMARY RAYS IN RAINBOWS

The formation of the primary rainbow is caused by two refractions and one internal reflection of the light rays from the sun (or moon or electric light). Entering each drop at (A), the light is refracted and dispersed, as in a prism; it impinges on the back of the drop at (B) and is reflected forward and outward at (C). Here, the light is refracted again before finally traveling to the observer. The original white light has been dispersed into a two-degree band of colors.

In the secondary bow, two refractions and two reflections occur. Here, the sunlight (or moonlight or electric light) is refracted as it enters from the lower part of the drop and is reflected from (B) to (C) to (D), where it is finally refracted in its travel to the observer. Supernumerary bows are the result of interference of light in the rays which enter and leave the drops, different parts of the beam being superposed.

At sunrise and sunset an observer will see the rainbow as a semicircular arc, because the axis of the rainbow cone is parallel to the horizon. When the sun's altitude is greater, the rainbow cone is correspondingly tilted and so is less than a semicircle. The center of the rainbow arc is, in degrees, as far below the observer's level as the sun is above it. If the sun is over 42° in altitude, no rainbow is seen. Except in high latitudes, rainbows cannot appear at noon because the sun's altitude is too great. Circular rainbows may be witnessed in the spray from waterfalls, garden hose, and other sources, and may be seen in atmospheric water vapor from aloft by balloonists and aviators when these observers are sufficiently elevated above the ground to avoid the cutoff from the earth. At sea, as many as twenty or more

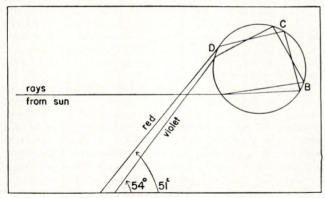

FORMATION OF SECONDARY RAYS IN RAINBOWS

marine rainbows, caused by wave crests perpetually turning into spray, may be in evidence simultaneously. Lunar rainbows are formed in a similar manner to the solar bows, though they occur much less frequently. They are comparatively pale in color, but because of their rarity and the night effect they afford a remarkable spectacle.

The question of the distance of the rainbow is interesting. Although the colored arc appears to lie in a two-dimensional plane, this is an illusion. It really has great depth and is to be considered as occupying the edges of a hollow cone, whose vertex is at the observer and whose axis is along a line from the sun to the observer and on to the rainbow center. The spectator is looking along the edges of this cone. No two persons can see exactly the same rainbow. Naturally, the same general effect may be witnessed, but the two bows have different positions and are formed by different water drops. Similarly, a rainbow observed by reflection, as in still water, is different from one sighted directly.

A fine rainbow is a magnificent phenomenon. When falling rain or spray is producing a rainbow, the beautiful effect is attained by a co-operative effort of all the droplets falling across the edges of the rainbow cone of the observer. The effect of each drop is extremely transitory. The surface of

the rainbow cone composes several layers; as each drop falls swiftly to a succession of critical points, it gives out momentarily the proper spectral colors in succession from red to violet. Each drop is succeeded by a multiplicity of other drops that do likewise, so that the rainbow as observed is continuous across the arc, as well as over the lengthwise extent of the rainbow's arch.

Halos. Halos are somewhat colorless arcs of light, produced either by refraction or reflection. The 22° halo is the

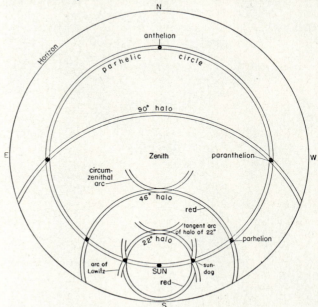

SKY PLAN OF THE MOST COMMON HALOS
Compass points are situated as shown in this sky view

one seen most frequently. This is a ring of indefinite colors around the sun (or moon) with a radius of approximately 22°, and possibly having a reddish color on the inner portion. Other spectral colors may be there in order, but usually they are practically unrecognizable. The halo is caused by refraction of light in crystals of ice or snow in the atmosphere. The crystals composing the halo are on a cone whose axis is the line of sight to the sun and whose vertex is at the observer. Under certain conditions the atmosphere is filled with small crystals, many of whose edges are at right angles to the plane through the sun, observer, and the crystals. These edges refract the light as it enters and leaves, with an effective deviation of 22°. The less common 46° halo is a circle of radius 46°, concentric with the 22° halo and outside of it. This also has a red tint on the inside of the ring. The cause here is likewise refraction of light but from crystal faces that make a right angle with each other. The halo's breadth is over 2½°, and the top and bottom of this and the 22° halo are apt to be brighter than other sections. The rare 90° halo is a faint, nearly colorless ring, concentric with the other two halos. When a color is apparent, it is the red, which appears on the side away from the sun. The cause of the halo appears to be imperfectly known, but is supposedly due to fortuitously directed bipyramidal crystals, both refraction and reflection operating in these ice prisms.

Parhelia and Arcs. The parhelic circle is a white ring of light having the zenith as its center and passing through the sun. It is parallel to the horizon and shows no spectral colors. It is caused by reflection of sunlight from the vertical faces of ice crystals. If the crystals are sufficiently well distributed in the air, a complete circle becomes evident. Parhelia (sundogs or mock suns) are bright spots roughly resembling the sun and formed at the intersection of the parhelic circle with halos of 22°, 46°, and 90°. The commonest and most intense is the one formed with the 22° halo, and it is often colored almost like a rainbow. Parhelia

COURTESY OF AMERICAN MUSEUM OF NATURAL HISTORY

BROCKEN SPECTER

at 46° and 90° occur much more rarely; the ones seen with the halo of 90° being known as paranthelia. The anthelion, a bright spot directly opposite the sun on the parhelic circle, occurs occasionally. It is supposed that this phenomenon is caused by double internal reflection of sunlight. The reflected ray has the same path as the incident ray but is in the opposite direction. The circumzenithal arc (also called, incorrectly, the upper tangent arc of halo of 46°) is an arc of 90° or less, with its center at the zenith, the arc being above the sun about 46°. It is seen only rarely and lasts but a few minutes. Its color is brilliant, the red being outside. The circumzenithal arc is remarkable because of the color, brightness, and the sharpness of the edges. Another curious and very rare halo effect is the arcs of Lowitz. These appear as extensions of the parhelia of 22° and go out obliquely, concave toward the sun. Columns of whitish light, as well as crosses of various kinds, are at times visible at sunrise and sunset, particularly in the polar regions, and may occur with either sun or moon. Lunar halos are occasionally seen, and the various phenomena are similar to those already described, the commonest lunar halo ("ring around the moon") being that of 22°. The parhelia here become paraselenae moondogs or mock moons).

Coronas. Coronas are small, concentric, colored rings surrounding the sun, moon, or other bright object, occurring at times when very thin clouds cover the light source. The radius of a corona is smaller than that of a halo by about 1° to 5°, and the blue or violet is nearest the sun. The corona is due to diffraction of light by small droplets of water. A bright area, the aureole, extends around the sun (or moon), ending in a reddish ring. This sometimes makes up the corona, and at other times two or more concentric rings are noticed beyond the aureole. If outer rings are present, their colors are faint. Iridescent clouds are an allied phenomenon in which, at times, very high clouds develop brightly colored edges. Although rarely seen, they are a noteworthy spectacle.

Glory; Brocken Specter. Certain odd phenomena of the atmosphere are produced under special conditions. When the place and atmosphere are exactly right, with the sun at the observer's back throwing a shadow on a near-by bank of mist or cloud, a glory—a circle of colored light around a person's head—may be witnessed. More commonly, a luminous aureole or glory circle around the head may be seen as reflected by droplets of dew which cover a grass lawn. In certain parts of the world the observer is situated on an eminence with the rising or setting sun behind, and the spectator's shadow is thrown onto a cloud bank a little distance away. The shadow acquires the unique and spectacular effect of a colossal figure of the observer. This is the famous Brocken specter, named from the type locality, the Brocken hill in the Harz Mountains, Germany, running through Hanover, where it is best observed. The phenomenon is due to reflection and diffraction of light from fine droplets of water in the mist. The appearance is extremely limited in place and time.

Mirages. A mirage is an optical illusion caused by refraction of light passing through layers of atmosphere of varying density. Objects in the distance may be raised above or depressed below their normal position and may be distorted into irregular, fantastic shapes. A mirage is often witnessed in warm climates, as for example over sandy plains. The form most commonly in evidence is the inferior mirage, in which the distant, nearly level desert surface may assume

COURTESY OF AMERICAN MUSEUM OF NATURAL HISTORY

DOUBLE SUPERIOR MIRAGE

the appearance of a sheet of water, especially if one observes from a slight elevation or simply from a point above the heated layer. The same illusion is apt to occur over a heated paved roadway, whereby the distant road is apparently a water surface. The latter is really an image of the sky. Below eye level in this "water" surface, objects, usually inverted, may appear. Over a hot surface of land, the air stands in layers nonhomogeneous in density; the hottest and the least dense layers are below and nearest the ground. The air layers near the surface are unduly rarefied and there exists a distortion of wave fronts because of varying speed of light as the density of the medium changes.

A superior mirage is less common and more spectacular than the inferior mirage. Distant objects (often over a sea horizon) are delineated in the sky upside down, and there may also be an erect image of the same object above the inverted one. The effect is typical of cold areas and of conditions where there is a strong temperature inversion, with warm strata of air above cooler layers. The effect is not, as commonly supposed, caused by reflection from a surface above the spectator. The explanation is complicated and involves the action of the wave fronts of light as they progress through strata of nonhomogeneous density. Occasionally very unusual and grotesque images are observed, especially in the polar regions. When the mirage is witnessed on land, all the trees and other landscape features are inverted, and in all cases of superior mirage the images are more clearly defined than in an inferior mirage. Sometimes lateral mirage is observed, where two layers of air are separated by a vertical plane. Such an effect takes place, for instance, in proximity to a large south-facing wall (in the Northern Hemisphere) that has acquired considerable heat.

Certain mirage effects have specific names. Looming is the appearance of objects ordinarily hidden below the horizon. The effect is apt to occur over water surfaces when the normal rate of decrease of air density with altitude is enhanced. A reversed effect, known as sinking, also occurs at sea when the opposite conditions take place. In this case shorelines and vessels which should be seen on the horizon are caused to sink below it and become invisible. In the phenomenon called towering, because of irregular refraction, the light rays are curved downward, those from the top of the object more so than the lower ones; and so the observer apparently sees the objects more elevated than they should be, and magnified in a vertical direction. If, however, the light rays from the top of the distant object are curved downward less than the bottom rays, there appears to be a contraction vertically, called stooping. This vertical shortening of horizon objects is frequently observed with the sun and moon when they are rising or setting. Along with stooping itself of the sun and moon, one often sees exceptional distortion of the disk, caused by abnormal density effects of the lower strata of the atmosphere. Under certain conditions of irregular and unstable temperature and density conditions of the air, some curious and fantastic mirages may appear, particularly over water. The famous fata morgana occurs, for example, over the Strait of Messina, between Calabria and Sicily. These are deformed and complex images due to refractions and reflections, exhibiting hundreds of pilasters, towers, castles, ships, and buildings, in extraordinary patterns. The spectacle is said to occur mostly on very calm mornings.

St. Elmo's Fire. Atmospheric optical phenomena may be luminous. Several such effects are electrical. The commonest example is lightning, which is meteorological. St. Elmo's fire is much more unusual—a faint blue or violet flame that may be one to several feet in extent, sometimes involving an acre or more. It is observed typically on the tops and yardarms of masts on vessels at sea. Or the rigging of a ship may appear as if suffused with phosphorus. St. Elmo's fire is occasionally seen on mountaintops, also on the spires and sharp corners of tall buildings. The phenomenon

is actually a "brush discharge" that takes place on the ends of electric generators and conductors, the conditions for its formation being an exceptional potential gradient in the atmosphere. The electric charge on the conductor supposedly takes place when the surrounding air mass is highly electri-

ST. ELMO'S FIRE

fied. St. Elmo's fire may even be seen, though rarely, playing over a person's body or his clothes and various objects held; more than once it has been said that the entire body has been observed radiating with light.

The *ignis fatuus* (will-o'-the-wisp, jack-o'-lantern, *feu follet*) is a faint bluish or greenish light sometimes discovered in swamps, moors, cemeteries, and burying vaults. Different forms of the flame are assumed; often it appears like a candle flame, but about a foot or so high, seemingly burning in a quiet and heatless manner and hovering momentarily over an object. It is described as singularly elusive, and at the approach of the observer may appear to remove itself to another spot. Decay of organic matter is the cause of this manifestation, and spontaneous combustion of marsh gas (methane, CH_4) or of phosphine (PH_3) takes place. These *ignes fatui* are variable in form, sometimes being globular.

Noctilucent Clouds. Noctilucent clouds are very rare night clouds in the lower ionosphere regions of the atmosphere. They are somewhat luminous and occur ordinarily within subpolar latitudes, and at an elevation of about 50 mi., being thus much farther from the surface than any other clouds, and probably illuminated by sunshine. The clouds are extremely tenuous and may be white, yellowish, or bluish. The nature of noctilucent clouds is uncertain, but it is supposed that they are made of particles of cosmic dust from outer space. Some observers have asserted that they travel at extraordinary speeds.

Green Flash. The green flash is a momentary flash of sunlight—a blue-green ray occasionally witnessed as the last bit of the solar disk sinks below the far horizon in a very clear atmosphere. Or it may appear as the first portion of the disk rises in the east. It is not a common phenomenon, since atmospheric conditions must be favorable, and the sun must not be too red. Besides, the observer must be watching carefully, as the duration is only one or two seconds. The colored ray is caused by atmospheric refraction. As the last of the sun sinks over the horizon, the red components of the white light, being the least refrangible, disappear first, the other colors following in order, with the blue (the most refrangible) the last; moreover, the effect is noticed only when but a minute part of the disk is in sight, since otherwise there is a blending of colors.

Crepuscular Rays. Crepuscular rays are radiating beams of sunlight made visible, with a low morning or afternoon sun, by the illuminated dust in the distant atmosphere, and being delimited by clouds—that is, cloud shadows form the darkened areas between which the rays extend. The effect is popularly ascribed to the sun's drawing water, but the notion is altogether erroneous. The seeming divergence is an illusion due to the effects of perspective. *See also* AURORA BOREALIS AND AURORA AUSTRALIS; LIGHTNING; OPTICS.

H. S. R.

ATOLL [æ'tɒl; ətɒ'l], a roughly circular coral reef surrounding a body of water. These are found in tropical and subtropical seas, especially the Pacific and Indian oceans. These reefs, which commonly project above the surface as chains of islets, are usually called atolls, from the name used in an Oceanic language. The lakelike bodies of water inside them are termed lagoons, doubtless from the Spanish word *laguna*. Ordinarily the islets are only a very few feet (up to 15) above sea level; the reefs are awash, except for occasional deep passages, and the lagoons quite deep, generally 60 to 100 or even 300 ft.

Composition. The basic material of which the reefs are composed is limestone of organic origin, formed by the accumulation of the calcareous skeletons of marine animals and plants, mainly corals and coralline algae. The islets characteristically scattered along the reefs are commonly made up of broken or pulverized limestone thrown up by wave action and often piled in small dunes by wind. The distribution of this material from the outer or seaward beach to the inner or lagoon beach is of interest. The outer shores of most atoll islands are made up of rather narrow fringing reefs, often with smooth rose-colored rims of massive calcareous algae and with a steep, narrow beach of broken or wave-rounded limestone fragments. Inside the crest of the beach the material changes to rubble, which becomes finer, changing to gravel. In the center of the islet is often a brackish depression with a mucky soil. The inner half is ordinarily a coarse coral sand, or fine gravel, and the inner beach is of fine calcareous sand. On some atolls these materials are loose, while in others they may be cemented into a crumbly rock. If the atoll is at all raised above sea level, the limestone is usually weathered to an incredibly rough surface

called *makatea*. The water table is, naturally, very near the surface, and shallow wells are often dug at or near the center. If the islet is large or the rainfall high, the water will tend to be fresh; if it is small or in a less rainy region, the water will be brackish or salty.

Flora. The most obvious surface feature of atolls is the vegetation. The flora is sparse, mostly of a few widely distributed strand plants and trees. The vegetation is arranged in definite zones, from the outer shores to the inner. These may be described in general terms for the Indo-Pacific region, where atolls are abundant and the flora rather uniform. The outer zone is a scrub made up largely of *Scaevola frutescens*. Next is a halophytic forest, largely of the tree heliotrope (*Messerschmidia argentea*) and *Pandanus tectorius*. Inward, this becomes less halophytic, with the addition of *Cordia, Pisonia grandis, Ochrosia,* etc. In the center, on more mesophytic islets, the original vegetation was probably of such trees as *Guettarda speciosa, Hibiscus tiliaceus, Ficus, Pisonia, Pandanus, Barringtonia asiatica, Terminalia,* and others. This forest has been replaced on most islands by forests of coconut and breadfruit, planted by man. Although the coconut palm is commonly thought of as the characteristic plant of atolls, its original home is unknown. Wherever it is found, it is thought to have been planted by man. On the inner beach is usually a thin fringe of trees of *Hernandia, Calophyllum, Pandanus, Thespesia, Cordia,* etc. On sand spits between islets, *Suriana maritima* and *Scaevola* are common; on rock outcrops, *Pemphis acidula*. Here and there in the interior are wet depressions. In some islets these are rocky and contain several species of trees elsewhere characteristic of mangrove swamps. On others they are marshy and open, with grasses and sedges as the dominant vegetation. On inhabited islets the marshes are often excavated and enlarged, filled with decomposing vegetable debris, and used as taro patches, where *Colocasia, Cyrtosperma,* sugar cane, and other food plants are raised. Owing to the high salinity, few food plants other than those mentioned thrive on low coral islets. Taros, breadfruit, and coconuts form the principal vegetable food, while coconuts also furnish drinking water.

Other Products. The great majority of atolls are inhabited and under as intensive cultivation as their sterile, saline soils will support. Other than subsistence crops, coconuts, the dried meat of which is exported as copra, form the principal culture. The principal foods, other than those from plants, are fish and shellfish, which abound in the lagoons, on the reefs, and in the adjacent open sea. Articles of commerce, other than copra, are guano, pearls, shells for buttons, and a dried holothurian commonly called *bêche-de-mer,* or sea cucumber, which is exported to China and used as food.

The fertility of atolls is much greater on the larger islets, on those in very rainy regions, and especially on those that rise above the level of the sea. This is reflected in greater luxuriance of vegetation, more extensive flora, and much more diversified agriculture. The reason for this is believed to be decreased salinity. On raised atolls, too, there are often extensive deposits of phosphate rock, probably derived from prehistoric guano accumulations. These have been extensively mined on the islands of Makatea, Nauru, Ocean, and Angaur, all raised atolls, and exported for use as fertilizer in phosphate-deficient areas. The guano deposits on many atoll islets are made by the large numbers of sea birds, chiefly gannets, tropic birds, frigate birds, and terns, which breed there. Other than these birds, land crabs, and coconut crabs, the terrestrial fauna is sparse. Rats are prevalent, and in the western Pacific fruit bats are conspicuous. In the water are turtles, spiny lobsters, giant clams, innumerable kinds of fish, and a rich reef fauna which includes many kinds of invertebrates.

Theories of Origin. The curious form of atolls has led to much speculation as to their origin. At one time it was thought that they represented the crater rims of volcanoes which had not quite reached the surface of the ocean, but this explanation was clearly an absurdity. Charles Darwin, on the famous voyage of the *Beagle,* made the observations which led to his formulation of the theory which, with modifications resulting from further information, has since been generally regarded as outlining the essential facts of their formation.

Darwin's Theory. Darwin's theory depends upon the relationships between fringing reefs, barrier reefs, and atolls. It may be readily observed that there is a gradation between typical fringing reefs and typical barrier reefs. Some reefs are hard to classify. The fact that the shore line back of a well-developed barrier reef is deeply embayed at the mouths of valleys indicates that subsidence has taken place, that the land has been lowered in relation to sea level. The indications are that a fringing reef will gradually become a barrier reef as subsidence of the shore line takes place. The coral growth is usually able to keep pace with the subsidence at its outer edge, where growth is most rapid and where there is no drainage of fresh water to produce unfavorable conditions. The slower growth toward shore accounts for the lagoon behind the barrier. That the same process does not stop with the production of a barrier is plain from the existence of a perfect series of examples of every stage, from barrier reef surrounding a volcanic island to "almost atolls," with just the tops of the peaks showing above the surface of the lagoon, to true atolls, with no trace left of the original island except the outline marked by the periphery of the atoll. The islets found on barrier reefs surrounding islands or along continental coasts are in every respect like those on atoll reefs. Though Darwin's theory has satisfied most students up to the present time, it did not go unchallenged. Several workers have favored the idea that atolls have grown up on pre-existing submarine platforms. Daly suggested that during the glacial period the seas were several hundred feet lower and the water was much colder; hence the corals did not form reefs to protect the islands. This permitted the action of waves to truncate a vast number of islands down to sea level; then, when the oceans rose again with the melting of the glaciers, reefs grew up on the platforms thus produced. According to both of these theories, the lagoon is produced by the failure of the coral growth in the center to keep pace with that on the periphery, where the water is more agitated and food and dissolved gases more abundant.

Theory of Subsidence. However, there are many facts that are not so well explained by those theories as by that of subsidence, especially the developmental series that exist from fringing reefs to barriers to atolls. The principal difference between the original subsidence theory, as propounded by Darwin, and that generally accepted at the present time is in the extent of the areas affected by subsidence. Darwin believed that subsidence on a continental scale had taken place. Now it seems more probable that the subsidence is generally local, perhaps resulting from the lack of isostatic adjustment between the weight of material poured out, when an island is built up by volcanic action, and the underlying section of the earth's crust. Thus an island would tend to sink gradually of its own weight. The rise in sea level resulting from the melting of the glaciers is also generally taken into account. The acceptance of the idea that what are now atolls were once high islands is of great significance in understanding the distribution of plants and animals in insular regions.

Important Atolls. The most important groups of atolls are the Maldive and Laccadive islands in the Indian Ocean; the Caroline, Marshall, and Gilbert groups in Micronesia; the Tuamotu and Pacific Equatorial islands in Polynesia; and the large numbers of atolls scattered through Melanesia. In the Atlantic there are several atolls in the Lesser Antilles, and the Bahamas contain some rather atypical atolls. The largest atoll in land area is Christmas Island, in the central Pacific. It has a relatively small lagoon. The largest lagoon is probably that of Kwajalein Atoll, in the Marshalls, though some others are almost as large. *See also* CORAL REEFS.   F. R. F.

ATOMIC AND NUCLEAR MOMENTS. The term moment when applied to atoms and atomic nuclei includes any one of the following: (1) the moment of momentum or spin angular momentum, (2) the magnetic dipole moment, (3) the electrical quadrupole moment, or (4) the higher electrical or magnetic multipole moments. The existence of a resultant angular momentum and of a magnetic moment for an atom was implied in the Bohr theory of the atom, formulated in 1913, and was in agreement with the observations first made by Pieter Zeeman in 1896 of the effects of magnetic fields on spectral lines. A relatively direct measurement of the magnetic moment of an atom was first made by Otto Stern and Wahlter Gerlach in 1921 by observing the effect of an inhomogeneous magnetic field in deflecting a beam of silver atoms. On the basis of a study of the fine structure of spectral lines, George Uhlenbeck and Samuel A. Goudsmit in 1925 suggested that the electron has an intrinsic spin angular momentum and a magnetic moment. The first suggestion of a spin angular momentum and magnetic moment for an atomic nucleus was made by Wolfgang Pauli in 1924 in an effort to account for hyperfine structure of spectral lines. The first evidence for a nuclear electrical quadrupole moment was obtained by H. Schüler and Th. Schmidt in 1935. Extensive measurements of nuclear moments have been made by studies of spectral lines; by studies with the molecular beam technique of Stern, Isidor Rabi, and their co-workers; and by the radiofrequency resonance absorption methods developed by Rabi, E. M. Purcell, F. Bloch, and others in 1937 and 1946.

Types of Moments. *Spin Angular Momentum.* The spin angular momentum or spin of an atom or atomic nucleus is a measure of the property of the atom or nucleus which is similar to that which characterizes a spinning top or gyroscope. The angular momentum of a rigid body rotating about an axis is defined as the sum of the angular movements of all the particles of which the body is composed. The angular momentum for each particle is as follows; the product of the mass of the particle, its linear velocity, and the shortest distance from the axis of rotation to the particle. The angular momentum is considered as a vector quantity parallel to the axis of rotation and in the direction that a right-handed screw-thread would advance under the rotation. In atoms and nuclear spin, angular momenta are measured in units of $h/2\pi$ where h is Planck's constant, equal to 6.62×10^{-27} erg-seconds. In such units it is found experimentally that, in agreement with the formalism of quantum mechanics, the observable components along a given direction of all spin angular momenta are either integral or half integral, i.e., either 1, 2, 3 . . . or 1/2, 3/2, 5/2 . . . The maximum value which the component can have is taken as the spin for the atom or nucleus concerned. For example, if a nucleus has a spin of 5/2, the largest measurable component of the spin in any direction is $5/2 \times h/2\pi$ erg-seconds.

Magnetic Dipole Moment. The magnetic dipole moment of an atom or nucleus is a measure of the property of the atom or nucleus analogous to that which characterizes a compass needle. In other words, the magnetic dipole moment measures the tendency of the atom or nucleus to rotate in a magnetic field. The dipole moment is a vector quantity, μ, whose direction and sense is that of an external field, for which the dipole moment would be in stable equilibrium, and whose magnitude is one half the difference in the potential energy when the dipole moment is directed oppositely to a magnetic field of 1 gauss and when it is directed parallel to a field of this magnitude. Magnetic moments of atoms are usually measured in units of Bohr magnetons, where the Bohr magneton $= \mu_0 = \dfrac{eh}{4\pi mc} = 0.927$

$\times 10^{-20}$ erg/gauss, where e is the charge of the electron, h is Planck's constant, m is the mass of the electron, and c is the velocity of light. Magnetic moments of nuclei, on the other hand, are usually measured in units of nuclear magnetons, where the nuclear magneton is defined as the Bohr magneton divided by the ratio of the proton mass to the electron mass, this ratio being experimentally determined as 1836.

Electric Quadrupole Moment. The electrical quadrupole moment of an atomic nucleus is a measure of the departure of the nuclear electrical charge from spherical symmetry. Quantitatively it is defined as

$$Q = Z\left(\overline{3z^2 - r^2}\right), \qquad (1)$$

when the spin vector of the nucleus has its maximum possible component along the z axis of a rectangular co-ordinate system whose origin is at the center of the nucleus. In this, Z is the nuclear charge or atomic number, z is the z co-ordinate of a point in the nucleus, r is the distance of that point from the center of the nucleus, and the bar above the quantity in parenthesis means that the quantity is averaged according to charge density over all parts of the nucleus. It can readily be shown that $Q = 0$ in the case of spherical symmetry.

ATOMIC MOMENTS

Study by Zeeman Effect. One of the earliest and most effective means of studying atomic moments was the so-called Zeeman effect, based on the effects of external magnetic fields on the spectral lines of the atom concerned. If a discharged tube giving rise to an atomic spectrum is placed in an external magnetic field, the spectral lines will be split into several different components. Typical illustrations of these splittings are shown in Fig. 1. The spacing of these components is determined by the interaction energies of the atomic moments with the external magnetic fields. Since these interaction energies depend on the magnetic moments of the atoms, measurements of the splittings yield information on the magnitudes of the magnetic moments. The numbers of spectral lines indicate the magnitudes of the spin angular momenta.

Stern and Gerlach Method. A particularly clear, significant, and direct measurement of atomic magnetic moments was first made in an entirely different way by Stern and Gerlach in 1921. Their method was based on the deflection of atoms with magnetic moments when passing through an inhomogeneous magnetic field. Such a magnetic moment would not be deflected in a homogeneous magnetic field, since, essentially, the north pole of the magnet would be pushed northward equally as strongly as the south pole would be pushed southward. Consequently, no net deflection of the center of gravity of the atom would occur, and there would be merely a tendency for a rotation about the center of gravity of the atom. In an inhomogeneous magnetic field, however, the result would be different, since, due to the variation of the magnetic field over the finite size of the magnet, one pole would be pushed harder

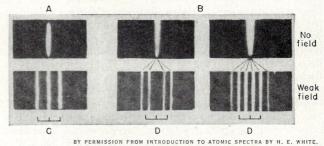

Fig. 1—NORMAL AND ANOMALOUS ZEEMAN EFFECTS, VIEWED PERPENDICULAR TO MAGNETIC FIELD.

(A) Zinc singlet; (B) Sodium principal doublet; (C) Normal triplet; and (D) Anomalous patterns.

in one direction than the other pole would be pushed in the opposite direction, so that a net deflection would take place.

The experiments were performed by heating the atoms in an oven and allowing them to escape between narrow slit jaws into an evacuated chamber, where the beam of atoms was accurately collimated and allowed to strike a plate on which the atoms accumulated for detection. An inhomogeneous magnetic field was then produced across the path of the beam, and the deflection of the atoms was observed. A different deflection should have been observed for each different possible component along the field of the magnetic moment and spin angular momentum. In classical physics, a continuous distribution of components should have been possible, and, consequently, the trace obtained on the detection plate should have been smoothly spread out. In quantum mechanics, however, only certain discrete components are ob-

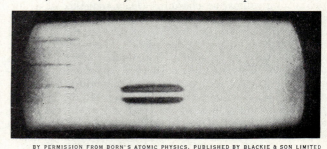

Fig. 2—Magnetic splitting of the trace at the detector of a lithium beam by the method of Stern and Gerlach.

servable, and, consequently, the observed pattern, instead of being a continuous one, should be broken up into two or more parts, with the number of parts being $2j + 1$, where j is the atomic angular momentum in the units defined above. A typical result of this experiment is shown in Fig. 2, where the pattern is split into two distinct parts in agreement with quantum mechanics and in complete disagreement with classical mechanics. The atomic angular momentum j can be determined from the number of components, since the number of components equal $2j + 1$. The magnetic moments can be obtained from the spacing of the components.

Results of Experiments. The results of the above and

related experiments are all consistent with the following assumption concerning angular momenta and magnetic moments in atomic structure:

(a) Each electron, by virtue of its motion in a Bohr orbit, will have an angular momentum l and an associated magnetic moment

$$\mu_l = \mu_0 l \qquad (l \text{ is in units of } h/2\pi) \qquad (2)$$

(b) Each electron has an intrinsic spin angular momentum of s, where the magnitude of s is $1/2$. Associated with this is a magnetic moment

$$\mu_s = 2\mu_{0s} = \mu_0 \qquad (3)$$

That is, in the case of the electron spin, the ratio of the magnetic moment to the angular momentum is double that of orbital angular momentum.

(c) The resultant contribution of the electrons to the angular momentum and magnetic moment of the atom is a suitable vector sum of the above orbital and spin contributions. The method of forming this appropriate vector sum varies in different cases. For a large and important class of atoms, the so-called Russell-Sounders coupling holds, for which the orbital and spin angular momenta are first separately added together and then combined.

NUCLEAR MOMENTS

Nuclear moments have been measured in a number of different ways. One of the earliest and most important was the careful study of the so-called hyperfine structure of atomic spectra. The spin may be inferred from the number of the component spectral lines or from the relative intensities of the lines. The spins, magnetic moments, and electrical quadrupole moment interaction can be determined from the spacings of the components or from the effects of magnetic

By suitable adjustments of the magnetic fields and by a study of the deflection pattern or the refocusing of the atomic beam, the nature of the coupling between the nuclear moments and the electron moments can be inferred. Nuclear spins, nuclear magnetic moment interactions, and nuclear quadrupole moment interactions have been measured in this way.

The study of the absorption of radiofrequency and microwave frequency radiations by atoms and molecules has probably been the most effective means so far discovered for investigating nuclear moments. As in optical spectroscopy absorption of radiation by a molecule will take place at a frequency ν such that

$$h\nu = \Delta E, \qquad (4)$$

where ΔE is the energy difference between two energy states of the molecule between which a transition is allowed. In the case of a simple nuclear magnetic moment of magnitude μ associated with a spin I in a magnetic field H, the value of ΔE may be easily evaluated theoretically, with the result that the resonance occurs at a frequency ν such that

$$h\nu = \frac{M}{I}\mu_N H, \qquad (5)$$

where μ is the nuclear magneton previously defined. This shows that since h and μ_N are known physical constants, a measurement of the field H and the corresponding oscillator frequency ν gives the ratio of the magnetic moment to the spin. If the molecular interactions are more complicated, (4) will no longer reduce to (5), and absorption of the radiation will occur at frequencies other than those given by (5). One type of such an additional interaction may occur if the nucleus has an electrical quadrupole moment, since such

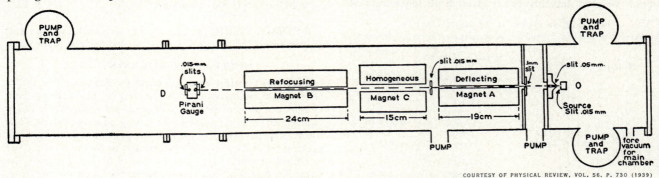

COURTESY OF PHYSICAL REVIEW, VOL. 56, P. 730 (1939)

Fig. 3—SCHEMATIC DIAGRAM OF MOLECULAR BEAM RESONANCE ABSORPTION APPARATUS.

fields on the lines (the so-called Zeeman effect in hyperfine structure).

Molecular Beam Method. The molecular beam methods developed by Stern and Rabi and their collaborators have been particularly effective in investigating nuclear moments. A number of different molecular beam methods have been used. One, used by Stern in the case of hydrogen and deuterium, employs molecules H_2 in a molecular beam apparatus, similar in principle to that described above in the Stern and Gerlach experiment. Since, however, the major part of the electron magnetic moments in H_2 exactly cancel, the deflection is due chiefly to the nuclear magnetic moment. Consequently, the nuclear magnetic moment can be inferred from a measurement of the deflection pattern. A different variety of beam experiments conducted by Rabi and his coworkers used atoms with a resultant electron magnetic moment to form the beam of atoms which passes through one or two deflecting magnetic fields of the Stern-Gerlach type.

an electrical quadrupole moment can interact with the inhomogeneous electric field, arising from the other charges of the molecules in which the nucleus is located. In this case, the magnitude of the nuclear electrical quadrupole moment interaction can be inferred from the frequencies at which absorption occurs.

This method of radiofrequency-radiation absorption was first used successfully by Rabi and his co-workers in 1937. As a means of detecting the existence of the absorption, Rabi studied the effect of the absorption on the deflection of molecules in a molecular beam. A typical apparatus of this type is shown in Fig. 3. The molecules emerge from the oven O into an evacuated chamber containing two inhomogeneous magnetic fields A and B, with directions of inhomogeneity reversed. The paths of the molecules are deflected by magnet A, as in the Stern and Gerlach experiment, and then refocused by magnet B to fall on the detector D, provided that the constituent magnetic moments of the molecule are oriented the same way in B as in A. If, however, any constituent moment is reoriented in the region C, the refocusing will no longer occur and the beam intensity will drop. Consequently, a homogeneous magnetic field and an oscillating radiofrequency field is applied in the region C, and absorption of the radiofrequency radiation is detected by a reduction of beam intensity. A typical result for a molecule of heavy hydrogen is shown in Fig. 4, in which the beam intensity is plotted as a function of the homogeneous magnetic field C. The deepest central minimum of beam intensity corresponds to a frequency and field given by (2), and consequently, the ratio of the magnetic moment to the spin may be determined from this measurement. The separations of the smaller, subsidiary, resonance minima are due to the electrical quadrupole interaction, so, from a measurement of their positions, the electrical quadrupole moment of the heavy hydrogen nucleus, or deuteron can be inferred.

Other Experiments. In 1946 Purcell and Bloch first successfully used the resonance-absorption technique without molecular beams but by employing the effect of the absorption on the radiation field as the means of detection. Since then a number of other workers have undertaken similar experiments, including absorption experiments at microwave frequencies, in which the rotational state of the molecule is changed in the transition. Methods similar to the molecular, beam-resonance absorption method have been applied to the measurement of the magnetic moment of the neutron. Also, in addition to the above general methods, information on nuclear moments has been obtained by a number of more specialized methods such as the study of band spectra, specific heat, etc.

The values of the nuclear moments of isotopes whose atomic weight is less than 24 are given in the following table:

TABLE OF NUCLEAR MOMENT VALUES

Nucleus	Spin in Units of $h/2$	Magnetic Moment In Nuclear Magnetons	Quadrupole Moment In Square Centimeters
$_0n^1$	(1/2)	−1.9103	......
$_1H^1$	1/2	2.7896	0
$_1H^2$	1	0.85647	2.73×10^{-27}
$_1H^3$	1/2	2.9754	......
$_2He^3$	(1/2)	.....	......
$_2He^4$	0	.....	......
$_3Li^6$	1	0.8214	......
$_3Li^7$	3/2	3.2535	$\neq 0$
$_4Be^9$	3/2	−1.176	......
$_5Be^{10}$	(1)	0.598	......
$_5Be^{11}$	(3/2)	2.687	......
$_6C^{12}$	(0)	.....	......
$_6C^{13}$	(1/2)	0.701	......
$_7N^{14}$	1	0.403	......
$_7N^{15}$	1/2	±0.280	......
$_8O^{16}$	(0)	.....	......
$_9F^{19}$	1/2	2.627	......
$_{10}Ne^{20}$	0	.....	......
$_{11}Na^{23}$	3/2	2.217	$\neq 0$

(Quantities in parentheses are theoretical predictions not measurements)

The following results are particularly noteworthy because of their important implications on the theories of nuclear forces:

1. The proton ($_1H^1$) and neutron ($_0n^1$) have magnetic moments that differ from one nuclear magneton, despite the prediction of several theories that it should be exactly one nuclear magneton.

2. The difference between the deuteron ($_1H^2$) magnetic moment and the sum of the proton and neutron ($_0n^1$) mo-

ments is small but finite (3 per cent). This means that the neutron and proton moments are not simply additive in the deuteron.

3. The magnetic moment of ($_1H^3$) differs from that of ($_1H^1$) by 6.6 per cent, despite the predictions of certain theories that they should be identical.

4. The deuteron has an electrical quadrupole moment, i.e., it departs from spherical symmetry like an American

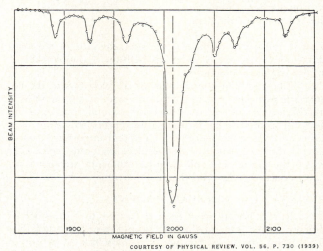

COURTESY OF PHYSICAL REVIEW, VOL. 56, P. 730 (1939)

Fig. 4—RESONANCE CURVE FOR HEAVY HYDROGEN (D₂) MOLECULES.

football, despite the predictions of the theories prior to this discovery that the deuteron would be spherically symmetric. *See also* ELECTRICITY AND MAGNETISM; MECHANICS; QUANTUM MECHANICS; SPECTROSCOPY.   N. F. R.

ATOMIC ENERGY, the energy released by the rearrangement of the particles making up the nucleus of an atom.

NUCLEAR ENERGY CONTENT

Surface-Tension and Disruptive Forces. The nuclei of different atoms can be considered as being built from various numbers of protons and neutrons (collectively called "nucleons") bound together by strong cohesive forces. The constituent parts of the nucleus are packed tightly together, making the nuclear model very similar to the classical picture of a fluid droplet. Just as in the case of ordinary liquids, the attractive forces of cohesion between the nucleons try to reduce the free surface to the minimum, thus giving to the nucleus the form of a sphere.

If the surface-tension forces were the only forces acting in the nucleus, two nuclei coming into contact would always fuse in the same manner as do small droplets of mercury, since the surface of one comparatively large droplet is smaller than the sum of the surfaces of two smaller ones. It must be remembered, however, that since about one-half of the nuclear particles are protons, each nucleus carries a large electric charge. The forces of electric repulsion between the charged parts of the nucleus tend to break it up into two or more separate parts, in a fission process, working against the cohesive forces that try to hold the nucleus in one piece. Thus the nuclear stability is determined by the balance between the nuclear surface-tension forces and the disruptive forces due to its electric charge. One can easily write the expression for the total internal energy of atomic nucleus as a function of its atomic weight A and atomic number Z. Since each nucleon interacts only with its immediate neighbors because of the short-range nature of nuclear forces, the main term in the energy expression will be proportional to the total number of nucleons (that is, to the atomic weight) and can be written in the form $-aA$, where a is a constant and A is the atomic weight. This term must be amended by the surface-energy term, which accounts for the fact that the nucleons located at the surface have only half as many neighbors as those located in the interiors. Hence

$$- (aA - \sigma S) = -aA + \sigma S,$$

where S is the nuclear surface and σ the surface-tension constant. Since, according to the droplet model, nuclear density remains constant throughout the natural sequence of elements, the nuclear radius can be written

$$r = r_0 A^{1/3},$$

where $r_0 = 1.45 \times 10^{-13}$ cm.,

and the nuclear surface can be written

$$S = 4\pi r^2 = 4\pi r_0^2 A^{2/3}.$$

The coulomb energy of the nucleus can be calculated by using the classical formula for the uniformly charged spherical condenser, according to which this energy is equal to $\frac{5}{3}$ L of the square of the charge divided by the radius. This gives, for the last term in the energy expression,

$$\frac{5}{3}\frac{(eZ)^2}{r} = \frac{5}{3}\frac{(eZ)^2}{r_0 A^{1/3}}.$$

Energy Liberation by Fission and Fusion. With all terms combined, the total internal energy of the nucleus with atomic weight A and atomic number Z is expressed by

$$E = -aA + 4\pi r_0^2 \sigma A^{2/3} + \frac{5}{3}\frac{e^2 Z^2}{r_0 A^{1/3}},$$

which can be used for the calculation of the energy balance corresponding to different nuclear transformations. For the particular case of nuclear fission into two equal parts, the results indicated graphically in Fig. 1 are obtained. Here the energy curve crosses the zero axis in the region of atomic

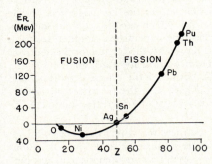

Fig. 1—ENERGY LIBERATION BY FUSION AND FISSION

(E_R) *Reaction energy in millions of electron volts; (Z) Atomic number of respective elements indicated along curve; (O) Oxygen; (Ni) Nickel; (Ag) Silver; (Sn) Tin; (Pb) Lead; (Th) Thorium; and (Pu) Plutonium.*

number corresponding to that of silver, so that for the nuclei of the first half of the natural system, the energy balance of fission is negative; that is, energy must be put in to break the nucleus into two halves. It follows that, in the region of lighter elements, nuclear energy cannot be obtained through the fission process, but rather through the fusion of two small nuclei into a bigger one. For the elements of the second half of the natural sequence, the energy balance is positive, showing that in this region the nuclear fission is the energy-liberating process. The important conclusion is that, by either the fusion or the fission process, energy can be liberated from the nuclei of practically any chemical element. The maximum amount of energy per unit mass of the material can be obtained either

by fission of the heaviest elements or by fusion of the lightest ones; for elements near the middle of the periodic system, where the energy curve of Fig. 1 crosses the zero axis, the conditions for energy liberation are least favorable. Numerically, the amount of nuclear energy that can be liberated by a given amount of material exceeds the corresponding amounts of ordinary chemical energy by a factor of many millions. Thus the fission of a kilogram of uranium can liberate 2×10^{13} cal., which is equivalent to the energy liberation of several thousand tons of the best chemical fuels.

Activation Energy. Since practically every material is overloaded with such tremendous amounts of nuclear energy, why does this energy not get free by itself, and why does all

Fig. 2—ACTIVATION ENERGIES FOR FUSION AND FISSION

(E_{AC}) *Activation energy in millions of electron volts; (Z) Atomic number; (O) Oxygen; (Sn) Tin; (Pb) Lead; (Th) Thorium; and (Pu) Plutonium.*

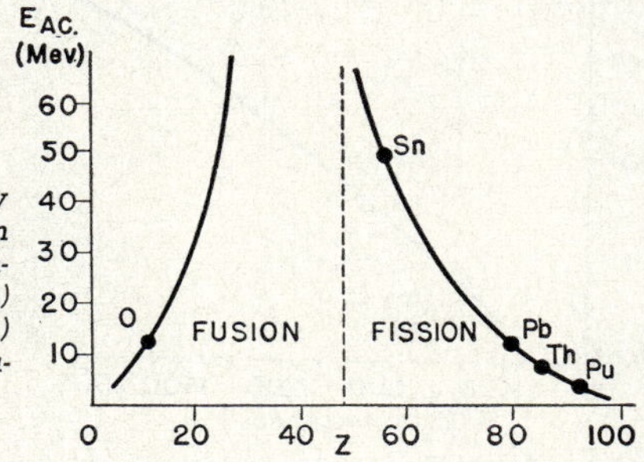

the matter of the universe not turn instantaneously into middleweight elements in one tremendous atomic explosion? The reason for the apparent nuclear stability of matter is very similar to that which prevents a piece of coal from spontaneous ignition, or a charge of TNT from spontaneous explosion. To make two light nuclei fuse, we must first bring them into contact against the repulsive forces between their electric charges, which requires a considerable amount of energy. Similarly, in order to produce the fission of a heavier nucleus, we must first put in a considerable amount of energy in order to deform the nucleus beyond its "breaking point." The amount of external energy that must be first put in to start the energy-liberating reaction is known as the activation energy. Because of the strong binding of the nucleus, nuclear activation energies are larger than ordinary chemical activation energies, in about the same proportion as the liberation of nuclear energy is larger than liberation of chemical energy. The activation energies for the fusion of lighter elements, and for the fission of heavier ones, can be calculated on the basis of the nuclear droplet model; they are shown graphically in Fig. 2. These values, as well as those shown in Fig. 1, are given in energy units known as electron volts. For comparison, the energy liberation in a TNT explosion is equal to 10 electron volts, whereas its activation energy is only 3 electron volts.

Hence nuclear reactions are, in a way, very similar to ordinary chemical reactions, with the difference, however, that the difficulty of starting and maintaining such reactions, as well as the amount of energy which can be obtained from them, exceeds the corresponding quantities in ordinary chemistry by factors of several millions.

LARGE-SCALE NUCLEAR REACTIONS

Thermal Method. In complete similarity with the ordinary chemical reactions, nuclear reactions can be induced by heating the material in question to a sufficiently high temperature. Since, however, nuclear excitation energies exceed those of chemical reactions by a factor of several millions, the ignition temperatures required in this case are correspondingly much higher. Thus, whereas most chemical reactions would go at the temperature of several hundred degrees centigrade, a temperature of at least a million degrees is required to start the most favorable nuclear reaction. The curve in Fig. 2 shows that nuclear activation energies have the smallest values at the two extreme ends of the natural sequence of elements; that is, for fusion of the lightest nuclei and for fission of the heaviest ones.

Although the high temperatures required for the maintenance of such thermonuclear reactions can hardly be obtained

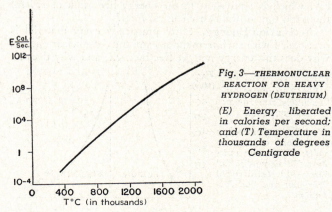

Fig. 3—THERMONUCLEAR REACTION FOR HEAVY HYDROGEN (DEUTERIUM)

(E) Energy liberated in calories per second; and (T) Temperature in thousands of degrees Centigrade

under laboratory conditions, knowledge concerning nuclear processes has progressed sufficiently to permit theoretical calculation of the rates of energy liberation for different possible thermonuclear reactions. The results for the case of the "easiest" fusion reaction

$$H^2 + H^2 \rightarrow He^3 + n^1$$

are shown in Fig. 3. Even in this case, an appreciable energy liberation begins only when the temperature approaches one million degrees. An important case of the above-described thermonuclear reactions is presented by the so-called carbon cycle, which comprises the following series of individual reactions:

$$C^{12} + H^1 \rightarrow N^{13}$$
$$N^{13} \rightarrow C^{13} + e^+$$
$$C^{13} + H^1 \rightarrow N^{14}$$
$$N^{14} + H^1 \rightarrow O^{15}$$
$$O^{15} \rightarrow N^{15} + e^+$$
$$N^{15} + H^1 \rightarrow He^4 + C^{12}$$
etc.

This reaction cycle, which finally transforms hydrogen into helium, proceeds at an appreciable rate only at temperatures of tens of millions of degrees, and is principally responsible for the energy production in stars.

Chain Reactions. Since the thermal method of inducing nuclear reactions, though actually taking place in the cosmos, requires temperatures that are almost prohibitively large for man-made experiments, some other method must be used for achieving the same end. Such an alternative is presented by the possibility of the so-called branching chain reactions, which are familiar from many examples of ordinary chemistry. A chain reaction can take place if a transformation process gives rise to several "active fragments" which in their turn are able to produce similar transformations on coming into contact with other particles of the material in question. Since every elementary transformation results in several directly induced transformations of the same kind, the rate of reaction increases exponentially, and the process usually terminates in an explosion. TNT and other high explosives are examples of such chain-reacting materials in the realm of ordinary chemistry.

The nuclear analogy of the chemical chain reactions is pre-

sented by the case of fission of heavy nuclei, where the fragments produced in one fission process can cause several similar fission processes in the surrounding material. It must be remembered, however, that the two heavy fission fragments, each representing about one half of the broken nucleus and carrying most of the liberated energy, cannot produce further fission processes because they are electrically charged and are thus prevented from direct bodily collisions with other nuclei by strong forces of electric repulsion. The situation is helped, however, by the fortunate fact that the fission process in heavy nuclei is accompanied by the emission of several neutrons, which in this case play the role of active fragments serving to perpetuate the chain of transformations. The number of these so-called fission neutrons varies from element to element, parallel with the total energy liberated in the fission process. Whereas for the elements just beyond the fission point (silver in Fig. 1), there may be only one fission neutron per many fission processes, the number of neutrons per fission becomes equal to 2 and more for the elements near the end of the natural sequence. Since neutrons carry no electric charge, they can penetrate without any difficulty into the nuclei of other neighboring atoms and, causing the fission of these nuclei, can carry on the process of branching chain reaction.

Reproduction Factor. It must not be thought, however, that each neutron which penetrates into a heavy nucleus will necessarily cause fission; in fact, in some cases the neutron can be captured by the nucleus, releasing the excess energy in the form of a gamma-ray; again, a neutron can escape from the nucleus without causing any damage at all. From the theory of nuclear structure one can conclude, however, that the chance of nuclear fission being produced by the impact of a neutron increases with increasing atomic number of the element bombarded. This is quite natural, since the heavier nuclei are more unstable than the lighter ones. If the number of neutrons per fission is denoted by v, and if the probability that the neutron entering the nucleus will cause its fission is denoted by ω, the mean number of secondary neutrons produced by a single primary neutron is given by the product $\eta = v\omega$. This number is known as the theoretical reproduction factor, in the case of an infinite amount of pure material where the neutron losses due to escape through the surface or to absorption in possible impurities are neglected. In the case of samples of finite size, which can also contain some ingredients that absorb the fission neutrons, another factor, α must be introduced; this represents the fraction of the neutrons remaining after absorption and escape through the surface. This factor leads to the notion of the effective reproduction factor; $K_{(eff)} = \eta\alpha$. If $K_{(eff)} < 1$, the reaction will rapidly die out; if $K_{(eff)} > 1$, it will rapidly increase, following the exponential law.

Critical Size. The substances for which the theoretical reproduction factor η is larger than unity are known as fissionable materials. When these materials are used in small amounts (small α because of the large probability of neutron escape through the surface) or in the form of a mixture with other nonfissionable substances (small α because of strong neutron absorption), they are perfectly stable and can be handled without any danger whatsoever. However, in the case of samples in which $\eta\alpha > 1$, the first stray neutron which enters into the sample will start a progressive chain reaction which will result in an almost instantaneous explosion. The size of the sample for which $\eta\alpha = 1$ is known as critical size, and no chain reaction can be started in a smaller amount of fissionable material. It can be easily understood on the basis of the above discussion that the critical size depends on the shape of the sample and on the amount of foreign material, as well

U. S. ARMY AIR FORCES

(Above) The Bikini explosion reaches its peak as the giant bomb cloud mushrooms high above the atoll. Although the 73-ship fleet was almost completely wiped out, outstanding consequence of the bomb action was radioactivity. This picture was taken more than a dozen miles from the explosion.

(Left) On July 1, 1946, the fourth atom bomb was exploded at Bikini Atoll, Marshall Islands, in an Army-Navy A-bomb test.

as on the nature of the fissionable material used (the value of η).

Delayed Neutrons. It may seem from the above discussion that pure fissionable materials are very poorly adapted for the purposes of steady energy production, since they do not react at all in subcritical sizes, and lead to an explosion as soon as this critical size is exceeded. Fortunately, however, the fission process possesses one additional feature that permits a comparatively easy control of this primarily explosive nuclear reaction. The point is that, whereas most of the fission neutrons are emitted instantaneously at the moment of nuclear breakup ("prompt neutrons"), a small fraction of them come out from the fission fragments with a considerable delay ("delayed neutrons"). Thus, in the case of uranium fission, 0.7 per cent of the neutrons are emitted with a delay of at least 0.6 sec., and about 0.03 per cent with a delay of more than 1 min. This phenomenon permits adjusting the size of the fissionable sample in such a way that it would be subcritical for prompt neutrons only, and overcritical when the delayed neutrons are also taken into account. It is easy to see that in such a case the development of a nuclear explosion will be comparatively slow, having the same period as the period of the delayed neutron emission. Thus there is an opportunity to control the chain reaction by bringing in some neutron-absorbing substances, called "control rods," before the fission chains develop beyond the danger point. This discussion will be resumed in the last section of this article, under Atomic Power Plants.

PREPARATION OF FISSIONABLE MATERIALS

Separation of U-235. The only natural substance satisfying the condition $\eta\alpha > 1$, which is necessary for the development of a nuclear chain reaction, is the lighter isotope of uranium, U^{235}. In natural conditions, this isotope is always mixed up with a much larger amount (99.3 per cent) of the nonfissionable heavier uranium isotope U^{238}, which prevents the development of a chain reaction in natural uranium. For use as an energy-producing substance, U^{235} must be separated from the heavier isotope, or at least increased in concentration from the original 0.7 per cent to a minimum of about 2 per cent, when the neutron absorption in U^{238} can no longer prevent the chain reaction from going on. Since all the isotopes of a given element possess identical chemical properties, such a separation or enrichment cannot be carried out by conventional chemical methods, and complete reliance must be placed on the physical differences between the isotopes arising from the difference in their atomic weights.

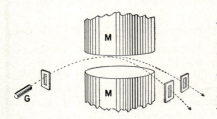

Fig. 4—DIAGRAMMATIC SKETCH OF A CALUTRON. (G) Uranium ion source; and (M) Magnet poles of electromagnet. Dotted lines show path of accelerated uranium ions and splitting of the original beam into two isotopes, U^{238} and U^{235}.

Mass-spectroscopic Method. The most straightforward method of isotope separation is the so-called mass-spectroscopic method, which utilizes the deflection of ion beams of the material in question in strong magnetic fields. This was the method originally used by F. W. Aston for the demonstration of the existence of isotopes and by means of which A. O. Nier was able in 1940 to produce the first portion of pure U^{235} (about 0.000000001 of a gram!) An apparatus known as the calutron has been developed to produce larger quantities of U^{235}. This machine, sketched in Fig. 4, consists of a giant

electromagnet with pole pieces 184 in. in diameter and an air gap of 72 in. between the poles. The beam of uranium ions from the ion source is accelerated by an electric field and enters the space between the magnet poles. Since the heavier atoms of U^{238} are deflected less than the lighter atoms of U^{235}, the beam splits in two, and the lighter isotope can be collected into a container placed near the exit. It must be remembered that, in order to obtain complete isotope separation by such a magnetic separator, it is necessary to use very thin slits, a method that reduces drastically the amount of material thus produced. The use of broad slits increases the efficiency of the apparatus considerably, but at the expense of the purity of the material (overlapping of the two beams).

Statistical Methods. The functioning of electromagnetic separators is based on the action of electromagnetic fields on the individual moving ions in the beams, thus leading to a reasonably complete separation of 235 and 238 isotopes. Another scheme, involving so-called statistical methods, depends upon the average behavior of large groups of atoms with different masses. Although statistical methods are much more efficient in dealing with a large number of individual particles, they lead only to the partial separation of the desired isotopes, and must thus be repeated a great many times if complete separation is desired.

One of these statistical methods, known as the centrifugal method, utilizes the principle often used in industry for separation of two fractions with different density. If a mixture of two substances is placed in a cylindrical vessel and subjected to rapid rotation, the heavier fraction, driven by centrifugal force, will accumulate near the walls of the vessel, whereas the lighter fraction collects closer to the center, as sketched in Fig. 5. However, owing to the small difference between the masses

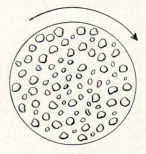

Fig. 5—CENTRIFUGAL METHOD OF SEPARATION OF ISOTOPES OF URANIUM.

of the two uranium isotopes, the difference between the concentrations will be very slight, and to obtain a reasonable separation the centrifuging of natural uranium must be repeated many times.

Another statistical separation method, sketched in Fig. 6, makes use of the process of gaseous diffusion through porous

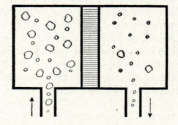

Fig. 6—GASEOUS DIFFUSION METHOD OF SEPARATION OF ISOTOPES OF URANIUM.

walls, and is based on the fact that speed of such diffusion is inversely proportional to the square root of molecular weight. Thus if uranium hexafluoride gas UF_6 is placed under comparatively high pressure on one side of a porous wall, and a vacuum is produced on the other side, the diffusion through the wall of the $U^{238}F_6$ and $U^{235}F_6$ molecules will proceed at different rates. Since the weights of the two molecules involved are 352 and 349, respectively, the ratio of the diffusion rates will be

$$\sqrt{\tfrac{352}{349}} = 1.0043$$

which represents the increase of concentration of the lighter isotope after a single diffusion process. To increase the concentration by a factor of 2, for example, the process must be repeated 160 times, since $(1.0043)^{160} = 2$.

Because of the slowness of the diffusion process, the production of a reasonably large amount of enriched uranium requires giant industrial facilities. At the isotope-separation plant in Oak Ridge, Tenn., which produced fissionable materials for the atomic bomb project, there were 175 large buildings (13,200 workers) devoted to the method of magnetic separation, and a giant four-story building ½ mi. long and ¼ mi. across (25,000 workers) in which the method of gaseous diffusion was used.

Artificial Fissionable Materials. By the magnetic or statistical methods described above for the separation of uranium isotopes, reasonable amounts of fissionable materials can be obtained for the construction of atomic power plants. It must be noted, however, that since uranium itself is a comparatively rare element, and since the lighter isotope forms only 0.7 per cent of natural uranium, the world's supply of U^{235} is rather meager. In fact, it has been estimated that the known uranium ore deposits in the Western Hemisphere contain only enough U^{235} to run United States industry for a few years. From the long-range point of view, then, the atomic power problem would present a rather discouraging prospect if U^{235} were to remain the only fissionable element usable for power production. Fortunately, however, other methods permit the production of much larger amounts of artificial fissionable materials by using only a small amount of natural U^{235}. The first step was the discovery and manufacture of plutonium in the so-called natural uranium piles.

Moderators. As stated above, a nuclear chain reaction involving U^{235} atoms cannot develop in natural uranium because these atoms, being in a small minority (0.7 per cent or $\frac{1}{140}$ of the total amount), have very little chance of capturing fission neutrons before these neutrons are caught by the much more abundant atoms of U^{238}. E. Fermi, however, indicated that the situation can be helped by slowing down the original fission neutrons before they have a chance to collide with other uranium nuclei. In fact, it is known that, in the case of slow neutrons, the nuclei of the light uranium isotope are 140 times more effective in a capture process than are those of the heavy isotope. It is easy to see that the nuclei of U^{235}, being 140 times less abundant and at the same time 140 times more effective in capturing slow neutrons, will now be given an even break in their competition with the U^{238} nuclei. Slowing down of fission neutrons can be accomplished by using natural uranium in the form of comparatively thin rods separated by some material that reduces the speed of neutrons emerging from one such rod before they enter into another. The substances used for the slowing down of fission neutrons, known as moderators, must satisfy certain conditions that limit their choice considerably: they must have a small atomic weight to take away a considerable part of neutron energy in each collision, and they must possess small absorptivity for slow neutrons. The best moderators are carbon, beryllium, and heavy water (deuterium).

Figure 7 is a schematic illustration of the functioning of the moderator in the natural uranium pile. Since in the natural uranium pile of the type described above, the U^{235} nuclei have only about a 50 per cent chance of capturing fission neutrons because of U^{238} competition, and since, on the other hand, the fission of a single U^{235} nucleus gives rise to only about two fission neutrons, the condition "one neutron off-spring per parent," necessary for the development of the chain reaction, can be satisfied here almost on the limit. If the moderating substance captures a few more neutrons than it should, or if a substantial number of neutrons can escape through the surface of the pile, the chain reaction will immediately die out. The fact that the natural uranium pile operates almost on the limit of possibility necessitates the use of extremely pure moderating substances, since a small amount of impurity will quench the reaction. Also, in order to reduce the number of neutrons escaping through the surface, it is necessary to make these piles extremely large, since the ratio of surface to volume decreases with the size of the body. The situation can be considerably improved by the use of uranium

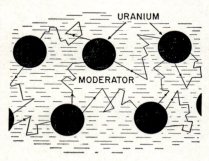

Fig. 7—SCHEMATIC ILLUSTRATION OF FUNCTIONING OF A MODERATOR IN A NATURAL URANIUM PILE.

enriched in its lighter isotope, instead of natural uranium. For example, by increasing the concentration of U^{235} from 0.7 to 2.1 per cent, the chances of neutron capture by the light isotope are increased from 50 to 75 per cent, since the U^{235} nuclei, being now only 40 times less abundant than U^{238} nuclei, are still 140 times more efficient. This condition permits considerably less care concerning the purity of the moderator, and also permits the use of piles of much smaller size. Enriched piles will be discussed further in the next section, in connection with the use of fissionable materials for power production.

Plutonium. Meanwhile, what is the fate of the neutrons which, instead of being captured by the U^{235} nuclei and thus serving for further development of the chain, are captured by the nuclei of the heavier uranium isotope? In this case no fission takes place, and the capture of the neutron results in the formation of still heavier isotope of uranium:

$$_{92}U^{238} + \text{neutron} \rightarrow {}_{92}U^{239}.$$

This, through the successive emission of two electrons, goes over into plutonium:

$$_{92}U^{239} \rightarrow {}_{93}Np^{239} + \text{electron}; \; {}_{93}Np^{239} \rightarrow {}_{94}Pu^{239} + \text{electron}.$$

Plutonium, which can be separated from original uranium by ordinary chemical methods, is an element even more fissionable than U^{235} itself. "More fissionable" means that the nucleus of Pu^{239} requires less activation energy to be broken up into two fragments, and also that the liberated energy as well as the number of neutrons emitted in the fission of the Pu^{239} nucleus is larger than in the case of U^{235}. The above described method of production and separation of Pu^{239} yields large amounts of pure fissionable material, and is in this sense much more convenient than the laborious procedure of isotope separation.

Uranium 233. In the same way that the nonfissionable U^{238} nuclei are transformed into the fissionable Pu^{239} nuclei by means of a chain reaction running in the natural (U^{235}; U^{238}) mixture, new artificial fissionable material can also be produced from another heavy radioactive element known as

Three scientists—representing Canada, Indonesia, and Uruguay—study a Cobalt-60 Therapy Unit displayed by Canada at the Conference.

ATOMS FOR PEACE

(Left) Delegates from seventy-two nations gathered in Geneva for the first International Conference on the Peaceful Uses of Atomic Energy, an outgrowth of President Dwight D. Eisenhower's Atoms for Peace program. Seated on the rostrum for the opening of the Conference are (left to right) Max Petitpierre, President of the Swiss Confederation; United Nations Secretary-General Dag Hammarskjold; Dr. Homi J. Bhabha of India, President of the Conference; and Professor Walter G. Whitman of the United States, Secretary-General of the Conference.

Several nations set up exhibits in the Palais des Nations. A model of an experimental boiling-water power reactor was part of the U.S. exhibit (below left), as was a display showing how atomic plant workers handle radioactive materials by remote-control tongs (below).

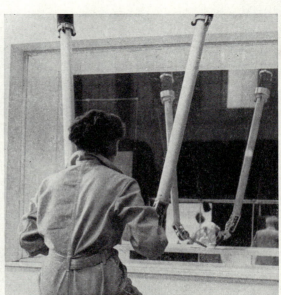

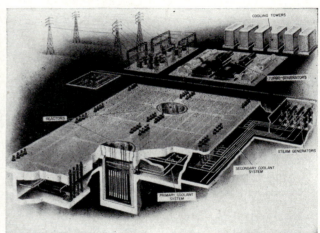

NEW USES OF ATOMIC ENERGY

(Above left) *A Geiger counter detects the arrival of radioactive material in an oil pipeline. The radioactive substance marks a change in the petroleum being transmitted and signals that a valve should be turned to switch the oil following it into the proper tank.*

(Above right) *The power plant pictured in the artist's sketch could produce about 200,000 kilowatts of electricity from atomic fission occurring in nuclear reactors (center and lower center). Heat from the fission process is transferred by liquid sodium through primary and secondary coolant systems to give steam in the steam generators (right). The steam powers turbo-generators (top) which produce the electricity for the power lines (top left).*

(Left) *Radioactive isotopes are employed at Oak Ridge National Laboratory to study the effects of irradiated soil on growing cotton plants.*

Pellets of radioactive iodine are fed to sheep to determine their effect on the thyroid gland, blood constituents, and future generations of the animals. The study was undertaken because stack gases at the Hanford Works in the state of Washington contain small amounts of radioactive iodine which falls into vegetation eaten by the animals there.

thorium. Since, however, natural thorium consists of only one isotope, Th^{232}, which does not possess the property of fission, it must be mixed up with small amounts of some previously produced fissionable substance such as U^{235} or Pu^{239} that will supply the neutrons necessary for such a transformation. In this case, the reaction runs according to the equations:

$$_{90}Th^{232} + neutron \rightarrow {}_{90}Th^{233}; \quad _{90}Th^{233} \rightarrow {}_{91}Pa^{233} + electron;$$
$$_{91}Pa^{233} \rightarrow {}_{92}U^{233} + electron.$$

The newly produced U^{233} isotope, normally nonexistent in nature, can be separated chemically from the original thorium and possesses all the necessary properties of fissionable material. The production of artificial fissionable nuclei Pu^{239} and U^{233} from the nonfissionable nuclei U^{238} and Th^{232} has the advantage that purification can be achieved by ordinary chemical methods, and also increases considerably the prospective supply of fissionable materials. In fact, since in good fissionable materials the number of neutrons per fission is larger than 2, and since only one of these neutrons is needed to continue the chain reaction, more than one extra neutron is left for turning neutral materials into fissionable ones.

For example, if some Pu^{239} or U^{233} is mixed with neutral U^{238} or Th^{232} isotopes, and the slow chain reaction is run in that mixture, larger amounts of fissionable nuclei will come out than were originally put in. This phenomenon opens the way of turning the entire supply of U^{238} and Th^{232} into their fissionable counterparts, Pu^{239} and U^{233}. If, besides U^{235}, available fission-energy sources include energy from the 140 times more abundant U^{238}, and also from thorium, which is three times more abundant in nature than uranium, the estimate must be increased by a factor of 560. This means that, in the case of complete industrial reconversion to atomic energy, there is enough "fuel supply" for at least a few thousand years. It may be also added here that, if worse comes to worse, fissionable elements can be extracted from ordinary materials, not only from rich uranium and thorium deposits. In fact, it is known that plain granite rocks contain 4 g. of uranium and 12 g. of thorium per ton. This seems very little, but it should be remembered that 1 g. of these materials can supply energy equivalent to that of 20 tons of coal. Thus 1 ton of granite rock contains the equivalent of 320 tons of ordinary fuel.

ATOMIC POWER PLANTS

Specifications for Nuclear Reactors. It has been shown that the process of nuclear chain reactions in fissionable materials is of essentially explosive nature, but such a reaction still can be maintained at a steady level by making use of the delayed neutrons, checking the reaction whenever it comes too close to the danger point. Thus, by using the proper control measures, a steady stream of energy can be obtained from a given sample of pure or moderated fissionable material, provided its size is large enough to prevent the escape of too many neutrons through its surface. What is the approximate amount of fissionable material needed for the construction of such a nuclear reactor? In the case of a reactor made from pure (nonmoderated) fissionable material, the chain branches each time the neutron collides with a nucleus standing in its way, since all nuclei forming the material are fissionable. Thus the length of each link of the chain is simply equal to the "free path" of fast neutrons, which in the case of heavy elements is known to be about 3 cm. Simple geometrical considerations show that, in order to have the chain develop completely within the sample of fissionable material, the diameter of the sample must be about three times larger than a link of the chain. Thus the critical diameter of a sample of pure fissionable material must be equal to about 10 cm. Its total volume will

be 500 cm.^{3}, and its weight (taking 20 for density of heavy elements) about 10 kg., or 22 lb.

In the case of a moderated reactor, the fission neutrons having an original energy of about one million electron volts are slowed down to thermal energies ($\frac{1}{40}$ electron volts) by collisions with moderating nuclei. The number of collisions required is the least for materials of low atomic weight, ranging from 17, in the case of hydrogen, to more than 100 for elements heavier than carbon. Since the possibility of a neutron escaping from the surface of the reactor increases with the required number of collisions, low atomic weight materials make the best moderators.

The use of a moderator takes advantage of the fact that fissionable nuclei are much more effective in capturing slow, or thermal, neutrons, than fast neutrons. Thus, the minimum requirement of fissionable material in a moderated reactor is considerably less than in the case of a fast reactor, being of the order of 1 kg. In systems of different fissionable materials (U^{235}, U^{233}, Pu^{239}) and different types of moderators (H_2O, D_2O, Be, C), the minimum requirement of fissionable material is roughly the same order of magnitude.

Although the minimum requirement is low, moderated reactors of practical significance often require amounts of fissionable material considerably in excess of the 1 kg. mentioned above. This is particularly true in reactors fueled with natural uranium, in which U-235 and U-238 compete on roughly equal terms for the capture of neutrons. In addition, amounts of fissionable material often have to be added to offset the absorption of neutrons by structural material and other substances in the reactor. The properties of some typical nuclear reactors are given as follows:

Reactor Designation	Fuel	Moderator	Diameter
North Carolina State..	U-235 (1 kg.)	H_2O (15 kg.)	1 ft.
Low Power Research (NAA)	{ 50% U-235 { 50% U-238	C (4 tons)	5 ft.
Norwegian	nat U (2 tons)	D_2O (7 tons)	7 ft.
Oak Ridge Graphite (X-10)	nat U (50 tons)	C (250 tons)	24 ft.

The above reactor dimensions apply only to the fuel-containing portion, or reactor core. It is usually advantageous to place a moderating material around the core to reflect neutrons which normally would escape. By reducing neutron leakage, the use of a reflector results in a considerable saving in fissionable material. The addition of such a reflector, however, plus a shield to protect personnel from radiation, increases the over-all diameter of even the smallest reactor to more than 10 ft.

Atomic reactors constructed according to the principles described above can be operated at any desirable temperature lower than the melting points of the materials used, and will supply a steady stream of heat which can then be transformed into mechanical work. Thus the heat developed in the reactor can be used to heat water or some other "working fluid," for the purpose of running a turbomotor, as in the closed-cycle turboengines of Fig. 8. For aircraft propulsion, the heat of the atomic reactor can be used to heat air, which is then ejected from the rear pipe, producing a powerful thrust, "jet propulsion," as in Fig. 9. It must be noticed, however, that the above-described simple solid-block reactor has too small an external surface to satisfy the necessary conditions for sufficiently rapid heat transfer from the reactor's body to the working fluid, so that it becomes necessary to drill a number of channels running through its entire body.

The system of such channels running through the body of the reactor necessitates the increase of its total size in order to satisfy the conditions necessary for a chain reaction. If, for example, the channels occupy 50 per cent of the reactor's

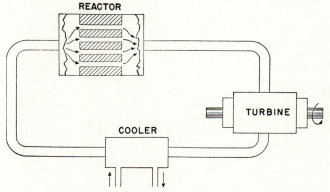

Fig. 8—ATOMIC REACTOR USED TO OPERATE A TURBINE.

volume, the mean free path of neutrons in the body of the reactor will be doubled. Therefore its linear dimension must be doubled and its volume increased by a factor of 8. Since, however, half of that volume is occupied by the channels, the total weight of the reactor, as well as the amount of fissionable material needed, increases only by a factor of 4. A reactor with 90 per cent channeling and only one-tenth solid material would

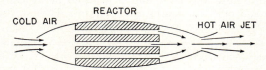

Fig. 9—ATOMIC REACTOR APPLIED TO AIRCRAFT PROPULSION.

be 10 times larger in all directions and would weigh 100 times more than the simple solid block.

Shielding Problem. In using atomic energy for propelling various types of vehicles, the most serious problem is the protection of crew and passengers from the powerful radiation emitted in any nuclear reaction. This radiation, consisting mostly of hard gamma rays and streams of fast neutrons, possesses very strong penetrative power through any type of material, and requires thick layers of protective shielding. For example, consider a large transport aircraft, which requires engine power of the order of 100,000 hp. or 75,000 kw. From the well-known data concerning the intensity of gamma radiation which accompanies the fission process, a reactor powering such an aircraft will emit radiation amounting to 3,000 roentgens per second at a distance of 10 meters. A person exposed to this radiation will receive a lethal dose within a fraction of a second. Since the usually accepted radiation tolerance amounts to 0.05 roentgen per day, or 10^{-6} roentgens per second, the radiation coming from the reactor must be reduced by a factor of 3.10^9. It is known that radiation intensity is halved by passing through 2 cm. of lead, from which it follows that the total number N of "2-cm. thicknesses" is determined by the equation $2^N = 3.10^9$. This yields $N = 30$, so that the total thickness of shielding material becomes about 0.6 meter or about 2 ft. The total weight of such lead shielding will run up to 1,000 tons, as compared with only a few tons for the weight of the reactor itself. In stationary power plants and in ship propulsion, the weight of additional shielding does not lead to any difficulties; in the latter case the reactor and

the motor can simply be surrounded by water-filled compartments. But the problem becomes serious in the case of aircraft. In fact, the weight of a properly shielded atomic-power motor will permit its use only for very large aircraft, somewhat larger than the biggest transport planes now in use. Of course, light unshielded reactors can be used in small, unmanned robot planes; in this case, however, the ionization of the surrounding air produced by the powerful radiation coming out of the reactor will make it difficult for radio signals to get through to the plane.

Space Ships. The most interesting problem arising from the possibility of liberating atomic energy is that of a space ship that can travel through empty space to the moon and even to the various planets. The only way of traveling through empty space lies in the employment of the rocket principle, which requires the use of some material heated by the atomic reactor and then ejected at high speed from a nozzle located at the rear of the vehicle, as sketched in Fig. 10. The necessity of carrying along the substance to be used for the jet reduces considerably the effectiveness of atomic-powered rockets, making them comparable with ordinary rockets, like the German V-2, which also have to carry along their own fuel. Thus,

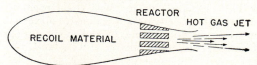

Fig. 10—ATOMIC REACTOR EMPLOYED IN A ROCKET.

under the most favorable conditions, the atomic-propelled rocket can hardly be expected to be more than a few times better than a good conventional rocket. Even this limited improvement, however, may be of great importance in the space-rocket problem. In fact, it is known that the best chemical rocket fuels fall short by a factor of only a few units from communicating to the rocket the speed of 11 km. per second necessary to escape from the gravity of the earth. Of course the problem can still be solved by using the so-called step rocket consisting of several conventional rockets of gradually decreasing size, which are shot consecutively from one another during the flight. In this case, however, the first step rocket may have to be as big as a battleship in order to enable a rather small last step rocket to get out into space. If the use of atomic power will permit the improvement of rocket properties only by a factor of 2 or 3, escape from the earth's gravity can be made in one single step. However, just as with aircraft, the problem of the space rocket becomes much more difficult if it is to be manned, since then the huge weight of the necessary radiation shielding must be added. Moreover, it must not be supposed that, once the rocket had escaped from the gravity of the earth, it can travel unhindered all around the solar system. In fact, a rocket going out with a speed of 11 km. per second (thus escaping from the earth's surface) will remain bound to the earth's orbit around the sun. This condition would not prevent a trip to the moon, but for a trip to Mars, Venus, and other planets, the rocket would have to be fast enough to escape the gravitational force of the sun, which would mean an additional velocity of 42 km. per second. This rate, however, seems to lie outside the possibilities of atomic-powered rockets carrying their own exhaust material. The only way of building a rocket that would travel freely between the planets lies in getting rid of the exhaust-material method, utilizing directly the recoil of the particles produced in nuclear fission, and this method may well be beyond the realm of possibility.

G. G. and J. A. L.

ATOMIC NUMBER, the ordinal number of a chemical element in the periodic table. It was first shown by J. A. R. Newlands in 1865, and independently but much more completely by D. I. Mendelyeev in 1869, that if the elements are arranged in order of their atomic weights a striking periodicity is observed in which certain characteristic properties repeat themselves among the elements at definite intervals. The arrangement of the elements in this manner, with three slight exceptions, is known as the periodic table. The exceptions are the pairs potassium and argon, nickel and cobalt, and iodine and tellurium; for these pairs the correct periodic arrangement requires a reversal of the atomic weights, which in these cases differ by less than one unit.

The fundamental significance of the atomic number was first realized by H. G. J. Moseley, who studied the frequencies, i.e., reciprocal of wave lengths, of the characteristic X rays produced by a number of elements. He found that these frequencies are usually related in a very simple manner to the atomic numbers, although there is no such relationship between the frequencies and the atomic weights. In 1913 Moseley and A. van den Broek suggested that the atomic number of an element is equal to the net positive charge carried by the atomic nucleus. This theory was verified by J. Chadwick in 1920, from observations on the scattering of alpha particles, as a result of their passage through thin sheets of various metals. The alpha particles are known to carry two unit positive charges; and, by supposing that their scattering is due to electrical repulsion by the positively charged nuclei of the metal atoms, the charge of the latter could be calculated. The results obtained in a number of cases were identical, within experimental limits, with the known atomic numbers. It may thus be regarded as established that the atomic number of an element is equal to the number of unit positive charges in the nucleus, and hence to its number of protons. All isotopes of a given element carry the same nuclear charge, and hence have the same atomic number; in fact the name "isotope" was meant to imply that the elements occupied the same position in the periodic table. *See also* PERIODIC TABLE. S. Gl.

ATOMIC STRUCTURE, that branch of physics which deals with the arrangement and distribution of the elementary particles within the atom, such as electrons, protons, and neutrons. The structure of an atom is not to be regarded as a static affair but as a dynamic one, in which the elementary particles undergo energy changes either spontaneously or as the result of the interaction of the atom with external fields and particles. It is these energy changes which yield the greatest amount of information concerning the structure of atoms. Some of the energy changes occur during chemical reactions; hence chemistry supplies some information on atomic structure. Other types of energy changes accompany the emission and absorption of electromagnetic radiation; a great deal of information can therefore be obtained from the study of spectroscopy, both optical and X ray. Some energy changes result in the spontaneous emission of charged particles with a consequent change in the chemical nature of the atom, the so-called radioactive disintegration; evidence from the field of radioactivity will therefore be needed to obtain knowledge of the structure of the atom.

The subject of atomic structure is thus not an independent branch of physics but depends for its data largely upon work done in many other fields of physics and to some extent upon chemistry. A detailed discussion of basic theories, experiments, laws, and hypotheses governing the behavior of the component parts of the atom is presented in the following.

ATOMIC THEORY

Early Theories. The concept of atoms can be traced back to Leucippus and Democritus, two Greek philosophers of the fifth century B.C. It remained merely a philosophical concept without any experimental foundation until early in the nineteenth century. The word "atom" means indivisible, and until late in the nineteenth century it was used to designate the smallest indivisible particles of a substance. The atomic theory of matter as propounded by the Greek atomists was that all matter was composed of tiny indivisible atoms. Aristotle (384-322 B.C.), one of the greatest of the early scientists, did not accept the atomic theory. Since Aristotle's philosophy and science were accepted by the theologians of the later Middle Ages, the atomic theory remained dormant and was not revived in scientific speculations until after the Renaissance. Both Robert Boyle (1627-1691) and Sir Isaac Newton (1642-1727) used atomic theories in their speculations in chemistry and physics.

The scientific theory of atoms can be said to begin with the work of John Dalton (1766-1844), who in 1803 first formulated an atomic theory to explain the properties of gases, and in 1808 used the atomic theory to account for the formation of compounds from elements. Dalton used the term "atom" in a general sense, as the ultimate particle of an element or a compound. Dalton's work was extended by Jöns Jakob Berzelius (1779-1848), who made accurate determinations of the combining weights of elements and discovered many new elements.

Dalton's Laws. Dalton formulated two chemical laws which are at the basis of atomic theory. The first is the law of multiple proportions, which states that if two elements combine in more than one proportion to form different compounds, the weights of one of the elements which will unite with identical amounts of the second element are in the ratio of small integral numbers. For example, 16 grams of oxygen combine with 2.016 grams of hydrogen to form water (H_2O), whereas 32 grams of oxygen combine with 2.016 grams of hydrogen to form another compound, hydrogen peroxide (H_2O_2). Hence the weights of the oxygen in these two compounds which combine with equal amounts of hydrogen are in the ratio of 2:1. The second law is the law of definite proportions, which states that in any compound, the proportion by weight of the constituent elements is a constant.

Avogadro's Hypothesis. An extremely important hypothesis was advanced in 1811 by Amadeo Avogadro (1776-1856), who based his work upon the study of chemical reactions among gases by J. L. Gay-Lussac (1778-1850). In 1808 Gay-Lussac found that simple numerical relations exist between the volumes of the gases taking part in a chemical reaction. For example, 2 liters of hydrogen combine with 1 liter of oxygen to form 2 liters of water vapor. Also, 1 liter of hydrogen combines with 1 liter of chlorine to form 2 liters of hydrogen chloride. Using these results as a basis, Avogadro put forth the hypothesis that equal volumes of gases under the same conditions of temperature and pressure contain equal numbers of molecules. The term "molecule" is used here instead of "atom" to designate the smallest particle of a compound or of an element in the free state.

The above results can now be interpreted as follows: when 2 liters of hydrogen combine with 1 liter of oxygen to form 2 liters of water vapor, then two molecules of hydrogen and one molecule of oxygen combine to form two molecules of water vapor. This statement is expressed in the form of a chemical equation as follows:

$$2\,H_2 + O_2 \rightleftarrows 2\,H_2O.$$

In the second case mentioned above, the interpretation is that one molecule of chlorine combines with one molecule of hy-

TABLE I. DISTRIBUTION OF ELECTRONS IN THE ATOMS

X-Ray Notation			K	L		M			N				
Values of n, l			1, 0	2, 0	2, 1	3, 0	3,1	3, 2	4, 0	4, 1	4, 2	4, 3	
Spectral Notation			1s	2s	2p	3s	3p	3d	4s	4p	4d	4f	
Element	Atomic Number Z	First Ionization Potential in Volts											Lowest Spectral Term
H	1	13.529	1										$^2S_{1/2}$
He	2	24.465	2										$^1S_0$
Li	3	5.37	2	1									$^2S_{1/2}$
Be	4	9.281	2	2									$^1S_0$
B	5	8.28	2	2	1								$^2P_{1/2}$
C	6	11.217	2	2	2								$^3P_0$
N	7	14.48	2	2	3								$^4S_{3/2}$
O	8	13.550	2	2	4								$^3P_2$
F	9	18.6	2	2	5								$^2P_{3/2}$
Ne	10	21.47	2	2	6								$^1S_0$
Na	11	5.12	Neon configuration			1							$^2S_{1/2}$
Mg	12	7.61	10 electron core			2							$^1S_0$
Al	13	5.96				2	1						$^2P_{1/2}$
Si	14	8.12				2	2						$^3P_0$
P	15	10.9				2	3						$^4S_{3/2}$
S	16	10.3				2	4						$^3P_2$
Cl	17	12.96				2	5						$^2P_{3/2}$
A	18	15.69				2	6						$^1S_0$
K	19	4.32	Argon configuration						1				$^2S_{1/2}$
Ca	20	6.09	18 electron core						2				$^1S_0$
Sc	21	6.7						1	2				$^2D_{3/2}$
Ti	22	6.81						2	2				$^3F_2$
V	23	6.76						3	2				$^4F_{3/2}$
Cr	24	6.74						5	1				$^7S_3$
Mn	25	7.41						5	2				$^6S_{5/2}$
Fe	26	7.83						6	2				$^5D_4$
Co	27	8.5						7	2				$^4F_{9/2}$
Ni	28	7.606						8	2				$^3F_4$
Cu	29	7.68						10	1				$^2S_{1/2}$
Zn	30	9.36						10	2				$^1S_0$
Ga	31	5.97						10	2	1			$^2P_{1/2}$
Ge	32	8.09						10	2	2			$^3P_0$
As	33	10.						10	2	3			$^4S_{3/2}$
Se	34	9.5						10	2	4			$^3P_2$
Br	35	11.80						10	2	5			$^2P_{3/2}$
Kr	36	13.940						10	2	6			$^1S_0$

drogen to form two molecules of hydrogen chloride, thus:

$$H_2 + Cl_2 \rightleftarrows 2\ HCl.$$

The chemical symbols in the above equations also express the fact that in the free state a molecule of hydrogen, H_2, a molecule of oxygen, O_2, and a molecule of chlorine, Cl_2, consist of two atoms each; that is, they are diatomic molecules. Hydrogen chloride, HCl, is also composed of diatomic molecules, whereas water vapor, H_2O, is composed of triatomic molecules.

Atomic Weights. The relative weights of the elements in any compound can be found by chemical analyses; and since the atoms of elements combine in the ratio of small integral numbers, it is a comparatively straightforward process to assign a series of numbers to express the relative weights of the atoms of the elements. In modern chemistry the atomic weights of all elements are based upon the assignment of the number of 16.0000 for the atomic weight of oxygen. For example, it is known that 16 grams of oxygen combine with 2.016 grams of hydrogen to form 18.016 grams of water vapor. Since a molecule of water vapor contains one atom of oxygen and two atoms of hydrogen, the atomic weight of hydrogen is 2.016/2, or 1.008. The chemical atomic weights of the elements are listed in the Periodic Table (*q.v.*). These atomic weights are averages of the best experimental determinations; they are reviewed periodically and changed whenever necessary by the Committee on Atomic Weights of the International Union of Chemistry.

The term "chemical system of atomic weights" is used in order to differentiate it from another system, the physical system of atomic masses.

The Avogadro Number. Avogadro's hypothesis that equal volumes of gases at the same conditions of temperature and pressure have equal numbers of molecules has been amply verified by a variety of experiments, and the number of molecules in a given volume has been determined from the results of experiments on Brownian motion, black-body radiation, X-ray crystal structure analysis, and electrolysis. Of particular interest here is the relationship of the Avogadro hypothesis to atomic structure. Since the atomic weight of oxygen is 16.0000 and a molecule of oxygen in the free state consists of two atoms, the molecular weight of oxygen is 32.0000. The system of molecular weights is a set of numbers which express the molecular weights of elements and compounds relative to oxygen=32.0000 as the standard. Thirty-two grams of oxygen

TABLE I. DISTRIBUTION OF ELECTRONS IN THE ATOMS (*Continued*)

X-Ray Notation		K	L	M	N				O					P						Lowest Spectral Term
Values of n,l		1 1,0	2 0,1	3 0,1,2	4,0	4,1	4,2	4,3	5,0	5,1	5,2	5,3	5,4	6,0	6,1	6,2	6,3	6,4	6,5	
Spectral Notation		$1s$	s,p	s,p,d	$4s$	$4p$	$4d$	$4f$	$5s$	$5p$	$5d$	$5f$	$5g$	$6s$	$6p$	$6d$	$6f$	$6g$	$6h$	
Element	Atomic Number Z	First Ionization Potential in Volts																		
Rb	37	4.159	Krypton configuration							1											$^2S_{1/2}$
Sr	38	5.667								2											$^1S_0$
Y	39	6.5						1		2											$^2D_{3/2}$
Zr	40	6.92						2		2											$^3F_2$
Cb	41	—						4		1											^6D
Mo	42	7.35	36 electron core					5		1											$^7S_3$
Tc	43	—						6		1											$^6D_{9/2}$
Ru	44	7.7						7		1											$^5F_5$
Rh	45	7.7						8		1											$^4F_{9/2}$
Pd	46	8.3						10													$^1S_0$
Ag	47	7.54	Palladium configuration							1											$^2S_{1/2}$
Cd	48	8.96								2											$^1S_0$
In	49	5.76								2	1										$^2P_{1/2}$
Sn	50	7.30								2	2										$^3P_0$
Sb	51	8.5								2	3										$^4S_{3/2}$
Te	52	8.96	46 electron core							2	4										$^3P_2$
I	53	10.6								2	5										$^2P_{3/2}$
Xe	54	12.078								2	6										$^1S_0$
Cs	55	3.87	Xenon configuration												1						$^2S_{1/2}$
Ba	56	5.19	54 electron core												2						$^1S_0$
La	57	5.6	Shells $1s$ to $4d$ contain 46 electrons							2	6	1			2						$^2D_{3/2}$
Ce	58	6.54							1	2	6	1			2						$^3H_4$
Pr	59								2	2	6	1			2						$^4K_{11/2}$
Nd	60								3	2	6	1			2						$^5L_6$
Il	61								4	2	6	1			2						$^6L_{9/2}$
Sm	62								5	2	6	1			2						$^7F_0$
Eu	63	5.64							6	2	6	1			2						$^8S_{7/2}$
Gd	64	6.16							7	2	6	1			2						$^9D_2$
Tb	65								8	2	6	1			2						$^8H_{17/2}$
Dy	66								9	2	6	1			2						$^7K_{10}$
Ho	67								10	2	6	1			2						$^6L_{19/2}$
Er	68								11	2	6	1			2						$^5L_{10}$
Tm	69								13	2	6	0			2						$^2F_{7/2}$
Yb	70								14	2	6	0			2						$^1S_0$
Lu	71								14	2	6	1			2						$^2D_{3/2}$

occupy a volume of 22.4 liters at 0° C. and 76 cm. of mercury pressure. This volume is called the gram-molecular volume. The weight of a substance, in grams, equal numerically to its molecular weight, is called a mole. On the basis of Avogadro's hypothesis, a mole of any substance, either element or compound, contains the same number of molecules. This number is called the Avogadro number and will be denoted by the letter N.

Since N represents the number of molecules in a mole of an element, it must also represent the number of atoms in a gram-atomic weight of the element. In the case of elements with monatomic molecules, such as helium, neon, and argon, the atomic weight and molecular weight are identical; hence there are N atoms in a gram-atomic weight of such an element. In the case of elements with diatomic molecules, such as oxygen, hydrogen, and chlorine, the atomic weight is half the molecular weight; a gram-atomic weight of such an element thus contains $N/2$ molecules; but since each molecule consists of two atoms, there are N atoms in a gram-atomic weight of this type of element. This argument can be extended to all elements. Hence the Avogadro number N is the number of atoms in a gram-atomic weight of an element.

One of the best methods of determining the Avogadro number is from the data of electrolysis. The quantity of charge that must be transferred through an electrolytic solution to liberate a gram-atomic weight of a monovalent element, or an equivalent weight (atomic weight divided by valence) of any other element, is a constant and is called the faraday (F). Accurate measurements of the faraday yield the value

$$F = \frac{9{,}652.01 \text{ electromagnetic units (e.m.u.) of charge}}{\text{gram-atomic weight (physical scale)}}$$

Since each ion of a monovalent element carries a charge e equivalent to that of one electron and since there are N atoms in a gram-atomic weight, the total charge carried through the electrolyte by a gram-atomic weight of the element is Ne, or

$$F = Ne$$

In 1949 the accepted value of the electronic charge was

$$e = 4.8029 \times 10^{-10} \text{ electrostatic units (e.s.u.) of charge.}$$

If this value is converted to electromagnetic units of charge by dividing by the speed of light, then

$$e = 1.6021 \times 10^{-20} \text{ electromagnetic units (e.m.u.) of charge.}$$

If these values are substituted in the above equation, the resultant equation is

TABLE I. DISTRIBUTION OF ELECTRONS IN THE ATOMS (*Concluded*)

X-Ray Notation		K	L	M	N	O					P						Q		
Values of n, l		1	2	3	4	5,0	5,1	5,2	5,3	5,4	6,0	6,1	6,2	6,3	6,4	6,5	7,0	7,1	
Spectral Notation						5s	5p	5d	5f	5g	6s	6p	6d	6f	6g	6h	7s	7p	
Element	Atomic Number Z	First Ionization Potential in Volts																	Lowest Spectral Term
Hf	72								2			2								F_2
Ta	73		Shells						3			2								$F_{3/2}$
W	74	7.94	1s to 5p						4			2								D_0
Re	75		contain						5			2								$S_{5/2}$
Os	76		68 electrons						6			2								D_4
Ir	77								7			2								$F_{9/2}$
Pt	78	8.9							9			1								D_3
Au	79	9.2							10			1								$S_{1/2}$
Hg	80	10.38										2								S_0
Tl	81	6.07	Shells									2	1							$P_{1/2}$
Pb	82	7.38	1s to 5d									2	2							P_0
Bi	83	8.0	contain									2	3							$S_{3/2}$
Po	84		78 electrons									2	4							P_2
At	85											2	5							$^2P_{3/2}$
Rn	86	10.69										2	6							$^1S_0$
Fr	87											2	6					1		$^2S_{1/2}$
Ra	88											2	6					2		$^1S_0$
Ac	89											2	6	1				2		$^2D_{3/2}$
Th	90											2	6	2				2		$^3F_2$
Pa	91									2		2	6	1				2		$^4F_{3/2}$
U	92									3		2	6	1				2		$^5D_0$
Np	93									4		2	6	1				2		—
Pu	94									5		2	6	1				2		—
Am	95									6		2	6	1				2		—
Cm	96									7		2	6	1				2		—

$N = \mathrm{F}/e = 6.0247 \times 10^{23}$ atoms/gram-atomic weight. This is the accepted value of the Avogadro number.

Periodic Table. In the early days of the atomic theory, chemists sought some relationship between the atomic weights and the chemical properties of the elements. D. I. Mendeleev (1834–1907) discovered a periodicity in the chemical properties of the elements when they were arranged in the ascending order of atomic weights. In 1869 he produced a tabular arrangement of the elements in which those with similar chemical properties were put in the same vertical column; this arrangement has since become known as the periodic table. Some places in this table had to be left vacant, with the assumption that they would ultimately be filled by the discovery of the missing elements. One advantage of the periodic table was that the probable chemical properties of the missing elements could be inferred from the positions of the vacant spaces. Many of the elements missing in 1869 were discovered shortly afterward, and their chemical properties were found to be substantially those predicted. In 1955 there were 101 known elements, the last nine of which having been produced during atomic energy research from 1940 to 1955.

The positions of the elements in the periodic table have acted as a guide in the study of atomic structure on the assumption that elements with similar chemical properties should present certain similarities in the structure of their atoms. It will be shown that the chemical properties of an element are determined principally by the arrangement of the outer electrons of their atoms (*see* Table I).

Atomic Number. The atomic number of an element was originally used to represent its ordinal number when the elements were arranged in the order of increasing atomic weights, with numbers assigned to those elements which were still missing from the periodic table. Several discrepancies in this order baffled chemists for a long time, because there were pairs of elements in which the one with the larger atomic weight required the lower atomic number in order to fit into the periodic table. Tellurium, for example, has a larger atomic weight than iodine, but according to its chemical properties tellurium belongs to Group VI with oxygen, and should have a lower atomic number than iodine, which belongs in Group VII with fluorine.

Rutherford-Bohr Theory. This discrepancy was cleared up only after Rutherford advanced his theory of the nuclear structure of the atom in 1911. According to this theory, an atom is assumed to consist of a very small positively charged nucleus surrounded by a number of negatively charged electrons comparatively far removed from the nucleus. Since under ordinary conditions the atom is electrically neutral, the total positive charge of the nucleus is equal to the total negative charge carried by the electrons of a neutral atom. By a series of careful experiments on the scattering of alpha particles by nuclei (*see* section on The Nuclear Atom, below), Rutherford and his co-workers were able to show that the positive charge of a nucleus is equal to Ze, where Z is the atomic number of the element and e is the electronic charge. This idea was further confirmed in a series of experiments by H. G. J. Moseley in 1913 on the X-ray spectra of the elements (*see* section on Arrangement and Distribution of Electrons in Atoms, below). In 1913 Niels Bohr adopted the Rutherford nuclear theory of the atom in his explanation of the optical spectrum of hydrogen (*see* section on The Hydrogen Atom, below) and then extended this to explain the electronic structure of the heavier elements. According to this theory, a hydrogen atom consists of a positively charged nucleus, called a proton, and a single negative electron moving in some orbit about the proton. The Rutherford-Bohr theory of the structure of the atom, suitably modified by subsequent experiment and theory, remained in 1955 the accepted theory of the structure of the atom.

On the basis of the above experiments, the atomic number of an element designates the total number of electrons outside the nucleus of a neutral atom and also the total number of protons in the nucleus, since each proton has a charge equivalent to that of an electron.

THE ELECTRON

Discovery. The modern theory of the structure of the atom dates from the discovery of the electron by J. J. Thomson in 1897. The passage of electric currents through gases had been studied for some time prior to this, and it was known that, at very low pressures, charged particles came from the cathode, or negative terminal, in the tube. Thomson showed that these cathode rays, as they were called, are electrons. He measured the ratio of the charge e to the mass m of these cathode rays by deflecting them in electric and magnetic fields, and showed that all electrons have the same value of e/m no matter what their origin. In 1955 the accepted value of e/m was

$$e/m = 1.75888 \times 10^7 \text{ e.m.u./gram.}$$

The Millikan Oil-Drop Experiment. There were many early attempts to measure the charge of the electron. J. J. Thomson in 1898 and H. A. Wilson in 1903 succeeded in getting the right order of magnitude for the charge, but R. A. Millikan was the first to make an accurate determination of it. He developed the famous oil-drop experiment, in which a very small drop of oil was allowed to move in the air between the two horizontal plates of a capacitor. With no electric field on, the drop would fall with a uniform velocity v, which, according to Stokes' law, was proportional to the weight of the oil drop. When a difference of potential was applied to the plates of the capacitor, the velocity of the oil drop would change because of the additional force on it due to the electric field acting on the charge on the oil drop. The velocity of the oil drop was measured by timing its passage between two parallel cross hairs in a viewing telescope. The same oil drop could be observed for hours. Every once in a while its velocity would change abruptly, indicating that the charge on it had changed, because it had acquired an ion, either positive or negative, from the air through which it was moving. The air between the capacitor plates was sometimes ionized by the passage of X rays through it, or by allowing radiations from radioactive material to pass through it.

From these measurements, Millikan computed the changes in the charge, that is, the charges acquired or lost by the oil drop, and showed that the charge q, positive or negative, acquired or lost by the oil drop could be represented by

$$q = ne,$$

where n is an integer and e is the elementary charge equivalent to that of an electron. The value of e determined by Millikan in 1917 was 4.77×10^{-10} e.s.u. Its value as accepted in 1955 was

$$e = 4.80288 \times 10^{-10} \text{ e.s.u.}$$

THE DIVISIBLE ATOM

The discovery of the electron by J. J. Thomson in 1897, the discovery of X rays by W. C. Roentgen in 1895, and the discovery of natural radioactivity by Henri Becquerel in 1896 led to the abandonment of the concept of the indivisible atom and to the formulation of a new concept in which the atom consisted of positive and negative charges. The experiments initiated by these three discoveries led to the development of the modern nuclear theory of the atom.

Radioactivity Phenomena. Of particular interest is the light that is shed on the structure of the atom by the phenomena associated with radioactivity. The radiations emitted by radioactive elements have comparatively high energies and have been used as projectiles to disrupt other atoms. The modern nuclear theory of the atom arose from experiments in

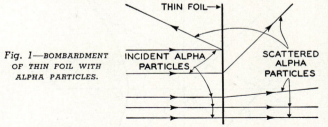

Fig. 1—BOMBARDMENT OF THIN FOIL WITH ALPHA PARTICLES.

which positively charged alpha particles shot out by radioactive particles were directed against thin foils; it was found that most alpha particles went straight through the foil with practically no deviations from their original paths (*see* Fig. 1). Some alpha particles were scattered through small angles. Occasionally some were scattered in the backward direction. The only plausible explanation for this behavior is that matter consists mostly of empty space, since most of the incident alpha particles go straight through the thin foils. The electric charges within the atoms must be very small in comparison with the size of the atom. Moreover, in order to account for the occasional backward scattering of an alpha particle, the positive charges of an atom must all be concentrated in a very small nucleus, since only when there is a very close approach between the incident alpha particle and a positively charged atomic nucleus will there be a sufficiently strong electric field to produce a large-angle deviation of the alpha-particle path.

THE NUCLEAR ATOM

Single Scattering of Alpha Particles. Guided by the experiments on the scattering of alpha particles, in 1911 Rutherford pictured a neutral atom as consisting of a very small, massive, positively charged nucleus of charge Ze, and Z electrons at comparatively great distances from the nucleus. Z is the atomic number of the element and e is the electronic charge. To establish the existence of the nuclear atom, Rutherford developed the theory of the single scattering of alpha particles by atomic nuclei and then inaugurated a series of experiments to verify the results of the theory. These were performed in his laboratory by Abraham Geiger, Ernest Marsden, and James Chadwick.

In developing this theory, Rutherford assumed that Coulomb's law held for the force F between the nucleus of charge Ze and the alpha particle of charge E, so that at a distance r from each other the force of repulsion would be

$$F = \frac{ZeE}{r^2}.$$

If the experiment is performed by directing the alpha particles against thin foils of the heavy elements, such as gold and platinum, then the nucleus may be considered stationary at some point C (*see* Fig. 2). Since the force varies inversely as the square of the distance between the particles, the path of the alpha particle must be a conic section; and since the force is one of repulsion, the path must be a hyperbola. In Fig. 2, AB represents the original direction of motion of the alpha particle, and p is the distance from the nucleus to this line. The alpha particle is projected toward the nucleus along the line *AB* and is deflected through an angle θ so that when it leaves the region of the nucleus it is traveling along the line *OD*. *AB* and *OD* are the asymptotes of the hyperbolic orbit of the alpha particle whose distance of closest approach to the nucleus is *CG*. The solution of the problem of motion under an inverse

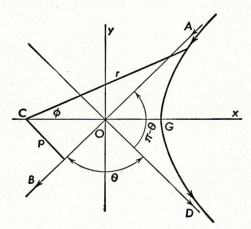

Fig. 2—PATH OF ALPHA PARTICLE IN A NUCLEAR FIELD

square law is well known, and only the results will be stated here. The eccentricity of the hyperbolic orbit of the alpha particle is

$$\epsilon = \sqrt{1 + \left(\frac{MV^2 p}{ZeE}\right)^2},$$

where M is the mass of the alpha particle and V is its initial speed. The angle of scattering θ is given by the equation

$$\cot \frac{\theta}{2} = \frac{MV^2}{ZeE} p.$$

Alpha particles will be scattered through an angle equal to or greater than θ if their original line of motion comes within a distance p of a nucleus. The probability that an alpha particle will be deflected through an angle equal to or greater than θ can be determined by imagining each nucleus surrounded by a sphere of radius p. If the stream of alpha particles is directed normally against the area A of the foil, and the thickness t is sufficiently small so that an alpha particle is scattered by one nucleus only, then the nuclei in the foil can be treated as having cross-sectional areas πp^2. If there are n atoms per unit volume of the foil, there will be ntA nuclei presenting an effective scattering area of $\pi p^2 ntA$ to the incident alpha particles. The probability f that an alpha particle will be scattered through an angle equal to or greater than θ will be the ratio of the area $\pi p^2 ntA$ to the total area A of the foil, or

$$f = \pi p^2 nt$$
$$= \pi nt \left(\frac{ZeE}{MV^2}\right)^2 \cot^2 \frac{\theta}{2}.$$

The probability that an alpha particle will be scattered through any angle whose value lies between θ and $\theta + d\theta$ is, therefore,

$$df = \pi nt \left(\frac{ZeE}{MV^2}\right)^2 \cot \frac{\theta}{2} \csc^2 \frac{\theta}{2} \, d\theta.$$

In the experiments of Geiger and Marsden, the alpha particles which were deflected through an angle were allowed to strike a fluorescent screen normally and the alpha particles were detected by the scintillations they produced on the screen. If Q alpha particles per unit time are directed against the foil, the number N per unit time deflected through an angle lying between θ and $\theta + d\theta$ is

$$N = Q \frac{nt(Ze)^2 E^2}{4r^2 (MV^2)^2 \sin^4 \frac{\theta}{2}},$$

in which r is the distance of the fluorescent screen from the foil.

The conclusions implied in the above equation were amply verified in a series of experiments on the scattering of alpha particles in which each of the quantities t, V, θ, and Z were varied in turn, the other quantities being held constant in the experiment. For example, it was shown that within the limits of error of the experiment, N varied directly with the thickness t of foil used, the other quantities being held constant. Also, N varied directly with $(Ze)^2$ with the other quantities held constant. The following table gives the results of Chadwick's experiments with copper, silver, and platinum foils as the scatterers:

Element	Nuclear Charge Ze	Atomic Number Z
Cu	29.3e	29
Ag	46.3e	47
Pt	77.4e	78

The results of the experiments on the scattering of alpha particles can be used to determine the radii of the scattering nuclei from the determination of the distance of closest approach, *GC*, in Fig. 2. In some experiments scattered alpha particles were observed at an angle of 150 deg. For the case of gold nuclei, $GC = 3.2 \times 10^{-12}$ cm.; for silver nuclei, $GC = 2 \times 10^{-12}$ cm. Since the alpha particle itself is the nucleus of helium, the distance *GC* may be considered as the distance between the centers of the two nuclei during a collision. The above distances therefore represent the upper limits to the radii of the respective nuclei.

These experiments laid the foundation for the modern theory of the atom as consisting of a very small, massive nucleus of charge Ze surrounded by Z electrons.

ISOTOPES

Dalton, in developing his atomic theory of the elements, introduced the hypothesis that the atoms of any one element are identical in all respects, including that of weight. Others suggested that the atoms need not be identical in weight and that the chemical atomic weights represent average values of the weights of the atoms of the particular elements. In 1815 William Prout put forth the hypothesis that all elements are composed of hydrogen atoms. This condition would mean that the atomic weights of the elements should have integral values based on 1 which is the atomic weight of hydrogen. At the time Prout presented his hypothesis, the atomic weights were known only to the nearest integer. More accurate determinations, however, showed that the atomic weights are not integral numbers relative to that of hydrogen. In the latter half of the nineteenth century, Prout's hypothesis was abandoned in favor of Dalton's. The discovery of radioactivity by Henri Becquerel in 1896 and the subsequent discovery and the analysis of the many radioactive elements, particularly by Pierre Curie, Marie Curie, Rutherford, and Frederick Soddy, made it apparent that there are many elements near the end of the periodic table, formed in the process of radioactive disintegration, that have identical chemical properties but different atomic weights. Several elements are identical with lead, others with bismuth, others with thallium, and so on. This means that such elements within one group must occupy the same position in the periodic table of elements. For example, the radioactive elements that are identical with lead and must occupy the same place as lead in the periodic table are the following:

Element	Atomic Weight
Radium B	214
Radium D	210
Radium G	206
Thorium B	212
Thorium D	208
Actinium B	211
Actinium D	207

(The atomic weight of lead is 207.21.)

In 1910 Soddy suggested the name "isotopes" for those elements which occupy the same place in the periodic table.

Concept of Whole Numbers. The fact that several elements have atomic weights that differ considerably from integral numbers suggested the idea that these elements also consist of isotopes whose individual atomic weights are whole numbers and that the atomic weight as determined by chemical means is a weighted average of these whole numbers. The concept of whole numbers has played an important role in atomic physics.

Positive Ray Analysis. The first investigation of the existence of isotopes among the nonradioactive elements was made by J. J. Thomson, who in 1910 investigated the element neon, the lightest element whose atomic weight, 20.2, differs appreciably from an integral number. The method consisted of allowing the positive ions of neon which were produced in a gas-discharge tube to pass simultaneously through parallel electric and magnetic fields in a highly evacuated tube. The ions were deflected by these fields, and after leaving them, the ions continued along the tube until they reached a photographic plate at the end of the tube. All the ions which had the same value of e/m, that is, ratio of charge to mass, struck the plate at some point along a common parabola. On examining the photographic plate, Thomson found two parabolas, one corresponding to a mass of 20 and the other to a mass of 22, showing the existence of two isotopes of neon. Several other elements were analyzed by this method and shown to consist of two or more isotopes. This method is known as positive ray analysis.

Mass Spectrographs. Thomson's method, though capable of showing the existence of isotopes, was not sufficiently accurate for the precise determination of the masses of these isotopes. F. W. Aston, working in Thomson's laboratory, redesigned the instrument so that it could be used for the precise determination of the masses of the isotopes and their relative abundance in a given sample of material. This type of instrument has come to be known as a mass spectrograph. Other mass spectrographs of somewhat different designs were developed in the United States by A. J. Dempster, K. T. Bainbridge, A. O. Nier, and others, and by J. J. Mattauch in Germany. All these instruments depend essentially upon the determination of e/m of positive ions of the element under investigation by deflecting these ions through one or more electric and magnetic fields. The mass spectrograph developed by Bainbridge and Jordan is shown in Fig. 3a, and two typical mass spectrograms obtained with this instrument are shown in the two photographs, or spectrograms (Figs. 3b and 3c), which give an idea of its resolving power.

The results of the investigations with mass spectrographs have shown that about 280 different isotopes are found in nature; their atomic weights differ slightly from whole numbers ranging from 1 to 238. A list of the stable isotopes and their relative abundance is given in Table II. It will be noted that most elements have more than one stable isotope, and it is

of great importance that oxygen, which is the standard for the determination of the chemical system of atomic weights, has three stable isotopes. Physicists have developed a new table of atomic masses in which to express the masses of the isotopes.

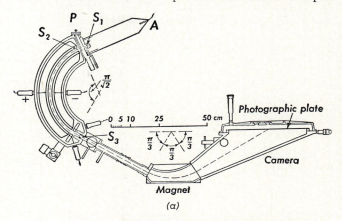

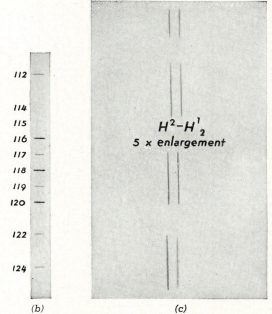

Fig. 3—MASS SPECTROGRAPH AND TYPICAL SPECTROGRAMS

(a) Mass spectrograph developed by Bainbridge and Jordan: (A) Gas discharge tube; (S_1, S_2, S_3) Slits.
(b) Spectrogram of ten isotopes of tin with mass numbers ranging from 112 to 124.
(c) Spectrogram of the ions of deuterium, H^2, and molecular hydrogen H^1_2.

This scale is known as the physical scale of atomic masses and uses the lightest isotope of stable oxygen of mass 16.0000 as the standard. Isotopic masses are shown in Table III.

Mass Number of an Isotope. A glance at Table III shows that the atomic mass of every isotope is almost an integral number. The term "mass number" is used to designate the integer nearest the value of the atomic mass of the isotope; this is represented by the letter A. Two particles of nuclear size are known, each of which has a mass very close to 1; these are the proton, which is the nucleus of the hydrogen isotope of mass number 1, and the neutron, an electrically neutral particle first discovered by Chadwick in 1932 in his experiments on artificial nuclear disintegration.

Table II. Stable Isotopes

Atomic No.	Atom	Mass No.	Relative Abundance (%)
1	H	1	99.98
	H	2	0.02
2	He	4	100.
3	Li	6	7.5
	Li	7	92.5
4	Be	9	100.
5	B	10	18.4
	B	11	81.6
6	C	12	98.9
	C	13	1.1
7	N	14	99.62
	N	15	0.38
8	O	16	99.76
	O	17	0.04
	O	18	0.20
9	F	19	100.
10	Ne	20	90.00
	Ne	21	0.27
	Ne	22	9.73
11	Na	23	100.
12	Mg	24	77.4
	Mg	25	11.5
	Mg	26	11.1
13	Al	27	100.
14	Si	28	89.6
	Si	29	6.2
	Si	30	4.2
15	P	31	100.
16	S	32	95.1
	S	33	0.74
	S	34	4.2
17	Cl	35	75.4
	Cl	37	24.6
18	A	36	0.307
	A	38	0.061
	A	40	99.632
19	K	39	93.38
	K	40	0.012
	K	41	6.61
20	Ca	40	96.96
	Ca	42	0.64
	Ca	43	0.15
	Ca	44	2.06
21	Sc	45	100.
22	Ti	46	7.95
	Ti	47	7.75
	Ti	48	73.45
	Ti	49	5.51
	Ti	50	5.34
23	V	51	100.
24	Cr	50	4.49
	Cr	52	83.78
	Cr	53	9.43
	Cr	54	2.30
25	Mn	55	100.
26	Fe	54	6.04
	Fe	56	91.57
	Fe	57	2.11
	Fe	58	0.28
27	Co	59	100.
28	Ni	58	67.4
	Ni	60	26.7
	Ni	61	1.2
	Ni	62	3.8
	Ni	64	0.9
29	Cu	63	70.13
	Cu	65	29.87
30	Zn	64	50.9
	Zn	66	27.3
	Zn	67	3.9
	Zn	68	17.4
	Zn	70	0.5
31	Ga	69	61.2
	Ga	71	38.8
32	Ge	70	21.2
	Ge	72	27.3
	Ge	73	7.9
	Ge	74	37.1
	Ge	76	6.5
33	As	75	100.
34	Se	74	0.9
	Se	76	9.5
	Se	77	8.3
	Se	78	24.0
	Se	80	48.0
	Se	82	9.3
35	Br	79	50.6
	Br	81	49.4
36	Kr	78	0.35
	Kr	80	2.01
	Kr	82	11.53
	Kr	83	11.53
	Kr	84	57.11
	Kr	86	17.47
37	Rb	85	72.8
	Rb	87	27.2
38	Sr	84	0.56
	Sr	86	9.86
	Sr	87	7.02
	Sr	88	82.56
39	Y	89	100.
40	Zr	90	48.
	Zr	91	11.5
	Zr	92	22.
	Zr	94	17.
	Zr	96	1.5
41	Cb	93	100.
42	Mo	92	14.9
	Mo	94	9.4
	Mo	95	16.1
	Mo	96	16.6
	Mo	97	9.65
	Mo	98	24.1
	Mo	100	9.25
44	Ru	96	5.68
	Ru	98	2.22
	Ru	99	12.81
	Ru	100	12.70
	Ru	101	16.98
	Ru	102	31.34
	Ru	104	18.27
45	Rh	103	100.
46	Pd	102	0.8
	Pd	104	9.3
	Pd	105	22.6
	Pd	106	27.2
	Pd	108	26.8
	Pd	110	13.5
47	Ag	107	51.9
	Ag	109	48.1
48	Cd	106	1.4
	Cd	108	1.0
	Cd	110	12.8
	Cd	111	13.0
	Cd	112	24.2
	Cd	113	12.3
	Cd	114	28.0
	Cd	116	7.3
49	In	113	4.5
	In	115	95.5
50	Sn	112	1.1
	Sn	114	0.8
	Sn	115	0.4
	Sn	116	15.5
	Sn	117	9.1
	Sn	118	22.5
	Sn	119	9.8
	Sn	120	28.5
	Sn	122	5.5
	Sn	124	6.8
51	Sb	121	56.
	Sb	123	44.
52	Te	120	< 1.
	Te	122	2.9
	Te	123	1.6
	Te	124	4.5
	Te	125	6.0
	Te	126	19.0
	Te	128	32.8
	Te	130	33.1
53	I	127	100.
54	Xe	124	0.094
	Xe	126	0.088
	Xe	128	1.90
	Xe	129	26.23
	Xe	130	4.07
54	Xe	131	21.17
	Xe	132	26.96
	Xe	134	10.54
	Xe	136	8.95
55	Cs	133	100.
56	Ba	130	0.101
	Ba	132	0.097
	Ba	134	2.42
	Ba	135	6.59
	Ba	136	7.81
	Ba	137	11.32
	Ba	138	71.66
57	La	139	100.
58	Ce	136	< 1.
	Ce	138	< 1.
	Ce	140	89.
	Ce	142	11.
59	Pr	141	100.
60	Nd	142	26.95
	Nd	143	13.0
	Nd	144	22.6
	Nd	145	9.2
	Nd	146	16.5
	Nd	148	6.8
	Nd	150	5.95
62	Sm	144	3.
	Sm	147	17.
	Sm	148	14.
	Sm	149	15.
	Sm	150	5.
	Sm	152	26.
	Sm	154	20.
63	Eu	151	49.1
	Eu	153	50.9
64	Gd	152	0.2
	Gd	154	2.86
	Gd	155	15.61
	Gd	156	20.59
	Gd	157	16.42
	Gd	158	23.45
	Gd	160	20.87
65	Tb	159	100.
66	Dy	158	0.1
	Dy	160	1.5
	Dy	161	22.
	Dy	162	24.
	Dy	163	24.
	Dy	164	28.
67	Ho	165	100.
68	Er	162	0.1
	Er	164	1.5
	Er	166	32.9
	Er	167	24.4
	Er	168	26.9
	Er	170	14.2
69	Tm	169	100.
70	Yb	168	0.06
	Yb	170	4.21
	Yb	171	14.26
	Yb	172	21.49
	Yb	173	17.02
	Yb	174	29.58
	Yb	176	13.38
71	Lu	175	97.5
	Lu	176	2.5
72	Hf	174	0.18
	Hf	176	5.30
	Hf	177	18.47
	Hf	178	27.13
	Hf	179	13.85
	Hf	180	35.14
73	Ta	181	100.
74	W	180	0.2
	W	182	22.6
	W	183	17.3
	W	184	30.1
	W	186	29.8
75	Re	185	38.2
	Re	187	61.8
76	Os	184	0.018
	Os	186	1.59
	Os	187	1.64
	Os	188	13.3
	Os	189	16.1
	Os	190	26.4
	Os	192	41.0
77	Ir	191	38.5
	Ir	193	61.5
78	Pt	192	0.8
	Pt	194	30.2
	Pt	195	35.3
	Pt	196	26.6
	Pt	198	7.2
79	Au	197	100.
80	Hg	196	0.15
	Hg	198	10.1
	Hg	199	17.0
	Hg	200	23.3
	Hg	201	13.2
	Hg	202	29.6
	Hg	204	6.7
81	Tl	203	29.1
	Tl	205	70.9
82	Pb	204	1.5
	Pb	206	23.6
	Pb	207	22.6
	Pb	208	52.3
83	Bi	209	100.
90	Th	232	100.
92	U	234	0.006
	U	235	0.71
	U	238	99.28

TABLE III. ISOTOPIC MASSES

Atomic No.	Atom	Mass No.	Mass	Atomic No.	Atom	Mass No.	Mass
1	H	1	1.00813	15	P	30	29.9885
	H	2	2.01473		P	31	30.98441
	H	3	3.01700		P	32	31.98436
2	He	3	3.01699	16	S	31	30.98965
	He	4	4.00386		S	32	31.98252
	He	5	5.01543		S	33	32.98200
	He	6	6.0209		S	34	33.97981
3	Li	6	6.01692	17	Cl	33	32.9875
	Li	7	7.01816		Cl	34	33.981
	Li	8	8.02497		Cl	35	34.9807
4	Be	7	7.01909		Cl	36	35.9799
	Be	8	8.00781		Cl	37	36.9777
	Be	9	9.01496		Cl	38	37.9800
	Be	10	10.01662	18	A	35	34.9865
5	B	9	9.01610		A	36	35.9792
	B	10	10.01617		A	38	37.97473
	B	11	11.01290		A	40	39.97459
	B	12	12.0168		A	41	40.97740
6	C	10	10.02086	19	K	41	40.9731
	C	11	11.01502	20	Ca	45	44.97075
	C	12	12.00388	21	Sc	45	44.96977
	C	13	13.00756		Sc	46	45.96909
	C	14	14.00774	22	Ti	48	47.96580
7	N	13	13.00990	23	Va	51	50.96035
	N	14	14.00753		Va	52	51.95857
	N	15	15.00487	24	Cr	52	51.948
	N	16	16.00645	26	Fe	56	55.9571
8	O	15	15.0078	28	Ni	58	57.942
	O	16	16.000000	30	Zn	64	63.935
	O	17	17.00450	33	As	75	74.934
	O	18	18.00485	34	Se	80	79.941
9	F	17	17.00758	35	Br	79	78.929
	F	18	18.00670		Br	81	80.926
	F	19	19.00454	36	Kr	78	77.926
	F	20	20.00654		Kr	80	79.926
10	Ne	19	19.00798		Kr	82	81.927
	Ne	20	19.99889		Kr	83	82.927
	Ne	21	21.00002		Kr	84	83.928
	Ne	22	21.99858		Kr	86	85.929
11	Na	22	22.00032	41	Cb	93	92.926
	Na	23	22.99644	42	Mo	98	97.946
	Na	24	23.99774		Mo	100	99.945
12	Mg	23	23.00055	50	Sn	120	119.912
	Mg	24	23.99300	52	Te	126	125.937
	Mg	25	24.99462	52	Te	128	127.936
	Mg	26	25.99012	53	I	127	126.932
	Mg	27	26.99256	54	Xe	134	133.929
13	Al	26	25.99446	55	Cs	133	132.933
	Al	27	26.99069	56	Ba	138	137.916
	Al	28	27.99077	73	Ta	181	180.927
	Al	29	28.9890	74	W	184	184.00
14	Si	27	26.99711	75	Re	187	186.981
	Si	28	27.98727	76	Os	190	189.981
	Si	29	28.98635		Os	192	191.981
	Si	30	29.98399	80	Hg	200	200.016
	Si	31	30.9866	81	Tl	203	203.036
15	P	29	28.9135		Tl	205	205.037

of any one element differ only in the number of neutrons they contain.

These two numbers, the atomic number Z and mass number A, completely identify the individual atoms. However, since there are chemical symbols in common use for the elements, a convention has been adopted for identifying the different isotopes by combining the numbers with the chemical symbol. The atomic number Z is written as a subscript at the lower left of the chemical symbol and the mass number A is written as a superscript on the upper right of this symbol; e.g., $_8O^{16}$, $_8O^{17}$, $_8O^{18}$ are the symbols used to represent the three stable isotopes of oxygen of mass numbers 16, 17, and 18. The atomic number of oxygen is 8.

Mass Defect. The atomic masses of the isotopes differ only slightly from whole numbers. The difference between the atomic mass M of any isotope and its mass number A is called the mass defect and is represented by the symbol Δ (delta); thus

$$\Delta = M - A.$$

The mass defect may be either positive, negative, or zero. As will be shown later, the mass defect has an important bearing on the binding energy of the particles in the nucleus.

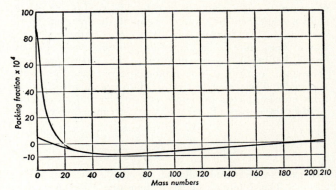

Fig. 4—PACKING FRACTIONS FOR STABLE ISOTOPES.

Packing Fraction. Another term useful in discussing nuclear energy changes, introduced by Aston, is the packing fraction P. It is defined by the equation

$$P = \frac{\Delta}{A} = \frac{M\text{-}A}{A}.$$

The packing fraction represents the mass defect per nuclear particle. Fig. 4 shows the packing fraction plotted against mass number for the stable isotopes. It will be observed that the packing fractions of isotopes whose mass numbers lie between 20 and 200 have small negative values; the packing fractions are positive for isotopes of mass numbers greater than 200 and less than 20. The packing fractions have large positive values for most of the light elements with the exception of $_2He^4$, $_6C^{12}$, and $_8O^{16}$. The packing fraction of $_8O^{16}$ is zero by definition.

Atomic-Mass Units. The physical scale of atomic masses is based on the assignment of 16.0000 for the atomic mass of $_8O^{16}$. The unit of atomic mass is one-sixteenth of an atom of $_8O^{16}$. This very convenient unit in atomic physics is denoted as 1 atomic-mass unit (a.m.u.). To convert atomic-mass units into grams, it is necessary only to remember that the Avogadro number is the number of atoms in a gram-atomic mass of an isotope, so that

$$1 \text{ a.m.u.} = \frac{1}{N} = \frac{1}{6.0247 \times 10^{23}} \text{grams} = 1.66 \times 10^{-24} \text{ grams.}$$

The mass of an electron is known independently from the determinations of the electronic charge $e = 4.8029 \times 10^{-10}$

Nuclear Constitution: Atomic Number and Mass Number. Two important integers are used to denote an atom of an element. The atomic number Z denotes the number of protons in the nucleus and also the number of electrons outside the nucleus of the neutral atom.

The accepted view concerning the constitution of the nucleus is that the nucleus of an atom consists of protons and neutrons and that the mass number A represents the total number of particles in the nucleus. Since the atomic number Z represents the number of protons in the nucleus, A − Z is the number of neutrons in the nucleus. The isotopes of any one element all have the same atomic number but have different mass numbers. This means that the nuclei of the isotopes e.s.u., and the specific electronic charge $e/m = 1.75888 \times 10^7$ e.m.u./gram, which, with $c = 2.99793 \times 10^{10}$ cm./sec., yields for the electronic mass,

$$m = 9.1085 \times 10^{-28} \text{ gram}$$
or
$$m = 0.000549 \text{ a.m.u.}$$

The mass of a hydrogen atom is

$$M_H = 1.00813 \text{ a.m.u.}$$
or
$$M_H = 1.664 \times 10^{-24} \text{ gram.}$$

Since a hydrogen atom of mass number 1 consists of a positively charged nucleus, the proton, and an electron outside the nucleus, the mass of a proton is

$$M_p = 1.00758 \text{ a.m.u.}$$
$$= 1.662 \times 10^{-24} \text{ gram.}$$

The ratio of the mass of the proton to that of the electron is about 1,840:1. The masses of all other isotopes can be expressed either in atomic mass units or converted into grams as above. The value of atomic mass of any isotope given in Table III is the sum of the masses of the nuclei and electrons in a.m.u.

Equivalence of Mass and Energy. From the values of the atomic masses listed in Table III, it is obvious that the atomic mass of an isotope is less than the sum of the masses of its protons, neutrons, and electrons in the free state. Since the mass of the electron is so small, its contribution to the atomic mass may be neglected in this discussion. For example, hydrogen of mass number 2, $_1H^2$, sometimes called deuterium, consists of one proton and one neutron in the nucleus, and one electron outside the nucleus. Hydrogen of mass number 1 consists simply of a proton and an electron. Adding the masses of $_1H^1$ and the neutron $_0n^1$ gives

$$_1H^1 = 1.00813$$
$$_0n^1 = \underline{1.00893}$$
$$2.01706$$

whereas the measured value of the atomic mass of $_1H^2$ is 2.01473. The difference between these two values is 0.00233 a.m.u. Similar results can be obtained for all other nuclei.

The difference in mass between the particles in the free state and the particles in the nucleus of an atom can be accounted for by using the principle of equivalence of mass and energy, first developed by Albert Einstein in 1905 as one of the consequences of the special theory of relativity. This principle states that mass and energy are equivalent to each other; it has the effect of enlarging the principle of conservation of energy to include mass as one form of energy. There are many different units for expressing energy, such as ergs, joules, calories, and kilowatt-hours; since mass and energy are equivalent, mass units can also be used for expressing quantities of energy. The conversion factor between mass units and energy units was derived by Einstein and takes the following form: when the mass m is expressed in grams and the energy $\mathcal{E}$ is expressed in ergs, the relationship between them is

$$\mathcal{E} = mc^2,$$

where c is the speed of light in centimeters per second. For most calculations it will be convenient to use

$$c = 3 \times 10^{10} \frac{\text{cm.}}{\text{sec.}}$$

A gram of mass is equivalent to

$$\mathcal{E} = 1 \text{ gram} \times 9 \times 10^{20} \frac{\text{cm}^2}{\text{sec}^2}$$
$$= 9 \times 10^{20} \text{ ergs}$$
$$= 9 \times 10^{13} \text{ joules}$$
$$= 25 \times 10^6 \text{ kw.-hr.}$$

Matter is thus simply a highly concentrated form of energy.

Means can be found to convert matter into energy, and conversely, energy can be converted into matter.

Binding Energy. To return to the immediate problem of the mass defect of atomic nuclei, it is evident that the difference between the mass of an atomic nucleus and the sum of the masses of its constituent particles in the free state must have been released in some other form of energy in the process or processes of formation of the nucleus. This decrease in mass, or the mass defect, represents the binding energy of the particles in the nucleus. The binding energy of a neutron and a proton in a deuterium nucleus is thus 0.00233 a.m.u.

It will be convenient at this stage to list a few conversion factors for the various energy units commonly used in atomic physics. It has been shown that

$$1 \text{ gram} = 9 \times 10^{20} \text{ ergs.}$$
Since
$$1 \text{ a.m.u.} = 1.66 \times 10^{-24} \text{ gram,}$$
$$1 \text{ a.m.u.} = 1.49 \times 10^{-3} \text{ ergs.}$$

Electron Volt. Another common energy unit is the electron volt, which is the kinetic energy required by an electron when it is accelerated in an electric field produced by a difference of potential of one volt. Since the work done upon an electron of charge e when moved through a difference of potential V is Ve,

$$1 \text{ electron volt} = 1 \text{ ev.} = 1.60 \times 10^{-12} \text{ erg,}$$
$$1,000 \text{ electron volts} = 1 \text{ kev.} = 1.60 \times 10^{-9} \text{ erg,}$$
$$1 \text{ million electron volts} = 1 \text{ Mev.} = 1.60 \times 10^{-6} \text{ erg.}$$

The conversion factor for a.m.u. to Mev. is

$$1 \text{ a.m.u.} = 931.04 \text{ Mev.}$$

The mass m of an electron, for example, is 9.1055×10^{-28} gram. When expressed in energy units this becomes

$$m = 8.18 \times 10^{-7} \text{ erg}$$
$$= 0.512 \text{ Mev.}$$
$$= 0.00055 \text{ a.m.u.}$$

Disintegration of the Deuteron. It was shown above that the binding energy of a neutron and proton in a deuterium nucleus is 0.00233 a.m.u. Using the conversion factor 1 a.m.u. = 931.04 Mev., this binding energy becomes 2.17 Mev. One interpretation of this result is that if an experiment is to be performed to distintegrate the deuteron, that is, the nucleus of deuterium, then an amount of energy at least equal to 2.17 Mev. will have to be supplied to the deuteron. One such experiment was performed by Chadwick and Goldhaber, who used the gamma rays from thorium C″, which have an energy of 2.62 Mev. The difference between these two values, 2.62−2.17, or 0.45 Mev., represents the kinetic energies of the neutron and proton which are separated in this disintegration process. The reaction which takes place can be written in the form of an equation as follows:

$$_1H^2 + h\nu \rightarrow (_1H^2) \rightarrow {}_1H^1 + {}_0n^1,$$

in which h is Planck's constant, ν the frequency of the gamma ray, and $h\nu$ the energy of the gamma-ray photon. The symbol $(_1H^2)$ represents the excited state of the deuteron that has absorbed the gamma-ray photon, just prior to its disintegration into a proton and a neutron.

The above reaction has also been produced with gamma rays from RaC with an energy of only 2.198 Mev., just slightly above the binding energy.

THE HYDROGEN ATOM

Structure. The structure of the hydrogen atom and the relationship of this structure to the emission and absorption of energy was worked out in great detail by Niels Bohr in 1913. Using Rutherford's nuclear theory of the atom, Bohr assumed that hydrogen, of mass number 1 and atomic number 1, consists of a single proton of charge Ze with $Z = 1$, and a single electron of charge $-e$ moving in a circular orbit with the nucleus at its center. Since the mass M of the nucleus is about 1,840 times the mass m of the electron, the nucleus may be considered stationary, at least to a first approximation.

Assuming Coulomb's law to hold, the force of attraction F between the proton and the electron is

$$F = \frac{e^2}{r^2}, \qquad (1)$$

where r is the radius of the circular orbit. F is also the centrifugal force which acts on the electron (which has an acceleration

$$a = \frac{v^2}{r} \qquad (2)$$

toward the center of the circle), so that

$$F = \frac{mv^2}{r}. \qquad (3)$$

Equating these two expressions for F yields

$$mv^2 = \frac{e^2}{r}, \qquad (4)$$

so that the kinetic energy of the electron becomes

$$\tfrac{1}{2}\,mv^2 = \tfrac{1}{2}\,\frac{e^2}{r}. \qquad (5)$$

The potential at a distance r from a positive charge $+e$ is e/r in a Coulomb field of force; hence the potential energy of the electron of charge $-e$ at a distance r from the proton is $-e^2/r$. The total energy $\mathcal{E}$ of the electron is therefore

$$\mathcal{E} = \tfrac{1}{2}\,\frac{e^2}{r} - \frac{e^2}{r} = -\tfrac{1}{2}\,\frac{e^2}{r}. \qquad (6)$$

It will be noted that the zero level of energy is taken at $r = \infty$, that is, when the atom is ionized by the removal of the electron from the field of force of the proton. As the electron moves toward the proton, the energy of the system becomes smaller, since $\mathcal{E}$ is negative. This result means that energy is given out by the system when the electron moves toward the proton and that energy must be supplied to the system to move the electron away from the nucleus. One mode of energy exchange is in the emission and absorption of radiation.

Spectrum. The spectrum of hydrogen is well known; it consists of a series of very sharp lines of definite wave lengths. Empirical relationships have been obtained among these wave lengths, particularly by Balmer in 1885 and by Rydberg in 1889. Expressed in modern notation, Balmer's equation becomes

$$\frac{1}{\lambda} = \bar{v} = R_H \left(\frac{1}{2^2} - \frac{1}{n^2} \right), \text{ where } n = 3, 4, 5 \ldots, \quad (7)$$

in which λ is the wave length of a spectral line; $\bar{v}$, the reciprocal of the wave length, is the wave number of this spectral line; n is an integer greater than 2; and R_H is an empirical constant known as the Rydberg constant for hydrogen. Its value is

$$R_H = 109,677.76 \text{ cm.}^{-1}. \qquad (8)$$

Substitution of different integers for n yields the wave numbers of those spectral lines of hydrogen which form the Balmer series. Several of the lines are in the visible spectrum (*see* Fig. 5). Most of the others in this series are in the ultraviolet portion of the spectrum; they crowd together toward the series limit, for which $n = \infty$ and $\bar{v} = R_H/4 = 27,419.44$ cm.$^{-1}$

Bohr's Postulates. In order to explain the emission of the sharp spectral lines, Bohr introduced two fundamental postulates. The first postulate states that of all possible electron orbits only those are permissible for which the angular momentum of the electon is a whole multiple of $h/2\pi$, where h is the Planck constant. Further, as long as the electron remains in such an orbit it does not radiate any energy; energy is radiated only when the electron goes from one permissible

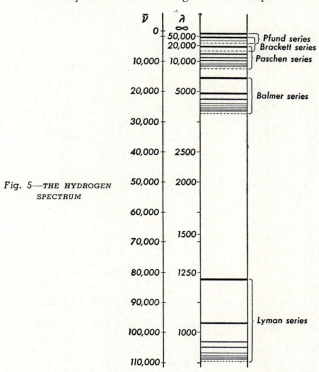

Fig. 5—THE HYDROGEN SPECTRUM

orbit to another. The second postulate states that whenever radiant energy is emitted or absorbed by an atom, the energy is emitted or absorbed in whole quanta, each of amount $h\nu$, where ν is the frequency of the radiation.

The first postulate leads to the equation

$$mvr = n\,\frac{h}{2\pi} \qquad (9)$$

in which mvr is the angular momentum of an electron moving with velocity v in a circle of radius r, and n is an integer, called the quantum number. Orbits which satisfy Eq. (9) are sometimes referred to as stationary orbits.

Bohr's second postulate leads to the equation

$$\mathcal{E}_i - \mathcal{E}_f = h\nu \qquad (10)$$

in which $\mathcal{E}_i$ is the energy in the initial stationary orbit and $\mathcal{E}_f$ is the energy in the final stationary orbit, and ν is the frequency of the radiation which is either emitted or absorbed, depending upon whether $\mathcal{E}_i$ is greater or less than $\mathcal{E}_f$.

The radii of the permissible orbits can be obtained by eliminating v from Eqs. (5) and (9), yielding

$$r = n^2\,\frac{h^2}{4\pi^2 m e^2}. \qquad (11)$$

The quantities h, m, and e are known physical constants hence the radius of any stationary orbit can be computed by assigning the appropriate value to n. For example, when $n = 1$,

$$r_1 = \frac{h^2}{4\pi^2 m e^2} = 0.529 \times 10^{-8} \text{ cm.} = 0.529\text{Å}. \qquad (12)$$

This is the radius of the first and smallest stationary orbit. Since the radius of the proton is about 2×10^{-13} cm., the radius of the first Bohr orbit is more than 10,000 times the radius of the hydrogen nucleus.

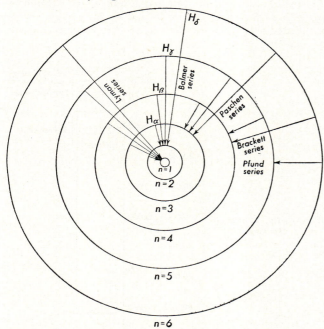

Fig. 6—STATIONARY ORBITS FOR AN ELECTRON

The radius of any other orbit of quantum number n is

$$r_n = n^2 r_1. \qquad (13)$$

That is, the radii of the stationary orbits vary as the square of the quantum number n (see Fig. 6).

The energy $\mathcal{E}_n$ of the electron, when it is in a stationary orbit of quantum number n, can be obtained by substituting the value of r from Eq. (11) into Eq. (6), obtaining

$$\mathcal{E}_n = -\frac{2\pi^2 m e^4}{n^2 h^2}. \qquad (14)$$

Using Bohr's second postulate, the frequency of the radiation emitted or absorbed when an electron goes from an initial orbit n_i to a final orbit n_f is

$$\nu = \frac{\mathcal{E}_i - \mathcal{E}_f}{h}. \qquad (15)$$

Substituting the appropriate values for $\mathcal{E}_i$ and $\mathcal{E}_f$ from Eq. (14), the frequency of the radiation can be expressed as

$$\nu = \frac{2\pi^2 m e^4}{h^3}\left(\frac{1}{n_f^2} - \frac{1}{n_i^2}\right). \qquad (16)$$

The frequency ν is related to the wave length λ by the equation

$$\nu = \frac{c}{\lambda} = c\bar{\nu}.$$

Hence $$\bar{\nu} = \frac{2\pi^2 m e^4}{ch^3}\left(\frac{1}{n_f^2} - \frac{1}{n_i^2}\right). \qquad (17)$$

Eq. (17) has exactly the same mathematical form as Eq. (7) for the Balmer series of spectral lines. These two will become identical with assignment of the following values:

$$n_f = 2, \qquad n_i = n, \qquad R_H = 2\pi^2 m e^4/ch^3.$$

The values of m, e, c, and h are known from other data, although not with the same precision as R_H. Substituting these known values yields

$$\frac{2\pi^2 m e^4}{ch^3} = 109{,}740 \text{ cm.}^{-1},$$

in good agreement with the value of R_H.

Quantum Number. Fig. 6 shows the stationary orbits for small values of the quantum number n; the nucleus, not shown, is assumed to be at the center. On the Bohr model, an electron may be in any one of the stationary orbits; under normal conditions it would be in the orbit of least energy, that is, the one for which $n = 1$. To get the electron into an orbit of larger quantum number, and hence higher energy, requires the addition of energy to the atom. This may be done by shining light of the proper frequency ν on it, by bombarding the hydrogen atom with electrons, or by raising the temperature of the hydrogen gas so that a sufficient amount of energy may be transferred to some atoms during collisions with other atoms. Atoms may also be raised to higher energy states by the passage of an electric current through a tube containing hydrogen at a low pressure. Some of the atoms are ionized and some of the ions recombine with electrons while the current is maintained in the tube.

The Balmer series of lines is emitted whenever the hydrogen atoms have been excited to high energy states for which $n > 2$, and return to the energy state for which $n = 2$. For example, the red line of the hydrogen spectrum, known as the H_a line, is emitted when the atom goes from an initial state $n_i = 3$ to the final state $n_f = 2$, and similarly for the other lines of the Balmer series.

The Bohr theory led to the prediction of the existence of other series of spectral lines in the ultraviolet and infrared regions. Lyman discovered the ultraviolet series, which is produced when the excited atoms go to the final state $n_f = 1$. L. C. Paschen found a series of lines in the infrared region produced by atoms that go from excited states for which $n_i > 3$ to the state $n_f = 3$.

Modifications of the Bohr Theory. Further details on the spectrum of hydrogen and the successes and limitations of the Bohr theory will be found in the article on Spectroscopy. A few important modifications of the original Bohr theory will be discussed here because of their importance to the subject of atomic structure.

One of the assumptions in the above theory is that the nucleus is at rest, which would be correct only if its mass were infinite. Since its mass M is finite, both the nucleus and the electron rotate about a common center of mass with a common angular velocity. The effect of this rotation is to make a slight change in the expression for the energy of the atom in any given quantum state. The expression for the energy now becomes

$$\mathcal{E} = -\frac{2\pi^2 \mu e^4}{h^2}\left(\frac{1}{n^2}\right), \qquad (18)$$

and the expression for the wave numbers of the spectral lines becomes

$$\bar{\nu} = \frac{2\pi^2 \mu e^4}{ch^3}\left(\frac{1}{n_f^2} - \frac{1}{n_i^2}\right), \qquad (19)$$

in which $$\mu = \frac{mM}{m+M} = \frac{m}{1 + \dfrac{m}{M}}. \qquad (20)$$

These equations differ from Eqs. (14) and (17), respectively, in that the electronic mass m is replaced by the reduced electronic mass μ.

Discovery of Deuterium. The modified Bohr theory of the hydrogen atom played an important part in the discovery of the hydrogen isotope of mass number 2, sometimes called deuterium. Aston, from his determination of atomic masses with the mass spectrograph, found an apparent discrepancy of about 2 parts in 10,000 in the atomic weight of hydrogen. Birge and Menzel in 1931 suggested that this discrepancy could be explained by assuming the existence of two isotopes of hydrogen H^1 and H^2 in the ratio of 4,500:1. If another isotope of hydrogen does exist, then from Eq. (19) each line of the hydrogen spectrum should actually be a double line, one comparatively very intense due to H^1 and the other very faint due to H^2. The separation of these components can be calculated from the equation and is found to be 1.793 Å for the H_α line and 1.326 Å for the H_β line, and so forth. Such separations can be readily observed with spectroscopes of good resolving power.

In 1932, Urey, Murphy, and Brickwedde performed a series of experiments in which the spectrum of hydrogen was photographed by using a concave diffraction grating of 21-ft. radius. Using ordinary tank hydrogen gas in the discharge tube, they obtained faint traces of the lines from deuterium as well as the regular Balmer series lines. They then prepared samples of hydrogen enriched with the heavier isotope by taking liquid hydrogen and allowing most of it to evaporate, using only the small residue. The basis for this process is that the lighter isotope evaporates at a faster rate than the heavier one. With the enriched sample in the discharge tube, they obtained lines of comparable intensities for the spectra of H^1 and H^2. The measured displacements of the two components agreed with the calculated values.

Neutron and Deuteron. Contemporaneously with the discovery of deuterium, Chadwick discovered the neutron, a particle of mass number 1 and zero charge. The neutrons were produced by the disintegration of beryllium nuclei that were bombarded with alpha particles. The nuclear reaction in this case is

$$_4Be^9 + _2He^4 \rightarrow (_6C^{13}) \rightarrow _6C^{12} + _0n^1.$$

Prior to the discovery of the neutron, the nucleus of an atom was assumed to consist of electrons and protons. Discrepancies began to appear between theory and experiment, particularly in the subject of hyperfine structure of spectral lines, which could only be reconciled by assuming that there were no electrons in the nucleus. The view presently accepted is that a nucleus consists of Z protons and $A - Z$ neutrons. The simplest nucleus, that of H^1, is simply a proton, with $A = Z = 1$. The nucleus of H^2, called the deuteron, consists of one proton and one neutron.

The year 1932 may be said to have ushered in a new era in the study of atomic structure; more particularly the study of nuclear structure and nuclear process. Until 1932, the radiations from radioactive elements were the most useful tools for the investigation of nuclear physics. The discovery of the neutron made a neutral particle available for bombarding the nucleus. The advantage of a neutron as a bombarding particle is that it is uninfluenced by the intense electric field of the nucleus and can penetrate nuclei very readily. With the development of high voltage sources such as the Van de Graaff electrostatic machine and the cyclotron developed by E. O. Lawrence and M. S. Livingston, physicists were provided with large quantities of high-energy projectiles for attack on the problem of nuclear structure and nuclear processes.

ARRANGEMENT AND DISTRIBUTION OF ELECTRONS IN ATOMS

Modifications of the Bohr Atomic Model. The Bohr theory was the first fairly successful attempt at correlating the spectrum of an element with its atomic structure. However, even in the case of hydrogen, it was not completely successful. For example, it failed to give an adequate account of the fine structure of the spectral lines. One of the first modifications of the Bohr theory was introduced by A. Sommerfeld, who generalized Bohr's first postulate so that it would be applicable to elliptic as well as circular orbits. This modification can be stated as

$$\int p_i dq_i = n_i h,$$

in which q_i is a co-ordinate which varies periodically, p_i is the corresponding value of the momentum, and n_i is an integer. $\int$ implies integration over a whole period of the motion.

For circular orbits, the Sommerfeld condition reduces to the original Bohr postulate. For elliptic orbits, two independent equations are needed:

$$\int p_\phi \, d\phi = n_\phi \, h$$
$$\int p_r \, dr = n_r h$$

where r is the radius vector of the ellipse and ϕ is the angle this vector makes with the major axis; n_ϕ is called the azimuthal quantum number and n_r the radial quantum number. When this problem of elliptic motion is solved it is found that n_r and n_ϕ satisfy the condition that

$$n = n_r + n_\phi$$

and

$$1 - \epsilon^2 = \frac{n^2 \phi}{n^2},$$

where n is the principal quantum number and ϵ is the eccentricity of the ellipse.

Although this solution yields several additional orbits, it does not lead to any new spectral lines, because the energy in an elliptic orbit is a function only of the semimajor diameter of the ellipse, and the length of the semimajor diameter depends only on the principal quantum number n.

Another modification introduced by Sommerfeld was to assume that the mass of the electron varied with its speed in the elliptic orbit, according to relativistic mechanics. This did lead to an additional energy term in Eq. (14), as follows:

$$\Delta \varepsilon = -\frac{2\pi^2 m e^4}{h^2} Z^4 \alpha^2 \left(\frac{n}{n_\phi} - \frac{3}{4} \right) \frac{1}{n^4}$$

where

$$\alpha = \frac{2\pi e^2}{ch} = 7.284 \times 10^{-3} \doteq \frac{1}{137},$$

known as the Sommerfeld fine-structure constant. The number of possible transitions is much greater than the number of fine-structure components observed for any spectral line. To bring observation and theory more nearly in agreement, certain of the transitions were ruled out by the introduction of a selection principle. The one chosen was that the azimuthal quantum can change only by $+1$ or -1.

The application of this selection rule brought about some improvement, but the agreement between theory and experiment remained somewhat unsatisfactory until the introduction of the hypothesis of electron spin in 1925 by Uhlenbeck and Goudsmit.

Another difficulty with the Bohr theory was that it could not be extended to the more complex atoms; it failed even with helium. This difficulty was not resolved until L. de Broglie, in 1924, introduced the hypothesis that material particles have a wave motion associated with them such that if a particle of mass m has a velocity v, then the wave length λ associated with it is given by

$$\lambda = \frac{h}{mv},$$

where h is the Planck constant. The velocity of this wave w and the velocity of the particle v are related by the equation

$$wv = c^2.$$

Since v is always less than c, the wave velocity w is always greater than c. E. Schroedinger incorporated this hypothesis in a new treatment of atomic physics which has come to be known as wave mechanics. At about the same time W. Heisenberg introduced a slightly different treatment known as quantum mechanics. The two different treatments were shown by Schroedinger to be equivalent. It is beyond the scope of this article to treat wave mechanics and quantum mechanics, but the results of these theories will be utilized in the following discussion.

Assignment of Quantum Numbers. The solution of Schroedinger's wave equation for the hydrogen atom leads to the natural occurrence of three numbers which are usually denoted by the letters n, l, and m_l. n is an integer; it may have any value greater than zero and is called the principal quantum number of the electron. l is another integer whose value may be any number from zero to $n-1$. It determines the orbital angular momentum of the electron. From the solution of the wave equation it is shown that the orbital angular momentum of an electron is

$$\sqrt{l(l+1)}\,\frac{h}{2\pi}.$$

Since angular momentum is a vector quantity, it is convenient to introduce what is termed the vector model of the atom in order to simplify the treatment. Instead of writing

$$\sqrt{l(l+1)}\,\frac{h}{2\pi},$$

it is more convenient to represent the angular momentum by the vector l in units of $h/2\pi$. In actual calculations, of course, the correct wave-mechanical value must be used.

The quantum number m_l is called the magnetic orbital quantum number and is related to the orbital quantum number by the limitation that the possible values of m_l are l, $l-1$, $\ldots 0, \ldots -l$, that is, there are $2l+1$ possible values of m_l. An interpretation of this result on the vector model can be obtained by imagining an external magnetic field of strength H to be impressed upon the atomic systems. The direction of H can be used as a reference axis for the vectors l and m_l. Since an electron moving in an orbit has a magnetic moment $\mu = iA$, where i is the current due to electronic motion and A is the area of the orbit, the effect of impressing an external magnetic field on the system is to cause the orbit to precess about the direction of the magnetic field as an axis (*see* Fig 7). This is the Larmor precession. The vector l representing the angular momentum of the orbit can be drawn perpendicular to the plane of the orbit acccording to the conventional right-hand rule. The results of the solutions of the

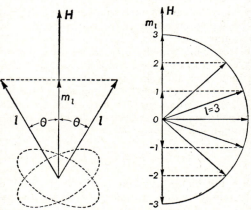

Fig. 7—(LEFT) ILLUSTRATION OF LARMOR PRECESSION
Fig. 8—(RIGHT) LIMITATIONS OF ANGULAR MOMENTUM
OF ORBIT

Schroedinger equation are interpreted as placing severe limitations upon the orientation of the vector l with respect to H.

These limitations can be stated as follows: that the angle θ between l and H must satisfy the equation

$$\cos\theta = \frac{m_l}{l},$$

where m_l has the values given above. This statement is illustrated in Fig. 8 for an electron with a value of $l = 3$.

Magnetic Moment of an Orbital Electron. The value of the magnetic moment $\mu = iA$ of an orbital electron can be evaluated in terms of physical constants by assuming some definite form, such as a circle or an ellipse, for the orbit and putting in the appropriate values for i and A. This will lead to the value

$$\mu = l\frac{eh}{4\pi mc}.$$

The quantity $eh/4\pi mc$ is called a Bohr magneton, and its numerical value is 9.27×10^{-21} erg gauss^{-1}.

Electron Spin. The concept of electron spin was introduced by Uhlenbeck and Goudsmit in 1925 to account for the anomalous Zeeman effect, that is, the splitting of a spectral line into several components when the source is placed in a magnetic field. The electron is assumed to rotate about an axis just as a top spins about an axis. The angular momentum of the electron due to its spin is

$$\sqrt{s(s+1)}\,\frac{h}{2\pi},$$

where s is called the spin quantum number and always has the value $\frac{1}{2}$. On the vector model of the atom the spin angular momentum is written simply as $s \times \dfrac{h}{2\pi}$.

An electron spinning about an axis behaves as a tiny magnet and has a magnetic moment μ_s. However, nothing is known about the distribution of charge on the electron, so that the only way of evaluating μ_s is to assign a value to it which will be in accord with experimental results. This assigned value is

$$\mu_s = 2\sqrt{s(s+1)}\,\frac{eh}{4\pi mc},$$

or on the simpler vector model,

$$\mu_s = 2s\frac{eh}{4\pi mc}.$$

Since $s = \frac{1}{2}$, the numerical value of μ_s is

$$\sqrt{3}\,\frac{eh}{4\pi mc} = 1.62 \times 10^{-20} \text{ erg gauss}^{-1}.$$

When an external magnetic field is applied to an atomic system, the electron can orient itself in one of two possible ways, either parallel to the magnetic field or antiparallel (that is, oppositely directed) to it. The projection of s on the magnetic field direction is denoted by m_s, the spin magnetic quantum number. From the above, the value of $m_s = \pm \frac{1}{2}$.

Total Angular Momentum of an Electron. Each electron in an atom has an orbital angular momentum l and a spin angular momentum s. The total angular momentum of a single electron, denoted by j, is the vector sum of these two; thus

$$j = l + s$$

with the restriction that j must be an odd multiple of $\frac{1}{2}$. Since $s = \frac{1}{2}$, j can have only two values for any electron, $(l + \frac{1}{2})$ and $(l - \frac{1}{2})$, except for the case $l = 0$, when $j = \frac{1}{2}$ only. Again, the wave-mechanical value of the total angular mo-

mentum is
$$\sqrt{j(j+1)}\frac{h}{2\pi}.$$

Pauli Exclusion Principle. There are now six quantum numbers that specify the state of an electron. Since there is one equation connecting j, l, and s, only five of these quantum numbers are needed to specify the state of an electron. A neutral atom of atomic number Z has Z electrons. Wave mechanics furnishes no guide for determining the state of each of these electrons. W. Pauli, in 1925, introduced what has since been known as the Pauli exclusion principle, for assigning quantum numbers to the electrons in an atom. This principle states that no two electrons in an atom can exist in the same state. This means that the group of numbers assigned to the five quantum numbers must be different for each electron in the atom.

It is not possible to determine the arrangement and distribution of the electrons in an atom by the use of the Pauli principle alone. Recourse must be had to the chemical and physical properties of the elements and in particular to their optical and X-ray spectra. Some generalities may be noted here. All electrons which have the same value of n are said to be in the same group or in the same energy level. These electrons which have the same value of l for a given value of n form a subgroup. An example of the application of the Pauli exclusion principle is given in Table IV, which shows the

TABLE IV. POSSIBLE NUMBER OF ELECTRONS IN A GIVEN GROUP

n	l	m_l	m_s	No. of Electrons in Subgroup	No. of Electrons in Completed Group
1	0	0	$+\frac{1}{2}$	2	2
1	0	0	$-\frac{1}{2}$		
2	0	0	$+\frac{1}{2}$	2	
2	0	0	$-\frac{1}{2}$		
2	1	-1	$+\frac{1}{2}$		8
2	1	-1	$-\frac{1}{2}$		
2	1	0	$+\frac{1}{2}$	6	
2	1	0	$-\frac{1}{2}$		
2	1	1	$+\frac{1}{2}$		
2	1	1	$-\frac{1}{2}$		
3	0	0	$+\frac{1}{2}$	2	
3	0	0	$-\frac{1}{2}$		
3	1	-1	$+\frac{1}{2}$		
3	1	-1	$-\frac{1}{2}$		
3	1	0	$+\frac{1}{2}$	6	
3	1	0	$-\frac{1}{2}$		
3	1	1	$+\frac{1}{2}$		
3	1	1	$-\frac{1}{2}$		18
3	2	-2	$+\frac{1}{2}$		
3	2	-2	$-\frac{1}{2}$		
3	2	-1	$+\frac{1}{2}$		
3	2	-1	$-\frac{1}{2}$		
3	2	0	$+\frac{1}{2}$	10	
3	2	0	$-\frac{1}{2}$		
3	2	1	$+\frac{1}{2}$		
3	2	1	$-\frac{1}{2}$		
3	2	2	$+\frac{1}{2}$		
3	2	2	$-\frac{1}{2}$		

maximum possible number of electrons in a given group for $n = 1, 2$, and 3, and the corresponding subgroups. Since $s = \frac{1}{2}$ for each electron, it has not been listed in the table; four other quantum numbers n, l, m_l, and m_s are listed. It will be noted that a subgroup is completed when the vector sum of m_l is

zero and the vector sum of m_s is zero. The maximum number of electrons in a subgroup is $2(2l+1)$. The maximum number of subgroups for a given value of n is n.

Distribution of Electrons in the Atoms. The distribution of electrons in the atoms as accepted in 1949 is given in Table I. Proceeding in the order of increasing atomic numbers, elements are built up successively by adding an electron outside the nucleus and a proton inside the nucleus. The number of neutrons that must be added to the nucleus to form successive elements does not follow such a simple rule; this number can be obtained from Table II.

It will be noted from Table I that for the first 18 elements the electrons are added to the lowest incomplete subgroup until it is complete. With element $Z = 19$, however, the nineteenth electron, instead of being added to the subgroup $n = 3$, $l = 2$, is placed in the subgroup $n = 4$, $l = 0$. The evidence for this reassignment is chemical and spectroscopic. Potassium, $Z = 19$, is in the same column of the periodic table as lithium, $Z = 3$, sodium, $Z = 11$; rubidium, $Z = 37$; and cesium, $Z = 55$. These elements must have the same outer electronic structure, since the chemical properties of an element are determined mostly by the outer electrons. Moreover, these elements have very similar optical spectra because of the energy changes of the outermost electron; the lowest spectral term for each one is a $^2S\frac{1}{2}$ term, which, in the spectroscopic notation, means that $l = 0$ for this electron.

It will be observed that the inert gases—helium $Z = 2$; neon, $Z = 10$; argon, $Z = 18$; krypton, $Z = 36$; xenon, $Z = 54$; and radon, $Z = 86$—have all their occupied subgroups complete. They all show the same type of optical spectra, so-called singlet and triplet series, and have identical lowest spectral terms, $^LS_0$.

The electron which is added to form the atom of the succeeding element is not always placed in the outer subgroup. In the case of scandium, $Z = 21$, for example, the twenty-first electron is placed in the subgroup $n = 3$, $l = 2$, instead of the subgroup $n = 4$, $l = 1$. In the rare-earth or lanthanide series, $Z = 57$ to $Z = 71$, the additional electrons are not added to the outer group $n = 6$, but to the inner groups. Lanthanum, the transition element of this series, has the additional electron in the subgroup $n = 5$, $l = 2$; beginning with cerium, $Z = 58$, the additional electrons are added to the subgroup $n = 4$, $l = 3$. The four outermost subgroups of this series, with two exceptions, are identical, and the elements of this series are known to have many similar chemical properties.

In the Transuranic Elements. G. T. Seaborg and his co-workers have studied the chemistry of thorium, uranium, and the transuranic elements neptunium, Np; plutonium, Pu; americium, Am; and curium, Cm. They conclude that these elements belong in a new series, the actinide series. Actinium, $Z = 89$, is the transition element for this series, just as lanthanum is the transition element for the lanthanide series. In the actinide series the successive electrons are added to the subgroup $n = 5$, $l = 3$, rather than to the subgroup $n = 6$, $l = 3$; thorium, $Z = 90$, is the exception to this rule, having two electrons in the $n = 6$, $l = 2$ subgroup and none in the $n = 5$, $l = 3$ subgroup.

Energy Changes. Energy changes involving the outermost electrons of an atom are comparatively small, as is indicated by the values of the first ionization potentials listed in Table I. It is the energy changes of these electrons that give rise to the optical spectra of the elements, those with lines in the visible, infrared, and ultraviolet regions. Energy changes of the innermost electrons give rise to the characteristic X-ray spectra of the elements.

X-Ray Spectra. Moseley first showed the similarities in the characteristic X-ray spectra of the elements. These spectra are generally classified as *K* series, *L* series, and *M* series. The similarity of the *K*-series lines for the different elements indicates similarity in origin. Since the innermost levels of most elements are completely filled with their quota of electrons, the only condition that permits electrons to go from one inner level to another is to have an electron missing from one of these levels. The usual method for producing X rays is to bombard an element with electrons. If an incident electron has sufficient energy it may succeed in knocking out an electron from the lowest level, $n = 1, l = 0$, of an atom. In X-ray notation, this level is called the *K* level; the one for which $n = 2$ is the *L* level; that for $n = 3$, the *M* level; and so on. If an electron is removed from the *K* level to the outside, the atom is ionized and one electron is missing from the *K* level. The atom is said to be in the *K* state and have an energy ε_K equal to the energy required to remove the electron from the *K* level (*see* Fig. 9). With an electron missing from the *K* level, the atom is in a state of high energy; an electron may therefore go from the *L* level to the *K* level. The atom is still left in an ionized state, with an electron missing from the *L* level. The energy state

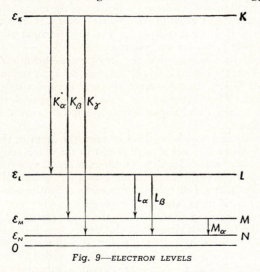

Fig. 9—ELECTRON LEVELS

of the atom is now ε_L; it is less than the energy ε_K. The difference between these two values of the energy of the atom was radiated in the form of X rays of frequency ν given by Bohr's second postulate,

$$\nu = \frac{\varepsilon_K - \varepsilon_L}{h}.$$

The X-ray spectral line emitted in this energy change is called the K_a line.

An electron need not go from the *L* level to the K level, if one is missing from the latter. Instead, an electron from the *M* level may go directly to the *K* level. This will still leave the atom in an ionized state with an energy ε_M less than ε_L and ε_K. When the electron goes from the *M* level to the *K* level a photon of frequency

$$\nu = \frac{\varepsilon_K - \varepsilon_M}{h}$$

is emitted by the atom. This is the K_β line. If an electron goes from the *N* level directly to the *K* level, the K_γ line is emitted with the atom left in the energy state ε_N. Or a sequence of events may be started when an electron is knocked out of the *K* level: an electron may go from *L* to *K* with the emission of

the K_a line, followed by another electron going from the M to the *L* level, with the emission of the L_a line of the *L* series, and this is followed by a third electron going from the *N* to the *M* level with the emission of the M_a line of the *M* series. X-ray spectra are much more complex than is indicated in the above discussion.

Moseley's work has played an important role in atomic structure because of the order it brought to the subject. Moseley found that the square root of the frequency of a character-

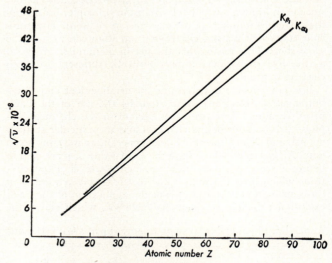

Fig. 10—MOSELEY DIAGRAM

istic line, say the K_a line, was directly proportional to the atomic number of the element emitting this line. A graph of this relationship is shown in Fig. 10. The K_a line, actually a doublet, was not resolved in Moseley's work. In order to obtain such a straight line, Moseley had to invert the order of nickel and cobalt, assigning the lower atomic number to cobalt, even though it has a higher atomic weight. The graph of Fig. 10 is usually referred to as a Moseley diagram. It has played an important role in the discovery of new elements and the assignment of electrons to the appropriate levels in the atoms of the elements. *See also* ATOMIC ENERGY; QUANTUM MECHANICS.   H. S.

ATOMIC VIBRATION. *See* KINETIC THEORY AND STATISTICAL MECHANICS.

ATOMIC VOLUME, the volume, in cubic centimeters, occupied by 1 gram atomic weight of an element; i.e., by 6.023×10^{23} of its individual atoms. If *A* is the atomic weight of the element and *d* is its density, in grams per cubic centimeter, in its normal state, then the atomic volume is *A/d* cc. In 1869 Lothar Meyer plotted the atomic volumes of the elements against their respective atomic weights and found that the points fell on six adjacent catenary curves forming a series of maxima where each curve joined the next one. Elements with similar properties appear on corresponding portions of these catenaries, thus indicating a definite periodicity analogous to that found in the periodic table of the elements. Elements which are gaseous or which melt or boil at relatively low temperatures appear on the ascending portions of each catenary, whereas those which melt or volatilize with difficulty are on the descending portions. The transitional elements, Group VIII, invariably appear at the bottom of each curve, and the alkali metals occupy the maxima.   S. Gl.

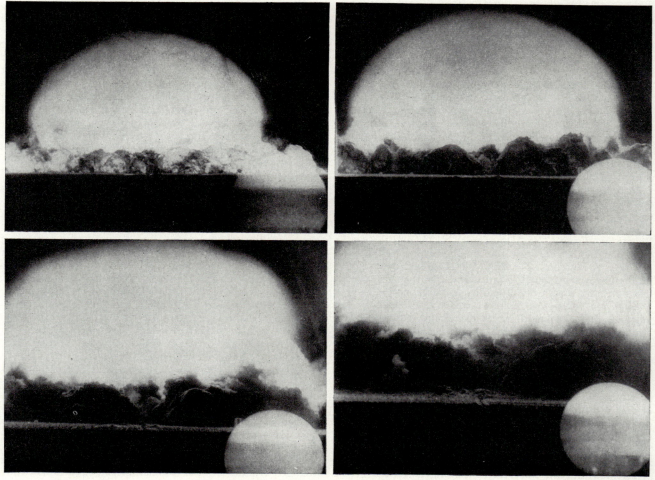

First atomic bomb explosion, occurring at Alamogordo, New Mexico. The sequence of photos (left to right) shows the progress of the explosion. (White circle in lower right corner of each photo is due to a camera reflection.)

ATOMIC WEAPONS. Atomic weapons resemble weapons of the more conventional type insofar as their explosive effect results from the very rapid liberation of a large quantity of energy in a relatively small space. But they differ from other weapons in three important respects: first, the amount of energy released by an atomic weapon is a thousand or more times as great as that produced by the most powerful TNT bombs; second, an atomic explosion is accompanied by highly-penetrating and deleterious invisible rays, in addition to intense heat and light; and third, the substances which remain after an atomic explosion are radioactive, emitting radiations capable of producing harmful consequences in living organisms.

Radiation Effects of an Atomic Weapon. An atomic weapon emits an enormous number of gamma rays at the instant it explodes. When an atom undergoes fission, not only are fragments and neutrons released but also some high-energy radiation. Everything in the vicinity of the explosion is exposed to what amounts to a severe overdose of radiation similar to X rays. People so exposed may eventually die in the following weeks as their tissues slowly disintegrate from the effects of the rays.

Fragments of the split atoms remaining after an atomic weapon has exploded are radioactive. They continue to emit radioactive rays for several months after being created. In Japan, the atomic bombs were exploded high in the air,

and the explosion materials were spread and dissipated by winds. Had these bombs been exploded near the ground, as in tests in New Mexico, the atomic fragments would have remained on the ground. In this event, rescue workers coming into the explosion area would have been exposed to the radiation from these fragments. The area would have remained uninhabitable for several weeks.

Chronology of Wartime Atomic Bomb Development in the U.S. The atomic bomb was achieved in a strategic race against time which, in effect, compressed a generation of effort into a mere five years. It was a race that could not have been won without a unique combination of fundamental scientific research, technical development in and out of the laboratory, mass production methods, and skillful management. It has been made clear that the atomic bomb is unlike any other weapon, in that each usage constitutes a full-scale military operation. As to the monumental effort that went into its perfection, the following timetable of events is significant:

October 11, 1939—President Roosevelt was advised of the possibilities of development of an atomic bomb; and he later appointed an Advisory Committee on Uranium, following confirmation in the United States of the fissionable properties of uranium, first reported from Europe. The committee's first meeting was held on Oct. 21, 1939.

August 13, 1942—The United States Army Corps of Engineers was first assigned to active participation in the development project. A special unit of the Corps became the Manhattan Engineer District, under command of Major General Leslie R. Groves, then a brigadier general.

September-December 1942—Sites were selected and construction was started on the three main installations of the Manhattan District. These were the Clinton Engineer Works at Oak Ridge, Tenn., where on a 60,000-acre tract were built the three main plants for separating U-235, by gaseous diffusion, thermal diffusion, and magnetic deflection; the Laboratory at Los Alamos, N. M., for bomb development on a 45,000-acre site; and the Hanford Engineer Works at Richland, Wash., 400,000-acre site of plants for the production of plutonium.

December 2, 1942—The first self-sustaining nuclear chain reaction was initiated and controlled beneath the west stands of Stagg Field, University of Chicago.

July 16, 1945—The first bomb was exploded in a test, known as "Trinity," at Alamogordo, N. M., and the results and conclusions were forwarded to President Truman, who was then at Potsdam. Ten days later the Potsdam surrender ultimatum was delivered to Japan and dismissed in a broadcast by Radio Tokyo as "unworthy of public notice."

August 6, 1945—An atomic bomb was dropped on the Japanese city of Hiroshima. Sixteen hours later President Truman disclosed to the world the nature of the bomb and the information that it had more explosive power than 20,000 tons of TNT and more than 2,000 times the blast power of the largest bomb used up to that time.

August 9, 1945—Nagasaki, another Japanese city, was hit by an atomic bomb. Five days later, after nearly four years of war and only eight days after the first atomic bomb was dropped on Hiroshima, the Japanese government accepted unconditionally the terms of the Potsdam Declaration.

Security will not yet permit disclosure of the number of atomic bombs available when the war ended.

The Manhattan District. Prefacing perfection of the atomic bomb were years of unremitting and always secret work by the Manhattan District and those who worked with it (nearly 500,000 persons at the peak of operations). Even before that, many years had been spent in preliminary research in all parts of the country.

The Manhattan District was not an ordinary district of the Corps of Engineers but one established solely to carry out the Atomic Bomb Project. Its work, beginning in August 1942 and terminating officially when its organization and facilities were taken over on Jan. 1, 1947, by the United States Atomic Energy Commission, may be divided generally into four major classifications:

1. Major problems of research and development included the production of two essential materials, one or the other of which was required for manufacture of the bomb, i.e., U-235 and plutonium. Laboratory methods had produced both materials in microscopic quantities, and the involved problems of quantity production not only remained unsolved when the Manhattan District began work, but it was unknown whether they were capable of solution by any method.

2. The design, construction, and operation of plants for the full-scale output of the required fissionable materials had yet to be carried out.

3. Once the foregoing difficulties were recognized and overcome, it remained necessary to design, construct, and test the actual bomb. This aspect of the work, carried out largely at Los Alamos, N. M., cannot yet be publicly discussed.

4. The maintenance of security and absolute secrecy in all phases and details of the undertaking.

The cost of the Manhattan District was set at $2,000,000,-000, of which nearly $1,500,000,000 was directly invested in physical facilities.

Postwar U.S. Atomic Weapons Tests. Through 1952 and part of 1953, the following atomic weapons tests were conducted by the United States: "Trinity" was conducted at Alamogordo, N.M., just before the end of World War II, in 1945, and was the first explosion of an atomic bomb. One bomb was detonated. "Crossroads" was conducted at Bikini in the Marshall Islands in 1946 with two bombs. "Sandstone" was conducted in the Marshall Islands in 1948 with three bombs. "Ranger" was conducted in the United States in early 1951 with five devices detonated. "Greenhouse" was conducted in the Marshall Islands in 1951. "Buster-Jangle" was conducted in the United States in the fall of 1951 with seven bombs exploded. In the spring of 1952, "Tumbler-Snapper" was conducted in the United States with eight shots fired. "Ivy" was conducted in the Marshall Islands in 1952. (Although never officially confirmed, this test might have been the experiment on the so-called thermonuclear weapon; i.e., hydrogen bomb.) "Upshot-Knothole" was conducted in the spring of 1953 at the Nevada Proving Ground. Eleven devices were exploded, including the first atomic shell from an artillery field piece. Operation "Castle," which took place in the Pacific in 1954, and, in 1955, "Teapot" in Nevada and an underwater blast sponsored by the U.S. Navy greatly strengthened our knowledge and military capabilities in the field of nuclear weapons.

In general, the purpose of atomic tests has been to advance the weapons-development program, both from the standpoint of improving design and performance and to increase the knowledge of effects of atomic explosions. Information gained from the tests can also be used by architects and engineers in the design of structures, and by civil defense authorities in preparing for emergencies.

Up through Operation Crossroads, atomic bomb tests were conducted jointly by the Manhattan Engineer District and the military. Starting with Operation Sandstone, the effort has been coordinated by the Department of Defense and the U.S. Atomic Energy Commission. The Commission, through its contractors, is generally responsible for test devices, and both the Commission and Department of Defense participate in scientific measurements. The armed forces take advantage of atomic detonations for indoctrination of personnel in the effects of atomic explosions, for simulated combat maneuvers, and in the study of blast and radiation effects on military equipment.

It is not possible to describe publicly the specific advances made in the atomic weapons program but details of the work are enumerated in classified reports to the Joint Committee on Atomic Energy of The Congress. Information on civilian defense measures pertaining to atomic explosions has been widely disseminated by the Federal Civil Defense Administration.

Radioactive "Fall-Out" from Atomic Tests. A phenomenon peculiar to atomic detonations is the "fall-out" of minute radioactive particles from the resulting atomic cloud. Most of the fall-out occurs within the vicinity of the target area. Atomic weapons are not tested unless atmospheric conditions are such that radiological safety can be assured. Weather conditions caused unscheduled delays between bomb detonations during Operation "Teapot." Some radioactive particles, however, are picked up by wind currents and deposited throughout the country. To detect and measure these particles, an extensive network of monitoring teams and fall-out collections stations has been organized. There have been few dangerous concentrations of radioactive fall-out in any part of the world outside of the controlled atomic weapons testing sites. With the cooperation of the U.S. Air Force, the U.S. Civil Aeronautics Authority, and the U.S. Weather Bureau, the monitoring activities are continuously being expanded.

The extensive monitoring operation, conducted before, during, and after every atomic test series, has four goals. Its primary purpose is to protect test personnel and the public by keeping a continuous and accurate record of the amount of radiation dispersed in the air at the time of a nuclear detonation and carried across the country by prevailing winds. The second important purpose is the collection of data for the evaluation of atomic weapons effects. Such data is used, in one instance, for the guidance of sensitive industries, such as the radiation instrument manufacturers to whom even minute increases above normal background radiation might be significant. The third and fourth purposes of the monitoring operation are for meteorological studies and weather data. Movements of large masses of air at varying altitudes can be studied. A cloud even minutely radioactive can be traced across the country and its reaction to other meteorological forces recorded.

The background radioactivity normal for any area varies geographically as well as from hour to hour during a given day. The continental atomic tests caused a temporary average increase in radioactivity across the country of a magnitude no greater than the normal background radioactivity in a community such as Denver, where the background radiation level is ordinarily five times greater than that of New York City or Washington, D.C. In isolated instances, and for short periods of time, higher levels have been measured; but generally the levels of radiation have been far below those considered to be of public health significance. It can be stated that at no time in any part of the country, outside of the controlled test area, has radiation from atomic tests seriously harmed human beings, animals, or crops.

Within an hour after an atomic test, airborne members of the test organization begin making measurements in the air above the immediate vicinity of "ground zero" (center of detonation of atomic weapon). Shortly thereafter, monitoring teams in jeeps enter the test area to carry out a more detailed survey. A few hours later, planes equipped with sample-collecting boxes attached to their wings circle through the radioactive cloud, and out as far as 600 mi., to make sure that commercial airways crossed by the cloud are safe.

The terrain survey is carried out by planes flying about 50 ft. above the ground. Attached to the outside of these planes is a 6-ft.-long tube through which samples of air can be drawn into an ion chamber. This instrument can differentiate between activity on the surface of the ground and that in the air at the level of the plane, thus making possible measurements of both locations for radiation.

Several hours after an atomic explosion, members of six mobile teams are flown in planes provided by the U.S. Air Force to locations within a 200- to 500-mi. radius of the test site, directly in the path predicted for the radioactive cloud. These teams are equipped with suction devices which draw air through a filter paper, causing dust particles to be deposited on the paper. Samples are collected continuously for periods of from 20 min. to 2 hr., during the first 48 hr. after the atomic explosion, and are spot-checked in the field with a Geiger counter to determine the general

radiation levels in the area. The filter papers are then flown to the Commission's New York Operations Office laboratory for more specific measurements and analysis. Automatic counting apparatus, designed and built by the Health and Safety Division Instrument Branch, has made possible the counting of 400 to 600 samples per day, since operations of this sort started early in 1952.

This 40,000-ft. cloud resulted from detonation of a nuclear device in Nevada in 1955. Streaks at right are rocket trails.

The roentgen, symbolized by r, is the unit used to measure the ionizing power of radiation, the factor causing damage to living things. Scientifically, one r, is the amount of radiation as neutrons, gamma rays, X rays, etc. which will produce one electrostatic unit of ions in a volume of one cu. cm. which is a direct function of the number of molecular disintegrations in a cu. cm. of human tissue. r is a cumulative unit and does not define a rate. The AEC's permissible dose for its workers is 15 r per year at a rate of 0.3 r per week. The average annual dosage for workers at Hanford and Oak Ridge, however, is less than one r per year each. Radiation dosage of 25-50 r for brief periods will produce detectable effects in the human body; exposures of 75-100 r and greater for brief periods will generally cause radiation sickness and nausea; serious illness will occur at the 200 r radiation level. It is generally believed that approximately 50 per cent of all human beings will die if exposed to 400 r whole-body radiation levels for even brief periods.

Radiation levels can be measured by the ionization chamber, Geiger counter, scintillation counter, and calorimetric detector. A new scintillation counter, the tissue radiation fluorimeter, is used in medicine.

In an ordinary nuclear bomb, for each 20,000 tons of TNT equivalent explosive power, about two pounds of radioactive materials are produced comprising some 90 different radioactive species. After detonation of the bomb these materials are intensely radioactive, but they immediately start decaying. After seven hours the radioactivity is 1/10th of what it was one hour after the explosion; two days later it is 1/100th of this value, and two weeks after detonation of the bomb, it is 1/1000th of what is was one hour after the explosion. During operation Castle in early 1954, one bomb contaminated 7,000 sq. mi. of the South Pacific to a dangerous level. Japanese fisherman some 80 mi. from the point of detonation received a total whole-body exposure of at least 200 r.

It is recommended that getting away from contaminated areas is the best defense against radioactive fallout. Three ft. of water, earth, or concrete will provide good protection from sources of radiation until natural decay to tolerable levels has occurred. An official report stated that the average contamination in the U.S. on January 1, 1955 corresponded to a dosage rate of 1/1,000 r per year. The total dosage from all atomic tests since 1945 for people in the U.S. averaged less than 1/10 r. Cosmic radiation bombards the whole bodies of human beings at an average level of at least 1/10 r per year. A routine chest X ray renders a *localized* radiation exposure from 0.5 to 5 r per exposure.

INTERNATIONAL CONTROL

Initial Proposals. The shock to the world of the disclosure at Hiroshima and Nagasaki of the unprecedented destructive power of the atomic bomb produced an immediate reaction, evidenced by plans for controlling the production of atomic energy through an external body and prohibiting the further use of atomic weapons in warfare. The first step toward such an international agreement was taken by the United States, Great Britain, and Canada, the three powers which had been associated in the atomic bomb project. On Nov. 15, 1945, a declaration was issued at Washington, signed by President Truman, Prime Minister Attlee, and Prime Minister Mackenzie King, proposing the establishment of a commission under the United Nations to prepare plans for an international atomic control agreement. In December 1945 the Council of Foreign Ministers, meeting in Moscow, endorsed these proposals, and the General Assembly of the United Nations, meeting in London, unanimously adopted a resolution, Jan. 24, 1946, setting up the United Nations Atomic Energy Commission.

This commission consisted of a member for each nation represented on the Security Council, plus Canada when Canada was not a member of the Council. The resolution charged the commission to make recommendations on the following subjects: (1) international exchange of scientific information for peaceful use; (2) control of atomic energy to insure its use only for peaceful ends; (3) elimination of atomic weapons and "other weapons of mass destruction" from national armaments; (4) effective safeguards by inspection and otherwise to protect complying states "against the hazards of violation or evasion."

Early in 1946 the United States government released a report on possible methods of effective international control of atomic energy, prepared by a committee headed by Dean Acheson, later Secretary of State, and David Lilienthal, later chairman of the United States Atomic Energy Commission. The Acheson-Lilienthal report proved a valuable guide and framework for the efforts of the United Nations Atomic Energy Commission when it first met in New York, June 14, 1946. Two plans were presented: (1) that of the United States delegation, headed by Bernard M. Baruch, which became widely known as the Baruch Plan, and (2) that of the Soviet delegation, headed by Andrei A. Gromyko, later Chief Deputy Foreign Minister of the Soviet Union.

American Plan. The American plan called for an Inter-national Atomic Development Authority exercising direct control of atomic activities in all countries, either by actual ownership, management, or supervision in the case of "dangerous" activities, or by licensing and inspection in other cases. This control system would be established by stages. After it was in operation, manufacture of atomic weapons would stop, existing weapons would be disposed of, and full powers over atomic information and development would be vested in the world authority. The United States proposal insisted that no veto power in the Security Council should apply to punishment of violators of the agreement.

Soviet Plan. The Soviet plan, in effect, called for destruction of all atomic weapons at once and discussion of controls afterward. The United States, supported by the majority of the other delegations, declined this act of unilateral disarmament until it could be assured of reasonable safeguards.

U.N. Action. The majority of the U.N. Atomic Energy Commission (all the members except the Soviet Union and its satellite, Poland) contended that prohibition of the manufacture and use of atomic weapons should form part of a comprehensive control plan, so that the application of safeguards, such as international inspection, should accompany the imposition of control and prohibition.

After long and futile discussion, the commission decided to examine scientific evidence to determine whether effective control of atomic energy was feasible. Scientists and engineers of all nations joined in a unanimous report that there existed no insurmountable technological barrier to success. This finding was included in the first report of the commission, approved Dec. 31, 1946, by a vote of 10 to 0, the Soviet and Polish delegations abstaining.

First U.N. Report. This report, among other matters, pointed out that the production of atomic energy depended on uranium and thorium; hence the commission recommended international inspection of all mines, mills, and refineries producing or processing these materials. As the materials assumed a more concentrated and therefore more dangerous form, the commission recommended stricter controls. Plants producing substantial quantities of fissionable materials, the commission recommended, should be placed under exclusive management of the world atomic authority. The commission continued its work during 1947 without coming closer to agreement between the majority viewpoint and that of the Soviet Union. The Soviet delegation, supported by a vigorous propaganda, constantly accused the United States of desiring to maintain "an atomic monopoly," and kept hammering away, from various angles, at its demand for the immediate destruction of all atomic weapons, with controls and safeguards to be taken up when that was done.

Second U.N. Report. The second report of the U.N. Atomic Energy Commission was approved and sent to the Security Council on Sept. 11, 1947. Ten nations voted in favor, the Soviet Union against, and Poland abstained. This report contained specific proposals as to the powers and duties of an international control agency. Special attention was given to making the agency truly responsible to United Nations authority by providing means by which, in various ways, the Security Council, the General Assembly, and the International Court of Justice might check any arbitrary practices and review complaints. The Soviet delegation objected, however, chiefly on the ground that the powers granted the agency, even thus limited, constituted a violation of national sovereignty. While Gromyko did accept the principle of international inspection, he seemed to mean by this merely periodic inspections rather than a continuous and careful system of supervision and a constant flow of information to the agency from international inspectors in all parts of the world, which the ten majority delegations agreed to be necessary for the common security. And the Soviet delegation still insisted that all violations should be dealt with by the Security Council, without impairment of the veto power.

The deadlock continued during the spring of 1948. The Working Committee of the commission devoted itself to a lengthy examination of the Soviet proposals (now reduced to the simple device of the simultaneous signing of two treaties providing for the immediate destruction of atomic weapons and the setting up of some sort of control system). A joint report by four delegations (Canada, China, France, and Great Britain) stated, on March 29, that the Soviet proposals "would not prevent the diversion of atomic material, provided no effective means for the detection of clandestine activities, and . . . no provision for prompt and effective enforcement action."

Third U.N. Report. Thereafter events moved swiftly and somberly toward a climax. On May 17, 1948, the commission approved (by a vote of 9 to 2) and sent to the Security Council its third report, which began: "The Atomic Energy Commission reports that it has reached an impasse." The concluding paragraphs of this report summarized the situation as it then stood:

"The new pattern of international co-operation and the new standards of openness in the dealings of one country with another that are indispensable in the field of atomic energy might in practice pave the way for international co-operation in broader fields, for the control of other weapons of mass destruction, and even for the elimination of war itself as an instrument of national policy.

"However, in the field of atomic energy, the majority of the Commission has been unable to secure the agreement of the U.S.S.R. to even those elements of effective control considered essential from the technical point of view, let alone

PRESS ASSOCIATION, INC.

Ruins of Mitsubishi Steel Works, Nagasaki, Japan, after atomic blast one mile away

its acceptance of the nature and extent of participation in the world community required of all nations in this field by the First and Second Reports of the Atomic Energy Commission. As a result, the Commission has been forced to recognize that agreement on effective measures for the control of atomic energy is itself dependent on co-operation in broader fields of policy.

"The failure to achieve agreement on the international control of atomic energy arises from a situation that is beyond the competence of this Commission. In this situation the Commission concludes that no useful purpose can be served by carrying on negotiations at the Commission level.

"The Commission, therefore, recommends that until such time as the General Assembly finds that this situation no longer exists, or until such time as the sponsors of the General Assembly Resolution of 24 January 1946, who are the permanent members of the Atomic Energy Commission, find, through prior consultation, that there exists a basis for agreement on the international control of atomic energy, negotiations in the Atomic Energy Commission be suspended.

"In accordance with its terms of reference, the Atomic Energy Commission submits this Report and recommendation to the Security Council for consideration, and recommends that they be transmitted, along with the two previous Reports of the Commission, to the next regular session of the General Assembly as a matter of special concern."

This report was the subject of extended debate in the Political Committee of the General Assembly, and in the Assembly itself, at its next meeting, which took place in Paris in the autumn of 1948. While no substantial change in the Soviet position was manifested during these debates, the Soviet delegation was unalterably opposed to the termination of the work of the Atomic Energy Commission. One Soviet suggestion was to scrap all the work that the Commission had done during more than two years of grueling effort, go back to the beginning and start all over again. It was difficult, as

WIDE WORLD PHOTOS

Devastation in Nagasaki, Japan, after atomic bomb blast one-quarter of a mile away

a French delegate observed, to tell whether the Soviet delegation wanted the Commission to go on working in the sincere hope that an agreement might be reached, or merely wished the discussion to be prolonged. Some of the smaller powers, however, supported the view that the Commission's labors should not be suspended; there was evident a small-power feeling that to give up would be to abandon hope for peace and security.

Recommendation of "Further Study." The United States and other major powers yielded to this anxiety, and on Oct. 20, 1948, the Political Committee, by a vote of 41 to 6, with 10 abstentions, passed a resolution which (1) approved the general findings and recommendations of the first report and the specific proposals of the second report as "the necessary basis for establishing an effective system for the international control of atomic energy," (2) expressed deep concern at the impasse as stated in the third report, (3) requested the six permanent members of the Atomic Energy Commission (the "Big Five" powers and Canada) to consult as to whether a basis for atomic agreement existed and to report to the Assembly at its next regular meeting, and finally (4) called on the Atomic Energy Commission, meanwhile, to resume its sessions and "proceed to the further study of such subjects . . . as it considers to be practicable and useful." On Nov. 4, 1948, the Assembly approved the committee's resolution by a vote of 40 to 6, with 4 abstentions. In both cases the only negative votes were cast by the Soviet bloc. The only hopeful note during the whole discussion was a remark of the Soviet delegate, Andrei Vishinsky, that "appropriate distribution of quotas of atomic fuel and distribution of raw materials among countries had not yet been sufficiently studied," and that "such a proposal might facilitate the reaching of agreement on a great number of other questions." It seemed likely at that time, therefore, that the next step in seeking atomic agreement would be a further study of the quota system and exploration of the possibility that assignment of definite quotas might produce a change in the Soviet attitude. However, nothing ever came of this proposal. Altogether, seventeen nations had participated in the work of the Atomic Energy Commission and fourteen had supported the reports of the commission. Only three—the Soviet Union, the Soviet Ukraine, and Poland—had refused to accept the proposals. In effect, therefore, the Soviet Union stood alone, with its satellites, in preventing international agreement on the control of atomic energy and the elimination of atomic weapons from national armaments.

This situation continued into 1949 when the Soviet Union balked at the acceptance of any agreement for the control of atomic energy as long as the representatives of Nationalist China were seated instead of those from Communist China. In 1950, the Soviet Union boycotted the meetings of the Atomic Energy Commission for the same reason and thus blocked all progress on the control of atomic energy and atomic weapons. The United States proposed combining controls of both atomic weapons and conventional armaments, but this was also rejected by the Soviet Union.

On Oct. 24, 1950, President Truman, following through on the idea of considering all armaments jointly, recommended that the separate commissions within the United Nations for atomic energy and conventional armaments be combined in a single commission. This recommendation was approved by a majority vote on Sept. 28, 1951, and, on Dec. 19, 1951, the combined commission, to be known as the Disarmament Commission, was voted by a majority. Subsequently, on Jan. 11, 1952, this commission formally replaced both the Atomic Energy Commission and the Commission for Conventional Armaments. On every vote in connection with the formation of the new commission, the Soviet Union and its satellites either voted against the idea or abstained from voting.

The Disarmament Commission was directed to prepare proposals for a treaty to regulate and limit armed forces and armaments, and to eliminate weapons of mass destruction, such as atomic weapons. The commission was to establish a plan of international inspections and control within the framework of the Security Council. Peaceful uses of atomic energy were to be promoted.

The Soviet Union still held out for prohibition of atomic weapons and use of existing atomic weapons for civilian purposes only. The United States, on the other hand, held out for complete disclosure of atomic weapons in the stockpiles of the various countries and regular inspections of atomic weapons developments and other armaments. The entire situation of international control of atomic weapons (and conventional armaments) therefore reached a complete stalemate.

STRATEGIC ASPECTS

The popular idea of the atomic bomb as an "absolute weapon" by means of which any conflict can be brought to a speedy termination is somewhat exaggerated. It is true that there was a dramatic conclusion of the war with Japan soon after the atomic bombing of Hiroshima and Nagasaki, but it is generally conceded that Japan was already a beaten nation.

The great military advantage of atomic weapons, so far as their explosive effect is concerned, is the complete destruction over a much wider area than can be accomplished with ordinary high-explosive bombs. Complete and final destruction of an industrial center, for example, is not easily achieved with high-explosive bombs; if accomplished at all, it must be done in piecemeal fashion in a series of continuous attacks. In between bombings, much can be done by the enemy in the way of repair and recovery, as Allied experience in bombing Germany in World War II proved. With the atomic bomb, destruction is complete in a single attack; there is no opportunity for repair or recovery. If such atomic attacks could be widely distributed against all major industrial centers of a nation within a short time, the nation would find it extremely difficult, if not entirely impossible, to continue to wage war.

Military and Civilian Defense. As long as only one nation possesses atomic weapons, it is obvious that this nation has a commanding military advantage. This was the position of the United States (with its Allies) until it was officially announced by President Truman on Sept. 23, 1949, that the Soviet Union had conducted an atomic explosion "during one of the recent weeks." Since that time, there has been the threat of an all-out atomic attack by the Soviet Union which might devastate all major cities and industrial centers of the United States in a single thrust of Soviet airplanes. In turn, a similar threat of an all-out atomic attack by the United States forces on Soviet centers has likely been instrumental in deterring Soviet leaders from increased aggression and possibly the starting of World War III.

Although there has been a limited release of information concerning the use of supersonic guided missiles to explode atomic bombs before they can hit their targets, the only realistic defense is apparently a defense against the vehicles used to transport the bombs to their targets. Radar screens, ground observation by civilian volunteers, and air patrols serve the purpose of detecting enemy airplanes and providing a warning before targets have been reached by the airplanes. Defense measures can also be taken against the possibility of delivery of an atomic attack by way of submarines or internal sabotage. Civilian defense rules, and practice of those rules, can serve to minimize the effects of an atomic attack and to speed recovery from such an attack.

Consideration of Radiation Effects. While the greater explosive force of atomic weapons is an important factor in the strategic considerations of atomic warfare, the effects of harmful radiation coincident with the release of atomic energy is a key factor. A large area surrounding the center of explosion of an atomic weapon remains radioactive for a considerable time after the explosion. This means that the attacked area will be uninhabitable until radiation has decreased to a safe level. Defensive forces cannot move in for reconstruction or possession of the area until it is safe. Similarly, an attacking army could not move into the area for some time. Over-all strategy and field tactics are thus quite different with the use of atomic weapons as compared with ordinary explosives.

have been an accidental explosion of atomic materials or it may have been a minor experiment leading to the development of an actual bomb. However, it is certain that at least an atomic explosion had taken place within the Soviet Union, since facts made public after the detonation of the first U.S. atomic bomb at Alamogordo made it a matter of general knowledge that an atomic explosion releases a cloud of radioactive materials which drift with the winds in the stratosphere and can be detected thousands of miles away.

Air view of Bikini underwater atom bomb test, showing disposition of ships and phenomena of blast.

Radiation also has another, indirect, effect on the strategy of atomic warfare. Atomic-energy-powered vehicles, such as aircraft carriers, submarines, and possibly aircraft are under consideration and development as a part of atomic warfare, since such vehicles would lend themselves to the high-power, long-distance operations involved. However, the radiation that is emitted with the operation of an atomic power plant presents a difficult problem of shielding and protection of personnel. Experience gained in the control of radiation during operation of stationary atomic reactors will, in time, serve to produce atomic powered craft that will attain relatively high speeds and long ranges of operation, thus affecting the entire strategic and tactical aspects of warfare.

FOREIGN ATOMIC WEAPONS DEVELOPMENT

Although little information has been published on the progress of foreign developments in the field of atomic weapons, official U.S. sources announced in 1949 that the Soviets had conducted an "atomic explosion." This was followed by two more Soviet "explosions" in 1951 and several more since then. Earlier the Soviet Union vaguely acknowledged that they had conducted an atomic explosion and more recently stated that the U.S. no longer possessed the monopoly of the H-Bomb.

There is no certainty that the Soviet atomic explosion represented an actual detonation of an atomic bomb; it may

In 1952, the British detonated their first atomic "device" in the vicinity of Australia at the Monte Bello Islands. *See also* HYDROGEN BOMB.   E. J. C.; W. S. P.; R. Ma.

ATOMIC WEIGHT, a number which expresses the weight of an atom relative to a chosen standard. This method is more convenient than referring to the actual weight of a single atom, which is very small indeed. At one time the weight of the hydrogen atom was used as the standard of reference, but for various reasons the oxygen atom has come to be taken as the standard, its weight being set at 16.0000. The atomic weight of any element is thus the weight of an atom of that element relative to the weight of the oxygen atom as 16.0000. The oxygen referred to in this definition is ordinary oxygen as present in the air; the significance of this point will be seen later. On the foregoing basis, the lightest element, hydrogen, has an atomic weight of 1.0080, whereas the heaviest element found in nature—at least in appreciable quantities—is uranium with an atomic weight of 238.07. The atomic weight of an element expressed in grams is called a gram-atomic weight or, more briefly, a gram atom. The actual weight of a single atom of any element is obtained by dividing the gram-atomic weight by the Avogadro number.

Valence. According to the atomic theory, elements unite with one another by whole numbers; since the weights in terms of which elements combine are proportional to their equivalent weights, it can be seen that the atomic weight of an element must be either equal to the equivalent weight or a simple integral multiple of it. The ratio of the atomic weight to the equivalent weight is called the valence of the element; hence

Atomic weight = equivalent weight × valence.

The earliest atomic weight estimates were based on equivalent weights of fair accuracy; but since the valences of the elements were uncertain, the atomic weights were often in error by a factor of 2 or more.

Cannizzaro's Method. The first reliable system of atomic weights was developed by S. Cannizzaro in 1858. Since an atom is the smallest portion of an element that can be found in a molecule of any of its compounds, it follows that the atomic weight is the smallest weight of the element which can be present in the molecular weight of a compound. By preparing a series of compounds of the given element, determining their molecular weights, and then analyzing the compounds, it is possible to find the weights of the element present in the molecular weights of the various compounds. If sufficient compounds have been used in this study, it is probable that at least one of them will contain only one atom of the particular element in the molecule. In this event, the smallest weight of the element present in the molecular weights of the several compounds will be identical with its atomic weight. In any case, since a molecule must contain a whole number of atoms, the highest common factor of the weights of the element in the molecular weights of its compounds will give the correct atomic weight. Working in this manner, Cannizzaro derived a number of atomic weights which are in close agreement with the latest accepted values.

Since the ratio of the atomic to the equivalent weight is a small integer, the valence, modern chemical methods of determining atomic weights are based mainly on accurate equivalent weights. Once the equivalent weight is known for any element, it is necessary to find only the integer by which it must be multiplied in order to obtain the accurate atomic weight. Thanks to past investigations, the valences of the elements are so well known that they do not have to be specially determined, but this has not always been the case. Brief reference will therefore be made to methods of the past.

Other Earlier Methods. In 1818, P. R. Dulong and A. T. Petit found that the atomic-heat capacities, i.e., the products of atomic weights and specific heats in calories per degree, of a number of solid elements have the approximately constant value of 6.4. This result has been found to apply, at ordinary temperatures, to nearly all solid elements, with the exception of carbon, boron, and silicon. The specific heats of these three elements increase rapidly with temperature, and an approximate limiting value of 6.4 is obtained for the atomic-heat capacities at high temperatures. Since, in general,

Atomic weight × specific heat = 6.4 (approx.),

it follows that an approximate value of the atomic weight of a solid element can be estimated, provided the specific heat is available. The accurate atomic weight can then be derived from the accurately known equivalent weight. The equivalent weight of lead, for example, is known accurately to be 103.605, and its specific heat is 0.031 cal. per degree. The approximate atomic weight is thus 6.4/0.031, i.e., about 206, and hence the exact atomic weight must be 2 × 103.605 = 207.21.

In some cases the valence of an element can be obtained by making use of Mitscherlick's law of isomorphism in the following form: Substances similar in crystalline form (i.e.,

isomorphous) and in chemical properties can usually be represented by similar formulas. Thus silver sulphide is known to be isomorphous with cuprous sulphide and to have properties similar to it. The formula of cuprous sulphide is Cu_2S, and consequently silver sulphide might be expected to be Ag_2S. This would make the valence of silver unity, or 1, so that its atomic weight is equal to its equivalent weight. The law of isomorphism is not always reliable, however, since lead sulphide (PbS) has the same crystalline form as silver sulphide (Ag_2S). Another procedure makes use of the periodic table of the elements. The product of the equivalent weight and the valence of an element must bring the atomic weight into a position that is in harmony with the known chemical properties of the element. The correct atomic weight of beryllium was first obtained in this manner; its valence, which had been regarded as 3, was shown actually to be 2.

A useful method for determining atomic weights, not involving equivalent weights, is based on the accurate molecular weight of a compound in which the weights of the other elements are known. The procedure has been applied to obtain the atomic weights of light elements, e.g., carbon, nitrogen, and fluorine, which form gaseous compounds whose molecular weights can be evaluated from density measurements. The accurate molecular weight of carbon dioxide (CO_2) is 44.010; if from this is subtracted 32.000, for the two oxygen atoms, the atomic weight of carbon is found to be 12.01.

The inert gases of the atmosphere, i.e., helium, neon, argon, krypton, and so on, do not form chemical compounds, and so none of the foregoing principles could be used to obtain their atomic weights. The latter could be derived from the molecular weights, calculated from the densities, if the number of atoms in the molecule, i.e., the atomicity, were known. Heat-capacity measurements show definitely that the molecules of these gases contain only one atom; i.e., the atom and molecule are identical. The atomic weights are thus the same as the molecular weights.

Mass-Spectrograph Method. A more fundamental approach to the problem of atomic weights has become available as a result of the development of the mass spectrograph. By comparing the position of the lines produced in this instrument by a given element with the position of that due to an element of known atomic weight, e.g., oxygen, it is possible to evaluate the atomic weight with an accuracy of 1 part in 10,000. If the element under consideration has only one isotopic form, the problem is simple, but if it consists of several isotopes it is necessary to determine the weight of each isotope as well as its proportion in the mixture. Both these quantities can be obtained with considerable accuracy in modern mass spectrographs. The element boron was found to consist of 1 part of the isotope of atomic weight 10.0163 and 4.0 parts of the 11.0129 isotope; the mean atomic weight is thus $(10.0163 + 4.0 × 11.0129)/5.0 = 10.814$.

There is a difference, for which allowance must be made, between atomic weights determined by the mass spectrograph and those obtained by the other methods. Ordinary atmospheric oxygen contains three isotopes, whose weights are close to 16, 17, and 18, and conventional "chemical" atomic weights are based on the postulate that the mean is exactly 16.0000. In the determination of "physical" atomic weights by the mass spectrograph, however, it is the atomic weight of the O-16 isotope which is given this value, so that the mean physical atomic weight of ordinary oxygen would be greater than 16.0000. From the known isotopic composition of atmospheric oxygen it is calculated that physical atomic weights should be divided by 1.00027 to give the chemical values. The conventional atomic weight of boron will thus be 10.814/1.00027 = 10.81, which may be compared with the accepted chemical value of 10.82.

International Atomic Weights. The International Union of Chemistry's Committee on Atomic Weights issues, from time to time, a report containing a critical survey of atomic-weight determinations published since the preceding report. The atomic weights recommended by the committee are referred to as the International Atomic Weights. *See also* PERIODIC TABLE.   S. Gl.

ATOMISM, an explanation of the world as made up of countless particles whose ever-shifting arrangement in space is the reality behind all appearances. Modern atomism began as a revival of Greek atomism, which was founded and completely developed, short of modern experimental methods, in the fifth century B.C. by Leucippus and Democritus. Their views, adopted with little change by Epicurus, reached the Latin poet Lucretius, whose *De rerum natura (On the Nature of Things)* is the fullest surviving version of ancient atomism. This tradition was revived in the seventeenth century by Gassendi, received attention from Boyle and Newton, and eventually provided a framework for the precise quantitative atomic theory of Dalton. Atomic theories were developed also by Arabian and Jewish philosophers of the Middle Ages, and by Indian materialistic philosophers of Jainism and Buddhism; but these seem not to have influenced the modern tradition.

The following features may be said to characterize the theory of atomism in all ages:

(1) *Analysis of matter into ultimate indivisible units moving in empty space.* In Greek theory, the atoms were viewed as indivisible *(a-tomon)*, impenetrably solid, and possessed of size, shape, and a certain original momentum which could be transferred to other atoms by impact. Indian theories endowed the atom with elementary sense qualities. The most consistent view, perhaps, was that of the Arabian school of Al-Ash'ari, and of the Jewish philosopher Maimonides, which conceived the atoms as infinitesimal points of impenetrable density, having no size and no shape, but merely position. In modern times the word "atom" has come to be applied to a unit of matter no longer conceived as indivisible. The units to which the name should traditionally refer would be whatever ultimate and unanalyzable components there may prove to be within the so-called chemical atoms.

(2) *Mechanistic determinism.* The only forces are those of matter in motion; the only kind of causation is that of the mechanical forces that join and separate atoms. No causal explanations are allowed in terms of thought or purpose, whether natural, human, or divine. The laws of motion have no exceptions, and nothing occurs uncaused. No particle of matter or of motion is ever lost, nor any ever gained, however these may be distributed in space. (Conservation of matter and motion.)

In Greek theory the forces of change were altogether those of *impact*. As clouds of particles swarmed through the reaches of infinite space, there came to be innumerable whorls—centers of evolving worlds—created by the contrasting motions of large slow atoms and small fast ones. Thereafter, the continuing clash and linkage of atoms moving round these centers account for the natural history of the universe. Atoms of like size and shape were sifted together. Certain stable patterns—such as air, fire, water, earth, flesh, light—and others, more complex, maintained themselves for shorter or longer periods.

When atomism was revived in modern physics, the concept of physical forces had changed, so that the ultimate particles were conceived as moving according to the new laws of motion established by Newton, with their notion of attractive force acting at a distance. Greeks and moderns agreed in banishing the gods from the natural world as explainers of the course of its history.

(3) *Geometric materialism.* All that is real is either atoms or some combination of atoms. Though things appear to come into existence and to perish, all that really happens is that certain atoms join together for a while in certain geometrical patterns, only to fall apart again in due course. When asked to account for the immense variety of the objects of sense and for such phenomena as sensation and thought, the Greek atomists sought the help of an idea original with the Pythagorean philosophers—an idea still at the core of physics and chemistry. On this view, each variety of substance was the appearance of a particular geometric arrangement of fixed numbers of atoms. Thoughts and sensations were viewed as in reality certain typical sequences of shifting patterns of atoms within the body.

In antiquity atomism lived as long as the school of Epicurus, whose views it was held to support by its denial of supernatural causes and of freedom of the will. Attacks came from other schools, particularly that of Aristotle and his successors during the Middle Ages, Albertus Magnus and St. Thomas Aquinas. Academic philosophy ever since has continued these attacks, treating atomism as the chief type of materialism, in its attempt to reduce the immense world of experience to an inexplicable appearance of a set of simple abstract entities and forces. In the eighteenth and nineteenth centuries, however, the prestige of physics and chemistry lent to materialism in general, and to atomism in particular, a widespread quasi-scientific popularity as a final metaphysical view, as exemplified in the works of Baron d'Holbach.

Atomism in its narrower scope, as one of many possible hypotheses about the structure of matter, denied rival theories asserting the continuity of matter, or the infinite divisibility of matter, or the nonexistence of completely empty space. Atomism, with its insistence that every point of space is either absolutely empty or absolutely full, was rejected alike by Parmenides and Descartes, by Aristotle and Leibniz. In the nineteenth century, atomism came to occupy a basic position in the highly fruitful theory of chemistry, which undertook a precise geometric analysis of matter. During the twentieth century, however, theories of space, time, and energy have advanced to a point where they could no longer be properly designated atomistic in the traditional sense, although atomism never ceased to be incorporated in them.

Any view which stresses the reality of ultimate simple parts and the unreality of any grouping of these parts may be called an atomistic view. Thus, the theories of Hobbes and his successors were called political atomism because they denied the dependence of the individual upon social institutions, these latter being changeable and dependent upon the individual and serving him. In modern logic, Bertrand Russell called his views logical atomism, as confining reality to ultimate irreducible simple facts in contrast to the unreality of any structure of thought into which these "atomic" facts might enter.   J. W. D.

ATONEMENT, the means by which broken communion between God and man is restored, or the condition and state of such a reconciliation. In primitive religions, atonement is made necessary because man breaks accepted taboos or fails to observe prescribed rituals; in the higher religions, man's disobedience is regarded under the more elaborate and subtle concept of sin. Atonement is thus at the very heart of all religion and, in general, synonymous with redemption or salvation.

In the Old Testament, atonement is intimately associated with sacrifice and the function and office of the priest. No detailed philosophy of atonement is worked out, but throughout Leviticus, for example, it may be seen how central the notion was. In the prophets there is considerable criticism of the abuses of the sacrificial system, and Micah warns that God requires not sacrifice but justice, mercy, and humility (vi:6-8). The climax of the Jewish ritual conception is reached in the Day of Atonement, celebrated the tenth day of the seventh month, when the sanctuary, the priest, and the people are cleansed of sin. The high priest entered the Holy of Holies, a scapegoat was sent into the wilderness to carry away the sins of the people, and the covenant relationship between God and Israel was reaffirmed. The most exalted conception of atonement in the Old Testament is found in Isaiah liii, which speaks of the "suffering servant," a passage which the Christian Church has consistently applied to Christ.

In the New Testament, there is no one word in general use for atonement, though in Romans v:11 Καταλλαγή is translated "atonement" in many English versions. The idea of reconciliation involved here has suggested to some that atonement should be conceived as at-one-ment. The New Testament writers are unanimous, however, in associating atonement with Christ's death, which is taken to be both the revelation of man's sin and the redemptive expression of God's holy love; this conception appears clearly in the words of Jesus regarding his death as "a ransom for many" (Mark x:45) and his blood as "shed for many" (Mark xiv:24). Paul's interpretation of atonement makes much of Christ's identification with the believer, who, as sinner, is judged righteous by God because of Christ's perfect righteousness. The whole theme of the Epistle to the Hebrews is that Christ has made a more perfect sacrifice for sin than was possible to the Old Testament priesthood.

In the history of the Church, many different theories of atonement have been advocated. For nearly a thousand years the most widely accepted view, known as the ransom theory, was that Christ's death was a ransom paid to Satan by means of which man was delivered from the bondage of sin. Anselm (died 1109) in his *Cur deus homo* gave classic expression to the satisfaction theory, by which Christ's death was interpreted as the satisfaction of God's justice and honor. Abelard (died 1142) rejected this view and insisted, formulating what is known as the moral influence theory, that the atonement was primarily an expression of God's love. The Protestant Reformers maintained that Christ bore on the Cross the punishment due our sins, an interpretation sometimes called the penal substitutionary theory.

In modern times there have been numerous attempts to restate these traditional theories, with a tendency to avoid the idea of God's reconciliation to man and to emphasize man's need to be reconciled to God.　　　　　　H. T. K.

ATONEMENT, DAY OF. *See* YOM KIPPUR.

ATREK [ɑ'trɛk], an affluent of the Caspian Sea on its Asiatic side, one of the few rivers of any size or importance in northeastern Iran, having its source in a spring, Kora Kazan, or "Black Cauldron," in the mountains northwest of Meshed, and flowing a meandering course generally westward to the sea. The main stream, which reaches an elevated plain (4,500 ft.) near Kuchan, traverses a straight-line distance of about 300 mi., but the river's actual course is much longer. The lower course of the river for a few miles forms the boundary between the southwestern part of the Turkmen Soviet Socialist Republic and northeastern Iran. There are no major cities on the Atrek's banks, but the Turkmen town of Tchikishliar on the Caspian Sea is about 15 mi. north of the river's mouth. The nearest Iranian city is Asterabad, about 50 mi. to the south.

ATREUS, HOUSE OF [e'trus], in Greek legend, the ruling family of Mycenae, whose tragic fate, the result of crime and violence, provided many themes for the Greek tragedians. Atreus, son of Pelops and Hippodamia and grandson of Tantalus, was, according to Homer, the father of Agamemnon and Menelaus, but a later tradition made Agamemnon and Menelaus the sons of Pleisthenes and, therefore, grandsons of Atreus. The variously reported crime of Tantalus against the gods and Pelops' treachery and violence to Myrtilus, who cursed him and all his family, provide the background for the crimes of Atreus and his brother, Thyestes. Having murdered their half-brother, Chrysippus, they fled to Mycenae, where Atreus became king after the death of Eurystheus; there Thyestes later seduced Aerope, Atreus' wife, and was driven from the kingdom. In one version, Thyestes then sought revenge for his exile by sending Pleisthenes, a son of Atreus whom he had reared, to kill Atreus. In this venture Pleisthenes was slain by his own father, but Atreus' revenge upon Thyestes was more horrible still; he killed Thyestes' sons and, pretending a reconciliation, invited their father to a banquet in which their flesh was served. When Thyestes discovered his inadvertent cannibalism, he again fled, cursing the House of Atreus. Thyestes had another son by his own daughter Pelopia, who later married Atreus. This son, named Aegisthus, was reared by Atreus, who later sent him to slay Thyestes; but the latter recognized the youth as his son and the two then killed Atreus. The curse on the house then passed on to the descendants of Atreus; Aegisthus conspired with Clytemnestra to kill Agamemnon, and Orestes, son of Agamemnon and Clytemnestra, avenged his father's death by slaying his guilty mother and her lover. The long series of crimes comes to an end when Orestes is finally acquitted of wrongdoing. *See also* AGAMEMNON; MENELAUS; ORESTES; PELOPS; TANTALUS. G. E. D.

ATRIPLEX [æ'trɪplɛks], about 180 herbs and low shrubs of the goosefoot family, many known as saltbush. They are native to temperate and subtropical regions, about sixty occurring in the United States, chiefly in the arid parts of the west. Most are mealy or silvery-hairy plants with clusters of inconspicuous green flowers. The orach, *A. hortensis*, native in Asia, is grown as a green in the Old World. *A. breweri* with silvery foliage is popular for hedges in southern California. Various Australian kinds called saltbush are grown for forage. Atriplex is also known as desert holly.

ATROPINE. *See* ALKALOIDS.
ATROPOS. *See* FATES.
ATTACCA. *See* MUSICAL TERMS.

ATTACHMENT, in law, in its ordinary modern usage imports the taking of property into the custody of an officer of the law by virtue of legal process issued by competent judicial authority. Attachment is a remedy ancillary to an action by which the plaintiff therein is enabled to acquire a lien upon property or effects of the defendant for satisfaction of the judgment which the plaintiff may obtain. It is a provisional and extraordinary remedy which generally may be invoked only upon a showing that the person whose property is to be attached is a nonresident, fraudulent, or absconding debtor.

The term "attachment" is at times also used to designate legal processes whereby a person is arrested and brought into court in connection with the civil administration of justice.

H. Si.

ATTAINDER, the extinction of civil rights after conviction of treason or felony. Under ancient practice, guilt might be established by confession or by verdict after trial. Normally attainder led to confiscation of the offender's real and personal estate and the "corruption" of his blood, so that nothing could pass to or through him by inheritance. In English constitutional history before the middle of the seventeenth century, judgment was not infrequently passed by a bill of attainder, that is, by an act of Parliament condemning the accused without the formalities of an ordinary judicial trial. A famous example was the attainder of the Earl of Strafford in the reign of Charles I. The practice was abolished after the Revolution of 1688, although what were known as bills of pains and penalties were enacted at rare intervals until well into the eighteenth century. In Great Britain, where Parliament is legally unlimited, there is nothing to prevent the revival of the procedure except the general sense of its iniquity. In the United States, bills of attainder are prohibited by the Constitution. As late as 1946 an act of Congress denying by name salaries to certain officials was declared void by the Supreme Court of the United States as a bill of attainder, the court affirming the proposition that "legislative acts, no matter what their form, that apply either to named individuals or to easily ascertainable members of a group in such a way as to inflict punishment on them without a judicial trial are bills of attainder prohibited by the Constitution."   L. W. L.

ATTALIDS [æ'təlɪdz], a dynasty of Hellenistic rulers whose capital was the city of Pergamum in Asia Minor. The founder of the dynasty was a eunuch named Philetaerus, who about 281 B.C. had absconded with the treasury of Lysimachus and joined forces with Lysimachus' enemy, Seleucus I. When Seleucus was killed in 281 B.C., Philetaerus set himself up at Pergamum as a vassal of Antiochus I, the son and successor of Seleucus. After Philetaerus died, he was succeeded by a nephew, Eumenes (263-241 B.C.), and later by a grand-nephew, Attalus (269-197 B.C.). Attalus was the first to take the title of King of Pergamum (about 241 B.C.), and his successors continued the monarchy for about a century. Pergamum enjoyed its greatest affluence and prosperity under the two successors of Attalus I, viz., Eumenes II (197-159 B.C.) and Attalus II (c.159-138 B.C.). The kingdom became a commercial and industrial center which dominated the political and economic life of western Asia Minor. The Attalids were famous as patrons of arts and letters, and the city of Pergamum was noted for its distinctive school of sculpture. Attalus and Eumenes also paid tribute to Athens as the home of Greek culture by erecting costly buildings. The advance of Rome into the eastern Mediterranean, however, gradually undermined the independence of the Hellenistic kingdoms. The last of the Pergamene kings was Attalus III (138-133 B.C.), who, when he died in 133 B.C. willed his kingdom to Rome.   T. B. J.

ATTALUS. *See* ATTALIDS.

'AṬṬĀR, FARĪD UD-DĪN [æ'tər] (died 1230), Persian poet, whose full name was Abū Hamid Muhammad ibn-Ibrāhīm; his surname 'Aṭṭār, "the druggist," refers to his father's trade, which he inherited. Born near Nisapur in the second half of the twelfth century, he died in 1230. Very little is known about his life, most of which he spent in retirement in a Sufi monastery, having become a follower of mysticism at an early age. He made a pilgrimage to Mecca, however, and traveled in Syria and Egypt, where he met many masters of mysticism, writing, as a result of his acquaintance with them, a biographical work, *Tadhkirat ul-awliyā'* ("The Memorial of the Saints"), a masterpiece of candor and penetration. 'Aṭṭār's reputation is due chiefly to his poetical achievements, and especially to his allegorical poem, *Manṭiq ul-ṭayr* ("The Speech of the Birds"), one of the most popular books in Persian literature. The old fable of the birds who want to elect a king is transformed into a symbol of the human soul in search of the supreme goal of mysticism, the absorption into God's essence, and the annihilation of the individual into His oneness. In a language in which the most abstruse concepts are realistically expressed with a rich and vivid imagery, 'Aṭṭār recounts the hardships and dangers of the birds' long journey to the mountain, Kaf, the abode of the divine bird, Sīmurgh, under the guidance of the Hoopoe (representing the teacher of mysticism), and the attainment of eternal life by the few who reached their goal.

G. L. V. D.

ATTENTION, in ordinary speech, is a faculty or power which can be focused and directed, like a searchlight, to bring objects or aspects of objects into full awareness. Various groups of psychologists have used the term in different ways. The Structuralists, in their effort to describe the contents of consciousness, had no place for the dynamic element. Hence they made attention synonymous with clearness, and considered such problems as the number of levels of clearness. Thus a person may be fully aware of the pencil in his hand, while dimly aware of a ticking clock, and completely unaware of other objects or sensations. The Functionalists, on the other hand, stressed the utility of attention. For them it was a force or process that was necessary for learning, or when old habits were inadequate. Thus one can attend to a conversation while he is walking along on a dry sidewalk, but he must shift his attention to his footsteps when he approaches a puddle. The Functional approach led to many facts that were useful in applied fields. For example, advertisers are interested in factors which will attract readers to their advertisements. Such factors, or "determiners," are size, movement, repetition, strangeness, certain colors, and relationship to strong interests. Many of these factors are relative, so that the actual attention-getting value of a specific advertisement must be determined by experimental test. Other applications are in the field of education. Here the effort is to tie new subjects to centers of the children's interest, thus using "derived primary" attention, rather than "secondary" or "forced" attention. The Behaviorists objected to the mentalistic connotations of the term attention, and frequently discarded it. But the material included under the term was too important to neglect. Therefore, most modern textbooks of psychology include a section or chapter on the subject, in which they present the traditional topics discussed above. The emphasis is on objective factors, such as eye movements and postural mechanisms. The problems of attention are closely related to neural processes of inhibition, facilitation, and integration. *See also* EXPERIMENTAL PSYCHOLOGY.   H. Sc.

ATTERBURY, FRANCIS [æ'tərbe'ri] (1662-1732), English prelate, was born in Buckinghamshire, near Newport-Pagnell, March 6, 1662. He received his education at

Westminster School and at Christ Church, Oxford. After service at St. Bride's, as lecturer and as royal chaplain, he became Dean of Carlisle in 1704; in 1712 he was made Dean of Christ Church, Oxford, having been a prolocutor in Convocation from 1710. In 1713 he was chosen Bishop of Rochester and also served as Dean of Westminster.

FRANCIS ATTERBURY

FROM AN ENGRAVING BY
H. T. RYALL FROM A
PAINTING BY
SIR GODFREY KNELLER

COURTESY OF THE NEW YORK
PUBLIC LIBRARY

As a vigorous supporter of the ecclesiastical authority, Bishop Atterbury soon found himself embroiled in difficulties with the state, and because of his sympathies with the Jacobites he took part in the movement which sought restoration of the Stuart dynasty. When the Hanoverian declaration of fidelity was promulgated in 1715, Atterbury was among those who declined to take the oath. This refusal combined with his support of the Jacobite plot for the Stuarts, brought

France, where he died on Feb. 22, 1732, in Paris. Atterbury was among the best-known opponents of the Hanoverians in the ecclesiastical sphere, and his deprivation and banishment caused considerable but ineffectual criticism in English circles. An account of his life and his politico-religious vicissitudes may be found in his *Memoirs and Correspondence,* published in London in 1869.   C. W. D.

ATTIC. *See* ARCHITECTURAL TERMS.

ATTICA [æ'tɪkə], the region around Athens, a triangular area jutting out from central Greece in a southeasterly direction into the Aegean Sea. To the northwest is Boeotia, and to the southwest, Megara. On the northern boundary of Attica are the Parnis Mountains, which slope down to the Athenian plain. The plain itself occupies the major portion of Attica and is bounded by Mt. Hymettus on the east, the Saronic Gulf on the south, and Mt. Aegaleus on the west. Across Mt. Aegaleus lay the road to the sacred city of Eleusis. Attica was noted in antiquity for its olive oil and for the fine honey from Mt. Hymettus. Silver was found on the tip of the peninsula at Laurium. The fine marble of Mt. Pentelicon and Mt. Hymettus was used to build the temples and other public buildings of Athens. Despite its long coastline, Attica has only one good seaport, Piraeus, which in the fifth century became the port serving Athens. The people of Attica in the classical period were related to the Ionians of Asia Minor. Attic, the Greek dialect of Attica and Athens, became the literary language of Greece. Pop. 1951, 1,553,815.   T. B. J.

ATTILA (ETZEL) [æ'tɪlə] (406-453), king of the Huns, was born in 406, the son of Mundsuk. In 434 he and

ATTILA AFTER THE BATTLE OF CHALONS

him into bad favor with the civil authorities, and in the year 1722 he was charged with treason and sent to the Tower of London. Parliament in a special bill deprived him of his offices, banished him from England, and refused him permission to return there during his lifetime. He went to

his brother succeeded to the throne of the Hunnic Empire, which stretched from the Caspian Sea to the Rhine River. Ten years later Attila had his brother killed and ruled alone. His raids on the Eastern Roman Empire gained him the title of "Scourge of God," and forced Theodosius II, the emperor at Constantinople, to pay an annual tribute in return for peace. In 450 Marcian, successor to Theodosius II, refused to pay tribute, and Attila, in order to retrieve his fortune, transferred his operations to Gaul. Aetius, commanding the troops of Valentinian III, with the help of the Visigoths, defeated the Huns at the battle of Châlons in 451. Subsequently, Attila invaded Italy, where he destroyed Aquileia, a city at the head of the Adriatic Sea. He also threatened Rome, but was dissuaded by an appeal made by Pope Leo I. Attila died in northern Italy in 453, and his empire soon disintegrated.   T. B. J.

ATTITUDE GYRO. *See* AIRCRAFT INSTRUMENTS.

ATTLEBORO [æ'təlbʌro], a city in Bristol Co., in southeastern Massachusetts, about 14 mi. northwest of Taunton. Settled in 1634, Attleboro was incorporated as a town in 1694 and as a city in 1914. A mayor and council administered the city in 1951. Among the colonial buildings that are of interest to the visitor is the Peck Homestead, which was built in 1706. The New York, New Haven and Hartford Railroad affords transportation for this industrial community. Attleboro is a noted center for the jewelry industry, which was established in the city in 1790. Other industries produce silverware, paper boxes, auto accessories, pressed steel, cotton machinery, and textiles. Pop. 1950, 23,809.

ATTLEE, CLEMENT RICHARD [æ'tli] (1883-   ), British political leader, was born in London, Jan. 3, 1883. Educated at Haileybury and University College, Oxford, he was admitted to the bar in 1905. From 1913 to 1923 he was

CLEMENT R. ATTLEE

COURTESY OF THE BRITISH
INFORMATION SERVICES

tutor and lecturer in social science at the London School of Economics. During this period Attlee engaged in social settlement work and lived in London's East End district. He served in World War I in the Tank Corps and attained the rank of major. In 1919 he was elected mayor of Stepney, and served as alderman from 1919 until 1927. He was elected to Parliament in 1922 as Labour Party member for the Limehouse division of Stepney, a seat he has held since, and in 1924 he was made Undersecretary of State for War. Attlee went to India in 1927 as a member of the Indian Statutory Commission under the chairmanship of Lord Simon, and since he supported self-government for India he dissented from the report of the Joint Select Committee in 1933. In the second Labour ministry he was Chancellor of the Duchy of Lancaster from 1929 to 1931, and Postmaster General in

1931. In 1931 he also was elected deputy leader of the Labour Party in the House of Commons but, with many of the Labour colleagues, he broke with Ramsay MacDonald when the latter formed the National Coalition government in 1931. In 1935 he succeeded George Lansbury as parliamentary leader of the Labour Party and leader of the opposition. Attlee opposed the policy of non-intervention in the Spanish Civil War, and denounced the Hoare-Laval Pact. When Winston Churchill became Prime Minister in 1940, Attlee joined his wartime coalition cabinet as Lord Privy Seal, and in 1942 he was made Secretary of State for the Dominions and Deputy Prime Minister. Attlee became Lord President of the Council in 1943. In 1945 he was a British delegate to the San Francisco Conference on World Security and was present at the Potsdam Conference in July of the same year. After the victory of the Labour Party in the elections of July 1945, he became Prime Minister.

As spokesman for his party, Attlee stated in a speech at Margate on May 27, 1947, that the chief problems which faced the British government at the end of World War II were the need for two transitions: (1) from a war to a peace economy, and (2) from a capitalism based on private enterprise and private property to a socialist economy based on the control and direction of the wealth and resources of the country in the interest of all the people. While the Labour Party under Attlee's leadership was in power, the Bank of England, the coal mining industry, the iron and steel industry, communications, gas and electricity production, and transportation were nationalized. A comprehensive system of social security came into force on July 5, 1948, as a consequence of the enactment of the National Insurance Act; the Industrial Injuries Act; the National Assistance Act, which abolished the last remnant of the old Poor Law; and the National Health Service Act, which provides that proper care and treatment shall not depend on financial resources, and with few exceptions provided for all hospitals to pass into the country's ownership. India, Pakistan, Ceylon, and Burma were given Commonwealth status, and the British mandate in Palestine was terminated. The agricultural industry was reorganized, and the Trade Disputes and Trade Unions Act of 1927 was repealed. In November 1948 Attlee stated that the European Recovery Program had helped to close the gap between imports and exports and to balance Great Britain's dollar account. He added that Great Britain was making a substantial contribution to the restoration of European economy under the inter-European payments scheme. Attlee approved the five-power treaty between the Benelux nations, and France and Great Britain signed at Brussels on Mar. 17, 1948. He was also a proponent of the North Atlantic Pact. The Labour Party survived the February 1950 elections by a narrow margin, but they were defeated in the close election of October 1951, and Attlee was succeeded as Prime Minister by Winston Churchill. Attlee is the author of *The Will and the Way to Socialism* and *The Labour Party in Perspective* (1937). E. R. A.

ATTRITION [ətrɪ'ʃən] (Lat. *attritio,* a rubbing upon), in ecclesiastical usage, a Scholastic technical synonym for imperfect contrition. Contrition is a sorrow of soul and a hatred of sin committed, linked with a firm purpose of not offending God in the future. Perfect contrition arises from the love of God; imperfect contrition (attrition) either from the turpitude of sin, or from the fear of hell and of punishment. The traditional Roman Catholic teaching, based on Scripture, was summarized in 1551 by the Council of Trent (Session XIV, Canon 5): If anyone says that attrition "is not a true and profitable sorrow; that it does not prepare the soul for grace, but that it makes a man a hypocrite . . . let him be anathema."   N. J. T.

ATTU [ættu'], the westernmost Aleutian island, located between the Bering Sea and the North Pacific Ocean, about 460 mi. east of the Kamchatka Peninsula of Siberia. The international date line makes a jog westward around Attu, which is so far west of North America that it is in the Eastern Hemisphere. Attu is a rocky, volcanic, almost

THE VILLAGE OF ATTU, ATTU ISLAND

barren island, with cool marine climate. Fog, drizzle, and rain predominate all year round. The summers are cool, and the winter temperature ranges around 30°-33°F. The island is sparsely inhabited by Aleuts, a branch of the Eskimos, who make a precarious living fishing and growing a few subsistence vegetables. Attu was invaded by Japanese on Apr. 8, 1942, and recaptured on May 11, 1943, by American and Canadian forces. American troops garrisoned it through the remainder of World War II as one of several Aleutian bases in the Alaskan defense system.   J. E. F.

ATWOOD, GEORGE (1746-1807), British mathematician, was born in 1746, entered Westminster School in 1759, and in 1765 received a scholarship to Trinity College, Cambridge. He graduated with a B.A. degree in 1769, becoming a fellow and tutor in the college. Three years later he received his M.A. degree. Atwood's lectures in the field of mathematics and "natural philosophy" were stimulating and effective, but his writings lacked these qualities, and have since been superseded. He is chiefly remembered for his original design of an apparatus for illustrating the accelerative action of gravity, known as "Atwood's machine." He became a fellow of the Royal Society in 1776. In 1784 Atwood left Cambridge to accept a sinecure position as a patent searcher of the customs, offered him by William Pitt, who had been an admirer of his lectures. In 1796 he was awarded the Copley Medal for an article on the mathe-

matical determinants governing the positions assumed by floating homogeneal bodies. He died in Westminster, July 7, 1807.   C. W. D.

ATWOOD, WALLACE WALTER (1872-1949), American geographer and geologist, was born in Chicago, Ill., Oct. 1, 1872, and was graduated from the University of Chicago in 1897. He taught at Lewis Institute, 1897 to 1899, at Chicago Institute, 1900 to 1901, at the University of Chicago, 1899 to 1913, and at Harvard University, 1913 to 1920. In 1920 he was appointed president of Clark University, where he established, and became the director of, the Graduate School of Geography. He was connected with the United States Geological Survey from 1901 to 1949. Collaborating with Rollin D. Salisbury, he published United States Geological Survey Professional Paper No. 60, *Interpretation of Topographic Maps* (1908), a study of the contour maps issued by the survey. The Atwood Geographical Textbook Series for public schools, numbering nearly one hundred, began in 1920; an advanced textbook for colleges, *The Physiographic Provinces of North America,* appeared in 1940, and for the general public he wrote *The Rocky Mountains* in 1945. In 1925 he founded and edited the journal *Economic Geography.* He retired as director of the Graduate School of Geography in 1946. He died at Annisguam, Mass., July 24, 1949.
         S. Van V.

ATYPICAL CHILDREN, a term in general use referring to children who deviate from the normal, physically, mentally, or socially, to such a degree that they require specialized educational planning and services. These deviant children are also commonly referred to as "exceptional." This term has won acceptance because it is broad enough to include the physically and mentally handicapped and the mentally superior, i.e., the gifted, as well as the mentally retarded.

Auxiliary education programs for exceptional children are required for approximately 12 per cent of the school population. The United States Office of Education classifies these children in the following groups, and estimates the incidence of each group as follows:*

ESTIMATED PERCENTAGE AND NUMBER OF EXCEPTIONAL CHILDREN IN THE UNITED STATES, 5 TO 19 YEARS OLD

(*On the basis of an estimated population of 33,604,000 children, 5 to 19 years of age, in 1945*)

Exceptional Children	Estimated Percentage	Estimated Number
Blind and partially seeing	0.2	67,208
Deaf and hard-of-hearing	1.5	504,060
Crippled	1.0	336,040
Delicate (of lowered vitality)	1.5	504,060
Speech-defective	1.5	504,060
Mentally retarded	2.0	672,080
Epileptic	.2	67,208
Mentally gifted	2.0	672,080
Behavior problems	2.5	840,100
Approximate total (estimate)	12.4	4,166,896

*Elise H. Martens, *Needs of Exceptional Children*, Leaflet No. 74, U. S. Office of Education (1944).

Educational services for exceptional children are administered on the state and local levels. The United States Office of Education provides consultation services through specialists, but does not administer programs. Approximately half of the states have one or more persons in the state department of education devoting time specifically to the administration of auxiliary education programs. Likewise the majority of the larger cities have personnel administering and supervising services for exceptional children.

Within a given state, the administration of the education for exceptional children is divided among several types of schools and agencies. In general, the typical publicly supported program includes: (1) state residential schools, (2) special schools and classes as part of the public-school program, (3) special commissions and agencies giving service to a specific type of handicapped child. Historically speaking, the state residential school is the oldest service, the first state-aided school for the deaf having made its appearance in Hartford, Conn., in 1817. The public school programs have developed within the present century, especially since 1920.

Every state makes some legislative provision for the education of its deaf and its blind children in residential schools, either within the state or in neighboring states. Every state also provides residential schools for socially maladjusted youth; and every state makes some provision for the institutionalization of its feeble-minded population. The Biennial Survey of Education (1938-40) gives the number of pupils reported in private and residential auxiliary schools in the United States as follows:

Blind	5,870
Deaf	14,673
Mentally deficient	21,800*
Delinquent	29,109

*Includes only children reported for school work.

The state departments of education usually have some official control of, or unofficial close, working relationship with, the schools for the deaf and the blind. Schools for the socially maladjusted and mentally retarded are administered, for the most part, by state institutional or welfare agencies. Residential schools are financed by state appropriations, and are under the immediate supervision of a superintendent. They all have well-organized educational programs, except for institutions for the mentally deficient, in which case custodial care tends to predominate.

Provision for auxiliary day-school classes is not nearly so common, though appropriate enactments are increasing with every session of the state legislatures. Approximately half of the states have one or more persons within the department of education devoting time to the administration and supervision of these classes. Great variation is found among the states in the types of children and types of provisions mentioned in their statutes. Physically handicapped children, that is, deaf and hard-of-hearing, blind and partially-seeing, and crippled children, are provided for most frequently. There is an increasing tendency to provide for mentally retarded children who have intelligence levels above those committed to state residential schools.

The education of mentally gifted children is not provided for in the auxiliary education statutes of any state. Several cities provide classes for such children as a part of their regular program. In general, however, school administrators in the United States have not favored this type of program, but have preferred plans which provide enrichment of the regular curriculum for intellectually superior children.

The day-school program is considered a financial obligation of the regular day-school district, or of the state supporting the district's program. Since the costs of educating the handicapped child are materially greater than the costs of the so-called normal child, the states provide extra assistance toward these excess costs. This assistance is distributed on a per-pupil basis, or as an extra allocation toward each teacher's salary.

The dates for the establishment of the first class held for each type of exceptional child are in dispute, but the following dates and cities are often quoted in literature on the subject: deaf (Boston) 1869; mentally retarded (Boston) 1896; orthopedic (Chicago) 1899; blind (Chicago) 1900; epileptic (Cleveland) 1906; speech therapy (Jersey City) 1911; sight saving (Boston and Cleveland) 1913.

Children who suffer from speech defects are served by specialists referred to as speech correctionists or speech pathologists. The correctionist travels from school to school and gives assistance on an individual or small group basis two or three times per week. The majority of defects found among school children are correctible through such assistance. Extreme cases must be referred to clinics for intensive remedial work.

Children who are homebound because of serious crippling conditions, or because they are convalescing from illness, are often provided with instruction by teachers who go to the home. Somewhat related to this service is the organized school program administered in children's hospitals, convalescent homes, and sanitaria. By means of these programs, many children keep up with their school work and often graduate with their classes when released from the hospital.

It is common practice for all handicapped children to be examined by appropriate specialists prior to assignment to special public school classes. Medical science in particular is given an opportunity to alleviate or minimize the handicap before the remedial program of the school is initiated. Class placement or assignment to a remedial program is considered a temporary measure for most children, and it is the goal of the school to return the child to the regular school program as soon as possible.

F. E. L.

AUBADE. *See* MUSICAL TERMS.

AUBE [o'b], a department in north-central France, with an area of 2,317 sq. mi., bounded by the departments of Marne on the north, Haute-Marne on the east, Côte d'Or and Yonne on the south, and Seine-et-Marne on the west. The surface is mostly level except in the southern portions. The southwest, in which the Forêt d'Othe is situated, is high, while the southeastern part of the department has greater elevation. The soil in the northwestern part of the department is poor, but on the more fertile soil in the south, in the chalky regions, rye and barley are grown. Potatoes are grown for home consumption and wine grapes and sugar beets are also cultivated. Sheep herding and dairy farming are important, and butter, cheese, and milk are sent to Paris markets. The Seine and its affluent, the Aube, are the principal rivers. Rayon and nylon fabrics are manufactured. Troyes, the prefecture, is a hat-manufacturing town; it is also rich in fifteenth-century to seventeenth-century works of art. At Bar-sur-Aube in 1440 Charles VII had the rebellious Bastard of Bourbon sewn into a sack and thrown into the river. Napoleon Bonaparte studied at the military school at Brienne le Château from 1779 to 1784. Because the town was partly destroyed by his artillery fire in January 1814, when he fought General Blücher there, Napoleon left the town a legacy of 1,000,000 francs; 400,000 francs of the legacy was finally paid to the town in 1854 by Napoleon III. The department was formed in 1790 from part of the department of Champagne and a small part of Burgundy. Pop. 1954, 240,797.   S. Van V.

AUBERVILLIERS [o'bɛ'rvi'lye'], a suburban city northeast of Paris, in the department of Seine-et-Oise, in northern France. It is an industrial suburb with factories chiefly manufacturing chemicals and metallurgical products. Aubervilliers was the headquarters of Henry IV when he besieged Paris. During the Middle Ages it was a place of pilgrimage to Notre Dame des Vertus. Pop. 1954, 58,740.   S. Van V.

AUBIGNAC, FRANÇOIS HÉDELIN, ABBÉ D' [o'bi'nya'k] (1604-1676), French dramatist and critic, was born in Paris, Aug. 4, 1604. He was reared in Nemours and became a self-taught lawyer at the age of twenty-three. Shortly thereafter he went to Paris, was ordained in the Church, and became tutor to Richelieu's nephew, for which he received the abbeys of Aubignac and Mainac. Piqued at not having been invited into the Académie Française, he founded his own "Little Academy" in 1654. He spent the last years of his life in Nemours, and died there July 20, 1676. Aubignac seems to have been arrogant and quarrelsome by nature, and took a violent part in many literary disputes of the day, particularly in that of the "Ancients" versus the "Moderns," siding with the latter. He wrote many sermons and four tragedies, *Cyminde* (1642), *La pucelle d'Orléans* (1642) ("The Maid of Orleans"), *Zénobie* (1647), and *Sainte Cathérine,* of which the original manuscript is lost, which served to illustrate his dramatic theories, but failed as drama. His most noted work, however, and an important historical landmark in the French theatre, is *La Pratique du théâtre* (1657) (*The Whole Art of the Stage,* 1684), written at the request of Richelieu. This work leans heavily on Aristotle, but advocates a greater degree of realism and adherence to the rule of the three "unities" for the dramatic poem. A posthumously published work, *Conjectures académiques sur l'Iliade* (1715), questions the existence of Homer, thus anticipating Wolf.   C. W. D.

AUBIGNÉ, THÉODORE AGRIPPA D' [o'bi'nye'] (1552-1630), French poet, soldier, and writer on historical, military and religious subjects, was born at Saint-Maury (Saintonge), Feb. 8, 1552. His education included Latin, Greek, Hebrew, Italian, and Spanish. Despite the considerable bulk of his published works, he was essentially a man

of action. Filled with fury, when eight years old, at the sight of Protestant skeletons hung from the battlements of Amboise, he became one of the fiercest, most ardent defenders of Protestantism. As aide-de-camp to Henry of Navarre, he took part in most of the important battles from 1573 to 1595. When Henry, as Henry IV of France, abjured the Protestant faith, D'Aubigné retired to his estates. He opposed the policies of Catherine de Médicis, and, in 1620, proscribed for his supposed part in an uprising under his friend Henri de Rohan, he fled to Geneva, where he died on April 29, 1630. A daughter of his son, Constant, became famous as Madame de Maintenon.

D'Aubigné's literary masterpiece, *Les Tragiques,* is a stirring, violent poem in seven cantos, much of it written in camp between battles. With pity and indignation D'Aubigné portrays the suffering of the peasants in their ravaged fields, satirizes the administration of justice and the royal court, and depicts the massacres on both sides in the religious wars, concluding with a powerful scene of the Last Judgment. His poetry is always forceful and eloquent, often obscure and diffuse, but picturesque in the details drawn from his own experiences and observations. When D'Aubigné's work was first published in 1616, François de Malherbe (1555-1628) had already proclaimed a new literary era and D'Aubigné's defects attracted the chief notice of contemporary critics. His very considerable merits were not recognized until the nineteenth century. In matters other than religion he exerted himself to be impartial and to give political, military, and historical details with accuracy. His most ambitious historical work is the *Histoire universelle depuis 1550 jusqu'à l'an 1601,* which appeared in three volumes between 1616 and 1619.
                    R. G. M.

AUBRIETIA [ɔbri'shiə], commonly known as the purple rock-cress. It is a genus of the cabbage family and is native to both southern Europe and Persia. One species, *A. deltoidea,* is much used as an edging or rock plant. It is an evergreen trailing perennial, two to twelve inches high, producing pale lavender flowers from March to June. Various garden varieties have been developed, such as the trumpet aubrietia with rose-lilac flowers.   J. C.Wis.

AUBURN [ɔ'bərn], a city in northeastern Indiana, the county seat of DeKalb Co., situated on Cedar Creek, 20 mi. northeast of Fort Wayne. Founded and established as the county seat in 1836, Auburn was incorporated as a city in 1900. In 1951 the government was of the mayor-council type. Transportation is furnished by the New York Central, the Pennsylvania, and the Baltimore & Ohio railroads. Local manufactures include auto parts, steel and lumber products, rubber soles and stamps, tires, metal products, and flour. Pop. 1950, 5,879.

AUBURN, a city of southwestern Maine, the county seat of Androscoggin Co., on the Androscoggin River opposite Lewiston, about 35 mi. north of Portland. In the surrounding region there are dairy and fruit farms, clay pits, and brickyards. Auburn, settled in 1786, adopted the city manager form of government in 1917. Transportation is supplied by the Northeast Airlines, the Maine Central, and the Grand Trunk railroads. Auburn, together with Lewiston, constitutes one of the largest manufacturing centers in Maine, women's shoes being Auburn's chief product. Pop. 1950, 23,134.

AUBURN, a town in Worcester Co., in central Massachusetts, 4 mi. south of Worcester, of which it is a residential suburb. Settled in 1714 and incorporated in 1914, it had the town meeting form of government in 1951. It is served by the New York, New Haven and Hartford Railroad. Pop. 1950, 8,840.

AUBURN, a city in central New York, the county seat of Cayuga Co., situated on the Owasco River, in the heart of the beautiful Finger Lakes region, about 25 mi. southwest of Syracuse. In 1793 Colonel John L. Hardenburgh laid out the settlement, which was called Hardenburgh's Corners. In 1805 the name was changed to Auburn, and the community was made the county seat. It was chartered as a city in 1848. Auburn Prison, which was built in 1816, is the oldest in the state and is famous for its Auburn system which combines solitary confinement at night with group work by day. The mansion of William H. Seward, Secretary of State under Lincoln, and the Cayuga Museum with its Indian relics are of special interest. Transportation is supplied by the New York Central and Lehigh Valley railroads. The surrounding fertile area produces grains, hay, and a variety of fruits. Auburn has a number of industries, the products of which are drop forgings, Diesel engines, ropes and twine, rugs, and agricultural implements. Pop. 1950, 36,722.

AUCASSIN ET NICOLETTE [o'ka'sæ' e ni'ko'lɛ't], a narrative, composed about 1200, partly in prose and partly in verse, and combining courtly idyl with feudal parody. The main action of the story takes place at the castle of Beaucaire, on the Rhône in Provence. Aucassin, only son of the Count of Beaucaire, is passionately in love with Nicolette, a girl who was captured in childhood by the Saracens and sold to a noble of Beaucaire. The Count's efforts to keep the lovers apart provoke Aucassin to various forms of defiance, including refusal to fight when an army is at the gates of Beaucaire, and end in the escape of Nicolette from the castle to the neighboring forest, where she is found by Aucassin. Further adventures by land and sea separate the lovers once more, but in the end they are reunited, Aucassin inherits his father's title, and Nicolette, who is discovered to be the daughter of the king of Carthage, is crowned Countess of Beaucaire.

The anonymous author of this piece, who probably came from Hainaut unless he was amusing himself by imitating a northern dialect, exhibits moods that elude the conventional classifications of scholars. The lovers' tribulations inspired him to authentic lyricism, but there are non-lyric passages that are more arresting. One such passage contains Aucassin's famous announcement that he prefers the glamor of Hell to the stodgy grimness of Paradise; another shows Aucassin so lost in dreams of Nicolette that he is listlessly indifferent to the perils of combat; still another describes the grotesque behavior of a king and queen encountered by Aucassin on his travels. In general, the work illustrates a type of medieval humor which has not received the imaginative interpretation it deserves.   E. B. H.

AUCHINLECK, SIR CLAUDE [ɔ'χɪnlɛ'k] (1884-   ), British soldier, was born in June 1884 at Aldershot, England. He graduated from Wellington College, and the Royal Military College, Sandhurst, and in 1904 was assigned to the Sixty-second Punjab Regiment as a second lieutenant. He served in India until the outbreak of World War I, when he went first to Egypt and then to Aden. In 1916 he was transferred to Mesopotamia, and during his three years' service there he was awarded the D.S.O., the O.B.E., and at the end of the war the Croix de Guerre. Auchinleck then returned to India with his regiment, and was on duty there as

an instructor at the Staff College; from 1930 to 1933 he taught at the Staff College at Quetta. In 1933 Auchinleck distinguished himself in an expedition against Afghan tribesmen at Khyber Pass; from 1936 to 1938 he served as deputy chief of the General Staff in India; and from 1938 to 1940, with the rank of colonel, he was commander of the Meerut District, India. Auchinleck, an exponent of armored warfare, is credited with having motorized the Indian Army. In May 1940, after the outbreak of World War II, he was sent to Norway as commander of the British Expeditionary Force. He captured and then lost Narvik. After withdrawing from Norway, Auchinleck became commander in chief of the Southern Command in England. In December 1940 he was appointed commander of the British Army in India, and in 1941 he replaced Gen. Archibald Wavell as commander in chief in the Middle East. In this post Auchinleck made plans for the British offensive which eventually drove the Germans out of northern Africa. In June 1943 he was succeeded by Sir Harold Alexander and returned to India as commander in chief, serving in that post until the realization of Indian independence in 1947. He was knighted in 1945, and on June 1, 1946, was promoted to field marshal.   S. D.

AUCKLAND [ɔ'klənd], a province and the capital city of that province, on North Island, in New Zealand.

The City. The city of Auckland is New Zealand's largest and principal city. It is located in the northwestern section of North Island, at 36° 52' S. lat. and 174° 46' E. long., on a low, narrow neck of land between Hauraki Gulf on the northeast and Manukau Harbor on the southwest. Auckland has a cool, humid, marine type of climate with an average annual temperature of 59° F. July is the coldest month and averages 51° F., while February, the warmest month, averages 67° F. The average annual rainfall is 44 in., and there is some rain every month. July is the wettest month, with an average of 5 in. of rain, and January the dryest, with 2 to 3 in. Auckland's favorable position and its excellent transportation facilities have been prime factors in its development as an export and import center and a manufacturing city. There are steamship and plane connections with the rest of New Zealand and the world, and it has rail and road connections with the important cities of North Island. The city's industries produce dairy products, lumber products, paper, rope, and brick.

Founded in 1840 by Governor William Hobson, Auckland was the capital of New Zealand until 1865, when the seat of government was moved to Wellington. The city is beautifully situated overlooking the harbor, one of the best in New Zealand. Queen Street, the main thoroughfare, is lined by the principal public buildings. Albert Park, directly fronting the harbor, has a fine bronze statue of Queen Victoria. There are other parks of note in and around the city. Of interest are two cathedrals, St. Mary's, Anglican, and St. Patricks, Roman Catholic. In the Auckland Museum there is an excellent collection of native Maori art. The city is the seat of Auckland University College, one of the four branches of the University of New Zealand. Other landmarks of the city include the "Old Windmill," the public library, and the art gallery. Outside the city is one of New Zealand's largest race tracks. Pop. 1947, 106,800.

The Province. Auckland Province occupies the northern half of North Island, and it is New Zealand's most northerly province. It contains approximately 25,400 sq. mi., including numerous islands off its northeastern coast. The northern part of the province is an elongated peninsula whose eastern coast is particularly indented by numerous bays and harbors.

The province contains a number of extinct volcanoes and two active ones, Ngauruhoe and Ruapehu. Auckland has many sites of natural beauty, and the thermal region about Rotorua is very scenic, with its geysers, pools of boiling mud, hot springs, sulphur springs, and curative baths. Coal is found in abundance, and it is mined in the Waikato District south of Auckland. Borings have been made for oil in the southeastern section of the province, but with little success. Quartz mining has replaced gold mining; the richest quartz deposits are found in the Waihi District.

Because of the year-round growing season and regular rainfall, farming flourishes. North of the city of Auckland

AUDE [o'd], a department in southern France bounded by the departments of Tarn on the north, Hérault on the northeast, Pyrénées-Orientales on the south, Ariège on the west, Haute-Garonne on the northwest, and the Gulf of Lions on the east. The department, 2,436 sq. mi. in area, has many hills and mountains, the massif of Madrès in the south, the Plantarel in the north, and the Corbières, which extend in a southwest-northeast direction. The Aude is the largest river, but is navigable only for rafts. There are iron mines and marble quarries. In the valleys and plains, more cereals are raised than are needed for local consumption, and vegetables and fruits, especially

COURTESY OF THE BRITISH PRESS SERVICE

AUCKLAND, NEW ZEALAND, SEEN FROM MT. EDEN

citrus and other fruits are the principal crops. There is some dairy farming, but it is in the Waikato District directly south of the city that dairy farming is the chief activity. This area is one of New Zealand's principal dairying regions. Sheep grazing is the principal occupation along the east coast of the province except around the Bay of Plenty, where corn growing is important. Pop. (est. 1947), 679,987.

                          J. E. F. and R. G. B.

AUCKLAND ISLANDS, a group of islands situated in the South Pacific Ocean, 290 mi. south of New Zealand, (50° 32′ S. lat. and 166° 13′ E. long.). The total area is approximately 234 sq. mi., the largest island in the group being 27 mi. long and 15 mi. wide. The islands have several good natural harbors, but the terrain is mountainous, with a maximum elevation of 2,000 ft.

Discovered by Captain Abraham Bristow of the whaling ship *Ocean* on Aug. 18, 1805, the islands were claimed by Great Britain and named for Lord Auckland. In 1847 the Aucklands were proclaimed outlying islands within the geographical boundaries of New Zealand. The Aucklands are uninhabited, although at various times they have been used as a temporary base for sealers plying the South Pacific and Antarctic waters. Several attempts to settle the islands have failed, and the meteorological station was closed in 1945. Supplies for shipwrecked seamen are cached on the islands.

AUCTION BRIDGE. *See* BRIDGE.

AUCTION COMPANIES. *See* MARKETING AND MERCHANDISING.

AUCTION PITCH. *See* CARD GAMES.

olives, are raised in the arrondissement of Narbonne. A large area is devoted to vineyards. Horses, mules, cattle, and sheep are raised in the prairies of Montagne Noire. Agricultural machinery is made at Narbonne and Carcassone. Carcassone, the prefecture, is divided by the Aude River, with the Ville Basse on the left bank and the Cité on the right bank, on a hill. This is a fortress dating from the fifth century, when Visigoths built there on Roman ruins. It was restored by the architect Viollet-le-Duc between 1855 and 1879. Narbonne, five miles from the Mediterranean and connected with it by the Canal de la Robine, is noted for its honey. The Romans used the mineral waters of Alet. The cathedral at Alet, the ruins of which still exist, was begun in 873, rebuilt in 1018, and eventually destroyed by the Protestants in 1577. The department was formed in 1790 from part of the old province of Languedoc. Pop. 1954, 268,254.   S. Van V.

AUDEN, WYSTAN HUGH [ɔ'dən] (1907-   ), Anglo-American poet, dramatist, and literary critic, was born Feb. 21, 1907, in York, England. He received his education at Gresham's School and Christ Church, Oxford, and after his graduation became the foremost of a group of leftist writers which included Stephen Spender, Christopher Isherwood, and Louis MacNeice. In his first book, *Poems* (1930), which combined ideas from Marx, Darwin, Freud, and Homer Lane, Auden celebrated in conversational rhythms the decay of middle-class society and his hopes for a new order; but his concern, unlike that of the Communists, with whom he was often confused, was with the gifted individual rather than with the masses. The social criticism implicit in this collection became explicit in his most Marxist poem, *The Dance of Death* (1933), a fantasia in doggerel verse, and in the three poetic plays he composed with Isherwood, of which *The Dog Beneath the Skin* (1935) and *The Ascent of F.6* (1936) are the most notable. The latter, successfully produced in London in 1937, is an expressionistic allegory of the gifted individual, torn between the pulls of right and left. This quandary, Auden's own and that of his generation, may also be detected in *Spain* (1937), the best of his political poems and one of the best of the many poems inspired by the Spanish Civil War. With MacNeice he wrote *Letters from Iceland* (1937) and with Isherwood, *Journey to a War* (1939), the latter an account of his visit to China. The poems of *Look, Stranger!* (1936) also prove him to be one of the best lyric poets of his time.

In 1939 Auden came to America where he lectured at the University of Michigan, Swarthmore, Barnard, and the New School for Social Research. After serving as a civilian attached to the United States Strategic Bombing Survey in 1945, he became a United States citizen on May 20, 1946. Poems published after his coming to America, *Another Time* (1940), *The Double Man* (1941), and *For the Time Being* (1944), are increasingly religious and philosophical. *The Collected Poetry* was issued in 1945, *The Age of Anxiety,* a "baroque" eclogue, in 1947, and *Nones* in 1951. He collaborated with Chester Kallman on the libretto for Stravinsky's opera *The Rake's Progress* (1953). Auden received the Bollingen Prize in Poetry for 1953. **W. Y. T.**

AUDHUMBLA [au′dhumlɑ], in Nordic mythology, a huge cow which came into existence together with the giant Ymir, progenitor of all the frost giants. She produced "streams of milk" to nourish Ymir. Audhumbla means "desert darkness," and the name probably refers to the cow's origin, for she sprang into existence when the warm winds met ice in the primeval "yawning chasm." Audhumbla nourished herself by licking salty ice-blocks. The licking also supposedly created the god Buri, father of Bor, who begot Odin, Vili, and Ve. **E. B. A.**

AUDIO-VISUAL AIDS, any apparatus or materials which give direct sensory experience, chiefly to the eye or ear, in order to make instruction or communication more realistic. Exclusively auditory aids are the radio, phonograph, public-address system, and sound recorder. Exclusively visual aids are the silent motion picture; still projections, such as slides, filmstrips, and opaques; flat pictures; maps and charts; and stereographs. Objects and models, sometimes called "mock-ups," involve three-dimensional experience. Auditory and visual experience are combined in the sound-film strip and the sound motion picture.

The use of audio-visual aids in entertainment, news dissemination, advertising, and propaganda was expanded enormously between World Wars I and II. Their use in education had a parallel development, but on a considerably smaller scale. Originally considered mere "aids" to learning, audio-visual apparatus and materials came to be recognized as highly effective tools for teaching. In particular, their influence upon social attitudes and patterns of conduct was clearly demonstrated. There was a growing recognition in library circles that many types of audio-visual material have values traditionally attributed only to books. Many libraries developed collections of phonograph records, motion picture films, and radio transcriptions. For the smaller schools, however, the cost of films remained prohibitive. The usual practice was to obtain films from rental libraries, generally in urban centers

or state universities. Under these circumstances, problems of distribution frequently hampered the school film program. During World War II the armed services training program brought about the use of audio-visual aids on a scale unimagined until then by any educator. It was estimated that during four years the armed forces created more than six times the quantity of audio-visual aids ever produced for educational purposes. Moreover, audio-visual aids were not regarded as mere auxiliaries, but were used in a great variety of training programs as the principal means of instruction. With the close of World War II, the impetus of the armed services training program began to be reflected in civilian education. Materials and equipment produced for military use were transferred to civilian schools in considerable quantity. Publishers began to produce films and recordings to accompany specific textbooks. Schools developed for themselves the simpler types of material in increasing quantities. With this went the realization that even a limited school library budget permits the development of valuable collections of phonograph records, flat pictures, miniature slides, and filmstrips. **M. L. S.**

AUDIT. *See* BUSINESS ORGANIZATION AND MANAGEMENT.

AUDITION, the faculty or sense of hearing. Audition depends upon: (1) the ear, which responds to sounds in the air surrounding it; (2) the auditory nerve, which is stimulated by the action of the ear; and (3) certain parts of the brain, in which the action of the auditory nerve produces awareness of the original sound stimulus.

Sounds may originate from any one of a number of sources, such as a violin string which has been bowed, the column of air pulsating in an organ pipe, or the vocal cords of a person speaking. The motion of each of these sources disturbs the surrounding air, first minutely compressing and then minutely decompressing it. From each source, consequently, there emanates a series of high-pressure and low-pressure waves which progress rapidly through the air. Such a moving train of waves constitutes a sound, the stimulus to audition.

Most of the sounds encountered in everyday life are very complex. Their sources execute very complicated movements, and the sound waves themselves are correspondingly complex. In experiments with audition the sound stimulus is usually made as simple as possible in order to clarify the experimental results. A great deal of care is taken to be sure that the sound source vibrates with the simple harmonic motion of a pendulum. The resulting train of sound waves, called a pure tone, shows a smooth, regular variation between high and low pressures.

Limits of Audibility. Pure tone is an ideal sound source which may be made to vibrate as slowly or as rapidly as one chooses. One of the primary questions in audition is that of how slowly or how rapidly the source may vibrate and still be heard by the human ear. The answer to this question has been determined experimentally. When the sound source is vibrating very slowly, at fewer than twenty complete vibratory cycles per second, one hears each individual sound wave separately; the experience is not one of hearing a continuous tone. As the frequency of vibration increases one begins to hear a continuous low tone much like that of the deepest bass pipe in a church organ. As frequency is further raised the tone becomes increasingly higher until, at a frequency of 1,000 cycles per second, one hears a note much like that of a soprano's high *C*. This note, however, is still far from the upper limit of human hearing. It is not until the frequency reaches the region of 20,000 cycles per second that the normal human ear gradually fails and then can no longer perceive the sound.

The ear is not equally sensitive to each of these frequencies of vibration. It is most sensitive to an intermediate range of frequencies, 1,000 to 4,000 cycles per second. Here, indeed, sensitivity is so extreme that any substantial increase would actually be disadvantageous; the ear would then detect the constant noise of molecules moving about at random in the air. As frequency decreases or increases from this central range of sensitivity, however, the acuity of the ear gradually diminishes. At the extremes of audible frequency a sound must be very powerful to be heard at all, so powerful that it may sometimes be physically felt before it can be heard.

Sound and Sensation. As has been implied, pure tones have two independent dimensions: (1) frequency, and (2) strength, or intensity. Frequency is measured by the number of complete vibratory cycles per second. Intensity is conveniently measured by the pressure-difference between the high-pressure waves and the low-pressure waves of the sound. It must be remembered that the terms "frequency" and "intensity" are used only in reference to sound, the external, physical stimulus to audition. The terminology applied in speaking of the sensation, the internal, subjective auditory experience, is somewhat different. Here, the highness or lowness of a heard sound is referred to as pitch, and the strength of the sensation as loudness. Generally speaking, pitch is the attribute of the sensation which varies closely with the frequency of the sound: higher frequencies have higher pitches. Likewise, in general, loudness of sensation varies directly with intensity of sound: more intense sounds seem louder. These relationships are not, however, invariable and absolute, as is often assumed. To some degree, pitch is affected by intensity and loudness by frequency. It is thus possible, for instance, to increase the frequency of a sound and yet prevent a corresponding increase in pitch by a judicious readjustment of the intensity of the sound.

"Just Noticeable Differences." A problem of considerable importance, both theoretical and practical, is that of "just noticeable differences" in frequency and intensity. By how much must the frequency or the intensity of a sound stimulus be changed before the change is just barely noticed by the listener? As it turns out, a certain proportionate change in the stimulus, rather than a certain absolute change, constitutes "a just noticeable difference." This statement is true both for changes in frequency and for changes in intensity.

The required proportionate change in frequency is not the same for sounds of all frequencies, nor is it the same even for sounds of the same frequency, but it is for those of different intensities. It can be said, however, that it approximates a constant value of 5 per cent over the wide range of frequencies from 1,000 to 12,000 cycles per second. The value increases somewhat for the higher frequencies, considerably for the lower frequencies. It is thus seen that the ear is less sensitive to changes in frequency at either end of the frequency scale than it is to changes in the intermediate range. This fact is often observed by those who play the piano; the high notes and low notes do not seem so far apart in pitch as the middle notes.

The situation with regard to just noticeable differences in intensity is somewhat different. A large relative change is required, a change of about 10 per cent in the difference between the pressure of the high-pressure waves and the pressure of the low-pressure waves. The required change is fairly constant for sounds of almost all frequencies and

intensities; however, when the intensity of the stimulus is low, the "just noticeable difference" increases considerably, especially, again, for the tones of lower frequency.

Overtones in the Ear. It is a peculiarity of almost any sound source that it vibrates, not with the simple harmonic motion which produces a single pure tone, but with a complicated motion which produces a complex of several simultaneous pure tones. Usually such a complex tone consists of a basic fundamental pure tone plus several overtones, pure tones whose respective frequencies are integral multiples of the fundamental frequency. Thus, an object vibrating at a fundamental frequency of 500 cycles per second may also produce overtones of 1,000 cycles, 1,500 cycles, 2,000 cycles, and so on. The human ear, in responding to a sound stimulus, behaves in much the same way. Its anatomical vagaries provide abundant opportunity for the energy of an incoming pure tone to be converted, at least partially, into overtones. Consequently, a careful listener may sometimes detect not only the fundamental tone, but a barely perceptible overtone or two, when a pure tone is directed into his ear.

The Interaction of Two Tones. When two pure tones are presented to the human ear, their combined effect may be one of several, depending upon the nature of the tones. The tones may mask each other. Masking is especially likely to occur when the tones are not widely disparate in frequency. The two tones also may combine. Combination tones are heard sounds whose frequency corresponds to the difference between the respective frequencies of the stimulating tones, or to the sum of those frequencies. When the two tones are made very nearly like in frequency, a single tone is heard, corresponding in pitch to the frequency being employed; that tone, however, waxes and wanes in loudness as the two slightly out-of-tune acoustic stimuli interact to reinforce and cancel one another.

Timbre. Objectively speaking, complex tones may differ in composition or complexity; the subjective attribute of sensation generally corresponding to this is called timbre. Thus, sensations from complex tones may be characterized not only by a certain pitch and loudness, but by a certain timbre as well; some seem rich and full, others do not. It is primarily by differences in timbre that one distinguishes among the sounds of the various musical instruments. The note *A*, as played on the piano, is easily differentiated from the same note as played on the violin; if, however, one contrives to filter away and silence all of the overtones from each instrument, the two notes become indistinguishable.

Localization of Sounds. Not only can the human ear distinguish among sounds and their sources, but both ears working together are capable of localizing rather accurately the direction from which a sound happens to be coming. Because the two ears are on opposite sides of the head, the stimulus that reaches one ear from a given source is, in general, slightly different from the stimulus which reaches the other ear. The human mind interprets such a minute difference rather effectively to determine the direction of the sound source. A sound source almost directly in front of the head is localized along the right-to-left dimension correctly within a few degrees, and localization when the source is farther to either side of the head is only somewhat less accurate; the distinctions between front and back, and between up and down, are more difficult.

Anomalous Audition and Animal Hearing. Although the normal stimulus to human audition is air-borne sound, the ear may be effectively stimulated in other ways. To hear under water is, for instance, a fairly common experience. Again, the application of a vibrating body to one of the bony parts of the head will often arouse sensation through bone-conduction of the sound. This latter fact has a great practical utility in some forms of deafness; if a small transmitter is applied directly to the mastoid process of the skull, immediately behind the ear, the afflicted individual is often able to hear sounds imparted to the skull by the transmitter.

Audition is, of course, not a uniquely human faculty. The ability to hear is found far down the animal scale, even among insects and fishes. The various species are sensitive to various ranges of frequencies of sound, some hearing a smaller range than man, some a larger. A notable example of the latter case is the dog, whose ear is sensitive to frequencies above those which can be heard by man. *See also* SOUND. K. R. S.

AUDITORY CANAL. *See* EAR.

AUDRAN [o'drã'], a family of French engravers. Charles (1594-1674) first made the house renowned. Benoît II the Younger (1698-1772) was last of the family. Others were Benoît I, Claude I the Elder, Claude II the Younger, Claude III, Gabriel, Germain, and Louis. Gérard and Jean were the most illustrious.

Gérard (or Girard) Audran (1640-1703), French engraver, was born at Lyon on Aug. 2, 1640. From his father, Claude the Elder, he learned the first principles of design and engraving, then perfected himself under the direction of his uncle Charles in Paris. At Rome in 1667 he studied under Carlo Maratti and Ciro Ferri, developing a picturesque and original style that placed him among the most eminent engravers. His engraving of a portrait of Pope Clement IX made him famous. Returning to Paris, he became engraver to the king and was lodged at the Gobelins. Gérard reproduced several paintings of Charles Le Brun. He went to Rome again about 1675. His engravings, other than portraits, are illustrative of the Old and New Testaments, Classical mythology, and history. He died at Paris on July 26, 1703.

Jean Audran (1667-1756), French engraver, was born at Lyon on Apr. 28, 1667. He learned the principles of engraving from his father, Germain, then studied with his celebrated uncle Gérard in Paris. At twenty he ranked among renowned artists. In 1707 he was named engraver to the king, pensioned, and lodged at the Gobelins. His subjects are similar to those of Gérard Audran. He died at Paris, June 17, 1756.

AUDUBON, JOHN JAMES [ɔ'dəbən] (1785-1851), ornithologist and artist, was born at Les Cayes, Santo Domingo, now Haiti, Apr. 26, 1785, the natural son of Jean Audubon, a native of Les Sables, La Vendée, France, and a Creole woman known as Mlle. Rabin. In 1794 he was legally adopted by his father, at Nantes, France, and at thirty years of age assumed his father's name. When four years old, he was taken by his father to France, where he later studied art under the famous painter, Jacques Louis David. His studies, however, were interrupted by the outbreak of the French Revolution and his subsequent induction into the French Navy. In 1803 he emigrated to the United States and settled near Philadelphia. There he married Lucy Bakewell in 1808, and, in the same year, went to Louisville, Ky., where he opened a general store. Becoming bankrupt in 1819, he traveled down the Mississippi River painting birds. Arriving in Louisiana, he worked as a tutor and drawing teacher at New Orleans and St. Francisville. The *Birds of America,*

to which he owes his fame, was published in four volumes, from 1827 to 1838; his *Ornithological Biography* was published in five volumes from 1831 to 1839; *Synopsis of the Birds of North America* was published in two volumes from 1845 to 1848.

A tireless student of nature, Audubon portrayed with scrupulous care not only the birds but the accessories and environment of which he considered the birds a part. The

JOHN JAMES AUDUBON

COURTESY OF THE AMERICAN
MUSEUM OF NATURAL HISTORY

tree limb from which he had shot an eagle was reproduced in one of his illustrations with the meticulous devotion to detail that he bestowed on the bird itself.

In his efforts to secure a publisher, and afterwards, while the volumes were going through the press, Audubon divided his time between England and the United States. In 1840 he settled in New York City, where he carefully revised his *Birds of America* and prepared *The Viviparous Quadrupeds of North America.* After 1847 his health began to fail and he gradually lost his mind. He died in New York City, Jan. 27, 1851. A. W. Gr.

AUDUBON, a borough in Camden Co., in southwestern New Jersey, 4 mi. southeast of Camden. Named after John J. Audubon, the ornithologist, it was incorporated in 1905. Although primarily a residential suburb of Camden and Philadelphia, Pa., Audubon produces leather goods and plumbing supplies. The Pennsylvania-Reading Seashore Line supplies transportation. Pop. 1950, 9,531.

AUDUBON SOCIETIES. The original Audubon Society, named after the great naturalist John James Audubon, was founded in New York City in February 1886 for the purpose of protecting American birds from total destruction in commercial ventures. At that time, indiscriminate slaughter threatened to render many species extinct. The movement began on a small scale and with little authority. In 1905, to achieve greater control, the well-financed National Audubon Society for the Protection of Birds, later the National Audubon Society, superseded the parent organization. Largely as a result of its activities, in 1918 a treaty between the United States, Great Britain, and Canada, by which most of the migratory birds were given governmental protection, was enacted. As a result, much "shooting" of birds is done with camera instead of with gun. The National Audubon Society, through its local units in the United States and Canada with a 1948 membership of 14,000 adults, is frequently affiliated with local or national scientific bodies such as the Chicago Academy of Sciences and the United States Fish and Wildlife Service.

Patrolled sanctuaries all over the United States and Canada

have been established, and beginning in 1911 Junior Audubon Clubs have been organized, chiefly in public schools. More than eight million schoolchildren have been enrolled. In 1948, 311,768 boys and girls in 12,559 clubs were active throughout the United States and Canada. The organization of Audubon Nature Camps was begun in Maine in 1936 and is spreading throughout the United States. *The Audubon Magazine* began publication in February 1887 but was discontinued in June 1888. In 1899, *Bird Lore,* which later became *The Audubon Magazine,* was begun; since 1934 this publication has been the property of the National Audubon Society. In 1946, the Society, in collaboration with the Fish and Wildlife Service, began bimonthly publication of *Audubon Field Notes,* a magazine devoted to bird watching. The headquarters of the National Audubon Society are at 1000 Fifth Avenue, New York City. In 1948 in the United States and Canada there were 31 independent branches and 150 affiliates, such as bird and garden clubs.

AUER, LEOPOLD [auʼər] (1845-1930), Hungarian violinist and teacher, was born June 7, 1845, at Veszprém. A pupil of Ridley Kohne, Jakob Dont, and Joseph Joachim,

LEOPOLD AUER

Auer built his reputation as soloist and pedagogue during a half century as professor at the Imperial Conservatory, St. Petersburg. In 1918, he took up residence in New York, where he spent most of the remainder of his lifetime. Among Auer's pupils were Jascha Heifetz, Mischa Elman, Efrem Zimbalist, and Nathan Milstein. He died near Dresden, July 17, 1930.   P. G. G.

AUERBACH, BERTHOLD [auʼərbɑχ] (1812-1882), German novelist, was born Feb. 28, 1812, in Nordstetten, a Black Forest village in Württemberg. His Swabian peasant-merchant family intended him for the rabbinate, but the study of law and philosophy at Tübingen, Munich, and Heidelberg diverted him to literature. His novels based on the history of Judaism and his translation of Spinoza's complete works (1841) were followed by the *Schwarzwälder Dorfgeschichten* (1843-1854) (*Black Forest Village Stories,* 1874). The refined realism and reflective idealism with which he here depicted peasant life won him European fame and many imitators. Further works of fiction included *Barfüssele* (1856) (*Little Barefoot,* 1913-1914), *Edelweiss* (1861), (English translation, 1869), the much-translated *Auf der Höhe* (1865) (*On the Heights,* 1912), and *Das Landhaus am Rhein* (1869) (*The Villa on the Rhine,* 1911). He died Feb. 8, 1882, at Cannes, France.   R. S. B.

AUERSPERG, ANTON ALEXANDER, GRAF VON [auʼərspɛrχ] (1806-1876), Austrian poet and statesman, pseudonym Anastatius Grün, was born at Laibach, Carniola, Apr. 11, 1806. In youth he inherited family estates, including the castle of Thurn-am-Hart. Auersperg studied law and philosophy at the universities of Graz and Vienna, after which he traveled in Italy, France, England, and Germany. In 1848 he was elected to the German *Vor-Parlament,* and later represented Laibach in the National Assembly, though he took no conspicuous part in the proceedings. After the violent deaths of two fellow members at Frankfurt, Sept. 18, 1848, he retired from public life, although he later sat in the House of Lords. Auersperg was regarded as the leader of the liberal party in Austria. In 1830 under his nom de plume he published *Blätter der Liebe* ("Leaves of Love"), a volume of poems, and *Der Letzte Ritter* ("The Last Knight"), a ballad-cycle based upon the life of Emperor Maximilian I (1459-1519). Distinctly a political—even a national—poem, it traced the origin and development of liberal monarchy. Pleading for civic liberties, it expressed love of "Old Austria" and resentment against the reactionary policies of her nineteenth-century rulers. Anastatius Grün immediately won wide celebrity. His fame increased with the appearance in 1831 of *Saunterings of a Vienna Poet,* a collection of thirty patriotic poems, which demanded a constitutional monarchy. His later works include *Schutt* ("Ruins"), *Gedichte* ("Poems"), *Nibelungen im Frack* ("Nibelungen in Evening Clothes"), and *Pfaff vom Kahlenberg* ("Priest of Bare Mountain"). None of his other poetry compares with his political verse. Grün, Georg Herwegh, and Ferdinand Freiligrath form the lyric triumvirate of the German Revolution of 1848-1849. An aristocrat, not a republican, Auersperg favored paternal monarchy, justice, and equal opportunity for all. He died at Graz on Sept. 12, 1876.   T. R.

AUFIDIUS. *See* Tullus Aufidius.

AUFRECHT, THEODOR [auʼfrɛχt] (1822-1907), German Indologist and linguist, was born at Heschwitz in Upper Silesia, Jan. 7, 1822. He studied in the University of Berlin from 1843 to 1847 with Franz Bopp, Karl Lachmann, August Böckh, A. Kirchhoff, Adalbert Kuhn, and Albrecht Weber and received his doctoral degree at Halle in 1847. He taught as *Privatdozent* in Berlin from 1850 to 1852, worked in the Bodleian library in Oxford from 1852 to 1862, accepted a call to Edinburgh in 1862, and in 1875 succeeded Christian Lassen at Bonn, continuing in this position until his retirement from teaching in 1889. Aufrecht founded in 1851, with Adalbert Kuhn, the *Zeitschrift für vergleichende Sprachforschung.* Among his many important works may be mentioned the first critical work on the Iguvinian tables, which were discovered at Iguvinium, Italy, in 1444, *Über die umbrischen Sprachdenkmäler* (with A. Kirchhoff, 2 vols., 1849-1851); the great standard edition of the whole *Rig-Veda* in transcription, *Die Hymnen des Rigveda* (1861-1863); the *Catalogus codicum sanscritorum postvedicorum* (1859-1864); *A Catalogue of Sanskrit Manuscripts in the Library of Trinity College* (1869); *Über die Paddhatī von Sārngadhara* (1873); *Aitareya Brāhmana* (1879); and especially the enormous *Catalogus catalogorum* (1891-1903), in three volumes, containing a detailed description of practically all Sanskrit manuscripts known at the time of publication. Aufrecht died in Bonn, Apr. 3, 1907.   G. B.

AUGEAN STABLES. *See* Heracles.

AUGIER, GUILLAUME VICTOR ÉMILE [o′zhye′] (1820-1889), French dramatist, was born at Valence (Drôme) on Sept. 17, 1820. The grandson of the novelist Pigault-Lebrun, Augier was a member of the upper middle class. He studied law, but did not practice, and in 1844 he wrote *La Ciguë* ("The Hemlock"), a verse play in two acts, the first work of his which was presented on the stage.

Augier shares with Alexandre Dumas *fils* the position as creator of the Realistic drama. His first plays, written in verse, attack the Romantic fictions still very popular in his time. Thus in *L'Aventurière* (1848) (*The Adventuress,* 1888), he exposes the guile of an adventuress who tries to marry into a respectable family, while in *Gabrielle* (1849) he denounces the favorite Romantic theme of the self-justification of passion. He defends again the sanctity of the family in *Le Mariage d'Olympe* (1855) (*The Marriage of Olympe,* 1915), which is directed against *La Dame aux camélias* of Alexandre Dumas *fils* and its romanticized portrait of a prostitute, but in *Madame Caverlet* (1876) he admitted the legitimacy of divorce. *Le Gendre de M. Poirier* (1854) (*Monsieur Poirier's Son-in-Law,* 1915) pokes fun at a bourgeois *nouveau riche* who marries his daughter to a

GUILLAUME VICTOR ÉMILE AUGIER

BY E. COTTINET

ruined nobleman who despises him. In *La Ceinture dorée* (1855) Augier condemns the unscrupulous acquisition of wealth; he attacks dishonest speculations in *Les Effrontés* (1861), and greed, even when cloaked with strict legality, in the powerful play, *Maître Guérin* (1864). *Le Fils de Giboyer* deals with the excesses of journalism, and *Lions et renards* (1869) with the intrigues of the clergy in politics. Augier has been one of the most successful of French dramatists: between 1845 and 1900 there were 2,656 performances of his plays at the Comédie Française. He withdrew from the stage at the height of his popularity, after *Les Fourchambault* (1878) (*The House of Fourchambault,* 1915), ending his dramatic career much as he had begun it, with a play devoted to the preservation of the integrity of the family. He died on Oct. 25, 1889, at Croissy.   F. V.

AUGITE. *See* PYROXENE GROUP.
AUGMENTATION. *See* MUSICAL TERMS.

AUGSBURG [au′ksburχ], a commercial and industrial city in Bavaria, southern Germany, 35 mi. northwest of Munich, at 48° 20′ N. lat., and 10° 53′ E. long. It lies at the confluence of the Wertach and Lech rivers on the high Bavarian plateau. Founded by the Romans about 15 B.C., it became a free imperial city in 1276 and the wealthy center of North European-Levantine trade in the fifteenth and six-

teenth centuries. The Confession of Augsburg, the most celebrated creed of the Lutheran churches, was read in the former Bishop's Palace in 1530. Fortifications, dismantled in 1703, became walks and boulevards. In 1806, the city became a part of Bavaria. Large aircraft factories drew severe World War II air raids which destroyed the city's medieval beauty, and damaged many old buildings, including the tenth-century cathedral, St. Anna Church, as well as St. Ulrich Church, town hall, and Fugger House. A rail and road junction, Augsburg was an important textile producing center, while other manufactures included machinery, chemicals, and paper. After World War II, Augsburg was placed in the United States occupation zone. Pop. 1953, 196,600.   C. C. H.

AUGSBURG CONFESSION, the earliest of many formal statements of belief prepared by Protestants, and still the chief standard of Lutherans. It was presented to the German Diet of Augsburg, June 25, 1530, in response to a request of Emperor Charles V, who hoped to effect thereby a reunion of religious parties in Germany. This circumstance, together with the recent failure of Martin Luther and Ulrich Zwingli to compose their differences in the Marburg Colloquy (1529), accounts in part for the document's conciliatory attitude toward Catholicism and its sharp repudiation of radical Protestantism. The irenical Philip Melanchthon was the author of the confession, but he prepared it in consultation with Luther and other theologians. Moreover, he based it on earlier statements, notably the Schwabach Articles (1529) and the Torgau Articles (1530).

The first part of the confession, consisting of twenty-one brief paragraphs, discusses such basic subjects as belief in God, belief in Christ, sin, justification, the Christian life, the Church, the ministry, the Sacraments, civil affairs, and the Last Judgment. The second part, comprising seven longer articles, treats abuses in the Church which the confessors claim to have corrected: the notion of merit, the Mass, confession, celibacy, monasticism, and episcopal authority.   T. G. T.

AUGUSTA [augu′stɑ], a small seaport and naval station at the northern end of the Gulf of Augusta on the east coast of Sicily, about 20 mi. north of Syracuse. It is situated on an island, once a peninsula, connected by bridge with the mainland. Between the island and the mainland to the west lies a well-protected bay 6 mi. long and 3 mi. wide, with a minimum depth of 45 ft., offering one of the largest and most secure anchorages in the Mediterranean Sea. Prior to and during World War II the Italian navy used it as a secondary base and supply point and as a principal station for naval aviation. These installations were heavily bombed by the Allies in 1942 and 1943. The port's commercial traffic has been small in relation to its potentialities.

The city owes its name and origin to the Emperor Augustus, who placed a Roman colony there in 42 B.C. Devastated by the barbarians and Saracens, it was rebuilt according to its existing regular plan by Frederick II after 1232 and provided with a tower. Under Spanish rule it was subject to Moorish attacks. Its fortifications were strengthened and the peninsula made into an island by digging a ditch. In 1649 the Knights of Malta were given rights to build warehouses and barracks and other buildings in Augusta to be used as a base, and this concession endured until the beginning of the nineteenth century. An earthquake destroyed the city in 1693, and it was long in recovering its importance. Another quake in 1848 wrecked two thirds of the city, but after the Unification of Italy it revived. Pop. 1936, 17,716.   R. G. W.

AUGUSTA [ɔgʌ'stə], a city in northeastern Georgia, the county seat of Richmond Co., 110 mi. northwest of Savannah, at the head of navigation on the Savannah River. The surrounding land is fertile farming country, producing cotton, corn, grains, peaches, and truck crops. Augusta's scenic location and mild climate has made it a popular winter resort.

The Cherokee Indians had a trading post on the city's site, and in 1735 General James Ogelthorpe established Fort Augusta. In 1798 the community was incorporated as a town, and in 1817 it became a city. In 1951 a mayor and council governed the city, which is rich in historical background. At the beginning of the American Revolution the inhabitants were Loyalists. The town was the meeting place of the Land Court which confiscated the Loyalist property in Georgia, and of the convention which ratified the Constitution of the United States. During the Civil War its factories produced military supplies for the Confederacy. The great fires of 1829 and 1916 destroyed many buildings of historic and architectural interest. Among those remaining are St. Paul's Church, founded in 1750; the Academy of Richmond County, established in 1783; the home of George Walton, a signer of the Declaration of Independence; a standing chimney of a Confederate powder mill; and the Manse, where Woodrow Wilson lived. Near by is the site of the first cotton gin built by Eli Whitney. Augusta's educational institutions include the State Medical College of the University of Georgia, Paine College for Negroes, and the Junior College of Augusta.

The Southern, the Atlantic Coast Line, the Augusta & Summerville, the Central of Georgia, the Charleston & Western Carolina, the Georgia, and the Georgia & Florida railroads, and Delta Air Lines provide transportation. Augusta is an important cotton center. In addition to cotton cloth and waste, the city's factory output includes bagging, textiles, cottonseed oil products, rayons, lumber and mill work, fire and building brick, tile, and fertilizers. Pop. 1950, 71,508.

AUGUSTA, the capital city of Maine, the county seat of Kennebec Co., 62 mi. northeast of Portland, on both banks of the Kennebec River. Records indicate a settlement in 1607 on the site of an Indian village. In 1627 a trading post of the Plymouth Colony was established there. It was incorporated as Harrington in 1797, the same year it was renamed Augusta. The community became the state capital in 1831 and was chartered as a city in 1849. A point of interest in the city is Fort Western, built in 1754 and restored as a museum in 1919. This landmark is associated with such historic names as Benedict Arnold, Aaron Burr, and Paul Revere. The executive mansion is the former home of James G. Blaine, who lived in Augusta for a large portion of his public life.

Transportation for the city is furnished by the Northeast Airlines and the Maine Central Railroad. Augusta serves as the trade center for the surrounding agricultural region. It is an industrial metropolis including among its industries printing and publishing and the manufacture of cotton goods, shoes, carbonated beverages, paper, lumber, paper tissue, and ice cream. Pop. 1950, 20,913.

AUGUSTANA COLLEGE, an accredited, coeducational private college of arts and sciences owned by the Lutheran Augustana Synod, at Rock Island, Ill. It started in 1860 at Chicago, moved to Paxton, Ill., in 1863, and to its present location in 1875. Until 1947 it was known as Augustana College and Theological Seminary. At that time the synod established separate boards for the operation of the institutions. Augustana College is located in the center of the Tri-Cities of Davenport, Iowa, and Moline and Rock Island, Ill.

Degrees of A.B., B.S., B.Mus., and B.Mus.Ed. are offered in the college of liberal arts, the school of nursing, and the school of music, respectively. The degrees of B.D. and M.S.Th. are offered in theology.

Special features include an amateur radio station operated by the college and administered by the speech department. Educational silent and sound films are used in classes, primarily in foreign languages and the natural sciences. An adult education program offering noncredit courses was inaugurated in 1931. Dormitory facilities are provided and out-of-town students must reside in the college dormitories. Scholarship and loan funds are available. *For statistics see* COLLEGES AND UNIVERSITIES. J. R. To.

AUGUSTANA COLLEGE, a coeducational, private institution, controlled by the Evangelical Lutheran Church, at Sioux Falls, S. D. Started in 1860 at Chicago as Augustana Seminary, the institution moved in 1863 to Paxton, Ill., and the present name was adopted there, one division being established for Swedish and one for Danish and Norwegian students. The Danish and Norwegian division then moved to Marshall, Wis., to become Marshall Academy. After a number of changes in name and location, determined by a desire of the church to keep the institution near the center of its membership, the college located in Sioux Falls and again became Augustana College. Only the A.B. degree is offered. Limited scholarship and loan funds are available to residents of South Dakota. Nonresident freshmen and sophomores reside in college dormitories insofar as possible; deans of men and women supervise rooming arrangements off the campus. *For statistics see* COLLEGES AND UNIVERSITIES. J. R. To.

AUGUSTAN AGE. *See* ENGLISH LITERATURE, HISTORY OF; LATIN LITERATURE.

AUGUSTA VICTORIA [ɔgʌ'stə vɪktɔ'riə] (German, Auguste Viktoria) (1858-1921), German empress, the daughter of Frederick VIII, duke of Schleswig-Holstein-Sonderburg-Augustenburg. In 1881 she married the prince who in 1888 became Emperor William II of Germany. Her simplicity and piety in her paternal home remained characteristic of her life as empress. She was the mother of six sons and one daughter.

AUGUSTE, JULES-ROBERT [o'gü'st] (1789-1850), French painter, known as Monsieur Auguste, was born on April 6, 1789, in Paris. On receiving the *Prix de Rome* in 1810, he left for Italy, and thence traveled to Greece, Syria, and Egypt, returning to Paris about 1820 with a vast collection of fabrics, costumes, and curios. Here he communicated his enthusiasm for orientalism to a group of painters and writers among whom were Jean Géricault, Ferdinand Delacroix, and Prosper Mérimée. Through modesty or indifference he attached little importance to his own works, and, after his death in Paris, April 15, 1850, was nearly forgotten until 1930, when an exhibition in the Paris *Orangerie* brought to light his Oriental pastels, and reinstated him in his true significance. K. B.

AUGUSTINE, ST. (AURELIUS AUGUSTINUS) [ɔ'gəstin; ɔgʌ'stɪn] (354-430), foremost of the Latin Church Fathers, was born at Tagaste in Roman North Africa on Nov. 13, 354.

Life. In the life and intellectual development of Augustine three periods may be distinguished, each of which reflects one of the three cultural traditions of antiquity which went into the formation of Western Christianity. As student and teacher of grammar and rhetoric, until the time of his conversion in 386, Augustine absorbed the civic and pagan culture represented by Roman liberal education. From 386 until his entrance into the priesthood in 391, he was primarily influenced by Greek speculative philosophy, in terms of which

ST. AUGUSTINE
FROM *CANONS OF ST. AUGUSTINE*, PRINTED BY MARTIN SCHOTT, 1490

he tended to interpret his newly embraced Christian faith. From 391 until his death in 430, his life and thought were dominated by a practical, dogmatic, and historical conception of Christianity, rooted in the Bible and the religious tradition of the Jews.

First Period (354-386). The story of Augustine's life, up to the time of his conversion and baptism, is told with moving simplicity in his great spiritual autobiography, the *Confessions.* Though his mother, Monica, was a devout Christian, his father, Patricius, was a pagan. At school Augustine showed aptitude at his studies, and his parents, aided by a wealthy citizen of Tagaste named Rominianus, stretched their modest resources to educate him for a career as a teacher. After studying grammar at the near-by city of Madaura, Augustine was sent to Carthage, at the age of seventeen, for his higher education in a school of rhetoric. Here he became acquainted with the pleasures and dissipations of a great city, forming an attachment to a mistress to whom he remained faithful for fourteen years, who bore him a son to whom he gave the name Adeodatus. After completing his studies, Augustine taught grammar at Tagaste for two years, and in 375 set up his own school of rhetoric at Carthage. The reading of Cicero's *Hortensius* aroused Augustine, at the age of nineteen, to a consciousness of his need of a philosophy that would give meaning and purpose to his life. He first turned to his mother's religion, but on reading the Bible he was repelled by the crudities of its style, and felt that the

teaching of the Old Testament was in contradiction to that of the Gospels. The sect of Manichaeans, who taught that God is opposed by an eternal principle of evil, seemed to Augustine to offer a more convincing explanation of the source of unhappiness and of sin than did his mother's faith, and to her great distress, he joined the Manichaeans, remaining outwardly a member of their sect until 384. Yet he soon became dissatisfied with their teachings, which he found inconsistent and superstitious. Despairing of certitude, he came to consider himself a skeptic of the Academic school, in the manner of Cicero.

In the autumn of 383 Augustine moved to Rome, where he hoped to achieve fame and fortune as a rhetorician. After a year of disappointment and illness, he was glad to accept a salaried post as professor of rhetoric at Milan. The most important personage at Milan was Ambrose, Catholic bishop and future saint. Augustine, listening to the bishop's sermons, was charmed by his Ciceronian eloquence and by his allegorical interpretations of the Bible. At this time he also read the works of the Neo-Platonic philosophers, Plotinus and Porphyry, which had been translated into Latin by Marius Victorinus, a famous rhetorician of the day, and he was through these influences brought to reconsider Christianity in the light of the Neo-Platonic doctrines of the immateriality of God and the soul, and of the unreality of evil when viewed as a mere privation of good. By 386 he was intellectually converted, but still unable to renounce a life of passion and pleasure. Dismissing his faithful mistress when his mother, who had joined him at Milan, persuaded him to arrange a suitable marriage, Augustine found continence impossible and promptly found another concubine. The end of his moral conflict, vividly described in the *Confessions,* came in July 386, through a sudden and complete conversion of will, which Augustine always felt to have been a miraculous intervention of the Holy Spirit. This personal experience undoubtedly influenced Augustine in his later opposition to Pelagianism.

Second Period (386-391). During the eight months, preceding his baptism by Ambrose in April 387, Augustine retired to a villa at Cassiciacum, near Milan, provided by a friend. Here, with the companionship of his mother, his brother Navigius, his son Adeodatus, and some young friends, he wrote a number of philosophical dialogues. The *Contra Academicos* was directed against the skepticism which he had previously professed; the *De ordine, De beata vita,* and *Soliloquia* were in large measure directed against his earlier Manichaeanism, and treated of the problem of evil, the immateriality and immortality of the soul, and the conception of happiness as consisting in the knowledge and love of God. Some of these dialogues were apparently stenographic records of actual conversations between Augustine and his companions, revised by him for publication. They exhibit the optimistic enthusiasm of a convert, convinced that he has found the answers to all the problems of philosophy and religion. A treatise, *De musica,* and some fragments intended to be treatises on grammar and dialectic, were commenced at this time, as part of a plan for replacing the pagan texts on the liberal arts with books suited for Christian education.

In the summer of 387 Augustine left Milan for Rome, there to take ship for Africa. While at Rome his mother died, after having enjoyed a spiritual companionship with her son, described in an unforgettable account of one of their last conversations, in Book IX of the *Confessions.* It is at this point that Augustine's story of his own life comes to an end. The external facts of his subsequent life are few and simple. After staying a short time at Carthage, he spent the years 388-391 in retirement at Tagaste, where he completed some writings which had been begun at Milan and Rome. These included the *De quantitate animae, De libero arbitrio, De magistro, De moribus ecclesiae catholicae,* and *De moribus Manichaeorum.*

Third Period (391-430). In 391, while on a visit to Hippo, Augustine was persuaded to become a priest, and to assist the aged Bishop Valerius in this provincial diocese of North Africa. Four years later he was made colleague-bishop of Hippo, becoming the sole bishop of the diocese when Valerius died a short time after. As bishop Augustine turned his immense energies and talents to strengthening the authority and organization of the Catholic Church, to combatting schism and heresy, and to subjecting the whole orbit of ancient culture to a profound and remorseless criticism grounded in a dogmatic, historical, and biblical approach to Christian doctrine. During these years he achieved great personal influence and prestige throughout the world of Latin Christendom. Through the great writings of his maturity, Augustine left his mark on the entire subsequent tradition of western Christianity, Protestant as well as Catholic. He died at Hippo on Aug. 28, 430, while the Vandals, who had devastated Spain and conquered most of Morocco and Algeria, were besieging the city.

Augustine's Writings. All of Augustine's works indicate an extraordinary personality, at once highly complex and profoundly simple. Passion and austerity, tenderness and severity, are fused in a nature of almost terrifying honesty and candor. While Augustine's literary powers were great, and his handling of the Latin language eloquent and impressive, the power of his writing stems from his extraordinary mind and personality. The Cassiciacum dialogues exhibit the less severe aspect—an active, sensitive mind, graced with humor and charm, exploring with optimistic enthusiasm the world of ordered perfections and beauties which his Neo-Platonic interpretation of Christianity had revealed. In the great works of his maturity, Augustine's charm and optimism recede into the background; looking beneath the veneer of pagan culture, he finds only moral corruption and spiritual suicide. His writings, marked by a prophetic urgency, are dedicated to the task of rescuing the souls of men from a corrupt civilization, for the sake of the "City of God" which is to be realized, not in this world, but in the next.

The major works of Augustine's maturity include the *Confessions* (written between 398 and 400), the *De Trinitate* (398-416), the *De doctrina christiana* (397-426), the *De Genesi ad litteram libri XII* (401-415), and the *De civitate Dei* (413-426). Most of these were composed at intervals during a long period of years, and bear traces of the interrupted manner of their composition. The *De Trinitate* is Augustine's principal work in systematic theology; by a profound and extremely rich dialectical analysis of the various levels of finite existence, construed as reflections of the infinite being of the Creator, he gave great metaphysical development to the Athanasian doctrine of the Trinity. In the *De doctrina christiana,* designed as a guide to the reading and interpretation of the Scripture, Augustine set forth a powerful and original theory of language and communication, influential in the history of philosophy. His *De Genesi ad litteram,* in twelve books, was an extensive commentary on the first chapter of Genesis; here he dealt with the themes of creation, of the beginning of matter and motion and time, and of the development and order of the created universe.

In many respects the most distinctive and original of Augustine's works is the *De civitate Dei* (*The City of God*). The writing of this work was occasioned by the sack of Rome in 410 by Alaric the Goth. Pagan critics of Christianity claimed that this calamity had fallen upon Rome as a result of the abandonment of the ancient gods who had protected the city in former times and made her mistress of the world. To answer these charges, Augustine undertook a detailed examination of the religious cults, idolatries, superstitions, and philosophies of the pagan culture; he revealed their human origins, their moral perversions and shortcomings, and their many contradictions and absurdities. These he associated with the "city of this world," the society of the children of Cain, corrupted by original sin and seeking a vain and illusory happiness in material possessions, worldly pleasure, and power; its history is that of the doomed empires of antiquity, founded in war and slavery, and successively destroyed by their own pride and corruption. With this worldly city he contrasts the City of God, whose history is traced in the Old Testament; this is the society of those chosen by God for the future Kingdom of Heaven, the society of the prophets and saints of Israel and of the faithful Christians under the new dispensation of the Gospels. The two communities are intermingled in the world, and cannot be identified with the civil state and the visible Church; they are communities of spiritual allegiance, with contrasted origin, development, and destiny. The *De civitate Dei* is a landmark in the history of philosophical literature. By its emphasis on the reality and irreversibility of time, its location of meaning and truth in concrete fact rather than abstract theory, and its emphasis on historical evolution and process, this work stands in sharp contrast to the Greek philosophical tradition, which had assigned no philosophical significance to the historical process.

As bishop of Hippo, Augustine carried on an active correspondence, much of which is preserved, and composed many sermons, exegetical writings, and treatises of polemical or controversial character. The latter were at first directed against the Donatists, a schismatic faction of the African Church. But after 412 Augustine was deeply involved in the Pelagian controversy and unceasingly attacked the Pelagian thesis that the baptized Christian is able, by the power of his own will, to stay free of mortal sin and merit eternal life. Augustine's position was extreme and scandalized many of his contemporaries; so jealous was he of any suggestion that man could have any claim on the will of God, that he came close to denying freedom and moral responsibility to man.

In his last work, the *Retractationes,* Augustine reviewed and censored his own earlier writings, the brunt of his criticism falling on the dialogues in which he had espoused Neo-Platonic doctrines of doubtful orthodoxy. His progressive criticisms of himself, throughout his life, were criticisms of the cultural aspects of the ancient world in which he had lived. In passing from Vergil and Cicero to Plotinus and Porphyry, and from these philosophers to the biblical and dogmatic viewpoint of his maturity, the earlier phases of Augustine's life and thought were absorbed and transformed into the later ones. The culture of western Christianity, during the thousand years following Augustine's death, passed through these phases in reverse: the theological Augustine dominated the earlier Middle Ages; the Neo-Platonism embedded in his works became influential in the twelfth and thirteenth centuries; and the literary and rhetorical aspects of his writing made a fresh appeal to the humanists of the Renaissance. With Luther and Calvin, the theological Augustine was again invoked, and in the seventeenth century Descartes, Malebranche, and Pascal drew philosophical inspiration from him, as St. Bonaventure had done in the thirteenth century. Augustine's influence has been recurrently important, in one or another aspect of Western culture, until the present time.   E. A. M.

AUGUSTINE, ST. (d. 604), first archbishop of Canterbury and Apostle of the English, was a monk of St. Andrew's in Rome when, in 595, he was chosen to head a group of some forty missionaries sent to England by Pope Gregory I (the Great). Ethelbert, king of Kent, established them at Canterbury, and was himself publicly baptized. On Christmas Day 597, over 10,000 persons were baptized, probably in the Swale, by the "First Archbishop of the English." Unsuccessful efforts to secure Catholic unity with the Celtic bishops and the constitution of a hierarchy for the Saxon Church occupied Augustine's last years. He died in 604 on May 26, his feast in England; the Roman calendar observes May 28.   W. C.

AUGUSTINIANS [ɔgəstɪ'niənz], in a broad sense, the members of any one of the several religious orders and congregations in the Roman Catholic Church that follow what is known as the rule of St. Augustine. Chief among these are the Canons Regular of St. Augustine (Austin Canons) and the Augustinian Hermits or Friars. The Canons, organized into various congregations in the fourteenth century, follow a life essentially clerical, engaging in the duties of pastoral care, but joining to this the monastic features of common life, religious vows, and choir. Thomas a Kempis belonged to the Windesheim (Netherlands) congregation of the Canons. The Reformation and the French Revolution took a toll of the order's houses, and at present the Canons are far less numerous than in former times.

The Hermits, more properly known as the Augustinians, are a mendicant order, gathered into a single society in 1256 from a number of monastic congregations of Italy; they spread rapidly throughout Europe and in the fifteenth century counted some thirty thousand friars. Today their numbers are fewer, but they still flourish, and in their parishes, schools, colleges, and missions they carry on their work of the cure of souls and the advancement of learning through teaching and research. Their prior-general resides at Rome; in the United States, where there are two provinces, one vicariate, and one vice-province, the mother house is at Villanova, Pa. The discalced branch of the Hermits (Augustinian Recollects) is a reform organization.

A later group of Augustinians is known as the Assumptionists, a congregation founded in France in 1843 and approved by papal brief Nov. 26, 1864, which devotes itself chiefly to scholarly pursuits and to the missions of the Near East. Congregations of women, living under the rule of St. Augustine, more or less modified, have been in existence since early times, and in the twentieth century there are still many convents of canonesses and hermitesses, as well as Assumptionist and other communities, engaged in works of education and mercy.   T. A. B.

AUGUSTULUS, ROMULUS. *See* ROMULUS AUGUSTULUS.

AUGUSTUS [ɔgʌ'stəs] (63 B.C.-A.D. 14), founder of the Roman Empire, was born in Rome, Sept. 23, 63 B.C. Augustus, meaning "the revered," is merely a title conferred in 27 B.C. upon Gaius Octavius, the grandnephew of Julius Caesar. When Caesar adopted Octavius as his son in 44 B.C., his name was changed to Gaius Julius Caesar Octavianus. For the next two decades he was known as Octavianus (anglicized, Octavian).

Triumvir. Octavian was only eighteen at the time of Caesar's death, Mar. 15, 44 B.C. When he went to Rome to claim his inheritance, Mark Antony refused to relinquish Caesar's property. However, after some fighting, he was able to carry out the will. Although Octavian had had little experience in public affairs, his position as Caesar's heir assured him of the support of the veterans who had served under the great commander. Therefore when Antony proved unfriendly, Octavian first sided with the Senate in the struggle against him. Later, however, because the Senate was not sufficiently grateful for his assistance, Octavian changed sides. In 43 B.C. he, Mark Antony, and Lepidus, Caesar's Master of the Horse, joined forces,

AUGUSTUS CAESAR

COURTESY OF THE
METROPOLITAN MUSEUM OF ART

overwhelmed the Senate, and ultimately became the members of the Second Triumvirate, the "committee of three for the settlement of the republic." In possession of the western provinces and Italy, the triumvirs moved into the Balkans, where they defeated Brutus and Cassius at the battle of Philippi in 42 B.C. The formal life of the Second Triumvirate extended over the decade from 43-33 B.C. Antony took charge of affairs in the East, Lepidus in Africa, and Octavian in Italy and the western provinces. Until 36 B.C. the necessity of dealing with the powerful opposition offered by Sextus Pompey held the triumvirs together. After Pompey was defeated, Lepidus began to fade into the background, while the world became too small for both Antony and Octavian. The apparent desire of Antony to create an empire in the East in the name of Cleopatra finally gave Octavian an excuse to declare war upon the Egyptian queen in 32 B.C. After the defeat of Antony and Cleopatra at Actium the following year, Octavian pursued them to Egypt, where both Antony and Cleopatra committed suicide. Egypt became a Roman province in 30 B.C.

Emperor. Octavian returned to Rome a year later as the undisputed master of the Roman world. After two years of peace and reconstruction, he announced "the restoration of the republic" and resigned the extraordinary powers which had been bestowed upon him during the years of crisis. Nevertheless, the republic could not be restored so easily. There was no one strong enough to replace Octavian; therefore means had to be discovered to retain him at the head of the state and yet reconcile his position with constitutional practice. Between 27 B.C. and 23 B.C. he continued to hold the consulship, and his authority in the provinces where troops were stationed was maintained by a special proconsular power. By a settlement made in 23 B.C., Octavian, by then honored with the title of Augustus, was able to sketch the broad outlines of a new form of government which was to endure for the next three centuries. Basing his power upon the proconsular imperium and the full power of a tribune, Augustus became the princeps (first citizen, or perhaps president) who theoretically joined with the Senate in the government of Rome and the empire. In this dyarchy, or joint rule of the princeps and Senate, the princeps enjoyed special powers in addition to those inherent in his proconsular imperium and tribunician power. He was commander in chief of the army, had the sole right to make war and peace, controlled the grain supply of Rome, spoke first in the Senate, nominated or approved the candidacy of Roman citizens for high public office, and, after the death of Lepidus in 12 B.C., stood at the head of the state religion as Pontifex Maximus (high priest). Although most people, perhaps even Augustus himself, at first thought that these measures were only temporary, it soon became clear that the new governmental form had come to stay. Moreover, since Augustus lived until A.D. 14, his reforms tended to take on a permanent character. This raised the problem of providing for a successor. Though Augustus had married three times, he left no son to succeed him. In the end it was decided that his second stepson, Tiberius Claudius Nero Caesar, a distinguished soldier, should be his heir.

Conquests and Social Changes. Although the efforts of Augustus in the direction of social reform and his attempts to revive the old religion were not successful, he did stabilize the administration of the provinces and brought about the formation of the senatorial and equestrian classes on a permanent basis. Wealth became the main criterion for membership in the two classes, and each class had its own place in the governmental system. The senators, of course, sat in the Senate and filled the old republican magistracies. The equestrians provided the men who occupied the new and important prefectures and served as governors in the imperial provinces. The Age of Augustus saw the completion of the conquest of Spain, the near conquest of Germany to the Elbe, and the addition of the new provinces Rhaetia, Noricum, Illyricum, and Pannonia. After the defeat in A.D. 9 of Quintilius Varus in Germany, the possibility of an Elbe frontier was abandoned, and the Rhine and the Danube were set as the Roman boundaries. In the East the new province of Egypt was organized, and buffer states under Roman influence were established between Roman territory and that of Parthia (now northeastern Iran).

Personal Attributes. Augustus himself inspired great devotion among most Romans. He is described as handsome and dignified, with a calm and modest manner. He never enjoyed robust health, and his diet was a sparing one with a distinct vegetarian slant. Many reformers, including Julius Caesar, might have been more successful if they had adhered to the favorite motto of Augustus: "Make haste slowly." Augustus died in Nola, Aug. 19, A.D. 14.   T. B. J.

AUK [ɔ'k], one of several species of web-footed sea birds of the family Alcidae, but especially the extinct great auk or garefowl, *Pinguinus impennis,* and the razor-billed auk, *Alca torda.*

The great auk stood over two feet high and was about the size of a domestic goose, but had wings so small that it could not fly; it was black above and white beneath, and had a conspicuous white patch on the side of the head. It bred on Funk Island off Newfoundland, on Iceland, and on

islands north of Scotland, and ranged southward in winter to New England and the British Isles. Owing to its fearlessness it was subjected to merciless slaughter by sealers, whalers, and others, and seems to have been exterminated by about 1844. That it was once very abundant is shown by the great number of bones that have been recovered from its former haunts.

The razor-billed auk is something over a foot long, and has a strongly compressed black bill, crossed by a white band;

COURTESY OF THE AMERICAN MUSEUM OF NATURAL HISTORY
GREAT AUK

its plumage is black above and white below. It is fairly common on the coasts and islands of the North Atlantic, both in Europe and America.   H. G. De.

AUKLET [ɔ'klət], one of the medium-sized to small, web-footed sea birds of the auk family, in the genera *Ptychoramphus, Cyclorrhynchus, Aethia,* and *Cerorhinca.* As a group, they occur on the coasts and islands of the northern Pacific from Alaska south to Japan and California, but some are common only on one or the other side of the ocean. Their plumages are various combinations of black, white, and grays,

BY DOUGLAS GRAY FOR U.S. FISH AND WILDLIFE SERVICE
CRESTED AUKLETS, AETHIA CRISTATELLA

but they are remarkable for their bright-colored and usually curiously formed bills. All except one, at least while breeding, have specialized feathers about the head, in the shape of filaments or plumes. The largest species, the rhinoceros auklet, *Cerorhinca monocerata,* during the breeding season, develops, in addition to two rows of white filaments on each side of the head, a prominent single horn above the nostrils, which is later lost.   H. G. De.

AUKRUST, OLAV [au'krust] (1883-1929), Norwegian poet, was born in the mountain valley of Lom, Gudbrandsdal, Jan. 1, 1883. His chief collections of poetry are loosely joined cycles dominated by certain basic ideas about the problems of national culture: *Himmelvarden* (1916) ("Cairn of Heaven"), *Hamar i Hellom* (1926) ("Hamar of the Rocks"), and *Solrenning* (1930) ("Sunrise"). Averse as he was to the dominant Dano-Norwegian urban culture, he sought in the folk life of the valleys a counterpoise made up of elements from saga, ballad, and folk tale. His chief concern was the living continuity of his people from ancient times to the present, and he sought to preserve it in rugged, many-faceted New Norse verse, humorous and melancholy in turn, richly varied and original in expression. He died Nov. 3, 1929.   E. H.

AULIYE-ATA. *See* Dzhambul.

AULULARIA (THE POT OF GOLD) [ɔ'lulɛ'əriə], a comedy by Plautus, written between 207 and 184 B.C. The plot centers around Euclio, a poor man who discovers a pot of gold in his house and endeavors to keep the treasure from being discovered. Amusing complications result when the gold is stolen and Lyconides, who has seduced Euclio's daughter, is accused of the theft. The ending of the play is lost, but Euclio apparently recovers his gold and permits Lyconides to marry his daughter. The most famous adaptation of this play is Molière's *L'Avare.*   G. E. D.

AUNIS [o'ni's], former French province in southwestern France, bounded by the provinces of Poitou on the north, and Saintonge on the east and south, and by the Bay of Biscay on the west. The ancient capital was La Rochelle. The surface is level, sloping to low land on the sandy coast, marshy in some places. It was occupied by the Celtic tribes, the Agesinates and the Santones, at the time of the Roman conquest. It was conquered by the Visigoths, and by the Franks under Clovis in 507. A succession of rulers reigned in the province, the Châtelaillons, and the duke of Aquitaine. The Plantagenets acquired it as part of the dowry brought by Eleanor of Aquitaine on her marriage to the English king Henry II in 1152. Louis VIII of France conquered La Rochelle in 1224 and united Aunis to France until 1360, when it was returned to England under the treaty of Brétigny. In 1371 Charles V of France defeated the English and Aunis again became part of France. Aunis and Saintonge were administered together until 1373, when the commercial importance of La Rochelle was so great that the two provinces were separated. It was the last stronghold of French Protestantism until 1628, when La Rochelle fell to Richelieu. In 1694 Aunis and Saintonge were reunited for administrative purposes as the generality of La Rochelle. In 1790 it became, with Saintonge, part of the department of Charente-Maritime. *See also* Charente-Maritime.
                                                    S. Van V.

AURA [ɔ'rə], a vaporous light or emanation surrounding the head or entire body of a person, representing his spiritual or astral aspect, supposedly visible to psychically sensitive persons. Belief in such a nimbus frequently obtains among members of cults preoccupied with occult phenomena. Theosophists claim to see auras having color and form surrounding the heads of persons, and they maintain that such auras are indicative of character traits. Belief in such auras is an instance of purely subjective phenomena, unverifiable as such.

Aura refers also to the inferred emanation of a volatile substance, particularly to so-called electrical aura and to air currents following electrical discharge.

Aura epileptica frequently precedes an epileptic fit. The aura may consist of a distressing sensation of fleeting duration, or pain in a limb or internal organ. The aura may also be confined to a motor or sensory center, shown by the contraction or trembling of an arm or leg muscle, or by the twitching of eyelids, or by the quivering of lips. The aura may be sufficiently distinct and prolonged to enable the patient to find security before the seizure.   A. L. H-Q.

AURANGABAD [aurʌ'ŋgɑbɑ'd], the capital city of the Aurangabad District of west central India, located in northwestern Hyderabad, about 175 mi. northeast of Bombay, at 19° 52′ N. lat. and 75° 20′ E. long. The city, situated on the Deccan Plateau, on a small tributary of the Godavari River, is in a rather dry region; only 10 to 30 in. of rain falls during the summer season, while almost no rain falls during the winter. In spite of the slight rainfall, the black soils of the district produce good crops of cotton, millet, wheat, and linseed. The manufacturing and commerce of Aurangabad are limited largely to cotton mills and to the processing and trading of grain. Aurangabad became a city about 1658, and under the direction of Aurangzeb, sixth emperor of Hindustan, it became an important commercial center, fortified by high stone walls. The old palace of Aurangzeb and the mausoleum of his favorite wife are within the city limits. Aurangabad declined in importance with the development of the Hyderabad-Secunderabad area. Pop. 1951, 66,636.
                                                    J. E. F.

AURELIANUS, LUCIUS DOMITIUS [ɔri'lie'nəs] (c. A.D. 213-275), generally known as Aurelian, a Roman emperor who reigned from 270 to 275. He was the principal general under Claudius Gothicus and upon the death of Claudius in 270 Aurelian was proclaimed emperor by the army. His claim to the throne was subsequently recognized by the Senate. The reign of Aurelian was remarkable for many brilliant military successes: he repelled the barbarians on the Danubian frontier, quelled a revolt in Egypt, and restored Gaul to the Roman Empire. In the East he destroyed the kingdom of Palmyra in two rapid campaigns and brought Queen Zenobia to Rome as his captive. In addition to restoring the unity of the Roman Empire, Aurelian fortified Rome with a strong wall 12 mi. in circumference, reformed the badly depreciated imperial currency, and made the widespread military cult of the sun the state religion. Aurelian was assassinated as the result of a conspiracy at court in 275.   T. B. J.

AURELIUS ANTONINUS, MARCUS. *See* Marcus Aurelius Antoninus.

AUREOMYCIN. *See* Antibiotics.

AURIC, GEORGES [ɔ'ri'k] (1899-   ), French composer, was born on Feb. 15, 1899, in Lodève, Hérault. He received his musical training at the Paris Conservatory, and at the Schola Cantorum, where he studied under Albert

Roussel and Vincent d'Indy. Under the influence of Erik Satie, Maurice Ravel, and Gabriel Fauré, he was a member of a group known as the "Six," the other five members of which were Louis Durey, Arthur Honegger, Darius Milhaud, Germaine Tailleferre, and Francis Poulenc. As a composer Auric belongs to the ultramodern school, and his early music was extremely harsh and dissonant. Later he came under the influence of Stravinsky, but his recent music has shown a greater emphasis on melody. He has been called a "musical hedonist," and his music is said to be inspired by the everyday lives and sounds of Paris. In 1946 he won the international prize of the Société des Auteurs, Compositeurs et Editeurs de Musique for the best musical score for films. He has composed songs; works for the piano; music for the films; an *opéra comique, Sous le masque* ("Behind the Mask"); and the music for several ballets, notably *Les Fâcheux* (1921-1923) ("The Bores") and *Les Matelots* (1924-1925) ("The Sailors").   C. W. D.

AURICLE. *See* EAR; HEART.

AURIGA [ɔraiˈgə], the Charioteer, a constellation discovered in ancient times, and centered at approximately right ascension, 6 hr.; declination, + 42°. It is visible from the entire Northern Hemisphere and much of the Southern. It includes the first-magnitude star Capella, and its western boundaries are in the Milky Way. Several fairly bright stars form with Capella a large oblong figure. A small triangle of third and fourth magnitude stars near Capella, usually known as the Kids, present an interesting asterism. There are several

AMERICAN MUSEUM OF NATURAL HISTORY
AURIGA

noteworthy telescopic objects in this constellation: M 37 and M 38, open clusters, are splendid, and many double stars of contrasting colors are also found. A fourth-magnitude nova appeared in Auriga in 1892.

No definite myth seems to be connected with Auriga. The group is often pictured as the driver of a chariot holding a mother goat on his shoulder and the kids in one hand. Capella is the heart of the mother goat. *See also* CAPELLA; EPSILON AURIGAE.   J. H. P.

AURIGNACIAN [ɔrɪgneˈshən], the name originally given by prehistorians to the blade and burin cultures of the Upper Paleolithic period, after the site of Aurignac in the Haute-Garonne, France; it is now usually restricted to denote what was formerly known as the Middle Aurignacian culture.

Type specimens include beaked burins and keeled scrapers showing a special fluted retouch and bone points with split bases. The culture is especially well developed in Palestine and probably originated somewhere in western Asia, whence it spread into western Europe by way of the Balkans.

AURIOL, VINCENT [ɔˈryɔˈl] (1884-   ), President of the French Republic, was born at Revel, Haute Garonne, Aug. 25, 1884. He studied at the University of Toulouse,

FRENCH EMBASSY, INFORMATION DIVISION
VINCENT AURIOL

where he received a doctorate in law. During his student days he had joined the Socialist Party, and in 1909 he became editor of *Le Midi Socialiste*. In 1914 he was elected to the Chamber of Deputies from the District of Muret, and thereafter was regularly re-elected. He was mayor of Muret and counselor-general of the Haute Garonne. From 1919 to 1936 Auriol served as secretary of the Socialist group in the National Assembly, and for a brief period in 1928-1929 replaced Léon Blum as leader of the French Socialists. Auriol has been regarded as an authority on economics and finance. He participated in the London Conference on German reparations in 1924, and was a member of the Caillaux delegation which discussed the settlement of the French war debt to the United States in 1925. He became a member of the finance commission of the Chamber of Deputies in 1924, was appointed minister of finance in the first Blum cabinet (1936-1937), served as minister of justice in the Chautemps cabinet which followed it, and became minister of state in the second Blum cabinet of 1938. He was one of the eighty representatives who voted against allowing Pétain full power after the defeat of France in 1940. He was imprisoned at Pellevoisin, but was later released for reasons of health and interned for the duration of the war. On Oct. 17, 1943, he managed to leave France and go to London, where he offered his services to General Charles De Gaulle, leader of the Free French movement. He later served as a member of the consultative assembly and as chairman of the committee of the interior at Algiers, to which the Free French government-in-exile had moved. When it convened in Paris in November 1944, Auriol was elected to head the foreign affairs committee of the Constituent Assembly in October 1945. He became a minister without portfolio in the Free French cabinet of General De Gaulle in November 1945. Following the restoration of the elected French government at the end of World War II, Auriol became chairman of the first and second Constituent Assemblies and was elected speaker of both. He served as a delegate from France to the United Nations General Assembly and Security Council in 1946. Auriol became president of the National Assembly in December 1946 after the first elections under the new constitution in France. He was elected president of the French Republic, Jan. 16, 1947, for a seven-year term. In 1951 Auriol paid the first formal visit to the United States ever made by a president of the French Republic. He was succeeded in the presidency by René Coty on Jan. 16, 1954. He is the author of *Hier-Demain* (2 vol., 1945).   S. D.

AUROCHS [ɔ'rɒks], *Bos primigenius,* an extinct species of wild cattle which in prehistoric times ranged widely over Europe and to Syria in Asia Minor. It persisted in Germany until 1409. The last wild aurochs, a cow, died near Warsaw, Poland, in 1627. Some authorities believe that English park cattle and certain other breeds are descended from aurochs that were domesticated before the Christian era. The aurochs stood at least six feet high, had a brownish-black coat, and long, tapering horns which grew outward, then forward and up.   V. H. C.

AURORA [ɔrɔ'rə], in Roman mythology, the goddess of the dawn. The word is also used metaphorically for the East. *See also* Eos.

AURORA, a town in York Co., Ontario, Canada, 25 mi. north of Toronto. It was incorporated as a village in 1863 and became a town in 1888. Near by are St. Andrews College and De La Salle College, both residential schools for boys. Pop. 1951, 3,358.   D. F. P.

AURORA, a city of northern Illinois, in Kane Co., on the Fox River, 38 mi. west of Chicago. Aurora was settled in 1834, incorporated in 1857, and is administered by a commission government. A point of interest near by is Mooseheart, famous child city, established by the Loyal Order of Moose for orphan children of its deceased members. Four railroads, the Chicago & Northwestern, the Chicago, Aurora & Elgin, the Elgin, Joliet & Eastern, and the Chicago, Burlington & Quincy, furnish transportation. The city is an active industrial center, producing such items as conveying and road-building machinery, pumps, pneumatic tools, clothing, electrical appliances, brushes, chemicals, alloy metals, and foundry products. Pop. 1950, 50,576.

AURORA BOREALIS and **AURORA AUSTRALIS** [ɔrɔ'rə bɔrie'lis; ɔstre'lis]. The polar auroras are beautiful displays of light in the sky, known in northern latitudes as aurora borealis or northern lights, and in southern latitudes as aurora australis or southern lights. These displays may take the form of arches, streamers, and curtains, or of various modifications or combinations of these. The polar auroras may occur at any time of year and at any time of night. There is, however, a correlation between these displays and sunspot activity; when there are few or no sunspots, they are

COURTESY OF THE AMERICAN MUSEUM OF NATURAL HISTORY
AURORA BOREALIS
FROM A PAINTING BY HOWARD RUSSELL BUTLER

neither intense nor frequent. This correlation has led to the general acceptance of the theory that the polar auroras are caused by electrified particles which are shot out from the sun, more abundantly at times of great sunspot activity. These particles, it is supposed, cause the glow by striking the upper regions of the air, where the gases are highly rarefied. Often there is color present, especially red and green, which are produced by the action of the electrified particles on rarefied nitrogen and oxygen respectively.

PAINTING—COURTESY OF THE AMERICAN MUSEUM OF NATURAL HISTORY
AURORAL CURTAIN SEEN IN THE NORTH

Ausable Chasm, in northeastern New York, cut by the Ausable River in its course from the Adirondack Mountains to Lake Champlain

The aurora borealis has been seen as far south as New Orleans, La., and Fort Myers in south Florida, but the zone of maximum occurrence is a circular one with a center east of the north magnetic pole, and with a radius of approximately 23.5°. The displays diminish in intensity and frequency northward or southward from this belt. Observers have reported a hissing, crackling, or swishing noise attending displays of the aurora borealis.

Auroral displays appear at heights of 50 to nearly 200 miles above the earth's surface in the atmospheric layer called the ionosphere and where radio-reflecting layers are approximately located. They have been observed at heights of over 600 miles above sea level, but these rare displays occur only in fairly low latitudes during very strong magnetic storms. The disturbances to radio, telegraph, and telephone communications which accompany an auroral display are not caused by the aurora, but rather by the magnetic storms that are responsible for the display. G. C. F.

AURORA COLLEGE, a privately controlled, fully accredited, coeducational college of liberal arts located 40 mi. west of Chicago in Aurora, Ill. Degrees granted are the Bachelor of Arts, the Bachelor of Science, and the Bachelor of Theology. The curriculum includes special affiliations with Copley Hospital (nursing and medical technology), the Illinois Institute of Technology (engineering), the University of Illinois (occupational therapy), and the Evangelical Theological Seminary (theology).

Aurora College admits without regard to race or religious background on a selective basis which considers scholastic record, character references, and the acceptance of the Christian purposes of the College. There are generous freshmen scholarships and excellent work opportunities. Campus students live in residence halls; off-campus students live at home. There are no fraternities or sororities. *For statistics see* COLLEGES AND UNIVERSITIES.

AUSABLE CHASM [ɔseˈbəl] is a gorge located on the boundary line between Clinton and Essex Counties in northeastern New York State. The chasm was formed by the Ausable River, which has two main branches. These branches rise in the Adirondack Mountains, and join at Ausable Forks to form one river, which flows into Lake Champlain. Just west of Lake Champlain the river has cut a two-mile-long zigzag gorge through Potsdam sandstone. The gorge is narrow and deep and varies in width from about 15 ft. to about 50 ft. and in depth from 100 to 200 ft. There are many geologic faults exposed in this chasm, and numerous potholes along the river bed. The whole area attracts many tourists. Keeseville, N. Y., is the nearest town. J. E. F.

AUSGLEICH [auˈsglaiχ], or Compromise of 1867, a treaty regulating the constitutional relationship of the Dual Monarchy (Austria-Hungary). Count Friedrich von Beust, Count Gyula Andrássy, and Ferencz Deák were the principal architects of this plan which divided the old Austrian Empire by the course of the Leith River into Cisleithania (Austria) and Transleithania (Hungary). These countries were united in the person of the Emperor of Austria, who was crowned Apostolic King of Hungary at Pest-Ofen, Jan. 8, 1867. Commercial and economic policies, the tariff, and the national debt were regulated by joint agreement. A ten-year period was stipulated for this and other renewable features of the compromise. Monetary contributions were set at seventy per cent for Austria and thirty per cent for Hungary, figures which were altered only slightly in 1907, the occasion of the last renewal. Each nation had its own parliament whose ministries were governed by a joint delegation.

While the problem of Hungarian political rights in the Austrian Empire was very old, earnest discussion of a constitutional settlement began in March 1866, when Deák secured the appointment of a parliamentary commission. Its terms were presented in June. The outcome of the Six Weeks' War in 1866 naturally sharpened the Hungarian demand for autonomy. The Austrian prime minister, Count Richard Belcredi, sought to stave off the Hungarians with a plan to federalize the entire empire, but his successor, Count Beust, won Francis Joseph I over to the Hungarian proposal. The Compromise of 1867 was included in Article 12 of the Hungarian constitution and in Austrian law on Dec. 27, 1867. Count Gyula Andrássy, first minister-president of Hungary, had much to do with the acceptance of dualism and with the establishment of the Hungarian government under it. Such Hungarian patriots as Lajos Kossuth still believed in independence. Yet, in addition to autonomy in their own country, the Hungarians enjoyed, after 1867, a large influence in the public affairs of the Dual Monarchy. This proved irritating to the Slavic peoples, especially the Czechs, who were anxious to win autonomy for themselves. No agreement to this effect was ever reached, although it was always a foremost issue of Austrian politics. Actually, dualism had broken down by 1897. A constitutional order giving larger political rights to the Slavs had become necessary.

Without essential revision since 1867, the governments of both Austria and Hungary were in need of reform. In

Austria the Crown was supreme, but in Hungary the Constitution was the supreme power. This produced many anomalies in the position of the joint ruler, and introduced legal technicalities which hindered the government. In addition, the growth of nationalism was rapid, and the demands of the Czechs, Slavs, Poles and other nationalities, whose rights were curtailed under the existing government, became more and more insistent. Between 1897 and 1907 the dual system became very confused, and it was renewed only because no acceptable alternative could be found. Concentration on foreign affairs after 1907 distracted attention from this fundamental issue; yet the compromise of 1867 was a model for the federalization of the empire along lines of nationality. The plan of Emperor Charles I to federate the Dual Monarchy was presented on Oct. 16, 1918, but it was then too late to save Austria-Hungary from dissolution.

W. O. S.

AUSSIG. *See* Usti Nad Labem.

AUSTEN, JANE (1775-1817), English novelist, was born in Hampshire, Dec. 16, 1775. Her father, a clergyman, passed his life as curate of two very small country parishes, but his income was comfortable, both he and his wife were talented and of well-established families, and the countryside abounded in manor houses where good company was in demand. Jane, the seventh of eight children, thus grew up in an atmosphere of lively wit at home and of frequent visits among the country families. This society naturally contained both cosmopolitan personalities and rather sorry provincials, but all alike cultivated conversation, either wit or at any rate gossip, and engaged in the inevitable social intrigues. The young Miss Austen came to know every aspect of this society thoroughly and sharpened her opinions of it by exposure to the mature judgment of her family. She was able to develop the attitude of a disinterested though amused observer and still to remain an amiably attached member of the group, popular as a young woman and respected in her middle age.

This was her whole life. She never cared to travel further than London, and she never married, though it seems likely that she fell in love with a man who died soon after their unannounced engagement. Even her writing began as a pastime for her family and never occupied her as a career; she published nothing before she was thirty-five, and though her authorship then became noised about her name never appeared on a novel during her lifetime. After her father's retirement and death she maintained a family life with her mother and her sister, Cassandra, living first in the small, fashionable cities of Bath and Southampton, and finally settling in 1809 in the Hampshire village of Chawton, about fifteen miles from Winchester. She died July 18, 1817, at Winchester, where she had gone after a lingering illness.

Before she was twenty, Jane Austen was already writing burlesques, but at the age of twenty-two she had in perhaps final form a novel called *First Impressions,* which now, under the title *Pride and Prejudice,* is among the best-known novels in English. By 1803, at the age of twenty-eight, she had written *Sense and Sensibility* and *Northanger Abbey.* No publisher was interested enough to print these books, however, and except for *The Watsons,* which was never finished, she wrote no more until 1812. From then until 1816, while *Sense and Sensibility* (1811) and *Pride and Prejudice* (1813) were at last being published, she wrote *Mansfield Park* (1814), *Emma* (1815), and *Persuasion* (published posthumously with *Northanger Abbey* in 1818).

Jane Austen's earlier novels, especially *Pride and Prejudice,* have sharper focus; the later ones, more richness of detail, deeper perception of human difficulties, and deeper sympathy. But broadly viewed, both groups are alike. All offer a delightful grasp of the subject matter which was her life, her own level of society. But while her knowledge of it seems complete in all of its conventions, fads, habits, daily details, and individual types, this knowledge never appears as an end in itself but merely as the medium in which she thinks. She reduces human conduct to a struggle for marriage or position, on one hand, and to an effort toward integrity, in love or in social life, on the other. She puts

JANE AUSTEN

BRITISH COUNCIL OVERSEAS
PRESS DEPARTMENT

both society and the individual under sly but strong judgments. Society she makes a joke, and a sorry one, when it cannot recognize and encourage the good in people. She is contemptuous of unthinking or hypocritical conformists, but she is also merrily skeptical of individualists, laughing at eccentrics and testing everyone, even her favorite heroines, for infatuations and other illusions in affairs of love or of self-love. Her style, witty, idiomatic, and unornamented, is always guided by her clarity of mind and never becomes impressionistic or wild; her stories take on carefully plotted patterns, in which each detail is eventually recognized to have been pointing toward the end. Always in her novels the end involves such a recognition: what is genuine and valid finally becomes apparent, freed at last from the perverse and the ridiculous.

S. K. W.

AUSTENITE. *See* Metallurgy, Physical.

AUSTERLITZ, BATTLE OF [ɑuˈstərlɪts; ɔˈstərlɪts] (Dec. 2, 1805), an engagement between the French troops under Napoleon and the combined Austrian and Russian armies under the command of General Weyrother, resulted in a great victory for Napoleon. Although the allied army consisted of more than 82,000 men, while the French could muster only 65,000, the French outmaneuvered their opponents. As the allied army was attempting to turn Napoleon's right flank, the French delivered a counterstroke which ultimately divided the opposing army. The French casualties did not exceed 10 per cent, but the allied army lost more than a quarter of its effective strength. The French victory compelled Emperor Francis I of Austria to sue for peace soon afterwards.

M. K.

AUSTIN, ALFRED (1835-1913), English poet, was born in Headingley, near Leeds, May 30, 1835. After completing his education at Stonyhurst and London University in 1853, he studied law for some four years, but thereafter devoted himself to writing. He was associated for some time with the *Standard* and the *National Review* as a political writer and published abundantly in verse, composing lyrics, satires, and light verse, but his attempts to deal with large themes were unsuccessful. His prose garden-diaries and his ventures into nature lyrics have been admired, but his major claim to distinction was his elevation to the post of poet laureate in 1896. Austin died near Ashford, Kent, June 2, 1913.

C. D.

AUSTIN, MARY (1868-1934), American writer, was born Mary Hunter, Sept. 9, 1868, at Carlinville, Ill. Although her many books and articles reveal a wide range of interests and an attachment to various causes, notably feminism, Mrs. Austin is best remembered for her sympathetic portrayal of the American Indian and his culture in such volumes as *The Land of Little Rain* (1903), *The Basket Woman* (1904), *Lost Borders* (1909), *The Arrow Maker,* a play (1911), and *The American Rhythm* (1923, 1930). A leader in the South-western regional movement, she lived after 1924 in Santa Fe, N. M., where she died Aug. 13, 1934. Her autobiography, *Earth Horizon,* was published in 1932.

K. B. T.

AUSTIN, ROBERT SARGENT (1895-   ), English etcher, was born June 23, 1895, in Leicester. He attended the Leicester Municipal School of Art from 1902 until 1913, and then went to the Royal College of Art, South Kensington, where he studied painting and etching under Sir Frank Short. In 1922 he received the scholarship of the British School at Rome, where he studied until 1925. After returning to England, he taught at the Royal College of Art. A Fellow of the Royal Society of Painter-etchers and Engravers since 1928, Austin is known as an etcher of carefully composed plates, principally of Italian peasants in religious attitudes, of beggars, wayside shrines, and landscapes.

J. S. By.

AUSTIN, STEPHEN FULLER (1793-1836), American pioneer, founder of the first legal settlement of English-speak-

STEPHEN FULLER AUSTIN

ing people in Texas, was born in Wythe County, Virginia, Nov. 3, 1793, but moved with his family to St. Louis in 1798. He attended Bacon Academy in Connecticut, and Transylvania University in Kentucky. He was a member of the territorial legislature of Missouri and a director of the Bank of St. Louis when his father, Moses Austin, lost his fortune in the 1819 panic. After the death of his father, who in January 1821 had obtained a grant of Texas land for

colonization purposes from Mexico, Austin set out for Texas by way of Arkansas. There he was offered, but declined, a judgeship, but after reaching New Orleans he remained for six months, studying law and doing editorial work for the Louisiana *Advertiser.* Arriving in Texas about July 1821, he founded a colony of 300 families near the Gulf of Mexico between the Brazos and Colorado rivers. The overthrow of the Spanish regime in Mexico and the new requirements for settlers made it necessary for him to go to Mexico City to have his grant confirmed. During his administration of the Texas colony Austin mapped and surveyed the area, fixed the land system, and in the interest of the slaveholders of the colony prevented the abolition of slavery by the Mexican government. He was imprisoned in 1833 by Mexico for treasonable statements, but upon his release in 1835 he secured aid from private sources in the United States to carry on the Texas revolution. After the establishment of the Republic of Texas, he was defeated for the presidency by Sam Houston. He then served briefly as secretary of state. Austin died in Texas on Dec. 27, 1836.

D. R.

AUSTIN, WARREN ROBINSON (1877-   ), American lawyer, statesman, and diplomat, was born in Highgate, Vt., Nov. 12, 1877. He was graduated from Brigham Academy in 1895 and from the University of Vermont in 1899. Austin studied law and was admitted to the Vermont bar in 1902. He was state's attorney for Franklin Co., 1904-1906; mayor of St. Albans, 1909; United States Commissioner, 1907-1915; and special counsel for Vermont in the boundary dispute with New Hampshire, 1925-1936. He was a delegate to the 1928, 1940, and 1944 Republican national conventions, and in 1944 wrote the international plank of the Republican platform. He served as United States Senator from Vermont, 1931-1947. During his service in the Senate he was an independent conservative in domestic affairs and a consistent internationalist in foreign affairs. As a member of the Senate Foreign Relations Committee, he supported the Dumbarton Oaks agreement and the charter of the United Nations. In June 1946 Austin was appointed permanent United States representative to the United Nations, with the rank of ambassador. He resigned from the Senate and officially took office, Jan. 14, 1947, serving until January 1953, when he retired from public life. In the United Nations he had also served on the Security Council, the U.N. Atomic Energy Commission, the Commission for Conventional Armaments, and the interim committee of the General Assembly. D. R.

AUSTIN, the county seat of Mower Co., southeastern Minnesota, on the Cedar River, 100 mi. south of Minneapolis. The city was settled in 1853, platted in 1856, and incorporated in 1876. It is the site of Austin Junior College. Dairying, the raising of grain, incubator chicks, and livestock are the commercial pursuits of the vicinity, and meat packing is the city's leading industry. It is also an important railway division point, and florists throughout the country are supplied with cut flowers and plants from Austin's greenhouses. Pop. 1950, 23,100.

AUSTIN, a city located on the Colorado River, 164 mi. northwest of Houston, in central Texas. It is the capital of the state and the county seat of Travis Co. and is governed by a mayor, manager, and commission. Austin lies in an agricultural region in which corn, cotton, cattle, poultry, and fruits are raised. It was settled in 1838 and incorporated in 1839. At that time its name was changed from Waterloo to Austin in honor of the American pioneer Stephen F. Austin. Among its buildings of historic interest are the legation built by the French government in the days of the Republic of Texas, the red granite state capitol, the O. Henry museum, in which are displayed many mementos of the famous writer, and the home of sculptor Elizabeth Ney, which houses many of her works. The Laguna Art Gallery and the Texas Fine Arts Association are also in Austin.

Austin is the seat of the University of Texas, St. Edward's University, Austin Presbyterian Theological Seminary, Huston-Tillotson College, Concordia College, and the Episcopal Theological Seminary of the Southwest. A number of state institutions are located in the city: Austin State School, Austin State Hospital, the Texas State School for the Deaf, and the Texas State School for the Blind.

The products of the city's many industries, which take power from five dams across the Colorado River, include cottonseed machinery, engines, brick and tile, building stone, food products, cottonseed oil, furniture, and pottery. Publishing activity centers in the University of Texas Press. Austin is served by the Missouri-Kansas-Texas, the Missouri Pacific, and the Southern Pacific railroads and Braniff International, Continental, and Trans-Texas air lines. Bergstrom Air Force Base, established in 1942, is a permanent military installation. Pop. 1950, 132,459.

AUSTRALASIA [ɔstrəle′zhə], a rather vaguely defined geographical designation for Australia, New Zealand, New Guinea, New Britain, and certain lesser islands in their immediate vicinity. The term "Australasia" appears to have been introduced by Charles de Brosses in his *Histoire des navigations aux terres australes* (1756). R. G. B.

AUSTRALIA, COMMONWEALTH OF, a self-governing dominion of the British Commonwealth of Nations and an island continent of the Southern Hemisphere, southeast of Asia. It is bounded by the South Pacific Ocean on the east and by the Indian Ocean on the west. It lies between 10° 41′ and 43° 39′ S. lat. and between 113° 9′ and 153° 39′ E. long. The total area, including the island of Tasmania, is 2,974,581 sq. mi., or slightly less than that of the United States. Its coastline, including Tasmania, is 12,210 mi. long, and it has two well-defined breaks, the Gulf of Carpentaria on the north and the Great Australian Bight on the south. The east-west extension of the continent is about 2,400 mi.; from north to south it is 1,970 mi. Australia is separated from Tasmania by the Bass Strait, 150 mi. wide, and from New Guinea by the Torres Strait, about 90 mi. wide. The distance between Australia and the United States is about 6,000 mi., and between England and Australia about 11,000 mi. Australia consists of six states: New South Wales, with an area of 309,433 sq. mi.; Victoria, 87,884 sq. mi.; Queensland, 670,500 sq. mi.; South Australia, 380,070 sq. mi.; Western Australia, 975,920 sq. mi.; and Tasmania, 26,215 sq. mi. Two mainland territories, the Northern Territory, with an area of 523,620 sq. mi., and the Australian Capital Territory, with an area of 939 sq. mi., are under the control of the federal government. External territories, administered through the Federal Department of the Territories, include Norfolk Island and Ashmore and Cartier islands. Nauru is administered under the United Nations trusteeship agreement, and Papua (90,540 sq. mi.), which was transferred to the federal government in 1906, is now jointly administered with the Trust Territory of New Guinea (91,000 sq. mi.). In February 1954 Australia established a permanent base at Mawson, on the Antarctic continent, where Australia's territory covers approximately 2,500,000 sq. mi. Bases are also maintained at the subantarctic islands of Heard and Macquarie.

GEOLOGY

The geological history of Australia roughly parallels that of Africa in that marine sedimentary rocks cover a smaller part of the continent, and vast areas have a bedrock of Pre-Cambrian metamorphic and igneous rocks, or of terrestrial sediments.

Present Physiographic Regions. The continent can be divided into five major physiographic regions, as follows: (1) The eastern highlands, composed of folded sedimentary rocks with small granitic intrusions. The sediments range from Silurian to Triassic in age. Ranges average 150 mi. in width and extend from Cape York Peninsula on the north to Tasmania on the south. (2) The central lowlands in the southeast central part of the continent, lying between the eastern highlands and the South Australian highlands. The region is the drainage basin of the Murray-Darling River systems. (3) The South Australian highlands, a series of block-faulted mountains extending northward from the south coast along the western margin of the central lowlands. (4) The Great Australian (Artesian) Basin, a low plateau sloping westward from the eastern highlands, extending from the Gulf of Carpentaria on the north to the north end of the central lowlands and the South Australian highlands on the south. (5) The western plateaus, extending from the South Australian highlands on the southeast and the Great Australian Basin on the east and northeast to the western margin of the continent; this is by far the largest of the regions.

Archeozoic and Proterozoic Eras. Outcrops of Archeozoic and Proterozoic rocks cover much of the western plateaus. After the deposition of thick Archeozoic sandstones, shales, and limestones, great folding, metamorphism, and intrusions of granite occurred. Following a period of erosion, the seas re-entered and Proterozoic sandstones and shales were deposited. At the end of the Proterozoic Era the region was folded again to produce the extensive western plateau or shield. Parts of this have been downwarped, permitting the entrance of epeiric seas for short periods of time in subsequent geologic eras, but in general the shield of Western Australia remained largely above water.

Paleozoic Era. At the beginning of the Paleozoic Era a large geosynclinal trough developed in eastern Australia along the trend of the present eastern highlands. This trough was submerged and received marine sediments throughout most of the era. A smaller trough extended northward from the south coast along the trend of the present south Australian highlands. This trough was submerged only during the Cambrian Period. The western shield remained above water until the Devonian, when parts of it were depressed to permit entrance of small epeiric seas. During the Carboniferous (Mississippian-Pennsylvanian) Period the sea oscillated in and out of the eastern trough. When emergent, the region was low and swampy, resulting in the accumulation of coal beds. At this time Western Australia received great thicknesses of continental deposits, corresponding roughly to the Karroo beds of Africa in their physical characters. The lower part of the formation is a consolidated glacial drift above which are beds of sandstone and shale containing plant and reptile remains.

At the end of the Paleozoic Era the sediments that had been accumulating in the eastern trough were folded to form the eastern highlands. In addition, the southern trough containing Cambrian sediments was uplifted and block-faulted to produce the South Australian highlands.

COURTESY OF THE AUSTRALIAN NEWS AND INFORMATION BUREAU

RUINED CASTLE ROCKS AT KATOOMBA IN THE BLUE MOUNTAINS, NEW SOUTH WALES

Mesozoic Era. In the Mesozoic Era a large epeiric sea extended southward from the Gulf of Carpentaria along the west flank of the eastern highlands, covering the region now known as the Artesian Basin. Thick beds of alternating sandstones and shales were deposited in this region between the Triassic and Cretaceous periods. At the end of the Cretaceous the region was elevated, more strongly toward the southeast, to produce a low plateau sloping northwestward. Rains falling on the elevated southeastern part seep underground and migrate along the porous sandstone layers, accumulating under pressure to the northwestward and producing the artesian water that gives the region its name. Minor overlaps of the sea occurred in Western Australia during the Mesozoic, but the sea covering the Artesian Basin was the only one of great size during the era.

Cenozoic Era. The major outlines of Australia were already established by the end of the Mesozoic Era, when the Artesian Basin was elevated. Throughout the Tertiary Period only minor overlaps of the sea occurred on the coastal margins. The most extensive submergence was along the south coast in the region of the Great Australian Bight, where a wide coastal plain is formed by Tertiary deposits.

Australia was not affected by continental glaciation during the Quaternary period, and deposits of this age are very limited on the continent, with the exception of alluvial deposits in the central lowlands. The most spectacular occurrence of this time was the development of the Great Barrier Reef. Slow subsidence of the east coast of Australia has produced the excellent embayed harbors in the region and also a broad, shallow continental shelf. Great masses of coral have been growing on the outer margin of this shelf since early Pleistocene time, producing a reef paralleling the east coast from the Cape York Peninsula southward for a distance of 1,250 mi. The reef averages 35 mi. in width and much

of it is above water at low tide. The growth of the reef has produced an inland passage from 30 to over 100 miles wide between the reef and the east coast.　　　　E. C. S.

TOPOGRAPHY

Australia, a kidney-shaped continent, is far removed from the great fold lines of the world. It is more level, proportionately, than any other continent, with only 5 per cent of its land surface above 2,000 ft. A huge plateau, mainly 600 to 1,500 ft. above sea level, covers the western half of the continent. The other two main features of the continent's topography are the eastern highlands, running parallel with the coast and generally from 50 to 150 mi. inland, and the great central plain that lies between these highlands and the western plateau. The central plains are made up of the Carpentaria, Lake Eyre, and Murray-Darling basins. In the extreme southeast of the continent the highlands swing westward. The coastal plains in the east are generally narrow.

Highlands. The Australian topography, on the whole, offers little variety and finds its most striking features in the eastern highlands, which cover about one sixth of the continent and contain about five sixths of the population. These highlands form a belt of flat-topped, warped, or domed plateaus running parallel to the eastern coast from the Cape York Peninsula to Tasmania and averaging about 150 mi. in width. Their seaward slopes are generally steeper than those on the western side, and they approach so close to the coast in some parts that their spurs form cliffed headlands. These highlands are referred to as the Great Dividing Range because they divide the coastal streams from those flowing west.

A lack of uniformity exists in the structure of the eastern highlands: granite masses buttress blocks of Carboniferous sediments near the Grampians in southwestern Victoria; slate

AUSTRALIA

Index to Physical Features and Points of Interest

TOPOGRAPHIC FEATURES

Islands, Peninsulas, Capes, Mountains, Plateaus, Valleys, etc.

Admiralty, islands . . . h12
Albert Edward, mountain, 13,000′ . . . k12
Arnhem, cape . . . B 6
Arnhem Land, region . . . B 5
Arunta, desert . . . D 6
Banks, island . . . B 7
Barrow, island . . . D 2
Bartle Frere, mountain, 5,438′ . . . C 7
Bathurst, island . . . B 5
Bismarck, archipelago . . . h12
Bismarck, range . . . k11
Blue, plateau . . . F 8
Bruce, mountain, 4,024′ . . . D 2
Buccaneer, archipelago . . . C 3
Byron, cape . . . E 9
Cape Barren, island . . . o15
Cape York, peninsula . . . B 7
Capoompeta, mountain, 5,100 . . . E 9
Chesterfield, island . . . C10
Cloates, point . . . D 1
Cobourg, peninsula . . . B 5
Cradle, mountain, 5,069′ . . . o15
Croker, island . . . B 5
Culver, point . . . F 3
Curtis, island . . . D 9
Dalrymple, mountain, 4,190′ . . . D 8
Dampier, archipelago . . . D 2
Darling, range . . . F 2
Daru, island . . . k11
D'Entrecasteaux, islands . . . k13
D'Entrecasteaux, point . . . F 2
Direction, cape . . . B 7
Dirk Hartog, island . . . E 1
Dorre, island . . . E 1
Dyaul, island . . . h13
Eighty Mile, beach . . . C 3
Emirau, island . . . h13
Everard, ranges . . . E 5
Eyre, peninsula . . . F 6
Flinders, island . . . F 5
Flinders, island . . . n15
Flinders, range . . . F 6
Fowler, point . . . F 5
Fraser (Great Sandy), island . . . E 9
Freycinet's, peninsula . . . o15
Furneaux, island . . . o15
Gawler, ranges . . . F 6
Gibson, desert . . . D 3
Great Artesian, basin . . . D 7
Great Barrier, reef . . . C 8
Great Dividing, range . . . C 7, F 8
Great Sandy, desert . . . D 3
Great Victoria, desert . . . E 4
Gregory, range . . . C 7
Grenville, cape . . . B 7
Grey, range . . . E 7
Grim, cape . . . o14
Groote Eylandt, island . . . B 6
Hamersley, plateau . . . D 2
Hann, mountain, 2,800′ . . . C 4
Hermit, islands . . . h12
Hinchinbrook, island . . . C 8
Hood, point . . . F 2
Howe, cape . . . G 9
Hunter, island . . . o14
Jaffa, cape . . . G 6
James, ranges . . . D 5
Kangaroo, island . . . G 6
Karkar, islands . . . h12
King, island . . . n14
King Leopold, range . . . C 4
Kosciusko, mountain, 7,305′ . . . G 8
Larrey, point . . . D 2
Leeuwin, cape . . . F 2
Leveque, cape . . . C 3
Limmen, bight . . . B 6
Londonderry, cape . . . B 4
Long, island . . . k12
Luitpold, mountain, 14,435′ . . . k12
MacDonnell, ranges . . . D 5
Manam, islands . . . h12
Mann, ranges . . . E 5
Manus, island . . . h12
Maria, island . . . o15
Melville, cape . . . B 7
Melville, island . . . B 5
Monte Bello, island . . . D 2
Moreton, island . . . E 9
Mulgrave, island . . . B 7
Murua, islands . . . k13
Musgrave, ranges . . . E 5
Naturaliste, cape . . . F 2
New Britain, island . . . k13
New Hanover, islands . . . h12
New Ireland, island . . . h13
Ninety Mile, beach . . . G 8
North Stradbroke, island . . . E 9
Northumberland, island . . . D 9
North West, cape . . . D 1
Nullarbor, plain . . . F 4
Otway, cape . . . n14
Owen Stanley, range . . . k12
Paseley, cape . . . F 3
Prince of Wales, island . . . B 7
Recherche, archipelago . . . F 3
Riche, cape . . . F 2
St. George, cape . . . h13
Sandy, cape . . . D 9
Sandy, desert . . . C 5
Seaview, mountain, 3,570′ . . . F 9
Simpson, desert . . . E 6
Sir Edward Pellew Group, island . . . C 6
Sir Samuel, mountain, 2,850′ . . . E 3
Sorell, cape . . . o15
South, cape . . . m12
South Bruny, island . . . o15
Southwest, cape . . . o15
Steep, point . . . E 1
Stuarts, range . . . E 5
Swain, reefs . . . D 9
Tabar, islands . . . h13
Tasman, peninsula . . . o15
Thursday, island . . . B 7
Trobriand, islands . . . k13
Ulawun, mountain, 7,546′ . . . k13
Van Diemen, cape . . . B 5
Victoria, mountain, 13,150′ . . . k12
Vitu, islands . . . h12
Wellesley, island . . . C 6
Wessel, island . . . B 6
West Cape Howe, cape . . . G 2
Wilhelm, mountain . . . k12
Wilson's promontory . . . n15
Woodroffe, mountain, 4,970′ . . . E 5
Yorke, peninsula . . . F 6
Ziel, mountain, 4,955′ . . . D 5

HYDROGRAPHIC FEATURES

Lakes, Rivers, Creeks, Bays, Straits, Seas, etc.

Amadeus, lake . . . D 5
Anson, bay . . . B 5
Arafura, sea . . . B 6
Archer, river . . . B 7
Ashburton, river . . . D 2
Austin, lake . . . E 2
Barcoo, river . . . D 7
Barlee, lake . . . E 2
Barwon, river . . . E 8
Bass, strait . . . n15
Belyando, river . . . D 8
Blue Mud, bay . . . B 6
Breaden, lake . . . E 4
Broad, sound . . . D 8
Buchanan, lake . . . D 8
Bulloo, river . . . E 7
Burdekin, river . . . C 8
Capricorn, channel . . . D 9
Carnegie, lake . . . E 3
Carpentaria, gulf . . . B 6
Clarence, strait . . . B 5
Coleman, river . . . B 7
Collier, bay . . . C 3
Condamine, river . . . E 8
Cooper's, creek . . . E 7
Coral, sea . . . D 9
Cowan, lake . . . F 3
Culgoa, river . . . E 8
Daly, river . . . B 5
Darling, river . . . F 7
Dawson, river . . . D 8
De Grey, river . . . D 2
Diamantina, river . . . D 7
Disappointment, lake . . . D 3
Drysdale, river . . . B 4
Dundas, lake . . . F 3
Dundas, strait . . . B 5
Encounter, bay . . . G 6
Everard, lake . . . F 5
Exmouth, gulf . . . D 1
Eyre, lake . . . E 6
Finke, river . . . E 5
Fitzroy, river . . . C 3
Fitzroy, river . . . D 8
Flinders, river . . . C 7
Fly, river . . . k11
Forest, lakes . . . E 4
Fortescue, river . . . D 2
Frome, lake . . . F 6
Gairdner, lake . . . F 6
Galilee, lake . . . D 8
Gascoyne, river . . . E 2
Geographe, bay . . . F 2
Geographe, channel . . . D 1
Georgina, river . . . D 6
Gilbert, river . . . C 7
Gillen, lake . . . E 3
Great Australian, bight . . . F 5
Great, lake . . . o15
Gregory, lake . . . E 6
Gregory, river . . . C 6
Halifax, bay . . . C 8
Hay, river . . . D 6
Hervey, bay . . . D 9
Huon, gulf . . . k12
Jacquinot, bay . . . k13
Jervis, bay . . . G 9
Joseph Bonaparte, gulf . . . B 4
King, sound . . . C 3
King George, sound . . . F 2
Lefroy, lake . . . F 3
Leichhardt, river . . . C 7
Macdonald, lake . . . D 4
Mackay, lake . . . D 4
Macquarie, river . . . F 8
Maranoa, river . . . E 8
Mitchell, river . . . C 7
Murchison, river . . . E 2
Murray, river . . . G 7
Murrumbidgee, river . . . F 8
Nabberu, lake . . . E 3
Namoi, river . . . F 8
Narran, river . . . E 8
Neales, river . . . E 6
Nicholson, river . . . C 6
Norman, river . . . C 7
Normanby, river . . . B 7
Nurrari, lakes . . . E 5
Papua, gulf . . . k11
Paroo, river . . . F 7
Port Jackson, bay . . . F 9
Port Musgrave, bay . . . B 7
Port Phillip, bay . . . n14
Princess Charlotte, bay . . . B 7
Queens, channel . . . B 4
Raeside, lake . . . E 3
Ramu, river . . . k11
Repulse, bay . . . D 8
Roebuck, bay . . . C 3
Roper, river . . . B 5
St. Vincent, gulf . . . G 6
Salt, lake . . . D 1
Sepik, river . . . h11
Serpentine, lakes . . . E 4
Shark, bay . . . E 1
Spencer, gulf . . . F 6
Strzelecki, creek . . . E 7
Sturt, creek . . . C 4
Sunday, strait . . . C 3
Swan, river . . . F 2
Tasman, sea . . . G 9
Thomson, river . . . D 7
Timor, sea . . . B 3
Todd, river . . . D 6
Torrens, lake . . . F 6
Torres, strait . . . A 7
Van Diemen, gulf . . . B 5
Victoria, river . . . C 5
Warburton, river . . . E 6
Warrego, river . . . E 8
Wells, lake . . . E 3
Wenlock, river . . . B 7
Woods, lake . . . C 5
Yamma Yamma, lake . . . E 7
Yeo, lake . . . E 3

SPECIAL POINTS OF INTEREST

Parks, Monuments, Ruins, Dams, Sites, Buildings, etc.

Aboriginal, reserve . . . E 4
Adelaide, University of, Adelaide, S. Australia . . . F 6
Captain James Cook's Cottage, Fitzroy Gardens, Melbourne, Victoria . . . G 8
First Permanent Settlement, Botany Bay, 1788, N. S. Wales . . . F 9
Henbury Craters, Henbury Station, Northern Territory . . . D 5
Hermannsburg Mission, Hermannsburg, Northern Territory . . . D 5
Melbourne, University of, Melbourne, Victoria . . . G 8
Prince's Park and Mulgrave Battery, Hobart, Tasmania . . . o15
Queen Victoria Museum, Launceston, Tasmania . . . o15
Queensland, University of, Brisbane, Queensland . . . E 9
Southernmost point on continent of Australia, Wilson's Promontory . . . G 8
Sydney, University of, Sydney, New South Wales . . . F 9
Tasmania, University of, Hobart, Tasmania . . . o15
Wentworth House, Vaucluse, New South Wales . . . F 9
Western Australia, University of, Perth, W. Australia . . . F 2
Wilpena Pound, South Australia . . . F 6

AUSTRALIA

Area....2,974,581 sq. m.
Population.....9,037,000

KEY TO MAP SYMBOLS

⊕ National Capital
☆ Divisional Capital
• Size of symbols and
• type indicates rela-
• tive population.

STATES

AUSTRALIAN CAPITAL
TERRITORY (Ter.) .G 8
Area.........939 sq. m.
Pop............30,000

NEW SOUTH WALES..F 8
Area.....309,433 sq. m.
Pop.........3,425,000

NORTHERN TERRITORY
(Ter.)...........C 5
Area.....523,620 sq. m.
Pop............30,000

QUEENSLAND.......D 7
Area.....670,500 sq. m.
Pop.........1,327,000

SOUTH AUSTRALIA....F 6
Area.....380,070 sq. m.
Pop...........801,000

TASMANIA...........o15
Area.....26,215 sq. m.
Pop...........309,000

VICTORIA..........G 7
Area.......87,884 sq. m.
Pop.........2,453,000

WESTERN AUSTRALIA .E 3
Area.....975,920 sq. m.
Pop...........662,000

CITIES AND TOWNS

Adelaide, 30,118
(*483,535).........F 6
Ajana, 80..........E 1
Albany, 8,265.......F 2
Albury, 16,736.......G 8
Alice Springs, 2,785...D 5
Aramac, 488........D 8
Ararat, 7,414....G 7, n14
Argyle Downs, 153....C 4
Arltunga..........D 5
Armidale, 8,662......F 9
Augusta, 142........F 2
Bairnsdale, 5,712..G 8, n15
Ballarat, 39,964
(*48,050).....G 7, n14
Barcaldine, 1,705.....D 8
Barrow Creek.......D 5
Bathurst, 16,090.....F 8
Beachport, 293......G 7
Bega, 3,518....G 8, n15
Benalla, 6,051.......G 8
Benanee...........F 7
Bendigo, 28,726
(*36,918).......G 7
Birdsville..........E 6
Birdum............C 5
Blackall, 1,885......D 8
Bombala, 1,258..G 8, n15
Borroloola..........C 6
Boulder, 6,279......F 3
Bourke, 2,642......F 8
Bowen, 3,571......C 8
Brewarrina, 903......E 8
Bridgewater, 267....o15
Brinkworth, 218......F 6
Brisbane, 502,353....E 9
Broken Hill, 31,387...F 7
Broome, 1,093.......C 3
Brunette Downs......C 6
Bunbury, 9,870......F 2
Bundaberg, 19,953...D 9
Burketown, 59......C 6
Burnie, 11,195......o15
Busselton, 2,449.....F 2
Cairns, 21,021......C 8
Camooweal, 192.....C 6
Canberra, 28,277....G 8
Carnarvon, 1,453....D 1
Ceduna, 570.......F 5
Cessnock, 14,417....F 9
Charleville, 4,517....E 8
Charlotte Waters.....E 5
Charters Towers, 6,960.D 8
Clermont, 1,587......D 8
Cloncurry, 1,955.....D 7
Cobar, 2,223.......F 8
Coen.............B 7
Collie, 8,668.......F 2
Condobolin, 2,843...F 8
Cook, 205.........F 5
Cooktown, 397......C 8
Coolgardie, 963.....F 3

AUSTRALIA

Statute Miles 100 0 100 200 300
Kilometers 100 0 100 200 300 400

Lambert Azimuthal Equal Area Projection
SCALE 1:16,000,000   1 Inch = 252 Statute Miles

8R56

Moora, 652 . . . . F 2
Moree, 5,501 . . . . E 8
Mount Gambier,
    10,334 . . . . G 7
Mount Isa, 7,432 . . . . . D 6
Mount Magnet, 631 . . . . E 2
Mount Morgan, 4,151 . . D 9
Mullewa, 627 . . . . E 2
Mungana . . . . C 7
Mungindi, 915 . . . . E 8
Muswellbrook, 5,638 . . . F 9
Nannine . . . . E 2
Naracoorte, 3,329 . . . . G 7
Narrabri, 3,720 . . . . . . F 8
Narrandera, 4,419 . . . . F 8
Narrogin, 3,768 . . . . . . F 2
Naryilco . . . . E 7
Newcastle, 134,094
    (*178,156) . . . . F 9
Newcastle Waters, 82 . C 5
Newdegate, 75 . . . . F 2
New Norfolk, 4,756 . . . o15
Normanton, 234 . . . . . . C 7
Nornalup . . . . F 2
Norseman, 2,538 . . . . . F 3
Northam, 5,725 . . . . . . F 2
Northampton, 626 . . . . E 1
Nullarbor . . . . F 5
Nymagee, 197 . . . . F 8

Nyngan, 2,257 . . . . F 8
Onslow, 180 . . . . D 2
Oodnadatta, 130 . . . . . E 6
Ooldea . . . . F 5
Orange, 18,248 . . . . . . F 8
Ouyen, 1,426 . . . . F 7
Palmerville . . . . C 7
Parachilna . . . . F 6
Pardoo . . . . D 2
Peak Hill, 46 . . . . E 2
Peebinga, 67 . . . . F 7
Penong, 118 . . . . F 5
Perth, 97,305
    (*348,596) . . . . F 2
Peterborough, 3,473 . . . F 6
Pimba, 56 . . . . F 6
Pine Creek, 91 . . . . B 5
Pooncarie, 66 . . . . F 7
Port Adelaide, 38,381 . . F 6
Port Augusta, 6,704 . . . F 6
Port Douglas, 122 . . . . C 8
Port Hedland, 328 . . . . D 2
Portland, 4,758 . . . . . . G 7
Port Lincoln, 5,871 . . . . F 6
Port Macquarie, 4,423 . . F 9
Port Pirie, 14,222 . . . . F 6
Port Wakefield, 429 . . F 6
Powell Creek . . . . C 5
Queenstown, 3,461 . . . o15

Quilpie, 640 . . . . E 7
Ravensthorpe, 116 . . . . . F 3
Rawlinna, 124 . . . . F 4
Renmark, 1,979 . . . . F 7
Richmond, 775 . . . . D 7
Rockhampton, 40,676 . . D 9
Rodingo . . . . D 5
Roebourne, 136 . . . . D 2
Roma, 4,248 . . . . E 8
Roto, 127 . . . . F 8
Roy Hill . . . . D 2
St. George, 1,698 . . . . . E 8
St. Lawrence, 264 . . . . D 8
Salmon Gums, 61 . . . . . F 3
Sandstone 101 . . . . E 2
Selwyn . . . . D 7
Sir Samuel . . . . E 3
Smithton, 2,506 . . . . . o15
South Coast, see
    Southport
Southern Cross, 760 . . . F 2
Southport (South Coast),
    19,818 . . . . E 9
Springsure, 719 . . . . . . D 8
Swan Hill, 5,198 . . . . . G 7
Sydney, 193,145
    (*1,863,217) . . . . F 9
Tailem Bend, 1,952 . . . G 6
Tambo, 404 . . . . D 8

Tamworth, 13,647 . . . . . F 9
Tanami . . . . D 4
Tarcoola, 225 . . . . F 5
Tempe Downs . . . . D 5
Tennant Creek, 567 . . . C 5
Tenterfield, 3,267 . . . . . E 9
Thargomindah, 96 . . . . E 7
Theodore, 386 . . . . D 9
Toowoomba, 43,152 . . . E 9
Townsville, 40,485 . . . . C 8
Ulverstone, 5,006 . . . . o15
Victoria River Downs . . C 5
Wagga Wagga,
    19,243 . . . . G 8
Walgett, 1,348 . . . . . . F 8
Wallal Downs . . . . C 3
Wallaroo, 2,403 . . . . . . F 6
Wanaaring, 76 . . . . E 7
Warrnambool,
    10,850 . . . . G 7, n14
Warwick, 9149 . . . . E 9
Wave Hill, 75 . . . . C 5
Welford . . . . E 7
Wentworth, 4,035 . . . . . F 7
Whyalla, 8,598 . . . . F 6
Wilcannia, 823 . . . . F 7
William Creek . . . . E 6
Wiluna, 576 . . . . E 3
Windorah, 48 . . . . E 7

Winning Pool . . . . D 1
Winton, 1,396 . . . . D 7
Wollongong, 90,829 . . . F 9
Wonthagai, 4,461 . G 8, n15
Woodside, 171 . . G 8, n15
Woomera, 4,500 . . . . . F 6
Wooramel . . . . E 1
Wyalong, 524 . . . . F 8
Wyndham, 458 . . . . . . C 4
Yanac, 252 . . . . G 7
Yaraka, 27 . . . . D 7
Yarraden . . . . B 7
York, 1,720 . . . . F 2

NEW GUINEA TERRITORY

Area . . . . . 91,000 sq. m.
Population 755,882
CITIES AND TOWNS

Aitape h11
Bibi k12
Gasmata k13
Kavieng h13
Kokopo h13
Lae, 948 . . . . k12
Lawagan h13

Madang, 379 . . . . k12
Morobe, 1,000 . . . . k12
Muliama h13
Namatanai h13
Rabaul, 2,950 . . . . h13
Sag Sag k12
Salamaua k12
Sialum k12
Talasea k13
Wewak h11

PAPUA

Area . . . . . . 90,540 sq. m.
Population 301,500
CITIES AND TOWNS

Abau m12
Baniara k12
Buna k12
Kaimare k11
Kerema k12
Kikori k11
Mugolo k11
Port Moresby, 2,503 . . . k12
Rigo k12
Samarai m13
Tatiarato k11
Tufi k12

* Population including suburbs.

VARIETIES OF CORAL FROM THE GREAT BARRIER REEF, QUEENSLAND

and granite form the dome of Kosciusko; and granite predominates in the New England highlands. Sedimentary formations, from the Lower Silurian to the Triassic, with varying axes of uplift, are present throughout.

In Queensland between the Gulf of Carpentaria and Townsville, on the eastern coast, is the Atherton Plateau, an area of 15,000 sq. mi. with an elevation of over 2,000 ft. The highest point in this area is Mount Bartle Frere, 5,438 ft. Much of the plateau is covered with thick forests of valuable timber, and there are some farms. The Burdekin River enters the sea between Bowen and Townsville, and the Fitzroy empties into Keppel Bay 35 mi. below Rockhampton.

South of Rockhampton, the highlands increase gradually in height, culminating in the New England massif, which lies between Brisbane and Newcastle. This area is the most extensive high-lying area in Australia, with an elevation between 3,000 and 5,000 ft. and an area of about 8,000 sq. mi. The New England massif is about 100 mi. wide, with broad offshoots extending toward the west; it also forms the divide between the Macintyre, Gwydir, and Namoi rivers on the west, and the Clarence, Macleay, and Manning on the east. Between the upland area and the Blue Mountains to the south lies the Liverpool Range. Here rises the Goulburn River which joins the Hunter to flow directly east to the sea from Cassilis Col or Gate, the lowest gap in the Great Dividing Range of southeastern Australia.

Behind Sydney, the Blue Mountain massif, a Triassic sandstone platform from 1,000 to 4,000 ft. high, is barren. This area long resisted the efforts of settlers to open a route to the west. The greater part of this area is drained by the main stream and tributaries of the Macquarie River. Near the source of the Macquarie are the Jenolan caves, fine examples of limestone erosion.

A narrow high-lying ridge, on which lies Lake George, separates the Blue Mountains from the Kosciusko massif to the south. The massif terminates in the granite boss of Mount Kosciusko, 7,328 ft. high, the highest point on the Australian continent. This region is drained on the north by the Murrumbidgee River, on the west by the Murray River, and on the south by the Snowy River. The granite mass of the Kosciusko massif turns west and continues across southern Victoria (known as the Victorian highlands) up to the boundary of South Australia. As far as Melbourne, the range retains an elevation of over 3,000 ft.; it then gradually declines near the Grampian highlands and the Glenelg River. Eastern Victoria has the largest number of peaks over 6,000 ft.: Hotham, 6,100 ft.; Feathertop, 6,300 ft.; and Bogong, 6,509 ft. These places have become important tourist and sporting centers. The Mitta Mitta, Ovens, and Goulburn rivers flow through this rugged country. In the central portion of the Victorian highlands, around Ballarat, some of the best-known Australian gold fields are located.

A continuation of the eastern highlands is found in the is-

Angorichina Hostel in the rugged Flinders Ranges, South Australia, established for veterans of World War I

land of Tasmania. The dominant feature is the central plateau, most of which is over 3,000 ft. On its western edge, the plateau rises to Mount Cradle, 5,069 ft. high, and to the west and south lie other isolated portions of the plateau such as Mount Elden, Mount Field West, and Mount Wellington; to the northeast is Legge's Peak, 5,160 ft., on the Ben Lomond Plateau, the highest peak in the state. There are many large but shallow lakes on the plateau; the Great Lake, 52 sq. mi. in area, is the island's largest. The rivers that drain the island are the Tamar-Macquarie stream in the northeast; the Pieman River on the west; and the Derwent, the main river, which receives the Clyde and Ouse rivers, in the southeast.

In the central portion of the main continent of Australia (South Australia and the Northern Territory) the principal highlands are the Mount Lofty Range, 2,334 ft., near Adelaide, and the Flinders Range, north of Adelaide. The Flinders Range runs roughly north and south for about 200 mi. and culminates in St. Mary's Peak, 4,000 ft. The MacDonnell and Musgrave ranges are near Alice Springs in central Australia, Mount Woodroffe, 5,200 ft., being in the Musgrave Range.

Western Australia lies almost entirely at altitudes of between 1,000 and 2,000 ft. Its greatest altitude is 4,024 ft. at Mount Bruce on the Hamersley Plateau, which is itself 3,000 ft. above sea level. In the north, by the Timor Sea, lies the Kimberley District of Western Australia, and there the highest point, Mount Hann, 2,800 ft. above sea level, is only 800 ft. above its plateau base. In the extreme south, the Stirling Range rises to 3,640 ft., whereas the Darling Range near Perth rises to a mere 1,000 ft.

Plains. The plains of Australia consist of (1) coastal lowlands that form a rim of varying width around the continent, and (2) large inland areas. The great inland plain consists of the central lowlands that lie between the eastern highlands and the western tablelands and extend from the Gulf of Carpentaria in the north to the Victorian highlands in the south. The central lowlands are divided into

the Murray-Darling lowlands in the southeast and the Great Australian Basin, which is further divided into the Artesian lowlands in the center and north, and the dry Lake Eyre Basin in the southwest.

The Murray-Darling lowlands are bounded by the Flinders Range in the west, the Kosciusko and Blue Mountain highlands in the east, the Victorian highlands in the south, and the Great Australian Basin in the north. The fall is extremely slight, and, consequently, the rivers are slow-moving and meandering. The Murray-Darling Basin is mainly at an elevation of less than 600 ft.; the Murray River, in the course of 1,366 mi. between the foot of the highlands and its mouth, falls less than 500 ft. In this area the longest river is the Darling, which flows 1,760 mi. from its source to its junction with the Murray. The latter, although not so long as the Darling, is the more important river, for the Darling dries up in long droughts. Other streams of the Murray network are the Lachlan, Murrumbidgee, Ovens, Goulburn, and Loddon.

The Great Australian Basin extends 1,200 mi. from the Gulf of Carpentaria to Dubbo on the Macquarie River in New South Wales and is about 300 mi. wide. The rock beneath the surface consists of solid shales above, and very porous, crumbly sandstones underneath. It is the largest artesian basin in the world, and it is into this basin that many of the inland rivers disappear. Its surface is rather monotonous, consisting of vast rolling plains at an elevation of less than 1,000 ft. Low ridges separate the broad, alluvial-filled valleys of the Diamantina, Thomson, and Paroo rivers, which flow only after heavy rains but then extend for many miles. The most important use of the artesian water is to augment the pluvial water supplies for grazing purposes. The water is obtained by sinking bores into the earth.

The Lake Eyre Basin, or the desert artesian region, lies northeast of the South Australian highlands and extends northward from the southern coast. It is connected with Lake Torrens, a salty expanse of water 150 mi. long, by a ridge, called the Torrens Rift Valley, which is only 176 ft.

above sea level. This rift was caused by the sinking of a strip of the earth's crust along the line of Spencer's Gulf. The basin has a watershed of nearly 500,000 sq. mi. It is practically uninhabited because of its location in one of the driest parts of Australia, where it receives only 5 in. of rain per year. The sills of the lake itself are 39 ft. below sea level, and the area about the saline lake is a vast salty plain formed from the alluvium carried down by the rivers, which enter it only in flood time. On the Eyres Peninsula, the rocks are chiefly granites and schists, and nearly all are covered with sandy soils.

The second large plain area in Australia is the Great Western Plateau, which comprises 54 per cent of the continent. In the south, it consists of a large area of ancient rocks, gneisses, schists, and quartzites. To the north of 25° S. lat. the rocks appear to be largely of Paleozoic age. The surface is covered thinly with soil and wind-blown dunes. It is a very ancient land-surface, which was brought about by the wearing away of almost all projections during countless centuries of erosion by rivers, rain, and wind. There are no rivers in the interior, and even where there is a heavy rain on the plateau, as in the tropical zone, it falls only a few months of the year. On the Nullarbor Plain, a low-lying section of the plateau bordering on the Great Australian Bight, the rainfall drains off into holes in the land's surface. The land is treeless and without grass, and only saltbrush is abundant.

The Western Plateau, described as a peneplain, is at an average elevation of 1,400 ft. There are few relieving features: the Hamersley and Ophthamia ranges in the northwest district of Western Australia; the MacDonnell and Musgrave ranges in central Australia, between which lies the great shallow sheet of salt water, Lake Amadeus; ranges in the Kimberley district in the northern part of Western Australia; and the Darling and Stirling ranges in the southwest corner of the state. The central part of the western peneplain is desert and was the last part of Australia to be explored.

One region of the Western Plateau, which is fertile, is Swanland, located in the southwest corner of Western Australia. Swanland is a triangular-shaped area of about 50,000 sq. mi. and is rich in timber and suited for agriculture. This section is the most thickly populated of the whole western plateau area.

Rivers and Lakes. There are two types of rivers in Australia: the perennial, which flows toward the coast, and the intermittent, which flows inland and disappears into the sand or breaks into chains of pools.

The main river system is formed by the Murray and its tributaries. It rises in the Snowy Mountains near Mount Kosciusko, and for 1,200 mi. it marks the boundary between the states of New South Wales and Victoria. The Murray Basin covers an area of 414,253 sq. mi. and is navigable for 900 mi. However, sandbars block its mouth, and these prevent coastal ships from utilizing the river. The Darling, main tributary of the Murray, is 1,760 mi. in length, but it often runs dry for as long a period as eighteen months. The Murrumbidgee rises in the main section of the Australian Alps, not far from the headwaters of the Murray, then forms a great arc, covering 1,050 mi., before entering the Murray. The Lachlan runs into the Murrumbidgee, which supports a number of anabranches as it crosses the plains. Rivers such as the Paroo and Warrego enter the Darling only during periods of heavy floods.

The rivers of the center and east central parts of Australia are generally late-mature or senile in character, and in the dry interior, rivers flow only during the short wet season. The rivers of the far north in Western Australia are tidal,

their main waters being "sweet" only in summer, and rapid streams such as the Fitzroy, Ord, and Victoria on the northwest coast flow in well-marked gorges. In the southeastern portion of Australia in Swanland, the rivers are perennial, as are those which empty into the Pacific Ocean.

Most of the lakes in Australia, like the rivers, disappear during dry weather. Lake George, 17 mi. northeast of Canberra, is at times the largest sheet of fresh water on the continent. At such times, boat races are held on it. After a

COURTESY OF THE AUSTRALIAN NEWS AND INFORMATION BUREAU

Along the bank of the Wollondilly River in the Lower Burragorang Valley, New South Wales

period of dry years, however, sheep are able to graze over the lake floor. Lake Eyre, 3,700 sq. mi., is often dry.

At an elevation of about 1,200 ft. in the southwestern sector of Western Australia is a granite peneplain, divided into many mesas. When rain falls, the water is collected in wide shallow depressions, called "saltpans," if small, or "lakes," if large. There are about 200 of these lakes or playas, which are arranged in more or less connected strings; after heavy rains, they may flow into each other. Some of these saltpans are used for commercial salt and gypsum production. Tasmania's Great Lake, 52 sq. mi. in area, is important because it is the island's principal source of hydroelectric power.

CLIMATE

Temperature. Australia experiences, on the whole, a relatively warm climate, with an average temperature of about 70° F., although light frosts are common in the interior in winter and temperatures below freezing prevail during the winter months in the higher mountain regions in the southeast. Summers are hot nearly everywhere except in the higher mountain regions and the extreme southern parts of the continent. At Marble Bar, Western Australia, in 1940-1941, there were over 140 consecutive days on which the temperature rose above 100° F. The summer months in Australia are December, January, and February, and the winter months, June, July, and August.

Rainfall. A low rainfall, combined with a relatively high rate of evaporation, is characteristic of much of Australia, especially the interior. This places rather severe limitations on soil moisture, plant growth, water supply, and hence also on land settlement. The average annual rainfall has little significance in relation to agricultural and pastoral activities, however, because of the wide variations in rainfall from one season to another and from one year to the next. Heavy rains at times and in places convert the dry country of the interior into rich pasture and cause the normally dry channels of streams to fill with water. At other times or places severe droughts cause the plants to wither and die, the streams may dry up completely, and pastoral industries may suffer heavy losses as a result. The lowest rainfall is received at Lake Eyre in South Australia, which has an average of 4 in., and the highest on the coast of Queensland, near Innisfail, which has over 160 in. Nearly 60 per cent of the continent is arid or semiarid. Practically all of the precipitation is in the form of rain. Snow is confined to the higher elevations in Tasmania and to the sum-

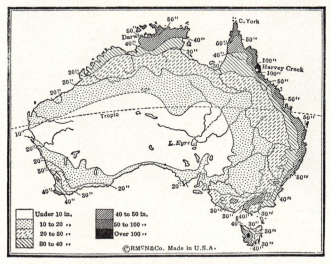

AVERAGE ANNUAL RAINFALL

mits of the Great Dividing Range between northeastern Victoria and southeastern Queensland. Hail is uncommon.

R. G. B.

SOILS

The geographical distribution of soil types throughout Australia is determined by three main features: present climate, past climate, and parent materials. It is the interplay of climate on the parent materials that determines the present nature of the soil and its natural fertility level as expressed by the native vegetation or the crops and pastures which have replaced this vegetation. Generally speaking, apart from those developed on basaltic parent material, the soils of Australia are relatively deficient in phosphate, and the use of superphosphate as a fertilizer is the basis of wheat and pasture production over much of the southern areas of Australia.

Soil surveys have been in progress since 1927. First attention was given to irrigation areas and to some of the wheat, fruit-growing, and forest areas. By 1953 some 4,660 sq. mi. of irrigated areas had been surveyed, and 296,362 sq. mi. in natural rainfall areas. In some areas of reasonably good rainfall where the land has been unproductive, it has been found that deficiencies of some of the so-called trace elements (such as copper, molybdenum, manganese, and zinc) exist. By the use of the necessary soil additives new prospects are opened up. Climate is important in soil formation in that the amount of rainfall, its seasonal distribution, and its effectiveness as controlled by run-off and evaporation determine the degree of leaching to which the soil is subjected. One third of Australia, or about 1,000,000 sq. mi., receives less than 10 in. of rainfall, and in this area the soils belong to a desert group which shows no leaching except in areas subject to occasional flooding. With increasing rainfall the soils begin to show the

effect of leaching, and such constituents as gypsum and calcium carbonate are washed down to greater depths until, with relatively high rainfall, they disappear completely from the soil profile.

Soils are classified in accordance with their characteristic profiles, and in soil surveys it is the profile which is described as a basis for defining the soil type. Throughout Australia there are many occurrences of laterite, expressed as a surface incrustation of ironstone or as abundant ironstone gravel in the profile. It is believed that these occurrences represent the result of leaching and weathering during former climatic cycles, probably in Pliocene times, followed by the normal processes of geological erosion. Laterites give soils which are frequently infertile, owing to deficiencies in trace elements. Natural soil erosion plays a very important part in determining the landscape and the distribution of soil types in the desert regions and in the tropical regions with markedly seasonal rainfall. In the more temperate parts of Australia, erosion has been accelerated through overstocking and cultivation, and there is now some form of soil conservation service to assist farmers and pastoralists in all the mainland states and in the internal territories controlled by the Commonwealth government. The definition of the major soil groups of Australia and their classification are based on the comparison of the soil profiles, a system which was first adopted in Russia and later in the United States. The most important soil groups which have so far been recognized are given below.

Soils of the Tablelands and Ranges. Soils of the tablelands and ranges of the semidesert and tropical regions of summer rainfall are very shallow and are frequently washed away. This type of soil is caused by the natural erosion of the soil after torrential rains following long dry periods.

Desert and Semidesert Soils. The desert and semidesert soils which are not subject to leaching are common to two types of region: the desert sandhill areas and the plains of the semidesert. Desert sandhills are usually covered with desert porcupine grass. There are three important areas of this type in the more arid parts of Australia. Plains of the semidesert include the mulga country, some of the stony deserts, and the Nullarbor Plain.

Soils Subject to Leaching. Certain soils are subject to leaching in varying degrees.

Brown soils of light texture usually contain lime but not gypsum. The best-known examples are the mallee soils of the lower Murray Valley and Western Australia. They are also important in the tropical regions.

Gray and brown soils of heavy texture are usually soils of the treeless plains and contain both lime and gypsum in the lower parts of the profile, since the leaching is not intense. Such soils are found in the Wimmera of Victoria, in the Riverina of New South Wales, in the Rolling Downs of Queensland, in the Barkly Tableland of the Northern Territory, and in the Kimberley region of Western Australia. These soils are very important from the pastoral point of view.

Red-brown earths also may contain lime in the lower layers, but the most striking feature is a heavy subsoil of red clay which has been washed down from the surface layer. This surface layer is usually brown and lighter in texture. The red-brown earths are the most important wheat soils in Australia and usually carry in their native condition an open woodland of eucalyptus or pines, with a grass ground cover, an association of plants known as a savannah woodland.

Black earths are soils of eastern Australia and are best

seen in Queensland. The profile is uniformly very dark gray or black for 3 or 4 ft., and there is usually free lime present. In their virgin state they carry an open grass-land, but in some cases trees such as eucalyptus or brigalow are also present. The black earths of Australia are akin to the black earths of southern Russia and of the southern parts of the United States, and have some relationship with the black cotton soils of India.

Podsolic soils have a gray-brown or dark gray surface layer, with usually a yellow or gray-yellow clayey sub-soil. There is no free lime in the profile. Podsols occur mostly in regions of high rainfall and carry eucalyptus forests or sometimes heaths on the poorer, sandier types.

Shallow peaty moor soils are found on the high plains of Victoria and on the plateaus of Tasmania. They are formed under cold wet conditions with little evaporation.

Red loams are the red basaltic soils occurring generally in the region of the podsols. They are usually very deep and very fertile and show few changes in the profile. They are important on the northwest coast of Tasmania and in parts of Victoria, of New South Wales, and of Queensland.

J. A. P.

FLORA

Ecology. An account of floristics cannot be divorced from an account of the ecology of the continent's vegetation, for correlation between these two aspects is marked. Climatic and soil factors determine the limits of the smaller plant areas, but the broad zones of vegetation—the formation types—show a close correlation with mean annual rainfall. The outstanding feature of Australian meteorology is the arid center, which is surrounded by concentric belts with progressively increasing rainfall. In amount the annual rainfall varies from 5 in. or less in the center to 40 in. or more in the coastal areas of eastern, northern, and parts of southern Australia; in the latter areas, locally the rainfall may be higher, reaching an annual maximum of 160 in. in parts of the eastern coast of tropical Queensland. Consequently there is a wide range of vegetation types, but generalizations can be made for areas classified with respect to annual rainfall as listed below.

(1) *Annual Rainfall Less Than 5 Inches*. Desert, chiefly sand-dune or sand-plain, occurs in this area. The dominant plants are hard-leaved perennial grasses belonging to the genera *Triodia*, and *Spinifex* dominates.

(2) *Annual Rainfall 5-10 Inches*. Semiarid regions of

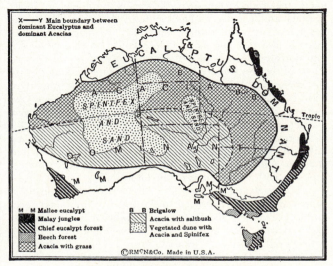

BOTANICAL ZONES OF AUSTRALIA

two main kinds occur. (a) Shrub-steppe, or treeless regions of small shrubs chiefly belonging to the genera *Atriplex* (saltbushes) and *Kochia* (bluebushes), dominates. Here plants are extremely drought-resistant. Some are palatable to stock. These areas are used for sheep grazing, and in appearance are similar to the sagebrush of the western United States. (b) Arid scrub occurs on sandy soils or rocky hills; these are dense growths of various small trees and shrubs

COURTESY OF THE AUSTRALIAN NEWS AND INFORMATION BUREAU
Unusual tree ferns grow in Australia's tropical areas

dominated by various species of *Acacia;* the most widespread is *A. aneura* (mulga). Both types of community show a wealth of annual plants after infrequent rains.

(3) *Annual Rainfall 10-20 Inches*. Two main vegetation types occur in this zone. In the south, where the rainy season is restricted to winter months, mallee scrub occurs. This is a dense assemblage of plants dominated by various dwarf species of *Eucalyptus* which have a characteristic habit in common, viz., the production of several stems from an under-ground rootstock and a restricted canopy of leaves at the ends of the branches. The term "mallee" is applied to this scrub. In northern and eastern Australia, with predominantly summer rainfall, grasslands occur. The dominants vary, but the most extensive and economically important are species of *Astrebla* (Mitchell grass) and *Iseilema* (Flinders grass).

(4) *Annual Rainfall 20-30 Inches*. In this zone occur sa-vannah grasslands. These are open, parklike regions dominated by different species of *Eucalyptus* in different parts of Australia, with essentially grassy or herbaceous undergrowth. These communities have been used extensively for pastoral purposes and for wheat growing. Their open nature has allowed ready colonization by aggressive alien weeds. Savannah grasslands occasionally occur within the sclerophyll forest zone, but always on soils of higher nutrient status than are generally found in a sclerophyll forest.

(5) *Annual Rainfall 30-50 Inches*. Sclerophyll forests are characteristic of this climatic zone. These are forest com-

munities dominated by various species of *Eucalyptus*, the trees growing close together and with a dense undergrowth of hard-leaved shrubs belonging to several characteristic Australian genera; grass is rare. On the drier side these forests merge into savannah woodlands and on the wetter side into rain forest. The drier sclerophyll forests resemble in appearance the chaparral of California. The greatest concentration of typical Australian species occurs in the

EUCALYPTUS FLOWERS

sclerophyll forests. Economically these forests are important as sources of hardwood timber.

(6) *Annual Rainfall Greater Than 50 Inches.* Rain forests are restricted to zones of higher rainfall and usually also to soils derived from basalt. They may be subdivided into tropical and temperate rain forests. The rain forests contain a varied tree vegetation, often with no specific dominant, including many creepers and luxuriant undergrowth. In the tropical rain forests the species are predominantly of Indo-Malayan origin; in the southern temperate rain forests an Antarctic element is prominent, notably in such genera as *Nothofagus* (Southern beech) and in conifers, such as *Dacrydium, Phyllocladus,* and *Arthrotaxus.*

Floristics. In his *Introductory Essay to the Flora of Tasmania,* J. D. Hooker points out that the Australian flora is characterized by a large number of genera and species which are restricted to Australia. Approximately 15,000 species of flowering plants are known today from Australia and about three quarters of these are indigenous. Hooker also first pointed out that floristic analysis showed that there were three main elements which had played major roles in the development of the present-day Australian flora, viz., an Antarctic element, an Indo-Melanesian element, and a native Australian element.

(1) *Antarctic Element.* The term Antarctic element is in general use to embrace species or allied species which are common to southeastern Australia, New Zealand, the sub-Antarctic islands and the southern Andes of South America. Examples of genera which show this distribution at the present day are *Nothofagus, Drimys, Lomatia, Araucaria, Gunnera,* and *Acaena.* These genera have also been found as fossils in the Early Tertiary of the now icebound Seymour Island and Graham Land. The aforementioned plants, as well as many others, today have a solely Antarctic distribution, and it has been suggested that these species spread to their present areas from an Antarctic continental center. Whether such plants originated in Antarctica or were derived from plants which originated in the Northern Hemisphere and migrated southward at some earlier date remains speculative. It is clear, however, that this Antarctic element, present today in southeastern Australia, was widespread in Australia during Early Tertiary times, for Oligocene deposits both in South Australia and Victoria show *Nothofagus* and *Lomatia* admixed with Australian genera such as *Eucalyptus, Banksia,* and *Hakea.* Today the Antarctic element is prominent in temperate rain forests. These considerations apply to the Antarctic element in the restricted sense defined above. The term is sometimes used to include larger groups of plants which today are restricted to the Southern Hemisphere and which are common to South Africa and Australia. Genera common to these two areas are *Caesia, Bulbine, Helichrysum,* and *Restio,* and there are tribes of families which have this distribution in common. Any connection between Australia and South Africa seems to be more remote than that with South America, and present opinion, necessarily speculative, suggests that the plants common to South Africa and Australia were derived from common ancestors which migrated from the north.

(2) *Indo-Melanesian Element.* This element finds expression in those plants which today are common to Australia, the Indo-Malayan region, and Melanesia. Floristic analysis reveals two well-marked streams, one derived from Indo-Malaya, the other from Melanesia, both of which are evident and mixed in New Guinea today. In Australia this element comprises Paleotropic members of many families, especially a host of tropical Sympetalae. The Indo-Malayan element in the Australian flora today shows close affinities with the flora of the Asiatic mainland, especially India, Malaya, and the Malay Archipelago. However, there has been little migration northward of the purely Australian element; two species of *Eucalyptus* and one of *Melaleuca* extend through the Malay Archipelago to Lombok and to the Philippines, but do not cross Wallaces's line (approximately the Asiatic continental shelf). The Melanesian element is shown most clearly in the ferns. The Indo-Melanesian element is a relatively old one in Australia, and it is probable that major migration and expansion occurred during the warm, moist climatic period of the Miocene. In Australia today the Indo-Melanesian element is restricted to moist habitats and usually to basaltic soils. It occurs along the northern Australian littoral, but finds its greatest development in the rain forests of Queensland, which extend also into northern New South Wales. These rain forests contain a host of species; *Rhododendron* and *Garcinia* (mangosteens) are interesting Asiatic genera. Some of the more important both from a vegetative and economic point of view are *Cedrela, Elaeocarpus, Eugenia, Ficus, Geissois, Sloanea, Tarrietia, Albizzia.* The flora of the arid and desert regions of Australia also show affinities with the Old World tropics, rather than with a native Australian element. Genera such as *Atriplex* and *Kochia* and many desert ephemeral plants are common with arid regions of the Old World.

(3) *Australian Element.* The Australian element includes genera and species restricted to Australia or attaining maximum development there; endemic families of plants are few and relatively unimportant. The great Australian genera, with more than 100 species each, are *Eucalyptus* (more than 500 species), *Acacia* (species belonging to the section Phyllodineae, with a simple, flattened, leaflike axis; about 500

species), *Grevillea, Hakea, Melaleuca, Pultenaea, Leucopogon, Goodenia,* and *Hibbertia.* Genera with more than 50 species each include *Banksia, Verticordia, Dryandra, Dodonaea, Persoonia, Daviesia, Baeckea, Boronia,* and *Pimelea.* The typical Australian flora is concentrated in two main regions, southwestern Australia and southeastern Australia. Hooker first pointed out the richness of southwestern Australia in characteristic Australian families, approximately six sevenths of which attain their maximum in that region, the remaining one seventh reaching maximum development in the southeast, with none reaching maximum development in the tropics. Difficulty has arisen in determining whether this element is a truly native one or whether it has been derived from earlier Paleotropic or Antarctic migrants. In any case, certain groups of plants today are entirely Australian in their distribution or, at most, poorly represented on adjacent islands, and their remarkable development in southwestern Australia has special significance.

The center of origin of the Australian element is unknown. The same general botanical features are shown in the Australian paleontological record as elsewhere. The first species of flowering plants are recorded from the late Cretaceous of Queensland, but there is no evidence of the typical Australian flora being widespread until the Oligocene, when such genera as *Eucalyptus, Banksia, Hakea,* and *Persoonia* were widespread throughout southern Australia, admixed, as mentioned earlier, with Antarctic species such as *Nothofagus.* From the concentration of family and generic peculiarities in southwestern Australia, Hooker was led to suggest that this region was the centrum in which the Australian element originated and from which it migrated eastward. Most of the work dealing with the origin and development of the Australian element has been concerned with an analysis of the present-day flora. It has been shown that the flora of southeastern Australia has strong affinities and is closely allied with that of southwestern Australia, and that the isolation of these areas is sufficient to account for the degree of endemism in the two areas today. The results of such an analysis might seem to suggest a Western origin for the flora, but it is dangerous to draw conclusions from the present-day distribution of a flora. The importance of parallel geological factors in its evolution and development must be taken into account.

The widespread Oligocene flora, with its characteristic Australian plants, provides a starting point. During the long period between the Cretaceous and the Miocene, Australia apparently enjoyed great stability and was reduced to a peneplain; the fossil record during this period suggests abundant rainfall and moderate temperatures. No physical barriers to plant migration can therefore be envisaged, and recent work suggests the existence of a pan-Australian flora during this period. During the Miocene, seas inundated much of southern Australia, and in addition to destroying much of the vegetation must have proved an effective barrier to migration, for floristically they isolated southeastern and southwestern Australia. Late in the Miocene, earth movements began which continued through to the Pleistocene. In eastern Australia these movements uplifted portions of the old peneplain (Kosciuszko Epoch) and initiated the cycle of erosion in the Great Dividing Range today; in South Australia blockfaulting caused elevation of a range system and the sunkland of the southern gulfs. By the close of the Pleistocene, the Miocene seas had withdrawn approximately to the position of those existing today. The earth movements provided habitat diversity and barriers to migration; in addition a major barrier was the great limestone deposits at the head

of the Great Australian Bight. These isolated the flora of southwestern Australia, which had developed and been selected on podsolic and lateritic soils.

During the Pleistocene, the general climatic pattern was apparently similar to that existing today; however, a major change occurred during the early mid-Recent. It was marked

COURTESY OF THE AUSTRALIAN NEWS AND INFORMATION BUREAU

A karri forest in Pemberton, Western Australia. These giant gum trees furnish one of the hardest woods in the world.

by a sharp decline in rainfall, which formed the sand-dune deserts of the center, left its mark on soil profiles, and in southern Australia caused a sharp contraction of the existing flora and the marked discontinuity of species distribution, which is an outstanding feature in southern Australia today. This did not affect, however, the broad pattern of distribution of the flora. In conclusion, it is found that the evidence suggests a widespread pan-Australian flora in southern Australia in the early Tertiary, followed by division into two groups in the Miocene; since that time physiographic and climatic influences have isolated floristically the southeastern and southwestern parts of Australia, and the southwest has preserved great floristic stability.

In the settled areas of southern and eastern Australia alien plants have established themselves, particularly in the more open communities, such as the savannah woodlands, where introduced grasses and herbs have supplanted the corresponding native species. More than half of these naturalized plants are natives of the Mediterranean region. Introductions from South Africa, which has a similar Mediterranean type of climate, are also prominent. The remainder, approximately a third of the total, are from Europe and western Asia.

Native plants fit for human consumption are insignificant, although they provided food for the aborigines. *Macadamia terrifolia* is cultivated for its edible nut, both in Australia and in Hawaii. There are no indigenous cereals. Fodder plants have been mentioned above. The most important grasses are species of *Danthonia, Iseilema,* and *Astrebla.* Species of

Atriplex (saltbushes) and *Kochia* (bluebushes) are important in arid areas. Materials for tanning are obtained from the barks of various species of *Acacia,* especially *A. pycnantha,* which is cultivated both in Australia and in South Africa.

Blackboys, so called because from a distance they resemble natives wearing tufts of grass, are strange plants of the Lily family. They grow on the sand plains near Moora, 100 miles from Perth.

COURTESY OF THE
AUSTRALIAN NEWS AND
INFORMATION BUREAU

Australia is rich in trees, both softwoods and hardwoods, whose timbers have many uses.   J. G. W.

FAUNA

Australia constitutes the major portion of the zoogeographical region of Australasia, which also includes Tasmania, New Zealand, New Guinea, and the adjacent islands of the Melanesian and Malaysian groups westward to Wallace's Line. This imaginary line, which forms the boundary of the truly typical Australian fauna, passes northward between the islands of Bali to the west and Lombok to the east, thence northward through Macassar Strait, between Borneo and Celebes, and finally northeastward between Serangani Island of the Philippine group and Palmas Island. Wallace's Line, although it separates closely adjacent islands throughout its length, is the eastern boundary of the Asiatic-Oriental fauna.

Mammals. Probably the most widely known fact of animal distribution is that pouched animals, as typified by the kangaroo, are natives of Australia. There is an almost unconscious recognition of the bizarre quality of the animal population in the land "down under," but the familiar kangaroo does not begin to do justice to the truly unique character of Australia's mammalian fauna.

The most primitive living subclass of the mammals, the Monotremata, is found in no other part of the world. The platypus (*Ornithorhynchus*) lays eggs, has a snout that startlingly resembles a duck's bill, is covered with hair, and suckles its young when they are hatched. It is relatively abundant, thanks to the forward-looking efforts of Australian conservationists. Its closely related cousin, the spiny anteater or echidna (*Tachyglossus*), looks rather like a porcupine, but it, too, lays eggs. Of these two monotremes, the

platypus is confined to Australia and Tasmania, whereas the echidnas (*Tachyglossus* and *Zaglossus*) are found in New Guinea as well.

In number and variety of species, however, the monotremes and the placental mammals are overwhelmed by the marsupials, that subclass which is characterized by the early, immature birth of the young, who are then transferred to the marsupium, or pouch, there to be nurtured until old enough to fend for themselves.

According to the most generally accepted theory of mammalian distribution, proposed by W. D. Matthew in his book

COURTESY OF THE AUSTRALIAN NEWS AND INFORMATION BUREAU

The kangaroo, Australia's national animal

Climate and Evolution (1915), the cradle of mammalian life has been in the northern continents, whence the primitive and usually less successfully specialized groups have been pushed slowly into the southern continents as new waves of more aggressive and successful mammals made their appearance. This general theory is well supported by the marsupials, since fossil evidences of their existence is widespread throughout the northern world in addition to the

COURTESY OF THE AUSTRALIAN NEWS AND INFORMATION BUREAU

Australian bandicoots, small marsupials, feed mainly on roots, bulbs, and tubers. They are particularly injurious to potato and grain crops.

extant North and South American remnants noted below. Once the monotremes and marsupials had been pushed back into the cul-de-sac of Australia, the connection between that region and the Asiatic mainland was cut off, and the two groups were free of serious competition with the later, more aggressive placental types.

These events served to set the stage for what happened to the Australian mammal fauna. Isolated as they were from competition, the marsupials flourished and blossomed forth into a great variety of types, sizes, habits, and adaptations, paralleling in many ways the subsequent history of the placentals in the northern continents. The marsupials of Australia include superficial counterparts of the carnivores, insectivores, rodents, and herbivores. Apart from the American opossums (Didelphyidae) and the peculiar South American *Caenolestes,* the marsupials are confined to the Australasian region.

The Dasyuridae and the Peramelidae are included in the polyprotodont marsupials, which have two or three lower incisors on each side. The Dasyuridae, or "native cats," include *Dasyurus,* the Tasmanian devil (*Sarcophilus*), and the arboreal and insectivorous members of the genus *Phascogale.* The latter genus is widespread throughout Australasia. Closely related to the dasyures is the Tasmanian wolf (*Thylacinus*), which has been recorded from the mainland of Australia as well. The banded anteater, *Myrmecobius,* has undoubtedly been derived from the dasyure-thylacine group, as has the pouched "mole," *Notoryctes,* of north and central Australia. The bandicoots (Peramelidae), a family that includes eight genera distributed throughout Australasia, occupy a place in the regional fauna analogous to that of the Insectivora in the northern world.

The diprotodont marsupials, characterized by having only one pair of lower incisors, are more widely known than the polyprotodonts. Their distribution is confined to Australasia. The most primitive of the diprotodont marsupials is the family Phalangeridae, which includes *Petaurus,* paralleling the flying squirrels; *Acrobates,* the pigmy flying phalanger;

COURTESY OF THE AUSTRALIAN NEWS AND INFORMATION BUREAU

The dingo, a wild dog destructive to Australia's sheep

and *Trichosurus,* the opossum of Australia. The koala (*Phascolarctus*), the prototype of the "Teddy bear," is a member of the phalanger family. The koala is the psychological counterpart of the sloth, and, indeed, its sleepy and slow reactions give it more than a superficial resemblance to the true sloth of South America. The wombat (*Phascolomys*), confined to Australia proper, is a relatively large, beaverlike derivative of the phalanger stock. The kangaroos and wallabies (Macropodidae) are found throughout the zoogeographic region. Living in the open forest is the most common of the kangaroos, *Macropus giganteus,* the great gray kangaroo. Other open-country types are *Petrogale, Peradorcas,* and *Palorchestes.* Among the interesting genera of this group should be mentioned *Dendrolagus,* the tree-climbing kangaroo, whose forefeet and hind feet are specialized for climbing.

That the marsupials have long held sway in Australia is amply demonstrated by the fossil remains of the giant wombat (*Diprotodon*) and the marsupial "lion," *Thylacoleo.*

Although the mammalian fauna is thus predominantly marsupial, there are a few indigenous rodents, such as *Anisomys, Conilurus, Crossomys, Hydromys*—all of the family Muridae. Of the bats, Australasia is well represented with numerous genera of Megachiroptera and Microchiroptera. Especially notable in the region is the flying fox, *Pteropus.* Only one other group of placental land mammals is represented in Australia. The Carnivora are present in the form of the dingo (*Canis dingo*), a true dog whose presence in Australia dates back to the Pleistocene. The entry of the dingo into Australia is believed to coincide with the advent of Pleistocene man in that continent.

As in New Zealand, the ecological balance has been somewhat upset by the white man's intentional or unintentional introduction of placental mammals, such as the rabbit and fox, into the local fauna.

Birds. The avifauna of Australia includes many species of great interest and importance. Among the flightless ratite birds are the emu (*Dromaius novae-hollandiae*) and the cassowary (*Casuarius casuarius*), a native of north Queensland. The Australian continent is very rich in ducks, which are represented by the shelduck (*Casarca*), and the musk

COURTESY OF THE AUSTRALIAN NEWS AND INFORMATION BUREAU

Koala bears, native to Australia and confined there by law

duck (*Biziura*). Birds of prey are represented by the wedge-tailed eagle (*Uroaetus audax*), the whistling eagle (*Haliastur sphenurus*), the peregrine falcon (*Falco peregrinus*), and the goshawk (*Astur fasciatus*). Australia is outstanding for the occurrence of the mound-builder mallee fowl (*Leipoa*) and brush turkey (*Alectura*); the bower birds; the

Cassowary, Casuarius casuarius, *found in tropical north Queensland, is a flightless bird about 5 ft. tall.*

birds of paradise; the honey eaters; the lyre bird; and the great abundance and variety of parrots, pigeons, and ducks with the total absence of vultures and woodpeckers. The Australian region is the center of radiation of the parrots and is populated by all of the subfamilies of the group. The region is also especially notable for the presence of the most primitive of the "song birds," the lyre bird (*Menura*) and the scrub birds (*Atrichornis*).

Reptiles. Australia has a widespread reptile fauna of snakes, crocodiles, lizards, and turtles. Of the approximately 150 species of Australian snakes, the taipan (*Oxyuranus scutellatus*) is the largest of the venomous group, and the Queensland python (*Python amethystinus*) attains a length of twenty feet. The crocodiles are represented by two species, the estuarine type (*Crocodilus porosus*) and the smaller river crocodile (*Crocodilus johnsoni*), both of which are represented in northern Australia and New Guinea. The turtles are represented by about ten species distributed between the genera *Chelodina* and *Emydura*. Noteworthy among the more than three hundred species of Australian lizards are the legless lizards (Pygopodidae), which are found in Australia and New Guinea, and the large monitor lizards (Varanidae), some of which reach seven feet in length.

Amphibians. The amphibian fauna of Australia is characterized by the absence of Urodeles, or tailed types, but there are numerous genera of toads and frogs. The Australian bufonid toads of the subfamily Criniinae, structurally the most primitive of the true toads, are typified by the genera *Crinia, Mixophyes,* and *Helioporus.* There are sixteen genera present in the region. Typical of New Guinea are the narrow-mouthed toads *Liophryne, Oxydactyla, Copiula, Callulops,* and *Xenobatrachus.*

Fish. Australia does not have a large or varied fresh-water fish fauna. There are no carps, killifishes, or salmon and only a few catfishes. Most of the fresh-water fauna are descendants of marine types—the Murray cod (*Oligorus*),

perches (*Percalates, Plectroplites, Macquaria*), grunters (*Therapon*), herrings (*Potamalosa*), garfish (*Hemirhamphus*), and gudgeons (*Gobiomorphus, Carassiops*). There are, however, two noteworthy exceptions—the Queensland lungfish (*Neoceratodus*) and the barramundi (*Scleropages*). As in New Zealand, there are a number of species of mountain trout (*Galaxias*) as well as the blackfish (*Gadopsis*).

G. M. C.

ETHNOLOGY AND POPULATION

Aborigines. The first human inhabitants of Australia were probably the Tasmanian natives, who arrived on the continent many thousands of years ago and whose descendants survived in Tasmania until 1876. Shortly after them came several waves of Australian blackfellows, whose descendants still inhabit parts of the interior and the northern fringe of Australia. Australian natives have been classified in various ways by anthropologists, but usually as a separate race (Australoid) or subrace, because of various anatomical characteristics that appear to set them apart from the Caucasoid, Mongoloid, and Negroid races. Their economy was formerly limited to hunting small game and gathering insects, roots, seeds, and berries. Many of them are now engaged as stockmen, earning a living on the northern cattle ranches.

Population. The population of Australia was 8,917,763, exclusive of about 47,000 full-blooded aborigines, according to official estimates at the end of December 1953. At that time the population by states and territories was as follows: New South Wales, 3,472,294; Victoria, 2,405,296; Queensland, 1,270,381; South Australia, 765,520; Western Australia, 633,531; Tasmania, 322,812; Australian Capital Territory, 30,983; and Northern Territory, 16,946. Density of population per square mile was 2.99 for Australia as a whole; 27.37 for Victoria; 32.99 for the Australian Capital Territory; 12.33 for Tasmania; 11.22 for New South Wales; 2.01 for South Australia; 1.89 for Queensland; and .03 for Northern Territory. By comparison the density of population in the United States in 1953 was 53 per square mile. The urban population of Australia constituted more than two thirds of the total, with about

ABORIGINES AT KURANDA, QUEENSLAND

half the Australians living in the state capitals. The population of these capitals was: Sydney, 1,621,040; Melbourne, 1,393,000; Brisbane, 469,000; Adelaide, 459,000; Perth, 346,000; and Hobart, 91,080. Canberra, the federal capital, had a population of 26,732, and Darwin, the largest city in Northern Territory, had a population of 7,836.

In the twenty-year period 1933-1953 Australia's population increased by approximately 33 per cent. During this time the tendency toward greater industrialization was reflected in the increased percentage of people engaged in manufacturing industries—a trend apparent since the foundation of the Commonwealth. In 1901, 30 per cent of the population of Australia was engaged in primary industries; by 1953 the proportion was down to 16.15 per cent. In the latter year 959,000 people were engaged in manufacturing industries, three fourths of them in New South Wales and Victoria.

The Australian birthrate in 1953 was 22.90 per 1,000 and the death rate, 9.08 per 1,000. The excess of births over deaths was 122,047. Between 1861 and 1929 migration had accounted for an average of 24.5 per cent of Australia's total population increase. Between 1929 and 1945 immigration and emigration had about balanced each other. Immediately after World War II Australia launched a large-scale immigration program which, by December 1953, had taken almost 800,000 new settlers to Australia. Of the immigrants, 49.6 per cent were British (including the United Kingdom, Eire, and Malta); 10.6, Italian; 8.9, Polish; 6.6, Dutch; 3.2, Yugoslav; 2.6, German; 2.6, Russian; 2.5, Latvian; 1.8, Hungarian; 1.7, Greek; 1.5, Czechoslovak; and 1.1, American. In the 1947 census religious affiliations were as follows: 2,957,032, Church of England; 1,569,726, Roman Catholic and other Catholic bodies; 871,425, Methodist; 743,540, Presbyterian; 113,527, Baptist; 71,771, Church of Christ; 66,891, Lutheran; 63,243, Congregational; and 32,019, Jewish.

Land Settlement. The policy of both the state and federal governments of Australia has been to encourage settle-

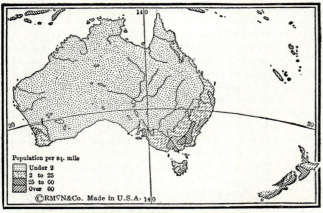

POPULATION DENSITY

ment on the land wherever the prospects appeared to be good. Immigration reached its peak during the days of the gold rush in the 1850's, but there was another wave in the early 1920's, when immigration and closer settlement were hailed as the cure-all for Australia's economic, social, and political problems. In many cases the land used for settlement projects was not adequately surveyed and assessed, the settlers were ill chosen, and intelligent planning and

organization was conspicuously absent. After World War II there was a more cautious attitude. With few exceptions, the areas of future promise for settlement appeared to lie within the area already occupied, i.e., the east and southwest, and it was thought that closer settlement in these areas would probably be of greater significance than new settlements beyond the present frontier.

R. M. Y.

GOVERNMENT AND POLITICS

Central Government. The legal basis of the Commonwealth government is the Commonwealth Act of 1900, which was passed by the British Parliament, received the royal assent on July 9, 1900, and came into effect Jan. 1, 1901. This measure enacted into imperial law the constitution submitted to it as a result of previous deliberations in Australia. The constitutional system is federal in nature and shows definite and conscious influence of the federal system in use in the United States.

Powers. The federal government possesses both exclusive and concurrent powers. The former include some that were once possessed by the separate colonies, such as the right to legislate for posts, telegraphs, and telephones, and for defense; some that were not formerly so possessed, such as external affairs and the relations with the islands of the Pacific; and some with respect to matters on which, under the Commonwealth Act, the states are forbidden to legislate, such as the provision of military forces, and coinage. In the field of concurrent legislation, federal law takes precedence over state law. Those powers not definitely delegated to the Commonwealth are reserved to the states. It was the purpose of the makers of the constitutional system to provide a central government that would represent the people of Australia to the world and at the same time take account of the obvious loyalty of the people to their respective colonial governments.

Federal Parliament. The constitution provides for the election of a House of Representatives on the basis of population for a three-year term, and a Senate in which each of the original states has six members. The members of the Senate are elected, one half each three years, by popular vote, each state being a single constituency. The two houses have equal legislative power except in the field of financial legislation, where the Senate is merely empowered to "suggest" that the House of Representatives pass certain amendments. The Senate may refuse to pass a money bill already passed by the House. In 1947 the Australian parliament passed an act to increase Senate membership from 36 to 60, each state to have 10 members instead of the previous 6. The House was to be correspondingly increased from 75 to 123. This change, which was made without formal constitutional amendment, went into effect at the 1949 federal general election.

Cabinet. The Commonwealth Act provided for an executive council, but made no mention of a cabinet as such. The cabinet system of government is practiced, of course, under the common understanding that members of the council, viz., the Cabinet, shall possess the confidence of the members of the House of Representatives. In the operation of the Australian party system the Governor-General has no influence in the choice of a prime minister to head the Cabinet. The Cabinet is responsible primarily to the House of Representatives. Its members must, within three months of appointment, secure seats in either the upper or lower house. The Commonwealth Act provides a method of dealing with deadlocks between the House and the Senate. If the House passes any bill and the Senate rejects it, and the same process is repeated in the same or in the next ses-

FEDERAL PARLIAMENT HOUSE, CANBERRA, AUSTRALIAN CAPITAL TERRITORY

sion, "the Governor-General may dissolve the Senate and the House of Representatives simultaneously." If the newly-elected House passes the proposed law and the new Senate rejects it, the Governor-General may convene a joint sitting of the two houses. If the bill is passed at the joint sitting by an absolute majority of the total membership of the two houses, it is taken to have been passed by both houses separately. This ingenious device was framed with a view to avoiding endless conflicts between two legislative bodies composed on different principles, as well as to providing a satisfactory basis for the operation of the British system of cabinet responsibility in a federal government where both houses carry mandates from the people.

High Court. The constitutional system set up in the Commonwealth Act provides for a supreme court known as the High Court of Australia; the state courts are invested with federal jurisdiction, and appeals may be made from state courts to the High Court. Under certain conditions, appeal may be made from the High Court to the Judicial Committee of the Privy Council in Great Britain. Room was thus left for the interpretation of the constitutional system through court action.

Civil Service. Australia has been called "overgoverned" by many of its citizens. The implication is that such a state of affairs is bad, but the increase in number of public servants in Australia is perhaps chiefly indicative of a trend that has been characteristic of most countries. In the depression year of 1934, one out of every five employed persons in Australia worked for the government, a far greater proportion than that in the United States.

Political Parties. In Australian history before 1901 the most important political questions had concerned the desire for white security, federation, and tariff protection. The first had been settled for each colony by action of the British Government; the second was to be settled by the creation of the Commonwealth; the individual states had decided the third according to their own presumed interests, Victoria practicing protection and New South Wales free trade. In the first Commonwealth parliament a cabinet favoring moderate protection committed the new government to a policy of protection; thus new issues naturally arose in the period of the Commonwealth. Political parties in Australia have been based on three particular economic interests: manufacturing, trade unions, and agrarian activity. These interests are to a considerable extent in conflict, but from time to time have been able to find certain areas of agreement. The following are the principal political groups or parties since 1901.

(1) *Protectionists.* Led by Sir Edmund Barton and Alfred Deakin, protectionism under the latter was accompanied by a willingness to pass advanced social legislation.

(2) *The Opposition.* Led by George Houston Reid, the opposition had free-trade leanings but could not bring about a return to that policy.

(3) *Liberal Party (Old).* Founded in 1909-1910 during the Deakin ministry, the old Liberal Party was protectionist and composed of all non-Labour elements.

(4) *Labor Party.* The Labour Party first elected representatives to colonial parliaments before 1890 and grew rapidly after 1891. Marxian ideas played but little part in its thought and activity. It believed in creating a society where all could live the "good life," and regarded protection and labor legislation as the means of making this possible. The Labour Party developed a system of party discipline that enabled it to act effectively in the attainment of its goals. In each electorate there is a party branch which names local candidates and chooses delegates to a conference of the State Labour League. The conference writes the platform. On the Commonwealth level there is also a conference with similar functions. Questions of parliamentary tactics are decided in a caucus of members of both the House of Representatives and the Senate.

By means of the caucus, the Labour Party is also able to determine the choice of premier and cabinet members. In State administrations Labour first came to power in 1899 in Queensland. In the federal sphere, the Labour government of John C. Watson (1904) was the first. Andrew Fisher led three Labour ministries (1908-1909, 1910-1913, and 1914-1915) and was succeeded by Labour administrations under William Morris Hughes (1915-1917) and later by James Scullin (1929-1932). A Labour government led by John Curtin took office in 1941 and won the 1943 elections. By 1946, when another general election returned Labour, the Party was under the leadership of Joseph B. Chifley. Labour lost the 1949 election to the Liberal-Country Party coalition.

(5) *Nationalist Party.* Founded in 1917 by a fusion of the Liberals with those Labourites who had been read out of the party for their promotion of conscription during war, the Nationalist Party favored protection and national development, and was forced, through the labor element in its ranks, to favor wage determination by governmental action. In the year 1931 it fused with supporters of one faction of the fallen Labour government to form the United Australia Party.

(6) *Country Party.* Founded in 1919 to defend agrarian interests, the Country Party, while critical of certain aspects of the tariff, has not strongly opposed protection. The party has worked for protection for the farmer by means of special aid, in addition to existing protection to industry and labor. Work has been done to promote the effective marketing of agricultural products. From 1923 to 1929 the Country Party co-operated with the Nationalists in the Bruce-Page ministry. After the 1949 general elections, the Country Party came to power with the Liberal Party, and the coalition retained office in the 1951 and 1954 elections.

(7) *United Australia Party.* Founded in 1931 by a fusion of a labor group under J. A. Lyons with the Nationalist Party, the United Australia Party was able in the next parliament to govern without the assistance of the Country Party. As a result of the elections of 1934 and 1937, however, a coalition government was necessary. In 1943 the United Australia Party went to the polls in alliance with the Country Party, but met defeat.

(8) *Liberal Party (New).* Because of dissatisfaction with the results achieved by the United Australia Party and because of a demand for a party that would include all non-labor elements, conferences were held in October and December 1944. Out of these came a new Liberal Party. While the Country Party chose to maintain its separate existence, it has worked closely with the new Liberal Party. The 1949 elections returned a Liberal-Country Party majority and Robert G. Menzies became Prime Minister in the coalition government which succeeded in the general elections in 1951 and 1954.

(9) *Communist Party.* The Communist Party in Australia is small and has slight influence, though it has tried to exert political power through control of trade unions.

Government in Action. The Commonwealth Act of 1900 contained no bill of rights, and none has since been added to the constitution. On the contrary the act gave to the federal parliament the right to make laws with respect to "the people of any race, other than the aboriginal race in any State, for whom it is deemed necessary to make special laws." *The Welfare State.* Australia has been energetic in developing social services of many kinds. Social welfare plays an important role in the political platform of all parties. Aid touches every aspect of life and includes child endowment for all children under 16, maternity allowances, widows'

pensions, invalid and old-age pensions, funeral benefits, and unemployment benefits. Under the Federal Government's National Health Service, which went into operation in 1953, provision is made for medical, hospital, and pharmaceutical benefits. Other aspects of the activity are tuberculosis allowances, free milk for school children, and financial aid to mental institutions. The 1953-1954 budget provided for an expenditure of £(A)184,052,000 for social services.

National Defense. During World War II, there were 727,152 enlistments in the Australian army, including 35,762 women. The absorption of most of these into civil life was hardly complete before a new defense program was inaugurated. The original five-year plan of 1948 was stepped up in 1950. Changes included the introduction of military training for all 18-year-olds, expansion and modernization of the Air Force, and a new naval construction program. Budgets in 1952 and 1953 provided for an annual defense expenditure of £(A)200,000,000. The strength of the Australian forces in March 1954 was as follows:

	Navy	Army	Air	Total
Permanent Forces	14,152	25,226	14,946	54,324
Citizens Forces	7,681	85,767	13,708	107,156
Totals:	21,833	110,993	28,654	161,480

The long-range weapons establishment at Woomera, South Australia, is a joint British-Australian project to develop and test pilotless aircraft and guided missiles. The British government in collaboration with the Australian government conducted atomic tests at the Monte Bello Islands off the west coast, in October 1952, and at the Woomera Rocket Range, South Australia, in October 1953. The Australian Atomic Energy Commission was established in 1952 to control Commonwealth activities in connection with uranium and atomic energy.

Public Finance. Postwar budgets of the federal government have provided for greatly increased expenditure and for the first time a £(A)1,000,000,000 (equivalent to $2,250,000,000) budget was presented for the fiscal year ending June 20, 1952. This compares with the £(A)100,-000,000 budget presented for 1939-1940. The rising budgets reflected the rising national income (up from £(A)852,-000,000 in 1939-1940 to £(A)3,579,000,000 in 1952-1953), and increased social service and defense expenditure. In the 1953-1954 budget, social service allocation was £(A)184,-052,000; defense allocation, £(A)200,000,000; and for capital works, £(A)101,548,000. Most postwar years have provided a reasonably large budget surplus and in no instances has there been more than a nominal deficit.

International reserves built up to £(A)843,000,000 in 1950-1951, falling to £(A)362,000,000 the next year, with a sharp rise in imports following on a record wool season. In 1952-1953 reserves again rose by £(A)186,000,000 to £(A)548,000,000.

The Australian pound remains tied to English sterling but is pegged at 125 Australian to 100 English pounds. The Commonwealth Bank of Australia issues paper currency and conducts the federal financial transactions. A trading section does general banking business. In 1947 a bill was passed to nationalize all private banking concerns, but the act was subsequently declared to be unconstitutional by the High Court of Australia.

National Debt. The federal and state public debt amounted to £(A)1,215,299,000 in June 1939 (£(A)174 per head of population) and in 1954 stood at £(A)3,431,863,000 (£(A)388/18/6 per head of population). During World War II the total public debt was more than doubled. The

A HERD OF MERINOS

two World Wars accounted for £(A)1,625,110,000 of the outstanding debt at June 1953. The proportion of the Australian debts repayable overseas has decreased, most loans having been floated within Australia since 1930. The outstanding debt payable in New York stood at $158,000,000 in June 1954.

By 1954 Australia had negotiated dollar loans amounting to $254,000,000 from the International Bank for purchase in the United States of capital goods and equipment.

Federal-State Relations. The respective powers of federal and state legislatures are set down in the Commonwealth Act of 1900 with its amendments. But much of the practice of federalism in Australia stems from other sources. Periodic meetings of the Australian prime minister with state premiers has resulted in much effective co-ordination of procedure and even policy. Similar meetings of ministers and deputy ministers concerned with some particular branch of government service, such as health, education, taxation, and statistics, have carried this process even further. The Australian Loan Council has long been an effective means of both guiding and supporting state finance policies. State loans made outside the state must secure its approval. The Commonwealth Grants Commission has had the function of recommending an equalizing of financial burdens among the states so as to keep the standard of government services to the people in the claimant states up to certain minimum levels. The acceptance by Australians of this type of co-ordination, as compared with their great reluctance to

vote in favor of constitutional amendments that would legally alter the relations of federal and state control, is striking.

External and British Commonwealth Relations. Before World War II Australia had no diplomatic representatives abroad. While vitally interested in both British Commonwealth and foreign affairs, Australians had been content to have any negotiations conducted through the diplomatic service of the United Kingdom. Since 1940, however, Australia has come to have wide representation overseas. Ambassadors have been appointed to the United States, France, Germany, Indonesia, Japan, and The Netherlands; ministers to Brazil, Burma, Egypt, Indo-China, Italy, the Philippines, and Thailand. Australia has High Commissioners in Britain, Canada, Ceylon, India, New Zealand, Pakistan, South Africa, and a Commissioner in Malaya. Australia is represented in the United Nations by a mission headed by a minister.

ECONOMIC RESOURCES AND ACTIVITIES

Pastoral Industries. Approximately one fifth of the national wealth is derived from pastoral production, which ranks second only to manufacturing as a source of income. Australia produces one fourth of the world's wool and 60 per cent of the world's marino wool. Wool accounted for 46 per cent of total exports in 1952-1953. About one third of the continent is good pastoral country except in times of severe drought. Additional handicaps include plagues of rabbits, grasshoppers, dingoes (wild dogs), blowflies, ticks, and other insects, while in some localities large tracts of land are overrun with noxious weeds. Widespread introduction in 1951 of the virus disease myxomatosis has decreased the rabbit menace and in three years was estimated to have cut rabbit numbers by half. As a result, harvests and the wool clips have increased. Some doubt exists about the long-range effectiveness of this form of control, however, since signs of immunity to the virus have appeared.

Sheep. Sheep have long been the mainstay of the Australian pastoral economy. In 1953 Australia had about one sixth of the world's sheep (123,000,000), and produced about one fourth of the world's wool. Most of the sheep are pastured well inland from the coast in the east and southeast, but other sheep-producing areas are located in the southwest and northwest. Merino sheep predominate in the drier country toward the interior of the continent and provide the finest wool, while cross-bred or "dual-purpose" sheep, such as the Corriedale, are found mainly in the humid margins of the sheep country, and provide both meat and wool.

Cattle. Cattle were second in importance to sheep in the pastoral economy of Australia in 1953; the numerical ratio between the two was about 8:1. Most of the cattle are produced in the southeastern and northeastern parts of the country, although important cattle-raising districts are also found in the southwestern and northwestern parts of Western Australia. The trend toward wheat and sheep production on the better land has forced cattle raising into the more remote and inferior country. Droughts have caused heavy losses of stock at times, and Australian pastoral industries have long suffered from various additional handicaps, such as high labor costs, long hauls to markets, high transportation costs, and competition from other meat-producing countries.

Dairying. Dairying is carried on mainly in the wetter coastal regions fairly close to urban markets and coastal ports. Although Australian consumption of dairy products is high, large quantities of butter and cheese are exported each year, chiefly to Great Britain.

Agriculture. Agriculture has ranked third among Australian industries for many years. It now accounts for about one eighth of the total value of production. About one per cent, or 20,000,000 acres, of the total area of the Commonwealth is under cultivation. Wheat occupies first place in the agricultural economy, with half of the total cultivated area sown to wheat. Most of the wheat is grown is the subhumid areas in the southeast and southwest where yields average up to 19 bu. per acre. About 40 per cent of the annual yield is normally exported to the United Kingdom. Other grain crops include oats, barley, maize, and rice. Root crops are not as important in the Australian economy as in the economy of northwest Europe. Sugar cane and a variety of tropical and subtropical fruits and vegetables have been introduced successfully in eastern Queensland. The 1953 crop of 1,270,000 tons of raw sugar was valued at £(A)50,-000,000. Tobacco growing has been encouraged in the southeast and southwest, but local production is insufficient for Australian requirements. Among the fruits grown in Australia are bananas, pineapples, papayas, currants, oranges, lemons, grapefruit, peaches, apricots, pears, plums, and cherries. Much of the fruit is produced in the irrigation districts along the Murray River and its tributaries in Victoria and South Australia, which also specialize in fodder, vineyards, dairying, and vegetable growing. Other fruit-growing areas are scattered along the east coast from Tasmania to northeastern Queensland as well as in southwestern Western Australia.

Mining. The mineral resources of Australia, although not so great as those of the United States or the U.S.S.R., are important. Australian mines have yielded large quantities of gold, silver, lead, zinc, coal, iron, copper, and tin, as well

DRIVING A HERD OF CATTLE ACROSS A RIVER IN QUEENSLAND

DISKING THE SOIL IN ONE OF THE EXTENSIVE VINEYARDS OF BAROSSA VALLEY NEAR ADELAIDE

as smaller amounts of other minerals. Mineral production in 1952 was valued at £(A)139,932,000 ($294,847,000). New South Wales and Western Australia together accounted for more than half the total. Western Australia was the chief gold-producing state, South Australia produced most of the iron ore, New South Wales accounted for most of the bituminous coal, and Victoria practically all of the brown coal. New South Wales and Queensland produced most of the silver, lead, and zinc ore; Tasmania, Queensland, and New South Wales accounted for most of the copper and tin. Important uranium deposits have been discovered. In 1953 an oil strike was made at Exmouth Gulf, Western Australia, giving promise of oil in commercial quantities.

Forests and Forest Products. The area of state forest preserves in 1947 was slightly more than 119,402 sq. mi., equivalent to four per cent of the total land area of Australia. Queensland and New South Wales accounted for most of the sawn softwood timber and Western Australia and Victoria for more than half of the hardwood timber. Forest products other than timber include eucalyptus oil, sandalwood and sandalwood oil, grass tree or yacca gum, and tanbarks. During World War II a process was dis-

covered for the manufacture of paper from certain Australian eucalyptus. Only about five per cent of the trees of Australia are softwoods, and Australia has had to rely on softwood imports from Canada, Norway, Sweden, and the United States. Since World War I, however, plantations of Monterey pine (*Pinus radiata*) and other softwood trees have been started in the southeast.

Fisheries. Little has been done to develop commercial fishing in Australian waters. The only organized developments are the pearl oyster, *bêche-de-mer* (trepang), and turtle fisheries in tropical waters off the northern shore of the continent, the oyster-breeding industry on the coast of New South Wales, and the crayfish industry in Western Australia and South Australia.

Manufacturing. Manufacturing ranks first among Australian industries in total value of production and is mainly concentrated in or near the six state capitals: Sydney, Melbourne, Adelaide, Brisbane, Perth, and Hobart. Almost all the power for manufacturing is derived from coal. The chief coal-producing states, New South Wales and Victoria, are also the most populous and keep the lead in manufacturing in the southeastern part of Australia. Production of manu-

STEEL WORKS AT NEWCASTLE, AUSTRALIA'S GREAT STEEL CITY

"THE GOLDEN MILE," A RICH GOLD MINING AREA IN KALGOORLIE, WESTERN AUSTRALIA

factured goods, despite the tremendous advances made during World War II and since, is still largely confined to the needs of the home market. Although there has been some advance in agricultural, pastoral, and mining industries, the striking rise in the manufacturing industry has tended to overshadow the others. It has chiefly taken two forms: the development of the processing industries and the growth of metal manufactures. The latter is indicated in the export of metal manufactures and machinery from £(A)10,058,000 in the fiscal year 1938-1939 to £(A)61,368,000 in 1952-1953.

Commerce. *Exports.* The total value of Australian exports rose from £(A)140,496,000 in 1938-1939 and £(A)309,029,000 in 1946-1947 to £(A)871,272,000 in 1952-1953. Much the most important item was wool, which (at £(A)402,871,000) accounted for 46 per cent of the total value of exports in 1952-1953. Next in importance were wheat and flour exports, valued at £(A)89,683,000. The value of exports to the United States amounted to £(A) 57,837,000 in 1952-1953.

Imports. The pattern of Australian imports is shown by the following figures: in 1938-1939, £(A)116,754,000; 1946-1947, £(A)209,485,000; 1951-1952,£(A)1,053,423,000; and 1952-1953, £(A)514,109,000. The sharp decline in 1952-1953 after the tremendous rise in imports in the previous fiscal year was due to restrictions placed on imports under a government licensing system. This was introduced when overseas balances were halved in a six-months' period. Progressive relaxation of the import restrictions began in April 1953.

Transportation. *Railroads.* Australia had in 1950 almost 28,000 miles of railway, of which 24,778 belonged to individual states, 2,201 to the Commonwealth, and the remainder to private corporations. The continent was first spanned from east to west in 1917, but a gap of over 525 direct miles between Birdum and Alice Springs, both in the Northern Territory, remains in the rail connection between Adelaide and Darwin. Completion of this north to south connection was provided for in the Railway Standardization Act of 1946. The same act made provision for the establishment of a uniform gauge throughout Australia of 4 ft. 8½

in. Hitherto this gauge has been used only in New South Wales, on the trans-Australian line between Port Augusta, South Australia, and Kalgoorlie, Western Australia, and on a small part of the Queensland system. This costly alteration was expected finally to eliminate the more costly transshipment of goods at break-of-gauge stations. Modernization of Australia's railways began in the postwar years with the introduction of diesel electric locomotives. Steam locomotives have been replaced on the trans-Continental run of 1,100 miles, between Port Augusta, South Australia, and Kalgoorlie, Western Australia, reducing running time from 38 hours to 24. Extensive adoption of diesels since 1951 has resulted in lowering of costs and in faster schedules. Australia's heaviest railway networks are to be found in the areas of greatest population concentration, in the southeast and southwest. As the states control most of the rail and all of the road traffic, there has been a disposition to place strict limits on motor traffic that might injure railway revenues.

Highways. With respect to motor roads, only the east and southwest areas of the continent are well serviced. World War II brought a long-delayed connecting link between Alice Springs, in the southern part of the Northern Territory, and Darwin, leading city and port on the northern coast. There were also a few other roadbuilding operations of local importance during the war.

Water Transportation. There are few navigable waterways in Australia, owing to the low rainfall of most of the continent, the irregular flow of water in most of the streams, and the short length and steep gradients of streams in the humid, coastal regions. River traffic on the Murray and Darling rivers, which formerly was important, fell off rapidly after the granting of preferential freight rates to the state-owned railroads. Much of the interstate traffic is carried by coastwise steamships. British ships call at the principal ports. American vessels are able to compete with the British in the direct traffic between Australia and the United States. Bulk commodities are handled in large quantities in coastwise and ocean traffic.

Coastal Shipping. Because the main centers of population are on the coast and widely separated, shipping remains the cheapest form of interstate transport. In 1954 there were 197 coastal trading vessels and 14 overseas vessels. During 1952-1953, 10,487,000 tons of cargo were handled in interstate trade. Overseas cargo handled in the same period consisted of 9,662,000 tons discharged and 7,497,000 shipped.

Airways. By 1939 Australia was fairly well provided with a network of air lines, and World War II brought many additional improvements. During 1953, domestic airlines operated 85,793 route miles, flying 718,354,850 passenger-miles and carrying 64,856 tons of freight. Fifteen domestic airlines operate in Australia. International services operated 56,459 route miles in 1953, flying 221,864,854 passenger miles. Government-owned Qantas Empire Airways took over the service between Sydney and San Francisco and Vancouver in 1954. Its Australia-England air services through the Far East are run in conjunction with services by B.O.A.C. A Qantas service to South Africa via the Cocos Islands and Mauritius was introduced in 1952. Australia operates the Tasman Empire Airways Ltd. (T.E.A.L.) service to New Zealand, jointly with that country. The airplane is doing for remote outposts in central and northern Australia what the railway, automobile, and ship have thus far failed to do—provide a fast, low-cost interconnecting system of transportation.   R. M. Y.

SOCIAL AND CULTURAL CONDITIONS

Labor. Following the gold rush of the 1850's came Australia's first great period of growth by immigration. Between 1876 and 1890, the net gain by migration was 328,153. Almost all of the immigrants at this time were from the United Kingdom, and many of them came from industrial areas where the labor movement was rapidly increasing in both numbers and organized strength. A sturdy labor movement in Australia was the result. Labour governments in power in states and in the Commonwealth and Labour parties holding a balance of power between contending parties naturally made the progress of labor organization easier. This was also furthered by the state and Commonwealth industrial arbitration courts which insisted on dealing only with organized labor unions. These conditions have resulted in the creation not only of urban but also of rural unions.

Standards of Living. By setting up certain standards of living, with procedures for adjustment of wages to correspond with changes in living costs, industrial courts have at once raised and stabilized Australian standards. The effects of their awards have been felt far beyond the limited area of particular awards. Provision is made, under the arbitration system of wage determination, for a judicially-fixed minimum wage, reviewed so as to provide at all times "the normal needs of an average employee, regarded as a human being living in a civilized community." The broadening of the country's economic base by the stimulation of secondary industries has, of late, been effective in stabilizing the standard of living at a high level.

Education. In Australia, as in the United States, education is controlled by the states. A Commonwealth Office of Education was established in 1945. Education is compulsory and free between the ages of 6 and 14 to 16, depending upon the state. Most of Australia's elementary schools are state-owned and nondenominational, but there is a substantial number of church schools. High schools are supplemented by technical and agricultural schools which are also free. There is a university at each of the state capitals, and a national university, for postgraduate studies, at Canberra, the federal capital. The educational system is supplemented by correspondence courses for children in the "outback." Approximately 15,000 children in remote areas are thus given adequate education. Agricultural colleges, teacher training colleges, Workers' Educational Association classes for adults, traveling libraries, National Film Board documentaries, and educational broadcasts of the Australian Broadcasting Commission and state broadcasting stations help to round out Australia's educational system.

Culture. The cultural life of Australia has been conditioned by a number of factors, the principal of which are the following: (1) the general nature of the physical habitat; (2) the English heritage brought by freemen and convicts to Australia; (3) the hardships involved in making a living on a new continent; (4) the lack of meaningful scenes and shrines, such as one would find in an old civilization; (5) the lack of distinct cultural minorities; (6) the lack of cultural contacts with continental Europe; (7) a "genteel tradition" that failed to appreciate cultural materials in the Australian milieu; and (8) the lack of adequate encouragement from a large and appreciative audience.

Literature. In the field of literature Australians have achieved more with the novel, the short story, and poetry than they have with the drama, though in none has their contribution been outstanding. In 1859 Henry Kingsley, brother of Charles Kingsley, published *Geoffrey Hamlyn,* which gave a vivid picture of life in the Australian bush of western Victoria. The book glorified the squatter class as a sort of transplanted English aristocracy. Marcus Clarke gave a gloomy picture, based on source material, of early convict establishments in *For the Term of His Natural Life* (1874), showing the literary influence of Dickens and Hugo. Thomas Alexander Browne, writing under the pen name of Rolfe Boldrewood, published *Robbery Under Arms* (1888), a perennially successful story of Australian bushranging. The principal characters and the setting of the book were truly Australian. In this and his other novels the author embodied his own experiences in the vivid and active life in the Australian bush. The struggle of the "selector," or small farmer, against the squatter was portrayed in *Such Is Life* (1903) by Joseph Furphy (pseudonym Tom Collins). The important novels of Henrietta Richardson, who wrote under the pen-name of Henry Handel Richardson (e.g., *Fortunes of Richard Mahony,* 1930) had Australian settings, but the author spent most of her life in England. Life in the bush was effectively portrayed also in the sketches in Henry Lawson's *While the Billy Boils* (1896), in which the typical characters of the region were described sympathetically against a background of hatred for a social system that the author thought favored the squatter. Among the more recent Australian novelists may be mentioned Katherine Pritchard, author of *Working Bullocks* (1926), *Coonardoo* (1929), and *The Roaring Nineties* (1946). While critical opinion is divided as to the worth of much Australian poetry, it is commonly agreed that early poetic literature is of slight value and that much time elapsed before Australian poets freed themselves from imitation of their English Romantic masters. Adam Lindsay Gordon (1833-1870), who long was considered the national poet of Australia, wrote in Byronic forms. Henry Kendall (1839-1882), held in high regard by Australians, was a lover of the sounds, scenes, and scents of the bush. The Australianism of Kendall was not characterized by race consciousness. A more definite Australian nationalism may be felt in Brunton Stephens' *The Dominion of Australia* (1877). The development of Australian poetry was aided by the founding of *The Sydney*

Bulletin in 1881 by John Feltham Archibald, who invited Australian writers to send him their contributions. The *Bulletin* became not only a medium of publication, but of literary criticism as well. Much of the poetic literature of the time was nationalistic, but stopped short of jingoism. Both pessimistic and gay notes may be found in the poetry of the period: the pessimism in Barbara Baynton, Henry Lawson, and Barcroft Boake, and the gaiety particularly in Andrew Barton Paterson (1864-1941), who is considered by one Australian authority to be "the most important and the most characteristic of the Australian balladists." For the more recent period, note should be taken of Christopher Brennan (1875-1932) for his sonorous intellectual poetry, and of Bernard O'Dowd (1866-1953), representing democracy in its intellectual aspect and warning Australia of the dangers of materialism. Mention should also be made of William Baylebridge (1883-1942), Mary Gilmore (1865-   ), Hugh McCrae (1876-   ), and John Shaw Neilson (1872-1942).

Drama and Music. Australian interest in the drama has expressed itself more in playgoing than in writing and has had to depend to a considerable extent on actors from overseas. In 1954 the Australian Elizabethan Theatre Trust was set up to aid theatrical ventures "of sufficient artistic standards" and to promote drama, opera, and ballet. In the musical field, Australia is known internationally through its singers, composers, and instrumentalists. Notable among them are Dame Nellie Melba, Florence Austral, Marjorie Lawrence, Peter Dawson, John Brownlee, Harold Williams and Horace Stevens (singers); Alfred Hill (composer and conductor); Percy Grainger and John Antill (composers); Lauri Kennedy ('cellist); and Eileen Joyce (pianist). In each state there is a conservatory of music. Those in Melbourne, Sydney, and Adelaide are part of the universities and provide courses for the degrees of bachelor and doctor of music. Many choral and orchestral societies are active, regularly presenting programs of solo, orchestral, and chamber music, choral works, and, occasionally, grand opera. These concerts are supplemented by visits of overseas artists. The Australian Broadcasting Commission maintains orchestras of very high standard in the capital cities, which give seasons of public symphony concerts as well as regular broadcast programs. Special orchestral concerts for school children are frequently presented.

Art and Sculpture. Achievement in painting was difficult during the first seventy-five years of Australian history, although some early scientific drawings showed much artistic skill, and a considerable amount of portrait and miniature painting was done for those who could afford it. Great interest was shown in water colors of Australian scenes. Early Australian paintings showed an interesting mixture of native and foreign elements, such as English castles in Australian landscapes. Emancipation from English tastes had not been achieved. The gold-rush period created an increased demand for artistic works, particularly those illustrating the incidents and actualities of life in Australia. The founding of artists' schools of design served to train future artists, while the well-endowed National Gallery of Victoria, founded in 1873, and other galleries provided both artists and the public with adequate collections. Foreign artists and teachers were attracted to Australia and brought Continental interests and tastes with them. The stage was thus set for the development of a native school of Australian painters who could use European technical knowledge on Australian materials. Impressionistic techniques were applied to the problem of painting Australian landscapes, whose flora and color tones

were distinctly non-European. Important among the artists of the Impressionist school were Tom Roberts, Arthur Streeton, Frederick McCubbin, and Charles Conder. Other painters, such as John Ford Paterson, David Davies, and Walter Withers, attempted to go beyond the technique of direct observation and endeavored to achieve a representation of the moods and emotional tones of Australian landscapes. Attention was also paid to genre painting, which was used to portray the growing democratic life and nationhood of Australia. George Lambert specialized in a portraiture that combined Impressionism with a severe academic discipline. Australian art has been influenced to some extent by modern tendencies, despite the bitter opposition of critics. From 1913 onward the influence came to be felt first in Sydney and then in Melbourne. It was not until the 1930's that abstract and constructional art had any devotees among painters. Surrealist influence may be seen in the work of James Gleeson. During World War II the attention of artists was turned to subject matter and away from design and construction. Some painters, such as Russell Drysdale, gave a realistic interpretation of Australian scenes, while others like Jean Bellette and David Strachan took a Romantic approach to their material. Australian contributions to art include etching and pen drawing. Among the best etchers are Sir Lionel Lindsay and H. van Raalte; prominent in pen drawing are Norman Lindsay, Phil May, and David Low. Sculpture has been hindered by the lack of adequate commissions. Among the principal sculptors are Sir Bertram Mackennal, Charles Web Gilbert (*The Critic,* Tate Gallery, London, and statue of Matthew Flinders in Melbourne). The work of Roynor Hoff (1894-1937) in architectural sculpture is considered outstanding, and the abilities of Lyndon Dadswell are also praised.   R. G. B. and R. V. S.

HISTORY

Discovery and Exploration. It is generally believed that Australia was first discovered by travelers from the Orient, possibly Chinese or Malays, but no definite dates or other facts are known. Its discovery by Europeans resulted from the need for charting new routes to the East Indies by way of both the Indian and Pacific oceans. In 1567 Alvaro de Mendaña discovered the Solomon Islands; in 1606 Luis de Torres touched the island of New Guinea, thinking that he had seen the "great southern continent." Meanwhile the Dutch, in constant strife with the Spanish, were entrenching themselves in the trade of the East Indies. Finding it difficult to get winds to carry them from the Cape of Good Hope to the Indies, they learned that by sailing due east from the Cape for 3,000 mi., they could then turn northward to Java. Following these directions, Dirk Hartog in 1616 landed on an island in Shark Bay, in present Western Australia, having gone farther than was necessary. He erected a post and nailed to it a plate to record the event. In 1642 Abel Tasman discovered the island that now bears his name—Tasmania; thence he sailed to New Zealand and the Friendly (Tonga) Islands, and arrived at Batavia after sailing along the northern shore of New Guinea. In 1644 he sailed into the seas between New Guinea and Australia but failed to find Torres Strait, the passage into the Pacific Ocean. The exact geographical relationship between Tasmania and Australia and between New Guinea and Australia had not been determined. In 1689 and 1699 William Dampier visited the west coast of Australia, but his voyages were not productive of immediate results. Much more important were the various expeditions of the famous English explorer, Captain James Cook. In 1768 the British government, in co-operation with the British

Royal Society, promoted an expedition to Pacific waters for both geographical and astronomical purposes. After witnessing the transit of Venus at the Friendly Islands, the expedition, under Captain Cook and Joseph Banks of the Royal Society, was to search for the southern continent. After the scientific work, the expedition rediscovered New Zealand and then sailed to the east coast of Australia, which was explored from Sydney Harbor to Torres Strait. The eastern seaboard was annexed under the name of New South Wales in 1770. Cook then sailed through Torres Strait and proceeded to England via the Cape of Good Hope.

Settlement of New South Wales. The British colonization of Australia was dependent on events in other parts of the world. When the American Revolution forced the exodus from the United States of thousands of persons loyal to the British crown, it was planned to settle some of them in Australia; the same revolution also made it impossible any longer to transport convicts to what had been an important portion of the British Empire in North America. In 1779 Sir Joseph Banks suggested that Australia would be a suitable place for settlement of convicts. Six years later a definite plan was submitted to the government for the settlement of both Loyalists and convicts. In the end, however, only the latter class was provided for. The immediate purpose of the government was to do something about the large number of condemned persons being kept in old vessels in the Thames River. The plan was adopted in 1786, and in January 1787 the formal announcement of the government's intention was made. The government showed no sign that it was aware of the great future possibilities of the plan of Australian colonization. The first fleet left England in May 1787 and arrived in January 1788 at Botany Bay. Captain Arthur Phillip disliked the location and soon discovered that a harbor somewhat to the north would prove much more satisfactory. A landing was made at Farm Cove, on Port Jackson, and the work of clearing land and constructing the necessary buildings was begun. A number of the more hardened criminals were sent to Norfolk Island, northeast of Port Jackson. The principal problems of the colony of New South Wales were the provision of an adequate food supply, the proper management of the convicts, and the policy to be adopted with regard to the latter when they became free. At first the new colony suffered from the lack of food and supplies. Although the soil at Port Jackson (Sydney) was not fertile, it was found that crops could be grown in the valleys of the Hawkesbury and Hunter rivers, with the result that the colony soon became self-sufficient in this regard. Despite the drawback of the convict system the early growth of Australia would have been more rapid had the aborigines been in the agricultural stage of development, as were the North American Indians when European settlers arrived on the Atlantic coast. But the native Australian was nowhere beyond a very primitive hunting stage. Wild native plants were found of little use, and the earliest settlers were almost wholly dependent on the importation of food, or of seeds which might or might not thrive in the new environment. The economic future of the colony was indicated when Captain John Macarthur proved that New South Wales could produce from Merino sheep a wool that commanded a premium in Europe.

Convict Problem. The convicts of New South Wales included disreputable characters as well as persons who had been sent to the colony for political crimes, and some who had been convicted of crimes that would not in more recent times demand a heavy penalty. Convicts were assigned individually or in groups to work under free persons as needed, and were paid nominal wages in kind and provided with the essentials of food, clothing, and housing. Masters were permitted to discipline these servants, but were forbidden to use cruel methods in dealing with them. Relations between masters and servants varied greatly. Unfortunately for the colony, rum became a most highly prized commodity. People commonly bartered highly essential articles for the available rum. From these earlier years the excessive drinking of spirits became characteristic of the colony, and the establishment of a brewery failed to achieve the desired result of a change of beverage. The unhappy situation of many convicts and the lack of a variety of forms of entertainment no doubt helped to bring about this undesirable situation. The increasing number of whalers only added to this and other evils. If a convict showed good conduct he might be freed from his servitude by the governor and allowed to join the emancipists. The governor also had the right to give "tickets of leave," which permitted convicts to work for themselves without being assigned to a specific person. Convicts whose terms of transportation expired naturally became free to work on their own account. Emancipists and expirees presented a social and political problem which became more acute with the passage of time. To what extent should they be socially accepted by those not bearing the stigma of a court conviction? Should they be given political rights if the colony should reach political maturity?

Early Governors. Governor Phillip took an optimistic view of the future of the colony and was capable in his handling of problems as they arose. Bad health forced him to leave for England in 1792, and for the next three years two temporary governors sought to administer the colony, with the aid of a police force known as the New South Wales Corps, recruited in England. Governor John Hunter, who served from 1795 to 1800, though conscientious, was not sufficiently ruthless to hold in check the officers who had learned to profit from the sale of rum. Lacking adequate support from the British government, he was recalled in 1800, being succeeded by Philip Gidley King, who governed from 1800 to 1806. King fought bravely against the officers and the traffic in rum, but the opposition was too great and toward the end of his administration he showed signs of disappointment in his dispatches to the home government. His successor, William Bligh, famous for his connection with the mutiny on H.M.S. *Bounty,* was unfortunate in his attempt to apply the rigors of naval discipline to the life of a colony. While possessing sufficient determination and will power, he lacked the suavity and decorum required of a successful governor. Bligh came into inevitable conflict with John Macarthur over the manufacture of rum and jailed him. People in the colony took sides in accordance with their own interests, and affairs moved on to a crisis. The commanding officer of the New South Wales Corps, Major Johnston, finally released Macarthur from jail; the latter wrote a request to Johnston asking him to place Bligh under arrest. Soldiers were sent to Government House for this purpose; Bligh was arrested, and the problem of insurrection was placed in the hands of the British government. Johnston was cashiered, and a regular successor to Bligh arrived in New South Wales in December 1809. Bligh was advanced in naval rank, but never again held civic office.

Colonel Lachlan Macquarie was governor of New South Wales from 1809 to 1821. He brought with him the Seventy-third Highland Regiment, and the members of the New South Wales Corps were sent to England. Macquarie, like the governors before him, had unlimited power and was ready to use it. He had the power of life and death, and combined in himself legislative, executive, and judicial functions. Fortunately for his sway, the British government was concerned with more immediate problems, and some former troublemakers had either left the colony or had submitted to the will of the governor. Macquarie caused considerable opposition, however, by his favorable attitude toward emancipists, whom he considered to be more satisfactory than free settlers. He much disliked the decision of the home government to allow free settlers to enter New South Wales. Despite a number of excellent aspects of his governorship, such as the encouragement of education and building, the restraint of unlawful persons, and the large growth of population, opposition to his rigorous regime rose, until it became necessary for the government to send out an investigator in the person of J. T. Bigge, a barrister. Criticism of Macquarie led to his resignation, and he was succeeded by Sir Thomas Brisbane.

Political Reforms. When Parliament had in hand sufficient information about Australian problems, it passed a number of moderate reform acts. The Judicature Act of 1823 provided for the creation of a legislative council of from five to seven appointive members. Legislative proposals were to be made by the governor, who was not required to accept the judgment of the council upon them, although he was required to obtain from the chief justice a statement that they were not contrary to English law. The act authorized the creation of a supreme court; trial by jury in civil cases could be had on the request of both parties. In 1825 the legislative council was separated from the executive council, and the chief justice ceased to be a member of the legislative body. Three years later a further act increased the membership of the legislative council to fifteen members, with an official majority, which received the power to reject the legislative proposals of the governor. Trial by jury in criminal cases, foreshadowed by the Imperial Act of 1828, was granted by an act of the legislative council of New South Wales in 1830.

Emancipists vs. Exclusionists. The reform acts of 1823-1828 were modest steps toward self-government in New South Wales. It was impossible to proceed rapidly so long as the differences between the emancipists and the exclusionists were unsettled. The former insisted on their right to participate in the processes of government, while the latter feared the grant of political privileges to those who had once been convicts. The advocates of representative government, led by Dr. John Dunmore Lang, W. C. Wentworth, and others, formed the Australian Patriotic Association in 1835 and maintained a parliamentary agent in England. An English parliamentary committee in 1837-1838 recommended the abandonment of the transportation of convicts. In 1840 the British government put the recommendation into effect for New South Wales. The deck was thus cleared for a further step toward colonial self-government. An act of 1842 granted to New South Wales a legislative council of 36 members, 24 of whom were to be elected and 12 appointed. Convicts, but not emancipists, were excluded from the franchise. The act was not democratic in the modern sense, inasmuch as a property qualification of almost $1,000 was set up for voters, and persons not owning a freehold of almost $10,000 were ineligible for the legislative council. Clauses in the act looked forward to the eventual separation of the Melbourne area from New South Wales. Matters such as the civil list, the crown lands, and the proceeds from the sale of land were still to be kept in the hands of the executive. Bills could be vetoed by the governor or sent to the British government for consideration.

Beginnings of Self-government. The cessation of transportation to New South Wales in 1840 resulted in the breakdown of the cleavage between exclusionists and emancipists, and both groups demanded the grant of responsible government. Fortunately for them, Earl Grey, British Secretary of State for War and the Colonies from 1846 to 1852, wanted to achieve the same result, although he differed in also wishing to bring about a federated Australia. The final result of many discussions was the Australian Colonies Government Act of 1850, by which the Port Phillip district (Victoria) was separated from New South Wales, the kind of representative government enjoyed by New South Wales was extended to the other Australian Colonies, and the colonial legislatures were permitted, subject to the consent of the British government, to frame new constitutions for themselves. On the basis of the Act of 1850, constitutions were, by 1855, framed by New South Wales, Victoria, South Australia, and Tasmania, convict transportation to this last point being abandoned only in 1853. The new colonial legislatures, bicameral in form, were granted power over crown lands, and were by constitutional usage allowed to practice responsible government in the British and Canadian manner. Queensland became organized into a separate colony in 1859. Western Australia, founded in 1829, was constitutionally retarded by the importation of convicts, at the colonists' request, between 1850 and 1868. It received representative institutions in 1870, but responsible government was not granted until 1890.

Later Exploration. Meanwhile further knowledge had been obtained about the nature and extent of the Australian continent. In 1813 Gregory Blaxland and others penetrated the Blue Mountains to the Bathurst Plains, where grassland was plentiful. In 1817 John Oxley traversed part of the course of the Lachlan River, and in 1818 followed the Macquarie River for about 150 mi. Further knowledge of the river system west of the Blue Mountains was gained by Hamilton Hume and William H. Hovell in a journey from Lake George to the western arm of Port Phillip in 1824. The expeditions of Captain Charles Sturt between 1828 and 1830 revealed the true nature of the river system that includes the Murrumbidgee, the Darling, and the Murray rivers. In 1823 John Oxley discovered the Brisbane River while searching for a suitable location for a convict settlement. Further knowledge of the southeast and south coasts of Australia and of the relation between Australia and Van Diemen's Land (Tasmania) was gained in 1796 and 1798 by Matthew Flinders and his surgeon, George Bass. In 1801 Flinders began the exploration and mapping of the southern coast of the Australian continent, thus proving that there was no separation between New South Wales and New Holland (Western Australia). In 1803 Flinders circumnavigated the continent and prepared a map showing it in its entirety. He urged that the term "Australia" should be used to denote the whole land mass. Australian exploration had by 1820 revealed the general configuration of the continent, and this, coupled with the fear of imminent French occupation of ports in the west and north, resulted in the annexation in 1824 of Bathurst and Melville islands in the north, of the area between 135° and 129° E. long. in 1825, and of the entire continent in 1829.

Gold Rush of 1851. In 1851 an event occurred that profoundly changed the trend of Australian history. It was the discovery of gold. In February of that year a squatter brought gold from near Bathurst to Sydney and was able to convince the governor that an announcement of the finding of gold would deter people from emigrating to California. Within a short time a few hundred miners were searching for nuggets and gold dust. The newly organized colony of

Victoria, wishing to participate in the movement, offered rewards to anybody who could find gold within 200 mi. of Melbourne. Results came quickly, and soon the Victoria diggings were found to be more productive than others. By the end of 1851 more than $5,000,000 worth of gold had been dug in Victoria. The gold fields first attracted large numbers from the towns and countryside of Victoria and New South Wales, leaving many economic activities short-handed. The usual problems of social control arose, but general conditions were not so bad as might have been

Digging for gold at the 100-foot level of a mine at Diamond Creek near Melbourne

expected. Despite the presence of many undesirable characters and the large sale of spirits, many of the diggers were men of democratic and reformist tendencies who deprecated conditions that easily develop in a mining frontier. Some non-British came to the gold area, but not in sufficient numbers to alter seriously the dominantly British population structure. The gold rush greatly stimulated economic activity, particularly in Victoria. It was necessary to provide cereals, meat, and dairy products for the increased population, and buildings and equipment had to be provided. Increased prices proved to be a boon for the producers of these products, and the acreage under cultivation doubled between 1850 and 1858.

Political Consequences. The movement of so large a number of people from town and country to the diggings had great political significance, as did the influx of European and English immigrants having revolutionary or Chartist convictions. Significant in this connection is the fact that universal manhood suffrage was conceded in the Australian colonies in the 1850's, and that secret voting by what has since been known as the Australian ballot was first adopted by Victoria in 1856. The democratic aspects of the Eureka Stockade incident may also be noted here.

The value of the gold produced in Victoria in the decade 1851-1861 varied greatly from year to year. The production of 1852, about $81,500,000, was never again reached, and the year 1861 saw a production of something less than $39,000,000. At the same time the number of diggers was increasing, and mechanical power and technology were coming more and more into use. The tendency was obviously against the interests of the individual miner who lacked funds for large-scale enterprise. Since many individual miners were forced to leave the gold fields for other activities, there developed a belief that government had a positive function in promoting the interests of the common man.

Growth of Democracy. The history of Australia after the adoption of constitutions in the 1850's shows a strong desire to achieve democracy in actual practice as far as possible. The constitutions embodied the principle of universal manhood suffrage, although woman suffrage had to wait for later adoption (South Australia, 1894; Western Australia, 1899; New South Wales, 1902; Tasmania, 1903; Queensland, 1905; Victoria, 1908). The secret ballot was adopted in Victoria in 1856. Four of the six colonies elected their legislative councils on a restricted franchise. In New South Wales and Queensland the members were at first appointed for life terms.

Legislative Changes. Considerable difficulty was experienced in Australia in the relations between assemblies and legislative councils, whether appointive or elective. In New South Wales a struggle arose over the passage of an assembly bill to promote "free selection" of land. When the council amended the bill, the governor named twenty-one new members to bring about the passage of the legislation in 1861. In Victoria, where the legislative council was elective, a dispute arose in 1865-1866 between the assembly and the legislative council over the adoption of protection for industry, the assembly desiring the change. In 1877-1878 a deadlock developed over the question of a permanent policy of salaries for members of parliament. As a result of pressure by the premier, the legislative council accepted the principle of salaries. In 1881 the term of the legislative council in Victoria was reduced from ten to six years and the property qualifications of members and electors were reduced, thus rendering the legislative council more responsive to popular demands. In the same year South Australia devised a solution to the problem of the relations between the two houses by providing that if the assembly twice passed a bill and an election followed, and if the council then rejected it, the governor might dissolve both houses or have additional members elected to the council.

Land Tenure. The desire to achieve democracy expressed itself also in economic matters, particularly in those of land tenure and labor relations. Numerous acts were passed in most of the colonies to enable persons to buy land for agriculture, despite the opposition of the squatter class. With the decline of gold mining in Australia, there was an increasing need to provide economic opportunity for many. The various governments desired to build up an independent farming class in Australia. Acts were passed in New South Wales, Victoria, and South Australia to promote agricultural freeholds, but the legislation by no means achieved the desired results. The purpose was to give to prospective buyers an opportunity to select freeholds from lands being used as sheep runs. The practice of "dummying" was used by the squatters to procure freeholds indirectly for themselves, with the result that the squatters eventually gained a full title to part of the land which they had been using. Sheep raising continued to be the leading rural activity, particularly in

New South Wales, Victoria, and in that part of Queensland west of the mountains. An illustration of the victory of pastoral industry over farming may be found in the fact that in 1883 a total of more than 8,000,000 acres of land in New South Wales was held by 96 persons. In South Australia the countryside came to present a mixed pattern of farm lands and sheep runs. A better balanced rural situation had been realized.

Both farmer and pastoralist came upon evil days in the last thirty years of the nineteenth century. The rabbit pest had to be met by the building of fences, world prices showed a downward trend, and lack of adequate rainfall hastened the development of "dust-bowl" conditions. Millions of acres of land were abandoned and the number of sheep declined by 33 per cent between 1891 and 1901. In eastern Queensland the sugar-cane industry attracted settlers and capital. Large numbers of Pacific Island laborers called Kanakas were brought by the planters to work in the fields under unsatisfactory conditions. There was much opposition in Queensland against such a system, but the planters insisted that they could not continue their operations if forced to use white labor. It was not until after the government of the Commonwealth went into effect that the problem was successfully resolved.

Labor Movement. The period of Australian history between the end of the gold rush and the adoption of federal government at the close of the nineteenth century was characterized by the growth of a labor movement and the corresponding development of a typically Australian form of democracy. Labor organization of the modern type is to be dated from the 1850's. Unions in the building trades began an agitation for the eight-hour day. While the early unions agitated for the eight-hour day or against Chinese labor, trade union congresses after 1879 worked for such political goals as pay for members of parliament. Trade unions were not, however, politically powerful until after 1890. By that time miners, seamen, dock workers, and sheep shearers were organized, and labor felt that it was in a position to exert effective pressure on employers. The maritime strike of 1890 became a crucial battle between labor and capital in Australia, labor standing for union supremacy and capital for the right to employ "free labor" through individual bargaining. The failure of the strike convinced Australian labor of the necessity of political action. Labor had already been stimulated by socialistic doctrines from Great Britain, William Lane, the Socialist leader, declaring "socialism in our time" as the goal to be reached. The Australian labor movement thus contained within itself two points of view: the desire for improved living standards through economic and political action and the belief that a complete socialistic system should be adopted.

Some typical legislative goals of Australian labor in the 1890's were: (1) restriction of immigration and the exclusion of Orientals, (2) the abolition of "sweated" industry, (3) factory legislation, (4) the adoption of systems of wage control and labor arbitration, and (5) old-age pensions. Labor was unable, with one brief exception, to attain political power in the Australian colonies before 1901, but was able to exert pressure on other political groups to bring about the passage of desired legislation. Victoria passed factory acts in 1885 and 1895 and provided for the creation of local minimum wage boards in 1896 to deal with the problem of "sweated" trades. Attempts to pass labor legislation were less successful elsewhere.

Tariff Protection. During the period from 1860 to 1900 all of the Australian colonies except New South Wales made some efforts to encourage industry by tariff protection. The decline in profits from placer gold mining created a large supply of unused labor which had to be provided for by either agriculture or industry. David Syme, editor of the *Melbourne Age,* used his journalistic skill to promote the doctrine of protection, with the result that Victoria became protectionist in 1864. The relations between Victoria and New South Wales became particularly estranged by vexatious frontier regulations to control commerce across their borders, and South Australia was to some extent concerned in the difficulties. Tasmania adopted a tariff system providing for rates that varied with the treatment of Tasmanian goods by the country of origin. It seems impossible to adduce proof that either protective tariffs or tariffs for revenue were primarily responsible for any degree of prosperity enjoyed by the Australian colonies in the thirty-five years before the Commonwealth.

"White Australia" Policy. By the end of the century the "White Australia" policy had become generally accepted, the country agreeing that the introduction of Chinese, Kanaka, or other low-priced labor would destroy the Australian standard of living and create difficult problems of morals and social control. Indeed the whole history of Australia with its continental extent and its sparse population can be adequately understood only against the background of its Oriental neighbors numbering well over 1,000,000,000.

The Making of the Commonwealth. *Federation Question.* While some interest in Australian federation had been shown in the 1850's and 1860's, it was not until the last two decades of the nineteenth century that the situation became favorable for it. A potential external danger was needed to bring about activity looking toward federation for the Australian colonies. The feeling of security from foreign influence was definitely shaken by the interest of European powers in the islands of the western Pacific. Convicts escaped from the French penal colony of New Caledonia into Australia, and many feared that France would annex the New Hebrides. Great fear was shown at the rumor that Germany had annexed the northeast part of New Guinea. Under the stress of such circumstances a convention was held at Sydney in 1883 to discuss the relations of the Australian colonies. Unwilling to go so far as to adopt full federation, the delegates endorsed a scheme which was enacted by the British Parliament as the Federal Council of Australia Act of 1885. A federal council representing the Australian colonies was empowered to legislate on a limited list of relatively unimportant subjects, but no provision was made for either an executive power or a revenue. The new system failed as a substitute for federation. The refusal of New South Wales to co-operate at all in the plan, and the inherent weakness of the plan itself, rendered its accomplishments ineffectual. By its very inadequacy, however, the Federal Council pointed the way to a more perfect union, in much the same way as the American Confederation led to the Federal Constitution of 1787.

Toward the end of the 1880's there developed a renewed interest in actual federation, again under the influence of foreign affairs. In 1888 the colonies agreed to contribute toward an Australian naval squadron; in 1889 General Bevan Edwards reported the unsatisfactory condition of Australian defenses and linked the problem of defense with the need for federation. In the same year Sir Henry Parkes opened a campaign for the calling of a convention to frame a federal constitution. He was able to bring about a meeting at Melbourne in 1890 of all of the Australian colonies and New Zealand, at which a resolution was passed calling for the summoning of a convention to draft a constitution for the Australian colonies. In 1891 there assembled at Sydney a total of forty-five representative statesmen, who proceeded to fashion a constitution.

Sydney Convention of 1891. Some of the members of the Sydney Convention were not only statesmen of ability, but students of constitutional law and history as well. The necessities of the situation required them to make use of the experience of other countries with federal government, particularly Switzerland, Canada, and the United States. The

*Turtle spearing in the Great Barrier Reef waters,
north Queensland*

recent publication of James Bryce's *The American Commonwealth* provided them with an excellent interpretative account of the functioning of federalism in the United States. The principal problem faced by the convention was the fashioning of a system of government that would be democratic and federal and could at the same time be operated on the basis of the British system of cabinet responsibility. The solution to the first was found in the examples of Switzerland and the United States, of a lower house representing population as such and an upper house representing the states. While there was no opposition to the creation of two chambers, there was considerable difference of opinion as to their relative powers. As was the case in the American Constitutional Convention of 1787, there developed a cleavage of opinion between small states and large states, the former wanting a strong upper house and the latter a strong lower house. The final settlement of their differences may be seen in the provisions of the Commonwealth Act of 1900.

After considerable debate on fundamental principles, the convention divided itself into three committees and in less than two weeks wrote a draft constitution, which in turn was accepted with few amendments by the convention itself. It was recommended that the constitution be submitted to the people of the various colonies in popular elections. Action did not follow, however, largely because of the political situation in New South Wales; and it was not until 1895 that action again got under way. In that year a number of premiers met in Hobart, Tasmania, where a plan was adopted

for the calling of another constitutional convention, the submission of the resulting constitution to the voters in the colonies, and, in the case of its acceptance, to the British Parliament for its enactment. After a delay of some months, New South Wales passed the act for the calling of the convention, and the other colonies, with the exception of Queensland, followed suit.

Adelaide Convention of 1897. The convention opened its session at Adelaide on Mar. 22, 1897. The draft constitution of 1891 was taken as the basis for the work of the convention and of its three committees. A new constitution was adopted on April 23, and the convention adjourned to give the legislatures of the various colonies an opportunity to study the document and make suggestions for amendment. The convention met again in Sydney in September and spent three weeks in discussing the most important aspects of the proposed constitution; it adjourned because of an election in Victoria and met for its final sessions at Melbourne in January 1898. In its debates the most important problem was that of the relation between the will of the majority of the voters and that of the majority of the state, the final disposition of which would determine the relative powers of the upper and lower houses and the means of resolving conflicts between them. The 1891 compromise, providing that the upper house could not amend money bills, but only reject them or request the lower house to amend them, was kept in the new draft. The question of the means of resolving a difference between the two houses was settled by the adoption of a plan whereby, as a last resort, a dissolution of both houses and a double election might be had, so that the will of the people might be known. Little difficulty was met in deciding on the list of powers to be assigned to the federal government under the new constitutional system. A clause was inserted that gave to the new federal parliament power with regard to "conciliation and arbitration for the prevention and settlement of industrial disputes extending beyond the limits of any one state."

Adoption of the Constitution. Large majorities for the constitution were received in Victoria, Tasmania, and South Australia, but in New South Wales it was not legally accepted because of the requirement that 80,000 votes be cast for it. After a political election in New South Wales the new premier, G. H. Reid, called a meeting of the premiers and persuaded them to accept a number of amendments. The proposed constitution was again submitted to the electorates and was accepted in all of the Australian colonies except Western Australia. The latter colony refrained from taking part in the election because of its fear of the loss of both revenue and protection for its industries. The next step was to receive the assent of the British Parliament for the proposed constitution. The British Colonial Secretary, Joseph Chamberlain, insisted on a number of amendments, the principal one of which protected the right of the Queen to grant special permission to appeal from the Australian High Court to the Judicial Committee of the Privy Council in certain cases. The bill for the enactment of the Australian constitution was passed without difficulty through the British Parliament and was signed July 9, 1900. Meanwhile the parliament of Western Australia had passed an enabling act, and on July 31 voted for federation. The way was thus cleared for a royal proclamation which set Jan. 1, 1901, as the date for the establishment of the Commonwealth of Australia.

Early Years of the Commonwealth, 1901-1914.
Economic and Social Issues. The political life of Australia between 1901 and 1914 shows forces similar to those which

existed before 1901. There were free-trade groups and protectionist groups, with labor holding the balance of power and gaining as much legislation for itself as possible. The unstable nature of the political situation may be noted in the fact that during the period 1901-1914 there were ten cabinets and six elections. The issue of protection was solved by the passage of the Tariff Act of 1902, with duties of from 8 to 25 per cent, heavier duties being levied by an act of 1908. Labor, at first divided on the issue, became convinced of the value of protection and gave ample support to the desired legislation. The principle of a "White Australia" was continued by Commonwealth legislation. Steps were taken to deport Kanaka laborers, and an immigration restriction law was passed requiring a literacy test in any European language. Because of Japanese objections the law was amended in 1905 to require a test in "any prescribed language," which in practice might be one of which the immigrant was ignorant. Note should be made of the connection between immigration restrictions and tariff protection, the latter supposedly guaranteeing the high standard of living that would justify the former. Among the other important types of legislation passed between 1901 and 1914 were those providing for woman suffrage, old-age pensions, and a system of conciliation and arbitration of labor disputes. The latter, enacted in 1906, was foreshadowed by a constitutional provision empowering the federal government to pass laws dealing with "conciliation and arbitration for the prevention and settlement of industrial disputes extending beyond the limits of any one State." Henry Bourne Higgins, first president of the court of conciliation and arbitration, ruled that laborers were entitled to a wage that would take care of "the normal needs of the average employee, regarded as a human being living in a civilized community." Labor would thus not be considered as a commodity and would be guaranteed a "just wage."

Growth of Federal Power. While a federal system of government was instituted by the Commonwealth Act, the general trend of the period was toward a strengthening of the central power at the expense of the states, principally because economic problems were increasingly national. Tariffs and immigration policy were handled by the federal government, and the commonwealth system of conciliation and arbitration inevitably assumed a superiority to similar state systems. The High Court of Australia gave considerable but not unlimited support to the increase of federal power. Customs duties brought large sums to the federal treasury; the federal government took over the existing debts of the states in 1909 and two years later provided for a payment of about $6 per head to the state governments for a period of ten years.

Foreign Policy and Defense. The government of Australia, despite its lack of independence in foreign and diplomatic affairs, showed decided interest in certain problems. The advance of Germany in the western Pacific in the 1880's caused great concern on the continent of Australia, particularly in Queensland. Fearing aggressive tendencies of any foreign power in the Australian area, the people in 1906 opposed the Anglo-French condominium in the New Hebrides. The interest of Australia in foreign and imperial affairs was shown in Australian representation at the Colonial Conference of 1902, at the Imperial Conferences of 1907 and 1911, and in the establishment of the Office of High Commissioner for Australia in London in 1909. The government of Australia made no claim to autonomy in the control of its own foreign affairs. It desired, however, to be able to state its wishes to the British government and to be

informed of British policies. Australia also showed considerable concern for military and naval defense. In 1905 a council of defense was created, and a federal act of 1909 adopted the principle of military training. At first the Swiss system was adopted, but in 1912 the defense forces were reorganized along British lines. A system was established whereby there was an exchange of officers between the British army and the Commonwealth staff. Similar interest was shown in naval matters. Three destroyers were ordered in 1909, and by 1914 the Australian navy included a battle cruiser, two light cruisers with a third under construction,

Shearing sheep in a woolshed

three destroyers, and two submarines. Just before the British declaration of war in 1914, Australia offered to turn over to Great Britain all of her naval vessels and personnel.

Economic Development. During the years 1901-1914 the population of Australia increased from 3,750,000 to almost 5,000,000. The economic development was highly encouraging, and optimism for the future was shown in government borrowing for public works, particularly railroads, of which some 5,000 mi. were constructed between 1901 and 1914. The number of factories and factory workers increased. Trade-union membership increased to the point that by 1914 the unions contained a larger percentage of the total population than was the case in any other country.

World War I. Australia was in the throes of an election at the time of the war crisis of 1914. The government of Joseph Cook could count on a majority of only one in the House of Representatives and had a minority of supporters in the Senate. When a conflict developed between the houses over two government bills, the prime minister advised the governor-general to dissolve both houses and thus bring about a general election. In the campaign that followed the dissolution of July 30, 1914, the leaders of both parties made it clear that they would support Great Britain in all eventualities. The Cook government fell and Andrew Fisher, Labour Party leader, became prime minister on September 14. On August 3, the day before war was declared by Great Britain, the government of Australia offered to make its navy available to the British government and to create an expeditionary force for foreign service. The offer was at once accepted and steps were taken to put it into effect. Owing to the threat of German naval squadrons, it was not until November 1 that Australian and New Zealand forces were able to sail from Western Australia under escort. Landing in Egypt, the Australian forces went into training.

Military and Naval Operations. During the course of the war, Australian military units took part in the Gallipoli campaign of 1915, saw action in France and Belgium at the Somme, Messines Ridge, Ypres, Passchendaele, and Cambrai, and in the advances of August-September 1918; they also had a part in the campaign for Palestine in 1916-1918. In the Pacific area Australian naval forces escorted the New Zealand contingent which captured German Samoa, as well as the Australian contingent that took Bismarck Archipelago and German New Guinea. The battle cruiser *Australia* later served as flagship to the Second Battle Cruiser Squadron in the North Sea. The cruisers *Sydney* and *Melbourne* were used in the North Atlantic patrol and later in the North Sea. Australian destroyers saw service in the Mediterranean. It may be said that Australian naval craft served on most of the seas of the world.

Political Effects. World War I had a profound effect on Australian political life. Andrew Fisher resigned the premiership in October 1915 and was succeeded in office by W. M. Hughes. The Hughes ministry at first took the attitude that no change from the policy of voluntary enlistment for foreign service was needed, in view of the fact that Australia had sent 100,000 men and had over 70,000 men in training camps. After his visit to England in 1916, however, Hughes became convinced of the need of increasing the number of men in war services by means of conscription. It was decided that the best way to get a decision on the matter would be through a referendum. In the balloting of Oct. 28, 1916, the proposal was defeated by 72,476 (1,087,557 affirmative, 1,160,033 negative). The decision of the Cabinet to promote conscription and the results of the referendum split the Labour Party. The party expelled the leaders who had sponsored the conscription move; a temporary Labour government was carried on by Hughes and his followers with the support of the Opposition; and on Feb. 17, 1917, Hughes offered the resignation of the Cabinet, with the advice to the governor-general that he should be allowed to form a new ministry. The result was the formation of a national war cabinet composed of five proconscription Labour ministers and six of the former Opposition. The "Nationalist" Party thus came into being. The new party won a mandate from the voters in the election of May 1917.

Governmental Powers. The necessities of war had forced the Commonwealth government to enlarge its scope of action in the legislative and executive fields. In 1915 the legislature passed two measures calling for a significant enlargement of the legislative power of the Commonwealth government in the fields of commerce and the control of corporations and labor. Because of opposition, it was decided, after a conference with state governments, that the states should, for the duration of the war and one year afterward, confer on the Commonwealth most of the powers included in the new laws and that the referenda should therefore be dropped. The states did not carry out their part of the agreement, but the situation was improved because of the fact that the High Court made a number of decisions that provided the Commonwealth government with adequate power to prosecute the war vigorously despite restraints. During the war the government fixed the prices of the necessities of life, formed a wheat pool, formed a Central Wool Committee for the appraisal of wool before it was sold to the British government, created an Australian Metal Exchange for control over the export of metals from Australia, instituted strict control over shipping and rates, and engaged in other economic control activities essential in time of war. At the close of the war Australia went through the experience of "decontrol" to bring itself back to a relatively free economy.

Peace Conference. Australia was permitted to have formal representation at the peace conference in Paris at the close of World War I. W. M. Hughes represented Australian interests with considerable asperity. Fearing the proximity to Australian territory of a potential enemy, he demanded that Australia be allowed to annex any lands that she had conquered during the war. He was opposed to the proposal that the former German colonies become mandates to be ruled under the general supervision of the League of Nations. In the end, Hughes had to be content to allow Japan to hold the former German Pacific possessions north of the equator.

Australian Mandates. The acquisition of mandated territories by Australia was closely associated with her fears of Japanese influence in the Pacific area. Not being able to secure the annexation of areas occupied during that war, Australia accepted a Class C mandate and became responsible for the administration of New Guinea, including the Bismarck Archipelago and the northern Solomon Islands. Labor relations were regulated under an indenture system minutely stating the obligations of employer and laborer. Much criticism was directed against the system for the effect it was said to have on native community and family life. By 1940 about one third of the natives who had been indentured had been transferred from indenture to the free-labor system. On the restoration of civil government at the close of military operations in 1945, alterations were made in the indenture system looking toward its abolition in about five years. Until 1941, education was largely in the hands of missionaries, native teachers being used for actual work with the natives. Missions have been a factor in the maintenance of law and order. Most mission staffs receive some training in anthropology. At the Paris Peace Conference of 1919 the Japanese delegates suggested the adoption of a "race equality" clause for the Covenant of the League of Nations. Such a statement, even in a mild form, seemed diametrically opposed to the traditional "White Australia" policy, and Hughes opposed it. A mild wording was finally adopted, but Woodrow Wilson ruled that it could not pass because the vote was not unanimous.

The Interwar Period. *Nationalist-Country Party Coalition.* Though Premier Hughes enjoyed a triumphal reception upon his return in August 1919, his popularity did not continue. Each component part of the coalition felt that its interests were being sacrificed. The election of December 1919 gave the Nationalist Party only 39 members out of a total of 75 in the lower house, and the Party returned only 22 members in 1922. The rural interests, since 1919 organized as the Country Party, gained 14 seats in 1922 and were thus able to hold the balance of power between the Nationalists and Labour. Their refusal to support a Nationalist government led by Hughes forced the prime minister's resignation in February 1923 and led to the formation of a Nationalist-Country Party coalition under the leadership of Stanley M. Bruce, Nationalist, and Dr. Earle Page, Country Party. The new coalition government remained in power after the elections of 1925 and 1928, but was unable to withstand increasing opposition to the adoption of a policy of financial retrenchment and thus was forced to turn over its power to the Labour Party under J. H. Scullin in 1929. In its six years of tenure the Nationalist-Country Party coalition brought about the moving of the federal capital to Canberra in 1927, executed plans for helping almost 35,000 war veterans to become established on the land, co-operated with the British government in bringing emigrants to Australia, gave the Commonwealth Bank the power to issue paper money and fix discount rates, and made it the depository for commercial banks. In 1927 an agreement was reached whereby the federal government would legally guarantee the payment of existing state debts and contribute annually toward interest charges a sum equal to the surplus revenue payable in 1926-1927 to the states under existing arrangements. The states gave legal recognition to an Australian Loan Council to regulate all future borrowing outside the territorial limits of each state.

"Protection All Around." The Bruce-Page government had strengthened the existing tariff laws. Special consideration was shown agrarian interests by prohibitive duties on certain imports and by export bounties on primary products, the necessary funds being procured by taxes to be paid on the same goods by Australian consumers. This method of granting protection all around meant that the Australian prices for certain goods were higher than corresponding world prices. The indices of Australian economic growth were favorable until shortly before the depression of the early 1930's, however, and the general optimism was shown in large increases in the public debt, both state and federal.

Labour Government. In the elections of 1928 the Labour Party gained enough parliamentary representation to make it an important political opposition. In 1929 the government proposed the repeal of federal legislation on industrial arbitration in order to enable state governments to enter the field. Hughes used the proposal as a means of bringing about the fall of the government. He and his followers thought they would be returned to leadership, but J. H. Scullin and the Labour Party achieved a smashing political victory. Scullin took office in October, the month of the Wall Street crash of 1929. Signs of financial difficulty were already in evidence in a budget deficit of more than $24,000,000 for 1928-1929, and the Australian Loan Council had been unable to negotiate a loan in London in April 1929. Being an important producer of primary commodities, Australia felt quickly the effect of falling prices from 1929 to 1931.

The Depression. Australian politics increasingly revolved around the problem of finding the best means of battling economic depression. The radical wing of the Labour Party wanted socialization of industry and the issuance of increased quantities of paper money. The Labour government desired to curb wages and governmental expenditures. The banking interests and conservative groups in general wanted the adoption of a policy of deflation: reductions in wages and governmental costs in harmony with the world fall in prices. Various methods were used to meet the situation. The Commonwealth Bank took over the gold reserves, and at once the export of gold was prohibited. In 1930 the sterling balances in England were ordered to be paid first for the interest on Australian bonds and only then for imports. In the same year the tariff rates were raised and the importation of certain articles was forbidden. Loan expenditures were reduced. Early in 1931 the arbitration court ordered a 10 per cent reduction in wages, and the federal government decided on a 20 per cent reduction in governmental salaries, a cut of 12½ per cent in pensions, and a scaling down of interest rates on bonds. The Australian pound was stabilized at the depreciated ratio of £125 Australian to £100 sterling.

Party Realignments. The Scullin government lost supporters because of its handling of depression problems. One section, under J. A. Lyons, joined with the Nationalists to form the United Australia Party. Another group followed J. T. Lang, radical labor premier of New South Wales, in his opposition to Scullin's policies. In December 1931 the United Australia Party elected 39 members to the House of

Representatives; the regular Labour group elected only 18 and the Country Party 16; 2 anti-Labour independents completed the membership of 75. The situation was complicated by the fact that Premier Lang of New South Wales refused to follow the deflationary program accepted by the other governments. He preferred, instead, a restoration of wages to their former levels and a reduction in the salaries of state officials. In April 1931 New South Wales defaulted in its payments on state bonds. The federal government intervened and paid the interest. In 1932 Lang was dismissed from

COURTESY OF THE AMERICAN MUSEUM OF NATURAL HISTORY

ALICE SPRINGS, NORTHERN TERRITORY

office by the governor. By means of a combination of policies —lower wages and salaries, reduced interest rates on government bonds, and restricted imports—Australia was able to achieve a favorable balance of trade for 1931-1932. The federal budget was balanced during the years from 1932 to 1939. The United Australia Party failed to hold its majority in the election of 1934 but formed a coalition government with the Country Party. This coalition won the election of October 1937. Upon the death of Lyons in 1939, Sir Earle Page was in control for a few months and was followed by R. G. Menzies, who became head of the United Australia Party and prime minister as well.

Commonwealth Status. During the 1920's Australia was more interested in domestic than in foreign affairs. Some attention was given, of course, to the problem of her position in the British Commonwealth of Nations. She did not have separate diplomatic representation abroad. Australia made no claim to the right of neutrality should the United Kingdom be at war. She failed at that time to approve the Statute of Westminster of 1931, which recognized the legislative autonomy of the British dominions. Without such acceptance of the statute by her federal legislature, Australia was theoretically subject to the older rule that an Australian enactment would be void if repugnant to those acts of the British Parliament which specifically applied to Australia. This legal power of the British Parliament was conditioned before 1931 by the convention that acts would not be passed to apply to a dominion without the consent of the dominion concerned. In 1942 the Australian Parliament passed the Statute of Westminster Adoption Act, under which certain sections of the Statute were accepted.

Defense Measures. At the close of World War I Australia joined the League of Nations and looked to the League for effective handling of international problems. She reduced her armaments and dropped universal military service. But the failure of later disarmament conferences, the aggressive tactics of Japan in Manchuria and China, and those of Italy in Ethiopia forced Australians to pay closer attention to defense problems. Australia co-operated with Great Britain in imposing sanctions on Italy in its war with Ethiopia. Australian response to the deterioration of international relations was reflected in the increase in defense expenditures from $15,543,000 in 1932-1933 to $56,115,000 in 1937-1938. After the Munich crisis a rearmament program was adopted. A special attempt was made to increase the production of airplanes and munitions. Particular attention was given to the fortification of Port Darwin as one of the more important naval bases in the Far East. It was also decided to build at Sydney a dock that would accommodate battleships. When war broke out in 1939 there was no question that Australia would enter.

World War II. *Army.* At the outbreak of war in September 1939 Australia possessed a partly trained militia force of 80,000 men, supplemented by a small force of permanent soldiers and a staff corps of trained officers. Recruitment of a special expeditionary force of volunteers, the Second Australian Imperial Force, began immediately. In November 1939 the compulsory provisions of the Defense Act were put into effect and the first class of eligible men was called up for full time duty for home defense. The first convoy of the A.I.F. sailed from Australia in January 1940 and began war training in Palestine. A corps comprising the Sixth, Seventh, and Ninth divisions was established in the Middle East where Australian forces took part in battles against the Axis forces in North Africa, especially at Bardia, Benghazi, Tobruk, and El Alamein; in Greece; and in Crete. Early in 1942 two of the three Middle East divisions returned to Australia to meet the Japanese threat to their country, and the third division returned in 1943. Earlier a fourth division had been stationed in Malaya; its troops were mostly lost as prisoners of war upon the collapse of Singapore. Australian forces also aided the Dutch in Java and Timor. In New Guinea Australian forces defeated the Japanese in battles at Eoribaiwa Ridge, Milne Bay, Salamana, Aitape, Madang, and Alexishafen and, with the assistance of United States forces, eliminated Japanese forces at Buna, Gona, Sanananda, and Lae. In the Solomons and New Britain Australian troops relieved United States forces late in 1944. The final campaign fought by Australian troops in the war was a successful attack by two divisions in Borneo against the Japanese. Total Army casualties were 78,417, including 19,686 killed or missing and presumed dead. Members of the Australian Army Nursing Service served in all theaters of war from 1940. Enlistment in the Australian Women's Army Service began in January 1942, and its members released men for service in the fighting units.

Navy. The Royal Australian Navy, at the outbreak of the war, had a small but balanced fleet comprising six cruisers, five destroyers, two sloops, a survey ship, and a depot ship, totaling approximately 60,000 tons. Construction of another two sloops had begun. The strength in ships was further increased during 1940 and 1941 by taking up for naval duties of various merchant ships and by the addition of four destroyers. These were later added to by three destroyers and the heavy cruiser *Shropshire*. By the end of the war the Royal Australian Navy numbered 57,000 men compared with its 5,440 men in 1939. In the six years of war ships of the R.A.N. fought in every major theater. By the end of 1939 five destroyers were in the Mediterranean

where the cruiser *Sydney* joined them. Between May 1940 and December 1941 there were never less than one cruiser and four destroyers serving the Mediterranean fleet at any one time. During May and June 1941—the period of evacuations of Greece and Crete, the Syrian campaign, and the siege of Tobruk, in all of which operations the R.A.N. ships were actively engaged—nine ships, including the *Perth,* seven destroyers, and a sloop were in the Mediterranean. Two destroyers were lost.

The *Sydney* played the principal role in the action of July 1940 in which two Italian cruisers were put to flight, one of which, the *Bartolomeo Colleoni,* was crippled by the *Sydney's* fire and later sank. The *Sydney* was lost in November 1941 while in the Indian Ocean, during an engagement with the German raider *Steiermark* in which the enemy vessel was sunk. The cruiser *Australia* was active in the Atlantic from June 1940 to February 1941. Elsewhere R.A.N. ships were in action in the Arabian and Red seas.

When the Pacific war opened in December 1941 eight R.A.N. ships were in Malayan waters. Six others arrived soon afterwards. The destroyer *Vampire* was sunk in April 1942, and the sloop *Yarra* was lost. Subsequently, the *Perth* was lost in Sundra Straight, in February 1942. The R.A.N. was active in the close defense of Australia. Troops and supplies were carried to Ambon, Dutch Timor, Papua, and New Guinea. The R.A.N. was responsible for all shipping movements, the supply of convoy escorts, and anti-submarine protection. Much of this work was carried out under heavy enemy air attack. The *Australia* and the *Hobart* were part of the Allied cruiser and destroyer task force which screened Port Moresby during the Coral Sea Battle in May 1942, in which United States aircraft smashed Japanese invasion forces and frustrated the enemy attempt on Port Moresby.

Throughout the period of the building up for, and the eventual mounting of, the offensive against Japan in the southwest Pacific, the Royal Australian Navy was responsible for the maintenance of essential sea communications between Australia and New Guinea. It was also responsible for the maintenance of the Australian coastal traffic. The corvettes and survey ships of the R.A.N. led the gradual encroachment of Allied power around the eastern tip of New Guinea and made possible the successful campaign which followed. The cruisers *Australia, Canberra,* and *Hobart* led the Allied attack on the Solomon Islands in August 1942, during which the *Canberra* was lost. Throughout the phase of amphibious operations, R.A.N. ships were operating with the United States Navy and supporting Australian Army operations. In all, Australian Navy casualties were 2,849, including 2,007 killed. In addition, over 500 Australians served in the Royal (British) Navy. The Women's Royal Australian Naval Service was formed in April 1941, and at the end of the war had a strength of 2,590 members. A nursing service, established in 1942, had 60 members when the war ended.

Air Force. At the outbreak of the war the Royal Australian Air Force had a strength of 310 officers and 3,179 men; there were 12 squadrons. First to see action was Squadron No. 10, equipped with Sunderlands, which was placed on R.A.F. Coastal Command Strength. There were also many Australians serving in the R.A.F.'s Fighter and Bomber Command squadrons. Zones of operations of the R.A.A.F. from 1943 on included the Egyptian and Libyan theaters, Italy, Tunisia, Corsica, Malta, Greece, and Crete. Squadrons operating in Britain flew a total of 65,841 sorties. In the Pacific war the main R.A.A.F. effort was in New Guinea and adjoining islands. Activity included supply dropping, reconnaissance, and direct support of land operations such as pre-assault bombardment. Destruction of enemy water-craft was an important role. From a circle of operational bases established on the Australian mainland squadrons kept watch on important shipping lanes. At its peak, in December 1944, the R.A.A.F. had a strength of 183,000. Total casualties suffered were 14,657, including 9,434 killed or missing and presumed dead.

War Economy. Immense strides were taken in Australia in the manufacture of war supplies and equipment. By 1943 there were more than 700,000 Australians engaged in industry, much of it for war purposes. Although the with-drawal from civilian pursuits of service men and women created a problem for the economy, Australia's wool and food production was kept at a high level throughout the war.

Australia provided the United States forces in the south-west Pacific with provisions, technical equipment, general stores, transportation, and other equipment and services. In June 1946 an agreement was signed by the two countries under which neither government would make any pay-ment for Lend-Lease and reciprocal aid supplied up to V-J Day and used in the achievement of common victory. The total value of United States lend-lease to Australia amounted to $1,500,000,000, while reciprocal aid to the United States amounted to $912,000,000. Australia's pay-ment of $27,000,000 for postwar value of capital equip-ment, machine tools, and transfer of surplus property settled outstanding war debts to the United States.

The Postwar Period. The chief problems facing the Labour government following the war were the demobiliza-tion of the armed forces, the conversion of war industries to a peace-time basis, the securing of adequate credit for international trade, and the establishment of security in the south Pacific. The transition from wartime to peace-time economy was effected with actual gain to industry. By 1947 more than 800,000 persons were engaged in the manufacturing industries. A major national undertaking in 1949 was the Snowy Mountain power and irrigation scheme, designed to conserve water high in the Australian Alps by the use of dams and the diversion of rivers and to yield hydroelectric power. The first power of the $1,-000,000,000 plan, scheduled for completion in 1975, was generated in 1954.

Following the war Australia joined with other interested countries in establishing a South Pacific Commission whose headquarters were set up in 1948 at Loumea in New Cale-donia. Australia became a charter member of the United Nations and its delegates took an active part in international discussions.

In internal political affairs, the government secured by referendum the transfer of the social services to federal control, although other proposed transfers were defeated. In addition, the federal welfare program was increased in existing fields and extended into new ones. In 1947 the Labour government passed an act for the absorption in the Commonwealth Bank of Australia of all private banking concerns. This act was later declared by the High Court to be unconstitutional and an appeal to the Privy Council confirmed the decision, but the issue of banking was a major one in the 1949 general election, when the Labour Party was swept from office by the Liberal-Country coalition.

The 1950's. The Liberal-Country party coalition govern-ment pressed forward with social welfare plans, maintained the large-scale immigration program, and supported major public works projects. A measure to outlaw the Communist Party in Australia was declared unconstitutional, and the government failed to gain a majority in its appeal by referendum for the necessary constitutional change.

In international affairs Australia was a major contributor to the Colombo Plan, designed to assist underdeveloped countries of Southeast Asia to raise their economic level. Australia's foreign policy continued to be based on its membership in the British Commonwealth and in the United Nations. In 1952 Australia's relationships were strengthened by the signing of the ANZUS Treaty linking Australia and New Zealand with the United States in a mutual defense pact.

During the Korean War the Royal Australian Air Force made a total of 18,000 sorties against the enemy; nine Royal Australian Navy ships saw active service; and almost 8,000 Army men served in Korea, with more than 4,000 based in Kure, Japan, in support. Total casualties were 1,391, of whom 263 were killed in action. Australia provided $4,500,000 for Korean rehabilitation.

In 1954 the 14,500-mile tour of Australia by Queen Eliza-beth II and her husband the Duke of Edinburgh marked the first visit ever to be made to Australia by a reigning British monarch.   R. V. S. and R. M. Y.

AUSTRALIAN ALPS, a geographical name commonly applied to the broad, undulating uplands and associated mountain peaks of that part of the eastern highlands of Australia overlapping northeastern Victoria and southeastern New South Wales. A considerable part of the region stands more than 3,000 ft. high, and Mt. Kosciusko, the highest point in Australia, is 7,328 ft. above sea level. In winter, when the higher elevations are blanketed by deep snows, the area serves as the commonwealth's winter sports center; the uplands support cattle and some sheep grazing in summer, and are the source of most of the water used in the irriga-tion projects westward along the Murray and Murrumbidgee rivers.   R. G. B.

AUSTRALIAN CAPITAL TERRITORY. *See* CAN-BERRA.

AUSTRALIAN LANGUAGES, the languages spoken on the Australian continent, the island of Tasmania, and several small islands close to Australia. In 1945, native speak-ers were still estimated at a few hundred thousand. At least two racial elements speak these languages, which are about 100 in number and seem to belong to one linguistic family. No outside relationship is certain. From northeastern Aus-tralia across Cape York Peninsula and across minor islands a transition in language structure into the Papuan pattern of New Guinea is noticeable. This phenomenon may be due to mixture or to slow assimilation.

An analysis of the known material suggests that the speak-ers of these languages came to their Australian settlements in not less than two waves of migration, the second of which, at least, is traceable to India. The language of the first migra-tion seems to have remained unadulterated in Tasmania; in 1834, eight to ten different languages were still spoken there, but none survived into the twentieth century. They were ex-tremely simple. Hissing consonants were absent, the vocabu-lary was poor and primitive, and there were pronouns only for the first person and the second person. The second wave covered Australia and resulted in various mixtures with the pre-existing dialects.

The main characteristics of Australian languages may be enumerated briefly. Their nouns are invariable, for, except in the case of the languages spoken from the eastern shore of King's Sound through the northern Kimberleys and along Western Arnhem Land, there is no gender, and number (singular, dual, often trial and plural) is indicated usually by suffixes. The varying origins of these suffixes suggest that the languages underwent development after they separated. Possession is indicated in very different ways, sometimes resembling Melanesian, sometimes Papuan, sometimes neither. The conjugation of the verb expresses tense and mood, and, in some languages, also person. The original numerals of most of the languages run no higher than 2 or 3. Papuan and Indonesian, in contrast with the Australian languages, usually have no number, and Papuan, unlike Australian, has no distinct adjective.   P. F.

AUSTRASIA [ɔstre′zhə], the eastern section of an ancient Frankish kingdom, with Metz as its capital. The remaining sections of the kingdom were Neustria and Burgundy, all three being united in 613 under the rule of Clotaire II. In 623 Austrasia was entrusted by Clotaire to his son Dagobert, with Pepin of Landen and Bishop Arnulf as his advisers. In 630 Dagobert also became ruler of Neustria, the western section of Clotaire's kingdom. However, after Dagobert's death, the two realms were again separated. Eventually the Mayors of the Palace, descended from both Arnulf and Pepin, became the real rulers of Austrasia and once more gained supremacy in Neustria, uniting the two realms under Austrasia. Charles Martel ruled as Mayor from 714 to 741 and was succeeded by his son Pepin the Short, who was formally elected as the first Carolingian king in 751. During Charlemagne's reign the name Austrasia was applied to the Frankish territories beyond the Rhine.   F. H.

AUSTRIA, a federal republic of 32,388 sq. mi., located between the Bohemian massif and the Alps, and traversed from west to east by the Danube, at the crossroads of Europe. South across the Brenner Pass is Italy; to the southeast, across the Ljubljana gap, is Yugoslavia; to the east stretches the great plain of Hungary; to the north lie the valleys and mountains of Czechoslovakia; to the northwest Germany is easily accessible through the broad Danube valley, and to the west passes through the Vorarlberg lead to Switzerland and Liechtenstein. The federal government comprises eight provinces: Burgenland, Carinthia, Lower Austria, Upper Austria, Salzburg, Styria, Tirol, and Vorarlberg; and the self-governing city of Vienna (Wien).

GEOGRAPHICAL FEATURES

Topography. Austria is a mountainous country. Only the northern third, situated in the Danube basin, is not dominated by the Alps. Vienna, the largest city and the capital, lies in a great plain in the northeast, overlooked on the west by an escarpment covered by the famous "Vienna Woods." Otherwise Austria lies entirely within the eastern Alps, consisting of three east-west ranges, separated by longitudinal valleys. In the north are the Noric Alps; in the center, the Rhaetian, Ötztaler, and Semmering ranges; and in the south, the Carnic and Karawanken Alps. Each affords spectacular scenery and numerous winter sports centers which help to sustain Austria's thriving tourist industry. The Alps of western, central, and southern Austria, particularly the Hohe Tauern, Ötztaler, and Algauer, rank with the Bernese Oberland of Switzerland and the Dolomites of Italy in scenic grandeur. Such cities as Salzburg and Innsbruck are overshadowed by towering mountains.

AUSTRIA
Statute Miles
25   0   25   50
Copyright by Rand McNally & Co., Chicago
Made in U.S.A.

Gross Glockner, a double-peaked mountain with a glacier at its base, is located between Tirol and Carinthia.

The Danube and its several Austrian tributaries, the Inn, Traun, Enns, Drava, and Leitha, provide drainage for most of the country. Only the southeastern part is in the Adriatic watershed, where the Piave and the Tagliamento drain the southern slopes of the Carnic Alps. Within Austria, the Danube alone is navigable. The largest lake in Austria, the Neusiedler See, lies southeast of the capital, a portion of it astride the Hungarian frontier.

Soil. The soils of the country are mainly gray-brown podsolic, which are not as leached as the true podsols farther north. Considerable leaching takes place on the mountain sides, but in the valleys the rich alluvial soils make possible extensive agriculture. The Vienna Basin is the most fertile part of Austria; other productive areas lie to the west, south of the Danube, as well as in the Klagenfurt and Graz basins, and eastern Burgenland.

Flora and Fauna. Some of the higher peaks, such as Gross Glockner, the highest point in Austria (12,457 ft.), are permanently snow-covered, but most mountain slopes are blanketed with broad-leafed hardwood trees, including oak, beech, elm, chestnut, and maple; poplar and willow are found in the lowlands, while at the higher elevations there are coniferous forests. Small fur-bearing animals such as foxes, lynx, wildcats, and martens are found throughout Austria. Deer and rabbits abound. A few chamois still remain in the high Alps.

Climate. Climatically, Austria lies in a transition zone between maritime northwest Europe and continental Russia, with hot, wet summers and cold, dry winters. The mean temperature of the coldest month ranges from 20° F. in Klagenfurt to 29° F. in Vienna, although, of course, temperatures considerably below these are reached in the mountains. In the summer the mean temperature of the warmest month has a range of from 65 to 70° F., being highest in the east near the Hungarian Plain. The average annual rainfall is between 25 and 30 in., the maximum coming in the early summer. This amount increases considerably on the higher slopes. In the winter the valleys are often covered with fog, while the higher slopes are clear and warmed by the sun, a factor which helps to popularize Austrian ski resorts.

ETHNOLOGY AND POPULATION

Racial Origins and Language. Austria is a Germanic country, 97.5 per cent of whose inhabitants speak either High German or dialects related to it. Slovenian and Croat are the languages of a Slavic minority found principally in Carinthia, Burgenland, and Styria.

The Austrians, like most Europeans, are of mixed racial ancestry. History, religion, and culture have played a larger role than race in creating the "Austrian type"; however, its most characteristic physical traits are those of the Alpine-Dinaric group.

The earliest traces of human habitation were left in Paleolithic time by the Neanderthal man and his successor the Aurignacian man. More abundant settlements were made in Neolithic time, for through the Danube Valley, the great natural passage of central Europe, flowed numerous peoples and cultures. Both Mediterranean and Germanic stocks have been identified in the several "Danubian migrations" which moved over Austria. In the east, Austria's

533

Neolithic inhabitants were mainly long-headed (dolichocephalic); toward the west, following the invasion of the Lake Dwellers, they were round-headed (brachycephalic). These people were probably the ancestors of the Alpine race, and their influence upon Austria and central Europe was immense, especially because many of the subsequent invaders were of the same race. By the end of Neolithic time racial amalgamation had taken place, and from the

EDELWEISS

COURTESY OF THE AUSTRIAN
STATE TOURIST DEPARTMENT

early Bronze Age (2200 B.C.) until the first millennium B.C. Austria's inhabitants were part of that central European culture known as Illyrian.

About 390 B.C. Austria was invaded by the Celts, the same people who overran Spain, Gaul, and the British Isles. The Celts not only advanced culture, since they introduced the later Iron Age, or La Tène period, in Austria, but the Alpine characteristics, especially round-headedness, became more firmly fixed. Most of the Celts seem to have been Alpines, and their culture flourished until the Romans conquered what is now Austria between 35 and 15 B.C. Almost four hundred years of Roman rule brought a strong Latin and Mediterranean influence to bear upon the people, but the most significant and enduring traces of the prolonged Roman occupation have been cultural rather than racial in nature.

With the collapse of the Roman Empire, waves of German tribes passed over Austria. The settlement of Austria by the Alemanni and the Baiuwarii insured its future character as a German nation. The Nordic and Alpine characteristics of the Germans were re-enforced by the steady westward movement of the Slavs, who form another important element in Austria's ethnic history. The Slavs were distinguished from the Germans chiefly by language and culture, and by paganism, which the Slavs retained until the ninth century. For three centuries before their conversion to Christianity the Slavs had colonized Lower Austria, Burgenland, Styria, East Tirol, and Carinthia. Charlemagne's conquests and his missionary activity made possible the gradual assimilation of German and Slav, and this mixture, primarily cultural rather than racial, gave Austria its peculiar ethnic quality.

Modern Austrians combine all the major European races, and Alpine, Nordic, and Mediterranean, and their combinations are well represented. Yet the principal racial character of the people is Alpine and its subgroup, Dinaric. Round heads, dark to light brown hair, brown eyes, and figures ranging from stocky for the Alpines to tall spareness for Dinarics are most frequently encountered. The proportion of brachycephalic (round) heads is greatest in the Tirol (81 per cent), but it is also high in Salzburg and Upper and Lower Austria. In some parts of Carinthia and Styria, however, dolichocephalic (long) heads prevail.

Religion. About 88 per cent of the people are Roman Catholics, while less than 6 per cent are Protestants. The Jewish population, which amounted to about 3 per cent before the Nazi occupation in 1938, had been reduced to 1.26 per cent a year later. Less than half of these Jews survived the war. Catholicism has had a deep influence on Austrian life and culture, providing one of the chief distinctions between the Austrian and the German nationality. There are two archdioceses (Vienna and Salzburg), and four dioceses (Linz, St. Pölten, Klagenfurt, and Graz).

Population. Austria's population according to the census of 1951 was 6,933,905, a figure that included about 400,000 German political refugees from areas behind the Iron Curtain. Nearly one fourth of the population lives in Vienna, which had a 1951 population of 1,616,125 (1,900,000 in the metropolitan area). Vienna, Lower (1,400,471) and Upper (1,108,720) Austria, and Styria (1,109,335) contain more than two thirds of the nation's population; these are the principal urban and industrial areas. Except for the cities of Salzburg and Innsbruck, the population is least dense in the mountainous provinces of Salzburg (327,232), Tirol (427,465), and Vorarlberg (193,657). The remaining two provinces, Carinthia and Burgenland, had 1951 populations of 474,764 and 276,136 respectively.

Graz (226,453), Linz (184,685), Salzburg (102,927), and Innsbruck (95,055) are the largest cities next to Vienna. Other urban centers are Klagenfurt (62,782), Wels (38,120), Steyr (36,818), Villach (30,066), Wiener-Neustadt (30,559), Baden (21,312), and Mödling (17,076).

TRIANGLE PHOTO SERVICE

Austrian girls in Wachau on the Danube

Austria's farmlands yield rye, wheat, hops, flax, and other crops

ECONOMIC RESOURCES AND ACTIVITIES

Agriculture and Forestry. About 40 per cent of the Austrian people engage in agriculture or forestry. Cereals, particularly rye and wheat, and potatoes and sugar beets are the principal crops. Hops and flax are raised in Upper Austria, and in the Tirol some tobacco is cultivated. Fruit trees flourish in the lowlands, and vineyards thrive, especially in the Danube valley and in eastern Styria. Dairying and beef production, the basic economy of the Alpine region, not only meet the domestic needs but provide an exportable surplus. Agriculture as a whole meets 85 per cent of the nation's food requirements.

The Austrian forests, after Sweden and Finland the largest in Europe, are carefully tended as a crop. They furnish lumber and wood pulp as well as invaluable protection to the soil.

Mining. Lignite (brown coal), iron ore, magnesite, and graphite are the principal mineral resources. Austria contributes substantially to the world's production of magnesite and graphite. Lignite is mined principally in Styria and Lower Austria. The Eisernerz-Vordernberg iron deposits in Styria are among the richest in Europe; the Erzberg (literally "ore mountain"), worked since Roman times, provides ore that is especially suited for making high-grade steel. Salt is another important mineral mined at many places in Austria. Copper, lead, zinc, sulphur, antimony, and mica are found in small quantities. The oil fields northeast of Vienna (discovered around Zistersdorf in 1932) have been augmented by new finds (the Matzen and Aderklaa fields)

so as to yield as much as 3,500,000 metric tons annually. Austrian domestic consumption of oil requires less than half that amount.

Hydroelectric Power. Austria's great potential hydroelectric power has been steadily developed since World War II. All electric power companies were nationalized in 1947, and Marshall Plan aid raised the output of kilowatt hours approximately 60 per cent over the 1939 level. An abundant source of electric power promises to spur the aluminum industry based on the great plant at Ranshofen in Upper Austria. Built by the Germans during World War II, this plant has the capacity to meet a substantial part of Europe's need for aluminum. Electric power also promises to diminish Austria's coal imports since domestic production meets only half the national requirement. The increasing availability of electric power is reflected in the 1955 index of industrial production which was 100 per cent above that for 1937.

Manufacturing. Lower Austria and Vienna are the chief centers of the fabricating and consumer-goods industries; the metallurgical and heavy-machine industries are found mainly in Styria. Oil refining is carried on adjacent to the oil fields in Lower Austria. Mountainous Vorarlberg, owing to intensive development of small-scale industries, has, in proportion to its population, the highest percentage of industrial workers. All productive facilities of the Austrian economy are government-operated, the basic industries, together with mining, transport and banking, having been nationalized in 1946.

Austria's main industrial products are iron and steel, machinery, electrical goods, textiles, aluminum, paper, wood products, synthetic fibers, chemicals, drugs, gasoline, and fuel oil. Rayon and other synthetic fibers are supplied to the textile industries from plants developed during World War II. Pig-iron and steel production each currently exceeds 1,000,000 metric tons annually. Pig-iron production is actually in excess of Austria's steel-making capacity, a consequence in part of Linz' expansion during World War II as

the Austrian economy. Tourism, systematically encouraged by the federal government, has steadily yielded more dollar earnings. Some $80,000,000 came from this source in 1954.

Transportation. Vienna, in accordance with its former position as the commercial and financial capital of the Austro-Hungarian Empire, remains the key transportation center of Central Europe. Although heavily damaged during World War II, the Austrian rail net (4,000 mi.) has been fully restored since 1948. The railroads are national prop-

Open-air mining in Styria, a province of Austria. This mine, the "Erzberg," has one of the largest iron-ore deposits in Europe.

an iron-smelting center rivalling the older centers in the Mur-Mürz Valley. Graz, Austria's second largest city is the urban center of this industrial and mining complex. Plants and mines in this area have been extensively retooled since World War II both by Marshall Plan aid and by Austrian investments. War industries spurred Wiener-Neustadt's growth so that it ranks high as a fabricating center. Vienna contains diversified industries although it remains essentially a commercial and governmental city. Still, Viennese luxury products such as toilet articles, fine furniture and rugs, and women's gloves, shoes, and high-fashion clothes remain world famous. Local crafts such as wood carving, lace making, and hand weaving thrive in most Alpine villages during the winter months. Brewing is carried on in most cities, with Europe's largest brewery located in Vienna. Wine making occurs mainly in Lower Austria and in Burgenland.

Commerce. Foreign trade is vital to Austria which must import coal and raw materials. Thanks to skilled workmanship Austrian foreign trade has grown steadily since the end of World War II. Between 1948-1954 the value of exports tripled, giving rise in 1953-1954 to a small favorable balance (worth $48,000,000 in 1954). This situation warranted the discontinuance of foreign aid in 1953. By that date Austria had found new markets outside the German economy of which Austria formed a part between 1938 and 1945. Switzerland, Italy, and Czechoslovakia were Austria's first important postwar customers. But Germany has regained first place by taking one fifth of Austria's exports. About one quarter of Austria's imports come from Germany. Nations of the European Payments Union buy one fifth of Austria's exportable products, for Austrian trade is now almost wholly oriented toward western Europe. The United States lags behind the United Kingdom as a market for Austrian goods, but American tourists contribute substantially to

erty, and the operating personnel belongs to the Austrian civil service. From Vienna express routes run over Linz and Passau toward Germany. Vienna also lies on the Orient Express route from Paris to Istanbul and on the main line from Prague to Budapest. Express trains also connect Vienna with Salzburg and Innsbruck where the Brenner route to Italy commences. From Innsbruck the Arlberg route via Feldkirch connects Austria with Switzerland and western Europe. Innsbruck also enjoys good connections with Munich. From Vienna express lines also run south over Graz to Yugoslavia and over Klagenfurt and Villach to Trieste and northern Italy. More than half of these routes have been electrified, an objective successfully fostered by Marshall Plan aid.

The Austrian road system (53,000 mi.) adequately serves the nation's limited number of automotive vehicles (about 65,000 automobiles and 55,000 trucks). The most modern portions of the road system were laid down before 1939 as part of Hitler's *Autobahnen*. Still, in the lofty Gross Glockner auto road traversing the Hohe Tauern Alps, Austrian engineers achieved spectacular results and added a valuable trans-Alpine route. Only since 1950 has the federal government seriously undertaken to expand and improve the road net. Since the end of World War II Danubian river commerce, which made Austria, and Vienna in particular, a focal point of Central European transport, has considerably diminished. From 1945 to 1955 the circumstance that the Soviet Union controlled the Danubian Shipping Co. and its assets together with the western powers discouragement of Austria's former east-west trade, limited Danube downstream traffic to coal imports from Germany and upstream traffic to iron ore and timber. Passenger traffic on the Danube is now largely limited to excursion steamers. The state treaty of May 15, 1955, permits Austria to redeem the Danubian Shipping Co. and when this is accomplished

Danube freight traffic may revive. Vienna, served by two major airports and twenty-one airlines, remains the hub of the nation's air transport, with regularly scheduled flights from all parts of the world. Salzburg, Innsbruck, and Linz are also served by international airways. Foreign companies supply most of Austria's air transport, although Austria's civil aviation may be expected to grow since the state treaty sets forth conditions for its development.

SOCIAL AND CULTURAL ACTIVITIES

Education. Austria, situated at the crossroads of Europe, has traditionally been open to cosmopolitan influences. Only the Nazi regime (1938-1945) excluded them. Since 1945 Vienna has regained its world eminence as a cultural and educational capital. The largest of the three Austrian universities (8,000 students) is located there; the others are at Graz and Innsbruck. After the German fashion, engineering and technical instruction are not provided by universities. A small agricultural college at Leoben and two advanced technical schools in Vienna meet this need. Only about 23,000 students are enrolled in higher education, since the mass of the people receive only a primary education followed by craft, commercial, or technical instruction. About 5,000 schools provide primary education to some 850,-000 pupils. Religious instruction is given them according to their parents' preference. A directive of September 1945 also requires primary education to instill Austrian patriotism and sympathy for democracy and humanity. Experiments in this direction have long characterized Austrian education. Otto Blockel, Minister of Education in the first republic, tried, with some success by 1926, to make the schools serve more democratic ends. Austria also has an active adult education movement, an ideal still unique in European countries. Vienna alone registers 35,000 adults in these courses. The program is served indirectly by a nation-wide net of some 1,500 People's Libraries. Shortly after World War II each of the occupying powers began to provide free libraries and information centers in the cities of its zone. The United States and France were the most zealous and successful in striving to re-establish the cosmopolitanism which alone could wipe out the baneful effects of the Nazi tyranny over Austria.

Cultural Features. Austria has long been the home of great music, opera, and drama. Mozart was born in Salzburg, and Beethoven, Haydn, Schubert, and Brahms lived and composed in Vienna. Johann Strauss made that city the waltz capital. The "Vienna School" of dramatists headed by Arthur Schnitzler created, around 1900, a new mood in European playwriting. In Hugo von Hofmannsthal, Austria had a lyric poet and dramatist of first rank. Starting in 1917 the Salzburg Festival became an annual showcase of the dramatic and musical arts. Max Reinhardt subsequently made Vienna famous as a center of dramatic training and created a unique "Vienna Style." The Vienna Philharmonic, under such famous composer-conductors as Gustav Mahler and Richard Strauss, won a world reputation for excellence as have the Vienna Choir Boys, the actual choir of St. Stephen's Cathedral.

These activities have traditionally found their focus in the State Opera and in the Burgtheater in Vienna. The latter burned late in World War II while the former suffered severe bomb damage. Nonetheless opera and drama revived quickly at the war's end. The Salzburg Festival regained its stature as an outstanding European cultural event, while in Vienna opera and music found a new home in the hallowed Theater an der Wien (where Beethoven's *Fidelio* had its première); drama and light opera were staged in variety halls and commercial theaters. Because the war had not scattered its personnel, the Vienna Philharmonic soon regained its old splendor.

Provincial theaters and orchestras also revived soon after World War II and although handicapped at first by lack of costumes, instruments, and production material, they soon brought the arts to the people throughout Austria. The Tirol *Landestheater* at Innsbruck has scored notable successes with classic and with modern drama and opera. Music festivals rivalling Salzburg have developed on a lesser scale in recent years at Graz, Bregenz, St. Florian, and Eisenstadt. Direct government subsidies support the theater in Austria with funds obtained by taxing cinema tickets and radios. The directors, actors, singers, musicians, and staff are in a sense civil servants, maintained, in keeping with princely tradition, for the national cultural welfare. Because music festivals stimulate the tourist trade, they are profitable investments. Many tourists have been attracted to Vienna because no other postwar European city continually offers such musical abundance.

Although the Museum of Art History in Vienna suffered severe war damage, the famous collection of pictures (which toured United States art galleries in 1950) survived intact. This collection together with the drawings and other objets d'art at the Albertina make Vienna an outstanding art capital.

The Belvedere and Schönbrunn Palaces in Vienna's suburbs, both newly repaired, remain outstanding examples of princely residences. Throughout the provinces there is a wealth of late Gothic, Baroque, and Rococo architecture. Melk, the Benedictine monastery on the Danube, and the Salzburg Cathedral are notable baroque edifices; both Innsbruck and Salzburg are veritable museums of architectural styles.

The past outweighs the present in Austria's intellectual life. Before 1914 Freud and Alder made Vienna the European center of psychoanalytic research. After 1918 the circle of logical positivists in Vienna achieved world-wide influence by their determined effort to think through the implications of scientific method for epistemology and metaphysics. Throughout these years Vienna University commanded respect for its medical research and medical education. The Austrian school of economists headed by Othmar Spann also won acclaim. Some measure of this intellectual vitality persists, however, since Austria currently ranks among the first six nations in the numbers of books produced annually.

Social Welfare. Only the Saar and West Germany exceed Austria in the scope and cost of the national security program. State welfare activity cushions the life of each citizen from the cradle (maternity care) to the grave (publicly controlled funerals). The present system has expanded the social legislation enacted after 1920 under the influence of Ferdinand Hanusch and Joseph Resch, the latter Austria's first Minister of Social Welfare. The coverage includes unemployment insurance, health and accident insurance and compensation pay, old age pensions, an eight-hour day, paid vacations, control of women's and children's employment, and extensive public housing. The latter has not kept pace with the actual postwar need nor has it matched the vast municipal apartments built in Vienna after World War I. Only Linz and Wiener-Neustadt have fulfilled noteworthy public-housing programs since World War II. Private rental properties have not been forthcoming in adequate amounts because of strict rent controls pegged to low personal income levels. Heavy income and inheritance taxes help to provide for social welfare costs as well as to distribute and equalize the national income. Each of the postwar wage-price agreements embodied a social welfare principle in attempting to maintain the workers' real wages in the face of an inflationary spiral. Since June 1948, agricultural and forestry workers have shared all the social benefits previously applied to industrial workers and civil servants. Other postwar bills have increased the amount of old-age pensions and have extended the paid vacation period. The Works Council Law of March 1947 extended the right of trade unionists to participate in management decisions, a right embodied in the initial Works Council Law of 1919 but never as fully developed in Austria as in West Germany.

GOVERNMENT AND POLITICS

Governmental Structure. Austria is a federal republic pledged to democratic institutions by the state treaty of May 15, 1955. The constitution resembles the one adopted by the first Austrian Republic in 1920 and subsequently modified in 1929. The legality of the present form of government was formally acknowledged by the Allied Council on Nov. 30, 1945. All citizens enjoy unabridged civil rights. Both male and female citizens exercise the suffrage in freely conducted electoral contests concluded by secret ballot. The president, elected by direct popular vote for a term of six years, is the nominal head of the government. Majority rule determines the outcome of presidential elections. If no candidate receives a majority, a run-off election is held between the two highest candidates. Substantial executive powers cloak the president's office; he may issue decrees having the force of law. There is a bicameral parliament. The upper house, or *Bundesrat,* represents the provinces and is chosen by their popularly elected assemblies. The lower house, or *Nationalrat,* represents the people and is chosen directly by them according to the principle of proportional representation. The ministry, or executive branch of the government, is chosen from the leading party or parties in the *Nationalrat.* This ministry assumes executive and ministerial functions in accordance with the practice of ministerial responsibility: its tenure depends upon the endorsement of its policies by the *Nationalrat.* In the provinces and in Vienna, assemblies elected according to proportional rule legislate for local affairs. The judiciary as a coordinate branch of the government is more than a mere branch of the civil service for administering justice. Civil law rests on the code of 1811; criminal law on that of 1852. Trial by jury was restored on Feb. 5, 1951.

Defense. The national defense, carried out from 1945 to 1955 by military forces of the occupying powers, is now vested in the federal republic. The state treaty does not limit the size of Austria's armed forces, but it does limit the type of arms that the republic may use and it specifically forbids the enlistment of former Nazis or the use of German and Japanese war material. Atom bombs and guided missiles are among the prohibited weapons. In view of the perpetual neutrality pledged by the Austrian Republic, only defense forces may be organized. Police forces are state-controlled.

Political Parties. Political opinion is free to develop and be organized into parties, except for Nazism. The state treaty pledges Austria to continue the victors' policy of denazification and to eliminate all traces of Nazism from Austrian political, economic, and cultural life. The major parties are the Austrian People's Party (formerly the Christian Social Party), supported mainly by the Catholics and by the rural population; and the Socialists (formerly the Social Democrats), the party of urban dwellers and of

workingmen. Since Vienna is a Socialist stronghold, Austrian politics often becomes a contest between town and country. Minor parties include the Union of Independents, appealing to refugees and other dissident elements; and the Communists, whose popularity has suffered from memories of Red Army brutality during its occupation of Austrian territory in 1945. The Communists have steadily declined since the first free elections of Nov. 25, 1945, when they received five and one-half per cent of the votes. Since those elections the ministry has usually represented a coalition of the People's and Socialist parties. A free press and the right of assembly assure vigorous campaigning; a compulsory voting law assures popular participation.

Finance. Austria's current financial stability contrasts with the unhappy situation after World War I when for six years the League of Nations administered the national finances. The stability finally achieved by deflation and lowering the standard of living broke down again in 1931 with the failure of the Credit-Anstalt, Austria's largest bank. Its failure led to the financial collapse of Central Europe. Although the schilling, the monetary unit first introduced by the League's fiscal reforms, had again become stable by 1937, personal savings and investment remained low. World War II, by leaving Austria with a swollen note issue and a ruined economy, threatened to repeat this story. Yet Austria's postwar fiscal policy has successfully steered between the extremes of deflation and inflation threatened by a far-reaching economic readjustment.

Currency and foreign exchange affairs are regulated through the Austrian Central Bank (re-established in July 1945). All phases of banking, including local commercial operations, have been nationalized since 1946. Two basic currency reforms (December 1945 and December 1947) reduced the swollen note issue and began to stabilize the schilling, which remains the national currency unit. Its 1955 value was 26.1 schillings per dollar. Monetary stability also gained from the policy, carried out between 1947 and 1951, of enforcing a national wage and price structure. Negotiations to fix the scale were carried out between the government, the farmers, and wage earners in 1947, 1948, and 1949. But both wages and commodity prices are now permitted to correspond to market conditions. Yet controlled domestic prices together with import restrictions helped to stabilize the schilling and minimize postwar budgetary deficits. Military occupation costs, which added 230 per cent to the civil budget in 1945-1946 and averaged about 15 per cent thereafter, enhanced these deficits. They would actually have been unmanageable save for foreign aid (especially UNRRA and ERP) which, in the first postwar years, covered Austrian food imports. In all, Austria had received some $1,500,000,000 from abroad when Marshall Plan assistance stopped in 1953. Federal fiscal policy embraces the rate of investment in the nationalized industries, transport, and communications systems; the annual budget includes these items as well as the heavy costs of Austria's extensive social welfare and pension systems. With industrial recovery Austria has regained its monetary autonomy as well as as a favorable credit balance in the European Payments Union.

W. O. S.

HISTORY

Early Tribes in Austria. Austrian history begins with the invasion of Celtic tribes, the Taurisci and Norici, about 390 B.C. The Celts introduced the Iron Age to Austria, and around their iron-working settlement at Noreia was established the earliest Austrian state, Noricum. It became part of the Roman Empire after the conquest of Raetia, in what is now eastern Austria, by the Roman legions in 15 B.C. Part of historic Austria was also included in the Roman province of Pannonia, organized in A.D. 10. Until the fourth century the Romans held these provinces and the Danube frontier against the German tribes. Meanwhile the Celtic inhabitants were Romanized and such towns as Flavia Solva, in modern Styria, and Vindobona, on the site of Vienna, were developed. The Emperor Marcus Aurelius died in Vindobona in A.D. 180. In the third century these provinces rose in importance, not only because the Illyrian soldier-emperor drew support there, but also because of the great pressure of the German barbarians on the Danubian frontier. Tribes like the Quadi and Marcomanni repeatedly invaded Roman territory, but Latin institutions and culture persisted through the fourth century. The first mention of Christianity in Austria occurs about 313 in Constantine's reign.

After Valentinian I's death in 375 the Roman watch on the Danube began to break down. Beside the Swabic Germans who had passed over Austria there now came the East Germans, such as the Visigoths, the Ostrogoths, Gepidae, Rugii, and Vandals. About 432 Pannonia was delivered to the Huns, a people of Mongolian origin. First of the Germans to take permanent possession of Austrian territory were the Alamanni, who settled between 450 and 500. They were followed by their kinsmen the Bajuwarii, or Bavarians, who provided political leadership until the eighth century.

Amid the turmoil caused by the collapse of Roman rule various Slavic tribes moved into Austria from the east. They were either impelled or carried along with the Avars, an Asiatic people, who, like the Huns, had only a transient effect on Austrian history. The Slavs became attached to the soil and by 590 had settled all of Styria, Lower Austria, and Carinthia and had crossed the mountains to Upper Austria and Salzburg. To the east the Slavic influence was paramount,

RULERS AND PRESIDENTS OF AUSTRIA

Dates of Reign		Name	Succession	Born	Died
			BABENBERG DYNASTY		
			As Margraves of Austria		
976	994	Leopold (Luitpold) I	Appointed by Holy Roman Emperor Otto II	?	994
994	1018	Henry (Heinrich) I	Son of Leopold I	?	1018
1018	1055	Adalbert	Younger son of Leopold I	?	1055
1055	1075	Ernest (Ernst)	Son of Adalbert	?	1075
1075	1095	Leopold II	Son of Ernest	?	1095
1095	1136	Leopold III the Pious	Son of Leopold II; canonized in 1485	1075	1136
1136	1141	Leopold IV	Son of Elizabeth, sister of Leopold III, and Ottokar, Margrave of Steyr	?	1141
1141	1156	Henry II	Younger brother of Leopold IV; Austria raised from margraviate to duchy by Holy Roman Emperor Frederick I (Barbarossa) in 1156	1114	1177
			As Dukes of Austria		
1156	1177	Henry II	(see above)	1114	1177
1177	1194	Leopold V	Son of Henry II	1157	1194
1194	1198	Frederick I	Son of Leopold V	?	1198
1198	1230	Leopold VI the Glorious	Younger son of Leopold V	1176	1230
1230	1246	Frederick II	Son of Leopold VI; last of the Babenbergs	1211	1246
			INTERREGNUM—1246-1251		
			BOHEMIAN DYNASTY		
1251	1276	Ottokar	Son of Wenceslaus I, King of Bohemia; elected by Estates of Austria; ousted by Rudolph of Hapsburg; killed in attempt to recover his possessions.	1230?	1278
			HOUSE OF HAPSBURG		
1276	1740	(See Holy Roman Empire)	As Holy Roman Emperors		
			HOUSE OF HAPSBURG-LORRAINE		
			As Sovereigns of Austria-Hungary		
1740	1780	Maria Theresa	Daughter of Emperor Charles VI, wife of Emperor Francis I; mother of Emperors Joseph II and Leopold II.	1717	1780
1780	1790	Joseph II	Son of Maria Theresa and Emperor Francis I; Holy Roman Emperor from 1765	1741	1790
1790	1792	Leopold II	Third son of Maria Theresa and Emperor Francis I	1747	1792
1792	1835	Francis I	Son of Leopold II; Holy Roman Emperor as Francis II until 1806 (end of Holy Roman Empire); assumed title of Emperor of Austria in 1804.	1768	1835
1835	1848	Ferdinand I	Son of Francis I; abdicated during revolution	1793	1875
1848	1867	Francis Joseph (Franz Josef) I	Son of Archduke Francis Charles; nephew of Ferdinand I	1830	1916
			As Emperors of Austria and Kings of Hungary (Dual Monarchy)		
1867	1916	Francis Joseph (Franz Josef) I	(see above)	1830	1916
1916	1918	Charles (Karl) I	Grandnephew of Francis Joseph; abdicated on defeat of Central Powers in World War I.	1887	1922
Terms of Office			**FIRST REPUBLIC OF AUSTRIA**		
1919	1920	Karl Seitz	Acting president	1869	1950
1920	1928	Michael Hainisch	Elected president	1858	1940
1928	1938	Wilhelm Miklas	Elected president; actual power in hands of chancellors Engelbert Dollfuss (from 1932 to 1934) and Kurt von Schuschnigg (1934 to 1938); resigned on German occupation.	1872	1956
			PART OF THIRD REICH (NAZI GERMANY)—1938-1945		
			SECOND REPUBLIC OF AUSTRIA		
1945	1950	Karl Renner	Elected president by National Assembly; Austria occupied by the Soviet Union, the United States, Great Britain, and France (1945-1955).	1870	1950
1951		Theodor Körner	Elected president	1873	

while to the west the German tribes were in control. Traces of a Romanized peasantry remained in both areas, however, and Latin customs long survived in the Tirol. Under their great king, Samo, the Slavs by 632 had won independence from the Avars. Among the Swabic Germans, however, the work of missionaries had strengthened feudal ties with the Franks. Among these missionaries was St. Rupert, who made Salzburg the fount of religion for both Austria and

TRIANGLE PHOTO SERVICE

Tirolese costumes from the Lower Inn Valley

Bavaria. Salzburg and Passau were the first dioceses in what is now Austria.

Beginning in the 740's the Bavarian dukes attempted to become free of Frankish authority, the greatest effort being made by Duke Tassilo after 763. Charlemagne, sole ruler of the Franks after 771, proved too strong, and Tassilo was forced to yield in 787-788 and retire to a monastery. Charlemagne went on to destroy the Avar power which still menaced Austria and to found there two great marks which were defensive outposts of his own empire. Under Charlemagne's encouragement the conversion of the Slavs to Christianity was begun (796), thus preparing for the amalgamation of German and Slav in Austria.

Birth of the "East Mark." Austria's origins as a political unit are found in the mark, or realm, established along the Danube about A.D. 800 to protect Charlemagne's empire lying to the west. From the name assigned to this region, *Österreich,* meaning "East Mark," has come the name Austria. This usage had begun by the end of the tenth century. In the later Middle Ages and in early modern times Austria has come to mean the state ruled by the Hapsburg archdukes of Austria. A state bearing the name Austria came into existence only in 1804, when Francis II, who ruled the country as Holy Roman Emperor, proclaimed himself Francis I, Emperor of Austria, in order to maintain the equality of his house with that of Napoleon Bonaparte. Austria, or the East Mark, played a defensive role under Charlemagne's successors, and the Carolingian influence in Austria was

short-lived, for the Hungarian invasion of the ninth century overthrew the margraves, or counts of the mark, and destroyed virtually all traces of their rule. Austria also served as a buffer in the policies of Otto the Great, Holy Roman Emperor who defeated the Hungarians on the Lechfeld in 955. Austria was assigned in 976 by Otto's son and successor, Otto II, to Leopold I of Babenberg, whose vigorous administration established Austria as a German state. The country's destiny was intertwined with this Franconian dynasty until 1246. Under its rulers both the territory and prestige of Austria increased; colonization and settlement advanced as far as the Leitha River; and the capital shifted eastward with this expansion, reaching Vienna about 1140. By 1156 Austria had become a duchy with very limited obligations to the German (Holy Roman) Empire. The later Babenbergs, without any strong bishops or imperial cities to oppose them, acted as independent sovereigns, making foreign treaties, controlling commerce, and absorbing the territory of weaker rulers. In this way Upper Austria, Styria, and Carniola were added to the Babenberg lands, and Vienna became one of the richest and most important German cities. The independence of the Babenberg rulers was shown by their policies toward Henry IV (1050-1106) and Frederick II (1194-1250), two of the strongest rulers of medieval Germany. Leopold II of Austria deserted Henry IV during the investiture struggle and maintained his control of Austria against Vratislav II, a usurper sanctioned by the Emperor. When Duke Frederick the Quarrelsome refused to appear in the Italian diet of Frederick II, his lands were declared vacant and Vienna was made an imperial city. None of these changes proved permanent, and Duke Frederick was soon in full authority. He was, however, the last of the Babenbergs, for he left no heir when killed in battle against the Hungarians in 1246. After a period of confusion in which Pope and Emperor both claimed the right to determine the ruler of Austria, the Austrian estates met in 1251 and chose a Bohemian, Ottokar, as their duke. Through his inheritance (he became King of Bohemia in 1253) and his military success, Austria's fortunes were temporarily associated with those of Bohemia. Ottokar also added Carinthia to the complex of lands included with Austria. This ruler's ambition proved his undoing, but his failure gave Austria the dynasty closely linked with its subsequent history, the Hapsburgs.

TRIANGLE PHOTO SERVICE

OPERA HOUSE, VIENNA

Expansion under the Hapsburgs: 1273-1547. Rudolph of Hapsburg, who had been elected Emperor in 1273, challenged Ottokar's claim to the lands which had once been controlled by Emperor Frederick II. While Rudolph acted in the name of the Empire, it is probable that he coveted the lands for himself and his heirs. An imperial ban was placed on Ottokar, who, unlike his Babenberg prede-

MALLNITZ, SURROUNDED BY THE ANKOGEL MOUNTAIN GROUP

cessors, could not maintain himself against the ill-will of the Emperor. In 1276 he submitted to Rudolph and surrendered the duchies of Austria, Styria, and Carinthia. The duchies were administered as imperial dependencies until Dec. 27, 1282, when the Emperor's sons, Albert and Rudolph, were invested with Austria and Styria. Carinthia passed temporarily out of Hapsburg control. Several members continued to rule jointly in the lands which made up Austria, since primogeniture was not yet a Hapsburg family rule. Several of Albert's sons became sovereigns in Austria after Albert's election as Emperor in 1298. While the Hapsburgs did not yet dominate the imperial office, in the struggle for that crown Hapsburg attention tended to be distracted from Austrian interests and problems. Rudolph IV tried to free the duchy from the Empire and did not refrain from a contest with the Empire to secure an electorate for Austria. When this was not granted in the Golden Bull of 1356, Rudolph claimed the title of archduke and declared Hapsburg lands indivisible. Neither the principles nor the title was immediately assumed by his successors. By founding the University of Vienna in 1365, Rudolph IV earned a lasting place in history. During the fourteenth century Hapsburg sway was once more extended over Carinthia, while Tirol, Trieste, and part of Istria were added to their family domain.

Internal Dissension. Disorders attending family quarrels over the Hapsburg patrimony made Austrian history turbulent in the fifteenth century. Frederick III, the weak-minded and irresponsible Emperor elected in 1440, became regent of Austria. A revolt against him in favor of the minor,

Ladislaus, developed among the estates and elements of the nobility. Ulrich Eitzing, a commoner, organized armed resistance to the regent and seized Vienna in 1451. The higher aristocracy gradually replaced Eitzing's popular appeal. Ladislaus' majority was compromised by Ulrich's shadowy influence. Austria's internal convulsions signified the growing dissatisfaction with a feudal rule which advanced family prestige at the expense of national unity, prosperity, and peace. National unification, the foremost political trend of the later Middle Ages, was delayed in Austria by the political interest of its rulers in the moribund Empire. Late in the fifteenth century the Hapsburg family fortunes were at low ebb. All the significance of Frederick III's solemn proclamation of an Austrian archduchy in 1453 was lost by 1487 in the complete conquest of Austria, Styria, and Carinthia by Matthias Corvinus, King of Hungary.

Leadership in Europe. Austria and the Hapsburg future were assured only by the energy and capacity of Maximilian I (1459-1519), Frederick III's son. He was the founder of Hapsburg greatness in modern history and the restorer of the traditional base of their power in Austria. His subsequent marriage alliances and the rich inheritance of his heirs gave the Hapsburgs the leading role not only in German affairs, but in the history of the principal European nations. Maximilian's first task was to wrest the Austrian lands from the Hungarians, a feat accomplished by 1491. Diplomacy and war brought the Tirol and Gradisca under his sway. A higher sense of Austrian unity was furthered by incorporation in an Imperial Circle in 1512 and by meetings of

the provincial estates at Innsbruck in 1518. These centralizing measures were made necessary by the military threat
of the Ottoman Turks, already dangerously near Vienna. Yet
centralization of government did not proceed as far in Austria as it did in western European monarchies, and Austria
long remained a loose collection of lands held together only
by a common sovereign. Maximilian's marriage in 1477 to
Mary of Burgundy, only daughter of Charles the Bold, secured rich parts of the Netherlands for the Hapsburgs, thereby raising new political problems such as the control of
the Flemish estates and rivalry with France. From this time
until the eve of the Seven Years' War (1756-1763) French
opposition to Austria was virtually continuous. The Netherlands did not divert Maximilian from consolidating the
Hapsburg control of traditional Austrian holdings or from
laying claim to the Empire, for he succeeded his father as
Emperor in 1493. Too grandiose schemes and a fanciful,
chivalric idea of politics, plus those personal qualities which
had earned Maximilian the name of "the last of the knights,"
caused his own plans to fail. His attempts to centralize administration both in Austria and in the Empire were pursued energetically, but without success. Other shortcomings
of his reign included an Italian policy which wasted men
and treasure and antagonized the Venetians, whose assistance was indispensable against the Turks. Yet Maximilian,
following the example set in his own marriage, arranged
matches for his heirs that augmented the Hapsburg domains. His son, Philip the Fair, married Joanna the Mad,
heiress to the Spanish throne; the marriage of Maximilian's
grandson, Ferdinand, gave the Hapsburgs a claim on Bohemia and Hungary. After Maximilian's time the Hapsburgs controlled the Holy Roman Empire, Austria, Bohemia,
the Netherlands, Spain, and Spain's overseas possessions.
Charles V, Maximilian's grandson, who was elected Emperor in 1519, was the first Hapsburg to enjoy the world-
wide prestige of his house. Government in Austria was
exercised after 1521, however, by Charles' brother, Ferdinand I (1503-1564). On the death in 1526 of Louis II, King
of Bohemia and Hungary, Ferdinand laid claim to his titles.
Only by promising the Bohemian estates large concessions
did Ferdinand receive their assent to his rule. The Hungarian estates were recalcitrant and elected John Zápolya of
Transylvania, who threw in his lot with Suleiman the Magnificent and the Turkish power which was then dominant in
central Europe. Not until 1547 did Hungarian claimants of
the crown yield to Ferdinand; but by then Hungary had
fallen almost completely under Turkish rule, and even Ferdinand had to pay tribute for his small share of that country.

Reformation and Counter Reformation. While his
brother, Charles V, struggled to maintain orthodoxy in Germany, Ferdinand in general exercised the same Catholic
policy in Austria. Nevertheless, the number of Protestants
in Austria grew appreciably during his reign. At the Council
of Trent (1545-1563) Ferdinand advanced views favoring a
reconciliation of Protestants and Catholics, and hence he
approved the settlement made at Augsburg in 1555. The
following year he was elected Emperor. Ferdinand built
upon the centralizing reforms of Maximilian and provided
a number of administrative organs common to the various
lands, provinces, and kingdoms that made up Austria.
Among these organs were the Privy Council, to make important state and foreign policy decisions; the General Court
of Chancery, to execute these decisions; the Court Council
of War, to administer military affairs and supply; and
the Court Treasury, to handle finances. Centralization did
not avail, since primogeniture had not yet been accepted by

the Hapsburgs. Even before Ferdinand's death in 1564 the
Hapsburg lands were divided among his heirs. Maximilian
II, the eldest heir, ruled as Emperor and King of Hungary
and Bohemia from 1564 to 1576. Wars with the Turks and
the religious issue occupied his reign. Partly because his
uncle, Charles V, gave the Spanish patrimony to his own
son, Philip II, and partly because Maximilian had Protestant
inclinations, he reacted against the Catholic policy which
had been espoused by the Hapsburgs. Maximilian's leniency
toward the Protestants enabled the Austrian Reformation to
make great strides, and by the 1570's the majority of his
subjects were Protestants. Only political motives connected
with the European interests of the dynasty kept Maximilian
within the Catholic Church. In his reign a *de facto* religious
liberty prevailed, although it was presently terminated by
his successor, Rudolph II (1552-1612), whose views were
Catholic, but whose energies were taken up by his collections,
by interest in the arts, and by the patronage of learned men.
Toward the end of his life insanity weakened his grasp of
the government. Steps to reconvert the Protestants were pursued mainly by his brothers. Jesuits associated with the University of Graz supplied the spiritual leadership, while zealots
such as Melchior Khlesl preached with great success among
the peasants. By their measures Protestanism was soon placed
on the defensive in Austria.

Bohemian and Hungarian Unrest. The same policies
failed to convert Bohemia, Moravia, and Hungary, where
the Reformation had made deep inroads among the nobles
and the people. The Hungarian Protestants made common
cause with the Turks, while an alliance of Bohemian Protestants and the estates made ready to defend religious
and political liberty. At this crisis the prestige and power
of the Hapsburgs was placed in jeopardy by the manifest
insanity of Rudolph II. His brothers proposed that his
brother Matthias be recognized as head of the house, a solution which Rudolph rejected, although expediency eventually
made necessary a division of the Austrian lands between
them (1606-1608). A settlement was arranged by negotiation with the various estates, which naturally insisted upon
safeguards for their political rights and a recognition of
Protestantism. Freedom for certain Protestant sects and a
substantial amount of political autonomy were included in
the constitution which Rudolph granted to the Bohemians in
1609. Such concessions, however, were no longer able to
win over dissident subjects. The Counter Reformation had
been pushed in Austria to a point short of open warfare.
Both Protestants and Catholics formed leagues which, with
their foreign attachments and connections, threatened the
Hapsburg realm with civil war and armed intervention.
Bohemia grew increasingly restless, while the Hungarians,
under Bethlen Gábor, openly disputed Matthias' rule. This
state of internal tension, unrest, and rebellion gave rise to
the events culminating in the Thirty Years' War.

The Thirty Years' War: 1618-1648. After Matthias'
brief rule (1612-1619), the Hapsburg mantle fell upon Ferdinand II (1578-1637), who had been recognized as the heir
by a general family agreement in 1617. He at once antagonized the Bohemians by violations of the privileges granted
them in 1609. Attacks upon local autonomy and the rights
of the estates, as well as an energetic prosecution of the
Counter Reformation, provoked a rebellion. The Bohemian
Kingdom rejected the Hapsburgs in 1619 and elected the
Count Palatine of the Rhine as Frederick V, known as "the
Winter King." His reign was short, since Ferdinand's armies
defeated the Bohemians at the White Mountain on Nov. 8,
1620. A stern policy was pursued against the Bohemians;

lands of the rebellious nobility were confiscated; local autonomy was suppressed by a new constitution issued in 1627. Together with the political repression a free hand was provided the Jesuits to convert the Bohemians. The policy pursued against the Hungarians was not so harsh for various reasons: the Turkish danger; the strength of the rebel, Bethlen Gábor; and the fear of deeper involvement while the religious-political issue was acute in Germany. Out of these circumstances there developed the Hapsburg policy of centralizing the German and Bohemian lands while permitting a large degree of independence to the Hungarians.

Rise and Fall of Wallenstein. With the success of his arms and those of his allies, Ferdinand's prestige rose during the early course of the Thirty Years' War. A fateful dependence upon the military and organizing talents of Duke Albrecht von Wallenstein was a disturbing note. In recognition of valiant services before Vienna, when that city was threatened by Bethlen Gábor, and for other military exploits, Wallenstein had been entrusted in 1626 with the raising of an entire army. The Emperor's dependence upon Wallenstein became all the more clear when the military balance was upset in 1630 by the intervention of Gustavus Adolphus of Sweden on the Protestant side. To check the Swedes, Ferdinand had to give Wallenstein a free hand in military affairs. After Gustavus Adolphus' death in 1632, Wallenstein turned increasingly to projects for unifying Germany under his own rule. His vast political ambition, which never went beyond the stage of plotting and negotiation, aroused the suspicion of the Emperor. Wallenstein was charged with high treason and by imperial order was assassinated in 1634.

Setback to Hapsburg Prestige. In the long stalemate which marked the subsequent course of the Thirty Years' War, the Hapsburgs could regret the enmity between their house and France, because the Bourbons joined the Protestant side in 1635. When, after protracted negotiations at Münster and Westphalia, peace was eventually made in 1648, the Hapsburg prestige in Europe had greatly diminished. Imperial territory was ceded to France, and the house of Bourbon, guided by Richelieu and Mazarin, was in the ascendancy. Increasingly after 1648 the Hapsburgs turned to their dynastic holdings rather than to Germany as a source of power. The end of the Thirty Years' War rapidly curtailed the international rule of the Hapsburgs. Various administrative changes under Ferdinand II had helped to establish the distinction between the imperial, or German, concerns and the dynastic, or Austrian, concerns of the ruling family. It became the lot of Ferdinand III (1608-1657), who became Emperor in 1637, to bring the war with France and Sweden to an end and in internal affairs to moderate his father's stern policy of centralizing and Catholicizing the realm. After the Peace of Westphalia, the individual states were so fortified in their rights and privileges that projects similar to those of Maximilian I were impossible. Hapsburg authority was momentarily checked, both in the Empire and in their own lands. It was never regained in the Empire, which from 1648 until its dissolution in 1806 remained a paradox of history: a government based on a constitutional system but lacking both sovereignty and an administration. From the Empire the Hapsburgs were forced to turn to their own archduchy of Austria and their hereditary lands, making these the basis of their power. Austria's fortunes and those of the Empire remained connected, however, because the Hapsburgs were loath to give up the prestige associated with the Emperor's title. With one exception, Charles VII (1697-1745), all subsequent emperors were of the Hapsburg or Hapsburg-Lorraine house. In both diplomacy and war the resources of the Empire were derived primarily from the lands grouped around the Hapsburgs' traditional center, the Archduchy of Austria.

Victories Over Turkey. Almost continuous warfare with the Turks and with Louis XIV of France marked the reign of Leopold I (1640-1705), who came to the throne in 1658. Yet he was the first who might be said to have ruled "Austria," since his success over the Turks and the defense of his rights against Louis XIV gave rise to greater political

Fenstergrün Castle with its old and new towers

unity and prestige. In 1683 the great siege of Vienna by the Turks was raised by the intervention of a Polish army led by King John Sobieski. From this time, the Turks were thrown upon the defensive, and one of the Hapsburgs' greatest projects became the relief of central Europe from Turkish rule. In thus meeting and overcoming the challenge of the Turks, the Hapsburgs served Europe's cause. Their own political gains were not incidental aspects of this crusade, however. After the capture of Budapest, the Hungarians, at the Diet of Pressburg in 1687, recognized the Hapsburgs as Hungarian kings and secured the succession of their male line. By 1699 the Turks were glad to make the Peace of Carlowitz and to cede Transylvania, territory between the Theiss and Danube rivers, and part of Slovenia. A leading part in these Turkish wars was taken by Prince Eugene of Savoy, who later distinguished himself in the wars with Louis XIV. Since the Empire was drawn into the numerous coalitions which tried to preserve the balance of power against Louis XIV, the rulers of Austria had great interest in European affairs. To restrain Louis, the Empire participated in warfare which was virtually continuous after 1667.

War of the Spanish Succession: 1701-1714. Even the Peace of Ryswick in 1697, which was a defeat for France, did not restrain Louis' ambition when he was presented with an opportunity to add Spain to the Bourbon possessions. In violation of his promises, Louis acted upon the will of Charles II, the deceased Spanish ruler, to claim Spain for his grandson. To prevent so formidable a concentration of power in Bourbon hands, a great coalition arose in 1701. In the subsequent War of the Spanish Succession, Austrian arms and leaders took a notable part. The English Duke of Marlborough and Prince Eugene won victories over the French at Blenheim and Malplaquet, but neither battle was decisive enough to unlock the French barrier fortresses. To the resulting military stalemate were added complications arising from the death of the Emperor Joseph I, who had ruled from 1705 to 1711. His younger brother, Charles, laid claim to the Austrian-Spanish inheritance, for in 1703 he had been proclaimed the lawful heir of Charles II of Spain in place of Philip V, the Bourbon grandson of Louis XIV. Since Charles proved obstinate about his Spanish claims, the maritime powers, Great Britain and Holland, were faced with the possible revival of the sixteenth century Hapsburg empire. The plan to combine Hapsburg authority in Germany, central Europe, and Spain seemed likely to create a state of affairs as distasteful to Austria's allies as the combination of Spain and France under the Bourbons, which they were then at war to prevent. This problem of Hapsburg succession, as well as domestic issues and political intrigue, inclined Great Britain to the peace signed at Utrecht in 1713. With reluctance Charles eventually yielded his Spanish claims and was crowned Emperor. As Charles VI he was memorable principally for the preparation of the Pragmatic Sanction. At the Peace of Rastatt in 1714 Charles gave up part of Alsace, but received the Spanish Netherlands, Naples, Milan, Sardinia, and part of Tuscany. Thenceforth the Hapsburgs had strong interests in Italy, while in western Europe they continually sought to link up the Netherlands with their older possessions in Austria.

Aftermath of the War. Charles VI's reign from 1711 to 1740, which had begun so inauspiciously, was dogged by misfortune. The Peace of Passarowitz with the Turks in 1718 merely rounded out annexations begun at Carlowitz in 1699. Some territorial gains were made at the expense of the Duke of Savoy, who ceded Sicily to the Emperor in exchange for Sardinia. Control of Sicily was short-lived, for Charles's support of the Saxon candidate for the Polish crown led to serious reverses. Without the support of Great Britain or Holland, Charles was not strong enough to defeat Savoy, France, and Spain. As a result, Naples, Sicily, Tuscany, Novara, and Tortona were lost; and only the duchies of Parma and Piacenza solaced the Hapsburg for his rash intervention in Polish and Italian affairs. In the Turkish wars the Austrian reverses threatened to undo the successes of Leopold I.

Bosnia, Serbia, and the two Wallachias were lost; and at the Peace of Belgrade in 1739 the Hapsburg ruler accepted severe limitations upon the Austro-Turkish frontier.

The Pragmatic Sanction. Before Charles VI's accession in 1711 a number of agreements had been reached conferring the Hapsburg succession upon the male members of that house. Joseph and Charles, the sons of Leopold I, had agreed to divide the Austrian and Spanish lands between them. International complications foiled Charles's hopes with respect to Spain; on Joseph's death he set to work to regulate anew the line of succession. All previous arrangements had been dynastic. Charles proposed to make them constitutional, that is, to secure the consent of the various estates in his realm. In 1713 Charles began to win their consent to the principle of primogeniture and, if male heirs were lacking, undivided inheritance by his eldest daughter. With the death of Charles's son in 1716, and for want of another male issue, this arrangement for the inheritance, known as the Pragmatic Sanction, began to occupy all his energies. All the important estates were pledged in some degree to honor this principle, and the assent of the foreign powers to it then became the first object of Charles's foreign policy. At length, secure in the belief that the Pragmatic Sanction was established in the constitutional law of his lands and accepted in international law by treaties, Charles VI died peacefully. He was succeeded in 1740 by his daughter, Maria Theresa. The remark of Prince Eugene that Charles's energies might have been better spent on the army than on paper guarantees was prophetic.

Reign of Maria Theresa: 1740-1780. While the estates recognized Maria Theresa and her husband, Francis of Lorraine, whom she had married in 1736, the powers of Europe did not. Bavaria, Saxony, and Spain at once laid claim to parts of the Hapsburg lands, while Prussia, moved by the energies of its young ruler, Frederick II (the Great), seized Silesia in a rapid invasion. This was the opening act in a series of hostilities over the Austrian succession.

LEOPOLDSBERG ON THE DANUBE RIVER

MELK, FAMOUS BENEDICTINE ABBEY ON THE DANUBE RIVER

Wars of the Austrian Succession. The Austrian defeat at Mollwitz encouraged other nations, and, in the First War of the Austrian Succession, Prussia, France, Bavaria, Spain, Saxony, and Sardinia attacked Austria, which was supported only by the maritime powers. At the Peace of Breslau in 1742 Maria Theresa ceded Silesia to Frederick. The war against his allies continued, and Austrian successes brought Prussia into the war once more. At Dresden in 1745 the cession of Silesia was again confirmed. A general end to hostilities, which eventually found France the most important Austrian opponent, did not come until the Peace of Aix-la-Chapelle in 1748. That Austria lost only Parma, Guastalla, and Piacenza in addition to Silesia can be attributed to the diplomacy of Maria Theresa and her ministers, and to the strength of the Austrian army at the end of the war. Changing relations among the great powers during Maria Theresa's forty-year reign contributed to a reversal of Austria's traditional foreign policy. France and Austria were being placed on the defensive by the expansionist policies of Great Britain and Prussia: the British tormented France in the colonial field; the Prussians irritated Austria upon the Continent.

Count Kaunitz, Maria Theresa's foreign minister, recommended and carried out a policy of alliance with France. Treaties confirmed in 1756 and 1757 brought to an end the historic rivalry of the Hapsburg and Bourbon dynasties.

The Seven Years' War. The alliance made possible the enlargement of the imperialist struggle between France and Great Britain, which had already broken out in America in the Ohio River valley. The result was the Seven Years' War (1756-1763). Since the British had made an alliance with Prussia, Frederick the Great was obliged to fight both Austria and France, as well as Russia, which presently joined in the war. This preponderance of arms and the improvement of the Austrian army saved Maria Theresa from a disastrous invasion like that of Silesia in 1740. After successfully defending Prague in 1756, the Austrians were overwhelmed on Dec. 4, 1757, at Leuthen in a battle which was a classic of Frederick's military art. In other hard-fought battles, such as at Torgau and Hochkirch, the Austrian army showed to better advantage. No Austrian leader proved the equal of Frederick, whose skillful conduct of the war in the face of great odds earned him the title of "The Great." Peace between Prussia and Austria was made at Hubertusburg in 1763 without any territorial alterations.

First Partition of Poland. On the death of her husband, Francis I, in 1765, Maria Theresa made her eldest son her co-ruler in the Hapsburg lands; he also was elected Emperor as Joseph II. Without success he pursued the policy so fascinating to the Hapsburgs since the Peace of Rastatt, namely, expansion at Bavarian expense. Diplomatic and military pressure by Frederick the Great blocked Joseph's ambitions, especially since his mother was unwilling to enter into new struggles with the Prussian king. The Polish partition momentarily satisfied the Hapsburg desire for more territory. As compensation for Russia's gains at Turkish expense, and as a solution for the rivalries among the eastern monarchs, Austria participated in the first partition of Poland in 1772 and received Zips, Galicia, and Lodomeria. The frontiers were also rounded out by acquiring Bukovina and part of Moldavia from Turkey in 1774-1775.

Internal Reforms. Maria Theresa undertook very extensive internal reforms, characterized chiefly by steady centralization and Germanization of the Hapsburg lands. She was the first ruler to break through the laws, customs, and particularisms of "Austria" and bring the Hapsburg authority to bear upon the people. A bureaucracy staffed principally by Germans was expanded; functions previously exercised by estates were entrusted to new agencies in Vienna. Policies for the Netherlands, Italy, and Hungary, as well as Bohemia and Austria, were formulated after 1760 in the new State Council. Other new organs were established for finance (*Hofkammer*) and for commerce (*Kommerzienrat*), while existing organs for military administration were strengthened. In the interests of absolutism the independence and privileges of the Catholic Church were curtailed, even by a monarch as pious as Maria Theresa. An antipapal sentiment known as Febronianism was the basis for measures establishing the government's interest in religious matters.

"Enlightened Despotism." Joseph II succeeded his mother in 1780 and embarked upon an even more vigorous program of enlightened reforms, centralization, and religious liberty. Financial and political administration was again reorganized to promote centralization; historic and traditional political rights were canceled in the interest of expediency and efficiency. Joseph's efforts to change the character of his nation by imposing reforms from above earned him a place among the "enlightened despots." Urban government, the judicial system, the legal codes, and taxation all felt the reorganizing hand of the monarch. Serfdom was abolished in Bohemia, Moravia, and Silesia in 1781; papal bulls were made subject to government scrutiny; appeals to Rome were forbidden; marriage was made a civil contract; numerous religious orders were dissolved. These reforms were by no means acceptable to Joseph's subjects. Hungarian and Bohemian resentment deepened because of the Germanizing tendencies of the program, while in the Netherlands the monarchial violations of the constitution provoked an armed rebellion in 1789. With an empty treasury and facing growing unrest and open revolt, Joseph at last yielded to his counsellors a year before his death in 1790 and moderated the ambitious reforms which had made him unique among Austria's rulers. Upon his brother, Leopold II (1747-1792), fell the responsibility for restoring tranquility at home and adopting a policy toward the French Revolution. As Grand Duke of Tuscany, Leopold had been an enlightened and reform-minded ruler, but the disturbed condition of Austria and the uneasy balance of power in Europe inclined him toward caution when he took over Joseph's au-

thority. Internal unrest was calmed by terminating virtually all of his brother's reforms. Restrictions on the estates were eased; Latin in place of German once more became the official language in Hungary. Only the Church remained subject to the strict control of the Hapsburg central government. But Leopold's timid and cautious policy toward France relieved the revolutionaries there of the fear of Austrian intervention. When war broke out among the powers, it was on terms imposed by France.

Coalition Against France. By 1792 both Austria and Prussia were aware of the dangers to monarchical absolutism in the program of the French Revolution. Leopold's sister, Marie Antoinette, the Queen of France, had secretly been importuning him for aid. While Prussia and Austria discussed intervention, France prepared to act. The French revolutionary government's declaration of war against Austria on April 20, 1792, began the wars of the French Revolution and of Napoleon which were to last, with brief interruptions, until 1815. Leopold's death placed great responsibilities upon his son, Francis II, who was destined to preside over the founding of the new Austrian Empire in 1804 and the dissolution of the Holy Roman Empire in 1806, when he became Francis I of Austria. Prosecution of the war against France was handicapped by suspicion between Austria and her ally, Prussia, especially over the latter's dealings with Russia for a renewed assault upon Poland. So it came about that Austria was excluded from the second Polish partition in 1792. Austrian military fortunes were at low ebb in this year. Under Dumouriez the French invaded the Austrian Netherlands and won a victory at Jemappes on Nov. 6, 1792. Only the formation of the First Coalition in 1793 rescued the Austrians. With new allies and bolstered by British money, the Austrians defeated the French at Neerwinden in March 1793, but not so severely as to permit the invasion of France. The allies, under an Austrian leader, Prince Josias of Saxe-Coburg, settled down to take the French barrier fortresses. New French armies organized by Carnot in 1793 held the allies at bay at Hondschoote and Wattignies. After Prussia concluded peace at Basel in 1795, Austria carried on the war virtually alone. Yet, in co-operation with Prussia and Russia, Austria partitioned Poland for the third time in 1795, receiving West Galicia. In the war against France the desultory fighting along the Rhine was relieved only by the brilliant campaign of Archduke Charles of Austria against Moreau and Jourdan in 1796. With inferior numbers the Archduke succeeded in driving the French over the Rhine by maneuvers which have secured his reputation as a great soldier and strategist.

The Napoleonic Wars. The real decision was reached in 1796 and 1797 in Italy, where Austrian armies opposed a young and yet untried general, Napoleon Bonaparte. His victories at Arcola and Rivoli shook the Austrian cause and led to an armistice which was the basis for the Peace of Campo Formio. Austria gave up the Netherlands as well as the duchies of Milan and Mantua to France. Almost all of Venice, including Venetian Istria and Dalmatia, was obtained in exchange. Austria also consented to French annexations up to the west bank of the Rhine, a cession arranged at Rastatt in the same year.

Campaigns in Germany and Italy. These terms were disputed by the War of the Second Coalition, which, owing to Napoleon's embarrassment in the Egyptian campaign, opened auspiciously for the allies in 1798. Russia and Great Britain joined Austria in attempting to improve the terms of Campo Formio and redress the balance of power in Europe. Their military forces, after meeting some initial successes, were destroyed by the brilliant strategy of Napoleon and his marshals. The principal seats of the war were in Germany and Italy. Italy was the scene of the Austrian defeat at Marengo in 1800. This blow at the Second Coalition was capped by another at Hohenlinden in Germany. There an Austrian army, bogged down by mud and weather, was cut to pieces by Napoleon's marshals. Once more Austria made peace, and at Lunéville in 1801 the provisions made earlier at Campo Formio were confirmed. In consequence of Napoleon's assumption of an imperial title in 1804, Francis II in the same year proclaimed himself Emperor of Austria and thus, for the first time, provided a common title for the lands grouped together under the authority of the Archduke of Austria. Francis' unilateral action, flouting the law of the Holy Roman Empire, of which he was the chief executive, foreshadowed the breakup of that ancient state by Napoleon. There was to be one more military adventure before this could be accomplished. In 1805 Austria joined Great Britain and Russia in the war which followed the short-lived peace made at Lunéville and at Amiens in 1802.

Battles of Ulm and Austerlitz. Since 1800 significant reforms and reorganizations had improved the Austrian army. It was still not a match for Napoleon, especially since its best commander, Archduke Charles, was dispatched to Italy, leaving Mack von Leiberich in Germany to meet Napoleon's intended advance upon Vienna. Mack's defensive strategy soon foundered, and at Ulm in 1805 his army was badly defeated. What remained of the Austrian army joined with the advancing Russians to defend Vienna. At Austerlitz in 1805 Napoleon again won a decisive victory, and the coalition raised against him was again broken up.

End of the Holy Roman Empire. Another humiliating peace was forced upon Austria at Pressburg on Dec. 26, 1805. All German and Italian holdings were relinquished, and Austria was forced to witness the dissolution of the Empire which for centuries had been a source of Hapsburg pride. Under Napoleon's protection sixteen German princes formed the Confederation of the Rhine, thus making France rather than Austria the guarantor of Germany's political order. On Aug. 6, 1806, Francis renounced the imperial title, and the thousand-year-old Holy Roman Empire stood dissolved.

Renewal of Hostilities. Until 1809 internal reforms, military reorganization, and the awakening of national hostility to Napoleon occupied Austrian leaders, especially Count Stadion, the foreign minister, and Archduke Charles, the war minister. The degree of nationalism awakened in Austria was less than in other countries, but popular affection for the dynasty and its cause was undoubtedly strong after 1809. Stadion favored a renewal of the war against Napoleon, a policy seconded by Metternich, then Austrian ambassador at Paris. With official encouragement Andreas Hofer, a Tirolean patriot, had begun to resist the Bavarians, to whom the Tirol had been ceded at Pressburg in 1805. Hofer's cause was abetted by the success of Stadion's war party, which insisted that Napoleon's discomfiture in Spain was an opportunity not to be overlooked. Austrian hopes were greatly encouraged by Archduke Charles's victory over Napoleon at Aspern, May 21-22, 1809, one of the Emperor's most serious defeats. Yet, with the resources of skill and energy so characteristic of him, Napoleon wrested the Archduke's laurels away by defeating him at Wagram on July 6. The disastrous end to the war brought about Stadion's retirement, and the conduct of foreign affairs after Oct. 9,

Riegersburg Castle, Graz, Styria

1809, was in Metternich's hands. The Peace of Schönbrunn on Oct. 14, 1809, imposed severe losses: Salzburg, the Inn district, and West Galicia were ceded. Emperor Francis, with disdain for the sacrifices made by his loyal subject, Andreas Hofer, permitted his capture by the French, who subsequently shot him.

The "Age of Metternich": 1815-1848. After 1809 Austria's destinies were guided by Metternich, who pursued an astute policy of building Austria's strength while preserving amicable but ever vigilant relations with France. Metternich proved to be the most distinguished minister ever to serve Austria, and under his direction Austria played a paramount role in European affairs. As a symbol of his country's friendship for France, Metternich arranged the marriage of Marie Louise, Francis' daughter, to Napoleon. No permanent affection of the Hapsburg house for the Corsican was thereby established. Partly to conceal the Austrian military preparations, Metternich consented to an alliance on March 14, 1812, guaranteeing Austrian participation in war against Russia. Some 30,000 Austrian troops fought on the side of Napoleon in 1812, and when most of them had been extracted from the disasters of that year Metternich returned to a policy of neutrality. Until summer Metternich bided his time, while both Napoleon and his enemies sought to impress him with their strength. Metternich's diplomacy was served by the virtual stalemate in the war, which made Austrian intervention the decisive factor. It is doubtful whether Metternich would ever have joined Napoleon, though in negotiations and at the farcical Congress of Prague in July 1813 he permitted Napoleon to think that he might do so.

Napoleon's Defeat at Leipzig. Meanwhile Metternich had decided to enter the Reichenbach agreements, which were the basis of the new coalition. At the expiration of the summer armistice on Aug. 10, Austria joined the coalition which included Great Britain and Sweden as well as the eastern monarchies. An Austro-Russian army was beaten at Dresden, but the allied powers eventually broke Napoleon's resistance at Leipzig ("The Battle of the Nations") on Oct. 16-18, 1813. Napoleon's military skill prolonged the war, but at length hostilities were halted temporarily by the Peace of Paris on May 30, 1814.

Congress of Vienna. Austrian influence at the Congress of Vienna, September 1814-July 1815, was insured by Metternich's eminence in diplomacy and by the leading role he had taken in arranging relations among the great powers, as in

MARKET STREET, FELDKIRCH, VORARLBERG

the Treaty of Chaumont in March 1814. Through the Quadruple Alliance arranged Nov. 20, 1815, Metternich established the policy of stabilizing European affairs by the action of the great powers in concert. Austria emerged from the Congress of Vienna as the leading power in both Germany and Italy. Although the Austrian Netherlands were surrendered, Venetia and part of Dalmatia were obtained in exchange. Because Metternich opposed the re-establishment of the Holy Roman Empire, a weak German confederation under Austrian control was set up instead. In what is called the "Age of Metternich" (1815-1848) Austria exerted for the last time a controlling influence in European affairs.

Suppression of Liberalism. After 1815 Metternich kept close watch on liberal and revolutionary tendencies in Europe, and by summoning congresses of the great powers he exercised his policy of armed intervention in behalf of the restoration governments. By stabilizing Europe he hoped to maintain a tranquil Austria. Although he underestimated the strength of both liberalism and nationalism, he rightly understood that both would disturb the political structure of Austria, with its numerous nationalities. Metternich maintained a rigid supervision of German political life, and through the Carlsbad Decrees of 1819 he attempted to regiment the German universities. His Balkan policy was conservative, and he tried to remain on friendly terms with Great Britain as a counterweight to Russia. For the police

and spy system in Austria, and for the severance of cultural and intellectual ties with the rest of Germany, Francis I, rather than Metternich, was mainly responsible. Metternich was not against reform under conservative auspices, but his projects were opposed by Francis and by such ministers as Kolowrat-Liebsteinsky. The governmental changes made in Francis I's regime were in the interest of absolutism. Common administrative and judicial organs were created for Bohemia, Austria, and the Italian territories, while a common economic policy was also upheld. None of these new organs had any interlocking connection, and public affairs continued to be exercised in a ponderous and inefficient way. Only the clumsiness of the Austrian government made its absolute principles bearable to the people. Yet the government tried to suppress new ideas and to imprison political malcontents. That Metternich recognized the shortcomings of an outright police regime is now generally conceded by historians. In Hungary, despite many previous manifestations of dissatisfaction with arbitrary rule, Francis I governed from 1813 until 1825 without convoking the Diet. It is not surprising that an intended reorganization of provincial administration failed.

Unrest Among Minorities. Ferdinand I, a weak-willed, incompetent ruler, succeeded Francis in 1835. The internal condition of Austria grew worse, and there were signs abroad that the system of Metternich was coming to an end. Dissolution of the reactionary governments in Europe was not far off, and Ferdinand's Conference of State, organized in 1836, served only as a forum for the disagreements between Metternich and the other ministers. Opposition to the Hapsburgs was organizing along national as well as liberal lines. This was true in Hungary of the party led by Count István Széchenyi, while in Bohemia a new nationalism based on Czech literature, language, and culture was being promoted. Among the south Slavs, the cry of "Illyrianism" was raised. Middle-class circles in Austria, despite ties of language and nationality with the Hapsburgs, began to stir under the repressive measures and to clamor for a liberal government. Among the peasants—and Austria was still an overwhelmingly agrarian nation—there was unrest over serfdom.

Revolt and Reform. The revolution of 1848, at first inspired by the uprising in Paris, was begun by Lajos Kossuth, who on March 3 urged the Hungarian Diet to revolt. Popular uprisings at Prague and Vienna followed within ten days, and these manifestations of ill will encouraged Metternich's aristocratic opposition to demand his resignation. After Metternich's withdrawal from the government on March 13, there was a flurry of liberal reforms: the end of censorship, a promise of a national constitution, a new government in Bohemia, and the end of serfdom in Galicia. Publication of the new constitution in April only brought about new remonstrances because of its monarchical origin and the limited suffrage. Great turbulence continued in Vienna, for the army and national guard were of dubious loyalty and none of the new liberal ministers enjoyed popular confidence. The imperial family withdrew to Innsbruck, leaving Archduke John as regent. Plans for establishing a popular monarchy were set in motion, and on July 22, 1848, delegates to the first Austrian parliament convened. Abolition of serfdom, one of the basic social issues, was accomplished Sept. 7, 1848.

Meanwhile the counterrevolution had been started by loyal elements of the imperial army. In Prague, General Windisch-Grätz had won control by June. On July 25 Radetzky badly defeated the Sardinian armies at Custozza, thus preventing the liberal and national uprising in Italy which the House of Savoy had hoped to lead. Clever manipulations, in which Slavic and Hungarian issues were opposed, broke the united front against the Hapsburgs. Yet in Vienna the German population showed its sympathy for the Hungarian bid for independence by interfering with troop movements. A popular revolt succeeded in taking over the capital on Oct. 7, and once more the court was forced to flee. A Croatian army under Josip Jelačić od Bužima, who had rejoined the Hapsburg cause out of distrust of the Hungarians, combined with Windisch-Grätz' forces in laying siege to the city, which surrendered Oct. 31. A reactionary government under Prince Felix von Schwarzenberg then prepared to deal with the revolutionary movement.

Reign of Francis Joseph: 1848-1916. To stabilize the regime, Ferdinand II was urged to abdicate. On Dec. 2, 1848, he was succeeded by his eighteen-year-old nephew, Francis Joseph I, but Schwarzenberg was the real head of the government from 1848 to 1852. To quiet the clamor for reforms and the transformation of Austria into a more modern and unified state, he published a constitution on Mar. 4, 1849. Meanwhile a Hungarian republic had been proclaimed, and, when Austrian armies failed to suppress it, Russian aid was sought at Schwarzenberg's insistence. Russian troops overran Hungary. Kossuth, the Hungarian patriot leader, escaped to America. In Italy the Austrian army was everywhere victorious over Sardinia, which was still at war to exploit the confusion of the revolutionary period. Without further opposition in Hungary or Italy, Schwarzenberg was able to press his solution of the German question at the Frankfurt Parliament, namely, a united Germany under Austrian leadership. While this plan was not successful, Schwarzenberg did momentarily check Prussian ambitions. At Olmütz in November 1850, Prussia gave up plans to unify Germany and re-entered the German Confederation, which was once more dominated by Austria.

Diplomatic and Military Reverses. Schwarzenberg's death in 1852 deprived Austria of his able leadership, without which Francis Joseph embarked on a personal rule. With Alexander von Bach as his minister, the constitution of 1849 was withdrawn and restrictions were placed on both the people and the press. Clerical influence multiplied, and in 1855 a new concordat gave a privileged place to the Catholic Church. Francis Joseph's conduct of foreign affairs proved vacillating and weak. Austrian neutrality in the Crimean War (1854-1856) alienated Russia and displeased the western powers. A diplomatic defeat at the Congress of Paris in 1856 was followed in 1859 by military reverses in Italy, where France and Sardinia combined to defeat Austria, thus paving the way for Italian unification. By the treaty of Villafranca in 1859 Austria lost Lombardy; the people of Parma, Modena, Tuscany, and the Romagna voted in plebiscites for union with Sardinia. Austria's role as an Italian power was drawing to an end, while in Germany the Prussians were reviving their own plans for German unification. Austrian leadership in German affairs was virtually brought to an end by Bismarck when he was able to prevent the King of Prussia from attending the congress called by Francis Joseph to meet at Frankfurt in 1863.

Internal Dissatisfaction. These failures had already given rise to dissatisfaction, especially in Hungary, with Francis Joseph's absolute rule. The "October Diploma" (Oct. 20, 1860), which divided legislative power between an Austrian *Reichsrat* and the various estates, did not please any party. Austria's governmental problems were steadily becoming more complex because of the divergent interests of the subject nationalities and the reluctance of the Austrians to concede autonomy to them. From the moderate federalism of the "October Diploma," the government swung back to centralization under the liberal guidance of Anton von Schmerling. His government issued a constitution on Feb. 21, 1861, providing for a bicameral legislature while diminishing the role of the estates. A restricted suffrage enabled the Germans and landed classes to dominate this government. Slavic, Hungarian, and Italian elements attacked the constitution for jeopardizing their national liberties and governmental aspirations. Ferencz Deák led the resistance in Hungary, where the Diet rejected the new constitution. By 1863 the Czechs had also withdrawn their delegation from the imperial government, and Austria's experiment with a liberal, centralized government was near an end. In 1865 the constitution was suspended, and the Austrian government drifted back to its traditional structure. Dissatisfaction was still very great in Hungary. Events abroad hastened the solution favorable to the Hungarian interest.

Seven Weeks' War. Since 1848 Austria and Prussia had been rivals in planning to unify Germany. As victors in the war with Denmark in 1864, they had been left with the responsibility of administering the Elbe duchies, Schleswig and Holstein. Under Bismarck's direction, Prussia moved swiftly toward a showdown with Austria, and the Elbe duchies afforded the pretext for war. The struggle for power in Germany was settled by the Seven Weeks' War, in which Prussia was overwhelmingly victorious. In what was actually a civil war among the German states, the Prussians soundly defeated the Austrians at Königgrätz (Sadowa) on July 3, 1866, and won the right to reorganize Germany. Austria defeated Prussia's ally, Italy, at Custozza and Lissa; but the Austrian defeat in the north led to the cession of Venetia to Italy. In 1866, therefore, Austria ceased to be a major influence in both Germany and in Italy, long traditional seats of Hapsburg power.

Birth of the Dual Monarchy. These circumstances naturally influenced the constitutional struggle and enabled the Hungarian leaders, Ferencz Deák and Gyula Andrássy, to obtain concessions. Friedrich von Beust, who became minister-president in 1867, believed that a compromise with the Hungarians was necessary. The result was the *Ausgleich* (compromise) of 1867, which made Austria a dual monarchy, Austria-Hungary, the two realms having a common monarch. These two parts were designated as Cisleithania (Austria) and Transleithania (Hungary). Foreign affairs, war, and commerce were handled jointly; monetary contributions were apportioned; and every ten years the financial, customs, and commercial relations were to be revised. Most Austrian liberals approved the compromise with Hungary, especially since a number of enactments in 1867 and 1868 made all citizens equal before the law, freed office-holders from religious tests, and provided for state-controlled education and civil marriage. Conservatives, clericals, and Slavs were conciliated to some degree by allowing the provincial diets to exercise reserved powers. Ministerial responsibility and an enlarged role for the supreme court were also concessions giving Austria the appearance of a constitutional state. Military and financial reforms completed the reorganization.

Disorders in Bohemia. Neither the belated reforms nor the compromise itself solved the fundamental problem of Austria, namely, the relation of the non-Germanic subject people to what was essentially a German government. The Slavic resentment deepened because of favored treatment accorded the Hungarians. The Italian provinces raised anew the cry for unification with Italy. The Czechs were the first to reject the compromise of 1867, for the following year the Bohemian deputies denied the authority of the Imperial Council. Disorders occurred throughout the Bohemian crown lands and even in Dalmatia in 1868 and 1869. Count Eduard von Taaffe, as minister-president, was not strong enough to achieve public tranquility, nor could his immediate successors find the formula which would satisfy the Czechs, who demanded recognition of their national rights. Amid these trying domestic issues, the Franco-Prussian War of 1870-1871 added new complications. There was an Austrian war party which was anxious to avenge the defeat of 1866 and renew

able to Austria because of the clash of Austrian and Russian interests in the Balkans. These were temporarily reconciled by the League of Three Emperors, organized by Bismarck in 1881 and renewed in 1884; but by 1887 tension between Austria and Russia had increased to such a degree because of the Bulgarian crisis that Bismarck was hard put to prevent war. Except for Russia, the other powers were on good terms with Austria. Italy joined Austria and Germany in 1882, creating the Triple Alliance, which was renewed in 1887. Conventions made with Great Britain and Italy in the same year pledged Austria to maintain the Mediterra-

LAKE ACHEN IN THE TIROL

Austrian prestige in both Germany and Italy. Beust and the military represented this view. Gyula Andrássy opposed intervention or participation, and Austria-Hungary remained neutral. Meanwhile continuous attempts were made to solve the problem of Bohemian autonomy; but an ambitious proposal of Count Karl Hohenwart, minister-president, and Albert Eberhard Schäffle, his minister of commerce, that Bohemia be given a status comparable to that of Hungary was rejected in 1871 by Francis Joseph. Only toward the Poles were the Austrians willing to make concessions; after 1871 Galicia was administered without central interference.

Successes of Andrássy. Relations with Russia and the new German Empire were handled skilfully by Andrássy, the foreign minister. Monarchs of the three countries agreed in 1872 on the preservation of peace and on the settlement of their interests in the Near East. When trouble developed between Russia and Turkey, Andrássy arranged with Russia in 1876-1877 for Austrian occupation of Bosnia and Herzegovina, small Turkish provinces adjacent to Austria. A mandate to administer these provinces under the suzerainty of Turkey was granted to Austria at the Congress of Berlin in 1878, but there was sharp fighting in Bosnia before Austrian rule was established. An alliance with Germany, signed Oct. 7, 1879, capped Andrássy's handling of foreign policy. Bismarck took the initiative in arranging the agreement, but Andrássy's conviction that Austria should develop a closer attachment to Germany became the new basis of Austrian diplomacy. The German alliance became increasingly valu-

nean *status quo,* a provision aimed wholly at possible Russian aggression. Both Serbia and Romania were within the Austrian orbit in the 1880's, and Austria enjoyed apparent security in the Balkans.

Slavic and Socialist Opposition. Domestic issues continued to be disturbing, however. Count Taaffe's ministry (1879-1893), which enjoyed support among conservatives, peasants, and the bureaucracy, granted concessions to the Czechs in the use of their language and in university education. The German and liberal parties, which represented the centralizing interests, were at this time divided over the question of Austria's future as a multinational state and also alarmed by the rise of anti-Semitism, which was being propagated in Vienna by Karl Lueger. This manifestation of social unrest was further complicated by the strengthening of socialist views among the urban workers. Without a part in the government or the legislature, the workers could make their opposition known only by riots and disorders. Settlement of the Czech issue was made even more difficult by the emergence of the Young Czech party, an intransigent group with extreme conceptions of Bohemian rights and autonomy. Without Czech support, Taaffe was obliged to turn increasingly to the German elements for backing. No solution was reached in Bohemia, and unrest was so great there that Prague was placed in a state of siege in 1893. Taaffe's ministry fell in that year over the issue of suffrage, when he proposed universal suffrage in place of the four-class electorate as a last attempt to reconcile the Slavic and socialist opposition to Austrian authority. Since the Emperor had considered him a bulwark against a parliamentary regime, Taaffe was dismissed; but the suffrage issue could not be ignored, and in 1896 some modifications were achieved which momentarily satisfied the opposition. From 1893 until 1907 the Dual Monarchy was in great turmoil. Count Kasimir Badeni, a Pole and ex-governor of Galicia, attempted as minister to rule as a *Kaiserminister,* that is, to establish a strong imperial authority based on historic rights of the nationalities. His language decrees of April 5, 1897, placing Czech and German languages on an equal official footing, were excellently conceived but touched off a violent storm among the German nationalists. Moreover, the compromise in 1867 was beginning to prove unmanageable; its renewal in 1897 was very difficult, and among the south Slavs there was an increasing restlessness. There were two basic problems which the Dual Monarchy seemed unable to solve: the Czech desire to achieve the autonomous status of the Hungarians and the rise of the socialist question among urban workers of every nationality. The concession of universal suffrage came too late to unite the nation. A succession of ministers attacked the suffrage problem, but only when Francis Joseph came to believe that it would strengthen the monarchy in the face of foreign dangers was universal manhood suffrage enacted in 1907. By that date the international scene was less favorable to Austria.

The Bosnian Crisis. After the Russo-Japanese War (1904-1905), Russia returned to her interests in the Balkans and with French support was pursuing a course dangerous to Austrian security. Serbia, which had once been friendly to Austria, was bitterly hostile after the change of dynasties in 1903. After 1900 Italy's remaining in the Triple Alliance was uncertain. In this precarious situation the foreign minister, Count Alois von Aehrenthal, resolved to secure outright possession of Bosnia and Herzegovina. The Young Turk revolution of 1908 afforded an occasion. Arrangements were made with the Russian foreign minister, Alexander Izvolsky, for the annexation in exchange for a Russian solution of the Dardanelles issue. Izvolsky promptly denied this arrangement when great protests arose from the western powers and from Serbia. With German diplomatic assistance, a compromise was eventually reached, and Austria was permitted in 1908 to annex Bosnia and Herzegovina. Serbian national feeling was outraged, while the Russians were piqued at their diplomatic defeat. The long crisis strained relations among the great powers and pushed Europe to the brink of war. Aehrenthal's peace policy won out, however, over the views of the Austrian chief of staff, Conrad von Hötzendorf, who favored a preventive war with Serbia. On the other hand, Count Leopold von Berchtold, who succeeded Aehrenthal in 1912, favored a strong representation of Austrian interests.

Prelude to War. During the ten years preceding World War I, the Czech autonomy issue, the question of federalizing the Dual Monarchy, and the demand for liberal political reforms all remained acute. Even the clerical party became estranged from the government because strong action was not taken against the *Los von Rom* movement, an anticlerical and modernist movement among Austrian Catholics which resulted in very substantial withdrawals from the Catholic Church. Pan-German agitators encouraged the movement in order to weaken the Church and strengthen Austrian ties to Protestant Germany. Uneasiness among the south Slavs over political and cultural rights steadily increased and was a serious danger to Austria, since Serbia nurtured hopes of building a great south Slav state. This ambition was the real source of Serbian enmity

for Austria. Neither the Hungarians nor the Austrians made any real attempt to solve the domestic aspects of the south Slav problem. In 1914 their attempt to solve it in foreign affairs by crushing Serbia developed into a general war which dragged Austria down to ruin. It was symptomatic of the tension in the Dual Monarchy that during the Sarajevo crisis of June-July 1914 the parliaments were not in session to give voice to the popular will.

World War I. On June 28, 1914, Archduke Francis Ferdinand, the heir apparent, and his wife were assassinated

TRIANGLE PHOTO SERVICE

CITY OF MATREI ON THE BRENNER PASS

in the Bosnian capital of Sarajevo. Apparent Serbian complicity enabled the Vienna war party to demand vigorous action. Berchtold, who handled the negotiations attending the ultimatum to Serbia on July 23, pursued a firm policy. Despite a conciliatory reply from Serbia, the war party in Austria gained control. With the assurance of German aid, and undismayed by the manifest Russian displeasure, Austria on July 28 declared war against Serbia. Within a fortnight all the great European powers except Italy were at war.

Austrian Reverses. Austria, facing Serbian and Russian armies, proved unable to deal decisively with either. The war in Serbia became a stalemate, while in Galicia in the late summer of 1914 Austrian armies suffered serious reverses at Russian hands. Italy's entry into the war in April 1915 added a new front for Austria, but until 1917 the warfare there was a continuous deadlock. Against Russia the Austrians could not prevail and had repeatedly to be saved from disaster by the Germans. The conquest of both Serbia and Romania was mainly a German achievement. Military reverses, lack of food, and the dissatisfaction of the various nationalities with Austrian rule all intensified the war weariness in Austria-Hungary. Austria therefore favored a joint statement of peace aims with Germany and the settlement of the war by negotiation. Before Francis Joseph's death on Nov. 21, 1916, no agreement with Germany had been reached on this point. His successor, the young Emperor Charles I, resolved to end the war by negotiation, but his efforts in the spring of 1917 only provoked ill-feeling in Germany and were not given serious consideration by the Allies. German military successes in the east and the beginning of unrestricted submarine warfare did not disillusion Charles about Austria-Hungary's ability to remain in the war, but his attempts to reconcile the nationalities and revive Austria as a nation proved futile. An effort to make peace on the basis of President Woodrow Wilson's Fourteen Points failed, and negotiations with Italy broke down; when Austria refused to consider a separate peace, she was committed to the same fate as Germany.

Last Days of the Monarchy. In an attempt to stave off disaster, sweeping social and political reforms were promised. These did not satisfy the Slavic people, who increasingly strove for complete independence. The Czechs took the lead in this movement, though even in Hungary the socialists advanced a program for independence. All these insurgent developments were influenced by the Russian Revolution in March 1917. As military reverses overwhelmed the Central Powers in September and October 1918, the Austrian government attempted eleventh-hour concessions to save the monarchy. After a recognition of national autonomy movements on October 1, the government decreed October 16 that Austria-Hungary would become a federal state, loosely organized under the Hapsburgs. Meanwhile, however, the subject nationalities had begun to form their own governments, which the Austrians were powerless to suppress. The breakup of the Hapsburg monarchy was nearly complete. On the Italian front, the severe defeat at Vittorio Veneto obliged the Austrian command to sue for an armistice, which was granted November 3. By November 12 an Austrian republic had been proclaimed, and its constitution announced union with Germany. With Austria's repudiation of the Hapsburgs, their authority in the Dual Monarchy came to an end.

First Austrian Republic. Hope that the Austrian Republic would include the German-speaking parts of Bohemia and Moravia was extinguished by the Treaty of St. Germain on Oct. 17, 1919. Union with Germany was also expressly forbidden, and the name "German-Austrian Republic" had to be changed to Austrian Republic. Work on a constitution was begun on Mar. 4, 1919, by a national constituent assembly divided between three parties: Social Democrats, which had 69 seats; Christian Socialists, which had 63; and the Nationalists, which had 26. A federal-republican government with a responsible ministry came into being. Under the control of the Social Democrats, this government was set in motion by the middle of March 1919. Karl Renner, who subsequently played a prominent role in the establishment of the Second Austrian Republic in 1945, was a leading figure in 1919. Problems of re-establishing the Austrian economy, now deprived of the resources of the old empire, settling the frontier issue, and reconciling the divergent interests of urban workers and the peasants confronted the government. However, Social Democrats defended Austria against heavy pressure from the Communist government briefly established in Hungary in 1919.

Reconstruction Crisis. Austria's economic plight in the postwar years was desperate. Vienna, a city of almost two million inhabitants, was an economic island cut off from the great hinterland which had nourished its growth before 1914. Inflation, lack of food, and a moribund trade made recovery and stabilization difficult. During the first ministry of Monsignor Ignaz Seipel in 1922, loans were negotiated abroad. The League of Nations in that year embarked on a program of financial reconstruction in Austria, which stabilized the currency and stimulated foreign trade. Internal political conditions, however, remained uneasy. To counter the *Schutzbund,* or private army of the Socialists, another private army, the *Heimwehr,* under conservative and clerical control, came into being. Clashes between these forces were frequent and sanguinary. Control of Austrian politics drifted into conservative, clerical, and nationalist hands, especially under President Miklas and with the rise of Prince Ernst von Starhemberg in the *Heimwehr.* Vienna continued to be a stronghold of the Socialists. An international crisis developed in 1930 over a proposed customs union with Germany. France protested bitterly against the plan as a violation of the St. Germain treaty, holding that it would be tantamount to a political union. Further financial aid to Austria was made a condition for abandoning the project.

Rise of Dollfuss. The Austrian financial crisis and the weakness of its major bank, the Credit Anstalt, brought prominence to a Christian Socialist financial expert, Engelbert Dollfuss (1892-1934), who became chancellor in 1932. The clericals and nationalists soon looked unfavorably upon union with Germany, for there, in 1933, the Nazis came into absolute power. Defense of Austrian independence became Dollfuss' first principle in foreign policy; from abroad his support came mainly from Fascist Italy. To meet the Nazi and also the Socialist threats, Dollfuss was armed by President Miklas with powers that made him a virtual dictator. Outlawing of the Nazi party was followed by dissolution of the Socialist *Schutzbund.* Dollfuss began to construct an autonomous, authoritarian regime in Austria based on Catholic and traditional principles of government. The *Heimwehr* under Starhemberg supported him. When all political parties were dissolved on Feb. 11, 1934, a Socialist revolt broke out which was crushed by the *Heimwehr.* Italian troops stood ready on the frontier to intervene if necessary. This Dollfuss victory was quickly followed by a new constitution on May 1, 1934, which proclaimed Austria a Christian corporative state.

Nazi Putsch of 1934. Alarmed by these rapid developments and by Dollfuss' energy, the Nazis attempted a *Putsch,* making use only of their followers in Austria. Although unsuccessful, in the confusion Nazis wearing Austrian uniforms gained entrance into the Chancellery on July 25, 1934, and shot Dollfuss, who died soon afterwards. Kurt Schuschnigg succeeded him as chancellor and was able to establish order and secure the adoption of the constitution which Dollfuss had introduced. In July 1936, Schuschnigg also reached an agreement with Germany in which guarantees of Austrian independence were given. Fascist Italy under Mussolini was now a partner of Nazi Germany and was accordingly less concerned with Austrian affairs.

German Seizure of Austria. The agreement with Germany did not restrain the Nazis from propagandizing Austria in behalf of *Anschluss,* or political union. Partly to offset the growing influence of the Nazi movement, and partly because of his own sympathies, Schuschnigg encouraged the Hapsburg supporters to carry on legitimist activities; but the showdown with Germany could not be long delayed. In February 1938, Hitler called Schuschnigg to Berchtes-

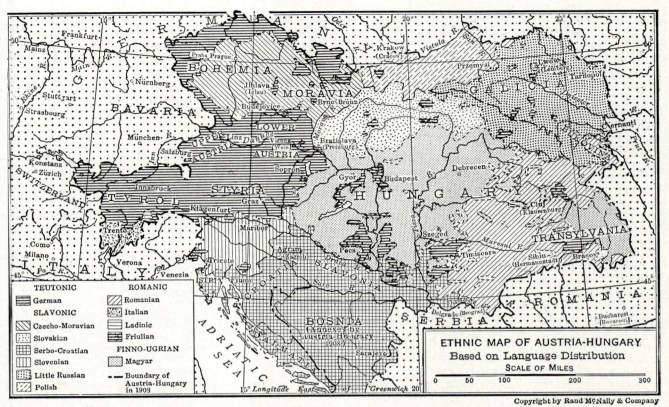

TEUTONIC   ROMANIC
■ German   ▨ Romanian
SLAVONIC   ▧ Italian
▨ Czecho-Moravian   ▤ Ladinic
▨ Slovakian   ▦ Friulian
▦ Serbo-Croatian   FINNO-UGRIAN
▥ Slovenian   ▨ Magyar
▨ Little Russian   – Boundary of
▨ Polish   Austria-Hungary
                                in 1903

ETHNIC MAP OF AUSTRIA-HUNGARY
Based on Language Distribution
SCALE OF MILES
0   50   100   200   300

DISTRIBUTION OF NATIONALITIES IN AUSTRIA-HUNGARY—19TH CENTURY

gaden and forced him to revise his government, giving important portfolios to Nazis. Schuschnigg, detained in Germany on Hitler's orders, attempted to parry this move by calling a plebiscite on the question of Austrian independence. Perhaps fearful of the outcome of a free election, Hitler precipitated a new crisis in which, to avoid a military decision, Schuschnigg was forced to resign. He was held in a German concentration camp until released by Allied troops in 1945. Artur von Seyss-Inquart, the Austrian Nazi minister of the interior, took over as chancellor. His first act, on Mar. 12, 1938, was to call for German intervention in order to "avoid bloodshed." This sealed the fate of Austria's independence, for the country was promptly annexed by Germany and renamed the *Ostmark*. Nazi laws and political methods soon went into effect in Austria. A plebiscite under Nazi auspices, held throughout Greater Germany on April 10, 1938, ratified the *Anschluss* by a majority of 99 per cent.

World War II. As part of Greater Germany, Austria contributed manpower and war material to the German war effort. Nonetheless, the Allies considered Austria a Nazi victim worthy of postwar liberation. In the Moscow Declaration of Oct. 31, 1943, the United States, Great Britain and Soviet Russia pledged themselves to restore an independent and sovereign Austrian republic. Austrian war losses were heavy; some 300,000 persons were killed. Eastern Austria and Vienna were severely damaged by bombing and ground fighting; the Red Army's siege of Vienna (April, 1945) laid waste to large areas within the city. Other cities, particularly key industrial and transportation centers, suffered repeatedly from American and British bombing raids. Wiener-Neustadt, a wartime center of munitions and aircraft factories, suffered more bomb damage than any other

Austrian city. Allied bombers struck hard at the railroads, their trackage as well as rolling stock. Seizures and requisitions of food, livestock, transport, machinery and even personal effects characterized the Red Army's advance. By May, 1945, Soviet control extended over Vienna, Lower Austria, and parts of Styria. U.S. soldiers had entered Tirol, while the British, striking from Italy, had occupied Carinthia. The end of the war and the collapse of Nazism left Austria's government and economy in chaos. To the native's plight was added that of about a million refugees who had fled before the Soviet invaders.

Postwar Reconstruction. Feeding the Austrian people, reconstituting republican government, and reviving the economy were the major problems facing the victorious allies. Although the occupying armies fed civilians from their own stocks, the national diet during 1945-1946 averaged less than 2,000 calories daily, with many urban dwellers surviving on less than half that amount. Malnutrition and disease doubled the normal death rate, while extensive black marketing made equitable distribution of food difficult and frustrated the initial economic controls. Food parcels from abroad and regular UNRRA food deliveries beginning in April 1946 gradually eliminated the worst shortages, but some hardship persisted until relieved by the good harvest and the initial ERP food imports in 1948. Rationing, except for a few basic commodities, was gradually dismantled in 1949-1950. Austrian agriculture now provides eighty-five per cent of the nation's food.

Soviet military authorities prevailed upon Dr. Karl Renner, Chancellor of the first Austrian Republic, to organize a provisional government (Apr. 27, 1945). Limited at first to the Russian controlled provinces, his government won recognition from all the occupying powers on Oct. 20, 1945.

Such pre-war Social Democratic leaders as Theodor Körner and Christian Socialists, such as Leopold Figl, together with some Communists took posts in this coalition government. Postwar Austrian politics, except for Communist intransigence, showed from the outset a spirit of moderation which had been lacking after World War I. The Catholic Church avoided direct political participation, thereby calming the Socialists whose fear of Soviet Communism made them willing to compromise with People's Party moderates. Each party also determined to uphold Austrian interests whatever policy the victors might pursue.

On July 4-9, 1945, the occupying powers, acting through the European Advisory Commission in London, established zones of military occupation and agreed on an Allied Council to sit in Vienna and supervise Austria's political and economic rehabilitation. The Allied Council was empowered to veto Austrian legislation; it also supervised the press and certified Austrian political parties. This assured the uniformity of Austrian law even in the Soviet zone where the government's authority was seriously jeopardized. The military zones corresponded to areas controlled by each power at the war's end: France took over Vorarlberg and Tirol; Great Britain had Carinthia and Styria; the U.S. occupied Salzburg and Upper Austria below the Danube; while the U.S.S.R. held Upper Austria above the Danube and all of Lower Austria and Burgenland. Vienna itself was divided among the four powers while the inner city remained under four-power occupation. Each power, except the Soviet Union, encouraged the provisional government toward autonomy in anticipation of an early peace treaty in keeping with the Moscow Declaration (1943). Most of Austria's postwar political troubles stemmed from the long delay in obtaining this treaty. The U.S.S.R. blocked it at the outset in order to conspire with Communists in the government and among the police to turn Austria into a "people's democracy" on the Hungarian or Romanian model.

The outcome of the first free elections on Nov. 25, 1945 showed the Communists' popular weakness. They polled only five and one-half per cent of the votes, while the remaining vote was shared between the People's Party and the Socialists with a slight advantage for the former. A new coalition government came into being under Leopold Figl (People's Party). At their first sitting both houses of the legislature then elected the venerable Karl Renner (Socialist Party) as President. Communist office holders were either dismissed or demoted. This popular verdict restored Austrian politics to its pre-war two-party pattern and dealt Soviet intrigues a hard blow. On June 28, 1946 the Allied Council recognized the government's legislative powers and reserved its approval only for constitutional amendments. Deputies of the occupying powers' foreign ministers met in London on Jan. 3, 1947 to prepare an Austrian peace treaty, but the foreign ministers' talks in Moscow (Mar. 10-Apr. 24, 1947) broke down because of excessive Soviet demands for reparations and war damage claims. Yugoslavia's persistent demand for southern Carinthia also proved troublesome, particularly since Yugoslavia as a Soviet satellite (until 1949) had Soviet diplomatic backing. Almost 300 fruitless conferences were to be held until a treaty satisfactory to the U.S.S.R. was finally drafted early in 1955.

To get the economy on its feet the Austrian government and the occupying powers set about rebuilding the transport and communications system, overcoming the food crisis, preventing runaway inflation, and reviving foreign trade. What recovery had been made up to 1947 was primarily due to the resilience of the artisans and small-scale

manufacturers, who were best able to extemporize in the use of substitute materials. Nonetheless, by 1947 the Austrian economy reached full employment for the first time in peace since the post-World War I inflation days. Commercial imports and exports, food production, fuel, and power supplies were still too low for the economy to function properly, however. And inflation, despite successive national wage and price agreements, threatened to undo even these modest achievements.

This economic crisis provided the background for the nationalization of Austria's basic industries—mining, transport, and banking—in 1946-1947. Private capital was lacking for the rebuilding and retooling of Austrian heavy industries, which had all been greatly expanded during the Nazi era to become the postwar backbone of the economy. Before *Anschluss* with Germany, Austria had emphasized consumer goods industries, whereas under national control it appeared that an over-all plan for economic recovery might be more effective.

Such a plan was forthcoming when in the summer of 1947 Austria agreed to participate in the Marshall Plan for European Recovery, a decision sharply protested by the Soviet High Commissioner on the Allied Council. Actual Marshall Plan aid did not begin until April 1948, and in the first year more than half of Austria's allocation went for food imports. Still, the ERP program in Austria undertook to rebuild the iron and steel industries and to stimulate coal and electric power production without destroying the balance of the Austrian economy between industry, commerce, and agriculture. Forestry, agriculture, and tourism received important consideration from ERP, but, by and large, the consumer-goods industries were not assisted. ERP aid went only to projects and industries located outside the Soviet zone, a political need which augmented the wartime shift of Austrian industry to the western provinces. Substantial ERP aid also went into developing the hydroelectric power industry. Of all the new power stations, that at Kaprun in Salzburg, a year-round reservoir installation, was the most valuable to the economy as a whole. Magnesite mines received special ERP attention because their output earned valuable dollar exchange. From the ERP Central Office in Vienna, foreign experts also advised Austrian industrialists about techniques for raising Austria's industrial productivity, which remains low in terms of the available plant capacity and man-hours of use.

Economic recovery suffered severely from the initial looting and seizure of German industrial assets by the Red Army, a loss estimated at more than $200,000,000, as well as from the Soviet attempts to exploit their zone for their own and their satellite states' benefit. Since the refineries and wells of the Austrian oil industry lay in Soviet-controlled Lower Austria it could be exploited at will. Under a special Soviet Mineral Oil Administration the bulk of oil production was diverted from the Austrian economy. Although production increased more than twofold over the wartime yield, Austria often had to purchase oil supplies abroad. Not until 1952-1953 did adequate amounts of Austrian-produced oil begin to reach the national market. Other German assets such as banks, landed estates, and factories were organized in a gigantic Soviet-managed trust (Administration for Soviet Property in Eastern Austria) which paid no taxes and undermined privately owned Austrian businesses. To these property seizures the Soviets added the threat of arrests and kidnappings. Foes of Communism were systematically abducted, many from within the Soviet Zone in Vienna. This regime of personal insecurity and economic exploitation contrasted sharply with the western powers' generously conceived plans for political and economic reconstruction.

By 1952-1953 the Soviets gradually relaxed their arbitrary methods as well as the policy of holding their zone apart from the national economy. The quickening of exports in the same years, the stabilization of currency and prices, and the mounting industrial productivity warranted the termination of ERP aid in 1953. Some $1,500,000,000 had been provided to Austria from foreign sources, including ERP, UNRRA, and British and Swiss grants-in-aid. Without it Austria might not have recovered its economic nor its political stability.

Recent History. Austrian politics from 1945 to 1955 lived under the shadow of the U.S.S.R.'s unwillingness to negotiate a peace treaty. Western statesmen in interminable conferences pressed the U.S.S.R. relentlessly though fruitlessly for agreeable peace terms. Want of national sovereignty appeared to make the Allied Council and the armies of occupation permanent fixtures. The danger of a Communist coup d'état also persisted; indeed, a dress rehearsal for one occurred in the fall of 1950 when Communist-led trade unionists, party agitators, and sympathizers demonstrated violently and temporarily seized communications and transport. Such violent measures failed to intimidate the Austrian people who continued to endorse the political status quo. Coalition government won a popular endorsement in the parliamentary elections of Oct. 9, 1949, which again gave the People's Party a slight edge over the Socialists. When the death of President Renner on Dec. 31, 1950 required a popular presidential election, the voting on May 6, 1951 gave the People's Party a rude shock. Their candidate, Heinrich Gleissner, was defeated by the Socialist, Theodor Körner.

Differences of opinion about economic policy also threatened Austria's coalition government. The People's Party favored the controlled inflation which had been the government's underlying fiscal policy, the growth of the export industries, and, with the help of private investment, the strengthening of free enterprise and competition. The Socialists looked to the increase of real wages, the growth of consumer goods industries, and the continued emphasis on state control and state investment in industry. A substantial reduction of the occupation forces in 1953 eased the burden on the civil budget and helped to preserve the spirit of compromise in Austrian government. Still, popular opinion swung toward the Socialists in the 1953 elections, obliging Figl's cabinet to resign in favor of one headed by Julius Raab (People's Party). Figl became Minister of Foreign Affairs, enjoying particular success in undertaking good will tours in Great Britain and the United States, which affirmed Austria's basic commitment to the west.

Even greater diplomatic success awaited Chancellor Raab, invited to Moscow on Mar. 24, 1955 to discuss peace terms with Molotov. Only the year before at the Big Four foreign ministers' conference in Berlin (January-February, 1954) Molotov had blocked treaty discussions. His readiness to come to terms with Raab complied with the Soviets' sudden policy shift away from aggressive toward conciliatory diplomatic tactics. Following up this opportunity, foreign ministers of the occupying powers swiftly drafted a state treaty embodying the Soviet concessions. The formal signing occurred on May 15, 1955 at the Belvedere Palace in Vienna. Molotov signed for the U.S.S.R.; Harold Macmillan for Great Britain; Antoine Pinay for France; John Foster Dulles for the U.S.; and Leopold Figl (as Foreign Minister) for Austria.

The state treaty (so-called because Austria was considered a forced partner of Nazi Germany, not a co-belligerent) re-established Austria's sovereignty and independence within the frontiers of Jan. 1, 1938. Economic or political union with Germany or a Habsburg restoration were expressly forbidden, although neither issue, unlike the situation after 1918, had aroused popular sympathy. Democratic institutions with full civil rights for all citizens and minority cultural groups were to be upheld. Nazism in all forms was legally proscribed. The treaty pledged Austria to perpetual neutrality in foreign affairs. A constitutional amendment will incorporate this policy in Austria's fundamental law. In the future neither military alliances nor foreign military bases may be maintained and the occupation armies must withdraw within ninety days of the treaty's ratification, or no later than Dec. 31, 1955. The size of Austria's armed forces remains unrestricted although the country may not possess certain types of arms, such as atom bombs or guided missiles. The treaty contained no war guilt clause, nor were any reparations demanded. Nonetheless, the state treaty placed Austria in debt to the Soviet Union for its claim to former German industrial assets as war booty. The other signatories waived their right to make similar claims. Article 22 gave the U.S.S.R. the right for thirty years to take up to sixty per cent of the oil output from the fields and refineries northeast of Vienna. Title to other former German industrial and agricultural assets was also transferred to the U.S.S.R. In addition, Austria agreed to pay the U.S.S.R. $150,000,000 within six years in order to redeem other unclaimed Nazi German industrial assets. Austria also agreed to redeem the Danubian shipping seized by the U.S.S.R. at the end of World War II.   W. O. S.

AUSTRIA-HUNGARY, also known as the Dual Monarchy, a central European power created by the *Ausgleich,* or Compromise of 1867, which gave the kingdom of Hungary a status of equality with the Austrian Empire under Hapsburg rule. The Dual Monarchy lasted for fifty-one years, collapsing at the end of World War I in 1918. During all but the last two years of its existence it was ruled by Emperor Francis Joseph I.

Austrian Dissension. The events leading to the formation of the Dual Monarchy are detailed in the preceding article on Austria. Two of the motivating factors, however, were of special importance in the light of subsequent developments. These were (1) the growing discontent of the numerous subject nationalities which composed Francis Joseph's patchwork empire and (2) the steadily declining prestige of Austria in the last half of the nineteenth century.

Nationalities. In ancient and medieval times it was not unusual for one empire to hold sway over vast areas of Europe and northern Africa, embracing many different races with varied cultures and traditions. Few modern states, however, have contained such a conglomeration of diverse nationalities as did the Austrian Empire in the latter part of the nineteenth century.

Twelve million Germans dominated a population of approximately 50,000,000 people. In the northern part of the empire were 17,500,000 north Slavs; these included 7,000,000 Czechs and Slovaks in Bohemia and Moravia and 5,000,000 Poles and 4,000,000 Little Russians (also called Ruthenians or Ukrainians) in Galicia. Hungary and Transylvania, occupying the eastern portion of the empire, contained 10,000,000 Magyars and 3,000,000 Romanians. Along the southern border lived 7,000,000 south Slavs (Serbs, Croats, and Slovenes in Croatia, Slavonia, and Bosnia) and a little less

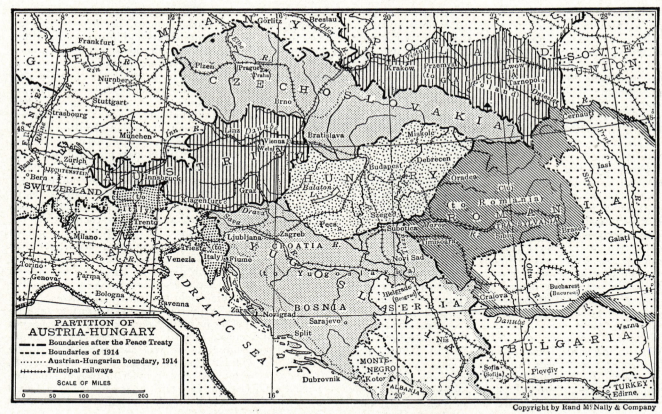

Copyright by Rand McNally & Company

STATES FORMED BY THE PARTITION OF AUSTRIA-HUNGARY AFTER WORLD WAR I

than 1,000,000 Italians in the Trentino and the peninsula of Istria. The 12,000,000 Austrians of German descent were concentrated in the west. There was constant jealousy and bickering among these diverse races. They were proud of their traditions, spoke their own languages, and refused to become Germanized. The Austrian Empire was, in fact, scarcely more than a geographical expression. There was no Austrian language, no distinct Austrian tradition, no separate Austrian culture.

Of the various subjects of the Hapsburgs, by far the most aggressive and influential were the Magyars of Hungary. After 1815 Metternich, the most powerful statesman in Europe, concerned himself almost solely with preserving his Continental System, leaving internal affairs to Emperor Francis I. That sovereign, strongly reactionary, began to develop an increasingly suspicious attitude toward the many non-German nationalities which were asserting their claims to a share in the government. A system of representation existed, but it rarely functioned effectively, and by the middle of the nineteenth century, Francis had transformed Austria into a police state, governed by an inept bureaucracy which refused to consider political and social reform.

When Louis Philippe of France was overthrown in 1848, Europe was shaken to its foundations. The revolutionary movement, sweeping eastward over the Continent, found Austria more than ready for insurrection. For a moment it appeared that the unwieldy empire would disintegrate completely. Metternich fled to London, the Magyars set up a constitutional government of their own in Budapest, there were riots in Vienna, the Italians revolted, the south Slavs formed a "liberal" government of their own at Agram, and the north Slavs held a "Pan-Slavic" congress at Prague. In this crisis the German ruling element followed the historic

policy which had proved so effective many times before: it played one nationality against another. The south Slavs were persuaded that an independent Hungary would be a greater menace to them than their Hapsburg rulers; as a result, they joined forces with the Austrians to suppress the rebellions in Hungary and northern Italy. The German element in Bohemia similarly co-operated in putting down the Czechoslovak insurrection. By 1849 the new emperor, Francis Joseph I, had regained complete control of the country.

Francis Joseph, who had ascended the throne in the revolution of 1848, had promised his subjects a new constitution in an effort to pacify them; but now, being firmly re-established in power, he was in a position to reconsider and reject all but one of these constitutional guarantees: the abolition of serfdom. Hungary, meanwhile, had found a new leader, Ferencz Deák. The Magyars had gained nothing by violent methods in the revolution of 1848-1849. Deák convinced them that the hodgepodge structure of the Austrian Empire could not last long; he counseled the Magyars to use peaceful methods and bide their time.

Decline of Austrian Prestige. Deák's counsel proved wise. Austria shortly suffered a disastrous loss of prestige in two brief wars which emphasized her weakness. The War of Italian Liberation in 1859, which found her arrayed against France and Sardinia, cost her Lombardy. The Seven Weeks' War with Prussia in 1866, over the Schleswig-Holstein dispute, shattered the German Confederation, which Austria had dominated, and ended her ascendancy to central Europe.

Compromise of 1867. During these troubles Deák had restrained the Magyars from a new revolt, and Francis Joseph was not ungrateful. He was convinced that the time had come to admit Hungary to equal partnership in the empire. The *Ausgleich,* or Compromise of 1867, was a series of treaties which implemented Hungary's chief demands: a constitution, internal administration, and parliament of its own, and equality in the conduct of foreign affairs, military policy, and finance of the empire.

Francis Joseph had hoped, by these concessions, to placate the most powerful of his subject peoples, but the partnership did not work as smoothly as he had expected. There were petty quarrels over the apportionment of the Dual Empire's joint expenses. The Hungarian kingdom, with its new sense of power, was as unsympathetic toward the Romanians and its other subject nationalities as the Germans had been, and it was especially repressive in the case of the south Slavs in Croatia and Slavonia, who had become Hungarian subjects under the *Ausgleich*.

To bolster Austria's steadily declining position in Europe, Francis Joseph sought to expand southward into the Balkans. Here he met a hard core of Slavic resistance. Serbia, backed by Russia, by this time had assumed regional leadership of the Slavs in the Balkans, and Austria-Hungary's annexation of the Turkish provinces of Bosnia and Herzegovina in 1908 blocked her way to the Adriatic Sea. Russia mobilized as if for war against the Dual Monarchy, but Germany announced she would aid Francis Joseph. Thus began the succession of Balkan crises that brought on World War I and the disintegration of Austria-Hungary as a political entity. *See also* AUSTRIA.   A. J.

AUSTRIAN SCHOOL, a neoclassical school of economists, also known as the psychological or marginal utility school. Its founder was Karl Menger (1840-1921), whose most prominent followers were Friedrich von Wieser (1851-1926) and Eugen von Böhm-Bawerk (1851-1914). The Austrian school was part of the widespread movement of the second half of the nineteenth century which sought to improve upon the classicism of Ricardo, Senior, and J. Mill. Although this new movement in economic thought had its antecedents in the work of economists like H. H. Gossen (1810-1858), it was not until the marginal utility concept was developed by W. S. Jevons, K. Menger, and M. E. L. Walras in the 1870's that the neoclassical movement became well established.

Theory of Marginal Utility. In developing its subjective economics the Austrian school begins with human wants and their satisfaction. When a good has the power to satisfy a human want, it is said to have use value or utility. If the good is both useful and scarce, it is an "economic" rather than a "free" good. In the case of economic goods, the classical economists had been unable to distinguish between the utility of the total supply and the utility of any one unit of the supply. Menger solved this difficulty by pointing out that the utility of the last unit added to a supply is determined by the least important use to which the good can be put. Thus, the utility of the total supply of bread is very great, but the utility of any one loaf, or the "marginal utility" of bread as Wieser described it, is very small because the use to which the marginal loaf is put is unimportant. The Austrians explained that the principle of marginal utility is fundamental to all exchanges, since the individual exchanges goods until all his relative marginal utilities are the same.

Primacy of Demand. The Austrian school made the concept of utility the foundation of their subjective theory of value. They accepted the view that values are affected by both supply and demand, but they held that demand, and hence utility, is of primary significance. Costs could limit the supply of goods but they could not give value to goods. According to their interpretation supply is a matter of costs, and costs in turn involve labor and capital. Labor and capital derive their value from the fact that they indirectly produce final or consumer goods. The casual flow was therefore said to be from utility to consumer goods, and then to labor and capital. In this manner, all values were alleged to be determined by utility to the final consumer.

Opportunity Cost Principle. In applying the marginal utility principle to the field of distribution, Menger, Wieser, and Böhm-Bawerk laid the foundation for the marginal productivity theory of distribution. They pointed out that the agents of production operate collectively in the creation of an output. The contribution of each agent, however, can be determined by observing the diminution of the total output brought about by withdrawing from use any one unit of labor or capital. At this point in their analysis the Austrian school introduced what later came to be known as the opportunity cost principle. With a given supply of capital goods the value of the product of any one capital good is determined by the least important use to which the capital good is put. Furthermore, in competitive circumstances capital goods are distributed along various lines until the values of their products are the same in all alternative uses. Just as consumers equate relative marginal utilities, producers equalize the marginal contributions of labor and capital goods by making the necessary substitutions.

Time-preference Theory of Interest. Böhm-Bawerk's contribution was primarily in applying the utility doctrine to the problem of interest. In developing his time-preference theory of interest Böhm-Bawerk made further use of the idea of choice or preference that underlies the utility doctrine developed by Menger and Wieser. He pointed out that goods have a greater utility in the present than in the future, and that to overcome an individual's preference for the present a premium or agio has to be offered. This premium can be paid because the capitalistic system of production is made more fruitful through the use of capital provided by saving.

Limitations. The Austrian school could arrive at its conclusions about value theory only by ignoring the long-run influence of objective cost factors, and by paying little attention to the social aspects of the valuation processes. It is true that, given a supply of goods, utility and not cost is of primary importance; but where the supply of goods is changing, costs also become factors of fundamental importance. From a broader viewpoint than that held by the Austrian school, values are seen to be determined by many subjective and objective factors. The Austrian school performed a service in pointing out the defects of the classical cost-of-production theory of value, but it was at fault in erecting its subjective economics on the basis of too narrow a theory of valuation. *See also* CLASSICAL SCHOOL OF ECONOMICS.   A. G. G.

AUSTRIAN SUCCESSION, WAR OF THE (1740-1748), a series of general European conflicts in which the defense of Austrian territorial unity and the maintenance of the balance of power were the paramount issues. The principal struggle occurred between Prussia and Austria over Silesia. In its early stages the war was a test of strength between Frederick the Great and Maria Theresa. Spain, France, and Bavaria joined Prussia in attempting to despoil Maria Theresa, whose accession in 1740 had been the signal for the outbreak of war. England and Holland supported her cause. Austria proved unable to dislodge Prussia from Silesia, seized in 1740, and made a separate peace at Breslau (June 11, 1742). The war against Prussia's allies continued. Austrian success alarmed Frederick the Great who re-entered the struggle while France openly declared war for the first time. The Netherlands, the Rhineland, Bohemia, and Italy became the seats of a general war. England, Holland, Austria, and Saxony formed a Quadruple Alliance on Jan. 8, 1745, a year which witnessed the greatest battles of the war. The first was at Fontenoy (May 11, 1745), a stubborn, hard-fought battle in which the French under Marshal Saxe defeated an Allied army. Impressive Prussian victories at Hohenfriedberg (June 4) and Kesselsdorf (Dec. 14) compelled Austria to yield, and Maria Theresa once more recognized the cession of Silesia in the Peace of Dresden (Dec. 24, 1745). Operations in Italy dominated the years 1745 to 1747, while in North America, the English colonists, in what they called King George's War, took the French fortress of Louisburg, Cape Breton (April 29-June 16, 1745). In Europe the end of the war was dominated by the brilliant campaigns of Marshal Saxe who repeatedly defeated the Austrians and Dutch. Peace was finally made at Aix-la-Chapelle on Oct. 18, 1748.   W. O. S.

AUSTROASIATIC LANGUAGES, a group of languages usually said to include the following major subgroups: (1) Mon-Khmer, further subdivided into Mon-Khmer proper, the Eastern group, the Malay Peninsula group, Nicobarese, and the Salowen Basin or Sikhasi languages; (2) Munda, with the Himalayan and the Chota-Nagpur languages; and (3) Annam-Muong, with Annamese and Muong. Sometimes the Austroasiatic languages are further combined with the Austronesian languages into one supergroup, Austric, but this Austric classification has been questioned, especially in view of the fact that the Austroasiatic languages as such are by no means to be classified as a true language family. The current Austroasiatic classification rests merely on some rather superficial resemblances in phonology and morphology. Mon-Khmer and Munda, for example, both use prefixation and infixation in a somewhat similar manner. But these similarities may also merely be the result of a general diffusion of typical linguistic features, and a true genetic classification must await a better description of the languages involved.
    T. A. S.

AUSTRONESIAN LANGUAGES. *See* Malayo-Polynesian Languages.

AUTHORIZED STOCK, the stock which a corporation is authorized to issue by the provisions of its charter or articles of incorporation. State incorporation laws require that the articles of incorporation, which are filed with the secretary of state or corresponding state official when a corporation is organized, stipulate the number of shares of stock, and par value if any, which the corporation is to be authorized to issue. Approval of the articles of incorporation by the secretary of state then confers upon the corporation authority to issue the stipulated number of shares, but no more. Authorized stock may be divided into classes having different rights and limitations, such as common stock and preferred stock. The rights and limitations of each class are set forth in the articles of incorporation. When a corporation has issued the entire amount of its authorized capital stock, it may not issue more or split that outstanding without obtaining new authority from the state of incorporation. An increase in the amount of authorized stock may be obtained, however, by amendment of the articles of incorporation. Such an amendment must be approved by the directors of the corporation, by a majority of the existing stockholders having voting rights, and by the appropriate state authority.   H. C. S.

AUTOBIOGRAPHY, a form of biography in which the subject is also the author; it is generally written in the first person and covers most or an important phase of the author's life. Autobiography has existed, in a sense, from antiquity, but the word itself was not coined until 1809 by Robert Southey.

Historical Evolution of Autobiography. Historically considered, the autobiographical tendency belongs chiefly to the modern rather than to the ancient world, for modern man is far more self-conscious than his Classical predecessor. Perhaps the beginnings of self-examination should even be sought not among the Classical peoples, but among the Old Testament psalmists and prophets and the writers of the New Testament Epistles. But autobiography requires a more narrative form than sheer self-examination. In the strict sense it has developed through four distinct stages, for in four periods of upheaval and transition, which pulled men this way and that and made them want to find their bearings, certain persons felt the self-recording urge and in consequence produced outstanding books in which the typical forms of autobiography were established.

The first of these periods of conflict occurred at the time of the breakup of the Classical world; and the first great autobiographer was St. Augustine (A.D. 354-430). The war in his own person that he experienced as the son of a hot-blooded father and a saintly mother, his intense inward Christianity, and the clash of opposites in his environment made him acutely aware of himself and found expression in the engrossing record of spiritual experiences that he set down in the *Confessions.*

From the time of St. Augustine onward there was no important autobiographical writing until the Renaissance and the Reformation. Both of these movements involved reaffirmations of individuality. Self-consciousness had been rare in the ancient Classical world, but the rediscovery of Classical thought and attitude at the time of the Renaissance seemed to release a new awareness of personality which encouraged the individual to assert himself, while the Reformation among Protestants, like the Counter Reformation among Catholics, demanded that the individual examine himself before God. There are three writers in particular who mark this autobiographical advance. They are Benvenuto Cellini (1500-1571), Jerome Cardan (1501-1576), and Michel de Montaigne (1533-1592). Only the first of them actually narrates his life, and indeed his fascinating autobiography is the first full-dress narrative of the events of a man's life to be written by himself. Whereas St. Augustine had concentrated on the inward, Cellini concentrated on the outward; he was highly self-conscious in the sense of having an inordinate vanity and self-satisfaction, but he was quite innocent of self-knowledge. Cardan and Montaigne had no stories to tell, but they are of first importance as self-portrayers. Cardan classifies all the attributes of man and proceeds to describe his own peculiarities under each head. He thus gives a regular inventory of his effects, physical, intellectual, and moral, down to the most absurd details. He had unquestionable powers of self-examination and was never guilty of deliberate falsehood, but his imagination frequently got the better of his judgment, and for long he lived under a kind of hallucination. Montaigne, on the other hand, was nothing if not sane. He was his own chief subject, and seldom has a man achieved such a balanced and reliable estimate of himself. He is quite unsystematic in his arrangement, but for that reason he is all the more convincing, since his innumerable flashes of insight obviously came unforced. Among the autobiographers of this second period the following may be added to those already mentioned: Margery Kempe (c.1373-c.1440), Desiderius Erasmus (1466-

1536), Robert Greene (c.1560-1592), Lord Herbert of Cherbury (1583-1648), and John Bunyan (1628-1688).

The third impulse to autobiography came with the opening of new mental horizons in the eighteenth century. The typical autobiographer of this period is Jean Jacques Rousseau (1712-1778). It is difficult to imagine a less accommodating nature than his; he determined to be himself and to live the life of his own choice, and his *Confessions* and their sequels show him as he was and provide a revelation so frank as to suggest spiritual exhibitionism. These books, however, have probably had more influence on subsequent autobiographies than any others before or since. Notable among the autobiographical writers of this and the following century are Colley Cibber, "George Psalmanazar," Benjamin Franklin, Carlo Goldoni, Giacomo Casanova, Edward Gibbon, J. W. von Goethe, William Cobbett, the Vicomte de Chateaubriand, Sir Walter Scott, Henri Beyle (Stendhal), Leigh Hunt, Thomas De Quincey, Benjamin Haydon, Silvio Pellico, Alphonse de Lamartine, J. H. Newman, Hector Berlioz, George Sand, J. S. Mill, Charles Darwin, Fanny Kemble, Alexander Herzen, Anthony Trollope, Henry Thoreau, John Ruskin, Ernest Renan, Count Leo Tolstoy, Joseph Jefferson, F. W. Nietzsche, and Richard Jefferies.

The twentieth century brought with it the fourth autobiographical stage. Undoubtedly one important factor in this revival was the development of psychology, which made more disturbingly obvious the complexity of the human personality, not only on the conscious but on the subconscious and unconscious levels. Moreover, as in the three previous epochs discussed, this was a period in which a new age was coming to birth. There were rival ideologies, and the wars were not only wars of ideas but wars in the literal sense and on a scale that made all previous conflicts look small by comparison. It is not surprising, then, that the autobiographies of the twentieth century are more numerous than the total of all the centuries before, but it would be difficult to take any as typical of their epoch. Some of the more notable autobiographers of the twentieth century are Henry Adams, G. K. Chesterton, Theodore Dreiser, Havelock Ellis, André Gide, Sir Edmund Gosse, Maxim Gorki, W. H. Hudson, Henry James, Siegfried Sassoon, Mark Twain, Booker T. Washington, H. G. Wells, and W. B. Yeats.

The Literary Variables. Looking at autobiographies from a literary rather than an historical point of view, one can detect a number of variables. They differ, first, in the proportion of physical to mental events: the space given to the things done and seen and the persons known on the one hand, and to the thoughts and emotions of the autobiographer on the other. Secondly, they differ in variety and breadth, according to the opportunities and experience of the author and the range of his interests and ideas. Thirdly, there is a moral variation with respect to certain related factors: the activity and reliability of the autobiographer's memory, his honesty and balance, and the candor of his disclosures and opinions. Lastly, there are artistic differences which arise from the varying skill with which the author selects the significant, disposes the material, appreciates the interrelation of cause and effect, and evokes from the multiplicity of life a unifying pattern.

Types and Motives. It can hardly be said that there is a single autobiographical type or anything like a common motive impelling autobiographers to make them take the world into their confidence. All kinds of men and women, acting from all kinds of motives, have written their own lives: the distinguished and the undistinguished; the extra-verts, or lookers-out on the world, and the introverts, or lookers-in on themselves; saints and sinners; self-condemners and self-justifiers; conformers and reformers; thinkers and doers; artistic creators and practical men of business or affairs; travelers and stay-at-homes; the balanced and the unbalanced. But probably all of them have acquired a certain detachment from the events they choose to record. There has been in their experience something in the nature of a conversion; or a change of environment; or an ambition attained or an undertaking completed; or something endured, such as failure, disillusionment, misunderstanding, injustice, imprisonment, prolonged illness, and poverty. Or perhaps they are moved to write by the realization of a mission, or by the maturing of a philosophy of life, or by merely the lapse of time from the activities of youth and middle life to the backward-looking reminiscences of old age.

Some Related Kinds. The aim of an autobiography, then, is to present a life, or some phase of it, viewed as a whole after the lapse of time has given the self-biographer a certain detachment and the events a certain coherence. Hence it differs from a diary or journal, such as those of John Evelyn, George Fox, Samuel Pepys, James Boswell, Henri Frédéric Amiel, and Edmond and Jules de Goncourt, which records day-to-day facts and impressions. It differs, too, from the memoir, though the two terms are often interchanged, in that the autobiography is the personal history of the author, whereas the memoir—as written, for example, by Jean de Joinville, the Emperor Baber, the Duc de Saint-Simon, Louis de Bourrienne, Ulysses S. Grant—is a familiar history of more-or-less public events in which the author may have played only a subordinate part.

Though autobiography is generally regarded as a department of prose literature, at least one great example, Wordsworth's *Prelude* (completed 1805), is a poem. An autobiographical strain, too, with or without disguise, is not infrequent in other poetry, such as Horace's *Satires* and *Epistles,* Dante's *Vita Nuova,* George Herbert's *Temple,* Byron's *Childe Harold,* and Tennyson's *In Memoriam.* A similar strain often shows in the familiar essays of Charles Lamb, William Hazlitt, R. L. Stevenson, Max Beerbohm, and others. Furthermore, the personal letter is largely autobiographical anecdote and comment in the piecemeal fashion of the diary or journal, as may be seen in such letters as those of Lady Mary Wortley Montagu, Horace Walpole, and William Cowper.

Fiction has sometimes assumed the guise of autobiography, as in Daniel Defoe's *Robinson Crusoe,* Jonathan Swift's *Gulliver's Travels,* Alain René Lesage's *Gil Blas,* Tobias Smollett's *Roderick Random,* Sir Walter Scott's *Rob Roy,* W. M. Thackeray's *Henry Esmond,* and many others. On the other hand, novelists have frequently drawn on their own experiences for those of their characters, notably in Henry Fielding's *Amelia,* Charles Dickens' *David Copperfield,* Benjamin Constant's *Adolphe,* George Sand's *Elle et lui* and other novels, Charlotte Brontë's *Jane Eyre,* Tolstoy's novels generally, W. H. White's *Autobiography of Mark Rutherford,* Thomas Hardy's *Jude the Obscure,* H. G. Wells's *Kipps,* Marcel Proust's *À la recherche du temps perdu,* and Somerset Maugham's *Of Human Bondage.* George Moore in *Confessions of a Young Man* and other books gives what purports to be his own life but is in fact a considerably fictionized version of it. A. M. Cl.

AUTOCRACY [ɔtɒˈkrəsi], a political system under which one man wields unlimited power, restricted by no constitutional provisions or effective political opposition. Usually, autocracy prevails in very backward communities which have been unable to develop political and legal institutions to protect the individual against the whims of the ruler. The more men mature, the less are they willing to submit unquestioningly to the arbitrary decisions of an autocrat. The ancient despotisms of the Babylonian and Assyrian empires, the Tsarist regime in Russia before 1917, and the Nazi and Fascist dictatorships that evolved in the twentieth century are samples of the autocratic pattern of government, in which the ruler remains above the law. The democratic tradition of the West, based upon ancient Athenian procedures, is opposed to autocracy.   W. E.

AUTO-DA-FÉ [ɔ′to də fe′] (Port., act of faith), the name later applied in the Roman Catholic Church to what was originally called the *sermo generalis,* the solemn ceremony wherein were promulgated the final sentences of the Inquisition. It was preceded by the reading, in brief and in the vernacular, of the charges, and by a summons to appear for the verdict. Early in the morning a short discourse or exhortation was pronounced. The secular authorities were then called on to vow that they would obey the inquisitor in all that concerned the suppression of heresy. Next were regularly read the so-called "decrees of mercy" (mitigations or removals of penalties previously imposed). The offences of the guilty were again recalled and due punishments assigned them, ending with the most severe, life imprisonment or death. Those condemned were thereupon delivered to the secular authorities. The term "auto-da-fé" applies also to the execution of the sentence, particularly to the burning of a heretic. The last auto-da-fé on record took place in Mexico in 1815. *See also* INQUISITION.   N. J. T.

AUTOGIRO. *See* ROTATING-WING AIRCRAFT.

AUTOINTOXICATION, a generalized condition said to be caused by the absorption of harmful products from the intestinal tract. There is little or no scientific evidence to show that such a condition exists. However, certain persons believe that, under abnormal circumstances, the symptoms of dull headache, lassitude, weakness, loss of appetite, and mild dizziness are due to the fact that the contents of the lower bowel are either retained longer than usually, are poorly digested, or undergo abnormal decomposition, and that, as a result, harmful poisons enter the blood stream and are carried to all parts of the body. This term, as a specific diagnosis, is usually omitted from modern textbooks.

                                    W. T. G., Jr.

AUTOMATIC PILOT, a mechanism for automatically steering an aircraft on a set course. It is used to relieve human pilots on long, straight flights. Although differing in details, it is similar in general principles of operation to the gyro pilot used on marine vessels. *See* GYRO PILOT.

                                    W. R. W.

AUTOMATIC WEAPONS. *See* FIREARMS, INFANTRY.

AUTOMATION, a contraction of the word *automatization.* It is the name that has been applied to an industrial movement which started in the U.S. at the beginning of the 1950's. In its relatively short existence, automation has become one of the important areas of industrial management. Other countries are now following this example, and automation is becoming a world-wide movement.

Although used in many specialized connotations, such as the automatic loading and unloading of machine tools,

automation most generally describes a concept of production which is unique to the decade of the 1950's in its technology and philosophy, as well as in the breadth of its application. It is an integration of machines with one another into a fully automatic and, in some cases, self-regulating system. It permits the partial or total manufacture and assembly of a product with a minimum of human intervention in the process. Automation is as much a concept of production as it is a technology. It is an innovation, as was the assembly line, in the way industrial and business processes are organized. Although its roots can be traced far back in our indus-

FORD MOTOR CO.

In this almost fully automatic process, pistons move from belt conveyors to machines for grinding, boring, and chucking. If a chute is full, the piston moves to the next open machine.

trial history and it makes use of old, as well as new, techniques, it is essentially a new way of approaching the problems of commerce and industry in manufacturing and processing, retailing, transportation, and communications.

Automation may be considered to be a new phase of the continuing Industrial Revolution because of the nature of its technology. It is providing machines to perform the functions of control. The first part of the Industrial Revolution could be described by the word mechanization. Its keyword was power, and its goal was to substitute inanimate energy for man's brawn. Within a single century, human and animal effort declined from 90 per cent of the total motive power in the economy to 10 per cent. Automation is not going to reduce that figure much further. Its impact is elsewhere. Most human beings no longer act as beasts of burden or as mere sources of power. Instead they are controllers of mechanical power, guides for inanimate energy, and links between mechanized operations. It is here that automation is making changes. By linking together machines into integrated systems and by controlling these systems and the machines within them, automation is providing fully, and partially, automatic processes for performing many kinds of work.

The first step in automation, a natural one in the development of both machine tools and the production line, is advanced mechanization. Automotive manufacturers have employed it extensively and have found it profitable. These manufacturers have not only eliminated the need for much human intervention in the machining process, but, by using ingenious transfer mechanisms and new automatic devices for handling materials, they have integrated their machinery into entirely automatic processes. To a company like Ford, in its highly automatic Cleveland and Buffalo plants, automation is primarily the linking together of production processes through the use of special-purpose machines. Electric and hydraulic controls permit the loading and unloading of special-purpose, multi-stage machine tools, while large transfer machines move workpieces from one operation to the next.

Feedback. If this were its only aspect, automation would be severely limited in application. Long runs of non-varying products would be necessary to justify the big investment in special-purpose machines, and in a consumer economy as dynamic as ours there is only a limited number of such products. Also, automation would be primarily a manufacturing, if not a fabricating, concept applicable perhaps to other fields in its philosophy, but not providing the means for applying the philosophy of integration in practice. It is because of the technology of feedback or machine self-correction that automation is having such a broad impact upon our economy. The technology of self-regulating control is the truly revolutionary characteristic of automation. Through feedback and the ability to handle information rapidly and automatically a wide variety of machines for office and plant are possible.

When James Watt harnessed heat energy and made possible the replacement of hand labor by power-driven machinery, the Industrial Revolution was inaugurated. James Watt's steam engine also contained the germ of automation, for Watt employed the principle of feedback in building the governor. This simple flyball device, invented in 1788, controlled the speed of the engine. As the load on the steam engine decreased, the engine speed naturally tended to increase. The weighted balls on the arms of the flyball governor were then driven apart and, through a mechanical linkage, the valve controlling the steam which drove the engine was closed. This action, using a small part of the energy output of the machine, regulated the speed of the machine and kept it constant.

Watt, however, was not the first to use feedback. The Dutch employed the principle to keep the sails of their early windmills facing into the wind by means of small sails placed at right angles to the large mill. A shift in the wind's direction rotated the miniature blades, which then swung the large mill into the wind. Even the ancient Romans employed feedback in the float control valves in their plumbing systems. The application of feedback before the 20th century was only sporadic, however, although Watt's governor found extensive use during the 19th century. By the middle of the 19th century, the feedback principle was being used in the steering engines of ships and, from time to time, in other devices, for example, bathroom plumbing. Until recently such use has always been traced to the ingenuity of an individual inventor, for there was no generally applicable theory of control.

The big change came with World War II. The speed and maneuverability of airplanes quickly outmoded traditional gun-laying techniques. For the sake of national survival, the scientific and engineering talent of both England and the U.S. was concentrated on developing new weapons to counter those of the enemy. The efforts of Gordon Brown, Donald Campbell, and Norbert Wiener of this country, and Arnold Tustin of England, and their associates, led to an entirely new field of engineering knowledge. In developing radar gear and servomechanisms, they produced a general theory of feedback control.

Feedback in itself is simple enough. But when coupled with such qualities as the ability to control a process from a distance at a low energy level—the pressure of a finger setting in motion thousands of horsepower by remote control—its possibilities become staggeringly large. Machines can be built which handle and store "information" in enormous quantity and which digest and use that information in a matter of micro-seconds. The result of linking machines that store information with those that count or calculate maxima and minima within fractions of seconds and those that are more sensitive to light and touch, for example, than any human being ever could be, is a machine that can carry out a whole sequence of operations with uncanny speed, precision, and "sensitivity."

Factory Applications. The process industries have been the first to avail themselves of feedback control. Certain refineries and several of the AEC plants are almost entirely automatic. Thus, they are truly representative of the new technology. In these plants machines not only regulate factors such as temperature, mixing and chemical rate of reaction, but—and this is a critical point—machines tell machines what to do. The entire operation is so complex, swift-moving, and delicate that only machines can possibly control it.

Feedback in machine tool control allows the flexibility necessary to machine pieces with varying specifications automatically, yet economically. Conventional automatic machine tools are controlled by mechanical devices, such as cams or levers, which cannot change from one product specification to another without costly and extensive adjustments. They can, therefore, machine automatically only long runs of identical products. This is the very situation that automation now promises to alter. Machines can be made versatile as well as automatic through feedback control. No longer must the benefits of automatic production be limited to large operations. Now the job and semi-production shop, which account for the largest volume of production, can enjoy the fruits of automation.

In a way this is perhaps the least interesting and significant part of automation's effect. Feedback control can and will make possible new levels of achievement. Atomic energy, for example, would not be possible were it not for feedback control. No man could operate valves or hand controls deep within the atomic reactor; remote feedback-controlled devices must perform such work. The manufacture of polyethylene, the plastic used to make squeezable bottles, would not be possible without feedback control. Exquisite operational precision is necessary to control the time, temperature, and pressure, lest the product turn out to be a useless wax.

Office Applications. Feedback control, through the medium of electronic data handling systems, is beginning to be applied to the office. In many communities, the Bell Telephone Company operates an Automatic Message Accounting System which records calls, assigns them to the right subscriber, and computes and prints the bills—all automatically. American Airlines keeps track of reservations on a magnetic drum; the Toronto Stock Exchange handles bid and asked quotations with a similar device; department stores record sales at the point of origin by electronic "tag readers."

General purpose computers, both large and small, are equally important. Their ability to process huge quantities of data at fantastic speeds, to control the sequence of their operations automatically according to variable instructions, and to store information for future reference makes them ideal for the handling and processing of business information. Early models of these machines were used to calculate and print payroll checks, to schedule materials for production, control inventory, distribute costs, and to calculate order load allocations for production machines. Such, however, are only a few examples of the useful services which computers can perform. The imagination and skill of the people using computers is the limiting factor and, as operating experience accumulates, more applications will be developed.

Computers make at least three major contributions to office automation. They provide better information about business operations, faster reports, and reduced clerical costs. Their use opens to management the possibility of an entirely new order of magnitude of control over business operations. Savings in clerical costs would be the smallest effect of automation on the business office; it is by providing management with better and far more current information that the electronic computers will score their greatest gains.

Social Effects. First and most obviously, automation means a new and fast-growing industry in America. There are more than 1,000 companies engaged wholly or partly in the manufacture of automatic control equipment. Their aggregate output last year totaled more than three billion dollars. Secondly, automation is going to mean new products for business. Industries that become automated do not merely turn out their old product more cheaply or in larger quantity. More often than not, automation is accompanied by a change in the product itself or by the economical manufacture of products which are currently impossible to make. The first effect of automation that will be felt, then, is going to be technological—new processes, new products, new cost figures, new production schedules, and new merchandising and sales problems.

But this will be the smallest of the many effects of automation! In an automated plant, we can expect labor to be upgraded. Fewer men will do routine jobs; more will perform supervisory or skilled maintenance work. Three-shift operation—or four-shift, if the work day is cut to six hours—can be expected, for machines work best 24 hours a day. Hence, the impact of automation will not be so much to use fewer men, as to use men for fewer hours at better work. A whole stratum of dull, repetitive, low-paid jobs, both in factories and offices, is going to be eliminated. What problems will this pose for the American economy?

J. D.

AUTOMATISM [ɔtɒˈmətɪzəm], a state in which the subject carries out activity without conscious knowledge of the fact. Thus, a patient with a catatonic form of schizophrenia (dementia praecox) may repeat a phrase over and over without being aware of the act. Automatisms are common occurrences in neurotic subjects who suffer fugues, that is, hallucinations of flight. Habit spasms and tics, such as a rhythmic flicking of eyelids, are regarded as automatisms. Eugen Bleuler observed: "Automatic actions are not directly noticed by the patient himself; he neither feels that he wishes to accomplish the action, nor that he executes it. If the action lasts for some time, he takes notice of it like a third person, by observing and listening."

In automatic obedience the patient, particularly the catatonic schizophrenic, completes the commands of others without critical or automatic judgment; for example, such a patient, when asked if he will stick out his tongue so that the examiner may pierce it with a pin, will promptly comply even though the warning of pain has been clearly made to him. As a corollary, command automatism is a condition in which the subject scrupulously obeys an order without exercising any critical judgment; such a state is commonly induced by hypnosis, a form of suggestion. Ambulatory automatism is a rhythmic form of automatic activity. Of another form of automatism, Charles Mercier states: "A very peculiar consequence which often follows epileptic convulsions, especially those in which the convulsion is but slight, and which are called *petit mal* (epilepsy without unconsciousness), is the occurrence of what is appropriately called 'post-epileptic automatism.'" After the occurrence of a convulsion, which may be so slight that the patient does not even fall, and which, if not closely observed, may be overlooked, the patient is found to be in a state in which he acts without any consciousness, apparently, of what he is doing, and certainly without any subsequent remembrance of what he has done. The acts done in this state are always what is termed "automatic" in character; from very long usage, they are performed with a minimum of deliberation, attention, and volition, and they are common in all normal, habitual pursuits. Such to the clerk is the act of writing; to the housemaid, of scrubbing; to the seamstress, of needlework; to the smith, of hammering; to everyone, of undressing.

A classical illustration of post-epileptic automatism was that of Vincent Van Gogh, the famous painter, who, in the last days of his illness, while incarcerated in a private institution, ran from the hospital one day while in a seizure; when he was found later, panting and exhausted, leaning against a tree miles from the sanitarium, the artist could give no explanation of how he had reached there, why he had come, or where he actually was. Thus, there is a close association between fugue and automatism. The former, in psychiatric parlance, is a flight from reality in the sense that the subject becomes more or less completely unmindful of his environment and frequently of himself. It is a so-called psychological amnesia, in which he seems to possess all his mental faculties, but in which careful questioning may reveal complete or partial lack of memory (amnesia) for certain experiences.

J. A. Br.

Automatization, a term which has two distinct meanings, referring, in the first place, to training that leads to the formation of desirable habits. The attention of the agent is first directed upon his act; with the growing perfection of the activity, his attention is permitted to lapse, either by himself or his instructor, and the action comes to be performed with less and less consciousness, until at last it can be said to be performed automatically. Automatization is, thus, no single science, but, in its most general sense, the whole of the educative process. On its more elementary level it includes the teaching of table manners to a child; on its more advanced, instruction in foreign languages and the abstract sciences.

In the second place, "automatization" refers to the creation of states during which automatic activities are performed in accordance with the unconscious, abnormal drives of the agent. The development of such states is not the result of teaching, but has usually emerged from the agent's response to his environment. Sleepwalking, fugues, and echolalia, the basic causes of which may sometimes be revealed by psychoanalysis, are among the many examples of automatism to which such automatization may give rise.

AUTOMEDON [ɔtʌˈmədən], in Greek mythology, the son of Dioreus and, according to Homer, the charioteer and companion of Achilles. Vergil said that he became the charioteer of Pyrrhus, Achilles' son, after the latter's death. Automedon commanded ten ships in the war against Troy.

AUTOMOBILE. *See* AUTOMOTIVE INDUSTRY; MOTOR VEHICLES.

AUTOMOBILE INSURANCE. *See* INSURANCE.

AUTOMOBILE RACING. *See* MOTOR VEHICLES.

AUTOMOTIVE ENGINEERING, a branch of engineering concerned with the design, manufacture, testing, and application of automotive vehicles and their component parts. Certain phases of aeronautical, marine, railroad, and industrial engineering are closely related to automotive engineering as, for example, in the case of engines, fuels, lubricants, instruments, and other items common to all. *See also* AUTOMOTIVE INDUSTRY.

AUTOMOTIVE INDUSTRY. The manufacture of motor vehicles is a typically American industrial development. It grew from relative insignificance in 1895 to become the largest producer of durable consumer goods in the country. In 1953, automotive retailer sales amounted to nearly $44,000,000,000, and motor vehicle traffic in this country approached 550 billion miles. About 32,000,000 families in the United States owned automobiles, and highway users paid nearly $6,000,000 in special taxes. Some 79 per cent of the world's passenger car production was in this country, with the United Kingdom, the world's second largest car producing area, contributing only 7⅓ per cent to the world production total. While there were only four registered passenger cars in the United States in 1895, in 1953 the number came to over 46,000,000. Motor travel today is an important source of revenue for almost all states, with 21 states deriving more than one third of their tax revenues from taxes on fuel and licenses, and only Louisiana and New York deriving less than one fifth from this source. Automo-

tive products rank high on this country's list of exports, with the total value of such exports over $1,000,000,000 in 1953.

Few inventions have had such enthusiastic acceptance as the automobile. In the history of manufacturing the automotive industry has no parallel. The import of the industry to the national economy is all the more significant because of its comparatively recent development. Of the three hun-

CHRYSLER CORPORATION

Typical early automobile, built by Carl Breer

dred automobiles owned in the United States in 1895, only four were made in this country. Of the more than 26,000,000 registered in 1939, all but a small fraction were manufactured in American plants. Before the war Germany and the United Kingdom were the competitors of the United States in the foreign sales of passenger cars and trucks. In 1938 the estimated world production of cars, trucks, and busses totaled a little over 4,000,000. The United States accounted for 62 per cent, and the United Kingdom and Germany, 11 per cent and 9 per cent, respectively. In 1953 the corresponding figures were 70, 8, and 4 per cent, with France just passing Germany's percentage.

WORLD MOTOR VEHICLE PRODUCTION, 1938 AND 1953

Country	1938	1953
United States	2,508,407	7,323,214
Canada	166,086	484,316
Austria	*	3,038
Belgium	1,665	1,786
Czechoslovakia	13,000	......†
Denmark	303	26
France	214,989	497,348
Germany	352,369	490,046
Hungary	790	......†
Italy	70,141	174,294
Japan	24,100	144,588
Poland	2,920	......†
Spain	......†	660
Sweden	7,046	29,427
Switzerland	600	1,500
United Kingdom	444,877	834,153
U.S.S.R.	210,731	......†

Source: U. S. Department of Commerce.

* Included with Germany.
† Not available.

FACTORY SALES TO DOMESTIC AND FOREIGN MARKETS

From Plants Located in the United States

YEAR	PASSENGER CARS, MOTOR TRUCKS, AND BUSES		
	Domestic Market	Foreign Market	Total
1921	1,552,500	63,619	1,616,119
1925	3,837,136	428,694	4,265,830
1929	4,671,830	665,257	5,337,087
1933	1,745,601	144,216	1,889,817
1937	4,323,569	496,650	4,820,219
1941	4,425,490	208,911	4,634,401
1945	322,132	38,869	361,001
1948	4,825,919	436,217	5,262,136
1949	5,941,155	287,775	6,228,930
1950	7,648,921	303,684	7,952,605
1951	6,124,467	470,549	6,595,016
1952	5,022,572	329,586	5,352,158
1953	6,864,245	325,203	7,189,448

Source: U.S. Dept. of Commerce and Automobile Manufacturers Ass'n.

Development of the Automobile. The invention of the automobile is not the product of a single mind, of a single country, or of a single generation in any country. Leonardo da Vinci saw the possibility of power-driven vehicles as early as the fifteenth century. Newton proposed a steam carriage to be powered by a "rearwardly directed jet of steam" in 1680. In 1769 Nicholas Joseph Cugnot, a captain in the French army, actually built a steam carriage. In England and America experimental vehicles powered by steam were built about the turn of the century. Soon after 1830 the interest of engineers and experimenters turned from the steam engine to the problem of the internal combustion engine. The advancement of the internal combustion engine to a stage of working efficiency in 1885 provided the imme-

Charles B. King (left) and J. Frank Duryea (right), early pioneers, in Duryea automobile

diate stimulus for the development of the automobile. The steam engine, the electric motor and battery, the hydrocarbon-type motor, and the internal combustion engine were all available between 1875 and 1890, and in the following decade experimenters succeeded in building practical, self-propelled road vehicles.

Pioneer Manufacturers. Étienne Lenoir in France and Gottlieb Daimler and Karl Benz in Germany were some of the pioneers who developed the automobile. Not only did foreign experiments antedate all American production, but American designers also copied foreign models extensively even after the industry was established here in the United States. American pioneers using steam, electric, or internal combustion motors were Charles Edgar Duryea, Ransom E. Olds, Elwood Haynes, Alexander Winton, Henry Ford, Charles B. King, John D. Maxwell, Elmer Apperson, Andrew L. Riker, Lewis B. Clarke, Francis Edgar Stanley, Walter White, and Herbert H. Franklin. All these men constructed automobiles between 1886 and 1899. In 1893 Duryea built the first successful gasoline motor vehicle in this country. The next year Ford and Haynes constructed and ran gasoline motor cars of their own design. At first the steam car developed much more rapidly than the gasoline car and by 1900 it appeared that steam would be the dominant form of motive power for motor vehicles. The total output of cars for that year consisted of 1,681 steam, 1,575 electric, and only 936 gasoline. The greater flexibility, ease of operation, and economy of the gasoline-powered motor vehicle brought about the shift from steam to gasoline.

Dependent Industries. The raw materials used in manufacturing motor vehicles come from every state in the Union and many of the countries of the world. A great variety of materials is required, and many of the purchases are the finished products of parts manufacturers.

The industry is one of the best customers of the aluminum, copper, zinc, machine tool, and chemical industries. It is also the foremost consumer of all forms of steel, plate glass, lead, nickel, rubber, and many other products. An estimate of the amount of some of the materials consumed in a year when production of motor vehicles reached five million units is as follows: 6,500,000 tons of steel, 155,000,000 sq. ft. of plate glass, 6,000,000 lbs. of mohair, 600,000 bales of cotton, 372,000 tons of malleable iron, 434,000 long tons of rubber, 25,000 tons of aluminum, 144,000 tons of copper, 12,000 long tons of tin, 214,000 tons of lead; 75,000 tons of zinc, and 11,500 tons of nickel. Metals account for about 90 per cent of the materials going into a vehicle. Deep-drawing sheet steel is used for body panels; frames, fenders, gasoline tanks, and many small pressed parts are made from low-carbon steel. Valve springs, leaf springs, and bumpers are made of high-carbon steels. Aluminum is an alloying element in certain steels. It is used by some manufacturers for pistons and cylinder heads in automobile engines, as well as for many small parts in stamped form. Chromium has taken the place of nickel for decorative plating on exposed parts. Zinc is used mainly for die-casting. Lead is used chiefly for storage batteries and in combination with tin for solder. Copper is used for wires, switches, and other electrical parts of the lighting, starting, and ignition systems. The radiator core and sometimes the fuel line are made of copper or brass. Bronze is used as a bearing material in the engine and in various parts of the chassis. Wood and plastics are also used, as are paints and varnishes.

Industrial Evolution. In the early stages of the industry there were many small automobile companies. Almost two hundred different manufacturers produced automobiles commercially between 1903 and 1926. The earliest producers were obliged to finance expansion through the reinvestment of profits rather than by borrowing. The working capital requirements were met in part by the funds received from dealers as deposits on orders, and in part by buying supplies and parts on credit. The business was primarily one of assembly, and relatively few parts were made within the manufacturer's plant.

HENRY FORD AND HIS FIRST AUTOMOBILE

Ford. The earliest companies produced a variety of models at a variety of prices. In 1908 the Ford Motor Company, organized in 1903, embarked on the quantity production of the universal, low-priced Model T. This car was noted for its ruggedness, ease of operation, and simplicity of construction. The low manufacturing costs brought about by product standardization constantly widened the market. Production of Model T's rose from 10,000 cars in 1909 to a peak of more than 2,000,000 in 1923. Most of the profits were ploughed back into the Ford Motor Company for further plant expansion. Starting with a capital investment of $100,000, the company grew to huge size. In the meantime numerous other companies were struggling to secure a foothold. The mortality was high, but nevertheless companies entered the field at a faster rate than they withdrew. After 1921 manufacturers became fewer as small companies fell by the wayside or were absorbed by larger companies. Large companies grew larger. General Motors, and later Chrysler, rose to challenge the undisputed leadership formerly held by Ford.

General Motors. General Motors, organized in 1908, was a consolidation of about two dozen existing companies, some of which had been motor companies and others accessory manufacturing companies. During the first year of its operations it produced more than 20 per cent of the industry's cars. Its magnitude was its biggest weakness, and sixteen years elapsed before General Motors outsold Ford. About 1921 a policy of consolidating numerous subsidiary units was put into effect. A centralized budget was installed and a system of centralized-decentralized administration was set up. The operating divisions are virtually autonomous units, but receive aid from General Motors in matters such as finance, engineering, and research. In 1927, based on volume of production, General Motors became the leading company of the industry. During the middle twenties consumers showed a marked preference for smartly-styled cars with the very latest mechanical improvements and accessories. After 1921 sales of the Model T began to decline relative to the total industry production. In 1927 Ford closed down his plant in order to design a new car before resuming production. During the eighteen-month shutdown General Motors obtained 40 per cent of the automobile business.

Chrysler. The first Chrysler car was designed and exhibited by Walter Chrysler in 1924. In the following years several models were added, giving Chrysler a price line almost as broad and complete as that of General Motors. In the

WALTER P. CHRYSLER AND HIS FIRST AUTOMOBILE

period 1930-1941, Chrysler produced about 25 per cent of the total automobile volume.

Distribution of Production. In 1953 there were 32 manufacturers of motor vehicles, some of which were divisions of a parent company. Passenger cars were made by 17 manufacturers, motor trucks by 18, and motor coaches or buses

by 11. Of the above, 7 made both passenger cars and trucks, and 3 made both motor trucks and coaches. Of the 17 producers of passenger cars, 11 were divisions of the General Motors Corporation, the Chrysler Corporation, or the Ford Motor Company. These three companies accounted for about 90 per cent of the passenger-car sales and about 85 per cent of total motor-vehicle sales in the period before World War II. Automobile production tended to become localized in a small number of centers, particularly in Michigan, early in its history. The homes of many of the early leaders were in this region, and the presence of automobile manufacturing soon led to the development in this area of a body of workmen skilled in the automotive trade and available for new enterprises. Thus automotive manufacturing became established as an almost local industry and it remains practically so, except as branch assembly plants have been placed near the chief markets of the country to save transportation costs. The Detroit area is the center of the industry.

MASS PRODUCTION

Adam Smith, in his *The Wealth of Nations,* published in 1776, described the workings of mass production in common pin manufacture. The most familiar modern application of this method is in automotive manufacturing, starting in 1909 with the Model T Ford, which within a decade was being turned out at a rate as high as 7,000 a day. Over the years, mass-production methods have been applied widely in all industries in which parts or products are made in large quantities. In the automotive industry, the process is closely allied with mechanical engineering, because the very design of each part must be so developed as to suit the manufacturing facilities of a given plant. Consequently, there must be close co-operation between engineering and production departments to assure a product of acceptable quality at the lowest possible cost.

Mass production involves many elements, including paced conveyor lines for carrying raw materials to machines and for transporting parts from one machine to another, feeder-line conveyors carrying finished parts and subassemblies to the final assembly lines, and pacemaking conveyors for final assembly lines. Then there are the machine lines with their specialized metal-cutting machinery and "process" lines for certain stages of fabrication—heat-treatment, painting, electroplating, and cleaning. Finally, the making of parts and delivering them to the final assembly lines in proper order and at the right time are co-ordinated and controlled by scheduling, which is really what makes the mass production system function. Scheduling is required to get the right raw materials of every description into the plant at the right time; it is responsible for the sequence in which parts are machined and shaped and painted; and finally, it produces the orderly flow of thousands of parts by various means to the final assembly line.

The secret of the process is the arranging of machine-shop lines and assembly lines to provide the shortest path from raw materials to the finished product. Machine shops are provided with metalworking machinery of the most advanced kind and capable of operating automatically. All that the operator has to do is to load raw parts and remove finished parts.

Usually the small plants or those which make parts in relatively small quantities are so laid out that parts move from one department to another until every operation has been completed. In such plants similar machines are grouped together. For example, lathes will be in one department, grinders in another, and drill presses, milling machines, turret lathes, in still other departments. Thus if a given part has to be turned, milled, drilled, and ground, it is moved progressively to the respective operation departments, and last to inspection. This is a reasonable way of working when parts are made in small lots and is still practiced in many industries.

In mass production, however, the greater volume justifies setting up of compact, self-contained machine lines for each

FORD MOTOR COMPANY

EARLY FORD CONVEYOR ASSEMBLY LINE

part or for families of similar parts. To take an engine piston as an example, all the machinery for turning, grinding, milling, and drilling is arranged in a single department and in the order in which such operations are to be performed. If the pistons are to be plated, an automatic electroplating machine will be installed right in the line. Instead of moving from one department to another, the piston comes to a self-contained machine line and moves from one operation to another in sequence. At the end of this line, it is ready to move to stock or directly to the engine assembly line.

Mass production is many-sided. It involves a mental process or slant that is brought to bear in the solution of manufacturing problems. It includes metalworking machinery of advanced type; it requires advanced materials handling to bring work to the machine and to carry it from one machine to another. It is the sum of many techniques designed to reduce handling of work, speed the flow of machine lines, and bring all necessary parts together at the assembly benches or assembly lines at the right time, in the right place, and along the shortest path. When added together properly, these result in low costs that bring the products within the reach of many people.

The automobile industry was built upon the dual basis of an already developed system of interchangeable parts manufacture and machine-tool development. The manufacture of separate parts in quantities and the assembly of the finished product from standard parts had been applied in factories making watches, agricultural implements, railroad cars, and other products between about 1850 and 1875. Between 1800 and 1875 machine tools were developed which laid the basis for the more recent developments of the late nineteenth and early twentieth centuries. Once the crudest experimental stages of the automobile were past, the attempt to produce on a large scale was made by American enterprise almost from the start. The first instance of anything approaching mass production occurred in 1898, when the Mitchell-Lewis Car Company in Wisconsin manufactured five hundred three-wheeled motor vehicles for the European market.

The Ford Model T. The American practice of specializing in the production of cars with interchangeable parts was

FORD MOTOR COMPANY

EARLY FORD BODY-DROP ASSEMBLY LINE

given impetus by the appearance on the market of Henry Ford's Model T in 1909. The manufacture of a single model whose parts fitted so accurately that not even the slightest adjustment was necessary in assembly was a radical departure from the manufacturing methods obtaining in other plants of the period. The production of 10,000 units of the Model T in 1909, an unprecedented achievement at that time, marked the real beginning of quantity production of low-priced cars. The highly successful production and marketing policies initiated by the Ford Motor Company were later put into practice by other manufacturers. Product standardization, specialized machine tools for use in the factories themselves, power-driven conveyor assemblies, and minute subdivision of labor became the bywords of automobile production.

Standardization. Although individual manufacturers had begun using interchangeable parts for their cars, there was a wide divergence between the demands of various companies

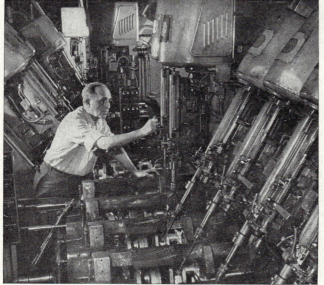

FORD MOTOR COMPANY

Drilling oil system into crankshaft in one operation

for parts and accessories. In 1910 the Society of Automotive Engineers formed its Standard Committee, which pointed the way to simplification of engineering practice. Industry-wide adoption of such standardized parts as wheel sizes, axles, screws, and many other minor parts was brought about, considerably lessening the price of parts going into the car. Today the manufacture of motor vehicles, resting on the fundamental principles of interchangeable parts and the assembly line, often is quoted as the classic example of mass production.

Stages of Production. *Design.* Designing is begun about a year before the model appears on the market. Upon final decision of style, specifications are drawn up for all component parts by the engineers. Experimental models are built and subjected to extensive laboratory and road tests. Corrections are made before the designs are released to the production departments. The patterns, dies, machine tools, and necessary fixtures are then made.

Pressing sheets to form part of car's body

Machining. Machining, the second step, requires extensive foundry equipment as well as special-purpose machine tools. The basic processes are metal cutting, casting, forging, stamping, welding, and heat treating. Castings are used to make a number of intricately shaped parts, from the cylinder block to the radiator ornament. Crankshafts, camshafts, gear blanks, connecting rods, valves, and steering-gear parts are usually forged from steel. Hundreds of the parts of a vehicle are formed by stamping in presses; these include body parts, fenders, frames, gasoline tanks, fans, wheels, crankcases, rear axle housings, lamp parts, and dust shields. Many stampings are welded to form the body and its parts. By heat treating, the crystalline structure of steel is changed to obtain the desired properties of hardness, toughness, and high strength. All of these form-making operations are physically segregated from the assembly lines.

Assembly. The third step, assembly of the motor vehicle, represents the industry's greatest achievement in mass-production techniques. After the parts have been completed and inspected, they are either shipped to distant assembly plants or carried by conveyor to points where they are assembled into the primary units of the car, such as the motor, frame, or body. These subassemblies, where the primary units are

FORD MOTOR COMPANY

ENGINE BLOCKS IN SUSPENSION
Arms of steel, hung from overhead monorail system of tracks, hold 180-pound overhead-valve engines as part of the moving assembly line.

fashioned, flow into the two or more final assembly lines. Each man along the line has a specific operation to perform on each car. The guiding principle is the saving of time, by bringing material to the worker instead of having the worker go to the material. Assembly of the car begins with the placing of the frame on the line in an inverted position. After such units as the rear and front springs, the rear-axle assembly, and the shock absorbers have been added, the frame is turned upright and other parts are added. In the meantime, the engine unit is being assembled. After the engine is formed and tested it goes to the overhead platform, where it is lowered and mounted on the waiting chassis. During this time, the body has been received on another assembly line. As it moves along, the dash is installed, the body is wired, and other parts such as the fenders, body hardware, and radiator case are added. The body is then raised from the body-conditioning line by an overhead cabin hoist, brought to the main assembly line, and lowered into its position on the chassis. Body bolts are tightened, the instruments are connected to the engine, and other parts—including the steering wheel, floor covering, and one-piece hood—are then installed. With gasoline and water poured in, the car runs off the assembly line under its own power. Economy is achieved through volume production. Owing to the nature of the production process, unit costs rise sharply as output decreases, and fall when production increases. Despite costly machines and dies that make overhead costs extremely high, costs per vehicle are comparatively small with volume production.

Division of Labor. The size of the labor force directly employed in the manufacture of motor vehicles, bodies, and parts grew from 2,500 workers in 1899 to 920,200 in 1953. Nowhere else has the principle of the division of labor been carried farther. Each worker has that bit of work to do for which he is particularly qualified, thus eliminating waste energy and waste motion. Practically all the construction of the parts of the car and some of the assembly work are done automatically by machine.

Types of Machines. *Single-Purpose.* The kinds of machines used in mass production depend entirely upon the number of pieces to be produced a day. At one time the larger manufacturers relied to a great extent on the so-called single-purpose machines. These are special, expensive machines, capable of machining only one part but turning out enormous quantities at extremely low cost. Their disadvantage is that they can produce one part and one only and cannot be changed over for another part or even a change in design of the same part. Apart from the risk of investing a great deal of money in a machine that may have to be junked long before it wears out, there is the greater disadvantage that its use fixes engineering design.

Unit Type. Although single-purpose equipment still is used and is justified in special instances, the more recent practice is to adopt an advanced type of machine—the so-called unit type. It is made up of separable sections much like units of modern furniture. In one form it is a single-purpose machine with the same scale of economy as a true single-purpose machine. But if the product is changed, it is possible to replace certain sections to suit the new part, or the machine may be adapted to an entirely different part by changing more of the sections and introducing some new elements. This kind of machine is much more flexible, lends itself to change-over, and permits change-over at reduced cost. It helps to unfreeze engineering design, permits the engineer to make even radical changes more frequently without facing the penalty of major expenditures for machinery.

Transfer Type. The transfer type of machinery is a still more advanced and complicated form of unit-type machine, combining a number of different functions within a single machine. Some units combine the functions of from six to a hundred different machines. The objective is to load a rough part at one end of the machine, have the part go through a number of stations, and then come out at the other end completely finished. A more practical variation in the case of large parts is to have a succession of transfer machines in a long line so that the part is completed at the end of the line. With transfer-type machinery, parts go through the complete cycle of operations automatically within each machine, and from one machine to another. Operators are required only for loading the first machine and unloading the last station, although long lines should have operators or inspectors between units to make sure of product quality before work is permitted to move from one machine into another.

Special Machines. Even in the automotive industry, some parts are made in relatively small lots. In some cases this problem is met by using simple machines with skilled operators. But even here the ingenuity of engineers has found applications of unit-type or special machines, capable of meeting the low-cost standards so necessary in this industry. By skillful planning and design, it is possible to develop machines capable of finishing a large number of similar parts or even of different parts that require the same kind of machining. The resultant basic machine is provided with a large number of fixtures for holding work and the tools for machining it. The technique of operation involves setting up the tooling for a given part in the largest quantity that

GENERAL MOTORS CORPORATION

TIRE-MOUNTING OPERATION

Wheel of proper color and tire of proper style, according to information on telautograph paper (at left), are coupled to meet chassis on the assembly line.

can be made at one time, then changing tools and fixtures for the next part and repeating the process for as many parts as may have been planned for the operation. Some plants machine as many as 150 different kinds of parts over a single special machine of this kind.

Conveyors and the Assembly Line. Conveyors used in mass production are of many kinds: overhead chains with hooks for carrying the work, chains in the floor for moving cars and trucks, endless belts for light assembly as well as for movement from one machine to another, inclined belts that serve as elevators, spiral conveyors, gravity rollers on which heavy work can be slid without much manual effort, and other variations and combinations. Each one has its

GENERAL MOTORS CORPORATION

Attaching rear leaf spring to car's frame

proper function, and it is the job of mechanical engineers to determine their best use.

The conveyor is a pacemaker for assembly operations, the means for feeding assembly lines, and the backbone of assembly. When used for subassembly or final assembly, the conveyor becomes a pacemaker, since its speed can be controlled at will to accommodate even hourly changes in production rate. Its principal role, however, is to maintain a smooth flow of parts and subassemblies along the assembly line so as to present the job progressively to the workers at each of a long row of stations. Assembly conveyors, in turn, are paced by other conveyor lines called feeder conveyors, which transport parts or subassemblies from departments in which they originate or from storerooms directly to the point at which they are required on the assembly line. Such conveyors range in length from a few hundred feet to several miles in their path through the plant. They move continuously and serve the added purpose of storage, since parts remain on the line until they are taken off.

Developments in materials handling include special means for making conveyor functions automatic even to the point of picking up work and delivering it at the right spot without the aid of an operator. This procedure has been worked out in different ways by a number of different manufacturers. On machine lines or press-shop lines, parts are moved automatically from one machine to another by belt conveyors. At each machine the belt will have a deflector bar, which forces parts to come off the belt and drop into a chute that carries the parts directly to the machine operation. This arrangement can be likened to a succession of funnels through which parts can drop from a large belt into individual hoppers.

Scheduling. The network of conveyors, in all their complication, may be considered as an orderly scheme for the scheduling of final assembly lines. By an apparent miracle of organization, the final assembly line in a motor-car plant alternately delivers a number of different models of cars, with a variety of bodies—sedans, coupés, convertibles, limousines—one a minute or one in three minutes or whatever the time cycle is in the plant. And this is only part of the complication, for each body may have a different color or color combination, and wheel size and color may vary. Yet they go together without fail although the assembler has no part in selecting the units he applies. How is it done? Each day, hour by hour, the department in charge of scheduling works out a jigsaw puzzle consisting of cars or trucks specified for delivery that day by the sales department. At the start of the day, each chassis is lined up in exact order of assembly. Bodies, sheet metal, and other parts are lined up the same way to fit the cars or trucks as they are to be built. Key stations in the plant have a copy of the same schedule. To meet the first car, the man on the body line sends on the first body of proper color and type. Similarly, the man in charge of fenders or wheels sends the right fenders or wheels in their proper order. Since the process is repeated for each vehicle to be built during the day, there is an orderly movement of bodies, wheels and tires, fenders, hoods, and the other parts. The feeder-line conveyors carrying these parts are adjusted in speed to match the speed of the final assembly conveyor. With the first car of the day, the tenth, and the thousandth, the right body and fenders and wheels arrive at just the proper time for assembly to the chassis.

PRODUCTION ENGINEERING

The automotive engineering discussed here is confined to what is commonly known in the industry as the product

Electronic machine which automatically balances crankshafts.

engineering department or section of a company, corporation, or major subsidiary of a large organization. The purpose of the product engineering section is to create, design, standardize, test, develop, and improve the products of the organization. To handle the work, the engineering section co-operates with purchasing, material control, inspection, tooling, manufacturing, planning, accounting, service, sales, and other departments of the organization, and with outside companies that supply component parts or assemblies.

Specialization. The automotive product engineering field has expanded and developed into a group of specialized sections that allow the engineer in charge of each group to devote his entire effort to a particular section of the vehicle. In contrast to the situation in the 1890's, when one or two men would design and build a complete automobile, the modern automotive vehicle is the end product of the combined efforts of engineering experts in the fields of chemistry, ceramics, electricity, mechanics, metallurgy, styling, and other fields. A large share of the combined effort comes about through the additional engineering done by the manufacturers of accessories and parts, such as carburetors, fuel pumps, generators, lamps, tubing, bearings, and tappets.

To name a few of the pioneers, Charles E. and J. Franklin Duryea built the first gasoline-engine-driven motor vehicle in America in 1892. In 1893, Elwood G. Haynes designed a car and had Elmer and Edgar Apperson build it for him. Henry Ford and Charles King built their first cars in 1894. In the late 1890's, G. B. Selden, R. E. Olds, Alexander Winton, John Wilkinson, Rollin White, J. W. Packard, and many others designed and produced their first cars.

Although these early cars seem relatively simple in retrospect, it was quite a feat for one or two men to design and build a car that would start and continue to run.

In 1900, production of automobiles totaled only 4,192 vehicles. In that year, the first national automobile advertising appeared and the first auto show was held in the old Madison Square Garden.

A Typical Organization. A typical modern automobile product engineering organization has three main divisions, all under the chief engineer. These are headed, respectively, by the experimental engineer, the design engineer, and the metallurgical engineer. The experimental engineer has charge of laboratory tests, road tests, shops, and records of experiments. The design engineer, who may be the assistant chief engineer, has charge of design drafting and of specification records, and heads the design divisions for the various components. The metallurgical engineer directs the activities of the laboratory. However, in any case the ultimate responsibility for costs, budgets, and procedures goes back to the chief engineer.

Such an organization would function equally well for truck or bus engineering. Even though product engineering departments of all automotive concerns have the same general functions, the organizations vary widely, depending upon the products, plant size, the engineers in charge, and numerous other controlling and related factors.

Grouping of Parts. To understand the typical organization better, it is advisable also to refer to a typical listing and grouping of automotive parts. A typical grouping is as follows: body, frame, front-wheel suspension, rear-wheel suspension, brakes, engine and clutch, transmission, fuel tank, exhaust system, wheels and tires, chassis sheet metal, electrical system and instruments, radiator, bumpers, and miscellaneous assembly items.

In multiple-plant companies, parts are grouped by their functions, to facilitate the uniformity and flow of records, releases, parts lists, cost reports, weight and material analyses, drawings, purchase orders, tool control, and material schedules. In single-plant concerns, the grouping is often built on a subassembly basis in accord with the method of assembly. Only the major groups are indicated in the preceding paragraph. For example, the body is further broken down into front end, floor, roof, doors, seats, and other subgroups; and the engine is further detailed into subgroups such as cylinder block, cylinder head, crankshaft, pistons and rods, and valve gear.

Functions of Automotive Engineering. Basically, present-day automotive engineering consists of (1) research to develop new products, (2) styling to create new bodies and appearance items, and (3) product engineering to refine and develop the new ideas and styles into designs suitable for production. The engineering group handling this third phase is by far the largest. Further responsibilities of this group are to check patents, carry on tests and development work, release new models, and help with the solution of any problems that may arise on current production.

Success of an engineering development requires the best efforts of each man to prove the new design. Many skills are required to make up a successful automotive engineering organization—the executive, engineer, designer, draftsman, metallurgist, modelmaker, machinist, experimental mechanic, laboratory technician, road tester, assembler, clerk, stenographer, analyst, and others.

Styling. After preliminary sketches and over-all specifications of a new model have been developed, the chief engineer discusses them with the general manager, the sales manager, and other executives. Stylists then proceed to make the small-scale clay models, which usually undergo numerous revisions. After the styling is agreed upon, full-size blackboard drawings are made and used to guide the modelmakers in their construction of a full-size model. When finished, this model has the outward appearance of a completed car even though it is made of wood, clay, and other materials that are easily worked by hand.

Presentation of this full-size model to the executive group is a major event for the stylists, modelmakers, and engineers. Changes are often made, and interest is at a high pitch until final approval is given for the engineers to proceed with the design for production.

Product Engineering. At this point the product engineering program swings into full force. Body and sheet-metal designers make their full-size layouts on coated aluminum sheets. These are used in making many of the templates (patterns) and detail drawings, and for checking purposes. Chassis designers complete their work on the frame, front and rear suspensions, brakes, steering gears, wheels, and other units. The engine, transmission, electrical, and accessory designers work out their problems in co-operation with each of the related groups. Advice is welcomed from all engineering personnel who can contribute constructive suggestions during the design program. Engineers who are especially familiar with production processes make suggestions that will facilitate manufacture. Men with service and field experience on existing models suggest changes to improve accessibility and reduce owner maintenance expense. The customer research group expresses the desires of the motoring public. Tool and process engineers contribute ideas beneficial to tooling, processing, or assembling. Such ideas may include use of a newer and lower-cost process, the replacing of a casting or forging with a lower-cost stamping of equal or greater strength, or developing more suitable production equipment which, because of its increased capacity, will lower manufacturing cost.

Laboratory Tests. While the design group makes the drawings, the experimental department is busy ordering and making parts for test and testing components. Frequently, accelerated laboratory tests are required to check new units

A body and a chassis, each built on a separate assembly line, converging at this point to form a matched unit

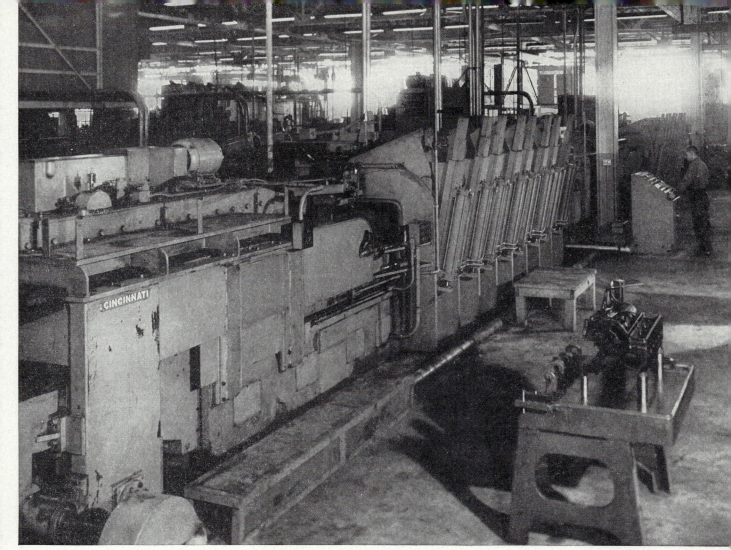

AUTOMATION IN THE AUTO INDUSTRY

A single workman watches controls, as broaching machine automatically cuts holes into cylinder blocks

before they are installed on the experimental road-test cars. Very often the experimental machine shop suggests improvements as a result of difficulties they encounter in fabrication of newly designed parts. Minor design errors sometimes are

Installing a V-8 engine on chassis

uncovered in both the experimental machine and assembly shops.

As the experimental test parts are accumulated, records of material analyses and various hardness tests are made for such items as front-wheel spindles, king pins, steering linkage, gears, axle shafts, and engine parts subject to wear, stress, or strain. These records provide important information in case experimental tests show excessive wear or undue fatigue. Accurate records of all drawings, changes, releases and tests are maintained.

Laboratory tests are made on some of the new or redesigned subassemblies to compare them with the corresponding existing production units. New engines are tested in the dynamometer laboratory for power and fuel-consumption characteristics. Spark-advance requirements, operating temperatures, balance, vibration, and many other characteristics are checked. Carburetion and manifold developments and tests are major projects, especially on a newly designed engine. Engine endurance tests run on the dynamometer stands need proper interpretation to compare the results with engine durability determined by actual road tests.

Checking after Completion. When the first experimental car is completed, the engineers check it for general performance, operating characteristics, ease of handling, and riding comfort. Changes may be needed to improve certain of these characteristics or to correct objectionable features that were not anticipated in the design. Assembly difficulties, interferences, and misalignments are reported. Specialists representing the accessory manufacturers work along with the car-development engineers on problems related to their particular units such as carburetors, fuel pumps, brakes, and shock absorbers. Cooling tests are often conducted in wind tunnels to determine whether the sheet metal and grille interfere with the proper flow of air through the radiator core.

Fixture indicating adjustments needed to fit body to frame

Road Tests. The second experimental car is usually scheduled for endurance testing. After a rapid break-in, the car is driven day and night by a road-test crew trained to drive at speeds and under conditions that represent severe owner usage. The endurance-test schedules are worked out, after considerable study, to include all types of roads and a wide range of speeds. It is not sufficient to do all road testing of the car at high speeds. Under normal driving conditions some difficulties may occur which are not encountered at top speed. If a car were designed to withstand continuous top-speed operation, many of the units would be far more costly than required for the average motorist, who only occasionally drives at top speed.

Complete records are kept of general performance—acceleration, speed, hill-climbing ability, fuel and oil consumption, tire mileage, unusual noises, operating defects, mechanical adjustments, and parts replacements. The engineers study the records and reports and check them against the specifications and the original standards. They also compare the records with like records of current models.

More up-to-the-minute changes are incorporated as each additional experimental car is tested. About the time the experimental program is well under way, several test cars incorporating all the latest changes are driven on a cross-country trip that enables the engineers to check general performance in desert country and at high altitudes.

One automobile manufacturing organization with extensive proving-ground facilities can, by use of three shifts of test drivers, complete 25,000-mi. endurance runs in four weeks. Durability cars are usually driven on a durability break-in schedule for approximately 2,000 mi. before the cars are run at maximum speed. After this break-in, the durability schedule includes all ranges of speeds on all types of roads. At regular intervals of approximately 5,000 mi.

the cars involved in the test are checked for performance and economy.

Performance tests include acceleration, hill climbing, maximum speed, idling and minimum speed for flexibility, braking, and "roadability." Economy tests are made at constant speeds to determine fuel consumption at 20, 30, 40, 50, 60 and 70 m.p.h. and at maximum speed. Normally once during the 25,000-mi. durability run, highway economy tests are made to determine fuel consumption under normal highway conditions. Compression-ratio measurements are made at any time during the tests if conditions indicate that they are desirable for engineering information. Other tests are run occasionally, depending on current engineering problems.

Tooling. From a manufacturing consideration, some of the new items must be released to the tool-and-die departments long before all car tests are completed. Body dies, for example, require almost a year to complete before production is started. Numerous other items require three to six months for tooling. Engineers work very closely with the tool-design section on the advance release of blueprints. In the automotive business it is considered good economy to proceed with the tooling even though it may later be necessary to discard some of the tools as a result of design changes.

Specifications and Records. The engineering specifications section, usually a part of the design department, issues releases, change notices, blueprints, stop orders, parts lists, and bills of material to all concerned. The specifications and records department handles the bulk of the paper work for the engineering section and frequently furnishes product information and technical data to the sales and advertising departments and to trade publications.

Checking and Experimental Cars. A section of the experimental assembly department is set aside to build a production and design check car. This group receives copies of all releases, blueprints, and bills of material ready for the production departments, from which they build a check car. The check car is kept up to date with all the latest design changes and consequently is used for numerous purposes. For example, engineers and specifications men need only to look at this car to tell what is short on their production releases.

As soon as possible, an experimental car is assigned to the service department, to allow them sufficient time to work out service procedures and establish flat-rate time for the

The Buick XP-300, an experimental convertible powered by a 300-hp engine designed to produce speeds of 150 hpm

The Bruetsch Dwarf, built by Egon Bruetsch of Stuttgart, Germany, is a three-wheeled vehicle of unconventional design, weighing 370 lb. It is powered by a one-cylinder, two-stroke, DKW engine and has a maximum speed of about 60 mph. (Right) The two seater; (left) the same model designed for one.

The Thunderbird 56, built by the Ford Motor Company, retains its classic lines but offers three power train options —a 225-hp engine with Fordomatic transmission, a 215-hp engine with overdrive, and a 202-hp engine with standard transmission. Safety equipment includes a concave steering wheel, safety belts, and shock absorbent cushioning for the instrument panel and sun visors.

Cadillac's Eldorado Seville sets a new trend in hardtop styling.

The "modern formal" Continental Mark II, introduced by Ford.

A Bel Air Series sports sedan, new in the Chevrolet line.

A 225-hp Spitfire V-8 engine is featured in the Chrysler Windsor.

The first of its kind in the world is the new General Motors XP-500, a free-piston engine car. This type of engine burns animal, vegetable, or mineral oils, and pumps hot gasses through a pipe to a turbine which drives the rear wheels of the vehicle. It is probably the engineering link between the internal combustion, piston compression engine of today and the gas turbine models of the near future.

AUTOMOBILES OF THE FUTURE

(Right above) A more realistic "dream car" is this Cadillac Eldorado Brougham Town Car. It marks the return of the classic Town Car body, with its comfortable privacy and chauffeured elegance. The interior of the air-conditioned, fibre-glass body has a radio-telephone and a women's fitted vanity compartment.

(Right center) The Ford Motor Company built this "dream car," naming it F-X Atmos (Future Experimental). While not proposed as a production vehicle, it is not entirely fantastic. Many of its features are within reasonable reach of realization with today's technological developments that anticipate the gas turbine engine of the future or even the more remote solar power.

(Right below) The Falcon, a low-slung (51 in. high) two-seater roadster, one of Chrysler Corporation's newest "Idea" cars that suggests automobile designing of the future. Note the laterally mounted, chrome-plated exhaust muffler and functional radiator grille, which reveal the European sports car influence. The car offers a fully automatic transmission, power-assisted steering and braking, and electric window lifts, for ease of operation.

(Below) The General Motors "Sunmobile" is one of the first ever built. It runs on electricity which the 12 photoelectric cells on top convert from the rays of the sun or other sources of light. While the car offers a glimpse of a possible future power source, it is still impractical for our present conception of a motor car.

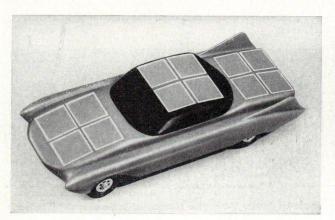

dealers' manuals. During the repeated disassembling and reassembling, the service department makes suggestions for changes that will improve accessibility and reduce servicing time.

Production Checking. Now production assembly of the new car begins, but the work of the engineering department on this model never ends until it is superseded by a new model. In the modern plant, engineering checks of production cars are made from time to time to make sure they meet the engineering specifications. This testing includes production control, checking units submitted by manufacturers under consideration as duplicate sources, experimentation with alternate materials, and further development and improvement. The engineering department continues the close scrutiny of field service reports from all types of users in various localities for information on any inherent weaknesses and to learn whether climatic or atmospheric conditions are adversely affecting the automobile or its components.

Because of this highly intensified effort on the part of the modern automotive engineering department, present-day automobiles have high standards of performance and are capable, with ordinary maintenance attention, of long service life.

Marketing of Motor Vehicles. Whereas production has been centralized, the automobile market has been nationwide. Geographically the largest section of the market for motor vehicles includes New England, the Middle Atlantic, and the East North Central divisions of the country. Almost half of all registered motor vehicles are in these regions. The East South Central, West South Central, and Mountain divisions combined account for less than one fifth. In 1953 California led in registrations with 4,713,917 privately-owned and publicly-owned vehicles, followed by New York State with 3,686,921.

Dealerships which distribute motor vehicles usually handle one manufacturer's product exclusively. The dealer's franchise is an agreement on the part of the manufacturer to let the dealer purchase and resell the product. As of January 1954 there were a total of 122,038 retail outlets, including dealers, repair shops, superservice stations, and wrecking and body establishments. Of these, 47,460 were passenger car and truck dealers.

The Industry in World War II. Production of finished passenger automobiles for civilian use was suspended in

KAISER - FRAZER CORPORATION
View of typical automobile assembling plant

February 1942 by order of the War Production Board. All the tremendous facilities of the industry were converted to produce war matériel. In 1943 the production of motor vehicles had dropped to 699,828 units, of which all but 139 were trucks, and less than 3,000 of these were for civilian use. The industry converted to war production with little reduction in the annual volume of shipments, and a sharp increase occurred in 1943. This increase was made possible in part by the large wartime expansion of the industry's facilities. To the production capacity of the prewar industry was added $1,100,000,000 in new plants. In addition, the capacity of the old plants was expanded with more than $800,000,000 of new facilities. Nearly $29,000,000,000 worth of military matériel was delivered by the automobile industry for the war effort. This included aircraft, engines, ammunition, guns, marine equipment, tanks, motor vehicles and many other products.

Postwar Production. Production of passenger cars for civilian use was resumed in July 1945 after a lapse of almost three and a half years, during which only a few units were assembled from parts on hand. Only 69,532 passenger cars were produced in 1945. The output in 1946 amounted to 2,148,677 units, or 57 per cent of the 1941 figure, but it surpassed the 1941 figure in 1948, and reached a peak of 6,665,863 cars in 1951. The peak of purchases of new cars was reached in 1950, with about 5,200,000 sales, but that for used cars continued to rise, reaching about 8,000,000 in 1953. Of all passenger cars in use in 1953, less than 7 per cent were new, more than half were at least 5 years old, and about one fourth at least 12 years old. These facts are related to the increased life expectancy of cars: average life of those scrapped in 1952 was 14.3 years, as compared with only 10.2 years in 1941 and 7 years in 1930.

Production for Export. Exports of motor vehicles in 1953 amounted to 154,459 passenger car units, valued at $276,020,000, and 134,435 truck and bus units, valued at $268,577,000. The leading export markets for passenger cars in 1953 were Canada, Venezuela, Mexico, and Belgium. Mexico, Colom-

MOTOR VEHICLE REGISTRATIONS IN THE UNITED STATES, 1900 TO 1953

YEAR	TOTAL	PRIVATE AND COMMERCIAL VEHICLES		
		Passenger cars	Trucks and truck tractors	Busses
1900	8,000	8,000	. . . . . .	. . . . . . *
1905	78,800	77,400	1,400	. . . . . . *
1910	468,500	458,377	10,123	. . . . . . *
1915	2,490,932	2,332,426	158,506	. . . . . . *
1920	9,239,161	8,131,522	1,107,639	. . . . . . *
1925	19,940,724	17,439,701	2,483,215	17,808
1927	23,139,559	20,142,120	2,969,780	27,659
1929	26,502,508	23,060,421	3,408,088	33,999
1931	25,862,038	22,330,402	3,489,756	41,880
1933	23,876,707	20,586,284	3,245,505	44,918
1935	26,229,743	22,494,884	3,675,865	58,994
1937	29,706,158	25,390,773	4,249,219	66,166
1939	30,615,087	26,139,526	4,406,702	68,859
1941	34,472,145	29,524,101	4,859,244	88,800
1943	30,499,608	26,912,730	4,480,176	106,702
1945	30,638,429	25,691,434	4,834,742	112,253
1949	44,139,951	36,312,380	7,692,569	135,002
1951	51,326,438	42,525,217	8,657,931	143,290
1952	52,644,317	43,646,343	8,853,535	144,439
1953	55,626,081	46,289,129	9,195,697	141,255

Source: United States Public Roads Administration.

* Not available

bia, and Venezuela were the leading markets for trucks in 1953. Various methods of reaching the export market have been employed by United States firms. Some have maintained branch factories abroad; others have established branch assembly plants outside the United States; still others have staffs of wholesalers in foreign countries, or deal directly with their distributors by mail and cable.

UNITED STATES PRODUCTION OF MOTOR VEHICLES
1895 TO 1954

Year	Total production	Passenger cars	Motor trucks and busses
1895	4	4	.....
1900	4,192	4,192	.....
1905	25,000	24,250	750
1910	187,000	181,000	6,000
1915	969,930	895,930	74,000
1920	2,227,349	1,905,560	321,789
1925	4,265,830	3,735,171	530,659
1927	3,401,326	2,936,533	464,793
1929	5,358,420	4,587,400	771,020
1931	2,389,738	1,973,090	416,648
1933	1,920,057	1,573,512	346,545
1935	3,946,934	3,252,244	694,690
1937	4,808,974	3,915,889	893,085
1939	3,577,202	2,866,796	710,496
1941	4,840,502	3,779,682	1,057,905
1943	699,828	139	699,689
1945	725,215	69,532	655,683
1949	6,253,651	5,119,466	1,134,185
1951	6,756,263	5,338,435	1,426,828
1952	5,538,959	4,320,794	1,218,165
1953	7,323,214	6,116,948	1,206,266
1954*	6,558,000	5,520,000	1,038,000

Sources: Bureau of the Census; Automobile Manufacturers Association.
*Preliminary.

Production Trend. Over 92,000,000 cars and trucks were produced in the United States between 1895 and 1946. The prewar peak year of production, 1929, was passed in 1949. The production trend has been generally upward, interrupted only by periods of war and of business depression. In 1953 over 55,625,000 motor vehicles were registered and, statistically speaking, every third person in the United States owned a passenger car. *See also* MOTOR VEHICLES; MOTOR TRANSPORT.   R. M., P. C. P., and J. G.

AUTONOMIC NERVOUS SYSTEM. *See* NERVOUS SYSTEM.

AUTOPSY [ɔ'tɒpsi], the opening and examination of the body, including the internal organs, after death; also known as post-mortem examination. A more descriptive and accurate word to describe this procedure is necropsy, since it is compounded from the Greek *nekros*, death, and *opsis*, view, rather than from *autos*, self, and *opsis*. The term autopsy came into use early in the history of modern medicine to distinguish the opening of the human body by human agents from the much commoner practice of dissecting animals.

Historical Background. Post-mortem examinations of some sort have probably been made since man first took a rational interest in disease. One of the first written records of a specific autopsy is that of one performed by William of Saliceto (c. 1201-1280) on the nephew of the Marchese Pallavicini. In many of the early reports it is apparent that the impetus to post-mortem examination was medico-legal. Pope Alexander V was autopsied in 1410 because of the suspicions arising from his sudden and unexplained death. Throughout the sixteenth and seventeenth centuries the prac-

tice became increasingly common, and by 1700 a number of collections of necropsy reports had been published. The best of these was the systematized collection of morbid anatomy of Théophile Bonet (1620-1689), *Sepulchretum anatomicum sive anatomica practica* (1679), which is said to have inspired the famous work of Giovanni Morgagni, *De sedibus et causis morborum per anatomen indigatis* (1761). This book inaugurated the method of investigation of disease based on autopsy findings that culminated in the atlas and text of Matthew Baillie, *The Morbid Anatomy of Some of the Most Important Parts of the Human Body* (1794), in spirit a modern textbook of pathology.

The development of the use of the compound microscope in the nineteenth century and Rudolf Virchow's (1821-1902) doctrine of cellular pathology added to the usefulness of the autopsy to medical science, so that since the mid-nineteenth century it has been the custom in the better hospitals to request permission for autopsies on all fatal cases.

Purpose and Value of Autopsy. Laws differ from place to place, but in general in the civilized world of today an autopsy can be performed only with the permission of the next of kin and by a qualified doctor of medicine who is usually especially trained in pathology, that branch of medical science which is concerned with the structural and functional changes caused by disease. The primary purpose of the autopsy is to further the knowledge of disease, and in his post-mortem examination the aim of the pathologist is threefold. He attempts to discover and describe all deviations from normal anatomy in the body and its various organs, and, if possible, to correlate these with each other by cause and effect. Secondly, he tries to explain the abnormal function manifested during life on the basis of anatomical alterations. And finally, he confirms or invalidates the clinical diagnosis made during life. The opportunity provided by the autopsy for the doctors who have treated the deceased to judge of their own diagnostic accuracy and therapeutic wisdom is invaluable to the progress of their medical knowledge and ability. Medical science in general, however, is more greatly benefited by the elucidation of disease processes that results from a long series of carefully conducted and accurately recorded examinations. The information obtained from such data frequently is irrelevant to the immediate cause of death in any one case. To the individual patient and his physician a lesion—an alteration toward the abnormal in structure—may be completely unimportant and even unsuspected, yet when thoroughly studied in conjunction with lesions of similar type from other cases it may result in an advance in medical knowledge. For instance, much of the present day conception of the pathology, the development, and even the epidemiology of pulmonary tuberculosis is based upon studies of the lungs of persons who had long since recovered from the disease, in whom it was in an arrested or quiescent state, and in whose fatal illness it played no part.

Procedure. An autopsy is performed as soon as possible after death so that the various putrefactive and other post-mortem changes that occur in the dead body may not be confused with the true pathological alterations that have brought about death. Since many diseases as well as violent injuries are evidenced by visible or palpable lesions of the body surfaces and superficial membranes of eyes, nose, and mouth, a very thorough external examination is first made. This is followed by an incision designed to give the greatest exposure of the viscera compatible with complete restoration of the normal outward appearance of the body. Thus no mark is made upon a part that is not customarily covered by clothing, and, if the skull is incised, the cut is placed above the hair line. When the peritoneal and thoracic cavities have been laid open, their contents and the relationship of the viscera to each other are noted. Then the various organs are removed either *en bloc* or separately and examined in detail. The thorough necropsy includes not only gross naked eye observations but also microscopic studies of the organs and tissue in histological preparation. The final diagnosis always depends on the microscope.

Legal Aspects of Autopsy. The autopsy also plays a large part in medical jurisprudence. In the United States, as in most civilized communities, there is a department of local government that is concerned with the investigation of deaths resulting from violence or poisoning, either accidental, homicidal, or suicidal, or in which the circumstances are so unusual as to raise a suspicion of foul play or to suggest legal action to recover damages. The officer in charge of this department, either a coroner elected by popular vote or a medical examiner appointed by the chief of local government, may in any such case perform an autopsy or order an autopsy performed by a pathologist. The purpose of the autopsy here is to provide evidence for legal action rather than to increase scientific knowledge, and therefore the chief concern of the examiner is the determination of the cause and time of death and the circumstances under which it occurred. Often external evidence—the appearance of the body, wounds or other traumatic injuries; its situation or position, or the nature of objects surrounding it—points to the cause of death, but frequently examination of the inside of the body reveals that the apparent external cause was secondary. An example of this is a sudden attack of heart failure which results in unconsciousness, a fall, and a head injury suggesting a fractured skull. Here the autopsy shows the fatal heart lesion and the absence of fatal damage to the brain. Acute alcoholic intoxication often leads to traumatic accidents that simulate homicidal or suicidal death. When chemical analysis of the brain removed at autopsy shows a high alcoholic content, the possibility of the accidental nature of the injuries is greatly increased. In sudden or unexplained deaths in which no fatal structural alteration of vital organs can be found, the pathologist relies on the toxicologist, who determines the presence of poison by chemical examination of the stomach contents, brain, or viscera.

Determination of Time of Death. In medical-legal cases the determination of the time of death is often of extreme importance but unfortunately it seldom can be made with any degree of accuracy. There are no fixed rules. The general configuration of the body, obese or emaciated, the clothing, the surrounding temperature of the air or, if submerged, the water, all must be taken into consideration when estimating the time of death. These are, however, postmortem changes that occur at successive intervals and provide a guide for an approximation of how long the subject has been dead. These are loss of body heat, lividity, rigor, and decomposition.

Temperature and Lividity. The body cools in from 3 to 12 hours, the rate obviously depending on the amount of clothing and the environmental temperature. Lividity, the purplish discoloration of the skin that is brought about by the gravitational sinking of the blood into dependent portions of the body, begins in one to four hours, depending on the amount of the blood in the vessels, and reaches its maximum extent in 12 hours. Lividity is probably more useful in indicating the position of the body and whether or not it has been moved than in determining the time of death.

Rigor Mortis. Rigor mortis, the stiffness that occurs in the muscles after death, begins at once and becomes complete in 2 or 3 hours, developing more rapidly in the head, neck, and upper extremities than in the lower. Although in general it lasts from 12 to 24 hours and gradually disappears, here again the external temperature and the degree of muscular development of the subject affect it markedly. Heat speeds both the onset and dissolution. Most authorities agree that cold delays both the onset and disappearance but it is said by some authorities that although rigor disappears later in the cold it is initiated earlier. In muscular persons the rigor comes on more slowly and lasts longer than in the nonmuscular.

Decomposition. Decomposition, if it is at all advanced, obviously indicates that the interval after death is long, but even here there is an extreme variation with the temperature and humidity. In a warm damp atmosphere an advanced state of decomposition may be reached in 48 hours, while in the cold dry air of a northern winter it may be delayed indefinitely. Submersion speeds the process. Burial in the ground retards it.

Stomach Contents. When the hour of the last meal is known, the extent of digestion of the food in the stomach and small intestine is helpful evidence, but the speed of digestion varies widely from person to person and with the amount and character of the food.

Hair Growth. Contrary to popular opinion, hair does not grow after death. If, then, the time of the last shave is known, the length of the beard indicates fairly accurately when demise occurred.

Social Attitude to Autopsy. Even in modern times there has been opposition to the autopsy, usually by the ill-informed and unreflective portion of the population. That this opposition is based on superstition, or misguided but perhaps understandable emotion, is indicated by the fact that neither the Christian, nor the Jewish, nor indeed any of the major religions of the world, with the exception of the Hindu, places any absolute prohibition on post-mortem examinations. Théophile Bonet in 1679 put into words the continuing attitude of intelligent and progressive medical men toward autopsies when he said "Let those who interdict the opening of bodies well understand their errors. When the cause of a disease is obscure, in opposing the dissection of a corpse which must soon become the food of worms, they do no good to the inanimate mass, and they cause a grave damage to the rest of mankind; for they prevent the physicians from acquiring a knowledge which may afford the means of great relief, eventually, to individuals attacked by a similar disease. No less blame is applicable to those delicate physicians, who, from laziness, or repugnance, love better to remain in the darkness of ignorance than to scrutinize, laboriously, the truth; not reflecting that by such conduct they render themselves culpable toward God, toward themselves and toward society at large." J. M. P.

AUTUN [o'tœ'], a city in east central France, at the juncture of the Ternin and Arroux rivers, about 55 mi. southwest of Dijon. It is the chief city of an arrondissement in the department of Saône-et-Loire and the seat of a bishopric. It was the capital of the Eudens, a Gallic tribe, and later it was a Roman city, the site of the residence of the prefect of Gaul. Autun went through a series of invasions and pillages at the hands of the Vandals in 406, the Burgundians in 414, the Huns in 451, the Franks in 534, the Saracens in 739, and the Normans in 895. In 1379 the city was burned by the English, and in 1494 and 1564 plagues all but wiped out the population. This city is one of the richest in Roman ruins in France, containing aqueduct walls, the Temple of Janus, the gates of Arroux and Saint André, and the remains of the temples of Apollo and Minerva. The Cathedral of St. Lazare dates partly from 1120. Autun is an important market center dealing in cattle, lumber, and grains. Pop. 1954, 14,399.   S. Van V.

AUVERGNE [o'vɛ'rny], a former province in southern France, with Bourbonnais on the north, Forez on the east, Languedoc on the southeast, Rouergue on the south, and Quercy, Limousin, Dordogne, and Marche on the west. Its capital was Clermont-Ferrand. Lower Auvergne, in the north, has fertile soil, especially in the valleys of the Allier and the Dore. Upper Auvergne, in the south, is covered by the remains of a volcanic mountain and the basaltic plateaus of Saint Flour, Mauriac, and Cézallier. The province took its name from the *Arverni*, a Gallic tribe whose leader, Vercingetorix, fought Caesar. Their capital, Gergovia, was destroyed and replaced by the colony of Augusto-Nemetum, which later became Clermont. Under the Romans it was included in Prima Aquitania. It was ceded to the Visigoths in 475 and conquered by the Frankish king, Clovis, in 507. Under the Merovingians it formed a countship dependent on Aquitaine, and later was the scene of battles between the dukes of Aquitaine and the Carolingians. After the death in 928 of Acfred, who was nephew and successor of William the Pious, first hereditary count, Auvergne passed to the Count of Toulouse and then to the Count of Poitiers. In the twelfth century Auvergne recognized the kings of England as its suzerains with the

and appanaged to the house of Orleans from the time of Louis XIII until the French Revolution. The duchy of Auvergne, created in 1360 by John II, was united to the crown when the domains of its last duke, Charles of Bourbon, were confiscated. The countship of Clermont was under the domination of the bishops of that city up to 1552. In 1790 the modern departments of Puy-de-Dôme, Cantal and part of Haute-Loire were formed from the province.   S. Van V.

AUXERRE [osɛ'r], the capital city of the department of Yonne, France, 101 mi. southeast of Paris on the Yonne River. In the city are Roman remains, a museum, library, college, and palace of justice. Also in the city are the thirteenth-century Gothic cathedral of Saint Étienne, the churches of Saint Germain (thirteenth and fourteenth centuries) and Saint Pierre (sixteenth and seventeenth centuries), and the episcopal palace, later a prefecture. Auxerre was inhabited by the Senones, a Celtic tribe. It has been the seat of a bishop since the third century. The city was a duchy of the Carolingian empire which later passed to the House of Nevers. It was bought by Charles V in 1370, ceded to Philip of Burgundy in 1435, and reunited to the French crown after the death of Charles the Bold in 1477. Auxerre is a center of cooperage, stockyards, lumber, and textiles, the distillation of excellent and famous wines, and the manufacture of ocher and machine tools. Pop. 1954, 26,583.   S. Van V.

AUXIN. *See* TROPISMS.
AVALANCHE. *See* LANDSLIDES.

AVALON HARBOR,
CATALINA ISLAND,
CALIFORNIA

marriage of Eleanor of Aquitaine, heiress of Auvergne, to Henry II, but the English were driven from France after the Hundred Years' War, and the country was divided into several large fiefs. The countship of Auvergne was united to the crown under Louis XIII, but was appanaged to the house of Bourbon until 1789. The Dauphiné d'Auvergne was confiscated by Francis I from the constable of Bourbon

AVALON [æ'vəlɒn], a city in Los Angeles Co., in southern California, situated on Avalon Bay at the southern end of Santa Catalina Island, 25 mi. southwest of Long Beach. The principal settlement and center of sports and tourist activities of the island, it lies at the mouth of a canyon, 27 mi. by ferryboat from Wilmington, and is also served by the United Air Lines. In 1542, Juan Rodriguez Cabrillo discovered and named the island San Salvador, but Sebastian Viscaino renamed it Avalon Harbor when he entered in 1602. Until Mexico won freedom from Spain in 1821, illicit trade was carried on with the mainland. Discovery of gold in 1834 caused a boom lasting until José Maria Corrubias purchased Santa Catalina in 1855. Prospecting miners ran tunnels out under the ocean floor, and different owners unsuccessfully attempted silver mining and resort building. In 1919 William Wrigley, Jr., bought the island and made Avalon a successful tourist center. In 1951, Avalon was governed by a mayor, council, and city manager. The city formed one terminus of the world's first commercial radio-telephone circuit in 1920 with Los Angeles as the other end. Submarine cables superseded the circuit in 1923. Avalon has excellent hotels and entertainment facilities as well as good climate, scenery, and fishing grounds. Points of interest include Avalon Casino, Avalon Bird Park, and Glidden Indian Museum. Catering to the transient population is the chief occupation of the permanent inhabitants of Avalon. Pop. 1950, 1,506.

AVALON, a residential borough of western Pennsylvania, situated in Allegheny Co., on the Ohio River, 6 mi. northwest of Pittsburgh, of which it is a suburb. The region is rich in coal, and there is also some oil and gas. Founded about 1771, Avalon was incorporated as a borough in 1871. Transportation is furnished by the Pennsylvania Railroad. Pop. 1950, 6,463.

AVAR. *See* Asiatic Tribes.

AVARE, L' [la'va'r], a five-act comedy in prose by Molière (Jean Baptiste Poquelin), first performed in Paris on Sept. 9, 1668. With borrowings from Plautus and from his French contemporaries, Pierre de Larivey and François de Boisrobert, Molière created a character play that has almost the breadth and depth of *Tartuffe*. Harpagon, the central figure of the play, is rich and he is in love, but his avarice corrupts all natural affections, and spoils his relations with his fellow men. His children turn against him, and rob and insult him. Thus, in spite of the fact that the play contains passages which recall Molière's most extravagant farces, the final impression conveyed by *L'Avare* is sad and painful. Rousseau, criticizing Molière for being immoral, quoted *L'Avare* to support his assertions. It seems obvious, however, that Molière does not side with the rebellious children against the father, whose loss of paternal authority is the result of his vice. The play got a cold reception in Molière's time. Since then, it has become a favorite of the French repertoire.

H. L. B.

AVARS [a'varz], originally Asiatic nomads of Mongolian or Turkish origin, who established themselves in the old Roman provinces of Dacia and Pannonia soon after the middle of the sixth century. Under their ruthless khan, Baian, they built up a great tributary empire of Slavs and Bulgars that stretched from the Baltic to the Black Sea. Relatively few in number, they lived by plunder and domination of others. They ravaged the Balkans at will, twice attacking the city of Constantinople and penetrating far into Greece. Hordes of Slavs were driven into these areas, or were settled there by the Avars. But before the end of the eighth century the Avar power had decayed, so that Charlemagne was able to defeat them and take the great rings or fenced enclosures—some of which were many miles in circumference—where the Avars lived and kept the treasures plundered from all of central Europe. A hundred years later the Avars had disappeared from history, having been amalgamated with a fresh horde of Asiatic nomads, the Magyars.

E. E. B.

AVE [e'vi; a've] (Lat., Hail!), the first word of the Hail Mary, or Angelical Salutation, which is the most familiar of the prayers addressed by the Roman Catholic Church to the Virgin Mother of God. Its present form is: "Hail (Mary) full of grace, the Lord is with thee, blessed art thou amongst women, and blessed is the fruit of thy womb (Jesus). Holy Mary, Mother of God, pray for us sinners now and at the hour of our death. Amen." The first part embodies the greeting of the Angel Gabriel to Mary (Luke i:28), the second part is taken from the greeting of St. Elizabeth (Luke i:42), and the third part is a petition added by the Church. "Full of grace" translates the Latin Vulgate version of the Greek original; the Authorized Version has "highly favoured"; a marginal alternative of the Revised Version reads, "endued with grace." The first part was early used as a salutation, the second part was added in the eleventh century, and the prayer thus constituted became very popular, its recitation being often accompanied by a genuflection and hence sometimes regarded as a penitential exercise. The addition of the name of Jesus is commonly ascribed to Pope Urban IV (1261). The complete Ave as now used was printed in 1495 and approved in 1568. In the canonical hours it is recited repeatedly, but never aloud. In some countries the words "Ave Maria" are applied to an evening bell rung about the hour of sunset.   N. J. T.

AVEBURY [e'vbəri; e'bəri], a small village on the downs of north Wiltshire in southern England. It is contained within part of the most gigantic prehistoric monument of Europe. This comprises a more or less circular area defined by a ditch and an outer bank, the height from the crest of the bank to the floor of the cleared ditch being approximately fifty feet. Defining the margin of the area enclosed by the amphitheater are remains of a circle some 1,100 ft. in diameter of upright sarsen stones of megalithic proportions. Within the great circle are traces of two smaller ones and excavation has disclosed traces of another on the line of the great ditch, which must therefore have been dug out at a later period. Remains of a double avenue of sarsen monoliths lead from the south to the monument which has an opening at this point. The avenue originally connected the Avebury circles with the concentric circles on Overton Hill a mile and two-fifths away. The construction of Avebury began near the close of the Neolithic Age, and the whole monument must have been complete about 2000 b.c. *See also* Megalithic Monuments.

AVEIRO [əve'ru], a district and the capital town of that district, in the province of Douro Litoral, in north central Portugal.

The Town. The district capital, which is also an episcopal see, is situated on the inland side of a salt-water lagoon (the Ria d'Aveiro) formed by the estuary of the Vouga River. It is 5 mi. from the sea and 140 mi. north of Lisbon. There is evidence that the town was founded by the Romans as the community of Talabriga, but of this community and its subsequent history little is known. The lagoon was formerly an arm of the sea, and during the sixteenth century Aveiro was an important port from which extensive commerce was carried on and expeditions sailed to Africa and America. Thereafter a bar was thrown across the mouth of the Vouga and malarial swamps developed. In 1808 a channel was constructed to connect the lagoon with the sea, thus draining a large part of the marshes. Rice is raised on the low ground, and salt is evaporated from the standing water. The lagoon is also rich in fish and oysters. Because of the canal from the lagoon to the sea. Aveiro became the fourth port in Portugal after World War I. It is the commercial center for the rich agricultural region surrounding it and lies on the main railway line from Lisbon to Oporto.

The old and new sections of the town are separated by the Barra Nova, the canal. The chief monuments include the cathedral, the Misericordia, the former Convent of Jesus (containing the tomb of St. Joanna, daughter of Alfonso V), São Domingos, and the remains of Santo Antonio. Pop. 1950, 13,423.

The District. The district contains 2,708 sq. mi. and consists mostly of coastal lowlands, together with a few hills in the interior along the Sierras de Caramullo and Gralheira. It is bounded on the north by the district of Porto, on the east by the district of Viseu, and on the south by the district of Coimbra. Farming (cereals, grapes for wine, and olives) and pasturing are the main occupations, with fishing and commerce of secondary importance. Industry is largely confined to small or handicraft enterprises. Other towns of regional importance other than the capital are Ilhavo and Ovar. Pop. 1950, 483,396.   R. G. W.

AVELLANEDA [aveˈlyaneˈtha], a port city in northern Argentina, situated across the Riachuelo River from Buenos Aires, in the province of Buenos Aires. It is the manufacturing suburb of the nation's capital. Its immense packing houses, extensive docks, and large textile industry make it one of the country's most important industrial centers. Practically every type of product manufactured in Argentina is represented in the factory output. The city's show places include a church in the Renaissance style, the city hall, and a monument to President Nicolás Avellaneda. Pop. 1947, 279,572.   S. G. I.

AVELLANEDA Y ARTEAGA, GERTRUDIS GÓMEZ DE [aˈvelyaneˈtha i aˈrteaˈga] (1814-1873), Spanish dramatist, novelist, and poet, was born at Puerto Príncipe (Camagüey), Cuba, on Mar. 23, 1814. She was self-educated and early showed a preference for the drama. She went to Spain in 1836 and spent 1838-1839 at Cádiz and Sevilla. At the latter she met Ignacio de Cepeda y Alcalde, whose influence on her work was enduring. Her first verses were published in *La Aureola* ("The Halo"), at Cádiz, in 1839 under the name of "La Peregrino" ("The Pilgrim"). In 1840 she went to Madrid, where she met many prominent literary personages. Her triumphs as a dramatist began at this period. In 1845 she won a gold laurel wreath, the poetry prize of the Madrid Liceo. In 1853 she applied for election to the Spanish Academy, which voted 14 to 6 against admission of a woman. In 1860 she returned to Cuba, and the Havana Liceo awarded her a golden wreath. She edited the literary review *El Album cubano* ("The Cuban Album"). In 1864 she visited the United States, England, Paris, and Madrid, finally settling in Sevilla, where she died on Feb. 1, 1873. Her dramas included *Leoncia,* presented in Sevilla June 6, 1840; *Alfonso Munio* and *El Príncipe de Viana,* both performed in Madrid in 1844; *Egilona,* 1846; the Biblical drama *Saúl,* 1849, only moderately successful; *Flavio Recaredo,* 1851; *La Verdad vence apariencias* ("Truth versus Appearances") and *Errores del corazón* ("Errors of the Heart"), both 1852; the popular comedy, *La Hija de los flores* ("The Daughter of the Flowers"), 1852; *La Aventurera* ("The Adventuress"), 1853; *La Sonambula* ("The Sonambulist"), 1854, which was

hostilely received; the comedies *Los Oráculos de Talía* ("The Oracles of Thalia"), *La Hija del Rey René* ("The Daughter of King René"), and *Simpatía y antipatía* ("Sympathy and Antipathy"), 1855; *Los tres amores* ("The Three Loves"), 1858, which was unsuccessful; and the Biblical drama, *Baltasar,* 1858, a success. Her first collection of poems was published in 1841, and a second edition appeared in 1850. Between 1841 and 1845 she published four novels, *Dos mujeres* ("Two Women"), *Espatolino, Guatimozín,* and *La Baronesa de Youx;* in 1849 *El Donativa del Diablo* ("The Gift of the Devil") appeared in the periodical *Semanario pintoresco* ("Picturesque Weekly"); and *Dolores* was published in 1851. From 1865 to 1871 La Avellaneda prepared a final five-volume edition of her works, the first volume of which, containing the poetry, appeared in 1869.   T. R.

AVELLINO [aˈvelliˈno], a province and also a capital city in the mountainous interior of Campania, southern Italy.

The City. Avellino is situated on a hill at an elevation of 1,150 ft. above sea level and at a distance of 2 mi. from the valley of the Sabato River and 28 mi. northeast of the city of Naples.

The older city clusters around the Cathedral, built in the tenth century. The modern city has spread east and west along the main highway, but is without notable monuments. Avellino has no industries of significance and derives its importance from its function as an administrative center and as a market place for the surrounding agricultural region. Avellino is on a branch of the state railways that connects with through lines at Benevento, Salerno, and Nocera.

Originally a Samnite town, Avellino became a Roman city of local importance, located in the valley of the Sabato. It was moved to its present site on the hill only in the Middle Ages, when it was under Lombard dominion (principalities of Benevento and Salerno). The city fell successively under Norman, Hohenstaufen, Aragonese, Spanish, and Bourbon rule but, from 1589 to 1844, was owned by a series of great feudal families ending with the Caracciolo. Avellino was the starting point for the insurrections of 1820-1821, which spread to all of southern Italy. During the heavy fighting in this area in World War II, Avellino was repeatedly bombed and finally captured by the Allies in the fall of 1943. Pop. 1947 (commune), 36,398.

The Province. The province of Avellino, comprising 113 communes, has an area of 1,109 sq. mi. The province extends from the eastern slope of the Apennines (valley of the Ofanto) to the edge of the Neapolitan plains in the west. It is thus pre-eminently a mountainous region, with the highest elevations in the south—Monte Terminio (5,800 ft.) and Monte Cervialto (5,900 ft.). Communication within the province is difficult, as there are few good highways or railway lines. Agriculture is the principal means of livelihood, with pastoral pursuits ranking second. In the west, the crops are more varied and of greater value than in the drier eastern part, where cereal and potato culture predominates. The western districts, in addition to cereals, are rich in olive and fruit trees of various sorts. Forests are extensive in the mountains and vegetable gardens in the lowlands. Sheep and swine lead among domestic animals. The only center of importance in the province, besides the city of Avellino, is Ariano Irpino (pop. 9,473 in 1936), a resort town in the northeast at an elevation of 2,600 ft. Pop. (est. 1947), 491,000.   R. G. W.

AVE MARIA. *See* AVE; MUSICAL TERMS.
AVENA. *See* OAT.

AVENARIUS, FERDINAND [ɑvənɑ'riʊs] (1856-1923), German poet, editor, and critic, was born at Berlin on Dec. 20, 1856. He resided most of his life at Dresden, but in his youth sojourned at length in Italy. His reputation rests primarily upon his unwearying activity in forming the artistic tastes of his period. He championed individual originality and refinement of expression. In 1887 Avenarius founded *Der Kunstwart* ("The Art Adviser"), one of the leading literary reviews of the day, which he edited until 1923. He was also a leader in the Dürerbund, founded in 1902, and in other cultural enterprises. His decided views won him the nickname *praeceptor Germaniae*. During World War I he was politically active in a nationalistic sense, publishing the cartoon collections *Das Bild als Verleumdung* (1917) ("Slanderous Pictures"), and *Das Bild als Narr* (1918) ("Jesting Pictures"). His *Wandern und Werden* (1881) ("Travel and Growth") and *Stimmen und Bilder* (1897) ("Voices and Pictures") are volumes of verse. He also published *Die Kinder von Wohldorf* (1885) ("The Children of Wohldorf") and the dramatic poems *Faust* (1919) and *Baal* (1920). His fame as an original poet has declined considerably. Avenarius died at Kampen, on the island of Sylt, on Sept. 22, 1923.

AVENS [e'vɛnz; e'vɪnz], any species of the genus *Geum,* which formerly included *Sieversia* of the rose family, a group of perennial herbs native to temperate and

PURPLE AVENS,
GEUM RIVALE

MILLSBAUGH

colder regions of both Northern and Southern Hemispheres. About ten species grow wild in the United States. Flowers of different species may be purple, red, orange, yellow, or white. The elongate styles are persistent, giving the spent blooms a bearded effect. *G. chiloense,* with scarlet flowers, has given rise to several attractive horticultural forms. Some of the European species have been hybridized for garden use. They flower in summer. The name comes from an obsolete French term for the plants, *avence.* In England, the related alpine plant, *Dryas octopetala,* is called mountain avens.   C. H. Wo.

AVENTURINE [əve'ntshərɪn], a variety of albite feldspar, a sodium aluminum silicate, $NaAlSi_3O_8$, is characterized by a display of sparkling red iridescent colors. The effect is particularly noticeable when the mineral is cut cabochon and given a high polish. Aventurine is a mineral containing numerous microscopic, thin, platelike inclusions of brown-red iron oxide, hematite. Incident light striking these heterogeneously oriented particles produce the aventurine optical effect. Aventurine has a hardness of 6-6.5 and a density of 2.65. Indices of refraction are low, namely, 1.531-1.540. Other varieties of feldspar, such as oligoclase, and even some species of quartz yield specimens akin to aventurine. The name sunstone is synonymous with aventurine. This semiprecious gem stone is obtained from several localities in Switzerland.   A. E. A.

AVERNUS [əvɜ'rnəs], a small lake, approximately 1½ mi. in circumference, located about 1½ mi. north of the popular health resort of Baiae, in Campania, Italy. Formed in the crater of an extinct volcano, Lake Avernus was regarded by the ancients as the entrance to Hades, the underworld, used by both Aeneas and Odysseus. Situated near the promontory between Cumae and Puteoli, Avernus has no natural outlet. In 37 B.C. Agrippa, then consul, converted it into a naval base connecting it with Lake Lacrine. In A.D. 1530, however, the volcano, Monte Nuovo, rising next to the lake, erupted, destroying not only the canal, but also the harbor. This left Lake Avernus in its original state, with no outlet.

AVERROËS [əve'roiz] (1126-1198), was born Abu'l-Walïd Muhammad ibn-Ahmad ibn-Rushd in Cordova, Spain. His family was eminent in the Mohammedan culture of the period, and Averroës, extremely gifted and versatile, was appointed to several important civil posts. Like his father and grandfather before him, Averroës served as cadi or judge of Cordova, and because of his great knowledge of medicine he was made physician to the court. For most of his life he had the advantages of status and the friendship of the ruling caliphs who liberally encouraged learning and inquiry. In these favorable circumstances he mastered the entire range of knowledge of his day and wrote important works, especially in the sciences and philosophy. His work, *Destructio destructionis,* was written in defense of the Greek philosophical tradition against an attack by the orthodox thinker, al-Ghazzali. In an effort to recover the true meaning of Aristotle's philosophy, Averroës wrote extensive commentaries on most of the works of Aristotle, and these brought him lasting fame and influence among Jewish and Christian philosophers. During the latter part of his life, he was a victim of a religious reaction against science and philosophy, and for a brief period he was exiled and imprisoned, although he was restored to favor shortly before his death in 1198. But though he was himself restored, the religious reaction was successful in bringing to an end any further influence that his views might have exercised in Mohammedan thought.

Within a few years after his death, Averroës' reputation was firmly established among Jewish and Christian philosophers, and by the end of the twelfth century, most of his works were available in Latin translation to the Christian world. The value of his commentaries on Aristotle was universally recognized, and he became known as the "Commentator." But in spite of the general esteem, one of the most important controversies of thirteenth-century Christian philosophy developed upon his theory of the relation of philosophy to theology, the basis of this controversy being, in all probability, the question that had caused Averroës' difficulties with his fellow Mohammedans. Philosophic truth, he held, is to be found in the philosophy of Aristotle; religious truth, on the other hand, is truth adapted to the understanding of the ordinary man. This was a direct challenge to religious authority, for it placed the philosopher in a position to claim access to truth outside the established religious sources.

This distinction was taken by some of Averroës' Christian followers to mean that there are two kinds of truth, a philosophic truth and a religious truth, which may be mutually contradictory and yet both be true. This theory became known as the theory of "double truth." Although this extreme formulation is not, strictly speaking, to be found in Averroës, it is nevertheless true that his thought led in this direction, and the doctrine of double truth afforded a convenient theory by which to justify unorthodox ideas.

Once the theory of double truth was assumed, Averroës' Christian followers had no difficulty in accepting his interpretations of Aristotle, even those which were most strikingly in contradiction with Christian doctrine; as, for example, when, with some justification, Averroës interpreted Aristotle as holding that the individual shares in a common, universal mind, that, in other words, the human soul (in its immortal aspects, at least) is not individual. This clearly denied the doctrine of the immortality of the individual as a knowing, conscious being, and to deny the immortality of the individual was to strike at the very heart of Christian doctrine.

Other interpretations of Aristotle, equally difficult to reconcile with Christian doctrine, were to be found in Averroës' commentaries. Even putting aside questions of the accuracy of their interpretation, it was soon recognized that Averroës' followers held unorthodox views, and this drew upon them the vigorous attacks of more orthodox thinkers. Insofar as Aristotle was claimed as the source of such ideas, Aristotle himself seemed to stand condemned, and this proved a decided embarrassment to all those thirteenth-century philosophers who were attempting to adapt the Aristotelian philosophy to Christian theology. Even the effort of Thomas Aquinas to develop and introduce the synthesis of Aristotle and Christian doctrine was seriously threatened.

Although Averroës' ideas were rejected and even officially condemned by the Pope in 1277, his followers kept alive both the doctrine of double truth and his interpretations of Aristotle. Throughout the later Middle Ages and the Renaissance, Averroës continued to inspire the notion of the necessity of the separation of philosophy and science from theology. This view had important repercussions, even in the sphere of political thought, for it was the Averroists in the fourteenth century who, by an extension of the theory of double truth, argued for the separation of church and state.

Besides his commentaries on the works of Aristotle, of which extensive portions are extant, there exist in Latin translation, as well as Arabic, works by Averroës on grammar, astronomy, medicine, and law.   J. Go.

AVERY, OSWALD THEODORE [e'vəri] (1877-1955), American physician and bacteriologist, was born in Halifax, Nova Scotia, Oct. 21, 1877. He was educated at Colgate University (A.B.) and Columbia University College of Physicians and Surgeons (M.D., 1904). He became a member of the Rockefeller Institute for Medical Research in the special field of investigating pneumonia. In 1947 Dr. Avery was one of the five initial winners of the Lasker Awards in Public Health given annually by the American Public Health Association. The honor was conferred upon him for his 30-year study of pneumococci (pneumonia germs), which aided in reducing deaths from pneumonia in the United States from 112,821 in 1917 to 58,000 in 1946. Dr. Avery received honorary degrees of D.Sc. from Colgate (1921) and LL.D. from McGill University (1935). Among the learned and scientific bodies of which he became a member are the National Academy of Sciences, the American Academy of Arts and Sciences, and the Society of American Bacteriologists. Dr. Avery died on Feb. 20, 1955, in Nashville, Tenn.   D. D. M.

AVES [e'viz], the scientific name for the birds. The group constitutes a class in the phylum Chordata. They are vertebrates, distinguished from all other members of the phylum by their possession of feathers. They are warm-blooded, a characteristic they share with mammals; but, as distinct from the mammals, the aorta, the main artery leading from the heart, arches to the right side instead of to the left, and the body cavity is not separated into two chambers by a respiratory diaphragm. In the Aves the primary active muscular motion in respiration is exhalation; inhalation is produced by a muscular relaxation. In mammals, inspiration is the active muscular phase of respiration, expiration being the relaxed period.

Aves as a group seem to be closely allied to the archosaurian reptiles, probably arising from the primitive Triassic Thecodontia, the group from which the dinosaurs also evolved.

The most ancient bird fossils were found in the Jurassic lithographic stone beds of Bavaria. They are described as two genera, *Archaeopteryx* and *Archaeornis*. Both these birds, which were about the size of a crow, show two features which are absent in modern birds. They possessed teeth and their tails had a long, jointed, bony axis from which feathers erupted laterally. This tail structure has in modern birds been reduced to a short bony element, the pygostyle, which supports the base of the tail feathers. These two birds would probably have been identified as reptiles if the impression of feathers had not been present with the bones.

COURTESY OF THE AMERICAN MUSEUM OF NATURAL HISTORY, NEW YORK

Great toothed diver, Hesperornis regalis, one of the fossil Aves

Two other fossil birds of great interest are from marine Cretaceous beds of Kansas. They are *Ichthyornis* and *Hesperornis*. *Ichthyornis* was about 8 in. tall, with a large head. It had a toothed jaw similar to that of earlier birds, but it had reduced tail elements. From its body form and proportions, it is reasonable to assume, the *Ichthyornis* was not greatly unlike a modern gull. *Hesperornis* was larger, about 2 ft. long, and quite like a modern loon; but from the size of its wings it is evident that the bird was flightless. However, the size and position of the feet indicate that *Hesperornis* was a powerful swimmer and diver.

Modern birds, as known today, probably came into existence at the close of the Cretaceous period. They are distinguished from ancient birds by several features: they have no teeth, the two halves of the lower jaw are fused at the tip, and in the pelvis the posterior portion of the ischium is fused with the ilium. Unfortunately the fossil record of birds is incomplete because most birds are slight and delicate, as compared with mammals and reptiles, and their bones do not fossilize well. *See also* BIRDS.   R. S. M.

AVESTA. *See* AVESTAN; ZOROASTRIANISM.

AVESTAN [əveˈstən], the language of the Avesta, the sacred book of the Zoroastrian religion. The exact date of this text is disputed; opinions on the date of the oldest part, the *Gathas,* vary from the tenth to the sixth century B.C., but it is probable that the great bulk of the rest belongs approximately to the period between 400 B.C. and A.D. 200. The language of the Avesta is clearly mixed, but for the most part it belongs to the northwestern group of the Iranian dialects, which corresponds to Northern Modern Persian. Thus the Avestan *zered* ("heart") corresponds to N.M.P. *zīrd,* where Southern Modern Persian has *dīl;* the Avestan *puθra* ("son") corresponds to N.M.P., *puhr,* as against S.M.P. *pus;* and the Avestan *vac* ("to say") corresponds to N.M.P. *va-čēd,* as against Old Persian *gaub* and S.M.P. *gōwēd.* There are also elements of the southwestern group of Iranian dialects in Avestan, however, and the Avestan *kerenav* ("to make") is thus to be compared with the S.M.P. *kun,* where N.M.P. has *kar-.* Finally, there is even a relationship between Avestan and the eastern Iranian dialects to be seen, for example, in the fricative treatment of the group *rt,* where *arta* becomes *aša,* a shift which also appears in ancient Afghan. Nevertheless, some of the connections of Avestan with the eastern group, such as the *-r* ending, which appears also in Sogdian, are merely archaisms preserved in both lateral areas and therefore do not justify a direct historical link. Without doubt, Avestan reflects the complicated history of the Zoroastrian religion, which was born in the Eastern zone, as, indeed, tradition asserts, and was then transplanted into Media in the West.

Among the Avestan texts, the *Gathas,* which was perhaps composed, at least in part, by Zoroaster, is the oldest. The language of this book presents certain characteristics which distinguish it from the other books of the Avesta; it is far more archaic, and very near to the Indic of the Rig-Veda. This fact is of little value for the establishment of the date, however, for religious texts in all countries regularly preserve very archaic forms of language.

In 1902, a distinguished scholar, C. F. Andreas who was later followed by J. Wackernagel, tried to prove that the original text of the Avesta had been written down first in the Arsacid period (c. 250 B.C.-A.D. 226). Both scholars argued that this text was originally written in the Pahlavi alphabet, which consisted of nineteen characters and almost no vowels, and was then transliterated into the elaborate Avestan script of forty-eight signs. If this were true, the Avesta would originally have had a very different aspect from the one which it now has, especially from the phonetic point of view, and all the work of the Iranologists, such as C. Bartholomae and H. Reichelt, as well as that of the Indo-Europeanists who used their material, would be of very little value. In 1942, however, W. B. Henning brought very strong arguments against the Andreas-Wackernagel transcription theory. *See also* IRANIAN.   G. B.

AVEYRON [aˈvɛˈrɔ̃ˈ], a department in south central France, with an area of 3,376 sq. mi., bounded by the departments of Cantal on the north, Lozère and Gard on the east, Hérault and Tarn on the south, Tarn-et-Garonne and Lot on the west. There is a deeply eroded basaltic plateau in the

north, an infertile plateau in the center, and fertile red earth valleys in the west and south. The principal rivers are the Lot, the Tarn, and the Aveyron. Animal raising is the usual form of agriculture. Horses, cattle, sheep, and mules are raised in the mountain areas. Fruit, truffles, mushrooms, grapes, and potatoes are more important crops than grains. More than 25,000 dairies make the famous ewes'-milk cheese which is ripened in the limestone caves at Roquefort. Coal, lead, zinc, and iron mines are operated in the region. There are many commercial wool-carding and weaving establishments, and large glove factories are situated at Millau, on the Tarn River. The prefecture is Rodez, noted for its devotion to the Protestant cause in the sixteenth century. Villefranche-de-Rouergue, founded in 1252 by Alphonse de Poitiers, Count of Toulouse, was occupied by the English during the Hundred Years' War. It was almost depopulated during the Black Death. The department was formed in 1790 from part of the province of Guyenne. The population in 1954 was 292,727.   S. Van V.

AVIATION, HISTORY OF. Aviation history divides naturally into two parts: (1) the development of lighter-than-air craft, and (2) the development of heavier-than-air craft. The first section covers the story of aerial navigation by means of balloons and airships, machines that float in the air by virtue of the lifting power of large volumes of lighter-than-air gases, such as hot air, hydrogen, and helium, and which float in the air in accordance with the law of Archimedes, that bodies lose in their weight the weight of the displaced element.

True flight, in the modern sense, involves machines which displace relatively little volume of air but which derive lift by virtue of the passage of air over properly shaped surfaces, such as wings, rotor blades, and propellers. Such flight depends wholly upon the relative motion of the air and the supporting surfaces. Since the action is dynamic, the general science of heavier-than-air flight is known as the science of aerodynamics.

The history of aerial navigation from 1783 to about 1890 was almost wholly concerned with aerostatics, which is the general science of lighter-than-air flight. Beginning in the last decade of the nineteenth century, however, when man began to try his wings in heavier-than-air gliders, the science of aerodynamics has become increasingly important. Today, the lighter-than-air craft, except for highly specialized military or research uses, has almost disappeared.

LIGHTER-THAN-AIR CRAFT

It was not until 1643 that man realized that atmospheric air possessed the same kind of specific physical properties, such as weight and density, as any gas or mixture of gases. Evangelista Torricelli (1608-1647), with his primitive barometer, first demonstrated in that year that the earth's atmosphere is more than mere nothingness. Once that fact was accepted, flight experimentation gradually progressed.

About 1650, a Jesuit monk, Francesco de Lana, suggested that a hollow sphere from which all air had been pumped should rise into the air, just as a bubble rises through water. The theory of the vacuum balloon is theoretically sound, but in practice, the improbability of finding a weightless container of almost infinite strength (to avoid complete collapse of the "balloon" from atmospheric pressure) precludes any actual demonstration. Over a hundred years passed before anyone thought to reverse the idea. Instead of attempting de Lana's impossible suggestion, more practical men finally conceived the idea of filling a lightweight container

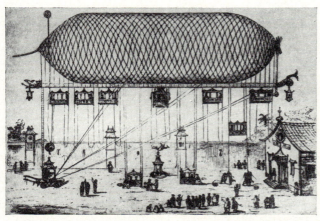

FIRST BALLOON ASCENSION IN CHINA

over heated air as a lifting gas were soon apparent. Fortunately, perhaps, the explosive nature of hydrogen was not fully realized at the time; otherwise men might not have been so willing to risk their lives. In December 1783, a French chemist, J. A. C. Charles (1746-1823), mixed a considerable quantity of iron filings and sulphuric acid, from which enough hydrogen was produced to fill a fair-sized balloon. He made a flight in it of almost two hours' duration which carried him some twenty-seven miles from his starting point, a really notable achievement that demonstrated the superiority of hydrogen beyond all doubt. Once the way had been shown, free ballooning advanced at a rapid pace. The hot-air balloon was generally abandoned by serious experimenters, and the more efficient hydrogen-filled type took its place. After World War I, helium was substituted for hydrogen in the United States. As a lifting gas it is less efficient, but it will not burn nor explode.

Blanchard. François Blanchard (1753-1809), another Frenchman, is considered the greatest of the early pioneers.

with some sort of gas that was inherently lighter than air. Even then the discovery came almost by accident.

FREE BALLOONS

History. *The Montgolfiers.* Two brothers, Joseph (1740-1810) and Étienne (1745-1799) Montgolfier, experimenting in Annonay, France, in 1782, found that if they held a light paper bag over their kitchen fire, it would fill out into a "balloon" and would rise into the air. They verified their discovery several times with small balloons. On June 5, 1783, they astonished the countryside (and possibly themselves) by sending up an unmanned hot-air balloon, some thirty feet in diameter and weighing altogether three hundred pounds! The balloon rose to a height exceeding a mile and descended about a mile and a half from the starting point.

BLANCHARD BALLOON
IN CHANNEL CROSSING

FROM AN OLD ENGRAVING

MONTGOLFIER BALLOON

FROM AN OLD ENGRAVING

In September of that year, a "Montgolfier" carried aloft a sheep, a rooster, and a duck. The animals returned to earth unharmed, and on Oct. 15, 1783, Jean-François Pilâtre de Rozier (1756-1785) made the first human ascent in history, rising to a height of 84 ft. and remaining aloft for 4 min., 24 sec.

Use of Hydrogen. Twenty years before, the British chemist, Henry Cavendish (1731-1810) had isolated a new and extremely light gas, hydrogen. The advantages of hydrogen

He made his first flight in Paris early in 1784 and subsequently demonstrated his balloons in almost every sizable city in Europe. He later made the first American balloon flight, in Philadelphia on Jan. 9, 1793. George Washington, then President of the United States, was present for the occasion. Blanchard's most famous flight, however, was his crossing of the English Channel on Jan. 17, 1785. On this trip, the first aerial crossing of the channel, he was accompanied by Dr. John Jeffries, an American physician. They carried the first international air mail on record.

Andrée. The most ambitious balloon flight of the nineteenth century was the Andrée expedition, which departed from Spitsbergen on July 11, 1897, in an effort to drift across the North Pole. Salomon Andrée (1854-1897), his crew of two and his balloon vanished from sight for over 33 years. In 1930, the frozen bodies of the aeronauts and the remains of their gear were discovered on an ice-bound island in the Arctic Ocean. Their records were intact, and even some of their photographic plates were successfully developed later.

Other Early Balloonists. Many other balloonists appeared during the nineteenth century: the Sadlers, father and son; Vincent Lunardi, who tried unsuccessfully to paddle his balloon about in the air with large oars; Richard Crosbie, an Irishman; Count Francesco Zambeccari of Italy; the Robertson brothers; Charles Green; Henry Coxwell; Felix Nadar; and many others. In balloons of various shapes and sizes they soared higher and higher into the earth's atmosphere. It was during this period that the possibilities of the parachute were recognized. Several balloonists saved themselves by descending from burst or burning balloons with the aid of these aerial umbrellas. Others were killed when their experimental parachutes failed to function.

Applications. In the early years of the twentieth century, free ballooning attained considerable standing as a sport. A number of annual balloon races, of which the Gordon Bennett was the most famous, were held until the outbreak of World War I. These races were international and were held in various countries from year to year.

During World War I tethered hydrogen balloons were used as observation posts by both Germany and the Allies. This was not, however, the first military use of balloons. Both the Union and the Confederate armies made limited use of balloons for observation during the American Civil War. In 1870, during the siege of Paris, balloons were used to maintain communications between the beleaguered city and the outside world.

Scientific. Following World War I, free ballooning was almost abandoned until the early 1930's. Then came a great revival of interest in the balloon as a means of exploring the upper reaches of the earth's atmosphere. Prior to 1930 the highest altitude ever attained by man was some 34,000 ft. The limiting factor had been the ability of the crews to exist at altitudes at which the oxygen content and the pressure of the air were below that required to sustain human life. Between 1930 and 1935, several successful expeditions were carried out with balloons equipped with sealed gondolas in which near-normal air pressure and oxygen content could be maintained artificially, and in which balloon crews could work comfortably and without danger. The first stratosphere flight, May 27, 1931, was made by Auguste Piccard and Charles Kipfer in Belgium, who reached an altitude of 51,793 ft. The following year, with the same balloon, Professor Piccard and his assistant, Max Cosyns, touched 53,672 ft. In November 1933, Captain C. L. Fordney, United States Marine Corps, and Lieutenant Commander T. G. Settle, United States Navy, in a similar balloon, reached 61,237 ft. from Akron, Ohio.

In 1934, the Goodyear Tire and Rubber Company built a balloon of 1,000,000 cu. ft. capacity for a high-altitude research project sponsored jointly by the National Geographic Society and the United States Army Air Corps. On the first attempt, the balloon, *Explorer I,* reached 60,000 ft., at which point it exploded. Its crew, Major W. E. Kepner, Captain A. W. Stevens and Captain O. A. Anderson of the U. S. Army, parachuted to safety. The following year the Goodyear Company built a new balloon, *Explorer II,* of almost 4,000,000 cu. ft. capacity. For this attempt, the explosive hydrogen gas was replaced by helium. After one unsuccessful attempt in July, a flight was made on Nov. 11, 1935, which carried Major Stevens and Captain Anderson to a record altitude of 72,395 ft., the highest so far attained by man. This flight yielded many data of scientific interest with respect to conditions of the upper atmosphere.

AIRSHIPS

It is obvious that as a practical vehicle, a balloon leaves much to be desired. Its speed and direction of flight must always depend on the speed and direction of the winds aloft.

History. *Nonrigid.* Very early in the history of aviation, balloon pilots began to give some thought to dirigibility. The ability to navigate a lighter-than-air craft to a desired point and back, at will, seemed highly desirable. Many schemes to accomplish this end were committed to paper between 1783 and 1884. The earliest concept of a true airship was that of a Frenchman, General Jean Meusnier, who sketched a dirigible balloon of surprisingly modern form in 1785. His greatest problem, however, and the obstacle that confronted all of his successors for many years, was lack of a suitable power plant. About seventy years later, Henri Giffard tested a small steam engine driving a primitive propeller, suspended on a platform below a streamlined gas bag. He took off from Paris and flew to Elancort on Sept. 24, 1852, but his machine lacked sufficient power to fly him back to his starting point. Finally, in 1884, two French army officers, Captain Charles Renard and Captain A. C. Krebs, built and flew the first true dirigible airship, *La France,* using an electric motor to drive their propeller. In spite of the great weight and low efficiency of their power plant, they were able to make flights over predetermined courses, returning always to the starting point. Their work marked the beginning of successful mechanical flight.

Alberto Santos-Dumont, a Brazilian millionaire living in France, built and flew a series of successful airships between

Santos-Dumont airship flying around Eiffel tower

1887 and 1904. He first flew around the Eiffel Tower in October 1901. Santos-Dumont's work stimulated airship development in Europe and the United States. By 1907, airship flights were popular events at fairs and exhibitions everywhere. The United States Army acquired its first military aircraft in 1909, a Baldwin nonrigid ship driven by a Curtiss gasoline engine.

Semirigid. The airships so far mentioned were all of the so-called nonrigid type, simply elongated gas bags with cars or gondolas for passengers and power plants suspended beneath. In the early 1900's a type in which the gas bag was partially reinforced by longitudinal framing (the so-called semirigid) attained some use. Lebaudy built several for the French army, and the Clement-Bayard airship made the first Channel crossing in 1910. Walter Wellman, an American, attempted an unsuccessful North Polar exploration in 1909, and an equally unsuccessful Atlantic crossing in 1910. Several large semirigid airships were built in Italy and in the United States during and after World War I, but the type

EARLY GERMAN ZEPPELIN   BROWN BROTHERS

EXPLOSION OF THE HINDENBURG   THE SHERMAN M. FAIRCHILD COLLECTION

was never particularly successful and was eventually abandoned in favor of the nonrigid, or fully rigid, airship.

Rigid. Count Ferdinand von Zeppelin of Germany became interested in airship possibilities between 1895 and 1900. In 1899 he built the first so-called rigid type of airship. This type, as contrasted with the nonrigids and the semirigids, has an external longitudinal and transverse framework surrounding the lifting gas cells. It was 155 ft. long and 44 ft. in diameter. Though not particularly successful, it was the direct ancestor of a long line of Zeppelin airships, the first of which

sister ships, the *Akron* and the *Macon,* each more than six times larger in cubic capacity than the wartime Zeppelins, were destroyed while on active duty with the United States Navy. The *Akron* went down in April 1933 off Barnegat Light, N.J., and the *Macon* was lost in February 1935 off Point Loma, Calif. The loss of the *Macon* marked the end of large airship development in the United States. During the following years, and particularly during the antisubmarine activity of World War II, the United States Navy built and used a large number of smaller nonrigid airships, which

THE GERMAN AIRSHIP GRAF ZEPPELIN

ACME PHOTO

flew successfully in 1900. The last to be seen outside Germany was the hydrogen-inflated *Hindenburg,* which exploded and burned at Lakehurst, N.J., in May 1937.

During the early years of World War I, the Zeppelin was the only available long-range bombing aircraft. Zeppelin attacks against London in 1914 and 1915 were stopped only by the rapid development of the military airplane. By 1916 the fast airplane had made all lighter-than-air craft obsolete for military purposes except for highly specialized and limited usage.

Applications. After World War I other countries, including the United States, undertook the development of large rigid airships. The British R-34 made the first transatlantic airship flight, between England and the United States, in July 1919. During the 1920's, the British built two large Zeppelin-type airships, R-100 and R-101. The effort terminated when the R-101 was destroyed near Beauvais, France, in October 1930, with the loss of many high-ranking civil and military air officers.

Experiments with large airships in the United States were no less disastrous, although the German-built *Los Angeles* (acquired as a part of German reparations) served the United States Navy for many years. The American-built *Shenandoah* was destroyed in a storm in Ohio in September 1925. Two

proved useful for offshore patrol and convoy duty. Altogether some hundreds of airships were used by the Navy during the war, but after the close of hostilities most of them were decommissioned and lighter-than-air craft became relatively inactive.

Army activity with airships was also disastrous. The Italian-built semirigid *Roma* exploded and burned at Hamp-

COURTESY OF CURTISS-WRIGHT CORP.

THE AIRSHIP MACON

ton, Va., in 1922 with considerable loss of life. In the twenty years following, the Army Air Forces concentrated on heavier-than-air craft. At its entry into World War II, the United States Army allocated practically all lighter-than-air craft operation to the Navy and transferred all its ships to the naval service.

HEAVIER-THAN-AIR CRAFT

Although lighter-than-air navigation dates back to 1783, it has long since been surpassed in importance by flight in heavier-than-air machines, whose active usage dates only

COURTESY OF THE GLENN L. MARTIN CO.

GLENN L. MARTIN'S FIRST PLANE

from 1903. But the heavier-than-air concept has a lengthy history. Long before the early philosophers even conceived of air as a gas in which objects lighter than air might be floated, they observed and sought to emulate the flight of birds, and it was a long time before the idea was abandoned. The key to successful flight by man was considered, by some, to be lightweight power, and it was not until the dawn of the twentieth century that the development of the internal-combustion engine put this key into men's hands. Other authoritative schools of thought advanced the opinion that the discovery of the principles of controllability was the main key to successful flight.

ORNITHOPTERS

Although no experimenter from Leonardo da Vinci (1452-1519) to date has ever flown successfully on flapping wings, speculation and experimentation in that direction led eventually to the conquest of the air. Mythology and religious lore are full of references to men with wings, and ancient history occasionally mentions philosophers who sought to fly with them. But the first real engineering analysis of the problem is Da Vinci's, about the year 1500. He wrote his ideas but never tried to build a machine.

The earliest experimental work on record dates from the late seventeenth century, when Robert Hooke, a British philosopher, reported an unsuccessful attempt to fly a man-carrying machine. Hooke was followed by Karl Meerwein in 1781, Sir George Cayley in 1800, Jacob Degen in 1809, Thomas Walker in 1810, Gustav Trouvé in 1870, Alphonse Pénaud in 1871, Vincent de Groof in 1874, Victor Tatin in 1875, Lawrence Hargrave in 1884, Otto and Gustav Lilienthal in the 1890's, and many others, all bent on being the first to solve the age-old problem.

These men produced many weird wing-flapping devices, but not one of them was capable of successful mechanical flight. Of the lot, de Groof was the first man to be killed in a heavier-than-air craft. He built a contrivance with flapping wings and had himself carried aloft with it attached to a balloon. When he cut himself loose, his flimsy machine collapsed.

In the middle 1890's, the brothers Otto and Gustav Lilienthal made the first really scientific approach to the problem. They first tried wing flapping but presently became con-

vinced that more was to be gained from gliding flight. As will be seen presently, Otto Lilienthal's gliding research in 1894 and 1895 led directly to the invention of the modern airplane.

Before dismissing the ornithopter, however, it must be noted that several serious attempts have been made recently to explore the idea further. The invention of the high-speed camera has made possible a study of the behavior of birds' wings in flight which has revealed many interesting phenomena. No man has yet succeeded in lifting himself off the ground by flapping wings, but several serious researchers are still attempting it. Possibly, after a further study of bird flight and with the aid of modern phototechniques, some solution may be found to the problem. Stranger things have happened in the history of aeronautics.

HELICOPTERS

Early Types. Before the commonest form of heavier-than-air craft, the fixed-wing airplane, is discussed, one other type should be considered, the rotating-wing machine, of which the helicopter is the most important form. It was first suggested by Da Vinci. He based his design on the behavior of the so-called Chinese top, a simple propeller-like device made of a cork and four feathers, rotated by a spring or a string. When spun rapidly, the top sails upward. It was such a top that suggested to the Wright brothers that they might soon find a method of flying. Although many curious designs for rotating-wing helicopters appeared between Da Vinci's time and the end of World War I, none developed into a practical machine. The principal drawback, as in the case of all early aircraft, was the lack of a compact lightweight power plant.

After World War I, when airplane engines had been developed to a reasonable degree, a number of helicopters were built which succeeded in rising off the ground. Emile and Henry Berliner built three machines at College Park, Md., between 1920 and 1923 that flew to some degree. De Bothezat made low-altitude test flights on a huge, ungainly machine at the Army's McCook Field, Dayton, Ohio, in 1922. In Europe between 1923 and 1930, a number of experimental flights were carried out on machines built by Oehmichen and by Pescara in France, and by d'Ascanio in Italy. In the United States, the Curtiss-Wright Corporation built a machine from designs by Bleecker in 1930, but it was not a success. As a matter of fact, none of these machines could be considered successful. Many of them could rise off the ground under their own power, but they could not carry much in the way of useful load, and they all lacked stability and controllability.

Successful Modern Types. The Germans under Hitler built the first successful helicopter. Between 1936 and 1940, a series of experimental machines were designed and built which tended to perform very creditably. Prior to the outbreak of the war in 1939, the German aviatrix, Hanna Rasche, flew a Focke-Achgelis machine cross-country from Bremen to Berlin at an average speed of 70 mph. A German test pilot, Ewald Rohlfs, climbed to nearly 12,000 ft. in a similar aircraft.

The success of the Focke-Achgelis machine stimulated interest elsewhere and led to very active helicopter development in the United States during and after World War II. The great airplane designer, Igor Sikorsky, had experimented unsuccessfully in Russia as early as 1910, but lack of a satisfactory power plant, and a shift in interest to the airplane, diverted his attention from helicopters until 1939 and 1940. In the spring of 1940 he demonstrated to the United States

Army a single-rotor helicopter which had astonishing performance for the time.

There was little helicopter development during World War II, but in the immediate postwar years, aided by Air Force and Navy development contracts, Sikorsky, Bell, Mc-Donnell, Piasecki, and other American manufacturers developed the idea rapidly. Within two or three years after

Early Sikorsky helicopter with Igor I. Sikorsky at controls

the war, a number of highly successful helicopter designs were available for both military and civilian use.

The outbreak of the Korean War in 1950 provided great impetus for the development of the military helicopter, which was ordered in increasing quantities by the Air Force, the Navy, and the Ground Forces and which proved extremely useful in evacuating the wounded, in re-supplying combat troops in difficult terrain, and in rescuing pilots forced down in enemy territory or at sea.

By 1952 every aircraft carrier on active duty with the United States fleets was provided with one or more helicopters for pilot rescue duty at sea. The United States Coast Guard has many helicopter units available for sea search and rescue, and the United States Marine Corps has developed new assault tactics for securing beachheads by helicopter-carried troops. All of the military services were interested in the development of very large helicopters for short-range transport of heavy equipment up to, and including, light tanks.

On the civilian side, the application of helicopters has been largely in the local transport of air mail. The first development of this kind was in Los Angeles, where helicopter pickup and delivery services cover a radius of about 100 mi. from the downtown post office. Similar programs were underway in Chicago and New York City. Special types of helicopters came into use for crop-pest control, forest-fire fighting, and pipe-line inspection.

AUTOGIROS

Another form of rotating-wing aircraft that closely resembles the helicopter is the autogiro. This craft differs from the helicopter in that its rotor is driven by air forces resulting from its own movement through the air. The rotor of the helicopter is driven directly by an engine, and thus supplies both the lift and thrust for vertical and horizontal flight.

The autogiro had a relatively brief history. It was flown successfully by its inventor, Juan de la Cierva, in Spain in

1923, and underwent active development between 1928 and 1940 in England and the United States. A considerable number were built, both for civil and experimental military use, but the type proved to be uneconomical and impractical, and was finally displaced by the helicopter.

GLIDERS

The immediate ancestor of the modern airplane was the glider. Just as a child learns to crawl before he walks, so man learned to glide before he flew.

The choice, however, was not deliberate. Until the introduction of a successful internal-combustion engine about 1900, no light and compact source of power was available. Some authorities believe that Otto Lilienthal probably knew enough about heavier-than-air flight by 1896 to have achieved success, had a satisfactory power plant then been available. It was not until the mechanical genius of the Wright brothers combined their knowledge of gliding with their own development of a suitable gasoline engine that the airplane became a reality.

Cayley. Sir George Cayley built a successful model glider as early as 1804. His little machine combined most of the aerodynamic elements of modern aircraft, but his experiments stopped when the problem of power was encountered. His work earned him a place in history as the father of British aeronautics. Cayley's results, although widely published, were not followed up immediately. It was not until the middle of the nineteenth century that other glider experiments appeared. A Frenchman, Le Bris, claimed that he had built a successful man-carrying glider in 1855. His own account of his flights is unconfirmed. In the following forty years, several people, among them F. H. Wenham of England and Louis Mouillard of France, built machines of various forms and tested them, with but indifferent success.

The Lilienthals. Serious study of gliding possibilities began with the brothers Otto and Gustav Lilienthal. Otto

Otto Lilienthal's first glider experiments in Germany

experimented from 1886 to 1896, making his first flight from the top of an artificial hill which he built near Anklam, Germany, about 1891. He built a series of gliders (both monoplanes and biplanes) from which he learned much about lift, stability, and control. More important, he recorded his observations in detail for the benefit of those who were to follow. Unfortunately, at the height of his career he was killed, in the summer of 1896, when one of his machines went out of control and crashed.

Chanute. The probability of flight, however, had been sufficiently demonstrated to encourage others. Lilienthal's work was carried on by Pilcher in England, who was killed in a crash in 1899; by Montgomery in California; and by the great experimenter, Octave Chanute (1832-1910).

Chanute, an engineer, took a thoroughly scientific approach to the problem of flight. His main contribution to the field, however, lay in his writings. Chanute corresponded widely with aeronautical experimenters all over the world and was responsible for the spreading of much valuable technical information. He was a personal friend of the Wrights and assisted them for a time in their experiment at Kitty Hawk.

became a military weapon. Air-borne assault troops, carried aboard large gliders towed behind powered aircraft, spearheaded the Allied assault against beachheads in France on D-Day. They were also employed in large numbers in many other tactical operations. Towed gliders for troop transport were also used by the Germans and the Japanese, but these tactics reached their highest development in the air forces of Great Britain and the United States.

With the end of hostilities, gliding resumed its role as a sport. Interest in motorless flight is again on the upswing in the United States. Many new and efficient glider designs

The Wright glider, forerunner of the first Wright airplane, in action at Kitty Hawk, North Carolina. Three seasons of experimenting with glider flight made possible the historic first successful heavier-than-air flight by the Wrights in 1903.

The Wrights. Wilbur and Orville Wright, bicycle manufacturers of Dayton, Ohio, had been following Lilienthal's work in Germany with great interest and resolved after his death to carry on his experiments. Their glider work from 1900 to 1902 is well known. Three years of kite flying and experimental gliding at Kill Devil Hill, Kitty Hawk, N. C., taught them to fly and prepared them for their first powered flight.

German Developments. The advent of the powered airplane in 1903 diverted interest in gliding, as such, to other fields for almost twenty years. It was the Treaty of Versailles that caused its revival. After World War I, defeated Germany was forbidden the use of powered aircraft. As a consequence, a tremendous development in motorless flying ensued in Germany between 1921 and 1933. This proved to be a means of keeping aircraft designs alive, and also provided training for thousands who later became the Luftwaffe pilots of 1939 to 1945. By the early 1930's, the Germans had developed strong, lightweight sail planes of great efficiency, capable of soaring to high altitudes and over long distances without the benefit of power. Altitudes of over 7,000 ft. and cross-country flights of better than a hundred miles were not uncommon. The art of aerodynamics was not the only beneficiary. Great strides were made, also, in the science of meteorology, for soaring to great heights and over long distances depends above all else on close study and proper interpretation of winds and weather. During the 1930's, the sport attracted considerable attention in the United States. German sail plane and soaring pilots came over to demonstrate and to compete in American glider meets. A number of excellent American designs were evolved, and American glider pilots were soon outflying their European teachers.

Troop Transport in World War II. During World War II, the glider progressed beyond a training device and

are appearing, and competition among glider pilots for altitude, speed, and distance has again become keen.

AIRPLANES

The real beginning of powered flight is to be found in the work of two Britishers, William Samuel Henson and John Stringfellow. They collaborated on the development of an "aerial steam carriage" in 1842. The Henson design of that period had incorporated many basic elements of the modern airplane, although it did not have ailerons for one thing. These inventors, however, lacked adequate knowledge of aerodynamic and structural principles to bring their work to a successful conclusion. Also, they lacked a suitable power plant. Their steam-engine-powered airplane was a good effort for the times, but it could not have flown. Even today, with all our advanced knowledge of materials and efficient equipment, steam still appears to be impractical as a motive power for aircraft. Henson and Stringfellow, however, are credited with the first powered model flight. In 1848 they built a batlike monoplane of 10-ft. span that made short sustained flights.

During the last half of the nineteenth century several other inventors in Europe and America tackled the problem of mechanical flight. Some of them came remarkably close to a solution. The problem appeared so hopeless of solution that even up to the day the Wrights flew, scientists could prove mathematically that powered flight was an impossibility.

Notable Contributors. Felix and Louis du Temple patented a steam-driven monoplane in 1857; Alphonse Pénaud designed a flying wing with many modern features in 1876; Thomas Moy and R. E. Shill, two British engineers, collaborated in 1874 on a large steam-driven model that left the ground at the end of a tether but never achieved free flight; Victor Tatin flew a tethered compressed-air-driven model in

1879; and M. A. Goupil, another French experimenter, built a birdlike steam-driven airplane in 1884 that allegedly was successful as a glider but never flew under power.

Maxim. By 1880, scientific research began to enter the picture. Men began to test wing sections and wing forms in one way or another to try to analyze the behavior of lifting

THE BETTMANN ARCHIVE

THE MAXIM FLYING MACHINE

surfaces. A literature of aeronautics began to develop. Horatio Phillips and Sir Hiram Maxim in England made large numbers of such tests under controlled conditions and recorded their data for future study. In 1894, Maxim constructed a monstrous, kitelike, steam-driven apparatus that ran on a circular track on his estate. He never attempted to fly it, but he

Langley Aerodrome poised on a houseboat for initial takeoff, October 7, 1903, after four years of preparation. This test ended in failure when the plane plunged into the Potomac River barely fifty yards from the takeoff.

BROWN BROTHERS

collected many data of the power and thrust of propellers that were later useful.

Ader. About the same time in France, Clement Ader made a determined bid to be the first man to fly. Between 1886 and 1897 he built several large bat-shaped steam-driven monoplanes. He claimed that in secret trials in 1886, 1891, and 1897 he actually got off the ground. Official witnesses disagreed, however, and history has failed to accept Ader's claims. It is possible that his last machine might have lifted off the ground, but it certainly was not capable of controlled flight, because the basic essentials for airplane stability and control were entirely lacking.

Hargrave. Inventors all over the world were now laboring seriously over ideas for mechanical flight. In New South Wales, Australia, a flier of kites left his mark. Lawrence Hargrave first experimented with flying models, powered by rubber bands and with steam. He then turned his attention to what he called three-dimensional kites, the now familiar box-kite idea. In June 1895 he was lifted off the ground by a string of four such kites in tandem. The biplane form of aircraft which attained its maximum development in the 1920's and which is still seen occasionally is the direct descendent of the Hargrave kite.

Langley. Samuel Pierpont Langley is the last in the long list of inventors who labored mightily but failed to achieve heavier-than-air flight. Langley was one of the first to attack the problem of flight by experimental work under exacting scientific conditions. His "whirling arm" for aerodynamic research was an interesting and valuable device. Because of his great contributions to early aerodynamic knowledge, the largest of the laboratories of the National Advisory Committee for Aeronautics now bears his name.

Langley's early work was carried out in Pittsburgh. In 1889 he moved to Washington to become assistant secretary of the Smithsonian Institution. After a long study of bird and other wing forms, Langley evolved a series of model aircraft which he called aerodromes (literally, air runners), which proved to his satisfaction that mechanical flight was possible. The first models refused to fly at all, but late in October 1894, *Aerodrome 5* made a flight of six or seven seconds. In May 1896, a model 16 ft. long, of 14-ft. span, weighing 25 lbs., and powered by a 1½ h.p. steam-engine, flew three complete circles and a total distance of over 3,000 ft.

The story of Langley's work in the following six years has been told in great detail in the *Memoir on Mechanical Flight,* published by the Smithsonian Institution. Assisted by Charles H. Manly, who developed a five-cylinder liquid-cooled engine, which produced 52.4 h.p. for a total weight of 125 lb., Langley built a full-scale aerodrome designed to be launched from a catapult mounted on top of a houseboat.

The work was supported by a War Department grant of $50,000 plus some $20,000 contributed by the Smithsonian. An attempt was made to launch the aerodrome on Oct. 7, 1903, but ended in failure when the launching mechanism faltered and plunged the aerodrome into the river. It was salvaged and rebuilt and another attempt was made on Dec. 8, 1903. The results were almost identical, but this time the

forced glider of the 1902 type, it powered the first successful airplane flight in history, on the morning of Dec. 17, 1903, at Kitty Hawk, N. C. Orville Wright was at the controls. His first flight, of 120 ft., lasted 12 seconds. On the third flight that day Wilbur flew for 59 seconds and 852 ft., but the machine was damaged on landing, and experimental work for that year ended. The Wrights returned to Dayton.

COURTESY OF CURTISS-WRIGHT CORP.

HISTORIC FIRST FLIGHT OF WRIGHT PLANE, KITTY HAWK, N. C.
Orville Wright is at the controls, while brother Wilbur runs alongside.

machine was damaged beyond repair and Langley's work was finished. Ironically enough, the airplane designed and built by the Wright brothers inaugurated the age of flight about a week after the crash of the Langley aerodrome.

The Wrights. The spotlight now focuses squarely on Orville and Wilbur Wright of Dayton, whose work began with gliders. For three years they experimented with wing models in a small wind tunnel, and with kites and gliders in flight. By the end of 1902 their results warranted the belief that they could fly if they could only secure a compact, lightweight power plant. They searched the growing automobile industry for a motor that would suit their needs. Their experience was the same as Langley's. There was none to be had, nor would any builder try to meet their proposed specifications. And so they designed and built their own engine. It was a clumsy four-cylinder affair which, by the fall of 1903, could deliver about 16 h.p. for a weight close to 200 lb. It proved to be satisfactory. Mounted in a rein-

During the next five years, working in a cow pasture near Dayton, the Wrights really learned to fly. They also improved the airplane and the engine. But public recognition of their achievement was slow. It was not until they demonstrated their military airplane to the United States Army at Fort Myer, Va., in September 1908, that people finally recognized the fact that flight by man was a reality. They proved their point beyond all doubt, but they also experienced a setback. An accident, in which Orville was severely injured and Lieutenant Thomas Selfridge was killed, eliminated the ma-

COURTESY OF CURTISS-WRIGHT CORP.

ORVILLE WRIGHT AT CONTROLS OF HIS 1909 PLANE

OFFICIAL U.S. AIR FORCE PHOTO

1908 WRIGHT MILITARY AIRPLANE IN FLIGHT

chine from Army consideration for that year. In July of the following year, however, a new machine passed all Army tests and the military history of the airplane began.

Although the United States Government was slow to recognize the work of the Wright brothers, they received considerable encouragement from abroad between 1906 and 1909. Wilbur demonstrated one of their machines in Europe in the summer of 1908 and, by 1909, had established a flying school

Historic flight of Claude Grahame-White, famed English aeronaut, in Washington, D.C., October 14, 1910. He took off in his Farman biplane from the narrow street between the State, Navy and War Department buildings.

WIDE WORLD PHOTO

and in the spring of that year Curtiss won a $10,000 prize posted by the *New York World* for a flight from Albany to New York City.

In America, other pioneer flights were made by Calbraith P. Rodgers and Kelly and Macready. Rodgers made the first coast-to-coast flight, from Sheepshead Bay, Long Island, to Long Beach, California, in 1911 in a Wright EX. His trip took 84 days. In 1923 Kelly and Macready piloted a

Early Curtiss flying boat during tests at Lake Keuka, Hammondsport, New York

COURTESY OF
CURTISS - WRIGHT CORP.

in France. The demonstration in Europe stimulated interest in flying in all parts of the world.

Pioneers. The first flight in Europe, a brief straightaway hop, was made in 1906 by Santos-Dumont. In the next two or three years many famous pilots appeared, among them Louis Blériot, Henri Farman, and Hubert Latham. Blériot made his flight across the English Channel in July 1909. In mid-summer of 1909 the world's first aviation meet was held at Reims, France, with thirty-eight airplanes entered. A speed record of 47.8 mph was set and the world's altitude record was increased to 508 ft. A non-stop flight of 118 miles won the Grand Prix. The speed record, at Reims in 1909, was set by Glenn H. Curtiss, an American, then a new name in aeronautics but destined to become one of this country's leading figures in airplane building. Following his return from France, Curtiss flew during the Hudson-Fulton Celebration in 1910, as did the Wrights,

Fokker T-2, an Army Air Service plane, in the first transcontinental non-stop flight; they flew from New York to San Diego in 26 hrs., 50 min.

Prizes. The *World* prize was one of a number for the encouragement of flying. Fame and sometimes fortune awaited those who risked their lives to fly farther, faster, or higher than others. In 1927, competition for the Orteig prize induced Charles A. Lindbergh to fly the Atlantic. In the same year the Dole prize started eight planes from Oakland to Honolulu; only two reached their destination. Every year competition for the Bendix and Thompson trophies sends the best speed pilots hurtling across the continent or around the grueling 300-mi. course at Cleveland. Awards have also been made for technical advances. The oldest is the Collier trophy, founded in 1911 by Robert J. Collier and now in the custody of the National Aeronautic Association. It is presented each year for "the greatest achievement in aviation

THE RECORD-MAKING U.S. NAVY NC-4

COURTESY OF CURTISS-WRIGHT CORP.

in the United States, the value of which has been demonstrated in actual use during the preceding year." Other medals and awards have been given for the same purpose, to recognize outstanding achievement among aeronautical engineers and scientists. Among those in the United States are: the Wright Brothers medal, awarded annually by the American Society of Mechanical Engineers; the Guggenheim medal, awarded by a joint board of the American Society of Mechanical Engineers, the Society of Automotive Engineers, and the Institute of the Aeronautical Sciences; and the Reed, Sperry, Losey, Bane, Jefferies, and Chanute awards of the Institute of the Aeronautical Sciences.

Later Developments. In the early years of the airplane, competition among designers sometimes led to bitter controversy and into the courts of law. Shortly after the Hudson-Fulton Celebration, at which the Wrights and Curtiss demonstrated their rival machines, a great battle was joined over their respective patent claims and patent rights, the repercussions of which were still reverberating thirty years later. The quarrel between the Wrights and Glenn Curtiss rose out of their different methods of achieving lateral control. One of the results of this dispute was the sending of the original Wright machine to England in 1928. It was returned in 1948 and is a permanent exhibit of the Smithsonian Institution.

Airplane Development During World War I. Before World War I the airplane was considered mainly as a sporting vehicle. Few could see much of a future for it as a military weapon or as a commercial carrier. At the outbreak of World War I, in 1914, no general staff had any understanding of the military potential of aircraft. At best, the airplane was looked upon as an auxiliary to the cavalry for scouting purposes. Except in an experimental way, no bomb had been dropped, nor had any guns been fired from aircraft in flight. An airplane was simply an airplane. It had no specialties. On the average, it could fly 60 to 70 mph for an uncertain 200-mi. range. Once the war was under way, special uses developed. Performance improved rapidly. Machine guns were mounted, and bombs of considerable size were fitted. By 1918 special categories for pursuit, bombardment, ob-

servation, and naval usage had been designed and were in quantity production by all the belligerent powers. In 1918, the best fighters were flying about 120 mph; bombers, 80 to 90 mph; and 15,000-ft. altitudes were commonplace. The poorest military machines of 1918 could have flown rings around any prewar planes.

First Transatlantic Flights. In 1919 three United States Navy flying boats attempted an Atlantic crossing. One of them, the NC-4, made it by way of the Azores in May of that year. The first nonstop transatlantic flight, from Newfoundland to Ireland, was accomplished a month later in a Vickers-Vimy biplane by Captain John Alcock and Lieutenant Arthur W. Brown of England. In 1924 a flight of the Army's Douglas bombers flew around the world.

Achievements During the 1920's. Following the war, the DH-4 biplane, the Martin biplane bomber, and the Thomas-

THE SHERMAN M. FAIRCHILD COLLECTION

EARLY CURTISS TRIPLANE

Morse Scout in America; the Bristol fighter, the Sopwith Pup and Camel pursuits, and the Handley-Page bomber in England; and the Bréguet bomber and the Spad fighter in France became the prototypes for the development of military aircraft during the early 1920's.

Germany was prohibited the use of powered aircraft but trained hundreds of potential pilots on gliders and sailplanes during that period. Germany also maintained the nucleus of design and development organizations in companies of neutral countries like Switzerland and Sweden. These were readily transplanted back to Germany in 1933 and produced the machines that equipped the Luftwaffe in the early stages of World War II.

It is impossible to trace here the development of individual airplane designs during the twenty-year interval between the wars. Generally speaking, however, the so-called "stick-and-wire" types (monoplane and biplane) that came out of the war were carried to a high level of development. Their characteristics were externally braced fabric-covered wings and tail surfaces, fixed landing-gears, and uncowled engines. Racing machines, built especially for the purpose, were nearing the 300 mph mark in the late 1920's. Altitudes up to 40,000 ft. had been attained, and flight ranges had been increased to the point where Lindbergh was able to fly nonstop from New York to Paris in 1927.

That was a period of great pioneering flights. The same year Lindbergh flew the Atlantic, Clarence Chamberlin and Richard E. Byrd also flew successfully from America to Europe, and three planes made flights from California to Honolulu. The British pilot Kingsford-Smith flew from San Francisco to Sydney, Australia. Donald B. MacMillan and Byrd surveyed many square miles of the Arctic by air in 1925, and in May 1926 Byrd and Floyd Bennett flew over the North Pole. In 1928, 1933, and 1939 Byrd made extensive use of the airplane in Antarctic exploration. He first flew over the South Pole on Nov. 29, 1929. Wiley Post and Harold Gatty flew around the world in 1931.

The All-Metal Plane. By the early 1930's, the limitations of the stick-and-wire type aircraft had become apparent. Research was progressing in new fields. Almost overnight, in 1931 and 1932, a new type of airplane emerged, the all-metal, smooth-skinned, internally-braced monoplane with every excrescence cowled or made retractable in flight. The Boeing B-100 bomber, a development of the experimental Boeing Monomail, could properly be considered the prototype. The Martin B-10 appeared almost simultaneously. Although improvements in detail and performance rapidly rendered these machines obsolete, they embodied practically all the elements of the most modern conventional airplanes.

FORD TRI-MOTOR ALL-METAL PLANE

During the early stages of the United States participation in World War II, designs were more or less "frozen" in the interest of high production, and the war was over before many of the newest designs had reached the production level. With two notable exceptions, the B-29 bomber and the P-61 night fighter, no military airplane was used in combat by United States air forces that had not been designed

and flown in prototype before Pearl Harbor. However, speed, range, and general efficiency were improved continuously throughout the war period and by the end of the war bombers weighing over 100,000 lb. were able to operate over combat radii of 1,500 to 2,000 mi. Single-seat fighters were capable of combat at flight speeds of 350 to 400 mph at altitudes up to 40,000 ft.

The DH-4, an early airmail plane

Jet Types. The first of the crop of truly postwar designs appeared in the fall of 1946 and the spring of 1947. The greatest changes were in the military types. In practically all the new high-performance fighters, and in many of the new high-speed bombers, jet power plants replaced the engine and propeller combinations that had been standard for all American aircraft before V-J Day.

In jet aircraft, the Germans had been first in the field with a practical fighter, the Me-262. The British were not far behind. It was not until 1946 that the United States Army Air Forces had enough Lockheed P-80 jet fighters to train pilots and to organize squadrons. During 1947, however, improved models came into service in some quantity, including the Republic Thunderjet (Army) and the McDonnell Phantom (Navy).

The United States rearmament program, touched off by the outbreak of the Korean War, speeded the design and manufacture of jet aircraft in the United States. Except for a few turbine-driven propeller aircraft for relatively long-range applications, practically all military specifications have been for jet-powered aircraft. Not only are the fighter types jet powered but also all the bombers up to, and including, the largest. As a consequence, all military combat speeds have shown a sharp rise. Single-seat fighters in the United States as well as in other countries are now capable of combat speeds in the neighborhood of 650 to 700 mph at altitudes upward of 50,000 ft. The largest bombers have almost the same combat capabilities. Certain military machines can now be flown in excess of the speed of sound, and many countries are now moving toward supersonic speeds for military aircraft. Research airplanes have been flown at speeds better than 1,200 mph to altitudes in the neighborhood of 80,000 ft. Such aircraft usually incorporate rocket-type power plants, similar to those used by the Germans in the V-2's of World War II.

Transport Types. In the transport category, the Boeing 247 (1933) was the prototype. It was followed in 1934 by the Douglas DC-2, which gained rapid acceptance with United States and foreign airlines. The Douglas DC-3 went into airline service in 1936. Under its military designation, C-47 (Army) and R4D (Navy), it carried the bulk of military cargo and air-borne assault troops throughout the war. After the war the DC-3 was used by airlines for

DE HAVILLAND JET-PROPELLED "COMET" CIVIL TRANSPORT

moderate-range service. In the four-engine, long-range class, the prototype of the Douglas DC-4 was first flown in 1938. As the Army C-54 (Navy R5D) it was widely used during the war for long-range, over-ocean transport. A greatly improved version, the DC-6, was introduced into commercial service in the spring of 1947. Another fast four-engine machine, the Lockheed Constellation, commenced operations in considerable numbers after the end of hostilities. Originally delivered to the Army, many were diverted to the airlines, which converted them for high-speed express service, both transcontinental and transoceanic.

By 1953 improved versions of the DC-6 and the so-called Super-Constellation, together with the Boeing double-decked Stratoliner, made up the bulk of the four-engined transport equipment in service on United States-operated airlines. A new series of 50-passenger, twin-engine transport aircraft, the Convair 240 and 340 and the Martin 2-0-2 and 4-0-4, had largely replaced the Douglas DC-3's in United States domestic service. All of these aircraft fly at speeds in the neighborhood of 300 mph or better. The four-engined machine can handle from 60 to 100 passengers, depending upon seating arrangements.

In 1953 there were approximately 1,200 transport airplanes in service on United States domestic and overseas airlines. The acceptance of aircraft as a normal mode of travel is indicated by the fact that more people ride in airplanes than ride in Pullman cars in the United States, and more people fly across the Atlantic Ocean than cross it in steamships. Early in 1953 there were no jet or turbojet transport aircraft in service in the United States, but a number of American manufacturers had designs for such machines and all United States operators were watching carefully the experiments of the British since the introduction of both jet and turboprop machines in their European service since 1952. The British De Havilland jet-propelled *Comet* was the first of its type in regular civil transport service.

Probable Trends. From a purely commercial point of

75-PASSENGER CLIPPER "AMERICA"

view, the value of extreme size or very high speed seems questionable. Power costs rise very rapidly as speed is increased, and the difficulties of handling very large aircraft on the ground are obvious.

In the military field the situation is quite different. High speeds can be justified on the grounds of military necessity, passenger comfort can generally be overlooked, and cost of operation is not a limiting factor.

The human factor may well prove to be the real limitation. The human body is ill-adapted to the physical and psychological strains of supersonic flight. Excessive heat due to air friction is one obstacle. It also seems probable

purchase these aircraft, and Congress usually appropriates funds on the basis of the international situation. If it appears that the U.S. will become involved in a war in the not too far distant future, Congress generally authorizes large sums to purchase aircraft; if peace seems likely, appropriations are usually sharply reduced, and the effect of these reductions is that aircraft orders are cut back.

The procedure which ultimately results in appropriation of funds for the purchase of military aircraft begins each year when the Joint Chiefs of Staff prescribe the roles, missions, and responsibilities of each of the services. Each service then carries out studies of the quantities of airplanes,

Supersonic research plane shown under wing of its carrier plane from which it is released while in flight

OFFICIAL U.S.
AIR FORCE PHOTO

that aircraft will shortly possess performance capacity beyond the capabilities of a human pilot to control. Techniques for the operation of aircraft by remote control are being studied, and it is not impossible that in the future, passenger and cargo aircraft, as well as bombers and guided missiles, may be dispatched and be brought to their ultimate destination entirely by automatic devices. The human pilot's job may thus, eventually, be reduced to supervising and monitoring the operation of the machine and its accessories.   S. P. J.

AVIATION INDUSTRY, the companies in the U.S. which are involved in the research and development, design, testing, construction, modification, and sale of airplanes. Their product is a heavier-than-air craft consisting of an airframe or fuselage, a wing, one or more engines, a landing gear, and instruments for navigation and communication. The industry, which had its origins in the flight of Orville and Wilbur Wright in the Kitty Hawk airplane on December 17, 1903, has been in existence for over 50 years. In this time, more than half a million airplanes have been built.

Ninety per cent or more of the business of the aviation industry is transacted with the Federal Government. Basically the industry is dependent on government contracts for its existence. This means that manufacturers can not plan for a mass market with millions of potential customers, as do other mass-production industries. The military services, in their turn, are dependent on Congress for the money to

airfields, equipment, and personnel which will be required to meet these objectives. This is followed by an estimate of the financial cost, the refinement of these amounts being included in the detailed Defense Department budget message presented to Congress each January. Before the President submits the budget, however, hearings are held by the Services, as well as by the Defense Department. The individual components in each service explain and defend the dollar figures they propose and the total is frequently cut, adjusted, changed, and otherwise modified many times before officials of the Bureau of the Budget and the Defense Department decide whether the sums being proposed by the three services are both legitimate and feasible. Frequently, other fiscal considerations cause a large reduction. When the appropriate House of Representatives and Senate subcommittees finally take up the request for new airplanes and other defense needs, they call dozens of military and civilian officials of the Defense Department to explain and justify the requests. These subcommittees then make recommendations to the full Senate and House Appropriations Committees, which, in turn, pass them along to the parent bodies. After both the House and Senate have passed their versions of the Defense Department's appropriations bill, conferees representing each group resolve any differences. A mutually acceptable measure passes both houses again and is signed by the President. The amount finally granted, usually late in June or July of each year, is frequently different from the sums originally asked in the budget message. In most cases it has been reduced, but there have been instances where Congress appropriated more than requested. Once the Army, Navy, and Air Force know the money available, they must arrange their programs to operate within the sums appropriated.

The Federal Government spends more money on the purchase of airplanes than for any other purpose. More than one dollar in every eight spent by the U.S. during 1954 and 1955 went to buy aircraft. This is roughly, the same percentage as in 1944, the height of World War II. In 1944, however, airplanes represented only 17 per cent of total spending for defense as compared to 25 per cent for the 1955 figure.

TABLE 1—TOTAL FEDERAL EXPENDITURES AND EXPENDITURES FOR MILITARY AIRCRAFT AND RELATED PROCUREMENT

(*Dollar Figures in Millions*)

Fiscal Year	Total Federal Expenditures	Total Military Expenditures	Expenditures for Aircraft	Percent Aircraft of Total Federal	Percent Aircraft of Total Military
1940	$9,183	$1,799	$ 205	2.2	11.4
1941	13,387	6,252	587	4.4	9.4
1942	34,187	22,905	2,915	8.5	12.7
1943	79,622	63,414	10,072	12.6	15.9
1944	95,315	75,976	12,828	13.5	16.9
1945	98,703	80,537	11,521	11.7	14.3
1946	60,703	43,151	1,649	2.7	3.8
1947	39,289	14,769	593	1.5	4.0
1948	33,791	11,983	703	2.1	5.9
1949	40,057	13,988	1,248	3.1	8.9
1950	40,156	13,440	1,705	4.2	12.7
1951	44,633	20,821	2,536	5.7	12.2
1952	66,145	38,967	5,712	8.6	14.7
1953	73,982	47,565	8,605	11.6	18.1
1954	67,772	40,336	9,247	13.6	22.9
1955 (estimate)	63,504	34,375	8,300	13.1	24.1

Design and Research. Airplanes are produced with one of two purposes in mind. They must either meet a military requirement and perform missions, such as training, intercepting, bombing, and patroling, better than similar craft of unfriendly nations or, if built for commercial sale, must be able to carry enough passengers economically so that the airlines can make a profit operating them. To design such aircraft, the aviation industry relies on its engineering personnel. These engineers and technicians perform the research from which it is concluded that an airframe of a given configuration, powered by an engine or engines of promised performance, will have specified characteristics, for example, that it will fly at a certain speed and carry a definite number of passengers or amount of cargo. Utilized in this research are devices, such as "electronic brains" into which data can be inserted for quick analysis and wind tunnels. The latter, which can simulate speeds up to 15 and 20 times the speed of sound, are virtually indispensable in present-day aeronautical research. Some are operated by aircraft companies at their own plants, others are located at several of the larger universities and at a few military and government installations. The high cost of these research installations was usually at least partially paid for by the military services. While much can be learned of an airplane's performance by the use of wind tunnels and electronic computers, it is only through actual flight testing that the aviation industry can find an airplane's faults so that they may be corrected before the plane goes into quantity production. For this reason, the military

services order one or more prototypes of a new aircraft and subject it to extensive testing.

Much basic data on new aircraft and engines is provided by the National Advisory Committee for Aeronautics, an independent government agency. Through co-operative efforts by NACA, the Navy and Air Force, and the aviation industry, it has been possible to finance the construction of research aircraft which test the ideas of aeronautical engineers and scientists. One such model, the X-1A, currently holds the unofficial world speed record of 1,650 mph and the record for altitude, 90,000 ft.

As much as 90 per cent of the research carried on by the aviation industry is performed under government contract. Aircraft companies, however, expend millions of dollars of their own money each year for research. Although their own research is aimed primarily at the development of commercial types, the industry frequently tries to anticipate military requirements, hoping that such investments will be returned in the form of military-sponsored contracts. Frequently, even when the product of company-financed research is purchased by either the military or airlines, the sale is not large enough to cover the investment in research, labor, and machinery. This was the experience of an aircraft company which developed a new two-engine piston airliner shortly after World War II and succeeded in selling 101 models to two airlines and two more of the transports to the U.S. Coast Guard. Because sales of this plane and its predecessor were not enough to warrant continued production in the hope that other airline or military purchases would follow, the firm ended the production line after 103 had been delivered. This meant a net loss for the year of more than $22 million. The high cost of tooling was not amortized by the sale of the 103 aircraft.

Production. Aircraft production has been characterized by large output in emergencies and wars and by a large cutback in production schedules in peacetime. In 1939, for example, when World War II began, U.S. aircraft manufacturers turned out a total of only 5,856 planes of which 2,196 were military models. The demands of friendly European nations and a request by President Franklin D. Roosevelt for 50,000 planes a year resulted in a sharp production upturn. The number of military aircraft made rose from 6,019 in 1940 to 96,318 in 1944. This figure not only represented more planes than had ever been made in any year by any nation, but also more than the entire world production prior to 1940. The surrender of Japan in August 1945 resulted in large-scale cancellations of orders, and, in 1946, only 1,669 military aircraft were built. A similar cycle was brought on by the outbreak of hostilities in Korea.

The aircraft industry uses all the techniques of mass production, including automation. Aircraft producers, however, must work to requirements and tolerances and with materials much more exacting than those of any other mass-production industry. The military airplane, for example, has been transformed from a vehicle moving at 250 mph to one which travels faster than the speed of sound in a period of less than 10 years. This change has created the need for new techniques, new tools, and new production processes. Many conventionally used materials, such as aluminum and stainless steel, can not withstand the high temperatures encountered at such speeds. Nickel alloys and titanium had to be found to replace them. Each advance brings problems and necessitates continuous research.

Aircraft manufacturers can not "freeze" designs to permit production economies. To stay ahead of aircraft developments by potential aggressors, changes must be made

The Navy's Grumman F11F-1 applies the principle of area rule which reduces wing drag that causes power loss at supersonic speed.

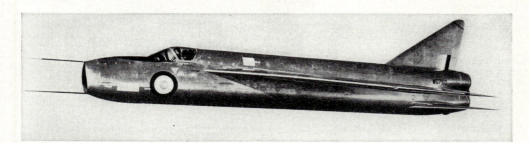

The buglike Electric P-1 interceptor fighter, the first British plane to top the speed of sound at level flight.

The Convair F-102A, an all-weather, supersonic jet interceptor in production for the U.S. Air Force as a day-or-night continental defense weapon, is powered by a J-57 jet engine.

An artist's sketch of the Douglas DC-8 flying over the Battery in New York City. The jet airliner, expected to be in service in 1959, is powered by 4 turbojet engines and will have a top speed of over 580 mph, enabling it to make the flight from Los Angeles to New York in under 5 hours.

(Above) *An artist's conception of the vertical-rising, disc-shaped aircraft which is being developed by the U.S. Air Force and resembling the popular conception of the "flying saucer."*

(Right) *The pilot controls horizontal flight of this one-passenger "Flying platform" by shifting his weight; it is the first aircraft using a ducted fan for lift and propulsion to attain free flight.*

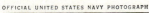

(Left) *An artist's conception of the "Flying Barrel" aircraft currently under development for the Office of Naval Research. It is designed to rise vertically like a helicopter or to fly horizontally like conventional craft, using either jets or propellers.*

(Below) *A lightweight, inflatable monoplane has been designed by the Goodyear Aircraft Corporation. Wing, tail assemblies, and pilot's seat are made of a nylon fabric, rubber-coated and shaped by thousands of dropped pile threads; the conical fuselage is of airship fabric. A 2-cycle, 40-hp engine powers the craft which when deflated, can be packed into the trunk compartment of a car.*

continually to take advantage of improvements in engines, radar equipment, and other devices. These improvements usually entail reworking the basic design and involve a delay in production. Production runs, therefore, are small and never firmly planned. One fighter plane now used in the U.S. and several friendly nations had a production run of nearly 5,000. Several thousand major and minor engineering changes, however, were made during the four years it was in production, and, at the peak of production, only 10 craft were turned out each working day.

TABLE 2—U.S. AIRCRAFT PRODUCTION
(*Number of aircraft*)

Year	Total	Military	Civil	Year	Total	Military	Civil
1912	45	16	29	1934	1,615	437	1,178
1913	43	14	29	1935	1,710	459	1,251
1914	49	15	34	1936	3,010	1,141	1,869
1915	178	26	152	1937	3,773	949	2,824
1916	411	142	269	1938	3,623	1,800	1,823
1917	2,148	2,013	135	1939	5,856	2,195	3,661
1918	14,020	13,991	29	1940	12,804	6,019	6,785
1919	780	682	98	1941	26,277	19,433	6,844
1920	328	256	72	1942	47,836	47,836	.....
1921	437	389	48	1943	85,898	85,898	.....
1922	263	226	37	1944	96,318	96,318	.....
1923	743	687	56	1945	49,761	47,714	2,047
1924	377	317	60	1946	36,670	1,669	35,001
1925	789	447	342	1947	17,717	2,100	15,617
1926	1,186	532	654	1948	9,586	2,284	7,302
1927	1,995	621	1,374	1949	6,089	2,544	3,545
1928	4,346	1,219	3,127	1950	6,520*	3,000*	3,520
1929	6,193	677	5,516	1951	7,877*	5,400*	2,477
1930	3,437	747	2,690	1952	12,509*	9,000*	3,509
1931	2,800	812	1,988	1953	15,134*	11,000*	4,134
1932	1,396	593	803	1954	12,989*	9,600*	3,389
1933	1,324	466	858	1955	12,000*	8,500*	3,500*

*Estimate.

Aircraft lead time, which is the period between the time a requirement is established for an aircraft capable of doing a specific job and the time it is delivered, is a highly technical but vital part of aviation manufacture. Since an airplane has thousands of parts and components and since each of these takes a different length of time to be produced, the lead time of any specified airplane is inevitably related to the lead time of the component which takes longest to deliver. Thus, while it may be possible for an airframe producer to fulfill an order in 15 months, two years may be needed to obtain the engine for that airframe and 30 months for electronic equipment, so that the lead time for complete aircraft is 30 months. Other complications affect the lead time, for example, formulation of requirements by military experts, the bidding for and awarding of contracts, building and testing experimental prototypes, preparations in tooling for the complete airplane and its individual components, testing the first production aircrafts, and then making any changes thus shown to be necessary.

The aviation industry does not expect to maintain its current rates of production after the three military services attain their scheduled goals on June 30, 1957, but if national policy remains unchanged reasonably high peacetime production levels will be necessary. Defense officials estimate that at least 25 per cent of the planes in military service will have to be replaced each year after June 30, 1957 to prevent the Air Force and Navy air arm from becoming obsolete. This would require an annual military aircraft production of 6,500—8,000 planes.

Aircraft Producers. Although the bulk of aircraft production is concentrated on the east and west coasts of the U.S., there is hardly a manufacturing city in any one of the 48 states that does not contribute to the nation's output of military and commercial aircraft. Production of large gas turbine (jet) and reciprocating aircraft engines is handled chiefly by five companies, three of which have their principal production sites located in the midwest. The others are on the east coast. Propeller output is dominated by three firms, two of which are on the east coast and one inland. Ever since World War II, the aviation industry has been encouraged to disperse inland instead of concentrating on the coast. The Defense Department has decreed that a company seeking a contract to produce aircraft or guided missiles will have to agree to erect any new facilities away from either coast.

During a war or a period of limited mobilization, the aviation industry is invariably confronted by many costly moves which are mandatory if production of warplanes is to be quickly increased. Wars or limited crises are normally followed by longer working hours for existing employees, an increase in the number of work shifts, the necessity for hiring and training inexperienced personnel, and the acquisition or construction of new plants and production equipment. The aviation industry was better prepared to cope with production when the Korean War began than it had been at the start of World War II, the amount of plant space having increased from 9.5 to 63.5 million sq. ft. in that period. During the World War II peak, in December 1943, the space used for aircraft production totaled 175 million sq. ft. Moreover, in 1950, a large number of government-owned plants were in standby condition. These and other facilities paid for by the military services and the aircraft industry during the Korean War resulted in the use of 135.8 million sq. ft. by mid-1953. Toward the end of 1954 some of the plants had gone out of production and this figure had dropped to 127.5 million sq. ft.

Profits in the aviation industry have consistently been much lower than in other U.S. manufacturing industries. Aircraft builders felt the excess profits tax more than most groups because the base years for the tax were the late 1940's, a low point as far as aviation sales and profits were concerned. When the excess profits tax expired at the end of 1953, earnings in the industry increased. In 1954, however, the average net profit was only 3.8 per cent after meeting federal and state taxes. In the five-year period from 1950 to 1954, the 12 principal airframe companies received average earnings after tax deductions of 3.1 per cent of their sales; the corresponding figure for all manufacturing industries was 6.1 per cent. Earnings have improved as a result of the so-called incentive-type contract in which the manufacturer and the contracting agency agree on a fair price for producing a specified number of aircraft or other items. The contract contains an arrangement whereby the company is permitted to keep a percentage of any amount saved, if by watching costs closely, it is able to produce the articles at a lower price.

During World War II, the aviation industry provided only $420 million of the nearly $3.9 billion in funds required for expansion of facilities and for purchase of new equipment, the remainder being paid by the military services. Expansion prompted by the Korean War amounted to almost the same sum, of which the industry provided nearly three times as much as it had in 1940-1945, or about $1.2 billion.

The principal aircraft manufacturers and their products are listed in Table 3. These are not the only companies in the aviation industry. Each company, for example, must buy steel, aluminum, and other fabrication and construction materials. Use is made of literally thousands of subcontractors to obtain parts and components which make up the finished products. The aviation industry spends about 50 cents of each sales dollar with its vendors, suppliers, and subcontractors. In addition, the governmental policy of having at least two sources of production for the aircraft, engines, and parts which would be critically needed in case a major war broke out has brought many of the large automotive companies into the aircraft industry. A similar program was in effect on a smaller scale during World War II. The Ford Motor Company, for example, made thousands of B-24 Liberator bombers at its Willow Run plant. Air Force planners have worked out details of the types of facilities and the machine tools which would be required for these second sources to enter aircraft production and have decided which automobile companies would best handle assignments.

TABLE 3—SOME AIRCRAFT MANUFACTURERS AND THEIR PRODUCTS

Manufacturer	Product
Beech Aircraft Corp.	Airframes
Bell Aircraft Corp.	Airframes
Boeing Airplane Co.	Airframes
Cessna Aircraft Co.	Airframes
Chance Vought Aircraft, Inc.	Airframes
Curtiss-Wright Corp., Propeller Div.	Propellers
Curtiss-Wright Corp., Wright Aeronautical Div.	Engines
Douglas Aircraft	Airframes
Fairchild Engine & Airplane Corp., Fairchild Engine Div.	Airframes
General Dynamics Corp., Convair Div.	Airframes
General Electric Co., Aircraft Gas Turbine Div.	Engines
General Motors Corp., Aeroproducts Operations Allison Div.	Propellers
General Motors Corp., Allison Div.	Engines
Grumman Aircraft Engineering Corp.	Airframes
Lockheed Aircraft Corp.	Airframes
The Glenn L. Martin Co.	Airframes
McDonnell Aircraft Corp.	Airframes
North American Aviation, Inc.	Airframes
Northrup Aircraft, Inc.	Airframes
Republic Aviation Corp.	Airframes
United Aircraft Corp., Hamilton-Standard Div.	Propellers
United Aircraft Corp., Pratt & Whitney Aircraft Div.	Engines
Westinghouse Electric Corp., Aviation Gas Turbine Div.	Engines

While there could be no aviation industry without the existence of the airframe, engine, and propeller producers, it is equally true that these basic firms could not survive without aircraft parts producers. Since no airplane is complete when it has a fuselage, engine, and propeller, many other companies have developed along with the aircraft industry proper. These companies produce such components as special aircraft spark plugs, radios, flexible hose lines to aircraft forgings, jet engine blades, landing gear, and nuts and bolts. They range in size from shops having only a dozen employees to huge industrial plants. The latter category includes divisions of some of the large corporations and companies which specialize in aviation products and derive more than 75 per cent of their incomes from the sale of products to the aircraft industry and the military services. Because the industry has grown so large in such a short time, there are not enough qualified aircraft parts suppliers in the country. As a result, new sources of auxiliary aircraft products have been found in companies which formerly dealt almost exclusively with the automobile industry. In recent years, moreover, stipulations have been made that the military services and large defense contractors must grant as many orders and subcontracts to "small business" as possible. The "small business" concern, which is by government definition one with fewer than 500 employees, has become prominent as an integral part of the aviation industry.

Aircraft Labor. Employment in the aircraft industry has paralleled the production curve. When World War I began in 1914, 200 people were employed in the infant industry. Four years later, the figure was estimated at 50,000. In 1919, the number had dropped to 4,200 and, in the following two years, a further decrease to 2,000 occurred. Although employment increased to 18,600 in 1929, the number fell off to 9,600 in 1933, the height of the depression. When World War II began in 1939, aircraft employment totaled nearly 64,000. Between January 1940 and the end of 1943, the employment levels in the aircraft industry multiplied 17 times; more persons were engaged in military aircraft production than in any other single manufacturing endeavor in history—more than 1,342,500 were employed directly by aircraft builders and another 650,000 were working for aircraft subcontractors and suppliers. In 1946, after the war ended, industry employment reached its postwar low of 219,100 as military orders were sharply curtailed.

Even when output is low, skilled management, research, and development personnel and production facilities must be maintained. The actual size of the manufacturing plant and the personnel on the payroll are not as important in preparing for advances in aviation as the background and experience of the technicians and managers of the company.

In 1954 the typical aircraft employee was working a 41-hour week, averaging $2.08 an hour, and grossing more than $85 each week for his efforts. He received a paid vacation and other fringe benefits, including seven or eight paid holidays a year, life and hospitalization insurance, and, in many cases, pension plans. The typical worker was a member of one of the two major aircraft unions, the AFL International Association of Machinists or the CIO United Automobile Workers. About 17 per cent of the work force were women.

Trends and Problems. During World War II free-flight rockets in the surface-to-air, air-to-air, air-to-surface, and surface-to-surface categories were developed, as were "guidance systems" for bomb- and plane-like devices. Toward the end of the war, the Germans developed the V-2, a hypersonic surface-to-surface missile, which might have changed the course of the war had it been evolved sooner. The trend, thus, is away from the inhabited airplane and toward the guided missile, which is frequently referred to as pilotless aircraft. Regardless of how a guided missile is employed, it is basically an aerial weapon. Therefore, the aircraft industry feels that guided missile activities logically complement airplane production. Because each missile is comprised of numerous electronic components, a large number of electrical and electronic firms are also deeply involved in missile research and production. Thus the possibility exists that a group other than the aviation industry will be primarily concerned with the production of guided missiles, and, even if airframe companies retain managerial responsibility for most of the missiles under development, they will not receive most of the money paid by the Armed Forces for missiles.

The helicopter, a rotary-wing aircraft capable of vertical flight, has become an increasingly more important industry since World War II. The vertical lift principle has been known since Leonardo da Vinci, 500 years ago, sketched a design for a helicopter-like vehicle. In 1907 Louis Breguet flew a four-rotor helicopter weighing half a ton. The first successful flight of a rotorcraft in the Western Hemisphere did not take place until Dr. Igor I. Sikorsky flew his VS-300 at Bridgeport, Connecticut in 1939. During World War II, the Army, Navy, and Marines used helicopters on a limited scale, principally for light emergency transport and rescue. In 1947, the Marines formed an experimental helicopter squadron to test new vertical-landing combat techniques. The following year the helicopter became a standard air rescue vehicle. Use of the helicopter has not been limited to military applications only. Newly created companies, using helicopters to haul passengers, cargo, and mail, are already operating in New York, Los Angeles, and Chicago, and this type of operation is scheduled to be expanded in other metropolitan areas as well. The first international helicopter passenger service has been inaugurated between Belgium, the Netherlands, France, and Germany; American carriers have also begun helicopter service. Larger helicopters are expected to replace transport planes on short-haul (up to 300 mi.) airline routes. An airline passenger traveling such a distance frequently spends as much or more time getting to and from the airports as he does aloft. A large helicopter capable of taking off and landing near the center of cities would present a definite time advantage.

As more uses are found for the helicopter, such as crop dusting, spraying, aerial survey work, mapping, prospecting, and patroling, manufacturing companies will expand. Several large aircraft companies, with an eye to the potential helicopter market, are considering buying existing companies or starting helicopter production. Those principally engaged in the production of rotary-wing aircraft include:

American Helicopter Division, Fairchild Engine and Airplane Corp.; Bell Aircraft Corp.; Doman Helicopters, Inc.; Hiller Helicopters; Kaman Aircraft Corp.; Piasecki Helicopter Corp.; Sikorsky Aircraft Div., United Aircraft Corp.

American-built transports fly the routes of virtually every airline in the world. It is estimated that about 80 per cent of the commercial airlines in use were built in this country. Several other nations, however, are challenging America's role as principal supplier of transports. Great Britain, for example, was the first nation to offer a jet-powered airliner. The Vickers Viscount turboprop airliner has been purchased by U.S. airlines in sizable quantities. The U.S. is the largest exporter of aviation products. Those exports represent only about five per cent of total American exports and less than 10 per cent of total aircraft production. The export market for aeronautical products is, therefore, one which presumably will be expanded.

Foreign nations have licensed U.S. companies to build their aircraft products. An example of this is in the field of jet engine manufacture. Great Britain emphasized research in jet propulsion during World War II and, as a result, British jet engine makers were far ahead of their American counterparts. U.S. engine producers consequently made licensing and/or technical assistance agreements with various British companies. Thus, the Rolls-Royce Nene and Tay turbojets have evolved into the Pratt & Whitney J42 and J48; the Armstrong-Siddeley Sapphire, into the Wright J65; the Bristol Olympus, into the Wright J67. When the U.S. Air Force needed a light jet bomber, it imported the English Electric Canberra which is being built by Martin as the B-57. The French, who perfected a series of small turbojets after World War II, licensed Continental Motors Corporation of Muskegon, Michigan, to produce many of them.

Various foreign aircraft components and techniques have also been imported by the American aviation industry. American production of equipment for the "probe and drogue" system of air-to-air refueling is thus possible. U.S. companies, of course, license the foreign manufacture of their products. The F-86 Sabre jet fighter is made in Canada, Australia, and Italy; the T-33 jet trainer and S2F anti-submarine plane are being produced in Canada; other U.S. aviation equipment is being built under license in countries as widely separated as Japan and Norway.

The aviation industry is seeking to develop two new models. One is a nuclear-powered bomber. The other is an intercontinental guided missile which, launched in the U.S., would travel at 15,000-20,000 mph as high as 800 mi. above the earth and hit a target 5,000 mi. or more away. Virtually every aircraft and engine company in the industry is working on the atomic-powered bomber. Almost all research in this field is financed by the Navy, Air Force, and the Atomic Energy Commission, and the National Advisory Committee for Aeronautics is making basic studies the findings of which are available to the industry. The greatest problem in the development of a nuclear airplane is the provision for crew members of adequate shielding against radiation. Under investigation is the use of water-based aircraft, such as large seaplanes, which would be able to release quantities of radioactive waste materials into the ocean when they landed. When the nuclear airplane finally appears, it will have cost almost half a billion dollars to develop and will weigh at least as much as the very heavy bombers in use by the Air Force or more than 350,000 lb. Aeronautical engineers feel that such an aircraft is completely feasible, once the shielding problem is solved, and cite the development of nuclear-powered submarines.

The intercontinental ballistics guided missile (ICBM) would feature a thermonuclear warhead which would explode a few hundred feet over the target area. Frequently it is called the "ultimate weapon," because there is no known defense against it. Because of the speeds at which the unmanned ICBM will travel, it will come very close to becoming an artificial moon. The principal task in this respect, therefore, is to regulate the speed so that the missile will reach a target 5,000 mi. away rather than end up as an earth satellite. A major problem is that of cooling the surface of the missile so that it does not disintegrate like a meteorite on re-entering the earth's atmosphere.

Still another major project undertaken by the aviation industry for the military is the development of devices which will eliminate the need for long runways. With the development of jet propulsion and larger warplanes, it has become necessary to lengthen airport runways. Commercial and military airports, however, are surrounded by housing developments in many cases, and the additional land required is often not available. The aviation industry is trying techniques, such as reverse thrust for turbojet engines—which is the same principle as reversing propellers on piston power plants—and deceleration parachutes which fly out of the tail of the airplane on landing, to create more "drag" when the aircraft touches down. This will shorten the runway length needed. To shorten take-off runs, the industry has developed RATO (rocket-assist-take-off) bottles, which are basically small expendable engines providing additional thrust just as the airplane becomes airborne. Also being tested is a trailer-like combination from which a fighter plane is catapulted directly into the air. Although the Navy has been using catapults to launch aircraft from ships for many years, the principle is now being tried on land with the same trailer as those used for the launching of a tactical guided missile. If successful, this technique would eliminate the need for a take-off runway. Other solutions include the design of such experimental aircraft as the Army-sponsored convertiplane, a combination fixed- and rotary-wing craft, and the Navy's vertical take-off fighter planes. Many such developments not only have immediate military applications but also potential commercial uses, for airliners have become larger, necessitating longer runways.

Noise caused by the whine and blast of turbojet engines is a leading problem. The turbojet is inherently a noisy power plant, far surpassing any reciprocating engine of comparable rating in the number of decibels emitted. The more powerful the jet engine, the more noise it makes. The use of an afterburner, a device fitted to the exhaust of the gas turbine engine to reburn the gases and produce additional pounds of thrust, increases the noise.

The aviation industry, therefore, is one which has been and will continue to be beset by a variety of problems including development of new types of aircraft and missiles, finances, shortages of qualified technical personnel, and the nation's apparent inability to decide whether it is willing to pay the cost of maintaining strong aircraft companies in peacetime. All have been overcome to some degree, and the industry is continually working toward their ultimate solution.   R. M. L.

AVIATION MEDICINE, the application of medical arts and sciences to the human problems engendered by piloted aircraft. This definition suggests three distinct but interrelated phases: (1) the basic research in various fields such as physiology and biophysics, (2) the formulation of human tolerances and the development of equipment for aviators, and (3) the practice of medicine in the clinical disorders of flying. Basic research, the least spectacular phase, is necessary to provide a fund of knowledge that will enable man to fly the machines of his invention. The development of new combat aircraft for high-altitude flight made it imperative that human factors be considered in engineering design, thereby focusing attention on the applied-research phase of aviation medicine. As a result of this impetus, tremendous advances were made in the application of basic research to the human problems of flying. The wide popularity of air travel during the 1930's added to the fund of knowledge concerning pathological conditions arising among passengers during flight. This increase, together with prior military and civilian research, provided the basis for the aviation medical research of World War II.

HISTORY

The medical implications of flying were known before the airplane. The first doctor to fly was John Jeffries, of Boston, who accompanied Blanchard on his famous crossing of the English Channel in a hydrogen-filled balloon in 1785. The systematic study of aviation medicine began in Europe, particularly with the French balloonists of the middle nineteenth century. Dr. Paul Bert (1833-1886) determined some of the effects of decreased atmospheric pressure on the human body and is credited with the discovery of the beneficial effects of oxygen inhalation.

In September 1908, Orville Wright was injured and Lt. Thomas Selfridge was killed in the first fatal airplane accident. U.S. Army doctors, realizing the human applications of flying, established strict physical standards by 1912. At this period most people had never seen an airplane.

Dr. William H. Wilmer headed the first American laboratory, established in 1918 at Mineola, L. I., New York. In the same year, General Pershing called for medical personnel to assist the Aviation Section of the Signal Corps overseas.

These doctors were praised in a report for their contribution to the increased military effectiveness of the fliers, as measured by increased flying hours and the establishment of a record of 4,436 flying hours without a fatal accident. In 1920 the research laboratory at Mineola was moved to Mitchel Field as a school for flight surgeons and from this small beginning evolved the U.S. Air Force School of Aviation Medicine at Randolph Field, Texas.

The period of 1920 to 1926 was the day of barnstorming by ex-service pilots in old "Jennies." These airplanes did not tax man's abilities. A tight belt, such as worn by motorcycle riders, and a scarf about the neck were part of the costume of aviators in those days. Their purpose was to overcome acceleration forces. The belt prevented accumulation of blood in the abdomen and the scarf could be knotted tightly to give a little extra protection against black-out when pulling out of a dive. In 1927, Charles A. Lindbergh flew across the Atlantic in the *Spirit of St. Louis,* and in 1929 Carl A. Spaatz and Ira C. Eaker stayed aloft for almost 51 hours in the *Question Mark*. These two events marked the end of the old carefree era of barnstorming.

In 1926, Congress had recognized civil aviation with a Bureau of Air Commerce in the Department of Commerce; a medical section was formed in this bureau under the direction of Dr. Louis H. Bauer. In 1929, Dr. Bauer founded the Aero Medical Association, a national organization of physicians interested in aviation medicine.

The early 1930's produced remarkable advances in engineering; airplanes like the Boeing B-9 were capable of sustained flight above 18,000 ft., where pilots required oxygen continuously.

The decade 1935 to 1945 witnessed the growth of great networks of commercial air lines carrying thousands of passengers daily, as well as a tremendous increase in the private use of airplanes for transportation and sport. Many of the clinical applications of aviation medicine came to the fore. The disorders peculiar to flying were recognized by the public and understood by the medical profession. The development of jet and rocket planes capable of flight at supersonic speeds, posed a host of additional human problems. In 1953, certification in the specialty of aviation medicine was undertaken.

RESPIRATION

The principal problems confronting man as he ascends into the sky are related to altitude and speed. As the flier ascends, the barometric pressure of the atmosphere surrounding him is radically decreased; and, as the old balloonists

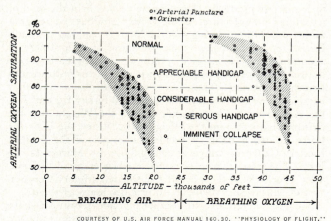

COURTESY OF U.S. AIR FORCE MANUAL 160.30, "PHYSIOLOGY OF FLIGHT."

Fig. 1—OXYGEN REQUIREMENTS IN FLIGHT

found, this phenomenon produces changes in the aviator's circulation and respiration. These changes will be considered individually, but first something should be said about the mechanism of respiration and circulation.

Breathing is simply an exchange of gases between an organism and its environment. An animal exchanges carbon dioxide produced by the body for oxygen from the inhaled air. This gas exchange, which takes place in the lungs, is termed external respiration. The average man at rest draws in 500 cu. cm. (30 cu. in.) of air about 12 to 16 times a minute; hence he ventilates his lungs at the rate of 6 to 8 liters of air each minute. Of course, the ventilation rate can be increased greatly, but it is limited by the amount of air that can be inhaled in one breath and by the number of breaths a minute. Air is principally nitrogen (79 per cent). Dry air is four-fifths nitrogen (by volume) and one-fifth oxygen, with 0.04 per cent carbon dioxide and traces of certain rare gases. The relative proportions of these gases do not change with altitude.

The gases in the tiny air sacs of the lungs (alveoli) pass through the cell walls into the blood flowing through the capillaries of the lungs. The blood carries oxygen principally in the red blood cells by means of a chemical combination with hemoglobin, which has an amazingly high affinity for oxygen at the pressures found in the alveoli and a correspondingly low affinity for oxygen at the pressures found in the tissues. The oxygen-dissociation curve explains the transportation of oxygen by means of circulating blood; the hemoglobin picks up oxygen in the alveolar capillaries and deposits it in the tissues.

The total amount of oxygen carried in the blood can be increased, of course, by speeding the circulation, but this increase is limited by the capacity of the heart, the number of red cells in the circulating blood, and the ability of the tissues themselves to pick up and utilize the oxygen from the blood.

PROBLEMS OF ALTITUDE

Man lives on the floor of an "ocean" of air at least 600 mi. in thickness. This sea of atmosphere is usually considered as comprising three layers: the troposphere up to 7 mi., the stratosphere 8 to 50 mi., and then the ionosphere. These layers are not uniform in thickness, being thinnest at the poles and thickest over the equator. At 40° N. lat. the United States standard atmosphere fixes the lower limit of the stratosphere at 35,000 ft. Combat operations of World War II ranged up to altitudes of 30,000 ft., a mere 6 mi. above the earth. Commercial flights invade the lower regions of the stratosphere. The ionosphere has been pierced by V-2 rockets which reached an altitude of 160 mi. The principal realm of activity is still the troposphere. Even in this lowest atmospheric layer, however, there are many problems in maintaining human flight.

Hypoxia. Anoxia means, literally, absence of oxygen. Hypoxia, or undersupply of oxygen, is a more exact term. It refers to the lowering of the blood oxygen saturation.

There are three levels to consider in oxygen requirements: 10,000 ft., 38,000 ft., and 50,000 ft. At 10,000 ft. some individuals require supplemental oxygen in order to maintain maximum efficiency, and upon reaching 14,000 ft. almost everyone needs extra oxygen. It is true that mountain climbers remain at higher altitudes for considerable periods, but this ability is made possible by the process of acclimatization, which requires days to acquire and hence is of no value to the aviator who ascends in a few minutes. The blood oxygen saturation can be maintained at 90 to 95 per cent, an efficient working level, by inhalation of oxygen up to an alti-

tude of 38,000 ft.—roughly the upper limit of the troposphere. Above 38,000 ft., even pure oxygen (administered by masks) is insufficient to maintain the blood oxygen saturation at optimum levels. Figure 1 shows the percentile saturation of arterial blood at altitudes up to 44,800 ft., with subjects breathing pure oxygen. The curves on the left show the range of performance among persons breathing air. Curves on the right show the range of performance among persons breathing pure oxygen.

In order to maintain satisfactory blood-oxygen levels at altitudes above 40,000 ft., oxygen must be introduced into the lungs under pressure because of increased water-vapor pressure and the carbon dioxide in the lungs. Although these factors remain constant (47 mm. Hg and 40 mm. Hg, respectively), these pressures become relatively larger with the decreasing atmospheric pressure until the latter is 87 mm. Hg at 50,000 ft. when the sum of the carbon dioxide pressure and water vapor pressure equals the pressure outside the lungs. Respiration under these conditions is impossible.

Man cannot breathe unaided above 50,000 ft. Air pumps to pressurize the cabins for pilots and passengers are a solution of the problem. By appropriate pressurization, the atmospheric pressure inside the cabin may be adjusted to a much lower equivalent altitude.

The cerebral cortex is particularly sensitive to hypoxia. The initial effect produced is that of mild intoxication, with a feeling of exhilaration and a lack of critical judgment. Special skills such as writing, addition, and multiplication decrease rapidly. Vision, also, is sensitive to hypoxia, and night vision is extremely poor in subjects who are hypoxic, i.e., have below 90 per cent blood-oxygen saturation. For this reason, pilots of unpressurized airplanes were advised to inhale oxygen from the ground up during night flying. Fortunately, hypoxia is a completely reversible physiological phenomenon. Immediate complete recovery is the rule.

Decompression Sickness. This disease, popularly known as bends or chokes, is similar to the well-known condition of caisson disease. It results from vaporization of the gases dissolved in blood and the body tissues. Nitrogen is not utilized by the tissues in respiration while oxygen is consumed in the chemical process of metabolism. At sea level the pressure of air surrounding the human organism (14.6 lb. per square inch) holds the nitrogen in solution in the body; however, at altitudes above 30,000 ft. the decrease in pressure surrounding the body allows the nitrogen to come out of solution very much as opening a bottle of soda pop causes the release of thousands of tiny bubbles of dissolved gases. (This is a working hypothesis; there are some experimental observations at variance with it.) These bubbles, principally of nitrogen, cannot be absorbed without recompression of the whole individual.

A principal symptom is bends—pain around large joints, sometimes so severe as to produce collapse. Usually there are multiple collections of gas and hence several sites of pain so severe that it becomes necessary for the individual to descend, where the increased atmosphere forces the gas back into solution in the body fluids. If nitrogen bubbles form within the blood vessels, serious effects (aeroembolism), may ensue since the bubbles act as plugs in the smaller blood vessels. Confused states, followed by paralysis and, on rare occasions, death, may result from aeroembolism of the blood vessels of the brain. An immediate descent to lower altitudes again causes re-solution of the gases and recovery.

Bends rarely occur below 30,000 ft. and are more easily produced by rapid ascents, cold environments, and physical exercise, or by remaining at a high altitude for periods of several hours. Circulatory collapse ("shock") may occur within twenty-four hours following exposure to low barometric pressure. Barometric pressure at 63,000 ft. is equal to the vapor pressure of the water in the lungs and in the body (47 mm. Hg). Not only do the dissolved gases come out of solution, but the body water itself vaporizes. Instantaneous death can be prevented only by increasing pressure on the outside of the body by wearing a pressure suit or by pressurizing the cabin of the aircraft.

Cold. However sweltering the heat may be at sea level, there is intense cold a scant 8 mi. up, even above the equator. A flight into the stratosphere will mean that temperatures of $-55°$ C. ($-67°$ F.) will be encountered.

At these temperatures fingers will freeze in a few moments, so that additional protection for the aviator in the form of cabin heating or electrically heated suits is required. All work of operating combat airplanes was done with the handicap of heavy gloves during World War II, because frostbite was an ever-present menace to combat crewmen flying at altitudes of 20,000 to 30,000 ft.

Explosive Decompression. Failure of a pressure cabin is equivalent to an extremely rapid ascent, since the individual is subjected to the change in atmospheric pressure almost instantly. At 30,000 ft. the gas contained in the intestines expands to four times its volume at sea level, causing considerable discomfort. Doctors working in altitude chambers (large steel enclosures equipped with air pumps to reduce the pressure to any desired partial vacuum and thus simulate the conditions of high-altitude flight) have determined that survival is possible under conditions of explosive decompression, provided oxygen masks are immediately available.

The period of useful consciousness during which time an individual can save himself decreases rapidly with higher altitudes. At 20,000 to 25,000 ft. the pilot has almost five minutes to remedy his hypoxic condition by inhalation of oxygen. At 35,000 ft., however, this time is down to 90 sec. before unconsciousness supervenes.

Escape at Altitude. The first human venture into the upper atmosphere was the balloon ascent of O. A. Anderson and A. W. Stevens, sponsored by the National Geographic Society and the United States Army Air Corps, reaching an altitude of 72,395 ft. on Nov. 11, 1935. Had they been required to leave their pressurized cabin, they would not have survived. The first high-altitude parachute jump on record is that of an Air Force doctor, William Randolph Lovelace II, who successfully leaped from 40,200 ft. in 1943. It took Colonel Lovelace 23 min. and 51 sec. to descend to ground level with open parachute. It is obvious from the discussion on hypoxia that, since he was above 25,000 ft. for 8 min., he would not have survived without carrying supplemental oxygen with him. Escape from an airplane flying at altitudes of 8 mi. or higher is virtually impossible without some means of supplying the aviator with oxygen until he has descended below 20,000 ft.

An additional consideration is the fact that the opening shock of a parachute opened at altitudes such as these might be great enough to rupture the parachute and produce serious bodily injury. The opening shock of a similar parachute at the same air speed but at a much lower altitude of 15,000 ft. is only 9.5 g. (The symbol g refers to the force of gravity. One g is the force acting upon a body at rest and is measured by the weight of that body. A human weighing 200 lb. weighs 400 lb. when he is under a force of two g's.) Flight surgeons advised aviators to fall free until below 20,000 ft. One solution to this problem was automatic opening devices to release parachute canopies at

a safe altitude without depending on the individual, who might be confused or unconscious.

PROBLEMS OF SPEED

Speed of itself produces no objective or subjective effects so long as the velocity and direction remain constant. With the

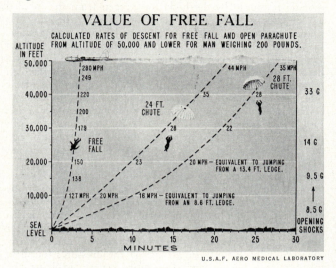

U.S.A.F. AERO MEDICAL LABORATORY

earth rotating once in 24 hours, everyone travels at approximately 1,000 mph while moving about on the surface. A passenger traveling in an airplane in a straight and level flight is not conscious of the sensation of speed.

Linear Acceleration. The human problems arise in getting the airplane up to a constant speed (acceleration) and in slowing it down (deceleration). The sensation experienced in an airplane launched by catapult is similar to that produced by sharp acceleration in an automobile. The postwar jet engines could produce a thrust of 1.5 to 3.0 g on take-off, which can be easily tolerated. It is possible to tolerate terrific speed if the increase in speed is gradual, and provided the force is applied over a considerable time and in the same direction.

There is no basis in fact for Jules Verne's romantic concept of passengers floating about in a space ship because of the absence of gravity. In order to maintain the usual sensation of gravity (1 g) it would be necessary merely to accelerate at a constant, calculated rate. The human occupants and all the contents of the space ship would be pressed toward the rear of the ship by inertia.

Linear Deceleration. The sudden deceleration produced by crash landing is the crucial problem in linear deceleration. The U.S. Navy in 1947 catapulted airplanes into an embankment at 100 mph and by careful instrumentation of dummies demonstrated that the maximum force or impact on the human body was approximately 170 g at that moderate speed. It is usually stated that the human body cannot stand large decelerative forces. There are, however, instances of falls from high buildings in which the human body has withstood terrific impact when the force was evenly distributed over the whole body. The problem of successful human deceleration is to provide a smooth, constant slowing over as long a time and as great a distance as possible. Using a rocket-powered sled, speeding along a pair of rails until it struck a series of brakes, Lt. Col. John P. Stapp, an Air Force flight surgeon, sustained a deceleration of 46.2 g for ¼ sec.—approximately equivalent to an automobile moving at 70 mph crashing into a brick wall and stopping in nine ft.

Curvilinear Acceleration. The force of g acts on the human body when a change of direction is made. In dive bombing during World War II it became evident that if the pilot pulled up from a dive when he was traveling at 200 to 300 mph, the inertia of his body tended to drag him down into the seat; the result was an effective increase of his weight. Pilots came to refer to pull-outs as 3 g, 5 g, or 9 g, and sometimes specifications were written to provide that the airplane should withstand a pull-out of 9 g.

It was early determined that the maximum human tolerance to this acceleration force is between 4 and 5 g for periods over 5 sec. In effect, the weight of the blood in the body increases along with the other body elements so that the heart is not capable of forcing blood up into the head. The first result is a loss of vision, called black-out, succeeded by loss of consciousness if the acceleration is continued long enough. It became apparent that in order for airplanes to travel at high speeds and yet be maneuverable, the pilot needed protection against the acceleration force produced by turns at high speeds. A jet fighter, for instance, required a turn of a 1,600-yards radius at 600 mph in order to avoid black-out of the pilot.

An "anti-g suit" was developed during World War II as a means of combating the adverse effects of acceleration forces. This suit was a series of distensible bladders arranged over the lower legs and lower abdomen. When the bladders were distended with air, they pressed on the lower portion of the body, thus enabling the heart to maintain the blood flow in the head. At the most, these suits were capable of increasing the g tolerance by 1.5 g's.

Escape from High-Speed Aircraft. As aircraft attained speeds in the range of 300 to 400 mph it became increasingly difficult for pilots to jump clear of the tail structure. As a partial answer to this problem, the Germans during World War II developed a method of ejecting the pilot in his seat by an explosive charge. The pilot shot into the air stream with sufficient force (a velocity of 60 ft. per second), so that he would be well clear of the tail. It was shown in 1947 that downward ejection of the pilot is far more satisfactory; since there are no large structures to be cleared, the force of ejection can be much less. The ejection seat was only a partial answer to the question of escape from high-performance aircraft since wind blast at high speed and hypoxia at high altitudes presented great problems after clearing the airplane.

Wind Blast. The German aviation medical group showed during World War II that human facial tissues are grossly distorted by wind blast of 400 mph, and they guessed that wind blast might inflict fatal injuries at speeds of roughly 500 mph. With supersonic jet and rocket aircraft, the problem of wind blast called for the development of some sort of pilot escape enclosure. Efforts were made to disconnect the pilot's portion of the airplane, or perhaps to eject the cockpit with its own oxygen system and parachute.

Cockpit Heating. The Bell X-1 rocket plane was designed for a top speed of 1,500 mph when traveling in the lower stratosphere. This speed is equivalent to Mach 2, or twice the speed of sound. (The speed of sound is not constant. At sea level, it travels roughly 761 mph; at 40,000 ft., it is approximately 663 mph. Because of this variation, airplane engineers compute the speed of aircraft relative to Mach 1, which is the speed of sound.) When an airplane flies at supersonic speeds, ram air compression heats the airplane surfaces or skin. At 1,500 mph or Mach 2, the cockpit temperature exceeds 300° F. Efficient refrigeration devices to render cockpits habitable are therefore necessary.

HUMAN PROBLEMS OF THE GROUP

Personnel selection is a problem common to both civilian and military aviation. Physical requirements vary with the type of flying, but the principal physical considerations are eyesight, hearing, and muscular co-ordination. In addition, psychological aptitude for flying is important. The Army Air Forces developed extensive test procedures during World War II for the selection of applicants who would be successful in pilot training, thus avoiding lost time in training.

Anthropometric studies of thousands of air crewmen established the basic measurements for cockpits and seat heights. Head sizes and face sizes were determined in order to fit helmets and oxygen masks properly, and clothing and equipment were checked against these extensive measurements.

INDIVIDUAL HUMAN PROBLEMS

Fatigue. As flights of greater duration became possible, the problem of fatigue came to the fore. The use of two pilots was an effort to share the work and to simplify the job of piloting, but this expedient was not always sufficient when craft capable of sustained flights greater than 24 hours' duration came into use. Pilots must be at peak efficiency to make a successful landing, and hence flights of long duration place a greater strain on the pilot than the same number of hours spent at intervals in the air. The radar operators, navigators, and engineers face a similar problem. An extensive psychological research project was begun to determine the periods of time during which a man can perform a given complex task with maximum efficiency. A concomitant problem was the investigation of control knobs, instrument displays, and all types of devices designed for use of aviators, with a critical evaluation of the human requirements. This study indicated in each case whether it was necessary for the equipment to be redesigned so that it could be used with greater efficiency and with less fatigue.

Vibration and Noise. Airplanes have always been noisy; this fact has been recognized as one of the occupational hazards of flying. A reduction in hearing for higher tones is a common finding in experienced aviators. A principal component of noise in conventional airplanes is the sound wave produced by the propeller tips.

The development of jet engines in 1944 intensified the noise problem not only for the aircrews, but also for the maintenance crews who work at or near the engines. As the power of the jet engine increases, its noise production mounts. Vibration is another facet of the same problem, since low-frequency mechanical vibrations of high energy are alleged to disturb the sympathetic nervous system and to produce sickness and fatigue.

Motion Sickness. Probably everyone who has flown has experienced an attack of slight nausea and an uncomfortable feeling from the strange motions produced by rough air. Motion sickness has been the subject of a considerable amount of research. It can be separated into at least two distinct entities. Some people have a predisposition to motion sickness; they become carsick or trainsick as well as airsick and seasick. Little if anything can be done for these people, who, fortunately, comprise only a small number of the population. The other form of motion sickness arises primarily from apprehension and is commonly found in novice air travelers and student pilots. It disappears as experience and confidence increase and is to be regarded as a normal occurrence.

PROBLEMS OF THE FUTURE

"The sky is the limit" applies particularly to research in aviation medicine. The sights have been raised to the stratosphere. Rocket planes can operate in the upper atmosphere since no oxygen is needed for rocket propulsion.

Pressure. Pressure cabins, of course, may be so perfected that they will maintain sufficient atmospheric pressure to permit occupancy at great altitudes, but at approximately 80,000 ft. the density of the atmosphere is so low that it would require impossibly large compression pumps to keep the cabin pressurized. Furthermore, the ozone found in the upper stratosphere would be toxic if pumped into the cabin. A sealed cabin which contains an atmosphere under sufficient pressure is needed for upper atmosphere flight. For emergencies the individual must be given some additional protection.

Temperature. One interesting phenomenon of the upper atmosphere is the fact that temperature increases; temperatures above 300° F. may exist. There is a theoretical question in designing an ionosphere vehicle—the problem of heat exchange between the scorching hot side exposed to the sun and the intensely cold shaded portion of the vehicle. Space vehicles will require excellent insulation and a very rapid heat transfer around their periphery.

Radiation. The problem of biological effects of cosmic or other solar radiation is in the realm of speculation, but in an ascent to the ionosphere the high-energy radiation encountered will require an effective shielding of the passengers.

Speed. In all probability, supersonic planes will travel in the stratosphere or higher. The heat exchange will become more important as speeds increase until it is possible to fly above the atmosphere, where aerodynamic heating will be no problem. How high this may be is indicated by the fact that meteors (shooting stars) are heated to an incandescent temperature while traveling at 25,000 mph over 50 mi. above the earth. It may be necessary to go beyond the atmosphere to eliminate the heat from skin friction.

Space Flight. Flight in vacuo is theoretically possible. Several difficulties must be overcome, however, before flight beyond the earth's atmosphere is feasible. Any change, of course, in direction at supersonic speed would produce very high accelerative forces upon the occupants. Changes in velocity and direction would necessarily be made in extremely small increments.

Disease. Returning to more mundane problems of the future, the mass movement of peoples by air between continents will become commonplace. This rapid transfer of vast numbers of people will require the elimination of the various scourges and pestilences from the earth. Smallpox, for example, occurs endemically in India and China. In order to prevent its spread over the entire globe, at least 50 per cent of the total world population will need to be vaccinated.

Typhus fever, cholera, and all the other exotic diseases could easily be brought into the United States in a few hours. Patients suffering from the usual contagious diseases could be transported halfway around the world while still in the incubation period of their disease, while they themselves would not know they were ill. The revision of quarantine regulations and the provision of uniform sanitation laws are needed for future international air travel. The transportation of insect pests by air, some of them vectors of disease and others dangerous to domestic agriculture, poses a similar problem.

Disaster Relief. The airplane provides the most efficient means available of handling disasters, such as earthquakes, floods, fires, and famine. The future of disaster relief depends on an adequate recognition of the position of air evacuation in the handling of injured people, and also a realization of the rapidity by which a medical rescue team can be brought to the scene of disaster. The airplane may prove one of man's greatest boons as well as an instrument capable of loosing death and injury on hundreds of thousands of people at a single stroke.   V. M. D.

AVIATION SAFETY. The Civil Aeronautics Board defines an aircraft accident as follows: "An aircraft accident is considered to be any occurrence while the aircraft is operating as such, which results in fatal or serious injury to persons or appreciable damage to the aircraft. The aircraft is considered to be operating as such from the time the engine(s) is (are) started for purposes of flight until the flight is completed; in the case of gliders, while they are under tow or gliding. Propeller accidents to persons are arbitrarily included in the above . . . "

The Civil Aeronautics Board requires: "Report and notification of accidents. A written report shall be made without delay to the Civil Aeronautics Board at its nearest branch office of every accident involving a civil aircraft which occurs within the United States and every accident involving a certificated aircraft of the United States, without regard to where it occurs. Such report shall be made upon an accident report form furnished by the Civil Aeronautics Board. In addition, the Civil Aeronautics Board, or the Administrator of Civil Aeronautics, shall be notified immediately in person or by cable, telegraph, telephone, or radio, of the occurrence of any air carrier accident, or accident resulting in serious or fatal injury to any person, or accident known or believed to have resulted from a structural failure in flight. This requirement of immediate notification shall apply to every such accident involving civil aircraft which occurs within the United States and every such accident involving air-carrier aircraft without regard to where it occurs. The pilot in command of a nonair-carrier aircraft involved in the accident shall make the report and notification of the accident as required by this section unless he is incapacitated, in which event the operator of the aircraft shall make such report and notification. The operator of an air-carrier aircraft involved in an accident shall make such report and notification."

In these regulations, "United States" means the states, the territories and possessions, and the territorial waters surrounding them, unless a different meaning is specifically indicated. "Operator" includes the owner or lessee or any other persons who cause or authorize the operation of aircraft.

SAFETY IN AIR-CARRIER FLYING

Scheduled Domestic Air-Carrier Operations. The yardstick commonly used to measure air-carrier safety is the rate of passenger fatalities per 100,000,000 passenger-miles flown. During 1953, the domestic scheduled airlines carried some 25 million passengers approximately 15.3 billion passenger-miles with a passenger fatality rate of 0.56 per 100 million passenger-miles. This compares with rates of 0.4 in 1952 (this year having the best safety record to date), 1.3 in 1951, and 1.1 in 1950. In 1953, there were 31 accidents in scheduled passenger operations, of which four were fatal, involving the deaths of 86 passengers and 15 crew members. The total number of plane-miles flown by the domestic airlines was 505,074,347 in 1953, and there were 126,268,587 plane-miles of travel for each fatal accident. The percentage of passengers fatally injured in these accidents was 0.0003, as compared with 0.0002 in 1952 and 0.0006 in 1951.

Plane miles flown per accident is significant, as distinguished from fatal accidents because accident frequency is

TABLE I. ACCIDENTS IN SCHEDULED DOMESTIC PASSENGER-CARRYING AIR-CARRIER OPERATIONS
(Calendar Years)

	1943	1944	1945	1946	1947	1948	1949	1950	1951	1952	1953[a]
Total accidents	14	24	33	31	36	53	29	35	37	36	31
Fatal accidents	2	3	7	9	5	5	4	4	8	5	4
Passenger fatalities..	22	48	76	75	199	83	93	96	142	46	86
Crew fatalities:											
Pilot	2	3	4	8	4	4	3	4	6	2	4
Copilot	2	3	4	8	5	4	3	4	6	2	4
Other	4†	2	3	6	8	7	5	5	12	2	7
Total fatalities	30	56	87	97	216	98	104	109	166	52	105

Source: Civil Aeronautics Board.

* Including trunk, feeder, and territorial carriers. These statistics exclude all propeller accidents to persons. † Includes company employee riding in jump seat. [a] Preliminary figures.

usually a more satisfactory index than severity in determining accident trends. Also, the difference between a fatal and a nonfatal accident in aviation is often a matter of chance. William W. Moss, an airline pilot of great experience, has shown that the parameter of plane miles is more representative of the pilot's problem than the rates based on passenger miles. The pilot's primary responsibility is to bring the aircraft and passengers safely to destination, without regard to number of passengers.

International Air-Carrier Safety. In international scheduled passenger-carrying service in 1953 there were five accidents, two of which were fatal, causing the deaths of two passengers and no crew members. Plane-miles aggregated 105,081,124, giving a rate of 52,540,562 plane-miles per fatal accident and a percentage of passengers fatally injured of 0.0001. These figures for 1953 are only preliminary (as are all the other 1953 figures in this article), but they would suggest that the safety record for this year is by far the best to date.

Irregular Air-Carriers. The so-called "non-scheduled" carriers have extended the scope of their operations in both domestic and international trade. Because of the fact that their mileage records are not as complete, their accident records are not directly comparable with those of the scheduled lines.

In 1953, the large "irregular" domestic and international air carriers had 13 accidents, of which five were fatal, involving the deaths of 141 passengers and 20 crew members. These figures include eight accidents in military charter service, of which three were fatal, causing 86 passenger fatalities and 20 fatalities among crew members. In 1952, the "irregular" domestic airlines had seven accidents. Two of these were fatal, involving the deaths of 26 passengers and five crew members. In the same year, the "irregular" international carriers had three accidents, but none of these proved to be fatal.

Types and Causes of Air-Carrier Accidents. Table IV gives a recapitulation of the number and severity of ac-

TABLE II. ACCIDENTS IN U.S.A. INTERNATIONAL PASSENGER-CARRYING AIR CARRIER OPERATIONS
(Calendar Years)

	1939	1947	1948	1949	1950	1951	1952	1953[a]
Thousands of plane miles flown	7,578	83,126	93,920	99,039	90,287	99,366	99,099	105,081
Fatal accidents.....................	1	3	1	0	2	1	3	2
Passenger fatalities	10	20	20	0	48	31	94	2
Crew fatalities:								
Pilot	1	2	1	0	1	1	1	0
Copilot	1	2	1	0	1	1	1	0
Other	2	9	8	0	6	7	7	0
Total fatalities	14	33	30	0	56	40	103	2

[a] Preliminary figures.

Source: Civil Aeronautics Board.

TABLE III. COMPARATIVE AIR-CARRIER PASSENGER-CARRYING ACCIDENT STATISTICS
(Calendar Years)

	U.S.A. INTERNATIONAL			U.S.A. DOMESTIC		
	1951	1952	[a]1953	1951	1952	[a]1953
Passenger fatalities per 100,000,000 passenger miles..	1.1	3.0	....	1.3	0.4	....
Per cent passengers fatally injured..................	0.0015	0.0040*	0.0001*	0.0006*	0.0002*	0.0003*
Plane miles flown per fatal accident.................	93,366,512	33,032,977	52,540,562	49,199,327	89,431,698	126,268,587
Plane miles flown per accident.....................	9,336,651	11,010,992	21,016,225	10,637,692	12,421,069	16,292,721

* Based on revenue passengers only
[a] Preliminary figures.

Source: Civil Aeronautics Board.

TABLE IV. AIR-CARRIER AIRCRAFT ACCIDENTS IN BOTH SCHEDULED AND IRREGULAR OPERATIONS, EXCLUSIVE OF GROUND ACCIDENTS AND MISHAPS, BY CLASSES OF ACCIDENT AND TYPES OF FLYING, DURING CALENDAR YEAR 1952

| | SCHEDULED OPERATORS | | | | | | IRREGULAR OPERATORS | | | | | | ALASKAN OPERATORS | | | Grand Total |
| | DOMESTIC | | | INTERNATIONAL | | | DOMESTIC | | | INTERNATIONAL | | | | | | |
	Passenger	Other	Total	Passenger	Other	Total	Passenger	Other	Total	Passenger	Other	Total	Passenger	Other	Total	
Total accidents	36	13	49	9	4	13	2	5	7	0	3	3	17	15	32	104
Degree of injury:¶																
Fatal	46	26	72	127	12	139	26	5	31	0	0	0	3	1	4	246
Serious	47	13	60	2	2	4	0	0	0	0	0	0	0	4	4	68
Minor or none..........	793	158	951	236	54	290	54	17	71	0	10	10	36	32	68	1390
Degree of damage:																
Destroyed	‡	‡	6	‡	‡	3	‡	‡	2	‡	‡	1	‡	‡	8	20
Substantial	‡	‡	33	‡	‡	8	‡	‡	5	‡	‡	2	‡	‡	24	72
Minor or none..........	‡	‡	10	‡	‡	3	‡	‡	0	‡	‡	0	‡	‡	0	13
Type of accident:																
Landing, take-off, and taxiing	‡	‡	33	‡	‡	8	‡	‡	4	‡	‡	2	‡	‡	37	84
Spin-stall	‡	‡	1	‡	‡	1	‡	‡	0	‡	‡	0	‡	‡	4	6
Airframe failure	‡	‡	4	‡	‡	1	‡	‡	0	‡	‡	0	‡	‡	8	13
Collision (other aircraft) ...	‡	‡	4	‡	‡	0	‡	‡	1	‡	‡	0	‡	‡	0	5
Collision (other objects)....	‡	‡	5	‡	‡	1	‡	‡	2	‡	‡	0	‡	‡	8	16
Fire	‡	‡	3	‡	‡	0	‡	‡	0	‡	‡	0	‡	‡	0	3
Other	‡	‡	6	‡	‡	3	‡	‡	0	‡	‡	0	‡	‡	0	9
Cause of accident:																
Pilot error	‡	‡	18	‡	‡	4	‡	‡	4	‡	‡	2	‡	‡	12	40
Personnel (other than pilot)	‡	‡	5	‡	‡	5	‡	‡	0	‡	‡	0	‡	‡	2	12
Structural failure†	‡	‡	7	‡	‡	1	‡	‡	2	‡	‡	0	‡	‡	5	15
Power-plant failure	‡	‡	4	‡	‡	0	‡	‡	1	‡	‡	1	‡	‡	3	9
Weather	‡	‡	7	‡	‡	3	‡	‡	0	‡	‡	0	‡	‡	2	12
Terrain	‡	‡	1	‡	‡	0	‡	‡	0	‡	‡	0	‡	‡	8	9
Undetermined	‡	‡	2	‡	‡	0	‡	‡	0	‡	‡	0	‡	‡	0	2
Miscellaneous	‡	‡	1	‡	‡	0	‡	‡	0	‡	‡	0	‡	‡	0	1

Source: Civil Aeronautics Board.

¶ Number of persons. "Other" includes crew members. ‡ Not reported separately. † Includes airframe, landing gear equipment and accessories. Note: Scheduled Intra-state carriers counted with Scheduled Domestic. One non-certificated carrier counted with Irregular Domestic.

cidents in the different classes of service, covering both scheduled and irregular air-carriers in domestic, international, and Alaskan territories for 1952. Table V gives an analysis of the causes of air-carrier accidents in 1952.

TABLE V. CAUSES OF AIR-CARRIER ACCIDENTS 1952
(Percent of total scheduled, irregular, and Alaskan carriers)

Personnel errors	49.1
Pilot	37.8
Other personnel	11.3
Material failures	
Structural failures and handling qualities....................	14.2
Power plant	8.5
Miscellaneous causes	0.9
Weather	11.3
Airport terrain or water.............................	9.5
Undetermined	1.8
In process	4.7

Source: "CAA Statistical Handbook of Civil Aviation," Civil Aeronautics Administration.

Personnel error continued to account for nearly half of all accidents, with more than one third of the total attributed to error by the pilot. Material failure was a close second, amounting to nearly 23 per cent, of which structural failure and handling qualities accounted for nearly twice the number of accidents charged to power-plant failure. Weather and terrain were responsible for a smaller number of accidents, amounting to over 11 and 9 per cent respectively.

Table VI sets forth what happened due to the human factor or material failure, in which a pattern can be traced.

Pilots and their organizations frequently criticize the term "pilot error," claiming that more thorough analysis of causes might reveal circumstances forcing an action by the pilot against his will or better judgment and not an actual error on his part. "Pilot action" is now considered a better term.

Because numerous accidents have taken the lives of all persons aboard, leaving no direct testimony of what took place, efforts are being made to develop an automatic sound recorder that would make a record of the instrument readings and other data, constructed so that it would not be destroyed by impact, explosion, or fire.

Material Factors. Aircraft accidents usually result from a combination of causes, but Table VI shows that failure of the human element overbalances failure of the machine. Although in most cases accidents would not have occurred if the facilities at hand had been properly used, further technological improvement is necessary to reduce this cause of accidents.

Ditching at Sea. Ditching at sea presents the double hazard of the dangers of a forced landing plus the low chances for survival if the occupants must leave the aircraft for life rafts. Further improvement in the record of ditching accidents should result from current efforts to provide better crew training and techniques for preparing passengers for ditching: better life jackets and other equipment in more accessible locations, improved methods for search and rescue, and greater co-ordination with rescue procedures of merchant and naval vessels.

Fire. The multiplication of electrical accessories and the complexity of power-plant installations, combined with large quantities of fuel, hydraulic oils, or other flammable material, have introduced a serious fire-prevention problem in air-transport operation. Fire detectors in nacelles and smoke detectors in baggage compartments have proved to be of uncertain value. The installation of valves to shut off the flow of fuel or oil to engine compartments, fire-resistant materials in critical locations, the elimination of fabrics where they can absorb flammable fluids, the reduction of flue effects within the structure, isolation of fuel flow, improved fire-extinguisher installation, and improvements in the possibility of passenger escape have all provided a partial solution.

Ice. The hazards of flying through weather conditions in which ice is deposited on aircraft wings, tail, propellers, and other surfaces have been fairly well attacked by thermal methods. Heat produced by specially designed combustion heaters or from the exhaust of the power plants through heat-transfer radiators extends the icing limits in which aircraft can operate safely. Heated air or electrical-type heating elements are used to keep ice from windshields. Injection-type carburetion has reduced the possibilities of icing trouble within the power plant, and electrical heating elements serve a similar purpose on propellers.

Electronic Improvements. The development and installation of electronic equipment such as reliable radio altimeters and radar should reduce the incidence of accidents by giving the pilot positive data on height above terrain and obstructions that lie in his path. Radar installation on the ground and in the airplane will also be of material benefit in air traffic control, and both radar alone and instrument landing systems using vertical and horizontal radio wave patterns will give positive guidance to the runway. High-intensity lights on the ground extending from each end of the runway will relieve the pilot of the searching tenseness involved in the final part of an instrument approach.

Other Technical Improvements and Problems. The installation of recording devices and flight analyzers will act as a powerful control over safety and economy of flight, and will serve as a challenge to the pilot to operate within his proposed flight plan. These records should give important clues in accident investigations, reduce collision hazards between aircraft, and show management and pilots where errors that might lead to accidents are being made. These, together with improved radio and navigational developments, are important material developments that should lead to greater safety and reduce the more significant hazards of flying. Numerous other safety problems are being studied, such as turbulence, electrical static, accumulation of ice on radio antenna and other projections, unpredictable weather, airport lighting, air-traffic control, cockpit design, cockpit lighting, and instrumentation.

Human Factors. Important as material factors may be in improving safety, their importance yields in the final analysis to human factors such as training, fatigue, emotional stress, mental attitude, and management control.

Physiologists, psychologists, and engineers are striving to simplify the operation of large air transports, since the growing complexity of controls and instruments increases the probability that a given pilot will meet a combination of circumstances with which he cannot cope successfully. Complexity demands more careful selection, training, and maintenance of proficiency by pilots and other crew members so that they will overlook nothing that increases safety and will be able to react quickly, decisively, and accurately when an emergency occurs. These are management problems of a high order and are being met by careful training and "checkout" procedures. Psychological studies have been initiated by both military and civilian agencies to determine the type of tests which should be given candidates for pilot and air crew positions. Many air lines have organized medical departments that guide and watch over their personnel so that pilots will be less apt to fly when in poor physical or mental condition.

Crew Safety. The accidental death rates for air crews

TABLE VI. TYPE OF ACCIDENT

Scheduled and Irregular Air-Carriers and Nonair-Carriers
Calendar Year 1952

TYPE	SCHEDULED AIR-CARRIERS		IRREGULAR AIR-CARRIERS		ALASKAN	NONAIR CARRIERS
	Domestic	International	Domestic	International		
Ground or water loop	1	1	0	0	2	249
Wing tips landing	0	0	0	0	0	4
Wheels up—down	3	0	2	1	3	95
Hard landing	4	0	0	1	1	279
Collapse of landing gear	6	2	1	0	0	36
Undershoot	3	3	0	0	0	84
Overshoot	4	0	1	1	0	156
Nose-up or over	1	0	0	0	6	463
Collision—two aircraft:						
Both airborne	1	0	1	0	0	12
One airborne	0	0	0	0	0	6
Both on ground	3	0	0	0	0	69
Collision—ground or water	1	1	2	0	3	231
Collision—objects	4	0	0	0	5	1,094
Stall	1	1	0	0	4	592
Fire on ground	0	0	0	0	0	5
Fire in flight	3	0	0	0	0	12
Airframe failure— air	3	1	0	0	0	19
Airframe failure— ground	1	0	0	0	9	198
Other	6	3	0	0	0	12
Undetermined	0	0	0	0	0	16
Powerplant failure	0	0	0	0	0	2
Propeller failure	0	0	0	0	0	2
Propeller blast	0	0	0	0	0	5
Propeller accidents to persons	0	1	0	0	0	16
In process	4	1	0	0	0	0
Totals	49	14	7	3	33	3,657

Source: *CAA Statistical Handbook*, Civil Aeronautics Administration.

TABLE VII. CREW LOSSES IN DOMESTIC SCHEDULED PASSENGER-CARRYING OPERATIONS

Year	Number pilots	Pilot fatalities	Number copilots	Copilot fatalities	Crew fatalities other than pilots	Number aircraft
1945	1,908	4	3,167	4	3	411
1946	2,677	8	3,123	8	6	562
1947	2,465	4	2,882	5	8	793
1948	7,762	4	‡	4	7	878
1949	9,025	3	‡	3	5	913
1950	5,785	4	‡	4	5	960
1951	6,688	6	‡	6	12	981
1952	7,209	2	‡	2	2	1,078

‡ Not reported separately.

in domestic scheduled operations have remained low in recent years despite steadily increasing mileage records.

In non-air carrier flying there is evidence also of a declining fatality rate since 1947, despite the severe hazards of some of the flying occupations classed in that group. These include instructional and agricultural flying, the latter being one of the most risky.

However, comparative rates based on the number of individuals holding pilot certificates, such as those in Table VII and VIII, are of limited practical value because not all of those holding certificates are actually actively engaged in flying. A better comparison would be one based on the miles or hours flown, but such figures as are available, especially in the nonair carrier field, are not sufficiently comprehensive to permit accurate calculation of rates.

TABLE VIII. PILOT FATALITIES IN NONAIR-CARRIER FLYING

Calendar year	Certified pilots total	Fatalities total	Rate per 1,000 pilots
1945	296,895	288	0.97
1946	400,061	623	1.56
1947	433,241	806	1.86
1948	491,306	769	1.56
1949	525,174	513	0.98
1950	‡	453	. . . . .
1951	580,574	407	0.70
1952	573,595	363	0.63

Source: *C.A.A. Statistical Handbook,* Civil Aeronautics Administration.
  ‡ Figure not reported.

Ground-Crew Safety. Although the larger air lines employ safety engineers who are expert at reducing injuries to ground personnel and damage to company property, air transport ranks among the hazardous industries. Natural hazards of weather, such as extreme heat or cold, dust, and wind, coupled with the hazards inherent in servicing, maintaining, and repairing aircraft, present the aviation safety engineer with new and unusual problems. Head injuries occur frequently because of the numerous projections on aircraft such as propellers, radio masts, and instruments. Falls from ladders and scaffolding are also frequent. The handling of cargo presents unusual problems in safety of personnel, especially in safe lifting and stowing. Ice, oil, and deposits of silt create dangerous conditions underfoot. Poor illumination at night contributes its share of ground accidents. In addition, there are also the usual hazards associated with the operation of shops, machinery, and automotive equipment. Progress has been made in recent years, and the record of the air-transport and aircraft-manufacturing industries compares favorably with that of many others. The severity rate for injuries to workers in air transport was reduced to 0.31 days per thousand man-hours in 1953, as compared with 1.15 in 1950. In aircraft manufacture this rate dropped from 0.61 in 1950 to 0.30 in 1953. The frequency rate of disabling injuries per million man-hours in air transport declined from 14.52 in 1950 to 12.80 in 1953, and in aircraft manufacture it fell from 4.17 in 1950 to 3.58 in 1953. These 1953 rates compare with the average severity rate of 0.83 and the average frequency rate of 7.44 for all industries.

Comparison of Aviation Safety with Other Forms of Transportation. The relative accident record for various forms of transportation for the years 1948 to 1950, from figures compiled by the National Safety Council, is given in Table IX.

SAFETY IN NONAIR-CARRIER FLYING

Nonair-carrier flying includes flying for private business or pleasure, commercial flying such as instruction, advertising, aerial photography, crop control, aerial survey, aerial patrol for pipe-line and power-line inspection, and so on.

Accident Statistics and Causes. An analysis of non-air-carrier accidents is presented in Tables X and XI.

It is impractical to determine the number of certificated aircraft which are used for a particular type of flying, such as student instruction, crop control, or charter, especially since one airplane may be used for many purposes during the year. Therefore it is difficult to obtain an actuarial basis for the analysis of accidents by use involving nonair-carrier aircraft. Tables XII and XIII show how the accidents were classified by the CAB in the calendar year 1952.

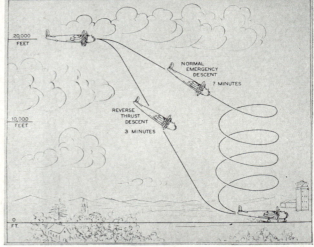

Reversible-pitch propeller (top) and its use in supplying reverse thrust "braking" for rapid emergency descent (bottom)

The greatest number of accidents in nonair-carrier flying in 1952 was due to collisions with objects on the surface. These totalled 1,094, while the number of accidents due to stalls dropped to 592, followed by those due to nose-up or nose-over causes, which came to 463. Hard landings accounted for 279 accidents, and those due to ground or water loops totalled 249. Collisions with the ground or water numbered 231, while airframe failure on the ground was responsible for 198 accidents.

Pilot error, largely due to inadequate training, lack of alertness, or reckless flying was the principal cause of these accidents, as in all recent years. Table XI gives the

TABLE IX. TRANSPORTATION ACCIDENT DEATH RATES 1951 TO 1953

	PASSENGER OPERATIONS			
	1953			1951-1953 average death rate
Kind of transportation	Passenger Miles	Deaths	Death rate per 100,000,000 passenger miles	
Passenger deaths in:				
Passenger automobiles and taxis*	820,000,000,000	23,500	2.9	2.9
Busses	55,000,000,000	70	0.13	0.16
Railroad passenger trains	31,690,000,000	50	0.16	0.21
Scheduled air-transport planes	15,340,000,000	86	0.56	0.70
All deaths† connected with the operation of:				
Passenger automobiles and taxis*	820,000,000,000	32,700	4.0	4.0
Busses	55,000,000,000	500	0.9	1.0
Railroad passenger trains	31,690,000,000	1,248	3.9	3.8
Scheduled air-transport planes	15,340,000,000	102	0.7	0.9

Source: *Accident Facts*, National Safety Council.

* Drivers of passenger automobiles are considered passengers.

† All persons (pedestrians, trespassers and others, as well as passengers) killed in the operation of the vehicles are included.

comparative figures. Further development of "spin-proof" aircraft, stall-warning indicators, and related instruments should have a favorable effect on accident rates.

Precautionary landings, forced landings, and other emergency landings are usually due to poor flight planning (running out of fuel, etc.), pilot error (taking off with cold engine, or inadvertent closing of the fuel valve), or improper maintenance or servicing (wrong grade of fuel, etc.).

Acrobatics carried on at low altitudes, zooming near objects close to the ground, and similar forms of exhibitionism or overconfidence constitute the majority of accidents in the reckless-flying category. Studies indicate that pilots under twenty-three years of age are the group most apt to succumb to the temptation of exhibitionism. The largest number of serious and fatal accidents in 1952 involved pilots in the age group from twenty-nine to thirty-nine, but the indications are that if a pilot maintains his skill with constant practice, his age is a minor accident factor.

In the numerous flying services that offer flying instruction and aircraft for rental or charter, the foundation of an accident-free record rests on the quality and continuity of supervision exercised by the manager. The quality of instruction is in turn reflected not only in the student's technical proficiency but also in his attitude toward safety. The

risks involved in renting aircraft are obviously high unless the owner is thoroughly familiar with the competence and character of the pilot.

Agricultural Flying. One of the most hazardous of occupations is agricultural flying, in which aircraft are used for spraying or dusting crops or trees to kill weeds or insects. It calls for flying at low altitudes, sometimes only a

TABLE X. NONAIR-CARRIER ACCIDENTS

	CALENDAR YEAR			
	1949	1950	¶1951	1952
Total number accidents*	5,459	4,505	3,824	3,657
Fatal	562	499	441	401
Percent fatal	10.3	11.0	11.5	11.0
Total fatalities	896	871	750	691
Nonair-carrier aircraft registered	‡	‡	‡	‡

* Collisions between two aircraft considered as one accident. Propeller accidents not included in totals.

‡ Figures not reported separately.

¶ Revised since preceding issue.

TABLE XI. CAUSES OF NONAIR-CARRIER ACCIDENTS

	1949	1950	1951	1952	Average 1951-1952
Pilot errors	4,092	3,519	2,949	2,706	76.1%
Other personnel	154	157	192	227	5.7%
Material failure	637	441	286	338	8.4%
Miscellaneous and undetermined	576	388	347	386	9.8%
Total accidents	5,459	4,505	3,774	3,657	100.0%

Source: *C. A. A. Statistical Handbook*, Civil Aeronautics Administration.

few feet above the ground, at low speeds, and in constant danger of collision. It requires a high degree of pilot skill and experience, imposing severe physical strain and the danger of poisoning from the chemicals used.

Crop-control flying is usually performed in the early morning and late afternoon, to take advantage of quiet wind conditions, and requires long working hours. The pilots are required to wear masks and protective clothing and should use approved shoulder harness.

Information regarding the exposure rate in crop-control flying supplied by the CAA shows that 707,277 hours were flown in 1952, with 49 fatal accidents, giving a fatal-accident rate of 0.69 per 10,000 hours flown. These figures compare with 708,129 hours flown in 1951, which year had 56 fatal accidents and a fatal-accident rate of 0.79 per 10,000 hours flown. The latest year for which exposure data are available for all commercial nonair-carrier flying exclusive of crop-control flying was 1951, when 1,037,876 hours were flown, with a fatal-accident rate of 0.15.

In 1952, there was a total of 376 accidents in crop-control flying, of which 49 (about 13 per cent) were fatal. Stall was the most frequent fatal-accident type, followed by collisions with surface objects. Pilot error was the primary cause of 81.6 per cent of the accidents.

In the past, the aircraft used in agricultural flying have not been of specialized design, generally being converted private or military craft purchased in secondary or surplus markets. In recent years, however, aircraft have been designed by agricultural colleges especially to meet the rigid requirements of agricultural flying. They give the pilot more favorable vision, better protection against collision or crash, proper shielding against the spray or dust materials, and adequate performance and control characteristics. With

TABLE XII. ACCIDENTS INVOLVING NONAIR-CARRIER AIRCRAFT, BY CLASSES OF ACCIDENT AND TYPES OF FLYING, CALENDAR YEAR 1952

Classes of accident	Instructional flying	Noncommercial flying	Passenger-carrying	Ferrying	Crop control	Power Line-Pipe Line	Testing Experimental	Exhibition-Demonstration	Cargo	Industrial and other	Advertising-Photography	Total commercial	Public and Miscellaneous	Grand total
			COMMERCIAL OTHER THAN AIR CARRIER											
Total accidents	788	2,254	56	4	376	1	1	1	17	14	13	483	132	3,657
Degree of injury:														
Fatal	43	269	11	2	49	1	1	1	3	2	2	72	17	401
Serious	36	165	6	0	41	0	0	0	2	0	2	51	17	269
Minor and none.............	709	1,820	39	2	286	0	0	0	12	12	9	360	98	2,987
Degree of damage:														
Destroyed	182	793	21	2	143	1	1	1	6	4	7	186	63	1,224
Substantial	604	1,443	35	2	230	0	0	0	11	10	6	294	69	2,410
Minor and none.............	2	18	0	0	3	0	0	0	0	0	0	3	0	23
Type of accident (operational phase):														
Landing, take-off, taxiing........	620	1,720	42	2	124	0	0	1	9	10	4	192	71	2,603
Stall	110	345	8	0	91	1	0	1	1	2	1	105	32	592
Structural failure¶	53	135	8	0	7	0	0	0	1	2	0	18	11	217
Collision (other aircraft).........	27	53	0	0	4	0	0	0	0	0	0	4	3	87
Collision (other objects).........	188	664	12	0	182	0	0	0	5	1	5	205	35	1,094
Fire on ground................	1	1	2	0	0	0	0	0	1	0	0	3	0	5
Fire in flight................	1	5	0	0	4	0	0	0	0	0	1	5	1	12
Propeller accidents to persons.....	2	14	0	0	0	0	0	0	0	0	0	0	0	16
Cause of accident:														
Pilot error	627	1,656	30	3	266	1	0	1	6	7	6	322	103	2,706
Personnel (other than pilot)......	44	145	6	0	25	0	0	0	2	0	0	33	5	227
Structural failure*	15	65	5	0	7	0	0	0	2	0	0	17	3	98
Power plant failure.............	39	134	4	0	44	0	0	0	3	2	6	59	8	240
Weather	37	111	6	0	14	0	0	0	2	3	0	23	8	187
Terrain	23	117	2	0	12	0	0	0	0	0	0	14	3	151
Undetermined	0	20	3	1	3	0	1	0	2	1	1	11	2	34
Miscellaneous	2	6	0	0	5	0	1	0	0	0	0	6	0	14
Class of pilot certificate involved:														
Student	513	0	‡	‡	‡	‡	‡	‡	‡	‡	‡	1	4	518
Private	111	1,697	‡	‡	‡	‡	‡	‡	‡	‡	‡	8	62	1,878
Commercial	160	528	‡	‡	‡	‡	‡	‡	‡	‡	‡	464	32	1,184
Air transport	4	29	‡	‡	‡	‡	‡	‡	‡	‡	‡	9	3	45
Unknown	0	0	‡	‡	‡	‡	‡	‡	‡	‡	‡	0	8	8
Miscellaneous:														
Continental United States	‡	‡	‡	‡	‡	‡	‡	‡	‡	‡	‡	‡	‡	‡
Outside continental United States ..	‡	‡	‡	‡	‡	‡	‡	‡	‡	‡	‡	‡	‡	‡
Day	751	2,065	52	2	374	1	1	1	12	14	13	470	115	3,401
Night	37	189	4	2	2	0	0	0	5	0	0	13	17	256
Accidents involving violations	‡	‡	‡	‡	‡	‡	‡	‡	‡	‡	‡	‡	‡	‡

Source: Civil Aeronautics Board.

* Includes airframe, landing gear, equipment, and accessories.   ‡ Not reported separately.   ¶ Airframe failures on ground and in air.

better aircraft and observation of the necessary precautions, safer crop-control flying is expected.

SAFETY BY DESIGN

For both air-carrier and nonair-carrier flying, greater safety can be attained by improving the design of the aircraft, its control equipment, and the airport facilities.

Designing Safer Airplanes. Safety begins in design. Engineers are continually striving to improve structure design, in order to strengthen the airplane against the various stresses encountered in flight. A fundamental precept is that the aircraft and its component parts be designed to "fail safely," that is, to possess enough strength to resist the shock of an accident, and to be capable of preventing the spread of whatever damage there may be to other parts of the structure. Fuselage, wings, and control surfaces are being strengthened, and instruments are being made more accurate, thanks to the many new electronic devices at the disposal of the designer.

Designing Against Pilot Error. William W. Moss has suggested two means whereby design can reduce pilot error. First, the controls should be so interconnected that it would be necessary to make two consecutive mistakes with different controls to cause an accident. He estimates that this would prevent 7.5 per cent of all accidents and 12.5 per cent of those attributed to pilot error. Second, he would make mandatory the use of reversible-pitch propellers on all airline aircraft, citing the record of some 62 accidents in a period of 13 years in which the aircraft ran off the field. He believes that their use would prevent 10 per cent of all accidents and 21 per cent of those attributed to pilot error.

Designing for Survival and Rescue. Another design problem is to build aircraft so that injuries would be minimized in the event of crash. Rearward-facing seats have been considered as a means for reducing the extent of injuries by supporting and cushioning the body during severe deceleration. However, there is still controversy on this point.

TABLE XIII. INJURY CLASSIFICATION FOR ALL PERSONS INVOLVED IN NONAIR-CARRIER FLYING
CALENDAR YEAR 1952

Kind of Flying	FATAL						SERIOUS						MINOR AND NONE						Grand total	Per cent of total persons
	Pilot	Student	Passenger	Crew	Total	Per cent of total fatalities	Pilot	Student	Passenger	Crew	Total	Per cent of total serious injuries	Pilot	Student	Passenger	Crew	Total	Per cent of total minor-and-none injuries		
Instructional*	6	40	18	0	64	9.3	4	31	15	0	50	11.7	163	730	67	1	961	18.8	1,075	17.2
Noncommercial	‡	‡	‡	‡	494	71.6	‡	‡	‡	‡	292	68.0	‡	‡	‡	‡	3,488	68.3	4,274	68.6
Commercial (other than aircarrier):																				
Passenger-carrying	‡	‡	‡	‡	29	4.2	‡	‡	‡	‡	14	3.3	‡	‡	‡	‡	142	2.8	185	3.0
Ferrying	‡	‡	‡	‡	3	0.4	‡	‡	‡	‡	0	0	‡	‡	‡	‡	2	0.04	5	0.08
Crop control	‡	‡	‡	‡	53	7.7	‡	‡	‡	‡	41	9.5	‡	‡	‡	‡	293	5.7	387	6.2
Power line-Pipe line ..	‡	‡	‡	‡	2	0.3	‡	‡	‡	‡	0	0	‡	‡	‡	‡	0	0	2	0.03
Testing-Experimental ..	‡	‡	‡	‡	2	0.3	‡	‡	‡	‡	0	0	‡	‡	‡	‡	0	0	2	0.03
Exhibition-Demonstration	‡	‡	‡	‡	2	0.3	‡	‡	‡	‡	0	0	‡	‡	‡	‡	2	0.04	4	0.06
Cargo	‡	‡	‡	‡	5	0.7	‡	‡	‡	‡	2	0.5	‡	‡	‡	‡	14	0.3	21	0.3
Advertising-Photography	‡	‡	‡	‡	3	0.4	‡	‡	‡	‡	3	0.7	‡	‡	‡	‡	17	0.3	23	0.4
Industrial and other ...	‡	‡	‡	‡	6	0.9	‡	‡	‡	‡	0	0	‡	‡	‡	‡	21	0.4	27	0.4
Total commercial	‡	‡	‡	‡	105	15.2	‡	‡	‡	‡	60	14.0	‡	‡	‡	‡	491	9.6	656	10.6
Public and miscellaneous flying:																				
Public flying	‡	‡	‡	‡	4	0.6	‡	‡	‡	‡	2	0.5	‡	‡	‡	‡	44	0.9	50	...
Miscellaneous	‡	‡	‡	‡	23	3.3	‡	‡	‡	‡	25	5.8	‡	‡	‡	‡	125	2.4	173	...
Total	...	...	...	...	27	3.9	...	...	...	...	27	6.3	...	...	...	...	169	3.3	223	3.6
Grand total	...	...	...	...	690	100.0	...	...	...	...	429	100.0	...	...	...	...	5,109	100.0	6,228	100.0

* Includes instructors and student pilots. ‡ Not reported separately.

Source: Civil Aeronautics Board.

DEMONSTRATION OF PILOT-SEAT EJECTOR IN A MODERN HIGH-SPEED FIGHTER PLANE

INTERNATIONAL NEWS PHOTO

The crash-injury research program of Cornell University has resulted in many valuable improvements. Aircraft occupants have been fatally injured in even mild accidents because of the inherent design of the cockpit or cabin. Projections such as radio knobs and switch handles or structural members have been located in line with the pilot's or passenger's skull and hence liable to pierce or crush it. Control-wheel rims have broken off in a crash, allowing the hub to pierce the chest of the pilot. Safety belts and anchorages have been inadequate but are being improved. The work of DeHaven and Hasbrook in improving the standards of cockpit and cabin design to reduce injury potentials is of great importance.

Designing for Ground Safety. Accidents at and near airports have resulted in injury and death for many non-flying persons. Much thought is being given to this problem, with a view toward improving the layout of runways to avoid residential areas, zoning to prevent the location of new housing developments in an established line of flight, and other measures. Planning for preferential runways, the use of unidirectional runways, and the dispersion of residential areas should tend to lessen this danger.

The aviation industry, for moral and economic reasons, must search for ways to improve safety. Three steps to accomplish this are, in order of importance: (1) increase the safety of flying; (2) by planning, reduce the danger to the public from falling aircraft; and (3) provide adequate equipment and trained personnel for crash-rescue work.

ORGANIZATIONS

Private. A number of active and influential organizations are endeavoring to improve safety practices. The air lines, through their Air Transport Association (ATA) collect and exchange vital information on maintenance and operations and call periodic meetings of key operators' personnel to exchange ideas and determine safety policy.

The Airline Pilots Association (ALPA) makes recommendations in relation to the improvement of safety practices and developments of interest to pilots.

The National Safety Council gives awards each year to airlines that establish outstanding safety records, and its Air Transport Section assists in reducing ground accidents.

The Aircraft Industry Association (AIA) has an engineering department that co-ordinates safety material for the manufacturers and works with the CAA and CAB on safety regulations, as do the ATA and ALPA.

The Aircraft Owners and Pilots Association (AOPA) contributes by special safety drives, special recognition of safety practices, and the financing of safety research.

Private non-profit organizations such as the Flight Safety Foundation, Inc. and Aviation Crash Injury Research have contributed greatly to the promotion of aviation safety and to the improved safety records achieved in recent years. Flight Safety Foundation was established in 1945 to anticipate flight safety problems, study flight safety procedures, and disseminate flight safety information. Other organizations study the causes of crashes in the attempt to reduce the accident rate.

Federal. Two Federal air agencies, the Civil Aeronautics Board (CAB) and the Civil Aeronautics Administration (CAA), provide the foundation of regulation, monitoring, and promotion of air safety. The Civil Aeronautics Board promulgates regulations and adjudicates violations; the Civil Aeronautics Administration interprets the regulations, enforces them, and in addition maintains the airways and has charge of the federally sponsored airport-development programs. Other governmental agencies, such as the Weather Bureau, the National Advisory Committee for Aeronautics, and the National Bureau of Standards are indirectly involved. The military services have contributed greatly to air safety by research and development of equipment and through operating practices.

In the United States, the philosophy underlying government safety regulation in aviation is based on the right of the individual to do what he pleases with his own safety so long as he does not endanger the lives or property of others. To protect the public, the Federal Government requires that pilots must be certificated on the basis of technical competence, medical standards, and knowledge of traffic regulations. It also requires periodic inspection and certification of aircraft and establishes the minimum equipment requirements for aircraft, such as lights for night flying. It also promulgates air-traffic rules and fixes minimum standards for aircraft operation. Since the average pilot does not possess the knowledge necessary to determine or assess the structural integrity, performance, and general airworthiness of aircraft, the government protects him and the public by requiring minimum standards of airworthiness to be met by the aircraft manufacturer. Safety regulations governing private flying, including flying for personal business, are less severe than for commercial flying.

Mechanics and other "airmen" (control-tower operators, parachute technicians, radio operators, and so on) are certificated as competent by the Federal Government to provide continuity of protection for the pilot and the public. Aircraft owners, pilots, mechanics, and other certificated airmen are subject to civil penalty by the Civil Aeronautics Administration for minor violations of the civil air regulations, or may have their certificates suspended or revoked by the Civil Aeronautics Board for more serious violations. In addition, penalties may be imposed by local governments if the offender violates local safety regulations.

State. Supplementing the Federal aviation regulatory bodies are the various state aviation agencies. Several state agencies have trained personnel to inspect aircraft, investigate accidents, and impose penalties. Their major objectives are to promote and develop aviation within the state by encouraging the establishment of new airports and improving old airports, to advise airport management, co-ordinate practice with Federal agencies, lay out airways, prepare aviation statistics, invite aviation industries to establish themselves within the state, and to advertise the state air attractions so that pilots from other states will be induced to use the state facilities on pleasure trips.

International. The International Civil Aviation Organization (ICAO) determines international standards for airworthiness, operational procedures, airmen, search, and rescue. This organization, having its headquarters in Montreal, is composed of fifty-seven nations. One of the several great accomplishments of ICAO is the establishment of international procedures for search for crashed or missing aircraft and rescue of occupants. This requires the positioning of stations to receive distress signals (in which are included a series of weather ships stationed across the oceans), uniform cockpit procedures and communications to alert rescue organizations, and thorough organization of search and rescue operations. The International Air Transport Association, also with headquarters in Montreal, provides international services, which are similar to the domestic services of the ATA.

An increase in airports, more easily controlled flying and landing characteristics of aircraft, improved electronic navigational and landing equipment, and more accurate weather forecasts, with a concurrent improvement in training of airmen, enforcement of safety rules, and improvement in management control of air carriers, airports, and airways, should enhance safety in all phases of flying. *See also* AIR TRANSPORT; AIRPLANE SAFETY DEVICES. J. L. and H. F. R.

AVIATION SPORTS, the use of aircraft for pleasure flying. Since the advent of the airplane, sport flying has been overshadowed by economic and military considerations. It has been difficult, therefore, to isolate that portion of flying activity which has been conducted purely for pleasure. Although a very small number of enthusiasts in the higher income brackets have been able to own and operate airplanes strictly for sport flying, many aircraft owners have justified the necessary expenditures by using their airplanes to some degree in the conduct of business.

GROWTH OF PLEASURE FLYING

Early Period. During the early days of flight the cost of aircraft ownership was so high that participation in pleasure flying was limited to a mere handful of wealthy sportsmen. After World War I the availability of a comparatively large volume of war-surplus training planes and engines broadened the base of sport-plane ownership. In fact, the low cost of this equipment opened the way for the creation in the United States of a branch of the aircraft manufacturing industry devoted largely to the production of pleasure planes.

The historic Curtiss "Jenny" (JN4D), a World War I trainer powered by the eight-cylinder water-cooled Curtiss OX-5 engine, was typical of the war-surplus planes used by sport fliers in the medium income brackets. Even many of these owners, however, found it necessary to use their planes in part for flight instruction, exhibition flying, and other aerial services in order to derive some income from them. The open-cockpit Jennys were underpowered, uncomfortable, and unsuited to family flying.

The excess supply of OX-5 engines over the available airplanes led to the design of somewhat refined versions of the original Jenny. Since a large part of the manufacturing cost of an airplane is that of its engine, the sale of newly produced power plants for small commercial planes was limited to a small group of considerably higher priced planes, some of which had closed cabins. To obtain a still greater degree of comfort and performance it was necessary to design very expensive planes powered by engines normally used in military craft. In the early period the manufacture of pleasure planes was frequently combined with military and transport plane production because the demand was too small to support a manufacturing organization.

Boom in the 1920's. The coincidence of the Lindbergh flight to Paris and a rising curve of inflation in 1927 developed an unfortunate boom in aviation manufacturing. The apparent prosperity of this period led many to the false assumption that the personal airplane was soon to achieve the popularity of the automobile, and manufacturers sought positions in the vanguard of the new industry. When the crash came in 1929 the number of so-called manufacturers approximated two hundred. Most were individuals who built aircraft in backyard shops, and only a few reached the stage where they produced more than one or two planes. Capital was easily available, however, and was eager to find its way into this new and promising industry. As a result, a few of the backyard builders reached small-volume production.

The most serious situation was created by the established manufacturers, who saw in waning military orders what

seemed to be an opportunity to build a substantial commercial business. Elaborate distributor organizations were set up and patterned along automotive merchandising lines; automobile manufacturers attempted to enter the field or watched it closely; and one large airplane manufacturer formed a subsidiary which bought up airports throughout the country at greatly inflated prices to develop a chain of sales and service bases. The collapse of the boom found many distributors overloaded with pleasure planes and a smaller number still in the hands of the manufacturers. All

WIDE WORLD PHOTOS

Popular "Jenny" plane of the 1920's used in early airmail flights, stunt flying, and aerial exhibitions

through the depression and afterward, the sport-plane business was making a painful recovery from the crash.

In those countries where money and fuel were less plentiful, the course of sport flying was somewhat more serene. In the moderate income groups flying for pleasure was conducted chiefly through government-subsidized flying clubs in France, Great Britain, and to some extent in Germany.

Gliding and Soaring. Germany, being engaged in systematic violation of peace treaty provisions, conducted sport flying on a limited basis, but sought to entertain and train its air-minded youth by promoting glider activities. As a result, that country became virtually the birthplace of gliding and soaring; other countries fell far behind. Mountainous country, where climatic conditions developed thermal (rising) air currents, was considered ideal in those days for motorless flight.

In the United States gliding progressed more slowly without government sponsorship and largely through gifts of a few interested benefactors. A number of suitable soaring sites was discovered, one of the best being in the hills just outside Elmira, N.Y. Here soaring activities have been popular since the early 1930's, and each year a national soaring meet has been conducted. Scientific students of soaring later discovered that thermal currents frequently are to be found along coast lines. Since prolonged soaring consists essentially of moving from one "thermal" to another with a minimum loss of altitude, they investigated the possibilities of long-range coastal soaring. The typically American preference for powered vehicles has made it difficult for motorless aircraft to gain a firm foothold in the United States. Even when the nation was still staggering from the economic blow of 1929, a few aircraft designers were attempting to develop light personal planes with small engines. The Guggenheim Safe Aircraft Competition of 1929 had produced a number of devices to increase flight safety, but these devices were not incorporated into the first light planes which appeared in the early 1930's.

Development in the 1930's. The manufacturers who began to produce light planes at that time had been concerned about the dwindling supply of inexpensive surplus OX-5 engines, but three engine builders had come to their rescue with relatively inexpensive engines of the four-cylinder opposed type. These engines developed a little less power and cost a little more than the OX-5. The personal airplane was therefore necessarily a two-seat vehicle with a range considerably limited by allowable weight for fuel. Most of the planes in this period found their way into the hands of

SMALL SEAPLANE IN ACTION

owners who were or became flight instructors. The small number purchased solely for pleasure flying changed ownership frequently as their owners grew tired of cruising around their home airports or of flying to the limited number of airports within their range. Then, too, a two-seater is inadequate for family flying. In spite of the lack of utility of the personal airplanes of the 1930's, production and sales grew slowly, and when World War II ended pleasure-plane production the annual American ouput had reached 6,597 planes. During the war the sports plane manufacturers devoted their facilities to the production of liaison planes for the armed forces and to subcontracting for the military plane manufacturers.

Postwar Problems. As the war drew to a close the military plane manufacturers took a look at the pleasure plane business. Some of them believed that the thousands of pilots trained for military flying would constitute a postwar sport plane market. Others thought that economic conditions, readjustment of the GI's to civilian life, and perhaps personal revulsion to flying as a result of war experience would cause the veterans to avoid aviation. For a time it seemed as if there would be a substantial postwar market for pleasure planes. Production and sales reached 33,254 units during the first year after the war. But the manufacturers of personal planes enjoyed only one boom year. One strictly military plane manufacturer, North American Aviation, entered the field at that time with a four-seat plane called the Navion. Later the project was abandoned, and the manufacturing rights were sold to the Ryan Aeronautical Corporation. The manufacturers seemed totally unaware that more than 70 per cent of their peak output was being used in the mushroom growth of flying schools which had occurred when flight instruction was included in the educational programs provided for veterans under the GI Bill of Rights. The impact of this situation came when sales began to decline; during 1947, production dropped sharply. Sales continued to decline and were at prewar levels before the advent of

the Korean War, which all but halted personal-plane production. Studies made after World War II of the personal-plane situation indicated that the pleasure airplane still lacked utility comparable with the automobile and that, since it could not replace the family car, its ownership was restricted to families of income levels high enough to maintain two automobiles. Even before these studies were made, there were attempts to increase the utility of pleasure craft by developing vehicles which could be operated from the home rather than from the airport. The roadable airplane and the helicopter were developed with that idea in mind.

"Flying Automobiles." The problem of designing a machine which is capable of flight and which also may be driven on the highway is a difficult one. Many compromises must be made to combine the characteristics of the airplane and automobile. The machine must be light enough to fly with reasonable power, yet sufficiently rugged to withstand road service and hazards. A transmission must be devised to drive both wheels and propeller unless two engines are used. One of the most serious problems is the disposition of wings when the machine is to be driven on the road. Several machines were designed with these ideas in mind, and some were successfully flown and driven on the road. The transmission problem was complicated, but not impossible of solution. A variety of methods of disposing of the wings was suggested. One idea was to leave the wings at the airport, but this involved attachment and detachment, entailing delays and the possibility of damage or carelessness in attachment. Some roadable plane designs were provided with folding wings, but they were cumbersome in highway use and increased risk of road damage to a vital part of the machine. One of the designs embodied a wing and tail structure with the automobile unit detachable. An extensive series of studies was made on flying automobiles by Consolidated Vultee and other manufacturers. The Convair project was abandoned in 1948, and the design rights reverted to the project engineer, Theodore Hall, one of the pioneers in this phase of development.

Helicopters. Helicopters reached a high stage of development in the middle 1940's, but the cost of machines of this type was prohibitive for the pleasure flier. Helicopters of the commercial type were then priced at approximately $10,000–$12,000 per seat. Some new manufacturers entered the field with the avowed intention of reducing manufacturing costs, but the problems were admittedly difficult. A substantial part of the production cost of helicopters is that of the engine, transmission, and rotor system. This led to the limited consideration of providing jet power units in the rotors, but this arrangement also posed problems. One experimental design was developed by the McDonnell Aircraft Corporation under Air Force sponsorship. This machine, known popularly as "Little Henry," was successfully test flown and proved the principle of jet-powered rotor blades for helicopters. There remained, however, several aerodynamic and other problems to be solved before commercial machines of this type could be developed. Apart from the cost problem, there is the difficulty of landing helicopters in most suburban areas. The practicability of operating these machines from private homes on tree-lined, wire-strewn streets is still in question, as is the possibility of storing them in the average private garage.

Airports. The small-airport problem was still important in the late 1940's. Some authorities believed that when small airports were more plentiful, there would be more pleasure flying. The Civil Airports Act provided for the

CROWD SCENE AT NATIONAL AIR RACES, CLEVELAND, OHIO

development of a national airport system in the United States, with the idea that funds provided equally by the Federal Government and local sources would increase the number of small airports. Actually, a large part of the funds went into larger airport projects. After the start of the Korean War, Federal funds were drastically reduced.

Another deterrent to the development of small airports was the reluctance of many local communities to allow them within their boundaries. Fear of real estate depreciation and the noise nuisance were factors in many cases. On the other hand, there was considerable evidence that airports had contributed to the economic health of some of the communities in which they were built. A classic example was that of Eldon, Mo., where an air park was built at a high per-capita cost to the small population. A substantial increase in business activity ensued, and was attributed in part to the availability of the airport. A movement to provide simple landing strips along main highways has been fostered for many years, but it has progressed very slowly. A project for more adequate marking of airways also has been attempted, but without outstanding success. A new air-marking project involving a simplified type of marker was under consideration by the National Association of State Aviation Officials before the beginning of the Korean War.

As an impetus to airport development prior to World War II, a number of local and national sport plane tours were conducted. One of the important annual events was the Light Plane Cavalcade, sponsored by oil companies and consisting of a week or more of cross-country flying by amateur pilots in a group over a prescribed route. During the early 1930's an outstanding annual event was the Ford Reliability tour. This pleasure plane cruise was sponsored by the aviation division of the Ford Motor Company, and usually brought out a reasonably large group of airplanes flown by pilot owners, many of whom brought their families along.

AIR MEETS, AIR SHOWS, AND BARNSTORMING

Air Meets. The period of 1910-1914 saw the birth of air meets and competitions. Probably the first important meet in America was held Jan. 10-20, 1910, at Los Angeles. There, Glenn Curtiss, with a passenger, established a world speed record of 55 m.p.h. and Louis Paulhan reached an altitude of 4,000 ft. On May 29, 1910, Curtiss made his famous flight down the Hudson from Albany to New York (150 mi. in 2 hr., 51 min. flying time) winning a $10,000 prize from the *New York Herald*. Other newspapers followed with prize offers for intercity flights, and several were won during that year. The second important American event was the Howard-Boston Meet held Sept. 3-17, 1910, at Squantum, Mass. Prize money totaling $82,950 was awarded. The largest share went to an English aviator, Claude Graham-White, who received $10,000 from the *Boston Globe* for a flight from Squantum to Boston Light and return. In his Blériot monoplane he flew the 33 mi. route in 34 min., 11 sec. An international air meet was held at Belmont Park, New York, Oct. 22-31, 1910, and forty American and French planes were exhibited. An altitude record of 8,471 ft. and speed records of approximately 60 m.p.h. were established. Thus began a long series of contests to achieve greater speed, range, and altitude for aircraft.

It was not until after World War I that passenger flying at air meets came into vogue. Added to these features were wing walking and parachute jumping. A typical week-end performance would begin with a hair-raising display of acrobatic flying to attract crowds. Next came the parachute jumps, followed by passenger flying. Pilots and mechanics usually were paid flat salaries and pilots received a percentage of the revenue from passenger trips. In some cases the mechanics increased their income by parachute jumping; in others, this part of the show was performed by volunteers. At some meets the only income for the jumper was derived by passing a hat to the audience.

National Air Races. During the 1920's air meets began to evolve into air races. The Lindbergh flight of 1927 set off a second series of races and contests. One of the important annual events became the National Air Races. For many years these were held in Cleveland, Ohio, where the municipal airport was sufficiently large to accommodate them without interruption of commercial traffic. Closed-course racing in various classes and long-distance races constituted the main events. Among the classics were the Thompson Trophy, Bendix Trophy, and Greve Trophy races. These events were interspersed with exhibition flights by individuals, as well as formation flights by the armed services. After World War II the National Air Races featured many contests in which jet-powered aircraft participated.

Air Shows. Early air shows and air meets were held together. As the plane manufacturing industry approached maturity, the need for trade shows became apparent. The Lindbergh flight and the economic boom of 1929 led to an outburst of industry shows all over the country. Some were officially sanctioned events, while others were organized by promoters who saw profit possibilities in them. The basic requirement of a national air show was a building sufficiently large to accommodate aircraft, with provisions to set up and remove exhibits without alteration of the building. Show locations have included the large Detroit City Airport Hangar, Cleveland Auditorium, Fisher Body plant at Cleveland Airport, and New York's Grand Central Palace. Before the full impact of the post-World War II recession in aircraft manufacturing was felt, an elaborate national show was held at Cleveland in the fall of 1946. The cost to exhibitors reached such proportions that the practice of holding such shows was suspended until a new and more justifiable formula for national exhibits could be found.

Barnstorming. The airport or fixed-base operations of today and even the great air-line systems had their beginnings in the period of the barnstormers. One of the first exhibition teams was organized by the Wright brothers, and included such pioneers as Arch Hoxsey, Ralph Johnstone, Al Welch, Walter Brookins, Phil Parmalee, and Frank Coffyn. This group toured the country giving shows at fairs, race tracks, and air meets. Their basic wage was $20 per week, plus traveling and living expenses and a bonus of $50 for each flight made. During the same period the pilot satellites of Glenn Curtiss were also on tour. Among them was Bud Mars, "the Curtiss Daredevil," whose well-developed routine often earned him as much as $5,000 per day. Thirty-seven early pilots died in crashes in 1910. Exhibition flying with lighter-than-air craft dates from approximately 1906, when Lincoln Beachey circled the Capitol dome in Washington in his "Rubber Cow." This machine was a one-man dirigible balloon having a treadway below the bag

JATO DEMONSTRATION
Three Lockheed F-80 Shooting Stars making a jet-assisted takeoff (JATO) at the National Air Races, Cleveland, Ohio

along which the pilot walked to preserve balance. Beachey later became a famous pilot of airplanes.

World War I interrupted the course of barnstorming, but when war-surplus planes became available in the early 1920's, the activity was resumed on a somewhat different basis. Both the rewards and the risks were materially reduced, and the practice of passenger hopping began again on a larger scale. A war-trained pilot would buy an airplane, set himself up in a field near a city or town, and carry passengers for what he could collect. The price dropped from $10 to $3 and by the early 1930's, as the passenger capacity of planes grew larger, the $1 ride became popular. There were hundreds of these gypsy fliers, and some were organized into groups. One of the most famous was the Gates Flying Circus, which continued until the death of Ivan Gates in the early 1930's. As the barnstormers became less itinerant, some would settle down to do business at one airport. They evolved later into the "fixed-base operators" of today. Sometimes they would conduct charter business; sometimes they tried to maintain regular operations between two or more points. A few were moderately successful in establishing regular services, some of which were consolidated later to form the basis for the present air-line systems.

AVIATION SPORTS ORGANIZATIONS

International. At the international level the Féderation Aéronautique International (F.A.I.) has cognizance and control of all phases of sport flying. It is one of the oldest organizations in the field, having been founded in 1905. No record is official unless it is made under conditions prescribed by the F.A.I. and approved by that organization. Almost every important country in the world has been a member of the F.A.I. through the federation of their national aero clubs. The group has included the United States, Argentina, Belgium, Bulgaria, Canada, Chile, Cuba, Denmark, Egypt, Finland, France, Germany, Great Britain, Greece, Hungary, Iceland, Italy, Japan, Lithuania, Luxemburg, Norway, the Netherlands, Poland, Portugal, Romania, Spain, Sweden, Switzerland, Turkey, Czechoslovakia, the Soviet Union, Uruguay, and Yugoslavia. The secretariat is in Paris, in the building of the Aero Club of France. More than forty international conventions of the F.A.I. have been held in various countries. One of its outstanding accomplishments is the creation of the international customs booklet called *Carnet de Passage en Douane,* which is comparable to that for automobiles issued by the International Association of Recognized Automobile Clubs. This device has greatly simplified the customs problem in international air touring. Prior to its creation, the speed of flight and the large number of small countries in Europe made touring extremely difficult because of the necessity of stopping for customs examination whenever a border was crossed.

American. The American member of the F.A.I., the National Aeronautic Association (N.A.A.), also dates back to ?, when it was founded as the Aero Club of America. Its ?ose was then and has continued to be the promotion of ?te and sport flying, safety, air defense, and airports. ?e official representative of the F.A.I., the N.A.A. su? s and homologates all official flight records in the ? States. No attempt to establish a record, even by ?med Services, can be official unless sanctioned by the ? and conducted under F.A.I. rules administered by ?A. Membership in the N.A.A. is truly representa? e users of aviation. It is divided into two classes: ?nd chapter. The membership reached a peak of ?1947 but dropped to about 5,000 by 1952, as a result

STUNT FLYING

Bevo Howard, stunt pilot, cutting a ribbon with an airplane wing at Miami All-American Air Maneuvers

of the decline in civil aviation and the advent of the Korean War, before once again beginning to increase. Officials are elected annually in a convention composed of delegates chosen directly by the membership.

In the spring of 1939 the Aircraft Owners and Pilots Association (A.O.P.A.) was founded under the laws of New Jersey, "to make flying more useful, less expensive, safer, and more fun." The membership is international and includes more than 30,000 persons concerned with the interests of noncommercial pilots. Its headquarters is in Washington, with local units located throughout the United States and Canada. Activities of the A.O.P.A. include programs for the improvement of airports and airport services, flight safety in all fields, crash injury research aimed toward better cockpit design, simplification of communication procedures and equipment, and reduction of government regulation and restrictions of personal flying.

A nonprofit membership organization, the Sportsman Pilots Association, was founded in 1930 and incorporated in 1945. Headquarters are in Chicago and there are branch organizations in more than one half of the states. The membership includes amateur pilots, and the purpose is to advance the use of private aircraft, improve landing fields and airways, and assist in the establishment and maintenance of fair, reasonable, and uniform laws governing the use of aircraft.

Although not concerned alone with sport flying, the National Association of State Aviation Officials (N.A.S.A.O.) has done much to promote personal flying through the state aviation commissions. The N.A.S.A.O. includes in its membership most of the leading officials in aviation at the state level. It was founded in 1931 by a group of state officials attending the National Air Races at Cleveland and has expanded steadily since then. The N.A.S.A.O. is divided into regional groups which conform with the regional subdivisions of the Civil Aeronautics Administration, and this geographical arrangement facilitates co-operation in the

NATIONAL AIR RACES, CLEVELAND, OHIO

Airplane rounding a pylon marker during a Goodyear Trophy Race

administrative work of both state and federal officials. Objectives include enforcement of safety regulations, licensing, and development of airports. Investigation of accidents to determine violations and study causes is also conducted by many states. Efforts have been made by member states to evolve uniform state laws and eliminate duplication or conflict between state and federal laws.

Women's Groups. Woman pilots have been represented since 1929 by the Ninety-Nines, which was organized at that time by 99 charter members to provide closer relationship among woman pilots and to unite them in any movement that may be for their benefit or for the benefit of aviation in general. There are more than 50 chapters, and total membership, including many individually affiliated members in other countries, is well over 1,000. Another organization of women is the Women's National Aeronautical Association of the United States. Its activities include sponsorship of the use of air mail, formation of model clubs, promotion of model meets, standardization of airport and air markings, and air safety. The Women Flyers of America encourages the participation of women in all air activities. It is a nonprofit educational organization whose stated purpose is to guide and prepare women in the various phases of aviation. It sponsors ground school courses and advanced ground training as well as flight instruction at reduced cost to members.

Soaring Society of America. To foster the art of gliding and soaring in the United States, the Soaring Society of America (S.S.A.) was organized in 1932. Membership in the society is approximately 1,000. The S.S.A. is the

American representative of the F.A.I. in gliding and soaring matters under the sponsorship of the N.A.A. Annual national soaring contests have been conducted by this organization since its foundation, with the exception of the war years 1942-1945 inclusive. Most of these contests have been held at Elmira, N.Y.

SPORTS PLANE RECORDS

Distance Records. A pleasure plane piloted by Captain William (Bill) Odom established a new world light plane nonstop distance record (First Category) Mar. 7-8, 1949, in a flight from Honolulu to the Teterboro, N.J., air terminal. The airplane was a Beech Bonanza Model 35, powered by a six-cylinder Continental engine rated at 185 hp. Although the actual flying distance was 5,273 mi., the great circle distance of 4,957.24 mi. was officially approved for the record. Elapsed time was 36 hr., 1 min. Captain Odom, on this flight, broke his own international and national distance record, made Jan. 12-13, 1949, in the same type of plane during the first light plane flight between Hawaii and the United States mainland. This flight, from Honolulu to Oakland, Calif., is recorded at 2,406.902 mi. It broke the record of 2,061.703 mi., made in a flight from Moscow to Krasnoyarsk, Sept. 23, 1937, by the Russian pilots A. Goussarov and V. Glebov in a Moskalev Airplane, Model M-11, powered by a 100-hp. engine. The First Category of light planes includes those having engines with cylinder displacement between 6.5 and 9 liters (397-549 cu. in.).

An international distance record in the Second Category (4-6.5 liters—244-397 cu. in.) was established in a flight made Nov. 30, 1937, between Istres (near Marseille) and Djibouti (French Somaliland) by Pilot Andre Jopy of France, flying a Caudron 600 Aiglon monoplane powered by a Renault Bengali Junior engine of 6.33 liters displacement. The distance was 3,168.365 mi.

In the Third Category (2-4 liters, or 132-244 cu. in.) an international record of 3,917.017 mi. was established Dec. 29-31, 1938, by Horat Pulkowski and Lieutenant R. Jenett of Germany in an Arado Ar 79 airplane with a Hirth HM 504 A2 engine of 3.984 liters. The flight was from Bengasi, Libya, to Gaya, British India. An American national record in the Third Category of 2,477.367 mi. was made Nov. 29-30, 1938, in a flight from Mines Field, Los Angeles, to Roosevelt Field, Mineola, N. Y., by J. M. Jones, flying a Aeronca C-50 monoplane having a Continental A-50 engine of 50 hp. and 2.80 liters.

In the Fourth Category (less than 2 liters, or 122 cu. in.) an international record of 1,186.713 mi. was made A 1939, by Heinz Gabler of Germany in an Erla 5D, D- airplane with Zundapp 91092, 52-hp. engine of 1.99

TYPICAL FAMILY

The Friedrichshafen-Vannes course was used. A Fourth Category American record of 1,014 mi. was established in a flight from Miami, Fla., to Camden, N.J., July 31, 1938, by Robert E. Bryant, flying an Aeronca C-3 monoplane with an Aeronca E-113-B engine of 1.86 liters.

Speed Records. Although most of the speed records are held by military planes or other craft outside the sport plane classes, speed records have been made in the Third and Fourth Categories. These records in general were made by specially designed and powered planes. S. J. Wittman established an international and American record Sept. 19, 1937, when he reached a speed of 238.225 m.p.h. with a plane in the Third Category. In the Fourth Category international and American speed records were made respectively by Georgio Parodi, Italy, on Aug. 27, 1929, at 243.940 m.p.h., and Clarence R. McArthur, United States, June 26, 1938, at 207.027 m.p.h.

Altitude Records. International and American altitude records in the Fourth Category were established by Herman Illg of Germany, July 7, 1939, at 29,773.560 ft., and by Grace Huntington of the United States, May 31, 1939, at 18,769.646 ft.

Glider Records. Among the many single-place glider records is the world straight-line distance flight mark of 535.169 mi., established by Richard H. Johnson in a flight from Odessa, Tex., to Salina, Kan., Aug 5, 1951. The world record for a distance flight with return to the point of departure, 242.334 mi., was made July 7, 1950, by Sixten Rudolf Laroy-Mansson of Sweden, who soared from Ljungbyed to Jonkoping and back. The American record is 229.189 mi. by Paul B. MacCready, Jr., who flew from Wichita Falls, Tex., to Anson, Tex., and back July 16, 1947. For a distance flight to a predetermined destination, the world record is 374.287 mi., established July 31, 1939, by P. Savtzov of the Soviet Union in a flight from Toula to Mikhailovka. The American record is 332.902 mi. by Wallace R. Wiberg, who flew from Odessa, Tex., to Guymon, Okla., Aug. 5, 1951. A world altitude-above-sea-level record was established Dec. 30, 1950 over Bishop, Calif., when William S. Ivans, Jr., attained a height of 42,100 ft. The world mark for a duration flight with return to the point of departure is 56 hr., 15 min., achieved over Romanin les Alphilles, France, Apr. 2-4, 1952, by Charles Atger of France. The American record, 21 hr., 34 min., was established by Lieutenant William Cocke, Jr., over Honolulu, Dec. 17-18, 1931.

Helicopter Records. Although inherently limited in speed, helicopters have established records in their own class for duration, distance, and altitude. An international and American record of 9 hr., 57 min. for closed circuit duration was made at Dayton, Ohio, Nov. 14, 1946, by Major D. H. Jensen and Major W. C. Dodds of the Air Force in a Sikorsky R-5A Helicopter powered by a Pratt and Whitney 450-hp. engine. For air-line distance an international and American record of 703.6 mi. was established May 22, 1946, in a flight from Dayton, Ohio, to Boston, Mass. The machine was a Sikorsky R-5 with 450-hp. Pratt and Whitney engine. The pilot was Major F. T. Caschman, and the copilot was Major W. E. Zins, both of the Air Force. An international and American altitude record of 19,167 ft. was established at Dayton, Ohio, Feb. 10, 1947, by Major E. M. Cassell of the Air Force, flying a Sikorsky R-5A with a Pratt and Whitney 450-hp. engine.

An unofficial helicopter speed record of 133.9 m.p.h. was claimed by the Bell Aircraft Corporation for one of its XH-12 machines in two level runs over the Niagara Falls, N.Y., airport, Mar. 25, 1949. A British helicopter, the Fairey Gyrodyne, reached a record speed of 124.3 m.p.h. piloted by Squadron Leader Basil Arkell, June 28, 1948.

Although no official records were made, a convincing demonstration of helicopter reliability was achieved in the transcontinental flight of Stanley Hiller, Jr., in a commercial machine of his own design. The flight began Jan. 24, 1949, at Palo Alto, Calif., made a first stop at Los Angeles, and then proceeded in short hops for a total distance of 5,200 mi., ending April 12 at New York's Wall Street Skyport. Demonstration flights were conducted at many stops along the way. Shortly before the arrival of the Hiller 360 machine in New York, a Coast Guard HO3S-1 helicopter built by Sikorsky Aircraft completed a coast-to-coast ferry flight of 3,750 mi. Flight time was 57.6 hr. over a 10½-day period. The pilot was Lieutenant Stewart R. Graham, executive officer of the Elizabeth City Coast Guard Rotary Wing Development unit. *See also* AERONAUTICAL EDUCATIONAL INSTITUTIONS; AERONAUTICAL SOCIETIES AND ORGANIZATIONS; AIRPLANES, PRIVATE; AIRPORTS; AVIATION, HISTORY OF; GLIDERS; ROTATING-WING AIRCRAFT.　　　L. E. N.

AVICENNA or **IBN SINA** [æ'vɪsɛ'nə, ɪ'bn si'na] (979-1037), generally regarded as the greatest of the Arabian philosophers and physicians, was born at Afskena, near Bukhara, in 979. Educated informally in the rudiments of arithmetic, geometry, and medicine, he knew the Koran thoroughly at the age of ten. His versatility was amazing and covered nearly every field of science. Avicenna's philosophy was Aristotelian. In 997 he secured an appointment as court physician and thus had access to the library of the Samanids. After the fall of the Samanid Dynasty in 1004, he traveled until he began lecturing on astronomy and logic at Jurjan, near the Caspian Sea. Later he went to Hamadan, Persia, where he occupied the office of vizier to Shams Addaula. He was forced to relinquish this position because of the opposition of the soldiery. Avicenna then went to Isfahan, Persia, where the ruler, Ala Addaula, made him his physician and scientific advisor. Avicenna spent the rest of his life in this capacity. He wrote about one hundred treatises; the most famous, his *Canon of Medicine,* was still in use as a medical textbook in the French universities of Montpellier and Louvain in the middle of the seventeenth century. Avicenna died in Hamadan in 1037.　　　H. N. A.

AVIGNON [a'vi'nyɔ̃'], the capital city of the department of Vaucluse, in southeastern France, located on the east bank of the Rhone River about 60 mi. northwest of Marseilles, at 43° 55' N. lat., and 4° 50' E. long. Situated in the middle of the Comtat Plain, it is often disturbed by the mistral winds. The palace of the popes, built between 1334 and 1392, is located in the northwest part of the city flanking the Doms rocks. The basilica of Notre Dame des Doms, begun in the twelfth century, contains the Gothic mausoleum of Pope John XXII. Originally a Gallic city, then a colony for the Roman veterans of the Gallic Wars, Avignon became a troubled city and changed sovereigns many times. It saw a succession of rulers—the dukes of Toulouse, the province of Provence, Louis VIII, and the popes—and it once had a quasi independence. Prosperity, culture, and splendor existed when it was the residence of the popes, beginning with Clement V, during the so-called Babylonian Exile, 1309 to 1377. The city remained a papal possession until it was annexed by the French National Assembly late in the eighteenth century. During the seventeenth and eighteenth centuries, there was another period of prosperity, when Avignon became the

Pont d'Avignon adjoining the Palace of the Popes, at Avignon, France

center for the manufacture of choice pottery and madder, a Turkey-red dye. In World War II, the city was almost totally destroyed by bombing. After World War II, the manufactures of Avignon included fertilizer, furniture, clothing, fruit conserves, and licorice. Early fruits, especially peaches, are grown in the suburbs. Pop. 1954, 62,768.   S. Van V.

ÁVILA [a'vila], a province and also the capital city of the province in Old Castile, north central Spain.

The City. Ávila, 53 mi. northwest of Madrid, is situated about midway between Madrid and Salamanca on the northern slopes of the Sierra de Ávila, at an elevation of some 3,700 ft. The city lies on an eminence overlooking the River Adaja from the east. It is connected by rail with Salamanca, Valladolid, and Madrid. It is the seat of a bishopric and serves as an administrative center and market place for the surrounding area.

Ávila's importance stemmed originally from its strategic position at the northern entrance of a pass leading to New Castile between the Sierras de Guadarrama and de Gredos. From 1550 to 1807 the city possessed a university, created from the Colegio de Santo Tomás. Ávila is the object of pilgrimages, since it is the native city of Santa Teresa de Jesús (1515-1582). A temple has been erected on the spot where the learned mystic was born. The city presents a most picturesque appearance. The medieval town is enclosed within a roughly rectangular circuit of granite walls (approximately 1,300 ft. by 1,900 ft.), marked by 8 gates and 86 semicircular towers. The streets are narrow, crooked, and often steep. The newer quarters are found to the east and south. The principal monuments include the fortified cathedral (begun in the twelfth century), containing several significant works of art and historic interest; the basilica of San Vicente (begun in 1020); the Gothic church of Santo Tomás; and several other religious edifices and habitations of medieval nobility.

Of possible Phoenician origin, Ávila passed successively to Roman, Visgothic and—in 767—Moorish rule. The latter was contested by the Christian monarchs, and the city changed hands several times until at the end of the eleventh century it had been definitively conquered by Castile. In 1466 it was the center of the nobles' conspiracy that dethroned Henry IV, and again in 1520 it participated actively in the revolt of the *comuneros,* the party which upheld Spanish liberty against the encroachments of Charles V. When first the Jews, and then the Moriscos (1609) were driven out, Ávila lost much of its economic importance and thereafter was in a state of decay. During the Spanish Civil War of 1936-1939, the city was early taken by the Rebels and held by them during the rest of the conflict. Pop. 1940, 19,590.

The Province. The province of Ávila has an area of 3,144 sq. mi. It straddles the Sierras de Guadarrama and de Gredos and thus lies within the upper basins of both the Tagus and the Duero rivers. In the north the land is less accidented, forming part of the Castilian Plain; in the highlands considerable areas are covered with pine forests. Sheep are raised in large numbers and, despite generally poor soils and the rugged terrain, some two fifths of the land is cultivated with wheat, rye, and other cereals. Grapes and olives grow only in certain favorable localities south of the mountains. Pop. 1940, 234,671; (est. 1946), 242,316.   R. G. W.

AVITUS, SAINT SEXTUS ALCIMUS ECDICIUS [əvai'təs] (c.450-c.520), Bishop of Vienne, France (Narbonian Gaul), was born, probably at Vienne, near the middle of the fifth century. He came of a distinguished Gallo-Roman family, originally from Auvergne, which was related to Emperor Marcus Avitus (455-456). He succeeded his father, who was also Bishop of Vienne, in 490. Avitus was a determined opponent of Arianism, Semipelagianism, and other heresies, and he successfully uprooted Arianism from Burgundy, winning over King Gundobald to his cause. He was a strong supporter of the papacy in Rome, and stood for a closer connection between southern Gaul and the Holy See. He was appointed apostolic vicar in Gaul and in 517 presided in that capacity over the Council of Epao, which planned to strengthen ecclesiastical discipline in Gaul. Avitus has been called the most distinguished of the Christian poets between the sixth and the eighth centuries. He was the author of *De spiritualis historiae gestes,* an account of the origin of man and his fall, the flood, and the Exodus. He also wrote numerous letters, sermons, and homilies, many of which have been preserved. These writings, especially the letters, are of much historical importance. Avitus died in Vienne, between 518 and 526, and in due course was canonized. R. Peiper prepared an edition of *Avitus' Works,* published in Berlin in 1883. In 1890, M. U. Chevalier published another edition in Lyon.   E. B. A.

AVOCADO [æ'voka'do], the tree, and the fruit of, *Persea americana,* of the laurel family, also known as the alligator pear. The name is probably derived from the Aztec name, *ahuacatl.* The fruit, which resembles a large plum more than a pear, has a soft, buttery flesh, with a bland, musty, and somewhat nutlike flavor. The center of the fruit has a large smooth stone; the skin has a coarse texture and may vary from a green to a maroon in color. The size of the fruit varies from 1 to 8 in. in length, with a weight of from 2 oz. to 4 lbs. The consistency of the flesh is smooth, which led to its being called by sailors "midshipman's butter." Avocados are frequently used in salads with French dressing.

There are three cultivated races of avocado, the Mexican, the Guatemalan, and the West Indian. The Mexican race, var. *drymifolia,* has a small, thin-skinned fruit and an anise

ÁVILA, SPAIN

color in the leaf when it is crushed. It is frost-resistant and hardy in subtropical regions. The Guatemalan race has a large, thick-skinned fruit, and is more tender and less frost-resistant than the Mexican. Forms are found in the wild which have characters intermediate between these two. The Fuerte avocado is a natural hybrid which is intermediate in both fruit characters and in its resistance to frost. The West Indian form is cultivated more in the tropical regions, since it is the least hardy of the three varieties. The tree may grow to a height of 60 ft. U.P.H.

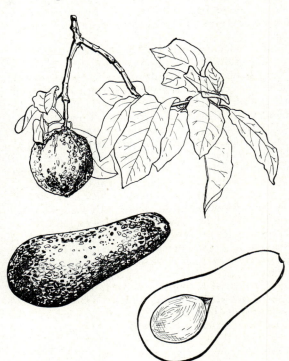

Stem, leaves, and fruit of an Avocado

AVOCET [æ′vosɛt], any one of four species of wading birds of the genus *Recurvirostra,* allied to the sandpipers and plovers and occurring in temperate and tropical regions of both the Old and New Worlds. They possess webbed feet,

AVOCET

U.S. FISH AND WILDLIFE SERVICE

fairly long legs, and a remarkably slender bill curving upward toward the tip. In the American form, *R. americana,* the head, neck, and breast are cinnamon and the rest of the plumage white, boldly marked with black. It breeds on inland sloughs and lagoons from southwestern Canada to the Mexican border and winters in similar places from the southwestern United States to Guatemala. H. G. De.

AVOGADRO, AMEDEO [ɑ′vogɑ′dro] (1776-1856), Italian physicist famous for his molecular hypothesis, was born June 8, 1776, in Turin and died there July 9, 1856. His complete name was Lorenzo Romano Amedeo Carlo Avogadro di Quaregna e di Cerreto. Descended from a line of ecclesiastical barristers, Avogadro received a degree in this profession in 1796. However, from 1800 to 1805 he studied mathematics and physics and was appointed professor at the Royal College of Vercelli in 1809. He later occupied the chair of mathematical physics at the University of Turin. Avogadro was lovable and modest personally, and a lifelong student. His contemporaries were reluctant to accept Avogadro's hypothesis, which assumes that equal volumes of all gases at the same temperature and pressure contain equal numbers of molecules. They accused him of unreality in declaring that there were simple and compound molecules, today called atoms and molecules. He was opposed by many of the leading scientists of his day, including John Dalton, W. H. Wollaston, and J. J. Berzelius, Dalton declaring, "No man can split an atom." Auguste Laurent and C. F. Gerhardt supported the hypothesis, but it finally remained for his fellow countryman S. Cannizzaro to bring about its adoption at a convention in Karlsruhe in 1860, where he presented the Avogadro law in pamphlet form so clearly that its opponents were won over. The inestimable value of this law was its clear distinction between molecules and atoms, paving the way to accurate calculation of atomic weights and to concepts of molecular structure in organic chemistry. Walter H. Nernst called it "a horn of plenty to chemists." The famous paper in which the hypothesis was published appeared in 1811 in the *Journal de physique,* entitled (translated) "An Essay on a Method of Determining the Relative Masses of the Elementary Molecules of Bodies."   H. N. A.

AVOGADRO'S NUMBER, the number of molecules in one gram-molecular weight of any substance. The accepted value of this number in 1947 was 6.023×10^{23}. Avogadro's Law states that equal volumes of different gases, at the same temperature and pressure, contain equal numbers of molecules. The number of individual molecules present in a volume of 22.414 liters of any (ideal) gas at $0°$ C. and one atmosphere of pressure, which is the volume occupied by one gram-molecular weight, is equal to the Avogadro number. Hence, the latter is actually the number of individual molecules present in a gram molecule of any substance; it is also the number of individual atoms in a gram atom of any

element. Many methods have been developed for calculating the Avogadro number, and the fact that completely different approaches have given results in close agreement provides support for their reliability and also tends to confirm the theory that molecules actually exist.

Loschmidt's Method. The first attempt at counting the number of molecules in a given volume of gas was made in 1865 by J. Loschmidt, who based his calculations on the assumption that when a gas is liquefied at low temperatures, it consists of closely packed spherical molecules. The approximate diameter, and hence the volume, of a single molecule can be derived from certain properties of the gas, such as viscosity; and hence the number of individual molecules in a known volume of liquid may be calculated. Knowing the volume of gas which gave that volume of liquid upon liquefaction, the number of molecules per unit volume of gas may be obtained. From these results the Avogadro number was found to be of the order of 10^{22}.

Perrin's Method. More accurate determinations were made in 1908 by J. Perrin, from studies of, among other things, the erratic movement, known as the Brownian motion or movement, exhibited by small solid or liquid particles suspended in either a gas or a liquid. By supposing the movement of these microscopically visible particles to be due to their continuous bombardment by the invisible molecules, Perrin was able to derive equations relating the various properties of the suspended particles to the Avogadro number. By a series of ingenious experiments, Perrin obtained the data necessary to calculate this constant. His work has been repeated by others using suspensions of different types; and, in every case, the value of the Avogadro number has been found to be about 6×10^{23}.

Other Methods. Two entirely different methods based on radioactive studies have been employed to obtain the Avogadro number. One involves the determination of the volume of helium and the number of alpha particles, i.e., helium nuclei, given off by radium in a given time; the other makes use of the half-life period of a radioactive element. Both methods give values in good agreement with those quoted above.

The two following methods, unlike those described previously, are capable of great accuracy. The first makes use of X rays of known wave length to determine the spacing between the layers of molecules or ions in a crystal, and the second utilizes the charge of an electron and the value of the faraday. The faraday may be taken as equal to the total charge carried by a gram molecule, i.e., the Avogadro number, of electrons. Hence, if it is divided by the charge of a single electron, the result will be the Avogadro number. The most reliable value of this constant is believed to be 6.023×10^{23}. Since this quantity of gas occupies 22.4 liters at $0°$ C. and 1 atmosphere of pressure, it can be seen that a liter of any gas under these conditions contains something like 30 billion billion individual molecules.

In order to determine the actual weight of a single atom or molecule in grams, the gram-atomic or gram-molecular weight, respectively, must be divided by 6.023×10^{23} or multiplied by 1.66×10^{-22}. The weight of a single oxygen molecule (molecular weight 32.00) is thus 53.1×10^{-22} gram, and it would require nearly 2×10^{20} individual oxygen molecules to weigh 1 gram. *See also* ATOMIC STRUCTURE; KINETIC THEORY AND STATISTICAL MECHANICS. S. Gl.

AVON [e'vən], the name of several rivers in England. The East or Hampshire Avon rises in Wiltshire, south of Marlborough, $2\frac{2}{3}$ mi. east of Devizes. Near Salisbury it is

STRATFORD-ON-AVON

BRITISH OFFICIAL PHOTOGRAPH

joined from the east by the Bourne and from the west by the Wylye; 2½ mi. from its mouth the Stour enters it from the west. It is 60 mi. long, with a total fall of 500 ft.; it enters the English Channel at Christchurch. The Lower or Bristol Avon rises on the eastern slopes of the Cotswold Hills in Gloucestershire, near Tetbury, and flows past Bristol to enter the Bristol Channel at Avonmouth. From Bristol to its mouth it is an important commercial waterway, offering the easiest route to the London Basin of any of the rivers flowing into the Bristol Channel. The Upper Avon, also called the Shakespeare or Warwickshire Avon, is a tributary of the Severn, entering it at Tewkesbury. Evesham, Arden Forest, Warwick Castle, and Stratford-on-Avon are famous historic spots along its course. The river is locked, but beyond Evesham it is little used. Its length is about 100 mi.

S. Van V.

AVRANCHES [a'vrɑ'sh], a French town at the base of the Cotentin Peninsula, on the estuary of the Sée River, and near the Bay of St. Michel. It is capital of an arrondissement in the department of Manche, is 85 mi. south of Cherbourg, and is one of the oldest towns in Normandy. Many ruins prove that Avranches was once the site of a Roman military station. It later became part of the province of Normandy and a stake in the rivalry between the Capetian House and the Plantagenets. During the Hundred Years' War the city was French from 1404 to 1418, then English. It was reconquered by Arthur III in 1438. In 1562 Avranches was devastated by the Calvinists, and in 1589 it refused to recognize Henry IV. An uprising occurred in 1639 against the exactions, principally the salt tax, of the Gabelle. In World War II the Germans planned to make a stand at Avranches to prevent the encirclement of their forces, but on July 31, 1944, the town fell to the United States Third Army sweeping eastward. As a result the town was partly destroyed. Avranches is a commercial center for agricultural products. Pop. 1954, 8,004.

S. Van V.

AWAJI [ɑ'wɑ'jɪ], one of the most thickly populated Japanese islands, having an area of 228.8 sq. mi. and located at 34° 20′ N. lat. and 134° 45′ E. long. between the islands of Honshu and Shikoku near the eastern end of the Inland Sea of Japan. It is bounded on the north by Akasi Strait, on the southeast by Osaka Bay and Osaka Strait, on the southwest by Naruto Pass, and on the northwest by the Harima Sea. The island is roughly triangular in shape, with the most acute angle stretching toward Kobe. The hilly northern and southern sections are composed of diorite, gneiss, granite, and old schists, with elevations rising to 1,692 ft. and wooded to the tops. The central section is a low fertile plain containing the bulk of the population, and here rice-growing dominates the land-use pattern. Fishing villages are strung along the coast and linked by a road which encircles Awaji close to the water's edge. Awaji wares made on the island are generally monochromatic, with a bright green or yellow glaze. Sumoto, on the eastern side of Awaji, is the administrative center and principal town (pop. 1940, 35,000). Other towns are Iwaya, Sensan, and Hukura. A railroad runs between Sumoto and Hukura. Strategically, the island dominates the eastern sea approach to Japan's vital Inland Sea and the industrial nerve centers and communication lines of southwest Honshu. During World War II, most of Awaji was in a restricted strategic area. Pop. 1940, 186,000.

R. G. B.

AXIOM [æ'ksiəm], a principle or proposition, as in philosophy or mathematics, accepted as true without proof. The word was in use both before and after Euclid's time; but he himself used the phrase κοινή ἔννοια, "common notion," i.e., a notion generally accepted (as true), for an axiom of general import; and the word αἴτημα, "a demand" (Lat. *postulatum*), i.e., a proposition the reader is asked to accept for the sake of the argument though he may reserve judgment, for a primitive proposition of specifically geometric content. This distinction is preserved to this day only in elementary mathematics. As will be seen, in higher mathematics the word postulate is used almost exclusively, in the sense of an assumed truth of purely logical import.

Although Euclid's postulates were early recognized as imperfect, they continued to be regarded as truly descriptive of the space of human experience. Jerome Saccheri (1667-1733) tried to prove the parallel postulate (through a point P not on a line L, one and only one parallel to L can be drawn); Nikolai Lobachevski (1793-1856) and Farkas Bolyai (1802-1860), independently of each other, created a different geometry by assuming that more than one line can be drawn through P parallel to L; while Georg Riemann (1826-1866) created still another by assuming that every line through P intersects L. In 1882, Moritz Pasch offered the first Euclidean geometry deduced from postulates without defining the elements point, line, and plane. In 1888, Giuseppe Peano began publishing the results of his efforts to reduce all mathematics to abstract systems deduced from explicitly stated postulates, expressed in precise symbolism and using as few undefined terms as possible. In 1899, David Hilbert published his *Grundlagen der Geometrie,* which established Euclidean geometry as an abstract, purely formal system, deduced from explicitly stated postulates about terms otherwise undefined.

Thus was launched the postulational era in mathematics. There are now postulates for geometry (Euclidean or non-Euclidean, metric or projective), for arithmetic, for algebra, and so on. The question of what intrinsic truth the postulates possess is no longer a relevant one, nor are the elements for which the postulates are concerned required to have any meaning other than that conferred on them by the postulates. Because of this enhanced importance of the postulates in a mathematical system, they are now scrutinized more closely than ever before. They are required, of course, to be consistent among themselves, but it is highly desirable that they also be independent of one another, and that they be as few as possible. In certain cases, they have to form a complete set. Roughly speaking, a postulate set is said to be complete if it is capable of deciding the truth or falsity of any proposition within the field of its applicability; or, putting it differently, if it is impossible to add new postulates about the same elements to the set without redundancy or contradiction.

G. C. V.

AXOLOTL [æ'ksolɒtəl], the name of the larval form of salamanders of the genus *Ambystoma*. Axolotls are remarkable because they reach sexual maturity and reproduce without metamorphosing into the adult form. This process is known as neoteny or neoteinia. Metamorphosis is controlled by the secretions of the thyroid gland. In these neotenic larvae there is a well-developed thyroid, but the tissues of the axolotl do not normally appear to be sensitive to its secretions. Axolotls are found in a few Mexican lakes, among them Xalco and Xochomilco. Adult forms of the genus *Ambystoma* are found in the cool parts of Mexico and northward into Canada. Both albino and brownish axolotls are known. The length in the adult stage ranges from 6 to 10 in. The most striking feature of the animal is the external gills, which in

A tiger salamander, Ambystoma tigrinum, or Axolotl, at the aquatic stage

other salamanders disappear on metamorphosis. The tail of the axolotl, as in the aquatic larvae of other salamanders, is flattened from side to side. In Mexico, axolotls are quite frequently sold in the markets as food.   A. Sv.

AXUM [ɑksu′m], the holy city of the Coptic Christians of Ethiopia and the ancient capital of an important kingdom that flourished from the fourth century B.C. to the ninth century A.D. It is located in the highlands of Tigré Province in northern Ethiopia at an elevation of 6,600 ft. It is 10 mi. southwest of Adua, 240 mi. from Gondar, and 112 mi. from Asmara, Eritrea, with all of which it is connected by highways. Axum and its environs are rich in historical structures, including the Cathedral Enda Mariam Zion, probably the most noted church in Ethiopia, erected by Emperor Fasilidas around 1665. It was in this church that for many generations the emperors of Ethiopia were crowned. Several other churches and religious edifices mark Axum as an ecclesiastical center. Also notable are the remains of the Axumite kingdom, including a number of giant steles, a necropolis, and the foundations of large-scale buildings. Almost all of the local population are Tigrinya-speaking adherents of the Coptic Church. Pop. (est. 1938), 10,000.
R. G. W.

AYACUCHO [ɑ′yɑku′tsho], the capital city of the department of Ayacucho, in central Peru, situated at 9,216 ft. above sea level, 360 mi. southeast of Lima, at 13° 7′ S. lat. and 74° 13′ W. long. The city is on the highway connecting Lima, Huancayo, and Cusco. It was founded by Francisco Pizarro in 1539, and until 1825 was known as Guamanga or Huamanga. Near by, at La Quinua, is the site of General Antonio José de Sucre's famous victory over the Spanish in 1824. The defeat and capture of the Spanish viceroy resulted in the independence of Peru and completed the emancipation of the Spanish colonies in South America. There are more than 25 churches in Ayacucho, the most noteworthy being the cathedral. Silver filigree, pottery, and rugs are the city's chief manufactures. Pop. (est. 1945), 22,000.

The department comprises 18,185 sq. mi. and consists of the seven provinces of Huamanga, Cangallo, Huanta, La Mar, Lucanas, Parinacochas, and Victor Fajardo. Both chains of the Cordilleras cross the department, and it is watered by numerous rivers. It is bounded by the departments of Junín, Cusco, and Apurimac on the north and east, by Arequipa on the south, and by Ica and Huancavelica on the west. Stock raising is important in the department, as is the mining of gold, silver, copper, and cobalt. Cacao, fruits, vegetables, grains, and alfalfa are grown in the fertile valleys. Pop. (est. 1947), 461,414.   S. G. I.

AYDIN or **AIDIN** [ɑidi′n], a city in southwestern Turkey, the chief city of the vilayet of the same name, situated in the fertile Meander River valley immediately north of the river, about 34 mi. east of the Aegean Sea, and about 70 mi. southeast of Smyrna. The city has short, cool, wet winters and long, hot, dry summers. The summer temperature average is between 70° and 80° F. The average annual rainfall is between 20 and 30 in. The vegetation is of a thorny, scrub type and includes many oleanders and myrtles. The mountains in the environs have some coniferous trees. Wheat, barley, tobacco, some cotton, grapes, figs, and olives are grown in the surrounding countryside, and there is some grazing in the region. Many of the grapes are dried and exported as raisins through Aydin; olive oil is also a local product of considerable importance. Aydin is a railroad and highway center.

Aydin was founded near the ancient city of Tralles, remnants of which are evident on the heights above Aydin. Turkish rule in Aydin dates from the late thirteenth century, when it was taken by the Seljuk Turks. A hundred years later, in 1390, while under the domination of Isa Bey, the city definitely acknowledged the suzerainty of the Ottomans. The city was damaged severely by an earthquake in 1899 and again by frequent assaults made on the city during the Greco-Turkish war of 1919-1922. Aydin has a mixed population of Turks, Greeks, Armenians, and Jews. It contains not only beautiful mosques, but churches, cathedrals, and synagogues. Pop. 1950, 20,421.   J. E. F.

AYE-AYE [ɑi′ɑi], a peculiar Madagascar lemur, *Daubentonia madagascariensis,* sole representative of a family. It has rodentlike incisor teeth, although the other teeth, the skull, the feet, and the internal anatomy show the aye-aye's true relationships with the lemurs. It is the size of a large cat, and is grizzled-blackish in color. It has a bushy tail, and large and naked ears. The great toe is opposable and bears a nail, the other digits being armed with claws. The middle

AYE-AYE

finger, which is slender and wirelike, is used to sound for wood-boring grubs, and then as a probe, to draw them out. The chisel-like incisors aid in this task, biting into the wood. In addition to insect food, the aye-aye feeds on fruit, eggs, and buds. Natives of Madagascar show a superstitious veneration for aye-ayes, believing them to be embodiments of their ancestors.   J. E. Hi.

AYLESBURY [e′lzbərɪ], a municipal borough and county town, in a valley near the source of the Thames, in the Aylesbury parliamentary division of Buckinghamshire, England, about 38 mi. northwest of London. Aylesbury was incorporated in 916, but the act was inoperative until 1117. In 1239 Henry III granted a fair; in 1554 Queen Mary made Aylesbury a free borough, allowing it a market. The Domesday Book reported the borough as having valuable lands. Aylesbury became a municipal borough in 1917. Statues honoring John Hampden and Benjamin Disraeli are in the town. Chief occupations are duck raising and dairying; others include lace making, printing, and straw braiding. The town has a considerable agricultural trade. Pop. 1952, 20,860. A. W.

AYLMER, a town in Elgin Co., Ontario, Canada, 25 mi. south of London, Ont., and 8 mi. north of Lake Erie. It is on the Canadian National Railways and Provincial Highway 3. It was incorporated as a town in 1887. The trading center for a rich and varied agricultural district, Aylmer has a large tobacco processing plant, canneries, frozen food, and dairy plants. Near by is a permanent Royal Canadian Air Force station. Pop. 1951, 3,483. D. F. P.

AYLMER, a town in Hull Co., Quebec, Canada, situated on the north bank of the Ottawa River, 8 mi. west of the city of Ottawa, of which it is a residential suburb. It is on Provincial Highway 8, and is served by the Canadian Pacific Railway. Founded in 1816, it was for many years a sawmilling center. It was incorporated as a village in 1847 and as a town in 1890. Pop. 1951, 4,375. D. F. P.

AYMARÁ. *See* INDIAN TRIBES, SOUTH AMERICAN.

AYR [ɛ′r], a royal, municipal burgh, seaport, resort, and county town, in the Ayr Burghs, a parliamentary division of Ayrshire, Scotland, situated at the mouth of the Ayr River, on the Firth of Clyde, 41½ mi. southwest of Glasgow. Ayr is the center of the Robert Burns country, and Tam o' Shanter Inn at Ayr is reputed to be the point from which Tam began his ride in Burns' poem *Tam o' Shanter*. Ayr is an active import and export center, and shipbuilding, commercial

fishing, and the manufacture of textiles and shoes are important industries. Pop. 1952, 43,247. A. W.

AYRES, LEONARD PORTER [ɛ′rz] (1879-1946), American educator, statistician, and economist, was born in Niantic, Conn., Sept. 15, 1879. He graduated from Boston University in 1902, began his career as a teacher in Puerto Rico the same year, and became general superintendent of the island schools in 1906. From 1908 to 1920 he was director of education and statistics for the Russell Sage Foundation. During World War I he was chief statistical officer of the United States Army and of the American Expeditionary Forces, with the rank of colonel on the General Staff. He also served as statistician on various important boards and commissions, and was awarded the Distinguished Service Medal. In 1920 he became vice-president of the Cleveland Trust Company, Cleveland, Ohio; in 1924 he was economic adviser on the Dawes Plan Commission. During World War II, from 1940 onward, Ayres was chief statistician for the War Department. He was noted for his studies of business cycles and for his forecasts of business conditions. He wrote numerous books, including *Economics of Recovery* (1933), *The Chief Cause of This and Other Depressions* (1935), *Inflation* (1936), and *Turning Points in Business Cycles* (1939). He died in Cleveland, Ohio, Oct. 29, 1946. J. E. Mo.

AYRSHIRE [ɛ′rshɪr], the largest county in southern Scotland, has an area of 1,131.6 sq. mi. It is bounded by Renfrewshire on the north, Lanarkshire and Dumfriesshire on the east, Kirkcudbrightshire and Wigtownshire on the south, and the Firth of Clyde on the west. There are mountains in the southwest. The principal rivers are the Garnock, Irvine, Ayr, Doon, Girvan, and Stinchar, none of which is navigable. Ayrshire is famous for its dairy products and its fine breed of cattle. The manufactures are valuable, and include woolens, cotton, iron, and earthenware. Coal, iron, limestone, and sandstone are all extensively worked. Robert

Rolling terrain, typical of that found near Kirkmichael in Ayrshire

Bruce was born in 1274 in Turnberry Castle, which became the starting point of his attempt to free his country. Kilmarnock, in northern Ayrshire, is associated with Robert Burns, whose poems were first published there in 1786. The county sends three members to Parliament. Pop. 1952, 321,977.

In 1782 the capital was moved to Bangkok, which soon surpassed Ayutthaya in importance. After Siam capitulated to Japan in December 1941, the city remained under Japanese domination until the end of the war in August 1945.

Ayutthaya contains many interesting ruins of all types of buildings, an archeological museum, and an old elephant

Native craft laden with produce crowd the river market at Ayutthaya, Siam.

AYU [a′yu], *Plecoglossus altivelis,* or sweetfish, is a dwarf salmonlike fish that enters rivers in Japan, Korea, and China and may become landlocked. It seldom grows to a length of more than one foot. It is an excellent food fish. The flesh is white, with little oil and no odor. In China and Japan tame cormorants, fitted with a harness and string and with a ring about the lower part of the neck, are used in fishing for ayu. Fishing is done at night by torchlight. The cormorants dive and fill their throats and gular pouches with fish. They are then pulled to shore and forced to give up their prey.

E. C. R.

AYUDHYA or **AYUTHIA.** *See* AYUTTHAYA.

AYUTTHAYA [ayu′tai′a], or Krum-Kao, the former capital city of Siam, 43 mi. north of Bangkok, on the Menam Chao Phraya, in the southern part of central Siam at 14° 28′ N. lat. and 100° 36′ E. long. It lies on a broad alluvial plain in a maze of small creeks and rivers; the original city was on an island. Ayutthaya is a market and trade center for the surrounding agricultural district and is an army division headquarters. It has government administrative buildings and a palace. Rice is the major crop of the area, and some subsistence crops are also grown. Manufacturing is limited to rice mills, a few teakwood sawmills, and the production of home necessities. A large part of the city is built on stilts because of the annual flood of the Menam, and there are many houseboats. The city was established about 1351 by Pra Chao U. T'Hong, and became a large and important capital city, but in 1559 it was destroyed by the Burmese. The city was rebuilt and flourished during the sixteenth century, but in 1767 it was again destroyed by the Burmese.

ring, or enclosure, which is used to hold wild elephants that are driven in from the neighboring area. Pop. (est. 1947), 25,000; (est. 1949), 50,000.

J. E. F.

MAULANA ABUL
KALAM AZAD

AZAD, MAULANA ABUL KALAM [aza′d] (1888-), Indian Moslem scholar and politician, was born at Mecca, Arabia, in 1888, moved to Calcutta in 1898, was tutored by Arabic scholars, and in 1905 entered Al-Azhar University in Cairo, Egypt. Returning to India in 1907, he became interested in the nationalist movement, learned English, and in 1912 founded the weekly *Al-Hilal,* which discussed social, political, and religious topics. During World War I his paper was confiscated; Azad was banished from Bengal and was interned at Ranchi until 1920. There he wrote his personal reminiscences, *Tazkira*. Azad was president of the Indian National Congress, 1923-1924, 1930-1932, and 1940-1941. He supported the July 15, 1942, resolution of the Congress Working Committee appealing for the withdrawal of British rule, and on Aug. 8, 1942, with other recalcitrant Indian leaders, he was arrested by the British authorities and jailed until the summer of 1945. He was a member of the so-called Indian interim government, and on Aug. 15, 1947, when the newly constituted Union of India cabinet was set up, he was made minister of education. Azad is the author of *Commentary on the Koran*.

AZALEA [əzeʹliə], the name now used commonly, but not botanically, for about forty species of rhododendron which have funnel-shaped instead of the typical bell-shaped flowers. Formerly they were classified as a distinct genus. Azaleas, native chiefly to Asia and eastern North America, are both evergreen and deciduous, hardy and tender, with a wide range of colors, white, pink, purple, red, and yellow. There

FROM EWING GALLOWAY

Azaleas in bloom

are many fine hybrids. Azaleas rank high as spring flowering ornamental shrubs. Among the best known American species are the flame azalea, *Rhododendron calendulaceum*, of the southern Appalachians; the pale pink pinxter bloom, *R. nudiflorum;* and the fragrant white swamp azalea, *R. viscosum,* which is commonly known as the swamp honeysuckle. The white azalea native to the Pacific coast is *R. occidentale*.   J. C. Wis.

AZAN [ɑzɑʹn] (Arabic *ādhān,* announcement), is the Moslem call to prayer, uttered by a muezzin (announcer) five times a day from a mosque or the top of a minaret. With minor variations, the *azan,* chanted in Arabic, follows this standard text: "Allah is great. I testify that Mohammed is the apostle of Allah. Come to prayer. Come to salvation. Allah is great. There is no God save Allah." *See also* MUEZZIN.   E. J. J.

AZAÑA Y DÍEZ, MANUEL [athaʹnya i diʹeth] (1880-1940), political leader and president of Spain, was born in

Alcalá de Henares, in Castile, on Jan. 10, 1880. He was educated at the college of the Augustinian Order at Escorial, and became one of the leading literary figures of Spain and, in 1930, president of the Madrid Ateneo. He organized the Republican Action Party, which helped overthrow King Alfonso XIII, and in the provisional government set up, Apr. 15, 1931, with Niceto Alcalá Zamora as premier, Azaña became war minister. As champion of a movement to restrict clerical power and dissolve the Jesuit Order, he replaced Alcalá Zamora as premier in October 1931. With the first election under the republican constitution, Alcalá Zamora became president in December 1931, and Azaña remained as premier. An increase in conservative sentiment forced Azaña's resignation in September 1933. He was suspected of involvement in the 1934 revolts of the Asturian miners and Catalan nationalists and organized a new Left Republican Party which dissociated itself from the Alcalá Zamora government. After Azaña's arrest in October 1934, and the abandonment of his trial in 1935, he became the leader of the Frente Popular, which achieved a significant electoral victory in February 1936. Again premier, Azaña rejected reconciliation with President Alcalá Zamora, whom he deposed and succeeded on May 10. In July the Civil War broke out, and the leadership of the republican government was assumed by a succession of premiers. In February 1939 Azaña sought asylum in Paris, and after the recognition of the Franco government by Britain and France he resigned as president on Mar. 1, 1939. He became reconciled to the Church during an illness which ended with his death at Montauban, France, on Nov. 4, 1940.

AZANDE. *See* AFRICAN PEOPLES.

AZEGLIO, MASSIMO TAPARELLI, MARCHESE D' [ɑdzɛʹlyo] (1798-1866), Italian novelist and statesman, was born in Turin, Oct. 24, 1798, the son of Marchese Cesare d'Azeglio. After serving in the Piedmontese army, he went to Rome to study art, becoming a successful painter. Going to Milan, he associated with the Romanticists, married Giulia, daughter of Alessandro Manzoni, and wrote two novels. In 1848 he joined the army of Pius IX and was wounded fighting against Austria. In 1849 Victor Emanuel II made him prime minister of Piedmont. His firm and intelligent policy, in collaboration with Cavour, was Italian, not narrowly Piedmontese, and helped prepare the liberation of Italy. Disapproving of violence and conspiracy, he gradually fell out of sympathy with the revolutionary movement and retired from political life. He died in Turin, Jan. 15, 1866.

D'Azeglio's two historical novels were among the most successful products of Italian Romanticism. The subject of the first, *Ettore Fieramosca, o la disfida di Barletta* (1833) was suggested by his painting of the contest at Barletta in 1503, in which thirteen Italian champions under Fieramosca defeated thirteen Frenchmen. *Niccolò de' Lapi* (1841) concerns the siege of Florence in 1530. D'Azeglio also wrote political tracts. His interesting memoirs, *I miei ricordi,* were left unfinished at his death.   K. McK.

AZERBAIDZHAN [ɑʹzərbaijɑʹn], a region lying partly within northern Iran and partly within the Soviet Union. It is also spelled Azerbaijan and Azerbaidjan.

Azerbaidzhan Soviet Socialist Republic. The Azerbaidzhan Soviet Socialist Republic came into being in 1936 as one of the sixteen constituent "republics" of the Union of

Soviet Socialist Republics. It occupies approximately 33,200 sq. mi. of the trans-Caucasian region of western Asia and southeastern Europe, extending northward from Iran to the mountain boundaries of the Daghestan Autonomous Soviet Socialist Region of the Russian Soviet Federated Socialist

KARADAG FISHERIES, AZERBAIDZHAN S. S. R.

Republic and westward from the Caspian Sea to the Armenian S. S. R. and the Georgian S. S. R.

Physically, Azerbaidzhan occupies the very broad, flat, tectonic Kura Depression and its encircling mountains, the main Caucasus ridge on the north, the Little Caucasus Mountains on the southwest, and the Talish Hills in the southeast. More than one third of the country lies in the Kura Basin, a structural depression filled with alluvial deposits and drained by the Kura River and the Araks River in the southeast. Below the Caucasus range and the 14,734-ft. peak, Mount Bazardyuze, Azerbaidzhan's broad plains are generally hot and dry in the summer and cold in the winter; but the terrain varies from the moist, cool slopes of the Caucasus, which make good summer pasture land, and the irrigable semi-deserts and cultivated valleys near the Kura River and the Araks, Azerbaidzhan's principal streams, to river marshlands and the wet Lenkoran coast of the Caspian Sea, a one-time malarial region which is responding to drainage. Azerbaidzhan is sparsely wooded, but the oak, elm, silver poplar, willow, and mulberry grow on the banks of the Kura and the elm, ash, oak, and maple on the Talish Hills in the southeast. The steppes of the Kura Basin support artemisia, salt shrubs, and similar desert brush, but little other natural plant life.

Except for the Russians settled in its urban centers and the Armenians and Kurds in its western highlands, the population of the Azerbaidzhan S. S. R., which was estimated at 3,300,000 in 1954, is largely of Turkic and Mongol stock. The vast oil deposits in or near the capital city and seaport, Baku, on the Apsheron Peninsula, have yielded 25,000,000 tons of petroleum annually, a very substantial part of the Soviet Union's total production. In Baku, which has a popu-

lation of over 800,000 and is the fourth largest Russian city, great oil refineries, chemical plants processing synthetic rubber and fertilizer, food plants, tool factories, and shipyards are responsible for three fourths of Azerbaidzhan's industrial output. These plants produce iodine and bromine; there are textile mills at Kirovabad and silk mills at Nukha. The mineral wealth includes salt, iron, corundum, copper, barite, and pyrites. Farms grow cotton, rice, wheat, and alfalfa in the irrigated plains along the Kura River; mulberries for silk-worm breeding, grapes, and walnuts in the north; and tea, tangerines, pomegranates, figs, and tobacco in the south. These activities make Azerbaidzhan an important manufacturing, mining, and agricultural area. Its farm holdings were 90 per cent collectivized by 1938. In 1939, 26 per cent of the population was illiterate, but the "republic" had 60 technical schools to train its industrial workers and 14 schools of college level. By 1945 its local branch of the Academy of Sciences of the U.S.S.R. had expanded enough to emerge as the Academy of Sciences of the Azerbaidzhan S.S.R. The principal cities include Baku; Kirovabad, formerly Gaudglia and Yelizavetpoe; Kuba; and Agdam. Included in Azerbaidzhan are the Nakhichevan Autonomous Soviet Socialist Republic and the Nagorno-Karabakh Autonomous Region.

History. The early Assyrian chronicles of more than 5,000 years ago mention the riches of the Azerbaidzhan region. It was then a part of an area known as Georgia, which was located in the territory between the Black and Caspian seas, generally south of an east-west line between Krasnodar and Astrakhan. Christianity came to the region in the second century, displacing the fire worship of Zoroaster, the Azerbaidzhan god. The legendary site of the Garden of Eden is frequently placed in this area. Located on the trade routes between the Black and Caspian seas and those southward into Persia (now Iran) and Turkey, Azerbaidzhan was an area of constant conflict.

In time, this region of Georgia came to be divided into four parts: North Caucasia, Georgia, Armenia, and Azer-

BUZOVNYEFT OIL FIELD, AZERBAIDZHAN S. S. R.

baidzhan. In the eleventh century Azerbaidzhan was colonized by Seljuk Turks, and from the thirteenth to the fifteenth centuries it was occupied by Mongolians and was a part of Tamerlane's empire. After the collapse of Mongolian control a number of independent khanates and sultanates sprang up. Early in the sixteenth century a struggle began between

Persia and the Ottoman Empire for the control of Azerbaidzhan, in which Persia was usually successful. For two hundred years, until about 1740, Persia controlled Azerbaidzhan without much challenge, but by the latter half of the eighteenth century Russian expansionist plans had turned south toward the Caucasus.

In 1801 Russia, by violation of a treaty made in 1783, gained control of Georgia. By 1813 Russian armies had compelled Persian recognition of Baku and a large part of eastern Transcaucasia as Russian. The Azerbaidzhanian people did not readily submit to Russian control. Fighting continued, and the khanates into which the country had been divided came together to fight the common menace, whether it was Russian, Turkish, or Persian. About 1825 a large part of Azerbaidzhan was seized by Persia and formed into a province with Favris as its capital. This seizure brought on war with Russia, 1826-1828, which culminated in the fixing of the boundary between the Russian and Persian areas of Azerbaidzhan at the Araks River, where it now is. The ten khanates remaining under Russian control, one after another, were forced to submit to Russian rule.

On Sept. 20, 1917, after the overthrow of the Imperial Russian government and the establishment of a revolutionary government under the Bolsheviks, a council of Transcaucasian peoples met at Tiflis. Armenia, Georgia, and Azerbaidzhan declared themselves to be the Transcaucasian Federal Republic within the Soviet Union. A council of government was formed on Nov. 15, 1917, and six months later, on Apr. 22, 1918, the newly formed republic declared its independence of Russia. As a result of this action, Transcaucasia became for some time a theatre of war, revolution, and international intrigue.

The Treaty of Brest-Litovsk, between the Soviet Union and Germany, ceded the southern part of Transcaucasia to Turkey, in spite of the protest of the Transcaucasian seim (Parliament). In May 1918 a German army occupied Georgia, and shortly afterward the Caucasian republics of Azerbaidzhan, Georgia, and Armenia came into existence. On

Mausoleum of Abu Muhammad Nizami, Persian poet, in Kirovabad, Azerbaidzhan S.S.R.

SOVFOTO

June 3, 1918, a treaty with Turkey was signed by each newly created republic, with boundaries identical to those stipulated in the Brest-Litovsk treaty. In November 1918, when the war ended, German troops were withdrawn and British troops marched in. The act of independence of Azerbaidzhan became effective Mar. 2, 1919, and was liberal in its provisions. Conditions in the region were not conducive to such movements, however. The Soviet Union attempted to

extend its control over the region, and sought to use the new republics against General Denikin and the White Russians. When the proposals of alliance were rejected, the Soviet Russian troops, on one pretext or another, moved into Azerbaidzhan in April 1920, seized Baku, the oil port on the Caspian Sea, and soon followed this by gradual occupation

SOVFOTO

Inspecting and packing caviar in a Kirovabad fishery, Azerbaidzhan S.S.R.

of the Transcaucasian republics. By the early part of 1921, the Soviet army was in full control of Azerbaidzhan. But in resisting the occupation, thousands of natives were killed and thousands more were maltreated and driven from their homes. As the result of a "revolution," Apr. 27-28, 1920, a Soviet regime was established in Azerbaidzhan and a Transcaucasian Federated Socialist Republic was set up Mar. 12, 1922, consisting of Georgia, Armenia, and Azerbaidzhan. Theoretically any country had the right to free withdrawal, but when Georgia attempted to exercise this privilege in October 1924 the Soviet government answered the request with bullets. Thousands were killed and much property destroyed. In 1936 the Federative Republic was dissolved, and Azerbaidzhan, Armenia, and Georgia each became an "independent" Soviet Socialist Republic.

During World War II German troops endeavored to penetrate into Transcaucasia to Baku, the capital, but were stopped short of their goal by Russian armies. At the close of the war the bitter controversy between the Soviet Union and Iran, each endeavoring to secure control of the Azerbaidzhan area held by the other, came to a head, and for a time conflict seemed certain. The basis of the difficulty is partition of a people with a common cultural, linguistic, and religious background. To this must be added the conflict over the rich oil resources of the area. The Soviet Union has secured marked preference through its program of industrial development, social benefits, and participation in local government by those willing to conform to the requirements of Communist standards.

The entire region of Transcaucasia is especially important to the Soviet Union, not only because of its resources in oil and other important products, but also because it gives access through Azerbaidzhan and Iran to the rich oil resources of the Near East and to the water route of the Persian Gulf.

Iranian Azerbaijan. The Iranian province of Azerbaijan at one time was united to the north with what is now the Azerbaidzhan Soviet Socialist Republic. It was colonized in the eleventh century by Seljuk Turks, and two centuries later was occupied by invading Mongolians from the east. Later the Arabs came from the west, bringing with them their religion of Islam. The people of Azerbaijan in Iran are preponderantly of Mongol and Turkic strain, and are generally known as Tatars.

For two hundred years before the eighteenth century all of Azerbaijan was controlled by Persia, but this control was challenged by Russia under Peter the Great and his successors. The present boundary between the Russian and Iranian regions was fixed after the 1826-1828 war with Russia, brought about by Iran's seizure of part of Azerbaidzhan.

Until World War I and the Russian Revolution, there was little or no change in the two areas. Although the Russian area became a member of the autonomous Caucasian republics and later the Azerbaidzhan S. S. R., the part of Azerbaijan in Persia remained a province of that country.

Towards the end of World War II Soviet efforts to gain control of Iranian Azerbaijan were renewed. In November 1945 a separatist movement, engineered by the Soviet Union, resulted in an attempt by the Azerbaijan Democratic Party to set up an autonomous government. Iranian troops, sent to quell the revolt were stopped by Soviet forces on a pretext. Thus protected, the autonomists took over the district.

Negotiations with the Soviet Union were begun by Iran looking to the withdrawal of Soviet troops from the province in accordance with the Tripartite Berlin Conference, Aug. 1, 1945. The Soviet government finally agreed to evacuate the province within six weeks, beginning on Mar. 24, 1946, but insisted on an agreement with the Iranian government providing for joint Soviet-Iranian exploitation of the oil reserves in Iranian Azerbaijan. Soviet troops began to leave on May 6, 1946. On Oct. 22, 1947, Iran repudiated this agreement. The Soviet government protested, Nov. 20, 1947, but four days later Iran rejected the protest.

Iranian troops had moved into the province as Soviet forces withdrew. On Aug. 17, 1948, the Iranian parliament approved an amnesty measure for the province, but many of the released prisoners went to the Azerbaidzhan S.S.R. to aid in the formation of a so-called government-in-exile. In 1949 there were reports of frontier clashes between Iranian and Soviet troops. Thus the Soviet Union exerted pressure upon Iran for an agreement with respect to this important frontier area. Though no oil-producing areas are now being exploited, it is believed that vast deposits of high-grade oil underlie the province.

W. S. V. and C. C. H.

AZERBAIJAN. *See* AZERBAIDZHAN.

AZERBAIJANI TURKS. *See* ASIATIC TRIBES.

AZEVEDO, ALUÍZIO DE [əzəve'thu] (1857-1913), Brazilian novelist, was born in São Luís de Maranhão. He followed a career in the diplomatic service, with literature as an avocation. His early work was strongly influenced by Romanticism, but in 1881, with the publication of *O Mulato* ("The Mulatto"), he identified himself with the French Naturalist school, and was the instigator of this tendency in Brazil. *O Mulato,* a passionate and powerful work, deals with the bitter racial problems of his native province. Azevedo, moved by a turbulent imagination which occasionally seems almost morbid, sometimes allows his early Roman-

ticism to divert him from the channels of pure Naturalism, while at other times his devotion to the precepts of Zola is carried to extremes. He is always a faithful Naturalist in respect to description and richness of detail, but his objectivity is often vitiated by his passionate identification with his theme. In his most famous novel, *O Cortiço* (1890) ("The Tenement House"), he demonstrates his gifts as an impressionist. His description of slum life in Rio de Janeiro and of Brazilian middle-class genteel vulgarity, both of which he knew at first hand, attain a high novelistic quality. A social rather than a psychological analyst, he achieves his best effects in the incisive description of exterior detail, in the representation of typical rather than individualized behavior, and in the projection of local dialect. Thus, he is primarily a novelist of manners, a collectivist who rarely creates a great character, but who presents prevailing social types with extraordinary exactness and intensity of characterization. In *O Cortiço, A Casa de Pensão* (1884) ("The Boarding House"), and *O Homem* (1887) ("The Man"), Azevedo, nevertheless, has left a rich impression of certain aspects of Brazilian society in his time.

E. G. Da C.

AZILIAN CULTURE. *See* MAS D'AZIL, LE.

AZIMUTH [æ'zɪməth]. **In Astronomy.** In astronomy, azimuth is the angular distance on the horizon from the south point to the foot of the celestial object's vertical circle, measured westward around the circle from 0° to 360°. Or it is the angle at the zenith from the southern half of the meridian westward to the object's vertical circle. Thus the west point is 90° in azimuth, the north point 180°, and so on.

In Navigation. In navigation, azimuth (also called bearing) is the angular distance from the north point, measured eastward and around the circle. Azimuth and altitude are co-ordinates of the horizon system of the celestial sphere.

In Surveying. In surveying, the azimuth of a line is the horizontal angle which the line makes with a north-and-south line, as measured clockwise, commonly from the south point.

H. S. R.

AZORES [əzɔ'rz], a group of islands, also known as the Western Islands, lying in the North Atlantic Ocean about 900 mi. west of Portugal, to which they belong. There are nine islands of varying size and several islets, totaling 922 sq. mi. in area. São Miguel is the largest, embracing 297 sq. mi., followed by Terceira, Pico, and São Jorge. Smaller islands are Fayal, Graciosa, Flores, Santa Maria, and Corvo. On several occasions this volcanic group has had earthquakes and eruptions. There are several hot springs, notably on São Miguel. The topography is mountainous, with heights rising to 7,613 ft. on Pico. The climate is temperate, varying little from season to season within a range of 50° to 80° F. Rainfall is heaviest in the cooler months but is by no means lacking in summer and varies from 35 to 45 in. Snow is encountered only on the high peaks. The native fauna is limited, but fishing, including whaling, is a major industry. The natural vegetation derives from Europe and is luxuriant because of the warm and wet climate. The original absence of taller trees has been modified by localized planting of various European varieties. Semitropical fruit trees, such as the orange and lemon, flourish. Agriculture is the economic mainstay of the people, aided by the equable climate and the generally fertile soil. The vineyards, formerly flourishing, have largely been destroyed by blight. Oranges, once an important item of export, were also hard hit by disease. In recent years the two chief agricultural exports have been the

"SEVEN CITIES," A GROUP OF SEVEN LAGOONS IN SÃO MIGUEL ISLAND, AZORES

banana and pineapple. Sugar cane and sugar beets are also grown, as are tea, tobacco, corn, and wheat. Cattle, sheep, and goats are pastured on the mountain slopes. The population of the archipelago was 318,558 in 1950, a density of over 300 per square mile, one of the highest in Portuguese territory. The inhabitants are basically Portuguese, with a mingling of Flemish, English, Scottish, Irish, and Moorish elements. The universal language is Portuguese, and a large majority of the population professes Roman Catholicism. Relatively heavy emigration, chiefly to the United States and Hawaii, occurred during the latter nineteenth and early twentieth centuries. This exodus accounted for a decrease of over 35,000 in population between 1881 and 1920.

The archipelago comprises a province, divided into three administrative districts, each of which sends a representative to the Assembly in Lisbon. The capitals of these districts and their populations are: Ponta Delgada, 22,448, on São Miguel Island; Angra do Heroismo, 9,435, on Terceira Island; and Horta, 8,184, on Fayal Island. The Azores are administered as an integral part of Portugal. Angra do Heroismo is the seat of a bishopric.

The Azores lie along several important ocean routes, such as those from New York to the Mediterranean and from northern Europe to the Caribbean, but provide no natural harbors. Ponta Delgada is the busiest port, though Angra has the best harbor. Horta is also a much frequented port.

The Carthaginians appear to have visited the islands, and some Arab navigators probably landed there in the Middle Ages. Italian vessels touched there early in the fourteenth century, but only in the following century, beginning in 1432, were the Azores definitively explored and annexed by the Portuguese. During the period when Portugal was part of the Spanish domain, from 1580 to 1640, the Azores provided a halfway station for the galleons returning to Spain from America. Hence the islands were the scene of various naval engagements with English vessels. After a temporary revival under the enlightened administration of the Marquis of Pombal in the latter part of the eighteenth century, the islands relapsed into a state of somnolence. They emerged momentarily into prominence during the conflict in Portugal between the reactionary government of Dom Miguel and the constitutionalist forces rallying around Maria II. Forces loyal to the latter occupied Terceira Island in 1820, and for several years Maria resided at Angra while her father, Dom Pedro I of Brazil organized the invasion of Portugal, which in 1834 put Maria on the throne. During World War II, Portugal granted her ancient ally, Great Britain, and the United States permission to use certain areas in the Azores for military purposes. The United States Air Force constructed a large air field on Santa Maria Island. In August 1946, it was announced that the Portuguese government had purchased this field and its various installations and equipment.

R. G. W.

AZORÍN [ɑ'thori'n], pseudonym of the Spanish writer and critic José Martínez Ruiz (1873-   ), born June 8, 1873, at Monóvar, Alicante. He was for many years a journalist, participated also in politics, and was elected to the Cortes several times during the monarchy. He is one of the outstanding figures of the "generation of '98," to which, indeed, he gave its name.

The works of Azorín are of three kinds: essays, novels, and plays, but above all he is an essayist. In his writing several phases can be distinguished. He began his career as a keen, hard-hitting critic who was, politically speaking, an anarchist. This phase is reflected in his *La Crítica literaria en España* (1893) ("Literary Criticism in Spain"), *Anarquistas literarios* (1895) ("Literary Anarchists"), and *Crítica discordante* (1897) ("Discordant Criticism"). By 1900, however, he had abandoned this aggressive but negative attitude and in this year published *El Alma castellana, 1600-1800* ("The Castilian Spirit, 1600-1800"), and *Los Hidalgos,* which are collections of essays of a more creative nature. In these volumes he turned to the theme that was to shape all his future works: Castile and the basic Spanish man, the peasant of Castile. This eventually led to such works of fiction as *La Voluntad* (1902) ("The Choice"), *Antonio Azorín* (1903), and *Las Confesiones de un pequeño filósofo* (1904) ("The Confessions of a Little Philosopher"), all three built around a single character, Antonio Azorín. Thereafter the author identified himself with his character, and was no longer José Martínez Ruiz, but simply Azorín, the pen name by which he is known throughout the Hispanic world. It was in these works, too, that Azorín found himself as an artist, and using his pseudonym, he published the following notable collections of essays: *Los Pueblos* (1904) ("The Villages"), *La Ruta de Don Quijote* (1905) ("The Itinerary of Don Quixote"), *España: hombres y paisajes* (1900) ("Spain: Men and Landscapes"), and *Castilla* (1912). Here he affirmed what had been outlined in his second period, and in these works one finds the most direct and complete statement of Azorín's national faith: the Castilian land has a soul, and to say Castile is to say Spain, with all its villages and its peoples. Azorín realized intensely that these people and these landscapes, the Spanish peasant and the land he plowed, represented the basic timelessness for which he was searching, and in describing them he attained a sense of the continuity of Spanish history. In American literature this feeling, which their author derived from Azorín, can be seen in *Rosinante to the Road Again* and *The Villages Are the Heart of Spain,* both by John Dos Passos.

Azorín's attempt to bring the past to life appears also in his later critical essays, which show an orientation very different from that of his first period. It is apparent in *Lecturas españolas* (1912), *Clásicos y modernos* (1913), *Los Valores literarios* (1913) ("Literary Values"), *Al margen de los clásicos* (1915) ("Marginalia on the Classics"), and *De Granada á Castelar* (1922). By the time the last was written, Azorín had become a conservative, politically speaking, and in 1924 was made a member of the Spanish Academy. At this time he seems to have taken new roads; he returned to the novel, but not to a realistic conception of it, for he appeared to be striving toward some mythical universality. In 1922 he published *Don Juan* (English translation, 1924), and in 1925 *Doña Inés.* In both novels Azorín tried, he explains, to "put a new soul, a soul of our time, into old characters." This basic artistic effort to bring the past into the present is also applied here to historical characters and even to supernatural beings, and one may also find this device in his later novels, *Félix Vargas* (1928) and *Superrealismo* (1929). Since 1939, Azorín seems to have returned to a concrete preoccupation with Spain as a past and a present inextricably interwoven; this is exemplified in his collections of essays, *Pensando en España* (1940) ("Thinking of Spain") and *Sintiendo á España* (1942) ("As I Feel Spain"). He has also been engaged in writing his memoirs.

Azorín is one of the greatest literary figures of contemporary Spain and has introduced into Spanish prose a very original style of neat, short sentences, which gives unity to all of his writings. His major literary discovery has been the poetic significance of daily life in the timelessness of its detail, and his intelligent presentation of this material has been a notable and much-needed contribution to the revitalization of the Spanish heritage. J. A. L. M.

AZOTE. *See* NITROGEN.

AZOV, SEA OF [ɑ′zof; azɔ′f], about 14,500 sq. mi., a northern extension of the Black Sea almost completely land-locked by the Crimean Peninsula on the west and the delta of the Kuban River on the east. Kerch Strait connects the Sea of Azov with the Black Sea. On the northeast is the long, narrow Gulf of Taganrog and there are several smaller bays, such as Beizugsku and Ashtersku. The Don River flows into the head of the Gulf of Taganrog, and Rostov on the Don is the most important city. Taganrog, Primarsko-Akhtarskaya, and Kerch are railroad terminals along the coast. Fishing and some trading are important on this sea. On the west a long narrow strip of land, the Tongue of Arabat, separates the Sea of Azov from the Sivash, or Putrid Sea. J. E. F.

AZRAEL [æ′zreɛl], the angel of death in the Jewish and Islamic religions. He watches over the dying, separates the soul from the body, and receives the spirits of the dead. The name "Azrael" is an adaptation of a Hebrew form meaning "God has helped." E. J. J.

AZTEC [æ′ztɛk], the name of the Indian tribe or nation which controlled a large part of Mexico at the time of the Spanish Conquest in A.D. 1520. The term Aztec is also used in alluding to the culture or civilization characteristic of this

AZTEC SACRIFICIAL STONE PHILIP D. GENDREAU

tribe and of many neighboring tribes from about A.D. 1300 to 1520. In conjunction with this usage, the Aztec tribe proper is sometimes referred to as the Tenochca. According to legends, the Tenochca entered the Valley of Mexico from the northwest sometime in the twelfth century. For a long time they were one of the lesser tribes there, culturally and politically. Their capital, the site of modern Mexico City, was located on an island in a lake. By a series of military alliances and conquests the Tenochca rose to a position of prominence in 1428, and in the ensuing decades became the dominant military power of Mexico. The last Tenochca or Aztec ruler, Montezuma II, was defeated, captured, and killed by Hernando Cortes and his Spanish soldiers in the campaign of 1519-1520. Aztec civilization was compounded of the centuries of cultural development which had preceded it in the Valley of Mexico and Middle America. Craftsmanship in stone, textiles, and ceramics was high. Literature was in process of formulation. The outstanding Aztec achievements, however, were in warfare and political organization.

In these the Aztecs were second only to the Incas of Peru. *See also* ARCHAEOLOGY; INDIAN TRIBES, NORTH AMERICAN; MEXICO. G. R. W.

AZUELA, MARIANO [ɑsue'lɑ] (1873-1952), Mexican novelist, was born in Lagos de Moreno, Jalisco, Jan. 1, 1873, the son of a small independent landholder. Azuela completed his education in 1899 with a degree in medicine from the University of Guadalajara, but had early demonstrated an active interest in both literature and politics. In 1896 he began writing newspaper articles and sketches and at the same time identified himself with student agitation against the regime of Porfirio Díaz. His education finished, Azuela returned to his native town to combine the practice of medicine with a career of intense literary production. By the time of the revolution of 1910, Azuela had published three novels treating of social corruption, but he had received no public recognition. He began to write his best-known work, *Los de abajo (The Underdogs,* 1929), while serving as an army doctor with the forces of Pancho Villa. After the defeat of Villa's forces by Venustiano Carranza and Álvaro Obregón in 1915, Azuela fled northward with the retreating troops. He finally finished his novel in El Paso, Texas, where he published it serially in a local Spanish-language newspaper. He continued writing but was still virtually unknown until 1924, when a quarrel of literary critics over the revolution's significance for literature brought his work to prominence. The hero of the novel is an imaginary revolutionary chieftain, Demetrio Macías, not completely barbarous but also without those ideals and that consciousness of human direction that would expose him to ordinary value judgments. As his career proceeds from minor leadership of a group of discontented Indians to the position of general under Villa, he comes to be identified with the organic growth and decline of the revolution itself. In Demetrio Macías there is something both alien to man and larger than any single member of the species; he awakens a feeling, not of sympathy nor hate, but, like Achilles, of elemental wonder. Beneath the novelistic exterior of *Los de abajo* there are many reminders of the epic tradition. Other well-known novels by Azuela are *Mala yerba* (1909) ("Weeds"), *Las Moscas* (1918) ("Flies"), *La Malhora* (1923), and *San Gabriel de Valdivias* (1938). Azuela died in Mexico City on Mar. 1, 1952. S. G.

AZURITE [æ'zhurait], a blue copper carbonate mineral, with the composition $2CuCO_3 \cdot Cu(OH)_2$. It is closely associated with the green copper carbonate, malachite, but is much less common. The color of azurite is deep azure blue; this property, plus its effervescence in acid, suffices to distinguish the mineral from all others. Azurite and malachite are oxidation products, formed by the alteration of primary copper minerals by percolating waters containing oxygen and carbon dioxide. Azurite occurs in various copper districts in the southwestern states. The finest crystals of this mineral come from Tsumeb, South-West Africa. K. K. L.

AZUSA [æ zu'sə], a city in southwestern California, situated in the East San Gabriel Valley section of Los Angeles Co., 22 mi. east of the city of Los Angeles. It was founded in 1887 by Jonathon S. Slauson and incorporated as a city in 1898. It has the council-mayor form of government. Azusa is a busy industrial center which manufactures guided missiles, aircraft components, beverages, rock products, plastics, clothing, chemicals, fertilizers, resins, steel and cement products, foundries, and wheel goods. It is also a shipping point for the orange, lemon, avocado, grapefruit, tangerine, and walnut crops grown in the vicinity.

Azusa is the home of the Rainbow Angling Club and its famous trout pool and the gateway to San Gabriel Canyon and its various recreational areas, including Crystal Lake Park. Fishing, in season, is permitted in the Canyon, which is part of the Sierra Madre. Citrus Junior College and Pacific Bible College are the city's institutions of higher learning. Pop. 1950, 11,042; 1954, 15,087.

B

B. Since the early origins of the alphabet, *B* has retained its second position in the series of letters. The Semitic forms ꟙ ꟙ have been, in the main, only slightly modified in the history of the alphabet. On the Moabite stone discovered in 1868 at Dhibon (in the present state of Jordan) and dating from the ninth century B.C., the form is ꟙ. Early Greek forms appeared as ꟙ ꟙ, but the better-known styles are ꟙ β , which recur unchanged in the Etruscan and obviously are closely similar to the modern *B*. The Hebrew form ꟙ, named *beth*, developed from an early Semitic symbol which suggested the ground-floor plan of a house, whence its name in *bēth'ēl*, "house of God." The Greek *beta* retains the Phoenician word form. The minuscule *b* is an abbreviated *B* and first appeared in the Latin cursive ꟷ, from which the Carolingian ꟷ of the ninth and tenth centuries was derived. The accompanying table notes the typical forms from early times.

Pronunciation. All over Europe, *b* has approximately the same sound that it had in Latin (voiced labial stop). In southern Germany, however, including Austria and German Switzerland, the sound represented by *b* frequently approaches *p* so nearly that the two are confused, and people there used to speak of *hartes* (hard) *p* and *weiches* (soft) *b,* for purposes of spelling; *burg* is pronounced more or less like *purk*. In Spain the sign *b* represents two different sounds (a labial occlusive stop *b* in absolute initial position and after a nasal, and a bilabial voiced fricative *b* with bar or *β* in every other position); this difference is exclusively phonetic, not phonemic, and therefore the average Spaniard cannot perceive the difference between French *vient* and *bien*. The same is true in great part for Sardinia, southern Italy, and Sicily. In Modern Greek, *β* has taken the sound of a voiced fricative (like the Spanish *b* in noninitial position), and for the sound *b* it has had recourse to the curious digraph *μπ* (=mp), used mostly in foreign words; for example, *bálla* is written *μπάλλα*. The Cyrillic alphabet, which is of late Greek origin, has consequently kept the sign "B" for *v* (labiodental voiced fricative) and has created for the sound *b* (very frequent in Slavic languages) the new sign Б.

Uses. Like the letter *A,* the second letter of the alphabet is widely used as a sign. Because of its second position, *B* signifies the quality of "good" in school marks, commercial products, and services. In algebra, *b* is the second known quantity, as in (*a* + *b*). In footwear, *B* indicates a size wider than *A*. Musical notation employs it as a name of a note on the keyboard and on the treble and bass clefs, as well as the signature of a scale, B-flat, for example. In the mystical cabalist system of Biblical interpretation, it denotes the numeral 2, and in Elizabethan systems it had the same numerical value. In the form of the Greek *β* (*beta*) it is a sign in the physical sciences, including aeronautics. In outlining, *B* is used to indicate the second co-ordinate item, and *b* and (*B*) are used as the second subordinate. As geometrical forms, *B* and *b* appear to have no significant application, except to denote an angle. In chemistry, B is the symbol for boron.

As the first consonant, its name "bee" or "be" indicates no specific sound value apart from an accompanying vowel. In music, the German system of notation employs H instead of B, and B signifies B-flat; the B minor scale is known as H *moll*. B-flat is the key of most clarinets and many brasses in military bands. The soprano, tenor, and bass saxophones are voiced in B-flat, a medium-length clarinet indicates the scale

Origin	Form
Egyptian Hieroglyphics	ꟙ ꟙ ꟙ ꟙ
Semitic	ꟙ ꟙ ꟙ
Phoenician	ꟙ
Cypro-Phoenician	ꟙ
Early Hebrew	ꟙ
Greek Ninth Century B.C.	ꟙ
Greek Eighth Century B.C.	ꟙ
Crete Seventh Century B.C.	ꟙ ꟙ
Greek Classical Capitals	B
Greek Classical Uncials	β Ᏸ
Etruscan	ꟙ
Latin Fourth Century B.C. Capitals . .	B
Latin Third Century A.D. Uncials . .	ꟷ ꟷ
Cyrillic	Б Б
German	ℬ ꟷ
English	B ℓ

of B-flat, and bass clarinets are usually voiced in B-flat or A. *See also* ABBREVIATIONS; ALPHABET; SIGNS AND SYMBOLS; WRITING.   O. W. H-Q. and G. B.

BAADER, FRANZ XAVER VON [ba′dər] (1765-1841), German scientist and Catholic philosopher, was born March 27, 1765, in Munich. His career in science began with the study of medicine at the universities of Ingolstadt and Vienna and culminated in his position as superintendent of mines for Bavaria from 1817 to 1820. His career in philosophy began while in England from 1792 to 1796 with his study of Hume's empiricism and Böhme's mysticism. Repelled by the former, Baader developed his own philosophy and speculative theology on the latter, publishing his *Fermenta Cognitionis* in 1822. His reputation grew with his publications and he was appointed professor of theology and philosophy at the university in Munich in 1826. The lectures of his first year were published in 1827 under the title of *Spekulative Dogmatik*. His career ended in 1838 when the state forbade the teaching of theological subjects by laymen.

Baader, who has come to be regarded as the greatest Catholic thinker of modern times, developed a system of philosophy which strengthen's the Church's position within contemporary society and the state and at a time of social change. The tenets of faith rest in mysticism, the application of them in life is in a state ruled by the Church, redemption is through God's love, and an individual's self-realization comes through identification with God. Baader's influence continues to broaden and the bibliography of his works to increase. His collected works were published in Leipzig from 1851 to 1860 in sixteen volumes and his selected works in two volumes in 1886 and 1887.

BAAL [beʹəl], the great active figure in the cults of ancient Syria-Palestine, who was represented by a multitude of local deities. The name is derived from a Canaanite-Phoenician word that means "owner" or "lord." Philo and the Ugarit texts refer to him as Haddu (Hadad), the storm-god and king of the gods. In the fourteenth century B.C., Baal had already won among the Phoenicians the title Baal Shamen (Lord of Heaven). He was one of the brothers of El (The God), head of the Canaanite group of deities.

Referred to as Aliyan (I Prevail), he triumphed over the champions he encountered in battle. He came to be distinguished by the name of the locality in which he was adored and by the special character or function attributed to him. Every major aspect of religious life could, moreover, develop the cult of its own Baal. In general, he was credited with being the male author of fertility in soil and flock, and offerings in kind were presented to him at proper festivals.

The Baal of Tyre, referred to in the Old Testament, was known as Melkarth. The sanctuaries and shrines of Baal were frequently called "high places." As a mountain-deity and storm-god, he was portrayed in appropriate imagery. Associated with the female, Anath, his consort, he bore a special tie to the clan and was remembered through personal names.

E. J. J.

BAALBEK [baʹlbɛk; balbeʹk], now a small town but anciently a splendid temple-city, located in Lebanon between the Lebanon and Anti-Lebanon mountains. The broad valley between the two mountain ranges is called El Bekaa or Lowland and was formerly known as Coele Syria or "hollow Syria." The city is 3,850 ft. above sea level and lies between the Leontes and Orontes rivers. It is in a very fertile region and on the caravan route from Damascus to Tyre.

History. The city is named Baalbeki in Assyrian and Egyptian inscriptions, doubtless because of the worship there of a god who was called Baal and was later identified with Jupiter. The Greeks knew the city as Heliopolis, and the Emperor Augustus made it a Roman colony with the name Colonia Julia Augusta Felix Heliopolitana.

Baalbek attained its greatest splendor in the Roman period, and was a renowned center of the worship not only of Jupiter Heliopolitanus but also of Bacchus and of Venus. In the early part of the fourth century, according to the church historian Eusebius, the Emperor Constantine suppressed the licentious worship which had prevailed in Heliopolis and erected there a large Christian church of great magnificence.

In A.D. 635 the city was taken by the Arabs under Abu Ubaida. Relatively unprotected hitherto because its fame was only that of a cult center, the city was now strongly fortified by the Arabs, and the temple district and acropolis were transformed into a citadel. As an important fortress, Baalbek had a varied history during the Middle Ages. 'Ali and Mu'awiya, rivals for the caliphate, fought there in A.D. 659. El-Welīd (died 715) is said to have taken a dome of brass from a Baalbek church to be set up in the Dome of the Rock at Jerusalem. Marwān II (died 750) destroyed the walls, and Tughtakin of Damascus brought Baalbek under the control of that city in 1110. In 1175 it was taken by Saladin; in 1260 it was destroyed by the Mongol Hulagu; and in the latter part of the thirteenth century it was rebuilt by the Sultan Kalāwūn. Sacked by Tamerlane in 1400, partially destroyed by Jezzār of Acre in the eighteenth century, and damaged from time to time by severe earthquakes, Baalbek, under the Turks, had sunk by the nineteenth century to a small and insignificant town. Today, with a population of approximately 9,000, it is a resort town of the republic of Lebanon.

Archaeology. Excavations were conducted at Baalbek by a German expedition in the years 1898 to 1905; and the results of these investigations were published by Theodor

Temple remains of the ancient city of Heliopolis, now the modern town of Baalbek, Lebanon

Wiegand in four large volumes, which appeared between 1921 and 1925. In 1933 and 1934, French archaeologists undertook restorations at Baalbek.

The ruins of the acropolis of the ancient city lie west of the modern town. The entrance to the temple precinct was from the east, where a great stairway led up to the propylaea or monumental gateway. Here there was a colonnade about 165 ft. wide, flanked by square towers nearly 100 ft. high. Behind the tall columns of this portico, a large central door and two small side doors opened into a hexagonal forecourt. This court, which was some 20 ft. higher than the ground outside, was surrounded by a double colonnade and had four rectangular recesses.

Beyond the forecourt, three large doorways gave access to the Court of the Altar, in the center of which there stood originally a large altar. Half of this altar still stands, but the rest of it was destroyed, probably in the fourth century when a Christian cathedral was built in the court. On both sides of the altar there were basins for washing. Around three sides of the court were fine colonnades, and behind these were ornamented semicircular recesses. At the west side of the Court of the Altar a stairway of sixteen steps approached the temple terrace proper. This terrace was very large and was elevated more than 20 ft. above the altar-court. It was surrounded by a wall, composed in part of stone blocks of extraordinary size. Three of these on the west side have respective lengths of 63, 63.75, and 64 ft., and are each 13 ft. high and 10 ft. thick. A similar enormous stone, 70 by 14 by 13 ft. in size and weighing 1,000 tons, may be seen partly quarried on the hillside half a mile southwest of the modern town.

On the terrace stood the great temple of Jupiter. It was a rectangular structure, built in line with the main axis of the entire temple. The base of the temple was 300 ft. long and 170 ft. wide, and around this area were over 50 beautiful columns, 7½ ft. in diameter and 65 ft. high. Six of these columns still stand in an unbroken row on the south side, giving a powerful impression of the vertical proportions of the ancient temple.

The temple of Bacchus was built on a lower terrace, to the south of the temple of Jupiter. It is smaller than the temple of Jupiter, but it is much better preserved and is regarded as the most beautiful Roman monument in Lebanon. Even its size is by no means unimpressive, for it has an area larger than that of the Parthenon, and the forty-six columns with which it was surrounded had a height of 57 ft. The columns were originally arranged with fifteen on each side and eight on the ends; and along the north side nine of them are still preserved in an unbroken row, while others, either intact or broken, stand, lean, or lie prostrate on other sides. A beautifully ornamented portal gives access to the cella or enclosed inner portion of the temple, which was 87 ft. long and 75 ft. wide. The interior likewise was lavishly decorated, and at the west end the cult statue of Bacchus undoubtedly stood.

The third temple, dedicated to Venus, stands 1,000 ft. to the east of the acropolis. Likewise well preserved, it was a circular structure, originally domed with stone, and ornamented in the manner of the buildings of the acropolis.

The temple of Jupiter probably dates from the first century A.D., that of Bacchus from the second century, and that of Venus from the third.   J. F.

BABA [baˊba], in the Slavonic languages, a word meaning "old woman." It was also the name given to an old witch, Yaga Baba, who very often appeared in Russian folk tales. Yaga Baba was known as Ienzababa in Poland, and as Jazi Baba by the Czechs. She was a small, ugly old witch with bony legs, long teeth, and disheveled hair. She could travel in the sky sitting in a mortar, and she used a pestle to bring the mortar down to earth. The trail Yaga Baba left behind she swept with a broom. She ate children and hoarded precious metals.

BABBITT, IRVING [bæˊbɪt] (1865-1933), American moralist and critic, was born Aug. 2, 1865, in Dayton, O., the son of a physician and the grandson of a Congregational clergyman. Aided financially by affluent relatives, he was graduated from Harvard in 1889 and, after teaching at the University of Montana, studied Sanskrit and Pali at the Sorbonne under Sylvian Lévi from 1891 to 1892. He returned to Harvard to study for his M.A. under Prof. C. R. Lanman, and, after obtaining the degree in 1893, he taught Romance languages for a year at Williams College. In 1894 he returned to Harvard as an instructor and remained there for the remainder of his life, becoming a full professor of French in 1912. Babbitt was notably successful as a teacher and was frequently invited as an exchange lecturer to other universities. In 1923 he served in this capacity at the Sorbonne and at other times appeared at Yale, Amherst, Stanford, and at other leading colleges and universities. He died in Cambridge, Mass., July 15, 1933.

Babbitt's interest in humanistic doctrine dominated his entire life and exerted a wide influence on and through his students throughout his career. *The Rational Study of the Classics,* a lecture delivered at the University of Wisconsin in 1895, was his apprentice critique of Naturalism and Romanticism, and this studied aversion he elaborated encyclopedically in *Literature and the American College* (1908), *The New Laokoön* (1910), *The Masters of Modern French Criticism* (1912), *Rousseau and Romanticism* (1919), *Democracy and Leadership* (1924), *On Being Creative* (1932), and *Spanish Character* (1940). As Paul Elmer More, his sensitive companion in humanistic doctrine, has suggested, Babbitt's view of life, from book to book, followed "a kind of rotary movement instead of a regular progression." Thus, the potential student of Babbitt's doctrine can discover the assumptions and discipline of his humanistic challenge in any of the several volumes. Babbitt's significance did not lie in the events of his life, but during his professional career he exerted a profound influence on his students by the humanistic criteria which he uttered and phrased with Attic clarity and prophetic conviction.

Babbitt's humanism is rooted in the assumption that man, "placed on this isthmus of a middle state," is as distinct from God as from nature. It assumes that man is a divided creature in whom there is perpetual war between his ethical and impulsive selves, between his active will and the sloth and lethargy of the senses, between the restraint that achieves decorum and the spontaneous expansiveness that leads to anarchy and decadence. It assumes that man's will can direct his experience toward what is universally human. Stressing assimilation rather than self-expression, Babbitt looked for an expression of his principles to "that golden chain of masterpieces," especially the literature of Greece and the Orient, which seemed to him to offer evidence of moral values that persist; in general, he looked to literature prior to the eighteenth century, a time that heralded such doctrines as man's natural goodness, humanitarianism, and infinite progress. Concerned with what is central, inner, and universal, Babbitt distrusted the efficacy of technological progress and humanitarian service; he thought them inadequate substitutes for the

Socratic self-knowledge and the Christian and Oriental humility that come from the study and imitation of the wisdom of the past. He desired to substitute inner self-control for the faith in external reform characteristic of his contemporaries. Babbitt's democracy idealized an aristocracy of intelligence and character even as it feared an aristocracy of birth and wealth; he employed all of his moral vigor in assaulting modern man's optimistic faith in the machine, science, indiscriminate sympathy, and impulsive emotionality unchecked by reason.   C. E. J.

BABBITT, ISAAC (1799-1862), American inventor, was born in Taunton, Mass., July 26, 1799. Early in life he was apprenticed to a goldsmith, and became interested in the production of alloys. He experimented with the manufacture of britannia ware, and in 1824 successfully cast the alloy and commenced marketing the first britannia ware ever produced in the United States. In partnership with William Crossman he built a factory in Taunton, Mass., in 1827, but when

BABBLERS, an enormous and ill-defined assemblage of small to medium-sized songbirds, commonly combined in the so-called family Timaliidae, but better treated as a mere subfamily of the insect eaters or Muscicapidae, which embraces also the great aggregations of Old World warblers, thrushes, and flycatchers. The babblers are widespread in the tropical and subtropical regions of Africa, Asia, and Australasia. The typical members of the group are poor fliers, but have strong bills and feet; they live on or near the ground in forests or thickets, and are inconspicuously clothed in black, white, grays, browns, and yellows. Other forms, probably incorrectly placed with them, are partly or wholly arboreal, and wear yellows, reds, and even blues, or striking combinations of black and white. The name is derived from the noisy chatter of many of the species.   H. G. De.

BABEL, TOWER OF [be′bəl], built, according to Biblical tradition, by the descendants of Noah in the land of Shinar (Babylonia). Its purpose was to reach heaven. God,

THE TOWER OF BABEL

FROM A PAINTING BY
PIETER BRUEGHEL THE ELDER

BY BURTON HOLMES
FROM EWING GALLOWAY

business declined a few years later they sold out to their apprentices and Babbitt went to work in Boston as superintendent of the South Boston Iron Works, also known as Cyrus Alger's Foundry. There he produced the first brass cannon ever cast in the United States, and in 1839 obtained a patent on a journal box of his design, which included the formula for a soft alloy to be used as a bearing metal for lining the boxes of axles. This latter relatively incidental detail proved to be the most valuable element of his invention, and is still used and referred to as Babbitt's metal. Babbitt received a gold medal from the Massachusetts Mechanical Society in 1841 for his invention, and in 1842 was voted a $20,000 reward by Congress. Later in life he was associated with a relative in the manufacture of soap. Babbitt's last days were spent at the McLean Asylum for the mentally ill in Somerville, Mass., where he died May 26, 1862.   C. W. D.

displeased with the aim and action of the builders, confused their tongues, so that they could not understand one another, and scattered them over the earth, all speaking different languages. The city where the tower was built was given the name *Babel,* a word derived, according to the etymology suggested in Genesis xi:1-9, from the Hebrew root *balal* meaning "to confuse." This Biblical narrative is an ancient attempt to explain the origin of the various languages of the world.

Historically considered, the city of Babel, situated on the banks of the Euphrates and the capital of Babylonia since the days of Hammurabi, was famous for its temple, *Sag-illa,* the name of which means "reaching to the clouds." This temple very likely was built by Hammurabi, who also built a temple, *Miti-ursagga,* whose "top he carried up as high as heaven." The name *Babel* comes from the Babylonian *bab-ilu,* meaning "gate of God."   M. A. G.

BAB EL MANDEB [ba'b ɛl ma'ndɛb; ba'b ɛl mɑ'ndɛb], a strait connecting the Red Sea and the Gulf of Aden. Yemen and the British Protectorate of Aden are on the eastern side; French Somaliland and Eritrea are on the western side. Perim Island lies in the strait, separating it into two channels; the western is 16 mi. wide; the eastern, 2 mi. The strait controls the southern approach to the Suez Canal. Bab el Mandeb has been nicknamed both "the Gate of Mourning," because of the danger of the passage to sailing ships, and "the Exile's Gate," because Europeans bound for the Orient and Australia must sail through it.   S. Van V.

BABENBERG, HOUSE OF [ba'bǝnbɛrχ], a family of ancient and noble origin which ruled Austria from 976 to 1246. Babenberg Castle, near the town of Bamberg in northern Bavaria, was the seat of this Franconian dynasty. Among the first Babenbergs of prominence was Poppo, Count Grabfeld, who lived in the ninth century, and who numbered among his sons Henry, duke and margrave of Franconia (d. 886), and Poppo, margrave of Thuringia. In 892, the Conradines, bitter rivals of the Babenbergs, ousted the younger Poppo from his possessions. This good fortune they owed to the patronage of the German king, Arnulf. In the feud which followed, Poppo's heirs were killed and the family sank into obscurity, not to rise again until 976 when Leopold I (Luitpold), Count in Donnegau, a descendant of the counts of Babenberg, was appointed margrave of Austria by Emperor Otto II. The Babenberg margraves (later dukes) of Austria proved able both in administrative and military affairs. The most famous member of the family was Leopold III the Pious (1075-1136), canonized in 1485, who reigned from 1095 to 1136 and who in 1125 refused the emperor's crown. When Richard I of England passed through Germany on his return from the Third Crusade, it was Leopold V (1177-1194) of this ducal line who took Richard, his personal enemy, captive and turned him over to Emperor Henry VI to be held for heavy ransom. The Babenberg family died out when Frederick II (1211-1246), duke of Austria and Styria, known as the Quarrelsome, was killed in battle in the sixteenth year of his reign. Their possessions passed to the Hapsburgs.
                    R. H. L.

BABER, BABUR, or **BABAR** [ba'bǝr] (1483-1530), conqueror of India and founder of the Mogul dynasty, was born in 1483. He was a descendant of the great Mongol emperor Genghis Khan through his second son, Jagatai, and from the equally renowned Turkish chieftain Timur, or Tamerlane. His name was Zahir ud-Din Muhammad, and his surname Baber, meaning "tiger," was derived from the Mongols. In 1495 he succeeded his father, Sheikh Omar Mirma, as king of Ferghana, a realm in western Turkestan, but was driven out by intrigues and revolts on the fringes of his domain. By 1501 he had lost almost all of his parental heritage, but through a series of daring military exploits he soon recaptured Kashgar, Kunduz, Kandahar, and Kabul—the last-named in 1504—as steps toward the subjection of Hindustan. Attempts to reconquer his capital at Samarkand having failed, he penetrated Hindustan in 1519-1524 and crossed the Indus River in 1525. He overthrew the Afghan sultan, Ibrahim Lodi, established his government at Delhi, and in 1527 won a decisive victory at Agra. The remaining years of Baber's life at Delhi were disturbed by insurrections. Nevertheless, his short reign in the Ganges valley was renowned for administrative reforms and the construction of great public works. He died Dec. 26, 1530, and was succeeded by his son, Humayun.   B. La.

BABINGTON PLOT [bæ'bɪŋtǝn] (1585), a conspiracy in 1585 to murder Queen Elizabeth and put Mary, Queen of Scots, upon the throne of England. The plot was largely the work of one of Mary's pages, Anthony Babington, and a Roman Catholic priest, John Ballard. They had secured promises of assistance from Philip II of Spain. From the beginning the plot was known to Sir Francis Walsingham, Elizabeth's secretary of state and spymaster. Babington's correspondence in code with Mary, who had long been imprisoned in England, passed through the hands of royal spies. It is probable that Walsingham actually encouraged the plotters in order to secure evidence against Mary. In 1586 Babington, Ballard, and others of the conspirators were arrested, tried, and executed. In 1587 Mary was beheaded at Fotheringay Castle as a result of her participation in the plot.
                    E. R. A.

BABIRUSA or **BABIROUSSA** [bæ'bɪru'sǝ], *Babirussa babirussa,* a wild hog of Celebes and other islands of the Malay Archipelago. The upper canine teeth of the male are

BABIRUSA

extraordinary. They grow vertically through the nose, emerge from the face, curve backward toward the eyes, and then may bend downward. Having no enamel, they continue to grow as long as the animal lives, and may exceed 16 in. in length. The lower canines grow upward, outside the upper jaw, and project an inch or more beyond the lips. These tusks may well have been useful during earlier stages of the animal's evolution, wearing down as fast as they grew. Now, however, they are nothing more than an excrescence. Slenderer and longer-legged than the domestic swine, the babirusa has a dark gray skin roughened by a labyrinth of wrinkles. The Celebes race is practically bare of hair, while that of Buru is well covered with gray hair. Perhaps because of its tusks, the babirusa does not root like other swine but feeds on green vegetation and fallen fruits. Standing up to 27 in. tall at the shoulder, it weighs as much as 128 lb. Its flesh is considered excellent for eating. The species has been depleted to a dangerously low level and may become extinct.   V. H. C.

BABISM [ba'bɪzǝm], a modern religious movement which was founded in Iran (Persia) in 1844 by Mirza Ali Mohammed ibn-Radhik of Shiraz (1819-1850). Ibn-Radhik believed himself to be the Imam and Bab (from the Arabic word meaning "gate") of revelation. Using the theory of progressive revelation, he preached that no ostensible truth was final. He adopted the title of Bāb-ud-Din ("Gate of the Faith") and forbade polygamy and concubinage, mendicancy, the use of intoxicants and drugs, and slave dealing.

Cast into jail, he was put to death in 1850 and the authorities then determined to exterminate the Babis.

Among the leaders of the early Babis was Mirza Husayn Ali, eldest son of a wealthy minister of state. Mirza Husayn, known to the believers as Bahā'u'llāh ("Glory of God"), eventually became founder of Baha'ism, another and more important offshoot of Islam. Persecuted at home, his believers settled in Baghdad, then in Constantinople, where they remained until they established a permanent home in Acre, Palestine. From Acre the teachings of Bahā'u'llāh (1817-1892) and his successor, Abdul Baha (1844-1921), were carried into many distant lands. The Babism of Bāb-ud-Din is significant, therefore, both for its own sake and because it was the precursor of international Baha'ism; Babism and Baha'ism are branches of Shiite Islam.

The first Babis withdrew from the Shiite community of Twelvers, beginning, like the more radical Ismailis, to speak about a manifestation of the godhead. Fadl'u'llāh, fourteenth-century founder of the Shiite Hurufis, indirectly influenced the Babis to find cabalistic, mystical meaning in combinations of letters; he had, also, proclaimed himself a manifestation of God. The Babi-Baha'i movement had its predecessors, therefore; its link with the Shiite heritage being close. Babism may be considered a reform sect within Islam, whereas the world-wide religion of the Baha'is in its present character is something unique. Baha'ism constitutes a union of many conflicting creeds and doctrines, many ideals and mystic philosophies; it is an attempt to establish a new religious synthesis for mankind. *See also* BAHA'I MOVEMENT, THE.   E. J. J.

BABITS, MIHÁLY [bɒ'bɪtsh] (1883-1941), Hungarian poet and author, born in Szekszárd, Nov. 26, 1883, was graduated from Budapest University. His literary activity began in 1907 with the appearance of his poems in the Nagy-varad anthology, *Holnap*. In 1908 he began to devote himself to writing, and he contributed regularly to the *Nyugat* ("West"), a magazine devoted to modern literature. After 1917 he edited *Nyugat* and raised its standards to a high level, his work influencing creative writing in Hungary. He was also successful with his novels and short stories, and master-fully translated Dante's *Inferno* and *Purgatorio*. Babits trans-lated portions of the works of Shakespeare, Oscar Wilde, Goethe, Charles Baudelaire, and Paul Verlaine, and published two volumes of these translations, *Peacock Feathers* (1920) and *Erato* (1921). Among his verse collections are *Recitative* (1916), *Leaves from Iris' Wreath* (1920), and *Valley of Restlessness* (1920). His novels are *Stork Caliph,* (1919), *The Card House* (1925), *Madonna of the Night* (1927), and his greatest book, *Sons of Death,* which presents a picture of social changes before and after World War I. Babits died Aug. 4, 1941.   L. A. V.

BABOL or **BABUL** [babu'l], formerly known as Bar-furush the largest town in Mazanderan Province, Iran, 15 mi. south of the Caspian Sea, on the east bank of the Babol River. It is 165 mi. northeast of Tehran by a modern motor road that traverses a high pass in the Elburz Mountains. Near-by Babolsar has air-line service. To the southeast of Babol, which was founded in the sixteenth century, are the remains of a royal garden constructed by Abbas the Great, shah from 1586 to 1628. Because of the heavy rainfall of the region, the houses are usually roofed with tile or thatch. Dense forests of the vicinity contrast with the bare hills and mountains of the arid Iranian Plateau. Riza Shah Pahlavi, ruler of Iran from 1925 to 1941 and a native of Mazanderan Province, did much to improve the port and highway facilities of Babol. The city is a center for business of the region and for export to the Soviet Union. There are several large establishments for the baling and shipping of cotton; citrus fruits and tobacco are also important items of trade. Pop. 1944, 33,656.   J. C. Wi.

BABOON, a doglike and principally terrestrial primate, *Papio* and related genera, inhabitating Africa and Arabia. The limbs of these animals are of approximately equal length, their muzzles of great size, and the nostrils terminal. The canine teeth of the males are particularly long. The tail is generally short, and, in some species, is almost completely absent. When long, the tail is carried arched at the base, the end hanging straight down. The naked skin areas, especially of the sex organs, are often brightly colored; bright yellow, blue, and rose are frequent.

Well-known species of baboon are the chacma, *P. comatus,*

STREET SCENE IN BABOL, IRAN

EWING GALLOWAY

a very large species of South Africa; the gelada, *Theropithecus gelada,* of Abyssinia, whose long, hairy mantle, tufted tail, and bare red chest (in the male) are familiar in zoological parks; the hamadryad, *Comopithecus hamadryas,* of North Africa, which was identified in ancient Egypt with the god Thoth; the Egyptian baboon, *P. doguera,* also deified by the Egyptians, but trained by them to gather figs for their masters; the West African drill, *Mandrillus leucophaeus;* and the mandril, *Mandrillus sphinx.*

Baboons live in droves of as many as 300, which forage over the ground, or in trees, for their varied food. These groups are led by one or more old males, and sentries guard the group. Bushbucks and wild pigs sometimes mingle with these bands, but separate when alarmed.

Baboons are savage by nature, and old individuals tend to be quite ferocious. The usual sound of alarm or anger is a bark or cough. The young hang on the underside of the females, and are solicitously tended.

Baboons are extremely destructive to field crops and fruit trees, which the large bands frequently raid. They move away only before an armed man, sometimes walking three-legged, carrying an armful of corn. The chacma, a particu-

BABOON   YLLA

larly large and destructive species of South Africa, is said to kill lambs and kids to obtain the milk in their stomachs.

Leopards use baboons as a staple item of diet, but in daylight the baboons can defend themselves and four or more will attack a leopard. Man is also a constant enemy, but baboons are dangerous to approach and have been known to mutilate unarmed persons.   R. T. H.

BABOON ROOT, a genus, *Babiana,* of the iris family comprising about fifty species, native to South Africa. They are bulbous plants having broad, veined leaves; the flower stalk rises as high as 12 in., and is crowned with clusters of fragrant flowers, usually red, blue, or purplish. *B. stricta* is the species usually grown as an ornamental. In mild climates it can be grown in gardens, but in the northern United States the bulbs are grown in pots under glass.   J. C. Wis.

BABSON, ROGER WARD (1875-   ), American statistician and economist, was born at Gloucester, Mass., on July 6, 1875. He attended the local schools and was graduated from Massachusetts Institute of Technology in

1898. After working for a Boston investment firm, Babson organized his own bond-selling business in New York, and later joined a public utility bond firm. He moved to Wellesley Hills, Mass., began to publish his analyses and tabulations of business reports for bankers, and in 1904 incorporated the Babson Business Statistical Organization, designed to

ROGER W. BABSON

WIDE WORLD PHOTO

inform and protect the investor in relation to the safe and profitable use of his funds. He invented the "Babsonchart," distributed the Babson Reports Service, and contributed a column "Be Right with Babson" to a New York newspaper. Early in World War I, Babson became secretary of the Society to Eliminate the Economic Causes of War and served as director general of information and education under the United States secretary of labor. He wrote *Why Are We Fighting?,* a booklet for the armed forces, in 1917. In 1919 he founded Babson Institute near Wellesley Hills, one of the first business schools of its kind, offering courses in finance, production, distribution, and personal efficiency. Webber College, a similar school for women, was founded at Babson Park, Fla., in 1927. In 1923 Babson formed his own newspaper syndicate service, Publishers Financial Bureau. He was moderator of the General Council of the Congregational Christian Churches of the United States of America, 1936-1938, and was unanimously nominated for the presidency by the American Prohibition Party in 1940. His autobiography, *Actions and Reactions,* appeared in 1935; he has published many other books and pamphlets, and his *Looking Ahead Fifty Years* appeared in 1942.

BABUL. *See* Babol.

BABY BLUE-EYES, *Nemophila menziesi,* a charming, low-growing annual of the waterleaf family, with vivid blue, cup-shaped flowers about 1 in. wide. It is a native of moist places in California and is cultivated in gardens. J. C. Wis.

BABY BONDS. *See* Banking, Investment.

BABYLON [bæ'bɪlən], the ancient and famous capital of Babylonia, located on the banks of the Euphrates River about 55 mi. south of modern Baghdad and just north of Hilla. Its old Semitic name was Bab-ilu, meaning "gate of god," a designation which became Babel in Hebrew, and Babylon in Greek and Latin. The original name was

RUINS OF THE OLD CITY OF BABYLON WHERE SCULPTURED ANIMALS EMBOSS THE ANCIENT BUILDING WALLS.

preserved through the centuries, and, in the form Babil, is still attached to the most northerly mound at the site. The excavation of the tremendous complex of ruins which represents the ancient city was undertaken in 1899 by the Deutsche Orientgesellschaft, under the direction of Robert Koldewey, and continued thereafter for many years.

Babylon emerges into the light of history in the Old Babylonian Period (c.1850-c.1600 B.C.). At the beginning of this period, the previously insignificant town of Bab-ilu in Akkad became the capital of a small kingdom ruled by a man who bore an Amorite name, Sumu-abu. While little is otherwise known of this king, he became the founder of the important First Dynasty of Babylon. His successors were Sumu-la-el, Sabum, Apil-Sin, Sin-muballit, and Hammurabi, a king formerly believed to have ruled about 1900 B.C. but more recently dated on good authority as late as 1700 B.C. Hammurabi was the greatest ruler of his period and was outstanding both in military accomplishment and in administrative work. By defeating Rim-Sin, of Larsa, Hammurabi became master of Sumer, in the lower Mesopotamian Valley, as well as of his own Akkad; and by destroying the city of Mari he extended the power of the Old Babylonian Kingdom far up the Euphrates. The effective administration of this kingdom is attested by numerous letters written by Hammurabi giving instructions relative to details of rule; and the king's work as a law giver is shown by the famous Code of Hammurabi, a copy of which was found at Susa.

Excavations in the central Merkes Mound at Babylon reached a stratum lying partly above and partly below the twentieth-century water level and dating from the time of the First Dynasty and of Hammurabi. The evidences are that the city was already planned with straight streets intersecting each other at right angles. The houses found had mud brick walls resting upon burnt brick foundations.

Samsuiluna, the immediate successor of Hammurabi, was threatened by an invasion of Kassites from the eastern mountains. He repelled them successfully for a time, but they continued to penetrate the country and eventually overthrew the First Babylonian Dynasty. The dynasty of the Kassites then ruled in Babylon for half a millennium (c.1600-c.1175 B.C.). The excavation of the Kassite stratum of the Merkes Mound showed that the arrangement of the city in streets and blocks of houses had remained practically the same as in the time of Hammurabi. The houses of this period were made of mud brick and generally lacked the burnt brick foundations characteristic of Hammurabi's city. The pottery was of a distinctively different kind, and particularly noteworthy was the abundance of jewelry and ornaments found.

The Kassite Dynasty was succeeded by the Pashe Dynasty, which held sway for over a century; its leading king, Nebuchadnezzar I, ruled with some brilliance. Thereafter, however, throughout the greater part of the Middle Babylonian Period the land was under the domination of Assyria. Sargon of Assyria built a thick wall with round corner tower at the southern citadel of Babylon, and left on its bricks an inscription which begins as follows: "To Marduk! the great Lord, the divine creator who inhabits Esagila, the Lord of Babil, his lord; Sargon the mighty king, King of the land of Ashur, King of all, Governor of Babil, King of Sumer and Akkad, the nourisher of Esagila and Ezida." Sennacherib completely destroyed the city because of its constant rebelliousness, and even deflected the Euphrates to wipe out large areas of it. Esarhaddon, however, pursued a policy of conciliation, and restored and rebuilt the city. His repair of Esagila is evidenced by a pavement still in place at the ruins of this temple.

The New Babylonian Empire (612-539 B.C.) was inaugurated when Nabopolassar, a Chaldean, seized the kingship of Babylon and joined with other allies to destroy Nineveh, capital of Assyria. He was succeeded by his son Nebuchadnezzar II (605-562 B.C.), under whom Babylon reached its greatest glory. A "colossal rebuilding of the entire city," as the German excavators put it, now took place. Marduk's temple Esagila, the ziggurat Etemenanki, the temple of Emach on the Citadel, and the older Ishtar temple in Merkes, all were rebuilt. The southern citadel was completed with the king's own palace, and a new palace was erected far to the north. Earlier city walls were restored, a great outer wall was constructed to surround the enlarged city, canals were dug, and the first stone bridge was built across the Euphrates. The Hanging Gardens came to be regarded as one of the wonders of the world, but modern excavations have failed to identify their ruins with certainty. Most splendid of all, as far as extant remains go, were the Ishtar Gate and the Procession Street, which were given their latest form and decorated with friezes of bulls, dragons, and lions executed in enameled colored brick. The colors of these bricks, as well as of those which provided ornamental patterns for the king's throne room, are still bright and beautiful. The last king of this period was Nabonidus (Nabū-na'id), who shared the rule of Babylon with his oldest son Belshazzar. The work of Nabonidus, revealed by the excavations, included the new Ishtar temple in Merkes and a strong fortification wall on the banks of the Euphrates.

Babylon fell to Cyrus the Great on Oct. 13, 539 B.C., as the Chronicle of Nabonidus and the Cylinder of Cyrus both record. We have descriptions of Babylon in the time of the Persian kings written by Herodotus and by Ctesias, physician to Artaxerxes II; from the reign of Artaxerxes II we have the ruins of a building on the southern citadel. Before the conquests of Alexander the Great, however, it is clear that the decline of Babylon had begun. Alexander proposed extensive restorations, but died before he could carry them out. The demolition of the ancient royal structures and the use of their bricks for other buildings commenced in the Greek and Parthian periods and continued through the centuries, until the once proud world capital was reduced to the vast complex of ruins which first met the gaze of modern archaeologists. J.F.

BABYLONIA AND ASSYRIA [bæbɪlo'niə, asɪ'riə]. Ancient Babylonia comprised the Tigris-Euphrates plain from modern Baghdad, in the northwest, to the Persian Gulf, in the southeast. Before the rise of the city of Babylon to political importance about 1850 B.C., the same area was known as Sumer (in the southeast) and Akkad (in the northwest). Assyria lay north of Babylon along the upper Tigris and the waters of the Great and Little Zab rivers; its modern boundaries would be Iran in the east, Turkey in the north, and Syria in the west. In general, modern Iraq, north of the Euphrates, includes most of the ancient territory of Babylonia and Assyria.

Sumerian Period. The Sumerians, the first civilized inhabitants of the Babylonian plain, took possession of the southeastern area around the Persian Gulf as early as 5000 B.C. There they drained the swamps, practiced flood control, and established agriculture on a permanent basis. Developing trade with surrounding areas and building up an industrial

(Left) *Babylon's one-time Triumphal Gateway of the Goddess Ishtar on the Processional Road of the God Marduk.* (Right) *A massive smooth-sculptured statue of the ancient city.*

economy which included metalworking and the manufacture of textiles and pottery, the Sumerians by 3500 B.C. had a complex culture, which was characterized by urban life, a well-developed region, and an efficient system of writing (cuneiform). Their civilization was adopted by the Semites (Akkadians) who lived in the northwestern part of the plain. The history of Sumer and Akkad between 2700-1850

administration of justice, the direction of agricultural production, and the collection of taxes. The clay tablets which were the business documents of the Babylonians show an economic life amazing in its complexity; among the classes of business records represented are receipts, loans, contracts, leases, transfers, inventories, and ledgers. Although private persons held large tracts of land, other land belonged to the

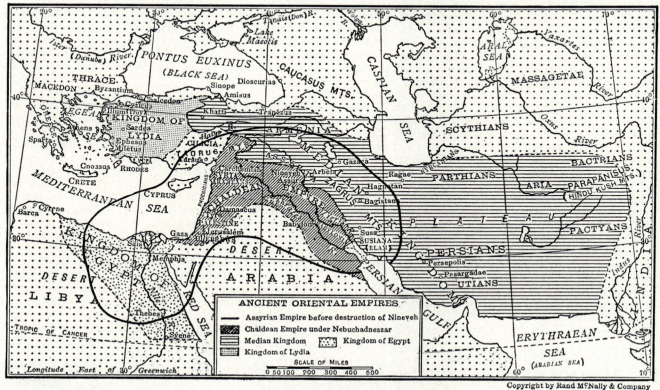

ANCIENT ORIENTAL EMPIRES

B.C. was largely one of conflict between the various Sumerian city-states themselves, and wars between Sumerians and Akkadians.

The Sumerian-Akkadian period came to an end about 1850 B.C., when a new Semitic people, the Amorites, invaded the plain and established themselves at Babylon. Gradually the city of Babylon extended its political influence over the Tigris-Euphrates valley until about 1700 B.C., when Hammurabi, the sixth Amorite king, completed the process of Babylonian expansion by the establishment of an empire which included Sumer, Akkad, Assyria, and perhaps Syria. The city of Babylon was the capital of this wide realm, and the area once called Sumer and Akkad was henceforth called Babylonia.

Complex Economy. Although the civilization of the Babylonians in the time of Hammurabi was based upon that of the early Sumerians, the official language became Semitic. The Sumerian elements in the population had lost their identity. There were three main social classes: an upper class composed of a feudal landed nobility, the civil and military officials of the bureaucracy, and the priests; a middle class of merchants, craftsmen, scribes, and professional men; and a lower class of small landholders, urban and rural workers, and a horde of slaves. Under Hammurabi, the Babylonian government was a well-organized bureaucracy headed by the king and his ministers. The government concerned itself with national defense, the

crown or the priests; the land was worked by free men, slaves, and serfs. There were also tenant farmers, who might be either renters or sharecroppers.

Many Babylonian craftsmen owned their shops, but others worked in the palaces and temples for board and wages. The apprentice system was universal, and the craftsmen were enrolled in guilds with others who plied the same trades. There was trade with Egypt, Syria, the northern hills, and India. In this trade the media of exchange were gold, silver, and copper, and the Babylonian system of weights and measures became standard throughout the Near East.

From this early Sumerian-Babylonian civilization have come many culture traits in our own modern civilization. These ancient people were the first to employ the seven-day week and the 24-hour day (with twelve double hours). Great advances were made (for calendrical purposes) in the study of astronomy, and astrology was of great importance. The Babylonians mastered the various arithmetical processes and the simpler geometric manipulations concerned with land measurement. Recent studies have shown also that Babylonian algebra was more advanced than that of the Greeks.

Kassite Rule. This early phase of Babylonian history came to an end about 1600 B.C., when Babylonia was subjected to attacks by Indo-European invaders from the north. The Hittites, who had established themselves firmly in Asia

Minor, sacked Babylon some years after the death of Hammurabi, and then the Kassites from Elam descended upon the plain to destroy the Amorite dynasty and replace it with kings drawn from the Kassite ranks.

With the Kassite occupation of Babylonia, the rise of Assyria as an independent state began. In the time of Hammurabi, Assyria had been a province of Babylonia, but the Kassites were unable to keep the Assyrians in subjection. Thus, along the upper Tigris, the warlike, predominantly

reached the Mediterranean Sea in the west, and penetrated Babylonia. Ashurnasirpal II, who boasted that he had "no rival among the princes of the Four Quarters of the World," campaigned against one or another enemy of Assyria almost every year of his long reign, and his successors followed his example. Nevertheless, a century of such sustained effort had its necessary reaction, and the Assyrian state collapsed into a temporary anarchy after an eclipse of the sun in 763 B.C.

THE HANGING GARDENS OF BABYLON

Semitic Assyrians began to lay the foundations for an empire larger than any of its predecessors.

Historical Periods. The history of Assyria after its first rise to national greatness falls into three main periods:

I. 1300-1100 B.C. The first problem of the Assyrians was to secure their frontiers. On the west were the once-powerful Mitannians, to the north the Urartu around Lake Van, to the east the Elamite tribes, and to the south the Kassites. During the first part of this period there was continuous fighting with the Mitannians and Urartu led by the great Assyrian king, Shalmaneser I, and his successors. By the end of the period, when defensible frontiers had been secured on the east, north, and west, the Assyrians were able, under Tiglath-pileser I, to turn their attention to the south in Babylonia, where the Kassite dynasty had recently fallen (1169 B.C.). At the end of the twelfth century B.C., Tiglath-pileser captured Babylon, but the Assyrians were unable to retain it after his death, when the pressure from the Hittites in Syria forced them to turn their attention once more to the west.

II. 885-763 B.C. After two centuries of confusion (1100-900 B.C.) following the death of Tiglath-pileser I, the Assyrians emerged at the beginning of the ninth century B.C. as a completely militarized state. Under three great warrior-kings—Ashurnasirpal II, Shalmaneser II, and Adadnirari III—whose reigns cover the period 885-783 B.C., the Assyrians once more secured their frontiers in the north and east,

III. 745-612 B.C. By 745 B.C. order in Assyria had been restored by Tiglath-pileser III, who also accomplished the reconquest of Babylonia and was crowned king in the ancient city of Hammurabi in 728. Under Sargon II, who established a new Assyrian dynasty in 722 B.C., the Assyrians began a truly imperial age. It was Sargon II who captured and deported the Israelites, destroyed the Hittite fortress of Carchemish, and extended his realm to the borders of Egypt. Sennacherib (705-681 B.C.) carried the Assyrian standards into Elam and also destroyed the city of Babylon after it had revolted in 689. Esarhaddon (681-669 B.C.) in 671 carried out the conquest of Egypt; and between 669 and 626 B.C., during the reign of his son Ashurbanipal, the Assyrian empire attained its greatest limits and began to disintegrate. New invasions of the Near East by the Cimmerians and Scythians and the rise of nationalism in Media and Babylonia saddened the last years of Ashurbanipal and sapped the military and financial reserves of Assyria. A combined force of Medes, Babylonians, and Scythians captured the Assyrian capital of Nineveh in 612 B.C., and thus brought the independence of Assyria to an end.

Assyrian Civilization. Assyrian civilization was patterned after the Babylonian, though the Assyrians were responsible for a number of important innovations. The formation of their empire has been called the first real attempt at political organization in the ancient world. Conquered territories were divided into provinces, and all paid tribute to the king. In remote areas the provinces retained their own local governments, with officials who were vassals of the Assyrian ruler; other areas maintained native governments with Assyrian governors and garrisons, while still others were kept in complete subjection. Many cities enjoyed municipal autonomy under charters granted by the king. The Assyrian army was better organized and more versatile than any which had preceded it. War chariots were employed; there were both heavy and light armed infantrymen, as well as bowmen and slingers. The Assyrian engineers developed efficient siege machinery which the best-fortified cities could not withstand.

Scientific Progress. In chemistry and medicine the Assyrians made considerable progress beyond the points attained by the Babylonians. They were expert at working leather and making dyes. In medicine the Assyrians employed almost four hundred vegetable and mineral drugs. Medical texts reveal the use of charms and incantations in the treatment of disease, although in many cases more efficacious remedies were employed; for example, physicians used cold baths to reduce fever, and recognized that dental infections were responsible for some illnesses. There are also examples of psychiatry and mental healing.

Terrorist Methods. The Assyrians were masters of psychological warfare. They deliberately encouraged stories of their ferocity in combat and their implacable punishment for those who dared to oppose them. As a result, their enemies often fled before them without striking a blow, and their subjects hesitated to raise the standard of revolt. The official Assyrian inscriptions are full of bloodthirsty accounts of battle and the punishments meted out to the enemy. A few lines from the Annals of Ashurnasirpal II will suffice to illustrate this point:

> "I slaughtered them, and with their blood I dyed the mountain like crimson wool. . . . . The heads of their warriors I cut off, and I piled them in a heap . . . . and their young men and their maidens I burned in the fire. . . . . I slaughtered their inhabitants in great numbers—and the cities I burned with fire. . . . . From some I cut off their hands and their fingers, and from others their noses and their ears."

Nebuchadnezzar. After the fall of Assyria, Babylonia enjoyed a period of independence down to its capture by the Persians in 539 B.C. This last Babylonian kingdom, the Neo-Babylonian, began with a revolt in 625 B.C., when Nabopolassar, an Assyrian general, broke away from Assyria and later combined with Cyaxares, the Median king, to destroy Nineveh in 612 B.C. Nabopolassar's son was the famous Nebuchadnezzar, who reigned in Babylon from 605 to 562 B.C. Nebuchadnezzar is remembered as the builder of the Hanging Gardens and the king who carried off the Jews into their Babylonian captivity (587-586 B.C.). A contemporary Babylonian relief supports the Biblical tradition that some Jews were thrown into "fiery furnaces."

Persian Invasion. The last of the Neo-Babylonian rulers was Nabonidus (556-539 B.C.), who was supported by his son Belshazzar. Nabonidus was an elderly scholar and antiquarian who seems to have lacked the energy or competence to direct his kingdom in a critical period when other states, Lydia and Media, were crumbling before the advance of Persia under Cyrus the Great. In 539 B.C., when Cyrus finally turned his attention to Babylonia, he encountered little resistance. In fact, there is ground for suspicion that the Babylonians, particularly the priests, were willing to exchange Nabonidus for Cyrus.

After 539 B.C., Babylonia and Assyria ceased to be independent and passed successively under the rule of the Per-

sians, Alexander the Great, the Seleucids, the Parthians, and the other later conquerors of the Near East. The city of Babylon itself remained an important administrative center for many centuries, but the old cities of Assyria were abandoned. When Xenophon passed by the Assyrian capital of Nineveh at the end of the fifth century B.C., only a huge mound of earth remained to mark the site of a once thriving urban center. *See also* ASHURNASIRPAL; CIMMERIANS; CYRUS THE GREAT; HAMMURABI; HITTITE EMPIRE; NEBUCHADNEZZAR; SARGON II; SUMERIANS.   T. B. J.

BABYLONIAN AND ASSYRIAN ART. For the student of ancient art and archaeology, the term "Babylonian" applies to the whole southern region of Iraq (Mesopotamia) from approximately 34° N. lat. to the Persian Gulf, and from the Syrian Desert to the Zagros Mountains. The time span takes in a period from c. 5000 B.C. to 539 B.C., when Babylon fell to the Persians.

Archaeological excavations of the first half of the twentieth century, especially those after World War I, yielded great stores of objects disclosing the long development of art in this area from the earliest Sumerian beginnings through the succeeding Semitic cultures. Almost every variety of artistic form is exhibited among these remains, filling virtually the whole range from crude painting and incising of pottery to highly decorative mural designs; from early essays in carving cylinder seals to mature achievements in bas-relief; from grotesque human and animal forms of modeled clay to colossal but often beautifully proportioned sculptured statues; and from almost formless cast metal trinkets to superbly wrought gold and silver jewelry and inlay work.

It will be convenient to follow the development of Babylonian and Assyrian art through five well-defined periods:

I. Earliest Prehistoric (Sumerian) to Dynasty of Akkad, c. 2400 B.C.
II. Akkad Dynasty to end of First Dynasty of Babylon, c. 1600 B.C.
III. Kassite Dynasty, to c. 1100 B.C.
IV. Golden Age of Art in Assyria, ninth to seventh century B.C.
V. Neo-Babylonian Art, 604 to 539 B.C.

BABYLONIAN

The lack of stone and wood in the alluvial plain of southern Mesopotamia compelled the adoption of clay, present in great abundance, as building material and as the artistic medium for modeled objects in the earliest period. Throughout Babylonian history, indeed, the common building material was sun-dried or baked bricks, with bitumen serving as mortar, and palaces and temples of colossal size were erected on immense brick platforms to protect them from the periodic floods. The earliest buildings, however, were marsh-dwellers' huts made of bundles of reeds lashed together to form walls, and plastered with claylike mud.

During the first of three clearly defined prehistoric cultures of southern Mesopotamia, the so-called Ubaidian (from the remains found at Tell el Ubaid, dating from the late fifth millennium to the mid-fourth millennium B.C.) clay bricks came into use and larger buildings appeared. Artistic mosaic-like effects were produced on the mud-plastered walls by the pressing in, at intervals, of slender cone-shaped "nails" with flat heads, which were painted black and red. Finely formed, graceful, and often quite thin-walled pottery, incised or painted with free geometric designs, as well as hand-modeled, crudely shaped figurines, human and animal, also appeared here.

During the next prehistoric culture, called "Warkan," from the ancient Mesopotamian city known in Sumerian as Uruk, dating from the late fourth millennium, and in modern times known as Warka, temple buildings became more complex. At Uruk was the first ziggurat, or pyramid tower, consisting of several stages of decreasing size, with a shrine at the top, to be reached by ramps. The ziggurat became henceforth the most characteristic type of temple architecture in Mesopotamia. Here also appeared the earliest-known cylinder seals, small hard stone cylinders on which were carved, in intaglio, designs of human and animal figures, mythological and ritual scenes, and aspects of daily life. The cylinder seals were used to impress the owner's property mark or signature on various objects; when the seals were rolled on a

jeweler's art, such as gold and silver ornaments, filigree work, dagger sheaths, gold cups, and bowls, as well as an elaborate pair of inlaid panels of three registers each, known as the "War and Peace Standard," their scores of human and animal figures made of shell set in a lapis lazuli background.

With the establishment by Sargon of the Semitic Dynasty of Akkad, a marked improvement in bas-reliefs occurred, the best example being the "Victory Stele" of Sargon's supposed son, Naram-Sin (c. 2400 B.C.), which contains finely proportioned human figures, and reveals dramatic feeling and a keen sense of balance in composition. Sculpture in the round also shows development, more attention being given to careful portrayal of muscles and contours, facial and

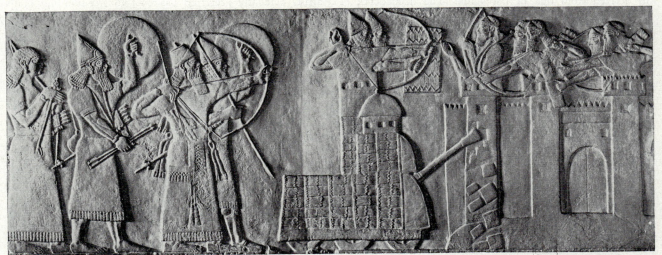

COURTESY OF THE METROPOLITAN MUSEUM OF ART

Alabaster bas-relief from the palace of Ashurnasirpal, King of Assyria (884-859 B.C.), at Nimrud, depicting the king attacking a city

soft clay surface, a small bas-relief was produced, which, if extended over a longer soft surface, could be used to execute a continuous frieze of indefinite length. This form of glyptic art became highly elaborated and perfected in later periods and constituted Babylonia's most original contribution to decorative art.

The third prehistoric culture, the Jemdet-Nazr, so called from the ruins found at that hill, near the site of the ancient city of Kish (end of fourth or beginning of third millennium B.C.), was in many respects inferior to its predecessor, but shows advances in the art of sculpture in stone, both in bas-relief and in the round, the latter being represented by a well-executed figure of a crouching wild boar.

In the early dynastic period (c. 2800 B.C.), metalwork assumed importance, as can be seen in surviving engraved metal vases, depicting scenes of the hunt and religious ceremonies involving men and deities. Animals were represented, sometimes in bas-relief, sometimes as protomas with heads disengaged, their eyes made of inlaid colored stones, with tongues of the same materials, and horns, if any, of gold. Sculpture in the round was mostly of human figures, but quite ill-proportioned and squat. Large bas-relief friezes, from Tell el Ubaid, depicting a milking scene and other domestic activities, and the famous "Vulture Stele" of King Eannatum of Lagash, showing the king attacking and vanquishing his enemies and burying the dead, illustrate the realism and vigor with which the artists of the early third millennium executed their work. The contemporary Royal Tombs at Ur have yielded some exquisite examples of the

other details. At this time there was a flowering of art that left its influence upon succeeding periods.

A brief Sumerian revival came in with Gudea of Lagash (c. 2350 B.C.) and the Third Dynasty of Ur, the principal monuments of which are the numerous black diorite statues of Gudea himself, rather rigid and heavy in form but with muscular and facial details well executed, and many other male and female statues, reliefs, and carved vases. There exists from this period one beautiful female head of ivory that shows great artistic skill.

A stele of Ur-Nammu (c. 2200 B.C.) of the Third Dynasty of Ur depicts in five registers the building of the famous ziggurat of Ur, the finest surviving example of this type of building in Mesopotamia. This stele presents the earliest-known portrayal of angels in art. The long lines of the Ur ziggurat are said to have been slightly curved to give the impression of beauty and lightness to the colossal structure.

A general decline in artistic ability marked the succeeding Semitic First Dynasty of Babylon, the Hammurabi Dynasty (c. 1800 B.C.), whose one outstanding monument is the well-known Stele of Hammurabi (Law Code), at whose top appears a bas-relief showing the king receiving the laws from the sun-god, Shamash, but the workmanship is stiff and clumsy. Other forms of art of this period show similar inferiority, statues in the round being generally poor in proportions, vase paintings and reliefs amateurish, seals less skillfully cut and often too crowded with figures.

The Kassite Dynasty (c. 1600 B.C.), consisting of barbaric invading tribes from the Zagros Mountain region, brought a decided retrogression in culture and art in Babylonia for more than five centuries. No originality or creativeness appears here, but simply a continuation, on a vastly inferior plane, of earlier Babylonian art. Cylinder seals show the deterioration of quality, lines being poorly cut, and inscribed incantations or prayers often added, as well as rows of prophylactic figures—frogs, lizards, and so on—indicating the lower state of religion during the period. Bas-reliefs were confined mostly to boundary stones on which were portrayed gods, royal persons, or others, together with symbols intended to drive away danger or damage from the stones.

ASSYRIAN

The art of Assyria, like most elements in Assyrian culture, was derived from that of Babylonia. The dependence of

(the head being protoma, disengaged, or sculptured in the round), an added leg gives the figure the appearance of a standing animal. Such guardians were placed at the doorways of palaces and temples alike.

A city like that of Sargon's gives evidence that Assyrian architects employed the round and pointed arch, the barrel vault, the dome, and, as can be learned from pictured representations on seals and bas-reliefs, the column.

The beginnings of Assyrian history go back to about 3000 B.C., but few objects of art earlier than c. 1000 B.C. survive, most of them coming from the ninth to the seventh centuries, the golden age of Assyria. Examples of sculpture in the round are very rare, the only perfect surviving one being that of Ashurnasirpal II (reigned 884-859 B.C.). The Assyrian artists evidently preferred bas-relief to free-standing sculp-

COURTESY OF THE METROPOLITAN MUSEUM OF ART

Limestone bas-relief from the palace of Ashurbanipal, King of Assyria (669-626 B.C.), at Nineveh, depicting the king and queen dining in a garden

Assyrian on Babylonian modes of art is particularly conspicuous in the architecture of Assyria, for although stone was readily available in the north the Assyrians persisted in copying their southern neighbors in using baked clay bricks in the construction of their buildings.

The great preoccupation of Assyrian kings with military conquests no doubt restricted development of art to some extent, and at the same time influenced the character and themes of Assyrian art. Sculpture and plastic art dwelt largely upon the depiction of the military exploits of the kings, or of scenes from the king's second favorite pursuit, the chase—civilians and women being almost entirely absent from Assyrian art. During peaceful interludes between wars, or when their conquered enemies were reduced to docility, many Assyrian monarchs were great builders of temples and immense palaces. The best example of such work is the new royal city of Sargon II (Dur-Sharrukin, "Sargonsburg," modern Khorsabad) constructed just north of the old capital, Nineveh, in 707 B.C. The palace complex covered some twenty-five acres and contained nearly one thousand rooms, numerous great courts, endless sculptured corridors, and, adjacent to the palace, a seven-storied ziggurat temple. Outside the main gates, colossal human-headed winged bulls and lions of alabaster stood guard. A unique feature of these "protectors of the gates" (*lamassu*) is that, viewed from the side (the bodies being carved in high relief), the four legs are seen in striding position, while viewed from the front

ture. Numerous single-figure, round-topped steles remain, depicting royal or divine personages. Many of these are found in outlying regions where they were set up by a king, pictured thereon, to proclaim his annexation of conquered territories. In the same manner, kings sometimes celebrated victories by erecting in their palaces obelisks containing bas-relief representations of various scenes of conquest. The best of these is the Black Obelisk of Shalmaneser II (859-825 B.C.), which, in five registers on each of its four faces, pictures the homage rendered to the king by five conquered nations.

The most numerous bas-reliefs, however, are those that cover the interior walls of royal palaces like "stone tapestry," illustrating military campaigns, hunting expeditions, ritual acts, and other everyday activities of king and people. Sometimes paints of dull shades (red, blue, black, and white) were used to emphasize details of these reliefs.

Characteristic of all these mural reliefs is a uniformly poor representation of human figures and a progressively more mature depiction of animals. Human beings, though strongly modeled and dignified, are stiff, expressionless, with conventional curled hair and beard, exaggerated muscles, and heavy garments—all quite lacking in grace. Facial features are almost identical in all the reliefs, showing that the Assyrian artist was not producing portraits of individuals. There is also an inability, like that of Egyptian artists, to foreshorten figures, which results in awkward attitudes in which legs, lower body, and head are in profile, with a full-shaped eye appearing in the profile face, while the chest is front view with both shoulders showing. With animals, however, the Assyrian artists attained a marvelously likelife quality in form and expression, the hunting scenes especially portraying beasts in all their pain, terror, and fury. There is perhaps nothing in all ancient art to match the two wonderful representations in Ashurbanipal's palace of a dying lion and a smitten lioness. The latter masterpiece caught the stricken beast in her final convulsions, hindquarters paralyzed, legs dragging helplessly, while she supports herself tremblingly for a lingering moment on her front paws; her half-opened jaws, upper lip drawn back in a snarl, show both agony and menace. This is a truly great work of creative artistic genius. Thus Assyrian art reached its apogee just before the nation's downfall, Ashurbanipal (669-626 B.C.) being the last great Assyrian monarch.

Of large-scale embossed metal work, the most notable example is the hammered-bronze gates of Balawat, southeast of Nineveh, erected by Shalmaneser II. Here are depicted with amazing skill and clarity varied scenes from the first nine years of the king's reign.

In the smaller arts—jewelry, carved ivories, glazed ware, embroidery, furniture—the Assyrians were skilled craftsmen. Gems and cylinder seals, delicately carved, continued to be made, with the same variety of motifs as in bas-reliefs.

The art of the Neo-Babylonian Empire can be almost wholly confined to the time of Nebuchadnezzar II (reigned 605-562 B.C.), who built up Babylon to a splendor never before known, with great temples, palaces, the famous Hanging Gardens, a broad triumphal street whose walls were decorated with colored enameled brick depicting animals and dragons of various kinds in brilliant blues, reds, and yellows. More such colored-tile reliefs adorned the great Ishtar gate of the city, while the throne room of the king was decorated with conventionalized borderwork of lotus blossoms and palms. This particular use of enameled tile or brick for bas-relief is thought to have originated at this time; it became so popular as virtually to displace other bas-relief. Only one large sculptured statue in the round remains from these last years of Babylon's greatness, a huge unfinished lion of dolerite shown in full stride with a man under his feet, symbolizing, perhaps, a victory over an enemy.

Minor arts were carried on even during the later periods of Persian, Greek, and Roman domination, almost to the beginning of the Christian era, but with little change and no distinctive features. J. W. F.

BABY ORCHID, *Odontoglossum grande,* a magnificent species of orchid native to Guatemala. It is an epiphyte, with two or three lance-shaped leaves about 5 in. long, and foot-long racemes bearing a few large brilliant yellow flowers, barred with cinnamon-brown 5 to 6 in. across. It blooms in autumn and is a greenhouse favorite.

BABY'S-BREATH, *Gypsophila paniculata,* a member of the pink family, is a tall, fine, multibranched perennial herb, a native of Europe and Asia, widely grown as a garden ornamental. It has many graceful clusters of tiny white flowers and is excellent as a cut flower. The name is also used for wild madder (*Galium mollugo*) and for Scotch mist (*G. sylvaticum*), natives of Europe but naturalized in the eastern United States. E. R. C.

BACCHAE, THE [bæ′ki], a tragedy by Euripides, produced probably in 405 B.C. Its subject is the impact of the god Dionysus and the Dionysiac religion upon the Greek city of Thebes, whose king and people refuse to recognize his divinity. In it there is a twofold conflict, that between Dionysus and King Pentheus, and that between two aspects of the god himself, the mild, gentle god of the first half of the play and the vengeful, cruel god of the latter half. The tragic result is Pentheus' dreadful death at the hands of his mother, Agave, and her sisters, who in a Dionysiac frenzy blindly tear him limb from limb. It is a strange, mysterious play full of wildly beautiful choral lyrics mingled with scenes of grim irony and awesome horror. One of the greatest works of antiquity, it is at the same time one of the most difficult to interpret. *See also* DIONYSUS. S. D. At.

BACCHANALIA [bækəne′liə], the Roman name for festivals of Bacchus (Dionysus), the god of wine. The rites were believed to include drunken orgies and gross debaucheries and were prohibited by a decree of the Roman senate in 186 B.C. *See also* DIONYSUS. G. E. D.

BACCHUS [bæ′kəs], a name applied by both the ancient Greeks and Romans to Dionysus, the god of wine. *See also* DIONYSUS.

BACCHYLIDES [bəkɪ′lɪdiz] (c. 517-c. 450 B.C.), Greek lyric poet, nephew of Simonides, born at Iulis in Ceos, was a younger contemporary of Pindar, probably closer to him in date than has been usually assumed. Until the publication in 1897 of an Egyptian papyrus containing several epinician and dithyrambic poems, his work was unknown save for some fragments of convivial and erotic poetry; other less significant papyri have been discovered since that year. It is clear from the fragments that Bacchylides was a rival of Pindar in many areas—Thessaly, Macedonia, Aegina, Athens, and especially Sicily. For Athens, Bacchylides wrote dithyrambs which, together with one composed for Ceos, are important in the history of that literary form. In the writing of epinicia his highest success lay in the commission to celebrate the chariot victory of Hiero of Syracuse at Olympia (468 B.C.), undoubtedly to the great disappointment of Pindar, whose treatment of Hiero's physical and political weaknesses had been less delicate than that of Bacchylides.

The influence of Simonides on his nephew must have been great, but we may also regard Bacchylides as a follower of Stesichorus, who made mythological narrative a highly significant part of choral lyric. The myths of Bacchylides are certainly closer to epic than the lyric narrative of Pindar. Longinus commends Bacchylides' polished elegance but considers it inferior to the somewhat unpredictable brilliance of Pindar; and this is a true appraisal. Bacchylides was a thoroughly reliable, even picturesque craftsman, but he lacked Pindar's inspiration and vigor. C. M. D.

BACCIO D'AGNOLO [ba′ttsho da′nyolo] (1462-1543), Italian architect and wood carver, was born in Florence on May 15, 1462. He learned wood carving from his father and from Bernardo della Cecca, Giuliano da Maiano, and Francione. Baccio did the wood carving in the choirs of the churches of Santa Maria Novella (1491-1496) in Florence and of Sant' Agostino (1502-1503) in Perugia. Having almost unwittingly achieved a mastery of architectural principles, he devoted the remainder of his career exclusively to architecture. About 1500 Baccio collaborated with Cronaca in constructing the Great Hall of the Palazzo Vecchio in Florence; he also designed the Palazzo Taddei, Florence, built in 1503-1504. From 1507 until 1515 he was *capo-*

maestro (master builder), in association with Cronaca and the brothers Sangallo, for the Cathedral in Florence. He designed the campaniles of Santo Spirito (1511) and San Miniato a Monte (1524-1527), the Palazzo Cocchi Serristori, and the façade of the Palazzo Bartolini-Salimbeni (1517-1520). Baccio's art had elegance and simplicity, yet possessed an admirable spontaneity. He died in Florence on May 6, 1543.

BACH [bɑ'χ], the name of a German family of outstanding importance in the history of music, members of which were amateur or professional musicians throughout more

JOHANN SEBASTIAN
BACH

FROM A DRAWING
BY LOUIS LUPAS

than two centuries. Its greatest member was Johann Sebastian Bach, now generally recognized as one of the foremost musicians and composers of all times.

Early Family History. The strongly Lutheran Bach family seems to have originated in Thuringia, and this state remained the center of its activities. Vitus Bach (c.1555-1619), a baker and miller and the earliest known ancestor of Johann Sebastian, spent part of his life in Hungary, and on this fact the later Bachs based a belief that the family was of Hungarian descent. Vitus liked music, and one of his sons had a certain amount of musical training. His three grandsons turned professional, and the fourth generation included Johann Christoph Bach (1642-1703), who was known as a "profound" composer; Johann Michael Bach (1648-1694), brother of the preceding, and known as an "able" composer; and, among their cousins, a pair of twins who "looked so much alike that even their wives could not tell them apart." Among the Thuringian town musicians the Bachs were so numerous that the family name became a synonym of the profession. A list of the musical members of the family with biographical notes compiled by Johann Sebastian in 1735 contains fifty-three entries.

Johann Sebastian Bach. Johann Ambrosius Bach (1645-1695), court and town musician in Eisenach and one of the twins mentioned above, had three surviving sons by his first marriage with Elizabeth Lëmmerhirt (d. 1694), daughter of an Erfurt council member. Of these, Johann Christoph (1671-1721) spent an uneventful life, largely as organist and schoolmaster in Ohrdruf, while Johann Jacob (1682-1722) entered the Swedish army as oboist, accompanied Charles XII during the Russian campaign and Turkish exile, and died in Stockholm.

The youngest son, Johann Sebastian, was born on March 21, 1685. After the death of his parents in his tenth year,

he went to live with Johann Christoph at Ohrdruf, but in 1700 his brother also died and Johann Sebastian then went to Lüneburg to join a well-known school choir. Three years later he secured his first position, that of court musician to Prince Johann Ernst, brother of the reigning duke, at Weimar, and in the same year he moved on to Arnstadt as organist of the New Church. In 1707 he assumed corresponding duties in the larger and richer church of St. Blasius in the Thuringian Mühlhausen, but in 1708 he returned to Weimar as chamber and court organist to Duke Wilhelm Ernst and in 1714 was given the additional rank of concertmaster. In 1717 he went as capellmeister and director of the "chamber" on secular music to the court of the genuinely musical and artistic Prince Leopold of Anhalt-Cöthen and in 1723, after several musicians of greater popularity had declined the post, he was elected music director and cantor at the Church and School of St. Thomas in Leipzig, a key position in Lutheran church music. In 1736 in Dresden he was given the honorary title of Royal Polish and Electoral Saxon Court Composer. He died in Leipzig from a stroke on July 28, 1750, his health undermined by unsuccessful surgical attempts to restore his failing eyesight.

Bach first married a second cousin, Maria Barbara Bach, daughter of the Johann Michael mentioned above, in 1707; she died suddenly in 1720, however, while her husband was accompanying his patron on a trip to Carlsbad, the Bohemian spa, and the following year Bach took as a second wife Anna Magdalena Wülcken, daughter of a Weissenfels court musician and herself a singer. Anna Magdalena died in poverty in 1760. Of seven children of the first marriage, three survived the father; of thirteen children of the second marriage, six. Both marriages produced sons of musical importance who are mentioned below.

Bach had a successful though not spectacular career, and during his life his fame rested primarily on his playing and improvisation, particularly on the organ. He appears to have been a good violinist and viola player as well, however, and he had a good, penetrating voice of wide range. Of his mature life he spent approximately sixteen years at court, and thirty-two in the service of church and church school. He made no contribution to opera, but he covered every other field of music with unique thoroughness and was an exceptional teacher of keyboard performance and of composition.

Bach's greatness rests on the intensity and finality of structure which he imparted to his works. His musical imagination was of the utmost complexity, yet it was at the same time flawlessly logical, so much so, indeed, that one is inclined to overestimate the intellectual and mathematical side of Bach's music. His greatest accomplishments are concentrated in the fields of counterpoint, harmony, and formal structure, and no other composer has possessed an equal ability to present simultaneously melodies of different or contrasting characters. He excelled also in his bold and fast-moving harmony, which was richer and more expressive than that of any predecessor, and although it has since been surpassed in dissonance it remains unique in power. His structural procedure was to assure unity of a composition through a more or less dense web of relationships between sectional elements; he was the greatest representative of this art, and his compositions are thus incomparably fascinating objects for analytical study.

Historically, Bach concluded the Baroque era, in which the interest in polyphonic writing still balanced that in harmony. He was a progressive musician but he never relinquished a basically contrapuntal concept of composition, and in fact his last works show an even greater interest in contrapuntal

FROM A PAINTING BY TOBY E. ROSENTHAL

COURTESY OF THE NEW YORK PUBLIC LIBRARY

MORNING PRAYERS IN THE FAMILY OF SEBASTIAN BACH

intricacy. The music of his time, on the other hand, moved with revolutionary speed toward a lighter, purely harmonic, style, and as a matter of course Bach's works fell into almost complete oblivion after his death. A deliberate revival began around 1800, however, and Bach's popularity has been growing steadily since that time.

The bulk of Bach's church music consists of the choral works for voices and instruments that we have come to call cantatas; close to two hundred of these compositions in several movements have survived. After some initial hesitation, Bach here came to employ the entire range of operatic forms, using them most effectively as expressions of religious feeling. The opening choruses of the cantatas are frequently fugues cast in *de capo* form; the concluding movements are generally chorales. In later years Bach liked to base entire cantatas on hymns of the Lutheran church, introducing the chorale melody in at least two of the movements.

Bach's church music culminates in a single complete Mass of gigantic proportions, known inaccurately as the "B-minor Mass"; two Passions, one according to St. John, the other, to St. Matthew; and a Christmas Oratorio, written originally as a set of six cantatas to be performed singly during the holy season. While the Mass introduces no extraneous texts, the Passions and Christmas Oratorio round out the Biblical narratives with hymns or chorales, as well as contemporary poetry.

Bach's instrumental music looms even larger today than does his output for voices with instruments, and in many fields he created the most monumental examples of definite types on record. Such claim may be made for his sonatas and partitas (suites) for a single unaccompanied violin or violincello; for his orchestral overtures which are likewise

suites; and for his concertos for several instruments, the *Concerti grossi,* written for a margrave of Brandenburg and hence known as "Brandenburg Concerto." Bach was the first to write concertos for one, two, three, and four harpsichords with orchestra, and the first to use the harpsichord consistently for fully written-out parts as in chamber music. His works for the secular keyboard instruments, where he generally uses the harpsichord and clavichord without distinction, consist mainly of three sets of suites; fifteen two-part inventions and a like number of three-part sinfonias written as studies for his son, Wilhelm Friedemann Bach; and preludes and fugues, mainly in two sets of twenty-four pieces, a prelude and fugue in each major and minor key, and called collectively *Das Wohltemperirte Klavier (The Well-Tempered Clavier).* His works for organ, the peak of achievement among compositions for this instrument, comprise fascinating settings of chorale melodies in his chorale preludes and chorale fantasies, magnificent toccatas, and a lovely set of sonatas, which were also written for Wilhelm Friedemann Bach.

Very few of Bach's works were published during his lifetime. Contemporary publications include four parts of the *Klavier Übung (Keyboard Practice),* containing, among other compositions, the "Goldberg Variations," named after a pupil of Bach; *Das musikalische Opfer (The Musical Offering),* dedicated to Frederick the Great, King of Prussia, who furnished the principal theme during a visit by Bach to Potsdam; and the posthumous *Die Kunst der Fuge (Art of the Fugue),* a collection of fugues and canons based on a common theme.

Bach's works were issued in a complete edition by the Bach Gesellschaft (46 vol., completed 1900; American facsimile edition, Ann Arbor, 1948). Numerous editions of separate works exist, most of them, unfortunately, with indiscriminate additions by the editors.

Sons of Johann Sebastian Bach. Four of Bach's surviving sons chose musical careers.

Wilhelm Friedemann (b. Weimar, 1710; d. Berlin, 1784), a greatly gifted musician, was carefully instructed by his father. He held positions as organist in Dresden and Halle, but, lacking discipline, he wasted his opportunities as well as his talent.

Karl Philipp Emanuel (b. Weimar, 1714; d. Hamburg, 1788) was for many years the accompanist of Frederick the Great of Prussia, and later became director of church music in Hamburg. His numerous works, marked by careful dynamic grading and fine thematic elaboration, paved the way for the classical style of Mozart and Haydn, who did not fail to acknowledge their indebtedness to him. His *Versuch über die wahre Art das Klavier zu spielen* (in two parts 1753, 1762) ("Essay on the True Manner of Playing the Clavier") is a comprehensive treatise of high quality and great historical interest.

Johann Christoph Friedrich (b. Leipzig, 1732; d. Bückeburg, 1795), a solid musician and composer, served a middle-German court for forty-five years.

Johann Christian (b. Leipzig, 1735; d. London, 1782) became in his time the most famous of all the Bachs. After his father's death, he was educated by his stepbrother, Karl Philipp Emanuel, but later went to Italy, joined the Roman Catholic Church, and was appointed organist at Milan Cathedral. In 1762 he moved to London where, music-master to the Queen, he was acclaimed as a teacher and composer of operas, symphonies, concertos, chamber music, and marches.. His delightful works largely anticipated the melodic and harmonic style of Mozart, who was his personal and artistic admirer.   H. T. D.

BACHE, BENJAMIN FRANKLIN [be'tsh] (1769-1798), American printer and journalist, was born in Philadelphia, Pa., Aug. 12, 1769. His father, Richard Bache, was a wealthy merchant and postmaster general, and his mother was Sarah, the daughter of Benjamin Franklin. Young Bache accompanied Franklin to Europe in 1776, and was educated by him in Paris and Geneva. He also learned printing under François A. Didot, the noted French printer. He returned to America in 1785, and graduated from the University of Pennsylvania in 1787. In 1790 he opened a printing shop in Philadelphia and commenced publishing the *General Advertiser,* which later became the *Aurora General Advertiser.* Originally devoted to the straightforward reporting of political, literary, and local information, the paper presently became involved in political controversies. Succeeding Philip Freneau's *National Gazette* as the Republican mouthpiece, the paper opposed the Federalists, who were represented by John Fenno's *Gazette of the United States.* Fenno hired William Cobbett to write for his paper, and the unrestrained duel of words between Bache and Cobbett produced the journalistic sensation of the day. No amount of virulent and personal abuse seemed too much for these men, and between 1796 and 1798 the *Aurora* became one of the most violent and bitter newspaper publications in the history of American journalism.

Bache's popularity did not increase when he was forced to attack George Washington in defense of his grandfather, Franklin. In 1795 the *Aurora's* premature publication of John Jay's treaty with France aroused public opposition to the signing of the treaty, although it was unsuccessful in

preventing it. In the face of a mounting war fever, Bache continued vehemently to attack the Federalists and to use the columns of his paper to denounce the clamor for war with France. On June 26, 1798, on the authority conferred by the Alien and Sedition Acts, Bache was arrested for libeling the President, but was released on parole. In *Truth Will Out* (1798) he accused his political enemies of attempting to ruin him. Bache died of yellow fever in Philadelphia, Sept. 10, 1798. After his death the *Aurora* was continued by his widow, assisted by William J. Duane, who later married her.   C. W. D.

BACHELOR'S BUTTON. *See* CORNFLOWER.

BACHOFEN, JOHANN JAKOB [ba'χofən] (1815-1887), Swiss anthropologist and historian, was born in Basel, Dec. 22, 1885. He was an orthodox Lutheran, a well-to-do patrician, a university professor, and a jurist in Basel. His thought was based on the German Romantic concept of antiquity, held by K. O. Müller, Friedrich Creuzer, and F. K. von Savigny. According to Bachofen every society, including those of Greece and Rome, shifted from an original promiscuity to a matriarchy, with the child belonging to the mother's family. This matriarchal life was characterized by a highly developed mystical insight into the essence of reality. This capacity, according to Bachofen, has been irrevocably lost due to the triumph of the paternal society with its intellectualism. This theory found some adherents; most historians rejected it, but evolutionistic anthropologists in Germany accepted parts of it. Moreover, Friedrich Engels incorporated it into the Marxian system with the addition that a shift from matrilinear to patrilinear society means simultaneously a change from collective to individual property. Neo-Romanticists such as Ludwig Klages espoused it, since it emphasized emotionalism. Anthropologists of cultural cyclical conviction, such as Wilhelm Schmidt and Wilhelm Koppers, incorporated matrilineal society into their system of spreading cultural cycles. This particular emphasis, while popular in Europe and Latin America, found much opposition in the United States. Bachofen died at Basel, Nov. 25, 1887.   P. H.

BACILLUS. *See* BACTERIOLOGY.

BACK BAY, a fashionable residential district in Boston, Massachusetts, on the filled land of what was an arm of the Charles River. The district maintains the name of the original body of water. In 1852 a state commission recommended that the area be filled in, since the water was polluted; the work began in 1858. The section extends south and east between the Common and the hills of Brookline as far as the Neck connecting Boston and Roxbury.

BACKGAMMON, a game for two played on a board with counters that are moved in accordance with the casting of dice. Originally, the board was marked with twelve parallel lines, but these lines have been supplanted by wedge-shaped "points," twelve of which project from each player's side of the board (Fig. 1). The play consists of advancing fifteen counters or "stones" across the points to a certain quarter of the board, known as the player's "home table," whence they are "borne off." The first player to bear off all his stones wins the game. If the loser has failed to bear off a single stone, he is "gammoned" and pays a double stake; if, in addition, the loser has any stone outside his home table, he is "backgammoned" and loses a triple stake.

The two players move their stones in opposite directions

along the same course of twenty-four points. Rules governing collision provide that any number of stones of one color may rest on a point; that no stone may rest or touch upon a point occupied by two or more adverse stones; that a single stone on a point is a "blot" and if "hit" by an adverse stone landing upon the same point is sent "to the bar," i.e., must begin again as though from a twenty-fifth point farthest away from the owner's home table.

Variants. In the English-speaking and many other countries, the stones are all on the board at the beginning of a game, in a standardized formation. In "Dutch" and "Rus-

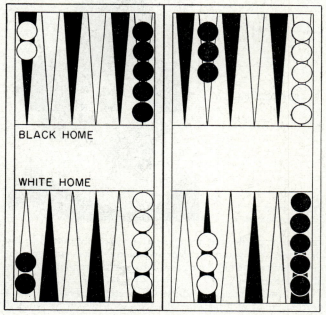

BLACK HOME

WHITE HOME

Fig. 1—A modern backgammon board with counters in position for start of game

sian" backgammon, all the stones commence off the board and have to be "entered." There are other widely played variants, such as "Acey-Deucey," in which the roll of 2-1 gives special privileges.

History. Backgammon probably grew out of parcheesi, which it greatly resembles. Boards, dice, and counters have been excavated at Babylon and elsewhere; a board from Ur of the Chaldees is believed to date from 3000 B.C. Whether this equipment was used for backgammon in the modern sense, or for parcheesi or some parent game, is mere conjecture. One of the earliest unmistakable references to backgammon occurs in Plato, *ludus duodecim scriptorum,* the "twelve-lined game."

Backgammon, together with hundreds of other games that lend themselves to betting, came into great popularity in France and England during the seventeenth century. It probably was the first of the games of skill to be analyzed with any degree of mathematical precision, the element of skill in backgammon being that exercised in choice of stones to move. Of five games described by Edmond Hoyle in 1743, backgammon is the only one in which his counsel of strategy is not obsolete. A wide revival of interest in backgammon occurred in the 1930's, when American players adopted a new rule as to doubling and redoubling the stakes, thereby accelerating the pace of the game.   G. M-S.

BACKS RIVER, in the northeastern region of the Northwest Territories of Canada. The river was formerly

called the Great Fish, but its name was changed to honor Sir George Back who, in 1834, explored its entire length. The Backs River rises in Sussex Lake in the District of Mackenzie and flows northeastward into a bay of the Arctic Ocean. The river has a total length of approximately 570 mi. and meanders a great deal. In its middle course the river enlarges to form several large, irregularly shaped lakes named, from west to east, Pelly, Garry, and Macdougall; near the mouth of the river is Lake Franklin, a somewhat smaller lake. The river is frozen all winter and is not of any commercial importance. A large number of ducks and also mosquitoes breed in this practically uninhabited sub-Arctic muskeg and tundra region during the summer months.

BACK TO METHUSELAH [məthyu'sələ], a set of five plays by George Bernard Shaw produced in 1921 and subtitled "A Metabiological Pentateuch." In conception and execution this pentalogy occupies in the Shavian drama a position comparable to that of the tetralogy *The Ring of the Nibelungs* in Wagnerian opera. Here, in full scope and elucidation, is Shaw's dramatization of the philosophy of Creative Evolution, from the Creation on into the future "as far as thought can reach." To some it is tedious, interminable and soporific; to others, in the words of Hermann Keyserling, it is the "loftiest contribution of the prophet Shaw . . . for its incorporation of fruitful human problems in witty episodes and expressions is the first work since Goethe comparable in content to *Faust.*"

The play is based on the Biblical narrative of the Garden of Eden and reveals the evolutionary struggle of man, as the agent of an imperfect, aspiring Life Force, "to rise above himself, to himself" (Friedrich Nietzsche). The clue to this progressive advance is the scientific extension of the life span, for longevity has become indispensable for the preservation of the race, and once this is universally recognized man will effectively will his own vital extension. Shaw presents the plausible hypothesis that though experience does not bring wisdom enough to counterbalance the recklessness produced by the shortness of our lives, an increase in our expectation of life would at once produce more serious, responsible, and farsighted conduct.   A. H.

BACOLOD [bɑko'lod], a chartered city 330 mi. southeast of Manila and the largest urban unit on the island of Negros, in the Philippine Islands. The capital of the province of Negros Occidental, the city lies on a shallow bay and is one of several urban communities along the northeastern coast of the island. This part of Negros is one of the major sugar-cane areas of the archipelago. Larger vessels must anchor about a mile offshore, and sugar from the *centrales* is transferred to them by lighters. Bacolod lies on the flat coastal plain amid rice paddies and cane fields and behind the coconut palms along the beach. A stone church and a convent are centrally located, and the large concrete capitol building and a 100-bed hospital are in the northern part of the town. The Bacolod sugar *central,* a well-constructed sheet-iron building on a concrete foundation, is 1½ mi. from the coast. There are many palatial residences owned by wealthy planters. The principal streets and the coastal highway are paved. Pop. 1939, 26,562.

BACON, AUGUSTUS OCTAVIUS (1839-1914), American politician and United States senator, was born in Bryan County, Ga., Oct. 20, 1839. He was graduated from the University of Georgia in 1859; during the Civil War he served in a Georgia regiment in the Confederate Army, attaining the rank of captain. He began the practice of law at Macon, Ga., in 1866, and after serving several terms in the state legislature was in 1894 elected to the United States Senate. After the death of Vice-President John Sherman in 1900, Bacon served as president *pro tempore* of the Senate. Three times re-elected, he died in Washington, D. C., Feb. 14, 1914.

BACON, DELIA SALTER (1811-1859), American author, was born in Tallmadge, Ohio, Feb. 2, 1811. She attended the school of Catherine Beecher in Hartford, Conn., until 1826. For the next four years she taught school. In 1831 she published a collection of short stories, *Tales of the Puritans,* followed in 1839 by *The Bride of Fort Edward: A Dramatic Story.* She then lectured on literature and history with remarkable success, infecting her audiences with her enthusiasm. By 1852 she became convinced that Shakespeare's plays were the work of a literary circle presided over by her namesake, Bacon, and by Raleigh and Spenser, and that this circle utilized the plays for the dissemination of a liberal political philosophy that could not be avowed openly. She devoted the remainder of her life to propagating this thesis. Emerson, temporarily converted, gave her a letter to Carlyle. She reached England in May 1853 and was kindly received by Carlyle. *Putnam's Magazine* contracted for a series of her articles, published the first, and rejected the remainder. Nathaniel Hawthorne, American consul at Liverpool, thought her thesis deserved a hearing, loaned her money, and found an English publisher for her book, *Philosophy of the Plays of Shakspere Unfolded,* which appeared in April 1857. Delia Bacon became violently insane shortly after the book's publication, and returned to America in 1858 with her nephew, George Bacon. Her book remains one of the curiosities of literature. Delia Bacon is credited with having given currency to what is perhaps the most popular of literary heresies, namely, that Shakespeare was not the author of the plays attributed to him. She died in Hartford, Conn., Sept. 2, 1859.

BACON, FRANCIS, Baron Verulam, Viscount St. Albans (1561-1626), English statesman, essayist, and philosopher, was born in London, Jan. 22, 1561, the youngest son of Sir Nicholas Bacon, Lord Keeper of the Great Seal. He attended Cambridge for two years, spent three years in France, and then, left without adequate means by the death of his father in 1579, began the study of law at Gray's Inn. He became a member of Parliament in 1584 and took a prominent part in the debates of every session of the House of Commons until 1614. From time to time he addressed letters of advice to Queen Elizabeth, notable for their unbiased presentation of the most expedient political action on the points under discussion; if his advice had been followed, some of the later troubles between the Crown and Parliament might have been avoided. But his ability as a statesman did not advance his fortunes, partly because he was opposed by Lord Burghley, who saw in his brilliance an obstacle to the ambitions of his own son, and partly because he lost the favor of Elizabeth by courageously opposing, on a point of principle, a bill for a royal subsidy. About 1592, with his brother Anthony, he became political adviser to the Earl of Essex, who rewarded him with generous gifts. He made it clear to his patron, however, that his chief loyalty would always be to his country, and when in 1601 Essex attempted to rouse the London populace to rebellion Bacon, in his official capacity as counsel for the Crown, was among those instrumental in securing the Earl's conviction for treason. He never held any important office under Elizabeth,

but with the accession of James I his fortunes prospered. In 1607 he was appointed solicitor general, in 1613 attorney general, and in 1618 lord chancellor, the highest legal post in the kingdom. He was knighted in 1603, created Baron Verulam in 1618, and made Viscount St. Albans in 1621. In the latter year he was accused of accepting bribes from clients who had cases pending before him for judgment. He admitted the charge but argued that he had never allowed "gifts" to influence his decision, an indication of the curious

FRANCIS BACON

FROM A PRINT
BY S. HOUBRAKEN

mixture of intellectual acuteness and moral obtuseness in his character. He was then deprived of his offices and temporarily banished from court, and he spent his remaining years in retirement.

The chief literary products of Bacon's experience as a practical man of affairs are the *Essays* on which he worked intermittently for twenty-eight years; he published ten in 1597 and by 1625 had revised and expanded the collection to fifty-eight. Written in a terse, sententious style ornamented with learned illustrations and brilliant metaphors, these essays are what Bacon called "dispersed meditations" on ambition, friendship, love, riches, studies, honor, reputation, and other fundamental aspects of human life. They contain coldly calculated advice, unbiased by considerations of sentiment or impracticable idealism, on how to get on in the world; the aphorisms "All rising to great place is by a winding stair" and "He that hath a wife and children hath given hostages to fortune" illustrate both their style and their content. Another of his works, *De sapientia veterum* (1609) (*The Wisdom of the Ancients,* 1619), is an allegorical interpretation of the hidden truths contained in ancient myths. His *History of the Reign of Henry VII* (1622) is notable for its vivid characterization and clear political analysis.

Despite his political and legal activities, Bacon's ruling interests were philosophy and science, and he grandly asserted, "I have taken all knowledge to be my province." Aristotelian deduction, the prevailing method of philosophical inquiry in his time, he found unsatisfactory, so he cast about for a new instrument of thought, or organon, with which to re-erect human learning on surer foundations. The general outline of his *Instauratio magna,* or great plan for the restoration of knowledge, was sketched by 1620 in the introduction to his *Novum organum.* It was to contain six parts: a general survey of the contemporary state of human learning, a description of a new method for acquiring true knowledge, an assemblage of empirical data, a discussion of topics for further investigation, provisional solutions, and the final philosophy itself. He succeeded only in producing preliminary sketches of the first two parts of this grandiose scheme. The sketch of the first part was *The Advancement of Learning* (1605), revised and greatly expanded in a Latin version, *De augmentis scientiarum* (1623). Here, in describing contemporary attitudes that impeded the advance of learning, he established a tripartite division of learning in accordance with the functions of the mind, classing history under memory, poetry under imagination, and philosophy (in which he included what we now call the sciences) under reason. He also surveyed the extent and nature of human knowledge attained in each of these categories, and, more important, he indicated what fields of investigation had been neglected and needed cultivation. The sketch of the second part was the *Novum organum,* and in his unfinished *New Atlantis* he described a utopian community of scientists engaged in collecting and analyzing data of all sorts in accordance with the third part of his great plan.

Bacon's opposition to the dependence upon authority and "logic chopping" of his time, his emphasis on the need for new methods if learning is to advance, and his insistence that investigation should begin with observable facts rather than with theories make him an important figure in the history of scientific thought. Actually, however, he made no new contribution of significance to scientific fact or theory, and his system of induction by the method of exclusions, which he thought would produce new knowledge "as if by machinery," is not the method experimental scientists have used in achieving their greatest discoveries. His importance results from the general stimulus, rather than from the specific direction, that he gave to scientific inquiry. He died Apr. 9, 1626, as the result of a chill contracted while stuffing a chicken with snow to see whether cold would halt decay; it is the only scientific experiment he is known to have conducted.   W. R.

BACON, HENRY (1866-1924), American architect, was born in Watseka, Ill., on Nov. 28, 1866. He studied architecture at the University of Illinois in 1884-1885, and entered the offices of McKim, Mead & White in New York in 1888. From 1889 to 1891 he was a Rotch Traveling Scholar in Europe. He then returned to his former employers until 1897; he was a member of the firm of Brite and Bacon from 1897 to 1903. Thereafter he practiced independently in New York City until his death. Bacon's best-known work is the Lincoln Memorial in Washington, D. C., completed in 1920. For this design he was awarded the gold medal of the American Institute of Architects, presented to him in an impressive ceremony in 1923 by President Warren G. Harding. Among other buildings designed by Bacon are the Public Library at Paterson, N. J., the Waterbury, Conn., General Hospital, the Lincoln Monument at Lincoln, Nebr., and the World War Memorial at Yale University. With Augustus Saint-Gaudens he designed the Parnell Monument in Dublin, Ireland. He died on Feb. 16, 1924, in New York City.   R. Ne.

BACON, JOHN (1740-1799), English sculptor, was born at Southwark, Nov. 24, 1740. At fourteen he was apprenticed to a Mr. Crispe for whom he modeled groups of figures. He was then employed at an artificial stone works. While still an apprentice, Bacon won a premium from the Society of Arts. In all he won this society's awards nine times. Upon the foundation of the Royal Academy in 1768, Bacon entered as a student. In 1769 he received from the hands of Joshua Reynolds the first gold medal for sculpture

awarded by the Academy. His winning subject was a bas-relief, *Aeneas Escaping from Troy.* A statue of Mars obtained the gold medal of the Society of Arts and caused his election in 1770 as associate of the Royal Academy. He then was given a commission for a bust of George III for the hall of Christ Church, Oxford. From then on Bacon enjoyed uninterrupted prosperity. He won fifteen of sixteen competitions that he entered. His works included monuments to Pitt in the Guildhall and in Westminster Abbey; to Dr. Johnson and the philanthropist John Howard in St. Paul's; to William Blackstone at All Souls College, Oxford; and a bronze statue of George III and a colossal figure symbolizing the *Thames* in Somerset House. Bacon was largely self-taught. He had little imagination but displayed delicacy of technique, simplicity, and good taste. Bacon died in London, Aug. 4, 1799.   T. R.

BACON, LEONARD (1802-1881), American Congregational clergyman, was born in Detroit, Mich. on Feb. 19, 1802. The family returned to Connecticut, and he was educated at Hartford Grammar School, was graduated from Yale in 1820, attended Andover Theological Seminary, and became minister of the First Church of New Haven on Mar. 9, 1825. He filled this pastorate for forty-one years and then was pastor emeritus until his death. His influence in the city and in Congregational councils was extraordinary. Bacon was acting professor of revealed theology at Yale Divinity School from 1866 to 1871, and lecturer on church polity and American church history from 1871 until his death. Some of his hymns, such as "O God, beneath Thy guiding hand" (1838), found a permanent place in hymnals. He was one of the most powerful polemical writers and speakers of American Congregationalism in his era. He wrote *Thirteen Historical Discourses* (1839) and *The Genesis of the New England Churches* (1874). From his *Slavery Discussed in Occasional Essays* (1846) Lincoln adapted the assertion "If slavery is not wrong, nothing is wrong." Bacon was an editor of the *Christian Spectator* from 1826 to 1838 and a founder and for twenty years editor of the *New Englander.* In 1848 he also founded and was senior editor of the *Independent,* a "free-soil" periodical.   T. R.

BACON, ROGER (c. 1214-1294), English medieval scholar noted for advocating experimental method in science, was born near Ilchester around 1214. Educated at Oxford and Paris, he became a friar around 1257 and lived thereafter at the Franciscan convent in Paris. Scornfully critical of the academic learning of his time, he conceived a plan and method for the reform of the sciences, and at the request of Pope Clement IV outlined his ideas in his best-known work, the *Opus maius.* The Pope meanwhile died, Bacon was accused of unorthodoxy, and in 1278 he was condemned to prison by his superiors. Released in 1292, he died two years later.

Most of Bacon's writings constitute an incomplete encyclopedia of knowledge, reflecting the traditional content of medieval learning. It is in the *Opus maius* that his distinctive philosophical ideas are expressed. The basic doctrine is thoroughly medieval—all wisdom stems from God through three channels of revelation: the written word of Scripture, the visible works of nature, and the interior illumination of the soul achieved in seven stages of "internal experience." Indispensable instruments for deciphering these three revelations are, respectively, mastery of languages, knowledge of mathematics, and the moral and spiritual disciplines. Knowledge is fulfilled and certified, however, only through "experimental science," which Bacon conceives as application of theory to practical works—to discoveries and inventions useful to material welfare, and to moral and spiritual works leading to eternal beatitude.

Bacon's fame rests on his eloquent plea for experimental method in science, but close study of his writings reveals that he had little grasp of experimental method in the modern sense, and no greater competence in the sciences than

ROGER BACON

many other men of his age. His writings, many of which were written in a secret cipher, had relatively slight influence on subsequent intellectual history.   E. A. M.

BACON'S REBELLION, 1676,

an uprising of small farmers in Virginia led by Nathaniel Bacon. During the first half century of its history, Virginia was primarily a land of small farmers where every adult male could vote. In England, after the restoration of Charles II in 1660, the group of politicians who surrounded him was interested in the colonies as places to make money. Gov. Sir William Berkeley of Virginia was connected with this group. He built up a political machine with the aid of the larger planters in the colony. A law was passed which allowed only property holders to vote. Heavy taxes were assessed to build up the town of Jamestown. The enforcement of the Navigation Acts, after the passage of the first one in 1660, lowered the price of tobacco and raised the cost of freight.

These economic factors, coupled with gradual destruction of self-government within the colony, led to very real discontent on the part of the people. They accused the rich men of controlling the whole colony for their selfish purposes. The discontent came to a head in the year 1676, when the Indians attacked the frontier and Governor Berkeley failed to defend the colony. Rumor had it that he and his friends were interested in trade with the Indians. Because he did nothing, frontier farmers took matters into their own hands. They elected Nathaniel Bacon, a young Englishman who had settled a frontier plantation, to lead them. Bacon's troops were successful in defeating the Indians, but the governor was furious and denounced Bacon and his followers as rebels.

Bacon and his men then descended on Jamestown. They forced the governor to call an election—none had been held in fifteen years. When the new Assembly met it repealed the laws limiting voting to property holders and provided that every free man could vote; it also provided punishment for sheriffs found stuffing ballot boxes; and ruled that none could hold more than one office at a time; it also ruled that mem-

bers of the governor's council should not be exempt from taxation. These and other measures were passed in an attempt to undo the work of Berkeley and his political supporters.

Bacon likewise received a commission to lead a force against the Indians, but after he commenced his campaign the governor again declared him a rebel. This time Bacon returned to Jamestown and burned the town. Governor Berkeley fled to Maryland. Bacon became the ruler of Virginia, but soon afterward he fell ill and died. Without his leadership, the rebellion collapsed. Berkeley and his followers returned, hunted down Bacon's followers, executed some of them, and confiscated their property. Additional troops and a commissioner were sent from England the next year. Berkeley was replaced and returned to England, and peace was restored.

This rebellion of small farmers against the rising planter aristocracy was the first of many such colonial outbreaks.
                                                                M. Je.

BACTERIA. *See* BACTERIOLOGY.

BACTERIN [bæ'ktərɪn]. A term used in veterinary medicine, designating a bacterial extract which is a standardized suspension of disease-producing bacteria killed by heat or chemicals. When injected into an animal, the dead bacteria create immunity to, and thereby afford protection against, the live bacteria. Bacterins are used to prevent such diseases as blackleg, malignant edema, and hemorrhagic septicemia (shipping fever).   C. R. S.

BACTERIOLOGY, a branch of biology, consisting of the study of the characteristics and activities of bacteria. The subject includes studies of the effects produced by bacteria. Microorganisms biologically similar to bacteria are often included under bacteriology.

History. The concept of corpuscular, independent, living elements antedates the first actual observations of microorganisms, including bacteria. Bacteria were described by Antony van Leeuwenhoek (1632-1723), a Dutch haberdasher, town official, and surveyor, whose hobby was grind-

Iron water pipe linings showing different types of bacterial corrosion

ing lenses and observing stagnant water and body fluids. He drew the general shapes of bacteria and described the paths traced by those which moved.

Improvements in the microscope firmly established the existence of bacteria during the eighteenth century but added surprisingly little to the concepts of their activities. The early arguments were principally concerned with the sources of bacteria—whether they were spontaneously formed from the inert ingredients of their environments, or whether the new cells were formed by the reproduction of old cells, with the original cells lost in antiquity. This argument over spontaneous generation was largely overcome by Louis Pasteur (1822-1895), who effectually connected bacteria with fermentation, spoilage, and, eventually, disease. By relating observations to concepts, he brought bacteria into the realm of biology. Pasteur's interest was primarily in the activities of bacteria rather than in their biological positions, a point of view that has consistently influenced the development of the subject. The steps taken by Pasteur include: first, the relating of bacteria to fermentative processes; second, the realization that spoilage was an undesirable fermentative or putrefactive process; and, third, the crystallization of the concept that certain diseases of animals and of man were essentially spoilage due to the growth of bacteria.

From 1880 to 1890, numerous discoveries of different kinds of bacteria responsible for infectious diseases were made under Robert Koch and many others. At the close of the decade, filtrates freed from the bacteria of diphtheria and of tetanus were found to be poisonous, or to contain toxins. Then filtrates free from bacteria were found to contain ferments or enzymes, which are substances capable of inducing chemical reactions and thereby furnishing clues to the chemical reactions causing bacteria to grow and produce changes. Filtrates free of bacteria were also found sometimes to contain viruses, originally called "filterable viruses," presumed to be relatively smaller microorganisms capable of multiplying like bacteria. Although most kinds of bacteria are not capable of causing disease, all known viruses develop on, or in, living cells. The existence of a class of viruses not so adapted has not been disproven; means of demonstration have been lacking.

Bacteriology has both expanded and added to its concepts since the rapid developments from 1880 to 1900. Serologic studies have provided analyses of both the chemical composition and structure of bacteria. The electron microscope has confirmed and extended morphological data. The restraining influences exerted by one microorganism on another, long known, led to the discovery of antibiotics, like penicillin, which is extremely helpful in understanding cellular metabolism. Vaccines, serums, and skin-test products used for man and animals have contributed much to the welfare of man, although, contrary to popular opinion, they are applicable to relatively few diseases. Knowledge of the location and manner of scattering of bacteria causing diseases of plants, animals, and man has permitted the development of methods of control for many diseases, while knowledge of bacterial activity has provided sound bases for the preservation of foods, for sanitation, and for the exploitation of useful bacteria.

BACTERIAL FORMS AND CHARACTERISTICS

Bacteria are regarded as the simplest forms of yeasts and molds, with which, as a group of simple plants containing no chlorophyll, they compose a large group commonly called fungi. In this group, bacteria are known as Schizomycetes, or fission fungi, because they multiply by transverse division into two cells. Yeasts and molds represent the simplest plants, and protozoa the simplest animals. Rickettsiae and some of the larger viruses have much in common with bacteria and are also less complex than yeasts and molds, or than protozoa. These elementary forms need not necessarily be placed in the animal or plant kingdoms; possibly some of them represent the neutral ground from which both kingdoms developed.

Within the group of bacteria there are, according to D. H. Bergey's *Manual of Determinative Bacteriology* (1947), seven major subdivisions or orders: true bacteria, moldlike bacteria, algalike and sheathed bacteria, algalike but gummy and unsheathed, sulphur bacteria, active forms resembling slime molds, and flexuous, thin forms. Bacteria are commonly designated only by the genus and the species, e.g., *Staphylococcus aureus* and *Bacillus subtilis*. There are only arbitrary relationships between species or major groups of bacteria. Evolutionary and biological relationships which define the classifications of botany and zoology are not evident. Definitive descriptions of bacteria can be accomplished by points of (1) morphology; (2) metabolism; (3) antigenic composition, or the presence of specific proteins and carbohydrates; and (4) pathogenicity, or the ability, if any, for the production of diseases in animals or plants.

Morphological Distinctions. Morphologically, bacteria fall into one of four categories: the approximately spherical form, or coccus; the rod or cylindrical form, with rounded ends, or bacillus; the rigid, helical, coiled rod, called a spirillum; and the flexible, thin, hairlike form, or spirochete.

The size of bacteria is usually within the limits of 0.5 to 2.0 micra (1 micron or $\mu = 0.001$ mm. $= 1/25,000$ in.) in width and 1.0 to 8.0 micra in length. There are bacteria barely within the resolving power of the most powerful standard microscope (about 0.3 micra) and a few which exceed 10 micra in length and are correspondingly broad. Some kinds of spirochetes may be 40 or 50 micra long, although they are thin. Within a species, variation in size may be considerable.

Bacteria are enclosed within as many as three membranes, an outer slimy capsule, composed chiefly of carbohydrate, an inner membrane, and possibly a sheath within that. Within these layers, the cytoplasm is not regularly differentiated. Most species lack differentiable nuclei, vacuoles, and granules. The existence of a nucleus in bacteria is presumed by analogy with other types of cells, by the presence of nucleoproteins, and by observations made with nuclear dyes and with the electron microscope.

Some species of bacteria, principally among the rod forms, may develop spores. Unlike the spores of molds and the seeds of higher plants, there is no excess of sporulation; one bacterium develops one spore, and, from that, one bacterium may develop. Within a sporulating species, the spore is formed regularly at a given position in the cell, at one end, in the center, or between these points. Spores are formed by condensation of cytoplasm, which becomes enclosed within a wall, after which the rest of the cell disintegrates. They are as wide as or wider than the cell; they germinate by rupture of the spore wall. The conditions responsible for the formation of spores are not known, but to call them adverse is considered presumptuous; species capable of sporulation may fail to produce spores under various conditions. Spores are exceptionally resistant to physical and chemical influences. Bacteria responsible for anthrax, tetanus, gas gangrene, and botulism are the only pathogenic sporulating bacteria.

The presence of flagella, or flexuous appendages much thinner than the bacterium but often longer, is responsible for the motion which occurs in some species of bacteria. Other species are not motile; motility by cilia or membranes is not known. Flagella are extensions of the outer membranes of bacteria, with perhaps a core of endoplasm. Some species of rods and most spirilla are capable of developing flagella. In a single species, the number and position of flagella is constant: single at one end, single at each end, scattered around the whole cell, or arranged as a brush at one end. Flagella are usually seen only by the use of special methods of staining; they are occasionally visible with dark-field illumination. The motion of cells is end-over-end, forward, and backward. Spirochetes have a flexing motion, a rotating movement around the long axis, and movement from place to place. All of their motion is probably not due to flagella.

Granules are observed in bacteria. They may appear regularly in each end of most rods of some species; in others they may be scattered irregularly, with one to five or more per cell. Granules usually develop in aging cells. They have no known significance, although specific substances found in some granules, especially in larger saprophytic bacteria, may be functional.

In the early days of bacteriology, the presence of conspicuous capsules on some species of bacteria was noted.

significance in man's environment. Metabolic reactions aid in the identification of bacteria; they also furnish clues to cellular growth.

Under conditions favorable to growth, bacteria multiply in geometric progression: 2,4,8,16,32,64 . . . . When transferred to a favorable environment, there is a period of adjustment followed by a multiplication of some cells, then of nearly all cells, and then a gradual cessation of multiplication until, finally, there is no net increase. During this process, bacteria have enlarged, produced various enzymes, changed some of the chemicals of their environment, and assimilated some substances already present or formed. From the energy acquired, they have synthesized elements from their environment into the complex proteins, carbohydrates, and lipide substances of their cytoplasm.

Nearly all known sorts of enzymes are produced by one or another kind of bacteria, and many not known outside of

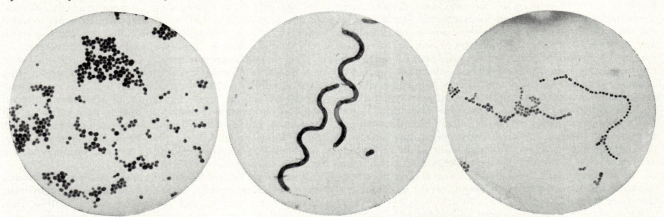

PHOTOMICROGRAPHS BY ROY M. ALLEN

(Left) Staphylococcus pyogenes aureus, a species of bacteria found on the skin and mucous membranes and causing suppuration (magnified 3200 X); (Center) Spirillum volutans, a saprophytic species and one of the largest known bacteria (magnified 1700 X); (Right) Streptococcus pyogenes, an organism which causes septicemia and acute pyogenic inflammations (magnified 2800 X)

They account for the sliminess of some masses of bacterial growth and are likely to disappear from species under artificial cultivation, depending somewhat on the chemical environment furnished. Improved methods of optical, chemical, and serologic study have led to the belief that most organisms may develop capsules that are not always visible.

Bacteria grown on a gel multiply in one spot, forming separated colonies. If the original cell or cells were of one species, the colony will contain only one species. Since organisms snap, pull, or slip apart after division or sometimes adhere in chains or packets, the mechanical forces of reproduction lead to the development of colonies distinctive for the species. They may be translucent or opaque; white, red, violet, yellow, or colorless; shiny or dull; convex, flat, or varied in cross section, even wavy, or fringed at the edges; and viscous, pasty, or crumbling in consistency. Colonies of a single species may be mucoid, smooth, or rough, due to hereditary changes in certain cells from which colonies are derived. These colonies or "strains" of the species are designated respectively as M, S, or R. The change is called dissociation and is probably a form of mutation. Because of the fact that growing bacteria usually divide at fifteen- to forty-minute intervals, changes of this sort can be readily studied.

Identification by Metabolism. Metabolic processes of bacteria have been extensively studied. Some knowledge of metabolism is needed to cultivate and thus to study bacteria. Chemical changes caused by huge numbers of bacteria have

bacteriology are formed. The elements required are principally carbon, hydrogen, oxygen, nitrogen, and phosphorus; in some species, other elements, such as sulphur, calcium, magnesium, and lesser amounts of many other elements, are of considerable significance. These elements may be utilized for growth, chiefly in the forms of nitrogenous salts, carbohydrates, and proteins (usually simplified and digested proteins called peptones). No organisms are known to be free of synthesized proteins, but some species do not utilize proteins in growth. Fats ordinarily are not utilized or affected by bacteria.

Respiration occurs in the growth of bacteria. It is similar to that of animals in that oxygen from the atmosphere is fixed by the bacteria and carbon dioxide is given off as gas. Under most conditions, the ratio is roughly four fifths as much carbon dioxide discharged as there has been oxygen consumed. Carbon dioxide sometimes affects the growth of organisms; gases discharged by some species include methane and hydrogen. Not all bacteria are able to utilize atmospheric oxygen; strict "anaerobes" will not grow unless the oxygen is removed. These organisms give off carbon dioxide and differ from aerobes in that their oxygen requirement can be met only by chemically combined oxygen, not by oxygen as a gas.

Bacteria, for growth, must have a suitable physical environment. Bacteria may grow in moderately strong acid, often pH 4 to 5, exceptionally at pH 2 or below; they tolerate alkaline environment less readily. They are relatively insensitive to osmotic pressure; a number of species will develop in brines as strong as 15 per cent salt or more, and in syrups. The fact that brines and syrups rarely "spoil" does not preclude the growth of some harmless or beneficial species. Organisms withstand temperatures several hundred degrees below zero. Some can multiply at temperatures a few degrees below freezing, while a majority grow well between room temperature and body temperature, from 20° to 37°C., or from 70° to 99°F., and organisms called thermophiles are found growing in hot springs and elsewhere at temperatures of very hot water, over 70°C. or 160°F.

In their development, bacteria may, through their intricate series of chemical reactions, produce heat. They may also produce cold light or phosphorescence strong enough to permit reading. Different species produce pigments, acids, alcohols, toxins, and countless chemical substances not so readily classified with daily existence. It is the accumulation of one or another of these products of growth which, in most instances, causes the cessation of growth after a short period of rapid multiplication. The cultivation of bacteria is accomplished by careful transfer of bacteria to tubes containing sterile culture media. These media are usually either broths or gels of varying consistency. Besides water, they contain small quantities of buffering salts to maintain an equilibrium with regard to acid and alkali, usually peptone, and often a carbohydrate, notably dextrose. The gels, more or less firm, are usually made with a complex polysaccharide, agar, a substance extracted from seaweed and itself affected by only a few species of bacteria. Bacteria may also be grown in milk, on gels made with the basic ingredients and gelatin, on carrots and potatoes, and on synthetic media in which all ingredients are purified chemical substances. Proteins are unimportant for some species; they may even be toxic for some organisms. Culture media for these organisms are usually of the synthetic type.

Serologic Identification. The antigenic components of bacteria are determined by serologic processes. Antigens are ordinarily complex proteins, with or without carbohydrates. Bacteria contain not one but several antigens. Antigens, when injected several times into an animal, stimulate the formation of a special protein, a globulin, in the liquid or noncellular part of the blood of the animal, known as the serum. This special globulin, called antibody, is specifically matched with the corresponding antigen; it will react specifically and demonstrably with this antigen and not with other antigens. If large numbers of bacteria of one species are injected into an animal, the blood will eventually contain antibodies for each antigen in the bacteria injected. This furnishes a convenient tool for the identification of antigenic substances. This serologic analysis is based upon changes which occur on the surfaces of antigens to which antibody has been specifically adsorbed. The result may be a precipitation of the antigen-antibody complex, a clumping of bacterial cells, called agglutination, a change in the permeability of the cell wall, called lysis, or a neutralization of the toxic property of antigenic toxins. An electrolyte is needed for all of these reactions; they are usually brought about in the presence of 0.85 per cent salt.

By serologic procedures, bacteria may be defined in terms of antigenic components in more detail than is possible by other means. Different species of bacteria may have antigenic components in common. It is not clear to what extent this should be a basis for defining a species, or to what extent it subdivides a species. Some groups of bacteria have been found in which there are many groups of antigens which overlap in different degrees. This may result in designations by common consent of a long series of closely related species; in others, especially those in which there are differences in the capsules, the practice is to assume that a single species has many types. This has been carried to the point of speaking of serologic groups within a species, and types within the groups. Serologic typing and grouping is based on seemingly stable characteristics of bacteria, but antigenic components, like metabolic reactions and morphology, are not rigid.

The development of antibodies is often regarded as a defensive mechanism on the part of the injected animal. This is considered a false concept. Antibodies occasionally play a role in counteracting toxins or infecting bacteria, and it is certain that they frequently fail to operate defensively. More significant to the argument, antibodies are regularly formed in response to injections of substances which qualify as antigens, whether these are harmless or harmful bacteria, or toxic or inert solutions of chemical substances. The formation of antibodies is a result of antigenic stimulus, not a reaction of defense.

Pathogenic Characterization. Characterization of bacteria by their pathogenicity is not pertinent for the many species which are not pathogenic and are in no way related to infection. The significance of the many species which can alter or destroy plants which human beings enjoy or on which they depend, animals which affect their lives, or their own existence and lives, makes the pathogenicity of bacteria a quality of considerable concern. Bacteria which may be pathogenic are isolated and studied more often than other types.

The growth of a microorganism on or in a plant, animal, or person, with some deleterious effect, constitutes an infection. The concept of the infectivity of bacteria cannot be dissociated from the concept of the receptivity of the organism infected. During an epidemic, or even within a family, the same exposure at the same time, presumably to the same strain of the same species of bacteria, does not lead to the same degrees of illness. This often is due to differences in constitution and in the immunity of the persons exposed to infection, and not to differences in the pathogenicity of the bacteria. Constitutional differences, the chance of proper exposure, the number of bacteria, and purely mechanical barriers may lead to differences in the degrees of illness—all with bacteria of the same pathogenicity. For example: the pneumococcus of pneumonia may reside in the throats of a hundred persons, yet the pneumococcus may reach the lungs of only one; a field of plants may be swept by millions of pathogenic bacteria, yet, although all the plants may be susceptible, the organisms may strike only 5 per cent in the right spot with the right amount of moisture and do injury.

The process of infection consists of the implantation of virulent bacteria in the susceptible host, in the right number, at a spot where they find an environment suitable for growth. Virulent pathogenic organisms are organisms which find the environment in the host suitable for multiplication. They may grow where they are implanted or they may be moved, by sap, lymph, or blood, to some other part where they may multiply. The disease is composed of two phases, after implantation occurs: first, establishment and multiplication; and, second, production of changes which affect the physiology of the affected parts of the host. Some bacteria produce mechanical difficulties by the extent of their growth, some produce cellular changes in the affected region which upset the functioning of that region, and some produce poisons or toxins which are disseminated to cause damage in areas where there is no actual infection.

The virulence of bacteria is a property which may be defined as the ability of an organism to establish itself, to multiply, and to produce disease in a susceptible plant or animal host. The virulence of pathogenic organisms is usually increased by either natural or artificial transfer through a susceptible host; it is usually reduced by a different environment, such as growth on culture media, growth at temperatures different from that of the host, growth in acid, or by old age. Virulence is usually measured in terms of the numbers of bacteria required to produce infection in a susceptible host. With two strains of growing bacteria of the same species, otherwise apparently equal, there may be a difference of as much as 100,000 times in the quantity needed to infect.

SIGNIFICANCE OF BACTERIA

Bacteria have considerable general significance in maintaining the balance of the world. Although they may spoil

dulant fever, and from man, directly or from a contaminated water supply, the bacteria of dysentery, typhoid fever, streptococcus sore throat, including scarlet fever, and diphtheria. Food poisoning may arise from milk or products containing it. The greatest protection against these bacteria is afforded by pasteurization, by heating milk at 142° to 145°F. for 30 minutes, or at 161° to 163°F. for 15 seconds. These temperatures kill pathogenic bacteria, although all bacteria are not killed by pasteurization. Milk is subjected to fermentations of several sorts. Spoilage, through decomposition of the proteins, is undesirable. Souring, through fermentation of the milk sugar, is often useful. The addition of "starter," a mixture of souring bacteria, is a common practice. By applying this to skimmed milk, and later adding butterfat, artificial buttermilk is made. When added to milk, whole or skimmed, an initial slight souring is followed by coagulation with rennin; then, by pressing out

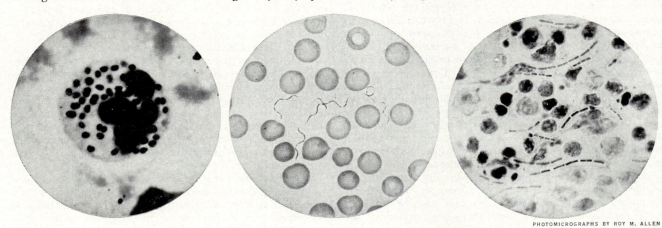

PHOTOMICROGRAPHS BY ROY M. ALLEN

(Left) Micrococcus gonorrheae *showing phagocytosis by polymorphonuclear leucocytes (magnified 4500 X); (Center)* Spirochaeta obermeieri, *the organism which causes European relapsing fever (magnified 2500 X); (Right)* Bacillus anthracis, *a bacterium of anthrax or splenic fever, in pus and showing capsule (magnified 1700 X)*

food, they also aid in the decomposition of vegetation, insects, and animals in the field, and the waste of cities. They may produce disease in cattle, but man is probably indebted to them for the aid they give in preserving a balance in the realm of plants, insects, animals, and, perhaps, even man. A perspective on this sort of influence of bacteria on history is presented in Hans Zinsser's *Rats, Lice, and History.*

Importance in Agriculture. Bacteria are important in nearly all phases of agriculture. They produce diseases in plants. They are transmitted by insects and through the air, by soil, by cuttings, and by seeds. They are sometimes overcome by isolation and burning, but often the development of resistant plants has been the safeguard. Viruses and molds cause more diseases of plants than bacteria. Bacteria produce many diseases in animals, causing losses of cattle, poultry, swine, sheep, and other animals. Veterinarians have problems of prevention and cure of infection similar to those of physicians and health officers. These problems concern sanitation and the preservation of valuable animals to promote the production of safe dairy and meat supplies.

In the production of dairy products, bacteria enter nearly all phases. They produce tuberculosis, undulant fever, which is a contagious abortion called brucellosis, and mastitis in cattle. Milk is a good culture medium for bacteria, usually harmless, which inevitably reach milk from the cow and the environment. Bacteria which produce disease in man include, from the cow, bacteria of tuberculosis and of un-

the liquid whey, cheese is formed. The countless flavors produced in the many varieties of cheese are due almost entirely to the combinations of bacteria and their influence, one on the other. Sour milk and sour cream have many uses. Drinks of fermented milk, containing 1 or 2 per cent of alcohol, have been made in various countries for many years. Occasionally, bacteria which cause coloration or excessive viscosity permeate a dairy, which must then be elaborately cleaned.

Effect on Soils. The soil may contain millions of bacteria per gram or billions per ounce. Harmful organisms are relatively rare in the soil. Collectively, they change millions of tons of the chemical elements of the soil. The decomposition processes which enrich the soil are of tremendous benefit. Alfalfa and clover, and the thousands of other varieties of leguminous plants, develop nodules on their roots due to bacteria which are capable of taking nitrogen from the air and fixing it in the soil as soluble salts beneficial to plants. Nitrogen is an essential element in fertile soil; it is continuously removed and only part of it is replaced directly, making the fixation of nitrogen a significant contribution to mankind's welfare.

Control and Use in Foods. Bacteria must also be considered in foods other than milk. Nicolas Appert (1749-1841) discovered in 1810, before Pasteur was born, that food could be preserved by heat. Spoilage of foods is usually caused by bacterial growth. Most bacteria are killed quickly at less than boiling temperatures, but those which form spores may survive many hours in boiling water. These include the spores of botulism, a disease which is usually fatal and a result of the toxin formed in canned foods, or foods sealed from air, rather than of infection by the organism. Modern canning processes specify heating well above the boiling point for all except decidedly acid foods, or those packed in decidedly strong brines. Preservation of foods by freezing, or partial preservation by refrigeration, is based on the prevention of multiplication of bacteria; the bacteria are not killed by the process and may start to develop as soon as the food is warmed.

Bacteria are also used in the production of foods. The countless varieties of alcoholic drinks are usually based on fermentations by yeasts, rather than by bacteria, but bacteria may play a role either in fermentation or in spoilage. A bacterial process may carry alcoholic fermentation into the acid stage, producing vinegar. The fermentation industries are based on inoculations and cultivations similar to those in the dairy and the bacteriologic laboratory. Inoculations, as in the production of sauerkraut, ensilage, hard cider, or wines, may be a natural rather than a deliberate process.

Industrial Uses. Industrial uses of bacteria, and difficulties from bacteria in industry, are scattered. Bacteria have some roles in the retting of flax, the curing of tobacco, and the tanning of leather. In the food industries, such as the manufacture of bread, wines, vinegars, and sauerkraut, yeasts and bacteria "make" and sometimes "break" the producer. The use of bacteria to produce chemical substances, utilizing their ability to formulate their own energy, is by no means exhausted. The processes ebb and flow as means are found for synthesis which obviate the need for biologic control. One industry, originating with penicillin made from a mold, is the production of antibiotic substances, such as streptomycin or tyrothricin. Bacteria furnish the basis for the production of vaccines, serums, and skin-test products used in the prevention and cure of disease.

Role in Medicine. The role of bacteriology in medicine centers in infectious diseases. In this respect, differentiation between bacteria, viruses, rickettsiae, yeasts, molds, and protozoa is often inconsequential, for infection is subject largely to the same rules in all cases.

Cycles of Infection. Infection is a process which is studied in terms of two cycles of events in the life of the disease-producing organism. One cycle is that which occurs outside the infected body; the other is that which occurs within the body after the incidence of infection and before the recovery or death of the patient.

Knowledge of the external cycle is important in maintaining public health. Some bacteria may be derived from the soil and infect wounds. Others may be carried by insects, accidentally, or because the insect is essential in the cycle of development. Disease-causing bacteria may be derived from the bite or contact of animals, or from their milk or meat. They often are carried only directly from person to person by droplets of saliva, dried nuclei, or dust, with a short period of survival outside the body. With venereal infection, and with wounds, organisms are directly inoculated. Foods and water may be a means of introducing contaminating pathogenic bacteria into the body. The life of bacteria outside the body may be complicated and long or simple and limited. The inoculation into the body must be adapted to the organism: the bacteria of tetanus may be swallowed safely but not inoculated into a wound; the bacteria of typhoid fever may be inoculated into a wound but not swallowed.

The internal cycle, after organisms are introduced to the right spot, may be equally simple, or it may be complicated.

The inoculation of a cluster of spherical bacteria, called staphylococci, into the skin through a hair follicle may lead to the formation of a boil. The same staphylococcus, or a chain of cocci, called streptococci, may enter the skin through an injury and reach the blood stream, producing a general infection or septicemia, which, before the advent of sulpha drugs and antibiotics, usually led to death. The bacteria of tuberculosis may lodge in several spots, frequently the lungs, and develop slowly in the spot of inoculation, gradually ceasing to grow in most cases, but sometimes continuing until other foci of infection occur and until functional disturbance kills the patient. Bacteria of diphtheria, which are club-shaped rods, grow in the throat, but the disease is more than a sore throat, because of the potent toxin produced and diffused throughout the body.

Control of Infections. The rules of infection are relatively simple, but infections are not easy to control. The nursing profession is concerned with disinfection and isolation, so that remedial measures for the patient may not lead to transmission to well persons, including the nurse. Laboratory diagnosis of infections includes, besides biochemical tests and examinations of blood cells, the isolation and identification of the causative or suspected bacteria. Sometimes the serum of patients' blood is examined for the presence of antibodies produced by the organism of infection, e.g., the Wassermann test for syphilis and its many variations. The health officer, and his corps of inspectors and epidemiologists, is concerned with the location of a case of infection, its isolation, and tracing the source to protect the rest of the population. He is also concerned with vaccination and sanitation, to prevent the occurrence of infection by blocking bacteria and other infecting agents at some point in their external cycles. The sanitary inspector operates on the principle that cleanliness will not only improve aesthetics and appearance, but will also prevent spoilage and the transmission of pathogenic microorganisms. The physician is concerned primarily with the detection of the kind of infection and where it is located in the body, with restricting its spread, with remedy of the damage done, and with the prevention of its recurrence. He also has his share in preventing dissemination and, by vaccination in the few instances in which this is reasonable, in preventing the disease.   M. S. M.

BACTRIA, the ancient name of what is now the northeastern part of Afghanistan. Bactria extended from the Hindu Kush on the south to the Amu Darya (Oxus River) on the north; the old capital was on the site of the modern city of Balkh. Bactria rose as an independent kingdom, but was captured by Cyrus the Great and made a satrapy of the Persian Empire. *See also* AFGHANISTAN.

BADAGAS. *See* ASIATIC TRIBES.

BADAJOZ [ba'thaho'th], the name of a province and the capital city of that province, in western Spain, located in the Estremadura region.

The City. The city is situated on the Guadiana River, approximately 130 mi. northwest of Sevilla. It occupies a strategic location near the Spanish-Portuguese frontier, and, as a consequence, it was heavily fortified in previous centuries. In addition to serving as an administrative center, civil, military, and ecclesiastical, Badajoz is a transit point for Spanish-Portuguese trade and possesses a few local industries producing chiefly liquors, soap, and crude textiles. It is the last Spanish station on the Madrid-Ciudad Real-Lisbon line. The city, surrounded by a wall studded with eight bastions, is overlooked by a hill crowned with an imposing castle of Arab origin. The river is spanned by the granite Puente de las Palmas, protected at both ends. On the north bank of the river, the fortifications are completed by the Fort of San Cristóbal. The massive Cathedral of San Juan, erected in the thirteenth century, also presents a fortresslike appearance.

Badajoz became the capital of a small Moorish kingdom (Aftasid dynasty) in the eleventh century after the fall of the caliphate of Córdoba. It later was part of the Almoravid and Almohad empires. Though occupied by Alfonso I of Portu-

and swine. Large land holdings are the rule and do not conduce to the support of a big agricultural population. Industries are few and small, and operate essentially for the local market. Trade is of some importance but is handicapped by inadequate transport facilities, both rail and highway.

Cities of consequence, with their populations in 1940, are: Mérida (22,440); Almendralejo (21,071), agricultural market place; Don Benito (20,163), farming and small industrial center on the Guadiana; Villanueva de la Serena (16,060), farming center; Azuaga (15,413), livestock market; and

Pack mules on a hilly street in Badajoz, Spain

gal in 1169, it was not definitively delivered from Moslem rule until 1227 by Alfonso IX of León. Portuguese rule was briefly re-established four times between the fourteenth and early eighteenth centuries, and the city acquired the sobriquet "Key to Portugal."

During the Napoleonic Era the French failed to capture it in 1808 and 1809, but finally succeeded in taking the city through bribery in 1811. A year later the Duke of Wellington besieged the city and took it after a singularly bloody battle, following which the British soldiery subjected the city to three days of pillage. Nationalist troops occupied the city in the opening days of the Civil War of 1936-1939 and butchered a large number of pro-government sympathizers. Pop. 1940, 32,604.

The Province. The province of Badajoz has an area of 8,349 sq. mi., the largest in Spain, but it has one of the country's lowest densities of population with an estimated 92 persons per sq. mi. in 1947. It is bounded on the north by the province of Cáceres, east by the region of New Castile, south by the region of Andalucia, and west by Portugal.

The Guadiana River flows from east to west through the northern part and then follows the Portuguese frontier southward for approximately 30 mi. In the northwest corner lies the low Sierra de San Pedro, and in the south is the Sierra Morena culminating in the Sierra de Tudia (3,450 ft.). The terrain is predominantly hilly; the soil varies widely in fertility, and the rainfall is scanty.

The fertile Tierra de Barros district in the center of the province produces large amounts of cereals. Grapes are another important crop. Certain other zones of the province are cultivated, but wide areas are left to pasture for sheep, goats,

Jérez de los Caballeros (12,486), surrounded by a Moorish wall and the home of Núñez de Balboa, discoverer of the Pacific. Pop. province 1940, 742,547.   R. G. W.

BADAKHSHAN [baˈdaxshaˈn], a province of Afghanistan, is located in the extreme northeastern part of the country, within a large bend of the upper Amu Darya (Oxus River), which forms the northern and eastern boundaries of the province. The Tadzhik Soviet Socialist Republic is north and east of the river. High ranges of the Hindu Kush form a barrier along the southern boundary. This relatively isolated and unknown province of Afghanistan has cold, snowy winters and hot, dry summers. There is a small amount of local agriculture, and some lapis lazuli and rubies are found, but pastoral nomadism is the major economic activity; fat-tailed sheep and goats are the most common animals, while yaks and camels are the beasts of burden. Some of the region is forested, and there are numerous wild animals such as leopards, bears, mountain goats, and sheep. The people are entirely Moslem and are called Badakhchis. The capital city of Faizabad is connected with the rest of Afghanistan by trail, or by very poor road.

In ancient times a caravan route from India to the Oxus crossed the province by way of the Kocha River. This area was included in the region of ancient Bactria of the Greeks; legend associates Alexander the Great with the early kings of the district. Chinese explorers visited the region about A.D. 630, and Marco Polo was there in 1272. The district has undergone invasions and numerous local feuds and uprisings, but since 1859 has been ruled by the Afghan royal family.   J. E. F.

BADARIAN [bədɑ′riən], a very early culture thought to have prevailed in Lower and Middle Egypt in predynastic times. It was named after El Badari, a site on the east bank of the Nile at approximately 27° N. lat. investigated between 1922 and 1925. The Badarians supported life in part by hunting and fishing, but mainly by cultivating emmer wheat and breeding cattle, sheep, and goats. The technology was chiefly based on flint, from which they chipped beautiful arrowheads and daggers; although copper was hammered into beads and malachite was used for painting round the eyes, there is no evidence of true metallurgy. The dead were buried contracted in simple trench graves dug in the sand, and climatic conditions have preserved the bodies exceptionally well. The men were either clean-shaven or beardless and wore their hair long; the women wore theirs in plaits and had curly fringes down to the eyes. Undergarments were made from a linenlike substance, strips of which were also wrapped round the head. Outer garments were of animal skins, the hairy side generally being worn innermost for warmth. J.G.D.C.

BADEN, an Austrian watering place situated about 15 mi. south of Vienna, on the Schwechat River in the foothills of the Wienerwald. The thermal springs at Baden have been known since Roman times, when they were called the Thermae Pannoniae. The baths were destroyed by the Hungarians and the Turks but have since been restored. Parks and promenades are a feature of the town, which is a favorite excursion point from Vienna. Near by is the Calvarienberg, whose summit dominates the city. Pop. 1951, 21,312. S. Van V.

BY BURTON HOLMES FROM EWING GALLOWAY
Entrance to State Park, Baden, Austria

BADEN [bɑ′dən], a region in southwestern Germany bordering on Alsace and Switzerland. Made a duchy in 1806, in 1919 it became a state under the Weimar Republic. The area of Baden is 15,071 sq. km., or 5,822 sq. mi., and it had a population in 1953 of 2,996,400. The eastern area is a mountainous region containing the Black and Odin Forests; the western section is a broad valley, bordered by the Rhine River from Basel to Mannheim, a distance of about 140 mi. The Danube (Donau) River rises in southern Baden, about 12 mi. northeast of Freiburg; in this area is also the lower Neckar valley. The principal towns are Karlsruhe, Mannheim (the capital), Heidelburg, Freiburg, Pforzheim, Baden-Baden, and Konstanz, on the Lake of Constance or Bodensee, through which the Rhine flows. The western section of Baden has the mildest climate in Germany and a very fertile soil. Among the agricultural products are wheat, potatoes, oats, rye, tobacco, and wine

grapes. The forested mountain region yields both timber and minerals, including copper, silver, cobalt, lead, iron, cadmium, coal, alum, sulphur, and salt. The principal manufactures are textiles, jewelry, paper, leather goods, mirrors, clocks, machinery, and wines. There are evidences of Roman occupation throughout Baden; the Baden-Baden mineral springs were used in Roman times, and the town was a fashionable health resort for centuries. The Freiburg minster is one of the finest examples of Gothic buildings in Germany. Baden's early history is that of its cities, as there was no national consciousness, only that of the rulers, who held their strongholds against enemies. The *Markgrafen* (margraves) who ruled for the longest period of time were those descended from Conrad of Zähringen (duke 1122-1152), who founded Freiburg in 1120 and whose ancestor Berthold or Berzelin was related to the house of Staufen (Hohenstaufen). Berthold's son, Berthold I, was given the title of Duke of Kärnthen in 1061 and later Margrave of Verona. He died in 1087, and the family divided into two branches. The younger son, Berthold II, inherited the larger share of the ancestral domains and reigned until 1111. The older son, Margrave Hermann II, the head of the House of Baden, founded the dynasty which ruled Baden until 1918. During the Middle Ages, Baden was divided and reunited several times as the ruling house divided into a number of branches and later various of these branches died out. In 1806, Napoleon, trying to establish an empire similar to that of Charlemagne, created the grand duchy of Baden as part of the Confederation of the Rhine in return for the support of the incumbent ruler of Baden, Charles Frederick. The latter was succeeded in 1811 by his grandson, Charles Louis Frederick, who, although married to Napoleon's adopted daughter, Eugenie de Beauharnais, withdrew from the Confederation of the Rhine in 1813 when Napoleon's fortunes seemed on the wane and in 1815 joined the German Confederation. Thus he was able to retain his dukedom after Napoleon's downfall. Baden was little disturbed by the tide of revolutions that swept over Europe in 1830, but in 1848 Duke Leopold was driven out of Baden. He appealed to Prussia for aid, and an army led by Prince William of Prussia (later William I of Germany) restored him to his dukedom. In 1852 Leopold died and his son, Frederick, succeeded him as regent and became Duke Frederick I in 1856. In 1856 Frederick married Louise, Prince William's daughter. Nevertheless, Baden allied itself with Austria in the Austro-Prussian War (1866). In 1870, however, Frederick took the lead in advocating the entrance of the South German states into the North German Confederation and thus helped to bring about the unification of Germany in 1871. Frederick was succeeded in 1907 by his son, Frederick II, who abdicated in 1918. Baden then joined the Weimer Republic as a state. When France and Belgium invaded the Ruhr, France also took over part of Baden. After World War II, Baden was divided between the zones assigned to the United States and France. The United States governed the patchwork of states consisting of Würtemburg-Baden, Greater Hesse, and Bavaria until the zones of Great Britain, France, and the United States were united in 1948. R.H.L.

BADEN-BADEN [bɑ′dən bɑ′dən] (so called to distinguish it from spas with similar names in Austria and Switzerland), a resort town in central Baden, in southwestern Germany, 18 mi. southwest of Karlsruhe. It lies at an elevation of 600 ft. in the Oos River Valley, in the picturesque, well-wooded, northwest Black Forest. Its warm springs were known in Roman times, when a Roman colony called Civitas Aurelia Aquensis was established near by, and the salubrious climate and springs have made the town Germany's most popular luxury watering place, rivaled only by Wiesbaden. There are numerous hotels and baths, ruins of an old castle on a height commanding an excellent view of the Rhine Valley, an imposing *Konversationshaus,* and fine parks and promenades. Baden-Baden suffered little damage during World War II, and at the close of the war was included in the French zone of occupation. The population in 1953 was 40,400.   C. C. H.

BADEN-POWELL, ROBERT STEPHENSON SMYTH [be'dən po'əl] (1857-1941), first Baron of Gilwell, was born in London, Feb. 22, 1857, the sixth son of Prof. H. G. Baden-Powell of Oxford. Educated at Charterhouse, in 1876 he began his military career as an adjutant in the 13th Hussars, serving in South Africa and the East. Stationed at Malta from 1890 to 1893, he acted as assistant military secretary, and, in 1895, was appointed to a command in Ashanti, British Africa. In the Matabele campaign of 1896-1897, Baden-Powell was chief staff officer, and, as lieutenant colonel, to which rank he was promoted in 1897, he won considerable fame and the rank of major general for his 215-day defense of Mafeking (Oct. 12, 1899 to May 17, 1900) in the Boer War. In the years which followed the war, Baden-Powell's organization of the South African Constabulary brought him the post of inspector general of that police force. His last command was that of the Northumbrian Territorial Division. He retired in 1910 with the rank of lieutenant general.

The Boy Scout and Girl Guide movements, which he and his sister Agnes founded in 1908 and 1910, respectively, and to which he devoted the rest of his life, were adopted in many countries of the world. Baden-Powell, as Chief Scout, continued active in this work until his death on Jan. 8, 1941, in Nyeri, Kenya Colony, Africa.

Baden-Powell received a baronetcy in 1921 and was elevated to the peerage in 1929, taking his title from a Boy Scout training center, Gilwell Park. Other countries also honored him for his work among the youth of the world: France made him a Commander of the Legion of Honor in 1922 and in 1936 he received the Grand Cordon of the Legion of Honor. In 1928, Baden-Powell became a Knight of the Grand Cross of the British Order of St. Michael and St. George. He also received decorations from Afghanistan, Austria, Belgium, Chile, Czechoslovakia, Denmark, Estonia, Greece, Hungary, Holland, Latvia, Lithuania, Luxembourg, Romania, and Sweden.

Baden-Powell was the author of many books; these included *The Matabele Campaign* (1896), *Scouting for Boys* (1908), *My Adventures as a Spy* (1915), *Girl Guiding* (1917), *Lessons from the 'Varsity of Life* (1933), *Adventures and Accidents* (1936), and *Paddle Your Own Canoe* (1939).
                                      L. W. B.

BADGER, a large, squat member of the weasel family, Mustelidae. The badger's upper parts and short tail are covered with long, shaggy, grizzled hairs, and the distinctive white face has a large, brown crescent on the cheeks. The short forelimbs are armed with heavy claws, which are efficient tools for digging out the ground squirrels and other rodents on which the animal chiefly feeds. Badgers occur over much of North America, from the Pacific Coast as far

PANORAMA OF BADEN-BADEN, FAMOUS SPA OF GERMANY'S BLACK FOREST REGION

EWING GALLOWAY

NORTH DAKOTA BADLANDS, NEAR MEDORA

east as Ohio. Their favorite habitat is situated in the prairie states and the mountainous areas of the West. During the coldest months of the year, badgers remain in a comatose condition, seldom venturing from their burrows while frigid temperatures prevail. Full-grown badgers weigh over 20 lbs. The fur is used chiefly in trimmings and shaving brushes

BADGER, TAXIDEA TAXUS

and for "pointing" more valuable pelts. The American badger is technically known as *Taxidea taxus,* while the European form is placed in the genus *Meles.* There are several Asiatic species, but these have little commercial value.

W. J. Ha.

BADLANDS, a descriptive term adopted from common usage for regions of the earth that have been severely dissected and eroded, and have weird and fantastic geologic forms. Badland regions are usually formed in semiarid areas, where soft material such as clays and horizontally bedded sandstones or shales are exposed and unprotected by soil and vegetation. When precipitation occurs in this area, particularly on slopes, the water runs off rapidly, eroding the soft surface and cutting numerous deep gullies which become deeper and steeper until the area is eroded into a badland of pinnacles and steep buttes and is useless for human settlement or cultivation. Some of the badland areas are in regions of multicolored clays and sandstones, and the resultant color

and shapes have made them tourist centers. One badland area is along the Greybull River in the Big Horn Basin of Wyoming, and the largest region is the Big Badlands of southwestern South Dakota. The Big Badlands along the White and Cheyenne rivers cover an area about 100 mi. long and from 25 to 40 mi. wide on the eastern and southern edges of the Black Hills. This region is famous for the large number of fossils exposed by the erosion. There are similar regions in Asia and South America. J. E. F.

BADMINTON [bæ'dmɪntən], a game played with light, strong rackets, which are used to strike a shuttlecock (a feathered, cork missile) back and forth across a net within a rectangular-shaped court (Fig. 1).

The game derives much of its fascination from the fact that an extremely varied repertory of strokes is involved, from the most vicious smash to the most delicate of drop shots. There are few games in which it is possible to develop so much deception and variety of attack and to mask for such a length of time the intention of the striker. This fact derives from the lightness of the rackets which are used, so that the wrist can be used much more than in most other tennis-type games; and even more from the peculiarities in the flight of the shuttlecock or bird which, because of its sixteen feathers and light cork base, decelerates with extreme rapidity after being forcefully struck. The game as played by experts is very strenuous and requires great stamina. There is general agreement that badminton is not a particularly good outdoor game because of the influence of the lightest breeze upon the flight of the bird.

History. There is little agreement about the historical originals of badminton, although most authorities seem to feel that the game was developed from a pastime of antiquity known as battledore and shuttlecock, which intrigued British Army officers stationed in India and was brought to England about 1870. A British woman player reports that in the early days of the game, following the founding of the English Badminton Association in 1893, the court was shaped like an hourglass and the feathers on the shuttlecock were curved in such a way that the bird was barrel-shaped.

657

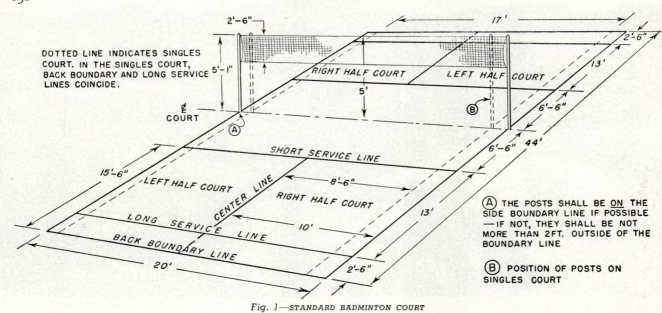

DOTTED LINE INDICATES SINGLES
COURT. IN THE SINGLES COURT,
BACK BOUNDARY AND LONG SERVICE
LINES COINCIDE.

Ⓐ THE POSTS SHALL BE ON THE
SIDE BOUNDARY LINE IF POSSIBLE
—IF NOT, THEY SHALL BE NOT
MORE THAN 2FT. OUTSIDE OF THE
BOUNDARY LINE

Ⓑ POSITION OF POSTS ON
SINGLES COURT

Fig. 1—STANDARD BADMINTON COURT

It is generally conceded that the oldest badminton club in the world with a continuous existence is the Badminton Club of the City of New York, which was founded in 1878 by two gentlemen enthusiasts who settled there—one having arrived from England, the other from India, and each having learned the game in the country from which he came. However, the game did not become widely popular in the United States until the middle 1930's. The American Badminton Association was formed in 1936. There had been a flourishing association in Canada for the previous fifteen years. The International Badminton Federation, an organization founded in 1934, lists approximately twenty national badminton associations among its members.

Play. The game of singles is played by two persons in a series of innings. One inning lasts as long as the server continues to score points. Failure to score a point on the serve or in the following play forfeits the service to the opponent. The serve must be delivered so that it would fall into the correct service court were it allowed to touch the floor. When the server's score is even, the service is delivered from the right service court to any part of the opponent's left service court. In badminton the shuttlecock is always played in the air, and play on any point terminates, or service changes, when the shuttlecock strikes the court.

Scoring. A standard game consists of fifteen or twenty-one points as may be decided, the usual game being fifteen. For women, eleven points constitutes a game. In case the score is tied at thirteen or fourteen all, the player first reaching that score has the option of "setting" the game at five or three points more, rather than concluding when the score reaches fifteen. In case the game is "set" at five, the first to score eighteen points is the winner. In case the game is set at three, seventeen points are necessary to win.

Championships. The American Badminton Association is the governing body so far as United States championships are concerned. There are a large number of state and regional associations representing clubs in practically all parts of the United States. In 1940, the International Badminton Federation adopted a set of regulations for determining the International Badminton Championship to be played for the Thomas Cup donated by Sir George Thomas, president of the federation.

UNITED STATES BADMINTON CHAMPIONS

MEN'S

	Singles	Doubles
1937	Walter R. Kramer	Chester Goss—Donald Eversoll
1938	Walter R. Kramer	Hamilton Law—Richard Yeager
1939	David G. Freeman	Hamilton Law—Richard Yeager
1940	David G. Freeman	David G. Freeman—Chester Goss
1941	David G. Freeman	David G. Freeman—Chester Goss
1942	David G. Freeman	David G. Freeman—Chester Goss
1943—1946 No tournaments		
1947	David G. Freeman	David G. Freeman—Webb Kimball
1948	David G. Freeman	David G. Freeman—Wynn Rogers
1949	Marten Mendez	Barney McCay—Wynn Rogers
1950	Marten Mendez	Barney McCay—Wynn Rogers
1951	Joe Alston	Joe Alston—Wynn Rogers
1952	Marten Mendez	Joe Alston—Wynn Rogers

WOMEN'S

	Singles	Doubles
1937	Mrs. Del Barkhuff	Mrs. Del Barkhuff—Zoe G. Smith
1938	Mrs. Del Barkhuff	Mrs. Roy Bergman—Helen Gibson
1939	Mary E. Whittemore	Mrs. Del Barkhuff—Zoe G. Smith
1940	Evelyn Boldrick	Elizabeth Anselm—Helen Zabriski
1941	Thelma Kingsbury	Janet Wright—Thelma Kingsbury
1942	Evelyn Boldrick	Janet Wright—Evelyn Boldrick
1943—1946 No tournaments		
1947	Ethel Marshall	Janet Wright—Thelma Kingsbury Scovil
1948	Ethel Marshall	Janet Wright—Thelma Kingsbury Scovil
1949	Ethel Marshall	Janet Wright—Thelma Kingsbury Scovil
1950	Ethel Marshall	Janet Wright—Thelma Kingsbury Scovil
1951	Ethel Marshall	Loma Smith—Dorothy Hann
1952	Ethel Marshall	Ethel Marshall—Bea Massman

MIXED DOUBLES

1937	Mrs. Del Barkhuff—Hamilton Law
1938	Mrs. Del Barkhuff—Hamilton Law
1939	Zoe G. Smith—Richard Yeager
1940	Sally L. Williams—David G. Freeman
1941	Sally L. Williams—David G. Freeman
1942	Sally L. Williams—David G. Freeman
1943—1946 No tournaments	
1947	Virginia Hill—Wynn Rogers
1948	Mrs. Patsy Stephens—Clinton Stephens
1949	Loma Smith—Wynn Rogers
1950	Loma Smith—Wynn Rogers
1951	Loma Smith—Wynn Rogers
1952	Helen Tibbetts—Wynn Rogers

L. T. R.

BADOGLIO, PIETRO [bɑdɔ'lyo] (1871-), marshal of Italy, was born in Grazzano Montferrato in the province of Piedmont, Sept. 28, 1871. After his graduation from a military school in Turin, he participated in the East African campaign as an artillery lieutenant from 1895 to 1896. He attended the War College in 1899. In the course of the Libyan Campaign, 1911-1912, he was promoted to the rank of major. During World War I, he fought the Austrians, first as a lieutenant colonel, then as a colonel and chief of staff of the Sixth

PIETRO BADOGLIO

WIDE WORLD PHOTO

Army Corps. He soon became a general and was placed in command of the Second Army. He counterattacked on the Piave after the disaster at Caporetto and is credited with the victory at Vittorio Veneto in November 1918. At the end of the war he was in supreme command of the Italian forces. He was appointed leader of the Italian Commission that negotiated the armistice with the Austrians. In recognition of services rendered during the war, he was appointed chief of the general staff and senator for life. In 1921, he was sent as envoy extraordinary to Romania and the United States. A convinced monarchist, he was completely opposed at first to the Fascist forces of Benito Mussolini. But for his intervention, Mussolini probably would have seized the throne, thus destroying even the nominal rule of the king. In 1924, Badoglio was sent as ambassador to Brazil and, in 1925, he was again appointed chief of the general staff, a post he retained until 1940. From 1928 to 1933, Badoglio was also governor general of Libya. In 1926, he had been made a marshal of Italy, and, in 1929, he was further honored when he was created marquis of Sabotino. In 1935, he was appointed high commissioner in East Africa, and on May 5, 1936, led his victorious troops into Addis Ababa to complete Italy's conquest of Ethiopia. He was appointed viceroy of Ethiopia but soon asked that he be released from his post, whereupon he was created duke of Addis Ababa. When in June 1940, Italy declared war against the Allies, Badoglio was placed in command of all Italian forces. He resigned on Dec. 6, 1941, when he was blamed for the setback which Italian troops suffered in Greece. When Mussolini was forced to flee after the Allied invasion of Italy in the summer of 1943, Badoglio emerged from his retirement to head the government of his country. On September 3, he signed a secret armistice with the Allies, and five days later he announced to his people the unconditional surrender of Italy. It was Badoglio's government which declared war against Germany on Oct. 13, 1943. Badoglio resigned as premier of Italy on June 9, 1944. Since then he has lived in retirement. He has supported the Italian republic,

which replaced the monarchy, and has consistently opposed Communism. E. B. A.

BADUI. *See* INDONESIAN PEOPLES.

BADULLA [bədʌ'lə], the capital city of Uva Province, situated in the mountains of south central Ceylon, about 52 mi. southeast of Kandy, approximately 2,200 ft. above sea level, on the short Oya River in the Uva Basin. The Uva Basin is surrounded by steep and picturesque mountains, and the local mountain and forest scenery is unusually beautiful. Because of its elevation and protecting ring of mountains, Badulla and the Uva Basin have a comparatively dry and cool climate. The average annual temperature is about 72° F., and the average annual rainfall is between 70 and 80 in. Large sections of the basin were formerly planted with rice, but some of the paddy land has gone out of cultivation and become high grass and bush area. The hillsides around and above Badulla are planted in tea. A little rubber and cacao are grown in the region, as well as local vegetables. Ducks and water buffalo and bullocks are common farm animals. The city serves as the trade center for the district, and it is served by railroad. Pop. (est. 1943), 11,270.

BAEDEKER, KARL [be'dəkər] (1801-1859), German publisher, was born in Essen, Nov. 3, 1801. He received his early education in Essen and at The Hague and in 1817 went to Heidelberg to learn the printing business. He studied at Heidelberg University and from 1823 to 1825 worked in Berlin. After a year of travel he settled in Coblenz, where in 1829 he bought and almost wholly rewrote a *Traveler's Handbook for the Rhine,* by J. A. Klein, which had been published by Franz Röhling in Coblenz in 1828. As a result of his own travel experience, largely on foot, Baedeker learned that there was need for a guide that would give authentic information on hotels and inns, living and travel costs, the distance between places, and the best routes to follow. He included such facts, accordingly, and pointed out ways to economize. As the handbook did not carry any advertising, Baedeker was entirely free to use his own knowledge and to present information that was unaffected by commercial considerations. He refused all gifts or other financial support and by his freedom from outside influences created such an acceptance of his recommendations that his approval was widely sought. In 1839 Baedeker issued his yellow-backed *Rhine Handbook*. Traveling constantly, he wrote of a journey to Holland, and several years later, in 1842, he issued travel books on Germany, Austria, and northern Italy. In 1844 the *Handbook of Switzerland* appeared and soon became one of the most popular of his series. By 1842 Baedeker had adopted the familiar red cover for his series. The volumes, written primarily for the traveler of modest means, were compact, easy to handle, and contained accurately drawn maps and plans of cities. In 1845 Baedeker issued the fourth edition of *Traveler's Handbook of Conversations* in four languages: English, German, French, and Italian. In 1855 he issued his last publication, *Handbook of Paris and Its Environs.* Baedeker retired shortly afterward, turning his business over to his sons, Ernest (1833-1861) and Karl (1837-1911). Fritz Baedeker (1844-1925) became head of the firm in 1878. Karl Baedeker, the founder, died in Coblenz, Oct. 4, 1859. Fritz built the business to large proportions. In 1872 the publishing firm moved to Leipzig, continuing to issue its guide books in English, German, and French. The Leipzig establishment was destroyed by bombing during World War II, but in 1949 it was reported that

Karl, a great-grandson of the founder, had received a publishing license from British authorities in Germany and was planning to publish a guide to Schleswig-Holstein.

BAEKELAND, LEO HENDRIK [be′klənd; ba′kəlant] (1863-1944), inventor of Velox photographic paper and of the plastic, Bakelite, was born in Ghent, Belgium, on Nov. 14, 1863, and died in Beacon, N. Y., on Feb. 23, 1944. After graduating from the University of Ghent in 1882, he studied electrochemistry at the Polytechnicum, Charlottenburg, Ger-

LEO HENDRIK BAEKELAND

KEYSTONE VIEW

many. In 1889 he came to the United States, after teaching several years in Belgium. During the next few years Baekeland invented photographic paper, and in 1893 founded the Nepera Chemical Company in Yonkers, N. Y., for its manufacture. But in 1899 the rights were acquired by the Eastman Kodak Co., and Baekeland diverted his research into engineering fields. In 1906 he produced a new plastic by the interaction of phenol and formaldehyde and named it Bakelite. Because of its wide industrial applications where natural resins, rubber, or celluloid are not suitable, the discovery of Bakelite stimulated research in many synthetic organic fields and led to a variety of new plastics. For his important discoveries Baekeland was awarded the Nichols medal (1909), the John Scott medal of the Franklin Institute (1910), the Willard Gibbs medal (1913), the Chandler medal of Columbia University (1914), and the Perkin medal (1916). Baekeland served as president of the American Electro-Chemical Society, and of the American Institute of Chemical Engineers.   H. N. A.

BAEL FRUIT, a fruit allied to the orange, borne on a small tree (*Aegle marmelos*) of the rue family. It is native to India, and widely grown in tropical Asia. The trees are sometimes spiny, with three-parted leaves and fragrant white flowers. The hard-shelled yellow-green fruits, containing an orange-fragrant sweet pulp, are highly prized by the Hindus for food and for their medicinal qualities. The tree is sacred to Siva and is much planted in temple gardens.   J. C. Wis.

BAER, KARL ERNST VON [be′r] (1792-1876), distinguished Russian naturalist and geographer, known as the "father of modern embryology," was born at Piep, Estonia, Feb. 29, 1792. He attended school at Reval and, from 1810 to 1814, studied medicine at the University of Dorpat where he received his M.D. From 1814 to 1817 von Baer studied comparative anatomy at Würzburg. In 1817 he became prosector at the University of Königsberg and in 1819

was appointed professor of zoology and chief of the new zoological museum which he organized. In 1826 he began to teach anatomy and in 1828 he was appointed a member of the St. Petersburg Academy of Sciences. In 1829 he went to St. Petersburg to teach zoology, returning in 1830 to Königsberg. In 1834 he became librarian at the St. Petersburg Academy of Sciences, and engaged in research in zoology and anatomy. In 1851-1852 he was inspector of fisheries for the empire. In 1837 he visited Nova Zembla and during 1851-1856 studied the fisheries of Lake Peipus and the Baltic and Caspian seas. He remained with the Academy until 1867 when he retired to Dorpat as an honorary member of the Academy. Von Baer's contributions to science were pre-eminent and his influence far-reaching and lasting. Creator of modern embryology, discoverer of the human ovum and the notochord, he originated the germ-layer theory, formulated the law of embryonic development, exploded the animalcule doctrine, and founded the St. Petersburg Society for Geography and Ethnography and the German Anthropological Society. His honors included the Copley Medal of the Royal Society (1867). Following his discovery of the mammalian egg and the human ovum he published *Epistola de ovi mammalium et hominis genesi* (1827). His other major works were his *Entwickelungsgeschichte der Thiere* (part 1, 1828; part 2, 1837; and part 3, 1888) ("History of the Development of Animals"); and *Untersuchungen über die Entwickelung der Fische* (1835) ("Researches on the Development of Fishes"). In 1864 the Estonian nobles published for private circulation at their expense a de luxe edition of von Baer's *Autobiography,* which was reprinted in 1867 for public sale. He died at Dorpat, Nov. 28, 1876.   D. D. M.

BAEYER, JOHANN FRIEDRICH WILHELM ADOLF, VON [be′yər] (1835-1917), German organic chemist, was born in Berlin on Oct. 31, 1835. After completing some years of training in Heidelberg under R. W. Bunsen and F. A. Kekulé, von Baeyer received his doctor's degree in the laboratory of A. W. Hofmann in Berlin in 1858, becoming an assistant professor there in 1866. In 1872 he was appointed professor of chemistry and director of the chemical laboratories at Strasbourg. Three years later he succeeded Justus von Liebig at Munich, where he built the New Chemical Institute, in which two generations of distinguished organic chemists were trained under his tutelage. Here he investigated the properties of indigo, producing it synthetically. His researches were begun in 1865; and in 1880 his patents were acquired by the Badische Anilin and Soda Fabrik and the Hoechst Farbwerke, which had been carrying out researches for eighteen years at a cost of $5,000,000. Two processes were involved in the manufacture of indigo from coal-tar products: one commencing with benzene, the other with naphthalene. Synthetic indigo was later found to be impracticable commercially. He was the recipient of the Davy medal in 1881 and of the Nobel prize in chemistry in 1905. In this latter year, on the seventieth anniversary of his birth, his scientific papers were published in two volumes at Brunswick, Germany. The broad scope of these research papers testifies to his caliber as a scientist and to the tremendous influence he exerted in the rapid development of organic chemistry. The topics include the organic arsenic compounds, the uric acid group, indigo, pyrrole and pyridine bases, phthaleins, terpenes, nitroso compounds, furfural, aromatic peroxides, basic properties of benzene, aliphatic series, hydroaromatic compounds, and acetylene compounds. Von Baeyer died in Munich on Sept. 5, 1917.   H. N. A.

HUDSON'S BAY COMPANY POST, AT ARCTIC BAY, BAFFIN ISLAND

BAEYER, JOHANN JAKOB VON (1794-1858), Prussian soldier and geometrician and father of the chemist Adolf von Baeyer, was born at Muggelsheim, Nov. 5, 1794. Chief of the Berlin Geodetical Institute, he wrote treatises on the refraction of light in the atmosphere and on the size and form of the earth. He died in September 1858.   H. N. A.

BAFFIN, WILLIAM (1584-1622), English navigator, was born in 1584, probably in London. In 1612 he accompanied James Hall in his search for a northwest passage to the Pacific. On this trip they surveyed the west coast of Greenland up to 67° N. lat. In 1613 Baffin commanded an English whaling fleet in the arctic seas. He sailed north in the *Discovery* under Robert Bylot in 1615, and explored the inlet known as Baffin Bay. Baffin examined the Hudson Strait and the eastern coast of Southampton Island with such accuracy that his latitudes and notes agree with subsequent rigid observations. One of the first navigators to attempt to determine longitude at sea by astronomical observations, he observed the time of the moon's culmination and the lunar distance of the sun. He was killed in 1622 in the Anglo-Persian attack on the island of Qishm in the Persian Gulf.   S. Van V.

BAFFIN BAY, an oval body of water lying north of Davis Strait, bounded by Greenland on the east, Ellesmere, Devon and Baffin islands on the north and west. Polar ice enters the bay from the channels to the north and west, and drifts southward along the Baffin Island coast, where it is known as the "West Ice" or "Middle Pack" depending upon its location. Generally there is open water for navigation in August and September, especially in the southern part of the

bay. Baffin Bay was first entered by John Davis, English navigator, in 1585. Whaling fleets operated in this region throughout the nineteenth century.   S. Van V.

BAFFIN ISLAND, Canada's largest arctic island, west of Davis Strait and Baffin Bay, at the mouth of Hudson Bay. It is about 900 mi. from north to south and averages 200 to 300 mi. in width; the area is roughly 200,000 sq. mi. The east coast of Baffin Island is mountainous, with peaks rising to 8,000 and 10,000 ft. Several large icecaps discharge glaciers into long, narrow fiords. The southern part of the island is a barren rocky plateau about 2,500 ft. in elevation, sloping down to a flat tundra along the west coast. The northwestern part is a sedimentary plateau rising directly from the sea with elevations of about 1,000 ft. Several settlements of Eskimos, fur-trading posts, Royal Canadian Mounted Police detachments, meteorology stations, and mission churches, are located on sheltered inlets along the south, east, and north coasts. The island was first visited by Martin Frobisher, the English navigator, in 1576-1578.   S. Van V.

BAGATELLE [bægətɛ'l], a game, like billiards, played with balls and cues on a special table. A cushion at the head of the table is semicircular, and in the bed at the same end are nine or fifteen holes, numbered consecutively so that the higher numbers are in the center of the array. There are nine balls, two colored and seven white, of ivory or composition, somewhat smaller than carom billiard balls. Bagatelle tables vary in length from ten to fifteen feet. A string line parallel to the foot marks off an area within which balls are "dead." The player strikes a colored ball with his cue,

LINDSLEY HALL

RIVER STREET, BAGHDAD, IRAQ

endeavoring to drive the other colored ball and the white balls into the pockets. Scoring may be based solely on the number of balls pocketed, or on the numbers of the pockets also. In most games, no white ball may be struck directly by the cue ball; the other colored ball must be hit first.

According to *The American Hoyle* (1868), by William Dick, "Bagatelle is to Billiards, what Draughts is to Chess, and he who plays the superior game seldom practises much at the other." This quaint stricture, traditional but grossly false as to draughts, or checkers, is true enough as to bagatelle. The bagatelle table, invented in France, was designed to be a leveler of talents, and to give opportunity to the casual player lacking the skill for pocket and carom billiards. But interest in the game has greatly decreased, with the result that bagatelle tables are rare in billiard parlors.

The principle of bagatelle continues to flourish, however, in many games using modified equipment. Small wooden boards, on which marbles are driven by flicking the fingers, have been popular among children of many generations. A later elaboration, having steel or wooden balls driven by a bolt actuated by a spring, is the "pinball machine," outlawed by many cities and states as a gambling device.   G. M-S.

BAGATELLE. *See* MUSICAL TERMS.
BAGDAD. *See* BAGHDAD.

BAGEHOT, WALTER [bæ′jət] (1826-1877), English economist, editor, and critic was born in Langport, Feb. 3, 1826. He took an M.A. at University College, London, in 1848 and later studied for the bar, but he abandoned the practice of law to become a banker and shipowner. Later he was joint editor with R. H. Hutton of *The National Review* and editor of *The Economist* (1860-1877). Bagehot's versatile interests and his original and penetrating mentality are evidenced in his many works on a wide variety of subjects, eco

nomic, political, biographical, and literary. Of these works the best known are *The English Constitution* (1867), *Physics and Politics; or, Thoughts on the Application of the Principles of Natural Selection and Inheritance to Political Society* (1872), *Lombard Street: a Description of the Money Market* (1873), *Literary Studies* (1879), and *Biographical Studies* (1881). Whatever his subject, Bagehot wrote with wit, humor, and force; he was a master of epigram. As an essayist he was interested chiefly in the philosophical principles underlying the subjects which he treated. Of his literary essays, the most representative is *Wordsworth, Tennyson, and Browning; or, Pure, Ornate, and Grotesque Art in English Poetry*. Bagehot died in Langport, Mar. 24, 1877.   F. E. F.

BAGHDAD [bagdɑ′d], the capital and most important city of Iraq, located at 33° 15′ N. lat. and 44° 25′ E. long., in the central part of eastern Iraq, straddling the Tigris River, about 350 mi. from the Persian Gulf. It lies 220 ft. above sea level on a treeless, flat, sunbaked plain of fine sediment. There are practically no stones in the surrounding monotonous region, which has an arid to semiarid climate with a wide range of temperature. The average annual temperature is 73° F. Temperatures as high as 120 F. have been recorded, and the lowest recorded temperature has been 19° F. The average annual rainfall is 7 in., but it varies greatly, most of the rain occurring in the winter and early spring. The rest of the year is extremely dry. Baghdad is mostly hot and uncomfortable. The extremely low humidity helps make the heat bearable for the city's residents, but it also causes too rapid evaporation of moisture from the skin. The flat-topped roofs of some of the houses and hotels are used for sleeping quarters during the hot summer nights.

Grass, shrubs, and small spring-flowering plants are the district's common forms of natural vegetation. Agriculture is limited to areas where irrigation is possible. Palms and a few trees grow along the river and the canals and in Baghdad's watered spots. The small groves of trees extending along the Tigris at Baghdad have always been a refreshing sight to the desert traveler.

History. Old Baghdad, the fabulous city of *The Arabian Nights,* lies on the western bank on the Tigris, and the modern city is on the eastern bank. The two sections are connected by a pontoon bridge. The famous city is not as old as other Near Eastern cities. It was founded in A.D. 762 by the caliph, Al-Mansur. For 500 years it was the capital of the Moslem world and a center of Arabic art and learning, reaching its intellectual and economic peak in the ninth century during the reign of Harun al-Rashid. The trade routes from the Persian Gulf, India, Persia, the Mediterranean Sea, and the Levant coast met at Baghdad; consequently the city became a great trading center. The Mongols abolished the caliphate of Baghdad in 1258, and so thorough was the destruction wrought by them that hardly any traces remained of the city's spectacular palaces and other buildings. Thereafter Baghdad declined, but it remained a prize contested by warriors and rulers of the Orient. Tamerlane took it in 1392, and in the fifteenth century the Persians took control. For decades the city was the scene of strife between the Persians and Turks, the latter finally gaining control in the first half of the seventeenth century. It was retained by Turkey until 1917, when the Turks were driven out by the British during World War I. The city was the center of the British administration of Iraq after the war. In 1927 Baghdad became the capital of the independent kingdom of Iraq. During World War II British and Allied troops again occupied the city temporarily.

Transportation and Communication. The continuing warfare for the city after the Mongol invasion caused Baghdad's trade to drop off, but a more important reason for the decline was the shift of economic activity from the overland routes to the Orient to those of the Atlantic Ocean. The Baghdad trade route was adversely affected further by the opening of the Suez Canal in 1869. The transportation facilities which have been established in the twentieth century, linking the city more easily with the rest of the Orient and Europe, have made Baghdad once again a trade and transportation center of importance. The famous Berlin-to-Baghdad railroad, which was envisaged at the end of the nineteenth century to give Germany a direct overland route to

copper articles, tiles, bricks, felt, and carpets are made. Dates, carpets, textiles, hides, and gum are also exported.

Sites of Interest. The mud walls of the old suburb of Rusafa, which was founded on the eastern bank of the Tigris River during Harun al-Rashid's rule, enclose the nucleus of the modern city. Most of the city streets are very narrow dirt paths, but some have been broadened and paved, particularly in the newer city. The city's shops and bazaars are well stocked and are of particular interest to the visitor. Because of the Mongol destruction and the ensuing centuries of warfare, few remains of antiquity exist. The only ones of note in Rusafa are the famous college building of Al-Mustansir Billah, known as Mustansiriyah, and the Abbasside

THE KADHIMAIN MOSQUE IN BAGHDAD

BROWN BROTHERS

the Persian Gulf, did not become a reality until July 1940, when the first train ran between Baghdad and Ankara, the capital of Turkey, thus linking Baghdad with the European rail system. The city was connected by rail with the country's chief port, Basra, in 1920. There are also rail connections with Syria, with Israel, and Transjordan. In order to send supplies to the Soviet Union and to move troops in the Near East, the Allies extended the railroads during World War II, their chief headquarters being at Baghdad and Basra. Baghdad's airport is a stop on the air routes joining the leading cities of the Middle East, the Orient, and Europe. In addition, trucks, buses, and motor cars make constant use of the short route across the Syrian desert to Damascus, one of the old caravan routes.

Trade. Even in modern times Baghdad's manufactures are primarily silks. Wool, one of the chief exports, is cleaned, processed, and woven in the city. There are tanneries, rice and flour mills, and factories in which brass and

Palace in the citadel, whose ruins have been partially restored. The city's mosques, the minarets and domes of which break the flat-topped appearance of Baghdad, add a colorful aspect to the city. The Kadhimain Mosque contains the tombs of Imam Musa Al-Kadhim and Imam Mohammed Al-Jawad. The dome of each tomb is covered with pure gold sheet. In the Jewish quarter of Baghdad there are several outstanding synagogues, particularly the Great Synagogue and the Sheik Ishaq Synagogue.

Educational and Cultural Institutions. Baghdad is the Iraqi educational and cultural center. Its educational institutions include the Institute of Fine Arts, founded in 1936; Al-Shari's College; the Royal Staff College; a medical college established in 1927; law, engineering, and police-training schools; a teachers' college; and a military college. There are also the American School of Oriental Research; the British School of Archaeology in Iraq; and Baghdad College, a high school with a faculty of American Jesuits. The Iraq

Museum, founded in the 1920's, has a valuable collection of antiquities, some of which date from prehistoric times. Pop. 1947, 466,733.   J. E. F.

BAGLEY, WILLIAM CHANDLER (1874-1946), American educator and writer, was born in Detroit, Mich., Mar. 15, 1874. He graduated, B.S. (1895), from Michigan State College, from which he later (1940) received the honorary degree of LL.D. In addition, he obtained the following degrees: M.S. (1898), University of Wisconsin; Ph.D. (1900), Cornell University; Ed.D. (1919), Rhode Island State College. For a total of nine years (1895-1897 and 1901-1908), he taught in both normal and public schools. He was professor of education at the University of Illinois (1908-1917) and from 1917 to 1940 occupied the same position at Teachers' College, Columbia University, retiring (1940) as professor emeritus. He held important posts in the educational field, among them editor of the National Education Association *Journal* (1920-1925) and president of the National Council of Education (1931-1937). Dr. Bagley wrote or collaborated on more than twenty books, among them *The Educative Process* (1911), *Education, Crime and Social Progress* (1931), *Education and Emergent Man* (1934), and *America Yesterday and Today* (1938), in collaboration with R. F. Nichols and Charles A. Beard. From 1939 to 1946 he was editor of *School and Society*. He died in New York, N. Y., July 1, 1946.   A. S. M.

BAGOTVILLE, a town and port in Chicoutimi Co., Quebec, Canada, situated on the Saguenay River, 110 mi. north of Quebec. Founded in 1839 as a lumbering center, it was incorporated as a village in 1876 and as a town in 1920. It is the terminus for Canada Steamship Lines' cruises up the Saguenay. Pulpwood is exported from Bagotville. During World War II an important Royal Canadian Air Force station was located in the town. Pop. 1951, 4,136. D. F. P.

BAGPIPE, a musical instrument consisting of two or more reeded pipes and a flexible leather bag, the bag being inflated by the human lungs or by a bellows and used as a

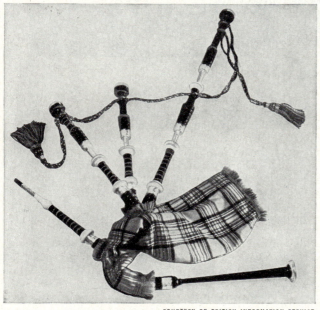

COURTESY OF BRITISH INFORMATION SERVICE

SCOTTISH BAGPIPE

reservoir for the wind supply. Normally one of these pipes, known as a "chanter," is melodic, and its pitch can be altered by means of finger-stopping; each of the others, known as "drones," plays only a single accompanying note. In rare instances two chanters have been employed. The bag of the bagpipe is carried under the arm, and the instrument is played by forcing air through the pipes by means of arm pressure.

The bagpipe probably originated in southwestern Asia, but it is first seen historically in Rome during the first century of the Christian Era, the notorious Emperor Nero being the earliest known player. In medieval Europe the simple breath-blown type with two or three pipes was popular with shepherd, soldier, and prince. The bellows, as a substitute for human lungs, was developed in seventeenth-century Ireland and in France, where the softly nasal musette, a small bagpipe, became the height of fashion and was even used by Lully in his opera orchestra. In the twentieth century, save for the shrill war pipes of Scotch and Irish regiments, the bagpipe survives only as a folk instrument, but one that is cultivated in many different varieties throughout most of Europe, the Middle East, and North America. Best known are the highland bagpipe of the Scotch, the union pipes of Ireland, and the Arabic ghaita.   W. Li.

BAGUIO [ba'gio'], a chartered city, resort community, and the summer capital of the Philippine Republic, located 125 air mi. northwest of Manila. It is also the capital of Benguet, a subdivision of Mountain Province, and the principal city of mountainous northern Luzon. Situated in rugged terrain about 5,000 ft. above sea level and with more than 60 mi. of winding streets and boulevards, it appears as a huge pine-covered mountain park. It is reached by a famous zigzag highway from the lowland plain. Baguio is the gateway to the northern mountain area; therefore, most of the commerce into or from Mountain Province passes through the city. It lies on the margin of the principal gold-mining district in the Far East. In prewar years there were fourteen well-developed mines near the city. These included the two largest ones in the Philippines (Benguet Consolidated and Balatoc Mines). Spaniards probably visited the site about 1829, but there was little development until after the United States occupation of the Philippines. The city was laid out in 1904 by D. H. Burnham, famous American architect and city planner Allied personnel were interned at Baguio by the Japanese during World War II. After heavy fighting and severe war damage, the city was recaptured by American forces in early May 1945. Reconstruction began at the end of hostilities. Pop. 1939, 24,117.   A. Cu.

BAHA AL-DIN, ABUL MAHASIN YUSUF IBN-SHADDAD [bæha' uddi'n] (1145-1234), Arabic historian and statesman, was born at Mosul, Mesopotamia, in 1145. After studying the Koran as well as Islamic tradition and law in his native town, he taught at the college of Nidham el Mulk in Baghdad. In 1174 he was appointed professor at Mosul. He went on a pilgrimage to Mecca in 1187, and decided to proceed to Jerusalem by way of Damascus. While in Damascus, he received an invitation to join Saladin (Salāh al-Dīn) who was then besieging Kaukab. The sultan and the learned professor soon became friends. Baha al-Din was entrusted with various embassies and other undertakings by the sultan. During that period he wrote a treatise entitled *The Laws and Discipline of Sacred War,* in which he presented the doctrines of the Prophet on the subject. He also was appointed judge (*cadi*) of the army and later judge of

Jerusalem. Following the death of Saladin in 1193, Baha al-Din attached himself to the third son, Malik uz Zahir, who received Aleppo as his share of his father's dominions. Baha al-Din was appointed judge at Aleppo. When Malik uz Zahir died, Baha al-Din served as chief regent during the minority of his successor. Baha al-Din was also the author of a *Life of Saladin*. Albert Schultens prepared a Latin translation of this work, *Vita et res gestae sultani Saladini* (Leiden 1732-1755), of which an English translation appeared in 1897. Baha al-Din died at Aleppo in 1234.

BAHA'I MOVEMENT, THE [baha'i]. A movement for world unity was launched in Iran in 1844 under the leadership of Ali Mohammed of Shiraz, known as The Bab ("The Gate"). He called for a reinvigoration of Islam and for freedom from the incrustations of a political religious organization. He also announced the imminent appearance of one far greater than he, who would free humanity from the limitations of old customs and prejudices and usher in a new era. The Bab's teaching reacted at once in all circles, rich and poor, and his adherents, calling themselves "Babis," multiplied so fast that both church and state took alarm. The Bab was cast into prison and died in the city of Tabriz six years after the declaration of his mission.

Mirza Husayn Ali, son of a wealthy minister of state, renounced his social standing by joining the Babis and, assuming the name of Bahā'u'llāh ("the Glory of God"), became one of the most powerful exponents of the new cause. He was imprisoned with other believers in an underground dungeon in Tehran, and it was there, while he was chained to a wall, that he came to see that he was the one whose coming had been foretold by The Bab.

At the request of the Russian ambassador, Bahā'u'llāh was not included in the general massacres which caused the streets of Tehran to run red with Babi blood. Instead he, with his wife and children and a few followers, was exiled to Turkey. When the new message began again to circulate among the people, Bahā'u'llāh was ordered to leave that country, too. On the eve of his departure from Baghdad in 1863, Bahā'u'llāh told his followers that he was the leader foretold by The Bab, and on that night the Babis took his name, calling themselves "Baha'is."

Bahā'u'llāh was exiled to Constantinople, to Adrianople and finally to Acre, prison city on the shore of Palestine, where, in 1892, he died.

Bahā'u'llāh's eldest son, Abbas (1844-1921), later known as Abdul Baha ("the Servent of Glory") was nine years old when the family was banished from Iran. He was sixty-five when the Young Turks overthrew the Ottoman government and release came to political prisoners throughout the empire. He then visited Europe and North America, carrying the Baha'i teachings, and established the Baha'i cause in the Western Hemisphere. In his lectures in churches, synagogues, schools, and before civic organizations, he summed up his father's teachings in a set of principles and offered them as basis for a new civilization. These are as follows:

(1) The oneness of the world of humanity.
(2) Independent investigation of truth.
(3) Abolition of all prejudices.
(4) Agreement between science and religion.
(5) Equality of the sexes.
(6) A universal auxiliary language.
(7) Education for all, everywhere.
(8) The spiritual solution of the economic problem.
(9) A universal faith based on the identity of the foundations of the great religions.
(10) A world union governed by the representatives of all peoples.

When Abdul Baha died in 1921, he left a will in which he appointed his grandson Shoghi Effendi as the guardian of the Baha'i movement. Under the guidance of Shoghi Effendi the Baha'is of North America have developed a system of administration, the headquarters of which is in Chicago. Wherever there exist nine or more Baha'is, an "Assembly" is formed. There are about ninety such Assemblies in the United States. Annual conventions of the delegates from the Assemblies are held in Chicago, and at them the general policies of the organization are discussed and decided upon. A Baha'i Temple stands at Wilmette, Ill., to which followers from all over the world have contributed, and the headquarters of the Baha'i organization is also in Wilmette.

In 1948 the Baha'i authorities claimed to have a membership in the United States of a little over 4,000. It would be impossible to give a census of the Baha'is in other parts of the world, for no such counting has ever been undertaken.

The Caravan of East and West, established in New York in 1930 by Mr. and Mrs. Lewis Stuyvesant Chanler and Mirza Ahmad Sohrab is an independent youth movement founded on the Baha'i principles. Hundreds of thousands of letters are exchanged among the members each year, regardless of frontier, race, nationality, or religion. The Caravan has approximately seventeen hundred chapters in forty-five countries. It publishes books and booklets on the Baha'i cause, as well as two periodicals, *The Caravan* and *Pen Friends Guide*. *See also* BABISM.　　　M. A. S.

BAHA'I TEMPLE, a temple located in Wilmette, Ill., and designed as the American center of the Baha'i faith. Each of its nine sides contains a portal through which may

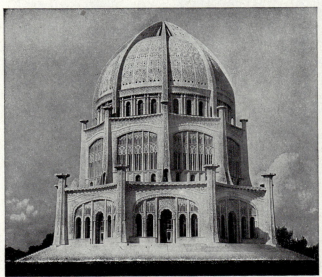

BAHA'I PUBLIC RELATIONS BUREAU

BAHA'I TEMPLE

pass adherents of the nine world religions into a brotherhood of man. The structure was designed in 1920 by Louis J. Bourgeois, an American architect of French birth. The outstanding feature of the temple, completed and dedicated in 1953, is a great pointed dome of lacelike reinforced concrete 162 ft. high. This stands upon a two-storied base 153 ft. in diameter. In the geometrical ornament with which the exterior is covered there are symbols of all the world's religions. Though original in outline and ornamentation, the building bears certain resemblances to Moslem architecture in Persia and India. This similarity is appropriate, since the founder

Nassau, capital of the Bahamas, showing the course of Bay Street along the sea

of the order, Mirza Husayn Ali (Bahā'u'llāh), and his son and successor, Abdul Baha, were born in Iran.   R. Ne.

BAHAMA ISLANDS [bəhɑ′mə; bəhe′mə], a chain of almost 700 islands and more than 2,000 cays and rocks lying northeast of Cuba between Hispaniola (Haiti and the Dominican Republic) and Florida. Most of them constitute the British Bahama Islands colony, but since 1848 the Turks and Caicos islands in the extreme southeast have formed a dependency of Jamaica. The total area of the colony is 4,375 sq. mi., and the length of the chain is about 550 mi. The more important islands from northwest to southeast are: Grand Bahama, Little and Great Abaco, the Biminis, the Berry Islands, Andros, New Providence, Eleuthera, Cat, San Salvador (Watling), Great Exuma, Rum Cay, Long, Crooked, Acklin, Mayaguana, the Caicos, and the Inaguas. Only about twenty of the islands are inhabited. Nassau, the capital, on New Providence, had a population in 1943 of 29,391, and the total population of the colony was then 68,846, about 85 per cent being Negro.

The Bahamas are composed of submarine banks of limestone on which sand was washed and blown, then consolidated into rock that can be sawed into blocks for building purposes. There is little soil development. The highest elevation, which occurs on Cat Island, is about 400 ft. above sea level. The rest of the islands vary from sea level to 200 ft. in elevation. The drainage pattern is an interior type, and there are numerous curious depressions and holes in the

limestone. The mean annual temperature is 77°F. August, the warmest month, has an average temperature of 83°F.; while January, the coldest month, averages about 72°F. The rainfall averages 46 in. a year, most of this occurring in the summer and early autumn. Hurricanes occasionally sweep over the Bahamas doing considerable damage, the hurricane season lasting from late August to November. Most of the islands are barren except for grass, palms, and bushes; some have stands of small pines, while Andros and Abaco islands are forested with mahogany, lignum vitae, and ironwood.

The colony's imports regularly exceed its exports. In 1946 the value of the former was about $11,360,000; the latter only $1,600,000. The economy of the colony is, however, balanced by the expenditures of an increasing number of winter tourists. The government consists of an appointed governor, executive council, legislative council, and an elected assembly.

In 1492, Columbus first landed on one of the Bahamas, probably Watling. The Spaniards depopulated the islands. In 1646 settlers came from Bermuda, and in 1647 the islands were granted to the London company of "Eleutherian Adventurers." After passing through various hands, the colony was finally placed under direct crown control in 1717. Its history was troubled, for not only were the islands attacked by enemy powers, but they were used, until 1718, as bases for piracy. After the American Revolution many Tories

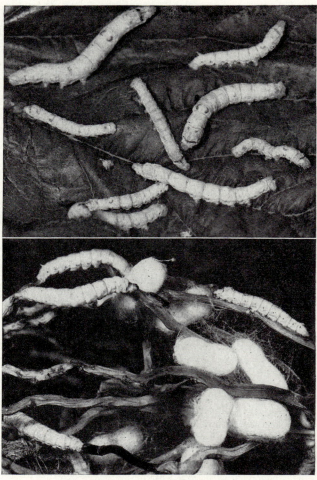

Silkworms feed on mulberry leaves at Nassau's silkworm farm (above) and (below) spin nut-shaped cocoons on a cradle of coconut palm fiber.

from the American mainland migrated to the Bahamas, more than doubling the population. The abolition of slavery in 1834 had an adverse effect on the economy of the islands. The American Civil War, on the other hand, brought sudden prosperity. Improvements in steam communication between the colony and both the United States and Canada made for steady improvement in trade, and the establishment of air communication between Miami and Nassau greatly increased the tourist trade. Although the local currency is based on sterling, United States currency is in wide circulation. Pop. 1943, 68,846.   J. E. F.

Sünde ("The Great Sin"). In 1890 he became coeditor of the Berlin periodical, *Die freie Bühne* ("The Private Theatre"). For some twenty years, beginning in 1892, he promoted all phases of the artistic life of Vienna. Bahr edited *Die Zeit* ("The Times") and was theatre critic for *Deutsche Zeitung* ("German Gazette"). His writings as a Vienna dramatic critic from 1892 to 1906 are collected in four volumes: *Wiener Theater* ("Vienna Stage"), *Premieren* ("Premieres"), *Rezensionen* ("Reviews"), and *Glossen* ("Comments"). He is best known for *Das Konzert* (1909) (*The Concert*) which was adapted and performed in New York by

THE BAHAMA ISLANDS AND THEIR POPULATION GROUPS

(Statistics based on census of 1943)

Island	European	African	Mixed	Mongolian	Others	Not Stated	Total
Abaco and Cays	1,311	2,138	....	3	9	....	3,461
Acklin Island	....	1,261	471	1	11	....	1,744
Andros Island	44	6,472	195	7	....	....	6,718
Berry Islands	15	388	....	....	....	....	403
The Biminis	64	592	62	....	....	....	718
Cat Island	5	3,843	21	1	....	....	3,870
Cay Lobos	....	7	....	....	....	....	7
Crooked Island	....	1,067	11	....	....	....	1,078
Eleuthera Island	620	5,530	257	23	....	....	6,430
Exuma and Cays	120	3,615	47	2	....	....	3,784
Grand Bahama Island	27	2,300	2	....	4	....	2,333
Harbour Island	234	517	....	6	12	....	769
Inagua Island	145	661	43	35	6	....	890
Long Cay	....	87	14	....	....	....	101
Long Island	641	2,886	1,037	....	....	....	4,564
Mayaguana Island	....	587	4	....	....	....	591
New Providence Island	3,950	24,234	1,036	100	71	....	29,391
Ragged Island and Cays	72	336	9	....	....	....	417
Rum Cay	....	219	....	....	....	....	219
San Salvador or Watling Island	21	600	....	....	5	67	693
St. George's Cay	654	6	5	....	....	....	665
Grand Total	7,923	57,346	3,214	178	118	67	68,846

BAHÍA. *See* SALVADOR.

BAHÍA BLANCA [baiˈa blaˈŋka], a city and port on the coast of eastern Argentina, in the province of Buenos Aires, the city itself being built back about 2½ mi. from the bank of the Naposta River, which empties into the bay for which the city is named. Bahía Blanca, which means white bay, lies about 397 mi. south of Buenos Aires, at 38° 43′ S. lat. and 62° 17′ W. long. A naval base and an important shipping point, it ranks close to Buenos Aires in commercial importance. It has extensive shipyards and one of the largest dry docks in the Southern Hemisphere. The chief industry of the surrounding region is sheep and cattle raising, and wheat is the main farm product. Immense quantities of wool and wheat are exported from the city, and petroleum products, lumber, and agricultural machinery are the chief imports. The city was founded in 1828, when a combined fort and trading post was established to guard against possible invasion by naval forces from Brazil, with which country Argentina was then at war over boundary claims. Bahía Blanca is connected by air, rail, and highway with Buenos Aires and other South American centers. Pop. (est. 1947), 93,122.   S. G. I.

BAHR, HERMANN [baˈr] (1863-1934), Austrian dramatist, critic, and essayist, was born at Linz on July 19, 1863. He studied Classics and law at the universities of Vienna and Berlin. Bahr resided in Paris in 1888-1889 and there wrote his first major work, the tragedy, *Die grosse*

Leo Ditrichstein in 1910. This was a light Viennese comedy about the love affairs of a famous pianist. *Der Franzl* ("Little Francis"), *Sanna,* a tragedy, and *Die Stimme* (1916) ("The Voice") are among his best dramas; *Himmelfahrt* ("Ascension") and *Die Rotte Korahs* ("The Company of Korah"), his finest novels. He resided in Salzburg from 1912 to 1921 and afterwards in Munich. *Selbstbildnis* ("Self-Portrait"), his autobiography, appeared in 1923. He published over thirty plays, eight novels, and several volumes of literary and philosophical essays. Bahr was brilliant and versatile and pioneered for three decades in every major artistic and literary movement in central Europe. He died in Munich, Jan. 15, 1934.

BAHRAL or **BUHREL.** *See* SHEEP.

BAHREIN [bareˈn], an independent Arab state, composed of eight islands which lie west of the Qatar Peninsula in the Gulf of Bahrein, an arm of the Persian Gulf, about 22 mi. off the eastern coast of Saudi Arabia. The largest island is Bahrein, which is 30 mi. long and 10 mi. wide. In addition there are Muharraq, Sitra, Hawar, and numerous other islets. Together they comprise about 500 sq. mi., and in 1941 had a population of 120,000. Manama, on Bahrein, is the capital city (30,000), followed in size by Muharraq (20,000), on the island of the same name. Most of the people live in small, walled-in villages.

The inhabitants are primarily Arabs; in addition, Negroes, Persians, and Hindus occupy the islands. The Arabs are equally divided between the Shiite and Sunnite sects; west-

MANAMA, ON BAHREIN ISLAND, LIES DIRECTLY ACROSS THE GULF OF SELWA FROM THE SAUDI ARABIAN MAINLAND.

ern Christianity is represented by a Dutch Reformed mission from the United States.

The islands are generally flat and sandy, but the oases permit cultivation of rice, wheat, sugar, tea, and many types of fruits, of which dates and citrons are famous. Both temperature and humidity are high, making living and working conditions difficult. Pearling and the oil industry are the principal economic activities. The Bahrein Islands have always been one of the world's leading pearling centers. As many as 20,000 men and 1,000 boats have been employed in the industry, and its annual income has been as high as $10,000,000; by 1949, however, it had dwindled to $200,000. Pearl divers go down as far as 60 ft. for the precious pearl oysters. The waters about the island abound with many kinds of fish. Oil which has replaced pearls as the most important economic asset, was discovered on Bahrein Island in 1932 and concessions are held by American companies.

Until the nineteenth century the islands were generally subject to the Arabs, who used them as naval bases against the Persians. In 1507 the Portuguese established commercial bases on them, only to be driven off a hundred years later. Since 1783 the islands have been under the nominal control of the al-Khalifa family, which came over from the mainland. The present ruler is Sheik Sir Suleiman ibn Hamad al-Khalifa. Since 1820 the islands have been a protectorate of Great Britain, which has maintained that position against the Turks, Arabs, and Persians. A British resident always holds an advisory position to the reigning sheik. H. C. K.

BAHR EL GHAZAL [baʹr ɛl gəzɑʹl], a tributary of the White Nile in southern Anglo-Egyptian Sudan. It rises in the swamps of Bahr Sudd Ghazal in the watershed between the Nile Basin and the Congo and flows north and west to its juncture with the Nile, or, more specifically, from Meshra el Rek, at 8° 25′ N. lat. and 29° 15′ E. long., to Lake No, at 9° 30′ N. lat. and 30° 30′ E. long., a distance of 125 mi. All along the river are large areas of swamp fed by a number of streams. The papyrus and other reeds flourish in these marshes, occasionally encroaching upon the river itself and often hiding the channel. It is necessary to clear away this growth in order to maintain navigation.

M. B. H.

BAHURIM [bəhuʹrɪm], a Biblical town near Jerusalem, on the way to the Jordan. Its exact site is unknown, though it has been suggested that it might be the site where the village of Almit now stands. When David commanded that Michal be brought to him, she was followed by her husband from Gallim to Bahurim. At that place Abner commanded the weeping husband to return. It was at Bahurim that David, in his flight from Absalom, was cursed by a native of that town named Shimei. Ahumaaz and Jonathan, who were acting as spies for David, hid in the well of a house at Bahurim to escape from the servants sent after them by Absalom.

BAHYA BEN JOSEPH IBN PAKUDA [baʹya ɪʹbn pəkuʹdɑ], eleventh-century Jewish philosopher, of whose life nothing is known except that he lived in Saragossa, Spain. He was the author of an important book in Arabic on Jewish ethics, *Al Hidayah ila Faraidi al-Kulub,* which is known in the Hebrew translation of Judah ibn Tibbon as *Hobot ha-Lebabot* ("Duties of the Heart"). He also wrote a number of liturgical poems.

In his book, Bahya, an original thinker of distinction, dealt with the fundamentals of Judaism, and attempted a systematization of Jewish ethical values. According to him, the essence of all spirituality is the recognition of God as the designer of all things. He considered it even more important for a man to own and love God in his heart than to seek to know Him through his intellect, and he opposed anthropomorphist conceptions of the Godhead. Bahya's book contains many quotations from the works of non-Jewish moral philosophers and reveals a vast knowledge of Arabic scientific and philosophical literature. **D. G.**

BAIAE [bai'i], fashionable watering-place of the ancient Romans, situated in the territory of Cumae, on the east side of the low volcanic range which extends southward from the citadel of Cumae to Capo Miseno and helps to delimit the Bay of Naples.

In modern times the place has been known as Baia. Baiae itself and its neighbor, Puteoli, stand like two sentinels at the entrance to the half-landlocked inner recess of the sea, the Bay of Puteoli; and this situation, combined with the numerous healing springs and vapors and the mild, soft climate, early attracted visitors from Rome in search of health and relaxation. The amenities of this lovely coast, and the often insidious allurements of the life that was lived there, became notorious, and they frequently appear in Latin literature. The hills and shores were chosen as places of sojourn by many Romans of the Republic, and eventually by members of the imperial house. The names of the generals and statesmen Marius, Pompey, and Julius Caesar, and of the men of letters Hortensius, Cicero, and Varro, are associated with this landscape; Nero's all-embracing building activities are recorded; both Marcellus, the adopted son of Augustus, and Hadrian died here.

The little bay as seen from Baiae preserves sinister memories. It was here that mad Caligula held his parade upon a bridge of boats that spanned the water from shore to shore, and it was here, also, that Nero attempted to do away with his mother Agrippina by means of a collapsible ship—an only partially successful device, for the unfortunate half-disabled victim had to be finished off on land after her desperate escape from peril by sea. Both the hillsides and the shores are full even today of the remains of sumptuous villas; but the two outstanding edifices, close to the water's edge, although they are traditionally known as the "Temple of Venus" and "Temple of Diana," belong to bath establishments. With their domical vaulting and their brick and concrete technique, they show the same general features that characterize the Pantheon in Rome and Hadrian's villa near Tivoli; they, too, are to be dated under Hadrian. **A. W. Van B.**

BAIE ST. PAUL [be'sæ'po'l; be'səntpɔ'l], a port and the county town of Charlevoix West Co., Quebec, Canada, on the north shore of the St. Lawrence Estuary opposite Ile-aux-Coudres at the mouth of Rivière du Gouffre, about 60 mi. northeast of the city of Quebec. The Canadian National Railways supplies transportation facilities. Founded in 1683, the village was long isolated, its inhabitants living by fishing and hunting. Later it exported firewood and timber. It was incorporated as a village in 1893. The first passable road to Quebec was completed in 1824 and was made a highway in 1925. The Canadian National Railways reached Baie St. Paul in 1914. A picturesque place with many old buildings, Baie St. Paul is a well-known tourist resort. It is a notable center of fox breeding in Quebec. Pop. 1951, 3,716. **D. F. P.**

BAILEY, IRVING WIDMER (1884-   ), American professor of plant anatomy, was born in Tilton, N.H., Aug. 15, 1884. He received degrees of A.B. in 1907, and M.F. in 1909 from Harvard University, where he remained as an assistant in botany. The following year he became an instructor in forestry and in 1927 a professor of plant anatomy. From 1914 to 1916 he was a member of the advisory board of the United States Forest Products Laboratory and in 1918 was placed in charge of the Wood Section, Materials Engineering Department, of the Bureau of Aircraft Production. Bailey was a member of the National Research Council from 1917 to 1932 and a research associate with the Carnegie Institution from 1930 to 1940. He was elected president of the Society of American Foresters and the Botanical Society of America in 1945 and in 1946 was appointed chairman of the Institute for Research in General Plant Morphology. He has written numerous articles and papers on botany and forestry and, in collaboration with H. A. Spoehr, wrote *The Role of Research in the Development of Forestry in North America* (1929). **C. W. D.**

BAILEY, LIBERTY HYDE (1858-1954), American botanist and horticulturist, one of the world's greatest authorities on garden plants, palm trees, and blackberry bushes, was born Mar. 15, 1858, at South Haven, Mich. Graduating from Michigan Agricultural College in 1882 he served as an assistant to Asa Gray at Harvard from 1882 to 1883. In 1885 he returned to Michigan Agricultural College as professor of horticulture and landscape gardening in the first such department in any American college. In 1888 he became professor of horticulture at Cornell University, and he became dean of the New York State College of Agriculture at Cornell in 1903. He retired from that position in 1913, at which time he was appointed dean and professor emeritus. After his retirement Dr. Bailey devoted his time to research, collecting over a quarter of a million plants, and writing and editing more than 100 books. He edited *The Cyclopedia of American Agriculture* (1907-1909), *The Standard Cyclopedia of Horticulture* (1914-1917), *Hortus* (1930), *Hortus Second* (1941), and other important works, and wrote *Plant-Breeding* (1897), *Manual of Gardening* (1910), and *Manual of Cultivated Plants* (1924). In 1935 Dr. Bailey presented to Cornell University his entire botanical collection and professional library, including the land and buildings in which they were housed. These were named the Liberty Hyde Bailey Hortorium, and Dr. Bailey remained as director until 1952. In 1948 the National Garden Institute announced an annual award of a medal in honor of Dr. Bailey to be presented to the winner of a horticultural competition. At the age of 91 Dr. Bailey undertook a palm-collecting expedition in the Caribbean area. He died Dec. 25, 1954, at Ithaca, N.Y. **J. C. Wis.**

BAILLIE, JOANNA [be'li] (1762-1851), Scottish poet and dramatist, was born Sept. 11, 1762, at Rothwell, Lanarkshire, Scotland. Her poems were collected in 1823 under the title *Poetic Miscellanies,* and her *Dramatic and Poetical Works* were published in 1851. Although she was most noted in her day as a talented poet, she was also the outstanding woman dramatist of the period. She published three series of *Plays on the Passions* (1798, 1802, 1812) and three volumes of *Dramas* (1836). As her knowledge of stagecraft was inadequate, their success as plays was slight, though critics acclaimed her sentiments and gifts. Her most powerful drama was *Le Montfort.* Most successful on the stage was *The Family Legend* (1810), with a Scottish national theme. The greater part of the poet's life was passed in London or with her sister in Hampstead, England, where she died Feb. 23, 1851.

BAILMENT, in law, a transfer of the possession of personal property from one person to another without transfer of ownership, made pursuant to an agreement between the parties, express or implied, obligating the person thus obtaining possession of the property to return it after the accomplishment of some contemplated purpose or object.

The person who thus holds chattels under the obligation to return them is called the bailee, and the person who has thus delivered his chattels to the bailee is called the bailor, all of these terms being derived from the French word *bailler,* meaning "to deliver."

Ancient codes of law treated the subject of bailments. Provisions respecting bailments appear in Roman law and, even earlier, in the Mosaic Codes and Babylonian Code of Hammurabi.

The modern law of bailments is indebted to the systematizing efforts of Sir William Jones in his treatise on bailment, in 1781, as well as to the opinion of Lord Holt in *Coggs* v. *Bernard,* in 1703.

It is now customary to classify bailments as (1) bailments for the sole benefit of the bailor, (2) bailments for the sole benefit of the bailee, and (3) bailments for the benefit of both parties. The rights and obligations of the bailor and the bailee, in any particular transaction, are governed in large measure by the classification in which such individual bailment falls.

In the case of a bailment for the sole benefit of the bailor, such as the storing of goods for another without compensation, the bailee is said to be liable for loss or destruction of the goods only if he has been grossly negligent. The care required of the gratuitous bailee in order to exonerate him from liability must necessarily be couched in broad and general terms. The law's criterion in this regard is not susceptible to precise definition. An approach to a ready standard appears in the decision of a Maine court that the gratuitous bailee who "keeps the goods as he keeps his own, though he keep his own negligently, (he) is not answerable for them." This ruling, however, appears to deviate somewhat from the concensus of authoritative opinion which holds that even the gratuitous bailee is guilty of actionable negligence if he fails to use such care as ordinarily prudent persons would exercise under like circumstances.

On the other hand, the bailee who has borrowed property for some use or object, solely for his own benefit, is bound to use extraordinary diligence in the care and safeguarding of the property lent to him.

In the absence of special contract or statute, the bailee, where a bailment is for mutual benefit of himself and the bailor, is required to exercise the care which a capable, skilled, as well as reasonably prudent person, engaged in the business of receiving such bailments, is likely to observe toward the object so entrusted to him.

The great bulk of bailments fall into this category of bailment for mutual benefit. Any instance in which goods are entrusted to another for a consideration constitutes the person receiving them a bailee for hire, and the transaction that of a bailment for mutual benefit. The transfer of goods for the purpose of their transportation, repair, or storage becomes a bailment for mutual benefit if the bailee charges for his services.

A pledge of articles to secure repayment of a loan or other performance of an agreement by their owner is deemed to constitute a bailment for mutual benefit. The matter of articles left by a customer in a shop or restaurant is more difficult to classify. The proprietor becomes a bailee only if the customer's articles are left in his custody. Where the customer does not avail himself of the particular facilities provided for his convenience, but deposits his effects elsewhere on the premises, it may be held that there has been no delivery at all into the custody of the proprietor and that hence no bailment has arisen.   H. Si.

BAILY'S BEADS, one of the features of a total solar eclipse; the name was given because of the descriptions by Francis Baily of the 1836 eclipse, observed from Scotland. Immediately before totality the thin disappearing crescent of the sun breaks up, showing a row of shining points, like a string of bright beads, because of the irregular surface of the approaching moon's limb, or edge. The effect appears in reverse just after the totality ends. Baily correctly explained the phenomenon as caused by irradiation. Spaces between the "beads" become black parallel lines connecting the limbs of the sun and moon, and these lines suddenly give way. This phase of the phenomenon is allied to the black-drop phenomenon witnessed at transits of Venus over the sun's disk.   H. S. R.

BAIN, ALEXANDER [be'n] (1818-1903), Scottish psychologist, logician, and writer on education, was born in Aberdeen, June 11, 1818. He graduated from Marischal College

ALEXANDER BAIN

in 1840; became assistant to Dr. Glennie, professor of moral philosophy, in 1841; and met John Stuart Mill, George Grote, and Thomas Carlyle in London in 1842. In 1845 he was appointed professor of mathematics and moral philosophy at Andersonian University, Glasgow, and in 1848 he became assistant secretary to the metropolitan sanitary commission of London. Bain also lectured at Beford College for Women until 1855, edited Paley's *Moral Philosophy* (1852), and published *The Senses and the Intellect* (1855), *The Emotions and the Will* (1859), and *The Study of Character* (1861). He received a royal appointment to the newly created professorship of logic and English at the University of Aberdeen, and began to improve the teaching of these subjects. He wrote an English grammar (1863), *English Composition and Rhetoric* (1866), *English Extracts,* and *Mental and Moral Science* (1868), a major work. With J. S. Mill and Grote, he edited James Mill's *Analysis of the Phenomena of the Human Mind* (1869); and he assisted George C. Robertson to edit Grote's *Aristotle* (1872). Bain's *Logic* appeared in 1870, *Mind and*

Body in 1872, and *Education as a Science* in 1879, and in 1876 he founded the philosophical journal *Mind*. Bain resigned his professorial chair in 1880 and became Lord Rector of Aberdeen University in 1881, serving two three-year terms. His later writings included *James Mill: A Biography; John Stuart Mill: A Criticism, with Personal Recollections* (1882); and *Autobiography* (published posthumously, 1904). Bain's major contribution was his work as a psychologist. He greatly advanced and popularized psychology, and in England pioneered in applying to it the results of physiological researches. He died in Aberdeen, Sept. 18, 1903.

BAIN, HARRY FOSTER (1871-1948), American mining engineer and geologist, was born in Seymour, Ind., Nov. 2, 1871. After his undergraduate work at Moore's Hill College, he obtained a Ph.D. degree from the University of Chicago in 1897. From 1893 to 1900 he was assistant state geologist of Iowa; a little later, from 1905 to 1909, while state geologist of Illinois and director of the Illinois Geological Survey, he performed outstanding work in the Wisconsin-Illinois zinc area. He resigned the latter position to enter professional work and subsequently assumed the editorship of leading American and British technical publications. In 1921 he was appointed director of the United States Bureau of Mines, where he remained until 1925. He was a chief witness for the government prosecution in the Teapot Dome and Elk Hills oil reserve lease cases. In 1926 he became executive secretary of the American Institute of Mining Engineers. While occupying this post, he made numerous examinations in foreign fields, including investigations of oil and mineral deposits for the governments of Colombia, Argentina, and Japan. In 1932 he was retained as managing director of the Copper and Brass Research Association. On a professional trip to the Orient, he met Manuel Quezon, then president of the Philippine Commonwealth, who persuaded him to become his mineral advisor, and he remained in that capacity until the outbreak of World War II. He was largely responsible for strengthening the mining industry of the Philippines, as well as instituting an enlightened government policy toward mining development that established it firmly in the country's economy. He was the author of several reference books on mining subjects, including *Ores and Industry in the Far East* and *Ores and Industry in South America*. On his return to the United States after the war, he was appointed a member of the National Engineers Committee to prepare a postwar plan for Japanese industry. He died in Manila, Mar. 9, 1948.

W. F. B.

BAINBRIDGE, WILLIAM (1774-1833), American naval officer, was born in Princeton, N. J., May 7, 1774. Educated privately, he went to sea at fifteen, became first mate at eighteen, and was in command of a vessel at nineteen. In 1798, when the United States Navy was organized, he was appointed to command the schooner *Retaliation*. He was defeated and captured by the French at Guadaloupe, in the West Indies. Returning to the United States after having diplomatically absolved himself and his country from acceding to French requests, Bainbridge was given command of the *Norfolk*. His reports of maltreatment of Americans by the French at Guadaloupe helped to secure enactment of the Retaliation Act by Congress in 1798. After naval experience in the West Indies, Bainbridge returned in 1800 to Philadelphia, where he was promoted to a captaincy. In command of the *George Washington*, he conveyed tribute to the Bey of Algiers, who claimed jurisdiction of the Mediterranean and who demanded that he proceed to Constantinople with presents

to the Sultan of Turkey. The forced voyage created friendly relations between Turkey and the United States and a cessation of tributes to Algiers. In May 1803, in command of the *Philadelphia*, he sailed to Gibraltar to defend American shipping against Tripolitan attacks. He was taken prisoner in Tripoli harbor and held in captivity until the end of the war in June 1805. In the fall of that year Bainbridge was put in

COURTESY OF THE NEW YORK PUBLIC LIBRARY

WILLIAM BAINBRIDGE

FROM AN ENGRAVING BY W. WELLSTOOD OF A PAINTING BY CHAPPEL

command of the New York Navy Yard. In 1808 he took over the *President* as commander. At the beginning of the War of 1812, Bainbridge, upon Isaac Hull's resignation, became commander of the *Constitution* ("Old Ironsides") and defeated the British frigate *Java*, Dec. 29, 1812, off the Brazilian coast. After the war Bainbridge superintended the construction of the battleship *Independence;* assumed command of the ship after its completion, and joined Commander Stephen Decatur's fleet at Algiers. When the Barbary States had bowed to American naval power, Bainbridge returned with the *Independence* to the United States. In the spring of 1820 he was placed in command of the eighty-gun ship *Columbus*. Bainbridge died in Philadelphia, July 27, 1833.

BAINBRIDGE, a city in southwestern Georgia, the county seat of Decatur Co., situated on the Flint River, about 150 mi. southwest of Macon. Peanuts, cotton, tobacco, corn, and truck crops are raised in the area. The region has deposits of fuller's earth. Founded in 1822, Bainbridge was incorporated as a city in 1829. In 1949 the government was the mayor-councilmanic type. Of historical interest is the site of Hernando de Soto's first encampment in Georgia, as well as Fort Recovery, built in 1812, and

Fort Hughes, built in 1817. Transportation is supplied by the Atlantic Coast Line and the Seaboard Air Line railroads. Local industrial establishments include sawmills, bottle-washing machinery factories, feed mills, peanut-shelling plants, and box and crate factories. Pop. 1950, 7,562.

BAIRAM [baira'm; bai'ram], a Turkish word meaning "festival," is applied to either one of the two major holidays of Islam. The first holiday is the 'Id al-Fitr ("Festival of Fast-Breaking"), which follows the month of fasting, Ramadan (ninth month of the Moslem calendar), taking place on the first three days of the tenth month, Shawwāl.

The second holiday is the 'Id al-Adha ("Festival of Sacrifice"), which falls on the tenth day and two or three following days of the twelfth month, Dhu-al-Hijja, when a pilgrimage is observed. Throughout the Moslem world the Sacrifice Festival is celebrated by the slaughter of an animal—ram, he-goat, cow, or camel—which is consumed by the family or shared with the poor.   E. J. J.

BAIRD, SPENCER FULLERTON (1823-1888), American naturalist, was born in Reading, Pa., Feb. 3, 1823. He graduated from Dickinson College, Carlisle, Pa., in 1840, and in 1843 received his M.A. degree. He was appointed professor of natural history at Dickinson College in 1845 and in 1848 received the first grant of the Smithsonian Institution for scientific exploration. Two years later he became assistant secretary of the Institution, a position he held until 1878, when he became secretary. From 1850 to 1860 Baird conducted explorations for the government in the Wyoming territory and prepared the Smithsonian *Instructions to Collectors.* When the United States Bureau of Fisheries was established in 1871, he was appointed the first commissioner. He was also a trustee of Columbia University and science editor of the Harper & Brothers' publications. He was one of the foremost men of the day in his field and was accorded many honors for his valuable work with the Smithsonian Institution. His work in ornithology was characterized by an insistence on accuracy of description, and his numerous scientific contributions include works on North American birds, reptiles, and mammals. He died in Woods Hole, Mass., on Aug. 19, 1888.   C. W. D.

BAIRSTOW, LEONARD [bɛ'rsto] (1880-   ), British pioneer in aerodynamics, was born in Halifax, Yorkshire, on June 25, 1880, and was educated at the Royal College of Science in London. In 1904 he joined the National Physical Laboratory, where he became superintendent of the aerodynamics laboratory and was active in the development of the wind tunnel for use in airplane design. His early work included contributions on the stability of airplanes and airships, and on the analysis of the disturbed or controlled motion of airplanes in flight. He joined the British Air Ministry in 1917 as superintendent of aerodynamic research and in 1920 became professor of aerodynamics at the Imperial College of Science and Technology in London. From 1923 to 1947 he was Zaharoff Professor of Aviation at the University of London and director of the School of Aviation. His *Applied Aerodynamics,* first published in 1919, was the first comprehensive textbook on the subject to be published in English. He served as vice-chairman of the Aeronautical Research Committee for many years. In 1935 he became dean of the engineering faculty of the University of London and in 1936, a member of the University senate. M. H. Sm.

BAIT CASTING. *See* FISHING.

BAJAZET. *See* BAYAZID.
BAJO. *See* ORANG LAUT.
BAKELITE. *See* PLASTICS.

BAKER, GEORGE PIERCE (1866-1935), American educator, was born in Providence, R. I., Apr. 4, 1866. Graduating from Harvard University, he taught English and founded a student dramatic laboratory, "The 47 Workshop," at the university. In 1925 he was appointed director of the Yale University Theatre. He proved the value of his methods of teaching playwriting through the success of his former pupils, notably Eugene O'Neill. He wrote several books on acting and the drama, among them *Development of Shakespeare as a Dramatist* (1907) and *Dramatic Technique* (1919). He retired in 1933 and died in New York City, Jan. 6, 1935.   M. Sr.

BAKER, NEWTON DIEHL (1871-1937), American lawyer and administrator, was born at Martinsburg, W. Va., Dec. 3, 1871. He was graduated from Johns Hopkins Uni-

NEWTON D. BAKER

versity in 1892 and from the law school of Washington and Lee University in 1894. In 1896 he was for a short time private secretary to Postmaster General William L. Wilson. He practiced law in Martinsburg, moving in 1899 to Cleveland, Ohio, where he continued in private practice. From 1902 to 1912 he served as city solicitor of Cleveland, and between 1912 and 1916 was mayor. In 1916, as a result of his progressive municipal administration and his political support of President Woodrow Wilson, he was appointed secretary of war, a position which he retained during the remainder of Wilson's presidency. As the director of the military policy of the United States, when the country became involved in World War I, Baker was the subject of much criticism; his acts were investigated in 1917 by a congressional committee. After the military successes of 1918, however, Baker's administration of the War Department was vindicated. In 1921 he returned to the private practice of law in Cleveland. At the Democratic national convention of 1924, Baker sought unsuccessfully to obtain support of the League of Nations as a part of the party's program. He was suggested at this and other Democratic conventions as a possible candidate for the presidency but was never actually nominated. In 1928, President Calvin Coolidge appointed Baker a member of the Permanent Court of Arbitration at The Hague. President Herbert Hoover, in 1929, appointed him to the National Law Enforcement Commission. Baker died in Cleveland, Ohio, Dec. 25, 1937.

R. T.

BAKER, RAY STANNARD (1870-1946), author and historian, was born Apr. 17, 1870, in Lansing, Mich. He graduated from Michigan State College in 1889 and studied law at the University of Michigan. Abandoning the law in favor of a literary career, he started work as a newspaper reporter, and his coverage of the march of Coxey's army in 1894 gained him the subeditorship of the Chicago *Record*. In 1897 he became managing editor of McClure's syndicate, and in 1899 one of the editors of *McClure's Magazine*. He accepted in 1906 an editorship on the *American Magazine*, where he remained until 1915. Meanwhile, under the pseudonym of "David Grayson," he wrote several books of philosophical essays. He covered World War I under the aegis of the State Department, acting as special commissioner to Great Britain, France, and Italy. In 1919 he served with the American Peace Commission under President Woodrow Wilson.

RAY STANNARD BAKER

WIDE WORLD PHOTO

Becoming closely associated with Wilson, he was made director of the press bureau of the American Commission to Negotiate Peace, a post he held until Wilson's death. At Wilson's request, Baker was made his official biographer. The first two volumes of his eight-volume work, *Woodrow Wilson, His Life and Letters,* appeared in 1927, and the final volumes were published in 1939. For this Baker was awarded the 1940 Pulitzer prize in biography. He had previously written *What Wilson Did at Paris* (1919), *Woodrow Wilson and World Settlement* (3 vols., 1922), and edited the *Public Papers of Woodrow Wilson* (6 vols.). His works include *Following the Color Line* (1908), *Adventures in Solitude* (1931), *Native American* (1941), and *American Chronicle* (1945). He died at Amherst, Mass., July 12, 1946.

M. E. McD.

BAKER, SIR SAMUEL WHITE (1821-1893), English explorer and author, was born in London, June 8, 1821. After study in England and Germany, Baker established an agricultural colony at Nuwara Eliya, Ceylon. After traveling to Constantinople and to the Crimea in 1856, he superintended the construction of a railway connecting the Danube with the Black Sea. In 1861, he went to Central Africa on a journey of exploration to find the sources of the Nile. He ascended the Nile to Gondokoro where he met John Hanning

Speke and James Augustus Grant returning from their discovery of Lake Victoria. From these two he learned of another large lake in the district, and on Mar. 14, 1864, he discovered Lake Albert. Baker in 1865 returned to England where he received many honors. He was knighted in August 1866. In 1869, he went back to Africa with the authority of the khedive of Egypt to suppress the slave trade, to open the way to commerce, and to annex large parts of the recently explored country. Baker remained four years and became its governor-general. He later traveled in America and Asia in search of big game. His writings include: *The Rifle and the Hound in Ceylon* (1854); *Eight Years Wanderings in Ceylon* (1855); *The Albert Nyanza* (1866); *The Nile Tributaries of Abyssinia* (1867); *Ismailia, A Narrative of the Expedition to Central Africa* (1874); *Cyprus As I Saw It* (1879); *True Tales for My Grandsons* (1883); and *Wild Beasts and Their Ways* (1890). He died at his estate of Sandford Orleigh in South Devon, Dec. 30, 1893.

S. Van. V.

BAKER, VALENTINE (1827-1887), British soldier, was a younger brother of Sir Samuel White Baker. He was educated at Gloucester and in Ceylon and selected the army as a career. He saw action in the Kaffir War of 1852-1853 and in the Crimean War. He had commanded the 10th Hussars for thirteen years when he was dismissed from the army in 1874 because of a scandal. He entered the service of Turkey and rapidly rose to the rank of lieutenant-general during the Russo-Turkish War of 1877-1878. After the war he went to Egypt to take over command of the Egyptian army, but instead was placed in command of the Egyptian police. In the Sudan War, Baker Pasha, as he was then known, attempted to relieve Tokar with 3,500 men, but was overwhelmingly defeated by Osman Digna at El Teb. Only a handful of officers escaped. British troops under Sir Gerald Graham were later guided by Baker to El Teb, where Baker was wounded in the ensuing battle. An attempt was made to secure his readmission into the British army, but Queen Victoria refused to approve his commission. He remained in command of the Egyptian police until his death at Tell el Kebir, Egypt, in 1887.

BAKER, a city in northeastern Oregon, the county seat of Baker Co., is situated in a farming, dairying, livestock, and timber area, near the Elkhorn Mountains, 338 mi. southeast of Portland. Natural resources of the region are gold, silver, copper, zinc, lead, manganese, chrome, and antimony. Baker became a county seat in 1865, soon after it had been settled, and was incorporated as Baker City in 1874. It was renamed Baker about forty years later. Baker is on the route of the Oregon Trail. Whitman National Forest is in the vicinity. Transportation is furnished by the Union Pacific Railroad and the Empire Air Lines. The city's industries include lumbering, foundries, cement factories, and dairy and meat-packing plants. Pop. 1950, 9,471.

BAKER, MOUNT, a dormant volcano, contained in the Cascade Range in northwestern Washington, about 30 mi. east of Bellingham. Formed in the Recent Period of geologic time on the Cascade peneplain, Mount Baker erupted in 1843, 1854, 1858, and again in 1870. The mountain rises to a height of 10,750 ft.

J. E. F.

BAKERSFIELD, a city of southern California, the county seat of Kern Co., 100 mi. northwest of Los Angeles. It is served by the Southern Pacific and the Atchison, Topeka and Santa Fe railroads and the United Airlines. Extensive oil deposits in the surrounding region make oil refining the chief industry of Bakersfield. Other natural resources are silver, gold, soda, and borax. The district is rich agriculturally, the principal crops being cotton, potatoes, alfalfa, and grapes. Pop. 1950, 34,784.

BAKER UNIVERSITY, an accredited coeducational institution under the control of the Methodist Church, situated in Baldwin City, Kan., a town in the farming district near Kansas City, Kan. It was chartered by the Kansas Territorial Legislature in 1858 and opened for instruction that year. The A.B. degree in liberal arts is offered, and a program of general education offers definite training in citizenship and churchmanship. Limited scholarship and student loan assistance is available. Dormitory facilities can accommodate about half of the women students and about 20 per cent of the men students, and such facilities are available also for married students. *For statistical information see* COLLEGES AND UNIVERSITIES.   J. R. To.

BAKHMUT. *See* ARTEMOVSK.
BAKING SODA. *See* SALTS.

BAKU [baku'], a petroleum center and the capital of the Azerbaidzan S. S. R., in the southwestern Soviet Union. It lies in a semi-arid region, on the southern edge of the Apsheron Peninsula, on the southwestern coast of the Caspian Sea. Baku is an old city of Persian origin, probably developed in about the fifth century. Definitely mentioned in the tenth century, it belonged to Persia from 1509 to 1723. Restored to Persia after twelve years of Russian rule, it became Russian once more in 1806. Petroleum was long known to exist in the vicinity, and in 1871 the first scientifically drilled wells gave great impetus to the development of the city. The city suffered a disastrous fire in 1901 and was damaged in the abortive 1905 revolution and in the 1917 revolution. On the west, Baku consists of an old town whose narrow, crooked streets give a distinct oriental atmosphere; however, most of the city is modern with tall buildings, blocks of flats, factories, offices, boulevards, and gardens. Of interest in the old section are a medieval mosque, the ruins of a khan's palace, and the Maiden's Tower, a massive cylindrical structure formerly used as a lighthouse. Baku possesses a state university, academy of sciences, institute of medicine, and art school.

Baku is connected with the Black Sea by two railways, and its port handles more tonnage, chiefly petroleum products, than any other Soviet port. A pipe line extends westward to Batumi on the Black Sea east coast. Baku is one of the world's great petroleum centers, the surrounding fields

yielding about 60 per cent of the Soviet production. While its economy is based chiefly on oil production, the city has large refineries, cotton mills, shipbuilding yards, and flour mills, and local factories manufacture tobacco, chemicals,

SOVFOTO

KIROV AVENUE, BAKU, CAPITAL OF THE AZERBAIDZAN, S.S.R.

metals, timber products, and machinery. It has extensive trade with Iran and is the Soviet's fifth largest city. Pop. (est. 1954), 890,000.   C. C. H.

BAKUNIN, MIKHAIL [bʌku'nyɪn] (1814-1876), Russian anarchist, of aristocratic family. He supplemented his education with travels in Germany, France, and Switzerland, where he decided to settle permanently, thus losing his property in Russia. He took part in the Revolution of 1848 in Germany, being active in the movement in Dresden. Later captured by the Austrian authorities, he was handed over to the Russians, who sentenced him in 1855 to exile in Siberia, from which he escaped in 1860. He lived in London and was a friend of Karl Marx and Frederich Engels and a member of the First International, from which he was expelled in 1872. He died June 13, 1876, in Berne. His influence, which continues to be very pronounced on certain sections of the revolutionary movement of the working class, notably in Spain, Italy, and Belgium, is derived from his writings, especially *God and the State* (1882), and from the closely co-ordinated organization of members devoted to their leaders to achieve the destruction of the state through open insurrection rather than political methods.   F. N. F.